THE NORTON ANTHOLOGY OF
WORLD
LITERATURE

FOURTH EDITION

VOLUME B

THE NORTON ANTHOLOGY OF

WORLD
LITERATURE

FOURTH EDITION

MARTIN PUCHNER, *General Editor*
HARVARD UNIVERSITY

SUZANNE AKBARI
UNIVERSITY OF TORONTO

WIEBKE DENECKE
BOSTON UNIVERSITY

BARBARA FUCHS
UNIVERSITY OF CALIFORNIA, LOS ANGELES

CAROLINE LEVINE
CORNELL UNIVERSITY

PERICLES LEWIS
YALE UNIVERSITY

EMILY WILSON
UNIVERSITY OF PENNSYLVANIA

VOLUME B

W. W. NORTON & COMPANY | New York · London

W. W. Norton & Company has been independent since its founding in 1923, when William Warder Norton and Mary D. Herter Norton first published lectures delivered at the People's Institute, the adult education division of New York City's Cooper Union. The firm soon expanded its program beyond the Institute, publishing books by celebrated academics from America and abroad. By midcentury, the two major pillars of Norton's publishing program—trade books and college texts—were firmly established. In the 1950s, the Norton family transferred control of the company to its employees, and today—with a staff of four hundred and a comparable number of trade, college, and professional titles published each year—W. W. Norton & Company stands as the largest and oldest publishing house owned wholly by its employees.

Editor: Peter Simon
Associate Editor: Gerra Goff
Project Editor: Christine D'Antonio
Manuscript Editor: Mike Fleming
Managing Editor, College: Marian Johnson
Managing Editor, College Digital Media: Kim Yi
Production Manager: Sean Mintus
Media Editor: Carly Fraser-Doria
Media Project Editor: Cooper Wilhelm
Assistant Media Editor: Ava Bramson
Editorial Assistant, Media: Joshua Bianchi
Marketing Manager, Literature: Kimberly Bowers
Art Direction: Rubina Yeh
Book Design: Jo Anne Metsch
Permissions Manager: Megan Schindel
Permissions Clearer: Margaret Gorenstein
Photo Editor: Catherine Abelman
Composition: Westchester Book Services
Manufacturing: Thomson Reuters

Permission to use copyrighted material is included in the backmatter of this book.

Library of Congress Cataloging-in-Publication Data

Names: Puchner, Martin, 1969- editor. | Akbari, Suzanne Conklin, editor. | Denecke, Wiebke, editor. | Fuchs, Barbara, 1970- editor. | Levine, Caroline, 1970- editor. | Lewis, Pericles, editor. | Wilson, Emily R., 1971- editor.
Title: The Norton anthology of world literature / Martin Puchner, general editor ; Suzanne Akbari, Wiebke Denecke, Barbara Fuchs, Caroline Levine, Pericles Lewis, Emily Wilson.
Description: Fourth edition. | New York : W. W. Norton & Company, [2018] | Includes bibliographical references and index.
Identifiers: LCCN 2017060699| ISBN 9780393602814 (pbk. : v. A) | ISBN 9780393602821 (pbk. : v. B) | ISBN 9780393602838 (pbk. : v. C) | ISBN 9780393602845 (pbk. : v. D) | ISBN 9780393602852 (pbk. : v. E) | ISBN 9780393602869 (pbk. : v. F)
Subjects: LCSH: Literature—Collections.
Classification: LCC PN6014 .N66 2018 | DDC 808.8—dc23 LC record available at https://lccn.loc.gov/2017060699

ISBN 978-0-393-60282-1 (pbk.)

W. W. Norton & Company, Inc., 500 Fifth Avenue, New York, NY 10110-0017
wwnorton.com
W. W. Norton & Company Ltd., 15 Carlisle Street, London W1D 3BS
    3   4   5   6   7   8   9   0

Contents

Preface

They arrive in boats, men exhausted from years of warfare and travel. As they approach the shore, their leader spots signs of habitation: flocks of goats and sheep, smoke rising from dwellings. A natural harbor permits them to anchor their boats so that they will be safe from storms. The leader takes an advance team with him to explore the island. It is rich in soil and vegetation, and natural springs flow with cool, clear water. With luck, they will be able to replenish their provisions and be on their way.

In the world of these men, welcoming travelers is a sacred custom, sanctioned by the gods themselves. It is also good policy among seafaring people. Someday, the roles may very well be reversed: today's host may be tomorrow's guest. Yet the travelers can never be certain whether a particular people will honor this custom. Wondering what to expect, the thirteen men enter one of the caves dotting the coastline.

The owner isn't home, but the men enter anyway, without any compunction. There are pens for sheep and goats, and there is plenty of cheese and milk, so the men begin eating. When the owner returns, they are terrified, but their leader, boldly, asks for gifts. The owner is not pleased. Instead of giving the intruders what they demand, he kills two of them and eats them for dinner. And then two more the next day. All the while, he keeps the men trapped in his cave.

A wily man, the leader devises a scheme to escape. He offers the owner wine, enough to make him drunk and sleepy. Once he dozes off, the men take a staff that they have secretly sharpened and they plunge it into the owner's eye, blinding him. Without sight, he cannot see the men clinging to the undersides of his prized sheep as they stroll, one by one, out of the cave to graze, and cleverly the men cling only to the male sheep, not the females, which get milked.

* * *

This story of hospitality gone wrong comes from *The Odyssey*, one of the best-known works in all of world literature. We learn of this strange encounter of Greek soldiers with the one-eyed Cyclops named Polyphemus from Odysseus, the protagonist of the epic, when he recounts his exploits at the court of another host, the king of the Phaeacians. Unsurprisingly, Polyphemus isn't presented in the best light. Odysseus describes the Cyclopes as a people without a "proper" community, without agriculture, without hospitality. Is Odysseus, who has been wined and dined by his current host, trying to curry favor with the king of the Phaeacians by telling him how terribly he was treated by these non-Greek others? Reading the passage closely, we can see that Polyphemus and the other Cyclopes are adroit makers of cheese, so they can't be all that lazy. When the blinded Polyphemus cries out for help, his associates come to help him as a matter of course, so they don't live quite as isolated from one another as Odysseus claims. Even though Odysseus asserts that Polyphemus is godless, the land is blessed by the gods with fertility, and Polyphemus's divine father comes to his aid when he prays. Odysseus says that the Cyclopes lack laws and custom, yet we are also shown the careful, regular, customary way that Polyphemus takes care of his household. In a touching scene toward the end of his encounter with Odysseus, after he is blinded, Polyphemus speaks gently and respectfully to his favorite ram, so he can't be all that monstrous. The one-eyed giants assist one another, they are shepherds and artisans, and they are capable of kindness. The passage's ambiguities suggest that perhaps it was partly Odysseus's fault that this encounter between cultures went so badly. Were he and his companions simply travelers badly in need of food, or were they looters hoping to enrich themselves? The passage suggests that it's a matter of narrative perspective, from whose point of view the story is told.

Scenes of hospitality (or the lack thereof) are everywhere in world literature, and questions about hospitality, about the courtesies that we owe to strangers and that strangers owe to us (whether we are guests or hosts), are as important today as they were in the ancient world. Although many writers and thinkers today are fond of saying that our era is the first "truly global" one, stories such as this episode from Homer's *Odyssey* remind us that travel, trade, exile, migration, and cultural encounters of all kinds have been features of human experience for thousands of years.

The experience of reading world literature, too, is a form of travel—a mode of cultural encounter that presents us with languages, cultural norms, customs, and ideas that may be unfamiliar to us, even strange. As readers, each time we begin to read a new work, we put ourselves in the role of a traveler in a foreign land, trying to understand its practices and values and hoping to feel, to some degree and in some way, connected to and welcome among the people we meet there. *The Epic of Gilgamesh*, for example, takes its readers on a tour of Uruk, the first large city in human history, in today's Iraq, boasting of its city walls, its buildings and temples with their stairways and foundations, all made of clay bricks. Like a tour guide, the text even lets its readers inspect the city's clay pits, over one square mile large, that provided the material for this miraculous city made from clay. The greatest marvel of them all is of course *The Epic of Gilgamesh* itself, which was inscribed on clay tablets—the first monument of literature.

Foundational Texts

From its beginnings, *The Norton Anthology of World Literature* has been committed to offering students and teachers as many complete or substantially represented texts as possible. This Fourth Edition emphasizes the importance of *foundational* texts as never before by offering new translations of some of the best-known and most-loved works in the history of world literature. *The Epic of Gilgamesh* stands first in line of these foundational texts, which capture the story of an entire people, telling them where they came from and who they are. Some foundational texts become an object of worship and are deemed sacred, while others are revered as the most consequential story of an entire civilization. Because foundational texts inspire countless retellings—as Homer did for the Greek tragedians—these texts are reference points for the entire subsequent history of literature.

Perhaps no text is more foundational than the one with which we opened this preface: Homer's *Odyssey*. In this Fourth Edition, we feature *The Odyssey* in a new translation by our classics editor, Emily Wilson. This version captures the fast pace and rhythmic regularity of the original and offers a fresh perspective on cultural encounters such as the one between Odysseus and Polyphemus that is described above. Astonishingly, Wilson's translation is the first translation of *The Odyssey* into English by a woman. For centuries, commentators have remarked that *The Odyssey* is unusually attuned to the lives of women, especially in its portrait of Odysseus's wife, Penelope, a compelling and powerful character who cunningly holds a rowdy group of suitors at bay. Wilson's translation pays special attention to the poem's characterization of this remarkable woman, who is every bit as intriguing as the "complicated man" who is the eponymous hero of the tale. Other female characters, too, are given a new voice in this translation. For example, Helen, wife of the Greek king Menelaus and (according to legend) possessor of "the face that launched a thousand ships," is revealed through Wilson's translation to speak of herself not as a "whore" for whose sake so many young Greek men fought, suffered, and died (as she does in most other translations) but instead as a perceptive, clever person, onto whom the Greeks, already eager to fight the Trojans, projected their own aggressive impulses: "They made my face the cause that hounded them," she says. The central conflicts of the epic, the very origin of the Trojan War, appear here in a startling new light.

We are also delighted to feature a new translation of the great Indian epic *The Mahabharata* by Carole Satyamurti, whose modern retelling captures the careful, patterned language of the original by rendering it in a fluent blank verse, a form familiar in English literature from Shakespeare to Wordsworth and also used in Wilson's *Odyssey*, a form particularly suitable to narrative. Readers used to older prose versions will find that the quest for honor and fame at the heart of this epic comes across as never before.

These two examples highlight an exciting dimension of our emphasis on new translations. The first several volumes of this anthology have always been dominated by male voices because men enjoyed privileged access to literacy and cultural influence in the centuries prior to modernity. Our focus on new translations has allowed us to introduce into these volumes many female voices—the voices of translators. So, for example, we present Homer's *Iliad* in a new translation by Caroline Alexander, Sophocles' *Antigone* in a recent translation by Ruby Blondell, and Euripides' *Medea* in a new, specially commissioned translation by Sheila H. Murnaghan, and we continue to offer work in the first volumes translated by female translators such as Laura Gibbs (Aesop's *Fables*), Dorothy Gilbert (Marie de France's *Lais*), Sholeh Wolpé (*The Conference of the Birds*), Wendy Belcher (*Kebra Nagast*), Sheila Fisher (Chaucer's *Canterbury Tales*), Rosalind Brown-Grant (Christine de Pizan's *Book of the City of Ladies*), and Pauline Yu (Wang Wei's poetry), among others. This commitment to featuring the work of female translators extends beyond these early centuries as well, for example in the brilliant new translation by Susan Bernofsky of a foundational text of literary modernity—Kafka's *Metamorphosis*. The result throughout the anthology is that these works now speak to today's readers in new and sometimes surprising ways.

Our emphasis in this edition on new translations is based on and amplifies the conviction expressed by the original editors of this anthology over fifty years ago: that world literature gains its power when it travels from its place of origin and speaks to people in different places. While purists sometimes insist on studying literature only in the original language, a dogma that radically shrinks what one can read, world literature not only relies on translation but actually thrives on it. Translation is a necessity; it is what enables a worldwide circulation of literature. It also is an art. One need only think of the way in which translations of the Bible shaped the history of Latin or English or German. Translations are re-creations of works for new readers. This edition pays keen attention to translation, featuring dozens of new translations that make classic texts newly readable and capture the originals in compelling ways. With each choice of translation, we have sought a version that would spark a sense of wonder while still being accessible to a contemporary reader.

Among other foundational texts presented in new translations and selections is the Qur'an, in a verse translation that is the product of a collaboration between M. A. Rafey Habib, a poet, literary scholar, and Muslim, and Bruce Lawrence, a renowned scholar of Islam. Their team effort captures some of the beauty of this extraordinary, and extraordinarily influential, sacred text. Augustine's *Confessions* are newly presented in a version by Peter Constantine, and Dante's *Inferno* is featured in the long-respected and highly readable translation by the American poet John Ciardi.

We have also maintained our commitment to exciting epics that deserve wider recognition such as the Maya *Popol Vuh*, the East African *Kebra Nagast*, and the *Sunjata*, which commemorates the founding of a West African empire in the late Middle Ages. Like *The Odyssey* and *The Mahabharata*, *Sunjata* was transmitted for centuries in purely oral form. But while *The Odyssey* was written down around 800 B.C.E. and *The Mahabharata* several hundred years later, the *Sunjata* was written down only in the twentieth century. We feature it here in a new prose translation by David C. Conrad, who personally recorded this version from a Mande storyteller, Djanka Tassey Condé, in 1994. In this way, *Sunjata* speaks to the continuing importance of oral storytelling, the origin of all foundational epics, from South Asia via Greece and Africa to Central America. Throughout the anthology, we remind readers that writing has coexisted with oral storytelling since the invention of literature and that it will continue to do so in the future.

A Network of Stories

In addition to foundational texts, we include in this edition a great number of story collections. The origins of this form of literature reach deep into the ancient world, as scribes collected oral stories and assembled them in larger works. We've substantially increased our offerings from what is undoubtedly the most famous of these collections, *The Thousand and One Nights*, to give readers a better sense of the intricate structure of this work, with its stories within stories within stories, all neatly framed by the overarching narrative of Shahrazad, who is telling them to her sister and the king to avoid being put to death. What is most notable about these story collections is how interconnected they are. Stories travel with striking ease from one collection to the next, appearing in *The Jataka*, one of the oldest Indian story collections framed by the

Buddha, and the *Pañcatantra*, an Indian collection put together for the education of princes, to *The Thousand and One Nights*, and, in Greece, Aesop's *Fables*. There existed a continent-spanning network of stories that allowed storytellers and scribes to recycle and reframe what they learned in ever new ways; it proved so compelling that later writers, from Marie de France to Chaucer, borrowed from it frequently. To give readers a sense of these connections, we have rethought our selection of stories by including those that appear in different collections, allowing readers to track the changes that occur when a story is told by the Buddha, by Shahrazad, or on a pilgrimage to Canterbury Cathedral.

Expanded Selections

Along with our focus on making foundational texts and story collections fresh and accessible, we have pruned the overall number of authors and were therefore able to increase our offerings from major texts that feature in many world literature courses. *Don Quixote* now includes the compelling "Captive's Tale," in which Cervantes draws on his own experiences as a slave in Algiers, where he spent five years after having been captured by pirates. Sor Juana Inés de la Cruz, whose significance is steadily increasing, is now represented by an additional selection from her mystery play, *The Divine Narcissus*, in Edith Grossman's elegant translation. Other major texts with increased selections include Machiavelli's *Prince* and, in the twentieth century, Lu Xun, who now can be introduced to students as the author not only of *Diary of a Madman* but also of *Ah Q—The Real Story*.

Despite this focus on foundational texts, story collections, and other major works, there are plenty of entirely new texts in this Fourth Edition. The Spanish Renaissance tale *The Abencerraje* tells of a Moorish knight who is taken prisoner by a Christian on his wedding day. Ultimately his captor relents and allows the knight to marry his beloved. This enormously popular tale speaks of the complex relations between Christianity and Islam in the early modern era and is featured here in a new translation by our Renaissance editor, Barbara Fuchs. Equally exciting is our representation of Korean literature. *The Tale of Hong Kiltong*, a story of a Korean Robin Hood endowed with magical powers, is a classic that we paired with excerpts from Lady Hyegyŏng's memoirs, which chronicle with deep psychological insight the horror and violence at the Korean royal court. These older Korean texts are complemented by a modern writer, Park Wansuh, whose work reflects the upheavals of the twentieth century on the Korean peninsula, from Japanese occupation and the Korean War to economic development. One of the first women to achieve critical success in modern Korea, Park offers readers keen insight into Korea's modern struggles.

We are particularly excited to now close the anthology with a story by the Nigerian writer Chimamanda Ngozi Adichie called "The Headstrong Historian," which, since its publication in 2008, has already become a favorite in world literature classrooms. This compact work introduces us to three generations of Nigerians as they navigate a complicated series of personal and cultural displacements. A thought-provoking exploration of the complex results of cultural contact and influence, this probing, searching journey seemed to us the most fitting conclusion to the anthology's survey of 4,000 years of literature.

Cultural Contact

Odysseus's encounter with the Cyclopes speaks not only to hospitality but also to the theme of cultural contact more generally. The earliest civilizations—those that invented writing and hence literature—sprang up where they did because they were located along strategic trading and migration routes. Contact was not just something that happened between fully formed cultures but something that made these cultures possible in the first place.

Committed to presenting the anthology's riches in a way that conveys this central fact of world literature, we have created sections that encompass broad contact zones—areas of intense trade in peoples, goods, art, and ideas where the earliest literatures emerged and intermingled. One of these is the Mediterranean Sea, whose central importance we visualize with four new maps. It was not just a hostile environment that could derail a journey home, as it did for Odysseus, or where nontravelers, like Polyphemus, might encounter violent invaders willing to attack and steal; it was also a connecting tissue, allowing for intense contact around its harbors. Medieval maps of the Mediterranean pay tribute to this fact: so-called portolan charts show a veritable mesh of lines connecting hundreds of ports. For this edition, we have further emphasized these contact zones, the location of intense conflict (including Cervantes's experience as a slave in North Africa) as well as friendly exchange. In a similar manner, the two major traditions of East Asia—China and Japan—are presented in the context of the larger region, including our new emphasis on Korea.

The importance of cultural contact and encounter is expressed not just in the overall organization of the anthology and the selection of material; it is also made visible in clusters of texts on the theme of travel and conquest, giving students access to documents related to travel, contact, trade, and conflict. For not all travel was voluntary. People traveled to escape wars and famine, plagues and environmental disasters. They were abducted, enslaved, and trafficked. Beginning with the early modern era, European empires dominated global politics and economics and accelerated the pace of globalization by laying down worldwide trade routes and communication networks, but old empires, such as China, continued to be influential as well. We added more material to our cluster "At the Crossroads of Empire," including a letter by Machemba, a chief in East Africa under German colonial control, and Mark Twain's trenchant soliloquy of Belgian King Leopold defending his brutal rule in Congo.

To these expanded clusters, we added a new one, "Poetry and Politics," which includes the Polish national poet Adam Mickiewicz and Latin American poet Rubén Darío's *To Roosevelt*, a powerful reminder of the crucial role poetry played in the gaining of national independence across the world. Poets captured the aspirations of nations and often enshrined those aspirations in national anthems, which also led us to include the Puerto Rican national anthem (one poet included in our anthology, Rabindranath Tagore, wrote not one but two national anthems, of both India and Bangladesh).

In the same volume, we also enhanced our cluster "Realism across the Globe," which traces one of the most successful global literary movements, one that found expression in France, Britain, Russia, Brazil, Mexico, and Japan. In keeping with our commitment to frequently taught authors, we increased our selection of Chekhov and present Tolstoy's *Death of Ivan Ilyich* in a new, acclaimed translation by Peter Carson.

The Birth of World Literature

In 1827, a provincial German writer, living in small-town Weimar, recognized that he was in the privileged position of having access not only to European literature but also to literature from much further afield, including Persian poetry, Chinese novels, and Sanskrit drama. The writer was Johann Wolfgang von Goethe, and in 1827, he coined a term to capture this new force of globalization in literature: "world literature." (We now include the "prologue" to Goethe's play *Faust*, which he wrote after encountering a similar prologue in the classical Sanskrit play *Śhakuntalā*, also included in the anthology.)

Since 1827, for less than 200 years, we have been living in an era of world literature. This era has brought many lost masterpieces back to life, including *The Epic of Gilgamesh*, which was rediscovered in the nineteenth century, and the *Popol Vuh*, which languished in a library until well into the twentieth century. Other works of world literature weren't translated and therefore didn't begin to circulate outside their sphere of origin until the last 200 years, including *The Tale of Genji*. With more literature becoming more widely available than ever before, Goethe's vision of world literature has become a reality today.

In presenting world literature from the dawn of writing to the early twenty-first century, and from oral storytelling to literary experiments of the avant-garde, this anthology raises the question not only of what world literature is but also of the nature of literature itself. We call attention to the changing nature of literature with thematic clusters on literature in the early volumes, to give students and teachers access to how early writers from different cultures thought about literature. But the changing role and nature of literature are visible in the anthology as a whole. Greek tragedy and comedy are experienced by modern students as literary genres, encountered in written texts; but for the ancient Athenians, they were primarily dramas, experienced live in an outdoor theater in the context of a religious and civic ritual. Other texts, such as the Qur'an or the Bible, are sacred pieces of writing, central to many people's religious faith, while others appreciate them primarily or exclusively as literature. Some texts, such as those by Laozi or Plato or Kant, belong in philosophy, while others, such as the Declaration of Independence, are primarily political documents. Our modern conception of literature as imaginative literature, as fiction, is very recent, about 200 years old. We have therefore opted for a much-expanded conception of literature that includes creation myths, wisdom literature, religious texts, philosophy, political writing, and fairy tales in addition to poems, plays, and narrative fiction. This answers to an older definition of literature as writing of high quality or of great cultural significance. There are many texts of philosophy or religion or politics that are not remarkable or influential for their literary qualities and that would therefore have no place in an anthology of world literature. But the works presented here do: in addition to or as part of their other functions, they have acquired the status of literature.

This brings us to the last and perhaps most important question: When we study the world, why study it through its literature? Hasn't literature lost some of its luster for us, we who are faced with so many competing media and art forms? Like no other art form or medium, literature offers us a deep history of human thinking. As our illustration program shows, writing was invented not for the composition of literature but for much more mundane purposes, such as the recording of ownership, contracts, or astronomical observations. But literature is writing's most glorious by-product. Literature can be reactivated with each reading. Many of the great architectural monuments of the past are now in ruins. Literature, too, often has to be excavated, as with many classical texts. But once a text has been found or reconstructed it can be experienced as if for the first time by new readers. Even though many of the literary texts collected in this anthology are at first strange, because they originated so very long ago, they still speak to today's readers with great eloquence and freshness. No other art form can capture the human past with the precision and scope of literature because language expresses human consciousness. Language shapes our thinking, and literature, the highest expression of language, plays an important role in that process, pushing the boundaries of what we can think and how we think it. This is especially true with great, complex, and contradictory works that allow us to explore different narrative perspectives, different points of view.

Works of world literature continue to elicit strong emotions and investments. The epic *Rāmāyana*, for example, plays an important role in the politics of India, where it has been used to bolster Hindu nationalism, just as the *Bhagavad-Gītā* continues to be a moral touchstone in the ethical deliberation about war. The so-called religions of the book, Judaism, Christianity, and Islam, make our selections from their scriptures a more than historical exercise as well. China has recently elevated the sayings of Confucius, whose influence on Chinese attitudes about the state had waned in the twentieth century, creating Confucius Institutes all over the world to promote Chinese culture in what is now called New Confucianism. World literature is never neutral. We know its relevance precisely by the controversies it inspires.

There are many ways of studying other cultures and of understanding the place of our own culture in the world. Archaeologists can show us objects and buildings from the past and speculate, through material remains, how people in the past ate, fought, lived, died, and were buried; scientists can date layers of soil. Literature is capable of something much more extraordinary: it allows us a glimpse into the imaginative lives, the thoughts and feelings of humans from thousands of years ago or living halfway around the world. This is the true magic of world literature as captured in this anthology, our shared human inheritance.

New Selections and Translations

Following is a list of the new translations, selections, and works in the Fourth Edition, in order:

VOLUME A

A new translation of Homer's *The Iliad* by Caroline Alexander • A new translation of Homer's *The Odyssey* by Emily Wilson, complete • Six new Aesop's *Fables*: "The Onager, the Donkey and the Driver," "The Eagle and the Farmer," "The Dung Beetle and the Eagle," "The Fox, the Donkey, and the Lion Skin," "Aesop and His Lamp," and "The Lion, the Fox, and the Deer" • New translations of Sappho's poetry by Philip Freeman, including ten new poems • New translations of *Oedipus the King* by David Grene, *Antigone* by Ruby Blondell, *Medea* by Sheila H. Murnaghan, and *Lysistrata* by Jeffrey Henderson • Benjamin Jowett's translation of *Symposium*, new to this edition • New translations of Catullus's poetry by Charles Martin • A new selection from *The Aeneid* from "The Kingdom of the Dead" • A new translation of *The Mahabharata* by Carole Satyamurti, including new selections from "The Book of Drona" and "Books 17 and 18: The Books of the Final Journey and the Ascent to Heaven" • New selections from *Zhuangzi* from "The Way of Heaven," "Outer Things," and "Of Swords"

VOLUME B

A new translation of Augustine's *Confessions* by Peter Constantine with a new selection from "Book XI [Time]" • A new translation of the Qur'an by M. A. Rafey Habib and Bruce Lawrence with new selections from "Light," "Ya Sin," and "The Sun" • A new translation of Marie de France's *Lais* by Dorothy Gilbert, including the new selection "Bisclavret" • A selection from *Vis and Ramin* translated by Dick Davis • A new translation of *The Conference of the Birds* by Sholeh Wolpé • A new translation and selection of Rumi's poetry, including six new poems: "[The nights I spend with you]," "[Like blood beneath my skin]," "[Profession, profit, trade]," "[A rose is still a rose]," "[How marvelous, that moment]," and "[On death's day]," as well as selections from *The Masnavi* translated by Dick Davis: "[On the Prohibition of Wine]," "[This World as a Dream]," "[On Men's Behavior with Women]," "[Man's Life Compared to That of an Embryo in the Womb]," and "[Moses and the Shepherd]" • John Ciardi's translation of *The Divine Comedy*, newly included, supplemented by two additional translations from Canto 3 of *Inferno* by Clive James and Mark Musa • A new translation of *Kebra Nagast* by Wendy Belcher and Michael Kleiner, including a new chapter, "About How King Solomon Swore an Oath to the Queen" • Seven new tales from *The Thousand and One Nights*: "[The Story of the Porter and the Three Ladies]," "[The First Dervish's Tale]," "[The Second Dervish's Tale]," "[The Tale of the Envious and the Envied]," "[The Third Dervish's Tale]," "[The Tale of the First Lady]," and "[The Tale of the Second Lady]" • "The Nun's Priest's Tale" from *The Canterbury Tales* • Three new tales from the *Pañcatantra*: "The Bird with Golden Dung" and "The Ass in the Tiger Skin" translated by Arthur W. Ryder and "The Ass without Ears or a Heart" translated by Patrick Olivelle • New selections from *The Tale of Genji*: "Sakaki: A Branch of Sacred Evergreens," "Maboroshi: Spirit Summoner," "Hashihime: The Divine Princess at Uji Bridge," "Agemaki: A Bowknot Tied in Maiden's Loops," "Yadoriki: Trees Encoiled in Vines of Ivy," and "Tenarai: Practicing Calligraphy"

VOLUME C

A new prose translation of *Sunjata: A West African Epic of the Mande* by David C. Conrad • New selections from *The Prince*: "[Liberality and Parsimony]," "[Love and Fear]," "[Dissimulation]," "[Contempt and Hatred]," "[Princely Devices; Fortresses]," "[The Excellent Prince]," "[Flatterers]," and "[The Princes of Italy]" • "The Abencerraje" translated by Barbara Fuchs, Larissa Brewer-García, and Aaron J. Ilika • A new selection from *Don Quixote*, "[A Story of Captivity in North Africa, Told to Don Quixote at the Inn]" • A revised *Fuenteovejuna* translated by G. J. Racz

VOLUME D

A new translation of "What Is Enlightenment?" by Mary C. Smith • A new translation of Sor Juana Inés de la Cruz's work translated by Edith Grossman, including three new sonnets, "[O World, why do you wish to persecute me?]," "[I adore Lisi but do not pretend]," and "[Because you have died, Laura, let affections]," as well as *Loa* to the Mystery Play *The Divine Narcissus: An Allegory* translated by Edith Grossman • Hŏ Kyun's "The Tale of Hong Kiltong" translated by Marshall R. Pihl • A selection from Lady Hyegyŏng's *The Memoirs of Lady Hyegyŏng* translated by JaHyun Kim Haboush

VOLUME E

A new selection from *Faust*, "Prelude in the Theatre" • Machemba's "Letter to Major von Wissmann" translated by Robert Sullivan and Sarah Lawall • A selection from Mark Twain's "King Leopold's Soliloquy" • A new cluster, "Poetry and Politics," including four new works, Adam Mickiewicz's "The Prisoner's Return" translated by Jerzy Peterkiewicz and Burns Singer, Speranza's (Lady Jane Wilde's) "A Lament for the Potato" and "The Exodus," and Lola Rodríguez de Tió's "The Song of the Borinquen" translated by José Nieto, as well as the new translation of "Guantanamera" by Elinor Randall • A new translation of *The Death of Ivan Ilyich* by Peter Carson • A new translation of "The Cane" by Margaret Jull Costa • José López Portillo y Rojas's "Unclaimed Watch" translated by Roberta H. Kimble • Anton Chekhov's "The Lady with the Dog" translated by Ivy Litvinov

VOLUME F

A new translation of *The Metamorphosis* by Susan Bernofsky • Lu Xun's "Ah Q—The Real Story" translated by William A. Lyell • Eric Bentley's translation, new to this edition, of Pirandello's *Six Characters in Search of an Author* • A new translation of "The Dancing Girl of Izu" by J. Martin Homan • Jorge Luis Borges's "The Library of Babel" translated by James E. Irby • M. D. Herder Norton's translations of Rainer Maria Rilke's poems, newly included • A new translation of "Lament for Ignacio Sánchez Mejías" by Pablo Medina • A new translation of "Matryona's Home" by Michael Glenny • Derek Walcott's "Sea Grapes" • Park Wansuh's "Mother's Hitching Post, Part 2" • Yu Hua's "On the Road at Eighteen" • Chimamanda Ngozi Adichie's "The Headstrong Historian"

Resources for Students and Instructors

Norton is pleased to provide students and instructors with abundant resources to make the teaching and study of world literature an even more interesting and rewarding experience.

We are pleased to launch the new *Norton Anthology of World Literature* website, found at digital.wwnorton.com/worldlit4pre1650 (for volumes A, B, C) and digital.wwnorton.com/worldlit4post1650 (for volumes D, E, F). This searchable and sortable site contains thousands of resources for students and instructors in one centralized place at no additional cost. Following are some highlights:

- A series of eight brand-new video modules are designed to enhance classroom presentation and spark student interest in the anthology's works. These videos, conceived of and narrated by the anthology editors, ask students to consider why it is important for them to read and engage with this literature.
- Hundreds of images—maps, author portraits, literary places, and manuscripts—are available for student browsing or instructor download for in-class presentation.
- Several hours of audio recordings are available, including a 10,000-term audio glossary that helps students pronounce the character and place names in the anthologized works.

The site also provides a wealth of teaching resources that are unlocked with an instructor's log-in:

- "Quick read" summaries, teaching notes, discussion questions, and suggested resources for every work in the anthology, from the much-praised *Teaching with* The Norton Anthology of World Literature: *A Guide for Instructors*
- Downloadable Lecture PowerPoints featuring images, quotations from the texts, and lecture notes in the notes view for in-class presentation

In addition to the wealth of resources in *The Norton Anthology of World Literature* website, Norton offers a downloadable Coursepack that allows instructors to easily add high-quality Norton digital media to online, hybrid, or lecture courses—all at no cost. Norton Coursepacks work within existing learning management systems; there's no new system to learn, and access is free and easy. Content is customizable and includes over seventy reading-comprehension quizzes, short-answer questions, links to the videos, and more.

Acknowledgments

The editors would like to thank the following people, who have provided invaluable assistance by giving us sage advice, important encouragement, and help with the preparation of the manuscript: Sara Akbari, Alannah de Barra, Wendy Belcher, Jodi Bilinkoff, Daniel Boucher, Freya Brackett, Psyche Brackett, Michaela Bronstein, Rachel Carroll, Sookja Cho, Kyeong-Hee Choi, Amanda Claybaugh, Lewis Cook, David Damrosch, Dick Davis, Burghild Denecke, Amanda Detry, Anthony Domestico, Megan Eckerle, Marion Eggert, Merve Emre, Maria Fackler, Guillermina de Ferrari, Alyssa Findley, Karina Galperín, Stanton B. Garner, Kimberly Dara Gordon, Elyse Graham, Stephen Greenblatt, Sara Guyer, Langdon Hammer, Emily Hayman, Iain Higgins, Paulo Lemos Horta, Mohja Kahf, Peter Kornicki, Paul W. Kroll, Peter H. Lee, Sung-il Lee, Lydia Liu, Bala Venkat Mani, Ann Matter, Barry McCrea, Alexandra McCullough-Garcia, Rachel McGuiness, Jon McKenzie, Mary Mullen, Djibril Tamsir Niane, Johann Noh, Felicity Nussbaum, Andy Orchard, John Peters, Michael Pettid, Daniel Taro Poch, Daniel Potts, Megan Quigley, Payton Phillips Quintanilla, Catherine de Rose, Imogen Roth, Katherine Rupp, Ellen Sapega, Jesse Schotter, Stephen Scully, Kyung-ho Sim, Sarah Star, Brian Stock, Tomi Suzuki, Joshua Taft, Sara Torres, J. Keith Vincent, Lisa Voigt, Kristen Wanner, Emily Weissbourd, Karoline Xu, Yoon Sun Yang, and Catherine Vance Yeh.

All the editors would like to thank the wonderful people at Norton, principally our editor Pete Simon, the driving force behind this whole undertaking, as well as Marian Johnson (Managing Editor, College), Christine D'Antonio and Kurt Wildermuth (Project Editors), Michael Fleming (Copyeditor), Gerra Goff (Associate Editor), Megan Jackson (College Permissions Manager), Margaret Gorenstein (Permissions), Catherine Abelman (Photo Editor), Debra Morton Hoyt (Art Director; cover design), Rubina Yeh (Design Director), Jo Anne Metsch (Designer; interior text design), Adrian Kitzinger (cartography), Agnieszka Gasparska (timeline design), Carly Fraser-Doria (Media Editor), Ava Bramson (Assistant Editor, Media), Sean Mintus (Production Manager), and Kim Bowers (Marketing Manager, Literature). We'd also like to thank our Instructor's Guide authors: Colleen Clemens (Kutztown University), Elizabeth Watkins (Loyola University New Orleans), and Janet Zong (Harvard University).

This anthology represents a collaboration not only among the editors and their close advisers but also among the thousands of instructors who teach from the anthology and provide valuable and constructive guidance to the publisher and editors. *The Norton Anthology of World Literature* is as much their book as it is ours, and we are grateful to everyone who has cared enough about this anthology to help make it better. We're especially grateful to the professors of world literature who responded to an online survey in 2014, whom we have listed below. Thank you all.

Michelle Abbott (Georgia Highlands College), Elizabeth Ashworth (Castleton State College), Clinton Atchley (Henderson State University), Amber Barnes (Trinity Valley Community College), Rosemary Baxter (Clarendon College), Khani Begum (Bowling Green State University), Joyce Boss (Wartburg College), Floyd Brigdon (Trinity Valley

Community College), James Bryant-Trerise (Clackamas Community College), Barbara Cade (Texas College), Kellie Cannon (Coastal Carolina Community College), Amee Carmines (Hampton University), Farrah Cato (University of Central Florida), Brandon Chitwood (Marquette University), Paul Cohen (Texas State University), Judith Cortelloni (Lincoln College), Randall Crump (Kennesaw State University), Sunni Davis (Cossatot Community College), Michael Demson (Sam Houston State University), Richard Diguette (Georgia Perimeter College, Dunwoody), Daniel Dooghan (University of Tampa), Jeff Doty (West Texas A&M University), Myrto Drizou (Valdosta State University), Ashley Dugas (Copiah-Lincoln Community College), Richmond Eustis (Nicholls State University), David Fell (Carroll Community College), Allison Fetters (Chattanooga State Community College), Francis Fletcher (Folsom Lake College), Kathleen D. Fowler (Surry Community College), Louisa Franklin (Young Harris College), James Gamble (University of Arkansas), Antoinette Gazda (Averett University), Adam Golaski (Central Connecticut State University), Anissa Graham (University of North Alabama), Eric Gray (St. Gregory's University), Jared Griffin (Kodiak College), Marne Griffin (Hilbert College), Frank Gruber (Bergen Community College), Laura Hammons (Hinds Community College), Nancy G. Hancock (Austin Peay State University), C. E. Harding (Western Oregon University), Leslie Harrelson (Dalton State College), Eleanor J. Harrington-Austin (North Carolina Central University), Matthew Hokom (Fairmont State University), Scott Hollifield (University of Nevada, Las Vegas), Catherine Howard (University of Houston, Downtown), Jack Kelnhofer (Ocean County College), Katherine King (University of California, Los Angeles), Pam Kingsbury (University of North Alabama), Sophia Kowalski (Hillsborough Community College), Roger Ladd (University of North Carolina at Pembroke), Jameela Lares (University of Southern Mississippi), Susan Lewis (Delaware Technical Community College), Christina Lovin (Eastern Kentucky University), Richard Mace (Pace University), Nicholas R. Marino (Borough of Manhattan Community College, CUNY), Brandi Martinez (Mountain Empire Community College), Kathy Martinez (Sandhills Community College), Matthew Masucci (State College of Florida), Kelli McBride (Seminole State College), Melissa McCoy (Clarendon College), Geoffrey McNeil (Notre Dame de Namur University), Renee Moore (Mississippi Delta Community College), Anna C. Oldfield (Coastal Carolina University), Keri Overall (Texas Woman's University), Maggie Piccolo (Rutgers University), Oana Popescu-Sandu (University of Southern Indiana), Jonathan Purkiss (Pulaski Technical College), Rocio Quispe-Agnoli (Michigan State University), Evan Radcliffe (Villanova University), Ken Raines (Eastern Arizona College), Jonathan Randle (Mississippi College), Kirk G. Rasmussen (Utah Valley University), Helaine Razovsky (Northwestern State University of Louisiana), Karin Rhodes (Salem State University), Stephanie Roberts (Georgia Military College), Allen Salerno (Auburn University), Shannin Schroeder (Southern Arkansas University), Heather Seratt (University of Houston, Downtown), Conrad Shumaker (University of Central Arkansas), Edward Soloff (St. John's University), Eric Sterling (Auburn University Montgomery), Ron Stormer (Culver-Stockton College), Marianne Szlyk (Montgomery College), Tim Tarkington (Georgia Perimeter College), Allison Tharp (University of Southern Mississippi), Diane Thompson (Northern Virginia Community College), Sevinc Turkkan (College at Brockport, State University of New York), Verne Underwood (Rogue Community College), Patricia Vazquez (College of Southern Nevada), William Wallis (Los Angeles Valley College), Eric Weil (Elizabeth City State University), Denise C. White (Kennesaw State University), Tamora Whitney (Creighton University), Todd Williams (Kutztown University of Pennsylvania), Bertha Wise (Oklahoma City Community College), and Lindsey Zanchettin (Auburn University).

THE NORTON ANTHOLOGY OF

WORLD

LITERATURE

FOURTH EDITION

VOLUME B

I

Circling the Mediterranean: Europe and the Islamic World

The word "Mediterranean" comes from Latin, meaning "in the middle of the lands." From antiquity through the Middle Ages, the centrally located Mediterranean Sea—also called by those who lived along its shores *Mare nostrum,* or "our sea"—facilitated trade and exchange. Not only commodities but also stories and songs continually circulated from place to place, crisscrossing the water to link nations in Europe, North Africa, and the Near and Middle East. Port cities all around the Mediterranean were sites of particularly intense cultural and economic interaction, collectively making up a single complex web that knit together distant lands.

While earlier generations of historians have tended to see the diverse cultures of the Mediterranean region in monolithic terms, conceiving of an Islamic world and a Christian world that were fundamentally opposed, more recent research has unearthed the intimate links between the various cultures of the region. There was both a great deal of interaction *between* the cultural spheres conventionally marked as "Europe" and "the Islamic world" and, on the other hand, a great deal of diversity *within* each one of these apparently undifferentiated units. "Europe," as a multinational concept, almost never appeared during the Middle

A fourteenth-century image of the Venetian trader Marco Polo, embarking from Venice.

3

Ages; people referred to themselves as "English," "Franks," "Normans," and "Lombards," not as "Europeans." "The Islamic world" was similarly divided by rival efforts to lead the Muslim community in the caliphates of Damascus, Baghdad, and Cairo, as well as by the Mongol invasions of the thirteenth century. The opposition of "the Islamic world" and "Europe" is a modern invention: it was not the way medieval people described themselves or the world they lived in.

The false division between Europe and the Islamic world enabled a misleading view of history in which Christian Europe was seen as the sole heir to a rich legacy of Greco-Roman philosophy and literature, uncontaminated by Arabic or Persian influences—an unin-terrupted cultural bloodline, so to speak, reaching back from Aquinas to **Aristotle**, from **Dante** to **Virgil**. Nothing could be further from the truth. The Arabic translations of ancient Greek philosophy and science that made the work of **Plato**, Aristotle, and Ptolemy available to Europeans as they slowly emerged from a long period of intellectual dormancy were not just passive vessels that transmitted ancient knowledge to an awakening Europe on the cusp of the Renaissance: on the contrary, the cultural ferment of the Islamic world was an essential element in the emergence of the early modern West. The story of premodern history and literature is, therefore, above all a story of connections, interaction, and mutual influence.

This image, from an illuminated thirteenth-century Arabic manuscript, depicts the Greek philosopher Socrates discoursing with his students.

CHRISTIANITY AND PLATONISM

By the year 100, broad changes were under way in the lands circling the Mediterranean Sea. The Roman Empire, which had reached its pinnacle of cultural and military supremacy during the reign of Augustus Caesar, had expanded to the point that unrest in the eastern provinces was a perpetual worry. In the Roman-ruled province of Judea (roughly, modern Israel), the suppression by the civil authorities of a loosely organized rebellion culminated in the destruction of Jerusalem and scattering (or "diaspora") of the Jewish community in 70 C.E. Those exiled from the region included the Jewish followers of James and John who had embraced the message of the gospel, as well as those mixed Jewish and Gentile communities that took up the intensely hellenized brand of Christianity developed by Paul and his followers, which drew on the philosophy of Plato as well as of mystical Neoplatonists such as Plotinus and Porphyry. Not until about three centuries later would this heterogeneous collection of new religious orientations become codified as a single Christian doctrine, encapsulated in Jerome's production of the Latin (or "Vulgate") **Bible** and in **Augustine**'s masterful synthesis of Christian doctrine and Greek philosophy.

Augustine's autobiography, the **Confessions**, pays tribute to the theologian's engagement with the philosophy and literature of the Roman world: he paraphrases Seneca and Cicero, and movingly describes the tears he shed while reading Virgil's account of Dido in the **Aeneid**. These moments illustrate the imaginative pull of classical literature, which persisted during the period of Christianity's emergence. The values of Rome, its celebration of the arts and worldly pleasures, were very much at odds with a Christian ethic that demanded a rejection of the things of this world. Music, art, and poetry were to be avoided, unless they were explicitly in the service of God: liturgical music, as part of the act of communal worship, along with painted images of the crucified Christ, the Virgin Mary, and apostles, became increasingly important in early Christianity, while the classical principles of poetic composition were applied to new types of writing such as religious hymns and saints' lives. Writers found that poetry could be made to serve Christ, in the same way that figurative parables could disseminate the eternal truths of scripture. Jesus had told illustrative anecdotes, such as the parable of the Sower or the parable of the Wise and Foolish Virgins: preachers therefore believed that they too were authorized to use fictions, as long as the effort was wholly in the service of the Lord and not intended to seduce the soul with bodily pleasures.

The yearning for a mystical faith that would provide a sense of purpose was ubiquitous in the late Roman Empire, as can be seen, for example, in the devotion to the cult of Isis described so vividly by **Apuleius**. Christianity was just one of a number of religious cults that had fashioned a kind of cultural compromise with the philosophical orientation of the period; but it thrived as no other religion did, ultimately becoming the state religion of the Roman Empire under the rule of Constantine in the fourth century. While the Italian city of Rome remained the seat of imperial power in the West, the capital city of Byzantium (modern Istanbul, in Turkey) represented Rome in the East. Renamed "Constantinople" (Constantine's city) by the Christian emperor of Rome, the city would be simply known as "al-Rum" (Rome) to speakers of Arabic and Persian. An empire stretched so widely that it had two capitals, one in the West and one in the East, was ripe for dissolution: sooner or later in the history of every empire, things fall

This Byzantine mosaic in the monastery church in Hosios Loukas, Greece, depicts Christ saving Adam, Eve, King David, and King Solomon, who had been confined in limbo.

apart. The waves of invasion of Italy by Germanic tribes came to a head in the fifth century, when Rome endured a series of weak rulers. The eastern Roman capital of Constantinople, by contrast, remained intact until the end of the Middle Ages, though during that time its character had changed very substantially from what it had been in the age of the Caesars. Both Augustine and Boethius, writing in the fifth and sixth centuries, bear witness to the decay of Rome—and to the birth of something entirely new, as a Christian culture, various and diffuse, rose out of the ashes of empire.

The diaspora—literally, "scattering" (Greek)—of Jews from Jerusalem in 70 C.E. not only facilitated the spread of Christianity throughout the Roman Empire but also created a new cultural environment that would lead to the development of rabbinic Judaism. The simultaneous emergence of rabbinic Judaism and Christianity can be described as a kind of twin birth, both of them formed in the crucible of Roman aggression in the first century. Beyond the physical experience of exile, the figurative concept of diaspora—like the ancient paradigm of the mass movement of people described in Exodus, which recounts the migration of the Jewish nation from Egypt to the promised land after many years of exile—provided an enormously powerful model for thinking about the movement of peoples in the early Middle Ages. Whereas the Jewish people were thought to be consigned to a permanent state of diaspora, endlessly wandering in the desert of the wide world, other communities sometimes claimed for themselves the role of the "true Israel": for medieval Christians, thinking of themselves as the true Israel meant identifying themselves as a chosen people. But their promised land was not to be found on the earth—it was the Heavenly Jerusalem, whose pleasures would be enjoyed only in the afterlife. National histories, too, made the history of the Jewish people into a template for their own myths of origin: this can be seen in medieval chronicles that liken accounts of the Trojans, who fled the ruins of Troy to found the great city of Rome, to accounts of the Jews in the diaspora. A similar national myth of origins can be found in the East African *Kebra Nagast*, which draws on the founding stories of the Jewish peoples to claim for Ethiopian Christians a place in the same lineage, identifying their rulers as the offspring of Solomon and Sheba and asserting that they preserved the original ark of the covenant in Ethiopia.

THE SPREAD OF ISLAM

Like the emergence of Christianity in the wake of the Jewish diaspora, the dissemination of the **Qur'an** by Muhammad and his followers in the seventh century and the subsequent formation of an Islamic community had a dramatic effect on the development of Mediterranean culture. In his account of Muhammad's life, the early biographer Ibn Ishaq describes a community struggling to form itself not only in accord with the explicit dictates found in its holy book, the Qur'an, but also in conformity with the exemplary life led by its prophet, Muhammad. These two models, the revealed book and the life perfectly led, were the religious guidelines of an empire that grew almost overnight to dominate large swathes of the Middle East and North Africa: in 750, little more than a century after Muhammad

began delivering the Qur'an in 610, Islamic rule extended westward through Spain into southern France and eastward through Persia (modern Iran) into India. The spread of Islam took place not only through cultural and religious means but also through direct military conquest, such as the assault on the Byzantine Christian empire that culminated in the Battle of Yarmūk in 636: after that time, the southern regions of Anatolia (modern Turkey) and virtually the whole of the Levant (modern Near East) were under the control of the armies of Islam. In spite of its military successes and dynamic expansion, this new empire was far from monolithic: after the fall of the Umayyad caliphate (literally, "headship") that had been based in Damascus, the Abbasid caliphate was established at Baghdad, where it endured for more than five hundred years until the Mongol invasions from Central Asia in the mid-thirteenth century. Even after their fall from power in the East, however, the Umayyads retained control in the West, where they continued to rule the Spanish provinces they had named "al-Andalus."

In addition to the political divisions centered on the caliphates, religious divisions also cut across the nations gathered under Islamic rule. The most important of these is the division of Sunni from Shi'a Islam: the former centers on a strict conformity to the exemplary life of the Prophet Muhammad and a literal reading of the Holy Book; the latter instead prescribes a special veneration of the family of the Prophet, especially his daughter Fatima, her husband (who was also the Prophet's cousin) Ali, and their sons Hasan and Hussain. The highly emotional, affective quality of Shi'a Islam is expressed in devotional stories and plays chronicling the martyrdom of the members of the Prophet's family, as well as in the later medieval emergence of Sufi mysticism; the mystics used figurative poetic language to

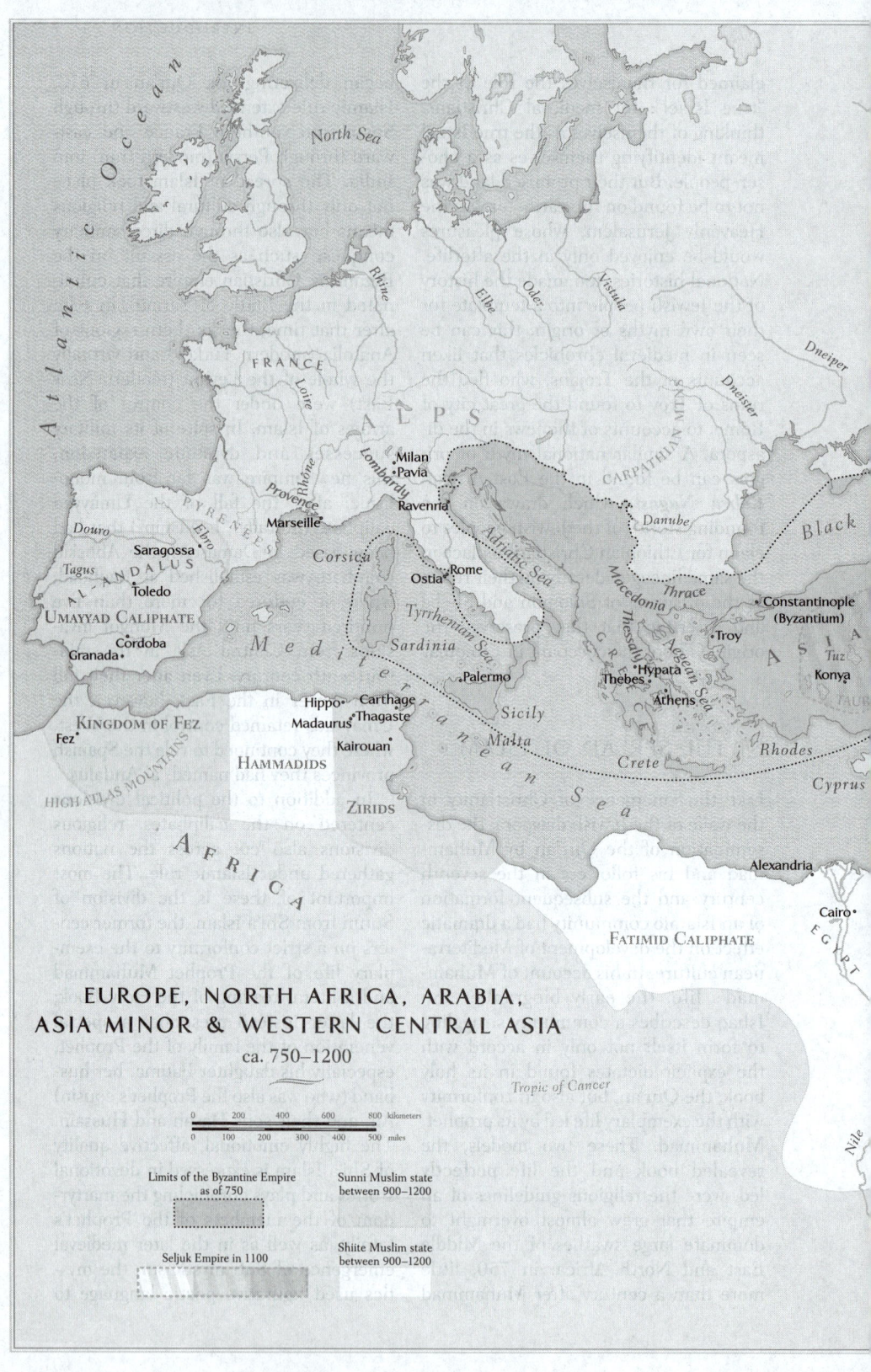

North Sea

Atlantic Ocean

FRANCE

Loire

Rhine

Elbe

Oder

Vistula

Dnieper

Dniester

ALPS

CARPATHIAN MTNS.

Rhône

Provence

Lombardy • Milan

• Pavia

Ravenna

Danube

Black

PYRENEES

Marseille •

Douro

Saragossa •

Ebro

Tagus

AL-ANDALUS

• Toledo

UMAYYAD CALIPHATE

• Córdoba

Granada •

Corsica

Mediterranean Sea

Ostia • • Rome

Sardinia

Adriatic Sea

Tyrrhenian Sea

Macedonia

Thessaly

Thrace

Constantinople
(Byzantium)

• Troy

ASIA

Tuz

Konya

Aegean Sea

• Hypata

Thebes • Athens •

Palermo

Sicily

Malta

Crete

Rhodes

Cyprus

KINGDOM OF FEZ

Fez •

Hippo •

Madaurus •

Carthage •

Thebaste

Kairouan •

HAMMADIDS

ZIRIDS

Alexandria

Cairo •

FATIMID CALIPHATE

EGYPT

AFRICA

Nile

EUROPE, NORTH AFRICA, ARABIA,
ASIA MINOR & WESTERN CENTRAL ASIA

ca. 750–1200

Tropic of Cancer

| 0 | 200 | 400 | 600 | 800 kilometers |

| 0 | 100 | 200 | 300 | 400 | 500 miles |

Limits of the Byzantine Empire
as of 750

Sunni Muslim state
between 900–1200

Seljuk Empire in 1100

Shiite Muslim state
between 900–1200

Lake Balkash

Aral
Sea

QARAKHANIDS

Oxus

Samarkand

Bukhara

K H O R A S A N

Caspian
Sea

Balkh

Merv

Kabul

Tus

Nishapur

Ghazna

Lahore

GHAZNAVID EMPIRE

Sea

Prut

M I N O R

Mosul

Hamadan

Aleppo

Tigris

Euphrates

BUYID SULTANATE

Baghdad

P E R S I A

I N D I A

Indus

Babylon

Tyre Damascus

Shiraz

Nazareth

Jerusalem
Bethlehem
Gaza

Persian Gulf

Sinai

Arabian Sea

A R A B I A

Medina

Red Sea

Mecca

Tropic of Cancer

I n d i a n   O c e a n

Axum

Aden

ETHIOPIA

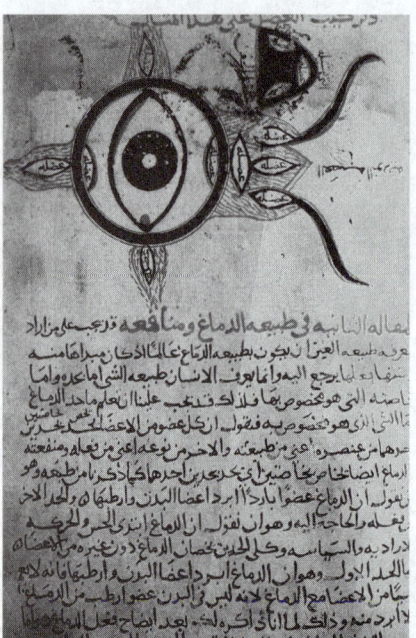

A twelfth-century copy of a ninth-century Arabic manuscript by Hunayn Ibn Ishaq on the anatomy of the eye. Ibn Ishaq wrote a wide variety of medical and scientific treatises under the patronage of the Abbasid caliphate.

convey the soul's experience of the divine. Both Shi'a veneration of the family of the Prophet and Sufi poetic expressions of religious devotion were regarded with suspicion wherever Sunni practice was the norm; the literature of Shi'a and Sufi piety, however, has continued to be widely popular not only in the Arabic and Persian-speaking populations of the Near and Middle East but also—in translation—throughout the world.

Divisions, both political and religious, persisted throughout the lands of medieval Islam: in response to the alienation of the Shi'a community by the Abbasids who ruled from Baghdad, a separate Fatimid caliphate that was Shi'a in orientation arose in Cairo. Internal squabbling finally gave way to utter chaos with the invasion of the Mongols in the early thirteenth century and their seizure of Baghdad in 1258.

The Mongols soon converted to Islam, following the same pattern of rule through assimilation that led to their long domination of East Asia, centered on the powerful regional force of China. Successive Islamic dynasties ended, at last, when the Ottomans invaded and consolidated their power in the eastern Mediterranean with the conquest of Constantinople in 1453. The Ottomans remained in a position of strength in the region: their siege of Vienna in 1683 was an assault on the gates of early modern Europe, and they went on to establish diplomatic relations with several European nations.

Regardless of where the dominant caliphate was based—Damascus, Baghdad, or Cairo—the various nations yoked under Islamic rule shared one crucial element: the Arabic language. It served not only as the standard language of administration but also as the language of religious observance (all Muslims were urged to memorize the Qur'an, at least short sections that could be recited within the daily prayers), as well as the common vernacular that straddled national borders. Arabic was the standard language of conversation, administration, and poetic composition not only for Muslims but also for Christians and Jews who lived in regions under Islamic rule, such as al-Andalus. In this way, the Arabic language served to unify diverse populations, in much the same way as Greek had done in the ancient eastern Mediterranean and Latin would do in medieval Europe. Poetic traditions in Arabia before the revelation of the Qur'an had placed special value on recitation and the musical quality of verse, its rhythmic repetitions and use of end rhyme. Because the Qur'an itself conformed to many of these pre-Islamic norms, it became a standard model for poetic excellence while maintaining its preeminent theological value.

As Islamic influence spread further

eastward, the historically powerful and culturally dominant civilization of Persia came within its orbit. The effect was transformative, both for Persian culture, which developed a particularly rich strand of mystical Islam, and for Islamic culture more broadly, which assimilated much of the poetic richness offered by Persian literature. Even though Arabic quickly became the language of administration and religion in Persia, the Persian language remained predominant in poetry and common in both philosophy and the natural sciences. In addition, the complex and vivid mythology of the indigenous religion of Persia, Zoroastrianism, persisted well after the advent of Islamic rule, as can be seen in the **Shahnameh** or *Book of Kings*, the national epic composed by **Ferdowsi**. Persian influence continued to be felt throughout the Islamic world, especially after the Mongol invasions and the establishment of Ottoman rule at Constantinople (renamed Istanbul). The Ottomans held Persian language, art, and poetics in high esteem, and imported painters as well as writers to serve their imperial court. Finally, the marriage of religious devotion and an exquisite poetic sensibility, so finely expressed in the lyrics of **Attar**, **Rumi**, and **Hafez**, would come to be a crucial part of the literary legacy of Islam, widely disseminated not only among the community of Muslim readers but also among the diverse modern audiences of world literature.

The influence of Islamic literature was felt not only through the exalted union of philosophy and theology with poetics but also on a more mundane, vernacular level. The vibrant tradition of frame-tale narratives, in which an outer layer organizes a series of nested narratives that are contained within the frame like the layers of an onion, had a long history in the Mediterranean region: writers as early as **Ovid** and **Apuleius**, in the first and second centuries, had relied on nested narratives. But with the arrival of more elaborate frame-tale models—especially *Kalila wa Dimna*, a series of animal fables based on the Indian **Pañcatantra**—the genre took off in Persian and Arabic literatures. Perhaps the best known example of the frame tale, **The Thousand and One Nights**, survives in its earliest versions in the Persian language; these were soon supplemented by a range of retellings in Arabic. The *Nights* circulated about the Mediterranean, with bits and pieces of it finding its way into other collections and its frame-tale form serving as the inspiration for many European manifestations of the genre, including **Boccaccio's *Decameron*** and **Chaucer's *Canterbury Tales***.

THE INVENTION OF THE WEST

For writers in the Islamic world, "the West" (*al-maghrib*) was the northern coast of Africa and al-Andalus, a region that was recognized as at once part of the Islamic sphere of influence and yet culturally and regionally distinctive. The idea of the West as a synonym for Christian Europe—which seems so natural and familiar to modern readers— did not even begin to emerge until the late Middle Ages. Medieval inhabitants of Europe instead categorized themselves in different ways: in terms of their ethnic origin or "nation," in terms of their primary language, and—above all—in terms of their religion. Unlike in the areas under Islamic rule, where Jews and Christians were tolerated albeit subject to special taxation and restrictions (so-called *dhimmi* rule), in Christian Europe Jews were only sporadically tolerated, and Muslims were virtually unknown. We can thus infer that Europe exhibited much

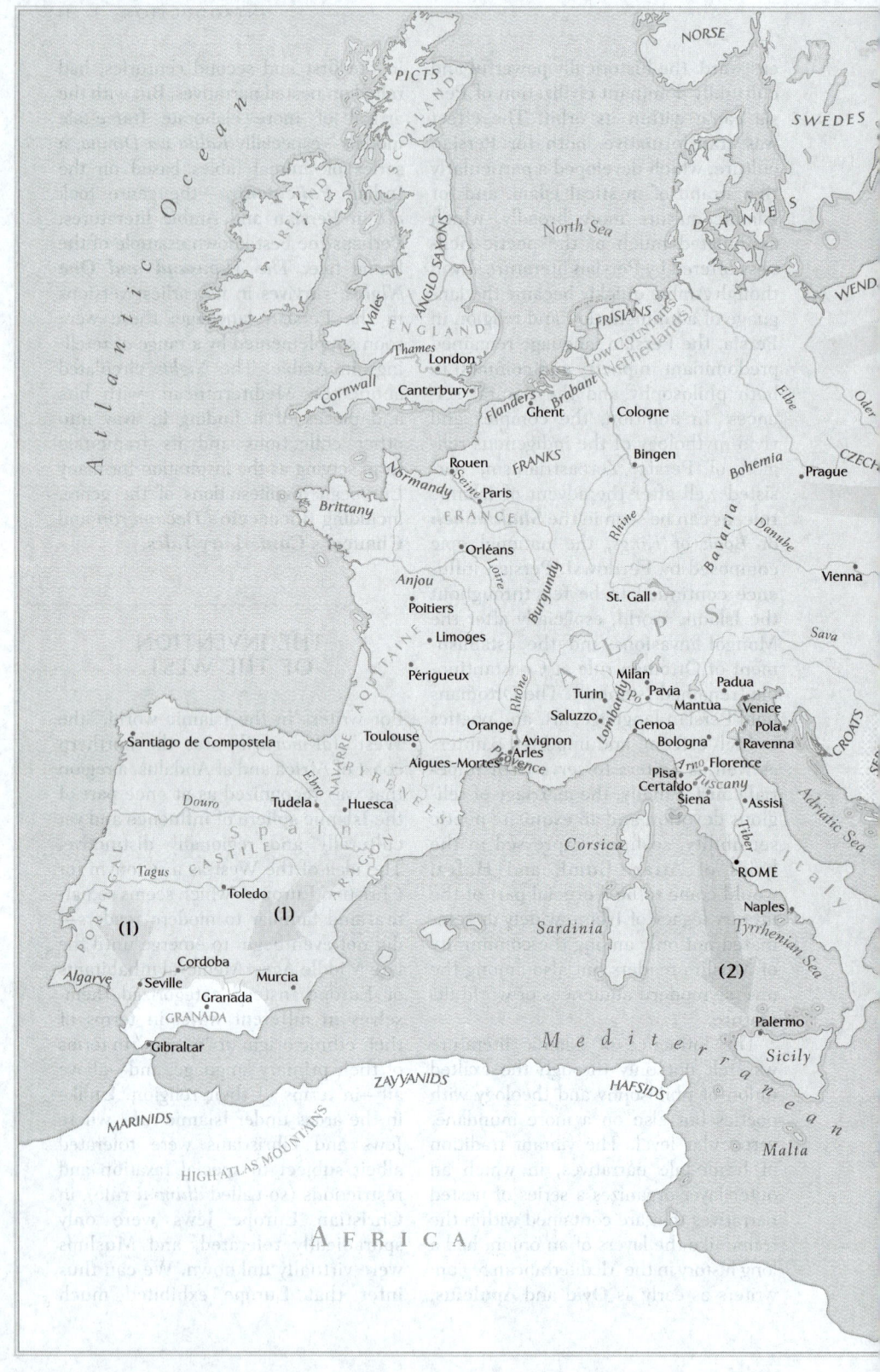

EUROPE
ca. 1300

FINNS

ESTONIANS

Baltic Sea

LETTS

TEUTONIC ORDER

LITHUANIANS

POLES

Vistula

SLOVAKS

MAGYARS

CARPATHIAN MOUNTAINS

Danube

BULGARS

BYZANTINE EMPIRE

Athens

Chiarenza

Morea

Aegina

Chios

Aegean Sea

Sea

Crete

Novgorod

•Novgorod

RUSSIANS

(3)

(3)

• Kiev

Dneiper

Dneister

Prut

Approximate line of
division between Roman
Catholics and Orthodox
Christians in the 14th century

Approximate line of division
between Christendom and
the Muslim world in 1300

Volga

Black Sea

Trebizond

• Constantinople

S E L J U K   S T A T E S

S E L J U K   A S I A   M I N O R

CAPPADOCIA

TAURUS MOUNTAINS

MESOPOTAMIA

Tigris

Euphrates

Smyrna (Izmir)

Rhodes

Paphos•   Cyprus

(4)

• Aleppo

Antioch

• Damascus

CRUSADER STATES

Syrian Desert

Jerusalem

Alexandria

MUMLAKS

0	200	400	600	800	kilometers
0	100	200	300	400	500	miles

General directions of the expansion of Latin Christendom
from the 7th to the 15th centuries—
(1) through the Spanish Reconquista
(2) through the Norman conquest of Sicily
(3) through migration and conquest in eastern and northern Europe
(4) through the Crusades

The so-called Hereford Mappamundi, ca. 1300. Jerusalem sits at the center of this medieval map; Asia occupies most of the top half; and Europe is in the lower-left quadrant.

more religious homogeneity, at least until the first glimmerings of early Protestant reform impulses in the late fourteenth century. Uniformity of religion was further strengthened by uniformity of language, as Latin was used not only for all religious but also all political and administrative purposes, just as Arabic was in the Islamic world. Indeed, Latin's cultural hold was stronger: medieval Christians used it exclusively to compose their philosophical and scientific works, while both Arabic and Persian functioned as languages of literature and learning for Muslims. Beginning in the ninth century, however, and with increasing frequency from the twelfth century onward, vernacular languages such as English, French, German, Italian, and Spanish became more common vehicles for poetic composition.

Medieval people defined themselves first of all by their religious orientation and next by ethnic origin, relying not at all on the categories familiar to modern readers. This perspective on the place of the self in the world is well illustrated on the medieval world maps, or *mappae-mundi*, that were used not as practical guides to navigation but rather as abstract overviews of both the literal shape of the world and its metaphorical meaning. Accordingly, such maps conventionally place Jerusalem at the exact center, marking the site of Christ's crucifixion as the fixed point about which the whole world revolves. The mappamundi itself is almost always oriented toward the east (Latin *oriens*), rather than toward the north as on modern maps, so that its easternmost point, the Garden of Eden, appears—appropriately—as both the beginning of space and the beginning of time. Asia, Europe, and Africa, the three known continents, are depicted symmetrically on the map. Asia takes up twice as much space as the other two, dominating the top half of the world sphere; Europe is tucked away at the lower left; and "the West" (Latin *occidens*) lies, rather forlornly, at the bottom.

The medieval map, with its deeply religious imaginative geography and central focus on Jerusalem, illumi-

A detail from a page of the Luttrell Psalter (ca. 1300) depicts Richard I and Saladin jousting during the Third Crusade. Saladin is drawn with a grotesque blue face—a rendering that makes it all the easier for the psalter's Christian readers to see the conflict as a clearly defined battle between good and evil.

nates the ways in which the repeated cycles of European warfare around the Mediterranean and into the Middle East—called "Crusades," after the cross (Latin *crux*) sewn by the warriors onto their garments—functioned not just as actual military campaigns but also as symbolic assaults designed to reclaim control of the spiritual homeland of the medieval Christian. The First Crusade, launched in 1095, included a violent assault on Jerusalem that ended with the slaughter of most of the city's inhabitants and the establishment of the "Latin Kingdom of Jerusalem": a significant outpost of Europeans occupying Jerusalem itself together with additional European fortifications in adjoining towns along the coast (most importantly Acre, which remained in European hands until 1291). Although expeditions continued to be launched intermittently until the end of the Middle Ages—including the dramatic Third Crusade, which united the English army of Richard the Lion-Hearted with the armies of Philip of France and Frederick Barbarossa of Germany—no later military successes matched those of the First Crusade that began them all. The Crusades functioned mainly as opportunities for economic development and international cooperation among the nations of Europe, helping to unify these disparate Christian nations through their shared opposition to the Muslim enemy. The passions stirred by this effort to stimulate political unity through religious fervor came at a high price: with each successive call to crusade, violent attacks were made on the only locally available non-Christian populations within the cities of Europe—that is, the Jews. Anti-Muslim violence in the form of crusade was therefore closely linked with the persecution of Jews and the early emergence of anti-Semitism.

The opposition of Christian and non-Christian, so fundamental to the ideology of crusade, permeates the epic literature of the Middle Ages. It is especially visible in the poetry of the eleventh century, such as the **Song of Roland**, which is often described as the national epic of France: "Christian" and "pagan" are set against one another throughout the work, as the conflict is cast as white versus black, right versus wrong. The ultimate triumph of the Christian forces of Charlemagne over the Muslims at Saragossa literally takes place in medieval Spain; metaphorically, however, the victory of Christian over pagan is presented as a template for all holy war—including the First Crusade, which was being launched at the very moment that *Roland* (originally an oral poem) was committed to the page.

The epic genre began to emerge, originally in oral form and subsequently in written texts, by the ninth century. Like the Persian *Shahnameh* of Ferdowsi, the Anglo-Saxon *Beowulf* describes a shadowy era in which myth and history are intertwined; both works also have a similar complicated relationship to the religions that had become obligatory in their cultures but were anachronisms in the mythic worlds that they evoked. For Ferdowsi, Islam was an overlay that covered over but did not obscure the indigenous Persian myth that animates the epic of kings; for the anonymous author of *Beowulf*, Christianity is likewise an innovation applied as a veneer, here on a pagan Germanic past. The Germanic notion of *wyrd* or fate is aligned, by the *Beowulf*-poet, with Christian notions of divine providence, but it remains clear that the two concepts are far from identical. Epic, whether in England or in Persia, thus creates a sense of national identity by evoking a common historical origin, but it also grafts upon the rootstock of native myth new forms of identity—especially religious forms imported from outside the borders of the nation.

Epic is often opposed to romance: the former is portrayed as a masculine genre dedicated to the deeds of knights and the matter of war, the latter as a feminine genre that focuses on the relations of the lady and her lover, confined to the domestic sphere of the court. However, both genres, which rose to prominence in the twelfth century, share the idealized image of the knight: if he expresses his chivalry on the field of battle, the work is epic, but if his prowess is displayed in the private space of the bedchamber, the work is romance. The romances of Chrétien de Troyes, like the shorter romance works or *lais* of his predecessor, **Marie de France**, highlight this idealized role of the knight, which is also seen in the later medieval English, German, and Italian romances that were adapted from French originals. The French origins of the romance genre are also closely tied to the emergence of French as a literary language. Latin was unquestionably the primary language of scholarly learning, whether theological, philosophical, or scientific, but vernacular or spoken languages increasingly came to be the first choice for poetic composition. In the twelfth century, French was the first of the European languages to be elevated in this way; by the fourteenth century, other vernaculars had also begun to be widely used. Explicitly, in his treatise on languages (*De vulgari eloquentia*), and implicitly, in his **Divine Comedy**, Dante Alighieri stakes a claim for the local Florentine dialect of Italian as the "most illustrious vernacular," while Chaucer will make similar claims for English in his *Canterbury Tales*.

In spite of this ongoing shift, Latin experienced an important revival in the fourteenth century. Paradoxically at just the moment when literature in the vernacular was reaching new levels of sophistication with works such as Boccaccio's *Decameron* and Chaucer's *Canterbury Tales*, classical forms of Latin were being championed in humanistic circles under the guiding hand of **Petrarch**. Ambivalence about the competing claims of a revived classical Latin, on the one hand, and the potent spontaneity of the vernacular, on the other hand, is evident in the work of Petrarch himself: the author of several Latin treatises and a powerful advocate for classical scholarship, his exquisite lyrics in Italian would exert a powerful influence on the rise of Renaissance lyric not only in Italy but also in France and England. This paradox is reflected in modern scholarship, which tends to label Petrarch, who wrote in the early fourteenth century, as a "Renaissance" poet and his friend and disciple Boccaccio, who wrote in the mid-fourteenth century, as a "medieval" writer. The example of these two contemporaries illustrates the ways in which period divisions, like geographical divisions, sometimes obscure the profound continuities that underlie literary history.

Though Boccaccio wrote his masterwork, the *Decameron*, in Italian, he also composed (at the encouragement of Petrarch) several treatises in Latin. Chaucer did not write in Latin, but he shared Boccaccio's consciousness of the importance of the legacy of Roman antiquity and Latin literature; he produced several English translations of Latin works, including Boethius's *Consolation of Philosophy*. In late medieval French circles too, as illustrated in the mythographic works of **Christine de Pizan** written under the influence of Boccaccio, the Greco-Roman past loomed large. In all three of these major writers, the yearning for a revival of classical antiquity reveals the extent to which the wholehearted embrace of the ancient past that we tend to associate exclusively with the Renaissance was amply foreshadowed in the work of at least some late medieval authors, especially those whose perspective was particularly cosmopolitan, rooted in the experience of the city as a cultural, economic, linguistic, and—above all—literary crossroads.

While we can read Boccaccio, Chaucer, and Christine de Pizan in the context of the emergence of Latin humanism, they can also be seen as central participants in the late medieval European flowering of the frame-tale genre. Transmitted from India to Persia and then disseminated throughout the Islamic world and across the Mediterranean, frame-tale narratives such as the *Thousand and One Nights* were widely popular, both in written and in oral form. One of the first medieval examples of the genre to cross over from the Islamic world into Europe is the twelfth-century ***Disciplina Clericalis*** (*Scholar's Guide*) of **Petrus Alfonsi**, an Andalusi Jew who had converted to Christianity and spent the later part of his life in England and northern France. His own experience of moving between cultures, religious communities, and linguistic groups bears a striking resemblance to the frame-tale genre itself, which shows an almost uncanny ability to slip through the borders that separate national literatures. Petrus Alfonsi's work is just one of the first in a long series of frame-tale narratives, including Marie de France's *Lais* and the work of Boccaccio and Chaucer, and it is ample testimony to the cultural flux so strongly expressed in medieval Spain, and more broadly throughout the Mediterranean world.

The age of Boccaccio and Chaucer also witnessed the rise of yet one more genre centered on the crossing of cultural boundaries: the travel narrative. Early in the thirteenth century **Marco Polo** had already committed to paper an account of his journeys along the Silk Road as far as the east coast of China, but it was not until the fourteenth century that travel literature won general popularity with the wide diffusion of such works as ***The Book of John Mandeville***, which begins with a conventional pilgrimage itinerary to Jerusalem but then goes on to a wildly speculative journey through Asia in search of Prester John's Land. Columbus carried copies of both Marco Polo and Mandeville on his journey in search of a westward passage to the Indies, where he stumbled across a new land that would alter the shape of the old world maps and offer new horizons for conquest, thus bringing the medieval age to a close.

THE CHRISTIAN BIBLE
THE NEW TESTAMENT GOSPELS
ca. first century c.e.

For some readers, the Bible is to be read as sacred history and divine revelation, as a book whose truth is grounded by religious faith. For others, it is a rich trove of cultural history, sometimes supported by archaeology and other corroborating evidence, sometimes not. Beginning in the nineteenth century, however, readers started to also think of the Bible as a work of literature, analyzing it in terms of genre and poetics and comparing it to other literary works written around the same time. The Gospels of Matthew, Mark, and Luke, for instance, all of which retell the life of Jesus, can be read as examples of Greco-Roman biography as practiced around the Mediterranean during the first century c.e. The metaphorical language of the Gospel of John reflects the strong influence of Platonic philosophy on Jewish communities within the Roman Empire. This literary approach to the Bible has inspired recent generations of modern intellectuals, writers, and artists—sometimes from a devout perspective, sometimes not. Yet it is crucial to realize that considering the Christian Bible as literature is not a modern novelty: over the past two thousand years, poets have constantly quoted and paraphrased the Gospels in order to enrich their own work with the resonant, messianic tone and powerful turns of phrase that appear in what is arguably the single most influential text of world literature.

CHRISTIAN CULTURE IN THE
ROMAN EMPIRE

Jesus was born in the town of Bethlehem, a town located in the province of Judea in the eastern part of the Roman Empire. While Latin was the language mainly used in Rome itself, in far-off Judea the language of administration was Greek. For most local inhabitants, however, the vernacular was Aramaic, a language related to Hebrew but sufficiently different from it that Aramaic speakers would not necessarily have understood Hebrew. The polyglot nature of the region was mirrored in the wide range of ethnicities and religious orientations found there. Judea and the surrounding lands had formerly been part of the vast empire established by Alexander the Great, under whose influence the local Jewish population—especially the more affluent and educated classes—had embraced Greek literature and philosophy. This religious and cultural ferment gave rise to a variety of religious groups; some became marginalized and died out, but others (including Christianity and rabbinic Judaism) would live on.

From Roman administrative records, we know that there was a historical Jesus, a disruptive rabble-rouser who attracted the attention of the local authorities and was ultimately executed. Yet the Jesus of the gospel accounts is something far more complex, more a phenomenon than a man. It is clear that the events of his life rapidly led to the establishment of not just a single community but a number of communities organized around the symbolic significance that could be assigned to this man, his words, and his deeds. These included both Jewish communities, for whom Jesus was to be identified with the long-awaited Messiah, and non-Jewish (or "Gentile") communities around the Mediterranean Sea. The dating system we use today reflects the fundamental break in time that early Christians believed had taken place. Dates in the Roman Empire were ordinarily based on the number of the year in the reign of the individual ruler, but Christians viewed Jesus as a divine lord whose authority surmounted that of any earthly kingdom or empire. Consequently, they began to number the years "A.D."— that is, *Anno Domini*, or "In the year of the Lord." Today, we more often use the more inclusive abbreviation C.E. for the Common Era, but we continue to number years from the birth of Jesus—a practice that reflects the early Christians' profound sense of a temporal rupture, the belief that a new age had dawned.

WORK

Together with the Gospel of Mark, the three books of the Bible excerpted here—the Gospels of Matthew, Luke, and John—form the core of the collection of twenty-seven books that Christians call the New Testament. This label, taken with the "Old Testament," encapsulates the Christian perspective on the relationship of Jesus' mission to the history of the Jewish people recounted in the **Hebrew Bible**, comprising the Pentateuch (the first five books, or Torah), the books of prophets and history, and the poetic books. For Christians, the covenant established by God with Noah after the flood, and reestablished with Abraham, was merely a prefiguration, the first stage of a process that would be fulfilled only with the advent of Jesus and subsequent rise of Christianity. In some ways, this perspective honors and elevates the role of the Jewish people; in other ways, it denigrates Judaism, relegating it to a subordinate position in the divine plan for humanity.

Although the Gospels present themselves as eyewitness testimony to events in the life of Jesus, they were actually committed to written form decades after his death. The earliest of them, the Gospel of Mark, probably dates to about 70 C.E.; the latest, the Gospel of John, dates to about 100 C.E. The sequence of four gospels was established relatively early on, as was the authoritativeness of their testimony. The second-century theologian Irenaeus of Lyons declared that there are only four gospels, just as there are only four corners of the earth, and four winds in the heavens. This declaration served to exclude the many alternative accounts of the life of Jesus that were also in circulation, and to give a more specific structure to the teachings of Jesus and his authorized followers; the final result was a codified form of the New Testament and, ultimately, Christian theology. The Gospels of Matthew, Mark, and Luke are called the Synoptic Gospels, because they give a panorama or overview (synopsis) of the life of Jesus, all telling the same story but from rather distinctive perspectives. The Gospel of John also recounts the life of Jesus, but with a very different narrative line and a deep concern to integrate Platonic philosophy and mysticism into the expression of divinity in the person of Jesus Christ, identified as the Word of God.

The Synoptic Gospels have a number of episodes in common, of which the most important are the Sermon on the Mount, the Last Supper, and the crucifixion and resurrection of Jesus. Yet each of the three gospels also has its own individual character: Luke tells us the most about the childhood and parentage of Jesus, and his work is closely related to the noncanonical tradition of "infancy gospels"—stories about the life of Jesus as a child that survive in Arabic as well as in Greek and Syriac versions. Mark provides the tightest and most focused account, placing special emphasis on the death of Jesus and recounting his biography in simpler, more primitive language. Mark appears to be addressing a Gentile audience, and his gospel is sometimes associated with the early foundation of Christian communities in Rome or, at least, in the regions of the Roman Empire lying to the west of Judea. Matthew, conversely, clearly directs his biography at an audience that is quite familiar with the Hebrew Bible: he gives a very detailed account of Jesus' preaching mission and his role as the long-awaited Messiah. Matthew exhibits a special interest in the ways in which Jewish history is fulfilled in the coming of Jesus Christ, and in the ways in which the old covenant established between God and man is renewed in and superseded by the new covenant established with the sacrifice of Christ in the crucifixion.

Matthew also displays a central concern with the ways in which Jesus preached, especially his use of parables: little stories that reveal profound spiritual truths through metaphorical, even allegorical language. The excerpts presented here include parables of Jesus as recounted both by Matthew and by Luke, passages of the Gospels that are among those with the most profound literary influence on writers throughout the Middle Ages. The figurative, philosophical language of the Gospel of John would also go on to be highly influential, disseminated through a wide range of poetic evocations of the divine nature. John's account of the birth of Christ, excerpted here, seemingly describes the same transformative event narrated in the infancy chapters of Luke. Yet the two accounts could not be more different, as they represent two totally different perspectives on the nature of Jesus Christ, understood as that deepest of all para-

doxes, the being who is at once both God and man. For John, Christ is the Word through which God creates all things, a mediator between matter and spirit, the temporal and the eternal. For Luke, he is Jesus of Nazareth, whose divine nature smoothly coexists with his human status, rooted in the cultural norms and social structures of first-century Judea.

The Gospels as we have them today reflect a complex and intertwined linguistic history: Jesus and his apostles would have spoken Aramaic, which we hear when Jesus cries out on the crucifix, "Eli, eli, lama sabachthani?" ("My God, my God, why have you forsaken me?" [Matthew 27.46]). However, the Gospels were written down in koine Greek, the vernacular that was the lingua franca of the eastern Mediterranean. This was a language meant to travel, and so the Gospels did: they were swiftly passed on in both oral and written form across the Mediterranean Sea, through Asia, Europe, and northern Africa. Latin translations of the Gospels soon began to be produced, and in 382 Pope Damasus asked the theologian Jerome to prepare a full, authorized translation into Latin. This version, known as the Vulgate, would become the standard version of the Bible read for more than a thousand years in the West, until new versions of the sacred text began to be produced at the dawn of the Reformation. Over the five hundred years since then, translations of the Bible have multiplied exponentially, as every spoken language has produced its own version of holy scripture. Most recently, modern writers and artists have moved the Bible into new formats such as the graphic novel, used by devout Christians to educate their children and enjoyed by a wide range of nonreligious readers.

The Bible: The New Testament Gospels[1]

Luke 2

[The Birth and Youth of Jesus]

It happened in those days that a decree went forth from Augustus Caesar[2] that all the world should be enrolled in a census. This was the first census, when Quirinius was governor of Syria. And all went to be enrolled, each to his own city. And Joseph also went up from Galilee,[3] from the city of Nazareth, to Judaea, to the city of David[4] which is called Bethlehem, because he was of the house and family of David; to be enrolled with Mary his promised wife, who was pregnant. And it happened that while they were there her time was completed, and she bore a son, her first-born, and she wrapped him in swaddling clothes and laid him in a manger, because there was no room for them in the inn. And there were shepherds in that region, camping out at night and keeping guard over their flock. And an angel of the Lord stood before them, and the glory of the Lord shone about them, and they were afraid with a great fear. The angel said to them: Do not be afraid; behold, I tell you good news, great joy which shall be for all the people; because this day there has been born for you in the city of David a savior who is Christ the Lord. And here is a sign for you; you will find a baby wrapped in swaddling clothes and lying in a manger. And suddenly with the angel there was a multitude of the heavenly host, praising God and saying: Glory to God in the highest and peace on earth among men of good will. And it happened that after the angels had gone off from them into the sky, the shepherds began saying to each other: Let us go to Bethlehem and see this thing which has happened, which the Lord made known to us; and they went, hastening, and found Mary and Joseph, and the baby lying in the manger; and when they had seen, they spread the news about what had been told them concerning this baby. And all who heard wondered at what had been told them by the shepherds; and Mary kept in mind all these sayings as she pondered them in her heart. And the shepherds returned, glorifying and praising God over all they had heard and seen, as it had been told them.

And when eight days were past, for his circumcision, his name was called Jesus, as it was named by the angel before he was conceived in the womb.

And when the days for their purification[5] according to the Law of Moses had been completed, they took him up to Jerusalem to set him before the Lord, as it has been written in the Law of the Lord: Every male child who opens the womb shall be called sacred to the Lord; and to give sacrifice as it is stated in the Law of the Lord, a pair of turtle doves or two young pigeons. And behold, there was a man in Jerusalem whose name was Simeon, and this man was righteous and virtuous and looked forward to the consolation of Israel, and the Holy Spirit was

---

1. Translated by Richmond Lattimore.
2. Gaius Julius Caesar (63 B.C.E.–14 C.E.), who took the title Augustus as the first Roman emperor.
3. The region surrounding the Sea of Galilee, in the Roman province of Judea (modern Israel).

4. Second king of Israel, according to the Hebrew Bible; he was anointed king in Bethlehem, his traditional birthplace.
5. The ritual cleansing following childbirth (prescribed in Leviticus 12).

upon him; and it had been prophesied to him by the Holy Spirit that he should not look upon his death until he had looked on the Lord's Anointed. And in the spirit he went into the temple; and as his parents brought in the child Jesus so that they could do for him what was customary according to the law, Simeon himself took him in his arms and blessed God and said: Now, Lord, you release your slave, in peace, according to your word; because my eyes have looked on your salvation, what you made ready in the presence of all the peoples; a light for the revelation to the Gentiles, and the glory of your people, Israel. And his father and his mother were in wonder at what was being said about him. And Simeon blessed them and said to Mary his mother: Behold, he is appointed for the fall and the rise of many in Israel; and as a sign which is disputed; and through your soul also will pass the sword; so that the reasonings of many hearts may be revealed. And there was Anna, a prophetess, the daughter of Phanuel, of the tribe of Asher. And she was well advanced in years, having lived with her husband seven years from the time of her maidenhood, and now she was eighty-four years a widow. And she did not leave the temple, serving night and day with fastings and prayers. And at this same time she came near and gave thanks to God and spoke of the child to those who looked forward to the deliverance of Jerusalem.

And when they had done everything according to the Law of the Lord, they went back to Galilee, to their own city, Nazareth.

And the child grew in stature and strength as he was filled with wisdom, and the grace of God was upon him.

Now his parents used to journey every year to Jerusalem for the feast of the Passover.[6] And when he was twelve years old, when they went up according to their custom for the festival and had completed their days there, on their return the boy Jesus stayed behind in Jerusalem, and his parents did not know it. And supposing that he was in their company they went a day's journey and then looked for him among their relatives and friends, and when they did not find him they turned back to Jerusalem in search of him. And it happened that after three days they found him in the temple sitting in the midst of the masters, listening to them and asking them questions. And all who heard him were amazed at his intelligence and his answers. And they were astonished at seeing him, and his mother said to him: Child, why did you do this to us? See, your father and I have been looking for you, in distress. He said to them: But why were you looking for me? Did you not know that I must be in my father's house? And they did not understand what he had said to them. And he returned with them and came to Nazareth, and was in their charge. And his mother kept all his sayings in her heart. And Jesus advanced in wisdom and stature, and in the favor of God and men.

6. The holiday (Heb. *Pesach*) commemorating the liberation of the people of Israel, led by Moses, from bondage in Egypt.

Matthew 5–7

[*The Sermon on the Mount*]

And seeing the multitudes he went up onto the mountain, and when he was seated, his disciples came to him, and he opened his mouth and taught them, saying:

Blessed are the poor in spirit, because theirs is the Kingdom of Heaven.

Blessed are they who sorrow, because they shall be comforted.

Blessed are the gentle, because they shall inherit the earth.

Blessed are they who are hungry and thirsty for righteousness, because they shall be fed.

Blessed are they who have pity, because they shall be pitied.

Blessed are the pure in heart, because they shall see God.

Blessed are the peacemakers, because they shall be called the sons of God.

Blessed are they who are persecuted for their righteousness, because theirs is the Kingdom of Heaven.

Blessed are you when they shall revile you and persecute you and speak every evil thing of you, lying, because of me. Rejoice and be glad, because your reward in heaven is great; for thus did they persecute the prophets before you.

You are the salt of the earth; but if the salt loses its power, with what shall it be salted? It is good for nothing but to be thrown away and trampled by men. You are the light of the world. A city cannot be hidden when it is set on top of a hill. Nor do men light a lamp and set it under a basket, but they set it on a stand, and it gives its light to all in the house. So let your light shine before men, so that they may see your good works and glorify your father in heaven.

Do not think that I have come to destroy the law[1] and the prophets. I have not come to destroy but to complete. Indeed, I say to you, until the sky and the earth are gone, not one iota or one end of a letter must go from the law, until all is done. He who breaks one of the least of these commandments and teaches men accordingly shall be called the least in the Kingdom of Heaven; he who performs and teaches these commandments shall be called great in the Kingdom of Heaven. For I tell you, if your righteousness is not more abundant than that of the scribes and the Pharisees,[2] you may not enter the Kingdom of Heaven.

You have heard that it was said to the ancients: You shall not murder. He who murders shall be liable to judgment. I say to you that any man who is angry with his brother shall be liable to judgment; and he who says to his brother, fool, shall be liable before the council; and he who says to his brother, sinner, shall be liable to Gehenna.[3] If then you bring your gift to the altar, and there remember that your brother has some grievance against you, leave your gift before the altar, and go first and be reconciled with your brother, and then go and offer your gift. Be quick to be conciliatory with your adversary at law when you are in the street with him, for fear your adversary may turn you over to the judge, and the judge to the officer, and you be thrown into prison. Truly I tell you, you cannot come out of there until you pay the last penny.

---

1. That is, the Torah, the five books of the law that begin the Hebrew Bible.
2. A major Jewish sect that emphasized strict observance of Jewish law; they were instrumental in the development of rabbinic Judaism.
3. Hell (Heb. *gehinnom*); figurative use of the name of a valley outside Jerusalem where children were sacrificed to pagan gods.

You have heard that it has been said: You shall not commit adultery. I tell you that any man who looks at a woman so as to desire her has already committed adultery with her in his heart. If your right eye makes you go amiss, take it out and cast it from you; it is better that one part of you should be lost instead of your whole body being cast into Gehenna. And if your right hand makes you go amiss, cut it off and cast it from you; it is better that one part of you should be lost instead of your whole body going to Gehenna. It has been said: If a man puts away his wife, let him give her a contract of divorce. I tell you that any man who puts away his wife, except for the reason of harlotry, is making her the victim of adultery; and any man who marries a wife who has been divorced is committing adultery. Again, you have heard that it has been said to the ancients: You shall not swear falsely, but you shall make good your oaths to the Lord. I tell you not to swear at all: not by heaven, because it is the throne of God; not by the earth, because it is the foot-stool for his feet; not by Jerusalem, because it is the city of the great king; not by your own head, because you cannot make one hair of it white or black. Let your speech be yes yes, no no; more than that comes from the evil one.

You have heard that it has been said: An eye for an eye and a tooth for a tooth. I tell you not to resist the wicked man; but if one strikes you on the right cheek, turn the other one to him also; and if a man wishes to go to law with you and take your tunic, give him your cloak also, and if one makes you his porter for a mile, go with him for two. Give to him who asks, and do not turn away one who wishes to borrow from you. You have heard that it has been said: You shall love your neighbor and hate your enemy. I tell you, love your enemies and pray for those who persecute you, so that you may be sons of your father who is in heaven, because he makes his sun rise on the evil and the good, and rains on the just and the unjust. For if you love those who love you, what reward do you have? Do not even the tax collectors do the same? And if you greet only your brothers, what do you do that is more than others do? Do not even the pagans do the same? Be perfect as your father in heaven is perfect.

Take care not to practice your righteousness publicly before men so as to be seen by them; if you do, you shall have no recompense from your father in heaven. Then when you do charity, do not have a trumpet blown before you, as the hypocrites do in the synagogues and the streets, so that men may think well of them. Truly I tell you, they have their due reward. But when you do charity, let your left hand not know what your right hand is doing, so that your charity may be in secret; and your father, who sees what is secret, will reward you. And when you pray, you must not be like the hypocrites, who love to stand up in the synagogues and the corners of the squares to pray, so that they may be seen by men. Truly I tell you, they have their due reward. But when you pray, go into your inner room and close the door and pray to your father, who is in secret; and your father, who sees what is secret, will reward you. When you pray, do not babble as the pagans do; for they think that by saying much they will be heard. Do not then be like them; for your father knows what you need before you ask him. Pray thus, then:[4] Our father in heaven, may your name be hal-lowed, may your kingdom come, may your will be done, as in heaven, so upon

---

4. The following verses, commonly known as the Lord's Prayer, are central to Christian religious practice.

earth. Give us today our sufficient bread, and forgive us our debts, as we also have forgiven our debtors. And do not bring us into temptation, but deliver us from evil. For if you forgive men their offenses, your heavenly father will forgive you; but if you do not forgive men, neither will your father forgive you your offenses. And when you fast, do not scowl like the hypocrites; for they make ugly faces so that men can see that they are fasting. Truly I tell you, they have their due reward. But when you fast, anoint your head and wash your face, so that you may not show as fasting to men, but to your father, in secret; and your father, who sees what is secret, will reward you.

Do not store up your treasures on earth, where the moth and rust destroy them, and where burglars dig through and steal them; but store up your treasures in heaven, where neither moth nor rust destroys them, and where burglars do not dig through or steal; for where your treasure is, there also will be your heart. The lamp of the body is the eye. Thus if your eye is clear, your whole body is full of light; but if your eye is soiled, your whole body is dark. If the light in you is darkness, how dark it is. No man can serve two masters. For either he will hate the one and love the other, or he will cling to one and despise the other; you cannot serve God and mammon.[5] Therefore I tell you, do not take thought for your life, what you will eat, or for your body, what you will wear. Is not your life more than its food and your body more than its clothing? Consider the birds of the sky, that they do not sow or harvest or collect for their granaries, and your heavenly father feeds them. Are you not preferred above them? Which of you by taking thought can add one cubit to his growth? And why do you take thought about clothing? Study the lilies in the field, how they grow. They do not toil or spin; yet I tell you, not even Solomon[6] in all his glory was clothed like one of these. But if God so clothes the grass of the field, which grows today and tomorrow is thrown in the oven, will he not much more clothe you, you men of little faith? Do not then worry and say: What shall we eat? Or: What shall we drink? Or: What shall we wear? For all this the Gentiles study. Your father in heaven knows that you need all these things. But seek out first his kingdom and his justice, and all these things shall be given to you. Do not then take thought of tomorrow; tomorrow will take care of itself, sufficient to the day is its own evil.

Do not judge, so you may not be judged. You shall be judged by that judgment by which you judge, and your measure will be made by the measure by which you measure. Why do you look at the straw which is in the eye of your brother, and not see the log which is in your eye? Or how will you say to your brother: Let me take the straw out of your eye, and behold, the log is in your eye. You hypocrite, first take the log out of your eye, and then you will see to take the straw out of the eye of your brother. Do not give what is sacred to the dogs, and do not cast your pearls before swine, lest they trample them under their feet and turn and rend you. Ask, and it shall be given you; seek, and you shall find; knock, and the door will be opened for you. Everyone who asks receives, and he who seeks finds, and for him who knocks the door will be opened. Or what man is there among you, whose son shall ask him for bread, that will give him

---

5. Wealth (an Aramaic word transliterated into Greek); the personification of Mammon as a god became a common trope in later Christian literature.

6. King of Israel and son of David, famed for his wisdom and for building the First Temple in Jerusalem.

a stone? Or ask him for fish, that will give him a snake? If then you, who are corrupt, know how to give good gifts to your children, by how much more your father who is in heaven will give good things to those who ask him. Whatever you wish men to do to you, so do to them. For this is the law and the prophets.

Go in through the narrow gate; because wide and spacious is the road that leads to destruction, and there are many who go in through it; because narrow is the gate and cramped the road that leads to life, and few are they who find it. Beware of the false prophets, who come to you in sheep's clothing, but inside they are ravening wolves. From their fruits you will know them. Do men gather grapes from thorns or figs from thistles? Thus every good tree produces good fruits, but the rotten tree produces bad fruits. A good tree cannot bear bad fruits, and a rotten tree cannot bear good fruits. Every tree that does not produce good fruit is cut out and thrown in the fire. So from their fruits you will know them. Not everyone who says to me Lord Lord will come into the Kingdom of Heaven, but he who does the will of my father in heaven. Many will say to me on that day: Lord, Lord, did we not prophesy in your name, and in your name did we not cast out demons, and in your name did we not assume great powers? And then I shall admit to them: I never knew you. Go from me, for you do what is against the law.

Every man who hears what I say and does what I say shall be like the prudent man who built his house upon the rock. And the rain fell and the rivers came and the winds blew and dashed against that house, and it did not fall, for it was founded upon the rock. And every man who hears what I say and does not do what I say will be like the reckless man who built his house on the sand. And the rain fell and the rivers came and the winds blew and battered that house, and it fell, and that was a great fall.

And it happened that when Jesus had ended these words, the multitudes were astonished at his teaching, for he taught them as one who has authority, and not like their own scribes.

Luke 15

[Parables]

All the tax collectors and the sinners kept coming around him, to listen to him. And the Pharisees and the scribes muttered, saying: This man receives sinners and eats with them. But he told them this parable, saying: Which man among you who has a hundred sheep and has lost one of them will not leave the ninety-nine in the wilds and go after the lost one until he finds it? And when he does find it, he sets it on his shoulders, rejoicing, and goes to his house and invites in his friends and his neighbors, saying to them: Rejoice with me, because I found my sheep which was lost. I tell you that thus there will be joy in heaven over one sinner who repents, rather than over ninety-nine righteous ones who have no need of repentance. Or what woman who has ten drachmas,[1] if she loses one drachma, does not light the lamp and sweep the house and search diligently until she finds it? And finding it she invites in her friends

1. Greek silver coins, each roughly equivalent in value to a manual laborer's wages for one day.

and neighbors, saying: Rejoice with me, because I found the drachma I lost. Such, I tell you, is the joy among the angels of God over one sinner who repents.

And he said: There was a man who had two sons. And the younger of them said to his father: Father, give me my appropriate share of the property. And the father divided his substance between them. And not many days afterward the younger son gathered everything together and left the country for a distant land, and there he squandered his substance in riotous living. And after he had spent everything, there was a severe famine in that country, and he began to be in need. And he went and attached himself to one of the citizens of that country, who sent him out into the fields to feed the pigs. And he longed to be nourished on the nuts that the pigs ate, and no one would give to him. And he went and said to himself: How many hired servants of my father have plenty of bread while I am dying of hunger here. I will rise up and go to my father and say to him: Father, I have sinned against heaven and in your sight, I am no longer worthy to be called your son. Make me like one of your hired servants. And he rose up and went to his father. And when he was still a long way off, his father saw him and was moved and ran and fell on his neck and kissed him. The son said to him: Father, I have sinned against heaven and in your sight, I am no longer worthy to be called your son. But his father said to his slaves: Quick, bring the best clothing and put it on him, and have a ring for his hand and shoes for his feet, and bring the fatted calf, slaughter him, and let us eat and make merry because this man, my son, was a dead man and came to life, he was lost and he has been found. And they began to make merry. His older son was out on the estate, and as he came nearer to the house he heard music and dancing, and he called over one of the servants and asked what was going on. He told him: Your brother is here, and your father slaughtered the fatted calf, because he got him back in good health. He was angry and did not want to go in. But his father came out and entreated him. But he answered and said to his father: Look, all these years I have been your slave and never neglected an order of yours, but you never gave me a kid so that I could make merry with my friends. But when this son of yours comes back, the one who ate up your livelihood in the company of whores, you slaughtered the fatted calf for him. But he said to him: My child, you are always with me, and all that is mine is yours; but we had to make merry and rejoice, because your brother was a dead man and came to life, he was lost and has been found.

From Matthew 13

[*Why Jesus Teaches in Parables*]

On that day Jesus went out of the house and sat beside the sea; and a great multitude gathered before him, so that he went aboard a ship and sat there, and all the multitude stood on the shore. And he talked to them, speaking mostly in parables: Behold, a sower went out to sow. And as he sowed, some of the grain fell beside the way, and birds came and ate it. Some fell on stony ground where there was not much soil, and it shot up quickly because there was no depth of soil, but when the sun came up it was parched, and because it had no roots it dried away. Some fell among thorns, and the thorns grew up and stifled it. But some fell upon the good soil and bore fruit, some a hundred-fold, some sixtyfold, some thirtyfold. He who has ears, let him hear. Then his disciples came to him and said: Why do you talk to them in parables? He answered them and said: Because it is given to you to understand the secrets of the Kingdom of Heaven, but to them it is not given. When a man has, he shall be given, and it will be more than he needs; but when he has not, even what he has shall be taken away from him. Therefore I talk to them in parables, because they have sight but do not see, and hearing but do not hear or understand. And for them is fulfilled the prophecy of Isaiah,[1] saying: With your hearing you shall hear and not understand, and you shall use your sight and look but not see. For the heart of this people is stiffened, and they hear with difficulty, and they have closed their eyes; so that they may never see with their eyes, or hear with their ears and with their hearts understand and turn back, so that I can heal them.

Blessed are your eyes because they see, and your ears because they hear. Truly I tell you that many prophets and good men have longed to see what you see, and not seen it, and to hear what you hear, and not heard it. Hear, then, the parable of the sower. To every man who hears the word of the Kingdom and does not understand it, the evil one comes and seizes what has been sown in his heart. This is the seed sown by the way. The seed sown on the stony ground is the man who hears the word and immediately accepts it with joy; but he has no root in himself, and he is a man of the moment, and when there comes affliction and persecution, because of the word, he does not stand fast. The seed sown among thorns is the man who hears the word, and concern for the world and the beguilement of riches stifle the word, and he bears no fruit. And the seed sown on the good soil is the man who hears the word and understands it, who bears fruit and makes it, one a hundredfold, one sixtyfold, and one thirtyfold.

He set before them another parable, saying: The Kingdom of Heaven is like a man who sowed good seed in his field. And while the people were asleep, his enemy came and sowed darnel in with the grain, and went away. When the plants grew and produced a crop, the darnel was seen. Then the slaves of the master came to him and said: Master, did you not sow good grain in your field? Where does the darnel come from? He said to them: A man who is my enemy did it. His slaves said: Do you wish us to go out and gather it? But he said: No, for fear that when you gather the darnel you may pull up the grain with it. Let them both grow until harvest time, and in the time of harvest I shall say to the harvesters: First gather the darnel, and bind it in sheaves for burning, but store the grain in my granary.

He set before them another parable, saying: The Kingdom of Heaven is like a grain of mustard, which a man took and sowed in his field; which is the smallest of all seeds, but when it grows, it is the largest of the greens and grows into a tree, so that the birds of the air come and nest in its branches.

He told them another parable: The Kingdom of Heaven is like leaven, which a woman took and buried in three measures of dough, so that it all rose.

All this Jesus told the multitudes in parables, and he did not talk to them except in parables; so as to fulfill the word spoken by the prophet, saying: I will open my mouth in parables, and pour out what has been hidden since the creation. Then he sent away the multitudes and went to the house. And his

1. See Isaiah 6.9–10.

disciples came to him and said: Make plain to us the parable of the darnel in the field. He answered them and said: The sower of the good seed is the son of man; the field is the world; the good seed is the sons of the Kingdom; the darnel is the sons of the evil one, and the enemy who sowed it is the devil; the harvest time is the end of the world, and the harvesters are angels. Then as the darnel is gathered and burned in the fire, so it is at the end of the world. The son of man will send out his angels, and they will gather from his Kingdom all that misleads, and the people who do what is not lawful, and cast them in the furnace of fire; and there will be weeping and gnashing of teeth. Then the righteous men will shine forth like the sun in the Kingdom of their father. He who has ears, let him hear. The Kingdom of Heaven is like a treasure hidden in the field, which a man found and hid, and for joy of it he goes and sells all he has and buys that field. Again, the Kingdom of Heaven is like a trader looking for fine pearls; he found one of great value, and went and sold all he had and bought it. Again, the Kingdom of Heaven is like a dragnet cast into the sea and netting every kind of fish; and when it is full they draw it out and sit on the beach and gather the good ones in baskets, but the bad they throw away. So will it be at the end of the world. The angels will go out and separate the bad from the midst of the righteous, and cast them in the furnace of fire; and there will be weeping and gnashing of teeth. Do you understand all this? They said to him: Yes. And he said to them: Therefore every scribe who is learned in the Kingdom of Heaven is like a man who is master of a house, who issues from his storehouse what is new and what is old.

Matthew 27–28

[*Crucifixion and Resurrection*]

When morning came, all the high priests and elders of the people held a meeting against Jesus, to have him killed. And they bound him and took him away and gave him over to Pilate the governor.[1]

Then when Judas, who had betrayed him, saw that he had been condemned, he repented and proffered the thirty pieces of silver back to the high priests and the elders, saying: I did wrong to betray innocent blood. They said: What is that to us? You look to it. And he threw down the silver pieces in the temple and went away, and when he was alone he hanged himself. The high priests took up the silver pieces and said: We cannot put them in the treasury, since it is blood money. Then they took counsel together and with the money they bought the potter's field[2] to bury strangers in. Therefore that field has been called the Field of Blood, to this day. Then was fulfilled the word spoken by Jeremiah the prophet,[3] saying: I took the thirty pieces of silver, the price of him on whom a price was set, whom they priced from among the sons of Israel, and I gave the money for the field of the potter, as my Lord commanded me.

---

1. Pontius Pilate, imperial administrator of the Roman province of Judea (26–36 C.E.).
2. A place where clay was dug to make pottery; after the Gospels, a common term for a burying place for the poor.

3. Alluding perhaps to the purchase of a field in Jeremiah 32, or to the potter of Jeremiah 18–19 (though the citation is to Zechariah 11.13).

Now Jesus stood before the governor; and the governor questioned him, saying: Are you the King of the Jews? Jesus answered: It is you who say it. And while he was being accused by the high priests and the elders he made no answer. Then Pilate said to him: Do you not hear all their testimony against you? And he made no answer to a single word, so that the governor was greatly amazed.

For the festival, the governor was accustomed to release one prisoner for the multitude, whichever one they wished. And they had at that time a notorious man, who was called Barabbas.[4] Now as they were assembled Pilate said to them: Which one do you wish me to release for you, Barabbas, or Jesus, who is called Christ? For he knew that it was through malice that they had turned him over. Now as he was sitting on the platform, his wife sent him a message, saying: Let there be nothing between you and this just man; for I have suffered much today because of a dream about him. But the high priests and the elders persuaded the crowd to ask for Barabbas and destroy Jesus. Then the governor spoke forth and said to them: Which of the two shall I give you? They answered: Barabbas. Pilate said to them: What then shall I do with Jesus, who is called Christ? They all said: Let him be crucified. But Pilate said: Why? What harm has he done? But they screamed all the more, saying: Let him be crucified. And Pilate, seeing that he was doing no good and that the disorder was growing, took water and washed his hands before the crowd, saying: I am innocent of the blood of this man. You see to it. And all the people answered and said: His blood is upon us and upon our children. Then Pilate gave them Barabbas, but he had Jesus flogged, and gave him over to be crucified.

Then the soldiers of the governor took Jesus to the residence, and drew up all their battalion around him. And they stripped him and put a red mantle about him, and wove a wreath of thorns and put it on his head, and put a reed in his right hand, and knelt before him and mocked him, saying: Hail, King of the Jews. And they spat upon him and took the reed and beat him on the head. And after they had mocked him, they took off the mantle and put his own clothes on him, and led him away to be crucified. And as they went out they found a man of Cyrene, named Simon. They impressed him for carrying the cross.

Then they came to a place called Golgotha, which means the place of the skull, and gave him wine mixed with gall to drink. When he tasted it he would not drink it. Then they crucified him, and divided up his clothes, casting lots, and sat there and watched him. Over his head they put the label giving the charge against him, where it was written: This is Jesus, the King of the Jews. Then there were crucified with him two robbers, one on his right and one on his left. And those who passed by blasphemed against him, wagging their heads, and saying: You who tear down the temple and rebuild it in three days, save yourself, and come down from the cross, if you are the son of God. So too the high priests, mocking him along with the scribes and the elders, said: He saved others, he cannot save himself. He is King of Israel, let him come down from the cross and we will believe in him. He trusted in God, let him save him now, if he will; for he said: I am the son of God. And the robbers who were crucified with him spoke abusively to him in the same way.

---

4. Bar-Abbas, meaning "son of Abbas" (literally, "son of the Father"). John 18.40 calls Barabbas a "bandit" (lēstēs), a term often applied to the Jewish revolutionaries who defied Roman rule (Mark 15.7 refers to his involvement in "sedition").

But from the sixth hour there was darkness over all the earth until the ninth hour. But about the ninth hour Jesus cried out in a great voice, saying: *Elei elei lema sabachthanei?*[5] Which is: My God, my God, why have you forsaken me? But some of those who were standing there heard and said: This man calls to Elijah.[6] And at once one of them ran and took a sponge, soaked it in vinegar and put it on the end of a reed, and gave it to him to drink. But the rest said: Let us see if Elijah comes to save him.

Then Jesus cried out again in a great voice, and gave up his life. And behold, the veil of the temple[7] was split in two from top to bottom, and the earth was shaken, and the rocks were split, and the tombs opened and many bodies of the holy sleepers rose up; and after his resurrection they came out of their tombs and went into the holy city, and were seen by many. But the company commander and those with him who kept guard over Jesus, when they saw the earthquake and the things that happened, were greatly afraid, saying: In truth this was the son of God. And there were many women watching from a distance there, who had followed Jesus from Galilee, waiting on him. Among them were Mary the Magdalene, and Mary the mother of James and Joseph, and the mother of the sons of Zebedee.

When it was evening, there came a rich man of Arimathaea, Joseph by name, who also had been a disciple of Jesus. This man went to Pilate and asked for the body of Jesus. Then Pilate ordered that it be given up to him. And Joseph took the body and wrapped it in clean linen, and laid it in his new tomb, which he had cut in the rock, and rolled a great stone before the door of the tomb, and went away. But Mary the Magdalene and the other Mary were there, sitting before the tomb. On the next day, which is the day after the Day of Preparation, the high priests and the Pharisees gathered in the presence of Pilate, and said: Lord, we have remembered how that impostor said while he was still alive: After three days I shall rise up. Give orders, then, that the tomb be secured until after the third day, for fear his disciples may come and steal him away and say to the people: He rose from the dead. And that will be the ultimate deception, worse than the former one. Pilate said to them: You have a guard. Go and secure it as best you can. And they went and secured the tomb, sealing it with the help of the guard.

Late on the sabbath, as the light grew toward the first day after the sabbath, Mary the Magdalene and the other Mary came to visit the tomb. And behold, there was a great earthquake, for the angel of the Lord came down from heaven and approached the stone and rolled it away and was sitting on it. His look was like lightning, and his clothing white as snow. And those who were on guard were shaken with fear of him and became like dead men. But the angel spoke forth and said to the women: Do not you fear; for I know that you look for Jesus, who was crucified. He is not here. For he rose up, as he said. Come here, and look at the place where he lay. Then go quickly and tell his disciples

---

5. These words are in Aramaic, a Semitic language commonly spoken in the region (closely related to Hebrew and Syriac); the rest of the gospel is in vernacular Greek.
6. The prophet who was bodily taken up to heaven in a chariot of fire (2 Kings 2.8–11);

his return was prophesied to herald the coming of the Messiah (Malachi 3.1; 4:5).
7. The veil covering the door of the inner sanctuary of the Temple (Exodus 26.31–34), where God was said to appear (Leviticus 16.2).

that he has risen from the dead, and behold, he goes before you into Galilee. There you will see him. See; I have told you. And quickly leaving the tomb, in fear and great joy, they ran to tell the news to his disciples. And behold, Jesus met them, saying: I give you greeting. They came up to him and took his feet and worshipped him. Then Jesus said to them: Do not fear. Go and tell my brothers to go into Galilee, and there they will see me. And as they went on their way, behold, some of the guards went into the city and reported to the high priests all that had happened. And they met with the elders and took counsel together, and gave the soldiers a quantity of money, saying: Say that the disciples came in the night and stole him away while we were sleeping. And if this is heard in the house of the governor, we shall reason with him, and make it so that you have nothing to fear. And they took the money and did as they were instructed. And this is the story that has been spread about among the Jews, to this day.

Then the eleven disciples went on into Galilee, to the mountain where Jesus had given them instructions to go; and when they saw him, they worshipped him; but some doubted. And Jesus came up to them and talked with them, saying: All authority has been given to me, in heaven and on earth. Go out, therefore, and instruct all the nations, baptizing them in the name of the Father and the Son and the Holy Spirit, teaching them to observe all that I have taught you. And behold, I am with you, all the days until the end of the world.

John 1

[The Word]

In the beginning was the word, and the word was with God, and the word was God. He was in the beginning, with God. Everything came about through him, and without him not one thing came about. What came about in him was life, and the life was the light of mankind; and the light shines in the darkness, and the darkness did not understand it.

There was a man sent from God; his name was John. This man came for testimony, to testify concerning the light, so that all should believe through him. He was not the light, but was to testify concerning the light. The light was the true light, which illuminates every person who comes into the world. He was in the world, and the world came about through him, and the world did not know him. He went to his own and his own people did not accept him. Those who accepted him, he gave them power to become children of God, to those who believed in his name, who were born not from blood or from the will of the flesh or from the will of man, but from God.

And the word became flesh and lived among us, and we have seen his glory, glory as of a single son from his father, full of grace and truth. John bears witness concerning him, and he cried out, saying (for it was he who was speaking): He who is coming after me was before me, because he was there before I was; because we have all received from his fullness, and grace for grace. Because the law was given through Moses; the grace and the truth came through Jesus Christ. No one has ever seen God; the only-born God who is in the bosom of his father, it is he who told of him.

And this is the testimony of John, when the Jews sent priests and Levites[1] from Jerusalem to ask him: Who are you? And he confessed, and made no denial, but confessed: I am not the Christ. And they asked him: What then? Are you Elijah? And he said: I am not. Are you the prophet? And he answered: No. Then they said to him: Who are you? So that we can give an answer to those who sent us. What do you say about yourself? He said: I am the voice of one crying in the desert: Make straight the way of the Lord; as Isaiah the prophet said. Now they had been sent by the Pharisees. And they questioned him and said to him: Why then do you baptize, if you are not the Christ, or Elijah or the prophet? John answered them saying: I baptize with water; but in your midst stands one whom you do not know, who is coming after me, and I am not fit to untie the fastening of his shoe. All this happened in Bethany beyond the Jordan,[2] where John was baptizing.

The next day he saw Jesus coming toward him and said: See, the lamb of God who takes away the sinfulness of the world. This is the one of whom I said: A man is coming after me who was before me, because he was there before I was. And I did not know him. But so that he might be made known to Israel, this was why I came baptizing with water. And John bore witness, saying: I have seen the Spirit descending like a dove from the sky, and it remained upon him; and I did not know him, but the one who sent me to baptize with water was the one who said to me: That one, on whom you see the Spirit descending and remaining upon him, is the one who baptizes with the Holy Spirit. And I have seen, and I have borne witness that this is the son of God.

The next day John was standing with two of his disciples, and he saw Jesus walking about and said: See, the lamb of God. His two disciples heard what he said and followed Jesus. Jesus turned about and saw them following him and said: What are you seeking? They said to him: Rabbi (which translated means master), where are you staying? He said to them: Come and see. So they came, and saw where he was staying, and stayed with him for that day. It was about the tenth hour. Andrew, one of the two who heard Jesus and followed him, was the brother of Simon Peter. He went first and found his brother Simon and said to him: We have found the Messiah (which is, translated, the Christ). He took him to Jesus. Jesus looked at him and said: You are Simon, the son of John. You shall be called Cephas[3] (which means Peter).

The next day Jesus wished to go out to Galilee. And he found Philip and said to him: Follow me. Philip was from Bethsaida, the city of Andrew and Peter. Philip found Nathanael and said to him: We have found the one of whom Moses wrote in the law, and the prophets: Jesus the son of Joseph, from Nazareth. And Nathanael said to him: Can anything good come from Nazareth? Philip said to him: Come and see. Jesus saw Nathanael coming toward him and said of him: See, a true son of Israel, in whom there is no guile. Nathanael said to him: How is it that you know me? Jesus answered and said to him: I saw you when you were under the fig tree, before Philip called you. Nathanael answered: Master, you are the son of God, you are the King of Israel. Jesus

---

1. Members of the tribe of Levi (one of the sons of Jacob), who formed a hereditary subordinate priesthood (see Numbers 18.1–6).
2. The river that forms the border between modern Israel and, to the east, Jordan and Syria.
3. *Kêfâ* (Aramaic), meaning "rock" or "stone" (Greek *petros*).

answered and said to him: Because I told you I saw you under the fig tree, you believe? You will see greater things than that. And he said to him: Truly truly I tell you, you will see the heaven open and the angels of God ascending and descending to the son of man.[4]

4. Compare Jacob's vision of the ladder at Bethel (Genesis 28.10–17).

APULEIUS
ca. 125–ca. 180

The Golden Ass is a wildly miscellaneous stew of elements. It is a novel, but has stories embedded within it, like a frame-tale narrative; it features processions and theatrical settings, as does a play, but also has a dreamlike, almost hallucinatory quality. The work's alternative title, *Metamorphoses*, points to the main literary model for this work: the human and animal transformations in the **Metamorphoses** of **Ovid**. But while the Roman poet features the classical gods, such as Jupiter and Apollo, Apuleius introduces us to the exotic cult of Isis, which originated in Egypt, and the dangerous allure of witchcraft. We follow our hero, Lucius, through a series of erotic encounters, comic catastrophes, and exotic transformations and finally—like Lucius—we reflect on what lessons might be learned from a life so extravagantly led.

We have two sources of information about Apuleius: what he tells himself in his four surviving works, and what his African countryman **Augustine** wrote about him (rather disapprovingly) two centuries later. Apuleius was born in Madaurus (near modern Mdaourouch, in Algeria), the same town where Augustine would be educated before moving on to Carthage and Rome. The Roman provinces that made up Apuleius's Africa were in a state of cultural flux; Carthaginian culture strongly persisted and the Punic language remained in use, while the greater Roman Empire still was a political and economic power. Madaurus was a city of four languages: the local vernaculars of Punic and Libyan plus Latin and Greek, the administrative and elite languages of the empire. Apuleius says he spoke Greek as a mother tongue, though he also pursued it at an advanced level during his study abroad in Athens, and his novel is composed in remarkably eloquent Latin. In one sense, Apuleius is a product of Roman culture, although he lived in the provinces; yet Apuleius himself makes much of his African background and takes a native pride in the region. Born to a family of wealth and status, with a father who, as a *duumvir* (colonial magistrate), held the highest political office in the region and who left his two sons a vast fortune, Apuleius was lavishly educated, first in Carthage and then in Athens and Rome. His travels and education identify him clearly as a member of the cosmopolitan Roman Empire.

Although we do not know when Apuleius wrote *The Golden Ass*, we do have a firm date for one of his other works, the

Apology: Apuleius delivered this defense orally at his trial in 158, after he was charged with practicing black magic in order to seduce his wealthy older wife, Pudentilla, and then poisoning her son (and Apuleius's former best friend) Pontianus. Apuleius was acquitted and went on to serve as orator and politician at Carthage. The author of a huge number of works, though only four survive, he wrote in many genres, including speeches, novels, poems, philosophical dialogues, and histories; the subjects of his prose treatises ranged from arithmetic to love to zoology. His capacious and synthetic mind enabled Apuleius to collate and disseminate a huge array of information, as well as to compose the most extraordinarily heterogeneous literary work of the premodern age.

The *Apology* is useful in providing not only information about Apuleius's life and times but also an intriguing context for reading *The Golden Ass*, whose narrator Lucius also experiences a traumatic court trial, is drawn in by the appeal of transgressive romantic liaisons, and discovers the dangers of magic. The eleven books of *The Golden Ass* take the reader on a whirlwind of adventure. At times Lucius is trapped in the position of a slave, his position hopeless; then a sudden reversal of fortune sets him free and another cycle of wild adventure begins. The excerpts provided here center on Lucius's magical transformation, which takes place during his stay at the city of Hypata in Thessaly (Greece). At the marketplace, Lucius meets an old family friend, Byrrhena, who warns him about his host, Milo, and the secret powers of seduction possessed by Pamphile, Milo's wife. More intrigued than alarmed, Lucius decides to try to learn more about Pamphile with the aid of her equally attractive maid, Photis—with disastrous and comic results.

The style of *The Golden Ass* is highly episodic, as our hero undergoes a series of adventures—some sordid, some titillating. He is a young man of privileged background and limited experience, and his transformation into a beast of burden leads him to experience the underbelly of society as lived in the eastern cities of the Roman Empire. Lucius meets thieves and beggars, prostitutes and slave women, and while in their company he hears the everyday comic and scurrilous tales that were fundamental to the oral culture of the second century—a culture that is largely invisible to modern readers, because ancient writers tended to stick to more elevated subject matter. Though *The Golden Ass* is based on an earlier Greek novel by one Lucius of Patras (perhaps Lucian of Samosata), Apuleius does much more than simply translate the story into Latin. He reduces the Greek cultural framework significantly, placing his narrator instead in the heterogeneous world of the Roman Empire as he moves through Asia Minor (modern Turkey), Greece, Egypt, and Italy. Beyond adding a great deal of local detail about daily life in various cultural centers, Apuleius creates an entirely new ending set not in Greece but in Rome. Yet this is an Orientalized Rome, where the narrator becomes a devotee of the religion of Isis, an Egyptian goddess whose cult had taken hold in the imperial center.

The Golden Ass was popular in its own time, circulating especially in North Africa and the eastern Mediterranean, where it was read eagerly by the student populations that Augustine describes with such contempt in his *City of God* and *Confessions*. Interest in it reawakened in the Renaissance, reflected in the hybrid jackass-man Nick Bottom in **Shakespeare**'s *Midsummer Night's Dream*, and its influence has persisted in modernist fiction, including the hideously transformed Gregor Samsa of Franz Kafka's *Metamorphosis* and the hapless companions of the hero, turned into donkeys, in Carlo Collodi's novel *The Adventures of Pinocchio*.

From The Golden Ass[1]

FROM BOOK 2

[*Lucius in Hypata*]

As soon as the darkness was dispelled and a new sun ushered in the day, I rose from my couch the moment I awoke from sleep, for I was generally buoyed up, and most eager to discover the weird and wonderful features of the place. I recalled that I was in the heart of Thessaly,[2] the source of those spells of the magic art which are famed by common consent through the entire world. I remembered too that the tale recounted by Aristomenes, that best of companions,[3] had its origin in this city. So in expectation and enthusiasm alike I was quite alert, and I studied each feature with some care. I did not believe that anything which I gazed on in the city was merely what it was, but that every single object had been transformed into a different shape by some muttered and deadly incantation. I thought that the stones which caused me to trip were petrified persons, that the birds which I could hear were feathered humans, that the trees enclosing the city-limits were people who had likewise sprouted foliage, that the waters of the fountains were issuing from human bodies. I imagined that at any moment the statues and portraits would parade about, that the walls would speak, that oxen and other cattle would prophesy, that the very sky and the sun's orb would suddenly proclaim an oracular message.

In this trance, or rather hypnosis, induced by such tortured longing, I went round examining everything, but without finding a suggestion or even a trace of what I passionately sought. I wandered from door to door like a man seeking some extravagant and dissolute diversion, and all unknowing I suddenly found myself at the food-market. I caught sight of a woman walking through it, surrounded by a sizeable retinue, and I quickened my step and overtook her. Her jewellery was gold-inlaid and her clothes gold-embroidered, undoubtedly signalling that she was an upper-class matron. Walking close to her side was a man of advanced years. As soon as he set eyes on me he exclaimed: 'Heavens, it's Lucius!' and he gave me a kiss of greeting. At once he whispered something in the lady's ear which I could not overhear. 'This is your aunt,' he said. 'You must approach her yourself, and greet her.' 'I'm shy of doing that', I said, 'for I do not know her.' Whereupon I blushed all over, and kept my distance with my head bowed.

The lady then turned to stare at me. 'My goodness,' she said, 'he has the manners of a gentleman. He gets them from his mother Salvia who is a model of goodness. And damn me if his appearance generally isn't just right! He is tall, but not lofty; he's slim, but there is spunk there; his colour is moderately ruddy, his hair is blonde but not foppish; his green eyes have a watchful look, quick to focus, sharp as an eagle's. His face looks healthy from every angle, and his walk is pleasing and natural.'

Then she added: 'Lucius, these hands of mine reared you. That was as it should be, for not only am I your mother's blood relation, but we were brought up together. We are both descended from Plutarch's household, we had the same wet-nurse, and we grew up together as inseparable sisters. The one thing

---

1. Translated by P. G. Walsh.
2. A region of northern Greece, traditionally
associated with sorcery.
3. Met by Lucius in book 1.

that distinguishes us is our social standing. She contracted marriage with a prominent public figure, whereas I married a private citizen. I'm called Byrrhena; you may recall the name through mention of it among those who brought you up. So don't be shy of accepting our hospitality; in fact our house is yours.'

These remarks of hers had given me time to disguise my blushes, and I spoke up in reply. 'Dear aunt,' I said, 'I could hardly bid my host Milo goodbye without his feeling aggrieved. I shall make every effort to do what I can, short of breaching my obligation to him. Whenever any occasion for a journey this way arises in future, I shall always lodge with you.' In the course of these and similar exchanges, the short journey we had made on foot brought us to Byrrhena's house.

The reception-area was very fine. Pillars stood at each corner, supporting statues representing the goddess Victory. In these representations, her wings were outspread but motionless, and her dewy feet stood on tiptoe on the slippery surface of a revolving sphere, momentarily joined to it but giving the impression of imminent flight. But the notable feature was Parian marble chiselled into the likeness of Diana,[4] which occupied the centre of the whole atrium, and was raised off the ground. The statue gleamed spectacularly; with her garment breeze-blown, her lively figure was hastening forward as if to confront the incomer with the august majesty of her godhead. Hounds, likewise executed in marble, escorted the goddess on both flanks. Their eyes were threatening, their ears pricked up, their nostrils flaring, their maws savage. If barking sounded loudly from anywhere near at hand, you would think that it issued from those mouths of marble. But the highest feat of craftsmanship achieved by that genius of a sculptor was that the hounds were rearing breast-high, and their hind legs were braking while their forelegs were in rapid motion.

To the rear of the goddess rose a rock forming a cave. Out of the stone sprouted moss, green plants, foliage and brushwood; vines on one side were set off against miniature trees on the other. Within the cave the reflection of the statue shone out because of the smooth brightness of the marble. Apples and grapes hung from the lower edge of the rock; their highly artistic finish, depicted with a skill rivalling nature's, made them lifelike, so that you could imagine that some of them could be plucked for eating once the maturing autumn endowed them with the colour of ripeness. If you bent low and gazed into the water which skirted the goddess's feet as it lapped in gentle waves, you would think that the bunches of grapes hanging from the rock possessed the faculty of movement as well as other lifelike qualities. In the middle of the marble foliage a statue of Actaeon[5] was visible, fashioned in marble and reflected in the water; his neck craned forward as he gazed with curiosity towards the goddess. He was already animal-like, on the point of becoming a stag as he waited for Diana to take her bath.

As I repeatedly ran my eye over this scene with intense delight, Byrrhena remarked: 'All that you see is yours.' After saying this, she had a private word with all the others, and asked them to leave us. When they had all been sent away, she said to me: 'Dearest Lucius, I swear by the goddess here; I am troubled and

---

4. Roman goddess of virginity, the moon, and the hunt (and thus often depicted with her hunting dogs).
5. In Greek myth, a hunter who saw Diana/ Artemis bathing in the woods; after the furious goddess transformed him into a stag, he was devoured by his own hunting dogs (see Ovid, *Metamorphoses* 3.138–52).

fearful for you. Since you are my cherished son, I should like to give you warning well in advance. Watch out for yourself. Take stringent precautions against the wicked arts and evil enticements of the notorious Pamphile, the wife of Milo, who you say is your host. She is reputed to be a witch of the first rank, a specialist in all forms of necromancy. She has only to breathe on twigs, pebbles, and common objects of that kind, and she can plunge all this light of day which descends from the starry heavens into the lowest depths of Tartarus,[6] reducing it to the chaos of old. Then as soon as she catches sight of any handsome young man, she is captivated by his charms, and at once focuses her eyes and her attention on him. She sows the seeds of allurements, dominates his will, and proceeds to imprison him in eternal bonds of deep love. If those who are less amenable prove worthless to her because they scorn her, she transforms them in a trice into stones or cattle or any animal you can think of, while others she utterly destroys. These are the fears I have for you, and I think that you should be on your guard against them, for she is constantly ablaze with desire, and your youth and handsome bearing make you a suitable target for her.' These were the troubled thoughts which Byrrhena shared with me.

But I was already disposed to curiosity, and as soon as I heard mention of the art of magic which I had always prayed for, so far from taking precautions against Pamphile, I was eager even without compulsion to undergo such schooling willingly, and to pay a heavy price for it. In short, I was all for taking a running jump and landing myself headlong in those murky depths. So with lunatic haste I freed myself from Byrrhena's detaining hand as if from a confining chain, and bade her a hasty farewell. I then flew off at top speed to Milo's lodging. As I redoubled my steps like one demented, I said to myself: 'Lucius, look alive, and keep your wits about you. This is the chance you were praying for. You will be able to achieve that long-standing ambition of yours, and obtain your heart's content of wonderful stories. Dismiss your childish fears, come to grips with the issue at close quarters and without cowardice. You must steer clear of any love-relationship with your hostess, and scrupulously respect the good Milo's marriage-bed. Make a bee-line instead for the maidservant Photis. She is attractive, she has amusing ways, and she is quite sharp. Last night when you retired to sleep, she genially escorted you to your room, fussed over you in getting you to your bed, tucked you in quite affectionately, kissed your forehead, and showed by her face her unwillingness to leave. In fact she kept halting and looking back. So even though it has its hazards, Photis must be your target. The best of luck in your endeavours.'

These were the arguments occupying my mind as I made for Milo's door. I voted with my feet, as the expression goes. I found neither Milo nor his wife at home, but only my dear Photis. She was cooking minced pork for stuffing, and slices of meat, and some very spicy sausage of which I had already caught a whiff. She was wearing an elegant linen dress, with a bright red belt fastened up supporting her breasts. As she turned the casserole-dish round and round with her petal-like fingers, and shook it repeatedly in its circular motion, she simultaneously rotated her body. Her hips moved lightly in rhythm, and as she wiggled her supple spine, her person rippled most attractively. I was spellbound at the sight, and stood there lost in admiration. The parts of me that

6. In classical myth, the part of the underworld in which the wicked are punished.

were asleep before now stood to attention. Finally I managed to speak to her; 'My dear Photis,' I said, 'how lusciously and attractively you wiggle that wee pot, and your bottom with it! That's a succulent dish you have in readiness there! How lucky a fellow would be if you let him stick his finger in—he'd be on top of the world!'

That pert and witty girl at once replied: 'Keep clear, poor boy, keep clear as far as possible from this stove of mine. If once my little flame shoots out and as much as sears you, you will be all ablaze inside, and I'll be the only one who can put your fire out. The spices which I incorporate are sweet. I'm an expert at pleasurably shaking a bed as well as a pot.'

With these words she looked me in the eye, and grinned. I did not leave her presence until I had carefully studied all the features of her appearance. Of her other charms I need say nothing, for it has always been my one obsession first to examine a person's head of hair thoroughly and openly outside, and then to take pleasure in it privately indoors. I have a secure and well-established justification for preferring this criterion of beauty. First comes the fact that the head is the outstanding part of the body; it is exposed and prominent, and is the first feature to meet the eye. Secondly, whereas the other physical parts are made attractive by the gay colour of bright clothing, it is the head's own natural sheen which achieves this. Lastly, most women when they wish to demonstrate their personal attractions disrobe and remove all their clothes in their eagerness to show off their naked beauty, seeking to please the eye more with the rosy blush of their skin than with the golden colour of their dress. But if you were to scalp some lady of outstanding beauty, and thus rob her face of its natural adornment—this is a sacrilegious suggestion, and I pray that so grisly an illustration of my point may never materialize—it would not matter if she came down from heaven, or rose from the sea, or was sprung from the waves. In other words, it would not matter if she were Venus[7] herself, flanked by a whole choir of Graces, accompanied by the entire body of Cupids, wearing that belt of hers around her waist, diffusing the scent of cinnamon and bedewing the air with balsam; if she appeared without her hair, she would not give pleasure even to her Vulcan.

How enchanting is a woman's hair when its pleasing colour and glossy sheen shines out! When it faces the sun's rays, it is enlivened and flashes fire, or gently reflects the sunlight. Sometimes it offers contrasting pleasures by varying its appearance. Hair with a golden glow subsides into the soft shaded colour of honey. Hair which is raven-black seeks to rival the ultramarine necks of doves. Hair oiled with drops of Arabian perfume, parted with the fine teeth of a sharp comb, and gathered at the back, serves as a mirror when it confronts the lover's eyes, and affords him a more flattering reflection. Sometimes numerous strands are combined to form a thick wedge on top of the head, or they flow down the back, extending in a long plait. Such in fact is the lofty status of a woman's hair that she can appear before us adorned with gold, fine clothes, jewellery and the rest of her finery, but unless she has ordered her hair she cannot be regarded as well-groomed.

My Photis, however, had not fussed over hers, and yet its tousled arrangement lent her added charm. Her abundant hair had been let hang soft and free

7. The beautiful Roman goddess of love, mother of Cupid (Eros, god of love) and wife of Vulcan, god of the forge; she was closely associated with the Graces, personifications of grace and beauty.

down from her head over her neck, and having rested briefly on the golden border of her dress, it had finally been gathered and fastened in a knot on top of her head.

I could no longer endure the fierce torture of my extreme pleasure. I leaned over her, and implanted the sweetest of honeyed kisses where her hair reached the crown of her head. She then twisted her neck to face me, and gave me a sidelong look with devouring eyes. 'Hey there, schoolboy,' she said, 'the savoury dish you're sampling is bitter as well as sweet. Just watch out; that honey which tastes so sweet may bring on a lengthy attack of bitter bile.'

'How can you say that, light of my life?' I asked. 'I am ready to be laid and grilled on this fire of yours, once you have roused me with one little kiss.' As I spoke I grasped her tightly in my arms, and started to kiss her. In a moment she was as abandoned as I was, as she rose to the same heat of passion. With unrestrained desire she showed her longing for me; the breath from her open lips was like cinnamon, and the thrust of her tongue was like nectar as it met mine. I said to her: 'This is killing me! Indeed, I'm already dead unless you take pity on me.' She gave me another long kiss, and answered: 'Don't worry. That longing which we share makes me your slave, and our pleasure will be postponed no longer. As soon as the first lamp is lit, I'll be in your bedroom. So be off with you, and make your preparations. I shall engage you in an all-night battle with the strength of passion.'

FROM BOOK 3

[Metamorphosis]

Eventually my Photis came in, after having seen her mistress to bed. Her demeanour was quite different from before, for she did not look cheerful, nor was her conversation spiced with wit. She wore a sombre look, wrinkling her face into a frown.

At last she spoke hesitantly and timidly. 'I have to confess', she said, 'that I caused this discomfiture of yours.' As she spoke, she produced a strap from under her dress, and handed it to me. 'Take your revenge, I beg you,' she said, 'on a woman who has betrayed you, or exact some punishment even greater than this. But I implore you not to imagine that I deliberately planned this painful treatment for you. God forbid that you should suffer even the slightest vexation on my account. If anything untoward threatens you, I pray that my life-blood may avert it. It was because of a mischance that befell me, when ordered to perform a different task, that the damage was inflicted on you.'

Impelled by my habitual curiosity and eager to have the hidden cause of the incident of the previous night revealed, I then replied: 'This is a wicked and most presumptuous strap, since you have allotted it the task of beating you. I shall destroy it by cutting it up or by slashing it to pieces rather than have it touch your skin, which is soft as down and white as milk. But tell me truthfully: what action of yours was attended by the perversity of savage Fortune, and resulted in my downfall? I swear by that head of yours which is so dear to me that I can believe no one, and you least of all, in the suggestion that you laid any plan for my undoing. In any case, a chance happening, or even a detrimental occurrence, cannot convert innocent intentions into guilty deeds.' As I finished speaking, I thirstily applied my mouth to the moist and trembling eyes of my Photis, which were languid with uncontrolled desire, and were now half-closed as I pressed hungry kisses upon them.

Her high spirits now restored, 'Please wait a moment,' she said, 'until I carefully close the bedroom door. I don't wish to commit a grievous error by carelessly and sacrilegiously letting my tongue run free.' As she spoke, she thrust home the bolts and fastened the hook securely. Then she came back to me, and took my neck in both her hands. In a low and quite restrained voice, she said: 'I am fearful and mortally terrified of revealing the secrets of this house, and of exposing the hidden mysteries wrought by my mistress. But I have considerable trust in you and your learning. In addition to the noble distinction of your birth and your outstanding intellect, you have been initiated into several sacred cults, and you are certainly aware of the need for the sacred confidentiality of silence. So all that I entrust to the sanctuary of your pious heart you must for ever enclose and guard within its confines, and thus repay the ingenuous trust of my revelations with the steadfast security of your silence. The love which holds me fast to you compels me to reveal to you things which I alone know. You are now to gain acquaintance with the entire nature of our household, with the wondrous and secret spells of my mistress. To these the spirits hearken and the elements are enslaved, and by them the stars are dislocated and the divine powers harnessed. But for no purpose does my mistress have recourse to the power of this art so much as when she eyes with pleasure some young man of elegant appearance, and indeed this is a frequent practice of hers.

'At the moment she is passionately obsessed with a young and extremely handsome Boeotian,[8] and she eagerly deploys every device and every technique of her art. Only this evening I heard her with my own ears threatening the sun itself with cloud cover and unbroken darkness because it had not retired from the sky quickly enough, and had yielded to nightfall too late for her to practise the enticements of magic. Yesterday, when she was on her way back from the baths, she happened to catch sight of the young man sitting in the barber's, and she ordered me to remove secretly his hair which had been snipped off by the scissors and was lying on the floor. As I was carefully and unobtrusively gathering it, the barber caught me at it. Now we in this city have a bad name for practising the art of sorcery, so he grabbed me brusquely and rebuked me. "You brazen hussy, is there no end to your repeatedly stealing the hair of eligible young men? If you don't finally stop this criminal practice, I'll have you up at once before the magistrates." He followed up his words with action; he thrust his hands between my breasts, felt around, and angrily extracted some hair which I had already hidden there. I was extremely concerned at this turn of events, remembering my mistress's usual temper. She often gets quite annoyed if she is frustrated in this way, and she takes it out on me most savagely. I actually thought of running away from her, but the thought of you at once caused me to reject the idea.

'I was just returning dispirited and afraid to go back empty-handed from the barber's, when I saw a man paring some goatskins with scissors. Once I watched the skins inflated, tightly tied, and hanging up, and the hair from them lying on the ground and of the same blonde colour as that of the young Boeotian, I abstracted a quantity of it and passed it to my mistress, concealing

8. A native of Boeotia, a region of central Greece northwest of Athens.

its true provenance. So it was that in the first hours of darkness, before you returned from your dinner, my mistress Pamphile in a fit of ecstatic madness climbed up towards the overlapping roof. On the far side of the house there is an area which is uncovered and exposed to the elements. It commands every view on the eastern side, as well as those in other directions. So it is especially convenient for those magical arts of hers, and she practises them there in secret. First of all she fitted out her infernal laboratory with the usual supplies, including every kind of aromatic plant, metal strips inscribed with unintelligible letters, the surviving remains of ill-omened birds, and a fairly large collection of corpses' limbs, earlier mourned over by relatives and in some cases even buried. Noses and fingers were in a heap in one place, and in another, nails from the gibbet to which there still clung flesh from the men hanged there. In yet another place the blood of slaughtered men was kept, and also gnawed skulls, torn from the fangs of wild beasts.

'Then, after chanting spells over quivering entrails, she poured propitiating offerings of various liquids—now spring-water, now cow's milk, now mountain-honey; she also poured out mead. She twisted and entwined the locks of hair with each other, and placed them on live coals to be burnt with a variety of fragrant plants. Immediately, through this combination of the irresistible power of her magic lore and the hidden energy of the harnessed deities, the bodies from which the hair was crackling and smoking acquired human breath, and were able to feel and walk. They headed for the place to which the stench from the hair they had shed led them, and thus they took the place of the Boeotian youth in barging at the doors, in their attempt to gain entrance. At that moment you appeared on the scene, drunk with wine and deceived by the darkness of the sightless night. You drew your short sword, and armed yourself for the role of the mad Ajax.[9] But whereas he inflicted violence on living cattle and lacerated whole herds, you much more courageously dealt the death-blow to three inflated goat-skins. Thus you laid low the enemy without shedding a drop of blood, so that I can embrace not a homicide but an utricide.'[1]

This elegant remark of Photis made me smile, and I responded in the same joking spirit. 'Well then,' I said, 'I can regard this as the first trophy won by my valour, in the tradition of Hercules' twelve labours,[2] for I can equate the body of Geryon which was in triplicate, or the three-formed shape of Cerberus, with the like number of skins that I slew. But to obtain as you desire my forgiveness willingly for the entire error by which you involved me in such great distress, you must grant me the favour which is my dearest wish. Let me watch your mistress when she sets in train some application of her supernatural art. Let me see her when she summons the gods, or at any rate when she changes her shape. I am all agog to witness magic from close up. Mind you, you yourself do not seem to be a novice wholly innocent of such things. I have come to be quite convinced

---

9. One of the greatest Greek warriors at Troy. Driven mad by Athena, he killed animals, believing that he was attacking the Greek leaders who had refused to give him the armor of the dead Achilles; returned to sanity, he killed himself in shame.
1. A skin-slayer; in Latin, a *uter* is a bag or bottle made of animal hide.

2. The tasks undertaken by the greatest hero of classical mythology as part of his purification after he killed his wife and children in a fit of madness; they included stealing the cattle of Geryon, who had the bodies of three men joined at the waist, and capturing Cerberus, the monstrous three-headed dog of the lord of the underworld.

of this, for your flashing eyes and rosy cheeks, your shining hair, your kisses with parted lips, and your fragrant breasts hold me fast as your willing slave and bondsman, whereas previously I always spurned the embraces of matrons. So now I have no thought of returning home or planning my departure there; there is nothing which I count better than spending a night with you.'

'Lucius,' she replied, 'I should dearly love to grant your wish, but her surly disposition aside, Pamphile invariably seeks solitude and likes to perform such secret rites when no one else is present. However, I shall put your wish before my personal danger. I shall watch out for a favourable occasion, and carefully arrange what you seek. My only stipulation, as I said at the beginning, is that you must promise to maintain silence in this momentous matter.'

As we chatted away, our desire for each other roused the minds and bodies of both of us. We threw off the clothes we wore until we were wholly naked, and enjoyed a wild love-orgy. When I was wearied with her feminine generosity, Photis offered me a boy's pleasure. Finally this period of wakefulness caused our eyes to droop; sleep invaded them, and held us fast until it was broad daylight.

After we had spent a few nights in such pleasurable pursuits, one day Photis came hurrying to me trembling with excitement. Her mistress, she said, was having no success in her love-affair by other means, and so she intended on the following night to invest herself with a bird's plumage, and to join her beloved by taking wing. I should accordingly be ready to observe with due circumspection this astonishing feat. So just as darkness fell, Photis led me silently on tiptoe to that upper chamber, and instructed me to witness what was happening there through a chink in the door.

Pamphile first divested herself of all her clothing. She then opened a small casket and took from it several small boxes. She removed the lid from one of these, and extracted ointment from it. This she rubbed for some time between her hands, and then smeared it all over herself from the tips of her toes to the crown of her head. She next held a long and private conversation with the lamp, and proceeded to flap her arms and legs with a trembling motion. As she gently moved them up and down, soft feathers began to sprout on them, and sturdy wings began to grow. Her nose became curved and hard, and her nails became talons. In this way Pamphile became an owl; she uttered a plaintive squawk as she tried out her new identity by gradually forsaking the ground. Soon she rose aloft, and with the full power of her wings quitted the house.

This was how Pamphile deliberately changed her shape by employing techniques of magic. I too was spellbound, but not through any incantation. I was rooted to the ground with astonishment at this event, and I seemed to have become something other than Lucius. In this state of ecstasy and riveted mindlessness, I was acting out a waking dream, and accordingly I rubbed my eyes repeatedly in an effort to discover whether I was awake. Finally I returned to awareness of my surroundings, and seizing Photis' hand I placed it on my eyes. 'While the chance allows,' I begged her, 'do please allow me one great and unprecedented boon bestowed by your affection. Get me, my honey-sweet, a little ointment from that same box—by those dear breasts of yours I beg you. Bind me as your slave for ever by a favour which I can never repay, and in this way ensure that I shall become a winged Cupid,[3] drawing close to my Venus.'

3. Cupid was conventionally depicted with wings.

'Is that what you're after, my foxy lover?' she asked. 'Are you trying to force me to apply an axe to my own limbs? When you are in that vulnerable state, I can scarcely keep you safe from those two-legged Thessalian wolves! And where shall I seek you, when shall I see you, once you become a bird?'

'The gods preserve me from perpetrating such an outrage,' I replied. 'Even if I were to fly through the entire heavens on the soaring wings of an eagle, as the appointed messenger or happy squire of highest Jove,[4] would I not sweep down from time to time from the enjoyment of such distinction on the wing to this fond nest of mine? I swear by this sweet knot that binds your hair and has enmeshed my heart, there is no other girl I prefer to my dear Photis. A second thought comes to my mind: once I have smeared myself and have become a bird like that, I shall have to keep a safe distance from all habitations. What a handsome and amusing lover I should make for matrons to enjoy when I'm an owl! If those night-birds do get inside a house, the residents, as we see, take care to catch them and nail them to their doors, to expiate by their sufferings the threatened destruction to the household occasioned by their ill-omened flight. But I almost forgot to ask: what word or action do I need to discard those feathers and to return to my being Lucius?' 'You have no worries in ensuring that,' she answered, 'for my mistress has shown me each and every substance that can restore to human form those who have adopted such shapes. Do not imagine that she did this out of mere goodwill; it was so that I could aid her with an efficacious remedy on her return. Observe with what cheap and everyday herbs such a great transformation is achieved. You wash yourself with water in which a sprig of dill and some bay-leaves have been steeped, and drink some of it.'

She made this claim repeatedly, and then with great apprehension she crept into the chamber, and took a box from the casket. First I hugged and kissed it, and prayed that it would bring me happy flying hours. Then I hastily tore off all my clothes, dipped my hands eagerly into the box, drew out a good quantity of the ointment, and rubbed all my limbs with it. I then flapped my arms up and down, imitating the movements of a bird. But no down and no sign of feathers appeared. Instead, the hair on my body was becoming coarse bristles, and my tender skin was hardening into hide. There were no longer five fingers at the extremities of my hands, for each was compressed into one hoof. From the base of my spine protruded an enormous tail. My face became misshapen, my mouth widened, my nostrils flared open, my lips became pendulous, and my ears huge and bristly. The sole consolation I could see in this wretched transformation was the swelling of my penis—though now I could not embrace Photis.

As I helplessly surveyed the entire length of my body, and came to the realization that I was not a bird but an ass, I tried to complain at what Photis had done to me. But I was now deprived of the human faculties of gesture and speech; all I could do by way of silent reproach was to droop my lower lip, and with tearful eyes give her a sidelong look. As soon as she saw what I had become, she beat her brow with remorseful hands and cried: 'That's the end of poor me! In my panic and haste I made a mistake; those look-alike boxes deceived me. But the saving grace is that the remedy for this transformation is quite easy and available. Just chew some roses, and you will stop being an ass and at once become my Lucius again.'

---

4. Another name for Jupiter, whose bird was the eagle.

AUGUSTINE
354–430

When Augustine lay dying in August of 430, Vandal armies were besieging the African city of Hippo (modern Annaba, Algeria), where Augustine was the spiritual leader of a vibrant community of Christians living under the rule of the Roman Empire. Within weeks, Hippo would fall; the great city of Rome itself would be captured within thirty years. Born into the culture of antiquity but laying the foundations for the medieval millennium that was just about to begin, Augustine stands with one foot in each world. His monumental autobiography, the *Confessions*, constantly draws on the rich literature of the Roman orators and prose writers, especially Cicero. Yet it also reaches forward, innovatively exploring the ways in which the reader—like Augustine himself—might find that the Word of God has all along been lodged within his innermost soul.

LIFE AND TIMES

Augustine was a native of the northern African regions that were part of the Roman Empire. Yet the empire was in a gradual state of collapse throughout Augustine's lifetime: strong military leaders were running the government in all but name from 395 onward, and the final Roman emperor would be deposed by rebellious mercenary troops in 476. It was a transitional period—a time of great instability and, simultaneously, cultural and religious ferment. Mystery and cult religions were particularly popular, as witnessed by Augustine's account of his years with the Manichaeans; **Apuleius** also captures this milieu in his description of the devotees of Isis

in *The Golden Ass*. Despite the instability and uncertainty of the period, the administrative and economic structures of the empire were still healthy enough to ease travel between its various parts, allowing Augustine to journey throughout northern Africa and Italy.

Augustine spent his early years in Africa, where there were several provincial cities of substantial size. Born at Thagaste (modern Souk-Ahras, Algeria), he had his first schooling at the nearby town of Madaurus and, later, at the sophisticated cultural capital of Carthage. There, Augustine became intrigued by Manichaeanism, a dualistic religion that resembled early Christianity in emphasizing the life of the mind and the drive toward increasing spiritual purity, though the two religions differed very significantly in their views of the nature of God. Augustine quickly rose to the top of his profession as an educator and public speaker, teaching grammar at his birthplace of Thagaste and, later, rhetoric at Carthage. These provincial successes impelled him to Rome, where he established a school of rhetoric; he was then invited to come to Milan, which had become a capital of the Western Roman Empire, to take on the chair of rhetoric and such duties as writing honorific speeches to be presented at court. At Milan, Augustine entered into a very sophisticated intellectual community, where he became deeply involved in Neoplatonism both as a philosophy and as a quasi-religious form of mysticism. He also came to know Ambrose, the Roman Catholic bishop of Milan. At the time, Augustine says, he told himself that he was attending Ambrose's sermons simply to judge his excellence as a public speaker. In fact, Augustine was becoming increasingly drawn to Christianity, a religion to which his mother, Monica, had vainly tried to introduce him since he was a young child.

The bond between Augustine and Ambrose was strengthened enormously by Monica, who had followed her son to Milan and become close to Ambrose; the bishop reciprocated, constantly telling his friend Augustine what a treasure he had in his faithful and devout mother. The *Confessions* shows that Monica played a major role in her son's spiritual growth, which culminated in Augustine's conversion and baptism on Easter 386, at the age of thirty-two. This was a moment of complete change for Augustine, not just spiritually but also practically: he gave up his chair in rhetoric at the imperial court of Milan, withdrew from his engagement to marry, and went with his mother to the port of Ostia to return to Africa. But before they could sail from Italy, Monica died, as did Augustine's son, Adeodatus, who had been born in Carthage to Augustine's longtime mistress, traveled to Italy with Augustine, and undergone baptism alongside his father. Alone back in Thagaste, Augustine surrounded himself with spiritual brothers—members of the growing Christian community in the region—and transformed his family home into a monastery. When he paid a visit to a friend at Hippo in 391, Augustine found that his reputation as a spiritual leader had preceded him. The community at Hippo begged Augustine to remain with them, and he was ordained a priest at their request. By 396, he was bishop of Hippo, a position he held until his death.

WORK

Augustine probably began work on the *Confessions* in 397, when he was forty-three years old. He seems to have been suffering from a terrible case of writer's block, with several half-finished pieces of

work on hand. The experience of writing the *Confessions* apparently cured it, for almost immediately after completing it Augustine went on to produce an extraordinarily large number of works. The *Confessions* is, as the name suggests, autobiographical, the story of one man's life in his own words. But it is also confessional in the sense of being a full account of one's sins; a story addressed first of all to God, the hearer who is able to forgive the transgressions that Augustine recounts. At the same time, the *Confessions* has a secondary addressee, as Augustine himself acknowledges: other would-be Christians who might be able to trace the path of their own spiritual journey as a result of having read about the struggles of another. Of the thirteen books of the *Confessions*, only the first nine are autobiographical, covering the period from Augustine's early childhood memories to his stay in Ostia in 387, as he waits for the boat that would take him home. The autobiographical genre, almost without precedent in this period, is perhaps Augustine's greatest literary legacy. We hear nothing from Augustine about his later years in Africa; instead, the final books of the *Confessions* are an analysis of the account of creation in Genesis, along with a sustained meditation on the nature of time and memory. The overall effect of the *Confessions* is to turn the reader inward, away from the individual journey of Augustine and toward the collective journey of humanity toward the divine.

Surprisingly for a book dedicated to the relationship of the soul to God, the most moving parts of the *Confessions* focus on Augustine's relationship to other human beings—not just his mother, Monica, who was so instrumental to Augustine's conversion to Christianity, but also his beloved son, Adeodatus, and the unnamed mistress who was Augustine's companion from age seventeen (when he first went to Carthage) until his mother persuaded him to enter into an arranged marriage in 385, shortly before his conversion. This woman, whom Augustine simply calls "the One," faithfully followed him on his journeys, first to Rome and then to Milan. When Augustine finally renounced his relationship with her, she returned to Africa, "vowing before you never to know any other man." All of these human relationships, however passionate, are in the end subsumed within Augustine's all-consuming relationship with God. He addresses God familiarly throughout the *Confessions*, as if he were an intimate friend who knew all Augustine's secrets, but who also had the terrifying capacity to destroy, inspiring both adoration and fear.

Augustine writes frankly about his self-fashioning within the various communities to which he belonged, from his involvement in a gang of undisciplined youths to his immersion in the Manichaean community at Carthage, his time among the Neoplatonists in Milan, and his final place of rest among the Christian community at Hippo. His journey is, at a deep level, a search for the self, which he comes to find only after long struggle, and only through the companionship of others. Augustine comes home first spiritually, with a conversion inspired by the supernatural voice of a child, and then physically, sailing from Ostia to Thagaste, where he will make a new spiritual home filled with Christian believers among the bricks and mortar of his childhood house. Desire and longing structure the narrative of the *Confessions*, from Augustine's heady days in Carthage, at the theater by day and in the arms of his mistress by night, to his patient vigil at the port of Ostia, consumed at once by sorrow for the death of Monica and joy in his discovery of Christ. Caught between his love for human beings and his longing for the divine, Augustine is never more present to us than when, shortly before his conversion, he cries out to God, "Grant me chastity and continance, only not yet." Augustine's painstaking examination of his innermost self, racked with contradictions and unexplained desires, had a profound influence not only on the medieval Christians who sought, like Augustine, to purge their souls of sin but also on the secular self-examination of early modern writers such as **Montaigne** and **Rousseau**.

From Confessions[1]

FROM BOOK I

[Childhood]

[6. 7] For what do I wish to say, Lord, except that I do not know from where I came into what I call this dying life, or living death; I do not know. But the consolation of Your mercies uplifted me, as I heard from the father and mother of my flesh, out of whom and in whom You formed me at the appropriate time, for I do not remember it myself. I was embraced by the comforts of human milk, but neither my mother nor my nurses filled their own breasts for me. It was You Who through them gave me the food of my infancy according to Your ordinance and the riches spread throughout the essence of all things. You also granted me to want no more than You gave, and granted that my nurses wanted to give me what You had given them, for they sought to give me by divine ordination what they had received in abundance from You. But the good that came

1. Translated by Peter Constantine. Paragraph numbering throughout refers to the Latin text.

to me from them was also good for them, though it did not come from them but through them; for from You, O God, come all good things, and from my God is my entire salvation.[2] This I learned only later, when, through all the inner and outer things You bestow, You called to me; for then I only knew how to suckle, content in what was pleasurable and crying at what offended my flesh, and nothing more.

[6. 8] Later I began to smile—first in sleep, then waking. At least that is what I was told about myself and I believe it, for this is what we see in infants, though I do not remember it about myself. Gradually I began to perceive where I was, and to want to express my needs to those who could fulfill them; but I could not express them, for the needs were inside me, and the other people outside; nor were they able with any of their senses to enter my soul. So I kicked and shouted; these were the few signs I could make that resembled my wishes, though they did not really resemble them. And when I was not obeyed, either because I was not understood or because what I wanted might harm me, I became indignant with the adults for not submitting to me, indignant with those who were not my slaves for not serving me, and avenged myself by crying. That is how infants are, as I learned from those I have been able to observe; the infants who knew nothing showing me better than my experienced nurses that I too had been like that.

* * *

[8. 13] On my way to the present I passed from infancy to boyhood. Or is it not that boyhood came to me, succeeding infancy? Not that infancy departed, for where would it have gone? Yet suddenly it was no more, for I was no longer an infant who could not talk but had become a boy speaking.[3] This I remember; but how I learned to speak I found out only later. I was not taught to speak by adults presenting me with words in a certain fixed order, as they would do somewhat later with letters. But with the mind that You gave me, my God, I myself learned through cries and all kinds of sounds and motions of my limbs, to express the feelings of my heart so that my wishes would be fulfilled. But I was not able to express everything I wanted to express to whomever I wanted. I managed to remember whenever adults called a thing something; and when, along with their voice, they moved their bodies toward a certain object I would see and retain the sounds with which they expressed the object. Moreover, what they wanted to express was clear from their gestures, which are the natural language of all races and are expressed in the face, the eyes, and movements of the limbs, and tones of voice that indicate the state of a person's mind as it strives toward, takes hold of, rejects, or shuns a thing. In this way, by repeatedly hearing words as they were positioned in various sentences, I gradually connected them with the things they signified, and so trained my mouth to express my desires through these signs. In this way I communicated the signs of my desires to the people I was among, and so entered into the tempests of society; yet I was still dependent on the authority of my parents and the will of the adults around me.

2. Throughout the *Confessions* Augustine quotes liberally from the Bible. When a quotation bears on Augustine's situation, it is annotated.
3. The English word *infant* comes from the Latin *infans*, "speechless."

[9. 14]   O God, my God, what miseries I now experienced, what follies, when as a boy it was put before me that the only way of living right was to obey those who were instructing me to excel in this world by using the skill of language[4] to secure worldly honors and spurious wealth. I was sent to school to learn to read and write, the uses of which, poor wretch that I was, I did not know, and whenever I lagged in my studies I was beaten. This was extolled by adults, many previous generations having laid out the difficult path we were made to tread, increasing the toil and suffering of the sons of Adam. But, Lord, we also came upon men who prayed to You, and from them we learned, as far as we were able, to imagine You as some great being who, though we could not see You, would hear and help us. Thus I began as a boy to pray to You, my aid and refuge, and invoking You unraveled the knots of my tongue, a small boy but with great love, praying to You that I not be beaten in school.[5] And when You did not hear me—which saved me from the folly of praying to You for trifles—the adults, including my parents, laughed, though not unkindly, at the beatings I received, which at the time were a great and heavy sorrow to me.

[9. 15]   Is there anyone, O Lord, any mind so great, so close to You in powerful love? Is there anyone, I ask, so close to You in piety and magnanimous love that he will think lightly (and not because his wits are dull) of the racks and hooks[6] and other torments that men in this world pray to You with such dread to escape, but who mock the torments they so bitterly fear, just as our parents mocked the torments our tutors inflicted on us as boys? For we did not fear our torments less, nor did we pray less to You to escape them. But still we transgressed, for we wrote, read, and studied less than was demanded of us. Not that we lacked the ability or memory, O Lord, which You willed us to have in ample measure for our age. But we delighted in amusements, for which we were punished by those who also delighted in amusements—yet the amusements of adults are called "business," while those of children are punished by the adults, and no one pities either the children or the adults. Perhaps some fine arbiter might approve of my having been beaten because my playing with a ball hindered the pace of the learning that I was to use as an adult to play reprehensible games. Was he who flogged me any better? If a fellow tutor should trump him on some trifling matter, was he any the less angry or jealous than I was when a playmate beat me at ball?

* * *

[12. 19]   Yet even in childhood, when my family feared less for me than in my youth, I did not like to study, and hated being forced to do so. But I was forced, and it was good for me. Not that it was I who was doing good, because I would not have studied had I not been compelled to. No one does good when he does it against his will, even if he is doing a good thing—yet neither were they who were forcing me doing good. What was good came to me from You, my God, for they did not consider how I should later use what they forced me to learn

---

4. I.e., the study of rhetoric, which was the passport to eminence in public life.
5. Augustine recognizes the necessity of this rigorous training; that he never forgot its harshness is clear from his remark in the *City of God* (21.14): "If a choice were given him between suffering death and living his early years over again, who would not shudder and choose death?"
6. The instruments of torture and public execution.

other than to satiate the insatiable desires of an impoverished wealth and an ignominious glory. But You, Who number the hairs of our head,[7] used for my good the error of all those who urged me to learn; and You used my own error in not wanting to learn to punish me, a punishment I deserved, so small a boy and yet so great a sinner. You did me good through those who did not do good, and for my own sin You exacted a just retribution: for You have commanded, and it is so, that every disordered soul will be its own punishment.

[13. 20]   I have still not managed to fathom the reasons why I hated Greek,[8] which I studied as a boy. Yet Latin I truly loved; not what my first masters taught me, but what I later learned from the men we call grammarians. For I considered my first lessons of reading, writing, and arithmetic as great a burden and punishment as any Greek lesson. And yet, as I was flesh, a passing breath that does not return, did this not come from the sin and vanity of life? The first lessons were in fact better than the later ones, because they were more sound. Through them I acquired, and still retain, the ability to read whatever I find written and to write whatever I want; whereas in my later lessons I was forced to retain the strayings of an Aeneas[9] I did not know, forgetting my own, and to weep over a dead Dido[1] who killed herself for love; while I, without a tear, was prepared to pitiably die away from You through such works, my God, my life.

[13. 21]   What is more pitiable than a pitiful being who does not pity himself but weeps at the death of Dido for love of Aeneas; a pitiful being who does not weep over the death he is suffering because he does not love You, O God, light of my heart, bread of the mouth deep within my soul, vigor that impregnates my mind and the vessel of my thoughts. I did not love You, and fornicated against You,[2] and as I did so I heard from all around cries of "Well done! Well done!," for the friendship of this world is fornication against You; and "Well done! Well done!" is what they shout in order to shame a man who is not like them. For all this I did not weep, but wept for Dido, "who with a dagger did the lowest ends pursue,"[3] just as I, having forsaken You, pursued the lowest of Your creations, dust turning to dust. Had I been forbidden to read these works I would have suffered at not being able to read what made me suffer. And such foolishness is considered a higher and better education than that by which I learned to read and write.

[13. 22]   But now may my God call out in my soul, Your truth proclaiming to me, "This is wrong, this is wrong! Your first lessons were better by far!" For I would readily forget the strayings of Aeneas rather than forget how to read and write. The doors of the grammarians' schools are indeed hung with precious curtains,[4] but this is not so much a sign of high distinction as a cloak for their errors. Let not those whom I no longer fear cry out against me while I

---

7. I.e., who knows and attends to the smallest detail of each life (cf. Matthew 10.30).
8. The study of Greek was important not only for gaining knowledge of Greek literature but also because it was the official language of the Eastern Roman Empire. Augustine never really mastered Greek, though his remark elsewhere that he had acquired so little Greek that it amounted to practically none is overmodest.
9. Virgil's *Aeneid* 3.
1. Queen of Carthage whose unrequited love

for the Trojan warrior Aeneas ended in her untimely death; Aeneas was obliged to pursue his destiny to be the founding father of Rome (Virgil, *Aeneid*, esp. book 4).
2. Here, metaphorically.
3. Virgil, *Aeneid* 6.457.
4. In Augustine's time, school entrances were covered by veils with an attendant standing by to make sure that only those who paid tuition were admitted; the veil was also a symbol of the hidden knowledge that lay beyond the threshold.

confess to You what my soul seeks, finding peace in condemning my evil ways and loving Your good ways. Let not the sellers and buyers of high learning cry out against me. If I ask them whether it is true that Aeneas once came to Carthage, as the poet says, the less learned will reply that they do not know, while the more learned will say that he never did. But if I ask with what letters the name "Aeneas" is written, everyone who has learned this will answer me correctly, according to the agreement and decision that men have reached concerning these signs. Likewise, if I should ask which was the greater inconvenience, forgetting how to read and write or forgetting those poetic fictions, who would not know what answer someone in possession of his senses would give? Thus as a boy I sinned, preferring empty learning to learning that was more useful, going so far as to love the former and hate the latter. "One plus one is two, two plus two is four" was a hateful incantation, while the sweetest dream of my vanity was the wooden horse filled with armed men, the burning of Troy, and even the ghost of Creusa.[5]

* * *

[17. 27]   Permit me, my God, also to say something about my innate talent, Your gift, and the foolishness on which I squandered it. I was set a task that greatly worried me because of the prospect of praise or shame, and the dread of being beaten: the task was to speak the words of Juno as she raged and grieved, unable as she was to "keep the Prince of Troy from seeking the shores of Italy,"[6] even though I knew she had never spoken such words. But we were forced to go astray in the footsteps of those poetic creations, and to say in plain speech what Virgil had said in verse. The declaimer who was most praised was the one who best brought forth, shrouded in the most fitting words, the grandeur of the feigned characters in their passion of rage and grief. What is it to me, my God and true life, that my declamation was applauded over that of so many of the pupils of my age and in my class? Is all this not smoke and wind? Was there nothing else on which to exercise my talent and my tongue? Your praises, Lord, Your praises through Your Scriptures, would have trellised the young vines of my heart, and foolish nonsense would not have snatched at it, vile prey for winged scavengers. There is more than one way for man to pay homage to fallen angels.

* * *

FROM BOOK II

[The Pear Tree]

[1. 1]   I recall my past impurity and the carnal corruptions suffered by my soul, not because I love them but so that I may love You, my God. It is out of love for Your love that in the bitterness of my memory I seek to recall the most

5. While at a feast held in his honor by Dido, Aeneas tells the story of the fall of Troy and his escape from the burning city, during which he lost his wife, Creusa (Virgil, *Aeneid*, book 2, esp. 2.772).
6. Augustine was assigned the task of delivering a prose paraphrase of Juno's angry speech in

Aeneid 1. In it she complains that her enemies, the Trojans under Aeneas, are on their way to their destined goal in Italy in spite of her resolution to prevent them. Rhetorical exercises such as this were common in the schools, because they served the double purpose of teaching both literature and rhetorical composition.

terrible things I did, so that Your sweetness will flow into me, O God, O Sweet One Who never fails, Sweet One serene and untroubled, Who gathered up the pieces into which I had been scattered when I turned away from You, the One, only to waste myself among the many. For in my youth I burned fervently to satisfy my hellish desires, wallowing in sensual and shadowy loves, my beauty wasting away; before Your eyes I was putrid, while I sought pleasure for myself and to please the eyes of others.

[2. 2] What was it that I delighted in, if not loving and being loved? But there was no path from soul to soul, no luminous links of friendship, it was only vapors rising from the slimy lusts of the flesh and the gushings of puberty that beclouded my heart, so that I was not able to discern the bright serenity of love from the hazy mists of lust. Both love and lust raged in turmoil within me, dragging me in my weak youth into the chasms of sin, plunging me into the raging abyss of disgrace. Your wrath was growing, though I did not know it. The clanking chains of my mortal flesh had rendered me deaf, punishing me for the pride of my soul, and I strayed ever further from You, and You let me. I was hurled and scattered in all directions, dissipating myself in my fornications, while You, O my belated joy, were silent! You were silent then, and in proud degradation and restless despondence I strayed ever further from You, the seed of my sorrow ever more sterile.

* * *

[2. 4] Where was I, how far was I exiled from the delights of Your House, in that sixteenth year of the age of my flesh? The madness of lust raised its scepter over me and I had relinquished myself to it entirely, condoned as it was by the turpitude of man, yet forbidden by Your laws. Meanwhile, my family did not seek through marriage to keep me from plunging into the abyss; their only concern was that I should learn to excel in discourse and be persuasive as an orator.

* * *

[4. 9] Your law punishes theft, O Lord, as does the law written in the hearts of men that even wickedness cannot erase, for what thief will gladly bear another thief robbing him, even if he is rich and the one robbing him is in need? But I wanted to steal and I did, driven not by any need, but by a lack of regard for justice and an abundance of wickedness. For I stole something of which I had plenty and far better; nor did I seek to enjoy what I had stolen, only the theft and the sin itself. Near our vineyard was a pear tree heavy with fruit that did not tempt with either color or taste. Late one night, I and some wicked youths, still seeking fun in our usual haunts, as was our foul habit, set about to shake the pears off the tree and carry them away, taking with us a huge load, not to eat, but to throw to the pigs. If we ate a few of the pears it was only to relish the wrongness of what we had done. Such was my heart, O God, such was my heart, which You took pity on in the profoundest depths of the abyss. Let my heart tell You now what it sought there, being wicked for no reason and having no cause to do ill except wickedness itself. It was detestable, but I delighted in it. I delighted in my undoing, I delighted in my eclipse, not that for which I was eclipsed but the eclipse itself, a depraved soul falling from Your firmament to its destruction, not seeking anything through my shamefulness but shame itself.

[5. 10]   Just as beauty can be seen in lovely objects, in gold and silver and such things, and just as the harmony of objects is vital to our sense of touch, each of our other senses have their own response. Transient honor too, such as the powers of ruling and command, has its splendor, which also give rises to man's urge to claim his rights. And yet in our quest for these things we must not depart from You, O Lord, nor deviate from Your law. The life we live in this world also has its appeal through a certain beauty of its own and a harmony with all the beautiful things here below, as does friendship, tied with its sweet and precious knot that unites many souls. Yet all of this can lead to sin when through an unrestrained urge for good things that are the lowest things of Your creation, forsaking things that are better and higher, forsaking You, our Lord God, Your truth, and Your law. For the lower things have their delights, but not like my God, Who made all things, and in Whom those who are righteous delight, and Who is the joy of those upright in heart.

[5. 11]   When we ask why a crime was committed, we tend not to believe the answer unless there seems to have been a desire to obtain—or a fear of losing— some of the things I have called a lower good. This lower good is beautiful and appealing, though when compared with higher and blessed good, it is base and vile. A man has committed a murder; why did he do it? Perhaps he loved the murdered man's wife, or his property, or he robbed the man to secure his livelihood, or feared that he might be robbed of his livelihood by the man he murdered; or, wronged, he burned to be avenged. Would anyone commit murder for no reason, simply delighting in murder? Who would believe such a thing? Yet it has been said[7] of a certain crazed man of boundless cruelty that he was cruel and evil without cause, though a reason was also cited: Lest through idleness his hand or heart should wilt. And yet, we should ask why was this man so cruel? It was so that through his acts of crime he might seize Rome and attain honors, power, and wealth, and free himself from fear of the laws, the dangers of poverty, and the offenses he had committed. Hence not even this man, Catiline, loved his deeds, but loved something else for the sake of which he did them.

[6. 12]   Wretch that I was, what did I love in you, my theft, O deed committed in that night of my sixteenth year? It is not that you were beautiful, for you were a theft. Are you even a thing, that I can speak to you? Beautiful were the fruits we stole, for they were Your creation, O Most Beautiful of all, Creator of all, O God that is good, God the highest Good and my true Good. Beautiful were those fruits, but it was not them that my wretched soul desired, for I had plenty better, and the ones I plucked I plucked only so that I might steal. No sooner had I plucked them than I threw them away, my sin being the only feast I rejoiced in. And the few bites of fruit that did enter my mouth were seasoned with sin. And now, O Lord my God, I ask You what it was in that theft that delighted me. It had no beauty: I do not mean beauty as in the beauty of justice or judiciousness, nor such beauty as is in the mind of man, in the memory, the senses, or blossoming life; nor as the stars are beautiful and splendid in the sky, nor as the earth and sea are filled with new life, through birth replacing what has died; not even the false beauty lurking in shadows that belongs to vice.

---

7. By the Roman historian Sallust (*Catiline* 16). Cataline was a Roman politician whose conspiracy against the state was foiled by the consul Cicero in 63 B.C.E.

[6. 13]   This too is the way that pride imitates lofty elegance, whereas You alone are God, exalted above all. What does vanity seek but honors and glory, whereas You alone are to be honored and glorious in eternity. The cruelty of powerful men aims to be feared, but who is to be feared other than the one and only God? What can be seized or robbed of his power—when, where, how, or by whom? Tender caresses aim to spark love, yet nothing is more tender than Your love, nor is anything loved with more wholesomeness than Your truth, beautiful and bright above all. Curiosity poses as a desire for knowledge, whereas You Who are above all know all. Ignorance and foolishness hide behind the names of simplicity and innocence, but there is no greater simplicity than You, no greater innocence, for sinners are harmed by their own deeds. Idleness poses as a desire for calm, but what calm is there other than the Lord? Extravagance strives to be called abundance and plenty, but You are plenitude and the unfailing plenteousness of imperishable delight. Prodigality seeks to array itself in the glow of generosity, but it is You Who are the supremely abundant giver of all good. Greed seeks to possess much, but You possess all. Jealousy strives for excellence, but what is more excellent than You? Anger seeks revenge, but who avenges with greater justice than You? Fear recoils from things that are unaccustomed and unexpected, things that endanger what is beloved, and fear takes precautions for the safety of what it loves. But to You what is unaccustomed? What is unexpected? Who can take from You what You love? Where other than with You is enduring safety? Sadness pines for things lost in which cupidity delighted, insisting that nothing be taken from it, just as nothing can be taken from You.

[6. 14]   Thus the soul that turns away from You fornicates, seeking outside You that which is clear and pure, but which it can only find when it returns to You. All those have erred who seek to imitate You perversely, having distanced themselves from You and extolling themselves in pride against You. But even by seeking to imitate You they admit that You are the creator of the entire universe and that it is not possible for them to distance themselves from You entirely. What then did I love in that theft, and how did I, albeit perversely and in error, imitate my Lord? Did I delight in breaking Your law at least furtively, as I lacked power, like a slave who steals with impunity, attaining a shadowy semblance of omnipotence? Behold the servant fleeing his Lord and seeking a shadow! O putridness! O monstrous life and chasm of death! Was I drawn to what was forbidden just because it was forbidden?

* * *

FROM BOOK III

[Student at Carthage]

[1. 1]   I came to Carthage[8] and was immersed in a seething cauldron of illicit loves. I had not yet loved but was burning to experience love, and, consumed by an inner craving, was vexed at myself for not craving more. In love with love, I sought an object of love, but shunned a path that had no snares. I was consumed by hunger, deprived of inner food, deprived of You, my God, and yet it

8. The provincial capital city (in modern-day Tunisia), where Augustine went to study rhetoric.

was not for You that I hungered; I lacked all desire for incorruptible sustenance, not because I was sated by it, but the emptier I was the more I disdained it. And so my soul sickened, and, covered in pustules, gushed forth,
wretchedly striving to be soothed by sensual objects. Yet if these objects had
not had a soul they would not have been objects of love. To love and be loved
was all the sweeter to me if I could delight in the body of the beloved. So I sullied the clear spring of friendship with the filth of carnality, dulling its brightness with infernal lust, and though I was base and vile, in my vanity I paraded
myself as refined and urbane. So I flung myself into that love by which I so
longed to be seized. My God, my Mercy! In Your goodness how much gall
did You sprinkle on that sweetness! For I was loved, and secretly attained
the fetters of delight, rejoicing in being enmeshed in the tangle of misery, to
be scourged with the burning rods of jealousy, suspicion, fear, anger, and
contention.

[2. 2] I was captivated by theatrical spectacles filled with images of my
miseries, which poured fuel on my fire. Why is it that man wants to sorrow by
watching distressing and tragic things that he would not want to endure? And
yet he wants to endure this sorrow as a spectator, and this sorrow is his delight.
What is this if not utter folly? Indeed, the more a man is moved by such suffering, the less free he is of it himself, for when one is suffering it is called misery,
while when one feels sympathy for the suffering of others it is called compassion. But what sort of compassion is this for things that are feigned and staged?
The spectator is not summoned to help but only to grieve, and the more he
grieves the more he applauds the actor of these representations. But if the misfortunes, whether of ancient times or invented, are acted in such a way that
the spectator does not grieve, he leaves the theater filled with disappointment
and anger, but if he does grieve he delights in his tears.

[2. 3] Thus sorrows are also loved. But people want to enjoy themselves; no
one likes to be miserable, even if he likes to commiserate: so do we love sorrows because commiserating cannot exist without misery?

* * *

[3. 6] My supposedly respectable studies[9] had the aim of achieving excellence in the courts of litigation, where the greater the deceit, the greater the
praise. Such is the blindness of men that they glory in blindness. And I was the
foremost pupil in the school of rhetoric. I was puffed up with pride and rejoiced
in vanity, though I was more restrained by far than my fellow students, Lord, as
You know, keeping my distance from the destructiveness of the *Destroyers*,[1] who
sported this sinister and devilish name as a sign of urbanity. I lived among them
shamelessly ashamed that I was not like them. I was with them, and at times
enjoyed their friendship, though I always abhorred the deeds with which
they shamelessly persecuted shy new students, attacking them and jeering
at them for no reason, feeding their own malicious delight. Nothing resembles
the actions of devils more than theirs, so what better name can there be for them
than "the Destroyers," destroyed and corrupted as they are by the deceitful

9. That is, his rhetorical studies.
1. In the Latin original *eversores*, which means
"overturners," a group of students who prided

themselves on their wild behavior and lack of
discipline.

spirits that secretly deride and waylay them with the same deeds with which they taunt and deceive others.

[4. 7] Its was among them, at my tender age, that I studied the books of eloquence by which I longed to distinguish myself, driven by delight in human vanity, a damnable and empty aim. In the course of my studies I had come upon a book by a certain Cicero, whose tongue[2] almost everyone admires, though not so much his heart. The book is called *Hortensius*,[3] and contains an exhortation to study philosophy. It altered my state of mind and my prayers, making them turn to You, Lord, changing my longings and desires. Suddenly every vanity became worthless, and with a fire raging in my heart I longed for the immortality of wisdom, rousing me to return to You. I did not immerse myself in this book to perfect my style, something I was pursuing in those days when I was nineteen with my mother's funds, as my father had died two years before. No, it was not to perfect my style, for it was not the book's style that swayed me but its words.

* * *

[5. 9] I was therefore determined to apply my mind to the Holy Scripture in order to see what it was, and what I saw was something not discernible by the proud, nor open to the young, its entrance modest but its inner halls exalted and veiled with mysteries. I was not one who was able to enter or to bow my head and proceed. I did not feel then when I approached the Scripture what I feel now, but it struck me as unworthy of comparison to the distinction of a Cicero. My strutting pride shunned the simplicity of the Scripture, my eye not keen enough to penetrate its interior. Yet the Scripture is such that it grows with those who are simple.[4] But I disdained the thought of being simple, and, swollen with pride, perceived myself as great.

* * *

FROM BOOK V

[Augustine Leaves Carthage for Rome]

[8. 14]   You led me so that I should be persuaded to go to Rome, to teach there what I was teaching in Carthage, and I will not omit confessing to You how I was persuaded to this, because in that, too, Your most profound recesses and Your mercy most present to us must be reflected on and confessed. I did not want to go to Rome simply because my friends urged me to, assuring me that in Rome I would garner greater profit and honor, though those things did influence my mind at the time. My main, and almost my only, reason was that I had heard that young men studied there more peaceably and were subjected to more rigorous discipline, not all rushing wildly into the class of a master whose

---

2. I.e., rhetorical style. "Cicero": Marcus Tullius Cicero (106–43 B.C.E.), Roman philosopher, politician, and lawyer. Augustine's admiration of Cicero is obvious; calling him "a certain Cicero" is a rhetorical convention; Augustine uses the same formulation to refer to the Apostle Paul.
3. Cicero's *Hortensius*, written in 45 B.C.E.

and now lost, was an analysis of the sources of happiness, which Cicero concluded lay in the pursuit of wisdom.
4. A reference not only to the rhetorical simplicity of Jesus' teachings but also to his interest in teaching children; cf. Matthew 19.14: "For of such is the kingdom of heaven."

pupils they were not; in Rome they were not even admitted into a class without a master's permission. In Carthage, on the other hand, there is an uncouth and unruly excess among pupils. They brazenly interrupt classes, and with crazed rowdiness bring turmoil to the order that the masters have established for the good of their students. With surprising foolishness they wreak mayhem that would be punishable by law if custom did not protect them, and they are the more wretched in that they do as lawful what will never be lawful by Your eternal law; and they believe that they are doing this with impunity, whereas they are punished with the blindness by which they do it, and suffer incomparably worse consequences than what they wreak. Such practices, which as a student I had refused to engage in, I had to endure in others as a teacher, and so I was happy to go to a place where those who knew assured me that such things were not done. But it was in truth You, my hope and my portion in the land of the living, who wanted me to change my earthly dwelling for the salvation of my soul, and in Carthage You goaded me so that I would tear myself away from it, and for Rome You placed before me enticements that would draw me there with the advice of Manichean friends who loved a dead life, doing mad things in this life, hoping for vain things in the next. To set my steps aright, You secretly used their and my perverseness; for those who disturbed my calm were blinded by a disgraceful frenzy, while those who summoned me away loved only this world. Yet I, who detested true misery here, sought false happiness there.

[8. 15]   You knew, God, why I left Carthage and went to Rome, but You did not reveal the reason either to me or my mother, who bitterly lamented my leaving and followed me as far as the shore.[5] She clung to me in desperation, seeking either to keep me there or to come with me, but I deceived her, pretending that I had a friend I was seeing off with whom I had to wait until he had a good wind to sail. I lied to my mother—lied to such a mother—and so escaped. This too You have mercifully forgiven me, I who was filled with abhorrent foulness, preserving me from the waters of the sea for the waters of Your grace that would cleanse me[6] and dry my mother's streaming eyes, with which she daily watered before You the ground on which she stood. But she refused to return home without me, and I barely managed to persuade her to stay that night in a place near our ship where there was a sanctuary in memory of the blessed Saint Cyprian.[7] But that night I secretly departed without her as she remained behind, weeping and praying. What was she asking of You with so many tears, my God, but that You would not let me sail? Yet You, in Your high mindfulness, hearing the core of her desire, did not heed what she was asking, so that You could make out of me exactly what she had always asked. The wind blew and swelled our sails and the shore receded from our sight, and on the following morning my mother came there raving with sorrow, filling Your ears with complaints and lamentations to which You paid no heed, while You

---

5. Augustine's mother, Monica of Hippo (322–387), has long been venerated as a saint in the Roman Catholic Church. Here, Monica and Augustine are in the roles of Dido and Aeneas; see Virgil, *Aeneid*, book 4.
6. A reference to the ritual of immersion in water to signify the cleansing of the soul from

sin; in Augustine's day, baptism was often put off until death was near, even by relatively observant Christians.
7. Bishop of Carthage, Christian writer, local martyr, and saint (c. 200–258) who was especially popular among North African Christians.

allowed me to be transported by my desires in order to extinguish those desires, and my mother's earthly longing for me was rightly chastened by the scourge of sorrow. For she loved my being with her, as mothers do, though much more than many others, and she did not know what great joy You were preparing for her by my absence. She did not know, which is why she wept and sobbed, and through these torments she manifested the inheritance of Eve, seeking as she did with pain what with pain she had brought forth. And yet, after accusing me of deception and cruelty, she again turned to interceding for me with You, and went back home while I went on to Rome.

* * *

FROM BOOK VI

[Earthly Love]

Strong in her piety, my mother had now come to me, following me over sea and land, confident in You in every danger she faced, and even on the perilous sea she comforted the sailors, who are more used to reassuring frightened passengers unaccustomed to the sea. She promised them a safe arrival, for You had assured her of this in a vision. She found me in great peril and in despair that I would ever find truth, though when I revealed to her that I was no longer a Manichean[8] though not yet a true Christian, she did not leap with joy as if my words were unexpected. But she was now reassured concerning that part of my misery for which she had wept over me as one dead, though to be reawakened by You, and on a bier of her thoughts she offered me to You that You might say to the son of this widow, "Young man, I say to you, arise!"[9] And her son would come to life again and begin to speak, and You would deliver him to his mother.

* * *

[13. 23]   I was continually being urged to take a wife. I made a proposal and it was accepted, largely through my mother's efforts, for she hoped that once I was married baptism with its salvation would cleanse me,[1] and she was delighted that I was more receptive with every day, and she saw that her prayers and Your promises were being fulfilled in my faith. At my bidding and through her longing she begged of You every day, with cries from her heart, that You reveal to her in a vision something about my future marriage, but You never did. What she saw were empty and fantastic visions fueled by the passion of the human spirit striving for answers; she told me about these visions, discounting them, as she did not have the same confidence in them that she had when it was You Who sent them. For she said that she could discern by some

8. Augustine had for nine years been a member of this religious sect, which followed the teaching of the Babylonian mystic Mani (216–277). The Manicheans believed that the world was a battleground for the forces of good and evil; redemption in a future life would come to the elect, who renounced worldly occupations and possessions and practiced a severe asceticism (including abstention from meat). Augus-

tine's mother, Monica, was a Christian, and lamented her son's Manichean beliefs.
9. Luke 7.14, recounting one of Christ's miracles.
1. Augustine could not be baptized while living in sin with his mistress, a liaison that resulted in the birth of a son, Adeodatus, who later accompanied his father to Italy.

strange sensation, which she could not explain in words, the difference between Your revelations and the dreams of her own soul. Nevertheless, the pressure on me to marry continued and a maiden was asked for in marriage; she was two years under marriageable age, but as she was thought suitable all were prepared to wait.[2]

[14. 24] We were a group of several friends who detested the turbulence and trouble of life, and we discussed and debated and had almost resolved to live in contemplation far removed from the bustling crowd, and this was how we intended to attain such a life: we would bring together whatever each of us was able to contribute, and from that create a single household, so that in our true friendship nothing would belong only to one person or another but would be a single possession gathered from all, and as a whole would belong to each, and all to all. We concluded that we could bring some ten men into this fellowship, some of whom were very wealthy, especially our townsman Romanianus, whom the burdensome tangle of his affairs had brought to the courts, and who from childhood had been a close friend of mine. He was the most zealous advocate of this plan, and his voice was of great weight because his wealth far exceeded that of any of us. We had also decided that two of us would be elected every year, the way magistrates are, to attend to everything, the rest of the group remaining free from such cares. But when we began to give thought as to whether wives, which some of us already had and others were hoping to attain, would agree to what we were planning with such care, it fell to pieces in our hands, and, our plans crushed, we cast them aside. And so we returned to our sighs and laments, our steps following the broad and well-trodden paths of the world,[3] for many thoughts were in our hearts, but Your counsel abides in all eternity. And yet through that counsel You laughed at our designs and prepared Your own to grant us nourishment in due season and fill our souls with blessing.

[15. 25] In the meantime my sins were multiplying, and when the woman with whom I shared my bed was torn from my side for being an impediment to my marriage,[4] my heart that clung to her was rent and bled. She returned to Africa, vowing before You never to know any other man, leaving with me the natural son I had had by her. But wretch that I was, I could not follow that woman's example. Impatient at the delay of my marriage, since it would be two years before I could have what I wanted, I procured for myself another woman, though not a wife; for I was not a lover of marriage but a slave to lust, so that the sickness of my soul was sustained and prolonged, remaining intact, even heightened, so that my habit could be guarded and tended until I reached the state of matrimony. Nor had the wound made by the parting with my former lover healed, but after inflammation and piercing pain it festered, and though the pain dulled, it also became more desperate.

* * *

2. Under Roman law, the minimum age for marriage was twelve, so the girl that Monica arranged for Augustine to marry must have been around ten. Augustine was in his early thirties at the time.

3. Cf. Matthew 7.13: "Broad is the way that leadeth to destruction," that is, to damnation.
4. This woman had been Augustine's companion since he was seventeen and had accompanied him from Carthage to Rome.

FROM BOOK VIII

[*Conversion*]

[11. 25]   This was how ill and tormented I was, accusing myself more bitterly than ever, twisting and wrenching to break free of my chains that were easing but still held me fast. And You, Lord, penetrated my hidden depths with severe mercy, redoubling the lashes of fear[5] and shame lest I should succumb and not break the last frail fetters that remained, allowing them to grow strong once more and bind me all the tighter. And I said to myself deep inside, "Act now, the time to act is now." In my words I was already resolved. I almost acted, but did not; however, I did not fall back into my former state, but kept close and recovered my breath. I tried once more and came even closer, and closer, I could almost touch it, almost take hold of it, yet I could not reach it, neither touching nor taking hold of it, hesitating to die to death and to live to life. Greater was the sway of the evil to which I was accustomed than the goodness to which I was unaccustomed, and the more the moment neared in which I was to become another man, the more I was struck by horror; yet horror did not strike a decisive blow, nor did it turn me away, but held me suspended.

[11. 26]   I was being held in check by vain trifles and trifling vanities, my longstanding paramours tearing at my garment of flesh and whispering: "Will you send us away? From that moment on we shall never again be with you. From that moment on you will never again be allowed this and that." And what they meant by "this and that"! What were they suggesting, my God! Let Your mercy repulse it from Your servant's soul! What filth they were proposing, what infamy! Now I less than half heard them, and they did not dare come out to contradict me openly but muttered as if behind my back, plucking at me almost furtively so I would turn and look; but they managed to hold me back and delay me from tearing myself away and shaking myself free from them, and making the leap to where I was being summoned, while the force of my habits called out to me, "Do you think you can bear being without them?"

[11. 27]   But the force of my habit said this now quite faintly, for in the direction to which I had turned my face and to which I feared to go, Continence[6] had now appeared before me, chaste and dignified, serene, cheerful though without allurements, beckoning me with sincerity to come and not to doubt, her holy hands reaching out to receive and embrace me with a profusion of honest examples: so many youths and maidens, so many people of every age, sober widows and aged virgins, and among them stood Continence herself, not barren but a fertile mother of children, with joys granted her by You, Lord, her Husband. And she smiled, both teasing and encouraging me, as if she were saying: "Can you not do what these youths and maidens can? Do you think they managed on their own without the help of the Lord their God? The Lord their God gave me to them. Why do you persist on your own where you cannot persist? Cast yourself upon Him, do not be afraid. He will not withdraw and let you fall. Cast yourself upon Him without fear—He will receive and will heal you." I truly blushed, for I was also still listening to the whisperings of frivolity, and so lingered and delayed, and again it was as if Continence were

5. Virgil, *Aeneid* 5.547.
6. Self-control or abstinence, especially with regard to sexuality; here personified as a woman.

saying: "Shut your ears to your impure limbs that are upon the earth, so that they will be mortified. They speak to you of delights, but not as does the law of the Lord your God." This dispute within my heart was merely myself battling myself, and Alypius,[7] who was at my side, waited in silence for the end of my unusual agitation.

[12. 28]   From hidden depths a profound introspection had gathered together and amassed all my misery before my heart's eye, and now a violent tempest arose within me, bringing a mighty shower of tears, and I got up and hastened away from Alypius so that my storm could gush forth with all its sounds and voices. Solitude seemed to me more fit for weeping, and I moved far enough away from him so that his presence would not burden me. That was the state I was in, and Alypius sensed it, for as I got up I think I said something in which my voice was choked with tears. Confounded, Alypius remained where we had sat. I collapsed beneath a fig tree, I do not remember how, and let my tears flow, streams pouring from my eyes, an acceptable sacrifice to You, and I said many things to You, not in these exact words, but to this purpose: "But You, O Lord, for how long? For how long, Lord? Will You be angry forever? Remember not our former iniquities."[8] For I felt that these iniquities were holding me in their grip. I uttered these wretched words: "How long, how long? Ever tomorrow and tomorrow? Why not right away? Why cannot my baseness come to an end this instant?"

[12. 29]   I was speaking and weeping in the most bitter contrition of my heart, when I suddenly heard from a nearby house a voice—that of a boy or a girl, I could not tell—repeating in a singsong, "Pick up and read, pick up and read." That instant, my countenance changed and I began to wonder intently whether there could be some kind of game in which children sang such words, but I could not remember there being such a game. I checked the torrent of my tears and rose, concluding that these words were clearly a divine command that I open the Book and read the first line I found. I had heard how Saint Anthony[9] had come upon a reading of the Gospel and had understood the words he heard being read out as an admonition, as if they were being spoken to him: "Go, sell all you have and give it to the poor, and you will have treasure in heaven; and come, follow me."[1] With these divine words he was immediately converted to You. So I hastened back to the place where Alypius was sitting, for it was there that I had laid down the volume of the Apostle[2] when I had arisen. I seized it, opened it, and in silence read the verse upon which my eyes first fell: "Not in revelry and drunkenness, not in lewdness and lust, not in strife and envy. But put on the Lord Jesus Christ, and make not provision for the flesh in its concupiscences." I neither wished nor needed to read further. Instantly, at the end of

---

7. A student of Augustine's at Carthage; he had joined the Manicheans with Augustine, followed him to Rome and Milan, and now shared his desires and doubts. After converting to Christianity along with Augustine, Alypius eventually became a bishop in North Africa in 394.
8. Cf. Psalm 79.5–8; here, Augustine compares his spiritual despair with that of captive and subjugated Israel.
9. St. Anthony the Great, also called Anthony

of the Desert (ca. 251–356), a Coptic Christian saint whose biography by Athanasius of Alexandria was widely circulated throughout the Mediterranean and was credited with many conversions.
1. Luke 18.22.
2. The Apostle Paul; Augustine is reading Paul's letter to the Romans. Compare with *Inferno* V:134–5 on pg 418.

these lines, it was as if a light of serenity was pouring into my heart, and all the darkness of uncertainty dispersed.

[12. 30] I shut the Book, putting my finger or some other mark between the pages, and with a calm countenance told Alypius what had happened. But he also apprised me of the change within him, of which I had not been aware. He asked to see what verse I had read. I showed it to him and he read it, and read further than I had; I did not know the verse that followed. What followed was, "Receive one who is weak in the faith," and Alypius told me that he was applying this to himself. This admonition gave him strength in his pious resolution and purpose, which truly corresponded to his character, in which he had always very much differed from me for the better, and without turbulent hesitation he joined me. We go inside to my mother, we tell her, she rejoices; we recount how it had come to pass; she exults, jubilates, and praises You Who are able to do beyond that which we desire or understand. She saw that You had granted her far more for me than she had begged for in her sad and tear-filled laments to You, for You had converted me to you so that I now sought neither a wife nor any ambition of this world, and stood firm upon that rule of faith as You had shown me to my mother in a dream so many years before.[3] And You converted her mourning into joy even more abundantly than she had hoped, and in a way that was much more precious and pure than she had sought in having grandchildren of my flesh.

* * *

FROM BOOK IX

[Death of His Mother]

[8. 17] We were together, and were resolved to dwell together in our holy cause. In seeking a place where we could serve You to the best purpose, we all decided to return to Africa. We had just reached Ostia,[4] by the mouth of the Tiber, when my mother died. I have passed over so much, as I have written in haste—receive my avowals and my gratitude, my God, for the countless things about which I have been silent—but I will not pass over all that my mind can bring forth concerning Your handmaid who brought me forth, both in the flesh so that I might be born into this temporal light, and in the soul so that I might be born to eternal light. I will not speak of her gifts, but of Your gifts to her, for neither did she create nor raise herself. It was You Who created her; nor did her father and mother know who it was that had been born to them, and it was the rod and the staff of Your Christ that had reared her in holy fear—the discipline of Your only Son—in her father's Christian household at the hand of a certain virtuous member of Your Church. She commended her mother's attentiveness for the devout training she received, but commended even more the training she received from a very old servant, who had carried her father on her back when he had been a child, in the way that children used to be carried by

3. At Carthage, when Augustine was still a Manichean, Monica had dreamed that she was standing on a wooden ruler weeping for her son and then saw that he was standing on the same

ruler as herself.
4. On the southwest coast of Italy; it was the port of Rome and the point of departure for Africa.

girls who were a little older. For this reason, and because of the servant's great age and excellent morals, she was greatly respected by the masters of that Christian household, which also accounted for the daughters of the house being left in her care. This task she undertook with great diligence, disciplining the girls with ardent and holy severity when it was necessary, and training them with profound attention. For example, beyond the hours in which they were fed with great moderation at their parents' table, though they might be burning with thirst she would not allow them to drink even water, thus forestalling an evil habit and adding these wise words: "You want to drink water now because you do not have recourse to wine, but when you come to be married and are made mistresses of your own pantries and cellars, you will dislike water, but still your habit of drinking it will remain." By this kind of instruction and the authority with which she commanded, she restrained the gluttony of tender years, and tempered the very thirst of the girls to such excellent moderation that they did not strive for anything that was not seemly.

[8. 18]   And yet my mother's love for wine, as she, Your handmaid, confided in me her son, her love for wine had crept up on her, for when her parents, believing her to be a temperate girl, sent her to draw wine out of the barrel, she would hold the bowl under the spigot and, before pouring the wine into the pitcher, would take a little sip with pursed lips, for more than a sip she found repellent. And yet she had not done this out of a passion for drink but out of the ebullience of youth, in which the kind of playful impulses boil over that are usually kept in check by the authority of elders. But by always adding a little more to that daily sip—for one who despises small things will fall little by little—she had fallen into the habit of drinking entire cups of unmixed[5] wine. Where then was that watchful old woman with her strict restraint? But there would have been no remedy against this hidden disease if Your healing, Lord, did not preside over us. When father, mother, and nurses are away, You are present, You Who created us, who call us, who through those placed above us induce the salvation of our souls. What did You do then, my God? How did You cure her? How did You heal her? Did You not bring forth from the soul of another a sharp reproach, like a surgeon's knife from Your secret store, and with a single slash remove all the festering putrescence? A servant with whom she used to go to the barrel happened to quarrel with her little mistress when they were alone, deriding her for her deeds with bitter insult, calling her a drunken sot. The insult stung the little girl to the quick, and she reflected on the shameful thing she had done, instantly condemning and abandoning her habit. Just as flattering friends lead to ruin, so accusing enemies often lead to reform. Yet it is not for what You do through people that You reward them, but for what people do of their own volition. The servant in her anger had sought to hurt her young mistress, not to mend her ways, and she spoke her words in secret, either in the heat of quarrel or because she might be called to account for not having said anything earlier. But You, Lord, Ruler of heaven and earth, turn to Your purposes the course of the deepest torrents, and order the turbulence of the tide of time. Through the affliction of one soul You gave health to another, and all who hear this must realize that they must not attribute a person's reform to

5. I.e., unmixed with water.

their own powers, when someone whom they wish to reform is reformed through words they have spoken.

[9. 19]   So my mother was brought up in modesty and sobriety, and she was made obedient by You to her parents rather than being made obedient by her parents to You, so that as soon as she was of full age to be a bride she was bestowed upon a man whom she served as her lord. And she did everything in her power to win this man over to You, speaking to him of You through the qualities by which You had made her beautiful, filling her husband with respect and love for her as well as admiration. She tolerated his infidelity so that there would never be any animosity between them, for she was awaiting Your mercy upon him, that in believing in You he might become chaste. Furthermore, he was as exceptionally kind as he was hot-tempered, but she had learned not to cross an angry husband in word or deed. It was only when his temper had settled, and he was calm and approachable, that she would explain her actions if he had happened to be too quick to flare up in anger. Many other wives who had gentler husbands bore shameful marks of beatings on their faces, and among their friends would blame their husbands' ways. But she would blame the women's tongues, giving the women as if in jest the solemn advice that the instant they had heard the marriage contract read out to them, they should have recognized that they were now slaves, and, remembering their station, it would have been more fitting for them not to take on airs before their lords. When her friends found out what a violent husband she had, they were amazed that nobody had ever heard of Patricius[6] raising his hand to her or that she never bore the marks of a beating, and that there had never been discord among them even for a day. Asked how this could be, she told her friends her custom of responding to her husband's ire which I have mentioned above. The women who followed her example were to thank her, while those who did not suffered and remained oppressed.

[9. 20]   Her mother-in-law had initially been incited against her by the insinuations of malicious servants, but was assuaged by the young wife's gentle, yielding manner and her steadfast forbearance, so that she herself revealed to her son that meddling tongues had disrupted the peace in the home, causing trouble between her and her daughter-in-law, and she insisted that he punish the wrongdoers. Patricius respected his mother's wish, ensuring that discipline and peace returned to his home, and he had the maids whipped as his mother had asked, and she promised the same payment to any servant seeking to ingratiate herself by saying evil things about her daughter-in-law. As no servant now dared speak ill of her, they all lived pleasantly and amicably together.

[9. 21]   To this good handmaid of Yours in whose womb You created me, my God, my Mercy, You granted her another great gift, that of being a peacemaker to quarreling people whenever she could. When she heard bitter words bursting forth from both sides in bilious anger, when a friend spewed out acrid rage against an absent enemy, she would only reveal to either one whatever words might lead to their reconciliation. I might have considered this a minor gift had I not had the painful experience of encountering so many people, who by some horrendous and rampant pestilence of sin not only disclose to an irate

6. Augustine's father, believed to have been a Roman citizen and a pagan until, he converted to Christianity on his deathbed.

person what their irate enemy said about them, but add things that were never said, whereas it ought to be clear to any humane person that he must not incite hostility between people through hostile words, if he cannot bring himself to use benign words to extinguish the hostility. That was how she was, for You had been the inner Teacher in the school of her heart.

[9. 22]   Finally, toward the very end of her husband's life on earth, she converted him to You, and once he was a believer he no longer gave her cause to lament what she had had to bear before he had become a believer. She was also the servant of Your servants, of whom all who knew her greatly praised and honored and loved You in her; they felt Your presence in her heart, which was attested by the fruits of her devout comportment, for she had been the wife of one man, had honored her debt to her parents and run her house piously, had testimony for her good works, and she had brought up children, of whom she labored as if in birth whenever she saw them straying from You.[7] Lastly she took care of all of us,[8] Your servants, Lord, for Your gift allows me to speak on behalf of us all, who, before she closed her eyes in sleep, all lived united in You since we had received the grace of Your baptism. She cared for us as though she had given birth to us all, yet served us as though she had been the daughter of every one of us.

[10. 23]   With the day looming on which she was to depart this life, a day that You knew but we did not, Your hidden ways arranged that she and I would stand alone gazing out of a window that overlooked the garden of the house in which we were staying in Ostia, by the mouth of the Tiber. In this house, far from all the noise and commotion, we were recuperating from the exertions of our long journey before we set sail across the sea. She and I were talking alone, in sweet conversation, forgetting the past and reaching out for what lay ahead, she and I wondering in the presence of the Truth, which You are, what the eternal life of saints would be like, which neither eye has seen nor ear has heard, nor has it entered into the heart of man. The mouth of our hearts opened wide to drink in those celestial streams of Your fountain, the fountain of life, which is with You, so that fortified to the extent that we could be, we might to some degree contemplate such a profound matter.

[10. 24]   And when in our conversation we reached the conclusion that the greatest delight of the bodily senses, the greatest corporeal light, is not worthy of comparison to the sweetness of the eternal life of saints, not worthy even of mention, we were lifted with a greater glowing love toward God, the Selfsame.[9] We rose by degrees past everything corporeal to the very heaven where sun and moon and stars shine upon the earth, and ascended even higher with our thoughts and words, with our marveling at Your works, reaching these in our minds and transcending them, coming to that region of unceasing plenty where You feed Israel in eternity with the food of truth,[1] where life is the Wisdom through which all these things are made, all things that have been and shall be. But Wisdom is not made: Wisdom is as it has been and ever shall be. For there

---

7. Augustine is paraphrasing Paul's description of the duties of a widow, enumerated in 1 Timothy 5.
8. I.e., Augustine and his fellow converts.
9. Reality, the divine principle. This ecstasy of Augustine and Monica is described throughout in philosophical terms in which God is Wisdom.
1. Reference to the manna that fed the Israelites in the desert during their flight from Egypt; see Exodus 16.11–35.

is no *was* or *will be* in Wisdom, only *being*, as Wisdom is eternal. For *was* and *will be* are not eternal. While we were discussing and longing for Wisdom, we touched it lightly with the most ardent effort of our hearts, and we sighed and left behind us the first-fruits of the Spirit, returning to the mere sounds of our mouths, where words have a beginning and an end, and how can these words be compared to Your Word, our Lord, who remains in Himself without age and renews all things?

[10. 25]   So we said: "If the commotion of the flesh were to fall silent in a man, silent the images of the earth and the waters and the air, and silent the heavens, and the soul were silent to itself and by not thinking of itself would surpass itself, if all dreams and imaginary revelations were silent, and silent every tongue and every sign and all that exists only transiently, since if anyone could hear these things then this is what they all would say: 'We did not make ourselves, but He who abides in eternity made us.' If having said this they fell silent, having led us to open our ears to Him who made these things, and He alone would speak through Himself and not through them so that we would hear His Word not through a tongue of flesh, nor through an Angel's voice, nor through the thundering sound from the clouds, nor through an obscure enigma,[2] but we might hear Him whom in these things we love, hear Him without these things, just as we now reached out and in swift thought touched the Wisdom that abides over all things in eternity. If this could continue, and other visions that were far inferior could be withdrawn, and could this vision ravish and absorb and envelop its beholder in inward joys, so that eternal life would be like that one moment of understanding for which we longed, then would this not mean: 'Enter into the joy of your Lord'? And when would that be? When we shall all rise again, though we shall not all be changed?"[3]

[10. 26]   Such were the things that I was saying, and even if not exactly in this way or with those words, yet, Lord, You know that it was on that day when we were speaking, and, as she and I spoke, this world with all its delights became contemptible to us, and she said, "My son, as for me, I no longer delight in anything in this life anymore. I do not know what I am still doing here, or why I am here now, since my hopes in this world have all expired. The one thing for which I wanted to linger a while longer in this life was that I might see you a true Christian before I died, but my God has granted my wish in greater abundance than I had sought, for I now see that you despise earthly happiness and have become His servant. What am I doing here?"

[11. 27]   I do not remember what I answered, but within five days, not much more, she fell sick of a fever, and one day in her illness she fainted and for a moment lost consciousness. We rushed to her side, but she was soon revived, and seeing me and my brother near her, asked, "Where was I?" And then, looking straight at us as we stood there stunned with grief, she said, "It is here that you will bury your mother." I remained silent, refraining from tears, but my brother spoke, saying he would be happier if she did not die in a strange land but in her own. Hearing his words she looked at him anxiously, her eyes

2. Cf. Luke 8.10: "Unto you it is given to know the mysteries of the kingdom of God: but to others in parables; that seeing they might not see, and hearing they might not understand."

3. Cf. 1 Corinthians 15.52: "the trumpet shall sound, and the dead shall be raised incorruptible, and we shall be changed," referring to the Last Judgment.

admonishing him because such things were still important to him, and then looking at me said, "Do you hear what your brother says?" and turning to us both, "Bury this body anywhere, and do not worry about such trifles. The only thing I ask of you is that wherever you may be, you will remember me at the Lord's altar." And having expressed her feeling in such words as she could still utter, she fell silent, overwhelmed by her growing illness.

[11. 28]   But as I thought of Your gifts, O invisible God, which You plant in the hearts of those faithful to You and from which wondrous fruits spring, I rejoiced and gave thanks to You, recalling the worry that had burned within her about arranging and preparing a tomb next to her husband's body. Since they had lived together in great harmony, she had also wished to have this addition to that happiness and to have this commemorated among men—so slightly is the human mind able to embrace divine things—wishing that after her pilgrimage beyond the sea the same earth should cover her and her husband's earthly remains. I did not know when, through the wealth of Your goodness, these empty trifles had begun to subside in her heart, but I rejoiced, surprised at what she had divulged to me, even if in our conversation by the window, when she had said, "I do not know what I am still doing here," she no longer appeared to desire to die in her own country. I was to hear later, too, that while we were at Ostia she had one day, when I was absent, spoken with a mother's confidence to some of my friends about her contempt for this life and the goodness of death. Amazed at the courage You had given to a woman, they had asked whether she was not afraid to leave her body so far from her own city, to which she replied: "Nothing is far away from God, nor is it to be feared that at the ends of the earth He would not know from where He should resurrect me." Then on the ninth day of her illness, in the fifty-sixth year of her life and the thirty-third of mine, that pious and religious soul was freed from her body.

[12. 29]   I closed her eyes, and pouring into my heart was a vast sorrow that overflowed into tears, though my eyes, under the strict command of my mind, redrank the fountain dry, the struggle causing great strife within me. At her last breath my son Adeodatus[4] broke into laments, but, checked by us all, fell silent. In the same way, the child within me strove toward weeping but was checked and silenced by the voice of my heart, for we did not think it was fitting to celebrate the funeral with tearful cries and lamentations, as in this way so many people lament the misery of the state of death, or death as complete eradication, whereas she was neither unhappy in her death, nor entirely dead: of this we were certain because of the evidence of the life she had led and her unfeigned faith.

[12. 30]   What was it that was hurting me so grievously within if not the fresh wound caused by the sudden shattering of the sweetest and most beloved custom of our life together? I was delighted with her words when, in her final illness, she countered my attentions with endearments and said that I was an affectionate son, avowing with great emotion and love that she had never heard from my mouth a single harsh or reproachful word against her. And yet, my God Who has made us, what comparison could there be between the esteem I showed her and her selfless servitude to me? My soul was wounded, losing

---

4. Adeodatus was then about fifteen or sixteen years old.

such a great solace in her. It was as if my life was torn in two, since her life and mine had been as one.

[12. 31]   My son having been stopped from weeping, Euodius took up the Psalter and began to chant, our whole household answering him: "I will sing of mercy and justice to You, O Lord."[5] The news spread and many brethren and religious women gathered, and while those whose office it was began to prepare the burial, I withdrew to another part of the house where, with friends who deemed I should not be left alone, I could aptly speak about matters suitable to the moment. The balm of truth soothed my torment that was known to You but unknown to them, and they listened to me intently, supposing that I felt no sorrow. But in Your ears, where none of them could hear, I blamed the weakness of my feelings and restrained my flow of grief, which for a while ceded to my will; yet its force overcame me once more, though not as tears bursting forth or my countenance changing. But I knew what I was suppressing within my heart. I was extremely unhappy with myself that these human matters, which in the due order and lot of our condition inevitably fall to us, could have such power over me and with new grief I grieved over my grief, and so was consumed by a double sorrow.

[12. 32]   When her body was carried out for burial, we went and returned without tears. I did not weep during the prayers we poured forth to You when the sacrifice of our redemption[6] was offered for her, nor during the prayers when her body was placed beside the tomb before being interred, as is the custom; but the entire day I was profoundly sad within, and with troubled mind prayed to You as best I could that You would heal my sorrow, though You did not, impressing by this lesson upon my memory, I believe, the strength of the chains of habit upon the mind, even when it does not feed on deceit. It seemed also good to me to go and bathe, having heard that the Latin word for bath, *balneum*, had its name from the Greek *balaneion*,[7] casting anguish from the mind. This too I avow to Your mercy, Father of orphans, that I bathed and was the same as I had been before I bathed, for the bitterness of sorrow did not exude from my heart. Then I slept, woke up, but found that my grief had not softened at all. Alone as I lay in my bed, I remembered those true verses of Your Ambrose,[8] for You are

> God, Creator of all things,
> Ruler of Heaven who vests
> The day with beauteous light
> The night with reposing sleep
> Loosening man's limbs in rest
> Restoring them, refreshed for labor
> Relieving the minds of the wearied
> Untangling the sorrows of the distressed.

[12. 33]   Then gradually I returned to my former thoughts of Your handmaid, remembering her pious attachment to You and the holy helpfulness and

---

5. Cf. Psalm 101.1. "Euodius": one of Augustine's community of Christian converts.
6. Perhaps a communion service.
7. Augustine evidently derives *balaneion* ("bath") from the words *ballō* ("cast away")

and *ania* ("sorrow").
8. Ambrose (ca. 337–397), bishop of Milan and mentor to Augustine, was the author of many theological works as well as poetic hymns.

tenderness to us of which I was suddenly deprived: and I wanted to weep in Your sight for her and on her account, for myself and on my account. And I released the tears I had restrained, letting them pour forth, strewing them out so that my heart could rest in them, and my heart found repose for it was in Your ears, not in those of man who would have eyed my tears with scorn. And now, Lord, I confess this to You in writing: let him read it who will and interpret it how he may, and if he finds it to be sinful that I wept for my mother for a few minutes, the mother who was now dead to my eyes and who for many years had wept for me that I might live in Your eyes, let him not scorn me, but rather if he is a man of great love, let him weep for my sins before You, the Father of all the brethren of Your Christ.

[13. 34]   Now, my heart healed of that wound in which I could be blamed of a fleshly state of mind, before You, our God, I shed very different tears for Your maidservant, tears flowing from a spirit shaken by the thoughts of the danger every soul that dies in Adam faces,[9] though she had been made alive in Christ even before she was released from the flesh; for she had lived so that Your name would be praised in her faith and the life she led. But I do not dare claim that from the moment You regenerated her through baptism no word against Your precepts issued from her mouth. Your Son, the Truth, has said, "Whoever shall say to his brother 'you fool' shall be in danger of the fire of Gehenna."[1] And woe even to commendable lives of men, if You should examine their lives casting mercy aside. But because You do not fiercely scrutinize our sins, we hope with confidence to find some place with You. But whoever enumerates his real merits to You is merely enumerating Your gifts. If only men would know themselves to be but men, and that he who glories would glory in the Lord.

[13. 35]   Therefore, God of my heart, my Praise and my Life, laying aside for a while my mother's good deeds for which I give thanks to You with joy, I now beseech You for her sins. Hear me by the Healer of our wounds[2] Who hung upon the cross and sits at Your right hand interceding with You on our behalf! I know that she always acted with compassion, and from her heart forgave her debtors their debts. Forgive her debts too, Lord, if she contracted any in the many years since she received the water of salvation. Forgive, Lord, forgive, I beseech You, and enter not into judgment with her. May mercy exalt above justice, since Your words are true and You have promised mercy to the merciful. That the merciful be so was Your gift to them, You Who will have mercy on whom You will have mercy and will have compassion on whom You have compassion.

[13. 36]   And I believe that You have already done what I am begging of You, but accept, Lord, the willing offerings of my mouth, for as the day of her release was imminent she gave no thought to having her body sumptuously wrapped or embalmed with perfumes, nor did she ask for an excellent monument or seek to be buried in her native land. She did not enjoin us to do these things, but asked only to be remembered at Your Altar at which she had served without missing a single day, for she knew that it is there that the holy sacrifice

9. I.e., with the curse of Adam not nullified through baptism in Jesus Christ and conformity with his teachings.
1. From Matthew 5.22, Jesus' Sermon on the

Mount. He is preaching a more severe moral code than the traditional one that whoever kills shall be liable to judgment. "Gehenna": hell.
2. Jesus.

is dispensed through which the handwriting of the decree against us is blotted out.[3] It is there that the enemy summing up our sins and seeking with what to charge us is vanquished, finding nothing in Him in Whom we are victors. Who will restore to Him His innocent blood? Who will repay Him the price with which He bought us and so take us from Him? To the Sacrament of this price Your handmaid bound her soul by the bond of faith. Let none sever her from Your protection. Let neither the lion nor the dragon[4] interpose themselves by force or trickery. She will reply that she owes nothing, lest she be refuted and seized by the wily accuser. She will reply that her debts have been forgiven her by Him to Whom none can repay the price that He, Who owed nothing, paid for us.

[13. 37]   So may she rest in peace with the husband before and after whom she had no other, whom she served bringing forth with patience fruit unto You, that she might also gain him for You. Inspire, my Lord, my God, inspire Your servants my brethren, Your sons my masters, whom I serve with voice and heart and pen, that all who read this may at Your altar remember Monnica Your maidservant, with Patricius who was once her husband, by whose flesh You brought me into this life, how I do not know.[5] May they all remember with pious affection those who were my parents in this transient light and all my brethren under You our Father in our mother the Christian Church, and my fellow-citizens in that eternal Jerusalem[6] for which Your wandering people are yearning from their exodus to their return. This way my mother's last request of me will, through my confessions, be far more abundantly fulfilled by the prayers of many, than by my prayers alone.

* * *

FROM BOOK XI

[*Time*]

[14. 17]   Hence there was no time when you had not made something, because You had made time itself. And no times are coeternal with You, because You abide, but if they were to abide they would not be times. For what is time? Who can explain this simply and in a few words? Who can comprehend it in thought so as to express it in words? And yet, when we converse, do we ever speak of anything with greater familiarity than of time? And we know what time is when we speak of it, just as we do when we hear another speak of it. So what is time? If no one asks me this, then I know; but if I am forced to explain it to someone who asks, then I do not know, though I will boldly maintain that I do know: that if nothing passed there would be no past time, and if nothing were to come then there would be no future, and if nothing is, then there would be no present time. So how do those two times—the past and the future—exist if the past does not exist now and the future does not yet exist? As for the present, if it were always present and never passed into the past, it would be not time, but

---

3. An allusion to Christ's redemption of humanity from the curse of Adam through the Crucifixion.
4. Cf. Psalm 91.13: "Thou shalt tread upon the lion and the adder: the young lion and the dragon shalt thou trample under feet, which invokes

God's protection of the godly."
5. I.e., Augustine does not understand the seemingly miraculous process by which the fetus grows in the womb.
6. That is, heaven.

eternity. Thus if the present, in order to be time, only comes into being because it passes into the past, how can we maintain that it exists if the aim of its being is that it will not be. Can we in truth maintain that time exists because its aim is not to exist?

* * *

[18. 23]   Permit me, my Lord and my Hope, to seek further. Let not my quest be confounded. For if past and future things exist I want to know where they are, which if I am still unable to know, at least I know that wherever they are, they are not there as future or past, but as present; for if they are also there as future, they are not yet there, and if they are also there as past, they are no longer there. Thus wherever and whatever they are, they only exist as present. When true things are recounted from the past, it is not the past things themselves that are brought forth from the memory, but words generated from their images that, as they passed through the senses, were fixed as imprints in the mind. Hence my childhood, which now no longer exists, is in the past that now no longer exists: but as I recall and recount its image, I behold it in the present because it still exists in my memory. Whether there is a similar process in foretelling things of the future, if one can preview the images of things that do not yet exist, I confess, my God, I do not know. What I do know is that we often first think our future actions through, and that this thinking through is present, but the action we are thinking through does not yet exist because it is a future action. It is only once we have embarked on this action, and have begun to do what we were thinking through, that this action exists, because then it is no longer future, but present.

[18. 24]   Whatever the nature of this mysterious sensing of future things, nothing can be seen that does not exist. But what now exists is not future, but present. Thus when things of the future are said to be seen, it is not the actual things that are seen, which do not yet exist—that is, which are future—but perhaps what is seen is their causes or signs that already exist. Hence these things are not future but are present to those who see the things from which the future, being generated in the mind, is foretold. Such generated things already exist, and those who foretell the future behold them as present before them. Let me take one example from a great number of examples: I see daybreak and predict the rising of the sun. What I see is present, what I foresee is future—not the sun being future, as it already exists, but its rising, which has not yet occurred. If I could not imagine in my mind the rising itself, as I do now in speaking of it, I would not be able to foretell it. Yet the daybreak that I see in the sky is not the sunrise, though it precedes it, just as the imagining of it in my mind is not the sunrise either. Both of these are discerned as present, so that the future sunrise can be foretold. Hence future things do not yet exist, and if they do not yet exist, they do not exist and cannot be seen. But they can be foretold from things that are present, which do exist and so can be seen.

* * *

[20. 26]   What is now clear and plain is that neither future things nor things of the past exist, nor can one rightly say, "There are three times: past, present, and future," though one might rightly say, "There are three times: a present of things past, a present of things present, and a present of things future." These three do in some way exist in the mind, for I do not see them anywhere else: The present of things past is memory, the present of things present is what I am seeing, and the present of things future is expectation. If I can express myself in these terms, I see three times, and I acknowledge that there are three. But we can actually say, "There are three times: past, present, and future." It is wrong, but that is how we say it. I do not take offense or find fault with what is said in this way if it is understood to mean that neither the future nor the past are present now. There is so little that we name correctly—most things we do not—but we do manage to impart what we mean.

* * *

[26. 33]   Does not my soul confess to You in all truth that I measure time? Is it, my God, that I am measuring and do not know what I am measuring? If I am measuring the movement of a body in time, am I not measuring time itself? Would I be able to measure the movement of a body, the duration of the movement, and how long it takes to move from one place to another, without measuring the time in which it moves? So how do I measure time itself? Do we use a shorter time to measure a longer time, the way we measure the length of a crossbar in cubits? We also tend to use the length of a short syllable to measure the length of a long syllable, calling it twice as long. We measure the length of poems by the length of the lines, and the length of the lines by the length of the feet, and the length of the feet by the length of the syllables, and the length of long syllables by the length of short. We do not measure the poem by its pages, for that way we would be measuring space, not time, but once we have declaimed the poem's words and they pass on, we say, "It is a long poem, because it is made up of so many lines; the lines are long, because they are made up of so many feet; they are long feet, since they stretch over so many syllables; it is a long syllable because it is twice as long as the syllable that is short." But even in this way we cannot determine a precise measurement of time, because it could be that a shorter line is spoken with more gravity and so takes up more time than a longer line declaimed with urgency. The same is true for a poem, a foot, a syllable. This has led me to believe that time is simply a distention, but of what I do not know, though it would be surprising if it were not of the mind itself. For I beseech You, my God, what is it that I am measuring, when I say either indefinitely, "This time is longer than that time," or definitely "This time is twice that"? I know that I measure time, but I do not measure the future, because it does not yet exist, nor do I measure the present, because it does not extend over any expanse, nor do I measure the past, because it no longer exists. So what is it that I am measuring? Perhaps the passing times, not those that have passed? This is what I have said before.

* * *

[31. 41]   Lord my God, how deep are the recesses of Your mysteries, and how far from them have I been cast by the consequences of my errors! Heal my eyes so that with Your Light I can rejoice! If a mind existed that was graced with such great knowledge and prescience so as to know all things past and future, the way I know a well-known hymn, that mind would be most miraculous and awe-inspiring, for nothing that has taken place and nothing that is to come in future ages would elude this mind, just as when I sing that hymn it would not elude me how much of it had passed since I had begun singing, and what and how much of the hymn still remained. But far be it that You, the Creator of the universe, the Creator of minds and bodies, far be it that You should know all things future and past in that way: You know them far more wonderfully and mysteriously. Someone who sings or hears a hymn he knows will feel his perception change and expand as he anticipates the words to come and remembers the words that have past. But this is not so with You Who are unchangeably eternal, the eternal Creator of minds. Just as You knew in the Beginning the heaven and the earth without any change of Your knowledge, so You made in the Beginning the heaven and the earth without Your action expanding. Let him who understands confess to You, and let him who does not understand confess to You. How exalted You are and yet You dwell in those who are humble in heart! You raise up all who are cast down, and those whose sublimity you are do not fall.

THE QUR'AN

610–632

The word *qur'an* literally means "the recitation." For Muslims, the Qur'an is not so much a book as a living and vibrant act of speech that has been passed down through an unbroken chain of human beings from the time of Muhammad, who with his companions in seventh-century Arabia formed the first community of Muslims. At the same time, the Qur'an is also conceived of as a book: not a literal object on the shelf but a divine work that exists only in the heavenly realm of paradise. Any physical copy of the Arabic text is thought of as a pale reflection of that ideal book, a tool to enable the reader to memorize and then recite the Qur'anic text. As divine speech, moreover, the Qur'an can never be rendered perfectly in the medium of the human voice, a deficiency that testifies to its fundamental inimitability, or *i'jaz*. In accord with this view of the nature of the Qur'an, no translation into any other language is thought of as actually being the holy book itself. The most that any translation can be, for the believer, is an aid to understanding the original.

The Qur'an presents itself as the last of a sequence of revealed holy books, including the Torah (in Arabic, Tawrat), the Psalms (Zabur), and the Gospels (Injil). Similarly, Muhammad is presented as one in a lineage of prophets (that is, those who have received communications directly from God) that begins with the first man, Adam. Earlier holy books each have an associated prophet: for the Torah, Moses; for the Psalms, David; and for the Gospels, Jesus and also Mary—who, despite being female, is also recognized as part of the prophetic lineage. Indeed, a minority of classical Muslim scholars, including Ibn Hazm (d. 1065), considered her to be a prophet outright. Stories and characters from Jewish and Christian scripture reappear in the Qur'an, as seen in the chapters (or surahs) on Joseph and Mary. When hearing these verses, the earliest converts to Islam, drawn from the local Christian and Jewish communities located in Arabia, would have marveled at the different perspective brought to bear on familiar stories by this new revelation. The Qur'an recognizes the followers of other monotheistic religions, such as Jews and Christians, as "people of the Book"—those who follow the word of God as revealed by his prophets. From the point of view of Islam, the people of the Book who lived before the revelation of the Qur'an were also followers of *islam*, in the literal sense of "submission" to God's will. Those who continued to reverence their own, pre-Islamic holy books, such as Jews and Christians, could be tolerated within the Muslim community, but this inclusiveness of monotheism had its limits. Muslims generally viewed their Prophet as the last of his kind, "the seal of prophets," and the Qur'an as the last holy book that would ever be revealed to humanity. The Torah and the Gospels, while divine in their inspiration, had become corrupt over time. Only through submission to the divine will as revealed in the Qur'an, Muslims believed, could the faithful be sure they would enter into paradise and avoid the punishments of hell.

Only from the nineteenth century on has the **Bible** begun to be read as a work of literature as well as a divinely inspired text, and so too this dual focus on the Qur'an has been recent. From the Middle Ages to the twenty-first century, Western readers of the Qur'an have all too often condemned what they saw as its theological deviance and narrative incoherence. As a result, Muslims have hesitated to offer up the Qur'an for study within the framework of literary history or to allow it to move beyond the conservative framework of faith-based perspectives. This attitude has begun to change, however, because of innovative approaches to Qur'anic interpretation

on the part of Muslim communities and an increasing willingness to place the Qur'an into dialogue with other sacred scriptures. The Qur'an itself invites comparison with other literary traditions—most explicitly, the rich traditions of oral poetry found in pre-Islamic Arabia. In that context, it appears as a marvel of literature whose divine inspiration is manifest in the form of lyrical chant and resonant verse. Reading the Qur'an on the page, in translation, weakly conveys its virtue, which can be appreciated only in the musical oral recitation (*tajwid*) that reveals the rhythmic quality of the verse and the haunting repetition of syllables at the ends of successive lines. It is possible to get a sense of this music in the repeated refrain of the surah "The All-Merciful" ("Ar Rahman"), translated below.

The Qur'an is divided into 144 surahs, some of which are quite short; others are very long, resembling a biblical book in form. Each surah is made up of a number of verses (*ayat*; singular *aya*). The Qur'an is also conventionally divided up into thirty sections (*ajza'*; singular *juz'*) of roughly equal length to facilitate recitation of the entire work over the period of one month. Because of the emphasis placed on its oral recitation, which must be performed as part of the five daily prayers, Muslims begin to memorize the Qur'an at a young age; they start with the introductory surah, "The Opening" ("Al-Fatiha"), and continue on with the short Meccan surahs that are concentrated near the end of the Qur'an, including "Purity" ("Al-Ikhlas"). Instead of being arranged in the order that Muhammad received them, the surahs are arranged as Muhammad said he had been instructed by God. Some of the surahs were revealed at Mecca, when the Muslim community was starting to develop, and others at Medina, where the persecuted community took refuge; the two types tend to differ not only in length but also in subject matter and in tone.

Instead of being carefully separated, however, the Meccan and Medinan surahs are intermingled, and many of the Meccan surahs dating from early in Muhammad's prophetic mission appear near the end of the text. The effect is one of fragments arranged in a mosaic—yet that mosaic has a very clearly defined form, delineated by strands running throughout. The repetition of phrases and motifs across surahs, often from different periods, creates a pattern as intricate as a woven tapestry.

With the exception of "Light" and "The All-Merciful," which were revealed at Medina, the excerpts reproduced here are Meccan surahs, which tend to be relatively short. Our aim was to provide entire chapters rather than abbreviated selections, so that the highly structured nature of the surahs could be grasped. The tightly ordered form illustrated on the level of the individual surah is also evident more generally in the Qur'an, in which the parts all contribute to make up the whole, but each part can also stand for the whole. Several of the surahs are known by another name, reflecting this part–whole relationship: "The Opening," which is the first surah, is also known as "The Mother of the Book," while surah "Ya Sin" is sometimes called "The Heart of the Qur'an." One of the last surahs, "Purity," was described by Muhammad himself as being "one-third of the Qur'an," because its highly condensed verses on the unity of God encapsulate the very core of Islamic theology. Other surahs, such as "Joseph" and "Mary," illuminate the extent to which the Qur'an is intertwined with Jewish and Christian faith traditions. Similarly, "Light" provides an Islamic vision of the divine that resonates with both the Neoplatonic concept of intellectual illumination and the Zoroastrian veneration of fire.

The Qur'an was received by Muhammad through the mediation of the angel Gabriel (Jibreel) over a period of about twenty-three years, beginning when he was forty years old and ending with his death in 632. During that time, the Qur'an existed as an oral recitation, repeated both by Muhammad himself and by the growing community of Muslims. After Muhammad's death, the community recognized the need to record the oral text to ensure that errors not creep into the recitation. The closest companions of Muhammad, under the supervision of the first caliph (or ruler) of the Muslim community, Abu Bakr, assembled the Qur'an in written form. The third caliph, Uthman, supervised the finalized version of the text, which was completed in 651, and then ordered all imperfect copies to be destroyed. It is this version of the Qur'an that we read today. Translations began to be produced almost immediately, beginning with a rendering of "The Opening" into the Persian language by Salman, one of the companions of the Prophet Muhammad. A full Persian translation of the Qur'an was made in the ninth century, attesting to the rapid embrace of Islam by the inhabitants of Persia (modern Iran). As is the case today, these translations were not made with the purpose of substituting Qur'anic verses in the local vernacular for the Arabic originals during prayer; instead, they were aids to understanding intended to enable fuller assimilation of the Arabic scripture within a new culture. Western audiences started to read the Qur'an in the Middle Ages, beginning with Robert of Ketton's Latin translation in 1143. The Qur'an is never accompanied by pictorial illustrations, in keeping with the Islamic practice of iconoclasm (the prohibition of any representation of living things, thereby avoiding the temptation of idolatry). It is, however, often rendered in elaborate calligraphy, a style of writing so ornate that it becomes art, fusing word with image in the aural masterpiece that is the Qur'an.

The Qur'an

Surah 1: The Opening[1]

1. In the Name of God,
   the All-Merciful, Ever-Merciful:[2]
2. All praise to God, Lord of the universe,[3]
3. the All-Merciful, Ever-Merciful;
4. Ruler on the Day of Reckoning
5. You alone we worship; and You alone
   we implore for help.
6. Guide us to the straight path,
7. the path of those whom You have favoured, not
   of those who have incurred Your wrath, nor
   of those who have gone astray.

Surah 12: Yusuf, or Joseph[1]

In the Name of God, the All-Merciful, Ever-Merciful

I

1. *Alif Lam Ra.*[2]
   These are the verses
   of the Manifest Book.

2. We[3] have sent it
   as an Arabic Qur'an,
   so you might
   understand.

3. We narrate to you
   the sublimest of narratives
   in revealing to you
   this Qur'an,
   though before this, you
   were indeed
   among the heedless.

1. Translated by M. A. R. Habib and Bruce B. Lawrence.
2. Though it appears at the outset of every chapter in the 114 chapters of the Qur'an except one (Q 9), it is only here that the *basmala*—"In the Name of God"—is treated as a verse. Its importance is underscored by its two qualifiers, "All-Merciful, Ever-Merciful" (*ar-Rahman* and *ar-Rahim*), derived from *ar-rahmah* (the mercy), which in turn derives from *ar-raham* (the womb).
3. Literally, "the worlds, or all worlds" ('*Alamin*,

pl. of '*alam*), including both Jinn and angels (see multiple references in the Qur'an, especially Q55 below on the Jinn).
1. Cf. Genesis 37.9–11.
2. *Alif Lam Ra* are an instance of what is known as the disaggregated or disconnected letters. They occur in 29 chapters, always at the beginning, and include about one half, or 14, of the 28 letters in the Arabic alphabet.
3. Throughout the Qur'an, "We" is used to express the voice of God (in Arabic "Allah").

4. When Joseph said
to his father: "My father,
I saw, in a dream, eleven stars
and the sun and moon:
I saw them bowing down
before me,"

5. he replied: "My son,
don't narrate this dream
to your brothers, lest they
plan a plot against you;
for surely Satan is
a manifest adversary
to humankind."

6. "Thus will your Lord choose you,
and teach you
the deeper meaning of events,
and perfect His favor
upon you and the family
of Jacob, as He
perfected it
before, upon your fathers
both, Abraham and Isaac[4]
for truly your Lord is
the Knowing, the Wise."

II

7. Surely, in [the story
of] Joseph and his brothers
are signs for those
who ask.

8. [His brothers] said: "Joseph
and his brother are dearer
to father than we,
though we are a larger body;
our father is in manifest error."

9. "Kill Joseph or cast him out
in some far land,
so your father will
turn his face to you alone;
and after this, you can be
a righteous community."

---

4. Isaac is Jacob's father, and Abraham is his grandfather; all three are recognized as prophets in Islam.

10. One of them said: "Don't kill
Joseph; if you must
act on this, throw him down
to the well's dark depth, so
some caravan will pick him up."

11. They said: "Father,
why won't you trust
us with Joseph?
For truly, we have
good will for him."

12. "Send him tomorrow with us;
so he'll enjoy himself and play,
and we'll be sure we
guard him well."

13. [Jacob] said: "It truly grieves me
that you take him, for I fear
the wolf might eat him
while you're not heeding him."

14. They said: "If the wolf
should eat him
—though we are a large body—
we would surely be among the lost."

15. So they took him,
and they all agreed
to throw him down
to the well's dark depth.
But We inspired him: "You will surely
in time apprise them of this deed of theirs
when they have grown unaware."

16. They came, then,
to their father
in the evening,
weeping.

17. They said: "Father,
we went racing, and left
Joseph with our things; then
the wolf devoured him.
You won't believe us,
even though we speak the truth.

18. They showed his shirt, soiled
with false blood. "No!" He cried,
"Your minds have enticed
you to some misdeed.
But patience is beautiful

and [I invoke] the help of God
against what you plead."

19. And a caravan came, travelers,
who sent to the well their water-carrier,
and he lowered his bucket.
"What good luck," he cried,
"Here is a boy!"
And they stowed him
in their merchandise. And God
is Aware of what they do.

20. They sold him
for a low price,
for a few silver coins,
such low regard
they had for him.

III

21. The man—Egyptian—
who bought him
told his wife: "Make easeful
his lodging; perhaps he'll
profit us or we'll
adopt him as a son."
And so We settled
Joseph in the land,
that We might teach him
the deeper meaning of events.
And so God prevails
in His affairs; but most
people do not know.

22. When he reached his prime,
We endowed him
with sound judgment and knowledge:
so We reward those who do good.

23. The woman, in whose house
he stayed, tried to seduce him;[5]
she secured the doors
and said, "Come close!"
"God forbid!" he said,
"He is my lord; he made
pleasant my lodging. Those
who do wrong will
surely not prosper."

5. Cf. Genesis 39.7–41.45.

24. She lusted
for him, and he
would have lusted for her, had he
not seen proof
from his Lord; so We kept
evil and unclean deeds
away from him, for he
was one of Our pure servants.

25. And they both raced
for the door, and she
tore his shirt from
behind, and they both
found her husband by the door.
"What penalty can there be,"
she cried, "for one
who designed evil against your wife,
but prison or torture?"

26. [Joseph] said: "It was she
who tried to seduce me."
Someone from her family
bore witness:
"If his shirt is torn
from the front, then
she speaks truthfully
and he is a liar."

27. "But if his shirt
is torn from behind,
then she is lying,
and he is truthful."

28. So when [the husband] saw his shirt
torn from behind, he said:
"This is your women's guile,
your guile is great indeed."

29. "Joseph, let this pass,
and wife, beg forgiveness
for your wrong; you
surely are a sinner."

IV

30. Women gossiped in the city:
"The governor's wife sought
to seduce her manservant
who has inflamed her
with love: we see her
openly straying."

31. When she heard
their gossip, she sent for them
and prepared for them
a banquet. She gave each of them
a knife; and said to Joseph:
"Come before them!"
When they saw him,
they so marveled at him,
they cut their hands, remarking:
"God save us! This is
no mortal—this is none other
than a noble angel!"

32. She said: "This
is the man on whose account
you reproved me!
Yes, I tried to seduce him
but he refused.
Yet, if he does not do
what I command, he'll be
thrown into prison,
ignominious."

33. He said: "My Lord,
prison is dearer to me
than what they call me to;
unless You turn away
their guile from me,
I might succumb to them,
in ignorance."

34. So his Lord answered him
and turned their guile
away from him. He is indeed
the Hearing, the Knowing.

35. Then it occurred to them,
after they had seen the signs
[of his virtue],
to imprison him awhile.

V

36. Entering the prison with him
were two young men. One of them
said: "I dreamt that I
was pressing wine." The other
said: "I dreamt that I
was carrying, on my head,
some bread, which birds
were pecking.

Tell us the deeper meaning
for we see you are
one of those who do good."

37. He said: "Surely, no food will
come to sustain you
before I inform you
of the dreams' deeper meaning.
This is part of what
my Lord has taught me.
I have left the creed
of a people who
disbelieve in God and who
deny the hereafter."

38. "And I follow the creed
of my forefathers, Abraham,
Isaac, and Jacob; it is not for us
to ascribe to God partners
of any kind—through God's
Grace upon us, and upon
humankind, though most
of humankind are ungrateful."

39. "My fellow prisoners,
which is better: many lords
differing among themselves,
or the One God,
the Omnipotent?"

40. "Besides Him, you worship nothing
but names—named by you—
you and your forefathers—
for which God has revealed
no sanction. Judgment belongs
to none but God. He
commands that you worship
none but Him. This is
the right religion, though
most of humankind
do not know.

41. "Fellow prisoners, one
of you will serve his lord
with wine; the other
will be crucified, and birds
will peck at his head.
This is the decree
in the matter on which
you both inquired."

42. And he said to the one
he thought would go free,
"Mention me to your lord."
But Satan made him forget
to mention him to his lord.
So [Joseph] remained in prison
a few years more.

VI

43. The king said:
"I saw, in a dream,
seven fat cows, which
seven lean ones devoured;
and seven ears of corn, green,
and seven others, withered.
Counselors, explain to me
my dream, if you can indeed
interpret dreams."

44. They said: "A confusing miscellany
of dreams; and we are not
versed in the deeper meaning
of dreams."

45. He, of the two, who was freed
now remembered, after all this time,
and said: "I shall disclose to you
its deeper meaning.
Dispatch me, then [to visit Joseph,
whom he then asked]:

46. "Joseph, you who
are truthful, explain
to us the meaning [of a dream]
of seven fat cows
which seven lean ones
devour, and of seven
ears of corn, green,
and seven others, withered,
so I may return
to the people, so they
may know."

47. He replied: "You will sow,
as usual, for seven years,
and what you reap, you will store,
leaving it in the ear, all
but a little, from which
you will eat."

48. "After that shall come
seven harsh years
which shall consume
what you have prepared
for them, all
but a little, which
you will preserve."

49. "Then after that shall come
a year in which the people
shall have abundant rain
and will press grapes."

VII

50. So the king said:
"Bring him to me."
But when the envoy
came to [Joseph, Joseph] said:
"Return to your lord,
and ask him the mind
of the women who
cut their hands.
Surely my Lord is
Aware of their guile."

51. The king said to the women:
"Tell me of the time
when you tried to seduce
Joseph?" They said:
"God forbid, we learned
nothing evil about him."
The governor's wife said:
"Now the truth is out:
It was I who tried to seduce him;
and he, without doubt, is telling the truth."

52. [Joseph said;][6]
"By this, my master may know
that I never was faithless to him
in his absence, and that God
will not guide the guile
of the treacherous."

53. "And I do not absolve
my own soul; the soul
is ever prone to evil,
unless my Lord affords

6. Some translators attribute these words to the governor's wife.

mercy. My Lord
is Forgiving,
Ever-Merciful."

54. And the king said:
"Bring him to me;
so I may keep him
for myself."
So when he had spoken
with him, he said:
"Today, we confer on you
power and trust."

55. Joseph said: "Let me
oversee the granaries
of the land: I will be
a wary custodian."

56. So We gave Joseph
power in the land, to live
wherever he wished. We bestow
Our mercy on whom
We will, nor will We forsake
the reward of those
who do good.

57. But the reward
of the Hereafter
is better, for those
who believe and are
mindful of God.

VIII

58. And the brothers of Joseph
arrived, and came before him,[7]
and he recognized them,
but they did not know him.

59. And when he had
provided them with supplies,
he said: "Bring to me
a brother of yours,
born of your own father.[8] Do you
not see that I trade fairly,
in full measure, and that I
am most gracious as a host?"

7. Cf. Genesis 42.3–46.7.
8. Benjamin, Joseph's full brother; his other brothers have different mothers.

60. "But if you don't
bring him to me,
you'll have no further
measure of corn from me, nor
shall you come near [me]."

61. They replied: "We'll
try to wrest him from
his father; we'll surely do that."

62. And Joseph told his servants:
"Place the goods they bartered
back in their saddle-bags,
so they'll recognize them
when they return to their people,
so they might come back."

63. And when they returned
to their father, they said:
"Father, we've been denied
any further measure of corn;
send with us our brother,
so we may procure our measure;
we'll be sure to protect him."

64. He said: "Shall I trust you
with him, as I trusted you
with his brother before?
Yet God is the Best
of Protectors, and He is
the Most Merciful
of the merciful."

65. And when they opened
their baggage, they found
their goods returned to them.
They said: "Father, what more
can we want? Our goods here
are returned to us:
we'll get food for our household,
we'll protect our brother;
and we'll get an extra camel-load
of grain, an easy load!"

66. Jacob answered: "Never
will he be sent with you,
until you make a pledge
to me—by God—that you'll bring him
to me, unless you're beseiged."
So when they had made their pledge,

he said: "God is Custodian
over all we say."

67. And: "My sons, don't
enter by one gate, but various
gates; yet I can't help you
in any way against [the Will of] God.
Judgment belongs to God alone:
in Him I put my trust,
and let all who trust
trust in Him."

68. And when they entered
from where their father
had directed, it helped them
in no way against [the Will of] God, for it was
but a need in Jacob, which
he fulfilled. For he possessed
knowledge, on account of what
We taught him. But most
of humankind does not know.

IX

69. And when they came
before Joseph, he drew
his brother to him: "I am
your own brother! So
don't grieve over
what they've been doing."

70. And while he was
preparing their supplies,
he planted a drinking cup
in his brother's saddle-bag.
Then a town-crier cried aloud:
"You, in the caravan!
You are surely thieves!"

71. They said, turning towards them:
"What are you missing?"

72. They said: "We're missing
the chalice of the king; whoever
brings it will be given
a camel-load, I pledge."

73. [The brothers] said: "By God!
You well know, we
haven't come to make mischief
in the realm, nor are we thieves!"

74. They said: "Then what
penalty should there be for this,
should you be lying?"

75. [The brothers] said:
"As penalty, the person who's
found with it in his saddle-bag,
should be held to account. That's how
we punish wrongdoers."

76. So Joseph began with
their bags, before searching
the bag of his brother; at length,
he lifted it out of his
brother's bag. So We
contrived things for Joseph, else he
could not detain his brother
within the law of the king,
without God's will. We
raise in station whom We will;
over all who know
is the All-Knowing.

77. They said: "If he has stolen,
well, he has a brother who stole
before him." But Joseph
said to himself, not
disclosing it to them:
"Your status is one
of evil,[9] and God knows best
concerning what you claim."

78. They said: "Governor,
he has a father, truly
advanced in age; so take
one of us in his place;
for we can see, truly,
you are one of those
who do good."

79. He said: "God forbid
we detain any but the one
on whom we found our possession;
we would then be doing wrong."

X

80. So when they lost hope
with him, they conferred

9. Literally, "in the worst place or situation."

in private. The eldest spoke:
"Do you not know
your father took a pledge
from you, in the name of God,
and before this, you were careless
with Joseph? I shall not
leave this land until my father
gives me leave or God decrees
thus for me, for He
is the Best of Judges."

81. "[As for the rest of you]
Go back to your father,
and say, 'Father of ours, your
son has been stealing.
We are witnesses only
to what we know; and
we could hardly guard
against the unforeseen.'

82. 'Ask in the town where
we were, and the caravan
we came with; for we
are telling the truth.'"

83. [When they said this
to their father]
Jacob replied: "No, your minds
have enticed you to some
misdeed. But
patience is beautiful;
perhaps God will bring them
all back to me. For He is
the Knowing, the Wise."

84. And he turned away
from them, and sighed:
"How great is my grief
over Joseph!" His eyes
grew white in sorrow,
and he grieved inside,
in silence.

85. They said: "By God,
will you not cease
to remember Joseph
till you reach
the frailest edge of illness, or
till you are deceased?"

86. He said: "I complain only
of my grief, my sorrow,

to God, and I know from God
what you do not."

87. "My sons, go,
inquire after Joseph
and his brother, and don't
despair of God's Grace.
None despairs of God's
Grace, except unbelievers."

88. So when they came
before Joseph, they entreated:
"Governor, adversity
has touched us, our family.
We bring but meager wares, yet
remit a full measure to us,
show charity to us, for God
surely rewards the charitable."

89. He said: "Do you know
what you did with Joseph
and his brother, in your
ignorance?"

90. They said: "Are you
Joseph, really?" [He replied]:
"I am Joseph, and
this is my brother:
God has been gracious
toward us. For those
who are pious and patient,
He does not forsake
the reward of those
who do good."

91. They said: "By God!
God surely has preferred
you over us, and we
have been sinners."

92. He said: "Let no
reproach weigh upon you
this day. May God forgive you,
for He is the Most Merciful
of the merciful."

93. "Go, with this shirt of mine,
and throw it over
my father's face: sight
will light up his eyes.
Then come back with
your entire family."

XI

94. After the caravan had journeyed,
their father said: "I detect
the scent of Joseph, though you
might think me a dotard."

95. [People] said: "By God,
you're still indeed in your
old error."

96. Then, when the bearer
of good news came,
he threw [the shirt]
over Jacob's face; he regained
his vision, saying:
"Did I not say to you,
I know from God
what you do not?"

97. They said: "Father,
ask forgiveness
for our sins, for we
have done wrong."

98. He said: "I shall
ask my Lord to
forgive you, for
He is indeed
Forgiving, Ever-Merciful."

99. So when they came
before Joseph, he embraced
his parents, saying:
"Enter into Egypt, in safety,
if it be the will of God."

100. And he raised his parents, both,
on the throne, and all of them
fell down, bowing before him.
"My dear father, here is
the deeper meaning of my dream
of long ago. My Lord has brought it
into being. Truly, he was good to me
when He brought me
out of prison
and brought you
out of the desert,
after Satan had sown
discord between me
and my brothers.

My Lord is Subtle
in what He wills.
He is the Knowing, the Wise.

101. "My Lord, you have
given me dominion, and you have
taught me the deeper meaning
of events. Maker
of the heavens and earth, you are
my Protector, in this world
and the hereafter. Receive me,
as one who submits to Your will,
and unite me with the righteous."

102. This is from the chronicles
of the Unseen,[1] which we reveal
to you [Muhammad]. You were not
with them when they
concocted together
their abominable plot.

103. And most of humankind,
however ardently you strive,
will not believe.

104. And you, do not seek reward
from them for this. This is no less
than a reminder to all worlds.

XII

105. And how many signs
in the heavens and earth
do they pass by, turning
away.

106. And most of them
do not believe in God
without ascribing partners
to Him.

107. Do they feel secure, then,
from the darkening calamity
of God's punishment, or
from the sudden descending
of the Hour, while they
are unaware?

1. "Unseen" (Arabic al-Ghaib), that is, That which is is both Invisible and Unknowable.

108. Say: "This is my way;
I call to God, with clear vision,
I, and whoever follows me.
Glory be to God, that I am
not of those who ascribe
partners to Him."

109. And we sent before you
only men whom we inspired,
from the people of the cities.
Did they not travel
the earth, and behold
the end of those before them?
Surely, the abode of the hereafter
is finer for those who are
mindful of God. Will you, then,
not understand?

110. When the messengers
despaired, thinking [the people] had
denied, Our help came to them;
We saved whom We will.
But Our wrath will never be
turned from wicked people.

111. In their stories, there is
a lesson for people
of understanding. This is not
an invented tale, but confirmation
of what came before,
an exposition
of all things, a Guide
and a Mercy to
a believing people.

Surah 19: Mary

In the Name of God, the All-Merciful, Ever-Merciful

I

1. *Kaf. Ha. Ya. 'Ain. Sad.*[1]

2. A reminder of the mercy of your Lord
toward His servant Zachariah:[2]

3. When he called to his Lord
with a secret call:

---

1. See "Joseph" fn. 2, above.   2. Cf. Luke 1.5–64.

4. "My Lord, my bones are grown frail,
and my hair is ablaze with grey,
yet never has my prayer
to You, my Lord, been vain."

5. "I fear [I shall have no]
future kin, when I am gone, for
my wife is barren.
So grant me—from Yourself—
an heir

6. to bear my legacy³
and the legacy
of Jacob's family;
and let him, my Lord,
be well-pleasing."

7. [God said]:
"Zachariah, We give you
glad news of a son,
whose name will be John,
a name we gave
to none before him."

8. "My Lord, he said,
how can I have a son,
when my wife is barren
and I have come to wither
with age?"

9. He replied: "These are the words
of Your Lord: 'It is easy for Me.
Indeed, I created you
before, when you were nothing.'"

10. He said: "My Lord,
give me a sign."

"Your sign is this:
you will not speak
to people
for three successive nights."

11. So he ventured out
to his people
from his sanctuary,
urging them [by gestures],
to glorify God
morning and evening.

---

3. "Legacy" refers here not to wealth but prophethood.

12. "John," [We said]
Hold, steadfast, to the Book,"
and We endowed him
with sound judgment, while yet a child,

13. and with tenderness,
from Ourself,
and purity. He was
mindful of God,

14. solicitous of his parents,
and never imperious[4]
or disobedient.

15. And peace be upon him
the day he was born,
the day he dies,
and the day he
will be raised
alive.

II

16. And mention in the Book
Mary, of when she withdrew
from her people
to a place in the East.

17. She veiled herself
from them.[5] Then We sent
Our spirit, appearing
to her fully
in the form of a man.

18. She said: "I seek refuge
with the Most Merciful
from you: [withdraw][6]
if you fear Him."

19. He said: "I am only
a messenger from your Lord,
granting you a pure son."

20. "How shall I
have a son," she said, "for

4. "Imperious" (Arabic al-Jabbar) is also one of the 99 names of Allah, usually translated as "The Compeller." See also v. 32 below, where the same attribute is negatively imputed to Jesus.
5. Literally, "She placed a screen between herself and them." In this context, the screen (Arabic hijab)—which refers to anything which blocks the sight or view of something—is metaphorical, referring to Mary's seclusion from her people.
6. The word "withdraw" is implied but not stated in the Arabic text.

no man has touched me,
for I have not been unchaste?"

21. He replied: "This is what
your Lord has said:
'Easy it is for Me; We
will make him
a sign for humankind,
and a mercy from Us.
It is a thing
ordained.'"

22. So she conceived him,
and withdrew with him
to a place far away.

23. And the pains of labor
drove her to the trunk
of a date-palm. She cried:
"I wish I had died
before this, and been
wholly forgotten!"

24. But [a voice] called to her
from beneath: "Do not grieve;
surely your Lord
has set beneath you
a stream."

25. "And shake the trunk
of the date-palm toward you,
to let fresh, ripe dates
fall upon you."

26. "So eat and drink
and be comforted; and
if you see anyone, say:
"I have vowed to the Most Merciful
a fast, and today I shall speak
with no-one."

27. Then she came with him
to her people, carrying him.
They said: "Mary, you bring
truly an unheard-of thing."

28. "Sister of Aaron,
your father was not
a wicked man, and
your mother was not
unchaste."

29. Then she pointed to [the child];
they said: "How can we
talk with a child in the cradle?"

30. [The child] said: "I am
a servant of God;
He has given me the Book
and has made me
a prophet."

31. "And He made me blessed
wherever I may be,
and enjoined upon me
prayer and charity as long
as I live."

32. "And He made me solicitous
toward my mother, not
imperious or sullen."

33. "And peace be upon me
the day I was born,
the day I die,
and the day
I will be raised
alive."

34. This was Jesus, son
of Mary: the Word
of truth, about which
they dispute.

35. It is not for God
to bear a child. Glory be to Him:
when He decrees
something, He says
to it only "Be"
and it is.

36. For truly God is my Lord
and your Lord: therefore
worship Him. This is
the straight path.

37. But the sects differed
among themselves; and woe
will be to those who disbelieve
—from the testimony
of a momentous day.

38. How keenly will they see
and how keenly will they hear

on the Day they come
to Us. But today
the wrongdoers are
manifestly astray.

39. And warn them of the Day
of remorse, when
the matter will be decided
while they are heedless,
while they do not believe.

40. It is We who will inherit
the earth, and all those
upon it, and to Us
they will be returned.

III

41. And mention in the Book
Abraham: he was
a man of truth,
a prophet.

42. He said to his father:
"Father, why do you
worship what cannot hear
and cannot see, and can
profit you in nothing?"

43. "Father, knowledge has come
to me which has not come
to you. Therefore, follow me,
I will guide you
to a level path."

44. "Father, do not worship
Satan, for truly Satan is
a rebel against the
Most Merciful."

45. "Father, I fear
punishment will
befall you from the
Most Merciful
and you will become
an ally of Satan."

46. [His father] replied:
"Do you refuse my gods,
Abraham? If you don't desist

in this, I shall stone you.
Now be gone from me."

47. Abraham said: "Peace
be upon you; I shall ask
my Lord to forgive you,
for He has been ever Gracious
toward me."

48. "But I will turn away from
you and what you call upon
besides God, and I will call upon
my Lord. Perhaps, in
my prayer, I will not
be disappointed."

49. So when he turned away
from them and those they
worshipped besides God,
We bestowed upon him Isaac
and Jacob, and We made
each of them a prophet.

50. And We bestowed
Our Mercy upon them,
and We exalted them
in truthfulness.

IV

51. And mention in the Book
Moses: he was sincere,
and he was a messenger,
a prophet.[7]

52. And We called him
from the right side
of Mount [Sinai],
and We drew him
near for private communion.

53. And We granted him
from Our Mercy
his brother Aaron
as a prophet.

7. The distinction between "prophet" (*nabi*) and "messenger" (*rasul*) is still disputed: most agree that prophets were divinely inspired and taught what had already been revealed, while messengers brought forth a new scripture from God.

54. And mention in the Book
Ismail:[8] he was true
to his promise, and was
a messenger, a prophet.

55. He would always enjoin
upon his people prayer
and charity, and he would always
be pleasing to his Lord.

56. And mention in the Book
Idris:[9] he was
a man of truth, a prophet:

57. And We raised him
to an exalted rank.

58. These were among the prophets
whom God favored, from
the descendants of Adam, and
whom We carried
with Noah, and from
the descendants of Abraham and Israel,
whom We guided and chose.
When the verses of the Most Merciful
were recited to them,
they would fall prostrate,
in tears.

59. But there followed them
successors who neglected
prayer and followed their
desires. Soon, they will face
a pit of Hell.

60. Except those who turn
to repent, and believe
and do good works.
These will enter the Garden
and will not be wronged
in any way.

61. Eternal Gardens, which
the Most Merciful has promised
to His servants, in the Unseen.
His promise inexorably
will come to be.

---

8. The first son of Abraham, the older half-brother of Isaac.
9. Unlike the earlier prophets mentioned above in this surah, Idris appears in neither the Hebrew Bible nor the Gospels.

62. There, they will not hear
vain discourse, only
"Peace." And there,
will have sustenance
morning and evening.

63. This is the Garden
We shall bequeath
to our servants who were
mindful of Us.

64. [The angels say:]
"We descend only
by command of your Lord.
To Him belongs what lies
before us and what lies
behind us, and what lies
between. And your Lord
is never forgetful."

65. "Lord of the heavens
and of the earth, and of all
between them: so worship Him,
and be steadfast in His worship.
Do you know of any
equal to Him?"

v

66. Man says:
"Shall I, once dead,
be brought to life?"

67. But does not Man
recall that We created him
before, when he was
nothing?

68. So, by your Lord,
We shall surely gather them,
and the devils, around Hell,
on their knees.

69. Then We shall surely
drag out from each sect
those who were most
obdurate against
the Most Merciful.

70. Then We surely know best
those who are most worthy
to be burned there.

71. And there is not one
of you who will not
come to it: a decree
from your Lord,
destined to be.

72. But We shall save those
who were mindful of God,
and We shall leave
the wrongdoers there,
on their knees.

73. When Our clear signs
are recited to them,
the unbelievers taunt those
who believe: "Which of the two
parties is better positioned,
and superior in sway?"

74. But how many generations
before them have We
destroyed, who were
superior in possessions
and in appearance?

75. Say: "Whoever is astray,
the Most Merciful prolongs
their straying, until they see
what was promised them, either
in punishment [here] or in the [coming] Hour.
Then they will know who
is in the worse position
and weaker in force."

76. "And God increases
in guidance those who would
be guided; and enduring
good deeds
are the best rewards
in the eyes of your Lord,
and best in their
recompense."

77. Have you then seen
the person who
denies Our signs, yet
says: "I shall surely
be given wealth and children?"

78. Has he fathomed
the Unseen, or secured
with the Most Merciful
a compact?

79. No. We shall record
what he says, and We
shall prolong his
punishment.

80. We shall inherit
all that he talks of,
and he shall come
before Us
alone.

81. Yet, they have taken
gods other than
God, to empower them.

82. However, [those gods]
will reject their worship,
and become their
adversaries.

VI

83. Do you not see:
We have sent
devils against the unbelievers,
inciting them to sin?

84. So make no haste
against them, for We
are only counting
for them their term.

85. On that day We shall
gather the God-fearing to
the Most Merciful,
as an assembly.

86. And We shall drive
the sinners to hell,
like thirsty cattle
to water.

87. None shall have power
of intercession, except
whoever secures with
the Most Merciful
a compact.

88. They say: "The Most Merciful
has begotten a child."[1]

89. Assuredly, you bring forward
a monstrous thing

90. at which the heavens
might be rent apart, and
the earth burst asunder, and
the mountains collapse
in utter ruin,

91. that they ascribe a child
to the Most Merciful.

92. For it is not for the Most Merciful
to bear a child.

93. There is none in the heavens
and earth who will not come
before the Most Merciful
as a servant.

94. Most certainly, He has
taken account of them,
and counted them,
every one.

95. And every one of them
will come before Him
on the Day of Resurrection
alone.

96. Surely, on those
who believed and did good works,
the Most Merciful will bestow
Love.

97. So We have made
[the Qur'an] easy for you,
in your own tongue, so with it
you might give glad news to
the God-fearing, and with it
you might warn
a people who are
obdurate.

---

1. A reference not to the Christian belief that Jesus is the Son of God—a view criticized elsewhere in the Qur'an—but to the belief in pre-Islamic Arabia that the angels were the daughters of God.

98. And, before them, how many
generations have we destroyed:
can you trace even one of them
or can you hear from them
even a whisper?

Surah 24 (Excerpt): Light

35. God is the Light[1]
of the Heavens and of the Earth;
His Light is a parable, of
a lamp within a niche; the lamp within a glass,
the glass haloed as a brilliant star, lit
from an olive tree, blessèd;
whose soil is neither East nor West;
its very oil would shine forth
though untouched by fire:
Light upon Light.
God guides to His Light whom He will;
He engenders parables for humankind, He
Whose knowing encompasses all things.

36. His Light abides in houses, sanctified by God
to be raised for the adoration of His Name.

37. There is He glorified, morning and evening
by those whom neither trade nor profit can
divert from remembrance of God
or steadfastness in charity and prayer;
whose fear is for the Day
when heart and vision will turn about,

38. that God might reward their finest deeds,
giving ever more from His Grace,
for God furnishes measurelessly
those whom He will.

39. As for the unbelievers:
their deeds are like a mirage
in the burning desert: the parched man's eyes see
water in the distance; approaching, he finds
nothing; before him, he finds
God, Who will give him
his due in full: God,
whose reckoning is swift.

---

1. "Light" (an-Nur): that is, divine guidance, knowledge, or power. Some interpretations asso- ciate it with the believer's heart, while the lamp is viewed as the Qur'an.

40. Or, like darkness on a fathomless ocean,
wave over wave, overcast by cloud:
darkness upon darkness;
if a man stretch out his hand,
he can scarce see it.
For those whom God deprives of Light
there is no Light.

Surah 36: Ya Sin

In the Name of God, the All-Merciful, Ever-Merciful

I

1. *Ya Sin.*[1]

2. By the wise Qur'an,

3. you [Muhammad] are truly
one of the messengers

4. on a straight path.

5. It is a revelation
sent down from
the Mighty,
the Ever-Merciful,

6. that you might warn
a people whose forefathers
had no warning, and so
are heedless.

7. The sentence has been pronounced
against most of them, for
they will not believe—

8. indeed We placed
around their necks yokes
drawn up to their chins,
forcing up their heads,

9. and before them a barrier,
and behind them a barrier,
and covered them up so
they cannot see.

10. It is the same to them
whether you warn them or not:
they will not believe.

1. See "Joseph," fn. 2. *Ya Sin* has at least once been translated as "O Thou Human Being."

11. You can warn only him
who follows the Message
and fears the All-Merciful
in the Unseen. So give
glad news to him, of forgiveness
and a noble reward.

12. Truly, We bring back
to life the dead, and We transcribe
all [the deeds] they send before them
and all that they leave behind,
and We have accounted all things
in a clear record.

13. Adduce for them
a parable, of a people
to whose town there came
messengers.

II

14. When We sent to them
two messengers,[2] they denied
them both. So We
reinforced them with a third,
and they declared:
"Truly, we have been sent
as messengers to you."

15. [The people] said: "You
are merely humans, like us,
and the All-Merciful
has not sent anything. You
are only lying."

16. They said: "Our Lord knows
that truly we have been sent
as messengers to you."

17. "And what is [laid] upon us is only
the clear conveyance [of the message]."

18. [The people] said:
"We augur that you
are an evil omen. If you
don't desist, we'll surely stone you:
a painful punishment from us
will surely reach you."

2. Perhaps Moses and Jesus.

19. They replied: "Your evil omen
is within yourselves. Is it because
you have been reminded?
Surely not: you are
a transgressive people."

20. And there came from
the outskirts of the city
a man running, who said:
"My people, follow
the messengers."

21. "Follow those who ask
no reward of you, and who
are rightly guided."

22. "And why should I
not worship Him
who created me? For to Him
you will be returned."

23. "Should I take other gods
besides Him? If the All-Merciful
intended harm for me,
their intercession could not
help in any way, nor
could they save me."

24. "I would truly be
in manifest error."

25. "Truly, I believe
in your Lord; so
hear me."

26. He was told: "Enter
the Garden." He said:
"If only my people knew

27. how my Lord has
forgiven me and has
set me among the honored."

28. And We did not send down
against his people, after him,
any hosts from heaven,
nor would We deign to:

29. there was but
one single blast,
and they were vanished.

30. Alas, for [My] servants;
whichever messenger comes to them,
they mock him.

31. Don't they see how many
generations before them
We destroyed, so none
would come back to them?

32. And every one,
all together, will be brought
before Us.

III

33. A sign for them
is the dead earth:
We bring her to life,
and bring from her
grain which they eat.

34. And We placed upon her
gardens, with palm-groves
and grape-vines, and We caused
springs to burst forth there,

35. so they might eat of its fruit,
and what their hands made;
will they not, then, be thankful?

36. Glory be to Him Who
created in pairs all that
the earth yields, and
their own selves, and
also things of which they
are unaware.

37. And a sign for them
is the night: we strip away from it
the light of day, so
they are left in darkness.

38. And the sun
courses through her sure path
by decree of the Almighty,
the All-Knowing,

39. and the moon,
for whom We ordained phases,
till it returns, like
a dried date-stalk of old.

40. The sun may not outrun
the moon, nor may the night
outstrip the day. Each glides
in [its own] orbit.

41. And a sign for them
is that We carried
their offspring in the loaded Ark
[through the Flood].

42. and We have created
for them the like [ships]
in which they sail.

43. And if We willed, We could
drown them, and they would
have no helper [to hear their cry],
nor would they be saved,

44. except by Our mercy,
as a reprieve for a while.

45. When they are told,
"Have fear of what lies before you
and what lies behind you,
that you might receive mercy,"

46. they turn away
from every sign that
comes to them
from their Lord;

47. and when they are told,
"Spend [in charity] from what God
has provided you," those who
disbelieve say to those who
believe, "Should we feed those whom,
if He willed, God Himself could have fed?
You are in manifest error."

48. And they say: "When
will this promise [of resurrection] come to pass,
if you are being truthful?"

49. But [unwitting] they are waiting only
for a single blast, which will
overtake them while
they are disputing.

50. They will be unable
to disburse any bequest,

or to return to
their own people.

IV

51. The trumpet shall be sounded,
and see, how then they will
hasten from their graves
to their Lord.

52. They will say: "Woe to us!
Who has raised us
from our place of sleep?"
[A voice will answer][3]
"This is what the All-Merciful
promised: the messengers
spoke the truth."

53. It will be but
a single blast, and then
they shall be brought, all,
before Us.

54. Then, on that Day,
no soul shall be
wronged in any way,
and you shall be
requited only for
what you have done.

55. Truly, on that Day,
the people of the Garden
shall find joy in all they do,

56. they and their spouses,
in the shade, reclining
on couches.

57. There, they shall have
[every] fruit,
and they shall have
all that they call for.

58. "Peace": the word [of welcome]
from a Lord Ever-Merciful.

---

3. There is a mandatory pause here in the Arabic to indicate that the subsequent lines reply to the question just posed, shown here by the parenthetical remark.

59. [And it will be said]:
"But you who are sinners,
stand apart this Day."

60. "Did I not enjoin you,
children of Adam, not
to worship Satan, for
he is your manifest enemy,

61. and to worship Me?
—this is a straight path."

62. "But he indeed led astray
a great multitude of you:
did you not, then,
use your reason?"

63. "This is Hell, of which
you were warned."

64. "Burn in it, this Day,
for you went on disbelieving."

65. This Day, We shall seal
their mouths; but their hands
shall speak to Us, and their feet
shall bear witness to what
they earned.

66. Had We willed, We could
surely have extinguished their sight,
then they would grope to find
the path, but how should they see?

67. And had We willed, We could
have transfixed them in their place,
unable to move on or go back.

V

68. And to whomever We grant
long life, We weaken
his capacities: will they not,
then, use their reason?

69. We have not taught
[the Prophet] poetry,[4] nor
is it fitting for him. This is

4. Although the Qur'an uses rhyme, it stops short of being "poetry," at least in the sense of 7th-century Arabia, where poetry, and poets, were linked to public self-advancement and commercial gain.

nothing other than a reminder
and a manifest Qur'an,

70. so those who are living
might be warned, and the sentence
pronounced against the disbelieving.

71. Don't they see that
We created for them
—among the things that
Our hands have made—
livestock, over which they
have dominion,

72. and which We made
tame for them,
some to ride and others to eat?

73. And they yield further
uses, and give drink.
Will they not then
be thankful?

74. Yet still they take
other gods besides God,
hoping they might be helped.

75. [Those gods] have no power
to save them, even if they
were brought before them
as a host.

76. So do not be grieved [Muhammad]
by what they say; surely, We know
what they conceal, and
what they reveal.

77. And does not man see
that it is indeed We who created him
from a drop of semen? Yet, see,
he is an open adversary"

78. and adduces allegories
about Us, forgetting his own
creation, asking: "who can bring
life to bones that have decomposed?"

79. Say [in reply]: "He will bring
life to them, who
composed them at first,
for He knows
every creation.

80. It is He who made fire
for you from the green tree,
and see, you light from it
your own fires."

81. Is not He who created
the heavens and earth
able to create the like
of them [human beings]? Indeed,
for He is the Creator,
the All-Knowing.

82. When He intends something,
His only command is to say
to it: "Be," and it is.[5]

83. Then glory be to Him
in whose hand is dominion
over all things; and to Him
you will be returned.

Surah 55: *The All-Merciful*

In the Name of God, the All-Merciful, Ever-Merciful

1. The All-Merciful:
2.   He taught the Qur'an,
3.   He created man,
4.   He taught him speech.

5. Both sun and moon, exact in their span,
6.   and stars and trees, bow down, both;

7. and the sky He raised high, and set down the Balance,
8.   that you might not infract what is due in balance;
9. then set up [your] weights justly,
         and do not fall short in balance.

10. And the earth He laid out for His creatures,
11.   with her fruit and date-palms, with clustered sheaths;
12.   and corn, with husks, and scented plants.

13. Which, then, of your Lord's favors would you both deny?

14. He created humankind from dry clay like earthen pots,
15.   and Jinn He created from smokeless fire.
16. Which of your Lord's favors would you both then deny?[1]

---

5. The same phrase is used elsewhere in the Qur'an, especially regarding the birth of Jesus (e.g., Q2:116: Q3:47).
1. Although in the Arabic this refrain is repeated exactly, the wording of the modern English trans-
lation varies in order to reflect the varied modes of intonation in the Arabic recitation. "Jinn": spiritual beings lower than angels and able to appear in human form (Arabic, source of English word *genie*).

17. Lord of the two Easts and Lord of the two Wests.[2]
18. And which of your Lord's favors would you both deny?

19. He let the two seas flow, so they might converge:
20.   between them a barrier, which they shall not transgress—
21. So which of your Lord's favors will you both deny?
22.   —out of them both come pearls and coral.

23. Which, then, of your Lord's favors will you both deny?

24. And His are the ships sailing high on the seas, like mountains.
25. So which of the favors of your Lord will you both deny?

26. All things upon [earth] shall perish,
27.   while the Face of your Lord abides, forever
        in Majesty and Munificence.

28. Which, then, of your Lord's favors will you both deny?

29. Whatever is in the heavens and earth beseeches Him,
        seeking each day His purpose.
30. Which of your Lord's favors will you then both deny?

31. Soon We shall settle with you, O hosts [of Jinn and humankind].
32. Then which of your Lord's favors will you both deny?
33. O company of Jinn and humankind: if you are able to pass
        beyond the realms of heaven and earth, then pass: yet you shall not pass
        without [Our] warrant.
34. And which of your Lord's favor will you both deny?
35. Against you both will be hurled a fiery flame, and smoke:
        you shall find no quarter.

36. Which, then, of your Lord's favors will you both deny?

37. When the sky is ripped asunder, turning crimson like red leather:
38. Which of your Lord's favors will you then both deny?
39. On that Day, none will be questioned about his sin,
        neither humans nor Jinn.
40. And which of your Lord's favors will you both deny?
41. The sinners shall be known by their marks, and shall be seized
        by their forelocks and feet.
42. Which, then, of your Lord's favors will you both deny?
43. This is Hell, which the sinners deny:
44.   they will wander in circles
        between it and boiling water.

45. Which, then, of your Lord's favors will you both deny?

2. The rising of the sun and the moon, or perhaps the farthest points of sunrise and sunset in summer and winter; an image of opposition and symmetry.

46. But for whoever fears [the Day] when he shall stand before his Lord:
      are two gardens—
47. So which of your Lord's favors will you both deny?
48.   —with spreading branches.
49. So which of your Lord's favors will you both deny?
50.   In them both will be two fountains, flowing.
51. So which of your Lord's favors will you both deny?
52.   In them both will be fruits of every kind, in pairs.
53. So which of your Lord's favors will you both deny?
54. Reclining on couches, lined in rich brocade, with fruit of both gardens
      within close reach.
55. So which of your Lord's favors will you both deny?
56.   In them will be females of modest glance, untouched before by human
      or Jinn—
57. So which of your Lord's favors will you both deny?
58.   —[In beauty] like rubies and coral.
59. So which of your Lord's favors will you both deny?
60.   What is the reward for goodness except goodness?

61. Which, then, of your Lord's favors will you both deny?
62.   And besides these two, shall be two more Gardens—[3]
63. Which, then, of your Lord's favors will you both deny?
64.   —both hued in deepest green.
65. And which of your Lord's favors will you both deny?
66.   In them both will be two fountains, overflowing.
67. Which, then, of your Lord's favors will you both deny?
68.   In them both will be fruit, date-palm, and pomegranate.
69. Which, then, of your Lord's favors will you both deny?

70.   In them will be maidens, virtuous and beauteous—
71. Which of your Lord's favors would you then both deny?
72.   —Houris,[4] dark-eyed, secluded in pavilions—
73. And which of your Lord's favors will you both deny?
74.   —untouched before by human or Jinn—
75. Which, then, of your Lord's favors will you both deny?
76.   —reclining on cushions of green and beauteous carpets.

77. Which, then, of your Lord's favors will you both deny?

78. Blessed is the Name of your Lord, forever
      in Majesty and Munificence.

---

3. The Islamic paradise has several ranks or levels, into which believers are to be placed after death according to their degree of merit; compare Dante's *Paradiso* for an adaptation of the structure of the Islamic paradise within a Christian framework.
4. Black-eyed maidens of Paradise (Arabic).

Surah 91: *The Sun*

In the Name of God, the All-Merciful, Ever-Merciful

1. By the sun
and her splendor;

2. by the moon
as he trails her;

3. by the day as he
displays her;

4. by the night as she
veils her;

5. by the heaven and He
Who framed her;

6. by the earth and He
Who extended her;

7. by the soul and He
Who perfected her;

8. for He inspired her
to know her [own] evil
and the piety within her;

9. he surely succeeds
who purifies her,

10. and he surely fails
who defiles her.

11. The nation of Thamud
denied [her prophet Salih],[1]
for she was a transgressor,

12. when she deputed her
most wicked offender [to denounce him].

13. God's messenger
advised them: "This is
a she-camel of God, so
provide drink for her.

---

1. This account appears in Q7:73–79, where it is compared with other histories, including that of Lot. "Thamud": ancient civilization of southern Arabia; Islamic legend holds that God sent the prophet Salih to warn the Thamudi to give up the decadence they had fallen into.

14. But they denied him
and hamstrung her.
So for their sin, their Lord
destroyed [their nation],
and levelled her.

15. Nor does He fear
what will become of her.

Surah 112: Purity [of Faith][1]

In the Name of God, the All-Merciful, Ever-Merciful

1. Say: He is God, the One,
2. God, the Absolute:
3. neither did He beget,
       nor was He begotten.
4. His like or equal there is none.

1. According to tradition, the Prophet Muhammad said that this chapter (surah) was equivalent to one-third of the Qur'an. The Persian poet **Rumi** also praises it: "Although these words are few in form, they are preferable to the lengthy chapter *Baqara* [Q2] by virtue of being to the point."

BEOWULF
ninth century

Surviving in a single tattered manuscript, its edges burned by fire, *Beowulf* provides a startlingly vivid glimpse into the early medieval past. Written in Old English, with a vocabulary that would have seemed old-fashioned even to its very first audience, the poem recalls a heroic age in which monsters stalked men by night, dragons guarded hoards of precious gems and heirloom swords, and heroes carried out great deeds of warfare that would later be commemorated by song and feasting. The bonds of family and clan give shape to the world of Beowulf and his companions, leading sometimes to the formation of new alliances, sometimes to the violent conflict of blood feud that lasted for generations. Like much Old English poetry, the poem is fundamentally elegiac, celebrating the beauty and mourning the disappearance of a culture that, by the year 1000, had already become part of the past.

The sole surviving copy of *Beowulf*

can be dated with some certainty to the years around 1000, a time of rich flowering of Anglo-Saxon literature and learning, expressed in both Old English and Anglo-Latin poetry. Yet this time was also the end of an era, just a few generations before English society would be completely transformed by the Norman Conquest of 1066. The poem thus sums up a particular form of English culture that would very soon vanish. Among the other works included in the manuscript containing *Beowulf* are saints' lives and exotic tales of the Orient: despite their varied genres, all are unified by a common theme of monsters and heroes. The three monsters of *Beowulf*—Grendel, Grendel's mother, and the dragon—and the superhuman hero who fights against them appear beside other examples of nonhuman nature, from the so-called monstrous races encountered by Alexander the Great in the extreme reaches of India to the dog-headed (or "cynocephalic") Saint Christopher. Read in this context, the poem sheds light on the nature of medieval English culture, especially on its ability to integrate pagan Germanic history within the framework of the Christian Middle Ages.

While we can date the manuscript of *Beowulf* to the years around 1000, the poem itself is almost certainly much older—a judgment based on the poem's old-fashioned vocabulary and certain genealogical allusions as well as the manuscript itself, whose copying errors suggest that a long history of transmission lies behind it. Yet the poem in its oral form is even older, drawing on a rich stock of myth and legend that was surely familiar among the northern Germanic peoples who inhabited the regions now known as Scandinavia, the Low Countries, and the British Isles. Those

who read *Beowulf* or heard it recited in the eleventh century would have likely recognized allusions to ancient blood feuds and tribal clashes that are only dimly comprehensible to modern readers. The poem appears to be set in the sixth century (in particular, we can date the death of Beowulf's lord, Hygelac, to around 520), and so the story would already have seemed like ancient history to the poem's earliest hearers. To the eleventh-century reader, the events of the poem are thus doubly removed into the past. Like **Homer**'s *Iliad*, whose written text codifies a much older oral form of the poem, *Beowulf* emerges as a written work of literature only at the end of generations of transmission as song.

Although we are accustomed to thinking of *Beowulf* as an "English" poem, its subject matter is not English people at all: Beowulf himself is a member of the tribe of the Geats, who live in the south of what is now Sweden, and he goes to serve in the court of Hrothgar, king of the Danes. In the period that the poem is set, England was only beginning to be settled by Germanic tribes, which had first invaded the island around 450. For the medieval English person reading the poem around 1000, therefore, the subject matter of the poem would have been at once strange and familiar—made up of persons and places that were remote in space and time from current-day England, but connected to the poem's audience by lines of heritage and descent. This simultaneous sense of strangeness and familiarity would have been heightened by *Beowulf*'s treatment of religion. While the readers and hearers of the poem, beginning in the ninth century and almost certainly earlier, would have brought a Christian perspective to the poem, the characters clearly belong to a pre-Christian world where *wyrd* (fate) governs the events that unfold in the lives of man. Yet the text is careful to maintain ambiguity regarding the role of Christianity in the world of the poem: the monstrous Grendel is said to be one of "Cain's clan," and is thus identified as an outcast from humanity in specifically biblical terms.

Grendel is only the first of three monsters that the hero Beowulf must confront. The initial single combat against this man-beast is quickly succeeded by a similar battle—this time carried out in the watery deeps of a distant wasteland—against Grendel's mother, an even more loathsome creature. After these successes, Beowulf's heroism is acclaimed, he is richly rewarded, and he returns to his own Geatish homeland to eventually become ruler of his people. Only decades later, in that homeland, does the third episode of combat take place, which pits Beowulf against a fierce dragon guarding a buried hoard of gems and shining weapons. Once again he enters battle alone, but before the struggle ends he is aided by his kinsman and companion Wiglaf. These clashes are among the most gripping scenes of the poem. First the hero wrestles with a dreadful monster who bites through his victim's bones, drinks his blood, and swallows his flesh in great chunks, consuming him "hand and foot." The horror of the confrontation with Grendel's vengeful mother is still greater: she is a "swamp-thing from hell." In Beowulf's final monstrous encounter, the dragon "billowed and spewed" venomous fire, at once burning and poisoning his victim.

Yet Beowulf's horrific enemies are more complex than they might first appear: Grendel is both monster and man, one of the family of Cain. Like Cain himself, he is said to be "God-cursed," and his status as an outcast, cut off from the community of men, makes him seem curiously forlorn, "spurned and joyless." Although he is undoubtedly a monster, Grendel shows human emotions; he is whipped into a blind and jealous fury against those able to enjoy the bonds of family and tribe, who sleep blissfully in the communal space of Heorot's great hall. Similarly, Grendel's mother is driven not just by her monstrous nature but also by a maternal desire to avenge the death of her son—and according to the codes of Germanic tribal society, revenge was an entirely appropriate motive. Even the fight with the dragon is not cast in simple terms: when Beowulf enters his cavernous lair, it is the hero—not the monster—who is identified as the invader, and the dragon is called the "hordweard," or guardian of the hoard. Although one is a man and one is a beast, both are said to be clad in armor, the hero bearing his shield and helm, the dragon his "enameled scales." As the line that separates human from nonhuman is blurred, every violent clash, whether man against man or man against monster, is couched in terms of equivalence and balance.

As vivid as these encounters are, the poem also has an important second level, concerned with the interpersonal ties of kinship and tribe, as well as the voluntary relationship of lord and warrior. We see Beowulf take on a series of roles within this social system. He begins among the Geats as a strong fighter of somewhat marginal status as a nephew of the king, Hygelac; he then is adopted with great honor into the household of Hrothgar, king of the Danes, after defeating Grendel and his mother; and finally Beowulf becomes ruler of the Geats, when Hygelac dies without a male heir. Beowulf appears first as a warrior in the service of his lord, and later as himself a lord—in the language of the poem, a "giver of rings" as well as one who receives them. The relationship of king and warrior is reciprocal, as the warrior provides service while his lord offers protection and distributes wealth, often in the form of armbands or neck torques ("rings"). Yet perhaps the most valuable gift that the lord grants is entrance into the community itself: in *Beowulf*, as in Old English poetry more generally, no burden is heavier than involuntary solitude. The warm bonds of fellowship nurture the warrior, and to be cut off from them is unimaginably bitter. Such isolation afflicts Grendel, as we have seen, and is memorably evoked in the poem's description of how the dragon's golden hoard came into being. It was the accumulated treasure of a long-ago people, the poet says, buried for safekeeping by the last of their line: "Death had come / and taken them all," leaving just one man "deserted and alone, lamenting his unhappiness / day and night." For the despairing survivor, there is "No trembling harp, / no tuned timber, no tumbling hawk / swerving through the hall." Bereft of the joys of the hall, the only man left alive can do little more than mourn as he waits for death.

The hall offers both the most secure and stable environment that a warrior can possibly inhabit and the culture's greatest point of vulnerability. Beowulf is given the opportunity to display his heroic nature in combat with Grendel because of the need to defend Heorot, the great hall of Hrothgar: the accursed monster has been sneaking into the hall by night, seizing and devouring warriors one by one. The threat is not simply to the lives of Hrothgar's men but to the very basis of the community, as the Danish war-

riors are reduced to fearful individuals, each concerned for his own life. The great hall of Heorot is a place of communal gathering and feasting, of goodwill and social bonds, where oaths of loyalty are sworn and golden rings are distributed, where heroic deeds are sung and the genealogies of kings recounted. Yet this idyllic space, representing the unity of the king and his people, is only temporary, for the danger posed to Heorot is not erased by the death of Grendel: other threats are darkly foreshadowed in the poem through allusions to the fate of the Danes after Hrothgar's reign ended. For the poem's medieval audiences, these passing references brought to mind the full story of the tragic downfall of Hrothgar's house and the burning of Heorot.

Swords and other weaponry appear throughout the poem, not just as tools of the warfare that punctuates the narrative at regular intervals but as a kind of social glue that links the community of warriors both in the present and across time and space. As treasures are shared, kings disburse weapons along with golden rings, items that are as precious for their ability to create interpersonal connections as for their physical material. Hrothgar's queen, Wealhtheow, rewards Beowulf with a golden collar that marks a new bond of affinity between the Geatish hero and the ruling house of the Danes, accompanying the sumptuous gift with the request that Beowulf do his best to support her young son in the future. The ring thus carries both material and social value, marking a bond of loyalty between persons and groups. Similarly, Hrothgar later rewards Beowulf with magnificent armor, which Beowulf goes on to deliver to his own Geatish lord, Hygelac, just as he also gives to Hygelac's queen, Hygd, the neck ring bestowed on him by Wealhtheow.

Beowulf's gifts unite the Danes and the Geats and thereby redouble his own honor. And the connections formed by heirloom weapons can extend far into the past. As Beowulf prepares to battle Grendel's mother, the Danish warrior Unferth lends him "a rare and ancient sword," and he in turn leaves his own weapon, a "sharp-honed, wave-sheened wonder-blade," with the Dane, who may keep it if he fails to return. In the muddy pool where Beowulf defeats Grendel's mother, he finds another blade, whose gold hilt is inscribed with "rune-markings" telling the name of the one "for whom the sword had first been made." This sword, "from the days of the giants," passes through time, wielded by men and by monsters, until it finally comes into the hands of Beowulf, who in turn delivers its remnants to the Danish king Hrothgar. The chain of descent confers glory on the hero, and unites the community of warriors across the ages.

Each of these three ancient swords is described as an heirloom or "ealde lafe": literally, an "old thing that is left," a remainder of past glory. The weapon is thus an instrument of warfare and a symbol of continuity, linking past, present, and future as successive men bear it. Such work of commemoration suffuses the poem, perhaps nowhere more movingly than in the songs of heroes that punctuate the communal celebrations and feasting held in Heorot. Like the "ealde

lafe," the heroic song recalls figures of the past and makes them live again as the warriors listen and join in the imagined community of the tribal nation and the symbolic space of the hall. After the defeat of Grendel, Hrothgar's minstrel sings a song of the Frisian king Finn and his Danish wife Hildeburh. The story is tragic, telling of the feud that destroyed their family, but the shared experience of the minstrel's music and tale brings Hrothgar's court together—a sense of community reawakened, perhaps, for the medieval audiences who heard Beowulf performed for them.

The translation here, by Seamus Heaney, seeks to reproduce the rhythmic quality of the Old English line—made up of two half-lines, each containing two beats. Coupled with the alliteration (repeated initial consonant sounds) that is prevalent in Old English poetry, the line produces a strong sense of rhythm, a recurrent thrumming sound that gives the poem its songlike quality, impossible to ignore even in written form. To give a clearer sense of the sound of the original work, reproduced at the top of page 124 are the closing lines (2262–69) of the lament of the last survivor, who long ago buried the hoard of treasure guarded by the dragon that is Beowulf's last and most dangerous enemy. Below these lines is a very literal, rhythmic translation that conveys the lines' aural quality more emphatically than does Heaney's version.

TRIBES AND GENEALOGIES

*1. The Danes (Bright-, Half-, Ring-, Spear-, North-, East-, South-, West-Danes;
Shieldings, Honor-, Victor-, War-Shieldings: Ing's friends).*

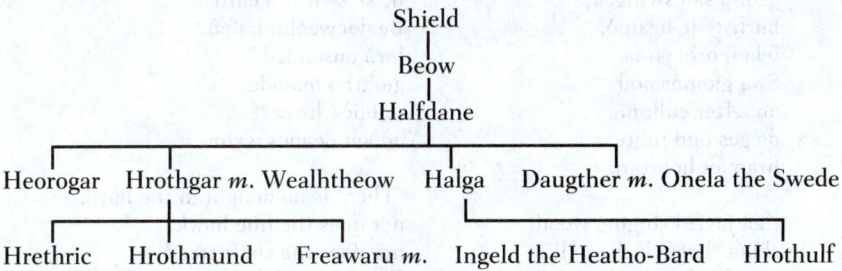

```
                          Shield
                            |
                          Beow
                            |
                        Halfdane
```

Heorogar   Hrothgar *m.* Wealhtheow   Halga   Daugther *m.* Onela the Swede

Hrethric   Hrothmund   Freawaru *m.*   Ingeld the Heatho-Bard   Hrothulf

2. The Geats (Sea-, War-, Weather-Geats).

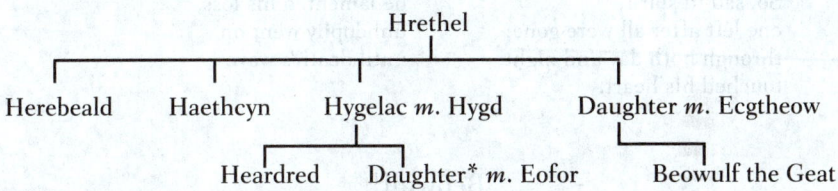

```
                          Hrethel
```

Herebeald   Haethcyn   Hygelac *m.* Hygd   Daughter *m.* Ecgtheow

Heardred   Daughter* *m.* Eofor   Beowulf the Geat

3. The Swedes

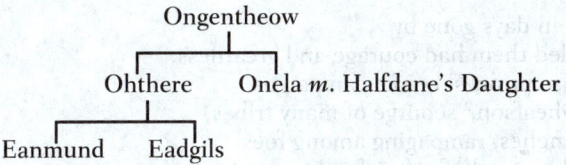

```
                        Ongentheow
```

Ohthere   Onela *m.* Halfdane's Daughter

Eanmund   Eadgils

*The daughter of Hygelac who was given to Eofor may have been born to him by a former wife, older than Hygd.

4. Miscellaneous.

A. The Half-Danes (also called Shieldings) involved in the fight at Finnsburg may represent a different tribe from the Danes described above. Their king Hoc had a son, Hnaef, who succeeded him, and a daughter Hildeburh, who married Finn, king of the Jutes.

B. The Jutes, or Frisians, are represented as enemies of the Danes in the fight at Finnsburg and as allies of the Franks at the time Hygelac the Geat made the attack in which he lost his life and from which Beowulf swam home. Also allied with the Franks at this time were the Hetware.

C. The Heatho-Bards (i.e., "Battle-Bards") are represented as inveterate enemies of the Danes. Their king Froda had been killed in an attack on the Danes, and Hrothgar's attempt to make peace with them by marrying his daughter Freawaru to Froda's son Ingeld failed when the latter attacked Heorot. The attack was repulsed, although Heorot was burned.

Beowulf, lines 2262–69[1]

"Næs hearpan wyn,
gomen gleobeames,   ne god hafoc
geond sæl swingeð,   ne se swifta mearh
burhstede beateð.   Bealocwealm hafað
fela feorhcynna   forð onsended."
Swa giomormod   giohtho mænde,
an æfter eallum,   unbliðe hwearf
dæges ond nihtes,   oððæt deaðes wylm
hran æt heortan.

"There is no delight in the harp,
that joyful singing wood,   nor does the fine hawk
shoot through the hall,   nor does the swift steed
beat his feet in the yard.   Baleful death has
sent out of this world   too many of our kind."
So, sad in spirit,   he lamented his loss,
one left after all were gone,   unhappily went on
through both day and night,   until death's wave
touched his heart.

Beowulf[1]

[Prologue: The Rise of the Danish Nation]

So. The Spear-Danes in days gone by
and the kings who ruled them had courage and greatness.
We have heard of those princes' heroic campaigns.
    There was Shield Sheafson,[2] scourge of many tribes,
a wrecker of mead-benches, rampaging among foes.   5
This terror of the hall-troops had come far.
A foundling to start with, he would flourish later on
as his powers waxed and his worth was proved.
In the end each clan on the outlying coasts
beyond the whale-road had to yield to him   10
and begin to pay tribute. That was one good king.
    Afterward a boy-child was born to Shield,
a cub in the yard, a comfort sent
by God to that nation. He knew what they had tholed,[3]
the long times and troubles they'd come through   15
without a leader; so the Lord of Life,
the glorious Almighty, made this man renowned.
Shield had fathered a famous son:
Beow's name was known through the north.
And a young prince must be prudent like that,   20

1. Translated by Suzanne Akbari.
1. Translated by Seamus Heaney.
2. Translates *Scyld Scefing*, which probably
means "son of Sheaf." Scyld's origins are
mysterious.
3. An Anglo-Saxon word that means "suf-

fered, endured" and that survives in the translator's native land of Northern Ireland. In
using this word, he also maintains an alliterative pattern similar to the original ("that . . .
they . . . tholed").

giving freely while his father lives
so that afterward in age when fighting starts
steadfast companions will stand by him
and hold the line. Behavior that's admired
is the path to power among people everywhere.   25

    Shield was still thriving when his time came
and he crossed over into the Lord's keeping.
His warrior band did what he bade them
when he laid down the law among the Danes:
they shouldered him out to the sea's flood,   30
the chief they revered who had long ruled them.
A ring-whorled prow rode in the harbor,
ice-clad, outbound, a craft for a prince.
They stretched their beloved lord in his boat,
laid out by the mast, amidships,   35
the great ring-giver. Far-fetched treasures
were piled upon him, and precious gear.
I never heard before of a ship so well furbished
with battle-tackle, bladed weapons
and coats of mail. The massed treasure   40
was loaded on top of him: it would travel far
on out into the ocean's sway.
They decked his body no less bountifully
with offerings than those first ones did
who cast him away when he was a child   45
and launched him alone out over the waves.[4]
And they set a gold standard up
high above his head and let him drift
to wind and tide, bewailing him
and mourning their loss. No man can tell,   50
no wise man in hall or weathered veteran
knows for certain who salvaged that load.

    Then it fell to Beow to keep the forts.
He was well regarded and ruled the Danes
for a long time after his father took leave   55
of his life on earth. And then his heir,
the great Halfdane, held sway
for as long as he lived, their elder and warlord.
He was four times a father, this fighter prince:
one by one they entered the world,   60
Heorogar, Hrothgar, the good Halga,
and a daughter,[5] I have heard, who was Onela's queen,
a balm in bed to the battle-scarred Swede.

    The fortunes of war favored Hrothgar.
Friends and kinsmen flocked to his ranks,   65
young followers, a force that grew
to be a mighty army. So his mind turned

---

4. Since Shield arrived with nothing, this sentence is a litotes or understatement, a characteristic of the laconic style of old Germanic poetry.

5. The text is faulty here, and the name of Halfdane's daughter has been lost. Halfdane: according to another source, Halfdane's mother was Swedish; hence his name.

to hall-building: he handed down orders
for men to work on a great mead-hall
meant to be a wonder of the world forever;   70
it would be his throne-room and there he would dispense
his God-given goods to young and old—
but not the common land or people's lives.[6]
Far and wide through the world, I have heard,
orders for work to adorn that wallstead   75
were sent to many peoples. And soon it stood there
finished and ready, in full view,
the hall of halls. Heorot[7] was the name
he had settled on it, whose utterance was law.
Nor did he renege, but doled out rings   80
and torques[8] at the table. The hall towered,
its gables wide and high and awaiting
a barbarous burning.[9] That doom abided,
but in time it would come: the killer instinct
unleashed among in-laws, the blood-lust rampant.   85

[Heorot Is Attacked]

  Then a powerful demon, a prowler through the dark,
nursed a hard grievance. It harrowed him
to hear the din of the loud banquet
every day in the hall, the harp being struck
and the clear song of a skilled poet   90
telling with mastery of man's beginnings,
how the Almighty had made the earth
a gleaming plain girdled with waters;
in His splendor He set the sun and the moon
to be earth's lamplight, lanterns for men,   95
and filled the broad lap of the world
with branches and leaves; and quickened life
in every other thing that moved.
  So times were pleasant for the people there
until finally one, a fiend out of hell,   100
began to work his evil in the world.
Grendel was the name of this grim demon
haunting the marches, marauding round the heath
and the desolate fens; he had dwelt for a time
in misery among the banished monsters,   105
Cain's clan, whom the Creator had outlawed
and condemned as outcasts.[1] For the killing of Abel

---

6. Apparently, slaves, along with pastureland used by all, were not in the king's power to give away.
7. That is, "hart," a symbol of royalty.
8. Golden bands worn around the neck.
9. The destruction by fire of Heorot—when the Heatho-Bard Ingeld attacked his father-in-law, Hrothgar—occurred at a later time than that of the poem's action. For a more detailed account of this feud and of Hrothgar's hope that it could be settled by the marriage of his daughter to Ingeld, see lines 2020–69.
1. Genesis 4.9–12.

the Eternal Lord had exacted a price:
Cain got no good from committing that murder
because the Almighty made him anathema   110
and out of the curse of his exile there sprang
ogres and elves and evil phantoms
and the giants too who strove with God
time and again until He gave them their reward.[2]
   So, after nightfall, Grendel set out   115
for the lofty house, to see how the Ring-Danes
were settling into it after their drink,
and there he came upon them, a company of the best
asleep from their feasting, insensible to pain
and human sorrow. Suddenly then   120
the God-cursed brute was creating havoc:
greedy and grim, he grabbed thirty men
from their resting places and rushed to his lair,
flushed up and inflamed from the raid,
blundering back with the butchered corpses.   125
   Then as dawn brightened and the day broke
Grendel's powers of destruction were plain:
their wassail was over, they wept to heaven
and mourned under morning. Their mighty prince,
the storied leader, sat stricken and helpless,   130
humiliated by the loss of his guard,
bewildered and stunned, staring aghast
at the demon's trail, in deep distress.
He was numb with grief, but got no respite
for one night later merciless Grendel   135
struck again with more gruesome murders.
Malignant by nature, he never showed remorse.
It was easy then to meet with a man
shifting himself to a safer distance
to bed in the bothies,[3] for who could be blind   140
to the evidence of his eyes, the obviousness
of the hall-watcher's hate? Whoever escaped
kept a weather-eye open and moved away.
   So Grendel ruled in defiance of right,
one against all, until the greatest house   145
in the world stood empty, a deserted wallstead.
For twelve winters, seasons of woe,
the lord of the Shieldings[4] suffered under
his load of sorrow; and so, before long,
the news was known over the whole world.   150
Sad lays were sung about the beset king,

2. The poet is thinking here of Genesis 6.2–8, where the Latin Bible in use at the time refers to giants mating with women who were understood to be the descendants of Cain and thereby creating the wicked race that God destroyed with the flood.

3. Outlying buildings; the word is current in Northern Ireland.

4. Hrothgar; as descendants of Shield, the Danes are called Shieldings.

the vicious raids and ravages of Grendel,
his long and unrelenting feud,
nothing but war; how he would never
parley or make peace with any Dane   155
nor stop his death-dealing nor pay the death-price.[5]
No counselor could ever expect
fair reparation from those rabid hands.
All were endangered; young and old
were hunted down by that dark death-shadow   160
who lurked and swooped in the long nights
on the misty moors; nobody knows
where these reavers from hell roam on their errands.

  So Grendel waged his lonely war,
inflicting constant cruelties on the people,   165
atrocious hurt. He took over Heorot,
haunted the glittering hall after dark,
but the throne itself, the treasure-seat,
he was kept from approaching; he was the Lord's outcast.

  These were hard times, heartbreaking   170
for the prince of the Shieldings; powerful counselors,
the highest in the land, would lend advice,
plotting how best the bold defenders
might resist and beat off sudden attacks.
Sometimes at pagan shrines they vowed   175
offerings to idols, swore oaths
that the killer of souls might come to their aid
and save the people.[6] That was their way,
their heathenish hope; deep in their hearts
they remembered hell. The Almighty Judge   180
of good deeds and bad, the Lord God,
Head of the Heavens and High King of the World,
was unknown to them. Oh, cursed is he
who in time of trouble has to thrust his soul
in the fire's embrace, forfeiting help;   185
he has nowhere to turn. But blessed is he
who after death can approach the Lord
and find friendship in the Father's embrace.

[The Hero Comes to Heorot]

  So that troubled time continued, woe
that never stopped, steady affliction   190
for Halfdane's son, too hard an ordeal.

---

5. According to Germanic law, a slayer could achieve peace with his victim's kinsmen only by paying them *wergild* ("man-price") as compensation for the slain man.
6. The poet interprets the heathen gods to whom the Danes make offerings as different incarnations of Satan. Naturally, the pagan Danes do not think of their gods in these biblical terms, but as the poet makes clear in the following lines, they have no other recourse.

There was panic after dark, people endured
raids in the night, riven by the terror.
  When he heard about Grendel, Hygelac's thane
was on home ground, over in Geatland.   195
There was no one else like him alive.
In his day, he was the mightiest man on earth,
highborn and powerful. He ordered a boat
that would ply the waves. He announced his plan:
to sail the swan's road[7] and seek out that king,   200
the famous prince who needed defenders.
Nobody tried to keep him from going,
no elder denied him, dear as he was to them.
Instead, they inspected omens and spurred
his ambition to go, whilst he moved about   205
like the leader he was, enlisting men,
the best he could find; with fourteen others
the warrior boarded the boat as captain,
a canny pilot along coast and currents.
  Time went by, the boat was on water,   210
in close under the cliffs.
Men climbed eagerly up the gangplank,
sand churned in surf, warriors loaded
a cargo of weapons, shining war-gear
in the vessel's hold, then heaved out,   215
away with a will in their wood-wreathed ship.
Over the waves, with the wind behind her
and foam at her neck, she flew like a bird
until her curved prow had covered the distance,
and on the following day, at the due hour,   220
those seafarers sighted land,
sunlit cliffs, sheer crags
and looming headlands, the landfall they sought.
It was the end of their voyage and the Geats vaulted
over the side, out on to the sand,   225
and moored their ship. There was a clash of mail
and a thresh of gear. They thanked God
for that easy crossing on a calm sea.
  When the watchman on the wall, the Shieldings' lookout
whose job it was to guard the sea-cliffs,   230
saw shields glittering on the gangplank
and battle-equipment being unloaded
he had to find out who and what
the arrivals were. So he rode to the shore,
this horseman of Hrothgar's, and challenged them   235
in formal terms, flourishing his spear:

7. That is, the sea. This is an example of a "kenning," a metaphoric phrase that is used to describe a common object. These kennings are very common throughout Anglo-Saxon poetry. See, for another instance, line 258, where the poet describes a man's capacity for speech as his "word-hoard."

"What kind of men are you who arrive
rigged out for combat in your coats of mail,
sailing here over the sea-lanes
in your steep-hulled boat? I have been stationed   240
as lookout on this coast for a long time.
My job is to watch the waves for raiders,
any danger to the Danish shore.
Never before has a force under arms
disembarked so openly—not bothering to ask   245
if the sentries allowed them safe passage
or the clan had consented. Nor have I seen
a mightier man-at-arms on this earth
than the one standing here: unless I am mistaken,
he is truly noble. This is no mere   250
hanger-on in a hero's armor.
So now, before you fare inland
as interlopers, I have to be informed
about who you are and where you hail from.
Outsiders from across the water,   255
I say it again: the sooner you tell
where you come from and why, the better."
    The leader of the troop unlocked his word-hoard;
the distinguished one delivered this answer:
"We belong by birth to the Geat people   260
and owe allegiance to Lord Hygelac.
In his day, my father was a famous man,
a noble warrior-lord named Ecgtheow.
He outlasted many a long winter
and went on his way. All over the world   265
men wise in counsel continue to remember him.
We come in good faith to find your lord
and nation's shield, the son of Halfdane.
Give us the right advice and direction.
We have arrived here on a great errand   270
to the lord of the Danes, and I believe therefore
there should be nothing hidden or withheld between us.
So tell us if what we have heard is true
about this threat, whatever it is,
this danger abroad in the dark nights,   275
this corpse-maker mongering death
in the Shieldings' country. I come to proffer
my wholehearted help and counsel.
I can show the wise Hrothgar a way
to defeat his enemy and find respite—   280
if any respite is to reach him, ever.
I can calm the turmoil and terror in his mind.
Otherwise, he must endure woes
and live with grief for as long as his hall
stands at the horizon on its high ground."   285
    Undaunted, sitting astride his horse,

the coast-guard answered: "Anyone with gumption
and a sharp mind will take the measure
of two things: what's said and what's done.
I believe what you have told me, that you are a troop   290
loyal to our king. So come ahead
with your arms and your gear, and I will guide you.
What's more, I'll order my own comrades
on their word of honor to watch your boat
down there on the strand—keep her safe   295
in her fresh tar, until the time comes
for her curved prow to preen on the waves
and bear this hero back to Geatland.
May one so valiant and venturesome
come unharmed through the clash of battle."   300
    So they went on their way. The ship rode the water,
broad-beamed, bound by its hawser
and anchored fast. Boar-shapes[8] flashed
above their cheek-guards, the brightly forged
work of goldsmiths, watching over   305
those stern-faced men. They marched in step,
hurrying on till the timbered hall
rose before them, radiant with gold.
Nobody on earth knew of another
building like it. Majesty lodged there,   310
its light shone over many lands.
So their gallant escort guided them
to that dazzling stronghold and indicated
the shortest way to it; then the noble warrior
wheeled on his horse and spoke these words: 315
"It is time for me to go. May the Almighty
Father keep you and in His kindness
watch over your exploits. I'm away to the sea,
back on alert against enemy raiders."
    It was a paved track, a path that kept them   320
in marching order. Their mail-shirts glinted,
hard and hand-linked; the high-gloss iron
of their armor rang. So they duly arrived
in their grim war-graith[9] and gear at the hall,
and, weary from the sea, stacked wide shields   325
of the toughest hardwood against the wall,
then collapsed on the benches; battle-dress
and weapons clashed. They collected their spears
in a seafarers' stook,[1] a stand of grayish
tapering ash. And the troops themselves   330
were as good as their weapons.

---

8. Images of boars—a cult animal among the
Germanic tribes and sacred to the god Freyr—
were fixed atop helmets in the belief that they
would provide protection from enemy blows.

9. "Graith" is an archaic word for equipment
or armor.
1. An archaic word for a pile or mass.

       Then a proud warrior
questioned the men concerning their origins:
"Where do you come from, carrying these
decorated shields and shirts of mail,
these cheek-hinged helmets and javelins? 335
I am Hrothgar's herald and officer.
I have never seen so impressive or large
an assembly of strangers. Stoutness of heart,
bravery not banishment, must have brought you to Hrothgar."
  The man whose name was known for courage, 340
the Geat leader, resolute in his helmet,
answered in return: "We are retainers
from Hygelac's band. Beowulf is my name.
If your lord and master, the most renowned
son of Halfdane, will hear me out 345
and graciously allow me to greet him in person,
I am ready and willing to report my errand."
  Wulfgar replied, a Wendel[2] chief
renowned as a warrior, well known for his wisdom
and the temper of his mind: "I will take this message, 350
in accordance with your wish, to our noble king,
our dear lord, friend of the Danes,
the giver of rings. I will go and ask him
about your coming here, then hurry back
with whatever reply it pleases him to give." 355
  With that he turned to where Hrothgar sat,
an old man among retainers;
the valiant follower stood foursquare
in front of his king: he knew the courtesies.
Wulfgar addressed his dear lord: 360
"People from Geatland have put ashore.
They have sailed far over the wide sea.
They call the chief in charge of their band
by the name of Beowulf. They beg, my lord,
an audience with you, exchange of words 365
and formal greeting. Most gracious Hrothgar,
do not refuse them, but grant them a reply.
From their arms and appointment, they appear well born
and worthy of respect, especially the one
who has led them this far: he is formidable indeed." 370
  Hrothgar, protector of Shieldings, replied:
"I used to know him when he was a young boy.
His father before him was called Ecgtheow.
Hrethel the Geat[3] gave Ecgtheow

2. The Wendels or Vandals are another Germanic nation; it is not unusual for people to be members of nations different from the ones in which they reside. Hence Beowulf himself is both a Geat and a Waegmunding.

3. The leader of the Geats prior to his son Hygelac, who is the current leader. Note that Ecgtheow's marriage to Hrethel's daughter makes Beowulf part of the royal line.

his daughter in marriage. This man is their son, 375
here to follow up an old friendship.
A crew of seamen who sailed for me once
with a gift-cargo across to Geatland
returned with marvelous tales about him:
a thane,[4] they declared, with the strength of thirty 380
in the grip of each hand. Now Holy God
has, in His goodness, guided him here
to the West-Danes, to defend us from Grendel.
This is my hope; and for his heroism
I will recompense him with a rich treasure. 385
Go immediately, bid him and the Geats
he has in attendance to assemble and enter.
Say, moreover, when you speak to them,
they are welcome to Denmark."
                    At the door of the hall,
Wulfgar duly delivered the message: 390
"My lord, the conquering king of the Danes,
bids me announce that he knows your ancestry;
also that he welcomes you here to Heorot
and salutes your arrival from across the sea.
You are free now to move forward 395
to meet Hrothgar in helmets and armor,
but shields must stay here and spears be stacked
until the outcome of the audience is clear."
    The hero arose, surrounded closely
by his powerful thanes. A party remained 400
under orders to keep watch on the arms;
the rest proceeded, led by their prince
under Heorot's roof. And standing on the hearth
in webbed links that the smith had woven,
the fine-forged mesh of his gleaming mail-shirt, 405
resolute in his helmet, Beowulf spoke:
"Greetings to Hrothgar. I am Hygelac's kinsman,
one of his hall-troop. When I was younger,
I had great triumphs. Then news of Grendel,
hard to ignore, reached me at home: 410
sailors brought stories of the plight you suffer
in this legendary hall, how it lies deserted,
empty and useless once the evening light
hides itself under heaven's dome.
So every elder and experienced councilman 415
among my people supported my resolve
to come here to you, King Hrothgar,
because all knew of my awesome strength.
They had seen me boltered[5] in the blood of enemies
when I battled and bound five beasts, 420

---

4. That is, a warrior in the service of a lord like Hrethel or Hrothgar himself.   5. Clotted, sticky—a Northern Irish term.

raided a troll-nest and in the night-sea
slaughtered sea-brutes. I have suffered extremes
and avenged the Geats (their enemies brought it
upon themselves; I devastated them).
Now I mean to be a match for Grendel,   425
settle the outcome in single combat.
And so, my request, O king of Bright-Danes,
dear prince of the Shieldings, friend of the people
and their ring of defense, my one request
is that you won't refuse me, who have come this far,   430
the privilege of purifying Heorot,
with my own men to help me, and nobody else.
I have heard moreover that the monster scorns
in his reckless way to use weapons;
therefore, to heighten Hygelac's fame   435
and gladden his heart, I hereby renounce
sword and the shelter of the broad shield,
the heavy war-board: hand-to-hand
is how it will be, a life-and-death
fight with the fiend. Whichever one death fells   440
must deem it a just judgment by God.
If Grendel wins, it will be a gruesome day;
he will glut himself on the Geats in the war-hall,
swoop without fear on that flower of manhood
as on others before. Then my face won't be there   445
to be covered in death: he will carry me away
as he goes to ground, gorged and bloodied;
he will run gloating with my raw corpse
and feed on it alone, in a cruel frenzy
fouling his moor-nest. No need then   450
to lament for long or lay out my body:
if the battle takes me, send back
this breast-webbing that Weland[6] fashioned
and Hrethel gave me, to Lord Hygelac.
Fate goes ever as fate must."   455
    Hrothgar, the helmet of Shieldings, spoke:
"Beowulf, my friend, you have traveled here
to favor us with help and to fight for us.
There was a feud one time, begun by your father.
With his own hands he had killed Heatholaf   460
who was a Wulfing;[7] so war was looming
and his people, in fear of it, forced him to leave.
He came away then over rolling waves
to the South-Danes here, the sons of honor.
I was then in the first flush of kingship,   465
establishing my sway over the rich strongholds
of this heroic land. Heorogar,

6. The blacksmith of the Norse gods.   7. The Wulfings are another Germanic nation.

my older brother and the better man,
also a son of Halfdane's, had died.
Finally I healed the feud by paying: 470
I shipped a treasure-trove to the Wulfings,
and Ecgtheow acknowledged me with oaths of allegiance.

   "It bothers me to have to burden anyone
with all the grief that Grendel has caused
and the havoc he has wreaked upon us in Heorot,   475
our humiliations. My household-guard
are on the wane, fate sweeps them away
into Grendel's clutches—but God can easily
halt these raids and harrowing attacks!

   "Time and again, when the goblets passed   480
and seasoned fighters got flushed with beer
they would pledge themselves to protect Heorot
and wait for Grendel with their whetted swords.
But when dawn broke and day crept in
over each empty, blood-spattered bench,   485
the floor of the mead-hall where they had feasted
would be slick with slaughter. And so they died,
faithful retainers, and my following dwindled.
Now take your place at the table, relish
the triumph of heroes to your heart's content."   490

[Feast at Heorot]

   Then a bench was cleared in that banquet hall
so the Geats could have room to be together
and the party sat, proud in their bearing,
strong and stalwart. An attendant stood by
with a decorated pitcher, pouring bright   495
helpings of mead. And the minstrel sang,
filling Heorot with his head-clearing voice,
gladdening that great rally of Geats and Danes.

   From where he crouched at the king's feet,
Unferth, a son of Ecglaf's, spoke   500
contrary words.[8] Beowulf's coming,
his sea-braving, made him sick with envy:
he could not brook or abide the fact
that anyone else alive under heaven
might enjoy greater regard than he did: 505
"Are you the Beowulf who took on Breca
in a swimming match[9] on the open sea,
risking the water just to prove that you could win?
It was sheer vanity made you venture out

8. Unferth is Hrothgar's *thyle*, a kind of licensed spokesman who here engages Beowulf in a traditional "flytting" or verbal combat; see the note to line 1457. Ecglaf appears in the poem only as the father of Unferth.

9. The original Anglo-Saxon describing this contest can be interpreted in such a way that Breca and Beowulf are competing not in swimming but in rowing, which is more plausible.

on the main deep. And no matter who tried,   510
friend or foe, to deflect the pair of you,
neither would back down: the sea-test obsessed you.
You waded in, embracing water,
taking its measure, mastering currents,
riding on the swell. The ocean swayed,   515
winter went wild in the waves, but you vied
for seven nights; and then he outswam you,
came ashore the stronger contender.
He was cast up safe and sound one morning
among the Heatho-Reams,[1] then made his way   520
to where he belonged in Bronding[2] country,
home again, sure of his ground
in strongroom and bawn.[3] So Breca made good
his boast upon you and was proved right.
No matter, therefore, how you may have fared   525
in every bout and battle until now,
this time you'll be worsted; no one has ever
outlasted an entire night against Grendel."
    Beowulf, Ecgtheow's son, replied:
"Well, friend Unferth, you have had your say   530
about Breca and me. But it was mostly beer
that was doing the talking. The truth is this:
when the going was heavy in those high waves,
I was the strongest swimmer of all.
We'd been children together and we grew up   535
daring ourselves to outdo each other,
boasting and urging each other to risk
our lives on the sea. And so it turned out.
Each of us swam holding a sword,
a naked, hard-proofed blade for protection   540
against the whale-beasts. But Breca could never
move out farther or faster from me
than I could manage to move from him.
Shoulder to shoulder, we struggled on
for five nights, until the long flow   545
and pitch of the waves, the perishing cold,
night falling and winds from the north
drove us apart. The deep boiled up
and its wallowing sent the sea-brutes wild.
My armor helped me to hold out;   550
my hard-ringed chain-mail, hand-forged and linked,
a fine, close-fitting filigree of gold,
kept me safe when some ocean creature
pulled me to the bottom. Pinioned fast
and swathed in its grip, I was granted one   555

---

1. A people of southern Norway.
2. The Brondings are the nation to which
Breca belonged, but nothing is known of their
territory.

3. Fortified outwork of a court or castle. The
word was used by English planters in Ulster to
describe fortified dwellings they erected on lands
confiscated from the Irish [translator's note].

final chance: my sword plunged
and the ordeal was over. Through my own hands,
the fury of battle had finished off the sea-beast.
    "Time and again, foul things attacked me,
lurking and stalking, but I lashed out,   560
gave as good as I got with my sword.
My flesh was not for feasting on,
there would be no monsters gnawing and gloating
over their banquet at the bottom of the sea.
Instead, in the morning, mangled and sleeping   565
the sleep of the sword, they slopped and floated
like the ocean's leavings. From now on
sailors would be safe, the deep-sea raids
were over for good. Light came from the east,
bright guarantee of God, and the waves   570
went quiet; I could see headlands
and buffeted cliffs. Often, for undaunted courage,
fate spares the man it has not already marked.
However it occurred, my sword had killed
nine sea-monsters. Such night dangers   575
and hard ordeals I have never heard of
nor of a man more desolate in surging waves.
But worn out as I was, I survived,
came through with my life. The ocean lifted
and laid me ashore, I landed safe   580
on the coast of Finland.
                        Now I cannot recall
any fight you entered, Unferth,
that bears comparison. I don't boast when I say
that neither you nor Breca were ever much
celebrated for swordsmanship   585
or for facing danger on the field of battle.
You killed your own kith and kin,
so for all your cleverness and quick tongue,
you will suffer damnation in the depths of hell.[4]
The fact is, Unferth, if you were truly   590
as keen or courageous as you claim to be
Grendel would never have got away with
such unchecked atrocity, attacks on your king,
havoc in Heorot and horrors everywhere.
But he knows he need never be in dread   595
of your blade making a mizzle[5] of his blood
or of vengeance arriving ever from this quarter—
from the Victory-Shieldings, the shoulderers of the spear.
He knows he can trample down you Danes
to his heart's content, humiliate and murder   600

4. The manuscript is damaged here, and the
word "hell" may well be "hall": "You will suffer
condemnation in the hall" is an acceptable
translation of the line.
5. That is, drizzle.

without fear of reprisal. But he will find me different.
I will show him how Geats shape to kill
in the heat of battle. Then whoever wants to
may go bravely to mead,[6] when the morning light,
scarfed in sun-dazzle, shines forth from the south   605
and brings another daybreak to the world."
    Then the gray-haired treasure-giver was glad;
far-famed in battle, the prince of Bright-Danes
and keeper of his people counted on Beowulf,
on the warrior's steadfastness and his word.   610
So the laughter started, the din got louder
and the crowd was happy. Wealhtheow came in,
Hrothgar's queen, observing the courtesies.
Adorned in her gold, she graciously saluted
the men in the hall, then handed the cup   615
first to Hrothgar, their homeland's guardian,
urging him to drink deep and enjoy it
because he was dear to them. And he drank it down
like the warlord he was, with festive cheer.
So the Helming woman went on her rounds,   620
queenly and dignified, decked out in rings,
offering the goblet to all ranks,
treating the household and the assembled troop,
until it was Beowulf's turn to take it from her hand.
With measured words she welcomed the Geat   625
and thanked God for granting her wish
that a deliverer she could believe in would arrive
to ease their afflictions. He accepted the cup,
a daunting man, dangerous in action
and eager for it always. He addressed Wealhtheow;   630
Beowulf, son of Ecgtheow, said:
"I had a fixed purpose when I put to sea.
As I sat in the boat with my band of men,
I meant to perform to the uttermost
what your people wanted or perish in the attempt,   635
in the fiend's clutches. And I shall fulfill that purpose,
prove myself with a proud deed
or meet my death here in the mead-hall."
This formal boast by Beowulf the Geat
pleased the lady well and she went to sit   640
by Hrothgar, regal and arrayed with gold.
    Then it was like old times in the echoing hall,
proud talk and the people happy,
loud and excited; until soon enough
Halfdane's heir had to be away   645
to his night's rest. He realized
that the demon was going to descend on the hall,
that he had plotted all day, from dawn-light

6. An alcoholic drink made by fermenting honey and adding water.

until darkness gathered again over the world
and stealthy night-shapes came stealing forth
under the cloud-murk. The company stood   650
as the two leaders took leave of each other:
Hrothgar wished Beowulf health and good luck,
named him hall-warden and announced as follows:
"Never, since my hand could hold a shield   655
have I entrusted or given control
of the Danes' hall to anyone but you.
Ward and guard it, for it is the greatest of houses.
Be on your mettle now, keep in mind your fame,
beware of the enemy. There's nothing you wish for   660
that won't be yours if you win through alive."

[The Fight with Grendel]

    Hrothgar departed then with his house-guard.
The lord of the Shieldings, their shelter in war,
left the mead-hall to lie with Wealhtheow,
his queen and bedmate. The King of Glory   665
(as people learned) had posted a lookout
who was a match for Grendel, a guard against monsters,
special protection to the Danish prince.
And the Geat placed complete trust
in his strength of limb and the Lord's favor.   670
    He began to remove his iron breast-mail,
took off the helmet and handed his attendant
the patterned sword, a smith's masterpiece,
ordering him to keep the equipment guarded.
And before he bedded down, Beowulf,   675
that prince of goodness, proudly asserted:
"When it comes to fighting, I count myself
as dangerous any day as Grendel.
So it won't be a cutting edge I'll wield
to mow him down, easily as I might.   680
He has no idea of the arts of war,
of shield or sword-play, although he does possess
a wild strength. No weapons, therefore,
for either this night: unarmed he shall face me
if face me he dares. And may the Divine Lord   685
in His wisdom grant the glory of victory
to whichever side He sees fit."
    Then down the brave man lay with his bolster
under his head and his whole company
of sea-rovers at rest beside him.   690
None of them expected he would ever see
his homeland again or get back
to his native place and the people who reared him.
They knew too well the way it was before,
how often the Danes had fallen prey   695
to death in the mead-hall. But the Lord was weaving

a victory on His war-loom for the Weather-Geats.
Through the strength of one they all prevailed;
they would crush their enemy and come through
in triumph and gladness. The truth is clear: 700
Almighty God rules over mankind
and always has.
                Then out of the night
came the shadow-stalker, stealthy and swift.
The hall-guards were slack, asleep at their posts,
all except one; it was widely understood   705
that as long as God disallowed it,
the fiend could not bear them to his shadow-bourne.
One man, however, was in fighting mood,
awake and on edge, spoiling for action.
   In off the moors, down through the mist-bands   710
God-cursed Grendel came greedily loping.
The bane of the race of men roamed forth,
hunting for a prey in the high hall.
Under the cloud-murk he moved toward it
until it shone above him, a sheer keep   715
of fortified gold. Nor was that the first time
he had scouted the grounds of Hrothgar's dwelling—
although never in his life, before or since,
did he find harder fortune or hall-defenders.
Spurned and joyless, he journeyed on ahead   720
and arrived at the bawn. The iron-braced door
turned on its hinge when his hands touched it.
Then his rage boiled over, he ripped open
the mouth of the building, maddening for blood,
pacing the length of the patterned floor   725
with his loathsome tread, while a baleful light,
flame more than light, flared from his eyes.
He saw many men in the mansion, sleeping,
a ranked company of kinsmen and warriors
quartered together. And his glee was demonic,   730
picturing the mayhem: before morning
he would rip life from limb and devour them,
feed on their flesh; but his fate that night
was due to change, his days of ravening
had come to an end.
              Mighty and canny,   735
Hygelac's kinsman was keenly watching
for the first move the monster would make.
Nor did the creature keep him waiting
but struck suddenly and started in;
he grabbed and mauled a man on his bench,   740
bit into his bone-lappings,[7] bolted down his blood
and gorged on him in lumps, leaving the body

7. That is, joints.

utterly lifeless, eaten up
hand and foot. Venturing closer,
his talon was raised to attack Beowulf   745
where he lay on the bed, he was bearing in
with open claw when the alert hero's
comeback and armlock forestalled him utterly.
The captain of evil discovered himself
in a handgrip harder than anything   750
he had ever encountered in any man
on the face of the earth. Every bone in his body
quailed and recoiled, but he could not escape.
He was desperate to flee to his den and hide
with the devil's litter, for in all his days   755
he had never been clamped or cornered like this.
Then Hygelac's trusty retainer recalled
his bedtime speech, sprang to his feet
and got a firm hold. Fingers were bursting,
the monster back-tracking, the man overpowering.   760
The dread of the land was desperate to escape,
to take a roundabout road and flee
to his lair in the fens. The latching power
in his fingers weakened; it was the worst trip
the terror-monger had taken to Heorot.   765
And now the timbers trembled and sang,
a hall-session[8] that harrowed every Dane
inside the stockade: stumbling in fury,
the two contenders crashed through the building.
The hall clattered and hammered, but somehow   770
survived the onslaught and kept standing:
it was handsomely structured, a sturdy frame
braced with the best of blacksmith's work
inside and out. The story goes
that as the pair struggled, mead-benches were smashed   775
and sprung off the floor, gold fittings and all.
Before then, no Shielding elder would believe
there was any power or person upon earth
capable of wrecking their horn-rigged hall
unless the burning embrace of a fire   780
engulf it in flame. Then an extraordinary
wail arose, and bewildering fear
came over the Danes. Everyone felt it
who heard that cry as it echoed off the wall,
a God-cursed scream and strain of catastrophe,   785
the howl of the loser, the lament of the hell-serf
keening his wound. He was overwhelmed,
manacled tight by the man who of all men

8. In Hiberno-English the word "session" (*seissiún* in Irish) can mean a gathering where musicians and singers perform for their own enjoyment [translator's note]. In other words, the poet is making a laconic joke, since the main function of the hall is celebration and singing.

was foremost and strongest in the days of this life.
    But the earl-troop's leader was not inclined   790
to allow his caller to depart alive:
he did not consider that life of much account
to anyone anywhere. Time and again,
Beowulf's warriors worked to defend
their lord's life, laying about them   795
as best they could, with their ancestral blades.
Stalwart in action, they kept striking out
on every side, seeking to cut
straight to the soul. When they joined the struggle
there was something they could not have known at the time,   800
that no blade on earth, no blacksmith's art
could ever damage their demon opponent.
He had conjured the harm from the cutting edge
of every weapon.[9] But his going away
out of this world and the days of his life   805
would be agony to him, and his alien spirit
would travel far into fiends' keeping.
    Then he who had harrowed the hearts of men
with pain and affliction in former times
and had given offense also to God   810
found that his bodily powers failed him.
Hygelac's kinsman kept him helplessly
locked in a handgrip. As long as either lived,
he was hateful to the other. The monster's whole
body was in pain; a tremendous wound   815
appeared on his shoulder. Sinews split
and the bone-lappings burst. Beowulf was granted
the glory of winning; Grendel was driven
under the fen-banks, fatally hurt,
to his desolate lair. His days were numbered,   820
the end of his life was coming over him,
he knew it for certain; and one bloody clash
had fulfilled the dearest wishes of the Danes.
The man who had lately landed among them,
proud and sure, had purged the hall,   825
kept it from harm; he was happy with his nightwork
and the courage he had shown. The Geat captain
had boldly fulfilled his boast to the Danes:
he had healed and relieved a huge distress,
unremitting humiliations,   830
the hard fate they'd been forced to undergo,
no small affliction. Clear proof of this
could be seen in the hand the hero displayed
high up near the roof: the whole of Grendel's
shoulder and arm, his awesome grasp.   835

9. Grendel is magically protected from weapons.

[Celebration at Heorot]

Then morning came and many a warrior
gathered, as I've heard, around the gift-hall,
clan-chiefs flocking from far and near
down wide-ranging roads, wondering greatly
at the monster's footprints. His fatal departure   840
was regretted by no one who witnessed his trail,
the ignominious marks of his flight
where he'd skulked away, exhausted in spirit
and beaten in battle, bloodying the path,
hauling his doom to the demons' mere.[1]   845
The bloodshot water wallowed and surged,
there were loathsome upthrows and overturnings
of waves and gore and wound-slurry.
With his death upon him, he had dived deep
into his marsh-den, drowned out his life   850
and his heathen soul: hell claimed him there.
    Then away they rode, the old retainers
with many a young man following after,
a troop on horseback, in high spirits
on their bay steeds. Beowulf's doings   855
were praised over and over again.
Nowhere, they said, north or south
between the two seas or under the tall sky
on the broad earth was there anyone better
to raise a shield or to rule a kingdom.   860
Yet there was no laying of blame on their lord,
the noble Hrothgar; he was a good king.
    At times the war-band broke into a gallop,
letting their chestnut horses race
wherever they found the going good   865
on those well-known tracks. Meanwhile, a thane
of the king's household, a carrier of tales,
a traditional singer deeply schooled
in the lore of the past, linked a new theme
to a strict meter.[2] The man started   870
to recite with skill, rehearsing Beowulf's
triumphs and feats in well-fashioned lines,
entwining his words.
                    He told what he'd heard
repeated in songs about Sigemund's exploits,[3]
all of those many feats and marvels,   875
the struggles and wanderings of Waels's son,
things unknown to anyone

1. A lake or pool.
2. The singer or *scop* composes extemporane-
ously in alliterative verse.
3. According to Norse legend, Sigemund, the
son of Waels (or Volsung, as he is known
in Norse), slept with his sister Sigurth, who
bore a son named Fitela; Fitela was thus also

Sigemund's nephew, as he is described here.
The singer here contrasts Sigemund's bravery
in killing a dragon with the defeat of the Danish king Heremod, who could not protect his
people. For more on Heremod as a bad king,
see lines 1709–22.

except to Fitela, feuds and foul doings
confided by uncle to nephew when he felt
the urge to speak of them: always they had been   880
partners in the fight, friends in need.
They killed giants, their conquering swords
had brought them down.   *After his death*
Sigemund's glory   grew and grew
because of his courage   when he killed the dragon,   885
the guardian of the hoard.   Under gray stone
he had dared to enter   all by himself
to face the worst   without Fitela.
But it came to pass   that his sword plunged
right through   those radiant scales   890
and drove into the wall.   The dragon died of it.
His daring had given him   total possession
of the treasure-hoard,   his to dispose of
however he liked.   He loaded a boat:
Waels's son   weighted her hold   895
with dazzling spoils.   The hot dragon melted.
   Sigemund's name   was known everywhere.
He was utterly valiant   and venturesome,
a fence round his fighters   and flourished therefore
after King Heremod's   prowess declined   900
and his campaigns slowed down.   The king was betrayed,
ambushed in Jutland,   overpowered
and done away with.   The waves of his grief
had beaten him down,   made him a burden,
a source of anxiety   to his own nobles: 905
that expedition   was often condemned
in those earlier times   by experienced men,
men who relied   on his lordship for redress,
who presumed that the part   of a prince was to thrive
on his father's throne   and defend the nation,   910
the Shielding land   where they lived and belonged,
its holdings and strongholds.   Such was Beowulf
in the affection of his friends   and of everyone alive.
But evil entered   into Heremod.
   Meanwhile, the Danes kept racing their mounts   915
down sandy lanes. The light of day
broke and kept brightening. Bands of retainers
galloped in excitement to the gabled hall
to see the marvel; and the king himself,
guardian of the ring-hoard, goodness in person,   920
walked in majesty from the women's quarters
with a numerous train, attended by his queen
and her crowd of maidens, across to the mead-hall.
   When Hrothgar arrived at the hall, he spoke,
standing on the steps, under the steep eaves,   925
gazing toward the roofwork and Grendel's talon:
"First and foremost, let the Almighty Father

be thanked for this sight. I suffered a long
harrowing by Grendel. But the Heavenly Shepherd
can work His wonders always and everywhere.   930
Not long since, it seemed I would never
be granted the slightest solace or relief
from any of my burdens: the best of houses
glittered and reeked and ran with blood.
This one worry outweighed all others—   935
a constant distress to counselors entrusted
with defending the people's forts from assault
by monsters and demons. But now a man,
with the Lord's assistance, has accomplished something
none of us could manage before now   940
for all our efforts. Whoever she was
who brought forth this flower of manhood,
if she is still alive, that woman can say
that in her labor the Lord of Ages
bestowed a grace on her. So now, Beowulf,   945
I adopt you in my heart as a dear son.
Nourish and maintain this new connection,
you noblest of men; there'll be nothing you'll want for,
no worldly goods that won't be yours.
I have often honored smaller achievements,   950
recognized warriors not nearly as worthy,
lavished rewards on the less deserving.
But you have made yourself immortal
by your glorious action. May the God of Ages
continue to keep and requite you well."   955
    Beowulf, son of Ecgtheow, spoke:
"We have gone through with a glorious endeavor
and been much favored in this fight we dared
against the unknown. Nevertheless,
if you could have seen the monster himself   960
where he lay beaten, I would have been better pleased.
My plan was to pounce, pin him down
in a tight grip and grapple him to death—
have him panting for life, powerless and clasped
in my bare hands, his body in thrall.   965
But I couldn't stop him from slipping my hold.
The Lord allowed it, my lock on him
wasn't strong enough; he struggled fiercely
and broke and ran. Yet he bought his freedom
at a high price, for he left his hand   970
and arm and shoulder to show he had been here,
a cold comfort for having come among us.
And now he won't be long for this world.
He has done his worst but the wound will end him.
He is hasped and hooped and hirpling⁴ with pain,   975

4. That is, limping.

limping and looped in it. Like a man outlawed
for wickedness, he must await
the mighty judgment of God in majesty."
     There was less tampering and big talk then
from Unferth the boaster, less of his blather   980
as the hall-thanes eyed the awful proof
of the hero's prowess, the splayed hand
up under the eaves. Every nail,
claw-scale and spur, every spike
and welt on the hand of that heathen brute   985
was like barbed steel. Everybody said
there was no honed iron hard enough
to pierce him through, no time-proofed blade
that could cut his brutal, blood-caked claw.
     Then the order was given for all hands   990
to help to refurbish Heorot immediately:
men and women thronging the wine-hall,
getting it ready. Gold thread shone
in the wall-hangings, woven scenes
that attracted and held the eye's attention.   995
But iron-braced as the inside of it had been,
that bright room lay in ruins now.
The very doors had been dragged from their hinges.
Only the roof remained unscathed
by the time the guilt-fouled fiend turned tail   1000
in despair of his life. But death is not easily
escaped from by anyone:
all of us with souls, earth-dwellers
and children of men, must make our way
to a destination already ordained   1005
where the body, after the banqueting,
sleeps on its deathbed.
                         Then the due time arrived
for Halfdane's son to proceed to the hall.
The king himself would sit down to feast.
No group ever gathered in greater numbers   1010
or better order around their ring-giver.
The benches filled with famous men
who fell to with relish; round upon round
of mead was passed; those powerful kinsmen,
Hrothgar and Hrothulf, were in high spirits   1015
in the raftered hall. Inside Heorot
there was nothing but friendship. The Shielding nation
was not yet familiar with feud and betrayal.[5]
     Then Halfdane's son presented Beowulf

---

5. The poet here refers to the later history of
the Danes, when after Hrothgar's death his
nephew Hrothulf drove his son Hrethric from
the throne. For Wealhtheow's fear that this
betrayal will indeed come to pass, see lines
1168–90.

with a gold standard as a victory gift,   1020
an embroidered banner; also breast-mail
and a helmet; and a sword carried high,
that was both precious object and token of honor.
So Beowulf drank his drink, at ease;
it was hardly a shame to be showered with such gifts   1025
in front of the hall-troops. There haven't been many
moments, I am sure, when men exchanged
four such treasures at so friendly a sitting.
An embossed ridge, a band lapped with wire
arched over the helmet: head-protection   1030
to keep the keen-ground cutting edge
from damaging it when danger threatened
and the man was battling behind his shield.
Next the king ordered eight horses
with gold bridles to be brought through the yard   1035
into the hall. The harness of one
included a saddle of sumptuous design,
the battle-seat where the son of Halfdane
rode when he wished to join the sword-play:
wherever the killing and carnage were the worst,   1040
he would be to the fore, fighting hard.
Then the Danish prince, descendant of Ing,[6]
handed over both the arms and the horses,
urging Beowulf to use them well.
And so their leader, the lord and guard   1045
of coffer and strongroom, with customary grace
bestowed upon Beowulf both sets of gifts.
A fair witness can see how well each one behaved.
     The chieftain went on to reward the others:
each man on the bench who had sailed with Beowulf   1050
and risked the voyage received a bounty,
some treasured possession. And compensation,
a price in gold, was settled for the Geat
Grendel had cruelly killed earlier—
as he would have killed more, had not mindful God   1055
and one man's daring prevented that doom.
Past and present, God's will prevails.
Hence, understanding is always best
and a prudent mind. Whoever remains
for long here in this earthly life   1060
will enjoy and endure more than enough.
     They sang then and played to please the hero,
words and music for their warrior prince,
harp tunes and tales of adventure:
there were high times on the hall benches,   1065
and the king's poet performed his part
with the saga of Finn and his sons, unfolding

6. A Germanic deity and the protector of the Danes.

the tale of the fierce attack in Friesland
where Hnaef, king of the Danes, met death.[7]

Hildeburh
     had little cause   1070
to credit the Jutes:
     son and brother,
she lost them both
     on the battlefield.
She, bereft
     and blameless, they
foredoomed, cut down
     and spear-gored. She,
the woman in shock,
     waylaid by grief,   1075
Hoc's daughter—
     how could she not
lament her fate
     when morning came
and the light broke
     on her murdered dears?
And so farewell
     delight on earth,
war carried away
     Finn's troop of thanes   1080
all but a few.
     How then could Finn
hold the line
     or fight on
to the end with Hengest,
     how save
the rump of his force
     from that enemy chief?
So a truce was offered
     as follows: first   1085
separate quarters
     to be cleared for the Danes,
hall and throne
     to be shared with the Frisians.
Then, second:
     every day
at the dole-out of gifts
     Finn, son of Focwald,

7. This song recounts the fight at Finnsburg between the Dane Hengest and the Jute (or Frisian) Finn. The poet begins with the bereft Hildeburh, daughter of the Danish king Hoc and wife of the Jute Finn, whose unnamed son and brother Hnaef have already been killed in the first battle with Finn. He then tells how Hengest, the new leader of the Danes, is offered a truce by the weakened Finn, how together they cremate their dead, following which Hengest and the remaining Danes spend the winter with Finn and the Jutes. But with the coming of spring, the feud breaks out again and Finn and the Jutes are slaughtered by Hengest with the help of two other Danes, Guthlaf and Oslaf.

should honor the Danes,
                     bestow with an even   1090
hand to Hengest
                    and Hengest's men
the wrought-gold rings,
                    bounty to match
the measure he gave
                    his own Frisians—
to keep morale
                    in the beer-hall high.
Both sides then
                    sealed their agreement.   1095
With oaths to Hengest
                    Finn swore
openly, solemnly,
                    that the battle survivors
would be guaranteed
                    honor and status.
No infringement
                    by word or deed,
no provocation
                    would be permitted.   1100
Their own ring-giver
                    after all
was dead and gone,
                    they were leaderless,
in forced allegiance
                    to his murderer.
So if any Frisian
                    stirred up bad blood
with insinuations
                    or taunts about this,   1105
the blade of the sword
                    would arbitrate it.
A funeral pyre
                    was then prepared,
effulgent gold
                    brought out from the hoard.
The pride and prince
                    of the Shieldings lay
awaiting the flame.
                    Everywhere   1110
there were blood-plastered
                    coats of mail.
The pyre was heaped
                    with boar-shaped helmets
forged in gold,
                    with the gashed corpses
of wellborn Danes—
                    many had fallen.
Then Hildeburh

                    ordered her own
son's body
                    be burnt with Hnaef's
the flesh on his bones
                        to sputter and blaze
beside his uncle's.
                    The woman wailed
and sang keens,
                    the warrior went up.[8]
Carcass flame
                    swirled and fumed,
they stood round the burial
                        mound and howled
as heads melted,
                    crusted gashes
spattered and ran
                bloody matter.
The glutton element
                    flamed and consumed
the dead of both sides.
                        Their great days were gone.
Warriors scattered
                    to homes and forts
all over Friesland,
                    fewer now, feeling
loss of friends.
                    Hengest stayed,
lived out that whole
                    resentful, blood-sullen
winter with Finn,
                    homesick and helpless.
No ring-whorled prow
                    could up then
and away on the sea.
                    Wind and water
raged with storms,
                    wave and shingle
were shackled in ice
                    until another year
appeared in the yard
                    as it does to this day,
the seasons constant,
                    the wonder of light
coming over us.
                Then winter was gone,
earth's lap grew lovely,
                    longing woke
in the cooped-up exile

---

8. The warrior (Hildeburh's son) either goes up on the pyre or goes up in smoke. "Keens": an Irish word for funeral laments.

for a voyage home—
but more for vengeance,
　　　　　　　　some way of bringing　　　　　　　　1140
things to a head:
　　　　　　　　his sword arm hankered
to greet the Jutes.
　　　　　　　　So he did not balk
once Hunlafing[9]
　　　　　　　　placed on his lap
Dazzle-the-Duel,
　　　　　　　　the best sword of all,
whose edges Jutes
　　　　　　　　knew only too well.　　　　　　　　1145
Thus blood was spilled,
　　　　　　　　the gallant Finn
slain in his home
　　　　　　　　after Guthlaf and Oslaf[1]
back from their voyage
　　　　　　　　made old accusation:
the brutal ambush,
　　　　　　　　the fate they had suffered,
all blamed on Finn.
　　　　　　　　The wildness in them　　　　　　　　1150
had to brim over.
　　　　　　　　The hall ran red
with blood of enemies.
　　　　　　　　Finn was cut down,
the queen brought away
　　　　　　　　and everything
the Shieldings could find
　　　　　　　　inside Finn's walls—
the Frisian king's
　　　　　　　　gold collars and gemstones—　　　　1155
swept off to the ship.
　　　　　　　　Over sea-lanes then
back to Daneland
　　　　　　　　the warrior troop
bore that lady home.

The poem was over,
the poet had performed, a pleasant murmur
started on the benches, stewards did the rounds　　　1160
with wine in splendid jugs, and Wealhtheow came to sit
in her gold crown between two good men,
uncle and nephew, each one of whom
still trusted the other;[2] and the forthright Unferth,

9. A Danish follower of Hengest.
1. Danes who seem to have gone home in
order to bring reinforcements to Hengest. But
it is possible that these two have been with
Hengest all along and that "their voyage" is an
unrelated journey.
2. See p. 146, n. 5.

admired by all for his mind and courage   1165
although under a cloud for killing his brothers,
reclined near the king.
                              The queen spoke:
"Enjoy this drink, my most generous lord;
raise up your goblet, entertain the Geats
duly and gently, discourse with them,   1170
be open-handed, happy and fond.
Relish their company, but recollect as well
all of the boons that have been bestowed on you.
The bright court of Heorot has been cleansed
and now the word is that you want to adopt   1175
this warrior as a son. So, while you may,
bask in your fortune, and then bequeath
kingdom and nation to your kith and kin,
before your decease. I am certain of Hrothulf.
He is noble and will use the young ones well.   1180
He will not let you down. Should you die before him,
he will treat our children truly and fairly.
He will honor, I am sure, our two sons,
repay them in kind, when he recollects
all the good things we gave him once,   1185
the favor and respect he found in his childhood."
She turned then to the bench where her boys sat,
Hrethric and Hrothmund, with other nobles' sons,
all the youth together; and that good man,
Beowulf the Geat, sat between the brothers.   1190

    The cup was carried to him, kind words
spoken in welcome and a wealth of wrought gold
graciously bestowed: two arm bangles,
a mail-shirt and rings, and the most resplendent
torque of gold I ever heard tell of   1195
anywhere on earth or under heaven.
There was no hoard like it since Hama snatched
the Brosings' neck-chain and bore it away
with its gems and settings to his shining fort,
away from Eormenric's wiles and hatred,   1200
and thereby ensured his eternal reward.[3]
Hygelac the Geat, grandson of Swerting,
wore this neck-ring on his last raid;[4]
at bay under his banner, he defended the booty,
treasure he had won. Fate swept him away   1205
because of his proud need to provoke
a feud with the Frisians. He fell beneath his shield,
in the same gem-crusted, kingly gear

---

3. The legend alluded to here seems to be that Hama stole the golden necklace of the Brosings from Eormenric (a historical figure, the king of the Ostrogoths, who died ca. 375), and then gave it to the goddess Freya.

4. The poet here refers to the death of Hygelac while raiding the Frisian territory of the Franks. This raid and Hygelac's death are recorded by the historian Gregory of Tours (d. 594) as having taken place about 520.

he had worn when he crossed the frothing wave-vat.
So the dead king fell into Frankish hands.   1210
They took his breast-mail, also his neck-torque,
and punier warriors plundered the slain
when the carnage ended; Geat corpses
covered the field.   Applause filled the hall.
Then Wealhtheow pronounced in the presence of the company: 1215
"Take delight in this torque, dear Beowulf,
wear it for luck and wear also this mail
from our people's armory: may you prosper in them!
Be acclaimed for strength, for kindly guidance
to these two boys, and your bounty will be sure.   1220
You have won renown: you are known to all men
far and near, now and forever.
Your sway is wide as the wind's home,
as the sea around cliffs. And so, my prince,
I wish you a lifetime's luck and blessings   1225
to enjoy this treasure. Treat my sons
with tender care, be strong and kind.
Here each comrade is true to the other,
loyal to lord, loving in spirit.
The thanes have one purpose, the people are ready: 1230
having drunk and pledged, the ranks do as I bid."
    She moved then to her place. Men were drinking wine
at that rare feast; how could they know fate,
the grim shape of things to come,
the threat looming over many thanes   1235
as night approached and King Hrothgar prepared
to retire to his quarters? Retainers in great numbers
were posted on guard as so often in the past.
Benches were pushed back, bedding gear and bolsters
spread across the floor, and one man   1240
lay down to his rest, already marked for death.
At their heads they placed their polished timber
battle-shields; and on the bench above them,
each man's kit was kept to hand:
a towering war-helmet, webbed mail-shirt   1245
and great-shafted spear. It was their habit
always and everywhere to be ready for action,
at home or in the camp, in whatever case
and at whatever time the need arose
to rally round their lord. They were a right people.   1250

[Another Attack]

    They went to sleep. And one paid dearly
for his night's ease, as had happened to them often,
ever since Grendel occupied the gold-hall,
committing evil until the end came,
death after his crimes. Then it became clear,   1255

obvious to everyone once the fight was over,
that an avenger lurked and was still alive,
grimly biding time. Grendel's mother,
monstrous hell-bride, brooded on her wrongs.
She had been forced down into fearful waters,   1260
the cold depths, after Cain had killed
his father's son, felled his own
brother with a sword. Branded an outlaw,
marked by having murdered, he moved into the wilds,
shunned company and joy. And from Cain there sprang   1265
misbegotten spirits, among them Grendel,
the banished and accursed, due to come to grips
with that watcher in Heorot waiting to do battle.
The monster wrenched and wrestled with him,
but Beowulf was mindful of his mighty strength,   1270
the wondrous gifts God had showered on him:
he relied for help on the Lord of All,
on His care and favor. So he overcame the foe,
brought down the hell-brute. Broken and bowed,
outcast from all sweetness, the enemy of mankind   1275
made for his death-den. But now his mother
had sallied forth on a savage journey,
grief-racked and ravenous, desperate for revenge.

  She came to Heorot. There, inside the hall,
Danes lay asleep, earls who would soon endure   1280
a great reversal, once Grendel's mother
attacked and entered. Her onslaught was less
only by as much as an amazon warrior's
strength is less than an armed man's
when the hefted sword, its hammered edge   1285
and gleaming blade slathered in blood,
razes the sturdy boar-ridge off a helmet.
Then in the hall, hard-honed swords
were grabbed from the bench, many a broad shield
lifted and braced; there was little thought of helmets   1290
or woven mail when they woke in terror.

  The hell-dam was in panic, desperate to get out,
in mortal terror the moment she was found.
She had pounced and taken one of the retainers
in a tight hold, then headed for the fen.   1295
To Hrothgar, this man was the most beloved
of the friends he trusted between the two seas.
She had done away with a great warrior,
ambushed him at rest.
       Beowulf was elsewhere.
Earlier, after the award of the treasure,   1300
the Geat had been given another lodging.

  There was uproar in Heorot. She had snatched their trophy,
Grendel's bloodied hand. It was a fresh blow
to the afflicted bawn. The bargain was hard,

both parties having to pay   1305
with the lives of friends. And the old lord,
the gray-haired warrior, was heartsore and weary
when he heard the news: his highest-placed adviser,
his dearest companion, was dead and gone.
  Beowulf was quickly brought to the chamber: 1310
the winner of fights, the arch-warrior,
came first-footing in with his fellow troops
to where the king in his wisdom waited,
still wondering whether Almighty God
would ever turn the tide of his misfortunes.   1315
So Beowulf entered with his band in attendance
and the wooden floorboards banged and rang
as he advanced, hurrying to address
the prince of the Ingwins,[5] asking if he'd rested
since the urgent summons had come as a surprise.   1320
  Then Hrothgar, the Shieldings' helmet, spoke:
"Rest? What is rest? Sorrow has returned.
Alas for the Danes! Aeschere is dead.
He was Yrmenlaf's elder brother
and a soul-mate to me, a true mentor,   1325
my right-hand man when the ranks clashed
and our boar-crests had to take a battering
in the line of action. Aeschere was everything
the world admires in a wise man and a friend.
Then this roaming killer came in a fury   1330
and slaughtered him in Heorot. Where she is hiding,
glutting on the corpse and glorying in her escape,
I cannot tell; she has taken up the feud
because of last night, when you killed Grendel,
wrestled and racked him in ruinous combat   1335
since for too long he had terrorized us
with his depredations. He died in battle,
paid with his life; and now this powerful
other one arrives, this force for evil
driven to avenge her kinsman's death.   1340
Or so it seems to thanes in their grief,
in the anguish every thane endures
at the loss of a ring-giver, now that the hand
that bestowed so richly has been stilled in death.
  "I have heard it said by my people in hall,   1345
counselors who live in the upland country,
that they have seen two such creatures
prowling the moors, huge marauders
from some other world. One of these things,
as far as anyone ever can discern,   1350
looks like a woman; the other, warped
in the shape of a man, moves beyond the pale

5. The friends of the god Ing—that is, the Danes. See p. 147, n. 6.

bigger than any man, an unnatural birth
called Grendel by the country people
in former days. They are fatherless creatures,   1355
and their whole ancestry is hidden in a past
of demons and ghosts.[6] They dwell apart
among wolves on the hills, on windswept crags
and treacherous keshes, where cold streams
pour down the mountain and disappear   1360
under mist and moorland.

          A few miles from here
a frost-stiffened wood waits and keeps watch
above a mere; the overhanging bank
is a maze of tree-roots mirrored in its surface.
At night there, something uncanny happens: 1365
the water burns. And the mere bottom
has never been sounded by the sons of men.
On its bank, the heather-stepper halts:
the hart in flight from pursuing hounds
will turn to face them with firm-set horns   1370
and die in the wood rather than dive
beneath its surface. That is no good place.
When wind blows up and stormy weather
makes clouds scud and the skies weep,
out of its depths a dirty surge   1375
is pitched toward the heavens. Now help depends
again on you and on you alone.
The gap of danger where the demon waits
is still unknown to you. Seek it if you dare.
I will compensate you for settling the feud   1380
as I did the last time with lavish wealth,
coffers of coiled gold, if you come back."

[Beowulf Fights Grendel's Mother]

Beowulf, son of Ecgtheow, spoke:
"Wise sir, do not grieve. It is always better
to avenge dear ones than to indulge in mourning.   1385
For every one of us, living in this world
means waiting for our end. Let whoever can
win glory before death. When a warrior is gone,
that will be his best and only bulwark.
So arise, my lord, and let us immediately   1390
set forth on the trail of this troll-dam.
I guarantee you: she will not get away,
not to dens under ground nor upland groves
nor the ocean floor. She'll have nowhere to flee to.
Endure your troubles today. Bear up   1395
and be the man I expect you to be."

---

6. Note that Hrothgar doesn't know of the biblical genealogy of Grendel and his mother that the poet has given us in lines 102–14.

   With that the old lord sprang to his feet
and praised God for Beowulf's pledge.
Then a bit and halter were brought for his horse
with the plaited mane. The wise king mounted   1400
the royal saddle and rode out in style
with a force of shield-bearers. The forest paths
were marked all over with the monster's tracks,
her trail on the ground wherever she had gone
across the dark moors, dragging away   1405
the body of that thane, Hrothgar's best
counselor and overseer of the country.
So the noble prince proceeded undismayed
up fells and screes, along narrow footpaths
and ways where they were forced into single file,   1410
ledges on cliffs above lairs of water-monsters.
He went in front with a few men,
good judges of the lie of the land,
and suddenly discovered the dismal wood,
mountain trees growing out at an angle   1415
above gray stones: the bloodshot water
surged underneath. It was a sore blow
to all of the Danes, friends of the Shieldings,
a hurt to each and every one
of that noble company when they came upon   1420
Aeschere's head at the foot of the cliff.
   Everybody gazed as the hot gore
kept wallowing up and an urgent war-horn
repeated its notes: the whole party
sat down to watch. The water was infested   1425
with all kinds of reptiles. There were writhing sea-dragons
and monsters slouching on slopes by the cliff,
serpents and wild things such as those that often
surface at dawn to roam the sail-road
and doom the voyage. Down they plunged,   1430
lashing in anger at the loud call
of the battle-bugle. An arrow from the bow
of the Geat chief got one of them
as he surged to the surface: the seasoned shaft
stuck deep in his flank and his freedom in the water   1435
got less and less. It was his last swim.
He was swiftly overwhelmed in the shallows,
prodded by barbed boar-spears,
cornered, beaten, pulled up on the bank,
a strange lake-birth, a loathsome catch   1440
men gazed at in awe.
                              Beowulf got ready,
donned his war-gear, indifferent to death;
his mighty, hand-forged, fine-webbed mail
would soon meet with the menace underwater.
It would keep the bone-cage of his body safe: 1445

no enemy's clasp could crush him in it,
no vicious armlock choke his life out.
To guard his head he had a glittering helmet
that was due to be muddied on the mere bottom
and blurred in the upswirl. It was of beaten gold,   1450
princely headgear hooped and hasped
by a weapon-smith who had worked wonders
in days gone by and adorned it with boar-shapes;
since then it had resisted every sword.
And another item lent by Unferth   1455
at that moment of need was of no small importance:
the brehon[7] handed him a hilted weapon,
a rare and ancient sword named Hrunting.
The iron blade with its ill-boding patterns
had been tempered in blood. It had never failed   1460
the hand of anyone who hefted it in battle,
anyone who had fought and faced the worst
in the gap of danger. This was not the first time
it had been called to perform heroic feats.
      When he lent that blade to the better swordsman,   1465
Unferth, the strong-built son of Ecglaf,
could hardly have remembered the ranting speech
he had made in his cups. He was not man enough
to face the turmoil of a fight under water
and the risk to his life. So there he lost   1470
fame and repute. It was different for the other
rigged out in his gear, ready to do battle.
      Beowulf, son of Ecgtheow, spoke:
"Wisest of kings, now that I have come
to the point of action, I ask you to recall   1475
what we said earlier: that you, son of Halfdane
and gold-friend to retainers, that you, if I should fall
and suffer death while serving your cause,
would act like a father to me afterward.
If this combat kills me, take care   1480
of my young company, my comrades in arms.
And be sure also, my beloved Hrothgar,
to send Hygelac the treasures I received.
Let the lord of the Geats gaze on that gold,
let Hrethel's son take note of it and see   1485
that I found a ring-giver of rare magnificence
and enjoyed the good of his generosity.
And Unferth is to have what I inherited:
to that far-famed man I bequeath my own
sharp-honed, wave-sheened wonder-blade.   1490
With Hrunting I shall gain glory or die."
      After these words, the prince of the Weather-Geats
was impatient to be away and plunged suddenly:

---

7. One of an ancient class of lawyers in Ireland [translator's note]. The word is used to translate
the Anglo-Saxon *thyle*.

without more ado, he dived into the heaving
depths of the lake. It was the best part of a day 1495
before he could see the solid bottom.

   Quickly the one who haunted those waters,
who had scavenged and gone her gluttonous rounds
for a hundred seasons, sensed a human
observing her outlandish lair from above. 1500
So she lunged and clutched and managed to catch him
in her brutal grip; but his body, for all that,
remained unscathed: the mesh of the chain-mail
saved him on the outside. Her savage talons
failed to rip the web of his war-shirt. 1505
Then once she touched bottom, that wolfish swimmer
carried the ring-mailed prince to her court
so that for all his courage he could never use
the weapons he carried; and a bewildering horde
came at him from the depths, droves of sea-beasts 1510
who attacked with tusks and tore at his chain-mail
in a ghastly onslaught. The gallant man
could see he had entered some hellish turn-hole
and yet the water there did not work against him
because the hall-roofing held off 1515
the force of the current; then he saw firelight,
a gleam and flare-up, a glimmer of brightness.

   The hero observed that swamp-thing from hell,
the tarn-hag[8] in all her terrible strength,
then heaved his war-sword and swung his arm: 1520
the decorated blade came down ringing
and singing on her head. But he soon found
his battle-torch extinguished; the shining blade
refused to bite. It spared her and failed
the man in his need. It had gone through many 1525
a hand-to-hand fight, had hewed the armor
and helmets of the doomed, but here at last
the fabulous powers of that heirloom failed.

   Hygelac's kinsman kept thinking about
his name and fame: he never lost heart. 1530
Then, in a fury, he flung his sword away.
The keen, inlaid, worm-loop-patterned steel
was hurled to the ground: he would have to rely
on the might of his arm. So must a man do
who intends to gain enduring glory 1535
in a combat. Life doesn't cost him a thought.
Then the prince of War-Geats, warming to this fight
with Grendel's mother, gripped her shoulder
and laid about him in a battle frenzy:
he pitched his killer opponent to the floor 1540
but she rose quickly and retaliated,
grappled him tightly in her grim embrace.

8. A "tarn" is a small lake.

The sure-footed fighter felt daunted,
the strongest of warriors stumbled and fell.
So she pounced upon him and pulled out   1545
a broad, whetted knife: now she would avenge
her only child. But the mesh of chain-mail
on Beowulf's shoulder shielded his life,
turned the edge and tip of the blade.
The son of Ecgtheow would have surely perished   1550
and the Geats lost their warrior under the wide earth
had the strong links and locks of his war-gear
not helped to save him: holy God
decided the victory. It was easy for the Lord,
the Ruler of Heaven, to redress the balance   1555
once Beowulf got back up on his feet.
    Then he saw a blade that boded well,
a sword in her armory, an ancient heirloom
from the days of the giants, an ideal weapon,
one that any warrior would envy,   1560
but so huge and heavy of itself
only Beowulf could wield it in a battle.
So the Shieldings' hero hard-pressed and enraged,
took a firm hold of the hilt and swung
the blade in an arc, a resolute blow   1565
that bit deep into her neck-bone
and severed it entirely, toppling the doomed
house of her flesh; she fell to the floor.
The sword dripped blood, the swordsman was elated.
    A light appeared and the place brightened   1570
the way the sky does when heaven's candle
is shining clearly. He inspected the vault:
with sword held high, its hilt raised
to guard and threaten, Hygelac's thane
scouted by the wall in Grendel's wake.   1575
Now the weapon was to prove its worth.
The warrior determined to take revenge
for every gross act Grendel had committed—
and not only for that one occasion
when he'd come to slaughter the sleeping troops,   1580
fifteen of Hrothgar's house-guards
surprised on their benches and ruthlessly devoured,
and as many again carried away,
a brutal plunder. Beowulf in his fury
now settled that score: he saw the monster   1585
in his resting place, war-weary and wrecked,
a lifeless corpse, a casualty
of the battle in Heorot. The body gaped
at the stroke dealt to it after death:
Beowulf cut the corpse's head off.   1590
    Immediately the counselors keeping a lookout
with Hrothgar, watching the lake water,
saw a heave-up and surge of waves

and blood in the backwash. They bowed gray heads,
spoke in their sage, experienced way   1595
about the good warrior, how they never again
expected to see that prince returning
in triumph to their king. It was clear to many
that the wolf of the deep had destroyed him forever.
        The ninth hour of the day arrived.   1600
The brave Shieldings abandoned the cliff-top
and the king went home; but sick at heart,
staring at the mere, the strangers held on.
They wished, without hope, to behold their lord,
Beowulf himself.
                    Meanwhile, the sword   1605
began to wilt into gory icicles
to slather and thaw. It was a wonderful thing,
the way it all melted as ice melts
when the Father eases the fetters off the frost
and unravels the water-ropes, He who wields power   1610
over time and tide: He is the true Lord.
        The Geat captain saw treasure in abundance
but carried no spoils from those quarters
except for the head and the inlaid hilt
embossed with jewels; its blade had melted   1615
and the scrollwork on it burned, so scalding was the blood
of the poisonous fiend who had perished there.
Then away he swam, the one who had survived
the fall of his enemies, flailing to the surface.
The wide water, the waves and pools,   1620
were no longer infested once the wandering fiend
let go of her life and this unreliable world.
        The seafarers' leader made for land,
resolutely swimming, delighted with his prize,
the mighty load he was lugging to the surface.   1625
His thanes advanced in a troop to meet him,
thanking God and taking great delight
in seeing their prince back safe and sound.
Quickly the hero's helmet and mail-shirt
were loosed and unlaced. The lake settled,   1630
clouds darkened above the bloodshot depths.
        With high hearts they headed away
along footpaths and trails through the fields,
roads that they knew, each of them wrestling
with the head they were carrying from the lakeside cliff,   1635
men kingly in their courage and capable
of difficult work. It was a task for four
to hoist Grendel's head on a spear
and bear it under strain to the bright hall.
But soon enough they neared the place,   1640
fourteen Geats in fine fettle,
striding across the outlying ground
in a delighted throng around their leader.

In he came then, the thanes' commander,
the arch-warrior, to address Hrothgar:
his courage was proven, his glory was secure.   1645
Grendel's head was hauled by the hair,
dragged across the floor where the people were drinking,
a horror for both queen and company to behold.
They stared in awe. It was an astonishing sight.   1650

[Another Celebration at Heorot]

Beowulf, son of Ecgtheow, spoke:
"So, son of Halfdane, prince of the Shieldings,
we are glad to bring this booty from the lake.
It is a token of triumph and we tender it to you.
I barely survived the battle under water.   1655
It was hard-fought, a desperate affair
that could have gone badly; if God had not helped me,
the outcome would have been quick and fatal.
Although Hrunting is hard-edged,
I could never bring it to bear in battle.   1660
But the Lord of Men allowed me to behold—
for He often helps the unbefriended—
an ancient sword shining on the wall,
a weapon made for giants, there for the wielding.
Then my moment came in the combat and I struck   1665
the dwellers in that den. Next thing the damascened[9]
sword blade melted; it bloated and it burned
in their rushing blood. I have wrested the hilt
from the enemies' hand, avenged the evil
done to the Danes; it is what was due.   1670
And this I pledge, O prince of the Shieldings:
you can sleep secure with your company of troops
in Heorot Hall. Never need you fear
for a single thane of your sept[1] or nation,
young warriors or old, that laying waste of life   1675
that you and your people endured of yore."
      Then the gold hilt was handed over
to the old lord, a relic from long ago
for the venerable ruler. That rare smithwork
was passed on to the prince of the Danes   1680
when those devils perished; once death removed
that murdering, guilt-steeped, God-cursed fiend,
eliminating his unholy life
and his mother's as well, it was willed to that king
who of all the lavish gift-lords of the north   1685
was the best regarded between the two seas.
      Hrothgar spoke; he examined the hilt,
that relic of old times. It was engraved all over

---

9. Ornamented with inlaid designs.
1. An Irish term meaning a clan or division of a tribe.

and showed how war first came into the world
and the flood destroyed the tribe of giants. 1690
They suffered a terrible severance from the Lord;
the Almighty made the waters rise,
drowned them in the deluge for retribution.
In pure gold inlay on the sword-guards
there were rune-markings correctly incised, 1695
stating and recording for whom the sword
had been first made and ornamented
with its scrollworked hilt. Then everyone hushed
as the son of Halfdane spoke this wisdom:
"A protector of his people, pledged to uphold 1700
truth and justice and to respect tradition,
is entitled to affirm that this man
was born to distinction. Beowulf, my friend,
your fame has gone far and wide,
you are known everywhere. In all things you are even-tempered, 1705
prudent and resolute. So I stand firm by the promise of friendship
we exchanged before. Forever you will be
your people's mainstay and your own warriors'
helping hand.
                    Heremod was different,
the way he behaved to Ecgwela's sons.[2] 1710
His rise in the world brought little joy
to the Danish people, only death and destruction.
He vented his rage on men he caroused with,
killed his own comrades, a pariah king
who cut himself off from his own kind, 1715
even though Almighty God had made him
eminent and powerful and marked him from the start
for a happy life. But a change happened,
he grew bloodthirsty, gave no more rings
to honor the Danes. He suffered in the end 1720
for having plagued his people for so long:
his life lost happiness.
                    So learn from this
and understand true values. I who tell you
have wintered into wisdom.
                    It is a great wonder
how Almighty God in His magnificence 1725
favors our race with rank and scope
and the gift of wisdom; His sway is wide.
Sometimes He allows the mind of a man
of distinguished birth to follow its bent,
grants him fulfillment and felicity on earth 1730
and forts to command in his own country.
He permits him to lord it in many lands
until the man in his unthinkingness

2. That is, the Danes. Ecgwela was evidently a former king of the Danes.

forgets that it will ever end for him.
He indulges his desires; illness and old age   1735
mean nothing to him; his mind is untroubled
by envy or malice or the thought of enemies
with their hate-honed swords. The whole world
conforms to his will, he is kept from the worst
until an element of overweening   1740
enters him and takes hold
while the soul's guard, its sentry, drowses,
grown too distracted. A killer stalks him,
an archer who draws a deadly bow.
And then the man is hit in the heart,   1745
the arrow flies beneath his defenses,
the devious promptings of the demon start.
His old possessions seem paltry to him now.
He covets and resents; dishonors custom
and bestows no gold; and because of good things   1750
that the Heavenly Powers gave him in the past
he ignores the shape of things to come.
Then finally the end arrives
when the body he was lent collapses and falls
prey to its death; ancestral possessions   1755
and the goods he hoarded are inherited by another
who lets them go with a liberal hand.
    "O flower of warriors, beware of that trap.
Choose, dear Beowulf, the better part,
eternal rewards. Do not give way to pride.   1760
For a brief while your strength is in bloom
but it fades quickly; and soon there will follow
illness or the sword to lay you low,
or a sudden fire or surge of water
or jabbing blade or javelin from the air   1765
or repellent age. Your piercing eye
will dim and darken; and death will arrive,
dear warrior, to sweep you away.
    "Just so I ruled the Ring-Danes' country
for fifty years, defended them in wartime   1770
with spear and sword against constant assaults
by many tribes: I came to believe
my enemies had faded from the face of the earth.
Still, what happened was a hard reversal
from bliss to grief. Grendel struck   1775
after lying in wait. He laid waste to the land
and from that moment my mind was in dread
of his depredations. So I praise God
in His heavenly glory that I lived to behold
this head dripping blood and that after such harrowing   1780
I can look upon it in triumph at last.
Take your place, then, with pride and pleasure,
and move to the feast. Tomorrow morning
our treasure will be shared and showered upon you."

The Geat was elated and gladly obeyed   1785
the old man's bidding; he sat on the bench.
And soon all was restored, the same as before.
Happiness came back, the hall was thronged,
and a banquet set forth; black night fell
and covered them in darkness.
       Then the company rose   1790
for the old campaigner: the gray-haired prince
was ready for bed. And a need for rest
came over the brave shield-bearing Geat.
He was a weary seafarer, far from home,
so immediately a house-guard guided him out,   1795
one whose office entailed looking after
whatever a thane on the road in those days
might need or require. It was noble courtesy.

[Beowulf Returns Home]

 That great heart rested. The hall towered,
gold-shingled and gabled, and the guest slept in it   1800
until the black raven with raucous glee
announced heaven's joy, and a hurry of brightness
overran the shadows. Warriors rose quickly,
impatient to be off: their own country
was beckoning the nobles; and the bold voyager   1805
longed to be aboard his distant boat.
Then that stalwart fighter ordered Hrunting
to be brought to Unferth, and bade Unferth
take the sword and thanked him for lending it.
He said he had found it a friend in battle   1810
and a powerful help; he put no blame
on the blade's cutting edge. He was a considerate man.
 And there the warriors stood in their war-gear,
eager to go, while their honored lord
approached the platform where the other sat.   1815
The undaunted hero addressed Hrothgar.
Beowulf, son of Ecgtheow, spoke:
"Now we who crossed the wide sea
have to inform you that we feel a desire
to return to Hygelac. Here we have been welcomed   1820
and thoroughly entertained. You have treated us well.
If there is any favor on earth I can perform
beyond deeds of arms I have done already,
anything that would merit your affections more,
I shall act, my lord, with alacrity.   1825
If ever I hear from across the ocean
that people on your borders are threatening battle
as attackers have done from time to time,
I shall land with a thousand thanes at my back
to help your cause. Hygelac may be young   1830

to rule a nation, but this much I know
about the king of the Geats: he will come to my aid
and want to support me by word and action
in your hour of need, when honor dictates
that I raise a hedge of spears around you.   1835
Then if Hrethric should think about traveling
as a king's son to the court of the Geats,
he will find many friends. Foreign places
yield more to one who is himself worth meeting."
    Hrothgar spoke and answered him: 1840
"The Lord in his wisdom sent you those words
and they came from the heart. I have never heard
so young a man make truer observations.
You are strong in body and mature in mind,
impressive in speech. If it should come to pass   1845
that Hrethel's descendant dies beneath a spear,
if deadly battle or the sword blade or disease
fells the prince who guards your people
and you are still alive, then I firmly believe
the seafaring Geats won't find a man   1850
worthier of acclaim as their king and defender
than you, if only you would undertake
the lordship of your homeland. My liking for you
deepens with time, dear Beowulf.
What you have done is to draw two peoples,   1855
the Geat nation and us neighboring Danes,
into shared peace and a pact of friendship
in spite of hatreds we have harbored in the past.
For as long as I rule this far-flung land
treasures will change hands and each side will treat   1860
the other with gifts; across the gannet's bath,
over the broad sea, whorled prows will bring
presents and tokens. I know your people
are beyond reproach in every respect,
steadfast in the old way with friend or foe."   1865
    Then the earls' defender furnished the hero
with twelve treasures and told him to set out,
sail with those gifts safely home
to the people he loved, but to return promptly.
And so the good and gray-haired Dane,   1870
that highborn king, kissed Beowulf
and embraced his neck, then broke down
in sudden tears. Two forebodings
disturbed him in his wisdom, but one was stronger:[3]
nevermore would they meet each other   1875
face to face. And such was his affection
that he could not help being overcome:
his fondness for the man was so deep-founded,

---

3. We are not told what the other foreboding is, but it is probably the old man's awareness of the imminence of his own death.

it warmed his heart and wound the heartstrings
tight in his breast.
              The embrace ended 1880
and Beowulf, glorious in his gold regalia,
stepped the green earth. Straining at anchor
and ready for boarding, his boat awaited him.
So they went on their journey, and Hrothgar's generosity
was praised repeatedly. He was a peerless king 1885
until old age sapped his strength and did him
mortal harm, as it has done so many.
    Down to the waves then, dressed in the web
of their chain-mail and war-shirts the young men marched
in high spirits. The coast-guard spied them, 1890
thanes setting forth, the same as before.
His salute this time from the top of the cliff
was far from unmannerly; he galloped to meet them
and as they took ship in their shining gear,
he said how welcome they would be in Geatland. 1895
Then the broad hull was beached on the sand
to be cargoed with treasure, horses and war-gear.
The curved prow motioned; the mast stood high
above Hrothgar's riches in the loaded hold.
    The guard who had watched the boat was given 1900
a sword with gold fittings, and in future days
that present would make him a respected man
at his place on the mead-bench.
                  Then the keel plunged
and shook in the sea; and they sailed from Denmark.
    Right away the mast was rigged with its sea-shawl; 1905
sail-ropes were tightened, timbers drummed
and stiff winds kept the wave-crosser
skimming ahead; as she heaved forward,
her foamy neck was fleet and buoyant,
a lapped prow loping over currents, 1910
until finally the Geats caught sight of coastline
and familiar cliffs. The keel reared up,
wind lifted it home, it hit on the land.
    The harbor guard came hurrying out
to the rolling water: he had watched the offing 1915
long and hard, on the lookout for those friends.
With the anchor cables, he moored their craft
right where it had beached, in case a backwash
might catch the hull and carry it away.
Then he ordered the prince's treasure-trove 1920
to be carried ashore. It was a short step
from there to where Hrethel's son and heir,
Hygelac the gold-giver, makes his home
on a secure cliff, in the company of retainers.
    The building was magnificent, the king majestic, 1925
ensconced in his hall; and although Hygd, his queen,
was young, a few short years at court,

her mind was thoughtful and her manners sure.
Haereth's daughter[4] behaved generously
and stinted nothing when she distributed   1930
bounty to the Geats.
               Great Queen Modthryth
perpetrated terrible wrongs.[5]
If any retainer ever made bold
to look her in the face, if an eye not her lord's[6]
stared at her directly during daylight,   1935
the outcome was sealed: he was kept bound,
in hand-tightened shackles, racked, tortured
until doom was pronounced—death by the sword,
slash of blade, blood-gush, and death-qualms
in an evil display. Even a queen   1940
outstanding in beauty must not overstep like that.
A queen should weave peace, not punish the innocent
with loss of life for imagined insults.
But Hemming's kinsman put a halt to her ways
and drinkers round the table had another tale: 1945
she was less of a bane to people's lives,
less cruel-minded, after she was married
to the brave Offa,[7] a bride arrayed
in her gold finery, given away
by a caring father, ferried to her young prince   1950
over dim seas. In days to come
she would grace the throne and grow famous
for her good deeds and conduct of life,
her high devotion to the hero king
who was the best king, it has been said,   1955
between the two seas or anywhere else
on the face of the earth. Offa was honored
far and wide for his generous ways,
his fighting spirit and his farseeing
defense of his homeland; from him there sprang Eomer,   1960
Garmund's grandson, kinsman of Hemming,[8]
his warriors' mainstay and master of the field.

   Heroic Beowulf and his band of men
crossed the wide strand, striding along
the sandy foreshore; the sun shone,   1965
the world's candle warmed them from the south
as they hastened to where, as they had heard,
the young king, Ongentheow's killer[9]

4. That is, Hygd.
5. A Danish queen whose wickedness is being used as a foil to Hygd.
6. Probably her father, although the Anglo-Saxon word can also refer to a husband.
7. A legendary king of the Angles, one of the Germanic peoples who invaded England and established a kingdom named Mercia in the north of the country prior to the composition of *Beowulf*. Hemming is evidently a forebear of the Angles.
8. Garmund is Offa's father, Eomer his son.
9. Hygelac, king of the Geats; he led the attack against the Swedes, although a Geat named Eofor actually killed Ongentheow. This is the first reference to the feud between the Geats and the Swedes (or Shylfings); see below, lines 2379–96, 2468–89, 2922–98.

and his people's protector, was dispensing rings
inside his bawn. Beowulf's return   1970
was reported to Hygelac as soon as possible,
news that the captain was now in the enclosure,
his battle-brother back from the fray
alive and well, walking to the hall.
Room was quickly made, on the king's orders,   1975
and the troops filed across the cleared floor.
    After Hygelac had offered greetings
to his loyal thane in a lofty speech,
he and his kinsman, that hale survivor,
sat face to face. Haereth's daughter[1]   1980
moved about with the mead-jug in her hand,
taking care of the company, filling the cups
that warriors held out. Then Hygelac began
to put courteous questions to his old comrade
in the high hall. He hankered to know   1985
every tale the Sea-Geats had to tell:
"How did you fare on your foreign voyage,
dear Beowulf, when you abruptly decided
to sail away across the salt water
and fight at Heorot? Did you help Hrothgar   1990
much in the end? Could you ease the prince
of his well-known troubles? Your undertaking
cast my spirits down, I dreaded the outcome
of your expedition and pleaded with you
long and hard to leave the killer be,   1995
let the South-Danes settle their own
blood-feud with Grendel. So God be thanked
I am granted this sight of you, safe and sound."
    Beowulf, son of Ecgtheow, spoke:
"What happened, Lord Hygelac, is hardly a secret   2000
any more among men in this world—
myself and Grendel coming to grips
on the very spot where he visited destruction
on the Victory-Shieldings and violated
life and limb, losses I avenged   2005
so no earthly offspring of Grendel's
need ever boast of that bout before dawn,
no matter how long the last of his evil
family survives.
                    When I first landed
I hastened to the ring-hall and saluted Hrothgar.   2010
Once he discovered why I had come,
the son of Halfdane sent me immediately
to sit with his own sons on the bench.
It was a happy gathering. In my whole life
I have never seen mead enjoyed more   2015
in any hall on earth. Sometimes the queen

1. That is, Hygd.

herself appeared, peace-pledge between nations,[2]
to hearten the young ones and hand out
a torque to a warrior, then take her place.
Sometimes Hrothgar's daughter distributed   2020
ale to older ranks, in order on the benches:
I heard the company call her Freawaru
as she made her rounds, presenting men
with the gem-studded bowl, young bride-to-be
to the gracious Ingeld,[3] in her gold-trimmed attire.   2025
The friend of the Shieldings favors her betrothal:
the guardian of the kingdom sees good in it
and hopes this woman will heal old wounds
and grievous feuds.
              But generally the spear
is prompt to retaliate when a prince is killed,   2030
no matter how admirable the bride may be.
  "Think how the Heatho-Bards are bound to feel,
their lord, Ingeld, and his loyal thanes,
when he walks in with that woman to the feast:
Danes are at the table, being entertained,   2035
honored guests in glittering regalia,
burnished ring-mail that was their hosts' birthright,
looted when the Heatho-Bards could no longer wield
their weapons in the shield-clash, when they went down
with their beloved comrades and forfeited their lives.   2040
Then an old spearman will speak while they are drinking,
having glimpsed some heirloom that brings alive
memories of the massacre; his mood will darken
and heart-stricken, in the stress of his emotion,
he will begin to test a young man's temper   2045
and stir up trouble, starting like this:
'Now, my friend, don't you recognize
your father's sword, his favorite weapon,
the one he wore when he went out in his war-mask
to face the Danes on that final day?   2050
After Withergeld[4] died and his men were doomed,
the Shieldings quickly claimed the field;
and now here's a son of one or other
of those same killers coming through our hall
overbearing us, mouthing boasts,   2055
and rigged in armor that by right is yours.'
And so he keeps on, recalling and accusing,
working things up with bitter words
until one of the lady's retainers lies

2. Wealhtheow, Hrothgar's queen, is called a "peace-pledge between nations" because kings attempted to end feuds by marrying their daughters to the sons of the kings of enemy nations. But as we have already seen in the case of the marriage of the Dane Hildeburh to the Jute Finn, and as we shall shortly learn again, such a strategy seems rarely to have worked.
3. King of the Heatho-Bards, whose father, Froda, was killed by the Danes.
4. A Heatho-Bard warrior.

spattered in blood, split open   2060
on his father's account.[5] The killer knows
the lie of the land and escapes with his life.
Then on both sides the oath-bound lords
will break the peace, a passionate hate
will build up in Ingeld, and love for his bride   2065
will falter in him as the feud rankles.
I therefore suspect the good faith of the Heatho-Bards,
the truth of their friendship and the trustworthiness
of their alliance with the Danes.

                   But now, my lord,
I shall carry on with my account of Grendel,   2070
the whole story of everything that happened
in the hand-to-hand fight.
                  After heaven's gem
had gone mildly to earth, that maddened spirit,
the terror of those twilights, came to attack us
where we stood guard, still safe inside the hall.   2075
There deadly violence came down on Hondscio[6]
and he fell as fate ordained, the first to perish,
rigged out for the combat. A comrade from our ranks
had come to grief in Grendel's maw:
he ate up the entire body.   2080
There was blood on his teeth, he was bloated and dangerous,
all roused up, yet still unready
to leave the hall empty-handed;
renowned for his might, he matched himself against me,
wildly reaching. He had this roomy pouch,[7]   2085
a strange accoutrement, intricately strung
and hung at the ready, a rare patchwork
of devilishly fitted dragon-skins.
I had done him no wrong, yet the raging demon
wanted to cram me and many another   2090
into this bag—but it was not to be
once I got to my feet in a blind fury.
It would take too long to tell how I repaid
the terror of the land for every life he took
and so won credit for you, my king,   2095
and for all your people. And although he got away
to enjoy life's sweetness for a while longer,
his right hand stayed behind him in Heorot,
evidence of his miserable overthrow
as he dived into murk on the mere bottom.   2100
    "I got lavish rewards from the lord of the Danes
for my part in the battle, beaten gold
and much else, once morning came

---

5. A Danish attendant to Freawaru, whose father killed a Heatho-Bard in the original battle; this action is envisioned as taking place at Ingeld's court after the marriage.

6. A Geat who was accompanying Beowulf; his name means "glove."

7. The Anglo-Saxon word translated as "pouch" literally means "glove."

and we took our places at the banquet table.
There was singing and excitement: an old reciter,   2105
a carrier of stories, recalled the early days.
At times some hero made the timbered harp
tremble with sweetness, or related true
and tragic happenings; at times the king
gave the proper turn to some fantastic tale,   2110
or a battle-scarred veteran, bowed with age,
would begin to remember the martial deeds
of his youth and prime and be overcome
as the past welled up in his wintry heart.
        "We were happy there the whole day long   2115
and enjoyed our time until another night
descended upon us. Then suddenly
the vehement mother avenged her son
and wreaked destruction. Death had robbed her,
Geats had slain Grendel, so his ghastly dam   2120
struck back and with bare-faced defiance
laid a man low. Thus life departed
from the sage Aeschere, an elder wise in counsel.
But afterward, on the morning following,
the Danes could not burn the dead body   2125
nor lay the remains of the man they loved
on his funeral pyre. She had fled with the corpse
and taken refuge beneath torrents on the mountain.
It was a hard blow for Hrothgar to bear,
harder than any he had undergone before.   2130
And so the heartsore king beseeched me
in your royal name to take my chances
underwater, to win glory
and prove my worth. He promised me rewards.
Hence, as is well known, I went to my encounter   2135
with the terror-monger at the bottom of the tarn.
For a while it was hand-to-hand between us,
then blood went curling along the currents
and I beheaded Grendel's mother in the hall
with a mighty sword. I barely managed   2140
to escape with my life; my time had not yet come.
But Halfdane's heir, the shelter of those earls,
again endowed me with gifts in abundance.
        "Thus the king acted with due custom.
I was paid and recompensed completely,   2145
given full measure and the freedom to choose
from Hrothgar's treasures by Hrothgar himself.
These, King Hygelac, I am happy to present
to you as gifts. It is still upon your grace
that all favor depends. I have few kinsmen   2150
who are close, my king, except for your kind self."
Then he ordered the boar-framed standard to be brought,
the battle-topping helmet, the mail-shirt gray as hoar-frost,
and the precious war-sword; and proceeded with his speech:

"When Hrothgar presented this war-gear to me   2155
he instructed me, my lord, to give you some account
of why it signifies his special favor.
He said it had belonged to his older brother,
King Heorogar, who had long kept it,
but that Heorogar had never bequeathed it   2160
to his son Heoroward, that worthy scion,
loyal as he was.
                Enjoy it well."
    I heard four horses were handed over next.
Beowulf bestowed four bay steeds
to go with the armor, swift gallopers,   2165
all alike. So ought a kinsman act,
instead of plotting and planning in secret
to bring people to grief, or conspiring to arrange
the death of comrades. The warrior king
was uncle to Beowulf and honored by his nephew: 2170
each was concerned for the other's good.
    I heard he presented Hygd with a gorget,
the priceless torque that the prince's daughter,
Wealhtheow, had given him; and three horses,
supple creatures brilliantly saddled.   2175
The bright necklace would be luminous on Hygd's breast.
    Thus Beowulf bore himself with valor;
he was formidable in battle yet behaved with honor
and took no advantage; never cut down
a comrade who was drunk, kept his temper   2180
and, warrior that he was, watched and controlled
his God-sent strength and his outstanding
natural powers. He had been poorly regarded
for a long time, was taken by the Geats
for less than he was worth: and their lord too   2185
had never much esteemed him in the mead-hall.
They firmly believed that he lacked force,
that the prince was a weakling; but presently
every affront to his deserving was reversed.
    The battle-famed king, bulwark of his earls,   2190
ordered a gold-chased heirloom of Hrethel's[8]
to be brought in; it was the best example
of a gem-studded sword in the Geat treasury.
This he laid on Beowulf's lap
and then rewarded him with land as well,   2195
seven thousand hides;[9] and a hall and a throne.
Both owned land by birth in that country,
ancestral grounds; but the greater right
and sway were inherited by the higher born.

8. Hygelac's father and, through his daugh-   to be sufficient land to support a peasant and
ter, Beowulf's grandfather.   his family.
9. A "hide" varied in size, but was considered

[The Dragon Wakes]

A lot was to happen in later days   2200
in the fury of battle. Hygelac fell
and the shelter of Heardred's shield proved useless
against the fierce aggression of the Shylfings:[1]
ruthless swordsmen, seasoned campaigners,
they came against him and his conquering nation,   2205
and with cruel force cut him down
so that afterwards
                the wide kingdom
reverted to Beowulf. He ruled it well
for fifty winters, grew old and wise
as warden of the land
                   until one began   2210
to dominate the dark, a dragon on the prowl
from the steep vaults of a stone-roofed barrow[2]
where he guarded a hoard; there was a hidden passage,
unknown to men, but someone managed[3]
to enter by it and interfere   2215
with the heathen trove. He had handled and removed
a gem-studded goblet; it gained him nothing,
though with a thief's wiles he had outwitted
the sleeping dragon. That drove him into rage,
as the people of that country would soon discover.   2220
   The intruder who broached the dragon's treasure
and moved him to wrath had never meant to.
It was desperation on the part of a slave
fleeing the heavy hand of some master,
guilt-ridden and on the run,   2225
going to ground. But he soon began
to shake with terror; . . . . . . in shock
the wretch . . . .
           . . . . panicked and ran
away with the precious   2230
metalwork. There were many other
heirlooms heaped inside the earth-house,
because long ago, with deliberate care,
somebody now forgotten
had buried the riches of a highborn race   2235
in this ancient cache. Death had come
and taken them all in times gone by
and the only one left to tell their tale,
the last of their line, could look forward to nothing
but the same fate for himself: he foresaw that his joy   2240
in the treasure would be brief.

---

1. Hygelac died in the raid against the Franks (see p. 152, n. 4); Heardred died in the long feud against the Swedes or Shylfings (see p. 168, n. 9).
2. A burial mound.

3. In the single manuscript of *Beowulf*, the page containing lines 2215–31 is badly damaged, and the translation is therefore conjectural. The ellipses of lines 2227–30 indicate lines that cannot be reconstructed at all.

A newly constructed
barrow stood waiting, on a wide headland
close to the waves, its entryway secured.
Into it the keeper of the hoard had carried
all the goods and golden ware   2245
worth preserving. His words were few:
"Now, earth, hold what earls once held
and heroes can no more; it was mined from you first
by honorable men. My own people
have been ruined in war; one by one   2250
they went down to death, looked their last
on sweet life in the hall. I am left with nobody
to bear a sword or to burnish plated goblets,
put a sheen on the cup. The companies have departed.
The hard helmet, hasped with gold,   2255
will be stripped of its hoops; and the helmet-shiner
who should polish the metal of the war-mask sleeps;
the coat of mail that came through all fights,
through shield-collapse and cut of sword,
decays with the warrior. Nor may webbed mail   2260
range far and wide on the warlord's back
beside his mustered troops. No trembling harp,
no tuned timber, no tumbling hawk
swerving through the hall, no swift horse
pawing the courtyard. Pillage and slaughter   2265
have emptied the earth of entire peoples."
And so he mourned as he moved about the world,
deserted and alone, lamenting his unhappiness
day and night, until death's flood
brimmed up in his heart.   2270
                          Then an old harrower of the dark
happened to find the hoard open,
the burning one who hunts out barrows,
the slick-skinned dragon, threatening the night sky
with streamers of fire. People on the farms
are in dread of him. He is driven to hunt out   2275
hoards under ground, to guard heathen gold
through age-long vigils, though to little avail.
For three centuries, this scourge of the people
had stood guard on that stoutly protected
underground treasury, until the intruder   2280
unleashed its fury; he hurried to his lord
with the gold-plated cup and made his plea
to be reinstated. Then the vault was rifled,
the ring-hoard robbed, and the wretched man
had his request granted. His master gazed   2285
on that find from the past for the first time.
     When the dragon awoke, trouble flared again.
He rippled down the rock, writhing with anger
when he saw the footprints of the prowler who had stolen
too close to his dreaming head.   2290

So may a man not marked by fate
easily escape exile and woe
by the grace of God.
                    The hoard-guardian
scorched the ground as he scoured and hunted
for the trespasser who had troubled his sleep.   2295
Hot and savage, he kept circling and circling
the outside of the mound. No man appeared
in that desert waste, but he worked himself up
by imagining battle; then back in he'd go
in search of the cup, only to discover   2300
signs that someone had stumbled upon
the golden treasures. So the guardian of the mound,
the hoard-watcher, waited for the gloaming
with fierce impatience; his pent-up fury
at the loss of the vessel made him long to hit back   2305
and lash out in flames. Then, to his delight,
the day waned and he could wait no longer
behind the wall, but hurtled forth
in a fiery blaze. The first to suffer
were the people on the land, but before long   2310
it was their treasure-giver who would come to grief.
    The dragon began to belch out flames
and burn bright homesteads; there was a hot glow
that scared everyone, for the vile sky-winger
would leave nothing alive in his wake.   2315
Everywhere the havoc he wrought was in evidence.
Far and near, the Geat nation
bore the brunt of his brutal assaults
and virulent hate. Then back to the hoard
he would dart before daybreak, to hide in his den.   2320
He had swinged[4] the land, swathed it in flame,
in fire and burning, and now he felt secure
in the vaults of his barrow; but his trust was unavailing.
    Then Beowulf was given bad news,
the hard truth: his own home,   2325
the best of buildings, had been burned to a cinder,
the throne-room of the Geats. It threw the hero
into deep anguish and darkened his mood:
the wise man thought he must have thwarted
ancient ordinance of the eternal Lord,   2330
broken His commandment. His mind was in turmoil,
unaccustomed anxiety and gloom
confused his brain; the fire-dragon
had razed the coastal region and reduced
forts and earthworks to dust and ashes,   2335
so the war-king planned and plotted his revenge.
The warriors' protector, prince of the hall-troop,
ordered a marvelous all-iron shield

---

4. That is, singed, scorched.

from his smithy works. He well knew
that linden boards would let him down   2340
and timber burn. After many trials,
he was destined to face the end of his days,
in this mortal world, as was the dragon,
for all his long leasehold on the treasure.

    Yet the prince of the rings was too proud   2345
to line up with a large army
against the sky-plague. He had scant regard
for the dragon as a threat, no dread at all
of its courage or strength, for he had kept going
often in the past, through perils and ordeals   2350
of every sort, after he had purged
Hrothgar's hall, triumphed in Heorot
and beaten Grendel. He outgrappled the monster
and his evil kin.

                        One of his cruelest
hand-to-hand encounters had happened   2355
when Hygelac, king of the Geats, was killed
in Friesland: the people's friend and lord,
Hrethel's son, slaked a sword blade's
thirst for blood. But Beowulf's prodigious
gifts as a swimmer guaranteed his safety: 2360
he arrived at the shore, shouldering thirty
battle-dresses, the booty he had won.
There was little for the Hetware[5] to be happy about
as they shielded their faces and fighting on the ground
began in earnest. With Beowulf against them,   2365
few could hope to return home.

    Across the wide sea, desolate and alone,
the son of Ecgtheow swam back to his people.
There Hygd offered him throne and authority
as lord of the ring-hoard: with Hygelac dead,   2370
she had no belief in her son's ability
to defend their homeland against foreign invaders.
Yet there was no way the weakened nation
could get Beowulf to give in and agree
to be elevated over Heardred as his lord   2375
or to undertake the office of kingship.
But he did provide support for the prince,
honored and minded him until he matured
as the ruler of Geatland.

                        Then over sea-roads
exiles arrived, sons of Ohthere.[6]   2380
They had rebelled against the best of all

5. A Frankish tribe.
6. King of the Swedes or Shylfings; after his
death his sons, Eanmund and Eadgils, were
driven out by their uncle Onela. They were
taken in by Heardred, Hygelac's son, who was
then king of the Geats, who was then in turn
attacked and killed (along with Eanmund) by
Onela. At this point Beowulf became king of
the Geats and supported Eadgils in his successful attack on Onela.

the sea-kings in Sweden, the one who held sway
in the Shylfing nation, their renowned prince,
lord of the mead-hall. That marked the end
for Hygelac's son: his hospitality   2385
was mortally rewarded with wounds from a sword.
Heardred lay slaughtered and Onela returned
to the land of Sweden, leaving Beowulf
to ascend the throne, to sit in majesty
and rule over the Geats. He was a good king.   2390
    In days to come, he contrived to avenge
the fall of his prince; he befriended Eadgils
when Eadgils was friendless, aiding his cause
with weapons and warriors over the wide sea,
sending him men. The feud was settled   2395
on a comfortless campaign when he killed Onela.
    And so the son of Ecgtheow had survived
every extreme, excelling himself
in daring and in danger, until the day arrived
when he had to come face to face with the dragon.   2400
The lord of the Geats took eleven comrades
and went in a rage to reconnoiter.
By then he had discovered the cause of the affliction
being visited on the people. The precious cup
had come to him from the hand of the finder,   2405
the one who had started all this strife
and was now added as a thirteenth to their number.
They press-ganged and compelled this poor creature
to be their guide. Against his will
he led them to the earth-vault he alone knew,   2410
an underground barrow near the sea-billows
and heaving waves, heaped inside
with exquisite metalwork. The one who stood guard
was dangerous and watchful, warden of the trove
buried under earth: no easy bargain   2415
would be made in that place by any man.
    The veteran king sat down on the cliff-top.
He wished good luck to the Geats who had shared
his hearth and his gold. He was sad at heart,
unsettled yet ready, sensing his death.   2420
His fate hovered near, unknowable but certain:
it would soon claim his coffered soul,
part life from limb. Before long
the prince's spirit would spin free from his body.
    Beowulf, son of Ecgtheow, spoke: 2425
"Many a skirmish I survived when I was young
and many times of war: I remember them well.
At seven, I was fostered out by my father,
left in the charge of my people's lord.
King Hrethel kept me and took care of me,   2430
was openhanded, behaved like a kinsman.
While I was his ward, he treated me no worse

as a wean[7] about the place than one of his own boys,
Herebeald and Haethcyn, or my own Hygelac.
For the eldest, Herebeald, an unexpected   2435
deathbed was laid out, through a brother's doing,
when Haethcyn bent his horn-tipped bow
and loosed the arrow that destroyed his life.
He shot wide and buried a shaft
in the flesh and blood of his own brother.   2440
That offense was beyond redress, a wrongfooting
of the heart's affections; for who could avenge
the prince's life or pay his death-price?
It was like the misery felt by an old man
who has lived to see his son's body   2445
swing on the gallows. He begins to keen
and weep for his boy, watching the raven
gloat where he hangs: he can be of no help.
The wisdom of age is worthless to him.
Morning after morning, he wakes to remember   2450
that his child is gone; he has no interest
in living on until another heir
is born in the hall, now that his first-born
has entered death's dominion forever.
He gazes sorrowfully at his son's dwelling,   2455
the banquet hall bereft of all delight,
the windswept hearthstone; the horsemen are sleeping,
the warriors under ground; what was is no more.
No tunes from the harp, no cheer raised in the yard.
Alone with his longing, he lies down on his bed   2460
and sings a lament; everything seems too large,
the steadings and the fields.
                                Such was the feeling
of loss endured by the lord of the Geats
after Herebeald's death. He was helplessly placed
to set to rights the wrong committed,   2465
could not punish the killer in accordance with the law
of the blood-feud, although he felt no love for him.
Heartsore, wearied, he turned away
from life's joys, chose God's light
and departed, leaving buildings and lands   2470
to his sons, as a man of substance will.
    "Then over the wide sea Swedes and Geats
battled and feuded and fought without quarter.
Hostilities broke out when Hrethel died.
Ongentheow's sons[8] were unrelenting,   2475

---

7. A young child [translator's note]; a Northern Irish word.
8. Ohthere and Onela, who attacked the Geats
and killed Haethcyn; Haethcyn was then
avenged by his brother Hygelac, whose attack on
the Swedes resulted in the death of Ongentheow

at the hands of the Geat Eofor (described below
in lines 2922–98). These events took place
before those of lines 2379–96, which describe
the Geats' role in the struggle between Onela
and Ohthere's two sons after Ongentheow's
death.

refusing to make peace, campaigning violently
from coast to coast, constantly setting up
terrible ambushes around Hreosnahill.⁹
My own kith and kin avenged
these evil events, as everybody knows,   2480
but the price was high: one of them paid
with his life. Haethcyn, lord of the Geats,
met his fate there and fell in the battle.
Then, as I have heard, Hygelac's sword
was raised in the morning against Ongentheow,   2485
his brother's killer. When Eofor cleft
the old Swede's helmet, halved it open,
he fell, death-pale: his feud-calloused hand
could not stave off the fatal stroke.
    "The treasures that Hygelac lavished on me   2490
I paid for when I fought, as fortune allowed me,
with my glittering sword. He gave me land
and the security land brings, so he had no call
to go looking for some lesser champion,
some mercenary from among the Gifthas¹   2495
or the Spear-Danes or the men of Sweden.
I marched ahead of him, always there
at the front of the line; and I shall fight like that
for as long as I live, as long as this sword
shall last, which has stood me in good stead   2500
late and soon, ever since I killed
Dayraven the Frank in front of the two armies.
He brought back no looted breastplate
to the Frisian king but fell in battle,
their standard-bearer, highborn and brave.   2505
No sword blade sent him to his death:
my bare hands stilled his heartbeats
and wrecked the bone-house. Now blade and hand,
sword and sword-stroke, will assay the hoard."

[Beowulf Attacks the Dragon]

    Beowulf spoke, made a formal boast   2510
for the last time: "I risked my life
often when I was young. Now I am old,
but as king of the people I shall pursue this fight
for the glory of winning, if the evil one will only
abandon his earth-fort and face me in the open."   2515
    Then he addressed each dear companion
one final time, those fighters in their helmets,
resolute and highborn: "I would rather not
use a weapon if I knew another way

9. The place of the battle can be translated as   1. A tribe related to the Goths.
Sorrow Hill.

to grapple with the dragon and make good my boast   2520
as I did against Grendel in days gone by.
But I shall be meeting molten venom
in the fire he breathes, so I go forth
in mail-shirt and shield. I won't shift a foot
when I meet the cave-guard: what occurs on the wall   2525
between the two of us will turn out as fate,
overseer of men, decides. I am resolved.
I scorn further words against this sky-borne foe.
    "Men-at-arms, remain here on the barrow,
safe in your armor, to see which one of us   2530
is better in the end at bearing wounds
in a deadly fray. This fight is not yours,
nor is it up to any man except me
to measure his strength against the monster
or to prove his worth. I shall win the gold   2535
by my courage, or else mortal combat,
doom of battle, will bear your lord away."
    Then he drew himself up beside his shield.
The fabled warrior in his war-shirt and helmet
trusted in his own strength entirely   2540
and went under the crag. No coward path.
    Hard by the rock-face that hale veteran,
a good man who had gone repeatedly
into combat and danger and come through,
saw a stone arch and a gushing stream   2545
that burst from the barrow, blazing and wafting
a deadly heat. It would be hard to survive
unscathed near the hoard, to hold firm
against the dragon in those flaming depths.
Then he gave a shout. The lord of the Geats   2550
unburdened his breast and broke out
in a storm of anger. Under gray stone
his voice challenged and resounded clearly.
Hate was ignited. The hoard-guard recognized
a human voice, the time was over   2555
for peace and parleying. Pouring forth
in a hot battle-fume, the breath of the monster
burst from the rock. There was a rumble under ground.
Down there in the barrow, Beowulf the warrior
lifted his shield: the outlandish thing   2560
writhed and convulsed and viciously
turned on the king, whose keen-edged sword,
an heirloom inherited by ancient right,
was already in his hand. Roused to a fury,
each antagonist struck terror in the other.   2565
Unyielding, the lord of his people loomed
by his tall shield, sure of his ground,
while the serpent looped and unleashed itself.
Swaddled in flames, it came gliding and flexing
and racing toward its fate. Yet his shield defended   2570

the renowned leader's life and limb
for a shorter time than he meant it to:
that final day was the first time
when Beowulf fought and fate denied him
glory in battle. So the king of the Geats   2575
raised his hand and struck hard
at the enameled scales, but scarcely cut through:
the blade flashed and slashed yet the blow
was far less powerful than the hard-pressed king
had need of at that moment. The mound-keeper   2580
went into a spasm and spouted deadly flames:
when he felt the stroke, battle-fire
billowed and spewed. Beowulf was foiled
of a glorious victory. The glittering sword,
infallible before that day,   2585
failed when he unsheathed it, as it never should have.
For the son of Ecgtheow, it was no easy thing
to have to give ground like that and go
unwillingly to inhabit another home
in a place beyond; so every man must yield   2590
the leasehold of his days.
                        Before long
the fierce contenders clashed again.
The hoard-guard took heart, inhaled and swelled up
and got a new wind; he who had once ruled
was furled in fire and had to face the worst.   2595
No help or backing was to be had then
from his highborn comrades; that hand-picked troop
broke ranks and ran for their lives
to the safety of the wood. But within one heart
sorrow welled up: in a man of worth   2600
the claims of kinship cannot be denied.
    His name was Wiglaf, a son of Weohstan's,
a well-regarded Shylfing warrior
related to Aelfhere.[2] When he saw his lord
tormented by the heat of his scalding helmet,   2605
he remembered the bountiful gifts bestowed on him,
how well he lived among the Waegmundings,
the freehold he inherited from his father[3] before him.
He could not hold back: one hand brandished
the yellow-timbered shield, the other drew his sword— 2610
an ancient blade that was said to have belonged
to Eanmund, the son of Ohthere, the one
Weohstan had slain when he was an exile without friends.

2. Wiglaf is, like Beowulf, a member of the clan of the Waegmundings (see lines 2813–14), although both consider themselves Geats as well. See p. 132, n. 2. Nothing is known of Aelfhere. 3. Wiglaf's father is Weohstan, who, as we learn shortly, was the man who killed Eanmund, Ohthere's son, when he had taken refuge among the Geats (lines 2379–84). How Wiglaf then became a Geat is not clear, although it may have been when Beowulf helped Eanmund's brother Eadgils avenge himself on Onela, who had usurped the throne of the Swedes; Eadgils then became king.

He carried the arms to the victim's kinfolk,
the burnished helmet, the webbed chain-mail   2615
and that relic of the giants. But Onela returned
the weapons to him, rewarded Weohstan
with Eanmund's war-gear. He ignored the blood-feud,
the fact that Eanmund was his brother's son.[4]
Weohstan kept that war-gear for a lifetime,   2620
the sword and the mail-shirt, until it was the son's turn
to follow his father and perform his part.
Then, in old age, at the end of his days
among the Weather-Geats, he bequeathed to Wiglaf
innumerable weapons.

               And now the youth   2625
was to enter the line of battle with his lord,
his first time to be tested as a fighter.
His spirit did not break and the ancestral blade
would keep its edge, as the dragon discovered
as soon as they came together in the combat.   2630

    Sad at heart, addressing his companions,
Wiglaf spoke wise and fluent words:
"I remember that time when mead was flowing,
how we pledged loyalty to our lord in the hall,
promised our ring-giver we would be worth our price,   2635
make good the gift of the war-gear,
those swords and helmets, as and when
his need required it. He picked us out
from the army deliberately, honored us and judged us
fit for this action, made me these lavish gifts—   2640
and all because he considered us the best
of his arms-bearing thanes. And now, although
he wanted this challenge to be one he'd face
by himself alone—the shepherd of our land,
a man unequaled in the quest for glory   2645
and a name for daring—now the day has come
when this lord we serve needs sound men
to give him their support. Let us go to him,
help our leader through the hot flame
and dread of the fire. As God is my witness,   2650
I would rather my body were robed in the same
burning blaze as my gold-giver's body
than go back home bearing arms.
That is unthinkable, unless we have first
slain the foe and defended the life   2655
of the prince of the Weather-Geats. I well know
the things he has done for us deserve better.
Should he alone be left exposed
to fall in battle? We must bond together,
shield and helmet, mail-shirt and sword."   2660

4. That is, Onela ignored the fact that Weohstan had killed his nephew Eanmund since he in fact wanted Eanmund dead.

Then he waded the dangerous reek and went
under arms to his lord, saying only:
"Go on, dear Beowulf, do everything
you said you would when you were still young
and vowed you would never let your name and fame   2665
be dimmed while you lived. Your deeds are famous,
so stay resolute, my lord, defend your life now
with the whole of your strength. I shall stand by you."

   After those words, a wildness rose
in the dragon again and drove it to attack,   2670
heaving up fire, hunting for enemies,
the humans it loathed. Flames lapped the shield,
charred it to the boss, and the body armor
on the young warrior was useless to him.
But Wiglaf did well under the wide rim   2675
Beowulf shared with him once his own had shattered
in sparks and ashes.
                         Inspired again
by the thought of glory, the war-king threw
his whole strength behind a sword stroke
and connected with the skull. And Naegling snapped.   2680
Beowulf's ancient iron-gray sword
let him down in the fight. It was never his fortune
to be helped in combat by the cutting edge
of weapons made of iron. When he wielded a sword,
no matter how blooded and hard-edged the blade,   2685
his hand was too strong, the stroke he dealt
(I have heard) would ruin it. He could reap no advantage.

   Then the bane of that people, the fire-breathing dragon,
was mad to attack for a third time.
When a chance came, he caught the hero   2690
in a rush of flame and clamped sharp fangs
into his neck. Beowulf's body
ran wet with his life-blood: it came welling out.

   Next thing, they say, the noble son of Weohstan
saw the king in danger at his side   2695
and displayed his inborn bravery and strength.
He left the head alone,[5] but his fighting hand
was burned when he came to his kinsman's aid.
He lunged at the enemy lower down
so that his decorated sword sank into its belly   2700
and the flames grew weaker.
                       Once again the king
gathered his strength and drew a stabbing knife
he carried on his belt, sharpened for battle.
He stuck it deep in the dragon's flank.
Beowulf dealt it a deadly wound.   2705
They had killed the enemy, courage quelled his life;
that pair of kinsmen, partners in nobility,

5. That is, the dragon's flame-breathing head.

had destroyed the foe. So every man should act,
be at hand when needed; but now, for the king,
this would be the last of his many labors   2710
and triumphs in the world.
                            Then the wound
dealt by the ground-burner earlier began
to scald and swell; Beowulf discovered
deadly poison suppurating inside him,
surges of nausea, and so, in his wisdom,   2715
the prince realized his state and struggled
toward a seat on the rampart. He steadied his gaze
on those gigantic stones, saw how the earthwork
was braced with arches built over columns.
And now that thane unequaled for goodness   2720
with his own hands washed his lord's wounds,
swabbed the weary prince with water,
bathed him clean, unbuckled his helmet.
   Beowulf spoke: in spite of his wounds,
mortal wounds, he still spoke   2725
for he well knew his days in the world
had been lived out to the end—his allotted time
was drawing to a close, death was very near.
   "Now is the time when I would have wanted
to bestow this armor on my own son,   2730
had it been my fortune to have fathered an heir
and live on in his flesh. For fifty years
I ruled this nation. No king
of any neighboring clan would dare
face me with troops, none had the power   2735
to intimidate me. I took what came,
cared for and stood by things in my keeping,
never fomented quarrels, never
swore to a lie. All this consoles me,
doomed as I am and sickening for death;   2740
because of my right ways, the Ruler of mankind
need never blame me when the breath leaves my body
for murder of kinsmen. Go now quickly,
dearest Wiglaf, under the gray stone
where the dragon is laid out, lost to his treasure;   2745
hurry to feast your eyes on the hoard.
Away you go: I want to examine
that ancient gold, gaze my fill
on those garnered jewels; my going will be easier
for having seen the treasure, a less troubled letting-go   2750
of the life and lordship I have long maintained."
   And so, I have heard, the son of Weohstan
quickly obeyed the command of his languishing
war-weary lord; he went in his chain-mail
under the rock-piled roof of the barrow,   2755
exulting in his triumph, and saw beyond the seat
a treasure-trove of astonishing richness,

wall-hangings that were a wonder to behold,
glittering gold spread across the ground,
the old dawn-scorching serpent's den   2760
packed with goblets and vessels from the past,
tarnished and corroding. Rusty helmets
all eaten away. Armbands everywhere,
artfully wrought. How easily treasure
buried in the ground, gold hidden   2765
however skillfully, can escape from any man!
   And he saw too a standard, entirely of gold,
hanging high over the hoard,
a masterpiece of filigree; it glowed with light
so he could make out the ground at his feet   2770
and inspect the valuables. Of the dragon there was no
remaining sign: the sword had dispatched him.
Then, the story goes, a certain man[6]
plundered the hoard in that immemorial howe,[7]
filled his arms with flagons and plates,   2775
anything he wanted; and took the standard also,
most brilliant of banners.
                              Already the blade
of the old king's sharp killing-sword
had done its worst: the one who had for long
minded the hoard, hovering over gold,   2780
unleashing fire, surging forth
midnight after midnight, had been mown down.
   Wiglaf went quickly, keen to get back,
excited by the treasure. Anxiety weighed
on his brave heart—he was hoping he would find   2785
the leader of the Geats alive where he had left him
helpless, earlier, on the open ground.
   So he came to the place, carrying the treasure
and found his lord bleeding profusely,
his life at an end; again he began   2790
to swab his body. The beginnings of an utterance
broke out from the king's breast-cage.
The old lord gazed sadly at the gold.
   "To the everlasting Lord of all,
to the King of Glory, I give thanks   2795
that I behold this treasure here in front of me,
that I have been allowed to leave my people
so well endowed on the day I die.
Now that I have bartered my last breath
to own this fortune, it is up to you   2800
to look after their needs. I can hold out no longer.
Order my troop to construct a barrow
on a headland on the coast, after my pyre has cooled.
It will loom on the horizon at Hronesness[8]

6. That is, Wiglaf.   8. The name means "Whaleness."
7. An Irish word for dwelling.

and be a reminder among my people— 2805
so that in coming times crews under sail
will call it Beowulf's Barrow, as they steer
ships across the wide and shrouded waters."

Then the king in his great-heartedness unclasped
the collar of gold from his neck and gave it 2810
to the young thane, telling him to use
it and the war-shirt and gilded helmet well.
"You are the last of us, the only one left
of the Waegmundings. Fate swept us away,
sent my whole brave highborn clan 2815
to their final doom. Now I must follow them."

That was the warrior's last word.
He had no more to confide. The furious heat
of the pyre would assail him. His soul fled from his breast
to its destined place among the steadfast ones. 2820

[Beowulf's Funeral]

It was hard then on the young hero,
having to watch the one he held so dear
there on the ground, going through
his death agony. The dragon from underearth,
his nightmarish destroyer, lay destroyed as well, 2825
utterly without life. No longer would his snakefolds
ply themselves to safeguard hidden gold.
Hard-edged blades, hammered out
and keenly filed, had finished him
so that the sky-roamer lay there rigid, 2830
brought low beside the treasure-lodge.

Never again would he glitter and glide
and show himself off in midnight air,
exulting in his riches: he fell to earth
through the battle-strength in Beowulf's arm. 2835
There were few, indeed, as far as I have heard,
big and brave as they may have been,
few who would have held out if they had had to face
the outpourings of that poison-breather
or gone foraging on the ring-hall floor 2840
and found the deep barrow-dweller
on guard and awake.
                        The treasure had been won,
bought and paid for by Beowulf's death.
Both had reached the end of the road
through the life they had been lent.
                            Before long 2845
the battle-dodgers abandoned the wood,
the ones who had let down their lord earlier,
the tail-turners, ten of them together.
When he needed them most, they had made off.

Now they were ashamed and came behind shields,   2850
in their battle-outfits, to where the old man lay.
They watched Wiglaf, sitting worn out,
a comrade shoulder to shoulder with his lord,
trying in vain to bring him round with water.
Much as he wanted to, there was no way   2855
he could preserve his lord's life on earth
or alter in the least the Almighty's will.
What God judged right would rule what happened
to every man, as it does to this day.
  Then a stern rebuke was bound to come   2860
from the young warrior to the ones who had been cowards.
Wiglaf, son of Weohstan, spoke
disdainfully and in disappointment:
"Anyone ready to admit the truth
will surely realize that the lord of men   2865
who showered you with gifts and gave you the armor
you are standing in—when he would distribute
helmets and mail-shirts to men on the mead-benches,
a prince treating his thanes in hall
to the best he could find, far or near—   2870
was throwing weapons uselessly away.
It would be a sad waste when the war broke out.
Beowulf had little cause to brag
about his armed guard; yet God who ordains
who wins or loses allowed him to strike   2875
with his own blade when bravery was needed.
There was little I could do to protect his life
in the heat of the fray, but I found new strength
welling up when I went to help him.
Then my sword connected and the deadly assaults   2880
of our foe grew weaker, the fire coursed
less strongly from his head. But when the worst happened
too few rallied around the prince.
  "So it is good-bye now to all you know and love
on your home ground, the open-handedness,   2885
the giving of war-swords. Every one of you
with freeholds of land, our whole nation,
will be dispossessed, once princes from beyond
get tidings of how you turned and fled
and disgraced yourselves. A warrior will sooner   2890
die than live a life of shame."
  Then he ordered the outcome of the fight to be reported
to those camped on the ridge, that crowd of retainers
who had sat all morning, sad at heart,
shield-bearers wondering about   2895
the man they loved: would this day be his last
or would he return? He told the truth
and did not balk, the rider who bore
news to the cliff-top. He addressed them all:
"Now the people's pride and love,   2900

the lord of the Geats, is laid on his deathbed,
brought down by the dragon's attack.
Beside him lies the bane of his life,
dead from knife-wounds. There was no way
Beowulf could manage to get the better   2905
of the monster with his sword. Wiglaf sits
at Beowulf's side, the son of Weohstan,
the living warrior watching by the dead,
keeping weary vigil, holding a wake
for the loved and the loathed.
                     Now war is looming   2910
over our nation, soon it will be known
to Franks and Frisians, far and wide,
that the king is gone. Hostility has been great
among the Franks since Hygelac sailed forth
at the head of a war-fleet into Friesland: 2915
there the Hetware harried and attacked
and overwhelmed him with great odds.
The leader in his war-gear was laid low,
fell among followers: that lord did not favor
his company with spoils. The Merovingian king   2920
has been an enemy to us ever since.
   "Nor do I expect peace or pact-keeping
of any sort from the Swedes. Remember:
at Ravenswood, Ongentheow
slaughtered Haethcyn, Hrethel's son,   2925
when the Geat people in their arrogance
first attacked the fierce Shylfings.
The return blow was quickly struck
by Ohthere's father.[9] Old and terrible,
he felled the sea-king and saved his own   2930
aged wife, the mother of Onela
and of Ohthere, bereft of her gold rings.
Then he kept hard on the heels of the foe
and drove them, leaderless, lucky to get away
in a desperate rout into Ravenswood.   2935
His army surrounded the weary remnant
where they nursed their wounds; all through the night
he howled threats at those huddled survivors,
promised to axe their bodies open
when dawn broke, dangle them from gallows   2940
to feed the birds. But at first light
when their spirits were lowest, relief arrived.
They heard the sound of Hygelac's horn,
his trumpet calling as he came to find them,
the hero in pursuit, at hand with troops.   2945
   "The bloody swathe that Swedes and Geats
cut through each other was everywhere.

9. Ongentheow.

No one could miss their murderous feuding.
Then the old man made his move,
pulled back, barred his people in: 2950
Ongentheow withdrew to higher ground.
Hygelac's pride and prowess as a fighter
were known to the earl; he had no confidence
that he could hold out against that horde of seamen,
defend his wife and the ones he loved   2955
from the shock of the attack. He retreated for shelter
behind the earthwall. Then Hygelac swooped
on the Swedes at bay, his banners swarmed
into their refuge, his Geat forces
drove forward to destroy the camp.   2960
There in his gray hairs, Ongentheow
was cornered, ringed around with swords.
And it came to pass that the king's fate
was in Eofor's hands,[1] and in his alone.
Wulf, son of Wonred, went for him in anger,   2965
split him open so that blood came spurting
from under his hair. The old hero
still did not flinch, but parried fast,
hit back with a harder stroke:
the king turned and took him on.   2970
Then Wonred's son, the brave Wulf,
could land no blow against the aged lord.
Ongentheow divided his helmet
so that he buckled and bowed his bloodied head
and dropped to the ground. But his doom held off.   2975
Though he was cut deep, he recovered again.
    "With his brother down, the undaunted Eofor,
Hygelac's thane, hefted his sword
and smashed murderously at the massive helmet
past the lifted shield. And the king collapsed,   2980
the shepherd of people was sheared of life.
Many then hurried to help Wulf,
bandaged and lifted him, now that they were left
masters of the blood-soaked battle-ground.
One warrior stripped the other,   2985
looted Ongentheow's iron mail-coat,
his hard sword-hilt, his helmet too,
and carried the graith[2] to King Hygelac,
he accepted the prize, promised fairly
that reward would come, and kept his word.   2990
For their bravery in action, when they arrived home,
Eofor and Wulf were overloaded
by Hrethel's son, Hygelac the Geat,
with gifts of land and linked rings
that were worth a fortune. They had won glory,   2995

1. The killing of Ongentheow by Eofor is   2. Armor.
described in lines 2486–89.

so there was no gainsaying his generosity.
And he gave Eofor his only daughter
to bide at home with him, an honor and a bond.
    "So this bad blood between us and the Swedes,
this vicious feud, I am convinced,   3000
is bound to revive; they will cross our borders
and attack in force when they find out
that Beowulf is dead. In days gone by
when our warriors fell and we were undefended,
he kept our coffers and our kingdom safe.   3005
He worked for the people, but as well as that
he behaved like a hero.
                              We must hurry now
to take a last look at the king
and launch him, lord and lavisher of rings,
on the funeral road. His royal pyre   3010
will melt no small amount of gold:
heaped there in a hoard, it was bought at heavy cost,
and that pile of rings he paid for at the end
with his own life will go up with the flame,
be furled in fire: treasure no follower   3015
will wear in his memory, nor lovely woman
link and attach as a torque around her neck—
but often, repeatedly, in the path of exile
they shall walk bereft, bowed under woe,
now that their leader's laugh is silenced,   3020
high spirits quenched. Many a spear
dawn-cold to the touch will be taken down
and waved on high; the swept harp
won't waken warriors, but the raven winging
darkly over the doomed will have news,   3025
tidings for the eagle of how he hoked[3] and ate,
how the wolf and he made short work of the dead."
    Such was the drift of the dire report
that gallant man delivered. He got little wrong
in what he told and predicted.
                              The whole troop   3030
rose in tears, then took their way
to the uncanny scene under Earnaness.[4]
There, on the sand, where his soul had left him,
they found him at rest, their ring-giver
from days gone by. The great man   3035
had breathed his last. Beowulf the king
had indeed met with a marvelous death.
    But what they saw first was far stranger:
the serpent on the ground, gruesome and vile,
lying facing him. The fire-dragon   3040
was scaresomely burned, scorched all colors.

3. Rooted about, a Northern Irish word [adapted
from translator's note].

4. The place where Beowulf fought the dragon;
it means "Eagleness."

From head to tail, his entire length
was fifty feet. He had shimmered forth
on the night air once, then winged back
down to his den; but death owned him now, 3045
he would never enter his earth-gallery again.
Beside him stood pitchers and piled-up dishes,
silent flagons, precious swords
eaten through with rust, ranged as they had been
while they waited their thousand winters under ground. 3050
That huge cache, gold inherited
from an ancient race, was under a spell—
which meant no one was ever permitted
to enter the ring-hall unless God Himself,
mankind's Keeper, True King of Triumphs, 3055
allowed some person pleasing to Him—
and in His eyes worthy—to open the hoard.
     What came about brought to nothing
the hopes of the one who had wrongly hidden
riches under the rock-face. First the dragon slew 3060
that man among men, who in turn made fierce amends
and settled the feud. Famous for his deeds
a warrior may be, but it remains a mystery
where his life will end, when he may no longer
dwell in the mead-hall among his own. 3065
So it was with Beowulf, when he faced the cruelty
and cunning of the mound-guard. He himself was ignorant
of how his departure from the world would happen.
The highborn chiefs who had buried the treasure
declared it until doomsday so accursed 3070
that whoever robbed it would be guilty of wrong
and grimly punished for their transgression,
hasped in hell-bonds in heathen shrines.
Yet Beowulf's gaze at the gold treasure
when he first saw it had not been selfish. 3075
     Wiglaf, son of Weohstan, spoke:
"Often when one man follows his own will
many are hurt. This happened to us.
Nothing we advised could ever convince
the prince we loved, our land's guardian, 3080
not to vex the custodian of the gold,
let him lie where he was long accustomed,
lurk there under earth until the end of the world.
He held to his high destiny. The hoard is laid bare,
but at a grave cost; it was too cruel a fate 3085
that forced the king to that encounter.
I have been inside and seen everything
amassed in the vault. I managed to enter
although no great welcome awaited me
under the earthwall. I quickly gathered up 3090
a huge pile of the priceless treasures

handpicked from the hoard and carried them here
where the king could see them. He was still himself,
alive, aware, and in spite of his weakness
he had many requests. He wanted me to greet you   3095
and order the building of a barrow that would crown
the site of his pyre, serve as his memorial,
in a commanding position, since of all men
to have lived and thrived and lorded it on earth
his worth and due as a warrior were the greatest.   3100
Now let us again go quickly
and feast our eyes on that amazing fortune
heaped under the wall. I will show the way
and take you close to those coffers packed with rings
and bars of gold. Let a bier be made   3105
and got ready quickly when we come out
and then let us bring the body of our lord,
the man we loved, to where he will lodge
for a long time in the care of the Almighty."
    Then Weohstan's son, stalwart to the end,   3110
had orders given to owners of dwellings,
many people of importance in the land,
to fetch wood from far and wide
for the good man's pyre:
                        "Now shall flame consume
our leader in battle, the blaze darken   3115
round him who stood his ground in the steel-hail,
when the arrow-storm shot from bowstrings
pelted the shield-wall. The shaft hit home.
Feather-fledged, it finned the barb in flight."
    Next the wise son of Weohstan   3120
called from among the king's thanes
a group of seven: he selected the best
and entered with them, the eighth of their number,
under the God-cursed roof; one raised
a lighted torch and led the way.   3125
No lots were cast for who should loot the hoard
for it was obvious to them that every bit of it
lay unprotected within the vault,
there for the taking. It was no trouble
to hurry to work and haul out   3130
the priceless store. They pitched the dragon
over the cliff-top, let tide's flow
and backwash take the treasure-minder.
Then coiled gold was loaded on a cart
in great abundance, and the gray-haired leader,   3135
the prince on his bier, borne to Hronesness.
    The Geat people built a pyre for Beowulf,
stacked and decked it until it stood foursquare,
hung with helmets, heavy war-shields
and shining armor, just as he had ordered.   3140

Then his warriors laid him in the middle of it,
mourning a lord far-famed and beloved.
On a height they kindled the hugest of all
funeral fires; fumes of woodsmoke
billowed darkly up, the blaze roared   3145
and drowned out their weeping, wind died down
and flames wrought havoc in the hot bone-house,
burning it to the core. They were disconsolate
and wailed aloud for their lord's decease.
A Geat woman too sang out in grief;   3150
with hair bound up, she unburdened herself
of her worst fears, a wild litany
of nightmare and lament: her nation invaded,
enemies on the rampage, bodies in piles,
slavery and abasement. Heaven swallowed the smoke.   3155
    Then the Geat people began to construct
a mound on a headland, high and imposing,
a marker that sailors could see from far away,
and in ten days they had done the work.
It was their hero's memorial; what remained from the fire   3160
they housed inside it, behind a wall
as worthy of him as their workmanship could make it.
And they buried torques in the barrow, and jewels
and a trove of such things as trespassing men
had once dared to drag from the hoard.   3165
They let the ground keep that ancestral treasure,
gold under gravel, gone to earth,
as useless to men now as it ever was.
Then twelve warriors rode around the tomb,
chieftains' sons, champions in battle,   3170
all of them distraught, chanting in dirges,
mourning his loss as a man and a king.
They extolled his heroic nature and exploits
and gave thanks for his greatness; which was the proper thing,
for a man should praise a prince whom he holds dear   3175
and cherish his memory when that moment comes
when he has to be convoyed from his bodily home.
So the Geat people, his hearth-companions,
sorrowed for the lord who had been laid low.
They said that of all the kings upon earth   3180
he was the man most gracious and fair-minded,
kindest to his people and keenest to win fame.

ABOLQASEM FERDOWSI
940–1020

The *Shahnameh*, literally "book of kings," is sometimes called Persia's national epic. It is what the *Iliad* is to the Greeks, the *Aeneid* to the Romans, *Beowulf* to the English, or the *Song of Roland* to the French. But the label "epic" only begins to capture the scope and ambitions of Ferdowsi's capacious text, which opens with the creation of the world and ends with the lineage of medieval Persian kings; along the way, it includes fairies and jinns, flying horses and giant birds. Standing on the threshold of the fall of his Persian patrons to invading Turkish armies, Ferdowsi was writing with one eye on the glories of the past and one eye on the turbulent court politics of his own day.

Abolqasem Ferdowsi was born in Khorasan, a region encompassing what is now northeastern Iran and the adjoining regions of Afghanistan, Turkmenistan, and Uzbekistan, in a village near the city of Tus. He wrote his major work, the *Shahnameh*, under the patronage of the Iranian Samanid rulers of Khorasan (819–1005), who were eager to revive Persian literature and culture after a long period of dormancy following the Arab Islamic invasions of Persia that began in 633. The Samanid ruler Nuh ibn Mansur ordered that a prose compendium be produced of all the Persian literature that had been suppressed over the past centuries, drawing on oral and written sources of Persian mythology and the native monotheistic religion of Zoroastrianism. Ferdowsi tells us that the first poet told to turn this (now lost) prose account into an epic poem, Daqiqi-e Balkhi, died suddenly before he could finish more

than a thousand lines. Ferdowsi claims to have incorporated Daqiqi's verses into his own *Shahnameh*—but because he ascribes to Daqiqi the most un-Islamic part of the poem, centering on the life of the prophet Zoroaster and the religion he founded, it is possible that the attribution is not so much fact as a clever tactic aimed at self-preservation. While Ferdowsi was at work on the *Shahnameh*, his Samanid patron fell from power. Though the rulers of this new regime, the Ghaznavid Turks, were ethnically distinct from and more rigorously Islamic than the Persian Samanids, they valued Persian culture highly. Ferdowsi therefore continued his work on the poem, sending selections to Mahmoud, the new Ghaznavid ruler, along with short poems praising his generosity.

Although the *Shahnameh* is an epic, it encompasses other genres as well. It begins with the creation of the world, the creation of the first human beings, and an account of their lineage, and thus resembles texts like *Gilgamesh* or *Genesis*. It is national in its evocation of the great mythic heroes of the Persian past, juxtaposed with a historical account of Persian rulers up through the Middle Ages. Beyond myth and history, the *Shahnameh* also contains elements of romance, star-crossed lovers and tragic scenes of misrecognition, fantastical creatures and supernatural events. Further complicating all these diverse elements is their presentation, as the stories are told in intricately rhymed verse. In addition, the *Shahnameh* functions as a "mirror for princes"—that is, a guidebook for rulers: the exemplary kings appear as models to be emulated, while the deeds of bad rulers to be avoided. This aspect of the *Shahnameh* is most evident in the story of Alexander (Sekandar) but is woven throughout the text, especially in the repeated stories of father–son relationships that have gone tragically wrong.

The *Shahnameh* can be divided into three parts: a relatively brief opening section focusing on origin myths, a long second section on the heroes of Persian antiquity, and a third section on the history of the kings. The material becomes steadily more grounded in historical fact as the text goes on; heroic kings who live for several hundred years dominate the middle section, which makes up the bulk of the work, but rulers of normal life spans appear in the later ages. The figure of Alexander the Great, whose life story is excerpted here, is placed at the crucial junction linking the age of heroes with the history of the kings. Alexander appears as a transitional figure, as more than a man yet an integral part of the history of Persian rule. The description of the end of his reign is followed by an extremely brief overview of the dissolution of his empire into a number of small principalities before the rise of the Sassanid dynasty, whose royal lineage makes up the rest of the *Shahnameh*. The poem ends not in Ferdowsi's own times but instead with the last Sassanid ruler, Yazdgerd III, who was forced off his throne by the invading Arab Islamic armies in 651. This poetic celebration of the Persian mythic and historical heritage thus draws a discreet curtain over the period when the advent of Islam threatened to overwhelm the native culture. Moreover, the *Shahnameh* provides a powerful counternarrative to the history of conquest, a counternarrative that depends a great deal on the figure of Alexander the Great. For Persians, it is an article of faith that their nation has never been conquered, even though at times it may have adopted new customs, new religions, and new rulers. In keeping with this perspective, the figure of Alexander is presented in the *Shahnameh* not as a Macedonian invader but as a Persian prince. Instead of being the alien enemy of the Persian ruler, he is Darius's brother and rival.

The legends of Alexander the Great, who emerged from Macedonia to build an empire that stretched from Spain to India, were widely disseminated all around the Mediterranean Sea, reaching throughout Europe and much of Asia. The basic outline of the Alexander story as presented in the *Shahnameh* will be familiar to anyone who has read any one of the many versions of his legend, including the war against Darius (Dara), ruler of Persia; the battles against Porus (Foor), king of India; and the letters describing the marvels of the East exchanged by Alexander with his old teacher, the Greek philosopher Aristotle (Arestalis). Yet Ferdowsi faced a particular challenge in describing Alexander's journeys of conquest into the remotest reaches of the Orient, where he ultimately met his doom. For European readers, Alexander's adventures in Babylon were set in the exotic Orient; for Ferdowsi's readers, Babylon was just down the road. Ferdowsi therefore constructs an even more oriental Orient for his hero, sending Alexander as far as China in search of marvels. At the same time, Ferdowsi's Alexander is also made familiar to Persian readers, drawn into the fold of the lineage of Persian kings. The rivalry between Alexander and his brother ends in the death of Darius, who gives his kingdom to Alexander on the condition that Alexander marry his daughter and uphold the local religion of Zoroastrianism. Here, conquest is transformed into cultural assimilation, and the heroic age moves smoothly into the lists of Persian kings. Implicitly, the transition ushered in by Alexander foreshadows the greater transition that informs the last lines of the *Shahnameh*, which recount the rule of the Sassanid Yazdgerd III. He would be the last native ruler of Persia until the rise of the Samanid rulers of Khorasan—Ferdowsi's patrons—in 819.

The celebration of Persian identity so poetically expressed in the *Shahnameh* continues to be enormously popular not only within modern Iran but also in communities of Iranians throughout the world. Along with the lyric poetry of **Hafez**, Ferdowsi's narrative poetry is widely quoted and used for inscriptions. Unlike the delicate ghazals of Hafez, however, the *Shahnameh* has also been rendered as a popular series of graphic novels. The endurance of the *Shahnameh* is partly due to how little the Persian language (Farsi) has changed over the thousand years since Ferdowsi completed his epic work. Modern speakers of Persian can read Ferdowsi without difficulty, much as we might read Shakespeare's English. For them, Ferdowsi's Persian is a living language, as resonant in the present moment as at any time in the past millennium.

A NOTE ON TRANSLATION

The *Shahnameh* has repeatedly been translated into European languages, usually in the form of an excerpt taken from the tragic story of the hero Rostam and his doomed son Sohrab; one of the best-known examples is Matthew Arnold's poem "Sohrab and Rustum" (1853). This narrative appealed to nineteenth-century European readers not just because of its emotional power and beauty but also because the story line of a father destroying his son corresponded well with an Orientalist view of the decadent East. The translation by Dick Davis reproduced here, by contrast, makes a real effort to bring the Persian text to readers of English on its own terms. Davis's versions of Persian narrative and lyric poetry have been particularly popular among diasporic Iranians, who are eager to rediscover their national literature within new cultural environments. Davis, himself a poet, renders Ferdowsi's heroic couplets in a lyrical, rhythmic prose punctuated by short passages in verse that mark moments of great emotional tension.

From Shahnameh[1]

The Birth of Sekandar

One night this lovely moon,[2] arrayed in jewels and scents, lay sleeping beside the king. Suddenly she sighed deeply, and the king[3] turned his head away, offended by the smell of her breath. This bad odor sickened him, and he frowned, wondering what could be done about it. He sent knowledgeable doctors to her; one who was especially expert was able to find a remedy. There is an herb that burns the palate, which they call "Sekandar" in Greece, and he rubbed this against the roof of her mouth. She wept a few tears and her face turned as red as brocade, because it burned her mouth, but the ugly smell was gone. But although this beautiful woman's breath was now as sweet as musk, the king no longer felt any love for her. His heart had grown cold toward his bride, and he sent her back to Filqus. The princess grieved, because she was pregnant, but she told no one of this.

1. Translated by Dick Davis.
2. Nahid, daughter of Filqus (Philip), King of Macedon, sent to marry Darab, King of Persia.

In Persian poetry, the moon often symbolizes feminine beauty.
3. Darab (Darius), King of Persia.

When nine months had gone by she gave birth to a boy as splendid as the sun. Because of his stature and splendor, and the sweet smell that his flesh exhaled, she named him Sekandar, after the herb that had cured her of her malady. Her father the king told everyone that the boy was his and made no mention of Darab, because he was ashamed to tell people that Darab had rejected his daughter. The same night that Sekandar was born, a cream-colored mare in the royal stables, a huge warlike horse, gave birth to a gray foal with a lion-like chest and short pasterns.[4] Filqus took this as a good omen, raising his hands to the heavens in gratitude. At dawn the next day he had both the new-born child and the mare and her foal brought to him and passed his hands over the foal's eyes and chest, because he was exactly the same age as Sekandar.

So the heavens turned and the years passed. Sekandar grew to have a princely heart, and his speech was that of a warrior. Filqus treated him even more attentively than a son and loved to dress him as a champion. In a little while the boy gained in wisdom; he became adroit, intelligent, grave in his manner, and knowledgeable. He was made the kingdom's crown prince, and Filqus delighted in his presence. Sekandar learned the arts of kingship from his teachers, and it seemed he was born to administer justice, to occupy a throne, and to found an empire.

In Persia, after Nahid had returned to her father, Darab took another wife. She gave birth to a fine, princely son who was a year younger than Sekandar. On the day he was born he was named Dara, and it was hoped that his good fortune would be greater than his father's. Then, after twelve years, Darab's star declined: he grew sick and wasted away and knew he would be called to another place. He summoned his nobles and counselors and spoke to them at length about the business of government and kingship. Then he added: "Dara, my son, will guide you well. Listen to him and obey him, and may your souls know peace in obedience to his commands. This royal throne is no one's for long, and in the midst of pleasure we are called away. Strive to be kind and just, and rejoice when you remember me." Having said this he heaved a sigh from the depths of his being, and the rosy pomegranate petal turned as pale as fenugreek.[5]

* * *

Dara's Dying Words to Sekandar

Dara's counselors made their way to Sekandar and said, "Wise and victorious lord, we have killed your enemy: his days as king are over." When Sekandar heard Janushyar's words, he said to him and to Mahyar,[6] "Where is this enemy of mine whom you've cast aside in this way? Take me to him." The two led Sekandar, whose heart was bursting with rage, to where Dara lay with his chest covered in gore, and his face as pale as fenugreek. Sekandar gave orders that no one else should approach, and that Dara's two counselors be detained. Quick as the wind he dismounted and laid the wounded man's head on his thigh. He rubbed both his hands against Dara's face until he began to revive and speak. Then Sekandar removed the royal diadem from Dara's head and loosened his

---

4. Bucephalus, who is featured prominently in classical Greek biographies of Alexander the Great.
5. A light green herb.

6. Janushyar and Mahyar, Zoroastrians serving in the royal retinue, have fatally wounded Dara, Sekandar's half-brother and rival for the crown of Persia.

armor. No doctor was nearby, and when he saw Dara's wounds, a few tears dropped from Sekandar's eyes. "May this pass easily from you," he said, "and may the hearts of those who wish you ill tremble in terror! Get up, and let me lay you in a golden litter, or if you have the strength, sit yourself in the saddle. I will bring doctors from India and Greece, and I shall weep tears of blood for your pain. I shall restore your kingdom to you, and when you have recovered, we shall swear friendship. This instant I shall hang from a gibbet those who have injured you. When I heard last night what had happened, my heart filled with sorrow, my soul with anger. We are from the same stock, the same root, the same people: why should we destroy one another for ambition's sake?"

When he heard Sekandar, Dara said, "May wisdom always be your companion! I think that you will find the reward for what you have said from God himself. You said that Iran is mine, and that the crown and the throne of the brave are mine; but death is closer to me than the throne. The throne is over for me, and my luck has run out. So the high heavens revolve; their turning is toward sorrow, and their profit is pain. Look at me before you say 'I am exalted above all this great company of heroes.' Know that evil and good both come from God, and see that you remain grateful to him for as long as you live. My own state shows you the truth of what I say. Look how I, who had such sovereignty and glory and wealth, am now despised by everyone. I who never injured anyone, who had such armor and such armies, such splendid horses, such crowns and thrones, who had such sons and relatives, and so many allies whose hearts bore my brand. Earth and time were my slaves, and remained so while my luck held. But now I am separated from good fortune, and have fallen into the hands of murderers. I despair of my sons and family; the earth has turned dark for me, and my eyes are white like the eyes of a blind man. Our own people cannot help us; my one hope is in God the Creator. I lie here wounded on the earth, fallen into the trap of death, but this is the way of the heavens whether we are kings or heroes. Greatness too must pass: it is the prey, and its hunter is death."

Sekandar's pity made his face turn pale, and he wept for the wounded king, lying there stretched out on the earth. Dara said to him, "Do not weep, there is no profit in it. My part in the fires of life is now merely smoke. This was my fate from him who apportions our fates. This is the goal toward which the splendor of my earthly days has led me. Listen to the advice I shall give you, accept it into your heart, and remember it." Sekandar said, "It is for you to order me: I give you my word." Then Dara spoke quickly, going over his wishes and omitting nothing. He began by saying, "You have achieved fame, but see that you fear the world's Creator, who has made the heavens and the earth and time, and the strong and the weak. Look after my children and my family, and my veiled wise women. Ask for my daughter's hand in marriage, and keep her gently and in comfort in the court. Her mother named her Roshanak and saw that the world was always a place of happiness and delight for her. Do not despise my daughter, or let malevolent men speak badly of her. She has been brought up as a princess, and at our feasts she has always been the loveliest person present. It may be that you shall have a son with her, and that the name of Esfandyar[7] will be renewed in him,

---

7. A legendary Iranian hero, son of King Goshtasp; his battle with the mighty Rostam is recounted earlier in the *Shahnameh*.

that he will preserve the fires of Zoroastrianism and live by the Zend-Avesta,[8] keeping the Feasts of Sadeh and No-Ruz[9] and preserving our fire temples. Such a son will honor Hormozd[1] and the sun and moon, and wash his soul and face in the waters of wisdom; he will renew the ways of Lohrasp and Goshtasp,[2] treating men according to their station whether it be high or low; he will make our faith flourish and his days will be fortunate."

Sekandar answered him, "Your heart is pure and your words are wise, O king. I accept all that you have said, and I shall not stray from your words while I am within the borders of your kingdom. I shall accomplish the good deeds you recommend, and your wisdom will be my guide." The master of the world grasped Sekandar's hand and began to weep bitterly.

> He kissed Sekandar's palm and said, "I pray
> That God will keep and guide you on your way.
> I give my flesh to dust, to God my spirit,
> My sovereignty is yours now to inherit."

He spoke, and his soul rose up from his body. All those gathered nearby began to weep, and Sekandar rent his clothes and poured dust on the royal diadem. Sekandar made a splendid tomb for him according to local custom and, now that the time for Dara's eternal sleep had come, the blood was washed from his body with clear rosewater. His body was wrapped in brocade woven with gold and sewn with jewels; it was then covered with camphor, even his face, so that no one could see it. As Dara's corpse was placed within its golden coffin the bystanders wept, and then it was carried in procession, passed hand to hand by the mourners, with Sekandar leading the cortege on foot, and as he approached the tomb, it seemed as if his skin would split with sorrow. The king's coffin was placed within the tomb according to the ancient royal rites, and the huge doors of the building were sealed. Then Sekandar had two gibbets built, one bearing the name Janushyar and the other Mahyar, and the two regicides were strung up on them. The soldiers who were there took rocks in their fists and stoned them to death, as a warning to those who would kill a king. When the Persians saw how Sekandar honored Dara and mourned for him, they offered the young king their homage and loyalty.

* * *

Sekandar's Letter to Foor

Having hidden his treasure in this way,[3] Sekandar led his army out from Milad and bore down on Qanuj like the wind. He wrote a threatening, bellicose letter,

8. The sacred scripture of Zoroastrianism: a collection of hymns and liturgical texts, together with their theological interpretations. The religion was founded by the prophet Zoroaster in Iran in the 6th century B.C.E. and was the state religion at the time of Alexander's conquest and from the 3rd century C.E. until shortly before the adoption of Islam.
9. The Persian New Year, which takes place on the spring equinox (March 20 or 21);

Sadeh is a midwinter festival held fifty days earlier. Both festivals involve the celebration of light, especially fire.
1. An early Iranian god (also called Ahura Mazda), who was proclaimed the single uncreated God by Zoroaster and is the highest deity in Zoroastrianism.
2. Legendary Iranian kings.
3. A concealment just described in a passage not included here.

"From Sekandar, the son of Filqus, who lights the flames of prosperity and adversity, to Foor, the lord of India, favored by the heavens, commander of the armies of Sind."[4] The letter opened with praise of God the Creator who is eternal, saying that those to whom he gives victory never want for countries, crowns, and thrones, while those from whom he turns away become wretched, and the sun never shines on them. "You will have heard how God has given me *farr*,[5] victory, good fortune, crowns, thrones, and sovereignty over this dark earth. But none of this will last, and my days draw on; another will come after me to enjoy my conquests. My only ambition is to leave a good name and no disgrace behind me on this sublunar earth. When they bring this letter to you, free your dark soul from sorrow; descend from your throne, do not consult with your priests or advisors, but mount your horse and come to me asking for my protection. Those who try to trick me only prolong matters, and if for one moment you disobey me by choosing arrogance and warfare, I shall descend on your country like a fire, bringing an army of picked warriors, and once you see my cavalry you will regret your delay in submitting to me." The letter was sealed with Sekandar's mark, and a soldier who was eager for fame was chosen to take it. The messenger arrived at the court, and when Foor was told of his arrival he was summoned into the royal presence.

When Foor read Sekandar's letter he started up in rage and immediately wrote a furious reply, planting a tree in the garden of vengeance. "We should fear God, and not use such presumptuous language, because a boastful man will find himself friendless and with no resources. Have you no shame that you summon me like this? Isn't your wisdom disturbed by this kind of talk? If it were Filqus writing thus to Foor, that would be something, but you? You dare to stir up trouble in this way? Your victory over Dara has gone to your head, but the heavens had had enough of him, and fate deals in this way with people who won't listen to good advice. And you found your quarrel with Kayd[6] was like a feast, so now you think all kings are your prey to hunt down. The ancient kings of Iran never addressed us in this way. I am Foor, descended from the family of Foor, and we have never paid any attention to Caesars[7] from the west. When Dara asked for my help, I sent him war elephants to buy time, although I saw that neither his heart nor his fortune were as they should be. When he was murdered by a slave, good fortune deserted the Persians. If evil came to him from an evil counselor, is that any reason for you to lose your good sense? Don't be so eager for battle and so disrespectful toward me; soon enough you'll see my war elephants and armies crowding the way before you. All you think of is your own glory, but inside you are the color of Ahriman.[8] Don't sow these seeds of strife throughout the world; fear misfortune and the harm that will come to you. I mean well by this letter, and may it gratify your heart."

Sekandar Leads His Army Against Foor

After reading this letter, Sekandar immediately selected chieftains from his army, men who were worthy of command: old in their understanding but young in years. Then he led his men against Foor, and they were so numerous that

4. China. "Foor": the Persian form of the Greek Porus.
5. God-given glory.
6. An Indian king.
7. That is, emperors.
8. In Zoroastrian theology, the god of evil and darkness, fundamentally opposed to Hormozd.

the earth was like a heaving sea. They traveled by every pathway, so that there seemed to be no track that they didn't take, over mountains, along the seashores, and through the most difficult terrain. The army grew weary of harsh traveling and fierce battles, and one evening when they pitched camp, a group of them came before the king. They said,

> "Sovereign of Greece and of all Asia too,
> Earth cannot hold the massive armies you
> Lead out against the world: Foor will not fight,
> And China's emperor quails before your might.
> Why should your army's valiant soldiers die
> For worthless lands beneath an alien sky?
> In all our ranks we cannot find one horse
> That's fit for war; if we reverse our course
> The infantry and cavalry will stray
> By unfamiliar paths and lose their way.
> Before, we fought and gained our victories
> Against the strength of human enemies,
> But none of us desires to die in wars
> With mountains and the sea's infertile shores;
> Men do not fight with rocks and ocean tides,
> With barren plains and rugged mountain sides.
> Do not convert the glory of our fame
> To ignominious and ignoble shame."

Sekandar was angered by their words, and he made short work of their complaints. He said, "In the war with the Persians, no Greek soldier was injured; Dara was killed by his own slaves, and none of you suffered. I shall continue on my way without you, and place my foot on the dragon's heart alone. You will see that the wretched Foor will have no desire for either battles or banquets when I have dealt with him. My help comes from God and the Persian army, and I have no need of Greek goodwill." Frightened by his anger, the army begged him to pardon them and said, "We are all our Caesar's slaves, and we tread the earth only as he wills us to. We shall go on, and when there are no horses left, we shall fight on foot. If the earth becomes a sea with our blood, and the low places become hills of corpses, even if the heavens rain down mountainous rocks, no enemy will ever see our backs in battle. We are your slaves, here for you to command, and how could you suffer any injury from us?"

Sekandar then formed a new battle plan. He chose thirty thousand Persian warriors headed by experienced, well-armored chieftains. Behind them he placed forty thousand Greek cavalry, and behind them his warlike Egyptian cavalry, who fought with swords. Forty thousand of Dara's troops and men from the Persian royal family accompanied them. Sekandar picked out twelve thousand Greek and Egyptian cavalry to bring up the rear and scour the plains and valleys. With his army Sekandar had sixty astrologers and sages to advise him on the most auspicious days for combat.

When Foor became aware of the enemy's approach, he chose a place suitable for battle, and his troops crowded the plain for four miles, with elephants in the van and his warriors behind them. Meanwhile Sekandar's spies told him of the war elephants in Foor's army, and how with their overpowering trunks (that were under the protection of Saturn) they could destroy two miles of cavalry, who would be unable either to defeat them or to get back to their own ranks. The spies drew a picture of an elephant on a piece of paper and showed it to the king, who had a model of the animal made from wax. Then he turned to his advisors and said, "Who can think of some way to defeat this?" The wise men of his court pondered the problem and then gathered together, from Greece, Egypt, and Persia, a group of more than forty times thirty blacksmiths, all of whom were expert at their trade. They made a horse of iron, with an iron saddle and an iron rider; its joints were held together with nails and solder, and then they polished both the rider and his steed. It was mounted on wheels and filled with black oil. They pushed it in front of Sekandar, who was pleased by the device and saw that it would be very useful. He ordered that more than a thousand of these iron horses and riders be made. What king had ever seen an army of dappled, gray, bay, and black horses, all of them made of iron? The devices went forward on wheels, and looked exactly like cavalry prepared for war.

Sekandar's Battle Against the Indian Troops; He Kills Foor

As Sekandar approached Foor's forces, the two armies caught sight of each other; amid clouds of dust a great cry went up from each side, and the warriors advanced on each other eager for battle. Then Sekandar's men set fire to oil in the iron horses and routed Foor's forces. Flames flared out from the iron steeds, and as soon as the elephants saw this they plunged precipitately this way and that. Foor's army was in turmoil, and when the elephants wrapped their trunks around the burning horses, they were maddened by their wounds, and their mahouts were bewildered as to what to do. The whole Indian army, including its mighty elephants, began to flee, and Sekandar pursued his malicious enemies like the wind. As the air darkened at nightfall there was nowhere left for the army to fight. Sekandar and the Greeks halted at a place between two mountains and sent out scouts to keep their camp safe from the enemy.

When the sun rose like a gold ingot, making the world as bright as clear crystal, the din of trumpets, bugles, and fifes rang out, and the two armies, thrusting their lances into the heavens, prepared to fight again. Clutching his Greek sword, Sekandar came between the hosts and sent a horseman to shout from a distance to Foor,

> "Sekandar stands before his troops and seeks
> To talk with Foor, and hear the words he speaks."

When Foor heard this he hurried to the head of his troops. Sekandar said,

> "Two armies have been shattered on these plains
> Where feral scavengers eat human brains,
> And horses tread on bones. We're brave and young,
> Each of us is a noble champion—

Our warriors have been killed, or they have fled:
Why should they flee, or be left here for dead?
Why should two countries fight when combat can
Decide who is the victor, man to man?
Prepare to face me, one of us alone
Will live to claim these armies and this throne."

Foor agreed to his proposal, thinking that his own body was like a lion's and that his horse was the equal of any fierce dragon, while Sekandar was as thin as a reed, wore light armor, and rode an exhausted mount. He said,

"This is a noble custom: hand to hand
We will decide who's ruler of this land."

Grasping their swords, they advanced on one another in the space between the two hosts. When Sekandar saw his massive opponent, his fearsome sword in hand and mounted on a huge horse, he was astonished and almost despaired of his life. Nevertheless he went forward, and as he did so Foor was distracted by a cry that went up from the rear of his army and turned toward it. Like the wind then Sekandar bore down on him, and struck the lion-like warrior with a mighty sword blow. The blade sliced through Foor's neck and trunk, and he fell from his horse to the earth.

 The Greek commander was overjoyed and his warriors rushed forward; the earth and clouds re-echoed with the thunder of a lion-skin drum, and the blare of trumpets. The Indian warriors looked on Sekandar with fury and were ready to fight, but a voice rang out from the Greek ranks: "Foor's head lies here in the dust, his mammoth body is hacked and torn, who is it you wish to fight for, who will benefit from more sword blows and destruction? Sekandar has become to you as Foor was; it is he you must look to now for battles and banquets." With a roar the Indian warriors called out their agreement, and they came forward to gaze at Foor's hacked and bloody body. A wail of sorrow went up from their ranks, and they threw down their weapons. Fearfully they went before Sekandar, groaning and heaping dust on their heads, but Sekandar returned their weapons, and his words were welcoming: "One Indian has died here, but you should not grieve. I shall cherish you more than he did and try to drive sorrow from your lives. I will distribute his wealth among you, and make the Indians powerful with crowns and throne." Then he mounted Foor's throne; on the one side there was mourning and on the other feasting. But this is the way of the passing world, which brings sorrow to those who dwell in it.

 For two months Sekandar sat on the Indian throne, distributing wealth to the army; then he placed there as his regent an Indian nobleman called Savorg, saying to him, "Don't hide your gold away. Distribute and consume whatever comes to you, and put no faith in this passing world, which sometimes favors Sekandar, sometimes Foor, and sometimes gives us pain and rage, sometimes joy and feasting." Savorg too distributed gold and silver to the Indian warriors.

* * *

Sekandar Leads His Army to Egypt

When he returned from his pilgrimage he bestowed gold on Nasr,[9] enriching those who had been poor and obliged to find food by their own labors. Then he led his army to Jeddah, where he didn't stay long. The soldiers were set to work making ships and a number of boats, in which the world conqueror and his army set off for Egypt. The Egyptian king at that time was named Qaytun, and he possessed an unimaginably large army; when he heard that a victorious world conqueror was coming with a following wind from the shrine at Mecca, he set out with a large company of soldiers to welcome him and took coins, slaves, and crowns as presents. Sekandar was pleased to see him and stayed in Egypt for a year, until he and his troops were well rested.

Andalusia[1] was ruled over by a woman; she was wise, had innumerable troops at her disposal, and ruled in prosperity and happiness. The name of this generous and ambitious woman was Qaydafeh.[2] She sought out a painter from the ranks of her soldiers, someone who could make an accurate likeness, and said to him, "Go to Sekandar, and see that you make no mention of my country or of me. Look carefully at him, see what his complexion is, examine his face and stature, and then paint me a full-length portrait of him." The painter heard her and immediately mounted his horse, ready to carry out his sovereign's orders. As quick as a royal courier he made his way from Andalusia to Egypt and into the presence of Sekandar. He observed him when he gave audience and when he was in the saddle; then he took paper and Chinese ink,[3] drew his portrait exactly as he was in real life, and returned to Andalusia. Qaydafeh was moved when she saw Sekandar's face and sighed to herself, then hid the portrait away.

Sekandar asked Qaytun, "Who is Qaydafeh's equal in the world?"

> And King Qaytun replied, "In all the earth
> There's no one of her glory and her worth;
> Unless he were to read the muster rolls
> No one could count the soldiers she controls.
> You won't find anyone in any land
> Who has the wealth she's able to command,
> Who has her dignity, her eloquence,
> Her wisdom, goodness, and magnificence.
> She's built from stone a wide and wondrous town
> So strong no leopard's claws could tear it down—
> Four parasangs in length, no man can measure
> Its endless width. And if you ask for treasure,
> Hers is uncountable; for years there's been
> Talk in the world of this exalted queen."

---

9. An Arab descendant of Ishmael (the older son of Abraham and the legendary forefather of the Arab people); he welcomes Sekandar to the Hijaz (modern Arabia) and Yemen. While there, Sekandar makes a pilgrimage to the Ka'aba at Mecca (a site of worship even before the rise of Islam).
1. Andalusia (or, more accurately, al-Andalus) became the name of modern Spain during the period of Islamic rule, which began about a thousand years after Alexander died and extended well past Ferdowsi's own time.
2. Queen of Andalusia; she corresponds to Candace, queen of the White Ethiopians, in Greek, Latin, and European versions of the Alexander story (also compare Queen Makeda in the Ethiopian *Kebra Nagast*).
3. Very high quality ink.

Sekandar's Letter to Qaydafeh

Sekandar summoned a scribe and had a letter written on silk, from Sekandar, the slayer of lions and conqueror of cities, to Qaydafeh the wise, whose name is unequalled in glory. The letter opened by invoking God, who is generous and just and who bestows prosperity on those who merit it, and continued: "I have not rushed into war with you; rather, I have been weighing the reports of the splendor of your court. When they bring you this letter, may it enlighten your dark soul. Send tribute to me, and understand that you do not have the strength to oppose me. You are wise, so act with foresight, as a powerful and religious sovereign should. If you attempt any kind of trick against me, you will see nothing but adverse fortune come your way. You don't have to look far to learn this lesson: consider what happened to Dara and Foor." As soon as the ink had dried the letter was sealed with musk.

A quick messenger took the letter at Sekandar's command, and when Qaydafeh read it she was astonished at its language. Her answer was as follows: "Praise be to him who created the earth, who has made you victorious over Foor of India, over Dara, and over the nobles of Sind. Your victory over these warriors has made you willful. You have crowned yourself in victory, but how can you put me on their level? I am far greater than they were, in *farr* and in glory, in my armies, and in my royal wealth. How can I submit to a Greek overlord, and how can you expect me to tremble with fear because of your threats? My armies number more than a thousand thousand men, and princes command every one of those armies. Who are you that you should boast in this way? Your defeat of Dara has made you the prince of braggarts!" She placed her gold seal on the letter and dispatched the messenger, who rode like the wind.

The Greeks Capture Qaydafeh's Son

Sekandar read her letter and then he had the trumpets sounded and his army led out. They marched for a month until they reached the borders of Qaydafeh's lands. A king called Faryan reigned there, a man possessed of an army and wealth, and successful in his life. His city was built to withstand war, and its walls were so high that cranes could not overfly them. He and his army occupied this fortress, and Sekandar ordered that balistas and catapults be brought up to batter the walls. After a week of fighting his army entered the town, and the victor gave orders that no blood was to be spilled.

One of Qaydafeh's sons, named Qaydrus, was married to Faryan's daughter, and was in the city, as his father-in-law delighted in his company. Qaydrus and his wife, however, had been captured by a man named Shahrgir; Sekandar knew of this and looked for some way to free them. He summoned his vizier, a wise and reasonable man named Bitqun, and showed him his crown and throne, saying, "Qaydrus and his bride will come before you, and I shall call you Sekandar, the son of Filqus. You will be seated on the throne here like a king, and I will stand ready to serve you. You will give orders that Qaydrus's head is to be severed from his shoulders by the executioner. I will humble myself before you and plead for them; you will clear the audience hall of courtiers, and when I redouble my pleas, you will grant my request." The vizier was very troubled by all this, as he was unsure what it meant. Sekandar continued, "This business must remain secret. Call me in as an envoy and talk a little about Qaydafeh; then cordially send me off to her with ten horsemen, saying, 'Hurry and take this letter and bring me the answer.'" Bitqun replied, "I will do it: I'll carry out this deception according to your orders."

Dawn came, the sun drew its glittering dagger, and night fled away in fear. Bitqun sat on the royal throne, but there was shame in his face and anxiety in his heart. Sekandar stood before him as a servant: he had closed the doors to the court and opened the doors to deception. When Shahrgir led in Qaydafeh's weeping son as a captive, together with his young and beautiful wife, who was wringing her hands in grief, Bitqun quickly said, "Who is this man, who has cause to weep so much?" The young man answered, "Come to your senses! I am Qaydrus, Qaydafeh's son, and this is Faryan's daughter, my sole wife. I wish to take her home and cherish her like my own soul, but I am a prisoner in Shahrgir's hands, my soul wounded by the stars, my body by arrows." When Bitqun heard him he was distressed and angry. He started up and said to the executioner, "These two must be buried beneath the dust! Cut off their heads with your Indian sword: now, just as they are, in chains here."

Sekandar came forward and kissed the ground, and said, "Great king of royal lineage, if you will free them for my sake, I shall be able to hold my head up in any company. Why should you vengefully cut off the heads of innocent people? The world's Creator will not look well on us for this." Wise Bitqun answered him, "You have freed these two from death," and to Qaydrus he added, "You've kept your head, which was already leaving your shoulders! Now I shall send you and this man who has interceded for you to your mother, and he can explain what has happened. It would be good if she would then send us tribute: this would mean that no one will lose his skin in this quarrel. Look after this vizier of mine, who will offer your mother war with me or prosperity; act well toward him as he has done toward you, since a noble man's heart is moved to repay kindness. When he has received the queen's answer, send him safely back to me." Qaydrus replied,

> "I will not take my heart or ears or eyes
> From him: how could I treat him otherwise
> Since he has here restored to me my wife,
> My soul, the living sweetness of my life?"

Sekandar Goes as an Envoy to Qaydafeh

Sekandar selected ten suitable companions from among the Greeks: they were all privy to his identity and willing to keep his secret. He said to them, "On this journey address me as Bitqun." Qaydrus led the group, and Sekandar watched him and listened to him attentively. Their splendid horses galloped forward like fire, until the travelers came to a mountain made all of crystal, yet with fruit trees and many plants growing on its slopes. They continued into the queen's realm, and when Qaydafeh heard that her son, about whom she had been anxiously seeking news, was approaching, she went out to welcome him with a large escort of nobles. As soon as Qaydrus saw his mother he dismounted and made his obeisance before her. She told him to remount, and as they rode on together, she grasped his hand in hers. Qaydrus told her all that he had seen and heard, and he turned pale as he described his sufferings in Faryan's city, and how he was now bereft of his crown, throne, army, and wealth. And he added, "This man who has come with us saved my and my bride's lives; if he hadn't intervened, Sekandar would have ordered that my head be cut off and my body burned. Treat him well, and don't hold back with excuses that would make me break my promise to him."

Hearing her son's words, Qaydafeh was distraught with grief. She had the messenger summoned from her palace where he had been installed and motioned him to a fine throne. She questioned him closely and made much of him and saw that a special residence was set aside for his stay. There she sent fine foods, clothes, and carpets.

At dawn the next morning Sekandar made his way to the court to talk with the queen. Servants drew the curtain aside and let his horse enter. He stared in wonder at Qaydafeh on her ivory throne, with her crown studded with rubies and turquoise, wearing a Chinese cloak woven with gold, her many serving girls with their necklaces and earrings standing around her, her face shining like the sun, her throne supported on crystal columns, her gold dress woven with jewels and clasped with a precious black and white Yemeni stone. Under his breath he called on God repeatedly. He saw that her throne alone surpassed anything that Greece or Persia could provide. He came forward and kissed the ground, like a man anxious to make a good impression. Qaydafeh encouraged him by asking a number of questions; then, like the sun passing from the dome of the sky she declared that the audience for strangers was over, and summoned a meal, wine, and musicians. Tables made of teak and inlaid with gold on an ivory ground were brought in; various kinds of food were served, and wine was set out for when they had finished eating. Gold and silver trays were put before them; first they drank to Qaydafeh herself, and then, as she drank more deeply, the queen began to look closely at Sekandar. She said to her steward, "Bring me that shining silk with the charming face painted on it; bring it quickly, just as it is. Don't stand there wringing your hands, go!"

The steward brought the cloth and laid it before her. She stared at it for a long time and then looked at Sekandar's face: she saw no difference between them. Qaydafeh knew that her guest was the Greek king and the commander of his armies, that he had made himself his own messenger and bravely come into her presence. She said to him, "You seem a man well favored by fortune. Tell me, what message did Sekandar give to you?" And he replied, "The world's king spoke to me in the presence of our nobles. He said to tell the pure-hearted Qaydafeh, 'Pursue only honesty, pay attention to what I say, and do not turn your head aside from my orders. If your heart harbors any rebellion, I shall bring an army against you that will break it in pieces. I have found evidence of your greatness, and I have not hurried to declare war on you. Wisdom and modesty are yours, and your subtle policies maintain the world in safety. If you willingly pay me tribute, you need have no fear of me; if you refuse to go the way of rebellion and disaster, you will see from me nothing but kindness and righteousness.'"

Qaydafeh was infuriated when she heard this, but she thought that silence was the best policy. She said, "Go to your quarters now, and rest with your companions. When you come to me tomorrow, I shall give you my answer and some good advice for your return journey." Sekandar went to the building that had been assigned to him and spent the night considering what he should do. When the world's lamp appeared above the mountaintops, and the plains and foothills took on the appearance of glittering brocade, Sekandar made his way back to Qaydafeh's court; his lips were full of smiles, his heart of grief and anxiety. The chancellor recognized him as the foreign envoy and, after questioning him, led him into the queen's presence. The audience hall was full of strangers. The queen's throne was crystal patterned with agates and emeralds surrounding gems of royal worth; its base was sandal and aloes wood and it rested on pillars studded with turquoise. Sekandar was astonished at the splendor and glory he saw, and he thought, "This is indeed a throne room, and no God-fearing man ever saw its like." He came forward to the queen and was directed to a subsidiary golden throne. Qaydafeh said to him, "Well, Bitqun, why are you staring in this way? Is it that Greece can't produce the like of what you see here, in my humble country?"

Sekandar replied, "Your majesty, you should not speak contemptuously of this palace. It is far more glorious than the palaces of other kings and seems like a mine of precious stones." Qaydafeh laughed at his reaction, and she felt delight in her heart that she was able to tease him in this way. Then she cleared the court and motioned the envoy to come closer to her. She said to him,

> "Filqus's son, I see you're fashioned for
> Battles and royal banquets, peace and war!"

Sekandar turned pale at her words, and then blushed violently; his soul was filled with distress. He said, "Wise queen, such words are not worthy of you. I am Bitqun, don't say that I am a son of Filqus. I give thanks to God that there is no one of noble lineage here, because if he reported what you have said to my king my soul would soon be separated from my body." Qaydafeh replied,

> "Enough excuses! If with your own eyes
> You see yourself, then you must recognize
> The truth of what I say, and don't attempt
> Either to lie or treat me with contempt."

Then she produced the silk with the charming face painted upon it and laid it before him; if the painted face had moved at all you would have said that it was Sekandar himself. Sekandar saw it and he nervously chewed his lower lip; the day had suddenly turned as dark as night for him. He said, "A man should never go out in the world without a hidden dagger!" Qaydafeh answered, "If you had your sword belt on and stood before me with a dagger, you'd have neither the strength nor an adequate sword nor a place to fight nor a means of escape." Sekandar said, "A noble and ambitious man should not flinch at danger; a low-minded person will never rise in the world. If I had my arms and armor here, all your palace would be a sea of blood; I'd have killed you, or ripped open my own belly in front of those who hate me!"

Qaydafeh Gives Sekandar Some Advice

Qaydafeh laughed at his blustering manliness and his angry words. She said, "O lion-like king, don't let yourself be led astray by your male pride! The Indian king Foor wasn't killed because of your glory, and neither were Dara and the heroes of Sind. Their good fortune was at an end, and yours was in the ascendant; and now you're so full of your manly valor because you've become the greatest man on earth at the moment. But you should know that all good things come from God, and while you live you should be grateful to him. You say the world is yours because of your knowledge, but what you say does not seem true to me. What will knowledge avail you when you go into the maw of the dragon death? Acting as your own envoy is sewing your shroud while you are still young. I am not in the habit of shedding blood, nor of attacking rulers. When a monarch has power and is merciful and just, that is when he becomes knowledgeable. Know that whoever spills a king's blood will see nothing but fire as his reward. Be assured of your safety, and leave here with joy. But when you have gone change your habits: don't go acting as your own messenger again, because even the dust knows that you are Sekandar. And I'm not aware of any great hero whose portrait I don't possess, stored away with a reliable courtier. While you remain here I will call you Bitqun and seat you at court accordingly, so that no one will guess your secret or hear your name. I will send you on your way in safety, but you, my lord, must be reasonable and swear that you will never plot against my son, my country, or any of my people or allies, and that you will refer to me only as your equal, as the ruler of my own country."

Freed from the threat of being killed, Sekandar rejoiced to hear her words. He swore by the just God, by the Christian faith, and by the dust of battle that he would act only kindly and righteously toward her land, her son, and her noble allies, and that he would never plot their destruction. When she had heard his oath, Qaydafeh said, "There is one other piece of advice that should not be kept from you: know then that my son Taynush has little sense and pays scant attention to my knowledge and advice. He is Foor's son-in-law and he must not in any way suspect that you and Sekandar occupy the same skin, or even that you are friends. He is eager to avenge Foor, and to confound the earth and sky in war. Now, go joyfully and safely to your own quarters, and have no fear of the world's sorrows."

* * *

Sekandar Sees a Corpse in the Palace of Topazes

The king and his army marched onward for a month and were sorely tried by their journey. They came to a mountain, where they saw no sign of either wild or domestic animals. The mountain's crest was of lapis lazuli, and a palace stood there, made of topazes. It was filled with crystal chandeliers, and in its midst was a fountain of salt water. Next to this fountain was a throne for two people, on which was stretched a wretched corpse. He had a man's body, but his head was like that of a boar; there was a pillow of camphor beneath his head, and a brocade covering had been drawn up over his body. Instead of a lamp a brilliant red jewel shone there, illuminating the whole area; its rays twinkled like stars in the water, and all the chamber glowed as if in sunlight. Whoever went there to take something, or even simply set foot within the palace, found himself rooted to the spot; his whole body began to tremble, and he started to waste away.

A cry came from the salt water, saying, "O king, still filled with longing and desire, don't play the fool much longer! You have seen many things that no man ever saw, but now it's time to draw rein. Your life has shortened now, and the royal throne is without its king." Sekandar was afraid and hurried back to his camp as fast as wind-blown smoke. Quickly he led his army away, weeping and calling on God's name. From that mountain he headed toward the desert, afflicted with sorrow and concerned for his soul. And so he went forward, at the head of his troops, weeping and in pain.

Sekandar Sees the Speaking Tree

The desert road led to a city, and Sekandar was relieved when he heard human voices there. The whole area was one of gardens and fine buildings and was a place to delight any man. The city's noblemen welcomed him, calling out greetings and showering him with gold and jewels. "It is wonderful that you have come to visit us," they said. "No army has ever entered this town, and no one in it has ever heard the name of 'king.' Now that you have come our souls are yours, and may you live with bodily health and spiritual serenity." Sekandar was pleased by their welcome and rested from the journey across the desert. He said to them, "What is there here that's astonishing, that should be inquired into?" A guide said to him, "Victorious king, there is a marvel here, a tree that has two separate trunks together, one of which is female and the other male, and these splendid tree limbs can speak. At night the female trunk becomes sweet smelling and speaks, and when the daylight comes, the male speaks." Sekandar and his Greek cavalry, with the nobles of the town gathered around, listened and said, "When is it you say that the tree speaks in a loud voice?" The translator replied, "A little after day has disappeared one of the trunks begins to speak, and a lucky man will hear its voice; in the dark night the female speaks, and its leaves then smell like musk."

Sekandar answered, "When we go beyond the tree, what wonders are there on the other side?" The reply was, "When you pass the tree there is little argument about which way to take, as there is no place beyond there; guides say it is the world's end. A dark desert lies ahead of you, but no man is so weary of his own soul as to go there. None of us have ever seen or heard that there are any animals there, or that birds fly there." Sekandar and his troops went forward, and when they came near the speaking tree the ground throbbed with heat and the soil there was covered with the pelts of wild beasts. He asked his guide what the pelts were, and who it was that had skinned so many animals in this way. The man answered, "The tree has many worshippers, and when they come here to worship, they feed on the flesh of wild animals."

When the sun reached its zenith Sekandar heard a voice above him, coming from the leaves of the tree; it was a voice to strike terror and foreboding in a man. He was afraid and said to the interpreter, "You are wise and mean well, tell me what the leaves are saying, which makes my heart dissolve within me." "O king, favored by fortune, the leaves say, 'However much Sekandar wanders in the world, he has already seen his share of blessings: when he has reigned for fourteen years, he must quit the royal throne.'" At the guide's words Sekandar's heart filled with pain, and he wept bitterly. He was sad and silent then, speaking to no one, until midnight. Then the leaves of the other trunk began to speak, and Sekandar again asked the interpreter what they said. He replied, "The female tree says, 'Do not puff yourself up with greed; why torment your soul in this way? Greed makes you wander the wide world, harass mankind, and kill kings. But you are not long for this earth now; do not darken and deaden your days like this.'" Then the king said to the interpreter, "Pure of heart and noble as you are, ask them one question: Will this fateful day come in Greece; will my mother see me alive again, before someone covers my face in death?"

> The speaking tree replied, "Few days remain;
> You must prepare your final baggage train.
> Neither your mother, nor your family,
> Nor the veiled women of your land will see
> Your face again. Death will come soon: you'll die
> In a strange land, with strangers standing by.
> The stars and crown and throne and worldly glory
> Are sated with Sekandar and his story."

Sekandar left the tree, his heart wounded as if by a sword. When he returned to his camp, his chieftains went into the town to collect the gifts from the town's nobility. Among these was a cuirass that shone like the waters of the Nile and was as huge as an elephant skin: it had two long tusks attached to it and was so heavy it was hard to lift. There was other armor, as well as fine brocade, a hundred golden eggs each weighing sixty *man*,[4] and a rhinoceros made of gold and jewels. Sekandar accepted the gifts and led off his army, weeping bitter tears as he went.

Sekandar Visits the Emperor of China

Now Sekandar led his army toward China. For forty days they traveled, until they reached the sea. There the army made camp and the king pitched his brocade pavilion. He summoned a scribe to write a letter to the Chinese emperor from Sekandar, the seizer of cities. The message was filled with promises and threats, and when it was completed Sekandar himself went as the envoy, taking with him an intelligent companion who was one with him in heart and speech and who could advise him as to what to do and what not to do. He entrusted his troops to the army's commander and chose five Greeks as his escort.

When news reached the Chinese emperor that an envoy was approaching his country, he sent troops out to meet him. Sekandar reached the court and the emperor came forward in welcome, but his heart was filled with suspicious thoughts. Sekandar ran forward and made his obeisance to him, and then was seated in the palace for a long while. The emperor questioned him and made much of him and assigned him noble sleeping quarters. As the sun rose over the mountains, dying their summits gold, the envoy was summoned to court. Sekandar spoke at length, saying what was appropriate, and then handed over the letter. It was addressed from the king of Greece, possessor of the world, lord of every country, on whom other kings call down God's blessings. It continued, "My orders for China are that she remain prosperous, and that she

---

4. A Persian unit of weight, usually equivalent to about 9 lbs.

should not prepare for war against me; it was war against me that destroyed Foor, and Dara, who was the lord of the world, and Faryan the Arab, and other sovereigns. From the east to the west no one ignores my commands, the heavens themselves do not know the number of my troops, and Venus[5] and the sun could not count them. If you disobey any command of mine you will bring distress on yourself and your country. When you read my letter, bring me tribute; do not trouble yourself about this, or look for evil allies to make war on me. If you come you will see me in the midst of my troops, and when I see that you are honest and mean well I shall confirm you in the possession of your crown and throne, and no misfortune will come to you. If, however, you are reluctant to come before your king, send me things that are peculiar to China— your country's gold work, horses, swords, seal rings, clothes, cloth, ivory thrones, fine brocade, necklaces, crowns—that is, if you have no wish to be harmed by me. Send my soldiers back to me, and rest assured that your wealth, throne, and crown are safe."

When the emperor of China saw what was in the letter, he started up in fury, but then chose silence as a better course. He laughed and said to the envoy, "May your king be a partner to the heavens! Tell me what you know about him. Tell me about his conversation, his height and appearance, and what kind of a man he is." The envoy said, "Great lord of China, you should understand that there is no one else in the world like Sekandar. In his manliness, policy, good fortune, and wisdom he surpasses all that anyone could imagine. He is as tall as a cypress tree, has an elephant's strength, and is as generous as the waters of the Nile; his tongue can be as cutting as a sword, but he can charm an eagle down from the clouds." When he heard all this, the emperor changed his mind. He ordered that wine and a banquet be laid out in the palace gardens. He drank till evening brought darkness to the world, and the company became tipsy. Then he said to the envoy, "May your king be Jupiter's[6] partner. At first light I'll compose an answer to his letter, and what I write will make the day seem splendid to your eyes." Sekandar was half drunk, and he staggered from the garden to his quarters with an orange in his hand.

When the sun rose in Leo[7] and the heavens dispelled the darkness, Sekandar went to the emperor, and all suspicious thoughts were far from his heart. The emperor asked him, "How did you spend the night? When you left you were quite overcome with wine." Then he summoned a scribe, who brought paper, musk, and ambergris, and dictated a letter. He began with praise of God, the lord of chivalry, justice, and ability, of cultivated behavior, abstinence, and piety, and called down his blessings on the Greek king. Then he continued, "Your eloquent envoy has arrived, bringing the king's letter. I have read through the royal words and discussed its contents with my nobles. As for your claims concerning the wars against Dara, Faryan, and Foor, in which you were victorious, so that you became a shepherd whose flock consists of kings, you should not consider what comes about through the will of the Lord of the Sun and Moon as the result of your own valor and the might of your army. When a great

5. The morning and the evening star, as well as the Roman goddess of love.
6. In Roman mythology, the king of the gods.

7. Sekandar's birth sign (the sun rises in Leo in midsummer), viewed in astrology as fiery and masculine.

man's days are numbered, what difference does it make whether he dies in battle or at a banquet? If they died in battle with you this is because their fate was fixed for that day, and fate is not to be hurried or delayed. You should not pride yourself so much on your victories over them, because even if you are made of iron there is no doubt that you too will die. Where now are Feraydun, Zahhak, and Jamshid,[8] who came like the wind and left like a breath? I am not afraid of you and I will not make war against you, neither shall I puff myself up with pride as you are doing. It is not my habit to shed blood, and besides it would be unworthy of my faith for me to do evil in this way. You summon me, but to no purpose; I serve God, not kings. I send with this more riches than you have dreamed of, so that there shall be no doubting my munificence."

These words were an arrow in Sekandar's vital organs, and he blushed with shame. In his heart he said, "Never again shall I go somewhere disguised as my own envoy." He returned to his quarters and prepared to leave the Chinese court.

The proud emperor opened his treasuries' doors, since he was not a man who found generosity difficult. First he ordered that fifty crowns and ten ivory thrones encrusted with jewels be brought; then a thousand camel loads of gold and silver goods, and a thousand more of Chinese brocades and silks, of camphor, musk, perfumes, and ambergris. He had little regard for wealth, and it eased his heart to be bountiful in this way. He had ten thousand each of the pelts of gray squirrel, ermine, and sable brought, and as many carpets and crystal goblets, and his wise treasurer saw to their being loaded on pack animals. Then he added three hundred silver saddles and fifty golden ones, together with three hundred red-haired camels loaded with Chinese rarities. He chose as envoy an eloquent and dignified Chinese sage and told him to take his message to the Greek king with all goodwill and splendor, and to say that Sekandar would be warmly welcomed at the Chinese court for as long as he wished to stay there.

The envoy traveled with Sekandar, unaware that he was the Greek king. But when Sekandar's regent came forward and the king told him of his adventures, and the army congratulated him on his safe return and bowed to the ground before him, the envoy realized that he was indeed the Greek king and dismounted in consternation. Sekandar said to him, "There is no need for apologies, but do not tell your emperor of this!" They rested for a night, and the next morning Sekandar sat on the royal throne. He gave gifts to the envoy and said to him, "Go to your emperor and tell him that I say 'You have found honor and respect with me. If you wish to stay where you are, all China is yours, and if you wish to go elsewhere, that too is open to you. I shall rest here for a while, because such a large army as mine cannot be mobilized quickly.'" The envoy returned like the wind, and gave Sekandar's message to the emperor.

Sekandar Leads His Army to Babylon

Sekandar camped there for a month, and then led his army toward Babylon, and the air was darkened with the dust of their march. They pressed on for a month, and no one had any rest during this time. They came to a mountain range so high that its summit was hidden by dark clouds, as if it reached to

8. Legendary Persian heroic rulers whose stories appear earlier in the *Shahnameh*.

Saturn. The king and his army could see no way forward but over the mountains and so with difficulty they climbed up toward the crest. The climb exhausted them, but once there they saw a deep lake lying below them. Joyfully and praising God, they began their descent; there was game of all kinds on every side, and for a while the soldiers lived off what they hunted.

Then in the distance a wild man appeared. He was covered in hair, and his body beneath the hair was a dark blue color, and he had huge ears, as big as an elephant's. The soldiers captured him and dragged him to Sekandar, who called on God in his astonishment at being confronted by such a creature. He said, "What kind of a man are you? What is your name? What can you find to live off in this lake, and what do you want from life?" The man replied, "O king, my mother and father call me Pillow-Ears." Then the king asked what it was that he could see in the middle of the lake, over toward where the sun rises. The man answered, "O king, and may you always be renowned in the world, that's a town that is like heaven; you'd say that earth had no part in its making. You won't see a single building there that isn't covered with fish skins and fish bones. On the walls they've painted the face of Afrasyah,[9] and he looks more splendid than the sun itself; and warlike Khosrow's[1] face is there too, and you can see his greatness and generosity by looking at it. They're painted on bones; you won't see one bit of soil in the whole city! The people eat fish there; that's the only thing they have to nourish them. If the king orders me to, I'll go there, but without any of your soldiers." Sekandar said to the man with huge ears, "Go, and bring back someone from the town, so that we can see something new."

Pillow-Ears hurried off to the town and soon came back with some of its inhabitants. Seventy men crossed the water with him; some were young and some old, and they were dressed in various kinds of silks. The older, more dignified men each carried a golden goblet filled with pearls, and the young ones each carried a crown; they came before Sekandar with their heads reverently bowed. They made their obeisance to him, and he talked with them for a long time. The army stayed there that night, and at cockcrow next morning the din of drums rang out from the king's pavilion. Sekandar continued the march to Babylon, and the air was dark with the dust sent up by his soldiers.

Sekandar's Letter to Arestalis[2] and Arestalis's Reply

The king knew that death was close, and that his days were darkening, and he decided that no one of royal lineage should be left alive in the world: he wanted to ensure that no man would be able to lead an army against Greece. With his mind fixed on this arrogant scheme, he wrote a letter to Arestalis, saying he would invite everyone of royal lineage to his court, where they were to come unsuspecting of what was in store for them. When this letter was delivered to

9. King of Turan, the archenemy of Iran; a powerful warrior, he was the agent of the evil god Ahriman.
1. One of the greatest of the Persian kings (531–579), famous for military conquests, cultural achievements, and major building projects.

2. The Greek philosopher Aristotle (384–322 B.C.E.), who tutored Alexander the Great. A fictional exchange of letters between Alexander and Aristotle (sometimes called *Wonders of the East*) circulated widely in Europe and the Islamic world throughout the Middle Ages.

the Greek sage, his heart seemed to break in two. Immediately he wrote a reply, weeping as if his ink were tears. "The king of the world's missive arrived, and he should give up this evil design of his. As for the evil you have already done, think no more of it but distribute goods to the poor. For the future, abstain from evil and give your soul to God; sow nothing but seeds of goodness in the world. From birth we are all marked for death, and we have no choice but to submit. No one who dies takes his sovereignty with him; he leaves, and hands on his greatness to another. Live within limits and do not shed the blood of the great families, which will make you cursed until the resurrection. And if there is no army or king in Persia, armies will sweep in from Turkestan, India, Scythia, and China, and it would be no surprise if whoever took Persia then marched on the west. The descendants of the Persian kings should not be harmed so much as by a breath of wind. Summon them to your court, but be generous to them, feast them, and consult with them. Treat each according to his rank and see that their names are listed in your pension rolls, since it is from them that you took the world, paying nothing for it. Do not give any of them power over another, or refer to any of them as king of the world, but make these royal nobles a shield to protect the west against foreign invasion."

Sekandar changed his mind when he read this letter. He summoned the world's nobly born, all who were chivalrous by nature, to his court, and assigned them suitable places there. He wrote a charter, which designated the portion of each, with the stipulation that none was to encroach on another's power: these nobles he called "kings of the peoples."

That night Sekandar reached Babylon, where he was joyfully greeted by the local nobility. During the same night a woman gave birth to an astonishing child that had a lion's head, a human chest and human shoulders, a cow's tail, and hooves. The baby was stillborn, and it would have been better if the woman had had no offspring at all rather than such a monster. Immediately they brought the child to Sekandar, who took it as an omen, and ordered that it be buried. He told his astrologers of the child, who grew pensive and silent. He demanded their opinion, saying, "If you keep anything back from me I'll cut your heads from your bodies this minute, and your shroud will be a lion's maw." When the king stormed in this way, they said:

> "First then, as scribes have written, at your birth
> The lion's emblem, Leo, ruled the earth.
> You saw the dead child had a lion's head,
> Which means your majesty will soon be dead.
> The world will be a place of strife until
> A new king bends its peoples to his will."
> The king grew pensive, then replied, "I see
> Death comes, for which there is no remedy.
> I'm not long for this world, I know, but I
> Refuse to brood on this until I die.
> Death comes to us on the appointed day—
> We cannot make fate hurry, or delay."

Sekandar's Letter to His Mother

That day, in Babylon, he fell sick, and he knew that his end was approaching. He summoned an experienced scribe and dictated what was in his heart, in a letter to his mother. He said, "The signs of death cannot be hidden; I have lived the life allotted to me in this world, and we cannot hurry or delay our fate. Do not grieve at my death, for this is not a new thing in the world: all who are born must die, be they kings or paupers. I shall tell our chieftains that when they return from this land to Greece they must obey you alone. I have established those Persians who fought against our armies as lords over their realm, so that they shall have no desire to attack Greece; our country will be secure and at peace. See that my body is buried in Egypt, and that you fulfill all that I say here. Every year distribute ten thousand gold coins of my wealth to the peasantry. If Roshanak[3] bears a son, then my name will surely survive; no one but he must become king of Greece, and he will renew the country's prosperity. But if, when her labor pains come to her, she bears a daughter, marry the child to one of Filqus's sons and call him my son, not my son-in-law, so that my name shall be remembered in the world. As for Kayd's innocent daughter, send her back to her father in India, together with the crowns and silver and gold and all the dowry she brought. Now I have completed my affairs and have no choice but to prepare my heart for death. First, see that my coffin is of gold and that my body's shroud is worthy of me; let it be of Chinese silk impregnated with sweet scents, and see that no one neglects the offices due to me. The joints of my coffin should be sealed with pitch, as well as camphor, musk, and ambergris. Honey should be poured into the coffin, then a layer of brocade placed there, on which my body is to be laid; when my face has been covered there is no more to be said. When I have gone, wise mother, remember my words. As for the things that I have sent from India, China, Turan, Iran, and Makran, keep what you need and distribute the surplus. Dear mother, my desire is that you be sensible and serene in your soul; do not torment yourself on my behalf, since no one who lives in the world lives forever. When your days too draw to a close, my soul shall surely see yours again; patience is a greater virtue than love, and a person blown hither and thither by emotion is contemptible. For months and years you lovingly cared for my body; now pray to God for my soul; with these prayers you will still care for me. And consider, who is there in all the world whose soul is not cast down by death?"

He sealed the letter and ordered that it be taken with all speed from Babylon to Greece, to give news there that the imperial glory had been eclipsed.

Sekandar Dies in Babylon

When the army learned of the king's illness, the world grew dark before them. Their eyes turned toward the throne, and the world was filled with rumors. Knowing that he had few days left to live and hearing of his army's concern, Sekandar gave orders that his sickbed be taken from the palace out to the open plain. His saddened troops saw his face devoid of color, and the plain rang

---

3. Sekandar's wife, the daughter of Darab.

from end to end with lamentations, as if the soldiers were burning in flames; they cried, "It is an evil day when the Greeks lose their king: misfortune triumphs, and now our country will be destroyed. Our enemies have reached their hearts' desire, while for us the world has turned bitter, and we shall mourn publicly and in secret."

> Then in a failing voice their king replied,
> "Live humbly, fearfully, when I have died,
> And if you'd grow and prosper see that you
> Keep my advice henceforth, in all you do.
> This is your duty to me when I'm gone
> Lest time undo the work that I have done."
> He spoke, and then his soul rose from his breast:
> The king who'd shattered armies was at rest.

An earsplitting wail went up from his troops as they heaped dust on their heads and wept bitter tears. They set fire to the royal pavilion, and the very earth seemed to cry out in sorrow. They cut the tails of a thousand horses and set their saddles on them back to front, as a sign of mourning. As they brought the golden coffin their cries resounded in the heavens; a bishop washed the corpse in clear rosewater and scattered pure camphor over it. They shrouded their king in golden brocade, lamenting as they did so, then placed him beneath a covering of Chinese silk, his body soaked from head to toe in honey. The coffin lid was fastened, and the noble tree whose shade had spread so widely was no more.

They passed the coffin from hand to hand across the plain, and as they went forward, two opinions began to be heard. The Persians said, "He should not be buried anywhere but here: this is the land of emperors, what are they doing carrying the coffin about the world like this?" But a Greek guide said, "It would not be right to bury him here; if you hear my view you'll see that I'm right. Sekandar should be buried in the soil that nourished him." A Persian interrupted, "No matter how much you continue this conversation it won't get to the root of the matter. I'll show you a meadow near here that's been preserved since the time of our ancient kings: old folk call it Jorm. There is a wooded area there, and a lake; if you ask it a question, an answer will come from the mountain nearby. Take an old man there, together with the coffin, and ask your question; if the mountain answers, it will give you the best advice." As quickly as mountain sheep they made their way to the thicket called Jorm. And when they asked their question, the answer came, "What are you doing with this royal coffin? The dust of Sekandar belongs in Alexandria, the town he founded while he was alive." As soon as they heard this, the soldiers hurried from the area.

The Mourning for Sekandar

When Sekandar's body reached Alexandria the world was beset with new disputes. The coffin was set down on the plain, and the land was filled with rumor and gossip. As many as a hundred thousand children, men, and women flocked there. The philosopher Arestalis was there, his eyes filled with bitter tears; the world watched as he stretched out his hand to the coffin and said, "Where are your intelligence, knowledge, and foresight, now that a narrow coffin is your resting place? Why in the days of your youth did you choose the earth as your couch?"

The Greek sages crowded round, each speaking in turn, lamenting Sekandar's death. And then his mother came running, and placed her face on his chest, and said,

> "O noble king, world-conqueror, whose state
> Was princely, and whose stars were fortunate,
> You're far away from me and seem so near,
> Far from your kin, far from your soldiers here.
> Would that my soul were your soul's slave, that I
> Might see the hearts of those who hate you die."
> Then Roshanak ran grieving to his side,
> Crying, "Where are those kings now, and their pride?
> Where's Dara, who once ruled the world? Where's Foor?
> Where's Ashk? Faryan? The sovereign of Sharzoor,
> And all those other lords who put their trust
> In battle and were dragged down to the dust?
> You seemed a storm cloud charged with hail: I said
> That you could never die, that you had shed
> So much blood, fought so many wars, that there
> Must be some secret you would not declare,
> Some talisman that fate had given you
> To keep you safe whatever you might do.
> You cleared the world of petty kings, brought down
> Into the dirt an empire's ancient crown,
> And when the tree you'd planted was to bear
> Its fruits you died, and left me in despair."

When the sky's golden shield descended, the nobles were exhausted by their grief, and they placed the coffin in the ground. There is nothing in the world so terrible and fearful as the fact that one comes like the wind and departs as a breath, and that neither justice nor oppression are apparent in this. Whether you are a king or a pauper you will discover no rhyme or reason to it. But one must act well, with valor and chivalry, and one must eat well and rejoice: I see no other fate for you, whether you are a subject or a prince. This is the way of the ancient world: Sekandar departed, and what remains of him now is the words we say about him. He killed thirty-six kings, but look how much of the world remained in his grasp when he died. He founded ten prosperous cities, and those cities are now reed beds. He sought things that no man has ever sought, and what remains of him within the circle of the horizon is words, nothing more. Words are the better portion since they do not decay as an old building decays in the snow and rain. I have finished with Sekandar now, and with the barrier that he built may our days be fortunate and prosperous.

SONG OF ROLAND
eleventh century

"Pagans are wrong and Christians are right." This poetic refrain, dividing the world into right and wrong, good and bad, white and black, Christian and non-Christian, expresses the fundamental outlook of the *Song of Roland*, which tells the story of how the heroic rearguard of Charlemagne's army was wiped out in an ambush at the mountain pass of Roncesvalles following their military victories in northern Spain. Yet this dualism goes beyond the metaphorical white hats and black hats of the Christian warriors and their "Saracen" (Muslim) opponents: from the first words of the poem, which identify Charlemagne as being at once "king" of the French people and "emperor" of the entire Christian world, the poem continuously defines things and persons from two points of view. The poetic rhythms of the text reaffirm this dualism as well, both within individual lines and in the doubling of stanzas (or *laisses*), when a heroic encounter on the battlefield is recounted first in simple terms, and a second time more elaborately. Yet the work never feels slow or repetitive: instead, the sequence of double stanzas heightens the reader's sense of anticipation, as the epic battle moves inexorably toward its bloody climax.

LIFE AND TIMES

At the very end of the earliest surviving copy of the *Song of Roland*, the so-called Oxford manuscript, the writer names himself: "Ci falt la geste que Turoldus declinet" ("here ends the story that Turoldus tells"). His name, a Latinized version of the Norman name "Turold" (Old Norse "Thorvaldr"), along with the French dialect of the poem, suggests that the poet who wrote and the courtly audiences who read—or, more likely, listened to—the *Song of Roland* were members of the new Anglo-Norman elite who dominated England following the Norman Conquest of 1066. These were the descendents of those same knights who, according to the twelfth-century chronicles of William of Malmesbury and Wace, had marched on the Anglo-Saxon armies of Harold, the last English claimant to the throne, while listening to their minstrel Taillefer "sing a song of Roland." This advancing Norman army would not be the last to find inspiration in the narrative of Charlemagne's heroic knight: in modern times, the *Song of Roland* has come to be seen as the foundational national epic of the French nation and, during the early twentieth century, was even used as a form of political propaganda.

THE SONG OF ROLAND

Although the Oxford manuscript dates to the mid-twelfth century, we know from Latin sources that the *Song of Roland* must have circulated much earlier in a variety of different forms, all of which were likely sung or recited. There may have been earlier manuscripts, now lost, but the text presented here is undoubtedly among the first versions of the song to be written down and thus fixed in its permanent form. Its oral origins persist, however, in the enigmatic "AOI" refrain, which appears at the close of several of the long *laisses* and may reflect a sung musical phrase or a chord played on the harp to note moments of particular drama. In the *Song of Roland*, we see one of the first manifestations of the rise of the vernacular into the realm of literature; before that time, written texts were almost exclusively in Latin, and the language spoken in daily life was thought to be simply a convenient medium for conversation, or for the evening entertainments of songs and recited tales as performed by jongleurs or minstrels. But by the time of the Oxford *Roland*, such works were entering into the poetic mainstream, beginning to take their place alongside the epic tradition of **Virgil**'s *Aeneid* and the histories of Alexander the Great. Known as the *chansons de geste*, or "songs of great deeds," these popular epics would gradually develop into the romances of the later Middle Ages, such as **Sir Gawain and the Green Knight**.

In keeping with the thematic dualism that underlies the *Song of Roland*—its division of the world into "pagan" wrong and "Christian" right—the setting of time and place as recounted in the Oxford manuscript is likewise double. The poem explicitly tells the story of the aftermath of the Frankish campaign in Spain, when in the late summer of 778 the victorious army of Charlemagne was ambushed by a band of local inhabitants at the pass of Roncesvalles. But by describing the attackers as an overwhelmingly large "Saracen" force instead of scattered Basque guerrillas, the poem reinvents eighth-century history in terms of the eleventh-century present. The result was a story of Christian battle against Muslim armies, inseparable—for the medieval reader—from the waves of crusades then being launched by European nations in an effort to conquer the Holy City of Jerusalem. The *Song of Roland* thus simultaneously looks backward to an idealized past, when the mighty king and emperor Charlemagne built his Holy Roman Empire, and forward to an anticipated period of unified European Christian rule over Jerusalem and, by extension, the whole world.

The poem opens with Charlemagne contemplating his seven long years of armed assault on Spain and deciding to return to his kingdom north of the Pyrenees, to "the sweet land of France." His army has conquered all the cities of Spain with the exception of Zaragoza, but Charlemagne, weary of battle, decides that rather than attacking the city he will accept a pledge of loyalty from its Saracen king, Marsilion. This decision precipitates the two parallel plots of the *Song of Roland*, one centering on the conflict between Christian and Saracen armies and the other centering on dissension within Charlemagne's own retinue of noble knights—his *douzepers*, or company of "twelve peers." These two plots are linked by the shared theme of treachery, in the form both of the deceitful behavior of the Saracen Marsilion, who lies to Charlemagne and attacks his men as soon as the French army begins its retreat from Spain, and of the betrayal carried out by Ganelon, the noble knight appointed by Charlemagne (at the suggestion of Roland, Ganelon's stepson and rival) to serve as messenger to Marsilion. While the first plot is acted out on the grand scale of armies, nations, and religions, the second plot is carried out on a more intimate stage, as something of a family feud. Because Ganelon is married to Charlemagne's sister, Roland is Charlemagne's nephew; and though that position brings him honor, it also obliges him to avoid the appearance of favoritism and to constantly prove his bravery and loyalty—even if doing so requires the rashest of deeds.

Roland is the exemplar of the ethical code of knighthood that is repeatedly praised in the poem, a code that entails not just exhibiting the conventional chivalric virtues of truthfulness, bravery, and loyalty but also balancing their competing claims—a more complex task. Roland's death results precisely from his extreme expression of the knightly virtues: when the rearguard is suddenly ambushed, he refuses to sound the alarm that would call back the main forces of Charlemagne's army, because he believes that asking for aid would cause him shame and prefers death to disgrace. That Roland is excessive, almost reckless, in his bravery is highlighted by the contrast with Oliver, his closest companion and the brother of his fiancée, Aude. As the poet puts it while praising the shared excellence of the two knights, who are among the brightest lights in Charlemagne's retinue, "Roland is good [*proz*—literally, 'brave'], and Oliver is wise." Oliver's wisdom casts a shadow on Roland's more impetuous behavior: bravery is admirable, but taken to an extreme it leads not only to Roland's death but to the extermination of the entire rearguard. At the same time, it is important to stress that these deaths were not in vain, for it is the tragic fate of the rearguard that ultimately spurs Charlemagne to gather his forces and strike decisively at the Saracen armies of Spain. In this light, Roland's death appears as a necessary sacrifice, the loss that sets the stage for the greater victory.

The conflict of Muslim Spain and Christian France that erupts fully after Roland's death is initially played out between the armies of Marsilion and Charlemagne; after Marsilion is mortally wounded, however, the leadership of the Saracens shifts to Baligant, their "emir" (ruler), who suddenly appears in the poem. This thousand-line section of the text, about a quarter of the whole, is almost certainly a twelfth-century addition to the basic narrative of the *Song of Roland*. It gives the sense of the perpetual, ongoing nature of the "pagan" threat to Christendom, as another leader springs up almost immediately to replace his fallen predecessor. The pagan identity is reinforced by the assertion of Saracen idolatry, with "Apolin," "Tervagant," and "Mahun" (Muham-

mad) forming a kind of malevolent anti-Trinity. Yet in spite of the fundamental opposition of Christian and pagan, right and wrong, the code of knightly behavior informs the behavior of warriors on both sides. When Charlemagne's knights meet the Saracen Baligant on the field (as described in a passage not included below), they are struck not by his difference from them but by the ways in which he seems to belong to their own kind: "God, what a noble lord," they exclaim, "if only he were made a Christian." Indeed, religious conversion, held out as a possible means of bridging the gap separating pagan and Christian on the battlefield, is achieved after the final conquest of Zaragoza by the armies of Charlemagne. The French offer the choice of conversion or death to all the inhabitants, with one significant exception: the Saracen queen Bramimunde, widow of King Marsilion. Charlemagne insists that she be converted *pur amur*, that is, "through love." For the writer of the Oxford *Song of Roland*, this phrase appears to imply a sincere religious conversion, suggesting that Bramimunde—now renamed "Juliana"—embraces Christianity out of love for Jesus Christ. Other versions of this story feature a Saracen queen whose motivation is more personal: namely, erotic love for one of the Christian knights. Such fantasies encouraged medieval readers to believe that their victory in the ongoing series of Crusades was inevitable, not just because of European military might but because of the Christian West's innate desirability.

In keeping with the double plot of the *Song of Roland*, with its grand narrative of battling armies and its intimate story of interpersonal conflict within Charlemagne's company, the poem has two separate climactic scenes of narrative closure. After the mass conversion and slaughter in Zaragoza, resolving the first level of the plot, Charlemagne and his men turn to the second level of the plot:

the trial of Ganelon. The emperor finds that the peers are divided regarding the degree of Ganelon's culpability: on the one hand, his behavior can be understood as treachery; on the other hand, it is arguably an appropriate expression of independence on the part of a powerful noble within the conventional obligations of a feudal relationship. In the end, after a trial by combat in which his champion is slain, Ganelon is condemned, his efforts at autonomy denounced as treason, and his punishment decreed: he is to be torn to pieces by four horses. Ganelon's broken body symbolizes the bonds of community shattered by the act of treason. The kinsmen who had stood with Ganelon and bound themselves as hostages before the trial are also condemned to death, by hanging; as the poet blandly puts it, "A traitor brings death, on himself and on others."

Despite these repeated scenes of closure, from the conversion and slaughter at Zaragoza to the punishment carried out after Ganelon's trial, the last lines of the *Song of Roland* insist on the essentially open-ended nature of the Christian mission. The poem ends with Charlemagne, exhausted and sorrowful after his years in Spain and the loss of his beloved nephew Roland, in the grip of a visionary dream in which the angel Gabriel commands him to embark upon a new campaign, renewing the unending cycle of battle between Christian and pagan. The king weeps bitterly, crying out, "God! . . . the pains, the labors of my life!"; nonetheless, he obeys the call.

For medieval readers, the *Song of Roland* was not an isolated, singular text but rather one episode within a whole cluster of stories about Charlemagne and his men, a cluster that was itself one among several comparable "cycles" of epic poetry. In the twelfth century, these *chansons de geste* were heroic models of the distant past that helped both inspire and perpetuate the ongoing warfare carried out by Crusaders in their repeated attempts to seize Jerusalem. In the twenty-first century, they are vivid reminders of an age in which warfare was the highest expression of human virtue, when the will of God was the compass that determined the actions of mankind.

From Song of Roland[1]

1

Charles the King, our Emperor, the Great,
has been in Spain for seven full years,
has conquered the high land down to the sea.
There is no castle that stands against him now,
no wall, no citadel left to break down—
except Saragossa, high on a mountain.[2]
King Marsilion holds it, who does not love God,

5

1. Translated by Frederick Goldin. Many of Goldin's notes have been adapted for use here.
2. Saragossa, in northeastern Spain, is not actually on a mountaintop. The poet's geography is not always accurate.

who serves Mahumet and prays to Apollin.[3]
He cannot save himself: his ruin will find him there. AOI.[4]

2

King Marsilion was in Saragossa.   10
He has gone forth into a grove, beneath its shade,
and he lies down on a block of blue marble,
twenty thousand men, and more, all around him.
He calls aloud to his dukes and his counts:
"Listen, my lords, to the troubles we have.   15
The Emperor Charles of the sweet land of France
has come into this country to destroy us.
I have no army able to give him battle,
I do not have the force to break his force.
Now act like my wise men: give me counsel,   20
save me, save me from death, save me from shame!"
No pagan there has one word to say to him
except Blancandrin, of the castle of Valfunde.

3

One of the wisest pagans was Blancandrin,
brave and loyal, a great mounted warrior,   25
a useful man, the man to aid his lord;
said to the King: "Do not give way to panic.
Do this: send Charles, that wild, terrible man,
tokens of loyal service and great friendship:
you will give him bears and lions and dogs,   30
seven hundred camels, a thousand molted hawks,
four hundred mules weighed down with gold and silver,
and fifty carts, to cart it all away:
he'll have good wages for his men who fight for pay.
Say he's made war long enough in this land: 35
let him go home, to France, to Aix, at last—
come Michaelmas[5] you will follow him there,
say you will take their faith, become a Christian,
and be his man with honor, with all you have.
If he wants hostages, why, you'll send them,   40
ten, or twenty, to give him security.
Let us send him the sons our wives have borne.
I'll send my son with all the others named to die.
It is better that they should lose their heads[6]
than that we, Lord, should lose our dignity   45
and our honors—and be turned into beggars!" AOI.

---

3. The Greek god Apollo; but the poet is mistaken, for these people worship only one god, Allah. "Mahumet": Muhammad (ca. 570–632), founder of the Islamic religion.
4. These three mysterious letters appear at certain moments throughout the text, 180 times in all. No one has ever adequately explained them, though every reader feels their effect.

5. The feast of St. Michael, September 29. *Aix*: Aix-la-Chapelle, or Aachen, was the capital of Charlemagne's empire.
6. The speaker expects that the hostages will be killed by the French when the deception becomes clear. Sometime before, hostages sent by the French had been similarly slain (see lines 207–09).

4

Said Blancandrin: "By this right hand of mine
and by this beard that flutters on my chest,
you will soon see the French army disband,
the Franks will go to their own land, to France.
When each of them is in his dearest home,   50
King Charles will be in Aix, in his chapel.
At Michaelmas he will hold a great feast—
that day will come, and then our time runs out,
he'll hear no news, he'll get no word from us.   55
This King is wild, the heart in him is cruel:
he'll take the heads of the hostages we gave.
It is better, Lord, that they lose their heads
than that we lose our bright, our beautiful Spain—
and nothing more for us but misery and pain!"   60
The pagans say: "It may be as he says."

5

King Marsilion brought his counsel to end,
then he summoned Clarin of Balaguét,
Estramarin and Eudropin, his peer,
And Priamun, Guarlan, that bearded one,   65
and Machiner and his uncle Maheu,
and Joüner, Malbien from over-sea,
and Blancandrin, to tell what was proposed.
From the worst of criminals he called these ten.
"Barons, my lords, you're to go to Charlemagne;   70
he's at the siege of Cordres,[7] the citadel.
Olive branches are to be in your hands—
that signifies peace and humility.
If you've the skill to get me an agreement,
I will give you a mass of gold and silver   75
and lands and fiefs, as much as you could want."
Say the pagans: "We'll benefit from this!" AOI.

6

Marsilion brought his council to an end,
said to his men: "Lords, you will go on now,
and remember: olive branches in your hands;   80
and in my name tell Charlemagne the King
for his god's sake to have pity on me—
he will not see a month from this day pass
before I come with a thousand faithful;
say I will take that Christian religion   85
and be his man in love and loyalty.
If he wants hostages, why, he'll have them."
Said Blancandrin: "Now you will get good terms." AOI.

---

7. Córdoba, in southern Spain, at that time the seat of a Muslim dynasty.

7

King Marsilion had ten white mules led out,
sent to him once by the King of Suatilie,[8]   90
with golden bits and saddles wrought with silver.
The men are mounted, the men who brought the message,
and in their hands they carry olive branches.
They came to Charles, who has France in his keeping.
He cannot prevent it: they will fool him. AOI.   95

8

The Emperor is secure and jubilant:
he has taken Cordres, broken the walls,
knocked down the towers with his catapults.
And what tremendous spoils his knights have won—
gold and silver, precious arms, equipment.   100
In the city not one pagan remained
who is not killed or turned into a Christian.
The Emperor is in an ample grove,
Roland and Oliver are with him there,
Samson the Duke and Ansëis the fierce,   105
Geoffrey d'Anjou, the King's own standard-bearer;
and Gerin and Gerer, these two together always,
and the others, the simple knights, in force:
fifteen thousand from the sweet land of France.
The warriors sit on bright brocaded silk;   110
they are playing at tables to pass the time,
the old and the wisest men sitting at chess,
the young light-footed men fencing with swords.
Beneath a pine, beside a wild sweet-briar,
there was a throne, every inch of pure gold.   115
There sits the King, who rules over sweet France.
His beard is white, his hair flowering white.
That lordly body! the proud fierce look of him!—
If someone should come here asking for him,
there'd be no need to point out the King of France.
The messengers dismounted, and on their feet   120
they greeted him in all love and good faith.

9

Blancandrin spoke, he was the first to speak,
said to the King: "Greetings, and God save you,
that glorious God whom we all must adore.
Here is the word of the great king Marsilion: 125
he has looked into this law of salvation,
wants to give you a great part of his wealth,
bears and lions and hunting dogs on chains,
seven hundred camels, a thousand molted hawks,
four hundred mules packed tight with gold and silver,   130
and fifty carts, to cart it all away;

---

8. A subordinate king, owing allegiance to Marsilion.

and there will be so many fine gold bezants,[9]
you'll have good wages for the men in your pay.
You have stayed long—long enough!—in this land,
it is time to go home, to France, to Aix.   135
My master swears he will follow you there."
The Emperor holds out his hands toward God,
bows down his head, begins to meditate. AOI.

10

The Emperor held his head bowed down;
never was he too hasty with his words: 140
his custom is to speak in his good time.
When his head rises, how fierce the look of him;
he said to them: "You have spoken quite well.
King Marsilion is my great enemy.
Now all these words that you have spoken here—   145
how far can I trust them? How can I be sure?"
The Saracen: "He wants to give you hostages.
How many will you want? ten? fifteen? twenty?
I'll put my son with the others named to die.[1]
You will get some, I think, still better born.   150
When you are at home in your high royal palace,
at the great feast of Saint Michael-in-Peril,[2]
the lord who nurtures me will follow you,
and in those baths[3]—the baths God made for you—
my lord will come and want to be made Christian."   155
King Charles replies: "He may yet save his soul." AOI.

11

Late in the day it was fair, the sun was bright.
Charles has them put the ten mules into stables.
The King commands a tent pitched in the broad grove,
and there he has the ten messengers lodged;   160
twelve serving men took splendid care of them.
There they remained that night till the bright day.
The Emperor rose early in the morning,
the King of France, and heard the mass and matins.
And then the King went forth beneath a pine,   165
calls for his barons to complete his council:
he will proceed only with the men of France. AOI.

12

The Emperor goes forth beneath a pine,
calls for his barons to complete his council:
Ogier the Duke, and Archbishop Turpin,   170

9. Gold coins; the name is derived from Byzantium.
1. That is, if the promise is broken. "Saracen": the usual term for the enemy.
2. The epithet "in peril of the sea" was applied
to the famous sanctuary Mont-St.-Michel off

the Normandy coast because it could be reached
on foot only at low tide, and pilgrims were
endangered by the incoming tide. Eventually,
the phrase was applied to the saint himself.
3. Famous healing springs at Aix-la-Chapelle.

Richard the Old, and his nephew Henri;
from Gascony, the brave Count Acelin,
Thibaut of Reims, and his cousin Milun;
and Gerer and Gerin, they were both there,
and there was Count Roland, he came with them,   175
and Oliver, the valiant and well-born;
a thousand Franks of France, and more, were there.
Ganelon came, who committed the treason.
Now here begins the council that went wrong.[4] AOI.

13

"Barons, my lords," said Charles the Emperor,   180
"King Marsilion has sent me messengers,
wants to give me a great mass of his wealth,
bears and lions and hunting dogs on chains,
seven hundred camels, a thousand molting hawks,
four hundred mules packed with gold of Araby,   185
and with all that, more than fifty great carts;
but also asks that I go back to France:
he'll follow me to Aix, my residence,
and take our faith, the one redeeming faith,
become a Christian, hold his march[5] lands from me.   190
But what lies in his heart? I do not know."
And the French say: "We must be on our guard!" AOI.

14

The Emperor has told them what was proposed.
Roland the Count will never assent to that,
gets to his feet, comes forth to speak against it;   195
says to the King: "Trust Marsilion—and suffer!
We came to Spain seven long years ago,
I won Noples for you, I won Commibles,
I took Valterne and all the land of Pine,
and Balaguer and Tudela and Seville.   200
And then this king, Marsilion, played the traitor:
he sent you men, fifteen of his pagans—
and sure enough, each held an olive branch;
and they recited just these same words to you.
You took counsel with all your men of France;   205
they counseled you to a bit of madness:
you sent two Counts across to the Pagans,
one was Basan, the other was Basile.
On the hills below Haltille, he took their heads.
They were your men. Fight the war you came to fight!   210
Lead the army you summoned on to Saragossa!
Lay siege to it all the rest of your life!
Avenge the men that this criminal murdered!" AOI.

---

4. The poet anticipates that the plan adopted
at the council will prove to be a mistake and

that Ganelon will commit treason.
5. A frontier province or territory.

15

The Emperor held his head bowed down with this,
and stroked his beard, and smoothed his mustache down,   215
and speaks no word, good or bad, to his nephew.
The French keep still, all except Ganelon:
he gets to his feet and, come before King Charles,
how fierce he is as he begins his speech;
said to the King: "Believe a fool—me or   220
another—and suffer! Protect your interest!
When Marsilion the King sends you his word
that he will join his hands[6] and be your man,
and hold all Spain as a gift from your hands
and then receive the faith that we uphold—   225
whoever urges that we refuse this peace,
that man does not care, Lord, what death we die.
That wild man's counsel must not win the day here—
let us leave fools, let us hold with wise men!" AOI.

16

And after that there came Naimon the Duke—   230
no greater vassal in that court than Naimon—
said to the King: "You've heard it clearly now,
Count Ganelon has given you your answer:
let it be heeded, there is wisdom in it.
King Marsilion is beaten in this war,   235
you have taken every one of his castles,
broken his walls with your catapults,
burnt his cities and defeated his men.
Now when he sends to ask you to have mercy,
it would be a sin to do still more to him.   240
Since he'll give you hostages as guarantee,
this great war must not go on, it is not right."
And the French say: "The Duke has spoken well." AOI.

17

"Barons, my lords, whom shall we send down there,
to Saragossa, to King Marsilion?"   245
Naimon replies, "I'll go, if you grant it!
At once, my lord! give me the glove and the staff."[7]
The King replies: "You're a man of great wisdom:
now by my beard, now by this mustache of mine,
you will not go so far from me this year; or ever.   250
Go take your seat when no one calls on you."

18

"Barons, my lords, whom can we send down there,
to this Saracen who holds Saragossa?"

6. Part of the gesture of homage; the lord enclosed the joined hands of his vassal with his own.

7. Symbols of his commission from the Emperor Charles.

Roland replies: "I can go there! No trouble!"
"No, no, not you!" said Oliver the Count,   255
"that heart in you is wild, spoils for a fight,
how I would worry—you'd fight with them, I know.
Now I myself could go, if the King wishes."
The King replies: "Be still, the two of you!
Not you, not he—neither will set foot there.   260
Now by this beard, as sure as you see white,
let no man here name one of the Twelve Peers!"[8]
The French keep still, see how he silenced them.

19

Turpin of Reims has come forth from the ranks,
said to the King: "Let your Franks have a rest.   265
You have been in this land for seven years,
the many pains, the struggles they've endured!
I'm the one, Lord, give me the glove and the staff,
and I'll go down to this Saracen of Spain
and then I'll see what kind of man we have."   270
The Emperor replies to him in anger:
"Now you go back and sit on that white silk
and say no more unless I command it!" AOI.

20

"My noble knights," said the Emperor Charles,
"choose me one man: a baron from my march,   275
to bring my message to King Marsilion."
And Roland said: "Ganelon, my stepfather."
The French respond: "Why, that's the very man!
pass this man by and you won't send a wiser."
And hearing this Count Ganelon began to choke,   280
pulls from his neck the great furs of marten
and stands there now, in his silken tunic,
eyes full of lights, the look on him of fury,
he has the body, the great chest of a lord;
stood there so fair, all his peers gazed on him;   285
said to Roland: "Madman, what makes you rave?
Every man knows I am your stepfather,
yet you named me to go to Marsilion.
Now if God grants that I come back from there,
you will have trouble: I'll start a feud with you,   290
it will go on till the end of your life."
Roland replies: "What wild words—all that blustering!
Every man knows that threats don't worry me.
But we need a wise man to bring the message:
if the King wills, I'll gladly go in your place."   295

---

8. The elite knights who make up Charlemagne's inner circle.

21

Ganelon answers: "You will not go for me. AOI.
You're not my man, and I am not your lord.
Charles commands me to perform this service:
I'll go to Marsilion in Saragossa.
And I tell you, I'll play a few wild tricks   300
before I cool the anger in me now."
When he heard that, Roland began to laugh. AOI.

22

Ganelon sees: *Roland laughing at him!*
and feels such pain he almost bursts with rage,
needs little more to go out of his mind;   305
says to the Count: "I have no love for you,
you *made* this choice fall on me, and that was wrong.
Just Emperor, here I am, before you.
I have one will: to fulfill your command."

23

"I know now I must go to Saragossa. AOI.   310
Any man who goes there cannot return.
And there is this: I am your sister's husband,
have a son by her, the finest boy there can be,
Baldewin," says he, "who will be a good man.
To him I leave my honors, fiefs, and lands.   315
Protect my son: these eyes will never see him."
Charles answers him: "That tender heart of yours!
You have to go, I have commanded it."

24

And the King said: "Ganelon, come forward, AOI.
come and receive the staff and the glove.   320
You have heard it: the Franks have chosen you."
Said Ganelon: "Lord, it's Roland who did this.
In all my days I'll have no love for him,
or Oliver, because he's his companion,
or the Twelve Peers, because they love him so.   325
I defy them, here in your presence, Lord."
And the King said: "What hate there is in you!
You will go there, for I command you to."
"I can go there, but I'll have no protector. AOI.
Basile had none, nor did Basan his brother."   330

25

The Emperor offers him his right glove.
But Ganelon would have liked not to be there.
When he had to take it, it fell to the ground.
"God!" say the French, "What's that going to mean?
What disaster will this message bring us!"   335
Said Ganelon: "Lords, you'll be hearing news."

26

Said Ganelon: "Lord, give me leave to go,
since go I must, there's no reason to linger."
And the King said: "In Jesus' name and mine,"
absolved him and blessed him with his right hand.   340
Then he gave him the letter and the staff.

27

Count Ganelon goes away to his camp.
He chooses, with great care, his battle-gear,
picks the most precious arms that he can find.
The spurs he fastened on were golden spurs;   345
he girds his sword, Murgleis, upon his side;
he has mounted Tachebrun, his battle horse,
his uncle, Guinemer, held the stirrup.
And there you would have seen brave men in tears,
his men, who say: "Baron, what bad luck for you!   350
All your long years in the court of the King,
always proclaimed a great and noble vassal!
Whoever it was doomed you to go down there—
Charlemagne himself will not protect that man.
Roland the Count should not have thought of this—   355
and you the living issue of a mighty line!"
And then they say: "Lord, take us there with you!"
Ganelon answers: "May the Lord God forbid!
It is better that I alone should die
     than so many good men and noble knights.
You will be going back, Lords, to sweet France: 360
go to my wife and greet her in my name,
and Pinabel, my dear friend and peer,
and Baldewin, my son, whom you all know:
give him your aid, and hold him as your lord."
And he starts down the road; he is on his way. AOI.   365

28

Ganelon rides to a tall olive tree,
there he has joined the pagan messengers.
And here is Blancandrin, who slows down for him:
and what great art they speak to one another.
Said Blancandrin: "An amazing man, Charles!   370
conquered Apulia, conquered all of Calabria,
crossed the salt sea on his way into England,
won its tribute,[9] got Peter's pence[1] for Rome:
what does he want from us here in our march?"
Ganelon answers: "That is the heart in him.   375
There'll never be a man the like of him." AOI.

---

9. Although begun perhaps as early as the 8th
century, the tribute was not the result of any
effort of Charlemagne, who did not in fact
visit England.

1. A tribute of one penny per house "for the use
of Saint Peter," that is, for the pope in Rome.

29

Said Blancandrin: "The Franks are a great people.
Now what great harm all those dukes and counts do
to their own lord when they give him such counsel:
they torment him, they'll destroy him, and others."   380
Ganelon answers: "Well, now, I know no such man
except Roland, who'll suffer for it yet.
One day the Emperor was sitting in the shade:
his nephew came, still wearing his hauberk,
he had gone plundering near Carcassonne;   385
and in his hand he held a bright red apple:
'Dear Lord, here, take,' said Roland to his uncle;
'I offer you the crowns of all earth's kings.'
Yes, Lord, that pride of his will destroy him,
for every day he goes riding at death.   390
And *should* someone kill him, we would have peace." AOI.

30

Said Blancandrin: "A wild man, this Roland!
wants to make every nation beg for his mercy
and claims a right to every land on earth!
But what men support him, if that is his aim?"   395
Ganelon answers: "Why, Lord, the men of France.
They love him so, they will never fail him.
He gives them gifts, masses of gold and silver,
mules, battle horses, brocaded silks, supplies.
And it is all as the Emperor desires: 400
he'll win the lands from here to the Orient." AOI.

31

Ganelon and Blancandrin rode on until
each pledged his faith to the other and swore
they'd find a way to have Count Roland killed.
They rode along the paths and ways until,   405
in Saragossa, they dismount beneath a yew.
There was a throne in the shade of a pine,
covered with silk from Alexandria.
There sat the king who held the land of Spain,
and around him twenty thousand Saracens.   410
There is no man who speaks or breathes a word,
poised for the news that all would like to hear.
Now here they are: Ganelon and Blancandrin.

32

Blancandrin came before Marsilion,
his hand around the fist of Ganelon,   415
said to the King: "May Mahumet save you,
and Apollin, whose sacred laws we keep!
We delivered your message to Charlemagne:
when we finished, he raised up both his hands
and praised his god. He made no other answer.   420

Here he sends you one of his noble barons,
a man of France, and very powerful.
You'll learn from him whether or not you'll have peace."
"Let him speak, we shall hear him," Marsilion answers. AOI.

33

But Ganelon had it all well thought out.   425
With what great art he commences his speech,
a man who knows his way about these things;
said to the King: "May the Lord God save you,
that glorious God, whom we must all adore.
Here is the word of Charlemagne the King: 430
you are to take the holy Christian faith;
he will give you one half of Spain in fief.
If you refuse, if you reject this peace,
you will be taken by force, put into chains,
and then led forth to the King's seat at Aix;   435
you will be tried; you will be put to death:
you will die there, in shame, vilely, degraded."
King Marsilion, hearing this, was much shaken.
In his hand was a spear, with golden feathers.
He would have struck, had they not held him back. AOI.   440

34

Marsilion the King—his color changed!
He shook his spear, waved the shaft to and fro.
When he saw that, Ganelon laid hand to sword,
he drew it out two fingers from its sheath;
and spoke to it: "How beautiful and bright!   445
How long did I bear you in the King's court
before I died! The Emperor will not say
I died alone in that foreign country:
they'll buy you first, with the best men they have!"
The pagans say: "Let us break up this quarrel!"   450

35

The pagan chiefs pleaded with Marsilion
till he sat down once again on his throne.
The Caliph[2] spoke: "You did us harm just now,
served us badly, trying to strike this Frenchman.
You should have listened, you should have heard him out."   455
Said Ganelon: "Lord, I must endure it.
I shall not fail, for all the gold God made,
for all the wealth there may be in this land,
to tell him, as long as I have breath, all
that Charlemagne—that great and mighty King!—   460
has sent through me to his mortal enemy."
He is buckled in a great cloak of sable,
covered with silk from Alexandria:

2. A high official of King Marsilion.

he throws it down. Blancandrin picks it up.
But his great sword he will never throw down!   465
In his right fist he grasps its golden pommel.
Say the pagans: "That's a great man! A noble!" AOI.

36

Now Ganelon drew closer to the King
and said to him: "You are wrong to get angry,
for Charles, who rules all France, sends you this word: 470
you are to take the Christian people's faith;
he will give you one half of Spain in fief,
the other half goes to his nephew: Roland—
quite a partner you will be getting there!
If you refuse, if you reject this peace,   475
he will come and lay siege to Saragossa;
you will be taken by force, put into chains,
and brought straight on to Aix, the capital.
No saddle horse, no war horse for you then,
no he-mule, no she-mule for you to ride: 480
you will be thrown on some miserable dray;
you will be tried, and you will lose your head.
Our Emperor sends you this letter."
He put the letter in the pagan's right fist.

37

Marsilion turned white; he was enraged;   485
he breaks the seal, he's knocked away the wax,
runs through the letter, sees what is written there:
"Charles sends me word, this king who rules in France:
I'm to think of his anger and his grief—
he means Basan and his brother Basile,   490
I took their heads in the hills below Haltille;
if I want to redeem the life of my body,
I must send him my uncle: the Algalife.[3]
And otherwise he'll have no love for me."
Then his son came and spoke to Marsilion,   495
said to the King: "Ganelon has spoken madness.
He crossed the line, he has no right to live.
Give him to me, I will do justice on him."
When he heard that, Ganelon brandished his sword;
he runs to the pine, set his back against the trunk.   500

38

King Marsilion went forth into the orchard,
he takes with him the greatest of his men;
Blancandrin came, that gray-haired counselor,
and Jurfaleu, Marsilion's son and heir,
the Algalife, uncle and faithful friend.   505

3. The Caliph.

Said Blancandrin: "Lord, call the Frenchman back.
He swore to me to keep faith with our cause."
And the King said: "Go, bring him back here, then."
He took Ganelon's right hand by the fingers,
leads him into the orchard before the King.   510
And there they plotted that criminal treason. AOI.

39

Said Marsilion: "My dear Lord Ganelon,
that was foolish, what I just did to you,
I showed my anger, even tried to strike you.
Here's a pledge of good faith, these sable furs,   515
the gold alone worth over five hundred pounds:
I'll make it all up before tomorrow night."
Ganelon answers: "I will not refuse it.
May it please God to reward you for it." AOI.

40

Said Marsilion: "I tell you, Ganelon,   520
I have a great desire to love you dearly.
I want to hear you speak of Charlemagne.
He is so old, he's used up all his time—
from what I hear, he is past two hundred!
He has pushed his old body through so many lands,   525
taken so many blows on his buckled shield,
made beggars of so many mighty kings:
when will he lose the heart for making war?"
Ganelon answers: "Charles is not one to lose heart.
No man sees him, no man learns to know him   530
who does not say: the Emperor is great.
I do not know how to praise him so highly
that his great merit would not surpass my praise.
Who could recount his glory and his valor?
God put the light in him of such lordliness,   535
he would choose death before he failed his barons."

41

Said the pagan: "I have reason to marvel
at Charlemagne, a man so old and gray—
he's two hundred years old, I hear, and more;
he has tortured his body through so many lands,   540
and borne so many blows from lance and spear,
made beggars of so many mighty kings:
when will he lose the heart for making war?"
"Never," said Ganelon, "while his nephew lives,
he's a fighter, there's no vassal like him
under the vault of heaven. And he has friends.   545
There's Oliver, a good man, his companion.
And the Twelve Peers, whom Charles holds very dear,
form the vanguard, with twenty thousand knights.
Charles is secure, he fears no man on earth." AOI.

42

Said the pagan: "Truly, how I must marvel   550
at Charlemagne, who is so gray and white—
over two hundred years, from what I hear;
gone through so many lands a conqueror,
and borne so many blows from strong sharp spears,
killed and conquered so many mighty kings: 555
when will he lose the heart for making war?"
"Never," said Ganelon, "while one man lives: Roland!
no man like him from here to the Orient!
There's his companion, Oliver, a brave man.
And the Twelve Peers, whom Charles holds very dear,   560
form the vanguard, with twenty thousand Franks.
Charles is secure, he fears no man alive." AOI.

43

"Dear Lord Ganelon," said Marsilion the King,
"I have my army, you won't find one more handsome:
I can muster four hundred thousand knights!   565
With this host, now, can I fight Charles and the French?"
Ganelon answers: "No, no, don't try that now,
you'd take a loss: thousands of your pagans!
Forget such foolishness, listen to wisdom:
send the Emperor so many gifts   570
there'll be no Frenchman there who does not marvel.
For twenty hostages—those you'll be sending—
he will go home: home again to sweet France!
And he will leave his rear-guard behind him.
There will be Roland, I do believe, his nephew,   575
and Oliver, brave man, born to the court.
These Counts are dead, if anyone trusts me.
Then Charles will see that great pride of his go down,
he'll have no heart to make war on you again." AOI.

44

"Dear Lord Ganelon," said Marsilion the King,
"What must I do to kill Roland the Count?"   580
Ganelon answers: "Now I can tell you that.
The King will be at Cize,[4] in the great passes,
he will have placed his rear-guard at his back:
there'll be his nephew, Count Roland, that great man,   585
and Oliver, in whom he puts such faith,
and twenty thousand Franks in their company.
Now send one hundred thousand of your pagans
against the French—let them give the first battle.
The French army will be hit hard and shaken.   590
I must tell you: your men will be martyred.
Give them a second battle, then, like the first.
One will get him, Roland will not escape.

---

4. The pass through the Pyrenees.

Then you'll have done a deed, a noble deed,
and no more war for the rest of your life!" AOI.   595

45

"If someone can bring about the death of Roland,
then Charles would lose the right arm of his body,
that marvelous army would disappear—
never again could Charles gather such forces.
Then peace at last for the Land of Fathers!"[5]   600
When Marsilion heard that, he kissed his neck.
Then he begins to open up his treasures. AOI.

46

Marsilion said, "Why talk. . . .
No plan has any worth which one. . . .[6]
Now swear to me that you will betray Roland."   605
Ganelon answers: "Let it be as you wish."
On the relics in his great sword Murgleis
he swore treason and became a criminal. AOI.

47

There stood a throne made all of ivory.
Marsilion commands them bring forth a book: 610
it was the law of Mahum and Tervagant.[7]
This is the vow sworn by the Saracen of Spain:
if he shall find Roland in the rear-guard,
he shall fight him, all his men shall fight him,
and once he finds Roland, Roland will die.   615
Says Ganelon: "May it be as you will." AOI.

48

And now there came a pagan, Valdabrun,
he was the man who raised Marsilion.
And, all bright smiles, he said to Ganelon:
"You take my sword, there's no man has one better: 620
a thousand coins, and more, are in the hilt.
It is a gift, dear lord, made in friendship,
only help us to Roland, that great baron,
let us find him standing in the rear-guard."
"It shall be done," replies Count Ganelon.   625
And then they kissed, on the face, on the chin.

49

And there came then a pagan, Climborin,
and, all bright smiles, he said to Ganelon:
"You take my helmet, I never saw one better,

---

5. "Tere Majur," in the original; it can mean
either "the great land" or "the land of fathers,
ancestors." It always refers to France.
6. Parts of lines 603–04 are unintelligible in
the manuscript.
7. Or Termagent, a fictitious deity whom medieval Christians believed to be worshipped by
Muslims.

only help us to Roland, lord of the march, 630
show us the way to put Roland to shame."
"It shall be done," replied Count Ganelon.
And then they kissed, on the face, on the mouth. AOI.

50

And then there came the Queen, Bramimunde;
said to the Count: "Lord, I love you well, 635
for my lord and all his men esteem you so.
I wish to send your wife two necklaces,
they are all gold, jacinths, and amethysts,
they are worth more than all the wealth of Rome.
Your Emperor has never seen their like." 640
He has taken them, thrusts them into his boot. AOI.

51

The King calls for Malduit, his treasurer:
"The gifts for Charles—is everything prepared?"
And he replies: "Yes, Lord, and well prepared:
seven hundred camels, packed with gold and silver, 645
and twenty hostages, the noblest under heaven." AOI.

52

Marsilion took Ganelon by the shoulder
and said to him: "You're a brave man, a wise man.
Now by that faith you think will save your soul,
take care you do not turn your heart from us. 650
I will give you a great mass of my wealth,
ten mules weighed down with fine Arabian gold;
and come each year, I'll do the same again.
Now you take these, the keys to this vast city:
present King Charles with all of its great treasure; 655
then get me Roland picked for the rear-guard.
Let me find him in some defile or pass,
I will fight him, a battle to the death."
Ganelon answers: "It's high time that I go."
Now he is mounted, and he is on his way. AOI. 660

53

The Emperor moves homeward, he's drawing near.
Now he has reached the city of Valterne:
Roland had stormed it, destroyed it, and it stood
from that day forth a hundred years laid waste.
Charles is waiting for news of Ganelon 665
and the tribute from Spain, from that great land.
In the morning, at dawn, with the first light,
Count Ganelon came to the Christian camp. AOI.

54

The Emperor rose early in the morning,
the King of France, and has heard mass and matins. 670

On the green grass he stood before his tent.
Roland was there, and Oliver, brave man,
Naimon the Duke, and many other knights.
Ganelon came, the traitor, the foresworn.
With what great cunning he commences his speech;   675
said to the King: "May the Lord God save you!
Here I bring you the keys to Saragossa.
And I bring you great treasure from that city,
and twenty hostages, have them well guarded.
And good King Marsilion sends you this word: 680
Do not blame him concerning the Algalife:
I saw it all myself, with my own eyes:
    four hundred thousand men, and all in arms,
their hauberks on, some with their helms laced on,
swords on their belts, the hilts enameled gold,
who went with him to the edge of the sea.   685
They are in flight: it is the Christian faith—
they do not want it, they will not keep its law.
They had not sailed four full leagues out to sea
when a high wind, a tempest swept them up.
They were all drowned; you will never see them;   690
if he were still alive, I'd have brought him.
As for the pagan King, Lord, believe this:
before you see one month from this day pass,
he'll follow you to the Kingdom of France
and take the faith—he will take your faith, Lord,   695
and join his hands and become your vassal.
He will hold Spain as a fief from your hand."
Then the King said: "May God be thanked for this.
You have done well, you will be well rewarded."
Throughout the host they sound a thousand trumpets.   700
The French break camp, strap their gear on their pack-horses.
They take the road to the sweet land of France. AOI.

                    55
King Charlemagne laid waste the land of Spain,
stormed its castles, ravaged its citadels.
The King declares his war is at an end.   705
The Emperor rides toward the land of sweet France.
Roland the Count affixed the gonfanon,[8]
raised it toward heaven on the height of a hill;
the men of France make camp across that country.
Pagans are riding up through these great valleys,   710
their hauberks on, their tunics of double mail,
their helms laced on, their swords fixed on their belts,
shields on their necks, lances trimmed with their banners.
In a forest high in the hills they gathered:
four hundred thousand men waiting for dawn.   715
God, the pity of it! the French do not know! AOI.

8. Pennant.

56

The day goes by; now the darkness of night.
Charlemagne sleeps, the mighty Emperor.
He dreamt he was at Cize, in the great passes,
and in his fists held his great ashen lance.   720
Count Ganelon tore it away from him
and brandished it, shook it with such fury
the splinters of the shaft fly up toward heaven.
Charlemagne sleeps, his dream does not wake him.

57

And after that he dreamed another vision: 725
he was in France, in his chapel at Aix,
a cruel wild boar was biting his right arm;
saw coming at him—from the Ardennes—a leopard,
it attacked him, fell wildly on his body.
And a swift hound running down from the hall   730
came galloping, bounding over to Charles,
tore the right ear off that first beast, the boar,
turns, in fury, to fight against the leopard.
And the French say: It is a mighty battle,
but cannot tell which one of them will win.   735
Charlemagne sleeps, his dream does not wake him. AOI.

58

The day goes by, and the bright dawn arises.
Throughout that host. . . .⁹
The Emperor rides forth with such fierce pride.
"Barons, my lords," said the Emperor Charles,   740
"look at those passes, at those narrow defiles—
pick me a man to command the rear-guard."
Ganelon answers: "Roland, here, my stepson.
You have no baron as great and brave as Roland."
When he hears that, the King stares at him in fury;   745
and said to him: "You are the living devil,
a mad dog—the murderous rage in you!
And who will precede me, in the vanguard?"
Ganelon answers, "Why, Ogier of Denmark,
you have no baron who could lead it so well."   750

59

Roland the Count, when he heard himself named,
knew what to say, and spoke as a knight must speak:
"Lord Stepfather, I have to cherish you!
You have had the rear-guard assigned to me.
Charles will not lose, this great King who rules France,   755
I swear it now, one palfrey, one war horse—
while I'm alive and know what's happening—
one he-mule, one she-mule that he might ride,

9. The rest of the line is unintelligible in the manuscript.

Charles will not lose one sumpter, not one pack horse
that has not first been bought and paid for with swords."
Ganelon answers: "You speak the truth, I know." AOI.   760

60

When Roland hears he will lead the rear-guard,
he spoke in great fury to his stepfather:
"Hah! you nobody, you base-born little fellow,
and did you think the glove would fall from my hands
as the staff fell[1] from yours before King Charles?" AOI.   765

61

"Just Emperor," said Roland, that great man,
"give me the bow that you hold in your hand.
And no man here, I think, will say in reproach
I let it drop, as Ganelon let the staff drop[2]
from his right hand, when he should have taken it."   770
The Emperor bowed down his head with this,
he pulled his beard, he twisted his mustache,
cannot hold back, tears fill his eyes, he weeps.

62

And after that there came Naimon the Duke,
no greater vassal in the court than Naimon,   775
said to the King: "You've heard it clearly now:
it is Count Roland. How furious he is.
He is the one to whom the rear-guard falls,
no baron here can ever change that now.
Give him the bow that you have stretched and bent,   780
and then find him good men to stand with him."
The King gives him the bow; Roland has it now.

63

The Emperor calls forth Roland the Count:
"My lord, my dear nephew, of course you know
I will give you half my men, they are yours.   785
Let them serve you, it is your salvation."
"None of that!" said the Count. "May God strike me
if I discredit the history of my line.
I'll keep twenty thousand Franks—they are good men.
Go your way through the passes, you will be safe.   790
You must not fear any man while I live."

64

Roland the Count mounted his battle horse. AOI.
Oliver came to him, his companion.
And Gerin came, and the brave Count Gerer,

---

1. Ganelon had let fall a glove, not a staff (line
333). For this and other less objective reasons,
some editors have questioned the authenticity of
this *laisse* (stanza).

2. In this *laisse* a reviser tried to make the text
more consistent by adding the reference to the
staff.

and Aton came, and there came Berenger,   795
and Astor came, and Anseïs, fierce and proud,
and the old man Gerard of Roussillon,
and Gaifier, that great and mighty duke.
Said the Archbishop: "I'm going, by my head!"
"And I with you," said Gautier the Count,   800
"I am Count Roland's man and must not fail him."
And together they choose twenty thousand men. AOI.

65

Roland the Count summons Gautier de l'Hum:
"Now take a thousand Franks from our land, France,
and occupy those passes and the heights there.   805
The Emperor must not lose a single man." AOI.
Gautier replies: "Lord, I'll fight well for you."
And with a thousand French of France, their land,
Gautier rides out to the hills and defiles;
will not come down, for all the bad news, again,   810
till seven hundred swords have been drawn out.
King Almaris of the Kingdom of Belferne
gave them battle that day, and it was bitter.

66

High are the hills, the valleys tenebrous,
the cliffs are dark, the defiles mysterious.   815
That day, and with much pain, the French passed through.
For fifteen leagues around one heard their clamor.
When they reach Tere Majur, the Land of Fathers,
they beheld Gascony, their lord's domain.
Then they remembered: their fiefs, their realms, their honors,   820
remembered their young girls, their gentle wives:
not one who does not weep for what he feels.
Beyond these others King Charles is in bad straits:
his nephew left in the defiles of Spain!
feels the pity of it; tears break through. AOI.   825

67

And the Twelve Peers are left behind in Spain,
and twenty thousand Franks are left with them.
They have no fear, they have no dread of death.
The Emperor is going home to France.
Beneath his cloak, his face shows all he feels.   830
Naimon the Duke is riding beside him;
and he said to the King: "What is this grief?"
And Charles replies: "Whoever asks me, wrongs me.
I feel such pain, I cannot keep from wailing.
France will be destroyed by Ganelon.   835
Last night I saw a vision brought by angels:
the one who named my nephew for the rear-guard
shattered the lance between my fists to pieces.
I have left him in a march among strangers.
If I lose him, God! I won't find his like." AOI.   840

68

King Charles the Great cannot keep from weeping.
A hundred thousand Franks feel pity for him;
and for Roland, an amazing fear.
Ganelon the criminal has betrayed him;
got gifts for it from the pagan king,   845
gold and silver, cloths of silk, gold brocade,
mules and horses and camels and lions.
Marsilion sends for the barons of Spain,
counts and viscounts and dukes and almaçurs,
and the emirs,[3] and the sons of great lords: 850
four hundred thousand assembled in three days.
In Saragossa he has them beat the drums,
they raise Mahumet upon the highest tower:
no pagan now who does not worship him
and adore him. Then they ride, racing each other,   855
search through the land, the valleys, the mountains;
and then they saw the banners of the French.
The rear-guard of the Twelve Companions
will not fail now, they'll give the pagans battle.

69

Marsilion's nephew has come forward   860
riding a mule that he goads with a stick;
said—a warrior's laugh on him—to his uncle:
"Dear Lord and King, how long I have served you,
and all the troubles, the pains I have endured,
so many battles fought and won on the field   865
Give me a fief, the first blow at Roland.
I will kill him, here's the spear I'll do it with.
If Mahumet will only stand by me,
I will set free every strip of land in Spain,
from the passes of Aspre to Durestant.   870
Charles will be weary, his Franks will give it up:
and no more war for the rest of your life!"
King Marsilion gave him his glove, as sign. AOI.

70

The King's nephew holds the glove in his fist,
speaks these proud words to Marsilion his uncle: 875
"You've given me, dear Lord, King, a great gift!
Choose me twelve men, twelve of your noble barons,
and I will fight against the Twelve Companions."
And Falsaron was the first to respond—
he was the brother of King Marsilion: 880
"Dear Lord, Nephew, it's you and I together!
We'll fight, that's sure! We'll battle the rear-guard
of Charlemagne's grand army! We are the ones!
We have been chosen. We'll kill them all! It is fated." AOI.

3. All lords of high rank.

71

And now again: there comes King Corsablis, 885
a Berber, a bad man, a man of cunning;
and now he spoke as a brave vassal speaks:
for all God's gold he would not be a coward.
Now rushing up: Malprimis de Brigal,
faster on his two feet than any horse; 890
and cries great-voiced before Marsilion:
"I'm on my way to Rencesvals to fight!
Let me find Roland, I won't stop till I kill him!"

[Lines 894–993 continue the roll call of volunteers.]

79

They arm themselves in Saracen hauberks,
all but a few are lined with triple mail; 995
they lace on their good helms of Saragossa,
gird on their swords, the steel forged in Vienne;
they have rich shields, spears of Valencia,
and gonfanons of white and blue and red.
They leave the mules and riding horses now, 1000
mount their war horses and ride in close array.
The day was fair, the sun was shining bright,
all their armor was aflame with the light;
a thousand trumpets blow: that was to make it finer.
That made a great noise, and the men of France heard. 1005
Said Oliver: "Companion, I believe
we may yet have a battle with the pagans."
Roland replies: "Now may God grant us that.
We know our duty: to stand here for our King.
A man must bear some hardships for his lord, 1010
stand everything, the great heat, the great cold,
lose the hide and hair on him for his good lord.
Now let each man make sure to strike hard here:
let them not sing a bad song about us!
Pagans are wrong and Christians are right! 1015
They'll make no bad example of me this day!" AOI.

80

Oliver climbs to the top of a hill,
looks to his right, across a grassy vale,
sees the pagan army on its way there;
and called down to Roland, his companion: 1020
"That way, toward Spain: the uproar I see coming!
All their hauberks, all blazing, helmets like flames!
It will be a bitter thing for our French.
Ganelon knew, that criminal, that traitor,
when he marked us out before the Emperor." 1025
"Be still, Oliver," Roland the Count replies.
"He is my stepfather—my stepfather.
I won't have you speak one word against him."

81

Oliver has gone up upon a hill,
sees clearly now: the kingdom of Spain,
and the Saracens assembled in such numbers: 1030
helmets blazing, bedecked with gems in gold,
those shields of theirs, those hauberks sewn with brass,
and all their spears, the gonfanons affixed;
cannot begin to count their battle corps,
there are too many, he cannot take their number.   1035
And he is deeply troubled by what he sees.
He made his way quickly down from the hill,
came to the French, told them all he had seen.

82

Said Oliver: "I saw the Saracens,
no man on earth ever saw more of them—   1040
one hundred thousand, with their shields, up in front,
helmets laced on, hauberks blazing on them,
the shafts straight up, the iron heads like flames—
you'll get a battle, nothing like it before.
My lords, my French, may God give you the strength.   1045
Hold your ground now! Let them not defeat us!"
And the French say: "God hate the man who runs!
We may die here, but no man will fail you." AOI.

83

Said Oliver: "The pagan force is great;
from what I see, our French here are too few.   1050
Roland, my companion, sound your horn then,
Charles will hear it, the army will come back."
Roland replies: "I'd be a fool to do it.
I would lose my good name all through sweet France.
I will strike now, I'll strike with Durendal,   1055
the blade will be bloody to the gold from striking!
These pagan traitors came to these passes doomed!
I promise you, they are marked men, they'll die." AOI.

84

"Roland, Companion, now sound the olifant,[4]
Charles will hear it, he will bring the army,   1060
the King will come with all his barons to help us."
Roland replies: "May it never please God
that my kin should be shamed because of me,
or that sweet France should fall into disgrace.
Never! Never! I'll strike with Durendal,   1065
I'll strike with this good sword strapped to my side,
you'll see this blade running its whole length with blood.

---

4. A form of *elephant*, which means "ivory" or "a horn made of ivory." It is used specifically, almost as a proper name, to denote Roland's horn, made of an elephant's tusk and adorned with gold and jewels about the rim.

These pagan traitors have gathered here to die.
I promise you, they are all bound for death." AOI.

85

"Roland, Companion, sound your olifant now,   1070
Charles will hear it, marching through those passes.
I promise you, the Franks will come at once."
Roland replies: "May it never please God
that any man alive should come to say
that pagans—pagans!—once made me sound this horn: 1075
no kin of mine will ever bear that shame.
Once I enter this great battle coming
and strike my thousand seven hundred blows,
you'll see the bloody steel of Durendal.
These French are good—they will strike like brave men.   1080
Nothing can save the men of Spain from death."

86

Said Oliver: "I see no blame in it—
I watched the Saracens coming from Spain,
the valleys and mountains covered with them,
every hillside and every plain all covered,   1085
hosts and hosts everywhere of those strange men—
and here we have a little company."
Roland replies: "That whets my appetite.
May it not please God and his angels and saints
to let France lose its glory because of me—   1090
let me not end in shame, let me die first.
The Emperor loves us when we fight well."

87

Roland is good, and Oliver is wise,
both these vassals men of amazing courage:
once they are armed and mounted on their horses,   1095
they will not run, though they die for it, from battle.
Good men, these Counts, and their words full of spirit.
Traitor pagans are riding up in fury.
Said Oliver: "Roland, look—the first ones,
on top of us—and Charles is far away.   1100
You did not think it right to sound your olifant:
if the King were here, we'd come out without losses.
Now look up there, toward the passes of Aspre—
you can see the rear-guard: it will suffer.
No man in that detail will be in another."   1105
Roland replies: "Don't speak such foolishness—
shame on the heart gone coward in the chest.
We'll hold our ground, we'll stand firm—we're the ones!
We'll fight with spears, we'll fight them hand to hand!" AOI.

88

When Roland sees that there will be a battle,
it makes him fiercer than a lion or leopard;
shouts to the French, calls out to Oliver:
"Lord, companion: friend, do not say such things.
The Emperor, who left us these good French,
had set apart these twenty thousand men:
he knew there was no coward in their ranks.
A man must meet great troubles for his lord,
stand up to the great heat and the great cold,
give up some flesh and blood—it is his duty.
Strike with the lance, I'll strike with Durendal—
it was the King who gave me this good sword!
If I die here, the man who gets it can say:
it was a noble's, a vassal's, a good man's sword." 1110 1115 1120

89

And now there comes the Archbishop Turpin.
He spurs his horse, goes up into a mountain,
summons the French; and he preached them a sermon:
"Barons, my lords, Charles left us in this place.
We know our duty: to die like good men for our King.
Fight to defend the holy Christian faith.
Now you will have a battle, you know it now,
you see the Saracens with your own eyes.
Confess your sins, pray to the Lord for mercy.
I will absolve you all, to save your souls.
If you die here, you will stand up holy martyrs,
you will have seats in highest Paradise."
The French dismount, cast themselves on the ground;
the Archbishop blesses them in God's name.
He commands them to do one penance: strike. 1125 1130 1135

90

The French arise, stand on their feet again;
they are absolved, released from all their sins:
the Archbishop has blessed them in God's name.
Now they are mounted on their swift battle horses,
bearing their arms like faithful warriors;
and every man stands ready for the battle.
Roland the Count calls out to Oliver:
"Lord, Companion, you knew it, you were right,
Ganelon watched for his chance to betray us,
got gold for it, got goods for it, and money.
The Emperor will have to avenge us now.
King Marsilion made a bargain for our lives,
but still must pay, and that must be with swords." AOI. 1140 1145 1150

91

Roland went forth into the Spanish passes
on Veillantif, his good swift-running horse.

He bears his arms—how they become this man!—
grips his lance now, hefting it, working it,   1155
now swings the iron point up toward the sky,
the gonfanon all white laced on above—
the golden streamers beat down upon his hands:
a noble's body, the face aglow and smiling.
Close behind him his good companion follows;   1160
the men of France hail him: their protector!
He looks wildly toward the Saracens,
and humbly and gently to the men of France;
and spoke a word to them, in all courtesy:
"Barons, my lords, easy now, keep at a walk.   1165
These pagans are searching for martyrdom.
We'll get good spoils before this day is over,
no king of France ever got such treasure!"
And with these words, the hosts are at each other. AOI.

92

Said Oliver: "I will waste no more words.   1170
You did not think it right to sound your olifant,
there'll be no Charles coming to your aid now.
He knows nothing, brave man, he's done no wrong;
those men down there—they have no blame in this.
Well, then, ride now, and ride with all your might!   1175
Lords, you brave men, stand your ground, hold the field!
Make up your minds, I beg you in God's name,
to strike some blows, take them and give them back!
Here we must not forget Charlemagne's war cry."
And with that word the men of France cried out.   1180
A man who heard that shout: Munjoie! Munjoie![5]
would always remember what manhood is.
Then they ride, God! Look at their pride and spirit!
and they spur hard, to ride with all their speed,
come on to strike—what else would these men do?   1185
The Saracens kept coming, never fearing them.
Franks and pagans, here they are, at each other.

93

Marsilion's nephew is named Aëlroth.
He rides in front, at the head of the army,
comes on shouting insults against our French: 1190
"French criminals, today you fight our men.
One man should have saved you: he betrayed you.
A fool, your King, to leave you in these passes.
This is the day sweet France will lose its name,
and Charlemagne the right arm of his body."   1195
When he hears that—God!—Roland is outraged!
He spurs his horse, gives Veillantif its head.
The Count comes on to strike with all his might,

5. For the poet's derivation of this war cry, see *laisse* 183, below.

smashes his shield, breaks his hauberk apart,
and drives: rips through his chest, shatters the bones,   1200
knocks the whole backbone out of his back,
casts out the soul of Aëlroth with his lance;
which he thrusts deep, makes the whole body shake,
throws him down dead, lance straight out,[6] from his horse;
he has broken his neck; broken it in two.   1205
There is something, he says, he must tell him:
"Clown! Nobody! Now you know Charles is no fool,
he never was the man to love treason.
It took his valor to leave us in these passes!
France will not lose its name, sweet France! today.   1210
Brave men of France, strike hard! The first blow is ours!
We're in the right, and these swine in the wrong!" AOI.

94

A duke is there whose name is Falsaron,
he was the brother of King Marsilion,
held the wild land of Dathan and Abiram;[7]   1215
under heaven, no criminal more vile;
a tremendous forehead between his eyes—
a good half-foot long, if you had measured it.
His pain is bitter to see his nephew dead;
rides out alone, baits the foe with his body,   1220
and riding shouts the war cry of the pagans,
full of hate and insults against the French:
"This is the day sweet France will lose its honor!"
Oliver hears, and it fills him with fury,
digs with his golden spurs into his horse,   1225
comes on to strike the blow a baron strikes,
smashes his shield, breaks his hauberk apart,
thrusts into him the long streamers of his gonfalon,
knocks him down, dead, lance straight out, from the saddle;
looks to the ground and sees the swine stretched out,   1230
and spoke these words—proud words, terrible words:
"You nobody, what are your threats to me!
Men of France, strike! Strike and we will beat them!"
Munjoie! he shouts—the war cry of King Charles. AOI.

95

A king is there whose name is Corsablis,   1235
a Berber, come from that far country.
He spoke these words to all his Saracens:
"Now here's one battle we'll have no trouble with,
look at that little troop of Frenchmen there,
a few odd men—they're not worth noticing!   1240
King Charles won't save a single one of them."

6. The lance is held, not thrown, and used to
knock the enemy from his horse. To throw one's
weapons is savage and ignoble. See *laisses* 154

and 160 and the outlandish names of the things
the pagans throw at Roland, Gautier, and Turpin.
7. See Numbers 16.1–35.

Their day has come, they must all die today."
And Archbishop Turpin heard every word:
no man on earth he wants so much to hate!
digs with spurs of fine gold into his horse,   1245
comes on to strike with all his awful might;
smashed through his shield, burst the rings of his hauberk,
sent his great lance into the body's center,
drove it in deep, he made the dead man shake,
knocked him down, dead, lance straight out, on the road;   1250
looks to the ground and sees the swine stretched out;
there is something, he says, he must tell him:
"You pagan! You nobody! You told lies there:
King Charles my lord is our safeguard forever!
Our men of France have no heart for running.   1255
As for your companions—we'll nail them to the ground;
and then you must all die the second death.[8]
At them, you French! No man forget what he is!
Thanks be to God, now the first blow is ours";
and shouts Munjoie! Munjoie! to hold the field.   1260

[Lines 1261–1319 narrate a series of single combats, many of them similar.]

104

The battle is fearful and wonderful   1320
and everywhere. Roland never spares himself,
strikes with his lance as long as the wood lasts:
the fifteenth blow he struck, it broke, was lost.
Then he draws Durendal, his good sword, bare,
and spurs his horse, comes on to strike Chernuble,   1325
smashes his helmet, carbuncles shed their light,
cuts through the coif, through the hair on his head,
cut through his eyes, through his face, through that look,
the bright, shining hauberk with its fine rings,
down through the trunk to the fork of his legs,   1330
through the saddle, adorned with beaten gold,
into the horse; and the sword came to rest:
cut through the spine, never felt for the joint;
knocks him down, dead, on the rich grass of the meadow;
then said to him: "You were doomed when you started,   1335
Clown! Nobody! Let Mahum help you now.
No pagan swine will win this field today."

105

Roland the Count comes riding through the field,
holds Durendal, that sword! it carves its way!
and brings terrible slaughter down on the pagans.   1340
To have seen him cast one man dead on another,
the bright red blood pouring out on the ground,
his hauberk, his two arms, running with blood,

8. The death of the soul, eternal damnation (see Revelation 2.11, 20.14, 21.8).

his good horse—neck and shoulders running with blood!
And Oliver does not linger, he strikes! 1345
and the Twelve Peers, no man could reproach them;
and the brave French, they fight with lance and sword.
The pagans die, some simply faint away!
Said the Archbishop: "Bless our band of brave men!"
Munjoie! he shouts—the war cry of King Charles. AOI. 1350

106

Oliver rides into that battle-storm,
his lance is broken, he holds only the stump;
comes on to strike a pagan, Malsarun;
and he smashes his shield, all flowers and gold,
sends his two eyes flying out of his head, 1355
and his brains come pouring down to his feet;
casts him down, dead, with seven hundred others.
Now he has killed Turgis and Esturguz,
and the shaft bursts, shivers down to his fists.
Count Roland said: "Companion, what are you doing? 1360
Why bother with a stick in such a battle?
Iron and steel will do much better work!
Where is your sword, your Halteclere—that name!
Where is that crystal hilt, that golden guard?"
"Haven't had any time to draw it out, 1365
been so busy fighting," said Oliver. AOI.

107

Lord Oliver has drawn out his good sword—
that sword his companion had longed to see—
and showed him how a good man uses it:
strikes a pagan, Justin of Val Ferrée, 1370
and comes down through his head, cuts through the center,
through his body, his hauberk sewn with brass,
the good saddle beset with gems in gold,
into the horse, the backbone cut in two;
knocks him down, dead, before him on the meadow. 1375
Count Roland said: "Now I know it's you, Brother.
The Emperor loves us for blows like that."
Munjoie! that cry! goes up on every side. AOI.

108

Gerin the Count sits on his bay Sorél
and Gerer his companion on Passe-Cerf; 1380
and they ride, spurring hard, let loose their reins,
come on to strike a pagan, Timozel,
one on his shield, the other on his hauberk.
They broke their two lances in his body;
turn him over, dead, in a fallow field. 1385
I do not know and have never heard tell
which of these two was swifter, though both were swift.
Esperveris: he was the son of Borel

and now struck dead by Engeler of Bordeaux.
Turpin the Archbishop killed Siglorel, 1390
the enchanter, who had been in Hell before:
Jupiter brought him there, with that strange magic.
Then Turpin said: "That swine owed us his life!
Roland replies: "And now the scoundrel's dead.
Oliver, Brother, those were blows! I approve!" 1395

109

In the meantime, the fighting grew bitter.
Franks and pagans, the fearful blows they strike—
those who attack, those who defend themselves;
so many lances broken, running with blood,
the gonfanons in shreds, the ensigns torn, 1400
so many good French fallen, their young lives lost:
they will not see their mothers or wives again,
or the men of France who wait for them at the passes. AOI.
Charlemagne waits and weeps and wails for them.
What does that matter? They'll get no help from him. 1405
Ganelon served him ill that day he sold,
in Saragossa, the barons of his house.
He lost his life and limbs for what he did:
was doomed to hang in the great trial at Aix,
and thirty of his kin were doomed with him, 1410
who never expected to die that death. AOI.

110

The battle is fearful and full of grief.
Oliver and Roland strike like good men,
the Archbishop, more than a thousand blows,
and the Twelve Peers do not hang back, they strike! 1415
the French fight side by side, all as one man.
The pagans die by hundreds, by thousands:
whoever does not flee finds no refuge from death,
like it or not, there he ends all his days.
And there the men of France lose their greatest arms; 1420
they will not see their fathers, their kin again,
or Charlemagne, who looks for them in the passes.
Tremendous torment now comes forth in France,
a mighty whirlwind, tempests of wind and thunder,
rains and hailstones, great and immeasurable, 1425
bolts of lightning hurtling and hurtling down:
it is, in truth, a trembling of the earth.
From Saint Michael-in-Peril to the Saints,
from Besançon to the port of Wissant,
there is no house whose veil of walls does not crumble. 1430
A great darkness at noon[9] falls on the land,
there is no light but when the heavens crack.

9. As during the crucifixion of Jesus, according to the gospel accounts (Matthew 27.45, Mark 15.33, Luke 23.44).

No man sees this who is not terrified,
and many say: "The Last Day! Judgment Day!
The end! The end of the world is upon us!" 1435
They do not know, they do not speak the truth:
it is the worldwide grief for the death of Roland.

111

The French have fought with all their hearts and strength,
pagans are dead by the thousands, in droves:
of one hundred thousand, not two are saved. 1440
Said the Archbishop: "Our men! What valiant fighters!
No king under heaven could have better.
It is written in the Gesta Francorum:[1]
our Emperor's vassals were all good men."
They walk over the field to seek their dead, 1445
they weep, tears fill their eyes, in grief and pity
for their kindred, with love, with all their hearts.
Marsilion the King, with all his men
in that great host, rises up before them. AOI.

112

King Marsilion comes along a valley
with all his men, the great host he assembled: 1450
twenty divisions, formed and numbered by the King,
helmets ablaze with gems beset in gold,
and those bright shields, those hauberks sewn with brass.
Seven thousand clarions sound the pursuit,
and the great noise resounds across that country. 1455
Said Roland then: "Oliver, Companion, Brother,
that traitor Ganelon has sworn our deaths:
it is treason, it cannot stay hidden,
the Emperor will take his terrible revenge.
We have this battle now, it will be bitter, 1460
no man has ever seen the like of it.
I will fight here with Durendal, this sword,
and you, my companion, with Halteclere—
we've fought with them before, in many lands!
how many battles have we won with these two! 1465
Let no one sing a bad song of our swords." AOI.

113

When the French see the pagans so numerous,
the fields swarming with them on every side,
they call the names of Oliver, and Roland,
and the Twelve Peers: protect them, be their warranter. 1470
The Archbishop told them how he saw things:
"Barons, my lords, do not think shameful thoughts,
do not, I beg you all in God's name, run.
Let no brave man sing shameful songs of us:
let us all die here fighting: that is far better. 1475

---

1. The Deeds of the French (Latin), title of an account of these events that has not survived.

We are promised: we shall soon find our deaths,
after today we won't be living here.
But here's one thing, and I am your witness:
Holy Paradise lies open to you,
you will take seats among the Innocents."[2]   1480
And with these words the Franks are filled with joy,
there is no man who does not shout Munjoie! AOI.

114

A Saracen was there of Saragossa,
half that city was in this pagan's keeping,
this Climborin, who fled before no man,   1485
who took the word of Ganelon the Count,
kissed in friendship the mouth that spoke that word,
gave him a gift: his helmet and its carbuncle.
Now he will shame, says he, the Land of Fathers,
he will tear off the crown of the Emperor;   1490
sits on the horse that he calls Barbamusche,
swifter than the sparrowhawk, than the swallow;
digs in his spurs, gives that war horse its head,
comes on to strike Engeler of Gascony,
whose shield and fine hauberk cannot save him;   1495
gets the head of his spear into his body,
drives it in deep, gets all the iron through,
throws him back, dead, lance straight out, on the field.
And then he cries: "It's good to kill these swine!
At them, Pagans! At them and break their ranks!"   1500
"God!" say the French, "the loss of that good man!" AOI.

115

Roland the Count calls out to Oliver:
"Lord, Companion, there is Engeler dead,
we never had a braver man on horse."
The Count replies: "God let me avenge him";   1505
and digs with golden spurs into his horse,
grips—the steel running with blood—Halteclere,
comes on to strike with all his mighty power:
the blow comes flashing down; the pagan falls.
Devils take away the soul of Climborin.   1510
And then he killed Alphaïen the duke,
cut off the head of Escababi,
struck from their horses seven great Arrabites:
they'll be no use for fighting any more!
And Roland said: "My companion is enraged!   1515
Why, he compares with me! he earns his praise!
Fighting like that makes us dearer to Charles";
lifts up his voice and shouts: "Strike! you are warriors!" AOI.

[Lines 1519–1627 narrate another series of single combats.]

2. The infants slain by King Herod (see Matthew 2.16).

125

Marsilion sees his people's martyrdom.
He commands them: sound his horns and trumpets;
and he rides now with the great host he has gathered.   1630
At their head rides the Saracen Abisme:
no worse criminal rides in that company,
stained with the marks of his crimes and great treasons,
lacking the faith in God, Saint Mary's son.
And he is black, as black as melted pitch,   1635
a man who loves murder and treason more
than all the gold of rich Galicia,
no living man ever saw him play or laugh;
a great fighter, a wild man, mad with pride,
and therefore dear to that criminal king;   1640
holds high his dragon,[3] where all his people gather.
The Archbishop will never love that man,
no sooner saw than wanted to strike him;
considered quietly, said to himself:
"That Saracen—a heretic, I'll wager.   1645
Now let me die if I do not kill him—
I never loved cowards or cowards' ways." AOI.

126

Turpin the Archbishop begins the battle.
He rides the horse that he took from Grossaille,
who was a king this priest once killed in Denmark.   1650
Now this war horse is quick and spirited,
his hooves high-arched, the quick legs long and flat,
short in the thigh, wide in the rump, long in the flanks,
and the backbone so high, a battle horse!
and that white tail, the yellow mane on him,   1655
the little ears on him, the tawny head!
No beast on earth could ever run with him.
The Archbishop—that valiant man!—spurs hard,
he will attack Abisme, he will not falter,
strikes on his shield, a miraculous blow: 1660
a shield of stones, of amethysts, topazes,
esterminals,[4] carbuncles all on fire—
a gift from a devil, in Val Metas,
sent on to him by the Amiral Galafre.
There Turpin strikes, he does not treat it gently—   1665
after that blow, I'd not give one cent for it;
cut through his body, from one side to the other,
and casts him down dead in a barren place.
And the French say: "A fighter, that Archbishop!
Look at him there, saving souls with that crozier!"   1670

---

3. Banner.   4. Precious ornaments.

127

Roland the Count calls out to Oliver:
"Lord, Companion, now you have to agree
the Archbishop is a good man on horse,
there's none better on earth or under heaven,
he knows his way with a lance and a spear."
The Count replies: "Right! Let us help him then." 1675
And with these words the Franks began anew,
the blows strike hard, and the fighting is bitter;
there is a painful loss of Christian men.
To have seen them, Roland and Oliver, 1680
these fighting men, striking down with their swords,
the Archbishop with them, striking with his lance!
One can recount the number these three killed:
it is written—in charters, in documents;
the Geste tells it: it was more than four thousand. 1685
Through four assaults all went well with our men;
then comes the fifth, and that one crushes them.
They are all killed, all these warriors of France,
all but sixty, whom the Lord God has spared:
they will die too, but first sell themselves dear. AOI. 1690

128

Count Roland sees the great loss of his men,
calls on his companion, on Oliver:
"Lord, Companion, in God's name, what would you do?
All these good men you see stretched on the ground.
We can mourn for sweet France, fair land of France! 1695
a desert now, stripped of such great vassals.
Oh King, and friend, if only you were here!
Oliver, Brother, how shall we manage it?
What shall we do to get word to the King?"
Said Oliver: "I don't see any way. 1700
I would rather die now than hear us shamed." AOI.

129

And Roland said: "I'll sound the olifant,
Charles will hear it, drawing through the passes,
I promise you, the Franks will return at once."
Said Oliver: "That would be a great disgrace, 1705
a dishonor and reproach to all your kin,
the shame of it would last them all their lives.
When I urged it, you would not hear of it;
you will not do it now with my consent.
It is not acting bravely to sound it now— 1710
look at your arms, they are covered with blood."
The Count replies: "I've fought here like a lord."[5] AOI.

5. Some have found lines 1710–12 difficult. Oliver means, "We have fought this far—look at the enemy's blood on your arms: It is too late, it would be a disgrace to summon help when there is no longer any chance of being saved." But Roland thinks that that is the one time when it is not a disgrace.

130

And Roland says: "We are in a rough battle.
I'll sound the olifant, Charles will hear it."
Said Oliver: "No good vassal would do it.   1715
When I urged it, friend, you did not think it right.
If Charles were here, we'd come out with no losses.
Those men down there—no blame can fall on them."
Oliver said: "Now by this beard of mine,
If I can see my noble sister, Aude,   1720
once more, you will never lie in her arms!"[6] AOI.

131

And Roland said: "Why are you angry at me?"
Oliver answers: "Companion, it is your doing.
I will tell you what makes a vassal good:
it is judgment, it is never madness;   1725
restraint is worth more than the raw nerve of a fool.
Frenchmen are dead because of your wildness.
And what service will Charles ever have from us?
If you had trusted me, my lord would be here,
we would have fought this battle through to the end,   1730
Marsilion would be dead, or our prisoner.
Roland, your prowess—had we never seen it!
And now, dear friend, we've seen the last of it.
No more aid from us now for Charlemagne,
a man without equal till Judgment Day,   1735
you will die here, and your death will shame France.
We kept faith, you and I, we were companions;
and everything we were will end today.
We part before evening, and it will be hard." AOI.

132

Turpin the Archbishop hears their bitter words,   1740
digs hard into his horse with golden spurs
and rides to them; begins to set them right:
"You, Lord Roland, and you, Lord Oliver,
I beg you in God's name do not quarrel.
To sound the horn could not help us now, true,   1745
but still it is far better that you do it:
let the King come, he can avenge us then—
these men of Spain must not go home exulting!
Our French will come, they'll get down on their feet,
and find us here—we'll be dead, cut to pieces.   1750
They will lift us into coffins on the backs of mules,
and weep for us, in rage and pain and grief,
and bury us in the courts of churches;
and we will not be eaten by wolves or pigs or dogs."
Roland replies, "Lord, you have spoken well." AOI.   1755

6. Aude had been betrothed to Roland.

133

Roland has put the olifant to his mouth,
he sets it well, sounds it with all his strength.
The hills are high, and that voice ranges far,
they heard it echo thirty great leagues away.
King Charles heard it, and all his faithful men.   1760
And the King says: "Our men are in a battle."
And Ganelon disputed him and said:
"Had someone else said that, I'd call him liar!" AOI.

134

And now the mighty effort of Roland the Count:
he sounds his olifant; his pain is great,   1765
and from his mouth the bright blood comes leaping out,
and the temple bursts in his forehead.
That horn, in Roland's hands, has a mighty voice:
King Charles hears it drawing through the passes.
Naimon heard it, the Franks listen to it.   1770
And the King said: "I hear Count Roland's horn;
he'd never sound it unless he had a battle."
Says Ganelon: "Now no more talk of battles!
You are old now, your hair is white as snow,
the things you say make you sound like a child.   1775
You know Roland and that wild pride of his—
what a wonder God has suffered it so long!
Remember? he took Noples without your command:
the Saracens rode out, to break the siege;
they fought with him, the great vassal Roland.   1780
Afterwards he used the streams to wash the blood
from the meadows: so that nothing would show.
He blasts his horn all day to catch a rabbit,
he's strutting now before his peers and bragging—
who under heaven would dare meet him on the field?   1785
So now: ride on! Why do you keep on stopping?
The Land of Fathers lies far ahead of us." AOI.

135

The blood leaping from Count Roland's mouth,
the temple broken with effort in his forehead,
he sounds his horn in great travail and pain.   1790
King Charles heard it, and his French listen hard.
And the King said: "That horn has a long breath!"
Naimon answers: "It is a baron's breath.
There is a battle there, I know there is.
He betrayed him! and now asks you to fail him!   1795
Put on your armor! Lord, shout your battle cry,
and save the noble barons of your house!
You hear Roland's call. He is in trouble."

136

The Emperor commanded the horns to sound,
the French dismount, and they put on their armor: 1800
their hauberks, their helmets, their gold-dressed swords,
their handsome shields; and take up their great lances,
the gonfalons of white and red and blue.
The barons of that host mount their war horses
and spur them hard the whole length of the pass;   1805
and every man of them says to the other:
"If only we find Roland before he's killed,
we'll stand with him, and then we'll do some fighting!"
What does it matter what they say? They are too late.

137

It is the end of day, and full of light,   1810
arms and armor are ablaze in the sun,
and fire flashes from hauberks and helmets,
and from those shields, painted fair with flowers,
and from those lances, those gold-dressed gonfanons.
The Emperor rides on in rage and sorrow,   1815
the men of France indignant and full of grief.
There is no man of them who does not weep,
they are in fear for the life of Roland.
The King commands: seize Ganelon the Count!
and gave him over to the cooks of his house;   1820
summons the master cook, their chief, Besgun:
"Guard him for me like the traitor he is:
he has betrayed the barons of my house."
Besgun takes him, sets his kitchen comrades,
a hundred men, the best, the worst, on him;   1825
and they tear out his beard and his mustache,
each one strikes him four good blows with his fist;
and they lay into him with cudgels and sticks,
put an iron collar around his neck
and chain him up, as they would chain a bear;   1830
dumped him, in dishonor, on a packhorse,
and guard him well till they give him back to Charles.

138

High are the hills, and tenebrous, and vast, AOI.
the valleys deep, the raging waters swift;
to the rear, to the front, the trumpets sound: 1835
they answer the lone voice of the olifant.
The Emperor rides on, rides on in fury,
the men of France in grief and indignation.
There is no man who does not weep and wail,
and they pray God: protect the life of Roland   1840
till they come, one great host, into the field
and fight at Roland's side like true men all.
What does it matter what they pray? It does no good.
They are too late, they cannot come in time. AOI.

139

King Charles the Great rides on, a man in wrath,   1845
his great white beard spread out upon his hauberk.[7]
All the barons of France ride spurring hard,
there is no man who does not wail, furious
not to be with Roland, the captain count,
who stands and fights the Saracens of Spain,   1850
so set upon, I cannot think his soul abides.
God! those sixty men who stand with him, what men!
No king, no captain ever stood with better. AOI.

140

Roland looks up on the mountains and slopes,
sees the French dead, so many good men fallen,   1855
and weeps for them, as a great warrior weeps:
"Barons, my lords, may God give you his grace,
may he grant Paradise to all your souls,
make them lie down among the holy flowers.
I never saw better vassals than you.   1860
All the years you've served me, and all the times,
the mighty lands you conquered for Charles our King!
The Emperor raised you for this terrible hour!
Land of France, how sweet you are, native land,
laid waste this day, ravaged, made a desert.   1865
Barons of France, I see you die for me,
and I, your lord—I cannot protect you.
May God come to your aid, that God who never failed.
Oliver, brother, now I will not fail you.
I will die here—of grief, if no man kills me.   1870
Lord, Companion, let us return and fight."

141

Roland returned to his place on the field,
strikes—a brave man keeping faith—with Durendal,
struck through Faldrun de Pui, cut him to pieces,
and twenty-four of the men they valued most;   1875
no man will ever want his vengeance more!
As when the deer turns tail before the dogs,
so the pagans flee before Roland the Count.
Said the Archbishop: "You! Roland! What a fighter!
Now that's what every knight must have in him   1880
who carries arms and rides on a fine horse:
he must be strong, a savage, when he's in battle;
for otherwise, what's he worth? Not four cents!
Let that four-cent man be a monk in some minster,
and he can pray all day long for our sins."   1885
Roland replies: "Attack, do not spare them!"
And with that word the Franks began again.
There was a heavy loss of Christian men.

7. A gesture of defiance toward the enemy.

142

When a man knows there'll be no prisoners,
what will that man not do to defend himself! 1890
And so the Franks fight with the fury of lions.
Now Marsilion, the image of a baron,
mounted on that war horse he calls Gaignun,
digs in his spurs, comes on to strike Bevon,
who was the lord of Beaune and of Dijon; 1895
smashes his shield, rips apart his hauberk,
knocks him down, dead, no need to wound him more.
And then he killed Yvorie and Yvon,
and more: he killed Gerard of Rousillon.
Roland the Count is not far away now, 1900
said to the pagan: "The Lord God's curse on you!
You kill my companions, how you wrong me!
You'll feel the pain of it before we part,
you will learn my sword's name by heart today";
comes on to strike—the image of a baron. 1905
He has cut off Marsilion's right fist;
now takes the head of Jurfaleu the blond—
the head of Jurfaleu! Marsilion's son.
The pagans cry: "Help, Mahumet! Help us!
Vengeance, our gods, on Charles! the man who set 1910
these criminals on us in our own land,
they will not quit the field, they'll stand and die!"
And one said to the other: "Let *us* run then."
And with that word, some hundred thousand flee.
Now try to call them back: they won't return. AOI. 1915

143

What does it matter? If Marsilion has fled,
his uncle has remained: the Algalife,[8]
who holds Carthage, Alfrere, and Garmalie,
and Ethiopia: a land accursed;
holds its immense black race under his power, 1920
the huge noses, the enormous ears on them;
and they number more than fifty thousand.
These are the men who come riding in fury,
and now they shout that pagan battle cry.
And Roland said: "Here comes our martyrdom; 1925
I see it now: we have not long to live.
But let the world call any man a traitor
    who does not make them pay before he dies!
My lords, attack! Use those bright shining swords!
Fight a good fight for your deaths and your lives,
let no shame touch sweet France because of us! 1930
When Charles my lord comes to this battlefield
and sees how well we punished these Saracens,

---

8. The Caliph, Marsilion's uncle, whom Ganelon lied about to Charlemagne (see lines 680–91).

finds fifteen of their dead for one of ours,
I'll tell you what he will do: he will bless us." AOI.

144

When Roland sees that unbelieving race,   1935
those hordes and hordes blacker than blackest ink—
no shred of white on them except their teeth—
then said the Count: "I see it clearly now,
we die today: it is there before us.
Men of France, strike! I will start it once more."   1940
Said Oliver: "God curse the slowest man."
And with that word, the French strike into battle.

145

The Saracens, when they saw these few French,
looked at each other, took courage, and presumed,
telling themselves: "The Emperor is wrong!"   1945
The Algalife rides a great sorrel horse,
digs into it with his spurs of fine gold,
strikes Oliver, from behind, in the back,
shattered the white hauberk upon his flesh,
drove his spear through the middle of his chest;   1950
and speaks to him: "Now you feel you've been struck!
Your great Charles doomed you when he left you in this pass.
That man wronged us, he must not boast of it.
I've avenged all our dead in you alone!"

146

Oliver feels: he has been struck to death;   1955
grips Halteclere, that steel blade shining, strikes
on the gold-dressed pointed helm of the Algalife,
sends jewels and flowers crackling down to the earth,
into the head, into the little teeth;
draws up his flashing sword, casts him down, dead,   1960
and then he says: "Pagan, a curse on you!
If only I could say Charles has lost nothing—
but no woman, no lady you ever knew
will hear you boast, in the land you came from,
that you could take one thing worth a cent from me, 1965
or do me harm, or do any man harm";
then cries out to Roland to come to his aid. AOI.

147

Oliver feels he is wounded to death,
will never have his fill of vengeance, strikes,
as a baron strikes, where they are thickest,   1970
cuts through their lances, cuts through those buckled shields,
through feet, through fists, through saddles, and through flanks.
Had you seen him, cutting the pagans limb
from limb, casting one corpse down on another,
you would remember a brave man keeping faith.   1975

Never would he forget Charles' battle-cry,
Munjoie! he shouts, that mighty voice ringing;
calls to Roland, to his friend and his peer:
"Lord, Companion, come stand beside me now.
We must part from each other in pain today." AOI.   1980

148

Roland looks hard into Oliver's face,
it is ashen, all its color is gone,
the bright red blood streams down upon his body,
Oliver's blood spattering on the earth.
"God!" said the Count, "I don't know what to do,   1985
Lord, Companion, your fight is finished now.
There'll never be a man the like of you.
Sweet land of France, today you will be stripped
of good vassals, laid low, a fallen land!
The Emperor will suffer the great loss";   1990
faints with that word, mounted upon his horse. AOI.

149

Here is Roland, lords, fainted on his horse,
and Oliver the Count, wounded to death:
he has lost so much blood, his eyes are darkened—
he cannot see, near or far, well enough   1995
to recognize a friend or enemy:
struck when he came upon his companion,
strikes on his helm, adorned with gems in gold,
cuts down straight through, from the point to the nasal,[9]
but never harmed him, he never touched his head.   2000
Under this blow, Count Roland looked at him;
and gently, softly now, he asks of him:
"Lord, Companion, do you mean to do this?
It is Roland, who always loved you greatly.
You never declared that we were enemies."   2005
Said Oliver: "Now I hear it is you—
I don't see you, may the Lord God see you.
Was it you that I struck? Forgive me then."
Roland replies: "I am not harmed, not harmed,
I forgive you, Friend, here and before God."   2010
And with that word, each bowed to the other.
And this is the love, lords, in which they parted.

150

Oliver feels: death pressing hard on him;
his two eyes turn, roll up into his head,
all hearing is lost now, all sight is gone;   2015
gets down on foot, stretches out on the ground,
cries out now and again: *mea culpa!*[1]

9. The nosepiece protruding down from the   1. My guilt (Latin); a formula used in the
cone-shaped helmet.   confession of one's sins.

his two hands joined, raised aloft toward heaven,
he prays to God: grant him His Paradise;
and blesses Charles, and the sweet land of France, 2020
his companion, Roland, above all men.
The heart fails him, his helmet falls away,
the great body settles upon the earth.
The Count is dead, he stands with us no longer.
Roland, brave man, weeps for him, mourns for him, 2025
you will not hear a man of greater sorrow.

151

Roland the Count, when he sees his friend dead,
lying stretched out, his face against the earth,
softly, gently, begins to speak the regret:[2]
"Lord, Companion, you were brave and died for it. 2030
We have stood side by side through days and years,
you never caused me harm, I never wronged you;
when you are dead, to be alive pains me."
And with that word the lord of marches faints
upon his horse, which he calls Veillantif. 2035
He is held firm by his spurs of fine gold,
whichever way he leans, he cannot fall.

152

Before Roland could recover his senses
and come out of his faint, and be aware,
a great disaster had come forth before him: 2040
the French are dead, he has lost every man
except the Archbishop, and Gautier de l'Hum,
who has come back, down from that high mountain:
he has fought well, he fought those of Spain.
His men are dead, the pagans finished them; 2045
flees now down to these valleys, he has no choice,
and calls on Count Roland to come to his aid:
"My noble Count, my brave lord, where are you?
I never feared whenever you were there.
It is Walter: I conquered Maëlgut, 2050
my uncle is Droün, old and gray: your Walter
and always dear to you for the way I fought;
and I have fought this time: my lance is shattered,
my good shield pierced, my hauberk's meshes broken;
and I am wounded, a lance struck through my body. 2055
I will die soon, but I sold myself dear."
And with that word, Count Roland has heard him,
he spurs his horse, rides spurring to his man. AOI.

153

Roland in pain, maddened with grief and rage:
rushes where they are thickest and strikes again, 2060

2. What follows is a formal and customary lament for the dead.

strikes twenty men of Spain, strikes twenty dead,
and Walter six, and the Archbishop five.
The pagans say: "Look at those criminals!
Now take care, Lords, they don't get out alive,
only a traitor will not attack them now!   2065
Only a coward will let them save their skins!"
And then they raise their hue and cry once more,
rush in on them, once more, from every side. AOI.

154

Count Roland was always a noble warrior,
Gautier de l'Hum is a fine mounted man,   2070
the Archbishop, a good man tried and proved:
not one of them will ever leave the others;
strike, where they are thickest, at the pagans.
A thousand Saracens get down on foot,
and forty thousand more are on their mounts: 2075
and I tell you, not one will dare come close,
they throw, and from afar, lances and spears,
wigars and darts, mizraks, javelins, pikes.
With the first blows they killed Gautier de l'Hum
and struck Turpin of Reims, pierced through his shield, 2080
broke the helmet on him, wounded his head;
ripped his hauberk, shattered its rings of mail,
and pierced him with four spears in his body,
the war horse killed under him; and now there comes
great pain and rage when the Archbishop falls. AOI.   2085

155

Turpin of Reims, when he feels he is unhorsed,
struck to the earth with four spears in his body,
quickly, brave man, leaps to his feet again;
his eyes find Roland now, he runs to him
and says one word: "See! I'm not finished yet!   2090
What good vassal ever gives up alive!";
and draws Almace, his sword, that shining steel!
and strikes, where they are thickest, a thousand blows, and more.
Later, Charles said: Turpin had spared no one;
he found four hundred men prostrate around him,   2095
some of them wounded, some pierced from front to back,
some with their heads hacked off. So says the Geste,
and so says one who was there, on that field,
the baron Saint Gilles,[3] for whom God performs miracles,
who made the charter setting forth these great things 2100
in the Church of Laon. Now any man
who does not know this much understands nothing.

---

3. St. Gilles of Provence. These lines explain how the story of Rencesvals could be told after all who had fought there died.

156

Roland the Count fights well and with great skill,
but he is hot, his body soaked with sweat;
has a great wound in his head, and much pain,   2105
his temple broken because he blew the horn.
But he must know whether King Charles will come;
draws out the olifant, sounds it, so feebly.
The Emperor drew to a halt, listened.
"Seigneurs," he said, "it goes badly for us—   2110
My nephew Roland falls from our ranks today.
I hear it in the horn's voice: he hasn't long.
Let every man who wants to be with Roland
ride fast! Sound trumpets! Every trumpet in this host!"
Sixty thousand, on these words, sound, so high   2115
the mountains sound, and the valleys resound.
The pagans hear: it is no joke to them;
cry to each other: "We're getting Charles on us!"

157

The pagans say: "The Emperor is coming, AOI.
listen to their trumpets—it is the French!   2120
If Charles comes back, it's all over for us,
if Roland lives, this war begins again
and we have lost our land, we have lost Spain."
Some four hundred, helmets laced on, assemble,
some of the best, as they think, on that field.   2125
They storm Roland, in one fierce, bitter attack.
And now Count Roland has some work on his hands. AOI.

158

Roland the Count, when he sees them coming,
how strong and fierce and alert he becomes!
He will not yield to them, not while he lives.   2130
He rides the horse they call Veillantif, spurs,
digs into it with his spurs of fine gold,
and rushes at them all where they are thickest,
the Archbishop—that Turpin!—at his side.
Said one man to the other: "Go at it, friend.   2135
The horns we heard were the horns of the French,
King Charles is coming back with all his strength."[4]

159

Roland the Count never loved a coward,
a blusterer, an evil-natured man,
a man on horse who was not a good vassal.   2140
And now he called to Archbishop Turpin:
"You are on foot, Lord, and here I am mounted,
and so, here I take my stand: for love of you.

---

4. The lines could be spoken either by Roland and the archbishop or by the pagans.

We'll take whatever comes, the good and bad,
together, Lord: no one can make me leave you.   2145
They will learn our swords' names today in battle,
the name of Almace, the name of Durendal!"
Said the Archbishop: "Let us strike or be shamed!
Charles is returning, and he brings our revenge."

160

Say the pagans: "We were all born unlucky!   2150
The evil day that dawned for us today!
We have lost our lords and peers, and now comes Charles—
that Charlemagne!—with his great host. Those trumpets!
that shrill sound on us—the trumpets of the French!
And the loud roar of that Munjoie! This Roland   2155
is a wild man, he is too great a fighter—
What man of flesh and blood can ever hope
to bring him down? Let us cast at him, and leave him there."
And so they did: arrows, wigars, darts,
lances and spears, javelots[5] dressed with feathers;   2160
struck Roland's shield, pierced it, broke it to pieces,
ripped his hauberk, shattered its rings of mail,
but never touched his body, never his flesh.
They wounded Veillantif in thirty places,
struck him dead, from afar, under the Count.   2165
The pagans flee, they leave the field to him.
Roland the Count stood alone, on his feet. AOI.

161

The pagans flee, in bitterness and rage,
strain every nerve running headlong toward Spain,
and Count Roland has no way to chase them,   2170
he has lost Veillantif, his battle horse;
he has no choice, left alone there on foot.
He went to the aid of Archbishop Turpin,
unlaced the gold-dressed helmet, raised it from his head,
lifted away his bright, light coat of mail,   2175
cut his under tunic into some lengths,
stilled his great wounds with thrusting on the strips;
then held him in his arms, against his chest,
and laid him down, gently, on the green grass;
and softly now Roland entreated him: 2180
"My noble lord, I beg you, give me leave:
our companions, whom we have loved so dearly,
are all dead now, we must not abandon them.
I want to look for them, know them once more,
and set them in ranks, side by side, before you."   2185
Said the Archbishop: "Go then, go and come back.
The field is ours, thanks be to God, yours and mine."

5. Small spears or javelins.

162

So Roland leaves him, walks the field all alone,
seeks in the valleys, and seeks in the mountains.
He found Gerin, and Gerer his companion,   2190
and then he found Berenger and Otun,
Anseïs and Sansun, and on that field
he found Gerard the old of Roussillon;
and carried them, brave man, all, one by one,
came back to the Archbishop with these French dead,   2195
and set them down in ranks before his knees.
The Archbishop cannot keep from weeping,
raises his hand and makes his benediction;
and said: "Lords, Lords, it was your terrible hour.
May the Glorious God set all your souls   2200
among the holy flowers of Paradise!
Here is my own death, Lords, pressing on me,
I shall not see our mighty Emperor."

163

And Roland leaves, seeks in the field again;
he has found Oliver, his companion,   2205
held him tight in his arms against his chest;
came back to the Archbishop, laid Oliver
down on a shield among the other dead.
The Archbishop absolved him, signed him with the Cross.
And pity now and rage and grief increase;   2210
and Roland says: "Oliver, dear companion,
you were the son of the great duke Renier,
who held the march of the vale of Runers.
Lord, for shattering lances, for breaking shields,
for making men great with presumption weak with fright,   2215
for giving life and counsel to good men,
for striking fear in that unbelieving race,
no warrior on earth surpasses you."

164

Roland the Count, when he sees his peers dead,
and Oliver, whom he had good cause to love,   2220
felt such grief and pity, he begins to weep;
and his face lost its color with what he felt:
a pain so great he cannot keep on standing,
he has no choice, falls fainting to the ground.
Said the Archbishop: "Baron, what grief for you."   2225

165

The Archbishop, when he saw Roland faint,
felt such pain then as he had never felt;
stretched out his hand and grasped the olifant.
At Rencesvals there is a running stream:
he will go there and fetch some water for Roland;   2230

and turns that way, with small steps, staggering;
he is too weak, he cannot go ahead,
he has no strength: all the blood he has lost.
In less time than a man takes to cross a little field
that great heart fails, he falls forward, falls down;   2235
and Turpin's death comes crushing down on him.

166

Roland the Count recovers from his faint,
gets to his feet, but stands with pain and grief;
looks down the valley, looks up the mountain, sees:
on the green grass, beyond his companions,   2240
that great and noble man down on the ground,
the Archbishop, whom God sent in His name;
who confesses his sins, lifts up his eyes,
holds up his hands joined together to heaven,
and prays to God: grant him that Paradise.   2245
Turpin is dead, King Charles' good warrior.
In great battles, in beautiful sermons
he was ever a champion against the pagans.
Now God grant Turpin's soul His holy blessing. AOI.

167

Roland the Count sees the Archbishop down,   2250
sees the bowels fallen out of his body,
and the brain boiling down from his forehead.
Turpin has crossed his hands upon his chest
beneath the collarbone, those fine white hands.
Roland speaks the lament, after the custom   2255
followed in his land: aloud, with all his heart:
"My noble lord, you great and well-born warrior,
I commend you today to the God of Glory,
whom none will ever serve with a sweeter will.
Since the Apostles no prophet the like of you[6]   2260
arose to keep the faith and draw men to it.
May your soul know no suffering or want,
and behold the gate open to Paradise."

168

Now Roland feels that death is very near.
His brain comes spilling out through his two ears;   2265
prays to God for his peers: let them be called;
and for himself, to the angel Gabriel;
took the olifant: there must be no reproach!
took Durendal his sword in his other hand,
and farther than a crossbow's farthest shot   2270
he walks toward Spain, into a fallow land,
and climbs a hill: there beneath two fine trees

---

6. Cf. Deuteronomy 34.10, on the death of Moses: "And there arose not a prophet since in
Israel like unto Moses, whom the Lord knew face to face."

stand four great blocks of stone, all are of marble;
and he fell back, to earth, on the green grass,
has fainted there, for death is very near. 2275

169

High are the hills, and high, high are the trees;
there stand four blocks of stone, gleaming of marble.
Count Roland falls fainting on the green grass,
and is watched, all this time, by a Saracen:
who has feigned death and lies now with the others, 2280
has smeared blood on his face and on his body;
and quickly now gets to his feet and runs—
a handsome man, strong, brave, and so crazed with pride
that he does something mad and dies for it:
laid hands on Roland, and on the arms of Roland, 2285
and cried: "Conquered! Charles's nephew conquered!
I'll carry this sword home to Arabia!"
As he draws it, the Count begins to come round.

170

Now Roland feels: *someone taking his sword!*
opened his eyes, and had one word for him: 2290
"I don't know you, you aren't one of ours";
grasps that olifant that he will never lose,
strikes on the helm beset with gems in gold,
shatters the steel, and the head, and the bones,
sent his two eyes flying out of his head, 2295
dumped him over stretched out at his feet dead;
and said: "You nobody! how could you dare
lay hands on me—rightly or wrongly: how?
Who'll hear of this and not call you a fool?
Ah! the bell-mouth of the olifant is smashed, 2300
the crystal and the gold fallen away."

171

Now Roland the Count feels: his sight is gone;
gets on his feet, draws on his final strength,
the color on his face lost now for good.
Before him stands a rock; and on that dark rock 2305
in rage and bitterness he strikes ten blows:
the steel blade grates, it will not break, it stands unmarked.
"Ah!" said the Count, "Blessed Mary, your help!
Ah Durendal, good sword, your unlucky day,
for I am lost and cannot keep you in my care. 2310
The battles I have won, fighting with you,
the mighty lands that holding you I conquered,
that Charles rules now, our King, whose beard is white!
Now you fall to another: it must not be
a man who'd run before another man! 2315
For a long while a good vassal held you:
there'll never be the like in France's holy land."

172

Roland strikes down on that rock of Cerritania:
the steel blade grates, will not break, stands unmarked.
Now when he sees he can never break that sword,   2320
Roland speaks the lament, in his own presence:
"Ah Durendal, how beautiful and bright!
so full of light, all on fire in the sun!
King Charles was in the vales of Moriane
when God sent his angel and commanded him,   2325
from heaven, to give you to a captain count.
That great and noble King girded it on me.
And with this sword I won Anjou and Brittany,
I won Poitou, I won Le Maine for Charles,
and Normandy, that land where men are free,   2330
I won Provence and Aquitaine with this,
and Lombardy, and every field of Romagna,
I won Bavaria, and all of Flanders,
all of Poland, and Bulgaria, for Charles,
Constantinople, which pledged him loyalty,   2335
and Saxony, where he does as he wills;
and with this sword I won Scotland and Ireland,
and England, his chamber, his own domain—
the lands, the nations I conquered with this sword,
for Charles, who rules them now, whose beard is white!   2340
Now, for this sword, I am pained with grief and rage:
Let it not fall to pagans! Let me die first!
Our Father God, save France from that dishonor."

173

Roland the Count strikes down on a dark rock,
and the rock breaks, breaks more than I can tell,   2345
and the blade grates, but Durendal will not break,
the sword leaped up, rebounded toward the sky.
The Count, when he sees that sword will not be broken,
softly, in his own presence, speaks the lament:
"Ah Durendal, beautiful, and most sacred,   2350
the holy relics in this golden pommel!
Saint Peter's tooth and blood of Saint Basile,
a lock of hair of my lord Saint Denis,
and a fragment of blessed Mary's robe:
your power must not fall to the pagans,   2355
you must be served by Christian warriors.
May no coward ever come to hold you!
It was with you I conquered those great lands
that Charles has in his keeping, whose beard is white,
the Emperor's lands, that make him rich and strong."   2360

174

Now Roland feels: death coming over him,
death descending from his temples to his heart.
He came running underneath a pine tree

and there stretched out, face down, on the green grass,
lays beneath him his sword and the olifant. 2365
He turned his head toward the Saracen hosts,
and this is why: with all his heart he wants
King Charles the Great and all his men to say,
he died, that noble Count, a conqueror;
makes confession, beats his breast often, so feebly, 2370
offers his glove, for all his sins, to God. AOI.

175

Now Roland feels that his time has run out;
he lies on a steep hill, his face toward Spain;
and with one of his hands he beat his breast:
"Almighty God, *mea culpa* in thy sight,[7] 2375
forgive my sins, both the great and the small,
sins I committed from the hour I was born
until this day, in which I lie struck down."
And then he held his right glove out to God.
Angels descend from heaven and stand by him. AOI. 2380

176

Count Roland lay stretched out beneath a pine;
he turned his face toward the land of Spain,
began to remember many things now:
how many lands, brave man, he had conquered;
and he remembered: sweet France, the men of his line, 2385
remembered Charles, his lord, who fostered him:
cannot keep, remembering, from weeping, sighing;
but would not be unmindful of himself:
he confesses his sins, prays God for mercy:
"Loyal Father, you who never failed us, 2390
who resurrected Saint Lazarus from the dead,
and saved your servant Daniel from the lions:[8]
now save the soul of me from every peril
for the sins I committed while I still lived."
Then he held out his right glove to his Lord: 2395
Saint Gabriel took the glove from his hand.
He held his head bowed down upon his arm,
he is gone, his two hands joined, to his end.
Then God sent him his angel Cherubin[9]
and Saint Michael, angel of the sea's Peril; 2400
and with these two there came Saint Gabriel:
they bear Count Roland's soul to Paradise.

7. See Psalm 51.4: "Against thee, thee only,
have I sinned, and done this evil in thy sight."
8. See Daniel 6.12–23. For the raising of
Lazarus, see John 11.1–44.

9. The poet seems to have regarded this as the
name of a single angel, though "cherubim" is the
plural of "cherub."

177

Roland is dead, God has his soul in heaven.
The Emperor rides into Rencesvals;
there is no passage there, there is no track, 2405
no empty ground, not an elle,[1] not one foot,
that does not bear French dead or pagan dead.
King Charles cries out: "Dear Nephew, where are you?
Where is the Archbishop? Count Oliver?
Where is Gerin, his companion Gerer? 2410
Where is Otun, where is Count Berenger,
Yves and Yvoire, men I have loved so dearly?
What has become of Engeler the Gascon,
Sansun the Duke, and Anseïs, that fighter?
Where is Gerard the Old of Roussillon, 2415
and the Twelve Peers, whom I left in these passes?"
And so forth—what's the difference? No one answered.
"God!" said the King, "how much I must regret
I was not here when the battle began";
pulls his great beard, a man in grief and rage. 2420
His brave knights weep, their eyes are filled with tears,
twenty thousand fall fainting to the ground;
Duke Naimon feels the great pity of it.

178

There is no knight or baron on that field
who does not weep in bitterness and grief; 2425
for they all weep: for their sons, brothers, nephew,
weep for their friends, for their sworn men and lords;
the mass of them fall fainting to the ground.
Here Naimon proved a brave and useful man:
he was the first to urge the Emperor: 2430
"Look ahead there, two leagues in front of us,
you can see the dust rising on those wide roads:
the pagan host—and how many they are!
After them now! Ride! Avenge this outrage!"
"Oh! God!" said Charles, "look how far they have gotten! 2435
Lord, let me have my right, let me have honor,
they tore from me the flower of sweet France."
The King commands Gebuïn and Othon,
Thibaut of Reims and Count Milun his cousin:
"Now guard this field, the valleys, the mountains, 2440
let the dead lie, all of them, as they are,
let no lion, let no beast come near them,
let no servant, let no groom come near them,
I command you, let no man come near these dead
until God wills we come back to this field." 2445
And they reply, gently, and in great love:
"Just Emperor, dear Lord, we shall do that."
They keep with them a thousand of their knights. AOI.

---

1. That is, an ell (45 inches).

179

The Emperor has his high-pitched trumpets sound,
and then he rides, brave man, with his great host.
They made the men of Spain show them their heels,
and they keep after them, all as one man.
When the King sees the twilight faltering,
he gets down in a meadow on the green grass,
lies on the ground, prays to the Lord his God
to make the sun stand still for him in heaven,
hold back the night, let the day linger on.
Now comes the angel[2] always sent to speak with Charles;
and the angel at once commanded him:
"Charles, ride: God knows. The light will not fail you.
God knows that you have lost the flower of France.
You can take vengeance now on that criminal race."
The Emperor, on that word, mounts his horse. AOI.

180

God made great miracles for Charlemagne,
for on that day in heaven the sun stood still.
The pagans flee, the Franks keep at their heels,
catch up with them in the Vale Tenebrous,
chase them on spurring hard to Saragossa,
and always killing them, striking with fury;
cut off their paths, the widest roads away:
the waters of the Ebro lie before them,
very deep, an amazing sight, and swift;
and there is no boat, no barge, no dromond,[3] no galley.
They call on Tervagant, one of their gods.
Then they jump in, but no god is with them:
those in full armor, the ones who weigh the most,
sank down, and they were many, to the bottom;
the others float downstream: the luckiest ones,
who fare best in those waters, have drunk so much,
they all drown there, struggling, it is amazing.
The French cry out: "Curse the day you saw Roland!" AOI.

181

When Charlemagne sees all the pagans dead,
many struck down, the great mass of them drowned—
the immense spoils his knights win from that battle!—
the mighty King at once gets down on foot,
lies on the ground, and gives thanks to the Lord.
When he stands up again, the sun has set.
Said the Emperor: "It is time to make camp.
It is late now to return to Rencesvals;
our horses are worn out, they have no strength—
take off their saddles, the bridles on their heads,

2450

2455

2460

2465

2470

2475

2480

2485

2490

2. Gabriel. Cf. *laisses* 185, 291, and others.
3. A very large ship, with oarsmen and a single sail.

let them cool down and rest in these meadows."
The Franks reply: "Yes, as you well say, Lord." AOI.

182

The Emperor commands them to make camp.
The French dismount into that wilderness;   2495
they have removed the saddles from their horses,
and the bridles, dressed in gold, from their heads,
free them to the meadows and the good grass;
and that is all the care they can give them.
Those who are weary sleep on the naked earth;   2500
and all sleep, they set no watch that night.

183

The Emperor lay down in a meadow,
puts his great spear, brave man, beside his head;
he does not wish, on this night, to disarm:
he has put on his bright, brass-sewn hauberk,   2505
laced on his helm, adorned with gems in gold,
and girded on Joiuse, there never was its like:
each day it shines with thirty different lights.
There are great things that we can say about the lance
with which Our Lord was wounded on the Cross:[4]   2510
thanks be to God, Charles has its iron point,
he had it mounted in that sword's golden pommel.
For this honor, and for this mighty grace,
the name Joiuse[5] was given to that sword.
Brave men of France must never forget this: 2515
from this sword's name they get their cry Munjoie![6]
This is why no nation can withstand them.

184

The night is clear, the moon is shining bright,
Charles lies down in grief and pain for Roland,
and for Oliver, it weighs down on him hard,   2520
for the Twelve Peers, for all the men of France
whom he left dead, covered with blood, at Rencesvals;
and cannot keep from weeping, wailing aloud,
and prays to God: lead their souls to safety.
His weariness is great, for his pain is great;   2525
he has fallen asleep, he cannot go on.
Through all the meadows now the Franks are sleeping.
There is no horse that has the strength to stand:
if one wants grass, he grazes lying down.
He has learned much who knows much suffering.   2530

4. See John 19.34.   6. My joy!
5. Joyful.

185

Charlemagne sleeps, a man worn out with pain.
God sent Saint Gabriel to him that night
with this command: watch over the Emperor.
All through the night the angel stands at his head;
and in a vision he brought the King dread tidings   2535
of a great battle soon to come against him:
revealed to him its grave signification:
Charles raised his eyes and looked up to the sky,
he sees the thunder, the winds, the blasts of ice,
the hurricanes, the dreadful tempests,   2540
the fires and flames made ready in the sky.
And suddenly all things fall on his men.
Their lances burn, the wood of ash and apple,
and their shields burn down to their golden bosses,
the shafts of their sharp spears burst into pieces,   2545
then the grating of hauberks, helmets of steel.
He sees his warriors in great distress—
leopards and bears furious to devour them,
serpents, vipers, dragons, demons of hell,
swarms of griffins, thirty thousand and more,   2550
and all come swooping down upon the French;
and the French cry: "Charlemagne, come help us!"
The King is filled with rage and pain and pity,
wants to go there, but something blocks his way:
out of a wood a great lion coming at him,   2555
it is tremendous, wild, and great with pride:
seeks the King's very body, attacks the King!
and they lock arms, King and lion, to fight,
and still he cannot tell who strikes, who falls.
The Emperor sleeps, his dream does not wake him.   2560

186

And after this he was shown another vision:
he was in France, at Aix, on a stone step,
and two chains in his hands holding a bear;
from the Ardennes he saw thirty bears coming,
and each of them was speaking like a man;   2565
they said to him: "Lord, give him back to us,
you must not keep him longer, it is not right;
he is our kin, we must deliver him."
From his palace a greyhound now, running,
leaps on the greatest bear among them all,   2570
on the green grass beyond his companions,
there the King sees an amazing struggle
but cannot tell who conquers, who goes down.
These are the things God's angel showed this baron.
Charles sleeps until the morning and the bright day.   2575

187

King Marsilion flees to Saragossa,
dismounts in shadow beneath an olive tree,
gives up his sword, his helmet, his hauberk,
lies down in shame, on the green grass, outraged:
he has lost his right hand, cleanly cut off,   2580
faints from the loss of blood and chokes with pain.
And before him stands his wife Bramimunde,
who weeps and wails, the fury of her lament!
and thirty thousand men, and more, with her,
cursing King Charles and the sweet land of France.   2585
They rush into a crypt to Apolin
and rail at him, disfigure him to vileness:
"Eh! you bad god, the shame you have done us!
Why did you let our king be beaten to dishhonor?
You give bad wages to men who serve you well."   2590
They tear away his scepter and his crown,
lay hands on him atop a lofty column
and throw him to the ground beneath their feet,
and beat him with big sticks, smash him to pieces;
and tear from Tervagant his great carbuncle,   2595
and throw the god Mahum into a ditch,
and pigs and dogs bite him and befoul him.

[Lines 2598–3663 describe the death of Marsilion and Charlemagne's defeat of the army of
Baligant, the emir of Cairo and Marsilion's overlord.]

266

The day wears on, the night has gathered now,
the moon shines bright, the stars are all ablaze,   3665
the Emperor has taken Saragossa.
He sends a thousand French to search the city,
the synagogues, the mosques of Mahumet,
with iron mauls and hatchets in their hands,
they break the images, shatter all idols: 3670
there shall be no more magic and no more fraud.
The King believes in God, he has one will:
to serve the Lord; and his bishops bless the waters,
lead the pagans to the baptismal font:
if there is one who now refuses Charles,   3675
he has that man struck dead, or hanged, or burned;
and they baptized more than a hundred thousand
true Christians all, but not Queen Bramimunde:
she will be led, a captive, to sweet France:
the King wants her led to conversion by love.   3680

267

Night passes on, and the bright day appears.
Charles fortified the towers of Saragossa,
left a thousand knights there, fighting men all;
they guard the city in the Emperor's name.

Now the King mounts his horse, all his men mount,   3685
and Bramimunde, whom he leads prisoner,
though he has but one will: to do her good.
They turn toward home, in joy, in jubilation,
and pass in force, a mighty host, through Nerbone;
and Charles came to Bordeaux, that . . . city, sets[7]   3690
on the altar of the baron saint Sevrin
the olifant, filled with gold and pagan coins—
pilgrims passing can see it there today;
crosses the Gironde in great ships that lie there;
he has escorted as far as Blaye his nephew   3695
and Oliver, his noble companion,
and the Archbishop, who was so wise and brave;
and bids these lords be laid in white stone coffins:
at Saint-Romain the brave men lie there still;
the Franks leave them to the Lord and His Names.[8]   3700
And Charles rides over the valleys and the mountains,
would take no rest all the long way to Aix,
and rode until he dismounts at the steps.
When he is in his sovereign high palace,
he summons all his judges, sends messengers: 3705
Saxons, Bavarians, Frisians, men of Lorraine,
the Alemans, the men of Burgundy,
the Poitevins, the Normans, the Bretons,
the wisest men among the men of France.
And now begins the trial of Ganelon.   3710

268

The Emperor is home again from Spain,
and comes to Aix, best residence of France,
ascends to the palace; entered the hall.
And now comes Aude, fair maid, before the King;
and said to him: "Where is Roland the captain,   3715
who swore to me to take me for his wife?"
And Charlemagne feels the weight and grief of this,
tears fill his eyes, he weeps, pulls his white beard:
"Sweet friend, dear sister, you ask for a dead man.
I will give you a good man in his place,   3720
it is Louis, I cannot name a better—
he is my son, he will possess my marches."
And Aude replies: "How strange these words sound to me.
May it never please God or his angels or saints
that I should go on living after Roland";   3725
loses color, falls at Charlemagne's feet,
already dead, God take pity on her soul.
Brave men of France weep and lament for Aude.

---

7. The line is incomplete in the manuscript.
8. A reference to prayers containing some of
the many names (Adonai, Emmanuel, Yeho-
vah, and so on) by which God is called in
sacred writings. These prayers were considered
effective in times of danger.

269

Aude the fair maid is gone now to her end;
the King believes that she has only fainted;
and he is moved, the Emperor weeps for Aude,
takes her two hands; now he has raised her up,
her head sinks down, fallen upon her shoulders;
when Charlemagne sees she is dead in his arms,
he has four countesses sent for at once,
and Aude is borne to a minster of nuns;
all through the night till dawn they wake beside her,
then nobly buried her by an altar.
The King gave Aude great honors, the church great gifts. AOI.

3730

3735

270

The Emperor has come home again to Aix.
In iron chains, the traitor Ganelon
stands before the palace, within the city.
He has been bound, and by serfs, to a stake;
they tie his hands with deerhide straps and thongs,
and beat him hard, with butcher's hooks, with clubs—
for what better reward has this man earned?
There he stands, in pain and rage, awaiting his trial.

3740

3745

271

It is written in the ancient Geste
that Charles summons his vassals from many lands;
they are gathered in the chapel at Aix,
a high day this, a very solemn feast,
the feast, some say, of the baron saint Sylvester.[9]
Now here begin the trial and the pleadings
of Ganelon, who committed treason.
The Emperor has had this man brought forth. AOI.

3750

3755

272

"Barons, my lords," said Charlemagne the King,
"judge what is right concerning Ganelon.
He was with me, came in my army to Spain,
and took from me twenty thousand of my French,
and my nephew, whom you'll not see again,
and Oliver, brave man, born to the court,
and the Twelve Peers—betrayed them all for money."
Said Ganelon: "Let me be called a traitor
    if I hide what I did. It was Roland
who cheated me of gold and goods; and so I wanted
to make him suffer and die; and found the way.
But treason, no—I'll grant no treason there!"
The Franks reply: "We shall take counsel now."

3760

3765

9. The feast of Saint Sylvester, December 31.

273

And there Ganelon stood, before the King,
breathing power—that lordly color on his face:
the image of a great man, had he been loyal. 3770
He sees his judges, he sees the men of France,
and his kinsmen, the thirty with him there;
then he cried out, with that great ringing voice:
"Barons, hear me, hear me for the love of God!
I was in that army with the Emperor 3775
and served him well, in love and loyalty.
Then his nephew Roland began to hate me,
and he doomed me to die an outrageous death:
I was sent as messenger to King Marsilion.
I used my wits, and I came back alive. 3780
Now I had challenged Roland, that great fighter,
and Oliver, and all of their companions:
King Charles heard it, and all his noble barons.
I took *revenge*, but there's no treason there."
The Franks reply: "We shall go into council." 3785

274

When Ganelon sees that his great trial commences,
he got his thirty kinsmen all around him.
There is one man the others listen to:
it is Pinabel of the castle of Sorence,
a man who counsels well and judges well, 3790
a valiant fighter—no man can win his arms. AOI.
Said Ganelon: "In you, friend . . .¹
free me from death and from this accusation!"
Said Pinabel: "You will soon be out of this.
Let one Frenchman dare sentence you to hang: 3795
once the Emperor sets us down man to man,
I will give him the lie with this steel sword."
And Ganelon, the Count, falls at his feet.

275

Bavarians, Saxons have gone into council,
Poitevins and Normans and men of France, 3800
the Alemans, the Germans from the North,
men of Auvergne, the courtliest of all.
They keep their voices low, because of Pinabel;
said to each other: "Best to let it stop here—
let's leave this trial and then entreat the King 3805
to let Count Ganelon go free this time
and serve henceforth in love and loyalty.
Roland is dead: you won't see him again,
he will not come for gold or goods again:
only a fool would fight over this now." 3810

---

1. The line is incomplete in the manuscript.

All go along, no one there disagrees
except one man, Lord Gefrei's brother: Tierri. AOI.

276

The barons now come back to Charlemagne,
say to the King: "Lord, this we beg of you:
let Ganelon go free, renounce your claim,   3815
then let him serve you in love and loyalty:
let this man live, for his family is great.
Roland is dead: we'll not see a hair of him,
though we die for it, not a shred of his garment,
or get him back for gold or goods again."   3820
And the King said: "You are all my traitors." AOI.

277

When Charles perceives all have abandoned him,
he bowed his head with that and hid his face,
and in such pain calls himself wretched man.
But now we see: a warrior before him,   3825
Tierri, brother of Gefrei, a duke of Anjou—
the meager body on him, such a slight man!
his hair all black, and his face rather dark;
hardly a giant, but at least not too small;
said to the Emperor, as one born to the court: 3830
"Dear Lord and King, do not lament before us.
You know I have served you well: I have the right,
my forebears' right! to give this judgment here:
Whatever wrong Count Roland may have done
to Ganelon, he was in your service,
    and serving you should have protected him,   3835
Ganelon is a traitor: he betrayed Roland.
It's you he wronged when he perjured himself,
and broke faith. Therefore, I sentence him
to die, to hang . . . his body cast . . .²
like a traitor, a man who committed treason.   3840
If his kinsman wants to give me the lie,
here is my sword, girded on: and with this sword
I am ready to make my judgment good."
The Franks reply: "Now you have spoken well."

278

Now Pinabel has come before the King: 3845
a huge man of swift grace, a valiant man—
time has run out for the poor wretch he strikes!—
said to the King: "Lord, is this not your court?
Give orders then, tell them to stop this noise.
Here I see Tierri, who has given his judgment: 3850

2. The line is incomplete in the manuscript.

I declare it is false; I shall fight with him";
places his deerhide glove in Charles's fist.
Said the Emperor: "I must have good surety."
Thirty kinsmen go hostage for his loyalty.
Then the King said: "I shall release him then"; 3855
and has them guarded until justice is done. AOI.

279

When Tierri sees the battle will take place
he gave to Charles his own right glove as gage.
The Emperor sets him free, for hostages;
then has four benches set round that battle ground: 3860
there they will sit: the two men pledged to fight.
The others judge they have been duly summoned,
Oger of Denmark had settled every question.
And then they call for their horses and arms.

280

Now since both men have been brought forth for battle, AOI. 3865
they make confession and are absolved and blessed;
they hear their mass, receive the Sacrament,
lay down great offerings in these minsters.
Now the two men have come back before Charles.
They have fastened their spurs upon their feet, 3870
and they put on white hauberks, strong and light,
and laced their bright helmets glowing upon their heads,
gird on their swords, the hilts of purest gold;
hang their great quartered shields upon their necks,
take hold of their sharp spears in their right fists; 3875
now they are mounted upon their swift war horses.
And then a hundred thousand warriors wept,
moved for love of Roland to pity Tierri.
The Lord well knows how this battle will end.

281

Down below Aix there is a broad meadow; 3880
there the battle is joined between these barons.
They are brave men, great warriors keeping faith,
and their horses are swift and spirited.
They spur them hard, reins loosened all the way,
come on to strike, the great strength that is theirs! 3885
their two shields burst in that attack to pieces,
their hauberks tear, their saddle girths rip open,
the bosses turn, the saddles fall to earth.
A hundred thousand men, who watch them, weep.

282

Now the two warriors are on the ground, AOI. 3890
now on their feet, and with what speed! again—
the grace and lightness, the strength of Pinabel!—

fall on each other, they have no horses now,
strike with their swords, the hilts of purest gold,
and strike again on these helmets of steel   3895
tremendous blows—blows that cut through helms of steel!
The knights of France are wild with grief and worry.
"Oh, God," said Charles, "make the right between them clear!"

283

Said Pinabel: "Tierri, now give it up!
I'll be your man, in love and loyalty,   3900
I'll give you all I own, take what you please,
only make peace with the King for Ganelon."
Tierri replies: "I cannot hear of that,
call me traitor if I consent to that!
May God do right between us two today." AOI.   3905

284

Now Tierri spoke: "Pinabel, you are good,
the great body on you formed like a lord's;
your peers know you: all that a vassal should be;
let this battle go then, let it end here,
I will make peace for you with Charlemagne.   3910
But justice will be done on Ganelon,
such justice will be done on his body,
no day will pass that men do not speak of it."
Said Pinabel: "May the Lord God forbid!
I will stand up for all my kin, I'll fight,   3915
no man alive will make me quit my kin
and cry defeat and beg for his mercy,
I'd sooner die than be reproached for that."
And they begin to beat down with their swords
on these helmets beset with gems in gold,   3920
and the bright fires fly from that fight toward heaven;
and no chance now that these two can be parted:
it cannot end without one of them dead. AOI.

285

Pinabel of Sorence, that valiant man,
strikes Tierri now on that helm of Provence: 3925
the fire shoots out and sets the grass aflame;
and shows Tierri the point of that steel sword:
he brought it down. Pinabel brought it down
on his forehead, and down across his face,
the whole right cheek is bloody from that blow,   3930
his hauberk runs with blood down to his waist.
God protects him, he is not struck down dead. AOI.

286

And Tierri sees: he is struck on the face—
the bright blood falling on the grass in the meadow;
strikes Pinabel on his helm of bright steel,   3935

and shattered it, split it to the nosepiece,
struck his brain out spattering from his head;
and raised his sword; he has cast him down, dead.
That was the blow, and the battle is won.
The Franks cry out: "God has made a miracle!   3940
Now Ganelon must hang, it is right now,
and all his kin who stood for him in court." AOI.

287

Now when Tierri had won his great battle,
there came to him the Emperor Charlemagne,
and forty of his barons along with him,   3945
Naimon the Duke, and Oger of Denmark,
William of Blaye, and Gefrei of Anjou.
The King has taken Tierri into his arms,
he wipes his face with his great furs of marten,
throws them aside; they clasp new furs round him.   3950
Very gently, they disarm the warrior,
then they mount him on a mule of Araby,
and he comes home in joy among brave men.
They come to Aix, it is there they dismount.
It is the time now for the executions.   3955

288

Now Charlemagne summons his counts and dukes:
"What is your counsel regarding those I have held?
They came to court to stand for Ganelon,
bound themselves hostages for Pinabel."
The Franks reply: "Not one of them must live."   3960
The King commands his officer, Basbrun:
"Go, hang them all on the accursed tree,
and by this beard, by the white hairs in this beard,
if one escapes, you are lost, a dead man."
Basbrun replies: "What should I do but hang them?";   3965
leads them, by force, with a hundred sergeants.
They are thirty men, and thirty men are hanged.
A traitor brings death, on himself and on others. AOI.

289

Bavarians and Alemans returned,
and Poitevins, and Bretons, and Normans,   3970
and all agreed, the Franks before the others,
Ganelon must die, and in amazing pain.
Four war horses are led out and brought forward;
then they attach his two feet, his two hands.
These battle horses are swift and spirited,   3975
four sergeants come and drive them on ahead
toward a river in the midst of a field.
Ganelon is brought to terrible perdition,
all his mighty sinews are pulled to pieces,
and the limbs of his body burst apart;   3980

on the green grass flows that bright and famous blood.
Ganelon died a traitor's and recreant's death.
Now when one man betrays another,
it is not right that he should live to boast of it.

290

When the Emperor had taken his revenge,   3985
he called to him his bishops of France,
Bavaria, Germany: "In my household
there is a noble captive, and she has heard,
for so long now, such sermons and examples,
she longs for faith in God, the Christian faith.   3990
Baptize this Queen, that God may have her soul."
And they reply: "Let her be baptized now
by godmothers, ladies of noble birth."
At the baths of Aix there is a great crowd gathered,
there they baptized the noble Queen of Spain,   3995
and they found her the name Juliana;
she is Christian, by knowledge of the Truth.

291

When the Emperor had brought his justice to pass
and peace comes now to that great wrath of his,
he put the Christian faith in Bramimunde;   4000
the day passes, the soft night has gathered,
the King lay down in his vaulted chamber.
Saint Gabriel! come in God's name to say:
"Charles, gather the great hosts of your Empire!
Go to the land of Bire, with all your force,   4005
you must relieve King Vivien at Imphe,
the citadel, pagans have besieged it:
Christians are calling you, they cry your name!"
The Emperor would have wished not to go.
"God!" said the King, "the pains, the labors of my life!"; 4010
weeps from his eyes, pulls his white beard.

Here ends the song   that Turold composes, paraphrases, amplifies,[3]
                          that Turold completes, relates,
Here ends the tale   that Turold declaims, recounts, narrates,
                          that Turold copies, transcribes,
Here ends the geste   for Turold grows weak, grows weary, declines,
Here ends the written history,
Here ends the source   that Turold turns into poetry.

3. The last line of the poem reads "Ci falt la geste que Turoldus declinet." The meaning of the words *geste* and *declinet* and the syntax of *que* have never been finally settled, and no line in the poem contains so many possible meanings as the last one. Some of the interpretations that have been proposed are given here, and every one is plausible.

PETRUS ALFONSI
1062–after 1116

Petrus Alfonsi was a man of three worlds. Born a Sephardic Jew named Moses, he was educated in both Hebrew and Arabic and may have been a physician attached to one of the Islamic courts in al-Andalus (modern Spain). After migrating to England, Petrus made a strong impact on the history of science as well as literary history: the data he provided from Arabic sources played a vital role in the early development of astronomy, while his frame-tale narrative, the *Disciplina Clericalis* (*The Scholar's Guide*), was a conduit for the transmission of Eastern wisdom literature into Europe.

In 1106, Petrus converted to Christianity while living at Huesca, the capital of Aragon; he took his new first name from St. Peter, on whose feast day he was baptized, and his new second name from his godfather, King Alfonso I. Sometime during the decade following his conversion, he moved to England, where he was likely attached to the court of Henry I, King of England and Duke of Normandy. Living in both England and France, Petrus was a member of a circle of scientists and philosophers who were laying the foundation for the twelfth-century rebirth of scientific learning and, within the next century, the revival of Aristotelianism. He produced a translation into Latin from Arabic of astronomical tables, which provided the information needed to calculate the movement of the planets, eclipses of the sun and moon, and other cosmological phenomena.

Petrus wrote two major works, the *Disciplina Clericalis* and the *Dialogi contra Iudaeos* (*Dialogues against the Jews*). The latter work is a dialogue between Peter and himself—or, more precisely, between Moses (his old self, before his conversion) and the newly Christian Peter. Though there are only two parties in the dialogue, they debate three religious options: whether it is best to be a Jew, a Christian, or a Muslim. In this work, which greatly influenced later anti-Jewish polemics, Petrus Alfonsi displays a detailed knowledge of all three monotheistic religions.

His *Disciplina Clericalis* (sometimes translated as *The Scholar's Guide*), the work selected here, also takes the form of a dialogue, but the exchange is not confrontational: instead, it is the familiar and affectionate back-and-forth of an Arab father and his son, who also share the relationship of teacher and student. Like Petrus Alfonsi's earlier work, the *Disciplina Clericalis* displays an eclectic range of knowledge, but with a tone of tolerance rather than of religious polemic. It is the first frame-tale narrative to make its way from its Indian, Persian, and Arabic origins into the literature of the Latin West, paving the way for such later European story collections as **Boccaccio's *Decameron***, **Chaucer's *Canterbury Tales***, and **Christine de Pizan's *City of Ladies***. Drawing on story traditions found in the **Pañcatantra** and the **Thousand and One Nights**, the *Disciplina Clericalis* recounts fantastic narratives of magic and mundane animal tales, snippets of Oriental Wisdom literature and comic anecdotes. The settings of the stories include the far-off regions of Baghdad, Babylon, and Mecca, as well as the more commonplace settings of the local marketplace and household.

Many manuscripts of the *Disciplina Clericalis* survive, along with a tremendous range of adaptations into vernacular languages: we have medieval versions, both in verse and prose, in French, Spanish, Catalan, Gascon, Italian, German, English, and Icelandic. These stories appealed to readers on a number of levels: they could be adapted as exemplary illustrations of moral truths, to be used in preaching, or they could simply be enjoyed as delightful narratives. Many of them found their way into other collections of tales: for example, the collection of **Aesop**'s *Fables* published by the early English printer William Caxton includes stories from the *Disciplina Clericalis*.

Perhaps the most striking quality of the text, for modern readers as for medieval readers, appears in the correspondences between East and West that are threaded throughout the *Disciplina Clericalis*. When Petrus describes Balaam, a figure of the **Hebrew Bible** who also is found in Christian apocryphal traditions, he quickly adds that "in the Arabic language, he is called Luqman." Similarly, when he mentions the prophet Enoch, important in both Hebrew and Christian scripture, he explains that Enoch's other name is "Idris," the Islamic prophet described in sura 31 of the **Qur'an.** As a premodern figure standing at the crossroads of three religions and many cultures, Petrus Alfonsi offers a remarkable look into the complex and heterogeneous world of medieval Spain.

From The Scholar's Guide[1]

Prologue

Petrus Alfunsus, a servant of Jesus Christ and the author of this book, said: I give thanks to God, who is the first without beginning, the source of all good, the end without end, the fulfillment of all good, the all-knowing, who gives man knowledge and reason, who has favored us with His wisdom, enlightened us with the admirable clarity of His reason, and enriched us with the manifold grace of His Holy Spirit. And, because God has deigned to endow me, although a sinner, with wide learning, and so that the light entrusted to me may not remain hidden under a bushel,[2] inspired by the same Spirit, I have been impelled to compose this book for the benefit of many, begging Him to give a good end to this beginning of my little book and to guard me, lest anything be said in it which may displease His will. Amen. May God, therefore, who inspired me to compose this book and translate it into Latin, assist me in this modest work.

As I strove to know thoroughly the causes of the creation of man, frequently pondering them in my mind, I discovered that the human wit was intended, by order of its creator, to occupy itself, while it is in the world, in the study of holy philosophy, by means of which it acquires better and greater knowledge of its creator; that man should strive to live virtuously, guided by continence; learn to guard himself against the ever-present adversities; and walk in the path, in this world, which leads him to the Kingdom of Heaven. For, if he lives according to

1. Translated from the Latin by Joseph Ramon Jones and John Esten Keller.

2. See Matthew 5.14–16; Mark 4.21–22.

the aforementioned rule of holy discipline, he has fulfilled the end for which he was created and ought therefore to be called perfect.

I have also observed that the temperament of man is delicate; it must be instructed by being led, as it were, little by little, so that it will not become bored. I am mindful also of its hardness, which must to some extent be softened and sweetened, so that it may retain what it learns with greater facility, remembering that, as it is forgetful, it needs many things to help it remember what it tends to forget. For this reason I have compiled this small volume, taking it in part from the parables and counsels of the philosophers, in part from the parables and counsels of the Arabs, from tales and poems, and finally, from animal- and bird-fables. Nevertheless, I have taken pains to see that my writing may offer the readers and listeners a stimulus and an occasion to learn, knowing that if I should write more than is necessary, it might be a burden rather than an aid. The knowledgeable will remember what they have forgotten by means of the things which are contained here.

The title given to the book, taken from the subject itself, is THE SCHOLAR'S GUIDE, because it makes the scholar disciplined. And I have decided to avoid, as far as I am able, that anything should creep into my treatise which is contrary to our belief or repugnant to our faith. May God omnipotent, in whom I trust, help me in this task. Amen. If anyone examines this work with human and exterior eyes and finds in it something which human nature insufficiently guarded against, I advise him to read it again with sharper eye. And finally, I submit it for correction to him and to all those perfect in the Catholic faith. The philosopher believes that, in human writings, nothing is perfect.

ON THE FEAR OF GOD

The philosopher Enoch (who in Arabic is called Edric[3]), said to his son, "Let your concern be the fear of God, and wealth will come to you without toil."

Another wise man said, "All things fear him who fears God; he who does not fear God fears all things. He who fears God loves Him; he who loves Him, obeys Him."

An Arabic poet said, "You disobey God; you pretend, nevertheless, to love Him, which is incredible; for if you truly loved Him, you would obey Him; for he who loves, obeys."

ON HYPOCRISY

Socrates[4] said to his pupils, "Try not to be obedient and disobedient to God in the same matter."

They replied, "Explain your words."

And he answered them: "Avoid hypocrisy, which is pretending obedience to God in the sight of men and yet being disobedient in secret."

One of his disciples asked him, "Is there some other kind of hypocrisy which one should avoid?"

---

3. Idris; he is sometimes but not always (and certainly not in the Qur'an) identified with the Jewish prophet Enoch.

4. Greek philosopher (469–399 B.C.E.); his method of teaching through inquiry is recorded in Plato's dialogues.

Socrates answered, "There is the man who makes a show of obeying God in public as well as in private, in order to be taken for a saint by others and to be more honored by them. There is another cleverer than this one, who abandons this kind of hypocrisy in order to cultivate another greater kind: when he fasts or gives alms and someone asks whether he has done so, he will answer, 'God knows!' or, 'No,' in order to be held in greater reverence and so that people will say that he is not a hypocrite, since he does not want his good works known among men. I believe that there are very few who are not affected by some kind of hypocrisy. See to it that you are not seduced by it and deprived of the reward of your good works. To avoid this, do everything with pure intention, without seeking to acquire glory from your actions."

Another wise man says, "If you lean firmly on God, all things will prosper for you wherever you go."

THE ANT, THE COCK AND THE DOG

Balaam,[5] who is called Lucaman[6] in Arabic, said to his son, "Son, do not let the ant, who gathers in the summertime in order to have something to live on in winter, be wiser than you; do not let the cock, who wakes early in the morning while you sleep, be more vigilant than you; do not let the cock, who satisfies his ten wives, whereas you cannot control one, be stronger than you; do not let the dog, who does not forget his benefactors, though you forget yours, have a nobler heart than you; do not think that to have one enemy is a small number or a thousand friends too many. I will tell you a story:"

I. The Parable of the Half Friend

An Arab, on his deathbed, called his son and asked him, "How many friends have you acquired in your lifetime?"

The son answered, "I believe that I have a hundred friends."

The father said, "The wise man says, 'Do not praise your friend until you have tested him.' I was born before you, and I have scarcely acquired half a friend. How have you got a hundred? Go now and test them all, so that you may know whether any of them will turn out to be a whole friend."

The son asked, "How do you advise me to do it?"

The father said, "Kill a calf, cut it in pieces, and put it in a sack in such a way that the outside of the sack is bloodstained; and when you go to your friend, say, 'My good friend, I have killed a man by accident; I beg you to bury him secretly; no one will suspect you, and thus you will be able to save me.'"

The son did as his father commanded. The first friend to whom he went said to him, "Carry the dead man away on your own back. Since you did wrong, take your punishment. You will not enter my house."

---

5. The diviner or soothsayer in Numbers 22–24; his opposition to the people of Israel is largely ineffectual. Balaam does not appear by name in the Qur'an, but some commentators identify him with the man who fails to recog- nize the divine message at Qur'an 7.175–76. Few identify him with Luqman.

6. Traditional figure of wisdom, sometimes believed to be a prophet; sura 31 takes its name from him.

And when he did this to all his other friends, one by one, all gave him that same answer. He went back to his father and told him what he had done, and his father said, "It has happened to you as the wise man said: 'There are many who are called friends, but in time of necessity they are few.' And now go to my half friend and see what he says to you."

The son went to him and told him what he had told the others. The half friend said, "Come inside! This secret should be kept from the neighbors."

And then he sent his wife, with all his household, away, and he dug a grave. When the boy saw everything made ready, he revealed the truth of the matter to the half friend and thanked him earnestly. Then he recounted to his father what he had done.

The father said to him, "Regarding such a friend, the philosopher says, 'He who helps you when the world fails you is a true friend.'"

The son asked his father, "Have you ever seen a man who had a whole friend?"

The father: "I have not seen such a thing, but I have heard of it."

The son: "Tell me about it, in case I should acquire such a friend."

From II. *The Parable of the Whole Friend*

The father: Once there were two merchants, one in Egypt and another in Baldach.[7] They knew each other only by reputation, and they sent to each other by messenger for the things that they needed. It happened that the merchant from Baldach had to go to Egypt on business, and when the Egyptian merchant heard of his arrival, he ran out to meet him and received him into his house with great joy and served him in all things, as friends do, for eight days and entertained him with all sorts of music, which he maintained in his house.

At the end of the eight days, the merchant from Baldach fell sick. The master of the house, gravely worried about his friend, admitted all the doctors of Egypt to examine his guest. The doctors took his pulse and examined his urine again and again, but they could recognize no illness in him. And since they could find no bodily sickness in him, they knew that his suffering was due to love. When the Egyptian merchant learned this, he went to his friend and asked him if he were in love with some woman in the household.

The sick man said, "Show me all the women in your house, and if by chance I see her among them, I will point her out to you." When the Egyptian heard this, he brought out all the singers and serving women, but none pleased the friend. Then the Egyptian showed him all his daughters, but the friend rejected and ignored them completely, as he had the other women. The master, however, had in his house a young noblewoman whom he had been educating for some time, because he was planning to marry her. And he showed her to his sick friend.

The sick man, seeing her, said, "My death or life depends on her."

When he heard this, the Egyptian gave the young noblewoman to his friend for a wife, together with all the property which he himself would have received with her and with all the things which he would have given to the young woman if he had married her.

7. Baghdad.

When all these things had been accomplished, when the friend had married the girl and received all the things which came with her, and when he had finished his business, he returned to his own country.

Later, it happened that the Egyptian lost all that he had, and in great poverty, he decided to go to Baldach, so that his friend might have pity on him. Therefore naked and hungry, he made the journey to Baldach and arrived very late at night. Shame prevented his going to his friend's house, because he was afraid that if he were not recognized, he might perchance be driven out of the house. He therefore entered an ancient temple in order to pass the night there. And while he was there, unhappy and thinking many things to himself, near the temple in the city two men met and one killed the other and stealthily fled.

Many citizens, hearing the noise, came running and found the dead man. Seeking the person who had committed the murder, they entered the temple, expecting to find the murderer. There they found the Egyptian, and when they asked him who had killed the man, they heard from his own lips, "I killed him." (For he longed desperately to end his poverty at once by death.) They seized him and took him to jail.

When morning came, he was taken before the judges, and after he was condemned to death, he was led away to the cross. Many, as usual, had come to see the execution, and among them was the Egyptian's friend, the merchant on whose account he had come to Baldach. The merchant, looking at the condemned man closely, discovered that he was the friend whom he had left in Egypt. Realizing that if the Egyptian were to die, he would not be able to repay him, the merchant of Baldach determined to die in his place. He therefore exclaimed in a loud voice:

"Why do you condemn this innocent man? Where are you taking him? He does not deserve to die. I killed that man!"

And they seized him and led him, bound, to the cross and absolved the other from death.

But the murderer was in the crowd, observing these things and thinking to himself, "I killed that man and a guiltless man is condemned to death. This innocent man is sentenced to be punished, and I, a wicked man, enjoy freedom. What is the cause of this injustice? I do not know, unless it is God's patience. For God, the just judge, leaves no crime without punishment. I shall reveal myself as the perpetrator of this crime so that God will not punish me more severely at some later time. And thus, by freeing them from death, I shall atone for the sin which I committed."

He therefore exposed himself to danger, saying, "I did it, I did it! Free this innocent man!"

The judges, not a little amazed, bound the one and released the other. In doubt concerning the sentence, they brought the murderer and the other two who had already been freed, before the king. When they had told him everything, as it had happened, they caused even him to hesitate in judgment. On the advice of all, the king pardoned all three the crimes which they had committed, on the condition that they tell him the reason for their confessions. And they told the king the truth.

When all three had been released by common consent, the citizen of Baldach who had determined to die for his friend brought the Egyptian home and with every honor, according to custom, said to him: "If you agree to stay here with me, I will share all of my property with you, as is just. But if you should want to return to your country, we will divide equally all that I have."

And the Egyptian, who longed for his native land, accepted part of all the substance which his friend had offered him and then went back to his native land.

When the story had thus been told, the son said to the father, "Such a friend must be hard indeed to find!"

Another wise man said, concerning friends who have not been tested, "Guard yourself well from your enemies but a thousand times more carefully from your friends. For perhaps some day the friend may become an enemy, and then he will more easily be able to do you harm."

* * *

XI. The Parable of the Sword

It is told that a certain man, leaving on a journey, left his mother-in-law to guard his wife. The wife, however, was secretly in love with a young man and at once told her mother about it. The mother approved of the love affair and invited the young man to dinner. While they were eating, the husband returned and knocked at the door. The wife got up and went to open the door for her husband. The mother-in-law, remaining with her daughter's lover, did not know what to do, since there was no place to hide him. But while her daughter was opening the door for her husband, the old lady took an unsheathed sword, gave it to the young man, and ordered him to stand before the door where the husband would enter and not to answer if the husband said anything to him. He did as the old woman had ordered.

When the door had been opened and the husband saw the young man standing there, he stopped and asked, "Who are you?"

The young man did not answer, and the husband, who at first was surprised, began to be afraid.

The old lady said in a low voice, "Hush, dear son-in-law, so no one can hear you!" "What is it, dear lady?" he asked, even more amazed. The old lady: "My son, three men came here after this man, and we opened the door and let him come in with his sword until the men who wanted to kill him had left. He is afraid that you might be one of them, and he does not answer you for fright."

The husband replied to her, "You did well to save this man from death in that way."

And entering the house, he invited his wife's lover to sit down with him, and, reassuring him with pleasant conversation, he sent him on his way at night.

The pupil said, "You have told me surprising things about women, but what amazes me most is their presumptuous audaciousness. Nevertheless, if it is not too much trouble, I want you to tell me about their tricks. The more you tell me, the greater the reward you deserve."

To whom the teacher said, "Are these not enough for you? I have already told you three parables, and you still insist?"

The pupil replied, "When you say three parables, you exaggerate the number, for they were short ones. Now tell me a long story which will fill my ears and will thus satisfy me."

The teacher answered, "Be careful, so that what happened between a king and his story teller does not happen between us."

"What happened, dear teacher?"

"The following:"

XII. The Parable of the King and His Story Teller

A king had a story teller who usually told him five tales each night. It happened finally that the king, troubled with cares, could not sleep, and he ordered the story teller to tell him more tales. The story teller told him three more, but they were short, and the king asked for more. The story teller demurred because, as it seemed to him, he had already told a good many.

The king replied, "You have already told many, but they were very short. I want you to tell me a long one, and then I will let you go to bed."

The story teller agreed and began thus:

A peasant who had a thousand silver coins went to market and bought two thousand sheep, at six denarii[8] each. And when he was returning, it happened that the river was swollen with floodwaters, and he was not able to cross by the bridge or the ford. Worried, he began looking for a place where he could cross with his sheep. He finally found a small boat which would only hold two sheep and the shepherd at the same time. But driven by necessity, he put two sheep in the boat and crossed . . .

When the story teller had told this, he fell asleep.

The king woke him up so that he could finish the story that he had begun, and he said, "The river is very wide, the boat is very small, and the sheep are very numerous. Let the peasant ferry his sheep across first, and then I will finish the story."

And thus the story teller silenced the king who was eager to hear long tales.

"If you force me to invent more than the ones already told, I shall try to free myself by means of the stratagem of the tale just told."

Then the pupil said, "It is told in the ancient proverbs that he who weeps for pay does not feel the same grief as the man in bodily pain. And the story teller did not love the king as you love me. He wanted only to amuse him for a while with his stories, whereas you do not wish merely to amuse me, your pupil. Therefore I beg you not to stop the story-telling already begun but, on the contrary, to reveal women's tricks in detail."

From XIII. The Parable of the Weeping Bitch[9]

It is related that a nobleman had a very chaste and beautiful wife. He wanted to go to Rome to pray in the holy places, and he did not want to leave any other guardian for his wife but herself, trusting in her chaste habits and the honor of her uprightness. When the retinue was ready, he departed and the wife remained, living chastely and acting prudently in all things.

---

8. Silver Roman coins, reintroduced in the 8th century as the standard coin of Charle- magne's empire.

9. Female dog.

It happened that she needed something, and she left her own house and went to a neighboring house. As she came home after transacting her business, a young man saw her and fell madly in love with her. He, desiring to be loved by her for whom he burned so ardently, sent many messages to her. But she refused his messages and rejected him completely.

The young man seeing himself utterly scorned, grief-stricken, fell gravely ill; but nevertheless he would often go where he had seen his lady leave, hoping to meet her; but he was not able to effect it at all. Weeping for sorrow, he met an old woman wearing the habit of a nun, and she asked the cause of his unhappiness; but the young man was not very anxious to reveal what was going on in his mind.

The old woman said to him, "The longer a sick man delays in revealing his illness to the doctor, the more he will suffer from the illness."

Hearing this, he told her what had happened to him and his secret.

The old lady said to him, "With God's help I'll find a remedy for what you have told me."

And she left him and returned to her own house. She forced a little dog which she had at home to go without food for two days. On the third day she gave the hungry dog bread made with mustard, and as the dog ate the bread, its eyes began to water with the sharpness of the mustard. The old woman brought the little dog to the house of the chaste woman whom the young man loved, and the woman received her respectfully because of her very religious appearance. The little bitch was following the old woman. When the woman saw it weeping, she asked what was wrong with it and why it was crying.

The old woman said to her, "Dear friend, do not ask what is wrong, because the sorrow is so great that I can hardly talk about it."

And the woman begged her even more earnestly to tell her.

The old woman: "This little dog which you see was my daughter, who was very chaste and modest and was loved by a young man; but she was so chaste that she spurned him and rejected his love. The young man, pining away, became very ill. For her sin, my wretched daughter was turned into a little bitch." And so saying, the old lady burst into tears.

The decent woman said at this, "O dear lady, what shall I do? I am guilty of a similar crime; for a young man loves me, but because of my love of chastity I have disdained him, and he has also fallen ill."

"Dear friend, I advise you to have pity on him as quickly as possible and do what he asks, so that you may not be turned into a dog just as my daughter was. If I had known of the love between my daughter and the young man, my daughter would never have been transformed."

The chaste woman said to her, "I beg you to give me good advice, so that I may not be turned into a little bitch, deprived of my own form."

"Willingly," said the old woman, "for the love of God and the health of my soul and because I feel sorry for you, I will seek the young man, and if he can be found, I will bring him back to you."

The woman thanked her, and the wily old woman kept her word and brought back the young man, as she had promised and thus brought them together.

The pupil said to the teacher, "I have never heard anything so astounding, and I think it was done with black magic."

The teacher: "Have no doubt!"

The pupil: "I think that if any man is wise enough always to fear being deceived by women's tricks, perhaps he will be able to guard himself against them."

The teacher: "I know of a certain man who took great precautions to guard his wife; but he did not gain anything by it."

The pupil: "Tell me what he did, teacher, so I will be better able to guard my wife, if I ever marry."

MARIE DE FRANCE

1150?–1200?

"Marie ai num, si sui de France" (Marie is my name, and I am from France). With these words, the author of the *Lais* tells us her name and her homeland. Yet Marie was an English writer, composing in the Anglo-Norman dialect of French that had become the mother tongue of the English ruling classes following the Norman Conquest a century before. Her short, intense stories of love and loss reflect the complex cultural encounter of Celtic folktale, Anglo-French court setting, and English landscape, and they set the stage for the flowering of the romance genre in the last decades of the twelfth century.

We know little about Marie beyond what she herself tells us in the Prologue to her *Lais*, which is reprinted here, and in the closing lines of her collection of animal fables. She is likely to have been a nun—possibly an abbess in a position of authority within her community; in offering her collection of twelve *Lais* as a gift to Henry II, King of England and Duke of Normandy, she uses terms that presume some degree of familiarity, perhaps even a family relationship. It was not uncommon in twelfth-century Europe for the illegitimate female offspring of noble or royal figures to enter convents, less because these women were pious than because it was expedient to prevent them from marrying political rivals and bearing children who might complicate the smooth order of future succession. Marie's place in the world, attached at once to the cloister and to the court, may reflect some such family history.

In addition to her *Fables*, which she claims to have translated from a now-lost text by the Anglo-Saxon king Alfred, Marie's other surviving works include the mysterious journey to the afterlife recounted in *Saint Patrick's Purgatory* (adapted from a Latin original) and an account of the life and works of the English saint Audrey. Her poems stand at the intersection of oral and written forms of literature, as well as at the crossroads of cultures—not just English and French, but Welsh or Breton as well. Celtic cultures had survived the warfare of English and French barons, both in the mountains of Wales and in Cornwall, to the north of the English Channel, and in the upper regions of

Normandy and Brittany, to the south. In her Prologue, Marie describes her desire to preserve these Breton songs: having heard them sung, she writes, "I don't want to neglect or forget them." She expresses a similar sentiment in the epilogue to her *Fables*, in which she tells the reader her own name "pur remembrance," "for remembrance." Through the *Lais*, Marie has ensured that both she and the ancient songs she has written down will live on in memory.

The two lais included here, "Bisclavret" and "Laüstic," represent two very different types: the first, more elaborate, offers a very fully developed psychology of the main characters, while the second, shorter and jewel-like, crystallizes an essential truth about the nature of love in poetic form. In "Bisclavret," we find the tale of a man who has a secret: he spends part of each week wandering the forest in the form of a wolf, a *bisclavret*. His wife learns the truth and tricks him, condemning him to exile as an animal in the wild. **Ovid's** *Metamorphoses* (especially the story of Actaeon who, changed into a stag, is chased by hunting dogs) looms in the background of this tale of animal-human nature. The royal court where Bisclavret finds justice is echoed elsewhere in Marie's lais, in the court of King Arthur. Marie was the first to bring these oral Breton materials into the mainstream of European literature, setting a precedent for her French successor, Chrétien de Troyes (in his various Arthurian romances) and, later, for the anonymous English poet who wrote **Sir Gawain and the Green Knight** and Thomas Malory in his *Morte d'Arthur*.

The theme of vengeance that emerges in "Bisclavret" also haunts "Laüstic," though the final note of this short tale is the transcendence and ultimate triumph of love. The affair between a woman and her husband's friend comes to a brutal end when the beautiful nightingale, whose nighttime song fuels the dreams of lovers, is killed by the jealous husband. The body of the bird becomes a token of their forbidden passion, first wrapped by the lady in an embroidered shroud, and then preserved by her lover in a begemmed reliquary. The miniature lai, like the miniature sarcophagus, remains as a potent reminder of the power of love.

From The Lais[1]

Prologue

WHOM God has given intelligence
and the great gift of eloquence
must not conceal these, or keep still,
but share and show them with good will.   4
When much is heard of some good thing,
then comes its first fine flowering;
when many more have praise to give,
these blossoms flourish, spread, and thrive.   8
Among the ancients, custom was—
Priscian[2] can testify to this—

---

1. Translated by Dorothy Gilbert. Lines of Marie's poetry are numbered every four lines instead of the usual five to emphasise her use of couplets.
2. Latin grammarian (early 6th century C.E.), widely read in the Middle Ages.

that in their books they made obscure
much that they wrote; this would ensure 12
that wise folk of another day,
needing to know what these texts say,
could gloss these works, and with their sense
give all the more intelligence. 16
Savants and scholars were aware
that in their strivings, more and more
they sensed the works' great subtlety
increasingly, as time went by. 20
And thus, too, they knew how to guard
from error in time afterward.
He who would keep from vice and sin
must some great arduous work begin; 24
struggle and study, strive to know,
and doing so avoid much woe,
free from great suffering and regret.
Thus I began to give some thought 28
to telling some good story, that
taken from Latin, I would put
into French; but then I would win
no glory there; so much is done! 32
I thought of lais³ that I had heard
and did not doubt; I felt assured
that these first writers who began
these lais, who told them, made them known, 36
wished, for remembrance, to record
adventures, stories, they had heard.
I too have heard them; I do not
wish them abandoned, lost, forgot. 40
Thus I made rhymes and poetry
late into night-time, wakefully!

To honor you, most noble King,⁴
courtly and skilled in everything, 44
to whom all joy makes obeisance,
in whose heart roots all excellence,
to gather lais I undertook,
to rhyme, make, tell; this was my work. 48
I in my heart thought this I'd do,
fair Sire: present this work to you.
If it should please you to receive
my gift, for all the days I live 52
I shall be joyful; you shall give
great happiness. Do not believe
me proud, presumptuous; but hear
as I begin my tales; give ear. 56

---

3. Narrative poems of adventure and romance, written in octosyllabic couplets (French).

4. Henry II, king of England, who also held substantial territories in France.

Bisclavret

In crafting lays, I won't forget
—I mustn't—that of Bisclavret;
Bisclavret: so named in Breton;
But *Garwaf* in the Norman tongue.   4

One used to hear, in times gone by
—it often happened, actually—
men became werewolves, many men,
and in the forest made their den.   8
A werewolf is a savage beast;
in his blood-rage, he makes a feast
of men, devours them, does great harms,
and in vast forests lives and roams.   12
Well, for now, let us leave all that;
I want to speak of Bisclavret.

In Brittany[5] there lived a lord
—wondrous, the praise of him I've heard—   16
a good knight, handsome, known to be
all that makes for nobility.
Prized, he was, much, by his liege lord;
by all his neighbors was adored.   20
He'd wed a wife, a worthy soul,
most elegant and beautiful;
he loved her, and she loved him, too.
One thing she found most vexing, though.   24
During the week he'd disappear
for three whole days, she knew not where;
what happened to him, where he went
His household, too, was ignorant.   28
He returned home again one day;
high-spirited and happy. She
straightway proceeded to inquire:
"My fair sweet friend," she said, "fair sire,   32
if I just dared, I'd ask of you
a thing I dearly wish to know,
except that I'm so full of fear
of your great anger, husband dear."   36
When he had heard this, he embraced her,
drew her to him, clasped and kissed her.
"Lady," he said, "come, ask away!
Nothing you wish, dear, certainly   40
I will not tell you, that I know."
"Faith!" she said, "you have cured me so!
But I have such anxiety,
sire, on those days you part from me,   44
my heart is full of pain. I fear

5. A Celtic region of present-day northwestern France.

so much that I will lose you, dear.
Oh, reassure me, hastily!
If you do not, I soon will die.   48
Tell me, dear husband; tell me, pray,
What do you do? Where do you stay?
It seems to me you've found another!
You wrong me, if you have a lover!"   52
    "Lady," he said, "have mercy, do!
I'll have much harm in telling you.
I'd lose your love, if I should tell
and be lost to myself, as well."   56
    Now when the wife was thus addressed,
it seemed to her to be no jest.
Oftimes she begged, with all her skill,
coaxing and flattering, until   60
at last he told her all he did,
the tale entire; kept nothing hid.
    "Dame, I become a bisclavret.
in the great forest I'm afoot,   64
in deepest woods, near thickest trees,
and live on prey I track and seize."
    When he had told the whole affair,
she persevered; she asked him where   68
his clothes were; was he naked there?
    "Lady," he said, "I go all bare."
    "Tell me, for God's sake, where you put
your clothes!"
                        "Oh, I'll not tell you that: 72
I would be lost, you must believe,
if it were seen just how I live.
Bisclavret would I be, forever;
never could I be helped then, never,   76
till I got back my clothes, my own;
that's why their cache⁶ must not be known."
    "Sire," said his lady in reply,
"more than all earth I love you. Why   80
hide, why have secrets in your life?
Why, why mistrust your own dear wife?
That does not seem a loving thought.
What have I done? What sin, what fault   84
has caused your fear, in any way?
You must be fair! You have to say!"
    So she harassed and harried him
So much, he finally gave in.   88
    "Lady," he said, "just by the wood,
just where I enter, by the road,
there's an old chapel. Now, this place
has often brought me help and grace.   92

6. Hiding place (French).

There is a stone there, in the brush,
hollow and wide, beneath a bush.
In brush and under bush, I store
my clothes, till I head home once more." 96
 The lady was amazed to hear:
She blushed deep red, from her pure fear.
Terror, she felt, at this strange tale.
She thought what means she could avail 100
herself of how to leave this man.
She could not lie with him again.

 In these parts lived a chevalier[7]
who had long been in love with her. 104
Much did he pray and sue, and give
largesse in service to his love;
she had not loved him, nor had she
granted him any surety 108
that she, too, loved; but now she sent
this knight the news of her intent.
 "Friend," she wrote him, "rejoice, and know
that for which you have suffered so, 112
I grant you now without delay;
I'll not hold back in any way.
My body and my love I grant;
make me your mistress, if you want!" 116
 Kindly he thanked her, and her troth
accepted; she received his oath.
She told her lover how her lord
went to the wood, and what he did, 120
what he became, once he was there.
She told in detail how and where
to find the road and clothing cache;
and then she sent him for the stash. 124
 Thus was Bisclavret trapped for life;
ruined, betrayed, by his own wife.
Because his absences were known,
people assumed he'd really gone, 128
this time, for good. They searched around,
enough, but he could not be found,
for all their inquiries. At last
everyone let the matter rest. 132
The lady wed the chevalier
who'd been so long in love with her.

 A whole year, after this event,
thus passed. The king went out to hunt, 136
went to the forest straightaway,
there where the bisclavret now lay.

---

7. Knight (French).

The hunting dogs were now unleashed
and soon they found the changeling beast.   140
All day they flung themselves at him,
all day pursued, both dogs and men;
they almost had him. Now they'd rend
and tear him; now he'd meet his end.   144
His eye, distinguishing, could see
the king; to beg his clemency
he seized the royal stirrup, put
a kiss upon the leg and foot.   148
The king, observing, felt great fear.
Calling his men, he cried, "Come here!"
"Lords!" he said, "Come and look at this!
See what a marvel is this kiss,   152
this humble, gracious gesturing!
That's a man's mind; it begs the king
for mercy. Now, drive back the hounds!
See that none strike or give it wounds.   156
This beast has mind; it has intent.
Come, hurry up! It's time we went.
I'll give protection for this beast.
And for today, the hunt has ceased."   160

     The king had turned around, at that;
following him, the bisclavret
close by; he would not lose the king,
abandon him, for anything.   164
The king then led the beast, to bring
it to the castle, marvelling,
rejoicing at it, for he'd never,
seen such a wondrous creature, ever.   168
He loved the wolf and held it dear
and he charged every follower
that, for his love, they guard it well
and not mistreat the animal.   172
No one must strike it; and, he'd said,
it must be watered and well fed.
Gladly his men now guarded it.
Among the knights, the bisclavret   176
now lived, and slept close by the king;
everyone loved it, cherishing
its noble bearing and its charm.
It never wanted to do harm,   180
and where the king might walk or ride,
there it must be, just at his side,
wherever he might go or move;
so well it showed its loyal love.   184

     What happened after that? Now, hear.
The king held court; he had appear

all barons, vassals; gave commands
to all who held from him their lands,   188
to help a festival take place,
serving with elegance and grace.
Among those chevaliers was he
—so richly dressed, so splendidly!—   192
who'd wed the wife of Bisclavret.
Little he knew or thought just yet
that he would find his foe so near!
Soon as he came, this chevalier,   196
to court, and Bisclavret could see
the man, he ran up furiously,
sank in his teeth, and dragged him close.
Many the injuries and woes   200
he would have suffered, but the king
called out commands, while brandishing
his staff. The beast rushed, twice, that day,
to bite the man; all felt dismay,   204
for none had seen the beast display
toward anyone, in any way,
such viciousness. There must be reason,
the household said, for him to seize on   208
the knight, who must have done him wrong;
the wish for vengeance seemed so strong.
    And so they let the matter rest
till the conclusion of the feast.   212
The barons took their leave, each one,
each to his castle and his home.
All my good judgment counsels me
he who was first to leave was he   216
set upon by the bisclavret.
Small wonder the beast had such hate!

    Not too long after this occurred
—such is my thought, so I have heard—   220
into the forest went the king
—so noble and so wise a being—
where he'd first found the bisclavret.
The animal was with him yet.   224
The night of this return, the king
took, in this countryside, lodging.
And this the wife of Bisclavret
well knew. Dressed fetchingly, she set   228
out to have speech with him next day;
rich gifts were part of her display.
Bisclavret saw her come. No man
had strength to hold him as he ran   232
up to his wife in rage and fury.
Hear of his vengeance! Hear the story!
He tore her nose off, then and there.

What worse could he have done to her?   236
From all sides now, and full of threat
men ran and would have killed him, but
a wise man expeditiously
spoke to the king. "Listen to me!   240
He's been with you, this animal;
there is not one man of us all
who has not, long since, had to see
and travel with him, frequently,   244
and he has harmed no one, not once
shown viciousness nor violence
save just now, as you saw him do.
And by the faith I owe to you,   248
he has some bitter quarrel with her
and with her husband, her seigneur.
She was wife to that chevalier
whom you so prized, and held so dear,   252
who disappeared some time ago.
What happened, no one seems to know.
Put her to torture. She may state
something, this dame, to indicate   256
why the beast feels for her such hate.
Force her to speak! She'll tell it straight.
We've all known marvels, chanced to see
strange events, here in Brittany."   260
    The King thought this advice was fair;
and he detained the chevalier.
The lady, too, he held; and she
he put to pain and agony.   264
Part out of pain, part out of fear,
she made her former lord's case clear:
how she had managed to betray
her lord, and take his clothes away;   268
the story he had told to her,
what he became, and how, and where;
and how, when once his clothes were gone
—stolen—he was not seen again.   272
She gave her theory and her thought:
Surely this beast was Bisclavret.
    These spoils, these clothes, the king demanded;
whether she would or no, commanded   276
that she go back and find them, get
and give them to the bisclavret.

    When they were put in front of him
he didn't seem to notice them.   280
The king's wise man spoke up once more
—the one who'd counselled him before—
"Fair sire, this will not do at all!
We can't expect this animal,   284
in front of you, sire, to get dressed

and change his semblance of a beast.
You don't grasp what this means, my king!
—or see his shame and suffering.   288
Into your room have led this beast;
with him, his clothes. Let him get dressed;
For quite some time, leave him alone.
If he's a man, that is soon known!"   292
    The king himself led the bisclavret;
and on him all the doors were shut.
They waited. And then finally
two barons, with the king, all three,   296
entered. What a discovery!
There on the king's bed, they could see
asleep, the knight. How the king ran
up to the bed, to embrace his man,   300
kiss him, a hundred times and more!
    Quickly he acted to restore
his lands, as soon as possible;
more he bestowed than I can tell.   304
His wife was banished. She was chased
out of the country, and disgraced,
and chased out, travelling with her,
her mate and co-conspirator.   308

    Quite a few children had this dame,
who in their way achieved some fame
for looks, for a distinctive face;
numbers of women of her race   312
—it's true—were born without a nose.
Noseless they lived, the story goes.

    And this same story you have heard
truly occurred; don't doubt my word.   316
I made this *lai* of Bisclavret
so no one, ever, will forget.

Laüstic

    There's an adventure, I will say,
of which the Bretons made a *lai*.
Laüstic is the name it's called
in its own country, so I'm told.   4
In French it's "Rossignol," this tale;
in proper English, "Nightingale."
    Near St. Malo[1] there was a town

---

1. A seaport in northwest France, in Brittany.

that in that region had renown.   8
There lived two knights, and side by side
their mansions, strong and fortified.
For knightly valor each had fame,
and gave their city a good name.   12
One had a wife, an excellent
lady, wise, courtly, elegant;
a marvel was she, so *soignée*,[2]
and groomed with great propriety.   16
The other of these chevaliers,
a bachelor, was by his peers
well known for prowess, and great valor.
With pleasure he did deeds of honor.   20
Much he tourneyed; with much largesse
gave of what he himself possessed.
He loved his neighbor's wife, and he
begged and sued so persistently   24
and had such qualities, that she
above all, loved him ardently;
partly, for all the good she heard;
partly, he lived close by, this lord.   28

    Well these two loved, and prudently,
and with great care and secrecy,
making sure they were not detected,
hindered, or noticed, or suspected;   32
and this they could do easily
because their dwellings lay nearby.
Nearby, their mansions and their halls,
their keeps, their dungeons. But no walls,   36
no barrier, except for one,
a great high wall of dark-hued stone.
Still, in her bedroom, when she stood
right at the window, then she could   40
talk to her love, her chevalier,
she speak to him and he to her;
they could toss tokens to each other,
throw little gifts, lover to lover.   44
Nothing displeased them in that place,
they were at ease there, face to face,
except that they could only see—
not join in pleasure utterly,   48
for when he was at home, her lord
had his wife under close, strict guard.
Still they made opportunity;
and thus by night and thus by day   52
they met; they spoke; they found a way
and none who watched could say them nay

---

2. Well groomed and elegantly dressed (French).

when to their windows they would each
come, and there speak their loving speech.   56
   For a long time they loved each other,
until one summer, when the weather
had made the fields and forests green
and gardens, orchards, bloom again;   60
above the flowers, with great joy
small birds sang sweetest melody.
He whose desire for love is strong
—no wonder that he heeds their song!   64
The truth about this knight, I'll tell;
he heard the song; he heard it well;
the lady, too, heard in her place;
thus they could love; court; speak, and gaze.   68
When the moon shone, the lady would
rise often from her husband's bed,
rise from beside him, while he slept
and softly, in her mantle wrapped,   72
cautiously to the window go
to see her lover, whom she knew
lived as she did, lived for her sight.
She'd stay awake most of the night.   76
   In gazing thus was their delight,
since nothing more could be their fate.
Such was the case. So often she
arose, her husband angrily   80
demanded of her, frequently,
where did she go, what for, and why?
The lady answered with this word:
   "My sire: he who has never heard   84
the nightingale, has not known joy
ever, in all this world. That's why,
that's where. So sweetly I have heard
it sing at night, enchanting bird,   88
so great my longing, my delight,
I cannot close my eyes at night."
   When he had heard her answer thus,
he laughed, enraged and furious,   92
and he resolved that without fail
he would entrap the nightingale.
Now every squire within that house
put net or snare or trap to use   96
throughout the garden. Everywhere,
on hazel, chestnut, lay a snare
or gluey bird-lime. So they got
the nightingale; so it was caught.   100
   When they had tricked and trapped the bird
alive, they brought it to the lord.
Oh, he was happy when they came!
Right to the chamber of his dame   104

he hurried. "Lady, where are you?
Come talk to us, my lady, do!
I've trapped your nightingale, the one
that's kept you sleepless for so long.   108
Now, finally, you'll sleep in peace—
these night excursions now can cease."
    She understood, as he spoke thus,
and full of grief, and furious   112
asked for the bird. But her demands
were vain; in rage, with his two hands
he broke its neck. So this seigneur,
spiteful and vicious, like a boor   116
killed it. He threw the corpse at her.
It fell on her chemise and there
bloodied her breast a little bit.
He left the room; at once went out.   120
    She gathered up the little body,
weeping vehemently. The lady
cursed those who caught the bird and laid
snares, nets, devices, all they made.   124
What joy was taken, wrenched away!
    "Alas," she said, "Oh, wretched me!
No more shall I arise at night,
go to the window for a sight   128
of my dear love and find him there.
And one thing I do know for sure:
he'll think me weak and faint of heart.
I must act now. Let me take thought.   132
I'll send my love the nightingale,
make known to him this vicious tale."
    She found a piece of samite,[3] wrought
with gold, and writing worked throughout;   136
in it she wrapped the little bird.
One of her servants she gave word,
gave him her message, and he went
to her *ami*,[4] where it was sent,   140
So to the chevalier he came
and gave him greetings from his dame,
gave the full message, told the tale,
delivered up the nightingale.   144
When the full story was made known
—he gave it good attention!—
he felt much sorrow. This knight, though,
was not a boor, nor was he slow   148
of sense. A tiny reliquary
he soon had forged, for him to carry:
not iron; not steel; pure gold, with stones

3. Luxurious, heavy silk.   4. Lover (French).

most rare and precious, lovely ones;   152
a lid that was a perfect fit.
The little bird was placed in it,
the vessel sealed. The chevalier
carried it with him everywhere.   156
   This story, more and more, got known;
it was not secret very long.
Of it the Bretons made their lay;
It's called *Laüstic* to this day.   160

MEDIEVAL LYRICS

Lyric poetry gets its name from the lyre, a harplike musical instrument used to accompany the singing of verse in the ancient world; it was associated in Greek and Roman culture with the god Apollo, and connected in Jewish and Islamic culture with King David, supposed poet of the **Psalms.** Unlike narrative poetry, which features an extended story line and the development of complex characters, lyric poetry paints a brief, highly focused picture of a specific place, a particular moment, or an intense emotion. In some periods this poetry, like modern song lyrics, was conventionally set to music; at other times it was circulated in written form. But even on the page, it retains in its vividness and immediacy something of the spontaneous, performative quality of song.

The lyrics collected here span a wide range, in terms both of their thousand-year time period and of their geographical origin. Some are composed in elevated, learned languages spoken across national borders, such as Arabic, Hebrew, and Latin; others are written in the vernacular languages of Europe and the Islamic world, from the Old English of the extreme northwest to the Persian of the southeast. Yet certain themes appear repeatedly, like fragments of set melodies that are

played over many times, in different keys and at different tempos. The preminent focus is love, whether amorous love for an individual person or spiritual love for the divine. Other recurrent themes include the sense of familiar place or homeland, often associated with the poetry of exile or with the elegiac mode, as the poet mourns a time and a place that seems to be lost forever; warfare, whose brutal violence and pain are coupled with extraordinary displays of heroism and the firm friendship of comrades; and poetry itself, the topic of a number of lyrics that meditate self-reflectively on the very task of literary composition, weighing the competing claims of supernatural inspiration against the simple, devoted labor of the artisan whose medium is the word and whose tool is the pen.

From the first poem onward, the lyrics collected here betray a fundamental ambivalence about the passion of love. On the surface level, there would seem to be a clear distinction between the love of one person for another, which is expressed physically, and the love directed toward God, which is expressed spiritually. In Boethius's lyric on Orpheus, the mythological musician unrivaled among mortals, this ambiguity takes the form of a stark opposition, leading to Orpheus's tragic mistake as he looks backward at his beloved wife Eurydice—he should, according to Boethius, have kept his gaze fixed on the proper, higher object, the love of the good. Orpheus's failure

A detail from a late fifteenth-century illuminated manuscript of the thirteenth-century French poem *Le Roman de la Rose.*

reveals the inescapable weakness of the lover, as his irrational passion brings about not only his own downfall but that of his beloved.

In Persian poetry and in the Arabic lyrics of medieval Spain, however, erotic love increasingly came to be represented as capable of refining or even perfecting the individual. Instead of opposing human love, expressed through the body, and divine love, expressed through the soul, the tradition that came to be known in Europe as "courtly love" posited that the human beloved was actually a medium through which one might glimpse the divine. **Ibn Arabi** and **Hafez** (and elsewhere in this anthology, **Rumi**) evoke this mediating quality possessed by the "beloved" or the "friend," an object of love that can equally be read as a human being adored by the poet or as the transcendent presence of God becoming fully immanent in this world. Something similar appears in the poetry of medieval Provence, in which the sensation of love brings the individual to the point of self-effacement— a moment memorably captured in **Bernart de Ventadorn**'s image of the lark that stretches its wings out to the sun, fully absorbed within the brilliant ray. In the writing of **Dante**, the divine reemerges as the focus of amorous love somewhat as the figure of the "friend" functioned in the Persian and Arabic traditions that lay behind Romance vernacular expressions of courtly love. But for Dante, the specifically Christian theology of redemption adds an additional layer to the process of mediation. In serving as a pathway to God, his Beatrice directs the poet's amorous gaze toward yet another intermediary, Christ.

Perhaps the most striking feature of the lyrics collected here is their simultaneous variety and unity; drawn from very different times and places, they display a remarkable harmony or resonance on the levels of both form and content. This connection can be illustrated with special poignancy in the lyrics of two women represented here, **Jahan Khatun** of Persia (modern Iran) and **Christine de Pizan**, a native of Italy who spent her life in France. Both born in the fourteenth century, living in regions of the world that were geographically and culturally very distinct, they share an ability to put into words the bittersweet experience of love. Jahan Khatun describes the painful experience of being a "stranger" in the court of the once-attentive beloved, while Christine de Pizan embraces the solitude of the *seulete*, the widow who holds close the memory of her absent beloved. Here, the power of lyric appears as an almost invisible but profoundly strong cord that enables the poetic imagination to create links across culture, across language— perhaps even across time.

A NOTE ON TRANSLATION

With the exception of one poem reproduced in its original Middle English, a language still comprehensible to the modern reader, all of the lyrics collected here are in translation. Unlike fiction or even narrative poetry, lyric poetry poses a special challenge to the translator because of the concentrated, highly focused quality of its language. Assonance and alliteration, rhythm and rhyme all demand to be reflected in the English version, despite the great challenge of retaining these poetic devices while still reproducing the meaning of the original verses.

The following translations reflect two different approaches: some translators have rendered the original text very literally, while others have sought equivalences, believing that the best way to capture the essential meaning of the source text is to rely on poetic modes that are natural to modern English even when those differ from literary devices in the author's language. One particularly remarkable example of the latter approach is Yusef Komunyakaa's translation of the Old English poem "**The Ruin**": Komunyakaa accurately renders the elements of the Anglo-Saxon world so hauntingly evoked in the lyric, while not hesitating to rely on analogies to convey the tenth-century experience of loss and exile to his twenty-first-century audience. Another can be found in Barbara Newman's rendering of the devout lyrics of the abbess **Hildegard of Bingen**, as the translator captures the passionate, even ecstatic quality of the medieval poet within a distinctively modern idiom.

BOETHIUS

A ncius Manlius Severinus Boethius (480–524) was a philosopher and poet who rose to political eminence, fell into disfavor, and spent his last days in prison under sentence of death. While awaiting execution he wrote his *Consolation of Philosophy*, a mixture of philosophical prose alternating with lyrical interludes. His work was widely read for more than a thousand years and was translated into English by not one but two monarchs, the Anglo-Saxon King Alfred and the Tudor Queen Elizabeth. The verse reproduced here marks a turning point in the *Consolation*, when the narrator learns that he must turn his intellectual gaze toward higher things, yet it also stands on its own as an elegiac tribute to the archetypal poet of classical myth, Orpheus.

From The Consolation of Philosophy[1]

III.12

Happy was he who could look upon
The clear fount of the good;
Happy who could loose the bonds
Of heavy earth.
Of old the Thracian poet[2] mourned   5
His wife's sad death,
He who before had made the woods so nimbly run
And rivers stand
With his weeping measures,
And the hind's fearless flank   10
Lay beside savage lions,
Nor was the hare afraid to look upon
The hound, made peaceful by his song;

1. Translated from the Latin by Stephen J. Tester. 2. Orpheus; Thrace is northeast of Greece.

When grief burned yet more fierce and hot
His inmost heart,   15
And measures that subdued all else
Soothed not their master,
Complaining of inexorable gods above
He approached the halls below.
There modulating gentle songs   20
On the sounding lyre
All that he drew from the foremost springs
Of his goddess mother,[3]
All that his unquelled grief bestowed
And love, that doubles grief,   25
Make his laments; he moves Taenarian hearts,
And with sweet prayer
Asks pardon of the lords of Hades' shades.
Taken by his strange song the doorkeeper
Three-headed Cerberus[4] stands benumbed;   30
Goddess-avengers of men's crimes[5] who make
The guilty quake with fear
Now full of sadness melt in tears;
Ixion's swift wheel
No longer spins his head,   35
And Tantalus tormented by long thirst
Scorns stooping to the water;
The vulture, while he is filled with Orpheus' measures,
Stops tearing at Tityus' liver.[6]
At last 'We are overborne' in pity says   40
The ruler of the shades;[7]
'We grant the man his wife to go with him,
Bought by his song;
Yet let our law restrict the gift,
That, while he Tartarus[8] quits,   45
He shall not turn his gaze.'
Who can give lovers laws?
Love is a greater law unto itself.
Woe! By the very boundaries of Night
Orpheus his Eurydice   50
Saw, lost, and killed.
To you this tale refers,
Who seek to lead your mind
Into the upper day;
For he who overcome should turn back his gaze   55
Towards the Tartarean cave,
Whatever excellence he takes with him
He loses when he looks on those below.

---

3. Calliope, the muse of epic poetry.
4. The monstrous dog that guards the entrance
of the underworld.
5. The Furies.
6. Three of the most famous examples of
those condemned to eternal punishment by
Zeus, king of the gods.
7. Hades.
8. That is, the underworld.

NOTKER BALBULUS

Notker Balbulus (ca. 840–912) was a monk at the powerful and influential monastery of St. Gall (in modern Switzerland), a paradise of devout learning in a region that was just entering into a period of cultural and intellectual revival. Although his surname means "the Stammerer," Notker more than compensated for his lack of oral eloquence with his extraordinary writing ability; he produced a great number of hymns and other compositions, many of which he himself set to music. His "Hymn to Holy Women" centers on the powerful symbol of the ladder, connecting heaven and earth, and stresses the role of woman in mediating the ascent of the soul. Eve, who introduced sin to humankind in Eden, is counterbalanced by Mary, whose willingness to become the vessel of the Incarnation brings about the salvation of the world.

A Hymn to Holy Women[1]

1. A ladder stretching up to heaven,
    circled by torments—

2. At whose foot an attentive
    dragon
    stands on guard, forever
    awake,

3. So that no one can climb even
    to the first rung and not be
    torn—

4. The ascent of the ladder barred
    by an Ethiop,[2] brandishing
    a drawn sword, threatening
    death,

5. While over the topmost rung
    leans a young man, radiant,
    a golden bough in his hand—

6. This is the ladder the love of
    Christ
    made so free for women
    that, treading down the
    dragon
    and striding past the Ethiop's
    sword,

7. By way of torments of every kind
    they can reach heaven's
    summit
    and take the golden laurel
    from the hand of the strength-
    giving king.

8. What good did it do you,
    impious serpent,
    once to have deceived a
    woman,

9. Since a virgin brought forth
    God incarnate,
    only-begotten of the Father:

1. Translated from the Latin by Peter Dronke.   2. I.e., the devil.

10. He who took your spoils away
    and pierces your jaw with a hook[3]

11. To make of it an open gate
    for Eve's race, whom you long to
    hold.

12. So now you can see girls
    defeating you, envious one,

13. And married women now
    bearing sons who please
    God.

14. Now you groan at the loyalty
    of widows to their dead
    husbands,

15. You who once seduced a girl
    to disloyalty towards her
    creator.

16. Now you can see women made
    captains
    in the war that is waged against
    you,

17. Women who spur on their sons
    bravely to conquer all your
    tortures.

18. Even courtesans, your vessels,
    are purified by God,

19. Transmuted into a burnished
    temple for him alone.

20. For these graces let us now
    glorify him together,
    both the sinners and those who
    are just,

21. Him who strengthens those who
    stand
    and gives his right hand to
    the fallen,
    that at least after crimes we may
    rise.

3. See Job 40.20.

ANONYMOUS

This anonymous ninth-century lyric survives only in partial form in a single manuscript, a collection of miscellaneous poems and riddles known as the Exeter Book. Damaged by fire, the vellum page containing the poem has one significant gap near the beginning and is badly marred near the end. This fragmentary nature is, however, appropriate to the poem's focus: the Roman ruins that dotted the medieval Anglo-Saxon countryside. "The Ruin" testifies to the ravages of time, which breaks down stone walls into rubble and causes the human beings who erected those walls to dwindle into nothing but a faint memory.

The Ruin[1]

Look at the elaborate crests chiseled into this stone wall
shattered by fate, the crumbled city squares,
and the hue and cry of giants rotted away.
There are caved-in roofs, towers in shambles,
rime on the limy mortar,   5
a storm-wall tilted and scarred,
half-fallen, slumped by time.
An earthly embrace holds the royal architects
rotting in their graves and lost to the cruel grip
of the ground, while a hundred generations   10
passed away. This wall, mapped and veined by lichen,
stained with red, outlasted one kingdom
after another, long stood upright after storms:
lofty and broad, it has fallen. The rampart
hewn and wedged together, sharpened roughly   15
and polished, an ancient structure well-worked by men . . .
ringed with encrustations of soil
still prods the brain and draws up a fiery clue.
Clever in the forging of chains,
some bold-minded man bound together the ribs   20
of the wall with amazing cables.

There were bright city plots linked by bathhouses,
a wealth of high, towering gables,
much clamor of the multitude,
many mead halls filled with revelry,   25
until a mighty Lot changed that.
Far and wide people fell dead:
days of pestilence ran rampant
and death clobbered ranks of the infamous swordsmen.
Their fortress became a tomb; the city rotted away: 30
those who should have braced it up, the multitudes,
were bones on the ground. Then, the courts knelt in dust
and the wide red roof of vaulted beams was left shedding tiles.
This ritual-place fell into ruin and piled-up heaps,
where once stood those lighthearted with gold,   35
clothed in splendor, proud and lifted by wine,
shorn in war-gear, and gazed upon a treasure
of silver and inlaid-plated gems,
on wealth and property, on precious stones
and this glorious citadel of a stout kingdom;   40
and the stone courts stood upright,
and the warming stream spouted its whole surge,
and a wall hugged everything to its bosom,
where the baths were steamy in its heart.
Streams poured across hot gray stones   45
until the round pool heated. . . .
It is still a fitting thing for this city.

1. Translated from the Old English by Yusef Komunyakaa.

ANONYMOUS

This anonymous Latin verse from the eleventh century features a conventional description of the natural landscape understood in terms of the "book of nature"—a complex unity of symbols that, when properly read, reveals the hidden message of the Creator. Here, each species of bird gives voice to its own song, together contributing to the complex harmony that is the song of summer. The duration of the song is both limited, confined to the summer months, and perpetual, as it is endlessly renewed with the cycle of the seasons.

Song of Summer[1]

The woodlands clothe the slender shoots
of boughs, laden with fruits;
from high perches wood pigeons sing
    songs to one and all.
Here the turtledove moans, here the thrush resounds,   5
here the age-old song of blackbirds rings out,
and the sparrow, not silent, with its chatter
    takes possession of the heights beneath the elms.
Here the nightingale sings, delighting in leafy boughs,
pours out a long warbling through the breeze,   10
solemnly, and with tremulous voice the kite
    causes the sky to echo.
The eagle as it soars starward sings, upon the breezes
the lark sings and produces sounds in melodies.
From above it swoops, with a different melody   15
    as it touches ground.
The swift swallow ever makes its call,
the quail sings, the jackdaw resounds:
thus birds everywhere celebrate for everyone
    the song of summer.   20
None among the birds is like the bee,
who represents the ideal of chastity,
if not she who bore Christ in her womb
    inviolate.

---

1. Translated from the Latin by Jan Ziolkowski.

IBN ZAYDUN

bn Zaydun (1003–1071) was a native of Córdoba, the seat of Muslim rule in medieval al-Andalus (modern Spain), at a time when the Umayyad dynasty was divided by internal conflict and, increasingly, besieged by enemies on its borders. Ibn Zaydun quickly became famous for his mastery of the sophisticated poetic form of the *qasida* (an Arabic counterpart to the Latin ode), almost single-handedly raising the reputation of the regional literature of al-Andalus to the level of that pro-duced in the eastern cultural centers of Baghdad and Cairo. Several of his lyrics commemorate his tumultuous love for Wallada, the daughter of the Umayyad ruler of Córdoba who was herself a poet. After falling into political disfavor, Ibn Zaydun fled to Seville, where he wrote some of his most poignant verses on the experience of exile from his homeland, on those he had loved there, and on the beautiful "city of light" (*al-Zahra*), now only a shining memory.

From Al-Zahra[1]

With passion from this place
   I remember you.
      Horizon clear, limpid
The face of earth, and wind,
Come twilight, desists,   5
   A tenderness sweeps me
When I see the silver
   Coiling waterways
      Like necklaces detached
From throats. Delicious those   10
   Days we spent while fate
      Slept. There was peace, I mean,
And us, thieves of pleasure.
   Now only flowers
      With frost-bent stems I see;   15
At my eyes their vivid
   Centers pull, they gaze
      Back at me, seeing me
Without sleep, and a light
   Flickers through their cups,   20
      In sympathy, I think.
The sun-baked rose-buds in
   Bushes, remember
      How their color had lit

1. Translated from the Arabic by Christopher Middleton and Leticia Garza-Falcon.

Our morning air; and still   25
    Breaths of wind dispense
        At break of day, as then,
Perfume they gather up
    From waterlilies'
        Half-open drowsy eyes.   30
Such fresh memories
    Of you these few things
        Waken in my mind. For
Faraway as you are
    In this passion's grip   35
        I persist with a sigh
And pine to be at one
    With you. Please God no
        Calm or oblivion
Will occupy my heart,   40
    Or close it. Listen
        To the shiver of wings
At your side—it is my
    Desire, and still, still
        I am shaking with it [. . .]   45
Pure love we once exchanged,
    It was an unfenced
        Field and we ran there, free
Like horses. But alone
    I now can lay claim   50
        To have kept faith. You left,
Left this place. In sorrow
    To be here again,
        I am loving you.

ASAD GORGANI

Fakhraddin As'ad Gorgani was an eleventh-century Persian poet who was likely born in or near the town of Gorgan, east of the Caspian Sea. Below is an excerpt from *Vis and Ramin*, composed between 1050 and 1055, which is considered the first major Persian romance. Excerpts from this long narrative poem stand out as the equal of any short lyric in the corpus of Persian poetry, such as the poems of **Hafez** and **Jahan Khatun**. On one level, Gorgani's romance, like **Ferdowsi's Shahnameh**, recalls a pre-Islamic period when Persian political and social dominance in the region went unchallenged; on another level, it recounts the story of two lovers using the language of mystic union that would become central to Islamic devotional writing, such as that of the poet **Rumi**. The basic story may derive from the Parthian period (247 B.C.E.–224 C.E.), and so Gorgani's retelling contains many cultural layers, both Zoroastrian and Islamic. Stylistically, the poem interrupts the flow of narrative with long, hyperbolic speeches, as seen in the passage below—yet these interruptions, which include exquisite descriptions of intense emotion, are among the most vivid and moving passages in all of *Vis and Ramin*.

From Vis and Ramin[1]

Vis and Ramin then swore no force could sever
The love that bound the two of them forever.
Ramin spoke first: "I swear by God, and by
His sovereignty that rules the earth and sky,
I swear now by the sun, and by the light   5
The shining moon bestows on us at night,
I swear by Venus and by noble Jupiter,
I swear by bread and salt and flickering fire,
I swear by faith and God's omnipotence,
And by the soul and all its eloquence,   10
That while winds scour the wastelands and the mountains,
While waters flow in rivers and in fountains,
While night has darkness, and while streams have fishes,
While stars have courses, and while souls have wishes,
Ramin will not regret his love, or break   15
The binding oath that he and Vis now make;
He'll never take another love, or cease
To give his heart exclusively to Vis."

Vis promised love when Prince Ramin had spoken
And swore her promises would not be broken.   20
She gave him violets then and murmured, "Take
This pretty posy, keep it for my sake,
Keep it forever, so that when you see
Fresh violets blooming you'll remember me;
And may the soul that breaks this solemn vow   25
Darken and droop as these poor flowers do now.
Each time I see the spring's new flowers appear
I will recall the oaths we swore to here;
May anyone that breaks this oath decay
And wither as fresh flowers do—in a day."   30

---

1. Translated by Dick Davis.

WILLIAM IX

The earliest troubadour poet and the ninth Duke of Aquitaine, William (1071–1127) displayed the same aggressive spirit in his lyrics that he did on the field of battle. He passed his love of poetry on to his descendants, including his granddaughter Eleanor of Aquitaine, Queen of England and patron to several court poets, and her son Richard the Lion-Hearted, King of England and a poet in his own right. William appreciated the cultural treasures of poetry, song, and dance to be found in Muslim al-Andalus (Spain) and played a major role in their transmission into Occitan and French culture. In his audacious claim to write a verse "de dreit nien"—meaning both "about nothing at all" and "out of nothing at all"—William playfully puts himself in the position of the divine Creator, who made the world *ex nihilo*.

I'll make a verse of nothing at all[1]

I'll make a verse of nothing at all:
It won't be about me or about anyone else,
It won't be about love or about youthful joys,
    Or about anything else;
In fact, I wrote it while I was dozing   5
    On the back of my horse.

I don't know exactly when I was born,
I'm not happy-go-lucky or quick to anger,
I'm not a stranger and not a close friend,
    And I can't be any other way;   10
Because I was bewitched one dark night,
    On a lonely hilltop.

I don't know when I go to sleep,
Or when I wake up, unless someone tells me about it.
My heart's not broken, not a bit,   15
    By some sharp sad sorrow.
And I don't give a damn for that,
    By Saint Martial![2]

I'm sick, and I'm afraid to die,
And I only know what I've heard said about it;   20
I've got to find a doctor, one who understands me,
    But I don't know such a one.

1. Translated from the Occitan-Provençal by Suzanne Akbari.
2. Bishop of Limoges and Toulouse in southern France; his shrine at Limoges was a key pilgrimage site in the 12th century.

He'll be a good doctor, if he can cure me of this,[3]
    But if I get any worse, there's no hope.

I have a lovely girl, but I don't know who she is,   25
Because I've never seen her, I swear it's true!
She never does what pleases me, she never gives me peace,
    And I don't care,
Because I never have a Norman or a Frenchman[4]
    In my house.   30

I've never seen her, and I love her with all my heart,
And she never treats me right, and she never treats me wrong;
I'm just as happy if I never see her again,
    I don't give a damn.
Because I know a girl even more lovely and pretty,   35
    She's worth ten of the other one.

I've made the verse, I don't know what it's about,
But I'll send it on to that one
Who will in turn send it to someone else
    Over there, out by Anjou,[5]   40
And maybe he'll send back to me, out of his private pocket,
    The secret clue.[6]

---

3. Of lovesickness, a state of body as well as mind.
4. Northerners, often the political enemies of the lords of Provence (modern southern France).
5. Dukedom in the west of France; in William IX's time, the Duke of Anjou was Geoffrey V Plantagenet, whose son Henry (later Henry II of England) married William's granddaughter, Eleanor of Aquitaine.
6. The *contraclau* that will unlock the riddling poem is a common feature of troubadour verse, especially in the poetic mode of *trobar clus*, or "enigmatic verse" (literally, "closed verse").

ARNAUT DANIEL

Born in Périgord (in modern France) of a noble family in the twelfth century, Arnaut had the reputation of being something of a ne'er-do-well: the short prose biographies or *vidas* attached to his lyrics refer to him as a jokester, gambler, and perpetual student. He excelled, however, in the remarkable craftsmanship of his poems; most notably, Arnaut's invention of the intricate and difficult verse form of the sestina earned him the praise of poets through the ages from **Dante** and **Petrarch** to Ezra Pound and T. S. Eliot. Dante offers his fellow poet the highest praise imaginable in his *Purgatorio*, calling Arnaut "il miglior fabbro" (the better craftsman) and granting him the singular privilege of speaking his native Occitan tongue within the Italian epic.

The Art of Love[1]

To this sweet and pretty air
I set words that I plane and finish;
and every word will fit well,
once I have passed the file there,
for at once Love polishes and aureates   5
my song, which proceeds from her,
ruler and guardian of merit.

Each day I am a better man and purer,
for I serve the noblest lady in the world,
and I worship her, I tell you this in the open.   10
I belong to her from my foot to the top of my head;
and let the cold wind blow,
love raining in my heart
keeps me warm when it winters most.

I hear a thousand masses and pay to have them said,   15
I burn lights of wax and oil,
so may God give me good luck with her,
for no defense against her does me any good.
When I look at her golden hair,
her soft young spirited body,   20
if someone gave me Luserna,[2] I'd still love her more.

I love her and seek her out with a heart so full,
I think I am stealing her out of my own hands by too much wanting,
if a man can lose a thing by loving it well.
For the heart of her submerges   25
mine and does not abate.
So usurious is her demand,
she gets craftsman and workshop together.

I do not want the empire of Rome,
do not make me pope of it   30
so that I could not turn back to her
for whom the heart in me burns and breaks apart.
If she does not cure me of this torment
with a kiss before new year's,
she murders me and sends herself to hell.   35

But this torment I endure
could not make me turn away from loving well,
though it holds me fast in loneliness,
for in this desert I cast my words in rhyme.
I labor in loving more than a man who works the earth,   40

1. Translated from the Occitan-Provençal by   2. A city, probably in Spain.
Frederick Goldin.

for the Lord of Moncli did not love
N'Audierna an egg's worth more.[3]

I am Arnaut, who hoards the wind,
and chases the hare on an ox,
and swims against the tide.   45

---

3. Neither the Lord of Moncli nor his love, N'Audierna, have been identified.

YEHUDA HALEVI

Yehuda HaLevi (ca. 1075–1141) was born under Muslim rule, in a region of northern Spain that was conquered by Christian armies while he was still a child. He spent his mature years in the thriving Jewish community located in the Muslim stronghold of Granada, where he was famed both for his skills as a physician and as the most renowned writer of Hebrew verse since biblical times. Using Hebrew as a literary language in a period when Arabic was the standard written language for Muslims, Christians, and Jews alike, HaLevi reinvented Arabic literary forms into a distinctly Hebrew idiom. While the first of the selections reproduced here addresses a real person and the second a divine being, they share a common language of passion and desire that grows out of the Islamic devotional poetics of al-Andalus.

To Ibn al-Mu'allim[1]

Gently, my hard-hearted, slender one,
be gentle with me and I'll bow before you.
I've ravished you only in looking—
my heart is pure, but not my eyes:
They'd gather from your features   5
the roses and lilies mingled there.
I'd lift the fire from your cheeks
to put out fire with fire,
and then when I was thirsty,
it's there I'd look for water.   10
I'd savor the lip that glows like ruby—
like coals in the tongs of my jaws.
My life hangs by scarlet threads;

---

1. Both poems are translated from the Hebrew by Peter Cole.

326 | MEDIEVAL LYRICS

my death is now concealed in dusk. . . .
I find that nights have no end,   15
where once no dark divided my days:
For Time then was clay in my hands
and Fortune—the potter's wheel.[2]

Lord,

all my desire is here before you,
   whether or not I speak of it:
I'd seek your favor, for an instant, then die—
   if only you would grant my wish.
I'd place my spirit in your hand,   5
   then sleep—and in that sleep find sweetness.

I wander from you—and die alive;
   the closer I cling—I live to die.
How to approach I still don't know,
   nor on what words I might rely.   10
Instruct me, Lord: advise and guide me.
   Free me from my prison of lies.

Teach me while I can bear the affliction—
   do not, Lord, despise my plea;
before I've become my own burden   15
   and the little I am weighs on me,
and against my will, I give in
   as worms eat bones that weary of me.

I'll come to the place my forefathers reached,
   and by their place of rest find rest.   20
Earth's back to me is foreign;
   my one true home is in its dust.
Till now my youth has done what it would:
   When will I provide for myself?

The world He placed in my heart has kept me   25
   from tending to my end and after.
How could I come to serve my Lord,
   when I am still desire's prisoner?
How could I ask for a place on high,
   when I know the worm will be my sister?   30

How at that end could my heart be glad,
   when I do not know what death will bring?
Day after day and night after night
   reduce the flesh upon me to nothing.

---

2. The potter's wheel turns as does the wheel of Fortune, a common motif in medieval art.

Into the winds they'll scatter my spirit. 35
    To dust they'll return the little remaining.

What can I say—with desire my enemy,
    from boyhood till now pursuing me:
What is Time to me but your Will?
    If you're not with me, what will I be? 40
I stand bereft of any virtue:
    only your justice and mercy shield me.

But why should I speak, or even aspire?
    Lord, before you is all my desire.

HILDEGARD OF BINGEN

Although she lived within the walls of a cloister from early childhood, Hildegard of Bingen (1098–1179) was both powerful and prolific: elected head of the religious community at Bingen (in modern Germany), she founded two new monasteries at Rupertsberg and Eibingen, corresponded with two popes, and wrote a large number of works, including medical treatises, musical works, plays, and religious poems. Among her two most intriguing creations are *Scivias*, a vividly illustrated book recounting the divinely inspired visions she had experienced since the age of three, and the *lingua ignota*, or "unknown language," she invented for the private use of her fellow nuns at Bingen. The selections included here are songs of praise for the most special patron of the women enclosed at Bingen, playing on the double meaning of Mary's role as both verdant branch (*virga*) of the Lord and perpetual virgin (*virgo*).

Responsory for the Virgin[1]

Slender branch
from the stump of Jesse,[2]
God gazed at you like an eagle
staring into the sun.
Daughter of Zion![3] such daring! 5
the supernal father
saw a maiden's splendor
and her mortal flesh spoke his word.[4]

1. Both poems are translated from the Latin by Barbara J. Newman.
2. The father of David, who was the ancestor of Mary (see Matthew 1.1–16). The tree of Jesse was a common motif in medieval art, showing names of the patriarchs extending upward to its top, crowned with Jesus as a flower or fruit.
3. The promised land (literally, a section of Jerusalem).
4. For Jesus as the word of God made flesh, see John 1.1, 14.

In the depth of mystery her
mind was illumined   10
and bright was the rose[5] that
sprang from that maiden
when the supernal father
saw her virgin splendor
and her mortal flesh spoke his word.   15

Glorify the Father,
the Spirit and the Son.
As it was in the beginning
so it is now
and so be it ever.   20

The supernal father
saw a maiden's splendor
and her mortal flesh spoke his word.

Responsory for the Virgin

Priceless integrity!
Her virgin gate[1]
opened to none. But the Holy One
flooded her with warmth
until a flower sprang in her womb   5
and the Son of God came forth
from her secret chamber like the dawn.

Sweet as the buds of spring, her
son opened paradise
from the cloister of her womb.   10
And the Son of God came forth
from her secret chamber like the dawn.

5. A symbol of Mary.   1. That is, her unbroken hymen.

THE ARCHPOET

This author (d. 1165?) is known only by the nickname "Archipoeta" (literally, "chief of poets"), in the margin of the manuscripts containing his ten surviving poems. He was likely of German origin, attached to the traveling household of the archbishop of Cologne. Although the Archpoet's lyrics are commonly associated with the so-called Goliardic school of poetry, which was characterized by lewd drinking songs, political satire, and celebrations of the dissolute life of university students, they are likely not so much a pure expression of anarchy as the outpourings of a wanton persona invented in order to amuse his noble patron.

"His Confession" includes the playful refrain "May God be gracious to this drinker," a pun on a standard Christian prayer for salvation that substitutes *potatori* (drinker) for *peccatori* (sinner); the refrain lives on as a popular student drinking song.

His Confession[1]

Seething over inwardly
    With fierce indignation,
In my bitterness of soul,
    Hear my declaration.
I am of one element,   5
    Levity my matter,
Like enough a withered leaf
    For the winds to scatter.

Since it is the property
    Of the sapient   10
To sit firm upon a rock,
    It is evident
That I am a fool, since I
    Am a flowing river,
Never under the same sky,   15
    Transient for ever.

Hither, thither, masterless
    Ship upon the sea,
Wandering through the ways of air,
    Go the birds like me.   20
Bound am I by ne'er a bond,
    Prisoner to no key,
Questing go I for my kind,
    Find depravity.

Never yet could I endure   25
    Soberness and sadness,
Jests I love and sweeter than
    Honey find I gladness.
Whatsoever Venus[2] bids
    Is a joy excelling,   30
Never in an evil heart
    Did she make her dwelling.

Down the broad way do I go,
    Young and unregretting,

---

1. Translated from the Latin by Helen Waddell.
2. Roman goddess of love.

Wrap me in my vices up,   35
    Virtue all forgetting,
Greedier for all delight
    Than heaven to enter in:
Since the soul in me is dead,
    Better save the skin.   40

Pardon, pray you, good my lord,
    Master of discretion,
But this death I die is sweet,
    Most delicious poison.
Wounded to the quick am I   45
    By a young girl's beauty:
She's beyond my touching? Well,
    Can't the mind do duty?

Hard beyond all hardness, this
    Mastering of Nature: 50
Who shall say his heart is clean,
    Near so fair a creature?
Young are we, so hard a law,
    How should we obey it?
And our bodies, they are young,   55
    Shall they have no say in't?

Sit you down amid the fire,
    Will the fire not burn you?
To Pavia[3] come, will you
    Just as chaste return you?   60
Pavia, where Beauty draws
    Youth with finger-tips,
Youth entangled in her eyes,
    Ravished with her lips.

Let you bring Hippolytus,[4]   65
    In Pavia dine him,
Never more Hippolytus
    Will the morning find him.
In Pavia not a road
    But leads to venery,   70
Nor among its crowding towers
    One to chastity.

Yet a second charge they bring:
    I'm for ever gaming.
Yea, the dice hath many a time   75
    Stripped me to my shaming.
What an if the body's cold,
    If the mind is burning,

3. Italian city then known for its wild life.
4. In Greek mythology, the chaste son of Theseus, famously devoted to the virgin huntress goddess Artemis.

On the anvil hammering,
    Rhymes and verses turning? 80

Look again upon your list.
    Is the tavern on it?
Yea, and never have I scorned,
    Never shall I scorn it,
Till the holy angels come, 85
    And my eyes discern them,
Singing for the dying soul,
    Requiem aeternam.[5]

For on this my heart is set:
    When the hour is nigh me, 90
Let me in the tavern die,
    With a tankard by me,
While the angels looking down
    Joyously sing o'er me,
Deus sit propitius 95
    Huic potatori.[6]

'Tis the fire that's in the cup
    Kindles the soul's torches,
'Tis the heart that drenched in wine
    Flies to heaven's porches. 100
Sweeter tastes the wine to me
    In a tavern tankard
Than the watered stuff my Lord
    Bishop hath decanted.

Let them fast and water drink, 105
    All the poets' chorus,
Fly the market and the crowd
    Racketing uproarious:
Sit in quiet spots and think,
    Shun the tavern's portal, 110
Write, and never having lived,
    Die to be immortal.

Never hath the spirit of
    Poetry descended,
Till with food and drink my lean 115
    Belly was distended,
But when Bacchus[7] lords it in
    My cerebral story,
Comes Apollo[8] with a rush,
    Fills me with his glory. 120

5. Eternal rest (Latin), the opening words of the Catholic Mass for the dead.
6. May God be gracious to this drinker (Latin).
7. Roman god of the vine.
8. God of musical and artistic inspiration, of light and the sun; Artemis/Diana is his sister.

Unto every man his gift.
    Mine was not for fasting.
Never could I find a rhyme
    With my stomach wasting.
As the wine is, so the verse: 125
    'Tis a better chorus
When the landlord hath a good
    Vintage set before us.

Good my lord, the case is heard,
    I myself betray me,   130
And affirm myself to be
    All my fellows say me.
See, they in thy presence are:
    Let whoe'er hath known
His own heart and found it clean,   135
    Cast at me the stone.

AVRAHAM IBN EZRA

orn in Tudela, on the border of Christian Spain and Muslim al-Andalus, Avraham Ibn Ezra (ca. 1093–ca. 1167) spent much of his life in transit. After he was driven south by increasing violence and anti-Judaism, Avraham lived in Toledo and in Córdoba, where he was the friend of **Yehuda HaLevi**, another eminent Hebrew poet. Avraham's son later married HaLevi's daughter. Avraham Ibn Ezra produced a large number of translations of scientific and philosophical works in addition to his poetry. His verse maintains many of the traditional Andalusian metrical patterns even while moving in new thematic directions and embracing a new, biblically influenced style that avoids rhyme. Continued political discord caused Avraham to leave Spain: by 1140, he was in Rome, and later documentary evidence places him in France and England, together with many other Jews who had been displaced from Sefarad, their home within Muslim al-Andalus.

Elegy for a Son[1]

Come, father, approach and mourn,
for the Lord our God has distanced from you
your son, your one and only child—
    Isaac whom you always loved.

1. Translated from the Hebrew by Peter Cole.

"I am a man who has witnessed affliction 5
   and watched as joy was driven away.
The fruit of my loins has been taken from me—
   words I never imagined I'd say.
I'd always envisioned him offering comfort,
   and being near me as I aged, 10
but all my labor has been in vain,
   for I've given birth to my own dismay—
      and how can I rejoice again
when Isaac has breathed his last and died?

Moment by bitter moment I weep 15
   and send up a mournful cry and lament,
thinking of how, three years ago,
   he died alone, in a foreign land,
after he'd wandered from place to place.
   And so my soul for his spirit moaned 20
until I'd be able to bring him home;
   all night and day, alone, I grieved.
      What pain and suffering I knew then!
And this is the story of Isaac, my son.

Be kind to me now—bear with me, friends! 25
   The comfort you offer adds to my grief.
So do not speak of my heart's desire,
   or even utter his name to me.
Time has quenched my final ember:
   How could it do any worse to me, 30
having decreed my ruin forever,
   and taken from me the light of my life?
      Now my flesh and heart are failing,
as Isaac's heart gave way when he died."

Lord, in whose hands all is held, 35
   whose will extends through all creatures,
speak to the heart of this grieving father
   who held your name in awe as a child.
Waken the spirit of consolation
   and let it pass through a heart now broken. 40
He taught, with his wife, his son to fear you,
   so he would follow on the path they do:
      While he was a boy, you set it before him,
for the sake of your servant, Isaac, their son.

BERNART DE VENTADORN

The early biographies or *vidas* tell us that Bernart (ca. 1135–ca. 1195) was the son of a baker; blessed with the gift of poetry, he made the mistake of falling in love with the wife of his noble patron and was forced to flee for his life. Whether or not this is a romantic fantasy, it is certainly true that Bernart made his way from southern France to the English court of Eleanor of Aquitaine, whose grandfather **William IX** had been the first known troubadour poet. Many of the musical settings of Bernart's lyrics survive, providing rare evidence of the intricate way the troubadours united what Bernart calls "the words and the sounds." This poem, widely imitated not just by Occitan poets but by French and Italian writers as well, illustrates Bernart's ability to couple vivid descriptions of the natural world with sophisticated allusions to myth, raising the lyric mode to its highest pitch.

When I see the lark stretch out[1]

When I see the lark stretch out, for joy,
Its wings against the sun's ray,
So that it forgets, and lets itself fall
Because of the sweetness that spreads through its heart,
I feel such great envy well up in me   5
Toward the one I see filled with gladness;
I can't believe that this doesn't cause
My heart to melt with desire.

Oh, I thought I knew all about
Love—I didn't know anything at all!   10
Because I can't keep myself from loving
The one who's never offered me any reward.
She took all my heart, and she took all of me,
And took herself too, and the whole entire world,
And when she took herself away, there was nothing left for me: 15
Just the blind desire, and the willing heart.

I never was the master of myself
Nor was I my own man ever since the moment
She let me look into her eyes,
In that mirror that pleases me so much.   20
Mirror, ever since I mirrored myself in you,
The sighs from down deep have led me to death,

---

1. Translated from the Occitan-Provençal by Suzanne Akbari.

And I've lost myself, just as he was lost:
The lovely Narcissus,[2] in the depths of the fountain.

I've lost all faith in the ladies;   25
I'll never trust them again,
Because just as I used to adore them,
Now I don't care for them at all.
Since I see that not one of them lends a hand
With that one who destroys me, who strikes me down,   30
I hate them all and don't believe a word they say,
Because I know very well that every one of them's the same.

In this, it's clear that my lady is
A woman like the rest of them, and I'll tell her so,
She doesn't want the things she ought to want   35
And whatever she ought not to do, she does.
I've fallen into bad grace,
And I'm totally like the fool perched on the bridge;
And I don't know why this has happened to me—
I guess I tried to climb up too high.   40

I've lost all grace, for sure,
And so I've lost the thing I've never been able to grasp,
For she who should have it most of all
Doesn't have a bit of it, and where will I ever find it?
Oh, how little they see, when they look at her: 45
They don't see this wretch, filled with longing,
The one who, without her, will never have anything at all;
She lets him die—she won't help him at all.

Since for my lady nothing is enough,
Neither prayer nor mercy, nor the rights that I should have,   50
Nor will it ever come to please her
That I love her, I won't say the words to her again.
Instead I'll leave her, I'll give up;
She's put me to death, and with death I'll answer her,
And I'll go, since she won't have me,   55
A wretch, in exile, I don't know where.

Tristan,[3] you'll get nothing from me,
Because I'm going away, a wretch, I don't know where.
I give up singing, it's all finished now,
To joy and love, I say goodbye.   60

2. In classical mythology, a beautiful youth who fell in love with his own reflection, wasted away, and died (see Ovid, *Metamorphoses* 3.405–501).

3. Legendary lover, loosely connected with the Arthurian tradition, whose passion for the married Iseult led to his banishment and death.

BEATRICE OF DIA

The troubadours of southern France included in their number female poets, called *trobairitz*, who were enthusiastic and skilled participants in the group's poetic contests of words. One of these was Beatrice, Countess of Dia (ca. 1150–1200), who was married to Guilhem de Poitiers, Count of Viennois, but (according to the short *vidas* attached to her poems) was the lover of the troubadour Raimbaut of Orange. The striking similarity of some of Beatrice's lyrics to those of Raimbaut is not evidence of copying on the part of one or the other; rather, it reveals the poetic games of mimicry and emulation practiced within the troubadour community, whose members might treat each other's phrases like common melodic refrains. One of Beatrice's lyrics, set to the notes of a flute, is the only trobairitz poem to survive with its original musical setting.

A Lover's Prize[1]

I have been in great distress
for a knight for whom I longed;
I want all future times to know
how I loved him to excess
    Now I see I am betrayed—   5
he claims I did not give him love—
such was the mistake I made,
    naked in bed, and dressed.

How I'd long to hold him pressed
naked in my arms one night—   10
if I could be his pillow once,
would he not know the height of bliss?
    Floris was all to Blanchefleur,[2]
yet not so much as I am his:
I am giving my heart, my love,   15
    my mind, my life, my eyes.

Fair, gentle lover, gracious knight,
if once I held you as my prize
and lay with you a single night
and gave you a love-laden kiss—   20
    my greatest longing is for you
to lie there in my husband's place,
but only if you promise this:
    to do all I'd want to do.

1. Translated from the Occitan-Provençal by Peter Dronke.
2. Lovers in a popular medieval romance.

BERTRAN DE BORN

As Lord of Altaforte, a castle located on contested border territory in the south of France, Bertran (ca. 1140–ca. 1200) was inevitably drawn into regional disputes over Aquitaine waged by Henry II, King of England, and his sons. Bertran allied initially with Henry II's eldest son, Henry the Young King, in a rebellion against his father, and later with the Young King's brother, Richard the Lion-Hearted. His poetry reflects this life of warfare and political intrigue, centering on the clash of personal and regional loyalties, and exalting the values of masculine personal honor and fearlessness in battle. Although Bertran ended his days in the pious solitude of a Cistercian monastery, he continued to be remembered for his skillful political maneuvering: **Dante** places him in the depths of the *Inferno* as a sower of discord for his role in dividing father from son.

In Praise of War[1]

I love the joyful time of Easter,
that makes the leaves and flowers come forth,
and it pleases me to hear the mirth
of the birds, who make their song
resound through the woods,   5
and it pleases me to see upon the meadows
tents and pavilions planted,
and I feel a great joy
when I see ranged along the field
knights and horses armed for war.   10

And it pleases me when the skirmishers
make the people and their baggage run away,
and it pleases me when I see behind them coming
a great mass of armed men together,
and I have pleasure in my heart   15
when I see strong castles besieged,
the broken ramparts caving in,
and I see the host on the water's edge,
closed in all around by ditches,
with palisades, strong stakes close together   20

And I am as well pleased by a lord
when he is first in the attack,
armed, upon his horse, unafraid,
so he makes his men take heart
by his own brave lordliness.   25
And when the armies mix in battle,

1. Translated from the Occitan-Provençal by Frederick Goldin.

each man should be poised
to follow him, smiling,
for no man is worth a thing
till he has given and gotten blow on blow.   30

Maces and swords and painted helms,
the useless shields cut through,
we shall see as the fighting starts,
and many vassals together striking,
and wandering wildly,   35
the unreined horses of the wounded and dead.
And once entered into battle
let every man proud of his birth
think only of breaking arms and heads,
for a man is worth more dead than alive and beaten.   40

I tell you there is not so much savor
in eating or drinking or sleeping,
as when I hear them scream, "There they are! Let's get them!"
on both sides, and I hear riderless
horses in the shadows, neighing,   45
and I hear them scream, "Help! Help!"
and I see them fall among the ditches,
little men and great men on the grass,
and I see fixed in the flanks of the corpses
stumps of lances with silken streamers.   50

Barons, pawn your castles,
and your villages, and your cities
before you stop making war on one another.
Papiols,[2] gladly go
fast to my Lord Yes-and-No[3]   55
and tell him he has lived in peace too long.

2. Bertran's *joglar*, or minstrel, who will sing the lyric.
3. A mocking reference to Bertran's lord at the time, Richard the Lion-Hearted, whom he accuses of indecisiveness.

HEINRICH VON MORUNGEN

We know little about Heinrich (ca. 1150–1222), whose thirty-five surviving lyrics are among the earliest great examples of the German tradition of *Minnesang* (literally, "songs of love"), developed in response to the influence of the Occitan lyrics of the troubadours on the vernacular poetics of Europe. The figure of Minne, central to these poems, is rather different from the conventional depiction of the god of love found in Occitan, French, and Italian lyric: gendered female, Minne is in some ways similar to the mythical figure of Aphrodite or Venus from the Greco-Roman pantheon, but she has a dangerous, almost magical quality that emerges from Germanic folklore. In the lyric reproduced here, Heinrich vividly conjures up the torments of love, which consign the speaker not just to the pains of unrequited desire but even to a hellish—yet erotic—abyss.

The Wound of Love[1]

She has wounded me
    in my innermost soul,
within the mortal core,
when I told her
    that I was raving and anguished   5
in desire for her glorious lips.
Once I bade my own lips
    to commend me to her service,
    and to steal me
a tender kiss of hers,   10
    that I might for ever be well.

How I begin to hate
    her rose-red lips,
which I never yet forgot!
It troubles me still,   15
    that they once refused me
with such vehemence.
Thus I have grown so weak
    that I would far rather—alive—
burn in the abyss   20
of hell than serve her still,
    not knowing to what end.

1. Translated from the German by Peter Dronke.

WALTHER VON DER VOGELWEIDE

Walther's surname simply means "of the bird field" or "forest," telling us only that he was not of a noble landowning family and that he was from a region remote from any city. Walther himself (ca. 1170–ca. 1230) tells us that he learned "to sing and to recite" ("singen unde sagen") while in Austria, likely referring to the cultural center of the court at Vienna. From an entry in the household accounts of the bishop of Passau recording the purchase of a fur coat for the young poet, we know that Walther must have been a member of the bishop's household during his travels across Europe; we can infer that Walther probably depended for his livelihood on numerous patrons, each willing for a while to support his poetic endeavors. Walther was a prolific writer whose lyrics address a wide range of strikingly naturalistic (rather than idealized) topics, composed in a style that emerges from Occitan and French models but takes on an idiosyncratic, deeply personal voice. His lyrics were widely admired but had few imitators, perhaps because of the unusual individuality of their tone.

Dancing Girl[1]

"Lady, accept this garland"—
these were the words I spoke to a pretty girl:
"then you will grace the dance
with the lovely flowers crowning you.
If I had priceless stones,   5
they would be for your hair—
indeed you must believe me,
by my faith, I mean it truly!"

She took my offering
as a gently nurtured child would take it.   10
Her cheeks became as red
as the rose that stands beside the lilies.
Her shining eyes were lowered then in shame,
yet she curtsied graciously.
That was my reward—   15
if any more becomes mine, I'll hold it secret.

"You are so fair,
that I want to give you my chaplet now,
the very best I have.
I know of many flowers, white and red,   20
so far away, on the heath over there,
where they spring up beautiful,
and where the birds are singing—
let us pluck them together there."

I thought that never yet   25
had I known such bliss as I knew then.
From the tree the flowers
rained on us endlessly as we lay in the grass.
Yes, I was filled with laughter in sheer joy.
Just then, when I was so gloriously   30
rich in my dreaming,
then day broke, and I was forced to wake.

1. Translated from the German by Peter Dronke.

She has stirred me so
that this summer, with every girl I meet,
I must gaze deep in her eyes: 35
perhaps one will be mine: then all my cares are gone.
What if she were dancing here?
Ladies, be so kind,
set your hats back a little.
Oh, if only, under a garland, I could see that face!   40

IBN 'ARABI

The greatest poet of medieval al-Andalus, Ibn 'Arabi (1165–1240) was also one of its greatest philosophers—bested only by his countryman Averroës (Ibn Rushd), whose commentary on Aristotle transformed the history of thought in the West. Born in Murcia (in modern Spain), Ibn 'Arabi received the standard education in grammar and rhetoric appropriate to a son of a minor court official, without any specifically religious education. After a conversion experience in his early teens, however, Ibn 'Arabi devoted himself fully to his lifelong task: the integration of philosophy and theology through the medium of mystical devotion. This goal is evident in his poetry's language of passionate desire directed toward the divine: the lover seeks at once to possess the beloved completely and to be annihilated by the beloved, losing track of the self in the experience of the other.

Gentle Now, Doves[1]

Gentle now, doves of the thornberry
and moringa[2] thicket,
don't add to my heartache
your sighs.

Gentle now,   5
or your sad cooing
will reveal the love I hide,
the sorrow I hide away.

I echo back, in the evening,
in the morning, echo,   10
the longing of a love-sick lover,
the moaning of the lost.

1. Translated from the Arabic by Michael Sells.   2. Horseradish tree (of East India and Africa).

In a grove of Gháda,[3]
spirits wrestled,
bending the limbs down over me,   15
passing me away.

They brought yearning,
breaking of the heart,
and other new twists of pain,
putting me through it.   20

Who is there for me in Jám',
and the Stoning-Ground at Mína,
who for me at Tamarisk Grove,
or at the way-station of Na'mán?[4]

Hour by hour   25
they circle my heart
in rapture, in love-ache,
and touch my pillars with a kiss.

As the best of creation
circled the Ká'ba,[5]   30
which reason with its proofs
called unworthy.

He kissed the stones there—
and he was entrusted with the word!
What is the house of stone   35
compared to a man or woman?

They swore, how often!
they'd never change—piling up vows.
She who dyes herself red with henna
is faithless.   40

A white-blazed gazelle
is an amazing sight,
red-dye signaling,
eyelids hinting,

Pasture between breastbone   45
and innards.
Marvel,
a garden among the flames!

My heart can take on
any form: 50
for gazelles a meadow,
a cloister for monks,

---

3. A kind of tamarisk often featured in early Arabic love poetry.
4. All sites along the Muslim pilgrimage route leading to the shrine of the Ka'aba at Mecca.
5. The ritual circling of the Ka'aba is the climax of the pilgrimage.

For the idols, sacred ground,
Ka'ba for the circling pilgrim,
the tables of the Toráh,[6]   55
the scrolls of the Qur'án.

I profess the religion of love.
Wherever its caravan turns
along the way, that is the belief,
the faith I keep.   60

Like Bishr,
Hind and her sister,
love-mad Qays and the lost Láyla,
Máyya and her lover Ghaylán.[7]

6. The first five books of the Hebrew Bible   7. Famous pairs of lover and beloved from the
(traditionally written on a scroll).   Arabic and Persian tradition.

ALFONSO X

The King of Castile, León, and Galicia, Alfonso X (1221–1284) was both a political and an intellectual leader who transformed the status of Castilian (an early version of Spanish) by making it the standard literary and administrative language of his realm and commissioning the translation of numerous scientific, historical, and literary works from Arabic into Castilian: consequently, he was commonly called Alfonso el Sabio ("the Learned"). He was also a poet whose own compositions were written in Galician-Portuguese, a popular literary vernacular of the period; they included both devotional lyrics such as his *Cantigas de Santa Maria* (*Songs on the Virgin Mary*) and more secular works. In "The Scorpions," we get a rare insight into the complex position of the monarch who must rule by force, but who longs to escape into anonymous solitude.

The Scorpions[1]

I cannot find such great delight
in the song
of birds, or in their twittering,
in love or in ambition
or in arms—for I fear   5
that these indeed

1. Translated from the Galician-Portuguese by Peter Dronke.

344 | MEDIEVAL LYRICS

are fraught with danger—
as in a good galleon
that can take me speedily
from this demonic landscape   10
where the scorpions dwell;
for within my heart
I have felt their sting!

    And by the holy God I swear
I would wear   15
neither cloak nor beard,
nor would I involve myself in love
or arms, for injury
and lamentation
come from these at every season—   20
no, I'd pilot a merchant-ship
and sail across the ocean,
selling vinegar and flour,
and I would fly from the poison
of the scorpion, for I know   25
no other medicine against it.

    I can take no pleasure here
in tilting,
nor, God save the mark,[2]
in mock-tournaments;   30
as for going armed by night
or patrolling,
I do it without any joy—
for I find more enchantment in the sea
than in being a knight: 35
long ago I was a mariner,
and henceforth I long to guard
myself against the scorpion, and return
to what I was in the beginning.

    I must try to explain to you: 40
the demon
will never be able to trick me
now into speaking the language
of arms, for this is not my role—
(useless   45
for me to reason thus,
I have not even arms to try)—
rather, I long to go alone
and in a merchant's guise
to find some land   50
where they cannot strike at me:
the black scorpion, and the mottled.

2. An exclamation of scorn.

SHEM TOV ARDUTIEL

S hem Tov (late thirteenth century– after 1345) was a fluent writer in three languages, making him a valuable member of the court of Alfonso XI, King of Castile (modern Spain). He is known for his *Proverbios morales* (*Moral Proverbs*), a collection of edifying epigrams published under the Spanish form of his name, Santob de Carrión; for a number of translations from Arabic into Hebrew; and for his original compositions. His Hebrew masterwork is "The Battles of the Pen and Scissors," an elaborate fantasy in which the poet sits down to work on a cold day only to find his inkpot frozen. A debate ensues between the pen, who argues that it is best to write with ink, and the scissors, who claims that one should cut words out of paper. Is the work a thinly veiled political satire, a playful entertainment, or an allegory of poetics itself? In the ambiguity is the pleasure of the text.

From The Battles of the Pen and the Scissors[1]

I. WRITER, YOU HOLD

Writer, you hold a flame in your hand,
   or is it the blade of a sword or a spear—
the tree of knowledge of good and evil,
   or a staff to make wondrous signs appear?

II. TO PRAISE THE PEN

Are there words enough in all of song
   to praise the pen? Who else could bear
the burden of bringing back the past
   and preserving it then as though with myrrh?

It has no ear with which it might hear,
   or mouth with which to offer answers;
and yet the pen, in a single stroke,
   at once does both—observes and remembers.

III. TOMORROW I'LL WRITE

At night he says: "Tomorrow I'll write,"
but there's nothing at all to back up his words;
the heavens' frost laughs in his face,
and the cackling of mocking ice is heard.

Don't pride yourself on tomorrow's prize,
when you have no notion of what it hides.

1. Translated from the Hebrew by Peter Cole.

IV. ENTER THE SCISSORS

A body fully drawn and rotted through,
like clothes eaten by moths—but this one's written:
a man with his hand in wisdom brought it forth,
    forming hole after hole in its skin.

V. WORK I WAS CUT OUT TO DO

I'm precious to every soul and man,
and lacking matter am only form.

I'm purest spirit—my body's nothing,
riding clouds and wings of the wind.

VI. THE PEN FIGHTS BACK

If only someone would shut you up,
    or that might be your wisdom's will;
for hope deferred you'll finish writing
    just makes the heart and soul feel ill.

Your languor casts us into a torpor—
then leaves us holding shreds of paper.

VII. THE SCISSORS LONGED

The scissors longed to be joined at last,
leaving nothing in the way of division—
so that its two might then be one,
to cut through what might come between them.

HADEWIJCH OF BRABANT

We know little about Hadewijch (thirteenth century) beyond the fact that she was an important member of a beguinage—a secular community of devout women who gathered voluntarily to serve the poor and worship Christ—located in the region of Brabant (now on the border of Belgium and the Netherlands). Already in Hadewijch's day, the beguines were regarded with suspicion by church authorities, and in the early fourteenth century they were condemned and some were executed on charges of heresy for their unconventional way of worshipping Christ through service to the poor. Hadewijch's surviving writings include letters, prose accounts of her divinely inspired visions, and devotional lyrics, which stand out for the way in which she expresses religious experience using figurative language derived from secular romance. Her god of love at first looks like the Cupid figure of French and Latin poetry but ultimately reveals himself to be the Son of God, embodied Love.

The Cult of Love[1]

1

The birds have long been silent
that were blithe here before:
their blitheness has departed,
they have lost their summer now;
they would swiftly sing again   5
if that summer came again,
which they have chosen above all
and for which they were born:
one hears it in their voices then.

2

I'll say no more of birds' laments: 10
their joy, their pain, is quickly gone;
I have more grievous cause to moan:
Love, to whom we should aspire,
weighs us down with her noble cares,
so we chase after false delights   15
and Love cannot enfold us then.
Ah, what has baseness done to us!
Who shall erase that faithlessness?

3

The mighty ones, whose hand is strong,
it is on them I still rely,   20
who work at all times in Love's bond,
heedless of pain, grief, tragedy;
they want to ride through all the land
that lovers loving by love have found,
so perfect is their noble heart;   25
they know what Love can teach by love,
how Love exalts lovers by love.

4

Why then should anyone refuse,
since by loving Love can be won?
Why not ride, longing, through the storm,   30
trusting in the power of Love,
aspiring to the cult of Love?
Love's peerlessness will then be seen—
there, in the brightness of Love's dawn,
where for Love's sake is shunned no pain   35
and no pain caused by Love weighs down.

1. Translated from the Flemish by Peter Dronke.

5

Often I call for help as a lost one,
but then, when you come close, my dear one,
with new solace you bear me up
and with high spirit I ride on,   40
sport with my dear so joyously
as if north and south and east
and west all lands belonged to me!
Then suddenly I am dashed down.—
Oh, what use to tell my pain?   45

ANONYMOUS

This poignant quatrain appears, in its original Middle English, in the middle of the highly formal Latin prose of the *Speculum Ecclesie*, or *Mirror of the Church* (1240), inserted at the point where the Apostle John is asked by the suffering Christ to take the Virgin Mary as his own mother. This pitiful scene elicits an affective response from the reader, heightened both by the intimate tone of the vernacular lines and by the poem's delicate wordplay, which aligns the setting sun in the sky with the dying Son on the cross, and echoes the Virgin's name in the sorrowful refrain "me rueth."

Calvary

Now goeth sonne[1] under wood,
Me rueth, Mary, thy fair rood;[2]
Now goeth sonne under tree,
Me rueth, Mary, thy son and thee.

---

1. Both "sun" and "son."   2. Both "face" and "cross."

GUIDO GUINIZZELLI

Guido Guinizzelli (ca. 1240–1276) was the founder of a poetic lineage whose more famous members would be **Guido Cavalcanti** and **Dante Alighieri**. The *dolce stil nuovo*, or "sweet new style," influenced the development of medieval and Renaissance lyric more than any other movement since that of the Occitan troubadours. Guido served as a lawyer and judge in Bologna, where his political maneuvering ended with his exile in 1274, shortly before his death. Some twenty lyrics survive from Guido's pen; about ten more works exist in fragmentary form or are of doubtful authorship. Guido's masterpiece, "Love always repairs to the noble heart," became a kind of manifesto for the masters of the sweet new style, paraphrased by Dante in his **Purgatorio** and widely imitated by generations of poets. Perhaps the most striking feature of Guido's poetry is its philosophical quality—its ability to address profound intellectual truths within the ornate, sweet language of metaphor and allusion.

Love always repairs to the noble heart[1]

Love always repairs to the noble heart
    Like a bird winging back into its grove:
Nor was love made before the noble heart,
    Nor did nature, before the heart, make love.
For they were there as long as was the Sun,   5
    Whose splendor's ever bright;
Never did love before that shining come.
Love nestles deep inside nobility
    Exactly the way
One sees the heart within the fiery blaze.   10

Fire of love in noble heart is caught
    Like power gleaming inside a precious stone.
The value does not come down from the stars
    Until the Sun has blenched the stone all pure.
Only after the might of the Sun   15
    Has drawn out all that's vile
Does the star bestow its noble power.
Just so a heart transformed by nature pure,
    Noble and elect,
A woman starlike with her love injects.   20

    Love for this reason stays in noble heart

---

1. Translated from the Italian by James J. Wilhelm.

Like a waving flame atop a burning brand,
Shining, its own delight, subtle and bright;
 It is so proud, it knows no other way.
Yet a nature which is still debased   25
 Greets love as water greets the fire,
With the cold hissing against the heat.
Love in noble heart will find a haven
 Like the shine
Of a diamond glinting in ore within the mine.   30

Sun beats against the mud the livelong day;
 Mud it remains; Sun does not lose its ray;
The haughty one says: "I am noble by my tribe."
 He is the mud; Sun is the noble power.
Man must never believe   35
 That nobility exists outside the heart
In the grandness of his ancestry,
For without virtue, heart has no noble worth;
 It's a ray through a wave;
The heavens retain the sparkle and splendor they gave. 40

Shines among the powers of heaven
 God the creator, more than Sun in our eye;
Each angel knows the Maker beyond its sphere,
 And turning its circle, obeys God's noble power.
And thus it follows at once: 45
 The blesséd tasks of the Master transpire.
In the same way, in all truth, the beautiful lady
Should behave, for in her eyes reflects the desire
 Of a noble man
Who will turn his every thought to her command. 50

Lady, God will ask me: "Why did you presume?"
 When my soul stands before his mighty throne.
  "You passed the heavens, came all the way to me,
   And cheapened me in the light of profane love.
  To me is due all the praise   55
   And to the Queen of the Royal Realm[2]
  Who makes all fraudulence cease."
I'll tell him then: "She had an angel look—
  A heavenly face.
What harm occurred if my love in her was placed?" 60

2. The Virgin Mary.

GUIDO CAVALCANTI

rawing on the "sweet new style" developed by Tuscan poets such as **Guido Guinizzelli** but adding his own unique perspective on the ability of lyric to capture profound truths about the nature of the human soul, Guido Cavalcanti (ca. 1255–1300) paved the way for the flowering of Italian verse in **Dante** and **Petrarch**. An eager participant in the bitter Florentine political scene of the late thirteenth century, Guido was exiled from the city of his birth and died on the road while trying to return. His complex, intricate poems carry out a philosophical argument, progressing through logically connected stages whose startlingly vivid juxtaposed images convey the passions of the soul. In "Donna me prega" ("A lady asks me"), Guido uses the conventional figure of the beloved lady to instigate a philosophical discourse in eight parts on the nature of love; he ultimately concludes that the body's physical desires can be balanced with the demands of the intellect only through the rational effort to comprehend the power of love over the sense perceptions that knit together body and soul.

A lady asks me[1]

A lady asks me—and so I want to talk
About an accidental quality[2] that is all too often uncontrollable
And is so high and mighty that we call it "love."[3]
    If only he who denies that fact could feel its bitter truth!
And, for this case right here, I'd like to find someone who knows
        all about it,   5
Since I don't think that a man of lowly heart
    Could ever make sense of such an argument.
Because without a physical demonstration
I would never even try to claim to know
Where it can be found, and who first made it go,   10
    And what might be its power and its potency,
And, then, its inner nature, and every last one of its movements,
And the blissful biting pleasure that makes us call it "love,"[4]
And whether you can ever really make it open to the eye.

    In that region where memory is found   15
It finds its private place, formed with the same contours

---

1. Translated from the Italian by Suzanne Akbari.
2. A quality that is not essential to a thing (a philosophical term).
3. The only use of the noun "love" (*amore*) in the poem; every other reference is simply to "it."
4. Cavalcanti uses *amare*, a form of the verb "to love," and thus plays on the adjective *amaro* (bitter); this pun is also frequent in other romance vernacular poetry (French, Occitan).

Of airy lightness itself, by a circling darkness
    That comes from fiery Mars,[5] and stays right there.
It is a created thing, and has its own special name,
It's a habit of the soul, and the heart's willful flame.   20
    It rises up from a form that one has seen,
Which is taken up in the mind by the possible intellect[6]
As if it were a substance, and then it settles in that place.
There, it never has any power,
    Since that intellect does not descend any lower;   25
It just shines in itself, glowing in the eternal effect;
The mind doesn't take delight in this, but is rapt in contemplation,
And so does not create some empty idle image.

    It's not a power of the mind, but it comes from the faculty
That is perfection itself (so the wise men say);   30
It's not the power of reason but of the senses I'm speaking of.
    It keeps its role as judge, regardless of its strength,
Because strong intention always rules over reason:
It doesn't work so well in the one who tends toward vice.
    Its potency often brings death at its heels,   35
Because when the mind's power is impaired,
This pushes the mind down the wrong road;
But not because it is against Nature!
    When a man is—by chance—turned away from the highest good,
He can't say that he is truly alive,   40
Because he is not the master of himself.
The same thing happens when a man forgets about this.

    Its mode of being is such that, when desire is so very strong
That it goes beyond every limit imposed by Nature,
It doesn't pause to take a refreshing rest.   45
    It shifts about, changing color, drawing laughter out of tears,
And the form you see, out of fear, flies away from sight.
It doesn't stay long; beyond that, you will see
    That it's mostly found in those whose spirit is truly noble.
This new quality causes you to sigh   50
And makes you gaze intently at a place—a place you cannot see—
Fanning such an anger that it feels like flames
    (If you haven't felt it, you don't know what I mean),
And it doesn't let you reach out and touch what you want,
And it doesn't let you look around for another source of joy: 55
For sure, your mind doesn't know anything at all.

    It draws forth a quick glance from one who feels the same
And so it seems like pleasure's sure to follow:

---

5. Roman god of war; the dusky redness of his planet reflects the darkness of the lover's mind.

6. The storehouse of all possible ideas or concepts, according to medieval theories of the mind.

It can't stay hidden anymore, once the eye-beams meet.[7]
    The beautiful forms—not those lesser ones—are like arrows,   60
For the desire is lessened by the fear;
But the soul who is pierced gets just what he longs for.
    And it can never be truly known through the eye:
To be able to see the faintest color white won't help you see this sight,
And—now listen to me!—you can't see form at all: 65
Ever so much less, then, can you see what comes from this.
    Having no color, having no being in itself,
Placed in darkest shadows, it devours light itself.
Without any lying, I tell you, and you must believe me in this,
Only from this thing is true mercy born.   70

You can safely go, my song,
Wherever you want to go, because I've made you so pretty
That your clever argument will always be praised
By all those who have real understanding:
You don't want to hang around with anyone else.   75

7. The classical idea that love travels along the glance, sometimes identified with a dart, appears occasionally in medieval poetry and became a commonplace in the Renaissance.

DANTE ALIGHIERI

Dante's lyric poetry responds directly to his fellow poets of the "sweet new style," building on the concepts of nobility and gentility developed by **Guido Guinizzelli** and countering **Guido Cavalcanti**'s philosophical condemnation of love as a dangerous passion that must be controlled by reason. Before turning to the epic genre in his *Divine Comedy*, Dante (1265–1321) wrote a large body of short lyrics, many of which he embedded within a longer prose commentary in his early masterpiece, the *Vita Nuova* (*New Life*), in which he forcefully contradicts Cavalcanti's view of love as irrational and destructive, insisting that the love of woman is the only path to spiritual transcendence. In the first poem presented here, Dante imagines a community in which those who truly comprehend the power of love, both the male writers of lyric and the women they adore, inhabit an enchanted space outside of time; in the second, he elaborates Guinizzelli's conception of the "gentle heart" into an allegory of desire in which love of a woman can redeem the soul of a man, and—a shockingly innovative claim—the love of a man can do the same for a woman.

Guido, I wish[1]

Guido, I wish that you and Lapo[2] and I,
Spirited on the wings of a magic spell,
Could drift in a ship where every rising swell
Would sweep us at our will across the skies;
Then tempest never, or any weather dire   5
Could ever make our blissful living cease;
No, but abiding in a steady, blesséd peace
Together we'd share the increase of desire.

And Lady Vanna and Lady Lagia[3] then
And she[4] who looms above the thirty best[5]   10
Would join us at the good enchanter's[6] behest;
And there we'd talk of Love without an end
To make those ladies happy in the sky—
With Lapo enchanted too, and you and I.

Love and the gentle heart[1]

Love and the gentle heart are one thing,
even as the sage[2] affirms in his poem,
and so one can be without the other
as much as rational soul without reason.
Nature creates them when she is amorous: 5
Love as lord and the heart as his mansion,
in which, sleeping, he rests
sometimes a brief and sometimes a long season.
Beauty appears in a wise lady, then,
which so pleases the eyes that in the heart   10
is born a desire for that which pleases;
and so long it lasts sometimes therein
that it wakens the spirit of Love.
And the same to a lady does a worthy man.

---

1. Translated from the Italian by James J. Wilhelm.
2. Guido Cavalcanti; see pp. 351–353. Guido and Lapo Gianni were poets in Dante's literary circle.
3. Giovanna and Lagia were Guido's and Lapo's ladies.

4. Beatrice, Dante's beloved.
5. Dante wrote a poem naming the most beautiful women of Florence.
6. Merlin.
1. Translated from the Italian by Dino Cervigni and Edward Vasta.
2. Guido Guinizzelli; see p. 349.

ALEXANDER THE WILD

A vivid full-page illustration of a man mounted on a rearing horse labeled "der wilde Alexander" (the wild Alexander), juxtaposed with a few lyrics, gives this late thirteenth-century poet his name. Like **Walther von der Vogelweide**, Alexander was a wandering poet who made his living by attaching himself to various courtly patrons; his vocabulary suggests that he was of South German or Swiss origin. In their vocabulary and poetic motifs, Alexander's lyrics grow out of the tradition of *Minnesang*, or "songs of love," but in their strong emphasis on social and moral issues they depart from that earlier mode. In "Strawberry Picking," Alexander conceals a stern moral lesson about the dangers of sin behind the veil of a colorful, naturalistic evocation of the summer landscape of a remembered childhood whose innocence proves to have been more apparent than real.

Strawberry Picking[1]

Long ago, when we were children,
in the time that spanned the years
when we ran across the meadows,
over from those, now back to these,
there, where we at times   5
found violets,
you now see cattle leap for flies.

I remember how we sat
deep in flowers, and decided
which girl was the prettiest.   10
Our young looks were radiant then
with the new garland
for the dance.
And so the time goes by.

Look, there we ran to find strawberries,   15
ran to the beech from the fir-tree,
over sticks and stones,
as long as the sun shone.
Then a forester called out
through the branches   20
"Come along, children, go home!"

All our hands were stained,
picking strawberries yesterday;
to us it was nothing but play.
Then, again and again, we heard   25

1. Translated from the German by Peter Dronke.

our shepherd calling
and moaning:
"Children, the forest is full of snakes!"

One child walked in the tall grass,
started, and cried aloud: 30
"Children, right here there was a snake!
He has bitten our pony—
it will never heal;
it must always
remain poisoned and unwell."   35

"Come along then, out of the forest!
If you do not now make haste
it will happen as I say:
if you are not sure to be gone
from the forest while there is day,   40
you will lose your way
and your joy will become a moan."

Do you know that five young women
loitered in the meadow-lands
till the king locked up his hall?   45
Great were their moans and their distress—
for the bailiffs tore
their clothes away,
so that they stood naked, without a dress.[2]

2. Probably an allusion to the parable of the Five Foolish Virgins in the New Testament: see Matthew 25.1–13.

DAFYDD AP GWILYM

U niversally recognized as the out-standing Welsh poet of the Middle Ages, Dafydd (ca. 1310–1370) left a large corpus of almost two hundred lyrics on a variety of themes, ranging from the pains of love and the beauty of the natural world to dynamic scenes of village life and comic erotica: one of his popular (but rarely anthologized) lyrics is a encomium in praise of the penis ("Cywydd y gal"). Renowned for his popularization of the *cywydd* meter, a musical verse form that soon became standard among Welsh poets, Dafydd wrote during a time of political turmoil following the loss of Welsh independence in 1282—years that were also, paradoxically, a dynamic period of cultural revival. In "The Fox," Dafydd displays his two greatest strengths in portrayal: a natural landscape, conjured in vivid detail, and a sophisticated, highly individual subjectivity. For Dafydd, the subject is always the self, whose engagement with the world reveals both his own essential character and that of the world around him.

The Fox[1]

Yesterday was I, sure of purpose,
Under the trees (alas that the girl doesn't see it)
Standing under Ovid's[2] stems
And waiting for a pretty girl beneath the trees;
She made me weep on her way.   5
I saw when I looked there
(An ape's shape where I did not love)
A red fox (he doesn't love our hounds' place)
Sitting like a tame animal,
On his haunches near his den.   10

    I drew between my hands
A bow of yew there, it was brave,[3]
About, like an armed man,
On the brow of the hill, a stirring of high spirits,
Weapon for coursing along a district,   15
To hit him with a long, stout bolt.
I drew for a try a shaft
Clear past the jaw.
My grief, my bow went
In three pieces, luckless disaster.   20

    I got mad (I did not dread him,
Unhappy bear) at the fox.
He's a lad who'd love a hen,
A silly bird, and bird flesh;
He doesn't follow the cry of horns,   25
Rough his voice and his carol.

Ruddy is he in front of a talus[4] slope,
Like an ape among green trees.
At both ends of a field there turns up
A dog-shape looking for a goose.   30
Crows' beacon near the brink of a hill,
Acre-strider, color of an ember,
Likeness of a lure for crows and magpies at a fair,
Portent looking like a dragon.
Lord of excitement, chewer of a fat hen,   35
Of acclaimed fleece, glowing flesh.
An awl of hollowed-out fine earth,
Fire-dish at the edge of a shuttered window.
Copper bow of light feet,
Tongs like a beak of blood.   40

    Not easy for me to follow him,
And his dwelling toward Annwn.[5]

---

1. Translated from the Welsh by Richard Morgan Loomis.
2. Roman love poet (43 B.C.E.–17 C.E.).
3. Splendid; excellent.
4. A pile of rock fragments at the base of a cliff.
5. The otherworld of Welsh myth.

Red roamer, he was found to be too fierce,
He'd run ahead of a course of hounds.
Sharp his rushing, gorse-strider, 45
Leopard with a dart in his rump.

HAFEZ

Shams al-Din Muhammad (1350–1390), whose pen name, "Hafez," simply means "accomplished reciter of the Qur'an," was a native of Shiraz (a city in modern Iran). His poems continue to be extraordinarily popular among Persian speakers, who recite their lines much as English speakers spontaneously quote phrases from **Shakespeare**. Hafez's verses are notoriously difficult to translate, due largely to the nature of Persian poetry. It relies on modes of metaphor very different from those in the Western tradition, and the verse forms favored by Hafez have no English equivalent—in particular, the poem tends to have individual, free-standing lines rather than a complex interwoven sequence of lines. Hafez is sometimes viewed as a Sufi writer in the tradition of **Rumi**, but his poems are not as theologically oriented, though they can be read as allegories of devotion: Hafez celebrates the virtues of actual wine drinking and real, embodied friends just as much as the spiritual pleasures of the hereafter and union with the divine beloved.

Plant friendship's tree[1]

Plant friendship's tree—the heart's desire
Is the fruit it bears:

And uproot enmity—which brings
Sorrows and cares.

Be friendly, easy, with drunkards— 5
Good fellowship's theirs;

It's pride brings the hangover, not
The wine-seller's wares.

Talk with your friends, deep in the night,
And see how life fares 10

Since when we are gone the heavens
Will bring others our cares;

---

1. Both poems are translated from the Persian by Dick Davis.

And welcome the spring in your heart
    Since the world never spares

To provide for us roses and song birds,   15
    Whoever despairs.

And love your belovèd—the heavens require you
    To be one who bears

The grief of Majnun[2] all your life:
    God grant me my prayers!   20

Your heart is so tired! You feel caught
    In the weary world's snares

But sip at your wine, and hear in your heart
    The hope it declares:

That Hafez will sit in his orchard   25
    By the stream that he shares

With his cypress-slim love, God willing,
    In the place that is theirs.

Thanks be to God

Thanks be to God now that the wine-shop door
Is open, since it's there I'm heading for;

The jars are groaning with fermented wine,
With wine that's real, and not a metaphor,

That brings us drunkenness, and pride, and pleasure,   5
While we bring weakness, need, and not much more!

The secret I've not told, and won't, to others
I'll tell my friend—of him I can be sure.

It's not a short tale, it describes the twists
In my belovèd's hair, and lovers' lore,   10

Majnun's grief, Layli's curls, Ayaz's foot
That royal Mahmud's face bowed down before;[1]

And like a hawk I've seeled[2] my eyes to all
The world, to glimpse the face that I adore.

---

2. The protagonist (sometimes called "Qays") of a classical Arabic love story; he was driven mad by his love for Layli.
1. Pairs of famous lovers: Layli and Majnun, and the sultan Mahmud and his beloved slave Ayaz.
2. Closed (literally, "sewn shut," as was done in the process of taming hunting birds).

Whoever strays within your street, it is   15
   Your eyebrows' curve that he will pray before;[3]

O friends, to know the fire in Hafez' heart
   Ask candles what they're burning, melting, for.

3. The eyebrows' curve repeats the curve of the *mihrab*, the prayer niche used by a Muslim to orient his or her prayer toward Mecca.

JAHAN KHATUN

Jahan Khatun ("Lady Jahan") was the daughter of the ruler of Fars, the central province of Persia (modern Iran); she lived most of her life in its capital, Shiraz, the home of several other poets of the fourteenth century, including **Hafez**. More than just scattered lyrics survive from the pen of Jahan Khatun: she is the author of a *divan*, or cycle of collected poems, with an introduction written by herself—a particularly unusual accomplishment in a period when female authors are rare. Although contemporary accounts of Jahan say that her love poems refer to a fellow poet with whom she exchanged verses, several of them apparently mourn a beloved stepmother who died at an early age. The lyric reprinted here includes several of the Eastern poetic tropes that entered Western literature by way of the Arabic literature of al-Andalus (Spain) and the troubadours of Provence, such as the midnight garden, with its roses and nightingales, and the lovesickness that no physician can cure.

Heart, in his beauty's garden[1]

Heart, in his beauty's garden, I—
   Like nightingales—complain,
And of his roses now for me
   Only the thorns remain;

My friends have gathered flowers, but I,   5
   Because of all his harshness,
Can find no flowers to gather here
   And search for them in vain.

My heart is filled with suffering;
   And all my doctor says is,   10
"Sugar from him, and nothing else,
   Will lessen your heart's pain."

1. Translated from the Persian by Dick Davis.

I've filled the world with love for him,
  So why do I receive
Such cruelty from my dearest love,   15
  Again, and yet again?

My free-will's gone from me, so how
  Can my poor ears accept
All the advice my clever tutor's
  Homilies contain?   20

No, in the pre-dawn darkness, I
  Am like the nightingale
That in the orchards sings the rose
  Its old love-sick refrain.

I hear it's strangers whom you welcome,   25
  Whom you make much of now;
Let me then be a stranger in
  The kingdom where you reign.

CHRISTINE DE PIZAN

Born in Italy but raised in France, Christine de Pizan (ca. 1364–ca. 1431) has the distinction of being the first professional European writer. Her father was physician and adviser to Charles V of France, and her husband had a promising career in the government administration; when first one and then the other died, Christine found herself a widow at the age of twenty-four, solely responsible for three children, a niece, and an aged mother. She supported them all with her pen, writing histories, books of myth, advice to princes, and allegorical visions for a series of royal and noble patrons. Christine's last poem is an exuberant song of praise of the young national heroine, Joan of Arc, who was then at the very height of her triumphs; Christine's early poems, one of which is reproduced here, comment on the tragic loss of her husband and consequent withdrawal from the world of erotic exchange. By embracing the role of the *seulete* (a term difficult to translate: literally, "the little solitary one"), Christine acknowledges her loss of the protection and rule of a husband, with all the difficulties that her new status entails—and all the freedom.

All alone am I, and alone I wish to stay[1]

All alone am I, and alone I wish to stay;
All alone, my sweet friend[2] has gone away.
All alone, no companion and no master,
All alone, with sorrow everlasting.
All alone, in weeping unconsoled,   5
All alone, more than any desperate soul.
All alone, left behind without a friend.

All alone am I, at the window, at the door,
All alone, hidden away in the corner.
All alone, fed only by my tears,   10
All alone, weighed down by doubt and fear.
All alone—and nothing suits me quite so well.
All alone, shut up in my quiet cell,
All alone, left behind without a friend.

All alone am I, every time, in every place,   15
All alone, wherever I go, wherever I stay.
All alone, more than any soul under the sun,
All alone, abandoned by each one.
All alone, pushed down by painful years,
All alone, wept empty of my tears,   20
All alone, left behind without a friend.

Prince, now my sorrow truly has arrived:
All alone am I, devoured on each side;
All alone, darkness looming without an end,
All alone, left behind without a friend.   25

1. Translated from the French by Suzanne
Akbari.

2. Her husband, now dead.

ANONYMOUS

This fifteenth-century lyric is an especially moving example of the lament, a genre of religious poem widely popular at the close of the Middle Ages, reflecting the strong devotion to the Virgin that pervaded English poetry on the eve of the Reformation. Written from the perspective of the Virgin Mary herself instead of (as would be more usual) from the perspective of one of her devotees, the poem offers a firm yet loving lesson to the reader: Mary asks the female reader to look at her own child while remembering the suffering of Mary's son, and to weep the tears of compassion that will cleanse the soul.

Lament of the Virgin

Of all women that ever were born,
That bear children, abide and see,
How my son lies me before,
Upon my knee, taken from the tree.
Your children ye dance upon your knee.   5
With laughing, kissing and merry cheer;
Behold my child, behold now me,
For now lies dead my dear son dear.

O woman, woman, well is thee,
Thy child's cap thee dotes upon;   10
Thou picks his hair, beholds his ble,[1]
Thou wost[2] not well when thou hast done.
But ever, alas, I make my moan
To see my son's head as it is here;
I pick out thorns by one and one,   15
For now lies dead my dear son dear.

O woman, a chaplet chosen thou has
Thy child to wear, it does thee great liking;
Thou pins it on with great solace,
And I sit with my son sore weeping.   20
His chaplet is thorns' sore pricking,
His mouth I kiss with a careful[3] cheer;
I sit weeping and thou singing,
For now lies dead my dear son dear.

O woman, look to me again,   25
That plays and kisses your children's pappis.[4]
To see my son I have great pain,
In his breast so great a gap is.
And on his body so many swappis.[5]
With bloody lips I kiss him here,   30
Alas! full hard methink me happis,[6]
For now lies dead my dear son dear.

O woman, thou takes thy child by the hand
And says, "My son, give me a strake!"[7]
My son's hands are sorely bleeding;   35
To look on him me list not lake.[8]
His hands he suffered for thy sake
Thus to be bored with nail and spear;
When thou make mirth great sorrow I make,
For now lies dead my dear son dear.   40
Behold, women, when that ye play

---

1. Complexion.
2. Know, be aware of.
3. Woeful.
4. Breasts.

5. Wounds.
6. I suffer.
7. Stroke—i.e., caress.
8. Is no pleasure to me.

And have your children on knees dansand;[9]
You feel their feet, so feat[1] are they,
And to your sight well likand,[2]
But the most[3] finger of any hand,　　　　　　　　　45
Through my son's feet I may put here,
And pull it out sorely bledand,[4]
For now lies dead my dear son dear.

Therefore, women, by town and street,
Your children's hands when ye behold　　　　　　　50
Their breasts, their body, and their feet,
Then good it were on my son think you wolde,[5]
How care has made my heart full cold
To see my son, with nail and spear,
With scourge and thorns many-fold,　　　　　　　55
Wounded and dead, my dear son dear.

Thou hast thy son full whole and sound,
And mine is dead upon my knee;
Thy child is loose and mine is bound,
Thy child is alive and mine dead is he.　　　　　　60
Why was this ought[6] but for thee?
For my child trespassed never here.
Me thinks ye be holden[7] to weep with me,
For now lies dead my dear son dear.

Weep with me, both man and wife,　　　　　　　65
My child is yours and loves you well.
If your child had lost his life
You would weep at every mele.[8]
But for my son weep ye never a del.[9]
If you love yours, mine has no peer;　　　　　　　70
He sends yours both hap and hele[1]
And for you died my dear son dear.

Now all women that have your wit,[2]
And see my child on my knees dead,
Weep not for yours but weep for it,　　　　　　　75
And ye shall have full muchel mede.[3]
He would again for your love bleed
Rather than that ye damnéd were.
I pray you all to him take heed,
For now lies dead my dear son dear.　　　　　　　80
Farewell, woman, I may no more

9. Dancing.　　　　　　　7. Obliged.
1. Pretty.　　　　　　　　8. Occasion.
2. Liking.　　　　　　　　9. Not at all.
3. Largest.　　　　　　　　1. Both fortune and health.
4. Bleeding.　　　　　　　2. I.e., wits.
5. Would.　　　　　　　　3. A great reward.
6. At all.

For dread of death rehearse his pain.
Ye may laugh when ye list[4] and I weep sore,
That may ye see and ye look to me again.
To love my son and ye be fain,[5]   85
I will love yours with heart entere,[6]
And he shall bring your children and you, certain,
To bliss where is my dear son dear.

4. Wish.   6. Entire.
5. If you be willing.

CHARLES D'ORLEANS

Captured by the English during the Hundred Years' War, the young Duke of Orleans (1394–1465), close relative of the French king, was far too valuable a prisoner to be returned to his home: consequently, he spent the next twenty-four years in comfortable imprisonment in a series of English castles, becoming the valued friend and companion of English nobles and poets.

A skilled writer, Charles was the author of hundreds of lyrics composed in a variety of forms, including the very popular *balade*, a genre designed for musical performance in a court setting. "If you wish to sell your kisses" features a lover who offers to mortgage his heart in order to purchase his lady's embraces—an ironic exchange, in view of Charles's own status as royal hostage.

If you wish to sell your kisses[1]

If you wish to sell your kisses,
I will gladly buy some,
And in return you will have my heart as deposit.
To use them as inheritance,
By the dozens, hundreds, or thousands.   5
Don't sell them to me at as high a price
As you would to a total stranger
For you are receiving me as your liegeman.
    If you wish to sell your kisses,
    I will gladly buy some.   10
    And in return you will have my heart as deposit.
My complete wish and desire
Are yours in spite of all suspicion;
Allow, as a faithful and wise woman,
That for my reward and share   15
I may be among the first served,
    If you wish to sell your kisses.

1. Translated from the French by Sarah Spence.

FARID UD-DIN ATTAR

1145–1221

From the time of Goethe, *The Conference of the Birds* has been admired by Western readers captivated by Attar's ability to describe in poetic language the experience of divinity. Attar tells the story of a group of thirty birds who embark on a pilgrimage to find the mystical great bird, or "Simorgh," whose presence and leadership they long for. The Simorgh is a mythic creature taken from Persian heroic epic and folktale; it is described in such canonical texts as **Ferdowsi's Shahnameh**, where it is able to lift the hero up into the heavens. Attar turns this Simorgh into something quite different: a source of spiritual ascent. Although the Simorgh proves to be a manifestation of divinity, the birds finally discover it not in a remote location but within themselves. The Simorgh turns out to be *si morgh*—literally, "thirty birds." The spiritual journey of the *Conference*, like that told by **Augustine** in his *Confessions*, reaches its end in the depths of the individual's own soul.

LIFE AND TIMES

According to contemporary accounts, the poet's given name was Abu Hamid Muhammad ibn Abu Bakr Ibrahim, but he always was known by the name of his profession, pharmacist (*attar*). He was born in Nishapur, one of the two main cities in the region of Khorasan, which was also the homeland of the poets Ferdowsi, Omar Khayyam, and **Rumi**. Although Attar's life was long, it probably ended violently. The date of his death coincides with the demolition of Nishapur by the invading Mongol army and the massacre of every man, woman, and child within its walls. Despite Attar's subsequent great fame, in his own lifetime he seems to have been little known outside of his own city. A number of works have been attributed to him, but the only two whose authorship is certain are *The Conference of the Birds*, which internal evidence dates to 1177, and a prose account of holy men in the tradition of mystical Islam, the *Biographies of the Saints (Tazkirat al-Awliya)*.

The prose *Biographies* quickly became widely read, but Attar's poetry did not achieve general popularity until more than two centuries after his death. The increasing interest in Attar's poetry paralleled the rising popularity of the brand of mystical Islam espoused throughout his works, Sufism. This form of religious practice sought to build up Muslims' experience of divine presence through devout meditation (*dhikr*), such as the repeated invocation of the names of God or other acts of pious remembrance. There are many strands in Sufism, but they have in common a strong emphasis on the need to learn Sufi practice from others who have embarked on the same spiritual path, whether within an active community of Sufis, under the mentorship of an individual Sufi master, or from the writings of earlier Sufis. The bonds of affection that unite Sufis are described as loving friendships, and the ultimate "Friend" is God. The various strands of Sufism also agree on the goal of the practice: the total annihilation of the self in the experience of God. Paradoxically, this experience of self-annihilation re-creates the individual soul as a manifestation of God. Thus the famous Sufi Mansour al-Hallaj, according to Attar's account in the *Biographies of the Saints*, was once so enrapt in devout contemplation that he cried out ecstatically, "I am the Truth," perceiving himself as God. That Al-Hallaj was condemned for this apparently excessive claim and publicly crucified as a heretic demonstrates another aspect of Sufism. From one standpoint, Sufis could be seen as especially devout Muslims; but they could equally be seen as deviants from the straight path of Islam, dangerous innovators who were closer to the pious practices of Christian ascetics than to the exemplary life of moderation conducted by the Prophet Muhammad.

WORK

On its face, *The Conference of Birds* is a wondrous animal fable like the Greek tales of **Aesop** or the Indian *Pañcatantra*. Read within the framework of Sufi practice, however, the work immediately opens up as a figurative account of the soul's search for God, the Divine Friend. In some ways, this figurative language resembles the parables told by Jesus in the Gospels, here put to use in an extended literary form: the *Conference* uses the parable as a frame for a sequence of about one hundred shorter tales on saintly figures of Sufi tradition. The frame tale centers on a group of birds who set out on a pilgrimage in search of the Simorgh, the great bird who they hope will be their leader and Friend. Their search for the Simorgh is ultimately successful, but only for the thirty birds who persist until the very end. The others fall by the wayside, worn down by the difficulty of the struggle to purify the soul.

The story of Sheikh San'an is by far the longest of the exemplary tales

embedded in the story of the birds' pilgrimage. Sheikh San'an is a holy man even before the story begins, spending his life at Mecca in the shadow of the holiest site in Islam, the Ka'aba. His life is turned upside down by a dream in which he finds himself not at the eastern heart of Islam but the western heart of Christendom—"Rûm," the Islamic name for Constantinople. Instead of being at the threshold of the Ka'aba, he is in the sanctuary of a church, and instead of worshipping God, he is prostrated before a stone image. The sheikh wakes up terrified but is nonetheless impelled to go to the lands of the Christians, where he becomes enslaved by his devotion to a living idol, a beautiful woman whom he discovers as soon as he arrives at Rûm (Constantinople). She returns his love, but demands that he make sacrifices for her. He must drink wine, burn his Qur'an, and bow down to images. Sheikh San'an's all-consuming love for this woman seems to be the most horrible deviance imaginable. Yet we know a happy ending must be coming, because in Sufism all-consuming love is always the only path to the Friend, even if the way must pass through the filth of sacrilege.

A series of oppositions structure the story of Sheikh San'an: Mecca and Rûm (Constantinople), the Ka'aba and the church, the prayer niche (*mihrab*) and the idol. Through the power of love and the intervention of the Friend, who appears to Sheikh San'an's distressed followers in the form of a wise counselor, these seeming contradictions are resolved in unity. Complete submission to love ends in the soul becoming, in Attar's words, "a drop of water" returned to "the True Ocean." Thrilled by the story, the birds are set aflame with a similar desire to carry out their pilgrimage in search of the Simorgh, who is also the Friend. The opposition of Islam and Christianity in the story, which is often viewed simply as a contrast between the right path to God and a falling away from the path, has a deeper significance when read in the light of Sufism, which enables Attar to present Sheikh San'an's all-consuming love for the Christian woman as not a path away from God but a path toward him. Throughout his writings, Attar makes it clear that all paths that are paved by love are equally paths to the Friend.

The geography of the story of Sheikh San'an is a microcosm of the geography of *The Conference of Birds* as a whole. Just as the sheikh travels away from the sacred center of Mecca in a journey that paradoxically leads to God, so too the birds seem to journey in the wrong direction; they traverse a sequence of seven valleys in their quest for the Simorgh, who proves to have been within themselves all along. Sensitive readers of Attar's poem quickly recognized this geography as a spiritual map of the soul's journey to God. The lyric poet Rumi recalls the *Conference*'s seven valleys when he praises Attar, saying that he has "roamed through the seven cities of love while we have barely turned down the first street." Rumi, along with **Hafez** and **Jahan Khatun**, would be among the next generations of Persian poets who would take up Attar's journey of the soul.

From The Conference of the Birds[1]

The Hoopoe Advises the Birds

Whether you're an ascetic or a libertine,
when you fall in love
your heart becomes the enemy of your *self*
and you'll no longer care about yourself.

Therefore, let go of your ego;   5
it's the road's end anyway.
Ego is a dam that keeps you from the Path.

Give up your eyes so that you may see.
If you are told to abandon your faith
or commanded to give up your self,   10
who are you to refuse?
Renounce them both.

Naysayers say this is blasphemy.
Tell them: Love is above heresy and faith.

What does love have to do with belief or unbelief?   15
What do lovers have to do with life's trappings?

A true lover strikes a match to the whole harvest.
If a hatchet is lifted over a lover's head,
a lover of the Path will say: Do it.

1. Translated from the Persian by Sholeh Wolpé.

Love insists on the heart's bleeding pain.　20
Love demands a gnarled and arduous tale.

Wine-bearer, come pour heart-blood into the cup!
If you don't have any, borrow some from love.
True love comes with passion that burns away veils.
Sometimes it ravages the veil; at other times it mends it.　25

An iota of love is better than all the worlds.
A morsel of lovers' pain is better than the lovers themselves.

Love is the magnetic core that draws everything together,
but beware: There is no perfect love without pain.

Angels hold love but not the pain;　30
only mortals merit the pain of love.
If you become sure-footed in love, you'll transcend
everything, even blasphemy and belief.

Love opens the door to poverty;
poverty will steer you to breach faith and belief.　35
When you liberate yourself from all you believe

and don't believe,
that's when your ego disappears.
Only then will you deserve this journey,
only then will you deserve its mysteries.　40

Staunch your fear and step forward.
Leave faith and blasphemy behind. Don't worry.
Don't be childish. Don't hesitate.
Go on, be bold. Take the first step.
If a hundred tests rain down on you,　45
don't panic; expect them on this hard journey.

Parable of Sheikh[2] San'an in Love

THE SHEIKH HAS A DREAM

Sheikh San'an was a revered elder of his era whose wisdom and virtue surpassed all description. For fifty years he had resided in the holy city of Mecca, and had four hundred diligent disciples who studied with him day and night. The sheikh held learning and wisdom inseparable from actions, and he was privy to ancient knowledge as well as to new discoveries and mysteries. He had made fifty pilgrimages[3] on appointed holy days, but since he was also a resident of Mecca, he was always on pilgrimage anyway.

2. An honorific title meaning "wise" or "learned."
3. To Mecca. The pilgrimage to Mecca—the hajj—is one of the five fundamental obliga-

tions of Islam, and making it even once shows great commitment.

In strict observance of his Faith's laws and decrees, he prayed and fasted frequently. Many a great sheikh visited him and when they were in his presence they would lose all sense of themselves. Why? Because Sheikh San'an, that spiritual man, would elucidate for them in great depth the divine miracles in the Holy Book. His utterance would restore anyone whose soul was ill, to his rightful self. In short, he was a leader and a pillar for his people, both in joy and sorrow.

The sheikh was aware that he served as an exemplar to his followers and was therefore greatly alarmed when he found himself dreaming the same disturbing dream night after night. In this dream, he prostrated himself over and over, before an idol, inside a temple. Finally, one night that Awake One woke up and cried out, "Horror! Pity! The graceful Joseph[4] has fallen into the well; I have come upon a difficult passage in the Path. I do not know if I can survive this pain, for I would rather die than give up my faith."

No soul on earth walks the Path without coming to such a strait. If the Wayfarer cuts through the strait right away, the passage will light up all the way to the throne of the Almighty. But if he or she falls behind, the road will stretch out even longer than before.

At last that wise ancient confided to his followers: "Something terrible has befallen me. I must go to Rûm[5] to see what can be done about it."

THE SHEIKH FALLS IN LOVE

All of his four hundred worthy disciples set out and accompanied their master on the journey. They headed out from the Holy City toward Rûm, and when they reached their destination, they walked its every nook and cranny. Then, by fate, the sheikh's eyes fell upon a Christian girl, pious and spiritual in nature, sitting on a beautiful balcony. She was filled with the spirit of devotion to her Lord.

There she was, a never-setting orb in virtue's sky, where, in envy of her face, the sun waxed yellower than the girl's lovesick admirers. Whoever gave that imprisoner of hearts his heart, put on a Zon'nar[6] for her sake. Whoever fixed his soul on her ruby lips, took one step and gave up his life with the next.

When the morning breeze, imbued with the musky fragrance of her hair, wafted through the city, Rûm furrowed its face to breathe it in. Her eyes were agents of calamitous love; her eyebrows, twin arches of temptation. A single glance at her beauty stripped her lovers of reason.

Her brows were like halos around the two moons of her eyes whose pupils hunted hundreds of souls. Her face, beneath her curling locks, was a mischievous flaring fire, and her moist ruby lips kept a whole world parched. Her drunken-dreamy eyes bore a thousand daggers; if you came thirsty to her well, her every blink plunged a blade into your belly. Her mouth was as small as the eye of a needle, and her chin dimpled with a silver pool.

Since the girl spoke to no one, anyone who claimed to have spoken to her was a foolish liar. She wore a Zon'nar braided like her own hair. Her spirit was

4. The son of Jacob, cast into a pit and then sold into slavery by his brothers (Genesis 37.18–28; Qur'an 12.10–19).
5. Constantinople (present-day Istanbul), which was named the new capital of the Roman Empire by Emperor Constantine in 324 C.E.
6. Rope or fabric worn around the waist or neck by Christians to distinguish themselves from Muslims. They often hung a cross from it.

as quickening as Christ's words, and a hundred thousand blood-drenched hearts fell Joseph-like into her well.

She wore a jewel like a bright sun in her hair, the strands of which cascaded in a black veil over her face. When she pushed that veil aside, the sheikh burned from limb to limb, and even though he quickly averted his eyes, the love of that idol's face had cast its spell. The poor sheikh lost all his senses and fell. All that he once was, all he had possessed, vanished and was uprooted. Love's fire smoldered his heart into smoke, his passion for the girl plundered his soul and his belief was sullied by the beauty of her hair.

In this way, the old man exchanged his faith for a Christian girl; he sold his soul's welfare and purchased his own shame. Passion so invaded the sheikh that his heart disenchanted him and he felt queasy in his soul. He said to himself, *With faith gone, what use is the heart? Loving a Christian girl is arduous.*

When his disciples found him so afflicted, they realized that the terrible test their master had foretold had indeed come to pass. They were amazed, astonished, and confounded. No matter how much they counseled the sheikh, he paid no heed because to him there was no remedy for his pain. What distraught lover ever listens and obeys? What pain that burns its own remedy ever finds a cure?

And so the sheikh spent a long day sitting until nightfall with his mouth hanging open and his eyes glued to the girl's balcony. Night fanned out its dark hair and cloaked everything, the way sin cloaks faithlessness. Every star that lit the sky was fueled by the old sheikh's agonized heart. His love multiplied that night a hundredfold and he lost the entirety of who he used to be. He closed his heart to himself and to the world, and began to moan, rubbing his head in the road's dust. Cheated of sleep and tranquillity, he trembled with love and wailed in agony.

He cried: "Dear God, has this night no day? I have spent so many nights denying my ego, but not one of those nights tortured me like this. I am a wick—I have no rest because I burn. Nothing is left in me except my heart's blood. I am a candle that burns and melts through the night, only to be snuffed out at daybreak. I drown in my heart's blood and suffer night assaults. I don't know what the day will bring. Whoever spends a single such night will know unrelenting agony.

"All the days and nights I spent in feverish torment were to prepare me for a night such as this. Destiny molded me to endure this night. Dear Almighty, will this night have no day? Will the candle of the sky never arrive and burn? Is this a sign that the Day of Judgment is about to arrive? Or have I blown out Heaven's candle with my sighs? Maybe the sun has veiled itself in envy of that stealer of hearts. If the night wasn't as long and black as her hair, I'd die from lacking a piece of her. Tonight I burn in longing; I've no stamina for love's mayhem.

"Where is there enough time to count my grief and lament until my heart is satisfied? Where is patience to help me regain myself or bravely drain the poison wine? Where is good fortune to smile on me or aid me in my love? Where is reason to comfort me and lead me toward my goal? Where are the palms to scoop up dust and pour it on my head? Where are the hands to lift my head from under the dirt and blood? Where are the feet to walk me toward my love? Where are the eyes to gaze again on her face? Where is the Friend to ease me in my grief? Where is the comrade to give me a hand? Where is the strength to lament and cry? Where is the sense to feign sobriety? Gone is reason, gone patience, gone the Friend. What kind of love is this, what sort of pain? What any of this?"

THE SHEIKH'S DISCIPLES PLEAD WITH HIM

The sheikh's disciples gathered around him in sympathy and communed with him on that night of his misery.

One of them pleaded: "Rise up, great sheikh! Perform ablutions[7] against this satanic temptation."

But the sheikh replied: "You fool, tonight I have performed a hundred ablutions with my heart's blood."

Another reprimanded: "Where are your prayer beads, sheikh? How can you find yourself again without them?"

He replied: "I threw them away to free my hands to wrap infidelity's belt about my waist."[8]

Another cried: "Oh ancient one, if you have committed a sin, repent." The sheikh replied: "I have renounced modesty and all states of Sufi trance. I have repented being a sheikh, repented waiting for soul-ecstasy."

Another said: "Wise one, get up and reconcile by reciting prayers."

He replied: "Where is the face of that idol so that I can turn in her direction and pray?"

Another pleaded: "How much more of this talk? Get up and prostrate yourself before the Almighty."

He replied: "I will prostrate, but only before that idol's face."

Another asked: "Have you no regrets? No longing for the faith you have abandoned?"

He replied: "My greatest remorse is that I haven't been in love before."

Another said: "The devil has waylaid you, Sheikh. Your heart has been struck with the arrow of disgrace."

He replied: "If it's the devil that lies in ambush, tell him to strike, and strike swiftly and gracefully."

Another said: "Whoever hears of this will say, how that ancient lost his way."

He replied: "I don't care about fame or notoriety. I will smash the glass of hypocrisy with a rock."

Another lamented: "You have distressed your old friends and broken their hearts."

He replied: "If that Christian child is happy in her heart, my heart is unconcerned with your distress or anyone else's."

Another pleaded: "Come, Sheikh, make up with your friends, let's head back tonight toward Mecca."

He replied: "There is no such Holy City for me anymore; now there is only the monastery. I am sober in Mecca, but drunk in the temple."

Another pleaded: "Come and take to the road at once, let's go to the mosque where you can seek forgiveness."

He replied: "I will ask forgiveness only at the threshold of that sweet one. Leave me alone!"

Another warned: "This leads to Hell. A vigilant man does not go to Hell."

He replied: "If I am to reside in Hell, all the Seven Hells[9] will crisp black from just one of my sighs."

---

7. That is, ritual washing; Muslims perform ablution before obligatory prayers (five times daily).

8. I.e., the Zon'nar.

9. The Qur'an describes Hell as having seven levels that are more and more terrible.

Another pleaded: "Come repent this ugliness, and you can still hope for Heaven."

He replied: "Since my darling's face is heavenly, if it is Paradise I must have then it's right here on this street."

Another said: "Have shame before the Almighty. Be reverent toward the Exalted One."

He replied: "It is the Great Almighty who has cast this fire into my soul. I cannot uncast it of my own volition."

Another counseled: "Go be at rest. Find your faith."

He replied: "Do not seek anything but unbelief from this bewildered one. Don't ask faith from one who has lost it."

Since their words had no effect on the sheikh, his disciples fell into reverent silence for that sorrowful one. Their hearts billowed with grief and they wondered what was to become of their master. At last, night was beheaded by the golden sword of day and the glorious world flooded with the sun's sea of light. The sheikh prepared a corner for himself in the street of his loved one, fending off the neighborhood dogs.

For a long time, he sat like a hermit on the dirt, and as he waited and longed for the sun of his beloved's face, he grew thin as a strand of hair. Eventually he fell sick for lack of seeing her, yet still he refused to turn his gaze away from the threshold of her door. The dust of that idol's street became his bed and her doorstep his pillow.

THE SHEIKH GIVES UP HIS FAITH

The girl finally became aware of the sheikh's love and, pretending incomprehension of his state, came to him and asked: "Sheikh, what ails you? How can a Muslim ascetic sit at the threshold of a Christian? Are you drunk with the wine of a god other than your own? If you fixate on my locks, your every breath invites madness."

The sheikh replied: "You can clearly see from the wretched state I am in that you have cunningly stolen my heart. Either give it back or put up with me. You see how I long for you. Don't flirt; leave your coquettish ways and give up your pride. Look at this old man, in love, a stranger in this land.

"Beauty, my love for you is not a passing thing. Either cut off my head or surrender. I will give up my life at your command, and if you wish it, you can restore it back to me with your lips. Your mouth and hair are my loss and gain. Your face and street are my destination. Don't torture me with the toss of those locks. Don't make me swoon with those intoxicating eyes.

"My heart is on fire for you, my eyes are clouds full of rain. I'm friendless, alone and agitated, all for you. I've sold my soul and my world for you, sold it all for just a sackful of love for you. My eyes rain when they don't see yours. Looking at your face throws my heart into agitation. No one has suffered what I've endured because of your eyes. No one has endured what I've suffered. Nothing remains of my heart but the blood of grief. How long must I drink that blood, when no heart is left?

"Don't kick this poor wretch's soul anymore, don't trample him like a conqueror. My life has become this waiting and expecting, perchance to unite with you one day. Every night I ambush my own soul and brave my life in your street. I lay my life at your doorstep and will give it up cheap as mud. How long must I lament at your door? Open it. Lend me your company, if just for a moment.

"You are the sun, how can I stay away? I am a shadow, how can I exist without you? Yet, even as your shadow, I would leap in anguish to the windowsill of your sun. If you nod your head *yes* to this lost one, I'll draw the Seven Heavens[1] beneath my wings, I'll lie beneath the earth, soul aflame, and set fire to the entire world with my blazing heart. My hand is on my heart, my feet are stuck in clay. My life is a receding tide; how long will you hide from me?"

The girl replied: "Senile man, you have lost touch with the world. Your breath is almost cold and yet you seek intimacy? Shame on you! Go think about your camphor and burial cloth![2] You're an old man and you want to play lover? Better to concern yourself with choosing your shroud than obsessing over me. You seek kingship when you can't even find a loaf of bread to fill your stomach."

The sheikh said: "Say what you will, say it a hundred thousand times, but I have no other preoccupation than love's sorrow. What does it matter if one is old or young? Love strikes all hearts with equal weight."

The girl replied: "If you mean what you profess, there are four tasks you must perform: bow before an idol saint, burn your Holy Book, drink wine,[3] and finally, deny your faith."

The sheikh said: "I will lift up a cup of wine and drink to you, but I will not do the other three."

The girl replied: "If you want this affair, you must wash faith from your hands. If you don't bow to your beloved and take on her shade, your love is nothing but smoke and scent."

The sheikh acquiesced and said: "Then I will do whatever you ask. I will obey your command with my life and soul. My sweet silver-bodied love, for you I will wear a slave's ring in my ear and bow my neck for a collar made from a strand of your hair."

She replied: "Then rise, come with me and drink. Wine will boil and excite your blood." She then took the sheikh to the temple. His disciples followed clamorously, all wailing. There the sheik, that spiritual man, saw a new kind of gathering. The temple's host was infinitely beautiful and gracious. The fire of love melted away his faith's armor, and the locks of the Christian girl became his ruin. Not an iota of sense or reason remained in him, and so, silently he took a breath and drank a goblet of wine from his beloved's hand.

He drank and severed his heart from the past. Wine and love mingled in his body and soul, multiplied his passion a hundred-thousand-fold. When her ruby lips parted in laughter and he saw the luster of her teeth, a flame of longing blazed in his body and a raw torrent rushed his eyes.

He asked for more wine, drank and asked for more. He took a strand of her hair, made a ring from it, and like a slave wore it on his ear. When the wine reached his navel,[4] the man who knew hundreds of religious texts by heart, the sage who could recite the Holy Book from memory, threw everything he knew and claimed to be out the window. No more boasting. Whatever he knew, he

---

1. The Seven Heavens appear in accounts of Muhammad's miraculous night journey (or *mi'raj*), and are reflected in Dante's *Paradiso*.
2. Used in ritual preparations for burial.

3. Alcohol is forbidden to Muslims.
4. That is, the liver; in the medical writings of Avicenna (c. 980–1037), wine affected the mind after it reached the liver.

forgot. The wine erased his memory and whatever had once been his was washed from the tablet of his mind. Everything was cleared away except his love, which now grew even fiercer. The drunk sheikh's passion flared higher and his soul became rowdy as the sea. Drunk and befuddled, he utterly lost control and reached out to caress the girl's neck.

The girl drew back and said: "You are not man enough for any of this yet. You pretend love but do not know its inner meaning. If your love is solid and true, if you believe in my curly locks, you must convert to my faith. Love's labor is not superficial work. Safety is not compatible with love. Sacrifice and sacrilege proves the strength of love. If you convert to my religion, then you may touch my neck. If you don't want to convert, then get up and go. Here is your cane and there's your cape."

The lovesick sheikh had let his wayward heart lead him where it may. When his head had been unclouded by wine, he'd had no desire to live, but now that the lovelorn old man was drunk, he stumbled and all was lost. He didn't come back to himself and unabashedly bowed before idols, bringing shame upon himself. The wine was aged enough to do its magic. It made the sheikh dizzy as a twirling compass.

An old man, vintage wine, and vernal love—add a beloved to the mix and out goes self-restraint.

When that ancient was fully ruined (and for a lovesick drunk, all is lost anyway), he said: "I cannot bear this anymore. Tell me, my moon-face, what else do you require from this heart-consumed man? In sobriety I did not become a worshipper of idols, but now in my drunken state I will burn even my holy texts."

The girl replied: "Now you are my man. Now you are deserving of me. Before this, you were raw in your love, but now you are as good as well done."

When the news reached other Christians that a prominent sheikh had embraced their faith, they took him, still drunk, to the monastery and instructed him in the wearing of their belt. The sheikh put his body into the ring of that belt and threw his dervish cloak into fire. Thus, he joined their ranks and untethered his heart from his faith, the memory of Mecca, and his status as a sheikh. After many years of righteous faith, this is how he was washed clean of it all.

He cried: "Grace has finally abandoned this dervish. Love of a Christian girl has done its work. From here on, I will do whatever she commands. What else can I possibly do that would be worse than what I have just done? When sober, I did not bow before an idol; now that I am completely drunk, I have become an idolater. Many have abandoned their faith because of wine. No doubt alcohol must be the mother of all evil to have such power."

He then turned to the girl and asked: "Heart-stealer, what else? I did as you asked, what else is left to do? I drank wine and bowed before an idol. May no one suffer the pain I have for love, or lose himself in such disgrace! For fifty years I have walked the Path, the sea of my heart surging with mysteries. Then a spark of love ambushed me and whirled me back to page one. Love has done this to others and will always do so. It transfigures the faithful into the faithless, and will forever play this trick. Love ushers an alphabet-learner's hand on the slate of faith, and turns the knower of the Invisible into a vagabond lover. What is gone is lost, but tell me, when will you join with me? My union with you depended on all that you asked, and I did it all so that I could unite with you. How long must I burn in the fire of my separation from you?"

The girl said: "Captive old man, my bride price is high, and you are poor. I require gold and silver, witless man. Do you presume you would succeed in uniting with me without wealth? Since you don't have a single coin to your name, either take these alms from me and go, or like the leisurely self-sufficient sun, become independent. Have patience and behave like a man."

The sheikh replied: "My silver-breasted tall cypress, is this how you keep your promises? I no longer have anyone in this world but you, my beautiful idol. At least refrain from this bantering. You throw a new demand at me every chance you get. You flirt with me, then flout me. I tasted blood in my pining for you, trusted in your words and did whatever you asked of me.

"Everything is now gone for the sake of your love—faith and unbelief, loss and gain, all of it. How long will you keep me waiting and anxious? Didn't you make a deal with me? All my followers are about to return to Mecca. They turned their backs on this lost soul and are my enemies now. So much for them, and now you too? What is this betrayal? What should I do? When heart and soul are gone, where can I turn? Sublime woman, I'd rather be with you in Hell than without you in Paradise."

That moon-face felt the old man's pain in her heart and decided to accept him as her man. She said: "Imperfect man, for my bride price, you must herd my pigs for a year.[5] When the year is up, we will marry, for better or worse."

The sheikh did not flinch at this command, for he well knew he who rebels against his beloved will not prevail. So, that ancient of Mecca, that dignified elder, picked up a cane and made swineherding his profession for the coming year.

> A hundred swine linger in human nature;
> burn them, or else don the belt of faithlessness.
> Don't imagine such a treacherous fate
> has befallen only that sheikh.
> The beast skulks inside us all   5
> and rears up its head when you start the Journey.
>
> If you don't know the swine inside,
> go elsewhere; this Journey is not for you.
> But if you step into the Path, you will meet
> a hundred idols and swine on your way.   10
> In love's wilderness, slaughter the swine,
> burn the idol or else become
> like the luckless sheikh, disgraced in love.

The sheikh's conversion created much talk in Rûm. His followers despaired, helpless. When they saw how captive and entangled their master had become, they broke from him. At last, they decided to return to Mecca, but just as they were about to leave, a bold one among them went back to the sheikh and said: "You have been afflicted by weakness. We are leaving for Mecca today. Tell us what to do. Should we abandon our faith and take on the shame that you have? We worry about your aloneness. We will don the Zon'nar for your sake. But if you can't see us doing so, then we must flee without you, return to the Holy City in prayer and cut ourselves off from you."

5. In Islam, pigs are considered scavengers, and therefore unclean. The eating of pork is forbidden [translator's note].

The sheikh replied: "My soul brims over with pain. Go where you want but do it quickly. So long as there is life in me, this place is good enough for me, for this girl keeps my soul alive. As empathetic as you may be, you can't understand what hasn't happened to you. If for a single moment you felt what I feel, you would all become my companions again. Return home, dear friend, for I still don't know what else is in store for me.

"If they ask about me in Mecca, tell them honestly what happened to this vile soul. Tell them his eyes are bloodshot and his mouth full of poison. Tell them he has fallen into the jaws of fate's dragon. Not even an unbeliever in this world has made the transgressions fate has forced me to commit. Tell them the moment the sheikh saw the Christian girl's hair, reason, faith, and wisdom abandoned that ancient man. He wrapped a lock of her hair around his neck, wore it like a captive slave, and gave himself up to gossip. Tell them everything, and if anyone tries to blame me, say that many others have fallen away as I have from the Path. In a journey that has no head or tail, no one is immune to such snares and hazards."

The sheikh said this and turned away from his friends, a swineherder tending his pigs. His disciples were ripped by grief, but in the end walked away from him. Souls scorched and bodies in anguish, they headed back toward Mecca and left their master alone in Rûm, bereft of his faith because of a Christian girl.

THE SHEIKH'S FOLLOWERS LEAVE

Back in Mecca, cracked by shame, his followers hid in their own little corners. But the sheikh had one faithful friend in Mecca who had not accompanied them to Rûm. He was a wise man of great eminence, and the sincerest of them all. When he saw his friends return without the sheikh, he asked what had become of their master. They recounted all that had come to pass, how fate had piled misfortune on the ancient man, and what the Divine had decreed for the sheikh.

They said: "A Christian girl's hair ensnared him and blocked the path of his faith. He now makes love to her locks and beauty spot, his dervish robe burned into ash. He is a changed man. He has withdrawn from all our faith's commandments and is now herding swine. That grieving holy one has wrapped the belt of idolatry tightly around his waist four times. It's true that our sheikh was the wisest of all in matters of faith, but now he is no different from a pagan."

The sheikh's wise friend listened to this account in astonishment. His face turned yellow and he began to weep. He then said: "You lewd scoundrels, when it comes to loyalty, you are neither men nor women. This is the time when a soul needs a hundred thousand friends. If you were indeed true friends to our sheikh, why did you not behave like friends? Shame on you. You call yourselves his disciples? Is this how you pay your dues and show loyalty?

"When our sheikh donned the Zon'nar, you should all have done the same. You should not have deserted him. Christianity ought to have been for you all. There was no camaraderie or consistency in your action. You're all hypocrites. When you offer your friendship, you must offer it with sincerity, even at the cost of giving up what's dear to you. When you prosper, your friends number a hundred thousand, but when you are weak and in need, that's when true friends distinguish themselves. When the sheikh fell into the jaws of a crocodile, you all quickly ran for fear of infamy. But love's foundation is infamy. Whoever shies away from it is unschooled, green and crass in heart and head."

They replied: "Everything you now say to us, we repeatedly said to the sheikh. We even resolved to share his sorrows and joy, to sell our piety and buy disgrace, to jettison our religion and bow before idols. But the sheikh thought it best that we swiftly depart. He saw no use in our camaraderie and turned us back toward home. We came back by his command. Truly, we have told the whole story and held nothing back."

The faithful friend spoke again: "Were you true Wayfarers of the Path, you would have stationed yourselves at the door of the Almighty and kept vigil and competed with one another in begging that Great One to show grace to your sheikh and return him to you. When you abandoned your sheikh, why did you come to Mecca instead of going straight to the Almighty's door?" When the disciples heard this, they hung their heads in shame.

The wise friend then said: "What use is this disgrace? What has happened has happened. Let's rise up and hurry to our master's aid. Let us put on our plaintiff's garments and go to the court of the Beloved, rub our heads in dust and ask for justice."

With this said, they all set out toward Rûm, absorbed in prayers. They prayed all day and all night, and each one, in his own way, knocked a hundred thousand times on the Almighty's door, begging for intervention and tearfully asking for help. They spent forty days and nights in prayer and did not eat nor sleep, denying themselves bread and water.

The supplications of this pure tribe caused a frightful uproar in Heaven, and green-clad angels,[6] from high and low donned garments of mourning. At last the prayers of the disciple who was the purest of them all hit the target in the eye. At dawn a musk-laden breeze wafted and unveiled a mysterious world to his heart. He saw the Prophet walking toward him like the moon, a braided black lock hanging over each shoulder. The Almighty's shadow was a sun on the Prophet's face—may a hundred worlds of souls fall prostrate to a single strand of his hair. He walked leisurely toward the disciple, and a smile graced his face. If you gazed at him, you'd lose yourself and disappear.

The disciple jumped from his seat, took the Prophet's hand, and beseeched him for help, pleading: "You are our leader, the world's lodestar from the Celestial Court. Help us. Our sheikh has gone astray from the Path. I beg you, please lend him your hand!"

The Prophet replied: "Noble soul, go. I have released your sheikh from bondage. Your devotion and beseeching did its work. You did not falter until your sheikh was saved. For a long time, a dark haze lay between the sheikh and the truth. I have lifted that dusty haze from the Path and have raised him from darkness. I have drawn dews from the healing ocean and sprinkled it upon him. The mist has burned off; repentance has descended and sin has perished. Know that a hundred sins dissipate with a single repentance uttered by the mouth. When the ocean of benevolence surges, it washes away the misdeeds of every man and woman."

The disciple lost consciousness, and when he came to, he shouted with such vigorous joy that it shook the rafters of Heaven. He gave the disciples the good news and they hurried toward Rûm, crying and running until they reached their swineherding sheikh. They saw him ablaze like fire. Having regained his

6. Green is the traditional color of Islam.

old vigor, he had shed his Zon'nar and cast off the obligatory bells for swine-herding.

When the sheikh saw his old disciples approaching from afar, he thought of himself shockingly stripped of light. From shame, he rent his own clothes to shreds and fell to the ground, shedding a storm of bitter tears and tearing at his flesh. His sighs singed the curtains of Heaven. His blood burned from grief. Faith's wisdom and knowledge that had been washed away from his consciousness now suddenly flooded back. He fell prostrate on the ground, sweat and blood-tears of shame steeped him red as a rose.

When his disciples saw him in such a state, they were stunned with grief and bliss. They greeted him amazed and thankful. They said: "Fathomer of mysteries, clouds have lifted from the sun; infidelity has absconded, faith has come home. The idolater of Rûm is once again a worshipper of one Creator. Sheikh, the Almighty's ocean of acceptance has surged and washed away your indiscretions. Now is the time for thankfulness, not for such wailing grief. Be obliged to your Beloved who opened a glistening path across black tar. The Beloved knows night from light and listens to remorse for such sins. When the fire of contrition is kindled, all that must burn will ignite."

To make the story brief, they readied themselves for the journey back to Mecca. The sheikh performed his ablutions and once again put on a dervish cloak. Then they started back toward the Holy City.

THE GIRL HAS A DREAM

Now the girl had a dream. She saw the sun fall into her arms, and the glowing orb began to speak. It said: "Go after the sheikh, take on his faith and be as dust at his feet. You who sullied his faith, now be his pure one. He unwittingly adopted your way; now in all fairness you must take on his. You waylaid him from his Path; now walk the Path with him. You were his highway robber; now be his highway companion. How long will you stay oblivious? Wise up!"

When the girl woke up from this dream, light emanated from her like the sun. The pain of longing for the sheikh took hold of her inner being and unsettled her. A flame ignited in her soul and she reached for her heart, but her heart had taken flight.

She did not know what kind of seed had borne fruit in her impatient soul. Something had happened to her and she had no one in whom to confide. She suddenly found herself in a mysterious world, a world with no signposts, a world that left her mute because the tongue had no function there. Her arrogance and gaiety drained away from her like rain from a cloud.

She screamed and ran out tearing at her own garment, penitent and crying tears of despair. Heart overflowing with grief, she ran after the sheikh, ran like a blood-filled cloud, hand over foot. But she did not know which way he had gone or where to seek him. She ran through fields and deserts.

Lost and feeble, she wailed long and loud, rubbed her face on the soil in despair, crying: "Skilled master, I don't know what to do. I waylaid a Wayfarer of your Path; forgive me, for I did not know what I was doing. Calm the sea of your anger. I did what I did out of sheer ignorance. I erred, forgive me. Do not punish me for my deeds. I accept your Path, grant me your aid. I am dying and there is no one to help me, and my share of honor is nothing but abasement."

THE SHEIKH IS INFORMED OF THE GIRL'S STATE

The sheikh was informed by a voice from within: "The girl has become acquainted with our faith and adopted our Way. Return and reunite with your idol. Become her companion."

Upon hearing this, the sheikh turned around like the wind. Again, an agitation fell amongst his disciples. They said: "Sheikh, are you returning again? What was all that talk of regret? If you once again become her lover, your repentance will be nulled."

But the sheikh described the girl's condition. They listened and felt their hearts melt. So once again the sheikh and his disciples took off toward that heart-thief's home.

They found her, yellow as gold, hair covered with dust, barefoot and with her dress torn. She was laid out on the ground like a body empty of life. When that moon-face saw her sheikh, she fainted. The sheikh sprinkled her face with his tears and when she opened her eyes and saw his face, she cried like spring clouds as she looked at his spiritual face. She threw herself at his feet and said: "My soul burns from shame and I cannot bear to live inside my blindness a single moment longer. I want to cast aside the veil of ignorance; please teach me all about the Path, so that I can start my journey."

THE SHEIKH TEACHES THE GIRL THE WAYS OF THE PATH

The sheikh's disciples looked on full of excitement as he taught the girl the ways of the Path. When that idol-face joined the rank of the elect, tears of the disciples surged like a sea. When she saw the Way and tasted the sweetness of seeing the Path in her now wide-awake heart, she became impatient with excitement and was seized by the kind of yearning that has no remedy.

She said: "Sheikh, my endurance has run out and I cannot bear separation from what I now know. I am leaving this troubled world of dust. I will no longer be able to speak, so please forgive me and do not be angry. By your leave, sheikh of the world. Farewell."

Then that moon-face surrendered her last breath and offered up the half-life she still held, to the Beloved. The sun disappeared behind a cloud as her sweet life left her. She had been a drop of water in this sea of fantasy, but now she found her way to the True Ocean.

> We all leave this world like a breeze,
> depart it just as she did.
> Many have suffered like this in the path of love.
> If you grasp love, you will grasp what I just said.

> Whatever you can imagine is possible in the Wayfarer's Path.   5
> It is all compassion and despair, faith and faithlessness.
> The ego has no ear to hear such mysteries.
> Comprehension is based on capacity.

> If it has not been ordained, you cannot grab your share.
> Truth must be listened to by the heart and the soul,   10
> not by what is fabricated from water and clay.
> The battle between the ego and the heart flares hotter by the hour.
> Wail, mourn, and lament the sorrow it brings.

JALAL AL-DIN MUHAMMAD RUMI
1207–1273

Rumi was born in the easternmost regions of Persia, in the town of Balkh (in modern Afghanistan), but spent almost all his life far to the west, in Konya (in modern Turkey): the name "Rumi" means "inhabitant of Rûm," a term loosely used to designate the newly Islamicized regions formerly held by Christian Byzantium, the eastern capital of the Roman Empire. The son of a scholar and teacher, Rumi seemed about to follow in his father's footsteps, but he suddenly emerged as a prolific and extraordinarily powerful mystical poet, transformed by the first of three friendships that would help inspire him to give voice to his passionate spiritual impulses. Explicitly dedicated to his beloved friend and spiritual guide Shams-e-Tabrizi, the short quatrains collected in Rumi's *Divan* reflect the passionate, even erotic union of the human soul with the divine. This fusion of the language of carnal love with that of spiritual devotion is also found in other religious traditions, including the **Song of Songs** of the Hebrew Bible, but in the lyrics of Rumi this yearning, which is both physical and intangible, is expressed in specifically Islamic terms, with allusions to the Qur'an, Muhammad, and prophetic figures such as Joseph and Moses. Underlying this narrative of spiritual union is a repeated evocation of sensory experience: the scent of the rose, the rich taste of wine.

Rumi's major achievement is the *Masnavi*, a collection of six books of rhymed couplets that lead the reader on a kind of spiritual ascent; it is beloved by Persian readers, who regard it as one of the masterworks of their literary tradition. In spite of its length (over 25,000 lines), the *Masnavi* lacks a framing narrative: instead, a series of short stories, vivid images, and digressive meditations are gracefully linked to form a step-by-step passage toward enlightenment as it seeks to "light love's fire" in the soul of the reader. In narrating a spiritual ascent, the *Masnavi* clearly echoes **Attar's *Conference of the Birds***; unlike Attar's narrative poem, however, the *Masnavi* generates within the reader the experience of ascent instead of simply recounting that experience as undergone by other enlightened souls. The following short excerpts of the *Masnavi* provide a sampling of the intense, densely poetic fragments stitched together in Rumi's masterpiece. While the *Masnavi* is central to Persian readers' appreciation of Rumi, his shorter quatrains have been disseminated more widely in translation, making him the Middle Eastern poet most widely read in the Western world, not so much for the undeniable literary merit of his verses as for their powerful spiritual call. While many of the most popular adaptations of Rumi in the West today are versified renditions of existing translations, the short lyrics and *Masnavi* excerpts reproduced here are a fresh translation from the Persian by Dick Davis.

[The nights I spend with you][1]

The nights I spend with you, love will not let me sleep—
The nights I lie alone, I lie awake and weep;
With you or without you, God knows I stay awake—
But look what different forms a sleepless night can take!   4

[Like blood beneath my skin]

Like blood beneath my skin, within my veins, love came;
Now emptied of myself my friend fills all my frame;
My friend fills out my limbs, my life—he's all I am
And all that still remains of me in me's my name.   4

[Profession, profit, trade]

Profession, profit, trade are what we've burned;
Song, poetry, and verse are what we've learned;
We've given heart and soul and sight to love
And heart and soul and sight are what we've earned.   4

[A rose is still a rose]

A rose is still a rose, wherever it might grow,
And wine is always wine, wherever it might flow;
And if the sun should rise up in the western skies
The sun is still the sun, wherever it might rise.   4

[How marvelous, that moment]

How marvelous, that moment when we'll sit so splendidly—you and I
Two substances, two bodies, a single soul's identity—you and I

That moment when we enter in love's orchard, the colors
Of the flowers, the voices of the birds, will give us immortality—you and I.   4

The stars will come to gaze on us, and we shall show
The splendor of the moon to them in that immensity—you and I

1. The following poems were translated by
Dick Davis. Lines of Rumi's poetry are numbered every four lines instead of the usual five
to emphasize his use of couplets.

Then you and I, no longer you and I, will be united by our love,
Happy and safe, and from all foolishness set free—you and I   8

Oh how the throng of heaven's birds will sing to us
When we sit smiling, laughing there, so happily—you and I

And we'll be in two places then, surrounded here with sweetness,
And seated too in paradise, eternally—you and I.   12

[On death's day]

On death's day, when you see my coffin bear me,
Don't think that this world's pains can still ensnare me

Don't weep, don't say "Alas! Alas!" in your despair,
With that "Alas" you've tumbled in the devil's snare   4

And when you see my corpse, don't say, "He's lost, he's lost,"
Since that's when I'll be welcomed home, and found at last

And as you bury me don't say, "Farewell, farewell"—
The grave is but a veil to where our spirits dwell   8

And as you see me laid to rest, know I'll arise
Since sunset means the moon will soar into the skies

You see the sunset, but it is the dawn you see,
The tomb seems like a jail, but sets the spirit free   12

What seed goes in the ground and does not grow again?
Why should you think the seed of man is different then?

What bucket let down in a well does not rise full?
Why mourn the soul that waits like Joseph in its well?[2]   16

When you have ceased to grieve, employ your voice elsewhere
Since all your grieving means no more than empty air.

From The Masnavi

[*On the Prohibition of Wine*][3]

Evil won't always come
        From a loss of self-control,
Wine makes a person ruder

2. See Qur'an 12:10; also Genesis 37.24.   (lines of Persian poetry are much longer than
3. Corresponds to Book 4, lines 2156–58   those in English).

Who has rudeness in his soul;
A wise man when he drinks
    Will seem to grow more clever,
An evil-natured man
    Will turn out worse than ever;   8
But since most men's behavior's
    An absolute disgrace
Wine has become forbidden
    To everyone, just in case!   12

[This World as a Dream][4]

A man lives in a town for many years
But when he sleeps another town appears
Before his eyes, one full of good and bad,
And he forgets the former life he had—   4
He never thinks "Surely there's something wrong here,
This isn't my town, and I don't belong here,
I lived once in that other place . . ." Instead
He's certain here's where he was born and bred.   8
So it's not strange then if the soul's unable to
Recall where it once came to be and grew,
Since this world's like a sleep as deep as night
Or like a cloud that hides the stars from sight.   12

[On Men's Behavior with Women][5]

If outwardly you rule a woman
    Like water that has drowned her,
While inwardly you're ruled by her
    Struggling until you've found her   4

This is man's nature, animals
    Don't have such sentiments;
The Prophet said that women rule
    Those with intelligence,   8

While ignorant and stupid men
    Rule women when they can—
They're savage beasts within, and lack
    The qualities of man.   12

Kindness, affection—these are traits
    That show humanity,
While lust and anger are a sign
    Of bestiality.   16

4. Corresponds to Book 4, lines 3628–33.   5. Corresponds to Book 1, lines 2431–36.

A woman's not your love, she is
    God's light—this is her nature.
She's the Creator; you could say
    That she is not a creature.   20

[Man's Life Compared to That of an Embryo in the Womb]⁶

If someone told an embryo in the womb
"There's a wide world outside, with endless room,
Delightful and well ordered, and replete
With many different tasty things to eat;   4
Long roads and endless plains, oceans are there,
Orchards, gardens, meadows everywhere,
A sky that's high above and filled with light,
There's sunlight, moonlight, and the stars at night.   8
Its marvels can't be put in words, so why—
Instead of staying put here—don't you try
To get away from this dark prison where
You feed on blood and live beset with care?"   12
The embryo would say the man was trying
To trick him and deceive him with his lying—
It couldn't picture what it's told, its mind
And understanding are completely blind.   16
And so it is when saints describe to men
The other world that lies beyond their ken,
And say this world's a pit as dark as night
While that world's substanceless and filled with light,   20
Their ears won't take it in, their nature's being
Is a thick veil that prevents their seeing;
Just as the embryo longs to feed on blood
Since where it dwells now blood's its only food,   24
And fed by blood alone it stays deprived
Of knowledge of the world that lies outside.

[Moses and the Shepherd]⁷

Moses once came across a shepherd praying

And this is what he overheard him saying,

"Where are you, dearest God, where are you, where?
I want to patch your cloak and comb your hair,   4
To be your servant, kill the fleas that bite you,
To wash your clothes and bring milk to delight you,
To kiss your hands and massage your dear feet,
And make your little bedroom nice and neat . . ."   8

---

6. Corresponds to Book 3, lines 53–64.   7. Corresponds to Book 2, line 1720.

When Moses heard such talk he said, "Hey you,
Who is it that you think you're talking to?
Your words are drivel, wicked, rank and rotten,
You ought to stuff your foolish mouth with cotton;   12
Dimwitted friends are just like enemies—
God doesn't need your silly services."
The shepherd tore his clothes in shame, and sighed,
And set off through the barren countryside.   16

Then Moses heard God speak to him and say,
"He is my slave, you've driven him away;
Did you come here to bring together, or
To cut and tear apart for evermore?   20
I've placed his nature in each man's possession
And given him his manner of expression—
The way men speak in India's right for them,
The way men speak in Sind[8] is right for them.   24
It's not men's outside and their words I see
It is their inner state that interests me,
I look into the heart, and foolish chatter—
When hearts are pure and humble—doesn't matter.   28
Words, metaphors, should not be your concern,
It's burning that I want, and hearts that burn;
Light love's fire in your soul, and burn away
Your worries as to what a man might say.   32
Moses, some men know what is taught in schools,
But those with burning souls know different rules;
Love's people are God's people, and their creed
Needs no religions; God is all they need."   36

8. A province now in modern-day Pakistan, known for its Sufi shrines.

DANTE ALIGHIERI

1265–1321

"Midway in our life's journey, I went astray / from the straight road and woke to find myself / alone in a dark wood." With these opening words, Dante compels his reader to inhabit the point of view of a narrator who, halfway through not "my" but "our" lifetime, suddenly realizes that he is lost. His life is thus our life, and the ethical or righteous "straight road" that the narrator hopes to rediscover also comes to be the reader's own goal. Yet this identification of reader and narrator is countered, again and again in *The Divine Comedy*, by an insistence on the specific circumstances of Dante's own life: traveling into the underworld and into the other realms of the afterlife, we meet his old teacher, Brunetto Latini; the father of his close friend **Guido Cavalcanti**; his great-great-grandfather, Cacciaguida; and, most important, the beautiful Beatrice Portinari, whom Dante has loved (he tells us) since they were both children. In spite of the particularity of the details of this afterlife—or, perhaps, because of them—the reader constantly identifies with the narrator, experiencing the painful turns of the journey as well as the joyful expectation of heavenly bliss at the road's end.

LIFE AND TIMES

Dante Alighieri was born and raised in Florence, a northern Italian city that was at once central to his sense of identity and—as depicted in *The Divine Comedy*—a place that he loathed and despised, a degenerate community rife with corruption and discord. During the years around 1300, Florence, like other cities in northern Italy, was caught up in a large-scale confrontation between forces favoring the power of the church and those favoring the independence of city-states. Dante quickly became deeply involved with these issues, both as a member of the political governing body within the city of Florence and in his role as envoy from the city to the seat of the papal government in Rome. Dante's own view—expressed most explicitly in his *De Monarchia* (1318), a political treatise that in some ways anticipates **Machiavelli**'s *The Prince*—was that secular rule and ecclesiastical rule should be clearly divided. Dante argued that a strong ruler in the person of an idealized emperor was necessary for the church to appropriately exercise its moral and religious authority. Because it sought to place limitations on the exercise of political power by the church, *De Monarchia* was immediately condemned; it remained on the list (or "Index") of books that Catholics are forbidden to read until 1881.

Florence had taken a leading role in the disputes concerning secular and ecclesiastical power, split first into the factions of the Guelphs (who supported the pope) and the Ghibellines (who supported the Holy Roman Emperor). By the time Dante became involved in Florentine politics, the Guelphs had become dominant within the city, but an internal fracture soon developed between the Black Guelphs, who continued to support Pope Boniface VIII, and the White Guelphs, who had come to oppose his despotism. Dante was allied with the latter, and when he was in Rome on a diplomatic mission, the Black Guelphs seized control of the city. Dante was consequently forbidden from ever reentering the city of his birth, under penalty of death by burning at the stake. Even worse, the split into the White and Black parties divided Dante's family, as the Black Guelphs were led by the Donatis—relatives of his wife, Gemma Donati—and his wife and their four children remained in Florence.

Deeply embittered by the experience of exile, Dante spent the next twenty years wandering from city to city, all the while continuing with his political writing as well as his poetic efforts. The scandal arising from *De Monarchia* undoubtedly hampered Dante's efforts to return to Florence. In his *Divine Comedy*, he movingly recalls "how bitter as salt and stone / is the bread of others," and laments "how hard the way that goes / up and down / stairs that are never your own." Dante never saw his sentence of exile lifted; indeed, Florence's city council finally revoked it only in 2008. That the vote was not unanimous—the motion passed 19 to 5—suggests that the city's political divisions may have lingered for seven hundred years.

WORK

Dante himself called his monumental poem simply the *Commedia*, or "comedy"; the adjective "divine" was added later by **Giovanni Boccaccio**, author of *The Decameron*, the other great work of medieval Italian literature. Boccaccio thereby signaled not just the subject matter of the work—that is, the realm of the afterlife, including the domains of hell, purgatory, and heaven—but also the elevated style in which it was written. The claim of direct inspiration by God, which Dante makes explicitly throughout the work, was taken at face value by the first generations of commentators, who accepted the work as the faithful poetic record of a real visionary experience. The theological content of the *Comedy* is both dense and elaborate: perhaps the most ambitious aspect of the poem's theology centers on purgatory, a place where souls are able to do penance for their sins even after death, to which Dante devotes the second of the three parts of his work. Purgatory would not become official Christian doctrine until well after the *Comedy* was completed, but Dante was responding to contemporary popular beliefs in the ability of the prayers of the living to affect the condition of the souls of the dead. He also reflects contemporary theological views of the persistence of the union of body and soul even after death, especially in the way that the shades that populate the afterworld of *The Divine Comedy* retain their individual bodily features though their flesh has been replaced by empty form. For modern readers, the term "comedy" might seem peculiar, conditioned as we are to associate comedy with laughter, just as we associate tragedy with tears. For medieval readers, however, following classical notions of genre, a comedy was simply a story that ended on a high note, with joy and—in the case of *The Divine Comedy*—with the narrator literally being lifted up into the heavens.

The Divine Comedy is divided into three books; each charts a different realm of the afterlife, from the depths of Hell in the *Inferno*, up the mountain of Purgatory in the *Purgatorio*, and finally through the ever-higher spheres of Heaven in the *Paradiso*. The three parts form a single path, as the narrator traverses a rugged landscape marked by hills, ravines, treacherous pathways, and difficult stairways, relying throughout on the help of a guide. For the journey through Hell and Purgatory, he follows in the footsteps of **Virgil**. The Roman poet is more than the literal guide of the wanderer within the fiction of the poem, for his *Aeneid*, the epic account of the fall of Troy and the foundation of Rome by Aeneas, is the constant poetic underpinning of Dante's own epic enterprise. But Virgil, as a pagan, cannot accompany him in Paradise: there Dante is led by Beatrice Portinari, his idealized love since childhood, who died in 1290. Both of these guides, as well as others who aid Dante along his way (such as Saint Lucy, who appears in the form of a golden eagle), are sent by a benefactor whom Dante only gradually comes to know: the *donna gentil* or "gracious lady" of Heaven, the Virgin Mary.

However important the theological message of *The Divine Comedy*, it never overshadows the essential realism and tangibility of the world Dante describes. From the horrible landscape of the ruined City of Dis seen in Hell to the brilliant light of the planets in Paradise, the reader's senses are continually stimulated. This stimulation is especially acute in the *Inferno*, where the vividness of the landscape is mirrored in the emotional affect of the narrator: he is moved to tears of pity by the sight of Paolo and Francesca, whose crime was to have given themselves over to the experience of love, but he shows contempt for the traitor Bocca degli Abati, kicking him and pulling out tufts of his hair. In keeping with Christian doctrine, the souls in this underworld have no material bodies, yet their shades retain the appearance of the bodies they had in life, and the punishments they suffer in Hell leave marks on their flesh. In the circle of schismatics, whose sin is that they have divided the community of the faithful, Dante finds Muhammad, the Prophet of Islam, his body "split . . . from his chin" down through his entrails. In this wound, as in the quartered body of Ganelon in the *Song of Roland*, the wrongful division of society, whether the body politic or the religious community, is made manifest on the canvas of the human body.

The structure of Hell, like that of Purgatory and Heaven, is highly symmetrical and full of numerical significance. *The Divine Comedy* is made up of one hundred chapters that Dante calls *cantos* (literally, "songs"), divided into three groups of thirty-three; the extra is added to the *Inferno*, which opens with an introductory canto. The numerological structure of the poem is also revealed in the landscape of each part. Hell is divided into nine circles, each containing a different category of sinners receiving their own proper form of punishment. The mountain of Purgatory is divided into nine parts as well, its seven main terraces (corresponding to the Seven Deadly Sins) surrounded by the entranceway of Ante-Purgatory and capped, at its summit, by the Earthly Paradise of Eden. Finally, the seven spheres of Heaven that lie above the mountain are brought to nine by the addition of those of the Fixed Stars and of the Primum Mobile—the first mover that imparts motion to all the other heavenly spheres. Beyond these nine are found only God and his angels. The constant play on the number three and its cube, three times three, highlights the Trinitarian theology that underlies the spiritual world of *The Divine Comedy*. Christian revelation places the earth at the center of the universe, surrounded by the spheres of the planets and of the stars and itself wounded by the cavernous pit of hell. At the base of the infernal pit, at the very center of the earth, Satan appears not wrapped in flames but rather frozen in a lake of ice. In Dante's memorable phrase, Satan is "the Great Worm of Evil / which bores through the world" as if it were a rotten apple.

Climbing over the hairy body of Satan and twisting through a narrow passageway, Dante and his guide emerge from the bowels of the earth to the base of the mountain of Purgatory. A new mood infuses the work from this point on, as the hopefulness of the narrator reflects

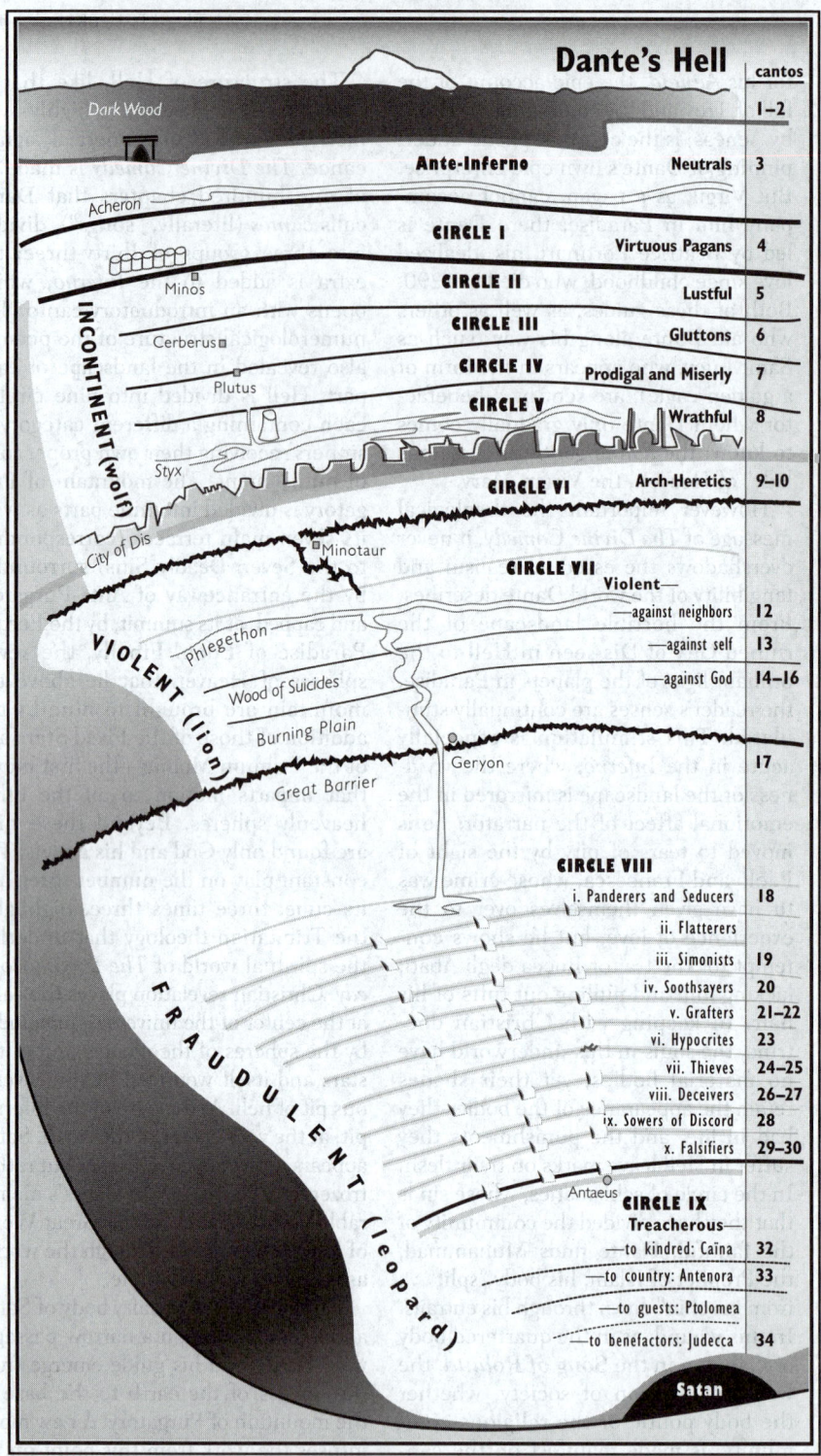

Dante's Hell

	cantos
Dark Wood	1–2
Ante-Inferno · Neutrals	3
Acheron	
CIRCLE I · Virtuous Pagans	4
Minos · CIRCLE II · Lustful	5
Cerberus · CIRCLE III · Gluttons	6
Plutus · CIRCLE IV · Prodigal and Miserly	7
CIRCLE V · Wrathful	8
Styx	
CIRCLE VI · Arch-Heretics	9–10
City of Dis · Minotaur · CIRCLE VII Violent—	
Phlegethon · —against neighbors	12
Wood of Suicides · —against self	13
Burning Plain · —against God	14–16
Great Barrier · Geryon	17
CIRCLE VIII	
i. Panderers and Seducers	18
ii. Flatterers	
iii. Simonists	19
iv. Soothsayers	20
v. Grafters	21–22
vi. Hypocrites	23
vii. Thieves	24–25
viii. Deceivers	26–27
ix. Sowers of Discord	28
x. Falsifiers	29–30
Antaeus · CIRCLE IX Treacherous—	
—to kindred: Caïna	32
—to country: Antenora	33
—to guests: Ptolomea	
—to benefactors: Judecca	34
Satan	

INCONTINENT (wolf)

VIOLENT (lion)

FRAUDULENT (leopard)

390

the very different circumstances of those who suffer pain in Purgatory. Here, unlike in Hell, suffering has a purpose, gradually redeeming the inhabitants from their former state of sin and enabling their souls to rise upward. At the summit of the mountain, Dante enters the Earthly Paradise of Eden, now hidden away in Purgatory to keep it from fallen humans. Here his wonder at a magnificent procession climaxes in a moment of staggering recognition: as he puts it, "I recognize / the tokens of the ancient flame." Here Dante is met by Beatrice, his first love and the soul who will lead him the rest of the way on his upward journey.

Moving through the spheres of Paradise entails progressive dematerialization: instead of the rugged landscape of Hell, we find instead a sequence of spheres—each of which eclipses the last, each adorned with a symbolic form. In the sphere of the Crusaders, we see a mighty eagle; in the exalted spheres of the Empyrean, a celestial rose, studded with saintly souls. One of the very last of these symbolic forms is the great book "bound by love," whose "scattered leaves" make up the universe. In this vivid image, the unity of divine revelation and of the written text of *The Divine Comedy* is complete. The love that binds the book reappears in the poem's last lines, as the narrator describes the endless motion of the heavens, turned by "the Love that moves the sun and the other stars." This earth-centered image of the cosmos would, two centuries after Dante, give way to a new worldview, with the sun at its center and with humanity placed in a very different relationship to its Creator.

To give a sense of different approaches to translation, reproduced here are the last lines of canto 3 of the *Inferno* as rendered by Mark Musa and Clive James, to be compared with the translation by John Ciardi that appears in the full text below. Here, Dante the pilgrim, led by Virgil, attempts to cross the River Acheron to enter the First Circle of Hell. Charon, the infernal boatman, notices that Dante is living and challenges him, but Virgil insists that they must pass through together. Although Dante the pilgrim collapses in weakness at the end of this passage, Dante the poet shows his strength: he beautifully reworks Virgil's double simile in *Aeneid* 6, comparing the souls of the dead to autumn leaves and winter birds. These lines thus provide particular insights into the task of the translator, where Dante the poet carries across (Latin: *translatio*) earlier material from Latin into Italian, and our translators then bring this passage into English in different ways.

From *Canto III*[1]

And then my Leader: "Charon, never fear:
All this is wanted there where what is willed
Is said and done, so more than that don't ask."
At these hard words the bristling jaws were stilled,   130
And the eyes blinked in the wrinkled, flame-red mask,
Of the ferry pilot of the pitch-black marsh:
But all those naked souls unhinged by fate
Changed colour when they heard that speech so harsh.
Clicking their bared, chipped teeth in hymns of hate,   135
They cursed their parents, God, the human race,
The time, the temperature, their place of birth,

1. Translated by Clive James.

Their mother's father's brother's stupid face,
And everything of worth or nothing worth
That they could think of. Then they squeezed up tight   140
Together, sobbing, on the ragged edge
That waits for all who hold God in despite.
Charon the demon, with hot coals for eyes,
Herds them yet closer with time-tested signs.
To anyone who lingers he applies   145
His oar, and as the autumn redefines
A branch by taking off its dead leaves one
By one until the branch looks down and knows
Its own dress, falling as it comes undone—
So Adam's bad seed, grain by bad grain, throws   150
Itself from that cliff not just at a run
But flying, as the falcon to the glove
Swoops home when signalled.[2] Out across the black
Water they flock, whereat the heights above
That they have left, without a pause go back   155
To being thick with people, a dark spring
Filling the branch for its next emptiness.
"My son, from many countries they take wing,"
My Master said, "but just the one distress
Collects them here. God's wrath, in which they died,   160
Came from His justice, which now turns their fear
Into desire to see the other side.
No soul worth saving ever comes through here,
So Charon's anger you can understand,
And understand why he spoke in that tone."   165
At which point the dark ground we stood on heaved
So violently the shock wave still can soak
My memory with sweat. As if it grieved,
The earth wept while it moved, and plumes of smoke
Went sideways with the wind. A red light shone.   170
My reeling senses gave out. I was gone.[3]

From *Canto III*[1]

And my guide, "Charon, this is no time for anger!
  It is so willed, there where the power is   95
  for what is willed; that's all you need to know.

These words brought silence to the woolly cheeks
  of the ancient steersman of the livid marsh,
  whose eyes were set in glowing wheels of fire.

2. These similes are drawn from *Aeneid* 5.56–60 (all line references are to the edition in this anthology).
3. Dante is describing an earthquake, which medieval science understood as the escape of vapors from within the earth; it is while he is unconscious that he crosses Acheron into Hell proper.
1. Translated by Mark Musa.

But all those souls there, naked, in despair,   100
  changed color and their teeth began to chatter
  at the sound of his announcement of their doom.

They were cursing God, cursing their mother and father,
  the human race, and the time, the place, the seed
  of their beginning, and their day of birth.   105

Then all together, weeping bitterly,
  they packed themselves along the wicked shore
  that waits for every man who fears not God.

The devil, Charon, with eyes of glowing coals,
  summons them all together with a signal,   110
  and with an oar he strikes the laggard sinner.

As in autumn when the leaves begin to fall,
  one after the other (until the branch
  is witness to the spoils spread on the ground),

so did the evil seed of Adam's Fall   115
  drop from that shore to the boat, one at a time,
  at the signal, like the falcon to its lure.

Away they go across the darkened waters,
  and before they reach the other side to land,
  a new throng starts collecting on this side.   120

"My son," the gentle master said to me,
  "all those who perish in the wrath of God
  assemble here from all parts of the earth;

they want to cross the river, they are eager;
  it is Divine Justice that spurs them on,
  turning the fear they have into desire.   125

A good soul never comes to make this crossing,
  so, if Charon grumbles at the sight of you,
  you see now what his words are really saying."

He finished speaking, and the grim terrain   130
  shook violently; and the fright it gave me
  even now in recollection makes me sweat.

Out of the tear-drenched land a wind arose
  which blasted forth into a reddish light,
  knocking my senses out of me completely,   135

and I fell as one falls tired into sleep.

FROM THE DIVINE COMEDY[1]

Inferno

Canto I

THE DARK WOOD OF ERROR

Midway in his allotted threescore years and ten, Dante comes to himself with a start and realizes that he has strayed from the True Way into the Dark Wood of Error (Worldliness). As soon as he has realized his loss, Dante lifts his eyes and sees the first light of the sunrise (the Sun is the Symbol of Divine Illumination) lighting the shoulders of a little hill (The Mount of Joy). It is the Easter Season, the time of resurrection, and the sun is in its equinoctial rebirth. This juxtaposition of joyous symbols fills Dante with hope and he sets out at once to climb directly up the Mount of Joy, but almost immediately his way is blocked by the Three Beasts of Worldliness: *The Leopard of Malice and Fraud, The Lion of Violence and Ambition*, and *The She-Wolf of Incontinence*. These beasts, and especially the She Wolf, drive him back despairing into the darkness of error. But just as all seems lost, a figure appears to him. It is the shade of *Virgil*, Dante's symbol of *Human Reason*.

Virgil explains that he has been sent to lead Dante from error. There can, however, be no direct ascent past the beasts: the man who would escape them must go a longer and harder way. First he must descend through Hell (The Recognition of Sin), then he must ascend through Purgatory (The Renunciation of Sin), and only then may he reach the pinnacle of joy and come to the Light of God. Virgil offers to guide Dante, but only as far as Human Reason can go. Another guide (*Beatrice*, symbol of *Divine Love*) must take over for the final ascent, for Human Reason is self-limited. Dante submits himself joyously to Virgil's guidance and they move off.

Midway in our life's journey.[2] I went astray
   from the straight road[3] and woke to find myself
   alone in a dark wood. How shall I say   3

what wood that was! I never saw so drear,
   so rank, so arduous a wilderness!
   Its very memory gives a shape to fear.   6

Death could scarce be more bitter than that place!
   But since it came to good, I will recount
   all that I found revealed there by God's grace.   9

How I came to it I cannot rightly say,
   so drugged and loose with sleep had I become[4]
   when I first wandered there from the True Way.[5]   12

---

1. Translated from the Italian by John Ciardi.
2. Born in 1265, Dante was 35 in 1300, the fictional date of the poem. The biblical span of human life is 70 (see Psalms 90.10 and Isaiah 23.15).
3. See Proverbs 2.13–14 and 4.18–19, and also 2 Peter 2.15.
4. See Romans 13.11–12.
5. See Psalms 23.3.

But at the far end of that valley of evil
   whose maze had sapped my very heart with fear
   I found myself before a little hill   15

and lifted up my eyes. Its shoulders glowed
   already with the sweet rays of that planet
   whose virtue leads men straight on every road,[6]   18

and the shining strengthened me against the fright
   whose agony had wracked the lake of my heart[7]
   through all the terrors of that piteous night.   21

Just as a swimmer, who with his last breath
   flounders ashore from perilous seas, might turn
   to memorize the wide water of his death—   24

so did I turn, my soul still fugitive
   from death's surviving image, to stare down
   that pass that none had ever left alive.[8]   27

And there I lay to rest from my heart's race
   till calm and breath returned to me. Then rose
   and pushed up that dead slope at such a pace   30

each footfall rose above the last.[9] And lo!
   almost at the beginning of the rise
   I faced a spotted Leopard, all tremor and flow   33

and gaudy pelt. And it would not pass, but stood
   so blocking my every turn that time and again
   I was on the verge of turning back to the wood.   36

This fell at the first widening of the dawn
   as the sun was climbing Aries with those stars
   that rode with him to light the new creation.[1]   39

Thus the holy hour and the sweet season
   of commemoration did much to arm my fear
   of that bright murderous beast with their good omen.   42

6. The sun, which in the astronomical system of Dante's time was thought to be a planet that revolves around the earth.
7. This phrase refers to the inner chamber of the heart, a cavity that in the physiology of Dante's time was thought to be the location of fear. Not coincidentally, Dante's last stop in the *Inferno* ends at the lake of Cocytus (see 31.123).
8. This simile of Dante as the survivor of a passage through the sea invokes the story of the escape of the Israelites from Egypt through the Red Sea, a central metaphor throughout the *Comedy* (see Exodus 14). There is also probably an allusion to the opening of the *Aeneid*, where Aeneas and his men survive a storm.
9. The pilgrim is limping because he suffers from the injury of original sin.
1. In the Middle Ages it was thought that the world was created in spring, when the sun is in the constellation Aries.

Yet not so much but what I shook with dread
　　at sight of a great Lion that broke upon me
　　raging with hunger, its enormous head　　　　　　　　　45

held high as if to strike a mortal terror
　　into the very air. And down his track,
　　a She-Wolf drove upon me, a starved horror　　　　　48

ravening and wasted beyond all belief.
　　She seemed a rack for avarice, gaunt and craving.
　　Oh many the souls she has brought to endless grief!　　51

She brought such heaviness upon my spirit
　　at sight of her savagery and desperation,
　　I died from every hope of that high summit.[2]　　　54

And like a miser—eager in acquisition
　　but desperate in self-reproach when Fortune's wheel
　　turns to the hour of his loss—all tears and attrition　　57

I wavered back; and still the beast pursued,
　　forcing herself against me bit by bit
　　till I slid back into the sunless wood.　　　　　　　60

And as I fell to my soul's ruin, a presence
　　gathered before me on the discolored air,
　　the figure of one who seemed hoarse from long silence.[3]　63

At sight of him in that friendless waste I cried:
　　"Have pity on me, whatever thing you are,
　　whether shade or living man." And it replied:　　　66

"Not man, though man I once was, and my blood
　　was Lombard, both my parents Mantuan.[4]
　　I was born, though late, *sub Julio*,[5] and bred　　　69

in Rome under Augustus in the noon
　　of the false and lying gods. I was a poet
　　and sang of old Anchises' noble son[6]　　　　　72

2. The meaning of the leopard, lion, and "she-wolf" is open to a number of interpretations, the most plausible being that they represent the three major forms of sin found in Hell, respectively fraud, violence, and incontinence or immoderation (see Canto 11 ff.). The structure of Hell indicates that the last is the least serious morally, but its role in this canto shows that it is the most difficult to overcome psychologically. Dante probably took the identities of these three beasts from a passage in Jeremiah 5.6.

3. The Roman poet Virgil's voice has not been heard since he died in 19 B.C.E.
4. Lombardy is the most northern area of Italy; Mantua is located to the east of Milan.
5. Virgil (70–19 B.C.E.) was born *sub Julio* (Latin), i.e., during the reign of Julius Caesar (assassinated in 44 B.C.E.), who was regarded by Dante as the founder of the Roman Empire.
6. Aeneas, the hero of Virgil's *Aeneid*. "Augustus": Julius Caesar's nephew and successor, who reigned as emperor from 27 B.C.E. to 14 C.E.

who came to Rome after the burning of Troy.
　　But you—why do *you* return to these distresses
　　instead of climbing that shining Mount of Joy　　　　75

which is the seat and first cause of man's bliss?"
　　"And are you then that Virgil and that fountain
　　of purest speech?" My voice grew tremulous:　　　　78

"Glory and light of poets! now may that zeal
　　and love's apprenticeship that I poured out
　　on your heroic verses serve me well!　　　　81

For you are my true master and first author,
　　the sole maker from whom I drew the breath
　　of that sweet style whose measures have brought me honor.　　　84

See there, immortal sage, the beast I flee.
　　For my soul's salvation, I beg you, guard me from her,
　　for she has struck a mortal tremor through me."　　　　87

And he replied, seeing my soul in tears:
　　"He must go by another way who would escape
　　this wilderness, for that mad beast that fleers　　　　90

before you there, suffers no man to pass.
　　She tracks down all, kills all, and knows no glut,
　　but, feeding, she grows hungrier than she was.　　　　93

She mates with any beast, and will mate with more
　　before the Greyhound comes to hunt her down.[7]
　　He will not feed on lands nor loot, but honor　　　　96

and love and wisdom will make straight his way.
　　He will rise between Feltro and Feltro,[8] and in him
　　shall be the resurrection and new day　　　　99

of that sad Italy for which Nisus died,
　　and Turnus, and Euryalus, and the maid Camilla.[9]
　　He shall hunt her through every nation of sick pride　　　　102

till she is driven back forever to Hell
　　whence Envy first released her on the world.
　　Therefore, for your own good, I think it well　　　　105

---

7. Dante's prediction of a modern political redeemer is so enigmatic that there can be no certainty of his identity. Most commentators think it is Cangrande (i.e., "Great Dog") della Scala of Verona, Dante's benefactor after his exile from Florence.

8. Feltre and Montefeltro are towns that roughly marked the limits of Cangrande's domains. But other interpretations are possible.
9. Characters in the *Aeneid* who die during Aeneas's conquest of Italy.

you follow me and I will be your guide
   and lead you forth through an eternal place.
   There you shall see the ancient spirits tried   108

in endless pain, and hear their lamentation
   as each bemoans the second death of souls.[1]
   Next you shall see upon a burning mountain   111

souls in fire and yet content in fire,
   knowing that whensoever it may be
   they yet will mount into the blessed choir.[2]   114

To which, if it is still your wish to climb,
   a worthier spirit shall be sent to guide you.[3]
   With her shall I leave you, for the King of Time,   117

who reigns on high, forbids me to come there
   since, living, I rebelled against his law.[4]
   He rules the waters and the land and air   120

and there holds court, his city and his throne.
   Oh blessed are they he chooses!" And I to him:
   "Poet, by that God to you unknown,   123

lead me this way. Beyond this present ill
   and worse to dread, lead me to Peter's gate
   and be my guide through the sad halls of Hell."   126

And he then: "Follow." And he moved ahead
in silence, and I followed where he led.

Canto II

THE DESCENT

It is evening of the first day (Friday). Dante is following Virgil and finds himself tired and despairing. How can he be worthy of such a vision as Virgil has described? He hesitates and seems about to abandon his first purpose.

    To comfort him Virgil explains how Beatrice descended to him in Limbo and told him of her concern for Dante. It is she, the symbol of Divine Love, who sends Virgil to lead Dante from error. She has come into Hell itself on this errand, for Dante cannot come to Divine Love unaided: Reason must lead him. Moreover, Beatrice has been sent with the prayers of the Virgin Mary (*Compassion*), and of Saint Lucia (*Divine Light*). Rachel (*The Contemplative Life*) also figures in the heavenly scene which Virgil recounts.

    Virgil explains all this and reproaches Dante: how can he hesitate longer when such heavenly powers are concerned for him, and Virgil himself has promised to

1. The second death is damnation; see Revelation 21.8.
2. The souls in Purgatory; the blessed are the saved in Paradise.
3. Beatrice.
4. Virgil "rebelled" against God because he was not a Christian.

lead him safely?
    Dante understands at once that such forces cannot fail him, and his spirits rise
in joyous anticipation.

The light was departing. The brown air drew down
    all the earth's creatures, calling them to rest
    from their day-roving, as I, one man alone,   3

prepared myself to face the double war
    of the journey and the pity, which memory
    shall here set down, nor hesitate, nor err.   6

O Muses! O High Genius! Be my aid!
    O Memory, recorder of the vision,
    here shall your true nobility be displayed!   9

Thus I began: "Poet, you who must guide me,
    before you trust me to that arduous passage,
    look to me and look through me—can I be worthy?   12

You sang how the father of Sylvius,[5] while still
    in corruptible flesh won to that other world,
    crossing with mortal sense the immortal sill.   15

But if the Adversary of all Evil
    weighing his consequence and who and what
    should issue from him, treated him so well—   18

that cannot seem unfitting to thinking men,
    since he was chosen father of Mother Rome
    and of her Empire by God's will and token.   21

Both, to speak strictly, were founded and foreknown
    as the established Seat of Holiness
    for the successors of Great Peter's throne.[6]   24

In that quest, which your verses celebrate,
    he learned those mysteries from which arose
    his victory and Rome's apostolate.   27

There later came the chosen vessel, Paul,
    bearing the confirmation of that Faith
    which is the one true door to life eternal.[7]   30

But I—how should I dare? By whose permission?
    I am not Aeneas. I am not Paul.
    Who could believe me worthy of the vision?   33

5. I.e., Aeneas, the father (or grandfather) of
Sylvius, who visited the underworld in *Aeneid* 6.
6. The Apostle Peter is considered by the
Roman Catholic Church to be the first pope.
7. St. Paul; see 2 Corinthians 212. Both Peter
and Paul were martyred in Rome.

How, then, may I presume to this high quest
   and not fear my own brashness? You are wise
   and will grasp what my poor words can but suggest."   36

As one who unwills what he wills, will stay
   strong purposes with feeble second thoughts
   until he spells all his first zeal away—   39

so I hung back and balked on that dim coast
   till thinking had worn out my enterprise,
   so stout at starting and so early lost.   42

"I understand from your words and the look in your eyes,"
   that shadow of magnificence answered me,
   "your soul is sunken in that cowardice   45

that bears down many men, turning their course
   and resolution by imagined perils,
   as his own shadow turns the frightened horse.   48

To free you of this dread I will tell you all
   of why I came to you and what I heard
   when first I pitied you. I was a soul   51

among the souls of Limbo, when a Lady
   so blessed and so beautiful, I prayed her
   to order and command my will, called to me.[8]   54

Her eyes were kindled from the lamps of Heaven.
   Her voice reached through me, tender, sweet, and low.
   An angel's voice, a music of its own: 57

'O gracious Mantuan whose melodies
   live in earth's memory and shall live on
   till the last motion ceases in the skies,   60

my dearest friend, and fortune's foe, has strayed
   onto a friendless shore and stands beset
   by such distresses that he turns afraid   63

from the True Way, and news of him in Heaven
   rumors my dread he is already lost.
   I come, afraid that I am too late risen.   66

Fly to him and with your high counsel, pity,
   and with whatever need be for his good
   and soul's salvation, help him, and solace me.   69

8. As we soon learn, the lady is Beatrice.

It is I, Beatrice, who send you to him.
   I come from the blessed height for which I yearn.
   Love called me here. When amid Seraphim[9]   72

I stand again before my Lord, your praises
   shall sound in Heaven.' She paused, and I began:
   'O Lady of that only grace that raises   75

feeble mankind within its mortal cycle
   above all other works God's will has placed
   within the heaven of the smallest circle;[1]   78

so welcome is your command that to my sense,
   were it already fulfilled, it would yet seem tardy.
   I understand, and am all obedience.   81

But tell me how you dare to venture thus
   so far from the wide heaven of your joy
   to which your thoughts yearn back from this abyss.'   84

'Since what you ask,' she answered me, 'probes near
   the root of all, I will say briefly only
   how I have come through Hell's pit without fear.   87

Know then, O waiting and compassionate soul,
   that is to fear which has the power to harm,
   and nothing else is fearful even in Hell.   90

I am so made by God's all-seeing mercy
   your anguish does not touch me, and the flame
   of this great burning has no power upon me.   93

There is a Lady in Heaven[2] so concerned
   for him I send you to, that for her sake
   the strict decree is broken. She has turned   96

and called Lucia[3] to her wish and mercy
   saying: 'Thy faithful one is sorely pressed;
   in his distresses I commend him to thee.'   99

Lucia, that soul of light and foe of all
   cruelty, rose and came to me at once
   where I was sitting with the ancient Rachel,[4]   102

9. Angels who dwell in "the blessed height," Paradise.
1. The sphere of the moon.
2. The Virgin Mary.
3. St. Lucy, a third-century martyr and the patron saint of those afflicted with poor or damaged sight.
4. Rachel signifies the contemplative life; see Genesis 29.16–17.

saying to me: 'Beatrice, true praise of God,
   why dost thou not help him who loved thee so
   that for thy sake he left the vulgar crowd?   105

Dost thou not hear his cries? Canst thou not see
   the death he wrestles with beside that river
   no ocean can surpass for rage and fury?'[5]   108

No soul of earth was ever as rapt to seek
   its good or flee its injury as I was—
   when I had heard my sweet Lucia speak—   111

to descend from Heaven and my blessed seat
   to you, laying my trust in that high speech
   that honors you and all who honor it.'   114

She spoke and turned away to hide a tear
   that, shining, urged me faster. So I came
   and freed you from the beast that drove you there,   117

blocking the near way to the Heavenly Height.
   And now what ails you? Why do you lag? Why
   this heartsick hesitation and pale fright   120

when three such blessed Ladies lean from Heaven
   in their concern for you and my own pledge
   of the great good that waits you has been given?"   123

As flowerlets drooped and puckered in the night
   turn up to the returning sun and spread
   their petals wide on his new warmth and light—   126

just so my wilted spirits rose again
   and such a heat of zeal surged through my veins
   that I was born anew. Thus I began: 129

"Blessèd be that Lady of infinite pity,
   and blessèd be thy taxed and courteous spirit
   that came so promptly on the word she gave thee.   132

Thy words have moved my heart to its first purpose.
   My Guide! My Lord! My Master! Now lead on:
   one will shall serve the two of us in this."   135

He turned when I had spoken, and at his back
I entered on that hard and perilous track.

---

5. These are the metaphoric waters of 1.22–24.

Canto III

The Opportunists

The Poets pass the Gate of Hell and are immediately assailed by cries of anguish. Dante sees the first of the souls in torment. They are *The Opportunists*, those souls who in life were neither for good nor evil but only for themselves. Mixed with them are those outcasts who took no sides in the Rebellion of the Angels. They are neither in Hell nor out of it. Eternally unclassified, they race round and round pursuing a wavering banner that runs forever before them through the dirty air; and as they run they are pursued by swarms of wasps and hornets, who sting them and produce a constant flow of blood and putrid matter which trickles down the bodies of the sinners and is feasted upon by loathsome worms and maggots who coat the ground.

The law of Dante's Hell is the law of symbolic retribution. As they sinned so are they punished. They took no sides, therefore they are given no place. As they pursued the ever-shifting illusion of their own advantage, changing their courses with every changing wind, so they pursue eternally an elusive, ever-shifting banner. As their sin was a darkness, so they move in darkness. As their own guilty conscience pursued them, so they are pursued by swarms of wasps and hornets. And as their actions were a moral filth, so they run eternally through the filth of worms and maggots which they themselves feed.

Dante recognizes several, among them *Pope Celestine V*, but without delaying to speak to any of these souls, the Poets move on to *Acheron*, the first of the rivers of Hell. Here the newly-arrived souls of the damned gather and wait for monstrous *Charon* to ferry them over to punishment. Charon recognizes Dante as a living man and angrily refuses him passage. Virgil forces Charon to serve them, but Dante swoons with terror, and does not reawaken until he is on the other side.

I AM THE WAY INTO THE CITY OF WOE.
I AM THE WAY TO A FORSAKEN PEOPLE.
I AM THE WAY INTO ETERNAL SORROW. 3

SACRED JUSTICE MOVED MY ARCHITECT.
I WAS RAISED HERE BY DIVINE OMNIPOTENCE,
PRIMORDIAL LOVE AND ULTIMATE INTELLECT.[6] 6

ONLY THOSE ELEMENTS TIME CANNOT WEAR
WERE MADE BEFORE ME, AND BEYOND TIME I STAND.
ABANDON ALL HOPE YE WHO ENTER HERE. 9

These mysteries I read cut into stone
   above a gate. And turning I said: "Master,
   what is the meaning of his harsh inscription?" 12

And he then as initiate to novice:
   "Here must you put by all division of spirit
   and gather your soul against all cowardice. 15

6. I.e., God as Father, Son, and Holy Ghost.

This is the place I told you to expect.
Here you shall pass among the fallen people,
souls who have lost the good of intellect."[7]   18

So saying, he put forth his hand to me,
and with a gentle and encouraging smile
he led me through the gate of mystery.   21

Here sighs and cries and wails coiled and recoiled
on the starless air, spilling my soul to tears.
A confusion of tongues and monstrous accents toiled   24

in pain and anger. Voices hoarse and shrill
and sounds of blows, all intermingled, raised
tumult and pandemonium that still   27

whirls on the air forever dirty with it
as if a whirlwind sucked at sand. And I,
holding my head in horror, cried: "Sweet Spirit,   30

what souls are these who run through this black haze?"
And he to me: "These are the nearly soulless
whose lives concluded neither blame nor praise.   33

They are mixed here with that despicable corps
of angels who were neither for God nor Satan,
but only for themselves.[8] The High Creator   36

scourged them from Heaven for its perfect beauty,
and Hell will not receive them since the wicked
might feel some glory over them." And I: 39

"Master, what gnaws at them so hideously
their lamentation stuns the very air?"
"They have no hope of death," he answered me,   42

"and in their blind and unattaining state
their miserable lives have sunk so low
that they must envy every other fate.   45

No word of them survives their living season.
Mercy and Justice deny them even a name.
Let us not speak of them: look, and pass on."   48

I saw a banner there upon the mist.
Circling and circling, it seemed to scorn all pause.
So it ran on, and still behind it pressed   51

---

7. "The good of intellect": i.e., God.
8. These "angels," not mentioned in the Bible but discussed by theologians throughout the Middle Ages, were those who declined to choose either side when Satan rebelled against God.

a never-ending rout of souls in pain.
    I had not thought death had undone so many
    as passed before me in that mournful train.   54

And some I knew among them; last of all
    I recognized the shadow of that soul
    who, in his cowardice, made the Great Denial.⁹   57

At once I understood for certain: these
    were of that retrograde and faithless crew
    hateful to God and to His enemies.   60

These wretches never born and never dead
    ran naked in a swarm of wasps and hornets
    that goaded them the more the more they fled,   63

and made their faces stream with bloody gouts
    of pus and tears that dribbled to their feet
    to be swallowed there by loathsome worms and maggots.   66

Then looking onward I made out a throng
    assembled on the beach of a wide river,
    whereupon I turned to him: "Master, I long   69

to know what souls these are, and what strange usage
    makes them as eager to cross as they seem to be
    in this infected light." At which the Sage: 72

"All this shall be made known to you when we stand
    on the joyless beach of Acheron."¹ And I
    cast down my eyes, sensing a reprimand   75

in what he said, and so walked at his side
    in silence and ashamed until we came
    through the dead cavern to that sunless tide.   78

There, steering toward us in an ancient ferry
    came an old man with a white bush of hair,²
    bellowing: "Woe to you depraved souls! Bury   81

here and forever all hope of Paradise:
    I come to lead you to the other shore,
    into eternal dark, into fire and ice.   84

And you who are living yet, I say begone
    from these who are dead." But when he saw me stand
    against his violence he began again: 87

9. This is Pope Celestine V, who was elected in July 1294 but abdicated five months later; Dante believed that this abdication ("the Great Denial) ushered in the corrupt papacy of Celestine's successor, Boniface VIII (see 19.49–57).
1. The first of the four rivers of Hell.
2. Charon; see *Aeneid* 6.

"By other windings and by other steerage
    shall you cross to that other shore. Not here! Not here!
    A lighter craft than mine must give you passage."[3]   90

And my Guide to him: "Charon, bite back your spleen:
    this has been willed where what is willed must be,
    and is not yours to ask what it may mean."   93

The steersman of that marsh of ruined souls,
    who wore a wheel of flame around each eye,
    stifled the rage that shook his woolly jowls.   96

But those unmanned and naked spirits there
    turned pale with fear and their teeth began to chatter
    at sound of his crude bellow. In despair   99

they blasphemed God, their parents, their time on earth,
    the race of Adam, and the day and the hour
    and the place and the seed and the womb that gave them birth.   102

But all together they drew to that grim shore
    where all must come who lose the fear of God.
    Weeping and cursing they come for evermore,   105

and demon Charon with eyes like burning coals
    herds them in, and with a whistling oar
    flails on the stragglers to his wake of souls.   108

As leaves in autumn loosen and stream down
    until the branch stands bare above its tatters
    spread on the rustling ground, so one by one   111

the evil seed of Adam in its Fall
    cast themselves, at his signal, from the shore
    and streamed away like birds who hear their call.[4]   114

So they are gone over that shadowy water,
    and always before they reach the other shore
    a new noise stirs on this, and new throngs gather.   117

"My son," the courteous Master said to me,
    "all who die in the shadow of God's wrath
    converge to this from every clime and country.   120

And all pass over eagerly, for here
    Divine Justice transforms and spurs them so
    their dread turns wish: they yearn for what they fear.   123

3. Charon knows that after death Dante will be taken not to Hell but to Purgatory in a "lighter craft" piloted by an angel; the arrival of the souls in Purgatory is described in *Purgatorio* 2.22–48. This is the first of several places in the *Commedia* where Dante predicts his own salvation.
4. These similes are drawn from *Aeneid* 6.56–60 (all line references are to the edition in this anthology).

No soul in Grace comes ever to this crossing;
  therefore if Charon rages at your presence
  you will understand the reason for his cursing."   126

When he had spoken, all the twilight country
  shook so violently, the terror of it
  bathes me with sweat even in memory: 129

the tear-soaked ground gave out a sigh of wind
  that spewed itself in flame on a red sky,
  and all my shattered senses left me. Blind,   132

like one whom sleep comes over in a swoon,
I stumbled into darkness and went down.[5]

Canto IV

CIRCLE ONE: LIMBO   *The Virtuous Pagans*

Dante wakes to find himself across Acheron. The Poets are now on the brink
of Hell itself, which Dante conceives as a great funnel-shaped cave lying
below the northern hemisphere with its bottom point at the earth's center.
Around this great circular depression runs a series of ledges, each of which
Dante calls a *Circle*. Each circle is assigned to the punishment of one category of sin.

  As soon as Dante's strength returns, the Poets begin to cross the *First Circle*.
Here they find the *Virtuous Pagans*. They were born without the light of Christ's
revelation, and, therefore, they cannot come into the light of God, but they are
not tormented. Their only pain is that they have no hope.

  Ahead of them Dante sights a great dome of light, and a voice trumpets through
the darkness welcoming Virgil back, for this is his eternal place in Hell. Immediately the great Poets of all time appear—*Homer, Horace, Ovid,* and *Lucan*. They
greet Virgil, and they make Dante a sixth in their company.

  With them Dante enters the Citadel of Human Reason and sees before his eyes
the Master Souls of Pagan Antiquity gathered on a green, and illuminated by the
radiance of Human Reason. This is the highest state man can achieve without
God, and the glory of it dazzles Dante, but he knows also that it is nothing compared to the glory of God.

A monstrous clap of thunder broke apart
  the swoon that stuffed my head; like one awakened
  by violent hands, I leaped up with a start.   3

And having risen; rested and renewed,
  I studied out the landmarks of the gloom
  to find my bearings there as best I could.   6

5. Dante is describing an earthquake, which medieval science understood as the escape of
vapors from within the earth; it is while he is unconscious that he crosses Acheron into Hell
proper.

And I found I stood on the very brink of the valley
    called the Dolorous Abyss, the desolate chasm
    where rolls the thunder of Hell's eternal cry,   9

so depthless-deep and nebulous and dim
    that stare as I might into its frightful pit
    it gave me back no feature and no bottom.   12

Death-pale, the Poet spoke: "Now let us go
    into the blind world waiting here below us.
    I will lead the way and you will follow."   15

And I, sick with alarm at his new pallor,
    cried out, "How can I go this way when you
    who are my strength in doubt turn pale with terror?"   18

And he: "The pain of these below us here,
    drains the color from my face for pity,
    and leaves this pallor you mistake for fear.   21

Now let us go, for a long road awaits us."
    So he entered and so he led me in
    to the first circle and ledge of the abyss.   24

No tortured wailing rose to greet us here
    but sounds of sighing rose from every side,
    sending a tremor through the timeless air,   27

a grief breathed out of untormented sadness,
    the passive state of those who dwelled apart,
    men, women, children—a dim and endless congress.   30

And the Master said to me: "You do not question
    what souls these are that suffer here before you?
    I wish you to know before you travel on   33

that these were sinless. And still their merits fail,
    for they lacked Baptism's grace, which is the door
    of the true faith *you* were born to. Their birth fell   36

before the age of the Christian mysteries,
    and so they did not worship God's Trinity
    in fullest duty. I am one of these.   39

For such defects are we lost, though spared the fire
    and suffering Hell in one affliction only:
    that without hope we live on in desire."   42

I thought how many worthy souls there were
    suspended in that Limbo, and a weight
    closed on my heart for what the noblest suffer.   45

"Instruct me, Master and most noble Sir,"
   I prayed him then, "better to understand
   the perfect creed that conquers every error: 48

has any, by his own or another's merit,
   gone ever from this place to blessedness?"
   He sensed my inner question and answered it:[6]   51

"I was still new to this estate of tears
   when a Mighty One descended here among us,
   crowned with the sign of His victorious years.   54

He took from us the shade of our first parent,[7]
   of Abel, his pure son, of ancient Noah,
   of Moses, the bringer of law, the obedient.   57

Father Abraham, David the King,
   Israel with his father and his children,
   Rachel, the holy vessel of His blessing,   60

and many more He chose for elevation
   among the elect. And before these, you must know,
   no human soul had ever won salvation."   63

We had not paused as he spoke, but held our road
   and passed meanwhile beyond a press of souls
   crowded about like trees in a thick wood.   66

And we had not traveled far from where I woke
   when I made out a radiance before us
   that struck away a hemisphere of dark.   69

We were still some distance back in the long night,
   yet near enough that I half-saw, half-sensed,
   what quality of souls lived in that light.   72

"O ornament of wisdom and of art,
   what souls are these whose merit lights their way
   even in Hell. What joy sets them apart?"   75

And he to me: "The signature of honor
   they left on earth is recognized in Heaven
   and wins them ease in Hell out of God's favor."[8]   78

And as he spoke a voice rang on the air:
   "Honor the Prince of Poets; the soul and glory
   that went from us returns. He is here! He is here!"   81

6. Dante's question is about the Harrowing of
Hell, when, according to Christian doctrine,
Christ descended into Hell after the crucifix-
ion and rescued the souls of the righteous of

Israel; see also 12.43–45.
7. Adam.
8. The "signature of honor" is "poet."

The cry ceased and the echo passed from hearing;
 I saw four mighty presences come toward us
 with neither joy nor sorrow in their bearing.   84

"Note well," my Master said as they came on,
 "that soul that leads the rest with sword in hand
 as if he were their captain and champion.   87

It is Homer, singing master of the earth.
 Next after him is Horace, the satirist,
 Ovid is third, and Lucan[9] is the fourth.   90

Since all of these have part in the high name
 the voice proclaimed, calling me Prince of Poets,
 the honor that they do me honors them."   93

So I saw gathered at the edge of light
 the masters of that highest school whose song
 outsoars all others like an eagle's flight.   96

And after they had talked together a while,
 they turned and welcomed me most graciously,
 at which I saw my approving Master smile.   99

And they honored me far beyond courtesy,
 for they included me in their own number,
 making me sixth in that high company.   102

So we moved toward the light, and as we passed
 we spoke of things as well omitted here
 as it was sweet to touch on there. At last   105

we reached the base of a great Citadel
 circled by seven towering battlements
 and by a sweet brook flowing round them all.[1]   108

This we passed over as if it were firm ground.
 Through seven gates I entered with those sages
 and came to a green meadow blooming round.[2]   111

There with a solemn and majestic poise
 stood many people gathered in the light,
 speaking infrequently and with muted voice.   114

Past that enameled green we six withdrew
 into a luminous and open height
 from which each soul among them stood in view.   117

9. Homer is the legendary epic poet of ancient Greece; Horace, Ovid, and Lucan are famous Roman poets.
1. Commentators have suggested that this is a Castle of Fame, its seven walls symbolizing the seven liberal arts, a system of knowledge developed in the classical period.
2. A locale reminiscent of the classical Elysian fields as described in *Aeneid* 6.468–73.

And there directly before me on the green
  the master souls of time were shown to me.
  I glory in the glory I have seen!   120

Electra stood in a great company
  among whom I saw Hector and Aeneas
  and Caesar in armor with his falcon's eye.[3]   123

I saw Camilla, and the Queen Amazon
  across the field. I saw the Latian King
  seated there with his daughter by his throne.[4]   126

And the good Brutus who overthrew the Tarquin:
  Lucrezia, Julia, Marcia, and Cornelia;
  and, by himself apart, the Saladin.[5]   129

And raising my eyes a little I saw on high
  Aristotle, the master of those who know,[6]
  ringed by the great souls of philosophy.   132

All wait upon him for their honor and his.
  I saw Socrates and Plato at his side
  before all others there. Democritus   135

who ascribes the world to chance, Diogenes,
  and with him there Thales, Anaxagoras,
  Zeno, Heraclitus, Empedocles.   138

And I saw the wise collector and analyst—
  Dioscorides I mean. I saw Orpheus there,
  Tully, Linus, Seneca the moralist,[7]   141

Eculid the geometer, and Ptolemy,
  Hippocrates, Galen, Avicenna,
  and Averrhoës of the Great Commentary.[8]   144

3. Julius Caesar. "Electra": the mother of Dardanus, the founder of Troy. "Hector": the leading warrior of the Trojans in the *Iliad*. "Aeneas": the hero of Virgil's Roman epic, the *Aeneid*.
4. Lavinia, heiress to King Latinus who ruled the area of Italy where Rome was later located and who married Aeneas. "Camilla": a female warrior in the *Aeneid*, where she is compared to Penthesilea, who fought for the Trojans against the Greeks.
5. Admired for his chivalry in fighting against the Crusaders, Saladin was sultan of Egypt and Syria and died in 1193. "Brutus": not the Brutus who killed Julius Caesar, but an earlier Roman who drove out the tyrant Tarquin. All four of the women mentioned were virtuous Roman matrons.
6. Aristotle (384–322 B.C.E.), Greek philosopher. The men mentioned in lines 134–38 are Greek philosophers of the 7th through the 4th centuries B.C.E.
7. Roman philosopher and dramatist, killed by Nero in 65 C.E. "Dioscorides": Greek physician (1st century C.E.). "Orpheus": mythical Greek poet. "Tully": Cicero (d. 43 B.C.E.), Roman orator.
8. Avicenna (d. 1037) and Averrhoës (d. 1198) were Islamic philosophers who wrote commentaries on Aristotle's works that were highly influential in Christian Europe. "Euclid": Greek mathematician (4th century B.C.E.). "Ptolemy": Greek astronomer and geographer (1st century C.E.) credited with devising the cosmological system that was accepted until the time of Copernicus in the 16th century (hence the term *Ptolemaic universe*). "Hippocrates and Galen": Greek physicians (4th and 2nd centuries B.C.E., respectively).

I cannot count so much nobility;
 my longer theme pursues me so that often
 the word falls short of the reality.   147

The company of six is reduced by four.
 My Master leads me by another road
 away from that serenity to the roar   150

and trembling air of Hell. I pass from light
into the kingdom of eternal night.

Canto V

CIRCLE TWO   *The Carnal*

The Poets leave Limbo and enter the *Second Circle*. Here begin the torments of
Hell proper, and here, blocking the way, sits *Minos*, the dread and semi-bestial
judge of the damned who assigns to each soul its eternal torment. He orders the
Poets back; but Virgil silences him as he earlier silenced Charon, and the Poets
move on.

 They find themselves on a dark ledge swept by a great whirlwind, which spins
within it the souls of the *Carnal*, those who betrayed reason to their appetites.
Their sin was to abandon themselves to the tempest of their passions: so they are
swept forever in the tempest of Hell, forever denied the light of reason and of
God. Virgil identifies many among them. *Semiramis* is there, and *Dido, Cleopatra,
Helen, Achilles, Paris,* and *Tristan*. Dante sees *Paolo* and *Francesca* swept together,
and in the name of love he calls to them to tell their sad story. They pause from
their eternal flight to come to him, and Francesca tells their history while Paolo
weeps at her side. Dante is so stricken by compassion at their tragic tale that he
swoons once again.

So we went down to the second ledge alone;
 a smaller circle of so much greater pain
 the voice of the damned rose in a bestial moan.   3

There Minos sits, grinning, grotesque, and hale.
 He examines each lost soul as it arrives
 and delivers his verdict with his coiling tail.[9]   6

That is to say, when the ill-fated soul
 appears before him it confesses all,
 and that grim sorter of the dark and foul   9

decides which place in Hell shall be its end,
 then wraps his twitching tail about himself
 one coil for each degree it must descend.   12

The soul descends and others take its place:
 each crowds in its turn to judgment, each confesses,
 each hears its doom and falls away through space.   15

---

9. Minos is described as judge of the underworld in *Aeneid* 6.207–11.

"O you who come into this camp of woe,"
   cried Minos when he saw me turn away
   without awaiting his judgment, "watch where you go   18

once you have entered here, and to whom you turn!
   Do not be misled by that wide and easy passage!"
   And my Guide to him: "That is not your concern;   21

it is his fate to enter every door.
   This has been willed where what is willed must be,[1]
   and is not yours to question. Say no more."   24

Now the choir of anguish, like a wound,
   strikes through the tortured air. Now I have come
   to Hell's full lamentation, sound beyond sound.   27

I came to a place stripped bare of every light
   and roaring on the naked dark like seas
   wracked by a war of winds. Their hellish flight   30

of storm and counterstorm through time foregone,
   sweeps the souls of the damned before its charge.
   Whirling and battering it drives them on,   33

and when they pass the ruined gap of Hell
   through which we had come, their shrieks begin anew,
   There they blaspheme the power of God eternal.   36

And this, I learned, was the never-ending flight
   of those who sinned in the flesh, the carnal and lusty
   who betrayed reason to their appetite.   39

As the wings of wintering starlings bear them on
   in their great wheeling flights, just so the blast
   wherries these evil souls through time foregone.   42

Here, there, up, down, they whirl and, whirling, strain
   with never a hope of hope to comfort them,
   not of release, but even of less pain.   45

As cranes go over sounding their harsh cry,
   leaving the long streak of their flight in air,
   so come these spirits, wailing as they fly.   48

And watching their shadows lashed by wind, I cried:
   "Master, what souls are these the very air
   lashes with its black whips from side to side?"   51

---

1. I.e., is willed in Heaven by God, who has the power to accomplish whatever he wills.

"The first of these whose history you would know,"
    he answered me, "was Empress of many tongues.
    Mad sensuality corrupted her so   54

that to hide the guilt of her debauchery
    she licensed all depravity alike,
    and lust and law were one in her decree.   57

She is Semiramis[2] of whom the tale is told
    how she married Ninus and succeeded him
    to the throne of that wide land the Sultans hold.   60

The other is Dido; faithless to the ashes
    of Sichaeus, she killed herself for love.
    The next whom the eternal tempest lashes   63

is sense-drugged Cleopatra.[3] See Helen there,
    from whom such ill arose. And great Achilles,
    who fought at last with love in the house of prayer.[4]   66

And Paris. And Tristan."[5] As they whirled above
    he pointed out more than a thousand shades
    of those torn from the mortal life by love.   69

I stood there while my Teacher one by one
    named the great knights and ladies of dim time;
    and I was swept by pity and confusion.   72

At last I spoke: "Poet, I should be glad
    to speak a word with those two swept together
    so lightly on the wind and still so sad."[6]   75

And he to me: "Watch them. When next they pass,
    call to them in the name of love that drives
    and damns them here. In that name they will pause." 78

Thus, as soon as the wind in its wild course
    brought them around, I called: "O wearied souls!
    if none forbid it, pause and speak to us."   81

2. Renowned for licentiousness, a mythical queen of Assyria and wife of Ninus, the legendary founder of Ninevah. Because both the capital of Assyria and Old Cairo were known as Babylon, her land is here confused with that ruled by the sultan of Egypt.
3. Dido, whose suicide for love of Aeneas is described in *Aeneid* 4.542–942, was the widow of Sichaeus. Cleopatra killed herself after the death of her lover, Mark Antony, in 30 B.C.E.
4. The medieval version of the Troy story described Achilles as enamored of a Trojan princess, Polyxena, and killed in an ambush set by Paris when he went to meet her. Helen's seduction by Paris (see line 67) was the cause of the Trojan War.
5. The lover of Iseult, wife of his lord King Mark.
6. Francesca da Rimini and her brother-in-law Paolo Malatesta.

As mating doves that love calls to their nest
  glide through the air with motionless raised wings,
  borne by the sweet desire that fills each breast—   84

Just so those spirits turned on the torn sky
  from the band where Dido whirls across the air;
  such was the power of pity in my cry.   87

"O living creature, gracious, kind, and good,
  going this pilgrimage through the sick night,
  visiting us who stained the earth with blood,   90

were the King of Time our friend, we would pray His peace
  on you who have pitied us. As long as the wind
  will let us pause, ask of us what you please.   93

The town where I was born lies by the shore
  where the Po descends into its ocean rest
  with its attendant streams in one long murmur.[7]   96

Love, which in gentlest hearts will soonest bloom
  seized my lover with passion for that sweet body
  from which I was torn unshriven to my doom.   99

Love, which permits no loved one not to love,
  took me so strongly with delight in him
  that we are one in Hell, as we were above.   102

Love led us to one death.[8] In the depths of Hell
  Caïna waits for him who took our lives."[9]
  This was the piteous tale they stopped to tell.   105

And when I had heard those world-offended lovers
  I bowed my head. At last the Poet spoke:
  "What painful thoughts are these your lowered brow covers?"   108

When at length I answered, I began: "Alas!
  What sweetest thoughts, what green and young desire
  led these two lovers to this sorry pass."   111

Then turning to those spirits once again,
  I said: "Francesca, what you suffer here
  melts me to tears of pity and of pain.   114

---

7. The river Po, in northern Italy, empties into the Adriatic Sea at Ravenna.
8. These seven lines (97–103) should be compared to the love sonnets by Guido Guinizzelli and Dante included in Medieval Lyrics (pp. 349–50 and 354).

9. Caïna is the circle of Cain (described in canto 32), where those who killed their kin are punished; the lovers were killed by Gianciotto Malatesta, Francesca's husband and Paolo's brother.

But tell me: in the time of your sweet sighs
    by what appearances found love the way
    to lure you to his perilous paradise?"   117

And she: "The double grief of a lost bliss
    is to recall its happy hour in pain.
    Your Guide and Teacher knows the truth of this.   120

But if there is indeed a soul in Hell
    to ask of the beginning of our love
    out of his pity, I will weep and tell: 123

On a day for dalliance we read the rhyme
    of Lancelot,[1] how love had mastered him.
    We were alone with innocence and dim time.   126

Pause after pause that high old story drew
    our eyes together while we blushed and paled;
    but it was one soft passage overthrew   129

our caution and our hearts. For when we read
    how her fond smile was kissed by such a lover,
    he who is one with me alive and dead   132

breathed on my lips the tremor of his kiss.
    That book, and he who wrote it, was a pander.
    That day we read no further."[2] As she said this,   135

the other spirit, who stood by her, wept
    so piteously, I felt my senses reel
    and faint away with anguish. I was swept   138

by such a swoon as death is, and I fell,
    as a corpse might fall, to the dead floor of Hell.

Canto VI

The Gluttons

Dante recovers from his swoon and finds himself in the *Third Circle*. A great
storm of putrefaction falls incessantly, a mixture of stinking snow and freezing rain,
which forms into a vile slush underfoot. Everything about this Circle suggests a
gigantic garbage dump. The souls of the damned lie in the icy paste, swollen and
obscene, and *Cerberus*, the ravenous three-headed dog of Hell, stands guard over
them, ripping and tearing them with his claws and teeth.

    These are the *Gluttons*. In life they made no higher use of the gifts of God than
to wallow in food and drink, producers of nothing but garbage and offal. Here

1. In Arthurian legend, the lover of Arthur's
wife, Guinevere.
2. Compare this line to Augustine's account

in *Confessions* of his conversion by reading a
passage in Paul's Epistle to the Romans.

they lie through all eternity, themselves like garbage, half-buried in fetid slush, while Cerberus slavers over them as they in life slavered over their food.

As the Poets pass, one of the speakers sits up and addresses Dante. He is *Ciacco, The Hog,* a citizen of Dante's own Florence. He recognizes Dante and asks eagerly for news of what is happening there. With the foreknowledge of the damned, Ciacco then utters the first of the political prophecies that are to become a recurring theme of the Inferno. The Poets then move on toward the next Circle, at the edge of which they encounter the monster Plutus.

My senses had reeled from me out of pity
   for the sorrow of those kinsmen and lost lovers.
   Now they return, and waking gradually,   3

I see new torments and new souls in pain
   about me everywhere. Wherever I turn
   away from grief I turn to grief again.   6

I am in the Third Circle of the torments.
   Here to all time with neither pause nor change
   the frozen rain of Hell descends in torrents.   9

Huge hailstones, dirty water, and black snow
   pour from the dismal air to putrefy
   the putrid slush that waits for them below.   12

Here monstrous Cerberus,[3] the ravening beast,
   howls through his triple throats like a mad dog
   over the spirits sunk in that foul paste.   15

His eyes are red, his beard is greased with phlegm,
   his belly is swollen, and his hands are claws
   to rip the wretches and flay and mangle them.   18

And they, too, howl like dogs in the freezing storm,
   turning and turning from it as if they thought
   one naked side could keep the other warm.   21

When Cerberus discovered us in that swill
   his dragon-jaws yawed wide, his lips drew back
   in a grin of fangs. No limb of him was still.   24

My Guide bent down and seized in either fist
   a clod of the stinking dirt that festered there
   and flung them down the gullet of the beast.   27

As a hungry cur will set the echoes raving
   and then fall still when he is thrown a bone,
   all of his clamor being in his craving,   30

---

3. For this creature as one of the guardians of Hell, see *Aeneid* 6. 190–97.

so the three ugly heads of Cerberus,
    whose yowling at those wretches deafened them,
    choked on their putrid sops and stopped their fuss.   33

We made our way across the sodden mess
    of souls the rain beat down, and when our steps
    fell on a body, they sank through emptiness.   36

All those illusions of being seemed to lie
    drowned in the slush; until one wraith among them
    sat up abruptly and called as I passed by:[4]   39

"O you who are led this journey through the shade
    of Hell's abyss, do you recall this face?
    You had been made before I was unmade."[5]   42

And I: "Perhaps the pain you suffer here
    distorts your image from my recollection.
    I do not know you as you now appear."   45

And he to me: "Your own city, so rife
    with hatred that the bitter cup flows over
    was mine too in that other, clearer life.   48

Your citizens nicknamed me Ciacco, The Hog:
    gluttony was my offense, and for it
    I lie here rotting like a swollen log.   51

Nor am I lost in this alone; all these
    you see about you in this painful death
    have wallowed in the same indecencies."   54

I answered him: "Ciacco, your agony
    weighs on my heart and calls my soul to tears;
    but tell me, if you can, what is to be   57

for the citizens of that divided state,
    and whether there are honest men among them,
    and for what reasons we are torn by hate."   60

And he then:[6] "After many words given and taken
    it shall come to blood; White shall rise over Black
    and rout the dark lord's force, battered and shaken.   63

4. A Florentine named Ciacco, known only through his appearance here.
5. I.e., "You were born before I died."
6. The enigmatic "prophecy" that follows refers first to the triumph of the Whites, or "the rustic party" (to which Dante was allied), in 1300, and then their defeat by the Blacks, aided by Pope Boniface ("one now gripped by many hesitations"), in 1302, at which time Dante was exiled.

Then it shall come to pass within three suns
   that the fallen shall arise, and by the power
   of one now gripped by many hesitations   66

Black shall ride on White for many years,
   loading it down with burdens and oppressions
   and humbling of proud names and helpless tears.   69

Two are honest,[7] but none will heed them. There,
   pride, avarice, and envy are the tongues
   men know and heed, a Babel of despair."   72

Here he broke off his mournful prophecy.
   And I to him: "Still let me urge you on
   to speak a little further and instruct me: 75

Farinata and Tegghiaio, men of good blood,
   Jacopo Rusticucci, Arrigo, Mosca,
   and the others who set their hearts on doing good—[8] 78

where are they now whose high deeds might be-gem
   the crown of kings? I long to know their fate.
   Does Heaven soothe or Hell envenom them?"   81

And he: "They lie below in a blacker lair.
   A heavier guilt draws them to greater pain.
   If you descend so far you may see them there.   84

But when you move again among the living,
   oh speak my name to the memory of men!
   Having answered all, I say no more." And giving   87

his head a shake, he looked up at my face
   cross-eyed, then bowed his head and fell away
   among the other blind souls of that place.   90

And my Guide to me: "He will not wake again
   until the angel trumpet sounds the day
   on which the host shall come to judge all men.[9]   93

Then shall each soul before the seat of Mercy
   return to its sad grave and flesh and form
   to hear the edict of Eternity."   96

7. The identity of these two is unknown.
8. Dante asks about famous Florentines; he
will find Farinata in canto 10, Tegghiaio and
Rusticucci in canto 16, and Mosca in canto

28. Arrigo does not appear.
9. Virgil refers to the Last Judgment, when
the dead will regain their bodies.

So we picked our slow way among the shades
   and the filthy rain, speaking of life to come.
   "Master," I said, "when the great clarion fades   99

into the voice of thundering Omniscience,
   what of these agonies? Will they be the same,
   or more, or less, after the final sentence?"   102

And he to me: "Look to your science again
   where it is written: the more a thing is perfect
   the more it feels of pleasure and of pain.   105

As for these souls, though they can never soar
   to true perfection, still in the new time
   they will be nearer it than they were before."[1]   108

And so we walked the rim of the great ledge
   speaking of pain and joy, and of much more
   that I will not repeat, and reached the edge   111

where the descent begins. There, suddenly,
we came on Plutus, the great enemy.[2]

Canto VII

CIRCLE FOUR   *The Hoarders and the Wasters*

CIRCLE FIVE   *The Wrathful and the Sullen*

Plutus menaces the Poets, but once more Virgil shows himself more powerful than the rages of Hell's monsters. The Poets enter the *Fourth Circle* and find what seems to be a war in progress.

The sinners are divided into two raging mobs, each soul among them straining madly at a great boulder-like weight. The two mobs meet, clashing their weights against one another, after which they separate, pushing the great weights apart, and begin over again.

One mob is made up of the *Hoarders*, the other of the *Wasters*. In life, they lacked all moderation in regulating their expenses; they destroyed the light of God within themselves by thinking of nothing but money. Thus in death, their souls are encumbered by dead weights (mundanity) and one excess serves to punish the other. Their souls, moreover, have become so dimmed and awry in their fruitless rages that there is no hope of recognizing any among them.

The Poets pass on while Virgil explains the function of *Dame Fortune* in the Divine Scheme. As he finishes (it is past midnight now of Good Friday) they reach the inner edge of the ledge and come to a Black Spring which bubbles murkily over the rocks to form the *Marsh of Styx*, which is the *Fifth Circle*, the last station of the *Upper Hell*.

---

1. They will be more perfect because body and soul will be reunited (a principle derived from Aristotelian science), which will only increase their pain.

2. Dante combines Pluto, the classical god of the underworld, with Plutus, the classical god of wealth.

Across the marsh they see countless souls attacking one another in the foul slime. These are the *Wrathful* and the symbolism of their punishment is obvious. Virgil also points out to Dante certain bubbles rising from the slime and informs him that below that mud lie entombed the souls of the *Sullen*. In life they refused to welcome the sweet light of the Sun (Divine Illumination) and in death they are buried forever below the stinking waters of the Styx, gargling the words of an endless chant in a grotesque parody of singing a hymn.

"Papa Satán, Papa Satán, aleppy,"[3]
   Plutus clucked and stuttered in his rage;
   and my all-knowing Guide, to comfort me: 3

"Do not be startled, for no power of his,
   however he may lord it over the damned,
   may hinder your descent through this abyss."   6

And turning to that carnival of bloat
   cried: "Peace, you wolf of Hell. Choke back your bile
   and let its venom blister your own throat.   9

Our passage through this pit is willed on high
   by that same Throne that loosed the angel wrath
   of Michael on ambition and mutiny."[4]   12

As puffed out sails fall when the mast gives way
   and flutter to a self-convulsing heap—
   so collapsed Plutus into that dead clay.   15

Thus we descended the dark scarp of Hell
   to which all the evil of the Universe
   comes home at last, into the Fourth Great Circle   18

and ledge of the abyss. O Holy Justice,
   who could relate the agonies I saw!
   What guilt is man that he can come to this?   21

Just as the surge Charybdis[5] hurls to sea
   crashes and breaks upon its countersurge,
   so these shades dance and crash eternally.   24

Here, too, I saw a nation of lost souls,
   far more than were above: they strained their chests
   against enormous weights, and with mad howls   27

rolled them at one another. Then in haste
   they rolled them back, one party shouting out:
   "Why do you hoard?" and the other: "Why do you waste?"   30

3. Virgil apparently understands this mysterious outburst regarding Satan, but commentators have remained baffled.
4. A reference to the battle in heaven between the Archangel Michael and Satan in the form of a dragon: see Revelation 12.7–9.
5. A famous whirlpool in the Strait of Messina, between Sicily and Italy, described in *Aeneid* 3.

So back around that ring they puff and blow,
    each faction to its course, until they reach
    opposite sides, and screaming as they go   33

the madmen turn and start their weights again
    to crash against the maniacs. And I,
    watching, felt my heart contract with pain.   36

"Master," I said, "what people can these be?
    And all those tonsured[6] ones there on our left—
    is it possible they *all* were of the clergy?"   39

And he: "In the first life beneath the sun
    they were so skewed and squint-eyed in their minds
    their misering or extravagance mocked all reason. 42

The voice of each clamors its own excess
    when lust meets lust at the two points of the circle
    where opposite guilts meet in their wretchedness. 45

These tonsured wraiths of greed were priests indeed,
    and popes and cardinals, for it is in these
    the weed of avarice sows its rankest seed."   48

And I to him: "Master, among this crew
    surely I should be able to make out
    the fallen image of some soul I knew."   51

And he to me: "This is a lost ambition.
    In their sordid lives they labored to be blind,
    and now their souls have dimmed past recognition. 54

All their eternity is to butt and bray:
    one crew will stand tight-fisted, the other stripped
    of its very hair at the bar of Judgment Day.   57

Hoarding and squandering wasted all their light
    and brought them screaming to this brawl of wraiths.
    You need no words of mine to grasp their plight.   60

Now may you see the fleeting vanity
    of the goods of Fortune for which men tear down
    all that they are, to build a mockery.   63

Not all the gold that is or ever was
    under the sky could buy for one of these
    exhausted souls the fraction of a pause."   66

6. The tonsure—a shaving of part of the head—was a mark of clerical status.

"Master," I said, "tell me—now that you touch
  on this Dame Fortune—what *is* she, that she holds
  the good things of the world within her clutch?"   69

And he to me: "O credulous mankind,
  is there one error that has wooed and lost you?
  Now listen, and strike error from your mind:[7]   72

That king whose perfect wisdom transcends all,
  made the heavens and posted angels on them
  to guide the eternal light that it might fall   75

from every sphere to every sphere the same.
  He made earth's splendors by a like decree
  and posted as their minister this high Dame,   78

the Lady of Permutations. All earth's gear
  she changes from nation to nation, from house to house,
  in changeless change through every turning year.   81

No mortal power may stay her spinning wheel.
  The nations rise and fall by her decree.
  None may foresee where she will set her heel: 84

she passes, and things pass. Man's mortal reason
  cannot encompass her. She rules her sphere
  as the other gods rule theirs. Season by season   87

her changes change her changes endlessly,
  and those whose turn has come press on her so,
  she must be swift by hard necessity.   90

And this is she so railed at and reviled
  that even her debtors in the joys of time
  blaspheme her name. Their oaths are bitter and wild,   93

but she in her beatitude does not hear.
  Among the Primal Beings of God's joy
  she breathes her blessedness and wheels her sphere.   96

But the stars that marked our starting fall away.
  We must go deeper into greater pain,
  for it is not permitted that we stay."[8]   99

7. Virgil now explains that each area of life is presided over by a "guide," a kind of angel, under the ultimate authority of God. The classical goddess Fortune—the "minister" of line 78—who was thought to distribute the world's goods capriciously is here described as acting under God's supervision.

8. The stars that were rising at the start of the journey (1.37–39) are now setting: Good Friday has passed, and the time is now the early hours of Holy Saturday.

And crossing over to the chasm's edge
   we came to a spring that boiled and overflowed
   through a great crevice worn into the ledge.   102

By that foul water, black from its very source,
   we found a nightmare path among the rocks
   and followed the dark stream along its course.   105

Beyond its rocky race and wild descent
   the river floods and forms a marsh called Styx,[9]
   a dreary swampland, vaporous and malignant.   108

And I, intent on all our passage touched,
   made out a swarm of spirits in that bog
   savage with anger, naked, slime-besmutched.   111

They thumped at one another in that slime
   with hands and feet, and they butted, and they bit
as if each would tear the other limb from limb.   114

And my kind Sage: "My son, behold the souls
   of those who lived in wrath. And do you see
   the broken surfaces of those water-holes   117

on every hand, boiling as if in pain?
   There are souls beneath that water. Fixed in slime
   they speak their piece, end it, and start again: 120

'Sullen were we in the air made sweet by the Sun;
   in the glory of his shining our hearts poured
   a bitter smoke. Sullen were we begun;   123

sullen we lie forever in this ditch.'
   This litany they gargle in their throats
   as if they sang, but lacked the words and pitch."   126

Then circling on along that filthy wallow,
   we picked our way between the bank and fen,
   keeping our eyes on those foul souls that swallow   129

the slime of Hell. And so at last we came
to the foot of a Great Tower that has no name.[1]

---

9. The second river of Hell.
1. This watchtower guards the entrance to lower Hell or the city of Dis—another name for Pluto, the classical god of the underworld, that is throughout the *Inferno* applied to Satan (see 11.65 and 34.20).

Canto VIII

CIRCLE FIVE: STYX   *The Wrathful, Phlegyas*

CIRCLE SIX: DIS   *The Fallen Angels*

The Poets stand at the edge of the swamp, and a mysterious signal flames from the great tower. It is answered from the darkness of the other side, and almost immediately the Poets see *Phlegyas*, the Boatman of Styx, racing toward them across the water, fast as a flying arrow. He comes avidly, thinking to find new souls for torment, and he howls with rage when he discovers the Poets. Once again, however, Virgil conquers wrath with a word and Phlegyas reluctantly gives them passage.

As they are crossing, a muddy soul rises before them. It is *Filippo Argenti*, one of the Wrathful. Dante recognizes him despite the filth with which he is covered, and he berates him soundly, even wishing to see him tormented further. Virgil approves Dante's disdain and, as if in answer to Dante's wrath, Argenti is suddenly set upon by all the other sinners present, who fall upon him and rip him to pieces.

The boat meanwhile has sped on, and before Argenti's screams have died away, Dante sees the flaming red towers of Dis, the Capital of Hell. The great walls of the iron city block the way to the Lower Hell. Properly speaking, all the rest of Hell lies within the city walls, which separate the Upper and the Lower Hell.

Phlegyas deposits them at a great Iron Gate which they find to be guarded by the *Rebellious Angels*. These creatures of Ultimate Evil, rebels against God Himself, refuse to let the Poets pass. Even Virgil is powerless against them, for Human Reason by itself cannot cope with the essence of Evil. Only Divine Aid can bring hope. Virgil accordingly sends up a prayer for assistance and waits anxiously for a Heavenly Messenger to appear.

Returning to my theme, I say we came
    to the foot of a Great Tower; but long before
    we reached it through the marsh, two horns of flame   3

flared from the summit, one from either side,
    and then, far off, so far we scarce could see it
    across the mist, another flame replied.   6

I turned to that sea of all intelligence
    saying: "What is this signal and counter-signal?
    Who is it speaks with fire across this distance?"   9

And he then: "Look across the filthy slew:
    you may already see the one they summon,
    if the swamp vapors do not hide him from you."   12

No twanging bowstring ever shot an arrow
    that bored the air it rode dead to the mark
    more swiftly than the flying skiff whose prow   15

shot toward us over the polluted channel
    with a single steersman at the helm who called:
    "So, do I have you at last, you whelp of Hell?"   18

"Phlegyas, Phlegyas,"[2] said my Lord and Guide,
  "this time you waste your breath: you have us only
  for the time it takes to cross to the other side."   21

Phlegyas, the madman, blew his rage among
  those muddy marshes like a cheat deceived,
  or like a fool at some imagined wrong.   24

My Guide, whom all the fiend's noise could not nettle,
  boarded the skiff, motioning me to follow:
  and not till I stepped aboard did it seem to settle   27

into the water. At once we left the shore,
  that ancient hull riding more heavily
  than it had ridden in all of time before.[3]   30

And as we ran on that dead swamp, the slime
  rose before me, and from it a voice cried:
  "Who are you that come here before your time?"   33

And I replied: "If I come, I do not remain.
  But you, who are *you*, so fallen and so foul?"
  And he: "I am one who weeps." And I then: 36

"May you weep and wail to all eternity,
  for I know you, hell-dog, filthy as you are."
  Then he stretched both hands to the boat, but warily   39

the Master shoved him back, crying, "Down! Down!
  with the other dogs!" Then he embraced me saying:
  "Indignant spirit, I kiss you as you frown.   42

Blessed be she who bore you.[4] In world and time
  this one was haughtier yet. Not one unbending
  graces his memory. Here is his shadow in slime.   45

How many living now, chancellors of wrath,
  shall come to lie here yet in this pigmire,
  leaving a curse to be their aftermath!"   48

And I: "Master, it would suit my whim
  to see the wretch scrubbed down into the swill
  before we leave this stinking sink and him."   51

And he to me: "Before the other side
  shows through the mist, you shall have all you ask.
  This is a wish that should be gratified."   54

2. A mythological figure condemned to Hell
for setting fire to the temple of Apollo in
revenge for the god's seduction of his daughter;
Dante found him in *Aeneid* 6.714–17.

3. Because of the unaccustomed weight of
the living Dante.
4. See Luke 11.27, where these words are
applied to Jesus.

And shortly after, I saw the loathsome spirit
    so mangled by a swarm of muddy wraiths
    that to this day I praise and thank God for it.   57

"After Filippo Argentil"[5] all cried together.
    The maddog Florentine wheeled at their cry
    and bit himself for rage. I saw them gather.   60

And there we left him. And I say no more,
    But such a wailing beat upon my ears,
    I strained my eyes ahead to the far shore.   63

"My son," the Master said, "the City called Dis
    lies just ahead, the heavy citizens,
    the swarming crowds of Hell's metropolis."   66

And I then: "Master, I already see
    the glow of its red mosques, as if they came
    hot from the forge to smolder in this valley."   69

And my all-knowing Guide: "They are eternal
    flues to eternal fire that rages in them
    and makes them glow across this lower Hell."   72

And as he spoke we entered the vast moat
    of the sepulchre. Its wall seemed made of iron
    and towered above us in our little boat.   75

We circled through what seemed an endless distance
    before the boatman ran his prow ashore
    crying: "Out! Out! Get out! This is the entrance."   78

Above the gates more than a thousand shades
    of spirits purged from Heaven for its glory[6]
    cried angrily: "Who is it that invades   81

Death's Kingdom in his life?" My Lord and Guide
    advanced a step before me with a sign
    that he wished to speak to some of them aside.   84

They quieted somewhat, and one called, "Come,
    but come alone. And tell that other one,
    who thought to walk so blithely through death's kingdom,   87

he may go back along the same fool's way
    he came by. Let him try his living luck.
    You who are dead can come only to stay."   90

5. A Florentine contemporary of Dante; Dante's acquaintances recounted great enmity between them, mainly as a result of Dante's exile from Florence.
6. The rebel angels, cast out of Heaven; see Luke 10.18 and Revelation 12.9.

Reader, judge for yourself, how each black word
    fell on my ears to sink into my heart:
    I lost hope of returning to the world.   93

"O my beloved Master, my Guide in peril,
    who time and time again have seen me safely
    along this way, and turned the power of evil,   96

stand by me now," I cried, "in my heart's fright.
    And if the dead forbid our journey to them,
    let us go back together toward the light."   99

My Guide then, in the greatness of his spirit:
    "Take heart. Nothing can take our passage from us
    when such a power has given warrant for it.   102

Wait here and feed your soul while I am gone
    on comfort and good hope; I will not leave you
    to wander in this underworld alone."   105

So the sweet Guide and Father leaves me here,
    and I stay on in doubt with yes and no
    dividing all my heart to hope and fear.   108

I could not hear my Lord's words, but the pack
    that gathered round him suddenly broke away
    howling and jostling and went pouring back,   111

slamming the towering gate hard in his face.
    That great Soul stood alone outside the wall.
    Then he came back; his pain showed in his pace. 114

His eyes were fixed upon the ground, his brow
    had sagged from its assurance. He sighed aloud:
    "Who has forbidden me the halls of sorrow?"   117

And to me he said: "You need not be cast down
    by my vexation, for whatever plot
    these fiends may lay against us, we will go on.   120

This insolence of theirs is nothing new:
    they showed it once at a less secret gate[7]
    that still stands open for all that they could do— 123

the same gate where you read the dead inscription;
    and through it at this moment a Great One comes.
    Already he has passed it and moves down   126

ledge by dark ledge. He is one who needs no guide,
and at his touch all gates must spring aside."

7. A reference to Christ's descent into Hell, after the crucifixion, for the "harrowing"; see above, 4.53.

Canto IX

The Heretics

At the Gate of Dis the Poets wait in dread. Virgil tries to hide his anxiety from Dante, but both realize that without Divine Aid they will surely be lost. To add to their terrors *Three Infernal Furies*, symbols of Eternal Remorse, appear on a nearby tower, from which they threaten the Poets and call for *Medusa* to come and change them to stone. Virgil at once commands Dante to turn and shut his eyes. To make doubly sure, Virgil himself places his hands over Dante's eyes, for there is an Evil upon which man must not look if he is to be saved.

But at the moment of greatest anxiety a storm shakes the dirty air of Hell and the sinners in the marsh begin to scatter like frightened Frogs. *The Heavenly Messenger* is approaching. He appears walking majestically through Hell, looking neither to right nor to left. With a touch he throws open the Gate of Dis while his words scatter the Rebellious Angels. Then he returns as he came.

The Poets now enter the gate unopposed and find themselves in the Sixth Circle. Here they find a countryside like a vast cemetery. Tombs of every size stretch out before them, each with its lid lying beside it, and each wrapped in flames. Cries of anguish sound endlessly from the entombed dead.

This is the torment of the *Heretics* of every cult. By Heretic, Dante means specifically those who did violence to God by denying immortality. Since they taught that the soul dies with the body, so their punishment is an eternal grave in the fiery morgue of God's wrath.

My face had paled to a mask of cowardice
    when I saw my Guide turn back. The sight of it
    the sooner brought the color back to his.   3

He stood apart like one who strains to hear
    what he cannot see, for the eye could not reach far
    across the vapors of that midnight air.   6

"Yet surely we were meant to pass these tombs,"
    he said aloud. "If not . . . so much was promised . . .
    Oh how time hangs and drags till our aid comes!"   9

I saw too well how the words with which he ended
    covered his start, and even perhaps I drew
    a worse conclusion from that than he intended.   12

"Tell me, Master, does anyone ever come
    from the first ledge, whose only punishment
    is hope cut off, into this dreary bottom?"[8]   15

I put this question to him, still in fear
    of what his broken speech might mean; and he:
    "Rarely do any of us enter here.   18

---

8. I.e., "Has anyone from Limbo ever descended into lower Hell before?"

Once before, it is true, I crossed through Hell
    conjured by cruel Erichtho[9] who recalled
    the spirits to their bodies. Her dark spell   21

forced me, newly stripped of my mortal part,
    to enter through this gate and summon out
    a spirit from Judaïca. Take heart,   24

that is the last depth and the darkest lair
    and the farthest from Heaven which encircles all,[1]
    and at that time I came back even from there.   27

The marsh from which the stinking gasses bubble
    lies all about this capital of sorrow
    whose gates we may not pass now without trouble."   30

All this and more he expounded; but the rest
    was lost on me, for suddenly my attention
    was drawn to the turret with the fiery crest   33

where all at once three hellish and inhuman
    Furies[2] sprang to view, bloodstained and wild.
    Their limbs and gestures hinted they were women.   36

Belts of greenest hydras wound and wound
    about their waists, and snakes and horned serpents
    grew from their heads like matted hair and bound   39

their horrid brows. My Master, who well knew
    the handmaids of the Queen of Woe,[3] cried: "Look:
    the terrible Erinyes of Hecate's crew.   42

That is Megaera to the left of the tower.
    Alecto is the one who raves on the right.
    Tisiphone stands between." And he said no more.   45

With their palms they beat their brows, with their nails they clawed
    their bleeding breasts. And such mad wails broke from them
    that I drew close to the Poet, overawed.   48

And all together screamed, looking down at me:
    "Call Medusa[4] that we may change him to stone!
    Too lightly we let Theseus[5] go free."   51

9. A legendary sorceress. The story of Virgil's prior descent into Hell is apparently Dante's own invention, although in the Middle Ages Virgil had the reputation of being a magician.
1. Judecca, the last subdivision of the last circle of Hell, where Judas is punished.
2. Three mythological monsters who represent the spirit of vengeance, known in Greek as the Erinyes (see below, line 42, and lines 43–45 for their individual names); they figure prominently in the *Aeneid* and other Latin poetry.
3. In classical mythology the queen of Hell is Hecate, or Proserpina, the wife of Pluto.
4. A mythological figure known as a Gorgon (line 56), so frightful in appearance that she turned those who gazed on her into stone.
5. Theseus, a legendary Athenian hero, descended into the underworld in order to try to rescue Proserpina, whom Pluto had abducted, and was rescued by Hercules.

"Turn your back and keep your eyes shut tight;
   for should the Gorgon come and you look at her,
   never again would you return to the light."   54

This was my Guide's command. And he turned me about
   himself, and would not trust my hands alone,
   but, with his placed on mine, held my eyes shut.   57

Men of sound intellect and probity,
   weigh with good understanding what lies hidden
   behind the veil of my strange allegory![6]   60

Suddenly there broke on the dirty swell
   of the dark marsh a squall of terrible sound
   that sent a tremor through both shores of Hell;   63

a sound as if two continents of air,
   one frigid and one scorching, clashed head on
   in a war of winds that stripped the forests bare,   66

ripped off whole boughs and blew them helter skelter
   along the range of dust it raised before it
   making the beasts and shepherds run for shelter.   69

The Master freed my eyes. "Now turn," he said,
   "and fix your nerve of vision on the foam
   there where the smoke is thickest and most acrid."   72

As frogs before the snake that hunts them down
   churn up their pond in flight, until the last
   squats on the bottom as if turned to stone—   75

so I saw more than a thousand ruined souls
   scatter away from one who crossed dry-shod
   the Stygian marsh into Hell's burning bowels.[7]   78

With his left hand he fanned away the dreary
   vapors of that sink as he approached;
   and only of that annoyance did he seem weary.   81

Clearly he was a Messenger from God's Throne,
   and I turned to my Guide; but he made me a sign
   that I should keep my silence and bow down.   84

Ah, what scorn breathed from that Angel-presence!
   He reached the gate of Dis and with a wand
   he waved it open, for there was no resistance.   87

6. Dante here reminds us of the need to interpret his poetry, although the lesson of this particular episode is far from self-evident.
7. This is an angel, although described in a way reminiscent of Mercury, the classical messenger of the gods. "Stygian": from the river Styx.

"Outcasts of Heaven, you twice-loathsome crew,"
    he cried upon that terrible sill of Hell,
    "how does this insolence still live in you?   90

Why do you set yourselves against that Throne
    whose Will none can deny, and which, times past,
    has added to your pain for each rebellion?   93

Why do you butt against Fate's ordinance?
    Your Cerberus, if you recall, still wears
    his throat and chin peeled for such arrogance."[8]   96

Then he turned back through the same filthy tide
    by which he had come. He did not speak to us,
    but went his way like one preoccupied   99

by other presences than those before him.
    And we moved toward the city, fearing nothing
    after his holy words. Straight through the dim   102

and open gate we entered unopposed.
    And I, eager to learn what new estate
    of Hell those burning fortress walls enclosed,   105

began to look about the very moment
    we were inside, and I saw on every hand
    a countryside of sorrow and new torment.   108

As at Arles where the Rhone sinks into stagnant marshes,
    as at Pola by the Quarnaro Gulf, whose waters
    close Italy and wash her farthest reaches,   111

the uneven tombs cover the even plain—
    such fields I saw here, spread in all directions,
    except that here the tombs were chests of pain:[9]   114

for, in a ring around each tomb, great fires
    raised every wall to a red heat. No smith
    works hotter iron in his forge. The biers   117

stood with their lids upraised, and from their pits
    an anguished moaning rose on the dead air
    from the desolation of tormented spirits.   120

And I: "Master, what shades are these who lie
    buried in these chests and fill the air
    with such a painful and unending cry?"   123

8. According to classical mythology, Hercules
dragged Cerberus into the daylight.
9. Arles, located on the river Rhone in southern
France, and Pola, located on the bay of Quarnero
in what is now Yugoslavia, were sites of Roman
cemeteries.

"These are the arch-heretics of all cults,
   with all their followers," he replied, "Far more
   than you would think lie stuffed into these vaults.   126

Like lies with like in every heresy,
   and the monuments are fired, some more, some less;
   to each depravity its own degree."   129

He turned then, and I followed through that night
between the wall and the torments, bearing right.

Canto X

CIRCLE SIX   *The Heretics*

As the Poets pass on, one of the damned hears Dante speaking, recognizes him as
a Tuscan, and calls to him from one of the fiery tombs. A moment later he
appears. He is *Farinata degli Uberti*, a great war-chief of the Tuscan Ghibellines.
The majesty and power of his bearing seem to diminish Hell itself. He asks
Dante's lineage and recognizes him as an enemy. They begin to talk politics, but
are interrupted by another shade, who rises from the same tomb.

This one is *Cavalcante dei Cavalcanti*, father of Guido Cavalcanti, a contemporary poet. If it is genius that leads Dante on his great journey, the shade
asks, why is Guido not with him? Can Dante presume to a greater genius than
Guido's? Dante replies that he comes this way only with the aid of powers Guido
has not sought. His reply is a classic example of many-leveled symbolism as well
as an overt criticism of a rival poet. The senior Cavalcanti mistakenly infers from
Dante's reply that Guido is dead, and swoons back into the flames.

Farinata, who has not deigned to notice his fellow-sinner, continues from the
exact point at which he had been interrupted. It is as if he refuses to recognize
the flames in which he is shrouded. He proceeds to prophesy Dante's banishment
from Florence, he defends his part in Florentine politics, and then, in answer to
Dante's question, he explains how it is that the damned can foresee the future
but have no knowledge of the present. He then names others who share his tomb,
and Dante takes his leave with considerable respect for his great enemy, pausing
only long enough to leave word for Cavalcanti that Guido is still alive.

We go by a secret path along the rim
   of the dark city, between the wall and the torments.
   My Master leads me and I follow him.   3

"Supreme Virtue, who through this impious land
   wheel me at will down these dark gyres,"[1] I said,
   "speak to me, for I wish to understand.   6

Tell me, Master, is it permitted to see
   the souls within these tombs? The lids are raised,
   and no one stands on guard." And he to me: 9

1. Circular turns.

"All shall be sealed forever on the day
   these souls return here from Jehosaphat
   with the bodies they have given once to clay.[2]   12

In this dark corner of the morgue of wrath
   lie Epicurus[3] and his followers,
   who make the soul share in the body's death.   15

And here you shall be granted presently
   not only your spoken wish, but that other as well,
   which you had thought perhaps to hide from me."[4]   18

And I: "Except to speak my thoughts in few
   and modest words, as I learned from your example,
   dear Guide, I do not hide my heart from you."   21

"O Tuscan, who go living through this place
   speaking so decorously, may it please you pause
   a moment on your way, for by the grace   24

of that high speech in which I hear your birth,
   I know you for a son of that noble city
   which perhaps I vexed too much in my time on earth."   27

These words broke without warning from inside
   one of the burning arks. Caught by surprise,
   I turned in fear and drew close to my Guide.   30

And he: "Turn around. What are you doing? Look there:
   it is Farinata[5] rising from the flames.
   From the waist up his shade will be made clear."   33

My eyes were fixed on him already. Erect,
   he rose above the flame, great chest, great brow;
   he seemed to hold all Hell in disrespect.   36

My Guide's prompt hands urged me among the dim
   and smoking sepulchres to that great figure,
   and he said to me: "Mind how you speak to him."   39

And when I stood alone at the foot of the tomb,
   the great soul stared almost contemptuously,
   before he asked: "Of what line do you come?"   42

2. According to the Bible, the Last Judgment when the dead will again receive their bodies will take place in the Valley of Jehosaphat; see Joel 3.2 and 3.12, and Matthew 25.31–32. 3. Greek philosopher (d. 270 B.C.E.) who rejected the idea of the immortality of the soul. 4. Presumably Dante's desire to see the Florentines who inhabit this circle. 5. Farinata degli Uberti (d. 1264), a leader of the Ghibelline faction in Florence.

Because I wished to obey, I did not hide
  anything from him: whereupon, as he listened,
  he raised his brows a little, then replied: 45

"Bitter enemies were they to me,
  to my fathers, and to my party, so that twice
  I sent them scattering from high Italy."   48

"If they were scattered, still from every part
  they formed again and returned both times," I answered,[6]
  "but yours have not yet wholly learned that art."[7]   51

At this another shade rose gradually,
  visible to the chin. It had raised itself,
  I think, upon its knees, and it looked around me[8]   54

as if it expected to find through that black air
  that blew about me, another traveler.
  And weeping when it found no other there,   57

turned back. "And if," it cried, "you travel through
  this dungeon of the blind by power of genius,
  where is my son? why is he not with you?"   60

And I to him: "Not by myself am I borne
  this terrible way. I am led by him who waits there,
  and whom perhaps your Guido held in scorn."[9]   63

For by his words and the manner of his torment
  I knew his name already, and could, therefore,
  answer both what he asked and what he meant.   66

Instantly he rose to his full height:
  "He *held*? What is it you say? Is he dead, then?
  Do his eyes no longer fill with that sweet light?"[1]   69

And when he saw that I delayed a bit
  in answering his question, he fell backwards
  into the flame, and rose no more from it.   72

6. Dante's family were Guelphs, who were driven out of Florence twice, in 1248 and 1260.
7. The Ghibellines were exiled in 1280, never to return.
8. This is Cavalcante de Cavalcanti, father of Dante's friend and fellow poet Guido (pp. 351–53); a Guelph, Guido married the daughter of Farinata in an unsuccessful attempt to heal the feud. In June 1300—after the fictional date of this conversation—Guido was exiled to a part of Italy where he caught the malaria from which he died in August. Dante was at that time a member of the governing body that made the decision to exile Guido.

9. The passage is ambiguous in the original Italian: as translated here, "him" refers to Virgil; but the Italian word can also be translated to refer to Beatrice, so that these two lines would then read: "that one waiting over there guides me through here, / to her whom your Guido perhaps held in scorn."
1. In line 63 Dante used a verbal form known in Italian as the remote past, which leads Cavalcante to believe, wrongly, that now, in April 1300, Guido is dead—although, ironically, in about four months he will indeed die, as Dante knew when he was writing this canto.

But that majestic spirit at whose call
  I had first paused there, did not change expression,
  nor so much as turn his face to watch him fall.   75

"And if," going on from his last words, he said,
  "men of my line have yet to learn that art,
  that burns me deeper than this flaming bed.   78

But the face of her who reigns in Hell[2] shall not
  be fifty times rekindled in its course
  before you learn what griefs attend that art.[3]   81

And as you hope to find the world again,
  tell me: why is that populace so savage
  in the edicts they pronounce against my strain?"   84

And I to him: "The havoc and the carnage
  that dyed the Arbia[4] red at Montaperti
  have caused these angry cries in our assemblage."   87

He sighed and shook his head. "I was not alone
  in that affair," he said, "nor certainly
  would I have joined the rest without good reason.   90

But I *was* alone at that time when every other
  consented to the death of Florence; I
  alone with open face defended her."   93

"Ah, so may your soul sometime have rest,"
  I begged him, "solve the riddle that pursues me
  through this dark place and leaves my mind perplexed: 96

you seem to see in advance all time's intent,
  if I have heard and understood correctly;
  but you seem to lack all knowledge of the present."   99

"We see asquint, like those whose twisted sight
  can make out only the far-off," he said,
  "for the King of All still grants us that much light.   102

When things draw near, or happen, we perceive
  nothing of them. Except what others bring us
  we have no news of those who are alive.   105

So may you understand that all we know
  will be dead forever from that day and hour
  when the portal of the Future is swung to."[5]   108

---

2. Proserpina, who is also the goddess of the moon.
3. Farinata here predicts Dante's own exile.
4. A stream near the hill of Montaperti, where the Ghibellines defeated the Guelphs in 1260.
5. The damned can see the future but not the present; after the Last Judgment, when human time is abolished, they will know nothing.

Then, as if stricken by regret, I said:[6]
   "Now, therefore, will you tell that fallen one
   who asked about his son, that he is not dead,   111

and that, if I did not reply more quickly,
   it was because my mind was occupied
   with this confusion you have solved for me."   114

And now my Guide was calling me. In haste,
   therefore, I begged that mighty shade to name
   the others who lay with him in that chest.   117

And he: "More than a thousand cram this tomb.
   The second Frederick[7] is here, and the Cardinal
   of the Ubaldini.[8] Of the rest let us be dumb."   120

And he disappeared without more said, and I
   turned back and made my way to the ancient Poet,
   pondering the words of the dark prophecy.[9]   123

He moved along, and then, when we had started,
   he turned and said to me, "What troubles you?
   Why do you look so vacant and downhearted?"   126

And I told him. And he replied: "Well may you bear
   those words in mind." Then, pausing, raised a finger:
   "Now pay attention to what I tell you here: 129

when finally you stand before the ray
   of that Sweet Lady[1] whose bright eye sees all,
   from her you will learn the turnings of your way."   132

So saying, he bore left, turning his back
   on the flaming walls, and we passed deeper yet
   into the city of pain, along a track   135

that plunged down like a scar into a sink
which sickened us already with its stink.

---

6. See note 1 to line 69 above.
7. Frederick II, Holy Roman Emperor from 1215 until his death in 1250; he reputedly denied that there was life after death.
8. Ottaviano degli Ubaldini (d. 1273), who is reputed to have said, "If I have a soul, I have lost it for the Ghibellines."
9. That is, Farinata's prediction of his exile.
1. Beatrice.

Canto XI

The Poets reach the inner edge of the *Sixth Circle* and find a great jumble of
rocks that had once been a cliff, but which has fallen into rubble as the result of
the great earthquake that shook Hell when Christ died. Below them lies the *Seventh Circle*, and so fetid is the air that arises from it that the Poets cower for
shelter behind a great tomb until their breaths can grow accustomed to the
stench.

Dante finds an inscription on the lid of the tomb labeling it as the place in Hell
of *Pope Anastasius*.

Virgil takes advantage of the delay to outline in detail *The Division of the Lower
Hell*, a theological discourse based on *The Ethics* and *The Physics* of Aristotle
with subsequent medieval interpretations. Virgil explains also why it is that the
Incontinent are not punished within the walls of Dis, and rather ingeniously sets
forth the reasons why Usury is an act of violence against Art, which is the child of
Nature and hence the Grandchild of God. (By "Art," Dante means the arts and
crafts by which man draws from nature, i.e., Industry.)

As he concludes he rises and urges Dante on. By means known only to Virgil,
he is aware of the motion of the stars and from them he sees that it is about two
hours before Sunrise of Holy Saturday.

We came to the edge of an enormous sink
   rimmed by a circle of great broken boulders.
   Here we found ghastlier gangs. And here the stink   3

thrown up by the abyss so overpowered us
   that we drew back, cowering behind the wall
   of one of the great tombs; and standing thus,   6

I saw an inscription in the stone, and read:
   "I guard Anastasius, once Pope,
   he whom Photinus led from the straight road."[2]   9

"Before we travel on to that blind pit
   we must delay until our sense grows used
   to its foul breath, and then we will not mind it,"   12

my Master said. And I then: "Let us find
   some compensation for the time of waiting."
   And he: "You shall see I have just that in mind.   15

My son,"[3] he began, "there are below this wall
   three smaller circles, each in its degree
   like those you are about to leave, and all   18

2. Pope Anastasius (d. 498) was thought,
wrongly, to have accepted a heresy promoted by
the 5th-century theologian Photinus that Christ
was not divine but only human.
3. Virgil now describes the three remaining
circles of Hell: the seventh, eighth, and ninth.

The seventh is for the violent and is divided
into three parts; the eighth and ninth are for the
fraudulent—the eighth for those who deceive
generally, the ninth for those who betray those
who love them. For the scheme of Hell as a
whole, see the diagram on p. 390.

are crammed with God's accurst. Accordingly,
   that you may understand their sins at sight,
   I will explain how each is prisoned, and why.   21

Malice is the sin most hated by God.
   And the aim of malice is to injure others
   whether by fraud or violence. But since fraud   24

is the vice of which man alone is capable,
   God loathes it most. Therefore, the fraudulent
   are placed below, and their torment is more painful.   27

The first below are the violent. But as violence
   sins in three persons, so is that circle formed
   of three descending rounds of crueler torments.   30

Against God, self, and neighbor is violence shown.
   Against their persons and their goods, I say,
   as you shall hear set forth with open reason.   33

Murder and mayhem are the violation
   of the person of one's neighbor: and of his goods;
   harassment, plunder, arson, and extortion.   36

Therefore, homicides, and those who strike
   in malice—destroyers and plunderers—all lie
   in that first round, and like suffers with like.   39

A man may lay violent hands upon his own
   person and substance; so in that second round
   eternally in vain repentance moan   42

the suicides and all who gamble away
   and waste the good and substance of their lives
   and weep in that sweet time when they should be gay.   45

Violence may be offered the deity
   in the heart that blasphemes and refuses Him
   and scorns the gifts of Nature, her beauty and bounty.   48

Therefore, the smallest round brands with its mark
   both Sodom and Cahors,[4] and all who rail
   at God and His commands in their hearts' dark.   51

Fraud, which is a canker to every conscience,
   may be practiced by a man on those who trust him,
   and on those who have reposed no confidence.   54

4. In the Middle Ages, the names of Sodom (see Genesis 18.20–19.29) and Cahors, a city in southern France, became synonymous with sodomites and usurers, respectively. Usury, forbidden by the medieval church, is charging interest on loans; the logic of this prohibition—based on the argument that usury, like sodomy, is unnatural—is explained in lines 97–111 below.

The latter mode seems only to deny
   the bond of love which all men have from Nature;
   therefore within the second circle lie   57

simoniacs,[5] sycophants, and hypocrites,
   falsifiers, thieves, and sorcerers,
   grafters, pimps, and all such filthy cheats.   60

The former mode of fraud not only denies
   the bond of Nature, but the special trust
   added by bonds of friendship or blood-ties.   63

Hence, at the center point of all creation,
   in the smallest circle, on which Dis[6] is founded,
   the traitors lie in endless expiation.   66

"Master," I said, "the clarity of your mind
   impresses all you touch; I see quite clearly
   the orders of this dark pit of the blind.   69

But tell me: those who lie in the swamp's bowels,
   those the wind blows about, those the rain beats,
   and those who meet and clash with such mad howls—   72

why are *they* not punished in the rust-red city
   if God's wrath be upon them? and if it is not,
   why must they grieve through all eternity?"   75

And he: "Why does your understanding stray
   so far from its own habit? or can it be
   your thoughts are turned along some other way?   78

Have you forgotten that your *Ethics*[7] states
   the three main dispositions of the soul
   that lead to those offenses Heaven hates—   81

incontinence, malice, and bestiality?
   and how incontinence offends God least
   and earns least blame from Justice and Charity?   84

Now if you weigh this doctrine and recall
   exactly who they are whose punishment
   lies in that upper Hell outside the wall,   87

you will understand at once why they are confined
   apart from these fierce wraiths, and why less anger
   beats down on them from the Eternal Mind."   90

5. Simony is the sin of selling a spiritual good, such as a church office or a sacrament like confession, for material gain. It is named after Simon Magus, a magician who sought to buy from the Apostles the power of baptism; Acts 8.9–24.
6. Dis is Satan, who is found at the bottom of Hell (see canto 34).
7. Aristotle's *Nicomachean Ethics*.

"O sun which clears all mists from troubled sight,
　　such joy attends your rising that I feel
　　as grateful to the dark as to the light.　　　　　　　93

Go back a little further," I said, "to where
　　you spoke of usury as an offense
　　against God's goodness. How is that made clear?"　　96

"Philosophy makes plain by many reasons,"
　　he answered me, "to those who heed her teachings,
　　how all of Nature,—her laws, her fruits, her seasons,—　99

springs from the Ultimate Intellect and Its art:[8]
　　and if you read your *Physics*[9] with due care,
　　you will note, not many pages from the start,　　　102

that Art strives after her by imitation,
　　as the disciple imitates the master;
　　Art, as it were, is the Grandchild of Creation.　　105

By this, recalling the Old Testament
　　near the beginning of Genesis,[1] you will see
　　that in the will of Providence, man was meant　　108

to labor and to prosper. But usurers,
　　by seeking their increase in other ways,
　　scorn Nature in herself and her followers.[2]　　　111

But come, for it is my wish now to go on:
　　the wheel turns and the Wain lies over Caurus,
　　the Fish are quivering low on the horizon,[3]　　　114

and there beyond us runs the road we go
down the dark scarp into the depths below."

Canto XII

CIRCLE SEVEN: ROUND ONE　　　　　　*The Violent against Neighbors*

The Poets begin the descent of the fallen rock wall, having first to evade the
Minotaur, who menaces them. Virgil tricks him and the Poets hurry by.

　　Below them they see the *River of Blood*, which marks the First Round of the
Seventh Circle as detailed in the previous Canto. Here are punished the *Violent
against Their Neighbors*, great war-makers, cruel tyrants, high-waymen—all who
shed the blood of their fellow men. As they wallowed in blood during their lives,

8. The laws of nature are determined by God.
9. Aristotle's *Physics*, which argues that human
art should follow natural laws.
1. In Genesis 3.17–19, God decrees that
because of the Fall people must toil, supporting themselves by the sweat of their brows.

2. The usurer makes money not from labor
but from money itself, which is an unnatural
and therefore illicit art.
3. The position of stars shows that it is now
about 4:00 a.m. on Holy Saturday.

so they are immersed in the boiling blood forever, each according to the degree of his guilt, while fierce Centaurs patrol the banks, ready to shoot with their arrows any sinner who raises himself out of the boiling blood beyond the limits permitted him. *Alexander the Great* is here, up to his lashes in the blood, and with him *Attila, the Scourge of God.* They are immersed in the deepest part of the river, which grows shallower as it circles to the other side of the ledge, then deepens again.

The Poets are challenged by the Centaurs, but Virgil wins a safe conduct from *Chiron*, their chief, who assigns *Nessus* to guide them and to bear them across the shallows of the boiling blood. Nessus carries them across at the point where it is only ankle deep and immediately leaves them and returns to his patrol.

The scene that opened from the edge of the pit
   was mountainous, and such a desolation
   that every eye would shun the sight of it: 3

a ruin like the Slides of Mark[4] near Trent
   on the bank of the Adige, the result of an earthquake
   or of some massive fault in the escarpment—   6

for, from the point on the peak where the mountain split
   to the plain below, the rock is so badly shattered
   a man at the top might make a rough stair of it.   9

Such was the passage down the steep and there
   at the very top, at the edge of the broken cleft,
   lay spread the Infamy of Crete,[5] the heir   12

of bestiality and the lecherous queen
   who hid in a wooden cow. And when he saw us,
   he gnawed his own flesh in a fit of spleen.   15

And my Master mocked: "How you do pump your breath!
   Do you think, perhaps, it is the Duke of Athens,
   who in the world above served up your death?[6]   18

Off with you, monster; this one does not come
   instructed by your sister,[7] but of himself
   to observe your punishment in the lost kingdom."   21

As a bull that breaks its chains just when the knife
   has struck its death-blow, cannot stand nor run
   but leaps from side to side with its last life—   24

4. A famous landslide on a mountain on the river Adige near Trent, a city in northern Italy.
5. The Minotaur, half man and half bull, was conceived when Pasiphaë, the wife of King Minos of Crete, had a wooden cow built within which she placed herself so as to have intercourse with a bull. The story of the Minotaur is told by Ovid, *Metamorphoses* 8.

6. Virgil is referring to Theseus, who killed the Minotaur in the labyrinth in which it was imprisoned.
7. Ariadne, daughter of Minos and Pasiphaë, who taught Theseus how to escape from the labyrinth within which the Minotaur was imprisoned.

so danced the Minotaur, and my shrewd Guide
cried out: "Run now! While he is blind with rage!
Into the pass, quick, and get over the side!"   27

So we went down across the shale and slate
of that ruined rock, which often slid and shifted
under me at the touch of living weight.   30

I moved on, deep in thought; and my Guide to me:
"You are wondering perhaps about this ruin
which is guarded by that beast upon whose fury   33

I played just now. I should tell you that when last
I came this dark way to the depths of Hell,
this rock had not yet felt the ruinous blast.   36

But certainly, if I am not mistaken,
it was just before the coming of Him who took
the souls from Limbo, that all Hell was shaken[8]   39

so that I thought the universe felt love
and all its elements moved toward harmony,
whereby the world of matter, as some believe,   42

has often plunged to chaos.[9] It was then,
that here and elsewhere in the pits of Hell,
the ancient rock was stricken and broke open.   45

But turn your eyes to the valley; there we shall find
the river of boiling blood in which are steeped
all who struck down their fellow men." Oh blind!   48

Oh ignorant, self-seeking cupidity[1]
which spurs us so in the short mortal life
and steeps us so through all eternity!   51

I saw an arching fosse[2] that was the bed
of a winding river circling through the plain
exactly as my Guide and Lord had said.   54

A file of Centaurs[3] galloped in the space
between the bank and the cliff, well armed with arrows,
riding as once on earth they rode to the chase.   57

---

8. Because of the earthquake that accompanied
Christ's death, which occurred just before his
descent to Hell and the "harrowing," Christ's
rescue of the virtuous Israelites from the First
Circle (see above, canto 4.52–63).
9. A reference to a theory of the Greek philosopher Empedocles that the universe is held
together by alternating forces of love and hate,
and that if either one predominates the result
is chaos. This classical theory is not consistent
with the Christian belief that the universe is
created and organized by God's love.
1. Desire for wealth.
2. Ditch.
3. Mythological creatures that are half man
and half horse.

And seeing us descend, that straggling band
   halted, and three of them moved out toward us,
   their long bows and their shafts already in hand.   60

And one of them cried out while still below:
   "To what pain are you sent down that dark coast?
   Answer from where you stand, or I draw the bow!"   63

"Chiron[4] is standing there hard by your side;
   our answer will be to him. This wrath of yours
   was always your own worst fate," my Guide replied.   66

And to me he said: "That is Nessus,[5] who died in the wood
   for insulting Dejanira. At his death
   he plotted his revenge in his own blood.   69

The one in the middle staring at his chest
   is the mighty Chiron, he who nursed Achilles:
   the other is Pholus,[6] fiercer than all the rest.   72

They run by that stream in thousands, snapping their bows
   at any wraith who dares to raise himself
   out of the blood more than his guilt allows."   75

We drew near those swift beasts. In a thoughtful pause
   Chiron drew an arrow, and with its notch
   he pushed his great beard back along his jaws.   78

And when he had thus uncovered the huge pouches
   of his lips, he said to his fellows: "Have you noticed
   how the one who walks behind moves what he touches?   81

That is not how the dead go." My good Guide,
   already standing by the monstrous breast
   in which the two mixed natures joined,[7] replied: 84

"It is true he lives; in his necessity
   I alone must lead him through this valley.
   Fate brings him here, not curiosity.   87

From singing Alleluia the sublime
   spirit who sends me came.[8] He is no bandit.
   Nor am I one who ever stooped to crime.[9]   90

---

4. A centaur renowned for wisdom who educated many legendary Greek heroes, including Achilles.
5. Nessus fell in love with Deianira, wife of Hercules, who killed him; while dying, Nessus poisoned with his own blood a robe that killed Hercules when he put it on.
6. Another centaur, killed by Hercules, whose rage is typical of these creatures.
7. When standing, Virgil reaches to the centaur's chest, where his human and animal natures join.
8. Beatrice.
9. Virgil is answering the question of lines 62–63, which assumes that they are condemned spirits.

But in the name of the Power by which I go
    this sunken way across the floor of Hell,
    assign us one of your troop whom we may follow,   93

that he may guide us to the ford, and there
    carry across on his back the one I lead,
    for he is not a spirit to move through air."   96

Chiron turned his head on his right breast
    and said to Nessus: "Go with them, and guide them,
    and turn back any others that would contest   99

their passage." So we moved beside our guide
    along the bank of the scalding purple river[1]
    in which the shrieking wraiths were boiled and dyed.   102

Some stood up to their lashes in that torrent,
    and as we passed them the huge Centaur said:
    "These were the kings of bloodshed and despoilment.   105

Here they pay for their ferocity.
    Here is Alexander. And Dionysius,
    who brought long years of grief to Sicily.[2]   108

That brow you see with the hair as black as night
    is Azzolino:[3] and that beside him, the blonde,
    is Opizzo da Esti, who had his mortal light   111

blown out by his own stepson."[4] I turned then
    to speak to the Poet but he raised a hand:
    "Let him be the teacher now, and I will listen."   114

Further on, the Centaur stopped beside
    a group of spirits steeped as far as the throat
    in the race of boiling blood, and there our guide   117

pointed out a sinner who stood alone:
    "That one before God's altar pierced a heart
    still honored on the Thames."[5] And he passed on.   120

We came in sight of some who were allowed
    to raise the head and all the chest from the river,
    and I recognized many there. Thus, as we followed   123

1. A river of blood, which we later learn is named Phlegethon (see 14.110).
2. Alexander the Great (d. 323 B.C.E.) and Dionysius of Syracuse in Sicily (d. 367 B.C.E.).
3. Azzolino III (d. 1259), a brutal ruler in northern Italy.
4. Opizzo II d'Este (d. 1293), another cruel northern Italian tyrant, reputedly murdered by his son, here called "stepson" either because of the unnaturalness of the crime or because Opizzo suspected his wife of adultery.
5. Guy de Montfort (d. 1298), who killed his cousin Prince Henry of Cornwall during a church service ("before God's altar") in the Italian city of Viterbo. Nessus's image of the blood dripping from the victim's heart indicates his focus on the fact that the murder is still unavenged. "Race": flow; stream.

along the stream of blood, its level fell
    until it cooked no more than the feet of the damned.
    And here we crossed the ford to deeper Hell.   126

"Just as you see the boiling stream grow shallow
    along this side," the Centaur said to us
    when we stood on the other bank, "I would have you know   129

that on the other, the bottom sinks anew
    more and more, until it comes again
    full circle to the place where the tyrants stew.   132

It is there that Holy Justice spends its wrath
    on Sextus and Pyrrhus[6] through eternity,
    and on Attila,[7] who was a scourge on earth: 135

and everlastingly milks out the tears
    of Rinier da Corneto and Rinier Pazzo,[8]
    those two assassins who for many years   138

stalked the highways, bloody and abhorred."
And with that he started back across the ford.

Canto XIII

CIRCLE SEVEN: ROUND TWO   *The Violent against Themselves*

Nessus carries the Poets across the river of boiling blood and leaves them in the Second Round of the Seventh Circle, *The Wood of the Suicides*. Here are punished those who destroyed their own lives and those who destroyed their substance.

The souls of the Suicides are encased in thorny trees whose leaves are eaten by the odious *Harpies*, the overseers of these damned. When the Harpies feed upon them, damaging their leaves and limbs, the wound bleeds. Only as long as the blood flows are the souls of the trees able to speak. Thus, they who destroyed their own bodies are denied a human form; and just as the supreme expression of their lives was self-destruction, so they are permitted to speak only through that which tears and destroys them. Only through their own blood do they find voice. And to add one more dimension to the symbolism, it is the Harpies—defilers of all they touch—who give them their eternally recurring wounds.

The Poets pause before one tree and speak with the soul of *Pier delle Vigna*. In the same wood they see *Jacomo da Sant' Andrea*, and *Lano da Siena*, two famous *Squanderers* and *Destroyers of Goods* pursued by a pack of savage hounds. The hounds overtake *Sant 'Andrea*, tear him to pieces and go off carrying his limbs in

---

6. Sextus, the son of the Roman consul Pompey, became a pirate (1st century B.C.E.); Pyrrhus, Achilles' son, killed the aged Priam at the fall of Troy, as described in *Aeneid* 2.595–704.
7. Attila the Hun (d. 453), who led repeated attacks against the Eastern and Western Roman Empires.
8. Both Riniers were bandits of Dante's day; they are now weeping from pain, whereas in life they never wept for their sins.

their teeth, a self-evident symbolic retribution for the violence with which these sinners destroyed their substance in the world. After this scene of horror, Dante speaks to an *Unknown Florentine Suicide* whose soul is inside the bush which was torn by the hound pack when it leaped upon Sant' Andrea.

Nessus had not yet reached the other shore
    when we moved on into a pathless wood
    that twisted upward from Hell's broken floor.   3

Its foliage was not verdant, but nearly black.
    The unhealthy branches, gnarled and warped and tangled,
    bore poison thorns instead of fruit. The track   6

of those wild beasts that shun the open spaces
    men till between Cecina and Corneto[9]
    runs through no rougher nor more tangled places.   9

Here nest the odious Harpies[1] of whom my Master
    wrote how they drove Aeneas and his companions
    from the Strophades with prophecies of disaster.   12

Their wings are wide, their feet clawed, their huge bellies
    covered with feathers, their necks and faces human.
    They croak eternally in the unnatural trees.   15

"Before going on, I would have you understand,"
    my Guide began, "we are in the second round
    and shall be till we reach the burning sand.[2]   18

Therefore look carefully and you will see
    things in this wood, which, if I told them to you
    would shake the confidence you have placed in me."   21

I heard cries of lamentation rise and spill
    on every hand, but saw no souls in pain
    in all that waste; and, puzzled, I stood still.   24

I think perhaps he thought that I was thinking
    those cries rose from among the twisted roots
    through which the spirits of the damned were slinking   27

to hide from us. Therefore my Master said:
    "If you break off a twig, what you will learn
    will drive what you are thinking from your head."[3]   30

---

9. Two towns that mark the limits of the Maremma, a desolate area in Tuscany.
1. Birds with the faces of women and clawed hands; in *Aeneid* 3 they drive the wandering Trojans from their refuge in the Strophades Islands and predict their future suffering.

2. The "burning sand" is in the third ring or "round" of the seventh circle, described in the next canto.
3. I.e., "Your thoughts that the moans come from people concealed among the trees will cease or 'break off.'"

Puzzled, I raised my hand a bit and slowly
    broke off a branchlet from an enormous thorn:
    and the great trunk of it cried: "Why do you break me?"[4]   33

And after blood had darkened all the bowl
    of the wound, it cried again: "Why do you tear me?
    Is there no pity left in any soul?   36

Men we were, and now we are changed to sticks;
    well might your hand have been more merciful
    were we no more than souls of lice and ticks."   39

As a green branch with one end all aflame
    will hiss and sputter sap out of the other
    as the air escapes—so from that trunk there came   42

words and blood together, gout by gout.
    Startled, I dropped the branch that I was holding
    and stood transfixed by fear, half turned about   45

to my Master, who replied: "O wounded soul,
    could he have believed before what he has seen
    in my verses only, you would yet be whole,[5]   48

for his hand would never have been raised against you.
    But knowing this truth could never be believed
    till it was seen, I urged him on to do   51

what grieves me now; and I beg to know your name,
    that to make you some amends in the sweet world
    when he returns, he may refresh your fame."   54

And the trunk: "So sweet those words to me that I
    cannot be still, and may it not annoy you
    if I seem somewhat lengthy in reply.[6]   57

I am he who held both keys to Frederick's heart,
    locking, unlocking with so deft a touch
    that scarce another soul had any part   60

---

4. This episode derives from *Aeneid* 3, where Aeneas and his Trojan companions, stopping in their search for a new home, discover Polydorus transformed into a bush. Sent out by Priam during the war to solicit aid from the Thracians, Polydorus had been murdered by his hosts, and the javelins with which his body had been pierced had grown into the bush from which Aeneas breaks off a branch that bleeds. See also Ovid, *Metamorphoses* 2.
5. I.e., had Dante been able to believe the story of Polydorus recounted in the *Aeneid*.
6. This is the soul of Pier della Vigna (ca. 1190–1249), who had risen to become minister to the Emperor Frederick II (on whom see n. 7 on 10.119); Frederick is referred to here as "Caesar" and "Augustus" because he sought to imitate the imperial court of Rome. Pier's name means "Peter of the Vine," probably because his father had been a simple worker in a vineyard.

in his most secret thoughts. Through every strife
    I was so faithful to my glorious office
    that for it I gave up both sleep and life.   63

That harlot, Envy, who on Caesar's face
    keeps fixed forever her adulterous stare,
    the common plague and vice of court and palace,   66

inflamed all minds against me. These inflamed
    so inflamed him that all my happy honors
    were changed to mourning. Then, unjustly blamed,   69

my soul, in scorn, and thinking to be free
    of scorn in death, made me at last, though just,
    unjust to myself.[7] By the new roots of this tree   72

I swear to you that never in word or spirit
    did I break faith to my lord and emperor
    who was so worthy of honor in his merit.   75

If either of you return to the world, speak for me,
    to vindicate in the memory of men
    one who lies prostrate from the blows of Envy."   78

The Poet stood. Then turned. "Since he is silent,"
    he said to me, "do not you waste this hour,
    if you wish to ask about his life or torment."   81

And I replied: "Question him for my part,
    on whatever you think I would do well to hear;
    I could not, such compassion chokes my heart."   84

The Poet began again: "That this man may
    with all his heart do for you what your words
    entreat him to, imprisoned spirit, I pray,   87

tell us how the soul is bound and bent
    into these knots, and whether any ever
    frees itself from such imprisonment."   90

At that the trunk blew powerfully, and then
    the wind became a voice that spoke these words:
    "Briefly is the answer given: when   93

out of the flesh from which it tore itself,
    the violent spirit comes to punishment,
    Minos assigns it to the seventh shelf.   96

7. I.e., "I unjustly committed suicide even though I was innocent of the accusations brought against me."

It falls into the wood, and landing there,
 wherever fortune flings it, it strikes root,
 and there it sprouts, lusty as any tare, 99

shoots up a sapling, and becomes a tree.
 The Harpies, feeding on its leaves then, give it
 pain and pain's outlet simultaneously. 102

Like the rest, we shall go for our husks on Judgment Day,
 but not that we may wear them, for it is not just
 that a man be given what he throws away. 105

Here shall we drag them and in this mournful glade
 our bodies will dangle to the end of time,
 each on the thorns of its tormented shade." 108

We waited by the trunk, but it said no more;
 and waiting, we were startled by a noise
 that grew through all the wood. Just such a roar 111

and trembling as one feels when the boar and chase
 approach his stand, the beasts and branches crashing
 and clashing in the heat of the fierce race. 114

And there on the left, running so violently
 they broke off every twig in the dark wood,
 two torn and naked wraiths went plunging by me.[8] 117

The leader cried, "Come now, O Death! Come now!"
 And the other, seeing that he was outrun,
 cried out: "Your legs were not so ready, Lano, 120

in the jousts at the Toppo."[9] And suddenly in his rush,
 perhaps because his breath was failing him,
 he hid himself inside a thorny bush 123

and cowered among its leaves. Then at his back,
 the wood leaped with black bitches, swift as greyhounds
 escaping from their leash, and all the pack 126

sprang on him; with their fangs they opened him
 and tore him savagely, and then withdrew,
 carrying his body with them, limb by limb. 129

Then, taking me by the hand across the wood,
 my Master led me toward the bush. Lamenting,
 all its fractures blew out words and blood:[1] 132

8. Lano of Siena and Giacomo da Sant' Andrea of Padua, two Italians of a generation earlier than Dante's; both were reputed to be spendthrifts.

9. Lano was killed at a battle on the river Toppo in 1287.

1. Nothing is known about this suicide, who hanged himself from his own house.

"O Jacomo da Sant' Andrea!" it said,
  "what have you gained in making me your screen?
  What part had I in the foul life you led?"   135

And when my Master had drawn up to it
  he said: "Who were you, who through all your wounds
  blow out your blood with your lament, sad spirit?"   138

And he to us: "You who have come to see
  how the outrageous mangling of these hounds
  has torn my boughs and stripped my leaves from me,   141

O heap them round my ruin! I was born
  in the city that tore down Mars and raised the Baptist.[2]
  On that account the God of War has sworn   144

her sorrow shall not end. And were it not
  that something of his image still survives
  on the bridge across the Arno,[3] some have thought   147

those citizens who of their love and pain
  afterwards rebuilt it from the ashes
  left by Attila, would have worked in vain.[4]   150

I am one who has no tale to tell:
  I made myself a gibbet of my own lintel."

Canto XIV

CIRCLE SEVEN: ROUND THREE   *The Violent against God, Nature, and Art*

Dante, in pity, restores the torn leaves to the soul of his countryman and the
Poets move on to the next round, a great *Plain of Burning Sand* upon which
there descends an eternal slow *Rain of Fire*. Here, scorched by fire from above
and below, are three classes of sinners suffering differing degrees of exposure to
the fire. The *Blasphemers* (The Violent against God) are stretched supine upon
the sand, the *Sodomites* (The Violent against Nature) run in endless circles, and the
Usurers (The Violent against Art, which is the Grandchild of God) huddle on the
sands.

The Poets find *Capaneus* stretched out on the sands, the chief sinner of that
place. He is still blaspheming God. They continue along the edge of the Wood of
the Suicides and come to a blood-red rill which flows boiling from the Wood and
crosses the burning plain. Virgil explains the miraculous power of its waters and
discourses on the *Old Man of Crete* and the origin of all the rivers of Hell.

The symbolism of the burning plain is obviously centered in sterility (the desert
image) and wrath (the fire image). Blasphemy, sodomy, and usury are all unnatural

---

2. Florence; when the Florentines converted
to Christianity, John the Baptist replaced Mars
as patron of the city, and therefore Mars would
forever persecute the city with civil war.

3. The river that runs through Florence.
4. According to legend, Attila the Hun destroyed
Florence when he invaded Italy in the 5th
century.

and sterile actions: thus the unbearing desert is the eternity of these sinners; and thus the rain, which in nature should be fertile and cool, descends as fire. Capaneus, moreover, is subjected not only to the wrath of nature (the sands below) and the wrath of God (the fire from above), but is tortured most by his own inner violence, which is the root of blasphemy.

Love of that land that was our common source
   moved me to tears; I gathered up the leaves
   and gave them back. He was already hoarse.   3

We came to the edge of the forest where one goes
   from the second round to the third,[5] and there we saw
   what fearful arts the hand of Justice knows.   6

To make these new things wholly clear, I say
   we came to a plain whose soil repels all roots.
   The wood of misery rings it the same way   9

the wood itself is ringed by the red fosse.
   We paused at its edge: the ground was burning sand,
   just such a waste as Cato[6] marched across.   12

O endless wrath of God: how utterly
   thou shouldst become a terror to all men
   who read the frightful truths revealed to me!   15

Enormous herds of naked souls I saw,
   lamenting till their eyes were burned of tears;
   they seemed condemned by an unequal law,   18

for some were stretched supine upon the ground,
   some squatted with their arms about themselves,
   and others without pause roamed round and round.   21

Most numerous were those that roamed the plain.
   Far fewer were the souls stretched on the sand,
   but moved to louder cries by greater pain.   24

And over all that sand on which they lay
   or crouched or roamed, great flakes of flame fell slowly
   as snow falls in the Alps on a windless day.   27

Like those Alexander met in the hot regions
   of India, flames raining from the sky
   to fall still unextinguished on his legions: 30

5. The third ring of the seventh circle is surrounded by the second ring of the woods through which Dante has just passed and the first ring of the river of blood described in canto 12.
6. Roman general (1st century B.C.E.) who campaigned in Libya.

whereat he formed his ranks, and at their head
  set the example, trampling the hot ground
  for fear the tongues of fire might join and spread—[7]   33

just so in Hell descended the long rain
  upon the damned, kindling the sand like tinder
  under a flint and steel, doubling the pain.   36

In a never-ending fit upon those sands,
  the arms of the damned twitched all about their bodies,
  now here, now there, brushing away the brands.   39

"Poet," I said, "master of every dread
  we have encountered, other than those fiends
  who sallied from the last gate of the dead—   42

who is that wraith who lies along the rim
  and sets his face against the fire in scorn,
  so that the rain seems not to mellow him?"[8]   45

And he himself, hearing what I had said
  to my Guide and Lord concerning him, replied:
  "What I was living, the same am I now, dead.   48

Though Jupiter wear out his sooty smith[9]
  from whom on my last day he snatched in anger
  the jagged thunderbolt he pierced me with;   51

though he wear out the others one by one
  who labor at the forge at Mongibello[1]
  crying again 'Help! Help! Help me, good Vulcan!'   54

as he did at Phlegra;[2] and hurl down endlessly
  with all the power of Heaven in his arm,
  small satisfaction would he win from me."   57

At this my Guide spoke with such vehemence
  as I had not heard from him in all of Hell:
  "O Capaneus, by your insolence   60

you are made to suffer as much fire inside
  as falls upon you. Only your own rage
  could be fit torment for your sullen pride."   63

7. Dante is here following an account by the philosopher Albertus Magnus (d. 1280) of a legendary adventure that befell Alexander the Great in his conquest of India.
8. Capaneus, one of the seven legendary kings who besieged Thebes as described in the *Thebaid* by Statius (d. 95 C.E.). He was struck with a thunderbolt when he boasted that not even Jupiter could stop him.
9. Vulcan, Roman god of fire, volcanoes, and the forge; equivalent of Greek Hephaestus.
1. The Sicilian name for Mt. Etna, thought to be Vulcan's furnace; "the others" are the Cyclopes, Vulcan's helpers.
2. Jove defeated the rebellious Titans at the battle of Phlegra (see 31.42).

Then he turned to me more gently. "That," he said,
  "was one of the Seven who laid siege to Thebes.
  Living, he scorned God, and among the dead 66

he scorns Him yet. He thinks he may detest
  God's power too easily, but as I told him,
  his slobber is a fit badge for his breast. 69

Now follow me; and mind for your own good
  you do not step upon the burning sand,
  but keep well back along the edge of the wood." 72

We walked in silence then till we reached a rill
  that gushes from the wood; it ran so red
  the memory sends a shudder through me still. 75

As from the Bulicame[3] springs the stream
  the sinful women keep to their own use;
  so down the sand the rill flowed out in steam. 78

The bed and both its banks were petrified,
  as were its margins; thus I knew at once
  our passage through the sand lay by its side. 81

"Among all other wonders I have shown you
  since we came through the gate denied to none,
  nothing your eyes have seen is equal to 84

the marvel of the rill by which we stand,
  for it stifles all the flames above its course
  as it flows out across the burning sand." 87

So spoke my Guide across the flickering light,
  and I begged him to bestow on me the food
  for which he had given me the appetite. 90

"In the middle of the sea, and gone to waste,
  there lies a country known as Crete," he said,
  "under whose king the ancient world was chaste.[4] 93

Once Rhea chose it as the secret crypt
  and cradle of her son; and better to hide him,
  her Corybantes raised a din when he wept.[5] 96

3. A hot sulphurous spring that supplied water to brothels in an area of northern Italy.
4. Saturn, mythical king of Crete during the Golden Age.
5. Jupiter was hidden by his mother, Rhea, from his father, Saturn, who tried to devour all his children to thwart a prophecy that he would be dethroned by one of them. So that Saturn would not hear the infant's cries, Rhea had her servants, the Corybantes (or Bacchantes), cry out and beat their shields with their swords.

An ancient giant stands in the mountain's core.
    He keeps his shoulder turned toward Damietta,[6]
    and looks toward Rome as if it were his mirror.   99

His head is made of gold; of silverwork
    his breast and both his arms, of polished brass
    the rest of his great torso to the fork.   102

He is of chosen iron from there down,
    except that his right foot is terra cotta;
    it is this foot he rests more weight upon.[7]   105

Every part except the gold is split
    by a great fissure from which endless tears
    drip down and hollow out the mountain's pit.   108

Their course sinks to this pit from stone to stone,
    becoming Acheron, Phlegethon, and Styx.
    Then by this narrow sluice they hurtle down   111

to the end of all descent, and disappear
    into Cocytus.[8] You shall see what sink that is
    with your own eyes. I pass it in silence here."   114

And I to him: "But if these waters flow
    from the world above, why is this rill met only
    along this shelf?" And he to me: "You know   117

the place is round, and though you have come deep
    into the valley through the many circles,
    always bearing left along the steep,   120

you have not traveled any circle through
    its total round; hence when new things appear
    from time to time, that hardly should surprise you."   123

And I: "Where shall we find Phlegethon's course?
    And Lethe's?[9] One you omit, and of the other
    you only say the tear-flood is its source."   126

"In all you ask of me you please me truly,"
    he answered, "but the red and boiling water
    should answer the first question you put to me,[1]   129

6. A city in Egypt. The Old Man has been interpreted as an emblem of the decline of human
history.
7. The four metals and the clay represent the
degeneration of history; Dante took this image
from Daniel 2.31–35.

8. The frozen lake at the bottom of Hell: see
32.22–30 and 34.52.
9. Lethe, the river of forgetting, is crossed when
Dante passes into the Earthly Paradise on the
top of Mount Purgatory.
1. See note 9 to 12.101.

and you shall stand by Lethe, but far hence:
   there, where the spirits go to wash themselves
   when their guilt has been removed by penitence."   132

And then he said: "Now it is time to quit
   this edge of shade: follow close after me
   along the rill, and do not stray from it;   135

for the unburning margins form a lane,
and by them we may cross the burning plain."

Canto XV

                The Violent against Nature

Protected by the marvelous powers of the boiling rill, the Poets walk along its
banks across the burning plain. The *Wood of the Suicides* is behind them; the
Great Cliff at whose foot lies the *Eighth Circle* is before them.

They pass one of the roving bands of *Sodomites*. One of the sinners stops
Dante, and with great difficulty the Poet recognizes him under his baked features
as *Ser Brunetto Latino*. This is a reunion with a dearly loved man and writer, one
who had considerably influenced Dante's own development, and Dante addresses
him with great and sorrowful affection, paying him the highest tribute offered to
any sinner in the *Inferno. Brunetto* prophesies Dante's sufferings at the hands of
the Florentines, gives an account of the souls that move with him through the
fire, and finally, under Divine Compulsion, races off across the plain.

We go by one of the stone margins now
   and the steam of the rivulet makes a shade above it,
   guarding the stream and banks from the flaming snow.   3

As the Flemings in the lowland between Bruges
   and Wissant,[2] under constant threat of the sea,
erect their great dikes to hold back the deluge;   6

as the Paduans along the shores of the Brent[3]
   build levees to protect their towns and castles
   Jest Chiarentana drown in the spring torrent—   9

to the same plan, though not so wide nor high,
   did the engineer, whoever he may have been,
   design the margin we were crossing by.   12

Already we were so far from the wood
   that even had I turned to look at it,
   I could not have made it out from where I stood,   15

2. Cities that, for Dante, mark the two ends of
the dike that protects Flanders from the sea.
3. A river that flows through Padua, fed by the
melting snows in the mountains of the province
of Chiarentana (modern Carinthia in Austria).

when a company of shades came into sight
  walking beside the bank. They stared at us
  as men at evening by the new moon's light   18

stare at one another when they pass by
  on a dark road, pointing their eyebrows toward us
  as an old tailor squints at his needle's eye.   21

Stared at so closely by that ghostly crew,
  I was recognized by one who seized the hem
  of my skirt and said: "Wonder of wonders! You?"   24

And I, when he stretched out his arm to me,
  searched his baked features closely, till at last
  I traced his image from my memory   27

in spite of the burnt crust, and bending near
  to put my face closer to his, at last
  I answered: "Ser Brunetto,[4] are you here?"   30

"O my son! may it not displease you," he cried,
  "if Brunetto Latino leave his company
  and turn and walk a little by your side."   33

And I to him: "With all my soul I ask it.
  Or let us sit together, if it please him
  who is my Guide and leads me through this pit."   36

"My son!" he said, "whoever of this train
  pauses a moment, must lie a hundred years
  forbidden to brush off the burning rain.   39

Therefore, go on; I will walk at your hem,
  and then rejoin my company, which goes
  mourning eternal loss in eternal flame."   42

I did not dare descend to his own level
  but kept my head inclined, as one who walks
  in reverence meditating good and evil.   45

"What brings you here before your own last day?
  What fortune or what destiny?" he began.
  "And who is he that leads you this dark way?"   48

"Up there in the happy life I went astray
  in a valley," I replied, "before I had reached
  the fullness of my years. Only yesterday   51

4. Brunetto Latini (ca. 1220–1294), active in Florentine politics and the author of—among other works—two books: a prose encyclopedia in French called the *Trésor*, which emphasizes the qualities needed for civic duty, and a shorter allegorical poem in Italian called the *Tesoretto*, which combines autobiography with philosophy.

at dawn I turned from it. This spirit showed
    himself to me as I was turning back,
    and guides me home again along this road."   54

And he: "Follow your star, for if in all
    of the sweet life I saw one truth shine clearly,
    you cannot miss your glorious arrival.   57

And had I lived to do what I meant to do,
    I would have cheered and seconded your work,
    observing Heaven so well disposed toward you.   60

But that ungrateful and malignant stock
    that came down from Fiesole[5] of old
    and still smacks of the mountain and the rock,   63

for your good works will be your enemy.
    And there is cause: the sweet fig is not meant
    to bear its fruit beside the bitter sorb-tree.[6]   66

Even the old adage calls them blind,
    an envious, proud, and avaricious people:
    see that you root their customs from your mind.   69

It is written in your stars, and will come to pass,
    that your honours shall make both sides hunger for you:
    but the goat shall never reach to crop that grass.[7]   72

Let the beasts of Fiesole devour their get
    like sows, but never let them touch the plant,
    if among their rankness any springs up yet,   75

in which is born again the holy seed
    of the Romans who remained among their rabble
    when Florence made a new nest for their greed."   78

"Ah, had I all my wish," I answered then,
    "you would not yet be banished from the world
    in which you were a radiance among men,   81

for that sweet image, gentle and paternal,
    you were to me in the world when hour by hour
    you taught me how man makes himself eternal,[8]   84

---

5. A hill town north of Florence whose rustic inhabitants were supposed to have joined with noble Romans in the founding of Florence, creating an unstable mixture.
6. The "bitter sorb-tree" are the Florentines descended from Fiesole; the "sweet fig" is Brunetto's term for the aristocratic Dante.

7. "I.e., Either both parties will ask you to join them or both parties will want to devour you—but keep yourself apart."
8. In the *Trésor*, Brunetto says that earthly glory gives man a second life through an enduring reputation.

lives in my mind, and now strikes to my heart;
  and while I live, the gratitude I owe it
  will speak to men out of my life and art.   87

What you have told me of my course, I write
  by another text I save to show a Lady[9]
  who will judge these matters, if I reach her height.   90

This much I would have you know: so long, I say,
  as nothing in my conscience troubles me
  I am prepared for Fortune, come what may.   93

Twice already in the eternal shade
  I have heard this prophecy; but let Fortune turn
  her wheel as she please, and the countryman his spade."[1]   96

My guiding spirit paused at my last word
  and, turning right about, stood eye to eye
  to say to me: "Well heeded is well heard."   99

But I did not reply to him, going on
  with Ser Brunetto to ask him who was with him
  in the hot sands, the best born and best known.   102

And he to me: "Of some who share this walk
  it is good to know; of the rest let us say nothing,
  for the time would be too short for so much talk.   105

In brief, we all were clerks and men of worth,
  great men of letters, scholars of renown;
  all by the one same crime defiled on earth.[2]   108

Priscian moves there along the wearisome
  sad way, and Francesco d'Accorso,[3] and also there,
  if you had any longing for such scum,   111

you might have seen that one the Servant of Servants
  sent from the Arno to the Bacchiglione
  where he left his unnatural organ wrapped in cerements.[4]   114

I would say more, but there across the sand
  a new smoke rises and new people come,
  and I must run to be with my own band.   117

---

9. Beatrice.
1. The traditional image of Fortune and her wheel is here compared to the rustic image of the peasant turning the soil with his hoe.
2. Sodomy, condemned in the Middle Ages as unnatural.
3. Priscian was a Greek grammarian (6th century C.E.); Francesco d'Accorso a Florentine law professor (d. 1293).
4. Andrea de' Mozzi, bishop of Florence (1287–1295), transferred by Pope Boniface (designated here by an official title for the pope, "the Servant of [Christ's] Servants") from Florence to Vicenza; the Arno runs through Florence, the Bacchiglione through Vicenza.

Remember my *Treasure*, in which I still live on:
  I ask no more." He turned then, and he seemed,
  across that plain, like one of those who run   120

for the green cloth[5] at Verona; and of those,
  more like the one who wins, than those who lose.

Canto XVI

The Poets arrive within hearing of the waterfall that plunges over the *Great Cliff*
into the *Eighth Circle*. The sound is still a distant throbbing when three wraiths,
recognizing Dante's Florentine dress, detach themselves from their band and
come running toward him. They are *Jacopo Rusticucci*, *Guido Cuerra*, and *Teg-
ghiaío Aldobrandi*, all of them Florentines whose policies and personalities Dante
admired. Rusticucci and Tegghiaio have already been mentioned in a highly com-
plimentary way in Dante's talk with Ciacco (canto VI).

The sinners ask for news of Florence, and Dante replies with a passionate lament
for her present degradation. The three wraiths return to their band and the Poets
continue to the top of the falls. Here, at Virgil's command, Dante removes a *Cord*
from about his waist and Virgil drops it over the edge of the abyss. As if in answer to
a signal, a great distorted shape comes swimming up through the dirty air of the pit.

We could already hear the rumbling drive
  of the waterfall in its plunge to the next circle,
  a murmur like the throbbing of a hive,   3

when three shades turned together on the plain,
  breaking toward us from a company
  that went its way to torture in that rain.   6

They cried with one voice as they ran toward me:
  "Wait, oh wait, for by your dress you seem
  a voyager from our own tainted country."[6]   9

Ah! what wounds I saw, some new, some old,
  branded upon their bodies! Even now
  the pain of it in memory turns me cold.   12

My Teacher heard their cries, and turning to,
  stood face to face. "Do as they ask," he said,
  "for these are souls to whom respect is due;   15

and were it not for the darting flames that hem
  our narrow passage in, I should have said
  it were more fitting you ran after them."[7]   18

5. A footrace run at Verona on the first Sunday in Lent, the prize being a piece of green
cloth. For the race to be run by the Christian,
see 1 Corinthians 9.24–25. *"Treasure"*: i.e.,

Latini's encyclopedia, the *Trésor* (French).
6. Florence.
7. To hurry was considered undignified.

We paused, and they began their ancient wail
   over again, and when they stood below us
   they formed themselves into a moving wheel.   21

As naked and anointed champions do
   in feeling out their grasp and their advantage
   before they close in for the thrust or blow—[8]   24

so circling, each one stared up at my height,
   and as their feet moved left around the circle,
   their necks kept turning backward to the right.   27

"If the misery of this place, and our unkempt
   and scorched appearance," one of them began,
   "bring us and what we pray into contempt,   30

still may our earthly fame move you to tell
   who and what you are, who so securely
   set your live feet to the dead dusts of Hell.   33

This peeled and naked soul who runs before me
   around this wheel, was higher than you think
   there in the world, in honor and degree.   36

Guido Guerra[9] was the name he bore,
   the good Gualdrada's grandson. In his life
   he won great fame in counsel and in war.   39

The other who behind me treads this sand
   was Tegghiaio Aldobrandi,[1] whose good counsels
   the world would have done well to understand.   42

And I who share their torment, in my life
   was Jacopo Rusticucci;[2] above all
   I owe my sorrows to a savage wife."   45

I would have thrown myself to the plain below
   had I been sheltered from the falling fire;
   and I think my Teacher would have let me go.   48

But seeing I should be burned and cooked, my fear
   overcame the first impulse of my heart
   to leap down and embrace them then and there.   51

"Not contempt," I said, "but the compassion
   that seizes on my soul and memory
   at the thought of you tormented in this fashion—   54

8. The three naked Florentines form a circle and are compared to oiled wrestlers (a sport practiced in Dante's time).
9. A leading participant in the civil strife in Florence (d. 1272).
1. An ally of Guido (see 6.76).
2. An ally of Tegghiaio who blames his wife for his sodomy (see 6.77).

it was grief that choked my speech when through the scorching
 air of this pit my Lord announced to me
 that such men as you are might be approaching. 57

I am of your own land, and I have always
 heard with affection and rehearsed with honor
 your name and the good deeds of your happier days. 60

Led by my Guide and his truth, I leave the gall
 and go for the sweet apples of delight.[3]
 But first I must descend to the center of all." 63

"So may your soul and body long continue
 together on the way you go," he answered,
 "and the honor of your days shine after you— 66

tell me if courtesy and valor raise
 their banners in our city as of old,
 or has the glory faded from its days? 69

For Borsiere,[4] who is newly come among us
 and yonder goes with our companions in pain,
 taunts us with such reports, and his words have stung us."[5] 72

"O Florence! your sudden wealth and your upstart
 rabble, dissolute and overweening,
 already set you weeping in your heart!" 75

I cried with face upraised, and on the sand
 those three sad spirits looked at one another
 like men who hear the truth and understand. 78

"If this be your manner of speaking, and if you can
 satisfy others with such ease and grace,"
 they said as one, "we hail a happy man. 81

Therefore, if you win through this gloomy pass
 and climb again to see the heaven of stars;
 when it rejoices you to say 'I was,' 84

speak of us to the living." They parted then,
 breaking their turning wheel, and as they vanished
 over the plain, their legs seemed wings. "Amen" 87

could not have been pronounced between their start
 and their disappearance over the rim of sand.
 And then it pleased my Master to depart. 90

---

3. I.e., leave Hell and head for Paradise.
4. An elegant member of Florentine society.
5. An account of the recent dissension within

the city, to which Dante himself was soon to
fall victim.

A little way beyond we felt the quiver
   and roar of the cascade, so close that speech
   would have been drowned in thunder. As that river—   93

the first one on the left of the Apennines[6]
   to have a path of its own from Monte Veso
   to the Adriatic Sea—which, as it twines   96

is called the Acquacheta from its source
   until it nears Forli, and then is known
   as the Montone in its further course—   99

resounds from the mountain in a single leap
   there above San Benedetto dell'Alpe
   where a thousand falls might fit into the steep;   102

so down from a sheer bank, in one enormous
   plunge, the tainted water roared so loud
   a little longer there would have deafened us.   105

I had a cord bound round me like a belt[7]
   which I had once thought I might put to use
   to snare the leopard with the gaudy pelt.[8]   108

When at my Guide's command I had unbound
   its loops from about my habit, I gathered it
   and held it out to him all coiled and wound.   111

He bent far back to his right, and throwing it
   out from the edge, sent it in a long arc
   into the bottomless darkness of the pit.   114

"Now surely some unusual event,"
   I said to myself, "must follow this new signal
   upon which my good Guide is so intent."   117

Ah, how cautiously a man should breathe
   near those who see not only what we do,
   but have the sense which reads the mind beneath![9]   120

He said to me: "You will soon see arise
   what I await, and what you wonder at;
   soon you will see the thing before your eyes."   123

---

6. Dante compares the roar of Phlegethon to the river Montone in the Apennine Mountains of northern Italy, whose course he traces in the next nine lines.

7. While commentators disagree, it seems likely that this cord is a reference both to Job 41.1, where God says he can draw Leviathan up with a hook and bind his tongue with a cord, and to Francis of Assisi, who wore a cord as a sign of humility and obedience. As a layman, Dante may have had a connection with the Franciscan friars, a common circumstance at the time.

8. The leopard of canto I, representing fraud.

9. Dante now realizes that Virgil can read his thoughts.

To the truth which will seem falsehood every man
　who would not be called a liar while speaking fact
　should learn to seal his lips as best he can. 126

But here I cannot be still: Reader, I swear
　by the lines of my Comedy—so may it live—
　that I saw swimming up through that foul air 129

a shape to astonish the most doughty soul,
　a shape like one returning through the sea
　from working loose an anchor run afoul 132

of something on the bottom—so it rose,
　its arms spread upward and its feet drawn close.

Canto XVII

CIRCLE SEVEN: ROUND THREE　　　　　*The Violent against Art. Geryon*

The monstrous shape lands on the brink and Virgil salutes it ironically. It is *Geryon*, the *Monster of Fraud*. Virgil announces that they must fly down from the cliff on the back of this monster. While Virgil negotiates for their passage, Dante is sent to examine the *Usurers* (The Violent against Art).

These sinners sit in a crouch along the edge of the burning plain that approaches the cliff. Each of them has a leather purse around his neck, and each purse is blazoned with a coat of arms. Their eyes, gushing with tears, are forever fixed on these purses. Dante recognizes none of these sinners, but their coats of arms are unmistakably those of well-known Florentine families.

Having understood who they are and the reason for their present condition, Dante cuts short his excursion and returns to find Virgil mounted on the back of Geryon. Dante joins his Master and they fly down from the great cliff.

Their flight carries them from the Hell of the *Violent and the Bestial* (The Sins of the Lion) into the Hell of the *Fraudulent and Malicious* (The Sins of the Leopard).

"Now see the sharp-tailed beast that mounts the brink.
　He passes mountains, breaks through walls and weapons.
　Behold the beast that makes the whole world stink."[1] 3

These were the words my Master spoke to me;
　then signaled the weird beast to come to ground
　close to the sheer end of our rocky levee. 6

The filthy prototype of Fraud drew near
　and settled his head and breast upon the edge
　of the dark cliff, but let his tail hang clear. 9

1. Geryon, the embodiment of fraud. For this figure Dante drew upon classical literature, where Geryon had not three natures—human, reptilian, and bestial—combined into one, as here, but three bodies and three heads.

His face was innocent of every guile,
  benign and just in feature and expression;
  and under it his body was half reptile.   12

His two great paws were hairy to the armpits;
  all his back and breast and both his flanks
  were figured with bright knots and subtle circlets: 15

never was such a tapestry of bloom
  woven on earth by Tartar or by Turk,
  nor by Arachne[2] at her flowering loom.   18

As a ferry sometimes lies along the strand,
  part beached and part afloat; and as the beaver,[3]
  up yonder in the guzzling Germans'[4] land,   21

squats halfway up the bank when a fight is on—
  just so lay that most ravenous of beasts
  on the rim which bounds the burning sand with stone.   24

His tail twitched in the void beyond that lip,
  thrashing, and twisting up the envenomed fork
  which, like a scorpion's stinger, armed the tip.   27

My Guide said: "It is time now we drew near
  that monster." And descending on the right
  we moved ten paces outward to be clear   30

of sand and flames. And when we were beside him,
  I saw upon the sand a bit beyond us
  some people crouching close beside the brim.   33

The Master paused. "That you may take with you
  the full experience of this round," he said,
  "go now and see the last state of that crew.   36

But let your talk be brief, and I will stay
  and reason with this beast till you return,
  that his strong back may serve us on our way."   39

So further yet along the outer edge
  of the seventh circle I moved on alone.
  And came to the sad people of the ledge.   42

Their eyes burst with their grief; their smoking hands
  jerked about their bodies, warding off
  now the flames and now the burning sands.   45

2. A woman in classical literature famous for
weaving, who was turned into a spider: see Ovid,
Metamorphoses 6.
3. Which was thought to catch fish by putting

its tail into the water.
4. Accusing Germans of drunkenness was a
tradition going back to the Romans.

Dogs in summer bit by fleas and gadflies,
   jerking their snouts about, twitching their paws
   now here, now there, behave no otherwise.   48

I examined several faces there among
   that sooty throng, and I saw none I knew;
   but I observed that from each neck there hung   51

an enormous purse, each marked with its own beast
   and its own colors like a coat of arms.
   On these their streaming eyes appeared to feast.[5]   54

Looking about, I saw one purse display
   azure on or, a kind of lion; another,
   on a blood-red field, a goose whiter than whey.   57

And one that bore a huge and swollen sow
   azure on field argent said to me:
   "What are you doing in this pit of sorrow?   60

Leave us alone! And since you have not yet died,
   I'll have you know my neighbor Vitaliano
   has a place reserved for him here at my side.[6]   63

A Paduan among Florentines, I sit here
   while hour by hour they nearly deafen me
   shouting: 'Send us the sovereign cavalier[7]   66

with the purse of the three goats!'" He half arose,
   twisted his mouth, and darted out his tongue
   for all the world like an ox licking its nose.   69

And I, afraid that any longer stay
   would anger him who had warned me to be brief,
   left those exhausted souls without delay.   72

Returned, I found my Guide already mounted
   upon the rump of that monstrosity.
   He said to me: "Now must you be undaunted: 75

this beast must be our stairway to the pit:
   mount it in front, and I will ride between
   you and the tail, lest you be poisoned by it."[8]   78

5. These are usurers, men who lent money for interest, which was forbidden by the Catholic Church in the Middle Ages (although often practiced). Each has a coat of arms on his purse by which he can be identified; all are Italians.

6. The speaker is from Padua and here maliciously identifies another Paduan who will soon be joining him.
7. A prominent Florentine banker.
8. Virgil protects Dante from Geryon's scorpion's tail.

Like one so close to the quartanary chill
   that his nails are already pale and his flesh trembles
   at the very sight of shade or a cool rill—   81

so did I tremble at each frightful word.
   But his scolding filled me with that shame that makes
   the servant brave in the presence of his lord.   84

I mounted the great shoulders of that freak
   and tried to say "Now help me to hold on!"
   But my voice clicked in my throat and I could not speak.   87

But no sooner had I settled where he placed me
   than he, my stay, my comfort, and my courage
   in other perils, gathered and embraced me.   90

Then he called out: "Now, Geryon, we are ready:
   bear well in mind that his is living weight
   and make your circles wide and your flight steady."   93

As a small ship slides from a beaching or its pier,
   backward, backward—so that monster slipped
   back from the rim. And when he had drawn clear   96

he swung about, and stretching out his tail
   he worked it like an eel, and with his paws
   he gathered in the air, while I turned pale.   99

I think there was no greater fear the day
   Phaeton[9] let loose the reins and burned the sky
   along the great scar of the Milky Way,   102

nor when Icarus,[1] too close to the sun's track
   felt the wax melt, unfeathering his loins,
   and heard his father cry "Turn back! Turn back!"—   105

than I felt when I found myself in air,
   afloat in space with nothing visible
   but the enormous beast that bore me there.   108

Slowly, slowly, he swims on through space,
   wheels and descends, but I can sense it only
   by the way the wind blows upward past my face.   111

Already on the right I heard the swell
   and thunder of the whirlpool. Looking down
   I leaned my head out and stared into Hell.   114

9. Son of Apollo, Phaeton tried to drive the chariot of the sun, but when it got out of control it scorched both Earth and the heavens, creating the Milky Way (Ovid, *Metamorphoses* 2).

1. Flying with wings made of wax and feathers, Icarus, the son of Daedalus, went too near the sun and fell (Ovid, *Metamorphoses* 8).

I trembled again at the prospect of dismounting
   and cowered in on myself, for I saw fires
   on every hand, and I heard a long lamenting.   117

And then I saw—till then I had but felt it—
   the course of our down-spiral to the horrors
   that rose to us from all sides of the pit.   120

As a flight-worn falcon sinks down wearily
   though neither bird nor lure has signalled it,
   the falconer crying out: "What! spent already!"—   123

then turns and in a hundred spinning gyres
   sulks from her master's call, sullen and proud—[2]
   so to that bottom lit by endless fires   126

the monster Geryon circled and fell,
   setting us down at the foot of the precipice
   of ragged rock on the eighth shelf of Hell.   129

And once freed of our weight, he shot from there
into the dark like an arrow into air.

Canto XVIII

CIRCLE EIGHT (MALEBOLGE)	*The Fraudulent and Malicious*
BOLGIA ONE	*The Panderers and Seducers*
BOLGIA TWO	*The Flatterers*

Dismounted from Geryon, the Poets find themselves in the *Eighth Circle*, called *Malebolge* (The Evil Ditches). This is the upper half of the *Hell of the Fraudulent and Malicious*. Malebolge is a great circle of stone that slopes like an amphitheater. The slopes are divided into ten concentric ditches; and within these ditches, each with his own kind, are punished those guilty of *Simple Fraud*.

A series of stone dikes runs like spokes from the edge of the great cliff face to the center of the place, and these serve as bridges.

The Poets bear left toward the first ditch, and Dante observes below him and to his right the sinners of the first bolgia, the *Panderers* and *Seducers*. These make two files, one along either bank of the ditch, and are driven at an endless fast walk by horned demons who hurry them along with great lashes. In life these sinners goaded others on to serve their own foul purposes; so in Hell are they driven in their turn. The horned demons who drive them symbolize the sinners' own vicious natures, embodiments of their own guilty consciences. Dante may or may not have intended the horns of the demons to symbolize cuckoldry and adultery.

The Poets see *Venedico Caccianemico* and *Jason* in the first pit, and pass on to the second, where they find the souls of the *Flatterers* sunk in excrement, the true

2. Unless it sights prey or is called back with a lure by its master, a trained falcon will continue flying until exhaustion compels it to descend.

equivalent of their false flatteries on earth. They observe *Alessio Interminelli* and *Thaïs*, and pass on.

There is in Hell a vast and sloping ground
    called Malebolge, a lost place of stone
    as black as the great cliff that seals it round.   3

Precisely in the center of that space
    there yawns a well extremely wide and deep.
    I shall discuss it in its proper place.[3]   6

The border that remains between the well-pit
    and the great cliff forms an enormous circle,
    and ten descending troughs are cut in it,   9

offering a general prospect like the ground
    that lies around one of those ancient castles
    whose walls are girded many times around   12

by concentric moats. And just as, from the portal,
    the castle's bridges run from moat to moat
    to the last bank; so from the great rock wall   15

across the embankments and the ditches, high
    and narrow cliffs run to the central well,
    which cuts and gathers them like radii.   18

Here, shaken from the back of Geryon,
    we found ourselves. My Guide kept to the left
    and I walked after him. So we moved on.   21

Below, on my right, and filling the first ditch
    along both banks, new souls in pain appeared,
    new torments, and new devils black as pitch.   24

All of these sinners were naked; on our side
    of the middle they walked toward us; on the other,
    in our direction, but with swifter stride.   27

Just so the Romans, because of the great throng
    in the year of the Jubilee,[4] divide the bridge
    in order that the crowds may pass along,   30

so that all face the Castle as they go
    on one side toward St. Peter's, while on the other,
    all move along facing toward Mount Giordano.   33

3. The last, or ninth, circle of Hell, described in cantos 31–34.
4. The year 1300 was declared the first-ever Jubilee Year by Pope Boniface, and Dante here describes the crowd control on the bridge that ran between the Castle of St. Angelo and St. Peter's Basilica in Rome.

And everywhere along that hideous track
   I saw horned demons with enormous lashes
   move through those souls, scourging them on the back.   36

Ah, how the stragglers of that long rout stirred
   their legs quick-march at the first crack of the lash!
   Certainly no one waited a second, or third!   39

As we went on, one face in that procession
   caught my eye and I said: "That sinner there:
   It is certainly not the first time I've seen that one."[5]   42

I stopped, therefore, to study him, and my Guide
   out of his kindness waited, and even allowed me
   to walk back a few steps at the sinner's side.   45

And that flayed spirit, seeing me turn around,
   thought to hide his face, but I called to him:
   "You there, that walk along with your eyes on the ground—   48

if those are not false features, then I know you
   as Venedico Caccianemico of Bologna:
   what brings you here among this pretty crew?"   51

And he replied: "I speak unwillingly,
   but something in your living voice, in which
   I hear the world again, stirs and compels me.   54

It was I who brought the fair Ghisola 'round
   to serve the will and lust of the Marquis,
   however sordid that old tale may sound.   57

There are many more from Bologna who weep away
   eternity in this ditch; we fill it so
   there are not as many tongues that are taught to say   60

'sipa'[6] in all the land that lies between
   the Reno and the Saveno, as you must know
   from the many tales of our avarice and spleen."   63

And as he spoke, one of those lashes fell
   across his back, and a demon cried, "Move on,
   you pimp, there are no women here to sell."   66

Turning away then, I rejoined my Guide.
   We came in a few steps to a raised ridge
   that made a passage to the other side.   69

5. This is Venedico Caccianemico, a man from Bologna who was reputed to have turned his sister Ghisolabella over to the Marquis of Este.

6. *Sipa* is a word for "yes" in the dialect spoken in the territory between the rivers Savena and Reno, which comprise the boundaries of Bologna.

This we climbed easily, and turning right
   along the jagged crest, we left behind
   the eternal circling of those souls in flight.   72

And when we reached the part at which the stone
   was tunneled for the passage of the scourged,
   my Guide said, "Stop a minute and look down   75

on these other misbegotten wraiths of sin.
   You have not seen their faces, for they moved
   in the same direction we were headed in."   78

So from that bridge we looked down on the throng
   that hurried toward us on the other side.
   Here, too, the whiplash hurried them along.   81

And the good Master, studying that train,
   said: "Look there, at that great soul that approaches
   and seems to shed no tears for all his pain—   84

what kingliness moves with him even in Hell!
   It is Jason,[7] who by courage and good advice
   made off with the Colchian Ram. Later it fell   87

that he passed Lemnos, where the women of wrath,
   enraged by Venus' curse that drove their lovers
   out of their arms, put all their males to death.   90

There with his honeyed tongue and his dishonest
   lover's wiles, he gulled Hypsipyle,
   who, in the slaughter, had gulled all the rest.   93

And there he left her, pregnant and forsaken.
   Such guilt condemns him to such punishment;
   and also for Medea is vengeance taken.   96

All seducers march here to the whip.
   And let us say no more about this valley
   and those it closes in its stony grip."   99

We had already come to where the walk
   crosses the second bank, from which it lifts
   another arch, spanning from rock to rock.   102

Here we heard people whine in the next chasm,
   and knock and thump themselves with open palms,
   and blubber through their snouts as if in a spasm.   105

---

7. Jason led the Argonauts on the voyage to the island of Colchis, where they stole the Golden Fleece. He seduced and abandoned Hypsipyle, who had hidden her father when the other women of Lemnos were killing all the males. He also married and later abandoned Medea, the daughter of the king of Colchis. For his story, see Ovid, *Metamorphoses* 7.

Steaming from that pit, a vapour rose
  over the banks, crusting them with a slime
  that sickened my eyes and hammered at my nose.   108

That chasm sinks so deep we could not sight
  its bottom anywhere until we climbed
  along the rock arch to its greatest height.   111

Once there, I peered down; and I saw long lines
  of people in a river of excrement
  that seemed the overflow of the world's latrines.   114

I saw among the felons of that pit
  one wraith who might or might not have been tonsured—
  one could not tell, he was so smeared with shit.   117

He bellowed: "You there, why do you stare at me
  more than at all the others in this stew?"
  And I to him: "Because if memory   120

serves me, I knew you when your hair was dry.
  You are Alessio Interminelli da Lucca.[8]
  That's why I pick you from this filthy fry."   123

And he then, beating himself on his clown's head:
  "Down to this have the flatteries I sold
  the living sunk me here among the dead."   126

And my Guide prompted then: "Lean forward a bit
  and look beyond them, there—do you see that one
  scratching herself with dungy nails, the strumpet   129

who fidgets to her feet, then to a crouch?
  It is the whore Thaïs[9] who told her lover
  when he sent to ask her, 'Do you thank me much?'   132

'Much? Nay, past all believing!' And with this
let us turn away from the sight of this abyss."

Canto XIX

The Simoniacs

Dante comes upon the *Simoniacs* (sellers of ecclesiastic favors and offices) and his
heart overflows with the wrath he feels against those who corrupt the things of
God. This *bolgia* is lined with round tube-like holes and the sinners are placed
in them upside down with the soles of their feet ablaze. The heat of the blaze is
proportioned to their guilt.

8. A prominent citizen of Lucca, in northern
Italy.

9. A character in a play by the Roman writer
Terence (c. 186–c. 159 B.C.E.).

The holes in which these sinners are placed are debased equivalents of the baptismal fonts common in the cities of Northern Italy and the sinners' confinement in them is temporary: as new sinners arrive, the souls drop through the bottoms of their holes and disappear eternally into the crevices of the rock.

As always, the punishment is a symbolic retribution. Just as the Simoniacs made a mock of holy office, so are they turned upside down in a mockery of the baptismal font. Just as they made a mockery of the holy water of baptism, so is their hellish baptism by fire, after which they are wholly immersed in the crevices below. The oily fire that licks at their soles may also suggest a travesty on the oil used in Extreme Unction (last rites for the dying).

Virgil carries Dante down an almost sheer ledge and lets him speak to one who is the chief sinner of that place, *Pope Nicholas III*. Dante delivers himself of another stirring denunciation of those who have corrupted church office, and Virgil carries him back up the steep ledge toward the *Fourth Bolgia*.

O Simon Magus![1] O you wretched crew
  who follow him, pandering for silver and gold
  the things of God which should be wedded to   3

love and righteousness! O thieves for hire,
  now must the trump of judgment sound your doom[2]
  here in the third fosse of the rim of fire!   6

We had already made our way across
  to the next grave, and to that part of the bridge
  which hangs above the mid-point of the fosse.   9

O Sovereign Wisdom, how Thine art doth shine
  in Heaven, on Earth, and in the Evil World!
  How justly doth Thy power judge and assign!   12

I saw along the walls and on the ground
  long rows of holes cut in the livid stone;
  all were cut to a size, and all were round.   15

They seemed to be exactly the same size
  as those in the font of my beautiful San Giovanni,[3]
  built to protect the priests who come to baptize;   18

(one of which, not so long since, I broke open
  to rescue a boy who was wedged and drowning in it.
  Be this enough to undeceive all men.)   21

---

1. Because in the Bible Simon Magus tried to buy spiritual power from the apostles (Acts 8.9–24), the selling of any spiritual good for material gain was known in the Middle Ages as simony. The most common form of simony was the selling of church offices.
2. Dante is here applauding the artfulness of divine justice because the simoniacs, who cared most for their purses, are here stuffed into fiery "purses" hewn into the rock; see line 69 below.
3. The baptistery in Florence where Dante himself was baptized. The subsequent personal reference has never been satisfactorily explained.

From every mouth a sinner's legs stuck out
  as far as the calf. The soles were all ablaze
  and the joints of the legs quivered and writhed about.   24

Withes and tethers would have snapped in their throes.
  As oiled things blaze upon the surface only,
  so did they burn from the heels to the points of their toes.   27

"Master," I said, "who is that one in the fire
  who writhes and quivers more than all the others?
  From him the ruddy flames seem to leap higher."[4]   30

And he to me: "If you wish me to carry you down
  along that lower bank, you may learn from him
  who he is, and the evil he has done."   33

And I: "What you will, I will. You are my lord
  and I know I depart in nothing from your wish;
  and you know my mind beyond my spoken word."   36

We moved to the fourth ridge, and turning left
  my Guide descended by a jagged path
  into the strait and perforated cleft.   39

Thus the good Master bore me down the dim
  and rocky slope, and did not put me down
  till we reached the one whose legs did penance for him.   42

"Whoever you are, sad spirit," I began,
  "who lie here with your head below your heels
  and planted like a stake—speak if you can."   45

I stood like a friar who gives the sacrament
  to a hired assassin, who, fixed in the hole,
  recalls him, and delays his death a moment.[5]   48

"Are you there already, Boniface? Are you there
  already?" he cried. "By several years the writ
  has lied. And all that gold, and all that care—   51

are you already sated with the treasure
  for which you dared to turn on the Sweet Lady[6]
  and trick and pluck and bleed her at your pleasure?"   54

---

4. Pope Nicholas III (r. 1277–80). He mistakenly believes that one of his successors, Boniface VIII, has come to be squeezed into the
hole (line 49). Like all damned souls, Nicholas
has foreknowledge, and because Boniface did
not die until 1303 Nicholas is surprised at

what he thinks is his appearance in 1300.
5. Hired murderers were occasionally executed
by being placed head-down in a ditch and then
buried alive.
6. The Church.

I stood like one caught in some raillery,
　　not understanding what is said to him,
　　lost for an answer to such mockery.　　　　　　　57

Then Virgil said, "Say to him: 'I am not he,
　　I am not whom you think.'" And I replied
　　as my good Master had instructed me.　　　　　　60

The sinner's feet jerked madly; then again
　　his voice rose, this time choked with sighs and tears,
　　and said at last: "What do you want of me then?　　63

If to know who I am drives you so fearfully
　　that you descend the bank to ask it, know
　　that the Great Mantle was once hung upon me.　　66

And in truth I was a son of the She-Bear,[7]
　　so sly and eager to push my whelps ahead,
　　that I pursed wealth above, and myself here.　　　69

Beneath my head are dragged all who have gone
　　before me in buying and selling holy office;
　　there they cower in fissures of the stone.　　　　　72

I too shall be plunged down when that great cheat
　　for whom I took you comes here in his turn.
　　Longer already have I baked my feet　　　　　　　75

and been planted upside-down, than he shall be
　　before the west sends down a lawless Shepherd[8]
　　of uglier deeds to cover him and me.　　　　　　　78

He will be a new Jason[9] of the Maccabees;
　　and just as that king bent to his high priests' will,
　　so shall the French king do as this one please."　　81

Maybe—I cannot say—I grew too brash
　　at this point, for when he had finished speaking
　　I said: "Indeed! Now tell me how much cash　　　84

our Lord required of Peter in guarantee
　　before he put the keys into his keeping?
　　Surely he asked nothing but 'Follow me!'[1]　　　　87

7. The arms of Nicholas's family (the Orsini) included a "she-bear."
8. Clement V (c. 1264–1314), who became pope in 1305 after agreeing with the French king to remove the papacy to Avignon in France. He is "from the West" because he was born in western France.

9. Jason became high priest of the Jews by bribing the king: see 2 Maccabees 4.7–9.
1. See Matthew 16.18–19; the keys are the Church's power to bind (condemn) and to loose (absolve). For "follow me," see Matthew 4.18–19.

Nor did Peter, nor the others, ask silver or gold
  of Matthew when they chose him for the place
  the despicable and damned apostle sold.[2]   90

Therefore stay as you are; this hole well fits you—
  and keep a good guard on the ill-won wealth
  that once made you so bold toward Charles of Anjou.[3]   93

And were it not that I am still constrained
  by the reverence I owe to the Great Keys
  you held in life, I should not have refrained   96

from using other words and sharper still;
  for this avarice of yours grieves all the world,
  tramples the virtuous, and exalts the evil.   99

Of such as you was the Evangelist's[4] vision
  when he saw Her who Sits upon the Waters
  locked with the Kings of earth in fornication.   102

She was born with seven heads, and ten enormous
  and shining horns strengthened and made her glad
  as long as love and virtue pleased her spouse.   105

Gold and silver are the gods you adore!
  In what are you different from the idolater,
  save that he worships one, and you a score?   108

Ah Constantine,[5] what evil marked the hour—
  not of your conversion, but of the fee
  the first rich Father took from you in dower!"   111

And as I sang him this tune, he began to twitch
  and kick both feet out wildly, as if in rage
  or gnawed by conscience—little matter which.   114

And I think, indeed, it pleased my Guide: his look
  was all approval as he stood beside me
  intent upon each word of truth I spoke.   117

---

2. Matthias was chosen by lot to fill the place of Judas (Acts 1.23–26).
3. Nicholas was believed to be involved in a plot against Charles of Anjou (1226–1285), ruler of Naples and Sicily.
4. John, author of Revelation, who in the Middle Ages was identified with the author of the Gospel according to John; for this passage, which was originally interpreted as referring to pagan Rome but which Dante applies to the corrupt Church, see Revelation 17.1–18. The "seven heads" are the seven Sacraments; the "ten . . . horns," the Ten Commandments; the "spouse," God.
5. Roman emperor (r. 306–337) who was the supposed author of a document—known as the Donation of Constantine—in which he granted temporal power and the right to acquire wealth to Pope Sylvester I, "the first rich Father" of this passage. The document was proved to be a forgery in the 15th century.

He approached, and with both arms he lifted me,
  and when he had gathered me against his breast,
  remounted the rocky path out of the valley,   120

nor did he tire of holding me clasped to him,
  until we reached the topmost point of the arch
  which crosses from the fourth to the fifth rim   123

of the pits of woe. Arrived upon the bridge,
  he tenderly set down the heavy burden
  he had been pleased to carry up that ledge   126

which would have been hard climbing for a goat.
Here I looked down on still another moat.

Canto XX

CIRCLE EIGHT: BOLGA FOUR   *The Fortune Tellers and Diviners*

Dante stands in the middle of the bridge over the *Fourth Bolgia* and looks down at
the souls of the *Fortune Tellers* and *Diviners*. Here are the souls of all those who
attempted by forbidden arts to look into the future. Among these damned are:
Amphiareus, Tiresias, Aruns, Manto, Eurypylus, Michael Scott, Guido Bonatti, and
Asdente.

Characteristically, the sin of these wretches is reversed upon them: their
punishment is to have their heads turned backwards on their bodies and to be
compelled to walk backwards through all eternity, their eyes blinded with tears.
Thus, those who sought to penetrate the future cannot even see in front of
themselves; they attempted to move themselves forward in time, so must they
go backwards through all eternity; and as the arts of sorcery are a distortion of
God's law, so are their bodies distorted in Hell.

No more need be said of them: Dante names them, and passes on to fill the
canto with a lengthy account of the founding of Virgil's native city of Mantua.

Now must I sing new griefs, and my verses strain
  to form the matter of the Twentieth Canto
  of Canticle One, the Canticle of Pain.   3

My vantage point permitted a clear view
  of the depths of the pit below: a desolation
  bathed with the tears of its tormented crew,   6

who moved about the circle of the pit
  at about the pace of a litany procession.[6]
  Silent and weeping, they wound round and round it.   9

And when I looked down from their faces, I saw
  that each of them was hideously distorted
  between the top of the chest and the lines of the jaw;   12

6. A "litany" is a form of public prayer, often recited during stately "processions" in the church.

for the face was reversed on the neck, and they came on
    backwards, staring backwards at their lions,
    for to look before them was forbidden. Someone,   15

sometime, in the grip of a palsy may have been
    distorted so, but never to my knowledge;
    nor do I believe the like was ever seen.   18

Reader, so may God grant you to understand
    my poem and profit from it, ask yourself
    how I could check my tears, when near at hand   21

I saw the image of our humanity
    distorted so that the tears that burst from their eyes
    ran down the cleft of their buttocks. Certainly   24

I wept. I leaned against the jagged face
    of a rock and wept so that my Guide said: "Still?
    Still like the other fools? There is no place   27

for pity here. Who is more arrogant
    within his soul, who is more impious
    than one who dares to sorrow at God's judgment?[7]   30

Lift up your eyes, lift up your eyes and see
    him the earth swallowed before all the Thebans,
    at which they cried out: 'Whither do you flee,   33

Amphiareus?[8] Why do you leave the field?'
    And he fell headlong through the gaping earth
    to the feet of Minos, where all sin must yield.   36

Observe how he has made a breast of his back.
    In life he wished to see too far before him,
    and now he must crab backwards round this track.   39

And see Tiresias,[9] who by his arts
    succeeded in changing himself from man to woman,
    transforming all his limbs and all his parts;   42

later he had to strike the two twined serpents
    once again with his conjurer's wand before
    he could resume his manly lineaments.   45

7. This is a rebuke to Dante, who errs by showing sympathy for the damned.
8. A priest swallowed up by the Earth in a battle against the Thebans as described in Statius's *Thebaid* (see note 7 to 14.45). For Minos, see 5.4.

9. A soothsayer of Thebes, he struck two coupling serpents with his rod and was transformed into a woman. Seven years later he repeated the action and was changed back into a man. See Ovid, *Metamorphoses* 3.

And there is Aruns,[1] his back to that one's belly,
   the same who in the mountains of the Luni
   tilled by the people of Carrara's valley,   48

made a white marble cave his den, and there
   with unobstructed view observed the sea
   and the turning constellations year by year.   51

And she whose unbound hair flows back to hide
   her breasts—which you cannot see—and who also wears
   all of her hairy parts on that other side,   54

was Manto,[2] who searched countries far and near,
   then settled where I was born. In that connection
   there is a story I would have you hear.   57

Tiresias was her sire. After his death,
   Thebes, the city of Bacchus,[3] became enslaved,
   and for many years she roamed about the earth.   60

High in sweet Italy, under the Alps that shut
   the Tyrolean gate of Germany, there lies
   a lake known as Benacus[4] roundabout.   63

Through endless falls, more than a thousand and one,
   Mount Apennine from Garda to Val Camonica,[5]
   is freshened by the waters that flow down   66

into that lake. At its center is a place
   where the Bishops of Brescia, Trentine, and Verona
   might all give benediction with equal grace.   69

Peschiera,[6] the beautiful fortress, strong in war
   against the Brescians and the Bergamese,
   sits at the lowest point along that shore.   72

There, the waters Benacus cannot hold
   within its bosom, spill and form a river
   that winds away through pastures green and gold.   75

1. An Etruscan soothsayer from the city of Luni, in the area of Carrara where marble is quarried, is described by the Roman poet Lucan (39–65 C.E.) in his *Pharsalia*.
2. Another Theban soothsayer described by Roman poets.
3. Bacchus (Dionysus) was the son of Jupiter and a mortal woman, Semele, daughter of the king of Thebes.
4. The present-day Lake Garda in northern Italy, located in terms of an island where the boundaries of the three dioceses of Trent, Brescia, and Verona meet.
5. Garda is a town by the lake and Val Camonica a valley below it.
6. Peschiera is a town on the south shore of the lake; the Brescians and the Bergamese are inhabitants of two towns to the northwest of Peschiera.

But once the water gathers its full flow,
  it is called Mincius rather than Benacus
  from there to Governo,[7] where it joins the Po.   78

Still near its source, it strikes a plain, and there
  it slows and spreads, forming an ancient marsh
  which in the summer heat pollutes the air.   81

The terrible virgin, passing there by chance,
  saw dry land at the center of the mire,
  untilled, devoid of all inhabitants.   84

There, shunning all communion with mankind,
  she settled with the ministers of her arts,
  and there she lived, and there she left behind   87

her vacant corpse. Later the scattered men
  who lived nearby assembled on that spot
  since it was well defended by the fen.   90

Over those whited bones they raised the city,
  and for her who had chosen the place before all others
  they named it—with no further augury—   93

Mantua.[8] Far more people lived there once—
  before sheer madness prompted Casalodi
  to let Pinamonte play him for a dunce.[9]   96

Therefore, I charge you, should you ever hear
  other accounts of this, to let no falsehood
  confuse the truth which I have just made clear."[1]   99

And I to him: "Master, within my soul
  your word is certainty, and any other
  would seem like the dead lumps of burned out coal.   102

But tell me of those people moving down
  to join the rest. Are any worth my noting?
  For my mind keeps coming back to that alone."   105

And he: "That one whose beard spreads like a fleece
  over his swarthy shoulders, was an augur
  in the days when so few males remained in Greece   108

---

7. A town some 30 miles south of Peschiera.
Presumably Virgil provides this detailed geography to illustrate that he is a native of this
region.
8. Virgil's native city.
9. A reference to the internal intrigues of the
rulers of Mantua in the 13th century.

1. Dante's Virgil contradicts the account of
Mantua's founding in *Aeneid* 10.198–200. It
is not clear why Dante has Virgil contradict
his own poem unless he is trying to clear Virgil
of any taint of himself being a magician (see
note 9 to 9.20).

that even the cradles were all but empty of sons.
   He chose the time for cutting the cable at Aulis,
   and Calchas[2] joined him in those divinations.   111

He is Eurypylus. I sing him somewhere
   in my High Tragedy; you will know the place
   who know the whole of it. The other there,   114

the one beside him with the skinny shanks
   was Michael Scott,[3] who mastered every trick
   of magic fraud, a prince of mountebanks.   117

See Guido Bonatti there; and see Asdente,[4]
   who now would be wishing he had stuck to his last,
   but repents too late, though he repents aplenty.   120

And see on every hand the wretched hags[5]
   who left their spinning and sewing for soothsaying
   and casting of spells with herbs, and dolls, and rags.   123

But come: Cain[6] with his bush of thorns appears
   already on the wave below Seville,
   above the boundary of the hemispheres;   126

and the moon was full already yesternight,
   as you must well remember from the wood,
   for it certainly did not harm you when its light   129

shone down upon your way before the dawn."
And as he spoke to me, we traveled on.

Canto XXI

CIRCLE EIGHT: BOLGIA FIVE   *The Grafters*

The Poets move on, talking as they go, and arrive at the *Fifth Bolgia*. Here the
Grafters are sunk in boiling pitch and guarded by *Demons*, who tear them to
pieces with claws and grappling hooks if they catch them above the surface of the
pitch.

   The sticky pitch is symbolic of the sticky fingers of the Grafters. It serves also
to hide them from sight, as their sinful dealings on earth were hidden from

---

2. Calchas and Eurypylus were prophets (or
augurs) involved in the Trojan War; here Virgil
says that they determined when the Greeks were
to set out for the war from the island of Aulis,
although *Aeneid* 2 gives a different account.
3. A famous scientist, philosopher, and astrologer from Scotland, Scott spent many years at
the court of Frederick II (10.119) in Palermo
and died in 1235.
4. A shoemaker famous as a soothsayer in

13th-century Italy. "Guido Bonatti": an astrologer at the court of Guido da Montefeltro (see
canto 27).
5. Common soothsayers and potion makers.
6. Popular belief held that God placed Cain
in the moon after the murder of Abel; "Cain
with his bush of thorns" means the moon with
its spots, which is now setting at the western
edge of the Northern Hemisphere. Overhead,
in Jerusalem, it is the dawn of Holy Saturday.

men's eyes. The demons, too, suggest symbolic possibilities, for they are armed
with grappling hooks and are forever ready to rend and tear all they can get their
hands on.

The Poets watch a demon arrive with a grafting *Senator of Lucca* and fling him
into the pitch where the demons set upon him.

To protect Dante from their wrath, Virgil hides him behind some jagged rocks
and goes ahead alone to negotiate with the demons. They set upon him like a pack
of mastiffs, but Virgil secures safe conduct from their leader, *Malacoda*. Thereupon
Virgil calls Dante from hiding, and they are about to set off when they discover that
the *Bridge across the Sixth Bolgia* lies shattered. Malacoda tells them there is
another further on and sends a squad of demons to escort them. Their adventures
with the demons continue through the next canto.

These two cantos may conveniently be remembered as the *Gargoyle Cantos*. If
the total *Commedia* is built like a cathedral (as so many critics have suggested), it
is here certainly that Dante attaches his grotesqueries. At no other point in the
Commedia does Dante give such free rein to his coarsest style.

Thus talking of things which my Comedy does not care
   to sing, we passed from one arch to the next
   until we stood upon its summit. There 3

we checked our steps to study the next fosse
   and the next vain lamentations of Malebolge;
   awesomely dark and desolate it was. 6

As in the Venetian arsenal,[7] the winter through
   there boils the sticky pitch to caulk the seams
   of the sea-battered bottoms when no crew 9

can put to sea—instead of which, one starts
   to build its ship anew, one plugs the planks
   which have been sprung in many foreign parts; 12

some hammer at a mast, some at a rib;
   some make new oars, some braid and coil new lines;
   one patches up the mainsail, one the jib— 15

so, but by Art Divine and not by fire,
   a viscid pitch boiled in the fosse below
   and coated all the bank with gluey mire. 18

I saw the pitch; but I saw nothing in it
   except the enormous bubbles of its boiling,
   which swelled and sank, like breathing, through all the pit. 21

And as I stood and stared into that sink,
   my Master cried, "Take care!" and drew me back
   from my exposed position on the brink. 24

7. The huge shipyard at Venice was called the Arsenal.

I turned like one who cannot wait to see
   the thing he dreads, and who, in sudden fright,
   runs while he looks, his curiosity   27

competing with his terror—and at my back
   I saw a figure that came running toward us
   across the ridge, a Demon huge and black.   30

Ah what a face he had, all hate and wildness!
   Galloping so, with his great wings outspread
   he seemed the embodiment of all bitterness.   33

Across each high-hunched shoulder he had thrown
   one haunch of a sinner, whom he held in place
   with a great talon round each ankle bone.   36

"Blacktalons of our bridge," he began to roar,
   "I bring you one of Santa Zita's Elders![8]
   Scrub him down while I go back for more: 39

I planted a harvest of them in that city:
   everyone there is a grafter except Bonturo.[9]
   There 'Yes' is 'No' and 'No' is 'Yes' for a fee."   42

Down the sinner plunged, and at once the Demon
   spun from the cliff; no mastiff ever sprang
   more eager from the leash to chase a felon.   45

Down plunged the sinner and sank to reappear
   with his backside arched and his face and both his feet
   glued to the pitch, almost as if in prayer.   48

But the Demons under the bridge, who guard that place
   and the sinners who are thrown to them, bawled out:
   "You're out of bounds here for the Sacred Face: 51

this is no dip in the Serchio:[1] take your look
   and then get down in the pitch. And stay below
   unless you want a taste of a grappling hook."   54

Then they raked him with more than a hundred hooks
   bellowing: "Here you dance below the covers.
   Graft all you can there: no one checks your books." 57

---

8. "Blacktalons" (*Malebranche*: in Italian—
"evil claws") is the generic name for the devils
in this ditch; each has a proper name as well
(lines 79, 107, 118–22). The elders of Santa
Zita in Lucca (a town near Florence) were ten
citizens who ran the government.

9. A current official in Lucca, Bonturo Datí
was in fact known as the most corrupt of all;
the devil is being ironic.
1. A river near Lucca. The Sacred Face of
Lucca was a venerated icon.

They dipped him down into that pitch exactly
   as a chef makes scullery boys dip meat in a boiler,
   holding it with their hooks from floating free.   60

And the Master said: "*You* had best not be seen
   by these Fiends till I am ready. Crouch down here.
   One of these rocks will serve you as a screen.   63

And whatever violence you see done to me,
   you have no cause to fear. I know these matters:
   I have been though this once and come back safely."[2]   66

With that, he walked on past the end of the bridge;
   and it wanted all his courage to look calm
   from the moment he arrived on the sixth ridge.   69

With that same storm and fury that arouses
   all the house when the hounds leap at a tramp
   who suddenly falls to pleading where he pauses—   72

so rushed those Fiends from below, and all the pack
   pointed their gleaming pitchforks at my Guide.
   But he stood fast and cried to them: "Stand back!   75

Before those hooks and grapples make too free,
   send up one of your crew to hear me out,
   then ask yourselves if you still care to rip me."   78

All cried as one: "Let Malacoda[3] go."
   So the pack stood and one of them came forward,
   saying: "What good does he think *this* will do?"   81

"Do you think, Malacoda," my good Master said,
   "you would see me here, having arrived this far
   already, safe from you and every dread,   84

without Divine Will and propitious Fate?
   Let me pass on, for it is willed in Heaven
   that I must show another this dread state."   87

The Demon stood there on the flinty brim,
   so taken aback he let his pitchfork drop;
   then said to the others: "Take care not to harm him!"   90

"O you crouched like a cat," my Guide called to me,
   "among the jagged rock piles of the bridge,
   come down to me, for now you may come safely."   93

2. Virgil may be referring to his difficulties with the devils in 8.82–128, when he and Dante tried to enter the city of Dis. **3.** "Evil-Tail."

Hearing him, I hurried down the ledge;
   and the Demons all pressed forward when I appeared,
   so that I feared they might not keep their pledge.   96

So once I saw the Pisan infantry
   march out under truce from the fortress at Caprona,
   staring in fright at the ranks of the enemy.[4]   99

I pressed the whole of my body against my Guide,
   and not for an instant did I take my eyes
   from those black fiends who scowled on every side.   102

They swung their forks saying to one another:
   "Shall I give him a touch in the rump?" and answering:
   "Sure, give him a taste to pay him for his bother."   105

But the Demon who was talking to my Guide
   turned round and cried to him: "At ease there, Snatcher!"
   And then to us: "There's no road on this side: 108

the arch lies all in pieces in the pit.[5]
   If you *must* go on, follow along this ridge;
   there's another cliff to cross by just beyond it.[6]   111

In just five hours it will be, since the bridge fell,
   a thousand two hundred sixty-six years and a day;
   that was the time the big quake shook all Hell.[7]   114

I'll send a squad of my boys along that way
   to see if anyone's airing himself below:
   you can go with them: there will be no foul play.   117

Front and center here, Grizzly and Hellken,"
   he began to order them. "You too, Deaddog.
   Curlybeard, take charge of a squad of ten.   120

Take Grafter and Dragontooth along with you.
   Pigtusk, Catclaw, Cramper, and Crazyred.
   Keep a sharp lookout on the boiling glue   123

as you move along, and see that these gentlemen
   are not molested until they reach the crag
   where they can find a way across the den."   126

---

4. A battle outside Florence in 1289, in which Dante may have taken part.
5. The bridge across the fifth ditch was smashed, as Malacoda explains, by the earthquake that occurred at the time of the crucifixion.
6. As the travelers discover, this is a lie.

7. According to medieval tradition, Christ's death on the cross occurred on Good Friday at noon, in his thirty-third year, which would be 34 C.E.; the time at which Dante and Virgil are in this fifth ditch of Malebolge is 7:00 a.m. of Holy Saturday, 1300, which is 1266 years plus one day, less five hours later.

"In the name of heaven, Master," I cried, "what sort
    of guides are these? Let us go on alone
    if you know the way. Who can trust such an escort!   129

If you are as wary as you used to be
    you surely see them grind their teeth at us,
    and knot their beetle brows so threateningly."   132

And he: "I do not like this fear in you.
    Let them gnash and knot as they please; they menace only
    the sticky wretches simmering in that stew."   135

They turned along the left bank in a line;
    but not before they had formed a single rank
    and stuck their pointed tongues out as a sign   138

to their Captain that they wished permission to pass;
and he had made a trumpet of his ass.

Canto XXII

CIRCLE EIGHT: BOLGIA FIVE   *The Grafters*

The poets set off with their escorts of demons. Dante sees the *Grafters* lying in
the pitch like frogs in water with only their muzzles out. They disappear as
soon as they sight the demons and only a ripple on the surface betrays their
presence.

   One of the Grafters, *An Unidentified Navarrese*, ducks too late and is seized by
the demons who are about to claw him, but *Curlybeard* holds them back while
Virgil questions him. The wretch speaks of his fellow sinners, *Friar Gomita* and
Michel Zanche, while the uncontrollable demons rake him from time to time with
their hooks.

   The Navarrese offers to lure some of his fellow sufferers into the hands of the
demons, and when his plan is accepted he plunges into the pitch and escapes.
Hellken and *Grizzly* fly after him, but too late. They start a brawl in mid-air and
fall into the pitch themselves. Curlybeard immediately organizes a rescue party
and the Poets, fearing the bad temper of the frustrated demons, take advantage of
the confusion to slip away.

I have seen horsemen breaking camp. I have seen
    the beginning of the assault, the march and muster,
    and at times the retreat and riot. I have been   3

where chargers trampled your land, O Aretines![8]
    I have seen columns of foragers, shocks of tourney,
    and running of tilts. I have seen the endless lines   6

march to bells, drums, trumpets, from far and near.
    I have seen them march on signals from a castle.
    I have seen them march with native and foreign gear.   9

---

8. The people of Arezzo, a city south of Florence.

But never yet have I seen horse or foot,
   nor ship in range of land nor sight of star,
   take its direction from so low a toot.   12

We went with the ten Fiends—ah, savage crew!—
   but "In church with saints; with stewpots in the tavern,"[9]
   as the old proverb wisely bids us do.   15

All my attention was fixed upon the pitch:
   to observe the people who were boiling in it,
   and the customs and the punishments of that ditch.   18

As dolphins surface and begin to flip
   their arched backs from the sea, warning the sailors
   to fall to and begin to secure ship—[1]   21

So now and then, some soul, to ease his pain,
   showed us a glimpse of his back above the pitch
   and quick as lightning disappeared again.   24

And as, at the edge of a ditch, frogs squat about
   hiding their feet and bodies in the water,
   leaving only their muzzles sticking out—   27

so stood the sinners in that dismal ditch;
   but as Curlybeard approached, only a ripple
   showed where they had ducked back into the pitch.   30

I saw—the dread of it haunts me to this day—
   one linger a bit too long, as it sometimes happens
   one frog remains when another spurts away;   33

and Catclaw, who was nearest, ran a hook
   through the sinner's pitchy hair and hauled him in.
   He looked like an otter dripping from the brook.   36

I knew the names of all the Fiends by then;
   I had made a note of them at the first muster,
   and, marching, had listened and checked them over again.   39

"Hey, Crazyred," the crew of Demons cried
   all together, "give him a taste of your claws.
   Dig him open a little. Off with his hide."   42

And I then: "Master, can you find out, please,
   the name and history of that luckless one
   who has fallen into the hands of his enemies?"   45

9. A popular proverb.
1. It was a common medieval belief that dolphins warned sailors of approaching storms.

My Guide approached that wraith from the hot tar
  and asked him whence he came. The wretch replied:
  "I was born and raised in the Kingdom of Navarre.[2]   48

My mother placed me in service to a knight;
  for she had borne me to a squanderer
  who killed himself when he ran through his birthright.   51

Then I became a domestic in the service
  of good King Thibault. There I began to graft,
  and I account for it in this hot crevice."   54

And Pigtusk, who at the ends of his lower lip
  shot forth two teeth more terrible than a boar's,
  made the wretch feel how one of them could rip.   57

The mouse had come among bad cats, but here
  Curlybeard locked arms around him crying:
  "While I've got hold of him the rest stand clear!"   60

And turning his face to my Guide: "If you want to ask him
  anything else," he added, "ask away
  before the others tear him limb from limb."   63

And my Guide to the sinner: "I should like to know
  if among the other souls beneath the pitch
  are any Italians?" And the wretch: "Just now   66

I left a shade who came from parts nearby.
  Would I were still in the pitch with him, for then
  these hooks would not be giving me cause to cry."   69

And suddenly Grafter bellowed in great heat:
  "We've stood enough!" And he hooked the sinner's arm
  and, raking it, ripped off a chunk of meat.   72

Then Dragontooth wanted to play, too, reaching down
  for a catch at the sinner's legs; but Curlybeard
  wheeled round and round with a terrifying frown,   75

and when the Fiends had somewhat given ground
  and calmed a little, my Guide, without delay,
  asked the wretch, who was staring at his wound: 78

"Who was the sinner from whom you say you made
  your evil-starred departure to come ashore
  among these Fiends?" And the wretch: "It was the shade   81

2. The identity of this sinner is not known, but he was employed in the household of Thibault II of Champagne, a man renowned for his honesty who was also king of Navarre, the area of Spain that is now Basque country.

of Friar Gomita of Gallura,[3] the crooked stem
　　of every Fraud: when his master's enemies
　　were in his hands, he won high praise from them.　　84

He took their money without case or docket,
　　and let them go. He was in all his dealings
　　no petty bursar, but a kingly pocket.　　87

With him, his endless crony in the fosse,
　　is Don Michel Zanche of Logodoro;[4]
　　they babble about Sardinia without pause.　　90

But look! See that fiend grinning at your side!
　　There is much more that I should like to tell you,
　　but oh, I think he means to grate my hide!"　　93

But their grim sergeant wheeled, sensing foul play,
　　and turning on Cramper, who seemed set to strike,
　　ordered: "Clear off, you buzzard. Clear off, I say!"　　96

"If either of you would like to see and hear
　　Tuscans or Lombards," the pale sinner said,
　　"I can lure them out of hiding if you'll stand clear　　99

and let me sit here at the edge of the ditch,
　　and get all these Blacktalons out of sight;
　　for while they're here, no one will leave the pitch.　　102

In exchange for myself, I can fish you up as pretty
　　a mess of souls as you like. I have only to whistle
　　the way we do when one of us gets free."　　105

Deaddog raised his snout as he listened to him;
　　then, shaking his head, said, "Listen to the grafter
　　spinning his tricks so he can jump from the brim!"　　111

And the sticky wretch, who was all treachery:
　　"Oh I am more than tricky when there's a chance
　　to see my friends in greater misery."　　114

Hellken, against the will of all the crew,
　　could hold no longer. "If you jump," he said
　　to the scheming wretch, "I won't come after you　　117

at a gallop, but like a hawk after a mouse.
　　We'll clear the edge and hide behind the bank:
　　let's see if you're trickster enough for all of us."　　120

3. A friar who was chancellor of the Gallura district on the island of Sardinia. He was hanged by his master, a lord of Pisa, when it was discov-ered that he had sold prisoners their freedom. 4. Little is known of this sinner, except that he too was a Sardinian.

Reader, here is new game! The Fiends withdrew
 from the bank's edge, and Deaddog, who at first
 was most against it, led the savage crew.   123

The Navarrese chose his moment carefully:
 and planting both his feet against the ground,
 he leaped, and in an instant he was free.   126

The Fiends were stung with shame, and of the lot
 Hellken most, who had been the cause of it.
 He leaped out madly bellowing: "You're caught!"   129

but little good it did him; terror pressed
 harder than wings; the sinner dove from sight
 and the fiend in full flight had to raise his breast.   132

A duck, when the falcon dives, will disappear
 exactly so, all in a flash, while he
 returns defeated and weary up the air.   135

Grizzly, in a rage at the sinner's flight,
 flew after Hellken, hoping the wraith would escape,
 so he might find an excuse to start a fight.   138

And as soon as the grafter sank below the pitch,
 Grizzly turned his talons against Hellken,
 locked with him claw to claw above the ditch.   141

But Hellken was sparrowhawk enough for two
 and clawed him well; and ripping one another,
 they plunged together into the hot stew.   144

The heat broke up the brawl immediately,
 but their wings were smeared with pitch and they could not rise.
 Curlybeard, upset as his company,   147

commanded four to fly to the other coast
 at once with all their grapples. At top speed
 the Fiends divided, each one to his post.   150

Some on the near edge, some along the far,
 they stretched their hooks out to the clotted pair
 who were already cooked deep through the scar   153

of their first burn. And turning to one side
we slipped off, leaving them thus occupied.

Canto XXIII

The Hypocrites

The Poets are pursued by the Fiends and escape them by sliding down the sloping bank of the next pit. They are now in the *Sixth Bolgia*. Here the *Hyprocrites*, weighted down by great leaden robes, walk eternally round and round a narrow track. The robes are brilliantly gilded on the outside and are shaped like a monk's habit, for the hypocrite's outward appearance shines brightly and passes for holiness, but under that show lies the terrible weight of his deceit which the soul must bear through all eternity.

The Poets talk to *Two Jovial Friars* and come upon *Caiaphas*, the chief sinner of that place. Caiaphas was the High Priest of the Jews who counseled the Pharisees to crucify Jesus in the name of public expedience. He is punished by being himself crucified to the floor of Hell by three great stakes, and in such a position that every passing sinner must walk upon him. Thus he must suffer upon his own body the weight of all the world's hypocrisy, as Christ suffered upon his body the pain of all the world's sins.

The Jovial Friars tell Virgil how he may climb from the pit, and Virgil discovers that Malacoda lied to him about the bridges over the Sixth Bolgia.

Silent, apart, and unattended we went
   as Minor Friars[5] go when they walk abroad,
   one following the other. The incident   3

recalled the fable of the Mouse and the Frog
   that Aesop tells.[6] For compared attentively
   point by point, "pig" is no closer to "hog"   6

than the one case to the other. And as one thought
   springs from another, so the comparison
   gave birth to a new concern, at which I caught   9

my breath in fear. This thought ran through my mind:
   "These Fiends, through us, have been made ridiculous,
   and have suffered insult and injury of a kind   12

to make them smart. Unless we take good care—
   now rage is added to their natural spleen—
   they will hunt us down as greyhounds hunt the hare."   15

Already I felt my scalp grow tight with fear.
   I was staring back in terror as I said:
   "Master, unless we find concealment here   18

5. Franciscan friars, who were known as "minor" or "lesser" friars because Francis of Assisi, the founder of the order, insisted upon humility.
6. The fable that Dante seems to be referring to tells how a frog offers to ferry a mouse across a river, then halfway over tries to drown him, only to be seized by a kite (a hawklike bird of prey) while the mouse escapes.

and soon, I dread the rage of the Fiends: already
   they are yelping on our trail: I imagine them
   so vividly I can hear them now." And he: 21

"Were I a pane of leaded glass, I could not
   summon your outward look more instantly
   into myself, than I do your inner thought.   24

Your fears were mixed already with my own
   with the same suggestion and the same dark look;
   so that of both I form one resolution: 27

the right bank may be sloping: in that case
   we may find some way down to the next pit
   and so escape from the imagined chase."   30

He had not finished answering me thus
   when, not far off, their giant wings outspread,
   I saw the Fiends come charging after us.   33

Seizing me instantly in his arms, my Guide—
   like a mother wakened by a midnight noise
   to find a wall of flame at her bedside   36

(who takes her child and runs, and more concerned
   for him than for herself, does not pause even
   to throw a wrap about her) raised me, turned,   39

and down the rugged bank from the high summit
   flung himself down supine onto the slope
   which walls the upper side of the next pit.   42

Water that turns the great wheel of a land-mill
   never ran faster through the end of a sluice
   at the point nearest the paddles—as down that hill   45

my Guide and Master bore me on his breast,
   as if I were not a companion, but a son.
   And the soles of his feet had hardly come to rest   48

on the bed of the depth below, when on the height
   we had just left, the Fiends beat their great wings.
   But now they gave my Guide no cause for fright;   51

for the Providence that gave them the fifth pit
   to govern as the ministers of Its will,
   takes from their souls the power of leaving it.   54

About us now in the depth of the pit we found
   a painted people, weary and defeated.
   Slowly, in pain, they paced it round and round.   57

All wore great cloaks cut to as ample a size
    as those worn by the Benedictines of Cluny.[7]
    The enormous hoods were drawn over their eyes. 60

The outside is all dazzle, golden and fair;
    the inside, lead, so heavy that Frederick's capes,
    compared to these, would seem as light as air.[8] 63

O weary mantle for eternity!
    We turned to the left again along their course,
    listening to their moans of misery, 66

but they moved so slowly down that barren strip,
    tired by their burden, that our company
    was changed at every movement of the hip. 69

And walking thus, I said: "As we go on,
    may it please you to look about among these people
    for any whose name or history may be known." 72

And one who understood Tuscan cried to us there
    as we hurried past: "I pray you check your speed,
    you who run so fast through the sick air: 75

it may be I am one who will fit your case."
    And at his words my Master turned and said:
    "Wait now, then go with him at his own pace." 78

I waited there, and saw along that track
    two souls who seemed in haste to be with me;
    but the narrow way and their burden held them back. 81

When they had reached me down that narrow way
    they stared at me in silence and amazement,
    then turned to one another, I heard one say: 84

"This one seems, by the motion of his throat,
    to be alive; and if they are dead, how is it
    they are allowed to shed the leaden coat?" 87

And then to me "O Tuscan, come so far
    to the college of the sorry hypocrites,
    do not disdain to tell us who you are." 90

And I: "I was born and raised a Florentine
    on the green and lovely banks of Arno's waters,
    I go with the body that was always mine. 93

7. One of the largest monasteries in Europe, located in Burgundy in France; the Benedictines are monks who follow the Rule of St. Benedict (d. 587), one of the founders of monasticism.

8. Frederick II (see note 7 to 10.119) was reported to have punished traitors by encasing them in lead and throwing them into heated cauldrons.

But who are *you*, who sighing as you go
   distill in floods of tears that drown your cheeks?
   What punishment is this that glitters so?"   96

"These burnished robes are of thick lead," said one,
   "and are hung on us like counterweights, so heavy
   that we, their weary fulcrums, creak and groan.   99

Jovial Friars and Bolognese were we.
   We were chosen jointly by your Florentines
   to keep the peace, an office usually   102

held by a single man; near the Gardingo⁹
   one still may see the sort of peace we kept.
   I was called Catalano, he, Loderingo."   105

I began: "O Friars, your evil . . ."—and then I saw
   a figure crucified upon the ground
   by three great stakes, and I fell still in awe.¹   108

When he saw me there, he began to puff great sighs
   into his beard, convulsing all his body;
   and Friar Catalano, following my eyes,   111

said to me: "That one nailed across the road
   counselled the Pharisees that it was fitting
   one man be tortured for the public good.   114

Naked he lies fixed there, as you see,
   in the path of all who pass; there he must feel
   the weight of all through all eternity.   117

His father-in-law² and the others of the Council
   which was a seed of wrath to all the Jews,
   are similarly staked for the same evil."   120

Then I saw Virgil marvel for a while
   over that soul so ignominiously
   stretched on the cross in Hell's eternal exile.   123

Then, turning, he asked the Friar: "If your law permit,
   can you tell us if somewhere along the right
   there is some gap in the stone wall of the pit   126

---

9. A district in Florence that was destroyed by a civil war incited by their meddling in Florentine affairs. "Jovial Friars": a military and religious order in Bologna called the Knights of the Blessed Virgin Mary, or popularly the "Jovial Friars" because of the laxity of the order's rules. The members were meant to fight only in order to protect the weak and enforce peace. Cata-lano and Loderingo were two citizens of Bologna who were involved in founding the Jovial Friars in 1261.

1. This is Caiaphas, the Jewish high priest under Pontius Pilate who advised that Christ be crucified (John 11.47–52).

2. Annas: see John 18.13.

through which we two may climb to the next brink
    without the need of summoning the Black Angels
    and forcing them to raise us from this sink?"   129

He: "Nearer than you hope, there is a bridge
    that runs from the great circle of the scarp
    and crosses every ditch from ridge to ridge,   132

except that in this it is broken; but with care
    you can mount the ruins which lie along the slope
    and make a heap on the bottom." My Guide stood there   135

motionless for a while with a dark look.
    At last he said: "He lied about this business,
    who spears the sinners yonder with his hook."[3]   138

And the Friar: "Once at Bologna I heard the wise
    discussing the Devil's sins; among them I heard
    that he is a liar and the father of lies."[4]   141

When the sinner had finished speaking, I saw the face
    of my sweet Master darken a bit with anger:
    he set off at a great stride from that place,   144

and I turned from that weighted hypocrite
to follow in the prints of his dear feet.

Canto XXIV

CIRCLE EIGHT: BOLGIA SEVEN   *The Thieves*

The Poets climb the right bank laboriously, cross the bridge of the *Seventh Bolgia* and descend the far bank to observe the Thieves. They find the pit full of monstrous reptiles who curl themselves about the sinners like living coils of rope, binding each sinner's hands behind his back, and knotting themselves through the loins. Other reptiles dart about the place, and the Poets see one of them fly through the air and pierce the jugular vein of one sinner who immediately bursts into flames until only ashes remain. From the ashes the sinner reforms painfully.

These are Dante's first observations of the Thieves and will be carried further in the next canto, but the first allegorical retribution is immediately apparent. Thievery is reptilian in its secrecy; therefore it is punished by reptiles. The hands of the thieves are the agents of their crimes; therefore they are bound forever. And as the thief destroys his fellowmen by making their substance disappear, so is he painfully destroyed and made to disappear, not once but over and over again.

The sinner who has risen from his own ashes reluctantly identifies himself as *Vanni Fucci*. He tells his story, and to revenge himself for having been forced to reveal his identity he utters a dark prophecy against Dante.

3. See 21.111.
4. For this description of the devil, see John 8.44.

In the turning season of the youthful year,
    when the sun is warming his rays beneath Aquarius[5]
    and the days and nights already begin to near   3

their perfect balance; the hoar-frost copies then
    the image of his white sister on the ground,[6]
    but the first sun wipes away the work of his pen.   6

The peasants who lack fodder then arise
    and look about and see the fields all white,
    and hear their lambs bleat; then they smite their thighs,   9

go back into the house, walk here and there,
    pacing, fretting, wondering what to do,
    then come out doors again, and there, despair   12

falls from them when they see how the earth's face
    has changed in so little time, and they take their staffs
    and drive their lambs to feed—so in that place   15

when I saw my Guide and Master's eyebrows lower,
    my spirits fell and I was sorely vexed;
    and as quickly came the plaster to the sore: 18

for when he had reached the ruined bridge, he stood
    and turned on me that sweet and open look
    with which he had greeted me in the dark wood.   21

When he had paused and studied carefully
    the heap of stones, he seemed to reach some plan,
    for he turned and opened his arms and lifted me.   24

Like one who works and calculates ahead,
    and is always ready for what happens next—
    so, raising me above that dismal bed   27

to the top of one great slab of the fallen slate,
    he chose another saying: "Climb here, but first
    test it to see if it will hold your weight."   30

It was no climb for a lead-hung hypocrite:
    for scarcely we—he light and I assisted—
    could crawl handhold by handhold from the pit;   33

and were it not that the bank along this side
    was lower than the one down which we had slid,[7]
    I at least—I will not speak for my Guide—   36

5. January 21–February 21.
6. I.e., snow.
7. Because the whole of the eighth circle is tilted downward, the downside wall of each ditch is lower than that on the upside.

would have turned back. But as all of the vast rim
    of Malebolge leans toward the lowest well,
    so each succeeding valley and each brim   39

is lower than the last. We climbed the face
    and arrived by great exertion to the point
    where the last rock had fallen from its place.   42

My lungs were pumping as if they could not stop;
    I thought I could not go on, and I sat exhausted
    the instant I had clambered to the top.   45

"Up on your feet! This is no time to tire!"
    my Master cried. "The man who lies asleep
    will never waken fame, and his desire   48

and all his life drift past him like a dream,
    and the traces of his memory fade from time
    like smoke in air, or ripples on a stream.   51

Now, therefore, rise. Control your breath, and call
    upon the strength of soul that wins all battles
    unless it sink in the gross body's fall.   54

There is a longer ladder yet to climb:[8]
    this much is not enough. If you understand me,
    show that you mean to profit from your time."   57

I rose and made my breath appear more steady
    than it really was, and I replied: "Lead on
    as it pleases you to go: I am strong and ready."   60

We picked our way up the cliff, a painful climb,
    for it was narrower, steeper, and more jagged
    than any we had crossed up to that time.   63

I moved along, talking to hide my faintness,
    when a voice that seemed unable to form words
    rose from the depths of the next chasm's darkness.   66

I do not know what it said, though by then the Sage
    had led me to the top of the next arch;
    but the speaker seemed in a tremendous rage.   69

I was bending over the brim, but living eyes
    could not plumb to the bottom of that dark;
    therefore I said, "Master, let me advise   72

8. Both the climb from the pit of Hell back to Earth and then the climb up Mount Purgatory.

that we cross over and climb down the wall:[9]
    for just as I hear the voice without understanding,
    so I look down and make out nothing at all."   75

"I make no other answer than the act,"
    the Master said: "the only fit reply
    to a fit request is silence and the fact."   78

So we moved down the bridge to the stone pier
    that shores the end of the arch on the eighth bank,
    and there I saw the chasm's depths made clear;[1]   81

and there great coils of serpents met my sight,
    so hideous a mass that even now
    the memory makes my blood run cold with fright.[2]   84

Let Libya boast no longer, for though its sands
    breed chelidrids, jaculi, and phareans,
    cenchriads, and two-headed amphisbands,   87

it never bred such a variety
    of vipers, no, not with all Ethiopia
    and all the lands that lie by the Red Sea.   90

Amid that swarm, naked and without hope,
    people ran terrified, not even dreaming
    of a hole to hide in, or of heliotrope.[3]   93

Their hands were bound behind by coils of serpents
    which thrust their heads and tails between the loins
    and bunched in front, a mass of knotted torments.   96

One of the damned came racing round a boulder,
    and as he passed us, a great snake shot up
    and bit him where the neck joins with the shoulder.   99

No mortal pen—however fast it flash
    over the page—could write down *o* or *i*
    as quickly as he flamed and fell in ash;   102

and when he was dissolved into a heap
    upon the ground, the dust rose of itself
    and immediately resumed its former shape.   105

9. Into the seventh ditch.
1. They cross the bridge over the seventh ditch and then climb down the wall between the seventh and eighth ditches.
2. The following list of exotic serpents derives from a description by the Roman poet Lucan (39–65 C.E.) of the plagues of Libya.
3. I.e., bloodstone, a mineral that was believed to make the bearer invisible.

Precisely so, philosophers declare,
    the Phoenix dies and then is born again
    when it approaches its five hundredth year.[4]   108

It lives on tears of balsam and of incense;
    in all its life it eats no herb or grain,
    and nard and precious myrrh sweeten its cerements.   111

And as a person fallen in a fit,
    possessed by a Demon or some other seizure
    that fetters him without his knowing it,   114

struggles up to his feet and blinks his eyes
    (still stupefied by the great agony
    he has just passed), and, looking round him, sighs—   117

such was the sinner when at last he rose.
    O Power of God! How dreadful is Thy will
    which in its vengeance rains such fearful blows.   120

Then my Guide asked him who he was. And he
    answered reluctantly: "Not long ago
    I rained into this gullet from Tuscany.   123

I am Vanni Fucci, the beast.[5] A mule among men,
    I chose the bestial life above the human.
    Savage Pistoia was my fitting den."   126

And I to my Guide: "Detain him a bit longer
    and ask what crime it was that sent him here;
    I knew him as a man of blood and anger."   129

The sinner, hearing me, seemed discomforted,
    but he turned and fixed his eyes upon my face
    with a look of dismal shame; at length he said: 132

"That you have found me out among the strife
    and misery of this place, grieves my heart more
    than did the day that cut me from my life.   135

But I am forced to answer truthfully:
    I am put down so low because it was I
    who stole the treasure from the Sacristy,   138

4. The "phoenix" is a mythical bird that is supposed to burn to death in its own nest every five hundred years, after which either itself or its son is reborn from the ashes; for these details, including its diet of exotic herbs and its funeral preparations (lines 109–11), see Ovid, *Metamorphoses* 15. In medieval mythography the phoenix was often taken as a symbol of Christ.

5. The illegitimate son of a noble father of Pistoia, a town just north of Florence; he was known as "the beast" because of the extravagance of his misbehavior. He reputedly robbed a church in Pistoia, a crime for which a similarly named man was wrongly hanged.

for which others once were blamed. But that you may
    find less to gloat about if you escape here,
    prick up your ears and listen to what I say:[6]   141

First Pistoia is emptied of the Black,
    then Florence changes her party and her laws.
    From Valdimagra the God of War brings back   144

a fiery vapor wrapped in turbid air:
    then in a storm of battle at Piceno
    the vapor breaks apart the mist, and there   147

every White shall feel his wounds anew.
    And I have told you this that it may grieve you."

Canto XXV

CIRCLE EIGHT: BOLGIA SEVEN   *The Thieves*

Vanni's rage mounts to the point where he hurls an ultimate obscenity at God, and the serpents immediately swarm over him, driving him off in great pain. The Centaur, *Cacus*, his back covered with serpents and a fire-eating dragon, also gives chase to punish the wretch.

Dante then meets *Five Noble Thieves of Florence* and sees the further retribution visited upon the sinners. Some of the thieves appear first in human form, others as reptiles. All but one of them suffer a painful transformation before Dante's eyes. Agnello appears in human form and is merged with *Cianfa*, who appears as a six-legged lizard. *Buoso* appears as a man and changes form with *Francesco*, who first appears as a tiny reptile. Only *Puccio Sciancato* remains unchanged, though we are made to understand that his turn will come.

For endless and painful transformation is the final state of the thieves. In life they took the substance of others, transforming it into their own. So in Hell their very bodies are constantly being taken from them, and they are left to steal back a human form from some other sinner. Thus they waver constantly between man and reptile, and no sinner knows what to call his own.

When he had finished, the thief—to his disgrace—
    raised his hands with both fists making figs,[7]
    and cried: "Here, God! I throw them in your face!"   3

Thereat the snakes became my friends, for one
    coiled itself about the wretch's neck
    as if it were saying: "You shall not go on!"   6

6. Vanni Fucci now prophesies, in the enigmatic terms appropriate to the genre, that the party of the Blacks (of which he was a member) will first be expelled from Pistoia by the Whites, but that then the Whites of Florence (Dante's party) will be defeated. The prophecy refers to events that occurred in either 1302 or 1306.

7. An obscene gesture made by thrusting a protruding thumb between the first and second fingers of a closed fist.

and another tied his arms behind him again,
  knotting its head and tail between his loins
  so tight he could not move a finger in pain.   9

Pistoia! Pistoia! why have you not decreed
  to turn yourself to ashes and end your days,
  rather than spread the evil of your seed!8   12

In all of Hell's corrupt and sunken halls
  I found no shade so arrogant toward God,
  not even him who fell from the Theban walls!9   15

Without another word, he fled; and there
  I saw a furious Centaur race up, roaring:
  "Where is the insolent blasphemer? Where?"   18

I do not think as many serpents swarm
  in all the Maremma1 as he bore on his back
  from the haunch to the first sign of our human form. 21

Upon his shoulders, just behind his head
  a snorting dragon whose hot breath set fire
  to all it touched, lay with its wings outspread.   24

My Guide said: "That is Cacus.2 Time and again
  in the shadow of Mount Aventine he made
  a lake of blood upon the Roman plain.   27

He does not go with his kin by the blood-red fosse
  because of the cunning fraud with which he stole
  the cattle of Hercules. And thus it was   30

his thieving stopped, for Hercules found his den
  and gave him perhaps a hundred blows with his club,
  and of them he did not feel the first ten."   33

Meanwhile, the Centaur passed along his way,
  and three wraiths came. Neither my Guide nor I
  knew they were there until we heard them say: 36

"You there—who are you?" There our talk fell still
  and we turned to stare at them. I did not know them,
  but by chance it happened, as it often will,   39

8. The most important founder of Pistoia was Catiline, who was a traitor against the Roman Republic in the 1st century B.C.E.
9. Capaneus (see 14.43–69).

1. A region infested with snakes; see 13.8.
2. A monster who lived in a cave on Mount Aventine in Rome and was killed by Hercules, from whom he had stolen cattle; see *Aeneid* 8.

one named another. "Where is Cianfa?"[3] he cried;
  "Why has he fallen back?" I placed a finger
  across my lips as a signal to my Guide.   42

Reader, should you doubt what next I tell,
  it will be no wonder, for though I saw it happen,
  I can scarce believe it possible, even in Hell.   45

For suddenly, as I watched, I saw a lizard
  come darting forward on six great taloned feet
  and fasten itself to a sinner from crotch to gizzard.   48

Its middle feet sank in the sweat and grime
  of the wretch's paunch, its forefeet clamped his arms,
  its teeth bit through both cheeks. At the same time   51

its hind feet fastened on the sinner's thighs:
  its tail thrust through his legs and closed its coil
  over his loins. I saw it with my own eyes!   54

No ivy ever grew about a tree
  as tightly as that monster wove itself
  limb by limb about the sinner's body;   57

they fused like hot wax, and their colors ran
  together until neither wretch nor monster
  appeared what he had been when he began: 60

just so, before the running edge of the heat
  on a burning page, a brown discoloration
  changes to black as the white dies from the sheet.   63

The other two cried out as they looked on:
  "Alas! Alas! Agnello,[4] how you change!
  Already you are neither two nor one!"   66

The two heads had already blurred and blended;
  now two new semblances appeared and faded,
  one face where neither face began nor ended.   69

From the four upper limbs of man and beast
  two arms were made, then members never seen
  grew from the thighs and legs, belly and breast.   72

Their former likenesses mottled and sank
  to something that was both of them and neither;
  and so transformed, it slowly left our bank.   75

3. A noble Florentine, reputedly a thief.   4. Another noble Florentine thief.

As lizards at high noon of a hot day
   dart out from hedge to hedge, from shade to shade,
   and flash like lightning when they cross the way,   78

so toward the bowels of the other two,
   shot a small monster; livid, furious,
   and black as a peppercorn. Its lunge bit through   81

that part of one of them from which man receives
   his earliest nourishment; then it fell back
   and lay sprawled out in front of the two thieves.   84

Its victim stared at it but did not speak:
   indeed, he stood there like a post, and yawned
   as if lack of sleep, or a fever, had left him weak.   87

The reptile stared at him, he at the reptile;
   from the wound of one and from the other's mouth
   two smokes poured out and mingled, dark and vile.   90

Now let Lucan be still with his history
   of poor Sabellus and Nassidius,[5]
   and wait to hear what next appeared to me.   93

Of Cadmus and Arethusa[6] be Ovid silent.
   I have no need to envy him those verses
   where he makes one a fountain, and one a serpent: 96

for he never transformed two beings face to face
   in such a way that both their natures yielded
   their elements each to each, as in this case.   99

Responding sympathetically to each other,
   the reptile cleft his tail into a fork,
   and the wounded sinner drew his feet together.   102

The sinner's legs and thighs began to join:
   they grew together so, that soon no trace
   of juncture could be seen from toe to loin.   105

Point by point the reptile's cloven tail
   grew to the form of what the sinner lost;
   one skin began to soften, one to scale.   108

The armpits swallowed the arms, and the short shank
   of the reptile's forefeet simultaneously
   lengthened by as much as the man's arms shrank.   111

5. Two soldiers bitten by serpents in Lucan's *Pharsalia*.
6. See *Metamorphoses* 4.

Its hind feet twisted round themselves and grew
   the member man conceals; meanwhile the wretch
   from his one member generated two.   114

The smoke swelled up about them all the while:
   it tanned one skin and bleached the other; it stripped
   the hair from the man and grew it on the reptile.   117

While one fell to his belly, the other rose
   without once shifting the locked evil eyes
   below which they changed snouts as they changed pose   120

The face of the standing one drew up and in
   toward the temples, and from the excess matter
   that gathered there, ears grew from the smooth skin;   123

while of the matter left below the eyes
   the excess became a nose, at the same time
   forming the lips to an appropriate size.   126

Here the face of the prostrate felon slips,
   sharpens into a snout, and withdraws its ears
   as a snail pulls in its horns. Between its lips   129

the tongue, once formed for speech, thrusts out a fork;
   the forked tongue of the other heals and draws
   into his mouth. The smoke has done its work.   132

The soul that had become a beast went flitting
   and hissing over the stones, and after it
   the other walked along talking and spitting   135

Then turning his new shoulders, said to the one
   that still remained: "It is Buoso's[7] turn to go
   crawling along this road as I have done."   138

Thus did the ballast of the seventh hold
   shift and reshift; and may the strangeness of it
   excuse my pen if the tale is strangely told.   141

And though all this confused me, they did not flee
   so cunningly but what I was aware
   that it was Puccio Sciancato[8] alone of the three   144

that first appeared, who kept his old form still.
The other was he for whom you weep, Gaville.[9]

---

7. The identity of this Buoso is uncertain.
8. This third thief is also a noble Florentine.
9. The "small monster" of line 80 above is now identified as Francesco de Cavalcanti, a Flo-rentine nobleman who lived in Gaville, a town south of Florence. When he was murdered by his townsmen, his kinsmen took brutal revenge.

Canto XXVI

CIRCLE EIGHT: BOLGIA EIGHT   *The Evil Counselors*

Dante turns from the Thieves toward the *Evil Counselors* of the next Bolgia, and between the two he addresses a passionate lament to Florence prophesying the griefs that will befall her from these two sins. At the purported time of the Vision, it will be recalled, Dante was a Chief Magistrate of Florence and was forced into exile by men he had reason to consider both thieves and evil counselors. He seems prompted, in fact, to say much more on this score, but he restrains himself when he comes in sight of the sinners of the next Bolgia, for they are a moral symbolism, all men of gift who abused their genius, perverting it to wiles and stratagems. Seeing them in Hell he knows his must be another road: his way shall not be by deception.

So the Poets move on and Dante observes the *Eighth Bolgia* in detail. Here the *Evil Counselors* move about endlessly, hidden from view inside great flames. Their sin was to abuse the gifts of the Almighty, to steal his virtues for low purposes. And as they stole from God in their lives and worked by hidden ways, so are they stolen from sight and hidden in the great flames which are their own guilty consciences. And as, in most instances at least, they sinned by glibness of tongue, so are the flames made into a fiery travesty of tongues.

Among the others, the Poets see a great doubleheaded flame, and discover that *Ulysses* and *Diomede* are punished together within it. Virgil addresses the flame, and through its wavering tongue Ulysses narrates an unforgettable tale of his last voyage and death.

Joy to you, Florence, that your banners swell,
   beating their proud wings over land and sea,
   and that your name expands through all of Hell!   3

Among the thieves I found five who had been
   your citizens,[1] to my shame; nor yet shall you
   mount to great honor peopling such a den!   6

But if the truth is dreamed of toward the morning,
   you soon shall feel what Prato[2] and the others
   wish for you. And were that day of mourning   9

already come it would not be too soon.
   So may it come, since it must! for it will weigh
   more heavily on me as I pass my noon.   12

We left that place. My Guide climbed stone by stone
   the natural stair by which we had descended
   and drew me after him. So we passed on,   15

1. Cianfa (25.40), Agnello (25.65), Buoso (25.137), Puccio (25.144), and Francesco (25.149) are all Florentines.

2. A town just north of Florence, on the way to Pistoia. The reason for this threat is unclear.

and going our lonely way through that dead land
   among the crags and crevices of the cliff,
   the foot could make no way without the hand.   18

I mourned among those rocks, and I mourn again
   when memory returns to what I saw:
   and more than usually I curb the strain   21

of my genius, lest it stray from Virtue's course;
   so if some star, or a better thing, grant me merit,
   may I not find the gift cause for remorse.   24

As many fireflies as the peasant sees
   when he rests on a hill and looks into the valley
   (where he tills or gathers grapes or prunes his trees)   27

in that sweet season when the face of him
   who lights the world rides north, and at the hour
   when the fly yields to the gnat and the air grows dim.—   30

such myriads of flames I saw shine through
   the gloom of the eighth abyss when I arrived
   at the rim from which its bed comes into view.   33

As he[3] the bears avenged so fearfully
   beheld Elijah's chariot depart—
   the horses rise toward heaven—but could not see   36

more than the flame, a cloudlet in the sky,
   once it had risen—so within the fosse
   only those flames, forever passing by   39

were visible, ahead, to right, to left;
   for though each steals a sinner's soul from view
   not one among them leaves a trace of the theft.   42

I stood on the bridge, and leaned out from the edge;
   so far, that but for a jut of rock I held to
   I should have been sent hurtling from the ledge   45

without being pushed. And seeing me so intent,
   my Guide said: "There are souls within those flames;
   each sinner swathes himself in his own torment."   48

"Master," I said, "your words make me more sure,
   but I had seen already that it was so
   and meant to ask what spirit must endure   51

---

3. Elisha, an Old Testament prophet, was mocked by children, who were then attacked by bears. He saw the ascent to heaven of the prophet Elijah in his chariot and continued Elijah's mission: 2 Kings 2.1–25.

the pains of that great flame which splits away
    in two great horns, as if it rose from the pyre
    where Eteocles and Polynices lay?"[4]   54

He answered me: "Forever round this path
    Ulysses and Diomede[5] move in such dress,
    united in pain as once they were in wrath;   57

there they lament the ambush of the Horse
    which was the door through which the noble seed
    of the Romans[6] issued from its holy source;   60

there they mourn that for Achilles slain
    sweet Deidamia[7] weeps even in death;
    there they recall the Palladium in their pain."   63

"Master," I cried, "I pray you and repray
    till my prayer becomes a thousand—if these souls
    can still speak from the fire, oh let me stay   66

until the flame draws near! Do not deny me:
    You see how fervently I long for it!"
    And he to me: "Since what you ask is worthy,   69

it shall be. But be still and let me speak;
    for I know your mind already, and they perhaps
    might scorn your manner of speaking, since they were Greek."[8]   72

And when the flame had come where time and place
    seemed fitting to my Guide, I heard him say
    these words to it: "O you two souls who pace   75

together in one flame!—if my days above
    won favor in your eyes, if I have earned
    however much or little of your love   78

in writing my High Verses, do not pass by,
    but let one of you be pleased to tell where he,
    having disappeared from the known world, went to die."   81

---

4. Eteocles and his brother, Polynices, were the sons of Oedipus; cursed by their father for their imprisonment of him, they engaged in a civil war over Thebes, killed each other, and were cremated on the same pyre, the flame of which divided into two as a sign of their enmity.
5. Two of the Greek leaders in the Trojan War. They devised the trick of the Trojan horse and stole the Palladium, a statue of Pallas Athena that protected the city. Their villainy is described by Aeneas in *Aeneid* 2.
6. The Trojan survivors, who founded Rome.
7. Achilles' lover, who tried to prevent him from going to the Trojan War but was thwarted by Ulysses.
8. Virgil may assume that Greeks would disdain anyone who, like Dante, did not know Greek (and was therefore a "barbarian"); or that because he derives from the classical world he is the more appropriate interlocutor.

As if it fought the wind, the greater prong
  of the ancient flame began to quiver and hum;
  then moving its tip as if it were the tongue 84

that spoke, gave out a voice above the roar.
  "When I left Circe,"[9] it said, "who more than a year
  detained me near Gaeta long before 87

Aeneas came and gave the place that name,[1]
  not fondness for my son, nor reverence
  for my aged father, nor Penelope's[2] claim 90

to the joys of love, could drive out of my mind
  the lust to experience the far-flung world
  and the failings and felicities of mankind. 93

I put out on the high and open sea
  with a single ship and only those few souls
  who stayed true when the rest deserted me. 96

As far as Morocco and as far as Spain
  I saw both shores; and I saw Sardinia
  and the other islands of the open main. 99

I and my men were stiff and slow with age
  when we sailed at last into the narrow pass
  where, warning all men back from further voyage,[3] 102

Hercules' Pillars rose upon our sight.
  Already I had left Ceuta on the left;
  Seville now sank behind me on the right. 105

'Shipmates,' I said, 'who through a hundred thousand
  perils have reached the West, do not deny
  to the brief remaining watch our senses stand 108

experience of the world beyond the sun.
  Greeks! You were not born to live like brutes,
  but to press on toward manhood and recognition! 111

With this brief exhortation I made my crew
  so eager for the voyage I could hardly
  have held them back from it when I was through; 114

9. Ulysses speaks here of the sorceress Circe, who turned his shipmates into swine and took Ulysses as her lover. Dante places Circe's home near Gaeta, on the coast of Italy north of Naples.
1. Aeneas named it after his nurse Caieta, who died there; see *Aeneid* 7.
2. Ulysses' faithful wife.

3. The Strait of Gibraltar, with the Spanish region that includes Seville on the European side and the Spanish city of Ceüta on the African. According to myth, Hercules separated a single mountain into two to mark the point beyond which human beings should not venture.

and turning our stern toward morning, our bow toward night,
    we bore southwest out of the world of man;[4]
    we made wings of our oars for our fool's flight.   117

That night we raised the other pole ahead
    with all its stars, and ours had so declined
    it did not rise out of its ocean bed.[5]   120

Five times since we had dipped our bending oars
    beyond the world, the light beneath the moon
    had waxed and waned, when dead upon our course   123

we sighted, dark in space, a peak so tall
    I doubted any man had seen the like.[6]
    Our cheers were hardly sounded, when a squall   126

broke hard upon our bow from the new land:
    three times it sucked the ship and the sea about
    as it pleased Another to order and command.   129

At the fourth, the poop rose and the bow went down
till the sea closed over us and the light was gone."

Canto XXVII

CIRCLE EIGHT: BOLGIA EIGHT   *The Evil Counselors*

The double flame departs at a word from Virgil and behind it appears another which contains the soul of *Count Guido da Montefeltro*, a Lord of Romagna. He had overheard Virgil speaking Italian, and the entire flame in which his soul is wrapped quivers with his eagerness to hear recent news of his wartorn country. (As Farinata has already explained, the spirits of the damned have prophetic powers, but lose all track of events as they approach.)

    Dante replies with a stately and tragic summary of how things stand in the cities of Romagna. When he has finished, he asks Guido for his story, and Guido recounts his life, and how Boniface VIII persuaded him to sin.

When it had finished speaking, the great flame
    stood tall and shook no more. Now, as it left us
    with the sweet Poet's license, another came   3

along that track and our attention turned
    to the new flame: a strange and muffled roar
    rose from the single tip to which it burned.   6

4. According to the geography of Dante's day, the Southern Hemisphere was made up entirely of water, with the only land being Mount Purgatory. "Our bow toward night" means to follow a westward course.
5. They had crossed the equator and could see only the stars of the Southern Hemisphere.
6. This is Mount Purgatory.

As the Sicilian bull—that brazen spit
    which bellowed first (and properly enough)
    with the lament of him whose file had tuned it—[7]   9

was made to bellow by its victim's cries
    in such a way, that though it was of brass,
    it seemed itself to howl and agonize: 12

so lacking any way through or around
    the fire that sealed them in, the mournful words
    were changed into its language. When they found   15

their way up to the tip, imparting to it
    the same vibration given them in their passage
    over the tongue of the concealed sad spirit,   18

we heard it say:[8] "O you at whom I aim
    my voice, and who were speaking Lombard,[9] saying:
    'Go now, I ask no more,' just as I came—   21

though I may come a bit late to my turn,
    may it not annoy you to pause and speak a while:
    you see it does not annoy me—and I burn.   24

If you have fallen only recently
    to this blind world from that sweet Italy
    where I acquired my guilt, I pray you, tell me: 27

is there peace or war in Romagna? for on earth
    I too was of those hills between Urbino
    and the fold from which the Tiber springs to birth."   30

I was still staring at it from the dim
    edge of the pit when my Guide nudged me, saying:
    "This one is Italian: *you* speak to him."   33

My answer was framed already; without pause
    I spoke these words to it: "O hidden soul,
    your sad Romagna is not and never was   36

without war in her tyrants' raging blood;
    but none flared openly when I left just now.
    Ravenna's[1] fortunes stand as they have stood   39

7. According to classical legend, Phalaris, the tyrant of Agrigentum in Sicily, had an artisan build a brazen bull in which he roasted his victims alive, their shrieks emerging as the sounds of a bull's bellowing. His first victim was the artisan himself, Perillus.
8. The speaker is Guido da Montefeltro (d. 1298), a nobleman deeply involved in the constant warfare of 13th-century Italy but who became a friar two years before his death (see lines 64–65).
9. The dialect of northern Italy. Dante believed that since Virgil came from Mantua, his spoken language would be not Latin but this dialect.
1. The major city of Romagna, ruled at the time by the Polenta family, who also controlled the small city of Cervia.

these many years: Polenta's eagles brood
    over her walls, and their pinions cover Cervia.
    The city[2] that so valiantly withstood   42

the French, and raised a mountain of their dead,
    feels the Green Claws again. Still in Verrucchio
    the Aged Mastiff and his Pup,[3] who shed   45

Montagna's blood, raven in their old ranges.
    The cities of Lamone and Santerno[4]
    are led by the white den's Lion, he who changes   48

his politics with the compass. And as the city[5]
    the Savio washes lies between plain and mountain,
    so it lives between freedom and tyranny.   51

Now, I beg you, let us know your name;
    do not be harder than one has been to you;
    so, too, you will preserve your earthly fame."   54

And when the flame had roared a while beneath
    the ledge on which we stood, it swayed its tip
    to and fro, and then gave forth this breath: 57

"If I believed that my reply were made
    to one who could ever climb to the world again,
    this flame would shake no more. But since no shade   60

ever returned—if what I am told is true—
    from this blind world into the living light,
    without fear of dishonor I answer you.   63

I was a man of arms: then took the rope
    of the Franciscans, hoping to make amends:
    and surely I should have won to all my hope   66

but for the Great Priest[6]—may he rot in Hell!—
    who brought me back to all my earlier sins;
    and how and why it happened I wish to tell   69

in my own words: while I was still encased
    in the pulp and bone my mother bore, my deeds
    were not of the lion but of the fox: I raced   72

2. Forli, which defeated French invaders but then fell under the control of the tyrannical Ordelaffi family, which had green paws on its coat of arms.
3. Malatesta de Verrucchio and his son Mala-testino were tyrants of Rimini who killed their enemy Montagna.
4. The cities of Faenza and Imola, on the Lamone and Santerno Rivers respectively, governed by an unreliable ruler who had a lion on a white ground on his coat of arms.
5. Cesena, located on the Savio River, was a free municipality although its politics were dominated by a single family.
6. Pope Boniface VIII.

through tangled ways; all wiles were mine from birth,
   and I won to such advantage with my arts
   that rumor of me reached the ends of the earth. 75

But when I saw before me all the signs
   of the time of life that cautions every man
   to lower his sail and gather in his lines, 78

that which had pleased me once, troubled my spirit,
   and penitent and confessed, I became a monk.
   Alas! What joy I might have had of it! 81

It was then the Prince of the New Pharisees drew
   his sword and marched upon the Lateran—
   and not against the Saracen or the Jew,[7] 84

for every man that stood against his hand
   was a Christian soul: not one had warred on Acre,[8]
   nor been a trader in the Sultan's land. 87

It was he abused his sacred vows and mine:
   his Office and the Cord I wore, which once
   made those it girded leaner.[9] As Constantine 90

sent for Silvestro to cure his leprosy,[1]
   seeking him out among Soracte's cells;
   so this one from his great throne sent for me 93

to cure the fever of pride that burned his blood.
   He demanded my advice, and I kept silent
   for his words seemed drunken to me. So it stood 96

until he said: 'Your soul need fear no wound;
   I absolve your guilt beforehand; and now teach me
   how to smash Penestrino[2] to the ground. 99

The Gates of Heaven, as you know, are mine
   to open and shut, for I hold the two Great Keys
   so easily let go by Celestine.'[3] 102

7. Boniface was struggling to retain the papacy against the challenge of another Roman family, the Colonnas.
8. City (now known as Akko) in the Holy Land, captured by the Crusaders and then recaptured by the Saracens.
9. Guido refers to the rough cord worn as a belt by Franciscan friars, a symbol of both obedience and poverty (hence it would make the wearer "leaner"); for another reference to this cord, see 16.106.

1. According to legend, the Emperor Constantine (r. 306–337) was cured of his leprosy by Pope Sylvester, who was hiding on Mount Soracte, some 20 miles north of Rome; see 19.109.
2. The fortress of the Colonnas.
3. The keys are those of damnation and absolution, given by Christ to Peter; see 19.85–86. Celestine V, Boniface's predecessor, resigned after five months as pope; see 3.56–57.

His weighty arguments led me to fear
  silence was worse than sin. Therefore, I said:
  'Holy Father, since you clean me here   105

of the guilt into which I fall, let it be done:
  long promise and short observance is the road
  that leads to the sure triumph of your throne.'   108

Later, when I was dead, St. Francis[4] came
  to claim my soul, but one of the Black Angels
  said: 'Leave him. Do not wrong me. This one's name   111

went into my book the moment he resolved
  to give false counsel. Since then he has been mine,
  for who does not repent cannot be absolved;   114

nor can we admit the possibility
  of repenting a thing at the same time it is willed,
  for the two acts are contradictory.'[5]   117

Miserable me! with what contrition
  I shuddered when he lifted me, saying: 'Perhaps
  you hadn't heard that I was a logician.'[6]   120

He carried me to Minos:[7] eight times round
  his scabby back the monster coiled his tail,
  then biting it in rage he pawed the ground   123

and cried: 'This one is for the thievish fire!'
  And, as you see, I am lost accordingly,
  grieving in heart as I go in this attire."   126

His story told, the flame began to toss
  and writhe its horn. And so it left, and we
  crossed over to the arch of the next fosse   129

where from the iron treasury of the Lord
the fee of wrath is paid the Sowers of Discord.

Canto XXVIII

CIRCLE EIGHT: BOLGIA NINE   *The Sowers of Discord*

The Poets come to the edge of the *Ninth Bolgia* and look down at a parade of
hideously mutilated souls. These are the *Sowers of Discord*, and just as their sin
was to rend asunder what God had meant to be united, so are they hacked and
torn through all eternity by a great demon with a bloody sword. After each mutila-

4. Francis of Assisi (c. 1181–1226), founder
of the order of friars joined by Guido. As patron
saint of Italy, Francis is venerated for his compassion and humility.
5. Guido wanted forgiveness for his sin of guile
at the same time as he was committing it; in

willing the sin he showed that he was not truly
repentant, the precondition for forgiveness.
6. The devil is referring to the logical law of
noncontradiction.
7. For Minos, see 5.4–12.

tion the souls are compelled to drag their broken bodies around the pit and to return to the demon, for in the course of the circuit their wounds knit in time to be inflicted anew. Thus is the law of retribution observed, each sinner suffering according to his degree.

Among them Dante distinguishes three classes with varying degrees of guilt within each class. First come the *Sowers of Religious Discord*. Mahomet (Muhammad) is chief among them, and appears first, cleft from crotch to chin, with his internal organs dangling between his legs. His son-in-law, Ali, drags on ahead of him, cleft from topknot to chin. These reciprocal wounds symbolize Dante's judgment that, between them, these two sum up the total schism between Christianity and Mohammedanism. The revolting details of Mahomet's condition clearly imply Dante's opinion of that doctrine. Mahomet issues an ironic warning to another schismatic, *Fra Dolcino*.

Next come the *Sowers of Political Discord*, among them *Pier da Medicina*, the Tribune *Curio*, and *Mosca deí Lamberti*, each mutilated according to the nature of his sin.

Last of all is *Bertrand de Born, Sower of Discord Between Kinsmen*. He separated father from son, and for that offense carries his head separated from his body, holding it with one hand by the hair, and swinging it as if it were a lantern to light his dark and endless way. The image of Bertrand raising his head at arm's length in order that it might speak more clearly to the Poets on the ridge is one of the most memorable in the *Inferno*. For some reason that cannot be ascertained, Dante makes these sinners quite eager to be remembered in the world, despite the fact that many who lie above them in Hell were unwilling to be recognized.

Who could describe, even in words set free
  of metric and rhyme and a thousand times retold,
  the blood and wounds that now were shown to me!   3

At grief so deep the tongue must wag in vain;
  the language of our sense and memory
  lacks the vocabulary of such pain.   6

If one could gather all those who have stood
  through all of time on Puglia's fateful soil
  and wept for the red running of their blood   9

in the war of the Trojans;[8] and in that long war
  which left so vast a spoil of golden rings,
  as we find written in Livy,[9] who does not err;   12

along with those whose bodies felt the wet
  and gaping wounds of Robert Guiscard's[1] lances;
  with all the rest whose bones are gathered yet   15

---

8. Puglia is in southern Italy; Dante refers here to those killed when the Trojans conquered it in the *Aeneid* 7–12.
9. Roman historian (d. 17 C.E.; he chronicled the Second Punic War (218–201 B.C.E.) between Rome and Carthage under Hannibal.

After the Battle of Cannae (216) the victorious Carthaginians displayed rings taken from fallen Romans.
1. A Norman conqueror (1015–1085) who fought the Greeks and Saracens for control of Sicily and southern Italy in the 11th century.

at Ceperano[2] where every last Pugliese
    turned traitor; and with those from Tagliacozzo[3]
    where Alardo won without weapons—if all these   18

were gathered, and one showed his limbs run through,
    another his lopped off, that could not equal
    the mutilations of the ninth pit's crew.   21

A wine tun when a stave or cant-bar starts
    does not split open as wide as one I saw
    split from his chin to the mouth with which man farts. 24

Between his legs all of his red guts hung
    with the heart, the lungs, the liver, the gall bladder,
    and the shriveled sac that passes shit to the bung.   27

I stood and stared at him from the stone shelf;
    he noticed me and opening his own breast
    with both hands cried: "See how I rip myself!   30

See how Mahomet's[4] mangled and split open!
    Ahead of me walks Ali in his tears,
    his head cleft from the top-knot to the chin.   33

And all the other souls that bleed and mourn
    along this ditch were sowers of scandal and schism:
    as they tore others apart, so are they torn.   36

Behind us, warden of our mangled horde,
    the devil who butchers us and sends us marching
    waits to renew our wounds with his long sword   39

when we have made the circuit of the pit;
    for by the time we stand again before him
    all the wounds he gave us last have knit.   42

But who are you that gawk down from that sill—
    probably to put off your own descent
    to the pit you are sentenced to for your own evil?"   45

"Death has not come for him, guilt does not drive
    his soul to torment," my sweet Guide replied.
    "That he may experience all while yet alive   48

2. A town that the barons of Puglia were pledged to defend for Manfred, the natural son of Frederick II (10.119), but whom they betrayed; he was then killed at the battle of Benevento in 1266.
3. A town where in 1268 Manfred's nephew Conradin was defeated by the strategy rather than the brute force of Alardo de Valery.
4. Muhammad, founder of Islam (570–632), regarded by some medieval Christians as a renegade Christian and a creator of religious disunity. Ali was his nephew and son-in-law, and his disputed claim to the rulership (or caliphate) divided Islam into Sunni and Shi'a sects.

I, who am dead, must lead him through the drear
    and darkened halls of Hell, from round to round:
    and this is true as my own standing here."   51

More than a hundred wraiths who were marching under
    the sill on which we stood, paused at his words
    and stared at me, forgetting pain in wonder.   54

"And if you do indeed return to see
    the sun again, and soon, tell Fra Dolcino[5]
    unless he longs to come and march with me   57

he would do well to cheek his groceries
    before the winter drives him from the hills
    and gives the victory to the Novarese."   60

Mahomet, one foot raised, had paused to say
    these words to me. When he had finished speaking
    he stretched it out and down, and moved away.   63

Another—he had his throat slit, and his nose
    slashed off as far as the eyebrows, and a wound
    where one of his ears had been—standing with those   66

who stared at me in wonder from the pit,
    opened the grinning wound of his red gullet
    as if it were a mouth, and said through it: 69

"O soul unforfeited to misery
    and whom—unless I take you for another—
    I have seen above in our sweet Italy;   72

if ever again you see the gentle plain
    that slopes down from Vercelli to Marcabò,
    remember Pier da Medicina[6] in pain,   75

and announce this warning to the noblest two
    of Fano,[7] Messers Guido and Angiolello:
    that unless our foresight sees what is not true   78

they shall be thrown from their ships into the sea
    and drown in the raging tides near La Cattolica
    to satisfy a tyrant's treachery.   81

5. In 1300 Fra Dolcino was head of a reformist order known as the Apostolic Brothers that was condemned as heretical by the pope. He and his followers escaped to the hills near the town of Novara, but starvation forced them out and many were executed.
6. The town of Medicina lies in the Po Valley between Vercelli and Marcabò. Nothing certain is known of Pier da Medicina.
7. A town on the Adriatic coast of Italy; its two leaders—named in the same line—were drowned in 1312 by the one-eyed tyrant Malatestino of Rimini (see note 3 to 27.45) near the promontory of Focara (see line 90) after he had invited them to the town of La Cattolica for a parley.

Neptune never saw so gross a crime
   in all the seas from Cyprus to Majorca,
   not even in pirate raids, nor the Argive[8] time.   84

The one-eyed traitor,[9] lord of the demesne
   whose hill and streams one who walks here beside me
   will wish eternally he had never seen,   87

will call them to a parley, but behind
   sweet invitations he will work it so
   they need not pray against Focara's wind."   90

And I to him: "If you would have me bear
   your name to time, show me the one who found
   the sight of that land so harsh, and let me hear   93

his story and his name." He touched the cheek
   of one nearby,[1] forcing the jaws apart,
   and said: "This is the one; he cannot speak.   96

This outcast settled Caesar's doubts that day
   beside the Rubicon by telling him:
   'A man prepared is a man hurt by delay.'"   99

Ah, how wretched Curio seemed to me
   with a bloody stump in his throat in place of the tongue
   which once had dared to speak so recklessly!   102

And one among them with both arms hacked through
   cried out, raising his stumps on the foul air
   while the blood bedaubed his face: "Remember, too,   105

Mosca dei Lamberti,[2] alas, who said
   'A thing done has an end!' and with those words
   planted the fields of war with Tuscan dead."   108

"And brought about the death of all your clan!"
   I said, and he, stung by new pain on pain,
   ran off; and in his grief he seemed a madman.   111

I stayed to watch those broken instruments,
   and I saw a thing so strange I should not dare
   to mention it without more evidence   114

8. Cyprus and Majorca are islands at the eastern and western ends of the Mediterranean. Neptune is the classical god of the sea; Argive is another name for Greek.
9. Caius Curio, whose story is told in lines 94–102.
1. Caius Curio, a Roman of the 1st century B.C.E., was bribed by Julius Caesar to betray his friends; he urged Caesar to cross the Rubi-con and invade the Roman Republic, starting a civil war.
2. A Florentine noble, who in 1215 started the civil strife that tore the city apart by advising a father to avenge the slight to his daughter by killing the man who had broken his engagement to her. Mosca's own family was a victim of the strife some 60 years later.

but that my own clear conscience strengthens me,
  that good companion that upholds a man
  within the armor of his purity.   117

I saw it there; I seem to see it still—
  a body without a head, that moved along
  like all the others in that spew and spill.   120

It held the severed head by its own hair,
  swinging it like a lantern in its hand;
  and the head looked at us and wept in its despair.   123

It made itself a lamp of its own head,
  and they were two in one and one in two;
  how this can be, He knows who so commanded.   126

And when it stood directly under us
  it raised the head at arm's length toward our bridge
  the better to be heard, and swaying thus   129

it cried:[3] "O living soul in this abyss,
  see what a sentence has been passed upon me,
  and search all Hell for one to equal this!   132

When you return to the world, remember me:
  I am Bernard de Born, and it was I
  who set the young king on to mutiny,   135

son against father, father against son
  as Achitophel set Absalom and David;
  and since I parted those who should be one   138

in duty and in love, I bear my brain
  divided from its source within this trunk;
  and walk here where my evil turns to pain,   142

an eye for an eye to all eternity:
thus is the law of Hell observed in me."[4]

Canto XXIX

CIRCLE EIGHT: BOLGIA TEN   *The Falsifers*
     (Class I, Alchemists)

Dante lingers on the edge of the Ninth Bolgia expecting to see one of his kinsmen, *Geri del Bello*, among the Sowers of Discord. Virgil, however, hurries him
on, since time is short, and as they cross the bridge over the *Tenth Bolgia*, Virgil

3. This is Bertran de Born, a Provençal nobleman and poet, who reputedly advised the son
of Henry II of England to rebel against his
father. For Achitophel's similar scheming
between David and his son Absalom, see 2
Samuel 15–17. A poem by Bertran is included
in Medieval Lyrics (pp. 337–38).
4. In Dante's hell, the sinner is punished by
having to commit his sin for all of eternity.

explains that he had a glimpse of Geri among the crowd near the bridge and that he had been making threatening gestures at Dante.

The Poets now look into the last *Bolgia* of the Eighth Circle and see *The Falsifiers*. They are punished by afflictions of every sense by darkness, stench, thirst, fifth, loathsome diseases, and a shrieking din. Some of them, moreover, run ravening through the pit, tearing others to pieces. Just as in life they corrupted society by their falsifications, so in death these sinners are subjected to a sum of corruptions. In one sense they figure forth what society would be if all falsifiers succeeded—a place where the senses are an affliction (since falsification deceives the senses) rather than a guide, where even the body has no honesty, and where some lie prostrate while others run ravening to prey upon them.

Not all of these details are made clear until the next canto, for Dante distinguishes four classes of Falsifiers, and in the present canto we meet only the first class, *The Alchemists*, the Falsifiers of Things. Of this class are *Griffolino D'Arezzo* and *Capocchio*, with both of whom Dante speaks.

The sight of that parade of broken dead
   had left my eyes so sotted with their tears
   I longed to stay and weep, but Virgil said: 3

"What are you waiting for? Why do you stare
   as if you could not tear your eyes away
   from the mutilated shadows passing there?   6

You did not act so in the other pits.
   Consider—if you mean perhaps to count them—
   this valley and its train of dismal spirits   9

winds twenty-two miles round.[5] The moon already
   is under our feet; the time we have is short,[6]
   and there is much that you have yet to see."   12

"Had you known what I was seeking," I replied,
   "you might perhaps have given me permission
   to stay on longer." (As I spoke, my Guide   15

had started off already, and I in turn
   had moved along behind him; thus, I answered
   as we moved along the cliff.) "Within that cavern   18

upon whose brim I stood so long to stare,
   I think a spirit of my own blood mourns
   the guilt that sinners find so costly there."   21

And the Master then: "Hereafter let your mind
   turn its attention to more worthy matters
   and leave him to his fate among the blind;   24

5. The reason for this exact measurement is not known. At 30.86 we are told that the circumference of the ninth circle is 11 miles, showing that Hell is shaped like a funnel.

6. This means that the sun (which they cannot see) is over their heads, and the time is about 2:00 p.m. The journey to the center of Hell lasts 24 hours, so only 4 hours are left.

for by the bridge and among that shapeless crew
  I saw him point to you with threatening gestures,
  and I heard him called Geri del Bello.[7] You   27

were occupied at the time with that headless one
  who in his life was master of Altaforte,[8]
  and did not look that way; so he moved on."   30

"O my sweet Guide," I answered, "his death came
  by violence and is not yet avenged
  by those who share his blood, and, thus, his shame. 33

For this he surely hates his kin, and, therefore,
  as I suppose, he would not speak to me;
  and in that he makes me pity him the more."   36

We spoke of this until we reached the edge
  from which, had there been light, we could have seen
  the floor of the next pit. Out from that ledge   39

Malebolge's final cloister lay outspread,
  and all of its lay brethren might have been
  in sight but for the murk; and from those dead   42

such shrieks and strangled agonies shrilled through me
  like shafts, but barbed with pity, that my hands
  flew to my ears. If all the misery   45

that crams the hospitals of pestilence
  in Maremma, Valdichiano, and Sardinia
  in the summer months when death sits like a presence[9] 48

on the marsh air, were dumped into one trench—
  that might suggest their pain. And through the screams,
  putrid flesh spread up its sickening stench.   51

Still bearing left we passed from the long sill
  to the last bridge of Malebolge. There
  the reeking bottom was more visible.   54

There, High Justice, sacred ministress
  of the First Father, reigns eternally
  over the falsifiers in their distress.   57

I doubt it could have been such pain to bear
  the sight of the Aeginian[1] people dying
  that time when such malignance rode the air   60

---

7. First cousin to Dante's father; his death at the hands of a member of another Florentine family initiated a feud between the two families that lasted some 50 years.
8. Bertran de Born (see 28.134).
9. The region of Maremma, the river valley of Val di Chiana, and the island of Sardinia were all plagued by malaria.
1. A mythical island that was infected by Juno with a pestilence that killed all its inhabitants and was then repopulated when Jupiter turned ants into men; see Ovid, *Metamorphoses* 7.

that every beast down to the smallest worm
    shriveled and died (it was after that great plague
    that the Ancient People, as the poets affirm,   63

were reborn from the ants)—as it was to see
    the spirits lying heaped on one another
    in the dank bottom of that fetid valley.   66

One lay gasping on another's shoulder,
    one on another's belly; and some were crawling
    on hands and knees among the broken boulders.   69

Silent, slow step by step, we moved ahead
    looking at and listening to those souls
    too weak to raise themselves from their stone bed.   72

I saw two there like two pans that are put
    one against the other to hold their warmth.[2]
    They were covered with great scabs from head to foot.   75

No stable boy in a hurry to go home,
    or for whom his master waits impatiently,
    ever scrubbed harder with his currycomb[3]   78

than those two spirits of the stinking ditch
    scrubbed at themselves with their own bloody claws
    to ease the furious burning of the itch.   81

And as they scrubbed and clawed themselves, their nails
    drew down the scabs the way a knife scrapes bream[4]
    or some other fish with even larger scales.   84

"O you," my Guide called out to one, "you there
    who rip your scabby mail as if your fingers
    were claws and pincers; tell us if this lair   87

counts any Italians among those who lurk
    in its dark depths; so may your busy nails
    eternally suffice you for your work."   90

"We both are Italian whose unending loss
    you see before you," he replied in tears
    "But who are you who come to question us?"   93

"I am a shade," my Guide and Master said,
    "who leads this living man from pit to pit
    to show him Hell as I have been commanded."   96

---

2. The image is of pans leaned against one another before a kitchen fireplace.

3. A brush used to groom horses.
4. A large fish like a carp.

The sinners broke apart as he replied
   and turned convulsively to look at me,
   as others did who overheard my Guide.   99

My Master, then, ever concerned for me,
   turned and said: "Ask them whatever you wish."
   And I said to those two wraiths of misery: 102

"So may the memory of your names and actions
   not die forever from the minds of men
   in that first world, but live for many suns,   105

tell me who you are and of what city;
   do not be shamed by your nauseous punishment
   into concealing your identity."   108

"I was a man of Arezzo," one replied,
   "and Albert of Siena had me burned;
   but I am not here for the deed for which I died.[5]   111

It is true that jokingly I said to him once:
   'I know how to raise myself and fly through air';
   and he—with all the eagerness of a dunce—   114

wanted to learn. Because I could not make
   a Daedalus of him—for no other reason—
   he had his father burn me at the stake.   117

But Minos, the infallible, had me hurled
   here to the final bolgia of the ten
   for the alchemy[6] I practiced in the world."   120

And I to the Poet: "Was there ever a race
   more vain than the Sienese? Even the French,
   compared to them, seem full of modest grace."   123

And the other leper answered mockingly:[7]
   "Excepting Stricca, who by careful planning
   managed to live and spend so moderately;   126

and Niccolò, who in his time above
   was first of all the shoots in that rank garden
   to discover the costly uses of the clove;   129

5. Griffolino of Arezzo cheated Albero (Albert) of Siena by promising to teach him the art of Daedalus—flying. The bishop of Siena, father of the illegitimate Albero, had Griffolino burned as a heretic.
6. A practice that sought to turn base metals like lead into gold. Alchemy was not condemned outright by the Catholic Church (and in fact alchemy was practiced by many prominent clerics), but its association with the occult and with sheer greed made alchemy morally suspect.
7. The speaker is Capocchio, a Florentine burned in 1293 for alchemy, which he here admits was mere counterfeiting. The people he names were rich young noblemen of Siena who joined a "Spendthrifts' Club" and sought to outdo each other in profligacy. For another member of this club, Lano of Siena, see 13.120.

and excepting the brilliant company of talents
    in which Caccia squandered his vineyards and his woods,
    and Abbagliato displayed his intelligence.   132

But if you wish to know who joins your cry
    against the Sienese, study my face
    with care and let it make its own reply.   135

So you will see I am the suffering shadow
    of Capocchio, who, by practicing alchemy,
    falsified the metals, and you must know,   138

unless my mortal recollection strays
how good an ape I was of Nature's ways."[8]

Canto XXX

    *The Falsifiers (The Remaining Three Classes:
Evil Impersonators, Counterfeiters, False Witnesses)*

Just as Capocchio finishes speaking, two ravenous spirits come racing through the pit; and one of them, sinking his tusks into Capocchio's neck, drags him away like prey. Capocchio's companion, Griffolino, identifies the two as *Gianni Schicchi* and *Myrrhe*, who run ravening through the pit through all eternity, snatching at other souls and rending them. These are the *Evil Impersonators*, Falsifiers of Persons. In life they seized upon the appearance of others, and in death they must run with never a pause, seizing upon the infernal apparition of these souls, while they in turn are preyed upon by their own furies.

Next the Poets encounter *Master Adam*, a sinner of the third class, a Falsifier of Money, i.e., a *Counterfeiter*. Like the alchemists, he is punished by a loathsome disease and he cannot move from where he lies, but his disease is compounded by other afflictions, including an eternity of unbearable thirst. Master Adam identifies two spirits lying beside him as *Potiphar's Wife* and *Sinon the Greek*, sinners of the fourth class, *The False Witnesses*, i.e., Falsifiers of Words.

Sinon, angered by Master Adam's identification of him, strikes him across the belly with the one arm he is able to move. Master Adam replies in kind; and Dante, fascinated by their continuing exchange of abuse, stands staring at them until Virgil turns on him in great anger, for "The wish to hear such baseness is degrading." Dante burns with shame, and Virgil immediately forgives him because of his great and genuine repentance.

At the time when Juno took her furious
    revenge for Semele,[9] striking in rage
    again and again at the Theban royal house,

8. By calling himself "an ape . . . of Nature's ways," Capocchio means that he merely imitated change in his alchemical displays rather than actually accomplishing it.
9. Daughter of the king of Thebes, Semele was loved by Jupiter (their union produced Bacchus, the god of wine) and therefore incited the wrath of Juno, who drove her brother-in-law Athamas insane. While mad, Athamas thought his wife, Ino, and his two sons, Learchus and Melicertes, were a lioness and two cubs: he killed Learchus, and Ino drowned herself and Melicertes. See Ovid, *Metamorphoses* 4.

King Athamas, by her contrivance, grew
   so mad, that seeing his wife out for an airing
   with his two sons, he cried to his retinue: 6

"Out with the nets there! Nets across the pass!
   for I will take this lioness and her cubs!"
   And spread his talons, mad and merciless,   9

and seizing his son Learchus, whirled him round
   and brained him on a rock; at which the mother
   leaped into the sea with her other son and drowned.   12

And when the Wheel of Fortune spun about
   to humble the all-daring Trojan's pride[1]
   so that both king and kingdom were wiped out;   15

Hecuba—mourning, wretched, and a slave—
   having seen Polyxena sacrificed,
   and Polydorus dead without a grave;   18

lost and alone, beside an alien sea,
   began to bark and growl like a dog
   in the mad seizure of her misery.   21

But never in Thebes nor Troy were Furies seen
   to strike at man or beast in such mad rage
   as two I saw, pale, naked, and unclean,   24

who suddenly came running toward us then,
   snapping their teeth as they ran, like hungry swine
   let out to feed after a night in the pen.   27

One of them sank his tusks so savagely
   into Capocchio's neck, that when he dragged him,
   the ditch's rocky bottom tore his belly.   30

And the Aretine,[2] left trembling by me, said:
   "That incubus, in life, was Gianni Schicchi;[3]
   here he runs rabid, mangling the other dead."   33

"So!" I answered, "and so may the other one
   not sink its teeth in you, be pleased to tell us
   what shade it is before it races on."   36

---

1. Parallel to the fate of Thebes is that of Troy, which is here represented by the madness into which Queen Hecuba fell when she saw her daughter Polyxena sacrificed on Achilles' tomb and the unburied body of her betrayed son Polydorus. See Ovid, *Metamorphoses* 13.

2. Griffolino (see 29.111).
3. A Florentine who impersonated Buoso Donati (line 44), who had just died, and dictated a new will that gave him Buoso's best beast ("the fabulous lead-mare" of line 43).

And he: "That ancient shade in time above
    was Myrrha,[4] vicious daughter of Cinyras
    who loved her father with more than rightful love.   39

She falsified another's form and came
    disguised to sin with him just as that other
    who runs with her, in order that he might claim   42

the fabulous lead-mare, lay under disguise
    on Buoso Donati's deathbed and dictated
    a spurious testament to the notaries."   45

And when the rabid pair had passed from sight,
    I turned to observe the other misbegotten
    spirits that lay about to left and right.   48

And there I saw another husk of sin,
    who, had his legs been trimmed away at the groin,
    would have looked for all the world like a mandolin.   51

The dropsy's[5] heavy humors, which so bunch
    and spread the limbs, had disproportioned him
    till his face seemed much too small for his swollen paunch.   54

He strained his lips apart and thrust them forward
    the way a sick man, feverish with thirst,
    curls one lip toward the chin and the other upward.   57

"O you exempt from every punishment
    of this grim world (I know not why)," he cried,
    "look well upon the misery and debasement   60

of him who was Master Adam.[6] In my first
    life's time, I had enough to please me; here,
    I lack a drop of water for my thirst.   63

The rivulets that run from the green flanks
    of Casentino to the Arno's flood,
    spreading their cool sweet moisture through their banks,   66

run constantly before me, and their plash
    and ripple in imagination dries me
    more than the disease that eats my flesh.   69

---

4. Myrrha impersonated another woman in order to sleep with her father; see Ovid, *Metamorphoses* 10.
5. A disease in which fluid ("humors") gathers in the cells and the affected part becomes grotesquely swollen.
6. A counterfeiter, burned in 1281, who made coins stamped with the image of John the Baptist, the patron saint of Florence, that contained 21 rather than 24 carats of gold (see line 90); he worked for a noble family of Romena (individual members are mentioned in lines 76–77), a town in the Florentine district of Casentino.

Inflexible Justice that has forked and spread
   my soul like hay, to search it the more closely,
   finds in the country where my guilt was bred   72

this increase of my grief; for there I learned,
   there in Romena, to stamp the Baptist's image
   on alloyed gold—till I was bound and burned.   75

But could I see the soul of Guido here,
   or of Alessandro, or of their filthy brother,
   I would not trade that sight for all the clear   78

cool flow of Branda's fountain.[7] One of the three—
   if those wild wraiths who run here are not lying—
   is here already. But small good it does me   81

when my legs are useless! Were I light enough
   to move as much as an inch in a hundred years,
   long before this I would have started off   84

to cull him from the freaks that fill this fosse,
   although it winds on for eleven miles
   and is no less than half a mile across.   87

Because of them I lie here in this pig-pen;
   it was they persuaded me to stamp the florins
   with three carats of alloy." And I then: 90

"Who are those wretched two sprawled alongside
   your right-hand borders, and who seem to smoke
   as a washed hand smokes in winter?" He replied: 93

"They were here when I first rained into this gully,
   and have not changed position since, nor may they,
   as I believe, to all eternity.   96

One is the liar who charged young Joseph wrongly:
   the other, Sinon, the false Greek from Troy.[8]
   A burning fever makes them reek so strongly."   99

And one of the false pair, perhaps offended
   by the manner of Master Adam's presentation,
   punched him in the rigid and distended   102

belly—it thundered like a drum—and he
   retorted with an arm blow to the face
   that seemed delivered no whit less politely,   105

7. A fountain near Romena.
8. The "liar" is Potiphar's wife, who falsely accused Joseph of trying to lie with her (Gen- esis 39.7–20); Sinon is the Greek priest who persuaded the Trojans to accept the wooden horse (*Aeneid* 2).

saying to him: "Although I cannot stir
   my swollen legs, I still have a free arm
   to use at times when nothing else will answer."   108

And the other wretch said: "It was not so free
   on your last walk to the stake, free as it was
   when you were coining." And he of the dropsy: 111

"That's true enough, but there was less truth in you
   when they questioned you at Troy." And Sinon then:
   "For every word I uttered that was not true   114

you uttered enough false coins to fill a bushel:
   I am put down here for a single crime,
   but you for more than any Fiend in Hell."   117

"Think of the Horse," replied the swollen shade,
   "and may it torture you, perjurer, to recall
   that all the world knows the foul part you played."   120

"And to you the torture of the thirst that fries
   and cracks your tongue," said the Greek, "and of the water
   that swells your gut like a hedge before your eyes."   123

And the coiner: "So is your own mouth clogged
   with the filth that stuffs and sickens it as always;
   if I am parched while my paunch is waterlogged,   126

you have the fever and your cankered brain;
   and were you asked to lap Narcissus' mirror[9]
   you would not wait to be invited again."   129

I was still standing, fixed upon those two
   when the Master said to me: "Now keep on looking
   a little longer and I quarrel with you."   132

When I heard my Master raise his voice to me,
   I wheeled about with such a start of shame
   that I grow pale yet at the memory.   135

As one trapped in a nightmare that has caught
   his sleeping mind, wishes within the dream
   that it were all a dream, as if it were not—   138

such I became: my voice could not win through
   my shame to ask his pardon; while my shame
   already won more pardon than I knew.   141

---

9. Narcissus saw his reflection in a pool of water, referred to here as a "mirror" (Ovid, *Metamorphoses* 3).

"Less shame," my Guide said, ever just and kind,
   "would wash away a greater fault than yours.
   Therefore, put back all sorrow from your mind;   144

And never forget that I am always by you
   should it occur again, as we walk on,
   that we find ourselves where others of this crew   147

fall to such petty wrangling and upbraiding.
   The wish to hear such baseness is degrading."

Canto XXXI

THE CENTRAL PIT OF MALEBOLGE   *The Giants*

Dante's spirits rise again as the Poets approach the Central Pit, a great well, at
the bottom of which lies Cocytus, the Ninth and final circle of Hell. Through the
darkness Dante sees what appears to be a city of great towers, but as he draws
near he discovers that the great shapes he has seen are the Giants and Titans who
stand perpetual guard inside the well-pit with the upper halves of their bodies
rising above the rim.

   Among the Giants, Virgil identifies *Nimrod*, builder of the Tower of Babel;
Ephialtes and *Briareus*, who warred against the Gods; and *Tityos* and *Typhon*,
who insulted Jupiter. Also here, but for no specific offense, is *Antaeus,* and his
presence makes it clear that the Giants are placed here less for their particular
sins than for their general natures.

   These are the sons of earth, embodiments of elemental forces unbalanced by
love, desire without restraint and without acknowledgment of moral and theological law. They are symbols of the earth-trace that every devout man must clear
from his soul, the unchecked passions of the beast. Raised from the earth, they
make the very gods tremble. Now they are returned to the darkness of their origins, guardians of earth's last depth.

   At Virgil's persuasion, Antaeus takes the Poets in his huge palm and lowers
them gently to the final floor of Hell.

One and the same tongue had first wounded me
   so that the blood came rushing to my cheeks,
   and then supplied the soothing remedy.   3

Just so, as I have heard, the magic steel
   of the lance that was Achilles' and his father's
   could wound at a touch, and, at another, heal.[1]   6

We turned our backs on the valley and climbed from it
   to the top of the stony bank that walls it round,
   crossing in silence to the central pit.   9

---

1. Achilles' father, Peleus, gave him a lance that would heal any wound it inflicted.

Here it was less than night and less than day;
  my eyes could make out little through the gloom,
  but I heard the shrill note of a trumpet bray   12

louder than any thunder. As if by force,
  it drew my eyes; I stared into the gloom
  along the path of the sound back to its source.   15

After the bloody rout when Charlemagne[2]
  had lost the band of Holy Knights, Roland
  blew no more terribly for all his pain.   18

And as I stared through that obscurity,
  I saw what seemed a cluster of great towers,
  whereat I cried: "Master, what is this city?"   21

And he: "You are still too far back in the dark
  to make out clearly what you think you see;
  it is natural that you should miss the mark: 24

you will see clearly when you reach that place
  how much your eyes mislead you at a distance;
  I urge you, therefore, to increase your pace."   27

Then taking my hand in his, my Master said:
  "The better to prepare you for strange truth,
  let me explain those shapes you see ahead: 30

they are not towers but giants. They stand in the well
  from the navel down; and stationed round its bank
  they mount guard on the final pit of Hell."   33

Just as a man in a fog that starts to clear
  begins little by little to piece together
  the shapes the vapor crowded from the air—   36

so, when those shapes grew clearer as I drew
  across the darkness to the central brink,
  error fled from me; and my terror grew.   39

For just as at Montereggione[3] the great towers
  crown the encircling wall; so the grim giants[4]
  whom Jove still threatens when the thunder roars   42

---

2. In *The Song of Roland* (laisse 133), Roland blows his horn to alert Charlemagne to the fact that the rear guard Roland commands has been slaughtered.
3. A castle surrounded by towers, built to pro-

tect Siena from attack by Florence.
4. These "giants" are the mythological Titans, monsters born of the Earth who assaulted Olympus and were defeated and imprisoned by Jupiter (Jove).

raised from the rim of stone about that well
    the upper halves of their bodies, which loomed up
    like turrets through the murky air of Hell.   45

I had drawn close enough to one already
    to make out the great arms along his sides,
    the face, the shoulders, the breast, and most of the belly.[5]   48

Nature, when she destroyed the last exemplars
    on which she formed those beasts, surely did well
    to take such executioners from Mars.   51

And if she has not repented the creation
    of whales and elephants, the thinking man
    will see in that her justice and discretion: 54

for where the instrument of intelligence
    is added to brute power and evil will,
    mankind is powerless in its own defense.   57

His face, it seemed to me, was quite as high
    and wide as the bronze pine cone in St. Peter's[6]
    with the rest of him proportioned accordingly: 60

so that the bank, which made an apron for him
    from the waist down, still left so much exposed
    that three Frieslanders[7] standing on the rim,   63

one on another, could not have reached his hair;
    for to that point at which men's capes are buckled,
    thirty good hand-spans[8] of brute bulk rose clear.   66

"Rafel mahee amek zabi almit,"[9]
    began a bellowed chant from the brute mouth
    for which no sweeter psalmody was fit.   69

And my Guide in his direction: "Babbling fool,
    stick to your horn[1] and vent yourself with it
    when rage or passion stir your stupid soul.   72

Feel there around your neck, you muddle-head,
    and find the cord; and there's the horn itself,
    there on your overgrown chest." To me he said: 75

---

5. This is Nimrod, described as "a mighty hunter before the Lord" (Genesis 10.9) and understood by medieval commentators to be a giant. He ruled over Babylon, where the tower of Babel was built (Genesis 11.1–9).
6. This bronze pine cone, over 12 feet high, stood outside St. Peter's Cathedral in Dante's time; today it can be seen in the papal gardens in the Vatican.

7. Inhabitants of the northernmost province of what is now the Netherlands, considered the tallest men of the time.
8. About 15 feet.
9. Appropriately for the builder of Babel, he speaks an incomprehensible language.
1. Nimrod has a "horn" because in the Bible he is described as a hunter (Genesis 10.9).

"His very babbling testifies the wrong
   he did on earth: he is Nimrod, through whose evil
   mankind no longer speaks a common tongue.   78

Waste no words on him: it would be foolish.
   To him all speech is meaningless; as his own,
   which no one understands, is simply gibberish."   81

We moved on, bearing left along the pit,
   and a crossbow-shot away we found the next one,[2]
   an even huger and more savage spirit.   84

What master could have bound so gross a beast
   I cannot say, but he had his right arm pinned
   behind his back, and the left across his breast   87

by an enormous chain that wound about him
   from the neck down, completing five great turns
   before it spiraled down below the rim.   90

"This piece of arrogance," said my Guide to me,
   "dared try his strength against the power of Jove;
   for which he is rewarded as you see.   93

He is Ephialtes, who made the great endeavour
   with the other giants who alarmed the Gods;
   the arms he raised then, now are bound forever."   96

"Were it possible, I should like to take with me,"
   I said to him, "the memory of seeing
   the immeasurable Briareus."[3] And he: 99

"Nearer to hand, you may observe Antaeus[4]
   who is able to speak to us, and is not bound.
   It is he will set us down in Cocytus,   102

the bottom of all guilt. The other hulk
   stands far beyond our road. He too, is bound
   and looks like this one, but with a fiercer sulk."   105

No earthquake in the fury of its shock
   has ever seized a tower more violently,
   than Ephialtes, hearing, began to rock.   108

Then I dreaded death as never before;
   and I think I could have died for very fear
   had I not seen what manacles he wore.   111

2. This is Ephialtes, a Titan who with his twin brother Otus tried to attack Olympus by piling Mount Ossa on Mount Pelion; see *Aeneid* 6.
3. Another Titan.
4. A Titan born too late to participate in the rebellion against Jupiter and therefore not chained; he was known for eating lions (line 118) and was defeated by Hercules in a wrestling match (line 132).

We left the monster, and not far from him
  we reached Antaeus, who to his shoulders alone
  soared up a good five ells[5] above the rim.   114

"O soul who once in Zama's fateful vale—[6]
  where Scipio became the heir of glory
  when Hannibal and all his troops turned tail—   117

took more than a thousand lions for your prey;
  and in whose memory many still believe
  the sons of earth would yet have won the day   120

had you joined with them against High Olympus—
  do not disdain to do us a small service,
  but set us down where the cold grips Cocytus.[7]   123

Would you have us go to Tityos or Typhon?—[8]
  this man can give you what is longed for here:
  therefore do not refuse him, but bend down.   126

For he can still make new your memory:
  he lives, and awaits long life, unless Grace call him
  before his time to his felicity."   129

Thus my Master to that Tower of Pride;
  and the giant without delay reached out the hands
  which Hercules had felt, and raised my Guide.   132

Virgil, when he felt himself so grasped,
  called to me: "Come, and I will hold you safe."
  And he took me in his arms and held me clasped.   135

The way the Carisenda[9] seems to one
  who looks up from the leaning side when clouds
  are going over it from that direction,   138

making the whole tower seem to topple—so
  Antaeus seemed to me in the fraught moment
  when I stood clinging, watching from below   141

as he bent down; while I with heart and soul
  wished we had gone some other way, but gently
  he set us down inside the final hole   144

whose ice holds Judas and Lucifer[1] in its grip.
Then straightened like a mast above a ship.

---

5. About 19 feet.
6. The "vale" of the Bagradas River in Tunisia, where the Roman Scipio defeated the Carthaginian Hannibal in the Battle of Zama in 202 B.C.E.
7. The frozen lake of Cocytus is in the ninth and last circle of Hell.
8. Two more Titans.
9. A leaning tower of Bologna: when a cloud passes over it, moving opposite to the tower's slant, it appears to be falling away from the sky.
1. Two of the inhabitants of Cocytus.

Canto XXXII

CIRCLE NINE: COCYTUS

ROUND ONE: CAÏNA

ROUND TWO: ANTENORA

Compound Fraud

The Treacherous to Kin

The Treacherous to Country

At the bottom of the well Dante finds himself on a huge frozen lake. This is *Cocytus*, the *Ninth Circle*, the fourth and last great water of Hell, and here, fixed in the ice, each according to his guilt, are punished sinners guilty of *Treachery against Those to Whom They Were Bound by Special Ties*. The ice is divided into four concentric rings marked only by the different positions of the damned within the ice.

This is Dante's symbolic equivalent of the final guilt. The treacheries of these souls were denials of love (which is God) and of all human warmth. Only the remorseless dead center of the ice will serve to express their natures. As they denied God's love, so are they furthest removed from the light and warmth of His Sun. As they denied all human ties, so are they bound only by the unyielding ice.

The first round is *Caïna*, named for Cain. Here lie those who were treacherous against blood ties. They have their necks and heads out of the ice and are permitted to bow their heads—a double boon since it allows them some protection from the freezing gale and, further, allows their tears to fall without freezing their eyes shut. Here Dante sees *Alessandro* and *Napoleone degli Alberti*, and he speaks to *Camicion*, who identifies other sinners of this round.

The second round is *Antenora*, named for Antenor, the Trojan who was believed to have betrayed his city to the Greeks. Here lie those guilty of *Treachery to Country*. They, too, have their heads above the ice, but they cannot bend their necks, which are gripped by the ice. Here Dante accidentally kicks the head of *Bocca degli Abbati* and then proceeds to treat him with a savagery he has shown to no other soul in Hell. Bocca names some of his fellow traitors, and the Poets pass on to discover two heads frozen together in one hole. One of them is gnawing the nape of the other's neck.

If I had rhymes as harsh and horrible
   as the hard fact of that final dismal hole
   which bears the weight of all the steeps of Hell,   3

I might more fully press the sap and substance
   from my conception; but since I must do
   without them, I begin with some reluctance.   6

For it is no easy undertaking, I say,
   to describe the bottom of the Universe;
   nor is it for tongues that only babble child's play.   9

But may those Ladies of the Heavenly Spring[2]
   who helped Amphion wall Thebes, assist my verse,
   that the word may be the mirror of the thing.   12

2. The Muses who helped the legendary musician Amphion raise the walls of Thebes with the music of his lyre.

O most miscreant rabble, you who keep
   the stations of that place whose name is pain,
   better had you been born as goats or sheep!   15

We stood now in the dark pit of the well,
   far down the slope below the Giant's feet,
   and while I still stared up at the great wall,   18

I heard a voice cry: "Watch which way you turn:
   take care you do not trample on the heads
   of the forworn and miserable brethren."   21

Whereat I turned and saw beneath my feet
   and stretching out ahead, a lake so frozen
   it seemed to be made of glass.[3] So thick a sheet   24

never yet hid the Danube's winter course,
   nor, far away beneath the frigid sky,
   locked the Don up in its frozen source: 27

for were Tanbernick[4] and the enormous peak
   of Pietrapana to crash down on it,
   not even the edges would so much as creak.   30

The way frogs sit to croak, their muzzles leaning
   out of the water, at the time and season
   when the peasant woman dreams of her day's gleaning—   33

just so the livid dead are sealed in place
   up to the part at which they blushed for shame,
   and they beat their teeth like storks.[5] Each holds his face   36

bowed toward the ice, each of them testifies
   to the cold with his chattering mouth, to his heart's grief
   with tears that flood forever from his eyes.   39

When I had stared about me, I looked down
   and at my feet I saw two clamped together
   so tightly that the hair of their heads had grown   42

together. "Who are you," I said, "who lie
   so tightly breast to breast?"[6] They strained their necks,
   and when they had raised their heads as if to reply,   45

---

3. The water for this lake derives from the crack in the Old Man of Crete (14.106–8).

4. Probably Mount Tambura, close to Mount Pietrapana in the Italian Alps. The Danube, in Central Europe, and the Don, in Russia, represent rivers of the north.

5. A harsh, clacking sound. The "part at which they blushed" is the face.

6. These are the two sons of Count Alberto degli Alberti of Florence; when he died (ca. 1280), they killed each other over politics and their inheritance.

the tears their eyes had managed to contain
   up to that time gushed out, and the cold froze them
   between the lids, sealing them shut again   48

tighter than any clamp grips wood to wood,
   and mad with pain, they fell to butting heads
   like billy goats in a sudden savage mood.   51

And a wraith who lay to one side and below,
   and who had lost both ears to frostbite, said,
   his head still bowed: "Why do you watch us so?   54

If you wish to know who they are who share one doom,
   they owned the Bisenzio's[7] valley with their father,
   whose name was Albert. They sprang from one womb,   57

and you may search through all Caïna's[8] crew
   without discovering in all this waste
   a squab more fit for the aspic than these two;   60

not him whose breast and shadow a single blow
   of the great lance of King Arthur pierced with light;[9]
   nor yet Focaccia; nor this one fastened so   63

into the ice that his head is all I see,
   and whom, if you are Tuscan, you know well—
   his name on the earth was Sassol Mascheroni.[1]   66

And I—to tell you all and so be through—
   was Camicion de' Pazzi.[2] I wait for Carlin[3]
   beside whose guilt my sins will shine like virtue."   69

And leaving him, I saw a thousand faces
   discolored so by cold, I shudder yet
   and always will when I think of those frozen places.   72

As we approached the center of all weight,[4]
   where I went shivering in eternal shade,
   whether it was my will, or chance, or fate,   75

7. A river north of Florence.
8. Named after Cain; this first of the four subdivisions of Cocytus is where those who betrayed their kin are imprisoned.
9. "Not him . . . light": This is Mordred, Arthur's nephew and son; when Arthur pierced him with a sword, he created a wound so large that the sun shone through, thus creating a hole in Mordred's shadow. Focaccia in the next line is a nobleman of Pistoia who killed his cousin.
1. A Florentine nobleman who murdered a relative.
2. A Florentine who killed his kinsman.
3. A Florentine who has betrayed a castle belonging to his party. When he dies (sometime after 1300) he will therefore be sent to the next subdivision, Antenora, for those who committed treachery against their country, city, or party—a harsher punishment, beside whose guilt Camicion says "my sins will shine like virtue."
4. The "center of all weight" is where gravity is strongest and toward which all material things are drawn.

I cannot say, but as I trailed my Guide
   among those heads, my foot struck violently
   against the face of one.[5] Weeping, it cried: 78

"Why do you kick me? If you were not sent
   to wreak a further vengeance for Montaperti,
   why do you add this to my other torment?"   81

"Master," I said, "grant me a moment's pause
   to rid myself of a doubt concerning this one,
   then you may hurry me at your own pace."   84

The Master stopped at once, and through the volley
   of foul abuse the wretch poured out, I said:
   "Who are you who curse others so?" And he: 87

"And who are *you* who go through the dead larder
   of Antenora[6] kicking the cheeks of others
   so hard, that were you alive, you could not kick harder?"   90

"I *am* alive," I said, "and if you seek fame,
   it may be precious to you above all else
   that my notes on this descent include your name."   93

"Exactly the opposite is my wish and hope,"
   he answered. "Let me be; for it's little you know
   of how to flatter on this icy slope."   96

I grabbed the hair of his dog's-ruff[7] and I said:
   "Either you tell me truly who you are,
   or you won't have a hair left on your head."   99

And he: "Not though you snatch me bald. I swear
   I will not tell my name nor show my face.
   Not though you rip until my brain lies bare."   102

I had a good grip on his hair; already
   I had yanked out more than one fistful of it,
   while the wretch yelped, but kept his face turned from me;   105

when another[8] said: "Bocca, what is it ails you?
   What the Hell's wrong? Isn't it bad enough
   to hear you bang your jaws? Must you bark too?"   108

5. Bocca degli Abati (his name is betrayed by one of the fellows damned in line 106); Bocca betrayed his party at the battle of Montaperti in 1260.
6. Dante and Virgil have moved into the second subdivision of Caïna, which is named after Antenor, a Trojan who betrayed the city to the Greeks; it is the location of those who betrayed their country.
7. The hair at the nape of the neck.
8. This is Buoso da Duera, who betrayed Manfred, the ruler of Naples, to his enemy Charles of Anjou in 1265.

"Now filthy traitor, say no more!" I cried,
   "for to your shame, be sure I shall bear back
   a true report of you." The wretch replied: 111

"Say anything you please but go away.
   And if you *do* get back, don't overlook
   that pretty one who had so much to say   114

just now. Here he laments the Frenchman's price.
   'I saw Buoso da Duera,' you can report,
   'where the bad salad is kept crisp on ice.'   117

And if you're asked who else was wintering here,
   Beccheria,[9] whose throat was slit by Florence,
   is there beside you. Gianni de' Soldanier[1]   120

is further down, I think, with Ganelon,
   and Tebaldello, who opened the gates of Faenza
   and let Bologna steal in with the dawn."   123

Leaving him then, I saw two souls together
   in a single hole, and so pinched in by the ice
   that one head made a helmet for the other.   126

As a famished man chews crusts—so the one sinner
   sank his teeth into the other's nape
   at the base of the skull, gnawing his loathsome dinner.   129

Tydeus[2] in his final raging hour
   gnawed Menalippus' head with no more fury
   than this one gnawed at skull and dripping gore.   132

"You there," I said, "who show so odiously
   your hatred for that other, tell me why
   on this condition: that if in what you tell me   135

you seem to have a reasonable complaint
   against him you devour with such foul relish,
   I, knowing who you are, and his soul's taint,   138

may speak your cause to living memory,
   God willing the power of speech be left to me."

9. Tesauro de' Beccheria, a churchman executed for treason in Florence in 1258.
1. Gianni Soldanier was a Florentine nobleman who switched political parties; Ganelon
(line 121) is the betrayer of Roland in the *Song
of Roland*; Tebaldello (line 122) was the citizen of Faenza (a town east of Florence) who
betrayed it to its enemies.
2. In the war against Thebes, Tydeus was mortally wounded by Menalippus, whom he killed
and whose skull he gnawed in fury while dying.

Canto XXXIII

CIRCLE NINE: COCYTUS	*Compound Fraud*
ROUND TWO: ANTENORA	*The Treacherous to Country*
ROUND THREE: PTOLOMEA	*The Treacherous to Guests and Hosts*

In reply to Dante's exhortation, the sinner who is gnawing his companion's head looks up, wipes his bloody mouth on his victim's hair, and tells his harrowing story. He is *Count Ugolino* and the wretch he gnaws is *Archbishop Ruggieri*. Both are in Antenora for treason. In life they had once plotted together. Then Ruggieri betrayed his fellow plotter and caused his death, by starvation, along with his four "sons." In the most pathetic and dramatic passage of the *Inferno*, Ugolino details how their prison was sealed and how his "sons" dropped dead before him one by one, weeping for food. His terrible tale serves only to renew his grief and hatred, and he has hardly finished it before he begins to gnaw Ruggieri again with renewed fury. In the immutable Law of Hell, the killer-by-starvation becomes the food of his victim.

The Poets leave Ugolino and enter *Ptolomea*, so named for the Ptolomaeus of *Maccabees*, who murdered his father-in-law at a banquet. Here are punished those who were *Treacherous against the Ties of Hospitality*. They lie with only half their faces above the ice and their tears freeze in their eye sockets, sealing them with little crystal visors. Thus even the comfort of tears is denied them. Here Dante finds *Friar Alberigo* and *Branca d'Oria*, and discovers the terrible power of Ptolomea: so great is its sin that the souls of the guilty fall to its torments even before they die, leaving their bodies still on earth, inhabited by Demons.

The sinner raised his mouth from his grim repast
    and wiped it on the hair of the bloody head
    whose nape he had all but eaten away. At last   3

he began to speak: "You ask me to renew
    a grief so desperate that the very thought
    of speaking of it tears my heart in two.   6

But if my words may be a seed that bears
    the fruit of infamy for him I gnaw,
    I shall weep, but tell my story through my tears.   9

Who you may be, and by what powers you reach
    into this underworld, I cannot guess,
    but you seem to me a Florentine by your speech.   12

I was Count Ugolino,[3] I must explain;
    this reverend grace is the Archbishop Ruggieri:
    now I will tell you why I gnaw his brain.   15

That I, who trusted him, had to undergo
    imprisonment and death through his treachery,
    you will know already. What you cannot know—   18

---

3. Ugolino, a governor of Pisa who was betrayed by his enemy Archbishop Ruggieri in 1288. His own crime is obliquely explained by his narrative.

that is, the lingering inhumanity
    of the death I suffered—you shall hear in full:
    then judge for yourself if he has injured me.   21

A narrow window in that coop of[4] stone
    now called the Tower of Hunger for my sake
    (within which others yet must pace alone)   24

had shown me several waning moons already
    between its bars, when I slept the evil sleep
    in which the veil of the future parted for me.   27

This beast appeared as master of a hunt
    chasing the wolf and his whelps across the mountain[5]
    that hides Lucca from Pisa. Out in front   30

of the starved and shrewd and avid pack he had placed
    Gualandi and Sismondi and Lanfranchi[6]
    to point his prey. The father and sons had raced   33

a brief course only when they failed of breath
    and seemed to weaken; then I thought I saw
    their flanks ripped open by the hounds' fierce teeth.   36

Before the dawn, the dream still in my head,
    I woke and heard my sons, who were there with me,
    cry from their troubled sleep, asking for bread.   39

You are cruelty itself if you can keep
    your tears back at the thought of what foreboding
    stirred in my heart; and if you do not weep,   42

at what are you used to weeping?—The hour when food
    used to be brought, drew near. They were now awake,
    and each was anxious from his dream's dark mood.   45

And from the base of that horrible tower I heard
    the sound of hammers nailing up the gates:
    I stared at my sons' faces without a word.   48

I did not weep: I had turned stone inside.
    They wept. 'What ails you, Father, you look so strange,'
    my little Anselm, youngest of them, cried.   51

4. A cage for birds; the prison in Pisa where Ugolino and his relatives were confined became known as the Torre de Fame or Tower of Hunger.
5. Mount San Giuliano lies between Pisa and Lucca. "The wolf and his whelps": Ugolino and his four sons. Ugolino was imprisoned with two sons (who were grown men) and two adolescent grandsons.
6. Pisan families of the political party opposed to that of Ugolino.

But I did not speak a word nor shed a tear:
    not all that day nor all that endless night,
    until I saw another sun appear.   54

When a tiny ray leaked into that dark prison
    and I saw staring back from their four faces
    the terror and the wasting of my own,   57

I bit my hands in helpless grief. And they,
    thinking I chewed myself for hunger, rose
    suddenly together. I heard them say: 60

'Father, it would give us much less pain
    if you ate us: it was you who put upon us
    this sorry flesh; now strip it off again.'[7]   63

I calmed myself to spare them. Ah! hard earth,
    why did you not yawn open? All that day
    and the next we sat in silence. On the fourth,   66

Gaddo, the eldest, fell before me and cried,
    stretched at my feet upon that prison floor:
    'Father, why don't you help me?'[8] There he died.   69

And just as you see me, I saw them fall
    one by one on the fifth day and the sixth.
    Then, already blind, I began to crawl   72

from body to body shaking them frantically.
    Two days I called their names, and they were dead.
    Then fasting overcame my grief and me."   75

His eyes narrowed to slits when he was done,
    and he seized the skull again between his teeth
    grinding it as a mastiff grinds a bone.   78

Ah, Pisa! foulest blemish on the land
    where "si" sounds sweet and clear,[9] since those nearby you
    are slow to blast the ground on which you stand,   81

may Caprara and Gorgona[1] drift from place
    and dam the flooding Arno at its mouth
    until it drowns the last of your foul race!   84

For if to Ugolino falls the censure
    for having betrayed your castles,[2] you for your part
    should not have put his sons to such a torture: 87

7. See Job 1.21.
8. See Matthew 27.46.
9. I.e., Italy, where *si* means "yes."
1. Islands belonging to Pisa that lie close to

the mouth of the Arno, which flows through
Pisa.
2. In 1285 Ugolino conveyed three Pisan castles
to Lucca and Florence.

you modern Thebes![3] those tender lives you spilt—
   Brigata, Uguccione, and the others
   I mentioned earlier—were too young for guilt!   90

We passed on further, where the frozen mine
   entombs another crew in greater pain;
   these wraiths are not bent over, but lie supine.[4]   93

Their very weeping closes up their eyes;
   and the grief that finds no outlet for its tears
   turns inward to increase their agonies: 96

for the first tears that they shed knot instantly
   in their eye-sockets, and as they freeze they form
   a crystal visor above the cavity.   99

And despite the fact that standing in that place
   I had become as numb as any callus,
   and all sensation had faded from my face,   102

somehow I felt a wind begin to blow,
   whereat I said: "Master, what stirs this wind?
   Is not all heat extinguished here below?"[5]   105

And the Master said to me: "Soon you will be
   where your own eyes will see the source and cause
   and give you their own answer to the mystery."   108

And one of those locked in that icy mall
   cried out to us as we passed: "O souls so cruel
   that you are sent to the last post of all,   111

relieve me for a little from the pain
   of this hard veil; let my heart weep a while
   before the weeping freeze my eyes again."   114

And I to him: "If you would have my service,
   tell me your name; then if I do not help you
   may I descend to the last rim of the ice."   117

"I am Friar Alberigo,"[6] he answered therefore,
   "the same who called for the fruits from the bad garden.
   Here I am given dates for figs full store."   120

3. In classical mythology, Thebes was notorious for its internecine violence, such as the story of Oedipus, his father, Laius, and his sons, Eteocles and Polynices (see 26.54).
4. Virgil and Dante pass into the third subdivision of Cocytus, called Ptolomea (line 124) after Ptolemy, governor of Jericho, who killed his father-in-law, Simon, and two of his sons while they were dining with him (1 Maccabees 16.11–17). In Ptolomea those who have betrayed their guests are punished.
5. Since the sun's heat was thought to cause wind, Dante wonders why he feels wind in this cold place. The answer will be given in 34.46–52.
6. A member of the Jovial Friars (see 23.100), he killed two of his relatives during a banquet at his house, signaling the assassins with an

"What! Are you dead already?" I said to him.
  And he then: "How my body stands in the world
  I do not know. So privileged is this rim   123

of Ptolomea, that often souls fall to it
  before dark Atropos[7] has cut their thread.
  And that you may more willingly free my spirit   126

of this glaze of frozen tears that shrouds my face,
  I will tell you this: when a soul betrays as I did,
  it falls from flesh, and a demon takes its place, 129

ruling the body till its time is spent.
  The ruined soul rains down into this cistern.
  So, I believe, there is still evident   132

in the world above, all that is fair and mortal
  of this black shade who winters here behind me.
  If you have only recently crossed the portal   135

from that sweet world, you surely must have known
  his body: Branca D'Oria[8] is its name,
  and many years have passed since he rained down." 138

"I think you are trying to take me in," I said,
  "Ser Branca D'Oria is a living man;
  he eats, he drinks, he fills his clothes and his bed." 141

"Michel Zanche had not yet reached the ditch
  of the Black Talons," the frozen wraith replied,
  "there where the sinners thicken in hot pitch,   144

when this one left his body to a devil,
  as did his nephew and second in treachery,
  and plumbed like lead through space to this dead level. 147

But now reach out your hand, and let me cry."
  And I did not keep the promise I had made,
  for to be rude to him was courtesy.   150

Ah, men of Genoa! souls of little worth,
  corrupted from all custom of righteousness,
  why have you not been driven from the earth?   153

---

order to bring the fruit. In saying that he is now being served dates instead of figs, he is ironically complimenting God for his generosity, since a date would be more valuable than a fig.
7. One of the mythological figures known as the Fates, she is the one who cuts the thread of life.
8. A nobleman of Genoa, who with a "nephew" (line 146) killed his father-in-law, Michel Zanche (line 142), at a banquet in 1275.

For there beside the blackest soul of all
   Romagna's evil plain, lies one of yours
   bathing his filthy soul[9] in the eternal   156

glacier of Cocytus for his foul crime,
   while he seems yet alive in world and time!

Canto XXXIV

NINTH CIRCLE: COCYTUS	*Compound Fraud*
ROUND FOUR: JUDECCA	*The Treacherous to Their Masters*
THE CENTER	*Satan*

"On march the banners of the King," Virgil begins as the Poets face the last depth. He is quoting a medieval hymn, and to it he adds the distortion and perversion of all that lies about him. "On march the banners of the King—of Hell." And there before them, in an infernal parody of Godhead, they see Satan in the distance, his great wings beating like a windmill. It is their beating that is the source of the icy wind of Cocytus, the exhalation of all evil.

All about him in the ice are strewn the sinners of the last round, *Judecca*, named for Judas Iscariot. These are the *Treacherous to Their Masters*. They lie completely sealed in the ice, twisted and distorted into every conceivable posture. It is impossible to speak to them, and the Poets move on to observe Satan.

He is fixed into the ice at the center to which flow all the rivers of guilt; and as he beats his great wings as if to escape, their icy wind only freezes him more surely into the polluted ice. In a grotesque parody of the Trinity, he has three faces, each a different color, and in each mouth he clamps a sinner whom he rips eternally with his teeth. *Judas Iscariot* is in the central mouth: *Brutus* and *Cassius* in the mouths on either side.

Having seen all, the Poets now climb through the center, grappling hand over hand down the hairy flank of Satan himself—a last supremely symbolic action—and at last, when they have passed the center of all gravity, they emerge from Hell. A long climb from the earth's center to the Mount of Purgatory awaits them, and they push on without rest, ascending along the sides of the river Lethe, till they emerge once more to see the stars of Heaven, just before dawn on Easter Sunday.

"On march the banners of the King of Hell,"[1]
   my Master said. "Toward us. Look straight ahead:
   can you make him out at the core of the frozen shell?"   3

Like a whirling windmill seen afar at twilight,
   or when a mist has risen from the ground—
   just such an engine rose upon my sight   6

9. That is, Friar Alberigo (line 118); Romagna is the part of Italy from which he and Branca come.

1. The first few words—"On march the banners of the King"—are opening lines of a 6th-century Latin hymn traditionally sung during Holy Week to celebrate Christ's Passion. Dante has added the last word, *Inferni*—"On march the banners of the King of Hell"—in order to apply the words to Satan.

stirring up such a wild and bitter wind
  I cowered for shelter at my Master's back,
  there being no other windbreak I could find.   9

I stood now[2] where the souls of the last class
  (with fear my verses tell it) were covered wholly;
  they shone below the ice like straws in glass.   12

Some lie stretched out; others are fixed in place
  upright, some on their heads, some on their soles;
  another, like a bow, bends foot to face.   15

When we had gone so far across the ice
  that it pleased my Guide to show me the foul creature
  that once had worn the grace of Paradise,[3]   18

he made me stop, and, stepping aside, he said:
  "Now see the face of Dis![4] This is the place
  where you must arm your soul against all dread."   21

Do not ask, Reader, how my blood ran cold
  and my voice choked up with fear. I cannot write it:
  this is a terror that cannot be told.   24

I did not die, and yet I lost life's breath:
  imagine for yourself what I became,
  deprived at once of both my life and death.   27

The Emperor of the Universe of Pain
  jutted his upper chest above the ice;
  and I am closer in size to the great mountain   30

the Titans make around the central pit,
  than they to his arms. Now, starting from this part,
  imagine the whole that corresponds to it!   33

If he was once as beautiful as now
  he is hideous, and still turned on his Maker,
  well may he be the source of every woe!   36

With what a sense of awe I saw his head
  towering above me! for it had three faces:[5]
  one was in front, and it was fiery red;   39

2. This is the last and lowest subdivision of Caïna, known as Judecca after Judas; the sinners here are those who betrayed their benefactors.
3. Lucifer, the "light-bearer," was the most beautiful of angels before he rebelled and was renamed Satan.
4. A classical name for Pluto, here applied to Satan (see also 11.65).
5. Satan's three faces (and much else) make him an infernal parody of the Trinity.

the other two, as weirdly wonderful,
  merged with it from the middle of each shoulder
  to the point where all converged at the top of the skull; 42

the right was something between white and bile;
  the left was about the color one observes
  on those who live along the banks of the Nile.[6] 45

Under each head two wings rose terribly,
  their span proportioned to so gross a bird:
  I never saw such sails upon the sea. 48

They were not feathers—their texture and their form
  were like a bat's wings—and he beat them so
  that three winds blew from him in one great storm: 51

it is these winds that freeze all Cocytus.
  He wept from his six eyes, and down three chins
  the tears ran mixed with bloody froth and pus. 54

In every mouth he worked a broken sinner
  between his rake-like teeth. Thus he kept three
  in eternal pain at his eternal dinner. 57

For the one in front the biting seemed to play
  no part at all compared to the ripping: at times
  the whole skin of his back was flayed away. 60

"That soul that suffers most," explained my Guide,
  "is Judas Iscariot, he who kicks his legs
  on the fiery chin and has his head inside. 63

Of the other two, who have their heads thrust forward,
  the one who dangles down from the black face
  is Brutus:[7] note how he writhes without a word. 66

And there, with the huge and sinewy arms, is the soul
  of Cassius,[8]—But the night is coming on
  and we must go, for we have seen the whole." 69

Then, as he bade, I clasped his neck, and he,
  watching for a moment when the wings
  were opened wide, reached over dexterously 72

6. I.e., Ethiopians (Dante refers to those who live near the Nile's source). The significance of these three colors is not certain; it has been suggested that they represent hatred, impotence, and ignorance as the opposites of the divine attributes of love, omnipotence, and wisdom (see 3.5–6).

7. One of murderers of Julius Caesar in 44 B.C.E. and thus for Dante a betrayer of the empire.

8. The other murderer of Caesar.

and seized the shaggy coat of the king demon;
    then grappling matted hair and frozen crusts
    from one tuft to another, clambered down.   75

When we had reached the joint where the great thigh
    merges into the swelling of the haunch,
    my Guide and Master, straining terribly,   78

turned his head to where his feet had been
    and began to grip the hair as if he were climbing;
    so that I thought we moved toward Hell again.[9]   81

"Hold fast!" my Guide said, and his breath came shrill
    with labor and exhaustion. "There is no way
    but by such stairs to rise above such evil."   84

At last he climbed out through an opening
    in the central rock, and he seated me on the rim;
    then joined me with a nimble backward spring.   87

I looked up, thinking to see Lucifer
    as I had left him, and I saw instead
    his legs projecting high into the air.   90

Now let all those whose dull minds are still vexed
    by failure to understand what point it was
    I had passed through, judge if I was perplexed.   93

"Get up. Up on your feet," my Master said.
    "The sun already mounts to middle tierce,[1]
    and a long road and hard climbing lie ahead."   96

It was no hall of state we had found there,
    but a natural animal pit hollowed from rock
    with a broken floor and a close and sunless air.   99

"Before I tear myself from the Abyss,"
    I said when I had risen, "O my Master,
    explain to me my error in all this: 102

where is the ice? and Lucifer—how has he
    been turned from top to bottom: and how can the sun
    have gone from night to day so suddenly?"   105

9. Virgil's reversal marks the point at which the two travelers pass from the Northern to the Southern Hemisphere. They began by climbing down Satan's body, but now reverse directions and climb up from the Earth's center (hence when they have passed through the center Dante sees Satan's legs sticking up [line 90]). Note that the travelers pass through the glassy ice, a passage that probably echoes 1 Corinthians 13.12: "For now we see through a glass, darkly; but then face to face."
1. About 7:30 a.m. on Holy Saturday. Dante has added 12 hours to his scheme so that the travelers will emerge from the Earth and arrive at the shore of Mount Purgatory just before the sunrise on the next day, Easter Sunday.

And he to me: "You imagine you are still
  on the other side of the center where I grasped
  the shaggy flank of the Great Worm of Evil   108

which bores through the world—you *were* while I climbed down,
  but when I turned myself about, you passed
  the point to which all gravities are drawn.[2]   111

You are under the other hemisphere where you stand;[3]
  the sky above us is the half opposed
  to that which canopies the great dry land.   114

Under the midpoint of that other sky
  the Man who was born sinless and who lived
  beyond all blemish, came to suffer and die.   117

You have your feet upon a little sphere
  which forms the other face of the Judecca.
  There it is evening when it is morning here.[4]   120

And this gross Fiend and Image of all Evil
  who made a stairway for us with his hide
  is pinched and prisoned in the ice-pack still.   123

On this side he plunged down from heaven's height,[5]
  and the land that spread here once hid in the sea
  and fled North to our hemisphere for fright;   126

and it may be that moved by that same fear,
  the one peak that still rises on this side
  fled upward leaving this great cavern here."   129

Down there, beginning at the further bound
  of Beelzebub's[6] dim tomb, there is a space
  not known by sight, but only by the sound   132

---

2. The center of the Earth, which is for Dante the center of the universe, and therefore the place where gravity is the strongest. Being furthest from Heaven, it is also the place which is most material and least spiritual.

3. I.e., under the Southern Hemisphere, exactly opposite Jerusalem where Christ ("the Man whose birth and life were free of sin") was crucified. Jerusalem is the center of the Northern Hemisphere (see Ezekiel 5.5) and is located directly over the cavity of Hell.

4. The "little sphere" upon which they stand is the other side of Judecca, which is a hollow. The sun is now over the Southern Hemisphere, and therefore it is night in the Northern, where Hell is located.

5. The land that was in the Southern Hemisphere before Satan fell fled to the Northern to avoid him; hence the Southern Hemisphere is composed of water. The exception is that when Satan plunged into the center of the world, the earth close to his body in the Northern Hemisphere moved "with that same fear" (line 127) to the Southern Hemisphere and became Mount Purgatory. The "cavern" (line 129) refers to Hell; Mount Purgatory is thus comprised of the land displaced by Satan in his fall. This elaborate explanation for medieval geography is Dante's own poetic scheme.

6. Another name for Satan.

of a little stream[7] descending through the hollow
   it has eroded from the massive stone
   in its endlessly entwining lazy flow.   135

My Guide and I crossed over and began
   to mount that little known and lightless road
   to ascend into the shining world again.   138

He first, I second, without thought of rest
   we climbed the dark until we reached the point
   where a round opening brought in sight the blest   141

and beauteous shining of the Heavenly cars.
And we walked out once more beneath the Stars.[8]

From Purgatorio

Canto I

ANTE-PURGATORY: THE SHORE OF THE ISLAND   *Cato of Utica*

The Poets emerge from Hell just before dawn of Easter Sunday (April 10, 1300), and Dante revels in the sight of the rediscovered heavens. As he looks eagerly about at the stars, he sees nearby an old man of impressive bearing. The ancient is *Cato of Utica*, guardian of the shores of Purgatory. Cato challenges the Poets as fugitives from Hell, but Virgil, after first instructing Dante to kneel in reverence, explains Dante's mission and Beatrice's command. Cato then gives them instructions for proceeding.

The Poets have emerged at a point a short way up the slope of Purgatory. It is essential, therefore, that they descend to the lowest point and begin from there, an allegory of Humility. Cato, accordingly, orders Virgil to lead Dante to the shore, to wet his hands in the dew of the new morning, and to wash the stains of Hell from Dante's face and the film of Hell's vapors from Dante's eyes. Virgil is then to bind about Dante's waist one of the pliant reeds (symbolizing Humility) that grow in the soft mud of the shore.

Having so commanded, Cato disappears. Dante arises in silence and stands waiting, eager to begin. His look is all the communication that is necessary. Virgil leads him to the shore and performs all that Cato has commanded. Dante's first purification is marked by a miracle: when Virgil breaks off a reed, the stalk immediately regenerates a new reed, restoring itself exactly as it had been.

---

7. This stream must flow down from Purgatory, perhaps from Lethe. It finds its source in "a space" (line 131) on Mount Purgatory; thus it is "at the further bound of Beelzebub's dim tomb"—that is, it is located on the surface of the Southern Hemisphere, which since Satan is at the center of the earth is the same distance from him as Hell (his "tomb") is deep.

When Dante has Virgil say that it is "down there" (line 130), he must be writing from the perspective of the Northern Hemisphere, since Mount Purgatory is at this moment above the travelers.
8. Each of the three parts of the *Divine Comedy* end with the word "stars" as an affirmation of God's benevolent order.

For better waters now the little bark
    of my indwelling powers raises her sails,
    and leaves behind that sea so cruel and dark.[1]   3

Now shall I sing that second kingdom given
    the soul of man wherein to purge its guilt
    and so grow worthy to ascend to Heaven.   6

Yours am I, sacred Muses! To you I pray.
    Here let dead poetry rise once more to life,
    and here let sweet Calliope[2] rise and play   9

some far accompaniment in that high strain
    whose power the wretched Pierides once felt
    so terribly they dared not hope again.[3]   12

Sweet azure of the sapphire of the east
    was gathering on the serene horizon[4]
    its pure and perfect radiance—a feast   15

to my glad eyes, reborn to their delight,
    as soon as I had passed from the dead air
    which had oppressed my soul and dimmed my sight.   18

The planet whose sweet influence strengthens love[5]
    was making all the east laugh with her rays,
    veiling the Fishes,[6] which she swam above.   21

I turned then to my right and set my mind
    on the other pole, and there I saw four stars
    unseen by mortals since the first mankind.[7]   24

The heavens seemed to revel in their light.
    O widowed Northern Hemisphere, bereft
    forever of the glory of that sight![8]   27

As I broke off my gazing, my eyes veered
    a little to the left, to the other pole
    from which, by then, the Wain[9] had disappeared.   30

1. The metaphor of the poem as a ship ("bark") is traditional; "better waters" refers to Purgatory, while "that sea so cruel" is Hell.
2. The Muse of epic poetry.
3. The nine daughters of Pierus—the Pierides—challenged the Muses to a singing contest and having lost, were turned into magpies; see Ovid, *Metamorphoses* 5.
4. The time is just before sunrise on Easter Sunday, 1300.
5. Venus, the morning star, although in fact on this date Venus would have been visible only after sunrise.
6. The constellation Pisces, in which Venus would have been located if it had risen before the sun on this date.
7. Prior to their expulsion from Eden, which is located on the summit of Mount Purgatory, Adam and Eve saw four stars about the South Pole. These stars symbolize the four cardinal virtues: prudence, temperance, justice, and fortitude.
8. Dante is lamenting the corruption of his present compared to the perfection of life before the Fall.
9. The constellation Ursa Major, which never disappears from northern skies but is not visible to an observer in the Southern Hemisphere. "The other pole": the celestial North Pole.

I saw, nearby, an ancient man,[1] alone.
His bearing filled me with such reverence,
no father has had more from any son.   33

His beard was long and touched with strands of white,
as was his hair, of which two tresses fell
over his breast. Rays of the holy light   36

that fell from the four stars made his face glow
with such a radiance that he looked to me
as if he faced the sun. And standing so,   39

he moved his venerable plumes and said:
"Who are you two who climb by the dark stream[2]
to escape the eternal prison of the dead?   42

Who led you? or what served you as a light
in your dark flight from the eternal valley,
which lies forever blind in darkest night?   45

Are the laws of the pit so broken? Or is new counsel
published in Heaven that the damned may wander
onto my rocks from the abyss of Hell?"   48

At that my Master laid his hands upon me,
instructing me by word and touch and gesture
to show my reverence in brow and knee,   51

then answered him: "I do not come this way
of my own will or powers. A Heavenly Lady[3]
sent me to this man's aid in his dark day.   54

But since your will is to know more, my will
cannot deny you; I will tell you truly
why we have come and how. This man has still   57

to see his final hour, though in the burning
of his own madness he had drawn so near it
his time was perilously short for turning.   60

As I have told you, I was sent to show
the way his soul must take for its salvation;
and there is none but this by which I go.   63

1. Cato (95–46 B.C.E.), a Roman known as "Cato the Younger (to distinguish him from his famous great-grandfather) and renowned for his uncompromising morality and love of liberty; rather than submit to what he saw as Julius Caesar's tyranny, he committed suicide in Utica, a city in North Africa. Dante is here influenced by Virgil's treatment of Cato in the underworld, where he is presented not as a suicide but as the lawgiver to the righteous (see *Aeneid* 6).
2. Lethe (see *Inferno* 34.133–35).
3. Beatrice.

I have shown him the guilty people. Now I mean
　　to lead him through the spirits in your keeping,
　　to show him those whose suffering makes them clean.　66

By what means I have led him to this strand
　　to see and hear you, takes too long to tell:
　　from Heaven is the power and the command.　69

Now may his coming please you, for he goes
　　to win his freedom; and how dear that is
　　the man who gives his life for it best knows.　72

You know it, who in that cause found death sweet
　　in Utica where you put off that flesh
　　which shall rise radiant at the Judgment Seat.[4]　75

We do not break the Laws: this man lives yet,
　　and I am of that Round not ruled by Minos,
　　with your own Marcia,[5] whose chaste eyes seem set　78

in endless prayers to you. O blessed breast
　　to hold her yet your own! for love of her
　　grant us permission to pursue our quest　81

across your seven kingdoms. When I go
　　back to her side I shall bear thanks of you,
　　if you will let me speak your name below."　84

"Marcia was so pleasing in my eyes
　　there on the other side," he answered then
　　"that all she asked, I did. Now that she lies　87

beyond the evil river, no word or prayer
　　of hers may move me. Such was the Decree
　　pronounced upon us when I rose from there.[6]　90

But if, as you have said, a Heavenly Dame
　　orders your way, there is no need to flatter:
　　you need but ask it of me in her name.　93

Go then, and lead this man, but first see to it
　　you bind a smooth green reed[7] about his waist
　　and clean his face of all trace of the pit.　96

4. See *Inferno* 5.4.
5. Cato's wife, now in Limbo (see *Inferno* 4.128); according to a story told by the Roman poet Lucan (39–65 C.E.), Cato ceded Marcia to his friend Hortensius, but on Hortensius's death Marcia's entreaty to Cato that he remarry her was granted.
6. Cato was freed during the Harrowing of Hell (see *Inferno* 4.53) and is now unmoved by the sufferings of those left behind. "The evil river": Acheron.
7. The reed is a symbol of humility.

For it would not be right that one with eyes
   still filmed by mist should go before the angel
   who guards the gate: he is from Paradise.   99

All round the wave-wracked shoreline, there below,
   reeds grow in the soft mud. Along that edge
   no foliate nor woody plant could grow.   102

for what lives in that buffeting must bend.
   Do not come back this way: the rising sun
   will light an easier way you may ascend."   105

With that he disappeared; and silently
   I rose and moved back till I faced my Guide,
   my eyes upon him, waiting. He said to me: 108

"Follow my steps and let us turn again:
   along this side there is a gentle slope
   that leads to the low boundaries of the plain."   111

The dawn, in triumph, made the day-breeze flee
   before its coming, so that from afar
   I recognized the trembling of the sea.   114

We strode across that lonely plain like men
   who seek the road they strayed from and who count
   the time lost till they find it once again.   117

When we had reached a place along the way
   where the cool morning breeze shielded the dew
   against the first heat of the gathering day,   120

with gentle graces my Sweet Master bent
   and laid both outspread palms upon the grass.
   Then I, being well aware of his intent,   123

lifted my tear-stained cheeks to him, and there
   he made me clean, revealing my true color
   under the residues of Hell's black air.   126

We moved on then to the deserted strand
   which never yet has seen upon its waters
   a man who found his way back to dry land.   129

There, as it pleased another, he girded me.
   Wonder of wonders! when he plucked a reed
   another took its place there instantly,   132

arising from the humble stalk he tore
so that it grew exactly as before.

Canto II

ANTE-PURGATORY:

THE SHORE OF THE ISLAND

The Angel Boatman •
Casella • Cato of Utica

It is dawn. Dante, washed, and girded by the reed, is standing by the shore when he sees a light approaching at enormous speed across the sea. The light grows and becomes visible as *The Angel Boatman* who ferries the souls of the elect from their gathering place at *The Mouth of the Tiber* to the shore of Purgatory.

The newly arrived souls debark and, taking the Poets as familiars of the place, ask directions. Virgil explains that he and Dante are new arrivals but that they have come by the dark road through Hell. The newly arrived souls see by his breathing that Dante is alive and crowd about him. One of the new souls is *Casella*, a musician who seems to have been a dear friend of Dante's. Dante tries three times to clasp him to his bosom, but each time his arms pass through empty air. Casella explains the function of the Angel Boatman and then, at Dante's request, strikes up a song, one of Dante's own *canzone* that Casella had set to music. Instantly, *Cato* descends upon the group, berating them, and they break like startled pigeons up the slope toward the mountain.

The sun already burned at the horizon,[8]
   while the high point of its meridian circle
   covered Jerusalem, and in opposition   3

equal Night revolved above the Ganges
   bearing the Scales that fall out of her hand
   as she grows longer with the season's changes: 6

thus, where I was, Aurora in her passage
   was losing the pale blushes from her cheeks
   which turned to orange with increasing age.   9

We were still standing by the sea's new day
   like travelers pondering the road ahead
   who send their souls on while their bones delay;   12

when low above the ocean's western rim,
   as Mars, at times, observed through the thick vapors
   that form before the dawn, burns red and slim;   15

just so—so may I hope to see it again!—
   a light appeared, moving above the sea
   faster than any flight. A moment then   18

I turned my eyes to question my sweet Guide,
   and when I looked back to that unknown body
   I found its mass and brightness magnified.   21

---

8. The opening nine lines designate the time by reference to Jerusalem (where the sun is setting), the Ganges (where it is midnight, and where the constellation Libra—the Scales—is in the sky), and Mount Purgatory (where the dawn—Aurora—is gradually reddening).

Then from each side of it came into view
    an unknown something-white; and from beneath it,
    bit by bit, another whiteness grew.   24

We watched till the white objects at each side
    took shape as wings, and Virgil spoke no word.
    But when he saw what wings they were, he cried: 27

"Down on your knees! It is God's angel comes!
    Down! Fold your hands! From now on you shall see
    many such ministers in the high kingdoms.   30

See how he scorns man's tools: he needs no oars
    nor any other sail than his own wings
    to carry him between such distant shores.   33

See how his pinions tower upon the air,
    pointing to Heaven: they are eternal plumes
    and do not moult like feathers or human hair."   36

Then as that bird of heaven closed the distance
    between us, he grew brighter and yet brighter
    until I could no longer bear the radiance,   39

and bowed my head. He steered straight for the shore,
    his ship so light and swift it drew no water;
    it did not seem to sail so much as soar.   42

Astern stood the great pilot of the Lord,
    so fair his blessedness seemed written on him;
    and more than a hundred souls were seated forward,   45

singing as if they raised a single voice
    in exitu Israel de Aegypto.[9]
    Verse after verse they made the air rejoice.   48

The angel made the sign of the cross, and they
    cast themselves, at his signal, to the shore.
    Then, swiftly as he had come, he went away.   51

The throng he left seemed not to understand
    what place it was, but stood and stared about
    like men who see the first of a new land.   54

The Sun, who with an arrow in each ray
    had chased the Goat out of the height of Heaven,[1]
    on every hand was shooting forth the day,   57

---

9. "When Israel went out of Egypt" (Latin). This is the first verse of Psalm 113 (114 in Protestant Bibles), which is a song of thanksgiving for the liberation of the Israelites from Egypt. Christians understood this liberation as prefiguring the salvation of sinners through Christ. That the day is Easter Sunday gives the psalm special relevance.

1. The constellation Capricorn can now not be seen because of the growing light.

when those new souls looked up to where my Guide
  and I stood, saying to us, "If you know it,
  show us the road that climbs the mountainside."   60

Virgil replied: "You think perhaps we two
  have had some long experience of this place,
  but we are also pilgrims, come before you   63

only by very little, though by a way
  so steep, so broken, and so tortuous
  the climb ahead of us will seem like play."   66

The throng of souls, observing by my breath
  I was still in the body I was born to,
  stared in amazement and grew pale as death.   69

As a crowd, eager for news, will all but smother
  a messenger who bears the olive branch,
  and not care how they trample one another—   72

so these, each one of them a soul elect,
  pushed close to stare at me, well-nigh forgetting
  the way to go to make their beauty perfect.   75

One came forward to embrace me, and his face
  shone with such joyous love that, seeing it,
  I moved to greet him with a like embrace.   78

O solid seeming shadows! Three times there
  I clasped my hands behind him, and three times[2]
  I drew them to my breast through empty air.   81

Amazed, I must have lost all color then,
  for he smiled tenderly and drew away,
  and I lunged forward as if to try again.   84

In a voice as gentle as a melody
  he bade me pause; and by his voice I knew him,
  and begged him stay a while and speak to me.   87

He answered: "As I loved you in the clay
  of my mortal body, so do I love you freed:
  therefore I pause. But what brings you this way?"   90

"Casella mine, I go the way I do
  in the hope I may return here," I replied.[3]
  "But why has so much time been taken from you?"   93

---

2. In his visit to the underworld in book 6 of the *Aeneid*, Aeneas also tries three times to embrace his father Anchisës.
3. He journeys now so that after death he may return to Purgatory. Casella, a Florentine musician, was said to have set some of Dante's lyrics to music. The question that follows assumes that Casella died well before the present moment.

And he: "I am not wronged if he whose usage
   accepts the soul at his own time and pleasure
   has many times refused to give me passage: 96

his will moves in the image and perfection
   of a Just Will:[4] indeed, for three months now
   he has taken all who asked, without exception.[5]   99

And so it was that in my turn I stood
   upon that shore where Tiber's stream grows salt,[6]
   and there was gathered to my present good.   102

It is back to the Tiber's mouth he has just flown,
   for there forever is the gathering place
   of all who do not sink to Acheron."[7]   105

"If no new law has stripped you of your skill
   or of the memory of those songs of love
   that once could calm all passion from my will,"   108

I said to him, "Oh sound a verse once more
   to soothe my soul which, with its weight of flesh
   and the long journey, sinks distressed and sore."   111

"Love that speaks its reasons in my heart,"[8]
   he sang then, and such grace flowed on the air
   that even now I hear that music start.   114

My Guide and I and all those souls of bliss
   stood tranced in song; when suddenly we heard
the Noble Elder[9] cry: "What's this! What's this!   117

Negligence! Loitering! O laggard crew,
   run to the mountain and strip off the scurf
   that lets not God be manifest in you!"   120

Exactly as a flock of pigeons gleaning
   a field of stubble, pecking busily,
   forgetting all their primping and their preening,   123

will rise as one and scatter through the air,
   leaving their feast without another thought
   when they are taken by a sudden scare—   126

4. I.e., the angel who chooses the souls to cross in his boat is directed by God.
5. Pope Boniface proclaimed 1300—the year of the poem's action—a Jubilee or Holy Year, when those making pilgrimage to Rome were granted release from punishments for their sins (see *Inferno* 18.28–29). Dante follows popular belief in assuming that this grant applies to the souls awaiting transport to Purgatory as well as to the living.
6. At Ostia, where the river Tiber enters the sea.
7. I.e., Hell.
8. "Love that speaks its reasons in my heart" is the first line of a lyric that Dante included in his prose philosophical work, the *Convivio*, which he left incomplete.
9. Cato.

so that new band, all thought of pleasure gone,
  broke from the feast of music with a start
  and scattered for the mountainside like one   129

who leaps and does not look where he will land.
  Nor were my Guide and I inclined to stand.

Canto XXI

THE FIFTH CORNICE   *The Hoarders and Wasters (The Avaricious)*

Statius

Burning with desire to know the cause of the "shock and shout," Dante hurries
after Virgil along the narrow way. Suddenly they are overtaken by a figure that
salutes them. Virgil answers, and the new soul, taking the Poets to be souls who
may not enter Heaven, expresses astonishment at finding them in this place.

Virgil explains his and Dante's state and asks the explanation of the earthquake
and of the great cry. The new soul explains that these phenomena occur only
when a soul arises from its final purification and begins its final ascent to Heaven.
The newcomer then reveals that he is *Statius* and recites his earthly history, ending with a glowing statement of his love for the works of Virgil. To have lived in
Virgil's time, says Statius, he would have endured another year of the pains he has
just ended.

Virgil warns Dante, with a glance, to be silent, but Dante cannot suppress a
half smile, which Statius notices, and asks Dante to explain. He thus learns that
he is, in fact, standing in the presence of Virgil. Immediately he kneels to embrace
Virgil's knees, but Virgil tells him to arise at once, for such earthly vanities are out
of place between shades.

The natural thirst that nothing satisfies
  except that water the Samaritan woman
  begged of Our Lord,[1] as St. John testifies,   3

burned me; haste drove me on the encumbered way
  behind my Guide, and I was full of grief
  at the just price of pain those spirits pay;   6

when suddenly—just as Luke lets us know
  that Christ, new risen from the tomb, appeared
  to the two travelers on the road[2]—just so   9

as we moved there with bowed heads lest we tread
  upon some soul, a shade appeared behind us;[3]
  nor did we guess its presence till it said: 12

---

1. I.e., the thirst for knowledge can be
quenched only by divine revelation. In the previous canto, Dante has heard a cry of exulta-
tion and felt Mount Purgatory shake; it is the
meaning of these events that he wishes to
know. For the woman of Samaria, see John

4.5–29.
2. Luke 24.13–31.
3. The avaricious are punished at this level of
Purgatory by being bound prone to the Earth,
since they worshipped earthly things in life.

"Brothers, God give you peace." My Guide and I
  turned quickly toward his voice, and with a sign
  my master gave the words their due reply.   15

Then he began: "May the True Court's behest,
  which relegates me to eternal exile,
  establish you in peace among the blest."   18

"But how, if you are souls denied God's bliss,"
  he said—and we forged onward as he spoke—
  "have you climbed up the stairs as far as this?"   21

My Teacher then: "You cannot fail to see,
  if you observe the Angel's mark upon him,
  that he will reign among the just.[4] But she   24

whose wheel turns day and night has not yet spun
  the full length of the thread that Clotho winds
  into a hank for him and everyone.[5]   27

Therefore, his soul, sister to yours and mine,
  since it cannot see as we do, could not
  climb by itself. And, therefore, Will Divine   30

has drawn me out of the great Throat of Woe
  to guide him on his way, and I shall lead him
  far as my knowledge gives me power to go.   33

But tell me, if you can, what was the shock
  we felt just now? And why did all the mountain
  cry with one voice down to its last moist rock?"   36

He struck the needle's eye of my desire
  so surely with his question, that my thirst,
  by hope alone, lost something of its fire.   39

The shade began: "The holy rules that ring
  the mountain round do not permit upon it
  any disordered or unusual thing,   42

nor any change. Only what Heaven draws
  out of itself into itself again—
  that and nothing else—can be a cause.[6]   45

4. Before Dante entered Purgatory proper, an angel traced seven *P*s upon his forehead, one for each deadly sin (*peccatum* in Latin); see *Purgatorio* 9.112–14. The marks disappear one by one as he climbs the mountain and passes through each of the seven terraces appointed for the purgation of sin.
5. According to classical mythology, the three

Fates determine the span of a person's life: Clotho holds the spool, Lachesis spins the thread, and Atropos cuts it at the predestined time.
6. Purgatory is free from any earthly influence, and therefore any change must be caused by motion from above.

Therefore, there never can be rain nor snow,
   nor hail, nor dew, nor hoarfrost higher up
   than the little three-step stairway there below.[7]   48

Neither dense clouds nor films of mist appear,
   nor lightning's flash, nor Thaumas' glowing daughter,[8]
   who shifts about from place to place back there;   51

nor can dry vapors raise their shattering heat
   above the top of these three steps I mentioned
   upon which Peter's vicar[9] plants his feet.   54

Shocks may occur below, severe or slight,
   but tremors caused by winds locked in the earth
   —I know not how—do not reach to this height.   57

It trembles here whenever a soul feels
   so healed and purified that it gets up
   or moves to climb; and then the great hymn peals.   60

The soul, surprised, becomes entirely free
   to change its cloister, moved by its own will,
   which is its only proof of purity.   63

Before purgation it does wish to climb,
   but the will High Justice sets against that wish
   moves it to will pain as it once willed crime.   66

And I, who in my torments have lain here
   five hundred years and more, have only now
   felt my will free to seek a better sphere.   69

It was for that you felt the mountain move
   and heard the pious spirits praise the Lord—
   ah may He call them soon to go above!"   72

These were the spirit's words to us, and mine
   cannot express how they refreshed my soul,
   but as the thirst is greater, the sweeter the wine.   75

And my wise Leader: "Now I see what snare
   holds you, how you slip free, why the mount trembles,
   and why your joint rejoicing fills the air.   78

7. To reach the gate of Purgatory proper one must climb three steps, which represent the three stages of penance: contrition of heart, confession of mouth, and satisfaction by deeds.

8. Iris, goddess of the rainbow.
9. The angel who guards the entrance to Purgatory and who marked Dante's forehead.

Now it would please me greatly, if you please,
  to know your name and hear in your own words
  why you have lain so many centuries."[1]   81

"In the days when the good Titus, with the aid
  of the Almighty King, avenged the wounds
  that poured the blood Iscariot betrayed,[2]   84

I lived renowned back there," replied that soul,
  "in the most honored and enduring name,
  but still without the faith that makes us whole.[3]   87

My verses swelled with such melodious breath
  that, from Toulouse,[4] Rome called me to herself,
  and there I merited a laurel wreath.   90

Statius my name, and it still lives back there.
  I sang of Thebes, then of the great Achilles,
  but found the second weight too great to bear.   93

The sparks that were my seeds of passion came
  from that celestial fire which has enkindled
  more than a thousand poets; I mean the flame   96

of the *Aeneid*, the mother that brought forth,
  the nurse that gave suck to my song. Without it
  I could not have weighed half a penny's worth.   99

And to have lived back there in Virgil's time
  I would agree to pass another year
  in the same banishment from which I climb."   102

Virgil, at these last words, shot me a glance
  that said in silence, "Silence!" But man's will
  is not supreme in every circumstance: 105

for tears and laughter come so close behind
  the passions they arise from, that they least
  obey the will of the most honest mind.   108

I did no more than half smile, but that shade
  fell still and looked me in the eye—for there
  the secrets of the soul are most betrayed.   111

1. The spirit reveals himself to be Statius (d. 96 C.E.), a Roman poet who composed an epic on the story of Thebes called the *Thebaid* and an unfinished epic on Achilles, the *Achilleid*. 2. The destruction of Jerusalem in 70 C.E. by the Roman emperor Titus in response to a rebellion was understood by Christians to be a divine punishment for the betrayal (by Judas Iscarot) and subsequent crucifixion of Christ. 3. I.e., he was a poet but not yet a Christian. 4. A city in southern France; Statius actually came from Naples, but Dante is following a medieval tradition.

"So may the road you travel lead to grace,"
  he said, "what was the meaning of the smile
  that I saw flash, just now, across your face?"   114

Now am I really trapped on either side:
  one tells me to be still, one begs me speak.
  So torn I heave a sigh, and my sweet Guide   117

understands all its meaning. "Never fear,"
  he says to me, "speak up, and let him know
  what he has asked so movingly to hear."   120

At which I said: "Perhaps my smiling thus
  has made you marvel, Ancient Soul; but now
  listen to something truly marvelous: 123

this one who guides my eyes aloft is he,
  Virgil, from whom you drew the strength to sing
  the deeds of men and gods in poetry.   126

The only motive for my smiling lay
  in your own words. If you conceived another,
  as you love truth, pray put the thought away."   129

He was bending to embrace my Teacher's knee,
  but Virgil said: "No, brother. Shade you are,
  and shade am I. You must not kneel to me."   132

And Statius, rising, said: "So may you find
  the measure of the love that warms me to you
  when for it I lose all else from my mind,   135

forgetting we are empty semblances
and taking shadows to be substances."

Canto XXII

THE ASCENT TO THE SIXTH CORNICE

THE SIXTH CORNICE   *The Gluttons*

The Tree • The Whip of Gluttony

The Poets have passed the Angel who guards the ascent, and Dante has had one
more *P* removed from his forehead. So lightened, he walks easily behind Virgil
and Statius despite their rapid ascent, listening eagerly to their conversation.

   Virgil declares his great regard for Statius, and Statius explains that he was on
the Fifth Cornice for Wasting rather than for Hoarding. He adds that he would
certainly have been damned, had Virgil's poetry not led him to see his error. For
Virgil, he acknowledges, not only inspired his song, but showed him the road to
faith, whereby he was baptized, though secretly, for fear of the persecutions—a
lukewarmness for which he spent four hundred years on the Fourth Cornice.

Statius then names his favorite poets of antiquity and asks where they are. Virgil replies that they are with him in Limbo. He then cites many who have not been mentioned before as being among his eternal companions.

At this point the Poets arrive at *The Sixth Cornice* and, moving to the right, come upon *An Enormous Tree* laden with fruits. From its foliage a voice cries out the examples of abstinence that constitute *The Whip of Gluttony*.

We had already left behind by now
    the Angel who directs to the Sixth Round.
    He had erased a stigma from my brow,[5]   3

and said that they who thirst for rectitude
    are blessèd, but he did not say "who hunger"
    when he recited that Beatitude.[6]   6

I, lighter than on any earlier stairs,[7]
    followed those rapid spirits, and I found it
    no strain at all to match my pace to theirs.   9

Virgil began: "When virtue lights in us
    a fire of love, that love ignites another
    within the soul that sees its burning.[8] Thus,   12

ever since Juvenal[9] came down to be
    one of our court in the Infernal Limbo,
    and told me of your great regard for me,   15

my good will toward you has been of a sort
    I had not felt for any unseen person;
    such as will make the climb ahead seem short.   18

But tell me—and if I presume too much
    in slackening the rein this way, forgive me
    as a friend would and answer me as such: 21

how, amid all the wisdom you possessed—
    and which you won to by such diligence—
    could Avarice find a place within your breast?"   24

At these words Statius let a brief smile play
    across his lips, and fade. Then he replied:
    "I hear love's voice in every word you say.   27

---

5. The "stigma" is a scar in the shape of a *P* for avarice, the sin cleansed on the previous terrace.
6. The angel quotes the beginning of the Fourth Beatitude from the Sermon on the Mount. "Blessed are they which do hunger and thirst after righteousness: for they shall be filled" (Matthew 5.6). He mentions only "thirst" (*sitiunt* in Latin), omitting hunger, which will appear at the end of the journey through the sixth terrace, where gluttony is purged.

7. Dante grows lighter as he is gradually relieved of the sins, symbolized by the *P*s on his forehead, weighing him down.
8. Virtuous love, such as Statius displayed at the end of canto 21, will elicit a similar response.
9. A Roman poet, contemporary with Statius but who outlived him (dying about 140 C.E.), located with Virgil in Limbo, as described in *Inferno* 4.

Often, indeed, appearances give rise
   to groundless doubts in us, and false conclusions,
   the true cause being hidden from our eyes.   30

Seeing me on the ledge from which I rose,
   you have inferred my sin was Avarice;
   an inference your question clearly shows.   33

Know then that my particular offense
   was all too far from Avarice: I wept
   thousands of months for riotous expense.   36

Had I not turned from prodigality[1]
   in pondering those lines in which you cry,
   as if you raged against humanity: 39

'To what do you not drive man's appetite
   O cursèd gold-lust!'[2]—I should now be straining
   in the grim jousts of the Infernal night.[3]   42

I understood then that our hands could spread
   their wings too wide in spending, and repented
   of that, and all my sins, in grief and dread.   45

How many shall rise bald to Judgment Day
   because they did not know this sin to grieve it
   in life, or as their last breaths slipped away![4] 48

For when the opposite of a sin, as here,
   is as blameworthy as the sin itself,
   both lose their growth together and turn sere.   51

If, then, I lay so long in my distress
   among the Avaricious where they weep,
   it was to purge the opposite excess."   54

"But when you sang of the fierce warfare bred
   between the twin afflictions of Jocasta,"[5]
   the singer of the sweet *Bucolics*[6] said,   57

1. Prodigality is a vice opposite to Avarice but its counterpart: both involve an excess in the use of money. In *Inferno* 7 the avaricious and the prodigal are punished together.
2. Statius is quoting from *Aeneid* 3.
3. I.e., by being punished in the fourth circle of Hell, described in *Inferno* 7.
4. The close-cropped heads of the prodigal are described in *Inferno* 7.57.
5. Statius's *Thebaid* deals with the history of Thebes: Jocasta's husband, Laius, was unwit-
tingly killed by their son, Oedipus, who then—again in ignorance—married Laius's widow, Oedipus's own mother. Their sons, Polynices and Eteocles, imprisoned their father in a dungeon and then fought over the throne of Thebes in a war in which they killed each other. It is this fratricidal war, in which Jocasta lost both her sons at once, to which Virgil refers.
6. Virgil's *Bucolics* contain his *Georgics* and *Eclogues*, which is quoted in lines 67–69.

"from what you said when Clio[7] tuned your strain,
  it would not seem that you had found the faith
  without the grace of which good works are vain.[8]   60

If that be so, what sun or beacon shone
  into your mist that you set sail to follow
  the Fisherman?"[9] And that long-waiting one: 63

"You were the lamp that led me from that night.
  You led me forth to drink Parnassian waters;[1]
  then on the road to God you shed your light.   66

When you declared, 'A new birth has been given.
  Justice returns, and the first age of man.
  And a new progeny descends from Heaven'[2]—   69

you were as one who leads through a dark track
  holding the light behind—useless to you,
  precious to those who followed at your back.   72

Through you I flowered to song and to belief.
  That you may know all, let me stretch my hand
  to paint in full what I have sketched in brief.   75

The world, by then, was swollen with the birth
  of True Belief sown by those messengers
  the Everlasting Kingdom had sent forth.[3]   78

Those words of yours I quoted, so agreed
  with the new preachers', that I took to going
  to where they gathered to expound the Creed.   81

In time, they grew so holy in my eyes
  that in the persecutions of Domitian[4]
  the tears burst from me when I heard their cries.   84

And long as I remained upon the vexed
  shores of that life, I helped them, and they taught me,
  by their strict ways, to scorn all other sects.   87

Before my poem[5] sang how the Greeks drew near
  the Theban rivers, I had been baptized,
  but kept my faith a secret, out of fear,   90

7. The Muse of history, whom Statius invokes in the *Thebaid*.
8. I.e., Christianity.
9. I.e., followed Peter, a fisherman who became "a fisher of men" (see Mark 1.17).
1. Dante follows a tradition that takes Parnassus, a mountain in Greece, as the home of the Muses.
2. A slightly altered citation from Virgil's Fourth Eclogue. A pastoral poem written about 40 B.C.E., it celebrated the birth of the son of an important Roman politician but was taken by medieval Christians as a prophecy of the birth of Christ.
3. The apostles.
4. Roman emperor, 81–96 C.E., thought by early Christian historians to have persecuted Christians.
5. The *Thebaid* described how six Greek rulers joined with Polynices to invade Thebes and topple Eteocles from the throne.

pretending to be pagan as before;
  for which lukewarmness I was made to circle
  the Ledge of Sloth[6] four hundred years and more.   93

Now may you please to tell me—you who rent
  the veil that hid me from this good I praise—
  while we have time to spare in the ascent,   96

where is our ancient Terence now? and where
  Caecilius, Varro, Plautus?[7]—are they damned?
  and if they are, what torments must they bear?"   99

—"All these are there with Persius and the rest,
  myself among them, who surround that Greek
  who outsucked all men at the Muses' breast.   102

All walk the first ledge of the dark of Hell;
  and we speak often of the glorious mountain
  on which the Nine[8] who suckled us still dwell.   105

Euripides is with us, Antiphon,
  Athenian Agathon, Simonides,
  and many more who wore the laurel crown.[9]   108

And there, of your own people, one may see
  Ismene, mournful as she was before,
  Deiphyle, Argia, Antigone,   111

Hypsipyle, who led to Langia's water,
  Thetis, Deidamia with her sisters,
  and there, too, one may see Tiresias' daughter."[1]   114

We stepped from the walled stairs to level ground,
  and both the Poets now had fallen still,
  attentive once again to look around.   117

Of the day's handmaids,[2] four had fallen back,
  and now the fifth stood at the chariot's pole,
  pointing the bright tip on its upward track,   120

when Virgil said: "I think we ought to go
  with our right shoulders to the outer edge,
  circling the slope as we have done below."[3]   123

6. Where Sloth, which is the cause of the failure to perform religious duties, is purged.
7. These men and Persius (line 100) are
Roman poets now in Limbo with Homer (lines
101–2).
8. The Muses walk on Mount Parnassus.
9. Greek dramatists and poets.
1. Characters from Statius's *Thebaid* and

Achilleid, which Dante considered historical
epics.
2. The hours, the fifth of which is guiding the
chariot of the sun; hence, it is between 10:00
and 11:00 a.m.
3. Mount Purgatory is climbed by turning to
the right; the travelers descended deeper into
Hell by turning to the left.

So custom served to guide us, and we went
  as Virgil said, with all the more assurance
  since Statius' silence gave us his consent.   126

They walked ahead and I came on behind
  treasuring their talk, which was of poetry,
  and every word of which enriched my mind.[4]   129

But soon, in mid-road, there appeared a tree
  laden with fragrant and delicious fruit,
  and at that sight the talk stopped instantly.   132

As fir trees taper up from limb to limb,
  so this tree tapered down; so shaped, I think,
  that it should be impossible to climb.   135

From that side where the cliff closed-off our way
  a clear cascade fell from the towering rock
  and broke upon the upper leaves as spray.   138

The poets drew nearer, reverent and mute,
  and from a center of the towering tree
  a voice cried: "You shall not eat of the fruit!"   141

Then said: "Mary thought more of what was due
  the joy and honor of the wedding feast
  than of her mouth, which still speaks prayers for you.   144

Of old, the mothers of Rome's noble blood
  found joy in water. And great wisdom came
  to holy Daniel in despising food.   147

Bright as pure gold was mankind's state at first:
  then, hunger seasoned acorns with delight,
  and every rill ran sweet to honest thirst.   150

No wine nor meat were in the wilderness.
  Honey and locusts—that and nothing more
  nourished the Baptist in his holiness;   153

and to that fact is his great glory due,
as the Gospel clearly testifies to you."

---

4. The canto continues with a new episode, not relevant to the literary issues that have so far occupied it.

From *Canto XXIV*

THE SIXTH CORNICE   *The Gluttons*

The Tree of Knowledge • The Rein of Gluttony

[*The Pilgrim and Virgil are now on the sixth terrace, where Gluttony is punished. Among other sinners, they meet Bonagiunta Orbicciana, a Florentine poet who was acquainted with Dante. This selection from this canto begins with Bonagiunta citing one of Dante's most famous sonnets* (canzioni *in Italian*).]

But is this really the creator of
   those new *canzoni*, one of which begins
   'Ladies who have the intellect of Love'?"[5]   51

And I: "When Love inspires me with delight,
   or pain, or longing, I take careful note,
   and as he dictates in my soul, I write."   54

And he: "Ah, brother, now I see the thong
   that held Guittone, and the Judge, and me
   short of that sweet new style[6] of purest song.   57

I see well how your pens attained such powers
   by following exactly Love's dictation,
   which certainly could not be said of ours.   60

And if one scan the two styles side by side,
   that is the only difference he will find."
   With that he fell still, as if satisfied.   63

From *Canto XXVI*

THE SEVENTH CORNICE   *The Lustful*

The Rein of Lust

[*Dante and Virgil are now on the seventh terrace, where Lechery is punished. Here they meet another of Dante's literary contemporaries and continue the discussion of literary issues. As the selection begins, Dante has just asked one of the shades to identify himself.*]

"Your wish to know mine shall be satisfied:
   I am Guido Guinizelli,[7] here so soon
   because I repented fully before I died."   93

5. The first line of the first lyric in Dante's *Vita Nuova* (*New Life*), which tells the story in poetry and prose of his transformation by his love for Beatrice.
6. The "sweet new style" (*dolce stil novo*) that Dante saw as characterizing his own poetry was first defined for him by Guido Guinizelli, whom he will meet in canto 26. The Judge (Giacomo

da Lentini) and Guittone d'Arezzo, like Bonagiunta, were Italian poets of the generation before Dante's.
7. Bolognese poet (d. ca. 1276), considered the greatest Italian poet prior to Dante. A poem by him is included in Medieval Lyrics (pp. 349–50).

In King Lycurgus' darkest hour, two sons
   discovered their lost mother:[8] I was moved
   as they had been (but could not match their actions)   96

when I heard his name, for he had fathered me
   and all the rest, my betters, who have sung
   sweet lilting rhymes of love and courtesy.   99

Enraptured, I can neither speak nor hear
   but only stare at him as we move on,
   although the flames prevent my drawing near.   102

When at last my eyes had fed, I spoke anew;
   and in such terms as win belief, I offered
   to serve him in whatever I could do.[9]   105

And he to me then: "What you say has made
   such a profound impression on my mind
   as Lethe[1] cannot wash away, nor fade.   108

But if the words you swore just now are true,
   let me know why you show by word and look
   such love as I believe I see in you?"   111

And I to him: "Your songs so sweet and clear
   which, for as long as modern usage lives,
   shall make the very ink that writes them dear."   114

"Brother," he said, "that one who moves along
   ahead there," (and he pointed[2]) "was in life
   a greater craftsman of the mother tongue.   117

He, in his love songs and his tales in prose,
   was without peer—and if fools claim Limoges
   produced a better,[3] there are always those   120

who measure worth by popular acclaim,
   ignoring principles of art and reason
   to base their judgments on the author's name.   123

So, once, our fathers sent Guittone's[4] praise,
   and his alone, bounding from cry to cry,
   though truth prevails with most men nowadays.   126

---

8. In an episode in Statius's *Thebaid*, a woman condemned to death by the warrior Lycurgus is saved at the last moment by the arrival of her twin sons.
9. Evidently Dante here swears an oath to Guinizelli to which the reader is not given access.
1. The river of forgetfulness that the fully purged souls will pass through in order to renounce their earthly lives.
2. Guinizelli is indicating Arnaut Daniel (d. ca. 1210), a Provençal poet. A poem by him is included in Medieval Lyrics (pp. 349–50).
3. The reference is to Giraut de Borneil (d. ca. 1220), another Provençal poet.
4. See *Purgatorio* 24.56.

And now, if you enjoy such privilege
    that you are free to go up to that cloister
    within which Christ is abbot of the college,   129

say an Our Father[5] for me in that host,
    as far as it may serve us in this world
    in which the very power to sin is lost."   132

With that, perhaps to yield his place with me
    to someone else he vanished through the fire
    as a fish does to the dark depths of the sea.   135

I drew ahead till I was by that shade
    he had pointed to, and said that in my heart
    a grateful place to feast his name was laid.   138

And he replied at once and willingly:[6]
    "Such pleasaunce have I of thy gentilesse,
    that I ne can, ne will I hide from thee.   141

Arnaut, am I, and weepe and sing my faring.
    In grievousnesse I see my follies past;
    in joie, the blistful daie of my preparing.   144

And by the eke virtue, I thee implour,
    that redeth thee, that thou amount the staire,
    be mindful in thy time of my dolour."   147

Then he, too, hid himself within the fire
that makes those spirits ready to go higher.

From *Canto XXVII*

       The Angel of Chastity

The Wall of Fire

       The Angel Guardian

[*The sun is near setting when the poets leave the souls of the Lustful and encounter the angel of Chastity, singing the beatitude "Blessed are the Pure of Heart." The angel tells them that they can go no farther without passing through the flames, but, numb with fear, the Pilgrim hesitates for a long time. Finally Virgil prevails upon him and they make the crossing through the excruciating heat. As they emerge on the other side, they hear the invitation "Come O ye blessed of my Father," and an angel exhorts them to climb as long as there is still daylight. But soon the sun sets and the poets are overcome by sleep. Toward morning the Pilgrim dreams of Leah*

5. The Lord's Prayer, which begins with the words "Our Father" (Matthew 6.9–13).
6. Arnaut speaks not in Italian but in Provençal. Ciardi renders Arnaut's Provençal in an old-fashioned English to reflect the relationship between the vernacular of the troubadours and Dante's own Florentine vernacular.

and Rachel, who represent the active and contemplative lives, respectively. When he awakens, he is refreshed and eager, and races up the remaining steps. In the last few lines, included here, Virgil describes the moral development achieved by the Pilgrim—such that he no longer needs his guidance. These are the last words that Virgil will speak in the poem.]

Now eastward the new day rayed Heaven's dome
 (the sweeter to the returning wanderer
 who wakes from each night's lodging nearer home),   111

and the shadows fled on every side as I
 stirred from my sleep and leaped upon my feet,
 seeing my Lords already standing by.   114

"This is the day your hungry soul shall be
 fed on the golden apples men have sought
 on many different boughs so ardently."[7]   117

These were the very words which, at the start,
 my Virgil spoke to me, and there have never
 been gifts as dear as these were to my heart.   120

Such waves of yearning to achieve the height
 swept through my soul, that at each step I took
 I felt my feathers growing for the flight.   123

When we had climbed the stairway to the rise
 of the topmost step, there with a father's love
 Virgil turned and fixed me with his eyes.   126

"My son," he said, "you now have seen the torment
 of the temporary and the eternal fires;[8]
 here, now, is the limit of my discernment.   129

I have led you here by grace of mind and art;
 now let your own good pleasure be your guide;
 you are past the steep ways, past the narrow part.   132

See there the sun that shines upon your brow,
 the sweet new grass, the flowers, the fruited vines
 which spring up without need of seed or plow.   135

Until those eyes come gladdened which in pain
 moved me to come to you and lead your way,[9]
 sit there at ease or wander through the plain.   138

7. On this day Dante will enter the Earthly Paradise and find Beatrice, who will conduct him through Paradise.

8. I.e., Purgatory and Hell.
9. See *Inferno* 2.55–74.

Expect no more of me in word or deed:
  here your will is upright, free, and whole,
  and you would be in error not to heed   141

whatever your own impulse prompts you to:
  lord of yourself I crown and mitre you."

From *Canto XXX*

Beatrice

Virgil Vanishes

The procession halts and the Prophets turn to the chariot and sing "Come, my bride, from Lebanon." They are summoning *Beatrice*, who appears on the left side of the chariot, half-hidden from view by showers of blossoms poured from above by *A Hundred Angels*. Dante, stirred by the sight, turns to Virgil to express his overflowing emotions, and discovers that *Virgil Has Vanished*.

Because he bursts into tears at losing Virgil, *Dante Is Reprimanded by Beatrice*. The Angel Choir overhead immediately breaks into a Psalm of Compassion, but Beatrice, still severe, answers by detailing Dante's offenses in not making proper use of his great gifts. It would violate the ordering of the Divine Decree, she argues, to let Dante drink the waters of Lethe, thereby washing all memory of sin from his soul, before he had shed the tears of a real repentance.

Time and again at daybreak I have seen
  the eastern sky glow with a wash of rose
  while all the rest hung limpid and serene,   24

and the Sun's face rise tempered from its rest
  so veiled by vapors that the naked eye
  could look at it for minutes undistressed.   27

Exactly so, within a cloud of flowers
  that rose like fountains from the angels' hands
  and fell about the chariot in showers,[1]   30

a lady came in view: an olive crown
  wreathed her immaculate veil, her cloak was green,
  the colors of live flame played on her gown.[2]   33

My soul—such years had passed since last it saw
  that lady and stood trembling in her presence,
  stupefied by the power of holy awe[3]—   36

now, by some power that shone from her above
  the reach and witness of my mortal eyes,
  felt the full mastery of enduring love.   39

1. Beatrice appears in a chariot accompanied by messengers of eternal life.
2. The colors are symbolic: white signifies hope; green, faith; red, charity.
3. Beatrice died in 1290, so it has been 10 years since Dante saw her.

572 | DANTE ALIGHIERI

bodyThe instant I was smitten by the force,
   which had already once transfixed my soul
   before my boyhood years[4] had run their course,   42

I turned left with the same assured belief
   that makes a child run to its mother's arms
   when it is frightened or has come to grief,   45

to say to Virgil: "There is not within me
   one drop of blood unstirred. I recognize
   the tokens of the ancient flame."[5] But he,   48

he had taken his light from us. He had gone.
   Virgil had gone. Virgil, the gentle Father
   to whom I gave my soul for its salvation![6]   51

Not all that sight of Eden lost to view
   by our First Mother[7] could hold back the tears
   that stained my cheeks so lately washed with dew.   54

"Dante,[8] do not weep yet, though Virgil goes.
   Do not weep yet, for soon another wound[9]
   shall make you weep far hotter tears than those!"   57

As an admiral takes his place at stern or bow
   to observe the handling of his other ships
   and spur all hands to do their best—so now,   60

on the chariot's left side, I saw appear
   when I turned back at the sound of my own name
   (which, necessarily is recorded here),   63

that lady who had been half-veiled from view
   by the flowers of the angel-revels. Now her eyes
   fixed me across the stream, piercing me through.   66

And though the veil she still wore, held in place
   by the wreathed flowers of wise Minerva's leaves,[1]
   let me see only glimpses of her face,   69

her stern and regal bearing made me dread
   her next words, for she spoke as one who saves
   the heaviest charge till all the rest are read.   72

body4. Dante was 9 when he fell in love with Beatrice.
5. A quotation from Virgil's *Aeneid* 4; it is Dido's response upon first seeing Aeneas.
6. This tercet echoes Virgil's *Georgics* 4.525–27, in which Orpheus looks back and laments the loss of Eurydice.
7. Eve, who caused the loss of the Eden in which Dante is now located.
8. This is the only time Dante's name appears in the *Commedia*.
9. The sharp words Beatrice will now speak.
1. Olive leaves, sacred to Minerva, the Roman goddess of wisdom.

"Look at me well. I am she. I am Beatrice.
    How dared you make your way to this high mountain?
    Did you not know that here man lives in bliss?"   75

I lowered my head and looked down at the stream.
    But when I saw myself reflected there,
    I fixed my eyes upon the grass for shame.   78

I shrank as a wayward child in his distress
    shrinks from his mother's sternness, for the taste
    of love grown wrathful is a bitterness.   81

* * *

From Paradiso

Canto XXXIII

THE EMPYREAN   *St. Bernard* • *Prayer to the Virgin* •
                                                        The Vision of God

St. Bernard offers a lofty *Prayer to the Virgin*, asking her to intercede in Dante's
behalf, and in answer Dante feels his soul swell with new power and grow calm in
rapture as his eyes are permitted the Direct Vision of God.

There can be no measure of how long the vision endures. It passes, and Dante
is once more mortal and fallible. Raised by God's presence, he had looked into
the Mystery and had begun to understand its power and majesty. Returned to
himself, there is no power in him capable of speaking the truth of what he saw.
Yet the impress of the truth is stamped upon his soul, which he now knows will
return to be one with God's Love.

"Virgin Mother, daughter of thy son;
    humble beyond all creatures and more exalted;
    predestined turning point of God's intention;   3

thy merit so ennobled human nature
    that its divine Creator did not scorn
    to make Himself the creature of His creature.   6

The Love that was rekindled in Thy womb
    sends forth the warmth of the eternal peace
    within whose ray this flower[1] has come to bloom.   9

Here, to us, thou art the noon and scope
    of Love revealed; and among mortal men,
    the living fountain of eternal hope.   12

1. In *Paradiso* 30, Dante saw the blessed souls arranged in a vast rose, to which St. Bernard now
refers.

Lady, thou art so near God's reckonings
   that who seeks grace and does not first seek thee
   would have his wish fly upward without wings.   15

Not only does thy sweet benignity
   flow out to all who beg, but oftentimes
   thy charity arrives before the plea.   18

In thee is pity, in thee munificence,
   in thee the tenderest heart, in thee unites
   all that creation knows of excellence!   21

Now comes this man who from the final pit
   of the universe up to this height has seen,
   one by one, the three lives of the spirit.   24

He prays to thee in fervent supplication
   for grace and strength, that he may raise his eyes
   to the all-healing final revelation.   27

And I, who never more desired to see
   the vision myself than I do that he may see It,
   add my own prayer, and pray that it may be   30

enough to move you to dispel the trace
   of every mortal shadow by thy prayers
   and let him see revealed the Sum of Grace.   33

I pray thee further, all persuading Queen,
   keep whole the natural bent of his affections
   and of his powers after his eyes have seen.   36

Protect him from the stirrings of man's clay;
   see how Beatrice and the blessèd host
   clasp reverent hands to join me as I pray."   39

The eyes that God reveres and loves the best
   glowed on the speaker, making clear the joy
   with which true prayer is heard by the most blest.   42

Those eyes turned then to the Eternal Ray,
   through which, we must indeed believe, the eyes
   of others do not find such ready way.   45

And I, who neared the goal of all my nature,
   felt my soul, at the climax of its yearning,
   suddenly, as it ought, grow calm with rapture.   48

Bernard then, smiling sweetly, gestured to me
   to look up, but I had already become
   within myself all he would have me be.   51

Little by little as my vision grew
   it penetrated further through the aura
   of the high lamp which in itself is true.   54

What then I saw is more than tongue can say.
   Our human speech is dark before the vision.
   The ravished memory swoons and falls away.   57

As one who sees in dreams and wakes to find
   the emotional impression of his vision
   still powerful while its parts fade from his mind—   60

just such am I, having lost nearly all
   the vision itself, while in my heart I feel
   the sweetness of it yet distill and fall.   63

So, in the sun, the footprints fade from snow.
   On the wild wind that bore the tumbling leaves
   the Sybil's oracles were scattered so.[2]   66

O Light Supreme who doth Thyself withdraw
   so far above man's mortal understanding,
   lend me again some glimpse of what I saw;   69

make Thou my tongue so eloquent it may
   of all Thy glory speak a single clue
   to those who follow me in the world's day;   72

for by returning to my memory
   somewhat, and somewhat sounding in these verses,
   Thou shalt show man more of Thy victory.   75

So dazzling was the splendor of that Ray,
   that I must certainly have lost my senses
   had I, but for an instant, turned away.   78

And so it was, as I recall, I could
   the better bear to look, until at last
   my vision made one with the Eternal Good.   81

Oh grace abounding that had made me fit
   to fix my eyes on the eternal light
   until my vision was consumed in it!   84

I saw within Its depth how It conceives
   all things in a single volume bound by Love,
   of which the universe is the scattered leaves;   87

2. In *Aeneid* 3, Virgil describes how the Sibyl of Cumae writes down the future on leaves that the wind then scatters.

substance, accident, and their relation[3]
   so fused that all I say could do no more
   than yield a glimpse of that bright revelation. 90

I think I saw the universal form
   that binds these things, for as I speak these words
   I feel my joy swell and my spirits warm. 93

Twenty-five centuries since Neptune saw
   the Argo's keel[4] have not moved all mankind,
   recalling that adventure, to such awe 96

as I felt in an instant. My tranced being
   stared fixed and motionless upon that vision,
   ever more fervent to see in the act of seeing. 99

Experiencing that Radiance, the spirit
   is so indrawn it is impossible
   even to think of ever turning from It. 102

For the good which is the will's ultimate object
   is all subsumed in It; and, being removed,
   all is defective which in It is perfect. 105

Now in my recollection of the rest
   I have less power to speak than any infant
   wetting its tongue yet at its mother's breast; 108

and not because that Living Radiance bore
   more than one semblance, for It is unchanging
   and is forever as it was before; 111

rather, as I grew worthier to see,
   the more I looked, the more unchanging semblance
   appeared to change with every change in me. 114

Within the depthless deep and clear existence
   of that abyss of light three circles[5] shown—
   three in color, one in circumference: 117

the second from the first, rainbow from rainbow;
   the third, an exhalation of pure fire
   equally breathed forth by the other two. 120

3. In the philosophical tradition followed by Dante, a "substance" is that which subsists in and of itself, an "accident" exists only as a quality or an attribute of a substance, and their "relation" is the way substances and accidents are bound together.

4. The voyage of Jason and the Argonauts after the Golden Fleece was thought to have occurred about 1300 B.C.E.; see *Inferno* 18.86–87.

5. Signifying the Trinity.

But oh how much my words miss my conception,
   which is itself so far from what I saw
   that to call it feeble would be rank deception!   123

O Light Eternal fixed in Itself alone,
   by Itself alone understood, which from Itself
   loves and glows, self-knowing and self-known;   126

that second aureole which shone forth in Thee,
   conceived as a reflection of the first—
   or which appeared so to my scrutiny—   129

seemed in Itself of Its own coloration
   to be painted with man's image.[6] I fixed my eyes
   on that alone in rapturous contemplation.   132

Like a geometer wholly dedicated
   to squaring the circle, but who cannot find,
   think as he may, the principle indicated[7]—   135

so did I study the supernal face.
   I yearned to know just how our image merges
   into that circle, and how it there finds place;   138

but mine were not the wings for such a flight.
   Yet, as I wished, the truth I wished for came
   cleaving my mind in a great flash of light.   141

Here my powers rest from their high fantasy,[8]
   but already I could feel my being turned—
   instinct and intellect balanced equally   144

as in a wheel whose motion nothing jars—
   by the Love that moves the Sun and the other stars.[9]

6. The "second aureole" in the "abyss of light" is Jesus Christ, the human incarnation of God.

7. The problem of constructing a square equal in area to a circle is a proverbially insoluble mathematical problem.

8. By "fantasy," Dante means the capacity of the mind to form images; it is "high" because it is capable of representing in visible form invisible truths.

9. As in the *Inferno* and the *Purgatorio*, the last word of the *Paradiso* is "stars," returning us to the perspective of the human gazing up at that which is beyond the human.

KEBRA NAGAST

Fourteenth century

The *Kəbrä Nägäśt* (hereafter *Kebra Nagast*), or *The Glory of the Kings*, is revered as a true account by many Ethiopians and African diasporic peoples throughout the world. The book relates how the Queen of Sheba, whose story is first told in the Bible, was actually an Ethiopian queen who had a son with the Israelite King Solomon. Imaginatively expanding on the laconic biblical account, the *Kebra Nagast* tells how Solomon tricked the Queen of Sheba into sleeping with him and how their son eventually took the Ark of the Covenant from Israel to Ethiopia, thus transferring God's blessings to a new chosen people. Ever since, Ethiopian tradition claims, the kings of Ethiopia have descended from the Middle Eastern King Solomon and the African Queen of Sheba. The transfer of the ark from Jerusalem to Ethiopia, like the transfer of the sacred images of the gods from Troy to Rome in **Virgil's** *Aeneid*, anchors the Christian Ethiopian nation's claim to spiritual supremacy and its kings' claims to dominion over other kings.

THE TEXT IN CONTEXT: MEDIEVAL CHRISTIAN ETHIOPIA

The Christian communities of Ethiopia date their origins to the fourth century. By the medieval period at the latest, however, Ethiopian Christianity had come to claim an older relationship with another biblical religion—Judaism. Ethiopians expressed this connection creatively, through texts such as the *Kebra Nagast,* first written down in Ethiopia shortly before 1322 C.E. in the ancient language of Ge'ez (or Classical Ethiopic, as it is often called outside Ethiopia), an Afro-Asiatic language spoken and written in Ethiopia throughout the first millennium C.E. and still used in the Ethiopian Church today. The Ethiopians also modeled the architecture of a medieval capital, Lalibela, on Jerusalem and their churches on Solomon's temple. They even claimed that the Aksumite church of Our Lady Mary of Zion housed the very same Ark of the Covenant that the Jews carried with them through the desert on their way to the Promised Land, as recounted in Exodus, and that later found its way to Ethiopia. Many passages in the *Kebra Nagast* celebrate the beauty and divine power of the ark, which is called "Our Lady Zion" in the text. The story of Solomon, an Ethiopian Queen of Sheba, and the Ark of the Covenant in Ethiopia has not yet been definitively proven or disproven. Every church in Ethiopia houses a replica of the ark, and it is the heart of parish life.

WORK

The *Kebra Nagast* begins with a broad overview of the book's own purpose and origins, followed by a brief account of world geography. But the main thread of the narrative is a love story— that of Solomon, king of the Jews and ruler of Jerusalem, and the lovely and accomplished Queen of Sheba. Although she is often called Makedda in Ethiopia today, this name does not appear in the *Kebra Nagast*. After learning from a traveling merchant about the profound wisdom of Solomon, the queen decides to travel to Jerusalem. There, she is as enraptured by Solomon's wisdom as he is by her beauty, and she converts from her people's traditional worship of the sun, moon, and stars to instead revering the "God of Israel." The blissful union of Solomon and Sheba results in the birth of a child who will be heir to the Ethiopian throne. His name is given as Bäynä Ləhkəm, meaning Son of the Wise man, simplified below to Bayna Lihkim. Although Solomon adores the queen as well as the firstborn son she has given him, it is impossible for him to install Bayna Lihkim as his heir in Jerusalem. But as a sign of his special favor, Solomon determines to ensure that his son will carry with him back to Ethiopia a very special treasure: the luxurious cloth used to cover the Ark of the Covenant holding the tablets of the law, which had been carefully preserved in the great temple. When Bayna Lihkim is on the journey homeward, however, he makes an extraordinary discovery. The young men of Jerusalem that Solomon has sent along to accompany his son to Ethiopia have brought with them not only the ceremonial cloth but the Ark itself.

The Kebra Nagast is remarkable for the extraordinary variety of literary and theological sources on which it draws, ranging from the Hebrew Scriptures and the New Testament to rabbinic commentaries, Christian apocrypha, Islamic texts, and Syriac legends. The hybrid national and racial identity crystalized in the Kebra Nagast has

been mirrored in the work's reception in later periods, especially its central role among the Rastafari communities. The Kebra Nagast is the foundation of their claim that Emperor Haile Selassie (1892–1975) was divine, a Christian king descended from biblical kings and related to Christ. Also, the movement of the ark from Israel to Ethiopia is seen as a model for their own migration into the New World, and their anticipated return—whether in body or in spirit—to Africa.

Although brief versions of the story of the Kebra Nagast began circulating in Europe very early, the whole of it was unknown there until the late eighteenth century, when the Scottish explorer James Bruce carried home from Ethiopia a collection of valuable manuscripts, including two copies of the Kebra Nagast. In 1905, the German scholar Carl Bezold published the first full scholarly edition (and German translation) of the Kebra Nagast text, based on seven Ge'ez manuscripts. The Bezold edition was the basis for the Kebra Nagast's first English translation, which E. A. Wallis Budge published in 1922. The new 2017 translation provided here is from a forthcoming book by Wendy Laura Belcher and Michael Kleiner. Their translation follows the Ge'ez text closely, except that they have sometimes inserted words or short phrases for the sake of readability.

The Glory of the Kings[1]

17. About the Glory of Zion

For Zion, the ark of his law, God first founded heaven.[2] Then, God was pleased that Zion should be the residence for his splendor on earth. Having wished it, God brought Zion down to earth and gave her to Moses, so that Moses would make a copy of her.

1. Translated by Wendy Laura Belcher and Michael Kleiner.
2. The stone tablets on which the Ten Commandments are inscribed are inside the Ark of

the Covenant, which is inside the Tent of the Testimony. These are described in Exodus 25 and elsewhere in the Hebrew Bible.

God said to Moses, "Make an ark from worm-resistant wood. Then, you will plate it with pure gold and place in it the words of the law of the covenant, which I have written with my own fingers, so that the two tablets of the covenant may preserve my law."

Wondrous are the appearance and workmanship of the heavenly, spiritual Zion! She is like jasper and shining gemstone, topaz and pearl, crystal and light itself. She ravishes the eye, she stupefies and enraptures the mind—fashioned by God's mind, not by the hands of a human artisan! Rather, God himself created her as the residence for his splendor. Zion is a spiritual being full of compassion; Zion is a heavenly being, full of light. Zion is noble and free, the residence of the divine that is in the heavens, its residence indeed. However, she walks about on earth too[3] and dwells among humans and angels—a friend of humanity, redemption! She is the residence of the Holy Spirit.

In addition, inside Zion lies a golden vessel, full to the brim with manna descended from heaven,[4] and the staff of Aaron, which blossomed even though it was dry wood and nobody had watered it.[5] Aaron then broke his staff twice so that it became three, all the while remaining one.

So, Moses coated Zion with pure gold and made carrying poles and rings for her.[6] Then, Zion was carried before the people until she was brought into the land of Israel's inheritance, that is, Jerusalem, the City of Zion.

When the Israelites were crossing the Jordan, with the priests carrying Zion, the water stood still like a wall until all the people had crossed over. After all had crossed, the priests crossed, carrying the ark. Then Zion was placed in the capital city of Judea, Jerusalem, in the land of their inheritance.

In the Tent of the Testimony,[7] prophets were appointed as leaders over the children of Israel; priests wore the ephod[8] to serve the Tent of the Testimony; and High Priests offered up sacrifices to implore for forgiveness for their sins and the sins of the people.

Then God ordered Moses and Aaron to prepare holy utensils for the Tent of the Testimony, to be set up in the Holy of Holies: golden vessels of bowls, chalices, and pitchers; tables, grates, and column tops; lanterns and lamp-filling vessels; snuffers of menorahs and their staves; pond- and sea-sized basins; garments of brocade and ordinary clothing; priestly turbans and vestments; purples and blues; carpets and scarlet curtains; oils for anointing to the priesthood and to the kingship; violet and ruby garments; doubly twined linen cloth and sea silk; goat-hair curtains and tanned sheepskins; and stones of carnelian, jasper, sapphire, and emerald—all placed in the Tent of the Testimony, where dwells Zion, the residence of God's splendor.[9]

Furthermore, God ordered Moses and Aaron to make a big chest for Zion and the two tablets written with God's fingers; Zion will dwell in them:

---

3. The Israelites carried the Ark of the Covenant with them on their way through the desert to the Holy Land.
4. Exodus 16.16–35.
5. Numbers 17.8.
6. Exodus 25.10–16; 37.1–6.
7. The Tent of the Testimony was one of the temporary structures that the Israelites set up

for worship in the wilderness while on their way from Egypt to the Promised Land. It contained the Ark of the Covenant with the Ten Commandments (Exodus 26.13).
8. The ephod is an overgarment worn by Jewish priests, a visible sign of their authority.
9. The temple objects as listed here are an amalgam from Exodus 31:7–9, 36:8–38; 37:1–29.

THE GLORY OF THE KINGS | 581

"Moses, you will make an ark of worm-resistant wood for her, where Zion shall dwell. It will be two and a half cubits long and one and a half cubits wide. You will plate it, inside and outside, with pure gold. You will make its moldings and coating with pure gold. As to the rings on the sides of it, you will make four loops into the ark's four feet. You will make its carrying poles from worm-resistant wood and plate them with pure gold. With those carrying poles, you Israelites will carry the ark of the law."

In this way, God gave his orders to Moses on Mount Sinai, and showed him how the tabernacle, that is, the ark, should be made, arranged, and colored, so that Moses would be able to make her. She was greatly revered and exalted in Israel, and accepted by God as the residence for his splendor. God himself descended from his mountain of his holiness and spoke to his chosen ones, the Jewish people. He released deliverance to them, rescuing them from their enemies. He spoke to them from a pillar of cloud, so that they would keep his laws and his precepts and walk according to God's commands.

* * *

19. About Where This Book Was Found

Domitius, the archbishop of Constantinople,[1] said: I personally found the book about the queen's visit to Solomon in the Hagia Sophia church,[2] among other royal books and treasures. The book declares that dominion over the whole world belongs to the monarch of Byzantium and the monarch of Ethiopia.[3]

20. About the Division of the Earth

The monarch of Byzantium's share extends from the middle of Jerusalem toward the north and northeast, and the monarch of Ethiopia's share from the middle of Jerusalem toward the south and southwest as well as to western India.[4] For both of them are descendants of Shem, the son of Noah; then descendants of Abraham, then descendants of David, and then descendants of Solomon. Truly, God conferred honor on the descendants of Shem because he blessed their father Noah. The monarch of Byzantium is a son of Solomon and the monarch of Ethiopia is a son of Solomon, but the monarch of Ethiopia is the firstborn and elder one.

21. About the Queen of the South and How That Son Came to Be Born

I, Domitius, found recorded in this book: "The Evangelists spoke as follows about this woman, the Queen of the South, 'Our Lord Jesus Christ reprimanded

1. No Domitius is attested as archbishop of Constantinople; Ethiopianist scholarship now generally regards the name as a corruption of Methodius.
2. Built in the sixth century under emperor Justinian I, the Hagia Sophia (Holy Wisdom) was the main church of Constantinople and of the Byzantine Empire as a whole.
3. Chapters 19–94 are ostensibly those read from this book by Domitius.
4. "Western India" here refers to the lands on the western and northwestern shores of the Indian Ocean and the Red Sea. The term *India* was used loosely in antiquity and the Middle Ages; sometimes it was even applied to Ethiopia.

the Jews, that generation of crucifiers, saying, "The Queen of the South will rise up on Judgment Day and take to court and conquer this generation, who did not listen to my preaching; for she herself came from the ends of the earth to listen to Solomon's wisdom."'[5]

The expression "Queen of the South" means the Queen of Ethiopïa, and it says "the ends of the earth" because of the weak nature of women, yet she endured the long journey, the burning sun, the hunger, and the thirst for water.

The Queen of the South was most beautiful in appearance and splendor, in knowledge and insight which God had given her so that she would go to Jerusalem to listen to Solomon's wisdom;[6] her visit happened due to God's will, and because it pleased him.

The Queen of the South was also very wealthy, due to the status and the riches that God had given her: gold and silver, luxurious garments, camels, and servants, as well as merchants who traded for her on sea and on land, as far as India and Aswan.[7]

22. About the Merchant Tamreen

There was a smart and prominent merchant whose name was Tamreen. He was so successful that he could load up 520 camels, and he owned seventy-three ships.

At that time, King Solomon wanted to build God's Temple, so he sent for all the traders, east and west, north and south, to come and receive gold and silver from him in exchange for the required materials for the task. Solomon was then told about this wealthy Ethiopian merchant. So he sent Tamreen a message, that he should procure for him the required red gold, worm-resistant black wood, and sapphires from the land of the Arabs.[8] Therefore, the merchant whose name was Tamreen, the merchant of the Queen of Ethiopia, went to King Solomon with these goods. The king took from Tamreen everything he required, and paid him what Tamreen wanted, spending generously from his wealth.

The merchant was very smart, so he observed Solomon's wisdom, marveled at it, and was careful to pay attention to Solomon's responses, to his justice, his eloquence and pleasant speech; to his conduct, his sitting-down and standing-up, his deeds, his affectionate ways; as well as to his administration, his banquets, and his laws. Solomon commanded in a friendly and mild manner those to whom he gave orders, and if they transgressed, he pardoned them because he ruled his house with wisdom and in the fear of God. He gently rebuked the ignorant, and gently assigned the maidservants their tasks. He spoke in parables, his words sweeter than honeycomb. His entire manner was pleasant, and his entire being charming. Truly, wisdom is appreciated by people of understanding, but rejected by the ignorant.

When the merchant had observed all this, he wondered and marveled greatly. For those who witnessed Solomon up close, he became their passion and teacher; and those who visited did not want to tear themselves away from him because of

5. Matthew 12.42; Luke 11.31.
6. 1 Kings 10.1–13; 2 Chronicles 9.1–12.
7. Aswan, located near the First Cataract of the Nile, has been identified as the southern-

most city of Egypt for millennia.
8. These tributary "Arabs" lived in the vicinity of Solomon's kingdom, between the Sinai in the south and southern Syria in the north.

his wisdom and attractiveness. His pleasant speech was like water for the thirsty, bread for the hungry, medicine for the sick, a garment for the naked, and a father for the orphaned. He judged justly and was not partial to anyone. He possessed great glory, as well as riches that God had given him in abundance—gold, silver, gems, and costly garments, plus livestock and wild game without number. In King Solomon's days, gold was as common as copper and silver as lead; with copper, lead, and iron as plentiful as the trees of the wilderness and the reeds of the sea; and furthermore, cedar wood was everywhere—due to the glory and riches and wisdom and favor that God had given Solomon, the likes of which had never been before him and will never be after him.

23. In Which the Merchant Returns to Ethiopia

Then the merchant Tamreen wanted to return to his country. So he went to King Solomon, prostrated himself before him, then stood again, and saluted him, saying: "Hail to your greatness! Permit me to go home, to my lady. I have stayed too long, attending to your glory and wisdom, and eating the many dishes you graciously served me. But now, I must return to my lady. I wish I could stay with you as one of your lowliest servants: Blessed are those who can listen to your words and carry out your commands! Yes, I wish I could stay here and not leave you, but, unfortunately, I must ask you to send me to my lady to honor my pledge to hand her earnings over to her, for I am her servant."

So, Solomon proceeded to Tamreen's house and handed over all that was due, respectful of the country of Ethiopia, and bid him farewell in peace.

Tamreen prostrated himself and then left Jerusalem. He went on his way, eventually reaching his queen and handing over to her all the earnings he brought. Then he told her how he had gone to Jerusalem, the capital city of Judea, and to King Solomon. He told her everything he had heard and seen there: How Solomon would dispense justice, how he would speak with integrity, how he would order the right thing done in all the cases he examined. Solomon replied gently to all; there was no falsehood in him. Tamreen told her how Solomon would appoint overseers over the laborers who carried loads of timber, over each group of 700, and over the stonemasons, over each group of 800; how he would question all the merchants and sellers about their skills and practices; how he would take, but give twofold in return. Every move and deed of his was done with insight.

Every morning Tamreen would tell the queen about all of Solomon's wisdom: How he would dispense justice, how he would do right, how he would host guests, how he would hold banquets, how he would teach wisdom, how he would give instructions to his servants, and how everything was governed by his judgements—how everybody lived by his word. There, nobody would cheat anybody else, and nobody would violate a neighbor's possessions. Indeed, in Solomon's day, there were no more robbers and thieves because he would wisely suss out those who had gone astray, then punish and scare them, so that they would not do evil again but live in peace out of fear of the king.

All this Tamreen told the queen; each morning he would recall what he had seen at the king's court and relate it to her. She was amazed by what she heard from her servant the merchant, and in her heart would ponder whether to visit Solomon. She would weep from the intensity of her love for what Tamreen told her, longing to meet Solomon. And she would entertain thoughts of visiting Solomon, but then would decide that the trip was too lengthy and too difficult.

But then she would inquire again, and Tamreen would tell her again, and she would long to visit Solomon in order to listen to his wisdom, see his face, greet him, and pay homage to his rule. Therefore, she finally determined to travel to him, although it was God who gave her this desire and caused her to make this decision to go.

So, she began to set her house in order, instructing her manservants, admonishing her maidservants, and organizing her properties and wealth. She then sought out everything needed for the trip, including those things needed as gifts for the king, for giving to her lords, and for remunerating her maidservants. She further assembled camels, mules, horses, and donkeys, as well as ships and rafts, panniers and bridles, supplies of food and drink, and carrying equipment. Thus she got ready to travel, also ordering all the lords under her to prepare for a trip of up to six months so that they would take along enough supplies of food and put their houses in order, because the land where they were going was far away.

* * *

25. How the Queen Came to Visit King Solomon

The queen arrived in Jerusalem and presented the king with the many gifts, the honor that he was due. As for him, he was delighted and bestowed honors on her, assigning her a royal palace near his own as a residence. In addition, he sent her luncheon and dinner every day—fifteen *qoré* measures[9] of ground wheat flour cooked with plenty of oil and sauce, and thirty *qoré* measures of crushed wheat flour, enough to make bread for 350 people, complete with the requisite plates and bowls; furthermore, ten fattened cows, five bulls, and fifty sheep, not to mention the wild goats, the mountain goats, the gazelles, and the fattened poultry; as well as a vat of new wine containing eighty *girret* measures,[1] and a vat of aged wine containing thirty *girret* measures, along with the cupbearers, twenty-five men and twenty-five women; and honeycomb and sweets—from the food and drink that he himself ate and drank.

Each day Solomon would dress up in eleven ravishing garments, and then went to be comfortable in the queen's company. The queen, too, went to be comfortable in his company. She witnessed his wisdom, his justice, his glory, his benevolence, and his pleasant conversation. She marveled at it all in her heart, was delighted by it in her mind, considered it with her reason, and observed it with her eyes, as was right. All in all, she was completely amazed by what she saw and heard in Solomon's presence: how he was fully at ease, wise in thought, joyfully gracious, and handsome in majesty. Furthermore, his words were cogent, his lips eloquent, his orders regal, and his replies peaceable and God-fearing. She saw all this and was amazed at the magnitude of Solomon's wisdom. Nothing whatsoever was lacking in his words and speech; rather, everything he spoke was perfect.

9. A measure of volume. In the Bible, a *kor* is a dry measure comprising somewhere between 200 and 400 liters.

1. Probably around 10 liters.

Meanwhile, Solomon worked on constructing God's Temple. He would rise up and walk to the right and to the left, to the front and to the back of the construction site—showing the workers how to use the measuring tools, the scales, and the saws; telling the smiths how to use the hammer, chisel, and bellows; and showing the stonecutters how to use the square edge, compass, and mallet. Everything was carried out according to Solomon's command; nobody transgressed it.

Truly, the light of Solomon's mind was like a lamp in the dark, and his wisdom as copious as grains of sand. Of the language of wild beasts and birds—none of it was unintelligible to him; he even subjugated the demonic spirits[2] through his wisdom. Solomon did everything through the talents that God had given him when he had asked for them. Indeed, Solomon had asked neither for victory over his enemies, nor for riches and glory. Rather, he had asked God to give him the wisdom and insight to govern his people with, build God's Temple, and make his deeds pleasing to God, through all the wisdom and insight that God would give him.

* * *

28. About How Solomon Instructed the Queen

The king replied to her:[3] "Truly, everyone should worship God, who has fashioned everything: heaven and earth, the sea and the dry land, the sun and the moon, the stars and other shining celestial bodies, the trees and the stones, the mammals and the birds, the land predators and the crocodiles, the fish and the whales, the hippopotamuses and the turtles, lightning and thunderstorms, clouds and thunder, and good as well as bad people. Him alone should we worship, with fear and trembling, with joy and happiness, for he is Lord over everything, the creator of angels and human beings. He puts to death and he brings to life, he punishes and he forgives; he raises the poor man from the dust and lifts the wretched man from the mud; he afflicts and he delights; and he raises up and casts down. Nobody can reproach him because he is Lord over everything; nobody can say to him: 'What have you done?!' He deserves praise and thanksgiving from the angels and from humanity.

"As to what you said before—'God has given you, Israel, an ark with the law'—yes, we have been given an ark from the Lord of Israel, which has been created before all creation through the resolve of the Divine Splendor. Having written his Ten Commandments, God then sent them down to us so that we would know his laws and rules, those which he ordained on the mountain of his holiness."

The queen replied, "From now on, I won't worship the sun, but only the sun's creator, the Lord of Israel! The ark of the Lord of Israel shall be my lady, as well as of my descendants after me, and of all the people of my dominion, those who are under my rule. For this purpose have I found grace before you

2. Literally, *aganent* ("the demons"), corresponding to the *jinn* of Arabic. See Qur'an 27:16–17 and 34:12.
3. In the preceding chapter (27), the queen had asked whom it was right to worship,

explaining that she and the majority of her people worshipped the sun, while others adored stones, trees, or statues made of silver and gold; but she had heard that Israel had a different god.

and before the Lord of Israel, my creator, who has brought me to you, let me hear your words, shown me your face, and let me grasp your instructions."

Then she returned to her residence. But, time and again, she would go over to listen to Solomon's wisdom and preserve it in her heart. Solomon, too, would go to her to answer everything she asked him. Soon she would return to him, asking him even more questions, and he would teach her about everything she desired.

After the queen had stayed in Jerusalem for six months, she wished to return to her country. So she sent a message to Solomon: "Although I personally desire to stay with you, I need to return to my country for the sake of my entire people. As to what I have heard from you, may God make it bear fruit in my heart as well as in the hearts of all those who heard it together with me! Truly, the ear never becomes too full with listening to your wisdom, and the eye too full with looking at it."

Further, it was not only she who visited Solomon, but many from the cities and the countryside, from near and far, because in those days there was nobody equal to Solomon in wisdom. And not only humans visited him, but also wild animals and birds, who listened to his words, marveled at his wisdom, conversed with him, and then returned home. Everybody marveled at Solomon's wisdom, at what they saw and heard.

After the queen had sent the message to Solomon that she planned to go home, he thought in his heart: "A woman of such beauty has come to me from the ends of the earth—will not God perhaps give me descendants in her?" As it says in the Book of Kings, "King Solomon loved women, and married some from among the Hebrews, Egyptians, Canaanites, Edomites, and Moabites," from among the delta Egyptians and the Georgians, the people of Damascus and of Tyre, as well as from among those beautiful women he had been told about— there were 400 queens and 600 concubines.[4] Now, Solomon did not do this out of lustfulness, but because he was exercising the wisdom that God had given him and remembering what God had said to Abraham: "I will make your descendants as abundant as the stars of the sky and as the grains of the sea's sand."[5] Consequently, Solomon said in his heart, "Perhaps God will give me male children, one from each of these women." Thus, cleverly, he acted like this, thinking: "My children will inherit the lands of my enemies and will eradicate those who worship idols."

The first people of God, the Jews, they lived by the law of the flesh because they had not yet been given the grace of the Holy Spirit; but those after Christ have been given the gift to live with a single woman in lawful marriage. For them the apostles decreed as follows: "Those who have partaken of Christ's flesh and blood in Holy Communion are all brothers. The Church is their mother, God is their father. Together with Christ, whom they have received, they will shout out, 'Our Father Who Art in Heaven.'" But, as for Solomon, nothing had been decreed for him regarding women, so no transgression accrued to him due to his marriages. Christian believers, by contrast, have been gifted the law, and the command, not to have multiple wives, according to what Paul said, "Those who marry multiple women seek out punishment for themselves, but he who marries

---

4. 1 Kings 11.1–3 speaks of 700 wives and 300 concubines.
5. Genesis 22:17.

one wife is without sin."[6] The law of the sister: "We have forbidden it, with respect to procreation," say the apostles in the *Sinodos*.[7]

* * *

29. About the 318 Nicene Bishops

We, too, the 318 Nicene Bishops,[8] have decreed regarding marriage as did the apostles, for we are aware of what the apostles, who preceded us, have spoken. We, the 318 establishers of the faith! Christ, being with us—he has established for us how we should teach and practice the faith.

29A. HOW THE QUEEN DINED WITH SOLOMON

Now King Solomon sent a message to the queen, with the following words: "After you have come all this way, why do you want to leave before you have seen how my government works; how banquets are held for the kingdom's dignitaries as if they were the righteous ones of God; and how the gentiles are hounded as sinners? By witnessing this, you will acquire wisdom. Come, follow me, and stay with my majesty in the tents—in this way I will complete your instruction, and you will come to understand the administration of my kingdom. For you love wisdom and it will remain with you until your last day, and beyond." Truly, these were prophetic words by Solomon.

Now the queen once again sent a message to him: "I was ignorant; now I have become wise through emulating your wisdom. I was disdained by the Lord of Israel; now I have become a chosen one through the faith in my heart. From now on, I will not worship anyone other than him! As for that which you say you desire—to improve me in wisdom and worth—I will come, just as you wish."

Solomon was happy when he heard this message. He clothed his dignitaries in finery, doubled the fare on his table, and commanded his entire household to be set in order—for days, King Solomon's house was suitably prepared. Over those days, he prepared it with great pomp—full of joy, at ease, with wisdom and mild disposition, as well as perfectly humble and gentle.

Then the king's table of guests was ordered according to the custom of the kingdom, and the queen, radiant and splendid, entered a hidden chamber in the palace through a back door and sat directly behind Solomon, where she could see, have things shown to her, and observe everything while being hidden. She marveled greatly at what she saw and heard. In her heart she praised the Lord of Israel, and, stupefied, she admired the magnificence of the palace. Indeed, she could see everything, but nobody could see her, due to how Solomon had cleverly arranged things for her. He had adorned her chamber, covering it with purple cloth and laying out fine carpets, as well as installing a disguised window

---

6. While this is not a direct quote, the Apostle Paul regularly wrote about the need for monogamy; see Romans 7.1–4; 1 Corinthians 6.15–17, 7.1–2; 1 Timothy 3.1–2; and Titus 1.5–6.
7. The *Sinodos* or *Senodos* (from Greek *synodos*, meaning council or assembly) is the Ethiopian Orthodox Church's most important

collection of ecclesiastical law and liturgy.
8. The Council of Nicaea in 325 was the first ecumenical council of the Church, said to have been attended by 318 bishops, who are often regarded as a group of saints in the Ethiopian Orthodox Church.

of marble and precious stones, sprinkling perfumes, scattering myrrh and cinnamon, and daubing the room with galbanum and frankincense. When one entered this room, its fragrance was delightful, and its sweet smell satiated one even before eating any dishes.

Now Solomon cleverly and cunningly sent the queen thirst-inducing cuisine, such as tart drinks, salty fish, and spicy dishes. He did this, giving it to the queen, so that she would eat from it. After the king's banquet had been completed three times, or seven times, and after the stewards, councilors, male youths, and the servants had gone home, the king stood up, went to the hidden chamber of the queen and, the two of them being alone, said to her, "Find comfort here, for the sake of love, until the morning."

She replied to him, "Swear an oath to me by your Lord, the Lord of Israel, that you will not take me unlawfully by force![9] If I, a maiden, strayed from the sanctions of society, I would fall into hardship, suffering, and misfortune on my way home if visibly pregnant."

30. About How King Solomon Swore an Oath to the Queen

The king replied to her, "I swear to you that I will not take you unlawfully by force—but you, too, swear to me that you will not take unlawfully by force anything that is in my home."

In reaction to this, the queen laughed and said to Solomon, "Why do you speak like a fool even though you are wise? Why would I steal or rob anything from the palace that the king has not given me? My lord, do not think that I came here for the love of riches: My kingdom is also rich, and I lack none of the things I desire. Rather, I came in search of your wisdom!"

Solomon countered, "Since you made me swear an oath, you swear an oath to me, too: An oath is appropriate for both of us, so that neither side will be wronged. If you had not made me swear an oath, I would not make you swear an oath either!"

Now the queen said to him, "Swear to me again that you will not take me unlawfully by force, then I will also swear that I will not take your possessions unlawfully by force."

So Solomon swore this to her again, but also extracted an oath from the queen.

Now the king ascended to his bed on one side of the room, while a bed was prepared also for her on the other side. While this was happening, Solomon said to a servant boy, "Rinse out the cups, and set out a pitcher of water as the queen watches. Then, lock the doors, and go to sleep yourself." But he said this in another language, one that the queen did not understand.

The servant boy did as ordered and then went to sleep. Yet, as for the king, he did not sleep, although he pretended to be asleep; instead, he observed the

9. *Ge'ez tahayyala* (to take by force, to overpower, to take unlawfully). Here and in the following chapter, this verb when used with reference to Solomon means potentially forcing the queen to have intercourse with him. Conversely, when it is used with reference to the queen it means her potentially taking any-

thing of Solomon's possessions unlawfully. As the parallelism of the Ge'ez usage, essential for the overall narrative, would be lost if we used two different translations for *tahayyala* according to the context, we have opted for "to take unlawfully by force" throughout.

queen closely. Fortunately, King Solomon's palace was as bright at night as during the day, since cleverly he had built pearls into the ceilings of his palace, which shone like the sun, the moon, and the stars.

As for the queen, she slept a little, and when she woke up, her mouth was completely dry from thirst because Solomon, cannily, had had thirst-inducing dishes served to her. Now she was intensely thirsty, with her mouth being completely dry. She sucked her mouth for moisture, but could not find any. Therefore, she thought about drinking the water that she had seen set out. She looked toward King Solomon and observed him closely. It appeared to her that he was fast asleep. Yet he was not asleep, but rather waiting until she would get up to stealthily take the water for which she thirsted.

So, the queen got up and, careful not to make any sound with her feet, tiptoed over to the water in the pitcher. She raised it up so as to drink—but at that moment, and before she had been able to drink any water, Solomon seized her arm and said to her: "Why are you breaking the oath that you have sworn, that you would not take unlawfully by force anything that is in my home?"

She replied timidly, "Does drinking water amount to breaking my oath?"

The king replied, "Have you seen anything more precious under the sky than water?"

So the queen said, "I have transgressed against my oath, so you are free from yours. But let me drink some water to quench my thirst!"

Yet Solomon asked again, "Am I indeed free from the oath you made me swear to you?"

The queen replied, "Be free from the oath—but let me drink some water!"

So Solomon let her drink the water, and after she had drunk it, he had his way with her, and they slept together.

But, then, after King Solomon had fallen asleep, a brilliant sun appeared to him, descending from the skies and shining brightly over Israel. Later, however, after remaining there for a long time, it suddenly withdrew and soared away until it came to the land of Ethiopia. Then, it shone brightly there, and will for eternity, because it loved to dwell there.

[*The remainder of the chapter tells of additional dream visions that Solomon had, and of the departure of the queen to return to Ethiopia, lavishly endowed with Solomon's gifts.*]

31. About the Token That Solomon Gave the Queen

The queen was delighted with these gifts and set out to leave, with Solomon preparing a magnificent farewell. He took her aside so that they were alone, removed a ring from his little finger, and gave it to the queen with these words:

"Take it so that you don't forget me! Also, if I should happen to receive a child from inside you, this shall be a token for that child; and if it is a boy, he should come to me. May the peace of God now be with you!

"By the way, while I slept next to you, I saw a multitude of visions in my dreams, such as the sun, after having risen in Israel, withdrawing and soaring away, and shining for Ethiopia. I don't know whether your country will be blessed through you—only God knows it. But, as for you, you should heed what I have told you, so that you will worship God with all your heart and do his will. Behold, he punishes the haughty and shows mercy to the meek; he tears down the thrones of the mighty and makes the lowly great! Death and life come from God, wealth and poverty are allotted according to his will. Everything belongs to him, nobody can resist his command or his condemnation, be it in heaven or on earth, in the sea or the deepest valley. May God be with you—now go in peace!"

Then they bade farewell to each other.

32. How the Queen Gave Birth and Reached Her Country

So the queen set forth and, nine months and five days after having been sent off by Solomon, reached the city of Bala Zadisarya.[1] Now labor pains gripped her, and she gave birth to a baby boy. She handed the infant over to a wet nurse with great reverence and joy, while she herself stayed in the birth chamber until the days of her purification were over.[2] Then she returned to her country, in great majesty. Those lords of hers who had remained behind presented their lady with gifts and prostrated themselves before her to do homage. All the provinces rejoiced about the queen's return. As for her, she outfitted the distinguished among the lords with fine clothes. To some she even gave gold and silver, as well as violet and ruby garments. She gave everybody the appropriate gift.

Then she set her kingdom in order, with nobody daring to disobey her commands. Truly, she loved wisdom, and God strengthened her rule.

Meanwhile, the child grew, and the queen gave him the name of Bayna Lihkim.[3] When he was twelve years old, he asked his young friends and his tutors, "Who is my father?" to which they replied, "King Solomon!"

So, he went to his mother, the queen, and said to her: "O Queen, tell me, who is my father?"

The queen replied angrily, trying to frighten him so that he would not want to go see Solomon, "Why are you asking me about a father? I am your father and your mother, don't look for any other parent!"

So the boy withdrew, but remained persistent, asking the queen a second and third time, and pressing her to answer. Therefore, one day she told him, with these words, "His country is far away, and the journey there is difficult, so don't even think about going there!"

Regarding the boy Bayna Lihkim, he was handsome. His entire stature and body, down to the way he held his head, resembled King Solomon, his father; also his eyes and legs, even the way he walked, resembled King Solomon. When Bayna Lihkim was twenty-five years old, he had learned all about combat, horse riding, the hunting of wild animals, and everything else that is customary for a

---

1. Not identified. According to Ethiopian tradition, the Queen of Sheba gave birth in Ethiopia.
2. Following the prescriptions of Leviticus 12.2–5, the Ethiopian Orthodox Church traditionally taught that a woman was unclean for forty days after giving birth to a male child, and for eighty after giving birth to a female

infant. She was required to remain separated from her community during that time.
3. The name *Bayna Lihkim*, meaningless in Ge'ez, results from corruption of an original Arabic *Ibn al-Hakīm* (The Son of the Wise Man), suggesting that at least parts of the *Kebra Nagast*, and certainly this chapter, were translated from an Arabic original.

young man. At that point, he told the queen: "I will go to see my father! But I will return here, God the Lord of Israel willing."

33. How the King of Ethiopia Descended to Israel

So the queen summoned Tamreen, her head merchant, and instructed him, "Prepare for another trip of yours and take this son of mine to his father, for night and day he has been pestering me to allow him to go visit Solomon. Take him to the king and then bring him back here safe and sound, God the Lord of Israel willing."

The queen then prepared provisions fit for the travelers' wealth and status, as well as all the equipment required for their journey, the gifts to be given to the king, and comforts that ease the journey. She had it all prepared to send off her son, and also provided for the lords who would accompany him, giving them the considerable funding required for the journey. In addition, she commanded them not to leave her son behind in Israel, but rather to compel the king, Solomon, to let him go; and that they should return her son to her, and that Solomon should also appoint him to the rule of her country. For it had long been the order of the country of Ethiopia that a chaste, unmarried woman ruled over it.[4]

So, the queen wrote to Solomon, "From now on a man from your lineage shall rule Ethiopia—no woman shall ever rule in the stead of your lineage and descendants, not for eternity! You shall write this down in a document, in the brass book of their prophets,[5] and you shall deposit it in God's Temple that you are building as a reminder of the past and a warning for future days, and so that people will not worship the sun or the bejeweled sky, nor the mountains, groves, stones, or trees of the wilderness, nor the depths of the seas and what is in their waters, nor idols and golden images, nor the flying birds; nor shall they interpret the flight of birds as omens or revere them. This decree shall remain valid forever—if someone transgresses it, your descendants shall punish him forevermore! In addition, give us a piece from the hem of the cloth of holy, heavenly Zion, the ark of God's law, so that we can salute and revere it. Hail to the power of your kingdom and to the shining wisdom that God, the Lord of Israel, our creator, has given you!"

Now the queen took her son aside alone and gave him the token that Solomon had given her, the ring that had been on his finger, so that by it Solomon would recognize his son and recall the queen's pledge—the covenant she had entered into—that all her life she, and all those under her rule, would worship God, with all that God had given her. Then she sent her son forth in peace.

He and his retinue set out on their journey, traveling and eventually reaching the borders of the district of Gaza,[6] the territory that King Solomon had given to the Queen of Ethiopia, as, in the Acts of the Apostles, Luke wrote of the Ethiopian

4. We possess no evidence so far that queens ruled in ancient Ethiopia (Aksum).
5. It makes little sense to speak to Solomon about the prophets of Israel as "their" instead of "your" prophets, so perhaps the text is cor-rupt here.
6. On the coastal road between Egypt and Israel, Gaza was a major city on the southern border of Solomon's kingdom (1 Kings 4:24).

official:[7] "He was her administrator for the entire district of Gaza, the eunuch of the Queen Hindaké[8] who believed in the word of Luke the Apostle."[9]

34. How Bayna Likhim Arrived at His Mother's Territory of Gaza

When Bayna Likhim arrived in his mother's city of Gaza, he delighted in the honors and the welcome he received there. For when the people of Gaza saw him, they thought he resembled King Solomon exactly and therefore prostrated themselves before him, shouting: "Hail! Long live the royal father!" They brought him gifts and offerings, fattened cows and rich meals, as if he was their king. The entire region of Gaza, up to the border with Judea, was in tumult, exclaiming, "This is King Solomon!" Yet some replied, "But the king is in Jerusalem building his Temple!" For Solomon had not yet finished the construction of God's Temple. Others, however, affirmed, "This is King Solomon, the son of David!"

They were in such tumult, quarreling with each other, that they finally sent swift messengers to Jerusalem, men on horses, who inquired whether King Solomon was really there or whether he was with them in Gaza. The swift messengers came to the guards at the gates of Jerusalem and in the city found King Solomon. They prostrated themselves before him and said to him: "Hail! Long live the royal father! Indeed, Gaza is in tumult because a traveler has come who resembles you in looks and appearance, without anything missing or being different. He resembles you in radiance and beauty, in build and attractiveness, without any shortcoming or deviation from you. His eyes are joyful like those of a man intoxicated from wine, his legs are lean, and the column of his neck rises like the tower of your father David. He resembles you in everything; his entire body is like yours!"

The king replied, "So then, where does that traveler intend to go?"

The messengers answered, "We did not dare to inquire about it from him directly because he is as majestic as you are. However, when we asked his retinue, 'Where have you come from, and where are you going?' they replied, 'We have come from the lands of India and Ethiopia,[1] and are going to the land of Judea, to King Solomon.'" When King Solomon heard this, his feelings got stirred up and his spirit rejoiced because at that time he did not have any sons, except for a small boy of seven years named Rehoboam. As Paul put it, "Truly, God has turned the wisdom of this world into foolishness,"[2] namely, as when Solomon had decided in his worldly wisdom to boast, "From 1,000 women, I will sire a thousand male children; through them I will inherit the cities of my enemies and destroy their idols." However, God gave Solomon only three male children, including his eldest son, the King of Ethiopia, the Queen of Ethiopia's son, the firstborn. For this is what God said in a prophecy,[3] "God swore a truthful oath to David, and will not go back on it: 'Truly, I will put one from among

---

7. The Ethiopia of Acts 8 is the state of Meroë in Nubia, in today's northern Sudan.
8. In Acts 8.27 *Kandakē* (Candace) is given as the name of the queen of "Ethiopia," i.e., Meroë.
9. Acts 8 relates that the apostle Philip converted the Ethiopian eunuch, not "Luke the Apostle," and it characterizes the eunuch as the Ethiopian (i.e., Meroitic) queen's treasurer,

not her governor of Gaza.
1. In antiquity and the Middle Ages, the Horn of Africa was identified as both "India" and "Ethiopia."
2. 1 Corinthians 2.
3. The text here lacks coherence and continuity.

the fruit of your loins on your throne!'"[4] Therefore, God let his servant David find favor with him, and gave him a descendant who would sit on the Divine Throne. In the flesh, that descendant, Christ, was from the Virgin, and on Judgment Day he will judge the living and the dead, repaying everybody according to his deeds: Praise be to our lord Jesus Christ in eternity, amen!

In addition, on earth God gave David a descendant, one who would be king over the ark of His law, the holy, heavenly Zion—this is the King of Ethiopia! Regarding those who rule as kings of Ethiopia but who are not Israelites, it is a transgression of the divine law and a provision that does not please God.

> [Chapter 35 relates how Solomon sent his right-hand man Joas to Gaza with a stately retinue to welcome Bayna Lihkim and escort him to Jerusalem, so as to find out whether he truly was his son.]

* * *

36. In Which King Solomon Meets His Son

So Joas, the son of Yodahé, went out and ushered Bayna Lihkim in. When King Solomon saw Bayna Lihkim, he rose to welcome him. Then, he opened the clasp of his cloak at the shoulder;[5] embraced him; pulled him to his chest; kissed him on the mouth, forehead, and eyes; and exclaimed, "Behold, my father David, restored to youthful manliness, has risen from the dead!"

Then, he turned to those who had told him about Bayna Lihkim, saying "You said to me, 'He looks like you,' yet this is not my build but rather the build of my father David in his youth. He looks much better than I do!"

> [The text goes on to relate how Solomon outfits his son with precious regal garments. Emerging with him again from his private chambers, Solomon then addresses his court dignitaries:]

"Among yourselves, you disparage me, saying that I have no sons. But look! This is my son, the fruit of my loins, whom God the Lord of Israel has given to me from where I didn't expect it!"

Solomon's lords replied, "May the mother who has given birth to this young man be blessed, and may the day be blessed on which you joined yourself to this young man's mother."

[The dignitaries of Israel now heap praise on Bayna Lihkim and also present him with gifts. But Bayna Lihkim has a gift, too, for his father.]

Bayna Lihkim presented to his father the ring that his mother had handed over to him in private, and said to Solomon, "Take this ring, and remember the words you exchanged with the queen. Now, let us have a piece from the hem of the cloth covering the ark of God's law, so that we, and all who are under us and fall under the rule of the queen, may worship Zion all our lives."

The king replied to him, "Why do you give me this ring as a piece of evidence?! Even without you giving me this token, I spotted that your appearance was my exact likeness: You truly are my son!"

---

4. Psalm 132.11.
5. Solomon taking off his cloak (lebs, literally "clothing") is a sign of intimacy, a signal that he receives Bayna Lihkim not as a monarch but as a father.

Now the merchant Tamreen also spoke to Solomon, "O king, listen to the message that your maidservant and my lady, the queen, sent me to deliver: 'Anoint this child, consecrate and bless him, and appoint him as king over our land, Ethiopia. In addition, decree that no woman shall ever again rule in Ethiopia. Then send him off in peace.

"'Hail to the might of your rule and to your shining wisdom! As for me, I did not want Bayna Lihkim to come to you—but he pressed me quite a bit to let him go. As for me, I was worried about him, that he might fall sick and die during the trip, either through thirst or through the sun's intense heat, and that, in my old age, I might go down to the grave in grieving. Therefore, I entrusted myself to the protection of the holy, heavenly Zion, the ark of God's law, so that you would not use your cleverness to hold him there.'"

[The queen goes on to describe the attraction of Solomon's personality even to his courtiers, despite their constant proximity to him. Therefore, her son, who experiences it for the first time, might feel that attraction all the more, thus her fears that he might stay behind at Jerusalem.]

"'Therefore, because I was afraid, I entrusted myself to Zion, so that you would not make him stay there, but rather send him to me in peace, without him suffering any illness or pain, in love and in peace, so that my heart could rejoice upon receiving him back."

The king replied to the queen's messenger Tamreen, "What claim does a woman have on a son—apart from suffering the pain of labor and nursing him as a baby? A daughter belongs to the mother, but a son belongs to the father! God cursed Eve when he said, 'Give birth in anguish and pain, and with a sorrowful heart! Then, after you have given painful birth, you will yet return to your husband. While giving birth you swear an oath against sex—but after having sworn, you will nonetheless return to your husband.'[6] This young man is my son! I will not give him back to the queen but rather will make him king over Israel. Truly, he is my firstborn, the first fruit of my rod, whom God has given me."

From then on, each morning and evening, Solomon would send Bayna Lihkim tasty foods, precious garments, gold, and silver, claiming that, "Truly, it is better to live here in our country, where God's Temple and the ark of God's law are, and where God dwells with us!"

But, his son would send messages back, "Gold and silver and fine garments are not lacking in our country. Rather, I came to listen to your wisdom, see your face, greet you, do homage to your rule, and bow down to you. But, now, you should send me back to my mother and my country. For nobody hates the place where he was born, and everybody loves his country's language."

[Bayna Lihkim goes on to explain how he prefers his own country's food to the delicacies served at Solomon's court; how the mountains of Ethiopia delight his heart; and how Ethiopia now also worships the one true God and Zion.]

So despite all Solomon did, he could not persuade his son to remain.

* * *

6. Genesis 3.16.

45. About How Those Sent Away Wept and Plotted

[In previous chapters, Solomon ordered the eldest sons of his priestly and secular nobility to accompany his own son to Ethiopia, so as to create a mirror image of his court there.]

The sons of the lords of Israel, who had been ordered to go to Ethiopia with King Solomon's son, jointly started to plot, "What should we do? We are about to leave our country and birthplace, our kin and the people of our country. So let's make a pact among only us, one that our relatives won't know about, that there, in Ethiopia, we will love and support each other. None of us will rush and none will hesitate regarding our pact. Let's not be afraid or half-hearted, for God is here and God is there. So, may God's will be done! Praise be to him for all eternity, amen."

Now Azariah and Elmiyas,[7] the sons of priests, spoke, "We won't let that other matter, that our relatives have rejected us, sadden us. Rather, we should be sad because they are making us leave our Lady Zion. For through her, we have been entrusted to God, and up until now, we have served her. Only, we are sad because they are making us leave her. Because of this, then, they make us weep for abandoning her."

Now the others spoke, saying to Azariah and Elmiyas, "Truly, she is our Lady, our hope, and our pride! We have grown up under her protection—how can we leave Zion, our Lady, behind?! Indeed, we have been given to her—but what can we do? If we refuse Solomon's order, the king will kill us. Also, we cannot disobey the words of our fathers and the order of the king. So what shall we do about Zion, our Lady?"

Azariah, the son of Zadok the priest, answered, "I will advise you about what we shall do—but first make a pact with me, valid until your last breath, and swear an oath to me that you will not speak about it, whether we die or live, whether we are apprehended or walk free."

So they swore the oath to him—by the name of God the Lord of Israel; by heavenly Zion, the ark of God's law; by what God had promised to Abraham;[8] by Isaac's innocence and goodness;[9] and by God multiplying Jacob's children and riches and giving him a foreign land as his inheritance as well as the inheritance of his descendants after him. When they had sworn this oath to Azariah, he said to them, "So, now, let's carry our Lady Zion away! I will even tell you how we can do it. Carry out my plan; then, God willing, we will be able to take our Lady with us! But, if they find us out and kill us, it will not sadden us because we will die for our Lady Zion."

At this point, they all rose and kissed Azariah's head, face, and eyes, with these words, "We will do everything you have advised us to do! We will die with

7. This character mostly appears as "Elmiyas" in the *Kebra Nagast*, but in chapter 43 his name is given as "Elyas," and in chapter 48 as "Elmeyanos."
8. In Genesis 17, God promises to make Abraham the ancestor of many nations, to bless him with many descendants (some of whom would become kings), to remain their faithful God, and to give the land of Canaan to him and his descendants.
9. Isaac was Abraham's son by Sarah, whom Abraham offered to God as a sacrifice (Genesis 22.1–19).

you or live with you for our Lady Zion. If we die, it will not sadden us, but if we live, that means what God wished will have happened."

One of them, Joas's son, whose name was Zechariah, said, "As for me, I cannot sit still thanks to the great joy in my heart—so, tell me the plan, Azariah. If anybody can, you can take Zion away. It is not a boast, since you can walk freely within God's Temple, substituting for your father. Also, the keys to the Temple are always in your hands. Now, before they get taken away from you due to our departure, consider closely what we suggest in return. You know the secret passageways that King Solomon built into the Temple. None of the other priests can go in there, only your father can go in once a year, to sacrifice in the Holy of Holies, on behalf of himself and the people. So, be ready, think carefully, and then don't fall asleep on the job, but be prepared to take away Zion. Then, we can go away with her, faithful to how we were entrusted to her, and so that there may be happiness for us, but sadness for our fathers, due to Zion coming with us to Ethiopia."

After hearing this advice, Azariah instructed them, "Do as I tell you, then we shall succeed! Each of you, give me ten double drachmas.[1] I will then give that money to a carpenter so that, for the love of silver, he may quickly make good wooden planks for me in the dimensions—the height, breadth, and length—of my Lady Zion. I will give him those dimensions after having measured Zion myself, and will deceitfully say to him, 'Make me a set of planks so that I can turn them into rafts, for we want to go to sea, and if the ship is wrecked, I can mount a raft and save myself from the sea.' I will then take away the planks individually, unassembled, and only there, in the Temple, will I combine those planks and put them in Zion's place. Finally, I will drape the assembled planks with Zion's cloth coverings. But I will take away the real Zion, dig a hole in the earth, and place her in it until we leave and take her with us. As for my lord the king, I won't tell him about it until we will have journeyed far away."

So, each one of them gave Azariah ten double drachmas, for a total of 140 double drachmas. Azariah took that money and gave it to the carpenter, who immediately did a good job for him, using the leftover wood of the Temple construction. Azariah was quite satisfied and showed the planks to his brothers.

* * *

48. In Which They Carry Away Zion

[In chapter 46, God's angel appeared to Azariah in a vision while he was asleep, instructing him to sacrifice to the Lord in penance for the coming theft of Zion. At the same time, the angel assured Azariah that God was angry with Israel, and that ultimately the theft of Zion would accomplish his will.]

And behold, God's angel once again appeared to Azariah in a vision, shining like a column of fire above him and filling the house with light. The angel shook Azariah and said to him, "Get up, be strong, and wake up your brother Elmiyas, as well as Abisa and Makeri. Then, pick up and carry those wooden planks, and

---

1. A Greek monetary unit, which in antiquity spread over the entire eastern Mediterranean world, but never had any currency in Ethiopia.

I myself will open the gates of the Temple for you. Then, carry away the real ark of God's law. You will be able to handle Zion without illness or suffering afflicting you; for I myself have been commanded by God to remain with Zion and to be your guide in transporting her away."

So, Azariah immediately got up and woke his three brothers. They took the planks and went to God's Temple, where they found all the gates open, from the outer gates to the inner gates open gates all the way, to the place where you come to Zion, the ark of God's law. There, Zion let herself be carried away easily, in the twinkling of an eye, because God's angel was in charge of her. If God had not willed it, Zion would not have let herself be carried away easily.

So, the four of them carried Zion away and took her to Azariah's house. Then, they returned to God's Temple, assembled the planks and put them in Zion's place, draped them with Zion's cloth coverings, and locked the gates. Then, they returned home. There they took some lamps and set them up in the real Zion's hiding place. In addition, they sacrificed a sheep, burnt incense, and spread purple cloth over her. Afterward, they moved Zion into another secret shelter for seven days and seven nights.

THE THOUSAND AND ONE NIGHTS
(ALF LAYLA WA-LAYLA)
fourteenth century

A text built from many texts, *The Thousand and One Nights* is an extraordinarily flexible and capacious storytelling machine, one that has absorbed stories from a range of cultures across Asia and North Africa and then cast them back out again into the world in many new forms, including theater, opera, film, cartoons, video games, fashion, children's toys, and, of course, other texts. Considered in light of the work's many manifestations, the "nights" are not "one thousand and one"—they are innumerable.

THE TEXT IN CONTEXT

The Thousand and One Nights was written by many unknown authors, scattered over many centuries and countries of the Middle East. The first document bearing any physical evidence of *The Thousand and One Nights* was a single piece of very rare old Syrian paper that dates from 879 C.E. Discovered in 1948 by a scholar studying in a Cairo archive, the page contained, among various other scrawls and jottings, a signature, a date, and a few words from the opening lines of the *Nights*. The next trace of the *Nights* appears in the tenth century, when Ibn al-Nadim, a book dealer in Baghdad, mentions in his catalogue a number of story collections; among them is a book of tales concerning "Shahrazad," which, he notes, is adapted from a Persian original called *Hazar Afsan*, or *Thousand Tales*. Another tenth-century writer, al-Mas'udi, also mentions Shahrazad and the now-lost Persian *Hazar Afsan*, and adds the title of the Arabic version of the work: *Alf Layla*, or *Thousand Nights*. The title that comes down to us in the earliest complete manuscript, a Syrian text dating from the fourteenth century, is the familiar *Alf Layla wa-Layla*, or *Thousand and One Nights*. The number—one thousand and one—seems precise, and in fact the first generation of Western readers took it literally, assuming that the manuscript, which contained far fewer than one thousand stories, must be incomplete. But its sense is instead symbolic: adding one more to a thousand implies an unending abundance. There is always one more tale to be told.

The Thousand and One Nights is an Arabic text, but one derived from a Persian source (reflected in the Persian names of the characters of the frame story—Shahrazad and her sister Dunyazad, King Shahrayar and his brother Shahzaman). Behind both the Arabic and the Persian texts may lie a Sanskrit original, just as the Indian *Pañcatantra* lies behind the other widely disseminated Arabic story collection, *Kalila and Dimna*; but this original, if it exists, has never been discovered. Whatever its early sources, the *Nights* quickly swelled with new stories from Arab traditions as its influence spread. One cluster of stories centers on Baghdad and its early ninth-century ruler, Harun al-Rashid, and his vizier, Ja'far al-Barmaki. Other groups of stories, which entered the collection at a later date, reflect the culture of medieval Cairo; still others allude to the itinerant heritage of the Bedouin of the Arabian Peninsula. The text of the *Nights*—if we can call such a flexible and changeable organism a "text"— was above all an inspiration for sharing stories, and was thus subject to change with each new telling.

Though the content of the *Nights* is unique, its literary form—the frame tale—is common in Eastern and Western traditions. The frame tale is an open-ended genre, in which an outer story or "frame" provides a structure within which other, shorter stories can be told. Frame tales are among the most popular of literary forms, surviving in the major works of **Boccaccio** and **Chaucer** as well as in the writings of **Apuleius, Petrus Alfonsi, Marie de France**, and many others. The genre most likely has its origins in India, in textual traditions such as Somadeva's *Kathāsaritsāgora*. The *Pañcatantra*, a Sanskrit collection of animal stories, is among the world's best-known and oldest frame tales, and it was the inspiration for the Arabic *Kalila and Dimna*, which was quickly disseminated throughout medieval Europe. While *Kalila and Dimna* was popular in the West because of the didactic and edifying quality of the tales (they each conclude, as do **Aesop**'s *Fables*, with a moral), *The Thousand and One Nights* were avidly read by Europeans for less noble reasons: they believed the *Nights* could offer insights into the duplicitous and irrational character of "the Oriental," and they found pleasure in the tales' sensuous details and often unrestrained sexuality. The long history of "Orientalist" approaches to *The Thousand and One Nights* in the West takes nothing away from our own enjoyment of the tales, but it is certainly a reminder of the dangers of interpreting any text as somehow embodying the culture in which it originated.

WORK

The overall frame of *The Thousand and One Nights* centers on a good king who has become a tyrant. After discovering the secret promiscuity of his wife, King Shahrayar decides that he will avoid the deception of women forever by taking a new bride every night and putting her to death in the morning. The deaths rapidly mount, the kingdom is filled with mourning parents—and to the horror and despair of the faithful royal vizier, his daughter, Shahrazad, volunteers to marry the king. He tries to dissuade her, but Shahrazad has a plan. By telling a story to the king every night, each one more marvelous and entrancing than the last, Shahrazad will continually defer the doom that awaits his bride. Yet she also has another goal, beyond self-preservation or even the salvation of her countrywomen. By telling stories that repeatedly address the problems of rule—both the rule of oneself and the rule of others—she will teach the king how to restore order in his own realm, as well as in his own soul.

Even among frame tales, *The Thousand and One Nights* is unique for its enchantingly intricate nested structure. Very often, a character in a tale will pause to tell yet another tale, with one story inside the next inside the next, like Russian nested dolls. In "The Story of the Merchant and the Demon," for example, three old men tell stories, each more fantastic than the last, to the dangerous jinn in their sucessful effort to purchase the merchant's freedom. "The Story of the Fisherman and the Demon" even more elaborately nests smaller stories within the larger one, always with a strong focus on the irresistibility of storytelling, as characters within the larger tale express their eagerness to hear every new story. When the fisherman comments offhandedly on finding himself in a situation "like that of King Yunan and the sage Duban," the jinn cannot resist asking, "What is their story?" Once his curiosity is piqued, the delightful power of the tale quickly defuses his potential for evil. And within that story, King Yunan himself tells "The Tale of the Husband and the Parrot." This structure makes *The Thousand and One Nights* an unusually playful text, seemingly spontaneous and improvisational even on the page, and wonderfully suited to public

entertainment and oral performance.

Perhaps the *Nights* is most extraordinary for the persistence of its fertile, regenerative quality even after being taken up by Western readers and rendered in a host of European and, later, American translations and adaptations. This process began in 1704, with the publication in French (by Antoine Galland) of a selection of tales from the earliest surviving complete manuscript. Readers were immediately captivated by the work: an unauthorized English translation of the French version appeared in 1706, and Galland himself quickly produced additional volumes for publication. When he ran out of tales to translate from the Syrian manuscript (which, like all the early collections, contains only about 280), Galland turned to other sets of Arabic tales, including the famous stories of Aladdin and Ali Baba. As he sought to reach the target number of one thousand and one, Galland even added some tales for which there were no written Arabic sources but only oral versions picked up from Arab visitors to Paris. The tremendous European appetite for *The Thousand and One Nights* led to the production of composite Arabic story collections in Cairo during the eighteenth and nineteenth centuries, and subsequently these versions were published in Arabic editions and translated. We can thus think of two separate lineages for the modern reception of the *Nights*: one can be traced back to the earliest complete text, the fourteenth-century Syrian manuscript translated by Galland, and the other to the later composite texts assembled in eighteenth- and nineteenth-century Cairo. The selections reproduced here come from the Syrian manuscript, but it would be wrong to think of these as the "authentic" tales and to dismiss those in the Cairo versions as unimportant innovations. Instead, the Syrian manuscript can best be thought of as a snapshot, an image captured of the

Nights at a certain moment in time, in a certain cultural location. The Cairo manuscripts also represent a specific time and place in the life of the *Nights*— one intimately connected with the history of French and, later, British rule in Egypt.

Western reception of *The Thousand and One Nights* has been uniformly enthusiastic, and yet wildly heterogeneous—a good example of the changing fortunes in the relations between Europe and the Middle East. This heterogeneity can be seen, for example, in the nineteenth-century English translations of the *Nights*, all of which were based on the enlarged Cairo compilations. The earliest of these was by Edward Lane, an Englishman living in Cairo; it tries to conjure up an entire way of life through the medium of the *Nights*. For Lane, the stories are not so much an end in themselves as a way for him to re-create the daily experiences of a nineteenth-century Egyptian who might have listened to such stories as they were performed in the coffeehouse. The translation of the philologist John Payne, published for a very limited audience of specialists, sought to use the *Nights* to construct an ethnographic portrait of Egyptian society, while the sexually explicit, extensively footnoted, and deliberately archaic translation by the extraordinary explorer Sir Richard Burton is in a category by itself. The variety of these encounters with the *Nights*, all so different yet all produced in the same language over the span of a few decades, was wittily summed up by a nineteenth-century commentator in the *Edinburgh Review* who states that

each version has "its proper destination: Galland for the nursery, Lane for the library, Payne for the study, and Burton for the sewers."

The influence of *The Thousand and One Nights* continued to spread out across the globe. Thus late nineteenth-century portrait photography in Japan shows a fascination with the "Arabian Nights" theme, which had become fashionable in stage costume and dress styles, theater and opera, music and ballet. Today, reflections of the *Nights* are visible in films and graphic novels for adults as well as cartoons and even coloring books for children. In the modern Middle East, however, attitudes toward *The Thousand and One Nights* are more ambivalent; they have even at times led to censorship, whether because of the text's graphic language or, more likely, because of the complicated history of the *Nights* in shaping European fantasies about the Orient.

While Eastern studies of the *Nights* have tended to consider the work in the context of folklore and oral storytelling, Western scholars are often preoccupied with the effort to nail down the work's point of origin. They want to know: Which is the original version? When was it composed? Is *The Thousand and One Nights* an Arab text? a Persian text? Indian? These questions ultimately slip away, because what the text *is* turns out to be much less interesting than what it *does*. *The Thousand and One Nights* has its life in transit—always becoming something new, leaving its reader in a perpetual state of anticipation. It is less a collection of stories than a machine that makes stories possible.

From The Thousand and One Nights[1]

Prologue

[*The Story of King Shahrayar and Shahrazad, His Vizier's[2] Daughter*]

It is related—but God knows and sees best what lies hidden in the old accounts of bygone peoples and times—that long ago, during the time of the Sasanid dynasty,[3] in the peninsulas of India and Indochina, there lived two kings who were brothers. The older brother was named Shahrayar, the younger Shahza-man. The older, Shahrayar, was a towering knight and a daring champion, invincible, energetic, and implacable. His power reached the remotest corners of the land and its people, so that the country was loyal to him, and his sub-jects obeyed him. Shahrayar himself lived and ruled in India and Indochina, while to his brother he gave the land of Samarkand[4] to rule as king.

Ten years went by, when one day Shahrayar felt a longing for his brother the king, summoned his vizier (who had two daughters, one called Shahrazad, the other Dinarzad) and bade him go to his brother. Having made preparations, the vizier journeyed day and night until he reached Samarkand. When Shahza-man heard of the vizier's arrival, he went out with his retainers to meet him. He dismounted, embraced him, and asked him for news from his older brother, Shahrayar. The vizier replied that he was well, and that he had sent him to request his brother to visit him. Shahzaman complied with his brother's request and proceeded to make preparations for the journey. In the meantime, he had the vizier camp on the outskirts of the city, and took care of his needs. He sent him what he required of food and fodder, slaughtered many sheep in his honor, and provided him with money and supplies, as well as many horses and camels.

For ten full days he prepared himself for the journey; then he appointed a chamberlain in his place, and left the city to spend the night in his tent, near the vizier. At midnight he returned to his palace in the city, to bid his wife good-bye. But when he entered the palace, he found his wife lying in the arms of one of the kitchen boys. When he saw them, the world turned dark before his eyes and, shaking his head, he said to himself, "I am still here, and this is what she has done when I was barely outside the city. How will it be and what will happen behind my back when I go to visit my brother in India? No. Women are not to be trusted." He got exceedingly angry, adding, "By God, I am king and sovereign in Samarkand, yet my wife has betrayed me and has inflicted this on me." As his anger boiled, he drew his sword and struck both his wife and the cook. Then he dragged them by the heels and threw them from the top of the palace to the trench below. He then left the city and going to the vizier ordered that they depart that very hour. The drum was struck, and they set out on their journey, while Shahzaman's heart was on fire because of what his wife had done to him and how she had betrayed him with some cook, some kitchen boy. They journeyed

1. All selections translated from the Arabic by Husain Haddawy except for "The Third Old Man's Tale," translated from the Arabic by Jerome W. Clinton.
2. Literally, "one who bears burdens" (Arabic):

the highest state official or administrator under a caliph or shah.
3. The last pre-Islamic dynasty (226–652).
4. A city and province in central Asia, now in Uzbekistan.

hurriedly, day and night, through deserts and wilds, until they reached the land of King Shahrayar, who had gone out to receive them.

When Shahrayar met them, he embraced his brother, showed him favors, and treated him generously. He offered him quarters in a palace adjoining his own, for King Shahrayar had built two beautiful towering palaces in his garden, one for the guests, the other for the women and members of his household. He gave the guest house to his brother, Shahzaman, after the attendants had gone to scrub it, dry it, furnish it, and open its windows, which overlooked the garden. Thereafter, Shahzaman would spend the whole day at his brother's, return at night to sleep at the palace, then go back to his brother the next morning. But whenever he found himself alone and thought of his ordeal with his wife, he would sigh deeply, then stifle his grief, and say, "Alas, that this great misfortune should have happened to one in my position!" Then he would fret with anxiety, his spirit would sag, and he would say, "None has seen what I have seen." In his depression, he ate less and less, grew pale, and his health deteriorated. He neglected everything, wasted away, and looked ill.

When King Shahrayar looked at his brother and saw how day after day he lost weight and grew thin, pale, ashen, and sickly, he thought that this was because of his expatriation and homesickness for his country and his family, and he said to himself, "My brother is not happy here. I should prepare a goodly gift for him and send him home." For a month he gathered gifts for his brother; then he invited him to see him and said, "Brother, I would like you to know that I intend to go hunting and pursue the roaming deer, for ten days. Then I shall return to prepare you for your journey home. Would you like to go hunting with me?" Shahzaman replied, "Brother, I feel distracted and depressed. Leave me here and go with God's blessing and help." When Shahrayar heard his brother, he thought that his dejection was because of his homesickness for his country. Not wishing to coerce him, he left him behind, and set out with his retainers and men. When they entered the wilderness, he deployed his men in a circle to begin trapping and hunting.

After his brother's departure, Shahzaman stayed in the palace and, from the window overlooking the garden, watched the birds and trees as he thought of his wife and what she had done to him, and sighed in sorrow. While he agonized over his misfortune, gazing at the heavens and turning a distracted eye on the garden, the private gate of his brother's palace opened, and there emerged, strutting like a dark-eyed deer, the lady, his brother's wife, with twenty slave-girls, ten white and ten black. While Shahzaman looked at them, without being seen, they continued to walk until they stopped below his window, without looking in his direction, thinking that he had gone to the hunt with his brother. Then they sat down, took off their clothes, and suddenly there were ten slave-girls and ten black slaves dressed in the same clothes as the girls. Then the ten black slaves mounted the ten girls, while the lady called, "Mas'ud, Mas'ud!" and a black slave jumped from the tree to the ground, rushed to her, and, raising her legs, went between her thighs and made love to her. Mas'ud topped the lady, while the ten slaves topped the ten girls, and they carried on till noon. When they were done with their business, they got up and washed themselves. Then the ten slaves put on the same clothes again, mingled with the girls, and once more there appeared to be twenty slave-girls.

Mas'ud himself jumped over the garden wall and disappeared, while the slave-girls and the lady sauntered to the private gate, went in and, locking the gate behind them, went their way.

All of this happened under King Shahzaman's eyes. When he saw this spectacle of the wife and the women of his brother the great king—how ten slaves put on women's clothes and slept with his brother's paramours and concubines and what Mas'ud did with his brother's wife, in his very palace—and pondered over this calamity and great misfortune, his care and sorrow left him and he said to himself, "This is our common lot. Even though my brother is king and master of the whole world, he cannot protect what is his, his wife and his concubines, and suffers misfortune in his very home. What happened to me is little by comparison. I used to think that I was the only one who has suffered, but from what I have seen, everyone suffers. By God, my misfortune is lighter than that of my brother." He kept marveling and blaming life, whose trials none can escape, and he began to find consolation in his own affliction and forget his grief. When supper came, he ate and drank with relish and zest and, feeling better, kept eating and drinking, enjoying himself and feeling happy. He thought to himself, "I am no longer alone in my misery; I am well."

For ten days, he continued to enjoy his food and drink, and when his brother, King Shahrayar, came back from the hunt, he met him happily, treated him attentively, and greeted him cheerfully. His brother, King Shahrayar, who had missed him, said, "By God, brother, I missed you on this trip and wished you were with me." Shahzaman thanked him and sat down to carouse with him, and when night fell, and food was brought before them, the two ate and drank, and again Shahzaman ate and drank with zest. As time went by, he continued to eat and drink with appetite, and became lighthearted and carefree. His face regained color and became ruddy, and his body gained weight, as his blood circulated and he regained his energy; he was himself again, or even better. King Shahrayar noticed his brother's condition, how he used to be and how he had improved, but kept it to himself until he took him aside one day and said, "My brother Shahzaman, I would like you to do something for me, to satisfy a wish, to answer a question truthfully." Shahzaman asked, "What is it, brother?" He replied, "When you first came to stay with me, I noticed that you kept losing weight, day after day, until your looks changed, your health deteriorated, and your energy sagged. As you continued like this, I thought that what ailed you was your homesickness for your family and your country, but even though I kept noticing that you were wasting away and looking ill, I refrained from questioning you and hid my feelings from you. Then I went hunting, and when I came back, I found that you had recovered and had regained your health. Now I want you to tell me everything and to explain the cause of your deterioration and the cause of your subsequent recovery, without hiding anything from me." When Shahzaman heard what King Shahrayar said, he bowed his head, then said, "As for the cause of my recovery, that I cannot tell you, and I wish that you would excuse me from telling you." The king was greatly astonished at his brother's reply and, burning with curiosity, said, "You must tell me. For now, at least, explain the first cause."

Then Shahzaman related to his brother what happened to him with his own wife, on the night of his departure, from beginning to end, and concluded,

"Thus all the while I was with you, great King, whenever I thought of the event and the misfortune that had befallen me, I felt troubled, careworn, and unhappy, and my health deteriorated. This then is the cause." Then he grew silent. When King Shahrayar heard his brother's explanation, he shook his head, greatly amazed at the deceit of women, and prayed to God to protect him from their wickedness, saying, "Brother, you were fortunate in killing your wife and her lover, who gave you good reason to feel troubled, careworn, and ill. In my opinion, what happened to you has never happened to anyone else. By God, had I been in your place, I would have killed at least a hundred or even a thousand women. I would have been furious; I would have gone mad. Now praise be to God who has delivered you from sorrow and distress. But tell me what has caused you to forget your sorrow and regain your health?" Shahzaman replied, "King, I wish that for God's sake you would excuse me from telling you." Shahrayar said, "You must." Shahzaman replied, "I fear that you will feel even more troubled and careworn than I." Shahrayar asked, "How could that be, brother? I insist on hearing your explanation."

Shahzaman then told him about what he had seen from the palace window and the calamity in his very home—how ten slaves, dressed like women, were sleeping with his women and concubines, day and night. He told him everything from beginning to end (but there is no point in repeating that). Then he concluded, "When I saw your own misfortune, I felt better—and said to myself, 'My brother is king of the world, yet such a misfortune has happened to him, and in his very home.' As a result I forgot my care and sorrow, relaxed, and began to eat and drink. This is the cause of my cheer and good spirits."

When King Shahrayar heard what his brother said and found out what had happened to him, he was furious and his blood boiled. He said, "Brother, I can't believe what you say unless I see it with my own eyes." When Shahzaman saw that his brother was in a rage, he said to him, "If you do not believe me, unless you see your misfortune with your own eyes, announce that you plan to go hunting. Then you and I shall set out with your troops, and when we get outside the city, we shall leave our tents and camp with the men behind, enter the city secretly, and go together to your palace. Then the next morning you can see with your own eyes."

King Shahrayar realized that his brother had a good plan and ordered his army to prepare for the trip. He spent the night with his brother, and when God's morning broke, the two rode out of the city with their army, preceded by the camp attendants, who had gone to drive the poles and pitch the tents where the king and his army were to camp. At nightfall King Shahrayar summoned his chief chamberlain and bade him take his place. He entrusted him with the army and ordered that for three days no one was to enter the city. Then he and his brother disguised themselves and entered the city in the dark. They went directly to the palace where Shahzaman resided and slept there till the morning. When they awoke, they sat at the palace window, watching the garden and chatting, until the light broke, the day dawned, and the sun rose. As they watched, the private gate opened, and there emerged as usual the wife of King Shahrayar, walking among twenty slave-girls. They made their way under the trees until they stood below the palace window where the two kings sat. Then they took off their women's clothes, and suddenly there were ten slaves, who mounted the ten girls and made love to them. As for the lady, she called, "Mas'ud, Mas'ud," and a black slave jumped from the tree to the ground, came to her, and said, "What do you want, you slut? Here is Sa'ad al-Din Mas'ud." She laughed and fell on her back, while the slave mounted her and like the others did his business with her. Then the black slaves got up, washed themselves, and, putting on the same clothes, mingled with the girls. Then they walked away, entered the palace, and locked the gate behind them. As for Mas'ud, he jumped over the fence to the road and went on his way.

When King Shahrayar saw the spectacle of his wife and the slave-girls, he went out of his mind, and when he and his brother came down from upstairs, he said, "No one is safe in this world. Such doings are going on in my kingdom, and in my very palace. Perish the world and perish life! This is a great calamity, indeed." Then he turned to his brother and asked, "Would you like to follow me in what I shall do?" Shahzaman answered, "Yes. I will." Shahrayar said, "Let us leave our royal state and roam the world for the love of the Supreme Lord. If we should find one whose misfortune is greater than ours, we shall return. Otherwise, we shall continue to journey through the land, without need for the trappings of royalty." Shahzaman replied, "This is an excellent idea. I shall follow you."

Then they left by the private gate, took a side road, and departed, journeying till nightfall. They slept over their sorrows, and in the morning resumed their day journey until they came to a meadow by the seashore. While they sat in the meadow amid the thick plants and trees, discussing their misfortunes and the recent events, they suddenly heard a shout and a great cry coming from the middle of the sea. They trembled with fear, thinking that the sky had fallen on the earth. Then the sea parted, and there emerged a black pillar that, as it swayed forward, got taller and taller, until it touched the clouds. Shahrayar and Shahzaman were petrified; then they ran in terror and, climbing a very tall tree, sat hiding in its foliage. When they looked again, they saw that the black pillar was cleaving the sea, wading in the water toward the green meadow, until it touched the shore. When they looked again, they saw that it was a black demon, carrying on his head a large glass chest with four steel locks. He came out, walked into the meadow, and where should he stop but under the very tree where the two kings were hiding. The demon sat down and placed the glass chest on the ground. He took out four keys and, opening the locks of the chest, pulled out a full-grown woman. She had a beautiful figure, and a face like the full moon, and a lovely smile. He took her out, laid her under the tree, and looked at her, saying, "Mistress of all noble women, you whom I carried away on your wedding night, I would like to sleep a little." Then he placed his head on the young woman's lap, stretched his legs to the sea, sank into sleep, and began to snore.

Meanwhile, the woman looked up at the tree and, turning her head by chance, saw King Shahrayar and King Shahzaman. She lifted the demon's head from her lap and placed it on the ground. Then she came and stood under the tree and motioned to them with her hand, as if to say, "Come down slowly to me." When they realized that she had seen them, they were frightened, and they begged her and implored her, in the name of the Creator of the heavens, to excuse them from climbing down. She replied, "You must come down to me." They motioned to her, saying, "This sleeping demon is the enemy of mankind. For God's sake, leave us alone." She replied, "You must come down, and if you don't, I shall wake the demon and have him kill you." She kept gesturing and pressing, until they climbed down very slowly and stood before her. Then she lay on her back, raised her legs, and said, "Make love to me and satisfy my need, or else I shall wake the demon, and he will kill you." They replied, "For God's sake, mistress, don't do this to us, for at this moment we feel nothing but dismay and fear of this demon. Please, excuse us." She replied, "You must," and insisted, swearing, "By God who created the heavens, if you don't do it, I shall wake my husband the demon and ask him to kill you and throw you into the sea." As she persisted, they could no longer resist and they made love to her, first the older brother, then the younger. When they were done and withdrew from her, she said to them, "Give me your rings," and, pulling out from the folds of her dress a small purse, opened it, and shook out ninety-eight rings of different fashions and colors. Then she asked them, "Do you know what these rings are?" They answered, "No." She said, "All the owners of these rings slept with me, for whenever one of them made love to me, I took a ring from him. Since you two have slept with me, give me your rings, so that I may add them to the rest, and make a full hundred. A hundred men have known me under the very horns of this filthy, monstrous cuckold, who has imprisoned me in this chest, locked it with four locks, and kept me in the middle of this raging, roaring sea. He has guarded me and tried to keep me pure and chaste, not realizing that nothing can prevent or alter what is predestined and that when a woman desires something, no one can stop her." When Shahrayar and Shahzaman heard what the young woman said, they were greatly amazed, danced with joy, and said, "O God, O God! There is no power and no strength, save in God the Almighty, the Magnificent. Great is women's cunning." Then each of them took off his ring and handed it to her. She took them and put them with the rest in the purse. Then sitting again by the demon, she lifted his head, placed it back on her lap, and motioned to them, "Go on your way, or else I shall wake him."

They turned their backs and took to the road. Then Shahrayar turned to his brother and said, "My brother Shahzaman, look at this sorry plight. By God, it is worse than ours. This is no less than a demon who has carried a young woman away on her wedding night, imprisoned her in a glass chest, locked her up with four locks, and kept her in the middle of the sea, thinking that he could guard her from what God had foreordained, and you saw how she has managed to sleep with ninety-eight men, and added the two of us to make a hundred. Brother, let us go back to our kingdoms and our cities, never to marry a woman again. As for myself, I shall show you what I will do."

Then the two brothers headed home and journeyed till nightfall. On the morning of the third day, they reached their camp and men, entered their tent, and sat on their thrones. The chamberlains, deputies, princes, and viziers came to attend King Shahrayar, while he gave orders and bestowed robes of honor, as well as other gifts. Then at his command everyone returned to the city, and he went to his own palace and ordered his chief vizier, the father of the two girls Shahrazad and Dinarzad, who will be mentioned below, and said to him, "Take that wife of mine and put her to death." Then Shahrayar went to her himself, bound her, and handed her over to the vizier, who took her out and put her to death. Then King Shahrayar grabbed his sword, brandished it, and, entering the palace chambers, killed every one of his slave-girls and replaced them with others. He then swore to marry for one night only and kill the woman the next morning, in order to save himself from the wickedness and cunning of women, saying, "There is not a single chaste woman anywhere on the entire face of the earth." Shortly thereafter he provided his brother Shahzaman with supplies for his journey and sent him back to his own country with gifts, rarities, and money. The brother bade him good-bye and set out for home.

Shahrayar sat on his throne and ordered his vizier, the father of the two girls, to find him a wife from among the princes' daughters. The vizier found him one, and he slept with her and was done with her, and the next morning he ordered the vizier to put her to death. That very night he took one of his army officers' daughters, slept with her, and the next morning ordered the vizier to put her to death. The vizier, who could not disobey him, put her to death. The third night he took one of the merchants' daughters, slept with her till the morning, then ordered his vizier to put her to death, and the vizier did so. It became King Shahrayar's custom to take every night the daughter of a merchant or a commoner, spend the night with her, then have her put to death the next morning. He continued to do this until all the girls perished, their mothers mourned, and there arose a clamor among the fathers and mothers, who called the plague upon his head, complained to the Creator of the heavens, and called for help on Him who hears and answers prayers.

Now, as mentioned earlier, the vizier, who put the girls to death, had an older daughter called Shahrazad and a younger one called Dinarzad. The older daughter, Shahrazad, had read the books of literature, philosophy, and medicine. She knew poetry by heart, had studied historical reports, and was acquainted with the sayings of men and the maxims of sages and kings. She was intelligent, knowledgeable, wise, and refined. She had read and learned. One day she said to her father, "Father, I will tell you what is in my mind." He asked, "What is it?" She answered, "I would like you to marry me to King Shahrayar, so that I may either succeed in saving the people or perish and die like the rest." When the vizier heard what his daughter Shahrazad said, he got angry and said to her, "Foolish one, don't you know that King Shahrayar has sworn to spend but one night with a girl and have her put to death the next morning? If I give you to him, he will sleep with you for one night and will ask me to put you to death the next morning, and I shall have to do it, since I cannot disobey him." She said, "Father, you must give me to him, even if he kills me." He asked, "What has possessed you that you wish to imperil yourself?" She replied, "Father, you must give me to him. This is absolute and final." Her father the vizier became furious and said to her, "Daughter, 'He who misbehaves, ends up in trouble,' and 'He who considers not the end, the world is not his friend.' As the popular saying goes, 'I would be sitting pretty, but for my curiosity.' I am afraid that what happened to the donkey and the ox with the

merchant will happen to you." She asked, "Father, what happened to the donkey, the ox, and the merchant?" He said:

[The Tale of the Ox and the Donkey]

There was a prosperous and wealthy merchant who lived in the countryside and
labored on a farm. He owned many camels and herds of cattle and employed
many men, and he had a wife and many grown-up as well as little children. This
merchant was taught the language of the beasts, on condition that if he revealed
his secret to anyone, he would die; therefore, even though he knew the language of every kind of animal, he did not let anyone know, for fear of death.
One day, as he sat, with his wife beside him and his children playing before
him, he glanced at an ox and a donkey he kept at the farmhouse, tied to adja-
cent troughs, and heard the ox say to the donkey, "Watchful one, I hope that
you are enjoying the comfort and the service you are getting. Your ground is
swept and watered, and they serve you, feed you sifted barley, and offer you
clear, cool water to drink. I, on the contrary, am taken out to plow in the middle
of the night. They clamp on my neck something they call yoke and plow, push
me all day under the whip to plow the field, and drive me beyond my endurance
until my sides are lacerated, and my neck is flayed. They work me from nighttime to nighttime, take me back in the dark, offer me beans soiled with mud
and hay mixed with chaff, and let me spend the night lying in urine and dung.
Meanwhile you rest on well-swept, watered, and smoothed ground, with a
clean trough full of hay. You stand in comfort, save for the rare occasion when
our master the merchant rides you to do a brief errand and returns. You are
comfortable, while I am weary; you sleep, while I keep awake."

When the ox finished, the donkey turned to him and said, "Greenhorn, they
were right in calling you ox, for you ox harbor no deceit, malice, or meanness.
Being sincere, you exert and exhaust yourself to comfort others. Have you not
heard the saying 'Out of bad luck, they hastened on the road'? You go into the
field from early morning to endure your torture at the plow to the point of
exhaustion. When the plowman takes you back and ties you to the trough, you
go on butting and beating with your horns, kicking with your hoofs, and bellowing for the beans, until they toss them to you; then you begin to eat. Next
time, when they bring them to you, don't eat or even touch them, but smell
them, then draw back and lie down on the hay and straw. If you do this, life
will be better and kinder to you, and you will find relief."

As the ox listened, he was sure that the donkey had given him good advice.
He thanked him, commended him to God, and invoked His blessing on him,
and said, "May you stay safe from harm, watchful one." All of this conversation
took place, daughter, while the merchant listened and understood. On the following day, the plowman came to the merchant's house and, taking the ox,
placed the yoke upon his neck and worked him at the plow, but the ox lagged
behind. The plowman hit him, but following the donkey's advice, the ox, dis-
sembling, fell on his belly, and the plowman hit him again. Thus the ox kept
getting up and falling until nightfall, when the plowman took him home and
tied him to the trough. But this time the ox did not bellow or kick the ground
with his hoofs. Instead, he withdrew, away from the trough. Astonished, the
plowman brought him his beans and fodder, but the ox only smelled the fodder

and pulled back and lay down at a distance with the hay and straw, complaining till the morning. When the plowman arrived, he found the trough as he had left it, full of beans and fodder, and saw the ox lying on his back, hardly breathing, his belly puffed, and his legs raised in the air. The plowman felt sorry for him and said to himself, "By God, he did seem weak and unable to work." Then he went to the merchant and said, "Master, last night, the ox refused to eat or touch his fodder."

The merchant, who knew what was going on, said to the plowman, "Go to the wily donkey, put him to the plow, and work him hard until he finishes the ox's task." The plowman left, took the donkey, and placed the yoke upon his neck. Then he took him out to the field and drove him with blows until he finished the ox's work, all the while driving him with blows and beating him until his sides were lacerated and his neck was flayed. At nightfall he took him home, barely able to drag his legs under his tired body and his drooping ears. Meanwhile the ox spent his day resting. He ate all his food, drank his water, and lay quietly, chewing his cud in comfort. All day long he kept praising the donkey's advice and invoking God's blessing on him. When the donkey came back at night, the ox stood up to greet him saying, "Good evening, watchful one! You have done me a favor beyond description, for I have been sitting in comfort. God bless you for my sake." Seething with anger, the donkey did not reply, but said to himself, "All this happened to me because of my miscalculation. 'I would be sitting pretty, but for my curiosity.' If I don't find a way to return this ox to his former situation, I will perish." Then he went to his trough and lay down, while the ox continued to chew his cud and invoke God's blessing on him.

"You, my daughter, will likewise perish because of your miscalculation. Desist, sit quietly, and don't expose yourself to peril. I advise you out of compassion for you." She replied, "Father, I must go to the king, and you must give me to him." He said, "Don't do it." She insisted, "I must." He replied, "If you don't desist, I will do to you what the merchant did to his wife." She asked, "Father, what did the merchant do to his wife?" He said:

[The Tale of the Merchant and His Wife]

After what had happened to the donkey and the ox, the merchant and his wife went out in the moonlight to the stable, and he heard the donkey ask the ox in his own language, "Listen, ox, what are you going to do tomorrow morning, and what will you do when the plowman brings you your fodder?" The ox replied, "What shall I do but follow your advice and stick to it? If he brings me my fodder, I will pretend to be ill, lie down, and puff my belly." The donkey shook his head, and said, "Don't do it. Do you know what I heard our master the merchant say to the plowman?" The ox asked, "What?" The donkey replied, "He said that if the ox failed to get up and eat his fodder, he would call the butcher to slaughter him and skin him and would distribute the meat for alms and use the skin for a mat. I am afraid for you, but good advice is a matter of faith; therefore, if he brings you your fodder, eat it and look alert lest they cut your throat and skin you." The ox farted and bellowed.

The merchant got up and laughed loudly at the conversation between the donkey and the ox, and his wife asked him, "What are you laughing at? Are you making fun of me?" He said, "No." She said, "Tell me what made you laugh."

He replied, "I cannot tell you. I am afraid to disclose the secret conversation of the animals." She asked, "And what prevents you from telling me?" He answered, "The fear of death." His wife said, "By God, you are lying. This is nothing but an excuse. I swear by God, the Lord of heaven, that if you don't tell me and explain the cause of your laughter, I will leave you. You must tell me." Then she went back to the house crying, and she continued to cry till the morning. The merchant said, "Damn it! Tell me why you are crying. Ask for God's forgiveness, and stop questioning and leave me in peace." She said, "I insist and will not desist." Amazed at her, he replied, "You insist! If I tell you what the donkey said to the ox, which made me laugh, I shall die." She said, "Yes, I insist, even if you have to die." He replied, "Then call your family," and she called their two daughters, her parents and relatives, and some neighbors. The merchant told them that he was about to die, and everyone, young and old, his children, the farmhands, and the servants began to cry until the house became a place of mourning. Then he summoned legal witnesses, wrote a will, leaving his wife and children their due portions, freed his slave-girls, and bid his family good-bye, while everybody, even the witnesses, wept. Then the wife's parents approached her and said, "Desist, for if your husband had not known for certain that he would die if he revealed his secret, he wouldn't have gone through all this." She replied, "I will not change my mind," and everybody cried and prepared to mourn his death.

Well, my daughter Shahrazad, it happened that the merchant kept fifty hens and a rooster at home, and while he felt sad to depart this world and leave his children and relatives behind, pondering and about to reveal and utter his secret, he overheard a dog of his say something in dog language to the rooster, who, beating and clapping his wings, had jumped on a hen and, finishing with her, jumped down and jumped on another. The merchant heard and understood what the dog said in his own language to the rooster, "Shameless, no-good rooster. Aren't you ashamed to do such a thing on a day like this?" The rooster asked, "What is special about this day?" The dog replied, "Don't you know that our master and friend is in mourning today? His wife is demanding that he disclose his secret, and when he discloses it, he will surely die. He is in this predicament, about to interpret to her the language of the animals, and all of us are mourning for him, while you clap your wings and get off one hen and jump on another. Aren't you ashamed?" The merchant heard the rooster reply, "You fool, you lunatic! Our master and friend claims to be wise, but he is foolish, for he has only one wife, yet he does not know how to manage her." The dog asked, "What should he do with her?"

The rooster replied, "He should take an oak branch, push her into a room, lock the door, and fall on her with the stick, beating her mercilessly until he breaks her arms and legs and she cries out, 'I no longer want you to tell me or explain anything.' He should go on beating her until he cures her for life, and she will never oppose him in anything. If he does this, he will live, and live in peace, and there will be no more grief, but he does not know how to manage." Well, my daughter Shahrazad, when the merchant heard the conversation between the dog and the rooster, he jumped up and, taking an oak branch, pushed his wife into a room, got in with her, and locked the door. Then he began to beat her mercilessly on her chest and shoulders and kept beating her until she cried for mercy, screaming, "No, no, I don't want to know anything.

Leave me alone, leave me alone. I don't want to know anything," until he got tired of hitting her and opened the door. The wife emerged penitent, the husband learned good management, and everybody was happy, and the mourning turned into a celebration.

"If you don't relent, I shall do to you what the merchant did to his wife." She said, "Such tales don't deter me from my request. If you wish, I can tell you many such tales. In the end, if you don't take me to King Shahrayar, I shall go to him by myself behind your back and tell him that you have refused to give me to one like him and that you have begrudged your master one like me." The vizier asked, "Must you really do this?" She replied, "Yes, I must."

Tired and exhausted, the vizier went to King Shahrayar and, kissing the ground before him, told him about his daughter, adding that he would give her to him that very night. The king was astonished and said to him, "Vizier, how is it that you have found it possible to give me your daughter, knowing that I will, by God, the Creator of heaven, ask you to put her to death the next morning and that if you refuse, I will have you put to death, too?" He replied, "My King and Lord, I have told her everything and explained all this to her, but she refuses and insists on being with you tonight." The king was delighted and said, "Go to her, prepare her, and bring her to me early in the evening."

The vizier went down, repeated the king's message to his daughter, and said, "May God not deprive me of you." She was very happy and, after preparing herself and packing what she needed, went to her younger sister, Dinarzad, and said, "Sister, listen well to what I am telling you. When I go to the king, I will send for you, and when you come and see that the king has finished with me, say, 'Sister, if you are not sleepy, tell us a story.' Then I will begin to tell a story, and it will cause the king to stop his practice, save myself, and deliver the people." Dinarzad replied, "Very well."

At nightfall the vizier took Shahrazad and went with her to the great King Shahrayar. But when Shahrayar took her to bed and began to fondle her, she wept, and when he asked her, "Why are you crying?" she replied, "I have a sister, and I wish to bid her good-bye before daybreak." Then the king sent for the sister, who came and went to sleep under the bed. When the night wore on, she woke up and waited until the king had satisfied himself with her sister Shahrazad and they were by now all fully awake. Then Dinarzad cleared her throat and said, "Sister, if you are not sleepy, tell us one of your lovely little tales to while away the night, before I bid you good-bye at daybreak, for I don't know what will happen to you tomorrow." Shahrazad turned to King Shahrayar and said, "May I have your permission to tell a story?" He replied, "Yes," and Shahrazad was very happy and said, "Listen":

[The Story of the Merchant and the Demon]
THE FIRST NIGHT

It is said, O wise and happy King, that once there was a prosperous merchant who had abundant wealth and investments and commitments in every country. He had many women and children and kept many servants and slaves. One day, having resolved to visit another country, he took provisions, filling his saddlebag with loaves of bread and with dates, mounted his horse, and set out on his journey. For many days and nights, he journeyed under God's care until he reached his destination. When he finished his business, he turned back to his home and family. He journeyed for three days, and on the fourth day, chancing to come to an orchard, went in to avoid the heat and shade himself from the sun of the open country. He came to a spring under a walnut tree and, tying his horse, sat by the spring, pulled out from the saddlebag some loaves of bread and a handful of dates, and began to eat, throwing the date pits right and left until he had had enough. Then he got up, performed his ablutions, and performed his prayers.

But hardly had he finished when he saw an old demon, with sword in hand, standing with his feet on the ground and his head in the clouds. The demon approached until he stood before him and screamed, saying, "Get up, so that I may kill you with this sword, just as you have killed my son." When the merchant saw and heard the demon, he was terrified and awestricken. He asked, "Master, for what crime do you wish to kill me?" The demon replied, "I wish to kill you because you have killed my son." The merchant asked, "Who has killed your son?" The demon replied, "You have killed my son." The merchant said, "By God, I did not kill your son. When and how could that have been?" The demon said, "Didn't you sit down, take out some dates from your saddlebag, and eat, throwing the pits right and left?" The merchant replied, "Yes, I did." The demon said, "You killed my son, for as you were throwing the stones right and left, my son happened to be walking by and was struck and killed by one of them, and I must now kill you." The merchant said, "O my lord, please don't kill me." The demon replied, "I must kill you as you killed him—blood for blood." The merchant said, "To God we belong and to God we turn. There is no power or strength, save in God the Almighty, the Magnificent. If I killed him, I did it by mistake. Please forgive me." The demon replied, "By God, I must kill you, as you killed my son." Then he seized him, and throwing him to the ground, raised the sword to strike him. The merchant began to weep and mourn his family and his wife and children. Again, the demon raised his sword to strike, while the merchant cried until he was drenched with tears, saying, "There is no power or strength, save in God the Almighty, the Magnificent." Then he began to recite the following verses:

> Life has two days: one peace, one wariness,
> And has two sides: worry and happiness.
> Ask him who taunts us with adversity,
> "Does fate, save those worthy of note, oppress?
> Don't you see that the blowing, raging storms   5
> Only the tallest of the trees beset,
> And of earth's many green and barren lots,
> Only the ones with fruits with stones are hit,
> And of the countless stars in heaven's vault
> None is eclipsed except the moon and sun?   10
> You thought well of the days, when they were good,
> Oblivious to the ills destined for one.
> You were deluded by the peaceful nights,
> Yet in the peace of night does sorrow stun."

When the merchant finished and stopped weeping, the demon said, "By God, I must kill you, as you killed my son, even if you weep blood." The merchant asked, "Must you?" The demon replied, "I must," and raised his sword to strike.

But morning overtook Shahrazad, and she lapsed into silence, leaving King Shahrayar burning with curiosity to hear the rest of the story. Then Dinarzad said to her sister Shahrazad, "What a strange and lovely story!" Shahrazad replied, "What is this compared with what I shall tell you tomorrow night if the king spares me and lets me live? It will be even better and more entertaining." The king thought to himself, "I will spare her until I hear the rest of the story; then I will have her put to death the next day." When morning broke, the day dawned, and the sun rose; the king left to attend to the affairs of the kingdom, and the vizier, Shahrazad's father, was amazed and delighted. King Shahrayar governed all day and returned home at night to his quarters and got into bed with Shahrazad. Then Dinarzad said to her sister Shahrazad, "Please, sister, if you are not sleepy, tell us one of your lovely little tales to while away the night." The king added, "Let it be the conclusion of the story of the demon and the merchant, for I would like to hear it." Shahrazad replied, "With the greatest pleasure, dear, happy King":

THE SECOND NIGHT

It is related, O wise and happy King, that when the demon raised his sword, the merchant asked the demon again, "Must you kill me?" and the demon replied, "Yes." Then the merchant said, "Please give me time to say good-bye to my family and my wife and children, divide my property among them, and appoint guardians. Then I shall come back, so that you may kill me." The demon replied, "I am afraid that if I release you and grant you time, you will go and do what you wish, but will not come back." The merchant said, "I swear to keep my pledge to come back, as the God of Heaven and earth is my witness." The demon asked, "How much time do you need?" The merchant replied, "One year, so that I may see enough of my children, bid my wife good-bye, discharge my obligations to people, and come back on New Year's Day." The demon asked, "Do you swear to God that if I let you go, you will come back on New Year's Day?" The merchant replied, "Yes, I swear to God."

After the merchant swore, the demon released him, and he mounted his horse sadly and went on his way. He journeyed until he reached his home and came to his wife and children. When he saw them, he wept bitterly, and when his family saw his sorrow and grief, they began to reproach him for his behavior, and his wife said, "Husband, what is the matter with you? Why do you mourn, when we are happy, celebrating your return?" He replied, "Why not mourn when I have only one year to live?" Then he told her of his encounter with the demon and informed her that he had sworn to return on New Year's Day, so that the demon might kill him.

When they heard what he said, everyone began to cry. His wife struck her face in lamentation and cut her hair, his daughters wailed, and his little children cried. It was a day of mourning, as all the children gathered around their father to weep and exchange good-byes. The next day he wrote his will, dividing his

property, discharged his obligations to people, left bequests and gifts, distributed alms, and engaged reciters to read portions of the Qur'an in his house.
Then he summoned legal witnesses and in their presence freed his slaves and
slave-girls, divided among his elder children their shares of the property,
appointed guardians for his little ones, and gave his wife her share, according
to her marriage contract. He spent the rest of the time with his family, and
when the year came to an end, save for the time needed for the journey, he
performed his ablutions, performed his prayers, and, carrying his burial shroud,
began to bid his family good-bye. His sons hung around his neck, his daughters
wept, and his wife wailed. Their mourning scared him, and he began to weep,
as he embraced and kissed his children good-bye. He said to them, "Children,
this is God's will and decree, for man was created to die." Then he turned away
and, mounting his horse, journeyed day and night until he reached the orchard
on New Year's Day.

He sat at the place where he had eaten the dates, waiting for the demon,
with a heavy heart and tearful eyes. As he waited, an old man, leading a deer on
a leash, approached and greeted him, and he returned the greeting. The old
man inquired, "Friend, why do you sit here in this place of demons and devils?
For in this haunted orchard none come to good." The merchant replied by telling him what had happened to him and the demon, from beginning to end. The
old man was amazed at the merchant's fidelity and said, "Yours is a magnificent
pledge," adding, "By God, I shall not leave until I see what will happen to you
with the demon." Then he sat down beside him and chatted with him. As they
talked . . .

*But morning overtook Shahrazad, and she lapsed into silence. As the day dawned,
and it was light, her sister Dinarzad said, "What a strange and wonderful story!"
Shahrazad replied, "Tomorrow night I shall tell something even stranger and
more wonderful than this."*

THE THIRD NIGHT

*When it was night and Shahrazad was in bed with the king, Dinarzad said to her
sister Shahrazad, "Please, if you are not sleepy, tell us one of your lovely little tales
to while away the night." The king added, "Let it be the conclusion of the merchant's story." Shahrazad replied, "As you wish":*

I heard, O happy King, that as the merchant and the man with the deer sat
talking, another old man approached, with two black hounds, and when he
reached them, he greeted them, and they returned his greeting. Then he asked
them about themselves, and the man with the deer told him the story of the
merchant and the demon, how the merchant had sworn to return on New
Year's Day, and how the demon was waiting to kill him. He added that when he
himself heard the story, he swore never to leave until he saw what would
happen between the merchant and the demon. When the man with the two dogs
heard the story, he was amazed, and he too swore never to leave them until he
saw what would happen between them. Then he questioned the merchant, and
the merchant repeated to him what had happened to him with the demon.

While they were engaged in conversation, a third old man approached and greeted them, and they returned his greeting. He asked, "Why do I see the two of you sitting here, with this merchant between you, looking abject, sad, and dejected?" They told him the merchant's story and explained that they were sitting and waiting to see what would happen to him with the demon. When he heard the story, he sat down with them, saying, "By God, I too like you will not leave, until I see what happens to this man with the demon." As they sat, conversing with one another, they suddenly saw the dust rising from the open country, and when it cleared, they saw the demon approaching, with a drawn steel sword in his hand. He stood before them without greeting them, yanked the merchant with his left hand, and, holding him fast before him, said, "Get ready to die." The merchant and the three old men began to weep and wail.

But dawn broke and morning overtook Shahrazad, and she lapsed into silence. Then Dinarzad said, "Sister, what a lovely story!" Shahrazad replied, "What is this compared with what I shall tell you tomorrow night? It will be even better; it will be more wonderful, delightful, entertaining, and delectable if the king spares me and lets me live." The king was all curiosity to hear the rest of the story and said to himself, "By God, I will not have her put to death until I hear the rest of the story and find out what happened to the merchant with the demon. Then I will have her put to death the next morning, as I did with the others." Then he went out to attend to the affairs of his kingdom, and when he saw Shahrazad's father, he treated him kindly and showed him favors, and the vizier was amazed. When night came, the king went home, and when he was in bed with Shahrazad, Dinarzad said, "Sister, if you are not sleepy, tell us one of your lovely little tales to while away the night." Shahrazad replied, "With the greatest pleasure":

THE FOURTH NIGHT

It is related, O happy King, that the first old man with the deer approached the demon and, kissing his hands and feet, said, "Fiend and King of the demon kings, if I tell you what happened to me and that deer, and you find it strange and amazing, indeed stranger and more amazing than what happened to you and the merchant, will you grant me a third of your claim on him for his crime and guilt?" The demon replied, "I will." The old man said:

[The First Old Man's Tale]

Demon, this deer is my cousin, my flesh and blood. I married her when I was very young, and she a girl of twelve, who reached womanhood only afterward. For thirty years we lived together, but I was not blessed with children, for she bore neither boy nor girl. Yet I continued to be kind to her, to care for her, and to treat her generously. Then I took a mistress, and she bore me a son, who grew up to look like a slice of the moon.[5] Meanwhile, my wife grew jealous of my mistress and my son. One day, when he was ten, I had to go on a journey. I entrusted my wife, this one here, with my mistress and son, bade her take good

---

5. The moon is a symbol of beauty for men and women.

care of them, and was gone for a whole year. In my absence my wife, this cousin of mine, learned soothsaying and magic and cast a spell on my son and turned him into a young bull. Then she summoned my shepherd, gave my son to him, and said, "Tend this bull with the rest of the cattle." The shepherd took him and tended him for a while. Then she cast a spell on the mother, turning her into a cow, and gave her also to the shepherd.

When I came back, after all this was done, and inquired about my mistress and my son, she answered, "Your mistress died, and your son ran away two months ago, and I have had no news from him ever since." When I heard her, I grieved for my mistress, and with an anguished heart I mourned for my son for nearly a year. When the Great Feast of the Immolation[6] drew near, I summoned the shepherd and ordered him to bring me a fat cow for the sacrifice. The cow he brought me was in reality my enchanted mistress. When I bound her and pressed against her to cut her throat, she wept and cried, as if saying, "My son, my son," and her tears coursed down her cheeks. Astonished and seized with pity, I turned away and asked the shepherd to bring me a different cow. But my wife shouted, "Go on. Butcher her, for he has none better or fatter. Let us enjoy her meat at feast time." I approached the cow to cut her throat, and again she cried, as if saying, "My son, my son." Then I turned away from her and said to the shepherd, "Butcher her for me." The shepherd butchered her, and when he skinned her, he found neither meat nor fat but only skin and bone. I regretted having her butchered and said to the shepherd, "Take her all for yourself, or give her as alms to whomever you wish, and find me a fat young bull from among the flock." The shepherd took her away and disappeared, and I never knew what he did with her.

Then he brought me my son, my heartblood, in the guise of a fat young bull. Then my son saw me, he shook his head loose from the rope, ran toward me, and, throwing himself at my feet, kept rubbing his head against me. I was astonished and touched with sympathy, pity, and mercy, for the blood hearkened to the blood and the divine bond, and my heart throbbed within me when I saw the tears coursing over the cheeks of my son the young bull, as he dug the earth with his hoofs. I turned away and said to the shepherd, "Let him go with the rest of the flock, and be kind to him, for I have decided to spare him. Bring me another one instead of him." My wife, this very deer, shouted, "You shall sacrifice none but this bull." I got angry and replied, "I listened to you and butchered the cow uselessly. I will not listen to you and kill this bull, for I have decided to spare him." But she pressed me, saying, "You must butcher this bull," and I bound him and took the knife . . .

But dawn broke, and morning overtook Shahrazad, and she lapsed into silence, leaving the king all curiosity for the rest of the story. Then her sister Dinarzad said, "What an entertaining story!" Shahrazad replied. "Tomorrow night I shall tell you something even stranger, more wonderful, and more entertaining if the king spares me and lets me live."

---

6. The Feast of Sacrifice, celebrated throughout the Muslim world at the end of the pilgrimage to Mecca; to commemorate Abraham, who was willing to sacrifice his son Isaac when commanded by God but was allowed to offer a ram instead, Muslims sacrifice animals to God.

The following night, Dinarzad said to her sister Shahrazad, "Please, sister, if you are not sleepy, tell us one of your little tales." Shahrazad replied, "With the greatest pleasure":

I heard, dear King, that the old man with the deer said to the demon and to his companions:

I took the knife and as I turned to slaughter my son, he wept, bellowed, rolled at my feet, and motioned toward me with his tongue. I suspected something, began to waver with trepidation and pity, and finally released him, saying to my wife, "I have decided to spare him, and I commit him to your care." Then I tried to appease and please my wife, this very deer, by slaughtering another bull, promising her to slaughter this one next season. We slept that night, and when God's dawn broke, the shepherd came to me without letting my wife know, and said, "Give me credit for bringing you good news." I replied, "Tell me, and the credit is yours." He said, "Master, I have a daughter who is fond of soothsaying and magic and who is adept at the art of oaths and spells. Yesterday I took home with me the bull you had spared, to let him graze with the cattle, and when my daughter saw him, she laughed and cried at the same time. When I asked her why she laughed and cried, she answered that she laughed because the bull was in reality the son of our master the cattle owner, put under a spell by his stepmother, and that she cried because his father had slaughtered the son's mother. I could hardly wait till daybreak to bring you the good news about your son."

Demon, when I heard that, I uttered a cry and fainted, and when I came to myself, I accompanied the shepherd to his home, went to my son, and threw myself at him, kissing him and crying. He turned his head toward me, his tears coursing over his cheeks, and dangled his tongue, as if to say, "Look at my plight." Then I turned to the shepherd's daughter and asked, "Can you release him from the spell? If you do, I will give you all my cattle and all my possessions." She smiled and replied, "Master, I have no desire for your wealth, cattle, or possessions. I will deliver him, but on two conditions: first, that you let me marry him; second, that you let me cast a spell on her who had cast a spell on him, in order to control her and guard against her evil power." I replied, "Do whatever you wish and more. My possessions are for you and my son. As for my wife, who has done this to my son and made me slaughter his mother, her life is forfeit to you." She said, "No, but I will let her taste what she has inflicted on others." Then the shepherd's daughter filled a bowl of water, uttered an incantation and an oath, and said to my son, "Bull, if you have been created in this image by the All-Conquering, Almighty Lord, stay as you are, but if you have been treacherously put under a spell, change back to your human form, by the will of God, Creator of the wide world." Then she sprinkled him with the water, and he shook himself and changed from a bull back to his human form.

As I rushed to him, I fainted, and when I came to myself, he told me what my wife, this very deer, had done to him and to his mother. I said to him, "Son, God has sent us someone who will pay her back for what you and your mother and I have suffered at her hands." Then, O demon, I gave my son in marriage to the shepherd's daughter, who turned my wife into this very deer, saying to me, "To me this is a pretty form, for she will be with us day and night, and it is better to turn her into a pretty deer than to suffer her sinister looks." Thus she stayed with us, while the days and nights followed one another, and the months and years went by. Then one day the shepherd's daughter died, and my son went to the country of this very man with whom you have had your encounter. Some time later I took my wife, this very deer, with me, set out to find out what had happened to my son, and chanced to stop here. This is my story, my strange and amazing story.

The demon assented, saying, "I grant you one-third of this man's life."

Then, O King Shahrayar, the second old man with the two black dogs approached the demon and said, "I too shall tell you what happened to me and to these two dogs, and if I tell it to you and you find it stranger and more amazing than this man's story will you grant me one-third of this man's life?" The demon replied, "I will." Then the old man began to tell his story, saying . . .

But dawn broke, and morning overtook Shahrazad, and she lapsed into silence. Then Dinarzad said, "This is an amazing story," and Shahrazad replied, "What is this compared with what I shall tell you tomorrow night if the king spares me and lets me live!" The king said to himself, "By God, I will not have her put to death until I find out what happened to the man with the two black dogs. Then I will have her put to death, God the Almighty willing."

THE SIXTH NIGHT

When the following night arrived and Shahrazad was in bed with King Shahrayar, her sister Dinarzad said, "Sister, if you are not sleepy, tell us a little tale. Finish the one you started." Shahrazad replied, "With the greatest pleasure":

I heard, O happy King, that the second old man with the two dogs said:

[The Second Old Man's Tale]

Demon, as for my story, these are the details. These two dogs are my brothers. When our father died, he left behind three sons, and left us three thousand dinars,[7] with which each of us opened a shop and became a shopkeeper. Soon my older brother, one of these very dogs, went and sold the contents of his shop for a thousand dinars, bought trading goods, and, having prepared himself for his trading trip, left us. A full year went by, when one day, as I sat in my shop, a beggar stopped by to beg. When I refused him, he tearfully asked, "Don't you recognize me?" and when I looked at him closely, I recognized my brother. I embraced him and took him into the shop, and when I asked him about his plight, he replied, "The money is gone, and the situation is bad." Then I took him to the public bath, clothed him in one of my robes, and took him home with me. Then I examined my books and checked my balance, and found out that I had made a thousand dinars and that my net worth was two thousand dinars. I divided the amount between my brother and myself, and said to him, "Think as if you have never been away." He gladly took the money and opened another shop.

---

7. Gold coins; the basic Muslim money units [translator's note].

Soon afterward my second brother, this other dog, went and sold his merchandise and collected his money, intending to go on a trading trip. We tried to dissuade him, but he did not listen. Instead, he bought merchandise and trading goods, joined a group of travelers, and was gone for a full year. Then he came back, just like his older brother. I said to him, "Brother, didn't I advise you not to go?" He replied tearfully, "Brother, it was foreordained. Now I am poor and penniless, without even a shirt on my back." Demon, I took him to the public bath, clothed him in one of my new robes, and took him back to the shop. After we had something to eat, I said to him, "Brother, I shall do my business accounts, calculate my net worth for the year, and after subtracting the capital, whatever the profit happens to be, I shall divide it equally between you and myself." When I examined my books and subtracted the capital, I found out that my profit was two thousand dinars, and I thanked God and felt very happy. Then I divided the money, giving him a thousand dinars and keeping a thousand for myself. With that money he opened another shop, and the three of us stayed together for a while. Then my two brothers asked me to go on a trading journey with them, but I refused, saying, "What did you gain from your ventures that I can gain?"

They dropped the matter, and for six years we worked in our stores, buying and selling. Yet every year they asked me to go on a trading journey with them, but I refused, until I finally gave in. I said, "Brothers, I am ready to go with you. How much money do you have?" I found out that they had eaten and drunk and squandered everything they had, but I said nothing to them and did not reproach them. Then I took inventory, gathered all I had together, and sold everything. I was pleased to discover that the sale netted six thousand dinars. Then I divided the money into two parts, and said to my brothers, "The sum of three thousand dinars is for you and myself to use on our trading journey. The other three thousand I shall bury in the ground, in case what happened to you happens to me, so that when we return, we will find three thousand dinars to reopen our shops." They replied, "This is an excellent idea." Then, demon, I divided my money and buried three thousand dinars. Of the remaining three I gave each of my brothers a thousand and kept a thousand for myself. After I closed my shop, we bought merchandise and trading goods, rented a large seafaring boat, and after loading it with our goods and provisions, sailed day and night, for a month.

But morning overtook Shahrazad, and she lapsed into silence. Then her sister Dinarzad said, "Sister, what a lovely story!" Shahrazad replied, "Tomorrow night I shall tell you something even lovelier, stranger, and more wonderful if I live, the Almighty God willing."

THE SEVENTH NIGHT

The following night Dinarzad said to her sister Shahrazad, "For God's sake, sister, if you are not sleepy, tell us a little tale." The king added, "Let it be the completion of the story of the merchant and the demon." Shahrazad replied, "With the greatest pleasure":

I heard, O happy King, that the second old man said to the demon:

For a month my brothers, these very dogs, and I sailed the salty sea, until we came to a port city. We entered the city and sold our goods, earning ten dinars for every dinar. Then we bought other goods, and when we got to the seashore to embark, I met a girl who was dressed in tatters. She kissed my hands and said, "O my lord, be charitable and do me a favor, and I believe that I shall be able to reward you for it." I replied, "I am willing to do you a favor regardless of any reward." She said, "O my lord, marry me, clothe me, and take me home with you on this boat, as your wife, for I wish to give myself to you. I, in turn, will reward you for your kindness and charity, the Almighty God willing. Don't be misled by my poverty and present condition." When I heard her words, I felt pity for her, and guided by what God the Most High had intended for me, I consented. I clothed her with an expensive dress and married her. Then I took her to the boat, spread the bed for her, and consummated our marriage. We sailed many days and nights, and I, feeling love for her, stayed with her day and night, neglecting my brothers. In the meantime they, these very dogs, grew jealous of me, envied me for my increasing merchandise and wealth, and coveted all our possessions. At last they decided to betray me and, tempted by the Devil, plotted to kill me. One night they waited until I was asleep beside my wife; then they carried the two of us and threw us into the sea.

When we awoke, my wife turned into a she-demon and carried me out of the sea to an island. When it was morning, she said, "Husband, I have rewarded you by saving you from drowning, for I am one of the demons who believe in God.[8] When I saw you by the seashore, I felt love for you and came to you in the guise in which you saw me, and when I expressed my love for you, you accepted me. Now I must kill your brothers." When I heard what she said, I was amazed and I thanked her and said, "As for destroying my brothers, this I do not wish, for I will not behave like them." Then I related to her what had happened to me and them, from beginning to end. When she heard my story, she got very angry at them, and said, "I shall fly to them now, drown their boat, and let them all perish." I entreated her, saying, "For God's sake, don't. The proverb advises 'Be kind to those who hurt you.' No matter what, they are my brothers after all." In this manner, I entreated her and pacified her. Afterward, she took me and flew away with me until she brought me home and put me down on the roof of my house. I climbed down, threw the doors open, and dug up the money I had buried. Then I went out and, greeting the people in the market, reopened my shop. When I came home in the evening, I found these two dogs tied up, and when they saw me, they came to me, wept, and rubbed themselves against me. I started, when I suddenly heard my wife say, "O my lord, these are your brothers." I asked, "Who has done this to them?" She replied, "I sent to my sister and asked her to do it. They will stay in this condition for ten years, after which they may be delivered." Then she told me where to find her and departed. The ten years have passed, and I was with my brothers on my way to her to have the spell lifted, when I met this man, together with this old man with the deer. When I asked him about himself, he told me about his encounter with you, and I resolved not to leave until I found out what would happen between you and him. This is my story. Isn't it amazing?

8. According to the Qur'an, God created both humans and demons (jinns), some of whom accepted Islam.

The demon replied, "By God, it is strange and amazing. I grant you one-third of my claim on him for his crime."

Then the third old man said, "Demon, don't disappoint me. If I told you a story that is stranger and more amazing than the first two would you grant me one-third of your claim on him for his crime?" The demon replied, "I will." Then the old man said, "Demon, listen":

But morning overtook Shahrazad, and she lapsed into silence. Then her sister said, "What an amazing story!" Shahrazad replied, "The rest is even more amazing." The king said to himself, "I will not have her put to death until I hear what happened to the old man and the demon; then I will have her put to death, as is my custom with the others."

THE EIGHTH NIGHT

The following night Dinarzad said to her sister Shahrazad, "For God's sake, sister, if you are not sleepy, tell us one of your lovely little tales to while away the night." Shahrazad replied, "With the greatest pleasure":

[The Third Old Man's Tale][9]

The demon said, "This is a wonderful story, and I grant you a third of my claim on the merchant's life."

The third sheikh approached and said to the demon, "I will tell you a story more wonderful than these two if you will grant me a third of your claim on his life, O demon!"

To which the demon agreed.

So the sheikh began:

O sultan and chief of the demons, this mule was my wife. I had gone off on a journey and was absent from her for a whole year. At last I came to the end of my journey and returned home late one night. When I entered the house I saw a black slave lying in bed with her. They were chatting and dallying and laughing and kissing and quarreling together. When she saw me my wife leaped out of bed, ran to the water jug, recited a spell over it, then splashed me with some of the water and said, "Leave this form for the form of a dog."

Immediately I became a dog and she chased me out of the house. I ran out of the gate and didn't stop running until I reached a butcher's shop. I entered it and fell to eating the bones lying about. When the owner of the shop saw me, he grabbed me and carried me into his house. When his daughter saw me, she hid her face and said, "Why are you bringing this strange man in with you?"

"What man?" her father asked.

"This dog is a man whose wife has put a spell on him," she said, "but I can set him free again." She took a jug of water, recited a spell over it, then splashed a little water from it on me, and said, "Leave this shape for your original one."

9. Translated by Jerome W. Clinton. Because the earliest manuscript does not include a story for the third sheikh, later narrators sup- plied one. This brief anecdote comes from a manuscript found in the library of the Royal Academy in Madrid.

And I became myself again. I kissed her hand and said, "I want to cast a spell on my wife as she did on me. Please give me a little of that water."

"Gladly," she said, "if you find her asleep, sprinkle a few drops on her and she will become whatever you wish."

Well, I did find her asleep, and I sprinkled some water on her and said, "Leave this shape for the shape of a she-mule." She at once became the very mule you see here, oh sultan and chief of the demons."

The demon then turned to him and asked, "Is this really true?"

"Yes," he answered, nodding his head vigorously, "it's all true."

When the sheikh had finished his story, the demon shook with laughter and granted him a third of his claim on the merchant's blood.

Then the demon released the merchant and departed. The merchant turned to the three old men and thanked them, and they congratulated him on his deliverance and bade him good-bye. Then they separated, and each of them went on his way. The merchant himself went back home to his family, his wife, and his children, and he lived with them until the day he died. But this story is not as strange or as amazing as the story of the fisherman.

Dinarzad asked, "Please, sister, what is the story of the fisherman?" Shahrazad said: . . .

[The Story of the Fisherman and the Demon]

It is related that there was a very old fisherman who had a wife and three daughters and who was so poor that they did not have even enough food for the day. It was this fisherman's custom to cast his net four times a day. One day, while the moon was still up, he went out with his net at the call for the early morning prayer. He reached the outskirts of the city and came to the seashore. Then he set down his basket, rolled up his shirt, and waded to his waist in the water. He cast his net and waited for it to sink; then he gathered the rope and started to pull. As he pulled little by little, he felt that the net was getting heavier until he was unable to pull any further. He climbed ashore, drove a stake into the ground, and tied the end of the rope to the stake. Then he took off his clothes, dove into the water, and went around the net, shaking it and tugging at it until he managed to pull it ashore. Feeling extremely happy, he put on his clothes and went back to the net. But when he opened it, he found inside a dead donkey, which had torn it apart. The fisherman felt sad and depressed and said to himself, "There is no power and no strength save in God, the Almighty, the Magnificent," adding, "Indeed, this is a strange catch!" Then he began to recite the following verses:

> O you who brave the danger in the dark,
> Reduce your toil, for gain is not in work.
> Look at the fisherman who labors at his trade,
> As the stars in the night their orbits make,
> And deeply wades into the raging sea,
> Steadily gazing at the swelling net,
> Till he returns, pleased with his nightly catch,
> A fish whose mouth the hook of death has cut,

5

And sells it to a man who sleeps the night,
Safe from the cold and blessed with every wish.   10
Praised be the Lord who blesses and withholds:
This casts the net, but that one eats the fish.

*But morning overtook Shahrazad, and she lapsed into silence. Then her sister
Dinarzad said, "Sister, what a lovely story!" Shahrazad replied, "Tomorrow night
I shall tell you the rest, which is stranger and more wonderful, if the king spares
me and lets me live!"*

THE NINTH NIGHT

*The following night Dinarzad said to her sister Shahrazad, "Sister, if you are
not sleepy, finish the fisherman's story." Shahrazad replied, "With the greatest
pleasure":*

I heard, O happy King, that when the fisherman finished reciting his verses, he
pushed the donkey out of the net and sat down to mend it. When he was done,
he wrung it out and spread it to dry. Then he waded into the water and, invoking
the Almighty God, cast the net and waited for it to sink. Then he pulled the rope
little by little, but this time the net was even more firmly snagged. Thinking that it
was heavy with fish, he was extremely happy. He took off his clothes and, diving
into the water, freed the net and struggled with it until he reached the shore, but
inside the net he found a large jar full of nothing but mud and sand. When he saw
this, he felt sad and, with tears in his eyes, said to himself, "This is a strange day!
God's we are and to God we turn," and he began to recite the following verses:

O my tormenting fate, forbear,
Or if you can't, at least be fair.
I went to seek my daily bread,
But they said to me it was dead.
And neither luck nor industry   5
Brought back my daily bread to me.
The Pleiads[1] many fools attain,
While sages sit in dark disdain.

Then the fisherman threw the jar away, washed his net, and, wringing it out,
spread it to dry. Then he begged the Almighty God for forgiveness and went
back to the water. For the third time, he cast the net and waited for it to sink.
But when he pulled it up, he found nothing inside but broken pots and bottles,
stones, bones, refuse, and the like. He wept at this great injustice and ill luck
and began to recite the following verses:

Your livelihood is not in your own hands;
Neither by writing nor by the pen you thrive.
Your luck and your wages are by lot;
Some lands are waste, and some are fertile lands.
The wheel of fortune lowers the man of worth,   5

---

1. Cluster of stars in the constellation of Taurus.

> Raising the base man who deserves to fall.
> Come then, O death, and end this worthless life,
> Where the ducks soar, while the falcons are bound to earth.
> No wonder that you see the good man poor,
> While the vicious exults in his estate.   10
> Our wages are alloted; 'tis our fate
> To search like birds for gleanings everywhere.
> One bird searches the earth from east to west,
> Another gets the tidbits while at rest.

Then the fisherman raised his eyes to the heavens and, seeing that the sun had risen and that it was morning and full daylight, said, "O Lord, you know that I cast my net four times only. I have already cast it three times, and there is only one more try left. Lord, let the sea serve me, even as you let it serve Moses."[2] Having mended the net, he cast it into the sea, and waited for it to sink. When he pulled, he found that it was so heavy that he was unable to haul it. He shook it and found that it was caught at the bottom. Saying "There is no power or strength save in God, the Almighty, the Magnificent," he took off his clothes and dove for the net. He worked at it until he managed to free it, and as he hauled it to the shore, he felt that there was something heavy inside. He struggled with the net, until he opened it and found a large long-necked brass jar, with a lead stopper bearing the mark of a seal ring.[3] When the fisherman saw the jar, he was happy and said to himself, "I will sell it in the copper market, for it must be worth at least two measures of wheat." He tried to move the jar, but it was so full and so heavy that he was unable to budge it. Looking at the lead stopper, he said to himself, "I will open the jar, shake out the contents, then roll it before me until I reach the copper market." Then he took out a knife from his belt and began to scrape and struggle with the lead stopper until he pried it loose. He held the stopper in his mouth, tilted the jar to the ground, and shook it, trying to pour out its contents, but when nothing came out, he was extremely surprised.

After a while, there began to emerge from the jar a great column of smoke, which rose and spread over the face of the earth, increasing so much that it covered the sea and rising so high that it reached the clouds and hid the daylight. For a long time, the smoke kept rising from the jar; then it gathered and took shape, and suddenly it shook and there stood a demon, with his feet on the ground and his head in the clouds. He had a head like a tomb, fangs like pincers, a mouth like a cave, teeth like stones, nostrils like trumpets, ears like shields, a throat like an alley, and eyes like lanterns. In short, all one can say is that he was a hideous monster. When the fisherman saw him, he shook with terror, his jaws locked together, and his mouth went dry. The demon cried, "O Solomon,[4] prophet of God, forgive me, forgive me. Never again will I disobey you or defy your command."

2. That is, by parting and returning at his command (Exodus 14.21–29); like Jews and Christians, Muslims view Moses as a prophet.
3. A ring set with an engraved stone, commonly used to imprint an authenticating mark; or it might be engraved with talismanic words and used as a charm.
4. Solomon (Suleiman), king of Israel (see 1 Kings 1–11), is mentioned as a prophet in the Qur'an.

But morning overtook Shahrazad, and she lapsed into silence. Then Dinarzad said, "Sister, what a strange and amazing story!" Shahrazad replied, "Tomorrow night I shall tell you something stranger and more amazing if I stay alive."

THE TENTH NIGHT

The following night, when Shahrazad was in bed with King Shahrayar, her sister Dinarzad said, "Please, sister, finish the story of the fisherman." Shahrazad replied, "With the greatest pleasure":

I heard, O happy King, that when the fisherman heard what the demon said, he asked, "Demon, what are you saying? It has been more than one thousand and eight hundred years since the prophet Solomon died, and we are now ages later. What is your story, and why were you in this jar?" When the demon heard the fisherman, he said, "Be glad!" The fisherman cried, "O happy day!" The demon added, "Be glad that you will soon be put to death." The fisherman said, "You deserve to be put to shame for such tidings. Why do you wish to kill me, I who have released you and delivered you from the bottom of the sea and brought you back to this world?" The demon replied, "Make a wish!" The fisherman was happy and asked, "What shall I wish of you?" The demon replied, "Tell me how you wish to die, and what manner of death you wish me to choose." The fisherman asked, "What is my crime? Is this my reward from you for having delivered you?" The demon replied, "Fisherman, listen to my story." The fisherman said, "Make it short, for I am at my rope's end."

The demon said, "You should know that I am one of the renegade, rebellious demons. I, together with the giant Sakhr, rebelled against the prophet Solomon, the son of David, who sent against me Asif ibn-Barkhiya, who took me by force and bade me be led in defeat and humiliation before the prophet Solomon. When the prophet Solomon saw me, he invoked God to protect him from me and my looks and asked me to submit to him, but I refused. So he called for this brass jar, confined me inside, and sealed it with a lead seal on which he imprinted God's Almighty name. Then he commanded his demons to carry me and throw me into the middle of the sea. I stayed there for two hundred years, saying to myself, 'Whoever sets me free during these two hundred years, I will make him rich.' But the two hundred years went by and were followed by another two hundred, and no one set me free. Then I vowed to myself, 'Whoever sets me free, I will open for him all the treasures of the earth,' but four hundred years went by, and no one set me free. When I entered the next hundred years, I vowed to myself, 'Whoever delivers me, during these hundred years, I will make king, make myself his servant, and fulfill every day three of his wishes,' but that hundred years too, plus all the intervening years, went by, and no one set me free. Then I raged and raved and growled and snorted and said to myself, 'Whoever delivers me from now on, I will either put him to the worst of deaths or let him choose for himself the manner of death.' Soon you came by and set me free. Tell me how you wish to die."

When the fisherman heard what the demon said, he replied, "To God we belong and to Him we return. After all these years, with my bad luck, I had to set you free now. Forgive me, and God will grant you forgiveness. Destroy me, and God will inflict on you one who will destroy you." The demon replied, "It must be. Tell me how you wish to die." When the fisherman was certain that he was going to die, he mourned and wept, saying, "O my children, may God not deprive us of each other." Again he turned to the demon and said, "For God's sake, release me as a reward for releasing you and delivering you from this jar." The demon replied, "Your death is your reward for releasing me and letting me escape." The fisherman said, "I did you a good turn, and you are about to repay me with a bad one. How true is the sentiment of the following lines:

> Our kindness they repaid with ugly deeds,
> Upon my life, the deeds of men depraved.
> He who the undeserving aids will meet
> The fate of him whom the hyena saved."

The demon said, "Be brief, for as I have said, I must kill you." Then the fisherman thought to himself, "He is only a demon, while I am a human being, whom God has endowed with reason and thereby made superior to him. He may use his demonic wiles on me, but I will use my reason to deal with him." Then he asked the demon, "Must you kill me?" When the demon replied, "I must," the fisherman said, "By the Almighty name that was engraved on the ring of Solomon the son of David, will you answer me truthfully if I ask you about something?" The demon was upset and said with a shudder, "Ask, and be brief!"

But morning overtook Shahrazad, and she lapsed into silence. Then Dinarzad said, "Sister, what an amazing and lovely story!" Shahrazad replied, "What is this compared with what I shall tell you tomorrow night if the king spares me and lets me live! It will be even more amazing."

THE ELEVENTH NIGHT

The following night Dinarzad said to her sister Shahrazad, "Sister, if you are not sleepy, finish the story of the fisherman and the demon." "Shahrazad replied, "With the greatest pleasure":

I heard, O King, that the fisherman said, "By the Almighty name, tell me whether you really were inside this jar." The demon replied, "By the Almighty name, I was imprisoned in this jar." The fisherman said, "You are lying, for this jar is not large enough, not even for your hands and feet. How can it be large enough for your whole body?" The demon replied, "By God, I was inside. Don't you believe that I was inside it?" The fisherman said, "No, I don't." Whereupon the demon shook himself and turned into smoke, which rose, stretched over the sea, spread over the land, then gathered, and, little by little, began to enter the jar. When the smoke disappeared completely, the demon shouted from within, "Fisherman, here I am in the jar. Do you believe me now?"

The fisherman at once took out the sealed lead stopper and hurriedly clamped it on the mouth of the jar. Then he cried out, "Demon, now tell me how you wish to die. For I will throw you into this sea, build a house right here, and sit here and stop any fisherman who comes to fish and warn him that there is a demon here, who will kill whoever pulls him out and who will let him choose how he wishes to die." When the demon heard what the fisherman said and found himself imprisoned, he tried to get out but could not, for he was prevented by the seal of Solomon the son of David. Realizing that the fisherman had tricked him, the demon said, "Fisherman, don't do this to me. I was only joking with you." The fisherman replied, "You are lying, you the dirtiest and meanest of demons," and began to roll the jar toward the sea. The demon shouted, "Don't, don't!" But the fisherman replied, "Yes, yes." Then in a soft and submissive voice the demon asked, "Fisherman, what do you intend to do?" The fisherman replied, "I intend to throw you into the sea. The first time you stayed there for eight hundred years. This time I will let you stay until Doomsday. Haven't I said to you, 'Spare me, and God will spare you. Destroy me, and God will destroy you'? But you refused, and persisted in your resolve to do me in and kill me. Now it is my turn to do you in." The demon said, "Fisherman, if you open the jar, I will reward you and make you rich." The fisherman replied. "You are lying, you are lying. Your situation and mine is like that of King Yunan and the sage Duban." The demon asked, "What is their story?" The fisherman said:

[The Tale of King Yunan and the Sage Duban]

Demon, there was once a king called Yunan, who reigned in one of the cities of Persia, in the province of Zuman.[5] This king was afflicted with leprosy, which had defied the physicians and the sages, who, for all the medicines they gave him to drink and all the ointments they applied, were unable to cure him. One day there came to the city of King Yunan a sage called Duban. This sage had read all sorts of books, Greek, Persian, Turkish, Arabic, Byzantine, Syriac, and Hebrew, had studied the sciences, and had learned their groundwork, as well as their principles and basic benefits. Thus he was versed in all the sciences, from philosophy to the lore of plants and herbs, the harmful as well as the beneficial. A few days after he arrived in the city of King Yunan, the sage heard about the king and his leprosy and the fact that the physicians and the sages were unable to cure him. On the following day, when God's morning dawned and His sun rose, the sage Duban put on his best clothes, went to King Yunan and, introducing himself, said, "Your Majesty, I have heard of that which has afflicted your body and heard that many physicians have treated you without finding a way to cure you. Your Majesty, I can treat you without giving you any medicine to drink or ointment to apply." When the king heard this, he said, "If you succeed, I will bestow on you riches that would be enough for you and your grandchildren. I will bestow favors on you, and I will make you my companion and friend." The king bestowed robes of honor on the sage, treated him kindly, and then asked him, "Can you really cure me from my leprosy without any medicine to drink or ointment to apply?" The sage replied, "Yes, I will cure you externally." The king was astonished, and he began to feel respect as well as great affection for the sage. He said, "Now, sage, do what you have promised." The sage replied, "I hear and obey. I will do it tomorrow morning, the Almighty God willing." Then the sage went to the city, rented a house, and

5. Modern-day Armenia.

there he distilled and extracted medicines and drugs. Then with his great knowledge and skill, he fashioned a mallet with a curved end, hollowed the mallet, as well as the handle, and filled the handle with his medicines and drugs. He likewise made a ball. When he had perfected and prepared everything, he went on the following day to King Yunan and kissed the ground before him.

But morning overtook Shahrazad, and she lapsed into silence. Then her sister Dinarzad said, "What a lovely story!" Shahrazad replied, "You have heard nothing yet. Tomorrow night I shall tell you something stranger and more amazing if the king spares me and lets me live!"

THE TWELFTH TIGHT

The following night Dinarzad said to her sister Shahrazad, "Please, sister, finish the rest of the story of the fisherman and the demon." Shahrazad replied, "With the greatest pleasure":

I heard, O King, that the fisherman said to the demon:

The sage Duban came to King Yunan and asked him to ride to the playground to play with the ball and mallet. The king rode out, attended by his chamberlains, princes, viziers, and lords and eminent men of the realm. When the king was seated, the sage Duban entered, offered him the mallet, and said, "O happy King, take this mallet, hold it in your hand, and as you race on the playground, hold the grip tightly in your fist, and hit the ball. Race until you perspire, and the medicine will ooze from the grip into your perspiring hand, spread to your wrist, and circulate through your entire body. After you perspire and the medicine spreads in your body, return to your royal palace, take a bath, and go to sleep. You will wake up cured, and that is all there is to it." King Yunan took the mallet from the sage Duban and mounted his horse. The attendants threw the ball before the king, who, holding the grip tightly in his fist, followed it and struggled excitedly to catch up with it and hit it. He kept galloping after the ball and hitting it until his palm and the rest of his body began to perspire, and the medicine began to ooze from the handle and flow through his entire body. When the sage Duban was certain that the medicine had oozed and spread through the king's body, he advised him to return to his palace and go immediately to the bath. The king went to the bath and washed himself thoroughly. Then he put on his clothes, left the bath, and returned to his palace.

As for the sage Duban, he spent the night at home, and early in the morning, he went to the palace and asked for permission to see the king. When he was allowed in, he entered and kissed the ground before the king; then, pointing toward him with his hand, he began to recite the following verses:

> The virtues you fostered are great;
> For who but you could sire them?
> Yours is the face whose radiant light
> Effaces the night dark and grim.
> Forever beams your radiant face;

5

That of the world is still in gloom.
You rained on us with ample grace,
As the clouds rain on thirsty hills,
Expending your munificence,
Attaining your magnificence.   10

When the sage Duban finished reciting these verses, the king stood up and embraced him. Then he seated the sage beside him, and with attentiveness and smiles, engaged him in conversation. Then the king bestowed on the sage robes of honor, gave him gifts and endowments, and granted his wishes. For when the king had looked at himself the morning after the bath, he found that his body was clear of leprosy, as clear and pure as silver. He therefore felt exceedingly happy and in a very generous mood. Thus when he went in the morning to the reception hall and sat on his throne, attended by the mamluks[6] and chamberlains, in the company of the viziers and the lords of the realm, and the sage Duban presented himself, as we have mentioned, the king stood up, embraced him, and seated him beside him. He treated him attentively and drank and ate with him.

But morning overtook Shahrazad, and she lapsed into silence. Then her sister Dinarzad said, "Sister, what a lovely story!" Shahrazad replied, "The rest of the story is stranger and more amazing. If the king spares me and I am alive tomorrow night, I shall tell you something even more entertaining."

THE THIRTEENTH NIGHT

The following night Dinarzad said to her sister Shahrazad, "Sister, if you are not sleepy, tell us one of your lovely little tales to while away the night." Shahrazad replied, "With the greatest pleasure":

I heard, O happy King who is praiseworthy by the Grace of God, that King Yunan bestowed favors on the sage, gave him robes of honor, and granted his wishes. At the end of the day he gave the sage a thousand dinars and sent him home. The king, who was amazed at the skill of the sage Duban, said to himself, "This man has treated me externally, without giving me any draught to drink or ointment to apply. His is indeed a great wisdom for which he deserves to be honored and rewarded. He shall become my companion, confidant, and close friend." Then the king spent the night, happy at his recovery from his illness, at his good health, and at the soundness of his body. When morning came and it was light, the king went to the royal reception hall and sat on the throne, attended by his chief officers, while the princes, viziers, and lords of the realm sat to his right and left. Then the king called for the sage, and when the sage entered and kissed the ground before him, the king stood up to salute him, seated him beside him, and invited him to eat with him. The king treated him intimately, showed him favors, and bestowed on him robes of honor and many other gifts. Then he spent the whole day conversing with him, and at the end of the day he

6. Literally, "slaves"; here, members of a military class who were originally slaves from the Caucasus region.

ordered that he be given a thousand dinars. The sage went home and spent the night with his wife, feeling happy and thankful to God the Arbiter.

In the morning, the king went to the royal reception hall, and the princes and viziers came to stand in attendance. It happened that King Yunan had a vizier who was sinister, greedy, envious, and fretful, and when he saw that the sage had found favor with the king, who bestowed on him much money and many robes of honor, he feared that the king would dismiss him and appoint the sage in his place; therefore, he envied the sage and harbored ill will against him, for "nobody is free from envy." The envious vizier approached the king and, kissing the ground before him, said, "O excellent King and glorious Lord, it was by your kindness and with your blessing that I rose to prominence; therefore, if I fail to advise you on a grave matter, I am not my father's son. If the great King and noble Lord commands, I shall disclose the matter to him." The king was upset and asked, "Damn you, what advice have you got?" The vizier replied, "Your Majesty, 'He who considers not the end, fortune is not his friend.' I have seen your Majesty make a mistake, for you have bestowed favors on your enemy who has come to destroy your power and steal your wealth. Indeed, you have pampered him and shown him many favors, but I fear that he will do you harm." The king asked, "Whom do you accuse, whom do you have in mind, and at whom do you point the finger?" The vizier replied, "If you are asleep, wake up, for I point the finger at the sage Duban, who has come from Byzantium." The king replied, "Damn you, is he my enemy? To me he is the most faithful, the dearest, and the most favored of people, for this sage has treated me simply by making me hold something in my hand and has cured me from the disease that had defied the physicians and the sages and rendered them helpless. In all the world, east and west, near and far, there is no one like him, yet you accuse him of such a thing. From this day onward, I will give him every month a thousand dinars, in addition to his rations and regular salary. Even if I were to share my wealth and my kingdom with him, it would be less than he deserves. I think that you have said what you said because you envy him. This is very much like the situation in the story told by the vizier of King Sindbad[7] when the king wanted to kill his own son.

But morning overtook Shahrazad, and she lapsed into silence. Then her sister Dinarzad said, "Sister, what a lovely story!" Shahrazad replied, "What is this compared with what I shall tell you tomorrow night! It will be stranger and more amazing."

THE FOURTEENTH NIGHT

The following night, when the king got into bed and Shahrazad got in with him, her sister Dinarzad said, "Please, sister, if you are not sleepy, tell us one of your lovely little tales to while away the night." Shahrazad replied, "Very well":

I heard, O happy King, that King Yunan's vizier asked, "King of the age, I beg your pardon, but what did King Sindbad's vizier tell the king when he wished to kill his own son?" King Yunan said to the vizier, "When King Sindbad, provoked by an envious man, wanted to kill his own son, his vizier said to him, 'Don't do what you will regret afterward.'"

---

7. Not to be confused with Sindbad the Sailor.

[The Tale of the Husband and the Parrot]

I have heard it told that there was once a very jealous man who had a wife so splendidly beautiful that she was perfection itself. The wife always refused to let her husband travel and leave her behind, until one day when he found it absolutely necessary to go on a journey. He went to the bird market, bought a parrot, and brought it home. The parrot was intelligent, knowledgeable, smart, and retentive. Then he went away on his journey, and when he finished his business and came back, he brought the parrot and inquired about his wife during his absence. The parrot gave him a day-by-day account of what his wife had done with her lover and how the two carried on in his absence. When the husband heard the account, he felt very angry, went to his wife, and gave her a sound beating. Thinking that one of her maids had informed her husband about what she did with her lover in her husband's absence, the wife interrogated her maids one by one, and they all swore that they had heard the parrot inform the husband.

When the wife heard that it was the parrot who had informed the husband, she ordered one of her maids to take the grinding stone and grind under the cage, ordered a second maid to sprinkle water over the cage, and ordered a third to carry a steel mirror and walk back and forth all night long. That night her husband stayed out, and when he came home in the morning, he brought the parrot, spoke with it, and asked about what had transpired in his absence that night. The parrot replied, "Master, forgive me, for last night, all night long, I was unable to hear or see very well because of the intense darkness, the rain, and the thunder and lightning." Seeing that it was summertime, during the month of July, the husband replied, "Woe unto you, this is no season for rain." The parrot said, "Yes, by God, all night long, I saw what I told you." The husband, concluding that the parrot had lied about his wife and had accused her falsely, got angry, and he grabbed the parrot and, taking it out of the cage, smote it on the ground and killed it. But after the parrot's death, the husband heard from his neighbors that the parrot had told the truth about his wife, and he was full of regret that he had been tricked by his wife to kill the parrot.

King Yunan concluded, "Vizier, the same will happen to me."

But morning overtook Shahrazad, and she lapsed into silence. Then her sister Dinarzad said, "What a strange and lovely story!" Shahrazad replied, "What is this compared with what I shall tell you tomorrow night! If the king spares me and lets me live, I shall tell you something more amazing." The king thought to himself, "By God, this is indeed an amazing story."

THE FIFTEENTH NIGHT

The following night Dinarzad said to her sister Shahrazad, "Please, sister, if you are not sleepy, tell us one of your lovely little tales, for they entertain and help everyone to forget his cares and banish sorrow from the heart." Shahrazad replied, "With the greatest pleasure." King Shahrayar added, "Let it be the remainder of the story of King Yunan, his vizier, and the sage Duban, and of the fisherman, the demon, and the jar." Shahrazad replied, "With the greatest pleasure":

I heard, O happy King, that King Yunan said to his envious vizier, "After the husband killed the parrot and heard from his neighbors that the parrot had told him the truth, he was filled with remorse. You too, my vizier, being envious of this wise man, would like me to kill him and regret it afterward, as did the husband after he killed the parrot." When the vizier heard what King Yunan said, he replied, "O great king, what harm has this sage done to me? Why, he has not harmed me in any way. I am telling you all this out of love and fear for you. If you don't discover my veracity, let me perish like the vizier who deceived the son of the king." King Yunan asked his vizier, "How so?" The vizier replied:

[The Tale of the King's Son and the She-Ghoul]

It is said, O happy King, that there was once a king who had a son who was fond of hunting and trapping. The prince had with him a vizier appointed by his father the king to follow him wherever he went. One day the prince went with his men into the wilderness, and when he chanced to see a wild beast, the vizier urged him to go after it. The prince pursued the beast and continued to press in pursuit until he lost its track and found himself alone in the wilderness, not knowing which way to turn or where to go, when he came upon a girl, standing on the road, in tears. When the young prince asked her, "Where do you come from?" she replied, "I am the daughter of an Indian king. I was riding in the wilderness when I dozed off and in my sleep fell off my horse and found myself alone and helpless." When the young prince heard what she said, he felt sorry for her, and he placed her behind him on his horse and rode on. As they passed by some ruins, she said, "O my lord, I wish to relieve myself here." He let her down and she went into the ruins. Then he went in after her, ignorant of what she was, and discovered that she was a she-ghoul, who was saying to her children, "I brought you a good, fat boy." They replied, "Mother, bring him to us, so that we may feed on his innards." When the young prince heard what they said, he shook with terror, and fearing for his life, ran outside. The she-ghoul followed him and asked, "Why are you afraid?" and he told her about his situation and his predicament, concluding, "I have been unfairly treated." She replied, "If you have been unfairly treated, ask the Almighty God for help, and He will protect you from harm." The young prince raised his eyes to Heaven . . .

But morning overtook Shahrazad, and she lapsed into silence. Then her sister Dinarzad said, "What a strange and lovely story!" Shahrazad replied, "What is this compared with what I shall tell you tomorrow night! It will be even stranger and more amazing."

THE SIXTEENTH NIGHT

The following night Dinarzad said, "Please, sister, if you are not sleepy, tell us one of your lovely little tales." Shahrazad replied, "I shall with pleasure":

I heard, O King, that the vizier said to King Yunan:

When the young prince said to the she-ghoul, "I have been unfairly treated," she replied, "Ask God for help, and He will protect you from harm." The young prince raised his eyes to Heaven and said, "O Lord, help me to prevail upon my enemy, for 'everything is within your power.'" When the she-ghoul heard his invocation, she gave up and departed, and he returned safely to his father and told him about the vizier and how it was he who had urged him to pursue the beast and drove him to his encounter with the she-ghoul. The king summoned the vizier and had him put to death.

The vizier added, "You too, your Majesty, if you trust, befriend, and bestow favors on this sage, he will plot to destroy you and cause your death. Your Majesty should realize that I know for certain that he is a foreign agent who has come to destroy you. Haven't you seen that he cured you externally, simply with something you held in your hand?" King Yunan, who was beginning to feel angry, replied, "You are right, vizier. The sage may well be what you say and may have come to destroy me. He who has cured me with something to hold can kill me with something to smell." Then the king asked the vizier, "My vizier and good counselor, how should I deal with him?" The vizier replied, "Send for him now and have him brought before you, and when he arrives, strike off his head. In this way, you will attain your aim and fulfill your wish." The king said, "This is good and sound advice." Then he sent for the sage Duban, who came immediately, still feeling happy at the favors, the money, and the robes the king had bestowed on him. When he entered, he pointed with his hand toward the king and began to recite the following verses:

> If I have been remiss in thanking you,
> For whom then have I made my verse and prose?
> You granted me your gifts before I asked,
> Without deferment and without excuse.
> How can I fail to praise your noble deeds,   5
> Inspired in private and in public by my muse?
> I thank you for your deeds and for your gifts,
> Which, though they bend my back, my care reduce.

The king asked, "Sage, do you know why I have had you brought before me?" The sage replied, "No, your Majesty." The king said, "I brought you here to have you killed and to destroy the breath of life within you." In astonishment Duban asked, "Why does your Majesty wish to have me put to death, and for what crime?" The king replied, "I have been told that you are a spy and that you have come to kill me. Today I will have you killed before you kill me. 'I will have you for lunch before you have me for dinner.'" Then the king called for the executioner and ordered him, saying, "Strike off the head of this sage and rid me of him! Strike!"

When the sage heard what the king said, he knew that because he had been favored by the king, someone had envied him, plotted against him, and lied to the king, in order to have him killed and get rid of him. The sage realized then that the king had little wisdom, judgment, or good sense, and he was filled with regret, when it was useless to regret. He said to himself, "There is no power and no strength, save in God the Almighty, the Magnificent. I did a good deed but was rewarded with an evil one." In the meantime, the king was shouting at the executioner, "Strike off his head." The sage implored, "Spare me, your Majesty, and God will spare you; destroy me, and God will destroy you." He repeated the statement, just as I did, O demon, but you too refused, insisting on killing me. King Yunan said to the sage, "Sage, you must die, for you have cured me with a mere handle, and I fear that you can kill me with anything." The sage replied, "This is my reward from your Majesty. You reward good with evil." The king said, "Don't stall; you must die today without delay." When the sage Duban became convinced that he was going to die, he was filled with grief and sorrow, and his eyes overflowed with tears. He blamed himself for doing a favor for one who does not deserve it and for sowing seeds in a barren soil and recited the following verses:

> Maimuna was a foolish girl,
> Though from a sage descended,
> And many with pretense to skill
> Are e'en on dry land upended.

The executioner approached the sage, bandaged his eyes, bound his hands, and raised the sword, while the sage cried, expressed regret, and implored, "For God's sake, your Majesty, spare me, and God will spare you; destroy me, and God will destroy you." Then he tearfully began to recite the following verses:

> They who deceive enjoy success,
> While I with my true counsel fail
> And am rewarded with disgrace.
> If I live, I'll nothing unveil;
> If I die, then curse all the men,   5
> The men who counsel and prevail.

Then the sage added, "Is this my reward from your Majesty? It is like the reward of the crocodile." The king asked, "What is the story of the crocodile?" The sage replied, "I am in no condition to tell you a story. For God's sake, spare me, and God will spare you. Destroy me, and God will destroy you," and he wept bitterly.

Then several noblemen approached the king and said, "We beg your Majesty to forgive him for our sake, for in our view, he has done nothing to deserve this." The king replied, "You do not know the reason why I wish to have him killed. I tell you that if I spare him, I will surely perish, for I fear that he who has cured me externally from my affliction, which had defied the Greek sages, simply by having me hold a handle, can kill me with anything I touch. I must kill him, in order to protect myself from him." The sage Duban implored again, "For God's sake, your Majesty, spare me, and God will spare you. Destroy me, and God will destroy you." The king insisted, "I must kill you."

Demon, when the sage realized that he was surely going to die, he said, "I beg your Majesty to postpone my execution until I return home, leave instructions for my burial, discharge my obligations, distribute alms, and donate my scientific and medical books to one who deserves them. I have in particular a book entitled *The Secret of Secrets*, which I should like to give you for safekeeping in your library." The king asked, "What is the secret of this book?" The sage replied, "It contains countless secrets, but the chief one is that if your Majesty has my head struck off, opens the book on the sixth leaf, reads three lines from the left page, and speaks to me, my head will speak and answer whatever you ask."

The king was greatly amazed and said, "Is it possible that if I cut off your head and, as you say, open the book, read the third line, and speak to your head, it will speak to me? This is the wonder of wonders." Then the king allowed the sage to go and sent him home under guard. The sage settled his affairs and on the following day returned to the royal palace and found assembled there the princes, viziers, chamberlains, lords of the realm, and military officers, as well as the king's retinue, servants, and many of his citizens. The sage Duban entered, carrying an old book and a kohl[8] jar containing powder. He sat down, ordered a platter, and poured out the powder and smoothed it on the platter. Then he said to the king, "Take this book, your Majesty, and don't open it until after my execution. When my head is cut off, let it be placed on the platter and order that it be pressed on the powder. Then open the book and begin to ask my head a question, for it will then answer you. There is no power and no strength save in God, the Almighty, the Magnificent. For God's sake, spare me, and God will spare you; destroy me, and God will destroy you." The king replied, "I must kill you, especially to see how your head will speak to me." Then the king took the book and ordered the executioner to strike off the sage's head. The executioner drew his sword and, with one stroke, dropped the head in the middle of the platter, and when he pressed the head on the powder, the bleeding stopped. Then the sage Duban opened his eyes and said, "Now, your Majesty, open the book." When the king opened the book, he found the pages stuck. So he put his finger in his mouth, wetted it with his saliva, and opened the first page, and he kept opening the pages with difficulty until he turned seven leaves. But when he looked in the book, he found nothing written inside, and he exclaimed, "Sage, I see nothing written in this book." The sage replied, "Open more pages." The king opened some more pages but still found nothing, and while he was doing this, the drug spread through his body—for the book had been poisoned—and he began to heave, sway, and twitch.

But morning overtook Shahrazad, and she lapsed into silence. Then her sister Dinarzad said, "Sister, what an amazing and entertaining story!" Shahrazad replied, "What is this compared with what I shall tell you tomorrow night if the king spares me and lets me live!"

THE SEVENTEENTH NIGHT

The following night Dinarzad said to her sister Shahrazad, "Please, sister, if you are not sleepy, tell us one of your lovely little tales to while away the night." The king added, "Let it be the rest of the story of the sage and the king and of the fisherman and the demon." Shahrazad replied, "Very well, with the greatest pleasure":

8. An ancient cosmetic used to darken the eyelids and as mascara, long employed by women in the Middle East.

I heard, O King, that when the sage Duban saw that the drug had spread through the king's body and that the king was heaving and swaying, he began to recite the following verses:

> For long they ruled us arbitrarily,
> But suddenly vanished their powerful rule.
> Had they been just, they would have happily
> Lived, but they oppressed, and punishing fate
> Afflicted them with ruin deservedly,   5
> And on the morrow the world taunted them,
> "'Tis tit for tat; blame not just destiny."

As the sage's head finished reciting the verses, the king fell dead, and at that very moment the head too succumbed to death. Demon, consider this story.

But morning overtook Shahrazad, and she lapsed into silence. Then her sister Dinarzad said, "Sister, what an entertaining story!" Shahrazad replied, "What is this compared with what I shall tell you tomorrow night if I live!"

THE EIGHTEENTH NIGHT

The following night, Dinarzad said to her sister Shahrazad, "Please, sister, if you are not sleepy, tell us one of your lovely little tales to while away the night." The king added, "Let it be the rest of the story of the fisherman and the demon." Shahrazad replied, "With the greatest pleasure":

I heard, O King, that the fisherman said to the demon, "Had the king spared the sage, God would have spared him and he would have lived, but he refused and insisted on destroying the sage, and the Almighty God destroyed him. You too, demon, had you from the beginning agreed to spare me, I would have spared you, but you refused and insisted on killing me; therefore, I shall punish you by keeping you in this jar and throwing you into the bottom of the sea." The demon cried out, "Fisherman, don't do it. Spare me and save me and don't blame me for my action and my offense against you. If I did ill, you should do good. As the saying goes, 'Be kind to him who wrongs you.' Don't do what Imama did to 'Atika." The fisherman asked, "What did Imama do to 'Atika?" The demon replied, "This is no time and this narrow prison is no place to tell a story, but I shall tell it to you after you release me." The fisherman said, "I must throw you into the sea. There is no way I would let you out and set you free, for I kept imploring you and calling on you, but you refused and insisted on killing me, without any offense or injury that merits punishment, except that I had set you free. When you treated me in this way, I realized that you were unclean from birth, that you were ill-natured, and that you were one who rewards good with ill. After I throw you into the sea, I shall build me a hut here and live in it for your sake, so that if anyone pulls you out, I shall acquaint him with what I suffered at your hands and shall advise him to throw you back into the sea and let you perish or languish there to the end of time, you the dirtiest of demons." The demon replied, "Set me free this time, and I pledge never to bother you or harm you, but to make you rich." When he heard this, the fisherman made the demon pledge and covenant that if the fisherman released him and let him out, he would not harm him but would serve him and be good to him.

After the fisherman secured the demon's pledge, by making him swear by the Almighty Name, he opened the seal of the jar, and the smoke began to rise. When the smoke was completely out of the jar, it gathered and turned again into a full-fledged demon, who kicked the jar away and sent it flying to the middle of the sea. When the fisherman saw what the demon had done, sure that he was going to meet with disaster and death, he wet himself and said, "This is a bad omen." Then he summoned his courage and cried out, "Demon, you have sworn and given me your pledge. Don't betray me. Come back, lest the Almighty God punish you for your betrayal. Demon, I repeat to you what the sage Duban said to King Yunan, 'Spare me, and God will spare you; destroy me, and God will destroy you.'" When the demon heard what the fisherman said, he laughed, and when the fisherman cried out again, "Demon, spare me," he replied, "Fisherman, follow me," and the fisherman followed him, hardly believing in his escape, until they came to a mountain outside the city. They climbed over to the other side and came to a vast wilderness, in the middle of which stood a lake surrounded by four hills.

The demon halted by the lake and ordered the fisherman to cast his net and fish. The fisherman looked at the lake and marveled as he saw fish in many colors, white, red, blue, and yellow. He cast his net, and when he pulled, he found four fish inside, one red, one white, one blue, and one yellow. When he saw them, he was full of admiration and delight. The demon said to him, "Take them to the king of your city and offer them to him, and he will give you enough to make you rich. Please excuse me, for I know no other way to make you rich. But don't fish here more than once a day." Then, saying, "I shall miss you," the demon kicked the ground with his foot, and it opened and swallowed him. The fisherman, O King, returned to the city, still marveling at his encounter with the demon and at the colored fish. He entered the royal palace, and when he offered the fish to the king, the king looked at them . . .

But morning overtook Shahrazad, and she lapsed into silence. Then Dinarzad said, "Sister, what an amazing and entertaining story!" Shahrazad replied, "What is this compared with what I shall tell you tomorrow night if the king spares me and lets me live!"

THE NINETEENTH NIGHT

The following night Dinarzad said to her sister Shahrazad, "Sister tell us the rest of the story and what happened to the fisherman." Shahrazad replied, "With the greatest pleasure":

I heard, O King, that when the fisherman presented the fish to the king, and the king looked at them and saw that they were colored, he took one of them in his hand and looked at it with great amazement. Then he said to his vizier, "Take them to the cook whom the emperor of Byzantium has given us as a present." The vizier took the fish and brought them to the girl and said to her, "Girl, as the saying goes, 'I save my tears for the time of trial.' The king has been presented these four fish, and he bids you fry them well." Then the vizier went back to report to the king, and the king ordered him to give the fisherman four hundred dirhams.[9] The vizier gave the money to the fisherman, who, receiving it, gathered it in the folds of his robe and went away, running, and as he ran, he stumbled and kept falling and getting up, thinking that he was in a dream. Then he stopped and bought some provisions for his family.

So far for the fisherman, O King. In the meantime the girl scaled the fish, cleaned them, and cut them into pieces. Then she placed the frying pan on the fire and poured in the sesame oil, and when it began to boil, she placed the fish in the frying pan. When the pieces were done on one side, she turned them over, but no sooner had she done this than the kitchen wall split open and there emerged a maiden with a beautiful figure, smooth cheeks, perfect features, and dark eyes. She wore a short-sleeved silk shirt in the Egyptian style, embroidered all around with lace and gold spangles. In her ears she wore dangling earrings; on her wrists she wore bracelets; and in her hand she held a bamboo wand. She thrust the wand into the frying pan and said in clear Arabic, "O fish, O fish, have you kept the pledge?" When the cook saw what had happened, she fainted. Then the maiden repeated what she had said, and the fish raised their heads from the frying pan and replied in clear Arabic, "Yes, yes. If you return, we shall return; if you keep your vow, we shall keep ours; and if you forsake us, we shall be even." At that moment the maiden overturned the frying pan and disappeared as she had come, and the kitchen wall closed behind her.

When the cook came to herself, she found the four fish charred, and she felt sorry for herself and afraid of the king, saying to herself, "'He broke his lance on his very first raid.' " While she remonstrated with herself, the vizier suddenly stood before her, saying, "Give me the fish, for we have set the table before the king, and he is waiting for them." The girl wept and told the vizier what she had seen and witnessed and what had happened to the fish. The vizier was astonished and said, "This is very strange." Then he sent an officer after the fisherman, and he returned a while later with the fisherman. The vizier shouted at him, saying, "Bring us at once four more fish like the ones you brought us before, for we have had an accident with them." When he followed with threats, the fisherman went home and, taking his fishing gear, went outside the city, climbed the mountain, and descended to the wilderness on the other side. When he came to the lake, he cast his net, and when he pulled up, he found inside four fish, as he had done the first time. Then he brought them back to the vizier, who took them to the girl and said, "Fry them in front of me, so that I can see for myself." The girl prepared the fish at once, placed the frying pan over the fire, and threw them in. When the fish were done, the wall split open, and the maiden appeared in her elegant clothes, wearing necklaces and other jewelry and holding in her hand the bamboo wand. Again she thrust the wand into the frying pan and said in clear Arabic, "O fish, have you kept the pledge?" and again the fish raised their heads and replied, "Yes, yes. If you return, we shall return; if you keep your vow, we shall keep ours; and if you forsake us, we shall be even."

9. Small silver coins.

But morning overtook Shahrazad, and she lapsed into silence. Then Dinarzad said, "What an entertaining story!" Shahrazad replied, "What is this compared with what I shall tell you tomorrow night if I live, the Almighty God willing!"

THE TWENTIETH NIGHT

The following night Dinarzad said to her sister Shahrazad, "Please, sister, if you are not sleepy, tell us one of your lovely little tales to while away the night." Shahrazad replied, "With the greatest pleasure":

I heard, O happy King, that after the fish spoke, the maiden overturned the frying pan with the wand and disappeared into the opening from which she had emerged, and the wall closed behind her. The vizier said to himself, "I can no longer hide this affair from the king," and he went to him and told him what had happened to the fish before his very eyes.

The king was exceedingly amazed and said, "I wish to see this with my own eyes." Then he sent for the fisherman, who came after a little while, and the king said to him, "I want you to bring me at once four more fish like the ones you brought before. Hurry!" Then he assigned three officers to guard the fisherman and sent him away. The fisherman disappeared for a while and returned with four fish, one red, one white, one blue, and one yellow. The king commanded, "Give him four hundred dirhams," and the fisherman, receiving the money, gathered it in the folds of his robe and went away. Then the king said to the vizier, "Fry the fish here in my presence." The vizier replied, "I hear and obey," and he called for a stove and a frying pan and sat to clean the fish. Then he lit the fire and, pouring the sesame oil, placed the fish in the frying pan.

When they were almost done, the palace wall split open, and the king and vizier began to tremble, and when they looked up, they saw a black slave who stood like a towering mountain or a giant descendant of the tribe of 'Ad.[1] He was as tall as a reed, as wide as a stone bench, and he held a green palm leaf in his hand. Then in clear but unpleasant language, he said, "O fish, O fish, have you kept the pledge?" and the fish raised their heads from the frying pan and said, "Yes, yes. If you return, we shall return; if you keep your vow, we shall keep ours; and if you forsake us, we shall be even." At that moment, the black slave overturned the frying pan, in the middle of the hall, and the fish turned into charcoal. Then the black slave departed as he had come, and the wall closed behind him. When the black slave disappeared, the king said, "I cannot sleep over this affair, for there is no doubt a mystery behind these fish." Then he bade the fisherman be brought before him again.

When the fisherman arrived, the king said to him, "Damn you, where do you catch these fish?" The fisherman replied, "My lord, I catch them in a lake that lies among four hills, on the other side of the mountain." The king turned to the vizier and asked, "Do you know this lake?" The vizier replied, "No, by God, your Majesty. For sixty years, I have hunted, traveled, and roamed far and wide, sometimes for a day or two, sometimes for a month or two, but I have

---

1. Tribe supposedly destroyed by God's wrath (Qur'an 41.15).

never seen or known that such a lake existed on the other side of the mountain." Then the king turned to the fisherman and asked him, "How far is this lake from here?" The fisherman replied, "King of the age, it is one hour from here." The king was astonished, and he ordered his soldiers to be ready. Then he rode out with his troops, behind the fisherman, who led the way under guard, muttering curses on the demon as he went.

They rode until they were outside the city. Then they climbed the mountain, and when they descended to the other side, they saw a vast wilderness that they had never seen in all their lives, as well as the four hills and the lake in whose clear water they saw the fish in four colors, red, white, blue, and yellow. The king stood marveling; then he turned to the vizier, princes, chamberlains, and deputies and asked, "Have any of you ever seen this lake before?" They replied, "Never." He asked, "And none of you knew where it was?" They kissed the ground before him and replied, "By God, your Majesty, till now we have never in our lives seen this lake or known about it, even though it is close to our city." The king said, "There is a mystery behind this. By God, I shall not return to the city until I find the answer to the mystery behind this lake and these fish in four colors." Then he ordered his men to halt and pitch the tents, and he dismounted and waited.

When it was dark, he summoned the vizier, who was an experienced and wise man of the world. The vizier came to the king, without being seen by the soldiers, and when he arrived, the king said, "I wish to reveal to you what I intend to do. At this very hour, I shall go all by myself to look for an answer to the mystery of this lake and these fish. Early tomorrow morning you shall sit at the entrance of my tent and tell the princes that the king is indisposed and that he has given you orders not to let anyone be admitted to his presence. You must not let anyone know about my departure and absence, and you must wait for me for three days." The vizier, unable to disobey him, abided by the order, saying, "I hear and obey."

Then the king packed, prepared himself, and girded himself with the royal sword. Then he climbed one of the four hills, and when he reached the top, he journeyed on for the rest of the night. In the morning, when the sun rose and steeped the mountaintop with light, the king looked and sighted a dark mass in the distance. When he saw it, he was glad, and he headed in its direction, saying to himself, "There may be someone there to give me information." He journeyed on, and when he arrived, he found a palace, built under a lucky star, with black stones and completely overlaid with iron plates. It had double doors, one open, one shut. Pleased, the king knocked gently at the door and waited patiently for a while without hearing any reply. He knocked again, this time more loudly than before, but again waited without hearing any reply or seeing anyone. He knocked for the third time and kept knocking repeatedly but once more waited without hearing any reply or seeing anyone. Then he said to himself, "There is no doubt that there is no one inside, or perhaps the palace is deserted." Summoning his courage, he entered and shouted from the hallway, "O inhabitants of the palace, I am a stranger and a hungry traveler. Have you any food? Our Lord will requite you and reward you for it." He shouted a second and a third time but heard no reply. Feeling bold and determined, he advanced from the hallway into the center of the palace and looked around, but saw no one.

But morning overtook Shahrazad, and she lapsed into silence. Then Dinarzad said, "Sister, what an amazing and entertaining story!" Shahrazad replied, "What is this compared with what I shall tell you tomorrow night if I live, the Almighty God willing!"

THE TWENTY-FIRST NIGHT

The following night Dinarzad said to her sister Shahrazad, "For God's sake, sister, if you are not sleepy, tell us one of your lovely little tales to while away the night." Shahrazad replied, "With the greatest pleasure":

I heard, O King, that the king walked to the center of the palace and looked around, but saw no one. The palace was furnished with silk carpets and leather mats and hung with drapes. There were also settees, benches, and seats with cushions, as well as cupboards. In the middle there stood a spacious courtyard, surrounded by four adjoining recessed courts facing each other. In the center stood a fountain, on top of which crouched four lions in red gold, spouting water from their mouths in droplets that looked like gems and pearls, and about the fountain singing birds fluttered under a high net to prevent them from flying away. When the king saw all this, without seeing anyone, he was astonished and regretted that he found none to give him any information. He sat pensively by one of the recessed courts, when he heard sad moans and lamentations and the following plaintive verses:

> My soul is torn between peril and toil;
> O life, dispatch me with one mighty blow.
> Lover, neither a bankrupt nor a noble man
> Humbled by love's law do you pity show.
> Ev'n from the breeze I jealously used to guard you,   5
> But at the blow of fate the eyes blind go.
> When, as he pulls to shoot, the bowstring breaks
> What can the bowman facing his foes do?
> And when the foes begin to congregate
> How can he then escape his cruel fate?   10

When the king heard the lamentation and the verses, he rose and moved toward the source of the voice until he came to a doorway behind a curtain, and when he lifted the curtain, he saw at the upper end of the room a young man sitting on a chair that rose about twenty inches above the floor. He was a handsome young man, with a full figure, clear voice, radiant brow, bright face, downy beard, and ruddy cheeks, graced with a mole like a speck of amber, just as the poet describes it:

> Here is a slender youth whose hair and face
> All mortals envelope with light or gloom.
> Mark on his cheek the mark of charm and grace,
> A dark spot on a red anemone.

The king greeted the seated young man, pleased to see him. The young man wore a long-sleeved robe of Egyptian silk with gold embroidery, and on his head he wore an Egyptian conical head covering, but his face showed signs of grief and sorrow. When the king greeted him, the young man greeted him back courteously and said, "Pardon me, sir, for not rising, for you deserve even a greater honor." The king replied, "Young man, you are pardoned. I myself am your guest, having come to you on a serious mission. Pray tell me the story behind the lake and the colored fish, as well as this palace and the fact that you sit alone and mourn with no one to console you." When the young man heard this, his tears began to flow over his cheeks until they drenched his breast. Then he sang the following *Mawwaliya* verses:[2]

> Say to the man whom life with arrows shot,
> "How many men have felt the blows of fate!"
> If you did sleep, the eyes of God have not;
> Who can say time is fair and life in constant state?

Then he wept bitterly. The king was astonished and asked, "Young man, why do you cry?" The young man replied, "Sir, how can I refrain from crying in my present condition?" Then he lifted the skirt of his robe, and the king saw that while one half of the young man, from the navel to the head, was human flesh, the other half, from the navel to the feet, was black stone.

But morning overcame Shahrazad, and she lapsed into silence. Then King Shahrayar thought to himself, "This is an amazing story. I am willing to postpone her execution even for a month, before having her put to death." While the king was thinking to himself, Dinarzad said to her sister Shahrazad, "Sister, what an entertaining story!" Shahrazad replied, "What is this compared with what I shall tell you tomorrow night if I live, the Almighty God willing!"

THE TWENTY-SECOND NIGHT

The following night Shahrazad said:

I heard, O King, that when the king saw the young man in this condition, he felt very sad and sorry for him, and said with a sigh, "Young man, you have added one more worry to my worries. I came to look for an answer to the mystery of the fish, in order to save them, but ended up looking for an answer to your case, as well as the fish. There is no power and no strength save in God, the Almighty, the Magnificent. Hurry up, young man, and tell me your story." The young man replied, "Lend me your ears, your eyes, and your mind." The king replied, "My ears, my eyes, and my mind are ready." The young man said:

[The Tale of the Enchanted King]

My story, and the story of the fish, is a strange and amazing one, which, if it could be engraved with needles at the corner of the eye,[3] would be a lesson to

---

2. Poem in colloquial language, often sung to the accompaniment of a reed pipe.
3. I.e., if a master calligrapher could by a miracle of his art write the entire story at the corner of an eye, it would then be read as a double miracle: one for the extraordinary events, one for the extraordinary art.

those who would consider. My lord, my father was the king of this city, and his name was King Mahmud of the Black Islands. For these four hills were islands. He ruled for seventy years, and when he died, I succeeded him and married my cousin. She loved me very much, so much so that if I was away from her even for a single day, she would refuse to eat and drink until I returned to her. In this way, we lived together for five years until one day she went to the bath and I ordered the cook to grill meat and prepare a sumptuous supper for her. Then I entered this palace, lay down in this very spot where you are sitting now, and ordered two maids to sit down, one at my head and one at my feet, to fan me. But I felt uneasy and could not go to sleep. While I lay with my eyes closed, breathing heavily, I heard the girl at my head say to the one at my feet, "O Mas'uda, what a pity for our poor master with our damned mistress, and him so young!" The other one replied, "What can one say? May God damn all treacherous, adulterous women. Alas, it is not right that such a young man like our master lives with this bitch who spends every night out." Mas'uda added, "Is our master stupid? When he wakes up at night, doesn't he find that she is not by his side?" The other replied, "Alas, may God trip the bitch our mistress. Does she leave our master with his wits about him? No. She places a sleeping potion in the last drink he takes, offers him the cup, and when he drinks it, he sleeps like a dead man. Then she leaves him and stays out till dawn. When she returns, she burns incense under his nose, and when he inhales it, he wakes up. What a pity!"

My lord, when I heard the conversation between the two maids, I was extremely angry and I could hardly wait for the night to come. When my wife returned from the bath, we had the meal served but ate very little. Then we retired to my bed and I pretended to drink the contents of the cup, which I poured out, and went to sleep. No sooner had I fallen on my side than my wife said, "Go to sleep, and may you never rise again. By God, your sight disgusts me and your company bores me." Then she put on her clothes, perfumed herself with burning incense and, taking my sword, girded herself with it. Then she opened the door and walked out. My lord, I got up . . .

But morning overtook Shahrazad, and she lapsed into silence. Then Dinarzad said, "O my lady, what an amazing and entertaining story!" Shahrazad replied, "What is this compared with what I shall tell you tomorrow night!"

THE TWENTY-THIRD NIGHT

The following night Dinarzad said to her sister Shahrazad, "Please, sister, if you are not sleepy, tell us one of your lovely little tales." Shahrazad replied, "With the greatest pleasure":

It is related, O King, that the enchanted young man said to the king:

Then I followed her, as she left the palace and traversed my city until she stood at the city gate. There she uttered words I could not understand, and the locks fell off and the gate opened by itself. She went out, and I followed her until she slipped through the trash mounds and came to a hut built with palm leaves, leading to a domed structure built with sun-dried bricks. After she entered, I

climbed to the top of the dome, and when I looked inside, I saw my wife standing before a decrepit black man sitting on reed shavings and dressed in tatters.
She kissed the ground before him and he raised his head and said, "Damn you,
why are you late? My black cousins were here. They played with the bat and
ball, sang, and drank brewed liquor. They had a good time, each with his own
girlfriend, except for myself, for I refused even to drink with them because you
were absent."

My wife replied, "O my lord and lover, don't you know that I am married to
my cousin, who finds me most loathsome and detests me more than anyone
else? Were it not for your sake, I would not have let the sun rise before reducing his city to rubble, a dwelling place for the bears and the foxes, where the
owl hoots and the crow crows, and would have hurled its stones beyond Mount
Qaf."[4] He replied, "Damn you, you are lying. I swear in the name of black chivalry that as of tonight, if our cousins visit me and you fail to be present, I will
never befriend you, lie down with you, or let my body touch yours. You cursed
woman, you have been playing with me like a piece of marble, and I am subject
to your whims, you cursed, rotten woman." My lord, when I heard their conversation, the world started to turn black before my eyes, and I lost my senses.
Then I heard my wife crying and imploring, "O my lover and my heart's desire,
if you remain angry at me, whom else have I got, and if you turn me out, who
will take me in, O my lord, my lover, and light of my eye?" She kept crying and
begging until he was appeased. Then, feeling happy, she took off her outer garments, and asked, "My lord, have you anything for your little girl to eat?" The
black man replied, "Open the copper basin," and when she lifted the lid, she
found some leftover fried rat bones. After she ate them, he said to her, "There
is some brewed liquor left in that jug. You may drink it." She drank the liquor
and washed her hands and lay beside the black man on the reed shavings.
Then she undressed and slipped under his tatters. I climbed down from the top
of the dome and, entering through the door, grabbed the sword that my wife
had brought with her, and drew it, intending to kill both of them. I first struck
the black man on the neck and thought that I had killed him.

*But morning overtook Shahrazad, and she lapsed into silence. Then Dinarzad
said, "Sister, what an entertaining story!" Shahrazad replied, "Tomorrow night I
shall tell you something more entertaining if I live!"*

THE TWENTY-FOURTH NIGHT

*The following night Dinarzad said to her sister Shahrazad, "For God's sake, sister, if
you are not sleepy, tell us one of your lovely little tales." Shahrazad replied, "With
the greatest pleasure":*

I heard, O King, that the enchanted young man said to the king:

My lord, I struck the black man on the neck, but failed to cut the two arteries.
Instead I only cut into the skin and flesh of the throat and thought that I had
killed him. He began to snort violently, and my wife pulled away from him. I

---

4. Legendary mountain cited for its remoteness.

retreated, put the sword back in its place, and went back to the city. I entered the palace and went to sleep in my bed till morning. When my wife arrived and I looked at her, I saw that she had cut her hair and put on a mourning dress. She said, "Husband, don't reproach me for what I am doing, for I have received news that my mother has died, that my father was killed in the holy war, and that my two brothers have also lost their lives, one in battle, the other bitten by a snake. I have every reason to weep and mourn." When I heard what she said, I did not reply, except to say, "I don't reproach you. Do as you wish."

She mourned for an entire year, weeping and wailing. When the year ended, she said to me, "I want you to let me build inside the palace a mausoleum for me to use as a special place of mourning and to call it the house of sorrows." I replied, "Go ahead." Then she gave the order, and a house of mourning was erected for her, with a domed mausoleum and a tomb inside. Then, my lord, she moved the wounded black man to the mausoleum and placed him in the tomb. But, although he was still alive, from the day I cut his throat, he never spoke a word or was able to do her any good, except to drink liquids. She visited him in the mausoleum every day, morning and evening, bringing with her beverages and broth, and she kept at it for an entire year, while I held my patience and left her to her own devices. One day, while she was unaware, I entered the mausoleum and found her crying and lamenting:

> When I see your distress,
> It pains me, as you see.
> And when I see you not,
> It pains me, as you see.
> O speak to me, my life,　　　　　　　　　　5
> My master, talk to me.

Then she sang:

> The day I have you is the day I crave;
> The day you leave me is the day I die.
> Were I to live in fear of promised death,
> I'd rather be with you than my life save.

Then she recited the following verses:

> If I had every blessing in the world
> And all the kingdom of the Persian king,
> If I see not your person with my eyes,
> All this will not be worth an insect's wing.

When she stopped crying, I said to her, "Wife, you have mourned and wept enough and further tears are useless." She replied, "Husband, do not interfere with my mourning. If you interfere again, I will kill myself." I kept quiet and left her alone, while she mourned, wept, and lamented for another year. One day, after the third year, feeling the strain of this drawn-out, heavy burden, something happened to trigger my anger, and when I returned, I found my wife in the mausoleum, beside the tomb, saying, "My lord, I have not had any word from you. For three years I have had no reply." Then she recited the following verses:

O tomb, O tomb, has he his beauties lost,
Or have you lost yourself that radiant look?
O tomb, neither a garden nor a star,
The sun and moon at once how can you host?

These verses added anger to my anger, and I said to myself, "Oh, how much longer shall I endure?" Then I burst out with the following verses:

O tomb, O tomb, has he his blackness lost,
Or have you lost yourself that filthy look?
O tomb, neither a toilet nor a heap of dirt,
Charcoal and mud at once how can you host?

When my wife heard me, she sprang up and said, "Damn you, dirty dog. It was you who did this to me, wounded my beloved, and tormented me by depriving me of his youth, while he has been lying here for three years, neither alive nor dead." I said to her, "You, dirtiest of whores and filthiest of all venal women who ever desired and copulated with black slaves, yes it was I who did this to him." Then I grabbed my sword and drew it to strike her. But when she heard me and realized that I was determined to kill her, she laughed and said, "Get away, you dog. Alas, alas, what is done cannot be undone; nor will the dead come back to life, but God has delivered into my hand the one who did this to me and set my heart ablaze with the fire of revenge." Then she stood up, uttered words I could not understand, and cried, "With my magic and cunning, be half man, half stone." Sir, from that instant, I have been as you now see me, dejected and sad, helpless and sleepless, neither living with the living nor dead among the dead.

But morning overtook Shahrazad, and she lapsed into silence. Then Dinarzad said, "Sister, what an amazing and entertaining story!" Shahrazad replied, "Tomorrow night I shall tell you something more entertaining if the king spares me and lets me live!"

THE TWENTY-FIFTH NIGHT

The following night Dinarzad said to her sister Shahrazad, "Sister, if you are not sleepy, tell us one of your lovely little tales to while away the night." Shahrazad replied, "With the greatest pleasure":

It is related, O King, that the enchanted young man said to the king:

"After my wife turned me into this condition, she cast a spell on the city, with all its gardens, fields, and markets, the very place where your troops are camping now. My wife turned the inhabitants of my city, who belonged to four sects, Muslims, Magians,[5] Christians, and Jews, into fish, the Muslims white, the Magians red, the Christians blue, and the Jews yellow. Likewise, she turned the islands into four hills surrounding the lake. As if what she has done to me and the city is not enough, she strips me naked every day and gives me a hundred lashes with the

5. Priests of Zoroastrianism, a dualistic religion (emphasizing the cosmic struggle between good and evil) that was dominant in Persia before Islam.

whip until my back is lacerated and begins to bleed. Then she clothes my upper half with a hairshirt like a coarse rug and covers it with these luxurious garments." Then the young man burst into tears and recited the following verses:

> O Lord, I bear with patience your decree,
> And so that I may please you, I endure,
> That for their tyranny and unfair use
> Our recompense your Paradise may be.
> You never let the tyrant go, my Lord;   5
> Pluck me out of the fire, Almighty God.

The king said to the young man, "Young man, you have lifted one anxiety but added another worry to my worries. But where is your wife, and where is the mausoleum with the wounded black man?" The young man replied, "O King, the black slave is lying in the tomb inside the mausoleum, which is in the adjoining room. My wife comes to visit him at dawn every day, and when she comes, she strips me naked and gives me a hundred lashes with the whip, while I cry and scream without being able to stand up and defend myself, since I am half stone, half flesh and blood. After she punishes me, she goes to the black slave to give him beverages and broth to drink. Tomorrow at dawn she will come as usual." The king replied, "By God, young man, I shall do something for you that will go down in history and commemorate my name." Then the king sat to converse with the young man until night fell and they went to sleep.

The king got up before dawn, took off his clothes, and, drawing his sword, entered the room with the domed mausoleum and found it lit with candles and lamps and scented with incense, perfume, saffron, and ointments. He went straight to the black man and killed him. Then he carried him out and threw him in a well inside the palace. When he came back, he put on the clothes of the black man, covered himself, and lay hiding at the bottom of the tomb, with the drawn sword hidden under his clothes.

A while later, the cursed witch arrived, and the first thing she did was to strip her husband naked, take a whip, and whip him again and again, while he cried, "Ah wife, have pity on me; help me; I have had enough punishment and pain; have pity on me." She replied, "You should have had pity on me and spared my lover."

But morning overtook Shahrazad, and she lapsed into silence. Then Dinarzad said, "Sister, what an amazing and entertaining story!" Shahrazad replied, "What is this compared with what I shall tell you tomorrow night if I live!" King Shahrayar, with a mixture of amazement, pain, and sorrow for the enchanted youth, said to himself, "By God, I shall postpone her execution for tonight and many more nights, even for two months, until I hear the rest of the story and find out what happened to the enchanted young man. Then I shall have her put to death, as I did the others." So he said to himself.

THE TWENTY-SIXTH NIGHT

The following night Dinarzad said to Shahrazad, "Sister, if you are not sleepy, tell us one of your lovely little tales to while away the night." Shahrazad replied, "With the greatest pleasure":

I heard, O King, that after the witch punished her husband by whipping him until his sides and shoulders were bleeding and she satisfied her thirst for revenge, she dressed him with the coarse hairshirt and covered it with the outer garments. Then she headed to the black man, with the usual cup of drink and the broth. She entered the mausoleum, reached the tomb, and began to cry, wail, and lament, saying, "Lover, denying me yourself is not your custom. Do not be stingy, for my foes gloat over our separation. Be generous with your love, for forsaking is not your custom. Visit me, for my life is in your visit. O my lord, speak to me; O my lord, entertain me." Then she sang the following verses of the *Mufrad*[6] variety:

> For how long is this cruel disdain,
> Have I not paid with enough tears?
> O lover, talk to me,
> O lover, speak to me,
> O lover, answer me.   5

The king lowered his voice, stammered, and simulating the accent of black people, said, "Ah, ah, ah! There is no power and no strength save in God the Almighty, the Magnificent." When she heard him speak, she screamed with joy and fainted, and when she came to herself, she cried, "Is it true that you spoke to me?" The king replied, "Damn you, you don't deserve that anyone should speak to you or answer you." She asked, "What is the cause?" He replied, "All day long you punish your husband, while he screams for help. From sunset till dawn he cries, implores, and invokes God against you and me, with his deafening and enervating cries that deprive me of sleep. If it had not been for this, I would have recovered a long time ago, and this is why I have not spoken to you or answered you." She said, "My lord, if you allow me, I shall deliver him from his present condition." He replied, "Deliver him and rid us of his noise."

She went out of the mausoleum, took a bowl, and, filling it with water, uttered a spell over it, and the water began to boil and bubble as in a caldron over fire. Then she sprinkled the young man with the water and said, "By the power of my spell, if the Creator has created you in this form, or if he has turned you into this form out of anger at you, stay as you are, but if you have been transformed by my magic and cunning, turn back to your normal form, by the will of God, Creator of the world." The young man shook himself at once and stood up, erect and sound, and he rejoiced and thanked God for his deliverance. Then his wife said to him, "Get out of my sight and don't ever come back, for if you do and I see you here, I shall kill you." She yelled at him, and he went away.

Then she returned to the mausoleum and, descending to the tomb, called out, "My sweet lord, come out and let me see your handsome face." The king replied in a muffled voice, "You have rid me of the limb, but failed to rid us of the body." She asked, "My sweet lord, what do you mean by the body?" He replied, "Damn you, cursed woman, it is the inhabitants of this city and its four islands, for every night at midnight, the fish raise their heads from the lake to implore and invoke God against me, and this is why I do not recover. Go to them and deliver them at once; then come back to hold my hand and help me rise, for I am beginning to feel better already." When she heard him, she

---

6. Literally "single," a verse form.

rejoiced and replied joyfully, "Yes, my lord, yes, with God's help, my sweet-heart." Then she rose, went to the lake, and took a little of its water.

But morning overtook Shahrazad, and she lapsed into silence. Then Dinarzad said, "What an amazing and entertaining story!" Shahrazad replied, "What is this compared with what I shall tell you tomorrow night if the king spares me and I live!"

THE TWENTY-SEVENTH NIGHT

The following night Dinarzad said to her sister Shahrazad, "If you are not sleepy, tell us one of your lovely little tales to while away the night." Shahrazad replied, "With the greatest pleasure":

It is related, O King, that the wife uttered some words over the lake, and the fish began to dance, and at that instant the spell was lifted, and the townspeople resumed their usual activities and returned to their buying and selling. Then she went back to the palace, entered the mausoleum, and said, "My lord, give me your gracious hand and rise." The king replied in a muffled voice, "Come closer to me." She moved closer, while he urged her "Come closer still," and she moved until her body touched his. Then he pushed her back and with one stroke of the sword sliced her in half, and she fell in two to the ground.

Then the king went out and, finding the enchanted young man waiting for him, congratulated him on his deliverance, and the young man kissed his hand, thanked him, and invoked God's blessing on him. Then the king asked him, "Do you wish to stay here or come with me to my city?" The young man replied, "King of the age, and Lord of the world, do you know the distance between your city and mine?" The king replied, "It is a half-day journey." The young man said, "O King, you are dreaming, for between your city and mine it is a full year's journey. You reached us in half a day because the city was enchanted." The king asked, "Still, do you wish to stay here in your city or come with me?" The young man replied, "O King, I shall not part from you, even for one moment." The king was happy and said, "Thank God who has given you to me. You shall be a son to me, for I have never had one." They embraced, holding each other closely, and felt happy. Then they walked together back to the palace, and when they entered the palace, the enchanted young king announced to the eminent men of his kingdom and to his retinue that he was going on a journey.

He spent ten days in preparation, packing what he needed, together with the gifts that the princes and merchants of the city had given him for his journey. Then he set out with the king, with his heart on fire to be leaving his city for a whole year. He left, with fifty Mamluks and many guides and servants, bearing one hundred loads of gifts, rarities, and treasures, as well as money. They journeyed on, evening and morning, night and day, for a whole year until God granted them safe passage and they reached their destination. Then the king sent someone to inform the vizier of his safe return, and the vizier came out with all the troops and most of the townspeople to meet him. Having given him up for lost, they were exceedingly happy, and the city was decorated and its streets were spread with silk carpets. The vizier and the soldiers dismounted and, kissing the ground before the king, congratulated him on his safety and invoked God's blessing on him.

Then they entered the city, and the king sat on his throne and, meeting with the vizier, explained to him why he had been absent for an entire year. He told him the story of the young man and how he, the king, had dealt with the young man's wife and saved him and the city, and the vizier turned to the young man and congratulated him on his deliverance. Then the princes, viziers, chamberlains, and deputies took their places, and the king bestowed on them robes of honor, gifts, and other favors. Then he sent for the fisherman, who was the cause of saving the young man and the city, and when the fisherman stood before the king, the king bestowed on him robes of honor, and then asked him, "Do you have any children?" The fisherman replied that he had one boy and two girls. The king had them brought before him, and he himself married one of the girls, while he married the other to the enchanted young man. Moreover, the king took the fisherman's son into his service and made him one of his attendants. Then he conferred authority on the vizier, appointing him king of the city of the Black Islands, supplied him with provisions and fodder for the journey, and ordered the fifty Mamluks, who had come with them, as well as a host of other people, to go with him. He also sent with him many robes of honor and many fine gifts for all the princes and prominent men there. The vizier took his leave, kissed the king's hand, and departed. The king, the enchanted young man, and the fisherman lived peacefully thereafter, and the fisherman became one of the richest men of his time, with daughters married to kings.

But morning overtook Shahrazad, and she lapsed into silence. Then Dinarzad said, "What an amazing and entertaining story!" Shahrazad replied, "What is this compared with what I shall tell you tomorrow night if the king spares me and lets me live!"

THE TWENTY-EIGHTH NIGHT

The following night Dinarza said to her sister Shahrazad, "Sister, if you are not sleepy, tell us one of your lovely tales." Shaharazad replied, "With greatest pleasure":

[The Story of the Porter and the Three Ladies]

I heard, O happy King, that once there lived in the city of Baghdad[7] a bachelor who worked as a porter. One day he was standing in the market, leaning on his basket, when a woman approached him. She wore a Mosul[8] cloak, a silk veil, a fine kerchief embroidered with gold, and a pair of leggings tied with fluttering laces. When she lifted her veil, she revealed a pair of beautiful dark eyes graced with long lashes and a tender expression, like those celebrated by the poets. Then with a soft voice and a sweet tone, she said to him, "Porter, take your basket and follow me." Hardly believing his ears, the porter took his basket and hurried behind her, saying, "O lucky day, O happy day." She walked before him until she stopped at the door of a house, and when she knocked, an old Christian came down, received a dinar from her and handed her an olive-green jug

---

7. Then and now capital of Iraq, at that time capital of the Abbasid caliphate and its empire, situated on the Tigris River. It is the scene of several of the stories of the *Nights*.
8. Then and now an important city in northern Iraq.

of wine. She placed the jug in the basket and said, "Porter, take your basket and follow me." Saying, "Very well, O auspicious day, O lucky day, O happy day," the porter lifted the basket and followed her until she stopped at the fruit vendor's, where she bought yellow and red apples, Hebron peaches and Turkish quinces, and seacoast lemons and royal oranges, as well as baby cucumbers. She also bought Aleppo jasmine and Damascus lilies, myrtle berries and mignonettes, daisies and gillyflowers, lilies of the valley and irises, narcissus and daffodils, violets and anemones, as well as pomegranate blossoms. She placed everything in the porter's basket and asked him to follow her.

Then she stopped at the butcher's and said, "Cut me off ten pounds of fresh mutton." She paid him, and he cut off the pieces she desired, wrapped them, and handed them to her. She placed them in the basket, together with some charcoal, and said, "Porter, take your basket and follow me." The porter, wondering at all these purchases, placed his basket on his head and followed her until she came to the grocer's, where she bought whatever she needed of condiments, such as olives of all kinds, pitted, salted, and pickled, tarragon, cream cheese, Syrian cheese, and sweet as well as sour pickles. She placed the container in the basket and said, "Porter, take your basket and follow me." The porter carried his basket and followed her until she came to the dry grocer's, where she bought all sorts of dry fruits and nuts: Aleppo raisins, Iraqi sugar canes, pressed Ba'albak figs, roasted chick-peas, as well as shelled pistachios, almonds, and hazelnuts. She placed everything in the porter's basket, turned to him, and said, "Porter take your basket and follow me."

The porter carried the basket and followed her until she came to the confectioner's, where she bought a whole tray full of every kind of pastry and sweet in the shop, such as sour barley rolls, sweet rolls, date rolls, Cairo rolls, Turkish rolls, and open-worked Balkan rolls, as well as cookies, stuffed and musk-scented kataifs, amber combs, ladyfingers, widows' bread, Kadi's tidbits, eat-and-thanks, and almond pudding. When she placed the tray in the basket, the porter said, to her, "Mistress, if you had let me know, I would have brought with me a nag or a camel to carry all these purchases." She smiled and walked ahead until she came to the druggist's, where she bought ten bottles of scented waters, lilywater, rosewater scented with musk, and the like, as well as ambergris, musk, aloewood, and rosemary. She also bought two loaves of sugar and candles and torches. Then she put everything in the basket, turned to the porter, and said, "Porter, take your basket and follow me." The porter carried the basket and walked behind her until she came to a spacious courtyard facing a tall, stately mansion with massive pillars and a double door inlaid with ivory and shining gold. The girl stopped at the door and knocked gently.

But morning overtook Shahrazad, and she lapsed into silence. Then her sister said, "Sister, what a lovely and entertaining story!" Shahrazad replied, "What is this compared with what I shall tell you tomorrow night if the king spares me and lets me live! May God grant him long life."

THE TWENTY-NINTH NIGHT

The following night Dinarzad said to her sister Shahrazad, "Sister, if you are not sleepy, tell us one of your little tales to while away the night." Shahrazad replied, "I hear and obey":

I heard, O wise and happy King, that as the porter stood with the basket, at the door, behind the girl, marveling at her beauty, her charm, and her elegant, eloquent, and liberal ways, the door was unlocked, and the two leaves swung open. The porter, looking to see who opened the door, saw a full-bosomed girl, about five feet tall. She was all charm, beauty, and perfect grace, with a forehead like the new moon, eyes like those of a deer or wild heifer, eyebrows like the crescent in the month of Sha'ban,[9] cheeks like red anemones, mouth like the seal of Solomon, lips like red carnelian, teeth like a row of pearls set in coral, neck like a cake for a king, bosom like a fountain, breasts like a pair of big pomegranates resembling a rabbit with uplifted ears, and belly with a navel like a cup that holds a pound of benzoin ointment. She was like her of whom the poet aptly said:

> On stately sun and full moon cast your sight;
> Savor the flowers and lavender's delight.
> Your eyes have never seen such white in black,
> Such radiant face with hair so deeply dark.
> With rosy cheeks, Beauty proclaimed her name,
> To those who had not yet received her fame.
> Her swaying heavy hips I joyed to see,
> But her sweet, slender waist brought tears to me.

When the porter saw her, he lost his senses and his wits, and the basket nearly fell from his head, as he exclaimed, "Never in my life have I seen a more blessed day than this!" Then the girl who had opened the door said to the girl who had done the shopping, "Sister, what are you waiting for? Come in and relieve this poor man of his heavy burden." The shopper and the porter went in, and the doorkeeper locked the door and followed them until they came to a spacious, well-appointed, and splendid hall. It had arched compartments and niches with carved woodwork; it had a booth hung with drapes; and it had closets and cupboards covered with curtains. In the middle stood a large pool full of water, with a fountain in the center, and at the far end stood a couch of black juniper wood, covered with white silk and set with gems and pearls, with a canopylike mosquito net of red silk, fastened with pearls as big as hazelnuts or bigger. The curtain was unfastened, and a dazzling girl emerged, with genial charm, wise mien, and features as radiant as the moon, She had an elegant figure, the scent of ambergris, sugared lips, Babylonian eyes, with eyebrows as arched as a pair of bent bows, and a face whose radiance put the shining sun to shame, for she was like a great star soaring in the heavens, or a dome of gold, or an unveiled bride, or a splendid fish swimming in a fountain, or a morsel of luscious fat in a bowl of milk soup. She was like her of whom the poet said:

> Her smile reveals twin rows of pearls
> Or white daisies or pearly hail.
> Her forelock like the night unfurls;
> Before her light the sun is pale.

The third girl rose from the couch and strutted slowly until she joined her sisters in the middle of the hall, saying, "Why are you standing? Lift the load

9. The eighth month of the lunar Muslim year.

off this poor man." The doorkeeper stood in front of the porter, and the shopper stood behind him, and with the help of the third girl, they lifted the basket down and emptied its contents, stacking up the fruits and pickles on one side and the flowers and fresh herbs on the other. When everything was arranged, they gave the porter one dinar and said . . .

But morning overtook Shahrazad, and she lapsed into silence. Then Dinarzad said to her sister Shahrazad, "What an amazing and entertaining story!" Shahrazad replied, "If I am alive tomorrow night, I shall tell you something stranger and more amazing than this."

THE THIRTIETH NIGHT

The following night Dinarzad said to her sister Shahrazad, "Sister, tell us the rest of the story of the three girls." Shahrazad replied, "With the greatest pleasure":

I heard, O King, that when the porter saw how charming and beautiful the girls were and saw how much they had stacked of wine, meat, fruits, nuts, sweets, fresh herbs, candles, charcoal, and the like for drinking and carousing, without seeing any man around, he was very astonished and stood there, hesitant to leave. One of the girls asked him, "Why don't you go? Do you find your pay too little?" and, turning to her sister, said, "Give him another dinar." The porter replied, "By God, ladies, my pay is not little, for I deserve not even two dirhams, but I have been wondering about your situation and the absence of anyone to entertain you. For as a table needs four legs to stand on, you being three, likewise need a fourth, for the pleasure of men is not complete without women, and the pleasure of women is not complete without men. The poet says:

> For our delight four things we need, the lute,
> The harp, the zither, and the double flute,
> Blending with the scent of four lovely flowers,
> Roses, myrtles, anemones, and gillyflowers.
> Only in four such things join together,   5
> Money, and wine, and youth, and a lover.

You are three and you need a fourth, a man." His words pleased the girls, who laughed and said, "How can we manage that, being girls who keep our business to ourselves, for we fear to entrust our secrets where they may not be kept. We have read in some book what ibn al-Tammam[1] has said:

> Your own secret to none reveal;
> It will be lost when it is told.
> If your own breast cannot conceal,
> How can another better hold?"

When the porter heard their words, he replied, "Trust me; I am a sensible and wise man. I have studied the sciences and attained knowledge; I have read and learned, and presented my knowledge and cited my authorities. I reveal the

---

1. Actually Abu-Tamman, an Arab poet of the ninth century, and author of the *Hamasa*.

good and conceal the bad, and I am well-behaved. I am like the man of whom the poet said:

> Only the faithful does a secret keep;
> None but the best can hold it unrevealed.
> I keep a secret in a well-shut house
> Of which the key is lost and the lock sealed."

When the girls heard what he said, they replied, "You know very well that this table has cost us a lot and that we have spent a great deal of money to get all these provisions. Do you have anything to pay in return for the entertainment? For we shall not let you stay unless we see your share; otherwise you will drink and enjoy yourself with us at our expense." The mistress of the house said, '"Without gain, love is not worth a grain.'" The doorkeeper added, "Have you got anything, my dear? If you are emptyhanded, go emptyhanded." But the shopper said, "Sisters, stop teasing him, for by God, he served me well today; no one else would have been as patient with me. Whatever his share will come to, I shall pay for him myself." The porter, overjoyed, kissed the ground before her and thanked her, saying, "By God, it was you who brought me my first business today and I still have the dinar you gave me; take it back and take me, not as a companion but as a servant." The girls replied, "You are very welcome to join us."

Then the shopper, girding herself, began to arrange this and that. She first tidied up, strained the wine, stacked up the flasks, and arranged the bowls, goblets, cups, decanters, plates, and serving spoons, as well as various utensils in silver and gold. Having prepared all the requisites, she set the table by the pool and laid it with all kinds of food and drink. Then she invited them to the banquet and sat down to serve. Her sisters joined her, as did the porter, who thought that he was in a dream. She filled the first cup and drank it, filled the second and offered it to one of her sisters, who drank it, filled a third and gave it to the other sister to drink, and filled a fourth and gave it to the porter, who held it in his hand and, saluting with a bow, thanked her and recited the following verses:

> Drink not the cup, save with a friend you trust,
> One whose blood to noble forefathers owes.
> Wine, like the wind, is sweet if o'er the sweet,
> And foul if o'er the foul it haply blows.

Then he emptied his cup, and the doorkeeper returned his salute and recited the following verses:

> Cheers, and drink it in good health;
> This wine is good for your health.

The porter thanked her and kissed her hand. After the girls had drunk again and had given the porter more to drink, he turned to his companion, the shopper, saying, "My lady, your servant is calling on you," and recited the following verses:

> One of your slaves is waiting at your door,
> With ample thanks for your ample favor.

She replied "By God, you are welcome. Drink the wine and enjoy it in good health, for it relieves pain, hastens the cure, and restores health." The porter emptied his cup and, pouring out another, kissed her hand, offered it to her, and proceeded to recite the following verses:

> I gave her pure old wine, red as her cheeks,
> Which with red fire did like a furnace glow.
> She kissed the brim and with a smile she asked,
> "How can you cheeks with cheeks pay what you owe?"
> I said, "Drink! This wine is my blood and tears,   5
> And my soul is the fragrance in the cup."
> She said, "If for me you have shed your blood,
> Most gladly will I on this red wine sup."

The girl took the cup, drank it off, then sat by her sister.

Thus receiving the full and returning the empty, they went on drinking cup after cup until the porter began to feel tipsy, lost his inhibitions, and was aroused. He danced and sang lyrics and ballads and carried on with the girls, toying, kissing, biting, groping, rubbing, fingering, and playing jokes on them, while one girl thrust a morsel in his mouth, another flirted with him, another served him with some fresh herbs, and another fed him sweets until he was in utter bliss. They carried on until they got drunk and the wine turned their heads. When the wine got the better of them, the doorkeeper went to the pool, took off her clothes, and stood stark naked, save for what was covered of her body by her loosened hair. Then she said, "Whee," went into the pool, and immersed herself in the water.

But morning overtook Shahrazad, and she lapsed into silence. Then Dinarzad said, "What an amazing and entertaining story!" Shahrazad replied, "What is this compared with what I shall tell you tomorrow night!"

THE THIRTY-FIRST NIGHT

The following night Dinarzad said, "Sister, if you are not sleepy, tell us one of your lovely little tales to while away the night." Shahrazad replied, "With the greatest pleasure":

I heard that the doorkeeper went into the pool, threw water on herself, and, after immersing herself completely, began to sport, taking water in her mouth and squirting it all over her sisters and the porter. Then she washed herself under her breasts, between her thighs, and inside her navel. Then she rushed out of the pool, sat naked in the porter's lap and, pointing to her slit, asked, "My lord and my love, what is this?" "Your womb," said he, and she replied, "Pooh, pooh, you have no shame," and slapped him on the neck. "Your vulva," said he, and the other sister pinched him, shouting, "Bah, this is an ugly word." "Your cunt," said he, and the third sister boxed him on the chest and knocked him over, saying, "Fie, have some shame." "Your clitoris," said he, and again the naked girl slapped him, saying, "No." "Your pudenda, your pussy, your sex tool," said he, and she kept replying, "No, no." He kept giving various other names, but every time he uttered a name, one of the girls hit him and asked,

"What do you call this?" And they went on, this one boxing him, that one slapping him, another hitting him. At last, he turned to them and asked, "All right, what is its name?" The naked girl replied, "The basil of the bridges." The porter cried, "The basil of the bridges! You should have told me this from the beginning, oh, oh!" Then they passed the cup around and went on drinking for a while.

Then the shopper, like her sister, took off all her clothes, saying, "Whee," went into the pool, and immersed herself completely in the water. Then she washed herself under the belly, around the breasts, and between the thighs. Then she rushed out, threw herself in the porter's lap, and asked, "My little lord, what is this?" "Your vulva," said he, and she gave him a blow with which the hall resounded, saying, "Fie, you have no shame." "Your womb," said he, and her sister hit him, saying, "Fie, what an ugly word!" "Your clitoris," said he, and the other sister boxed him, saying, "Fie, fie, you are shameless." They kept at it, this one boxing him, that one slapping him, another hitting him, another jabbing him, repeating, "No, no," while he kept shouting, "Your womb, your cunt, your pussy." Finally he cried, "The basil of the bridges," and all three burst out laughing till they fell on their backs. But again all three slapped him on the neck and said, "No, this is not its name." He cried, "All right, what is its name?" One of them replied, "Why don't you say 'the husked sesame'?" He cried out, "The husked sesame! Thank God, we are finally there." Then the girl put on her clothes and they sat, passing the cup around, while the porter moaned with sore neck and shoulders.

They drank for a while, and then the eldest and fairest of the three stood up and began to undress. The porter touched his neck and began to rub it with his hand, saying, "For God's sake, spare my neck and shoulders," while the girl stripped naked, threw herself into the pool, and immersed herself. The porter looked at her naked body, which looked like a slice of the moon, and at her face, which shone like the full moon or the rising sun, and admired her figure, her breasts, and her swaying heavy hips, for she was naked as God had created her. Moaning "Oh, oh," he addressed her with the following verses:

> If I compare your figure to the bough,
> When green, I err and a sore burden bear.
> The bough is fairest when covered with leaves,
> And you are fairest when completely bare.

When the girl heard his verses, she came quickly out of the pool, sat in his lap and, pointing to her slit, asked, "O light of my eyes, O sweetheart, what is the name of this?" "The basil of the bridges," said he, but she replied, "Bah!" "The husked sesame," said he, and she replied, "Pooh!" "Your womb," said he, and she replied, "Fie, you have no shame," and slapped him on the neck. To make a long story short, O King, the porter kept declaring, "Its name is so," and she kept saying "No, no, no, no." When he had had his fill of blows, pinches, and bites until his neck swelled and he choked and felt miserable, he cried out, "All right, what is its name?" She replied, "Why don't you say the Inn of Abu Masrur?" "Ha, ha, the Inn of Abu Masrur," said the porter. Then she got up, and after she put on her clothes, they resumed their drinking and passed the cup around for a while.

Then the porter stood up, took off his clothes, and, revealing something dangling between his legs, he leapt and plunged into the middle of the pool.

But morning overtook Shahrazad, and she lapsed into silence. Then Dinarzad said to her sister Shahrazad, "Sister, what a lovely and entertaining story!" Shahrazad replied, "What is this compared with what I shall tell you tomorrow night if the king spares me and lets me live!" The king said to himself, "By God, I will not have her put to death until I hear the rest of the story. Then I shall do to her what I did to the others."

THE THIRTY-SECOND NIGHT

The following night Dinarzad said to her sister Shahrazad, "Sister, if you are not sleepy, tell us one of your lovely little tales." Shahrazad replied, "With the greatest pleasure":

I heard, O King, that when the porter went down into the pool, he bathed and washed himself under the beard and under the arms; then he rushed out of the pool, planted himself in the lap of the fairest girl, put his arms on the lap of the doorkeeper, rested his legs in the lap of the shopper and, pointing to his penis, asked, "Ladies, what is this?" They were pleased with his antics and laughed, for his disposition agreed with theirs, and they found him entertaining. One of them said, "Your cock," and he replied, "You have no shame; this is an ugly word." The other said, "Your penis," and he replied, "You should be ashamed; may God put you to shame." The third said, "Your dick," and he replied, "No." Another said, "Your stick," and he replied "No." Another said, "Your thing, your testicles, your prick," and he kept saying, "No, no, no," They asked, "What is the name of this?" He hugged this and kissed that, pinched the one, bit the other, and nibbled on the third, as he took satisfaction, while they laughed until they fell on their backs. At last they asked, "Friend, what is its name?" The porter replied, "Don't you know its name? It is the smashing mule." They asked, "What is the meaning of the name the smashing mule?" He replied, "It is the one who grazes in the basil of the bridges, eats the husked sesame, and gallops in the Inn of Abu Masrur." Again they laughed until they fell on their backs and almost fainted with laughter. Then they resumed their carousing and drinking and carried on until nightfall.

When it was dark, they said to the porter, "Sir, it is time that you get up, put on your slippers, and show us your back." The porter replied, "Where do I go from here? The departure of my soul from my body is easier for me than my departure from your company. Let us join the night with the day and let each of us go his way early tomorrow morning." The shopper said, "By God, sisters, he is right. For God's sake and for my sake, let him stay tonight, so that we may laugh at him and amuse ourselves with him, for who will live to meet with one like him again? He is a clever and witty rogue." They said, "You cannot spend the night with us unless you agree to abide by our condition, that whatever we do and whatever happens to us, you shall refrain from asking for any explanation, for 'speak not of what concerns you not, lest you hear what pleases you not.' This is our condition; don't be too curious about any action of ours." He replied, "Yes, yes, yes, I am dumb and blind." They said, "Rise, then, go to the entrance, and read what is inscribed on the door and the entrance." He got up, went to the door, and found on the door and the entrance the following inscription written in letters of gold, "Whoever speaks of what concerns him not hears what pleases him not." The porter came back and said, "I pledge to you that I will not speak of what concerns me not."

Then the shopper went and prepared supper, and after they had something to eat, they lighted the lamps, and, sticking the aloewood and ambergris into the wax, they lighted the candles, and the incense burned, rose, and filled the hall. Then they changed the plates, laid the table with wine and fresh fruits, and sat to drink. They sat for a long time, eating, drinking, engaging in refined conversation, bantering, and laughing, and joking, when suddenly they heard a knocking at the door. Without showing much concern, one of the girls rose, went to the door, and returned after a while, saying, "Sisters, if you listen to me, you will spend a delightful night, a night to remember." They asked, "How so?" She replied, "At this very moment, three one-eyed dervishes[2] are standing at the door, each with a shaven head, shaven beard, and shaven eyebrows, and each blind in the right eye. It is a most amazing coincidence. They have just arrived in Baghdad from their travel, as one can see from their condition, and this is their first time in our city. Night overtook them and, being strangers with no one to go to and unable to find a place to sleep, they knocked at our door, hoping that someone would give them the key to the stable or offer them a room for the night. Sisters, each one of them is a sight, with a face that would make a mourner laugh. Would you agree to let them in for this one time, so that we may amuse ourselves with them tonight and let them go early tomorrow morning?" She continued to persuade her sisters until they consented, saying, "Let them in, but make it a condition that they 'speak not of what concerns them not, lest they hear what pleases them not.'"

Pleased, she disappeared for a while and returned, followed by three one-eyed dervishes, who greeted them, bowed, and stood back. The three girls rose to greet them, extended welcomes, expressed delight at their visit, and congratulated them on their safe arrival. The three dervishes thanked them and again saluted with bows, and when they saw the beautiful hall, the well-set table laden with wine, nuts, and dried fruits, the burning candles, the smoking incense, and the three girls, who had thrown off all restraint, they exclaimed with one voice, "By God, this is fine." When they turned and looked at the porter, who, sore from the beating and slapping and intoxicated with the wine, lay almost unconscious, they said, "Whether an Arab or a foreigner, he is a brother dervish." The porter sat up and, fixing his eyes on them, said, "Sit here without meddling. Haven't you read the inscription on the door, which is quite clearly written, 'Speak not of what concerns you not, lest you hear what pleases you not'? Yet as soon as you come in you wag your tongues at us." They replied, "O mendicant, we ask for God's forgiveness. Our heads are in your hands." The girls laughed and made peace between the dervishes and the porter; then the shopper offered the dervishes something to eat, and after they ate, they all sat down to carouse and drink, with the doorkeeper replenishing the cups as they passed them around. Then the porter asked, "Friends, can you entertain us with something?"

2. Members of a Muslim order of mendicant monks, vowed to a life of poverty.

But morning overtook Shahrazad, and she lapsed into silence. Then her sister Dinarzad said, "Sister, what a lovely and entertaining story!" Shahrazad replied, "What is this compared with what I shall tell you tomorrow night if I live!"

THE THIRTY-THIRD NIGHT

The following night Dinarzad said to her sister Shahrazad, "Sister, if you are not sleepy, tell us one of your lovely little tales to while away the night." Shahrazad replied, "With the greatest pleasure":

I heard, O King, that the dervishes, heated with the wine, called for musical instruments, and the doorkeeper brought them a tambourine, a flute, and a Persian harp. The dervishes rose, and one took the tambourine, another the flute, another the Persian harp, tuned their instruments, and began to play and sing, and the girls began to sing with them until it got very loud. While they were thus playing and singing, they heard a knocking at the door and the doorkeeper went to see what was the matter.

Now the cause of that knocking, O King, was that it happened on that very night that the Caliph Harun al-Rashid and Ja'far[3] came into the city, as they used to do every now and then, and as they walked through, they passed by the door and heard the music of the flute, the harp, and the tambourine, the singing of the girls, and the sounds of people partying and laughing. The caliph said, "Ja'far, I would like to enter this house and visit the people inside." Ja'far replied, "O Prince of the Faithful, these are people who are intoxicated and who do not know who we are, and I fear that they may insult us and abuse us." The caliph said, "Don't argue; I must go in and I want you to find a pretext to get us in." Ja'far replied, "I hear and obey." Then Ja'far knocked at the door, and when the doorkeeper came and opened the door, he stepped forward, kissed the ground before her, and said, "O my lady, we are merchants from the city of Mosul, and we have been in Baghdad for ten days. We have brought with us our merchandise and have taken lodgings at an inn. Tonight a merchant of your city invited us to his home and offered us food and drink. We drank and enjoyed ourselves and sent for a troop of musicians and singing women and invited the rest of our companions to join us. They all came and we had a good time, listening to the girls blow on the flutes, beat the tambourines, and sing, but while we were enjoying ourselves, the prefect of the police raided the place, and we tried to escape by jumping from walls. Some of us broke our limbs and were arrested, while some escaped safely. We have come now to seek refuge in your house, for, being strangers in your city, we are afraid that if we continue to walk the streets, the prefect of the police will stop us, discover that we are intoxicated, and arrest us. If we go to the inn, we shall find the door locked for, as is the rule, it is not to be opened till sunrise. As we passed by your house, we heard the sounds of music and the noise of a lovely party and hoped that you would be kind enough to let us join you to enjoy the rest of the night, giving us the chance to pay you

---

3. Harun al-Rashid was the fifth Abbasid caliph, who ruled from 786 to 809 c.e.; his rule is considered to be the golden age of the Arab empire, and his court in Baghdad is idealized in the *Nights*. Ja'far al-Barmaki was Harun al-Rashid's vizier and frequent companion, to whose family Harun delegated the administrative duties of the empire until, grown suspicious of their rising power, he had Ja'far and virtually the entire clan exterminated.

for our share. If you refuse our company, let us sleep in the hallway till the morning, and God will reward you. The matter is in your magnanimous hands and the decision is yours, but we will not depart from your door."

After the doorkeeper had listened to Ja'far's speech, looked at their dress, and seen that they were respectable, she went back to her sisters and repeated Ja'far's story. The girls felt sorry for them and said, "Let them in," and she invited them to come in. When the caliph, together with Ja'far and Masrur,[4] entered the hall, the entire group, the girls, the dervishes, and the porter, rose to greet them, and then everyone sat down.

But morning overtook Shahrazad, and she lapsed into silence. Then Dinarzad said, "What a lovely and entertaining story!" Shahrazad replied, "What is this compared with what I shall tell you tomorrow night if I stay alive!"

THE THIRTY-FOURTH NIGHT

The following night Dinarzad said to her sister Shahrazad, "Please, if you are not sleepy, tell us the rest of the story of the three girls." Shahrazad replied, "Very well":

It is related, O King, that when the caliph, together with Ja'far and Masrur, entered and sat down, the girls turned to them and said, "You are welcome, and we are delighted to have you as our guests, but on one condition." They asked, "What is your condition?" The girls replied, "That you will be eyes without tongues and will not inquire about whatever you see. You will 'speak not of what concerns you not, lest you hear what pleases you not.'" They replied, "Yes, as you wish, for we have no need to meddle." Pleased with them, the girls sat to entertain them, drinking and conversing with them. The caliph was astonished to see three dervishes, all blind in the right eye, and he was especially astonished to see girls with such beauty, charm, eloquence, and generosity, in such a lovely place, with a music band consisting of three one-eyed dervishes. But he felt that at that moment he could not ask any questions. They continued to converse and drink, and then the dervishes rose, bowed, and played another round of music; then they sat down and passed the cup around.

When the wine had taken hold, the mistress of the house rose, bowed, and, taking the shopper by the hand, said, "Sister, let us do our duty." Both sisters replied, "Very well." The doorkeeper got up, cleared the table, got rid of the peels and shells, replenished the incense, and cleared the middle of the hall. Then she made the dervishes sit on a sofa at one side of the hall and seated the caliph, Ja'far, and Masrur on another sofa at the other side of the hall. Then she shouted at the porter, saying, "You are very lazy. Get up and lend us a hand, for you are a member of the household." The porter got up and, girding himself, asked, "What is up?" She replied, "Stand where you are." Then the shopper placed a chair in the middle of the hall, opened a cupboard, and said to the porter, "Come and help me." When the porter approached, he saw two black female hounds with chains around their necks. He took them and led them to the middle of the hall. Saying, "It is time to perform our duty," the mistress of the house came forward, rolled up her sleeves, took a braided whip, and called to the porter,

---

4. A black eunuch who was Harun al-Rashid's executioner and bodyguard.

"Bring me one of the bitches." The porter dragged one of the bitches by the chain and brought her forward, while she wept and shook her head at the girl. As the porter stood holding the chain, the girl came down on the bitch with hard blows on the sides, while the bitch howled and wept. The girl kept beating the bitch until her arm got weary. Then she stopped, threw the whip away, and, taking the chain from the porter, embraced the bitch and began to cry. The bitch too began to cry, and the two cried together for a long time. Then the girl wiped the bitch's tears with her handkerchief, kissed her on the head, and said to the porter, "Take her back to her place, and bring me the other." The porter took the bitch to the cupboard and brought the other bitch to the girl, who did to her as she had done to the first, beating her until she fainted. Then she took the bitch, cried with her, kissed her on the head, and asked the porter to take her back to her sister, and he took her back. When those who were present saw what happened, how the girl beat the bitch until the bitch fainted, and how she cried with the bitch and kissed her on the head, they were completely amazed and began to speak under their breath. The caliph himself felt troubled and lost all patience as he burned with curiosity to know the story of these two bitches. He winked to Ja'far, but Ja'far, turning to him, said with a sign, "This is not the time to inquire."

O happy King, when the girl finished punishing the two bitches, the door-keeper said to her, "My lady, go and sit on your couch, so that I in turn may fulfill my desire." Saying, "Very well," the girl went to the far end of the hall and seated herself on the couch, with the caliph, Ja'far, and Masrur seated in a row to her right and the dervishes and the porter, to her left, and although the lamps glowed, the candles burned, and the incense filled the place, these men were depressed and felt that their evening was spoiled. Then the doorkeeper sat on the chair.

But morning overtook Shahrazad, and she lapsed into silence. Then Dinarzad said to her sister, "Sister, what an amazing and entertaining story!" Shahrazad replied, "What is this compared with what I shall tell you tomorrow night if I live!"

THE THIRTY-FIFTH NIGHT

The following night, Dinarzad said to her sister Shahrazad, "Sister, if you are not sleepy, tell us one of your lovely little tales to while away the night." Shahrazad replied, "Very well":

I heard, O happy King, that the doorkeeper sat on the chair and said to her sister the shopper, "Get up and pay me my due." The shopper rose, entered a chamber, and soon brought back a bag of yellow satin with two green silk tassels ornamented with red gold and two beads of pure ambergris. She sat in front of the doorkeeper, drew a lute out of the bag, and with its side resting on her knee, held it in her lap. Then she tuned the lute and, plucking the strings with her fingertips, began to play and sing the following verses of the *Kan wa Kan* variety:[5]

---

5. A verse form in quatrains, which originated in Baghdad. At first the subject matter consisted of narratives that began with the word "kan," meaning "once upon a time"; later the form included love lyrics and maxims.

My love, you are my aim,
And you are my desire.
Your company is constant joy,
Your absence, hellish fire.
You are the madness of my life,   5
My one infatuation,
A love in which there is no shame,
A blameless adoration.
The shirt of agony I wore
Revealed my secret passion,   10
Betrayed my agitated heart
And left me in confusion.
My tears to all declared my love,
As o'er my cheeks they flowed,
My treacherous tears betrayed me   15
And all my secrets showed.
O, cure me from my dire disease;
You are the sickness and the cure,
But he whose remedy you are
Will suffer evermore.   20
Your brilliant eyes have wasted me,
Your jet-black hair has me in thrall,
Your rosy cheeks have vanquished me
And told my tale to all.
My hardship is my martyrdom,   25
The sword of love, my death.
How often have the best of men
This way ended their breath?
I will not cease from loving you,
Nor unlock what is sealed.   30
Love is my law and remedy,
Whether hid or revealed.
Blessed my eyes that gazed on you,
O treasured revelation;
Which has left me confused, alone,   35
In helpless adoration.

When the girl finished the poem, her sister let out a loud cry and moaned, "Oh, oh, oh!" Then she grabbed her dress by the collar and tore it down to the hem, baring her entire body, and fell down in a swoon. When the caliph looked at her, he saw that her whole body, from her head to her toe, bore the marks of the whip, which left it black and blue. Seeing the girl's condition and not knowing the cause, he and his companions were troubled, and he said to Ja'far, "By God, I will not wait a moment until I get to the bottom of this and ask for an explanation for what has happened, the flogging of the girl, the whipping of the two bitches, then the crying and the kissing." Ja'far replied, "My lord, this is not the time to ask for an explanation, especially since they have imposed on us the condition that we speak not of what concerns us not, for 'he who speaks of what concerns him not hears what pleases him not.'"

Then the shopper rose and, entering the chamber, came out with a fine dress that she put on her sister, replacing the one her sister had torn, and sat down. The sister said to the shopper, "For God's sake, give me some more to drink," and the shopper took the cup, filled it, and handed it to her. Then the shopper held the lute in her lap, improvised a number of measures, and sang the following verses:

> If I bemoan your absence, what will you say?
> If I pine with longing, what is the way?
> If I dispatch someone to tell my tale,
> The lover's complaint no one can convey.
> If I with patience try to bear my pain,   5
> After the loss of love, I can't endure the blow.
> Nothing remains but longing and regret
> And tears that over the cheeks profusely flow.
> You, who have long been absent from my eyes,
> Will in my loving heart forever stay.   10
> Was it you who have taught me how to love,
> And from the pledge of love never to stray?

When the sister finished her song, the girl cried out, "Oh, oh, oh!" and, overcome by passion, again grabbed her dress by the collar and tore it to the hem. Then she shrieked and fell down in a swoon. Again the shopper entered the chamber and came out with a dress even better than the first. Then she sprinkled her sister's face with rosewater, and when her sister came to herself, she put the dress on her. Then the sister said, "For God's sake, sister, pay me and finish off, for there remains only this one song." "With the greatest pleasure," replied the shopper, and she took the lute and began to play and sing the following verses:

> How long shall I endure this cruel disdain?
> Have I not paid enough with tears of woe?
> For how long suffer your willful neglect,
> As if it were a vengeful, envious foe?
> Be kind! Your cruel ways inflict a cruel pain,   5
> Master, 'tis time to me you pity show.
> O gentlemen, avenge this thrall of love,
> Who neither sleep nor patience does now know.
> Is it the law of love that one my love enjoys,
> While I alone do emptyhanded go?   10
> My lord, let him my unjust tyrant be;
> Many the toils and trials I undergo.

When she finished her song . . .

But morning overtook Shahrazad, and she lapsed into silence. Then Dinarzad said, "Sister, what an amazing and entertaining story!" Shahrazad replied, "Tomorrow night I shall tell you something stranger, more amazing, and more entertaining if the king spares me and lets me live!"

THE THIRTY-SIXTH NIGHT

The following night Dinarzad said to her sister Shahrazad, "Sister, tell us the rest of the girls' story." Shahrazad said:

It is related, O King, that when the girl heard the third song, she cried out, "By God, this is good." Then she grabbed her dress and tore it, and, as she fell down in a swoon, she revealed on her chest marks like welts from a whip. The dervishes muttered. "We wish that we had never entered this house, but had rather spent the night on the rubbish mounds outside the city, for our visit has been spoiled by such heartrending sights." The caliph turned to them and asked, "How so?" and they replied, "O distinguished gentleman, our minds are troubled by this matter." The caliph asked, "But you are members of the household; perhaps you can explain to me the story of these two black bitches and this girl." They replied, "By God, we know nothing and we have never laid eyes on this place until tonight." Surprised, the caliph said, "Then this man who sits beside you should know the explanation." They winked at the porter, questioning him, but he replied, "By the Almighty God, 'In love all are alike,' for even though I have been raised in Baghdad, never in my life have I entered this house until today. I did spend an amazing day with them. Still, I kept wondering that they were all women without men." They said to him, "By God, we took you to be one of them, but now we find that you are in the same predicament as we are."

Then the caliph said, "Adding Ja'far and Masrur, we are seven men, and they are only three women, without even a single man. Let us ask them for an explanation; if they don't answer by choice, they will answer by force." They agreed to proceed with this plan, but Ja'far said, "This is not right; let them be, for we are their guests and, as you know, they made a condition that we promised to keep. It is better to keep silent about this matter, for little remains of the night, and soon each of us will go his own way." Then he winked at the caliph and whispered to him, "O Commander of the Faithful, be patient for this one last hour of the night, and tomorrow morning I will come back and bring them before you to tell us their story." But the caliph yelled at him, saying, "Damn it, I can no longer wait for an explanation. Let the dervishes question them." Ja'far replied, "This is not a good idea." Then they talked at length and disputed as to who should first put the question, and at last all agreed on the porter.

When the girls heard their clamor, one of them asked, "Men, what is the matter?" The porter approached her and said, "My lady, these men express the wish that you acquaint them with the story of the two black bitches and why you punish them and then weep over them, and they wish to know the story of your sister and how it was that she got flogged with the whip, like a man. That is all; that is what they want to know." Turning to them, the girl asked, "Is it true what he says about you?" They all replied, "Yes," except Ja'far, who remained silent. When the girl heard their reply, she said, "O guests, you have wronged us. Have we not told you of our condition, that 'he who speaks of what concerns him not will hear what pleases him not'? We took you into our home and fed you with our food, but after all this you meddled and did us wrong. Yet the fault is not so much yours as hers who let you in and brought you to us." Then she rolled up her sleeves and struck the floor three times, crying out, "Come at once," and a door opened and out came seven black men, with drawn swords in their hands. Then with the palm of the sword, each man dealt one of the men a blow that threw him on his face to the ground, and in no time they had the seven guests tied by the hands and bound each to each. Then they led them in a single file to the center of the hall, and each black man stood with his sword drawn above the head of his man. Then they said to the girl, "O most honorable and most virtuous lady, permit us to strike off their heads." She replied, "Wait a while until I question them, before you strike off their heads." The porter cried, "God protect me. O lady, slay me not for another's sin. All these men have sinned and offended, except me. By God, we had a delightful day. If only we could have escaped these one-eyed dervishes, whose entrance into any city blights it, destroys it, and lays it waste!" Then he began to weep and recite the following verses:

> Fair is the forgiveness of mighty men,
> And fairest when to weakest men 'tis shown.
> Break off not the first friendship for the last,
> By the bond of the love that has between us grown.

The girl, despite her anger, laughed, and, coming up to the group, said, "Tell me who you are, for you have only one hour to live. Were you not men of rank or eminent among your people or powerful rulers, you would not have dared to offend us." The caliph said to Ja'far, "Damn it, tell her who we are, lest we be slain by mistake." Ja'far replied, "This is part of what we deserve." The caliph yelled at him, saying, "This is no time for your witticisms." Then the lady approached the dervishes and asked, "Are you brothers?" They replied, "No, by God, mistress, we are not, nor are we mendicants." Then she asked one of them, "Were you born blind in one eye?" and he replied, "No, by God my lady. It was an amazing event and a strange mischance that caused me to lose my eye, shave off my beard, and become a dervish. Mine is a tale that, if it were engraved with needles at the corner of the eye, would be a warning to those who wish to consider." Then she questioned the second dervish, and he said the same, and questioned the third, and again he replied like the other two. Then they added, "By God, lady, each one of us comes from a different city, and each one of us is the son of a king, a prince sovereign over land and people." The girl turned to the black men and said, "Whoever tells us his tale and explains what has happened to him and what has brought him to our place, let him stroke his head and go,[6] but whoever refuses, strike off his head."

But morning overtook Shahrazad, and she lapsed into silence. Then Dinarzad said to her sister, "What an amazing and entertaining story!" Shahrazad replied, "What is this compared with what I shall tell you tomorrow night if I stay alive!"

THE THIRTY-SEVENTH NIGHT

The following night Dinarzad said to her sister Shahrazad, "Sister, if you are not sleepy, tell us one of your lovely little tales to while away the night." Shahrazad replied, "With the greatest pleasure":

6. I.e., stroke your head in satisfaction, or in appreciation that you still have it, and go.

I heard, O King, that after the girl spoke, the first to come forth was the porter, who said, "Mistress, you know that the reason I came to this place was that I was hired as a porter by this shopper, who led me from the vintner to the butcher, and from the butcher to the greengrocer, and from the greengrocer to the fruit vendor, and from the fruit vendor to the dry grocer, then to the confectioner, to the druggist, and finally to this house. This is my tale." The girl replied, "Stroke your head and go." But he replied, "By God, I will not go until I hear the tales of the others."

Then the first dervish came forward and said:

[The First Dervish's Tale]

My lady, the cause of my eye being torn out and my beard being shaved off was as follows. My father was a king, and he had a brother who was also a king and who had a son and a daughter. As the years went by and we grew up, I used to visit my uncle every now and then, staying with him for a month or two and returning to my father. For between my uncle's son and myself there grew a firm friendship and a great affection. One day I visited my cousin, and he treated me with unusual kindness. He slaughtered for me many sheep, offered me clear wine, and sat with me to drink. When the wine got the better of us, my cousin said, "Cousin, I would like to acquaint you with something that I have been preparing a whole year for, provided that you do not try to hinder me." I replied, "With the greatest pleasure." After he made me take a binding oath, he got up and quickly disappeared, but a while later came back with a woman wearing a cloak, a kerchief, and a headdress, and smelling of a perfume so sweet as to make us even more intoxicated. Then he said, "Cousin, take this lady and go before me to a sepulcher in such and such a graveyard," describing it so that I knew the place. Then he added, "Enter with her into the sepulcher and wait for me there." Unable to question or protest because of the oath I had taken, I took the lady and walked with her until we entered the graveyard and seated ourselves in the sepulcher. Soon my cousin arrived, carrying a bowl of water, a bag of mortar, and an iron adze. He went straight to a tomb, broke it open with the adze, and set the stones to one side. Then he went on digging into the earth of the tomb until he came upon an iron plate, the size of a small door, that covered the length and width of the tomb. He raised the plate, and there appeared below it a vaulting, winding staircase. Then turning to the lady, he said with a sign, "Make your choice," and she went down the staircase and disappeared. Then he turned to me and said, "Cousin, there is one last favor to ask." I asked, "What is it?" He said, "After I descend into this place, place the iron plate and the earth back over us."

But morning overtook Shahrazad, and she lapsed into silence. Then her sister said, "Sister, what an entertaining story!" Shahrazad replied, "What is this compared with what I shall tell you tomorrow night!"

THE THIRTY-EIGHTH NIGHT

The following night Dinarzad said to her sister Shahrazad, "For God's sake, sister, if you are not sleepy, tell us one of your lovely little tales." King Shahrayar added,

"Tell us the rest of the story of the king's son." Shahrazad replied, "With the greatest pleasure":

I heard, O happy King, that the first dervish said to the girl:

After I followed his instructions, I returned, suffering from a hangover, and spent the night in one of my uncle's houses, which he had given me to use before he went on a hunting trip. When I woke up in the morning and recalled the events of the previous night, I thought that it was all a dream. Being in doubt, I inquired about my cousin, but no one could tell me anything about him. Then I went to the graveyard and searched for the sepulcher, but I could not find it or remember anything about it. I kept wandering from sepulcher to sepulcher and from tomb to tomb, without stopping to eat or drink, until night set in. I was getting worried about my cousin, and as I wondered where the vaulted staircase led to, I began to recall the events little by little, as one recalls what happens in a dream. Finally I went back to the house, ate a little, and spent a restless night. Having recollected everything he and I did that night, I returned the following morning to the graveyard and wandered about, searching till nightfall, without finding the sepulcher or figuring out a way that might lead me to it. I went back to the graveyard for a third day and a fourth and searched for the sepulcher from early morning till nightfall without success, until I almost lost my sanity with frustration and worry. At last, realizing that I had no other recourse, I resolved to go back to my father's city.

When I arrived there and entered the city gate, I was immediately set upon, beaten, and bound. When I inquired, asking, "What is the cause?" I was told, "The vizier has plotted against your father and betrayed him. Being in league with the entire army, he has killed your father and usurped his power and ordered us to lie in wait for you." Then they carried me off in a swoon and brought me before him. O great lady, it so happened that the vizier and I were bitter enemies, for I was the cause of tearing out one of his eyes. Being fond of shooting with the crossbow, I stood one day on my palace roof, when a bird alighted at the palace of the vizier, who by coincidence also stood on his palace roof. When I shot at the bird, the missile missed him and instead hit the vizier and pierced the corner of his eye, and that was the cause of his grudge against me; therefore, when they brought me before him, he thrust his finger into my eye, gouged it out, and made it ooze over my cheek. Then he bound me, placed me in a chest, and handed me over to my father's swordsman, saying, "Ride your horse, draw your sword, and take this one with you into the wilderness. Then kill him and let the beasts and vultures devour his flesh." The executioner followed the vizier's order and led me into the wilderness. Then he dismounted, taking me out of the chest, and looked at me and was about to kill me. I wept bitterly over what had happened to me until I made him weep with me. Then looking at him, I began to recite the following verses:

> My shield I deemed you from the foeman's dart,
> But you did prove to be that very dart.
> I counted on your aid in all mishaps,
> Just as the left hand comes to aid the right.
> Stand then as one absolved, away from me,
> And let the foes at me their arrows aim,
> For if our friendship you cannot maintain,
> Between yourself and me there is no claim.

5

When the executioner heard my verses, he felt pity for me, and he spared me and set me free, saying, "Run with your life and never return to this land, for they will kill you and kill me with you." The poet says:

> If you suffer injustice, save yourself,
> And leave the house behind to mourn its builder.
> Your country you'll replace by another,
> But for yourself, you'll find no other self.
> Nor with a mission trust another man,   5
> For none is as loyal as you yourself.
> And did the lion not struggle by himself,
> He would not prowl with such a mighty mane.

Hardly believing in my escape, I kissed his hand and thought that losing my eye was certainly better than dying.

Then I journeyed slowly until I reached my uncle's city. When I went to him and told him about my father's death and the loss of my eye, he said to me, "I too have enough woes, for my son is missing, and I do not know what has happened to him, nor do I have any news about him." Then he wept bitterly, reviving my old grief and arousing my pity. Unable to remain silent, I acquainted him with what his son had done, and he was exceedingly happy and said, "Come and show me the sepulcher." I replied, "By God, uncle, I have lost the way to it, and I no longer know which one it is." He said, "Let us go together." Then he and I went secretly to the graveyard, and when I came to the center, I suddenly recognized the sepulcher and was exceedingly happy at the prospect of finding out what lay below the staircase and what had happened to my cousin. We entered the sepulcher, opened the tomb, and, removing the earth, found the iron plate. My uncle led the way, and we descended about fifty steps, and as we reached the bottom of the staircase, we met a great cloud of smoke that almost blinded our eyes. My uncle cried, "There is no power and no strength, save in God, the Almighty, the Magnificent." Then we saw a hallway, and as we advanced a little, we came to a hall resting on pillars and lighted by very high skylights. We wandered about and saw a cistern in the center, saw large jars and sacks full of flour, grains, and the like, and at the end of the hall saw a bed covered with a canopy. My uncle went up to the bed, and when he lifted the curtain, he found his son and the lady who had gone down with him, lying in each other's arms, but saw that the two had turned to black charcoal. It was as if they had been cast into a raging fire, which burned them thoroughly until they were reduced to charcoal. When my uncle saw this spectacle, he expressed satisfaction and spat in his son's face, saying, "This is your punishment in this world, but there remains your punishment in the world to come." Then he took off his shoe and struck his son, hard on the face.

But morning overtook Shahrazad, and she lapsed into silence. Then her sister Dinarzad said to her, "Sister, what an entertaining story!" Shahrazad replied, "What is this compared with what I shall tell you tomorrow night if I stay alive!"

The following night Dinarzad said to her sister Shahrazad, "Sister, if you are not sleepy, tell us one of your lovely little tales to while away the night." The king added, "Let it be the completion of the first dervish's tale." Shahrazad replied, "With the greatest pleasure":

I heard, O happy King, that the first dervish said to the girl:

My lady, when my uncle struck his son's face with the shoe, as he and the lady lay there in a charred heap, I said to him, "For God's sake, uncle, don't make me feel worse; I feel worried and sorry for what happened to your son; yet as if he has not suffered enough, you strike him on the face with your shoe." He replied, "Nephew, you should know that this son of mine was madly in love with his sister, and I often forbade him from seeing her but went on saying to myself, 'They are only children.' But when they grew up, they did the ugly deed and I heard about it, hardly believing my ears. I seized him and beat him mercilessly, saying, 'Beware, beware of that deed, lest our story spread far and wide even to every remote province and town and you be dishonored and disgraced among the kings, to the end of time. Beware, beware, for this girl is your sister, and God has forbidden her to you.' Then, nephew, I secluded her from him, but the cursed girl was in love with him, for the devil had possessed her and made the affair attractive in her eyes. When they saw that I had separated them from each other, he built and prepared this subterranean place, dug up the well, and brought whatever they needed of provisions and the like, as you see. Then, taking advantage of my going to the hunt, he took his sister and did what you saw him do. He believed that he would be enjoying her for a long time and that the Almighty God would not be mindful of their deed." Then he wept, and I wept with him. Then he looked at me and said, "You are my son in his place," and when he thought of what had happened to his two children, his brother's murder, and the loss of my eye, he wept again and I wept with him over the trials of life and the misfortunes of this world. Then we climbed out of the tomb and I replaced the iron plate cover over my cousin and his sister, and without being detected by anyone, we returned home.

But hardly had we sat down when we heard the sounds of kettledrums, little drums, and trumpets, the din of men, the clanking of bits, the neighing of horses, and the orders to line up for battle, while the world became clouded with dust raised by the galloping of horses and the tramping of men. We were bewildered and startled, and when we asked, we were told that the vizier who had usurped my father's kingdom had levied his soldiers and prepared his armies, and taking a host of bedouins[7] into service, had invaded us with armies like the desert sand, whom no one could count and no one could withstand. They took the city by surprise, and the citizens, being unable to oppose them, surrendered the place to the vizier. My uncle was slain and I escaped to the outskirts of the city, thinking to myself, "If I fall into the vizier's hands, he will kill me and kill Sayir, my father's swordsman." My sorrows were renewed and my anxiety grew, as I pondered over what had happened to my uncle and my cousins and over the loss of

7. Arab nomads of the desert.

my eye, and I wept bitterly. I asked myself, "What is to be done? If I show myself in public, the people of my city and all my father's soldiers will recognize me as they recognize the sun and will try to win favor with the vizier by killing me." I could think of no way to escape and save my life except to shave my beard and eyebrows. I did so, changed my clothes for those of a mendicant, and assumed the life of a dervish. Then I left the city, undetected by anyone, and journeyed to this country, with the intention of reaching Baghdad, hoping that I might be fortunate to find someone who would assist me to the presence of the Commander of the Faithful, the Vice Regent of the Supreme Lord,[8] so that I might tell him my tale and lay my case before him. I arrived this very night, and as I stood in doubt at the city gate, not knowing where I should go, this dervish by my side approached me, showing the signs of travel, and greeted me. I asked him, "Are you a stranger?" and when he replied, "Yes," I said, "I too am a stranger." As we were talking, this other dervish by our side joined us at the gate, greeted us, and said, "I am a stranger." We replied, "We are strangers, too." Then the three of us walked as night overtook us, three strangers who did not know where to go. But God drove us to your house, and you were kind and generous enough to let us in and help me forget the loss of my eye and the shaving off of my beard.

The girl said to him, "Stroke your head and go." He replied, "By God, I will not go until I hear the tales of the others."

But morning overtook Shahrazad, and she lapsed into silence. Then Dinarzad said, "Sister, what an entertaining story!" Shahrazad replied, "What is this compared with what I shall tell you tomorrow night if the king spares me and lets me live!" The king said to himself, "By God, I shall postpone her execution until I hear the tales of the dervishes and the girls, then have her put to death like the rest."

THE FORTIETH NIGHT

The following night Dinarzad said to her Shahrazad, "Sister, if you are not sleepy, tell us one of your lovely little tales." Shahrazad replied, "With the greatest pleasure":

It is related, O happy King, that those who were present marveled at the tale of the first dervish. The caliph said to Ja'far, "In all my life I have never heard a stranger tale." Then the second dervish came forward and said:

[The Second Dervish's Tale]

By God, my lady, I was not born one-eyed. My father was a king, and he taught me how to write and read until I was able to read the Magnificent Qur'an in all the seven readings. Then I studied jurisprudence in a book by al-Shatibi[9] and commented on it in the presence of other scholars. Then I turned to the study of classical Arabic and its grammar until I reached the height of eloquence, and I

8. Both of these honorifics apply to a caliph, the powerful leader of a Muslim community such as Baghdad or Cairo.
9. Well-known writer on Muslim jurispru-

dence. "Seven readings": a "reading" is a distinct manner of reciting, punctuating and vocalizing a text of the Qur'an.

perfected the art of calligraphy until I surpassed all my contemporaries and all the leading calligraphers of the day, so that the fame of my eloquence and calligraphic art spread to every province and town and reached all the kings of the age.

One day the king of India sent my father gifts and rarities worthy of a king and asked him to send me to him. My father fitted me with six riding horses and sent me along with the posted couriers. I bade him good-bye and set out on my journey. We rode for a full month until one day we came upon a great cloud of dust, and when a little later the wind blew the dust away and cleared the air, we saw fifty horsemen who, looking like glowering lions in steel armor . . .

But morning overtook Shahrazad, and she lapsed into silence. Then her sister said, "Sister, what an amazing and entertaining story!" Shahrazad replied, "What is this compared with what I shall tell you tomorrow night if I stay alive!"

THE FORTY-FIRST NIGHT

The following night Dinarzad said, "Sister, if you are not sleepy, tell us one of your lovely little tales to while away the night." Shahrazad replied, "Very well":

I heard, O happy King, that the second dervish, the young son of the king, said to the girl:

When we looked at them closely, we discovered that they were highwaymen, and when they saw that we were a small company with ten loads of goods—these were gifts—they thought that we were carrying loads of money, drew their swords, and pointed their spears at us. We signaled to them, saying, "We are messengers to the great king of India; you cannot harm us." They replied, "We are neither within his dominions nor under his rule." Then they killed all my men and wounded me. But while the highwaymen were scrambling for the gifts that were with us, I escaped and wandered away without knowing where I was heading or in which direction to go. I was mighty and became lowly; I was rich and became poor.

But morning overtook Shahrazad, and she lapsed into silence. Then her sister said, "What a strange and entertaining story!" Shahrazad replied, "What is this compared with what I shall tell you tomorrow night if the king spares me and lets me live!"

THE FORTY-SECOND NIGHT

The following night Shahrazad said:

I heard, O happy King, that the second dervish said to the girl:

After I was robbed, I fared on, and when night approached, I climbed the side of a mountain and took shelter for the night in a cave till daybreak. Then I journeyed till nightfall, feeding on the plants of the earth and the fruits of the trees, and slept till daybreak. For a month I traveled in this fashion until I came to a fair, peaceful, and prosperous city, teeming with people and full of life. It was the time when winter had departed with its frost and spring had arrived with its roses. The streams were flowing, the flowers blooming, and the birds singing. It was like the city of which the poet said:

> Behold a peaceful city, free from fear,
> Whose wonders make it a gorgeous heaven appear.

I felt both glad and sad at the same time, glad to reach the city, sad to arrive in such a wretched condition, for I was so tired from walking that I was pale with exhaustion. My face and my hands and feet were chapped, and I felt overwhelmed with worry and grief. I entered the city, not knowing where to go, and chanced to pass by a tailor sitting in his shop. I greeted him, and he returned my greeting, and detecting in me traces of better days, he welcomed me and, inviting me to sit with him, talked freely to me. He asked me who I was, and I told him about myself and what had happened to me. He felt sad for me and said, "Young man, do not reveal your secret to anyone, for the king of this city is your father's greatest enemy, and there is a blood feud between them." Then he brought some food, and we ate together. When it was dark, he gave me a recess next to his in the shop, and brought me a blanket and other necessities.

I stayed with him for three days; then he asked me, "Don't you have any skill with which you can earn your living?" I replied, "I am a jurist, a man of letters, a poet, a grammarian, and a calligrapher." He said, "Such skills are not much in demand in our city." I replied, "By God, I have no other skills, save what I have mentioned to you." He said, "Gird yourself, take an axe and a rope, and go and hew wood in the wilderness for your livelihood. But lest you perish, keep your secret to yourself and don't let anyone know who you are, until God sends you relief." Then he bought me an axe and a rope and put me under the charge of certain woodcutters. I went out with them, cut wood all day long, and came back, carrying my bundle on my head. I sold the wood for half a dinar and brought the money to the tailor. In such work I spent an entire year.

One day I went out into the wilderness, and having penetrated deep, I came to a thick patch of trees in a meadow irrigated by running streams. When I entered the patch, I found the stump of a tree, and when I dug around it with my axe and shoveled the earth away, I came upon a ring that was attached to a wooden plank. I raised the plank and beneath it I found a staircase. I descended the steps, and as I reached the bottom, I came to a subterranean palace, solidly built and beautifully designed, a palace so splendid that a better one I have never seen. I walked inside and saw a beautiful girl who looked as radiant as a brilliant pearl or the shining sun and whose speech banished all sorrow and captivated even the sensible and the wise. She was about five feet tall, with a beautiful figure, firm breasts, soft cheeks, and a fair complexion. Through the night of her tresses, her face beamed, and above her smooth bosom, her mouth gleamed, as the poet said of one like her:

> Four things that never meet do here unite
> To shed my blood and to ravage my heart,
> A radiant brow and tresses that beguile
> And rosy cheeks and a glittering smile.

But morning overtook Shahrazad, and she lapsed into silence. Then Dinarzad said, "Sister, what a strange and entertaining story!" Shahrazad replied, "What is this compared with what I shall tell you tomorrow night if the king spares me and lets me live!"

THE FORTY-THIRD NIGHT

The following night, Dinarzad said to her sister Shahrazad, "Sister, if you are not sleepy, tell us one of your lovely little tales to while away the night." Shahrazad replied, "Very well":

I heard, O happy King, that the second young dervish said to the girl:

When the girl looked at me, she asked, "What are you, a man or a demon?" I replied, "I am a human being." She asked, "What brought you here? I have lived in this place for twenty-five years without ever seeing any human being." I said—for I found her words sweet and touching and she captivated my heart—"My good fortune brought me here to dispel my care, or perhaps your good fortune, to banish your sorrow." Then I related to her my mishaps, and she felt sad for me and said, "I too shall tell you my tale. I am the daughter of Aftimarus, king of the Ebony Island. He married me to one of my cousins, but on my wedding night a demon snatched me up, flew away with me, and a while later set me down in this place. Then he brought me all I needed of food and drink and sweets and the like. Once every ten days he comes to spend a night with me—for he took me after he had already a family. If ever I need him for anything by night or by day, I have only to touch the two lines engraved on the doorstep, and he will be with me before I lift my fingers. He has been away for four days, so there remain only six days before he comes again. Would you like to spend five days with me and leave on the day before he arrives?" I replied, "Yes, indeed, 'if only dreams were true!'"

She was pleased and she rose and took me by the hand through an arched doorway that led to a bath. She took off my clothes and took off hers and, entering the bath, she bathed me and washed me. When we came out, she dressed me with a new gown, seated me on a couch, and, giving me a large cup of juice to drink, sat conversing with me for a while. Then she set some food before me, and I ate my fill. Then she offered me a pillow, saying, "Lie down and rest, for you are tired." I lay down and slept, forgetting every care in the world and regaining my energy. When I awoke, some time later, I found her massaging me. I sat up, thanked her, and commended her to God, feeling very much refreshed. Then she asked, "Young man, are you ready to drink?" I replied, "Yes, let us drink," and she went to a cupboard and took out a sealed flask of old wine and, setting a sumptuous table, began to sing the following lines:

> Had we known of your coming, our dark eyes
> Or throbbing heart for you we would have spread,
> Or with our cheeks would have covered the earth,
> So that over the eyelids you might tread.

My love for her began to possess my whole being and my sorrow departed. We sat drinking till nightfall, and I spent with her a delightful night the like of which I never spent in all my life. When we awoke, delight followed delight till midday, and

I was so drunk that I almost lost consciousness and began to stagger right and left. I said, "My beautiful one, let me carry you up and deliver you from this prison." She laughed and replied, "O my lord, sit still, hold your peace, and be content, for of every ten days only one is for the demon and nine for you." I said—as drink had got the better of me—"This very instant I shall smash the doorstep with the engraved inscription and let the demon come, so that I may kill him, for I am used to killing demons by the tens." When she heard my words, she grew pale and said, "No, for God's sake, don't do it." Then she recited the following lines:

> You, who seek separation, hold your reins,
> For its horses are much too swift and free.
> Hold, for betrayal is the rule of life
> And severance the end of amity.

But in my drunkenness, I kicked the step with my foot.

But morning overtook Shahrazad, and she lapsed into silence. Then Dinarzad said, "What a strange and entertaining story!" Shahrazad replied, "What is this compared with what I shall tell you tomorrow night if the king spares me and lets me live!"

THE FORTY-FOURTH NIGHT

The following night Dinarzad said, "Sister, if you are not sleepy, tell us one of your lovely little tales to while away the night." Shahrazad replied, "Very well":

It is related, O happy King, that the second dervish said to the girl:

As soon as I kicked the step, there was thunder and lightning, and the earth began to tremble and everything turned dark. I became sober at once and cried out to her, "What is happening?" She replied, "The demon is coming. O my lord, get up and run for your life." I fled up the staircase, but in my great terror I left my sandals and my iron axe behind. I had not reached the top when I saw the palace floor split asunder and the demon appear, saying, "What disaster has led you to trouble me like this?" She replied, "My lord, today I felt depressed and took a little wine to lighten my heart. Then I got up to go and relieve myself, but I felt tipsy and fell against the step." The demon cried, "You are lying, you whore," and, looking about, saw my sandals and my axe, and asked, "Whose are these?" She replied, "I have never set eyes on them till this moment. They must have stuck to your clothes and you brought them with you." The demon said, "I will not be deceived by this ruse, you slut." Then he seized her, stripped her naked and, binding her hands and feet to four stakes, proceeded to torture her and make her confess."

O lady, it was not easy for me to hear her cries, but trembling with fear, I climbed the staircase slowly until I was outside. Then I placed the trapdoor as it was before and covered it with earth. I felt very sad and extremely sorry, as I thought of the girl, her beauty, her kindness, and her generous treatment, how she had lived quietly for twenty-five years and how in one night I had brought her this calamity. And when I remembered my father and my country, how life turned against me and I became a woodcutter, and how for a brief moment it befriended me and punished me again, I wept bitterly, blamed myself, and repeated the following verses:

My fate does fight me like an enemy
And pursues helpless me relentlessly.
If once it chooses to treat me kindly,
At once it turns, eager to punish me.

Then I walked on until I came to my friend the tailor, whom I found most anxiously waiting for me. He was glad to see me and asked, "Brother, where did you stay last night? I was worried about you; praise be to God for your safety." I thanked him for his friendly concern and, retiring to my recess, sat thinking about what had happened to me, blaming myself for my rashness, for had I not kicked the step, nothing would have happened. As I sat, absorbed in such thoughts, my friend the tailor came to me and said, "There is outside an old Persian gentleman, who has your iron axe and your sandals. He had taken them to the woodcutters, saying, 'I went out this morning to answer the call to prayer and stumbled on this axe and these sandals. Take a look at them and tell me to whom they belong and where I may find him.' The woodcutters recognized your axe and told him where to find you, saying, 'This axe belongs to a young man, a foreigner who lives with the tailor.' At this very moment he is sitting at the entrance of the shop. Go to him and take your axe from him." When I heard what he said, I felt faint and turned pale and, while we stood there talking, the floor of my recess split asunder and there emerged the old Persian gentleman, who was that very demon. He had tortured the girl almost to her death, but she did not confess. So he took the axe and the sandals, saying, "If I am truly the son of Satan's daughter, I shall bring you back the owner of the axe." Then he assumed the guise of a Persian gentleman and came to find me. When the ground split asunder and he emerged . . .

But morning overtook Shahrazad, and she lapsed into silence. Then Dinarzad said, "Sister, what a strange and entertaining story!" Shahrazad replied, "What is this compared with what I shall tell you tomorrow night if the king spares me and lets me live!"

THE FORTY-FIFTH NIGHT

The following Night Dinarzad said to her sister Shahrazad, "Sister, if you are not sleepy, tell us one of your little tales." Shahrazad replied, "Very well":

It is related, O King, that the second dervish said to the girl:

As soon as the demon emerged, he snatched me up from my recess, soared high in the sky, and flew away with me. When he landed a while later, he kicked the ground with his foot, split it asunder, and, carrying me in a swoon, plunged under the earth and emerged with me in the middle of the palace where I had spent the night. There I saw the girl stripped naked, her limbs tied, and her sides bleeding, and my eyes filled with tears. The demon untied her and, covering her, said, "You slut, isn't it true that this man is your lover?" Looking at me, she replied, "I don't know this man at all and I have never laid eyes on him till this very moment." He said, "Damn you, all this torture, and you refuse to confess!" She said, "I don't know this man, and I cannot tell lies about him and let you kill him." He replied, "If you don't know him, take this sword then and strike off his head." She took the sword and, coming up to me, stood facing me. I signaled her with my eyes, and she understood and winked back, meaning, "Aren't you the one who has brought all this upon us?" I signaled again, "This is the time for forgiveness," and she replied with words written with tears on her cheeks:

> My eyes spoke for my tongue to let him know,
> And love betrayed what I tried to conceal.
> When we last met and shed our thoughts in tears,
> Tongue-tied, I let my eyes my heart reveal.
> He signed with his eyes, and I understood;   5
> I winked, and he knew what my eyes did say.
> Our eyebrows carried out our task so well,
> As mute we stood and let love have its sway.

Then the girl threw the sword away and stepped back, saying, "How can I strike the neck of one I do not know and be guilty of his blood?" The demon said, "You cannot bear to kill him because he has slept with you. You have suffered all this torture, yet you have not confessed. It is clear that only like feels for and pities like." Then he turned to me and said, "You human being, do you too not know this woman?" I replied, "Who may she be, for I have never laid eyes on her till this very moment?" He said, "Then take this sword and strike her head off, and I will believe that you do not know her and let you go free." I replied, "I will do it," and I took the sword and sprang toward her.

But morning overtook Shahrazad, and she lapsed into silence. Then Dinarzad said, "Sister, what an entertaining story!" Shahrazad replied, "What is this compared with what I shall tell you tomorrow night if I stay alive!"

THE FORTY-SIXTH NIGHT

The following night Dinarzad said to her sister Shahrazad, "Tell us the rest of the story." Shahrazad replied, "Very well":

I heard, O happy King, that the second dervish said to the girl:

When I took the sword and went up to her, she winked at me, meaning, "Bravo! This is how you repay me!" I understood her look and pledged with my eyes, "I will give my life for you." Then we stood for a while, exchanging looks, as if to say:

> Many a lover his beloved tells
> With his eyes' language what is in his heart.
> "I know what has befallen," seems to say,
> And with a glance he does his thoughts impart.
> How lovely are the glances of the eyes,   5
> How graceful are the eyes with passion fraught.
> One with his looks a lover's message writes,
> Another with his eyes reads what his lover wrote.

I threw the sword away, stepped back, and said, "Mighty demon, if a woman, who is befuddled, thoughtless, and inarticulate, refuses to strike off the head of a man she does not know, how can I, a man, strike off the head of a woman I do not know? I can never do such a deed, even if I have to die for it." The demon replied, "You two are conniving against me, but I am going to show you the result of your misdeeds." Then he took the sword and struck the girl, severing her arm from her shoulder and sending it flying. Then he struck again and severed the other arm and sent it flying. She looked at me, as she lay in the throes of death, and with a glance bade me good-bye. O my lady, at that moment I longed for death, and for a moment I fell into a swoon. "This is the punishment of those who deceive," said the demon and, turning to me, added, "O human being, it is in our law that if a wife deceives her husband, she is no longer lawful to him, and he must kill her and get rid of her. I snatched this woman away on her wedding night, when she was merely a girl of twelve who knew no man but myself. I used to come to her every ten days in the semblance of a Persian gentleman, to spend a night with her. When I became certain that she had deceived me, I killed her, for she was no longer lawful to me. As for you, even though I am not certain whether you are the culprit, I cannot let you go unharmed. Tell me into what animal you wish me to turn you with my magic, a dog, an ass, or a lion. Do you prefer to be a bird or a beast?" I replied, hoping that he might spare me, "O demon, it is more befitting to you to pardon me, even as the envied pardoned the envier." The demon asked, "And how was that?" and I began to tell him:

[The Tale of the Envious and the Envied]

It is related, O demon, that there lived in a certain city two men who dwelt in adjoining houses separated by a common wall. One of them envied the other, gave him the evil eye, and did his utmost to hurt him. He was so obsessed that his envy grew until he could hardly eat or enjoy the pleasure of sleep. But the envied did nothing but prosper, and the more the envious strove to injure him, the more he throve and flourished. At last the envy and malice of his neighbor came to his attention, and he left the neighborhood and moved to another city, saying, "By God, because of him, I will even depart from this world." There he bought himself a piece of land that had an old irrigation well, built a hermitage that he furnished with straw mats and other necessities, and devoted himself to the worship of the Almighty God. The mendicants began to flock to him from every quarter, and his fame spread throughout the city.

Soon the news reached his envious neighbor, how he had prospered and how even the eminent men of the city called on him. So the neighbor journeyed to that city, and when he entered the hermitage, the envied received him with cheerful greetings, warm welcome, and great respect. Then the envious said, "I would like to acquaint you with something that has caused me to come to you. Let us walk aside in the hermitage, so that I may tell you what it is." The envied got up, and as the envious held him by the hand, they walked to the far end of the hermitage. Then the envious said, "Friend, bid your mendicants enter their cells, for I will not tell you, except in private, so that none may hear us." Accordingly, the envied said to the mendicants, "Retire to your cells," and they did so. Then the envious said, "Now, as I was telling you, my tale . . ." and he walked with him slowly until they reached the edge of the old well. Suddenly the envious pushed the envied and, without being seen by anyone, sent him tumbling into the well. Then he left the hermitage and went away, believing that he had killed him.

But morning overtook Shahrazad, and she lapsed into silence. Then Dinarzad said, "Sister, what a strange and entertaining story!" Shahrazad replied, "What is this compared with what I shall tell you tomorrow night if I stay alive!"

THE FORTY-SEVENTH NIGHT

The following night Dinarzad said to her sister Shahrazad, "Sister, if you are not sleepy, tell us what happened to the envious after he pushed the envied into the well." Shahrazad replied, "Very well":

It is related, O King, that the second dervish said to the girl that he told the demon:

Demon, I heard that the envious threw the envied into the ancient well. That well happened to be haunted by a group of demons who caught him and, letting him down little by little, seated him on a rock. Then they asked each other, "Do you know who this man is?" and the answer was "No." But one of them said, "This man is the envied who, flying from the envious, came to live in our city, built this hermitage, and has ever since delighted us with his litanies and his recitals of the Qur'an. But the envious journeyed until he rejoined him, tricked him, and threw him into this well where you now are. It so happens that this very night the fame of this man has come to the attention of the king of this city, and he is planning to visit him tomorrow morning, on account of his daughter." Someone asked him, "What is the matter with her?" He replied, "She is possessed, for the demon Maimun ibn-Damdam is madly in love with her, but if this man knew the remedy, her cure would be as easy as can be." One of them asked, "What is the remedy?" He replied, "This man has in the hermitage a black cat with a white spot the size of a dirham at the end of his tail. If he plucks seven white hairs from the white spot, burns them, and fumigates her with the smoke, the demon will depart from her head, never to return, and she will be cured that very instant." O demon, all of this conversation took place while the envied listened. When the day dawned, the mendicants came out in the morning and found the holy man climbing out of the well, and he grew even greater in their esteem. Then the envied endeavored to look for the black cat and, when he found it, he plucked seven hairs from the white spot on its tail and kept them with him.

In the meantime hardly had the sun risen when the king arrived with his troops. He dismounted with the lords of the realm, bidding the rest of his troops stand outside. When he entered the hermitage, the envied welcomed him and, seating him by his side, asked, "Shall I tell you the cause of your visit?" The king replied, "Yes." The envied continued: "You have come to visit me with the intention of consulting me about your daughter." The king said, "O man of God, you're right." The envied said, "Send someone to fetch her, and God the Almighty willing, she will recover presently." The king gladly sent for his daughter, and they brought her in, bound and fettered. The envied made her sit behind a curtain and, taking out the hairs, burned them and fumigated her with the smoke. At that moment he who was in her head cried out and departed from her, and she instantly recovered her sanity and, veiling her face, asked, "What has happened to me and who brought me here?" The king felt unequaled joy, and he kissed his daughter's eyes and kissed the holy man's hand. Then turning to the great lords of the realm, he asked, "What do you say to this, and what does he who has cured my daughter deserve?" They answered, "He deserves to have her for a wife." The king said, "You are right." Then he married her to him, and the envied became son-in-law to the king. A short time later the vizier died, and the king asked, "Whom shall I make vizier?" They answered, "Your son-in-law," and the envied became vizier. And a short time later, the king also died, and his men asked each other, "Whom shall we make king?" The answer was, "The vizier," and the envied became a monarch, a sovereign king.

One day, as he was riding with his equipage . . .

But morning overtook Shahrazad, and she lapsed into silence. Then Dinarzad said, "What a strange and entertaining story!" Shahrazad replied, "What is this compared with what I shall tell you tomorrow night if the king spares me and lets me live!"

THE FORTY-EIGHTH NIGHT

The following night Dinarzad said, "Sister, if you are not sleepy, tell us what happened to the envious and the envied." Shahrazad replied, "Very well":

I heard, O King, that the second dervish said to the girl that he told the demon:

One day, as the envied rode with his royal equipage at the head of his princes, viziers, and lords of the realm, his eyes fell on the envious. He turned to one of his viziers and commanded, "Bring me that man, but do not alarm him or frighten him." The vizier left and came back with the envious neighbor. The king said, "Give him one thousand weights of gold from my treasury, provide him with twenty loads of goods he trades in, and send him with an escort to his own town." Then the envied bade him farewell and went away without reproaching him for what he had done to him.

I said to the demon, "O demon, consider the mercy of the envied on the envious, who had envied him from the beginning, borne him great malice, pursued him, followed him, and thrown him into the well to kill him. Yet the envied did not respond in kind, but instead of punishing the envious, he forgave him and treated him magnanimously." Then, O my lady, I wept until I could weep no more and recited the following verses:

> Pardon my crime, for every mighty judge
> Is used to mercy some offenders show.
> I stand before you guilty of all sins,
> But you the ways of grace and mercy know.
> For he who seeks forgiveness from above,   5
> Should pardon the offenders here below.

The demon replied, "I will not kill you, but in no way will I pardon you and let you go unharmed. I have spared you from death, but I will put you under a spell." Then he snatched me up and flew with me upward until the earth appeared like a white cloud. Soon he set me down on a mountain and, taking a little dust, mumbled some incantation and sprinkled me with the dust, saying, "Leave your present form and take the form of an ape." At that very instant, I became an ape, and he flew away and left me behind.

When I saw that I was an ape, I wept for myself and blamed life, which is fair to none. Then I descended the mountain and found a vast desert, over which I journeyed for a month until I reached the seashore. As I stood on the shore, looking at the sea, I saw in the offing a ship sailing under a fair wind and cleaving the waves. I went to a tree and, breaking off a branch, began to signal the ship with it, running back and forth and waving the branch to and fro, but being unable to speak or cry out for help, I began to despair. Suddenly the ship turned and began to sail toward the shore, and when it drew near, I found that it was a large ship, full of merchants and laden with spices and other goods. When the merchants saw me, they said to the captain, "You have risked our lives and property for an ape, who brings bad luck with him wherever he goes." One of them said, "Let me kill him." Another said, "Let me shoot him with an arrow." And a third said, "Let us drown him." When I heard what they said, I sprang up and held the hem of the captain's gown like a suppliant, as my tears began to flow over my face. The captain and all the merchants were amazed, and some of them began to feel pity for me. Then the captain said, "Merchants, this ape has appealed to me for protection, and I have taken him under my care. Let none of you hurt him in any way, lest he become my enemy." Then he treated me kindly, and I understood whatever he said and did his bidding, although I could not respond to him with my tongue.

For fifty days the ship sailed on before a fair wind until we came to a great city, vast and teeming with countless people. No sooner had we entered the port and cast anchor than we were visited by messengers from the king of that city. They boarded the ship and said, "Merchants, our king congratulates you on your safe arrival, sends you this roll of paper, and bids each of you write one line on it. For the king's vizier, a man learned in state affairs and a skilled calligrapher, has died, and the king has sworn a solemn oath that he will appoint none in his place, save one who can write as well as he could." Then they handed the merchants a roll of paper, ten cubits long and one cubit wide, and each of the merchants who knew how to write wrote a line. When they came to the end, I snatched the scroll out of their hands, and they screamed and scolded me, fearing that I would throw it into the sea or tear it to pieces, but I signed to them that I wanted to write on it, and they were exceedingly amazed, saying, "We have never yet seen an ape write." The captain said to them, "Let him write what he likes, and if he merely scribbles, I will beat him and chase him away, but if he writes well, I will adopt him as my son, for I have never seen a more intelligent or a better-behaved ape. I wish that my son had this ape's understanding and good manners." Then I held the pen, dipped it in the inkpot, and in Ruqa' script[1] wrote the following lines:

> Time's record of the favors of the great
> Has been effaced by your greater favor.
> Of you your children God will not deprive,
> You, being to grace both mother and father.

---

1. The scripts named are all calligraphic varieties of the cursive, curvilinear Arabic script.

Then under these, in Muhaqqiq script I wrote the following lines:

> His pen has showered bounty everywhere
> And without favor favored every land.
> Yet even the Nile, which destroys the earth,
> Cannot its ink use with such mighty hand.

And in Raihani script I wrote the following lines:

> I swore, whoever uses me to write,
> By the One, Peerless, Everlasting God,
> That he would never any man deny
> With one of the pen's strokes his livelihood.

Then in Naskhi script I wrote the following lines:

> There is no writer who from death will flee,
> But what his hand has written time will keep.
> Commit to paper nothing then, except
> What you would like on Judgment Day to see.

Then in Thuluth script I wrote the following lines:

> When the events of life our love condemned
> And painful separation was our end,
> We turned to the inkwell's mouth to complain,
> And voiced with the pen's tongue our parting's pain.

Then in Tumar script I wrote the following lines:

> When you open the inkwell of your boon
> And fame, let the ink be munificence and grace.
> Write good and generous deeds while write you can;
> Both pen and sword such noble deeds will praise.

Then I handed them the scroll, and they took it back in amazement.

But morning overtook Shahrazad, and she lapsed into silence. Then Dinarzad said, "Sister, what an amazing and entertaining story!" Shahrazad replied, "What is this compared with what I shall tell you tomorrow night if I stay alive!"

THE FORTY-NINTH NIGHT

The following night Dinarzad said, "Sister, tell us the rest of the story." Shahrazad replied, "Very well":

It is related, O happy King, that the second dervish said to the girl:

The messengers took the scroll and returned with it to the king, and when he looked at it, my writing pleased him and he said, "Take this robe of honor and this she-mule to the master of these seven scripts." The men smiled, and seeing that their smiling had made the king angry, they said, "O King of the age and sovereign of the world, the writer of these lines is an ape." The king asked, "Is it true what you say?" They replied, "Yes, by your bounty, the writer is an ape." The king was greatly amazed and said, "I wish to see this ape." Then he dispatched his messengers with the she-mule and the robe, "Dress him with this robe, place him on the she-mule, and bring him to me, together with his master."

As we sat on board, we saw the king's messengers suddenly appear again. They took me from the captain, dressed me with the robe, and, placing me on the she-mule, walked behind me in a procession, which caused a great commotion in the city. Everyone came out, crowding to gaze at me and enjoy the spectacle. By the time I reached the king, the whole city was astir, and the people were saying to each other, "The king has taken an ape for vizier."

When I entered into the presence of the king, I prostrated myself and then stood up and bowed three times. Then I kissed the ground once, before the chamberlains and statesmen and knelt on my knees. Those who were present marveled at my fine manners, most of all the king himself, who said, "This is a wonder." Then he gave permission to his retinue to leave, and everyone left, save for the king, one servant, one little Mamluk, and myself. Then, he ordered a table of food set before him, and motioned to me to eat with him. I rose, kissed the ground before him, and, after I washed my hands seven times, I sat back on my knees and, as good manners require, took only a little to eat. Then I took a pen and an inkwell and over a board wrote the following lines:

> Wail for the crane well stewed in tangy sauce;
> Mourn for the meat, either well baked or fried;
> Cry for the hens and daughters of the grouse
> And the fried birds, even as I have cried.
> Two different kinds of fish are my desire,   5
> Served on two loaves of bread, zestful though plain,
> While in the pan that sizzles o'er the fire
> The eggs like rolling eyes fry in their pain.
> The meat when grilled, O what a lovely dish,
> Served with some pickled greens; that is my wish.   10
> 'Tis in my porridge I indulge at night,
> When hunger gnaws, under the bracelets' light.
> O soul, be patient, for our fickle fate
> Oppresses one day, only to elate.

The king read the verses and pondered. Then they removed the food, and the butler set before us a choice wine in a glass flagon. The king drank first and offered me some. I kissed the ground before him, took a sip, and wrote the following lines over the flagon:

> For my confession they burned me with fire
> And found that I was for endurance made.
> Hence I was borne high on the hands of men
> And given to kiss the lips of a pretty maid.

When the king read the verses, he marveled and said, "If a man had such cultivation, he would excel all the men of his time." Then he set before me a chessboard and with a sign asked, "Do you play?" I kissed the ground before him and nodded "Yes." Then the two of us arranged the pieces on the board and played a game, and it was a draw. We played a second game, and I won. Then we played for the third time, and I attacked and won again, and the king marveled at my skill. Once more I took the inkwell and the pen and over the chessboard wrote the following lines:

> Two armies all day long with arms contend,
> Bringing the battle always to a head.
> But when night's cover on them does descend
> The two go sleeping in a single bed.

As the king read these lines, he was overwhelmed with admiration and delight, and said to the servant, "O Muqbil, go to your lady, Sitt al-Husn, and tell her that her father the king summons her to come and look at this strange ape and enjoy this wonderful spectacle."

The eunuch disappeared and came back a while later with the king's daughter. When she entered and saw me, she veiled her face and said, "O father, have you lost your sense of honor to such a degree that you expose me to men?" Astonished, the king asked, "Daughter, there is no one here, save this little Mamluk, this your mentor who brought you up, and I your father. From whom do you veil your face?" She replied, "From this young man who has been cast under a spell by a demon who is the son of Satan's daughter. He turned him into an ape after he killed his own wife, the daughter of Aftimarus, king of the Ebony Island. This whom you think an ape is a wise, learned, and well-mannered man, a man of culture and refinement." The king was amazed and, looking at me, asked, "Is it true what my daughter said?" I replied with a nod, "Yes." Then he turned to his daughter and asked, "For God's sake, daughter, how did you know that he is enchanted?" She replied, "O father, there was with me from childhood a wily and treacherous old woman who was a witch. She taught me witchcraft, and I copied and memorized seventy domains of magic, by the least of which I could within the hour transport the stones of your city beyond Mount Qaf and beyond the ocean that surrounds the world." The king was amazed and said to his daughter, "O daughter, may God protect you. You have had such a complete power all this time, yet I never knew it. By my life, deliver him from the spell, so that I may make him vizier and marry you to him." She replied, "With the greatest pleasure." Then she took a knife . . .

But morning overtook Shahrazad, and she lapsed into silence. Then Dinarzad said, "Sister, what a strange and entertaining story!" Shahrazad replied, "What is this compared with what I shall tell you tomorrow night, if the king spares me and lets me live!"

THE FIFTIETH NIGHT

The following night Dinarzad said to her sister Shahrazad, "Sister, if you are not sleepy, tell us one of your lovely little tales." Shahrazad replied, "Very well":

I heard, O King, that the second dervish said to the girl:

The king's daughter took a knife engraved with names in Hebrew characters and, drawing a perfect circle in the middle of the palace hall, inscribed on it names in Kufic letters,[2] as well as other talismanic words. Then she muttered charms and uttered spells, and in a short time the world turned dark until we could no longer see anything and thought that the sky was falling on our heads. Suddenly we were startled to see the demon descending in the semblance of a lion as big as a bull, and we were terrified. The girl cried, "Get away, you dog!" The demon replied, "You traitor, you have betrayed me and broken the oath. Have we two not taken an oath that neither would cross the other?" She said, "Cursed one, how could I keep a pledge with one like you?" The demon cried, "Then take what you have brought on yourself," and with an open mouth he rushed toward the girl, who quickly plucked a hair from her head and as she waved the hair in the air and muttered over it the hair turned into a keen sword blade with which she struck the lion, cutting him in half. But while the two halves went flying, the head remained and turned into a scorpion. The girl quickly turned into a huge serpent, and the two fought a bitter battle for a long time. Then the scorpion turned into a vulture and flew outside the palace, and the girl changed into an eagle and flew after the vulture. The two were gone for a long time, but suddenly the ground split asunder, and there emerged a pie-bald tomcat, which meowed, snorted, and snored. He was followed by a black wolf, and the two battled in the palace for a long time, and when the cat saw that he was losing to the wolf, he screamed, turned into a worm, and crept into a pomegranate that was lying beside the fountain. The pomegranate swelled until it was as big as a striped watermelon, and the wolf turned immediately into a snow white rooster. The pomegranate flew in the air and fell on the marble floor of the raised hall, breaking to pieces, and as the seeds scattered everywhere, the rooster fell to picking them. He picked them all, save for one that lay hidden at the edge of the fountain. Then the rooster began to cry and crow, flap his wings, and motion with his beak, as if to ask us, "Are there any seeds left?" But we did not understand, and he let out such a loud shriek that we thought that the palace was falling on our heads. Then the rooster chanced to turn and saw the seed at the edge of the fountain. He rushed to pick it . . .

But morning overtook Shahrazad, and she lapsed into silence. Then Dinarzad said, "Sister, what an amazing and entertaining story!" Shahrazad replied, "What is this compared with what I shall tell you tomorrow night if the king spares me and lets me live!"

THE FIFTY-FIRST NIGHT

The following night Dinarzad said to her sister Shahrazad, "Sister, if you are not sleepy, tell us the rest of the story." Shahrazad replied, "With the greatest pleasure":

I heard, O King, that the second dervish said to the girl:

O lady, the rooster, glad to see the seed, rushed to pick it, when it rolled into the fountain, became a fish, and dove into the water. The rooster turned immediately into a bigger fish and plunged after it, and the two disappeared into the bottom of the fountain for a very long time. Then we heard loud shouts, shrieks, and howls,

2. The rectilinear Arabic script characteristic of the early Qur'ans.

which made us tremble, and a while later the demon came out as a burning flame, followed by the girl, who was also a burning flame. The demon blew fire and sparks from his mouth, nostrils, and eyes and battled the girl for a long time until their flames engulfed them, and the smoke filled the palace until we were resigned to suffocate, as we stood stricken by fear for our lives, certain of disaster and perdition, and, as the fire raged and became more intense, we cried, "There is no power and no strength save in God, the Almighty, the Magnificent." Suddenly, before we could notice, the demon darted as a flame out of the fire, and with one leap stood in the hall before us, blowing fire in our faces, and the girl pursued him, with a loud cry. As the demon blew fire at us, the sparks flew, and, as I stood there in the semblance of an ape, one of them hit my right eye and destroyed it. A second spark hit the king, burning half of his face, including his beard and chin, and knocking out a row of his teeth. A third spark hit the servant in the chest and killed him instantly. At that moment, as we felt certain of destruction and gave ourselves up for lost, we heard a cry, "God is great, God is great! He has conquered and triumphed; He has defeated the infidel." It was the cry of the king's daughter, who had at that very moment defeated the demon. We looked and saw a heap of ashes.

Then the girl came up to us and said, "Bring me a bowl of water," and crying, "In the name of the Almighty God and His covenant, be yourself again," she sprinkled me with the water, and I shook and stood "a full-fledged man." Then she cried out, "The fire! The fire! O father, I am going to miss you, for I have been wounded by one of the demon's arrows, and I shall not live much longer. Although I am not used to fighting demons, I had no trouble until the pomegranate broke to pieces and I became a rooster. I picked all the seeds but overlooked the one that contained the very soul of the demon. Had I picked it up, he would have died instantly, but I overlooked it. I fought him under the earth and I fought him in the sky, and every time he initiated a domain of magic, I countered with a greater domain and foiled him until I opened the domain of fire. Few open it and survive, but I exceeded him in cunning, and with God's help I killed him. God will protect you in my place." Then she implored again, "The fire! The fire!"

But morning overtook Shahrazad, and she lapsed into silence. Then Dinarzad said, "Sister, what an entertaining story!" Shahrazad replied, "What is this compared with what I shall tell you tomorrow night if I stay alive!"

THE FIFTY-SECOND NIGHT

The following night Dinarzad said to her sister Shahrazad, "Sister, if you are not sleepy, tell us one of your little tales." Shahrazad replied, "Very well":

I heard, O King, that the second dervish said to the girl:

When the king's daughter implored, "The fire! The fire!" her father said, "Daughter, it would be a wonder if I too do not perish, for this your servant died instantly, and this young man has lost an eye." Then he wept and made me weep with him. Soon the girl implored again, "The fire! The fire!" as a spark shot at her legs and burned them, then flew to her thighs, then to her bosom, while she kept crying out, "The fire! The fire!" until all of her body burned to a heap of ashes. By God, mistress, I grieved sorely for her, wishing to have been a dog, an ape, or even a dead man, instead of seeing that girl fight, suffer, and burn to ashes. When the father saw that his daughter was dead, he beat his face, and as I did likewise and cried, the statesmen and the servants came in and were amazed to see two heaps of ashes and the king in a bad way. Then they attended him, and when he regained consciousness and told them about his daughter's calamity, their grief grew greater and they mourned for her for seven days. Then the king bade a vaulted tomb be built over his daughter's ashes, but the demon's ashes he bade be scattered to the wind.

Then the king lay ill for a full month, but when God granted him recovery and he regained his health and his beard grew again, he summoned me before him and said, "Young man, listen to what I have to say to you, and don't disobey me, lest you perish." I replied, "My lord, tell me, for I shall never disobey an order of yours." He said, "We have enjoyed the happiest of lives, safe from misfortunes of the world, until you came with your black face and brought disaster with you. My daughter died for your sake, my servant perished, and I myself barely escaped destruction. You were the cause of all this, for ever since we laid eyes on you, we have been unfortunate. Would that we never saw you, for we have paid for your deliverance with our destruction. Now I want you to leave our city and depart in peace, but if I ever see you again, I will kill you." Then he yelled at me, and I went forth from his presence, dumbfounded and deaf and blind to everything.

Before leaving the city, I went to the bath and shaved off my beard and eyebrows, and when I came out, I put on a black woolen robe and departed. I left the king's capital in dismay and tears, not knowing where I should go, and when I recalled everything that had happened to me, how I had entered the city and in what condition I was leaving it, my grief grew worse. O mistress, every day I ponder my misfortune, the loss of my eye and the death of the two girls. I weep bitterly and repeat these verses:

> The Lord of Mercy sees me stand perplexed,
> Beset by ills, whence came I cannot see.
> I will endure until I patience tire
> And God fulfills my wish by His decree.
> I will endure until God sees that I   5
> Bitterness worse than aloes have endured.
> Nor would I have tasted such bitterness,
> Had my weak patience such a teste endured.
> Nor would I have endured such bitterness,
> Had my weak patience endured such decree.
> He who says that life is made of sweetness   10
> A day more bitter than aloes will see.

Then I journeyed through many regions and visited many countries, with the intention of reaching Baghdad and the hope of finding someone there who would help me to the presence of the Commander of the Faithful, so that I might tell him my tale and acquaint him with my misfortune. I arrived here this very night and found this man my brother standing about. I greeted him and asked, "Are you a stranger?" and he replied, "Yes, I am a stranger." Soon this other man joined us and said, "I am a stranger," and we replied, "We too are strangers like you." Then the three of us walked on, as night descended on us, until God brought us to your house. Such then is the cause of losing my eye and shaving off my beard.

The girl said to him, "Stroke your head and go," but he replied, "By God, I will not leave until I hear the tales of the others." Then the black men untied him, and he stood by the side of the first dervish.

But morning overtook Shahrazad, and she lapsed into silence. Then her sister said, "Sister, what a strange and entertaining story!" Shahrazad replied, "What is this compared with what I shall tell you tomorrow night if I stay alive!"

THE FIFTY-THIRD NIGHT

The following night Dinarzad said, "Please, sister, if you are not sleepy, tell us a tale to while away the night." The king added, "Finish the dervishes' tale." Shahrazad replied, "Very well":

It is related, O King, that the third dervish said:

[The Third Dervish's Tale]

O great lady, the story behind the shaving off of my beard and the loss of my eye is stranger and more amazing than theirs, yet it is unlike theirs, for their misfortune took them by surprise, whereas I knowingly brought misfortune and sorrow upon myself. My father was a great and powerful king, and when he died, I inherited the kingdom. My name is 'Ajib ibn-Khasib, and my city stood on the shore of a vast sea that contained many islands. My fleet numbered fifty merchantmen, fifty small pleasure boats, and one hundred and fifty ships fitted for battle and holy war. One day I decided to go on an excursion to the islands, and I carried with me a month's supply and went there, enjoyed myself, and came back. A while later, driven by a desire to give myself to the sea, I fitted ten ships, carried two months' supply, and set out on my voyage. We sailed for forty days, but on the night of the forty-first, the wind blew from all directions, the sea raged with fury, buffeting our ships with huge waves, and a dense darkness descended upon us. We gave ourselves up for lost and said, "'Even if he escapes, the foolhardy deserves no praise.'" We prayed to the Almighty God and implored and supplicated, but the blasts continued to blow and the sea continued to rage till dawn. Then the wind died down, the waves subsided, and the sea became calm and peaceful, and when the sun shone on us, the sea lay before us like a smooth sheet.

Soon we came to an island, where we landed and cooked and ate some food. We rested for two days and we set out again and sailed for ten days, but as we sailed, the sea kept expanding before us and the land kept receding behind us. The captain was puzzled and said to the lookout man, "Climb to the masthead and look." The lookout man climbed, and after he looked for a while, came down and said, "I looked to my right and saw nothing but sky and water, and I looked to my left and saw something black looming before me. That is all I saw." When the captain heard what the lookout man said, he threw his turban to the deck, plucked out his beard, beat his face, and said, "O King, I tell you that we are all going to perish. There is no power and no strength save in God, the Almighty, the Magnificent," and he began to weep and made us weep with him. Then we said to him, "Captain, explain the matter." He replied, "My lord, we lost our course on the night of the storm, and we can no longer go back. By midday tomorrow, forced by the currents, we will reach a black mountain of a metal called the magnetic stone. As soon as we sail below the mountain, the ship's sides will come apart and every nail will fly out and stick to the mountain, for the Almighty God has endowed the magnetic stone with a mysterious virtue that makes the iron love it. For this reason and because of the many ships that have been passing by for a long time, the mountain has attracted so much iron that most of it is already covered with it. On the summit facing the sea, there is a dome of Andalusian brass, supported by ten brass pillars, and on top of the dome there is a brass horse with a brass horseman, bearing on his breast a lead tablet inscribed with talismans. O King, it is none but this rider who destroys the people, and they will not be safe from him until he falls from his horse." Then, O my lady, the captain wept bitterly, and certain that we would perish, we too wept for ourselves with him. We bade each other good-bye, and each of us charged his friend with his instructions, in case he was saved.

We never slept a wink that night, and in the morning we began to approach the magnetic mountain, so that by midday, forced by the currents, we stood below the mountain. As soon as we arrived there, the planks of the ship came apart, and the nails and every iron part flew out toward the mountain and stuck together there. Some of us drowned and some escaped, but those who did escape knew nothing about the fate of the others. As for me, O my lady, God spared me that I might suffer what He had willed for me of hardship and misery. I climbed on one of the planks of the ship, and it was thrown immediately by the wind at the foot of the mountain. There I found a path leading to the summit, with steps carved out of the rock.

But morning overtook Shahrazad, and she lapsed into silence. Then Dinarzad said, "Sister, what a strange and entertaining story!" Shahrazad replied, "What is this compared with what I shall tell you tomorrow night if I stay alive!"

THE FIFTY-FOURTH NIGHT

The following night Dinarzad said to her sister Shahrazad, "Please, sister, if you are not sleepy, tell us the rest of the story of the third dervish." Shahrazad replied, "Very well":

O my lord, I heard that the third dervish said to the girl:

When I saw the path on the side of the mountain, I invoked the name of the Almighty God, hung against the rock, and began to climb little by little. And the Almighty God bade the wind be still and helped me with the ascent, so that I reached the summit safely and went directly to the dome. Glad at my safe escape, I entered the dome, performed my ablutions, and prayed, kneeling down several times in thanksgiving to the Almighty God for my safety. Then I fell asleep under the dome overlooking the sea and heard in a dream a voice saying, "O 'Ajib, when you wake from your sleep, dig under your feet, and you will find a brass bow and three lead arrows inscribed with talismans. Take the bow and arrows and shoot at the horseman to throw him off the horse and rid mankind of this great calamity. When you shoot at him, he will fall into the sea, and the horse will drop at your feet. Take the horse and bury it in the place of the bow. When you do this, the sea will swell and rise until it reaches the level of the dome, and there will come to you a skiff carrying a man of brass (a man other than the man you will have thrown), holding in his hands a pair of paddles. Ride with him, but do not invoke the name of God. He will row you for ten days until he brings you to the Sea of Safety. Once there, you will find those who will convey you to your native land. All this will be fulfilled, providing that you do not invoke the name of God."

Then I awoke and eagerly sprang up to do the voice's bidding. I shot at the horseman, and he fell from the horse into the sea, while the horse dropped at my feet, and when I buried the horse in the place of the bow, the sea swelled and rose until it came up to me. Soon I saw a skiff in the offing, coming toward me, and I praised and thanked the Almighty God. When the skiff came up to me, I saw there a man of brass, bearing on his breast a lead tablet inscribed with names and talismans. I climbed into the skiff without uttering a word, and the boatman rowed with me through the first day and the second and on to the ninth, when I happily caught sight of islands, hills, and other signs of safety. But in my excess of joy, I praised and glorified the Almighty God, crying, "There is no god but God." No sooner had I done that than the skiff turned upside down and sank, throwing me into the sea. I swam all day until my shoulders were numb with fatigue and my arms began to fail me, and when night fell and I was in the middle of nowhere, I became resigned to drown. Suddenly there was a violent gust of wind, which made the sea surge, and a great wave as tall as a mountain swept me and with one surge cast me on dry land; for God had willed to preserve my life. I walked ashore, wrung out my clothes, and spread them to dry. Then I slept the whole night.

In the morning I put on my clothes and went to scout and see where I was. I came to a cluster of trees, circled around them, and as I walked further, I found out that I was on a small island in the middle of the sea. I said, "There is no power and no strength save in God, the Almighty, the Magnificent," and while I was thinking about my situation, wishing that I was dead, I suddenly saw in the distance a ship with human beings on board, making for the island. I climbed a tree and hid among the branches. Soon the ship touched land, and there came ashore ten black men, carrying shovels and baskets. They walked on until they reached the middle of the island. Then they began to dig into the ground and to shovel the earth away until they uncovered a slab. Then they returned to the ship and began to haul out sacks of bread and flour, vessels of cooking butter and honey, preserved meat, utensils, carpets, straw mats, couches, and other pieces of furniture—in short, all one needs for setting up house. The black men kept going back and forth and descending through the trapdoor with the articles until they had transported everything that was in the ship. When they came out of the ship again, there was a very old man in their middle. Of this man nothing much was left, for time had ravaged him, reducing him to a bone wrapped in a blue rag through which the winds whistled east and west. He was like one of whom the poet said:

> Time made me tremble; ah! how sore that was
> For with his might does time all mortals stalk.
> I used to walk without becoming tired;
> Today I tire although I never walk.

The old man held by the hand a young man who was so splendidly handsome that he seemed to be cast in beauty's mold. He was like the green bough or the tender young of the roe, ravishing every heart with his loveliness and captivating every mind with his perfection. Faultless in body and face, he surpassed everyone in looks and inner grace, as if it was of him that the poet said:

> With him to make compare Beauty they brought,
> But Beauty hung his head in abject shame.
> They said, "O Beauty, have you seen his like?"
> Beauty replied, "I have ne'er seen the same."

My lady, they walked until they reached the trapdoor, went down, and were gone for a long time. Then the old man and the black men came out without the young man and shoveled the earth back as it was before. Then they boarded the ship, set sail, and disappeared.

I came down from the tree and, going to the spot they had covered, began to dig and shovel away. Having patiently cleared the earth away, I uncovered a single millstone, and when I lifted it up, I was surprised to find a winding stone staircase. I descended the steps, and when I came to the end, I found myself in a clean, white washed hall, spread with various kinds of carpets, beddings, and silk stuffs. There I saw the young man sitting on a high couch, leaning back on a round cushion, with a fan in his hand. A banquet was set before him, with fruits, flowers, and scented herbs, as he sat there all alone. When he saw me, he started and turned pale, but I greeted him and said, "My lord, set your mind at ease, for there is nothing to fear. I am a human being like you, my dear friend, and like you, the son of a king. God has brought me to you to keep you company in your loneliness. But tell me, what is your story, and what causes you to dwell under the ground?"

But morning overtook Shahrazad, and she lapsed into silence. Then Dinarzad said, "Sister, what a strange and entertaining story!" Shahrazad replied, "What is this compared with what I shall tell you tomorrow night if I stay alive!"

THE FIFTY-FIFTH NIGHT

The following night Dinarzad said to her sister Shahrazad, "Please, sister, if you are not sleepy, tell us the rest of the story of the king's son and the young man under the ground." Shahrazad replied, "With the greatest pleasure":

I heard, O King, that the third dervish said to the girl:

My lady, when I asked the young man to tell me his story, and he was assured that I was of his kind, he rejoiced and regained his composure. Then he made me draw near to him and said, "O my brother, my case is strange and my tale is amazing. My father is a very wealthy jeweler, who deals even with kings and who has many black and white slaves as well as traders who travel on ships to trade for him. But he was not blessed with a child. One night he dreamt that he was going to have a son who would be short-lived, and he woke up in the morning, feeling depressed. My mother happened to conceive on the following night, and my father noted the date of her conception. When the months passed and her time came, she gave birth to me, and my father was exceedingly happy. Then the astrologers and wise men, noting my birth date, read my horoscope and said, 'Your son will live fifteen years, after which there will be a conjunction of the stars, and if he can escape it, he will live. For there stands in the salty sea a mountain called the magnetic mountain, on top of which stands a brass horseman riding on a brass horse and holding in his mouth a lead tablet. Fifty days after this horseman falls from the horse, your son will die, and his killer will be the man who will have thrown the horseman off the horse, a man named 'Ajib, son of King Khasib.' My father was stricken with grief. But he raised me and educated me as the years went by until I was fifteen. Ten days ago, the news reached my father that the brass horseman has been thrown into the sea by a man called King 'Ajib, son of King Khasib. When my father heard the news, he wept bitterly at our impending separation and became like a madman. Then for fear that 'Ajib, son of King Khasib, would kill me, my father built me this house under the ground and brought me in the ship with everything I need for the duration of fifty days. Ten days have already passed, and there remain only forty days until the conjunction of the stars is over and my father comes back to take me home. This is my story and the cause of my loneliness and isolation."

My lady, when I heard his narrative and strange tale, I said to myself, "I am the one who overthrew the brass horseman, and I am 'Ajib, son of King Khasib, but by God, I will never kill him." Then I said to him, "O my lord, may you be spared from death and safe from harm. God willing, there is nothing to worry about or fear. I will stay with you to serve you and entertain you these forty days. I will help you and go home with you, and you in turn will help me to return to my native land, and God will reward you." My words pleased him, and I sat to chat with him and entertain him.

When night came, I got up and, lighting a candle, I filled and lit three oil lamps. Then I offered him a box of sweets, and after we both ate and savored some, we sat and chatted most of the night. When he fell asleep, I covered him, and then I too lay down and slept. When I woke up in the morning, I heated some water for him and gently woke him up, and when he awoke, I brought him the hot water, and he washed his face and thanked me saying, "God bless you, young man. By God, when I escape the man who is called 'Ajib, son of Khasib, and God saves me from him, I will make my father reward you and grant you every favor." I replied, "May all your days be free from harm, and may God set my appointed day before yours!" Then I offered him something to eat, and after the two of us ate I rose and cut pieces of wood for checkers and set the pieces on the checkerboard. We diverted and amused ourselves, playing and eating and drinking till nightfall. Then I rose, lit the lamps, and offered him some sweets, and after we ate and savored some, we sat and chatted, then went to sleep.

My lady, in this way we passed many days and nights, and I became an intimate friend of his, felt a great affection for him, and forgot my cares and sorrows. I said to myself, "The astrologers lied when they told his father, 'Your son will be killed by one called 'Ajib, son of Khasib,' for by God, this is I and in no way will I kill him," and for thirty-nine days I kept serving him, entertaining him, and carousing with him through the night. On the night of the fortieth day, feeling glad at his safe escape, he said, "Brother, I have now completed forty days. Praise be to God who has saved me from death by your blessed coming. By God, I shall make my father reward you and send you to your native land. But, brother, kindly heat some water for me, so that I may wash my body and change my clothes." I replied, "With the greatest pleasure." Then I rose, heated some water, and took the young man into a little room where I gave him a good bath and put on him fresh clothes. Then I spread for him a high bed, covered with a leather mat, and there he lay down to rest, tired from his bath. He said to me, "Brother, cut me up a watermelon and sweeten the juice with sugar." I rose and, bringing back a fine watermelon, set it on a platter, saying, "My lord, do you know where the knife is?" He replied, "Here it is, on the high shelf over my head." I sprang up and, reaching over him in haste, drew the knife from the sheath, and as I stepped back, I slipped on the leather mat, as had been foreordained, and fell prostrate on the young man, and the knife, which was in my hand, pierced his heart and killed him instantly. When I saw that he was dead and realized that it was I who had killed him, I let out a loud scream, beat my face, tore my clothes, and cried, "O people, O God's creatures, there remained for this young man only one day out of the forty, yet he still met his death at my hand. O God, I ask for your forgiveness, wishing that I had died before him. These my afflictions I suffer, draught by bitter draught, 'so that God's will may be fulfilled.'"

But morning overtook Shahrazad, and she lapsed into silence. Then Dinarzad said, "What a strange and entertaining story!" Shahrazad replied, "What is this compared with what I shall tell you tomorrow night if I stay alive!"

THE FIFTY-SIXTH NIGHT

The following night Dinarzad said to her sister Shahrazad, "Sister, if you are not sleepy, tell us the rest of the story of the third dervish." Shahrazad replied, "With the greatest pleasure":

I heard, O King, that the third dervish said to the girl:

My lady, when I was sure that I had killed him, as the God above had foreordained, I rose and, ascending the stairs, replaced the trapdoor and covered it with earth. Then I looked toward the sea and saw the ship that had brought him, cleaving the waters toward the island to fetch him. I said to myself, "The moment they come and see their boy slain and find that I am his slayer, they will surely kill me." I headed toward a nearby tree and, climbing it, hid among the branches, and hardly had I done so when the ship reached the island and touched the shore, and the black servants came out with the old father of the young man I had killed. They came to the spot, and when they removed the earth, they were surprised to find it soft. They went down and found the young man lying down, with his face still glowing after the bath, dressed in clean clothes and the knife deep in his heart. When they examined him and found that he was dead, they shrieked, beat their faces, wept, wailed, and invoked awful curses on the murderer. His father fell into such a deep swoon that the black servants thought that he was dead. At last he came to himself, and they wrapped the young man in his clothes and carried him up, together with the old man. Then one of the slaves went and came back with a seat covered with silk, and they carried the old man, laid him there, and sat by his head. All this took place under the tree in which I hid, watching everything they did and listening to everything they said. My heart felt hoary before my head turned gray because of the afflictions, misfortunes, calamities, and sorrows I had suffered. O my lady, the old man remained in a swoon till close to sunset. When he came to himself, looked at his son, and recalled what had happened—that what he feared had come to pass—he wept, beat his face, and recited the following verses:

> By my life, hurry; they have gone away,
> And my tears from my eyes profusely flow.
> Their resting place is far, O far away;
> What shall I say of them, what shall I do?
> I wish that I had never seen their sight.   5
> Helpless I stand and no solution know.
> Comfort and consolation can I find
> When burning sorrow sets my heart aglow?
> O luck, off with me to their dwelling place;
> Cry out to them about my tears that flow.   10
> They died and left my heart with burning pain,
> The fire that in the loving breast did glow.
> I wish that death would take me to their place;
> Forever lasts the bond between us two.
> For God's sake, luck, be careful with our fate,   15
> Our pending union, careful be and slow.
> How blessed we lived together in one home
> A life of bliss that did no hindrance know
> Until with parting's arrow we were shot,
> And who can of such arrows bear the blow?   20
> By death was felled the noblest of the tribe,
> The age's pearl, with beauty on his brow.
> I mourned or silently I seemed to say,
> "I wish that death had not hastened the blow.
> On me and mine did envy fix his eye,   25
> O son, I'd have given my life for you.
> How can I meet you soon, my only one,
> My son, for whom I would my soul bestow?
> Your gifts you lavished like the bounteous moon,
> And like the moon your fame did rise and grow.   30
> If moon I call you, no, the moon goes down,
> And if I call you sun, the sun sinks low.
> O you, whose beauties were on every tongue,
> You whom the virtues did with grace endow,
> For you I will forever grieve and mourn;   35
> No other love but you I'll ever know.
> Longing for you your father has consumed,
> But helpless now he stands since death felled you.
> Some evil eyes on you have had their feast,
> Would they were pierced or black and blind did grow."   40

Then the old man took a breath, and with a deep sigh his soul left his body. The black servants shrieked and, throwing dust on their heads and faces, wailed and cried bitterly. Then they carried the old man and his son to the ship and laid them down side by side. Soon they set sail and vanished from my sight. Then I descended from the tree and went back to the underground dwelling. When I entered, I saw some of the young man's belongings, which reminded me of him, and I repeated the following verses:

> I see their traces and with longing pine
> In their empty dwelling, and my tears flow.
> And Him who has their loss decreed I beg,
> That He may on me their return bestow.

But morning overtook Shahrazad, and she lapsed into silence. Then her sister said, "Sister, what a strange and entertaining story!" Shahrazad replied, "What is this compared with what I shall tell you tomorrow night if I stay alive!"

THE FIFTY-SEVENTH NIGHT

The following night Dinarzad said to her sister Shahrazad, "If you are not sleepy, tell us the rest of the dervish's story." Shahrazad said:

I heard, O King, that the third dervish said to the girl:

My lady, for a month I lived on the island, spending my day in the open and my night in the underground hall, until one day I noticed that the water on the west side of the island was receding little by little. By the end of the month dry land appeared on the east side, and I felt happy and certain of my safety. I waded through the shallow water, and when I reached permanent dry land, I saw nothing but sand as far as the eye can see. Then I noticed a great fire raging in the distance, and I gathered my energy and braved the sand toward the fire, saying to myself, "Someone must surely have kindled such a fire, and there perhaps is where I can find help," and I repeated the following verses:

> Perhaps my fate will his own bridle turn
> And bring good fortune, O my fickle fate,
> Replacing past ills with present good deeds,
> My needs to answer and my hopes elate.

When I drew near, I found out that the fire was in reality a palace overlaid with copper plates that, as the sun shone on them, glowed and from a distance appeared like a fire. I was glad to see the palace and sat down to rest, but hardly had I done so when I was approached by ten neatly dressed young men accompanied by an old man, and I was astonished to see that each young man was blind in the right eye, and marveled at this coincidence. When they saw me, they greeted me, delighted to see me, and when they asked me about myself, I told them about my misfortunes. Marveling at my tale, they took me into the palace, where I saw ranged around the hall ten couches, each with blue bedding and blue coverlet, with a smaller couch in the middle, covered likewise in blue. We entered and each young man took his seat on a couch, and the old man seated himself on the smaller couch in the middle, saying to me, "Young man, sit down on the floor and do not inquire about our situation or the loss of our eyes." Then he rose and one by one set before each of them his own food and did the same for me. After we ate, he offered us wine, each in his own cup, and they sat to carouse and ask me about my extraordinary case and strange adventures, and I told them my tale until most of the night was gone. Then the young men said to the old man, "Old man, will you give us our due, for it is time to go to bed?" The old man rose, entered a chamber, and came back, carrying on his head ten trays, each covered with a blue cover. He set a tray before each young man and, lighting ten candles, stuck one on each tray. Then he drew off the covers, and there appeared on each tray nothing but ashes, powdered charcoal, and kettle soot. Then, rolling up their sleeves, every young man blackened his face and smeared his clothes with soot and ashes, beat his breast and face, and wept and wailed, crying out again and again, "We would be sitting pretty but for our curiosity.'" They carried on like this until it was close to sunrise. Then the old man rose and heated some water for them, and the young men ran, washed themselves, and put on clean clothes.

My lady, when I saw what the young men had done and how they had blackened their faces, I was filled with bewilderment and curiosity and forgot my own misfortunes. Unable to remain silent, I asked them, "What brought this on, after we frolicked and enjoyed ourselves? You seem, God be praised, perfectly sane, and such actions befit only madmen. I ask you by all that is dearest to you to tell me your tale and the cause of losing your eyes and smearing your faces with soot and ashes." They turned to me and said, "Young man, don't let our youth and our behavior deceive you. It is better for you not to ask." Then they laid out some food, and we began to eat, but my heart was still on fire and I burned with curiosity to find out the cause of their action, especially after having eaten and drunk with them. Then we sat to converse until late afternoon, and when it got dark, the old man offered us wine, and we sat drinking till past midnight. Then the young men said, "Give us our due, old man, for it is time to go to bed." The old man rose, disappeared, then came back a while later with the same trays, and the young men repeated what they had done the previous night.

My lady, to make a long story short, I stayed with them for a full month, and every night they did the same thing and washed themselves early in the morning, while I watched, marveling at their action, until my curiosity and my anxiety increased to the point that I was no longer able to eat or drink. At last I said to them, "Young men, if you don't relieve me and tell me why you blacken your faces and repeat, 'We would be sitting pretty but for our curiosity,' let me relieve myself of such sights by leaving you and going home, for as the saying goes, 'Better for me and meet to see you not, for if the eye sees nought, the heart grieves not.'" When they heard my words, they came up to me and said, "Young man, we have kept our secret from you only out of pity for you, so that you would not suffer what we have suffered." I replied, "You must tell me." They said, "Young man, listen to our advice and don't ask, lest you become one-eyed like us." I repeated, "I must know the secret." They replied, "Young man, when you find out the secret, remember that we will no longer harbor you nor let you stay with us again."

Then they fetched a ram, slaughtered it, skinned it, and made the skin into a sack. Then they said, "Take this knife and get into the sack, and we shall sew you up in it. Then we shall go away and leave you alone. Soon a bird called

Rukh[3] will pick you up with his talons, fly with you high in the air for a while; then you will feel that he has set you down on a mountain and moved away from you. When you feel that the bird has done so, rip the skin open with this knife and come out, and when the bird sees you, he will fly away. Proceed immediately and walk for half a day, and you will see before you a towering palace, built with sandal- and aloewood and covered with plates of red gold, studded with emeralds and all kinds of precious stones. Enter the palace, and you will have your wish, for we have all entered that palace, and that was the cause of losing our eyes and blackening our faces. It would be too tedious to tell you the whole story, for each of us has his own tale for losing his right eye."

But morning overtook Shahrazad, and she lapsed into silence. Then Dinarzad said, "Sister, what a strange and entertaining story!" Shahrazad replied, "What is this compared with what I shall tell you tomorrow night if I stay alive!"

THE FIFTY-EIGHTH NIGHT

The following night Dinarzad said to her sister Shahrazad, "Please, sister, if you are not sleepy, tell us the rest of the story of the third dervish." Shahrazad replied, "With the greatest pleasure":

It is related, O King, that King 'Ajib, the third dervish, said:

When the young men finished their explanation, they let me into the skin sack, sewed me up, and returned to the palace. Soon I felt the white bird approach, and snatching me up with his talons, he flew away with me for a while and set me down on the mountain. I ripped the skin open and came out, and when the bird saw me, he flew away. I proceeded immediately to walk until I reached the palace and found it to be exactly as they had described it. The door stood open, and when I entered, I found myself in a spacious and lovely hall as vast as a playground. It was surrounded by forty chambers with doors of sandal- and aloewood, covered with plates of red gold and graced with silver handles. At the far end of the hall, I saw forty girls, sumptuously dressed and lavishly adorned. They looked like moons, so lovely that none could tire of gazing on them. When they saw me, they said in one voice, "O lord, welcome, O master, welcome! and good cheer to you, lord! We have been expecting one like you for months. Praised be God who has sent us one who is as worthy of us as we are of him." Then they raced toward me and made me sit on a high couch, saying, "This day, you are our lord and master, and we are your maids and servants, at your beck and call." Then while I sat marveling at their behavior, they rose, and some of them set food before me; others warmed water and washed my hands and feet and changed my clothes; others mixed juice and gave me to drink; and they all gathered around me, joyful at my coming. Then they sat down to converse with me and question me till nightfall.

But morning overtook Shahrazad, and she lapsed into silence. Then Dinarzad said, "Sister, what a strange and entertaining story!" Shahrazad replied, "What is this compared with what I shall tell you tomorrow night if the king spares me and lets me live!"

---

3. The phoenix, a mythological bird.

THE FIFTY-NINTH NIGHT

The following night Dinarzad said to her sister Shahrazad, "Sister, if you are not sleepy, tell us the rest of the story." Shahrazad replied, "Very well":

It is related, O King, that the third dervish said to the girl:

My lady, the girls sat around me, and when night came, five of them rose and set up a banquet with plenty of nuts and fragrant herbs. Then they brought the wine vessels and we sat to drink, with the girls sitting all around me, some singing, some playing the flute, the psaltery, the lute, and all other musical instruments, while the bowls and cups went round. I was so happy that I forgot every sorrow in the world, saying to myself, "'This is the life; alas, that it is fleeting.'" I enjoyed myself with them until most of the night was gone and we were drunk. Then they said to me, "O our lord, choose from among us whomever you wish to spend this night with you and not return to be your bedfellow again until forty days will have passed." I chose a girl who had a lovely face and dark eyes, with black hair, joining brows, and a mouth with slightly parted teeth. Perfect in every way, like a willow bough or a stalk of sweet basil, her beauty struck the eye and bewildered the mind. She was like the one of whom the poet said,

> She bent and swayed like a ripe willow bough,
> O more lovely, sweet, and delicious sight!
> She smiled and her glittering mouth revealed
> The flashing stars that answered light with light.
> She loosened her black tresses, and the morn   5
> Became a dusky, black, and darkling night,
> And when her radiant face shone in the dark,
> From east to west the gloomy world turned bright.
> 'Tis foolish to compare her to a roe;
> How can such fledgling thing such beauties show,   10
> Such lovely body, such honeydew lips,
> Such sweet nectar to drink, such joy to know,
> Such wide eyes that with the arrows of love
> The tortured victim pierce; how can the roe?
> I loved her madly like a pagan boy,   15
> No wonder when with love one is laid low.

That night I slept with her and spent the best of nights.

But morning overtook Shahrazad, and she lapsed into silence. Then her sister said, "Sister, what a strange and entertaining story!" Shahrazad replied, "What is this compared with what I shall tell you tomorrow night if I stay alive!"

THE SIXTIETH NIGHT

The following night Dinarzad said to her sister Shahrazad, "Please, sister, tell us the rest of the story of the third dervish." Shahrazad replied, "Very well":

I heard, O King, that the third dervish said to the girl:

When it was morning, the girls took me to a bath in the palace, and after they bathed me, they dressed me in fine clothes. Then they served food, and after we ate they served wine, and as the cup was passed around, we drank into the night. Then they said, "Choose from among us whomever you wish to spend the night with; we are your maids, awaiting your command." I chose a girl with a lovely face and a soft body, like her of whom the poet said:

> I saw two caskets on her bosom fair,
> Shielded with musk seals from lovers' embrace.
> Against assault she guarded them with darts
> And arrowy glances from her lovely face.

I spent with her a lovely night, and when morning came, I bathed and put on new clothes.

My lady, to make a long story short, for a full year I lived with them a carefree life, eating and drinking, carousing, and spending every night with one of them. But one day, at the beginning of the new year, they began to wail and cry, bidding me farewell, clinging to me, and weeping. Amazed at their behavior, I asked, "What is the matter, for you are breaking my heart?" They replied, "We wish that we had never known you, for we had lived with many men but never met one more pleasant than you. May God never deprive us of you," and they wept. I asked, "Why do you weep, for to me your tears are gall?" They replied with one voice, "The reason is our separation from you, of which none other than you yourself is the cause. If you listen to us, we will not be separated, but if you disobey us, we will. Our hearts tell us that you will not obey and that it will happen, and this is the cause of our weeping." I said, "Explain the matter." They replied, "Our lord and master, we are the daughters of kings, and we have lived together here for many years. It has been our custom to go away once a year for forty days and return to live here for the rest of the year, eating and drinking and taking our pleasure and enjoying ourselves here. Now this is how you will disobey us. We are about to leave for forty days. We commit to you now all the keys to this palace, which contains one hundred chambers. Eat and drink and enjoy looking around in every chamber, for each one you open will occupy you a full day, but there is one chamber you must never open or even approach, for it is its opening that will cause our separation. You have ninety-nine chambers to open and to enjoy looking at what is in them as you please, but if you open the one with the door of red gold, that will cause our separation."

But morning overtook Shahrazad, and she lapsed into silence. Then Dinarzad said, "Sister, what a strange and entertaining story!" Shahrazad replied, "What is this compared with what I shall tell you tomorrow night if I stay alive!"

THE SIXTY-FIRST NIGHT

The following night Shahrazad said:

I heard, O happy King, that the third dervish said to the girl:

My lady, the forty girls said, "O our lord, the cause of our separation is in your hand. For God's sake and for our sake, enjoy looking into all ninety-nine chambers, but don't open the hundredth, lest we be separated. Be patient for forty days, and we shall come back to you." Then one of them came up to me, embraced me, wept, and repeated the following verses:

> When she drew near to bid adieu, her heart
> Burning with love and longing in her breast,
> Her tears and mine, wet pearls and carnelians,
> A necklace made for her and came to rest.

I bid her farewell, saying, "By God, I will never open that door." Then the girls left, shaking at me admonishing fingers.

When they departed and I was left alone in the palace, I said to myself, "By God, I will never open that door and never cause our separation." Then I went and opened the first chamber, and when I entered, I found myself in a garden with streams, trees, and abundant fruits. It was a garden like Paradise, with tall trees, intertwining branches, ripe fruits, singing birds, and running waters. Pleased with the sight, I walked through the trees, enjoying the perfume of the flowers and the song of the birds, which hymned together the glory of the Almighty One. I saw apples like those of which the poet said:

> Two colors, in one apple joining, seemed
> Two cheeks in the embrace of love's desire,
> Two cheeks that, as from sleep they startled stood,
> One yellow turned with fright, one burned with fire.

And I saw pears sweeter than sugar and rosewater and more aromatic than musk and ambergris and saw quinces like those of which the poet said:

> The quince has gathered every pleasing taste,
> Thereby the queen of fruits she has been crowned.
> Her taste is wine, a waft of musk her scent.
> Her hue is gold, her shape, like the moon, round.

And I saw plums so lovely that they dazzled the eyes like polished rubies. At last I went out of the garden and closed the door.

The following day I opened another door, and when I entered, I found myself in a large field full of palm trees and encircled by a running stream whose banks were covered with roses, jasmine, mignonettes, irises, daffodils, narcissus, violets, daisies, gillyflowers, and lilies of the valley; and as the breeze blew over these aromatic plants, the whole field was filled with the sweet aroma. After I enjoyed and diverted myself there for a while, I went out and closed the door. Then I opened a third door and found myself in a large hall covered with all kinds of colored marble, rare metals, and precious stones and hung with cages of aloe- and sandalwood, full of all kinds of singing birds, such as nightingales, thrushes, pigeons, ringdoves, turtledoves, silver doves, and Nubian doves. There I enjoyed myself, felt happy, and forgot my cares.

Then I went to sleep, and in the morning I opened a fourth door and found myself in a large hall, surrounded by forty chambers whose doors stood open. I entered every chamber and found them full of jewels, such as pearls, emeralds, rubies, corals, and carbuncles, as well as gold and silver. I was amazed at such abundance and said to myself, "Such wealth could belong only to the greatest of kings, for no ordinary monarch could assemble such a fortune, not even if all the monarchs of the world joined together." I felt happy and carefree, saying to myself, "I am the king of the age, for these jewels and this wealth are mine, and these girls belong to me and to me alone." O my lady, I enjoyed myself in chamber after chamber until thirty-nine days had passed and there remained only one day and one night. During that time, I had opened all ninety-nine chambers, and there remained only the hundredth, the one the girls had cautioned me not to open.

But morning overtook Shahrazad, and she lapsed into silence. Then Dinarzad said to her sister, "Sister, what an amazing and entertaining story!" Shahrazad replied, "What is this compared with what I shall tell you tomorrow night if the king spares me and lets me live!"

THE SIXTY-SECOND NIGHT

The following night Shahrazad said:

I heard, O happy King, that the dervish said:

There remained only that one chamber to complete the hundred, and I began to feel obsessed and tempted with it, as Satan urged me to open it and cause my undoing. Even though there remained but one night for the appointed time for the girls to return and spend a whole year with me, I was no longer able to restrain myself and, succumbing to the devil, at last opened the door plated with gold. As soon as I entered, I was met by a perfume that, as I smelled it, sent me reeling to the floor and made me swoon for a long time. When I came to myself, I summoned my courage and entered the chamber. I found the floor strewn with saffron and saw lamps of gold and silver, fed with costly oils, and saw fragrant candles burning with aloes and ambergris. I also saw two incense burners, each as large as a kneading bowl, full of glowing embers in which burned the incense of aloewood, ambergris, musk, and frankincense, and as the incense burned, the smoke rose to blend with the odors of the candles and the saffron, filling the chamber with perfume.

O my lady, I then saw a deep-black horse as black as the darkest night, bridled and ready with a saddle of red gold, as it stood before two mangers of clear crystal, one filled with husked sesame, the other with rosewater scented with musk. When I saw the horse, I was exceedingly amazed, and said to myself, "There is something of great importance about this horse." Then the devil took hold of me again, and I took the horse from his place and led him outside the palace. I got on his back and tried to ride him, but he refused to move. I kicked him, but he did not stir. Then I took the whip and hit him angrily, and as soon as he felt the blow, he neighed with a sound like roaring thunder and, spreading a pair of wings, flew up with me and disappeared in the sky. A while later he landed on the roof of another palace and, throwing me off his back, lashed my face with his tail with a blow so hard that it gouged out my eye and made it roll on my cheek, leaving me one-eyed. I cried, "There is no power and no strength save in God, the Almighty, the Magnificent. I have taunted the one-eyed young men until I became one-eyed like them."

I looked down from the terrace of the palace and saw again the ten couches with the blue bedding and realized that the palace was the same one that belonged to the ten one-eyed young men who had admonished me and whose admonition I had refused to follow. I went down from the roof and sat down amid the couches, and hardly had I done so when I saw the young men and their old companion approaching. When they saw me, they cried, "You are not welcome or wanted here. By God, we will not let you stay. May you perish." I replied, "All I wanted to know was why you smeared your faces with blue and black soot." They said, "Each of us suffered the same misfortune as you did. We all lived the best of lives in bliss, feeding on chicken, sipping wine from crystal cups, resting on silk brocade, and sleeping on the breasts of fair women. We had to wait one more day to gain a year of pleasures, such food and drink and such entertainment, but because of our curious eyes, we lost our eyes, and now, as you see, we are left to mourn our misfortune." I said, "Do not blame me for what I did, for I have become like you. Indeed, I want you to bring me all ten black trays to blacken my face," and I burst into bitter tears. They replied, "By God, by God, we will never harbor you or let you stay with us. Get out of here, go to Baghdad, and find someone to help you there."

When I saw that there was no avail against their harsh treatment and when I recalled the miseries written on my forehead, how I killed the young man and how 'I would be sitting pretty but for my curiosity,' I could no longer stand it. I shaved off my beard and eyebrows, renounced everything, and roamed the world, a one-eyed dervish. Then God granted me safe passage and I reached Baghdad on the evening of this very night. Here I met these two men standing at a loss, and I greeted them and said, "I am a stranger," and they replied, "We are strangers like you." We formed an extraordinary group, for by coincidence, all three of us happened to be blind in the right eye. This, my lady, was the cause of losing my eye and shaving off my beard.

It is related, O happy King, that after the girl heard the dervishes' tales, she said to them, "Stroke your heads and go your way," but they replied, "By God, we will not go until we hear our companions' tales." Then, turning to the caliph, Ja'far, and Masrur, the girl said, "Tell us your tales." Ja'far stood forth and said, "O my lady, we are citizens of Mosul who have come to your city for trade. When we arrived here, we took lodgings in the merchants' inn and we traded and sold our goods. Tonight a merchant of your city held a party and invited all the merchants in the inn, including our group, to his house, where we had a good time, with choice wine, entertainment, and singing girls. Then there was argument and yelling among some of the guests, and the prefect of police raided the place. Some of us were arrested and some escaped. We were among those who escaped, and when we went to the inn, late at night, we found the door locked, not to be opened again till sunrise. We wandered helplessly, not knowing where to go, for fear that the police would catch up with us, arrest us, and humiliate us. God drove us to your house, and when we heard the beautiful singing and the sound of carousing, we knew that there was a company having a party inside and said to ourselves that we would enter at your service and spend the rest of our night with you to entertain you and to make our pleasure complete. It pleased you to offer us your hospitality and to be generous and kind. This was the cause of our coming to you."

The dervishes said, "O our lady and mistress, we wish you to grant us as a favor the lives of these three men and to let us depart with gratitude." Looking at the entire group, the girl replied, "I grant you your lives, as a favor to all." When they were outside the house, the caliph asked the dervishes, "Men, where are you going, for it is still dark?" They replied, "By God, sir, we do not know where to go." He said, "Come and sleep at our place." Then, turning to Ja'far, the caliph said, "Take these men home with you for the night and bring them before me early tomorrow morning, so that we may chronicle for each his adventure that we have heard tonight." Ja'far did as the caliph bade him, while the caliph returned to his palace. But the caliph was agitated and stayed awake, pondering the mishaps of the dervishes and how they had changed from being sons of kings to what they were now, and burning with curiosity to hear the stories of the flogged girl and the other with the two black bitches. He could not sleep a wink and waited impatiently for the morning.

No sooner had the day dawned than he sat on his throne, and when Ja'far entered and kissed the ground before him, he said, "This is no time for dawdling. Go and bring me the two ladies, so that I may hear the story of the two bitches, and bring the dervishes with you," yelling at him, "Hurry!" Ja'far withdrew and came back soon with the three girls and the three dervishes. Then placing the dervishes next to him and the girls behind a curtain, he said, "Women, we forgive you because of your generosity and kindness to us. If you do not know who is the one sitting before you, I shall introduce him. You are in the presence of the seventh of the sons of 'Abbas, al-Rashid, son of al-Mahdi son of al-Hadi and brother of al-Saffah son of Mansur. Take courage, be frank, and tell the truth and nothing but the truth, and do not lie, for 'you should be truthful even if the truth sends you to burning Hell.' Explain to the caliph why you beat the two black bitches, why you weep after you beat them, and why they weep with you."

But morning overtook Shahrazad, and she lapsed into silence. Then Dinarzad said, "Sister, what a strange and amazing story!" Shahrazad replied, "What is this compared with what I shall tell you tomorrow night if the king spares me and lets me live!"

THE SIXTY-THIRD NIGHT
The following night Shahrazad said:

I heard, O happy King, that when the girl who was the mistress of the house heard what Ja'far said to her on behalf of the Commander of the Faithful, she said:

[The Tale of the First Lady, the Mistress of the House]

My case is so strange and my tale is so amazing that were it engraved with needles at the corner of the eye, it would be a lesson for those who wish to consider. The two black bitches are my sisters by the same mother and father. These two girls, the one whose body bears the marks of the rod and the other who is the shopper are sisters by another mother. When our father died and the inheritance was divided, the three of us lived with our mother, while the other two sisters lived with their own mother. After a while, our mother also died, leaving us three thousand dinars, which we divided equally among ourselves. Since I was the youngest of the three, my two sisters prepared their dowries and got married before me.

The husband of the eldest sister bought merchandise with his money and hers, and the two of them set out on their travels. They were absent for five years, during which time he threw away and wasted all her money. Then he deserted her, leaving her to wander alone in foreign lands, trying to find her way back home. After five years she returned to me, dressed like a beggar in tattered clothes and a dirty old cloak. She was in a most miserable plight. When I saw her, I was stunned, and I asked her, "Why are you in this condition?" She replied, "Words are useless, for 'the pen has brought to pass that which had been decreed.'" O Commander of the Faithful, I took her at once to the bath, dressed her with new clothes, prepared for her some broth, and gave her some wine to drink. I took care of her for a month, and then I said to her, "Sister, you are the eldest, and you have now taken the place of our mother. You and I will share my wealth equally, for God has blessed my share of the inheritance, and I have made much money by spinning and producing silk." I treated her with the utmost kindness, and she lived with me for a whole year, during which time our minds were on our other sister. Shortly she too came home in a worse plight than the first. I treated her just as I had treated the other, clothing her and taking care of her.

A little later, they said to me, "Sister, we would like to get married, for it is not fitting that we live without husbands." I replied, "Sister, there is little good in marriage, for it is hard to find a good man. You got married, but nothing good came of it. Let us stay together and live by ourselves." But, O Commander of the Faithful, they did not listen to my advice and married again without my consent. This time I was obliged to provide them with dowries from my own pocket. Soon their husbands betrayed them; they took what they could, cleared out, and left their wives behind. My two sisters came to me with apologies, saying, "Sister, although you are younger than the two of us in years, you are older in wisdom. We will never mention marriage again. Take us back, and we shall be your servants to earn our upkeep." I replied, "Sisters, none is dearer to me than you." I took them in and treated them even more generously than before. We spent the third year together, and all that time my wealth kept increasing, and my circumstances kept getting better and better.

One day, O Commander of the Faithful, I resolved to take my merchandise to Basra.[4] I fitted a large ship and loaded it with merchandise, provisions, and other necessities. Then we set out, and for many days we sailed under a fair wind. Soon we discovered that we had strayed from our course, and for twenty days we were lost on the high seas. At the end of the twentieth day, the lookout man, climbing the masthead, cried out, "Good news!" Then he joyfully came down, saying, "I have seen what seems to be a city that looks like a fat pigeon." We were happy, and in less than an hour our ship entered the harbor, and I disembarked to visit the city. When I came to the gate, I saw people standing there with staves in their hands, but as I drew nearer, I saw that they had been turned by a curse into stone. I went into the city and saw that all the people in their shops had been turned into stone. Not one of them breathed or gave a sign of life. I walked through the streets and found out that the entire city had been turned into hard stone. When I came to the upper end of the city, I saw a

4. Then and now a port city in southern Iraq, situated on the Shat al-Arab, a waterway formed by the confluence of the Tigris and the Euphrates and going into the Arabian, or Persian, Gulf.

door plated with red gold, draped with a silk curtain, and hung with a lamp. Saying to myself, "By God, this is strange! Can it be that there are human beings here!" I entered through the door and found myself in a hall that led to another and then another, and as I kept going from hall to hall all alone, without meeting anyone, I became apprehensive. Then I entered the harem quarters and found myself in an apartment bearing the royal insignia and hung throughout with drapes of gold brocade. There I saw the queen, the king's wife, wearing a dress decorated with opulent pearls, each as big as a hazelnut, and a crown studded with precious stones.

But morning overtook Shahrazad, and she lapsed into silence. Then Dinarzad said to her sister, "Sister, what an entertaining story!" Shahrazad replied, "What is this compared with what I shall tell you tomorrow night if the king spares me and lets me live!"

THE SIXTY-FOURTH NIGHT

The following night Shahrazad said:

I heard, O King, that the girl who was the mistress of the house said to the caliph:

O Commander of the Faithful, the queen wore a crown studded with all kinds of gems, and the apartment was spread with silk tapestries embroidered with gold. In the middle of the hall I saw an ivory bed plated with burnished gold, set with two bosses of green emeralds, and draped with a canopylike net strung with pearls. I saw something glitter, sending rays through the net, and when I approached and put my head in, I saw there, O Commander of the Faithful, set on a pedestal, a gem as big as an ostrich egg, with an incandescent glow and a brilliant light that dazzled the eyes. I also saw silk bedding and a silk coverlet, and beside the pillow, I saw two lighted candles. But there was nobody in the bed. I marveled at the sight, and astonished to find the gem and the two lighted candles, I said to myself, "Someone must have lighted these candles." Then I proceeded to other rooms and came to the kitchen, then the wine cellar, then the king's treasure chambers. I continued to explore the palace, going from room to room, absorbed in the wonderful sights and the amazing state of the city's inhabitants, until I forgot myself and was surprised by the night. I searched for the gate of the castle, but I lost my way and could not find it, and for a long time I wandered in the dark without finding a place of refuge save the canopied bed with the candles. I lay down there, covered myself with the coverlet, and tried to go to sleep, but I could not.

At midnight I heard a sweet voice chanting the Qur'an. I rose, glad to hear someone, and followed the voice until I came to a chamber, whose door stood ajar. I peered through and saw what looked like a place of worship and recitation, with a prayer niche lighted with hanging lamps and two candles. On a prayer carpet stood a section of the Qur'an set on a stand, and on the carpet sat a handsome young man reciting the Holy Book. I was amazed to find that this young man was the only one among the people of the city to have escaped the curse and thought that there was a mystery behind this. I opened the door and, entering the chamber, greeted him and said, "Blessed be God who has granted you to me, to be the cause of our deliverance and help our ship return to our native land. O holy man, by the Holy Book you are reciting, answer my question." He looked at me with a smile and said, "O good woman, tell me first what caused you to come here, and I shall relate to you what happened to me and to the people of this city and why they were cursed while I was not." I told him our story and how our ship had strayed for twenty days. Then I questioned him again about the city and its people, and he replied, "O sister, be patient, and I shall tell you." Then he closed the Qur'an, put it aside, and seated me, O Commander of the Faithful . . .

But morning overtook Shahrazad, and Dinarzad said, "O sister, what a strange and entertaining story!" Shahrazad replied, "Sister, what is this compared with what I shall tell you tomorrow night if the king spares me and lets me live!"

THE SIXTY-FIFTH NIGHT

The following night Shahrazad said:

It is related, O happy King, that the girl who was the mistress of the house said to the caliph:

O Commander of the Faithful, the young man placed the Qur'an in the prayer niche and seated me by his side. When I looked at him, I saw a face as beautiful as the full moon, like the one of whom the poet said:

> The stargazer one night charted the stars
> And saw his fair form shining like a moon
> Who vied in brilliance with the hiding sun
> And left in darkness the bewildered moon.

It was a face on which the supreme God has bestowed the robe of beauty, which was embroidered with the grace of his perfect cheeks. He was like the one of whom the poet said:

> By his enchanting eyelids and his slender waist,
> By his beguiling eyes so keen, so fair,
> By his sharp glances and his tender sides,
> By his white forehead and his jet black hair,
> By eyebrows that have robbed my eyes of sleep   5
> And made me subject to their mighty will,
> By lovely sidelocks that curl, coil, and charm
> And all rejected lovers with their beauty kill,
> By the soft myrtle of his rosy cheeks,
> By his carnelian lips and mouth of pearls,   10
> Which sends the fragrance of the honey breath,
> And the sweet wine which in its sweetness purls,
> By his graceful neck and his boughlike frame,
> Which bears two pomegranates on the breast,
> By his charming, tender, and slender waist,   15
> And hips that quiver while they move or rest,
> By his soft silky skin and charming touch
> And all the beauty that his own does seem,

> By his open hand and his truthful tongue,
> And noble pedigree and high esteem, 20
> By these I swear that his life-giving breath
> Gives the musk being and perfumes the air,
> That the sun pales before him and the moon
> Is nothing but a paring of his nail; I swear.

O Commander of the Faithful, I looked at him and sighed, for he had captivated my heart. I said to him, "O my dear lord, tell me the story of your city." He said, "O woman of God, this city is the capital of my father the king whom you must have seen turned into black stone inside this cursed palace, together with my mother the queen whom you found inside the net. They and all the people of the city were Magians[5] who, instead of the Omnipotent Lord, worshiped the fire, to which they prayed and by which they swore. My father, who had been blessed with me late in life, reared me in affluence, and I grew and throve. It happened that there lived with us a very old woman who used to teach me the Qur'an, saying, '"You should worship none but the Almighty God,"' and I learned the Qur'an without telling my father or the rest of my family. One day we heard a mighty voice proclaiming, 'O people of this city, leave your fire worship and worship the Merciful God.' But they refused to obey. A year later the voice cried out again and did the same the following year. Suddenly one morning the city turned into stone, and none was saved except myself. Here I sit now, as you see, to worship God, but I have grown weary of loneliness, for there is none to keep me company."

I said to him (for he had captured my heart and mastered my life and soul), "Come with me to the city of Baghdad, for this girl standing before you is the head of her family, mistress over servants and slaves, and a businesswoman of considerable wealth, part of which is on the very ship that, after straying, now anchors outside your city, by the will of God who drove us here that I might meet you." I continued to press him, O Commander of the Faithful, until he consented. I spent that night, hardly believing my fortune, asleep at his feet. When morning dawned, we rose and, taking from his father's treasure chambers whatever was light in weight and great in worth, the two of us went from the castle to the city and found the captain, my sisters, and my servants looking for me. When they saw me, they were happy, and when I related to them the story of the young man and the city, they were amazed. But when my two sisters, these very bitches, saw the young man with me, they envied me, O Commander of the Faithful, and harbored ill feelings toward me. Then we went aboard, all of us feeling happy at our gain, most of all I, because of the young man, and sat waiting for the wind to blow before setting sail.

But morning overtook Shahrazad, and she lapsed into silence. Then Dinarzad said, "O sister, what a strange and entertaining story!" Shahrazad replied, "What is this compared with what I shall tell you tomorrow if the king spares me and lets me live!"

5. Zoroastrian priests.

The following night Shahrazad said:

It is related, O happy King, that the girl who was the mistress of the house said to the caliph:

O Commander of the Faithful, when the wind began to blow, we set sail, and, as we sat chatting, my sisters asked me, "Sister, what will you do with this young man?" I replied, "I will make him my husband." Then I turned to him and said, "O my lord, I want you to follow my wish that when we reach Baghdad, our native city, I offer you myself in marriage as your maidservant, and we will be husband and wife." The young man replied, "Yes, indeed, for you are my lady and my mistress, and I will obey you in everything." Then I turned to my sisters and said, "Whatever goods we have brought are yours; my only reward is this young man; he is mine and I am his." But my sisters turned green with envy over him and harbored ill feelings toward me. We sailed on under a fair wind until we entered the Sea of Safety and began to approach Basra. When night came, and the young man and I fell asleep, my two sisters, who had been waiting patiently, carried me with my bed and threw me into the sea. They did the same thing to the young man. He drowned, but I was saved; I wish that I had drowned with him. I was cast on a raised island, and when I came to myself and saw myself surrounded by water, I realized that my sisters had betrayed me, and I thanked God for my safety. Meantime, the ship sailed on like a flash of lightning, while I stood alone through the night.

When morning dawned, I saw a dry strip of land connecting the island to the shore. I crossed it; then I wrung out my clothes and spread them to dry in the sun. When they were dry, I ate some dates and drank some fresh water I had found there; then I proceeded to walk until there remained only two hours between me and the city. As I sat to rest, I suddenly saw a long serpent, as thick as the trunk of a palm tree, gliding sideways and sweeping the sand in her way, as she speeded toward me. When she drew near, I saw that she was being pursued by a long and slender serpent, as slender as a spear and as long as two. He had seized her by the tail, while she, with a tongue about ten inches long, rolling in the dust, and eyes streaming with tears, wriggled right and left, trying to escape. Feeling pity for her, O Commander of the Faithful, I ran toward a big stone, picked it up, and calling on God for help, hit him with it and killed him. As soon as he rolled dead, the serpent opened a pair of wings, flew up, and disappeared from my sight.

Then I sat down to rest and dozed off, and when I awoke, I saw a black girl, together with two bitches, sitting at my feet, massaging them. Sitting up, I asked, "O friend, who are you?" She replied, "How soon you have forgotten me. I am she for whom you have done the good deed and sowed the seed of gratitude. I am the serpent who was in distress until it pleased you, with the help of the Almighty God, to kill my foe. In order to reward you, I hurried after the ship and carried to your house everything that belonged to you. Then I ordered my attendants to sink the ship, for I knew how you had been kind to your sisters all your life and how they had treated you, how out of envy over the young man, they threw you both into the sea and caused him to drown. Here they are, these two black bitches, and I swear by the Creator of the heavens that if you disobey my command, I will take you and imprison you under the earth." Then the girl shook and, turning into a bird, picked up me and my two sisters and flew up with us until she set us down in my house, where I found all my property, which she had brought from the ship. Then she said to me, "I swear by 'Him who made the two seas flow'—this is my second oath—that if you disobey my command, I will turn you into a bitch like them. I charge you to give them every night three hundred blows with the rod, as a punishment for what they did." I replied, "I shall obey," and she departed and left me. Since that time, I have been forced to punish them every night until they bleed. I feel very sorry for them, and, knowing that I am not to blame for their punishment, they forgive me. This is the cause of my beating them and crying with them, and this is my story and the end of my history.

When she finished, the caliph was greatly amazed. Then the Commander of the Faithful ordered Ja'far to ask the second girl to explain to them the cause of the rod marks on her sides and chest. She said:

O Commander of the Faithful, when my father died . . .

But morning overtook Shahrazad, and she lapsed into silence. Then her sister said, "O sister, what an entertaining story!" Shahrazad replied, "What is this compared with what I shall tell you tomorrow night if the king spares me and lets me live!"

THE SIXTY-SEVENTH NIGHT

The following night Shahrazad said:

I heard, O happy King, that the flogged girl said to the Commander of the Faithful:

[The Tale of the Second Lady, the Flogged One]

When my father died, he left me a great deal of money. Shortly thereafter, I married the wealthiest man in Baghdad, and for a year I lived with him the happiest of lives. Then he too died and left me my legal share of the inheritance, which was ninety thousand dinars. I lived a prosperous life, buying so much gold jewelry, clothes, and embroideries that I had ten complete changes of clothes, each costing one thousand dinars, and my reputation spread in the city. One day, as I was sitting at home, an old woman came to me, and what an old woman she was, with a pallid, scabby skin; a bent body; matted gray hair; a gray, freckled face; broken teeth; plucked-out eyebrows; hollow, bleary eyes; and a runny nose. She was like the one of whom the poet said:

> Seven defects are planted in her face,
> The least of which is but the curse of fate
> A bleary frown that covers all the face,
> A mouth full of stones, or a mowed-down pate.

She greeted me and, kissing the ground before me, said, "My lady, I have an orphan daughter, and tonight is her unveiling and wedding night, but we are brokenhearted, for we are strangers in this city, and we do not know anyone. If you come to her wedding, you will earn a reward in Heaven, for when the ladies of this city will hear that you are coming, they too will come, and you shall honor us with your presence and make her happy." Then the old woman repeated the following verses:

> We own that your visit is an honor
> That cannot be performed by another.

She wept and implored me until I felt pity for her and agreed to her request. I said, "Yes, I shall do it for the sake of the Almighty God, and she will not be unveiled to her bridegroom, save in my clothes, ornaments, and jewelry." Overjoyed, the old woman bent and kissed my feet, saying, "May God reward you and comfort you, as you have comforted me, but my lady, do not trouble yourself yet. Be ready at suppertime, and I shall come and fetch you." When she left, I proceeded to string the pearls, assemble the embroideries, and pack the ornaments and jewelry, not knowing what God had in store for me. At nightfall the old woman arrived with a happy smile and, kissing my hand, said, "Most of the ladies of the city are already assembled in our house, and they are waiting for you and looking forward to your coming." I rose, put on my outer garment, and, wrapping myself in my cloak, followed the old lady with my maids behind me. We walked on until we came to a well-swept and watered alley and stood before a door draped with a black curtain hung with a lamp covered with gold filigree, bearing the following inscription in letters of gold:

> I am the house of mirth
> And eternal laughter.
> Inside a fountain flows
> With a healing water,
> With myrtle, daisy, rose,   5
> And clove pink for border.

The old woman knocked at the door, and when it was opened we entered and saw silk carpets covering the floor and saw two rows of lighted candles that formed an avenue leading from the door to the upper end of the hall. There stood a couch of juniper wood, encrusted with gems and hung with a canopylike red-speckled silk curtain. Suddenly, O Commander of the Faithful, a girl came out from behind the curtain, shining like the half moon. Indeed, her face was as radiant as the full moon or the rising sun, just like her of whom the poet said:

> To her inferior Caesar she was sent,
> A gift nobler than all her Persian kings.
> The roses blossomed on her rosy cheeks,
> Staining with crimson dye such lovely things.
> Slender and sleepy-eyed and languorous,   5
> She won from Beauty all of Beauty's ploys,
> As if her forelock sat upon her brow
> A night of gloom before a dawn of joys.

The girl came down from the couch and said to me, "Welcome and greetings to my dear and illustrious sister." Then she recited the following verses:

> If the house could know who has visited,
> It would rejoice and kiss the very dust,
> As if to say, "Only the generous
> Has by his gifts such welcome merited."

Then she came up to me, O Commander of the Faithful, and said, "O my lady, I have a brother who is more handsome by far than I. He has noticed you at some wedding feasts and other festive occasions, and, seeing your great beauty and charm and hearing that, like him, you are the head of your clan, he has decided that he would like to tie his knot with you, so that you may become husband and wife." I replied, "Yes, I hear and obey." O Commander of the Faithful, no sooner had I uttered these words than she clapped her hands and a door opened and out came a finely dressed young man in the bloom of youth, all beauty and perfect grace. He was sweetly coquettish, with a fine figure, eyebrows arching like a bow, and eyes that bewitched the heart with their holy magic. He was like him of whom the poet said:

> He has a face as bright as the young moon,
> And joys as pearls he scatters as a boon.

As soon as I looked at him, I was attracted to him. He sat beside me and chatted with me for a while; then the girl clapped her hands a second time, and a door opened and out came a judge and four witnesses, who sat and wrote the marriage contract. Then the young man made me pledge that I would not look at any other man, and he was not satisfied until I took a solemn oath. I was feeling very happy and impatient for the night to come. When it finally came, we retired to our room, and I spent with him the best of nights. In the morning he slaughtered many sheep in thanksgiving, showed me favors, and treated me lovingly. For a full month thereafter, I lived with him a most happy life.

One day, wishing to buy certain fabric, I asked him for permission to go to the market. He consented, and I went with the old woman and two maids. When we entered the silk-mercers' market, the old woman said, "O my lady, here is a very young merchant who has a large stock of goods and every kind of fabric you may desire, and no one in the market has better goods. Let us go into his shop, and there you can buy whatever you wish." We entered his shop, and I saw that he was slender, handsome, and very young, like him of whom the poet said:

> Here is a slender youth whose hair and face
> All mortals envelope with light or gloom.
> Mark on his cheek the mark of charm and grace,
> A dark spot on a red anemone.

I said to the old lady, "Let him show us some nice fabric." She replied, "Ask him yourself." I said, "Don't you know that I have sworn not to speak to any man except my husband?" So she said to him, "Show us some fabric," and he showed us several pieces, some of which I liked. I said to the old woman, "Ask him for the price." When she asked him, he replied, "I will sell them for neither silver nor gold but for a kiss on her cheek." I said, "God save me from such a thing." But the old woman said, "O my lady, you needn't talk to him or he to you; just turn your face to him and let him kiss it; that is all there is to it." Tempted by her, I turned my face to him. He put his mouth on my cheek and bit off with his teeth a piece of my flesh. I fainted, and when I came to myself, a long time later, I saw that he had locked the shop and departed, while the old woman, in a display of grief, sorrowed over my bleeding face.

But morning overtook Shahrazad, and she lapsed into silence.

THE SIXTY-EIGHTH NIGHT

The following night Shahrazad said:

I have heard, O happy King, that the flogged girl said to the Commander of the Faithful:

The old woman, expressing anguish, grief, and sorrow, said, "O my lady, God has saved you from something worse. Take heart and let us go, before the matter becomes public. When you get home, pretend to be sick, and cover yourself up, and I will bring you powders and plasters that will heal your cheek within three days." I rose, and we walked slowly until we reached the house, where I collapsed on the floor with pain. Then I lay in bed, covered myself up, and drank some wine.

In the evening my husband came in and asked, "O my darling, what is the matter with you?" I replied, "I have a headache." He lighted a candle and, coming close to me, looked at my face and, seeing the wound on my cheek, asked, "What caused this?" I replied, "When I went today to the market to buy some fabric, a camel driver with a load of firewood jostled me in a narrow passage, and one of the pieces tore my veil and cut my cheek, as you see." He said, "Tomorrow I shall ask the governor of the city to hang every camel driver in this city." I replied, "O my lord, this does not warrant hanging innocent men and bearing the guilt of their death." He asked, "Then who did it?" I replied, "I was riding a rented donkey, and when the donkey driver drove it hard, it stumbled and threw me to the ground, and I fell on a piece of glass that happened to be there and cut my cheek." He said, "By God, I shall not let the sun rise before I go to Ja'far the Barmakid[6] and ask him to hang every donkey driver and every sweeper in this city." I said, "By God, my lord, this is not what really happened to me. Don't hang people because of me." He asked, "What then is the real cause of your wound?" I replied, "I suffered what God had foreordained for me." He kept pressing me relentlessly, and I kept mumbling and resisting him until he drove me to speak rudely to him. At that moment, O Commander of the Faithful, he cried out and a door opened and out came three black slaves who, at his bidding, dragged me out of my bed and threw me down on my back in the middle of the room. Then he ordered one slave to sit on my knees, the other to hold my head, and the third to draw his sword, saying to him, "You, Sa'd, strike her and with one blow cut her in half and let each of you carry one half and throw it into the Tigris river for the fish to feed upon. This is the punishment of those who violate the vow." Then he grew angrier and recited the following verses:

6. Harun al-Rashid's vizier.

> If there be one who shares the one I love,
> I'll kill my love even though my soul dies,
> Saying, "Better nobly to die, O soul,
> Than share a love for which another vies."

Then he ordered the slave to strike me with the sword. When the slave was sure of the command, he bent down to me and said, "O my lady, have you any wish, for this is the last moment of your life?" I replied, "Get off me, so that I may tell him something." I raised my head and, thinking of my condition and how I had fallen from high esteem into disgrace and from life into death, I wept bitterly and choked with sobs. But my husband looked at me angrily and recited the following verses:

> Tell her who for another lover left,
> Bored with me, and repaid me with disdain,
> That even though I suffered first, I found
> Contentment in what was between us twain.

When I heard his words, O Commander of the Faithful, I wept and, looking at him, replied with the following verses:

> You set my poor heart burning with your love
> And left my eyes to smart and went to sleep,
> While all alone I thought of you and wept
> And in my sorrow did a vigil keep.
> You promised to be faithful to the end,
> But when you had my heart, you broke the vow.
> I loved you in all childish innocence;
> Kill not that love, for I am learning now.

But when he heard my verses, O Commander of the Faithful, he grew even angrier and, giving me a furious look, recited the following verses:

> 'Twas not boredom that bid me leave my love,
> But a sin that imposed such fate on me.
> She wished to let another share our love,
> But faith forbade me such a blasphemy.

I wept and implored and, looking at him, recited the following verses:

> You left me burdened with the weight of love,
> Being too weak even a shirt to wear.
> I marvel not that my soul wastes away
> But that my body can your absence bear.

When he heard my words, he cursed me and scolded me. Then looking at me, he recited the following verses:

> You left me to enjoy another love
> And showed disdain, a deed I could not do.
> If you dislike my presence, I will leave

> And rue the end of love, as you did rue,
> And take another lover for myself,   5
> For love was killed not by me but by you.

Then he yelled at the slave, saying, "Cut her in half and rid me of her, for her life is worthless." O Commander of the Faithful, as we argued in verse, I grew certain of death and gave up myself for lost, but suddenly the old woman rushed in and, throwing herself at my husband's feet, said tearfully, "O son, by the rights of rearing you up, by the breasts that nursed you, and by my service to you, pardon her for my sake. You are still young, and you should not bear the guilt of her death, for as it is said, 'Whoever slays shall be slain.' Why bother with such a worthless woman? Drive her out of your hearth and heart." She kept weeping and imploring until he relented and said, "But I must brand her and leave a permanent mark on her." Then he ordered the slaves to strip me of all my clothes and stretch me on the floor, and when they sat on me to pin me down, he rose and, fetching a quince rod, fell with blows on my sides until I despaired of life and lost consciousness. Then he bade the slaves take me to my own home as soon as it was dark and let the old woman show them the way.

Following their master's command, they took me away, threw me into my house, and departed. I remained unconscious till the morning. Then I treated myself with ointments and drugs, but my body remained disfigured from the beating and my sides bore the marks of the rod. I lay sick in bed for four months, and when I recovered and was able to get up, I went to look for my husband's house but found it in ruin. The entire alley, from beginning to end, was torn down, and on the site of the house stood piles of rubbish. Unable to find out how this had come about, I went to this woman, my sister on my father's side, and found her with these two black bitches. I greeted her and told her my story, and she said, "O my sister, who is safe from the accidents of life and the misfortunes of the world?" Then she repeated the following verses:

> Such is the world; with patience it is best
> The loss of wealth or loss of love to breast.

Then, O Commander of the Faithful, she told me her story, what her sisters had done to her, and what had become of them.

We lived together without thinking of any man, and every day, this girl, the shopper, would come by and go to the market to buy for us what we needed for the day and the night. We lived like this for a long time until yesterday, when our sister went to shop as usual and returned with the porter, whom we allowed to stay to divert us. Less than a quarter of the night had passed when these three dervishes joined us, and we sat to converse, and when a third of the night had gone by, three respectable merchants from Mosul joined us and told us about their adventures. We had pledged the guests to accept a condition, and when they broke the pledge, we treated them accordingly. Then we questioned them about themselves, and when they told us their tales, we pardoned them and they departed. This morning we were unexpectedly summoned to your presence. This is our story.

The caliph, O happy King, marveled at their tales and their adventures.

But morning overtook Shahrazad, and she lapsed into silence. Then Dinarzad said, "O sister, what a strange, amazing, and entertaining story!" Shahrazad replied, "What is this compared with what I shall tell you tomorrow night if the king spares me and lets me live!"

THE SIXTY-NINTH NIGHT

The following night Shahrazad said:

It is related, O glorious King, that the caliph, marveling at these adventures, turned to the first girl and said, "Tell me what happened to the demon serpent who had cast a spell on your sisters and turned them into bitches. Do you know her whereabouts, and did she set with you the date of her return to you?" The girl replied, "O Commander of the Faithful, she gave me a tuft of hair, saying 'Whenever you need me, burn two of the hairs, and I will be with you at once, even if I am beyond Mount Qaf.'" The caliph asked, "Where is the tuft of hair?" She brought it, and he took it and burned the entire tuft. Suddenly the whole palace began to tremble, and the serpent arrived and said, "Peace be with you, O Commander of the Faithful! This woman has sown with me the seed of gratitude, and I cannot reward her amply enough, for she killed my enemy and saved me from death. Knowing what her sisters had done to her, I felt bound to reward her by avenging her. At first, I was about to destroy them once and for all, but I feared that their deaths would be hard on her; therefore, I cast a spell on them and turned them into bitches. Now, if you wish me to release them, O Commander of the Faithful, I will do it gladly, for your wish is my command, O Commander of the Faithful!" The caliph replied, "O spirit, release them and let us deliver them from their misery. After you release them, I will look into the case of this flogged girl, and may the Almighty God help me and make it easy for me to solve her case and discover who wronged her and usurped her rights, for I am sure that she is telling the truth." The she-demon replied, "O Commander of the Faithful, not only will I release these two bitches, but I will also reveal to you who abused and beat this girl. In fact, he is the nearest of all men to you." Then she took, O King, a bowl of water, and muttering a spell over it in words no one could understand, sprinkled the two sisters with the water and turned them back into their original form.

Then the she-demon said, "O Commander of the Faithful, the man who beat this girl is your son al-Amin brother of al-Ma'mun. He had heard of her beauty and charm, and he tricked her into a legal marriage. But he is not to blame for beating her, for he pledged her and bound her by a solemn oath not to do a certain thing, but she broke the pledge. He was about to kill her but, reflecting on the sin of murder and fearing the Almighty God, contented himself with flogging her and sending her back to her home. Such is the story of the second girl, and God knows all." When the caliph heard what the she-demon said and found out who had flogged the girl, he was exceedingly amazed and said, "Praise be to the Almighty God who has blessed me and helped me to release these two women and deliver them from sorcery and torture and who has blessed me a second time and revealed to me the cause of that woman's misfortune. By God, I am now going to do a deed by which I will be remembered." Then the caliph, O King, summoned his son al-Amin and questioned him to confirm the truth of the story. Then he assembled together the judge and witnesses, the three dervishes, the first girl and her two sisters who had been cast under a spell, and the flogged girl and the shopper. When they were all assembled, he married the first girl and her sisters who had been cast under a spell to the three dervishes, who were the sons of kings. He made the three dervishes chamberlains and members of his inner circle, giving them money, clothes, horses, a palace in Baghdad, and everything they needed. He married the flogged girl to his son al-Amin, under a new marriage contract, showered her with wealth and ordered the house to be rebuilt and made even better than before. Then the commander of the Faithful himself married the third girl, the shopper. The people marveled at the caliph's wisdom, tolerance, and generosity and, when all the facts were revealed, recorded these stories.

GIOVANNI BOCCACCIO
1313–1375

In 1362, Boccaccio had a midlife crisis: told by a monk that his death was approaching and that he must renounce his frivolous devotion to poetry, he decided to sell or throw away all his books. His intimate friend, **Petrarch**, urged him to reconsider; but if Boccaccio insisted on getting rid of his books, Petrarch added eagerly, "I am indeed grateful that you have offered them to me." Just two years later, Boccaccio again fell into a dark mood, this time almost led by his admiration of Petrarch's Latin masterworks to burn all of his own writings composed in the "low" language of Italian in order to clear the ground for the revival of a pure, classical Latin. Thankfully, Boccaccio did not give in to his urge, for today's readers have all but forgotten the learned encyclopedic compendia that he was certain would endure the test of time. Instead, modern audiences respond with a delighted sense of familiarity to the "medieval" Boccaccio of the *Decameron*, whose unruly and uncouth tales much more accurately

represent the chaos of everyday life than would be allowed by the strictures of Renaissance art and religion. In this work overflowing with multiple narratives of priests and sailors, merchants and princesses, Boccaccio disregarded all conceivable rules of decorum in order to celebrate the variety and fecundity of Mediterranean culture.

LIFE AND TIMES

Boccaccio was born in 1313, the illegitimate son of a merchant associated with the powerful Bardi banking family. Boccaccio's father arranged for his son's education, which included the study of accounting, doubtless hoping that the boy would enter his own line of work. When the young Boccaccio became restless during his apprenticeship in the countinghouses of the Bardi family, his father obligingly arranged for him to study law instead, but all Boccaccio wanted to do was to become a poet. He found a temporary outlet for his literary ambitions in the household of Robert of Anjou, a stimulating environment rich in art and culture. In his letters, Boccaccio describes these as the happiest days of his life, and it was with regret that he left Naples in 1340 to seek more permanent employment in Florence, where he spent most of the rest of his life.

At this time, an extraordinary movement was just beginning in mid-fourteenth-century Italy that would spread across both northern and southern Europe. Humanism would affect language, literature, philosophy, and theology, but in its foundational moment, it centered on the role of language: in response to the late medieval flowering of vernacular literature found in the French of the *Song of Roland*, in the Provençal of troubadour lyric, and, above all, in the "illustrious vernacular" of **Dante**'s *Divine Comedy*, a new generation of writers became determined to restore Latin to its ancient glory and to create a neo-classical literature that would follow in the footsteps of Virgil, Ovid, and—most particularly—the orator Cicero. The self-proclaimed leader of this movement was Petrarch, who, only a few years older than Boccaccio, was nonetheless recognized by the younger poet as his mentor and superior. Under Petrarch's guidance, Boccaccio turned away from his early narrative poems in the Italian language, such as the *Teseida* (the source of **Chaucer**'s Knight's Tale), *Diana's Hunt* (*Caccia di Diana*), and *Amorous Vision* (*Amorosa visione*), which nevertheless inspired a wide range of Renaissance poetry in France and England as well as in Italy. His embrace of Latin entailed not only a change of language but also a change of literary form, leading Boccaccio to produce learned Latin encyclopedias, such as an account of the rise and fall of famous men on the wheel of Fortune (*De casibus virorum illustrium*)

and a genealogy of the Greek and Roman gods (*De genealogia deorum gentilium*). Boccaccio enthusiastically signed on to Petrarch's project, both by producing his own Latin literary works and by participating in the humanist effort to revive ancient Greek poetry— most directly in his effort to produce a Latin translation of Homer's *Iliad* and *Odyssey*. Finding his own command of Greek too limited for such an important undertaking, Boccaccio had to content himself with hiring a native Greek speaker to carry out the work.

At exactly this moment of linguistic and cultural transition, an event took place that transformed the landscape of medieval Europe: from 1348 to 1351, the Black Death swept through the region, killing a third of the population. Mortality rates were particularly high in cities; indeed, in some locations half or even three-quarters of the population died. This event is the setting of Boccaccio's *Decameron*, which opens with a harrowing account of the effects of plague—not just the direct effects of the disease on individuals' bodies but its indirect effects on the body politic of Florence, torn apart and almost destroyed by the ravages of illness so horrific that, in Boccaccio's words, "brother abandoned brother" and, "almost unbelievable, fathers and mothers neglected to tend and care for their children, as if they were not their own." The two main forces of social order in the time of plague were the city governments, which sought to control the spread of disease and limit its impact on public health, and the church, which tried to reassure vulnerable citizens that at least their immortal souls would come through the pestilence unscathed. The role of the church as a source of social order and civic harmony is parodied in the *Decameron*'s playful account of rogues who deceive their confessors, nuns who allow the convent gardener to "cultivate their gardens," and priests who care more for their earnings than for the welfare of their flock. But despite its sometimes satirical tone, the *Decameron* does not depict a world in which the authority of the church is rejected: on the contrary, the church is seen as a regulating force in society like any other, and therefore similarly vulnerable to corruption and abuse.

WORK

Written before Boccaccio's first meeting with Petrarch in 1350 but after plague first struck Florence in 1348, the *Decameron* marks a pivotal point both in literary history and in Boccaccio's own life. Because its vernacular prose captures the rhythms of everyday speech and renders the voice of the carpenter or merchant as vividly as that of the priest or great lord, the *Decameron* brings to life the bustling life of medieval Florence, a city where trade and banking flourished. Not only the hubbub of the city but also the broader panorama of Mediterranean interconnections emerge in the tales that recount travel to North Africa, to Muslim-held regions of Spain, to Sicily, to Greece. In some tales, such as that of the Muslim princess Alatiel, action takes place aboard ship, representing powerfully the dynamic cultural and economic exchanges occurring in the Mediterranean.

The cross-cultural interactions prominently depicted in the tales also inform the genre of the *Decameron*, which follows the frame-tale model of Indo-Persian works such as the *Pañcatantra* and *The Thousand and One Nights*. Its framing story of seven young women and three young men who have fled Florence in the time of the Black Death

contains within it a series of short tales written in a wide range of genres, styles, and moods. The young people deliver their tales in a light and playful tone that belies the desperation engendered by their flight from the plague-ridden city, much as the storyteller Shahrazad, in *The Thousand and One Nights*, tells of marvels and wonders even as the threat of execution hangs over her head. Although written models for the frame-tale structure did make their way from Asia to Europe, influencing such works as **Petrus Alfonsi's** *Disciplina Clericalis*, oral sources are more likely to have been the principal inspiration behind Boccaccio's collection. These include not only the stories of traders and sailors that circulated throughout the Mediterranean region but also the folktales that had long been part of European tradition, as evidenced in such collections as the scatological and highly sexualized comic fabliaux surviving in French manuscripts.

The community of ten young men and women who recount the stories of the *Decameron* flee the city in the time of plague out of a concern for more than their own personal health. The stories that they tell are a kind of medicine concocted to heal both the individual spirit and the collective social fabric, focused on everyday themes such as how happiness follows misfortune, how women deceive their husbands, the power of the witty retort, and the value of generosity. The urgency and panic caused by pestilence is reflected but contained in the frame narrative, which begins with the group selecting as their leader Pampinea, the eldest of the young women, so that the community will be united under a single will. The leadership then rotates among them over a ten-day period, allowing each of the men and women to serve as "king" or "queen" of the day. Dioneo, the young man who tells the most unsavory and sexualized of the tales, claims for himself the privilege of telling the last tale of each day. Thus, through a series of comic inversions, the usual order of things is turned upside down: instead of a single male ruler, the group is governed first by a woman and then by a rotation of leaders, and a special status is awarded to the man who poses the loudest challenge to proper norms of behavior. Yet this chaotic quality does not escape the orderly structure: when the ten days come to an end, the community chooses to return to Florence, restored by the medicine of laughter and fellowship and determined to do all they can to rebuild a society in peril.

The *Decameron* includes many tales of the European fabliau type, but others have origins that are more broadly Mediterranean. The Mediterranean scope of the *Decameron* appears, for example, in the story of Alatiel, a Muslim princess who has a string of erotic adventures on her way to marry the Sultan of Algarve—that is, the ruler of *al-Gharb*, which literally means "the West." The distinctions between East and West that are almost second nature to modern readers are foreign to the world of the *Decameron*, where the West can be home to Islam just as easily as the East can be the natural turf of Italian merchants, as comfortable in the cities of Asia as they are in the cities of their native land. This interpenetration of worlds also appears in the two stories devoted to the Sultan Saladin, who displays an impartial wisdom in the story of the Three Rings, in which the comparative merits of Judaism, Christianity, and Islam are assessed, and in the story of Messer Torello, in which Saladin visits Italy disguised as a merchant and reveals himself to be an exotic paragon of munificence.

The informality of the prose in many of the tales is countered by what might be called the "high style" of the frame narrative, as well as by the care with which the work is structured. For example, the "Valley of Ladies" is a luscious verdant landscape that marks the transition between the Sixth and Seventh Days of the *Decameron*, but its concentric circles also provide a resonant symbolic echo of Dante's underworld, suggesting that the delightful feminine "valley" might prove to be less an erotic paradise than a torturous hell. Similarly, the numerical skeleton of the *Decameron*—ten tales told on each of the ten days of the expedition— reinforces an underlying sense of order and symmetry that flies in the face of the spontaneity and dynamism of the tales' content and tone. Chaos, in the *Decameron*, is consistently subordinated to order, reaffirming the ability of humanity to surmount any disruption, even the upheaval wrought by pestilence. By insisting that the triumph of order can be achieved through human effort, the *Decameron* contradicts its most important predecessor and model: Dante's *Divine Comedy*, in which God is repeatedly identified as the only source of form and harmony in the universe. The hundred cantos of the *Divine Comedy* represent the perfect order of divine creation; the hundred tales of the *Decameron*, in contrast, represent the fertile creativity of the human mind.

In a letter to his friend Boccaccio, Petrarch gently criticizes the low vernacular of the *Decameron* but praises the quality of the collection's last tale, the story of patient Griselda. In order that the story might survive the passage of time, Petrarch writes, "I attacked this story of yours," rendering it into immortal Latin. Ironically, Petrarch's effort to preserve Boccaccio's story by translating it into Latin reveals more about the limited shelf life of Latin humanism than it does about the defects of the vernacular: it is Boccaccio's own version, along with Chaucer's translation of the Griselda story into English in his Clerk's Tale, that continues to enchant readers today.

From Decameron[1]

Day 1, Story 1

Ser Cepparello deceives a holy friar with a false confession and dies, and although he was one of the worst of men during his life, he is reputed after his death to be a saint and is called Saint Ciappelletto.

Dearest ladies, it is fitting that everything man does should take as its origin the wonderful and holy name of Him who was the maker of all things. Thus, since I am the first and must begin our storytelling, I intend to start off with one of His marvelous works so that, once you have heard it, our hope in Him, as in that which is immutable, will be strengthened, and we will forever praise His name. Now, it is clear that the things of this world are all transitory and fading, so that both in themselves and in what they give rise to, they are filled with suffering, anguish, and toil, as well as being subject to countless dangers. We, who live in the midst of these things and are a part of them, would certainly not be able to resist and defend ourselves against them, if the special grace of God did not lend us strength and discernment. It is wrong to believe that this grace descends to us and enters us because of any merit of our own. Rather, it is sent by His loving kindness and is obtained through the prayers of those who, though mortal like us, truly followed His will while they were alive and now enjoy eternal bliss with Him. To them, as to advocates informed by experience of our frailty, we offer up prayers about our concerns, perhaps because we do not dare to present them personally before the sight of so great a judge. And yet in Him, who is generous and filled with pity for us, we perceive something more. Although human sight is not sharp enough to penetrate the secrets of the divine mind in any way, it some- times happens that we are deceived by popular opinion into making someone our advocate before Him in all His majesty whom He has cast into eternal exile. And yet He, from whom nothing is hidden, pays more attention to the purity of the supplicant than to his ignorance or to the damned state of his intercessor, listen- ing to those who pray as if their advocate were actually blessed in His sight. All of this will appear clearly in the tale I intend to tell—clearly, I say, not in keeping with the judgment of God, but with that of men.

The story is told that Musciatto Franzesi,[2] an extremely rich and celebrated merchant in France, who had been made a knight, was once supposed to move to

1. Translated from the Italian by Wayne Reb- horn.
2. Musciatto di Messer Guido Franzesi (d. 1310), a merchant from Tuscany who became rich while serving as counselor to King Philip of France; he advised the king to falsify his coinage and to confiscate funds from the Italian mer- chants living in France. Many of *The Decamer- on's* tales refer to historical persons.

Tuscany with Lord Charles Sans Terre, the King of France's brother, whom Pope Boniface[3] had sent for and was encouraging to come. Musciatto recognized that his affairs, as those of merchants often are, were tangled up here and there and could not be put right quickly and easily, but he thought of a number of different people to whom he could entrust them and thus found a way to take care of everything. There was, however, one exception. He was unsure whom he could leave behind to recover the loans he had made to quite a few people in Burgundy.[4] The reason for his uncertainty was that he had heard the Burgundians were a quarrelsome lot, evil by nature and untrustworthy, and he could think of no one he could rely on who would be sufficiently wicked that his wickedness would match theirs. After he had given the matter a great deal of thought, there came to mind a certain Ser Cepparello da Prato, who was often a guest in his house in Paris. Because the man was small of stature and dressed like a dandy, the French, not knowing what "Cepparello" signified and thinking it meant "hat," that is, "garland," in their language, called him, because he was small as we have said, not Ciappello, but Ciappelletto. And so, he was called Ciappelletto everywhere, while only a select few knew he was really Ser Cepparello.[5]

Let me tell you about the kind of life this Ciappelletto led. A notary, he would feel the greatest shame if even one of the very few legal documents he drew up was found to be other than false. He had composed as many of these phony ones as people requested, and he did so for free more willingly than someone else would have done for a sizable payment. Furthermore, he supplied false testimony with the greatest delight, whether it was asked for or not, and since people in France in those days placed the greatest trust in oaths, and since he did not care if his were false, he won a great many law cases through his wickedness whenever he was asked to swear upon his oath to tell the truth. Because it gave him real pleasure, he went to great lengths to stir up bad feelings, hatred, and scandals among friends and relations and everyone else, and the greater the evils he saw arise as a result, the greater his happiness. Invited to be an accomplice in a murder or some other criminal act, he would never refuse to go. Indeed, he would do so with a ready will and often found himself happily wounding or killing men with his own hands. He was the greatest blasphemer of God and the Saints, and since he would do so at the slightest provocation, he came off as the most irascible man alive. He never went to church and used abominable words to mock all its sacraments as being beneath contempt. On the other hand, he happily spent time in taverns and frequented other places of ill repute. Of women, he was as fond as dogs are of being beaten with a stick, and he took more delight in their opposite than any degenerate ever did. He would rob and steal with a conscience like that of a holy man

3. Boniface VIII (ca. 1235 or 1240–1303; pope, 1294–1303). "Tuscany": the region in northern Italy surrounding Florence.
4. Large, wealthy region in central France.
5. Cepparello da Prato's name appears in documents of the period as a tax collector for King Philip. The "Ser" before his name (short for "Messer") is an honorific (like "Sir"), and his first name is the diminutive (-ello) of Ciapo,

short for Jacopo (James), although Boccaccio plays with the fact that ceppo meant "log" or "stump." "Cepparello" could thus be translated "Little Log." The French-speaking Burgundians transform his name into "Ciappelletto," a double diminutive, which in their language would be the rather precious nickname "Little Garland of Flowers."

giving alms. He was a total glutton and a great drinker, so much so that some-times it would make him disgustingly ill. Plus, he was a devout cardsharp and gambled with loaded dice. But why do I lavish so many words on him? He was perhaps the worst man who had ever been born. For a long time his wicked-ness had preserved the wealth and rank of Messer Musciatto who often pro-tected him from both private persons, who were frequently the victims of his abuse, and from the courts, which always were.

Thus, when this Ser Cepparello crossed the mind of Messer Musciatto, who was well acquainted with his life, he thought to himself that this would be just the man he needed to deal with the wickedness of the Burgundians. He there-fore had Ciappelletto sent for and spoke to him as follows:

"Ser Ciappelletto, as you know, I am about to leave here for good, and since, among others, I have to deal with the Burgundians, who are full of tricks, I know of no one more qualified than you to recover my money from them. Since you're not doing anything at present, if you take care of this business for me, I intend to obtain the favor of the court for you here and to award you a fair por-tion of what you recover."

Ser Ciappelletto, who was indeed unemployed and in short supply of worldly goods, saw the man who had long been his refuge and defense about to depart, and so, without a moment's hesitation, constrained, as it were, by necessity, he made up his mind and said he would be more than willing to do what Musci-atto wanted. The two of them then worked out the details of their agreement, and Ser Ciappelletto received Musciatto's power of attorney as well as letters of introduction from the King. Soon after Messer Musciatto's departure, Ciap-pelletto went off to Burgundy, where almost no one knew him. There, in a kind and gentle manner quite beyond his nature, as though he were holding back his wrath till the end, he began recovering Musciatto's money and taking care of what he had been sent to do.

Before long, while he was lodging in the house of two Florentine brothers who lent money at interest and who treated him with great respect out of love for Messer Musciatto, he happened to fall ill. The two brothers immediately sent for doctors and servants to take care of him and to provide him with every-thing he might need to recover his health. All their help was in vain, however, for, in the opinion of the doctors, the good man, who was already old and had lived a disorderly life, was going from bad to worse every day, as people did who had a fatal illness. The two brothers were very upset about this, and one day, right next to the bedroom in which Ser Ciappelletto lay sick, they began talking together.

"What are we going to do about this guy?" said the one of them to the other. "We've got a terrible mess on our hands on account of him, because if we kick him out of our house, as sick as he is, people would condemn us for doing it. Plus, they'd really think we're stupid since we didn't just take him in at first, but also went to great lengths to find servants and doctors for him, and now, although he couldn't have done anything to offend us, they see him suddenly kicked out of our house when he's deathly ill. On the other hand, he's been such a bad man that he won't want to make his confession or receive any of the sacraments of the Church, and if he dies without confession, no church will want to receive his body, and they'll wind up tossing him into some garbage pit like a dog. But if he goes ahead and makes his confession, the same thing will happen. Since his sins are so many and so horrible, no friar or priest will be willing or able to absolve him, and so, without absolution, he'll be tossed into a garbage pit just the same. And when that happens, the people of this town—both because of our profession, which they think is truly wicked and which they bad–mouth all day long, and because of their desire to rob us—well, they'll rise up and riot when they see it. And as they come running to our house, they'll be screaming, 'These Lombard dogs[6] that the Church refuses to accept, we won't put up with them any longer!' And maybe they won't just steal our stuff, but on top of that, they'll take our lives. So, no matter how things work out, it'll be bad for us if this guy dies."

Ser Ciappelletto, who, as we said, was lying close to where they were talking, and whose hearing was sharp, as it often is in those who are sick, caught every word they were saying about him and reacted by sending for them to come to him.

"I don't want you to fear anything on my account," he told them, "or to be afraid you'll be harmed because of me. I heard what you were saying about me, and I'm very sure that the outcome will be exactly what you've predicted if things happen the way you've been imagining them. However, it's all going to turn out differently. I've done the Lord God so many injuries during my lifetime that doing Him one more at the hour of my death won't make a difference to Him one way or the other. So go and arrange for the holiest and worthiest friar you can find to come to me—if such a one exists—and leave everything to me, for I'm sure I can set both your affairs and my own in order so that all will be well and you'll be satisfied with the result."

Although the two brothers didn't derive much hope from this, they nevertheless went off to a monastery and asked for a wise and holy man to hear the confession of a Lombard who was sick in their house. They were assigned an elderly friar, a grand master of the Scriptures, who had lived a good and holy life and was a very venerable figure towards whom all the townspeople felt an immense special devotion, and they took this man back home with them.

When the friar reached the bedroom where Ser Ciappelletto was lying, he seated himself beside the sick man, and after speaking some words of comfort, asked him how much time had passed since he had made his last confession. Ser Ciappelletto, who had never been to confession, replied to him:

"Father, it used to be my custom to go to confession at least once a week, without counting the many weeks in which I went more often. Since I've been sick for about a week now, the truth is that the suffering I've endured from my illness has been so great that it has prevented me from going to confession."

"My son," said the friar, "you've done well, and you should continue that practice in the future. Considering how often you've made your confession, I don't think it will be a lot of trouble for me to hear it and to examine you."

"Messer Friar," said Ser Ciappelletto, "don't speak like that. Although I've gone to confession many, many times, I've always had a longing to make a general confession of all the sins I could remember, starting from the day of my

6. I.e., Italian bankers (Lombardy is a region in northern Italy).

birth and coming right down to the present. Therefore, my good father, I beg you to examine me point by point about everything just as if I'd never been to confession. And don't be concerned about me because I'm sick, for I would much rather mortify this flesh of mine than indulge it by doing something that might lead to the perdition of my soul, which my Savior redeemed with His precious blood."

These words pleased the holy man immensely and seemed to him to argue a well-disposed mind. Consequently, after commending Ser Ciappelletto warmly for making frequent confessions, he began by asking him if he had ever committed the sin of lust with a woman.

"Father," Ser Ciappelletto replied with a sigh, "I'm ashamed to tell you the truth on this subject for fear I might be committing the sin of pride."

"Don't be afraid to speak," said the holy friar. "Telling the truth was never a sin either in confession or anywhere else."

"Since you give me such reassurance," said Ser Ciappelletto, "I'll go ahead and tell you: I'm as much a virgin today as when I came forth from my mama's body."

"Oh, God's blessings on you!" said the friar. "What a good man you've been! In fact, by acting as you have, you are all the more meritorious, because, if you had wanted to, you had more freedom to do the opposite than we and others like us do, since we are bound by the vows of religion." Next, he asked Ciappelletto if he had displeased God through the sin of gluttony. Breathing a heavy sigh, Ser Ciappelletto replied that he had done so many times. For although it was his habit to fast on bread and water at least three days a week, in addition to doing so during the periods of fasting that devout people observed on holy days throughout the year, he had nevertheless drunk that water with as much delight and gusto as any great wine-drinker ever drank his wine, and especially if he was exhausted from performing acts of devotion or making a pilgrimage. Moreover, he was often filled with a longing to have those little salads of baby field greens that women fix when they go to the country, and sometimes, as he ate them, doing so seemed better to him than it should have seemed to someone, like himself, who fasted out of piety, which was the precise reason why he was fasting.

"My son," replied the friar, "these sins are natural and quite trivial, so I don't want you to burden your conscience with them any more than necessary. No matter how truly holy a man may be, eating after a long fast and drinking after hard work will always seem good to him."

"Oh, father," said Ser Ciappelletto, "don't say that just to console me. Surely you must realize that I know how every act we perform in the service of God has to be done wholeheartedly and with an unspotted soul, and how anybody who does otherwise is committing a sin."

Feeling quite content, the friar said: "I am overjoyed that you think like this. It pleases me greatly that on this topic your conscience is pure and good. But tell me: have you committed the sin of avarice by desiring more than what was proper or by keeping what you should not have kept?"

"Father," said Ser Ciappelletto, "I don't want you to suspect me of this because I'm living in the house of these usurers. I'm not here to do business. On the contrary, I've come with the intention of admonishing and chastising them and of leading them away from their abominable moneymaking. What is more, I think I would have succeeded if God had not visited this tribulation upon me. Now, you should know that although my father left me a rich man, I gave away the greater part of what he had to charity after his death. Then, however, in order to sustain my life and to be able to aid Christ's poor, I've done a little bit of trading, and in doing so, I did indeed desire to make money. But I've always divided what I earned down the middle with God's poor, devoting my half to my needs, and giving the other half to them, and my Creator has aided me so well in this that my business has continually gotten better and better."

"Well done," said the friar. "But say, how often have you gotten angry?"

"Oh," said Ser Ciappelletto, "that's something, just let me tell you, that's happened to me a lot. For who could restrain himself, seeing the disgusting things men do all day long, neither observing God's commandments, nor fearing His chastisement? There've been many days when I would have preferred to die rather than live to listen to young people swearing and forswearing themselves, and to watch them pursuing vanities, frequenting taverns rather than going to church, and following the ways of the world rather than those of God."

"My son," said the friar, "this is righteous anger, and for my part, I cannot impose any penance on account of it. But was there ever a case in which your anger led you to commit murder or to hurl abuse at anyone or to do them any other sort of injury?"

Ser Ciappelletto answered him: "Alas, sir, how can you, who appear to be a man of God, speak such words? If I'd had even the teeniest little thought about doing any one of the things you've mentioned, do you think I'd believe that God would have shown me so much favor? Those are things that thugs and criminals would do, and whenever I've come upon a person of that sort, I've always said, 'Be gone! And may God convert you.'"

"God bless you, my son!" said the friar. "Now tell me: have you ever borne false witness against anyone or spoken ill of others or taken things from them without their permission?"

"Yes, sir," replied Ser Ciappelletto, "I really have spoken ill of others. Because once I had a neighbor who, without the least justification, was forever beating his wife, and so one time, I criticized him to his wife's family because of the great pity I felt for the wretched creature. Whenever he'd had too much to drink, God alone could tell you how he used to smack her around."

"Well, then," said the friar, "you tell me you've been a merchant. Have you ever deceived anyone, as merchants do?"

"Yes, sir, by gosh," replied Ser Ciappelletto, "but I don't know who he was, except that he was a man who brought me money he owed me for some cloth I'd sold him, and I put it in a box without counting it. Then, a good month later, I discovered that there were four more pennies in it than there should have been. Well, I kept them for an entire year with the intention of returning them to him, but when I never saw him again, I gave them away to charity."

"That was a trifle," said the friar, "and you did well to have acted as you did."

On top of this, the holy friar went on to ask him about many other things and got the same kind of reply in each case. But then, just as he was about to proceed to absolution, Ser Ciappelletto said: "I still have a sin or two more, sir, that I haven't told you about."

The friar asked him what they were, and Ciappelletto replied: "I remember how one Saturday I didn't show proper reverence for the Holy Sabbath because after nones[7] I had my servant sweep the house."

"Oh, my son," said the friar, "that's a trifle."

"No," said Ser Ciappelletto, "don't call it a trifle, for the Sabbath cannot be honored too much, seeing that it was on just such a day our Savior came back to life from the dead."

Then the friar asked: "Have you done anything else?"

"Yes, sir," replied Ser Ciappelletto. "Once, not thinking about what I was doing, I spat in the house of God."

The friar smiled and said: "My son, that's nothing to worry about. We, who are in holy orders, spit there all day long."

"And what you're doing is vile," said Ser Ciappelletto, "for nothing should be kept as clean as the Holy Temple in which we offer sacrifice to God."

In brief, he told the holy friar many things of this sort, until he finally began sighing and then burst into tears—for he was someone who knew only too well how to do this when he wanted to.

"My son," said the holy friar, "what's wrong?"

"Alas, sir," Ser Ciappelletto replied, "there's still one sin of mine remaining that I've never confessed because I feel so much shame in speaking about it. As you can see, every time I remember it, it makes me weep, and I think there can be no doubt that God will never have mercy on me because of it."

"Come on now, son," said the holy friar, "what are you talking about? If all the sins that have ever been committed by all of humanity, or that will be committed by them as long as the world lasts, were united in one single man, and yet he were as penitent and contrite as I see you are, then truly the benignity and mercy of God are so great that if that man were to confess them, he would be forgiven willingly. Therefore, don't be afraid to speak."

Ser Ciappelletto continued to weep violently as he replied: "Alas, father, my sin is so great that I can hardly believe God will ever pardon it unless you use your prayers on my behalf."

"Speak freely," said the friar, "for I promise I'll pray to God for you."

Ser Ciappelletto just kept on crying and refusing to talk about it, and the friar went on encouraging him to speak. Then, after Ser Ciappelletto had kept the friar in suspense with his weeping for a very long time, he heaved a great sigh and said: "Father, since you've promised to pray to God for me, I will tell you about it. You should know that when I was a little boy, I once cursed my mama." And having said this, he started weeping violently all over again.

"Oh, my son," said the friar, "does this seem such a great sin to you? Why, men curse God all day long, and yet He freely pardons anyone who repents of having cursed Him. And you don't think that He will pardon you for this? Don't weep and don't worry, for surely, even if you had been one of those who

7. One of the canonical hours, at which prescribed prayers were offered daily and which thus served to divide the day: nones was the service at about 3 P.M.

placed Him on the cross, He would pardon you because of the contrition I see in you."

"Alas, father," replied Ser Ciappelletto, "what are you saying? My sweet mama, who carried me in her body, day and night, for nine months, and who held me in her arms more than a hundred times—I was too wicked when I cursed her! My sin is too great! And if you don't pray to God for me, it will not be forgiven."

When the friar saw that there was nothing left to say to Ser Ciappelletto, he absolved him and gave him his blessing, taking him to be a very holy man, for he fully believed that what Ser Ciappelletto had said was true—and who would not have believed it, seeing a man at the point of death speak like that?

Then, after all this, the friar said to him: "Ser Ciappelletto, with the help of God you'll soon be well, but if it should happen that God calls that blessed, well-disposed soul of yours to Him, would you like to have your body buried at our monastery?"

"Yes, sir," replied Ser Ciappelletto. "In fact, I wouldn't want to be anywhere else, since you've promised to pray to God for me, not to mention the fact that I have always been especially devoted to your order. Therefore, when you return to your monastery, I beg you to have them send me that most true body of Christ that you consecrate upon the altar every morning,[8] for, although I'm unworthy of it, I would like, with your permission, to partake of it, and afterward, to receive Holy Extreme Unction[9] so that if I have lived a sinner, at least I may die a Christian."

The holy man said he was greatly pleased that Ser Ciappelletto had spoken so well and told him that he would arrange for the Host to be brought to him right away. And so it was.

The two brothers, who were afraid that Ser Ciappelletto was going to deceive them, had placed themselves near a partition that divided the room where he was lying from the one they were in, and as they eavesdropped, they were able to understand everything he said to the friar. Upon hearing him confess the things he had done, they sometimes had such a desire to laugh that they almost burst, and from time to time they would say to one another: "What kind of man is this, whom neither old age, nor sickness, nor the fear of death, which is imminent, nor the fear of God, before whose judgment he must stand in just a short while, could induce him to give up his wickedness and want to die any differently than he lived?" But, seeing as how he had spoken in such a way that he would be received for burial in a church, everything else was of no consequence to them.

A little later Ser Ciappelletto took Communion, and as his condition was rapidly deteriorating, he received Extreme Unction and then died just a little after vespers[1] of the day on which he had made his good confession. Using Ser Ciappelletto's own money, the two brothers took care of all the arrangements necessary for him to be given an honorable burial and sent word to the friars'

---

8. I.e., the consecrated bread that Catholics consume in the Eucharist, as the body of Christ.

9. The Catholic sacrament administered to the sick who are in danger of dying.

1. A canonical hour, about 6 P.M.

house that they should come in the evening to perform the customary wake and take away the body in the morning.

The holy friar who had confessed Ser Ciappelletto, having heard that he had passed away, came to an understanding with the Prior of the monastery, and after the chapterhouse bell had been rung and the friars were gathered together, he explained to them how Ser Ciappelletto had been a holy man, according to what he had deduced from the confession he had heard. And in the hope that the Lord God was going to perform many miracles through Ser Ciappelletto, he persuaded the others to receive the body with the greatest reverence and devotion. The credulous Prior and the other friars agreed to this plan, and in the evening they all went to the room where Ser Ciappelletto's body was laid and held a great and solemn vigil over it. Then, in the morning, they got dressed in their surplices and copes, and with their books in their hands and the cross before them, they went for the body, chanting along the way, after which they carried it to their church with the greatest ceremony and solemnity, followed by almost all the people of the city, men and women alike. Once the body had been placed in the church, the holy friar who had confessed Ser Ciappelletto mounted the pulpit and began to preach marvelous things about him, about his life, his fasts, his virginity, his simplicity and innocence and sanctity, recounting, among other things, what he had confessed to him in tears as his greatest sin, and how he had scarcely been able to get it into his head that God would forgive him for it. After this, the holy friar took the opportunity to reprimand the people who were listening. "And you, wretched sinners," he said, "for every blade of straw your feet trip over, you blaspheme against God and His Mother and all the Saints in Paradise."

Besides this, the holy friar said many other things about Ser Ciappelletto's faith and purity, so that in short, by means of his words, which the people of the countryside believed absolutely, he managed to plant the image of Ser Ciappelletto so deeply inside the minds and hearts of everyone present that when the service was over, there was a huge stampede as the people rushed forward to kiss Ser Ciappelletto's hands and feet. They tore off all the clothing he had on, each one thinking himself blessed if he just got a little piece of it. Furthermore, the body had to be kept there all day long so that everyone could come to see him. Finally, when night fell, he was given an honorable burial in a marble tomb located in one of the chapels. The next day people immediately began going there to light candles and pray to him, and later they made vows to him and hung up *ex-votos*[2] of wax in fulfillment of the promises they had made. So great did the fame of Ciappelletto's holiness and the people's devotion to him grow that there was almost no one in some sort of difficulty who did not make a vow to him rather than to some other saint. In the end, they called him Saint Ciappelletto, as they still do, and claim that God has performed many miracles through him and will perform them every day for those who devoutly entrust themselves to him.

Thus lived and died Ser Cepparello da Prato who, as you have heard, became a saint. Nor do I wish to deny the possibility that he sits among the Blessed in

2. Votive offerings (*ex voto* means "out of a vow"; Lat.).

the presence of God. For although his life was wicked and depraved, it is possible that at the very point of death he became so contrite that God took pity
on him and accepted him into His kingdom. However, since this is hidden
from us, what I will say in this case, on the basis of appearances, is that he is
more likely in the hands of the Devil down in Hell than up there in Paradise.
And if that is so, then we may recognize how very great God's loving kindness
is toward us, in that He does not consider our sinfulness, but the purity of our
faith, and even though we make our intercessor one of His enemies, thinking
him His friend, God still grants our prayers as if we were asking a true saint to
obtain His grace for us. And therefore, so that all of us in this merry company
may, by His grace, be kept safe and sound during our present troubles, let us
praise His name, which is what we began with, and venerate Him, commending ourselves to Him in our need, in the certain knowledge that we will be
heard.

And at this point he[3] fell silent.

Day 2, Story 7

*The Sultan of Babylon sends one of his daughters to be married to the King of
Algarve,[4] and in a series of misadventures spanning a period of four years, she
passes through the hands of nine men in various places, until she is finally
restored to her father as a virgin and goes off, as she was doing at the start, to
marry the King of Algarve.*

If Emilia's tale had gone on perhaps just a little bit longer, the pity the young
ladies were feeling for Madam Beritola because of her misfortunes would have
made them weep. But since the tale had come to an end, it was the Queen's[5]
pleasure to have Panfilo continue the storytelling. Most obedient, he began as
follows:

It is difficult, charming ladies, for us to know what is truly in our best interest. For, as we have frequently observed, there are many who have thought that
if only they were rich, they would be able to lead secure, trouble-free lives, and
they have not just prayed to God for wealth, but have made every effort to
acquire it, sparing themselves neither effort nor danger in the process. However, no sooner did they succeed than the prospect of a substantial legacy led
to their being murdered by people who would never have considered harming
them before then. Others have risen from low estate to the heights of power,
passing through the dangers of a thousand battles and shedding the blood of
their brothers and friends to get there, all because of their belief that to rule
was felicity itself. And yet, as they could have seen and heard for themselves, it

3. Panfilo, one of the young men of the
brigata or "group" of storytellers; he recounts
the first story.
4. Medieval Islamic kingdom in present-day
southern Portugal (conquered in 1253 by the
Christian Alfonso III) and, across the Mediterranean, in the northern part of modern

Morocco; *al-Gharb* in Arabic means "the
West." "Babylon": the name commonly
applied to Cairo in the Middle Ages.
5. The ruler of the day; each day of the
Decameron has an appointed king or queen
from among the *brigata*.

was a felicity fraught with endless cares and fears, and when it cost them their lives, they finally realized that at the tables of royalty chalices may contain poison, even though they are made of gold. Again, there have been many who have ardently yearned for physical strength and beauty, while others have sought bodily ornaments with equal passion, only to discover that the things they unwisely desired were the cause of misery or even death.

But to avoid reviewing every conceivable human desire, let me simply affirm that no person alive can choose any one of them in complete confidence that it will remain immune from the vicissitudes of Fortune.[6] Thus, if we wish to live upright lives, we should resign ourselves to acquiring and preserving whatever is bestowed on us by the One who alone knows what we need and has the ability to provide it for us. However, just as there are myriad ways in which men are driven to sin because of their desires, so you, gracious ladies, sin above all in one particular way, namely, in your desire to be beautiful, for finding that the attractions bestowed on you by Nature are insufficient, you make use of the most extraordinary art trying to improve on them. And therefore, I would like to tell you a tale about a Saracen[7] girl's unfortunate beauty, which in the space of about four years turned her into a newly-wed nine separate times.

A long time ago Babylon was ruled by a Sultan named Beminedab,[8] in whose reign very little happened that went contrary to his wishes. Among his many children of both sexes, he had a daughter named Alatiel[9] who was at that time, according to what everyone said who saw her, the most beautiful woman in the world. The Sultan had been recently attacked by a huge army of Arabs, but thanks to the timely assistance of the King of Algarve, he had been able to defeat them decisively. Consequently, when, as a special favor, the King asked to be given Alatiel as his wife, the Sultan agreed, and after having seen her aboard a well-armed, well-equipped ship and having provided her with an honorable escort of men and women as well as with many elegant and expensive trappings, he commended her to God's protection and sent her on her way.

When the sailors saw that the weather was favorable, they unfurled their sails into the wind, and for some while after leaving the port of Alexandria,[1] their voyage prospered. One day, however, after they had already passed Sardinia and seemed close to their journey's end, crosswinds suddenly arose that were so violent and buffeted the ship so badly that time and again not only the lady, but the crew thought they were done for. Nevertheless, they held out valiantly, and by marshaling all their skill and all their strength, they resisted the onslaught of the heavy seas for two days. As night approached for the third time since the start of the storm, however, not only did it not abate, but rather, it kept growing stronger, until they felt the ship beginning to break apart.

6. The goddess whose wheel—ready to turn an individual from high to low at a moment—was often invoked in the Middle Ages.
7. Muslim (the term usually refers to an Arab, but sometimes to a European convert).
8. A fictitious name, though "Amminadab" is mentioned in passing in Numbers (1.7, 7.12) and in the genealogy of Jesus (Matthew 1.4).
9. A fictitious name, which may be a punning anagram of "La Lieta" (The Happy One).
1. In northern Egypt, not far from Cairo.

Although they were not far to the north of Majorca, the sailors had no idea of their location, and because it was a dark night and the sky was covered with thick clouds, they were unable to determine their position either by using nautical instruments or by making visual observations.

It now became a case of every man for himself, and the officers, seeing no other means of escape, lowered a dinghy into the water and jumped into it, choosing to put their faith in it rather than in the foundering ship. Right behind them, however, came all the other men on board, leaping down into the boat one after the other, despite the fact that those who had gotten there first were trying, knife in hand, to fend them off. Although they all thought this was the way to escape death, they actually ran right into it, for the dinghy, not built to hold so many people in such weather, went down, taking everyone with it.

Meanwhile, the ship, though torn open and almost completely filled with water, was being blown swiftly along by a fierce wind that finally drove it aground on a beach on the island of Majorca. At this point the only people remaining on board were the lady and her female attendants, all of whom lay prostrate, looking as if they were dead, overcome by both the tempest and their fear. The ship's impetus had been so great that it had thrust itself deep into the sand almost a stone's throw from the shore, where, now that the wind could no longer make it budge, it remained all night long, relentlessly pounded by the sea.

By daybreak the tempest had calmed down considerably, and the lady, who was feeling half dead, raised her head and, weak though she was, began calling to her servants one after the other. She did so in vain, however, because they were too far away to hear her. Puzzled when she got no reply and could see no one about, she began to feel quite panic-stricken, staggered to her feet, and finally discovered her ladies-in-waiting as well as all the other women who were lying about everywhere. As she went from one to the other, she called and shook them repeatedly. Few, however, showed any sign of life, most having died from a combination of terror and horrible stomach convulsions, a discovery that only served to intensify the lady's fears. Since she was all alone there and had no idea of her whereabouts, she felt a desperate need of assistance and prodded those who were still alive until she got them to their feet. But when she realized that no one knew where the men had gone and saw that the boat was stuck in the sand and full of water, she began weeping and wailing along with all the rest of them.

The hour of nones was already upon them before they saw anyone on the shore or elsewhere in the vicinity who might be moved to pity them and come to their assistance, for by chance, at that very hour, a nobleman named Pericone da Vislago,[2] who was returning from one of his estates, happened to come riding by on horseback, accompanied by several of his servants. The instant he saw the ship, he figured out what had happened and ordered one of his men to climb aboard without delay and to report what he discovered there. Although the servant had to struggle, he managed to get onto the ship, where he found

2. A fictitious character; his first name is a diminutive of the Catalan name "Pere" (Peter), and his last name refers to a castle in Majorca, a large island south of Catalonia (the northeast corner of modern Spain).

the young noblewoman, frightened out of her wits, hiding with her few remaining companions under the end of the bowsprit. On seeing him, they started weeping and repeatedly begged him for mercy, although when they realized he could not understand them, nor they him, they tried to explain their misfortune by means of gestures.

Once he had assessed the situation to the best of his ability, the servant reported what he had discovered up there to Pericone, who promptly had his men bring the women down, along with the most valuable objects they could salvage from the ship. Then he escorted the women to one of his castles where he arranged for them to be fed and allowed to rest in order to restore their spirits. From their rich attire he deduced that he had stumbled across some great lady, and he quickly recognized which one she was by the deference that the other women paid to her alone. Although she was pallid and extremely disheveled because of her exhausting experiences at sea, her features still struck Pericone as extremely beautiful, and for this reason he resolved on the spot to take her to wife if she had no husband, and if marriage were out of the question, to make her his mistress.

Quite a robust man with a commanding presence, Pericone had her waited on hand and foot, and when, after a few days, she had recovered completely, he found her to be more beautiful than he could have imagined. Although it pained him that they could not understand one another and he could not determine who she was, nevertheless, her beauty had set him all ablaze, and he tried, by means of pleasant, loving gestures, to coax her to give in to his desires without a struggle. But it was all in vain: she kept refusing to let him get on familiar terms with her, and in the meantime, Pericone's passion just got hotter and hotter.

The lady had no idea where she was, but she guessed, after having observed the local customs for a few days, that she was among Christians and in a place where she saw that there was little to be gained by revealing her identity, even if she had known how to do so. She recognized what was going on with Pericone, and although she concluded that eventually either force or love was going to make her satisfy his desires whether she liked it or not, nevertheless, she proudly resolved to rise above her wretched predicament. To her three remaining women, she gave orders never to reveal their identities to anyone unless they found themselves in a place where doing so would clearly help them gain their freedom. Beyond that, she implored them to preserve their chastity, declaring that she herself was determined to let no one except her husband ever enjoy her favors. Her women commended her resolve and said they would do their utmost to follow her instructions.

Pericone's passion was burning more fiercely from day to day, growing hotter and hotter as he got closer to the object of his desire and it was ever more firmly denied him. When he saw that his flattering her was getting him nowhere, he sharpened his wits and decided to make use of deception, keeping force in reserve as a last resort. On several occasions he had noticed that the lady liked wine, which she was unaccustomed to drinking because the laws of her religion forbade it, and by using it as Venus's[3] assistant, he thought he would be able to have his way with her. Thus, one evening, pretending not to care about

3. The Roman goddess of love.

the very thing for which she had shown such distaste, he arranged for a splendid supper in the manner of a holiday celebration, which the lady attended. Since the meal was graced with a wide array of dishes, he ordered the man who was serving her to give her a variety of different kinds of wine to drink with them. The man did his job extremely well, and the lady, caught off guard and carried away by the pleasures of drinking, consumed more wine than was consistent with her honor. Forgetting all the adversities she had been through, she became positively merry, and when she saw other women doing Majorcan dances, she herself did one in the Alexandrian manner.

On seeing this, Pericone thought he was getting close to what he wanted, and calling for more food and drink he prolonged the banquet into the wee hours of the night. Finally, after the guests were gone, he accompanied her, alone, to her bedroom. There, unhindered by any feeling of shame, and more heated by the wine than restrained by her sense of honor, she undressed in front of him as if he were one of her women, and got into bed. Pericone was not slow to follow her, and after extinguishing the lights, he quickly got in from the other side. Lying down beside her, he took her in his arms, and with no resistance whatsoever on her part, began playing the game of love with her. Up until that moment, she had no conception of the kind of horn men do their butting with, but once she did, she almost regretted not having given in to Pericone's solicitations. And from then on, she would no longer wait for an invitation to enjoy such sweet nights, but often issued the invitation herself, not by means of words, since she did not know how to make herself understood, but by means of actions.

Fortune, however, was not content to have made the wife of a king into the mistress of a lord, but was preparing a crueler alliance for the lady in place of the very pleasurable one she had with Pericone. For Pericone had a twenty-five-year-old brother named Marato, fair and fresh as a rose, who had seen the lady and felt powerfully attracted to her. As far as he could judge from her reactions, it seemed very likely to him that he stood in her good graces, and since he thought the only thing between him and what he desired was the strict watch that Pericone kept over her, he devised a cruel plan that he quickly turned into a terrible reality.

There happened to be a ship down in the port just then that was loaded up with merchandise and bound for Chiarenza in Romania.[4] Although it had already hoisted sail, ready to depart with the first favorable wind, Marato made a deal with its two young Genoese masters for them to take himself and the lady on board the following night. With this out of the way, Marato made up his mind about how he would proceed, and as soon as night fell, he wandered unobserved over to Pericone's house, taking along with him several of his most trusted companions whom he had enlisted specifically to help him carry out his plan. Since Pericone had no reason to be on his guard, Marato was able to hide himself inside the house just as he had told his men he was going to do. Then, in the dead of night, he opened the door and led them to the room in

4. Another name used by the medieval Italians for Morea, or the Peloponnese (southern Greece); Chiarenza (also "Klarenza") was a main seaport in Achaea, a region of the northwest Peloponnese.

which Pericone and the lady were sleeping. They slew Pericone in his bed and seized the lady, now wide awake and in tears, threatening to kill her if she made any noise. Then, after taking many of Pericone's most precious possessions, they left the house without being heard and hurried down to the harbor where Marato and the lady immediately boarded the ship while his companions returned to the city. The crew set sail, and with a good, fresh wind behind them, began their voyage.

The lady grieved bitterly over this second misfortune, just as she had over the first one, but Marato made good use of Saint Grows-in-the-Hand, God's gift to all of us, and began consoling her in such a way that she was soon on intimate terms with him and forgot all about Pericone. Things thus seemed to be going pretty well for her, but Fortune, not content it seems with the lady's previous tribulations, was already preparing her a new one. For what with her beauty, which was, as we have said many times before, quite stunning, and her extremely refined manners, the two young masters of the ship contracted such a violent love for her that they forgot about everything else and sought only to serve her and provide for her pleasures, at the same time, however, making sure that Marato never caught on to what they were doing.

When they discovered they were both in love with her, they talked things over in secret and agreed to make the acquisition of her love a joint venture—as if love could be shared like merchandise or money. The fact that Marato kept a close watch on her hindered their plan, but one day, when the ship was sailing ahead at full speed and he stood at the stern gazing out to sea, never suspecting that there was a plot against him, they both crept up on him, grabbed him quickly from behind, and threw him into the water. By the time anyone noticed that he had fallen overboard, they were already more than a mile away. When the lady heard what had happened and realized that there was no way of going to his rescue, she began filling the ship once more with the sound of her mourning.

Her two lovers came straightway to console her, and with the aid of sweet words and the most extravagant promises, of which she understood very little, they worked at getting her to calm down. She was really lamenting her own misfortune more than the loss of Marato, and when, after their lengthy speeches, which they repeated twice over, she seemed much less distressed to them, the pair had a private discussion to decide who would be the first one to take her to bed with him. Each man wanted that honor, and failing to reach an agreement, they started a violent argument about it. Their words kept fanning the flames of their anger until they reached for their knives and in a fury hurled themselves at one another, and before any of the ship's crew could separate them, they had both been stabbed repeatedly. One of them died instantly from his wounds, and although the other survived, he was left with serious injuries to many parts of his body.

The lady was very upset over what had happened, for she could see that she was all alone there now, with no one to turn to for aid or advice, and she was terrified that the relations and friends of the two masters would take their anger out on her. However, partly because of the injured man's pleas on her behalf and partly because the ship quickly reached Chiarenza, she escaped the danger of being killed. Upon arriving, she disembarked with the injured man and went to stay with him at an inn, from which rumors of her stunning beauty spread throughout the city, eventually reaching the ears of the Prince of Morea[5] who was living in Chiarenza at the time. He insisted on seeing her, and once he had, not only did he find that her beauty surpassed anything he had heard about it, but he immediately fell in love with her so passionately that he could think of nothing else.

Having learned about the circumstances of her arrival in the city, he saw no reason why he should not be able to have her, and in fact, while he was still trying to figure out a way to do so, the family of the injured man discovered what he was up to and sent the lady to him without a moment's hesitation. The Prince was absolutely delighted by this turn of events, as was the lady, who felt she had escaped a very dangerous situation, indeed. Observing that she was endowed with refined manners as well as beauty, the Prince concluded, not having any other way to determine her identity, that she had to be a noble woman, which had the effect of redoubling his love for her and led not only to his keeping her in high style, but to his treating her more like a wife than a mistress.

When the lady compared her present situation with the awful experiences she had been through, she considered herself pretty well off, and now that she had recovered fully and felt happy again, her beauty flowered to such an extent that all of Romania seemed to be talking about nothing else. And that is why the Duke of Athens,[6] a handsome, well-built youth, who was a friend and relative of the Prince, was moved by a desire to see her. And so, under the pretext that he was just paying a visit to the Prince, as he used to do on occasion, he arrived in Chiarenza at the head of a splendid, noble retinue, and was received there with honor amid great rejoicing.

A few days later, the two men fell to talking about the lady's beauty, and the Duke asked if she was really so marvelous an object as people said. "Far more so!" replied the Prince. "But rather than take my word for it, I'd prefer it if you judged with your own eyes."

The Prince invited the Duke to follow him, and together they went to the place where she was staying. Having already been informed of their approach, she welcomed them with the greatest civility, her face glowing with happiness. They had her sit down between them, but took no pleasure in conversing with her since she understood little or nothing of their language. Instead, as if she were some marvelous creature, they wound up simply gazing at her, and especially the Duke, who could hardly bring himself to believe she was a mere mortal. He did not realize he was drinking down the poison of Love through his eyes as he stared at her, and although he may have believed he could satisfy his desire simply by looking, the wretch was actually being caught up in the snare of her beauty and was falling passionately in love with her. After he and the Prince had taken their leave and he had had some time for reflection, he concluded that the Prince was the happiest of men in having such a beautiful creature at his beck and call. Many and varied were his thoughts on the subject until his burning passion finally overcame his sense of honor, and he decided

5. A fictional character.
6. Also a fictional character; but Boccaccio was acquainted with a real Duke of Athens, Walter of Brienne, who became ruler of Florence in 1342–43.

This page from the Codex Amiatinus (ca. 8th century C.E.), the earliest surviving manuscript
of the Latin Vulgate Bible, depicts the Jewish scribe Ezra. Ezra is traditionally credited with

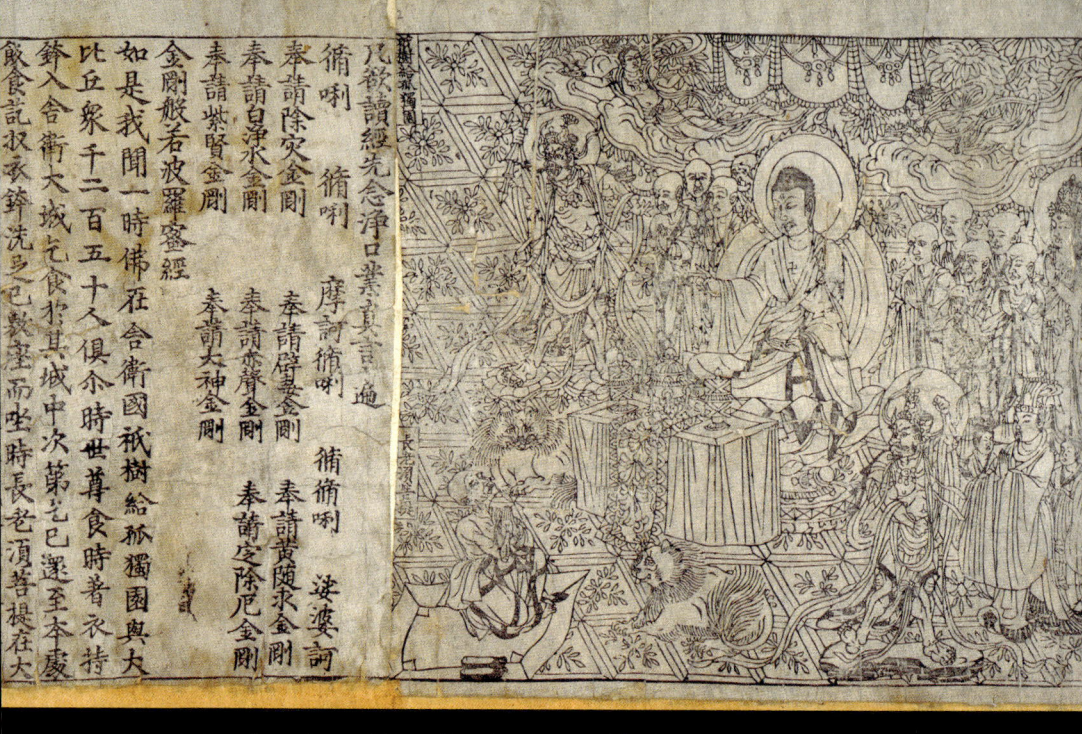

Frontispiece from the world's earliest dated printed book: a Chinese translation of the Buddhist *Diamond Sūtra*. This translation, consisting of a series of woodblock prints on a sixteen-foot scroll, was printed in 868 C.E.

A fragment of the Qur'an (specifically, the beginning of sura 33) written in Kufic script, the oldest calligraphic form of Arabic script. This parchment manuscript, decorated with designs in black and red ink and gold leaf, dates from the ninth or tenth century C.E.

The Old English poem *Beowulf* survives in only one manuscript copy, a page of which is pictured here. Though the poem is set in sixth-century Scandinavia, the date of its composition isn't known. This manuscript was copied sometime in the early eleventh century.

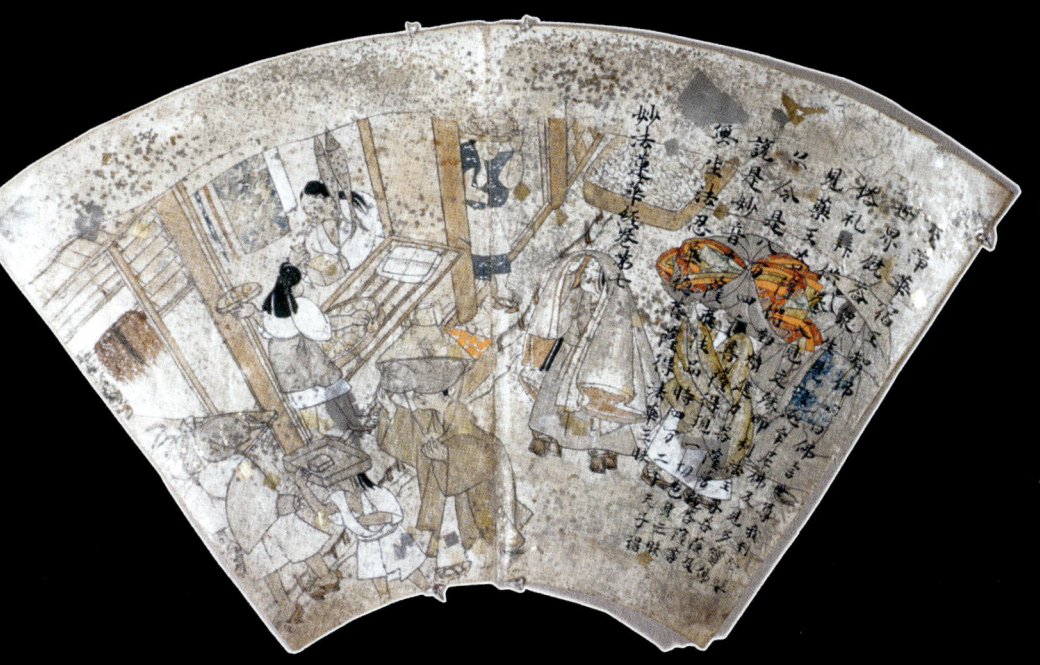

A single leaf from a fan-shaped album of excerpts from the Buddhist *Lotus Sūtra* that was produced near the end of the Heian Period in Japan (i.e., sometime during the late twelfth century). In addition to the calligraphic excerpt on the right, this page features a genre painting of servants performing their duties. The illustrations in these fan-shaped albums were typically unrelated to the quoted sutra.

A page from perhaps the most famous printed book of all time: the Gutenberg Bible (ca. 1453–56). Printed in Mainz, Germany, this Bible was one of the first books (and certainly the most notable one) to be printed in Europe using a movable-type printing press. Only

Typographus. Der Buchdrucker.

A Rte mea reliquas illuſtro Typographus artes,
Imprimo dum varios ære micante libros.
Quæ prius aucta ſitu, quæ puluere plena iacebant,
Vidimus obſcura noct̄e ſepulta premi.

Hæc veterum renouo neglecta volumina Patrum
Atq̃ ſcolis curo publica facta legi.
Artem prima nouam reperiſſe Moguntia fertur,
Vrbs grauis, & multis ingenioſa modis.
Qua nihil vtilius videt, aut precioſius orbis,
Vix melius quicquam ſecla futura dabunt.

A page from an illuminated manuscript of the Persian epic *Shahnameh*. This version is attributed to Muzaffar Ali, a famous Persian miniaturist who thrived during the reign of Shah Tahmasp (1525–76).

that, whatever the consequences, he would do everything in his power to deprive the Prince of that happiness and make it his own.

Determined to move with dispatch, he set aside all considerations of reason and justice, concentrating entirely on his treachery, and one day, in furtherance of his wicked plan, made arrangements with one of the Prince's most trusted servants, a man named Ciuriaci, to have his horses and baggage secretly readied for a sudden departure. When night fell, Ciuriaci, whom we have just mentioned, silently let him and an accomplice, both fully armed, into the Prince's chamber. It was a very hot night, and while the lady lay sleeping, the Duke saw the Prince standing completely naked next to a window that faced the sea, enjoying a light breeze coming from that direction. The Duke, who had told his accomplice what to do ahead of time, stole quietly across the room to the window and thrust a dagger into the Prince's back with such force that it went straight through him, after which he quickly picked him up and hurled him out of the window. The palace stood high above the sea, and the window by which the Prince had been standing overlooked a cluster of houses that had been reduced to ruins by the pounding of the waves. People went there seldom, if ever, and consequently, as the Duke had foreseen, no one noticed the Prince's body as it fell, for there was no one there to see it.

When the Duke's accomplice saw that the deed was done, he quickly took out a noose he had brought with him for the purpose, and while pretending to embrace Ciuriaci, threw it around his neck, and drew it so tight that the man could not make a sound. The Duke then came over, and together they strangled Ciuriaci before throwing him down where the Prince had just been thrown. Once this was done, and they were absolutely certain that neither the lady nor anyone else had heard them, after which the Duke took up a lantern, carried it over to the bed, and quietly took all the covers off of her as she lay there sound asleep. Looking her over from head to toe, he was enraptured, and if he had found her attractive when dressed, now that she was naked, his admiration knew no bounds. The flames of the Duke's desire were burning even more fiercely than before, and unperturbed by the crime he had just committed, he lay down beside her, his hands still bloody, and made love to her, while she, half-asleep, thought he was the Prince.

After a while, having enjoyed himself to the limit with her, the Duke got up and summoned a few of his men whom he ordered to hold the lady in such a way that she could not make a sound and to carry her out through the secret door by which he had entered. Then, making as little noise as possible, they put her on a horse, and the Duke led them all in the direction of Athens. Since he already had a wife, however, he did not take this unhappiest of ladies to Athens itself, but to an extraordinarily beautiful villa he had, not far from the city, that overlooked the sea. There he kept her hidden away, but ordered that she be treated with respect and given everything she needed.

The next day the Prince's courtiers waited until nones for him to get up, but when they still heard no sound coming from his room, they pushed open the doors, which were unlocked, only to discover that no one was there. Working on the assumption that he had gone off somewhere in secret to spend a few days in the happy company of his beautiful mistress, they did not give the matter a second thought.

Things stood thus until the next day, when a madman who had wandered into the ruins where the bodies of the Prince and Ciuriaci were lying, dragged Ciuriaci out by the rope around his neck, and walked about, pulling the body behind him. When people recognized who it was, they were dumbfounded and managed to coax the madman into taking them to the place from which he had brought the body. There, to the immense sorrow of the entire city, they found the dead Prince. After burying him with full honors, they opened an investigation to discover who was responsible for the heinous crime, and when they learned that the Duke of Athens, who had departed in secret, was nowhere to be found, they concluded correctly that he was the culprit and that he must have taken the lady away with him. After hastily choosing a brother of their dead Prince as their new ruler, they urged him with all the eloquence at their command to seek revenge. And when yet more evidence appeared, confirming that their suspicions were true, the new Prince summoned his friends, and servants from various places to support his cause, quickly assembling a splendid, large, and powerful army, with which he set out to wage war against the Duke of Athens.

The moment the Duke heard what was happening, he, too, mobilized his entire army for his defense. Many noblemen came to his aid, including two who were sent by the Emperor of Constantinople, namely his son Constantine and his nephew Manuel,[7] who arrived at the head of a fine large force. They were warmly welcomed by the Duke, and even more so by the Duchess, who was Constantine's sister.

As war came closer day by day, the Duchess found a convenient moment to invite the two young men to her room, where she told them the entire story in great detail. Weeping copiously as she explained the causes of the war, she complained bitterly about the disrespect the Duke was showing her by having some woman as his mistress, whose existence he thought he was managing to keep hidden from her, and she begged them, for the sake of the Duke's honor and her own happiness, to take whatever measures were necessary to set things right. Since the young men already knew the whole story, they did not ask her very many questions, but did their best to comfort her and give her every reason to be hopeful. Then, after being informed as to where the lady was staying, they took their leave of her.

Since they had often heard the lady praised for her marvelous beauty, they were actually quite eager to see her and begged the Duke to present her to them. He promised he would, forgetting what had happened to the Prince for having done something similar. And the next morning, after arranging to have a magnificent banquet served in a lovely garden that was on the estate where the lady was staying, he took the two young men, along with a few other companions, to dine with her there. Sitting down next to her, Constantine stared at her in wonder, vowing to himself that he had never seen anything so lovely and that no one would blame the Duke, or anybody else, for resorting to treachery and other dishonest means in order to gain possession of so beautiful an object. And as he looked her over again and again, each time he admired her more than the time before, until finally the same thing happened to him that had

7. Names that appear repeatedly among the Christian rulers of the Byzantine Empire, whose capital was Constantinople (renamed Istanbul after it fell to the Ottoman Turks in 1453), the former seat of the Eastern Roman Empire.

happened to the Duke. As a result, by the time he left, he was so much in love with her that he abandoned any thought of going to war and concentrated on how he might take her away from the Duke, all the while doing a very good job of concealing his passion from everyone.

As Constantine was burning in this fire, the moment arrived to march against the Prince, who had by now almost reached the Duke's territories. In accordance with their strategic plan, the Duke, Constantine, and all the others left Athens and went to take up positions along certain stretches of the frontier where they intended to block the Prince's advance. While they waited there for several days, Constantine, whose thoughts and feelings were entirely focused on the lady, fancied that since the Duke was no longer anywhere near her, he now had an excellent opportunity to get what he wanted. Pretending to be seriously ill in order to have a pretext for returning to Athens, he got permission from the Duke, handed his command over to Manuel, and went back to stay with his sister in the city. Several days later, after he got her talking about the disrespect she thought the Duke was showing her with his kept woman, he told her that if she wanted, he could certainly be of considerable assistance to her in this business, for he could have the woman removed from where she was staying and taken elsewhere. Thinking that Constantine was prompted by his love for her rather than for the lady, the Duchess said that it would please her very much, provided it was done in such a way that the Duke never found out she had given her consent to the scheme. Constantine reassured her completely on this point, and accordingly, the Duchess gave him permission to proceed in whatever way he thought best.

Constantine had a swift boat fitted out in secret, and one evening, after giving those of his men who were on board their instructions, he sent it to a spot near the garden on the estate where the lady was staying. Then, with another group of men, he went to her villa, where he was warmly received by her servants and by the lady herself, who at his request, went with him and his men to take a walk in the garden, accompanied by her servants.

Pretending he wanted to speak to her on behalf of the Duke, he led her down toward a gate overlooking the sea that had been unlocked earlier by one of his crew. There, at a given signal, the boat pulled up, and Constantine had his men seize her and quickly put her on board. Then he turned to her servants and said: "Don't anyone move or make a sound unless you want to be killed. My intention here is not to steal the Duke's mistress, but to take away the shame he's inflicted on my sister."

Seeing that no one dared to respond to him, he boarded the boat with his men, and sitting down beside the weeping lady, he ordered them to put their oars into the water and get under way. They did not row so much as fly along, arriving at Aegina[8] just before dawn the next day.

Disembarking there in order to rest, Constantine had his fun with the lady, who did nothing but lament her unlucky beauty. Then they boarded the boat once again and in just a few days reached Chios,[9] where Constantine decided to put up, thinking he would be safe there both from his father's reprimands

8. An island less than 25 miles southwest of Athens.

9. An island almost directly east of Athens, just off the coast of Turkey; Alatiel is steadily moving eastward.

and from the possibility that someone might take away from him the lady he himself had stolen. For several days the beauty bewailed her misfortune, but eventually, thanks to Constantine's unremitting efforts to console her, she began to enjoy, as she had every other time, the lot that Fortune had assigned her.

This was the state of affairs when Osbech,[1] at that time the King of the Turks, who was constantly at war with the Emperor, chanced to come to Smyrna,[2] where he learned that Constantine was leading a dissolute life on Chios with some woman of his whom he had abducted and that he had consequently not bothered to set up any defenses there. Arriving one night with a squadron of light warships, Osbech quietly entered the town with his men, capturing many people in their beds before they were even aware that the enemy was upon them, and killing those who awoke in time to run and get their weapons. They then set fire to the town, loaded their booty and their prisoners onto the ships, and went back to Smyrna. Upon reviewing their spoils after their return, the young Osbech was delighted to discover the beautiful lady, whom he recognized as being the one he had captured in bed together with Constantine as they lay sleeping. He married her on the spot, and after the wedding spent the next several months very happily sleeping with her.

In the period before these events occurred, the Emperor had been negotiating a pact with Basano, the King of Cappadocia,[3] to have his forces attack Osbech from one direction while the Emperor assaulted him from the other. He had not yet brought their negotiations to a conclusion, however, because he would not agree to some of Basano's demands that he found quite unreasonable. But on hearing what had happened to his son, the Emperor was so distraught that he accepted the King of Cappadocia's terms at once and urged him to attack Osbech as soon as he possibly could, while he himself made preparations to come down on Osbech from the other direction.

When Osbech heard about all this, rather than let himself get caught in the middle between two powerful rulers, he assembled his army and marched against the King of Cappadocia, leaving the lovely lady at Smyrna under the protection of a loyal retainer and friend. Some time later, he confronted the King of Cappadocia and attacked him, but in the battle his army was defeated and put to flight, and he himself was killed. Unopposed, the victorious Basano then marched on Smyrna, and as he went, all the peoples along the way submitted to him as their conqueror.

The retainer in whose care Osbech had left the lovely lady, a man named Antioco, was so taken with her beauty that he betrayed the trust of his friend and master, and despite his advanced years, fell in love with her. It pleased her immensely that he knew her language, because for a number of years she had been forced to live as if she were a deaf-mute, incapable of understanding others or getting them to understand her. Spurred on by love, in the first few

---

1. Uzbek was in fact the Mongol khan of the Golden Horde (ruled ca. 1312–ca. 1342) in what is now southern Russia. Boccaccio turns him into the King of the Turks, a separate ethnic group, and invents his war with Constantinople.
2. A city on the western coast of Turkey (modern Izmir), opposite Chios; by the early 14th century it was no longer under Christian control.
3. A region in central modern Turkey; though Christians lost control of the area during the 12th century, the Italian-sounding name of the fictional character "Basano" implies Christian rule.

days Antioco began taking so many liberties with her that before long they had cast aside any concern for their master, who was away fighting in the war, and became not merely friends, but lovers who gave one another the greatest pleasure imaginable over and over again as they lay together between the sheets.

When they heard that Osbech had been defeated and killed, however, and that Basano was on his way, carrying everything before him, they were of one mind in deciding to leave rather than wait for his arrival. Taking with them a substantial quantity of Osbech's most valuable possessions, they fled together in secret to Rhodes,[4] where they had not been very long before Antioco contracted a fatal illness. At the time he happened to have a Cypriot[5] merchant staying in his house, a very close friend whom he loved dearly, and as Antioco felt the end approaching, he decided to leave his friend both his possessions and his beloved lady. And so, when he felt his death was imminent, he summoned the two of them and said:

"I have no doubt that my strength is failing, which saddens me because my life has never been as happy as it's been of late. Truthfully, though, there's one thing that reconciles me to my death, and it's that since I'm going to die, I will do so in the arms of the two people I love more than anyone else in the world, that is, in your arms, my dear dear friend, and in those of this lady, whom I've loved more than I love myself for as long as I've known her. But still, what really continues to trouble me is that when I die, she'll be left all alone here in a strange land, with no one to turn to for help or counsel. And this worry would weigh on me even more than it does if I didn't have you here, because I believe that, out of love for me, you will take good care of her just as you would of me. Consequently, in the event of my death, I commit her, together with all my worldly goods, to your charge, and I entreat you as earnestly as I can to make use of them in whatever way you think will offer my soul some measure of consolation. And as for you, my dearest lady, I beg you not to forget me after my death, for then I can boast up there that I have been loved down here by the most beautiful woman ever fashioned by Nature. And now, if both of you will just reassure me on these two points, you may have no doubt but that I will die content."

Both Antioco's merchant friend and the lady wept as they listened to his words, and when he was finished, they comforted him and swore on their honor to do what he requested if he should happen to die. And not long after this, he did, in fact, pass away, and they saw to it that he was given an honorable burial.

A few days later, when the Cypriot merchant had taken care of all his business in Rhodes, he decided to take ship on a Catalan merchant vessel then in port that was about to sail to Cyprus. He asked the lady what she wanted to do, in light of the fact that he was compelled to return to Cyprus, and she replied that if he had no objection, she would gladly go with him, because she hoped that, out of love for Antioco, he would think of her like a sister and would treat her accordingly. The merchant said he would be happy to do whatever she wished, and in order to protect her from any harm that might befall her before they reached Cyprus, he told everyone she was his wife. When they got on

---

4. An island off the southwest coast of Turkey (southeast of Chios and Smyrna), and a much-disputed military stronghold.

5. Native of Cyprus, a large island in the north-eastern Mediterranean (south of Turkey).

board, they were, consequently, assigned a small cabin in the stern, and to ensure that their actions were consistent with their words, he slept in the same narrow little bunk with her. What happened next was something that neither one of them had intended when they left Rhodes. Stimulated by the darkness as well as by the warmth and comfort of the bed, which are forces not to be underestimated, they were both seized by the same desires, and forgetting all about the loyalty and love they owed Antioco, before long they were fondling one another, with the inevitable result that even before they reached Paphos,[6] the Cypriot's hometown, they were sleeping together like a regular married couple. Indeed, for quite some time after they reached their destination, she went on living with the merchant in his house.

By chance, a gentleman named Antigono happened to come to Paphos on some business or other at a time when the Cypriot merchant was away on a trading mission in Armenia. An elderly man, Antigono had acquired even more wisdom than years, albeit very little wealth in the process, because every time he had undertaken a commission in the service of the King of Cyprus, Fortune had always been his enemy. One day, as he was passing by the house where the lovely lady was staying, he happened to catch sight of her at one of the windows. He just could not stop staring at her, not only because she was so beautiful, but also because he had a vague recollection that he had seen her at some other time, although he could by no means remember where that had been.

For a long while, the lovely lady had been Fortune's plaything, but the moment was approaching when her sufferings would be over. Observing Antigono, she recalled having seen him in Alexandria where he had served her father in a position of some importance, and all of a sudden she was filled with hope that there might be some possibility of her returning once more to her royal station with the help of this man's advice. Since her merchant was out of the way, she sent for the old counselor at the first opportunity, and when he arrived, she asked him shyly if he was, as she thought, Antigono di Famagosto. Antigono replied that he was, adding: "My lady, I think I've seen you before, but I can't, for the life of me, remember where. Please be good enough, therefore, unless you have some objection, to remind me who you are."

When the lady heard that he was indeed Antigono, to his complete astonishment she burst into tears and threw her arms about his neck. Then, after a moment, she asked him if he had ever seen her in Alexandria. The instant Antigono heard her question, he recognized that she was Alatiel, the Sultan's daughter, who everybody thought had died at sea. He tried to bow to her as court etiquette required, but she would not permit it, inviting him, instead, to sit down beside her for a while. When he was seated, he asked her with due reverence how and when and from where she had come to Cyprus, for all of Egypt was convinced that she had drowned at sea many years before.

"I really wish that had happened," replied the lady, "instead of my having led the sort of life I've led. Furthermore, I think my father would agree with me if he ever found out about it." Then, having said this, she began weeping prodigiously once again.

6. In classical times, a major center of the worship of Aphrodite, Greek goddess of love.

"My lady, don't distress yourself unnecessarily," said Antigono. "Tell me about your misfortunes, if you like, and about the life you've led. Perhaps things can be handled in such a way that, with God's help, we'll be able to find a solution for your problem."

"Antigono," said the lovely lady, "when I first saw you here, I felt I was look-ing at my own father, and although I could have concealed my identity from you, I was moved to reveal it by the same love and tender affection I am bound to feel for him. Actually, there are few people I would have been as happy to have seen here as I am to have seen you, and therefore, I'm going to reveal to you, as to a father, the story of my terrible misfortunes, which I've always kept hidden from everyone else. If, after you've heard it, you can see any means of restoring me to my pristine condition, I implore you to make use of it. If not, I beg you never to tell anyone that you've either seen me or heard anything about me."

This said, she gave him an account, without ever ceasing to weep, of every-thing that had happened to her from the day she was shipwrecked off Majorca up to the present moment. Her story made Antigono start weeping himself out of pity for her, and after pondering the matter awhile, he said: "My lady, since no one ever knew who you were during all your misadventures, have no doubt but that I can restore you, more precious than ever, first to your father and then, as his bride, to the King of Algarve."

Questioned by her as to how he would manage this, he explained in detail just what she had to do. Then, to prevent anything from happening that might cause a delay, Antigono returned at once to Famagosto where he presented himself before the King. "My lord," he said, "if it please you, you can do some-thing at very little cost that will greatly redound to your honor, while simulta-neously being of inestimable benefit to me, who have grown poor while I've been in your service."

When the King asked how this might be done, Antigono answered: "The beautiful young daughter of the Sultan, who was long thought to have drowned at sea, has turned up in Paphos. For many years she has suffered through extreme hardships in order to preserve her honor, and now she is living here in poverty and wants to return to her father. If it should be your pleasure to send her back to him under my escort, it would greatly enhance your honor and would mean a rich reward for me. It is, moreover, inconceivable that the Sul-tan would ever forget such a service."

Moved by regal feelings of magnanimity, the King said that it was indeed his pleasure to send the lady home, and he dispatched an honor guard to accompany her to Famagosto where he and the Queen received her with the most incredible pomp and circumstance. When they asked her about her adventures, she replied by recounting the whole story just as Antigono had taught her to tell it.

A few days later, at her request, the King sent her back to the Sultan under Antigono's protection and with a splendid retinue of distinguished gentlemen and ladies. No one need ask how warm a welcome she got there or how Ant-igono and her entire entourage were received. After letting her rest awhile, the Sultan wanted to know how it had come about that she was still alive, where she had been living for all that time, and why she had never sent him word about her situation.

The lady, who had memorized Antigono's instructions to the letter, answered the Sultan as follows: "Father, some twenty days after I left you, our ship foundered in a fierce storm and ran aground one night on some beach or other in the West near a place called Aigues–Mortes.[7] I never found out what happened to the men who were on board. All I do remember is that when dawn arrived, I felt as though I was rising from the dead and returning to life. Some peasants, who had spotted the wrecked ship, came running from all over to plunder it. When I was put ashore with two of my women, they were instantly snatched up by some young men who then fled, carrying them off in different directions, and I have never discovered what became of them. As for me, although I tried to fight them off, two young men grabbed me and started to drag me away by my hair. I was weeping violently the whole time, but then, just as they started heading down a road in the direction of a very dense forest, four horsemen happened to come riding by, and the instant my abductors caught sight of them, they let go of me and immediately fled away.

"When they saw what was happening, the four horsemen, who seemed like persons of some authority, galloped over to me. They asked me a lot of questions, and I gave them a lot of answers, but it was impossible for us to understand one another. Then, after a long consultation among themselves, they put me on one of their horses and led me to a convent of women who practiced these men's religion. I have no idea what they said there, but the women gave me a very kind welcome and always treated me with respect. While I was in the convent, I joined them in reverently worshipping Saint Grows-in–the-Deep-Valley,[8] to whom the women of that country are passionately devoted. After I'd lived there awhile and had learned something of their language, they asked me who I was and what country I'd come from. Knowing where I was, I feared that if I told them the truth, they might expel me as an enemy to their religion, and so I replied that I was the daughter of an important nobleman of Cyprus, who had been sending me to be married in Crete when, unfortunately, we were driven onto their shores by a storm and shipwrecked.

"Fearful of a worse fate, I made a regular habit of observing their customs of every sort until, eventually, I was asked by the women's superior, whom they call their Abbess, whether I wanted to return to Cyprus, and I replied that there was nothing I desired more. Out of concern for my honor, however, she was unwilling to entrust me to just anyone coming to Cyprus, at least up until about two months ago, when certain French gentlemen, some of whom were related to the Abbess, arrived there with their wives. When she heard that they were going to Jerusalem to visit the Sepulcher, where the man they consider their God was buried after the Jews had killed Him, she placed me in their care and asked them to hand me over to my father in Cyprus.

"It would make too long a story if I were to describe how much I was honored and how warm a welcome I was given by these noblemen and their wives.

7. Literally, "dead [i.e., stagnant] waters" (Lat. *Aquae Mortuae*), named from the marshes on which this fortified city was built. On the southern coast of modern France, it was linked by trade routes with the Italian cities of Florence and Genoa.

8. Although the saint's name here appears to be a clever invention, there actually was a shrine of San Cresci in Valcava ("Saint Grows in Deep Valley") located about 15 miles north of Florence.

Suffice it to say that we all took ship and in just a few days reached Paphos, where it suddenly hit me that I'd come to a place where I didn't know anyone and thus had no idea what to tell the noblemen who wanted to follow the venerable lady's instructions and hand me over to my father. Perhaps God took pity on me, however, for he arranged to have Antigono there on the shore at Paphos at the precise moment we were getting off the ship. I called out to him at once, using our own language so as not to be understood by the noblemen and their wives, and told him to welcome me as his daughter. He grasped my meaning instantly and made a tremendous fuss over me. After entertaining those noblemen and their wives as well as his limited means allowed, he took me to the King of Cyprus, and I couldn't begin to describe how much he honored me, not only with the welcome he gave me there, but by sending me back here to you. If anything else remains to be said, I leave it to Antigono, for he has heard me recount my adventures time and time again."

"My lord," said Antigono, turning to the Sultan, "she has now told you exactly the same story she's recounted to me many times and what the noblemen who were accompanying her told me as well. There's only one part that she's left out, which I think she omitted because it would not be appropriate for her to talk about it, and that is how much praise the gentlemen and ladies with whom she was traveling lavished on her not just because of the honest life she'd led with the pious women, but also because of her virtue and her laudable character. She also failed to mention how all of them, the men as well as the women, grieved and wept bitter tears when the time came to say farewell to her and place her in my charge. Were I to recount in detail everything they told me on this subject, I'd be talking not only all day, but all night, too. Let it suffice for me to say just this much, that from what their words have revealed to me, and from what I myself have been able to see, you may boast of having a daughter who is far lovelier, chaster, and more courageous than that of any monarch wearing a crown today."

The Sultan was absolutely overjoyed to hear these things, and he repeatedly asked God to grant him the grace to bestow proper rewards on all those who had treated his daughter so honorably, and in particular on the King of Cyprus who had sent her home with such pomp and ceremony. A few days later, having ordered the most lavish gifts for Antigono, he gave him leave to return to Cyprus, sending letters and special envoys along with him to convey his most sincere gratitude to the King for what he had done for his daughter. Then, since he wanted to bring what he had started long before to its conclusion, namely to make her the wife of the King of Algarve, he wrote to the King, explaining everything that had happened, and adding that if he still wished to have her, he should send his envoys to fetch her. The King of Algarve was quite delighted by this proposition, sent an honorable escort for her, and gave her a joyous welcome. Thus, although she had slept with eight men perhaps ten thousand times, she not only came to the King's bed as if she were a virgin, but made him believe she really was one, and for a good many years after that, lived a perfectly happy life with him as his Queen. And that is the reason why we say:

A mouth that's been kissed never loses its charm,
But just like the moon, it's forever renewed.

Day 4, Story 9

Messer Guiglielmo Rossiglione slays his wife's lover, Messer Guiglielmo Guardastagno,[9] and gives her his heart to eat, but when she finds out about it later, she throws herself down to the ground from a high window, and after her death, is buried with her beloved.

Neifile's story had inspired great feelings of pity in the entire company, and when it was finished, the King, who had no intention of infringing on Dioneo's privilege, saw that there was no one else left to speak. Consequently, he began as follows:

Considering how much you are saddened, my most compassionate ladies, by lovers' misfortunes, the tale that presents itself to me will make you feel at least as much pity as the last one did, since the people involved in the events I am about to relate were of loftier rank and met with a crueler fate than those of whom we have already spoken. You must know, then, that according to the people of Provence, there were once two noble knights living in that region, each of whom had a castle and a large number of vassals under him. One was named Messer Guiglielmo Rossiglione and the other Messer Guiglielmo Guardastagno, and since both excelled in feats of arms, they used to arm themselves from head to toe, and not only would they go together to tournaments and jousts and other contests involving martial prowess, but they would do so wearing exactly the same device.[1]

Although the castles in which the two of them resided were a good ten miles apart, Messer Guiglielmo Guardastagno chanced to fall madly in love with Messer Guiglielmo Rossiglione's very beautiful and charming wife, and despite all the affection and camaraderie the men shared, he made use of one means and then another to make her aware of his feelings. The lady, knowing him to be a most gallant knight, was pleased by this and soon became so infatuated with him that there was nothing she burned and yearned for more, until the only thing she was still waiting for was to have him proposition her. Nor was it very long before he did, after which they met with some frequency and made passionate love together.

Since they were not very discreet in their encounters, one day her husband chanced to discover them and became so deeply incensed that the great love he felt for Guardastagno was transformed into mortal hatred. Better at keeping it hidden, however, than the two lovers had been with their affair, he decided, no matter what, that he would kill the man.

With Rossiglione in this frame of mind, a grand tournament happened to be announced in France. He immediately sent word of it to Guardastagno, asking him if he would like to come to his castle where the two of them could decide together whether they wanted to go and how they would get there. Quite delighted, Guardastagno replied that he would come without fail the next day and have supper with him.

---

9. The love triangle appears to be fictitious, but the names refer to the Provençal troubadour poet Guilhem de Cabestaing (1162–1212) and his lord Raimon de Castel-Rossillon (d. 1209).

1. The individual emblem, worn on armor or carried as a banner, that enabled a knight to be recognized on the field of battle.

When he received Guardastagno's message, Rossiglione thought the time had come to kill him. The next day, after arming himself, he got on his horse, and with a few of his men he went about a mile away from his castle, where he set up an ambush in a wood through which Guardastagno was bound to pass. After a long wait, he caught sight of him approaching, unarmed, followed by two servants, who were likewise unarmed, because he never thought for a moment that he might need to protect himself against his friend. When Rossiglione saw that Guardastagno had reached the spot he had chosen, he rushed out at him, with murder and vengeance in his heart, holding his lance above his head and shouting, "Traitor, you're a dead man!" And before the words were even out of his mouth, he thrust his lance straight through Guardastagno's chest.

Unable to defend himself, let alone even utter a word, Guardastagno fell, impaled on the lance, and died almost instantly, at which point his servants, without waiting to see who had killed him, turned their horses' heads around and fled back to their master's castle as fast as they could.

After dismounting from his horse, Rossiglione cut open Guardastagno's chest with a knife, tore out the heart with his own hands, and wrapping it up in a banderole, told one of his men to take it with him. Having given them all strict instructions not to dare to say so much as a word about what had happened, he got back on his horse and returned to his castle, by which time it was nightfall.

The lady, who had heard that Guardastagno was supposed to come to supper, was waiting for him with the greatest impatience. When he did not show up with her husband, she was quite surprised and asked him: "How is it, sir, that Guardastagno hasn't arrived?"

"Wife," replied her husband, "I've received word from him that he can't be here until tomorrow"—a statement that left her feeling somewhat perturbed.

After he had dismounted, Rossiglione had his cook summoned and said to him: "Take this boar's heart and make sure that you prepare the finest, most delectable dish you can with it. Then, when I'm seated at table, send it to me on a silver serving plate."

The cook took the heart, and calling upon all his knowledge and all his skill, he minced it, seasoned it with a number of savory spices, and made a very tasty dish out of it indeed.

When it was time to eat, Messer Guiglielmo sat down at the table with his wife. The meal was served, but he was preoccupied with the crime he had committed and ate very little. The cook then sent him the special dish, and he had it placed before the lady, saying he had no appetite that evening. He heartily commended the dish, however, and the lady, who did have an appetite, started to eat it, and finding it quite tasty, consumed every last morsel.

When the knight saw that his wife had finished the whole thing, he asked her: "Wife, what did you think of the dish?"

"In good faith, my lord," she replied, "I liked it very much."

"So help me God," said the knight, "I do believe you did. But I'm really not surprised that you liked it dead, because you liked it when it was alive more than anything else in the world."

Upon hearing these words, the lady hesitated a moment. Then she asked: "How's that? What's this thing you've had me eat?"

"What you ate," said the knight, "was actually the heart of Messer Guiglielmo Guardastagno, whom you, like the faithless woman you are, were so infatuated with. And you may rest assured that it really was his, because I ripped it out of his chest myself, with these hands, just a little while before I came back here."

When she heard what had happened to the man she loved more than anything else in the world, there's no need to ask if she was grief stricken. After a brief pause, she said:

"In doing what you did, you've behaved like a wicked, faithless knight, for if I was not forced into it by him, but freely chose to abuse you by making him the master of my love, then you should have punished me for it, not him. But now that I've eaten such a noble dish, made from the heart of so gallant and courteous a knight as Messer Guiglielmo Guardastagno, God forbid that any food should ever pass my lips again."

Then she stood up, and going to a window right behind her, without the slightest hesitation she let herself fall backward out of it. Because it was so high above the ground, the lady did not merely die, but was completely dashed to pieces.

Messer Guiglielmo was profoundly shaken by what he had witnessed and conscience-stricken over having done wrong. Moreover, he feared what his fellow-countrymen and the Count of Provence might do. Consequently, he had his horses saddled and rode away.

By the next morning, news of what had happened had spread throughout the entire region, and people came from both Messer Guiglielmo Guardastagno's castle and that of the lady's family to gather up the two bodies, which were taken, amid a great outpouring of grief and lamentation, to the chapel inside the lady's castle and buried there in a single tomb together. Upon it there was an inscription in verse, indicating who was buried inside and the manner as well as the cause of their deaths.

Day 10, Story 9

Disguised as a merchant, Saladin[2] is honorably entertained by Messer Torello, who, when a Crusade is launched, establishes a time period for his wife to wait before she remarries. He is taken prisoner, but because of his skill in training falcons, he comes to the attention of the Sultan, who recognizes him, reveals himself in turn, and entertains him lavishly. Having fallen ill, Messer Torello is transported by magic in a single night to Pavia, where his wife's second marriage is about to be celebrated. She recognizes him, and he then returns with her to his house.

Filomena had brought her story to a close, and when one and all had finished heaping praise on Titus for his magnificent act of gratitude, the King, who was reserving the last place for Dioneo,[3] began speaking as follows:

2. Salah ah-Din Yusuf ibn Ayyub (1138–1193), Sultan of Egypt and Syria, who led Muslim campaigns against the Christians in Palestine and recaptured Jerusalem in 1187. Although he was the Crusaders' greatest opponent, in European literature he was represented as a paragon of chivalry and generosity.
3. Dioneo requests and is granted the privilege of speaking last on each day of the *Decameron*; his tales are usually among the most bawdy.

Pretty ladies, not only is what Filomena says about friendship undoubtedly true, but she was right to complain in her final comments about how little regard people have for it nowadays. If we had come here to correct the errors of the world, or even to criticize them, I would follow up on what she said with a substantial discourse of my own. But since our purpose is different, it occurs to me to tell you a story, long perhaps but enjoyable from start to finish, that concerns one of the generous deeds performed by Saladin. Thus, even though our defects may prevent us from winning the deepest sort of friendship with another person, by imitating the things you will hear about in my tale, we may at least derive a certain delight from being courteous to others and hope that sooner or later we will receive our reward for doing so.

Let me begin by saying, then, that during the reign of Emperor Frederick I,[4] according to a number of accounts, the Christians launched a great Crusade to recover the Holy Land. Saladin, a most worthy lord who was then the Sultan of Babylon, having heard about what was happening some time in advance, decided to go in person and see what preparations the Christian leaders were making so that he would be better prepared to protect himself from them. Consequently, having settled all his affairs in Egypt, he pretended he was going on a pilgrimage[5] and set out disguised as a merchant, taking with him only three servants and two of his wisest senior counselors. After they had inspected many Christian kingdoms, one evening close to vespers, as they were riding through Lombardy on their way to cross the mountains, they happened to come upon a gentleman on the road between Milan and Pavia. He was named Messer Torello di Stra da Pavia,[6] and he was going, together with his servants, his dogs, and his falcons, to stay at a beautiful estate he owned on the banks of the Ticino.

As soon as Messer Torello caught sight of them, he concluded that they were foreigners of gentle birth and he was eager to offer them some sort of honorable entertainment. So, when Saladin asked one of Messer Torello's servants how much further it was to Pavia and whether they could still reach it in time to enter the city, Messer Torello prevented the man from saying a word by replying himself: "Gentlemen, by the time you reach Pavia, it'll be too late for you to get in."

"Then," said Saladin, "since we're strangers here, would you be so kind as to tell us where we can find the best lodging."

"I'll do so gladly," said Messer Torello. "I was thinking just now that I would send one of these servants of mine on an errand to a spot not too far from Pavia. I'll have him go with you, and he'll take you to a place where you'll find quite suitable accommodations."

Messer Torello then went up to the most discreet of his servants, told him what to do, and sent him off with Saladin's party. Meanwhile, he himself quickly rode on to his estate where he arranged for the best possible supper to be prepared and for tables to be set up in one of his gardens, after which he went to wait for his guests at the entrance. The servant, conversing with the

---

4. Also called Frederick Barbarossa (1122–1190); Holy Roman Emperor, 1152–90; he joined two kings, Richard the Lion-Hearted of England and Philip of France, in leading the Third Crusade in 1189–92. The Crusades were military campaigns against the Muslims to gain possession of the Holy Land.

5. Because pilgrimage is central to both Muslim and medieval Christian worship, Saladin's alibi would work well for both Muslim and Christian audiences.

6. That is, Torello whose hometown was Stra in the province of Pavia, a town south of Milan, on the east bank of the Ticino River.

gentlemen about various subjects, took them on a roundabout route, leading them along various byroads, until he had brought them, without their suspecting it, to his master's estate.

As soon as Messer Torello saw them, he went out on foot to meet them and said with a laugh: "Gentlemen, you are very welcome here, indeed."

An extremely astute man, Saladin realized that the knight had not invited them there when they first met, for fear they would have turned him down, and that he had cleverly arranged to have them brought to his house so they could not refuse to spend the evening with him. Thus, after returning Messer Torello's greeting, he said:

"Sir, were it possible to lodge a complaint against courteous people, we would lodge one against you, for even leaving aside the fact that you have taken us somewhat out of our way, you have more or less constrained us to accept this noble courtesy of yours when the only thing we did to deserve your goodwill was to exchange a single greeting with you."

"Gentlemen," replied the knight, who was both wise and well-spoken, "if I may judge from your appearance, the courtesy you are going to receive from me is a poor thing in comparison with what you deserve. Truth to tell, however, you could not have found decent lodging outside of Pavia, and that's why I hope you won't be upset to have gone somewhat out of your way in exchange for a little less discomfort here."

While he was speaking, his servants gathered around Saladin's party, and as soon as they had dismounted, took charge of the horses. Messer Torello then led the three gentlemen to the rooms that had been prepared for them. There, after they had been helped off with their boots, he offered them some deliciously cool wine as a refreshment and detained them with pleasant conversation until such time as they might go to supper.

Since Saladin and his companions and servants all knew Italian, they had no difficulty understanding Messer Torello or making themselves understood, and they were all of the opinion that this knight was the most agreeable and well-mannered gentleman and a better conversationalist than anyone they had ever encountered. For his part, Messer Torello concluded that they were all quite eminent men, much more distinguished than he had originally thought, and he regretted deeply that he could not entertain them in company that evening or offer them a more elaborate banquet. He therefore resolved to make amends the next morning, and having told one of his servants what he wanted him to do, he sent the man off to Pavia, which never locked its gates and was not that far away, bearing a message for his wife, a woman of great intelligence and exceptional spirit. This done, he led his guests into the garden and politely asked them who they were, where they had come from, and what their destination was.

"We are Cypriot merchants," replied Saladin. "We've just arrived from our country, and now we're heading to Paris on business."

"Would to God," said Messer Torello, "that this country of ours bred gentlemen comparable to the merchants I see coming from Cyprus."

On these and other matters they chatted for a while until it was time for supper. Messer Torello then asked them if they would do him the honor of being seated at his table, and although it was an impromptu meal, the food was quite good and the service, excellent. Nor had the tables long been cleared away before

Messer Torello, seeing how tired his guests were, showed them to the very comfortable beds that had been prepared for them to sleep in, following which, a little while later, he too retired for the night.

Meanwhile, the servant sent to Pavia delivered his message to Messer Torello's wife, who, in a spirit more like a queen's than an ordinary woman's, promptly summoned a large number of his friends and servants, and had all the preparations for a magnificent banquet set in motion. She had invitations delivered by torchlight to many of the most important nobles in the city, saw to it that a supply of fine clothes and silks and furs was at the ready, and took care of everything else, down to the very detail, that her husband had asked her to do.

The next day, after the gentlemen had risen, Messer Torello set out on horse-back with them, and having called for his falcons, he led the group to a nearby stretch of shallow water where he showed off how his birds could fly. Then, when Saladin asked if there was someone who could escort them to Pavia and direct them to the best inn in the city, Messer Torello replied, "I'll do it myself, because I'm obliged to go there anyway." They took him at his word and hap-pily set off down the road together, reaching the city just after tierce.[7] Thinking they were being escorted to the finest inn available, they arrived, instead, at Messer Torello's mansion where they found a good fifty of the leading citizens of Pavia who had assembled there to receive them and who immediately gath-ered around them in order to hold their reins and stirrups for them.

When Saladin and his companions saw this, they realized only too well what it all meant.

"Messer Torello," they said, "this isn't what we asked you to do for us. You treated us so very well last night, much better than we deserve, which is why it would have been quite proper for you to have just let us go on our way."

"Gentlemen," replied Messer Torello, "with regard to the service that was done for you last night, I am more indebted to Fortune than to you, for it was she who overtook you on the road at an hour when you had no choice but to come to my humble abode. However, with regard to the service that will be done for you this morning, I will be beholden only to you, as will all these gentlemen you see here about you, although if you think it courteous to decline an invitation to dine with them, then you are certainly at liberty to do so."

Acknowledging defeat, Saladin and his companions dismounted and were welcomed by the gentlemen who happily led them to a richly furnished set of rooms that had been prepared for them. After they had removed their traveling clothes and taken a little refreshment, they made their way to the great hall, where everything was magnificently arranged. Having washed their hands, they were seated at the table with great pomp and circumstance and were served so many courses in such splendid style that if the Emperor himself had been pres-ent, it would have been impossible to honor him more highly. In fact, even though Saladin and his companions were great lords and were accustomed to the grandest displays of opulence, they were nevertheless overcome with won-der at their treatment here, which, considering the position of the knight, whom they knew to be no ruler, but just a private citizen, seemed to them about as fine as anything they had ever experienced.

7. A canonical hour, about 9 A.M.

Once the meal was over and the tables cleared away, they discussed serious affairs for a while until, at Messer Torello's suggestion, the weather being quite hot, the gentlemen from Pavia all went off to take a nap, leaving him alone with his three guests. To make sure they got to see all of his most precious possessions, he escorted them into another room and sent for his good lady. A tall, strikingly beautiful woman, she presented herself before them, decked out in her rich garments and flanked by her two little children, who looked like a pair of angels, and welcomed them cordially to her home. The moment the three men saw her, they rose to their feet, gave her a most respectful greeting in return, and invited her to sit down with them, all the while making a great fuss over her beautiful little children. After starting a pleasant conversation with them, during which Messer Torello left the room for a while, she graciously asked them where they were from and where they were going, to which they gave her the same answer they had given her husband.

"Then I see that my woman's intuition may well be useful," said the lady, with a smile, "for I want to ask you a special favor, namely that you will neither refuse nor look down on the little trifling gift I'm going to have them bring for you. Instead, you should bear in mind that women, with their tiny hearts, give tiny presents, and consequently, you should judge what you are going to get more by the good intentions of the giver than the size of the gift."

She then sent for two pairs of robes for each of the guests, one lined with silk and the other with fur—all of them more suitable for lords than for private citizens or merchants—as well as three doublets of taffeta and a number of undergarments.

"Take these robes," she said. "They're just like the ones I've always dressed my husband in. As far as the other things are concerned, although they're of no great value, you may find they'll come in handy, considering how far away you are from your wives, not to mention the fact that you've come a long way and still have a long way to go, and I know how you merchants always like to be neat and trim."

The gentlemen were astonished, for it had become abundantly clear that Messer Torello was intent upon showing them every conceivable courtesy. Considering how magnificent the robes were and how unlike the ones any merchant would wear, they were afraid that he had recognized who they really were, but one of them nevertheless replied to his wife:

"My lady, these things are exquisite and should not be accepted lightly, but we feel compelled to do so because of your prayers, to which we cannot say no."

Thus they took her gifts, and since Messer Torello had now returned, the lady, having said goodbye to them, left the room and went away to see that their servants were supplied with similar gifts according to their rank. In response to Messer Torello's repeated entreaties, the gentlemen agreed to spend the entire day with him, and after they had slept for a while, they got dressed in their robes and rode through the city with him until it was time for supper, at which point they sat down to a magnificent feast in the company of many noble guests.

In due course they went to bed, and when they arose at daybreak, they discovered that they now had three fine, sturdy palfreys in place of their tired old nags and that their servants had likewise been provided with fresh, strong horses. Upon seeing all this, Saladin turned to his companions and said:

"I swear to God there's never been a more perfect gentleman than this, or one who is more courteous and considerate. If the kings of Christendom are as good at being kings as this man is at being a knight, the Sultan of Babylon will be unable to resist even one of them, let alone all those we've seen preparing to descend on him."

Knowing there was no way for them to refuse Messer Torello's gifts, they thanked him most politely and mounted their horses.

Messer Torello, together with many of his companions, escorted them quite some distance down the road leading out of the city. Finally, even though it weighed heavily on Saladin that he had to part company from his host, to whom he had formed a deep attachment, he felt he could not delay his departure any longer and begged him to turn back. Messer Torello, who found it just as hard to part from his guests, said:

"Since you want me to go, gentlemen, that's what I'll do. But there's one thing I must tell you: I don't know who you are, nor do I wish to know more than you care to reveal, but whoever you may be, you cannot make me believe you are merchants. Now, that said, I bid you Godspeed."

Saladin, who had already taken leave of Messer Torello's companions, turned to face him.

"Sir," he said, "we may yet have the chance to show you some of our merchandise and make a believer out of you. In the meantime, may God be with you."

Saladin then rode off with his companions, utterly determined that, if he managed to survive the war he was facing and avoid defeat, he would show Messer Torello no less hospitality than Messer Torello had shown him. As they went on, he talked to his companions about the gentleman and his wife and about all his gifts and favors and acts of kindness, praising them ever more highly each time he returned to the subject. But finally, when he had with no little labor surveyed all of the West, he put to sea and returned with his companions to Alexandria, where, now that he had all the information he needed, he prepared his defenses. As for Messer Torello, he went back to Pavia, and although he pondered at length who the three men might be, he never arrived at the truth or even came anywhere near it.

When the time came for the Crusade to begin and great preparations for it were under way everywhere, Messer Torello, despite the tears and entreaties of his wife, was fully determined to go with them. He therefore got everything ready, and just as he was about to ride off on his horse, he said to his wife, whom he loved deeply:

"As you can see, my lady, I'm joining this Crusade, both for the sake of my personal honor and for the salvation of my soul. I'm placing our good name and our possessions in your care. And since I feel less assurance about my return than about my departure, considering the thousand accidents that can occur, I would ask this favor of you: no matter what happens to me, even if you don't have any trustworthy news that I'm still alive, I nevertheless want you to wait for a year and a month and a day before you get married again, starting from this, the day of my departure."

"Messer Torello," replied the lady, who was weeping bitterly, "I don't know how I'm going to bear the sorrow you'll be leaving me in after you're gone, but if I'm strong enough to survive it, and if anything should happen to you, you may live and die in the certain knowledge that for the rest of my days, I shall remain wedded to Messer Torello and his memory."

"My lady," said Messer Torello, "I feel confident that you'll do everything in your power to keep your promise, but you're a beautiful young woman who comes from an important family, and everyone knows what a wonderful person you are. Consequently, I haven't the slightest doubt that if there's the least suspicion of my death, many fine gentlemen will come asking your brothers and kinsmen for your hand, and that no matter how much you try to resist, they'll subject you to so much pressure that you'll eventually be forced to comply with their wishes. And that's the reason why I'm not asking you to wait any longer than the time limit I've set for you."

"I'll do whatever I can to keep my promise," said the lady, "and even if I'm forced to act otherwise, I'll certainly follow those instructions you've given me. But I pray to God that neither you nor I ever have to deal with such extremities."

When she finished speaking, the lady wept and embraced Messer Torello. She then removed a ring from her finger and gave it to him, saying: "If I should happen to die before I see you again, remember me whenever you look at it."

Messer Torello took the ring, and having mounted his horse, he said farewell to everyone and went on his way. Upon reaching Genoa with his company, he boarded a galley and set sail, arriving at Acre in short order, where he met up with the rest of the Christian forces.[8] Almost immediately, however, a deadly epidemic broke out that overwhelmed the army, in the course of which, whether because of his skill or his good fortune, Saladin had no difficulty in capturing almost all the Christians who survived, and whom he divided up and sent away to be incarcerated in various cities. Among those taken was Messer Torello, who was led off to prison in Alexandria. No one recognized him there, and being afraid to reveal his true identity, he had no choice but to apply himself to the training of hawks. Since he was a past master of this art, his abilities soon brought him to the notice of Saladin, who had him released from prison and appointed him his falconer.

Neither man recognized the other, and Messer Torello, whom Saladin referred to simply as "the Christian," thought of nothing except Pavia and tried many times to escape, but always without success. Consequently, when a group of emissaries from Genoa, who had come to Saladin to ransom certain fellow citizens of theirs, were about to depart, Messer Torello decided he would write to his wife, letting her know that he was alive and would return to her as soon as possible, and asking her to wait for him. When he finished the letter, he earnestly begged one of the emissaries, whom he knew, to see that it got into the hands of his uncle, who was the Abbot of San Pietro in Ciel d'Oro.[9]

---

8. Acre, also called Saint John of Acre, was the main European stronghold in the region of Jerusalem. The city was captured by Christian Crusaders in 1104, retaken by Saladin in 1187, and then attacked by Christian armies in 1189 (the "Siege of Acre") and captured in 1191. Its reconquest by Muslims in 1291 marks the fall of the "Latin Kingdom of Jerusalem."

9. The church of San Pietro (St. Peter) stands in the center of Pavia.

This, then, is how things stood with Messer Torello until one morning, as Saladin was speaking with him about his birds, he just so happened to smile, moving his mouth in a way that the Sultan had noted in particular when he was staying at Messer Torello's house in Pavia. It put Saladin in mind of his former host, and after staring intently at him for a while, he felt pretty sure he knew who it was. He thus dropped the subject they had been discussing, and said: "Tell me, Christian, what country do you come from in the West?"

"My lord," answered Messer Torello, "I'm a poor man of humble condition, and I come from a city in Lombardy called Pavia."

When Saladin heard this, he was now almost completely certain that what he suspected was correct, and he happily said to himself, "God has given me a chance to show this man how much I appreciated his hospitality." He did not say another word on the subject, however, but had them put all of his robes on display in another room, and took Messer Torello there to see them.

"Have a look at these clothes, Christian," he said, "and tell me whether you've ever come across any of them before?"

Messer Torello began inspecting them, and albeit he spotted the garments his wife had given to Saladin, it was inconceivable to him that they could possibly be the same ones. Nevertheless, he replied: "My lord, I don't recognize any of them, although it's certainly true that these two look like robes I once wore myself, as did three merchants who happened to come to my house."

Saladin could no longer restrain himself and embraced Messer Torello tenderly.

"You are Messer Torello di Stra," he said, "and I am one of the three merchants to whom your wife gave these robes. And the time has now come for me to show you exactly what kind of merchandise I have, something I said when I left you, might well happen one day."

Upon hearing this, Messer Torello felt both overjoyed and ashamed, overjoyed to have had such a distinguished guest, and ashamed because he thought he had entertained him poorly. But then Saladin went on:

"Messer Torello, since God has sent you to me, from now on you should consider yourself, and not me, the master here."

After much mutual rejoicing at their reunion, Saladin had him dressed in regal robes, and having presented him to a gathering of his greatest lords, and spoken at length in praise of him as a most worthy gentleman, he ordered all those who valued his favor to honor Messer Torello's person as they did his own. And from then on, that is what everyone did, and especially the two lords who had accompanied Saladin when he stayed at Messer Torello's house.

For a while Messer Torello's sudden elevation to the heights of glory took his mind off his affairs in Lombardy, all the more so because he had no doubt that his letters had reached his uncle.

On the day that the crusaders had been captured by Saladin, however, there was a Provençal knight of little account named Messer Torello di Dignes[1] who had died and been buried on the battlefield, or rather in the Christian camp itself, and since Messer Torello di Stra was well known for his nobility throughout the army, whenever anyone heard people saying "Messer Torello is dead," it was assumed they were referring to Messer Torello di Stra and not the man

---

1. Also "Digne," a town in the French Alps at one time controlled by the rulers of Naples.

from Dignes. Before those who had been deceived had a chance to be unde-
ceived, however, Messer Torello was taken prisoner, and as a result, many Italians returned home bearing the news of his death with them, including some
who were so presumptuous that they did not hesitate to say they had seen his
corpse and been present at the burial. When the story finally reached his wife
and family, it was the cause of the most intense, inexpressible sorrow not just
for them, but for everyone who had known him.

It would take a long time, indeed, to describe the nature and the depth of
the lady's grief, the sadness and the woe she experienced. After she had
mourned for several months straight in utter misery, however, her sorrow
showed signs of abating, and since many of the most influential men in Lombardy were seeking her hand, her brothers and the rest of her relatives began
urging her to get married. Although she repeatedly refused to do so, always
amid floods of tears, her resistance was overcome in the end, and she agreed
to give them what they wanted, but only on the condition that she could
refrain from taking a husband until the period of time she had promised to
wait for Messer Torello was up.

This, then, was how things stood with the lady in Pavia when, about a week
or so before the date when she was supposed to be married, Messer Torello
happened to catch sight one day in Alexandria of a man he had seen embarking
with the Genoese emissaries on the galley that was taking them home. He
therefore sent for him and asked him how their trip had been and when it was
that they had reached Genoa.

"My lord," the man replied, "I was left behind in Crete, where I later learned
that the galley had had a disastrous voyage. As it was approaching Sicily, a furious northerly gale arose, driving it onto the Barbary reefs, so that no one managed to escape, including two of my brothers who perished along with the
rest."

Messer Torello had no reason to doubt the man's account, which was only
too true, and when he realized that there were just a few days left until the end
of the time period he had asked his wife to wait and that nothing was known in
Pavia about his present situation, he was absolutely convinced that she was
going to be getting married again. So deep was the despair into which he fell
that he lost his appetite, lay down on his bed, and resolved to die.

As soon as Saladin, who loved Messer Torello with great tenderness, heard
what had happened, he came to see him. Having discovered, after earnest and
repeated entreaties, the reason for his grief and his sickness, he scolded him
severely for not having told him about it before. Then, however, the Sultan
begged him to take heart, assuring Messer Torello that if he did so, he would
arrange for him to be in Pavia on the date prescribed. Saladin then went on to
explain how this would be done.

Messer Torello took him at his word, and since he had often heard that such
things were possible and had actually happened on numerous occasions, he
began to feel more optimistic and urged Saladin to take care of it at once. The
Sultan therefore ordered one of his necromancers, a man whose skill he had
already tested, to find a way to transport Messer Torello on a bed to Pavia in a
single night. The magician replied that it would be done, but that for Messer
Torello's own good, he would first put him to sleep.

When all this was arranged, Saladin returned to Messer Torello, whom he still found fully determined either to be back in Pavia by the date prescribed, if it were possible, or to die, if it were not.

"Messer Torello," he said, "God knows I can't blame you in the least for loving your wife so passionately and being so fearful of losing her to another. For I believe that of all the women I've ever seen, she's the one whose way of life, whose manners, and whose demeanor—to say nothing of her beauty, which will fade like a flower—seem to me most precious and commendable. Since Fortune has brought you here to me, I should have liked nothing better than for the two of us to have spent the rest of our lives together, ruling as equals over this realm of mine. God has not granted me this wish, however, and now that you've made up your mind to die unless you can return to Pavia by the appointed date, I really would have preferred to have known about all this in time for me to have sent you home with all the honor and pomp, as well as the splendid escort, your virtues deserve. But since even this has not been granted to me, and you, moreover, are set upon going there at once, I will do what I can to get you to Pavia in the manner I've described to you."

"My lord," replied Messer Torello, "apart from your words, your actions have given me sufficient proof of your goodwill toward me, which is far, far above anything I've merited, so that even if you'd said nothing, I should have lived and died utterly convinced that what you say is true. But seeing as how my mind's made up, I beg you to act quickly and do what you promised me, because tomorrow is the last day she's still going to be waiting for me."

Saladin assured him that everything had been taken care of, and on the next day, it being his intention to send Messer Torello off that same night, he had a very beautiful, luxurious bed set up in one of his great halls. Its mattresses were all covered in the Eastern fashion with velvet and cloth of gold, and on top of them there lay a quilt embroidered with enormous pearls and the rarest of precious stones arranged in oval patterns—the quilt was later considered a priceless treasure in these parts—as well as two pillows selected to match the bedding. When this was ready, he ordered them to dress Messer Torello, who had by now recovered his strength, in a robe of the Saracen fashion, the richest and most beautiful thing anyone had ever seen, while they took one of his longest turbans and wrapped it around his head in their usual style.

It was already late when Saladin, with many of his lords in attendance, went to Messer Torello's room and sat down beside him.

"Messer Torello," he began, practically in tears, "the hour is approaching for you to be separated from me, and since I cannot accompany you myself or send anyone with you, because the nature of the journey you have to make won't permit it, I must take my leave of you here in this room to which I've come for that purpose. But before I bid you Godspeed, I beg you, in the name of the love and friendship that exists between us, not to forget me, and if it's possible, before our days have ended, to come and see me at least one more time after you've taken care of your affairs in Lombardy. For not only will I rejoice to see you again, but I'll be able to compensate then for the delight I must now forego because of your hasty departure. Until such time as that should occur, I hope it won't be a burden for you to visit me by means of your letters and to ask me for whatever you please, because there is certainly no man alive I would serve more gladly than you."

Unable to hold back his own tears, Messer Torello only managed to utter a few words, declaring that it would be impossible for him ever to forget Saladin's kind deeds and noble spirit and that he would, without fail, do what Saladin requested if he were given the opportunity. Saladin embraced him and kissed him tenderly. Then, weeping copiously, he said "Godspeed" and left the room, after which the other lords all took their leave of him and accompanied Saladin into the hall where the bed had been set up.

It was getting late, and since the magician was anxious to send him quickly on his way, a doctor arrived with a potion that he got Messer Torello to drink, persuading him that it would enable him to keep up his strength. Soon afterward he fell asleep, and as he slept, he was carried at Saladin's command and laid upon the beautiful bed where the Sultan placed a large, exquisite, and extremely valuable crown, which he marked in such a way that later on everyone saw clearly that it was a present from him to Messer Torello's wife. Then, onto Messer Torello's finger he slipped a ring containing a ruby that gleamed like a lighted torch and whose value could scarcely be assessed. Next, he had him girded with a sword so richly ornamented that its value, too, would be difficult to determine, and in addition, he had them fasten a brooch on his chest that was studded both with pearls, the like of which had never been seen, and with many other precious stones. Finally, Saladin had them fill two enormous golden bowls with doubloons and set them on either side of him, while all around him were strewn numerous strings of pearls, plus rings and belts and other things that would take too long to describe. When they were done, he kissed Messer Torello one more time, and he had hardly finished telling the magician to hurry up when the bed and Messer Torello were suddenly whisked away right before his eyes, leaving Saladin behind still talking with his lords about his departed friend.

As he requested, Messer Torello was set down in the Church of San Pietro in Ciel d'Oro in Pavia, with all the jewels and finery that have been mentioned, and he was still fast asleep when the hour of matins was rung and the sacristan entered the church with a light in his hand. He immediately caught sight of the opulent bed, and after his initial amazement, he was so terrified that he turned on his heels and fled back the way he had come. The Abbot and the other monks were equally amazed to see him running away, and they asked him for an explanation, which he then produced.

"Come on," said the Abbot, "you're not a child anymore, and you're hardly a newcomer to this church, either, so you shouldn't get frightened so easily. Let's all go now and see what gave you such a scare."

After lighting a number of lanterns, the Abbot entered the church with his monks, where they saw this amazing, luxurious bed on which the knight lay sleeping. Then, as they were casting a wary and timorous eye over all the princely jewels, while staying far away from the bed, the effect of the potion just happened to wear off, Messer Torello woke up, and a great sigh escaped his lips. Upon seeing this, the monks were terrified, as was the Abbot, and they all ran away screaming "Lord, help us!"

When he opened his eyes and looked about him, Messer Torello discovered, to his immense satisfaction, that he was in the very place where he had asked to be taken. Although he had been aware of Saladin's generosity in the past, after he sat up now and observed, one by one, the treasures around him, he was all the more conscious of it and judged it now to be even greater than he had thought it was before. He could hear the monks running away, however, and divining the reason why, he did not make another move, but began calling the Abbot by name, telling him not to be afraid, as it was only Torello, his nephew.

Hearing these words, the Abbot became even more frightened, because for many months he had thought that Messer Torello was dead. But after a while, reassuring himself with rational arguments, as he continued to hear his name being called, he made the sign of the holy cross, and went up to him.

"O my father," said Messer Torello, "what are you afraid of? I'm alive, by the grace of God, and I've come back here from across the sea."

Although Messer Torello had a full beard and was dressed in Arab clothing, after a little while the Abbot managed to recognize him. Now, feeling thoroughly reassured, he took him by the hand and said, "Welcome home, my son."

"Our fear shouldn't surprise you," he continued, "because there's no one in this city who isn't firmly convinced that you're dead. What's more, I can tell you that your wife, Madonna Adalieta, has been overcome by the threats and the pleading of her relatives, and has been forced to remarry against her will. In fact, this is the very morning when she's to go to her new husband, and they've made all the necessary preparations there for the nuptials and the wedding feast."

Messer Torello got up off the luxurious bed, and after warmly embracing the Abbot and the monks, he begged them, each and every one, to say nothing about his return to anybody until he had taken care of some business of his. Next, having put all of the rich jewels in a safe place, he gave the Abbot an account of everything that had happened to him up to then. Delighted by his good fortune, the Abbot joined him in giving thanks to God. When they were done, Messer Torello asked him for the name of his wife's new husband, and the Abbot told him what it was.

"Before anyone learns of my return," said Messer Torello, "I intend to see how my wife conducts herself at these nuptials. And so, even though it's not customary for the religious to attend such festivities, I'd ask you, for my sake, to make arrangements for the two of us to go there."

The Abbot said he would be happy to oblige him, and right after daybreak, he sent a message to the new bridegroom, saying that he wished to attend the nuptials with a companion of his. In reply, the gentleman declared he would be quite delighted to see them.

When the hour for the banquet arrived, Messer Torello, still wearing the clothes he had arrived in, went with the Abbot to the bridegroom's house, where everyone who saw him stared at him in amazement, although none of them managed to recognize who he was. The Abbot told them all that Messer Torello was a Saracen who was being sent by the Sultan as his ambassador to the King of France. Accordingly, Messer Torello was seated at a table directly across from his wife, whom he gazed at with the utmost pleasure, thinking all the while that, from the look on her face, she was none too happy about this marriage. From time to time, she, too, glanced over at him, not because she recognized him in any way—for his great beard, his foreign dress, and her own firm belief that he was dead made this impossible—but because of the unusual clothes he had on.

Finally, when Messer Torello felt the time was right to put his wife to the test and see if she remembered him, he took the ring she had given to him at his departure, and holding it in his hand, called over a young man who was waiting on her.

"Tell the new bride on my behalf," he said, "that in my country, whenever a stranger, like me, is attending the wedding feast of a newly married woman, like her, it's customary for the bride to take a cup from which she herself has been drinking, fill it with wine, and send it to him as a token of her appreciation for his coming there to dine with her. Then, when the stranger has drunk his fill, he puts the cover back on, and the bride drinks up what remains."

The young man delivered this message to the lady, who, being both wise and well mannered, and believing that she was dealing with an important dignitary, hastened to show him how pleased she was that he had come. Accordingly, she ordered that a large gold cup, which stood on the table before her, should be washed, filled with wine, and taken over to the gentleman.

They carried it to Messer Torello, who had placed his wife's ring in his mouth, and he drank in such a way as to let it fall into the cup without anyone noticing. Then, when there was only a tiny bit of wine left in it, he replaced the cover and sent it back to the lady. In deference to the custom of his country, she took it, removed the lid, and put it to her lips. At that moment, she caught sight of the ring. After gazing at it for some time without saying a word, she identified it as the one she had given Messer Torello when he left her. She then picked it up and stared intently at the man she had assumed was a stranger. Now that she could see who it really was, she seized the table in front of her and hurled it to the ground, shouting as if she had gone mad:

"This is my lord, this is really Messer Torello."

Then she dashed over to where he was sitting, and without giving a thought to her clothing or any of the things on the table, she flung herself across it as far as she could and hugged him to her in a tight embrace. Nor could she be induced to let go of his neck for anything the people there could say or do, until Messer Torello himself told her to exercise a little self-control, for she would have plenty of time to embrace him later on.

The lady accordingly stood back up, and although by now the wedding feast was in total disarray, the return of so distinguished a knight actually made it happier than ever. Then, at Messer Torello's request, everyone grew silent, and he told them the story of what had happened to him from the day of his departure up to that very hour. He concluded by saying that the gentleman who, in the belief that he was dead, had married his wife could hardly take offense if he now reclaimed her as his own, since he was alive after all.

Though somewhat embarrassed, the bridegroom freely replied in a friendly manner that Messer Torello was at liberty to dispose of that which belonged to him in whatever way he pleased. The lady accordingly returned the ring and the crown her new bridegroom had given her and put on the ring she had taken from the cup as well as the crown that the Sultan had sent her. They then left the house they were in, and with all the pomp of a wedding procession, they made their way to Messer Torello's estate, where the merrymaking went on for hours, lifting the spirits of his unhappy friends and relations and all the townspeople, who considered his return something verging on a miracle.

After giving away some of his precious jewels to the gentleman who had paid for the wedding-feast as well as to the Abbot and to numerous others, Messer Torello sent more than one messenger to Saladin with word of his happy homecoming, declaring himself to be the Sultan's friend and servant. And for many years after that, he lived with his worthy wife, behaving in a more courteous manner than ever.

This, then, was how the tribulations of Messer Torello and his beloved wife came to an end, and how they were rewarded for their prompt and cheerful acts of courtesy. There are many people who strive to do the like, but although they have the wherewithal, they perform such deeds so ineptly that before they are finished, those who receive them wind up paying more for them than they are worth. And so, if such people get no credit for what they do, neither they nor anyone else should be surprised.

Day 10, Story 10

Induced by the entreaties of his vassals to take a wife, the Marquis of Saluzzo,[2] wanting to choose one his own way, selects the daughter of a peasant. After he has had two children with her, he makes it look to her as though they have been put to death. Later on, pretending to have grown weary of her, he claims he has married another woman and arranges to have his own daughter brought home as though she were his bride, meanwhile having turned his wife out of doors wearing nothing but her shift. On finding that she has borne everything with patience, however, he takes her back home again, dearer to him than ever, shows her their grown-up children, and honors her as Marchioness and causes everyone else to do so as well.

When the King had finished his long story, which everyone seemed to have really enjoyed, Dioneo laughed and said: "The good man who was looking forward to raising and lowering the bogeyman's tail the next night[3] would have given less than two cents for all the praise you are bestowing on Messer Torello." But then, knowing that he was the only one left to speak, he began as follows:

My gentle ladies, the way I see it, we have given this entire day over to kings and sultans and people of that ilk, and therefore, lest I stray too far away from the path you are on, I want to tell you about a Marquis whose behavior was not an example of magnanimity, but of senseless brutality. And even though things turned out well for him in the end, I would not recommend that you follow his lead, because it is a real shame that he derived any benefit from it at all.

A long time ago, there was a young man named Gualtieri who, as the head of the family, had succeeded to the Marquisate of Saluzzo, and being unmarried and childless, spent all of his time out hawking and hunting. He never gave a thought to finding a wife and starting a family, for which he should have been considered very wise, but his vassals were not content with this and repeatedly begged him to get married so that he would not be left without an heir and they without a lord. Moreover, they offered to find him a woman whose character and parents were

2. An Italian town south of Turin, in the foothills of the Alps; a marquis (lord) of Saluzzo named Gualtieri is named in a document dated 1174–75.
3. An allusion to the bawdy first tale told on day seven.

such that there would be every reason to feel hopeful about the match and he could expect to be quite happy with her. In response Gualtieri said:

"My friends, you are forcing me to do something I had absolutely resolved never to do, considering how hard it is to find a person whose character will be a fit for your own, how very many of the other sort there are out there, and how miserable life will be for a man if he stumbles upon a wife who is not well suited to him. Furthermore, it's foolish of you to believe that you can figure out what daughters will be like by considering how their fathers and mothers behave and on that basis to argue that you are going to find one who will please me. For I don't know how you can get any information about the fathers, let alone find out the secrets of the mothers, and even if you could, daughters are often very different from either one of their parents. But look, since you want to bind me in these chains, I'm willing to do it. Nevertheless, so that I won't have anybody to blame except myself if it turns out badly, I want to be the one who's responsible for finding her. And let me assure you that no matter what woman I choose, if you fail to honor her as your lady, you will learn to your great misfortune just how serious a matter it was for you to have begged me to take a wife against my will."

The gentlemen replied that they were satisfied, as long as he was amenable to taking a wife.

For quite some time Gualtieri had been impressed with the behavior of a poor girl who lived in a village not far from his home, and since she was also very beautiful, he thought that life with her ought to be rather agreeable. Thus, without searching any further, he resolved to marry her, and having summoned her father, who was very poor indeed, he made arrangements with him to take her as his wife.

This done, Gualtieri called all his friends in the area together and said to them:

"My friends, since it continues to be your pleasure that I should agree to take a wife, I'm prepared to do it, though more to gratify you than from any interest I have in getting married. You know what you promised me, namely, that you would be content with whatever woman I chose and would honor her as your lady. Now the time has arrived for me to keep my promise to you and for you to keep yours to me. I've located a young woman after my own heart who lives quite close by, and just a few days from now I intend to marry her and lead her home as my bride. So, see to it that the wedding feast is splendid and that you give her an honorable reception. That way I'll be able to pronounce myself satisfied that you've kept your word to me just as you'll be satisfied that I've kept mine to you."

The gentlemen all replied joyfully that they were very pleased with this decision and that no matter whom he chose, they would accept her as their lady and would honor her as such in every way they could. After that, they got everything ready so that the feast would be as grand and lavish and happy as possible, and Gualtieri did likewise, arranging for the most magnificent and beautiful wedding, to which he invited a host of his friends and relations as well as many great noblemen and others from the area round about. In addition, he had them make a fair number of beautiful dresses out of expensive material, all tailored to fit a girl who seemed to him the same size as the one he intended to marry. Finally, he ordered belts and rings, a lovely, costly crown, and everything else a new bride would require.

On the day set for the wedding, halfway between prime and tierce,[4] Gualtieri mounted his horse, as did all those who had come to honor him, and after everything necessary had been seen to, he announced, "Gentlemen, it's time to go and fetch the new bride." Then off he rode with the entire company. Before long they reached the little village, and when they got to the house belonging to the girl's father, they spotted her carrying water back from the spring, hurrying so that she could go with the other women to see Gualtieri's spouse as she arrived. The moment Gualtieri saw her, he called her by her name, which was Griselda,[5] and asked her where her father was, to which she bashfully replied, "He's in the house, my lord."

Gualtieri dismounted and told everyone to wait for him while he went into the hovel by himself. There he found her father, whose name was Giannucole, and said to him: "I've come to marry Griselda, but first, here in your presence, there are certain things I need to find out from her." Then he asked her whether, if he were to wed her, she would do her best to please him and never get upset at anything he ever said or did, and whether she would be obedient, and many other things of this sort, to all of which she replied that she would.

At this point Gualtieri, taking her by the hand, led her outside and in the presence of his entire company as well as all the other people living there, he had her stripped naked. Then he called for the clothing and shoes he had ordered for her and quickly had them dress her, after which he had them place a crown on her hair, disheveled though it was. And as everyone looked on in wonder, he proclaimed: "My lords, this is the woman I intend to take as my wife, provided that she wants to marry me." Then, turning to her as she stood there, feeling stunned and quite embarrassed, he asked her: "Griselda, will you have me as your husband?"

"Yes, my lord," she replied.

"And I," he said, "will take you as my wife." Then, right there, in the presence of the entire assembly, he married her, after which he had her seated on a palfrey[6] and led her, honorably attended, to his house where the wedding was celebrated in as beautiful, festive, and magnificent a style as if he had married the daughter of the King of France.

The young bride appeared to change her mind and her manners along with her clothes. As we have already said, she had a fine figure and lovely features, and in keeping with her beauty, she now became so charming, so pleasant, and so well-mannered that she did not seem like a shepherdess and the daughter of Giannucole, but like the child of some noble lord, leading everyone who had known her earlier to marvel at her transformation. Moreover, she was so obedient and attentive to her husband that he thought himself the happiest, most contented man in the world. At the same time she was so gracious and kind to her husband's subjects that they all loved her with utter devotion, honored her of their own free will, and prayed for her well-being, her prosperity, and her advancement. And whereas they used to say that Gualtieri had shown some lack of discretion in marrying her, now they declared him to be the wisest, most discerning man on earth because no one else could have ever perceived her lofty virtues, which were hidden under the poor rags of her peasant's clothing. In short, she comported herself so well that

4. Two canonical hours: about 7:30 A.M.
5. This name seems to have been invented by Boccaccio, perhaps as an ironic variation of Criseida, the aristocratic romance heroine of

his courtly poem *Il Filostrato*.
6. A horse for riding (as opposed to a warhorse), especially one used by ladies.

before long she had everyone talking, not only in her husband's domain, but far and wide, about how fine her character was and how virtuous her behavior, and she got people to change their minds if they had ever criticized her husband on her account at the time of his marriage.

She had not lived with Gualtieri very long before she became pregnant and in time, to his great happiness, gave birth to a little girl. But a little while later the strange idea popped into his head to test her patience by subjecting her to constant tribulations and generally making life intolerable for her. Consequently, he started by goading her with words, pretending to be angry and telling her that his vassals were thoroughly disgruntled with her because of her base origin, especially now that they saw her bearing children, and that, furthermore, they were upset about the little girl who had just been born and were doing nothing but grumbling about it.

The lady did not change her expression or show the least resentment when she heard these words. "My lord," she said, "do with me whatever you think best for your honor and your peace of mind, and I will be entirely content with it, for I know that I'm socially inferior to your vassals are and that I'm unworthy of the honor that you have so graciously bestowed on me." This reply was very gratifying to Gualtieri, for he realized that she had not gotten puffed up with pride because of the honors that he or the others had paid her.

Some time later, having already given her to understand in general terms that his subjects could not endure the little girl she had given birth to, he gave certain instructions to one of his servants and sent him to her.

"My lady," said the servant, with the most sorrowful expression on his face, "if I don't want to be put to death, I have to do what my lord has commanded, and he has commanded me to take this daughter of yours and to . . ." And at this point he could say no more.

When the lady heard the servant's words and saw his face, and when she recalled what her husband had said to her, she concluded that the man had been ordered to put her child to death. In response, although she was desperately sick at heart, she immediately took her daughter from the cradle, and without ever changing her expression, she kissed her and blessed her and placed her in the servant's arms. "There," she said to him, "do exactly what your lord, who is my lord as well, has ordered, but don't leave her to be devoured by the beasts and the birds unless he's told you to do so."

The servant took the child and reported what the lady had said to Gualtieri, who, marveling at her constancy, sent him away with the baby to one of his relatives in Bologna, asking her to raise and educate the child with some care, but never to reveal whose daughter she was.

Shortly afterward, the lady became pregnant once again, and when she came to term, she gave birth to a baby boy, which made Gualtieri very happy. Nevertheless, not content with what he had already done, he wounded his wife even more deeply. One day, glowering at her with feigned fury, he said:

"Woman, ever since you gave birth to this boy, I've found it completely impossible to live with my vassals, so bitterly do they complain that one of Giannucole's grandsons is to succeed me as their lord. So, if I don't want to be deposed by them, I'm afraid that I'll have to do in this case what I did in the other one, and that I'll also eventually have to leave you and find another wife."

The lady listened patiently, and her only reply was: "My lord, you should think about your own happiness and about how to satisfy your desires. Don't waste another thought on me, for nothing is of any value to me unless I see that it gives you pleasure."

Not many days after that, Gualtieri sent for his son the same way he had for his daughter, and having likewise pretended to have him put to death, he sent him to be brought up in Bologna just as he had done with the girl. In response, his wife said nothing more and did not change the expression on her face any more than she had in her daughter's case, all to Gualtieri's great astonishment, who told himself that no other woman could do what she did. And if it were not for the fact that he saw her treat the children with the utmost tenderness as long as he permitted her to do so, he would have concluded that she acted as she did because she had stopped caring for them. He knew, however, that her behavior was the product of her wisdom.

Since Gualtieri's subjects believed he had arranged to have his two children murdered, they condemned him, blaming it all on his cruelty, whereas they felt nothing but the most profound pity for his wife. But to the women who mourned with her for her children because they had suffered such a death, she never said anything except that if such was the pleasure of the man who had conceived them, then it was her pleasure as well.

Finally, many years after the birth of his daughter, Gualtieri decided the time had come to put his wife's patience to the ultimate test. Accordingly, he spoke with a large company of his vassals and told them that under no circumstances could he put up with Griselda as his wife any longer. He said that he had come to realize just how bad and immature a decision he had made when he chose her, and that he would therefore do everything he could to procure a dispensation from the Pope so that he could leave Griselda and take another wife. A large number of the worthy men took him to task over this plan, but his only reply was that it had to be done that way.

Upon learning of her husband's intentions, the lady grieved bitterly inside, for it seemed to her that what she had to look forward to was returning to her father's house and perhaps tending his sheep as she had done before, while being forced to see the man she loved with all her heart in another woman's embrace. But still, just as she had borne all of Fortune's other afflictions, she was determined to keep her countenance unchanged and endure this one as well.

A little later Gualtieri arranged to have counterfeit letters sent to him from Rome and led his subjects to believe that they contained the Pope's dispensation, which allowed him leave Griselda and take another wife. Hence, he summoned her to appear, and in the presence of a large number of people, he said to her: "Woman, through the concession granted me by the Pope I am now free to leave you and choose another wife. Since my ancestors have always been great noblemen and rulers in these parts, whereas yours have always been peasants, I no longer want you as my wife. You should return to Giannucole's house with the dowry you brought me, and I will bring home another woman I've found who is a more appropriate match for me."

When she heard these words, the lady managed to hold back her tears only by making an enormous effort that went well beyond the normal capacity of women.

"My lord," she said, "I have always known that my lowly condition and your nobility were in no way suited to one another, just as I have acknowledged that the position I have held with you was a gift from you and from God, nor have I taken what was given to me and treated it as if it were my own rather than as something lent to me. So, if it pleases you to have it back, then it must also please me—and it does—to return it to you. Look here's the ring with which you married me: take it. As for your ordering me to carry away the dowry I brought here, to do that will not require a paymaster on your part, nor a purse, let alone a packhorse, on mine, for I haven't forgotten that I was completely naked when you took me.[7] And if you think it proper to let everybody see this body that bore the children you sired, I will depart naked as well, but I beg you, in return for the virginity I brought here and cannot take away again, that it may please you to let me take away at least one single shift in addition to my dowry."

Although Gualtieri had a greater desire to weep than anything else, he maintained his stony expression and said: "You may take a shift with you."

The people standing about there begged him to give her a dress so that the woman who had been his wife for thirteen years or longer should not suffer the shame of leaving his house wearing only a shift like a pauper. All their pleading was in vain, however, and thus she left the house in her shift, barefoot, and with nothing to cover her head.[8] After having said goodbye to them all, she returned to her father's home, accompanied by the weeping and wailing of everyone who saw her.

Since Giannucole never really believed it possible for his daughter to last very long as Gualtieri's wife, he had been expecting just such a development every day and had kept the clothes that she had taken off the morning Gualtieri married her. He brought them to her, and after she had put them on, she devoted herself to all the menial chores in her father's house just as she had been accustomed to do, bravely enduring the fierce assault of a hostile Fortune.

As soon as he had sent Griselda away, Gualtieri led his vassals to believe that he had chosen as his wife a daughter of one of the counts of Panago.[9] And having ordered great preparations to be made for the wedding, he sent for Griselda to come to him. When she appeared, he said to her:

"I'm going to bring home the lady whom I have recently chosen to marry, and I want her to be given an honorable reception the moment she arrives. Since you know that I don't have any women in my house who can prepare the rooms properly and do many of the things that a festive occasion of this sort requires, and since you understand such household matters better than anyone else, I want you to see to it that all the arrangements are taken care of and that you invite as many ladies as you think necessary and receive them as though you were the mistress of the house. Then, when the wedding celebration is over, you can return home."

Gualtieri's words pierced Griselda's heart like so many knives, for she had not been able to put aside the love she bore him in the same way that she had relinquished the good fortune she once had. Nevertheless, she replied: "My lord, I am ready and willing."[1] And so, clad in homespun garments of coarse wool, she entered the house, which only a little while before she had left in a shift.

7. Compare Job 1.21: "Naked came I out of my mother's womb, and naked I shall return thither: the Lord gave, and the Lord hath taken away; blessed be the name of the Lord." Readers of Boccaccio's tale of Griselda (notably, his friend Petrarch) strongly associated her experiences with the biblical character of Job.
8. Only very poor (or very immodest) women would go out without a shawl or veil to cover their head.
9. Also "Panico," a city near Bologna ruled by counts of the Alberti family.
1. Compare Luke 1.38, "Behold the handmaid of the Lord." The Latin of the Vulgate, "Ecce ancilla Dei," was commonly written out in medieval pictures of the Annunciation.

Then she began sweeping and tidying up the rooms, had bed curtains and bench coverings put in place throughout the great halls, got the kitchen ready to go, and turned her hand to everything just as if she were some little household serving wench, never stopping until it was all as neat and trim as the occasion called for. Finally, after having invitations sent to all the women in those parts on Gualtieri's behalf, she stopped and waited for the celebration to begin. When the wedding day arrived, though the clothes she had on were poor, she displayed the spirit and bearing of a lady, receiving, with a happy smile on her face, all the women who came to the feast.

Gualtieri had seen to it that his children were brought up with care in Bologna by his kinswoman, who had been married into the house of the counts of Panago. His daughter, who had now reached the age of twelve, was the most beautiful creature ever seen, and his son was six. Gualtieri sent word to his kinswoman's husband, asking him if he would be so kind as to accompany his daughter and her brother to Saluzzo, to arrange a noble, honorable escort for her, and not to reveal to anyone who she was in reality, but simply to tell them that he was bringing her there as Gualtieri's bride.

The nobleman did everything the Marquis requested, and a few days after he set out on his journey with the girl and her brother and their noble retinue, he reached Saluzzo, arriving around the dinner hour, where he found that all the people there, as well as many others from neighboring communities, were waiting for Gualtieri's new bride. She was received by the ladies, and as soon as she entered the hall where the tables were set up, Griselda, dressed just as she was, happily went to meet her, and said: "You are welcome here, my lady."

The ladies had begged Gualtieri, earnestly but in vain, either to have Griselda remain in another room or to lend her one of the dresses that had once been hers, so that she would not appear in front of the guests looking as she did. But she was nevertheless seated at the tables along with all the rest of them, after which dinner was served. As everyone stared at the girl, they said that Gualtieri had done well by the exchange, and Griselda joined in, praising her warmly, and her little brother, too.

It seemed to Gualtieri that he had now seen as much as he could have ever desired of his wife's patience, for he had observed that no event, however outrageous, had produced any sort of change in her at all. Moreover, he felt sure that her reaction was not the result of obtuseness, since he knew just how wise she was. He therefore decided that it was time to deliver her from the bitter sorrow he guessed she was keeping hidden beneath her impassive exterior, and having summoned her, he smiled and asked her in the presence of all the assembled people: "What do you think of our bride?"

"My lord," replied Griselda, "she seems very fine to me, and if, as I believe, her wisdom matches her beauty, I have no doubt whatsoever that living with her will make you the happiest gentleman in the world. However, I beg you with all my heart not to inflict on her the same wounds you once gave the other spouse you used to have, because I find it hard to believe she'll be able to endure them, considering how much younger she is and also how refined an upbringing she has had, whereas the other one experienced continual hardships from the time she was a little girl."

Seeing that she firmly believed the girl was going to be his wife, and yet had nothing but good things to say, Gualtieri had her sit down beside him.

"Griselda," he said, "the time has finally come both for you to taste the fruit of your long patience, and for those who have thought me cruel, unjust, and brutish to realize that what I've done I've done with a deliberate end in view. For I wanted to teach you how to be a wife, to teach them how to manage one, and at the same time to beget for myself perpetual peace and quiet for the rest of my life with you. When I was at the point of taking a wife, I really feared I'd have no peace, and that's why I decided to choose one by means of a test and have, as you know, inflicted so much pain and suffering on you.

"And since I've never seen you deviate from my wishes in either word or deed, and since it seems to me that you will provide me with all the happiness I've desired, I intend to restore to you in an instant that which I took from you over such a long time, and with the sweetest of cures to heal the wounds I gave you. Receive this girl, then, with a glad heart, the one you believed to be my wife, along with her brother, for they are, in fact, our children, yours as well as mine, the very ones whom you and many others believed for a long time I had cruelly ordered to be put to death. And I am your husband, who loves you more than anything else, since I believe I may boast that there is no one else who could be as content with his wife as I am with you."

When he finished speaking, he embraced her and kissed her, and while she wept for joy, they both got up and went over to where their daughter sat, listening in amazement to what they were saying. Both of them embraced her and her brother tenderly, thus dispelling any confusion that they, like many others present, were feeling. The ladies were overjoyed, and getting up from the tables, they went with Griselda into a chamber where, with a more auspicious view of her future, they divested her of her old clothes and dressed her in one of her own stately gowns. Then, like the lady of the castle, which she always appeared to be even when clad in rags, they led her back into the hall, where her rejoicing with her children was simply wonderful. Indeed, everyone was so happy about what had happened that the feasting and the celebrating were redoubled and continued unabated for many more days. They all declared that Gualtieri was very wise, although they thought that the tests to which he had subjected his wife were harsh and intolerable, but they considered Griselda to be the wisest of them all.

A few days later the Count of Panago returned to Bologna, and Gualtieri, having taken Giannucole away from his drudgery, set him up in a position befitting the man who was his father-in-law, so that he was treated with honor and lived in great comfort during his last remaining years. As for Gualtieri himself, having arranged a noble match for his daughter, he lived a long, contented life with Griselda, always honoring her in every way he could.

What more is there left to say except that divine spirits may rain down from the heavens even into the houses of the poor, just as there are others in royal palaces who might be better suited to tending pigs than ruling men. Who, aside from Griselda, would have suffered, not merely dry eyed, but with a cheerful countenance, the cruel, unheard-of trials to which Gualtieri subjected her and not have her face streaked with tears? Perhaps it would have served him right if, instead, he had run into the kind of woman who, upon being thrown out of the house in her shift, would have found some guy to give her fur a good shaking and got a nice new dress in the bargain.

GEOFFREY CHAUCER

1340?–1400

While there was plenty of literature in English before Chaucer, later generations of writers would identify his *Canterbury Tales* as the foundation of the English poetic tradition. Chaucer was the first to conceive of poetry in English not as the product of an isolated, provincial nation located in an obscure corner of Europe but as a vital agent in the fourteenth-century emergence of the vernacular as a literary language. For this reason, Chaucer's models and rivals were not so much the English authors of *Beowulf* and *Sir Gawain and the Green Knight* as the Europeans **Dante**, **Petrarch**, and **Boccaccio**. Queen Elizabeth's tutor, Roger Ascham, recognized Chaucer's foundational role by calling him "our English **Homer**." The sentiment was reiterated by Dryden, who translated several of the tales alongside selections from Ovid's *Metamorphoses*, declaring "I hold him in the same degree of veneration as the Grecians held Homer or the Romans Virgil." In his *Faerie Queene*, Spenser calls Chaucer the "well of English undefiled," a stream of poetic influence still visible in the opening lines of T. S. Eliot's *The Waste Land*. For these writers, Chaucer's vivid, naturalistic English was the firm ground on which they could anchor a national literature.

LIFE

Chaucer's family origins were solidly middle class. His father and grandfather had been wine merchants, and by placing the youthful Chaucer as a servant at the royal court they set in motion a social transition that would ultimately lead to the family's participation in the upper classes of English society. Chaucer's granddaughter, Alice de la Pole, married a duke, and her grandson was named as the heir to his uncle, Richard III (though he never reached the throne). Chaucer's own family history is an example of the increasing social fluidity of late medieval English culture, in which status could change dramatically over just a few generations. Unlike many premodern poets who were supported by wealthy patrons, Chaucer was obliged to hold a mundane day job for most of his career. He had the time-consuming and tedious position of record keeper at the customs authority in London, and later supervised a number of building projects in his role as clerk of public works. In his *House of Fame*, Chaucer describes poring over his financial ledgers all day, and his books of poetry and fiction all night.

Chaucer's entry into the bureaucracy of English government followed from his early placement in a series of households within the royal family, beginning as a page in the retinue of the Countess of Ulster, daughter-in-law of King Edward III. In fact, the very first documentation of the poet's existence appears in a record of clothes purchased for the then-teenage Chaucer when he was attached to the countess's household. Later in his career, Chaucer was directly rewarded for his work for the court by Edward's grandson, King Richard II, and had the support of Edward's son John of Gaunt, the Duke of Lancaster (who, through a late third marriage, also became Chaucer's brother-in-law). Chaucer had a genius for keeping on the right side of power in a difficult and competitive era, a time characterized by civil unrest, international war, and, ultimately, seizure of the throne in 1399 by John of Gaunt's son and Richard II's cousin, Henry IV. Chaucer appears to have seamlessly transferred his loyalty from Richard to the new king, addressing one of his final lyrics, "A Complaint to His Purse," to the "conqueror of Brutus's Albion, who by lineage and free election is the true king." His subtle and politically astute poetry is as much the product of social and economic turmoil as is Dante's *Divine Comedy*: unlike Dante, however, who ended his days in exile, Chaucer knew how to play all sides against each other in order to protect himself.

As a soldier in the Hundred Years' War and, later, a diplomatic envoy for the English government, Chaucer traveled repeatedly to France, Spain, and—most importantly—Italy; there he encountered the work of Dante, Petrarch, and Boccaccio, which became central to his own writing. French literature had already had a strong impact on English writers of the period, but Italian literature was something new and exciting: through Chaucer, the humanist tradition championed by Petrarch began to be felt in England, along with the high allegorical mode of Dante and the story collections of Boccaccio. While the exact chronology of Chaucer's works is uncertain, they are often divided roughly into three periods: the so-called French phase, which includes the *Book of the Duchess*, an elegiac dream vision that owes much to the *Romance of the Rose* and the poetry of Machaut and Froissart; the Italian phase, which features the *Parliament of Fowls* and the *House of Fame*, both of which refer explicitly to Dante's *Divine Comedy*; and the English phase, during which Chaucer composed his *Canterbury Tales*. This sequence has many faults—most seriously, it tends to privilege the final, culminating period of the poet's career as specifically "English." Yet despite simplifying, it provides a useful way to contextualize a series of major works, each of which represents a significant innovation beyond what had come before.

In addition to the literature of his French and Italian contemporaries, Chaucer was deeply indebted to the major classical authors, especially Ovid and Virgil. A more particular influence, however, was the late antique philosophical poem of **Boethius**, the *Consolation of Philosophy*. Chaucer was a penetrating reader of the *Consolation*, which he translated into English, and he repeatedly turned to Boethian themes such as the competing roles of Fortune and Providence, the place of free will in the human soul, and the role of love as source of both chaos and order. In his dream visions and *Troilus and Criseyde*, Chaucer ostentatiously displays his classical learning and makes continual reference to the poems of his French and Italian contemporaries. But in the *Canterbury Tales*, Chaucer suddenly begins to wear his learning much more lightly: allusions become indirect and often parodic, and the focus of the poetry shifts instead to the landscape of society and, especially, to the relationship between the nature of a storyteller and the story he or she tells.

TIMES

Chaucer's England was the crucible of Reformation: the last years of the fourteenth century witnessed the emergence of religiously unorthodox communities loosely grouped under the term "Lollardy," an originally derogatory term used to identify such would-be reformers as dangerous heretics who sowed discord in the church. Lollard preachers argued that the Bible should be available in the vernacular language so that each person could know scripture at first hand, that images were really idols leading away from rather than toward God, and that pilgrimages were nothing more than social gatherings thinly disguised as devotional practice. In Chaucer's day, such unorthodox views were regarded with suspicion but were not yet as energetically suppressed as they would be just a few years after his death, when those suspected of Lollardy might be burned in the public square along with their unauthorized translations. Chaucer's Parson, who recounts a penitential treatise as the concluding story of the *Canterbury Tales*, is mocked by the Host, who exclaims, "I smell a Lollard in the wind." This kind of mockery, still just barely playful in the last decade of the fourteenth century, would soon evolve into denunciation and persecution. After this violent suppression, the aims of the Lollards would reemerge more successfully in the sixteenth century.

The same impulse that led medieval English men and women to want to read the Bible in English also led to other expressions of religious piety, including the tremendously popular stories of the lives of saints (two of which appear in the *Canterbury Tales*, in the Prioress's Tale and the Second Nun's Tale) and autobiographies of devout women such as Julian of Norwich and Margery Kempe. Chaucer's Wife of Bath is far less focused on heavenly goals than were these women: for her, pilgrimage is less about retracing the pathway to God than about "wandering by the way." Like Margery Kempe, however, the Wife of Bath is a strong female representative of the emerging bourgeois class whose wealth was built on local industries such as brewing (Margery Kempe) and weaving (the Wife of Bath), and whose independence was expressed physically through the act of travel both within England and abroad. Chaucer's pilgrims exem-

plify the late medieval English eagerness to find the right path to God, whether through the unmediated experience of scripture, as advocated by the Lollards, or through the highly overdetermined mediation of pardons (certificates from Rome that guaranteed the devout buyer a shorter stay in purgatory).

The same instability that had come to threaten the church's control of the Christian flock in England, through the rise of Lollardy, also affected the smooth working of government. The reign of Richard II, who had ascended the throne as a child in 1377 following the death of his grandfather Edward III, was marked by capricious rule, discord between the king's advisers and the major lords of the realm, and repeated heavy taxation necessitated by the ongoing war between England and France. Discord within the capital city of London itself was particularly intense, as the burghers of the city became increasingly involved in the disputes between Parliament and the king. The greatest disruption took place in 1381, as a popular uprising broke out in the countryside in response to the imposition of yet another heavy tax. The Peasants' Revolt, as it was later called, moved rapidly through the towns and fields outside London, entering the city with violence. When the archbishop of Canterbury confronted the mob, urging the peasants to return to their homes, he was decapitated and his head impaled on a pike on London Bridge. The peasants rampaged through the streets, sacking and burning the palace of the king's uncle and chief adviser, John of Gaunt. Gaunt was connected to Chaucer both as his main patron and through family ties, but the revolt struck still closer to home for Chaucer: the mob slaughtered a group of Flemish immigrant workers in a London street where Chaucer had lived as a boy, and it entered the city through a major gate—Aldgate—above which Chaucer had his lodgings. Although Chaucer must have witnessed this violence at first hand, his allusions to social unrest are always oblique and, above all, cautious.

WORK

The Canterbury Tales is a frame-tale poem; like *The Thousand and One Nights* and Boccaccio's *Decameron*, it has a beginning and ending within which a series of tales are related. Unlike *The Thousand and One Nights*, which has (for the most part) a single storyteller, and the *Decameron*, which has a relatively homogenous company of noble young narrators, *The Canterbury Tales* revels in the extraordinary range of possible tales and possible tale-tellers. From the humble Miller to the chivalric Knight, from the bossy Wife of Bath to the effete Pardoner, Chaucer's diverse pilgrims span the range of medieval English life. The pilgrims are, in a way, types or ideals of each manner of life available to the individual: the company includes a nun, a lawyer, a squire, a sailor, and so on. But each teller is also an individual, characterized as such not only in the prefatory prologues that introduce each tale but also in the manner in which the tale itself is told. Petty rivalries, as between the Miller and the Reeve or between the Friar and the Summoner, are played out during the interludes between tales; tale-tellers pay back or "quite" one another by telling stories that indirectly comment on their fellows, causing sometimes argument and discord, sometimes laughter, or sometimes—as at the end of the Pardoner's Tale—both.

Chaucer's Wife of Bath is endowed with a vivid personality and a complex inner life that she herself tells us all about. In her Prologue, she sets her female experience against the misogynist stereotypes of women as lawless, sexually voracious, and manipulative creatures, a view promoted by certain traditions of medieval religious thought. Yet the reader is forced to ask if the Wife's frank celebration of her own sexuality, and her account of the torment she has inflicted on her three old husbands, does not in fact confirm those stereotypes. An answer is suggested by the Wife's claim that she is only playing: indeed, at one point she speaks as if she were showing her almost exclusively male audience how she would conduct a kind of school for wives. She seems, in other words, to be putting on a performance, pretending to reveal to her fascinated audience the secrets that women share among themselves and thereby letting men witness the intimate life of a woman. Yet as the Prologue proceeds we feel that her playful dramatics give way to a more serious, more authentic self-revelation. We learn that not only have her husbands suffered in marriage but that she has too, that she is unavoidably (if cheerfully) aware of her advancing years, and that what she seems to value most is neither money nor the sex she so aggressively celebrates but the companionship and love she comes finally to share with her fifth husband. In the same way, her tale gradually reveals itself to be more than simply a nostalgic wish fulfillment for the return of youth and beauty. When the criminal knight tries to learn what women most desire, he is offered a series of misogynist answers; but when forced to marry he discovers, through the moral lecture his old wife delivers, that she possesses a wisdom that he himself lacks. This is why he leaves the final decision about what form she will assume up to her, and in granting her mastery he is rewarded not merely with youth and beauty but with a marriage of mutual affection. It is through this experience, then, rather than by relying on the authority of time-honored opinions, that the knight comes to learn about the true nature of women.

Unlike most of the tales recounted by the Canterbury pilgrims, the Nun's Priest's Tale is told by an enigmatic figure: although his title tells us that he travels as part of the Prioress's group, he does not appear in the portraits of the company embedded in the General Prologue, and we therefore have very little sense of what to expect when his tale begins. What we do recognize almost immediately, however, is the genre of tale he tells—an animal fable, a type of literature popular from the ancient world onward, surviving in such forms as the fables of **Aesop**, the **Panchatantra**, and *Kalila and Dimna*. The story opens with the anatomy of a household, including a widow and her two daughters, their three pigs, three cows, and "a sheep named Moll." The domestic detail of the sheep's name, together with a detailed account of the "brown bread" and other simple foods that make up their farmers' diet, establishes a setting that is at once humble and earthy. The addition of more members of the farmyard household, the rooster Chanticleer and his seven "wives," fleshes out the company.

Yet the tale takes a strange turn when Chanticleer is troubled by bad dreams, which his favorite chicken-wife Pertelote tries to remedy. Chanticleer responds to her efforts to medicate him by recounting examples of prophetic dreams that have come true in the past, from the biblical examples of Joseph and Daniel to the ancient writings of the Latin Macrobius. This learned disquisition, put in the mouth of the gorgeous (and vain) golden rooster, underlies the absurdity of this parodic animal fable. When the fateful dream comes true and Chanticleer's life hangs in the balance, the whole barnyard family is drawn into the melee—in a violent scene of chaotic "noise" that Chaucer explicitly likens to the most terrifying social upheaval of late medieval England, the Peasants' Revolt of 1381. This simple animal tale proves to have an unnerving social message hidden below the veil of the playful text.

CHAUCER'S LANGUAGE

Chaucer's Middle English strikes the present-day reader as both familiar and strange, separated from Modern English by peculiarities of pronunciation and word order, but recognizable as its ancestor through names and terms that have remained essentially unchanged. Unlike the Old English of *Beowulf*, which must be learned as though it were a foreign language, Middle English is usually approached as if it were a dialect or an idiom—close to home, but still uncannily strange. We reproduce below the first eighteen lines of the General Prologue to the *Tales*, not only to illustrate the gap between English of the fourteenth century and the twenty-first, and to provide a frame of reference for the modern English translation that follows, but also to give a taste of the unfamiliar familiar tongue of the father of English poetry.

Whan that Aprill with his shoures soote
The droghte of March hath perced to the roote,
And bathed every veyne in swich licour
Of which vertu engendred is the flour;
Whan Zephirus eek with his sweete breeth
Inspired hath in every holt and heeth
The tender croppes, and the yonge sonne
Hath in the Ram his halve cours yronne,
And smale foweles maken melodye,
That slepen al the nyght with open ye
(So priketh hem nature in hir corages);
Thanne longen folk to goon on pilgrimages,
And palmeres for to seken straunge strondes,

To ferne halwes, kowthe in sondry londes;
And specially from every shires ende
Of Engelond to Caunterbury they wende,
The hooly blissful martir for to seke,
That hem hath holpen whan that they were seeke.

FROM THE CANTERBURY TALES[1]

The General Prologue

Here begins the Book of the Tales of Canterbury.

When April comes and with its showers sweet
Has, to the root, pierced March's drought complete,
And then bathed every vein in such elixir
That, by its strength, engendered is the flower;
When Zephirus[2] with his sweet breath   5
Inspires life anew, through grove and heath,
In tender shoots, and when the spring's young sun
Has, in the Ram,[3] full half its course now run,
And when small birds begin to harmonize
That sleep throughout the night with open eyes   10
(So nature, stirring them, pricks up their courage),
Then folks, too, long to go on pilgrimage,
And palmers hope to seek there, on strange strands,[4]
Those far-off shrines well known in many lands;
And especially, from every shire's end   15
Of England, to Canterbury they wend;
The holy, blessed martyr[5] they all seek,
Who has helped them when they were sick and weak.
      It happened, in that season, on a day
In Southwark,[6] at the Tabard as I lay   20
Ready to start out on my pilgrimage
To Canterbury, with true, devoted courage,
At night, there came into that hostelry,[7]
Fully nine-and-twenty in a company
Of sundry folks, as chance would have them fall   25
In fellowship, and pilgrims were they all,

---

1. Translated from Middle English by Sheila Fisher.
2. Zephyr, the west wind.
3. Aries, the first sign of the zodiac in the solar year (March 21–April 20).
4. Shores, beaches. "Palmers": pilgrims who had returned from the Holy Land (they carried palm fronds in imitation of Jesus and his apostles during their entry into Jerusalem).
5. St. Thomas Becket (ca. 1118–1170), killed by assailants loyal to King Henry II of England as he stood before the altar of his church at Canterbury; until the Reformation, the site was something of a national center of religious devotion.
6. A suburb of London, south of the Thames, where theaters, brothels, and other businesses of dubious repute set up shop beyond the reach of the city's laws.
7. I.e., the Tabard.

Who, toward Canterbury, wished to ride.
The chambers and the stables were all wide,
And we were put at ease with all the best.
And, shortly, when the sun went to its rest,   30
I had so spoken with them, every one,
That I was in their fellowship anon,
And to rise early I gave them my vow,
To make our way, as I will tell you now.
    But, nonetheless, while I have time and space,   35
Before much further in this tale I pace,
It seems quite right and proper to relate
To you the full condition and the state
Of each of them, just as they seemed to me,
And what they were, and of what degree,   40
And also of the clothes they were dressed in,
And with a knight, then, I will first begin.
    A KNIGHT there was, and that, a worthy man,
Who, from the time when he first began
To ride to war, he loved most chivalry,   45
Truth and honor, largesse and courtesy.
Full worthy he, to fight in his lord's war,
No other man had ridden half so far,
As much in Christian as in heathen lands,
And all honor his worthiness commands;   50
At Alexandria[8] he was, when it was won.
At banquets, he was many times the one
Seated with honor above all knights in Prussia;
In Lithuania, he'd raided, and in Russia,
Unrivalled among knightly Christian men.   55
In Granada, at the siege, he'd also been
Of Algeciras; he rode at Belmarin.
At Ayas and at Adalia he had been
When they fell; and then in the Great Sea[9]
At fine armed conquests, he fought worthily.   60
In fifteen mortal battles had he been,
And thrice he fought for God at Tlemcen
Alone in lists, and always slew his foe.
And this same worthy knight had been also
At one time fighting alongside Balat's lord   65
Against another Turkish heathen horde;
And always was his fame a sovereign prize.
Not only was he was worthy, he was wise,
And in his bearing, meek as is a maid.
In all his life, no rude word had he said   70
To any man, however much his might.
He was a true and perfect gentle knight.

8. A city in northern Egypt, sacked by Peter I of Cyprus in 1365. The following places named, ranging from eastern Europe to the Muslim-held regions in southern Spain and North Africa, demonstrate both the large number and the wide variety of the Knight's campaigns.
9. The Mediterranean.

But now to tell you about his array,
His horse was good, but his dress was not gay.
His tunic was of fustian, coarse and plain, 75
Which by his rusty mailcoat was all stained,
For just lately he'd come from his voyage,
And now he went to make his pilgrimage.
    With him there was his son, a young SQUIRE,
A lover and in arms, a bachelor, 80
His locks waved like they'd seen a curling press.
About twenty years of age he was, I guess.
In his stature, he was of average length,
And wonderfully deft, and of great strength.
He'd ridden sometimes with the cavalry 85
In Flanders, in Artois, and Picardy,[1]
And fared quite well, within small time and space,
In hope of standing in his lady's grace.
Embroidered was he, as if he were a bed
All full of fresh spring flowers, white and red. 90
Singing he was, or fluting, all the day;
He was as fresh as is the month of May.
Short was his gown, its sleeves hung long and wide.
Well could he sit his horse, and nicely ride.
And also he wrote songs, both verse and note, 95
He jousted and he danced, he drew and wrote.
So hotly loved he that when nighttime came,
The nightingale and he slept both the same.[2]
Courteous and meek, to serve, quite able,
He carved before his father at the table.[3] 100
    A YEOMAN[4] had he—no servants beside,
For at this time, that's how he chose to ride,
And he was clad in coat and hood of green.
A sheaf of peacock arrows, bright and keen,
Under his belt, he bore quite properly 105
(For he could tend his gear quite yeomanly;
His arrows did not droop with feathers low),
And in his hand he bore a mighty bow.
A close-cropped head had he, a face well browned.
No man more skilled in woodcraft might be found. 110
Upon his arm he wore a gay wrist guard,
And by his side a small shield and a sword,
By his other side, a bright, gay dagger fell,
As sharp as a spear's point, and sheathed up well;
On his breast, a silver Christopher[5] was seen. 115

1. Regions in modern Belgium and northern France.
2. That is, not at all. In Persian, Arabic, Occitan, and French poetry, the nightingale was a symbol of erotic love.
3. One of the duties of a squire, and also a sign of obedience and loyalty.
4. A superior grade of servant in a noble household.
5. A medal bearing the image of the patron saint of travelers.

He bore a horn, its baldric was of green;
A forester, he was, truly, as I guess.
    There was also a Nun, a PRIORESS,
Who in her smiling was simple and gracious;
Her greatest oath was "by Saint Eligius";[6]   120
And she was known as Madame Eglentine.[7]
Quite well she sang the liturgy divine,
Intoning it in her nose quite properly;
And French she spoke quite well and elegantly,
After the school of Stratford-at-the-Bow,[8]   125
Because Parisian French she did not know.
In dining, she was well taught overall;
She let no morsel down from her lips fall,
Nor wet her fingers in her sauce so deep;
Deftly she could lift up a bite, and keep   130
A single drop from falling on her breast.
In courtesy, she found what pleased her best.
Her upper lip she wiped so nice and clean
That in her cup no single speck was seen
Of grease, because she drank her drink so neat.   135
Quite daintily, she reached out for her meat.
And truthfully, she was so very pleasant,
And amiable, her manners excellent;
She pained herself to imitate the ways
Of court, and to be stately all her days,   140
And to be held worthy of reverence.
But, now, to speak about her conscience,
She was so full of pity and charity,
That she'd cry for a mouse that she might see
Caught in a trap, if it bled or was dead.   145
With her, she had her small hounds, which she fed
With roasted flesh, or milk and pure white bread.[9]
Sorely she wept if one of them were dead,
Or if men smote it so hard it would smart;
With her, all was conscience and tender heart.   150
Quite properly, her pleated wimple draped,
Her eyes blue gray as glass, her nose well-shaped,
Her mouth quite small, and also soft and red.
But, certainly, she had a fair forehead;
It was almost a span[1] in breadth, I own;   155
For, truth to tell, she was not undergrown.
Quite elegant, her cloak, I was aware.
Made of small corals on her arm she'd bear,
A rosary, set off with beads of green,
And thereon hung a broach of golden sheen,   160

6. The patron saint of goldsmiths, said to have been a remarkably attractive man.
7. The name of a kind of wild rose (more appropriate to a romance heroine than a nun).
8. A village 2 miles from London.

9. A diet enjoyed only by the wealthy; in this period, most ate black or brown bread, with little meat.
1. A handspan (a wide forehead was a sign of beauty).

On which the letter "A," inscribed and crowned
With "Amor vincit omnia"[2] was found.
     Another NUN riding with her had she,
Who was her secretary, and priests three.
     A MONK there was, the handsomest to see,   165
An outrider, who most loved venery,[3]
A manly man, to be an abbot able.
Many a striking horse had he in stable,
And when he rode, men might his bridle hear
Jingling in a whistling wind as clear   170
And just as loud as tolls the chapel bell
Of the house where he was keeper of the cell.
The rule of Saints Maurus and Benedict,[4]
Because it was so old and somewhat strict—
This same Monk let the old things pass away   175
And chose the new ways of the present day.
For that text he'd not give you one plucked hen
That said that hunters are not holy men,
Or that a monk who disobeys his order
Is likened to a fish out of the water—   180
That is to say, a monk out of the cloister.
But that text, he held not worth an oyster.
And I said his opinion was good.
What! Should he study, and make himself mad should
He, always poring over books in cloister,   185
Or should he work with his hands and labor
As Augustine bids?[5] How shall the world be served?
For Augustine, let this work be reserved!
A fine hard-pricking spursman he, all right;
He had greyhounds as swift as birds in flight;   190
In pricking and in hunting for the hare,
Lay all his lust; for no cost would he spare.
I saw his sleeves were fur lined at the hand
With rich, gray squirrel, the finest in the land;
And to fasten his hood beneath his chin,   195
He had, all wrought from gold, a fancy pin;
A love knot on the larger end was cast.
His head was bald, and it shone just like glass,
His face shone, too, as though he'd been anointed.
He was a lord full fat and well appointed;   200
His eyes rolled in his head and shone as bright
As fires under furnace pots, cast light;
His boots were supple, his horses strong and fit;
Now, certainly, he was a fair prelate;

2. "Love conquers all" (Latin).
3. Hunting; also, sexual pleasure (Latin, *veneria*). "Outrider": here, the monk whose duty was to look after the lands belonging to the monastery.
4. The founder (d. 547) of the Benedictine order; Maurus (d. 584) was his disciple and founded an abbey in France.
5. The rule of St. Augustine of Hippo (354–430), author of the *Confessions*, requires that monks engage in manual labor.

He was not pale like a tormented ghost.   205
A fat swan[6] loved he best of any roast.
His palfrey was as brown as is a berry.
    A FRIAR there was, a wanton one, and merry,
A limitor,[7] quite an important man.
In all four orders[8] is no one who can   210
Talk quite so smoothly, with such winning speech.
Many marriages made he in the breach
For young women and at his own expense.
In him, his order found a fine defense.
Quite well beloved and on close terms was he   215
With the franklins[9] all throughout his country,
And with all the town's most worthy women,
For he had the right to hear confession,
As he said, more than a curate surely,
For, by his order, he was licensed fully.   220
So, quite sweetly, would he hear confession,
And quite pleasant was his absolution:
He was an easy man in giving penance,
Where he knew he'd get more than a pittance.
If to a poor order one has given,   225
It's a sure sign that one's been well shriven;
If a man gave, he knew well what it meant:
He dared to boast that this man would repent.
For many a man is just so hard of heart,
He may not weep, though he may sorely smart.   230
Therefore, instead of giving tears and prayers,
Men must yield up their silver to poor friars.
His hood's tip always was stuffed full of knives
And pins, for him to give out to fair wives.
Certainly his merry voice was pleasing: 235
And he could play the fiddle well and sing;
For ballads, he took first prize utterly.
His neck was white as is the fleur-de-lis.[1]
A strong champion was he in a brawl.
The taverns in each town, he knew them all;   240
Each in keeper and every barmaid, too,
More than lepers[2] or beggar girls, he knew,
Because, for such a worthy man as he,
It would not do, with his ability,
With sick lepers to have an acquaintance.   245
It is not right; it hardly can advance
Him if he has to spend time with the poor,

---

6. An expensive and rare delicacy; ordinarily, monks abstained from eating meat.
7. A friar licensed to beg in a specific territory.
8. In the 14th century, Franciscans, Augustinians, Carmelites, and Dominicans. Friars, unlike monks, circulated among the people.

9. Upper-middle-class landowners, ranked below the gentry.
1. A lily (in heraldry, the royal arms of France).
2. Shunned through antiquity and the Middle Ages, but healed by Jesus (see Mark 1.40–45; Luke 17.11–19).

Just with the rich and victualers, for sure.
And over all, where profit should arise,
Polite was he, and served in humble guise.   250
No man was so effective anywhere:
He was, in his house, the best beggar there.
For private begging turf, he laid out rent;
None of his brothers came there where he went;
And although one were a shoeless widow,   255
So charming was his "In principio,"[3]
A farthing he would get before he went.
His income was much higher than his rent.
And he could rage just like a little whelp.
On love-days,[4] like a judge, well could he help,   260
For there, he was not like a cloisterer
In a threadbare cloak, like a poor scholar,
But like a master or the pope as well.
Of double worsted, rounded as a bell
Fresh from the casting, was his short, rich cloak.   265
With affectation, he lisped when he spoke,
To make his English sweet upon his tongue;
In his harping, whenever he had sung,
His eyes would twinkle in his head as bright
As do the stars upon a frosty night.   270
This worthy limitor was named Huberd.

    A MERCHANT was there, too, with a forked beard,
In mixed-hued clothes; high on his horse he sat;
Upon his head, a Flemish beaver hat,
And his fair boots were fastened stylishly.   275
He uttered his ideas quite solemnly,
Sounding always increase in his winning.
He wished the sea safe, more than anything,
Between the ports of Middleburgh and Orwell.[5]
Well could he in exchange his florins sell.[6]   280
This worthy man quite deftly used his wit:
Were he in debt, no one would know of it,
So stately was he in his management
Of borrowing, buying, selling where he went.
Surely, he was a worthy man, in all,   285
But, truth to say, I don't know what he's called.

    A CLERK from Oxford[7] was with us also,
Whose work in logic started long ago.
As skinny was his horse as is a rake,
And he was not so fat, I undertake;   290
He looked hollow, and thus, grave and remote.

3. "In the beginning" (Latin), the opening words of the Vulgate translation of the Gospel of John, whose first fourteen verses were used by friars in devotions and in greetings.
4. Days when disputes were judged out of court.
5. Cities in the Netherlands and England, respectively.
6. I.e., he also profited in currency exchange. Florins were gold coins minted in Florence, Italy.
7. A student.

Quite threadbare was his outermost short coat;
He had as yet no clerical appointment,
And wasn't made for secular employment.
For he would rather have, at his bed's head,   295
Twenty books, all well bound in black or red,
Of Aristotle[8] and his philosophy
Than rich robes, or fiddle, or gay psaltery.
But, for all that he was a philosopher,
He had little gold piled in his coffer;[9]   300
For, anything that his friends to him lent,
On books and on his learning, it got spent.
Busily, for the souls of them he prayed
Who, so that he could go to school, had paid.
Of his studies, he took most care and heed.   305
Not one word spoke he more than he had need,
And that was said with dignity and respect,
And short, and quick, and full of intellect;
Resounding in moral virtue was his speech,
And gladly would he learn, and gladly teach.   310
    A SERGEANT OF THE LAW,[1] wary and wise,
Who often in Saint Paul's court[2] did advise,
There was also, quite rich in excellence.
Dignified and judicious in each sense—
Or he seemed such, his words were all so wise.   315
He was often a judge at the assize,[3]
With full commission—and through royal consent.
For all his learning and his fame's extent,
Fees and robes, he did have, many a one.
So great a land buyer elsewhere was none: 320
He would directly buy up the estate;
His purchase, no one could invalidate.
Nowhere was such a busy man as he;
He seemed busier than he was, actually.
He knew the precedents for everything   325
The law had done since William was the king.[4]
Fine legal texts, thus could he draft and draw
In which no one could find a single flaw;
Every statute, he could recite by rote.
He rode there in a simple mixed-hued coat.   330
A striped silk belt around his waist he wore;
About his dress, I won't tell any more.
    A FRANKLIN rode there in his company,
And his beard was white as is the daisy;

8. The rediscovered works of Aristotle (384–
322 B.C.E.) were widely read and commented
on in medieval universities, especially his
works on logic and science.
9. A joke that relies on understanding "philosopher" as also meaning "alchemist" (one
who sought to create gold out of base metals).
1. A judge.

2. By St. Paul's Cathedral, a meeting place
for lawyers and their clients.
3. Circuit court, presided over by itinerant
judges.
4. I.e., since modern law was established by
William I, the Norman who conquered England in 1066.

His mood was sanguine,[5] his face rosy red.　　　　　　335
Well loved he, in the morning, wine-soaked bread;
To live in sheer delight was his one care,
For he was Epicurus's[6] own heir,
Who thought that to lead life in all its pleasure
Was true perfect bliss beyond all measure.　　　　　　340
A householder, and a full great one, was he;
A Saint Julian[7] he was, in his country.
His bread, his ale, were always very fine;
No other man had better stocks of wine.
His house was never lacking in baked meat,　　　　　　345
Or fish or flesh, in plenty so complete
That it snowed, in his house, with food and drink,
With any dainties of which men could think.
According to the seasons of the year,
New dishes on his table would appear.　　　　　　350
Fat partridges in coops, when he did like;
He kept his fish pond stocked with bream and pike.
And woe unto his cook if he'd not got
His gear set and the sauce, spicy and hot.
Covered and ready did his table stay　　　　　　355
Set up for meals within the hall all day.
At county courts, he was the lord and sire;
And went to Parliament to serve his shire.
A two-edged dagger and a purse of silk
Hung from his girdle, white as morning's milk.　　　　　　360
A sheriff had he been, an auditor,[8]
And nowhere such a worthy landholder.
　　A Haberdasher and a Carpenter,
A Weaver, Dyer, and a Tapestry Maker—
They were all clothed in the same livery　　　　　　365
Of one great parish guild fraternity.[9]
All fresh and newly furbished was their gear;
On their knives no brass mountings were found here,
But only silver; fashioned just as fit,
Their girdles and their purses, every bit.　　　　　　370
Each of them seemed such a worthy burgess[1]
He might sit in the guildhall on the dais.
And each, with all the wisdom that he can,
Was suited to be made an alderman.
Income had they enough, and property,　　　　　　375
To this their wives would certainly agree;
Or else, quite surely, they would all be blamed.
It is quite nice "My Lady" to be named,

5. In medieval physiology, the dominance of blood (one of the four bodily humors), indicated by his red face, was believed to explain a cheerful disposition.
6. Greek philosopher (340–270 B.C.E.), viewed in the Middle Ages as a proponent of hedonism.
7. The legendary patron saint of innkeepers.
8. An official responsible for verifying accounts.
9. A trade group whose purposes were social, religious, and economic.
1. Propertied citizen.

At feasts and vigils, to march first in line,
And have, borne royally, a mantel[2] fine.   380

  For this trip, a COOK rode with them then
To boil the marrowbones up with the hens,
Along with spices tart and galingale.[3]
Well did he know a draught of London ale.
He could both roast and simmer, boil and fry,   385
Make stews and hash and also bake a pie.
But it was a real shame, it seemed to me,
That on his shin, a pus-filled sore had he.
A milky pudding made he with the best.

  A SHIPMAN was there, who lived in the west;   390
He came from Dartmouth,[4] for all that I guessed.
To ride a packhorse he did try his best,
In a gown of coarse wool cloth cut to the knee.
A dagger hanging on a strap had he
Around his neck, under his arm coming down.   395
The hot summer had turned his skin all brown.
And certainly, he was a good fellow.
So many draughts of fine wine from Bordeaux[5]
Had he drawn, while the merchants were asleep.
In a good conscience, small stock did he keep.   400
If, when he fought, he had the upper hand,
He sent them all, by water, back to land.
But in the art of reckoning the tides,
The currents and all perils near, besides,
The moon and piloting and anchorage,   405
No one was so skilled from Hull to Carthage.[6]
Hardy and wise in what was undertaken,
With many tempests had his beard been shaken.
He knew well all the harbors that there were,
Stretching from Gotland to Cape Finisterre,[7]   410
And each inlet from Brittany to Spain;
His sailing ship was called the "Magdalene."[8]

  With us was a DOCTOR OF MEDICINE;
No one was like him, all the world within,
To speak of medicine and surgery,   415
For he was schooled well in astrology.
Through natural magic,[9] he gave patients hope
By keeping close watch on their horoscope.
He could divine when planets were ascendant

2. I.e., a mantle (Chaucer's spelling, now
obsolete).
3. Aromatic root, also used as a powder.
4. Port on the southwest coast of England.
5. A center of the wine trade, in southwest
France.
6. I.e., from northern England to North Africa
(Carthage) or Spain (Cartagena; Chaucer has
"Cartage"); the Shipman is widely traveled.

7. From an island off the coast of Sweden to
the west coast of Spain.
8. Named after Mary Magdalen, Jesus' disciple; according to a French tradition, she, her
brother Lazarus, and some companions came
to the port city of Marseille in the south of
France and converted all of Provence.
9. As opposed to black magic.

To aid the star signs governing his patient. 420
Of every malady, he knew the source
In humors hot, cold, moist, or dry, of course,
And where they were engendered, from which humor.[1]
He was a perfect, true practitioner.
The cause and root known of the malady, 425
At once he gave the sick their remedy.
Quite ready had he his apothecaries
To send him their drugs and electuaries,[2]
For each made profit for the other one—
Their friendship had not recently begun. 430
Well knew he his old Aesculapius,[3]
Dioscorides, and also Rufus,
Old Hippocrates, Hali, and Galen,
Rhazes, Avicenna, Serapion,
Averroes, Damascien, Constantinus, 435
Bernard, Gaddesden, Gilbertus Anglicus.
Of his own diet, moderate was he,
For it contained no superfluity,
But was nourishing and digestible.
His study was but little on the Bible. 440
In blood red and in blue he was all clad,
A lining of two kinds of silk he had.
Yet he was quite cautious with expenses;
He saved what he earned in pestilences.
In medicine, gold[4] works well for the heart, 445
Therefore, he'd loved gold from the very start.
　　　A good WIFE was there from nearby to BATH;
It was a pity she was deaf by half.
In cloth-making she had such a talent
She far passed those from Ypres and from Ghent.[5] 450
And throughout all her parish, there was no
Wife who might first to the offering go
Before her; if one did, so mad was she
That she lost any sense of charity.
Her coverchiefs of fine linen were found; 455
I dare swear that they weighed a full ten pounds,
The ones that, Sundays, sat upon her head.
Her stockings were all fine and scarlet red,
Quite tightly laced, her shoes quite soft and new.[6]
Bold was her face, and fair, and red of hue. 460
All her life, she was a worthy woman,
Husbands at the church door, she'd had five then,

---

1. According to humoral physiology, illness was caused by imbalance in the four humors— the different combinations of the four qualities (hot, cold, moist, dry).
2. Medicinal pastes.
3. Greek god of healing. The list that follows names medical authors from ancient Greece, the Arabic world (including Avicenna), and medieval England (John of Gaddesden [d. 1348/49] and Gilbert the Englishman [d. ca. 1250]).
4. Used as a medicine in the Middle Ages.
5. Two cities in Flanders (modern Belgium) renowned for cloth production.
6. I.e., of good quality, supple leather.

Not counting other company in youth—
No need to speak of that now, to tell the truth.
And thrice she had been to Jerusalem;[7]   465
Many a foreign sea, she'd covered them;
At Rome she'd been, and also at Boulogne,
At Saint James in Galicia and Cologne.
She knew much of wandering by the way.
Gap toothed[8] she was, it is the truth to say.   470
Quite easily on her ambling horse, she sat,
Wearing a wimpled headdress and a hat
Like a buckler or a shield as broad and round;
A foot-mantle about her large hips wound,
And on her feet a pair of sharp spurs poked.   475
In fellowship, quite well she laughed and joked.
The remedies of love she knew by heart,
For of that old dance, she knew all the art.
    A good man was there of religion,
Of a town, he served as the poor PARSON.   480
But he was rich in holy thought and work.
He was also a learned man, a clerk,
And Christ's gospel truthfully he would preach;
His parishioners devoutly he would teach.
Gracious he was, a wonder of diligence,   485
And in adversity, he had such patience,
And in this, he had often tested been.
For tithes, he found it loathsome to curse men,
But he would rather give, there is no doubt,
To his poor parishioners, round about,   490
From Mass offerings and his own pay, too.
With little, he could easily make do.
Wide was his parish, the houses far asunder,
But he would not leave them, for rain or thunder,
If sickness or if trouble should befall   495
The farthest in his parish, great or small,
He'd go on foot; his staff in hand he'd keep.
This noble example he gave to his sheep:
That first he wrought, and afterward, he taught.
Out of the Gospels, those words he had caught,   500
And his own metaphor he added, too:
If gold should rust, then what will iron do?
For if a priest is foul, in whom we trust,
No wonder that a foolish man should rust;
And it's a shame, if care he does not keep—   505
A shepherd to be shitty with clean sheep.
Well should a priest a good example give,
By his own cleanness, how his sheep should live.

---

7. The major pilgrimage site for medieval Christians; lesser popular pilgrimage sites—in Italy, France, Spain, and Germany, respectively—follow.

8. According to medieval lore, a sign of a tendency to wander, associated especially with sexual excess.

His parish, he would not put out for hire
And leave his sheep encumbered in the mire   510
To run to London to Saint Paul's[9] to switch
And be a chantry priest[1] just for the rich,
Nor by guild brothers would he be detained;[2]
But he stayed home and with his flock remained,
So that the wolf would not make it miscarry;   515
He was a shepherd, not a mercenary.
And though he holy was, and virtuous,
To sinners, he was not contemptuous,
Not haughty nor aloof was he in speech,
With courtesy and kindness would he teach.   520
To draw folks up to heaven with his fairness,
By good example: this was all his business.
But if there were a person who was stubborn,
Whoever he was, high or low rank born,
Then he would scold him sharply, at the least.   525
There is nowhere, I know, a better priest.
He waited for no pomp or reverence;
For him, no finicky, affected conscience,
But the words of Christ and his apostles twelve
He taught: but first, he followed them himself.   530
　　　With him, his brother who was a PLOWMAN rode;
Of dung, this man had hauled out many a load;
A true laborer, and a good one was he,
Living in peace and perfect charity.
God loved he best with all of his whole heart   535
At all times, though it caused him joy or smart,
And next, his neighbor, just as he loved himself.
He would thresh, dig ditches, and also delve,
For Christ's sake and the sake of each poor man,
And without pay, he'd do all that he can.   540
His tithes, with all due fairness, he'd not shirk,
But paid from what he owned and with his work.
In a workman's smock, he rode on a mare.
　　　A REEVE and a MILLER were also there,
A SUMMONER and then a PARDONER,   545
A MAN and myself—that's all there were.
　　　The MILLER was a stout churl, it is true;
Quite big he was in brawn, and in bones, too.
That stood him in good stead; for where he came,
He'd win the ram[3] in every wrestling game.   550
He was short necked and broad, a thick-thewed thug;
There was no door around he couldn't lug
Right off its hinges, or break with his head.

9. The largest cathedral in medieval England.
1. A priest supported by an endowment to
say daily mass for the souls of particular individuals (usually wealthy men or their family
members).

2. I.e., he would not take the lucrative position of priest for a guild.
3. I.e., the prize for the winner of a village
wrestling contest.

His beard, just like a sow or fox, was red,[4]
And also broad, as though it was a spade.   555
Right up atop his nose's ridge was laid
A wart; on it, a tuft of hairs grew now,
Red as the bristles in ears of a sow;
His nostrils were quite black, and also wide.
A sword and buckler bore he by his side.   560
His mouth was as great as a great cauldron.
A jangling goliard, he was quite the one—
Of sin and harlotries, he most would tell.
He made three times his pay and stole corn well;
And yet, he had a thumb of gold, all right.[5]   565
A blue hood wore he, and a coat of white.
A bagpipe he knew how to blow and play.
And sounding it, he led us on our way.
    A good MANCIPLE[6] did business for a law school;
All food buyers could follow well his rule   570
For prudent buying; it would earn them merit;
For, whether he paid straight or took on credit,
In buying, he watched carefully and waited,
So he was in good shape and well ahead.
Now, is it not from God a sign of grace   575
That this unlearned man's wit can outpace
The wisdom of a heap of learned men?
Of his masters, he had more than thrice ten,
Who were quite skilled and expert in the law,
And in that house, a full dozen one saw   580
Worthy to be stewards of rents and land
For any lord who dwells now in England,
To make him live within the means he had
In debtless honor (unless he were mad),
Or as frugally as he could desire,   585
And able thus to help out all the shire
In any circumstance that may befall:
And yet this Manciple hoodwinked them all.
    The REEVE was a slender, choleric[7] man.
He shaved his beard as closely as one can;   590
His hair, short and up by his ears, he'd crop,
And, like a priest's, he'd dock it on the top.
Quite long his legs were; they were also lean,
And just like sticks; no calf was to be seen.
He could well guard the granary and bin;   595

---

4. His coloration, together with the description of his nostrils and mouth, would suggest to medieval readers a temperament given to strong displays of temper or rage.
5. "An honest miller has a golden thumb" was a proverb expressing the general belief that all millers were dishonest (either because no such miller existed or because millers cheated their customers with a heavy thumb on the scale).
6. Agent responsible for buying supplies and paying bills, especially for a college or monastery.
7. Dominated by choler, the humor associated with irascibility. "Reeve": farm or estate manager.

No auditor around could with him win.
He knew well, by the drought and by the rain,
The yieldings of his seed and of his grain.
His lord's sheep, his cattle, and his dairy,
His swine and horses, his livestock and poultry   600
Were wholly under this Reeve's governing,
And by his contract, he gave reckoning,
Because his lord, in age, was twenty years.
No man alive could bring him in arrears.[8]
No bailiff, herdsman, worker there might be   605
But he knew all their tricks and treachery;
As they feared death, of him they were all scared.
His dwelling place upon a heath was fair;
All shaded with green trees on every hand.
He could, much better than his lord, buy land.   610
Quite richly had he stocked up, privately.
And he could please his lord so cleverly
That he'd lend to him from his lord's own goods,
And have his thanks, then, plus a coat and hood.
When he was young, he had learned a fine trade,   615
A good wright, a skilled carpenter he made.
The Reeve on his stout farm horse sat that day,
Which was called Scot and was a dapple gray.
His overcoat was long, of darkish blue,
And by his side, a rusty blade hung, too.   620
From Norfolk[9] was this Reeve, of whom I tell,
From near a town that men call Baldeswell.
Like a friar's, he tucked his coat up fast.
In our company, he always rode the last.

    A SUMMONER[1] was with us in that place,   625
Who had a fiery-red cherubic face,
Pimply was he, with eyes swollen and narrow.
Hot he was and lecherous as a sparrow,[2]
With scabbed black brows; his beard had lost some hair.
And of his visage, children were quite scared.   630
Not lead monoxide, mercury, or sulphur,
Not borax, white lead, or cream of tartar—
No single ointment that would cleanse or bite—
Could help him to remove those pustules white,
Nor cure the pimples sitting on his cheeks.   635
Well loved he garlic, onions, also leeks,[3]
And drinking blood red wine, strongly fermented;
Then he would speak and cry as though demented.
And when of this good wine he'd drunk his fill,

8. I.e., convict him of having unpaid debts.
9. County northeast of London.
1. An officer of the ecclesiastical courts who served summonses to individuals charged with offenses against canon law.
2. A proverbially lecherous bird; this behavior is a manifestation of the Summoner's "hot" temperament.
3. These foods, according to medieval medicine, would increase the heat of the body and thus also cause lust, outbursts of fury, and outbreaks of the skin.

No words but Latin from his mouth would spill.   640
A few such terms he knew, like two or three,
That he had learned by hearing some decree—
It's no wonder, for he heard it all day;
And thus you know full well how any jay[4]
Can call out "Walter" as well as the pope.   645
But whoever might on other matters grope,
Then his philosophy was spent thereby;
Always, "Questio quid iuris,"[5] cry he would.
He was a noble rascal in his kind;
A better fellow men would never find.   650
And he would suffer, for a quart of wine,
A good fellow to have his concubine
A full year, and excuse him thus completely;
For he himself could pluck a finch[6] discreetly.
If he found a good fellow anywhere,   655
Then he would quickly teach to him that there
Was no need to fear archdeacons' curses,[7]
Unless men's souls were found in their purses;
For in their purses, they will punished be.
"The purse is the archdeacon's hell," said he.   660
He downright lied, I know, in what he said;
Excommunication guilty men should dread.
Absolving saves, but cursing slays indeed;
Of *Significavit,*[8] men should well take heed.
Under his thumb, he had, as it did please   665
Him, the young girls there of the diocese;
He counseled all who told him things in secret.
A garland he had fashioned and then set,
Big as an ale-house sign, upon his head.
He'd made a buckler from a loaf of bread.   670
      With him, there rode a gentle PARDONER
Of Roncevalles,[9] and good, close friends they were.
He'd come straight from the papal court at Rome,
And loudly sang, "Come hither, love, to me!"
With a stiff bass, the Summoner sang along;   675
No trumpet's sound was ever half so strong.
This Pardoner had hair yellow as wax,
But smooth it hung as does a hank of flax;
In skinny strands, the locks hung from his head,
And with them, he his shoulders overspread;   680
But thin it lay; its strands hung one by one.
For stylishness, a hood he would wear none,

---

4. A popinjay, or parrot.
5. "The question [is], what [point] of law [applies]" (Latin); a phrase familiar to the Summoner from the ecclesiastical courts.
6. To trick or blackmail; to have sexual relations.
7. I.e., excommunication.

8. Literally, "he has signified" (Latin): the writ issued for the arrest of an excommunicated person.
9. A church-affiliated hospital in London, supported in part by the sale of pardons—papal indulgences purchased to shorten the time spent by souls in purgatory.

Since it was trussed up within his wallet.
He thought he wore the latest fashions yet;
With loose hair, his head save for his cap was bare.   685
Such staring eyes he had, just like a hare.
A veronica[1] he'd sewn on his cap.
His wallet lay before him in his lap,
With pardons hot from Rome stuffed to the brim.
A voice high as a goat's came out of him.   690
No beard had he, nor should he wait for one;
His face smooth like his shaving'd just been done.
I think he was a gelding or a mare.
But, in his craft, from Berwick down to Ware,[2]
No pardoner like him in all the land.   695
In his bag was a pillowcase on hand,
And he declared it was Our Lady's[3] veil;
He said he had a big piece of the sail
Saint Peter used upon his boat when he,
Before Christ took him, had gone out to sea.   700
He had a fake gold cross bedecked with stones,
A glass he had that carried some pig bones.[4]
But with these relics, whenever he spied
A poor parson out in the countryside,
On that day, much more money would he make   705
Than, in two months, the poor parson might take;
And thus, with his feigned flattery and japes,
He made the parson and people his apes.
But to tell the whole truth, now, finally,
In church, a noble ecclesiastic was he.   710
Well could he read a lesson or a story,
But best of all, he sang the offertory;
For well he knew, when that song had been sung,
Then he must preach and smoothly file his tongue
To win his silver, as quite well could he;   715
Therefore, he sang quite loud and merrily.
    Now, I have told you truly, in a clause,
The rank, the dress, the number, and the cause
That brought together all this company
In Southwark, at this noble hostelry   720
That's called the Tabard, next door to the Bell.
But now it's time that to you I should tell
How that we all behaved on that same night
When we should in that hostelry alight;
Afterward, I will tell of our voyage   725

---

1. A reproduction of Jesus' features, as were said to have been miraculously impressed on the cloth offered to him by St. Veronica on his way to his crucifixion. The veronica was also a key point of reference for medieval artists who wished to claim a divine origin for their craft.

2. I.e., from northernmost England to the south.
3. The Virgin Mary.
4. The Pardoner has a variety of false saints' relics; such relics were believed to possess the saints' spiritual power and thus found eager buyers.

And all the rest about our pilgrimage.
But first I pray you, by your courtesy,
That you not blame my own vulgarity,
Although I might speak plainly in this matter,
When I tell you their words and their demeanor,   730
Or if I speak their words, exact and true.
For this you all know just as well as I do:
Whoever tells a tale after a man,
He must repeat, as closely as he can,
Every last word, if that is his duty,   735
Even if he has to speak quite rudely,
Or otherwise, he makes his tale untrue,
Or makes things up, or finds words that are new.
He may not spare, though that man were his brother;
He might as well say one word as another.   740
Christ himself plainly spoke in Holy Writ;
You know no vulgarity is in it.
And Plato says, whoever can him read,
That words must be the cousin to the deed.[5]
Also, I pray you that you will forgive me   745
Although I've not ranked folks by their degree
Here in this tale, the way that they should stand.
My wit is short, you may well understand.

    Our Host put us at ease with his great cheer;
At once, he set up supper for us here.   750
He served us all with victuals that were fine;
It pleased us well to drink his good, strong wine.
An impressive man our HOST was, all in all;
He could have been a marshal in a hall.
A large man he, with eyes both bright and wide—   755
No fairer burgess anywhere in Cheapside[6]—
Bold in his speech, and wise, and quite well taught.
And in his manhood, he did lack for naught.
Moreover, he was quite a merry man;
After supper, to amuse us, he began,   760
And spoke of pleasure, among other things,
When we had settled up our reckonings.
He then said thus: "Now, my good lords, truly,
To me, you are quite welcome, heartily;
For, by my word, if that I shall not lie,   765
So merry a company, this whole year, I
Have not seen in this inn, as I see now.
I'd gladly make you happy, knew I how.
I've just thought what would be entertaining;
It'd please you, and it wouldn't cost a thing.   770
    You go to Canterbury—bless the Lord,

---

5. Apparently an allusion to Plato's *Timaeus*
29B, borrowed by Chaucer from Boethius's
Consolation of Philosophy (ca. 525 C.E.) or
from the *Roman de la Rose* (ca. 1275).
6. A major business district in London.

May the blissful martyr pay you your reward!
I know well, as you travel by the way,
You all intend to tell tales and to play;
For truly, comfort and mirth both have flown   775
If you ride on the way dumb as a stone;
Now, I know a way I can divert you,
As I have said, and give you comfort, too.
And if it pleases you to give assent
So you all agree to trust my judgment,   780
And to do according to what I say,
Tomorrow, when you all ride by the way,
Now, by the soul of my father who is dead,
Unless you're merry, I'll give you my head!
Hold up your hands, now, without further speech."   785
      All our assent took not long to beseech.
It did not seem worthwhile to make a fuss,
For we did not need more time to discuss,
And we told him to give his verdict then.
"My lords," said he, "this plan is best. Now, listen. 790
But take it not, I pray you, with disdain.
This is the point, to speak now, short and plain:
Each one of you, to help shorten our way,
Along this journey, two tales you will say,
Toward Canterbury, as I mean you to,   795
And homeward, you'll tell us another two,
Of adventures that in old times did befall.
The one who bears himself the best of all—
That is to say, the one of you who might
Tell tales that have most meaning and delight—   800
Shall have a supper paid for by us all,
Sitting right near this post here in this hall,
When we all come again from Canterbury.
And to make you all even more merry,
I will myself quite gladly with you ride,   805
Right at my own expense, and be your guide.
Whoever will my judgment now gainsay
Shall pay for all we spend along the way.
If it be so, and all of you agree,
Without more words, at once, now you tell me,   810
And I'll make myself ready long before."
      This thing was granted, and our oaths we swore
With quite glad hearts, and we prayed him also
That he fully would agree to do so,
And that he would become our governor,   815
And of our tales, the judge and record keeper,
And set the supper at a certain price,
And we would all be ruled by his advice
In all respects; and thus, with one assent
We were all accorded with his judgment.   820

And thereupon, the wine was fetched in fast;
We drank, and to our rest we went at last,
Without us any longer tarrying.
    In the morning, as day began to spring,
Up rose our Host, and was, for us, the cock,   825
And gathered us together in a flock;
With slow gait, we started on our riding,
Till we came to Saint Thomas's Watering;[7]
And there, our Host began to stop his horse
And said, "Lords, listen—if you please, of course.   830
Let me remind you that you gave your word.
If evening-song and morning-song accord,[8]
Let see now who shall tell us the first tale.
As ever may I drink of wine or ale,
Whoso now rebels against my judgment   835
Shall pay for all that by the way is spent.
Now let's draw straws, and then we shall depart;
Whoever has the shortest straw will start.
Sir Knight, my master and my lord," he said,
"Now you draw first, for thus I have decided.   840
Come near," said he, "my lady Prioress.
And you, sir Clerk, leave off your bashfulness.
Don't study now. Lay hands to, every man!"
At once, to draw straws, everyone began;
To quickly tell the way it did advance,   845
Were it by fortune or by luck or chance,
The truth is this: the draw fell to the Knight,
For which we were quite glad, as it was right;
By agreement and arrangement, now he must
Tell us his tale, as it was only just,   850
As you have heard; what more words need be spent?
And when this good man saw the way it went,
Because he wise was, and obedient
To keep the word he gave by free assent,
He said, "Now, since I shall begin the game,   855
What, welcome is this straw, in the Lord's name!
Now, let us ride, and hearken what I say."
And with that word, we rode forth on our way,
And he began with then a merry cheer
His tale at once, and said as you may hear.   860

7. A spring dedicated to St. Thomas (not far   8. I.e., if your intention at night matches
from the inn).   what you promised in the morning.

The Wife of Bath's Prologue and Tale

The Wife of Bath's Prologue

"Experience, though no authority
Were in this world, is right enough for me
To speak of the woe that is in marriage;
For, my lords, since I was twelve years of age,[1]
Thanks be to God, eternally alive,   5
Husbands at the church door, I have had five—
If quite so often I might wedded be—
And all were worthy men in their degree.
But it was told me not so long ago,[2]
That since just once our Christ did ever go   10
To a wedding, in Cana in Galilee,[3]
That by that same example, he taught me
That only one time I should wedded be.
Lo, listen, what a sharp word then spoke he,
Beside a well when Jesus, God and man,   15
Spoke in reproof of the Samaritan:[4]
"Thou hast had five husbands,' then said he,
'And that same man here who now hath thee
Is not thy husband,' said he by the well.
But what he meant thereby, I cannot tell;   20
Except I ask, why is it the fifth man
Was not husband to the Samaritan?
How many might she have in marriage?
Yet I've never heard tell, in all my age,
About this, any number definite.   25
Up and down, men gloss[5] and guess about it,
But well I know, expressly, it's no lie,
That God bade us to wax and multiply;[6]
This gentle text, I can well understand.
Also, well I know, he said my husband   30
Should leave mother and father and cleave to me.[7]
But of no number a mention made he,
Of bigamy, or of octogamy;[8]
Why then should men speak of it villainy?
    Lo, here is the wise king, Don[9] Solomon;   35
I think he had some wives, well more than one.
Now would to God it lawful were for me

---

1. The minimum age of marriage, in canon law.
2. Many of the biblical sources cited by the Wife of Bath in the argument that follows can be found in St. Jerome's *Adversus Jovinianum* (392 C.E.), a polemical diatribe that is highly critical of both women and marriage.
3. See John 2.2.
4. A woman from Samaria (see John 4.7–18).
5. Interpret.
6. Genesis 1.28.
7. Genesis 2.24.
8. Marriage to two or to eight. Usually, *bigamy* involves concurrent marriages (as below, in references to biblical figures), but the Wife of Bath often instead means consecutive marriages.
9. Master. The biblical king Solomon was proverbially renowned for his great wisdom and for his hundreds of wives and concubines (see 1 Kings 11.3).

To be refreshed here half so much as he!
A gift from God had he with all his wives!
No man has such a gift who's now alive.   40
This noble king, God knows, as I would judge it,
That first night had many a merry fit
With each of them, so well was he alive.
Blessèd be God that I have wedded five!
Of whom I have picked out the very best,   45
For both their nether purse[1] and money chest.
Different schools can turn out perfect clerks,
And different practices in sundry works
Make the workman perfect, it's no lie;
From my five husbands, studying am I.   50
Welcome the sixth, when he shall come along.
In truth, I won't keep chaste for very long.
And when my husband from this world has passed,
Another Christian man will wed me fast;
Then the apostle[2] says that I am free   55
To wed, by God, where it most pleases me.
He says to be wedded is not sinning;
Better to be wedded than be burning.
What do I care if folks speak villainy
About accursed Lamech's bigamy?[3]   60
Abraham was a holy man, I know;
And as I understand it, Jacob also;
And each of them had wives now, more than one,
As many other holy men have done.
Where, can you say, in any kind of age,   65
That our high God has forbidden marriage
Expressly, in a word? I pray, tell me.
Or where did he command virginity?
I know as well as you, or else you should,
The apostle, when he speaks of maidenhood,   70
Said that a precept for it he had none.[4]
Men may counsel a woman to be one,
But counseling does not make a commandment.
All of it he left to our own judgment;
For if our God commanded maidenhood,   75
Then wedding with the deed, he'd damn for good.
And surely, if no seed were ever sown,
From what, then, would virginity be grown?
And at the least, Paul never dared demand
A thing that his own Master won't command.   80
The prize is set up for virginity;
Catch it who may; who runs the best, let's see.
    To everyone, this word does not apply,

1. I.e., scrotum.
2. St. Paul; see 1. Corinthians 7.39, 9.
3. See Genesis 4.19. Lamech (cursed as a murderer) is the first man in the Bible said to

have had more than one wife (or a wife and a concubine) at the same time, but he was hardly the last, as the Wife of Bath points out.
4. 1 Corinthians 7.25.

But only where God's might wants it to lie.
I know the apostle was a virgin; 85
Nonetheless, although he wrote and said then
He wished that everyone was such as he,
This is but counsel to virginity.[5]
He gave me leave to be a wife, all the same,
With his permission, so it is no shame, 90
If my mate dies, to go then and wed me,
Without objections about bigamy.
Though it may be good not to touch women[6]—
In his bed or on his couch, he meant then—
Fire and flax together make peril so— 95
What this example resembles, you all know.
The sum is this: he held virginity
More perfect than to wed from frailty.
Frailty I call it, unless he and she
Wished to lead all their lives in chastity. 100
　　　I grant it well that I have no envy,
Though maidenhood's preferred to bigamy.
To be clean pleases them, body and spirit;
Of my state, I make no boast about it,
For you well know, a lord in his household, 105
He has not every vessel made of gold;[7]
Some come from wood, and serve their lord withal.
In sundry ways, folks to him God does call,
Each has God's special gift while he must live,
Some this, some that, it pleases God to give.[8] 110
　　　Virginity thus is great perfection,
And also continence spurred by devotion,
But Christ, who of perfection is the well,
Bade not that every person should go sell
All that he has and give it to the poor, 115
And follow in his footsteps thus, for sure.
He spoke to those who would live perfectly,[9]
And my lords, by your leave, that is not me.
I will bestow the flower of my life
In married acts and fruits, and be a wife. 120
　　　Tell me, for what purpose and conclusion
Were the members[1] made for generation,
And by so perfectly wise a maker wrought?
Trust it well now: they were not made for nought.
Say what you will, or hedge it by glossing, 125
That they were made simply for the purging
Of urine; and both our small things also
Were made so male from female we could know,
And for no other cause—do you say no?
Experience well knows it is not so. 130

---

5. 1 Corinthians 7.8.　　　　　　　　8. See 1 Corinthians 7.7.
6. 1 Corinthians 7.1.　　　　　　　　9. See Matthew 19.21.
7. See 2 Timothy 2.20.　　　　　　　1. I.e., sexual organs.

So the clerks will not be angry at me,
They were made for both: I say this truly.
That is, to do our business and for ease
In engendering, where God we don't displease.
Why should men otherwise in their books set   135
It down that man should yield his wife her debt?[2]
Now how to her should he make his payment,
Unless he'd used his silly[3] instrument?
Thus, they were bestowed upon a creature
To purge urine, and so we could engender.   140
    But I don't say that each one's obligated,
Who has the harness that I've just related,
To go and use it for engendering.
Then for chastity, men wouldn't care a thing.
Christ was a maiden and shaped like a man,   145
And many saints, since first the world began;
They lived forever in perfect chastity.
I won't envy any virginity.
Let them be bread of wheat that's been refined,
As barley bread, let us wives be defined;   150
And yet, with barley bread, as Mark can tell,
Our Lord has refreshed many men quite well.[4]
In whatever rank God's called to us,
I'll persevere; I'm not fastidious.
In wifehood, I will use my instrument   155
As freely as my Maker has it sent.
If I'm aloof, then God send me dismay!
My husband can well have it, night and day,
When it pleases him to come and pay his debt.
A husband I will have—I won't stop yet—   160
Who shall be both my debtor and my slave,
With tribulation, unless he behaves,
Upon his flesh while I may be his wife.
I have the power, during all my life
Over his own body, and not he.   165
Thus the Apostle has told this to me,
And bade our husbands they should love us well.[5]
This meaning, I like more than I can tell"—
    Up the Pardoner starts, immediately;
"Now, Madame, by God and Saint John," said he,   170
"You are a noble preacher on this strife.
Alas! I was about to wed a wife.
Why on my flesh now pay a price so dear?
I'd rather not wed any wife this year!"
    "Just wait! My tale is not begun," said she.   175
"No, you'll drink from another cask, you'll see,
Before I go, that will taste worse than ale.

2. The marital debt, mutually owed;   4. See not Mark but John 6.9–13.
see 1 Corinthians 7.3–4.   5. Ephesians 5.25.
3. Innocent.

And when I will have told you all my tale
Of the tribulation that's in marriage—
About which I'm an expert in my age—   180
That is to say that I have been the whip—
Then you can choose if you might want to sip
Out of the cask that I will open here.
Beware of it, before you come too near;
For I shall give examples, more than ten.   185
'Whoever won't be warned by other men,
By him will other men corrected be.'
Those same words were written by Ptolemy;[6]
Read his *Almageste,* and there you'll find it still."
        "Madame, I pray you, if it be your will,"   190
Said this Pardoner, "now as you began,
Tell forth your tale, and don't spare any man;
Teach us young men all about your practice."
        "Gladly," said she, "since you might well like this;
But yet I pray to all this company,   195
If I speak after my own fantasy,
Do not be aggrieved by what I say,
For my intent is only now to play.
        And now, sir, now I'll tell on with my tale.
As ever I might drink of wine or ale,   200
I'll tell the truth; those husbands that I had,
Some three of them were good, and two were bad.
The three who were good men were rich and old;
And so they barely could the statute hold
Through which they all had bound themselves to me.   205
By God, you know what I mean, certainly!
So help me God, I laugh to remember
How pitifully at night I made them labor!
In faith, I set no store by their pleasure.
To me, they had given land and treasure;   210
No longer need I use my diligence
To win their love or do them reverence.
They loved me so well that, by God above,
I set no value then upon their love!
A wise woman will be the busy one   215
To get herself love, yes, where she has none.
But since I had them wholly in my hand,
And since to me they'd given all their land,
Why should I take care that I should them please
Unless it were for my profit and my ease?   220
I set them so to hard work, by my lights,
That they sung "Wey-la-way!" on many nights.
I don't think the bacon was meant for them now

6. Greek astronomer and mathematician (2nd century C.E.); his textbook, the *Almagest,* dominated astronomy for more than a thou-sand years; a preface containing proverbial wisdom attributed to Ptolemy was later added to the text.

That some men win in Essex at Dunmowe.[7]
I governed them so well, after my law,   225
That each of them was eager, as I saw,
To bring me home some gay things from the fair.
They were glad when my speech to them was fair;
I scolded them, as God knows, spitefully.
    Now, listen how I acted properly,   230
You wise wives, who can so well understand.
Thus should you accuse falsely, out of hand.
For half so boldly knows no living man
How to swear and lie just as a woman can.
This statement about wise wives, I don't make—   235
Unless it be when they've made some mistake.
A wise wife, who knows what's good for her,
Will swear the tattling crow is mad for sure,[8]
And make sure that her maid has assented
As her witness. But hear now what I said: 240
    'Sir old dotard, is this your array?
Why is it that my neighbor's wife's so gay?
She is honored everywhere she goes;
I sit at home; I have no decent clothes.
What do you do at my neighbor's house there?   245
Are you so amorous? Is she so fair?
What do you whisper to our maid? Bless me!
Sir old lecher, now let your jokes be!
If, without guilt, I have a chum or friend,
Just like a fiend, you scold me without end   250
If I should play or walk down to his house!
But you come home as drunken as a mouse,
And then preach from your bench, no proof from you!
And it's great mischief, as you tell me too,
A poor woman to wed, for the expense;   255
If she's rich and born to lofty parents,
Then you say that a torment it will be
To bear her pride and sullen melancholy.
And if she should be fair, you horrid cur,
You say every lecher soon will have her;   260
For she can't long in chastity abide,
Who is always assailed on every side.
    You say some folk want us for our richness,
Some for our figure, and some for our fairness,
Some because she can either dance or sing,   265
Some for gentility and socializing;
And some because their hands and arms are small;
By your lights, to the devil thus goes all.
You say men cannot defend a castle wall
When it's so long assailed by large and small.   270

---

7. A village ca. 35 miles northeast of London. In the 13th century, the custom began of awarding a side of bacon to the couple who swore not to have quarreled or regretted their marriage during the first year after their wedding.

8. The talking bird who reveals a wife's infidelity by repeating words it has heard is a common motif in folktales.

And if she should be ugly, you say she
Will covet every man that she may see,
For like a spaniel, she will on him leap
Until she finds a man to buy her cheap.
No goose goes out there on the lake so gray   275
That she will be without a mate, you say.
You say it's hard for men to have controlled
A thing that no man willingly would hold.
Thus you say, scoundrel, when you go to bed,
That no wise man has any need to wed,   280
Nor one who toward heaven would aspire.
With wild thunder claps and lightning's fire
May your old withered neck break right in two!
     You say that leaky houses, and smoke too,
And scolding wives all cause a man to flee   285
Out of his own house; ah now, God bless me!
What can ail such an old man, who must chide?
You say that we wives will our vices hide
Till we're hitched, and then we show them to you—
Well may that be the proverb of a shrew!   290
     You say horses, hounds, asses, and oxen
At different times can be tried out by men;
Wash bowls and basins, spoons and stools, you say,
All household things men try before they pay;
The same thing goes for clothes and gear and pots;   295
But to try out a wife, a man may not
Till they are wedded—you old dotard shrew!—
And then we show our vices, so say you.
     You say also that it displeases me
Unless you will always praise my beauty,   300
Or else always pore over my face,
And call me "Fair Madame" in every place.
Unless you make a feast upon the day
That I was born, and dress me fresh and gay;
Unless to my nurse, you do all honor,   305
And to the chambermaid within my bower,[9]
And to my father's folk and kin all day—
Old barrelful of lies, all this you say!
     Yet of Jenkin, who is our apprentice,
Whose curly hair shines just like gold—for this,   310
And because he will squire me around,
A cause for false suspicions, you have found.
I don't want him, though you should die tomorrow!
     Tell me: why do you hide, to my sorrow,
The keys now of your chest[1] away from me?   315
They are my goods as well as yours, bless me!
Will you make an idiot of your dame?
Now, by that good lord who is called Saint James,
You will not, though it might make you crazy,
Be master of both my goods and body;   320

9. Bedroom.   1. Strongbox.

One of them you'll forgo, to spite your eyes.
What good is it to ask around and spy?
I think you want to lock me in your chest!
You should say, "Wife, go where you think is best;
Enjoy yourself; I'll believe no tales of this. 325
I know you for my own true wife, Dame Alice."
We love no man who will take heed or charge
Of where we go; we want to be at large.
    And of all men, quite blessèd must he be,
That wise astrologer, Don Ptolemy, 330
Who says this proverb in his *Almageste,*
"Of all men, his wisdom is the highest
Who never cares who holds the world in hand."
By this proverb, you should well understand,
If you have enough, why then should you care 335
How merrily some other folks might fare?
For certainly, old dotard, by your leave,
You'll have some quaint things sure enough come eve.
He is too great a niggard who would spurn
A man to light a candle at his lantern; 340
By God, from that, he doesn't have less light.
If you've enough, complaining isn't right.
    You also say if we make ourselves gay
With our clothing and with precious array,
That it is peril to our chastity; 345
Woe to you—you then enforce it for me,
And say these words in the Apostle's name:
"In clothing made from chastity and shame
You women all should dress yourselves," said he,
"Not with well-coifed hair and with gay jewelry, 350
Not with rich clothes, with pearls, or else with gold."[2]
With your text and your rubric,[3] I don't hold,
Or follow them as much as would a gnat.
    You said this: that I was just like a cat;
Whoever wanted to singe a cat's skin 355
He could be sure the cat would then stay in;
And if the cat's skin were so sleek and gay,
She'd not stay in the house for half a day;
Forth she'd go, before the day was dawning,
To show her skin and to go caterwauling. 360
That is to say, if I am gay, sir shrew,
I'll run to put my poor old clothes on view.
    Sir old fool, what help is it if you spy?
Though you prayed Argus[4] with his hundred eyes
To be my bodyguard, as he'd know best, 365
He'd not guard me till I let him, I'll be blessed.
I'd hoodwink him, as I am prospering!

---

2. See I Timothy 2.9–10.
3. Direction written in red.
4. In classical myth, a monster used by

Hera/Juno, queen of the gods, to watch over
one of her husband's paramours.

Yet you also say that there are three things,
And that these same things trouble all this earth,
And that no man might yet endure the fourth.[5]   370
Oh, dear sir shrew, Jesus shorten your life!
Yet you will preach and say a hateful wife
Is one of these misfortunes that you reckon.
Aren't there other kinds of comparison
That, for all your parables, you could use,   375
Unless a poor wife were the one you'd choose?
      You liken, too, a woman's love to hell,
To barren land where water may not dwell.
You liken it also to a wild fire;
The more it burns, the more it has desire   380
To consume everything that burned will be.
You say that just as worms destroy a tree,
A wife destroys her husband, you have found;
This, they well know who to wives have been bound.'
      My lords, right thus, as you can understand,   385
I stiffly[6] kept my old husbands in hand
And swore they said thus in their drunkenness;
And all was false; except I took witness
On Jenkin there, and on my niece, also.
Oh Lord! The pain I did them and the woe.   390
And, by God's sweet pain, they were not guilty!
For, like a horse, I could bite and whinny.
I knew how to complain well even when
I had the guilt, or I'd been ruined then.
Whoever comes first to the mill, first grinds;   395
Complaining first, our war stopped, I did find.
They were glad to excuse themselves quite quickly
For things of which they never had been guilty.
Of wenches, I'd accuse them out of hand
When, in their sickness, they could hardly stand.   400
      Yet it tickled his heart, because then he
Thought that I had for him such great fancy!
I swore that all my walking out at night
Was to spy on wenches he was holding tight;
Using that cover, I enjoyed much mirth.   405
For all such wit is given us at birth;
Deceit, weeping, and spinning God did give
To women by nature, all the time they live.
And thus of one thing, I can surely boast:
In the end, I'm the one who won the most   410
By tricks or force or by some other thing
As much as constant grumbling and grousing.
Namely, then, they would have bad luck in bed:
I did them no pleasure, and I chided;
I would no longer in the bed abide,   415
If I felt his arm come over my side,

5. See Proverbs 30.21–23.   6. Firmly.

Till he had paid his ransom down to me;
Then I'd suffer him to do his foolery.
Therefore, to every man this tale I tell:
Win whoso may, for all is there to sell; 420
With empty hands men may no hawks then lure.
For profit, I would all their lust endure,
And I would fake it with feigned appetite;
And yet in bacon,[7] I had no delight.
That was the reason I would always chide them, 425
For though the pope were sitting right beside them,
At their own table, I would never spare.
In truth, I repaid them word for word there.
So help me, oh true God omnipotent,
If now I made my will and testament, 430
There was not one unpaid word I did owe.
By my own wit, I brought it all about so
That they must give it up, and for the best,
Or otherwise, we never would have rest;
Though he looked as crazy as a lion, 435
He would fail at gaining his conclusion.
　　　Then I would say to him, 'Sweetheart, take heed—
See how meek our sheep Willie looks, indeed!
Come near, my spouse, and let me kiss your cheek!
Truly you should be all patient and meek, 440
And have, too, a carefully spiced conscience,
Since you always preach about Job's patience.[8]
Suffer always, since you can so well preach;
Unless you do, for sure we shall you teach
That it's nice to have a wife in peace now. 445
Doubtless, one of the two of us must bow,
And so, since man is more reasonable
Than woman, to suffer you are able.
What ails you now that thus you grouse and groan?
Do you just want my quaint thing[9] for your own? 450
Why, take it all! Lo, have it through and through!
You love it well, by Peter,[1] curse on you;
For if I wanted to sell my *belle chose*,[2]
Then I could walk as fresh as is a rose;
But I will keep it just for your own tooth. 455
You are to blame, by God! I tell the truth.'
These are the kinds of words I had on hand.
And now I will speak of my fourth husband.
　　　My fourth husband was a reveler—
That is to say, he had a paramour— 460
And young and full of wantonness was I,
Stubborn, strong and jolly as a magpie.
How I'd dance when the small harp was playing;

7. I.e., preserved (old) meat; or perhaps a reference to the prize at Dunmow.
8. Proverbial; see the book of Job.
9. Genitals.
1. St. Peter.
2. Pretty thing (French).

Like a nightingale's was all my singing,
When I had drunk my draught of fine sweet wine!   465
Metellius, the foul churl, the swine,
Who, with a staff, bereft his wife of life,
Because she drank wine,[3] if I were his wife,
He wouldn't frighten me away from drink!
And after wine, on Venus[4] I must think,   470
For just as sure as cold engenders hail,
A lecherous mouth must have lecherous tail.
In wine-drunk women, there is no defence—
This, lechers know from their experience.
        But—Lord Christ!—when memories come back to me, 475
About my youth and all my jollity,
It tickles me right down to my heart's root.
To this day, it does my heart good, to boot,
That I have had my world right in my time.
But age, alas, that poisons what is prime,   480
Has bereft me of my beauty and my pith.[5]
Let it go. Farewell! The devil go therewith!
The flower's gone; there is no more to tell;
The bran, as I best can, now must I sell;
But yet to be right merry I have planned.   485
And now I will tell of my fourth husband.
        I say, I had in my heart a great spite
That he in any other took delight.
By God and Saint Judocus,[6] he's repaid!
Of the same wood, a cross for him I made;   490
Not in a foul manner with my body,
But I made folks such cheer that certainly
I made him fry enough in his own grease
Because his jealous anger would not cease.
By God, on earth I was his purgatory,   495
For which, I hope his soul will be in glory.
God knows, he often sat and sang "Alack"
When his shoe so bitterly pinched him back.
There was no man who knew, save God and he,
In what ways I twisted him so sorely.   500
When I came from Jerusalem, he died;
Buried beneath the cross's beam,[7] he lies.
His tomb is not fancy or curious
As was the sepulcher of Darius,
Which Appelles had formed so skillfully;[8]   505
A waste to bury him expensively.

3. One of the historical anecdotes compiled in the rhetorical handbook by Valerius Maximus (1st century C.E.), which presents Metellius's act as justified.
4. Roman goddess of love.
5. Energy.
6. St. Judoc or Josse, a 7th-century Breton saint (never canonized) whose emblem was the pilgrim's staff.
7. I.e., in a place of honor within the church itself.
8. According to the (fictional) account in Walter of Châtillon's 12th-century Latin epic, *Alexandreis*, the famous painter Apelles (4th c. B.C.E.) decorated the tomb of the Persian king Darius (d. 486 B.C.E.).

Let him fare well. God rest his soul, I ask it!
He is now in his grave and in his casket.
    Now of my fifth husband I will tell.
May God let his soul never go to hell! 510
Yet to me he was the biggest scoundrel;
On my whole row of ribs, I feel it still,
And ever shall until my dying day.
But in our bed, he was so fresh and gay,
And he knew so well just how to gloss me 515
When he wanted my *belle chose,* as you'll see;
Although he'd beaten me on every bone,
Quickly he'd win back my love for his own.
I believe that I loved him best since he
Could be standoffish with his love for me. 520
We women have, and no lie this will be,
In this matter, our own quaint[9] fantasy:
Whatever thing won't lightly come our way,
Then after it we'll cry and crave all day.
Forbid us something, and that desire we; 525
Press on us fast, and then we're sure to flee.
With standoffishness, we spread out all our wares;
Great crowds at market make the goods dear there,
Too great a bargain isn't thought a prize;
And this knows every woman who is wise. 530
    My fifth husband—now God his soul should bless—
Whom I took for love and not for richness,
Formerly, he was a clerk at Oxford,
And had left school, and went back home to board
With my close friend who in our town did dwell. 535
God save her! Her name's Alison, as well.
She knew both my heart and my privacy
More than our parish priest did, so help me!
With her, I shared my secrets one and all.
For had my husband pissed upon a wall, 540
Or done a thing that should have cost his life,
To her and to another worthy wife,
And to my niece, whom I did love so well,
All of his secrets I'd be sure to tell.
God knows too that I did this quite often 545
So I made his face both red and hot then
From shame itself. He blamed himself that he
Had ever shared with me his privacy.
    And so it happened that one time in Lent—
For often times to my close friend I went, 550
Because I always did love being gay,
And to walk out in March, April, and May,
From house to house, and sundry tales to hear—

---

9. "Queynt," meaning "quaint" in the modern
English sense and also a pun on the slang
word for the female sex organ; the pun is espe-

cially likely coming a few lines after the last
reference to Wife's *"belle chose"* (510).

Jenkin the clerk, Alison, my friend dear,
And I myself, into the fields all went.   555
My husband was at London all that Lent;
More leisure for my playing, I then had,
To see and to be seen (and I was glad)
By lusty folks. Did I know where good grace
Was destined to find me, or in what place?   560
Therefore, I made all my visitations
To vigils and also to processions,
To preachings and to these pilgrimages,
To miracle plays[1] and to marriages,
And always wore my gowns of scarlet bright.   565
Neither the worms nor moths nor any mites,
On my soul's peril, had my gowns abused.
Do you know why? Because they were well used.
      Now I'll tell you what happened then to me.
I say that out into the fields walked we,   570
Till truly, we had such a flirtation,
This clerk and I, that I made due provision
And spoke to him, and said to him how he,
Were I a widow, should be wed to me.
For certainly—and I'm not boasting here—   575
I have not ever lacked provisions clear
For marriage, or for such things, so to speak.
I hold a mouse's heart not worth a leek
Who's only got one hole where it can run,
And if that fails, then everything is done.   580
      I made him think he had enchanted me—
My mother taught me all that subtlety—
And said I had dreamed this of him all night:
As I lay on my back he'd slain me quite,
And I dreamed full of blood then was my bed;   585
'But yet I hope you'll do me good,' I said,
'For blood betokens gold, as was taught me.'
And all was false; I had no dream, you see,
But I always followed my mother's lore,
In this as well as other things before.   590
      But now, sirs, let's see what I shall say then.
Aha! By God, I've got my tale again.
      When my fourth husband lay up on his bier,
I wept quite long and made a sorry cheer,
As wives must, for it is common usage.   595
With my coverchief, I hid my visage,
But since I was provided with my next mate,
I didn't weep much—this to you I'll state.
      To church was my husband borne next morning
With the neighbors, who for him were mourning;   600
And there Jenkin, our clerk, was one of those.

---

1. Medieval dramas focused on the lives and acts of the saints or on events from the Bible (also
called "mystery plays"); performed in the vernacular, they were extremely popular.

So help me God, when I saw how he goes
Behind the bier, I thought he had a pair
Of legs and feet that were so clean and fair,
I gave him all my heart for him to hold.   605
He was, I think, just twenty winters old,
And I was forty, if I tell the truth;
But yet I always had a coltish tooth[2]
Gap toothed was I, and that became me well;
With Venus's seal[3] I'm printed, I can tell.   610
So help me God, I was a lusty one,
And fair and rich and young and well begun,
And truly, as my husbands all told me,
I had the best *quoniam*[4] there might be.
For certainly, I'm all Venerian   615
In feeling, and my heart is Martian.[5]
Venus gave me my love and lecherousness,
And Mars gave me my sturdy hardiness;
My ascendant sign's Taurus,[6] with Mars therein.
Alas! Alas! That ever love was sin!   620
I always followed my inclination
By virtue of my stars' constellation;
Thus I could not withdraw—I was made so—
My chamber of Venus from a good fellow.
Yet I have Mars's mark[7] upon my face,   625
And also in another private place.
For as God so wise is my salvation,
I have never loved in moderation,
But I always followed my appetite,
Should he be long or short or black or white;   630
I took no heed, so long as he liked me,
Of how poor he was, or of what degree.
    What should I say, but at the month's end, he,
This pretty clerk, this Jenkin, so handy,[8]
Has wedded me with great solemnity,   635
And I gave him all the land and property
That ever had been given me before.
But after, I was made to rue that sore;
My desires he would not suffer to hear.
By God, he hit me once upon the ear,   640
Because, out of his book, a leaf I rent,
And from that stroke, my ear all deaf then went.
But, like a lionness, I was stubborn,
And with my tongue, I was a jangler[9] born,
And I would walk around, as I once did,   645
From house to house, although he did forbid;

2. I.e., youthful appetites.
3. An alluring birthmark.
4. Literally, "whereas" (Latin): another slang form for female genitals.
5. Belonging to Mars, the Roman god of war.
6. Sign of the zodiac (April 21–May 20) in which Venus is dominant.
7. Probably a red birthmark.
8. Clever; courteous.
9. Chatterer.

Because of this, quite often he would preach,
And from old Roman stories, he would teach;
How one Simplicius Gallus[1] left his wife,
And her forsook for the rest of his life,   650
Because one day, and for no reason more,
Bareheaded she was looking out the door.
    Another Roman he told me by name,
Who, since his wife was at a summer's game
Without his knowledge, he then her forsook.   655
And then he would into his Bible look
For the proverb of Ecclesiasticus[2]
Where he commands, and he does forbid thus:
That man shall not suffer wife to roam about.
Then would he say right thus, without a doubt: 660
    'Whoever builds his house up all from willow
And pricks his blind horse over fields so fallow,
And lets his wife go seeking shrines so hallowed,
Is worthy to be hanging on the gallows!'
But all for nought: I didn't give a straw   665
For all his old proverbs or for his saws,
Nor by him would I then corrected be.
I hate him who my vices tells to me,
And so do more of us, God knows, than me.
This drove him mad about me, utterly;   670
For I wouldn't bear with any of this.
    I'll tell you the truth now, by Saint Thomas,[3]
Why once out of his book a leaf I rent,
For which he hit me so that deaf I went.
    He had a book that, gladly, night and day,   675
For his pleasure, he would be reading always;[4]
It's called Valerius and Theophrastus;
He always laughed as he read it to us.
And also there was once a clerk at Rome,
A cardinal, who was called Saint Jerome,   680
Who made a book against Jovinian;
In which book was also Tertullian,
Crisippus, Trotula, and Heloise,
An abbess near to Paris, if you please,
And too the Parables of Solomon,   685

1. This story and the next (lines 647–49) are found in Valerius Maximus.
2. See Ecclesiasticus 25.25–26.
3. Thomas Becket, to whose shrine the pilgrims are traveling.
4. This single anthology contains a number of works, all hostile or cast as hostile to women: *Letter of Valerius Concerning Not Marrying*, by Walter Map (12th century); *Against Jovinian* (a 4th-century monk), by the Church Father Jerome (d. 420), which mentions a lost *Golden Book of Marriage* by the Greek philosopher Theophrastus (d. 285 B.C.E.) and writings by the Church Father Tertullian (d. ca. 220) and Crisippus (otherwise unknown); Trotula, a legendary 11th-century Italian female doctor; Heloise (d. 1164), a participant in a scandalous love affair who wrote that philosophers should never marry; the biblical book of Proverbs; and the *Art of Love* by Ovid (43 B.C.E.–17 C.E.), a how-to book on seduction.

Ovid's *Ars,* and more books, many a one,
And all of these in one volume were bound,
And every night and day, some time he found
When he had some leisure and vacation
From his other worldly occupation,   690
To read then in this book of wicked wives.
He knew of them more legends and more lives
Then there are of good wives in the Bible.
For trust it well, it is impossible
For any clerk to speak some good of wives,   695
Unless he speaks about holy saints' lives:
This for no other women will he do.
Now who painted the lion, tell me who?[5]
By God, if women had written stories,
Like clerks do within their oratories,   700
They would have written of men more wickedness
Than all the mark of Adam could redress.
The children of Venus and Mercury[6]
In their actions are always contrary;
Mercury loves both wisdom and science;   705
Venus, revelry and extravagance.
Because of their different dispositions,
Each falls in the other sign's exaltation.
And thus, God knows, Mercury's despondent
In Pisces,[7] when Venus is ascendant,   710
And Venus falls where Mercury is raised.
Therefore, no woman by a clerk is praised.
The clerk, when he is old and may not do
Of Venus's work what's worth his old shoe,
Then he sits down and writes in his dotage   715
That women cannot keep up their marriage!
    But now to my purpose, why I told you
That I was beaten for a book, it's true!
One night Jenkin, who was our lord and sire,
Read in this book, as he sat by the fire,   720
Of Eve first: because of her wickedness,
All mankind was brought into wretchedness,
And thus Jesus Christ himself was slain then,
Who bought us with his own heart's blood again.
Lo, here, expressly, of woman you find   725
That woman was the loss of all mankind.
    He read to me how Samson lost his hair:
His lover cut it while he did sleep there;
And through this treason, he lost both his eyes.[8]
    And then he read to me, if I don't lie,   730

---

5. In one of Aesop's fables, a lion argues that the representation of a man killing a lion did not prove the man's superiority: if a lion could create an artwork, it would depict the opposite.
6. Winged messenger of the Roman gods, the god of commerce and trickery.
7. Sign of the zodiac (February 20–March 20).
8. See Judges 13–16 for the story of Delilah and Samson, whose superhuman strength lay in his hair.

About Dianyra and Hercules;[9]
She made him set himself on fire, if you please.
    Nor forgot he the woe throughout his life
That Socrates[1] endured from his two wives,
How Xantippa cast piss upon his head.   735
This foolish man sat still like he were dead;
He wiped his head and no more dared say plain,
But 'Before thunder stops, there comes the rain!'
    Of Pasiphaë, who was the queen of Crete,
From evilness, the tale seemed to him sweet;   740
Fie! Speak no more—it is a grisly thing—
Of her lust and horrible desiring.[2]
    Of Clytemnestra, who, from lechery,
Falsely made her husband die,[3] you see,
He read out that tale with great devotion.   745
    He told me also on what occasion
Amphiaraus at Thebes had lost his life.[4]
My husband had a legend of his wife,
Eriphyle, who, for a brooch of gold
Has privately unto the Greeks then told   750
Where her husband had kept his hiding place,
And thus at Thebes he suffered sorry grace.
    Of Livia and Lucia,[5] then heard I:
How both of them had made their husbands die,
The one for love, the other one for hate.   755
This Livia, for sure, one evening late,
Poisoned her husband for she was his foe;
Lecherous Lucia loved her husband so
That, to make sure he'd always on her think,
She gave to him such a kind of love-drink   760
He was dead before it was tomorrow;
And thus, always, husbands have had sorrow.
    Then he told me how one Latumius
Complained once to his fellow Arrius
That in his garden there grew such a tree   765
On which, he said, that all of his wives three
Hung themselves with spite, one then another.
Said this Arrius, 'Beloved brother,
Give me a shoot from off that blessèd tree,

---

9. The greatest hero of classical mythology, who died because his wife unwittingly gave him a poisoned cloak. (Many of the following exempla are drawn from myth.)
1. The Greek philosopher (469–399 B.C.E.) immortalized in the dialogues of his pupil Plato; Xantippa is protrayed as a shrew in ancient biographies.
2. The union of Pasiphaë with a bull produced the Minotaur.
3. Conspiring with her lover, the queen of Mycenae murdered her husband, Agamem-

non, when he returned from leading the Greeks in the Trojan War.
4. He was forced to join the war against Thebes, whose disastrous outcome he foresaw, by his wife, who had been bribed.
5. According to Jerome, Livia, who had a lover, deliberately poisoned her husband, Drusus (d. 23 C.E.), whose father later became the Roman emperor Tiberius, and Lucia (Lucilla) accidentally poisoned her husband, the poet Lucretius (d. 55 B.C.E.), with a love potion.

And in my garden, planted it will be.'[6]   770
    And later on, about wives he has read,
And some had slain their husbands in their bed,
And let their lechers hump them all the night,
While on the floor the corpses lay upright.
And some have driven nails into the brain,   775
While they did sleep, and thus they had them slain.
And some did give them poison in their drink.
He spoke more slander than the heart can think,
And on top of it, he knew more proverbs
Than in this world there can grow grass and herbs.   780
'Better,' he said, 'that your habitation
Be either with a lion or foul dragon,
Than with a woman who is used to chide.
Better,' said he, 'high on the roof abide,
Than down in the house with an angry wife;[7]   785
They're so wicked and contrary all their lives,
That they hate what their husbands love always.'
He said, 'A woman casts her shame away,
When she casts off her shift.' He spoke more so:
'A fair woman, unless she's chaste also,   790
Is just like a gold ring in a sow's nose.'[8]
Who would imagine, or who would suppose
The woe that in my heart was, and the pain?
    And when I saw he never would refrain
From reading on this cursèd book all night,   795
Then suddenly, three leaves I have ripped right
Out of his book, as he read, and also
With my fist, I took him on the cheek so
That backward in our fire, right down fell he.
He starts up like a lion who's gone crazy,   800
And with his fist, he hit me on the head
So on the floor I lay like I were dead.
And when he saw how still it was I lay,
He was aghast, and would have fled away,
Till, at last, out of my swoon I awoke.   805
'Oh! Hast thou slain me, false thief?' then I spoke,
'And for my land, hast thou now murdered me?
Before I'm dead, yet will I still kiss thee.'
    And fairly he knelt down when he came near,
And he said, 'Alison, my sister dear,   810
Never more will I hit you, in God's name!
If I've done so, you are yourself to blame.
I pray you, your forgiveness now I seek.'
And right away, I hit him on the cheek,
And said, 'Thief, now this much avenged am I;   815
I may no longer speak, now I will die.'
But then, at last, after much woe and care,

6. A story told in the *Letter of Valerius*.   8. Proverbs 11.22.
7. Proverbs 21.9.

We two fell into an agreement there,
He gave me all the bridle in my hand
To have the governing of house and land,   820
And of his tongue, and of his hands, then, too;
I made him burn his book without ado.
And when I had then gotten back for me,
By mastery, all the sovereignty,
And when he said to me, 'My own true wife,   825
Do as you like the rest of all your life;
Keep your honor, and keep my rank and state'—
After that day, we never had debate.
God help me so, there's no wife you would find
From Denmark to India who was so kind,   830
And also true, and so was he to me.
I pray to God, who sits in majesty,
To bless his soul with all his mercy dear.
Now will I tell my tale, if you will hear."

Behold the words between the Summoner and the Friar.

    The Friar laughed, when he had heard all this;   835
"Madame," said he, "so have I joy or bliss,
This is a long preamble to a tale!"
The Summoner had heard his windy gale,
"By God's two arms," the Summoner said, "lo!
Always will a friar interfere so.   840
Lo, good men, a fly and then a friar
Will both fall in every dish and matter.
Of preambulation, what's to say of it?
What! Amble, trot, keep still, or just go sit!
You're hindering our sport in this manner."   845
    "You say so, sir Summoner?" said the Friar;
"Now, by my faith, I shall, before I go,
Tell a tale of a summoner, you know,
That all the folks will laugh at in this place."
    "Now, elsewise, Friar, I do curse your face,"   850
Said this Summoner. "And I curse myself, too,
Unless I tell some tales, at least a few,
Of friars before I come to Sittingbourne[9]
So that, be sure, I will make your heart mourn.
I know full well that you're out of patience."   855
    Our Host cried out, "Peace now! And that at once!"
And he said, "Let the woman tell her tale.
You act like folks who are all drunk on ale.
Do, madame, tell your tale, and all the rest."
    "All ready, sir," said she, "as you think best,   860
If I have license of this worthy Friar."
    "Yes, madame," said he, "tell on. I will hear."

Here the Wife of Bath ends her Prologue.

9. A town on the road to Canterbury, 40 miles from London.

The Wife of Bath's Tale

Here begins the Tale of the Wife of Bath.

In the olden days of good King Arthur,
Of whom Britons still speak with great honor,
This whole land was all filled up with fairies.   865
The elf queen, with her pretty company,
Went dancing then through many a green mead.
I think this was the old belief, indeed;
I speak of many hundred years ago.
But now no one sees elves and fairies go,   870
For now all the charity and prayers
Of limitors[1] and other holy friars,
Who haunt through every land and every stream
As thick as motes floating in a sun beam,
Blessing halls and chambers, kitchens, bowers,   875
Cities, boroughs, castles, and high towers,
Barns and villages, cowsheds and dairies—
This is the reason why there are no fairies.
For there where once was wont to walk an elf,
Now there the begging friar walks himself   880
In the afternoons and in the mornings,
He says his matins[2] and his holy things
As he walks all throughout his begging grounds.
Now women may go safely all around.
In every bush and under every tree,   885
There is no other incubus[3] but he,
And he'll do them no harm but dishonor.
     So it happened that this good King Arthur
Once had a lusty knight, a bachelor,
Who, one day, came riding from the river,   890
And it chanced that, as he was born, alone,
He saw a maiden walking on her own,
From which maid, then, no matter what she said,
By very force, he took her maidenhead;
This oppressive violence caused such clamor,   895
And such a suit for justice to King Arthur
That soon this knight was sentenced to be dead,
By the course of law, and should have lost his head—
By chance that was the law back long ago—
Except the queen and other ladies also   900
So long had then prayed to the king for grace
Till he had granted his life in that place,
And gave him to the queen, to do her will,
To choose whether she would him save or kill.
     The queen then thanked the king with all her might,   905

---

1. Friars licensed to beg in a specific territory.
2. I.e., morning prayers.

3. An evil spirit believed to have sex with women as they sleep.

And after this, thus spoke she to the knight,
When, on a day, she saw that it was time.
"You stand," she said, "in this state for your crime:
That of your life, you've no security.
I grant you life, if you can tell to me   910
What thing it is that women most desire.
Keep your neck-bone from the ax now, sire!
And if, at once, the answer you don't know,
Still, I will give you leave so you can go
A twelvemonth and a day, to search and learn   915
Sufficient answer before you return;
Before you leave, I'll have security
That here you'll surrender up your body."

    Woe was this knight, and he sighs sorrowfully;
But what! He can't do all he likes completely.   920
And at last, he decided that he'd wend
His way and come back home at the year's end,
With such an answer as God would convey;
He takes his leave and goes forth on his way.

    He seeks in every house and every place   925
Where he has hopes that he'll find some good grace
To learn the thing that women love the most,
But he could not arrive on any coast
Where he might find out about this matter,
Two creatures who agreed on it together.   930

    Some said that all women best loved richness,
Some said honor, and some said jolliness,
Some, rich array, and some said lust in bed,
And often times to be widowed and wed.

    Some said that our hearts were most often eased   935
When we could be both flattered and well pleased.
He got quite near the truth, it seems to me.
A man shall win us best with flattery,
Solicitude, and eager busyness.
Thus we are captured, both the more and less.   940

    And some said that the best of all love we
To do what pleases us, and to be free,
And that no man reproves us for our folly,
But says that we are wise and never silly.
For truly, there is not one of us all,   945
If any one will claw us where it galls,
That we won't kick when what he says is true.
Try, and he'll find it so who will so do;
For, be we ever so vicious within,
We want to be held wise and clean of sin.   950

    And some say that we find it very sweet
To be thought dependable and discreet,
And in one purpose steadfastly to dwell,
And not betray a thing that men us tell.
A rake handle isn't worth that story.   955
We women can't keep secrets, by God's glory;

See Midas—will you hear the tale withal?[4]
    Once Ovid, among some other things small,
Said Midas covered up with his long hair,
On his head two ass's ears that grew there,   960
And this flaw he did hide as best he might
Quite cleverly from every mortal's sight,
So that, save for his wife, no one did know.
He loved her most, and trusted her also;
He prayed her that to no other creature   965
She would tell how he was so disfigured.
    She swore to him, "No"; all this world to win,
She would not do that villainy or sin,
To make her husband have so foul a name.
She wouldn't tell because of her own shame.   970
But, nonetheless, it seemed to her she died
Because so long she must that secret hide;
She thought it swelled so sorely near her heart
That some word from her must, by needs, depart;
Since she dared not tell it to any man,   975
Down to the marsh that was nearby, she ran—
Until she got there, her heart was on fire—
And as a bittern[5] bellows in the mire,
Down by the water, she did her mouth lay:
"Thou water, with your sound do not betray: 980
To thee I tell, and no one else," she said;
"My husband has long ass ears on his head!
Now is my heart all whole; now is it out.
I could no longer keep it, without doubt."
Here you see, if a time we might abide,   985
Yet it must out; we can no secret hide.
If of this tale you want to hear the rest,
Read Ovid, and there you will learn it best.
    This knight, about whom my tale is concerned,
Seeing that the answer he'd not learned—   990
That is to say, what women love the best—
Sorrowful was the spirit in his breast.
But home he goes; no more might he sojourn;
The day had come when homeward he must turn.
And on his way, it happened he did ride,   995
With all his cares, near to a forest's side,
Where he saw come together for a dance,
Some four and twenty ladies there by chance;
Toward which dance he eagerly did turn,
In hopes some wisdom from them he might learn.   1000
But truly, before he had arrived there,
The dancing ladies vanished—who knew where.
No creature saw he left there who bore life,
Save on the green, he saw sitting a wife[6]—

---

4. See Ovid, *Metamorphoses* 11.172–93 (where Midas's secret is discovered by a servant, not by his wife).

5. A wading bird with a deep, booming call.
6. A woman.

A fouler creature, none imagine might.   1005
This old wife then arose to meet the knight.
"Sir knight, there's no road out of here," said she.
"What you are seeking, by your faith, tell me.
Perhaps, then, you'll be better prospering."
She said, "These old folks can know many things."   1010
    "Beloved mother," said this knight, "it's fate
That I am dead unless I can relate
What thing it is that women most desire.
Could you tell me, I'd well repay your hire."
    "Pledge me your troth," said she, "here in my hand,   1015
And swear to me the next thing I demand,
You shall do it if it lies in your might,
And I'll tell you the answer before night."
    "I grant," he said, "you have this pledge from me."
    "Then, sire, I dare well boast to you," said she,   1020
"Your life is safe, and I will stand thereby;
Upon my life, the queen will say as I.
Let see who is the proudest of them yet
Who wears either a coverchief or hairnet
Who dares say 'Nay' to what I will you teach.   1025
Let us go forth without a longer speech."
Then she whispered a message in his ear,
And bade him to be glad, and have no fear.
    When they came to the court, this knight did say
That, as he'd pledged, he had held to his day,   1030
And he said his answer was ready then.
Many noble wives and many maidens
And many widows, because wise are they,
With the queen sitting as the judge that day,
Were all assembled, his answer to hear;   1035
And then this knight was told he should appear.
    It was commanded that there should be silence
And that the knight should tell in audience
The thing that worldly women love the best.
The knight did not stand like a beast at rest;   1040
At once to his question then he answered
With manly voice, so all the court it heard:
    "My liege lady, generally," said he,
"Women desire to have sovereignty
As well over their husbands as their loves,   1045
And to be in mastery them above.
This is your greatest desire, though me you kill.
Do as you like; I am here at your will."
In all the court, there was no wife or maiden
Nor widow who denied what he had said then,   1050
But they said he was worthy of his life.
And with that word, then, up jumps the old wife,
Whom the knight had seen sitting on the green:
"Mercy," said she, "my sovereign lady queen!
Before your court departs, by me do right.   1055

I taught this very answer to this knight;
For which he pledged to me his troth and hire,
So that the first thing I'd of him require,
This he would do, if it lay in his might.
Before the court, then I pray you, sir knight," 1060
Said she, "that you now take me for your wife,
For well you know that I have saved your life.
Upon my faith, if I say false, say 'nay.'"

    This knight answered, "Alas, and well away!
I know that was my promise, I'll be blessed. 1065
But for God's love now, choose a new request!
Take all my goods, and let my body go."

    "Oh no," said she, "I curse us both then so!
For though I may be foul and poor and old,
I'd not want all the metal, ore, or gold 1070
That's buried in the earth or lies above,
Unless I were your lady and your love."

    "My love?" said he, "oh, no, my damnation!
Alas, that one of my birth and station
Ever should so foully disparaged be!" 1075
But all for naught; the end is this, that he
Constrained was here; by needs, he must her wed,
And take his old wife, and go off to bed.

    Now here some men would want to say perhaps
That I take no care—so it is a lapse— 1080
To tell you all the joy and the array
That at the wedding feast was on that day:
To which, my answer here is short and small:
I say there was no joy or feast at all.
Only sorrow and heaviness, I say. 1085
For privately he wedded her next day,
And all day after, he hid like an owl,
For woe was he that his wife looked so foul.

    Great was the woe the knight had in his thoughts,
When he was with his wife to their bed brought; 1090
He wallows and he writhes there, to and fro.
His old wife just lay smiling, even so,
And said, "Oh husband dear, God save my life!
Like you, does every knight fare with his wife?
Is this the law here in the house of Arthur? 1095
Is each knight to his wife aloof with her?
I am your own love, and I am your wife;
And I am she who has just saved your life.
Surely, toward you I have done only right;
Why fare you thus with me on this first night? 1100
You're faring like a man who's lost his wits,
What's my guilt? For love of God, now tell it,
And it will be amended if I may."

    "Amended?" said this knight, "Alas! No way!
It will not be amended, this I know. 1105
You are so loathly, and so old also,

And come from such low lineage, no doubt,
Small wonder that I wallow and writhe about.
I would to God my heart burst in my breast!"
     "Is this," said she, "the cause of your unrest?" 1110
     "Yes," said he, "no wonder is, that's certain."
     "Sir," said she, "I could mend this again,
If I liked, before there'd passed days three,
If you might now behave well toward me.
     But since you speak now of such gentleness[7] 1115
As descends to you down from old richness,
So that, because of it, you're gentle men,
Such arrogance is just not worth a hen.
See who is most virtuous all their lives,
In private and in public, and most strives 1120
To always do what gentle deeds he can:
Now take him for the greatest gentle man.
Christ wills we claim from him our gentleness,
Not from our elders and from their old richness.
Though they leave us their worldly heritage, 1125
And we claim that we're from high lineage,
Yet they may not bequeath a single thing
To us here of their virtuous living,
Which is what made them be called gentle men;
This is the path they bade us follow then. 1130
     Well can he, the wise poet of Florence,
Who's named Dante,[8] speak forth with this sentence.
Lo, Dante's tale is in this kind of rhyme:
'Seldom up his family tree's branches climbs
A man's prowess, for God, in his goodness, 1135
Wills that from him we claim our gentleness';
For, from our elders, we may no thing claim
But temporal things that may hurt us and maim.
     And every man knows this as well as me,
If gentleness were planted naturally 1140
In a certain lineage down the line, yet
They'd not cease in public or in private,
From gentleness, to do their fair duty;
They might not then do vice or villainy.
     Take fire and bring it in the darkest house, 1145
From here to mountains of the Caucasus,[9]
And let men shut the doors and go return;
Yet still the fire will lie as fair and burn
Like twenty thousand men might it behold;
Its natural duty it will always hold, 1150
On my life, till extinguished it may be.

---

7. Gentility; nobility.
8. Dante Alighieri (1265–1321), Florentine poet whose *Divine Comedy* had a significant influence on Chaucer; the following lines echo *Purgatorio* 7.121–23.
9. The mountain range on the southwest border of Russia, between the Black and Caspian Seas.

Here, may you well see how gentility
Is not connected to one's possessions,
Since folks don't follow its operation
Always, as does the fire, lo, in its kind.   1155
For, God knows it, men may well often find
That a lord's son does shame and villainy;
And he who wants praise for his gentility,
Since a gentle house he was born into,
And had elders full of noble virtue,   1160
And who will not himself do gentle deeds,
And dead gentle ancestors hardly heeds,
He is not gentle, be he duke or earl;
A villain's sinful deeds do make a churl.
For such gentleness is only fame   1165
From your elders' high goodness and their name,
Which is a thing your person does not own.
Your gentleness must come from God alone.
Thus our true gentleness must come from grace;
It's not a thing bequeathed us with our place.   1170
    Think how noble, as says Valerius,
Was this one Tullius Hostillius,[1]
Nobility did poverty succeed.
Read Seneca, and Boethius[2] read;
There you shall see expressly that, indeed,   1175
The man is gentle who does gentle deeds.
And therefore, my dear husband, I conclude:
Though my ancestors were humble and rude,
Yet may the high God, and for this I pray,
Grant me grace to live virtuously each day.   1180
I am gentle, whenever I begin,
To live virtuously and to waive sin.
    You reproach me for poverty, indeed,
High God above, on whom we base our creed,
In willing poverty did live his life.   1185
And certainly each man, maiden, or wife
May understand that Jesus, heaven's king,
Would not choose a vicious way of living.
Glad poverty's an honest thing, it's true;
Thus Seneca and other clerks say, too.   1190
He who sees he's well paid by poverty,
Though he had no shirt, he seems rich to me.
He is a poor man who can only covet,
For he wants what he lacks power to get;
He who has naught, and does not covet, too,   1195
Is rich, though he a peasant seems to you.
True poverty, it sings out properly;

1. Third king of Rome (7th century B.C.E.);
according to legend, he began life as a herdsman.
2. Christian Roman philosopher (d. 474),
whose *Consolation of Philosophy*, written in
prison before his execution, was translated
from Latin by Chaucer. Seneca the Younger
(d. 65 C.E.), Roman Stoic moralist and dramatist who committed suicide by order of the
emperor Nero.

Now Juvenal[3] says of it merrily:
'The poor man, when he should go by the way,
Before the thieves, this man can sing and play.'   1200
Poverty is a hateful good, I guess,
A great encouragement to busyness;
Great improver of wisdom and good sense
For him who can suffer it with patience.
Poverty, though miserable seems its name,   1205
Is a possession no one else will claim.
Poverty often, when a man is low,
Can make him both his God and himself know.
Poverty's an eyeglass, it seems to me,
Through which he might his good and true friends see.   1210
And sire, now, if I don't grieve you, therefore
For poverty don't blame me anymore.

    Now, sire, with old age you have reproached me;
And truly, sire, though no authority
Were in books, you gentlemen of honor   1215
Say folks to an old man should show favor
And call him father, in your gentleness;
And I shall find authorities, I guess.

    Now, since you say that I am foul and old,
You don't have to fear to be a cuckold;   1220
For filth and age, so far as I can see,
Are great wardens upon one's chastity.
But, nonetheless, since I know your delight,
I shall fulfill your worldly appetite.

    Choose now," said she, "of these things, one of two: 1225
Till I die, to have me foul and old, too,
And be to you a true and humble wife,
And never displease you in all my life,
Or else you can have now a fair, young thing,
And take your chances with the visiting   1230
That happens at your house because of me,
Or in some other place, as well may be.
Choose yourself whichever one will please you."

    This knight now ponders and sighs sorely, too,
But finally, he said in this way here: 1235
"My lady and my love and wife so dear,
I put myself in your wise governing;
Choose yourself which one may be most pleasing
And most honor to both you and me too.
I do not care now which one of the two;   1240
What pleases you suffices now for me."

    "Then have I got mastery from you," said she,
"Since I may choose and govern all the rest?"

      "Yes, truly, wife," said he, "I think it best."

      "Kiss me," said she, "we are no longer angry,   1245

---

3. Roman poet (d. ca. 120 C.E.); the quotation is from *Satire* 10.22.

For, by my troth,[4] to you I will both be—
Yes, now both fair and good, as will be plain.
I pray to God that I might die insane,
Unless to you I'm also good and true
As any wife's been, since the world was new.   1250
Unless tomorrow I'm as fair to see
As any queen or empress or lady,
Who is between the east and then the west,
Do with my life and death as you think best.
Cast up the curtain; how it is, now see."   1255
    And when the knight saw all this verily,
That she now was so fair and so young, too,
For joy he seized her within his arms two,
His heart was all bathed in a bath of bliss.
A thousand times in a row, he did her kiss,   1260
And she obeyed him then in everything
That was to his pleasure or his liking.
    And thus they both lived until their lives' end
In perfect joy; and Jesus Christ us send,
Husbands meek and young and fresh in bed,   1265
And the grace to outlive those whom we wed;
I pray that Jesus may shorten the lives
Of those who won't be governed by their wives;
And old and stingy niggards who won't spend,
To them may God a pestilence soon send!   1270

The Nun's Priest's Prologue and Tale

The Prologue Of The Nun's Priest's Tale

"Whoa!" said the Knight, "good sire,[1] no more, I pray!
What you have said is just enough today,
And so much more; for a little sadness
Is quite enough for many folks, I guess.
I say, for me, it causes great unease,
When men have lived in both great wealth and ease,   5
To hear about their sudden fall, alas!
The contrary is great joy and solace,
As when a man of a poor rank has been,
And he can climb and wax fortunate then,   10
And rest on high in great prosperity.
Such a thing is pleasing, it seems to me.
Of such a thing it would be good to tell."
"Yes," said our Host, "now by Saint Paul's own bell!
You tell the truth; this Monk, he chatters loud.   15
He said how Fortune covered with a cloud

4. I.e., "I swear."
1. The Knight interrupts the Monk, whose tale consists of a number of short, tragic stories.

I know not what; and also tragedy
Right now you heard, and God, no remedy
It is now to lament or to complain
About what's done, and also, it's a pain,
As you have said, hearing about sadness.   20
        Sir Monk, no more of this, may God you bless!
Your tale's annoying all the company.
Such talking is not worth a butterfly,
For therein is found neither sport nor game.
And thus, sir Monk, Don Piers, as is your name,   25
Something else, heartily I pray, now tell;
If it weren't for the clinking of your bells
That on your bridle hang on every side,
By heaven's king, who for us all has died,
I should before have fallen down asleep,   30
Although the mud had never been so deep;
Then your tale would have been all told in vain.
For certainly, as these clerks do explain,
When there's a man who has no audience,
It doesn't help that his tale has substance.   35
        And well I know, the meaning's clear for me,
When anything shall well reported be.
Sire, tell something of hunting, I you pray."
        "No," said this Monk, "I have no urge to play.   40
Now let another tell, for my tale's told."
Then our Host spoke with his speech rude and bold,
And said right to the Nun's Priest,[2] "Now, come on!
Come near, you priest, come hither, you, sir John!
To cheer our hearts, you should tell us something.   45
Be happy, though on a nag you're riding.
So what if your horse is both foul and lean?
If he serves you, don't count it worth a bean.
See your heart merry while you are alive."
        "Yes, sir," said he, "yes, Host, so may I thrive,   50
Unless I'm merry, I'm a scolded man."
And right away, his tale then he began,
And spoke to each of us as we rode on,
This sweet priest and this goodly man, sir John.

It ends.

The Nun's Priest's Tale

*Here begins the Nun's Priest's Tale of the Cock and Hen,
Chanticleer and Pertelote.*

A poor woman, somewhat stooped down with age,   55
Once was dwelling in a narrow cottage,
Beside a grove there, standing in a dale.

2. I.e., the Prioress's chaplain.

This widow, about whom I tell my tale,
Since that day when she was last a wife,
In patience led a very simple life, 60
For small were her income and her chattel.
By husbanding what God has sent her well,
For herself and two daughters she provides.
Three large sows had she, and no more besides,
Three cows, and then also a sheep named Moll. 65
Quite sooty were her bower and her hall,
In which she ate many a slender meal.
With tangy sauce she didn't need to deal.
No dainty morsel through her throat did get,
For her small farm did dictate her diet. 70
Overindulgence never made her sick;
Temperate diet was her only physic,
Exercise, and a heart that was content.
From dancing, the gout did her not prevent,
And apoplexy did not hurt her head. 75
No wine did she drink, neither white nor red;
Her table was served most with white and black—
Milk and brown bread—in which she found no lack,
Smoked bacon, and sometimes an egg would do,
Because she was a dairywoman, too. 80
      A yard she had, enclosed on every side
With sticks, and a dry ditch on the outside,
In which she had a cock named Chanticleer.
For crowing, in this land, he had no peer,
With his voice merrier than the merry organ 85
Whose notes, on mass-days, in the church began.
When he crowed in his shed, surer was he
Than a clock or timepiece of an abbey.
By nature, he knew each revolution
Of hours as they rose in their ascension, 90
For when fifteen degrees had ascended,[3]
He crowed so it could not be amended.
His comb's redder than the finest coral,
And crenellated like a castle wall;
His bill is black, and just like jet, it glows; 95
Azure like lapus are his legs and toes;
His nails, whiter than the lily flower,
And like burnished gold is all his color.
This gentle cock had in his governing
Full seven hens to do his pleasuring, 100
His sisters, concubines, and paramours,
Wonderfully like him in their colors;
The one whose hue was fairest on her throat
Was called "The Fair Demoiselle Pertelote."
Courteous she was, gracious, debonnaire, 105
Obliging, and she bore herself so fair

---

3. The number of degrees figured to be in a clock hour [translator's note].

Since on the day that she was seven nights old
That truly, she has all the heart to hold
Of Chantecleer, locked up in every limb;   110
He loved her so that all was well with him.
But such a joy it was to hear them sing,
When first the bright sun up began to spring,
In sweet harmony, "My love's left the land!"—
For at that time, as I do understand,
All beasts and birds back then could speak and sing.   115
          So it happened when the day was dawning,
As Chantecleer there among his wives all
Sat on his perch, which was placed in the hall,
And next to him sat his fair Pertelote,
Chantecleer began groaning in his throat,   120
Like a man who, in dreams, has troubles sore.
And when his Pertelote thus heard him roar,
She was aghast and said, "O, my heart dear,
What ails you to groan in this manner here?
You are such a sound sleeper! For shame! Fie!"   125
          "Madame," he said, and thus he answered, "I
Pray to you that from this you take no grief.
By God, I dreamed that I was in such mischief
Right now that my heart still is sore with fright.
Now God," said he, "my dream interpret right,   130
And out of foul prison my body keep!
I roamed around, as I dreamed in my sleep,
Within our yard, when there I saw a beast
Like a hound, who'd have made arrest at least
On my body, or would have had me dead.   135
His color was between yellow and red;
Tipped was his tail and both of his ears there
With black, unlike the rest of all his hairs;
His snout was small; and glowing was his eye.
Yet, from his look, for fear, almost I die.   140
This caused me my groaning, it is doubtless."
          "Shame!" said she, "fie on you, coward spineless!
Alas," said she, "for, by that God above,
Now have you lost my heart and all my love!
By my faith, I cannot love a coward!   145
Surely, as any woman's said or heard,
We all desire, if it might ever be,
Husbands bold and wise, generous and free,
Also discreet—and no niggard or fool,
Nor one afraid of each weapon and tool,   150
Nor a boaster, by the good God above!
How dare you say, for shame, right to your love
That there is anything that you have feared?
Have you no man's heart, but still have a beard?
Alas! Aghast of dreams can you now be?   155
God knows, nothing's in dreams but vanity.

Dreams are engendered from satiation,
From gas and bodily disposition,
When your humors abound more than is right.
Surely this dream, which you have had tonight,   160
Comes straight from the great superfluity
Of red choleric humor, as you see,
Which causes folks within their dreams to dread
Both sharp arrows and then fire with flames red,
And red beasts, too, which they fear will them bite,   165
And strife and dogs, both great and small in might;
Just as the humor of melancholy
Makes many men in sleep cry openly
For fear both of black bears and of bulls black,
Or of black devils who might take them back.   170
Of other humors could I tell also
That work so men have sleep that's full of woe;
But I'll pass them by lightly as I can.
        Lo! See Cato,[4] who was so wise a man,
Said he not thus: 'Pay no heed now to dreams'?   175
Sire," said she, "when we fly down from these beams,
For God's love, now, please take some laxative.
By my soul's peril while here I may live,
I advise for the best—no lies from me—
That both of choler and melancholy   180
You purge yourself; and so you won't tarry,
Though in this town there's no apothecary,
To certain herbs I myself shall you lead
For both your health and benefit, indeed;
And in our yard, those herbs for you I'll find   185
Whose properties, by nature of their kind,
Can purge you both below and then above.
Don't you forget all this, by God's own love!
You're choleric in your disposition;
Watch out that the sun, in its ascension,   190
Won't find you filled up with hot humors yet.
And if it does, a groat I'd dare well bet
You shall have a reoccurring fever,
Or an ague that proves to be a killer.
For a day or two, you'll have digestives   195
Of worms, before you take your laxatives
Made from spurge laurel and fumitory,
From hellebore growing here and centaury,
From caper spurge, or else then from rhamus,
From ground ivy growing in our yard thus;   200
Peck them right where they grow and eat them in.
Be merry, husband, by your father's kin!
And dread no dream; I can tell you no more."
        "Madame," said he, "all thanks be for your lore."

4. Third- or fourth-century author of a Latin schoolbook of proverbs.

Nonetheless, regarding good Don Cato, 205
Who, for wisdom has great renown, I know,
Though he bade us that no dreams should we dread,
By God, in many old books, men have read
From many men of more authority
Than Cato, may I thrive prosperously, 210
Who say the reverse of his evidence,
And who have well found through experience
That dreams become the significations
Both of the joys and the tribulations
That folks here endure in this life present. 215
Of this, we need now make no argument;
The very proof of it shows in the deed.
    Of the greatest authorities men read,
One has said thus: that once two fellows went
On pilgrimage, with quite a good intent. 220
It happened, this was the situation:
In a town with such a congregation
Of people, and with few places to stay,
Not so much as a small cottage found they
In which the two of them might sheltered be. 225
Therefore they must, out of necessity,
For that one night, both part their company;
And each of them goes to his hostelry,
And took his lodging, whereso it might fall.
And one of them was lodged within a stall, 230
Far in a yard, with the plow and oxen;
That other man was lodged well enough then,
As was his fortune or his luck and chance,
That holds the world in common governance.
    So it happened, long before it was day, 235
This man dreamed in his bed, right where he lay,
How his fellow began on him to call,
And said, 'Alas, for in an ox's stall
This night I shall be murdered where I lie!
Now help me, brother dear, or else I'll die,' 240
He said, 'In all haste, now come to me here!'
From his sleep, this man started up in fear;
But when he'd wakened from his sleep indeed,
Over he turned and took of this no heed.
He thought his dream was only vanity. 245
Twice thus while he was sleeping, dream did he;
The third time his friend came, he did explain,
It seemed to him, and said, 'I am now slain.
Behold my wounds bloody and wide and deep!
Tomorrow rise up early from your sleep, 250
And at the west gate of the town,' said he,
'A cart there full of dung then you will see,
In which my body's hidden privately,
And at once have this same cart seized boldly.

My gold has caused my murder, the truth's plain.' 255
In detail he told him how he was slain,
With a piteous face all pale of hue.
And trust it well; his dream he found quite true.
In the morning, as soon as it was day,
Right to his fellow's inn, he took his way; 260
And when he came up to this oxen's stall,
After his fellow, he began to call.

      The innkeeper answered him directly,
And he said, 'sir, your fellow's gone, you see.
As soon as day came, out of town he went.' 265

      The man suspicious got of what he meant,
Remembering what his three dreams did say,
And forth he goes—he'd no longer delay—
To the town's west gate, and he found at hand
A dung cart set up to manure the land, 270
Which was arrayed in the exact same way
As you heard the dead man describe and say.
With an emboldened heart aloud cried he
For a just vengeance on this felony:
'My fellow has been murdered this same night; 275
In this cart, he lies there, gaping upright.
I cry out to the magistrates,' said he,
'Who should both protect and rule this city.
Harrow! Alas! Here lies my fellow slain!'
What should I more about this tale explain? 280
Out people ran and cast the cart to ground,
And in the middle of the dung they found
The dead man there, who murdered was all new.

      O blissful God, who is so just and true,
Lo, how you'll reveal a murder always! 285
Murder will out, as we see day by day.
Murder loathsome and abominable
To God, who's so just and reasonable,
That he won't suffer it concealed to be,
Though it should wait a year or two or three. 290
Murder will out; this is my conclusion.
The town's ministers, without hesitation,
Seized the carter and sorely did him torture,
And the innkeep sorely on the rack for sure;
Their wickedness they did confess and own, 295
And both then were hanged right by the neck bone.

      So here may men see that dreams are to dread.
And certainly, in the same book, I read,
Right there in the next chapter after this—
I'm not lying, may I have joy or bliss— 300
Of two men wanting to go out to sea,
For a reason, into a far country,
If the wind had not blown up contrary,
Making them then in a city tarry

That stood there by a harbor pleasantly;   305
But one day, before evening shortly,
The wind did change, and blew as they liked best.
Jolly and glad, they went right to their rest,
And they made plans quite early to set sail.
Hark! One man had a great marvel prevail: 310
For one of them, there sleeping as he lay,
A wondrous dream had early in the day.
It seemed a man was standing at his bedside,
Commanding him that his time he should bide,
And told him thus: 'If tomorrow you sail,   315
You shall be drowned; that's the end of my tale.'
He woke and told his friend what he dreamed then,
And prayed him this voyage to abandon;
And for that day, he prayed, his time to bide.
His fellow, who's lying by his bed's side,   320
Began to laugh, and heaped the scorn on fast.
'No dream,' said he, 'makes my heart so aghast
That I will hesitate to do my things.
I don't give a straw for all your dreamings,
For dreams are only vanities and japes.   325
All day men can dream of owls and apes,
And such sources of amazement plenty;
Men dream about things that shall never be.
But, now since you'll wait here, as I see,
And willingly waste your time slothfully,   330
Lord, it makes me sorry. Have a good day!'
And thus he took his leave and went his way.
But before half of his course he had sailed,
I don't know why or what bad luck it ailed,
But, by chance, the ship's bottom was all rent,   335
And ship and man beneath the water went
In sight of other ships there alongside,
Which were sailing with them on the same tide.
Therefore, I say, my dear, fair Pertelote,
That from such old examples, you may note   340
And learn that no man should be so heedless
Of his dreams; for as I tell you, doubtless,
There are many sad dreams that should cause dread.
        Lo, in the life of Saint Kenelm[5] I read—
He who was Kenwulf's son, the noble king   345
Of Mercia—how Kenelm had dreamed a thing.
A bit before he was murdered, one day,
His murder in a vision came his way.
His nurse expounded in every respect
His dream to him, and told him to protect   350
Himself from treason; but, seven years old,
Of his dreams, little notice did he hold,

5. Legendary Anglo-Saxon boy-king (9th century), venerated in the Middle Ages.

His heart so holy thought dreams could not hurt.
By God! I would for this give up my shirt,
If you had read this legend, just like me.   355
     Dame Pertelote, I say to you so truly,
Macrobius,[6] who wrote the vision so
In Africa of worthy Scipio,
Has affirmed dreams, because they are, says he,
Warnings of things that afterwards men see.   360
And furthermore, I pray you to look well
In the Old Testament, about Daniel,
If he believed that dreams were vanity.
Moreover, read Joseph,[7] and there you'll see
Whether dreams are sometimes—I don't say all—   365
Warnings of things that later should befall.
Look at Egypt's king, at that Don Pharoah,
And his baker and his butler also,
And see if dreams' effects can overwhelm.
Whoso seeks histories of sundry realms   370
Reads about dreams many a wondrous thing.
Lo Croesus, who of Lydia was king,
Dreamed he not he was sitting on a tree,
Which signified that he soon hanged would be?
Lo here Andromache, good Hector's wife,   375
On the same day that Hector,[8] lost his life,
She did dream on the very night before
How soon that Hector's life would be no more,
For on that day in battle he would fail.
She warned him well, but it was no avail;   380
He went to fight despite all of her pleas.
But at once he was slain by Achilles.
But this same tale is far too long to tell,
And it is almost day; I may not dwell.
Shortly I say, to make my conclusion,   385
That I shall have because of this vision
Adversity; and I say furthermore
That in these laxatives, I set no store;
They are venemous and well I know it;
Them I defy; I love them not one bit!   390
     Now, let us speak of mirth, and stop all this.
Madame Pertelote, so may I have bliss,
In one thing, God has sent to me much grace;
For when I see the beauty of your face—
You are so scarlet red about your eyes—   395

6. Fifth-century author believed in Chaucer's day to have written *Commentary on the Dream of Scipio*, a fictional, dream vision of Scipio Aemilanus, the Roman general who defeated Carthage in 146 B.C.E.
7. Figures associated with prophetic dream visions in the Bible. See Daniel 7 and Genesis 37 [translator's note].
8. Eldest son of Priam, King of Troy, and his wife; while the *Iliad* was unknown to Chaucer, the Troy story was popular.

It makes it so that all my dread just dies;
For just as surely as *In principio,*
Mulier est hominis confusio[9]—
Madame, the meaning of the Latin's this,
'Woman is man's joy and all his bliss.'   400
For when I feel at night your soft, warm side—
Although right then on you I cannot ride,
Since our perch is made too narrow, alas—
I am so full of both joy and solace
That I shall defy both vision and dream."   405
    And with that word, he flew down from his beam—
For it was day—and also his hens all,
And with a cluck, then to them he did call,
For he found corn that in the yard had laid.
Regal he was; he was no more afraid.   410
Full twenty times he feathered Pertelote,
And before prime tread her as much, you'll note.
He looks like he were the grimmest lion,
As he is roaming, his tiptoes upon;
He didn't deign set his foot on the ground.   415
He clucks whenever some corn he has found,
And to him run his wives then, one and all.
Thus royal, like a prince is in his hall,
This Chantecleer I leave in his pasture,
And after, I'll tell of his adventure.   420
    When the month in which the world began,
Which is called March, when first God had made man,[1]
Was all complete, and then there had passed too,
Since March was over, thirty days and two,
It happened Chantecleer in all his pride—   425
His seven wives were walking by his side—
Cast his eyes upward toward the bright sun,
That in the sign of Taurus then had run
Twenty degrees plus one, and somewhat more,
And knew by instinct, and no other lore,   430
It was nine, and crowed with blissful sound then.
"The sun," he said, "has climbed in the heaven
Forty degrees plus one, and more than this.
Madame Pertelote, of my world, my bliss,
Hark to these blissful birds and how they sing,   435
And see here the fresh flowers, how they spring;
Revelry fills my heart, and contentment!"
But quickly to him came a sad event;
Always the later end of joy is woe.
God knows that soon all worldly joy does go;   440
If a rhetorician could tell fairly,
In a chronicle, he might write safely

---

9. In the beginning, woman is the confusion of man (Latin).
1. Common medieval belief held that God cre-
ated the world on the first day of spring (March 20 or 21).

This is a sovereign fact quite notable.
Now, each wise man, hark, if he is able;
This story is as true, I undertake,   445
As is the book of Lancelot of the Lake,[2]
That women hold in such great reverence.
To tell my meaning, I'll now recommence.
     A black-tipped fox of sly iniquity,
Who, in the grove, had dwelled fully years three,   450
By high imagination as forecast,
Throughout the very hedges that night passed
Into the yard where Chanticleer the fair
With his wives was accustomed to repair;
And in a bed of cabbages, he lay   455
Till it was past midmorning of that day,
Biding his time, on Chanticleer to fall,
As gladly do these homicidals all
Who lie in waiting just to murder men.
O false murderer, lurking in your den!   460
O new Iscariot, new Ganelon,
False dissimulator, O Greek Sinon,[3]
Who brought Troy utterly to sorrowing!
O Chantecleer, accursed be that morning
That you into the yard flew from the beams!   465
You were full well forewarned then by your dreams
This very day would come perilously;
But all that God foreknows, thus it need be—
This opinion of a certain clerk is.
Witness on him who a perfect clerk is,   470
That in schools is a great altercation
In this matter, and great disputation,
And has been for a hundred thousand men.
I don't know how to sift it to the bran, then,
As can the holy doctor Augustine,   475
Boethius, or Bishop Bradwardine,[4]
About whether God's worthy foreknowing
Constrains me needfully to do a thing—
"Needfully" I call plain necessity;
Or else, if free choice is granted to me   480
To do that same thing, or just to do naught,
Though God foreknows the deed before it's wrought;
Or if his knowing constrains me not at all
Except by necessity conditional.
I won't deal with such matter, it is clear;   485
My tale's about a cock, as you may hear,
Who took his wife's counsel, to his sorrowing,

---

2. Figure of Arthurian romance; compare *Sir Gawain and the Green Knight*.
3. Betrayers of Christ, Roland and Charlemagne, and Troy, respectively [translator's note].

4. All philosophers and theologians who wrote about the state of the human will. Augustine's *Confessions* and an excerpt from Boethius's *Consolation of Philosophy* appears in this volume.

To walk in the yard that very morning
When he had dreamed the dream that I've you told.
These women's counsels are fatal and cold;   490
These women's counsels brought us first to woe
And from Paradise, they made Adam go,
Though he'd been merry and well at his ease.
But since I don't know whom it might displease,
If I these women's counsel wished to blame,   495
Pass over it; I said it in my game.
Read authorities who make such matters clear,
And what they say of women, you may hear.
For these are the cock's words; they are not mine;
In women, I can no harm divine.   500
　　　　To bathe herself merrily in the sand,
Lies Pertelote, with sisters near at hand;
Chanticleer, in the sun, noble and free,
Sang more merrily than mermaids in the sea
(For Physiologus[5] says certainly   505
How mermaids sing both well and merrily).
And so it happened, as he cast his eye
Among cabbages on a butterfly,
He was aware of this fox, lying low.
Nothing at all made him then want to crow;   510
He cried at once, "Cock! Cock!" and up does start
Like men who are quite frightened in their heart.
For naturally, a beast desires to flee
From his enemy, if he can it see,
Even if he'd never seen it with his eye.   515
　　　　This Chanticleer, when there he did him spy,
He would have fled, but to him the fox said,
"Now, gentle sire, alas, where do you head?
Are you afraid of me, who am your friend?
Now, certainly, may I meet a fiend's end,   520
If to you harm or villainy wished I!
I have not come on your secrets to spy,
But, it is true, the cause of my coming
Was only so I could hear how you sing.
In truth, you have a voice as merry then   525
As an angel who is up in heaven.
And thus, you in music have more feeling
Than Boethius[6] or any who can sing.
My lord your father—may God his soul bless—
And your mother, out of noble gentleness,   530
Have both been in my house to my great ease;
And, surely, sire, quite gladly I'd you please.

---

5. Name of an anonymous second-century Greek book or author of a bestiary or group of stories about real and mythological animals that were given Christian allegorical meanings.

The mermaids were interpreted as sirens in the Middle Ages [translator's note].
6. Boethius's works include a textbook on music theory.

But, since men speak of singing, I will say—
So might I use my two eyes well today—
Except for you, I never heard man sing   535
Like your father first thing in the morning.
True, when he sang, from his heart came his song.
And so that he could make his voice more strong,
He would so pain himself that with both eyes
He then must wink, so loud would be his cries,   540
And he'd step up upon his tiptoes tall,
And stretch forth his neck, which was long and small.
And moreover, he had such discretion
That there was no man in any region
Who him in song or wisdom might surpass.   545
I have well read in *Don Burnel the Ass*,[7]
Among his verses, how there was a cock,
Who, since a priest's son did give him a knock
On the leg when he was young and dumb thus,
He made it so he lost his benefice.   550
But, surely, here, there's no comparison
Between the wisdom and the discretion
Of your father, with all his subtlety.
Now sing, good sire, for holy charity,
Let see: can you your father counterfeit?"   555
        This Chanticleer was beating his wings yet,
Like a man who could not this treason see,
So was he ravished by this flattery.
        Lo, you lords, many a false flatterer
Is in your courts, and many a *losengeour*,[8]   560
Who pleases you much more, as I would guess,
Than he who speaks to you with truthfulness.
Read Ecclesiastes on flattery;
Be wary, you lords, of their treachery.
        This Chanticleer stood high upon his toes,   565
Stretching his neck, and his eyes tight did close,
For the occasion, he crowed quite loudly.
Don Russell the fox started up quickly,
And by the throat seized Chanticleer right there,
And on his back, him toward the woods did bear,   570
For there was no one yet who him pursued.
        O destiny that may not be eschewed!
Alas, that Chanticleer flew from those beams!
Alas, his wife cared not a bit for dreams!
On a Friday fell this misadventure.   575
        Alas, Venus, you goddess of pleasure,
Since your own servant was this Chanticleer,
Who in your service did all he might here,

---

7. *Don Burnel the Ass: The Mirror of Fools*, a
satiric work containing many stories in which
members of the clergy are lampooned as don-

keys, written in the late twelfth century by the
monk Nigel de Longchamps.
8. Liar or flatterer [translator's note].

More for delight than the world to multiply,
Why on your own day would you let him die? 580
    O dear sovereign master, you Sir Geoffrey,[9]
Who, when slain was King Richard so worthy
With an arrow, mourned for his death so sore,
Why have I not your wisdom and your lore,
Like you did to chide Friday, as we see? 585
For, on a Friday, truly, slain was he.
Then I would show you how I could complain
About Chanticleer's dread and for his pain.
    Surely, neither cry not lamentation
Did ladies ever make when Ilion 590
Was won, and when, with his sword drawn by him,
Pyrrhus, by the beard, had seized king Priam,
And slain him, as it says in the *Aeneid*,[1]
As in the yard there all of those hens did,
When they the sight of Chanticleer did see. 595
But Dame Pertelote did shriek supremely,
Much more loudly than did Hasdrubal's[2] wife,
When her own husband there had lost his life
And the Romans burned Carthage to the ground.
She was so filled by torment's rage profound, 600
Into the fire willingly she did start
And burned herself up with a steadfast heart.
    O woeful hens, you all cried exactly
The way, when Nero had burned the city
Of Rome, then cried all the senators' wives 605
Because their husbands guiltless lost their lives—
Nero slew them all as the city burned.
Now back again to my tale I will turn.
    This widow and her two daughters also,
Unknowing, heard these hens cry and make woe; 610
Immediately out of doors they drove,
And saw the fox then going toward the grove,
Who bore upon his back the cock away,
And they cried, "Out! Harrow and wey-la-way!
Ha! Ha! The fox!" and after him they ran, 615
And then, with staves, many another man.
Colle, our dog ran, and Talbot and Garland,
And Malkyn, with her distaff in her hand;
Ran cow and calf, and even ran the hogs,
So frightened by the barking of the dogs 620
And the shouts that the men and women make;
They ran so fast they thought their hearts would break.

9. Geoffrey of Vinsauf, 13th-century Anglo-Norman author whose *Poetria nova* includes a lament on the death of Richard I (1157–1199). 1. See Virgil's *Aeneid* 2, which describes the death of Priam, king of Troy (Ilion), at the hands of Pyrrhus, the son of Achilles. 2. King of Carthage in 146 B.C.E., at the time the Romans under Scipio destroyed it [translator's note].

They yowled just like fiends do down in hell;
The ducks cried like they would be killed as well;
The geese, for fear, flew up over the trees;   625
Out of the hive there came the swarm of bees.
So hideous was the noise—God bless me!—
That surely Jack Straw[3] and his company
Never made shoutings that were half as shrill
When any Flemish they did look to kill,   630
As that day at the fox all of them would.
They brought trumpets made of brass and boxwood,
And horns of bone, in which they puffed and blew,
And with those they shrieked out, and they whooped, too.
It seemed as though right down heaven would fall.   635
And now, good men, I pray you, listen all:
        Lo, see how Fortune does turn suddenly
The hope and pride both of the enemy!
This cock that on the fox's back did lay,
For all his dread, right to the fox did say,   640
And he spoke thus, "Sire, now, if I were you,
I should say, as wise God would help me to,
'Turn back again, you proud churls there, you all!
May a true pestilence upon you fall!
Now right to the woods' side, I have come near;   645
No matter what you do, the cock stays here.
I will eat him, in faith, and quickly, too!'"
        The fox answered, "In faith, that's what I'll do."
And as he spoke that word, all suddenly
This cock broke from his mouth quite agilely,   650
And up into a tree at once did fly.
When the fox saw the cock sit there up high,
"Alas!" said he, "O Chanticleer, alas!
For I have to you done a great trespass.
I made you afraid, catching you off guard,   655
When I seized you and brought you from the yard.
Sire, I did it with no wicked intent.
Come down now, and I'll tell you what I meant;
So God help me, I'll tell the truth to you!"
        "No, then," said he, "I'd curse both of us two.   660
And first, I'd curse myself, both blood and bone,
If you tricked me more than one time alone.
Through flattery, now no more will you try
To make me sing and then wink with closed eye;
For he who winks, when he with eyes should see,   665
Purposely, nevermore shall prosper he!"
        "No," said the fox, "but God give him mischance,
Who's so indiscreet in self-governance
That he jangles when he should be silent."

3. This is one of Chaucer's few references to the Peasants' Revolt of 1381 [translator's note].

Lo, thus it is to be so negligent   670
And reckless, and to trust in flattery,
        But you who think this tale just a folly,
About a fox, or else a cock and hen,
Take from it the morality, good men.
Saint Paul says that all that which is written,   675
For our teaching is truly written, then;[4]
Take the fruit, and let the chaff be still.
        Now, good God, if it should be your will,
As says my Lord, so make us all good men,
And bring us all to his high bliss! Amen.   680

Here is ended the Nun's Priest's Tale.

The Epilogue

"Sir Nun's Priest," our Host said to him quickly,
"Blessed may both your stones[5] and britches be!
A merry tale of Chanticleer we heard.
But, if you were a layman, by my word,
You would be a good treading-fowl, all right.   685
If you've got heart and vigor like you might,
You'd need some hens, if you know what I mean,
Yea, much more than seven times seventeen.
See now what brawn here has this gentle priest,
So great a neck, such a large breast, at least!   690
He looks like a sparrow hawk with his eye;
No need for him his color now to dye
With red hues made of grains from Portugal.
Sire, for your tale, may good luck you befall!"
And after that he, with quite merry cheer,   695
Said to another one, as you shall hear.

---

4. Romans 15.4: "For whatsoever things were written aforetime were written for our learning, that we through patience and comfort of the scriptures might have hope."
5. Testicles.

SIR GAWAIN AND THE GREEN KNIGHT
late fourteenth century

In spite of its modern popularity, and the wider dynamism of the Arthurian tradition, *Sir Gawain and the Green Knight* seems to have largely disappeared for more than four hundred years, until its rediscovery in the early nineteenth century. Surviving in a single manuscript from around 1400, *Sir Gawain and the Green Knight* is a particularly well-written example of the chivalric romance, a genre that was extremely popular in the late Middle Ages. Deeds of knights, both on the tournament field and in the private space of the castle chambers, are at the fore as Gawain ventures out from the court of King Arthur to a peculiar border territory. There, Gawain encounters a mysterious yet affable host and his overly friendly wife, procures a magical device that can save him from harm, and fights with a monstrous Green Knight who wields a terrifying great axe. These extraordinary twists and turns of the plot, coupled with a bold poetic voice, enable *Sir Gawain and the Green Knight* to captivate its twenty-first-century readers as fully as it did those first generations of medieval readers living on the English borderlands.

LIFE AND TIMES

We know very little about the author of *Sir Gawain and the Green Knight*, but we can infer a good deal about his place of origin, the environments within which he moved, and the kinds of books he read. The sole surviving manuscript of the poem, Cotton Nero A.x, contains three other poems that appear from their style and language to have been written by the same author:

Cleanness, a poem that relates the story of Sodom and Gomorrah in order to urge its readers toward spiritual and bodily purity; *Patience*, a retelling of the story of Jonah and his forty days in the belly of the whale; and *Pearl*, an allegorical account of love, loss, death, and the promise of eternal life with Christ. These three works reveal the poet's deep knowledge of the Bible and Christian theology, as well as his familiarity with the practical details of life, such as the parts of a sailing ship described in *Patience*.

In *Sir Gawain and the Green Knight*, the poet's experience in the life of the court is even more fully on display, not just in the account of knight's equipment but also in the terminology used for the practice of hunting, descriptions of the layout of the typical fourteenth-century English castle, and references to the routines of the servants of a castle household. We must in the end recognize this poet as a man of two worlds, one who clearly had an ecclesiastical education whether or not he was himself a priest, but who also engaged with courtly culture. He was as at home with the Bible as with the romances of knights and their ladies—perhaps he was a chaplain in an aristocratic household, or a courtier himself with a strong sense of his Christian soul. That the narrator of *Pearl* alludes specifically to a beloved daughter who has recently died does not argue against the author's having been a clergyman, since it was not uncommon for a man to enter holy orders after the death of a spouse.

Like **Geoffrey Chaucer**, his contemporary, the writer of *Sir Gawain* *and the Green Knight* lived at a time of great social mobility, when the devastation of the Black Death in the mid-fourteenth century had caused dramatic shifts in labor markets and had increased social movement between city and countryside. Unlike Chaucer, however, he was not attached to the royal household of Richard II or to the administrators running the government offices in London. Though some have suggested that the Gawain-poet may have been writing in London for a community of readers who shared his rural background, we can be far more certain about that background—he came from the northwestern Midlands of England, near the border with northern Wales. This border territory seems to have powerfully informed the poet's sense of the geography of the Arthurian world, situated between an idealized, imagined past and the concrete realities of late fourteenth-century society, between the Celtic realm of oral folktales and the English environment of written poetic composition.

SIR GAWAIN AND THE GREEN KNIGHT

By the fourteenth century, romances written both in English and in Anglo-French had become enormously popular in the British Isles. The earliest readers of romance, in the twelfth and thirteenth centuries, had been members of noble households; by the later Middle Ages, however, an increasingly mobile middle class had come to make up a greater share of their readership. *Sir Gawain and the Green Knight* resembles these popular romances but stands out for the orderly exposition of its narrative and the beauty of its language. Written in alliterative rhyme, the poem harks back to earlier, Old English models of poetic composition; but its use of figurative language and of tropes of courtly love places it within the French-influenced literature of the

late Middle Ages. The notations found in the manuscript divide the poem into four sections or "fitts" in this symmetrical structure, parts 1 and 4 (both dedicated to Gawain's encounter with the monstrous Green Knight) surround the two central fitts devoted to Gawain's visit to the castle of Sir Bertilak. The symmetrical structure of the fitts is complemented by the thematic structures of time and space, as the poem begins and ends with King Arthur's court at Camelot in the Christmas season. This symmetry persists in the inner two fitts as well; the three days of hunting at Bertilak's castle are mirrored in the three visits of Bertilak's attentive lady to the reluctant Gawain in his bed-chamber, and reflected once again in the three blows inflicted on Gawain by the Green Knight in the closing fitt of the poem. Beyond these formal principles based on number and symmetry, the symbolism of Gawain's ornate shield, adorned with a pentagram, and the magical qualities of the green girdle given to Gawain by Bertilak's lady add to the poem's mythic resonance.

In the end, Gawain demonstrates his knightly virtues, but he also shows his limits. By failing to uphold the highest standards of truth and honor, he exposes the weakness that will ultimately destroy the court of Arthur. Yet this earnest questioning of the Arthurian ideal is juxtaposed with a repeated focus on the essential playfulness of the knightly endeavor, ranging from the daily "game" that Bertilak imposes on his guest to the elaborate tricks that are revealed at the poem's end. Its juxtaposition of the earnest and the playful is perhaps the aspect of *Sir Gawain and the Green Knight* that brings it closest to the literary domain of Chaucer and **Boccaccio**. At the same time, the poem also expresses the poignant, elegiac quality seen in the other works found in the Cotton manuscript, especially the prayerful praise of the virtuous dead girl who is the central figure in *Pearl*. In his closing words to Gawain, the Green Knight might be speaking of the Pearl-maiden herself when he tells the selfless knight, "I declare you purged, as polished and as pure / as the day you were born, without blemish or blame."

Sir Gawain and the Green Knight[1]

FITT I

Once the siege and assault of Troy had ceased,
with the city a smoke-heap of cinders and ash,
the traitor who contrived such betrayal there
was tried for his treachery,[2] the truest on earth,
Aeneas, it was, with his noble warriors   5
who went conquering abroad, laying claim to the crowns
of the wealthiest kingdoms in the western world.
Mighty Romulus[3] quickly careered towards Rome
and conceived a city in magnificent style
which from then until now has been known by his name.   10
Ticius constructed townships in Tuscany
and Langobard did likewise building homes in Lombardy.[4]
And further afield, over the Sea of France,
Felix Brutus[5] founds Britain on broad banks
      most grand.   15
   And wonder, dread and war
   have lingered in that land
   where loss and love in turn
   have held the upper hand.

After Britain was built by this founding father   20
a bold race bred there, battle-happy men
causing trouble and torment in turbulent times,
and through history more strangeness has happened here
than anywhere else I know of on Earth.
But most regal of rulers in the royal line   25
was Arthur, who I heard is honored above all,
and the inspiring story I intend to spin
has moved the hearts and minds of many—
an awesome episode in the legends of Arthur.

1. Translated from Middle English by Simon Armitage.
2. According to one medieval tradition, the unnamed Trojan traitor was Antenor—a neutral character in Virgil's *Aeneid*, which ties the founding of Rome to the noble warrior Aeneas, who escaped the fall of his city. Another tradition blames Aeneas himself. Medieval historians invented additional Trojan genealogies for other European nations.
3. The legendary founder of Rome, along with his brother Remus; traditionally he is Aeneas's descendant, not his contemporary.
4. Two regions in northern Italy; Ticius and Langobard are other "Trojan" founders.
5. Great-grandson of Aeneas. "Felix": literally, "happy" or "fortunate" (Latin).

So listen a little while to my tale if you will   30
and I'll tell it as it's told in the town where it trips from
            the tongue;
    and as it has been inked
    in stories bold and strong,
    where loyal letters linked,   35
    have lasted loud and long.

It was Christmas at Camelot[6]—King Arthur's court,
where the great and the good of the land had gathered,
the right noble lords of the ranks of the Round Table
all roundly carousing and reveling in pleasure.   40
Time after time, in tournaments of joust,
they had lunged at each other with leveled lances
then returned to the castle to carry on their caroling,
for the feasting lasted a full fortnight and one day,
with more food and drink than a fellow could dream of.   45
The hubbub of their humor was heavenly to hear:
pleasant dialogue by day and dancing after dusk,
so house and hall were lit with happiness
and lords and ladies were luminous with joy.
With all the wonder in the world they gathered there as one: 50
the most chivalrous and courteous knights known to Christendom;
the most wonderful women to have walked in this world;
the handsomest king to be crowned at court.
All these fair folk in their first age, together in
            that hall: 55
    most fortunate under heaven,
    with Arthur, that man of high will;
    no bolder band could ever
    be found on field or hill.

With New Year so young it still yawned and stretched   60
helpings were doubled on the dais[7] that day.
And as king and company were coming to the hall
the choir in the chapel fell suddenly quiet,
then a chorus erupted from the courtiers and clerks:
"Noel," they cheered, then "Noel, Noel,"   65
"New Year Gifts!" the knights cried next
as they pressed forwards to offer their presents,
teasing with frivolous favors and forfeits,
till those ladies who lost couldn't help but laugh,
and the undefeated were far from forlorn.[8]   70
Their merrymaking rolled on in this manner until mealtime,

6. Located by tradition in various places, but usually in southern England (often Cornwall) or southern Wales.
7. A raised platform (the setting described here is not the famous Round Table but a conventional hall, in which those of highest rank sit at a table on the dais while the rest are at a long table or tables perpendicular to it).
8. Because the forfeit in this game is a kiss, both winners and losers are happy with the outcome.

when, worthily washed, they went to the table,
and were seated in order of honor, as was apt,
with Guinevere[9] in their gathering, gloriously framed
at her place on the platform, pricelessly curtained   75
by silk to each side, and canopied across
with tasteful tapestries of Toulouse and Turkestan,[1]
studded with stones and stunning gems
beyond pocket or purse, beyond what pennies
        could buy.   80
    But not one stone outshone
    the quartz of the queen's eyes;
    with hand on heart, no one
    could argue otherwise.

But Arthur would not eat until all were served.   85
He brimmed with ebullience, being almost boyish
in his love of life, and what he liked the least
was to sit still watching the seasons slip by.
His blood was busy and he buzzed with thoughts,
and the matter which played on his mind at that moment   90
was his pledge to take no portion from his plate
on such a special day until a story was told:
some far-fetched yarn or outrageous fable,
the tallest of tales, yet one ringing with truth,
like the action-packed epics of men-at-arms.   95
Or till some chancer had challenged his chosen knight,
dared him, with a lance, to lay life on the line,
to stare death face-to-face and accept defeat
should fortune or fate smile more favorably on his foe.
Within Camelot's castle this was the custom,   100
and at feasts and festivals when the fellowship
        would meet.
    With features proud and fine
    he stood there tall and straight,
    a king at Christmastime   105
    amid great merriment.

And still he stands there just being himself,
chatting away charmingly, exchanging views.
Good Sir Gawain is seated by Guinevere,
and on his other side Agravain the Hard Hand sits,   110
both nephews of the king and notable knights.
At the head of the board sat Bishop Baldwin,
with Ywain, son of Urien, to eat beside him.
First those sitting on the dais were splendidly served,
then those stalwarts seated on the benches to the sides.   115
The first course comes in to the fanfare and clamor
of blasting trumpets hung with trembling banners,

9. The wife of King Arthur.
1. A city in southern France and a region of Asia, respectively.

then pounding double-drums and dinning pipes,
weird sounds and wails of such warbled wildness
that to hear and feel them made the heart float free.   120
Flavorsome delicacies of flesh were fetched in
and the freshest of foods, so many in fact
there was scarcely space to present the stews
or to set the soups in the silver bowls on
            the cloth.   125
        Each guest received his share
        of bread or meat or broth;
        a dozen plates per pair—
        plus beer or wine, or both!

Now, on the subject of supper I'll say no more   130
as it's obvious to everyone that no one went without.
Because another sound, a new sound, suddenly drew near,
which might signal the king to sample his supper,
for barely had the horns finished blowing their breath
and with starters just spooned to the seated guests,   135
a fearful form appeared, framed in the door:
a mountain of a man, immeasurably high,
a hulk of a human from head to hips,
so long and thick in his loins and his limbs
I should genuinely judge him to be a half giant,   140
or a most massive man, the mightiest of mortals.
But handsome, too, like any horseman worth his horse,
for despite the bulk and brawn of his body
his stomach and waist were slender and sleek.
In fact in all features he was finely formed   145
            it seemed.
        Amazement seized their minds,
        no soul had ever seen
        a knight of such a kind—
        entirely emerald green.   150

And his gear and garments were green as well:
a tight fitting tunic, tailored to his torso,
and a cloak to cover him, the cloth fully lined
with smoothly shorn fur clearly showing, and faced
with all-white ermine, as was the hood,   155
worn shawled on his shoulders, shucked from his head.
On his lower limbs his leggings were also green,
wrapped closely round his calves, and his sparkling spurs
were green-gold, strapped with stripy silk,
and were set on his stockings, for this stranger was shoeless.   160
In all vestments he revealed himself veritably verdant!
From his belt hooks and buckle to the baubles and gems
arrayed so richly around his costume
and adorning the saddle, stitched onto silk.
All the details of his dress are difficult to describe,   165
embroidered as it was with butterflies and birds,

green beads emblazoned on a background of gold.
All the horse's tack—harness strap, hind strap,
the eye of the bit, each alloy and enamel
and the stirrups he stood in were similarly tinted,　170
and the same with the cantle and the skirts of the saddle,
all glimmering and glinting with the greenest jewels.
And the horse: every hair was green, from hoof
　　　　to mane.
　　　　A steed of pure green stock.　175
　　　　Each snort and shudder strained
　　　　the hand-stitched bridle, but
　　　　his rider had him reined.

The fellow in green was in fine fettle.
The hair of his head was as green as his horse,　180
fine flowing locks which fanned across his back,
plus a bushy green beard growing down to his breast,
which hung with the splendid hair from his head
and was lopped in a line at elbow length
so half his arms were gowned in green growth,　185
crimped at the collar, like a king's cape.
The mane of his mount was groomed to match,
combed and knotted into curlicues
then tinseled with gold, tied and twisted
green over gold, green over gold. . . .　190
The fetlocks were finished in the same fashion
with bright green ribbon braided with beads,
as was the tail—to its tippety-tip!
And a long, tied thong lacing it tight
where bright and burnished gold bells chimed clearly.　195
No waking man had witnessed such a warrior
or weird warhorse—otherworldly, yet flesh
　　　　and bone.
　　　　His look was lightning bright
　　　　said those who glimpsed its glow.　200
　　　　It seemed no man there might
　　　　survive his violent blow.

Yet he wore no helmet and no hauberk either,
no armored apparel or plate was apparent,
and he swung no sword nor sported any shield,　205
but held in one hand a sprig of holly—
of all the evergreens the greenest ever—
and in the other hand held the mother of all axes,
a cruel piece of kit I kid you not:
the head was an ell in length at least　210
and forged in green steel with a gilt finish;
its broad-edged blade brightly burnished,
it could shear a man's scalp and shave him to boot.
The handle which fitted that fiend's great fist
was inlaid with iron, end to end,　215

with green pigment picking out impressive designs.
From stock to neck, where it stopped with a knot,
a lace was looped the length of the haft,
trimmed with tassels and tails of string
fastened firmly in place by forest-green buttons.   220
And he kicks on, canters through that crowded hall
towards the top table, not the least bit timid,
cocksure of himself, sitting high in the saddle.
"And who," he bellows, without breaking breath,
"is governor of this gaggle? I'll be glad to know.   225
It's with him and no one else that I'll hold
          a pact."
          He held them with his eyes,
          and looked from right to left,
          not knowing, of those knights,   230
          which person to respect.

The guests looked on. They gaped and they gawked
and were mute with amazement: what did it mean
that human and horse could develop this hue,
should grow to be grass-green or greener still,   235
like green enamel emboldened by bright gold?
Some stood and stared then stepped a little closer,
drawn near to the knight to know his next move;
they'd seen some sights, but this was something special,
a miracle or magic, or so they imagined.   240
Yet several of the lords were like statues in their seats,
left speechless and rigid, not risking a response.
The hall fell hushed, as if all who were present
had slipped into sleep or some trancelike state.
          No doubt   245
          not all were stunned and stilled
          by dread, but duty bound
          to hold their tongues until
          their sovereign could respond.

Then the king acknowledged this curious occurrence,   250
cordially addressed him, keeping his cool.
"A warm welcome, sir, this winter's night.
My name is Arthur, I am head of this house.
Won't you slide from that saddle and stay awhile,
and the business which brings you we shall learn of later."   255
"No," said the knight, "by Him in highest heaven,
I'm not here to idle in your hall this evening.
But because your acclaim is so loudly chorused,
and your castle and brotherhood are called the best,
the strongest men to ever mount the saddle,   260
the worthiest knights ever known to the world,
both in competition and true combat,
and since courtesy, so it's said, is championed here,
I'm intrigued, and attracted to your door at this time.

Be assured by this holly stem here in my hand 265
that I mean no menace. So expect no malice,
for if I'd slogged here tonight to slay and slaughter
my helmet and hauberk wouldn't be at home
and my sword and spear would be here at my side,
and more weapons of war, as I'm sure you're aware; 270
I'm clothed for peace, not kitted out for conflict.
But if you're half as honorable as I've heard folk say
you'll gracefully grant me this game which I ask for
        by right."
        Then Arthur answered, "Knight 275
        most courteous, if you claim
        a fair, unarmored fight,
        we'll see you have the same."

"I'm spoiling for no scrap, I swear. Besides,
the bodies on these benches are just bum-fluffed bairns. 280
If I'd ridden to your castle rigged out for a ruck
these lightweight men wouldn't last a minute.
But it's Yuletide—a time of youthfulness, yes?
So at Christmas in this court I lay down a challenge:
if a person here present, within these premises, 285
is big or bold or red-blooded enough
to strike me one stroke and be struck in return,
I shall give him as a gift this gigantic cleaver
and the axe shall be his to handle how he likes.
I'll kneel, bare my neck and take the first knock. 290
So who has the gall? The gumption? The guts?
Who'll spring from his seat and snatch this weapon?
I offer the axe—who'll have it as his own?
I'll afford one free hit from which I won't flinch,
and promise that twelve months will pass in peace, 295
        then claim
        the duty I deserve
        in one year and one day.
        Does no one have the nerve
        to wager in this way?" 300

If flustered at first, now totally foxed
were the household and the lords, both the highborn and the low.
Still stirruped, the knight swiveled round in his saddle
looking left and right, his red eyes rolling
beneath the bristles of his bushy green brows, 305
his beard swishing from side to side.
When the court kept its counsel he cleared his throat
and stiffened his spine. Then he spoke his mind:
"So here is the House of Arthur," he scoffed,
"whose virtues reverberate across vast realms. 310
Where's the fortitude and fearlessness you're so famous for?
And the breathtaking bravery and the big-mouth bragging?
The towering reputation of the Round Table,

skittled and scuppered by a stranger—what a scandal!
You flap and you flinch and I've not raised a finger!"   315
Then he laughed so loud that their leader saw red.
Blood flowed to his fine-featured face and he raged
         inside.
    His men were also hurt—
    those words had pricked their pride.   320
    But born so brave at heart
    the king stepped up one stride.

"Your request," he countered, "is quite insane,
and folly finds the man who flirts with the fool.
No warrior worth his salt would be worried by your words,   325
so in heaven's good name hand over the axe
and I'll happily fulfill the favor you ask."
He strides to him swiftly and seizes his arm;
the man dismounts in one mighty leap.
Then Arthur grips the axe, grabs it by its haft   330
and takes it above him, intending to attack.
Yet the stranger before him stands up straight,
highest in the house by at least a head,
but stands there sternly, stroking his beard,
drawing down his coat, countenance undaunted,   335
about to be bludgeoned, but no more bothered
than a guest at the table being given a goblet
         of wine.
    By Guinevere, Gawain
    now to his king inclines   340
    and says, "I stake my claim.
    May this melee must be mine."

"Should you call me, courteous lord," said Gawain to his king,
"to rise from my seat and stand at your side,
politely take leave of my place at the table   345
and quit without causing offence to my queen,
then I would come to your counsel before this great court.
For I find it unfitting, as my fellow knights would,
when a deed of such daring is dangled before us
that you take on this trial—tempted as you are—   350
when brave, bold men are seated on these benches,
men never matched in the mettle of their minds,
never beaten or bettered in the field of battle.
I am weakest of your warriors and feeblest of wit;
loss of my life would be least lamented.   355
Were I not your nephew my life would mean nothing;
to be born of your blood is my body's only claim.
Such a foolish affair is unfitting for a king,
so, being first to come forward, it should fall to me.
And if my proposal is improper, let no other person   360
         stand blame."

The knighthood then unites
and each knight says the same:
their king can stand aside
and give Gawain the game.   365

So the sovereign instructed his knight to stand.
Getting to his feet he moved graciously forward
and knelt before Arthur, taking hold of the axe.
Letting go of it, Arthur then held up his hand
to give young Gawain the blessing of God   370
and hope he finds firmness in heart and fist.
"Take care, young cousin, to catch him cleanly,
use full-blooded force then you needn't fear
the blow which he threatens to trade in return."
Gawain, with the weapon, walked towards the warrior,   375
and they stood face-to-face, not one man afraid.
Then the green knight spoke, growled at Gawain:
"Before we compete, repeat what we've promised.
And start by saying your name to me, sir,
and tell me the truth so I can take it on trust."   380
"In good faith," said the knight, "Gawain is my name.
I heave this axe, and whatever happens after,
in twelvemonth's time I'll be struck in return
with any weapon you wish, and by you and you
        alone."   385
     The green man speaks again:
     "I swear on all I know,
     I'm glad it's you, Gawain,
     who'll drive the axe-head home."

"Gawain," said the green knight, "by God, I'm glad   390
the favor I've called for will fall from your fist.
You've perfectly repeated the promise we made
and the terms of the contest are crystal clear.
Except for one thing: you must solemnly swear
that you'll seek me yourself; that you'll search me out   395
to the ends of the earth to earn the same blow
as you'll dole out today in this decorous hall."
"But where will you be? Where's your abode?
You're a man of mystery, as God is my maker.
Which court do you come from and what are you called?   400
There is knowledge I need, including your name,
then I shall use all my wit to work out the way,
and keep to our contract, so cross my heart."
"But enough at New Year. It needs nothing more,"
said the warrior in green to worthy Gawain.   405
"I could tell you the truth once you've taken the blow;
if you smite me smartly I could spell out the facts
of my house and home and my name, if it helps,
then you'll pay me a visit and vouch for our pact.

Or if I keep quiet you might cope all the better,   410
loafing and lounging here, looking no further. But
          we stall!
       Now grasp that gruesome axe
       and show your striking style."
       He answered, "Since you ask,"   415
       and touched the tempered steel.

The green knight took his stance, prepared to be struck,
bent forward, revealing a flash of green flesh
as he heaped his hair to the crown of his head,
the nape of his neck now naked and ready.   420
Gawain grips the axe and heaves it heavenwards,
plants his left foot firmly on the floor in front,
then swings it swiftly towards the bare skin.
The cleanness of the strike cleaved the spinal cord
and parted the fat and the flesh so far   425
that the bright steel blade took a bite from the floor.
The handsome head tumbles onto the earth
and the king's men kick it as it clatters past.
Blood gutters brightly against his green gown,
yet the man doesn't shudder or stagger or sink   430
but trudges towards them on those tree-trunk legs
and rummages around, reaches at their feet
and cops hold of his head and hoists it high,
and strides to his steed, snatches the bridle,
steps into the stirrup and swings into the saddle   435
still gripping his head by a handful of hair.
Then he settles himself in his seat with the ease
of a man unmarked, never mind being minus
          his head!
       He wheeled his bulk about,   440
       that body which still bled.
       They cowered in the court
       before his speech was said.

For that scalp and skull now swung from his fist;
to the noblest at the table he turned the face   445
and it opened its eyelids, stared straight ahead
and spoke this speech, which you'll hear for yourselves:
"Sir Gawain, be wise enough to keep your word
and faithfully follow me until you find me,
as you vowed in this hall within hearing of these horsemen.   450
You're charged with getting to the Green Chapel,
to reap what you've sown. You'll rightfully receive
that what is due to be dealt to you as New Year dawns.
Men know my name as the Green Chapel knight,
and even a fool couldn't fail to find me.   455
So come, or be called a coward forever."
With a tug of the reins he twisted around
and, head still in hand, galloped out of the hall,

so the hooves brought fire from the flame in the flint.
Which kingdom he came from they hadn't a clue, 460
no more than they knew where he made for next.
                And then?
        Well, with the green man gone
        they laughed and grinned again.
        And yet such goings-on 465
        were magic to those men.

And although King Arthur was awestruck at heart
no sign of it showed. Instead he spoke
to his exquisite queen with courteous words:
"Dear lady, don't be daunted by this deed today, 470
it's in keeping that such strangeness should occur at Christmas
between sessions of banter and seasonal song,
amid the lively pastimes of ladies and lords.
And at least I'm allowed to eat at last,
having witnessed such wonder, wouldn't you say?" 475
Then he glanced at Gawain and spoke gracefully:
"Now hang up your axe[2]—one hack is enough."
So it dangled from the drape behind the dais
so that men who saw it would be mesmerized and amazed,
and give voice, on its evidence, to that stunning event. 480
Then the two of them turned and walked to the table,
the monarch and his knight, and men served the meal—
double dishes apiece, rare delicacies,
all manner of food—and the music of minstrels.
And they danced and sang till the sun went down 485
        that day.
        But mind your mood, Gawain,
        lest dread make you delay,
        or lose this lethal game
        you've promised you will play. 490

Fitt 2

This happening was a gift—just as Arthur had asked for
and had yearned to hear of while the year was young.
And if guests had no subject as they strolled to their seats,
now this serious concern sustained their chatter.
And Gawain had been glad to begin the game, 495
but don't be so shocked should the plot turn pear-shaped:
for men might be merry when addled with mead
but each year, short lived, is unlike the last
and rarely resolves in the style it arrived.
So the festival finishes and a new year follows 500
in eternal sequence, season by season.
After lavish Christmas come the lean days of Lent[3]

---

2. A punning phrase, as it applies both literally and figuratively—"stop what you're doing."

3. The forty days before Easter, a penitential period of prayer and restricted eating.

when the flesh is tested with fish and simple food.
Then the world's weather wages war on winter:
cold shrinks earthwards and the clouds climb;   505
sun-warmed, shimmering rain comes showering
onto meadows and fields where flowers unfurl;
woods and grounds wear a wardrobe of green;
birds burble with life and build busily
as summer spreads, settling on slopes as   510
      it should.
    Now every hedgerow brims
    with blossom and with bud,
    and lively songbirds sing
    from lovely, leafy woods.   515

So summer comes in season with its subtle airs,
when the west wind sighs among shoots and seeds,
and those plants which flower and flourish are a pleasure
as their leaves let drip their drink of dew
and they sparkle and glitter when glanced by sunlight.   520
Then autumn arrives to harden the harvest
and with it comes a warning to ripen before winter.
The drying airs arrive, driving up dust
from the face of the earth to the heights of heaven,
and wild sky wrestles the sun with its winds,   525
and the leaves of the lime lie littered on the ground,
and grass that was green turns withered and gray.
Then all which had risen over-ripens and rots
and yesterday on yesterday the year dies away,
and winter returns, as is the way of the world   530
      through time.
    At Michaelmas[4] the moon
    stands like that season's sign,
    a warning to Gawain
    to rouse himself and ride.   535

Yet he stayed until All Saints' Day[5] by his sovereign's side,
and they feasted in the name of their noble knight
with the revels and riches of the Round Table.
The lords of that hall and their loving ladies
were sad and concerned for the sake of their knight,   540
but nevertheless they made light of his load.
Those joyless at his plight made jokes and rejoiced.
Then sorrowfully, after supper, he spoke with his uncle,
and openly talked of the trip he must take:
"Now, lord of my life, I must ask for your leave.   545
You were witness to my wager. I have no wish
to retell you the terms—they're nothing but a trifle.
I must set out tomorrow to receive that stroke
from the knight in green, and let God be my guide."

4. The feast of St. Michael, September 29.   5. November 1.

Then the cream of Camelot crowded around: 550
Ywain and Eric and others of that ilk,
Sir Dodinal the Dreaded, the Duke of Clarence,
Lancelot, Lionel, Lucan the Good,
and Sir Bors and Sir Bedevere—both big names,
and powerful men such as Mador de la Port.[6]   555
This courtly committee approaches the king
to offer up heartfelt advice to our hero.
And sounds of sadness and sorrow were heard
that one as worthy and well liked as Gawain
should suffer that strike but offer no stroke in   560
        reply.
    Yet keeping calm the knight
    just quipped, "Why should I shy
    away? If fate is kind
    or cruel, man still must try."   565

He remained all that day and in the morning he dressed,
asked early for his arms and all were produced.
First a rug of rare cloth was unrolled on the floor,
heaped with gear which glimmered and gleamed,
and the stout knight steps onto it and handles the steel.   570
He tries on his tunic of extravagant silk,
then the neatly cut cloak, closed at the neck,
its lining finished with a layer of white fur.
Then they settled his feet into steel shoes
and clad his calves, clamped them with greaves,   575
then hinged and highly polished plates
were knotted with gold thread to the knight's knees.
Then leg guards were fitted, lagging the flesh,
attached with thongs to his thick-set thighs.
Then comes the suit of shimmering steel rings   580
encasing his body and his costly clothes:
well burnished braces to both of his arms,
good elbow guards and glinting metal gloves,
all the trimmings and trappings of a knight tricked out
        to ride: 585
    a metal suit that shone;
    gold spurs which gleam with pride;
    a keen sword swinging from
    the silk belt to his side.

Fastened in his armor he seemed fabulous, famous,   590
every link looking golden to the very last loop.
Yet for all that metal he still made it to mass,
honored the Almighty before the high altar.
After which he comes to the king and his consorts
and asks to take leave of the ladies and lords;   595
they escort and kiss him and commended him to Christ.

---

6. Literally, "of the Door" (French).

Now Gringolet is rigged out and ready to ride
with a saddle which flickered with fine gold fringes
and was set with new studs for the special occasion.
The bridle was bound with stripes of bright gold,   600
the apparel of the panels was matched in appearance
to the color of the saddlebows and crupper and cover,
and nails of red gold were arrayed all around,
shining splendidly like splintered sunlight.
Then he holds up his helmet and hastily kisses it;   605
it was strongly stapled and its lining was stuffed,
and sat high on his head, fastened behind
with a colorful cloth to cover his neck
embroidered and bejeweled with brilliant gems
on the broad silk border, and with birds on the seams   610
such as painted parrots perched among periwinkles
and turtle doves and true lover's knots, tightly entwined
as if women had worked at it seven winters
        at least.
    The diamond diadem   615
    was greater still. It gleamed
    with flawless, flashing gems
    both clear and smoked, it seemed.

Then they showed him the shining scarlet shield
with its pentangle[7] painted in pure gold.   620
He seized it by its strap and slung it round his neck;
he looked well in what he wore, and was worthy of it.
And why the pentangle was appropriate to that prince
I intend to say, though it will stall our story.
It is a symbol that Solomon once set in place[8]   625
and is taken to this day as a token of fidelity,
for the form of the figure is a five-pointed star
and each line overlaps and links with the last
so is ever eternal, and when spoken of in England
is known by the name of the endless knot.   630
So it suits this soldier in his spotless armor,
fully faithful in five ways five times over.
For Gawain was as good as the purest gold—
devoid of vices but virtuous, loyal
        and kind,   635
    so bore that badge on both
    his shawl and shield alike.
    A prince who talked the truth:
    known as the noblest knight.

First he was deemed flawless in his five senses;   640
and secondly his five fingers were never at fault;

7. I.e., a pentagram, a figure believed to have   king of the ancient Hebrews with mystic
mystical powers.   knowledge.
8. Folklore associated the proverbially wise

and thirdly his faith was founded in the five wounds
Christ received on the cross, as the creed recalls.
And fourthly, if that soldier struggled in skirmish
one thought pulled him through above all other things: 645
the fortitude he found in the five joys
which Mary had conceived in her son, our Savior.[9]
For precisely that reason the princely rider
had the shape of her image inside his shield,
so by catching her eye his courage would not crack.   650
The fifth set of five which I heard the knight followed
included friendship and fraternity with fellow men,
purity and politeness that impressed at all times,
and pity, which surpassed all pointedness. Five things
which meant more to Gawain than to most other men.   655
So these five sets of five were fixed in this knight,
each linked to the last through the endless line,
a five-pointed form which never failed,
never stronger to one side or slack at the other,
but unbroken in its being from beginning to end   660
however its trail is tracked and traced.
So the star on the spangling shield he sported
shone royally, in gold, on a ruby red background,
the pure pentangle as people have called it
        for years.   665
    Then, lance in hand, held high,
    and got up in his gear
    he bids them all good-bye
    one final time, he fears.

Spiked with the spurs the steed sped away   670
with such force that the fire-stones sparked underfoot.
All sighed at the sight, and with sinking hearts
they whispered their worries to one another,
concerned for their comrade. "A pity, by Christ,
if a lord so noble should lose his life.   675
To find his equal on earth would be far from easy.
Cleverer to have acted with caution and care,
deemed him a duke—a title he was due—
a leader of men, lord of many lands;
better that than being battered into oblivion,   680
beheaded by an ogre, through headstrong pride.
Whoever knew any king to take counsel of a knight
in the grip of an engrossing Christmas game?"
Warm tears welled up in their weepy eyes
as gallant Sir Gawain galloped from court   685
        that day.
    He sped from home and hearth

---

9. The events labeled by Christians the Annunciation (the announcement that Christ would
be born), the Nativity (Christ's birth), the Resurrection, the Ascension (of Christ into
heaven), and the Assumption (the bodily taking up of Mary into heaven).

and went his winding way
on steep and snaking paths,
just as the story says.   690

Now through England's realm he rides and rides,
Sir Gawain, God's servant, on his grim quest,
passing long dark nights unloved and alone,
foraging to feed, finding little to call food,
with no friend but his horse through forests and hills   695
and only our Lord in heaven to hear him.
He wanders near to the north of Wales
with the Isles of Anglesey[1] off to the left.
He keeps to the coast, fording each course,
crossing at Holy Head and coming ashore   700
in the wilds of the Wirral,[2] whose wayward people
both God and good men have quite given up on.
And he constantly enquires of those he encounters
if they know, or not, in this neck of the woods,
of a great green man or a Green Chapel.   705
No, they say, never. Never in their lives.
They know of neither a chap nor a chapel
          so strange.
     He trails through bleak terrain.
     His mood and manner change   710
     at every twist and turn
     towards that chosen church.

In a strange region he scales steep slopes;
far from his friends he cuts a lonely figure.
Where he bridges a brook or wades through a waterway   715
it's no surprise to find that he faces a foe
so foul or fierce he is bound to use force.
So momentous are his travels among the mountains
to tell just a tenth would be a tall order.
Here he scraps with serpents and snarling wolves,   720
here he tangles with wodwos[3] causing trouble in the crags,
or with bulls and bears and the odd wild boar.
Hard on his heels through the highlands come giants.
Only diligence and faith in the face of death
will keep him from becoming a corpse or carrion.   725
And the wars were one thing, but winter was worse:
clouds shed their cargo of crystallized rain
which froze as it fell to the frost-glazed earth.
Nearly slain by sleet he slept in his armor,
bivouacked in the blackness amongst bare rocks   730
where meltwater streamed from the snow-capped summits
and high overhead hung chandeliers of ice.

1. Off the northwest corner of Wales.   Wales, heads east.
2. A forest in the English county of Cheshire;   3. Wild men of the woods.
Gawain, after reaching the northern limits of

So in peril and pain Sir Gawain made progress,
crisscrossing the countryside until Christmas
           Eve. Then   735
     at that time of tiding,
     he prayed to highest heaven.
     Let Mother Mary guide him
     towards some house or haven.

Next morning he moves on, skirts the mountainside,   740
descends a deep forest, densely overgrown,
with vaulting hills to each half of the valley
and ancient oaks in huddles of hundreds.
Hazel and hawthorn are interwoven,
decked and draped in damp, shaggy moss,   745
and bedraggled birds on bare, black branches
pipe pitifully into the piercing cold.
Under cover of the canopy he girded Gringolet
through mud and marshland, a man all alone,
concerned and afraid in case he should fail   750
in the worship of our Deity, who, on that date
was born the Virgin's son to save our souls.
He prayed with heavy heart. "Father, hear me,
and Lady Mary, our mother most mild,
let me happen on some house where mass might be heard,   755
and matins in the morning; meekly I ask,
and here I utter my pater, ave
                and creed."[4]
     He rides the path and prays,
     dismayed by his misdeeds,   760
     and signs Christ's cross and says,
     "Be near me in my need."

No sooner had he signed himself three times
than he became aware, in those woods, of high walls
in a moat, on a mound, bordered by the boughs   765
of thick-trunked timber which trimmed the water.
The most commanding castle a knight ever kept,
positioned in a site of sweeping parkland
with a palisade of pikes pitched in the earth
in the midst of tall trees for two miles or more.   770
He stopped and stared at one side of that stronghold
as it sparkled and shone within shimmering oaks,
and with helmet in hand he offered up thanks
to Jesus and Saint Julian,[5] both gentle and good,
who had courteously heard him and heeded his cry.   775
"A lodging at last. So allow it, my Lord."
Then he girded Gringolet with his gilded spurs,

---

4. The Paternoster (Our Father), Ave Maria (Hail Mary), and Apostle's Creed—all foundational prayers said daily, as were mass and matins.

5. Julian the Hospitaller, legendary patron of travelers and innkeepers.

and purely by chance chose the principal approach
to the building, which brought him to the end of the bridge
      with haste. 780
    The drawbridge stood withdrawn,
    the front gates were shut fast.
    Such well-constructed walls
    would blunt the storm wind's blast.

In the saddle of his steed he halts on the slope 785
of the delving moat with its double ditch.
Out of water of wondrous depth, the walls
then loomed overhead to a huge height,
course after course of crafted stone,
then battlements embellished in the boldest style 790
and turrets arranged around the ramparts
with lockable loopholes set into the lookouts.
The knight had not seen a more stunning structure.
Further in, his eye was drawn to a hall
attended, architecturally, by many tall towers 795
with a series of spires spiking the air
all crowned by carvings exquisitely cut.
Uncountable chimneys the color of chalk
sprutted[6] from the roof and sparkled in the sun.
So perfect was that vision of painted pinnacles 800
clustered within the castle's enclosure
it appeared that the place was cut from paper.[7]
Then a notion occurred to that noble knight:
to seek a visit, get invited inside,
to be hosted and housed, and all the holy days 805
      remain.
    Responding to his call
    a pleasant porter came,
    a watchman on the wall,
    who welcomed Sir Gawain. 810

"Good morning," said Gawain, "will you go with a message
to the lord of this house to let me have lodging?"
"By Saint Peter,"[8] said the porter, "it'll be my pleasure,
and I'll warrant you'll be welcome for as long as you wish."
Then he went on his way, but came back at once 815
with a group who had gathered to greet the stranger;
the drawbridge came down and they crossed the ditch
and knelt in the frost in front of the knight
to welcome this man in a way deemed worthy.
Then they yielded to their guest, yanked open the gate, 820
and bidding them to rise he rode across the bridge.
He was assisted from the saddle by several men

6. I.e., sprouted.
7. Paper castles were sometimes used at elaborate feasts to decorate food.

8. An appropriate oath for a porter, since Jesus gave this apostle "the keys of the kingdom of heaven" (Matthew 16.19).

and the strongest amongst them stabled his steed.
Then knights, and the squires of knights, drew near,
to escort him, with courtesy, into the castle.   825
As he took off his helmet, many hasty hands
stretched to receive it and to serve this noble knight,
and his sword and his shield were taken aside.
Then he made himself known to nobles and knights
and proud fellows pressed forwards to confer their respects.   830
Still heavy with armor he was led to the hall
where a fire burned bright with the fiercest flames.
Then the master of the manor emerged from his chamber,
to greet him in the hall with all due honor,
saying, "Behave in my house as your heart pleases.   835
        To whatever you want you are welcome, do what
                you will."
        "My thanks," Gawain exclaimed,
        "May Christ reward you well."
        Then firmly, like good friends,   840
        arm into arm they fell.

Gawain gazed at the lord who greeted him so gracefully,
the great one who governed that grand estate,
powerful and large, in the prime of his life,
with a bushy beard as red as a beaver's,   845
steady in his stance, solid of build,
with a fiery face and fine conversation:
and it suited him well, so it seemed to Gawain,
to keep such a castle and captain his knights.
Escorted to his quarters the lord quickly orders   850
that a servant be assigned to assist Gawain,
and many were willing to wait on his word.
They brought him to a bedroom, beautifully furnished
with fine silken fabrics finished in gold
and curious coverlets lavishly quilted   855
in bright ermine and embroidered to each border.
Curtains ran on cords through red-gold rings,
tapestries from Toulouse and Turkistan
were fixed against walls and fitted underfoot.
With humorous banter Gawain was helped out   860
of his chain-mail coat and costly clothes,
then they rushed to bring him an array of robes
of the choicest cloth. He chose, and changed,
and as soon as he stood in that stunning gown
with its flowing skirts which suited his shape   865
it almost appeared to the persons present
that spring, with its spectrum of colors, had sprung;
so alive and lean were that young man's limbs
a nobler creature Christ had never created, they declared.
        This knight,   870
        whose country was unclear,
        now seemed to them by sight

a prince without a peer
in fields where fierce men fight.

In front of a flaming fireside a chair   875
was pulled into place for Gawain, and padded
with covers and quilts all cleverly stitched,
then a cape was cast across the knight
of rich brown cloth with embroidered borders,
finished inside with the finest furs,   880
ermine, to be exact, and a hood which echoed it.
Resplendently dressed he settled in his seat;
as his limbs thawed, so his thoughts lightened.
Soon a table was set on sturdy trestles
covered entirely with a clean white cloth   885
and cruets of salt and silver spoons.
In a while he washed and went to his meal.
Staff came quickly and served him in style
with several soups all seasoned to taste,
double helpings as was fitting, and a feast of fish,   890
some baked in bread, some browned over flames,
some boiled or steamed, some stewed in spices
and subtle sauces which the knight savored.
Four or five times he called it a feast,
and the courteous company happily cheered him   895
          along:
     "On penance plates you dine⁹—
     there's better board to come."
     The warming, heady wine
     then freed his mind for fun.   900

Now through tactful talk and tentative enquiry
polite questions are put to this prince;
he responds respectfully, and speaks of his journey
from the Court of Arthur, King of Camelot,
the royal ruler of the Round Table,   905
and he says they now sit with Gawain himself,
who has come here at Christmastime quite by chance.
Once the lord has gathered that his guest is Gawain
he likes it so well that he laughs out loud.
All the men of that manor were of the same mind,   910
being happy to appear promptly in his presence,
this person famed for prowess and purity,
whose noble skills were sung to the skies,
whose life was the stuff of legend and lore.
Then knight spoke softly to knight, saying   915
"Watch now, we'll witness his graceful ways,
hear the faultless phrasing of flawless speech;
if we listen we will learn the merits of language
since we have in our hall a man of high honor.

9. Because Christmas Eve is a fast day, he is served only fish, not meat.

Ours is a graceful and giving God   920
to grant that we welcome Gawain as our guest
as we sing of His birth who was born to save us.
        We few
    shall learn a lesson here
    in tact and manners true,   925
    and hopefully we'll hear
    love's tender language, too."[1]

Once dinner was done Gawain drew to his feet
and darkness neared as day became dusk.
Chaplains went off to the castle's chapels   930
to sound the bells hard, to signal the hour
of evensong, summoning each and every soul.
The lord goes alone, then his lady arrives,
concealing herself in a private pew.
Gawain attends, too; tugged by his sleeve   935
he is steered to a seat, led by the lord
who greets Gawain by name as his guest.
No man in the world is more welcome, are his words.
For that he is thanked. And they hug there and then,
and sit as a pair through the service in prayer.   940
Then she who desired to see this stranger
came from her closet with her sisterly crew.
She was fairest amongst them—her face, her flesh,
her complexion, her quality, her bearing, her body,
more glorious than Guinevere, or so Gawain thought,   945
and in the chancel of the church they exchanged courtesies.
She was hand in hand with a lady to her left,
someone altered by age, an ancient dame,
well respected, it seemed, by the servants at her side.
Those ladies were not the least bit alike: 950
one woman was young, one withered by years.
The body of the beauty seemed to bloom with blood,
the cheeks of the crone were wattled and slack.
One was clothed in a kerchief clustered with pearls
which shone like snow—snow on the slopes   955
of her upper breast and bright bare throat.
The other was noosed and knotted at the neck,
her chin enveloped in chalk-white veils,
her forehead fully enfolded in silk
with detailed designs at the edges and hems;   960
nothing bare, except for the black of her brows
and the eyes and nose and naked lips
which were chapped and bleared and a sorrowful sight.
A grand old mother, a matriarch she might
        be hailed.   965
    Her trunk was square and squat,
    her buttocks bulged and swelled.

1. Though Gawain is usually presented as a chaste and mighty knight, another tradition casts
him as a lover.

Most men would sooner squint
at her whose hand she held.

Then Gawain glanced at the gracious-looking woman,   970
and by leave of the lord he approached those ladies
saluting the elder with a long, low bow,
holding the other for a moment in his arms,
kissing her respectfully and speaking with courtesy.
They request his acquaintance, and quickly he offers   975
to serve them unswervingly should they say the word.
They take him between them and talk as they walk
to a hearth full of heat, and hurriedly ask
for specially spiced cakes, which are speedily fetched,
and wine filled each goblet again and again.   980
Frequently the lord would leap to his feet
insisting that mirth and merriment be made:
hauling off his hood he hoisted it on a spear—
a prize, he promised, to the person providing
most comfort and cheer at Christmastime.   985
"And my fellows and friends shall help in my fight
to see that it hangs from no head but my own."
So the laughter of that lord lights up the room,
and Gawain and the gathering are gladdened by games
            till late.   990
    So late, his lordship said,
    that lamps should burn with light.
    Then, blissful, bound for bed,
    Sir Gawain waved good night.

So the morning dawns when man remembers   995
the day our Redeemer was born to die,
and every house on earth is joyful for Lord Jesus.
Their day was no different, being a diary of delights:
banquets and buffets were beautifully cooked
and dutifully served to diners at the dais.   1000
The ancient elder sat highest at the table
with the lord, I believe, in the chair to her left;
the sweeter one and Gawain took seats in the center
and were first at the feast to dine; then food
was carried around as custom decrees   1005
and served to each man as his status deserved.
There was feasting, there was fun, and such feelings of joy
as could not be conveyed by quick description,
yet to tell it in detail would take too much time.
But I'm aware that Gawain and the beautiful woman   1010
found such comfort and closeness in each other's company
through warm exchanges of whispered words
and refined conversation free from foulness
that their pleasure surpassed all princely sports
            by far.   1015
    Beneath the din of drums

men followed their affairs,
and trumpets thrilled and thrummed
as those two tended theirs.

They drank and danced all day and the next   1020
and danced and drank the day after that,
then Saint John's Day[2] passed with a gentler joy
as the Christmas feasting came to a close.
Guests were to go in the grayness of dawn,
so they laughed and dined as the dusk darkened,   1025
swaying and swirling to music and song.
Then at last, in the lateness, they upped and left
toward distant parts along different paths.
Gawain offered his good-byes, but was ushered by his host
to his host's own chamber and the heat of its chimney,   1030
waylaid by the lord so the lord might thank him
profoundly and profusely for the favor he had shown
in honoring his house at that hallowed season
and lighting every corner of the castle with his character.
"For as long as I live my life shall be better   1035
that Gawain was my guest at God's own feast."
"By God," said Gawain, "but the gratitude goes to you.
May the High King of Heaven repay your honor.
Your requests are now this knight's commands.
I am bound by your bidding, no boon is too high   1040
        to say."
    At length his lordship tried
    to get his guest to stay.
    But proud Gawain replied
    he must now make his way.   1045

Then the lord of the castle inquired courteously
of what desperate deed in the depth of winter
should coax him from Camelot, so quickly and alone,
before Christmas was over in his king's court.
"What you ask," said the knight, "you shall now know.   1050
A most pressing matter prized me from that place:
I myself am summoned to seek out a site
and I have not the faintest idea where to find it.
But find it I must by the first of the year, and not fail
for all the acres in England, so the Lord help me.   1055
Consequently this inquiry I come to ask of you:
that you tell me, in truth, if you have heard the tale
of a green chapel and the ground where it stands,
or the guardian of those grounds who is colored green.
For I am bound by a bond agreed by us both   1060
to link up with him there, should I live that long.
As dawn on New Year's Day draws near,
if God sees fit, I shall face that freak

2. December 27 (celebrating the Apostle John).

more happily than I would the most wondrous wealth!
With your blessing, therefore, I must follow my feet. 1065
In three short days my destiny is due,
and I would rather drop dead than default from duty."
Then laughing the lord of the house said, "Stay longer.
I'll direct you to your rendezvous when the time is right,
you'll get to the green chapel, so give up your grieving. 1070
You can bask in your bed, bide your time,
save your fond farewells till the first of the year
and still meet him by midmorning to do as you might.
   So stay.
  A guide will get you there 1075
  at dawn on New Year's Day.
  The place you need is near,
  two miles at most away."

Then Gawain was giddy with gladness, and declared,
"For this more than anything I thank you thoroughly, 1080
and shall work to do well at whatever you wish,
until that time, attending every task."
The lord squeezed Gawain's arm and seated him at his side,
and called for the ladies to keep them company.
There was pleasure aplenty in their private talk, 1085
the lord delighting in such lively language,
like man who might well be losing his mind.
Then speaking to Gawain, he suddenly shouted:
"You have sworn to serve me, whatever I instruct.
Will you hold to that oath right here and now?" 1090
"You may trust my tongue," said Gawain, in truth,
"for within these walls I am servant to your will."
The lord said warmly, "You were weary and worn,
hollow with hunger, harrowed by tiredness,
yet joined in my reveling right royally every night. 1095
You relax as you like, lie in your bed
until mass tomorrow, then go to your meal
where my wife will be waiting; she will sit at your side
to accompany and comfort you in my absence from court.
   So lounge: 1100
  at dawn I'll rise and ride
  to hunt with horse and hound."
  The gracious knight agreed
  and, bending low, he bowed.

"Furthermore," said the master, "let's make a pact. 1105
Here's a wager: what I win in the woods will be yours,
and what you gain while I'm gone you will give to me.
Young sir, let's swap, and strike a bond,
let a bargain be a bargain, for better or worse."
"By God," said Gawain, "I agree to the terms, 1110
and I find it pleasing that you favor such fun."
"Let drink be served and we'll seal the deal,"

the lord cried loudly, and everyone laughed.
So they reveled and caroused uproariously,
those lords and ladies, for as long as they liked;   1115
then with immaculate exchanges of manners and remarks
they slowed and they stood and they spoke softly.
And with parting kisses the party dispersed,
footmen going forward with flaring torches,
and everybody was brought to their bed at long last,   1120
   to dream.
  Before they part the pair
  repeat their pact again.
  That lord was well aware
  of how to host a game.   1125

Fitt 3

Well before sunrise the servants were stirring;
the guests who were going had called for their grooms,
and they scurried to the stables to strap on the saddles,
trussing and tying all the trammel and tack.
The high-ranking nobles got ready to ride,   1130
jumped stylishly to their saddles and seized the reins,
then cantered away on their chosen courses.
The lord of that land was by no means last
to be rigged out for riding with the rest of his men.
After mass he wolfed down a meal, then made   1135
for the hills in a hurry with his hunting horn.
So as morning was lifting its lamp to the land
his lordship and his huntsmen were high on horseback,
and the canny kennel men had coupled the hounds
and opened the cages and called them out.   1140
On the bugles they blew three long, bare notes
to a din of baying and barking, and any dogs
which wandered at will where whipped back into line
by a hundred hunters, or so I heard tell,
   at least.   1145
  The handlers hold their hounds,
  the huntsmen's hounds run free.
  Each bugle blast rebounds
  between the trunks of trees.

As the cry went up the wild creatures quaked.   1150
The deer in the dale, quivering with dread
hurtled to high ground, but were headed off
by the ring of beaters who bellowed boisterously.
The stags of the herd with their high-branched heads
and the broad-horned bucks were allowed to pass by,   1155
for the lord of the land had laid down a law
that man should not maim the male in close season.[3]

3. I.e., the season closed to hunting.

But the hinds were halted with hollers and whoops
and the din drove the does to sprint for the dells.
Then the eye can see that the air is all arrows: 1160
all across the forest they flashed and flickered,
biting through hides with their broad heads.
What! They bleat as they bleed and they die on the banks,
and always the hounds are hard on their heels,
and the hunters on horseback come hammering behind   1165
with stone-splitting cries, as if cliffs had collapsed.
And those animals which escaped the aim of the archers
were steered from the slopes down to rivers and streams
and set upon and seized at the stations below.
So perfect and practiced were the men at their posts   1170
and so great were the greyhounds which grappled with the deer
that prey was pounced on and dispatched with speed
        and force.
    The lord's heart leaps with life.
    Now on, now off his horse   1175
    all day he hacks and drives.
    And dusk comes in due course.

So through a lime-leaf border the lord led the hunt,
while good Gawain lay slumbering in his sheets,
dozing as the daylight dappled the walls,   1180
under a splendid cover, enclosed by curtains.
And while snoozing he heard a slyly made sound,
the sigh of a door swinging slowly aside.
From below the bedding he brings up his head
and lifts the corner of the curtain a little   1185
wondering warily what it might be.
It was she, the lady, looking her loveliest,
most quietly and craftily closing the door,
nearing the bed. The knight felt nervous;
lying back he assumed the shape of sleep   1190
as she stole towards him with silent steps,
then cast up the curtain and crept inside,
then sat down softly at the side of his bed.
And awaited his wakening for a good long while.
Gawain lay still, in his state of false sleep,   1195
turning over in his mind what this matter might mean,
and where the lady's unlikely visit might lead.
Yet he said to himself, "Instead of this stealth
I should openly ask what her actions imply."
So he stirred and stretched, turned on his side,   1200
lifted his eyelids and, looking alarmed,
crossed himself hurriedly with his hand, as if saving
        his life.
    Her chin is pale, her cheeks
    are ruddy red with health;   1205
    her smile is sweet, she speaks
    with lips that love to laugh:

"Good morning, Sir Gawain," said the graceful lady,
"You sleep so soundly one might sidle in here.
You're tricked and trapped! But let's make a truce,   1210
or I'll bind you in your bed, and you'd better believe me."
The lady laughed, making light of his quandary.
"Good morning, madam," Gawain said merrily.
"I'll contentedly attend whatever task you set,
and in serving your desires I shall seek your mercy,   1215
which seems my best plan, in the circumstances!"
And he loaded his light-hearted words with laughter.
"But my gracious lady, if you grant me leave,
will you pardon this prisoner and prompt him to rise,
then I'll quit these covers and pull on my clothes,   1220
and our words will flow more freely back and forth."
"Not so, beautiful sir," the sweet lady said.
"Bide in your bed—my own plan is better.
I'll tuck in your covers corner to corner,
then playfully parley with the man I have pinned.   1225
Because I know your name—the knight Sir Gawain,
famed through all realms whichever road he rides,
whose princely honor is highly praised
amongst lords and ladies and everyone alive.
And right here you lie. And we are left all alone,   1230
with my husband and his huntsmen away in the hills
and the servants snoring and my maids asleep
and the door to this bedroom barred with a bolt.
I have in my house an honored guest
so I'll make the most of my time and stay talking   1235
                    a while.
        You're free to have my all,
        do with me what you will.
        I'll come just as you call
        and swear to serve you well."   1240

"In good faith," said Gawain, "such gracious flattery,
though I am not him of whom you speak.
I don't dare to receive the respect you describe
and in no way warrant such worthy words.
By God, I would be glad, if you agreed it fitting,   1245
to devote myself through speech or deed
to the prize of your praise—my joy in it would be pure."
Said the gracious lady, "Sir Gawain, in good faith,
how improper on my part if I were to imply
any slur or slight on your status as a knight.   1250
But what lady in this land wouldn't latch the door,
wouldn't rather hold you as I do here—
in the company of your clever conversation,
forgetting all grief and engaging in joy—
than hang on to half the gold that she owns?   1255
I praise the Lord who upholds the high heavens,
for I have what I hoped for above all else by

His grace."
That lovely looking maid,
she charmed him and she chased.
But every move she made   1260
he countered, case by case.

"Madam," said our man, "may Mary reward you,
in good faith, I have found your fairness noble.
Some fellows are praised for the feats they perform;   1265
I hardly deserve to receive such respect.
It is you who is genuinely joyful and generous."
"By Mary," she declared, "it's quite the contrary.
Were I the wealthiest woman in the world
with priceless pearls in the palm of my hand   1270
to bargain with and buy the best of all men,
then for all the signs you have shown me, sir,
of kindness, courtesy and exquisite looks—
a picture of perfection now proved to be true—
no person on this planet would be picked before you."   1275
"In fairness," said Gawain, "you found far better.
But I'm proud of the price you would pay from your purse,
and will swear to serve you as my sovereign lady.
Let Gawain be your servant and Christ your Savior."
Then they muse on many things through morning and midday, 1280
and the lady stares with a loving look,
but Gawain acts graciously and remains on guard,
and although no woman could be warmer or more winning,
he is cool in his conduct, on account of the scene he
       foresees: 1285
    the strike he must receive,
    as cruel fate decrees.
    The lady begs her leave—
    at once Gawain agrees.

She glanced at him, laughed and gave her good-bye,   1290
then stood, and stunned him with astounding words:
"May the Lord repay you for your prize performance.
But I know that Gawain could never be your name."
"But why not?" the knight asked nervously,
afraid that some fault in his manners had failed him.   1295
The beautiful woman blessed him, then rebuked him:
"A good man like Gawain, so greatly regarded,
the embodiment of courtliness to the bones of his being,
could never have lingered so long with a lady
without craving a kiss, as politeness requires,   1300
or coaxing a kiss with his closing words."
"Very well," said Gawain, "Let it be as you wish.
I shall kiss at your command, as becomes a knight,
and further, should it please you, so press me no more."
The lady comes close, cradles him in her arms,   1305
leans nearer and nearer, then kisses the knight.

Then they courteously commend one another to Christ,
and without one more word the woman is away.
Rapidly he rises and makes himself ready,
calls for his chamberlain, chooses his clothes,   1310
makes himself ready then marches off to mass.
Then he went to a meal which was made and waiting,
and was merry and amused till the moon had silvered
       the view.
    No man felt more at home   1315
    tucked in between those two,
    the cute one and the crone.
    Their gladness grew and grew.

And the lord of the land still led the hunt,
driving hinds to their death through holts and heaths,   1320
and by the setting of the sun had slaughtered so many
of the does and other deer that it beggared belief.
Then finally the folk came flocking to one spot
and quickly they collected and counted the kill.
Then the leading lords and their loyal men   1325
chose the finest deer—those fullest with fat—
and ordered them cut open by those skilled in the art.
They assessed and sized every slain creature
and even on the feeblest found two fingers worth of fat.
Through the sliced-open throat they seized the stomach   1330
and the butchered innards were bound in a bundle.
Next they lopped off the legs and peeled back the pelt
and hooked out the bowels through the broken belly,
but carefully, being cautious not to cleave the knot.
Then they clasped the throat, and clinically they cut   1335
the gullet from the windpipe, then garbaged the guts.
Then the shoulder blades were severed with sharp knives
and slotted through a slit so the hide stayed whole.
Then the beasts were prized apart at the breast,
and they went to work on the gralloching[4] again,   1340
riving open the front as far as the hind fork,
fetching out the offal, then with further purpose
filleting the ribs in the recognized fashion.
And the spine was subject to a similar process,
being pared to the haunch so it held as one piece   1345
then hoisting it high and hacking it off.
And its name is the numbles,[5] as far as I know, and
       just that.
    Its hind legs pulled apart
    they slit the fleshy flaps,   1350
    then cleave and quickly start
    to break it down its back.

---

4. Disemboweling (from a Gaelic term).   5. Organs of a deer that can be eaten.

Then the heads and necks of hinds were hewn off,
and the choice meat of the flanks chopped away from the chine,
and a fee for the crows was cast into the copse.   1355
Then each side was skewered, stabbed through the ribs
and heaved up high, hung by its hocks,
and every person was paid with appropriate portions.
Using pelts for plates, the dogs pogged out
on liver and lights and stomach linings   1360
and a blended sop of blood and bread.
The kill horn was blown and the bloodhounds bayed.
Then hauling their meat they headed for home,
sounding howling wails on their hunting horns,
and as daylight died they had covered the distance   1365
and had come to the castle where the knight was ensconced,
          adjourned
     in peace, with fires aflame.
     The huntsman has returned,
     and when he greets Gawain   1370
     warm feelings are confirmed.

Then the whole of the household was ordered to the hall,
and the women as well with their maids in waiting.
And once assembled he instructs the servants
that the venison be revealed in full view,   1375
and in excellent humor he asked that Gawain
should see for himself the size of the kill,
and showed him the side slabs sliced from the ribs.
"Are you pleased with this pile? Have I won your praise?
Does my skill at this sport deserve your esteem?"   1380
"Yes indeed," said the other. "It's the hugest haul
I have seen this seven years in the winter season."
"And I give it all to you, Gawain," said the master,
"for according to our contract it is yours to claim."
"Just so," said Gawain, "and I'll say the same,   1385
for whatever I've won within these walls
such gains will be graciously given to you."
So he held out his arms and hugged the lord
and kissed him in the comeliest way he could.
"You're welcome to my winnings—to my one profit,   1390
though I'd gladly have given you any greater prize."
"I'm grateful," said the lord, "and Gawain, this gift
would carry more worth if you cared to confess
by what wit you won it. And when. And where."
"That wasn't our pact," he replied. "So don't pry.   1395
You'll be given nothing greater, the agreement we have
          holds good!"
     They laugh aloud and trade
     wise words which match their mood.
     When supper's meal is made   1400
     they dine on dainty food.

Later, they lounged by the lord's fire,
and were served unstintingly with subtle wines
and agreed to the game again next morning
and to play by the rules already in place: 1405
any takings to be traded between the two men
at night when they met, no matter what the merchandise.
They concurred on this contract in front of the court,
and drank on the deal, and went on drinking
till late, when they took their leave at last,   1410
and every person present departed to bed.
By the third cackle of the crowing cock
the lord and his liegemen are leaping from their beds,
so that mass and the morning meal are taken,
and riders are rigged out ready to run as   1415
        day dawns.
     They leave the levels, loud
     with howling hunting horns.
     The huntsmen loose the hounds
     through thickets and through thorns.   1420

Soon they picked up a scent at the side of a swamp,
and the hounds which first found it were urged ahead
by wild-words and shrill shouting.
The pack responded with vigor and pace,
alert to the trail, forty lurchers[6] at least.   1425
Then such a raucous din rose up all around them
it ricocheted and rang through the rocky slopes.
The hounds were mushed with hollers and the horn,
then suddenly they swerved and swarmed together
in a wood, between a pool and a precipice.   1430
On a mound, near a cliff, on the margins of a marsh
where toppled stones lay scattered and strewn,
they coursed towards their quarry with huntsmen at heel.
Then a crew of them ringed the hillock and the cliff,
until they were certain that inside their circle   1435
was the beast whose being three bloodhounds had sensed.
Then they riled the creature with their rowdy ruckus,
and suddenly he breaks the barrier of beaters,
—the biggest of wild boars has bolted from his cover—
ancient in years and estranged from the herd,   1440
savage and strong, a most massive swine,
truly grim when he grunted. And the group were aggrieved,
for three were thrown down by the first of his thrusts;
then he fled away fast without further damage.
The other huntsmen bawled "hi" and "hay, hay,"   1445
blasted on their bugles, blew to regroup,
so the dogs and the men made a merry din,
tracking him nosily, testing him time and time

6. Hunting dogs.

again.

    The boar would stand at bay   1450
    and aim to maul and maim
    the thronging dogs, and they
    would yelp and yowl in pain.

Then the archers advanced with their bows and took aim,
shooting arrows at him which were often on target,   1455
but their points could not pierce his impenetrable shoulders
and bounced away from his bristly brow.
The smooth, slender shafts splintered into pieces,
and the heads glanced away from wherever they hit.
Battered and baited by such bombardment,   1460
in frenzied fury he flies at the men,
hurts them horribly as he hurtles past
so that many grew timid and retreated a tad.
But the master of the manor gave chase on his mount,
the boldest of beast hunters, his bugle blaring,   1465
trumpeting the tally-ho and tearing through thickets
till the setting sun slipped from the western sky.
So the day was spent in pursuits of this style,
while our lovable young lord had not left his bed,
and, cosseted in costly quilted covers, there he   1470
    remained.
    The lady, at first light,
    did not neglect Gawain,
    but went to wake the knight
    and meant to change his mind.   1475

She approaches the curtains, parts them and peeps in,
at which Sir Gawain makes her welcome at once,
and with prompt speech she replies to the prince,
settling by his side and laughing sweetly,
looking at him lovingly before launching her words.   1480
"Sir, if you truly are Gawain it seems wondrous to me
that a man so dedicated to doing his duty
cannot heed the first rule of honorable behavior,
which has entered through one ear and exited the other;
you have already lost what yesterday you learned   1485
in the truest lesson my tongue could teach."
"What lesson?" asked the knight. "I know of none,
though if discourtesy has occurred then blame me, of course."
"I encouraged you to kiss," the lady said kindly,
"and to claim one quickly when one is required,   1490
an act which ennobles any knight worth the name."
"Dear lady," said the other, "don't think such a thing,
I dare not kiss in case I am turned down.
If refused, I'd be at fault for offering in the first place."
"In truth," she told him, "you cannot be turned down.   1495
If someone were so snooty as to snub your advance,
a man like you has the means of his muscles."

"Yes, by God," said Gawain, "what you say holds good.
But such heavy-handedness is frowned on in my homeland,
and so is any gift not given with grace.
What kiss you command I will courteously supply,   1500
have what you want or hold off, whichever
                 the case."
          So bending from above
          the fair one kissed his face.   1505
          The two then talk of love:
          its grief; also its grace.

"I would like to learn," said the noble lady,
"and please find no offence, but how can it follow
that a lord so lively and young in years,   1510
a champion in chivalry across the country—
and in chivalry, the chiefmost aspect to choose,
as all knights acknowledge, is loyalty in love,
for when tales of truthful knights are told
in both title and text the topic they describe   1515
is how lords have laid down their lives for love,
endured for many days love's dreadful ordeal,
then vented their feelings with avenging valor
by bringing great bliss to a lady's bedroom—
and you the most notable knight who is known,   1520
whose fame goes before him . . . yes, how can it follow
that twice I have taken this seat at your side
yet you have not spoken the smallest syllable
which belongs to love or anything like it.
A knight so courteous and considerate in his service   1525
really ought to be eager to offer this pupil
some lessons in love, and to lead by example.
Why, are you, whom all men honor, actually ignorant,
or do you deem me too dull to hear of dalliances?
                 I come   1530
          to learn of love and more,
          a lady all alone.
          Perform for me before
          my husband heads for home."

"In faith," said Gawain, "may God grant you fortune.   1535
It gives me great gladness and seems a good game
that a woman so worthy should want to come here
and take pains to play with your poor knight,
unfit for her favors—I am flattered indeed.
But to take on the task of explaining true love   1540
or touch on the topics those love tales tell of,
with yourself, who I sense has more insight and skill
in the art than I have, or even a hundred
of the likes of me, on earth where I live,
would be somewhat presumptuous, I have to say.   1545
But to the best of my ability I'll do your bidding,

bound as I am to honor you forever
and to serve you, so let our Savior preserve me!"
So the lady tempted and teased him, trying
to entice him to wherever her intentions might lie. 1550
But fairly and without fault he defended himself,
no sin on either side transpiring, only happiness
   that day.
  At length, when they had laughed,
  the woman kissed Gawain. 1555
  Politely then she left
  and went her own sweet way.

Roused and risen he was ready for mass,
and then men sumptuously served the morning meal.
Then he loitered with the ladies the length of the day 1560
while the lord of the land ranged left and right
in pursuit of that pig which stampeded through the uplands,
breaking his best hounds with its back-snapping bite
when it stood embattled . . . then bowmen would strike,
goading it to gallop into open ground 1565
where the air was alive with the huntsman's arrows.
That boar made the best men flinch and bolt,
till at last his legs were like lead beneath him,
and he hobbled away to hunker in a hole
by a stony rise at the side of a stream. 1570
With the bank at his back he scrapes and burrows,
frothing and foaming foully at the mouth,
whetting his white tusks. The hunters waited,
irked by the effort of aiming from afar
but daunted by the danger of daring to venture 1575
   too near.
  So many men before
  had fallen prey. They feared
  that fierce and frenzied boar
  whose tusks could slash and tear. 1580

Till his lordship hacks up, urging on his horse,
spots the swine at standstill encircled by men,
then handsomely dismounts and unhands his horse,
brandishes a bright sword and goes bounding onwards,
wades through the water to where the beast waits. 1585
Aware that the man was wafting a weapon
the hog's hairs stood on end, and its howling grunt
made the fellows there fear for their master's fate.
Then the boar burst forward, bounded at the lord,
so that beast and hunter both went bundling 1590
into white water, and the swine came off worst,
because the moment they clashed the man found his mark,
knifing the boar's neck, nailing his prey,
hammering it to the hilt, bursting the hog's heart.
Screaming, it was swept downstream, almost slipping 1595

    beneath.
At least a hundred hounds
latch on with tearing teeth.
Then, dragged to drier ground,
the dogs complete its death.   1600

The kill was blown on many blaring bugle
and the unhurt hunters hollered and whooped.
The chief amongst them, in charge of the chase,
commanded the bloodhounds to bay at the boar,
then one who was wise in woodland ways   1605
began carefully to cut and carve up the carcass.
First he hacks off its head and hoists it aloft,
then roughly rives it right along the spine;
he gouges out the guts and grills them over coals,
and blended with bread they are tidbits for the bloodhounds.   1610
Next he fetches out the fillets of glimmering flesh
and retrieves the intestines in time-honored style,
then the two sides are stitched together intact
and proudly displayed on a strong pole.
So with the swine swinging they swagger home,   1615
the head of the boar being borne before the lord
who had fought so fiercely in the ford till the beast
        was slain.
    The day then dragged, it seemed,
    before he found Gawain,   1620
    who comes when called, most keen
    to countenance the claim.

Now the lord is loud with words and laughter
and speaks excitedly when he sees Sir Gawain;
he calls for the ladies and the company of the court   1625
and he shows off the meat slabs and shares the story
of the boar's hulking hugeness, and the full horror
of the fight to the finish as it fled through the forest.
And Gawain is quick to compliment the conquest,
praising it as proof of the lord's prowess,   1630
for such prime pieces of perfect pork
and such sides of swine were a sight to be seen.
Then admiringly he handles the boar's huge head,
feigning fear to flatter the master's feelings.
"Now Gawain," said the lord, "I give you this game,   1635
as our wager warranted, as well you remember."
"Certainly," said Sir Gawain. "It shall be so.
And graciously I shall give you my gains in exchange."
He catches him by the neck and courteously kisses him,
then a second time kisses him in a similar style.   1640
"Now we're even," said Gawain, "at this eventide;
the clauses of our contract have been kept and you have what
      I owe."

"By Saint Giles,"[7] the just lord says,
"You're now the best I know.
By wagering this way
your gains will grow and grow."   1645

Then the trestle tables were swiftly assembled
and cast with fine cloths. A clear, living light
from the waxen torches awakened the walls.   1650
Places were set and supper was served,
and a din arose as they reveled in a ring
around the fire on the floor, and the feasting party
made much pleasant music at the meal and after,
singing seasonal songs and carol dancing   1655
with as much amusement as a mouth could mention.
The young woman and Gawain sat together all the while.
And so loving was that lady towards the young lord,
with stolen glances and secret smiles
that the man himself was maddened and amazed,   1660
but his breeding forbade him rebuking a lady,
and though tongues might wag he returned her attention
            all night.
      Before his friends retire
      his lordship leads the knight,   1665
      heads for his hearth and fire
      to linger by its light.

They supped and swapped stories, and spoke again
of the night to come next, which was New Year's Eve.
Gawain pleaded politely to depart by morning,   1670
so in two days' time he might honor his treaty.
But the lord was unswerving, insisting that he stayed:
"As an honest soul I swear on my heart,
you shall find the Green Chapel to finish your affairs
long before dawn on New Year's Day.   1675
So lie in your room and laze at your leisure
while I ride my estate, and, as our terms dictate,
we'll trade our trophies when the hunt returns.
I have tested you twice and found you truthful.
But think tomorrow *third time throw best*.   1680
Now, a lord can feel low whenever he likes,
so let's chase cheerfulness while we have the chance."
So those gentlemen agreed that Gawain would stay,
and they took more drink, then by torchlight retired to
            their beds.   1685
      Our man then sleeps, a most
      reposed and peaceful rest.

7. A frequent subject of medieval art, always depicted with a hind.

As hunters must, his host
is up at dawn and dressed.

After mass the master grabs a meal with his men   1690
and asks for his mount on that marvelous morning.
All those grooms engaged to go with their lord
were high on their horses before the hall gates.
The fields were dazzling, fixed with frost,
and the crown of sunrise rose scarlet and crimson,   1695
scalding and scattering cloud from the sky.
At the fringe of the forest the dogs were set free
and the rumpus of the horns went ringing through the rocks.
They fall on the scent of a fox, and follow,
turning and twisting as they sniff out the trail.   1700
A young harrier yowls and a huntsman yells,
then the pack come panting to pick up the scent,
running as a rabble along the right track.
The fox scurries ahead, they scamper behind,
and pursue him at speed when he comes within sight,   1705
haranguing him with horrific ranting howls.
Now and then he doubles back through thorny thickets,
or halts and harkens in the hem of a hedge,
until finally, by a hollow, he hurdles a fence,
and carefully he creeps by the edge of a copse,   1710
convinced that his cunning has conned those canines!
But unawares he wanders where they lie in wait,
where greyhounds are gathered together, a group
                    of three.
          He springs back with a start,   1715
          then twists and turns and flees.
          With heavy, heaving heart
          he tracks towards the trees.

It was one of life's delights to listen to those hounds
as they massed to meet him, marauding together.   1720
They bayed bloodily at the sight of his being,
as if clustering cliffs had crashed to the ground.
Here he was ambushed by bushwhacking huntsmen
waiting with a welcome of wounding words;
there he was threatened and branded a thief,   1725
and the team on his tail gave him no time to tarry.
Often, in the open, the pack tried to pounce,
then that crafty Reynard[8] would creep into cover.
So his lordship and his lords were merrily led
in this manner through the mountains until midafternoon,   1730
while our handsome hero snoozed contentedly at home,
kept from the cold of the morning by curtains.

---

8. Conventional name for a fox (from the 12th-century beast fable *Roman de Renart*, whose hero was a fox).

But love would not let her ladyship sleep
and the fervor she felt in her heart would not fade.
She rose from her rest and rushed to his room   1735
in a flowing robe that reached to the floor
nor suppress the purpose which suppressed her heart.
Her head went unhooded, but heavenly gems
were entwined in her tresses in clusters of twenty.
She wore nothing on her face; her neck was naked,   1740
and her shoulders were bare to both back and breast.
She comes into his quarters and closes the door,
throws the window wide open and wakes Gawain,
right away rouses him with ringing words for
       his ear.   1745
    "Oh, sir, how can you sleep
    when morning comes so clear?"
    And though his dreams are deep
    he cannot help but hear.

Yes he dozes in a daze, dreams and mutters   1750
like a mournful man with his mind on dark matters—
how destiny might deal him a death blow on the day
when he grapples with the guardian of the Green Chapel;
of how the strike of the axe must be suffered without struggle.
But sensing her presence there he surfaces from sleep,   1755
comes quickly from the depths of his dreams to address her.
Laughing warmly she walks towards him
and finds his face with the friendliest kiss.
In a worthy style he welcomes the woman
and seeing her so lovely and alluringly dressed,   1760
every feature so faultless, her complexion so fine,
a passionate heat takes hold in his heart.
They traded smiles and speech tripped from their tongues,
and a bond of friendship was forged there, all blissful
       and bright.   1765
    They talk with tenderness
    and pride, and yet their plight
    is perilous unless
    sweet Mary minds her knight.

For that noble princess pushed him and pressed him,   1770
nudged him ever nearer to a limit where he needed
to allow her love or impolitely reject it.
He was careful to be courteous and avoid uncouthness,
and more so for the sake of his soul should he sin
and be counted a betrayer by the keeper of the castle.   1775
"I shall not succumb," he swore to himself.
With affectionate laughter he fenced and deflected
all the loving phrases which leapt from her lips.
"You shall bear the blame," said the beautiful one,
"if you feel no love for the lady you lie with,   1780
and wound her, more than anyone on earth, to the heart.

Unless, of course, there is a lady in your life
to whom you are tied and so tightly attached
that the bond will not break, as I must now believe.
So in honesty and trust now tell me the truth;   1785
for all the love alive, do not lessen the truth
            with guile."
        "You judge wrong, by Saint John,"
        he said to her, and smiled.
        "There is no other one   1790
        nor will be for this while!"

"Those words," said the woman, "are the worst of all.
But I asked, and you answered, and now I ache.
Kiss me as I wish and I shall walk away
in mourning like a lady who loved too much."   1795
Stooping and sighing she kisses him sweetly,
then withdraws from his side, saying as she stands,
"But before we part will you find me some small favor?
Give me some gift—a glove at least,
that might leaven my loss when we meet in my memory."   1800
"Well it were," said Gawain. "I wish I had here
my most precious possession as a present for your love,
for over and over you deserve and are owed
the highest prize I could hope to offer.
But I would not wish on you a worthless token,   1805
and it strikes me as unseemly that you should receive
nothing greater than a glove as a keepsake from Gawain.
I am here on an errand in an unknown land
without men bearing bags of beautiful things,
which my regard for you, lady, makes me regret;   1810
but man must live by his means, and neither mope
            nor moan."
        The pretty one replies:
        "Nay, knight, since you decline
        to pass to me a prize.   1815
        you must have one of mine."

She offers him a ring of rich, red gold,
and the stunning stone set upon it stood proud,
beaming and burning with the brightness of the sun;
what wealth it was worth you can well imagine.   1820
But he would not accept it, and said straight away,
"By God, no tokens will I take at this time;
I have nothing to give, so nothing will I gain."
She insists he receive it but still he resists,
and swears, on his name as a knight, not to swerve.   1825
Snubbed by his decision, she said to him then,
"You refuse my ring because you find it too fine,
and don't care to be deeply indebted to me;
so I give you my girdle, a lesser thing to gain."
From around her body she unbuckled the belt   1830

which fastened the frock beneath her fair mantle,
a green silk girdle trimmed with gold,
exquisitely edged and hemmed by hand.
And she sweetly beseeched Sir Gawain to receive it,
in spite of its slightness, and hoped he would accept. 1835
But still he maintained he intended to take
neither gold nor girdle, until by God's grace
the challenge he had chosen was finally achieved.
"With apologies I pray you be not displeased,
but end all your offers, for always against them 1840
      I am.
    For all your grace I owe
    a thousand thank-you's, ma'am.
    I shall through sun and snow
    remain your loyal man." 1845

"And now he spurns my silk," the lady responded,
"so simple in itself, or so it appears,
so little and unlikely, worth nothing, or less.
But the knight who knew of the power knitted in it
would pay a high price to possess it, perhaps. 1850
For the body which is bound within this green belt,
as long as it is buckled robustly about him,
will be safe against anyone who seeks to strike him,
and all the slyness on earth wouldn't see him slain."
The man mulled it over, and it entered his mind 1855
it might just be the jewel for the jeopardy he faced
and save him from the strike in his challenge at the chapel.
With luck, it might let him escape with his life.
So relenting at last he let her speak,
and promptly she pressed him to take the present, 1860
and he granted her wish, and she gave with good grace,
though went on to beg him not to whisper a word
of this gift to her husband, and Gawain agreed;
those words of theirs within those walls
        should stay. 1865
    His thanks are heartfelt, then.
    No sooner can he say
    how much it matters, when
    the third kiss comes his way.

Then the lady departed, leaving him alone, 1870
for no more merriment could be had from that man.
And once she has quit he clothes himself quickly,
rises and dresses in the richest of robes,
stowing the love-lace safely aside,
hiding it away from all hands and eyes. 1875
Then he went at once to the chapel of worship,
privately approached the priest and implored him
to allow his confession, and to lead him in life
so his soul might be saved when he goes to his grave.

Then fully and frankly he spoke of his sins,   1880
no matter how small, always seeking mercy,
beseeching the counselor that he receive absolution.
The priest declares him so clean and so pure
that the Day of Doom[9] could dawn in the morning.
Then in merrier mood he mingled with the ladies,   1885
caroling and carousing and carrying on
as never before, until nightfall. Folk feel
        and hear
     and see his boundless bliss
     and say, "Such charm and cheer;   1890
     he's at his happiest
     since his arrival here."

And long let him loiter there, looked after by love.
Now the lord of the land was still leading his men,
finishing off the fox he had followed for so long.   1895
He vaults a fence to flush out the victim,
hearing that the hounds are harrying hard.
Then Reynard scoots from a section of scrub
and the rabble of the pack rush right at his heels.
Aware of its presence the wary lord waits,   1900
then bares his bright sword and swishes at the beast,
which shirks from its sharpness, and would have shot away
but a hound flew forward before it could flee
and under the hooves of the horses they have him,
worrying the wily one with wrathful baying.   1905
The lord hurtles from his horse and heaves the fox up,
wrestles it from the reach of those ravenous mouths,
holds it high over head and hurrahs manfully
while the bloodthirsty bloodhounds bay and howl.
And the other huntsmen hurried with their horns   1910
to catch sight of the slaughter and celebrate the kill.
And when the courtly company had come together
the buglers blew with one mighty blast,
and the others hallooed with open throats.
It was the merriest music ever heard by men,   1915
that rapturous roar which for Reynard's soul
        was raised.
     The dogs, due their reward,
     are patted, stroked and praised.
     Then red fur rips—Reynard   1920
     out of his pelt is prised.

Then with night drawing near they headed homewards,
blaring their bugles with the fullness of their breath.
And at last the lord lands at his lovely home,
to find, by the heat of the fireside, his friend   1925
the good Sir Gawain, in glad spirits

9. Judgment Day.

on account of the company he had kept with the ladies.
His blue robe flowed as far as the floor,
his soft-furred surcoat suited him well,
and the hood which echoed it hung from his shoulders.   1930
Both hood and coat were edged in ermine.
He meets the master in the middle of the room,
greets him graciously, with Gawain saying:
"I shall first fulfill our formal agreement
which we fixed in words when the drink flowed freely."   1935
He clasps him tight and kisses him three times
with as much emotion as a man could muster.
"By the Almighty," said the master, "you must have had luck
to profit such a prize—if the price was right."
"Oh fiddlesticks to the fee," said the other fellow.   1940
"As long as I have given the goods which I gained."
"By Mary," said the master, "mine's a miserable match.
I've hunted for hours with nothing to my name
but this foul-stinking fox—fling its fur to the devil—
so poor in comparison with such priceless things,   1945
these presents you impart, three kisses perfect
            and true."
        "Enough!" the knight entreats,
        "I thank you through and through."
        The standing lord then speaks   1950
        of how the fox fur flew!

And with meals and mirth and minstrelsy
they made as much amusement as any mortal could,
and among those merry men and laughing ladies
Gawain and his host got giddy together;   1955
only lunatics and drunkards could have looked more delirious.
Every person present performed party pieces
till the hour arrived when revelers must rest,
and the company in that court heard the call of their beds.
And lastly, in the hall, humbly to his host,   1960
our knight says good night and renews his gratitude.
"Your uncountable courtesies have kept me here
this Christmas—be honored by the High King's kindness.
If it suits, I submit myself as your servant.
But tomorrow morning I must make a move;   1965
if you will, as you promised, please appoint some person
to guide me, God willing, towards the Green Chapel,
where my destiny will dawn on New Year's Day."
"On my honor," he replied. "With hand on heart,
every promise I made shall be put into practice."   1970
He assigns him a servant to steer his course,
to lead him through the land without losing time,
to ride the fastest route between forest
            and fell.[1]

---

1. A high field.

> Gawain will warmly thank
> his host in terms that tell;
> towards the womenfolk
> the knight then waves farewell.

It's with a heavy heart that guests in the hall
are kissed and thanked for their care and kindness,
and they respond with speeches of the same sort,
commending him to our Savior with sorrowful sighs.
Then politely he leaves the lord and his household,
and to each person he passes he imparts his thanks
for taking such trouble in their service and assistance
and such attention to detail in attendance of duty.
And every guest is grieved at the prospect of his going,
as if honorable Gawain were one of their own.
By tapering torchlight he was taken to his room
and brought to his bed to be at his rest.
But if our knight sleeps soundly I couldn't say,
for the matter in the morning might be muddying
        his thoughts.
> So let him lie and think,
> in sight of what he sought.
> In time I'll tell if tricks
> work out the way they ought.

Fitt 4

Now night passes and New Year draws near,
drawing off darkness as our Deity decrees.
But wild-looking weather was about in the world:
clouds decanted their cold rain earthwards;
the nithering[2] north needled man's very nature;
creatures were scattered by the stinging sleet.
Then a whip-cracking wind comes whistling between hills
driving snow into deepening drifts in the dales.
Alert and listening, Gawain lies in his bed;
his lids are lowered but he sleeps very little
as each crow of the cock brings his destiny closer.
Before day had dawned he was up and dressed
for the room was livened by the light of a lamp.
To suit him in his metal and to saddle his mount
he called for a servant, who came quickly,
bounded from his bedsheets bringing his garments.
He swathes Sir Gawain in glorious style,
first fastening clothes to fend off the frost,
then his armor, looked after all the while by the household:
the buffed and burnished stomach and breastplates,
and the rings of chain mail, raked free of rust,
all gleaming good as new, for which he is grateful

1975

1980

1985

1990

1995

2000

2005

2010

2015

2. Oppressing.

          indeed.   2020
    With every polished piece
    no man shone more, it seemed
    from here to ancient Greece.
    He sent then for his steed.

He clothes himself in the costliest costume: 2025
his coat with the brightly emblazoned badge
mounted on velvet; magical minerals
inside and set about it; embroidered seams;
a lining finished with fabulous furs. . . .
And he did not leave off the lady's lace girdle;   2030
for his own good, Gawain won't forget that gift.
Then with his sword sheathed at his shapely hips
he bound himself twice about with the belt,
touchingly wrapped it around his waist.
That green silk girdle truly suited Sir Gawain   2035
and went well with the rich red weaves that he wore.
But our man bore the belt not merely for its beauty,
or the appeal of its pennants, polished though they were,
or the gleam of its edges which glimmered with gold,
but to save his skin when presenting himself,   2040
without shield or sword, to the fatal swing of
         the axe.
    Now in his gear and gown
    he turns towards those ranks
    who served with such renown   2045
    and offers thorough thanks.

Then his great horse Gringolet was got up ready.
The steed had been stabled in comfort and safety
and snorted and stamped in readiness for the ride.
Gawain comes closer to examine his coat,   2050
saying soberly to himself, swearing on his word:
"There are folk in this castle who keep courtesy to the forefront;
their master maintains them—happiness to them all.
And let his lordship's lady be loved all her life.
If they choose, out of charity, to cherish a guest,   2055
showing kindness and care, then may heaven's King
who reigns over all reward them handsomely.
For as long as I live in the lands of this world
I shall practice every means in my power to repay him."
Then he steps in the stirrup and vaults to the saddle   2060
and his servant lifts his shield which he slings on his shoulder,
then he girds on Gringolet with his golden spurs
who clatters from the courtyard, not stalling to snort
        or prance.
    His man was mounted, too,   2065
    who lugged the spear and lance.
    "Christ keep this castle true,"
    he chanted. "Grant good chance."

The drawbridge was dropped, and the double-fronted gates
were unbarred and each half was heaved wide open.   2070
As he clears the planking he crosses himself quickly,
and praises the porter, who kneels before the prince
and prays that God be good to Gawain.
Then he went on his way with the one whose task
was to point out the road to that perilous place   2075
where the knight would receive the sorry stroke.
They scrambled up bankings where branches were bare,
clambered up cliff faces where the cold clings.
The clouds which had climbed now cooled and dropped
so the moors and the mountains were muzzy with mist   2080
and every hill wore a hat of mizzle³ on its head.
The streams on the slopes seemed to fume and foam,
whitening the wayside with spume and spray.
They wandered onwards through the wildest woods
till the sun, at that season, came skyward, showing   2085
          its hand.
     On hilly heights they ride,
     snow littering the land.
     The servant at his side
     then has them slow and stand.   2090

"I have accompanied you across this countryside, my lord,
and now you are near the site you have named
and have steered and searched for with such singleness of mind.
But there's something I should like to share with you, sir,
because upon my life, you're a lord that I love,   2095
so if you value your health you'll hear my advice:
the place you proceed to is held to be perilous.
In that wilderness lives a wildman, the worst in the world,
he is brooding and brutal and loves bludgeoning people.
He's more powerful than any person alive on this earth   2100
and four times the figure of any fighting knight
in Arthur's house, or Hector⁴ or any other hero.
He chooses the green chapel for his grim goings on,
and to pass through that place unscathed is impossible,
for he deals out death blows by dint of his hands,   2105
a man without measure who shows no mercy.
Be it chaplain or churl who rides by the chapel,
monk or priest, whatever man or person,
he loves murdering more than he loves his own life.
So I say, just as sure as you sit in your saddle,   2110
if you come there you'll be killed, of that there's no question.
Trust me, he could trample you twenty times over
          or more.
     He's lurked about too long
     engaged in grief and gore.   2115

3. Drizzle, light rain.   warrior; he was especially admired in the
4. Son of King Priam, and the greatest Trojan   Middle Ages.

His hits are swift and strong—
he'll fell you to the floor."

"Therefore, good Sir Gawain, let the man go,
and for God's sake travel an alternate track,
ride another road, and be rescued by Christ.   2120
I'll head off home, and with hand on heart
I shall swear by God and all his good saints,
and on all earthly holiness, and other such oaths,
that your secret is safe, and not a soul will know
that you fled in fear from the fellow I described."   2125
"Many thanks," said Gawain, in a terse tone of voice,
"and for having my interests at heart, be lucky.
I'm certain such a secret would be silent in your keep.
But as faithful as you are, if I failed to find him
and were to flee in fear in the fashion you urge,   2130
I'd be christened a coward, and could not be excused.
So I'll trek to the chapel and take my chances,
say my piece to that person, speak with him plainly,
whether fairness or foulness follows, however fate
            behaves.   2135
        He may be stout and stern
        and standing armed with stave,
        but those who strive to serve
        our Lord, our Lord will save."

"By Mary," said the servant, "you seem to be saying   2140
you're hell-bent on heaping harm on yourself
and losing your life, so I'll delay you no longer.
Set your helmet on your head and your lance in your hand
and ride a route through that rocky ravine
till you're brought to the bottom of that foreboding valley,   2145
then look towards a glade a little to the left
and you'll see in the clearing the site itself,
and the hulking person who inhabits the place.
Now God bless and good-bye, brave Sir Gawain;
for all the wealth in the world I wouldn't walk with you   2150
or go further in this forest by a single footstep."
With a wrench on the reins he reeled around
and heel-kicked the horse as hard as he could,
and was gone from Gawain, galloping hard
            for home.   2155
        "By Christ, I will not cry,"
        announced the knight, "or groan,
        but find my fortune by
        the grace of God alone."

Then he presses ahead, picks up a path,   2160
enters a steep-sided grove on his steed
then goes by and by to the bottom of a gorge
where he wonders and watches—it looks a wild place:

no sign of a settlement anywhere to be seen
but heady heights to both halves of the valley   2165
and set with saber-toothed stones of such sharpness
no cloud in the sky could escape unscratched.
He stalls and halts, holds the horse still,
glances side to side to glimpse the green chapel
but sees no such thing, which he thinks is strange,   2170
except at mid-distance what might be a mound,
a sort of bald knoll on the bank of a brook
where fell water surged with frenzied force,
bursting with bubbles as if it had boiled.
He heels the horse, heads for that mound,   2175
grounds himself gracefully and tethers Gringolet,
looping the reins to the limb of a lime.
Then he strides forwards and circles the feature,
baffled as to what that bizarre hill could be:
it had a hole at one end and at either side,   2180
and its walls, matted with weeds and moss,
enclosed a cavity, like a kind of old cave
or crevice in the crag—it was all too unclear to
        declare.
    "Green Church?" chunters the knight.   2185
    "More like the devil's lair
    where at the nub of night
    he dabbles in dark prayers."

"For certain," he says, "this is a soulless spot,
a ghostly cathedral overgrown with grass,   2190
the kind of kirk where that camouflaged man
might deal in devotions on the devil's behalf.
My five senses inform me that Satan himself
has tricked me in this tryst, intending to destroy me.
This is a haunted house—may it go to hell.   2195
I never came across a church so cursed."
With head helmeted and lance in hand
he scrambled towards skylight in that strange abyss.
Then he heard on the hillside, from behind a hard rock
and beyond the brook, a blood-chilling noise.   2200
What! It cannoned through the cliffs as if they might crack,
like the scream of a scythe being ground on a stone.
What! It whined and wailed, like a waterwheel.
What! It rasped and rang, raw on the ear.
"My God," cried Gawain, "that grinding is a greeting.   2205
My arrival is honored with the honing of an axe
        up there.
    Then let the Lord decide.
    'Oh well,' won't help me here.
    I might well lose my life   2210
    but freak sounds hold no fear."

Then Gawain called as loudly as his lungs would allow,
"Who has power in this place to honor his pact?

Because good Gawain now walks on this ground.
If anyone wants anything then hurry and appear   2215
to do what he needs—it's now or it's never."
"Abide," came a voice from above the bank.
"You'll cop for what's coming to you quickly enough."
Yet he went at his work, whetting the blade,
not showing until it was sharpened and stropped.   2220
Then out of the crags he comes, through the cave mouth,
whirling into view with a wondrous weapon,
a Danish-style axe[5] for dealing the dint,
with a brute of a blade curving back to the haft
filed on a stone, a four footer at least   2225
by the look of the length of its shining lace.
And again he was green, like a year ago,
with green flesh, hair and beard, and a fully green face,
and firmly on green feet he came stomping forwards,
the handle of that axe like a staff in his hand.   2230
At the edge of the water, he will not wade
but vaults the stream with the shaft, and strides
with an ominous face onto earth covered over
        with snow.
      Our brave knight bowed, his head   2235
      hung low—but not too low!
      "Sweet Sir," the green man said,
      "Your visit keeps your vow."

The green knight spoke again, "God guard you, Gawain.
Welcome to my world after all your wandering.   2240
You have timed your arrival like a true traveler,
honoring the terms that entwine us together.
Twelve months ago at this time you took what was yours,
and with New Year come you are called to account.
We're very much alone, beyond view in this valley,   2245
no person to part us—we can do as we please.
Pull your helmet from your head and take what you're owed.
Show no more struggle than I showed myself
when you severed my head with a single smite."
"No," said good Gawain, "by my life-giving God,   2250
I won't gripe or begrudge the grimness to come,
so keep to one stroke and I'll stand stock-still,
won't whisper a word of unwillingness, or one
        complaint."
      He bowed to take the blade   2255
      and bared his neck and nape,
      but, loath to look afraid,
      he feigned a fearless state.

Suddenly the green knight summons up his strength,
hoists the axe high over Gawain's head,   2260

5. A long-bladed battle-axe, as favored by the Vikings.

lifts it aloft with every fiber of his life
and begins to bring home a bone-splitting blow.
Had he seen it through as thoroughly as threatened
the knight, being brave, would have died from the blow.
But glimpsing the axe at the edge of his eye   2265
bringing death earthwards as it arced through the air,
and sensing its sharpness, Gawain shrank at the shoulders.
The swinging axman swerved from his stroke,
and reproached the young prince with some proud words:
"You are not Gawain," he goaded, "with his good name,   2270
"who faced down every foe in the field of battle
but now flinches with fear at the foretaste of harm.
Never could i hear such cowardice from that knight.
Did I budge or even blink when you aimed the axe,
or carp or quibble in King Arthur's castle,   2275
or flap when my head went flying to my feet?
But entirely untouched, you are terror struck.
I'll be found the better fellow, since you were so feeble
      and frail."
    Gawain confessed, "I flinched   2280
    at first, but will not fail.
    Though once my head's unhitched
    it's off once and for all!"

"So be brisk with the blow, bring on the blade.
Deal me my destiny and do it out of hand,   2285
and I'll stand the stroke without shiver or shudder
and be wasted by your weapon. You have my word."
"Take this then," said the other, throwing up the axe,
with a menacing glare like the gaze of a maniac.
Then he launches his swing but leaves him unscathed,   2290
withholds his arm before harm could be done.
And Gawain was motionless, never moved a muscle,
but stood stone-still, or as still as a tree stump
anchored in the earth by a hundred roots.
Then the warrior in green mocked Gawain again: 2295
"Now you've plucked up your courage I'll dispatch you properly.
May the honorable knighthood heaped on you by Arthur—
if it proves to be powerful—protect your neck."
That insulting slur drew a spirited response:
"Thrash away then, thug, your threats are hollow.   2300
Such huffing and fussing—you'll frighten your own heart."
"By God," said the green man, "since you speak so grandly
there'll be no more shilly-shallying, I shall shatter you,
      I vow."
    He stands to strike, a sneer   2305
    comes over lip and brow.
    Gawain is gripped by fear,
    no hope of rescue now.

Hoisted and aimed, the axe hurtled downwards,
the blade bearing down on the knight's bare neck,   2310

a ferocious blow, but far from being fatal
it skewed to one side, just skimming the skin
and finely snicking the fat of the flesh
so that bright red blood shot from body to earth.
Seeing it shining on the snowy ground   2315
Gawain leapt forward a spear's length at least,
grabbed hold of his helmet and rammed it on his head,
brought his shield to his side with a shimmy of his shoulder,
then brandished his sword before blurting out brave words,
because never since birth, as his mother's babe,   2320
was he half as happy as here and now.
"Enough swiping, sir, you've swung your swing.
I've borne one blow without backing out,
go for me again and you'll get some by return,
with interest! Hit out, and be hit in an instant,   2325
          and hard.
        One axe attack—that's all.
        Now keep the covenant
        agreed in Arthur's hall
        and hold the axe in hand."   2330

The warrior steps away and leans on his weapon,
props the handle in the earth and slouches on the head
and studies how Gawain is standing his ground,
bold in his bearing, brave in his actions,
armed and ready. In his heart he admires him.   2335
Then remarking merrily, but in a mighty voice,
with reaching words he rounded on the knight:
"Be a mite less feisty, fearless young fellow,
you've suffered no insulting or heinous incident
beyond the game we agreed on in the court of your king.   2340
One strike was promised—consider yourself well paid!
From any lingering loyalties you are hereby released.
Had I mustered all my muscles into one mighty blow
I would have hit more harshly and done you great harm.
But my first strike fooled you—a feint, no less—   2345
not fracturing your flesh, which was only fair
in keeping with the contract we declared that first night,
for with truthful behavior you honored my trust
and gave up your gains as a good man should.
Then I missed you once more, and this for the morning   2350
when you kissed my pretty wife then kindly kissed me.
So twice you were truthful, therefore twice I left
          no scar.
        The person who repays
        will live to feel no fear.   2355
        The third time, though, you strayed,
        and felt my blade therefore."

"Because the belt you are bound with belongs to me;
it was woven by my wife so I know it very well.
And I know of your courtesies, and conduct, and kisses,   2360

and the wooing of my wife—for it was all my work!
I sent her to test you—and in truth it turns out
you're by the far the most faultless fellow on earth.
As a pearl is more prized than a pea which is white,
in good faith, so is Gawain, amongst gallant knights.   2365
But a little thing more—it was loyalty that you lacked:
not because you're wicked, or a womanizer, or worse,
but you loved your own life; so I blame you less."
Gawain stood speechless for what seemed a great while,
so shocked and ashamed that he shuddered inside.   2370
The fire of his blood brought flames to his face
and he shrank out of shame at what the other had said.
Then he tried to talk, and finding his tongue, said:
"A curse upon cowardice and covetousness.
They breed villainy and vice, and destroy all virtue."   2375
Then he grabbed the girdle and ungathered its knot
and flung it in fury at the man before him.
"My downfall and undoing; let the devil take it.
Dread of the death blow and cowardly doubts
meant I gave in to greed, and in doing so forgot   2380
the freedom and fidelity every knight knows to follow.
And now I am found to be flawed and false,
through treachery and untruth I have totally failed," said
        Gawain.
    "Such terrible mistakes,   2385
    and I shall bear the blame.
    But tell me what it takes
    to clear my clouded name."

The green lord laughed, and leniently replied:
"The harm which you caused me is wholly healed.   2390
By confessing your failings you are free from fault
and have openly paid penance at the point of my axe.
I declare you purged, as polished and as pure
as the day you were born, without blemish or blame.
And this gold-hemmed girdle I present as a gift,   2395
which is green like my gown. It's yours, Sir Gawain,
a reminder of our meeting when you mix and mingle
with princes and kings. And this keepsake will be proof
to all chivalrous knights of your challenge in this chapel.
But follow me home. New Year's far from finished—   2400
we'll resume our reveling with supper and song.
        What's more
    my wife is waiting there
    who flummoxed you before.
    This time you'll have in her   2405
    a friend and not a foe."

"Thank you," said the other, taking helmet from head,
holding it in hand as he offered his thanks.
"But I've loitered long enough. The Lord bless your life
and bestow on you such honor as you surely deserve.   2410

And mind you commend me to your fair wife,
both to her and the other, those honorable ladies
who kidded me so cleverly with their cunning tricks.
But no wonder if a fool finds his way into folly
and be wiped of his wits by womanly guile—   2415
it's the way of the world. Adam fell because of a woman,
and Solomon because of several, and as for Samson,
Delilah was his downfall, and afterwards David
was bamboozled by Bathsheba and bore the grief.[6]
All wrecked and ruined by their wrongs; if only   2420
we could love our ladies without believing their lies.
And those were foremost of all whom fortune favored,
excellent beyond all others existing under heaven,"
        he cried.
    "Yet all were charmed and changed   2425
    by wily womankind.
    I suffered just the same,
    but clear me of my crime."

"But the girdle," he went on, "God bless you for this gift.
And shall wear it with good will, but not for its gold,   2430
nor its silks and streamers, and not for the sake
of its wonderful workmanship or even its worth,
but as a sign of my sin—I'll see it as such
when I swagger in the saddle—a sad reminder
that the frailty of his flesh is man's biggest fault,   2435
how the touch of filth taints his tender frame.
So when praise for my prowess in arms swells my pride,
one look at this love-lace will lessen my ardor.
But I will ask one thing, if it won't offend:
since I stayed so long in your lordship's land   2440
and was hosted in your house—let Him reward you
who upholds the heavens and sits upon high—
will you make known your name? And I'll ask nothing else."
"Then I'll treat you to the truth," the other told him,
"Here in my homelands they call me Bertilak de Hautdesert.   2445
And in my manor lives the mighty Morgan le Fay,[7]
so adept and adroit in the dark arts,
who learned magic from Merlin—the master of mystery—
for in earlier times she was intimately entwined
with that knowledgeable man, as all you knights know   2450
      back home.
    Yes, 'Morgan the Goddess'—
    I will announce her name.

---

6. A series of figures from the Hebrew Bible: in Gawain's telling, Adam was persuaded to sin by Eve, Solomon was led into sin by his many wives and concubines, Samson was tricked and betrayed by Delilah, and David was tempted to adultery and, in effect, murder by the beautiful Bathsheba.

7. Literally, "Morgan the Fairy"; in Arthurian tradition, the half-sister of Arthur. Having fallen in love with her, the sorcerer Merlin taught her.

There is no nobleness
　　she cannot take and tame." 2455

"She guided me in this guise to your great hall
to put pride on trial, and to test with this trick
what distinction and trust the Round Table deserves.
She imagined this mischief would muddle your minds
and that grieving Guinevere would go to her grave 2460
at the sight of a specter making ghostly speeches
with his head in his hands before the high table.
So that ancient woman who inhabits my home
is also your aunt—Arthur's half sister,
the daughter of the duchess of Tintagel; the duchess 2465
who through Uther, was mother to Arthur, your king.
So I ask you again, come and greet your aunt
and make merry in my house; you're much loved there,
and, by my faith, I am as fond of you my friend
as any man under God, for your great truth." 2470
But Gawain would not. No way would he go.
So they clasped and kissed and made kind commendations
to the Prince of Paradise, and then parted in the cold,
　　　　　that pair.
　　Our man, back on his mount 2475
　　now hurtles home from there.
　　The green knight leaves his ground
　　to wander who-knows-where.

So he winds through the wilds of the world once more,
Gawain on Gringolet, by the grace of God, 2480
under a roof sometimes and sometimes roughing it,
and in valleys and vales had adventures and victories
but time is too tight to tell how they went.
The nick to his neck was healed by now;
thereabouts he had bound the belt like a baldric— 2485
slantwise, as a sash, from shoulder to side,
laced in a knot looped below his left arm,
as a sign that his honor was stained by sin.
So safe and sound he sets foot in court,
and great joy came to the king in his castle 2490
when tidings of Gawain's return had been told.
The king kissed his knight and so did the queen,
and Gawain was embraced by his band of brothers,
who made eager enquiries, and he answered them all
with the tale of his trial and tribulations, 2495
and the challenge at the chapel, and the great green chap,
and the love of the lady, which led to the belt.
And he showed them the scar at the side of his neck,
confirming his breach of faith, like a badge
　　　　　of blame. 2500
　　He grimaced with disgrace,
　　he writhed in rage and pain.

Blood flowed towards his face
and showed his smarting shame.

"Regard," said Gawain, as he held up the girdle,   2505
"the symbol of sin, for which my neck bears the scar;
a sign of my fault and offence and failure,
of the cowardice and covetousness I came to commit.
I was tainted by untruth. This, its token,
I will drape across my chest till the day I die.   2510
For man's crimes can be covered but never made clean;
once sin is entwined it is attached for all time."
The king gave comfort, then the whole of the court
allow, as they laugh in lovely accord,
that the lords and ladies who belong to the Table,   2515
every knight in the brotherhood, should bear such a belt,
a bright green belt worn obliquely to the body,
crosswise, like a sash, for the sake of this man.
So that slanting green stripe was adopted as their sign,
and each knight who held it was honored ever after,   2520
as all the best books on romance remind us:
an adventure which happened in Arthur's era,
as the chronicles of this country have stated clearly.
Since fearless Brutus first set foot
on these shores, once the siege and assault at Troy   2525
            had ceased,
      our coffers have been crammed
      with stories such as these.
      Now let our Lord, thorn-crowned,
      bring us to perfect peace. AMEN.   2530

HONY SOYT QUI MAL PENCE[8]

8. I.e., "Honi soit qui mal y pense" (Middle French): "Shame on him who thinks ill of it." This closing phrase, added by a later scribe or reader of the poem, links the poem to the Order of the Garter, which was established around 1350 and which uses this phrase as its motto.

CHRISTINE DE PIZAN

ca. 1364–ca. 1431

"My head bowed as if in shame and my eyes full of tears, I sat slumped against the arm of my chair with my cheek resting on my hand. All of a sudden, I saw a beam of light, like the rays of the sun, shine down into my lap." Christine de Pizan's best-known allegory, *The Book of the City of Ladies*, opens with the narrator lamenting her female nature: she has been reading book after book about the character of women, learning that she, like all of her kind, is unfit for pursuing study, unable to perform meaningful work, and particularly likely to sin. Comforted by three crowned women, shining "goddesses" who embody Reason, Rectitude, and Justice, the narrator relearns the history of mankind—this time, through the lens of the feminine. From the stories of women of ancient times such as Dido and Lucrece to the lives of medieval saints, the goddesses work with the narrator to build the City of Ladies, stone by shining stone.

LIFE AND TIMES

Although Christine de Pizan lived almost her whole life in and around Paris, and wrote all of her works in the French language, she always remained (as she puts it in her *Book of Deeds of Arms and Chivalry*) "an Italian woman." Christine was the daughter of Tommaso da Pizzano, a doctor of medicine and of astrology, who moved from Italy to France to serve at the royal court of Charles V, and thus her fortunes were from childhood dependent on the favor and financial support of the ruling family. (The name "de Pizan," sometimes also spelled "de Pisan," reflects the family's landholdings in the town of Pizzano, on the outskirts of Bologna.) Her relationship to the royal household was reinforced after she wed Etienne de Castel, who worked as an administrative secretary and aide at the court. The marriage seems to have been a success: in her autobiographical writings, Christine refers to those ten years as the happiest of her life, and describes their abrupt end as the shattering of a ship tossed by a storm upon the rocks. Her ship had lost its "captain," and Christine had lost her "dearest friend." At the age of twenty-five, Christine found herself obliged to support herself, her three young children, a niece, and her widowed mother, at a time when few opportunities for paid work were available to women. Her solution: to live by her pen, becoming the first known female professional writer in European history.

The years around 1400 were tumultuous ones, especially for those near the royal court of France: the popular and effective ruler Charles V had died two decades before, leaving a son, Charles VI, who was at best erratic and at times descended into mental instability. His queen, Isabeau of Bavaria, attempted to maintain stable rule, aided by one of the king's brothers, but her efforts were thwarted by her own foreign birth and by rivalry on the part of other family members (especially Charles VI's uncle, the Duke of Burgundy). At the same time, the nation was engaged in repeated conflicts with England, in the course of the Hundred Years' War (1337–1453), and repeated bouts of plague following the devastating outbreak of the mid-fourteenth century roiled the country. Christine represents this political and social instability throughout her works, nowhere more memorably than in *Christine's Vision*, in which the "Crowned Dame" who represents the French nation laments the wicked children who tear her clothing and wound her body. By writing books of counsel and advice for the royal court, as well as works praising the virtues of the past king Charles V and the present queen Isabeau of Bavaria, Christine hoped to do her part in healing the body politic.

THE BOOK OF THE CITY OF LADIES

Christine de Pizan produced an extraordinary volume of writings, even compared with the prodigious output of her contemporaries **Petrarch, Boccaccio**, and **Chaucer**. She wrote hundreds of poems, both short lyrics and narrative works; allegorical visions, often incorporating autobiographical accounts of her life and times; and encyclopedic surveys of history and of myth. *The Book of the City of Ladies* is her most mature work, combining a remarkable ability to compile large amounts of information into a memorable form with the poetic gifts of metaphor and allegory: the city of ladies is a monumental edifice, built up piece by piece with "stones" made up of tales of individual women. Instead of being lofty, abstract figures, the goddesses of Reason, Rectitude, and Justice give Christine practical advice, urging her to wield "the pick of understanding" to dig out the badly shaped stones—that is, texts that describe women as ignorant and sinful—and instead to lay the foundations with the straight stones that are stories of great women of the past.

The three books of the *City of Ladies*, each supervised by a different goddess, demarcate progressive levels of the city-building project, moving upward from the foundations of book 1 to the walls of book 2 and finally to the houses and roofs of book 3. The first book, which is excerpted here, features women who ruled cities and empires, including Dido of Carthage and Semiramis of Babylon: these women, who had been condemned as lascivious and unstable by writers such as Virgil and **Dante**, become for Christine exemplars of the female ability to rule. Figures of myth also appear throughout book 1 as models for women's behavior: Ovid's Io, for example, is transformed from a foolish cow to a brilliant woman who gave the gift of learning and language to the Egyptians, while Minerva appears not as a goddess but as a woman who taught the Greeks their alphabet and ruled the city of Athens, where classical civilization flowered. The later books include historical examples of notable women of Christine's own time, both the lofty and the humble: not just duchesses and princesses but also Novella, the woman who sometimes lectured in the legal classroom of her father at the University of Bologna, and Anastasia, a brilliant painter of manuscript illustrations in medieval Paris.

Christine's works were quickly translated into other languages, and an English translation of the *City of Ladies* was read at the Tudor court. It is tempting to think of Christine's "city" as a hospitable home for the queens Mary I and Elizabeth, who would soon sit on the English throne. Although Christine's works were extremely popular during her lifetime and for more than a century after her death, they fell into neglect in subsequent generations. In the early 1970s, however, readers began to search out female authors of the premodern past. Along with **Marie de France**, Christine de Pizan is one of a long forgotten generation of medieval foremothers who laid the foundations for women writers of today.

From The Book of the City of Ladies[1]

FROM *PART ONE*

1. Here begins The Book of the City of Ladies

One day, I was sitting in my study surrounded by many books of different kinds, for it has long been my habit to engage in the pursuit of knowledge. My mind had grown weary as I had spent the day struggling with the weighty tomes of various authors whom I had been studying for some time. I looked up from my book and decided that, for once, I would put aside these difficult texts and find instead something amusing and easy to read from the works of the poets. As I searched around for some little book, I happened to chance upon a work which did not belong to me but was amongst a pile of others that had been placed in my safekeeping. I opened it up and saw from the title that it was by Matheolus.[2] With a smile, I made my choice. Although I had never read it, I knew that, unlike many other works, this one was said to be written in praise of women. Yet I had scarcely begun to read it when my dear mother called me down to supper, for it was time to eat. I put the book to one side, resolving to go back to it the following day.

The next morning, seated once more in my study as is my usual custom, I remembered my previous desire to have a look at this book by Matheolus. I picked it up again and read on a little. But, seeing the kind of immoral language and ideas it contained, the content seemed to me likely to appeal only to those who enjoy reading works of slander and to be of no use whatsoever to anyone who wished to pursue virtue or to improve their moral standards. I therefore leafed through it, read the ending, and decided to switch to some more worthy and profitable work. Yet, having looked at this book, which I considered to be of no authority, an extraordinary thought became planted in my mind which made me wonder why on earth it was that so many men, both clerks and others, have said and continue to say and write such awful, damning things about women and their ways. I was at a loss as to how to explain it. It is not just a handful of writers who do this, nor only this Matheolus whose book is neither regarded as authoritative nor intended to be taken seriously. It is all manner of philosophers, poets and orators too numerous to mention, who all seem to speak with one voice and are unanimous in their view that female nature is wholly given up to vice.

As I mulled these ideas over in my mind again and again, I began to examine myself and my own behaviour as an example of womankind. In order to judge in all fairness and without prejudice whether what so many famous men have said about us is true, I also thought about other women I know, the many princesses and countless ladies of all different social ranks who have shared their private and personal thoughts with me. No matter which way I looked at it and no matter how much I turned the question over in my mind, I could find no evidence from my own experience to bear out such a negative view of female nature and habits. Even so, given that I could scarcely find a moral work by any

---

1. Translated from the French by Rosalind Brown-Grant.
2. The French poet's Latin poem, *Liber Lamentationum* (ca. 1295), which became enormously

popular in its French translation by Jean le Fèvre as *The Lamentations of Matheolus* (ca. 1320), attacked women and marriage.

author which didn't devote some chapter or paragraph to attacking the female sex, I had to accept their unfavourable opinion of women since it was unlikely that so many learned men, who seemed to be endowed with such great intelligence and insight into all things, could possibly have lied on so many different occasions. It was on the basis of this one simple argument that I was forced to conclude that, although my understanding was too crude and ill-informed to recognize the great flaws in myself and other women, these men had to be in the right. Thus I preferred to give more weight to what others said than to trust my own judgement and experience.

I dwelt on these thoughts at such length that it was as if I had sunk into a deep trance. My mind became flooded with an endless stream of names as I recalled all the authors who had written on this subject. I came to the conclusion that God had surely created a vile thing when He created woman. Indeed, I was astounded that such a fine craftsman could have wished to make such an appalling object which, as these writers would have it, is like a vessel in which all the sin and evil of the world has been collected and preserved. This thought inspired such a great sense of disgust and sadness in me that I began to despise myself and the whole of my sex as an aberration in nature.

With a deep sigh, I called out to God: 'Oh Lord, how can this be? Unless I commit an error of faith, I cannot doubt that you, in your infinite wisdom and perfect goodness, could make anything that wasn't good. Didn't you yourself create woman especially and then endow her with all the qualities that you wished her to have? How could you possibly have made a mistake in anything? Yet here stand women not simply accused, but already judged, sentenced and condemned! I just cannot understand this contradiction. If it is true, dear Lord God, that women are guilty of such horrors as so many men seem to say, and as you yourself have said that the testimony of two or more witnesses is conclusive, how can I doubt their word? Oh God, why wasn't I born a male so that my every desire would be to serve you, to do right in all things, and to be as perfect a creature as man claims to be? Since you chose not to show such grace to me, please pardon and forgive me, dear Lord, if I fail to serve you as well as I should, for the servant who receives fewer rewards from his lord is less obligated to him in his service.'

Sick at heart, in my lament to God I uttered these and many other foolish words since I thought myself very unfortunate that He had given me a female form.

2. The three ladies

Sunk in these unhappy thoughts, my head bowed as if in shame and my eyes full of tears, I sat slumped against the arm of my chair with my cheek resting on my hand. All of a sudden, I saw a beam of light, like the rays of the sun, shine down into my lap. Since it was too dark at that time of day for the sun to come into my study, I woke with a start as if from a deep sleep. I looked up to see where the light had come from and all at once saw before me three ladies, crowned and of majestic appearance, whose faces shone with a brightness that lit up me and everything else in the place. As you can imagine, I was full of amazement that they had managed to enter a room whose doors and windows were all closed. Terrified at the thought that it might be some kind of apparition come to tempt me, I quickly made the sign of the cross on my forehead.

With a smile on her face, the lady who stood at the front of the three addressed me first: 'My dear daughter, don't be afraid, for we have not come to do you any harm, but rather, out of pity on your distress, we are here to comfort you. Our aim is to help you get rid of those misconceptions which have clouded your mind and made you reject what you know and believe in fact to be the truth just because so many other people have come out with the opposite opinion. You're acting like that fool in the joke who falls asleep in the mill and whose friends play a trick on him by dressing him up in women's clothing. When he wakes up, they manage to convince him that he is a woman despite all evidence to the contrary! My dear girl, what has happened to your sense? Have you forgotten that it is in the furnace that gold is refined, increasing in value the more it is beaten and fashioned into different shapes? Don't you know that it's the very finest things which are the subject of the most intense discussion? Now, if you turn your mind to the very highest realm of all, the realm of abstract ideas, think for a moment whether or not those philosophers whose views against women you've been citing have ever been proven wrong. In fact, they are all constantly correcting each other's opinions, as you yourself should know from reading Aristotle's *Metaphysics* where he discusses and refutes both their views and those of Plato and other philosophers.[3] Don't forget the Doctors of the Church either, and Saint Augustine[4] in particular who all took issue with Aristotle himself on certain matters, even though he is considered to be the greatest of all authorities on both moral and natural philosophy. You seem to have accepted the philosophers' views as articles of faith and thus as irrefutable on every point.

'As for the poets you mention, you must realize that they sometimes wrote in the manner of fables which you have to take as saying the opposite of what they appear to say. You should therefore read such texts according to the grammatical rule of *antiphrasis*, which consists of interpreting something that is negative in a positive light, or vice versa. My advice to you is to read those passages where they criticize women in this way and to turn them to your advantage, no matter what the author's original intention was. It could be that Matheolus is also meant to be read like this because there are some passages in his book which, if taken literally, are just out-and-out heresy. As for what these authors—not just Matheolus but also the more authoritative writer of the *Romance of the Rose*[5]—say about the God-given, holy state of matrimony, experience should tell you that they are completely wrong when they say that marriage is insufferable thanks to women. What husband ever gave his wife the power over him to utter the kind of insults and obscenities which these authors claim that women do? Believe me, despite what you've read in books, you've never actually *seen* such a thing because it's all a pack of outrageous lies. My

3. The influential Greek philosophers Plato (429–347 B.C.E.) and his student Aristotle (384–322 B.C.E.) were widely read in Latin translation in the Middle Ages.
4. Augustine of Hippo (354–430). Doctors of the Church: title given in the Middle Ages to certain saints who were also outstanding theologians.
5. A very popular French allegorical romance, written in two parts—by Guillaume de Lorris (ca. 1237) and by Jean de Meun (ca. 1275); Christine's objections are mainly to the continuation, which includes a number of misogynistic passages.

dear friend, I have to say that it is your naivety which has led you to take what they come out with as the truth. Return to your senses and stop worrying your head about such foolishness. Let me tell you that those who speak ill of women do more harm to themselves than they do to the women they actually slander.'

3. Christine recounts how the lady who had spoken to her told her who she was, what her function and purpose was, and how she prophesied that Christine would build a city with the help of the three ladies

On receiving these words from the distinguished lady, I didn't know which of my senses was the more struck by what she said: whether it was my ears as I took in her stirring words, or my eyes as I admired her great beauty and dress, her noble bearing and face. It was the same for the other ladies too: my gaze darted back and forth from one to the other since they were all so alike that you could hardly tell them apart. All except for the third lady, who was no less imposing than the other two. This lady had such a stern face that whoever glanced into her eyes, no matter how brazen they were, would feel afraid of committing some misdeed since she seemed to threaten punishment to all wrongdoers. Out of respect for the ladies' noble appearance, I stood up before them but was far too dumbfounded to utter a single word. I was extremely curious to know who they were and would have dearly loved to dare ask them their names, where they were from, why they had come, and what the priceless symbols were that each of them held like a sceptre in her right hand. Yet I didn't think myself worthy to put these questions to such honourable ladies as these, so I held my tongue and carried on gazing at them. Though still frightened, I was also in part reassured, for the lady's words had already begun to assuage my fears.

Presently, the wise lady who had addressed me first seemed to read my mind and began to answer my unspoken questions with these words: 'My dear daughter, you should know that it is by the grace of God, who foresees and ordains all things, that we, celestial creatures though we may be, have been sent down to earth in order to restore order and justice to those institutions which we ourselves have set up at God's command. All three of us are His daughters, for it was He who created us. My task is to bring back men and women when they drift away from the straight and narrow. Should they go astray but yet have the sense to know me when they see me, I come to them in spirit and speak to their conscience, instructing them in the error of their ways and showing them how exactly it is that they have done wrong. Then I teach them to follow the correct road and to avoid doing what is undesirable. Because it is my role to light their way to the true path and to teach both men and women to acknowledge their flaws and weaknesses, you see me here holding up a shining mirror like a sceptre in my right hand. You can be sure that whoever looks into this mirror, no matter who they may be, will see themselves as they truly are, such is its great power. Not for nothing is it encrusted with precious stones, as you can see. With the help of this mirror, I can determine the nature, quantity and essence of all things and can take full measure of them. Without this mirror, nothing can come to good. Since you obviously want to know what function my two sisters perform, each of them will shortly speak to you in turn and will add her weight to my words by giving you a clear explanation of both her name and her powers.

'First, however, I will tell you exactly why we are here. I want you to know that, as we do nothing without good reason, our appearance here today has a definite purpose. Though we do not attempt to be known in all places, since not everyone strives to acquaint themselves with us, we have none the less come to visit you, our dear friend. Because you have long desired to acquire true knowledge by dedicating yourself to your studies, which have cut you off from the rest of the world, we are now here to comfort you in your sad and dejected state. It is your own efforts that have won you this reward. You will soon see clearly why it is that your heart and mind have been so troubled.

'Yet we also have a further, more important reason for coming to visit you, which we'll now go on to tell you about. Our wish is to prevent others from falling into the same error as you and to ensure that, in future, all worthy ladies and valiant women are protected from those who have attacked them. The female sex has been left defenceless for a long time now, like an orchard without a wall, and bereft of a champion to take up arms in order to protect it. Indeed, this is because those trusty knights who should by right defend women have been negligent in their duty and lacking in vigilance, leaving womankind open to attack from all sides. It's no wonder that women have been the losers in this war against them since the envious slanderers and vicious traitors who criticize them have been allowed to aim all manner of weapons at their defenceless targets. Even the strongest city will fall if there is no one to defend it, and even the most undeserving case will win if there is no one to testify against it. Out of the goodness and simplicity of their hearts, women have trusted in God and have patiently endured the countless verbal and written assaults that have been unjustly and shamelessly launched upon them. Now, however, it is time for them to be delivered out of the hands of Pharaoh.[6] For this reason, we three ladies whom you see before you have been moved by pity to tell you that you are to construct a building in the shape of a walled city, sturdy and impregnable. This has been decreed by God, who has chosen you to do this with our help and guidance. Only ladies who are of good reputation and worthy of praise will be admitted into this city. To those lacking in virtue, its gates will remain forever closed.'

4. How, before the lady revealed her name, she spoke at greater length about the city which Christine was destined to build, and explained that she was entrusted with the task of helping her to construct the enclosure and external walls

'So you see, my dear daughter, that you alone of all women have been granted the honour of building the City of Ladies. In order to lay the foundations, you shall draw fresh water from us three as from a clear spring. We will bring you building materials which will be stronger and more durable than solid, uncemented marble. Your city will be unparalleled in splendour and will last for all eternity.

6. Like the Israelites from Egypt; in this comparison, Christine is implicitly cast as Moses.

'Haven't you read that King Tros founded the city of Troy with the help of Apollo, Minerva and Neptune,[7] whom the people of that time believed to be gods? Haven't you also heard of Cadmus, who created the city of Thebes at the gods' command?[8] Yet, in the course of time, even these cities fell into ruin and decay. However, in the manner of a true sibyl, I prophesy to you that this city which you're going to build with our help will never fall or be taken. Rather, it will prosper always, in spite of its enemies who are racked by envy. Though it may be attacked on many sides, it will never be lost or defeated.

'In the past, as the history books tell you, certain courageous ladies who refused the yoke of servitude founded and established the realm of Amazonia.[9] For many years afterwards, this realm was maintained under the rule of various queens, all of whom were noble ladies chosen by the women themselves, and who governed well and wisely, making every effort to keep their country safe. These women were very strong and powerful, having extended their rule over many of the lands of the east and having subjugated to their will all the neighbouring countries. They were feared by everyone, even the Greeks, who were the bravest nation in the world at that time. None the less, even the Amazons' power began to crumble in due course, as is the way with all earthly rulers. Now, the only trace that is left of that proud realm is its name.

'By contrast, the city which you're going to build will be much more powerful than these. As has been decided amongst the three of us, it is my task to help you begin by giving you tough, indestructible cement which you will need to set the mighty foundations and to support the great walls that you must raise all around. These walls should have huge high towers, solid bastions surrounded by moats, and outer forts with both natural and manmade defences. This is what a powerful city must have in order to resist attack. On our advice, you will sink these foundations deep in order to make them as secure as possible, and you will construct such high walls that the city inside will be safe from assault. Dear Christine, I have now told you all about why we have come. However, in order to convince you to give greater weight to my words, I'm going to reveal my name to you. The very sound of it should reassure you that, if you follow my instructions, you will find me to be an infallible guide to you in all your endeavours. I am called Lady Reason, so rest assured that you are in good hands. For the moment, I will say no more.'

* * *

14. More discussion and debate between Christine and Reason

'My lady, you have truly spoken well, and your words are like music to my ears. Yet, despite what we've said about intelligence, it's undeniable that women are by nature fearful creatures, having weak, frail bodies and lacking in physical

---

7. According to classical myth, the city of Troy (in modern-day Turkey) was founded by the son of Tros, aided by Apollo (god of the sun, prophecy, and music), Athena (called by the Romans Minerva, goddess of wisdom and war), and Poseidon (Neptune, god of the sea).
8. According to myth, the earliest inhabitants of the new city were men who grew from the dragon's teeth that Cadmus had sown in the ground on the instructions of Athena. Christine would have been most familiar with the verson of the story told in Ovid, *Metamorphoses* 3.1–137.
9. The country believed to be inhabited only by Amazons, the warrior women featured in several Greek myths; its location, a matter of dispute, was usually held to be somewhere near the Black Sea.

strength. Men have therefore argued that it is these things that make the female sex inferior and of lesser value. To their minds, if a person's body is defective in some way, this undermines and diminishes that person's moral qualities and thus it follows that he or she is less worthy of praise.'

Reason's reply was, 'My dear daughter, this is a false conclusion which is completely untenable. It is definitely the case that when Nature fails to make a body which is as perfect as others she has created, be it in shape or beauty, or in some strength or power of limb, she very often compensates for it by giving that body some greater quality than the one she has taken away. Here's an example: it's often said that the great philosopher Aristotle was very ugly, with one eye lower than the other and a deformed face. Yet, if he was physically misshapen, Nature certainly made up for it by endowing him with extraordinary intellectual powers, as is attested by his own writings. Having this extra intelligence was worth far more to him than having a body as beautiful as that of Absalom.

'The same can be said of the emperor Alexander the Great,[1] who was extremely short, ugly and sickly, and yet, as is well known, he had tremendous courage in his soul. This is also true of many others. Believe me, my dear friend, it doesn't necessarily follow that a fine, strong body makes for a brave and courageous heart. Courage comes from a natural, vital force which is a gift from God that He allows Nature to implant in some rational beings more than in others. This force resides in the mind and the heart, not in the bodily strength of one's limbs. You very often see men who are well built and strong yet pathetic and cowardly, but others who are small and physically weak yet brave and tough. This applies equally to other moral qualities. As far as bravery and physical strength are concerned, neither God nor Nature has done the female sex a disservice by depriving it of these attributes. Rather, women are lucky to be deficient in this respect because they are at least spared from committing and being punished for the acts of appalling cruelty, the murders and terrible violent deeds which men who are equipped with the necessary strength have performed in the past and still do today. It probably would have been better for such men if their souls *had* spent their pilgrimage through this mortal life inside the weak body of a woman. To return to what I was saying, I am convinced that if Nature decided not to endow women with a powerful physique, she none the less made up for it by giving them a most virtuous disposition: that of loving God and being fearful of disobeying His commandments. Women who don't act like this are going against their own nature.

'However, dear Christine, you should note that God clearly wished to prove to men that, just because *all* women are not as physically strong and courageous as men generally are, this does not mean that the entire female sex is lacking in such qualities. There are in fact several women who have displayed the necessary courage, strength and bravery to undertake and accomplish extraordinary deeds which match those achieved by the great conquerors and knights mentioned in books. I'll shortly give you an example of such a woman.

'My dear daughter and beloved friend, I've now prepared a trench for you which is good and wide, and have emptied it of earth which I have carried away in great loads on my shoulders. It's now time for you to place inside the trench

1. The greatest Greek general of antiquity (356–323 B.C.E.), renowned in the Middle Ages as an ideal of knighthood and the power to rule.

some heavy, solid stones which will form the foundations of the walls for the City of Ladies. So take the trowel of your pen and get ready to set to with vigour on the building work. Here is a good, strong stone which I want you to lay as the first of your city's foundations. Don't you know that Nature herself used astrological signs to predict that it should be placed here in this work? Step back a little now and let me put it into position for you.'

15. About Queen Semiramis

'Semiramis[2] was a truly heroic woman who excelled in the practice and pursuit of arms. Because of her great military prowess, the people of the time—who were all pagans—said that she was so invincible both on land and sea that she must be the sister of the great god Jupiter and the daughter of the old god Saturn whom they regarded as the rulers of these two domains. This lady was married to King Ninus, who named the city of Nineveh after himself. With the help of his wife Semiramis, who rode into battle at his side, this fine lord conquered the mighty city of Babylon, the vast land of Assyria and many other countries.

'When Semiramis was still quite young, it so happened that her husband Ninus was killed by an arrow during an assault on a city. Once he had been buried with all due ceremony as befitted a king, his wife didn't lay down her arms but rather took them up with renewed vigour and seized the reins of power over the kingdoms and territories that she and her husband had conquered together in battle. She gained full control over these lands, thanks to her military skills, and likewise accomplished so many other marvellous deeds that no man could match her in strength and ability. This supremely courageous lady had no fear of pain and was undaunted by anything. Semiramis confronted any type of danger with such courage that she crushed all her enemies who thought that, once she was widowed, they could overthrow her in the lands which she had conquered. However, she had such a fearsome reputation as a warrior that she not only kept all the lands she had already taken but even added others to her empire. Accompanied by vast numbers of troops, she attacked Ethiopia with such force that she defeated it completely. From there she set off with a huge army to conquer India, a country on which no one had ever dared wage war. She attacked this nation so ruthlessly that it fell entirely into her hands. To keep the tale short, she then went on to attack still more countries so that, in the end, the whole of the East came under her control. Thanks to these magnificent and mighty conquests, Semiramis was able to rebuild and fortify the city of Babylon which had been founded by Nimrod and the giants on the plains of Shinar.[3] Though the city was already powerful and fiercely protected, she strengthened it still further with more defences and deep moats all around.

'One time, Semiramis was sitting in her room surrounded by her handmaidens, who were busy combing her hair, when news suddenly came that one of her territories had rebelled against her. She jumped up immediately and swore

2. Legendary Assyrian queen, credited with conquering many lands but later conventionally associated with despotism and sexual appetites (specifically, incest; e.g., see Dante, *Inferno* 5.52–60). Christine's positive representation of Semiramis, identified during the Middle Ages as the Queen of Babylon, is unusual in the Middle Ages.
3. See Genesis 10.10.

on her kingdom that the half of her hair which had not yet been plaited would remain loose until she could avenge this outrage and take the country back into her control. Without further delay, she ordered huge numbers of her troops to prepare for battle and attacked the rebels with such ferocity and might that they submitted once more to her rule. These rebels and all her other subjects were so intimidated by her that none ever dared to revolt against her again. In memory of this great and noble deed, an enormous bronze statue of her, richly decorated in gold, was erected on a massive pillar in the middle of Babylon. This statue, which stood for many years, depicted a princess holding a sword in her hand with only one side of her hair plaited. Queen Semiramis founded and built several new cities and fortresses, and performed so many other notable feats that no man has ever been commemorated in the history books for having as much courage and for doing as many marvellous things as she did.

'It's true that some authors have criticized Semiramis—and rightly so, if she had been a Christian—for having married her own son whom she had borne to her husband, the lord Ninus. Yet she had two main reasons for doing so: firstly, she wanted no other crowned lady to share her empire with her, as would have been the case if her son had married another woman; and secondly, in her opinion, no other man than her son was worthy of her. This terrible transgression of hers can partly be excused by the fact that, at that time, there was no written law: people observed only the law of nature whereby they were free to do as they pleased without fear of committing a sin. There's no doubt that, since she was so proud and honourable, if she *had* thought she was doing anything wrong or that she might be subject to criticism for her actions, she would have refrained from doing as she did.

'The first foundation stone of our city is now in place, but we must follow it up with many more stones in order to raise high the walls of the building.'

16. About the Amazons

'There is a country near the land of Europe which lies on the Ocean,[4] that great sea that covers the whole world. This place is called Scythia, or the land of the Scythians. It once happened that, in the course of a war, all the noblest male inhabitants of this country were killed. When their womenfolk saw that they had lost all their husbands, brothers and male relatives, and that only very young boys and old men were left, they took courage and called together a great council of women, resolving that, henceforth, they would lead the country themselves, free from male control. They issued an edict which forbade any man from entering their territory, but decided that, in order to ensure the survival of their race, they would go into neighbouring countries at certain times of the year and return thereafter to their own land. If they gave birth to male children, they would send them away to be with their fathers, but the female children they would bring up themselves. In order to uphold this law, they chose two of the highest-born ladies to be queens, one of whom was called Lampheto and the other Marpasia. No sooner was this done than they expelled

---

4. On medieval maps, the name given to a sea that surrounded the entire landmass of the known world. The region known in classical times as Scythia includes areas of modern Ukraine, Russia, and Kazakhstan.

all the men who were left in the country. Next, they took up arms, women and girls together, and waged war on their enemies, laying waste to their lands with fire and sword and crushing all opposition until none remained. In short, they wreaked full revenge for their husbands' deaths.

'This is how the women of Scythia began to bear arms. They were later known as the Amazons, a name which means "they who have had a breast removed." It was their custom that, by a technique known only to this race of women, the most noble of them would have the left breast burnt off at a very early age in order to free them up to carry a shield. Those young girls who were of non-noble birth would lose the right breast so that they could more easily handle a bow. They took such pleasure in the pursuit of arms that they greatly expanded their territory by the use of force, thus spreading their fame far and wide. To get back to what I was saying, the two queens Lampheto and Marpasia each led a great army into various countries and were so successful that they conquered a large part of Europe and the region of Asia, subjugating many kingdoms to their rule. They founded many towns and cities including the Asian city of Ephesus,[5] which has long been justly renowned. Of these two queens, it was Marpasia who died first in battle and who was replaced by a young daughter of hers, a beautiful and noble maiden called Synoppe. This girl was so proud that she chose never to sleep with a man, preferring instead to remain a virgin until her death. Her only love and sole pleasure in life was the pursuit of arms: she never tired of going into battle and seizing new lands. She also avenged her mother's death fully by putting to the sword the entire enemy population and laying waste to their whole country, adding it to the others which she went on to conquer.'

17. About the Amazon queen, Thamiris

'As you will now go on to hear, the state founded by the Amazons flourished for a very long time, with a whole succession of valiant ladies becoming queen. Since it would be tedious to tell you all their names, I'll limit myself to the most famous individuals.

'One of the Amazon queens was the noble Thamiris, who was as brave as she was wise. Thanks to her intelligence, cunning and military prowess, she defeated and captured Cyrus,[6] a great and powerful king of Persia who had performed many marvellous feats, including the conquest of the mighty Babylon and a large part of the whole world. Having vanquished so many countries, Cyrus decided to attack the realm of the Amazons in an attempt to bring them too under his control. Once this wise queen had been informed by her spies that Cyrus was advancing towards her with an army big enough to defeat the entire world, she realized that there was no way to beat his troops by force and that she would have to use guile. So, like the battle-hardened leader she was, on learning that, as she had intended, Cyrus had now come well inside her territory having met no opposition, Thamiris ordered all her ladies to put on their armour and cleverly sent them off to set up strategic ambushes in the mountains and forests through which Cyrus would have to pass.

5. In Asia Minor, near the coast of the Aegean Sea (in modern Turkey).
6. The founder of the Persian Empire (d. 529 B.C.E), who conquered Babylon (but did not suffer the death described here).

'Hidden from view, Thamiris and her army waited for Cyrus and his men to move into the narrow passages and gullies between the trees and rocks where he had to pick his way. At the key moment, she had her horns sounded, taking Cyrus completely by surprise. To his dismay, he found his army attacked on all sides by ladies who were hurling down great piles of rocks to crush them. Because of the difficult terrain, his men could neither advance nor retreat: if they tried to go forwards or backwards, they were ambushed and killed as soon as they emerged at either end of the passages. All were crushed and slain, except Cyrus and his barons, who were taken prisoner by order of the queen. When the massacre was over, Thamiris had them brought before her pavilion, which she had ordered to be put up before the fighting began. She was so full of anger at Cyrus for having killed one of her beloved sons whom she had sent to his court that she decided to show no mercy. She had all his barons decapitated in front of him, saying: "Cyrus, you who were so cruel and bloodthirsty from killing other men, can now finally drink your fill." Thereupon she had his head cut off and thrown into a barrel in which all the blood of his barons had been collected.

'My sweet daughter and dear friend, I'm reminding you of these things because they are relevant to what we've been discussing, even though you are already familiar with them. Indeed, you yourself have recounted these stories elsewhere in your *Book of the Mutation of Fortune* and *Letter of Othea to Hector*. I'll now go on to tell you some more.'

18. How the mighty Hercules and his companion Theseus came from Greece to attack the Amazons with a great army and fleet of ships, and how the two maidens Menalippe and Hippolyta brought them down, horses and all, in a big heap

'What else shall I tell you about them? The ladies of Amazonia were so successful in warfare that they were feared and respected by all other nations. Their reputation for being invincible and their unquenchable thirst for conquering new lands which led them to lay waste any country which refused to surrender to them, spread even as far as the distant land of Greece. This made the Greeks very afraid that the Amazons would one day attempt to use force against them.

'Then living in Greece at the very height of his powers was the great and mighty Hercules.[7] In his day, he performed more feats of strength than any mortal man whose deeds are recorded in the history books, fighting with giants, lions, snakes and terrifying monsters, and beating them all. In short, the only man who ever matched him for strength was the magnificent Samson.[8] Hercules was of the opinion that the Greeks shouldn't wait for the Amazons to come to them but would be much better advised to invade them first instead. In order to execute this plan, he ordered ships to be made ready for war and gathered together a large group of young noblemen to go and attack the Amazons in numbers. When Theseus, the good and valiant king of Athens, heard what was happening, he declared that they wouldn't go without him. He joined forces with Hercules and they sailed off with a huge army towards the land of

7. The greatest hero of classical mythology; many of his feats were performed in connec- tion with his twelve famous labors.
8. See Judges 13–16.

the Amazons. When they were just off the coast, Hercules, despite his extraordinary strength and bravery and the fact that he had so many troops with him, did not dare to moor the ships and disembark during the daytime as he knew just how fierce and courageous the Amazons were. This would be an almost unbelievable thing to say were it not that so many history books have recounted how this man, who could not be beaten by any creature alive, was extremely wary of these women's strength. He and his army therefore waited until nightfall when, at that hour when all living things are fast asleep, they leapt out of their ships and ran ashore. They swept through towns, setting fire to everything and killing all those who were caught unawares and had no time to defend themselves. The news about what had happened spread like wildfire and, as soon as they could, the brave Amazons rushed over themselves to pick up their weapons and to head down in great waves to attack the enemy's ships.

'The queen of the Amazons at that time was called Orithyia, a very valiant lady who had conquered many lands. She was the mother of the good Queen Penthesilea, about whom I'll tell you more later. Orithyia had succeeded the courageous Queen Antiope who had ruled the Amazons and governed the country with superb military skill, achieving many great things in her time. Orithyia soon heard the news that the Greeks, entirely unprovoked, had landed like a pack of thieves in the night and were going around killing everyone. As you can imagine, she was livid with rage, and vowed that they would regret having made her so angry. Cursing her enemy, whom she didn't fear in the least, she immediately called her troops together for battle. You should have seen the ladies as they dashed about for their arms and lined up at their queen's side. By daybreak, all her battalions were ready.

'Two of the strongest and most courageous maidens, the finest and most valiant of all the Amazons, Menalippe and Hippolyta, who were closely related to the queen, decided not to wait for her order once they heard that her plan was to get all her ladies together and order them into battle formation. Instead, as quickly as they could, they threw on their arms and, with lances at the ready and shields of tough elephant hide slung round their necks, they headed off on their swift chargers directly towards the port. Boiling with the most terrible rage and fury, they lowered their lances and aimed straight for the leaders of the Greek army: Menalippe against Hercules and Hippolyta against Theseus. Despite the great strength, bravery and courage of their enemies, the women's anger soon bore fruit as each of them struck against her adversary with such power that the two knights were brought down, horses and all, in a big heap. The women too fell from their horses, but they immediately recovered themselves and attacked the knights with their swords.

'How can one praise these maidens highly enough for having brought down, completely unaided, two of the most valiant knights who ever lived? The story would be almost impossible to believe if so many reliable authors had not made mention of it in their works. Those writers who were themselves clearly amazed by the story attempted to find excuses for Hercules in particular, given his exceptional physical strength, claiming that he only fell because his horse stumbled on the impact of the blow, adding that he would never have been brought down if he had been on foot. These two knights were completely shamefaced to have been knocked off their horses by the two maidens. Although the women continued to fight long and hard with their swords in a drawn-out battle, they were eventually beaten by the two knights, which is hardly suprising given that there were no two other heroes like them in the whole world.

'Hercules and Theseus were so highly gratified at having taken the two maidens prisoner that they wouldn't have exchanged them for the wealth of an entire city. They returned to their ship to disarm and refresh themselves, for they were only too aware that the battle had been a hard one to win. The two knights treated their captives with the greatest of honour and, once the ladies had disarmed and revealed themselves in all their true splendour and beauty, they were even more delighted. As they feasted their eyes on the two ladies, it seemed to them that they had never won a prize which gave them greater pleasure.

'When Queen Orithyia heard that the two maidens had been captured, she advanced towards the Greeks with a huge army. She was deeply distressed by what had happened but, out of fear that more harm would come to the two prisoners if she attacked the Greeks, she called a halt and sent a couple of her baronesses to parley with the enemy and to tell them that whatever ransom they demanded for the return of the girls, she would pay it. Hercules and Theseus received the two messengers with great respect and courteously replied that if the queen chose to make peace with them and promise that she and her ladies would never wage war on the Greeks but would be their allies, they would make a reciprocal pact with her. As for the ransom, they were prepared to surrender the two women and keep only their arms as a token and reminder of the victory that they had won over them. Since Orithyia's only concern was to have the two maidens whom she loved dearly returned safely to her, she was obliged to agree to the Greeks' demands. Once all the negotiations were done and the terms accepted by both parties, the queen arrived unarmed to celebrate the peace treaty with a feast, accompanied by a whole host of ladies and girls who were more beautifully arrayed than any the Greeks had ever seen. This feast took place amidst much happiness and joy.

'Yet Theseus was extremely reluctant to let Hippolyta go as he had already fallen deeply in love with her. He therefore begged Hercules to ask Orithyia to allow him to marry Hippolyta and take her back to Greece with him, a request to which the queen gave her consent. After a magnificent wedding feast, the Greeks left for home with Hippolyta at Theseus's side. She later bore him a son called Hippolytus who became a famous knight of exemplary prowess and skill. When the people of Greece learnt that peace had been made with the Amazons, they were overjoyed because there was no other race in the world whom they feared more.'

19. About Queen Penthesilea and how she went to the rescue of the city of Troy

'This Queen Orithyia lived for a long time and died at a fine old age, having kept the realm of Amazonia in a flourishing state and expanded its dominion. The Amazons crowned as her successor her own daughter, the brave Penthesilea, who surpassed all others in intelligence, courage, prowess and virtue. She too was forever eager to take up arms and fight, increasing the Amazons' power further than ever before in her relentless pursuit of territory. She was so feared by her enemies that none dared approach her and so proud that she never slept with a man but preferred to remain a virgin all her life.

'It was during her reign that the terrible war between the Greeks and the Trojans broke out.[9] Because of the name that the great Hector had made for himself as the finest, bravest and most highly skilled knight in the world, Penthesilea, who was naturally drawn to him since they shared the same qualities, heard so much about him that she began to love him with a pure and noble heart and desired above all else to go and see him. In order to fulfil this wish, she left her country with a great host of noble ladies and maidens all expert in the arts of war and richly armed, setting off to the city of Troy which lay a great distance away. However, distances always seem shorter when one's heart is filled with a strong desire.

'Unfortunately, when Penthesilea arrived in Troy, it was already too late: she discovered that Hector had been killed by Achilles during a battle in which the flower of Trojan chivalry had been wiped out. Penthesilea was received with all honours by the Trojans—King Priam, Queen Hecuba and all the barons—yet she was inconsolable and heartbroken to find that Hector was dead. The king and queen, who never left off grieving for the death of their son, offered to show her his body since they had been unable to let her see him alive. They took her to the temple where his tomb had been prepared, truly the very noblest and finest sepulchre that has ever been recorded in the history books. There, in a beautiful, sumptuous chapel all decorated with gold and precious stones, sat the embalmed and robed body of Hector on a throne in front of the main altar dedicated to the gods. He appeared to be more alive than dead as he brandished a naked sword in his hand and his haughty face still seemed to be throwing out a challenge to the Greeks. He was draped in a long, full garment which was woven with fine gold and trimmed and embroidered with jewels. This garment came down to the floor, covering the lower half of his body, which lay completely immersed in a precious balm that gave off a most delicious scent. The Trojans worshipped this body, bathed in the dazzling light of hundreds of candles, as if it were one of their gods. A costlier tomb surely never was seen. Here they brought Queen Penthesilea, who no sooner glimpsed the body through the open chapel door than she fell on her knees in front of Hector and greeted him as if he were still alive. She then went up close towards him and gazed deeply on his face. Through her tears she cried out: "O flower of chivalry, the very epitome and pinnacle of bravery: who can dare to call themselves valiant or even strap on a sword now that the finest and most shining example of knighthood has gone? Alas, cursed be the day that he whose vile hand deprived the world of its greatest treasure was ever born! Most noble prince, why was Fortune so contrary as to prevent me from being by your side when this traitor was plotting your downfall? This never would have happened because I would not have allowed it. If your killer were still alive, I would surely avenge your death and thus extinguish the great sorrow and anger which are burning up my heart as I see you lifeless before me and unable to speak to me, as was my only desire. Yet, since Fortune decreed that it should be so and I can do nothing to gainsay her, I swear by the very highest gods of our faith and solemnly promise you, my dear lord, that as long as I have breath in my body I will make the Greeks pay for

9. The Trojan War, a central theme of classical literature; it was the subject of Homer's *Iliad* and the backdrop of Virgil's *Aeneid.* Hector was the greatest warrior among the Trojans; Achilles, the greatest among the Greeks.

your death." As she knelt before the corpse, Penthesilea's words reached the great crowd of barons, knights and ladies who were all gathered there and moved them to tears. She could barely drag herself away from the tomb but, finally, she kissed his hand that was holding the sword and took her leave, saying: "Most excellent knight, what must you have been like when you were alive, given that the mere image of you in death is so full of majesty!"

'Weeping tender tears, she left his side. As soon as she could, she put on her armour and, with her army of noble ladies, dashed out of the city to attack the Greeks who were holding Troy in a state of siege. To make a brief tale of it, she and her army set to with such vigour that, if she had lived longer, no Greek would ever again have set foot in Greece. She struck down and nearly killed Pyrrhus, Achilles's son, who was a very fine soldier. It was only with great difficulty that his men were able to rescue him and drag him, half-dead, back to safety. Thinking that he was unlikely to survive, the Greeks were distraught, for he had been their greatest hope. If Penthesilea felt hatred for the father, she certainly didn't spare the son.

'In short, though Penthesilea performed the most extraordinary feats, she finally succumbed after having spent several days with her army in the thick of battle. When the Greeks were at their lowest ebb, Pyrrhus, who had recovered from his wounds but was overcome with shame and sorrow that she had done him such grievous harm, ordered his valiant men to concentrate solely on surrounding Penthesilea and separating her from her companions. He wanted to kill her with his own hands and would pay a handsome reward to anyone who managed to trap her. Pyrrhus's men took a long time to do his bidding because Penthesilea dealt out such fearsome blows that they were extremely afraid of approaching her. However, in the end, after an enormous amount of effort on their part, they finally managed to encircle her one day and isolate her from her ladies. The Greeks attacked the other Amazons so fiercely that they were powerless to help their queen and Penthesilea herself was exhausted after having accomplished more in that time than even Hector himself could have done. Despite the astonishing strength with which she defended herself, the Greeks were able to smash all her weapons and tear off a good part of her helmet. When Pyrrhus saw her bare blonde head, he struck her such a blow that he split her whole skull in two. Thus died the great and good Penthesilea, a huge loss both to the Trojans and to her own countrywomen, who were immediately plunged into grief, which was understandable since from that day forth the Amazons never knew any other queen to rival her. With heavy hearts, they carried her dead body back home.

'So, you have now heard how the realm of Amazonia was founded and how it lasted for over eight hundred years. You can work this out by checking in the history books for the length of time it took from the beginning of their reign up to when Alexander the Great conquered the entire world, at which point they were still reckoned to be a powerful nation. The accounts of his exploits tell how he went to their country and was received by the queen and her ladies. Alexander lived a long time after the destruction of Troy and more than four hundred years after the founding of Rome,[1] which itself postdated the fall of Troy by a great deal. So, if you make the effort to compare these histories and calculate the timescale involved, you will see that the reign of the Amazons was

1. Generally given in legend as 753 B.C.E.

extremely long-lived. You'll also realize that, of all the kingdoms that lasted this long, there is none that could boast such a large number of illustrious rulers who accomplished such extraordinary deeds as this great nation could of its queens and ladies.'

* * *

33. Christine asks Reason if any woman has ever invented new forms of knowledge

I, Christine, on hearing Reason's words, took up this matter and said to her, 'My lady, I can clearly see that you are able to cite an endless number of women who were highly skilled in the arts and sciences. However, I'd like to ask you if you know of any woman who was ingenious, or creative, or clever enough to invent any new useful and important branches of knowledge which did not previously exist. It's surely less difficult to learn and follow a subject which has already been invented than it is to discover something new and unknown by oneself.'

Reason replied, 'Believe me, many crucial and worthy arts and sciences have been discovered thanks to the ingenuity and cleverness of women, both in the theoretical sciences which are expressed through the written word, and in the technical crafts which take the form of manual tasks and trades. I'll now give you a whole set of examples.

'First of all, I'll tell you about the noble Nicostrata, whom the Italians called Carmentis. This lady was the daughter of the king of Arcadia[2] whose name was Pallas. She was extraordinarily intelligent and endowed by God with special intellectual gifts, having such a vast knowledge of Greek literature and being able to write so wisely, elegantly and with such eloquence that the poets of the time claimed in their verse that she was loved by the god Mercury.[3] They similarly thought that her son, who was in his day equally renowned for his intelligence, was the offspring of this god, rather than of her husband. Because of various upheavals that occurred in her native land, Nicostrata, accompanied by her son and a whole host of other people who wanted to go with her, set off for Italy in a large fleet of ships and sailed up the River Tiber. It was here that she went ashore and climbed up a great hill which she named Mount Palatine after her father. On this hill, where the city of Rome was subsequently founded, she, her son and her followers built themselves a castle. As she found the indigenous population to be very primitive, she laid down a set of rules for them to observe and encouraged them to live a rational and just existence. Thus it was she who first established laws in this country that was to become so famous for developing a legal system from which all known laws would be derived.

'Amongst all the other attributes that this lady possessed, Nicostrata was particularly blessed with the gift of divine inspiration and prophecy. She was thus able to predict that her adopted country would one day rise above all others to become the most magnificent and glorious realm on earth. To her mind, therefore, it would not be fitting for this country which would outshine and conquer the rest of the world to use an inferior and crude set of alphabetical letters which

---

2. Region of central Greece, conventionally associated with pastoral poetry.
3. Messenger of the Roman gods; as a herald, he was a god of commerce and—especially important in the Middle Ages—skill in speaking and eloquence generally.

had originated in a foreign country. Moreover, Nicostrata wished to transmit her own wisdom and learning to future generations in a suitable form. She therefore set her mind to inventing a new set of letters which were completely different from those used in other nations. What she created was the ABC—the Latin alphabet—as well as the rules for constructing words, the distinction between vowels and consonants and the bases of the science of grammer. She gave this knowledge and this alphabet to the people, in the hope that they would become universally known. It was truly no small or insignificant branch of knowledge that this lady invented, nor should she receive only paltry thanks for it. This ingenious science proved so useful and brought so much good into the world that one can honestly say that no nobler discovery was ever made.

'The Italians were not lacking in gratitude for this great gift, and rightly so, since they heralded it as such a marvellous invention that they venerated her more highly than any man, worshipping Nicostrata/Carmentis like a goddess in her own lifetime. When she died, they built a temple dedicated to her memory, situated at the foot of the hill where she had made her home. In order to preserve her fame for posterity, they borrowed various terms from the science she had invented and even used her own name to designate certain objects. In honour of the science of Latin that she had invented, the people of the country called themselves Latins. Furthermore, because *ita* in Latin is the most important affirmative term in that language, being the equivalent of *oui* in French, they did not stop at calling their own realm the land of the Latins, but went so far as to use the name Italy to refer to the whole country beyond their immediate borders, which is a vast area comprising many different regions and kingdoms. From this lady's name, Carmentis, they also derived the Latin word *carmen*, meaning "song." Even the Romans, who came a long time after her, called one of the gates of the city the *Porta Carmentalis*. These names have not been changed since and are still the same today, no matter how the fortunes of the Romans have fared or which mighty emperor was in power.

'My dear Christine, what more could you ask for? Could any mortal man be said to have done anything so splendid? But don't think that she's the only example of a woman who invented many new branches of learning . . .'

34. About Minerva, who invented countless sciences, including the art of making arms from iron and steel

'Minerva, as you yourself have noted elsewhere, was a maiden from Greece who was also known as Pallas.[4] This girl was so supremely intelligent that her contemporaries foolishly declared her to be a goddess come down from the heavens, since they had no idea who her parents were and she performed deeds that had never been done before. As Boccaccio himself points out,[5] the fact that they knew so little about her origins meant that they were all the more astonished at her great wisdom, which surpassed that of every other woman of her time. She

---

4. An epithet of Athena.
5. In his *Genealogy of the Gentile Gods*, the Italian writer Giovanni Boccaccio (1313–1375) describes the descent of the gods, their evolution from actual human beings to divine figures, and the figurative significance of their names and deeds.

employed her skilfulness and her immense ingenuity not just in one domain but in many. First of all, she used her brilliance to invent various Greek letters called characters which can be used to write down a maximum number of ideas in a minimum number of words. This wonderfully clever invention is still used by the Greeks today. She also invented numbers and developed ways of using them to count and perform quick calculations. In short, she was so ingenious that she created many arts and techniques that had not previously been discovered, including the art of making wool and cloth. It was she who first had the idea of shearing sheep and developing the whole process of untangling, combing and carding the wool with various instruments, cleaning it, breaking down the fibres on metal spikes and spinning it on the distaff, whilst also inventing the tools needed for weaving it into cloth and making it into fine fabric.

'Likewise, she discovered how to make oil from pressing olives and how to extract the juice from other sorts of fruit.

'Likewise, she invented the art of building carts and chariots in order to carry things more easily from one place to another.

'Likewise, an invention of this lady's which was all the more marvellous for being such an unlikely thing for a woman to think of, was the art of forging armour for knights to protect themselves in battle and weapons of iron and steel for them to fight with. She taught this art first to the people of Athens, whom she also instructed in how to organize themselves into armies and battalions and to fight in serried ranks.

'Likewise, she invented flutes, pipes, trumpets and other wind instruments.

'This lady was not only extraordinarily intelligent but also supremely chaste, remaining a virgin all her life. It was because of her exemplary chastity that the poets claimed in their fables that she struggled long and hard with Vulcan, the god of fire,[6] but finally overcame and defeated him. This story can be interpreted to mean that she conquered the passions and desires of the flesh which so vigorously assail the body when one is young. The Athenians held this girl in the highest esteem, worshipping her as if she were a deity and calling her the goddess of arms and warfare because she was the first to invent these arts. She was also known as the goddess of wisdom, thanks to her great intelligence.

'After her death, the people of Athens built a temple dedicated to her, in which they placed a statue representing wisdom and warfare in the likeness of a girl. This statue had terrible fierce eyes to symbolize both the duty of a knight to enforce justice and the inscrutability of the thoughts of a wise man. The statue had a helmet on its head, to suggest the idea that a knight must be hardened in battle and have unfailing courage, and that the plans of a wise man should be shrouded in secrecy. It was also dressed in chainmail, to represent the power of the estate of knighthood as well as the foresight of a wise man who arms himself against the vicissitudes of Fortune. The statue held a great spear or lance as an emblem of the fact that a knight must be the rod of justice and that a wise man launches his attacks from a safe distance. Round the statue's neck hung a shield or buckler of crystal, meaning that a knight must always be vigilant and ready to defend the country and the people and that a wise man has a clear understand-

6. The Greek Hephaistos; according to one myth, he attempted to rape Athena/Minerva.

ing of all things. In the centre of this shield was the image of the head of a serpent known as a Gorgon,[7] to suggest the idea that a knight must be cunning and
stalk his enemies like a snake whilst a wise man must be wary of all the harm
that others might do to him. To guard the statue, they placed next to it a night
bird—an owl—to signify that a knight must be prepared, if needs be, to protect
the country both day and night, and that a wise man must be alert at all times
to do what is right. This lady Minerva was greatly revered for a long time and
her fame spread to many other countries, where they also dedicated temples to
her. Even centuries later, when the Romans were at the height of their powers,
they incorporated her image into their pantheon of gods.'

* * *

37. About all the great good that these ladies have brought into the world

'My lady, I'm delighted to hear from your lips that so much good has been
brought into the world thanks to the intelligence of women. Yet there are still
those men who go around claiming that women know nothing of any worth.
It's also a common way to mock someone for saying something foolish by telling them that they're thinking like a woman. On the whole, men seem to hold
the view that women have never done anything for humankind but bear children and spin wool.'

Reason's reply was: 'Now can you understand the terrible ingratitude of
those men who say such things? It's as if they're enjoying all the benefits without having any idea of where they come from or whom they should thank for
them. You can clearly see how God, who does nothing without good cause,
wanted to show men that they should no more denigrate the female sex than
they should their own sex. He chose to endow women's minds with the capacity not simply to learn and grasp all kinds of knowledge but also to invent new
ones by themselves, discovering sciences which have done more good and have
been more useful to humanity than any others. Just take the example of Carmentis, whom I told you about before. Her invention of the Latin alphabet
pleased God so much that He wished it to replace the Hebrew and Greek
alphabets which had been so prestigious. It was by His will that the alphabet
spread throughout most of Europe, a vast expanse of land, where it is used in
countless books and volumes in all disciplines which recall and preserve for
ever the glorious deeds of men and the marvellous workings of God, in addition to all the arts and sciences. But don't let it be said that I'm telling you
these things out of bias: these are the words of Boccaccio himself and thus the
truth of them is indisputable.

'One could sum up by saying that the good things that this Carmentis has
done are truly infinite, since it is thanks to her that men have been brought out
of their ignorant state and become civilized, even if they themselves have not
acknowledged this fact. Thanks to her, men possess the art of encoding their
thoughts and wishes into secret messages which they can send all over the

7. In classical mythology, one of three snake-
haired female monsters, the sight of which
turned viewers to stone; one was Medusa,
whose head was cut off by the hero Perseus
and then set in Athena's shield (see Ovid,
Metamorphoses 7.772–803).

world. They have the means to make their desires known and understood by others, and they have access to knowledge of past and present events as well as to some aspects of the future. Moreover, thanks to this lady's invention, men can draw up treaties and strike up friendships with people in faraway places; through their correspondence back and forth, they can get to know each other without ever meeting face to face. In short, it is impossible to count up all the advantages that the invention of the alphabet has brought: it is writing which allows us to describe and to know God's will, to understand celestial matters, the sea, the earth, all individuals and all objects. I ask you, then, was there ever a man who did more good than this?'

38. More on the same topic

'One might also ask if any man ever did as much for the benefit of humankind as this noble Queen Ceres,[8] whom I was telling you about before. Who could ever deserve more praise than she who led men, who were no better than savage primitives, out of the woods where they were roaming like wild beasts without any laws, and instead took them to dwell in towns and cities and taught them how to live a law-abiding existence? It was she who introduced men to far better nourishment than their previous diet of acorns and wild apples, giving them wheat and corn which makes their bodies more beautiful, their complexions clearer and their limbs stronger and more supple. This is much more suitable and substantial food for human beings to eat. It was she who showed men how to clear the land which was full of thistles, thorns, scrubby bushes and wild trees, and to plough the earth and sow seed by which means agriculture became a sophisticated rather than a crude process and could be used for the common good of all. It was she who enriched humankind by turning coarse primitives into civilized citizens and by transforming men's minds from being lazy, unformed and shrouded in ignorance to being capable of more suitable meditations and of the contemplation of higher matters. Finally, it was she who sent men out into the fields to work the land, men whose efforts sustain the towns and cities and provide for those inhabitants who are freed up to perform other tasks which are essential for human existence.

'Isis[9] is a similar example in terms of horticulture. Who could ever match the enormous benefits which she brought into the world when she discovered how to grow trees which bear fine fruit and to cultivate other excellent herbs which are so suitable for a human diet?

'Minerva too used her wisdom to endow human beings with many vital things such as woollen clothing, instead of the animal pelts which were all there was previously to wear. For the benefit of humankind, she invented carts and chariots to relieve men of the burden of carrying their possessions from place to place in their arms. Not to mention, my dear Christine, what she gave to noblemen and knights when she taught them the art and skill of making armour to give their bodies greater protection in battle, armour which was stronger, more

8. The Roman goddess of agriculture—the equivalent of Demeter, one of the most important of the Greek deities (described in a chapter not included here).

9. One of the principal Egyptian deities, the goddess of earth; she was credited with teaching the Egyptians how to cultivate wheat and barley.

practical and much finer than the leather hides which they had had to put on in the past.'

I answered Reason, saying, 'Indeed, my lady, from what you're telling me I've now realized the full extent to which those men who attack women have failed to express their gratitude and acknowledgement. They have absolutely no grounds for criticizing women: it's not just that every man who is born of woman receives so much from her, but also that there is truly no end to the great gifts which she has so generously showered on him. Those clerks who slander women, attacking them either verbally or in their writings, really should shut their mouths once and for all. They and all those who subscribe to their views should bow their heads in shame for having dared to come out with such things, considering that the reality is utterly different from what they've claimed. Indeed, they owe a huge debt of thanks to this noble lady Carmentis, for having used her fine mind to instruct them like a teacher with her pupils— a fact which they can't deny—and to endow them with the knowledge that they themselves hold in the highest regard, which is the noble Latin alphabet.

'But what about all the many noblemen and knights who go against their duty by launching their sweeping attacks on women? They too should hold their tongues, given that all their skills in bearing arms and fighting in orga- nized ranks, of which they're so inordinately proud, have come down to them from a woman. More generally, does any man who eats bread and lives in a civilized fashion in a well-ordered city or who cultivates the land have the right to slander and criticize women, as so many of them do, seeing all that has been done for them? Certainly not. It is women like Minerva, Ceres and Isis who have brought them so many advantages which they will always be able to live off and which will for ever enhance their daily existence. Are these things to be taken lightly? I think not, my lady, for it seems to me that the teachings of Aristotle, which have so greatly enriched human knowledge and are rightly held in such high esteem, put together with all those of every other philoso- pher who ever lived, are not worth anything like as much to humankind as the deeds performed by these ladies, thanks to their great ingenuity.'

Reason replied to me, 'These ladies were not the only ones to do so much good. There have been many others, some of whom I'll now go on to tell you about.'

* * *

46. About the good sense and cleverness of Queen Dido

'As you yourself pointed out earlier, good judgement consists of weighing up carefully what you wish to do and working out how to do it. To prove to you that women are perfectly able to think in this way, even about the most impor- tant matters, I'll give you a few examples of some high-born ladies, the first of whom is Dido.[1] As I'll go on to tell you, this Dido, whose name was originally Elissa, revealed her good sense through her actions. She founded and built a city in Africa called Carthage and was its queen and ruler. It was in the way that she established the city and acquired the land on which it was built that

1. The legendary founder of Carthage (a city that was located northeast of modern Tunis, in Tunisia); the dominant version of her story focuses on her love for the Trojan refugee Aeneas and her suicide after he leaves her to fulfill his destiny as forefather of the Roman people (see Virgil's *Aeneid*, esp. book 4).

she demonstrated her great courage, nobility and virtue, qualities which are indispensable to anyone who wishes to act prudently.

'This lady was descended from the Phoenicians, who came from the remotest regions of Egypt to settle in Syria where they founded and built several fine towns and cities. Amongst these people was a king named Agenor, who was a direct ancestor of Dido's father. This king, who was called Belus, ruled over Phoenicia and conquered the kingdom of Cyprus. He had only two children: a son, Pygmalion, and a daughter, Dido.

'On his deathbed, Belus ordered his barons to honour his children and be loyal to them, making them swear an oath that they would do so. Once the king was dead, they crowned his son Pygmalion and married the beautiful Elissa to a duke named Acerbas Sychaea, or Sychaeus, who was the most powerful lord in the country after the king. This Sychaeus was a high priest in the temple dedicated to Hercules, whom they worshipped, as well as being an extremely wealthy man. He and his wife loved each other very deeply and led a happy life together. But King Pygmalion was an evil man, the cruellest and most envious person you ever saw, whose greed knew no bounds. Elissa, his sister, was all too aware of what he was like. Seeing how rich her husband was and how well known for his fabulous wealth, she advised Sychaeus to be on his guard against the king and to put his treasure in a safe place where her brother couldn't lay his hands on it. Sychaeus followed his wife's advice but failed to watch his own back against possible attack from the king as she had told him to do. Thus it happened that, one day, the king had him killed in order to steal his great riches from him. Elissa was so distraught at his death that she nearly died of grief. For a long time, she gave herself over to weeping and wailing for the loss of her beloved lord, cursing her brute of a brother for having ordered his murder. However, the wicked king, whose wishes had been thwarted since he had only managed to recover a tiny part of Sychaeus's wealth, bore a deep grudge against his sister, whom he suspected of having hidden it all away.

'Realizing that her own life was in danger, Elissa's good sense told her to leave her native land and live elsewhere. Her mind made up, she carefully considered all that she needed to do and then steeled herself to put her plans into effect. This lady knew very well that the king did not enjoy the full support of his barons or his subjects because of his great cruelty and the excessive burdens he imposed on them. She therefore rallied to her cause some of the princes, townspeople and even the peasants. Having sworn them to secrecy, she outlined her plans to them in such persuasive terms that they declared their loyalty to her and agreed to go with her.

'As quickly and as quietly as she could, Elissa had her ship prepared. In the dead of night, she set sail with all her treasure and her many followers aboard, urging the sailors to make the ship go as fast as possible. Yet this lady's cleverness didn't end there. Knowing that her brother would send his men after her as soon as he learnt of her flight, she had great chests, trunks and boxes secretly filled up with heavy, worthless objects to make it look as if they contained treasure. The idea was that she would give these chests and boxes to her brother's men if they would only leave her alone and let her continue on her course. It all happened just as she planned, for they had not long been at sea when a whole host of the king's men came racing after her to stop her. In measured tones, she pointed out to them that as she was only setting out on a pilgrimage, they should allow her to sail on unhindered. However, seeing that they remained unconvinced by her explanation, she declared that if it was her treasure her brother was after, she would be prepared to give it to him, even though he had no right to interfere with her wishes. The king's men, who knew that this was his sole desire, forced her to part with it as that way they could do the king's bidding and she could appease her brother. With a sad face, as if it cost her dear, the lady made them load up all the chests and boxes on to their ships. Thinking that they had done well and that the king would be delighted with the news, his men immediately went on their way.

'Uttering not a single word of protest, the queen's only thoughts were of setting sail once more. They journeyed on, by day and night, until they came to the island of Cyprus, where they stopped for a short while to refresh themselves. As soon as she had made her sacrifices to the gods, the lady went back to the ship, taking with her the priest from the temple of Jupiter and his family. This priest had predicted that a lady would come from the land of the Phoenicians and that he would leave his country to join her. Casting off again, they left the island of Crete behind them and passed the island of Sicily on their right. They sailed along the whole length of the coast of Massylia until they finally arrived in Africa, where they landed. No sooner had they docked than the people living there rushed down to see the ship and to find out where those aboard were from.

'When they saw the lady and realized that she and her people had come in peace, they went and brought them food in abundance. Elissa talked to them in a very friendly way, explaining to them that she had heard such good things about their country that she wished to make her home there, if they had no objections. They replied that they were happy for her to do so. Insisting that she didn't want to establish a large colony on this foreign soil, the lady asked them to sell her a piece of land by the coast which was no bigger than what could be covered by the hide of a cow. Here she would build some dwellings for herself and her people. They granted her wishes and, as soon as the terms of the deal had been agreed upon, her cleverness and good sense came to the fore. Taking the cowhide, the lady had it cut into the tiniest strips possible, which were then tied together to form a rope. This rope was laid out on the ground by the seashore where it enclosed a huge plot of land. Those who had sold her the land were amazed and stunned by her cunning ruse, yet they had to abide by the deal they had struck with her.

'So it was that this lady took possession of all this territory in Africa. On her plot of land, a horse's head was discovered. This head, along with the movements and noises of the birds in the sky, they interpreted as prophetic signs that the city which they were about to found would be full of warriors who would excel themselves in the pursuit of arms. The lady immediately sent all over for workmen and spent her wealth freely to pay for their labour. The place which she had built was a magnificent and mighty city called Carthage, the citadel and main fortress of which were called Byrsa, which means "cowhide."[2]

'Just as she was beginning to build her city, she received news that her brother was coming after her and her followers for having made a fool of him

2. In Greek.

and tricked him out of his treasure. She told his messengers that she had most definitely given the treasure to the king's men for them to take back to him, but that perhaps it was they who had stolen it and replaced it with worthless objects instead. It was possibly even the gods who had decided to metamorphose the treasure and stop the king from having it because of the sin he had committed in ordering her husband's murder. As for her brother's threats, she had faith that, with the help of the gods, she could defend herself against him. Elissa therefore assembled all her fellow Phoenicians together and told them that she wanted no one to stay with her against their will nor suffer any harm for her sake. If any or all of them wanted to return home, she would reward them for their hard work and let them go. They all replied with one voice that they would live and die by her side, and would never leave her even for a single day.

'The messengers departed and the lady worked as fast as she could to finish the city. Once it was completed, she established laws and rules for her people to live an honest and just existence. She conducted herself with such wisdom and prudence that her fame spread all over the world and talk of her was on everyone's lips. Thanks to her bold and courageous actions and her judicious rule, she became so renowned for her heroic qualities that her name was changed to Dido, which means *"virago"*[3] in Latin: in other words, a woman who has the virtue and valour of a man. She lived a glorious life for many years, one which would have lasted even longer had Fortune not turned against her. As this goddess is wont to be envious of those she sees prosper, she concocted a bitter brew for Dido to drink, which I'll tell you about all in good time.'

* * *

48. About Lavinia, daughter of King Latinus

'Lavinia, queen of the Laurentines,[4] was similarly renowned for her good sense. Descended from the same Cretan king, Saturn, whom I've just mentioned, she was the daughter of King Latinus. She later wed Aeneas, although before her marriage she had been promised to Turnus, king of the Rutulians. Her father, who had been informed by an oracle that she should be given to a Trojan prince, kept putting off the wedding despite the fact that his wife, the queen, was very keen for it to take place. When Aeneas arrived in Italy, he requested King Latinus's permission to enter his territory. He was not only granted leave to do so but was immediately given Lavinia's hand in marriage. It was for this reason that Turnus declared war on Aeneas, a war which caused many deaths and in which Turnus himself was killed. Having secured the victory, Aeneas took Lavinia as his wife. She later bore him a son, even though he himself died whilst she was still pregnant. As her time grew near, she became very afraid that a man called Ascanius, Aeneas's elder son by another woman,[5] would attempt to murder her child and usurp the throne. She therefore went off to give birth in the woods and named the newborn baby Julius Silvius. Vowing never to marry again, Lavinia conducted herself with exemplary good judge-

3. Literally, "manlike woman" (Latin), in a heroic sense; while the English word sometimes retains this meaning, it also (and more often) came to mean "a shrew."
4. Inhabitants of Laurentum, on the coast of Latium just south of the mouth of the Tiber, where Aeneas and his men are said to have landed in Italy.
5. Aeneas's wife Creusa, who had died during the Greek sack of Troy.

ment in her widowhood and managed to keep the kingdom intact, thanks to her astuteness. She was able to win her stepson's affection and thus defuse any animosity on his part towards her or his stepbrother. Indeed, once he had finished building the city of Alba, Ascanius left to make his home there. Meanwhile, Lavinia ruled the country with supreme skill until her son came of age. This child's descendants were Romulus and Remus, who later founded the city of Rome. They in turn were the ancestors of all the noble princes who came after them.

'What more can I tell you, my dear Christine? It seems to me that I've cited sufficient evidence to make my point, having given enough examples and proofs to convince you that God has never criticized the female sex more than the male sex. My case is conclusive, as you have seen, and my two sisters here will go on to confirm this for you in their presentation of the facts. I think that I have fulfilled my task of constructing the enclosure walls of the City of Ladies, since they're all now ready and done. Let me give way to my two sisters: with their help and advice you'll soon complete the building work that remains.'

END OF THE FIRST PART OF *THE BOOK OF THE CITY OF LADIES*.

Travel and Encounter

Long before the early modern Age of Exploration, when Portuguese, Dutch, Spanish, and English sailors began to map out trade routes to East Asia and the Americas, medieval writers had begun to write travelers' accounts of eastward voyages. Some of these were largely fictional—entertainment for an audience eager to hear about exotic wonders. Others were based on real experience, offering practical knowledge concerning local languages and currencies and describing the safest and most lucrative routes a traveler might take. The three works collected here—the firsthand account of the merchant **Marco Polo**, the personal narrative of the learned and pious **Muhammad ibn Battuta**, and the half-fact, half-fantasy compilation that makes up the wildly popular *Book of John Mandeville*—represent both aspects of the travel genre.

Writing about travel in medieval Europe was at first centered on the practical experience of pilgrims, who made the difficult journey over land and sea to Jerusalem in order to retrace the footsteps of Jesus Christ. The fourth-century account of the nun Egeria, part of whose detailed letter recording her own visit to Jerusalem was copied and survived, illustrates the early popularity of this genre, which was both practical and inspirational—setting forth the spiritual journey behind the physical travel. People read such narratives not

just in order to plan their own itinerary but also to imagine voyages that they could never take in person, instead tracing the journey within their own souls. By the thirteenth century, the genre of the pilgrimage account had been taken up by traveling preachers (mainly Franciscan friars) who had voyaged to the distant East in order to bring new converts into the fold of Christianity. Figures such as the Italian Oderic of Pordenone and the Flemish William of Rubruck composed full descriptions of their journeys within India and China; intended to provide useful local information for subsequent waves of Christian missionaries, these works were also eagerly seized by other kinds of travelers who wished to undertake the difficult journey to East Asia.

Alongside the pious pilgrimage narratives and handbooks for missionaries a third genre developed, illustrated by Marco Polo's book: highly practical guides for merchants that provided the information on local customs, currencies, and commodities necessary to facilitate trade and exchange. And all three of these modes of travel writing stimulated the imaginations of armchair travelers who could enjoy vicarious journeys as they constructed a fantasy of the exotic East. The increasingly dynamic perspective on travel and exploration seen in these writings is also visible in medieval maps, especially in the shift away from the symbolic geography of the world map, or "mappamundi," oriented toward the east, with the Garden of Eden at the top and centered on Jerusalem. It was replaced by Ptolemaic

A page from an illustrated version of *The Book of John Mandeville*, produced in Bohemia ca. 1410, showing Mandeville on his way to Constantinople.

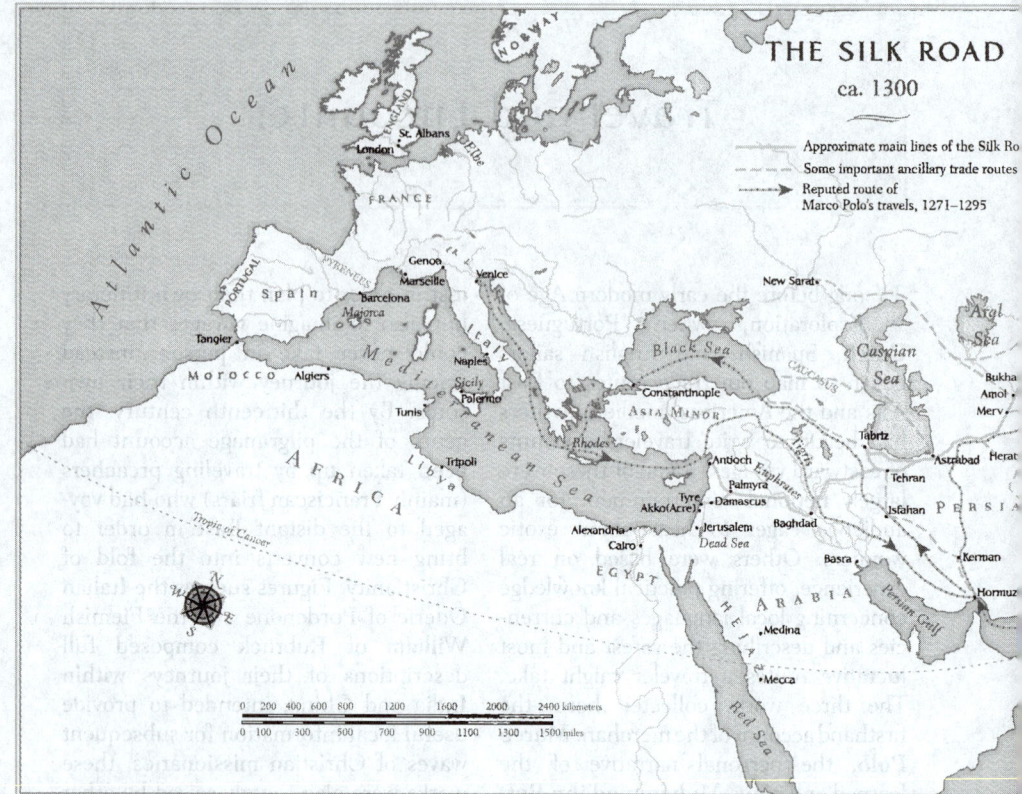

THE SILK ROAD
ca. 1300

maps, based on the empirical observations and instructions of the second-century C.E. Greek astronomer Ptolemy from a text rediscovered around 1400, and by late medieval portolan charts (from Italian *portolano*, "having to do with ports or harbors"). These were oriented toward the north, to aid navigation by the Pole Star, and included highly detailed renderings of coastlines and harbors as well as a series of crisscrossing lines indicating the various compass headings a navigator might use. This emphasis on navigation began to be reflected in monumental maps of the later Middle Ages, including the beautiful Catalan Atlas produced in 1375 by the Majorcan Jew Abraham Cresques. This extraordinarily detailed map, renowned for its accuracy and completeness, was almost immediately acquired by Charles V, King of France. Even earlier, however, Muslim cartographers had achieved a high degree of

Approximate limit of the Mongol ancestral homeland

MONGOLIA

Karakorum

Shangdu (Xanadu)

Dadu (Beijing)

Pacific Ocean

Yellow Sea

Yellow

Yangzhou

Hangzhou

Luoyang

GANSU

Hami

Suzhou

Anxi

Turfan

Dunhuang

Chang'an (Xi'an)

Lanzhou

Quanzhou

Gobi Desert

Orion Desert

Yangtze

Kulja

ake Balkash

Kuchā

TIAN SHAN

Kashgar

ashkent

Yarkand

Khotan

and

Taklamakan Desert

KUNLUN SHAN

Khanate of the Great Khan (Yuan Empire)

Guangzhou

TIBET

HINDU KUSH

niyan

Taxila

Peshawar

abul

Ghazni

ahar

Brahmaputra

HIMALAYAS

Ganges

Delhi

INDIA

Indus

Mandalay

Irrawaddy

Mekong

South China Sea

Bay of Bengal

Arabian Sea

Indian Ocean

Sumatra

Java

Sri Lanka (Ceylon)

realism in their maps, as can be seen in the so-called *Tabula Rogeriana* (*Book of Roger*; Latin), finished in 1154 by Muhammad al-Idrisi, an Arab map-maker and encyclopedist, at the request of Roger II, the Norman Christian ruler of Sicily. The volume contains seventy large maps, each highly detailed, that together constitute a single monumental world map. It was oriented toward the south (as is typical of medieval Islamic maps, and like the Catalan Atlas), and its division into seven latitudinal zones is in keeping with Ptolemaic conventions. The result was an exceptionally complete—and practical—vision of the world. In the *Book of Roger* we witness the mixing of cultures characteristic of the medieval Mediterranean. The Catalan Atlas of 250 years later, with its crisscrossed navigational lines, shows late medieval Europe poised on the threshold of a dynamic period of world exploration.

MARCO POLO

The Diversity of the World started out as story recounted by a merchant in an Italian jail. In 1298, Marco Polo (1254–1324) had just returned from an almost thirty-year journey through Asia, having spent years in the service of the Mongol emperor of China, Kublai Khan. The cell mate who listened to the traveler's story was a writer of romances, Rustichello of Pisa, and he transformed the merchant's detailed account of political and economic exchange into a tale of marvels that would captivate generations of readers. The original text, written in a hybrid French-Italian vernacular, was quickly translated into several other languages (including a popular Latin version). Although Marco Polo's work—like the writings of **Ibn Battuta** and **Mandeville**—is commonly known as his *Travels,* this is a modern name for a genre that was just beginning to emerge during the Middle Ages. The first generations to read Marco's story would have known it as *Le Devisement dou monde.* That title is translated here as *The Diversity of the World,* but the first word could also accurately be rendered as "division" or "description." This notion of diversity—exuberant, fertile heterogeneity—is key to Marco Polo's account, which highlights the tremendous range of cultures, peoples, and practices to be found along the trade routes winding from the Mediterranean Sea to the Indian Ocean and beyond.

The story opens by describing how Marco's father Niccolò and uncle Maffeo had traveled as far as China along the Asian trade route known as the Silk Road. After their return to Italy in 1269, they set forth again—this time joined by Marco. His extended journey throughout the Middle East and Asia would last almost three decades. The first excerpt below explains how Niccolò, Maffeo, and Marco came to the royal palace of the "Great Khan" (Kublai Khan), the ruler of China and the surrounding regions, and how Marco entered into his service. Marco learned a great deal about local customs and standard practices of the imperial administration as well as acquiring the local languages, and ultimately became a trusted envoy and diplomatic messenger. He remained, by his own account, seventeen years in the service of the Great Khan. In another excerpt, he provides a survey of "Lesser Java" (Sumatra) that is replete with an account of exotic wonders to be seen there, including wild elephants and elusive unicorns. Alongside these wonders, however, is practical information of interest to a merchant, such as a list of the spices and other trade-worthy goods that are plentiful in the region. Marco also supplies information useful to navigation, such as his note that the Pole Star—the main reference point in the Northern Hemisphere—"is not visible here." It is easy to see why Christopher Columbus carried a heavily annotated copy of Marco Polo's *Diversity of the World* with him on his voyages to the New World. In the final excerpted passage, Marco describes the virtuous and devout Brahmans of India, who eat and drink in extreme moderation and who so revere all living things that they refrain from killing even an insect. Some aspects of this account of the Brahmans are fanciful, in the tradition of "Wonders of the East" literature that began with ancient Greek writings on the eastern voyages of Alexander the Great. Yet other passages contain factual, detailed ethnographic description and offer a practical guide to exploration.

From The Diversity of the World[1]

FROM *PROLOGUE*

XIV. How the two brothers and Marc came to where the Great Khan was in the city of Clemeinfu

My lords Nicolau and Mafeu, and Marc, Nicolau's son, set out on the road and rode, winter and summer, until they came to the Great Khan, who was then in a large and very rich city called Clemeinfu.[2] What they found en route I won't mention now, for we will tell you about that later in the book, in due order. Know that it took them three and a half years' effort to get there; this was because of the snow, the rain, and the great rivers they had to cross, and because they couldn't ride as hard in winter as in summer. And he says in truth that when the Great Khan learned that my lords Nicolau and Mafeu were coming, he sent his messengers out forty days' journey to meet them, and they were well served and well honored in everything.

XV. How the two brothers and Marc went to the palace to meet the Great Khan

What should I tell you? When my lords Nicolau and Mafeu had arrived in this great city, they went to the chief palace, where they found the Great Khan with a great company of barons. They knelt before him and made every effort to humble themselves. The Great Khan had them stand and received them honorably, welcoming them with great joy and celebration. He kept asking them how they were and how they had done. And the two brothers told him that they had done very well, since they found him healthy and hale. Then they presented the warrants and letters the pope had sent him,[3] which made him very happy. Then they gave him the holy oil, which made him very happy and which he greatly prized. When the Great Khan saw Marc, who was a young man, he asked who he was. "Lord," said my lord Nicolau, "he is my son and your man." "He is welcome," said the Great khan. Why should I make a long tale of it? Know, in truth, that the arrival of these messengers brought great joy and celebration to the Great Khan and his entire court; they were well served and well honored in everything. They remained at court and were honored above all other barons.

XVI. How the Great Khan sent Marc as his messenger

Now it so happened that Marc, my lord Nicolau's son, learned the Tartars' customs, languages, and writing so well that it was a marvel: for I tell you truthfully that not long after coming to the great lord's court, he learned to read and write four languages. He was wise and exceedingly perspicacious, and the Great Khan was very well disposed toward him for the goodness and great valor he saw in him. When the Great Khan saw how wise Marc was, he sent

1. Translated by Sharon Kinoshita.
2. The summer residence of Kublai Khan (1215–1294), northwest of modern Beijing; also spelled *Kaipingfu* (literally, "Kaiping governmental capital"). Kublai Khan, a Mongol

emperor, conquered China and founded the Yuan dynasty.
3. On their earlier visit to China, Kublai Khan had asked Niccolò and Maffeo to go to Rome and deliver a message to the pope on his behalf.

him as an envoy to a land a good six months' distant. The young man fulfilled the embassy wisely and well. And having often seen and heard the Great Khan say that the messengers he had sent to different parts of the world were fools and ignoramuses (when they returned and reported on the missions they had been sent on but were unable to say anything else about the countries they had visited) and that he would rather hear about the news and the customs and practices of the foreign country than about the affairs for which he had sent them, Marco, well aware of all this, when he went on this mission, put a good deal of effort into being able to tell the Great Khan about all the novelties and oddities he had seen.

XVII. How Marc returned from his embassy and recounts his embassy to the Great Khan

When Marc had returned from his embassy, he went before the Great Khan and gave a complete report on his mission; and having accomplished this very well, he then told him of all the novelties and things he had seen on the way— so well and intelligently that the Great Khan and everyone who heard him marveled, saying to each other: if this young man lives, he will surely become a man of great wisdom and valor. What should I tell you? From the time of that embassy on, the young man was referred to as my lord Marc Pol—and so will he henceforth be called in our book. And this with good reason, for he was wise and accomplished.

Why should I make a long story of it? Know in truth that my lord Marc remained with the Great Khan a good seventeen years; and in all this time he never stopped going on embassies. For the Great Khan—seeing that my lord Marc brought him such news from all over and acquitted his missions so well—gave all the good, long embassies to my lord Marc. And he fulfilled his tasks very well and was able to relate many novelties and oddities. My lord Marc's conduct pleased the Great Khan so well that he was very favorably disposed toward him; he honored him and kept him so close to him that the other lords were very envious. This was how my lord Marc came to know more about things in that country than any other man: he looked around those foreign parts more than any man ever born, besides putting all his effort into this knowledge.

LESSER JAVA AND THE POLE STAR

CLXVI. Here the island of Lesser Java is described

On leaving the island of Pentain and heading southeast about 100 miles, you find the island of Lesser Java:[4] but know that it is not so small as to be any less than two thousand miles around. We will tell you the whole truth about this island.

Now, know that on this island there are eight kingdoms and eight crowned kings. On this island they are all idolators and have their own languages, for know that each kingdom has a language of its own. This island has the very

---

4. Modern Sumatra (which takes its name from the city-state described in the following chapter).

greatest abundance of treasure, costly spices, aloewood, and spikenard, and many other spices that never make it to our countries. Now I want to tell you about the customs of all these people, one at a time. First I'll tell you something that everyone will take as a marvel. Know in truth that this island is so far south that the North Star does not appear in the slightest. Now we'll return to men's customs and will tell you about the kingdom of Ferlec.

Know that this kingdom of Ferlec converted to Muhammad's law as a result of Saracen[5] merchants who often came there by ship: only the city people; the mountain people are like animals, for I tell you in truth that they eat human flesh and all other flesh—good and bad. They worship many things; for, when they get up in the morning, they worship the first thing they see. Now I've told you about Ferlec; next I'll tell you about the kingdom of Basma.

On leaving the kingdom of Ferlec you enter the kingdom of Basma. This Basma is its own kingdom; the people have their own language but no laws— they are like beasts. They call themselves subjects of the Great Khan but send him no tribute, for they are so far away that the Great Khan's people would not be able to get there. But all those on the island call themselves his subjects and sometimes send him oddities. They have wild elephants and lots of unicorns that are no smaller than elephants: they have hair like buffalo and feet like elephants, with a very thick, black horn in the middle of the forehead. And I tell you it doesn't do harm with its horn but with its tongue. For its tongue has very long spines, such that whatever harm it inflicts, it inflicts with its tongue. Its head is like that of a wild boar; it always carries its head bent down towards the ground and likes to stay in the mud and the muck. It's a very ugly beast to see. They are not as we say and describe here when they say that it lets itself be captured by a virgin. But I tell you it's just the opposite of what we all say it is like. They have a great abundance of swans of many different kinds; they have goshawks, black as crows; they are very large and hawk very well.

And I would tell you and have you know that those who bring little men from India are involved in a great lie and deception; for I tell you that those they call men are made on this island—I'll tell you how. It is true that on this island there's a kind of very small monkey whose faces are like men's: men take such monkeys and remove their hair, leaving the hair of their beards and chests. Then they dry them and shape them and rub them with camphor and other things so that they seem to have been human. This is a great deception, for they are made as you've just heard. For never in India or other, more savage parts have such little men as these seem to be ever been seen.

Now we won't tell you anything more of this kingdom, for there's nothing else there worth mentioning. Therefore we'll leave this and tell you about another kingdom called Sumatra.

CLXVII. Here the kingdom of Sumatra is described

Now, know that, leaving Basma, you find the kingdom of Sumatra, which is on the same island. I, Marc Pol, stayed there for five months, on account of the weather, which didn't allow us to continue on our way. Moreover, I tell you

---

5. The term generally used in the medieval West to mean "Muslim." "Muhammad's law": Islam.

that the North Star does not appear there; what's more, I tell you the Master constellation[6] doesn't appear at all. They are savage idolaters; their king is rich and powerful, and they call themselves subjects of the Great Khan. And here's how we stayed there five months: we disembarked from our ships and built castles out of wood and logs, then stayed in those castles for fear of those bestial men who eat men. They have the best fish in the world. They don't have any wheat but live on rice. They have no wine, except as I'll describe to you. Know in truth that they have a kind of tree; they cut its branches and put a large pot under the remaining stump; and I tell you that in a day and a night it fills up with wine that is very good to drink. The trees look like small date trees and have four branches; lop it off, and get the wine I've described to you, which is very good. I'll tell you something else as well: when this branch no longer give wine, they water the foot of the trees; and it doesn't take long for the branches to give wine which, I tell you, is white and red. They have a great quantity of Indian nuts, big and good. They eat every sort of flesh, good and bad.

BRAHMANS AND THE BUDDHA

CLXXVII. Concerning the island of Seilan

These Brahmans[7] live longer than anyone in the world because of how little they eat and for their great abstinence. They have very good teeth on account of an herb they're in the habit of eating, which is a great aid to digestion and is healthy for the human body. And know that these Brahmans are not bled from their veins nor have blood drawn from anywhere.

Among them there are some, living under a rule,[8] called Ciugui. They live longer than the others, for they live between 150 and 200 years. They are very able physically: they come and go wherever they want and fulfill all the services necessary to their church and their idols, and serve them as well as if they were younger. This is possible because of their great abstinence in eating little and good food, for they are in the habit of eating more rice and milk than anything else. Moreover, I tell you that these Ciugui, who live as long as I've told you, eat something I'll tell you about that will seem like a great thing to you: I tell you that they take quicksilver[9] and sulfur and mix them together into a beverage which they then drink. They say this prolongs their life, and they live quite long. I tell you that they do this twice a month. And know that these people drink this from childhood to live longer. And without fail those that live as long as I've described are accustomed to this sulfur-and-quicksilver drink.

Also in this kingdom of Maabar is a religion, also called Ciugui, involving such great abstinence and such a strong, tough life as I will describe to you. Know, truthfully, that they go around completely naked, wearing no covering, not covering their privates or any members. They worship cattle; and all of them wear a small cow, made of copper or gilded bronze, on their foreheads.

6. Ursa Major, or the Big Dipper.
7. Natives of India renowned for their virtuous mode of life in the ancient and medieval West, as described in the fictional letters exchanged between Alexander the Great and

their ruler, Didymus. They are loosely connected with the Brahmin caste.
8. A prescribed guide of conduct, as for a monastic "rule."
9. Mercury.

Understand that they have it tied to them. Moreover, I tell you that they burn cow's dung and make a powder of it, then anoint their bodies with it in several places, as reverentially as Christians do with holy water. They don't eat from bowls or trenchers, but eat their food off apple of paradise[1] or other big leaves— not green but dried. For they say the green ones have souls, and it would be a sin [to use them]. For I tell you that they refrain from harming all the world's creatures, for they believe that would be a sin and they would rather die than commit what they believe to be a sin. And when other men ask them why they go around naked, unashamed at showing their members, they say: "We go naked because we want nothing in this world, for we came into this world naked, without any clothing. The reason we are not ashamed to show our member is this: we do not sin with it, so we are no more ashamed of it than you would be to show your hand or face or other part with which you commit no lustful sin. It's because you've used your member sinfully and lustfully that you cover it and are ashamed of it; but we are no more ashamed of showing it than we would be to show a finger, for we do not sin with it." This is the explanation they give to men who ask them why they are unashamed to show their member. And I tell you that they kill no creatures or animals in the world—neither flies nor fleas nor lice nor worms—for they say they have souls and that they won't eat them for the sin they would incur. What's more, I tell you they eat nothing green—neither herbs nor roots—until they are dried, for they say anything green has a soul. And I tell you that they sleep on the ground completely naked, with nothing either under them or over them. And it's a great marvel that they don't die and that they live as long as I've described above. And they are very abstemious in their food, for they fast all year and drink nothing other than water.

And I'll tell you something else: they test those that live under a rule (those who live in their churches to serve their idols), as I shall tell you. They bring the maidens who have been offered to the idols and have them touch the men serving the idols. The maidens touch them here and there, all over their bodies. They fondle them and give them the world's greatest solace. And as for the man whom the maidens touch in the way I've told you: if his member doesn't move in any way more than before the maidens touched him, he is good and they keep him among them. As for the other whom the maidens touch, if his member moves and stands upright, they don't keep him: they expel him immediately and say they don't want a lustful man among them. And I'll tell you how cruel and perfidious their idols are. They say that this is why they burn their dead: they say that, if they didn't burn their dead, they would make worms.

CLXXVIII. The island of Seilan is described again

Seilan[2] is a big island, as I've described to you earlier in this book. Now it's true that on this island there's a very high mountain with cliffs so sheer that no one can climb it, except in this way: many iron chains hang from this mountain, arranged so that men can climb this chain to the top of the mountain. And I tell you that they say that on top of this mountain is the monument of Adam

---

1. The citron tree.　　　　2. Ceylon (modern Sri Lanka).

our first father. The Saracens say that this tomb is Adam's and the idolators say that it's the monument of Sergamoni Borcam.[3]

This Sergamoni was the first man in whose name idols were first made, for according to their customs he was the best man who ever lived among them. He was the first man they held holy and in whose name they made idols. He was the son of a great, wealthy, and powerful king. And this son of his had such a good life that he didn't want to hear about any worldly things nor did he want to become king. His father, seeing that his son didn't want to become king or hear about anything worldly, got very angry. He offered him very great things: he said he wanted to crown him king of the kingdom and that he could rule as he liked; what's more, he wanted to give up the crown, and would not rule over anything: he [his son] alone would be master. His son said that he didn't want a thing; when his father saw that he wanted nothing to do with earthly power, he got so angry that he almost died of affliction. And no wonder: for this was his only son, and he had no one to whom to leave his kingdom. So this is how the king reacted: he said to himself that he would make it so that his son would willingly return to earthly things and take up the crown and the kingdom. He put him in a very beautiful palace and gave him 30,000 beautiful serving maids, so that there were no men around him but only these maids. Maids put him to bed and served him at table and kept him company all day. They sang and danced before him, and made things as pleasant as possible, just as the king had ordered. And I tell you that all these maids were powerless to move the king's son to the least bit of lust: he remained more steadfast and chaste than before. He led a very good life, according to their customs. And I tell you that he was such a delicate young man that he had never left the palace—had never seen a dead man or anyone not completely healthy. For his father never allowed any elderly or infirm man into his presence. Now it happened that one day this young man was riding out on the road; then he saw a dead man. As someone who had never seen such a thing, he was completely stunned; he asked those accompanying him what it was, and they told him it was a dead man. "What?" said the king's son, "Then do all men die?" "Yes, truly," they replied. The young man didn't say a thing and rode on, lost in thought. After that, he hadn't ridden very far when he came across a very old man who couldn't move and had no teeth in his mouth, having lost them all on account of his great age. When the king's son saw this old man, he asked what this thing was and why he couldn't move. And those accompanying him said that old age kept him from moving and old age had made him lose his teeth. When the king's son had heard of the dead man and the old man, he returned to the palace, saying to himself that he would not remain in this bad world but would go seeking the one who had made it and did not die. Then he left the palace and his father; he went to some great, faraway mountains. And there he remained his whole life, simply and chastely, practicing great abstinence. And certainly, had he been Christian, he would have been a great saint with our lord Jesus Christ.

And when this king's son died, he was carried to his father the king. When he saw that the one he loved more than himself was dead, you needn't ask if he was

---

3. "Sergamoni" is probably a mistranscription of "Sakyamuni," one of the honorific names applied to Siddhartha Gautama (d. ca. 483 B.C.E.?), founder of Buddhism; "Borcam" may be a mistranscription of "Buddha."

vexed and distressed: he mourned greatly, and had a likeness made of pure gold and precious stones, and had all his subjects honor and worship him as a god. And they said he had died 84 times. For they said that when he first died, he became a cow; then he died again and became a horse; and thus they said he had died 84 times, each time becoming an animal—a dog or something else. But the 84th time he died, he became a god. And they hold idols to be the best and most powerful gods they have. And know that this was the idolaters' first idol; all the idols are descended from him. This was on the island of Seilan in India.

Now you have heard how about the earliest idol. And I tell you truly that idolaters come on pilgrimage from very distant parts, just as Christians go on pilgrimage to Saint James.[4] And the idolaters say that this monument, on this mountain, belongs to the king's son you've heard about, and that the teeth, hair, and bowl there also belonged to the king's son, whose name was Sergamoni Borcam, meaning "Saint Sergamoni." And the Saracens, who also come on pilgrimage here in great numbers, say that this is the monument of Adam our first father and that the teeth, hair, and bowl were also Adam's. Now you've heard how the idolaters say that this is the king's son who was their first idol and their first god, and how the Saracens say that it's Adam, our first father. But God knows who he is and who he was, for we do not believe that Adam is here in this place, because the Scripture of the Holy Church says that he's in another part of the world.

Now it happened that the Great Khan heard that Adam's monument was atop this mountain, along with his teeth, his hair, and the bowl he had eaten from; and he said to himself it was fitting that he should have these teeth and bowl and hair. So he sent a great embassy there: this was in the year 1284 of the Incarnation of Christ. What should I say of it? Know truly that the Great Khan's messengers set out on the road with a great entourage and traveled so far by land and by sea that they came to the island of Seilan. They went to the king and importuned him so much that they got the two molars, which were fat and large; and they also got the hairs and the bowl. The bowl was of very beautiful green porphyry. And when the Great Khan's messengers got these things I've told you about, they got on the road and returned to their lord. As they approached the great city of Ganbalu,[5] where the Great Khan was staying, they sent word that they were coming and that they were bringing what he had sent them to get. The Great Khan then ordered that everyone—the monks and others—should go to meet these relics that were understood to be Adam's. Why should I prolong my account? Know that, in truth, all the people of Ganbalu went to meet these relics; and the monks received it and brought it to the Great Khan, who received them with great joy, celebration, and reverence. And I tell you that they found in their writings that this bowl had such properties that if you filled it with food enough for one man, there would be enough for five; and the Great Khan said that he had tested it, and that it was true.

In such a way as you have heard, the Great Khan got the relics that you've heard about. And it cost him quite a great amount of treasure to acquire them.

Now we've told the whole truth of this whole story in order. From here we'll leave it and will tell you about other things. We'll tell you right away about the city of Cail.

4. St. James of Compostella (in Spain), perhaps the most important pilgrimage site in medieval Europe.

5. Also spelled *Khanbaliq* (literally, "great residence of the Khan"); modern Beijing.

IBN BATTUTA

Muhammad ibn Abdullah ibn Battuta (1304–1368/69) was born in Tangier, in what is now Morocco, to a Muslim Berber family. Well-educated and upper-class, Ibn Battuta was a member of a transnational urban elite that was relatively free to move about the Islamic world. His travels began in 1325, when he undertook the prescribed religious pilgrimage (or *hajj*) to Mecca and Medina; later, he would voyage to Africa's eastern coast, central Asia, and India. After a stay in Delhi, Ibn Battuta was sent by his patron on a diplomatic mission to the emperor of China. Upon his return to Morocco, Ibn Battuta's royal patron was amazed by the traveler's engrossing account of his experiences and commanded the court secretary, Muhammad ibn Juzayy, to write it down. Like the romancer Rustichello, who embroidered the practical report of the merchant **Marco Polo**, Ibn Juzayy embellished the account he was given. Specifically, he used Ibn Battuta's personal experiences as a foundation or framework to which he attached fragments of other, earlier travel narratives (such as that of Ibn Jubayr). Ibn Battuta's tale bears witness to the momentous events of his age: the increasing political chaos in India and Persia following the end of Mongol rule in 1336, the succession disputes that plagued Egypt after 1341, and the terrifying advent of the Black Death in 1348.

The geographical range of the excerpts from Ibn Battuta's account presented here stretches from areas of the Middle East under Islamic rule to the distant reaches of East Asia. His descriptions of the regions surrounding Jerusalem, including the Cave of the Patriarchs at Hebron, the site of Jesus' birth at Bethlehem, and "Lot's Lake" (the Dead Sea), are remarkable for the picture they summon up of an environment in which sites holy to Jews, Christians, and Muslims sit side by side, and where worshippers coexist in harmony. Ibn Battuta's account of the combined Jewish, Christian, and Muslim procession to the local shrine dedicated to Moses that took place in Damascus at the time of the Black Death is particularly striking, illustrating how a catastrophic event can bring a community together to worship, even across faiths. Nonetheless, he views Jerusalem not primarily in connection with Jewish history or with the lifetime of Jesus, but rather as the place where the Prophet Muhammad ascended into the heavens in his heavenly night journey, or *mi'raj*, leaving his footprint in the stone at the Dome of the Rock. Ibn Battuta also describes the imperial city of Constantinople (modern Istanbul), then still under Christian rule. He gives an overview of the geography of the city, the distribution of its different populations, and its most awe-inspiring monument: the cathedral of Hagia Sophia, "one of the greatest churches of the Greeks." Ibn Battuta is obliged to explain to his Muslim readers what a "monastery" is, because the life of renunciation undertaken by Christian monks and nuns would seem bizarre and unnatural to them. For these readers, Ibn Battuta's firsthand account of Christian life in Constantinople would have offered some of the most exotic ethnography of the entire work. Finally, Ibn Battuta recounts the marvels of Ceylon (Sri Lanka): priceless rubies, the Lake of Monkeys, the repulsive "flying leech," and the mountaintop shrine where one can see the rock containing the footprint of Adam, father of humankind. Marco Polo describes the same site, in an excerpt also reproduced in this cluster: but where Ibn Battuta sees a location holy to Abrahamic tradition, Marco finds only sordid evidence of the pagan origins of idolatry.

From Travels[1]

* * *

From Gaza I travelled to the city of Abraham [Hebron], the mosque of which is of elegant, but substantial, construction, imposing and lofty, and built of squared stones. At one angle of it there is a stone, one of whose faces measures twenty-seven spans. It is said that Solomon commanded the *jinn*[2] to build it. Inside it is the sacred cave containing the graves of Abraham, Isaac, and Jacob,[3] opposite which are three graves, which are those of their wives. I questioned the imám, a man of great piety and learning, on the authenticity of these graves, and he replied: "All the scholars whom I have met hold these graves to be the very graves of Abraham, Isaac, Jacob and their wives. No one questions this except introducers of false doctrines; it is a tradition which has passed from father to son for generations and admits of no doubt." This mosque contains also the grave of Joseph, and somewhat to the east of it lies the tomb of Lot,[4] which is surmounted by an elegant building. In the neighbourhood is Lot's lake [the Dead Sea], which is brackish and is said to cover the site of the settlements of Lot's people. On the way from Hebron to Jerusalem, I visited Bethlehem, the birthplace of Jesus. The site is covered by a large building; the Christians regard it with intense veneration and hospitably entertain all who alight at it.

We then reached Jerusalem (may God ennoble her!), third in excellence after the two holy shrines of Mecca and Madína,[5] and the place whence the Prophet was caught up into heaven.[6] Its walls were destroyed by the illustrious King Saladin[7] and his successors, for fear lest the Christians should seize it and fortify themselves in it. The sacred mosque is a most beautiful building, and is said to be the largest mosque in the world. Its length from east to west is put at 752 "royal" cubits[8] and its breadth at 435. On three sides it has many entrances,

1. Translated from the Arabic by H. A. R. Gibb.
2. See Qur'an 21.81–82, 34.12–13. "Jinn": in Islam, supernatural beings that, like angels and humans, are created by Allah.
3. Three Hebrew patriarchs, also revered by Muslims and Christians; Jacob was the son of Isaac, who was the son of Abraham.
4. Abraham's nephew; he escaped God's complete destruction of Gomorrah and Sodom, where he lived (see Genesis 19.1–29).
5. Islam's holiest sites: Mecca contains the Ka'aba, the building that Muslims face when they pray and that is the central point of the

pilgrimage prescribed as a religious duty; Medina, about 210 miles northwest, is where Muhammad and his followers fled to escape enemies in Mecca.
6. The *mi'raj*; this miraculous ascent of the Prophet Muhammad through the seven heavens is recounted in a number of Arabic and Persian texts.
7. Salah al-Din Yusuf ibn Ayyub (ca. 1138–1193), Sultan of Egypt and Syria. He successfully led Muslim campaigns against the Christians in Palestine, and his capture of Jerusalem in 1187 led to the Third Crusade.
8. About 1,630 by 940 feet.

but on the south side I know of one only, which is that by which the imám enters. The entire mosque is an open court and unroofed, except the mosque al-Aqsá, which has a roof of most excellent workmanship, embellished with gold and brilliant colours. Some other parts of the mosque are roofed as well. The Dome of the Rock is a building of extraordinary beauty, solidity, elegance, and singularity of shape. It stands on an elevation in the centre of the mosque and is reached by a flight of marble steps. It has four doors. The space round it is also paved with marble, excellently done, and the interior likewise. Both outside and inside the decoration is so magnificent and the workmanship so surpassing as to defy description. The greater part is covered with gold so that the eyes of one who gazes on its beauties are dazzled by its brilliance, now glowing like a mass of light, now flashing like lightning. In the centre of the Dome is the blessed rock from which the Prophet ascended to heaven, a great rock projecting about a man's height, and underneath it there is a cave the size of a small room, also of a man's height, with steps leading down to it. Encircling the rock are two railings of excellent workmanship, the one nearer the rock being artistically constructed in iron, and the other of wood.

Among the grace-bestowing sanctuaries of Jerusalem is a building, situated on the farther side of the valley called the valley of Jahannam [Gehenna] to the east of the town, on a high hill. This building is said to mark the place whence Jesus ascended to heaven. In the bottom of the same valley is a church venerated by the Christians, who say that it contains the grave of Mary. In the same place there is another church which the Christians venerate and to which they come on pilgrimage. This is the church of which they are falsely persuaded to believe that it contains the grave of Jesus. All who come on pilgrimage to visit it pay a stipulated tax to the Muslims, and suffer very unwillingly various humiliations. Thereabouts also is the place of the cradle of Jesus,[9] which is visited in order to obtain blessing.

I journeyed thereafter from Jerusalem to the fortress of Askalon,[1] which is a total ruin. Of the great mosque, known as the mosque of 'Omar, nothing remains but its walls and some marble columns of matchless beauty, partly standing and partly fallen. Amongst them is a wonderful red column, of which the people tell that the Christians carried it off to their country but afterwards lost it, when it was found in its place at Askalon. Thence I went on to the city of ar-Ramlah, which is also called Filastín [Palestine], in the *qibla* of those mosque they say three hundred of the prophets are buried. From ar-Ramlah I went to the town of Nábulus [Shechem],[2] a city with an abundance of trees and perennial streams, and one of the richest in Syria for olives, the oil of which is exported thence to Cairo and Damascus. It is at Nábulus that the carob-sweet is manufactured and exported to Damascus and elsewhere. It is made in this way: the carobs are cooked and then pressed, the juice that runs out is gathered and the sweet is manufactured from it. The juice itself too is exported to Cairo and Damascus. Nábulus has also a species of melon which is called by its name, a good and delicious fruit. Thence I went to Ajalún mak-

9. In the Church of the Nativity, located in Bethlehem (about 5 miles southwest of Jerusalem).
1. Former Crusader stronghold, demolished by the Muslims in 1270 (modern Ashkelon is a port city in Israel, just north of the Gaza Strip).
2. Modern Ramallah and Nablus, in the Palestinian West Bank.

ing in the direction of Ládhiqíya, and passing through the Ghawr,[3] followed the coast to 'Akká [Acre], which is in ruins. Acre[4] was formerly the capital and port of the country of the Franks in Syria, and rivalled Constantinople itself.

* * *

One of the celebrated sanctuaries at Damascus is the Mosque of the Footprints (al-Aqdám), which lies two miles south of the city, alongside the main highway which leads to the Hijáz, Jerusalem, and Egypt. It is a large mosque, very blessed, richly endowed, and very highly venerated by the Damascenes. The footprints from which it derives its name are certain footprints impressed upon a rock there, which are said to be the mark of Moses' foot. In this mosque there is a small chamber containing a stone with the following inscription "A certain pious man saw in his sleep the Chosen One [Muhammad], who said to him 'Here is the grave of my brother Moses.'" I saw a remarkable instance of the veneration in which the Damascenes hold this mosque during the great pestilence,[5] on my return journey through Damascus in the latter part of July 1348. The viceroy Arghún Sháh ordered a crier to proclaim through Damascus that all the people should fast for three days[6] and that no one should cook anything eatable in the market during the daytime. For most of the people there eat no food but what has been prepared in the market. So the people fasted for three successive days, the last of which was a Thursday, then they assembled in the Great Mosque, amírs, sharífs, qádís,[7] theologians, and all the other classes of the people, until the place was filled to overflowing, and there they spent the Thursday night in prayers and litanies. After the dawn prayer next morning they all went out together on foot, holding Korans in their hands, and the amírs barefooted. The procession was joined by the entire population of the town, men and women, small and large; the Jews came with their Book of the Law[8] and the Christians with their Gospel, all of them with their women and children. The whole concourse, weeping and supplicating and seeking the favour of God through His Books and His Prophets, made their way to the Mosque of the Footprints, and there they remained in supplication and invocation until near midday. They then returned to the city and held the Friday service, and God lightened their affliction; for the number of deaths in a single day at Damascus did not attain two thousand, while in Cairo and Old Cairo it reached the figure of twenty-four thousand a day.

* * *

The city[9] is enormous in size, and in two parts separated by a great river [the Golden Horn], in which there is a rising and ebbing tide. In former times there was a stone bridge over it, but it fell into ruins and the crossing is now made in boats. The part of the city on the eastern bank of the river is called Istambúl,

3. The Jordan Valley.
4. Site of the last Crusader stronghold in the region, which fell in 1291.
5. The outbreak of bubonic plague that began in Asia and by 1350 had killed more than a third of the population of Europe.
6. I.e., take no food or drink during daylight.

7. I.e., emirs (rulers), nobles, and judges.
8. The Torah (the first five books of the Bible).
9. Constantinople, modern Istanbul; Ibn Battuta later refers to its imperial quarter as "Istambul" (lit., "to the city"). The capital of the Byzantine Empire, the city came under Ottoman Muslim rule in 1453.

and contains the residence of the Emperor, the nobles and the rest of the population. Its bazaars and streets are spacious and paved with flagstones; each bazaar has gates which are closed upon it at night, and the majority of the artisans and sellers in them are women. The city lies at the foot of a hill which projects about nine miles into the sea, its breadth being the same or greater. On the top of the hill there is a small citadel and the Emperor's palace. Round this hill runs the city-wall, which is very strong and cannot be taken by assault from the sea front. Within its circuit there are about thirteen inhabited villages. The principal church is in the midst of this part of the city. The second part, on the western bank of the river, is called Galata, and is reserved to the Frankish Christians who dwell there. They are of different kinds, including Genoese, Venetians, Romans and people of France; they are subject to the authority of the king of Constantinople, who sets over them one of their own number of whom they approve, and him they call the *Comes*.[1] They are bound to pay a tax every year to the king of Constantinople, but often they revolt against him and he makes war on them until the Pope makes peace between them. They are all men of commerce and their harbour is one of the largest in the world; I saw there about a hundred galleys and other large ships, and the small ships were too many to be counted. The bazaars in this part of the town are good but filthy, and a small and very dirty river runs through them. Their churches too are filthy and mean.

Of the great church I can only describe the exterior, for I did not see its interior. It is called by them Ayá Súfiyá [St. Sophia],[2] and the story goes that it was built by Asaph, the son of Berechiah, who was Solomon's cousin. It is one of the greatest churches of the Greeks, and is encircled by a wall so that it looks as if it were a town. It has thirteen gates and a sacred enclosure, which is about a mile long and closed by a great gate. No one is prevented from entering this enclosure, and indeed I went into it with the king's father; it resembles an audience-hall paved with marble, and is traversed by a stream which issues from the church. Outside the gate of this hall are platforms and shops, mostly of wood, where their judges and the recorders of their bureaux sit. At the gate of the church there are porticoes where the keepers sit who sweep its paths, light its lamps and close its gates. They allow none to enter it until he prostrates himself to the huge cross there, which they claim to be a relic of the wood upon which the pseudo-Jesus was crucified.[3] This is over the gate of the church, set in a golden case whose height is about ten cubits, across which a similar golden case is placed to form a cross. This gate is covered with plaques of silver and gold and its two rings are of pure gold. I was told that the number of monks and priests in this church runs into thousands, and that some of them are descendants of the apostles, and that inside it is another church exclusively for women, containing more than a thousand virgins and a still greater number of aged women who devote themselves to religious practices. It is the custom of the king, the nobles and the rest of the people to come every morning to visit this

1. Companion (Latin); here, an attendant of the ruler.
2. Modern Hagia Sophia ("Holy Wisdom"; Greek); established as a Christian church in 360, it was converted to a mosque after the Ottoman conquest and is now a public museum.

3. A reference to the Muslim belief that Jesus, although miraculously born without a human father to the Virgin Mary and a prophet of God, was not crucified; instead, they believe, a substitute took his place before the execution.

church. The Pope comes to visit it once a year. When he is four days' journey from the town the king goes out to meet him, and dismounts before him and when he enters the city walks on foot in front of him. During his stay in Constantinople the king comes to salute[4] him every morning and evening.

A monastery is the Christian equivalent of a religious house or convent among the Muslims, and there are a great many such monasteries at Constantinople. Among them is the monastery which King George built outside Istambúl and opposite Galata, and two monasteries outside the principal church, to the right as one enters it. These two monasteries are inside a garden traversed by a stream of water; one of them is for men and the other for women. In each there is a church and they are surrounded by the cells of men and women who have devoted themselves to religious exercises. Each monastery possesses pious endowments for the clothing and maintenance of the devotees. Inside every monastery there is a small convent designed for the ascetic retreat of the king who built it, for most of these kings, on reaching the age of sixty or seventy, build a monastery and put on garments of hair,[5] investing their sons with the sovereignty and occupying themselves with religious exercises for the rest of their lives. They display great magnificence in building these monasteries, and construct them of marble and mosaic-work. I entered a monastery with the Greek whom the king had given me as a guide. Inside it was a church containing about five hundred virgins wearing hair-garments; their heads were shaved and covered with felt bonnets. They were exceedingly beautiful and showed the traces of their austerities. A youth sitting on a pulpit was reading the gospel to them in the most beautiful voice I have ever heard; round him were eight other youths on pulpits with their priest, and when the first youth had finished reading another began. The Greek said to me "These girls are kings' daughters who have given themselves to the service of this church, and likewise the boys who are reading [are kings' sons]." I entered with him also into churches in which there were the daughters of ministers, governors, and the principal men of the city, and others where there were aged women and widows, and others where there were monks, each church containing a hundred men or so. Most of the population of the city are monks, ascetics, and priests, and its churches are not to be counted for multitude. The inhabitants of the city, soldiers and civilians, small and great, carry over their heads huge parasols, both in winter and summer, and the women wear large turbans.

I was out one day with my Greek guide, when we met the former king George who had become a monk. He was walking on foot, wearing haircloth garments and a bonnet of felt, and he had a long white beard and a fine face, which bore traces of his austerities. Behind and before him was a body of monks, and he had a staff in his hand and a rosary on his neck. When the Greek saw him he dismounted and said to me "Dismount, for this is the king's father." When my guide saluted him the king asked him about me, then stopped and sent for me. He took my hand and said to the Greek (who knew the Arabic tongue) "Say to this Saracen (meaning Muslim) 'I clasp the hand which has entered Jerusalem and the foot which has walked within the Dome of the Rock and the great church of the Holy Sepulchre and Bethlehem,'" and he laid his hand upon my

4. Greet.
5. I.e., rough animal hair worn against the skin as penance.

feet and passed it over his face. I was astonished at their good opinion of one who, though not of their religion, had entered these places. Then he took my hand and as I walked with him asked me about Jerusalem and the Christians who were there, and questioned me at length. I entered with him the sacred enclosure of the church which we have described above. When he approached the principal gate, a party of priests and monks came out to salute him, for he is one of their chief men in monasticism, and on seeing them he let go my hand. I said to him "I should like to enter the church with you." Then he said to the interpreter, "Say to him 'He who enters it must needs prostrate himself before the great cross, for this is a rule which the ancients laid down and which cannot be contravened.' " So I left him and he entered alone and I did not see him again. After leaving the king I entered the bazaar of the scribes, where I was noticed by the judge, who sent one of his assistants to ask the Greek about me. On learning that I was a Muslim scholar he sent for me and I went up to him. He was an old man with a fine face and hair, wearing the black garments of a monk, and had about ten scribes in front of him writing. He rose to meet me, his companions rising also, and said "You are the king's guest and we are bound to honour you." He then asked me about Jerusalem, Syria, and Egypt, and spoke with me for a long time. A great crowd gathered round him, and he said "You must come to my house that I may entertain you." After that I went away, but I did not see him again.

* * *

In the island of Ceylon[6] rubies are found in all parts. The land is private property, and a man buys a parcel of it and digs for rubies. Some of them are red, some yellow [topazes], and some blue [sapphires]. Their custom is that all rubies of the value of a hundred *fanams* belong to the sultan, who pays their price and takes them; those of less value belong to the finders. A hundred *fanams* equal in value six gold dinars.[7]

We went on from Kunakár and halted at a cave called after Ustá Mahmúd the Lúrí, a pious man who dug out this cave at the foot of a hill beside a small lake. Thence we travelled to the Lake of Monkeys. There are in these mountains vast numbers of monkeys. They are black and have long tails, and their males are bearded like men. Shaykh 'Othmán and his sons and others as well told me that these monkeys have a chief, whom they obey as if he were a king. He fastens on his head a fillet of leaves and leans upon a staff. On his right and his left are four monkeys carrying staves in their hands. When the chief monkey sits down the four monkeys stand behind him, and his female and young come and sit in front of him every day. The other monkeys come and sit at a distance from him, then one of the four monkeys addresses them and all the monkeys withdraw. After this each one brings a banana or a lemon or some such fruit, and the monkey chief with his young and the four monkeys eat. One of the Yogis told me that he had seen the four monkeys in the presence of their chief beating a monkey with sticks and after the beating pulling out its

6. Modern Sri Lanka.
7. The dinar, used in the Muslim world, was about 4 grams of gold.

hair. We continued our journey to a place called "The Old Woman's Hut," which is the end of the inhabited part, and marched thence by a number of grottoes. In this place we saw the flying leech, which sits on trees and in the vegetation near water. When a man approaches it jumps out at him, and wheresoever it alights on his body the blood flows freely. The inhabitants keep a lemon in readiness for it; they squeeze this over it and it falls off them, then they scrape the place on which it alighted with a wooden knife which they have for the purpose.

The mountain of Sarandíb [Adam's Peak] is one of the highest in the world.[8] We saw it from the sea when we were nine days' journey away, and when we climbed it we saw the clouds below us, shutting out our view of its base. On it there are many evergreen trees and flowers of various colours, including a red rose as big as the palm of a hand. There are two tracks on the mountain leading to the Foot, one called Bábá track and the other Mámá track, meaning Adam and Eve. The Mámá track is easy and is the route by which the pilgrims return, but anyone who goes by that way is not considered by them to have made the pilgrimage at all. The Bábá track is difficult and stiff climbing. Former generations cut a sort of stairway on the mountain, and fixed iron stanchions on it, to which they attached chains for climbers to hold on by. There are ten such chains, two at the foot of the hill by the "threshold," seven successive chains farther on, and the tenth is the "Chain of the Profession of Faith," so called because when one reaches it and looks down to the foot of the hill, he is seized by apprehensions and recites the profession of faith for fear of falling. When you climb past this chain you find a rough track. From the tenth chain to the grotto of Khidr[9] is seven miles; this grotto lies in a wide plateau, and near by it is a spring full of fish, but no one catches them. Close to this there are two tanks cut in the rock on either side of the path. At the grotto of Khidr the pilgrims leave their belongings and ascend thence for two miles to the summit of the mountain where the Foot is.

The blessed Footprint, the Foot of our father Adam, is on a lofty black rock in a wide plateau. The blessed Foot sank into the rock far enough to leave its impression hollowed out. It is eleven spans long. In ancient days the Chinese came here and cut out of the rock the mark of the great toe and the adjoining parts. They put this in a temple at Zaytún,[1] where it is visited by men from the farthest parts of the land. In the rock where the Foot is there are nine holes cut out, in which the infidel pilgrims place offerings of gold, precious stones, and jewels. You can see the darwíshes,[2] after they reach the grotto of Khidr, racing one another to take what there is in these holes. We, for our part, found nothing in them but a few stones and a little gold, which we gave to the guide. It is customary for the pilgrims to stay at the grotto of Khidr for three days, visiting the Foot every morning and evening, and we followed this practice. When the three days were over we returned by the Mámá track, halting at a number of villages on the mountain. At the foot of the mountain there is an ancient tree whose leaves never fall, situated in a place that cannot be got at. I have never

---

8. In fact, the mountain is about 7,300 feet high.

9. An enigmatic figure, attested in the Qur'an (18.65) and venerated as a prophet in Islam.

1. In southeast China (modern Quanzhou), a great port in the Middle Ages.

2. I.e., dervishes, or ascetic Sufis (followers of a mystic form of Islam).

met anyone who has seen its leaves. I saw there a number of Yogis who never quit the base of the mountain waiting for its leaves to fall. They tell lying tales about it, one being that whosoever eats of it regains his youth, even if he be an old man, but that is false. Beneath the mountain is the great lake from which the rubies are taken; its water is a bright blue to the sight.

THE BOOK OF JOHN MANDEVILLE

The Book of John Mandeville (ca. 1360), today sometimes titled *Mandeville's Travels*, is almost exactly contemporary with but also quite different from Ibn Battuta's account: one is written by a Christian native of northern Europe, the other by a Muslim native of the Mediterranean coast of Africa; one is largely compiled from earlier books about the Orient, the other based primarily on personal experience of travel and cultural encounter. Yet the two have much in common—especially their evocation of the multicultural, multifaith environment of the major cities of the East. The author emphasizes the first-person quality of his work, beginning it with what can only be described as a claim of witness: "I, John Mandeville, knight, born and brought up in England in the town of St. Albans, have seen and gone around many lands, of which I will speak more fully." Ironically, this claim is not true, or at least not entirely true. There is no corroborating evidence of a John Mandeville of St. Albans; the text was written not in English but in French; and the work was most likely composed not in England but on the Continent. It was, however, written in a dialect of French (Anglo-Norman) that was spoken in the British Isles, and so the claim of authorship by an Englishman—especially in view of the text's rampant nationalism—is entirely plausible. The claim of actual experience of the

regions described is at least partially false: though the author may have visited some of these lands, including Constantinople and the regions around Jerusalem, the account of territories lying farther eastward is clearly adapted from earlier written sources. But the importance of *The Book of John Mandeville* lies not in the veracity of its ethnographic description, as in **Marco Polo**'s and **Ibn Battuta**'s works, but rather in its extraordinary popularity: more widely read than any other travel narrative of the period, "Mandeville's" book was translated, adapted, reprinted, and retold innumerable times.

Despite questions about its own authenticity, *The Book of John Mandeville* displays a strong interest in the practice of exploration, as can be seen in the account of navigation by the stars excerpted here. This chapter epitomizes the work's striking juxtaposition of information useful to the explorer and bizarre details designed to titillate the armchair traveler: we hear about the spherical shape of the world and the geography of eastern regions, on the one hand, and the practice of cannibalism on the other, as children are fattened up expressly to produce "the best and sweetest meat in the world." *The Book of John Mandeville* concludes with an account of the Great Khan, ruler of China—the same ruler sought by Ibn

Battuta on his mission to Beijing, and a descendant of Kublai Khan, who was served so loyally by Marco Polo. The *Book*'s last lines return to the opening claim of eyewitness testimony, as "John Mandeville" reassures us, once again, of the utter reliability of his half-truthful story of wonders. The influence of *The Book of John Mandeville* would continue to be felt for hundreds of years, across a wide range of genres, from the spiritual pilgrimage of Bunyan's *Pilgrim's Progress* (which alludes to Mandeville's "Valley Perilous") to the compilation of travels found in Hakluyt's *Principal Navigations*, and extending even as far as the fantastical "Xanadu" of Samuel Taylor Coleridge.

From The Book of John Mandeville[1]

XX. *About the evil customs used in the Isle of Lamory, and how the Earth and the Sea are of round form by proof of the Antarctic Star*

From this country one goes by the Ocean Sea and many diverse islands and many countries that would be too long to name and describe; and fifty-two days' journey from this land that I have spoken about, there is another land that is quite large and has the name Lamory.[2]

In this land there is a very great heat, and the custom is such that the men and the women all go naked. They jeer when they see any foreigner who is clothed, and they say that God who made Adam was naked—and [that] both Adam and Eve were made naked—and that people should not be ashamed to show themselves as God has made them, for nothing is ugly that comes from nature. And they say that those who are clothed are people of another era, or they are people who do not believe in God; and indeed they say that they believe in God who created the world and made Adam and Eve and all other things.

Since they have no married women, all the women of the country are thus common and refuse no man; and they say that they sin if they refuse men and that God commanded it of Adam and his descendents where he said: "*Crescite et multiplicamini et replete terram.*"[3] Therefore no man in all this country can say: "this is my wife." Nor can any woman say: "this is my husband." And when the women have children, they give them to those they like who have had sexual relations with them. The land is also common, for some hold it in one year and others in another, and each takes whatever part he wants; and also all the goods of the country are common, wheat and other things, for nothing is enclosed, nothing is locked up at all; each takes what he likes without restriction and one person is as rich as another. But they have an evil custom, for they more willingly eat human flesh than any other flesh. And the country abounds in wheat, meat, fish, gold, silver, and other goods. The merchants go there and take children with them for sale to the inhabitants, and the latter

1. Translated from the French by Iain Macleod Higgins.
2. Sumatra. The land just discussed is Coromandel, on the southeast coast of India.
3. "Increase and multiply and fill the Earth" (Genesis 1.28; Vulgate). Passages in Latin in Mandeville's text remained in that language in the many medieval vernacular translations, as here.

buy them; and if they are fat, they eat them right away, and if they are lean, they fatten them, and they say that this is the best and sweetest meat in the world.

In this land and in many others over there the Tramontane star[4] cannot be seen at all. It is the star of the sea that does not move which is towards the north. But one can see another star opposite it, towards the south, which is called Antarctic.[5] And just as sailors here take their bearings and steer themselves by that star to the north, so the sailors over there use this star to the south, which is never visible to us, and the one to the north is not visible to them.

Through this we can perceive that the earth and the sea are of round form, for the part of the firmament that appears in one country does not appear in another. And it can be easily discovered by experience and by clever research that, if a man found passage by ship and people who wanted to go explore the world, he could sail all around the world, both above and below. This thing I prove according to what I have seen, for I have been towards the regions of Brabant and seen with the astrolabe[6] that the Tramontane is 53 degrees high. And further forward in Germany and Bohemia it is 58 degrees, and further forward towards the northern regions it is 62 degrees and several minutes high, for I myself have measured it with the astrolabe.

Now you ought to know that opposite this Tramontane is the other star that is called Antarctic, as I have said above. And these two stars are not very mobile, and the whole firmament turns on them as a wheel turns on its axle, such that these stars divide the firmament into two equal parts so that there is as much below as above.

Afterwards, I went towards the meridional regions—that is, towards the south—and found that the Antarctic star is first seen in Libya, and the farther forward I went in those parts the higher I found this star, such that towards upper Libya it was 18 degrees and several minutes high (60 minutes make one degree). Then in going by sea and by land towards those regions that I have spoken about and to other islands and lands beyond this country, I found the Antarctic star 33 degrees and several minutes high.

If I had found company and ship to go further, I believe it to be certain that we would have seen the whole roundness of the firmament all around. For, as I told you above, half of the firmament is between these two stars. I have seen all of this half; and of the other half to the north under the Tramontane, I have seen 62 degrees and 10 minutes, and towards the meridional [southern] parts under the Antarctic I have seen 33 degrees and 16 minutes. Now half of the firmament in total has only 180 degrees, and of these 180 I have seen 62 of one part and 33 of the other, which is 95 degrees and almost half a degree. Thus I have not seen only 94 degrees and half a degree of the whole firmament; and that is not one quarter of the firmament, for a quarter of the roundness of the firmament is 90 degrees, and lacks 5 and a half degrees of the

4. The North Star.
5. Although no star in the Southern Hemisphere corresponds to the North Star in marking the celestial pole, navigators could steer by the Southern Cross.
6. An astronomical device, used for naviga-

tion, that was introduced to Europe from Islamic Spain; it quickly came into widespread use. "Brabant": a duchy in what is now the southern Netherlands and central and northern Belgium.

quarter. So I have seen three quarters of all the roundness of the firmament and 5 and a half degrees more. For this reason I say for certain that a man could travel around all the land in the world, both below and above, and return to his own country, if he had company and shipping and always found men, lands, and islands just as in this country.

For you know that those who are in the place of the Antarctic are exactly foot against foot[7] with those who live beneath the Tramontane, just as we and those who live under us are foot against foot: for all the parts of sea and land have their habitable and navigable opposites, and islands here as well as there. Know that according to what I can perceive and understand, the lands of Prester John,[8] Emperor of India, are under us. For in going from Scotland or England towards Jerusalem one is always climbing; for our land is in the low part of the earth to the west, and Prester John's land is the low part of the earth to the east, and they have day there when we have night, and just the opposite: they have night when we have day. For the earth and the sea are of round form, as I told you above, and as one climbs on one side one descends on the other.

Now you have heard said before that Jerusalem is in the middle of the world, and this can be shown over there by a spear fixed in the ground at the hour of noon at the equinox that casts no shadow on any side. That it is in the middle of the world David testifies in the Psalter, where he says *"Deus operatus est salutem in medio terre."*[9] Thus those who leave from these parts of the west to go towards Jerusalem take as many days of climbing to go all the way there as they would take from Jerusalem to the other ends of the earth's surface over there. And when one takes more days towards India and the farther islands, one is going around all the roundness of the land and the sea under our countries over here.

For this reason I have often recalled a thing I heard told when I was young: how a brave man once left from our regions to go explore the world. He passed India and the islands beyond India, where there are more than 5000 islands, and he went so far by sea and by land, and he went round so much of the world through many seasons that he found an island where he heard his own language spoken and the oxen called with the same words as in his own country. This amazed him very much. For he did not know how it could be. But I say that he had gone so far by land and by sea that he had gone around the whole earth, that he came back having gone right round to his own borderlands— and if he had gone forward he would have found his own country and his own knowledge. But he went back by the way he had come and lost much effort, as he himself said a great while after he had returned. For it happened afterwards that he was in Norway, and a storm on the sea caught him and he came to an island, and when he was on that island he recognized it as the island where he had heard his own language spoken in guiding the oxen pulling the plough.

7. I.e., at the Antipodes (literally, "having opposite feet"; Greek).
8. According to a legend invented in the 12th century, an Oriental (usually Indian) Christian ruler eager to join with the Christian nations of Europe to drive the Muslim forces out of the Holy Land. Voyagers looked for the Land of Prester John in Asia and elsewhere— especially Ethiopia, which had long been recognized as a Christian kingdom.
9. "God worked salvation in the middle of the Earth" (Psalm 74.12, slightly misquoted).

That was indeed a possible thing, although it seems to simple people that no one could go beneath the earth and that one must fall into the sky below. But this cannot be, any more than we could fall into the sky from the land where we are. For in whatever part of the earth one dwells, either above or below, it always seems to those living there that they walk more upright than any other people; and just as it seems to us that they are under us, so it seems to them that we are under them. For if one could fall from the earth to the firmament, [there is] all the more reason [to believe that] the earth and the sea—that are so large and so heavy—ought to fall right to the firmament. But that could not be, and this is why Our Lord says *"Non timeas me qui suspendi terram ex nichilo."*[1]

Although this is a possible thing that one could thus go around the whole world, nevertheless not one person in a thousand would travel the right way so as to return to his own country. For because of the large size of the earth and the sea, one could go by thousands of other ways, such that no one could return exactly to the regions from which he left, except by chance or God's true grace.

For the earth is very broad and very big, and is 20,425 miles in roundness and all around,[2] above and below, according to the opinion of the ancients. I do not reject their word, but according to my small intelligence, it seems to me that with all due respect it is larger. The better to understand what I mean, let there be imagined a figure of a large circle, and around the point of this large circle—the part called the centre—let there be another smaller circle. Then let the large circle be divided by lines into many parts, and let all the lines come together in the centre such that the small circle that is around the centre will be divided into as many parts as the large circle, although the spaces will be smaller. Now let the large circle stand for the firmament and the little circle for the earth. The firmament is divided by astronomers into twelve signs, and each sign is divided into thirty degrees; around the whole firmament there are 360 degrees. Now let the earth be divided into as many parts as the firmament, and each part will correspond to a degree of the firmament. Know that according to the authorities in astronomy, 600 stades[3] of the earth correspond to one degree of the firmament; there are 87,004 stades. Now let this be multiplied by 340 [360]; there will be 31,600 miles, each of eight stades, according to the miles of our country. Such is the earth in roundness and all around, according to my opinion and my understanding.

Know that, according to the opinion of the wise ancient philosophers and astronomers, our country, Ireland, Wales, Scotland, England, Norway, and the other islands bordering them are not on the earth's surface calculated above, as it appears in all the books of astronomy. For the surface of the earth is divided into seven parts by the seven planets, and these parts are called climates, and our parts are not in the seven climates.[4] For they descend to the

1. "Do not fear me, who suspended the Earth from nothing" (a somewhat garbled echo of Job 26.7).
2. The actual circumference of the earth is more than 24,000 miles.
3. The stade, or stadium, is one-eighth of a Roman mile (a little more than 600 feet).

4. Ancient and medieval astronomers (following the 2nd-century C.E. Greek astronomer Ptolemy) divided the Northern Hemisphere into seven zones of latitude or "climates"; the British Isles lie above the northernmost of the seven climates.

west owing to the roundness of the world, and the islands of India are there, and they are opposite us who are in the low part, and the seven climates extend all around the world.

From XXXIV. *About the customs of the kings and others dwelling on the islands near Prester John's Land, and about the honor that the son does to his dead father*

* * *

On this island they have a custom throughout the whole country that when someone's father dies and he wishes to greatly honor his father, he sends for all his friends and relatives and monks and priests and a great many minstrels. Then the body is carried onto a mountain with great ceremony and great joy, and when they have carried [it] all the way there, the greatest priest cuts off the head and sets it on a large platter made of gold or silver, if he is a rich man, and then delivers the head to the son, and the son and the other relatives chant many prayers to God. Then the priests and the monks cut all the flesh of the body into pieces, and then they say their prayers, and the birds of the country, which have long known this custom, come flying above—such as vultures, eagles, and all other birds that eat flesh—and the priests throw pieces of the flesh to them, and they carry it not far away and eat it. Then just as the chaplains over here chant "*Subvenite sancti Dei etc.*"[5] for the dead, so these priests there at this point chant aloud in their language, "See how worthy a man he was that God's angels seek him out and carry him to Paradise." At this point it seems to the son that he is very much honoured when the birds have eaten his father, and whoever has the greatest number of birds is the most honoured. Then the son takes his relatives and his friends back to his house and makes a great feast for them, and all the friends tell their story of how the birds came — five here, ten there, twenty here—and enjoy themselves most abundantly in the telling. When they are at the house the son has his father's head cooked and gives each of his most special friends a little of the flesh from it instead of a dish of something else, and from the skull he has a goblet made, and he drinks from it—and his relatives do too—with great devotion in memory of the holy man whom the birds have eaten. And the son will keep this goblet and drink from it all his life in his father's memory.

From this island after ten days on the return journey through the Great Khan's land, there is another very good island and large kingdom where there is a rich and strong king, and amongst the rich men of his country there is a very rich man who is neither prince, duke, commander, or count. But there are many who have their lands from him, and he is extremely rich, for each year he has in payment a good three thousand horses laden with wheat and rice, and he leads a very noble life according to the custom over there, for he has fifty maiden ladies-in-waiting who always serve him at meals and in going to bed and do whatever he likes. When he is eating a meal, they bring him his food five dishes at a time, and while carrying it in they sing a song. Then they cut his

5. Aid him, saints of God.

food up for him and put it in his mouth, for he touches nothing but just holds his hands in front of him on the table, for he has such long nails that he could not grasp or hold anything. It is a noble thing for men to have long nails and to let them always grow and be looked after as much as they can. There are many men in the country who let them grow so much that they encircle the whole hand, and it is a very noble thing; and the noble thing for women in this country is to have small feet. Therefore as soon as they are born, they have their feet bound so tightly that they grow only half as long as they should grow. These ladies-in-waiting always sing while he eats, and when he is no longer eating any of these five dishes, they bring him another five dishes and sing as before, and they do this right to the end of the meal. It is done this way every day, and this is how he spends his life, and so did his ancestors and so will those who come after him, without anyone doing a fair deed of arms, but he always lives like this in comfort like a pig that is being fattened. He has a very fine and very rich palace where he lives whose walls are a good two leagues in circumference, and he has inside it many beautiful gardens, and all the floors of the halls and the rooms are paved with gold and silver. In the middle of one of the gardens there is a small mountain where there is a meadow and in this meadow there is a little church with towers and pinnacles all of gold, and he often likes to sit in this little church both to take the air and to enjoy himself, for this church was made for no other purpose than for his pleasure alone.

From this country one goes by land through the Great Khan's land, about which I told you before, so no further account is needed.

Know that in all these countries about which I have spoken, and on all these islands, and amongst all these diverse peoples that I have described to you, and the diverse laws and the diverse beliefs they have, there is no people—because they have reason and understanding—who do not have some articles of our faith and some good points of our belief, and who do not believe in God who made the world, whom they call god of nature, according to the prophet, who said: "*Et metuent eum omnes fines terre.*" And elsewhere: "*Omnes gentes servient ei.*"[6]

But they do not know how to speak perfectly, for they have no one to explain it to them, except insofar as they understand it with their natural understanding. They do not know how to speak about the Son, nor about the Holy Spirit. But they all know how to speak about the Bible, especially about Genesis, the sayings of the prophets, and the books of Moses.

Indeed, they say that the creatures that they worship are not gods at all, but they worship them for the virtue that is in them, which could not exist without God's grace. About simulacra and idols, they say that there are no people who do not have simulacra, and they say this because we Christians have images of Our Lady and other saints that we worship. But they do not know what we worship: not the images of wood or stone, but the saints in whose name they are made. For just as the letter instructs and teaches the clergy what and how they should believe, so the images and the depictions teach the laity to think about and worship the saints in whose name they are made.

6. Respectively, "And all the ends of the Earth shall fear Him" (Psalm 67.7, slightly misquoted); "All nations shall serve Him" (Psalm 72.11).

They say also that God's angels speak to them in those idols, and that they perform great miracles; and they speak the truth that there is an angel within. But there are two kinds of angel, good and bad: Cacho [kakos] and Calo [kallos], as the Greeks say, and Cacho is bad and Calo is good.[7] But it is not the good angel, but the bad that is in the idols, to deceive them and keep them in their error.

There are many other diverse countries and many other wonders over there that I have not seen at all, and do not know how to speak properly about. And even in countries where I have been there are many diversities of which I have made no mention, for it would be a long thing to describe everything. Therefore what I have described for you about some countries should do you for now. For if I described as many things as there are over there, someone else who took the trouble and labored bodily to go into those far places and find out about the country would be hindered by my words from reporting on anything foreign, for he would have nothing new to say in which the listeners could take pleasure, and it is always said that new things give pleasure. Thus I shall keep quiet now without recounting any more diversities that exist over there, so that whoever wishes to go into those parts might find there enough to say.

And I, the above-named John Mandeville—who left our countries and crossed the sea in the year of grace 1322, who has since sought out many lands and many journeys and many countries, and who has been in much good company and in many a fine undertaking (although I never did any fair deed nor fine adventure), and now have come to rest, despite myself, because of arthritic gout, which constrains me—while taking pleasure in my miserable rest, in recording the time past, have compiled these things and put them into writing, such as I could remember, in the year of grace 1356, in the thirty-fourth year since I left our countries.

7. A difficult passage: the contrast is between the evil (Greek *kakos*) and the beautiful (Greek *kallos*) image.

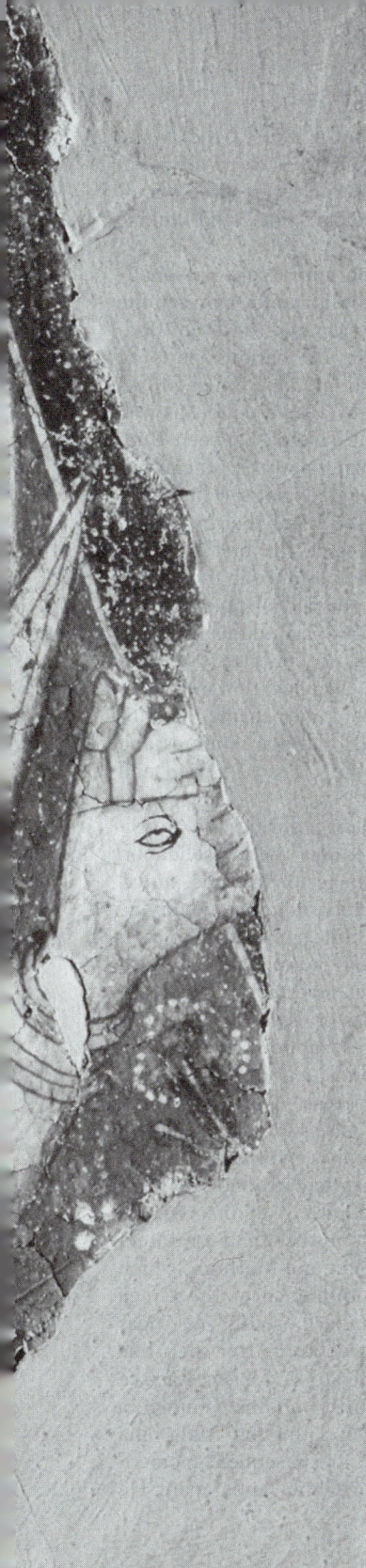

II

India's Classical Age

During the ancient period (ca. 1200 B.C.E.–400 C.E.), society on the Indian subcontinent evolved in several distinct stages. Beginning from agrarian villages, it developed a caste system and a religion centered on Vedic scripture and ritual; as the rural economy increasingly supported the growth of towns and cities, the first subcontinent-wide empires arose. The caste system grew more intricate, with five main categories that included so-called untouchables as well as numerous specific castes, even as the coexistence of monogamy, polygamy, and polyandry complicated the rules of social classification. The Vedic canon of scripture, commentaries, and code books came to articulate the concepts of *Brahman*, or undifferentiated godhead, and *ātman*, enduring individual self or soul; *mokṣa*, the soul's liberation from mundane existence, so that it can be reunited with godhead; and karma, or action and its consequences, as well as *dharma*, law and duty as defined by the gods. Vedic ritual, designed to please many deities and to increase its performer's chances of attaining *mokṣa*, was complemented by sophisticated debates about the nature of good and evil, morality and power, and ethics and justice, thereby laying the

This detail from a seventh-century Buddhist wall painting depicts the Hindu deity Indra kneeling in veneration before the Buddha.

947

foundation for Hinduism in the classical period. By the start of the Common Era, India was well-defined as a distinct cultural zone within Asia, characterized by its acceptance of pantheism and polytheism, its religious pluralism and tolerance, and its accommodation of social and cultural diversity.

THE TRANSITION TO THE CLASSICAL PERIOD

In the closing centuries of the ancient period, the subcontinent underwent several far-reaching changes that were part of a lengthy transition to the classical period (ca. 400–1100 C.E.). One major shift was a transformation of its political organization, which became evident under the Maurya dynasty (ca. 321–180 B.C.E.). Established immediately after Alexander the Great's invasion of India (327 B.C.E.), the Mauryan empire unified most of the country—then inhabited by about 50 million people—under a centralized administration and a single system of laws. The new empire interconnected its districts with highways, easing the movement of goods and people; and it established diplomatic and trade links with Greece, Rome, Egypt, Syria, and Central Asia. The visionary Mauryan emperor Aśoka (ruled 269–232 B.C.E.), in particular, influenced subsequent Indian and Asian history on a significant scale. He institutionalized the idea that a king "turns the wheel of *dharma*" on earth, and hence is fully responsible for his people's well-being under cosmic or universal law. His royal chancery standardized the Brahmi script system, which was used in his famous rock inscriptions, paving the way for the subcontinent's future literacy and the spread of writing throughout Southeast Asia. The standardization also emphasized multilingual pluralism, as Brahmi writing was simultaneously transcribed into the Greek and Kharosthī scripts (the latter a variant of the Aramaic), which were used widely along the ancient Silk Road linking Asia to Europe.

Equally important, Aśoka personally converted to Buddhism, patronized the Third Buddhist Council, and sent Buddhist embassies to various parts of Asia. Because of his adoption of *ahiṃsā* (nonviolence) as a state policy, as well as his unusual balance between Buddhist proselytizing and the official tolerance of many religions (Hinduism, Jainism, and Greek polytheism, among others), he became the first figure of transnational importance in the history of Buddhism; he is portrayed in the canon of Theravada Buddhism as second in importance only to Gautama Buddha. Aśoka's conception and practice of imperial rule became a multifaceted model for Indian empires and kingdoms in the classical period and later.

Another change during the transitional centuries was the consolidation of royal patronage for the arts, architecture and construction, and public works. Aśoka built many of the oldest, most venerated monuments of Buddhism, and he invested in hospitals, libraries, monasteries, and institutions of learning; his support initiated the growth and spread of Buddhist art and architecture across Asia over many centuries. A successor of the Mauryan state, the Kuṣāṇa empire (first–third century C.E.), particularly under Kaniṣka (ruled ca. 100 C.E.), sponsored the Indo-Greek sculpture and architecture of Gandhara and Mathura, which displayed the influence of the Greek colony Alexander established near Peshawar, Pakistan. After he, like Aśoka, converted to Buddhism, Kaniṣka hosted the Fourth Buddhist Council in Kashmir, which launched Mahāyāna Buddhism and its subsequent momentous spread to China and Japan. He patronized painters, musicians, and poets, including the poet-dramatist Aśvaghoṣa, whose *Buddhacarita* (*The Life of the Buddha,* second century C.E.) invented the style of Sanskrit *kāvya,* or poetry, that was to dominate the classical period.

SOCIAL AND POLITICAL CONTEXTS OF CLASSICAL LITERATURE

The "classical" phase—during which Indian literature achieved an exceptional degree of aesthetic balance, stylistic refinement, intellectual sophistication, and originality—began in the second century C.E.; it came to maturity during the Gupta empire (ca. 320–550), specifically under Candragupta Vikramāditya (ruled ca. 375–415). Despite turbulence in its latter half, the classical period lasted until the end of the eleventh century, after which Islam, having arrived from the Middle East, irreversibly transformed the subcontinent's politics, society, and economy.

Stretching across the whole of northern India, and building alliances with lesser powers to its south, the Gupta empire achieved a remarkable expansion and stabilization of the Indian economy. Agriculture and dairy farming yielded an array of grains, fresh produce, and milk products; at the same time, weaving and spinning guilds, salt and mineral mines, metalworks, jewelers' workshops, and specialized castes of artisans produced a wide range of luxury goods and items for everyday consumption. An efficient bureaucracy, regulated coinage, and banking led to an increase in travel and pilgrimage and the growth of shipping, ports, inland cities, and overland and maritime commerce. While trade with the Roman Empire declined, that with China and Southeast Asia—especially the Indonesian archipelago—flourished, creating prosperity across the countryside as well as in urban areas. The economic improvements of the Gupta empire continued, on a smaller scale, in the successor kingdoms of Harṣavardhana of Kannauj (seventh century, near Delhi) and of dynasties in central and eastern India (eighth–eleventh centuries).

The Gupta empire's prosperity and political stability had broad ramifications for the subcontinent's arts, religions, and literature. Like the Mauryas and Kuśānas before them, the Guptas had a pluralistic policy of supporting Hinduism, Jainism, and Buddhism, though more lavishly; but they themselves were Hindus, and their patronage powerfully aided the consolidation of what we now call classical Hinduism. Mainly because of their stimulus, Hinduism shifted from an elite focus on Vedic ritual and sacrifice to a more populist form of engagement, centered on pilgrimages to holy river sites and public worship in temples. It devalued many of the Vedic gods, who resembled the gods in the Greek and Roman pantheons, and elevated Viṣṇu (the god of preservation) and Śiva (the god of destruction) to the status of major deities. Moreover, it produced a vast new canon of theological and mythological works, called Purāṇas, focused on these gods; eventually, they significantly displaced the Vedas (ca. 1200–900 B.C.E.), the original revealed scripture, in the popular imagination. The Guptas aided this shift by financing temple architecture and construction on a grand scale; these edifices later served as models for temple complexes not only in India but also in Borobudur (Indonesia) and Angkor Wat (Cambodia). They also championed major advances in classical Indian stone and metal sculpture—examples are now widely represented in major museums around the world—which influenced the plastic arts throughout Asia.

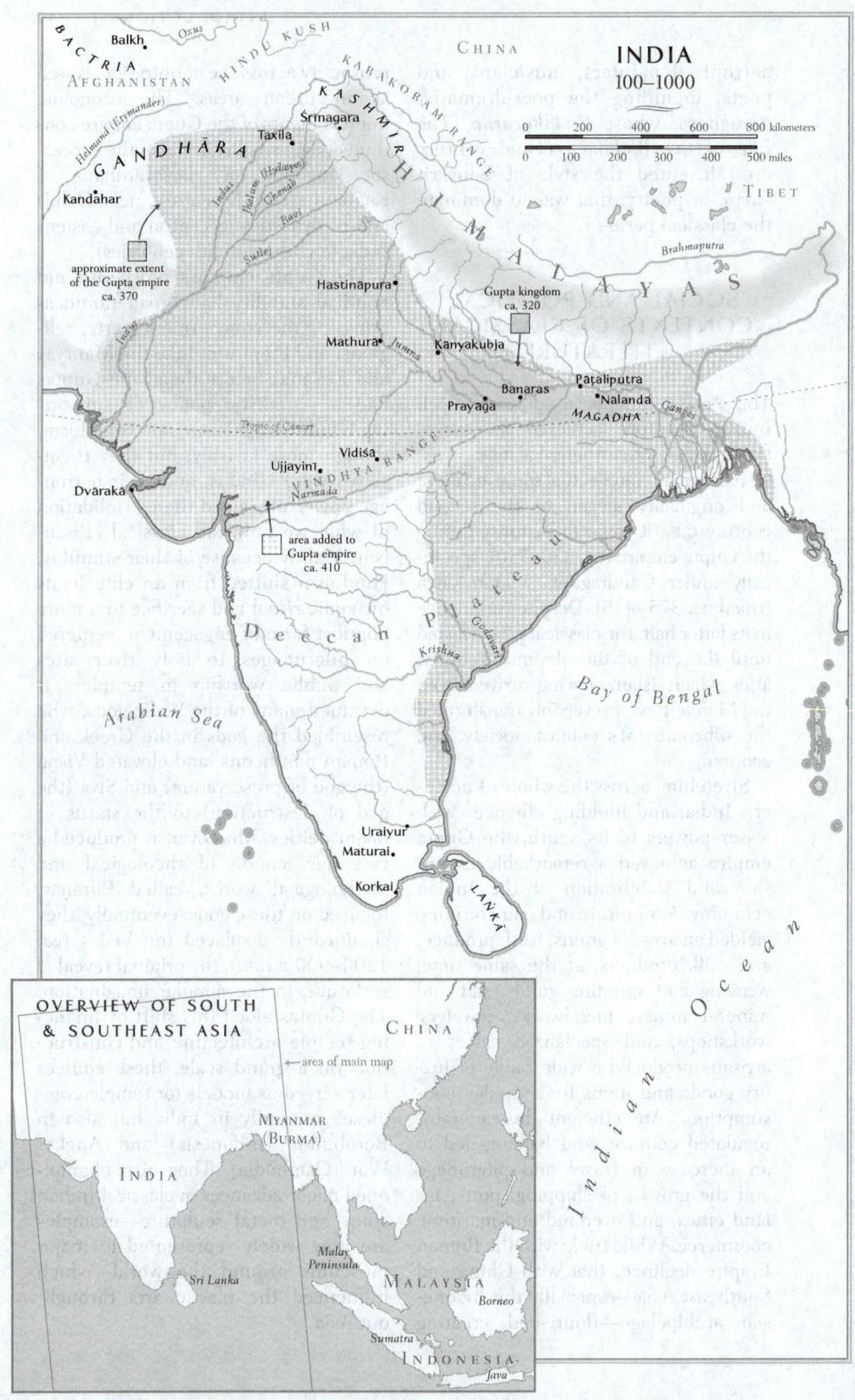

INDIA
100–1000

0   200   400   600   800 kilometers

0   100   200   300   400   500 miles

CHINA

BACTRIA

Balkh

Oxus

HINDU KUSH

AFGHANISTAN

KARAKORAM RANGE

TIBET

KASHMIR

Śrīnagara

HIMALAYAS

GANDHĀRA

Taxila

Helmand (Etymander)

Indus

Jhelum (Hydaspes)

Chenab

Ravi

Sutlej

Brahmaputra

Kandahar

approximate extent
of the Gupta empire
ca. 370

Hastinapura

Gupta kingdom
ca. 320

Mathurā

Jumna

Kanyakubja

Banaras

Prayāga

Pāṭaliputra

Nalanda

MAGADHA

Ganges

Tropic of Cancer

Indus

Vidiśā

Ujjayinī

VINDHYA RANGE

Narmadā

Dvāraka

area added to
Gupta empire
ca. 410

Deccan Plateau

Krishna

Godavari

Arabian Sea

Bay of Bengal

Uraiyur

Maturai

Korkai

LANKA

Indian Ocean

OVERVIEW OF SOUTH
& SOUTHEAST ASIA

CHINA

area of main map

INDIA

MYANMAR
(BURMA)

Sri Lanka

Malay
Peninsula

MALAYSIA

Borneo

Sumatra

INDONESIA

Java

The Dashavatar temple, dedicated to Viṣṇu, in Deogarh, India—characteristic of temple architecture during the height of the Gupta dynasty in the fifth century.

The Gupta dynasty extended patronage at their court to writers, scholars, and artists as well; they appointed a *rāja-kavi*, or poet laureate; and they maintained royal libraries. They initiated the tradition of underwriting the preparation and conservation of manuscripts by professional scribes, and the production of dramas and other entertainments. Kālidāsa's plays were written for and staged at the Gupta court; centuries later, the courtier-poet **Rā-jaśekhara** (one of the writers in our anthology) could draw on this tradition as he hosted play productions at his home. The Guptas also reinforced the older Mauryan and Kuṣāṇa practice of patronizing the writing and collection of manuscripts at monasteries and temples of various faiths. Among the classical authors represented here, **Kālidāsa** was probably the emperor Candragupta Vikramāditya's poet laureate, and **Bāṇa** was King Harṣa-vardhana's court poet and official biographer. **Somadeva** served the notable queen Sūryamati of Kashmir, whereas **Bhartṛhari**, **Bhavabhūtī**, and **Murāri** worked for lesser royal patrons. The poet **Dharmakīrti** and the editor Vidyākara, from whose classical anthology many of our Sanskrit lyrics are

drawn, were monks at Buddhist monasteries under Gupta-style patronage.

Most important, the Guptas' paradigm of royal patronage spread literacy and literature beyond the networks of the *brāhmaṇa* (priestly) caste, which had largely monopolized writing and scholarship in earlier Hindu society. Now, the caste groups of *kṣatriyas* (warriors) and *vaiśyas* (traders) were able to develop their own literate cultures, and the Buddhists and Jains— who had broken away around the sixth century B.C.E.—were able to extend and refine theirs. By the end of the Gupta empire, the Jains in particular had defined a cultural role for themselves that has proved central to Indian history: drawing on royal patronage from across the subcontinent, they became its informal "librarians," collecting and preserving manuscripts in virtually every language and period. Classical Tamil lyric poetry (called *caṅkam* poetry), for instance, whose canon was closed by the third century, was preserved for the next sixteen hundred years only in Jain monastic libraries. The Tamil people themselves rediscovered their classical heritage in the late nineteenth century, when, in a chance encounter, a Jain monk passed on a *caṅkam* manuscript to the leading Tamil scholar of the day.

CLASSICAL GENRES AND THE CLASSICAL POET

The classical period witnessed an expansion in how literature and the figure of the writer were understood. Sanskrit prose had appeared early in the ancient period, but during the first millennium B.C.E. its purposes were solely theological and practical. In the classical period, as prose became a medium with aesthetic qualities, it was used to compose fictional narratives in the genre of *kathā* (tale) or nonfictional narratives in the genre of *ākhyāyikā* (history, biography). Bāṇa (seventh century) is represented below by a few vignettes in verse, but his fame in Sanskrit *kāvya* is as the inventor of both *kathā* and *ākhyāyikā* in beautiful prose. His *Kādambarī* is the first novelistic fiction in Indian literature, an achievement that several modern languages of the subcontinent commemorate by using *kādambarī* as their term for "novel"; his *Harṣacarita* is the first biography, based on facts and legends about his patron, King Harṣavardhana.

In the ancient period, the *Rāmāyana* and the *Mahabharata* described themselves as *kāvyas*—that is, as epics in verse. The classical period, in both theory and practice, expanded the term's application to the full range of literary composition in verse, prose, and mixtures of verse and prose, whether oral or written. The category thus came to include drama, epics, tales, and lyrics, as well as didactic and nonfictional composition—but it contained only those works that displayed aesthetic qualities appropriate to their form and genre. Within classical *kāvya*, major forms, such as long poems in interwoven cantos, had equal footing with minor forms, such as topical satires, prayers, benedictions, and epigrams, which could be as short as a single verse. By the end of the first millennium C.E., Sanskrit literature had burgeoned, abandoning its original, narrow definition to refashion itself into a vast storehouse of texts in several dozen genres.

Whereas the *kavi* (poet) of the ancient period dealt primarily with oral transmission, the classical Indian author inhabited a more complex literary world permeated with orality, performance, and writing. His social life was also busy: as we know from the *Kāmasūtra* (fourth century) and other texts, the classical intellectual was a connoisseur of the arts and a man about town, with a taste for life's tangible pleasures. As a poet, he had to be trained in grammar, poetics, and philosophy; moreover, he had to command not just his mother tongue but also a regional lingua franca and Sanskrit. So that he could produce and interpret allusions, it was essential that *kāvya* as well as religious discourse and mythology (especially Hindu and Buddhist) be a part of his repertoire. A poet could not be original unless he knew what had been done in the past, and he could not be inventive unless he had mastered all the tools of his trade.

While classical society valued learning and versatility, these qualities were not sufficient to ensure greatness: an author had to display imagination and brilliance of conception (*pratibhā*) as well as urbane decorum (*aucitya*). And as the classical period progressed, he increasingly had to display his individuality. Among the writers we have selected, Kālidāsa and Bhartṛhari from the fifth century are shadowy figures; Murāri, Rājaśekhara, and Somadeva, several centuries later, have constructed more individuated literary personae. In the classical period, literature (*sāhitya*) by definition produced "mutual benefit" for the author and audience; a poet therefore had to employ his learning and skill to create something of moral or spiritual value for himself and for his readers and listeners. Most important, a classical *kavi* had to use all his resources to reach through and speak directly to his reader, a connoisseur who ideally was in sympathy with him—his true "companion at heart" (*sahṛdaya*). In a famous verse included in this anthology, the seventh-century poet-dramatist Bhavabhūtī memorably describes his search for the ideal reader:

The people in this world who
    scorn me
no doubt have a special wisdom,
so I don't write for them:

instead, I write with the thought
that since the world is wide and
    time is endless,
one day someone will be born

whose nature is the same as mine.

        (trans. Vinay Dharwadker)

As the classical era drew to a close, the corresponding ideal of the poet is conveyed by Kṣemendra, a minor Sanskrit writer of the twelfth century:

A poet should learn with his eyes
the forms of leaves
he should know how to make
people laugh when they are
    together
he should get to see
what they are really like
he should know about oceans
    and mountains
in themselves
and the sun and the moon and
    the stars
his mind should enter into the
    seasons
he should go
among many people
in many places
and learn their languages
        (trans. W. S. Merwin
        and J. Moussaieff Masson)

THE ROLE OF POETICS IN THE CLASSICAL PERIOD

One aspect of the new literary culture of the classical period was a fresh interest in theoretical reflection on the nature of beauty. Probably the result of imperial patronage of intellectual activity, poetics had a double relation to literature and the arts in classical India: it laid out both the ideals to which artistic practitioners should aspire, based on general considerations, and broad aesthetic rules, derived from the actual practice of past writers. Classical works of poetics and aesthetics therefore functioned simultaneously as philosophical expositions and as practical guides or manuals.

The earliest of these, and the broadest in its influence, was Bharata's *Nāṭyaśāstra* (*The Discipline of the Performing Arts*, second century B.C.E.–second century C.E.), which may have been composed during Kuṣāṇa imperial rule. A treatise on drama, stagecraft, dance, and music, it comprehensively charts their varieties, materials, techniques, and goals. It also provides guidelines for the training of performers, covering topics from acting, directing, set design, costume, and makeup to song and instrumental music. Within this framework, the *Nāṭyaśāstra* discusses ten main forms of drama, including the play in multiple acts; dramatic structure and language as well as types of character; and diction, versification, and meter.

According to Bharata, the overall goal of a literary work is to lead its audience to experience a *rasa*. *Rasa* is literally the taste, essence, or flavor of a human emotion, but it can be captured only via representation—that is, in works of art: the raw emotion of real life (called *bhāva*) is something quite different. A writer extracts the universal essence of an ordinary, specific *bhāva*; an actor or dancer on stage does the same, but instead of using words alone

This tenth-century sculpture of Śiva and his consort, Pārvatī, depicts the gods in a particular gesture and attitude that has a long history in Indian art and a specific name: "Uma Maheshvara."

he selects and combines all the elements of his craft, including song, gesture, movement, and melody. Through *rasa*, the audience experiences an emotion in its pure, sublime form, without the messiness that accompanies it in everyday life; such an experience refines the audience's aesthetic and moral sensibilities, thereby achieving the primary goal of "culture" or self-cultivation. A poet's aim therefore should be to take any one or more of the nine emotional states fundamental to human experience—love, joy, pity, anger, valor, terror, disgust, wonder, and peace—and transform them into the best words in the best order for a sublime effect on his readers or listeners. Bharata's analysis of the performing arts became the dominant poetic theory of the classical period, and its influence ultimately

spread throughout Southeast Asia, from Java and Bali to Thailand and Cambodia. Its greatest adherent in India was Kālidāsa.

The second major aesthetic theory appeared in Daṇḍin's *Kāvayādarśa* (*The Ideal of Poetry*, or *The Mirror of Literature*, sixth–seventh century), which limited itself to imaginative writing. A poet and theorist from the Tamil region in southern India, Daṇḍin asked a simple question: what makes a poem poetic? His answer, in effect, was that the poetic quality of poetry or the literariness of literature lies in a distinctive handling of language—in deviation from everyday speech and practical communication by the use of *alaṃkāra*, "embellishment." To achieve this deflection from the "normal," authors rely on a large repertoire of devices, falling broadly into the categories of figures of speech (such as alliteration, onomatopoeia, and rhyme) and figures of thought (such as metonymy, or association, and metaphor). Among the poets in our anthology, Bhavabhūtī and Murārī especially are masters of *alaṃkāra* in the Daṇḍin tradition, inventing superb metaphors with effortless skill. The first Indian work of poetics devoted exclusively to literature, Daṇḍin's exposition was widely celebrated in its time; within a few decades, it found its way to China, where, in translation, it became a theoretical template for T'ang and later Chinese poetry.

The third major aesthetic system of the classical period was articulated in Ānandavardhana's *Dhvanyāloka* (*The Radiance of Suggestion*, ninth century), a work produced in Kashmir. According to followers of this school of thought, the aesthetic effects of an artwork can largely be explained by how it conveys its meanings to an audience: they view such a conclusion as logical, since meaningless discourse (babble) fails to create beauty. In the perspective that Ānandavardhana adopts, meaning is grounded in language, and each word signifies at three levels: denotation, which supplies the word's literal or conventional meaning; connotation, which includes one or more secondary associative meanings; and suggestion, which produces a broader range of meanings evoked by the word's placement in a particular larger structure, such as a sentence, verse, or prose passage. For example, the word "village" by itself denotes "a small group of houses in a rural area"; it connotes life on a farm, a world with barnyard animals, a close-knit community, and a lack of urban amenities. In a phrase like "the village on the banks of the Ganges," however, the word suggests other, unexpected meanings: an exotic landscape, the cool-

ness and serenity of a river, timelessness and simplicity, peace and holiness. This last method of signification, called *dhvani*, is the principal device of poetry.

Persuaded by Ānandavardhana, many poets and readers of the late classical period and after came to believe that the beauty of poetry lies primarily in its power to create new meanings through the subtle use of suggestion. *Dhvanyāloka*, of course, also describes the technique of poetic suggestion as practiced by earlier writers; Bhartṛhari and Dharmakīrti are among the poets who exemplify the use of suggestion early in the classical period. But whichever theory or combination of theories they followed—*rasa, alaṃkāra*, or *dhvani*—classical authors and audiences alike found themselves engaged in unprecedented ways not only with the practice of literature but also with larger questions about its nature, function, and value.

Over a thousand years, between the transition from the ancient period and the arrival of Islam as a political power on the subcontinent, the varieties of literature in India gradually multiplied into an unprecedented diversity of texts and genres. Besides a voluminous body of *kāvya* in Sanskrit, the rich literary culture encompassed writing in regional Prakrits—languages such as Mahārāṣṭrī, Magadhī, and Śaurasenī—as well as the remarkable, completely different canon of *caṅkam* poetry in classical Tamil. A vital achievement of the period was the establishment of a reciprocal relation between literary theory and practice, which defined the materials, means, sources, and ends of poetry afresh and encouraged both authors and audiences to engage in sophisticated debates about the function and value of literature. Classical India thus radically altered the literary landscape it had inherited from the ancient period.

VIṢṆUŚARMAN

second or third century

Animal fables are among the earliest and most fundamental stories in world literature. A fable is usually a short tale with a moral, often involving supernatural events and nonhuman characters; its narrative is designed to teach a lesson, capture a general truth, or give practical advice, especially on conduct. Animal fables are particularly effective because they exploit the natural characteristics of various species to create parallels with humans, using wit and humor to make us laugh in recognition. We learn by identifying with the animals and taking pleasure in the identification.

According to its prologue, the *Pañcatantra*, the best-known ancient collection of Indian animal fables and folktales, was written with specific students in mind. Its author, a *brāhmaṇa* scholar named Viṣṇuśarman, was assigned the task of training three dull-headed and reluctant princes in the principles of statecraft. Viṣṇuśarman chose animal fables, practical in their wisdom and both entertaining and instructive, to teach the young men the arts of governance and diplomacy. The *Pañcatantra* is the collected record of this royal tutelage, and a delightful source on which storytellers throughout the world have drawn for millennia.

CONTEXT

Animal fables appeared in different parts of the ancient world between about 700 B.C.E. and 300 C.E.: among the Greeks, in **Aesop's Fables**; in India, among the Buddhists, in the **Jātaka** tales, and among the Hindus, in the *Pañcatantra* and the *Hitopdeśa*; and, among the Jews, in the Talmud.

These societies may have created such stories independently of each other; or fables invented in one or more places may have circulated widely through trade and conquest. The Indian and Arab traders who brought live peacocks to King Solomon in biblical times, or sold the subcontinent's muslin cloth to Egyptians (who used it to wrap the mummies interred in pyramids), may also have carried the Indian animal fables that are recorded in the Talmud. Likewise, the soldiers in Alexander's army who were left behind in a Greek colony in Gandhara (the Peshawar valley in modern Pakistan) around 327 B.C.E. may have retold Aesop's fables to their Indian contemporaries. In each of these places, animal fables caught the imagination of their audiences and quickly spread to other places, in oral and in written retellings.

WORK

Viṣṇuśarman probably composed his innovative work while serving a royal patron late in the transition from ancient to classical times. Its title, *Pañcatantra*, means "the five books, sciences, or rules of conduct," and it is divided into five large sections, each focusing on a single theme related to strategies for success in worldly affairs. Book 1, "The Loss of Friends," brings together tales about how two crafty jackals create conflict between a lion, the king of beasts, and a mighty bull, his competitor; book 2, "The Winning of Friends," tells stories of four animals in the forest who successfully pursue the ideals of friendship and harmony; book 3, "Crows and Owls," concentrates on tales about the perpetual war between two species of birds, sworn enemies of each other; and books 4 and 5, "Loss of Gains" and "Ill-Considered Action," contain stories warning against foolishness in financial transactions and everyday conduct.

The animal fables of the *Pañcatantra* are told in many different voices, but the stories are interlinked, one leading to another. The work as a whole is organized as a frame narrative, an older Indian invention: one story is told inside another, which in turn may be set inside another story, and so on. Each of the *Pañcatantra*'s five books has its own frame story, which concentrates on its main theme and introduces a number of characters, many of whom then in turn tell each other smaller stories, which ultimately lead back to the outer frame. Such a nesting of narratives emerged as a basic structural principle in the earlier Sanskrit epics, the *Rāmāyaṇa* and the *Mahabharata*, as well as in the Buddhist *Jātaka* tales composed in Pali.

The fables presented here are drawn from four different books of the *Pañcatantra*; the first three are from "The Loss of Friends," the fourth and fifth from "Crows and Owls," the next two from "Loss of Gains," and the last from "Ill-Considered Action." Each story has a particular animal narrator or set of narrators, and begins and ends with a short verse that summarizes the tale's lesson or moral; each animal narrator and character in the story has a name that highlights his or her moral quality or character trait. Thus, Rusty is the lion in "The Loss of Friends" who is in conflict with Lively the bull; Victor the jackal is the narrator of "Leap and Creep" and "The Blue Jackal," whereas Constance the plover is the narrator of "Forethought, Readywit, and Fatalist"; Red-Eye the owl tells "Mouse-maid Made Mouse"; and a group of judges collectively narrate "The Loyal Mungoose."

Each of the eight fables constructs an imaginative context for practical advice that is easy to grasp. In "Leap and Creep," for example, the main characters are a louse and a flea; the louse, who lives in the sheets of a king's bed, makes the mistake of accepting the flea as her guest. When he fails to heed her warning, the consequences for the louse are fatal. The moral of this tale is that one should never let a stranger share one's home. In contrast, "Mouse-maid Made Mouse" depicts a *brāhmaṇa* sage whose miraculous powers enable him to transform a mouse into a baby girl, as a gift for his childless wife. When the girl reaches puberty, the sage attempts to find her a bridegroom, but the girl finds flaws in and rejects each of the grand figures he suggests. When he presents a mouse, however, she is instinctively attracted to him, and the sage changes the mouse-maid back. The message, in this case, is that every type of creature has an inherent and unchangeable nature, which defines the creature's place in the world as well as his or her destiny. Several of these stories have direct parallels in other story collections. "The Bird with Golden Dung" is similar to the "Golden Goose" in the *Jātaka Tales* as well as to "The Man and the Golden Egg" in *Aesop's Fables*. "The Ass in the Tiger-Skin" is similar to Aseop's "The Ass in Lionskin," and "The Ass without Ears or a Heart" is reminiscent of Aesop's "The Lion, the Fox, and the Deer," among other parallels.

Over the centuries, the *Pañcatantra*'s fables have found many audiences. For all classes and ages, including children, they have offered a guide to prudent behavior in daily life; at the same time, they were used by leaders and rulers as a handbook on how to manage affairs of state. The tales were an extraordinary cultural success story in their own time and subsequently traveled far and wide: they appeared in early Persian and Syriac versions (sixth century); in a classic Arabic rendering, *Kalilah wa*

Dimnah (ca. 750); in Greek and Latin retellings; and then in early modern European versions, including the first renderings in German (1483) and English (1570), as well as the well-known fables of La Fontaine in French (late seventeenth century). By the end of the Renaissance, animal fables from ancient India, the Middle East, and Greece had become part of a transnational narrative culture that could no longer be traced back to any single point of origin, though the influence of the *Pañcatantra* remained preeminent.

FROM PAÑCATANTRA[1]

From Book I

The Loss of Friends

* * *

"With no stranger share your house;
Leap, the flea, killed Creep, the louse."

"How was that?" asked Rusty. And Victor[2] told the story of

LEAP AND CREEP

In the palace of a certain king stood an incomparable bed, blessed with every cubiculary virtue. In a corner of its coverlet lived a female louse named Creep. Surrounded by a thriving family of sons and daughters, with the sons and daughters of sons and daughters, and with more remote descendants, she drank the king's blood as he slept. On this diet she grew plump and handsome.

While she was living there in this manner, a flea named Leap drifted in on the wind and dropped on the bed. This flea felt supreme satisfaction on examining the bed—the wonderful delicacy of its coverlet, its double pillow, its exceptional softness like that of a broad, Gangetic sand-bank, its delicious perfume.[3] Charmed by the sheer delight of touching it, he hopped this way and that until—fate willed it so—he chanced to meet Creep, who said to him: "Where do *you* come from? This is a dwelling fit for a king. Begone, and lose no time about it." "Madam," said he, "you should not say such things. For

The Brahman reverences fire,[4]
Himself the lower castes' desire;
The wife reveres her husband dear;
But all the world must guests revere.

Now I am your guest. I have of late sampled the various blood of Brahmans, warriors, businessmen, and serfs, but found it acid, slimy, quite unwholesome. On the contrary, he who reposes on this bed must have a delightful vital fluid, just like nectar. It must be free from morbidity, since wind, bile, and phlegm are kept in harmony by constant and heedful use of potions prepared by physicians. It must be enriched by viands unctuous, tender, melting in the mouth; viands pre-

1. Translated by Arthur W. Ryder.
2. In the principal frame narrative of book 1, Victor the jackal tells this story to Rusty the lion.

3. This is a parody of the involved style of description found in the more ornate classical *kāvya* poems. "Gangetic": of the Ganges River.
4. A reference to the sacred fire of Hindu ritual.

pared from the flesh of the choicest creatures of land, water, and air, seasoned furthermore with sugar, pomegranate, ginger, and pepper. To me it seems an elixir of life. Therefore, with your kind permission, I plan to taste this sweet and fragrant substance, thus combining pleasure and profit."

"No," said she. "For fiery-mouthed stingers like you, it is out of the question. Leave this bed. You know the proverb:

> The fool who does not know
> His own resource, his foe,
> His duty, time, and place,
> Who sets a reckless pace,
> Will by the wayside fall,
> Will reap no fruit at all."

5

Thereupon he fell at her feet, repeating his request. And she agreed, since courtesy was her hobby, and since, when the story of that prince of sharpers, Muladeva,[5] was being repeated to the king while she lay on a corner of the coverlet, she had heard how Muladeva quoted this verse in answer to the question of a certain damsel:

> Whoever, angry though he be,
> Has spurned a suppliant enemy,
> In Shiva, Vishnu, Brahma,[6] he
> Has scorned the Holy Trinity.

Recalling this, she agreed, but added: "However, you must not come to dinner at a wrong place or time." "What is the right place and what is the right time?" he asked. "Being a newcomer, I am not *au courant*."[7] And she replied: "When the king's body is mastered by wine, fatigue, or sleep, then you may quietly bite him on the feet. This is the right place and the right time." To these conditions he gave his assent.

In spite of this arrangement, the famished bungler, when the king had just dozed off in the early evening, bit him on the back. And the poor king, as if burned by a firebrand, as if stung by a scorpion, as if touched by a torch, bounded to his feet, scratched his back, and cried to a servant: "Rascal! Somebody bit me. You must hunt through this bed until you find the insect."

Now Leap heard the king's command and in terrified haste crept into a crevice in the bed. Then the king's servants entered, and following their master's orders, brought a lamp and made a minute inspection. As fate would have it, they came upon Creep as she crouched in the nap of the fabric, and killed her with her family.

> "And that is why I say:
> With no stranger share your house, . . .

and the rest of it. And another thing. My lord and king does wrong in neglecting the servants who are his by inheritance. For

> Whoever leaves his friends,
> Strange folk to cherish,
> Like foolish Fierce-Howl, will
> Untimely perish."

"How was that?" asked Rusty. And Victor told the story of

5. A hero in the well-known Sanskrit romance *Bṛhatkathā* (*The Great Story*). See also Somadeva's *Kathāsaritsāgara* (p. 1076).
6. Gods of the Hindu triad: Śiva is the

destroyer, Viṣṇu is the preserver, and Brahmā is the creator.
7. Well informed; in the know (French).

THE BLUE JACKAL

There was once a jackal named Fierce-Howl, who lived in a cave near the suburbs of a city. One day he was hunting for food, his throat pinched with hunger, and wandered into the city after nightfall. There the city dogs snapped at his limbs with their sharp-pointed teeth, and terrified his heart with their dreadful barking, so that he stumbled this way and that in his efforts to escape and happened into the house of a dyer. There he tumbled into a tremendous indigo vat, and all the dogs went home.

Presently the jackal—further life being predestined—managed to crawl out of the indigo vat and escaped into the forest. There all the thronging animals in his vicinity caught a glimpse of his body dyed with the juice of indigo, and crying out: "What is this creature enriched with that unprecedented color?" they fled, their eyes dancing with terror, and spread the report: "Oh, oh! Here is an exotic creature that has dropped from somewhere. Nobody knows what his conduct might be, or his energy. We are going to vamoose. For the proverb says:

> Where you do not know
> Conduct, stock, and pluck,
> 'Tis not wise to trust,
> If you wish for luck."

Now Fierce-Howl perceived their dismay, and called to them: "Come, come, you wild things! Why do you flee in terror at sight of me? For Indra,[8] realizing that the forest creatures have no monarch, anointed me—my name is Fierce-Howl—as your king. Rest in safety within the cage formed by my resistless paws."

On hearing this, the lions, tigers, leopards, monkeys, rabbits, gazelles, jackals, and other species of wildlife bowed humbly, saying: "Master, prescribe to us our duties." Thereupon he appointed the lion prime minister and the tiger lord of the bedchamber, while the leopard was made custodian of the king's betel,[9] the elephant doorkeeper, and the monkey the bearer of the royal parasol. But to all the jackals, his own kindred, he administered a cuffing, and drove them away. Thus he enjoyed the kingly glory, while lions and others killed food-animals and laid them before him. These he divided and distributed to all after the manner of kings.

While time passed in this fashion, he was sitting one day in his court when he heard the sound made by a pack of jackals howling nearby. At this his body thrilled, his eyes filled with tears of joy, he leaped to his feet, and began to howl in a piercing tone. When the lions and others heard this, they perceived that he was a jackal, and stood for a moment shamefaced and downcast, then they said: "Look! We have been deceived by this jackal. Let the fellow be killed." And when he heard this, he endeavored to flee, but was torn to bits by a tiger and died.

> "And that is why I say:
> Whoever leaves his friends, ...

and the rest of it."

* * *

FORETHOUGHT, READYWIT, AND FATALIST[1]

In a great lake lived three full-grown fishes, whose names were Forethought, Readywit, and Fatalist. Now one day the fish named Forethought overheard pass-

---

8. The king of the gods.
9. A plant whose leaves are chewed as a digestive and stimulant in India.

1. In the frame story, Constance the plover tells this story to her mate, Sprawl.

ersby on the bank and fishermen saying: "There are plenty of fish in this pond. Tomorrow we go fishing."

On hearing this, Forethought reflected: "This looks bad. Tomorrow or the day after they will be sure to come here. I will take Readywit and Fatalist and move to another lake whose waters are not troubled." So he called them and put the question.

Thereupon Readywit said: "I have lived long in this lake and cannot move in such a hurry. If fishermen come here, then I will protect myself by some means devised for the occasion."

But poor, doomed Fatalist said: "There are sizable lakes elsewhere. Who knows whether they will come here or not? One should not abandon the lake of his birth merely because of such small gossip. And the proverb says:

> Since scamp and sneak and snake
> So often undertake
> A plan that does not thrive,
> The world wags on, alive.

Therefore I am determined not to go." And when Forethought realized that their minds were made up, he went to another body of water.

On the next day, when he had gone, the fishermen with their boys beset the inner pool, cast a net, and caught all the fish without exception. Under these circumstances Readywit, while still in the water, played dead. And since they thought: "This big fellow died without help," they drew him from the net and laid him on the bank, from which he wriggled back to safety in the water. But Fatalist stuck his nose into the meshes of the net, struggling until they pounded him repeatedly with clubs and so killed him.

"And that is why I say:

> Forethought and Readywit thrive;
> Fatalist can't keep alive."

* * *

From Book III

Crows and Owls

* * *

> "Though mountain, sun, and cloud, and wind
>   Were suitors at her feet.
> The mouse-maid turned a mouse again—
>   Nature is hard to beat."

"How was that?" asked Live-Strong. And Red-Eye told the story of

MOUSE-MAID MADE MOUSE[1]

The billows of the Ganges were dotted with pearly foam born of the leaping of fishes frightened at hearing the roar of the waters that broke on the rugged, rocky shore. On the bank was a hermitage crowded with holy men devoting their time to the performance of sacred rites—chanting, self-denial, self-torture, study, fasting, and sacrifice. They would take purified water only, and that in measured sips.

---

1. In the frame story of book 3, Red-Eye, the counselor of the king of the owls, tells this story to Live-Strong, the counselor of the king of the crows.

Their bodies wasted under a diet of bulbs, roots, fruits, and moss. A loin-cloth made of bark formed their scanty raiment.

The father of the hermitage was named Yajnavalkya. After he had bathed in the sacred stream and had begun to rinse his mouth, a little female mouse dropped from a hawk's beak and fell into his hand. When he saw what she was, he laid her on a banyan leaf, repeated his bath and mouth-rinsing, and performed a ceremony of purification. Then through the magic power of his holiness, he changed her into a girl, and took her with him to his hermitage.

As his wife was childless, he said to her: "Take her, my dear wife. She has come into life as your daughter, and you must rear her carefully." So the wife reared her and spoiled her with petting. As soon as the girl reached the age of twelve, the mother saw that she was ready for marriage, and said to her husband: "My dear husband, how can you fail to see that the time is passing when your daughter should marry?"

And he replied: "You are quite right, my dear. The saying goes:

> Before a man is gratified,
> These gods must treat her as a bride—
> The fire, the moon, the choir of heaven;
> In this way, no offense is given.
>
> Holiness is the gift of fire;   5
> A sweet voice, of the heavenly choir;
> The moon gives purity within:
> So is a woman free from sin.
>
> Before nubility, 'tis said
> That she is white; but after, red;   10
> Before her womanhood is plain,
> She is, though naked, free from stain.
>
> The moon, in mystic fashion, weds
> A maiden when her beauty spreads;
> The heavenly choir, when bosoms grow;   15
> The fire, upon the monthly flow.
>
> To wed a maid is therefore good
> Before developed womanhood;
> Nor need the loving parents wait
> Beyond the early age of eight.[2]   20
>
> The early signs one kinsman slay;
> The bosom takes the next away;
> Friends die for passion gratified;
> The father, if she ne'er be bride.
>
> For if she bides a maiden still,   25
> She gives herself to whom she will;
> Then marry her in tender age:
> So warns the heaven-begotten sage.
>
> If she, unwed, unpurified,
> Too long within the home abide,   30
> She may no longer married be:
> A miserable spinster, she.

2. Eight was considered a good age for marriage.

> A father then, avoiding sin,
> Weds her,[3] the appointed time within
> (Where'er a husband may be had)
> To good, indifferent, or bad.

Now I will try to give her to one of her own station. You know the saying:

> Where wealth is very much the same,
> And similar the family fame,
> Marriage (or friendship) is secure;
> But not between the rich and poor.

And finally:

> Aim at seven things in marriage;
> All the rest you may disparage;

But

> Get money, good looks,
> And knowledge of books,
> Good family, youth,
> Position, and truth.

"So, if she is willing, I will summon the blessèd sun, and give her to him." "I see no harm in that," said his wife. "Let it be done."

The holy man therefore summoned the sun, who appeared without delay, and said: "Holy sir, why am I summoned?" The father said: "Here is a daughter of mine. Be kind enough to marry her." Then, turning to his daughter, he said: "Little girl, how do you like him, this blessèd lamp of the three worlds?"[4] "No, father," said the girl. "He is too burning hot. I could not like him. Please summon another one, more excellent than he is."

Upon hearing this, the holy man said to the sun: "Blessèd one, is there any superior to you?" And the sun replied: "Yes, the cloud is superior even to me. When he covers me, I disappear."

So the holy man summoned the cloud next, and said to the maiden: "Little girl, I will give you to him." "No," said she. "This one is black and frigid. Give me to someone finer than he."

Then the holy man asked: "O cloud, is there anyone superior to you?" And the cloud replied: "The wind is superior even to me."

So he summoned the wind, and said: "Little girl, I give you to him." "Father," said she, "this one is too fidgety. Please invite somebody superior even to him." So the holy man said: "O wind, is there anyone superior to you?" "Yes," said the wind. "The mountain is superior to me."

So he summoned the mountain and said to the maiden: "Little girl, I give you to him." "Oh, father," said she. "He is rough all over, and stiff. Please give me somebody else."

So the holy man asked: "O kingly mountain, is there anyone superior even to you?" "Yes," said the mountain. "Mice are superior to me."

Then the holy man summoned a mouse, and presented him to the girl, saying: "Little girl, do you like this mouse?"

The moment she saw him, she felt: "My own kind, my own kind," and her body

---

3. Following the Indian tradition of arranged marriages, the father finds a suitable bride-groom for his daughter.
4. That is, heaven, earth, and the underworld.

thrilled and quivered, and she said: "Father dear, turn me into a mouse, and give me to him. Then I can keep house as my kind of people ought to do."

And her father, through the magic power of his holiness, turned her into a mouse, and gave her to him.

* * *

THE BIRD WITH GOLDEN DUNG

There was once a great tree on a mountain side. On it lived a bird in whose dung gold appeared.

One day a hunter came to the spot, and directly in front of him the bird dropped its dung, which at the moment of falling turned to gold. At this the hunter was amazed.

"Well, well!" said he. "For eighty years, man and boy, I have had bird-trapping on the brain, and I never once saw gold in a bird's dung." So he set a snare in the tree. And the bird, fool that he was, forgot the danger, and perched on the customary spot. Of course, he was caught immediately.

Then the hunter freed him from the snare, put him in a cage and took him home. But he reflected: "What am I to do with this bird of ill omen? If anybody should ever discover his peculiarity, it would be reported to the king. In that case my very life would be in genuine danger. I will take the bird and report to the king myself." And he did so.

Now when the king saw the bird, his lotus eyes blossomed and he felt supremely gratified. "Come now, guardsmen," said he. "Look after this bird with anxious care. Give him everything he wants to eat and drink."

Then a counselor said: "He was hatched from an egg. Why keep him? You have no evidence save the mere incredible assurance of a hunter. Is gold ever present in bird-dung? Take this bird from the cage and set him free."

So the king, taking the counselor's advice, freed the bird, who perched on the lofty arch of the doorway long enough to drop dung which was of gold. Then he recited the stanza:

> I played the fool at first; then he
> Who had me on his tether;
> And then the king and counselor—
> We all were fools together.

After which he took his carefree flight through the atmosphere.

> "And that is why I say:
> I played the fool at first, ...

and the rest of it."

* * *

From Book IV

Loss of Gains

THE ASS IN THE TIGER-SKIN

There was once a laundryman named Clean-Cloth in a certain town. He had a single donkey who had grown very feeble from lack of fodder.

As the laundryman wandered in the forest, he saw a dead tiger, and he thought: "Ah, this is lucky. I will put this tiger-skin on the donkey and let him loose in the barley fields at night. For the farmers will think him a tiger and will not drive him out."

When this was done, the donkey ate barley to his heart's content. And at dawn the laundryman took him back to the barn. So as time passed, he grew plump. He could hardly squeeze into the stall.

But one day the donkey heard the bray of a she-donkey in the distance. At the mere sound he himself began to bray. Then the farmers perceived that he was a donkey in disguise, and killed him with blows from clubs and stones and arrows.

"And that is why I say:
However skilful in disguise, ...

and the rest of it."

* * *

THE ASS WITHOUT EARS OR A HEART[5]

Once upon a time in a certain forest there lived a lion. He had one servant, a jackal. One day the lion came down with a stomach ailment and became too sick to do anything. The jackal became extremely hungry and said to the lion: 'Your Majesty, how can we sustain our lives if we wait like this doing nothing?'

The lion: 'This sickness, my friend, can only be cured with a medicine consisting of the ears and heart of an ass. It can't be cured otherwise. So, you should try your very best to get me an ass.'

'As my lord commands,' replied the jackal.

With that the jackal left, and coming near a city he saw an ass belonging to a washerman and said: 'My friend, why are you so lean?'

The ass: 'I spend every day, my friend, carrying huge loads of clothes. And this wicked man does not even give me any food.'

The jackal: 'Why undergo this torture? I will take you to a place where you will think you are in heaven.'

The ass: 'Tell me. How could that be?'

The jackal: 'That stretch of woods is watered by a river and full of emerald-green grass. In it live three lovely she-asses in the prime of their youth, the like of which you have never seen before. I think they have also run away, because they were similarly distressed. I will take you to them.'

When he heard that, the ass said, 'By all means,' and agreed to the proposal. So the jackal brought the foolish ass to the lion. Seeing the ass within striking distance, the lion sprang upon him in great delight. But he was too weak and the ass managed somehow to escape. With a terrified heart, he turned around and fled without ever looking back.

Then the jackal said to the lion: 'Come now! Is that the best blow you can deliver? You can't even kill an ass that has been brought to you! How will you be able to defeat your rival?'

The lion: 'That is undoubtedly true. But do bring him back. This time I will kill him.'

The jackal: 'Be ready for him. Even though he has seen your prowess, I will bring him back by the power of my cunning. But be sure that this time he does not run away like before.' With this he left laughing.

Then he went back to the ass and said: 'Why have you come back?'

5. Translated by Patrick Olivelle.

The ass: 'An awful thing happened to me. I don't know what it was, but a creature as large as a mountain peak jumped on top of me. It was not my time to die; that's probably why I managed to escape from him.'

The jackal: 'You misunderstood! As it is said:

> Now, usually when people in this world
> Desire to obtain the three goals of life,
> Even nonexisting impediments
> spontaneously rise up.

It was a she-ass. When she saw you, she was overcome with extraordinary lust, and she jumped at you passionately to embrace you. And you were such a coward that you ran away. But she could not bear to remain without you. So, as you were running away, she put out her arm to stop you. There is no other explanation for this. Why don't you come back?'

When he heard that, the ass said to him: 'I will go along with you.' The jackal then brought him back once again. And this time the lion caught hold of him and killed him.

After he killed the ass, the lion said to the jackal: 'This, my friend, is the way medicines should be taken. One should take them only after performing the appropriate rites, such as the worship of the gods. It is only then that medicines become effective. So, why don't you remain here out of sight and keep watch until I come back after taking my bath and performing my daily rites?' With this he left.

Once the lion was gone, the jackal became very greedy and ate the ears and the heart of the ass himself, thinking that it was a powerful medicine. After eating, he cleaned his mouth and paws well and remained there.

The lion returned after his bath, and as he was walking around the ass clockwise[6] he noticed that the ears and the heart were missing. So he asked the jackal: 'What happened here? Tell me, where are his ears and heart?'

The jackal: 'My lord, how can this fool have ears or a heart? Surely, if someone had ears and a heart, would he act like this?—

> He came and went back, he went and came back;
> .   .   .   .   '

Thereupon, the lion remained silent.

* * *

From Book V[1]

Ill-Considered Action

* * *

> Let the well-advised be done;
> Ill-advised leave unbegun;
> Else, remorse will be let loose,
> As with lady and mungoose.

---

6. It is an Indian custom to walk around a sacred object clockwise, keeping the object always to one's right, as a mark of respect. In the present case, the ass is viewed as a sacrificial victim and therefore sacred.

1. Translated by Arthur W. Ryder.

"How was that?" asked Jewel. And they told the story of

THE LOYAL MUNGOOSE[2]

There was once a Brahman named Godly in a certain town. His wife mothered a single son and a mungoose. And as she loved little ones, she cared for the mungoose also like a son, giving him milk from her breast, and salves, and baths, and so on. But she did not trust him, for she thought: "A mungoose is a nasty kind of creature. He might hurt my boy." Yes, there is sense in the proverb:

> A son will ever bring delight,
> Though bent on folly, passion, spite,
> Though shabby, naughty, and a fright.[3]

One day she tucked her son in bed, took a water-jar, and said to her husband: "Now, Professor,[4] I am going for water. You must protect the boy from the mungoose." But when she was gone, the Brahman went off somewhere himself to beg food,[5] leaving the house empty.

While he was gone, a black snake issued from his hole and, as fate would have it, crawled toward the baby's cradle. But the mungoose, feeling him to be a natural enemy, and fearing for the life of his baby brother, fell upon the vicious serpent halfway, joined battle with him, tore him to bits, and tossed the pieces far and wide. Then, delighted with his own heroism, he ran, blood trickling from his mouth, to meet the mother; for he wished to show what he had done.

But when the mother saw him coming, saw his bloody mouth and his excitement, she feared that the villain must have eaten her baby boy, and without thinking twice, she angrily dropped the water-jar upon him, which killed him the moment that it struck. There she left him without a second thought, and hurried home, where she found the baby safe and sound, and near the cradle a great black snake, torn to bits. Then, overwhelmed with sorrow because she had thoughtlessly killed her benefactor, her son, she beat her head and breast.

At this moment the Brahman came home with a dish of rice gruel which he had got from someone in his begging tour, and saw his wife bitterly lamenting her son, the mungoose. "Greedy! Greedy!" she cried. "Because you did not do as I told you, you must now taste the bitterness of a son's death, the fruit of the tree of your own wickedness. Yes, this is what happens to those blinded by greed. For the proverb says:

> Indulge in no excessive greed
> (A little helps in time of need)—
> A greedy fellow in the world
> Found on his head a wheel that whirled."[6]

---

2. A band of judges tells this story to Jewel the merchant. A mungoose (mongoose) is a small mammal and a natural enemy of snakes, which it can kill and eat.
3. A great value is placed on sons in the Indian family.

4. Priestly *brāhmaṇas* study the Vedas and other ritual texts.
5. *Brāhmaṇas* are entitled to live on alms: those priests without ritual commissions are obliged to live by begging.
6. This verse is the lead-in to the next story.

The Classical Tamil Lyric

Little-known outside India even in the early twenty-first century, the literature of the ancient Tamil people raises questions that are among some of the most intriguing for modern readers of world literature. How could a predominantly rural community, with no connection to an empire, create a body of poetry that has such range and depth in its representation of human experience? What makes it possible for classical Tamil poetry, composed by the beginning of the Common Era, to largely match in its qualities the classical poetry in imperial and urban languages such as Greek and Latin, Sanskrit and Mandarin?

CONTEXT

Ancient Tamil culture flourished in the southernmost region of the Indian peninsula, which has been the Tamil homeland ever since. Based mainly on agriculture, trade, and handicrafts, as well as hunting and fishing, its economy supported a network of small villages, market towns, and ports, governed by local chieftains in the countryside and by kings (ruling minor kingdoms) in a few larger cities. Yet the poets of this apparently unsophisticated society invented an aesthetic and a style of poetry able to richly explore the complexities of nature and culture, of human subjectivity in interaction with its environment, and of the impersonal forces at work in the cosmos. Their medium of expression was their mother tongue, Tamil, one of the twenty-three languages in the Dravidian language family; it acquired its classical form before the Common Era, and the poetry they composed in it became canonical between about 100 B.C.E. and 250 C.E. Used continuously since the ancient period, Tamil is one of India's two classical literary languages (the other is Sanskrit).

The Tamil people, most of whom still live in southern India, appear to have been visited by travelers from Rome and Greece in this early period; later they may have traveled to eastern Africa and they undoubtedly established contact with people and places across Southeast Asia, from Indonesia and Thailand to Cambodia and Vietnam. The Tamil script, derived from the Brahmi script that appeared on the subcontinent after about 500 B.C.E., influenced the development of the scripts of the Burmese, Thai, Khmer, and Lao languages, among others; and, since the early modern period, Tamil emigrants have settled in significant numbers in what are now Sri Lanka, Malaysia, Singapore, and Fiji.

WORK

Classical Tamil poetry, a body of work that was complete by the third century C.E., has been preserved and transmitted

This base relief is part of the Krishna Cave Temple, which was cut into rock at Mamallapuram, a bustling port city during the Pallavas dynasty (275 C.E.–897 C.E), in the south Indian state of Tamil Nadu. The central scene depicts a cowherd milking a cow.

in eight anthologies whose contents are mainly short and medium-length poems—most about love, war, and public and political life, but some also dealing with religion; in a set of ten long poems on love, war, cities, landscapes, and gods, some framed as guides, handbooks of advice, and vivid descriptions; and in a master work of grammar, linguistics, and rhetoric. The canon totals 2,381 poems, attributed to 473 poets known by their personal names or by poetic epithets (among them, twelve women) and to 102 poets who remain anonymous. Sixteen of the named poets are represented in the anthologies by substantial selections, others by only one poem each. The canon appears to have taken form through a centuries-long collective process of refinement rather than through the labor of any individual editor.

This entire body of poetry is known as *cankam* poetry—that is, poetry of the academy or fraternity (a community trained in grammar, rhetoric, poetics, and ethics). Its authors were called *puḷavārs*, scholars or wise men, and a seventh-century commentator claimed that they belonged to three distinct, successive *cankams*. According to the accompanying literary folklore, the works of the first have been lost; of the second, only the master work of grammar survives; and the eight anthologies and the ten long poems represent the third, most recent *cankam*. All three academies produced their work in a broadly secular framework, before the rise, spread, and consolidation of Hinduism in its classical form, and before the arrival of Buddhism and Jainism in southern India. As a result, classical Tamil poetry, as we have inherited it, differs fundamentally from classical Sanskrit poetry in its orientation. While a great deal of classical Sanskrit lyric, narrative, and dramatic poetry, from about the fourth century onward, takes Hindu, Buddhist, and even Jain ideas, beliefs, and practices for granted, clas-

sical Tamil poetry does not. The ancient Tamil scholar-poets, composing their poems before the third century, make no references to karma or *dharma*, caste or pollution, Śiva or Viṣṇu, the *Rāmāyaṇa* or the *Mahabharata*—or to *rasa* and Sanskrit poetics. *Cankam* poetry is thus "pre-Hindu" or even "pre-Sanskrit," and hence a truly alternative indigenous classical poetry of the Indian subcontinent.

The independence of *cankam* poetry is evident in its forms, genres, imagery, symbolism, figuration, and textual organization, as well as in its themes. Its canon is organized not by author but by genre: all the poems are classified and presented by theme, as either *akam* or *puṟam*. *Akam* means "interior," and this genre deals with the heart, love, self, the interiority of experience, home, family, the private and domestic spheres, and intimate emotions. In contrast, *puṟam* means "exterior," and poems within the genre convey an individual's experience of his or her public world—the shared world of war, social conflict, ethics, and community; of kings, heroes, poets, and ordinary citizens.

Within this broad distinction, the ancient Tamils conceived of an individual's inner or subjective world as consisting of five symbolic and figurative "interior landscapes," representing five principal phases of love. An individual in a specific phase of love is thought to inhabit a particular type of natural landscape, whose properties permeate all his or her experiences. The first phase is lovers' unions, which ideally take place at night on hillsides; the second phase is separation, anxious waiting, and secret meetings, which symbolically occur by the seashore at nightfall; the third phase is hardship, cast as the lovers' journey through a desert or wilderness in the heat of the sun; the fourth phase is happiness after marriage and patient waiting in domesticity, at home, on the edge of the forest in the evening; the fifth phase is unfaithfulness after marriage, imagined to occur in the agricultural lowland, where the loved one meets others working in the fields in the morning. By placing an individual as a character in the appropriate landscape, an *akam* lyric dramatizes his or her experience of, and emotions in, a particular situation. Since every character, emotion, and situation has many nuances, and the details of every interior landscape can vary, no two *akam* poems cover exactly the same terrain; and only when all the poems in the genre are taken together do they map out the full complexity of love and of human inner experience.

Having set up the facets and phases of love as a series of interior landscapes, the classical Tamil poets then turn to *puṟam* poetry as the "public" opposite of personal experience. These poems are often set in a town or city; they are about real people and real places, public issues and public events, common problems and common tragedies. They praise and attack kings, celebrate victories and criticize policies, reflect on ethical and economic principles, mourn the death of heroes and the destruction of cities, uphold virtues and values.

The thematic and rhetorical difference between *akam* and *puṟam* poems is quite sharp and deliberate. The love poems usually depict a young man, a young woman, and the young woman's girlfriend (who serves as a confidante and a go-between), often in the voice of one of the female characters (though the great majority of poets are male); that all are nameless enhances both the privacy and the universality of the inner world. In contrast, the public poems offer a wider range of social types and are articulated in a wider range of voices; those of supplicating poets, concerned citizens, grieving daughters, and bereaved mothers are especially common. At the same time, the two genres

complement each other by bringing love and war, as well as nature and culture, within the ambit of the ancient Tamils' agricultural way of life centered on small villages, with bustling market towns, port cities, and political capitals in the distance, on the horizon.

The poems we have selected, taken from only the shorter lyric poems in the classical Tamil anthologies, fall into two main parts, representing the *akam* and the *puṟam* genre, respectively. The *akam* poems are further subdivided into the five interior landscapes. Thus, the poems grouped under "The Hills" are all about lovers' unions; they consistently use images, symbols, and associations drawn from that landscape to evoke or dramatize various aspects of the first phase of love. Kapilar's "In His Country," for instance, depicts a young girl's longing for a dashing hunter who is still out of her reach; the same poet's "Forest Animals Walk There," in contrast, represents a young woman in a much later stage, as she grants her beloved permission to marry her. Kapilar's third poem in the section, "He Is from Those Mountains," portrays yet another type: the young woman whose joy is mixed with a great deal of anguish, because her lover is careless, insensitive, and lackadaisical. His fourth poem, "The Colors on the Elephant's Body," is a heady celebration, again from a woman's perspective, of a perfect match of desire and temperament.

The poems included in each of the other *akam* sections below likewise follow the conventions associated with their respective landscapes. The poems grouped under "Seashore" all deal with the phase of love that involves anxious waiting and secret meetings; this association of the seaside with love's trying circumstances is quite different from modern Euro-American conventions, which often present a seashore as an ideally "romantic" setting for lovers. The poems in the "Wasteland" section focus on the sufferings of the young lovers apart; in Auvaiyār's "The Round Blazing Sun," for example, a girl lies awake and imagines her lover crossing the wilderness alone, and she longs to bring him (and herself) the comfort of love. The selections in the "Forest" and "Lowland" sections then depict lovers' experiences of domestic happiness (as in Cīttalai Cattaṉār's "Rains in Season") and of the anguish of marital infidelity (as in the anonymous "From the Long Fronds"), respectively.

Finally, under the *puṟam* poems are lyrics that explore many different facets of public and social life in ancient Tamil society. Iḷam Peruvaḻuti's "This World Lives Because" presents an ethical ideal of conduct as a citizen, whereas Auvaiyār's "Earth's Bounty" pays homage to the land as well as its young men. In contrast, Poṉmuṭiyār's "A Young Warrior" captures the devastating tragedy of war. Complementing the preceding *akam* poems in both theme and tone, these writings on public events complete the unique imaginative accomplishment of *caṅkam* poetry: the depiction of the inner and outer worlds of the classical Tamil people.

Akam Poems[1]

Five Interior Landscapes[2]

1. The Hills: Lovers' Unions

[IN HIS COUNTRY]

What she said to her girl friend[3]

In his country,[4]

summer west wind blows
flute music
through bright beetle-holes in the waving bamboos.
The sweet sound of waterfalls is continuous,   5
dense as drums.
The urgent lowing voices of a herd of stags
are oboes,
the bees on the flowering slopes
become lutes.   10

Excited by such teeming voices,
an audience of female monkeys
watches in wonder

1. Translated by A. K. Ramanujan.
2. Imaginative landscapes that lovers supposedly inhabit, each evoking the emotions and experiences of a different phase of love. In this geography, hills are associated with lovers' unions; seashores, with anxious waiting and secret meetings; wastelands, with perilous journeys, separation, and hardship; the edge of forests, with patient waiting and happiness in marriage; and lowlands, with unfaithfulness after marriage.
3. An *akam* poem usually carries an initial statement, such as this, which identifies its speaker and characters and helps explain their feelings and actions.
4. Here, hill country; all the flora and fauna mentioned in this poem are characteristic of the uplands in the Tamil country.

the peacock in the bamboo hill
sway and strut
like a dancer
making an entrance
on a festival stage.

He had a garland on his chest,[5]
a strong bow in his grip,
arrow already chosen,
and he asked which way
the elephant went
with an arrow buried in its side.

He stood at the edge
of a ripe-eared millet field.

But, among all the people
who saw him standing there,
why is it
that I alone
lie in bed
in this harsh night,
eyes streaming,
arms growing lean?

Kapilar

[FOREST ANIMALS WALK THERE]

What she said

Forest animals walk there[6]
and elephants roam.
In the sky's high places
thunder rumbles.
But you come alone
in the night
along the narrow paths
of snakes and tigers,

O man of the mountain country,

that country of fruitful hills,
ancient conquests,
and wide spaces,
where the music of waterfalls

---

5. This young man not only belongs to the hill country but is also a local hero, which is why the young woman who is the speaker of the poem finds him irresistible.
6. The lower slopes of the hills, which often are forested.

mingles with bee sounds
as drums with lute-strings.[7]   15

If you wish to marry me, you can.[8]
But one thing: do not come
along those narrow paths;

though, if you must, please,
when you leave here   20
and reach your village in the hills,
think of us
living in anxiety here,
and get that long horn you use
to signal your hounds   25
and hunters
straying in the bamboo jungle,

and blow on it
a little.

                         Kapilar

                   [HE IS FROM THOSE MOUNTAINS]

                          What she said

He is from those mountains

        where the little black-faced monkey,
        playing in the sun,
        rolls the wild peacock's eggs
        on the rocks.   5

Yes, his love is always good
as you say, my friend,

but only for those strong enough
to bear it,

who will not cry their eyes out   10
or think anything of it

when he leaves.

                         Kapilar

7. Drums are associated with war and hunting;
lute strings, with music, emotion, and love.
8. In giving him permission to marry her, the
speaker is also proposing to the young man.

(Note the contrast with social conventions in
northern India, where marriages arranged by
couples' families became the norm in this
period.)

[THE COLORS ON THE ELEPHANT'S BODY]

What she said to her friend

The colors on the elephant's body
shine, as he grazes
with his herd
on bamboo shoots,
breaking down branches;   5
then, in thirst,
he goes to a watering place,
kills a crouching tiger
poised for attack.
Pouring rains   10
clean the tusks, wash down the blood on their tips,
as he walks slowly along slopes
of jagged rock.
He's arrogant
after finishing off a vicious enemy,   15
and with six-legged bees making lute-music
over the juices of his lust
he mounts his female,
then goes to sleep
in our man's banana groves.   20

    Friend,
    comforting me once, you said lovingly,
    "The man is just right
    for your rank and nature."
    Sweet words those, bless you,   25
    they've come true:
    garlands smell on him
    like nectar to people who crave it,
    his chest's embrace so tight
    there's no place   30
    even for the waist of a bee,
    and love
    is tireless still
    as on the very first day.

Kapilar

2. The Seashore: Anxious Waiting

[NEAR THE SALT PANS]

What her girl friend said to him

Near the salt pans
the clusters of neytal and blue lily[9]

9. Flowers of the Tamil coast. "*Neytal*": dark lily.

are closing for the day.
The sea restlessly
brings in the lapping tide,   5
the side-pincered crab
surfaces from its wet nest
of black clay,
and the seaside falls silent
in the absence of users.   10

Don't ask the charioteer
to yoke the thick-legged donkey,
          used to the crooked plow,
to your chariot strung with bells.

And for our lovely girl's sake,   15
her eyes cool as rain,
stay tonight
and go on tomorrow,
          man from the great waters.

In that shining big sea,   20
fishermen with big boats
          careless of the killer shark
dive for the right-spiralled oyster,

sound loud
the conch shells   25
that contain voices,

are met and welcomed
by bustling Koṟkai city[1]
as they disembark on the long sandy coasts.
There,   30
you'll see
our good little town.[2]

Centaṉ Kaṇṇaṉār

[ON THE NEW SAND]

What her girl friend said, the lover within earshot, behind a fence[3]

On the new sand
where fishermen,
          their big nets
          ripped apart by an angry sea,
dry their great hauls of fish   5

---

1. On the southeast tip of India.
2. By emphasizing her hometown's prosperity, the speaker seeks to impress the well-to-do young man, a visitor from a distant place.

3. This scenario—speech directed at one character but primarily meant to be overheard by another—is common in *akam* poems.

in a humming neighborhood
of meat smells,

a laurel tree blossoms
all at once in bright clusters
fragrant as a festival,   10

but this unfair town
is noisy with gossip.

And what with an unfair Mother too
keeping strict watch over us,

will our love just perish here   15
in sallow patches,

    this love for our man
    of the seashore

    where petals
    loosened by the traffic of birds   20
    mix with the mud of the backwaters,

    where the big-maned chariot horses galloping there
    are washed clean
    by the waves of the sea?

Ulōccaṇār

3. The Wasteland: Lovers' Hardships

[THE ROUND BLAZING SUN]

What she said, thinking of him crossing the wilderness alone

The round blazing sun
creeps in the sky,
raging as a fire
in the forest,

and the silk-cotton tree[4]   5
is leafless
yet in flower
without a bud,

    like a long array
    of red lamps   10
    in the month of Kārttikai[5]
    lit happily
    by bustling women,

4. A tree that tolerates a desert environment.　　5. Overlapping with November and December.

in the fruitless forest
where the pools are dry, dusty.   15

If only
he'd spend the time with me,
it would go fast,

if only he'd walk swiftly with me
on the dunes   20
overhung with flowering boughs,
all fragrant,
where the forest stream flows now
and the sand
is laid out like a woman's bodice,   25

       he could have what arms desire,
       loving embraces,
       body entering body,

and then my guiltless eyes
that now fill   30
ceaselessly like barren pools
fed by secret springs

could put aside
their daily sorrow
and find some sleep.   35

Auvaiyār

[A HEN-EAGLE BROODS, SICK]

What he said to his heart, arguing against further ambition and travel

A hen-eagle broods, sick
in the great branches
lifted to the sky,

in a neem tree[6]
with cracked trunk and dotted shade   5

       where unschooled children
       scratch their squares
       on a rock
       flat as a touchstone
       and play marbles with gooseberries   10

       in that wilderness
       with fierce little settlements

6. The margosa tree, common in India and Africa; because it thrives in arid environments, it is associated here with the wilderness or wasteland.

of marauders,
        the bow their only plow,

and as evening comes creeping in,   15
sapping my strength, what can I do
but think of her,

who is sweet as a deed
long wished for and done,

standing there   20
in this hour of memories
in front of a house lamp

blazing?

Iḷaṅkīraṉār

4. The Forest: Happiness after Marriage

[HER ARMS HAVE THE BEAUTY]

What he said

Her arms have the beauty
of a gently moving bamboo.
Her large eyes are full of peace.
She is faraway,
her place not easy to reach.   5

My heart is frantic
with haste,

        a plowman with a single plow
        on land all wet
        and ready for seed.   10

Ōrērulavaṉār
("The Poet of the Plowman with the Single Plow")[7]

[RAINS IN SEASON]

What he said to his charioteer, on his way back

Rains in season,
forests grow beautiful.
Black pregnant clouds
bring the monsoons, and stay.
Between flower and blue-gem   5
flower on the bilberry tree

7. The literal meaning of the poet's name (probably a literary pseudonym).

the red-backed moths multiply,
and fallen jasmines
cover the ground.[8]
   It looks like
a skilled man's work of art,   10
this jasmine country.

Friend, drive softly here.
Put aside the whip for now.
Slow down   15
these leaping pairs of legs,
these majestic horses
galloping in style
as if to music.

Think of the stag, his twisted antlers   20

     like banana stems
     after the clustering bud
     and the one big blossom
     have dropped,

think of the lovely bamboo-legged doe   25
ready in desire:

if they hear the clatter
of horse and chariot.
how can they mate
at their usual dead of night?   30

Cīttalai Cattaṉār

FROM SEVEN SAID BY THE FOSTER-MOTHER[9]

The way
they lay together

    like deer, mother-doe,
    and fawn.

with their boy   5
between them, was very sweet:

neither in this world
hugged by the wide blue sea
nor in the one above

is such a thing easy to get.   10

8. In *akam* poetry, fecundity is strongly associated with marriage and the interior landscape of the forest.

9. The young couple probably lives with the
husband's adoptive parents.

5. *The Lowland: Unfaithfulness*

[IN HIS COUNTRY]

What she said

In his country,

spotted crabs
born in their mother's death
grow up with crocodiles
that devour their young.[1]   5

Why is he here now?

And why does he
take those women,

     a jangle of gold bangles
     as they make love,   10

only to leave them?

Ōrampōkiyār

[FROM THE LONG FRONDS]

What her girl friend asked and what she replied regarding his return

"From the long fronds
of a deserted talipot tree
with clusters thick and hard
like an old date-palm's,

a male bird calls to its mate,   5
and the listening tiger
roars in echo

on those difficult roads
where hot winds blow—

     but then your lover who went there[2]   10
     has returned,
     has hugged you sweetly ever since
     and you've lain together
     inseparably
     in one place,   15

1. Predatory creatures of the lowland land-scape, underscoring its association with sexual predators and infidelity.

2. The wasteland or wilderness, associated with absence (perhaps the husband is a trader).

and yet
why do you look like a ruin,
why do you grieve, my girl?"

So you ask, friend.
It could look like that to someone
who doesn't know.   20
                What's the use
of longing faithfully
for his strong chest

        that's now like the cold beaches   25
        of Tonti city[3]
        famous in the mouths of many?

When love is gone,
what's copulation worth?

                        Anonymous

Puṟam Poems[1]

The Exterior Landscape[2]

[THIS WORLD LIVES BECAUSE]

This world lives
because

        some men
        do not eat alone,
        not even when they get
        the sweet ambrosia of the gods;   5

        they've no anger in them,
        they fear evils other men fear
        but never sleep over them;

        give their lives for honor,   10
        will not touch a gift of whole worlds

3. A port on the eastern coast, linked by the young woman with scandal and gossip. While imaginatively inhabiting the lowland, she invokes the seashore because her husband's unfaithfulness has given her cause for anxious waiting, typically associated in *akam* poetry with "cold beaches."
1. Translated by A. K. Ramanujan.
2. *Puṟam* poems are set in a single, shared "exterior landscape"; this public space contrasts with the five interior landscapes of *akam* poetry.

if tainted;

there's no faintness in their hearts
and they do not strive
for themselves.   15

Because such men are,
this world is.

Iḷam Peruvaḷuti

EARTH'S BOUNTY

Bless you, earth:

    field,
    forest,
    valley,
    or hill,   5

    you are only
    as good
    as the good young men
    in each place.

Auvaiyār

CHILDREN

Even when a man has earned much
of whatever can be earned,
shared it with many,
even when he is master of great estates,

if he does not have   5
children

    who patter on their little feet,
    stretch tiny hands,
    scatter, touch,
    grub with mouths   10
    and grab with fingers,
    smear rice and ghee
    all over their bodies,
    and overcome reason with love,

all his days   15
have come to nothing.

Pāṇṭiyaṉ Aṟivuṭai Nampi

A YOUNG WARRIOR

O heart
sorrowing
for this lad

once scared of a stick
lifted in mock anger   5
when he refused
a drink of milk,
            now
not content with killing
war elephants   10
with spotted trunks,

this son
of the strong man who fell yesterday

seems unaware of the arrow
in his wound.   15

his head of hair is plumed
like a horse's,

he has fallen
on his shield,

his beard still soft.[3]   20

                    Poṉmuṭiyār

A MOTHER'S LIST OF DUTIES

To bring forth and rear a son is my duty.
To make him noble is the father's.
To make spears for him is the blacksmith's.
To show him good ways is the king's.

And to bear   5
a bright sword and do battle,
to butcher enemy elephants,
and come back:

        that is the young man's duty.

                    Poṉmuṭiyār

---

3. I.e., still a teenager.

KĀLIDĀSA

fifth century

Kālidāsa's classical Sanskrit play *Śakuntalā and the Ring of Recollection*, composed around the fifth century, is the first romantic comedy in world drama. It gives us a fine-tuned account of the process of falling in love, from the first encounter to an impromptu wedding, with only the gods as the passionate couple's witnesses; and it shows us how the lovers reunite, after a terrible breakup and after overcoming impossible obstacles, to live happily ever after. When Goethe read the play in its first English translation by Sir William Jones, he fell in love with it; indeed, he adapted some of Kālidāsa's stage conventions for the prologue of his own *Faust*, Part I, a very different kind of play. The dramatic structure created for *Śakuntalā*, with some of its surprisingly modern themes, remains the stock formula for romantic comedy. Since the classical period, the play has also been considered the most perfect expression of the theory of *rasa*, a centerpiece of India's classical aesthetics.

LIFE

Kālidāsa probably lived in north-central India sometime between 390 and 470, early in the classical period. Legend suggests that he was born and raised in the countryside (possibly near the modern city of Ujjain), with few resources or opportunities and little education to nurture his imagination and talent for words. Nevertheless, he turned to poetry in his youth, and some believe that he gained a regional reputation as a nature poet in Sanskrit. He may then have found a royal patron in Candragupta Vikramāditya, the most famous ruler of the Gupta dynasty, which established ancient India's largest and most prosperous empire (320–550). According to one popular literary account, Kālidāsa moved to the imperial capital of Pataliputra (now Patna, in the modern Indian state of Bihar) as the court poet, married a Gupta princess, and perhaps even had a political career as governor of the province of Kashmir. Seven works are attributed to him: four long poems in different genres and three full-length plays, including *Śakuntalā*.

CONTEXT

The classical period of Sanskrit literature stretched from about the fourth to the twelfth century; during this time, the language itself achieved its classical form, when it was at its most "refined" (the literal meaning of *saṃskṛta*). The Sanskrit term for its classical (and epic) poetry is *kāvya*, and *kavi* is its related word for poet. *Kāvya* designates both "poetry to be heard" (in oral recitation) and "poetry to be seen" (in performance on stage); it encompasses prose and verse, narrative and lyric, epic and drama; and it can be composed in major and minor as well as continuous and discontinuous forms. Whatever shape it takes, *kāvya* by definition must be well-crafted: it uses language that is embellished with figures of speech and thought, such as metaphors, and its goal is to induce in its audience a heightened state or an experience of the sublime. Besides *alaṃkāra* (verbal ornamentation), *kāvya* also uses the power of *dhvani* (suggestion in language) to create imaginative effects beyond the levels of denotation (literal meanings) and connotation (secondary meanings). Even a simple phrase like "the village on the Ganges" works by suggestion: the phrase as a whole, understood in context, evokes an image of serenity, rustic beauty, holiness, and harmony with nature that far exceeds the denotations and connotations of its individual words.

Verse and prose (and mixtures of the two), drama and narrative, and epic and lyric are all equally capable of producing a sublime experience in a listener, viewer, or reader. According to the theory of *rasa* in classical Sanskrit poetics, the heightened experience conveyed by genuine poetry is based on the nine fundamental emotional states (called *bhāva*) that we experience in the course of our lives: love, joy, pity, anger, valor, terror, disgust, wonder, and peace. They are accompanied by more transitory, secondary feelings, such as dejection, jealousy, anxiety, excitement, pride, sorrow, and impatience (Sanskrit theorists usually list thirty-three of these), in different combinations. Each *bhāva* also has a characteristic physical manifestation in the person who experiences it.

The goal of a poem is to create a beautiful representation of one or more of the fundamental emotional states, so that its audience can experience each in its pure "essence," or *rasa* (which literally means juice, extract, essence, or flavor). Only works of art can create and communicate such an essence: they extract the full flavor of a *bhāva* by blending its characteristics with various subsidiary states and the physical signs associated with it. Thus, a love poem can give us the *rasa* of love by combining longing or desire with lovesickness ("I can't eat or sleep if I'm not with her"), anxiety ("Why hasn't he called me today?"), jealousy ("Is she

seeing someone else?"), or dejection ("He doesn't even notice me"), employing images such as a pallid face, sunken eyes, tears, a stunned look, and so on. The nine *rasas* created in art correspond exactly to the nine states found in real life. But for connoisseurs, the sublime experience of a *rasa* is superior to anything felt in the corresponding raw emotion and is essential to a refined sensibility. A high proportion of classical Sanskrit drama, poetry, and narrative (whether long or short, in prose or verse) was composed and understood in accordance with this aesthetic. Since his own times, Kālidāsa has been judged to be the best practitioner of the poetics of *rasa*, both in his long poems and in his plays, and the theory of *rasa* is thus closely linked with his work. *Śakuntalā* is universally viewed as his highest achievement in drama.

WORK

Abhijñānaśākuntalam, translated here as *Śakuntalā and the Ring of Recollection*, is classified in Indian poetics as a *nāṭaka*, the most important dramatic genre. A *nāṭaka* is a play in five to ten acts, with a prologue and interludes; its main characters are elevated figures, drawn from mythology or history— usually, a noble hero and a beautiful, extraordinary woman. Its secondary characters may come from different castes, social classes, and geographical regions. As a consequence, this type of play uses several regional languages while relying mainly on Sanskrit. It may employ verse as well as prose in its dialogue, and it contains music, song, and dance, which may be integral parts of the action or may provide entertainment in the prologue or interludes.

Śakuntalā follows this generic pattern quite closely. It is a multilingual play: the royal hero and his courtiers speak in Sanskrit, whereas women and lower-caste characters speak in various Prakrits (non-Sanskrit mother tongues, such as Magadhī and Śaurasenī, which were often regional and were considered relatively "unrefined"). It is divided into a prologue, interludes, and seven acts, which are arranged symmetrically around the fourth act, the longest and dramatically the most important. Its chief characters are a king and a woman of semidivine origin; they and their well-known story come from the *Mahabharata*, the Sanskrit epic that defines itself as a "poetic history of mankind" (though begun much earlier, it was probably taking its final shape around Kālidāsa's time). Besides a large number of named secondary characters from various social backgrounds, the play also features brief appearances by "celestial" characters who mediate between the human world and the gods.

Kālidāsa takes the basic story of Śakuntalā from *The Book of the Beginning*, the first major book of the *Mahabharata*, but adapts it substantially for his play; he reworks his epic material much as ancient Greek dramatists, such as **Aeschylus** and **Sophocles**, reshaped stories about Troy in plotting their tragedies. In the *Mahabharata*, the story of Duṣyanta and Śakuntalā is important because the son born of their liaison is Bharata, the prince who goes on to establish the great empire ruled by his dynasty. Indeed, the *Mahabharata* itself is literally "the great poem about the descendents of Bharata"; and today's Republic of India is officially called *Bhārata-varṣa*, "the land of Bharata's descendents." In the epic's Śakuntalā episode, Duṣyanta, a powerful king on a hunting expedition, encounters Śakuntalā in the ashram (hermitage) of her foster father, Kaṇva. Intensely attracted to Śakuntalā and taking advantage of Kaṇva's brief absence, Duṣyanta frankly propositions her. Somewhat surpris-

ingly, given her sheltered upbringing, Śakuntalā responds like a woman familiar with sexual negotiations: she agrees to "marry" Duṣyanta, but only if he promises to make any son born of their union the heir to his throne. The king eagerly agrees, they make love, and he leaves for his capital, promising to send for her soon. Kaṇva returns, already aware of what has transpired while he was gathering food, and gives Śakuntalā his blessing.

But Duṣyanta does not keep his word. Left in the ashram, Śakuntalā raises a handsome son; when the boy is six years old, she goes to the king's palace where, in the presence of courtiers, she reminds Duṣyanta of his promise. The king, fearing that this relationship may discredit him, refuses to recognize her or their son. Śakuntalā is enraged and confronts him, and he slanders her and casts doubt on his son's paternity. Śakuntalā leaves, humiliated and furious; but a "celestial voice" declares to the king and his courtiers that she has been faithful and that he is the father of her son. Following this divine intervention, Duṣyanta sends for Śakuntalā and explains his actions and makes amends, installing her as his lawful queen and anointing the boy as his heir.

In drawing on the *Mahabharata*, Kālidāsa views the story of Śakuntalā through the double lens of verisimilitude and of *aucitya*, (propriety, fitness, or decorum) a key concept in classical Indian morality and aesthetics. From his critical perspective, the epic offers a narrative unbecoming a great king: Duṣyanta's proposition to Śakuntalā is merely sexual, her response is much too calculated for an innocent country girl, and the swiftness of their "marriage" and Duṣyanta's departure is improbable. Moreover, the quarrel between Śakuntalā and the king at court is undignified and downright ugly, and Duṣyanta's subsequent reversal and explanation lack credibility.

So Kālidāsa imaginatively recasts most of the story in a new vein, in which Bharata must be conceived and born out of true love—rather than just a sexual transaction—between his parents, and the fundamental sequence of union–separation–reunion that binds them together must be tied to an emotional pattern that is true to human experience. Kālidāsa therefore invents much of his plot so that the audience could find Śakuntalā's story emotionally deeper, psychologically more plausible, and morally and aesthetically more appropriate in its outcome. At a pragmatic level, then, Kaṇva's absence from the ashram and his adoptive daughter must last for several days. Śakuntalā's entire character has to be reconceived in keeping with her upbringing apart from normal society: Kālidāsa presents her as an innocent teenager, untutored in the ways of men and seducers. Her encounter with the handsome king is a genuinely overwhelming experience of love at first sight (Act I), and she sees the impetuous "secret marriage" as a union of soul mates (Act III). Duṣyanta himself cannot be less than noble in his thoughts, intentions, and actions; hence, unlike the *Mahabharata*, which gives him no psychological depth, the play details his emotional entanglement with Śakuntalā (Acts II–III). Kālidāsa also eliminates the callousness, self-regard, and cynical manipulation that he displays in the original narrative by introducing the famous devices of the royal ring and the curse: when Duṣyanta and Śakuntalā part (Act III), he gives her a ring as a token of their bond; when she arrives, pregnant, at his court (Act V), a curse placed on her makes him forget their relationship; and because she has lost the ring, she cannot prove who she is.

The first half of the play thus sets up what has become a universal framework for romantic comedy ever since: after a brief initial union, the lovers are forced apart by their circumstances, and have to overcome seemingly insurmountable obstacles (imposed by their families, by society at large, or even by the gods) before they can happily come together once again. How Duṣyanta can remember and recognize Śakuntalā after the loss of the ring, whether he suffers any remorse for his cruelty when she presents herself at his palace, how—and whether—she survives when her companions at the ashram also turn her away after the king's rejection, and where and how the two can be plausibly reunited become the dramatic problems that Kālidāsa has to solve in the play's second half (Acts V–VII).

But while plot and characterization function superbly in Western poetic terms to drive the play forward—initial situation, complications, crisis, discovery, and reversal—Kālidāsa's handling of *rasa* is what affects the audience at every turn. Each act emphasizes one fundamental emotional state and combination of subsidiary emotions, or moves sequentially from one state to another. Act I, which depicts Duṣyanta and Śakuntalā's first meeting, foregrounds love, colored by excitement and infatuation; Act II, about Duṣyanta's feelings, combines love with joy and laughter, building up anticipation; Act III, which focuses on the lovers' intimacy, heightens the desire that leads to union. Act IV then portrays love under conditions of separation, associating it with distraction, impatience, and anxiety, while Act V evokes pity, fear, and anger in succession. In the final movement, Act VI combines pity with love, linking those emotions to dejection and tears, whereas Act VII moves from valor and wonder back to love, but now with sorrow as well as joy and peace. Kālidāsa thus takes us aesthetically through the entire range of our most basic emotions—from love and joy to pity, anger, terror, valor, and wonder, and then back to joy and on to peace—leaving out only the negative *rasa* of disgust. In the process, he also touches on all our important subsidiary or transitory emotions and their accompanying physical signs, from excitement and laughter to sorrow and tears, until we reach the powerful catharsis of the scene of reunion. *Śakuntalā* thus offers us a full experience of the drama of love with a happy ending—a romantic comedy, as generally understood.

Since about the sixth century, Kālidāsa and his plays and poems, especially *Śakuntalā*, have been constant points of reference in Indian literature: he is mentioned, quoted, or discussed by poets and dramatists as well as scholars and theorists across the subcontinent, in all its languages. Europeans discovered Kālidāsa and *Śakuntalā* in the late eighteenth century; since then,

the play has been translated into many of the world's languages, with new renderings appearing in English regularly since the nineteenth century. We know that it was produced in the classical period in India using the theatrical conventions and techniques of Sanskrit-based performance arts; but as courtly and public theater sharply declined in India under Muslim rule between the twelfth and eighteenth centuries, *Śakuntalā*, like other Sanskrit plays, disappeared from the stage. Even with the emergence of modern theater in India and with its dissemination abroad in translation, *Śakuntalā* is now rarely performed. Despite its remarkable survival and continuous influence over some 1,500 years, and its wide appeal to readers around the world, Kālidāsa's play seems better equipped to reveal its beauty and complexity as "drama" than as "theater."

Śakuntalā and the Ring of Recollection[1]

CHARACTERS

Players in the prologue:
DIRECTOR: *Director of the players and manager of the theater.*
ACTRESS: *The lead actress.*

Principal roles:
KING: *Duṣyanta, the hero; ruler of Hastināpura; a royal sage of the lunar dynasty of Puru.*
ŚAKUNTALĀ: *The heroine; daughter of the royal sage Viśvāmitra and the celestial nymph Menakā; adoptive daughter of the ascetic Kaṇva.*
BUFFOON: *Māḍhavya, the king's comical brahman companion.*

Members of Kaṇva's hermitage:
ANASŪYĀ and PRIYAṂVADĀ: *Two young female ascetics; friends of Śakuntalā.*
KAṆVA: *Foster father of Śakuntalā and master of the hermitage; a sage belonging to the lineage of the divine creator Marīci, and thus related to Mārīca.*
GAUTAMĪ: *The senior female ascetic.*
ŚĀRṄGARAVA and ŚĀRADVATA: *Kaṇva's disciples.*
Various inhabitants of the hermitage: a monk with his two pupils, two boy ascetics (named Gautama and Nārada), a young disciple of Kaṇva, a trio of female ascetics.

1. Translated by Barbara Stoler Miller.

Members of the king's forest retinue:
CHARIOTEER: *Driver of the king's chariot.*
GUARD: *Raivataka, guardian of the entrance to the king's quarters.*
GENERAL: *Commander of the king's army.*
KARABHAKA: *Royal messenger.*
Various attendants, including Greco-Bactrian bow-bearers.

Members of the king's palace retinue:
CHAMBERLAIN: *Vātāyana, chief officer of the king's household.*
PRIEST: *Somarāta, the king's religious preceptor and household priest.*
DOORKEEPER: *Vetravatī, the female attendant who ushers in visitors and presents messages.*
PARABHṚTIKĀ and MADHUKARIKĀ: *Two maids assigned to the king's garden.*
CATURIKĀ: *A maidservant.*

City dwellers:
MAGISTRATE: *The king's low-caste brother-in-law; chief of the city's policemen.*
POLICEMEN: *Sūcaka and Jānuka.*
FISHERMAN: *An outcaste.*

Celestials:
MĀRĪCA: *A divine sage; master of the celestial hermitage in which Śakuntalā gives birth to her son; father of Indra, king of the gods,*

whose armies Duṣyanta leads.
ADITI: *Wife of Mārīca.*
MĀTALI: *Indra's charioteer.*
SĀNUMATĪ: *A nymph; friend of Śakuntalā's mother Menakā.*

Various members of Mārīca's hermitage: two female ascetics, Mārīca's disciple Gālava.
BOY: *Sarvadamana, son of Śakuntalā and Duṣyanta; later known as Bharata.*

Offstage voices:
VOICES OFFSTAGE: *From the backstage area or dressing room; behind the curtain, out of view of the audience. The voice belongs to various players before they enter the stage, such as the monk, Śakuntalā's friends, the buffoon, Mātali; also to figures who never enter the stage, such as the angry sage Durvāsas, the two bards who chant royal panegyrics (vaitālikau).*
VOICE IN THE AIR: *A voice chanting in the air from somewhere offstage: the bodiless voice of Speech quoted in Sanskrit by Priyaṁvadā; the voice of a cuckoo who represents the trees of the forest blessing Śakuntalā in Sanskrit: the voice of Haṁsapadikā singing a Prakrit love song.*

The setting of the play shifts from the forest hermitage (Acts I–IV) to the palace (Acts V–VI) to the celestial hermitage (Act VII). The season is early summer when the play begins and spring during the sixth act; the passage of time is otherwise indicated by the birth and boyhood of Śakuntalā's son.

Act I

The water that was first created,
the sacrifice-bearing fire, the priest,
the time-setting sun and moon,
audible space that fills the universe,

what men call nature,[2] the source of all seeds,
the air that living creatures breathe—
through his eight embodied forms,
may Lord Śiva come to bless you![3]

Prologue

DIRECTOR: [*Looking backstage.*] If you are in costume now, madam,
please come on stage!

ACTRESS: I'm here, sir.[4]

DIRECTOR: Our audience is learned. We shall play Kālidāsa's new
drama called *Śakuntalā and the Ring of Recollection.* Let the players
take their parts to heart!

ACTRESS: With you directing, sir, nothing will be lost.

DIRECTOR: Madam, the truth is:

> I find no performance perfect
> until the critics are pleased;
> the better trained we are
> the more we doubt ourselves.

ACTRESS: So true . . . now tell me what to do first!

DIRECTOR: What captures an audience better than a song?
Sing about the new summer season and its pleasures:

> To plunge in fresh waters
> swept by scented forest winds
> and dream in soft shadows
> of the day's ripened charms.

ACTRESS: [*Singing.*]

> Sensuous women
> in summer love
> weave
> flower earrings
> from fragile petals
> of mimosa
> while wild bees
> kiss them gently.[5]

2. Here, earth.
3. This verse is a *nāndī* (benedictory verse)
recited at the beginning of a Sanskrit play,
immediately after the preparatory rituals performed before a dramatic performance in
ancient India. The benedictory verses of Sanskrit plays usually invoke the blessings of Śiva,
dancer of the cosmic dance of creation and
destruction as well as patron god of the drama.
In this verse, Kālidāsa praises Śiva as the cosmic divinity pervading the universe in his eight
manifest forms—the five elements (ether, air,

fire, water, and earth), the sun and moon, and
the sacrificing priest.
4. The prologues to many plays present the
actress as the director's wife.
5. Such verses are sung by women in Prakrit
and set to a melody, whereas the Sanskrit
kāvya verses of the play are recited or sung to a
simple tune that follows the rhythmic pattern
of the verse quarter. The women's songs
generally feature nature descriptions or the
nuances of love in natural settings.

DIRECTOR: Well sung, madam! Your melody enchants the audience. The silent theater is like a painting. What drama should we play to please it?

ACTRESS: But didn't you just direct us to perform a new play called *Śakuntalā and the Ring of Recollection*?   40

DIRECTOR: Madam, I'm conscious again! For a moment I forgot.

> The mood of your song's melody
> carried me off by force,
> just as the swift dark antelope
> enchanted King Duṣyanta.   45

[*They both exit; the prologue ends. Then the* KING *enters with his* CHARIOTEER, *in a chariot, a bow and arrow in his hand, hunting an antelope.*]

CHARIOTEER: [*Watching the* KING *and the antelope.*]

> I see this black buck move
> as you draw your bow
> and I see the wild bowman Śiva,
> hunting the dark antelope.[6]

KING: Driver, this antelope has drawn us far into the forest. There he   50
is again:

> The graceful turn of his neck
> as he glances back at our speeding car,
> the haunches folded into his chest
> in fear of my speeding arrow,   55
> the open mouth dropping
> half-chewed grass on our path—
> watch how he leaps, bounding on air,
> barely touching the earth.

[*He shows surprise.*]

Why is it so hard to keep him in sight?   60

CHARIOTEER: Sir, the ground was rough. I tightened the reins to slow
the chariot and the buck raced ahead. Now that the path is smooth,
he won't be hard to catch.

KING: Slacken the reins!

CHARIOTEER: As you command, sir. [*He mimes the speeding chariot.*]   65
Look!

> Their legs extend as I slacken the reins,
> plumes and manes set in the wind, ears angle back;
> our horses outrun their own clouds of dust,
> straining to match the antelope's speed.   70

---

6. The comparison is based on an ancient myth of Śiva's pursuit of the creator god Prajāpati,
who had taken the form of an antelope. The verse flatters the king.

KING: These horses would outrace the steeds of the sun.[7]

> What is small suddenly looms large,
> split forms seem to reunite,
> bent shapes straighten before my eyes—
> from the chariot's speed
> nothing ever stays distant or near.   75

CHARIOTEER: The antelope is an easy target now. [*He mimes the fixing of an arrow.*]

VOICE OFFSTAGE: Stop! Stop, king! This antelope belongs to our hermitage! Don't kill him!

CHARIOTEER: [*Listening and watching.*] Sir, two ascetics are protecting   80
the black buck from your arrow's deadly aim.

KING: [*Showing confusion.*] Rein in the horses!

CHARIOTEER: It is done!

> [*He mimes the chariot's halt. Then a* MONK *enters with* TWO PUPILS, *his hand raised.*]

MONK: King, this antelope belongs to our hermitage.

> Withdraw your well-aimed arrow! Your weapon should rescue victims,   85
> not destroy the innocent!

KING: I withdraw it. [*He does as he says.*]

MONK: An act worthy of the Puru dynasty's shining light!

> Your birth honors
> the dynasty of the moon![8]   90
> May you beget a son
> to turn the wheel of your empire![9]

THE TWO PUPILS: [*Raising their arms.*] May you beget a son to turn the wheel of your empire!

KING: [*Bowing.*] I welcome your blessing.   95

MONK: King, we were going to gather firewood.[1] From here you can see the hermitage[2] of our master Kaṇva on the bank of the Mālinī river. If your work permits, enter and accept our hospitality.

> When you see the peaceful rites of devoted ascetics,
> you will know how well your scarred arm protects us.[3]   100

KING: Is the master of the community there now?

MONK: He went to Somatīrtha,[4] the holy shrine of the moon, and put his daughter Śakuntalā in charge of receiving guests. Some evil threatens her, it seems.

---

7. The seven horses that draw the sun god's chariot.
8. Known as the "lunar dynasty," because it traces its descent to the moon god.
9. Any ancient Indian emperor is a *cakravartin*, a turner of the wheel of empire.
1. For the fire rituals and Vedic sacrifices per

formed at the hermitage.
2. It includes men and women and is organized like an extended family.
3. One of a king's chief duties is to protect hermits and ascetics.
4. A place of pilgrimage in western India.

KING: Then I shall see her. She will know my devotion and commend   105
me to the great sage.

MONK: We shall leave you now. [*He exits with his pupils.*]

KING: Driver, urge the horses on! The sight of this holy hermitage will
purify us.

CHARIOTEER: As you command, sir. [*He mimes the chariot's speed.*]   110

KING: [*Looking around.*] Without being told one can see that this is a
grove where ascetics live.

CHARIOTEER: How?

KING: Don't you see—

> Wild rice grains under trees   115
> where parrots nest in hollow trunks,
> stones stained by the dark oil
> of crushed iṅgudī nuts,[5]
> trusting deer who hear human voices
> yet don't break their gait,   120
> and paths from ponds streaked
> by water from wet bark cloth.[6]

CHARIOTEER: It is perfect.

KING: [*Having gone a little inside.*] We should not disturb the grove!
Stop the chariot and let me get down!   125

CHARIOTEER: I'm holding the reins. You can dismount now, sir.

KING: [*Dismounting.*] One should not enter an ascetics' grove in
hunting gear. Take these! [*He gives up his ornaments and his
bow.*] Driver, rub down the horses while I pay my respects to
the residents of the hermitage!   130

CHARIOTEER: Yes, sir! [*He exits.*]

KING: This gateway marks the sacred ground. I will enter.
[*He enters, indicating he feels an omen.*]

> The hermitage is a tranquil place,
> yet my arm is quivering . . .
> do I feel a false omen of love   135
> or does fate have doors everywhere?

VOICE OFFSTAGE: This way, friends!

KING: [*Straining to listen.*] I think I hear voices to the right of the grove.
I'll find out.
[*Walking around and looking.*]
Young female ascetics with watering pots cradled on their hips are   140
coming to water the saplings. [*He mimes it in precise detail.*] This
view of them is sweet.

---

5. These nuts are pressed by forest dwellers for oil.

6. Forest dwellers wear a cloth made of tree bark.

> These forest women have beauty
> rarely seen inside royal palaces—
> the wild forest vines far surpass
> creepers in my pleasure garden.

145

I'll hide in the shadows and wait.

[ŚAKUNTALĀ *and her two friends enter, acting as described.*]

ŚAKUNTALĀ: This way, friends!

ANASŪYĀ: I think Father Kaṇva cares more about the trees in the hermitage than he cares about you. You're as delicate as a jasmine, yet he orders you to water the trees.

150

ŚAKUNTALĀ: Anasūyā, it's more than Father Kaṇva's order. I feel a sister's love for them. [*She mimes the watering of trees.*]

KING: [*To himself.*] Is this Kaṇva's daughter? The sage does show poor judgment in imposing the rules of the hermitage on her.

155

> The sage who hopes to subdue
> her sensuous body by penances
> is trying to cut firewood
> with a blade of blue-lotus leaf.

Let it be! I can watch her closely from here in the trees.
[*He does so.*]

160

ŚAKUNTALĀ: Anasūyā, I can't breathe! Our friend Priyaṃvadā tied my bark dress too tightly! Loosen it a bit!

ANASŪYĀ: As you say. [*She loosens it.*]

PRIYAṂVADĀ: [*Laughing.*] Blame your youth for swelling your breasts. Why blame me?

165

KING: This bark dress fits her body badly, but it ornaments her beauty . . .

> A tangle of duckweed adorns a lotus,
> a dark spot heightens the moon's glow,
> the bark dress increases her charm—
> beauty finds its ornaments anywhere.

170

ŚAKUNTALĀ: [*Looking in front of her.*] The new branches on this mimosa tree are like fingers moving in the wind, calling to me. I must go to it! [*Saying this, she walks around.*]

PRIYAṂVADĀ: Wait, Śakuntalā! Stay there a minute! When you stand by this mimosa tree, it seems to be guarding a creeper.

175

ŚAKUNTALĀ: That's why your name means "Sweet-talk."[7]

KING: "Sweet-talk" yes, but Priyaṃvadā speaks the truth about Śakuntalā:

---

7. The characters of the two friends correspond to their names: Anasūyā (Without Envy) is a serious, straightforward, decisive young woman, while Priyaṃvadā (Sweet Talker) loves to tease and laugh and has a way with words. As noted above, the women speak Prakrit, whereas the king and other upper-class male characters speak Sanskrit.

Her lips are fresh red buds,
her arms are tendrils,
impatient youth is poised   180
to blossom in her limbs.

ANASŪYĀ: Śakuntalā, this is the jasmine creeper who chose the mango
tree in marriage,[8] the one you named "Forestlight." Have you forgotten
her?
ŚAKUNTALĀ: I would be forgetting myself! [*She approaches the creeper*   185
and examines it.] The creeper and the tree are twined together in
perfect harmony. Forestlight has just flowered and the new mango
shoots are made for her pleasure.
PRIYAṀVADĀ: [*Smiling.*] Anasūyā, don't you know why Śakuntalā looks
so lovingly at Forestlight?   190
ANASŪYĀ: I can't guess.
PRIYAṀVADĀ: The marriage of Forestlight to her tree makes her long to
have a husband too.
ŚAKUNTALĀ: You're just speaking your own secret wish. [*Saying this, she*
pours water from the jar.]
KING: Could her social class be different from her father's?[9] There's no   195
doubt!

She was born to be a warrior's bride,
for my noble heart desires her—
when good men face doubt,
inner feelings are truth's only measure.   200

Still, I must learn everything about her.
ŚAKUNTALĀ: [*Flustered.*] The splashing water has alarmed a bee. He is
flying from the jasmine to my face. [*She dances to show the bee's*
attack.]
KING: [*Looking longingly.*]

Bee, you touch the quivering
corners of her frightened eyes,   205
you hover softly near
to whisper secrets in her ear;
a hand brushes you away,
but you drink her lips' treasure—
while the truth we seek defeats us,   210
you are truly blessed.

---

8. In calling the jasmine creeper *svayaṁvara-*
vadhū (bride by her own choice), Anasūyā
refers to the public ceremony called *svayaṁvara*
(choosing one's own bridegroom) in which
women of the warrior class chose their own
husbands, thus foreshadowing Śakuntalā's
action later in the play.

9. Marrying outside one's class in the fourfold
Hindu scheme of classes (*varṇa*) is forbidden.
As the sage Kaṇva's daughter, Śakuntalā would
be a *brāhmaṇa*, and the king, being of the
kṣatriya (warrior) class, would not be allowed
to marry her.

ŚAKUNTALĀ: This dreadful bee won't stop. I must escape. [*She steps to one side, glancing about.*] Oh! He's pursuing me. . . . Save me! Please save me! This mad bee is chasing me!

BOTH FRIENDS: [*Laughing.*] How can we save you? Call King Duṣyanta.   215
The grove is under his protection.

KING: Here's my chance. Have no fear . . . [*With this half-spoken, he stops and speaks to himself.*] Then she will know that I am the king . . . . Still, I shall speak.

ŚAKUNTALĀ: [*Stopping after a few steps.*] Why is he still following me?   220

KING: [*Approaching quickly.*]

> While a Puru king rules the earth
> to punish evildoers,
> who dares to molest
> these innocent young ascetics?

[*Seeing the* KING, *all act flustered.*]

ANASŪYĀ: Sir, there's no real danger. Our friend was frightened when   225
a bee attacked her. [*She points to* ŚAKUNTALĀ.]

KING: [*Approaching* ŚAKUNTALĀ.] Does your ascetic practice go well?
[ŚAKUNTALĀ *stands speechless.*]

ANASŪYĀ: It does now that we have a special guest. Śakuntalā, go to our hut and bring the ripe fruits. We'll use this water to bathe his feet.[1]   230

KING: Your kind speech is hospitality enough.

PRIYAṀVADĀ: Please sit in the cool shadows of this shade tree and rest, sir.

KING: You must also be tired from your work.

ANASŪYĀ: Śakuntalā, we should respect our guest. Let's sit down. [*All*   235
sit.]

ŚAKUNTALĀ: [*To herself.*] When I see him, why do I feel an emotion that the forest seems to forbid?

KING: [*Looking at each of the girls.*] Youth and beauty complement your friendship.

PRIYAṀVADĀ: [*In a stage whisper.*] Anasūyā, who is he? He's so polite,   240
fine looking, and pleasing to hear. He has the marks of royalty.

ANASŪYĀ: I'm curious too, friend. I'll just ask him. [*Aloud.*] Sir, your kind speech inspires trust. What family of royal sages do you adorn? What country mourns your absence? Why does a man of refinement subject himself to the discomfort of visiting an ascetics' grove?[2]   245

ŚAKUNTALĀ: [*To herself.*] Heart, don't faint! Anasūyā speaks your thoughts.

KING: [*To himself.*] Should I reveal myself now or conceal who I am? I'll say it this way: [*Aloud.*] Lady, I have been appointed by the Puru king as the officer in charge of religious matters. I have come to this   250
sacred forest to assure that your holy rites proceed unhindered.

---

1. A traditionally mandated rite of hospitality.
2. Anasūyā uses the formal, florid style of courtly conversation.

ANASŪYĀ: Our religious life has a guardian now.

[ŚAKUNTALĀ *mimes the embarrassment of erotic emotion.*]

BOTH FRIENDS: [*Observing the behavior of* ŚAKUNTALĀ *and the* KING; *in a stage whisper.*] Śakuntalā, if only your father were here now!

ŚAKUNTALĀ: [*Angrily.*] What if he were?

BOTH FRIENDS: He would honor this distinguished guest with what he   255
values most in life.

ŚAKUNTALĀ: Quiet! Such words hint at your hearts' conspiracy. I won't
listen.

KING: Ladies, I want to ask about your friend.

BOTH FRIENDS: Your request honors us, sir.   260

KING: Sage Kaṇva has always been celibate, but you call your friend
his daughter. How can this be?

ANASŪYĀ: Please listen, sir. There was a powerful royal sage[3] of the
Kauśika clan . . .

KING: I am listening.   265

ANASŪYĀ: He begot our friend, but Kaṇva is her father because he
cared for her when she was abandoned.

KING: "Abandoned"? The word makes me curious. I want to hear her
story from the beginning.

ANASŪYĀ: Please listen, sir. Once when this great sage was practicing   270
terrible austerities on the bank of the Gautamī river, he became so
powerful that the jealous gods sent a nymph named Menakā to
break his self-control.[4]

KING: The gods dread men who meditate.

ANASŪYĀ: When springtime came to the forest with all its charm, the   275
sage saw her intoxicating beauty . . .

KING: I understand what happened then. She is the nymph's daughter.

ANASŪYĀ: Yes.

KING: It had to be!

No mortal woman could give birth to such beauty—   280
lightning does not flash out of the earth.

[ŚAKUNTALĀ *stands with her face bowed. The* KING *continues speaking to himself.*]
My desire is not hopeless. Yet, when I hear her friends teasing her
about a bridegroom, a new fear divides my heart.

PRIYAMVADĀ: [*Smiling, looking at* ŚAKUNTALĀ, *then turning to the* KING.]
Sir, you seem to want to say more.

[ŚAKUNTALĀ *makes a threatening gesture with her finger.*]

KING: You judge correctly. In my eagerness to learn more about your   285
pious lives, I have another question.

3. Viśvāmitra, who was born in the warrior class but acquired the spiritual powers of a *brāhmaṇa* sage.
4. A standard theme in classical Indian mythology, appearing in the narratives of the life of the Buddha as well. The gods feel threatened by the supernatural powers that ascetics amass through self-denial.

PRIYAṀVADĀ: Don't hesitate! Ascetics can be questioned frankly.
KING: I want to know this about your friend:

> Will she keep the vow of hermit life
> only until she marries . . .
> or will she always exchange
> loving looks with deer in the forest?   290

PRIYAṀVADĀ: Sir, even in her religious life, she is subject to her father,
but he does intend to give her to a suitable husband.
KING: [To himself.] His wish is not hard to fulfill.   295

> Heart, indulge your desire—
> now that doubt is dispelled,
> the fire you feared to touch
> is a jewel in your hands.

ŚAKUNTALĀ: [Showing anger.] Anasūyā, I'm leaving!   300
ANASŪYĀ: Why?
ŚAKUNTALĀ: I'm going to tell Mother Gautamī that Priyaṁvadā is talking nonsense.
ANASŪYĀ: Friend, it's wrong to neglect a distinguished guest and leave
as you like.[5]   305
[ŚAKUNTALĀ starts to go without answering.]
KING: [Wanting to seize her, but holding back, he speaks to himself.] A
lover dare not act on his impulsive thoughts!

> I wanted to follow the sage's daughter,
> but decorum abruptly pulled me back;
> I set out and returned again   310
> without moving my feet from this spot.

PRIYAṀVADĀ: [Stopping ŚAKUNTALĀ.] It's wrong of you to go!
ŚAKUNTALĀ: [Bending her brow into a frown.] Give me a reason why!
PRIYAṀVADĀ: You promised to water two trees for me. Come here and
pay your debt before you go! [She stops her by force.]   315
KING: But she seems exhausted from watering the trees:

> Her shoulders droop, her palms
> are red from the watering pot—
> even now, breathless sighs
> make her breasts shake;   320
> beads of sweat on her face
> wilt the flower at her ear;
> her hand holds back
> disheveled locks of hair.

5. Śakuntalā's failure here foreshadows her neglect of this duty and its consequences later in the play.

Here, I'll pay her debt!   325

[*He offers his ring. Both friends recite the syllables of the name on the seal and stare at each other.*][6]

Don't mistake me for what I am not! This is a gift from the king to identify me as his royal official.

PRIYAṀVADĀ: Then the ring should never leave your finger. Your word has already paid her debt. [*She laughs a little.*] Śakuntalā, you are freed by this kind man . . . or perhaps by the king. Go now!   330

ŚAKUNTALĀ: [*To herself.*] If I am able to . . . [*Aloud.*] Who are you to keep me or release me?

KING: [*Watching* ŚAKUNTALĀ.] Can she feel toward me what I feel toward her? Or is my desire fulfilled?

> She won't respond directly to my words,   335
> but she listens when I speak;
> she won't turn to look at me,
> but her eyes can't rest anywhere else.

VOICE OFFSTAGE: Ascetics, be prepared to protect the creatures of our forest grove! King Duṣyanta is hunting nearby!   340

> Dust raised by his horses' hooves
> falls like a cloud of locusts swarming
> at sunset over branches of trees
> where wet bark garments hang.
>
> In terror of the chariots, an elephant   345
> charged into the hermitage
> and scattered the herd of black antelope,
> like a demon foe of our penances—
> his tusks garlanded with branches
> from a tree crushed by his weight,   350
> his feet tangled in vines
> that tether him like chains.

[*Hearing this, all the girls are agitated.*]

KING: [*To himself.*] Oh! My palace men are searching for me and wrecking the grove. I'll have to go back.

BOTH FRIENDS: Sir, we're all upset by this news. Please let us go to our   355
hut.

KING: [*Showing confusion.*] Go, please. We will try to protect the hermitage.

[*They all stand to go.*]

BOTH FRIENDS: Sir, we're ashamed that our bad hospitality is our only excuse to invite you back.   360

KING: Not at all. I am honored to have seen you.

[ŚAKUNTALĀ *exits with her two friends, looking back at the* KING, *lingering artfully.*]

---

6. A clear indication that women were part of the literate courtly culture of classical India.

I have little desire to return to the city. I'll join my men and have
them camp near the grove. I can't control my feelings for Śakuntalā.

> My body turns to go,
> my heart pulls me back,
> like a silk banner
> buffeted by the wind.

365

[All exit.]

Act II

[The BUFFOON enters, despondent.]

BUFFOON: [Sighing.] My bad luck! I'm tired of playing sidekick to a
king who's hooked on hunting.[7] "There's a deer!" "There's a boar!"
"There's a tiger!" Even in the summer midday heat we chase from
jungle to jungle on paths where trees give barely any shade. We drink
stinking water from mountain streams foul with rusty leaves. At odd
hours we eat nasty meals of spit-roasted meat. Even at night I can't
sleep. My joints ache from galloping on that horse. Then at the
crack of dawn, I'm woken rudely by a noise piercing the forest.
Those sons of bitches hunt their birds then. The torture doesn't
end—now I have sores on top of my bruises. Yesterday, we lagged
behind. The king chased a buck into the hermitage. As luck would
have it, an ascetic's daughter called Śakuntalā caught his eye. Now
he isn't even thinking of going back to the city. This very dawn I
found him wide-eyed, mooning about her. What a fate! I must see
him after his bath. [He walks around, looking.] Here comes my
friend now, wearing garlands of wild flowers. Greek women carry his
bow in their hands.[8] Good! I'll stand here pretending my arms and
legs are broken. Maybe then I'll get some rest.

5

10

15

[He stands leaning on his staff. The KING enters with his retinue, as
described.]

KING: [To himself.]

> My beloved will not be easy to win,
> but signs of emotion revealed her heart—
> even when love seems hopeless,
> mutual longing keeps passion alive.

20

[He smiles.] A suitor who measures his beloved's state of mind by his
own desire is a fool.

7. The brāhmaṇa vidūśaka (buffoon), though
the king's constant companion, differs from him
in every respect, from his obsession with creature comforts and his cowardice to his coarse
language. A caricature of the learned brāhmaṇa
and Sanskrit scholar, the buffoon speaks only
Prakrit and is incapable of versifying.
8. In Kālidāsa's plays the king's bow bearers
are identified as yavanī (Greek women). North
Indian kings of the Gupta age and earlier
employed Bactrian Greek women as body-
guards and bow bearers.

> She threw tender glances   25
> though her eyes were cast down,
> her heavy hips swayed
> in slow seductive movements.
> she answered in anger
> when her friend said, "Don't go!"   30
> and I felt it was all for my sake . . .
> but a lover sees in his own way.

BUFFOON: [*Still in the same position.*] Dear friend, since my hands
can't move to greet you, I have to salute you with my voice.

KING: How did you cripple your limbs?   35

BUFFOON: Why do you ask why I cry after throwing dust in my eyes
yourself?

KING: I don't understand.

BUFFOON: Dear friend, when a straight reed is twisted into a crooked
reed, is it by its own power, or is it the river current?[9]   40

KING: The river current is the cause.

BUFFOON: And so it is with me.

KING: How so?

BUFFOON: You neglect the business of being a king and live like a
woodsman in this awful camp. Chasing after wild beasts every day   45
jolts my joints and muscles till I can't control my own limbs anymore.
I beg you to let me rest for just one day!

KING: [*To himself.*] He says what I also feel. When I remember Kaṇva's daughter, the thought of hunting disgusts me.

> I can't draw my bowstring   50
> to shoot arrows at deer
> who live with my love
> and teach her tender glances.[1]

BUFFOON: Sir, you have something on your mind. I'm crying in a
wilderness.[2]   55

KING: [*Smiling.*] Yes, it is wrong to ignore my friend's plea.

BUFFOON: Live long! [*He starts to go.*]

KING: Dear friend, stay! Hear what I have to say!

BUFFOON: At your command, sir!

KING: When you have rested, I need your help in some work that you 60
will enjoy.

BUFFOON: Is it eating sweets? I'm game!

KING: I shall tell you. Who stands guard?

---

9. Like Shakespeare's fools, the buffoon likes
to speak in riddles.

1. A comparison of women's eyes with the
eyes of deer, conventional in Sanskrit poetry.

2. A paraphrase of the Sanskrit proverbial
expression *aranyaruditām* (a cry in the wilderness); this is an expression of his puzzlement
at the king's behavior.

GUARD: [*Entering.*] At your command, sir!

KING: Raivataka! Summon the general!   65

[*The* GUARD *exits and reenters with the* GENERAL.]

GUARD: The king is looking this way, waiting to give you his orders. Approach him, sir!

GENERAL: [*Looking at the* KING.] Hunting is said to be a vice,[3] but our king prospers.

> Drawing the bow only hardens his chest,   70
> he suffers the sun's scorching rays unburned,
> hard muscles mask his body's lean state—
> like a wild elephant, his energy sustains him.

[*He approaches the* KING.]Victory, my lord! We've already tracked some wild beasts. Why the delay?   75

KING: Mādhavya's[4] censure of hunting has dampened my spirit.

GENERAL: [*In a stage whisper, to the* BUFFOON.] Friend, you stick to your opposition! I'll try to restore our king's good sense. [*Aloud.*] This fool is talking nonsense. Here is the king as proof:

> A hunter's belly is taut and lean,   80
> his slender body craves exertion;
> he penetrates the spirit of creatures
> overcome by fear and rage;
> his bowmanship is proved
> by arrows striking a moving target—   85
> hunting is falsely called a vice.
> What sport can rival it?

BUFFOON: [*Angrily.*] The king has come to his senses. If you keep chasing from forest to forest, you'll fall into the jaws of an old bear hungry for a human nose . . .   90

KING: My noble general, we are near a hermitage; your words cannot please me now.

> Let horned buffaloes plunge into muddy pools!
> Let herds of deer huddle in the shade to eat grass!
> Let fearless wild boars crush fragrant swamp grass!   95
> Let my bowstring lie slack and my bow at rest!

GENERAL: Whatever gives the king pleasure.

KING: Withdraw the men who are in the forest now and forbid my soldiers to disturb the grove!

---

3. The censure of hunting in Hindu law reflects the influence of the theory of karma and rebirth and the impact of nonviolent creeds. 4. The buffoon's.

Ascetics devoted to peace   100
possess a fiery hidden power,
like smooth crystal sunstones
that reflect the sun's scorching rays.

GENERAL: Whatever you command, sir!

BUFFOON: Your arguments for keeping up the hunt fall on deaf ears!   105
[*The* GENERAL *exits.*]

KING: [*Looking at his* RETINUE.] You women, take away my hunting
gear! Raivataka, don't neglect your duty!

RETINUE: As the king commands!
[*They exit.*]

BUFFOON: Sir, now that the flies are cleared out, sit on a stone bench
under this shady canopy. Then I'll find a comfortable seat too.   110

KING: Go ahead!

BUFFOON: You first, sir!
[*Both walk about, then sit down.*]

KING: Mādhavya, you haven't really used your eyes because you
haven't seen true beauty.

BUFFOON: But you're right in front of me, sir!   115

KING: Everyone is partial to what he knows well, but I'm speaking
about Śakuntalā, the jewel of the hermitage.

BUFFOON: [*To himself.*] I won't give him a chance! [*Aloud.*] Dear friend,
it seems that you're pursuing an ascetic's daughter.

KING: Friend, the heart of a Puru king wouldn't crave a forbidden   120
fruit . . .

The sage's child is a nymph's daughter,
rescued by him after she was abandoned,
like a fragile jasmine blossom
broken and caught on a sunflower pod.   125

BUFFOON: [*Laughing.*] You're like the man who loses his taste for dates
and prefers sour tamarind![5] How can you abandon the gorgeous
gems of your palace?

KING: You speak this way because you haven't seen her.

BUFFOON: She must be delectable if you're so enticed!   130

KING: Friend, what is the use of all this talk?

The divine creator imagined perfection
and shaped her ideal form in his mind—
when I recall the beauty his power wrought,
she shines like a gemstone among my jewels.   135

BUFFOON: So she's the reason you reject the other beauties!

KING: She stays in my mind:

_____

5. A fruit, the extract of which is used to flavor Indian sauces.

> A flower no one has smelled,
> a bud no fingers have plucked,
> an uncut jewel, honey untasted,   140
> unbroken fruit of holy deeds—
> I don't know who is destined
> to enjoy her flawless beauty.

BUFFOON: Then you should rescue her quickly! Don't let her fall into
the arms of some ascetic who greases his head with ingudī oil!   145
KING: She is someone else's ward and her guardian is away.
BUFFOON: What kind of passion did her eyes betray?
KING: Ascetics are timid by nature:

> Her eyes were cast down in my presence,
> but she found an excuse to smile—   150
> modesty barely contained the love
> she could neither reveal nor conceal.

BUFFOON: Did you expect her to climb into your lap when she'd barely
seen you?
KING: When we parted her feelings for me showed despite her mod-   155
esty.

> "A blade of kuśa grass[6]
> pricked my foot,"
> the girl said for no reason
> after walking a few steps away;   160
> then she pretended to free
> her bark dress from branches
> where it was not caught
> and shyly glanced at me.

BUFFOON: Stock up on food for a long trip! I can see you've turned that   165
ascetics' grove into a pleasure garden.
KING: Friend, some of the ascetics recognize me. What excuse can we
find to return to the hermitage?
BUFFOON: What excuse? Aren't you the king? Collect a sixth of their
wild rice as tax!   170
KING: Fool! These ascetics pay tribute that pleases me more than
mounds of jewels.

> Tribute that kings collect
> from members of society decays,
> but the share of austerity   175
> that ascetics give lasts forever.[7]

6. Used in Hindu sacred rites.
7. The king values the sacred power that the sages amass through self-denial.

VOICE OFFSTAGE: Good, we have succeeded!

KING: [*Listening.*] These are the steady, calm voices of ascetics.

GUARD: [*Entering.*] Victory, sir! Two boy ascetics are waiting near the gate. 180

KING: Let them enter without delay!

GUARD: I'll show them in. [*He exits; reenters with the boys.*] Here you are!

FIRST BOY: His majestic body inspires trust. It is natural when a king is virtually a sage.[8] 185

> His palace is a hermitage
> with its infinite pleasures,
> the discipline of protecting men
> imposes austerities every day—
> pairs of celestial bards praise 190
> his perfect self-control,
> adding the royal word "king"
> to "sage," his sacred title.

SECOND BOY: Gautama, is this Duṣyanta, the friend of Indra?[9]

FIRST BOY: Of course! 195

SECOND BOY:

> It is no surprise that this arm of iron
> rules the whole earth bounded by dark seas—
> when demons harass the gods, victory's hope
> rests on his bow and Indra's thunderbolt.

BOTH BOYS: [*Coming near.*] Victory to you, king! 200

KING: [*Rising from his seat.*] I salute you both!

BOTH BOYS: To your success, sir! [*They offer fruits.*]

KING: [*Accepting their offering.*] I am ready to listen.

BOTH BOYS: The ascetics know that you are camped nearby and send a petition to you. 205

KING: What do they request?

BOTH BOYS: Demons are taking advantage of Sage Kaṇva's absence to harass us.[1] You must come with your charioteer to protect the hermitage for a few days!

KING: I am honored to oblige. 210

BUFFOON: [*In a stage whisper.*] Your wish is fulfilled!

KING: [*Smiling.*] Raivataka, call my charioteer! Tell him to bring the chariot and my bow!

8. While Duṣyanta may appear worldly to a modern audience, his sacred royal office, his respect for the sages, and his disciplined adherence to the standards of *dharma* make him, in the sages' eyes, a person of tremendous self-control.

9. His friendship with Indra underscores the king's status as the earthly counterpart of the king of the gods.

1. The motif of a royal hero slaying demons who destroy the sacred rituals of forest sages is traditional.

GUARD: As the king commands! [*He exits.*]

BOTH BOYS: [*Showing delight.*]

> Following your ancestral duties   215
> suits your noble form—
> the Puru kings are ordained
> to dispel their subjects' fear.

KING: [*Bowing.*] You two return! I shall follow.

BOTH BOYS: Be victorious! [*They exit.*]   220

KING: Mādhavya, are you curious to see Śakuntalā?

BUFFOON: At first there was a flood, but now with this news of demons, not a drop is left.

KING: Don't be afraid! Won't you be with me?

BUFFOON: Then I'll be safe from any demon . . .   225

GUARD: [*Entering.*] The chariot is ready to take you to victory . . . but Karabhaka has just come from the city with a message from the queen.

KING: Did my mother send him?

GUARD: She did.   230

KING: Have him enter then.

GUARD: Yes. [*He exits; reenters with* KARABHAKA.] Here is the king. Approach!

KARABHAKA: Victory, sir! Victory! The queen has ordered a ceremony four days from now to mark the end of her fast. Your Majesty will   235 surely give us the honor of his presence.

KING: The ascetics' business keeps me here and my mother's command calls me there. I must find a way to avoid neglecting either!

BUFFOON: Hang yourself between them the way Triśaṅku[2] hung between heaven and earth.   240

KING: I'm really confused . . .

> My mind is split in two
> by these conflicting duties,
> like a river current split
> by boulders in its course.   245

[*Thinking.*] Friend, my mother has treated you like a son. You must go back and report that I've set my heart on fulfilling my duty to the ascetics. You fulfill my filial duty to the queen.

BUFFOON: You don't really think I'm afraid of demons?

KING: [*Smiling.*] My brave brahman, how could you be?   250

BUFFOON: Then I can travel like the king's younger brother.

KING: We really should not disturb the grove! Take my whole entourage with you!

BUFFOON: Now I've turned into the crown prince!

---

2. A mythic king who was left suspended between heaven and earth in a contest of power between the sage Viśvāmitra and the gods.

KING: [*To himself.*] This fellow is absent-minded. At any time he may   255
tell the palace women about my passion. I'll tell him this: [*Taking
the* BUFFOON *by the hand, he speaks aloud.*] Dear friend, I'm going
to the hermitage out of reverence for the sages. I really feel no desire
for the young ascetic Śakuntalā.

> What do I share with a rustic girl   260
> reared among fawns, unskilled in love?
> Don't mistake what I muttered
> in jest for the real truth, friend!

[*All exit.*]

Act III

[*A disciple of* KAṆVA *enters, carrying kuśa grass for a sacrificial rite.*]
DISCIPLE: King Duṣyanta is certainly powerful. Since he entered the
hermitage, our rites have not been hindered.

> Why talk of fixing arrows?
> The mere twang of his bowstring
> clears away menacing demons   5
> as if his bow roared with death.

I'll gather some more grass for the priests to spread on the sacrificial
altar. [*Walking around and looking, he calls aloud.*] Priyaṁvadā, for
whom are you bringing the ointment of fragrant lotus root fibers and
leaves? [*Listening.*] What are you saying? Śakuntalā is suffering   10
from heat exhaustion? They're for rubbing on her body? Priyaṁvadā,
take care of her! She is the breath of Father Kaṇva's life. I'll give
Gautamī this water from the sacrifice to use for soothing her.
[*He exits; the interlude ends. Then the* KING *enters, suffering from
love, deep in thought, sighing.*]
KING:

> I know the power ascetics have
> and the rules that bind her,
> but I cannot abandon my heart   15
> now that she has taken it.

[*Showing the pain of love.*] Love, why do you and the moon both
contrive to deceive lovers by first gaining our trust?

> Arrows of flowers and cool moon rays   20
> are both deadly for men like me—
> the moon shoots fire through icy rays
> and you hurl thunderbolts of flowers.

[*Walking around.*] Now that the rites are concluded and the priests
have dismissed me, where can I rest from the weariness of this   25
work? [*Sighing.*] There is no refuge but the sight of my love. I must
find her. [*Looking up at the sun.*] Śakuntalā usually spends the heat
of the day with her friends in a bower of vines on the Mālinī river-

bank. I shall go there. [*Walking around, miming the touch of breeze.*]
This place is enchanted by the wind.   30

> A breeze fragrant with lotus pollen
> and moist from the Mālinī waves
> can be held in soothing embrace
> by my love-scorched arms.

[*Walking around and looking.*]

> I see fresh footprints   35
> on white sand in the clearing,
> deeply pressed at the heel
> by the sway of full hips.

I'll just look through the branches. [*Walking around, looking, he
becomes joyous.*] My eyes have found bliss! The girl I desire is lying   40
on a stone couch strewn with flowers, attended by her two friends.
I'll eavesdrop as they confide in one another. [*He stands watching.
ŚAKUNTALĀ appears as described, with her two friends.*]

BOTH FRIENDS: [*Fanning her affectionately.*] Śakuntalā, does the breeze
from this lotus leaf please you?

ŚAKUNTALĀ: Are you fanning me?   45
[*The friends trade looks, miming dismay.*]

KING: [*Deliberating.*] Śakuntalā seems to be in great physical pain. Is
it the heat or is it what is in my own heart? [*Miming ardent desire.*]
My doubts are unfounded!

> Her breasts are smeared with lotus balm,
> her lotus-fiber bracelet hangs limp,   50
> her beautiful body glows in pain—
> love burns young women like summer heat
> but its guilt makes them more charming.

PRIYAMVADĀ: [*In a stage whisper.*] Anasūyā, Śakuntalā has been pining
since she first saw the king. Could he be the cause of her sickness?   55

ANASŪYĀ: She must be suffering from lovesickness. I'll ask her . . .
[*Aloud.*] Friend, I have something to ask you. Your pain seems so
deep . . .

ŚAKUNTALĀ: [*Raising herself halfway.*] What do you want to say?

ANASŪYĀ: Śakuntalā, though we don't know what it is to be in love,   60
your condition reminds us of lovers we have heard about in stories.
Can you tell us the cause of your pain? Unless we understand your
illness, we can't begin to find a cure.

KING: Anasūyā expresses my own thoughts.

ŚAKUNTALĀ: Even though I want to, suddenly I can't make myself tell   65
you.

PRIYAMVADĀ: Śakuntalā, my friend Anasūyā means well. Don't you see
how sick you are? Your limbs are wasting away. Only the shadow of
your beauty remains . . .

KING: What Priyamvadā says is true: 70

Her cheeks are deeply sunken,
her breasts' full shape is gone,
her waist is thin, her shoulders bent,
and the color has left her skin—
tormented by love,   75
she is sad but beautiful to see,
like a jasmine creeper
when hot wind shrivels its leaves.

ŚAKUNTALĀ: Friends, who else can I tell? May I burden you?
BOTH FRIENDS: We insist! Sharing sorrow with loving friends makes it   80
bearable.
KING:

Friends who share her joy and sorrow
discover the love concealed in her heart—
though she looked back longingly at me,
now I am afraid to hear her response.   85

ŚAKUNTALĀ: Friend, since my eyes first saw the guardian of the hermits'
retreat, I've felt such strong desire for him!
KING: I have heard what I want to hear.

My tormentor, the god of love,
has soothed my fever himself,   90
like the heat of late summer
allayed by early rain clouds.

ŚAKUNTALĀ: If you two think it's right, then help me to win the
king's pity. Otherwise, you'll soon pour sesame oil and water[3] on my
corpse . . .   95
KING: Her words destroy my doubt.
PRIYAṀVADĀ: [In a stage whisper.] She's so dangerously in love that
there's no time to lose. Since her heart is set on the ornament of the
Puru dynasty, we should rejoice that she desires him.
ANASŪYĀ: What you say is true.   100
PRIYAṀVADĀ: [Aloud.] Friend, by good fortune your desire is in harmony
with nature. A great river can only descend to the ocean. A jasmine
creeper can only twine around a mango tree.
KING: Why is this surprising when the twin stars of spring serve the
crescent moon?[4]   105
ANASŪYĀ: What means do we have to fulfill our friend's desire secretly
and quickly?

---

3. Offerings to the dead in Hindu funeral
rites. Śakuntalā and her friends have learned
of the king's real identity, because the hermits
have asked him to guard their hermitage from

demons.
4. The king refers metaphorically to the two
friends attending Śakuntalā as stars attending
a young moon that is waning.

PRIYAṀVADĀ: "Secretly" demands some effort. "Quickly" is easy.

ANASŪYĀ: How so?

PRIYAṀVADĀ: The king was charmed by her loving look; he seems thin 110
these days from sleepless nights.

KING: It's true . . .

> This golden armlet
> slips to my wrist
> without touching the scars 115
> my bowstring has made;
> its gemstones are faded
> by tears of secret pain
> that every night wets my arm
> where I bury my face. 120

PRIYAṀVADĀ: [Thinking.] Compose a love letter and I'll hide it in a
flower. I'll deliver it to his hand on the pretext of bringing an offering
to the deity.

ANASŪYĀ: This subtle plan pleases me. What does Śakuntalā say?

ŚAKUNTALĀ: I'll try my friend's plan. 125

PRIYAṀVADĀ: Then compose a poem to declare your love!

ŚAKUNTALĀ: I'm thinking, but my heart trembles with fear that he'll
reject me.

KING: [Delighted.]

> The man you fear will reject you
> waits longing to love you, timid girl— 130
> a suitor may lose or be lucky,
> but the goddess always wins.

BOTH FRIENDS: Why do you belittle your own virtues? Who would
cover his body with a piece of cloth to keep off cool autumn moonlight? 135

ŚAKUNTALĀ: [Smiling.] I'm trying to follow your advice. [She sits
thinking.]

KING: As I gaze at her, my eyes forget to blink.

> She arches an eyebrow,
> struggling to compose the verse—
> the down rises on her cheek,
> showing the passion she feels.[5] 140

ŚAKUNTALĀ: I've thought of a verse, but I have nothing to write it on.

PRIYAṀVADĀ: Engrave the letters with your nail on this lotus leaf! It's
as delicate as a parrot's breast.

---

5. Such quivering of the cheek is held to be a sign of inner emotion, which the actress is supposed to be able to represent.

ŚAKUNTALĀ: [*Miming what* PRIYAMVADĀ *described.*] Listen and tell me   145
  this makes sense!
BOTH FRIENDS: We're both paying attention.
ŚAKUNTALĀ: [*Singing.*]

> I don't know
> your heart,
> but day and night   150
> for wanting you,
> love violently
> tortures
> my limbs,
> cruel man.   155

KING: [*Suddenly revealing himself.*]

> Love torments you, slender girl,
> but he completely consumes me—
> daylight spares the lotus pond
> while it destroys the moon.

BOTH FRIENDS: [*Looking, rising with delight.*] Welcome to the swift   160
  success of love's desire!
       [ŚAKUNTALĀ *tries to rise.*]
KING: Don't exert yourself!

> Limbs lying among crushed petals
> like fragile lotus stalks
> are too weakened by pain   165
> to perform ceremonious acts.

ANASŪYĀ: Then let the king sit on this stone bench!
       [*The* KING *sits;* ŚAKUNTALĀ *rises in embarrassment.*]
PRIYAMVADĀ: The passion of two young lovers is clear. My affection for
  our friend makes me speak out again now.[6]
KING: Noble lady, don't hesitate! It is painful to keep silent when one   170
  must speak.
PRIYAMVADĀ: We're told that it is the king's duty to ease the pain of his
  suffering subjects.
KING: My duty, exactly!
PRIYAMVADĀ: Since she first saw you, our dear friend has been reduced   175
  to this sad condition. You must protect her and save her life.
KING: Noble lady, our affection is shared and I am honored by all you
  say.
ŚAKUNTALĀ: [*Looking at* PRIYAMVADĀ.] Why are you keeping the king
  here? He must be anxious to return to his palace.   180

---

6. Śakuntalā's modesty and good breeding prevent her from making her own declaration of love.

KING:

> If you think that my lost heart
> could love anyone but you,
> a fatal blow strikes a man
> already wounded by love's arrows!

ANASŪYĀ: We've heard that kings have many loves. Will our dear   185
friend become a sorrow to her family after you've spent time with
her?

KING: Noble lady, enough of this!

> Despite my many wives,
> on two the royal line rests—   190
> sea-bound earth
> and your friend.[7]

BOTH FRIENDS: You reassure us.

PRIYAMVADĀ: [Casting a glance.] Anasūyā, this fawn is looking for its
mother. Let's take it to her!   195
    [They both begin to leave.]

ŚAKUNTALĀ: Come back! Don't leave me unprotected!

BOTH FRIENDS: The protector of the earth is at your side.

ŚAKUNTALĀ: Why have they gone?

KING: Don't be alarmed! I am your servant.

> Shall I set moist winds in motion   200
> with lotus-leaf fans to cool your pain,
> or rest your soft red lotus feet[8]
> on my lap to stroke them, my love?

ŚAKUNTALĀ: I cannot sin against those I respect!
    [Standing as if she wants to leave.]

KING: Beautiful Śakuntalā, the day is still hot.   205

> Why should your frail limbs
> leave this couch of flowers
> shielded by lotus leaves
> to wander in the heat?

[Saying this, he forces her to turn around.]

ŚAKUNTALĀ: Puru king, control yourself! Though I'm burning with   210
love, how can I give myself to you?

KING: Don't fear your elders! The father of your family knows the law.
When he finds out, he will not blame you.

---

7. Royal polygamy was common in ancient
India; it served to make and cement political
alliances. Here the king speaks of the conventional ideal of a ruler's two "chief queens": the
royal consort, whose son will inherit the kingdom, and the earth, personified as the king's
spouse.
8. A common metaphor for feet in Indian
verse.

The daughters of royal sages often marry
in secret[9] and then their fathers bless them.   215

ŚAKUNTALĀ: Release me! I must ask my friends' advice!
KING: Yes, I shall release you.
ŚAKUNTALĀ: When?
KING:

Only let my thirsting mouth
gently drink from your lips,
the way a bee sips nectar   220
from a fragile virgin blossom.

[*Saying this, he tries to raise her face.* ŚAKUNTALĀ *evades him with a
dance.*]
VOICE OFFSTAGE: Red goose,[1] bid farewell to your gander! Night has
arrived!
ŚAKUNTALĀ: [*Flustered.*] Puru king, Mother Gautamī is surely coming   225
to ask about my health. Hide behind this tree!
KING: Yes.
[*He conceals himself and waits. Then* GAUTAMĪ *enters with a vessel
in her hand, accompanied by* ŚAKUNTALĀ's *two friends.*]
BOTH FRIENDS: This way, Mother Gautamī!
GAUTAMĪ: [*Approaching* ŚAKUNTALĀ.] Child, does the fever in your
limbs burn less?   230
ŚAKUNTALĀ: Madam, I do feel better.
GAUTAMĪ: Kuśa grass and water will soothe your body. [*She sprinkles*
ŚAKUNTALĀ's *head.*] Child, the day is ended. Come, let's go back to
our hut! [*She starts to go.*]
ŚAKUNTALĀ: [*To herself.*] My heart, even when your desire was within   235
reach, you were bound by fear. Now you'll suffer the torment of
separation and regret. [*Stopping after a few steps, she speaks aloud.*]
Bower of creepers, refuge from my torment, I say goodbye until our
joy can be renewed . . . [*Sorrowfully,* ŚAKUNTALĀ *exits with the other
women.*]
KING: [*Coming out of hiding.*] Fulfillment of desire is fraught with   240
obstacles.

Why didn't I kiss her face
as it bent near my shoulder,
her fingers shielding lips
that stammered lovely warning?   245

---

9. The *gāndharva* form of marriage, a secret
marriage of mutual consent, was permitted for
the warrior class. By the beginning of Act IV
this has taken place.

1. Also known as the sheldrake (*cakravāka*).
In Sanskrit poetry, separated lovers are symbolized by these birds, subject to a curse that
separates them from their mates every night.

Should I go now? Or shall I stay here in this bower of creepers that
my love enjoyed and then left?

> I see the flowers her body pressed
> on this bench of stone,
> the letter her nails inscribed   250
> on the faded lotus leaf,
> the lotus-fiber bracelet
> that slipped from her wrist—
> my eyes are prisoners
> in this empty house of reeds.   255

VOICE IN THE AIR: King!

> When the evening rituals begin,
> shadows of flesh-eating demons swarm
> like amber clouds of twilight,
> raising terror at the altar of fire.   260

KING: I am coming.
        [He exits.]

Act IV

[The two friends enter, miming the gathering of flowers.]

ANASŪYĀ: Priyaṁvadā, I'm delighted that Śakuntalā chose a suitable
husband for herself, but I still feel anxious.

PRIYAṀVADĀ: Why?

ANASŪYĀ: When the king finished the sacrifice, the sages thanked him
and he left. Now that he has returned to his palace women in the   5
city, will he remember us here?

PRIYAṀVADĀ: Have faith! He's so handsome, he can't be evil. But I
don't know what Father Kaṇva will think when he hears about what
happened.

ANASŪYĀ: I predict that he'll give his approval.   10

PRIYAṀVADĀ: Why?

ANASŪYĀ: He's always planned to give his daughter to a worthy husband. If fate accomplished it so quickly, Father Kaṇva won't object.

PRIYAṀVADĀ: [Looking at the basket of flowers.] We've gathered enough
flowers for the offering ceremony.   15

ANASŪYĀ: Shouldn't we worship the goddess who guards Śakuntalā?

PRIYAṀVADĀ: I have just begun. [She begins the rite.]

VOICE OFFSTAGE: I am here!

ANASŪYĀ: [Listening.] Friend, a guest is announcing himself.

PRIYAṀVADĀ: Śakuntalā is in her hut nearby, but her heart is far away.   20

ANASŪYĀ: You're right! Enough of these flowers!
        [They begin to leave.]

VOICE OFFSTAGE: So . . . you slight a guest . . .

> Since you blindly ignore
> a great sage like me,
> the lover you worship   25
> with mindless devotion
> will not remember you,
> even when awakened—
> like a drunkard who forgets
> a story he just composed!   30

PRIYAMVADĀ: Oh! What a terrible turn of events! Śakuntalā's distraction has offended someone she should have greeted. [*Looking
ahead.*] Not just an ordinary person, but the angry sage Durvāsas
himself cursed her and went away in a frenzy of quivering, mad
gestures. What else but fire has such power to burn?   35

ANASŪYĀ: Go! Bow at his feet and make him return while I prepare the
water for washing his feet!

PRIYAMVADĀ: As you say. [*She exits.*]

ANASŪYĀ: [*After a few steps, she mimes stumbling.*] Oh! The basket of
flowers fell from my hand when I stumbled in my haste to go. [*She*   40
mimes the gathering of flowers.]

PRIYAMVADĀ: [*Entering.*] He's so terribly cruel! No one could pacify
him! But I was able to soften him a little.

ANASŪYĀ: Even that is a great feat with him! Tell me more!

PRIYAMVADĀ: When he refused to return, I begged him to forgive a
daughter's first offense, since she didn't understand the power of   45
his austerity.

ANASŪYĀ: Then? Then?

PRIYAMVADĀ: He refused to change his word, but he promised that
when the king sees the ring of recollection, the curse will end. Then
he vanished.   50

ANASŪYĀ: Now we can breathe again. When he left, the king himself
gave her the ring engraved with his name. Śakuntalā will have her
own means of ending the curse.

PRIYAMVADĀ: Come friend! We should finish the holy rite we're performing for her.   55
  [*The two walk around, looking.*]
Anasūyā, look! With her face resting on her hand, our dear friend
looks like a picture. She is thinking about her husband's leaving,
with no thought for herself, much less for a guest.

ANASŪYĀ: Priyamvadā, we two must keep all this a secret between us.
Our friend is fragile by nature; she needs our protection.   60

PRIYAMVADĀ: Who would sprinkle a jasmine with scalding water?
  [*They both exit: the interlude ends. Then a* DISCIPLE *of* KAṆVA *enters,*
  just awakened from sleep.]

DISCIPLE: Father Kaṇva has just returned from his pilgrimage and
wants to know the exact time. I'll go into a clearing to see what
remains of the night. [*Walking around and looking.*] It is dawn.

The moon sets over the western mountain 65
as the sun rises in dawn's red trail—
rising and setting, these two bright powers
portend the rise and fall of men.

When the moon disappears, night lotuses
are but dull souvenirs of its beauty— 70
when her lover disappears, the sorrow
is too painful for a frail girl to bear.

ANASŪYĀ: [*Throwing aside the curtain and entering.*][2] Even a person
withdrawn from worldly life knows that the king has treated Śakuntalā badly. 75

DISCIPLE: I'll inform Father Kaṇva that it's time for the fire oblation.
[*He exits.*]

ANASŪYĀ: Even when I'm awake, I'm useless. My hands and feet don't
do their work. Love must be pleased to have made our innocent
friend put her trust in a liar . . . but perhaps it was the curse of
Durvāsas that changed him . . . otherwise, how could the king have 80
made such promises and not sent even a message by now? Maybe
we should send the ring to remind him. Which of these ascetics who
practice austerities can we ask? Father Kaṇva has just returned from
his pilgrimage. Since we feel that our friend was also at fault, we
haven't told him that Śakuntalā is married to Duṣyanta and is 85
pregnant. The problem is serious. What should we do?

PRIYAṂVADĀ: [*Entering, with delight.*] Friend, hurry! We're to celebrate
the festival of Śakuntalā's departure for her husband's house.

ANASŪYĀ: What's happened, friend?

PRIYAṂVADĀ: Listen! I went to ask Śakuntalā how she had slept. Father 90
Kaṇva embraced her and though her face was bowed in shame, he
blessed her: "Though his eyes were filled with smoke, the priest's
oblation luckily fell on the fire. My child, I shall not mourn for you
. . . like knowledge given to a good student I shall send you to your
husband today with an escort of sages." 95

ANASŪYĀ: Who told Father Kaṇva what happened?

PRIYAṂVADĀ: A bodiless voice was chanting when he entered the fire
sanctuary. [*Quoting in Sanskrit.*]

Priest, know that your daughter
carries Duṣyanta's potent seed 100
for the good of the earth—
like fire in mimosa[3] wood.

2. The *javanikā* (impeller), a curtain hung over two doors separating the backstage area from the stage of the ancient Indian playhouse. An agitated entrance was indicated when, as here, a character entered the stage by throwing aside the curtain.
3. Here, the *samī* tree, which Indians consider the repository of fire.

ANASŪYĀ: I'm joyful, friend. But I know that Śakuntalā must leave us today and sorrow shadows my happiness.

PRIYAMVADĀ: Friend, we must chase away sorrow and make this hermit   105
girl happy!

ANASŪYĀ: Friend, I've made a garland of mimosa flowers. It's in the coconut-shell box hanging on a branch of the mango tree. Get it for me! Meanwhile I'll prepare the special ointments of deer musk, sacred earth, and blades of dūrvā grass.[4]   110

PRIYAMVADĀ: Here it is!

[ANASŪYĀ *exits*; PRIYAMVADĀ *gracefully mimes taking down the box.*]

VOICE OFFSTAGE: Gautamī! Śārṅgarava and some others have been appointed to escort Śakuntalā.

PRIYAMVADĀ: [*Listening.*] Hurry! Hurry! The sages are being called to go to Hastināpura.   115

ANASŪYĀ: [*Reentering with pots of ointments in her hands.*] Come, friend! Let's go!

PRIYAMVADĀ: [*Looking around.*] Śakuntalā stands at sunrise with freshly washed hair while the female ascetics bless her with handfuls of wild rice and auspicious words of farewell. Let's go to her together.   120

[*The two approach as* ŚAKUNTALĀ *enters with* GAUTAMĪ *and other female ascetics, and strikes a posture as described. One after another, the female ascetics address her.*]

FIRST FEMALE ASCETIC: Child, win the title "Chief Queen" as a sign of your husband's high esteem!

SECOND FEMALE ASCETIC: Child, be a mother to heroes!

THIRD FEMALE ASCETIC: Child, be honored by your husband!

BOTH FRIENDS: This happy moment is no time for tears, friend.   125

[*Wiping away her tears, they calm her with dance gestures.*]

PRIYAMVADĀ: Your beauty deserves jewels, not these humble things we've gathered in the hermitage.

[*Two boy ascetics enter with offerings in their hands.*]

BOTH BOYS: Here is an ornament for you!

[*Everyone looks amazed.*]

GAUTAMĪ: Nārada, my child, where did this come from?

FIRST BOY: From Father Kaṇva's power.   130

GAUTAMĪ: Was it his mind's magic?

SECOND BOY: Not at all! Listen! You ordered us to bring flowers from the forest trees for Śakuntalā.

> One tree produced this white silk cloth,
> another poured resinous lac to redden her feet—   135
> the tree nymphs produced jewels in hands
> that stretched from branches like young shoots.[5]

---

4. Materials prepared by women for the ritual of farewell to a young woman moving from her father's to her husband's home.
5. The verse suggests that Śakuntalā is a kinswoman of the tree goddesses (*yakṣīs*), worshipped in popular cults. *Lac*: a substance secreted by a species of beetle, used by Indian women as a cosmetic dye for fingernails and toenails.

PRIYAṀVADĀ: [*Watching* ŚAKUNTALĀ.] This is a sign that royal fortune will come to you in your husband's house.

[ŚAKUNTALĀ *mimes modesty.*]

FIRST BOY: Gautama, come quickly! Father Kaṇva is back from bath-   140
ing. We'll tell him how the trees honor her.

SECOND BOY: As you say.

[*The two exit.*]

BOTH FRIENDS: We've never worn them ourselves, but we'll put these jewels on your limbs the way they look in pictures.

ŚAKUNTALĀ: I trust your skill.   145

[*Both friends mime ornamenting her. Then* KAṆVA *enters, fresh from his bath.*]

KAṆVA:

> My heart is touched with sadness
> since Śakuntalā must go today,
> my throat is choked with sobs,
> my eyes are dulled by worry—
> if a disciplined ascetic   150
> suffers so deeply from love,
> how do fathers bear the pain
> of each daughter's parting?[6]

[*He walks around.*]

BOTH FRIENDS: Śakuntalā, your jewels are in place; now put on the pair of silken cloths.   155

[*Standing,* ŚAKUNTALĀ *wraps them.*]

GAUTAMĪ: Child, your father has come. His eyes filled with tears of joy embrace you. Greet him reverently!

ŚAKUNTALĀ: [*Modestly.*] Father, I welcome you.

KAṆVA: Child,

> May your husband honor you   160
> the way Yayāti honored Śarmiṣṭhā.
> As she bore her son Puru,[7]
> may you bear an imperial prince.

GAUTAMĪ: Sir, this is a blessing, not just a prayer.

KAṆVA: Child, walk around the sacrificial fires![8]   165

[*All walk around:* KAṆVA *intoning a prayer in Vedic meter.*[9]]

6. A celebrated passage, prized for its convincing portrait of an Indian father's sorrow at losing his daughter to another household.
7. Yayāti and Puru are ancestors of Duṣyanta.
8. Holy objects, persons, and places are honored by ritually walking around them.
9. The version of the *triṣṭubh* meter used in the Vedic hymns, the oldest scriptures of the Hindu tradition.

Perfectly placed around the main altar,
fed with fuel, strewn with holy grass,
destroying sin by incense from oblations,
may these sacred fires purify you!

You must leave now! [*Looking around.*] Where are Śārṅgarava and   170
the others?
DISCIPLE: [*Entering.*] Here we are, sir!
KAṆVA: You show your sister the way!
ŚĀRṄGARAVA: Come this way!
        [*They walk around.*]
KAṆVA: Listen, you trees that grow in our grove!   175

Until you were well watered
she could not bear to drink;
she loved you too much
to pluck your flowers for her hair;
the first time your buds bloomed,   180
she blossomed with joy—
may you all bless Śakuntalā
as she leaves for her husband's house.

[*Miming that he hears a cuckoo's cry.*]

The trees of her forest family
have blessed Śakuntalā—   185
the cuckoo's melodious song
announces their response.

VOICE IN THE AIR:

May lakes colored by lotuses mark her path!
May trees shade her from the sun's burning rays!
May the dust be as soft as lotus pollen!   190
May fragrant breezes cool her way!

[*All listen astonished.*]
GAUTAMĪ: Child, the divinities of our grove love you like your family
and bless you. We bow to you all!
ŚAKUNTALĀ: [*Bowing and walking around; speaking in a stage whisper.*]
Priyaṁvadā, though I long to see my husband, my feet move with
sorrow as I start to leave the hermitage.   195
PRIYAṀVADĀ: You are not the only one who grieves. The whole her-
mitage feels this way as your departure from our grove draws near.

Grazing deer
drop grass,
peacocks   200

> stop dancing,
> vines loose
> pale leaves
> falling
> like tears.   205

ŚAKUNTALĀ: [*Remembering.*] Father, before I leave, I must see my sister, the vine Forestlight.

KAṆVA: I know that you feel a sister's love for her. She is right here.

ŚAKUNTALĀ: Forestlight, though you love your mango tree, turn to embrace me with your tendril arms! After today, I'll be so far away . . .   210

KAṆVA:

> Your merits won you the husband
> I always hoped you would have
> and your jasmine has her mango tree—
> my worries for you both are over.

> Start your journey here!   215

ŚAKUNTALĀ: [*Facing her two friends.*] I entrust her care to you.

BOTH FRIENDS: But who will care for us? [*They wipe away their tears.*]

KAṆVA: Anasūyā, enough crying! You should be giving Śakuntalā courage!
> [*All walk around.*]

ŚAKUNTALĀ: Father, when the pregnant doe who grazes near my hut   220
gives birth, please send someone to give me the good news.

KAṆVA: I shall not forget.

ŚAKUNTALĀ: [*Miming the interrupting of her gait.*] Who is clinging to my skirt?
[*She turns around.*]

KAṆVA: Child.   225

> The buck whose mouth you healed with oil
> when it was pierced by a blade of kuśa grass
> and whom you fed with grains of rice—
> your adopted son will not leave the path.

ŚAKUNTALĀ: Child, don't follow when I'm abandoning those I love! I   230
raised you when you were orphaned soon after your birth, but now
I'm deserting you too. Father will look after you. Go back! [*Weeping, she starts to go.*]

KAṆVA: Be strong!

> Hold back the tears that blind
> your long-lashed eyes—
> you will stumble if you cannot see   235
> the uneven ground on the path.

ŚĀRṄGARAVA: Sir, the scriptures prescribe that loved ones be escorted only to the water's edge. We are at the shore of the lake. Give us your message and return!   240

ŚAKUNTALĀ: We shall rest in the shade of this fig tree.
   [*All walk around and stop;* KAṆVA *speaks to himself.*]

KAṆVA: What would be the right message to send to King Duṣyanta?
   [*He ponders.*]

ŚAKUNTALĀ: [*In a stage whisper.*] Look! The wild goose cries in anguish when her mate is hidden by lotus leaves. What I'm suffering is much worse.   245

ANASŪYĀ: Friend, don't speak this way!

> This goose spends
> every long night
> in sorrow
> without her mate,   250
> but hope lets her
> survive
> the deep pain
> of loneliness.

KAṆVA: Śārṅgarava, speak my words to the king after you present   255
Śakuntalā!

ŚĀRṄGARAVA: As you command, sir!

KAṆVA:

> Considering our discipline,
> the nobility of your birth
> and that she fell in love with you   260
> before her kinsmen could act,
> acknowledge her with equal rank
> among your wives—
> what more is destined for her,
> the bride's family will not ask.   265

ŚĀRṄGARAVA: I grasp your message.

KAṆVA: Child, now I must instruct you. We forest hermits know something about worldly matters.

ŚĀRṄGARAVA: Nothing is beyond the scope of wise men.

KAṆVA: When you enter your husband's family: 270

> Obey your elders, be a friend to the other wives!
> If your husband seems harsh, don't be impatient!
> Be fair to your servants, humble in your happiness!
> Women who act this way become noble wives;
> sullen girls only bring their families disgrace.   275

But what does Gautamī think?

GAUTAMĪ: This is good advice for wives, child. Take it all to heart!

KAṆVA: Child, embrace me and your friends!

ŚAKUNTALĀ: Father, why must Priyaṃvadā and my other friends turn
back here?   280

KAṆVA: They will also be given in marriage. It is not proper for them
to go there now. Gautamī will go with you.

ŚAKUNTALĀ: [Embracing her father.] How can I go on living in a strange
place, torn from my father's side, like a vine torn from the side of a
sandalwood tree growing on a mountain slope?[1]   285

KAṆVA: Child, why are you so frightened?

> When you are your husband's honored wife,
> absorbed in royal duties and in your son,[2]
> born like the sun to the eastern dawn,
> the sorrow of separation will fade.   290

[ŚAKUNTALĀ falls at her father's feet.]
Let my hopes for you be fulfilled!

ŚAKUNTALĀ: [Approaching her two friends.] You two must embrace me
together!

BOTH FRIENDS: [Embracing her.] Friend, if the king seems slow to
recognize you, show him the ring engraved with his name!   295

ŚAKUNTALĀ: Your suspicions make me tremble!

BOTH FRIENDS: Don't be afraid! It's our love that fears evil.

ŚĀRṄGARAVA: The sun is high in the afternoon sky. Hurry, please!

ŚAKUNTALĀ: [Facing the sanctuary.] Father, will I ever see the grove
again?   300

KAṆVA:

> When you have lived for many years
> as a queen equal to the earth
> and raised Duṣyanta's son
> to be a matchless warrior,
> your husband will entrust him   305
> with the burdens of the kingdom
> and will return with you
> to the calm of this hermitage.[3]

GAUTAMĪ: Child, the time for our departure has passed. Let your father
turn back! It would be better, sir, if you turn back yourself. She'll   310
keep talking this way forever.

KAṆVA: Child, my ascetic practice has been interrupted.

ŚAKUNTALĀ: My father's body is already tortured by ascetic practices.
He must not grieve too much for me!

1. Śakuntalā's sorrow reflects the experience
of every Indian bride as she permanently
leaves the home of her birth to join the
extended family into which she has married.
2. The son, heir to the throne, will ensure an
honored place for Śakuntalā among the hitherto childless wives of King Duṣyanta.
3. It was a custom of Hindu kings and com-
moners of the three higher castes to retire to
the forest with their wives to concentrate on
the spiritual life.

KAṆVA: [Sighing.]

> When I see the grains of rice   315
> sprout from offerings you made
> at the door of your hut,
> how shall I calm my sorrow!

[ŚAKUNTALĀ *exits with her escort.*]

BOTH FRIENDS: [*Watching* ŚAKUNTALĀ.] Śakuntalā is hidden by forest trees now.   320

KAṆVA: Anasūyā, your companion is following her duty. Restrain yourself and return with me!

BOTH FRIENDS: Father, the ascetics' grove seems empty without Śakuntalā. How can we enter?

KAṆVA: The strength of your love makes it seem so. [*Walking around*   325
in meditation.] Good! Now that Śakuntalā is on her way to her husband's family, I feel calm.

> A daughter belongs to another man—
> by sending her to her husband today,
> I feel the satisfaction   330
> one has on repaying a loan.

[*All exit.*]

Act V

[*The* KING *and the* BUFFOON *enter; both sit down.*]

BUFFOON: Pay attention to the music room, friend, and you'll hear the notes of a song strung into a delicious melody . . . the lady Haṁsa-padikā is practicing her singing.

KING: Be quiet so I can hear her!

VOICE IN THE AIR: [*Singing.*]

> Craving sweet   5
> new nectar,
> you kissed
> a mango bud once—
> how could you
> forget her, bee,   10
> to bury your joy
> in a lotus?

KING: The melody of the song is passionate.

BUFFOON: But did you get the meaning of the words?

KING: I once made love to her. Now she reproaches me for loving   15
Queen Vasumatī. Friend Mādhavya, tell Haṁsapadikā that her words rebuke me soundly.

BUFFOON: As you command! [*He rises.*] But if that woman grabs my
hair tuft, it will be like a heavenly nymph grabbing some ascetic . . .
there go my hopes of liberation![4]   20

KING: Go! Use your courtly charm to console her.

BUFFOON: What a fate!
          [*He exits.*]

KING: [*To himself.*] Why did hearing the song's words fill me with such
strong desire? I'm not parted from anyone I love . . .

> Seeing rare beauty,   25
> hearing lovely sounds,
> even a happy man
> becomes strangely uneasy . . .
> perhaps he remembers,
> without knowing why,   30
> loves of another life
> buried deep in his being.[5]

[*He stands bewildered. Then the* KING'S CHAMBERLAIN *enters.*]

CHAMBERLAIN: At my age, look at me!

> Since I took this ceremonial bamboo staff
> as my badge of office in the king's chambers   35
> many years have passed; now I use it
> as a crutch to support my faltering steps.

A king cannot neglect his duty. He has just risen from his seat of
justice and though I am loath to keep him longer, Sage Kaṇva's
pupils have just arrived. Authority to rule the world leaves no time   40
for rest.

> The sun's steeds were yoked before time began,
> the fragrant wind blows night and day,
> the cosmic serpent always bears earth's weight,[6]
> and a king who levies taxes has his duty.   45

Therefore, I must perform my office. [*Walking around and looking.*]

> Weary from ruling them like children,
> he seeks solitude far from his subjects,

---

4. The buffoon is referring, in his own inimitable way, to the seduction of the ascetic by the courtesan and the thwarting of the former's quest for liberation from karma and rebirth. The buffoon's joke turns on the word *mokṣa*, which means "release," in the physical sense as well as in the spiritual one of liberation from karma.

5. An allusion to the power of art to revive buried memories of experiences from former lives.

6. According to Hindu mythology the earth rests on Śeṣa, the cosmic serpent. "Sun's steeds": horses for the sun god's chariot.

like an elephant bull who seeks cool shade
after gathering his herd at midday.   50

[*Approaching.*] Victory to you, king! Some ascetics who dwell in the
forest at the foothills of the Himālayas have come. They have women
with them and bring a message from Sage Kaṇva. Listen, king, and
judge!

KING: [*Respectfully.*] Are they Sage Kaṇva's messengers?   55
CHAMBERLAIN: They are.
KING: Inform the teacher Somarāta that he should welcome the ascet-
ics with the prescribed rites and then bring them to me himself. I'll
wait in a place suitable for greeting them.
CHAMBERLAIN: As the king commands. [*He exits.*]   60
KING: [*Rising.*] Vetravatī, lead the way to the fire sanctuary.
DOORKEEPER: Come this way, king!
KING: [*Walking around, showing fatigue.*] Every other creature is happy
when the object of his desire is won, but for kings success contains
a core of suffering.   65

High office only leads to greater greed;
just perfecting its rewards is wearisome—
a kingdom is more trouble than it's worth,
like a royal umbrella one holds alone.

TWO BARDS OFFSTAGE: Victory to you, king!   70
FIRST BARD:

You sacrifice your pleasures every day
to labor for your subjects—
as a tree endures burning heat
to give shade from the summer sun.

SECOND BARD:

You punish villains with your rod of justice,   75
you reconcile disputes, you grant protection—
most relatives are loyal only in hope of gain,
but you treat all your subjects like kinsmen.

KING: My weary mind is revived. [*He walks around.*]
DOORKEEPER: The terrace of the fire sanctuary is freshly washed and 80
the cow is waiting to give milk for the oblation. Let the king ascend!
KING: Vetravatī, why has Father Kaṇva sent these sages to me?

Does something hinder their ascetic life?
Or threaten creatures in the sacred forest?
Or do my sins stunt the flowering vines?   85
My mind is filled with conflicting doubts.

DOORKEEPER: I would guess that these sages rejoice in your virtuous
conduct and come to honor you.
     [*The ascetics enter;* ŚAKUNTALĀ *is in front with* GAUTAMĪ: *the* CHAM-
     BERLAIN *and the* KING'S PRIEST *are in front of her.*]
CHAMBERLAIN: Come this way, sirs!
ŚĀRṄGARAVA: Śāradvata, my friend: 90

          I know that this renowned king is righteous
          and none of the social classes follows evil ways,
          but my mind is so accustomed to seclusion
          that the palace feels like a house in flames.

ŚĀRADVATA: I've felt the same way ever since we entered the city.   95

          As if I were freshly bathed, seeing a filthy man,
          pure while he's defiled, awake while he's asleep,
          as if I were a free man watching a prisoner,
          I watch this city mired in pleasures.

ŚAKUNTALĀ: [*Indicating she feels an omen.*] Why is my right eye   100
twitching?
GAUTAMĪ: Child, your husband's family gods turn bad fortune into
blessings! [*They walk around.*]
PRIEST: [*Indicating the* KING.] Ascetics, the guardian of sacred order
has left the seat of justice and awaits you now. Behold him!   105
ŚĀRṄGARAVA: Great priest, he seems praiseworthy, but we expect no
less.

          Boughs bend, heavy with ripened fruit,
          clouds descend with fresh rain,
          noble men are gracious with wealth—   110
          this is the nature of bountiful things.

DOORKEEPER: King, their faces look calm. I'm sure that the sages have
confidence in what they're doing.
KING: [*Seeing* ŚAKUNTALĀ.]

          Who is she? Carefully veiled
          to barely reveal her body's beauty,   115
          surrounded by the ascetics
          like a bud among withered leaves.

DOORKEEPER: King, I feel curious and puzzled too. Surely her form
deserves closer inspection.
KING: Let her be! One should not stare at another man's wife!   120
ŚAKUNTALĀ: [*Placing her hand on her chest, she speaks to herself.*] My
heart, why are you quivering? Be quiet while I learn my noble husband's feelings.

PRIEST: [*Going forward.*] These ascetics have been honored with due
ceremony. They have a message from their teacher. The king   125
should hear them!
KING: I am paying attention.
SAGES: [*Raising their hands in a gesture of greeting.*] May you be vic-
torious, king!
KING: I salute you all!   130
SAGES: May your desires be fulfilled!
KING: Do the sages perform austerities unhampered?
SAGES:

> Who would dare obstruct the rites
> of holy men whom you protect—
> how can darkness descend   135
> when the sun's rays shine?

KING: My title "king" is more meaningful now. Is the world blessed by
Father Kaṇva's health?
SAGES: Saints control their own health. He asks about your welfare and
sends this message . . .   140
KING: What does he command?
ŚĀRṄGARAVA: At the time you secretly met and married my daughter,
affection made me pardon you both.

> We remember you to be a prince of honor;
> Śakuntalā is virtue incarnate—   145
> the creator cannot be condemned
> for mating the perfect bride and groom.

And now that she is pregnant, receive her and perform your sacred
duty together.
GAUTAMĪ: Sir, I have something to say, though I wasn't appointed to   150
speak:

> She ignored her elders
> and you failed to ask her kinsmen—
> since you acted on your own,
> what can I say to you now?   155

ŚAKUNTALĀ: What does my noble husband say?
KING: What has been proposed?
ŚAKUNTALĀ: [*To herself.*] The proposal is as clear as fire.
ŚĀRṄGARAVA: What's this? Your Majesty certainly knows the ways of
the world!   160

> People suspect a married woman who stays
> with her kinsmen, even if she is chaste—
> a young wife should live with her husband,
> no matter how he despises her.

KING: Did I ever marry you?   165

ŚAKUNTALĀ: [*Visibly dejected, speaking to herself.*] Now your fears are
real, my heart!

ŚĀRṄGARAVA:

> Does one turn away from duty in contempt
> because his own actions repulse him?

KING: Why ask this insulting question?   170

ŚĀRṄGARAVA:

> Such transformations take shape
> when men are drunk with power.

KING: This censure is clearly directed at me.

GAUTAMĪ: Child, this is no time to be modest. I'll remove your veil.
Then your husband will recognize you.   175
       [*She does so.*]

KING: [*Staring at ŚAKUNTALĀ.*]

> Must I judge whether I ever married
> the flawless beauty they offer me now?
> I cannot love her or leave her, like a bee
> near a jasmine filled with frost at dawn.

   [*He shows hesitation.*]

DOORKEEPER: Our king has a strong sense of justice. Who else would   180
hesitate when beauty like this is handed to him?

ŚĀRṄGARAVA: King, why do you remain silent?

KING: Ascetics, even though I'm searching my mind, I don't remember
marrying this lady. How can I accept a woman who is visibly pregnant when I doubt that I am the cause?   185

ŚAKUNTALĀ: [*In a stage whisper.*] My lord casts doubt on our marriage.
Why were my hopes so high?

ŚĀRṄGARAVA: It can't be!

> Are you going to insult the sage
> who pardons the girl you seduced   190
> and bids you keep his stolen wealth,
> treating a thief like you with honor?

ŚĀRADVATA: Śārṅgarava, stop now! Śakuntalā, we have delivered our
message and the king has responded. He must be shown some proof.

ŚAKUNTALĀ: [*In a stage whisper.*] When passion can turn to this, what's   195
the use of reminding him? But, it's up to me to prove my honor now.
[*Aloud.*] My noble husband . . . [*She breaks off when this is half-
spoken.*] Since our marriage is in doubt, this is no way to address
him. Puru king, you do wrong to reject a simple-hearted person
with such words after you deceived her in the hermitage.   200

KING: [*Covering his ears.*] Stop this shameful talk!

> Are you trying to stain my name
> and drag me to ruin—
> like a river eroding her own banks,
> soiling water and uprooting trees?   205

ŚAKUNTALĀ: Very well! If it's really true that fear of taking another
man's wife turns you away, then this ring will revive your memory
and remove your doubt.

KING: An excellent idea!

ŚAKUNTALĀ: [*Touching the place where the ring had been.*] I'm lost! The   210
ring is gone from my finger. [*She looks despairingly at* GAUTAMĪ.]

GAUTAMĪ: The ring must have fallen off while you were bathing in the
holy waters at the shrine of the goddess near Indra's grove.

KING: [*Smiling.*] And so they say the female sex is cunning.

ŚAKUNTALĀ: Fate has shown its power. Yet, I will tell you something   215
else.

KING: I am still obliged to listen.

ŚAKUNTALĀ: One day, in a jasmine bower, you held a lotus-leaf cup full
of water in your hand.

KING: We hear you.   220

ŚAKUNTALĀ: At that moment the buck I treated as my son approached.
You coaxed it with the water, saying that it should drink first. But
he didn't trust you and wouldn't drink from your hand. When I took
the water, his trust returned. Then you jested, "Every creature trusts
what its senses know. You both belong to the forest."   225

KING: Thus do women further their own ends by attracting eager men
with the honey of false words.

GAUTAMĪ: Great king, you are wrong to speak this way. This child
raised in an ascetics' grove doesn't know deceit.

KING: Old woman,   230

> When naive female beasts show cunning,
> what can we expect of women who reason?
> Don't cuckoos let other birds nurture
> their eggs and teach the chicks to fly?

ŚAKUNTALĀ: [*Angrily.*] Evil man! you see everything distorted by your   235
own ignoble heart. Who would want to imitate you now, hiding
behind your show of justice, like a well overgrown with weeds?

KING: [*To himself.*] Her anger does not seem feigned; it makes me
doubt myself.

> When the absence of love's memory   240
> made me deny a secret affair with her,
> this fire-eyed beauty bent her angry brows
> and seemed to break the bow of love.[7]

---

7. Of the love god Kāma.

[*Aloud.*] Lady, Duṣyanta's conduct is renowned, so what you say is
groundless.   245

ŚAKUNTALĀ: All right! I may be a self-willed wanton woman! But it was
faith in the Puru dynasty that brought me into the power of a man
with honey in his words and poison in his heart. [*She covers her face
at the end of the speech and weeps.*]

ŚĀRṄGARAVA: A willful act unchecked always causes pain.

> One should be cautious   250
> in forming a secret union—
> unless a lover's heart is clear,
> affection turns to poison.

KING: But sir, why do you demean me with such warnings? Do you
trust the lady?   255

ŚĀRṄGARAVA: [*Scornfully.*] You have learned everything backwards.

> If you suspect the word of one
> whose nature knows no guile,
> then you can only trust
> people who practice deception.   260

KING: I presume you speak the truth. Let us assume so. But what
could I gain by deceiving this woman?

ŚĀRṄGARAVA: Ruin.

KING: Ruin? A Puru king has no reason to want his own ruin!

ŚĀRADVATA: Śārṅgarava, this talk is pointless. We have delivered our   265
master's message and should return.

> Since you married her, abandon her or take her—
> absolute is the power a husband has over his wife.

GAUTAMĪ: You go ahead.
[*They start to go.*]

ŚAKUNTALĀ: What? Am I deceived by this cruel man and then   270
abandoned by you? [*She tries to follow them.*]

GAUTAMĪ: [*Stopping.*] Śārṅgarava, my son, Śakuntalā is following us,
crying pitifully. What will my child do now that her husband has
refused her?

ŚĀRṄGARAVA: [*Turning back angrily.*] Bold woman, do you still insist   275
on having your way?
[ŚAKUNTALĀ *trembles in fear.*]

> If you are what the king says you are,
> you don't belong in Father Kaṇva's family—
> if you know that your marriage vow is pure,
> you can bear slavery in your husband's house.   280

Stay! We must go on!

KING: Ascetic, why do you disappoint the lady too?

> The moon only makes lotuses open,
> the sun's light awakens lilies—
> a king's discipline forbids him   285
> to touch another man's wife.

ŚĀRṄGARAVA: If you forget a past affair because of some present
attachment, why do you fear injustice now?

KING: [To the PRIEST.] Sir, I ask you to weigh the alternatives:

> Since it's unclear whether I'm deluded   290
> or she is speaking falsely—
> should I risk abandoning a wife
> or being tainted by another man's?

PRIEST: [Deliberating.] I recommend this . . .

KING: Instruct me! I'll do as you say.   295

PRIEST: Then let the lady stay in our house until her child is born. If
you ask why: the wise men predict that your first son will be born
with the marks of a king who turns the wheel of empire.[8] If the child
of the sage's daughter bears the marks, congratulate her and
welcome her into your palace chambers. Otherwise, send her back to   300
her father.

KING: Whatever the elders desire.

PRIEST: Child, follow me!

ŚAKUNTALĀ: Mother earth, open to receive me!
[Weeping, ŚAKUNTALĀ exits with the PRIEST and the hermits. The KING,
his memory lost through the curse, thinks about her.]

VOICE OFFSTAGE: Amazing! Amazing!   305

KING: [Listening.] What could this be?

PRIEST: [Reentering, amazed.] King, something marvelous has
occurred!

KING: What?

PRIEST: When Kaṇva's pupils had departed,   310

> The girl threw up her arms and wept,
> lamenting her misfortune . . . then . . .

KING: Then what?

PRIEST:

> Near the nymph's shrine a ray of light
> in the shape of a woman carried her away.   315

[All mime amazement.]

KING: We've already settled the matter. Why discuss it further?

8. See p. 993, n. 9.

PRIEST: [*Observing the* KING.] May you be victorious! [*He exits.*]
KING: Vetravatī, I am bewildered. Lead the way to my chamber!
DOORKEEPER: Come this way, my lord! [*She walks forward.*]
KING:

> I cannot remember marrying   320
> the sage's abandoned daughter,
> but the pain my heart feels
> makes me suspect that I did.

[*All exit.*]

Act VI

[*The* KING's *wife's brother, who is city* MAGISTRATE, *enters with two policemen leading a* MAN *whose hands are tied behind his back.*]

BOTH POLICEMEN: [*Beating the* MAN.] Speak, thief! Where'd you steal this handsome ring with the king's name engraved in the jewel?
MAN: [*Showing fear.*] Peace, sirs! I wouldn't do a thing like that.
FIRST POLICEMAN: Don't tell us the king thought you were some famous priest and gave it to you as a gift!   5
MAN: Listen, I'm a humble fisherman who lives near Indra's grove.
SECOND POLICEMAN: Thief, did we ask you about your caste?
MAGISTRATE: Sūcaka, let him tell it all in order! Don't interrupt him!
BOTH POLICEMEN: Whatever you command, chief!
MAN: I feed my family by catching fish with nets and hooks.   10
MAGISTRATE: [*Mocking.*] What a pure profession![9]
MAN:

> The work I do
> may be vile
> but I won't deny
> my birthright—   15
> a priest
> doing his holy rites
> pities the animals
> he kills.

MAGISTRATE: Go on!   20
MAN: One day as I was cutting up a red carp, I saw the shining stone of this ring in its belly. When I tried to sell it, you grabbed me. Kill me or let me go! That's how I got it!
MAGISTRATE: Jānuka, I'm sure this ugly butcher's a fisherman by his stinking smell. We must investigate how he got the ring. We'll go   25
straight to the palace.
BOTH POLICEMEN: Okay. Go in front, you pickpocket!
[*All walk around.*]

---

9. Because their profession involves taking animal life, fishermen rank low in the caste system.

MAGISTRATE: Sūcaka, guard this villain at the palace gate! I'll report to the king how we found the ring, get his orders, and come back.

BOTH POLICEMEN: Chief, good luck with the king! 30

[*The* MAGISTRATE *exits.*]

FIRST POLICEMAN: Jānuka, the chief's been gone a long time.

SECOND POLICEMAN: Well, there are fixed times for seeing kings.

FIRST POLICEMAN: Jānuka, my hands are itching to tie on his execution garland.[1] [*He points to the* MAN.]

MAN: You shouldn't think about killing a man for no reason. 35

SECOND POLICEMAN: [*Looking.*] I see our chief coming with a letter in his hand. It's probably an order from the king. You'll be thrown to the vultures or you'll see the face of death's dog[2] again . . .

MAGISTRATE: [*Entering.*] Sūcaka, release this fisherman! I'll tell you how he got the ring. 40

FIRST POLICEMAN: Whatever you say, chief!

SECOND POLICEMAN: The villain entered the house of death and came out again. [*He unties the prisoner.*]

MAN: [*Bowing to the* MAGISTRATE.] Master, how will I make my living now? 45

MAGISTRATE: The king sends you a sum equal to the ring. [*He gives the money to the* MAN.]

MAN: [*Bowing as he grabs it.*] The king honors me.

FIRST POLICEMAN: This fellow's certainly honored. He was lowered from the execution stake and raised up on a royal elephant's back.

SECOND POLICEMAN: Chief, the reward tells me this ring was special 50 to the king.

MAGISTRATE: I don't think the king valued the stone, but when he caught sight of the ring, he suddenly seemed to remember someone he loved, and he became deeply disturbed.

FIRST POLICEMAN: You served him well, chief! 55

SECOND POLICEMAN: I think you better served this king of fish. [*Looking at the fisherman with jealousy.*]

MAN: My lords, half of this is yours for your good will.

FIRST POLICEMAN: It's only fair!

MAGISTRATE: Fisherman, now that you are my greatest and dearest friend, we should pledge our love over kadamba-blossom wine. Let's 60 go to the wine shop!

[*They all exit together; the interlude ends. Then a nymph named* SĀNUMATĪ *enters by the skyway.*]

SĀNUMATĪ: Now that I've performed my assigned duties at the nymph's shrine, I'll slip away to spy on King Duṣyanta while the worshipers are bathing. My friendship with Menakā makes me feel a bond with Śakuntalā. Besides, Menakā asked me to help her daughter. 65

[*Looking around.*] Why don't I see preparations for the spring festival in the king's palace? I can learn everything by using my mental

---

1. Condemned prisoners were taken to their executions dressed in robes and garlands, in the manner of sacrificial victims.   2. In Hindu myth two four-eyed dogs guard the path of the dead.

powers, but I must respect my friend's request. So be it! I'll make myself invisible and spy on these two girls who are guarding the pleasure garden.   70

[SĀNUMATĪ *mimes descending and stands waiting. Then a* MAID *servant named Parabhṛtikā, "Little Cuckoo," enters, looking at a mango bud. A* SECOND MAID, *named Madhukarikā "Little Bee," is following her.*]

FIRST MAID:

> Your pale green stem
> tinged with pink
> is a true sign
> that spring has come—
> I see you,   75
> mango-blossom bud,
> and I pray
> for a season of joy.

SECOND MAID: What are you muttering to yourself?
FIRST MAID: A cuckoo goes mad when she sees a mango bud.   80
SECOND MAID: [*Joyfully rushing over.*] Has the sweet month of spring come?
FIRST MAID: Now's the time to sing your songs of love.
SECOND MAID: Hold me while I pluck a mango bud and worship the god of love.   85
FIRST MAID: Only if you'll give me half the fruit of your worship.
SECOND MAID: That goes without saying . . . our bodies may be separate, but our lives are one . . . [*Leaning on her friend, she stands and plucks a mango bud.*] The mango flower is still closed, but this broken stem is fragrant. [*She makes the dove gesture with her hands.*]   90

> Mango-blossom bud,
> I offer you to Love
> as he lifts
> his bow of passion.
> Be the first   95
> of his flower arrows
> aimed at lonely girls
> with lovers far away!

[*She throws the mango bud.*]
CHAMBERLAIN: [*Angrily throwing aside the curtain and entering.*] Not now, stupid girl! When the king has banned the festival of spring,   100
how dare you pluck a mango bud!
BOTH MAIDS: [*Frightened.*] Please forgive us, sir. We don't know what you mean.
CHAMBERLAIN: Did you not hear that even the spring trees and the nesting birds obey the king's order?   105

The mango flowers bloom without spreading pollen,
the red amaranth buds, but will not bloom;
cries of cuckoo cocks freeze though frost is past,
and out of fear, Love holds his arrow half-drawn.

BOTH MAIDS: There is no doubt about the king's great power!   110
FIRST MAID: Sir, several days ago we were sent to wait on the queen by
Mitrāvasu, the king's brother-in-law. We were assigned to guard the
pleasure garden. Since we're newcomers, we've heard no news.
CHAMBERLAIN: Let it be! But don't do it again!
BOTH MAIDS: Sir, we're curious. May we ask why the spring festival   115
was banned?
SĀNUMATĪ: Mortals are fond of festivals. The reason must be serious.
CHAMBERLAIN: It is public knowledge. Why should I not tell them?
Has the scandal of Śakuntalā's rejection not reached your ears?
BOTH MAIDS: We only heard from the king's brother-in-law that the   120
ring was found.
CHAMBERLAIN: [To himself.] There is little more to tell. [Aloud.] When
he saw the ring, the king remembered that he had married Śakuntalā
in secret and had rejected her in his delusion. Since then the king has
been tortured by remorse.   125

> Despising what he once enjoyed,
> he shuns his ministers every day
> and spends long sleepless nights
> tossing at the edge of his bed—
> when courtesy demands that   130
> he converse with palace women,
> he stumbles over their names,
> and then retreats in shame.

SĀNUMATĪ: This news delights me.
CHAMBERLAIN: The festival is banned because of the king's melancholy.   135
BOTH MAIDS: It's only right.
VOICE OFFSTAGE: This way, sir!
CHAMBERLAIN: [Listening.] The king is coming. Go about your business!
BOTH MAIDS: As you say.
[Both maids exit. Then the KING enters, costumed to show his
grief, accompanied by the BUFFOON and the DOORKEEPER.]
CHAMBERLAIN: [Observing the KING.] Extraordinary beauty is   140
appealing under all conditions. Even in his lovesick state, the king is
wonderful to see.

> Rejecting his regal jewels,
> he wears one golden bangle
> above his left wrist;   145
> his lips are pale with sighs,
> his eyes wan from brooding at night—
> like a gemstone ground in polishing,
> the fiery beauty of his body
> makes his wasted form seem strong.   150

SĀNUMATĪ: [*Seeing the* KING.] I see why Śakuntalā pines for him
though he rejected and disgraced her.

KING: [*Walking around slowly, deep in thought.*]

> This cursed heart slept
> when my love came to wake it,
> and now it stays awake   155
> to suffer the pain of remorse.

SĀNUMATĪ: The girl shares his fate.

BUFFOON: [*In a stage whisper.*] He's having another attack of his
Śakuntalā disease. I doubt if there's any cure for that.

CHAMBERLAIN: [*Approaching.*] Victory to the king! I have inspected   160
the grounds of the pleasure garden. Let the king visit his favorite
spots and divert himself.

KING: Vetravatī, deliver a message to my noble minister Piśuna: "After
being awake all night, we cannot sit on the seat of justice today. Set
in writing what your judgment tells you the citizens require and send   165
it to us!"

DOORKEEPER: Whatever you command! [*She exits.*]

KING: Vātāyana, attend to the rest of your business!

CHAMBERLAIN: As the king commands! [*He exits.*]

BUFFOON: You've cleared out the flies. Now you can rest in some   170
pretty spot. The garden is pleasant now in this break between
morning cold and noonday heat.

KING: Dear friend, the saying "Misfortunes rush through any crack"
is absolutely right:

> Barely freed by the dark force   175
> that made me forget Kaṇva's daughter,
> my mind is threatened by an arrow
> of mango buds fixed on Love's bow.

BUFFOON: Wait, I'll destroy the love god's arrow with my wooden
stick.[3] [*Raising his staff, he tries to strike a mango bud.*]   180

KING: [*Smiling.*] Let it be! I see the majesty of brahman bravery.
Friend, where may I sit to divert my eyes with vines that remind me
of my love?

BUFFOON: Didn't you tell your maid Caturikā, "I'll pass the time in the
jasmine bower. Bring me the drawing board on which I painted a   185
picture of Śakuntalā with my own hand!"

KING: Such a place may soothe my heart. Show me the way!

BUFFOON: Come this way!
   [*Both walk around; the nymph* SĀNUMATĪ *follows.*]
The marble seat and flower offerings in this jasmine bower are
certainly trying to make us feel welcome. Come in and sit down!   190
   [*Both enter the bower and sit.*]

---

3. It is clear in the original that the buffoon's staff parodies Indra's rod (a symbol of virility) and
the phallic arrows of the god of love.

SĀNUMATĪ: I'll hide behind these creepers to see the picture he's drawn of my friend. Then I'll report how great her husband's passion is. [*She does as she says and stands waiting.*]

KING: Friend, now I remember everything. I told you about my first meeting with Śakuntalā. You weren't with me when I rejected her, but why didn't you say anything about her before? Did you suffer a loss of memory too? 195

BUFFOON: I didn't forget. You did tell me all about it once, but then you said, "It's all a joke without any truth." My wit is like a lump of clay, so I took you at your word . . . or it could be that fate is powerful . . . 200

SĀNUMATĪ: It is!

KING: Friend, help me!

BUFFOON: What's this? It doesn't become you! Noblemen never take grief to heart. Even in storms, mountains don't tremble.

KING: Dear friend, I'm defenseless when I remember the pain of my 205 love's bewilderment when I rejected her.

> When I cast her away, she followed her kinsmen,
> but Kaṇva's disciple harshly shouted, "Stay!"
> The tearful look my cruelty provoked
> burns me like an arrow tipped with poison. 210

SĀNUMATĪ: The way he rehearses his actions makes me delight in his pain.

BUFFOON: Sir, I guess that the lady was carried off by some celestial creature or other.

KING: Who else would dare to touch a woman who worshiped her 215 husband? I was told that Menakā is her mother. My heart suspects that her mother's companions carried her off.

SĀNUMATĪ: His delusion puzzled me, but not his reawakening.

BUFFOON: If that's the case, you'll meet her again in good time.

KING: How? 220

BUFFOON: No mother or father can bear to see a daughter parted from her husband.

KING:

> Was it dream or illusion or mental confusion,
> or the last meager fruit of my former good deeds?
> It is gone now, and my heart's desires are 225
> like riverbanks crumbling of their own weight.

BUFFOON: Stop this! Isn't the ring evidence that an unexpected meeting is destined to take place?

KING: [*Looking at the ring.*] I only pity it for falling from such a place.

> Ring, your punishment is proof 230
> that your face is as flawed as mine—
> you were placed in her lovely fingers,
> glowing with crimson nails, and you fell.

SĀNUMATĪ: The real pity would have been if it had fallen into some
other hand.   235
BUFFOON: What prompted you to put the signet ring on her hand?
SĀNUMATĪ: I'm curious too.
KING: I did it when I left for the city. My love broke into tears and
asked. "How long will it be before my noble husband sends news to
me?"   240
BUFFOON: Then? What then?
KING: Then I placed the ring on her finger with this promise:

> One by one, day after day,
> count each syllable of my name!
> At the end, a messenger will come   245
> to bring you to my palace.

But in my cruel delusion, I never kept my word.
SĀNUMATĪ: Fate broke their charming agreement!
BUFFOON: How did it get into the belly of the carp the fisherman was
cutting up?   250
KING: While she was worshiping at the shrine of Indra's wife, it fell
from her hand into the Gaṅgā.[4]
BUFFOON: It's obvious now!
SĀNUMATĪ: And the king, doubtful of his marriage to Śakuntalā, a
female ascetic, was afraid to commit an act of injustice. But why   255
should such passionate love need a ring to be remembered?
KING: I must reproach the ring for what it's done.
BUFFOON: [To himself.] He's gone the way of all madmen . . .
KING:

> Why did you leave her delicate finger
> and sink into the deep river?   260

Of course . . .

> A mindless ring can't recognize virtue,
> but why did I reject my love?

BUFFOON: [To himself again.] Why am I consumed by a craving for
food?   265
KING: Oh ring! Have pity on a man whose heart is tormented because
he abandoned his love without cause! Let him see her again!
[Throwing the curtain aside, the maid CATURIKĀ enters, with the
drawing board in her hand.]
CATURIKĀ: Here's the picture you painted of the lady. [She shows the
drawing board.]
BUFFOON: Dear friend, how well you've painted your feelings in this
sweet scene! My eyes almost stumble over the hollows and hills.   270

---

4. The Ganges River.

SĀNUMATĪ: What skill the king has! I feel as if my friend were before me.
KING:

> The picture's imperfections are not hers,
> but this drawing does hint at her beauty.

SĀNUMATĪ: Such words reveal that suffering has increased his modesty as much as his love. 275
BUFFOON: Sir, I see three ladies now and they're all lovely to look at. Which is your Śakuntalā?
SĀNUMATĪ: Only a dim-witted fool like this wouldn't know such beauty!
KING: You guess which one!
BUFFOON: I guess Śakuntalā is the one you've drawn with flowers falling 280 from her loosened locks of hair, with drops of sweat on her face, with her arms hanging limp and tired as she stands at the side of a mango tree whose tender shoots are gleaming with the fresh water she poured. The other two are her friends.
KING: You are clever! Look at these signs of my passion! 285

> Smudges from my sweating fingers
> stain the edges of the picture
> and a tear fallen from my cheek
> has raised a wrinkle in the paint.

Caturikā, the scenery is only half-drawn. Go and bring my paints! 290
CATURIKĀ: Noble Mādhavya, hold the drawing board until I come back!
KING: I'll hold it myself. [*He takes it, the maid exits.*]

> I rejected my love when she came to me,
> and how I worship her in a painted image—
> having passed by a river full of water, 295
> I'm longing now for an empty mirage.

BUFFOON: [*To himself.*] He's too far gone for a river now! He's looking for a mirage! [*Aloud.*] Sir, what else do you plan to draw here?
SĀNUMATĪ: He'll want to draw every place my friend loved.
KING:

> I'll draw the river Mālinī 300
> flowing through Himālaya's foothills
> where pairs of wild geese nest in the sand
> and deer recline on both riverbanks,
> where a doe is rubbing her left eye
> on the horn of a black buck antelope 305
> under a tree whose branches
> have bark dresses hanging to dry.

BUFFOON: [*To himself.*] Next he'll fill the drawing board with mobs of ascetics wearing long grassy beards.

KING: Dear friend, I've forgotten to draw an ornament that Śakuntalā   310
wore.

BUFFOON: What is it?

SĀNUMATĪ: It will suit her forest life and her tender beauty.

KING:

> I haven't drawn the mimosa flower on her ear,
> its filaments resting on her cheek,   315
> or the necklace of tender lotus stalks,
> lying on her breasts like autumn moonbeams.

BUFFOON: But why does the lady cover her face with her red lotus-bud
fingertips and stand trembling in fear? [*Looking closely.*] That son-of-
a-bee who steals nectar from flowers is attacking her face.   320

KING: Drive the impudent rogue away!

BUFFOON: You have the power to punish criminals. You drive him off!

KING: All right! Bee, favored guest of the flowering vines, why do you
frustrate yourself by flying here?[5]

> A female bee waits on a flower,   325
> thirsting for your love—
> she refuses to drink
> the sweet nectar without you.

SĀNUMATĪ: How gallantly he's driving him away!

BUFFOON: When you try to drive it away, this creature becomes   330
vicious.

KING: Why don't you stop when I command you?

> Bee, if you touch the lips of my love
> that lure you like a young tree's virgin buds,
> lips I gently kissed in festivals of love,   335
> I'll hold you captive in a lotus flower cage.

BUFFOON: Why isn't he afraid of your harsh punishment? [*Laughing,
he speaks to himself.*] He's gone crazy and I'll be the same if I go on
talking like this. [*Aloud.*] But, sir, it's just a picture!

KING: A picture? How can that be?   340

SĀNUMATĪ: When I couldn't tell whether it was painted, how could he
realize he was looking at a picture?

KING: Dear friend, are you envious of me?

> My heart's affection made me feel
> the joy of seeing her—   345
> but you reminded me again
> that my love is only a picture.

[*He wipes away a tear.*]

SĀNUMATĪ: The effects of her absence make him quarrelsome.

KING: Dear friend, why do I suffer this endless pain?

5. The king's preoccupation with the bee recalls the events of Act I.

Sleepless nights prevent our meeting in dreams;   350
her image in a picture is ruined by my tears.

SĀNUMATĪ: You have clearly atoned for the suffering your rejection
caused Śakuntalā.

CATURIKĀ: [*Entering.*] Victory, my lord! I found the paint box and
started back right away . . . but I met Queen Vasumatī with her maid   355
Taralikā on the path and she grabbed the box from my hand, saying,
"I'll bring it to the noble lord myself!"

BUFFOON: You were lucky to get away!

CATURIKĀ: The queen's shawl got caught on a tree. While Taralikā was
freeing it, I made my escape.   360

KING: Dear friend, the queen's pride can quickly turn to anger. Save
this picture!

BUFFOON: You should say, "Save yourself!" [*Taking the picture, he
stands up.*] If you escape the woman's deadly poison, then send word
to me in the Palace of the Clouds. [*He exits hastily.*]   365

SĀNUMATĪ: Even though another woman has taken his heart and he
feels indifferent to the queen, he treats her with respect.[6]

DOORKEEPER: [*Entering with a letter in her hand.*] Victory, king!

KING: Vetravatī, did you meet the queen on the way?

DOORKEEPER: I did, but when she saw the letter in my hand, she   370
turned back.

KING: She knows that this is official and would not interrupt my work.

DOORKEEPER: King, the minister requests that you examine the contents
of this letter. He said that the enormous job of reckoning the
revenue in this one citizen's case had taken all his time.   375

KING: Show me the letter! [*The girl hands it to him and he reads barely
aloud.*] What is this? "A wealthy merchant sea captain named
Dhanamitra has been lost in a shipwreck and the laws say that since
the brave man was childless, his accumulated wealth all goes to the
king." It's terrible to be childless! A man of such wealth probably had   380
several wives. We must find out if any one of his wives is pregnant!

DOORKEEPER: King, it's said that one of his wives, the daughter of a
merchant of Ayodhyā, has performed the rite to ensure the birth of
a son.[7]

KING: The child in her womb surely deserves his parental wealth. Go!   385
Report this to my minister!

DOORKEEPER: As the king commands! [*She starts to go.*]

KING: Come here a moment!

DOORKEEPER: I am here.

KING: Is it his offspring or not?   390

> When his subjects lose a kinsman,
> Duṣyanta will preserve the estates—
> unless there is some crime.
> Let this be proclaimed.

6. Royal polygamy called for elaborate courtesies.
7. This rite (*puṃsavana*) is performed in the third month of pregnancy.

DOORKEEPER: It shall be proclaimed loudly. [*She exits; reenters.*] The   395
king's order will be as welcome as rain in the right season.

KING: [*Sighing long and deeply.*] Families without offspring whose
lines of succession are cut off lose their wealth to strangers when the
last male heir dies. When I die, this will happen to the wealth of the
Puru dynasty.   400

DOORKEEPER: Heaven forbid such a fate!

KING: I curse myself for despising the treasure I was offered.

SĀNUMATĪ: He surely has my friend in mind when he blames himself.

KING:

> I abandoned my lawful wife, the holy ground
> where I myself planted my family's glory,   405
> like earth sown with seed at the right time,
> ready to bear rich fruit in season.

SĀNUMATĪ: But your family's line will not be broken.

CATURIKĀ: [*In a stage whisper.*] The king is upset by the story of the
merchant. Go and bring noble Mādhavya from the Palace of the   410
Clouds to console him!

DOORKEEPER: A good idea! [*She exits.*]

KING: Duṣyanta's ancestors are imperiled.

> Our fathers drink the yearly libation
> mixed with my childless tears,   415
> knowing that there is no other son
> to offer the sacred funeral waters.

[*He falls into a faint.*]

CATURIKĀ: [*Looking at the bewildered* KING.] Calm yourself, my lord!

SĀNUMATĪ: Though a light shines, his separation from Śakuntalā keeps
him in a state of dark depression. I could make him happy now, but   420
I've heard Indra's consort consoling Śakuntalā with the news that the
gods are hungry for their share of the ancestral oblations and will
soon conspire to have her husband welcome his lawful wife. I'll have
to wait for the auspicious time, but meanwhile I'll cheer my friend by
reporting his condition. [*She exits, flying into the air.*]   425

VOICE OFFSTAGE: Help! Brahman-murder![8]

KING: [*Regaining consciousness, listening.*] Is it Mādhavya's cry of pain?
Who's there?

DOORKEEPER: King, your friend is in danger. Help him!

KING: Who dares to threaten him?   430

DOORKEEPER: Some invisible spirit seized him and dragged him to the
roof of the Palace of the Clouds.

KING: [*Getting up.*] Not this! Even my house is haunted by spirits.

> When I don't even recognize
> the blunders I commit every day,   435
> how can I keep track
> of where my subjects stray?

VOICE OFFSTAGE: Dear friend! Help! Help!

---

8. Murder of a *brāhmaṇa* is among the most heinous sins.

KING: [*Breaking into a run.*] Friend, don't be afraid! I'm coming!

VOICE OFFSTAGE: [*Repeating the call for help.*] Why shouldn't I be 440
afraid? Someone is trying to split my neck in three, like a stalk of
sugar cane.

KING: [*Casting a glance.*] Quickly, my bow!

BOW-BEARER: [*Entering with a bow in hand.*] Here are your bow and
quiver. 445

    [*The KING takes his bow and arrows.*]

VOICE OFFSTAGE:

> I'll kill you as a tiger kills struggling prey!
> I'll drink fresh blood from your tender neck!
> Take refuge now in the bow Duṣyanta lifts
> to calm the fears of the oppressed!

KING: [*Angrily.*] How dare you abuse my name? Stop, carrion-eater! 450
Or you will not live! [*He strings his bow.*] Vetravatī, lead the way to
the stairs!

DOORKEEPER: This way, king.

    [*All move forward in haste.*]

KING: [*Searching around.*] There is no one here!

VOICE OFFSTAGE: Help! Help! I see you. Don't you see me? I'm like a 455
mouse caught by a cat! My life is hopeless!

KING: Don't count on your powers of invisibility! My magical arrows
will find you. I aim this arrow:

> It will strike its doomed target
> and spare the brahman it must save— 460
> a wild goose can extract the milk
> and leave the water untouched.[9]

    [*He aims the arrow. Then Indra's charioteer MĀTALI enters, having
released the BUFFOON.*]

MĀTALI: King!

> Indra sets demons as your targets:
> draw your bow against them! 465
> Send friends gracious glances
> rather than deadly arrows!

KING: [*Withdrawing his arrow.*] Mātali, welcome to great Indra's
charioteer!

BUFFOON: [*Entering.*] He tried to slaughter me like a sacrificial beast 470
and this king is greeting him with honors!

MĀTALI: [*Smiling.*] Your Majesty, hear why Indra has sent me to you!

KING: I am all attention.

MĀTALI: There is an army of demons descended from one-hundred-

---

9. The *hamsa*: in Sanskrit poetry this bird is said to have the ability to separate milk from the
water with which it has been diluted.

headed Kālanemi, known to be invincible . . .   475
KING: I have already heard it from Nārada, the gods' messenger.
MĀTALI:

> He is invulnerable to your friend Indra,
> so you are appointed to lead the charge—
> the moon dispels the darkness of night
> since the sun cannot drive it out.   480

Take your weapon, mount Indra's chariot, and prepare for victory!
KING: Indra favors me with this honor. But why did you attack
Mādhavya?
MĀTALI: I'll tell you! From the signs of anguish Your Majesty showed,
I knew that you were despondent. I attacked him to arouse your anger.   485

> A fire blazes when fuel is added;
> a cobra provoked raises its hood—
> men can regain lost courage
> if their emotions are aroused.

KING: [In a stage whisper.] Dear friend. I cannot disobey a command   490
from the lord of heaven. Inform my minister Piśuna of this and tell
him this for me:

> Concentrate your mind on guarding my subjects!
> My bow is strung to accomplish other work.

BUFFOON: Whatever you command!   495
[He exits.]
MĀTALI: Mount the chariot, Your Majesty!
[The KING mimes mounting the chariot; all exit.]

Act VII

[The KING enters with MĀTALI by the skyway, mounted on a chariot.]
KING: Mātali, though I carried out his command, I feel unworthy of
the honors Indra gave me.
MĀTALI: [Smiling.] Your Majesty, neither of you seems satisfied.

> You belittle the aid you gave Indra
> in face of the honors he conferred,   5
> and he, amazed by your heroic acts,
> deems his hospitality too slight.

KING: No, not so! When I was taking leave, he honored me beyond my
heart's desire and shared his throne with me in the presence of the
gods: 10

> Indra gave me a garland of coral flowers[1]
> tinged with sandalpowder from his chest,

---

1. The coral trees of heaven bear never-fading flowers.

> while he smiled at his son Jayanta,
> who stood there barely hiding h is envy.

MĀTALI: Don't you deserve whatever you want from Indra?   15

> Indra's heaven of pleasures has twice
> been saved by rooting out thorny demons—
> your smooth-jointed arrows have now done
> what Viṣṇu once did with his lion claws.[2]

KING: Here too Indra's might deserves the praise.   20

> When servants succeed in great tasks,
> they act in hope of their master's praise—
> would dawn scatter the darkness
> if he were not the sun's own charioteer?

MĀTALI: This attitude suits you well! [*He moves a little distance.*] Look   25
over there, Your Majesty! See how your own glorious fame has
reached the vault of heaven!

> Celestial artists are drawing your exploits
> on leaves of the wish-granting creeper[3]
> with colors of the nymphs' cosmetic paints,   30
> and bards are moved to sing of you in ballads.

KING: Mātali, in my desire to do battle with the demons, I did not
notice the path we took to heaven as we climbed through the sky
yesterday. Which course of the winds are we traveling?
MĀTALI:

> They call this path of the wind Parivaha—   35
> freed from darkness by Viṣṇu's second stride,
> it bears the Gaṅgā's three celestial streams[4]
> and turns stars in orbit, dividing their rays.

KING: Mātali, this is why my soul, my senses, and my heart feel calm.
[*He looks at the chariot wheels.*] We've descended to the level of the   40
clouds.
MĀTALI: How do you know?
KING:

> Crested cuckoos fly between the spokes,
> lightning flashes glint off the horses' coats,
> and a fine mist wets your chariot's wheels—   45
> all signs that we go over rain-filled clouds.

---

2. In his incarnation as half man, half lion, the god Viṣṇu slew a demon.
3. The *kalpalatā* vine that grows in Indra's heaven.
4. In heaven the Ganges flows with three streams before descending to earth. As the cosmic strider, Viṣṇu scattered the darkness from heaven.

MĀTALI: In a moment you'll be back in your own domain, Your Majesty.

KING: [*Looking down.*] Our speeding chariot makes the mortal world appear fantastic. Look!

> Mountain peaks emerge as the earth descends,   50
> branches spread up from a sea of leaves,
> fine lines become great rivers to behold—
> the world seems to hurtle toward me.

MĀTALI: You observe well! [*He looks with great reverence.*] The beauty of earth is sublime.   55

KING: Mātali, what mountain do I see stretching into the eastern and western seas, rippled with streams of liquid gold, like a gateway of twilight clouds?

MĀTALI: Your Majesty, it is called the "Golden Peak," the mountain of the demigods, a place where austerities are practiced to perfection.   60

> Mārīca, the descendant of Brahmā,
> a father of both demons and gods,
> lives the life of an ascetic here
> in the company of Aditi, his wife.

KING: One must not ignore good fortune! I shall perform the rite of   65
circumambulating the sage.

MĀTALI: An excellent idea!
[*The two mime descending.*]

KING: [*Smiling.*]

> The chariot wheels make no sound,
> they raise no clouds of dust,
> they touch the ground unhindered—   70
> nothing marks the chariot's descent.

MĀTALI: It is because of the extraordinary power that you and Indra both possess.

KING: Mātali, where is Mārīca's hermitage?

MĀTALI: [*Pointing with his hand.*]

> Where the sage stands staring at the sun,   75
> as immobile as the trunk of a tree,
> his body half-buried in an ant hill,
> with a snake skin on his chest,
> his throat pricked by a necklace
> of withered thorny vines,   80
> wearing a coil of long matted hair
> filled with nests of śakunta birds.

KING: I do homage to the sage for his severe austerity.

MĀTALI: [*Pulling hard on the chariot reins.*] Great king, let us enter Mārīca's hermitage, where Aditi nurtures the celestial coral trees.   85

KING: This tranquil place surpasses heaven. I feel as if I'm bathing in a lake of nectar.

MĀTALI: [*Stopping the chariot.*] Dismount, Your Majesty!

KING: [*Dismounting.*] Mātali, what about you?

MĀTALI: I have stopped the chariot. I'll dismount too. [*He does so.*] 90
This way, Your Majesty! [*He walks around.*] You can see the grounds
of the ascetics' grove ahead.

KING: I am amazed!

> In this forest of wish-fulfilling trees
> ascetics live on only the air they breathe 95
> and perform their ritual ablutions
> in water colored by golden lotus pollen.
> They sit in trance on jeweled marble slabs
> and stay chaste among celestial nymphs,
> practicing austerities in the place 100
> that others seek to win by penances.

MĀTALI: Great men always aspire to rare heights! [*He walks around,
calling aloud.*] O venerable Śākalya, what is the sage Mārīca doing
now? What do you say? In response to Aditi's question about the duties
of a devoted wife, he is talking in a gathering of great sages' wives.[5] 105

KING: [*Listening.*] We must wait our turn.

MĀTALI: [*Looking at the* KING.] Your Majesty, rest at the foot of this
aśoka tree. Meanwhile, I'll look for a chance to announce you to
Indra's father.

KING: As you advise . . . [*He stops.*] 110

MĀTALI: Your Majesty, I'll attend to this. [*He exits.*]

KING: [*Indicating he feels an omen.*]

> I have no hope for my desire.
> Why does my arm throb in vain?
> Once good fortune is lost,
> it becomes constant pain. 115

VOICE OFFSTAGE: Don't be so wild! Why is his nature so stubborn?

KING: [*Listening.*] Unruly conduct is out of place here. Whom are they
reprimanding? [*Looking toward the sound, surprised.*] Who is this child
guarded by two female ascetics? A boy who acts more like a man.

> He has dragged this lion cub 120
> from its mother's half-full teat
> to play with it, and with his hand
> he violently tugs its mane.

[*The* BOY *enters as described, with two female ascetics.*]

BOY: Open your mouth, lion! I want to count your teeth!

FIRST ASCETIC: Nasty boy, why do you torture creatures we love like 125
our children? You're getting too headstrong! The sages gave you
the right name when they called you "Sarvadamana, Tamer-of-
everything."

5. In Gupta society, the sages were teachers of *dharma* and of the norms of behavior for women
of the upper classes.

KING: Why is my heart drawn to this child, as if he were my own flesh?
I don't have a son. That is why I feel tender toward him . . .   130

SECOND ASCETIC: The lioness will maul you if you don't let go of her
cub!

BOY: [*Smiling.*] Oh, I'm scared to death! [*Pouting.*]

KING:

> This child appears to be
> the seed of hidden glory,   135
> like a spark of fire
> awaiting fuel to burn.

FIRST ASCETIC: Child, let go of the lion cub and I'll give you another
toy!

BOY: Where is it? Give it to me! [*He reaches out his hand.*]   140

KING: Why does he bear the mark of a king who turns the wheel of
empire?

> A hand with fine webs connecting the fingers
> opens as he reaches for the object greedily,
> like a single lotus with faint inner petals   145
> spread open in the red glow of early dawn.

SECOND ASCETIC: Suvratā, you can't stop him with words! The sage
Mārkaṇḍeya's son left a brightly painted clay bird in my hut. Get it
for him!

FIRST ASCETIC: I will! [*She exits.*]   150

BOY: But until it comes I'll play with this cub.

KING: I am attracted to this pampered boy . . .

> Lucky are fathers whose laps give refuge
> to the muddy limbs of adoring little sons
> when childish smiles show budding teeth   155
> and jumbled sounds make charming words.

SECOND ASCETIC: Well, he ignores me. [*She looks back.*] Is one of the
sage's sons here? [*Looking at the* KING.] Sir, please come here! Make
him loosen his grip and let go of the lion cub! He's tormenting it in
his cruel child's play.   160

KING: [*Approaching the* BOY, *smiling.*] Stop! You're a great sage's son!

> When self-control is your duty by birth,
> why do you violate the sanctuary laws
> and ruin the animals' peaceful life,
> like a young black snake in a sandal tree?   165

SECOND ASCETIC: Sir, he's not a sage's son.

KING: His actions and his looks confirm it. I based my false assumption on his presence in this place. [*He does what she asked; responding
to the* BOY's *touch, he speaks to himself.*]

> Even my limbs feel delighted
> from the touch of a stranger's son—
> the father at whose side he grew
> must feel pure joy in his heart.

170

SECOND ASCETIC: [*Examining them both.*] It's amazing! Amazing!

KING: What is it, madam?

SECOND ASCETIC: This boy looks surprisingly like you. He doesn't even know you, and he's acting naturally. 175

KING: [*Fondling the child.*] If he's not the son of an ascetic, what lineage does he belong to?

SECOND ASCETIC: The family of Puru.

KING: [*To himself.*] What? His ancestry is the same as mine . . . so this lady thinks he resembles me. The family vow of Puru's descendants is to spend their last days in the forest. 180

> As world protectors they first choose
> palaces filled with sensuous pleasures,
> but later, their homes are under trees
> and one wife shares the ascetic vows.

185

[*Aloud.*] But mortals cannot enter this realm on their own.

SECOND ASCETIC: You're right, sir. His mother is a nymph's child. She gave birth to him here in the hermitage of Mārīca.

KING: [*In a stage whisper.*] Here is a second ground for hope! [*Aloud.*] What famed royal sage claims her as his wife? 190

SECOND ASCETIC: Who would even think of speaking the name of a man who rejected his lawful wife?

KING: [*To himself.*] Perhaps this story points to me. What if I ask the name of the boy's mother? No, it is wrong to ask about another man's wife. 195

FIRST ASCETIC: [*Returning with a clay bird in her hand.*] Look, Sarvadamana, a śakunta! Look! Isn't it lovely?

BOY: Where's my mother?

BOTH ASCETICS: He's tricked by the similarity of names.[6] He wants his mother. 200

SECOND ASCETIC: Child, she told you to look at the lovely clay śakunta bird.

KING: [*To himself.*] What? Is his mother's name Śakuntalā? But names can be the same. Even a name is a mirage . . . a false hope to herald despair. 205

BOY: I like this bird! [*He picks up the toy.*]

FIRST ASCETIC: [*Looking frantically.*] Oh, I don't see the amulet-box on his wrist!

6. Śakunta, one of the Sanskrit and Prakrit words for "bird," is etymologically related to Śakuntalā (Woman of the Birds), who was so named because she was found in the forest in the company of birds. Now her son, Bharata, mistakes śakunta for śakuntalā. Like the women, the child speaks Prakrit, the "natural" language, but once he has entered the social world of men he must speak Sanskrit.

KING: Don't be alarmed! It broke off while he was tussling with the   210
lion cub. [*He goes to pick it up.*]

BOTH ASCETICS: Don't touch it! Oh, he's already picked it up! [*With
their hands on their chests, they stare at each other in amazement.*]

KING: Why did you warn me against it?

FIRST ASCETIC: It contains the magical herb called Aparājitā,[7] honored sir. Mārīca gave it to him at his birth ceremony. He said that if   215
it fell to the ground no one but his parents or himself could pick it up.

KING: And if someone else does pick it up?

FIRST ASCETIC: Then it turns into a snake and strikes.

KING: Have you two seen it so transformed?

BOTH ASCETICS: Many times.   220

KING: [*To himself, joyfully.*] Why not rejoice in the fulfillment of my
heart's desire? [*He embraces the child.*]

SECOND ASCETIC: Suvratā, come, let's tell Śakuntalā that her penances
are over.

        [*Both ascetics exit.*]

BOY: Let me go! I want my mother!   225

KING: Son, you will greet your mother with me.

BOY: My father is Duṣyanta, not you!

KING: This contradiction confirms the truth.

        [ŚAKUNTALĀ *enters, wearing the single braid of a woman in
        mourning.*]

ŚAKUNTALĀ: Even though Sarvadamana's amulet kept its natural form
instead of changing into a snake, I can't hope that my destiny will be   230
fulfilled. But maybe what my friend Sānumatī reports is right.

KING: [*Looking at* ŚAKUNTALĀ.] It is Śakuntalā!

> Wearing dusty gray garments,
> her face gaunt from penances,
> her bare braid[8] hanging down—   235
> she bears with perfect virtue
> the trial of long separation
> my cruelty forced on her.

ŚAKUNTALĀ: [*Seeing the* KING *pale with suffering.*] He doesn't resemble
my noble husband. Whose touch defiles my son when the amulet is   240
protecting him?

BOY: [*Going to his mother.*] Mother, who is this stranger who calls me
"son"?

KING: My dear, I see that you recognize me now. Even my cruelty to
you is transformed by your grace.   245

ŚAKUNTALĀ: [*To herself.*] Heart, be consoled! My cruel fate has finally
taken pity on me. It is my noble husband!

---

7. Meaning "invincible" or "unvanquished."
8. A woman separated from her lover

neglected her looks and wore her hair in a
single braid.

KING:

> Memory chanced to break my dark delusion
> and you stand before me in beauty,
> like the moon's wife Rohiṇī   250
> as she rejoins her lord after an eclipse.

ŚAKUNTALĀ: Victory to my noble husband![9] Vic . . . [*She stops when the word is half-spoken, her throat choked with tears.*]

KING: Beautiful Śakuntalā,

> Even choked by your tears,
> the word "victory" is my triumph   255
> on your bare pouting lips,
> pale-red flowers of your face.

BOY: Mother, who is he?

ŚAKUNTALĀ: Child, ask the powers of fate!

KING: [*Falling at* ŚAKUNTALĀ's *feet.*][1]

> May the pain of my rejection   260
> vanish from your heart;
> delusion clouded my weak mind
> and darkness obscured good fortune—
> a blind man tears off a garland,
> fearing the bite of a snake.   265

ŚAKUNTALĀ: Noble husband, rise! Some crime I had committed in a former life surely came to fruit and made my kind husband indifferent to me.

> [*The* KING *rises.*]

But how did my noble husband come to remember this woman who was doomed to pain?   270

KING: I shall tell you after I have removed the last barb of sorrow.

> In my delusion I once ignored
> a teardrop burning your lip—
> let me dry the tear on your lash
> to end the pain of remorse!   275

[*He does so.*]

ŚAKUNTALĀ: [*Seeing the signet ring.*] My noble husband, this is the ring!

KING: I regained my memory when the ring was recovered.

ŚAKUNTALĀ: When it was lost, I tried in vain to convince my noble husband who I was.

KING: Let the vine take back this flower as a sign of her union with   280
spring.

9. The traditional formula for greeting a royal husband.
1. In Sanskrit poetry, the repentant lover, regardless of his rank, must fall at the feet of his beloved, expressing his remorse and asking for her forgiveness.

ŚAKUNTALĀ: I don't trust it. Let my noble husband wear it!
[MĀTALI *enters.*]

MĀTALI: Good fortune! This meeting with your lawful wife and the
sight of your son's face are reasons to rejoice.

KING: The sweet fruit of my desire! Mātali, didn't Indra know about   285
all this?

MĀTALI: What is unknown to the gods? Come, Your Majesty! The
sage Mārīca grants you an audience.

KING: Śakuntalā, hold our son's hand! We shall go to see Mārīca
together.   290

ŚAKUNTALĀ: I feel shy about appearing before my elders in my husband's company.

KING: But it is customary at a joyous time like this. Come! Come!
[*They all walk around. Then* MĀRĪCA *enters with* ADITI: *they sit.*]

MĀRĪCA: [*Looking at the* KING.]

> Aditi, this is king Duṣyanta,
> who leads Indra's armies in battle;   295
> his bow lets your son's thunderbolt
> lie ready with its tip unblunted.

ADITI: He bears himself with dignity.

MĀTALI: Your Majesty, the parents of the gods look at you with affection reserved for a son. Approach them!   300

KING: Mātali, the sages so describe this pair.

> Source of the sun's twelve potent forms,
> parents of Indra, who rules the triple world,
> birthplace of Viṣṇu's primordial form,
> sired by Brahmā's sons,[2] Marīci and Dakṣa.   305

MĀTALI: Correct!

KING: [*Bowing.*] Indra's servant, Duṣyanta, bows to you both.

MĀRĪCA: My son, live long and protect the earth!

ADITI: My son, be an invincible warrior!

ŚAKUNTALĀ: I worship at your feet with my son.   310

MĀRĪCA:

> Child, with a husband like Indra
> and a son like his son Jayanta,
> you need no other blessing.
> Be like Indra's wife Paulomī!

ADITI: Child, may your husband honor you and may your child live   315
long to give both families joy! Be seated!
[*All sit near* MĀRĪCA.]

MĀRĪCA: [*Pointing to each one.*]

---

2. These references establish Aditi and Mārīca's status as primordial parents of the universe and
of the gods themselves.

> By the turn of fortune,
> virtuous Śakuntalā, her noble son,
> and the king are reunited—
> faith and wealth with order.   320

KING: Sir, first came the success of my hopes, then the sight of you.
Your kindness is unparalleled.

> First flowers appear, then fruits,
> first clouds rise, then rain falls,
> but here the chain of events is reversed—   325
> first came success, then your blessing.

MĀTALI: This is the way the creator gods give blessings.

KING: Sir, I married your charge by secret marriage rites. When her
relatives brought her to me after some time, my memory failed and I
sinned against the sage Kaṇva, your kinsman. When I saw the ring, I   330
remembered that I had married his daughter. This is all so strange!

> Like one who doubts the existence
> of an elephant who walks in front of him
> but feels convinced by seeing footprints,
> my mind has taken strange turns.   335

MĀRĪCA: My son, you need not take the blame. Even your delusion has
another cause. Listen!

KING: I am attentive.

MĀRĪCA: When Menakā took her bewildered daughter from the steps
of the nymph's shrine and brought her to my wife, I knew through   340
meditation that you had rejected this girl as your lawful wife because
of Durvāsas' curse, and that the curse would end when you saw the
ring.

KING: [Sighing.] So I am freed of blame.

ŚAKUNTALĀ: [To herself.] And I am happy to learn that I wasn't rejected   345
by my husband without cause. But I don't remember being cursed.
Maybe the empty heart of love's separation made me deaf to
the curse ... my friends did warn me to show the ring to my
husband ...

MĀRĪCA: My child, I have told you the truth. Don't be angry with your   350
husband!

> You were rejected when the curse
> that clouded memory made him cruel,
> but now darkness is lifted
> and your power is restored—   355
> a shadow has no shape
> in a badly tarnished mirror,
> but when the surface is clean
> it can easily be seen.

KING: Sir, here is the glory of my family! [*He takes the child by the hand.*]   360
MĀRĪCA: Know that he is destined to turn the wheel of your empire!

> His chariot will smoothly cross
> the ocean's rough waves
> and as a mighty warrior
> he will conquer the seven continents.   365
> Here he is called Sarvadamana,
> Tamer-of-everything;
> later when his burden is the world,
> men will call him Bharata, Sustainer.[3]

KING: Since you performed his birth ceremonies, we can hope for all   370
this.
ADITI: Sir, let Kaṇva be told that his daughter's hopes have been
fulfilled. Menakā, who loves her daughter, is here in attendance.
ŚAKUNTALĀ: [*To herself.*] The lady expresses my own desire.
MĀRĪCA: He knows everything already through the power of his   375
austerity.
KING: This is why the sage was not angry at me.
MĀRĪCA: Still, I want to hear his response to this joyful reunion.
Who is there?
DISCIPLE: [*Entering.*] Sir, it is I.   380
MĀRĪCA: Gālava, fly through the sky and report the joyous reunion to
Kaṇva in my own words: "The curse is ended. Śakuntalā and her son
are embraced by Duṣyanta now that his memory is restored."
DISCIPLE: As you command, sir! [*He exits.*]
MĀRĪCA: My son, mount your friend Indra's chariot with your wife   385
and son and return to your royal capital!
KING: As you command, sir!
MĀRĪCA: My son, what other joy can I give you?
KING: There is no greater joy, but if you will:

> May the king serve nature's good!   390
> May priests honor the goddess of speech!
> And may Śiva's dazzling power
> destroy my cycle of rebirths![4]
>
>   [*All exit.*]

3. Bharata is to become the emperor after whom ancient India (*Bhāratavarṣa*) is named. "Seven continents": those of the Hindu universe.
4. All Sanskrit plays end with a traditional verse called *bharatavākvya* (the utterance of [the sage] Bharata), in which the play's protagonist invokes the blessings of the gods on himself and the universal order.

The Classical Sanskrit Lyric

A short Sanskrit poem is like a snapshot—a vivid picture of a passing moment, created not in pixels but in words, seeking to forever capture an intensely emotional experience. Yet the numerous lyric poems preserved in classical Sanskrit also follow literary and social conventions that are quite different from those of lyric poetry in the European languages. One vital difference is that the Western lyric—from **Sappho** and **Catullus** to **Shakespeare** and Baudelaire—often allows a poet to speak in his or her individual voice, either directly or through a distinctive persona, to express unique personal feelings and private experiences. In contrast, the Sanskrit lyric usually requires a poet to represent even the most subjective emotions in an imaginative, impersonal, and universal form, at a remove from his or her actual personality and biography. This contrast is the result not of different values placed on the individual (as is often mistakenly assumed) but of very different conceptions of the nature and function of poetry.

The ten poets included in this cluster have long been recognized as "masters" of miniature poetry, and they all belong to the classical period of Sanskrit literature (the fourth to the eleventh century). They brought a wide range of personalities, life experiences,

and social backgrounds to their writing in varying historical circumstances. But each of them, including the three women poets—a rare and elusive category—display exceptional skill and imagination in the multifarious genre of short or lyric poetry.

The Sanskrit version of lyric poetry is called *subhāṣita*, something "beautifully expressed in language" within the limits of a single verse or condensed passage. There are two main types: poetry composed as a complete text in a short form, such as an epigram, a vignette, a eulogy, or a riddle, and poetry extracted from a longer work that can stand on its own, such as a description, a dramatic situation, a moment of epiphany, or even a piece of dialogue from a play. The most important criteria for recognizing a poem as a *subhāṣita* are that it be short (no longer than a verse or two or a few lines), self-contained (a complete thought, situation, or event), and well-crafted (the best and fewest words and images in the best order). At the same time, such a poem should capture a particular feeling, mood, or emotional state, using the power of suggestion to convey something larger than its literal meaning.

Since the middle of the first millennium, poets and scholars in Sanskrit have compiled large anthologies of brief poems and passages fitting this definition, drawing sometimes from a single author but more often from many authors. The chosen pieces may be composed in many different meters, genres, and styles; they usually cover a large variety of themes; and they capture different emotions and moods and their

This bronze sculpture (9th–10th century C.E., southern India) depicts Shakti, the Hindu goddess and Great Divine Mother, who personifies feminine powers, creation, and change (in Sanskrit, shak means "to be able" meaning "power").

many nuances. A short poem in Sanskrit, however, cannot represent the full essence of an emotional state. According to the classical Indian tradition, a fundamental emotional experience, like that of love or compassion or anger, is too large and complex to be conveyed in a single verse or passage; it can be properly expressed only when a work has enough room to spell out all its facets and stages. A lyric can do no more than give us a glimpse of a *rasa*, the state's essence, most often by creating a mood, suggesting a situation, or offering a single scene in an instant flash.

The lyric poems included here represent many features of Sanskrit *subhāṣita* poetry on a miniature scale. **Bhartṛhari**'s seven poems are drawn from a collection of his work, whereas the short poems by the other nine poets in this selection are all taken from a large multiauthor anthology—the *Subhāṣitaratnakośa* (*A Treasury of the Gems of Beautifully Crafted Verse*), compiled by the Buddhist monk Vidyākara just before 1100, probably at a monastery near today's India–Nepal border. A connoisseur of Sanskrit lyric in all its diversity, Vidyākara gathered 1,738 pieces by more than 200 poets, most of whom had lived during the preceding four centuries.

All the poems in our selection use indirect suggestion (*dhvani*) rather than mere description to create a mood or delineate a theme. The lyric poets of classical Sanskrit achieve their effects by focusing on the sensuous details of everyday experience, constructing verbal images that fully engage all the senses. For instance, **Bāṇa**'s "**The Horse Rises**" creates such an effective montage that we practically see a horse moving right before our eyes. The lyric poets also speak to us with wit and humor, combining precise observation—of the human and the natural worlds—with imaginative twists of language as well as thought or figuration (*alaṃkāra*). Their style is therefore realistic in its effects, even as it highlights the pleasures of perception, recognition, and remembrance.

BHARTṚHARI

Bhartṛhari (fifth century) was a court poet whose skill in composing short poems in various genres made him a model for subsequent generations. Collected soon after his lifetime, his poetry is preserved in the *Śatakatryam* (*The Three Centuries*, or *Three Hundred Poems*); it is celebrated most for its chiseled images, its melancholy tone, and its biting criticism of the ways of the world. The poems, complete in themselves (rather than excerpts from longer works), are grouped into three thematic sections or "centuries." In the original book, the poems in the first section deal with ethical and moral issues that arise in worldly affairs, those in the second focus on love and desire, while those in the third express disillusionment with the world and explore the complexities of renunciation. "I haven't been the cloud," for example, gives us unprecedented insight into a child's moral debt to its mother. "When she is out of sight" paints a small but exact picture of sexual attraction. And "For a moment he's a child" contemplates life's stages with the detachment of old age—foreshadowing **Shakespeare**'s image of "the seven ages of man" more than a thousand years later.

[I haven't been the cloud][1]

I haven't been the cloud
    that brings a rain of riches
to fields parched by lack of money;

I haven't been the powerful storm
    that devastates
a mountain-range of enemies;   5

I haven't even been the bee
    that buzzes around the lotus-faces
of sweet-eyed young women—

I've only been the axe   10
    that cut my mother's youth in two.

[When she's out of sight]

When she's out of sight,
    we desire to see her;
when we behold her,
    we want to hold her in a sweet embrace;
when this long-eyed beauty   5
    is in our arms,
we wish our separate bodies
    to be one at once—
without difference.

[When I knew little]

When I knew little,
I was like an elephant, blind in rut—
I know everything, I said,
    and proudly thought my mind was omniscient.

But when I kept the company   5
of wise people, little by little
I learned that *I'm a fool*—
    and the madness left me, like a fever.

To His Patron

You're the master of wealth,
of infinite means.
    I'm a master, too—
    of words and their infinite meanings.

---

1. Translated by Vinay Dharwadker. The poems are drawn from Bhartṛhari's *Śatakatryam*.

You're a great warrior—   5
   I'm a debater
   with limitless skill in the art
   of crushing my opponents' pride.
Those who serve you
are blinded by riches—   10
   but they also wish to hear me,
   to purify their minds.
You disregard me,
so I disregard you more—
   I'm gone, O king,   15
and greater than your presence at court
   is my absence from it.

[A human being]

A human being
is allotted a span
   of a hundred years.
Half of it
passes at night;   5
half of the other half
is consumed by childhood,
   old age;
the rest is spent
in serving others—   10
with illness, separation, grief
   for companions.
What's happiness, then,
for living things,
in a life that's like   15
   the bubbles in the froth
   on ocean waves?

[As the sun rises and sets]

As the sun rises and sets,
comes and goes,
life is whittled away
   day by day.
Engrossed in business,   5
weighed down by many tasks,
we don't know
   how time passes.
We witness birth, old age,
misfortune, death—   10

but they leave us
    unshaken.
The world has taken leave of its senses,
drunk on the heady wine
of worldliness   15
    and the gratification
    of the senses.

[For a moment he's a child]

For a moment he's a child—
for a moment, too, a youth—
a connoisseur of love and desire.

For a moment he's a beggar—
and—also for a moment—   5
a master of all wealth, all luxury.

At the end of his active life,
a man—his limbs wizened by age—
like an actor—his face painted with wrinkles—

retires behind the curtain of death.   10

THREE WOMEN POETS

VIKAṬANITAMBĀ

As is the case for the other women poets in classical Sanskrit and ancient Indian literature, we know practically nothing about Vikaṭanitambā beyond what we can infer from the few poetic pieces attributed to her. Her name indicates that she may have belonged to southern India; brief references by later poets and scholars provide evidence that she lived some- time between the fifth and seventh centuries. She treats erotic themes candidly, skillfully using images to show rather than tell and preferring the technique of suggestion over graphic description. In "As he came to bed," for example, she heightens the moment of passion by hinting at the act of love rather than providing dis- tracting details.

572[1]

As he came to bed the knot fell open of itself,
the dress held only somehow to my hips
by the strands of the loosened girdle.
So much I know, my dear;
but when within his arms, I can't remember who he was   5
or who I was, or what we did or how.

1. Translated by D. H. H. Ingalls. The number refers to the poem's position in Vidyākara's *Subhāṣitaratnakośa*.

BHĀVAKADEVĪ

Like Vikaṭanitambā, Bhāvakadevī probably belonged to the middle of the classical period of Sanskrit poetry, but we can surmise even less about her life or personality. Her literary name indicates that she was prized by her contemporaries and successors for her emotional sensitivity. In "At first our bodies knew," Bhāvakadevī memorably evokes her bitterness in marriage by referring only indirectly to its source in her husband's unfaithfulness.

646[1]

At first our bodies knew a perfect oneness,
but then grew two with you as lover
and I, unhappy I, the loved.
Now you are husband, I the wife,
what's left except of this my life,   5
too hard to break, to reap the bitter fruit,
your broken faith.

1. Translated by D. H. H. Ingalls. The number refers to the poem's position in Vidyākara's *Subhāṣitaratnakośa*.

VIDYĀ

Like Vikaṭanitambā and Bhāvakadevī, Vidyā is among the most frequently quoted women poets in classical Sanskrit, but only a few fragments of her poetry have survived. It is likely that she, too, lived between the fifth and the seventh centuries, but later than the other two women. Also like them, she is celebrated for her finely crafted love poems; they are explicitly set in the countryside, suggesting that she was more familiar with village life than with life at a royal court in a city. Her poem here is very oblique in its use of the technique of *dhvani*, or suggestion: a village housewife requests a neighbor to keep an eye on her hut while she goes out, ostensibly to fetch water from the river; but her expectation that she will return with visible scratches on her body indicates that she is really headed for a tryst with a lover on the riverbank.

807[1]

Good neighbor wife, I beg you
keep your eye upon my house a moment;
the baby's father hates to drink
the tasteless water from the well.
Better I go then, though alone, to the river bank   5
dark with *tamāla* trees and thick with canes,[2]
which with their sharp and broken stems
may scratch my breast.

1. Translated by D. H. H. Ingalls. The number refers to the poem's position in Vidyākara's *Subhāṣitaratnakośa*.
2. Vegetation characteristic of central India. In classical Sanskrit and later Indian lyric poetry, the riverbank—with shade and ground cover, not far from a village—is the favorite site for lovers' trysts, both before and after marriage.

BĀŅA

Bāṇa was a *brāhmaṇa* scholar and writer who served as the court poet of King Harsavardhana, the principal ruler in northern India (at Kannauj, near Delhi) during the first half of the seventh century. Bāṇa composed two works that were major turning points in Sanskrit literature: *Harṣacarita*, about his royal patron, the first full-length account of an Indian ruler by a contemporaneous biographer, and *Kādambarī*, the first work of novelistic fiction in an Indian language, written in poetic prose. Bāṇa's short poems are excerpted from longer works; they are noted for their careful craftsmanship, complicated figuration, and psychological realism.

1166[1]

The horse rises, stretches his hind legs,
lengthens his body by lowering his spine,
then arches his neck down, his head bent to his chest,
and shakes the dust from his mane;
his nostrils quiver under the muzzle, sniffing for grass;   5
he whinnies softly as he scrapes the ground with his hoof.

1174[2]

The puff of smoke from the forest fire,
black as the shoulder of a young buffalo,
curls slightly, spreads, is broken for a moment, falls;
then gathers its power gracefully, and rising thick,
it slowly lays upon the sky   5
its transient ornaments.

1305[3]

At evening having warmed himself to heart's content
before the public fire nor minded how he scorched his rags,
he then lies down to sleep on straw within the village shrine.
But the wind blows wet with sleet. His shivering
soon wakes him, for his half a cloak   5
is old and cold and full of holes. He moans,
huddling from one corner to the next.

---

1. The numbers assigned to Bāṇa's poems refer to their position in Vidyākara's *Subhā-ṣitaratnakośa*. This poem is translated by Vinay Dharwadker.
2. Translated by D. H. H. Ingalls.
3. Translated by D. H. H. Ingalls.

DHARMAKĪRTI

The poet Dharmakīrti (early seventh century) was a Buddhist; probably a monk in a monastery sponsored by a royal patron, he may have been the same person as the famous logician and philosopher of that name and time. His lyric pieces, which express specifically Buddhist values, stand out for their uncompromising wit, epigrammatic quality, and philosophical depth.

"Never to ask the wicked," for instance, is a perfect poetic expression of Buddhism's principles of moral firmness, mindfulness, and pursuit of the Middle Way, a path that avoids all extremes. But whether Hindu or Buddhist, the poet in classical India uses a short poem to create a specific mood, an aesthetic representation of a heightened emotional state. Thus, Dharmakīrti's "Your union with your lover" projects the mood of someone falling in love, highlighting the state of infatuation that occurs early in the process.

477[1]

Your union with your lover will be very brief,
like a dream or a magical illusion,
   and it will end in distaste:

I reflect on these truths a hundred times,
but my heart can't forget that girl   5
   with the eyes of a gazelle.

1213

Never to ask the wicked
for favors;
never to borrow
from a friend of meager means;

to be kind and loving in disposition,   5
just in action;
not to play foul
even at the hour of death;

to stand upright
in misfortune;   10
to follow in the footsteps
of the great:[2]

it's hard to do this—
as hard as it is to walk
on a sword's edge—   15

but good folks
don't need a sermon
about it.

1. Translated by Vinay Dharwadker. The numbers assigned to Dharmakīrti's poems refer to their position in Vidyākara's Subhā-ṣitaratnakośa.
2. Several core principles of Buddhism.

1729

There's no one riding ahead of me,[3]
there's no one behind me,
there are no fresh prints on this path:
    am I alone?

I see that the road   5
the ancients opened up long ago
is overgrown today:
    and I've definitely abandoned

that other—wide and easy—thoroughfare.

3. On the Buddhist monk's spiritual journey.

BHAVABHŪTĪ

Bhavabhūtī, a Hindu *brāhmaṇa*, was the best-known dramatist of the classical period after **Kālidāsa**. Most of the lyric verse with which he is represented in Sanskrit anthologies is taken from his two major poetic plays, *Mālatīmādhava* (*Mālatī and Mādhava*) and *Uttararāmacarita* (*King Rāma's Final Act*). He is celebrated for his individualism and experimentalism, for pushing his verse techniques and themes to an extreme, but he is especially renowned for his love poetry. "My love is married to me," which translates a single verse in Sanskrit, is a perfect example of Bhavabhūtī's originality and technical virtuosity: it projects the emotional state of a lover in a torrent of words and images resembling a modernist-style interior monologue, even as its content reminds us of a central theme in **Shakespeare**'s sonnets—a lover's desire for a complete and enduring "marriage of true minds" with his beloved. In thematic contrast, "The people in this world who scorn me" (one of the most frequently quoted lyrics in all of Sanskrit literature) gives us a unique image of a poet alienated from his own time and place who dreams of finding his ideal reader in posterity—a dream that this verse makes a reality for Bhavabhūtī himself. Many classical readers consider his "And as we talked together softly, secretly" to be the single most beautiful verse about love in Sanskrit poetry.

598[1]

And as we talked together softly, secretly,
cheek closely pressed to cheek
while our arms were busied in their tight embrace,
the night was gone without our knowing
the hours as they passed.   5

753[2]

A flood of tears blurs my vision time and again,
my limbs, numb from imagining her, are paralyzed,
my hand here breaks into a sweat, my fingers tremble,
as I try to paint my love:
                            tell me, how am I to do it?   5

783[3]

My love is married to me
as though she had melted into my mind

or was reflected in it or painted on it or sculpted in it
or set in it like a gem or cemented to it or engraved upon it

or as if she were nailed to it   5
by the five arrows of the god of love

or finely woven into the threads
of the very fabric of its thought

1731[4]

The people in this world who scorn me
no doubt have a special wisdom,
so I don't write for them:

instead, I write with the thought
that since the world is wide and time is endless,   5
one day someone will be born

whose nature is the same as mine.

1. The numbers assigned to Bhavabhūti's   2. Translated by Vinay Dharwadker.
poems refer to their positions in Vidyākara's   3. Translated by Vinay Dharwadker.
Subhāṣitaratnakośa. This poem is translated by 4. Translated by Vinay Dharwadker.
D. H. H. Ingalls.

YOGEŚVARA

Yogeśvara (ninth century) was a poet patronized by a king in eastern India in the late classical period. Probably from Bengal, he became the most celebrated lyric poet of "village and field"—of all aspects of country life—in Sanskrit. He captures the intangible qualities of village life and the countryside in several poems through a series of descriptions; but even when he seems to merely depict physical scenes in human and natural landscapes from a bird's-eye view, he succeeds in evoking powerful moods and emotions. Yogeśvara's range of emotions and situations is wider than we might expect: in "Now may one prize the peasant houses," we experience the sheer joy of harvest time; in "The warmth of their straw borne off by icy winds" we shiver with the peasants in the cold of incoming winter after threshing time; and in "When the rain pours down on the decrepit house" we feel deeply for the harried village wife struggling to survive in poverty.

257[1]

Now the great cloud cat,
darting out his lightning tongue,
licks the creamy moonlight
from the saucepan of the sky.

291

The days are sweet with ripening of sugar cane;
the autumn rice is high;
and brahmins, being overfed at feasts
to which the leading families invite them,
find that the heat grows hard to bear.[2]   5

314

Now may one prize the peasant houses
happy in the first harvest of the winter rice
and sweet with perfume from the jars of new-stored grain;
where the farmgirls take the pounder,
raise and shake and smoothly drop it,   5
their bracelets jingling as they raise their arms.

---

1. Translated by D. H. H. Ingalls. The numbers assigned to Yogeśvara's poems refer to their position in Vidyākara's *Subhāṣitaratnakośa*.

2. A satirical representation of the "parasitical" priestly caste. The poet is more sympathetic to the poor peasants in the countryside.

315

The fields where sesamum[3] has ripened
and now lies dry delight the doves;
the mustard turns to brown,
its flowers giving way to fruit;
the wind scatters the hemp   5
and makes the body shiver with its drops of sleet;
travelers, quarreling in empty argument,
huddle about the public fire.

318

The warmth of their straw borne off by icy winds,
time and again the peasants wake the fire
whose flame dies ever back, stirring with their sticks.
From the smoking bank of mustard chaff,
noisy with the crackling of the husks,   5
a penetrating odor spreads
to every corner of the threshing floor.

1163

The cat has humped her back;
mouth raised and tail curling,
she keeps one eye in fear upon the inside of the house;
her ears are motionless.
The dog, his mouthful of great teeth wide open   5
to the back of his spittle-covered jaws,
swells at the neck with held-in breath
until he jumps her.

1312

When the rain pours down on the decrepit house
she dries the flooded barley grits
and quiets the yelling children;
she bails out water with a potsherd
and saves the bedding straw.   5
With a broken winnowing basket on her head
the poor man's wife is busy everywhere.

3. Sesame.

MURĀRĪ

Like **Yogeśvara** before him, Murārī (mid-ninth century) was also a poet patronized by a king in eastern India. He may have belonged to Odisha or Orissa (the coastal region south of Bengal); without question he was a learned *brāhmaṇa* courtier, often praised for his highly elegant language, intricate craftsmanship, and wide-ranging literary allusions. His only surviving play is a dramatization of the *Rāmāyaṇa*, but his lyric poetry has also been preserved in quotations by later writers. Murārī's verses are dense and compact, full of surprising images and metaphors: in his two poems on moonlight, for example, he refers to "a group of carpenters" polishing "the tree of heaven," and to the power of a magnet to attract iron filings; in "My limbs are frail," he conjures up the idea that an aging man is "an actor in a farce," who is forced to wear "white hair / for makeup."

913[1]

Is the moonlight
      nothing but the powder
of the cleansing nut
      with which this sea of darkness
has been scrubbed bright,   5
      and its residue
precipitated to the bottom
      as shadows?
Or could the moon's rays
      be a group of carpenters   10
who polish the tree of heaven
      by planing it clean,
leaving its fallen bark
      for shadows?

958

As the moon ages,
      darkness covers the sky,
as if it were the smoke
      of opals about to burst into flames;
and though the sun   5

---

1. Translated by Vinay Dharwadker. The numbers assigned to Murārī's poems refer to their position in Vidyākara's *Subhāṣitaratnakośa*.

hasn't released its light as yet,
it draws out the bees
   imprisoned in the lotuses[2]
as a magnet attracts
   iron filings.   10

1019

O pearl free of flaws,
publish yourself—
   go furnish a house
or a king's necklace
   with your splendor,   5
bring your own virtues
   to fruit.
Why waste your life
   shut up in an oyster shell?
The ocean is enormous—   10
   who in this hole
can even calculate
   your worth?

1526

My limbs are frail,
my voice is weak,
   I suck up to the powerful—
I've been reduced
   to an actor in a farce.   5
I don't know
   in what new play
old age will cast me
   to play my part—
with this white hair   10
   for makeup.

1585

I remember this mountain,
I remember it well:
   here the jewels shine
so brightly at night

---

2. The lotus is photosensitive: its petals open at sunrise and close at sunset. The suggestion here is that if a bee happens to be feeding on a lotus at sundown, it may be "imprisoned" in the flower overnight when its petals close.

that the ravens gather 5
as if it were dawn,
and their cawing scares the owls
into the darkness of the caves;

here, when I took off
the wrap around your breasts, 10
you were so upset
that you tried to dress yourself
in the overhanging leaves,
and the forest-nymphs
amused themselves 15
by raising the branches
beyond your reach.

RĀJAŚEKHARA

Rājaśekhara (late ninth–early tenth century) was probably the son of a powerful court official in the Gurjara-Pratihara kingdom of north-central India. He was a poet and playwright composing in Sanskrit and in literary Prakrits, a theorist of literature, and a much-loved patron and friend of poets. He is especially famous because he publicly acknowledged his wife, Avantisundarī, as his equal in learning and taste, crediting her for his own literary success (the first Indian author to do so); he wrote his most famous play to please her, and she most likely hosted its first performance at their home. Rājaśekhara's short poems are verses taken from his plays; the best of them give us memorable images of the beauty of women and of the joys and intricacies of love. In "When people see her face," he pushes the technique of suggestion to an extreme with a clever inversion: he hints at a girl's extraordinary beauty by enumerating things to which her face, skin, eyes, eyebrows, and smile cannot be compared.

457[1]

When people see her face
    they stop talking about the moon;
when they see her skin,
    there's no more talk of gold.

1. The numbers assigned to Rājaśekhara's poems refer to their position in Vidyākara's *Subhā-ṣitaratnakośa*. This poem is translated by Vinay Dharwadker.

Waterlilies lose the contest   5
    against her eyes;
what's the nectar of moonlight
    when compared to her smile?
And the love god's bow is nothing
    when held up to her eyebrows.   10
But why say more—
    the truth is too well known,
that in the order of Creation
    the Creator shuns repetition.

336[2]

Youthfulness inscribes all her parts,
but is especially skillful in her eye's maturity,

for her gaze gathers all the expressions
of whichever man she chooses to look at,

and then conveys back to him   5
all that he feels as the one who looks at her,

whom she has found worthy of her gaze.

525[3]

The damsel of arched eyebrows,
gracefully circling as she whirls the yo-yo,
constructs three parasols:
with her skirt of southern silk,
with her beautiful pearl necklace,   5
and with her whirling braid of hair.

2. Translated by Vinay Dharwadker.   3. Translated by D. H. H. Ingalls.

SOMADEVA

eleventh century

How many different stories—truly different stories—have human beings invented? If we could read every story in the world and strip it down to its bare bones, how many distinct narrative cores would we find? Somadeva, a master storyteller from eleventh-century India, suggests that stories flow out of their tellers in streams and that all the streams, broadening into rivers, flow into an ocean of narrative that is potentially infinite.

LIFE

Somadeva was a *brāhmaṇa* scholar and courtier whose patron was Queen Sūryamati of Kashmir, an unusual woman with a strong interest in learning and the arts. In his prologue, he tells us that he compiled and composed the *Kathāsaritsāgara* to entertain the queen "when her mind had been wearied by the continuous study of the sciences." Trained in the traditional Indian disciplines of grammar, poetics and rhetoric, and philosophy (considered essential for any writer), he was exceptionally skilled in the crafts of both versification and narrative in the genre and style of Sanskrit *kāvya*.

Somadeva lived toward the end of the classical period of Indian literature, which stretched from about the fourth to the eleventh century. This period began with the establishment of the Gupta empire (320–550 C.E.) in northern India, and smaller imperial formations and kingdoms then emerged elsewhere on the subcontinent. The expansion of agriculture, mining and metallurgy, textile and handicraft production, and especially trade and commerce under the Gupta dynasty led to the rise of a wealthy and powerful merchant class and inaugurated several centuries of prosperity. Merchants became prominent citizens in busy port towns and cosmopolitan inland cities, investing in architecture and shipping; they crisscrossed the land on business and traveled widely overseas. Although they patronized pilgrimage sites and endowed temples and monasteries, their values were often secular and materialistic, focused on the acquisition and uses of wealth.

WORK

The large body of stories that Somadeva gathered in his *Kathāsaritsāgara* in the eleventh century reflected these developments. In contrast to earlier literature, which mostly emphasized frugality and otherworldliness in poorer economic conditions, the popular new tales of the classical period depicted a crowded world of traders, bankers, shopkeepers, con men, and thieves. Although the heroes and villains of these narratives are colorful characters, and their intrigues and wild schemes are often crooked, the stories themselves are concerned with more than the crass pursuit of wealth. Their recurrent concerns include the ancient Hindu themes of karma and rebirth, the memory of past lives and the power of curses, and *mokṣa*, the quest for liberation from worldly attachments. They also celebrate love and beauty in all their aspects, as well as the art of storytelling itself.

Somadeva brought together about 350 well-known stories, most of them transmitted from an earlier collection called *The Great Story* by Guṇāḍhya, which by the seventh century had been lost. Somadeva retold the tales in elegant Sanskrit couplets, in a heightened and distinctive style of verse narrative. The title, *Kathāsaritsāgara*, identifies the book as "the ocean into which the streams of narrative flow"; the work is thus intended to be, and has been received by generations of readers as, a large repository of all kinds of memorable stories. All the tales in the work are contained inside a main frame story, which recounts the adventures of Prince Naravāhanadatta, who becomes the king of the Vidyādharas (aerial spirits); the dominant themes of this narrative are the prince's acquisition of wealth and magical powers and his amorous relationships with several princesses and other beautiful women—including his great love, a courtesan he idealized. The nested short tales are told by various characters in the outer frame to amuse their friends, lovers, and spouses, in imitation of the stories that the great god Śiva is believed to tell his consort, Pārvatī, for her entertainment.

"The Red Lotus of Chastity," the story selected here, is a lively and entertaining example of the stories typically found in Somadeva's work and in classical literature in Sanskrit, as distinct from that language's earlier epic and religious narrative traditions. Though written much later, the story is set in the Gupta period of Indian history (probably in the fifth century); many of its characters belong to the wealthy merchant class of that time, and its action takes place in mainland India and on the islands of Indonesia. Its central theme is the value of fidelity in a marriage based on love, as it details the lengths to which a husband and a wife can go in order to remain faithful to each other.

The setup of the plot is unusual. A rich merchant of Bengal sails with his marriageable son to Indonesia to find a suitable bride for the young man in the community of wealthy Indian traders settled there. When they find a good match, however, the girl's father demurs because he does not want his beloved daughter to live far away, in India. But the girl has fallen completely in love and decides to marry the young man against her parents' wishes. Years later, after inheriting his father's trade in precious stones, the young husband decides to travel to another island in Indonesia; his wife, however, fears that he will be unfaithful to her during his long business trip abroad. To resolve their mutual anxieties, the couple appeals to the god Śiva, who gives them each a magical red lotus; if either of them commits adultery, then the lotus in the other's possession will wilt immediately.

What follows from this initial situation is a rollicking comedy of romantic love, sexual intrigue, and crafty worldliness. We encounter vivid characters—among them, the spoiled sons of a rich merchant, a corrupt Buddhist nun and her equally amoral protégée, and a wise and just king in a foreign land. The atmosphere is like that of a fairy tale, in which extraordinary events transform the destinies of ordinary people. But the characters themselves are realistically delineated and belong to social types that became standard figures both in India and abroad: Yogakaraṇḍikā and Siddhīkarī in "The Red Lotus of Chastity" are forerunners of the errant monks and nuns in later writing (such as **Chaucer's *Canterbury Tales***), and Yogakaraṇḍikā, who makes a career of procuring women for men, also foreshadows the bawd in European Renaissance literature. The story's heroine, Devasmitā, bravely disguises herself as a man and undertakes a perilous journey overseas to foil an evil plot, to prove her own fidelity, and to test the love of her husband, Guhasena. She reminds us of other women characters performing gender as a male to gain mobility that would otherwise be denied to a woman.

Like the earlier Buddhist *Jātaka* tales and Hindu animal fables of the **Pañcatantra**, the more secular and entertaining stories of the *Kathāsaritsāgara* migrated from India to the Middle East and later to Europe. Besides the examples mentioned above, characters, situations, and plots from Somadeva's narratives turn up in works ranging from **Boccaccio's** *Decameron* in the fifteenth century and **Shakespeare** at the end of the sixteenth century to Salman Rushdie's *Haroun and the Sea of Stories* (1990), which explicitly acknowledges its debt to the original "ocean of stories." Somadeva's eleventh-century work is especially famous as a model for *The Thousand and One Nights*.

From Kathāsaritsāgara[1]

The Red Lotus of Chastity

In this world is a famous port, Tāmraliptī,[2] and there lived a rich merchant whose name was Dhanadatta. He had no sons, so he assembled many brahmins, prostrated himself before them, and requested: "See to it that I get a son!"

"That is not at all difficult," said the priests, "for the brahmins can bring about everything on earth by means of the scriptural sacrifices.[3]

"For example," they continued, "long ago there was a king who had no sons, though he had one hundred and five women in his seraglio. He caused a special sacrifice for a son to be performed, and a son was born to him. The boy's name was Jantu, and in the eyes of all the king's wives he was the rising new moon. Once when he was crawling about on all fours, an ant bit him on the thigh, and the frightened child cried out. The incident caused a terrific disturbance in the seraglio, and the king himself lamented—'My son! O my son!'—like a commoner. After a while, when the ant had been removed and the child comforted, the king blamed his own anxiety on the fact that he had only one son.

" 'There must be a way to have more sons,' he thought, and in his grief he consulted the brahmins. They replied: 'Indeed, Your Majesty, there is one way by which you can have more sons. Kill the son you have and sacrifice all his flesh in the sacred fire. When the royal wives smell the burning flesh, they will all bear sons.' The king had everything done as they said and got as many sons as he had wives.

"Thus with the help of a sacrifice," concluded the brahmins, "we can bring you, too, a son."

So at the advice of the brahmins, merchant Dhanadatta settled on a stipend for their sacerdotal services, and the priests performed the sacrifice for him. Subsequently a son was born to the merchant. The boy, who was given the name Guhasena, grew up in due time, and his father Dhanadatta was seeking a wife for him. And the merchant voyaged with his son to the Archipelago[4] to find a bride, though he pretended that it was just a business expedition. In the Archipelago he asked the daughter of a prominent merchant, Dharmagupta, a girl named

---

1. Translated by J. A. B. van Buitenen.
2. During the Gupta era, an important port on the Bay of Bengal, a center for north India's trade
with south India and Southeast Asia.
3. That is, those described in the Vedas.
4. Islands of Southeast Asia and Indonesia.

Devasmitā, On-Whom-the-Gods-Have-Smiled, in marriage for his son Guhasena. Dharmagupta, however, did not favor the alliance, for he loved his daughter very much and thought that Tāmraliptī was too far away. But Devasmitā herself, as soon as she had set eyes on Guhasena, was so carried away by his qualities that she decided to desert her parents. Through a companion of hers she arranged a meeting with the man she loved and sailed off from the island at night with him and his father. On their arrival in Tāmraliptī they were married; and the hearts of husband and wife were caught in the noose of love.

Then father Dhanadatta died, and, urged by his relatives to continue his father's business, Guhasena made plans for a voyage to the island of Cathay.[5] Devasmitā, however, did not approve of his going, for she was a jealous wife and naturally suspected that he would love another woman. So with his relatives urging him on and his wife opposing, Guhasena was caught in the middle and could not get on with his business.

Thereupon he went to a temple and took a vow of fasting. "Let God in this temple show me a way out," he thought. Devasmitā came along, and she took the same vow. God Śiva[6] appeared to both of them in a dream. He gave them two red lotuses and spoke: "Each of you must keep this lotus in his hand. If one of you commits adultery while the other is far away, the lotus in the other's hand will wither away. So be it!" The couple woke up, and each saw in the other's hand the red lotus which was an image of the lover's heart.

So, carrying his lotus, Guhasena departed, and Devasmitā stayed home watching hers. Presently Guhasena reached Cathay and went about his business, trading in precious stones. But the lotus he carried around in his hands aroused the curiosity of four merchant's sons who noticed that the flower never seemed to fade. They tricked him into accompanying them home and gave him quantities of mead to drink: when he was drunk, they asked him about the lotus, and he told them. Calculating that the merchant's trade in precious stones would take a long time to be completed, the mischievous merchant's sons plotted together, and, their curiosity aroused, all four set sail at once for Tāmraliptī, without telling anybody, to see if they could not undo the chastity of Guhasena's wife. Reconnoitering in Tāmraliptī, they sought out a wandering nun,[7] Yogakaraṇḍikā, who lived in a Buddhist monastery. They ingratiated themselves with her and proposed, "Reverend Madam, if you can bring about what we wish, we shall reward you richly."

"Of course, you boys want some girl in town," said the nun. "Tell me. I shall see to it. I have no desire for money, because I have a clever pupil named Siddhīkarī,[8] and thanks to her I have amassed a great fortune."

"How is that? You have acquired great wealth through the favor of your pupil?" the merchant's sons asked.

"If you are curious to hear the story, my sons," said the nun, "I shall tell you. Listen.

"Some time ago a merchant came to town from the North. While he was staying here, my pupil, in disguise, contrived to get herself employed in his house as

---

5. Not China but an island in Southeast Asia or Indonesia.
6. The destroyer god (Śiva), one of the two great gods of Hinduism.
7. Buddhist monks and nuns must have no possessions and are required to live on alms, which they collect by wandering.
8. She Who Can Accomplish What One Desires.

a maid of all work; and as soon as the merchant had come to trust her, she stole all the gold he had in his house and sneaked away at dawn. A drummer[9] saw her leave town and, his suspicions aroused by her fast pace, started with his drum in his hand to pursue and rob her in turn. Siddhīkarī had reached the foot of a banyan tree when she saw the drummer approach, and the cunning girl called out to him in a miserable voice: 'I have quarreled with my husband, and now I have run away from home to kill myself. Could you fasten the noose for me, my friend?'

" 'If she is going to hang herself, then why should I kill the woman?' thought the drummer, and he tied a noose to the tree. He stepped on his drum, put his head through the noose, and said. 'This is the way to do it.' The same instant Siddhīkarī kicked the drum to pieces—and the drummer himself perished in the noose. But at that moment the merchant came looking for her, and from a distance he discerned the maid who had stolen his entire fortune. She saw him come, however, and immediately climbed up the tree and hid among the leaves. When the merchant came to the tree with his servants, he saw only the drummer dangling from the tree, for Siddhīkarī was nowhere in sight.

" 'Can she have climbed up the tree?' the merchant questioned, and immediately one of the servants went up.

" 'I have always loved you, and here you are, with me in a tree!' whispered Siddhīkarī. 'Darling, all the money is yours. Take me!' And she embraced him and kissed him on the mouth and bit the fool's tongue off with her teeth. Overcome with pain the servant tumbled out of the tree, spitting blood, and cried something unintelligible that sounded like 'la-la-la.' When he saw him, the merchant thought that the man was possessed by a ghost, and in terror he fled home with his servants. No less terrified, Siddhīkarī, my pupil, climbed down from the top of the tree and went home with all the money."

The nun's pupil entered just as her mistress finished, and the nun presented her to the merchant's sons.

"But now tell me the truth," resumed the nun, "which woman do you want? I shall prepare her for you at once!"

"Her name is Devasmitā," they replied, "Guhasena's wife. Bring her to bed with us!" The nun promised to do so and gave the young men lodging in her house.

The wandering nun ingratiated herself with the servants at Guhasena's house by giving them delicacies and so on, and thus she gained entrance to the house with her pupil. But when she came to the door of Devasmitā's chambers, a dog which was kept on a chain at the door barked at her, though never before had the bitch been known to bark. Then Devasmitā saw her, and wondering who the woman was that had come, she sent a servant girl to inquire and then herself conducted the nun into her chamber. When she was inside, the nun gave Devasmitā her blessing, and after courteous amenities for which she found a pretext, the wicked woman said to the chaste wife: "I have always had a desire to see you, and today I saw you in a dream.[1] That is why I have come to visit you. I see that you are separated from your husband, and my heart suffers for you; if youth and beauty are deprived of love's pleasures, they are fruitless."

---

9. A *domba*, an executioner or low-caste functionary in cemeteries.

1. Holy persons are thought to have supernatural gifts, such as the ability to dream true events and interpret them.

With such talk the nun gained Devasmitā's confidence, and after having chatted awhile she returned to her own home. The next day the nun took a piece of meat covered with sneezing powder and went to Devasmitā's house. She gave the meat to the dog at the door, and the animal at once swallowed it. The sneezing powder caused the dog's eyes to run, and the animal sneezed incessantly. Then the nun entered Devasmitā's apartment, and once she had settled down to her hostess' hospitality, the shrew began to weep. Pressed by Devasmitā she said, as if with great reluctance; "Oh, my daughter, go and look outside at your dog; she is crying. Just now she recognized me from a former life[2] when we knew each other, and she burst out in tears. Pity moved me to weep with her."

Devasmitā looked outside the door and saw the dog which seemed to be weeping. "What miracle is this?" she wondered for the space of a moment. Then the nun said: "Daughter, in a former life both she and I were the wives of a brahmin. Our husband had to travel everywhere at the king's orders as his envoy, and while he was gone, I carried on with other men as I pleased, to avoid frustrating the senses and the element. Our highest duty, you know, is to yield to the demands of sense and element. That is why I in this present life have the privilege of remembering past existences. But she in her ignorance guarded her chastity, and so she has been reborn a bitch, though she does remember her other life."

"What kind of moral duty is that?" thought Devasmitā, who was clever enough. "This nun has some crooked scheme afoot!" Then she said: "Reverend Madam, how long I have been ignorant of my real duty! You must introduce me to some handsome man!"

"There are some merchant's sons from the Archipelago who are staying in town," said the nun. "I shall bring them to you if you want."

Overjoyed the nun went home. And Devasmitā said secretly to her servant girls: "I am sure that some merchant's sons have seen the never-fading lotus which my husband carries in his hand, and out of curiosity they have asked him about it when he was drinking. Now the scoundrels have come here from their island to seduce me and have engaged that depraved nun as their go-between. Fetch me immediately some liquor loaded with Datura[3] drug and go and have a dog's-paw branding iron made." The maids did as their mistress told them, and one of them, at Devasmitā's instructions, dressed up as her mistress.

Meanwhile the nun selected one of the four merchant's sons, who each commanded to be taken first, and brought him, disguised as her own pupil, to Devasmitā's house. There she bade him go inside and went away unobserved. The maid who posed as Devasmitā gave the young merchant with all due courtesies the drugged liquor to drink, and the drink (as though it were his own depravity) robbed him of his senses. Then the girls stripped him of everything he wore and robed him monastically in air.[4] Thereupon they branded the dog's-paw iron on his forehead, dragged him outside, and threw him in a cesspool. In the last hours of night he came to his senses and found himself sunk in the cesspool—the very image of the Avīci hell[5] which his own wickedness had brought on! He got up, bathed, and, fingering the mark on his forehead, he returned naked to the nun's house.

2. The memory of past lives is a gift, enabling the rememberer to make amends for evil deeds of such lives.
3. A narcotic plant.

4. The Digambaras ("clad in air"), a major sect of Jaina monks, wander naked.
5. One of the many hells described in Hindu and Buddhist mythology.

"I won't be the only ridiculous one!" he thought, and so he told his brothers in the morning that he had been robbed on his way back. Pretending a headache from his long night and deep drinking, he kept his marked forehead wrapped in a turban's cloth.

The second merchant's son who went to Devasmitā's house that night was manhandled in the same way. He too came home naked and said that, despite leaving his jewelry at home, he had been stripped by robbers as he came back. And the next morning he too kept his head bandaged, supposedly because of a headache, to conceal the brand on his forehead. All four of them, though they dissimulated everything, were castigated, branded, plundered, and put to shame in the same fashion. Without disclosing to the nun how they had been maltreated ("Let the same thing happen to her!"), they departed.

The next day the nun, who thought that her plan had succeeded, went with her pupil to Devasmitā's house. With a show of gratitude Devasmitā courteously poured them drinks with Datura, and when the nun and her pupil had passed out, the chaste wife cut off their noses and ears[6] and tossed them outside in a sewage pit.

But then Devasmitā began to worry. "Might those merchant's sons now kill my husband in revenge?" She went to her mother-in-law and told her everything that had happened.

"Daughter," said her mother-in-law, "you have done well. But something bad may now happen to my son."

"Then I shall save him as Śaktimatī once saved her husband with her presence of mind!"

"And how did she save her husband?" asked her mother-in-law. "Tell me, my daughter."

"In my country," Devasmitā began, "we have a great Yakṣa[7] who is famous under the name of Maṇibhadra. He is very powerful, and our ancestors have built him a temple in our town. My countrymen come to this temple, each with his own presents, to offer them to Maṇibhadra in order to gain whatever it is they wish. There is a custom that any man who is found in this temple at night with another man's wife is kept with the woman in the sanctum of Maṇibhadra for the rest of the night, and the next morning they are brought to court, where they will confess to their behavior and be thrown in jail.

"One night a merchant named Samudradatta was caught in the act with another man's wife by one of the temple guards. The guard led the merchant away with the woman and threw them into the sanctum of the temple where they were securely chained. After a while the merchant's faithful wife, Śaktimatī, who was very ingenious, got to know what had happened. Immediately she took an offering for pūjā worship[8] and, disguised, went out into the night to the temple, full of self-confidence and chaperoned by her confidantes. When she came to the temple, the pūjā priest, greedy for the stipend she offered him, opened the gates for her, after informing the captain of the guard. Inside the temple she found her husband who was caught with the woman. She dressed the woman up to pass for

6. In Hindu law a punishment for women who commit adultery.
7. A type of demigod common to Hindu, Bud-
dhist, and Jaina mythologies.
8. The rite of worshipping holy or noble persons, guests, and images of gods and goddesses.

herself and told her to get out. The woman went out into the night in her disguise, and Śaktimatī herself stayed in the sanctum with her husband. When in the morning the king's magistrates came to examine them, they all saw that the merchant had only his wife with him. The king, on learning the fact, punished the captain of the guard and released the merchant from the temple as from the yawning mouth of death.

"So did Śaktimatī save her husband that time with her wits," concluded Devasmitā, and the virtuous wife added in confidence to her mother-in-law, "I shall go and save my husband with a trick, as she did."

Then Devasmitā and her maids disguised themselves as merchants,[9] boarded a ship on the pretext of business, and departed for Cathay where her husband was staying. And on her arrival she saw her husband Guhasena—reassurance incarnate!—in the midst of traders. Guhasena saw her too, from a distance, and drank deep of the male image of his beloved wife. He wondered what such a delicate person could have to do with the merchant's profession.

Devasmitā went to the local king and announced: "I have a message. Assemble all your people." Curious, the king summoned all citizens and asked Devasmitā, who still wore her merchant's disguise, "What is your message?"

"Among these people here," said Devasmitā, "are four runaway slaves of mine. May it please Your Majesty to surrender them."

"All the people of this town are assembled here," replied the king. "Look them over, and when you recognize your slaves, take them back."

Thereupon she arrested on their own threshold the four merchant's sons, whom she had manhandled before. They still wore her mark on their foreheads.

"But these are the sons of a caravan trader," protested the merchants who were present. "How can they be your slaves?"

"If you do not believe me," she retorted, "have a look at their foreheads. I have branded them with a dog's paw."

"So we shall," they said. They unwound the turbans of the four men, and they all saw the dog's paw on their foreheads. The merchants' guild was ashamed, and the king surprised.

"What is behind this?" the king asked, questioning Devasmitā in person, and she told the story, and they all burst out laughing.

"By rights they are your slaves, my lady," said the king, whereupon the other merchants paid the king a fine and the virtuous woman a large ransom to free the four from bondage. Honored by all upright people, Devasmitā, with the ransom she had received and the husband she had rejoined, returned to their city Tāmraliptī and never again was she separated from the husband she loved.

9. The motif of a woman disguising herself as a man, especially to perform a daring feat, is common in folk literature. Devasmitā bears a striking resemblance to more than one of Shakespeare's heroines.

III

Medieval China

The "Middle" in the European "Middle Ages" signifies the time between the Roman Empire and the Renaissance, a transitional period that has often been seen as a time of relative intellectual and cultural stagnation. In the case of China the situation is quite the reverse. If we use Western period terms, the *middle* of a Chinese "Middle Age" would mean "central." It is a period when Chinese thought and literature reached what many regard as their highest forms. During the medieval Period of Disunion (third through sixth centuries), a notoriously tumultuous age of political division, Buddhism, which had spread from India to China, took deep root in Chinese society, stimulating renewed interest in Daoist philosophy and the rise of religious Daoism. During the following two great medieval Chinese dynasties, the Tang and the Song (seventh through thirteenth centuries), classical Chinese poetry and prose reached an unprecedented height to which later ages would look back with awe and a sense that the achievements of its greatest writers could never be matched.

CHINA'S PERIOD OF DISUNION (220–589)

In the second century the Han Empire (206 B.C.E.–220 C.E.) was crumbling. Natural disasters, bad labor conditions, and political intrigues in the central

A Southern Song Dynasty hand scroll, "Streams and Mountains Under Fresh Snow," attributed to Liu Songnian, twelfth century.

government all helped weaken it. In 184 C.E. the leader of a Daoist religious cult called "Way of Great Peace" staged a major insurrection, gathering hundreds of thousands of followers who attacked local government offices throughout the country. Although the rebellion was suppressed by local armies initially encouraged by the Han government, it ultimately fostered the rise of warlords, often former Han generals, and eventually led to the division of China into three kingdoms: Shu in the west, Wu in the south, and Wei in the northern heartland under the Cao family. The battles of the "Three Kingdoms Period" (220–280) caught the Chinese imagination, and their heroes have lived on in poetry, prose romances, and, recently, epic film series. The empire was briefly reunified by the short-lived Western Jin Dynasty, but in 316 non-Chinese invaders raided the north and the great aristocratic clans fled to the area around Nanjing, where a new government was set up by a prince of the royal house. For the first time in Chinese history non-Chinese rulers took control of China's traditional northern heartland—around the old capitals of Chang'an and Luoyang—forcing the Chinese court aristocracy to flee to the southeastern hinterland. The émigrés from the north, which had been the center of Chinese civilization for more than fifteen hundred years, found themselves suddenly in the rustic southeastern provinces, while their ancestral graves and estates were taken over by northern "barbarians." In exile of sorts, the Chinese aristocracy developed a strong cultural pride and sense of "Chineseness." Cultural legitimacy came to be defined not by the occupation of a place (the North China plain) but by the possession of a portable tradition. Although the northern ruling houses were "barbarian" in the

eyes of the former Chinese aristocracy, they were no wild nomads. Their subjects were a largely Chinese population and some, like the Northern Wei Dynasty (386–534) of the Xianbei people, very astutely mixed tribal traditions with Chinese customs. China remained divided partly under foreign rule for centuries: China's north was split among various non-Chinese states and dynasties, while the south was ruled by a succession of short-lived Chinese dynasties.

NEW RELIGIONS OF SALVATION

The non-Chinese rulers of the north also understood that they needed a political tool to legitimate their governance over an ethnically mixed populace and to create harmony among peoples of various social and ethnic backgrounds—a tool that, ideally, was foreign like them: Buddhism. Buddhism originated in India around 500 B.C.E. when a prince of the Shakya clan in a small state in what today is south Nepal turned away in disgust from his privileged palace life, subjected himself to ascetic hardships, and eventually gained enlightenment. For the rest of his life he wandered and spread his teachings. In his first sermon he preached the "Four Noble Truths," central to all of the numerous schools of Buddhism that developed over time. He claimed that (1) pain, suffering, and anxiety are inevitable parts of human life; (2) they are caused by human desires and attachments; (3) it is possible for humans to overcome these attachments; and (4) humans can triumph over them by following the simple trajectory of the "Eightfold Path," a regime of psychological and physical self-control that enables individuals to leave the cycle of constant rebirths and reach "buddhahood," the passing into nirvana (nothingness), like the historical Buddha himself.

The extraordinary success of Buddhism in China and, spreading from there, throughout East Asia is one of the great surprises of Asian history. China became Buddhist even though there were no forced conversions imposed by missionaries and traditional Chinese Confucian values and Buddhist practices were often at odds. Becoming a Buddhist monk meant betraying on the personal and political levels the duties of Confucian filial piety: you gave up the chances to continue the family line, and by shaving your head you mutilated the body that you had received from your parents and that you needed to return to your ancestors unharmed when leaving the world; even worse, as a follower of the Buddha you could claim to be no longer subordinate to state power, the paternal authority of the political world.

Buddhism radically altered the face of China. Brought by merchants active in the east–west trade along the so-called Silk Road, Buddhism was a religion for the masses. Like Christianity, which was gaining believers around the same time at the other end of Eurasia, it promised personal salvation and escape from a world of suffering, and its soothing ethics of compassion and mercy included people of all social classes, men and women alike. Chinese cities became home to large temple complexes that hosted religious services and addressed the needs of education and charity; the countryside was suddenly dotted with monasteries and colossal Buddha statues carved in stone (images of deities in human form had not existed in China, and the Chinese found the innovation so strange that they called the new religion "the teaching of icons"). Buddhism mobilized

The Giant Wild Goose Pagoda in a Buddhist temple complex in Chang'an (modern-day Xi'an), China, was built during the Tang Dynasty. This is where the Chinese monk Xuanzang, whose adventure-filled trip to India found its way into the novel *Journey to the West* (included in Vol. D), deposited the Buddhist scriptures he had acquired in the homeland of Buddhism.

people as pilgrims set out on travels in search of holy places of Buddhism, scriptures, devotional objects, and wise teachers in China and even India. The new faith was welcomed by the people and patronized by rulers. Monasteries were not taxed, and monks and nuns were not required to perform labor service or military duty.

While Buddhism clashed with Confucian values, it resonated with Daoism in its promise of personal salvation from a corrupt world. Daoism was indigenous to China and took various forms before the arrival of Buddhism. Its intellectual foundations rested on two early Chinese "Master Texts," **Laozi** and **Zhuangzi**.

But Daoism also included a variety of practices, such as methods to promote longevity, certain breathing and sexual techniques, gymnastics, herbal medicine, and alchemy; and the leaders of some popular movements mobilized the underprivileged and poor for their own purposes under the banner of Daoist prophecies. The arrival of Buddhism in China transformed Daoism from an amorphous phenomenon into an organized religion and institution. Daoism now acquired a set of canonical texts (recorded from revelations), temples and monasteries with a celibate clergy, and a vast pantheon of Daoist gods, all on the model of the Buddhist canon of scriptures, the Buddhist monasteries, and the large pantheon of bodhisattvas (Buddhas who returned to the human world in order to help others attain buddhahood). Buddhism and Daoism were in fierce competition over patronage and audiences in part because their teachings were so similar. The closeness of Buddhist and Daoist ideas and teachings is evident from the frequency with which the earliest Chinese translations of Buddhist sutras—sermons of the Buddha recorded in Sanskrit and other Indian languages—used Daoist terminology to express new Buddhist concepts. This appropriation of Buddhism as a form of Daoism took a sudden turn in the fourth century when the brilliant Buddhist scholar and monk Kumārajīva (350–413), born of an Indian father and a Central Asian mother, was abducted by a Chinese ruler and set to work on translating Buddhist texts into Chinese; his abduction marked the beginning of large state-sponsored workshops that translated countless scriptures into Chinese. Kumārajīva rejected the earlier Daoist terminology, creating new words for the foreign Buddhist concepts out of transcriptions of the Sanskrit words into Chinese. Buddhism had become an independent cultural force in China.

The arrival of Buddhism and the emergence of the Daoist church led to a veneration of the ideal of the "recluse." Some recluses were true hermits, living far away from civilization; others, like the "Seven Sages of the Bamboo Grove," cultivated a form of libertine resistance to social norms; still others, such as the poet-recluse **Tao Qian**, decided to live on his family farm and not serve in government.

THE NEW COSMOPOLITAN EMPIRES OF THE SUI AND TANG (589–907)

In the long run it was a northern dynasty, the Sui (589–618), that reunified China; these rulers were quickly supplanted by another northern dynasty, the Tang (618–907). The two dynasties forged a new culture that combined northern and southern traditions. The Sui emperors razed the old southern capital near Nanjing and forced the southern aristocracy to relocate to the old northern capital of Chang'an. Between the Yangzi and the Yellow River they built a canal that became a crucial means to transport goods and people between the north and south, reconnecting territory that had been divided for more than three centuries. But its attempt to recover the possessions of the Han Empire, in particular repeated unsuccessful campaigns against Korea, brought down the dynasty. The Sui Dynasty was overthrown by a provincial governor who founded his own dynasty, the Tang.

The long Tang Dynasty was an age of cultural confidence and, initially, of expansion, as Tang armies pushed outward at every frontier. Particularly important was the expansion to the northwest and control of the trade routes to the west. Chang'an, an old capital now clothed in new splendor, mirrored the cosmopolitan empire it controlled. It was laid out on a grid pattern, with a mighty walled palace city at its north and two bustling markets to the south. The city teemed with foreigners, who came to the Chinese capital by the Central Asian land routes or the South Asian maritime trade routes as merchants, diplomatic envoys, pilgrims, monks, or adventurers. Nestorian Christians, Zoroastrians, Jews, and Arab merchants mingled with Japanese monks and Persian doctors. The people of Chang'an quickly adopted new hairstyles, new games such as polo, and new musical instruments, importing exotic melodies and dances from China's Central Asian "west."

The Tang was an age of innovation. Tea became a major commercial crop, and its consumption spread from China to East Asia via monks who used it to stay awake during long hours of meditation and sutra recitation. New Buddhist schools appeared, such as Chan (better known in its Japanese form, "Zen"), an iconoclastic form of Buddhism that espoused mind-to-mind transmission of truth, claiming that the study of scriptures was of no use. Poetry by one elusive recluse named **Hanshan** ("**Cold Mountain**"), whose very existence is shrouded in mystery, exemplified this new trend.

The most influential invention during the Tang Dynasty was printing. A printed copy of the Buddhist Diamond Sutra, dated 868, is considered the world's oldest printed book. Sealed in a cave in remote Dunhuang, a Silk Road oasis in northwest China some 1100 miles from Chang'an, it was discovered by archaeologists in the early twentieth century.

The Tang period is most famous for its poetry. The civil service examination used by the Tang in recruiting its elites for government service came to require the composition of poetry, and it also became an integral part of social life—a medium of social exchange. In few other places in the world has lyric poetry ever enjoyed such centrality, and a number of major poets emerged whose works have made them renowned in China to this day. A great poem might deal with large philosophical issues, but it was just as likely to describe a meeting with an old friend. Poetry was seen as a way to record both an individual's personality and a country's historic moments. The writings of **Wang Wei, Li Bo**, and **Du Fu** came to exemplify poetic perfection, in different styles. The Tang was also the first period to witness the flowering of prose tales, such as **Yuan Zhen**'s "**The Story of Yingying**," which became a fertile source for later Chinese stories and drama.

In the 750s, the confidence of the Tang Dynasty was broken during the reign of one its most splendid emperors, Xuanzong. Xuanzong gave military governors in frontier regions great powers, hoping thereby to strengthen the defense of the empire. An able administrator, patron of the arts, and even scholar in his own right—he wrote a commentary on *Laozi* and set up a school for examinations in Daoist scriptures—Xuanzong was greatly devoted to a concubine of lower status, Yang Guifei (or "Prized Consort Yang"), whose family increasingly began to occupy strategic official positions. An Lushan, an associate of Yang's kinsmen, rebelled in 755, took Chang'an, and put the emperor to flight. Threatened by his own armies, Xuanzong was forced to witness the execution of his beloved concubine. Although the rebellion was soon put down, the dynasty never quite regained its former authority. Later writers looked back with melancholy to Xuanzong's long and prosperous reign, and the tragic love of Xuanzong and Yang Guifei lived on in later literature such as **Bo Juyi**'s "**Song of Lasting Regret**."

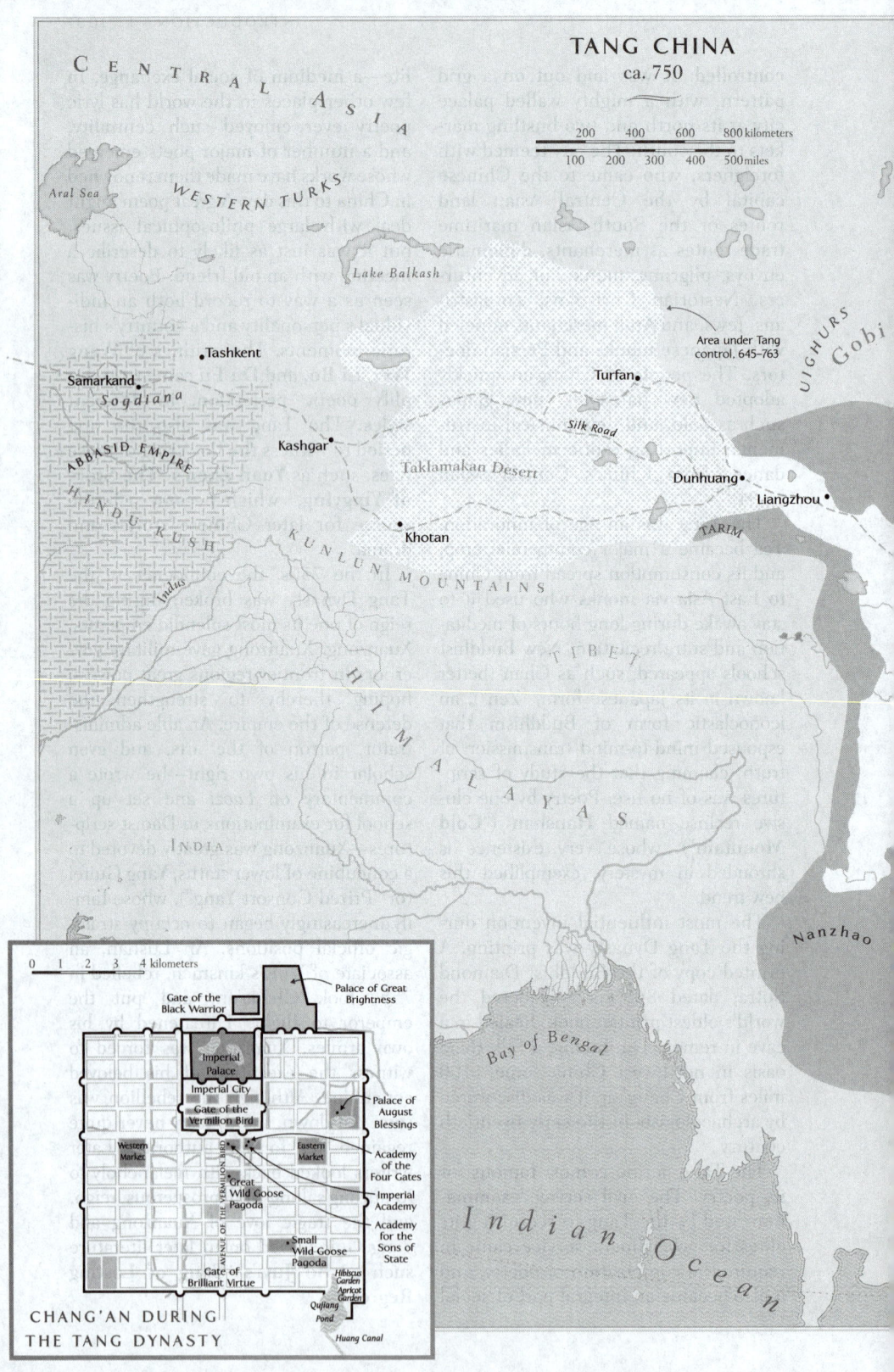

TANG CHINA
ca. 750

| 200 | 400 | 600 | 800 kilometers |
| 100 | 200 | 300 | 400 | 500 miles |

Area under Tang control. 645–763

CENTRAL ASIA

Aral Sea

WESTERN TURKS

Lake Balkash

UIGHURS

Gobi

Tashkent

Samarkand

Sogdiana

ABBASID EMPIRE

HINDU KUSH

Kashgar

Taklamakan Desert

Turfan

Silk Road

Dunhuang

Liangzhou

TARIM

Khotan

KUNLUN MOUNTAINS

Indus

TIBET

H I M A L A Y A S

INDIA

Nanzhao

Bay of Bengal

I n d i a n   O c e a n

CHANG'AN DURING THE TANG DYNASTY

| 0 | 1 | 2 | 3 | 4 kilometers |

Gate of the Black Warrior

Palace of Great Brightness

Imperial Palace

Imperial City

Gate of the Vermilion Bird

Palace of August Blessings

Western Market

AVENUE OF THE VERMILION BIRD

Great Wild Goose Pagoda

Eastern Market

Academy of the Four Gates

Imperial Academy

Academy for the Sons of State

Small Wild Goose Pagoda

Gate of Brilliant Virtue

Hibiscus Garden

Apricot Garden

Qujiang Pond

Huang Canal

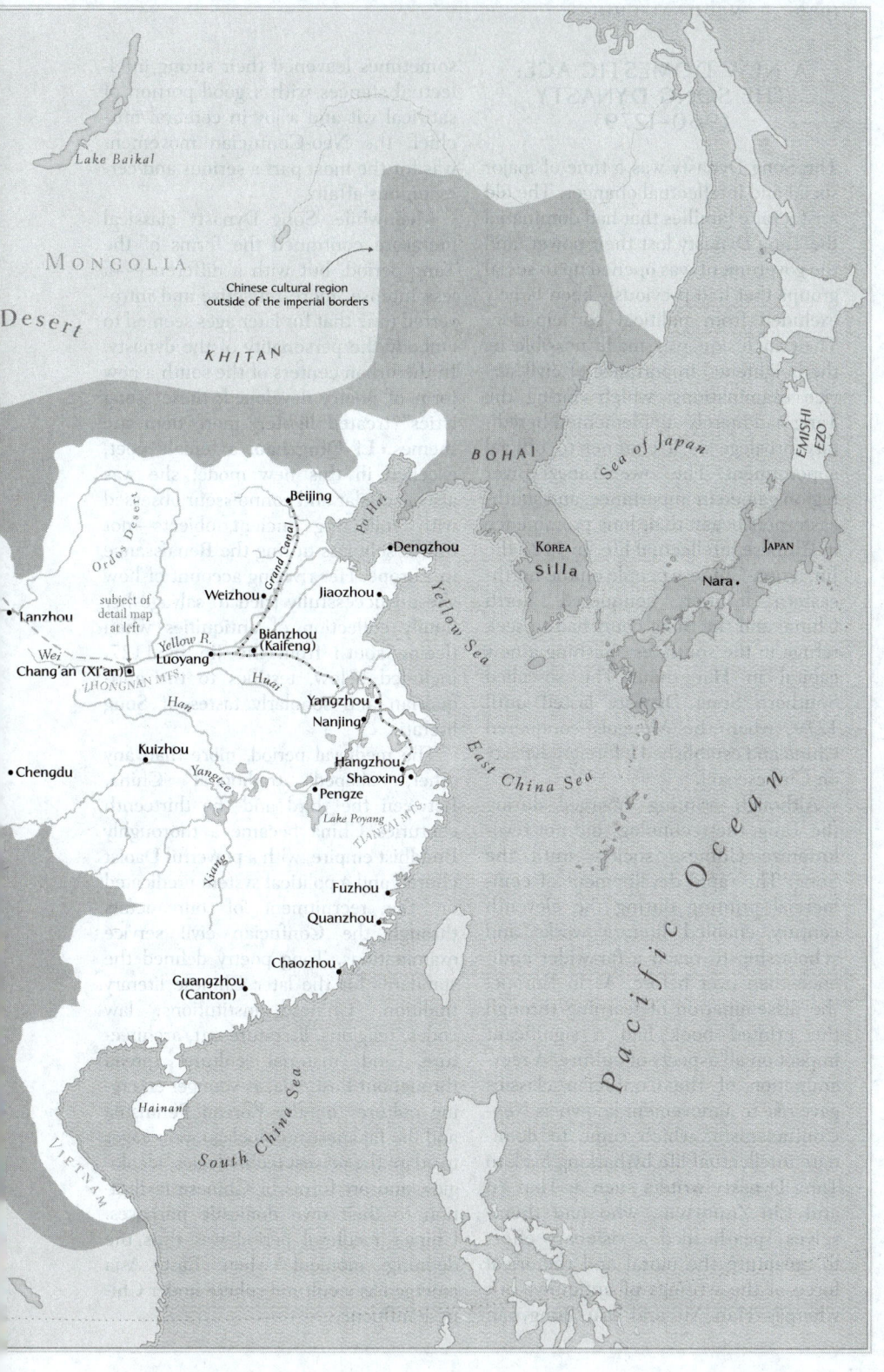

Lake Baikal

MONGOLIA

Desert

KHITAN

Chinese cultural region
outside of the imperial borders

BOHAI

Po Hai

Sea of Japan

EMISHI
EZO

Beijing

Grand Canal

Dengzhou

KOREA
Silla

JAPAN

Ordos Desert

subject of
detail map
at left

Weizhou

Jiaozhou

Nara

Lanzhou

Yellow R.

Bianzhou
(Kaifeng)

Yellow Sea

Wei

Luoyang

Chang'an (Xi'an)

ZHONGNAN MTS.

Huai

Han

Yangzhou

Nanjing

East China Sea

Kuizhou

Yangtze

Pacific Ocean

Chengdu

Hangzhou
Shaoxing

Xiang

Pengze

Lake Poyang

TIANTAI MTS.

Fuzhou

Quanzhou

Chaozhou

Guangzhou
(Canton)

Hainan

VIETNAM

South China Sea

A NEW DOMESTIC AGE: THE SONG DYNASTY (960–1279)

The Song Dynasty was a time of major social and intellectual changes. The old aristocratic families that had dominated the Tang Dynasty lost their power, and the government was opened up to social groups that had previously been largely excluded from political participation. Their inclusion was made possible by the heightened importance of civil service examinations, which during the Tang had merely supplemented hereditary privilege as a channel to official appointment. The lower Yangzi River region gained in importance, and southeasterners began their long prominence in Chinese intellectual life. In 1127 the Jin, a non-Chinese people on the northeastern frontier, conquered North China, and the Song court had to seek refuge in the south, establishing a new capital in Hangzhou. The so-called Southern Song Dynasty lasted until 1279, when the Mongols conquered China and established a foreign dynasty on Chinese soil.

Although printing emerged during the Tang, the technology did not revolutionize Chinese society until the Song. The rapid development of commercial printing during the eleventh century enabled literary works and scholarship to reach a far wider audience than ever before. As in Europe, the dissemination of learning through the printed book had a significant impact on all aspects of culture. A reexamination of the Confucian classics gave rise to a movement known as Neo-Confucianism, which came to dominate intellectual life by harking back to Tang Dynasty writers such as Han Yu and Liu Zongyuan, who had themselves spearheaded a visionary effort to recapture the moral and rhetorical force of the writings of antiquity. But whereas Han Yu and Liu Zongyuan sometimes leavened their strong intellectual stances with a good portion of satirical wit and a joy in cerebral mischief, the Neo-Confucian movement was for the most part a serious and ceremonious affair.

Meanwhile, Song Dynasty classical literature continued the forms of the Tang period, but with a difference—a less intense, more reflective and introverted tone that for later ages seemed to embody the personality of the dynasty. In the urban centers of the south a new form of poetry developed; these "song lyrics" treated lighter, more domestic themes. **Li Qingzhao**, a female poet, excelled in this new mode; she was also a scholar and connoisseur obsessed with collecting ancient objects—not unlike scholars during the Renaissance in Europe. Her riveting account of how she unsuccessfully tried to salvage her family collection of antiquities when fleeing south from the Jin in 1127, included below, testifies to the antiquarian and scholarly tastes of Song literati.

The medieval period, more than any other, shaped traditional China. Between the third and the thirteenth centuries China became a thoroughly Buddhist empire, with a powerful Daoist church and a political system predicated on the recruitment of bureaucrats through the Confucian civil service examinations. Tang poetry defined the standards for the later Chinese literary tradition. Chinese institutions, law codes, religions, literature, art, architecture, and material culture spread throughout East Asia, as younger emerging cultures on the Korean Peninsula and the Japanese archipelago were eager to adapt the newest technologies, ideologies, and art forms of Chinese civilization to their own domestic purposes. China's medieval period was thus the defining moment when East Asia emerged as a cultural sphere under Chinese influence.

TAO QIAN

365–427

"Whenever I have been involved in official life I was mortgaging myself to my mouth and belly." Thus Tao Qian (also known as Tao Yuanming) explains his decision to leave public office and return to his family farm. No Chinese poet before or after him captures with more immediate emotion the simple pleasures of country life, the value of being true to one's inner nature, and the necessity to make and unmake choices in life. He is one of the most beloved figures in the Chinese poetic tradition. Generations of readers have been enticed by Tao Qian's candor and his pursuit of personal integrity. Yet his poetry gains its depth and appeal from its roots in the tensions of his humble circumstances, reflecting the fear of failure and mortality.

Although Tao Qian talks much about himself in his poems and became the stuff of legend in later ages, very little is known about his life. His great-grandfather was a noted official and general, and initially Tao Qian followed in his footsteps, serving for thirteen years in several undistinguished official posts. But in 405, when he was magistrate of Pengze, a county seat some thirty miles from his hometown, he suddenly resigned. He had occupied the position for only about eighty days. Instead of living off the grain paid to government officials as their salary, he returned to his family farm to produce his own; self-sufficiency became the principle that would allow him to pursue his true inclinations and live out the last two decades of his life in peace and tranquillity.

Tao Qian lived during the so-called Period of Disunion, the four hundred years between two great empires, the Han (206 B.C.E.–220 C.E.) and the Tang (618–907). This was a time of unprecedented uncertainty, when a series of dynasties followed each other in quick succession. In 316, half a century before Tao Qian was born, non-Chinese tribes invaded northern China. In the ensuing turmoil many of the great aristocratic families and their retainers emigrated to the region south of the Yangzi River. For the first time in Chinese history, "China" no longer meant the territory of the traditional northern heartland; it was now a shared cultural heritage held dear and claimed by the émigrés in the new south. For Tao Qian's generation, the climate, food, and landscape of the south must still have been novelties, enticing people to seek the simple life in the countryside and capture it in poetry.

Also, during the Period of Disunion Buddhism spread to all classes of Chinese society, and the Daoist church (an institution whose founders based their claims to religious leadership on earlier Daoist philosophical texts) gained many supporters. Both Buddhism and Daoism sanctioned the retreat from public life; Confucianism, in contrast, valued active service in the state bureaucracy above all else and accepted withdrawal only in times of incompetent government. Even though Tao Qian described his decision to leave public life as a personal choice, he lived in an age in which political turmoil and new religions encouraged that choice.

Tao Qian's poetry celebrates the pleasures of wine, friendship, and gardening; the joys of composing poetry, reading books, and playing the zither;

and the desire for liberation from social strictures to pursue one's own inclinations. Poverty, hunger, and destitution do not call into doubt but rather throw into relief Tao Qian's decision to renounce public office. One grand theme of his poetry is the return to one's natural self, but it is unclear quite how far Tao Qian is willing to push this idea. To be sure, he renounces the pursuit of fame and official recognition and enjoys instead his wine and his garden. But he is also proud of his family line and seems deeply disappointed with his sons' lack of accomplishment. By the same token, writing and reading poetry was an exclusive domain of the educated elite, but the peasants in Tao Qian's poetry, his new neighbors, are apparently literate and he portrays them as sharing his literary interests.

Tao Qian despised worldly ambition, but no poet before him wrote so much about himself. "Substance, Shadow, and Spirit" dramatizes some of his inner tensions by staging a mock debate between three characters, each of whom proposes a different solution to how best to live life: to enjoy wine and forget mortality, as suggested by Substance; to strive to do good and precisely not to forget oneself, as endorsed by Shadow; or, as suggested by the conciliatory Spirit, to forget about both bodily pleasures and moral achievements and simply give oneself over "to the waves of the Great Change." "Biography of Master Five Willows" has been read as a self-portrait of Tao Qian, although he makes no direct reference to himself. In "Elegy" he seems to be coming back from the grave to imagine the scene of his own death and burial, an unprecedented use of a genre reserved for addressing the dead. Even "Peach Blossom Spring" is an autobiography of sorts, a tale about escape from oppressive rule (here from the First Emperor of the Qin Dynasty [221–206 B.C.E.], known in history for his extraordinary cruelty) to a land of self-sufficient happiness. It is also a parable of the impossibility of simply willing things to happen: the fisherman, an ambivalent figure who lives both in tune with nature and in contact with society, stumbles by chance upon the hidden cave while idly exploring an impressive grove of peach trees. After returning, the fisherman reports to the magistrate his spectacular discovery of a cave inhabited by a utopian society that managed to escape the vicissitudes of political turmoil. But to the official who sets out under orders to find the cave, the blissful cave of Peach Blossom Spring is forever beyond reach.

At first Tao Qian was admired as a recluse and man of principle, not as a poet. His straightforward style and simple diction contrast with the ornate imagery and sophisticated allusions in the poetry of his contemporaries. But a renewed interest in simplicity of expression during the Tang Dynasty propelled him to literary fame and has secured him a prominent position in the canon of Chinese poetry ever since. A sixth-century editor of Tao Qian's poetry praises him thus: "An extraordinary person rising above the crowd, Tao Qian followed his natural impulses and was content with his choices." An icon of self-fulfillment, whose poetry convinced people that reaching a state of contentment of sorts is possible, Tao Qian has timeless appeal.

The Peach Blossom Spring[1]

During the Taiyuan period of the Jin dynasty[2] a fisherman of Wuling once rowed upstream, unmindful of the distance he had gone, when he suddenly came to a grove of peach trees in bloom. For several hundred paces on both banks of the stream there was no other kind of tree. The wild flowers growing under them were fresh and lovely, and fallen petals covered the ground—it made a great impression on the fisherman. He went on for a way with the idea of finding out how far the grove extended. It came to an end at the foot of a mountain whence issued the spring that supplied the stream. There was a small opening in the mountain and it seemed as though light was coming through it. The fisherman left his boat and entered the cave, which at first was extremely narrow, barely admitting his body; after a few dozen steps it suddenly opened out onto a broad and level plain where well-built houses were surrounded by rich fields and pretty ponds. Mulberry, bamboo and other trees and plants grew there, and criss-cross paths skirted the fields. The sounds of cocks crowing and dogs barking could be heard from one courtyard to the next. Men and women were coming and going about their work in the fields. The clothes they wore were like those of ordinary people. Old men and boys were carefree and happy.

When they caught sight of the fisherman, they asked in surprise how he had got there. The fisherman told the whole story, and was invited to go to their house, where he was served wine while they killed a chicken for a feast. When the other villagers heard about the fisherman's arrival they all came to pay him a visit. They told him that their ancestors had fled the disorders of Qin times[3] and, having taken refuge here with wives and children and neighbors, had never ventured out again; consequently they had lost all contact with the outside world. They asked what the present ruling dynasty was, for they had never heard of the Han, let alone the Wei and the Jin.[4] They sighed unhappily as the fisherman enumerated the dynasties one by one and recounted the vicissitudes of each. The visitors all asked him to come to their houses in turn, and at every house he had wine and food. He stayed several days. As he was about to go away, the people said, "There's no need to mention our existence to outsiders."

After the fisherman had gone out and recovered his boat, he carefully marked the route. On reaching the city, he reported what he had found to the magistrate, who at once sent a man to follow him back to the place. They proceeded according to the marks he had made, but went astray and were unable to find the cave again.

A high-minded gentleman of Nanyang named Lui Ziji heard the story and happily made preparations to go there, but before he could leave he fell sick and died. Since then there has been no one interested in trying to find such a place.

---

1. All selections translated by James Robert Hightower except "Biography of Master Five Willows."
2. From 376 to 396 C.E.
3. During the first short-lived Chinese imperial dynasty (221–206 B.C.E.); the First Emperor was known for his megalomania and cruelty.
4. The dynasties that followed the Qin. The inhabitants did not know about anything that happened in the outside world between the third century B.C.E. up to the fourth century C.E.

The Ying clan[5] disrupted Heaven's ordinance
And good men withdrew from such a world.
Huang and Qi[6] went off to Shang Mountain
And these people too fled into hiding.
Little by little their tracks were obliterated   5
The paths they followed overgrown at last.
By agreement they set about farming the land
When the sun went down each rested from his toil.
Bamboo and mulberry provided shade enough.
They planted beans and millet, each in season.   10
From spring silkworms came the long silk thread
On the fall harvest no king's tax was paid.
No sign of traffic on overgrown roads,
Cockcrow and dogsbark within each other's earshot.
Their ritual vessels were of old design,   15
And no new fashions in the clothes they wore.
Children wandered about singing songs,
Graybeards went paying one another calls.
When grass grew thick they saw the time was mild,
As trees went bare they knew the wind was sharp.   20
Although they had no calendar to tell,
The four seasons still filled out a year.
Joyous in their ample happiness
They had no need of clever contrivance.
Five hundred years this rare deed stayed hid,   25
Then one fine day the fay retreat was found.
The pure and the shallow belong to separate worlds:
In a little while they were hidden again.
Let me ask you who are convention-bound,
Can you fathom those outside the dirt and noise?   30
I want to tread upon the thin thin air
And rise up high to find my own kind.

The Return

I was poor, and what I got from farming was not enough to support my family. The house was full of children, the rice-jar was empty, and I could not see any way to supply the necessities of life. Friends and relatives kept urging me to become a magistrate, and I had at last come to think I should do it, but there was no way for me to get such a position. At the time I happened to have business abroad and made a good impression on the grandees as a conciliatory and humane sort of person. Because of my poverty an uncle offered me a job in a small town, but the region was still unquiet and I trembled at the thought of going away from home. However, Pengze was only thirty miles from my native place, and the yield of the fields assigned the magistrate was sufficient to keep

5. That is, the clan of the First Emperor of Qin.
6. Virtuous men who went into reclusion in the mountains to protest the tyranny of the Qin emperor.

me in wine, so I applied for the office. Before many days had passed, I longed to give it up and go back home. Why, you may ask. Because my instinct is all for freedom, and will not brook discipline or restraint. Hunger and cold may be sharp, but this going against myself really sickens me. Whenever I have been involved in official life I was mortgaging myself to my mouth and belly, and the realization of this greatly upset me. I was deeply ashamed that I had so compromised my principles, but I was still going to wait out the year, after which I might pack up my clothes and slip away at night. Then my sister who had married into the Cheng family died in Wuchang, and my only desire was to go there as quickly as possible. I gave up my office and left of my own accord. From mid-autumn to winter I was altogether some eighty days in office, when events made it possible for me to do what I wished. I have entitled my piece 'The Return'; my preface is dated the eleventh moon of the year *yisi*.[1]

To get out of this and go back home!
My fields and garden will be overgrown with weeds—I must go back.
It was my own doing that made my mind my body's slave
Why should I go on in melancholy and lonely grief?
I realize that there's no remedying the past   5
But I know that there's hope in the future.
After all I have not gone far on the wrong road
And I am aware that what I do today is right, yesterday wrong.
My boat rocks in the gentle breeze
Flap, flap, the wind blows my gown;   10
I ask a passerby about the road ahead,
Grudging the dimness of the light at dawn.
Then I catch sight of my cottage—
    Filled with joy I run.
The servant boy comes to welcome me   15
    My little son waits at the door.
The three paths are almost obliterated
    But pines and chrysanthemums are still here.
Leading the children by the hand I enter my house
    Where there is a bottle filled with wine.   20
I draw the bottle to me and pour myself a cup;
Seeing the trees in the courtyard brings joy to my face.
I lean on the south window and let my pride expand,
I consider how easy it is to be content with a little space.
Every day I stroll in the garden for pleasure,   25
There is a gate there, but it is always shut.
Cane in hand I walk and rest
Occasionally raising my head to gaze into the distance.
The clouds aimlessly rise from the peaks,
The birds, weary of flying, know it is time to come home.   30
As the sun's rays grow dim and disappear from view
I walk around a lonely pine tree, stroking it.

Back home again!
May my friendships be broken off and my wanderings come to an end.

1. A year in the Chinese sixty-year cycle; eleventh month in this lunar calendar corresponds approximately to December.

The world and I shall have nothing more to do with one another. 35
If I were again to go abroad, what should I seek?
Here I enjoy honest conversation with my family
And take pleasure in books and zither to dispel my worries.
The farmers tell me that now spring is here
There will be work to do in the west fields. 40
Sometimes I call for a covered cart
Sometimes I row a lonely boat
Following a deep gully through the still water
Or crossing the hill on a rugged path.
The trees put forth luxuriant foliage, 45
The spring begins to flow in a trickle.
I admire the seasonableness of nature
And am moved to think that my life will come to its close.
    It is all over—
So little time are we granted human form in the world! 50
Let us then follow the inclinations of the heart:
Where would we go that we are so agitated?
I have no desire for riches
And no expectation of Heaven.
Rather on some fine morning to walk alone 55
Now planting my staff to take up a hoe,
Or climbing the east hill and whistling long
Or composing verses beside the clear stream:
So I manage to accept my lot until the ultimate homecoming.
Rejoicing in Heaven's command, what is there to doubt? 60

Biography of Master Five Willows[1]

We don't know what age the master lived in, and we aren't certain about his real name. Beside his cottage were five willow trees, so he took his name from them. He lived in perfect peace, a man of few words, with no desire for glory or gain. He liked to read but didn't try too hard to understand. Yet whenever there was something that caught his fancy, he would be so happy he would forget to eat. He had a wine-loving nature, but his household was so poor he couldn't always obtain wine. His friends, knowing how he was, would invite him to drink. And whenever he drank, he finished what he had right away, hoping to get very drunk. When drunk, he would withdraw, not really caring whether he went or stayed. His dwelling was a shambles, providing no protection against wind and sun. His coarse clothes were full of holes and patches; his plate and pitcher always empty; he was at peace. He forgot all about gain and loss and in this way lived out his life.

    Qianlou's[2] wife once said, "Feel no anxiety about loss or low station; don't be too eager for wealth and honor." When we reflect on her words, we suspect that Five Willows may have been such a man—swigging wine and writing poems to

1. Translated by Stephen Owen. "Master Five Willows" is Tao Qian's playful name for himself.
2. A figure of antiquity who preferred a life of poverty to serving in office.

satisfy his inclinations. Was he a person of the age of Lord No-Cares? Was he a person of the age of Getian?[3]

Substance, Shadow, and Spirit

Noble or base, wise or stupid, none but cling tenaciously to life. This is a great delusion. I have put in the strongest terms the complaints of Substance and Shadow and then, to resolve the matter, have made Spirit the spokesman for naturalness. Those who share my tastes will all get what I am driving at.

I

Substance to Shadow

Earth and heaven endure forever,
Streams and mountains never change.
Plants observe a constant rhythm,
Withered by frost, by dew restored.
But man, most sentient being of all,　　　　5
In this is not their equal.
He is present here in the world today,
Then leaves abruptly, to return no more.
No one marks there's one man less—
Not even friends and family think of him;　　　　10
The things that he once used are all that's left
To catch their eye and move them to grief.
I have no way to transcend change,
That it must be, I no longer doubt.
I hope you will take my advice:　　　　15
When wine is offered, don't refuse.

II

Shadow to Substance

No use discussing immortality
When just to keep alive is hard enough.
Of course I want to roam in paradise,
But it's a long way there and the road is lost.
In all the time since I met up with you　　　　5
We never differed in our grief and joy.
In shade we may have parted for a time,
But sunshine always brings us close again.
Still this union cannot last forever—
Together we will vanish into darkness.　　　　10
The body goes; that fame should also end
Is a thought that makes me burn inside.
Do good, and your love will outlive you;

3. Two legendary rulers of a golden age, before there were troubles in the world.

Surely this is worth your every effort.
While it is true, wine may dissolve care   15
That is not so good a way as this.

III

Spirit's Solution

The Great Potter[1] cannot intervene—
All creation thrives of itself.
That Man ranks with Earth and Heaven
Is it not because of me?
Though we belong to different orders,   5
Being alive, I am joined to you.
Bound together for good or ill
I cannot refuse to tell you what I know:
The Three August Ones[2] were great saints
But where are they living today?   10
Though Pengzu[3] lasted a long time
He still had to go before he was ready.
Die old or die young, the death is the same,
Wise or stupid, there is no difference.
Drunk every day you may forget,   15
But won't it shorten your life span?
Doing good is always a joyous thing
But no one has to praise you for it.
Too much thinking harms my life;
Just surrender to the cycle of things,   20
Give yourself to the waves of the Great Change
Neither happy nor yet afraid.
And when it is time to go, then simply go
Without any unnecessary fuss.

Returning to the Farm to Dwell

I

From early days I have been at odds with the world;
My instinctive love is hills and mountains.
By mischance I fell into the dusty net
And was thirteen years away from home.
The migrant bird longs for its native grove.   5
The fish in the pond recalls the former depths.
Now I have cleared some land to the south of town,
Simplicity intact, I have returned to farm.
The land I own amounts to a couple of acres
The thatched-roof house has four or five rooms.   10
Elms and willows shade the eaves in back,
Peach and plum stretch out before the hall.

---

1. The personified force of creation and
change in the cosmos.
2. Sage kings of antiquity, believed to have
lived to a fabulous old age.
3. A legendary figure who supposedly lived
eight hundred years.

Distant villages are lost in haze,
Above the houses smoke hangs in the air.
A dog is barking somewhere in a hidden lane,   15
A cock crows from the top of a mulberry tree.
My home remains unsoiled by worldly dust
Within bare rooms I have my peace of mind.
For long I was a prisoner in a cage
And now I have my freedom back again.   20

II

Here in the country human contacts are few
On this narrow lane carriages seldom come.
In broad daylight I keep my rustic gate closed,
From the bare rooms all dusty thoughts are banned.
From time to time through the tall grass   5
Like me, village farmers come and go;
When we meet we talk of nothing else
Than how the hemp and mulberry are growing.
Hemp and mulberry grow longer every day
Every day the fields I have plowed are wider;   10
My constant worry is that frost may come
And my crops will wither with the weeds.

Begging for Food

Hunger came and drove me out
To go I had no notion where.
I walked until I reached this town,
Knocked at a door and fumbled for words
The owner guessed what I was after   5
And gave it, but not just the gift alone.
We talked together all day long,
And drained our cups as the bottle passed.
Happy in our new acquaintance
We sang old songs and wrote new poems.   10
You are as kind as the washerwoman,
But to my shame I lack Han's talent.[1]
I have no way to show my thanks
And must repay you from the grave.[2]

On Moving House

I

For long I yearned to live in Southtown—
Not that a diviner told me to—

---

1. Han Xin, eventually a general of Liu Bang, the founder of the Han Dynasty (206 B.C.E.– 220 C.E.), was able to repay the kindness he received from the washerwoman who had given him food when he was a poor youth.
2. An allusion to the story of a ghost who repaid a debt of gratitude to Lord Huan of Wei by tripping his enemy.

Where many simple-hearted people live
With whom I would rejoice to pass my days.
This I have had in mind for several years   5
And now at last have carried out my plan.
A modest cottage does not need be large
To give us shelter where we sit and sleep.
From time to time my neighbors come
And we discuss affairs of long ago.   10
A good poem excites our admiration
Together we expound the doubtful points.

II

In spring and fall are many perfect days
For climbing high to write new poetry.
As we pass the doors, we hail each other,
And anyone with wine will pour us some.
When the farm work is done, we all go home   5
And then have time to think of one another—
So thinking, we at once throw on a coat
And visit, never tired of talk and jokes.
There is no better way of life than this,
No need to be in a hurry to go away.   10
Since food and clothing have to be provided,
If I do the plowing, it will not cheat me.

In the Sixth Month of 408, Fire

I built my thatched hut in a narrow lane,
Glad to renounce the carriages of the great.
In midsummer, while the wind blew long and sharp,
Of a sudden grove and house caught fire and burned.
In all the place not a roof was left to us   5
And we took shelter in the boat by the gate.

Space is vast this early autumn evening,
The moon, nearly full, rides high above.
The vegetables begin to grow again
But the frightened birds still have not returned.   10
Tonight I stand a long time lost in thought;
A glance encompasses the Nine Heavens.[1]
Since youth I've held my solitary course
Until all at once forty years have passed.
My outward form follows the way of change   15
But my heart remains untrammelled still.
Firm and true, it keeps its constant nature,
No jadestone is as strong, adamantine.
I think back to the time when East-Gate[2] ruled

---

1. That is, the entire sky; heaven was imagined as having nine layers.

2. A legendary ruler in the golden age, a time
of such plenty that no one bothered to steal.

When there was grain left out in the fields   20
And people, free of care, drummed full bellies,
Rising mornings and coming home to sleep.
Since I was not born in such a time,
Let me just go on watering my garden.

From Twenty Poems After Drinking Wine

Preface

Living in retirement here I have few pleasures, and now the nights are growing longer; so, as I happen to have some excellent wine, not an evening passes without a drink. All alone with my shadow I empty a bottle until suddenly I find myself drunk. And once I am drunk I write a few verses for my own amusement. In the course of time the pages have multiplied, but there is no particular sequence in what I have written. I have had a friend make a copy, with no more in mind than to provide a diversion.

V

I built my hut beside a traveled road
Yet here no noise of passing carts and horses.
You would like to know how it is done?
With the mind detached, one's place becomes remote.
Picking chrysanthemums by the eastern hedge   5
I catch sight of the distant southern hills:
The mountain air is lovely as the sun sets
And flocks of flying birds return together.
In these things is a fundamental truth
I would like to tell, but lack the words.   10

IX

I heard a knock this morning at my door
In haste I pulled my gown on wrongside out
And went to ask the caller, Who is there?
It was a well-intentioned farmer, come
With a jug of wine to pay a distant call.   5
Suspecting me to be at odds with the times:
'Dressed in rags beneath a roof of thatch
Is not the way a gentleman should live.
All the world agrees on what to do—
I hope that you will join the muddy game.'   10
'My sincere thanks for your advice, old man.
It's my nature keeps me out of tune.
Though one can learn of course to pull the reins,
To go against oneself is a real mistake.
So let's just have a drink of this together—   15
There's no turning back my carriage now.'[1]

1. That is, he has decided on the course of his life.

X

Once I made a distant trip
Right to the shore of the Eastern Sea
The road I went was long and far,
The way beset by wind and waves.
Who was it made me take this trip?   5
It seems that I was forced by hunger.
I gave my all to eat my fill
When just a bit was more than enough.
Since this was not a famous plan
I stopped my cart and came back home.   10

Finding Fault with My Sons

Over my temples the white hair hangs,
My wrinkled skin is past filling out.
Although five sons belong to me
Not one is fond of brush and paper.
Already Shu is twice times eight—   5
For laziness he has no match.
At Axuan's age one should study,
But love of letters is not in him.
Both Yong and Duan count thirteen years
And cannot add up six and seven.   10
Tongzi is getting on toward nine
And all he wants are pears and chestnuts.
If this is the way it is fated to be,
Just let me reach for the Thing in the Cup.[1]

From On Reading the Seas and Mountains Classic[1]

I

In early summer when the grasses grow
And trees surround my house with greenery,
The birds rejoice to have a refuge there
And I too love my home.
The fields are plowed and the new seed planted   5
And now is time again to read my books.
This out-of-the-way lane has no deep-worn ruts
And tends to turn my friends' carts away.
With happy face I pour the spring-brewed wine
And in the garden pick some greens to cook.   10

1. That is, wine.
1. An ancient book that provides a fabulous geography, describing the countries surround-ing China as inhabited by fantastic creatures and strange-looking human beings.

A gentle shower approaches from the east
Accompanied by a temperate breeze.
I skim through the *Story of King Mu*[2]
And view the pictures in the *Seas and Mountains Classic.*
A glance encompasses the ends of the universe—   15
Where is there any joy, if not in these?

Elegy

The year is *dingmao* of the cycle, the season that of the tone *wuyi,*[1] when days are cold and the nights long, when the wind blows mournfully as the wild fowl migrate, and leaves turn yellow and fall. Master Tao is about to depart from this lodging house to return for all time to his own home. Old friends are grieved and mourn for him: this evening they give him a farewell banquet, offering a sacrificial food, pouring libations of clear wine. They look, and his face is dim; listening, they no longer hear the sound of his voice.

Alas, alas, this vast clod, earth, that illimitable high firmament, together produce all things, even me who am a man. But from the time I attained human estate, my lot has been poverty. Rice-bin and wine-gourd have often been empty, and I have faced winters in thin clothes. Still I have gone happily to draw water from the brook and have sung as I walked under a load of firewood, going about my daily affairs in the obscurity of my cottage. As springs gave way to autumn, I have busied myself in my garden, hoeing, cultivating, planting or tending. I have rejoiced in my books and have been soothed by my zither. Winters I have warmed myself in the sun, summers I have bathed in the brook. There was little enough reward for my labor, but my mind enjoyed a constant leisure. Content with Heaven and accepting my lot, I have lived out the years of my life.

Men fear to waste their lives, concerned that they may fail to succeed. They cling to the days and lament passing time. During their life they are honored by the world, and after their death they still are mourned. But I have gone my own way, which is not their way. I take no glory in their esteem, nor do I feel defamed by their slander. I have lived alone in my poor house, drinking wine and writing poetry.

Aware of my destined end, of which one cannot be ignorant, I find no cause for regret in this present transformation. I have lived out my lifespan, and all my life I have desired quiet retirement. Now that I am dying, an old man, what have I left to wish for?

Hot and cold hasten on, one after the other.[2] The dead have nothing in common with the survivors. Relatives come in the morning, friends arrive in the evening, to bury me in the meadow and give comfort to my soul. Dark is my journey, desolate the grave. It is shameful to be buried extravagantly as was Huan Tui (whose stone coffin was three years a-making), and ridiculous to be parsimonious

---

2. The travel narrative of an early king of the Zhou Dynasty (ca. 1045–256 B.C.E.) who supposedly visited fantastic places outside of China.

1. Winter. "*Dingmao*": a cyclical date name (427 C.E.).
2. That is, the seasons pass.

like Yang Wangsun (who was buried naked), for after death there is nothing. Raise me no mound, plant me no grove; time will pass with the revolving sun and moon. I never cared for praise in my lifetime, and it matters not at all what eulogies are sung after my death. Man's life is hard enough in truth; and death is not to be avoided.

HANSHAN (COLD MOUNTAIN)

ca. 600–800

The Buddhist monk Hanshan may or may not have been a real person. The account included in the preface to his collected poems seems to be a sketch of a typical eccentric rather than the story of any individual. The Buddhist biographies tell us little about his life; instead, they feature Hanshan's extravagant conversations with his friend Shide and their master. Hanshan (literally, "Cold Mountain") is a mountain in the Tiantai mountain range in southeast China where a famous temple is located, but here it serves as a name around which a corpus of Buddhist poems gradually accumulated throughout the Tang period. The Hanshan poems were largely overlooked in China until modern times, when they were also admired in Japan and in the West thanks to the attention they received in the 1950s from the Beat poets, a group of American writers who experimented with drugs, unconventional forms of communal life and sexuality, and various Eastern religions.

The three hundred–odd poems that make up the Hanshan corpus are of very uneven quality. The best are among the finest expressions of Chan (Zen) Buddhism, a school of Buddhism that came to the fore during the Tang Dynasty and emphasizes paradox, madness, and austere meditation as means to enlightenment. The voice in the poems addresses outsiders, telling them about enlightenment. At times it seems to transcend all things human, but scriptures, books, or other people appear now and then. Since enlightenment cannot be put into words, the speaker can only point toward it in a series of figures; Cold Mountain becomes a landscape of the mind.

[Whoever reads my poems][1]

Whoever reads my poems
Must protect the purity in his mind.

---

1. Translated by Robert Hendricks.

Stinginess and greed must change into honesty day after day;
Flattery and deceit must *right now* become the upright!

Expel and banish, wipe out your bad karma;   5
Return to rely on, accept your true nature.

Today! You must attain the Buddha-body;[2]
Quickly! Quickly! Treat this just like it's imperial law![3]

[A thatched hut][4]

A thatched hut is home for a country man;
Horse or carriage seldom pass my gate:
Forests so still all the birds come to roost,
Broad valley streams always full of fish.
I pick wild fruit in hand with my child,   5
Till the hillside fields with my wife.
And in my house what do I have?
Only a bed piled high with books.

[A curtain of pearls][5]

A curtain of pearls hangs before the hall of jade
And within is a lovely lady,
Fairer in form than the gods and immortals,
Her face like a blossom of peach or plum.
Spring mists will cover the eastern mansion,   5
Autumn winds blow from the western lodge,
And after thirty years have passed,
She will look like a piece of pressed sugar cane.

[Here we languish][6]

Here we languish, a bunch of poor scholars,
Battered by extremes of hunger and cold.
Out of work, our only joy is poetry:
Scribble, scribble, we wear out our brains.
Who will read the works of such men?   5
On that point you can save your sighs.
We could inscribe our poems on biscuits
And the homeless dogs wouldn't deign to nibble.

[In my first thirty years][7]

In my first thirty years of life
I roamed hundreds and thousands of miles.
Walked by rivers through deep green grass

---

2. That is, gain enlightenment and become a Buddha.
3. A stock phrase used to conclude performances of ritual chants addressed to spirits or demons.

4. Translated by Burton Watson.
5. Translated by Burton Watson.
6. Translated by Burton Watson.
7. Translated by Gary Snyder, who was associated with the Beat Movement.

Entered cities of boiling red dust.
Tried drugs, but couldn't make Immortal;   5
Read books and wrote poems on history.
Today I'm back at Cold Mountain:
I'll sleep by the creek and purify my ears.

[Wonderful, this road to Cold Mountain][8]

Wonderful, this road to Cold Mountain—
Yet there's no sign of horse or carriage.
In winding valleys too tortuous to trace,
On crags piled who knows how high,
A thousand different grasses weep with dew   5
And pines hum together in the wind.
Now it is that, straying from the path,
You ask your shadow, "What way from here?"

[When people see the man of Cold Mountain][9]

When people see the man of Cold Mountain
They all say, "There's a crackpot!
Hardly a face to make one look twice,
His body wrapped in nothing but rags . . .
The things we say he doesn't understand;   5
The things he says we wouldn't utter!"
A word to those of you passing by—
Try coming to Cold Mountain sometime!

[High, high from the summit of the peak][1]

High, high from the summit of the peak,
Whatever way I look, no limit in sight!
No one knows I am sitting here alone.
A solitary moon shines in the cold spring.
Here in the spring—this is not the moon.   5
The moon is where it always is—in the sky above.
And though I sing this one little song,
In the song there is no Zen.

[I longed to visit the eastern cliff][2]

I longed to visit the eastern cliff
countless years until today
I finally grabbed a vine and climbed
but halfway there met mist and wind
the trail was too narrow for clothes   5
the moss too slick for shoes
I stopped beneath this cinnamon tree
and slept with a cloud for a pillow

8. Translated by Burton Watson.   1. Translated by Burton Watson.
9. Translated by Burton Watson.   2. Translated by Red Pine.

[On Cold Mountain there's a naked bug][3]

On Cold Mountain there's naked bug
its body is white its head is black
its hands hold two scrolls
in one is the Way in the other is Virtue
at home it makes no fire   5
for the road it packs no clothes
but always it carries the sword of wisdom
ready to strike troublesome foes

[Men ask the way to Cold Mountain][4]

Men ask the way to Cold Mountain
Cold Mountain: there's no through trail.
In summer, ice doesn't melt
The rising sun blurs in swirling fog.
How did I make it?   5
My heart's not the same as yours.
If your heart was like mine
You'd get it and be right here.

[My mind is like the autumn moon][5]

My mind is like the autumn moon
Shining clean and clear in the green pool
No, that's not a good comparison.
Tell me, how shall I explain?

[So Hanshan writes you these words][6]

So Hanshan writes you these words,
These words which no one will believe.
Honey is sweet; men love the taste.
Medicine is bitter and hard to swallow.
What soothes the feelings brings contentment,   5
What opposes the will calls forth anger.
Yet I ask you to look at the wooden puppets,
Worn out by their moment of play on stage!

[Do you have the poems of Hanshan in your house?][7]

Do you have the poems of Hanshan in your house?
They're better for you than sutra-reading!
Write them out and paste them on a screen
Where you can glance them over from time to time.

---

3. Translated by Red Pine.
4. Translated by Gary Snyder.
5. Translated by Burton Watson.

6. Translated by Burton Watson.
7. Translated by Burton Watson.

TANG POETRY

The poetry of the Tang Dynasty (618–907) is generally considered the high point of China's three-millennia-old history of poetry. Much compelling verse was written after the period, not least because the poetic giants of the Tang inspired later poets to write with self-conscious sophistication and skill. But later poets generally agreed that **Du Fu**, **Li Bo**, and their contemporaries had set a standard that could not be surpassed. For many centuries the elegant urgency and technical virtuosity with which these poets captured the world, as well as the scope of their poetic visions and themes, formed the basis for later poetic training and inspiration. The primacy of Tang poetry in the Chinese poetic canon continued until the early twentieth century, when Chinese intellectuals launched a revolutionary movement to replace the classical written idiom with vernacular spoken language. Today traditional poetry is popular once again, and the accomplishments of the Tang poets remain the high-water mark of what poetry can do.

Women under the Tang Dynasty were riding horses and even playing polo. This painting, inspired by a painting by Zhang Xuan, a court painter flourishing during the reign of Emperor Xuanzong, presumably depicts an outing of court women led by Lady Guo Guo. She was a sister of the emperor's beloved Prized Consort Yang, whom we see strangled before the emperor's eyes during a military rebellion in Bo Juyi's "The Song of Lasting Regret" (p. 1130).

POETRY AND TANG SOCIETY

Every educated Chinese during the Tang Dynasty was expected to be able to spontaneously dash off a poem with grace, or at least technical competence. Poetry was a form of social communication, not an arcane and highbrow art. The sheer mass of Tang poems still extant—close to 50,000, by some 2,200 authors—clearly indicates how common poetry was in everyday life. Many of those whose poems survived spent their lives in some official government position, after taking the civil service examination that qualified them for office. Whenever these scholar-officials were sent to a new post in the vast territory of the Tang Empire they would take leave from their colleagues and friends with a "farewell" poem and expect a poetic gift in return. In their new province, they would make friends by going on pleasure excursions or visiting temples and invariably writing poems about their journeys. They could also write poems to praise the imperial court or to criticize its policies. Poetry thus was a cultural custom, a craft that taught people how to pay attention to and share the significant moments in their lives—to find something lovely in a scene; to convey feelings about separation and friendship, painful and pleasurable events; to thank a host for a splendid evening party; or simply to express what would otherwise be awkward or impossible to say. Though the practice of writing poetry was general, only some thirty or forty truly talented poets achieved renown as artists of the highest caliber.

Yet some otherwise undistinguished writers produced a remarkable number of fine poems that would be read and memorized for the next thousand years.

THE ORIGIN OF TANG POETRY

Chinese literature began with the folk songs and ritual ballads about historical events preserved in the *Classic of Poetry* (ca. 600 B.C.E.). Most of the poems in that collection have stanzas of four to six lines containing four to six characters each, with end rhymes for every couplet. During the Han Dynasty (206 B.C.E.– 220 C.E.), about half a millennium after the compilation of the *Classic of Poetry*, a new genre of poetry emerged. Written in lines of five or seven characters and displaying a much more melodious and flexible rhythm, it became the basis for Tang poetry. During the century preceding the Tang Dynasty, poets began to experiment with introducing tonal patterns into their poems. Although variations in tone are common in many languages, including English, they are usually associated with sentence patterns. Chinese differs in attaching tones to individual syllables. Poets started to arrange the tones of each syllable of the poem—in modern Mandarin Chinese, a syllable can be pronounced in one of four different tones—in symmetrical patterns. This innovation led to the birth of so-called regulated poetry, a verse form that requires syllables to alternate "level" and "deflected" tones and demands training to master. The spread of Buddhism in the first half of the first millennium may have helped spark the development of regulated poetry. Chinese monks translating Sanskrit texts into Chinese must have been struck by the absence of tones in Sanskrit, and this new awareness of a defining feature of their own language perhaps inspired the introduction of rules mandating the alternation of tones in poetry. Whatever the reason, the emergence of regulated poetry (also called "recent-style" poetry, as earlier poetic forms such as those used by **Tao Qian** came to be called "old-style" poetry) radically changed the reading and writing of poetry. By imposing more rules on the game of poetry, it enabled readers to judge poetic craftsmanship more objectively.

Both the prominent place of poetry in social communication and everyday life and these new technical demands gave poetry an unprecedented status in Tang society. Poetry was introduced into the prestigious civil service examination; successful aspirants were awarded the "presented scholar" degree (*jinshi*), a prerequisite for a career as a government official. Although there were debates about whether the inclusion of poetry composition was appropriate for such exams, and was later abolished, the tight formal requirements of the regulated poem made it easier to judge and compare the candidates' relative worth. Also, the candidates were forced to learn how to compose succinctly and eloquently. This skill would be useful in their later careers in government service, as they drafted many complex official documents.

REGULATED POETRY OF THE TANG

The two basic forms of regulated poetry are in four lines (*jueju*) and eight lines (*lüshi*), although longer poems composed of several stanzas were also common. Regulated poetry placed a new emphasis on the couplet, a unit of two lines. For the ambitious Tang poet, couplets provided an opportunity to display virtuosity, as they provided a showcase for the parallelism required of the regulated poem. Consider **Du Fu's "Spring Prospect,"** which describes the fall of the Tang capital to rebels in 755 and the destruction of the great Tang Empire against the backdrop of innocent spring:

The nation shattered, mountains and rivers remain;
city in spring, grass and trees burgeoning.
Feeling the times, blossoms draw tears;
hating separation, birds alarm the heart.
Beacon fires three months in succession,
a letter from home worth ten thousand in gold.
White hairs, fewer for the scratching,
soon too few to hold a hairpin up.

Let us examine how this five-syllable regulated poem reads in classical Chinese. Some of the rhymes and tones are hardly recognizable in the modern Mandarin pronunciation of the characters given here, but they did rhyme and tonally harmonize during the Tang Dynasty. "Level tones" are marked with a hyphen (–); "deflected tones," with a straight line (|):

					FIRST COUPLET
國	破	山	河	在	(Chinese characters)
guó	pò	shān	hé	zài	(modern Mandarin pronunciation)
|	|	–	–	|	(tonal pattern)
nation	shattered	mountain	river	remain	(word-for-word translation)
城	春	草	木	深	
chéng	chūn	cǎo	mù	shēn(rhyme word)	
–	–	|	|	–	
city	spring	grass	tree	grow thick	
感	時	花	濺	淚	SECOND COUPLET
gǎn	shí	huā	jiàn	lèi	
|	–	–	|	|	
feel	time	blossom	shed	tear	
恨	別	鳥	驚	心	
hèn	bié	niǎo	jīng	xīn(rhyme word)	
|	|	|	–	–	
hate	separation	bird	alarm	heart	
烽	火	連	三	月	THIRD COUPLET

fēng	huǒ	lián	sān	yuè
|	|	–	–	|
beacon	fire	in succession	3	months

家	書	抵	萬	金
jiā	shū	dǐ	wàn	jīn(rhyme word)
–	–	|	|	–
home	letter	worth	10,000	gold

FOURTH COUPLET

白	頭	搔	更	短
bái	tóu	sāo	gèng	duǎn
–	–	–	|	|
white	head	scratch	even	shorter

渾	欲	不	勝	簪
hún	yù	bù	shēng	zān(rhyme word)
|	|	|	–	–
simply	want	not	hold	hairpin

The poem consistently relies on parallelism as it poignantly contrasts the stability of the natural cycle with the abrupt changes brought about by the rebellion. In the first couplet the capital Chang'an is taken by rebel forces, the emperor has fled to Sichuan Province and abdicated, and the "nation is shattered," yet, perversely, we see the "city in spring," untouched by the disaster of historic proportion. In the second couplet, even blossoms and birds appear startled by the human tragedy. The third couplet shows the economic costs of the rebellion: the rebels have cordoned off the capital so tightly that letters have become almost priceless, smuggled in and out only at risk of one's life. The last couplet lacks precise parallelisms but ends with thematic resonances and shows the poet in despair: the hairpin no longer secures his official cap to his head, because he has become too old and the dynasty he wanted to serve has fallen on hard times.

Parallelism in Tang poetry functioned on many levels beyond the grammatical, including thematic parallelism and contrast between lines or in the poem as a whole. Thus Tang writings on poetry distinguish many types. The parallel couplet was the central device of regulated poetry, and during the Tang people would write out their favorite couplets in lavish calligraphy on little hanging scrolls, which they could carry when traveling. Indeed, Tang poets compiled entire anthologies containing only beautiful couplets excerpted from famous poems. The emphasis on fashioning beautiful couplets created a huge market for practical manuals that explained how to avoid violating the tonal rules and how to come up with an impressive parallel. This approach later drew criticism from poets who saw artistic ambition and inspiration, rather than craft and training, as the keys to good poetry. But the attraction of Tang poetry lies precisely in the felicitous match of craft with inspiration. It was solid training in the rules of regulated poetry that enabled Tang poets to capture their experience of the world in memorable words. The ultimate art of Tang poetry is that it often hides its artfulness under the serene surface of natural imagery.

WANG WEI

One of the most prominent poets of his time, Wang Wei (ca. 699 to 761) was also a well-respected painter and musician. He confesses in one poem that he was a poet only "by mistake" and that he must have been a painter in an earlier life.

Wang Wei was born into an aristocratic family and passed the civil service examination at the age of twenty. He rose steadily in the ranks of the official bureaucracy but his career was interrupted in 755, when the frontier general An Lushan rebelled against the Tang—leading to the siege that occasioned **Du Fu's "Spring Prospect."** Although the emperor and his immediate entourage fled, many officials were captured by the rebels and forced to work for An Lushan's military government. When the revolt was put down, Wang Wei escaped charges of collaboration only thanks to the intervention of his brother, a high-ranking government official. Once rehabilitated, he served in office until his death.

The An Lushan Rebellion was the most catastrophic event in three centuries of Tang Dynasty rule (618–907). That a simple frontier general of Central Asian origin could bring down an empire that was at the time the largest and most efficiently administered in the world came as a profound shock to the Chinese and their East Asian neighbors; and it became a defining moment for Wang Wei's generation. Yet unlike many of his contemporaries, such as Du Fu, Wang Wei wrote almost nothing about it. The poem "While I Was Imprisoned in Puti Monastery" is unusual in this regard. Written when Wang Wei was held captive by An Lushan's rebels, it describes efforts of the former Tang court musicians to resist the rebel government's request to perform at its victory banquet. The poem was circulated after the rebellion as proof of Wang Wei's resistance to the rebel government, thereby aiding his rehabilitation.

Although he could write in an ornate style on public court occasions, Wang Wei is known mainly for his ability to evoke tranquil scenes of rural retreat and convey a sense of dispassionate detachment from the world. His vignettes of reclusive life combine simplicity and deliberate craft. He bought a retreat in the Zhongnan Mountains and later the "Wang River" estate outside the capital, which he and his friend Pei Di celebrated in a series of poems.

Wang Wei also painted the various scenic spots he mentions in his poetry. None of his original paintings are preserved, but the survival of many imitations suggests that they were very popular. Wang Wei is considered a pioneer of Chinese landscape art, known particularly for his monochrome painting, which uses black ink-wash on white paper; this technique allows the painter to depict landscapes dominated by white. His interest in snow scenes is also evident in "White Rock Rapids," in which he paints—in poetry—families washing white silk under bright moonlight, with white rocks and dark rushes implicit in the background.

Wang Wei's poetry echoes his friendship with Buddhist monks and recluses and his commitment to Buddhism. Whereas other poets celebrated the landscape as it appears to the senses, Wang Wei often represents an insubstantiality that corresponds to the notion of the "emptiness" of things—the fundamental Buddhist conviction that all we perceive is illusion.

Zhongnan Retreat[1]

In middle years I am rather fond of the Tao;
My late home is at the foot of Southern Mountain.
When the feeling comes, each time I go there alone.
That splendid things are empty, of course, I know.
I walk to the place where the water ends   5
And sit and watch the time when clouds rise.
Meeting by chance an old man of the forest,
I chat and laugh without a date to return.

In Response to Vice-Magistrate Zhang

In late years I care for tranquility alone—
A myriad affairs do not concern my heart.
A glance at myself: there are no long-range plans.
I only know to return to the old forest.
Pine winds blow, loosening my belt;   5
The mountain moon shines as I pluck my zither.
You ask about reasons for success and failure:
A fisherman's song enters the shore's deeps.

From Wang River Collection

Preface: My retreat is in the Wang River mountain valley. The places to walk to include: Meng Wall Cove, Huazi Hill, Grained Apricot Lodge, Clear Bamboo Range, Deer Enclosure, Magnolia Enclosure, Dogwood Bank, Sophora Path, Lakeside Pavilion, Southern Hillock, Lake Yi, Willow Waves, Luan Family Shallows, Gold Powder Spring, White Rock Rapids, Northern Hillock, Bamboo Lodge, Magnolia Bank, Lacquer Tree Garden, and Pepper Tree Garden. When Pei Di[2] and I were at leisure, we each composed the following quatrains.

* * *

Deer Enclosure

Empty mountain, no man is seen.
Only heard are echoes of men's talk.
Reflected light enters the deep wood
And shines again on blue-green moss.

---

1. All selections translated by and with notes adapted from Pauline Yu.

2. A fellow poet and minor official (b. 716), one of Wang Wei's closest friends.

Lake Yi

Blowing flutes cross to the distant shore.
At day's dusk I bid farewell to you.
On the lake with one turn of the head:
Mountain green rolls into white clouds.

Gold Powder Spring

Drink each day at Gold Powder Spring
And you should have a thousand years or more:
To soar on an azure phoenix with striped dragons,
And with plumes and tassels attend the Jade Emperor's
court.[3]

White Rock Rapids

Clear and shallow, White Rock Rapids.
Green rushes once could be grasped.
Families live east and west of the water,
Washing silk beneath the bright moon.

Written on Crossing the Yellow River to Qinghe

A boat sailing on the great river—
The gathered waters reach to the end of the sky.
Sky and waves suddenly split asunder:
A commandery city—a thousand, ten thousand homes.
Farther on I see a city market again;   5
There seems to be some mulberry and hemp.
Looking back at my old home country:
The water's expanse joins the clouds and mist.

While I Was Imprisoned in Puti Monastery, Pei Di Came to See Me. He Spoke of How the Rebels Ordered Music Played at Frozen Emerald Pond; after the Court Musicians Began to Play, Their Tears Fell. I Secretly Recited and Presented This to Pei Di[4]

From ten thousand homes of grieving hearts arises wild smoke.
The hundred officials—when will they again attend court?

3. Daoists often engaged in alchemical experiments, believing that gold could confer immortality. Both the Queen Mother of the West, who
rode on a phoenix chariot pulled by striped
dragons, and the Jade Emperor, supreme deity
in the Daoist pantheon, are associated with
immortality.

4. Probably Wang Wei's only expression of
political protest, written when he was imprisoned during the An Lushan rebellion in 756.
After An Lushan and his soldiers entered the
capital Chang'an, they forced members of the
imperial conservatory to perform at a victory
banquet for the rebels.

Autumn sophora leaves fall within the empty palace.
Next to Frozen Emerald Pond, music from pipes and strings.

Farewell

Dismounting I give you wine to drink,
And inquire where you are going.
You say you did not achieve your wishes
And return to rest at the foot of Southern Mountain.
But go—do not ask again: 5
White clouds have no ending time.

LI BO

Although Li Bo (also known as Li Po and Li Bai; 701–762) was raised in Sichuan in western China, speculations about his Turkic family background have enhanced his image as an exotic eccentric. Li Bo never attempted to take the civil service examination, which was the primary but not sole venue for advancement. Thanks to his connection with an influential Daoist at court, Li Bo gained a post at the eminent Hanlin Academy, an institution founded by Emperor Xuanzong to support unconventional intellectuals and literary talents. But Li Bo's drinking habits and unusual personality led to his dismissal only two years later. During the An Lushan Rebellion he joined the cause of a prince who attempted to establish an independent regime in southeast China, and after the rebellion was suppressed he was arrested for treason. Sentenced to exile, he was pardoned before he reached his remote destination; he died a few years later.

There are many legends about Li Bo's life, encouraged by the nonchalant poses projected in his poetry: according to one such legend, he drowned while trying to embrace the moon's reflection on the water. For someone who claimed in his poetry to converse and drink with the moon such an end was not implausible, though overindulgence in alcohol and Daoist longevity elixirs, which often contained mercury, might have played a role.

Much Tang poetry tends to treat the world at hand; Li Bo supplies an additional dimension by describing Daoist worlds beyond the world, evoking moments of history and legend, and even transforming everyday occasions into something miraculous. Because of his flair and capacity to see the world with fresh eyes, his contemporaries called him "the banished immortal"—an ethereal heaven-dwelling being exiled for a lifetime in the world of mortals as punishment for some extravagant misdemeanor.

Li Bo cultivated this reputation by writing poems that tell of encounters with immortals and of cloud-climbing excursions through the heavens.

Of the thousand-some poems by Li Bo that survive, many are written in the old verse form popular before the rise of regulated poetry during the Tang. Li Bo particularly liked to imitate folk songs and infuse his poetry with colloquial and bold language. In this way he could sometimes give voice to the common people's hardships: in "South of the Walls We Fought," for example, he echoes an older anonymous lament of soldiers fallen in battle, turning it into bitter criticism of the constant warfare of his time on the northern and northwestern frontier of Tang China against peoples such as the Tibetans.

Li Bo and **Du Fu** are considered the most important Tang poets, and readers and critics over the past millennium have devoted considerable effort to debating their relative merits and shortcomings. Quite apart from the greatness of their poetry, they made a particularly fitting couple, because they embody the two poles of poetic creativity that have been of greatest concern in the Chinese literary tradition: while Du Fu became the poet who captured, chronicled, and criticized reality within its limits, Li Bo came to stand for the poet who dedicated himself to breaking free from social convention and from the limits imposed by reality.

The Sun Rises and Sets[1]

The sun comes up from its nook in the east,
Seems to rise from beneath the earth,
Passes on through Heaven,
    sets once again in the western sea,
And where, oh, where, can its team of six dragons   5
    ever find any rest?
Its daily beginnings and endings,
    since ancient times never resting.
And man is not made of its Primal Stuff—
    how can he linger beside it long?   10
Plants feel no thanks for their flowering in spring's wind,
Nor do trees hate losing their leaves
    under autumn skies:
Who wields the whip that drives along
    four seasons of changes—   15
The rise and the ending of all things
    is just the way things are.

Xihe! Xihe![2]
Why must you always drown yourself
    in those wild and reckless waves?   20
What power had Luyang[3]

1. Translated by Stephen Owen.
2. Goddess who drove the sun's carriage.
3. According to legend, the lord of Luyang stopped the sun so that he could continue to fight in combat.

That he halted your course by shaking his spear?
This perverts the Path of things,
   errs from Heaven's will—
So many lies and deceits!   25
I'll wrap this Mighty Mudball of a world
   all up in a bag
And be wild and free like Chaos itself!

South of the Walls We Fought[4]

We fought last year at the Sanggan's source,
this year we fight on the Cong River road.
We washed weapons in the surf of Tiaozhi,
grazed horses on grass in Sky Mountain's snow.[5]
Thousands of miles ever marching and fighting: 5
until all the Grand Army grows frail and old.

The Xiongnu[6] treat slaughter as farmers treat plowing;
since bygone days only white bones are seen
   in their fields of yellow sand.
The House of Qin built the wall   10
   to guard against the Turk;
for the House of Han the beacon fires
   were blazing still.

Beacon fires blaze without ceasing,
the marching and battle never end.   15
They died in fighting on the steppes,
their vanquished horses neigh,
   mourning to the sky.
Kites and ravens peck men's guts,
fly with them dangling from their beaks   20
   and hang them high
      on boughs of barren trees.
The troops lie mud-smeared in grasses,
and the general acted all in vain.
Now I truly see that weapons   25
   are evil's tools:
the Sage will use them only
   when he cannot do otherwise.

---

4. Translated by Stephen Owen.
5. Four locations of Tang campaigns in the
north and northwest.

6. Formidable enemies of the Han Empire
(206 B.C.E.–220 C.E.).

Bring in the Wine[7]

Look there!
   The waters of the Yellow River,
   coming down from Heaven,
   rush in their flow to the sea,
   never turn back again   5
Look there!
   Bright in the mirrors of mighty halls
   a grieving for white hair,
   this morning blue-black strands of silk,
   now turned to snow with evening.   10
For satisfaction in this life
   taste pleasure to the limit,
And never let a goblet of gold
   face the bright moon empty.
Heaven bred in me talents,   15
   and they must be put to use.
I toss away a thousand in gold,
   it comes right back to me.
So boil a sheep,
   butcher an ox,   20
     make merry for a while,
And when you sit yourself to drink, always
   down three hundred cups.
   Hey, Master Cen,
   Ho, Danqiu,[8]   25
   Bring in the wine!
   Keep the cups coming!
And I, I'll sing you a song,
You bend me your ears and listen—
The bells and the drums, the tastiest morsels,   30
   it's not these that I love—
All I want is to stay dead drunk
   and never sober up.
The sages and worthies of ancient days
   now lie silent forever,   35
And only the greatest drinkers
   have a fame that lingers on!
Once long ago
   the prince of Chen
    held a party at Pingle Lodge.[9]   40
A gallon of wine cost ten thousand cash,
   all the joy and laughter they pleased.
    So you, my host,
How can you tell me you're short on cash?
Go right out!   45

7. Translated by Stephen Owen.
8. Two friends of Li Bo.
9. The scene of merry parties described by the
poet Cao Zhi (192–232), the brother of Cao Pi,
the author of "A Discourse on Literature."

Buy us some wine!
    And I'll do the pouring for you!
Then take my dappled horse,
    Take my furs worth a fortune,
Just call the boy to get them,   50
    and trade them for lovely wine,
And here together we'll melt the sorrows
    of all eternity!

Question and Answer in the Mountains[1]

They ask me why I live in the green mountains.
I smile and don't reply; my heart's at ease.
Peach blossoms flow downstream, leaving no trace—
And there are other earths and skies than these.

Summer Day in the Mountains[2]

Lazily waving a fan of white feathers,
Stripped naked here in the green woods,
I take off my headband, hang it on a cliff,
My bare head splattered by wind through pines.

Drinking Alone with the Moon[3]

A pot of wine among the flowers.
I drink alone, no friend with me.
I raise my cup to invite the moon.
He and my shadow and I make three.

The moon does not know how to drink;   5
My shadow mimes my capering;
But I'll make merry with them both—
And soon enough it will be Spring.

I sing—the moon moves to and fro.
I dance—my shadow leaps and sways.   10
Still sober, we exchange our joys.
Drunk—and we'll go our separate ways.

Let's pledge—beyond human ties—to be friends,
And meet where the Silver River ends.

1. Translated by Vikram Seth.   3. Translated by Vikram Seth.
2. Translated by Stephen Owen.

The Hardships of Traveling the Road I[4]

Clear wine in golden goblets, at ten thousand a peck:
Prized delicacies on jade plates, worth a myriad cash.
But I stopped the cup, threw down the chopsticks, was unable to eat:
I took out my sword, stared all around, my heart was blindly lost.
I wanted to cross the Yellow River, but ice blocked the waterway: 5
Was about to climb the Taihang range, but snow darkened the sky.
At my ease I let fall a line, sitting by the side of a stream;
Longed to be aboard ship again and dreamt of the realm of the sun.

    The hardships of traveling the road—hardships of traveling the road:
    So many branching roads!—and where now am I?   10
The long wind will smite the waves, and surely will come a time,
To hang straight the cloudy sail and cross the gray-blue sea!

Seeing Off Meng Haoran at Yellow Crane Tower, on His Way to Guangling[5]

My old friend bids farewell in the west at Yellow Crane Tower.[6]
Amid misty blossoms of the third month goes down to Yangzhou.
His lone sail's far shadow vanishes in the deep-blue void.
Now I see only the Long River flowing to the edge of the sky.

In the Quiet Night[7]

The floor before my bed is bright:
Moonlight—like hoarfrost—in my room.
I lift my head and watch the moon.
I drop my head and think of home.

Sitting Alone by Jingting Mountain[8]

The flocks of birds have flown high and away,
A solitary cloud goes off calmly alone.
We look at each other and never get bored—
Just me and Jingting Mountain.

---

4. Translated by Paul W. Kroll.
5. Translated by Paul W. Kroll.
6. A famous scenic spot in the southeastern

city of Hangzhou.
7. Translated by Vikram Seth.
8. Translated by Stephen Owen.

A Song on Visiting Heaven's Crone
Mountain in a Dream: On Parting[9]

Seafarers speak of that isle of Ying[1]—
but in blurred expanses of breakers and mist
   it is hard indeed to find.

Yue men tell of Heaven's Crone,[2]
appearing, then gone, it may be seen   5
   in the clouds and colored wisps.

Heaven's Crone reaches to sky
   and sideways runs to the sky,
its force stands over the Five Great Peaks,
   it casts Redwall in the shade.   10
Mount Tiantai[3] is forty and eight
   thousand yards high,
yet facing this it seems to tip,
   sagging southeastwardly.

And I, wishing to reach that place,   15
   once dreamed of Wu and Yue,
I spent a whole night flying across
   the moon in Mirror Lake.

The lake moon caught my reflection,
and went with me on to Shan Creek.   20
The place where Lord Xie spent the night
   is still to be found there now,
where green waters are ruffled in ripples,
   and the gibbon's wail is clear.

I put on the clogs of Lord Xie,[4]   25
and scaled that ladder into blue clouds.
Halfway up cliffside I saw sun in sea,
and heard in the air the Heaven-Cock crow.

A thousand peaks and ten thousand turns,
   my path was uncertain;   30
I was lost among flowers and rested on rock,
   when suddenly all grew black.

Bears roared and dragons groaned,
   making the cliff-streams quake,
the deep forests were shivering,—tiered ridges shook,   35

---

9. Translated by Stephen Owen.
1. One of the islands of immortals.
2. A mountain near the ancient southern state of Yue.
3. A sacred Buddhist mountain in southeast-

ern China (modern Zhejiang Province).
4. A 5th-century poet renowned for his landscape poetry, he was also famous for supposedly inventing special mountain-climbing shoes.

clouds hung blue,—portending rain,
troubled waters rolled,—giving off mists.

Thunder-rumbling in Lightning Cracks,
hill ridges split and fell;
then the stone doors of Caves to Heaven   40
swung open with a crash.
A billowing vast blue blackness
    whose bottom could not be seen,
where sun and moon were gleaming
    on terraces silver and gold.   45

Their coats were of rainbow,—winds were their steeds,
the lords of the clouds—came down in their hosts.
Tigers struck harps,—phoenixes drew coaches in circles,
those who are the Undying—stood in ranks like hemp.
All at once my soul was struck,—and my spirit shuddered,   50
I leapt up in dazed alarm,—and gave a long sigh.
I was aware only—of this moment's pillow and mat,
I had lost those mists and bright wisps—that had been here just
    before.

All pleasures in our mortal world   55
    are also just like this,
whatever has happened since ancient times
    is the water flowing east.

When I leave you now, you go,—when will you ever return?
just set a white deer out to graze   60
    upon green mountainsides,
and when I must go, I'll ride it
    to visit mountains of fame.

How can I pucker my brows and break my waist
    serving power and prestige?—   65
it makes me incapable
    of relaxing heart or face.

DU FU

Du Fu (712–770) failed in his political ambitions, and his poetry was not widely read during his lifetime. But during the Song Dynasty (960–1279) he rose to the top of the poetic canon because of his versatility and ability to capture the dramatic historical events and spirit of his age. Ever since that time, Du Fu, together with **Li Bo,** has maintained the reputation as the greatest of Chinese poets.

Du Fu was the grandson of a prominent court poet. Although he dreamed of an official career, that dream was dashed after he twice failed the civil service examination. When An Lushan rebelled in 755, the imperial court escaped but Du Fu was left behind in the capital. Eventually he slipped through the enemy lines and made his way to the court of the new emperor in exile. There he briefly held one of the court positions he had so much desired; but following the recapture of the capital, he was exiled to a minor provincial post. He soon quit in disgust and embarked on a lifetime of travels. He first went to seek the help of relatives in northwest China, and then took up residence in Chengdu in Sichuan Province. In his later years Du Fu moved to Kuizhou, where he produced his most admired poetry sequence, the "Autumn Meditations."

Du Fu is considered the "poet-historian" of Chinese literature, carrying out the Confucian duty to chronicle and criticize the events of his time. Prophetically, he grasped that the An Lushan Rebellion was an event of major historical proportions. But it was his ability to capture the rebellion's impact on his life and on the lives of the people around him that gave depth to his voice. In "Moonlight Night" Du Fu imagines his wife, whom he had managed to send to safety while he remained trapped in the occupied capital, watching the moon and worrying about him; "Qiang Village" conveys the riveting scene of reunion, after Du Fu has finally escaped from the capital and is reunited with his family. But the effects of the rebellion linger on even after it is quashed: a decade later, he devotes "Ballad of the Firewood Vendors" to the local working women in his new home in Kuizhou who despair that the loss of life has destroyed the marriage prospects of an entire generation.

The greatness of Du Fu's poetry lies in its extraordinary range of themes, styles, and observations. His poetic mastery is particularly visible in his preferred verse form, the regulated poem, in which he can be not just witty but also prophetic and visionary. Even when he is sober and humble, his everyday observations can reach cosmic proportions and take the unsuspecting reader by surprise.

Painted Hawk[1]

Wind-blown frost rises from plain white silk,
a gray falcon—paintwork's wonder.

Body strains, its thoughts on the cunning hare,
its eyes turn sidelong like a Turk in despair.

You could pinch the rays glinting on tie-ring,   5
its stance, to be called to the column's rail.

When will it strike the common birds?—
bloody feathers strewing the weed-covered plain.

Moonlight Night[2]

From her room in Fuzhou tonight,
all alone she watches the moon.

Far away, I grieve that her children
can't understand why she thinks of Chang'an.

Fragrant mist in her cloud hair damp,   5
clear lucence on her jade arms cold—

when will we lean by chamber curtains
and let it light the two of us, our tear stains dried?

Spring Prospect[3]

The nation shattered, mountains and rivers remain;
city in spring, grass and trees burgeoning.

Feeling the times, blossoms draw tears;
hating separation, birds alarm the heart.

Beacon fires three months in succession,   5
a letter from home worth ten thousand in gold.

White hairs, fewer for the scratching,
soon too few to hold a hairpin up.[4]

1. Translated by Stephen Owen.
2. Translated by Burton Watson. This poem
was written in 756, when Du Fu was held captive in the fallen capital of Chang'an during
the An Lushan Rebellion and his wife and family had fled to safety in Fuzhou in the north.

3. Translated by Burton Watson. This poem
was written when Du Fu was still a captive in
Chang'an.
4. Officials used hairpins to keep their caps in
place.

Qiang Village I[5]

Lofted and lifted, west of the clouds of red,
The trek of the sun descends to the level earth.
By the brushwood gate songbirds and sparrows chaffer,
And the homebound stranger from a thousand *li*[6] arrives.
Wife and children marvel that I am here: 5
When the shock wears off, still they wipe away tears.
In the disorders of the age was I tossed and flung;
That I return alive is a happening of chance.
Neighbors swarm up to the tops of the walls,
Touched and sighing, even they sob and weep.   10
The night wastes on, and still we hold the candle,
Across from another, as if asleep and in a dream.

My Thatched Roof Is Ruined by the Autumn Wind[7]

In the high autumn skies of September
    the wind cried out in rage,
Tearing off in whirls from my rooftop
    three plies of thatch.
The thatch flew across the river,   5
    was strewn on the floodplain,
The high stalks tangled in tips
    of tall forest trees,
The low ones swirled in gusts across ground
    and sank into mud puddles.   10
The children from the village to the south
    made a fool of me, impotent with age,
Without compunction plundered what was mine
    before my very eyes,
Brazenly took armfuls of thatch,   15
    ran off into the bamboo,
And I screamed lips dry and throat raw,
    but no use.
Then I made my way home, leaning on staff,
    sighing to myself.   20
A moment later the wind calmed down,
    clouds turned dark as ink,
The autumn sky rolling and overcast,
    blacker towards sunset,
And our cotton quilts were years old   25
    and cold as iron,
My little boy slept poorly,
    kicked rips in them.
Above the bed the roof leaked,
    no place was dry,   30

5. Translated by Paul W. Kroll. This poem was written in 757, when Du Fu finally rejoined his family after their separation during the tur- moil of the An Lushan Rebellion.
6. About 250 miles.
7. Translated by Stephen Owen.

And the raindrops ran down like strings,
    without a break.
I have lived through upheavals and ruin
    and have seldom slept very well,
But have no idea how I shall pass   35
    this night of soaking.
Oh, to own a mighty mansion
    of a hundred thousand rooms,
A great roof for the poorest gentlemen
    of all this world,   40
    a place to make them smile,
A building unshaken by wind or rain,
    as solid as a mountain,
Oh, when shall I see before my eyes
    a towering roof such as this?   45
Then I'd accept the ruin of my own little hut
    and death by freezing.

I Stand Alone[8]

A single bird of prey beyond the sky,
a pair of white gulls between riverbanks.

Hovering wind-tossed, ready to strike;
the pair, at their ease, roaming to and fro.

And the dew is also full on the grasses,   5
spiders' filaments still not drawn in.

Instigations in nature approach men's affairs—
I stand alone in thousands of sources of worry.

Spending the Night in a Tower by the River[9]

A visible darkness grows up mountain paths,
I lodge by river gate high in a study,

Frail cloud on cliff edge passing the night,
The lonely moon topples amid the waves.

Steady, one after another, a line of cranes in flight;   5
Howling over the kill, wild dogs and wolves.

No sleep for me. I worry over battles.
I have no strength to right the universe.

8. Translated by Stephen Owen.   9. Translated by Stephen Owen.

Thoughts while Travelling at Night[1]

Light breeze on the fine grass.
I stand alone at the mast.

Stars lean on the vast wild plain.
Moon bobs in the Great River's spate.

Letters have brought no fame.   5
Office? Too old to obtain.

Drifting, what am I like?
A gull between earth and sky.

Ballad of the Firewood Vendors[2]

Kuizhou women, hair half gray,
forty, fifty, and still no husbands;
since the ravages of rebellion, harder than ever
    to marry—
a whole life steeped in bitterness and long sighs.   5
Local custom decrees that men sit, women stand;
men mind the house door, women go out and work,
at eighteen, nineteen, off peddling firewood,
with money they get from firewood, making
    ends meet.   10
Till they're old, hair in two buns dangling to the neck,
stuck with wild flowers, a mountain leaf, a silver pin,
they struggle up the steep paths, flock to the market gate,
risk their lives for extra gain by dipping from salt wells.
Faces powdered, heads adorned, sometimes a trace   15
    of tears,
cramped fields, thin clothing, the weariness of
    stony slopes—
But if you say all are ugly as the women of Witch's
    Mountain,   20
how to account for Zhaojun,[3] born in a village to
    the north?

---

1. Translated by Vikram Seth.
2. Translated by Burton Watson. This poem, written in 766, describes local customs in Kuizhou, set on steep hillsides along the Yangzi River, where Du Fu had settled.
3. Wang Zhaojun, a stunningly beautiful court lady of the Han Dynasty (206 B.C.E.– 220 C.E.) who embodied the suffering of exile, because she was married off to a tribal chief of the fierce Xiongnu tribes as part of Han diplomacy on the unruly northern frontier. "Witch's Mountain": Wushan, near Kuizhou.

Autumn Meditations IV[4]

I've heard them say, Chang'an's like a chessboard;
sad beyond bearing, the happenings of these
    hundred years!
Mansions of peers and princes, all with new
    owners now;   5
in civil or martial cap and garb, not the same as before.
Over mountain passes, due north, gongs and
    drums resound;
wagons and horses pressing west speed the
    feather-decked dispatches.[5]   10
Fish and dragons sunk in sleep, autumn rivers cold;
old homeland, those peaceful times, forever in
    my thoughts!

4. Translated by Burton Watson. This poem comes from Du Fu's most famous poetic cycle, "Autumn Meditations."
5. Feathers attached to military dispatches marked the message as urgent; Uighurs were threatening from the north and Tibetans from the west.

BO JUYI

With more than 2,800 poems, Bo Juyi (or Bai Juyi; 772–846) stands out as the most prolific Tang poet. In "Last Poem" we see him on his deathbed, still busy scribbling poems to send back to his friends. Like no writer before him Bo Juyi recorded his daily life in poetry, considering such matters as his taste for fresh bamboo shoots, prices on the flower market, or the purchase of his beloved estate outside the capital. Seeking to write poetry as autobiography, he was also a highly self-conscious poet: in "On My Portrait" he laughs at himself, "some mountain man," and reads in his own face signs portending ruin rather than success.

Bo Juyi came from a modest scholar-official family, passed the civil service examination in his late twenties, and then embarked on a succession of government appointments, interrupted by several years in exile after he incurred the emperor's displeasure. While serving in powerful positions in the provinces away from the capital he became increasingly drawn to Buddhism and the joys of reclusive life.

Bo Juyi wrote in many styles and guises, but his "New Music Bureau Poetry," which drew attention to corrupt political practices and social abuses, was especially important to him. During the earlier Han Dynasty (206 B.C.E.–220 C.E.) the imperial Music Bureau was founded to collect songs from the people and provide musical performances. Its mission reflected the Confucian conviction that rulers should adjust their policies to the needs of their subjects and that song and poetry were particularly effective means of communicating the complaints of the people to the emperor and the ruling class. Bo Juyi revived this method of conveying grievances. The poem "Salt Merchant's Wife," for example, attacks the luxurious life that the imperial monopoly on iron and salt afforded salt merchants, who collected the imperial tax on iron and salt trading and often pocketed large profits.

Though Bo Juyi sternly castigated the abuse of power for private gains, he sympathized with a different kind of abuse of power that would have fatal consequences: the infatuation of Emperor Xuanzong (685–762) with "Prized Consort Yang" (Yang Guifei). The emperor's love for the consort enabled her clan to advance into positions of power at court on the eve of the An Lushan Rebellion. Although their connection with the rebellion is unclear, people held her and her clan responsible; and when the capital was overrun by rebels and Emperor Xuanzong tried to escape, the military demanded Yang Guifei's execution—so she was strangled before the emperor's eyes. Yang's taste for luxury and the exclusive attention the emperor lavished on her both fascinated and repelled people. This tale of fateful conflict between duty and love inspired many later poems, novels, and plays, but Bo Juyi's "Song of

Lasting Regret," composed half a century after the rebellion, became its most influential early treatment; his friend Chen Hong added a prose account to it. Though Bo Juyi and Chen Hong treat the same set of events, they differ markedly in how they structure the story, what significant details they choose to dramatize it, and how they judge the lovers. These differences go beyond a personal disagreement of opinion between two friends, also showing that poetry and prose had its distinct narrative logic and moral values regarding love affairs.

Bo Juyi achieved great fame during his lifetime. Copies of his poetry collection spread outside China to other East Asian countries, including Japan, where he became one of the most popular Chinese poets. His poetry was included in Japanese anthologies, his "New Music Bureau Poetry" became a basic primer for male and female students alike, and his song about the tragic love of Emperor Xuanzong and Yang Guifei was taken as the archetypal expression of impossible and tragic love; as such, it was frequently alluded to in the central masterpiece of Japanese literature, the eleventh-century *Tale of Genji* by the court lady **Murasaki Shikibu**.

The Song of Lasting Regret[1]

Monarch of Han, he doted on beauty, yearned for a bewitching temptress;
Through the dominions of his sway, for many years he sought but did
  not find her.
There was in the family of Yang a maiden just then reaching fullness,[2]
Raised in the women's quarters protected, unacquainted yet with others.   4
Heaven had given her a ravishing form, impossible for her to hide,
And one morning she was chosen for placement at the side of the
  sovereign king.
When she glanced behind with a single smile, a hundred seductions
  were quickened;
All the powdered and painted ones in the Six Palaces[3] now seemed   8
  without beauty of face.

---

1. Translated by and with notes adapted from Paul W. Kroll. The asterisks in this selection mark divisions, not excerptions.

2. The future Yang Guifei, the Emperor Xuanzong's "prized consort."

3. Residences of the imperial concubines.

In the coolness of springtime, she was permitted to bathe in the
    Huaqing pools,[4]
Where the slickening waters of the hot springs washed over her firm flesh.
Supported as she rose by a waiting-maid, she was so delicate, listless:
This was the moment when first she acceded to His favor   12
    and beneficence.

Cloud-swept tresses, flowery features, quivering hair-pendants of gold,
And behind the warmth of lotus-bloom drapings, they passed the
    springtime nights—
Springtime nights so grievously brief, as the sun rose again high!
From this time onward the sovereign king no longer held early court.   16

Taken with pleasure, she attended on the feasts, continuing without let;
Springtime followed springtime outing, evening after evening
    she controlled.

Of the comely beauties of the rear palace,[5] there were three thousand
    persons,
And preferments and affection for all three thousand were placed on   20
    her alone.
In her golden room, with makeup perfect, the Delicate One serves for
    the night;
In a tower of jade, with the feast concluded, drunkenness befits love in
    spring.

Her sisters and brothers, older or younger, all were enfeoffed[6] with land;
The most enviable brilliance and glory quickened their doorways and   24
    gates.
Then it came to pass, throughout the empire, that the hearts of fathers
    and mothers
No longer valued the birth of a son but valued the birth of daughters.

The high sites of Mount Li's palace reached into clouds in the blue,
And transcendent music, wafted on the wind, was heard there   28
    everywhere.

Measured songs, languorous dancing merged with sound of strings and
    bamboo,
As the sovereign king looked on all day long, never getting enough . . .
Until, out of Yuyang, horse-borne war-drums came, shaking the earth,
To dismay and smash the melody of "Rainbow Skirts and Feathered   32
    Vestments."[7]

* * *

4. Famous hot springs some fifteen miles outside of the Tang capital of Chang'an.
5. The women's quarters.
6. Deeded.
7. An exotic Central Asian dance melody;

Emperor Xuanzong rescored it, and Lady Yang
danced to it costumed as a moon maiden.
"Yuyang": the headquarters of the rebel An
Lushan, east of modern Beijing.

By the nine-layered walls and watchtowers, dust and smoke arose,
And a thousand chariots, ten thousand riders moved off to the southwest.[8]

The halcyon-plumed banners jounced and joggled along, moving and
    stopping again,
As they went forth westward from the metropolis' gates, something   36
    more than a hundred miles.
And then the Six Armies would go no farther—there was no other recourse,
But the fluently curved moth-eyebrows[9] must die before the horses.

Floriform filigrees were strewn on the ground, to be retrieved by no one,
Halcyon tailfeathers, an aigrette of gold, and hairpins made of jade.   40
The sovereign king covered his face—he could not save her;
When he looked back, it was with tears of blood that mingled in
    their flow.

                              *   *   *

Yellowish grit spreads and scatters, as the wind blows drear and doleful;
Cloudy walkways turn and twist, climbing Saber Gallery's[1] heights.   44
Below Mount Emei there are very few men who pass by;
Lightless now are the pennons and flags in the sun's dimmer aura.

Waters of Shu's[2] streams deepest blue, the mountains of Shu are green—
For the Paragon, the Ruler, dawn to dawn, night upon night, his   48
    feelings:
Seeing the moon from his transient palace—a sight that tears at his heart;
Hearing small bells in the evening rain—a sound that stabs his insides.

                              *   *   *

Heaven revolves, the days roll on, and the dragon carriage was turned
    around;[3]
Having reached the spot, faltering he haltered, unable to leave it again.   52
But amidst that muddy earth, below Mawei Slope,[4]
Her jade countenance was not to be seen—just a place of empty death.

Sovereign and servants beheld each other, cloaks wet from weeping;
And, looking east, to the metropolis' gates, let their horses take them   56
    homeward.

                              *   *   *

Returned home now, and the ponds, the pools, all were as before—
The lotuses of Grand Ichor Pool, the willows by the Night-is-Young Palace.

The lotus blossoms resemble her face, the willow branches her eyebrows;
Confronted with this, would it be possible that his tears should not fall?   60

---

8. The emperor and his retinue, fleeing from
An Lushan's rebel army.
9. That is, Lady Yang.
1. A sacred mountain in the southwestern
province of Sichuan.

2. An ancient name for the region.
3. That is, the emperor returned to the capital.
4. The site of Lady Yang's execution.

From the day that peach and plum flowers open, in the springtime breezes,
Until the leaves of the "we-together"[5] tree are shed in the autumn rain. . . .

The West Palace and the Southern Interior were rife with autumn grasses,
And fallen leaves covered the steps, their red not swept away.   64
The artistes, once young, of the Pear Garden have hair gone newly white;
The Pepper Room attendants and their budding nymphs are become
   aged now.

Fireflies flit through the hall-room at dusk, as he yearns in desolation;
When all the wick of his lone lamp is used, sleep still fails to come.   68
Ever later, more dilatory, sound the watch-drum and bell in the
   lengthening nights;
Fitfully sparkling, the River of Stars[6] streams onward to the dawn-
   flushed sky.

The roof-tiles, paired as love-ducks, grow chilled, and flowers of frost grow
   thick;
The halcyon-plumed coverlet is cold—whom would he share it with?   72
Dim-distanced, far-faded, are the living from the dead, parted more
   than a year ago;
Neither her soul nor her spirit have ever yet come into his dreams.

* * *

A Daoist adept from Linqiong, a visitor to the Hongdu Gate,[7]
Could use the perfection of his essential being to contact souls and   76
   spirits.
Because of his broodings the sovereign king, tossing and turning,
   still yearned;
So he set to task this adept of formulas, to search for her sedulously.

Cleaving the clouds, driving the ethers, fleeting as a lightning-flash,
Ascending the heavens, entering into the earth, he sought her out   80
   everywhere.
On high he traversed the sky's cyan drop-off, and below to the Yellow Springs;[8]
In both places, to the limits of vision, she was nowhere to be seen.

Of a sudden he heard rumor then of a transcendent mountain in the sea,
A mountain resting in void and nullity, amidst the vaporous seemings.   84

High buildings and galleries shimmer there brightly, and five-colored
   clouds mount up;
In the midst of this, relaxed and unhurried, were hosts of tender sylphs.
And in *their* midst was one, known as Greatest Perfection,[9]

---

5. A tree whose name sounds like the phrase "we together." The falling of the leaves reminds the emperor of his lost love.
6. The Milky Way.
7. An ancient name for the capital's gates.
8. A traditional name for the Chinese underworld. "Sky's cyan drop-off": the sky's blue reaches; also a Daoist technical term for a specific region in the "Heaven of Nascent Azure."
9. The religious name (Taizhen) adopted by Lady Yang when she briefly took orders as a Daoist priestess, before receiving a title as the emperor's consort.

Whose snow-white skin and flower-like features appeared to resemble   88
  hers.

In the western wing of the gatehouse of gold, he knocked at the jade bolting,
In turn setting in motion Little Jade who made report to Doubly Completed.[1]
When word was told of the Son of Heaven's envoy, from the House of Han,
Then, within the nine-flowered drapings, her dreaming spirit startled.   92

She searched for her cloak, pushed pillow aside, arose, walked forth
  distractedly;
Door-screens of pearl, partitions of silver, she opened out one after another.
With her cloud-chignon half-mussed to one side, newly awakened from sleep,
With flowered cap set awry, down she came to the ceremonial hall.   96

Her sylphine sleeves, puffed by a breeze, were lifted, flared and fluttering,
Just the same as in the dance of "Rainbow Skirts and Feathered Vestments."
But her jade countenance looked bleak, forlorn, crisscrossed with tears—
A single branch of pear blossom, in springtime laden with rain.   100

Restraining her feelings, focusing her gaze, she asked her sovereign king's
  indulgence:
"Once we were parted, both voice and face were lost to limitless vagueness.
There, within Zhaoyang Basilica, affection and favor were cut short,
While here in Penglai's[2] palaces, the days and months have   104
  lengthened.

"Turning my head and looking down to the sites of the mortal sphere,
I can no longer see Chang'an,[3] what I see is dust and fog.
Let me take up these familiar old objects to attest to my deep love:
The filigree case, the two-pronged hairpin of gold, I entrust to you to   108
  take back.

"Of the hairpin but one leg remains, and one leaf-fold of the case;
The hairpin is broken in its yellow gold, and the case's filigree halved.
But if only his heart is as enduring as the filigree and the gold,
Above in heaven, or amidst men, we shall surely see each other."   112

As the envoy was to depart, she entrusted poignantly to him words as well,
Words in which there was a vow that only two hearts would know:
"On the seventh day of the seventh month,[4] in the Hall of Protracted Life,
At the night's mid-point, when we spoke alone, with no one else around—   116

---

1. Two of Lady Yang's servants. "Doubly Completed" was the servant of a central Daoist goddess, the "Queen Mother of the West."
2. A Daoist island of the immortals in the eastern ocean (during Bo Juyi's time, sometimes associated with Japan).
3. The Tang capital.

4. According to popular legend, the only day when the constellation the Oxherd could cross the Milky Way to meet with his lover, the Weaver Maid; Lady Yang and the emperor had exchanged a love oath on that auspicious night. The festival is still celebrated today in East Asia as a Valentine's Day of sorts.

'In heaven, would that we might become birds of coupled wings!
On earth, would that we might be trees of intertwining limbs! . . .'"
Heaven is lasting, earth long-standing, but there is a season for their end;
This regret stretches on and farther, with no ending time.   120

Chen Hong, *An Account to Go with the "Song of Lasting Regret"*[5]

During the Kaiyuan Reign,[6] the omens of the Stair Stars showed a world at peace, and there were no problems throughout all the land within the four circling seas. Xuanzong, having been long on the throne, grew weary of having to dine late and dress while it was still dark for the dawn audience; and he began to turn over all questions of government, both large and small, to the Assistant Director of the Right, Li Linfu, while the Emperor himself tended either to stay deep in the palace or go out to banquets, finding his pleasure in all the sensual delights of ear and eye. Previously the Empress Yuanxian and the Consort Wuhui had both enjoyed His Majesty's favor, but each in turn had departed this world; and even though there were in the palace over a thousand daughters of good families, none of them really caught his fancy. His Majesty was fretful and displeased.

In those days every year in December the imperial entourage would journey to Huaqing Palace. The titled women, both from the inner palace and from without, would follow him like luminous shadows. And he would grant them baths in the warm waters there, in the very waves that had bathed the imperial sun. Holy fluids in a springlike breeze went rippling through those places. It was then that His Majesty's heart was smitten: for he had truly come upon the one woman, and all the fair flesh that surrounded him seemed to him like dirt. He summoned Gao Lishi to make a secret search for this woman in the palaces of the princes; and there, in the establishment of the Prince of Shou, he found the daughter of Yang Xuanyan. She had already become a mature woman. Her hair and tresses were glossy and well arranged; neither slender nor plump, she was exactly of the middle measure; and there was a sensuous allure in her every motion, just like the Lady Li of Emperor Wu of the Han. He ordered a special channel of the warm springs cut for her and commanded that it be offered to her gleaming fineness. When she came out of the water, her body seemed frail and her force spent, as if she could not even bear the weight of lace and gauze; yet she shed such radiance that it shone on all around her. His Majesty was most pleased. On the day he had her brought to meet him, he ordered the melody "Coats of Feathers, Rainbow Skirts" played to precede her. And on the eve when their love was consummated, he gave her, as proofs of his love, a golden hairpin and an inlaid box. He also commanded that she wear golden earrings and a hair-pick that swayed to her pace. The following year he had her officially listed as Guifei, Prized Consort, entitled to half the provision as an empress. From this point on she assumed a seductively coy manner and spoke wittily, suiting herself to His Majesty's wishes by thousands of fetching ways. And His Majesty came to dote on her ever more deeply.

5. Translated by Stephen Owen.
6. The golden years of Emperor Xuanzong's reign, from 713 to 741.

At this time the Emperor made a tour of his nine domains and offered the gold-sealed tablets in ceremonies on the Five Sacred Peaks. On Mount Li during snowy nights and in Shangyang Palace on spring mornings she would ride in the same palanquin as the Emperor and spend the night in the same apartments; she was the main figure of feasts and had his bedchambers all to herself when he retired. There were three Great Ladies, nine Royal Spouses, twenty-seven Brides of the Age, eighty-one Imperial Wives, Handmaidens of the Rear Palace, Women Performers of the Music Bureau—and on none of these was the Son of Heaven the least inclined to look. And from that time on, no one from the Six Palaces was ever again brought forward to the royal bed. This was not only because of her sensual allure and great physical charms, but also because she was clever and smart, artful at flattery and making herself agreeable, anticipating His Majesty's wishes—so much so that it cannot be described. Her father, her uncle, and her brothers were all given high honorary offices and were raised to ranks of Nobility Equal to the Royal House. Her sisters were enfeoffed as Ladies of Domains. Their wealth matched that of the royal house; and their carriages, clothes, and mansions were on a par with the Emperor's aunt, Princess Taichang. Yet in power and the benefits of imperial favor, they surpassed her. They went in and out of the royal palace unquestioned, and the senior officers of the capital would turn their eyes away from them. There were doggerel rhymes in those days that went:

> If you have a girl, don't feel sad;
> if you have a boy, don't feel glad.

and:

> The boy won't be a noble,
>   but the daughter may be queen;
> so look on your daughters now
>   as the glory of the clan.

To such a degree were they envied by people.

At the end of the Tianbao Reign,[7] her uncle Yang Guozhong stole the position of Chancellor and abused the power he held. When An Lushan led his troops in an attack on the imperial palace, he used punishing Yang Guozhong as his pretext. Tong Pass was left undefended, and the Kingfisher Paraphernalia of the imperial entourage had to set out southward.[8] After leaving Xianyang, their path came to Mawei Pavilion. There the Grand Army hesitated, holding their pikes in battle positions and refusing to go forward. Attendant officers, gentlemen of the court, and underlings bowed down before His Majesty's horse and asked that this current Chao Cuo[9] be executed to appease the world. Yang Guozhong then received the yak-hair hat ribbons and the pan of water, by which a great officer of the court presents himself to the Emperor for punishment, and he died there by the edge of the road. Yet the will of those who were with the Emperor was still not satisfied. When His Majesty asked what the problem was, those who dared speak out asked that the Prized Consort also be sacrificed to

---

7. Emperor Xuanzong's last reign period, from 742 to 756, leading up to the An Lushan Rebellion.
8. That is, the emperor fled west to Sichuan.
9. A Han Dynasty official, executed in 155 B.C.E. because he was blamed for helping to incite a rebellion.

allay the wrath of the world. His Majesty knew that it could not be avoided, and yet he could not bear to see her die, so he turned his sleeve to cover his face as the envoys dragged her off. She struggled and threw herself back and forth in panic, but at last she came to death under the strangling cord.

Afterward, Xuanzong came to Chengdu on his Imperial Tour, and Suzong accepted the succession at Lingwu.[1] In the following year the Monster himself [An Lushan] forfeited his head, and the imperial carriage returned to the capital. Xuanzong was honored as His Former Majesty and given a separate establishment in the Southern Palace, then transferred to the western sector of the Imperial Compound. As time and events passed, all joy had gone from him and only sadness came. Every day of spring or night of winter, when the lotuses in the ponds opened in summer or when the palace ash trees shed their leaves in autumn, the performers of the Pear Garden Academy would produce notes on their jade flageolets; and if he heard one note of "Coats of Feathers, Rainbow Skirts," His Majesty's face would lose its cheer, and all those around him would sob and sigh. For three years there was this one thing on his mind, and his longing never subsided. His soul sought her out in dream, but she was so far away he could not reach her.

It happened then that a wizard came from Shu; and knowing that His Majesty was brooding so much on Yang the Prized Consort, he said that he possessed the skills of Li the Young Lord, the wizard who had summoned the soul of Lady Li for Emperor Wu of the Han. Xuanzong was very pleased, and ordered him to bring her spirit. The wizard then used all his skills to find her, but could not. He was also able to send his spirit on journeys by riding vapors; he went up into the precincts of Heaven and sank down into the vaults of the Earth looking for her; but he did not meet her. And then again he went to the margins and the encircling wastelands, high and low, to the easternmost extreme of Heaven and the Ocean, where he strode across Fanghu.

He saw there the highest of the mountains of the Undying, with many mansions and towers; at the end of the western verandah there was a deepest doorway facing east; the gate was shut, and there was written "The Garden of Taizhen, Jade Consort." The wizard pulled out a hatpin and rapped on the door, at which a young maiden with her hair done up in a double coil came out to answer the door. The wizard was so flustered he couldn't manage to get a word out, so the maiden went back in. In a moment another servant girl in a green dress came out and asked where he was from. The wizard then identified himself as an envoy of the Tang Son of Heaven and conveyed the command he had been given. The servant said, "The Jade Consort has just gone to bed; please wait a while for her." Thereupon he was swallowed up in a sea of clouds with the dawn sun breaking through them as down a tunnel to the heavens; then the jasper door closed again and all was still and without a sound.

The wizard held his breath and did not move his feet, waiting at the gate with folded hands. After a long time, the servant invited him to come in and said, "The Jade Consort is coming out." Then he saw a person with a bonnet of golden lotuses, wearing lavender chiffon, with pendants of red jade hanging from her sash and phoenix slippers, and seven or eight persons in attendance on her. She greeted the wizard and asked, "Is the Emperor well?" Then she

1. Emperor Xuanzong abdicated to his successor, Emperor Suzong.

asked what had happened since the fourteenth year of the Tianbao Reign. When he finished speaking, she grew wistful and gestured to her servant to get a golden hairpin and inlaid box, each of which she broke in parts. She gave one part of each to the envoy, saying, "Express my gratitude to the Emperor and present him these objects as mementos of our former love."

The wizard received her words and these objects of surety; he was ready to go, but one could see in his face that something was troubling him. The Jade Consort insisted that he tell her what was the matter. Then he knelt down before her and said, "Please tell me something that happened back then, something of which no one else knew, so that I can offer to His Majesty as proof. Otherwise I am afraid that with the inlaid box and the golden hairpin I will be accused of the same kind of trickery that Xin Yuanping practiced on Emperor Wen of the Han."[2] The Jade Consort drew back lost in thought, as if there were something she were recalling with fondness. Then very slowly she said, "Back in the tenth year of the Tianbao Reign, I was attending on His Majesty, who had gone to the palace on Mount Li to escape the heat. It was autumn, in the seventh month, the evening when the Oxherd and the Weaver Star meet.[3] It was the custom of the people of Qin on that night to spread out embroidery and brocade, to put out food and drink, to set up flowers and melons, and to burn incense in the yard—they call this 'begging for deftness.' Those of the inner palace hold this custom in particularly high regard. It was almost midnight; and the guards and attendants in the eastern and western cloisters had been dismissed. I was waiting on His Majesty alone. His Majesty stood there, leaning on his shoulder, then looked up at the heavens and was touched by the legend of the Oxherd and Weaver Star. We then made a secret vow to one another, a wish that we could be husband and wife in every lifetime. When we stopped speaking, we held hands, and each of us was sobbing. Only the Emperor knows of this."

Then she said sadly, "Because of this one thought so much in my mind, I will be able to live on here no longer. I will descend again to the world below and our future destiny will take shape. Whether in Heaven or in the world of mortal men, it is certain that we will meet again and form our bond of love as before." Then she said, "His Former Majesty will not be long in the world of men. I hope that he will find some peace of mind and not cause himself suffering."

The envoy returned and presented this to His Former Majesty, and the Emperor's heart was shaken and much afflicted with grief. For days on end he could find no cheer. In the summer of that year, in the fourth month, His Majesty passed on.

In winter of the first year of the Yuanhe Reign, the twelfth month (February 807), Bo Juyi of Taiyuan left his position as Diarist in the Imperial Library to be the sheriff of Chou County. I, Chen Hong, and Wang Zhifu of Langya had our homes in this town; and on our days off we would go together visiting sites of the Undying and Buddhist temples. Our discussion touched on this story, and we were all moved to sighs. Zhifu lifted his winecup to Bo Juyi and said, "Unless such an event finds an extraordinary talent who can adorn it with colors, even

2. Xin Yuanping gained the favor of Emperor Wen of the Han Dynasty by producing fake omens, such as the miraculous appearance of a jade cup with an auspicious inscription.

When his frauds were discovered, he was executed.

3. See p. 1134, n. 4.

something so rare will fade away with time and no longer be known in the world. Bo Juyi is deeply familiar with poetry and has strong sentiments. Why doesn't he write a song on the topic." At this Bo Juyi made the "Song of Lasting Regret." It is my supposition that he was not only moved by the event, but he also wanted to offer warning about such creatures that can so enthrall a man, to block the phases by which troubles come, and to leave this for the future. When the song was finished, he had me write a prose account for it. Of those things not known to the general public, I, not being a survivor of the Kaiyuan, have no way to know. For those things known to the general public, the "Annals of the Reign of Xuanzong" are extant. This is merely an account for the "Song of Lasting Regret."

Salt Merchant's Wife (in hatred of profiteers)[1]

The salt merchant's wife[2]
has silk and gold aplenty,
but she does not work at farming,
    nor does she spin the silk.
From north to south to east to west   5
    she never leaves her home,
wind and waters, her native land,
    her lodging is the boat.
Once she came from Yangzhou,
    a humble family's child,   10
she married herself a merchant,
    a great one from Jiangxi.
Her glinting hair-coils have grown rich,
    there golden pins abound,
her gleaming wrists have gotten plump,   15
    her silver bracelets tight.

On one side she shouts to her servants,
    on the other, yells at her maids,
and I ask you, how does it happen
    that you come to live like this?   20
Her husband has been a salt merchant
    for fifteen years now,
attached to no county or province,
    attached to the Emperor.
Every year when salt profits   25
    are to enter official hands,
the lesser part goes to officials,
    the greater part goes to himself.
Official profits are meager,
    private profits are rich,   30

1. Translated by Stephen Owen.
2. Salt merchants were an intermediary social class; under the direct jurisdiction of the emperor, they enforced the state monopoly on iron and salt and were paid a percentage of the taxes they collected. In Bo Juyi's time, the imperial government had great difficulty enforcing the collection of taxes and staying on a sound fiscal footing.

the Secretary of Iron and Salt
   is far and does not know.

Better still, here on the river,
   where fish and rice are cheap,
with pink fillets and oranges   35
   and meals of fragrant rice.
Having eaten her fill, in thick make-up
   she leans by the cabin aft,
both of her rosy cheeks
   are buds about to bloom.   40
This salt merchant's wife
was lucky to marry a merchant:
All day long fine food to eat,
all year long good clothes.
But good clothes and fine food   45
   have to come from somewhere,
and she would be struck with shame
   before some Sang Hongyang.[3]
But Sang Hongyang
died many years ago;   50
this happened not in the Han alone,
   it happens also now.

On My Portrait[1]

I didn't even know my own face,
then Li Fang painted my portrait true.

Observe with dispassion the spirit and frame—
this has to be some mountain man!

Wood of willow and cane soon decay;   5
the heart of a deer is hard to tame;

Why then in the palace's red plazas
have I waited five years on His Majesty?

And worse, my too stiff and inflexible nature,
cannot join the world and wallow in its dirt.   10

These features not only foretell no honors,
I fear in them cause that will bring my ruin.

Best resign and depart, the sooner the better,
withdraw this body fit for clouds and streams.

3. Sang Hongyang (152–80 B.C.E.) was an exemplary manager of the salt and iron monopoly during the Han Dynasty (206 B.C.E.–220 C.E.); he ensured that the revenue went into the imperial treasury rather than into merchants' pockets.
1. Translated by Stephen Owen.

Last Poem[1]

They have put my bed beside the unpainted screen;
They have shifted my stove in front of the blue curtain.
I listen to my grandchildren reading me a book;
I watch the servants, heating up my soup.
With rapid pencil I answer the poems of friends,　　　　　5
I feel in my pockets and pull out medicine-money.
When this superintendence of trifling affairs is done,
I lie back on my pillows and sleep with my face to the South.

1. Translated by Arthur Waley.

YUAN ZHEN
779–831

The most important development in prose literature during the Tang was the emergence of the genre of so-called "classical tales" (*chuanqi*, literally "records of marvels"). Long fiction emerged late in Chinese literature; before the Tang Dynasty short anecdotes and parables were common. As tales became more popular, writers crafted longer narratives telling unusual stories of love and heroism, which sometimes included supernatural elements. Yuan Zhen's "The Story of Yingying" is the most famous and most enthralling example of this new genre.

Yuan Zhen's official career was a series of official appointments, followed by periods of exile caused by party politics, but he eventually rose to high office at court. He was the closest friend of **Bo Juyi**, with whom he exchanged many poems and shared, among much else, a fascination with tragic love affairs.

"The Story of Yingying," Yuan Zhen's only tale, may have been written while he was taking the civil ser-

vice examination. It was intended as a "warming scroll"—a piece of writing that candidates circulated informally in the hope of getting the attention of potential patrons. It sets out as a typical "talented scholar meets beautiful woman" tale, a popular theme. "The Story of Yingying" describes the seduction and rejection of the heroine Yingying by her distant cousin, an aspiring exam candidate. In this scenario, marriage would have been the obvious outcome. Yet the lovers, each in their own way, thwart the possibility of legitimate marriage and instead contribute to a story of heartbreak. One might see this as a thinly disguised account of the author's personal experiences. If it is indeed autobiographical, he is portraying himself in a most unflattering light. Is Yuan Zhen trying to justify the outrageous behavior of the faithless scholar? Might he have tried to absolve his guilt over a shabby deed by writing a confessionary tale about it? Does he bitterly mock the naiveté of the formulaic plot popular during his time, attempting to show that happy endings are rare in real life?

Not least because of its uncertain intent, "The Story of Yingying" became very popular, and it went through some drastic transformations in subsequent adaptations. The most famous later version was the thirteenth-century play *Romance of the Western Chamber*. Here all the troubling aspects of the work are smoothed over. The remarkably willful and cultivated Yingying is transformed into an ordinary, docile heroine, and the lovers are ultimately reunited to live happily ever after.

The Story of Yingying[1]

During the Zhenyuan period[2] there lived a young man named Zhang. He was agreeable and refined, and good looking, but firm and self-contained, and capable of no improper act. When his companions included him in one of their parties, the others could all be brawling as though they would never get enough, but Zhang would just watch tolerantly without ever taking part. In this way he had gotten to be twenty-three years old without ever having had relations with a woman. When asked by his friends, he explained, "Deng Tuzi[3] was no lover, but a lecher. I am the true lover—I just never happened to meet the right girl. How do I know that? It's because things of outstanding beauty never fail to make a permanent impression on me. That shows I am not without feelings." His friends took note of what he said.

Not long afterward Zhang was traveling in Pu,[4] where he lodged some ten *li*[5] east of the city in a monastery called the Temple of Universal Salvation. It happened that a widowed Mrs. Cui had also stopped there on her way back to Chang'an. She had been born a Zheng; Zhang's mother had been a Zheng, and when they worked out their common ancestry, this Mrs. Cui turned out to be a rather distant cousin once removed on his mother's side.

This year Hun Zhen[6] died in Pu, and the eunuch Ding Wenya proved unpopular with the troops, who took advantage of the mourning period to mutiny. They plundered the citizens of Pu, and Mrs. Cui, in a strange place with all her wealth and servants, was terrified, having no one to turn to. Before the mutiny Zhang had made friends with some of the officers in Pu, and now he requested a detachment of soldiers to protect the Cui family. As a result all escaped harm. In about ten days the imperial commissioner of inquiry, Du Que, came with full power from the throne and restored order among the troops.

Out of gratitude to Zhang for the favor he had done them, Mrs. Cui invited him to a banquet in the central hall. She addressed him: "Your widowed aunt with her helpless children would never have been able to escape alive from these rioting soldiers. It is no ordinary favor you have done us; it is rather as though you had given my son and daughter their lives, and I want to introduce them to you as their elder brother so that they can express their thanks." She

1. Translated by and with notes adapted from James Robert Hightower.
2. From 785 to 804.
3. An archetypal lecher.
4. Puzhou, a province northeast of Chang'an.
5. About 2½ miles.
6. The regional commander of Jiangzhou; he died in 799.

summoned her son Huanlang, a very attractive child of ten or so. Then she called her daughter: "Come out and pay your respects to your brother, who saved your life." There was a delay; then word was brought that she was indisposed and asked to be excused. Her mother exclaimed in anger, "Your brother Zhang saved your life. You would have been abducted if it were not for him—how can you give yourself airs?"

After a while she appeared, wearing an everyday dress and no makeup on her smooth face, except for a remaining spot of rouge. Her hair coils straggled down to touch her eyebrows. Her beauty was extraordinary, so radiant it took the breath away. Startled, Zhang made her a deep bow as she sat down beside her mother. Because she had been forced to come out against her will, she looked angrily straight ahead, as though unable to endure the company. Zhang asked her age. Mrs. Cui said, "From the seventh month of the fifth year of the reigning emperor to the present twenty-first year, it is just seventeen years."

Zhang tried to make conversation with her, but she would not respond, and he had to leave after the meal was over. From this time on Zhang was infatuated but had no way to make his feelings known to her. She had a maid named Hongniang with whom Zhang had managed to exchange greetings several times, and finally he took the occasion to tell her how he felt. Not surprisingly, the maid was alarmed and fled in embarrassment. Zhang was sorry he had said anything, and when she returned the next day he made shamefaced apologies without repeating his request. The maid said, "Sir, what you said is something I would not dare repeat to my mistress or let anyone else know about. But you know very well who Miss Cui's relatives are; why don't you ask for her hand in marriage, as you are entitled to do because of the favor you did them?"

"From my earliest years I have never been one to make any improper connections," Zhang said. "Whenever I have found myself in the company of young women, I would not even look at them, and it never occurred to me that I would be trapped in any such way. But the other day at the dinner I was hardly able to control myself, and in the days since, I walk without knowing where I am going and eat without hunger—I am afraid I cannot last another day. If I were to go through a regular matchmaker, taking three months and more for the exchange of betrothal presents and names and birthdates[7]—you might just as well look for me among the dried fish in the shop.[8] Can't you tell me what to do?"

"Miss Cui is so very strict that not even her elders could suggest anything improper to her," the maid replied. "It would be hard for someone in my position to say such a thing. But I have noticed she writes a lot. She is always reciting poetry to herself and is moved by it for a long time after. You might see if you can seduce her with a love poem. That is the only way I can think of."

Zhang was delighted and on the spot composed two stanzas of spring verses which he handed over to her. That evening Hongniang came back with a note on colored paper for him, saying, "By Miss Cui's instructions."

The title of her poem was "Bright Moon on the Night of the Fifteenth":

7. In order to determine an auspicious date for a wedding.
8. An allusion to the parable of help that comes too late, found in the early Chinese master text *Zhuangzi*.

> *I await the moon in the western chamber*
> *Where the breeze comes through the half-opened door.*
> *Sweeping the wall the flower shadows move:*
> *I imagine it is my lover who comes.*

Zhang understood the message: that day was the fourteenth of the second month, and an apricot tree was next to the wall east of the Cuis' courtyard. It would be possible to climb it.

On the night of the fifteenth Zhang used the tree as a ladder to get over the wall. When he came to the western chamber, the door was ajar. Inside, Hongniang was asleep on a bed. He awakened her, and she asked, frightened, "How did you get here?"

"Miss Cui's letter told me to come," he said, not quite accurately. "You go tell her I am here."

In a minute Hongniang was back. "She's coming! She's coming!"

Zhang was both happy and nervous, convinced that success was his. Then Miss Cui appeared in formal dress, with a serious face, and began to upbraid him: "You did us a great kindness when you saved our lives, and that is why my mother entrusted my young brother and myself to you. Why then did you get my silly maid to bring me that filthy poem? You began by doing a good deed in preserving me from the hands of ravishers, and you end by seeking to ravish me. You substitute seduction for rape—is there any great difference? My first impulse was to keep quiet about it, but that would have been to condone your wrongdoing, and not right. If I told my mother, it would amount to ingratitude, and the consequences would be unfortunate. I thought of having a servant convey my disapproval, but feared she would not get it right. Then I thought of writing a short message to state my case, but was afraid it would only put you on your guard. So finally I composed those vulgar lines to make sure you would come here. It was an improper thing to do, and of course I feel ashamed. But I hope that you will keep within the bounds of decency and commit no outrage."

As she finished speaking, she turned on her heel and left him. For some time Zhang stood, dumbfounded. Then he went back over the wall to his quarters, all hope gone.

A few nights later Zhang was sleeping alone by the veranda when someone shook him awake. Startled, he rose up, to see Hongniang standing there, a coverlet and pillow in her arms. She patted him and said, "She is coming! She is coming! Why are you sleeping?" And she spread the quilt and put the pillow beside his. As she left, Zhang sat up straight and rubbed his eyes. For some time it seemed as though he were still dreaming, but nonetheless he waited dutifully. Then there was Hongniang again, with Miss Cui leaning on her arm. She was shy and yielding, and appeared almost not to have the strength to move her limbs. The contrast with her stiff formality at their last encounter was complete.

This evening was the night of the eighteenth, and the slanting rays of the moon cast a soft light over half the bed. Zhang felt a kind of floating lightness and wondered whether this was an immortal who visited him, not someone from the world of men. After a while the temple bell sounded. Daybreak was near. As Hongniang urged her to leave, she wept softly and clung to him. Hongniang helped her up, and they left. The whole time she had not spoken a single word. With the first light of dawn Zhang got up, wondering, was it a dream?

But the perfume still lingered, and as it got lighter he could see on his arm traces of her makeup and the teardrops sparkling still on the mat.

For some ten days afterward there was no word from her. Zhang composed a poem of sixty lines on "An Encounter with an Immortal" which he had not yet completed when Hongniang happened by, and he gave it to her for her mistress. After that she let him see her again, and for nearly a month he would join her in what her poem called the "western chamber," slipping out at dawn and returning stealthily at night. Zhang once asked what her mother thought about the situation. She said, "She knows there is nothing she can do about it, and so she hopes you will regularize things."

Before long Zhang was about to go to Chang'an, and he let her know his intentions in a poem. Miss Cui made no objections at all, but the look of pain on her face was very touching. On the eve of his departure he was unable to see her again. Then Zhang went off to the west. A few months later he again made a trip to Pu and stayed several months with Miss Cui.

She was a very good calligrapher and wrote poetry, but for all that he kept begging to see her work, she would never show it. Zhang wrote poems for her, challenging her to match them, but she paid them little attention. The thing that made her unusual was that, while she excelled in the arts, she always acted as though she were ignorant, and although she was quick and clever in speaking, she would seldom indulge in repartee. She loved Zhang very much, but would never say so in words. At the time she was subject to moods of profound melancholy, but she never let on. She seldom showed on her face the emotions she felt. On one occasion she was playing her zither alone at night. She did not know Zhang was listening, and the music was full of sadness. As soon as he spoke, she stopped and would play no more. This made him all the more infatuated with her.

Some time later Zhang had to go west again for the scheduled examinations. It was the eve of his departure, and though he had said nothing about what it involved, he sat sighing unhappily at her side. Miss Cui had guessed that he was going to leave for good. Her manner was respectful, but she spoke deliberately and in a low voice. "To seduce someone and then abandon her is perfectly natural, and it would be presumptuous of me to resent it. It would be an act of charity on your part if, having first seduced me, you were to go through with it and fulfill your oath of lifelong devotion. But in either case, what is there to be so upset about in this trip? However, I see you are not happy and I have no way to cheer you up. You have praised my zither playing, and in the past I have been embarrassed to play for you. Now that you are going away, I shall do what you so often requested."

She had them prepare her zither and started to play the prelude to the "Rainbow Robe and Feather Skirt."[9] After a few notes, her playing grew wild with grief until the piece was no longer recognizable. Everyone was reduced to tears, and Miss Cui abruptly stopped playing, put down the zither, and ran back to her mother's room with tears streaming down her face. She did not come back.

9. An exotic Central Asian dance melody mentioned in Bo Juyi's famous "Song of Lasting Regret" (see p. 1133, n. 7).

The next morning Zhang went away. The following year he stayed on in the capital, having failed the examinations. He wrote a letter to Miss Cui to reassure her, and her reply read roughly as follows:

> I have read your letter with its message of consolation, and it filled my childish heart with mingled grief and joy. In addition you sent me a box of ornaments to adorn my hair and a stick of pomade to make my lips smooth. It was most kind of you; but for whom am I to make myself attractive? As I look at these presents my breast is filled with sorrow.
>
> Your letter said that you will stay on in the capital to pursue your studies, and of course you need quiet and the facilities there to make progress. Still it is hard on the person left alone in this far-off place. But such is my fate, and I should not complain. Since last fall I have been listless and without hope. In company I can force myself to talk and smile, but come evening I always shed tears in the solitude of my own room. Even in my sleep I often sob, yearning for the absent one. Or I am in your arms for a moment as it used to be, but before the secret meeting is done I am awake and heartbroken. The bed seems still warm beside me, but the one I love is far away.
>
> Since you said good-bye the new year has come. Chang'an is a city of pleasure with chances for love everywhere. I am truly fortunate that you have not forgotten me and that your affection is not worn out. Loving you as I do, I have no way of repaying you, except to be true to our vow of lifelong fidelity.
>
> Our first meeting was at the banquet, as cousins. Then you persuaded my maid to inform me of your love; and I was unable to keep my childish heart firm. You made advances, like that other poet, Sima Xiangru.[1] I failed to repulse them as the girl did who threw her shuttle.[2] When I offered myself in your bed, you treated me with the greatest kindness, and I supposed, in my innocence, that I could always depend on you. How could I have foreseen that our encounter could not possibly lead to something definite, that having disgraced myself by coming to you, there was no further chance of serving you openly as a wife? To the end of my days this will be a lasting regret—I must hide my sighs and be silent. If you, out of kindness, would condescend to fulfill my selfish wish, though it came on my dying day it would seem to be a new lease on life. But if, as a man of the world, you curtail your feelings, sacrificing the lesser to the more important, and look on this connection as shameful, so that your solemn vow can be dispensed with, still my true love will not vanish though my bones decay and my frame dissolve; in wind and dew it will seek out the ground you walk on. My love in life and death is told in this. I weep as I write, for feelings I cannot express. Take care of yourself; a thousand times over, take care of your dear self.
>
> This bracelet of jade is something I wore as a child; I send it to serve as a gentleman's belt pendant. Like jade may you be invariably firm and tender; like a bracelet may there be no break between what came before and what is to follow. Here are also a skein of multicolored thread and a tea roller of mottled bamboo. These things have no intrinsic value, but they are to signify

---

1. A bohemian poet (179–117 B.C.E.) who with his zither playing enticed the young widow Zhuo Wenjun to elope.

2. A neighbor girl repulsed the advances of Xie Kun (280–322) by throwing her shuttle in his face, knocking out two of his teeth.

that I want you to be true as jade, and your love to endure unbroken as a bracelet. The spots on the bamboo are like the marks of my tears,[3] and my unhappy thoughts are as tangled as the thread: these objects are symbols of my feelings and tokens for all time of my love. Our hearts are close, though our bodies are far apart and there is no time I can expect to see you. But where the hidden desires are strong enough, there will be a meeting of spirits. Take care of yourself, a thousand times over. The springtime wind is often chill; eat well for your health's sake. Be circumspect and careful, and do not think too often of my unworthy person.

Zhang showed her letter to his friends, and in this way word of the affair got around. One of them, Yang Juyuan, a skillful poet, wrote a quatrain on "Young Miss Cui":

> For clear purity jade cannot equal his complexion;
> On the iris in the inner court snow begins to melt.
> A romantic young man filled with thoughts of love.
> A letter from the Xiao girl,[4] brokenhearted.

Yuan Zhen[5] of Henan wrote a continuation of Zhang's poem "Encounter with an Immortal," also in thirty couplets:

> Faint moonbeams pierce the curtained window;
> Fireflies glimmer across the blue sky.
> The far horizon begins now to pale;
> Dwarf trees gradually turn darker green.
> A dragon song crosses the court bamboo;   5
> A phoenix air brushes the wellside tree.
> The silken robe trails through the thin mist;
> The pendant circles tinkle in the light breeze.
> The accredited envoy accompanies Xi wangmu;[6]
> From the cloud's center comes Jade Boy.[7]   10
> Late at night everyone is quiet;
> At daybreak the rain drizzles.
> Pearl radiance shines on her decorated sandals;
> Flower glow shows off the embroidered skirt.
> Jasper hairpin: a walking colored phoenix;   15
> Gauze shawl: embracing vermilion rainbow.
> She says she comes from Jasper Flower Bank
> And is going to pay court at Green Jade Palace.
> On an outing north of Luoyang's[8] wall,

3. An allusion to the legend of the two wives of the sage ruler Shun, who stained the bamboo with their tears when he died.
4. A term for any young woman (here, Yingying).
5. That is, the author.
6. The Queen Mother of the West, a central goddess in the Daoist pantheon; she dwells in the Kunlun Mountains in China's far west, in a huge palace inhabited by other immortals. Within its precincts grow the magic peach trees that bear the fruits of immortality once every three thousand years. This might be an allusion to Yingying's mother.
7. Perhaps an allusion to Yingying's brother.
8. Possibly a reference to the goddess of the Luo River, near the eastern capital of Luoyang.

By chance he came to the house east of Song Yu.[9]   20
His dalliance she rejects a bit at first,
But her yielding love already is disclosed.
Lowered locks put in motion cicada shadows;
Returning steps raise jade dust.
Her face turns to let flow flower snow   25
As she climbs into bed, silk covers in her arms.
Love birds in a neck-entwining dance;
Kingfishers in a conjugal cage.
Eyebrows, out of shyness, contracted;
Lip rouge, from the warmth, melted.   30
Her breath is pure: fragrance of orchid buds;
Her skin is smooth: richness of jade flesh.
No strength, too limp to lift a wrist;
Many charms, she likes to draw herself together.
Sweat runs: pearls drop by drop;   35
Hair in disorder: black luxuriance.
Just as they rejoice in the meeting of a lifetime
They suddenly hear the night is over.
There is no time for lingering;
It is hard to give up the wish to embrace.   40
Her comely face shows the sorrow she feels;
With fragrant words they swear eternal love.
She gives him a bracelet to plight their troth;
He ties a lovers' knot as sign their hearts are one.
Tear-borne powder runs before the clear mirror;   45
Around the flickering lamp are nighttime insects.
Moonlight is still softly shining
As the rising sun gradually dawns.
Riding on a wild goose she returns to the Luo River.
Blowing a flute he ascends Mount Song.   50
His clothes are fragrant still with musk perfume;
The pillow is slippery yet with red traces.
Thick, thick, the grass grows on the dyke;
Floating, floating, the tumbleweed yearns for the isle.
Her plain zither plays the "Resentful Crane Song";   55
In the clear Milky Way she looks for the returning wild goose.[1]
The sea is broad and truly hard to cross;
The sky is high and not easy to traverse.
The moving cloud is nowhere to be found—
Xiao Shi[2] stays in his chamber.   60

All of Zhang's friends who heard of the affair marveled at it, but Zhang had determined on his own course of action. Yuan Zhen was especially close to him and so was in a position to ask him for an explanation. Zhang said, "It is a general

9. In "The Lechery of Deng Tuzi," the courtier Song Yu tells of the beautiful girl next door who climbed up on the wall to flirt with him.

1. A goose might be carrying a message.
2. A well-known legendary flute player of early China.

rule that those women endowed by Heaven with great beauty invariably either destroy themselves or destroy someone else. If this Cui woman were to meet someone with wealth and position, she would use the favor her charms gain her to be cloud and rain or dragon or monster—I can't imagine what she might turn into. Of old, King Xin of the Shang and King You of the Zhou[3] were brought low by women, in spite of the size of their kingdoms and the extent of their power; their armies were scattered, their persons butchered, and down to the present day their names are objects of ridicule. I have no inner strength to withstand this evil influence. That is why I have resolutely suppressed my love."

At this statement everyone present sighed deeply.

Over a year later Cui was married, and Zhang for his part had taken a wife. Happening to pass through the town where she was living, he asked permission of her husband to see her, as a cousin. The husband spoke to her, but Cui refused to appear. Zhang's feelings of hurt showed on his face, and she was told about it. She secretly sent him a poem:

> Emaciated, I have lost my looks,
> Tossing and turning, too weary to leave my bed.
> It's not because of others I am ashamed to rise;
> For you I am haggard and before you ashamed.

She never did appear. Some days later when Zhang was about to leave, she sent another poem of farewell:

> Cast off and abandoned, what can I say now,
> Whom you loved so briefly long ago?
> Any love you had then for me
> Will do for the one you have now.

After this he never heard any more about her. His contemporaries for the most part conceded that Zhang had done well to rectify his mistake. I have often mentioned this among friends so that, forewarned, they might avoid doing such a thing, or if they did, that they might not be led astray by it. In the ninth month of a year in the Zhenyuan period, when an official, Li Gongchui, was passing the night in my house at the Pacification Quarter, the conversation touched on the subject. He found it most extraordinary and composed a "Song of Yingying" to commemorate the affair. Cui's child-name was Yingying, and Gongchui used it for his poem.

<hr>

3. Two ancient rulers whose infatuation with wicked concubines supposedly led to the end of their dynasties.

LI QINGZHAO

1084–ca. 1151

Li Qingzhao is one of the finest writers of Chinese song lyric (*ci*) and one of the most celebrated women poets of traditional China. Song lyric, a new poetic form that came to the fore during the Song Dynasty (960–1279), had begun as songs performed in the pleasure quarters of the bustling urban centers, but the genre eventually developed into a refined literary vehicle for delicately sketching mood and emotion. Li Qingzhao used the form with great virtuosity to capture her states of mind, displaying an effortless freshness that belies the precision of her poetic craftsmanship and her poems' emotional depth. She was also a true connoisseur of painting and antiquities in an age when the literary elite, like their European counterparts during the Renaissance, started to collect ancient artwork with great enthusiasm.

Born in northeastern China, in what is now Shandong Province, Li Qingzhao came from a distinguished literary family. Her father belonged to the literary circle of Su Shi, one of the greatest writers of the Song Dynasty, and after his appointment to the national academy in the capital, the family moved to Kaifeng. Her mother was also a poet, and Li Qingzhao was recognized as a promising poetic talent when still in her teens. In 1101, at age seventeen, she was married to Zhao Mingcheng, a student at the prestigious Hanlin Academy and son of a powerful official. Sharing an obsessive passion for books and learning, they began to amass a large collection of books, paintings, rubbings, and antiquities.

But the life they knew abruptly ended as the Song Dynasty lost its capital, the northern territories, and its emperor (himself an avid collector) to the invading Jin Tartars in 1126 and 1127. Li Qingzhao and her husband hastily fled south with part of their collection, but the pieces were gradually scattered and lost. Her husband left her due to an imperial summons and he soon fell ill and died. Li Qingzhao was now without a place of refuge and in constant flight from local rebellions. Finally she and the court settled in Hangzhou in the south in 1132. There has been much speculation as to whether Li Qingzhao married a second time in her late forties, then filed for divorce within a hundred days; a letter survives that accuses her second husband of greed and corruption, but many scholars deny its authenticity. Not much is known about her subsequent life, and even her year of death—1151 at the latest—is uncertain.

There is no better introduction to Li Qingzhao's remarkable world than her "Afterword" to her husband's study of early inscriptions, *Records on Metal and Stone*, a collection (now lost) of two thousand inscriptions from the second millennium B.C.E. to the tenth century C.E. Most prefaces and afterwords were stylized, scholarly, and relatively impersonal, but Li Qingzhao used the form to show the relationship between a work of scholarship and two lives. According to the "Afterword," the fate of Li Qingzhao and Zhao Mingcheng as a couple was mirrored in the fate of their collection of books and antiques: begun for their joint pleasure in the idyllic early years of their marriage, it increasingly grew into an obsession that dominated her husband's life, until at last both the collection and her husband's scholarly work reflected the differences between them. As she loses one piece after another of their shared possessions during her escape from the north, Li Qingzhao has to let go of her previous life and hopes. The residue of the collection represented many things to her. At one point it seemed to offer a way to purchase her husband's honor after a posthumous false accusation of treason; the books were also her companions as she ceaselessly fled from place to place, and the few pieces that ultimately remained became cherished mementos of the happier beginnings of her life. Throughout this short work Li Qingzhao returns again and again to the connection between people and their possessions, to the role of possessions in human relationships, and to the way in which such objects gain value and meaning.

The relatively few surviving song lyrics by Li Qingzhao, some of which are included here, are among the finest examples of the form. The ties between poetry and song in traditional China were old and complex. The works of poets were often set to music and were sometimes modified to answer musical needs. During the Tang period, however, an entirely new kind of music became popular: stanza-like melodies with musical lines of unequal length. In a language in which the pitch of a word (or "tone") is essential to understanding its meaning, Chinese song lyrics had to pay careful attention to the requirements of a particular melody—to be comprehensible, the pitch of the word had to match the pitch of the music. Tang poets began the practice of com-

posing lyrics for these popular irregular melodies, and this new poetic form came to be known as *ci*. These "song lyrics," which often concerned love, were frequently performed in the entertainment quarters of the great cities and at parties. By the early Song Dynasty the song lyric had evolved into a verse form whose character differed markedly from that of classical poetry. Primarily associated with delicate sensibility, it sought to evoke the passing mood.

In the lyrics to the melody "Note After Note" Li Qingzhao takes up the essential concerns of the form and one of the oldest questions in the Chinese tradition: the adequacy of language to express what occurs in the mind and heart. The lyric, which attempts to capture the essence of a particular moment, closes by wondering how the complex emotion she has evoked can be named by the simple word *sorrow*. Li Qingzhao had a genius for presenting scenes that could evoke feeling, as in the lyrics to "Southern Song," in which she describes changing from light summer clothes to a warmer autumn dress, decorated with scenes of a lotus pond. But the dress is old and its gilt lotus leaves are flaking off, giving the appearance of dying vegetation—a change she takes as both physical evidence and symbol of her own aging. It is at such moments that she answers in her own way the ancient question of how words can express the feeling of the moment, showing herself a true master not just of a particular poetic form but of verbal art generally.

From Records on Metal and Stone[1]

Afterword

What are the preceding chapters of *Records on Metal and Stone*?—the work of the governor, Zhao Defu.[2] In it he took inscriptions on bells, tripods, steamers, kettles, washbasins, ladles, goblets, and bowls from the Three Dynasties of high

---

1. All selections translated by Stephen Owen.
2. Sobriquet of Li Qingzhao's husband, Zhao Mingcheng.

antiquity all the way down to the Five Dynasties (immediately preceding our Song); here also he took the surviving traces of acts by eminent men and obscure scholars inscribed on large steles and stone disks. In all there were two thousand sections of what appeared on metal and stone. Through all these inscriptions, one might be able to correct historical errors, make historical judgements, and mete out praise and blame. It contains things which, on the highest level, correspond to the Way of the Sages, and on a lower level, supplement the omissions of historians. It is a great amount indeed. Yet catastrophe fell on Wang Ya and Yuan Zai alike: what did it matter that the one hoarded books and paintings while the other merely hoarded pepper? Changyou and Yuankai both had a disease—it made no difference that the disease of one was a passion for money, and of the other, a passion for transmission of knowledge and commentary. Although their reputations differed, they were the same in being deluded.

In 1101, in the first year of the Jianzhong Reign, I came as a bride to the Zhao household. At that time my father was a division head in the Ministry of Rites, and my father-in-law, later Grand Councilor, was an executive in the Ministry of Personnel. My husband was then twenty-one and a student in the Imperial Academy. In those days both families, the Zhaos and the Lis, were not well-to-do and were always frugal. On the first and fifteenth day of every month, my husband would get a short vacation from the Academy: he would "pawn some clothes"[3] for five hundred cash and go to the market at Xiangguo Temple, where he would buy fruit and rubbings of inscriptions. When he brought these home, we would sit facing one another, rolling them out before us, examining and munching. And we thought ourselves persons of the age of Getian.[4]

When, two years later, he went to take up a post, we lived on rice and vegetables, dressed in common cloth; but he would search out the most remote spots and out-of-the-way places to fulfill his interest in the world's most ancient writings and unusual characters. When his father, the Grand Councilor, was in office, various friends and relations held positions in the Imperial Libraries; there one might find many ancient poems omitted from the *Book of Songs*, unofficial histories, and writings never before seen, works hidden in walls and recovered from tombs. He would work hard at copying such things, drawing ever more pleasure from the activity, until he was unable to stop himself. Later, if he happened to see a work of painting or calligraphy by some person of ancient or modern times, or unusual vessels of the Three Dynasties of high antiquity, he would still pawn our clothes to buy them. I recall that in the Chongning Reign[5] a man came with a painting of peonies by Xu Xi and asked twenty thousand cash for it. In those days twenty thousand cash was a hard sum to raise, even for children of nobility. We kept it with us a few days, and having thought of no plan by which we could purchase it, we returned it. For several days afterward husband and wife faced one another in deep depression.

Later we lived privately at home for ten years, gathering what we could here and there to have enough for food and clothing. Afterward, my husband governed two provinces in succession, and he used up all his salary on "lead and wooden tablets" [for scholarly work].[6] Whenever he got a book, we would col-

---

3. All students at the Imperial Academy received an allowance of clothing.
4. A legendary emperor of the earliest times, when the world was still at peace.
5. From 1102 to 1106.
6. Throughout, the material in brackets is the translator's.

late it with other editions and make corrections together, repair it, and label it with the correct title. When he got hold of a piece of calligraphy, a painting, a goblet, or a tripod, we would go over it at our leisure, pointing out faults and flaws, setting for our nightly limit the time it took one candle to burn down. Thus our collection came to surpass all others in fineness of paper and the perfection of the characters.

I happen to have an excellent memory, and every evening after we finished eating, we would sit in the hall called "Return Home" and make tea. Pointing to the heaps of books and histories, we would guess on which line of which page in which chapter of which book a certain passage could be found. Success in guessing determined who got to drink his or her tea first. Whenever I got it right, I would raise the teacup, laughing so hard that the tea would spill in my lap, and I would get up, not having been able to drink anything at all. I would have been glad to grow old in such a world. Thus, even though we were living in anxiety, hardship, and poverty, our wills were not broken.

When the book collection was complete, we set up a library in "Return Home" hall, with huge bookcases where the books were catalogued in sequence. There we put the books. Whenever I wanted to read, I would ask for the key, make a note in the ledger, then take out the books. If one of them was a bit damaged or soiled, it would be our responsibility to repair the spot and copy it out in a neat hand. There was no longer the same ease and casualness as before. This was an attempt to gain convenience which led instead to nervousness and anxiety. I couldn't bear it. And I began to plan how to do away with more than one meat in our meals, how to do away with all finery in my dress; for my hair there were no ornaments of bright pearls or kingfisher feathers; the household had no implements for gilding or embroidery. Whenever we would come upon a history or the work of a major writer, if there was nothing wrong with the printing and no errors in the edition, we would buy it on the spot to have as a second copy. His family had always specialized in The Book of Changes and the Zuozhuan,[7] so the collection of works in those two traditions was most perfect and complete. Books lay ranged on tables and desks, scattered on top of one another on pillows and bedding. This was what took our fancy and what occupied our minds, what drew our eyes and what our spirits inclined to; and our joy was greater than the pleasure others had in dancing girls, dogs, and horses.

In 1126, the first year of the Jingkang Reign, my husband was governing Zechuan when we heard that the Jin Tartars were moving against the capital. He was in a daze, realizing that all those full trunks and overflowing chests, which he regarded so lovingly and mournfully, would surely soon be his possessions no longer. In the third month of spring in 1127, the first year of the Jianyan Reign, we hurried south for the funeral of his mother. Since we could not take the overabundance of our possessions with us, we first gave up the bulky printed volumes, the albums of paintings, and the most cumbersome of the vessels. Thus we reduced the size of the collection several times, and still we had fifteen cartloads of books. When we reached Donghai, it took a string of boats to ferry them all across the Huai, and again across the Yangzi to Jiankang. In our old mansion in Qingzhou we still had more than ten rooms of

7. Two works of the Confucian canon: a divination manual and the commentary to the Spring and Autumn Annals.

books and various items locked away, and we planned to have them all brought by boat the next year. But in the twelfth month Jin forces sacked Qingzhou, and those ten or so rooms I spoke of were all reduced to ashes.

The next autumn, the ninth month of 1128, my husband took charge of Jiankang Prefecture but relinquished the position in the spring of the following year. Again we put everything in boats and went up to Wuhu and Gushu intending to take up lodging on the River Gan. That summer in the fifth month we had reached Chiyang. At that point an imperial decree arrived, ordering my husband to take charge of Huzhou, and before he assumed that office, to proceed to an audience with the Emperor. Therefore he had the household stop at Chiyang from which he would go off alone to answer the summons. On the thirteenth day of the sixth month he set off to carry out his duty. He had the boats pulled up onto the shore, and he sat there on the bank, in summer clothes with his headband set high on his forehead, his spirit like a tiger's, his eyes gleaming as though they would shoot into a person, while he gazed toward the boats and took his leave. I was in a terrible state of mind. I shouted to him, "If I hear the city is in danger, what should I do?" He answered from afar, his hands on his hips: "Follow the crowd. If you can't do otherwise, abandon the household goods first, then the clothes, then the books and scrolls, then the old bronzes—but carry the sacrificial vessels for the ancestral temple yourself; live or die with them; don't give *them* up." With this he galloped off on his horse.

As he was hurrying on his journey, he suffered sunstroke from the intense heat, and by the time he reached imperial headquarters, he had contracted a malarial fever. At the end of the seventh month I received a letter that he was lying sick. I was much alarmed, considering my husband's excitable nature and how nothing had been able to prevent the illness deteriorating into fever; his temperature might rise even higher, and in that case he would have to take chilled medicines; then the sickness would really be something to be worried about. Thereupon I set out by boat and in one day and night traveled three hundred leagues. At the point when I arrived he was taking large doses of *chaihu* and yellow *qin*;[8] he had a recurring fever with dysentery, and the illness appeared terminal. I was weeping, and in such a desperate situation I could not bring myself to ask him what was to be done after his death. On the eighteenth day of the eighth month he could no longer get up; he took his brush and wrote a poem; when he finished, he passed away, with no thought at all for the future provision of his family.

When the funeral was over I had nowhere to go. His Majesty had already sent the palace ladies elsewhere, and I heard that crossings of the Yangzi were to be prohibited. At the time I still had twenty thousand *juan* of books, two thousand copies of inscriptions on metal and stone with colophons,[9] table service and mats enough to entertain a hundred guests, along with other possessions equaling those already mentioned. I also grew very sick, to the point that my only vital

---

8. Chinese herbal medicine.
9. Short essays containing the essential scholarly information on the inscriptions. These were Zhao Mingcheng's copies and rubbings of early inscriptions. "*Juan*": analogous to a book chapter, and used to measure the size of books or libraries.

sign was a rasping breath. The situation was getting more serious every day. I thought of my husband's brother-in-law, an executive in the Ministry of War on garrison duty in Hongzhou, and I dispatched two former employees of my husband to go ahead to my brother-in-law, taking the baggage. That winter in the twelfth month Jin invaders sacked Hongzhou and all was lost. Those books which, as I said, took a string of boats to ferry across the Yangzi were scattered into clouds of smoke. What remained were a few light scrolls and calligraphy pieces; manuscript copies of the collections of Li Bo, Du Fu, Han Yu, and Liu Zongyuan;[1] a copy of *A New Account of Tales of the World*;[2] a copy of *Discourses on Salt and Iron*; a few dozen rubbings of stone inscriptions from the Han and Tang; ten or so ancient tripods and cauldrons; a few boxes of Southern Tang manuscript editions—all of which I happened to have had removed to my chambers to pass the time during my illness—now a solitary pile of leftovers.

Since I could no longer go upriver, and since the movements of the invaders were unfathomable, I went to stay with my younger brother Li Hang, a reviser of edicts. By the time I reached Taizhou, the governor of the place had already fled. Proceeding on to Shan through Muzhou, we left the clothing and linen behind. Hurrying to Yellow Cliff, we hired a boat to take us toward the sea, following the fleeing court. The court halted a while in Chang'an, then we followed the imperial barge on the sea route to Wenzhou and Yuezhou.[3] In the twelfth month of the fourth year of the Jianyan Reign, early in 1131, all the officials of the government were released from their posts. We went to Quzhou, and then in the third month of spring, now the first year of the Shaoxing Reign (1131), we returned to Yuezhou, and in 1132, back again to Hangzhou.

When my husband had been gravely ill, a certain academician, Zhang Fei-qing, had visited him with a jade pot—actually it wasn't really jade but *min,* a stone like jade. I have no idea who started the story, but there was a false rumor that they had been discussing presenting it to the Jin as a tribute gift. I also learned that someone had made formal charges in the matter. I was terrified and dared say nothing, but I took all the bronze vessels and such things in the household and was about to turn them over to the imperial court. But by the time I reached Yuezhou, the court had already gone on to Siming. I didn't dare keep these things in the household any longer, so I sent them along with the manuscript books to Shan. Later, when the imperial army was rounding up defeated enemy troops, I heard that these had all been taken into the household of General Li. That "solitary pile of leftovers" of which I spoke had now been reduced by about fifty or sixty percent. All that remained were six or so baskets of books, painting, ink, and inkstones that I hadn't been able to part with. I always kept these under my bed and opened them only with my own hands.

At Kuaiji I chose lodging in a cottage belonging to a local named Zhong. Suddenly one night someone made off with five of the baskets through a hole

---

1. Four famous Tang Dynasty (617–907) writers of poetry and prose; see selections above.
2. A 5th-century book of anecdotes, some of which are included above in the "Hermits, Buddhists, and Daoists" grouping.

3. This itinerary follows the general route of the northerners to the southeast toward the sea, as they fled the threat of an invasion of South China by the Jin Tartars.

in the wall. I was terribly upset and offered a substantial reward to get them back. Two days later Zhong Fuhao next door produced eighteen of the scrolls and asked for a reward. By that I knew the thief was not far away.[4] I tried every means I could, but I still couldn't get hold of the rest. I have now found out that they were all purchased at a low price by the Circuit Fiscal Supervisor, Wu Yue. Now seventy or eighty percent of that "solitary pile of leftovers" is gone. I still have a few volumes from three or so sets, none complete, and some very ordinary pieces of calligraphy, but I still treasure them as if I were protecting my own head—how foolish I am!

Nowadays, when I chance to look over these books, it's like meeting old friends. And I recall when my husband was in the hall called "Calm Governance" in Laizhou: he had first finished binding the volumes, making title slips of rue leaves to keep out insects and tie-ribbons of pale blue silk, binding ten *juan* into one volume. Every day in the evening when the office clerks would go home, he would do editorial collations on two *juan* and write a colophon for one inscription. Of those two thousand items, colophons were written on five hundred and two. It is so sad—today the ink of his writing seems still fresh, yet the trees by his grave have grown to an armspan in girth.

Long ago when the city of Jiangling fell, Xiao Yi, Emperor Yuan of the Liang, did not regret the fall of his kingdom, yet destroyed his books and printings [unwilling to see them fall into the hands of his conquerors]. When his capital Jiangdu was sacked, Yang Guang, Emperor Yang of the Sui, wasn't concerned with his own death, only with recovering his books [his spirit overturning the boat in which they were being transported so that he could have his library in the land of the dead]. It must be that the passions of human nature cannot be forgotten, even standing between life and death. Or maybe it is Heaven's will that beings as insignificant as ourselves are not fit to enjoy these superb things. Or it might be that the dead too have consciousness, and they still treasure such things, give them their devoted attention, unwilling to leave them in the world of the living. How hard they are to obtain and how easy to lose!

From the time I was eighteen until now at the age of fifty-two—a span of thirty years—how much calamity, how much gain and loss I have witnessed! When there is possession, there must be lack of possession; when there is a gathering together, there must be a dissolution—that is the constant principle of things. Someone loses a bow; someone else happens to find a bow—what's worth noticing in that? The reason why I have so minutely recorded this story from beginning to end is to serve as a warning for scholars and collectors in later generations.

Written this second year of the Shaoxing Reign (1132), the eighth month, first day.

Li Qingzhao

---

4. That is, she knew that her landlord, Zhong Fuhao, was involved in the theft.

SONG LYRICS

To "Southern Song"

Up in heaven the star-river turns,
in man's world below
   curtains are drawn.
A chill comes to pallet and pillow,
   damp with tracks of tears.   5
I rise to take off my gossamer dress
and just happen to ask, "How late is it now?"

The tiny lotus pods,
   kingfisher feathers sewn on;
as the gilt flecks away   10
   the lotus leaves grow few.
Same weather as in times before,
   the same old dress—
only the feelings in the heart
are not as they were before.   15

To "Free-Spirited Fisherman"

Billowing clouds touch sky and reach
   the early morning fog,
the river of stars is ready to set,
   a thousand sails dance.
My dreaming soul moves in a daze   5
   to where the high god dwells—
I hear Heaven speak,
asking me with urgent concern
   where I am going now.

And I reply that my road is long,   10
   and, alas, twilight draws on;
I worked at my poems and for nothing have
   bold lines that cause surprise.
Into strong winds ninety thousand miles
   upward the Peng[1] now flies.   15
Let that wind never stop,
let it blow this tiny boat away
   to the Three Immortal Isles.[2]

1. A huge mythical bird described in the ancient Masters Text *Zhuangzi* (see Vol. A). Here it appears as a figure of greatness that smaller creatures cannot comprehend.
2. In the eastern sea, believed to be inhabited by immortals.

To "Like a Dream"

I will always recall that day at dusk,
   the pavilion by the creek,
and I was so drunk I couldn't tell
   the way home. My mood left me,
it was late when I turned back in my boat   5
and I strayed deep among lotuses—
how to get through?
how to get through?
and I startled to flight a whole shoal
   of egrets and gulls.   10

To "Drunk in the Shadow of Flowering Trees"

Pale fog, then dense clouds—
   gloomy all day long;
in the animal-shaped censer
   incense burns away.
Once again it is that autumn holiday: 5
to my jade pillow behind the gauze screen
at midnight the cold first comes.

By the eastern hedge I took wine in hand
   after twilight fell.
A fragrance filled my sleeves unseen.   10
Don't tell me this does not break your heart—
the west wind blowing up the curtains
and the person,
   as gaunt as the chrysanthemums.

To "Spring in Wuling"

The wind dies down, the fragrance in dirt,
   the flowers now are gone;
late afternoon, too weary to comb my hair.
Everything in the world is right; I am wrong;
   all that will happen is done;   5
before I can say it, tears come.

Yet I've heard it said that at Double Creek
   the spring is lovely still,
and I think I'll go boating there.
But then I fear   10
   those little boats of Double Creek
won't budge if they are made to bear
   this much melancholy.

To "Note After Note"

Searching and searching, seeking and seeking,
so chill, so clear,
dreary,
   and dismal,
     and forlorn.   5
That time of year
   when it's suddenly warm,
     then cold again,
now it's hardest of all to take care.
Two or three cups of weak wine—   10
how can they resist the biting wind
   that comes with evening?
The wild geese pass by—
that's what hurts the most—
and yet they're old acquaintances.   15

In piles chrysanthemums fill the ground,
looking all wasted, damaged—
who could pick them, as they are now?
I stay by the window,
how can I wait alone until blackness comes?   20
The beech tree,
   on top of that
     the fine rain,
on until dusk,
the dripping drop after drop.   25
In a situation like this
how can that one word "sorrow" grasp it?

IV

Japan's Classical Age

Although Japan consists of the four main islands of Hokkaidō, Honshū, Shikoku, and Kyūshū and about a thousand smaller islets, its contacts with the continent have always been close. In fact, much of what makes Japanese culture distinctive stems from the creative ways in which the Japanese adapted Chinese and Korean culture to their own circumstances. For example, the Japanese imported the Chinese writing system, but used it to produce their own distinct literature. They produced literature in two literary languages, one vernacular and the other Chinese-style, which differed strikingly in themes, rhetoric, and the gender of their authors. Some of the greatest works of Japanese literature were written by women in the vernacular language.

Much like the Romans confronting the older and more established civilization of the Greeks, early Japanese writers faced the challenging task of building their own literature on the sophisticated precedents of their mother culture while asserting their own originality. In addition to literature, Japan adopted crucial institutions and cultural practices from

Illustrated Biography of Prince Shōtoku, painted in 1069 by Hata no Chitei. This is part of a series of ten panels that depict the life of Prince Shōtoku (574–622), founder of Buddhism in Japan.

China, such as the concept of a state headed by a divine monarch, a government system based on administrative statutes and laws, Buddhism used as a state religion protecting the people's welfare, city planning, temple architecture, sacred sculpture, religious rituals, court music and elegant dances, imperial excursions, medicine, the culture of painting, calligraphy, and tea. But whereas Rome had conquered Greece and had its young elite educated by Greek slaves, early Japanese had relatively little actual contact with China and knew it mostly from books, thus feeling less self-conscious about their cultural identity. They believed in the numinous power of their language and their gods and were proud of the pristine simplicity of their earliest literature. Unlike parts of Korea and Vietnam, which at certain points in their history were conquered by China, Japan was never directly colonized by China; its inhabitants could admire their old neighbor at a safe distance.

CONTINENTAL CULTURE AND BI-LITERACY

The cultural dialogue with China resulted in one of the world's most complex literary traditions. Writing was invented in China some eighteen centuries before the Japanese learned how to read and write. Unlike Koreans and Vietnamese, who exclusively used Chinese-style writing for centuries, the Japanese used the Chinese writing system to produce texts in two literary languages: vernacular Japanese and Chinese-style writing (also called "Sino-Japanese," *kanbun*, or simply "Literary Chinese"). Chinese-style writing was transnational, enabling the Japanese court to participate in the diplomatic and cultural exchange with China and other states in the Chinese sphere of influence such as Korea and Vietnam; playing a

role similar to that of Latin in medieval Europe, it became the official language of the imperial administration and the Buddhist clergy, and was thus associated with high status, serious purpose, and male authorship. Although vernacular literature, in particular poetry, could serve similarly prestigious purposes at court, it became the preferred medium for emotional intimacy, romance, psychological sophistication, and fiction, all of which were associated with female sensibility.

Because the Chinese and Japanese languages belong to radically different language families, adopting Chinese characters to write Japanese required complex adjustments. Chinese is a noninflected language, with a "subject–predicate–object" word order; and literary Chinese is largely monosyllabic, meaning that most words consist of one or at most two syllables. Japanese, in contrast, is agglutinative, meaning that it strings short semantic elements together into long, complex words. It has highly inflected verbs and adjectives, which can carry a number of suffixes; these qualify such things as the mood, probability, or duration of an action or the social status of an agent. Moreover, Japanese has a "subject–object–predicate" word order and is polysyllabic—indeed, one word can sometimes fill an entire line of poetry. Chinese-style writing was written according to the Chinese word order and used the Chinese characters "logographically" for their meaning, each character representing a word. When Chinese-style writing was read out loud, the Japanese reader would perform a translation of sorts, adjusting the Chinese-style phrase to Japanese word order and adding inflections as needed. In contrast, vernacular Japanese writing mixed characters used for meaning with characters used "phonographically," for their sound value only. These characters functioned basically like a syllabic alphabet. As a result, in phonographic writing one word could require many Chinese characters.

Despite this complexity, Japan was not a bilingual culture; very few people learned spoken Chinese in addition to their native tongue. Japanese readers voiced Chinese texts in Japanese pronunciation. Their East Asian neighbors would be able to read the same text but would pronounce it in their languages and dialects. This led to a fascinating communicative paradox that can occur only in cultures with nonalphabetic writing systems. The Japanese ambassadors who visited China in order to present tribute gifts and bring home the newest law codes, Buddhist texts, musical instruments, and poetry collections could usually not ask for directions or the simplest things. Yet they could write sophisticated Chinese-style poetry for their Chinese hosts and communicate through so-called "brush talk": conversations through written messages in the shared Chinese script.

THE LITERATURE OF THE NARA COURT (710–784)

In early Chinese histories, the Japanese islands appear as a fabled realm of multiple polities, one of which—the Yamato clan—was ruled by a female monarch. During the fourth and fifth centuries the chieftains of the Yamato clan, based in western Japan south of modern-day Kyoto, managed to assert their local power over a broader territory. They sent tribute missions to China, benefiting in turn from the authority they gained from the titles and gifts that the Chinese emperors bestowed on them. By the eighth century the Yamato clan had established hegemony over most of Japan in the Nara Basin south of modern-day Kyoto. With the help of scribal specialists who had previously emigrated from Korea, the Yamato clan turned the medium of writing into a political tool that helped them enforce central control over an increasingly large territory. Rulers also realized that legitimate political authority required historical precedent. The two earliest longer texts produced in Japan were therefore historical chronicles that traced Yamato rule back to the age of the gods and their creation of the Japanese islands. *Records of Ancient Matters* (712), written in the vernacular, connected the Yamato clan to Amaterasu, the sun goddess, who is still worshipped today in the shrines at Ise as the ancestor of the reigning emperor. *Chronicles of Japan* (720), written in Chinese-style, also used Chinese yin-yang cosmology to explain the emergence of the Japanese archipelago.

In the process of state formation, Japan's early rulers relied on the beliefs and practices of the "Way of the Gods," the Buddhist law, and Confucian political ethics. The Way of the Gods, called Shinto in Japanese, is rooted in early Japanese folk religion and is concerned with the veneration of sacred sites in nature (such as mountains and rivers), the exorcism of evil-doing spirits, and the purification from polluting forces such as illness and death; it found expression in *Records of Ancient Matters* and thus also legitimated the rule of Amaterasu's descendants over Japan. Buddhism, which originated in India with the teachings of Buddha Shakyamuni and reached Japan via China and Korea, was adopted by Yamato rulers in the sixth century C.E. as a means to promote the welfare of the state. Buddhism promised above all the salvation of human beings from the suffering that comes with desires and attachments to the impermanent things of this world. But already in China it had turned into an instrument of statecraft, through which a sovereign could claim universal legitimacy and ask for protection of his or her realm. Buddhism also provided an important cultural link to Korea and China, as Japanese monks went to study the most recent Buddhist debates and schools on the continent. Confucianism, too, had broad appeal for the individual and the state. Confucius had propagated an ethics of benevolent behavior and self-cultivation. He emphasized the importance of social hierarchies and the value of filial devotion toward one's parents, a value that also applied to the head of state. Early Japanese rulers adopted the Chinese model of elite education and founded a state academy for the study of the Confucian Classics. Although in Japan the examination system was never used as a tool for government recruitment as in China, Japanese education until the modern period was based on the canonical Chinese texts. They have left their traces in the entire corpus of Japanese literature up until the twentieth century.

State building on the Chinese model and increasing literacy resulted in the first great period of Japanese literature during the late seventh and the eighth centuries. In 710 Nara became the first stable capital. Previously, capitals had often moved for each new reign, because people feared that the death of the ruler polluted the site. Nara was a radiant city, modeled on Chinese capitals with their quadrangular grid of large avenues and streets, a large palace complex to the north, and markets of various kinds. Its rulers commissioned the compilation of the earliest chronicles and of local gazettes. The Chinese-style poetry of Japan's earliest extant poetry anthology, *Florilegium of Cherished Airs* (751), describes imperial excursions, poetry banquets, and receptions for foreign diplomats who were entertained in the proud new capital and celebrated in verse. Slightly later, the earliest vernacular poetry anthology, **The Man'yōshū (Collection of Myriad Leaves)**, was compiled. Its prominent poets, including **Kakinomoto no Hitomaro, Ōtomo no Tabito,** and **Yamanoue no Okura,** developed a

The Tōdaiji Temple complex in Nara, Japan, was built in the eighth century and has been frequently repaired and reconstructed over the centuries. The building here, the "Great Buddha Hall," is today one of the largest wooden buildings in the world.

stunning breadth of themes and styles, ranging from ritual evocations of the divine imperial lineage to shattering death laments, from lighthearted praises of the powers of wine to desperate calls of support for the poor and oppressed. The literature of the Nara Period pulses with excitement over the new possibilities of technologies, such as writing and literature, and of active participation in the larger world of East Asia. Japan's new profile as an emerging state that had outgrown its tribal past did not go unnoticed among its neighbors. In the early eighth century it gained the new name "Nippon" ("at sun's root"), which signaled that Japan had been accepted as the eastern border of the Chinese sphere of influence.

HEIAN COURT CULTURE (794–1185)

As the result of struggles between the imperial court and the Buddhist clergy, the court moved to a new capital in 794: Heian-kyō ("the Capital of Peace"), modern-day Kyoto. Despite centuries of warrior rule and occasional civil wars, Kyoto would remain the seat of the imperial court until 1868. The four centuries of the Heian Period, when Kyoto was the sole political and cultural center of Japan, became in retrospect a golden age, viewed by subsequent ages as the pinnacle of culture. The literature produced by Kyoto's court aristocracy defined all later standards of taste and embodied a refinement of sensibilities that had timeless appeal.

Heian literature was mostly produced by and for the capital elite. There are descriptions of travel in the provinces, such as **Ki no Tsurayuki's** *Tosa Diary*, but Heian aristocrats found the countryside at best rustic and charming, at worst embarrassing and primitive. The capital was the center of all ambitions and

hopes: aristocrats eagerly awaited the promotion ceremonies that could secure them a higher rank and better post in the extensive court bureaucracy. In their court diaries, written in Chinese-style, they meticulously recorded the daily court routine. These diaries show mostly the official side of Heian life. For a picture of Heian after nightfall, we need to look at vernacular tales and women's diaries. Here we learn that men often had several wives and carried on several romantic affairs at once. They visited their lovers in the women's homes, plying them with allusive poetry or the tasteful calligraphy of a "morning-after note," written on a paper of just the right shade and adorned with just the right twig or blossom in season.

We get a remarkable close-up of the everyday lives, pleasures, and anxieties of Heian aristocratic women from works such as **Murasaki Shikibu's** *The Tale of Genji* and **Sei Shōnagon's** *The Pillow Book*. Heian women were dressed in a dozen layers of clothing whose shades carefully matched the season and occasion. They were hidden from view, spending their days in the dimly lit interiors of their residences waiting for welcome distractions: the banter of servants, an occasional outside caller with whom to exchange the latest gossip (if it was a man, the lady hid behind a screen as they talked), a love letter, or, even better, festivals or pilgrimages to nearby temples that broke the daily routine. Aristocratic women usually received a thorough education in *waka* poetry (classical Japanese verse composed in the set pattern of 5-7-5-7-7 syllables). They were also trained in music, dance, and often even the Chinese Classics, although Chinese scholarship was traditionally a male domain. Heian elite women had ample time to read and write and developed a subtle sense of propriety and distinction in social relations, clothing decorum, the delicate psychology of romantic affairs, and poetry exchanges.

This detail from a twelfth-century illustrated hand scroll of Lady Murasaki's diary gives us a glimpse of the dress and domestic situation of women at the Heian court.

By the tenth century, *waka* poetry was enshrined as the canonical court genre. *Waka* was both a way to parade one's literary sophistication and a simple form of everyday communication between men and women, who spent most of their time apart. A century earlier, two emperors with particularly Sinophile tastes had commissioned the compilation of Chinese-style poetry anthologies, which celebrated the cultural achievements of the court and its poets. But by the late ninth century the short and intimate *waka* form became popular: *waka* contests entertained the aristocracy and poets wrote *waka* on screen paintings in the imperial palace. Emperor Daigo's sponsorship of the first imperial *waka* anthology, **The Kokinshū** (*Collection of Ancient and Modern Poems*), in 905, first established the high status of *waka* at court. Between the tenth and fifteenth centuries Japanese emperors commissioned a total of twenty-one *waka* anthologies.

Having one's name included in one of these anthologies was the highest aspiration for generations of poets.

Waka relied heavily on a vast, but well-defined, vocabulary of seasonal phenomena and romantic love. Poets used this metaphorical and allusive imagery on public occasions in order to commemorate court events, praise the emperor, or participate in poetry contests. But they also used *waka* for more intimate purposes—to rekindle a love affair, to convey travel experiences, or to express feelings of longing, loneliness, or existential frustration with the impermanence of the world. Ki no Tsurayuki, the author of the "**Japanese Preface**" (or **Kana Preface**) to *The Kokinshū*, boldly claimed that *waka* originated in the age of the gods out of the universal human impulse to burst out in "song" in response to the outside world. Tsurayuki's preface became the foundational statement on the nature, history, and function of poetry and had a profound impact not just on literature but also on other traditional arts.

In addition to the establishment of *waka* at court, the ninth century saw the invention of the kana syllabary, which profoundly changed Japanese literature. Although the invention of the kana syllabary did not fundamentally alter how Japanese wrote, it introduced a script that became specifically associated with women: it was called "women's hand." Before the tenth century, both Chinese-style and vernacular texts were written in Chinese characters. In the new kana system, the characters used phonographically, for sound value, were replaced with a letter standing for a syllable: the curvier *hiragana* script was used for inflections and grammatical particles, while the square-shaped *katakana* script transcribed foreign loanwords such as Sanskrit terms and Buddhist vocabulary (and Western-language words in the modern period). The invention of these two kana scripts expanded Japan's rich vernacular prose literature, adding to the literary spectrum fictional tales, autobiographical diaries, and other genres that were associated with female sensibility, if not outright female authorship.

Of the world's prominent premodern literary traditions, Japan's is the only one in which women dominated certain areas. An important element in the flourishing of women's literature was the rise of the Fujiwara clan. The Fujiwara managed to gain a position of great influence by inserting themselves as regents between the emperor and the court administration. Fujiwara regents married their daughters into the imperial family, hoping that their grandsons would become future emperors. To that end, Fujiwara regents often lavished attention on their daughters, securing for them an education of the highest distinction and providing them with the most talented ladies-in-waiting. Because the emperor usually had several consorts and other lower-ranking women at his disposal, such polish was a way to attract the emperor's attention and gain a competitive advantage over rivals. Some of the greatest works of Japanese literature were written by prestigious ladies-in-waiting: Murasaki Shikibu and Sei Shōnagon served in the rival households of two Fujiwara daughters, empresses to Emperor Ichijō. The ambitions of the Fujiwara family to dominate the court and the imperial lineage created an environment in which female literary talent was instrumental in the success of the male members of the clan.

The political power of the Fujiwara clan also touched other aristocratic clans. **Sugawara no Michizane**, Japan's most celebrated Chinese-style poet, came from a prominent family of academy scholars. When he quickly rose in the ranks to one of the most prestigious court positions, a Fujiwara rival managed to have him demoted and exiled to distant Kyūshū, where he died in bitterness and misery. Despite these political maneuverings, the Heian Period was later considered a high point of cultural confidence and imperial rule.

MEDIEVAL JAPAN AND WARRIOR RULE

In the latter half of the twelfth century, the Heian world fell apart. The trigger was a protracted civil war between two warrior clans—the Heike and the Genji—vying for control over court and capital, a war that ultimately resulted in the establishment of a military government in Kamakura, southeast of today's Tokyo. Although the clans and the cities from where they ruled kept changing and a number of emperors attempted to reassert their imperial authority, Japan was dominated by

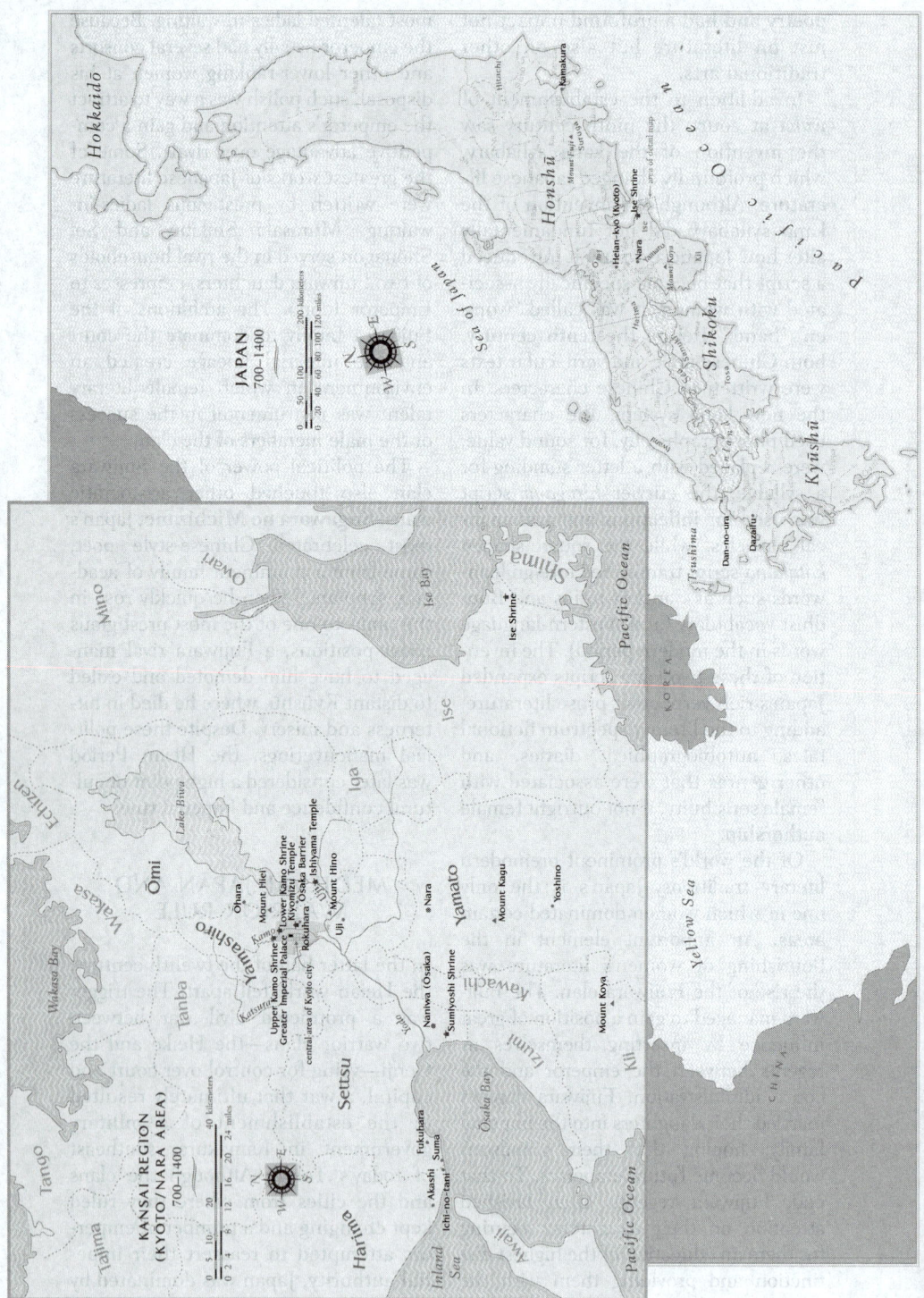

JAPAN
700–1400

Hokkaidō

Honshū

Sea of Japan

Pacific Ocean

Kamakura

Mount Fuji
Suruga

Hitachi

Heian-kyō (Kyoto)
Nara
Ise Shrine

Ōmi

Mount Kōya
Kii

Shikoku

Tosa

Kyūshū

Tsushima

Dan-no-ura
Dazaifu

area of detail map

0 50 100   200 kilometers
0 20 40 60 80 100 120 miles

KANSAI REGION
(KYOTO/NARA AREA)
700–1400

Wakasa Bay

Tango

Tajima

Tanba

Wakasa

Echizen

Ōmi

Lake Biwa

Mount Hiei
Ōhara
Kamo R.
Upper Kamo Shrine
Greater Imperial Palace
central area of Kyoto city
Katsura R.
Lower Kamo Shrine
Kiyomizu Temple
Rokuhara Ōsaka Barrier
Ishiyama Temple

Yamashiro

Tanba

Settsu

Fukuhara
Ichi-no-tani
Suma
Akashi

Inland
Sea

Harima

Mino

Owari

Ise Bay

Shima

Ise Shrine

Pacific Ocean

Iga

Ise

Uji
Mount Hino

Yamato

Nara

Mount Kagu

Yoshino

Kawachi

Naniwa (Osaka)
Sumiyoshi Shrine

Izumi

Mount Kōya

Kii

Ōsaka Bay

Yodo R.

Yura R.

Awaji

KOREA

Yellow Sea

CHINA

Pacific Ocean

0 5 10   20   40 kilometers
0 2 4 8 12 16 20 24 miles

military clans until 1868. Whereas the emperor—a symbolic figure of authority, often enjoying little actual power—remained in Kyoto with his court, military rulers, the so-called shoguns, in fact ruled the country through a feudal system of domain lords and their samurai. The civil war, which ushered in the medieval age in Japan, was so cataclysmic that Buddhist minstrels sang of the valiant deeds of the refined and courtly Heike—the eventual losers—and their wild and uncouth opponents from the east: the victorious Genji. Their chants were subsequently recorded in *The Tales of the Heike*. They infused what in reality had been a series of bloody wars with the Buddhist message that all power, splendor, and pride of this world must eventually fall before the law of impermanence. They endowed the Heike warriors with the elegance of the bygone Heian court to which medieval Japanese now looked back with nostalgia.

The medieval world was startlingly different from its Heian predecessor. Local shoguns, perhaps seeking their own cultural validation, became generous patrons of the arts, enabling cultural and literary production to flourish in new sites beyond the imperial court. They sponsored Zen monasteries, which became centers of Chinese scholarship and a new type of Chinese-style poetry. The shoguns also patronized theater performances and Noh

playwrights, including **Zeami Motokiyo**, the most important Noh dramatist, who wrote pieces that appealed to the warrior class such as *Atsumori*, a play based on the tragic death of a Heike noble.

Warrior rule also brought significant shifts in education and public values. Compared to the aristocratic Heian Period, now more people had access to basic education, and the austere warrior ethic valued honor, self-sacrifice, prowess, and loyalty to one's lord. Rather than depending largely on hereditary status within the administration of the imperial court, active involvement in government was now more haphazard and uncertain. Some responded by retreating from public life: they took Buddhist vows and settled outside the cities. **Kamo no Chōmei's "An Account of a Ten-Square-Foot Hut"** suggests that Buddhist faith or artistic pursuits can address the uncertainties of life and the desire for salvation.

Although the medieval world remained attached to the values encapsulated in the works of the Heian Period, it produced a literature more strongly influenced by the warrior ethos and the needs of a broader spectrum of society. Despite the profound differences between these two periods, both classical and medieval Japan created works that laid the foundation for the Japanese literary tradition and can thus together be considered the formative age of Japanese culture.

THE MAN'YŌSHŪ
(COLLECTION OF MYRIAD LEAVES)
ca. 759

As one of Japan's two oldest extant poetry anthologies, *The Man'yōshū* stands at the beginning of Japan's literary tradition. So influential on later traditions was this collection that its title was adopted as a name for Japan's earliest period of cultural flourishing during the late seventh and eighth centuries: the "Man'yō Age." Containing more than 4,500 poems, *The Man'yōshū* is a monumental compendium of poetic knowledge. Many of its poems give expression to the most elemental human experiences: love, separation, and mourning. Others celebrate public occasions at court and are designed to inspire and entertain. Some poems describe the political order and praise the gods and the imperial institution, while others deplore the injustices of the world. The poems frequently refer to myths and legends about the origin of names, human institutions, and customs, but they also include an encyclopedic array of plant and animal names and references to the natural world. Because Japan adopted the Chinese writing system and imported the rich store of Chinese literature, the earliest Japanese poets also rested on the shoulders of some nineteen centuries of China's literate tradition. But part of the fascination of *The Man'yōshū* lies in its having taken shape during a time of bold experimentation, when Chinese and native traditions were blended—a time that also saw the first flowering of Chinese-style poetry composition.

THE MAN'YŌ AGE

During the two centuries preceding the compilation of *The Man'yōshū*, the Japanese archipelago underwent changes more profound than any others it would experience before the modern period. Within this brief span, a loose confederation of competing clans, whose wealth was drawn from the cultivation of rice and whose principal cultural accomplishment was the erection of enormous burial mounds, had remade itself into a society with a national identity, a ruling imperial family, an elaborate government administration, a complex system of religious beliefs, and a command of letters and literature. The introduction of Buddhism from Korea in the mid-sixth century changed the face of Japan, bringing along with it a culture of writing and literature, temple architecture, sophisticated art and religious sculpture, and a religious model for the protection of the state based on the imperial patronage of Buddhism. By the mid-seventh century, the future Emperor Tenji (626–671) enhanced the power of the Yamato rulers by doing away with powerful rival lineages and instituting an incisive set of reforms designed to centralize power. Tenji is said to have established a state academy for Chinese learning; the earliest Chinese-style poetry was composed during banquets at his court.

Literature depended on court culture, and until the eighth century the location of the court changed with each sovereign to avoid the pollution believed to be caused by the previous ruler's death. Tenji attempted to move away from the heartland of Yamato, where earlier capitals had been, to the north, near Lake Biwa. But after only four years the new capital of Ōmi was abandoned by his brother and successor Emperor Tenmu, who moved his court back to Yamato. Empress Jitō (r. 687–96), his wife and successor, had court poets like the *Man'yōshū* poet Kakinomoto no Hitomaro sing her praises, and she built the first Chinese-style capital, with a spacious gridlock pattern centered on the palace complex—the residence of the newly important "heavenly sovereign" (*tennō*), as the former Yamato tribal chieftain was now called.

How could Japan catch up so swiftly with contemporary developments in China? From the seventh through ninth centuries, Japan sent about twenty diplomatic missions to the Chinese court. From the Chinese perspective, Japan was paying homage and tribute to China, like many other states in the Chinese influence sphere. On its part, the young and fledgling state of Japan looked to the venerable civilization of China with great admiration. The envoys and monks who had visited China came home with a rich harvest of experience—and a treasure trove of texts. They made recommendations to the Japanese emperor on how to adapt the most recent Chinese law codes, ritual manuals, Buddhist scriptures, medicinal literature, or poetry collections to the political, religious, and aesthetic needs of the Japanese court. During this period Kyūshū, the southernmost of the four main Japanese islands, served as the gateway to China and Korea. Despite its peripheral location, the flourishing government quarters at Dazaifu frequently hosted embassies going back and forth between Japan, Korea, and China, and it was therefore nicknamed "the distant capital." The officials who served in Dazaifu were in particularly close contact with new developments, and some of the greatest *Man'yōshū* poets owed their inspiration to mix indigenous and Chinese traditions to the time they spent there.

THE ANTHOLOGY

The Man'yōshū was slowly aggregated over the course of the eighth century. It is an anthology of anthologies, made up of parts of earlier poetry collections that have not survived. Portions of the first twenty volumes were already completed in the early eighth century, and its last poem dates from 759, but the entire collection probably reached its current form only in 785, when its final compiler, Ōtomo no Yakamochi, died. Most poems were composed between the mid-seventh and mid-eighth centuries. The poems are divided into three topical categories: "miscellaneous poems," composed during imperial excursions or on seasonal topics; "exchange poetry," songs exchanged between lovers, relatives, or friends; and "mourning poems" performed at the burial sites of sovereigns and princes or composed more generally on the subject of death, a particularly prominent topic in early Japanese poetry.

The Man'yōshū was compiled during the period when the new technology of writing was for the first time being used to produce longer texts. The anthology shows the ingenuity of early Japanese scribes in adapting the Chinese writing system to record the Japanese language. In the writing of the poems in *The Man'yōshū*, Chinese characters were used in three different ways: for their meaning, for their sound when read in Chinese, and for their sound when read in Japanese. The Chinese graph denoting "person," for instance, could naturally be used for its semantic value when the poet wanted to write the word "person." But it could also be used to approximate the sound of its Chinese pronunciation, which Japanese rendered *jin*, or *nin* (in modern Mandarin it is read *ren*). Or it could be used to represent the Japanese sound of its meaning: *hito*, the Japanese word for "person." For example, Hitomaro, the name of the first of the poets in the selections printed here, came to be written with the "person" character standing for the phonetic element "Hito." This system, which relied on thousands of Chinese characters working on three different levels, is daunting to master. But it allowed for a playfulness that still charms readers today and that is impossible in any language that, like English, relies solely on a phonetic alphabet.

The Man'yōshū also shows the variety of Japanese verse forms. In fact, it laid the groundwork for all later forms of poetry until haiku poetry, which came to the fore in the seventeenth century. Whereas the artistry of Chinese poetry is rooted in the dexterous use of rhyme and the tonal qualities of each syllable, the Japanese language has neither tones nor significant rhymes. Because the sound system of Japanese employs no stress accent, each syllable is pronounced with virtually equal emphasis; as a result the forms of meter based on stress that are familiar in English poetry are nonexistent in Japanese poetry. Moreover, because most Japanese syllables consist of a single vowel or consonants followed by a vowel, with only five vowel sounds, rhymes are so ubiquitous that they become meaningless to the ear. Instead, Japanese poetry depends on the rhythm created by alternating phrases of long and short syllable counts. Japan's most archaic songs employ this pattern, which originally varied from combinations of phrases with four syllables paired with those of six to alternations of five- and three-syllable phrases. By the mid-seventh century the accepted pattern became an alternation of five and seven syllables, establishing a rhythm that would prevail in Japanese poetry up to the present.

There are two main forms. The chōka, or long poem, consists of an indeterminate number of lines of alternating five- and seven-syllable phrases, culminating in a couplet of two seven-syllable phrases. The tanka, or short poem, is identical in form to the last five lines of a chōka: that is, it is a thirty-one-syllable poem arranged in lines whose syllable counts are 5, 7, 5, 7, 7. Approximately 4,200 of the 4,516 poems in the collection are tanka. Even most of the chōka have satellite tanka known as "envoys" that serve to sum up or expand on the theme of the original chōka. Although many of the chōka are the most memorable poems in the anthology, the form largely disappeared after the age of The Man'yōshū in favor of the thirty-one-syllable short verse, which became the dominant form of classical Japanese poetry.

The Man'yōshū was compiled at the imperial court and its prominent poets were literate and erudite, yet this earliest Japanese poetry anthology contains the voices of many people far from court, including simple peasants, soldiers guarding the eastern frontier against hostile tribes, and mothers seeing off their sons as they embark on dangerous missions to China. The collection transmits oral song traditions that were recorded owing to the new technology of writing, and almost two thousand poems of the collection are anonymous.

SELECTED POETS OF
THE MAN'YŌSHŪ

Attributed to Emperor Jomei (r. 629–41), a sovereign who ruled over a still largely preliterary realm, the second poem of the anthology (and the first poem included below) gives a vivid sense of the power of language that many poems in The Man'yōshū celebrate. The emperor gazes in satisfaction over his land, possibly performing the ritual of "land viewing," in which emperors would grace their territory symbolically with an imperial blessing while also asserting imperial control over it. The act of gazing draws its power from the act of naming parts of the divine landscape that the emperor sees from Mount Kagu, one of the three mountains of Yamato.

The poem by Princess Nukata (ca. 638–690s) leads us into the increasingly more literate world of Emperor Tenji's court. We know little about Nukata beyond her royal descent; she was one of those highly educated women in early Japan who distinguished themselves as poets, was at some point involved with the later Emperor Tenmu (r. 672–86), but then served his brother Emperor Tenji (r. 668–71). The occasion for the poem is courtly—an elegant competition to frame the better argument for the rival beauties of spring and autumn. Presenting a strong opinion on the topic, the poem is a famous example of the Chinese rhetoric of parallel couplets being put to new use in a Japanese vernacular poem.

Kakinomoto no Hitmaro (flourished ca. 680–700) is considered the foremost poet in *The Man'yōshū*. By the tenth century he was referred to as the "sage of poetry" and became a figure of religious veneration. He served Empress Jitō (r. 687–96), whom he accompanied on imperial excursions. He is the earliest poet whose poems have been preserved in large numbers on a wide range of topics. We know that there was a "Hitomaro poetry collection," which is now lost. Hitomaro could employ potent language of monumental simplicity: the *chōka* written at Yoshino, a numinous place situated in the mountains east of Yamato that since earliest times was associated with imperial visits, celebrates the power of the empress by comparing her to the pristine landscape. How he dealt with more ambivalent and risky topics can be seen in his poem on the ruins of Ōmi. Around 689 Hitomaro was in the retinue of Empress Jitō when passing the

capital where Emperor Tenji had ruled three decades earlier. Because Emperor Tenmu, Jitō's predecessor and husband, had violently deposed Tenji's son from his rule at Ōmi, the site was problematic for the Jitō court. In this poem the constancy of the place stands in ironic contrast to the disappearance of the ancient capital. The place-names express Hitomaro's ambivalence through the rhetorical device of poetic epithets (*makura kotoba*; literally, "pillow words"). These formulaic epithets, a feature of the Japanese poetic tradition, were attached to numinous place-names or the names of palaces and gods: Yamato, for example, is "sky-seen," while Tenji's cursed Ōmi is "far from heaven." Hitomaro's poetry expresses loss and transience with unique and poignant imagery. This power is especially evident in Hitomaro's many poems on death, represented in our selections by poems on the death of one of his wives and the death of a stranger, as well as Hitomaro's own deathbed poem.

The poetry of Ōtomo no Tabito (665–731) and Yamanoue no Okura (ca. 660–733) brings us into yet another world, when missions to the Chinese court had resumed after a hiatus of three decades, bringing a new wave of Chinese culture to Japan. Tabito held an official post in Dazaifu, on the southernmost island of Kyūshū, and his "Thirteen poems in praise of wine" pay homage to famous Chinese drinkers such as the bohemian "Seven Sages of the Bamboo Grove" and the recluse poet **Tao Qian**. The ironical verve with which the poet argues for the blessings of drunkenness is a poetic mode that was entirely new in Japanese poetry. Okura, possibly of Korean descent, spent several years in China as a member of a diplomatic mission. He infuses his poetry with novel themes such as reflections on moral and religious questions. A declaration of love to his children is couched as a playful jibe at the Buddha and his teaching that one should give up all worldly attachments. Using poetry to unmask injustices and failings in society was a tradition that ultimately went back to the Chinese *Classic of Poetry* (ca. 600 B.C.E.), and in his "Dialogue on Poverty" Okura puts this tradition to startling use: a plaint of a poor man is followed by one from a much poorer man, and in the end, although this "destitute man" has nothing left in his unused rice pot but spiderwebs, the village chief, whip in hand, appears to recruit him for forced government labor. The critical thrust of this poem—which might even be self-critical, given that Okura was himself a government

official—is unique in early Japanese poetry.

As often happens to periods that bear the weight of representing the origins of a culture, the Man'yō Age came to be associated with notions of emotional immediacy and sincerity—with innocence, vigor, and a seeming artlessness that stood in marked contrast to the controlled, more self-conscious polish that would define Japanese poetry throughout the subsequent classical era. And yet, a careful reading of *The Man'yōshū* reveals a work of great variety and considerable complexity, in which new confidence in the artistic effects of language and the new technology of writing take the place of preliterate beliefs in the incantatory power of words.

FROM THE MAN'YŌSHŪ[1] (COLLECTION OF MYRIAD LEAVES)

Emperor Jomei

A poem composed by the Emperor when he ascended Mount Kagu and viewed the land

In Yamato
There are crowds of mountains,
But our rampart
Is Heavenly Mount Kagu:[2]
When I climb it   5
And look out across the land,
Over the land-plain
Smoke rises and rises;
Over the sea-plain
Seagulls rise and rise.   10
A fair land it is,
Dragonfly Island,
The land of Yamato.

1. All selections translated by Edwin Cranston, with the exception of "Poem written by Kakinomoto Hitomaro when he parted from his wife in the land of Iwami," "Poem Written by Kakinomoto no Hitomaro upon seeing a dead man lying among the rocks on the island of Samine in Sanuki," and Ōtomo Tabito's

"Thirteen poems in praise of wine."
2. Mount Kagu was said to have descended from Heaven and settled among the hills in Yamato Province, the location of Jomei's court near the later capital of Nara. Yamato, like "Dragonfly Island," was also an ancient name for Japan.

Princess Nukata

When the Emperor [Tenji] commanded the Palace Minister, Fujiwara no Kamatari, to match the radiance of the myriad blossoms of the spring mountains against the colors of the thousand leaves of the autumn mountains, Princess Nukata decided the question with this poem:

> When spring comes forth
> That lay in hiding all the winter through,
>   The birds that did not sing
> Come back and sing to us once more;
>   The flowers that did not bloom   5
> Have blossomed everywhere again.
>   Yet so rife the hills
> We cannot make our way to pick,
>   And so deep the grass
> We cannot pluck the flowers to see.   10
>   But when on autumn hills
> We gaze upon the leaves of trees,
>   It is the yellow ones
> We pluck and marvel for sheer joy.
>   And the ones still green,   15
> Sighing, leave upon the boughs—
> Those are the ones I hate to lose.
> For me, it is the autumn hills.

Kakinomoto no Hitomaro

A poem composed by Kakinomoto no Hitomaro on passing the ruined capital of Ōmi

> From that hallowed age
> When the monarch Suzerain of the Sun
>   Reigned at Kashihara
> By Unebi, called the Jewel-sash Mount,[1]
>   Each and every god   5
> Made manifest in the world of men,
>   One by one in evergreen
> Succession like a line of hemlock trees,
>   Ruled under heaven
> All this realm with uncontested sway:[2]   10
>   Yet from sky-seen
> Yamato did one depart—

1. One of the Three Mountains of Yamato (Mount Kagu, mentioned in Jomei's poem above, is another). "Jewel-sash": a pillow word (formulaic epithet), literally ceremonial attire for worship.
2. Jimmu, the legendary first emperor of Japan and descendant of the sun goddess, ruled from Kashihara Palace in Yamato Province, the location of the courts of all subsequent emperors, gods "made manifest in the world of men."

Whatever may have been
The secret of his sage intent—
   And passed across   15
The slopes of blue-earth Nara Mountain
   To a land, remote
Beyond the distant heaven,
   The land of Ōmi
Where water dashes on the rocks,   20
   To the palace of Ōtsu
In Sasanami of the gently lapping waves;[3]
   And there, as it is said,
He[4] ruled this realm beneath the sky:
   That sovereign god,   25
August ancestral deity—
   His great palace stood
Upon this spot, as I have heard;
   Its mighty halls
Rose here, so all men say;   30
   Where now spring grasses
Choke the earth in their rife growth,
   And mists rise up
To hide the dazzling springtime sun;
   Now I view this site   35
Where once the mighty palace stood,
And it is sad to see.

ENVOYS

Still Cape Kara[5] stands
In Shiga of the gently lapping waves,
   Changeless from of old;   40
But it will wait in vain to see
The courtiers' boats row back.

Broad the waters stand
By Shiga of the gently lapping waves;
   The lake is still;   45
But how can it ever meet again
The men of long ago?

Poem composed by Kakinomoto no Hitomaro when the Sovereign went on an excursion to the palace at Yoshino[1]

Where our Sovereign reigns,
Ruling the earth in all tranquility,
   Under the heaven
Of this realm she holds in sway,

3. In 668 Emperor Tenji moved the capital north from Yamato to Ōtsu Palace in Ōmi, near Japan's largest lake (Lake Biwa). After his death in 671, his successor shifted the capital again to Yamato.
4. Emperor Tenji.
5. A scenic spot in Shiga Prefecture, which surrounds Lake Biwa.
1. A famous mountainous area that was known for its pristine and sacred beauty. Empress Jitō had a palace there, not far from the Yamato capitals, and Hitomaro visited it several times in her retinue.

Many are the lands, 5
But of their multitude,
  Seeing the clear pools
That form along this mountain stream,
  She gave her heart
To the fair land of Yoshino, 10
  And where blossoms fall
Forever on the fields of Akizu
  She planted firm
The mighty pillars of her palace halls.
  Now the courtiers, 15
Men of the palace of the hundred stones,
  Line up their boats
To row across the morning stream,
  Vie in their boats
To race upon the evening stream; 20
  And like the stream
This place shall last forever,
  Like these mountains
Ever loftier shall rise
  Beside the plunging waters 25
Of the torrent her august abode:
Long though I gaze, my eyes will never tire.

ENVOY

Long though I gaze,
Never shall I tire of Yoshino,
  Within whose stream 30
The water-moss grows smooth forever,
As I shall come to view these sights anew.

Poem written by Kakinomoto no Hitomaro when he parted from his wife in the land of Iwami and came up to the capital[1]

At Cape Kara
on the Sea of Iwami,
where the vines
  crawl on the rocks,
rockweed of the deep 5
grows on the reefs
and sleek seaweed
grows on the desolate shore.
As deeply do I
think of my wife 10
who swayed toward me in sleep
  like the lithe seaweed.
Yet few were the nights
we had slept together
before we were parted 15
like crawling vines uncurled.

1. Translated by Ian Hideo Levy.

And so I look back,
still thinking of her
with painful heart,
this clench of inner flesh,   20
but in the storm
of fallen scarlet leaves
on Mount Watari,[2]
crossed as on
    a great ship,   25
I cannot make out the sleeves
she waves in farewell.
For she, alas,
is slowly hidden
like the moon   30
    in its crossing
        between the clouds
over Yagami Mountain
just as the evening sun
coursing through the heavens   35
has begun to glow,
        and even I
who thought I was a brave man
find the sleeves
of my well-woven robe   40
drenched with tears.

ENVOYS

The quick gallop
of my dapple-blue steed
races me to the clouds,
passing far away   45
from where my wife dwells.

O scarlet leaves
falling on the autumn mountainside:
stop, for a while, the storm
your strewing makes, that I might glimpse   50
the place where my wife dwells.

*Poem composed by Kakinomoto no Hitomaro, sorely grieving with tears of blood,
after his wife died*

On the Karu Road,
Karu of the wing-filled sky,
    Was the village
Where she lived, my own dear wife,
    And to look at her   5
Was all I wanted in my heart:
    But had I always gone,

---

2. *Watari* means "crossing"; thus the leaves fall at the very spot where the poet might have
caught one last glimpse of his wife.

There were many eyes of men;
    Had I gone frequently
Others surely would have known.   10
    So, like branching vines,
After parting we would meet again,
    I thought, as confident
As one who rides in a great ship,
    And though ever yearning,   15
Kept our love secret, deep and still
    As a pool walled round with rock,
Gleaming softly like a glinting gem.
    But as the coursing sun
Goes down the sky to darkness,   20
    Or the radiant moon
Is lost to view within the clouds,
    So she who lay with me
As yielding as the seaweed to the wave
    Passed and was gone,   25
As leaves of autumn pass and are no more:
    It was a messenger,
Azusa-wood staff in hand, who brought the news.
    His words buzzed in my ears
Like a distant sound of *azusa*-wood bows:[1]   30
    Wordless, helpless,
Ignorant of all device,
    I could not bear to stand
Listening to the mere bruit of it,
    And so, imagining   35
Even the thousandth portion
    Of my longing
Might somehow be assuaged,
    I went where she
Had always gone to look about,   40
    To the market of Karu,
And there I lingered listening.
    On the hilltop
Of Unebi, called the Jewel-sash Mount,
    The birds were singing,   45
But I could not hear the voice I knew;
    Nor were there any
Passing on the jewel-spear road,
    Not even one,
Resembling her, of those that traveled there: 50
    In my helplessness
Crying my beloved's name,
I waved my useless sleeves.[2]

1. The twanging of these bows was believed to summon spirits from the world beyond. Also, messengers were said to carry staffs of *azusa* (catalpa) wood.
2. The waving of sleeves was associated with rituals to call back the spirits of the dead.

TWO TANKA

On the autumn hills
The trees are dense with yellow leaves— 55
　She has lost her way,
And I must go and search for her,
But do not know the mountain path.

Now that yellow leaves
Are scattering from the boughs, 60
　I see the messenger
With his *azusa*-wood staff,
And days with her return to mind.

Poem written by Kakinomoto no Hitomaro upon seeing a dead man lying among the rocks on the island of Samine in Sanuki[1]

The land of Sanuki,
　fine in sleek seaweed:
is it for the beauty of the land
that we do not tire
　to gaze upon it? 5
Is it for its divinity
that we deem it most noble?
Eternally flourishing,
　with the heavens
　　and the earth, 10
　with the sun
　　and the moon,
the very face of a god—
so it has come down
　　through the ages. 15

Casting off
from Naka harbor,
we came rowing.
Then tide winds
blew through the clouds; 20
on the offing
we saw the rustled waves,
on the strand
we saw the roaring crests.
Fearing the whale-hunted seas, 25
our ship plunged through—
we bent those oars!
Many were the islands
near and far,
but we beached on Samine— 30
　　beautiful its name—

1. Translated by Ian Hideo Levy. In Japan's creation myth, Sanuki (part of Shikoku, one of Japan's four main islands) was one of the first places born from the union of the creator couple, the gods Izanagi and Izanami.

and built a shelter
    on the rugged shore.

Looking around,
        we saw you   35
lying there
on a jagged bed of stones,
the beach
    for your finely woven pillow,
by the breakers' roar.   40
    If I knew your home,
I would go and tell them.
If your wife knew,
she would come and seek you out.
But she does not even know the road,   45
    straight as a jade spear.
Does she not wait for you,
    worrying and longing,
your beloved wife?

ENVOYS

If your wife were here,   50
she would gather and feed you
the starwort that grows
on the Sami hillsides,
but is its season not past?

Making a finely woven pillow   55
of the rocky shore
    where waves from the offing
           draw near,
you, who sleep there!

A poem composed by Kakinomoto no Hitomaro sorrowing over himself as he lay at the point of death in Iwami Province[1]

On Kamo Mountain
Embedded among boulders
    Here I rest my head—
Unknowing, my beloved wife
Must even now be waiting.   5

Two poems composed by his wife,[1] *a maiden of the Yosami, when Kakinomoto no Hitomaro died*

You for whom I wait
Day after day, do they not
    Say you lie mingled
With the shells, my love,
In the bed of Pebble River?   5

---

1. Hitomaro's deathbed poem. Iwami was a remote area on the western coast of Japan.

1. Probably the woman addressed in the previous poem.

To meet face to face—
We shall not meet so any more;
    Rise up, O clouds,
Stand along Pebble River—
I would gaze and remember.   10

Ōtomo no Tabito[1]

Thirteen poems in praise of wine by Lord Ōtomo Tabito, the Commander of the Dazaifu[2]

Rather than engaging
in useless worries,
it's better to down a cup
of raw wine.

Great sages of the past   5
gave the name of "sage"[3] to wine.
How well they spoke!

What the Seven Wise Men[4]
    of ancient times
wanted, it seems,   10
    was wine.

Rather than making pronouncements
    with an air of wisdom,
it's better to down the wine   15
and sob drunken tears.

What is most noble,
    beyond all words
    and beyond all deeds,
is wine.

Rather than be half-heartedly human,   20
I wish I could be a jug of wine
and be soaked in it!

How ugly!
    those men who,
        with airs of wisdom,   25
            refuse to drink wine.
Take a good look,
and they resemble apes.

How could even
a priceless treasure   30
be better than a cup
    of raw wine?

---

1. Translated by Ian Hideo Levy.
2. Government headquarters in Kyūshū, southernmost of the main islands of Japan, an important outpost for regulating contacts with China and Korea. In Tabito's time the city was nicknamed "the distant capital."
3. So called by those who drank it secretly during a short period of prohibition in China.

4. The so-called Seven Sages of the Bamboo Grove, Daoist-inspired intellectuals in 3rd-century China who stayed aloof from the unstable political establishment by writing poetry, drinking, philosophizing, and offending common taste. Some of their poems are included in the "Hermits, Buddhists, and Daoists" cluster in this volume.

How could even a gem
that glitters in the night
be as good as drinking wine   35
and cleansing the heart?

Here in this life,
on these roads of pleasure,
it is fun to sob drunken tears.

As long as I have fun   40
    in this life,
let me be an insect or a bird
    in the next.[5]

Since all who live
must finally die,   45
let's have fun
while we're still alive.

Smug and silent airs of wisdom
are still not as good
as downing a cup of wine   50
and sobbing drunken tears.

Yamanoue no Okura

Dialogue on Poverty

(THE POOR MAN)

On sodden nights
When rain comes gusting on the wind,
    On freezing nights
When snow falls mingled with the rain,
    Shivering helplessly   5
In the all-pervading cold,
    I take a lump
Of hardened salt and nibble on it
    While I sip diluted
Lees of *sake* from my cup.   10
    Clearing my throat,
Sniffling as my nose begins to run,
    Stroking the few hairs
Of my meager, scraggly beard,
    I puff myself up: 15
"What do people matter anyway,
    Aside from me?"
But still I'm cold, and so I take
    My hempen quilt
And pull it up around my shoulders.   20
    I put on every

5. According to Buddhism, bad actions in this life can result in rebirth into a lower state in the next.

Sleeveless homespun frock I own,
   Layer upon layer,
But the night is cold. And he,
   The man more destitute   25
Than even I, on such a night
   His father and mother
Must be starving, bodies chill and numb;
   His wife and children
Moaning softly in the dark: 30
   Yes, you—at times like these
How do you manage to go on,
How do you get through your life?

(THE DESTITUTE MAN)

   Although men say
That heaven and earth are vast,   35
   Have they not dwindled
To a narrow frame for me?
   Although men say
That the sun and moon are bright,
   Have they not refused   40
To grant their shining unto me?
   Are all men thus,
Or am I alone deprived?
   Though by rare chance
I was born into the world of men,   45
   And as any man
I toil to make my living on the land,
   Yet must I throw rags
About my shoulders, mere rotten
   Shreds of a sleeveless   50
Frock, hemp with no padding,
   Dangling like branches
Of sea pine over my bones;
   And in this crazy hut,
This flimsy, tumbling hovel,   55
   Flat on the ground
I spread my bedding of loose straw.
   By my pillowside
My father and my mother crouch,
   And at my feet   60
My wife and children; thus am I
   Surrounded by grief
And hungry, piteous cries.
   But on the hearth
No kettle sends up clouds of steam,   65
   And in our pot
A spider spins its web.
   We have forgotten
The very way of cooking rice;

Then where we huddle, 70
Faintly whimpering like *nue* birds,[1]
Deliberately,
As the saying goes, to cut
The end of what
Was short enough before, 75
There comes the voice
Of the village chief with his whip,
Standing, shouting for me,
There outside the place we sleep.
Does it come to this— 80
Is it such a helpless thing,
The path of man in this world?

Though we may think
Our lives are mean and frustrate
In this world of men, 85
We cannot fly into the air,
It being so we are not birds.

Respectfully presented with deep obeisance by Yamanoue no Okura

A poem of longing for his children; with preface

Shaka Nyorai preached truly with his golden mouth that he had equal
compassion for all beings, even as for Rāhula.[1] He also preached that there
is no love surpassing that for a child. The greatest sage still had the feeling
of love for his child. Who then of the green grass of the world would not
love his children?

When I eat melons
My children come to my mind;
When I eat chestnuts
The longing is even worse.
Where do they come from, 5
Flickering before my eyes,
Making me helpless
Incessantly night after night,
Not letting me sleep in peace?

ENVOY

What are they to me, 10
Silver, or gold, or jewels?
How could they ever
Equal the greater treasure
That is a child?

1. Ominous birds associated with loneliness
and melancholy.
1. Shaka Nyorai is the Japanese name for the
Buddha; Rāhula was the son he fathered while
still an Indian prince, before becoming an
ascetic and gaining enlightenment. Parental
love is generally considered an attachment
that prevents us from gaining enlightenment.

菅原道實

Poetry of the Heian Court

Japan has the world's oldest living tradition of court poetry. For more than 1,300 years, Japanese sovereigns have called on courtier-poets to compose praise poems and demonstrate their poetic sophistication; over about half of that time span, poetry collections representing the best and brightest courtier-poets of the realm were compiled at imperial command. The poetry of the Heian court constitutes the defining moment in this long tradition, and the selections that follow showcase the two genres that dominated at the Heian court: Chinese-style poetry, represented here by Sugawara no Michizane, Japan's foremost Chinese-style poet, and the thirty-one-syllable *waka* poem, which was enshrined as the main form of vernacular Japanese court poetry by **The Kokinshū (Collection of Ancient and Modern Poems)**, the first imperial *waka* collection. Although today the composition of poetry for events at the imperial court has been reduced to ritual formality, it continues a once proud tradition of refined entertainment that linked the writing of poetry to imperial power.

Court poetry is radically different from poetry as we know it today. First, it is panegyric, addressed to the sovereign and the political system that he embodies. It is performative: poets do not labor over their lines in isolation but recite their poetry publicly at court events. It is also "occasional" poetry, composed for specific social occasions including the large events of life and its passing pleasures. Lastly, court poetry is topic bound, composed on themes with fitting seasonal associations. Whether writing on simple topics such as "Cherry Blossoms" or creating visual vignettes such as "Fireflies Flutter among White Dew," the poet-courtiers had to come up with witty, fresh treatments of well-worn topics in order to impress the audience and build their reputation as both poets and courtiers.

Poetic mastery in the courtly tradition required astute variation, technical virtuosity, and poetic erudition. Poetry was so important in Heian Japan that to return from an outing when the cherries bloomed without having penned a suitable memento would quickly consign a courtier to social oblivion. A handsome, wellborn man who was inarticulate was no better than a boor. His career as a bureaucrat would stagnate, and his prospects for an interesting love life were nil.

A dramatic nineteenth-century portrait of Sugawara no Michizane, poet–official, god of scholarship, and god of thunder.

SUGAWARA NO MICHIZANE

The courtier, poet, and scholar Sugawara no Michizane (845–903) is considered the most outstanding Japanese poet of Chinese-style poetry. He used this traditional genre for trenchant observations and personal plaint as had no other poet before him.

Michizane came from a family of remarkable scholars, who had served as professors at the State Academy devoted to Chinese studies. Although the Sugawara clan was renowned for Chinese scholarship and Chinese-style poetry, its members had never held the highest offices at court. Alone in his family, Michizane eventually rose from the academy to the second-highest position in the state. Yet the spectacular series of promotions during the reign of Emperor Uda (r. 887–97), who favored Michizane, would eventually exact a heavy price. The powerful Northern branch of the Fujiwara clan regarded his career as a threat. In 886 a purge initiated by the Fujiwara sent Michizane off to a dreary governor post in the provinces, a demotion he deeply resented. But the most damaging hit came in 901, only two weeks after he had received yet another illustrious promotion in rank: on trumped-up charges, Michizane was suddenly banished to a minor post in faraway Kyūshū, the southernmost island of Japan. He died after two sorrowful years in exile, a broken man.

But the passing of the man Michizane was the birth of the god Tenjin. Some twenty years after his death, natural disasters and other inauspicious events at court were attributed to the wrath of his revengeful spirit. His reputation was rehabilitated and shrines to him in the guise of Tenjin were built to pacify the exiled poet's spirit. Today, he is revered at thousands of shrines throughout Japan as the god of scholarship (and a divine helping hand to students praying for academic success in the challenging university entrance exams).

Michizane identified strongly with the scholarly tradition of his family, as is evident in the selections in this anthology. Like the Chinese poet **Bo Juyi**, whom he admired greatly, he compiled his own literary collection, and he offered it to the emperor, together with the literary collections of his father and grandfather.

Plum blossoms, Michizane's emblem and the origin of many legends that grew around him, frame his poetic work. His first poem, "On Looking at the Plum Blossoms on a Moonlit Night," composed when he was eleven, shows his early training in writing on set topics and crafting parallel couplets, a distinctive feature of Chinese-style poetry. His last poem, "In Exile, Spring Snow," which also dwells on plum blossoms, shows that Michizane never lost hope of being recalled from exile. To the end he awaited liberation, pointing to famous examples of freed captives in classical Chinese literature, the books that had defined his life and identity.

On "Looking at Plum Blossoms on a Moonlit Night"[1]

Written when I was in my eleventh year. My father had Scholar Shimada test me. That's when I composed my first Chinese-style poem. Thus I include it as the beginning of my collection.[2]

Moon glistens like snow under brightened skies.
Plum blossoms seem like radiant stars.
Just lovely—this golden mirror turning
And in the courtyard the perfume of their jade calyces.

I Stop Practicing the Zither

No doubt: playing zither and reading books is an asset for a true scholar:
Under the window of my study rests my seven-stringed zither.[1]
Intense concentration shows no effect, in vain do I go over the score.
My finger technique is full of mistakes and I have to ask my teacher again
    and again.
In my "Deep Gorges"—no flow of an autumn torrent.   5
And my "Winter Crows"[2] never conveyed the desolation of cries at night.
The friends, who "know my tone,"[3] all say that I'm wasting my time for
    nothing.
Well, isn't my family tradition more in poetry composition?

The Hardships of Professors

My family is not one of generals,
With Confucian studies we make our living.
My venerable grandfather reached the third court rank
And my dear father served as high court noble.
They understood the power of studying the past   5
And bequeathed it for their descendants' glory.
The day I was promoted to the status of "advanced student"[1]
I eagerly wished to establish myself in our family trade.
The year I became professor at the state academy

---

1. All selections translated by Wiebke Denecke.
2. In 900, shortly before his exile, the aging Michizane compiled his own poetry collection and offered it up to the reigning Emperor Daigo, together with the collections of his father and grandfather, who had also been prominent scholar-officials and poets. This childhood poem was on a topic assigned for poetry practice by his tutor, Shimada.
1. In China this instrument had been associated with refinement and scholars.
2. Like "Deep Gorges," a musical piece from the zither repertoire.

3. "The one who knows the tone" became a stock expression for "a close friend." In a well-known anecdote, the brilliant zither player Bo Ya enjoys playing for his friend Zhong Ziqi, who is the only one who understands his playing and "knows his tone." After Zhong Ziqi's death Bo Ya never played his zither again.
1. The title of a student selected to prepare for the civil service examination, given to Michizane at the age of 23 (unusually young).

Luckily our lecture hall was rebuilt.   10
Everybody rushed to extend their congratulations
Only my father was startled.
Why was he so startled?
"Unfortunately you are our only child!
Certainly, the official rank of a professor[2] is not bad   15
And a scholar's salary is decent.
But I once also held this post
And learnt to be cautious, afraid of human emotions."
When I first heard his kind advice
I felt as if stepping on ice, unsure how to proceed.   20
In my fourth year the council decided
To have me teach all students.[3]
Hardly had I been at the lectern for three days
When slanderous rumors reached my ears.
This year, when recommending students for advancement,   25
The criteria for pass and fail were real clear.
But the first talentless student who failed
Badmouthed me and filed a complaint, demanding unearned promotion.
In my teaching there are no shortcomings
And in my selection for advancement I was fair.   30
How true! My father's advice
When he warned me before all this happened.

Note on My Library

There is a house in Senpū Ward in the eastern sector of the capital, a corridor in
the southwest corner of the house, and a room at the southernmost end of the
corridor. The room is hardly more than ten feet square: when setting foot there
those entering or leaving have to squeeze past each other and those getting up
and sitting down end up on tightly lined mats. Yet out of this room have emerged
about a hundred men who passed the "advanced student" and "presented scholar"
examinations. That's why scholars regard this room as a "Dragon Gate" of sorts.[1]
It goes also by the name of "Mountain Shade Pavilion," because it lies west of a
small hill. Near the entrance there is a plum tree and a few steps to the east there
are clumps of bamboo. Each time the plum tree is in bloom and the bamboo is
touched by the wind it heightens and brightens one's spirits and nourishes one's
mind.

    When I passed the "advanced student" examination my father said, "This room
has a famous reputation. Why not move in here, while you are studying hard for
the coming exams?" So I tidied up the room, shifting the blinds and mats around,
and moved my books to a safe place. But, oh my, when space conditions are

2. Sixth rank.
3. During Michizane's first three years as a
professor, the lectures were given by his senior
colleague, whose death gave Michizane the
opportunity to lecture.
1. "To climb the Dragon Gate" was a Chinese

expression for passing the civil service examinations; Michizane here is describing the private academy run by his father. "Presented
scholar" was the highest degree in the State
Academy in Kyoto; "advanced student," a step
toward it, was itself a title rarely bestowed.

cramped, people get edgy and distressed. Among my friends there are some I feel close to and some I don't know well. Some put on a friendly face, although they have no interest to connect on a deeper level, while others are annoying like some lowborn people but we are on familiar terms. Some claim to seek enlightenment, when they pry among my private books and notes, while others pretend to pay a courtesy call, only to barge in right when I am trying to rest.

Another thing: a brush and a scraper are implements for writing texts and erasing mistakes. But as for that flock of crows which descends on me, they have no idea what these things are used for. They wield the scraper, scratching and damaging the desks, and fiddle around with the brush until they have soiled and spoiled my books. Yet another thing: the foundation for proper study is excerpting and excerpting implies the production of notes. I am by nature not very organized and systematic, so I can't help sometimes stopping my brush (in the middle of study) and leave slips of paper strewn about with excerpted notes. That's when people sneak into my library—hard to know what they are really up to—and the clever ones, when they see the notes, fold them up and tuck them away into their gown, but the stupid ones simply snatch them up, tear them in two and throw them away! These kinds of things annoy me to the extreme, and there are countless other petty annoyances I could go on about.

One more thing. Sometimes a friend comes for some compelling reason on important business and enters the library, whereupon those sneaky intruders, not bothering to find out whether the person who is with me has important business, walk straight in with unimportant trifles. That's what makes me despair! Really, it makes me despair. That Dong Zhongshu let down his curtain and Master Xue[2] climbed over the wall was not only because they wanted to focus on their studies, they also wanted some peace of mind. When writing this piece today I don't mean it to be a treatise on how to break off relations. I simply want to pour out my worries in writing. I am especially ashamed that I did not establish a private academy that would attract talented men, but instead need to establish some rules for unwanted intruders of my library. This is for those who do not understand me, and those who do understand me number about three or so people. I hope that with the small net designed to keep out swallows and sparrows I don't end up driving phoenixes away.

Written in trepidation on the first day of the seventh month of 893.

Seeing the Plum Blossoms When Sentenced to Exile[1]

When the East Wind blows,
send me your fragrance
you plum blossoms!
With your master gone,
don't forget about spring.

2. Figures known for hiding from the throng of followers they attracted. Dong Zhongshu (ca. 179–104 B.C.E.), a leading Confucian thinker during the Han Dynasty, was said to lower the curtains of his room and lecture only to a select group of advanced students, letting them pass their lecture notes on to the beginners.

1. Michizane's most famous vernacular poem. Legend has it that the tree in his garden in Kyoto was so touched by this poem that it flew to be with him in Dazaifu, his place of exile in the south.

In Exile, Spring Snow

They fill the town, overwhelm the district: so many plum blossoms!
Just like blossoms early in the year, rustled by wind in the sunlight.
What I see sticking to the feet of the geese might be letters on cloth
And that, there, the white dots on the head of the crows, makes me
   hopeful that I will return home.[1]

---

1. Two Chinese allusions that express Michizane's hopes of returning from exile. A certain Su Wu, long held by northern tribes, was rescued when a Han emperor happened to shoot the goose to whose leg he had attached a message; and a prince of the state of Yan, held hostage by the king of Qin, was told he could return home when crows' heads turned white and horses grew horns—improbable events that came to pass, leading to his freedom. This was Michizane's last poem.

THE KOKINSHŪ

The age of *The Kokinshū*, the period around 900, was a turning point in Japanese history. Vernacular poetry gained public stature, and vernacular prose genres such as tales and diaries, which would culminate in **The Tale of Genji** and **The Pillow Book**, started to emerge. The flourishing of vernacular literature went hand in hand with the development of a new script—the kana syllabic alphabet, also called "women's hand"—which complemented the hitherto exclusive use of Chinese characters in writing Japanese. Politically, members of the Fujiwara family, which would dominate the court for the rest of the Heian Period, increasingly inserted themselves as powerful regents to the emperor, marrying their daughters into the imperial family.

Japan's earliest imperial poetry anthologies date from the early ninth century, when Emperor Saga, who was thoroughly trained in Chinese Classics and an avid poet himself, commissioned three anthologies of Chinese-style poetry. Following this tradition, Emperor Daigo commissioned *The Kokinshū* (a short form of *Kokinwakashū*, "Collection of Ancient and Modern Waka Poems"), the first anthology of vernacular *waka* poetry. The success of this collection helped enshrine the thirty-one-syllable *waka* poem (composed in a 5-7-5-7-7 pattern) as the dominant form, intended to represent the splendor of the reigning court.

Compiled by a team headed by **Ki no Tsurayuki** (ca. 868–945), a leading figure of the emerging vernacular literature (for his biography and his other pioneering work, see his **Tosa Diary**, excerpted in this volume), *The Kokinshū* contains more than one thousand poems, complete with a vernacular Japanese and a Chinese-style preface, and is arranged by topical categories in twenty books. The books on the four seasons and on "love" dominate the collection, but there are also books on topics such as "parting," "travel," "mourning," and "puns and wordplay."

The anthology and its books are arranged according to principles of association and progression into an overarching narrative that far exceeds the meaning of the individual poems. Sequences of poems with subtle variations on the same topic are the building blocks that make the anthology into a coherent text of its own. For example, the books on the seasons and on love lend themselves to a natural cycle of beginning, high point, and end or the familiar pattern of first glimpse of the beloved, courtship, passion, marriage (or liaison), disillusion, separation, loneliness, and despair. The compilers' ability to fashion a narrative out of poems composed by many different authors on different occasions is often stunning and would be much imitated. Though the principles of association and progression invented by the compilers of *The Kokinshū* would become increasingly sophisticated in later poetry anthologies, these structural devices are already fully realized in the first imperial anthology, demonstrating that one of the world's most compressed genres can transcend the apparent limitations of its form.

In contrast to collections such as *The Man'yōshū*—Japan's earliest poetry anthology, with its tones of archaic grandeur and simplicity best exemplified by **Hitomaro**'s writings—*The Ko-kinshū* values poetic elegance, intellectual twists, and erudite refinement. The contradiction between empirical evidence and conventional knowledge generates many of the clever conceits of *Kokinshū* poetry: a typical strategy is "elegant confusion," as when early plum blossoms at the beginning of spring are mistakenly interpreted as late snowflakes, or vice versa, and the discovery of the error—or the uncertainty about the real nature of white stuff on plum tree branches—becomes the main point of the poem. In addition to daring visual metaphor, the *waka* poetry in *The Kokinshū* relies on a variety of rhetorical figures that drastically condense poetic expression: "poetic pillows" (*utamakura*) are poetically evocative place-names, which in the space of a few syllables summon up a host of associations. An entire poetic geography of the Japanese archipelago developed that was based on these resonant names. "Pivot words" (*kakekotoba*) are phonetic puns, in which a sequence of syllables has two different meanings. Aided by the new phonetic kana syllabary, plays on double meaning apparently increased greatly during the Kokinshū age, showing a heightened awareness of the disjunction between phonetic sound and written character.

At least as influential as its poetry was Ki no Tsurayuki's "Japanese Preface" to *The Kokinshū* (also called "Kana Preface," because it used the vernacular syllabary). It is the canonical statement on the principles of *waka* poetry, grounding it in a universal instinct for song. Although Ki no Tsurayuki's vision of poetry ultimately relied on the Chinese **Classic of Poetry** and its **"Great Preface"** (included in Vol. A), he argued against the traditions of arduous training and sophisticated craftsmanship that characterized traditional Chinese-style poetry, favoring instead a spontaneous expression of human imagination. Originally conceived fairly narrowly as a polemic against the high status of Chinese-style poetry and an attempt to elevate vernacular *waka* poetry to a courtly art, Tsurayuki's statement became so influential in Japanese culture that it came to inform broad assumptions about how humans are moved to create works of art.

THE KOKINSHŪ

From The Japanese Preface[1]

by Ki no Tsurayuki

The seeds of Japanese poetry lie in the human heart and grow into leaves of ten thousand words. Many things happen to the people of this world, and all that they think and feel is given expression in description of things they see and hear. When we hear the warbling of the mountain thrush in the blossoms or the voice of the frog in the water, we know every living being has its song.

It is poetry which, without effort, moves heaven and earth, stirs the feelings of the invisible gods and spirits, smooths the relations of men and women, and calms the hearts of fierce warriors.

Such songs came into being when heaven and earth first appeared. However, legend has it that in the broad heavens they began with Princess Shitateru, and on earth with the song of Susano-o no mikoto.[2]

In the age of the awesome gods, songs did not have a fixed number of syllables and were difficult to understand because the poets expressed themselves directly, without polish. By the time of the age of humans, beginning with Susano-o no mikoto, poems of thirty-one syllables were composed.[3] Since then many poems have been composed when people were attracted by the blossoms or admired the birds, when they were moved by the haze or regretted the swift passage of the dew, and both inspiration and forms of expression have become diverse. As a long journey to distant places begins with one step and is completed after many months and years, and as a high mountain is created by the accumulation of dust and mire at its skirts and gradually reaches the trailing clouds of the heavens, so too has poetry been.

* * *

Nowadays because people are concerned with gorgeous appearances and their hearts admire ostentation, insipid poems, short-lived poems have appeared. Poetry has become a sunken log submerged unknown to others in the homes of lovers. Poems are not things to bring out in public places as openly as the opening blossoms of the pampas grass.

Japanese poetry ought not to be thus. Consider its origins: Whenever there were blossoms at dawn in spring or moonlit autumn nights, the generations of sovereigns of old summoned their attendants to compose poetry inspired by these beauties. Sometimes the poet wandered through untraveled places to use the image of the blossoms; sometimes he went to dark unknown wilderness lands to write of the moon. The sovereigns surely read these and distinguished the wise from the foolish.

* * *

1. Translated by Laurel Rasplica Rodd.
2. The naughty younger brother of Amaterasu, the sun goddess who is the ancestor of the Japanese emperors. "Princess Shitateru": an earthly deity who composed a dirge after her husband was killed.

3. The earliest historical chronicles of Japan credit the god Susano-o with the composition of the first *waka* poem ("poems of thirty-one syllables"), in praise of a new palace he had constructed for his wife.

This poetry has been handed down since days of old, but it is especially since the Nara period that it has spread far and wide. In that era the sovereign must truly have appreciated poetry, and during his reign Kakinomoto no Hitomaro of the Senior Third Rank was a sage of poetry.[4] Thus ruler and subjects must have been one.

On an autumn evening the crimson leaves floating on the Tatsuta River looked like brocade to the sovereign, and on a spring morning the cherry blossoms on Yoshino Mountain reminded Hitomaro of clouds.[5] There was also a man named Yamabe no Akahito. He was an outstanding and superior poet. Hitomaro cannot be ranked above Akahito, nor Akahito ranked below Hitomaro.

Aside from these, other great poets were heard, as generations succeeded each other like the segments of the black bamboo in a line unbroken as a twisted thread. Earlier poems were gathered in a collection called the *Man'yōshū*.

After that there were one or two poets who knew the ancient songs and understood the heart of poetry. However, each had strengths and weaknesses. Since that time more than one hundred years and ten generations have gone by. Of those who composed during this century, few have known the ancient songs and understood poetry. I would like to give some examples, but I will exclude those of poets of high rank and office, whom I cannot criticize lightly.

Among the others, one of the best known of recent times[6] was Archbishop Henjō, whose style is good but who lacks sincerity. His poetry is like a painting of a woman which stirs one's heart in vain.

> along slender threads
> of delicate twisted green
> translucent dewdrops
> strung as small fragile jewels—
> new willow webs in spring

* * *

Ariwara no Narihira has too much feeling, too few words. His poems are like withered flowers, faded but with a lingering fragrance.

> is this not that moon—
> is this spring not that spring we
> shared so long ago—
> it seems that I alone am
> unaltered from what was then

* * *

Fun'ya no Yashuhide used words skillfully but the expression does not suit the contents. His poetry is like a tradesman attired in elegant robes.

---

4. Hitomaro (flourished ca. 680–700) is one of the most famous poets in *The Manyōshū* (*Collection of Myriad Leaves*), an 8th-century compilation of this earliest flourishing of poetry.

5. The Tatsuta River was associated in poetry

with colorful autumn foliage; Yoshino was famous for its scenic beauty and its cherry blossoms.

6. This section offers judgments of the so-called Six Poetry Immortals, six famous poets who lived closer to Ki no Tsurayuki's time.

as soon as the gales
begin to rage   the trees and
field grass bend before
them   no wonder they call this
wind from the mountains Tempest

* * *

The poetry of Priest Kisen of Mount Uji is vague, and the logic does not run smoothly from beginning to end. Reading his poems is like looking at the autumn moon only to have it obscured by the clouds of dawn. Since few of his poems are known, we cannot make comparisons and come to understand them.

this is how I live
in my retreat southwest of
the capital   though
men call Uji Mountain[7] a
reminder of worldly sorrow

Ono no Komachi is a modern Princess Sotōri.[8] She is full of sentiment but weak. Her poetry is like a noble lady who is suffering from a sickness, but the weakness is natural to a woman's poetry.

* * *

I have sunk to the
bottom   and like the rootless
shifting water weeds
should the currents summon me
I too would drift away

* * *

Ōtomo no Kuronushi's songs are rustic in form; they are like a mountaineer with a bundle of firewood on his back resting in the shade of the blossoms.

* * *

well now   I'll go to
Mirror Mountain   gaze upon
it and then travel
on   for I wonder if I've
aged in all these years I've lived

There are others as well who are known, as numerous as the leaves of the trees of the forest, as widespread as the ivy which crawls in the fields, but they think anything they compose is poetry and do not know what poems are.

In the reign of the present sovereign[9] the four seasons have unfolded nine times. The boundless waves of his benevolence flow beyond the boundaries of the Eight Islands;[1] his broad compassion provides a deeper shade than Mount

---

7. The name puns on "grief"; the mountain is generally associated with gloom.
8. The consort of a 5th-century emperor. Ono no Komachi is the best woman poet in *The*

Kokinshū.
9. Emperor Daigo (r. 897–930).
1. The major islands of Japan.

Tsukuba. During his moments of leisure from the multifarious affairs of state, he does not neglect other matters: mindful of the past and desiring to revive the ancient ways, he wishes to examine them and to pass them on to future generations. On the eighteenth day of the Fourth Month of Engi 5 (905), he commanded Ki no Tomonori, Senior Secretary of the Ministry of Private Affairs, Ki no Tsurayuki, Chief of the Documents Division, Ōshikōchi no Mitsune, Former Junior Clerk of Kai Province, and Mibu no Tadamine, functionary in the Headquarters of the Palace Guards, Right Division, to present to him old poems not included in the *Man'yōshū* as well as our own. We have chosen poems on wearing garlands of plum blossoms, poems on hearing the nightingale, on breaking off branches of autumn leaves, on seeing the snow.[2] We have also chosen poems on wishing one's lord the lifespan of the crane and tortoise, on congratulating someone, on yearning for one's wife when one sees the autumn bush clover or the grasses of summer, on offering prayer strips on Ōsaka Hill, on seeing someone off on a journey, and on miscellaneous topics that cannot be categorized by season. These thousand poems in twenty books are called the *Kokinwakashū*. These collected poems will last as long as the waters flowing at the foot of the mountains; they are numerous as the grains of sand on the shore. There will be no complaints that they are like the shallows of the Asuka River;[3] they will give pleasure until the pebbles grow into boulders.

Now then, our poems have not the fragrance of spring blossoms, but a vain reputation lingers, long as the endless autumn night. Thus we fear the ear of the world and lack confidence in the heart of our poetry, but, whether going or staying like the trailing clouds, whether sleeping or rising like the belling deer, we rejoice that we were born in this generation and that we were able to live in the era when this event occurred.

Hitomaro is dead, but poetry is still with us. Times may change, joy and sorrow come and go, but the words of these poems are eternal, endless as the green willow threads, unchanging as the needles of the pine, long as the trailing vines, permanent as birds' tracks.[4] Those who know poetry and who understand the heart of things will look up to the old and admire the new as they look up to and admire the moon in the broad sky.

From Book 1. Spring

1[1]

Composed on a day when spring arrived within the old year

Spring has come
before the year's turning:
should I speak now

---

2. The preface here alludes to the different books of *The Kokinshū*, starting with the books on the four seasons.

3. A river famous for its shallowness (often used as an image of shallow love).

4. Or "handwriting," referring to the physical manuscript of *The Kokinshū*.

1. Poems 1–259 and 635–640 are translated by Lewis Cook; poems 495–500 and 553–658 are translated by Edwin Cranston.

of the old year
or call this the new year?[2]

Ariwara no Motokata

2

Composed on "the first day of spring"

Waters I cupped my
hands to drink, wetting
my sleeves, still frozen:
might this first day of
spring's wind thaw them?

Ki no Tsurayuki

3

Topic unknown

Where are the promised
mists of spring?
In Yoshino,[3] fair hills
of Yoshino, snow
falling still.

Anonymous

23

Topic unknown

Spring's robe of mist
is frail indeed—
its weft is sure
to be frayed by
the mountain winds

Ariwara no Yukihira

---

2. This poem, which opens *The Kokinshū* and its six books of poetry on the seasons (two books each for spring and autumn, one book each for summer and winter), plays on the discrepancy between the official lunar and the unofficial solar calendars. According to the solar calendar, the first day of spring always occurs in early February; in the lunar calendar, the new year begins in January or February. Thus the (lunar) first day of spring sometimes preceded (solar) New Year's Day.

Some commentators see this poem as alluding to the "old and new" poetry announced in the title of *The Kokinshū*.
3. A poetic place-name (*utamakura*), which by the time of *The Kokinshū* had become associated with heavy snowfall, cherry blossoms, and reclusion. Hitomaro, the leading *Manyōshū* poet, had praised its beauties and imperial landscape when visiting in the retinue of an empress (see p. 1176).

24

Presented at the Empress's poetry match in the reign of Kanpyō

Even the greens
of the evergreen pine
are refreshed
by the coming
of spring

Minamoto no Muneyuki

25

Composed in response to imperial command

My loved one's robes
stretched out to dry—
Each shower of spring[4]
deepens the greens
of the meadows

Ki no Tsurayuki

26

Composed in response to imperial command

Green threads
of the willows
spun by spring's wind
their tangled flowers
burst into bloom

Ki no Tsurayuki

27

On willow trees near the Great Western Temple

Their pale green threads
spun by the wind and
laced with gems
of white dew—
willows in spring

Archbishop Henjō

---

4. There is a pun on two meanings of the word *haru*, which can mean "to stretch" or the season "spring."

From Book 2. Spring

69

Topic unknown

On hills where mists of spring
trail, glowing faintly,
do the flowers' fading
colors foretell
their fall?[5]

Anonymous

70

Topic unknown

If saying "stay!"
would stop their
falling, could I hold
these blossoms
more dear?

Anonymous

71

Topic unknown

It's their falling without regret
I admire—
Cherry blossoms:
a world of sadness
if they'd stayed.

Anonymous

72

Topic unknown

I seem bound to sleep
in this village tonight:
led astray by falling
blossoms, I've forgotten
my way home.

Anonymous

---

5. This poem opens the second book of spring, marking the middle of the season. It is the first
of a sequence of twenty-one poems on the topic "falling cherry blossoms."

73

Topic unknown

Are they not like
this fleeting world?[6]
Cherry blossoms:
no sooner do they flower
than they fall.

                    Anonymous

From Book 6. Autumn

256

On seeing autumn leaves on Otowa Mountain while visiting Ishiyama

From that first day
the winds of autumn sounded,
the tips of trees on
Otowa Mountain's[7] peak
were turning color.

                    Ki no Tsurayuki

257

Composed for a poetry contest at the house of Prince Koresada

White dew
all of a single color:
how then does it dye
the leaves of autumn
a thousand different shades?[8]

                    Fujiwara no Toshiyuki

258

Composed for a poetry contest at the house of Prince Koresada

As the dew of autumn's night
settles in place,
will the falling tears
of wild geese
dye the fields yet deeper?

                    Mibu no Tadamine

6. Literally, "world of a cicada's discarded shell."
7. A pun on *oto*, "sound," exemplifying the rhetorical device of "pivot words" (*kakekotoba*), or puns, which abound in *The Kokinshū*. The

following four poems are from a 19-poem sequence on "autumn leaves."
8. The assumption here and in 258 and 259 is that dew causes the leaves to change color.

259

Topic unknown

Surely the autumn dew
must have its varied ways
to turn the mountain's leaves
so many shades
of color.

Anonymous

From Book 11. Love

495

Topic unknown

Memories revive
As on evergreen mountains
    Wild azalea flares:
Unspoken love burns stronger
For the silence where it dwells.

Anonymous

496

Topic unknown

Loving secretly
Is too hard for me to bear:
    I shall let my heart
Reveal to him its color,
The blush of the safflower.

Anonymous

497

Topic unknown

On the autumn fields,
Mingled with the plumegrass,
    Blossoming flowers—
Colors flaunted openly, I'll love;
If not, there is no way to meet.

Anonymous

498

Topic unknown

The warbler[9] singing
On the very topmost branch
    Of my garden plum:
Even such a cry as that
Will break forth from my yearning!

Anonymous

499

Topic unknown

Can the young cuckoo[1]
Singing in the footsore hills
    Be as sad as I,
Yearning for you all night long,
Unable to sleep a wink?

Anonymous

500

Topic unknown

The mosquito flares,[2]
Sputtering, fill the house with smoke,
    Now that summer's here—
How long must they still smolder on,
These fires in my stifled heart?

Anonymous

553

Topic unknown

Once I fell asleep
In a momentary doze, and saw
    Him for whom I long,
Since when I have begun to place
My trust in the things called dreams.

Ono no Komachi

---

9. A spring bird.
1. A bird associated with early summer.
2. One of the few annoying items of everyday life accepted in the refined vocabulary of the courtly *waka* tradition.

554

Topic unknown

When pressed with longing
Fiercely through desire's hour
    In the bead-black dark,
I slip off the robe of night
To lie with it inside out.[3]

Ono no Komachi

From Book 13. Love

635

Topic unknown

Autumn nights, long
only in name:
let's meet, we say,
yet dawn comes to part us
before we've begun.

Ono no Komachi

636

Topic unknown

For me, not long
enough at all:
autumn nights have always
taken their measure
from the depths of one's love.

Ōshikōchi no Mitsune

637

Topic unknown

Just as the morning sky
is brightening to dawn,
how sad that we must
sort our robes
and part.[4]

Anonymous

3. Wearing nightclothes inside out was believed to bring a desired dream. "Bead-black": a poetic epithet (*makurakotoba*) for night.
4. This and the following poems are from a sequence on "parting at dawn." With the arrival of dawn, marked by the crowing of a rooster, the lover must depart to avoid being seen.

638

Topic unknown

Dawn has come—
I resign myself to parting:
why then must thoughts
I can't find words for
cling to my heart?

Fujiwara no Kunitsune

639

From the empress's poetry contest in the Kanpyō era

Dawn has come—
on the path home from love
I am drenched:
rainfall swelling
my falling tears.

Fujiwara no Toshiyuki

640

Topic unknown

I begin to cry
regret for our parting
even before the rooster
crows the break
of dawn.

Utsuku

657

Topic unknown

Driven straight along
By a longing without bound,
I'll come by night,
For surely none will rebuke me
For trespass on the path of dreams.

Ono no Komachi

658

Topic unknown

Though on paths of dreams
With no resting for my feet
I run to and fro,
Such rendezvous are nothing
To one glimpse of you that's real.

Ono no Komachi

KI NO TSURAYUKI

ca. 868–945

Ki no Tsurayuki is a pioneering figure in the history of Japanese vernacular writing, which before him was reserved for poetry—almost all prose was composed in the official Chinese-style language. Already renowned as a prominent courtier-poet and as one of the four compilers of the first imperial anthology of Japanese poetry, *The Kokinshū* (*Collection of Ancient and Modern Poems*), Tsurayuki produced near the end of his life a prose work that captured what was distinctive about Japanese vernacular poetry and transplanted its innovations into a new form: the first prose diary in Japanese, *Tosa Diary*. Part memoir, based on his own travel experiences, and part imaginative fiction, Tsurayuki adopted the voice of a gentlewoman and used the new *kana* script (a syllabic alphabet associated with women's writing) to craft an extraordinary work.

Although Ki no Tsurayuki came from a relatively humble family, he obtained some minor government posts and began to gain renown as a court poet during staged poetry contests, a pastime that was just becoming popular in the 890s. These public competitions between two parties who composed and recited poems on set topics such as love or the four seasons were a sign that vernacular Japanese poetry was slowly gaining official recognition at court. During the ninth century, emperors had sponsored Chinese-style poetry, a genre of much higher status, and vernacular poetry had functioned mostly as a medium for expressing private sentiment and love. A crucial breakthrough for vernacular *waka* poetry (poetry of thirty-one syllables in a 5-7-5-7-7 pattern) came in 905, when the ruling emperor, Daigo, ordered Tsurayuki and three other leading poets to compile the first imperial anthology of Japanese poetry. Tsurayuki's preface to the anthology, the so-called "**Kana Preface**," laid the foundations for the principles of later *waka* poetry and helped enshrine *waka* as the leading courtly genre. Later, from 930 to 935, Tsurayuki received a middle-rank appointment as provincial governor of Tosa, a province on Shikoku, one of the four main islands of Japan. A decade later he died an official of undistinguished rank, but a poet renowned for his technical virtuosity and moving lyricism.

Tosa Diary, written around 935, is a day-by-day record of the travels of an unnamed governor of Tosa returning back to the capital after the conclusion of his appointment in the provinces. The diary, partially based on Tsurayuki's own experiences as the governor of Tosa, is written in the voice of a female attendant in the governor's retinue. This ironic distance between the author and the narrator is highlighted as the diary opens: "I wrote this wondering what it would be like for a woman to try her hand at one of those diaries that men are said to keep." There are many theories about why Tsurayuki assumed a female voice. Perhaps he wanted to break free from the constraints of male official diary writing, whose focus on court protocol and administrative matters left little space for poetry and the expression of moods and emotions. Adopting this fictional persona allowed him to say things that could be said only from a woman's perspective.

Poetry is central to the short diary, which features fifty-seven poems by the fictional lady, her travel companions, and locals on the scene. The company is stirred to poetry by the beauties of the scenery, by famous old poems, or by feelings of grief over events that have happened since their departure from the capital five years before—one woman, for example, had lost her child.

The contrast between the governor's retinue and the rustic locals they meet along the way is a source of humor and irony. Country bumpkins, who lack the education and refinement of the capital company, appear in embarrassing situations, but Tsurayuki also casts an ironic glance at the spoiled urbanites, who, for example, get frightened by rough weather at sea and are calmed only by the unperturbed sailors' songs—a more popular and far earthier type of verse than the elegant courtly *waka*.

Tsurayuki's *Tosa Diary* is a bold experiment in the expressive potential of vernacular Japanese prose, the literary contours of the female voice, and the power of *waka* poetry to capture and communicate the deepest human emotions. The tone of the diary, with its nostalgic yearning for the capital—the home of courtly tastes and lifestyles—echoes that of the "travel poems" in *The Kokinshū*, and in some ways the diary acts out the theoretical claims Tsurayuki had made in the "Kana Preface," thirty years earlier, about the nature of *waka*. But his *Tosa Diary* leads the reader into new territory, where song and poetry emerge from a much broader spectrum of society and where prose records memorable encounters between the sensibilities of courtier and commoner in Heian Japan's rustic countryside.

From Tosa Diary[1]

I wrote this wondering what it would be like for a woman to try her hand at one of those diaries that men are said to keep. One year, around eight in the evening of the twenty-first day of the Twelfth Month, I embarked on a journey. What follows are notes on some of the things that took place.

A certain person[2] had just received official clearance to return to the capital upon completing the usual term of four or five years in his provincial posting. We set out from the governor's mansion to the place where we were to board our boat, and people we knew and some we didn't came to see us off. Those who had come to know us well over the past few years were loath to see us go, and we spent the whole day, well into the night, in confusion, getting ready to depart. . . .

---

1. Translated by and with footnotes adapted from Gustav Heldt. All ellipses, marking omissions from the original, are Heldt's, as are bracketed additions.
2. Ki no Tsurayuki himself.

It is now the seventh [of the First Month], and we still are in the same harbor of Ōminato. I recall, in vain, that today the New Year's Presentation of White Horses[3] is held at court. The only white we can see here is that of the waves.

During the day, long chests were delivered to us from the home of someone who lives in a place called "Pond." Despite the name, there were no carp in them, but they were filled with many other foods, including perch and numerous other fish from both river and sea. The fresh greens reminded us of the New Year's plucking of shoots at home in the capital. The gifts came with this poem:

> A wild moor
> thick with weeds
> but no water:
> such is the "Pond" where I
> gathered these herbs.

How charming. The "Pond" of the poem is the name of the place. The poem was by a woman of rank who came to live with her husband in the provinces. The chests' contents were shared with everyone, including the children. When all had eaten their fill, the sailors drummed on their taut bellies. The sound was enough to startle even the sea god. No doubt we are in for waves.

Much else happened during the day. Someone came bringing lunch boxes. I'm sure his name will come back to me in a moment. It was clear that his heart was set on making a verse for the occasion. After talking about this and that for a while, he sighed mournfully and remarked, "Alas, the waves are rising," and then recited his poem:[4]

> Louder than the roar of the
> white-crested waves
> rising in your path
> will my cries resound
> when you depart.

He must have some voice. How could this poem compare with the things he had brought? We made a show of being impressed, but no one offered a poem in reply. Even though there was someone among them who was more than capable of replying, all we did was praise his poem and continue eating until nightfall.

Finally the man said, "Excuse me," and got up to leave. Just then, a child sitting in the back of our group whispered, "I'll offer a reply." Those of us near enough to hear were surprised and started to speak among ourselves, saying how charming this would be, and that if the girl was really going to compose something, she ought to do so at once. Hoping he might wait for the poem, we looked around for our erstwhile guest. But he had already left, no doubt because night had fallen.

3. The announcement of promotions and new appointments to official posts.
4. To offer departing travelers a poem predicting rough seas was inauspicious. The narrator pretends to have forgotten the versifier's name so that she can frankly report the embarrassing scene.

We still were curious. Someone asked the child to tell us what she had composed. She was shy and said nothing until pressed, then recited this poem:

> The sleeves of those who leave
> and those who stay
> are drenched in a stream of tears,
> swelling to soak them
> ever more.

What a fine verse—was it because the poet was so pretty that this seemed such a pleasant surprise? Still, what were we to do with a child's verse? An aunt or an uncle might put their signature on it. Not the right thing to do, perhaps. Someone suggested sending the verse to our visitor, but nothing was done, after all. . . .

The morning of the ninth [of the First Month]. We rowed out from Ōminato hoping to reach the harbor at Naha. Since we were leaving the bounds of the province, a great many people came to see us off. Fujiwara no Tokizane, Tachibana no Suehira, and Hasebe no Yukimasa in particular had been following us since the day we left the governor's mansion. These are truly men of feeling, their consideration as deep as the ocean before us.

We were about to leave the harbor and row into the offing, and these people had come to see us off. As we rowed out to sea, those who remained ashore receded into the distance, and those on the boat faded from their sight. Those on the shore must have had things left unsaid, and those of us on the boat felt the same, but there was no help for it. Nonetheless, I spoke this verse to myself before giving up such thoughts:

> I would send my feelings
> across the sea,
> but feelings not being words
> how could they know
> my thoughts?

We passed by the Uda Pines. Both the number of trees and the years they have grown there are beyond counting. The waves washed up near each root, and cranes flew above each branch. Unable to remain silent, someone on the boat composed this verse:

> I gaze across at the pines:
> the cranes that roost
> on every branch
> must take these evergreens
> for age-old companions.

The poem could hardly rival the sight itself. I watched the mountains and sea as we rowed into the gathering dusk. In the dark of night, I couldn't tell east from west, and we could only leave it to the captain to judge the weather. Even the men on board, not used to traveling at sea, were worried. As for the women, lying with their heads against the bilge, they could only weep aloud.

Feeling sorry for them, and not at all worried themselves, the crew and captain began singing boatmen's songs:

> In the fields in spring
> I weep aloud,
> my hands are cut
> by sharp blades of grass,
> the greens that I gather
> will be grabbed by his father,
> devoured by his mother.
> How I long to go home![5]

> Where's that girl
> who just last night
> begged for my money
> telling sweet lies
> buying on credit
> bringing no payment
> not even bringing herself?[6]

There were many others that I won't write down. They made us laugh, and though the sea was rough, our hearts were eased a bit. . . .

At daybreak on the thirteenth a little rain fell, then it stopped after a while. Several of the women got off the boat and went looking for a suitable place to bathe. Looking out at the sea, I composed this verse:

> All of the clouds
> look so like waves
> I wish for a diver,
> a girl I could ask
> "Which is the sea?"

Since it is past the tenth of the month, the moon in the dawn sky is charming. From the day we boarded the boat, the women have not once worn fine robes of red silk, fearful of catching the sea god's attention. Now, barely hidden by the cover of a few scant reeds, they have hitched up their skirts past their knees, carelessly showing the abalones and clams that go so well with sea squirts.[7] . . .

The twentieth. The weather is still unfavorable, and our boat stays in port. Everyone is complaining. Frustrated and anxious, I wonder how many days have passed since we set out. Has it been twenty? Thirty? Just counting them would hurt one's fingers. How dreary.

I stay awake all night. The moon of the twentieth rises in the sky, not from the rim of a mountain peak but straight from the sea. Was it a sight like this that was seen, in the distant past, by the man known as Abe no Nakamaro, who

---

5. The song supposedly expresses the plight of a young woman married to a farmer's son.
6. A comic song in the voice of a merchant deceived by a girl.

7. That is, male genitals; "abalones and clams" are female genitals. The sea god was believed to be ever-lustful.

had journeyed to the land of the Tang?[8] When he was readying to board a boat to return home, the people of that realm, reluctant to see him go, held a farewell party. They composed Chinese verses and, hesitating to part, lingered until the moon of the twentieth rose in the night sky. At the sight of the moon, Master Nakamaro said, "In my country, verses such as this were sung by the gods in their sacred age and, even today, are composed by people of all ranks—high, middle, and low—when they feel the regret of parting, or in celebration or in sadness," and he composed this:

> I look out
> across the wide blue sea
> and see the same moon
> that once rose over Mount Mikasa
> in distant Kasuga.[9]

Aware that the people of that country would be unable to understand the verse as recited, he sketched its meaning in Chinese characters[1] and explained it to someone there who had learned our language. They must have been able to understand his feelings, since they expressed immoderate praise for his poem. The speech of China and that of our country may differ, but the light of the moon is the same everywhere, and so it must be with the human heart.

Inspired by this story from the past, someone composed the following verse:

> The same moon I saw
> in the capital
> over the mountain rim
> now rises from the ocean's waves
> and sets there, too.

The fourth [of the Second Month]. The captain told us, "The weather looks very bad today," so we ended up staying in port. And in spite of that, there was not a single wind-tossed wave all day. Our captain is useless when it comes to predicting the weather.

The beach where we docked was covered with a variety of lovely shells and pebbles. Seeing them, someone on our boat who had lost a daughter composed this verse:

> Let the incoming waves
> bring to shore
> "forgetting shells"
> that I might gather
> to ease my longing for her.

---

8. Abe no Nakamaro (697–770) was 19 when he accompanied one of the regular diplomatic missions from Japan to China; he studied, passed the civil service examination, and served there in the Chinese government until his death.
9. Near Nara, which served as capital of Japan from 710 to 784. When Nakamaro left for China, the members of his embassy were seen off with prayers at the Kasuga shrine.
1. Literally, "men's letters"; using Chinese characters was a male prerogative, in contrast to the vernacular kana script associated with female writing.

Hearing this, someone else felt compelled to compose this to dispel the gloom of those on board:

> I'll not gather shells
> of forgetfulness—
> I'd rather keep
> my longing
> for that bright gem.[2]

The parent has been made weak as a child on account of her daughter. Someone may well ask, "Was she really as pretty as a gem?" Still, they say, "a dead child has a pretty face." . . .

The ninth [of the Second Month]. We were filled with impatience as our boat was towed upriver before daybreak, but since there isn't enough water in the river, we are reduced to a crawling pace. Eventually we came to a fork in the river called Wada no Tomari. Here, people begged for rice and fish and some was handed out.

As the boat was towed upstream, a place called Nagisa Villa came into view. Looking at it and thinking of its past, we realized that it was indeed a charming place. In the hills behind were pine trees, and inside the courtyard, plum trees were in bloom. People started talking. Long ago this was a famous place. This is where the middle captain, Ariwara no Narihira, in attendance on Prince Koretaka, composed that poem,

> If in this world
> no cherry flowers bloomed
> then would our hearts
> be at ease
> in springtime?

Then someone with us here and now composed a verse evoking the setting and its past:

> Though a thousand years
> may have passed,
> the chill in the sound
> of these pines
> hasn't changed.

And yet another person composed this:

> Longing for their lord,
> the plum blossoms
> of his ancient dwelling
> are as fragrant now
> as they were in the past.

---

2. That is, the child. The previous poem contains a play on "forgetting" (*wasure*) her by hurrying to the shore and gathering *wasuregai* clams.

And so we continued upstream, rejoicing as we drew nearer to the capital. Several of my fellow travelers were accompanied by children they had not had when they went down this same river, children born during their stay in the province of Tosa. Whenever the boat stopped, they would carry their children with them as they went ashore. Seeing this, the mother whose child had died was unable to contain her grief and sobbed as she composed this:

> Those who had none
> now return with theirs:
> others' children
> bring sorrow to one who
> has lost her own.

What must the father have felt as he heard this? Such overwhelming emotions, and the poems they provoke, are hardly matters of self-indulgence. It is said in China and here as well that poetry is an action one resorts to when feelings cannot be silenced. . . .

The sixteenth. This evening we made our way to the capital. . . .

We waited for night before entering the city,[3] and as we were taking our time, the moon came into view. We crossed the Katsura River under its brilliant light. Some of our party commented on how different this river was from the Asuka, notorious for varying between depths and shallows without warning. In response, someone composed this poem:

> The light of the moon
> on this river's waters
> remains as unchanged as
> its evergreen namesake,
> the moon's *katsura* tree.[4]

Someone responded with this:

> Once as distant
> as heaven's clouds,
> the Katsura River
> now soaks my sleeves
> as I cross.

Yet another person composed this verse:

> Though the Katsura River
> does not run through
> my heart,
> the depths
> of both must be the same.

So much joy on returning to the capital, hence so many poems.

---

3. Kyoto.
4. According to Chinese legends, the katsura laurel, an evergreen, grows on the moon.

As the night deepened, we could not tell one place from another. We are glad to be back in the capital! When we reached our residence and passed through the gate, we saw very clearly in the bright moonlight how things were. The house was far more dilapidated than we had been warned while away. The same must be true of the sensibilities of those we left in charge of the house. Though a fence divided our houses, we were as one family, and our neighbors offered to look after our place. To think that we had sent gifts every time we sent a message. Still, we did not raise our voices in complaint tonight. Unpleasant as it may be, we will have to offer a token of gratitude.

On the grounds of our residence, there is a depression filled with water, like a pond. It was surrounded by pine trees. During the past five or six years (it feels like a thousand), half of them have died, though some saplings have begun to grow among the surviving trees. Everything else was in ruin, and many sighs were heard. I recalled everything that had happened, and among the most painful were memories of the girl who, though born in this house, had not come back with us. Those who had traveled with us on the boat were playing noisily with their own children. There was one still unable to overcome her grief, and someone who understood quietly composed this:

> Even as a child born here
> does not return,
> how sad to see
> these pine saplings
> growing by our house.[5]

As though this were not enough, he composed another:

> If only I could have seen her
> for as long as the
> pine's thousand years
> and not known the sorrow
> of that distant parting.

I have much else to regret, much that is difficult to forget, but there is no end to writing such things. I should throw this away and be done with it.

---

5. The young trees are a reminder of the irreplaceability of the dead child.

SEI SHŌNAGON

ca. 966–1017

The gifted coterie of women writers who served as ladies-in-waiting to the Japanese imperial consorts of the late tenth and early eleventh centuries produced a number of superlative literary works that today stand at the center of the canon of Japanese literature. Next to **Murasaki Shikibu's** *The Tale of Genji* is *The Pillow Book* by Sei Shōnagon, who earned no kind words from Shikibu. In her diary she grumbled that Shōnagon was "dreadfully conceited" and "thought herself so clever, littering her writings with Chinese characters, but if one examined them closely, they left much to be desired." Shikibu was annoyed by Shōnagon's pretensions to break into the domain of Chinese learning, reserved at the time for male aristocrats. As ladies-in-waiting to two imperial consorts who maintained competing literary salons, Shikibu and Shōnagon were themselves engaged in an intense rivalry that spurred them to produce works to which later generations would look up with nostalgic awe. In design, form, and purpose, the two books are polar opposites. *The Tale of Genji* is an extensive, intricate, patient work of fiction. *The Pillow Book* is a slender catchall of personal observation, impressionistic and highly opinionated. Shōnagon has a sharp tongue, a keen eye, and a brush that moves masterfully between capturing lyrical moods and making pithy points. That she is both a supreme embodiment and a critical arbiter of Heian courtly tastes gives *The Pillow Book* a delightful depth.

SEI SHŌNAGON AND THE HEIAN COURT

Sei Shōnagon, whose actual name was probably Kiyohara Nagiko, was the daughter of a provincial governor noted for his poetry (in Heian Japan names were context-dependent, and a gentlewoman was usually named after the court title of a male relative). Although Shōnagon's father was a middle-ranking courtier with an appointment in the provinces, she seems to have spent all her life in the capital, the seat of the imperial court. Between 993 and 1000 she served Empress Teishi (977–1000), one of the consorts of Emperor Ichijō (980–1011). What we know about Shōnagon's life is mostly contained in *The Pillow Book*, which does not mention a husband or children, but other sources of the period suggest that she was briefly married to an undistinguished man named Tachibana no Norimitsu and had at least one child. In the *Pillow Book* Sei Shōnagon repeatedly mocks Norimitsu as a hopeless boor who lacks poetic sensibility, and the marriage apparently did not last long.

Shōnagon lived during the middle of the Heian Period, which was named after its capital, Heian-kyō, the "Capital of Peace and Tranquility" (present-day Kyoto). The Heian court, centered on the symbolic figure of the emperor, followed a complex aristocratic system. The large bureaucratic apparatus of ministries and offices reflected a strict hierarchy based on rank as well as an educational system whose focus was the study of the Chinese Classics. Although aristocratic women like Shōnagon received an excellent training in Chinese literature, they produced literature written only in vernacular Japanese; Chinese-style genres, which stood at the top of the literary hierarchy, were largely the domain of male aristocrats. Shōnagon particularly relished the moments when she succeeded in using her Chinese learning to outdo a man, even if she was bound to use vernacular Japanese and the vernacular *kana* script (called "woman's hand") in her sophisticated responses to his letters.

In the Heian court, where men and women were strictly segregated, letters exchanged between lovers, relatives, or friends played a crucial role in social relations. Although they spent their days participating in an extensive array of court ceremonies, receiving visitors and engaging in witty conversation, the women were generally hidden away, secured in their residences in spaces behind paper doors and screens through which they would usually speak with their visitors unseen. Writing provided an outlet, enabling them both to dispel their boredom and to express private sentiments that transcended or critiqued the swirl of rumors, whispers, and intrigue that defined their lives.

Aristocratic men enjoyed considerably more freedom. Men usually lived in or near the living quarters of their wives' parents, but they often pursued romantic interests elsewhere; they took several wives and installed them in separate residences, visited at their whim. Marriage arrangements were loose. Marriages could be established by a man's frequent visits; a cessation in visiting was equivalent to a divorce. If his visits became increasingly sporadic as he was drawn to romantic adventures elsewhere, the woman was left waiting and worrying about the future of their relationship.

Daughters were crucial pawns in the marriage politics of the Heian imperial

court. Beginning in the latter half of the tenth century, the northern branch of the powerful Fujiwara clan controlled the imperial succession through the so-called regent system. It became customary for a Fujiwara regent to rule on behalf of a child emperor and to marry his daughters into the imperial family. Thus, the Fujiwara regents became uncles and grandfathers of future emperors and were often more powerful than those emperors. Shōnagon lived during one of the most successful regencies of the Heian Period, that of Fujiwara no Michinaga (966–1027). Michinaga had his eldest daughter Shōshi appointed consort of Emperor Ichijō, to whom she bore two later emperors. While Murasaki Shikibu served in Shōshi's lively entourage, which featured several other prominent women writers, Shōnagon was lady-in-waiting to Shōshi's cousin, Teishi. Teishi was the daughter of Fujiwara no Michitaka, an elder brother and rival of Michinaga, who became regent in 990. After Michitaka unexpectedly died in an epidemic in 995 and, in the following year, Teishi's brother Korechika was sent into exile on the urging of their increasingly powerful uncle, Teishi lost her footing at court. Michinaga's daughter Sōshi advanced to the position of highest consort, and Teishi had to leave the palace. Although Shōnagon continued to serve Teishi until the young empress died in childbirth in 1000, these last few years must have been painful and humiliating, in stark contrast to the earlier, happier times at court that *The Pillow Book* evokes so vividly.

THE PILLOW BOOK AND HEIAN LITERATURE

The Pillow Book chronicles with wit and humor the moments of glamour and ennui, the obsessions and trivia, of Heian court life. It centers on questions of aristocratic taste, the paramount importance of learning and education, and the pleasures of experiencing the world through the refined languages of literature, art, and music. Over the course of *The Pillow Book*, as Shōnagon expounds on why some kinds of carriages should move faster than others, why priests should be handsome, or how a lover should make his good-byes, she emerges as an impatient and imperious figure. She is every inch the aristocrat, whose fastidious standards brook no slipshod behavior. So deft is she at homing in on human foibles and skewering the offender that the effect of her sharp sallies can be shattering. We chuckle at her delicious wit, but we are glad we are not the objects of her scrutiny. *The Pillow Book* is written in a compact and forceful style, which favors brevity and compression and produces surprising effects by means of unusual juxtapositions. Shōnagon's literary persona favors witty repartee, sly self-promotion, and occasional cutting insults. Her candor in admitting her hypercritical nature, and her display of ruthless honesty toward others and herself, gives her an irrepressible, magnetic voice. She is a presence.

The exact date of composition and the title of *The Pillow Book* have been subjects of much debate. It was probably finished around 1005, after Empress Teishi's death. Writing *The Pillow Book* in memory of her late patroness, Shōnagon focused exclusively on those happy years when Teishi's standing at court was at its height. That she was painfully aware, as she was composing the book, of the tragic fall that lay in store for Teishi and herself makes the work all the more poignant.

In the last section of our selections Shōnagon wants us to know that even the paper on which she wrote her original *Pillow Book* came from that happy period, before Teishi lost her place at court. Paper was a rare commodity and Teishi's brother Korechika, before his ignominious exile, had brought the empress a stack from the supply being used in the palace for copying the *His-*torical Records by the Chinese historian Sima Qian. We can be sure that this connection to China's canonical history—written eleven centuries earlier—certainly pleased her. Just as Sima Qian had chronicled the history of China up until his own time, the Han Dynasty, so Shōnagon understood herself as a chronicler of Heian court life.

Even more contested than *The Pillow Book's* date and title is its original format. The more than three hundred separate sections can be grouped into three basic types: diary-style entries describing datable events at court, catalogues of objects or attributes, and essayistic jottings on general topics. This mélange is unusual. Some moments in *The Pillow Book* exhibit the intimacy of a typical Heian women's diary, others evoke scenes that look as if they were taken from a Heian romantic tale such as *The Tale of Genji*, and yet other parts resemble the philosophical musings of the later essay genre (such as Yoshida Kenkō's famous *Essays in Idleness*). That *The Pillow Book* contains such variety in one book, sometimes even a single section, makes it unique. It is also a uniquely jumbled text: the earliest surviving copy of *The Pillow Book* dates to several hundred years after Shōnagon's time, and the text has come down to the present in four manuscript lineages that differ both in content and in the arrangement of individual sections. Two versions group the entries by type, while the version now considered more authentic and canonical (represented in the selection here) freely mixes the diary entries, catalogues, and essayistic sections.

Shōnagon's brush follows the rhythms of Heian court life with its cycle of annual festivals—occasions for sumptuous display for men and women alike—and its keen awareness of questions of rank and propriety. Section 2, "Times of Year," takes us through some of the annual highlights. In section 6,

"The Emperor's Cat," a cat receives court rank and the poor dog Okinamaro receives a beating, is expelled, and returns in humiliation. This story is often read as an allegory for Korechika's exile, throwing a critical light on the cruel workings of court politics and intrigue. The story in section 20 about an imperial consort who knew the entire *Kokinshū* (*Collection of Ancient and Modern Poems*) by heart shows the pleasures and pressures of court life: the ability to recite a famous poem, to render it in beguiling calligraphy, or to adapt it to a new occasion when poetry composition was a key aspect of living at court and to maintaining one's reputation. Shōnagon enjoys reporting the occasions when she succeeded in coming up with a witty solution to an unexpected challenge, though she often emphasized how badly things could have turned out without the stroke of her genius at the right moment. There can be no doubt that Shōnagon liked to emerge triumphant: in section 82, her overconfident claim that a snow mountain they had built in the garden of the palace would survive for an impossibly long time forces her to take hilarious measures in seeking to win her dispute with the Empress.

To receive favorable judgment and to pass astute judgment were highly desirable in the Heian court. Therefore, the vocabulary of judgment and taste is particularly central to *The Pillow Book*. The most important term is *okashi,* which can mean anything from "delightful," "intriguing," or "charming" to "engaging" or just "interesting" and occurs more than four hundred times in *The Pillow Book*. The word is so pervasive that the translator of our selections renders it nearly thirty different ways. In the book's famous opening section alone—"In spring, the dawn— when the slowly paling mountain rim is tinged with red, and wisps of faintly crimson-purple cloud float in the

sky"—it appears three times. Shōnagon's frequent outcries of *okashi* are much more than an indulgence in superficial pleasure or beauty. There is a delicacy in *The Pillow Book* that helps us see, hear, and feel the world around us with superior nuance. Whether representing changes in robes to match the cherry blossom season, a cuckoo's cry so faint that the hearer wonders whether it is actually heard or only imagined, or the thoughts piqued by various insects, the details in *The Pillow Book* capture the sensuous variety of life. *The Pillow Book* seems to prescribe a restrained cultivation of feeling—a responsiveness to the emotional environment—along with physical grace and a genuine appreciation of shape, proportion, color, and tone: an appreciation that includes the power to make subtle distinctions.

This cultivated aestheticism isn't always focused on things that are beautiful. In a world that values the matching of tastes, Shōnagon is quick to pinpoint moments when they clash. Ugly and repellent details—fleas dancing under ladies' skirts, houseflies alighting with their "damp little feet," silver tweezers that can pull out unsightly hair, or a slovenly looking woman making out in broad daylight with a "scrawny man with hair sprouting from his face"—also make occasional appearances in *The Pillow Book*. These mismatches appear not just in the list of "dispiriting" and "distressing things," or in "things that cannot be compared," but also in the diary section: Shōnagon's tale about the argument over the snow mountain is suggestively intertwined with the story of a bawdy begging nun who occasionally intrudes and scandalizes the company. In the midst of her sublime expressions of courtly taste and beauty, Shōnagon is also attracted to the grotesque, even as she castigates it.

Unlike other Heian classics such as *The Kokinshū, The Tales of Ise,* and *The Tale of Genji, The Pillow Book* did not become a canonical text in the medieval period. Its relative neglect is attributable in part to its containing far less poetry—the main focus of those studying these texts—than the other three works. In the early modern period it became the subject of parodies. *The Mongrel Pillow Book* of 1606 apes *The Pillow Book*'s aesthetics of lists: "Things that have ones hair stand on end . . . Putting on armor in winter without underclothes . . . Malaria. The prospect of an evening spent in conversation with one's boy favorite."

Shōnagon continues to fascinate readers, and its large number of translations and adaptations have made *The Pillow Book* into a favored work of world literature. Today Shōnagon's strong female voice inspires in her readers a kind of empathy with the world of an eleventh-century Japanese gentlewoman that she herself could never have dreamed of.

From The Pillow Book[1]

1 *In spring, the dawn*—when the slowly paling mountain rim is tinged with red, and wisps of faintly crimson-purple cloud float in the sky.

In summer, the night—moonlit nights, of course, but also at the dark of the moon, it's beautiful when fireflies are dancing everywhere in a mazy flight. And it's delightful too to see just one or two fly through the darkness, glowing softly. Rain falling on a summer night is also lovely.

In autumn, the evening—the blazing sun has sunk very close to the mountain rim, and now even the crows, in threes and fours or twos and threes, hurrying to their roost, are a moving sight. Still more enchanting is the sight of a string of wild geese in the distant sky, very tiny. And oh how inexpressible, when the sun has sunk, to hear in the growing darkness the wind, and the song of autumn insects.

In winter, the early morning—if snow is falling, of course, it's unutterably delightful, but it's perfect too if there's a pure white frost, or even just when it's very cold, and they hasten to build up the fires in the braziers and carry in fresh charcoal. But it's unpleasant, as the day draws on and the air grows warmer, how the brazier fire dies down to white ash.

2 *Times of year*—The first month; the third, fourth and fifth months; the seventh, eighth and ninth; the eleventh and twelfth—in fact every month according to its season, the year round, is delightful.

On the first day of the year, the sky is gloriously fresh and spring mists hang in the air. It's quite special and delightful the way people everywhere have taken particular care over their clothing and makeup, and go about exchanging New Year felicitations.

On the seventh day, people pluck the new shoots of herbs that have sprung up in the patches of bare earth amidst the snow[2]—they're wonderfully green and fresh, and it's charming just what a fuss is made over these herbs, which

---

1. Translated by and with notes adapted from Meredith McKinney.
2. In this passage Shōnagon describes some of the court festivals of the first four months of the year. The seventh day of the First Month is the Festival of Young Herbs, when various herbs are made into a gruel that is supposed to ward off evil spirits and to protect one's health throughout the year.

normally aren't to be seen at such close quarters. Those of good family who live outside the palace brighten up their carriages and set off to see the Parading of the Blue Roans. It's fun how, when the carriages are pulled over the big ground beam of the central palace gate, all the ladies' heads are jolted together so that your hair combs tumble out and can easily break if you aren't careful, and everybody laughs. I remember seeing a large group of senior courtiers and others standing about near the Left Gate Watch guardhouse, gaily snatching the attendants' bows and twanging them to startle the horses—also, peeping through the carriage blinds and delightedly glimpsing groundswomen and other serving ladies coming and going near one of the lattice fences further in. Witnessing such a scene, of course you sigh and wonder just what sort of people they must be, to manage to be so at ease in the 'nine-fold palace.' But when I actually saw them at such close quarters at the palace, the attendants' faces were all dark and blotchy where their white powder hadn't covered the skin properly, precisely like black patches of earth showing through where snow has half melted—a truly horrible sight. The horses' rearing and lunging was quite terrifying, so I retreated to the depths of the carriage, where I could no longer really see.

On the eighth day, there's a special thrill in the noise of all the carriages hurtling about as everyone who's received a promotion does the rounds to exchange felicitations.

On the fifteenth day, the day of the full moon, a delightful scene always takes place in the houses of the nobility after the festival food is served. Both the senior and junior gentlewomen of the house go about looking for a chance to strike each other with gruel sticks,[3] constantly glancing behind them to make sure they aren't hit themselves. It's marvellous fun when someone manages somehow to get in a strike, and everyone bursts into delighted peals of laughter— though you can certainly see why the poor victim herself feels upset.

A young man has recently begun to call on his new wife.[4] Now it's time for him to set off for the palace, and lurking in the background peeping out is one of her gentlewomen, gleefully self-important and struggling to contain herself till he leaves. The gentlewomen who are sitting gathered around the girl all smile, realizing perfectly well what's going on, but she secretly motions them to stay quiet. Meanwhile, the girl sits there innocently, seeming to have noticed nothing. Then up comes the gentlewoman, with some excuse such as 'I'll just pick this up,' darts over and strikes her and runs off, while everyone collapses in laughter. The young man doesn't take it amiss but smiles amiably, and as for the girl, it's quite charming to see that though she doesn't seem particularly surprised, she is nevertheless blushing slightly.

The gentlewomen strike each other too, and I gather men even get struck sometimes. It's also amusing to witness someone for some reason lose her temper and burst into tears, and roundly abuse whoever has struck her. Even the more exalted people in the palace join in the day's fun.

There's a charming scene in the palace at the time of the Spring Appointments List.[5] It's snowing and everything's icy, and men of the fourth and fifth

---

3. To mark the first full moon of the year, a special gruel that averted evil influences was served. It was believed that a woman whose loins were struck by sticks retrieved from the fire used to cook that gruel would soon give birth to a son.

4. It was common at the time for a young husband to be adopted into his wife's family and visit her at her parents' home, rather than move with her to a separate residence.

5. The time when court officials receive new appointments and promotions.

ranks are walking about holding their letters requesting promotion. The youthful, high-spirited ones inspire you with confidence in them, but there are also
old white-haired fellows who go around confiding in people, in hopes that this
will improve their chances. They approach some gentlewoman and obliviously
set about singing their own praises to her, and they can have no idea that some
of the younger gentlewomen are busy imitating them and laughing behind
their back. 'Do please mention me favourably to the Emperor or Empress,' they
implore us—and it's a fine thing if they actually gain the post they want, but
really most pathetic when they fail.

The third day of the third month is full of the soft sunshine of spring. Now is
the time when the peach trees begin to bloom, and of course the willows too are
particularly lovely at this time. It's charming to see the buds still cocooned in
their sheaths like silkworms—but on the other hand, once the leaves have
opened they're rather unpleasant.

If you break off a branch of splendidly flowering cherry and arrange it in a
large flower vase, the effect is delightful. And it's particularly charming if a
gentleman, be it one of Her Majesty's brothers or a normal guest, is seated
nearby engaged in conversation, wearing a cloak in the cherry-blossom combination with undersleeves displayed.

And how delightful it all is at the time of the Festival in the fourth month![6]
The court nobles and senior courtiers in the festival procession are only distin-
guishable by the different degrees of colour of their formal cloaks, and the
robes beneath are all of a uniform white, which produces a lovely effect of
coolness. The leaves of the trees have not yet reached their full summer abundance but are still a fresh young green, and the sky's clarity, untouched by
either the mists of spring or autumn's fogs, fills you with inexplicable pleasure.
And when it clouds a little in the evening or at night, how unbearably lovely
then to hear from far in the distance the muted call of a *hototogisu*,[7] sounding
so faint you almost doubt your ears.

It's delightful, as the day of the Festival approaches, to see the attendants
going to and fro carrying tight rolls of dark leaf-green or lavender fabric,[8]
wrapped lightly in just a touch of paper. Patterning effects such as graded dye
and dapple dye strike you as unusually beautiful at this time.

The little girls who will be in the procession are also enchanting. They've
already washed their hair and done it nicely, but they may still be wearing their
everyday threadbare and rumpled clothes, and they trot around full of excited
anticipation, crying 'Rethread my high clogs for me!' or 'Sew up the soles of my
shoes!' But for all their boisterous posturing and prancing, once they're dressed
up in their festival finery they suddenly begin parading about with great solemnity, like self-important priests at the head of some dignified procession, no
doubt starting to feel thoroughly nervous. It's also touching to see, in the festival procession, a parent or aunt or perhaps an older sister accompanying the
little girls and carefully tending their clothing as they walk.

When you see a man who's set his heart on becoming Chamberlain, but who's
in no position to achieve his goal just yet, dressed specially in the Chamberlain's

6. The Kamo Festival, still one of the most
important festivals of Kyoto; it includes a large
procession through the city from and back to
the Kamo Shrines.

7. A kind of cuckoo whose call is much
praised by Japanese poets.
8. Used to make up the robes worn at the festival.

green formal cloak[9] for the day of the Festival, you wish for his sake he didn't have to take it off again. It's a pity that it isn't damask like the real one, however.

4 *It breaks my heart to think* of parents sending a beloved son into the priesthood. Poor priests, they're not the unfeeling lumps of wood that people take them for. They're despised for eating that dreadful monastic food, and their sleeping arrangements are no better. A young priest must naturally be full of curiosity, and how could he resist the forbidden urge to peep into a room, especially if there's a woman in there? But this is criticized as disgraceful too.

Exorcist priests have an even harder life.[1] If they ever nod off, exhausted from their long labours, people complain that they do nothing but sleep. How constrained and miserable this must make them feel!

Well, this is how things used to be, anyway. These days, in fact, priests lead a much easier life.

* * *

6 *The Emperor's cat* had received the fifth rank, and was given the appropriate title-name 'Myōbu.' It was a charming creature, and the Emperor was quite devoted to it.

One day its carer, Muma no Myōbu,[2] found it lying basking on the veranda. 'How vulgar!' she scolded. 'Back you come inside.' But the cat continued to lie there asleep in the sun, so she decided to give it a fright. 'Okinamaro!' she cried to the dog. 'Here, boy! Come and get Myōbu!' The foolish dog couldn't believe its ears, and came rushing over, whereupon the terrified cat fled inside through the blind.

The Emperor was at that time in the Breakfast Room, and he witnessed this event with astonishment. He tucked the cat into the bosom of his robe, and summoned his men. When the Chamberlains Tadataka and Narinaka appeared, the Emperor ordered them, 'Give Okinamaro a thorough beating and banish him to Dog Island! Be quick about it!'

Everyone gathered and a noisy hunt ensued. The Emperor went on to chastise Muma no Myōbu, declaring that he would replace her as Myōbu's carer as she was completely untrustworthy, and thenceforth she no longer appeared in his presence. Meanwhile, they rounded up the dog, and had the guards drive it out.

We all pitied the poor thing. 'Oh dear,' we said, 'and to think how he used to swagger about the place as if he owned it.'

'Remember how on the third of the third month the Secretary Controller decked him out with a garland of willow and a peach-flower comb, and tied a branch of cherry blossom on his back? Who'd have guessed then that he'd meet with such a fate?'

'And the way he always attended Her Majesty at meal times. How we'll miss him!'

9. Usually only the Chamberlain could wear the color green, which was permitted to members of his office of lesser rank on this occasion.
1. Exorcizing a tenacious possession required that incantations and spells be performed for many hours.

2. A title for a gentlewoman of fifth rank. It was also applied to cats, and only cats of fourth and fifth rank were permitted in the emperor's palace.

Then around noon three or four days later, we heard a dog howling dreadfully. What dog could be howling on and on like this? we wondered, and as we listened dogs gathered from everywhere to see what was afoot. One of the cleaning women came running in. 'Oh, it's dreadful! Two of the Chamberlains are beating the dog! It's bound to die! His Majesty banished it, but apparently it came back, so they're teaching it a lesson.'

Alas, poor creature! It was Okinamaro. 'It's Tadataka and Sanefusa doing it,' someone said.

We sent someone to stop them, but at that point the dog finally ceased its howling. 'It's dead,' came the report, 'so they've thrown it outside the guardhouse.'

That evening as we were sorrowing over poor Okinamaro, up staggered a miserable trembling creature, terribly swollen and looking quite wretched. Can it be Okinamaro? we wondered. What other dog could be wandering around at this hour in such a state?

We called his name, but he didn't respond. 'It's him,' some of us declared, while others maintained that it wasn't, till Her Majesty said, 'Send for Ukon. She would recognize him.' We duly did so, and when she came Her Majesty showed her the dog and asked if it was indeed Okinamaro.

'There's certainly a likeness,' replied Ukon, 'but this dog looks simply revolting. And you only have to say his name and Okinamaro bounds happily up, but this dog doesn't respond at all. It must be a different dog. And they did say they'd killed him and thrown out the corpse, didn't they? How could he have survived after two men had beaten him like that?' This moved Her Majesty to fresh sorrow.

It grew dark. We gave the dog some food, but it didn't eat it, so we decided that it was indeed a different dog and left it at that.

The next morning, Her Majesty had performed her ablutions and had her hair combed, and I was holding the mirror for her to check that all was in order when I spied the dog, still there, crouching at the foot of a pillar. Seeing it I said aloud to myself, 'Oh poor Okinamaro, what a terrible beating he got yesterday! It's so sad to think he must be dead. I wonder what he'll be reborn as next time. How dreadful he must have felt!'

At this the dog began to tremble, and tears simply poured from its eyes. How extraordinary! I realized it was indeed Okinamaro! It was pitiful to recall how he'd avoided revealing himself the night before, but at the same time the whole thing struck me as quite marvellous. I set down the mirror and said, 'So you're Okinamaro, are you?' and he threw himself on the ground, whimpering and weeping.

Her Majesty laughed with relief, and sent for Ukon and told her the story. There was a great deal of laughter over it all, and the Emperor heard and came in to see what was happening. He laughed too, and observed, 'Isn't it odd to think a dog would have such fine feelings.' His gentlewomen also heard of it and gathered round, and this time when we called the dog he got up and came.

'His poor face is all swollen!' I cried. 'I do wish I could do something for it.'

'Now you're wearing your heart on your sleeve,' everyone teased me.

Tadataka heard from the Table Room, and sent saying, 'Is it really him? I must come and have a look.'

'Oh dear no, how awful!' I declared. 'Tell him it's not Okinamaro at all!'

'He's bound to be found out sooner or later,' came Tadataka's reply. 'You can't go on hiding him forever.'

Well, in due course Okinamaro was pardoned, and everything returned to normal. Now has there ever been such a delightful and moving moment as when Okinamaro began to tremble and weep at those pitying words of mine? Humans may cry when someone speaks to them sympathetically—but a dog?

* * *

20 *The sliding panels that close off the north-east corner* of the Seiryōden, at the northern end of the aisle, are painted with scenes of rough seas, and terrifying creatures with long arms and legs.[3] We have a fine time complaining about how we hate coming face to face with them whenever we open the door from the Empress's room.

On this particular day, a large green porcelain vase had been placed at the foot of the nearby veranda railing, with a mass of absolutely gorgeous branches of flowering cherry, five feet long or more, arranged in it with the flowers spilling out over the railing. His Excellency Korechika,[4] the Grand Counsellor, arrived around noon. He was wearing a rather soft and supple cloak in the cherry-blossom combination, over deep violet gathered trousers of heavy brocade and white under-robes, and he had arranged the sleeves of his wonderfully glowing deep scarlet-purple damask cloak for display. The Emperor was present, so His Excellency placed himself on the narrow veranda outside the door to converse.

Inside the blinds, we gentlewomen sat with our cherry-blossom combination Chinese jackets worn draped loosely back from the shoulders. Our robes were a fine blend of wisteria and kerria-yellow and other seasonal combinations, the sleeves all spilling out on display below the blinds that hung from the little half-panel shutters.

Suddenly, from the direction of the Imperial Day Chamber came the loud pounding of the attendants' feet as they arrived to deliver His Majesty's meal. The sound of the cry 'Make way!' reverberating through the scene of this gloriously serene spring day was utterly delightful. Then the Chamberlain arrived to report that he had delivered the last tray and the meal was in place, and His Majesty departed by the central door.

Korechika saw His Majesty on his way along the corridor, then returned to seat himself by the vase of blossoms once more. Her Majesty now moved aside her standing curtain and came out to the edge of the threshold near him to talk, and all those present were simply overcome with the sheer splendour of the scene. At this point Korechika languidly intoned the lines from the old poem:

> 'The months and years may pass,
> but let this remain unchanging
> as Mount Mimoro . . .'[5]

3. The frightening scenes from Chinese legends painted on the panels in the emperor's private residence, the Seiryōden, served as a protective device, required because the north-east was considered unlucky in geomancy.
4. The brother of Empress Teishi, whom Shōnagon served.
5. Part of a poem from *The Manyōshū* . Mount Mimoro, the site of an ancient Shinto shrine associated with the imperial line, figures here as an auspicious image of continuity.

—and most enchanting it was, for seeing her splendour we did indeed long for Her Majesty to continue just like this for a thousand years.

No sooner had those in charge of serving the Emperor's meal called the men to remove the trays than His Majesty returned.

Her Majesty now turned to me and asked me to grind some ink, but I was so agog at the scene before me that I could barely manage to keep the inkstick steady in its holder. Then Her Majesty proceeded to fold a piece of white paper, and said to us, 'Now I want each of you to write here the first ancient poem that springs to mind.'

I turned for help to the Grand Counsellor, who was sitting just outside. 'What on earth can I write?' I begged him, but he only pushed the paper back to me, saying, 'Quick, write something down yourself for Her Majesty. It's not a man's place to give advice here.'

Her Majesty provided us with the inkstone. 'Come on, come on,' she scolded, 'don't waste time racking your brains. Just quickly jot down any ancient poem that comes to you on the spur of the moment. Even something hackneyed will do.' I've no idea why we should have felt so daunted by the task, but we all found ourselves blushing deeply, and our minds went quite blank. Despite their protestations, some of the senior gentlewomen managed to produce two or three poems on spring themes such as blossoms and so forth, and then my turn came. I wrote down the poem:

> With the passing years
> My years grow old upon me
> yet when I see
> this lovely flower of spring
> I forget age and time.[6]

but I changed 'flower of spring' to 'your face, my lady.'

Her Majesty ran her eye over the poems, remarking, 'I just wanted to discover what was in your hearts.'

'In the time of Retired Emperor Enyū,'[7] she went on, 'His Majesty ordered the senior courtiers each to write a poem in a bound notebook, but it proved fearfully difficult, and some of them begged to be excused from the task. The Emperor reassured them that it didn't matter whether their calligraphy was skilful or otherwise, nor whether the poem was appropriate to the occasion, and finally after a great deal of trouble they all managed to produce something. Our present Regent,[8] who was Captain Third Rank at the time, wrote the following poem:

> "As the tide that swells
> in Izumo's Always Bay
> so always and always

---

6. Shōnagon cleverly adapts an old poem to the situation at hand. The original poem was written by an admiring father to his daughter; Shōnagon makes it into a compliment to the empress.

7. The father of the present emperor, Teishi's husband.
8. Michitaka, the father of Teishi and Korechika.

> oh how my heart swells and fills
> deep with love to think of you."

but he changed the last line to read "deep with trust in you, my lord," and His Majesty was full of praise for him.'

When I heard this, I felt a sudden sweat break out all over me. I do think, though, that that poem of mine isn't the sort of thing a young person could have come up with. Even people who can usually turn out a fine poem found themselves for some reason at a loss that day, and several made mistakes in their writing.

There was also the occasion when Her Majesty placed a bound book of *Kokinshū* poems in front of her, and proceeded to read out the opening lines of various poems and ask us to complete them. Why on earth did we keep stumbling over the answers, even for poems we'd engraved on our memories day in and day out? Saishō only managed about ten. Others could produce only five or six, and really, you'd think they could simply have admitted that they couldn't recall them. But no, they kept agonizing over the task. 'But we can't be so rude as to refuse point-blank to answer,' they wailed, 'when Her Majesty has been so good as to put the question to us,' which I found rather amusing.

Her Majesty then read out the complete poem for each of those that nobody had been able to answer, marking them with a bookmark, and everyone groaned, 'Oh of course I knew that one! Why am I being so stupid today?' Some of us had copied out the *Kokinshū* many times, and should really have known it all by heart.

'As I'm sure you are all aware,' Her Majesty began, 'the lady known as the Senyōden Consort, High Consort in the reign of Emperor Murakami,[9] was the daughter of the Minister of the Left, of the Smaller Palace of the First Ward. When she was still a girl, her father gave her the following advice: "First, you must study calligraphy. Next, you must determine to outshine everyone in your skill on the seven-stringed *kin*.[1] And you must also make it your study to commit to memory all the poems in the twenty volumes of the *Kokinshū*."

'Now the Emperor had learned of this, so one day, when he was kept from his usual duties by an abstinence,[2] he took a copy of the *Kokinshū* to the High Consort's quarters, and set up a standing curtain between them. She found this unusual behaviour rather odd, and when he opened a book and began asking her to recite the poem that so-and-so had written on such-and-such a date and occasion, she was intrigued to realize what he was up to—though on the other hand, she would also have been dreadfully nervous that there might be some which she would forget or misquote. He called in two or three of his gentlewomen who were well-versed in poetry, and had them extract the answers from her, and keep count of her mistakes with *go* counters. It must have been a wonderful scene to witness. I do envy them all, even the people who were merely serving on this occasion.

---

9. That is, 946–61; this story serves as an example of how admirable people were "in the old days."
1. A zitherlike instrument of the koto family,

particularly difficult to play; by Shōnagon's time it was somewhat old-fashioned.
2. A period of forced seclusion, prescribed by divination, to avoid evil influences.

'Well, he pressed her to go on answering, and she went through them making not a single mistake, though she cleverly gave just enough of each poem to show she knew it, and didn't try to complete them. His Majesty decided he would call a halt just as soon as she made a mistake, and as she went on and on he even began to get rather irritated, but they reached the tenth volume and still she hadn't made a single slip. "This has been quite futile," he finally declared, and he put a marker in the book and retired to another room to sleep. All very wonderful it was.

'When he awoke many hours later, he decided that it would never do to leave the matter hanging, and moreover it had better be done that day, since she might refresh her memory with another copy of the work if he left it till tomorrow. So he produced the remaining ten volumes, had the lamps lit and proceeded to work his way through the rest of the poems until long into the night. But she never made a single mistake.

'Meanwhile, word was sent to her father that the Emperor had returned to her quarters and that the test was continuing. The Minister flew into a panic with worry that she might fail the test; he ordered numerous sutras to be said for her,[3] while he placed himself facing the direction of the palace and spent the entire night in heartfelt prayer. Altogether a fascinating and moving story,' Her Majesty remarked in conclusion.

His Majesty too heard the tale with admiration. 'I wouldn't be able to manage more than three or four volumes myself,' he remarked.

'In the old days, even the most inconsequential people were impressive. You don't hear such stories these days, do you,' everyone agreed, and all the Empress's gentlewomen, and those who served the Emperor and were permitted to visit the Empress's quarters, gathered round and began talking. It was indeed a scene to fill the heart with ease and delight.

* * *

22 *Dispiriting things*—A dog howling in the middle of the day. The sight in spring of a trap for catching winter fish. Robes in the plum-pink combination, when it's now the third or fourth month. An ox keeper whose ox has died. A birthing hut where the baby has died. A square brazier or a hearth with no fire lit in it. A scholar whose wife has a string of daughters.[4]

A household that doesn't treat you hospitably, though you're there because of a directional taboo[5]—this is particularly dispiriting if it happens to be at one of the season changes.

A letter from the provinces that arrives without any accompanying gift. You might say the same for a letter sent from inside the capital, but this would contain plenty of things you wanted to hear about and interesting news, which makes it a very fine thing to receive in fact.

You've taken special care to send off a beautiful, carefully written letter, and you're eagerly awaiting the reply—time passes, it seems awfully long in coming,

3. That is, chanted by a priest to ensure her success.
4. Daughters would interrupt the continuous line in the family profession of scholarship, a male domain. "The plum-pink combination": the season for these colors lasted from the eleventh to the second month.
5. A ban on movement in a particular direction to avoid disturbing gods (whose movements were charted by divination), thereby temporarily halting the progress of a traveler.

and then finally your own elegantly folded or knotted letter is brought back, now horribly soiled and crumpled and with no sign remaining of the brush stroke that sealed it. 'There was no one in,' you're told, or 'They couldn't accept it on account of an abstinence.' This is dreadfully dispiriting.

A carriage is sent off to fetch someone you're sure is going to come. You wait, and finally there's the sound of the carriage returning. 'It must be her,' you think, and everyone in the house goes out to see—but the driver is already dragging the carriage back into its shed. He drops the shafts with a noisy clatter. 'What happened?' you ask. 'She's going somewhere else today, so she won't be coming,' he replies offhandedly, then he hauls out the harness and off he goes.

It's also very dispiriting when a man stops coming to visit his wife at her home. It's a great shame if he's gone off with a lady of good family who serves at court, and the wife sits moping at home, feeling ashamed and humiliated.

A little child's nurse has gone out, promising that she won't be long. You do your best to keep the child entertained and comforted, but when you send word saying 'please hurry,' back comes a message to the effect that she won't be able to return this evening. This is not just dispiriting, it's downright hateful.

It's even more dispiriting for a man when a woman fails to visit him.[6] And when the night has grown late at his house and suddenly he hears a subdued knock at the gate, and with beating heart he sends to find out who it is, only to have the servant return and announce the name of some other, boring person, well the word 'dispiriting' doesn't begin to cover it.

An exorcist priest comes to quell a spirit that has possessed a member of the household. With a confident air he hands the medium the rosary and the other paraphernalia to induce possession, and sets about his incantations in a high, strained, cicada-like chant. But there's no sign of the spirit shifting, and the medium fails to be possessed by the Guardian Deity.[7] Everyone who's gathered to pray, men and women both, begins to find this rather odd. The exorcist chants on until the change of watch two hours later, when he finally stops, exhausted. 'Get up,' he says to the medium as he retrieves the rosary. 'The spirit just won't budge,' and running his hand back from his forehead over his bald head he declares, 'Oh dear, the exorcism was quite futile.' Whereupon he lets out a yawn, leans back against some nearby object and falls asleep. It's truly awful for him when someone not especially important comes over to him, though he's feeling dreadfully sleepy, and prods him awake and forces him into a conversation.

Then there's the house of a man who has failed to receive a post in the recent Appointments List. Word had it that he was certain to get one this year, and all his former retainers, who have scattered far and wide or are now living off in the country-side somewhere, have gathered at his house in anticipation. His courtyard is crammed with the coming and going of their carriages and the tangle of their shafts; if he sets off on an excursion they all jostle to accompany him; and they eat, drink and clamour their way through the days as they wait[8]—but as the last day dawns, there's still no knock at the gate. 'How odd,' they

---

6. It was usual for men to visit women, who would be hidden away, waiting in their residences. Only under special circumstances could the roles be reversed.

7. The help of a Guardian Deity is required to transfer the spirit that is causing the illness.
8. The appointments were announced over a three-day period.

think, and as they sit straining to catch the sound, they hear the cries of the outriders as the court nobles emerge from the palace at the close of the Appointments ceremonies. The underlings who have spent a chilly night shivering outside the palace waiting to hear the news come trudging back dejectedly, and no one can even bring himself to ask them what happened. When some outsider inquires, 'What appointment did your master receive?' they always reply evasively, 'Oh, he's the former Governor of So-and-so.'

All those who really rely on him feel quite devastated. As morning comes, a few among the people who've been packed in together waiting begin to creep stealthily away. Those who've been many years in his service, however, can't bring themselves to leave his side so lightly. It's terribly touching to see them weaving solemnly about as they pace the room, hopefully counting on their fingers the Provincial Governorships due to come to the end of their term the following year.

There are also those times when you send someone a poem you're rather pleased with, and fail to receive one in reply. Of course there's no more to be done about it if it's to a man you care for.[9] Even so, you do lose respect for someone who doesn't produce any response to your tasteful seasonal references. It also dampens the spirit when you're leading a heady life in the swim of things and you receive some boring little old-fashioned poem that reeks of the longueurs of the writer, whose time hangs heavy on her hands.

You have a particularly fine fan intended for some ceremonial event, and you hand this precious thing to a person who you trust will treat it well, but when the day arrives it comes back to you with something quite unforeseen painted on it.

A messenger delivers a congratulatory birth gift or a farewell present, and isn't given any gift in repayment. Messengers should always be given something, such as decorative herbal balls or New Year hare-mallets,[1] even if they're only delivering some object of no permanent use. If he receives something when he's not expecting to, he will feel thoroughly pleased that he made the delivery. However, it's particularly dispiriting when he's come feeling sure he'll receive something for this errand, and his excited hopes are dashed.

A house where four or five years have passed since they brought in a husband but there's still been no joyous birth celebration is most depressing.

A couple has already produced numerous children, all now adult, and indeed of an age at which there could even be grandchildren crawling about, yet the two parents are indulging in a 'daytime nap.'[2] It's dispiriting for the children who witness this, with nowhere to turn while their parents are off behind closed doors.

The purificatory hot bath that you have to get up to take on New Year's Eve is not merely dispiriting, it's downright irritating.

Rain all day on New Year's Eve. Perhaps this is what's meant by the expression 'a single day of purificatory abstinence.'

* * *

9. Failure to respond to a love poem with a poem in reply signified rejection.
1. Protective charms given on the first hare

day (day 4 of the 12-day cycle) of the year.
2. That is, daytime sex.

30 *A priest who gives a sermon should be handsome.* After all, you're most aware of the profundity of his teaching if you're gazing at his face as he speaks. If your eyes drift elsewhere you tend to forget what you've just heard, so an unattractive face has the effect of making you feel quite sinful. But I'll write no further on this subject. I may have written glibly enough about sinful matters of this sort in my younger days, but at my age the idea of sin has become quite frightening.

I must say, however, from my own sinful point of view, it seems quite uncalled-for to go around as some do, vaunting their religious piety and rushing to be the first to be seated wherever a sermon is being preached.

An ex-Chamberlain never used to take up the vanguard of imperial processions, and once he retired from the post you'd no longer see him about the palace. These days things are apparently different. The so-called 'Chamberlain fifth-ranker' is actually kept in reasonably busy service, but privately he must nevertheless miss the prestige of his former post and feel at a loss how to fill his days, so once he tries going to these places and hears a few sermons he'll no doubt develop a taste for it and start to go along on a regular basis.

You'll find him turning up there with his summer under-robe prominently displayed beneath his cloak even in baking summer weather, and the hems of his pale lavender or blue-grey gathered trousers loose and trodden. He has an abstinence tag[3] attached to his lacquered cap, and he no doubt intends to draw attention to the fact that although it's an abstinence day and he shouldn't leave the house, this doesn't apply to him since his outing is of a pious nature. He chats with the officiating priest, even goes so far as to help oversee the positioning of the ladies' carriages, and is generally completely at home in the situation. When some old crony of his whom he hasn't seen recently turns up, he's consumed with curiosity. Over he goes, and they settle down together and proceed to talk and nod and launch into interesting stories, spreading out their fans and putting them to their mouths when they laugh, groping at their ornately decorated rosaries and fiddling with them as they talk, craning to look here and there, praising and criticizing the carriages, discussing how other priests did things this way or that in other Lotus Discourses[4] and sutra dedication services they've been to, and so on and so forth—and not listening to a word of the actual sermon they're attending. Indeed they would have heard it all so often before that they'd gain nothing from it anyway.

And then there's another type. The preacher has already seated himself when after a while up rolls a carriage, accompanied by only a couple of outriders. It draws to a halt, and the passengers step out—three or four slender young men, dressed perhaps in hunting costume or in cloaks more delicately gauzy than a cicada's wing, gathered trousers and gossamer silk shifts, and accompanied by a similar number of attendants. Those already seated move themselves along a little to make way for them when they enter. They seat themselves by a pillar near the preacher's dais and set about softly rubbing their rosaries as they listen to the sermon, and the preacher, who no doubt feels rather honoured to have them there, throws himself with fresh vigour into the task of putting his message

---

3. A label attached to the hat to signify that the wearer is under abstinence taboo (see p. 1226, n. 2).

4. Formal debates by priests on the Lotus Sutra, held on special ceremonial occasions.

across. The young men, however, far from casting themselves extravagantly to the floor as they listen, instead decide to leave after a decent amount of time has passed, and as they go they throw glances in the direction of the women's carriages and comment to each other, and you'd love to know what it was they were saying. It's funny how you find yourself watching them as they depart, interestedly identifying the ones you know, and speculating on the identity of those you don't.

Some people really take things to extremes, though. If someone mentions having been to a Lotus Discourse or other such event, another will say, 'And was so and so there?' and the reply is always, 'Of course. How could he not be?' Mind you, I'm not saying one should never show up at these places. After all, even women of low standing will apparently listen to sermons with great concentration. Actually, when I first started attending sermons, I never saw women going about here and there on foot to them. Occasionally you would find women in travelling attire, elegantly made up, but they were out as part of another excursion to some temple or shrine. You didn't often hear of women attending sermons and the like in this costume, though. If the ladies who went to sermons in those days had lived long enough to see the way things are today, I can just imagine how they would have criticized and condemned.

* * *

39 *Refined and elegant things*—A girl's over-robe of white on white over pale violet-grey. The eggs of the spot-billed duck. Shaved ice with a sweet syrup, served in a shiny new metal bowl. A crystal rosary. Wisteria flowers. Snow on plum blossoms. An adorable little child eating strawberries.

40 *Insects*—The bell cricket. The cicada. Butterflies. Crickets. Grasshoppers. Water-weed shrimps. Mayflies. Fireflies.

The bagworm[5] is a very touching creature. It's a demon's child, and the mother fears it must have the same terrible nature as its parent, so she dresses it in ragged clothes and tells it to wait until she returns for it when the autumn wind blows. The poor little thing doesn't realize that its mother has deserted it, and when it hears the autumn winds begin in the eighth month, it sets up a pitiable little tremulous cry for her.

The snap-beetle is also touching. Though it's a mere insect, it has apparently dedicated itself to the Buddhist Way, for it continually touches its forehead to the ground in prayer as it walks along. It's fascinating the way you find it wandering about in astonishingly dark places, making that clicking sound.

Nothing is more unlovely than a fly, and it properly belongs in the list of infuriating things. Flies aren't big enough to make them worth bothering to hate, but just the way they settle all over everything in autumn, and their damp little feet when they land on your face . . . And I hate the way the word is used in people's names.[6]

Summer insects[7] are quite enchanting things. I love the way they'll fly round above a book when you've drawn the lamp up close to look at some tale. Ants

5. A small insect thought to resemble a demon and to utter cries of despair.
6. Sometimes "fly" (*hae*) was used in the names of people of the lower classes.
7. Insects such as moths or mayflies that are attracted to flames.

are rather horrible, but they're wonderfully light creatures, and it's intriguing to see one running about over the surface of the water.

* * *

68 *Things that can't be compared*—Summer and winter. Night and day. Rainy days and sunny days. Laughter and anger. Old age and youth. White and black. People you love and those you hate. The man you love and the same man once you've lost all feeling for him seem like two completely different people. Fire and water. Fat people and thin people. People with long hair and those with short hair.

The noisy commotion when crows roosting together are suddenly disturbed by something during the night. The way they tumble off their perches, and flap awkwardly about from branch to branch, squawking sleepily, makes them seem utterly different from daytime crows.

* * *

71 *Rare things*—A son-in-law who's praised by his wife's father. Likewise, a wife who's loved by her mother-in-law.

A pair of silver tweezers that can actually pull out hairs properly.

A retainer who doesn't speak ill of his master.

A person who is without a single quirk. Someone who's superior in both appearance and character, and who's remained utterly blameless throughout his long dealings with the world.

* * *

82 *Once when Her Majesty was in residence* in the Office of the Empress's Household, a Continuous Sutra Reading[8] took place in the western aisle. A scroll of the Buddha's image was set up, and of course the monks were seated as usual.

Two days into the ceremony, we heard below the veranda a queer voice saying, 'Would there be any distribution of the offerings[9] for me?' and a monk was heard to reply, 'Come come, what can you be thinking? The ceremony's not over yet.'

Wondering who this person was, I went over to have a look, and discovered the voice belonged to a nun well past her prime, dressed in horribly grimy clothes and looking like a little monkey.

'What is it she wants?' I asked.

At this, she replied herself in a carefully affected tone, 'I am a disciple of the Buddha, come to ask for the altar offerings, and these monks are refusing to give them to me.'

Her voice was remarkably bright and elegant for a beggar. What a pity someone like her should have sunk to this, I thought, yet at the same time I couldn't help feeling there was something unpleasantly pretentious and flamboyant about her, given her circumstances.

'So altar offerings are the only thing you'll eat, are they? This is wonderfully pious of you,' I remarked.

---

8. A ritual recitation that would continue through several days and nights.

9. Offerings of food on Buddhist altars were generally handed out after the ceremony.

She was reading me carefully. 'No one's saying I won't eat other things,' she said slyly. 'It's because there's nothing else that I'm asking for offerings.'

I put together some snacks and rice cakes and gave the bundle to her, whereupon she became extremely friendly, and began to chatter about all manner of things.

Some young gentlewomen then came out, and all set about questioning the woman about where she lived, and whether she had a man, and children. She produced such entertaining replies, elaborating them with jokes and suchlike, that everyone kept drawing her out with endless questions, such as whether she sang and danced, until she set about singing,

> 'Who oh who shall I sleep with tonight?
> I think I'll sleep with "Hitachi no Suke"
> for I love the silk touch of her skin in bed . . .'

with much more besides. She also sang,

> 'The peak of Man Mountain[1] stands proud in fame.
> Its scarlet tip has quite a name!'

waving her head about as she sang in a manner that was utterly grotesque. The ladies all laughed in disgust and cried, 'Away with you! Away with you!'

'Poor thing,' I said. 'What shall we give her?'

At this point Her Majesty intervened. 'You've been making the woman act in a way that I've really found very difficult to have to overhear. I simply had to block my ears. Give her this gown[2] and send her on her way immediately.'

'Here's a generous gift from Her Majesty. Your own gown's filthy, so make yourself nice and clean with this one,' we said, and tossed the gown to her. She abased herself in thanks, and then lo and behold she proceeded to drape the gown over her shoulder and perform a dance! She really was disgusting, so we all withdrew inside again and left her to it.

This apparently gave her a taste for visiting, because after this she was often to be seen wandering about drawing attention to herself. We took to calling her 'Hitachi no Suke,' after her song. Far from wearing the nice clean gown, she still went about in her filthy one, which made us wonder with considerable annoyance what she'd done with the one we gave her.

One day Ukon paid us a visit, and Her Majesty told her about the woman. 'They have tamed her and more or less installed her. She's always coming around now,' she said, and she had Kohyōe take up the tale and give an imitation of Hitachi no Suke.

'I'd love to see her,' said Ukon, laughing. 'Do show her to me. You all seem to be great fans of hers. I promise I won't entice her away from you.'

A little later, another much more refined beggar nun turned up at the palace. We called her over and questioned her in the same way, and were touched by how shamefaced and piteous she was. Her Majesty gave her a gown, and she

---

1. A mountain outside the capital, famous for its autumn colors. The "peak" here refers both to the mountain and to the tip of a penis.

2. Payments or gifts were usually made in clothing.

abased herself in thanks and retreated, overcome with tears of joy. This was all very well, but Hitachi no Suke happened to come along and catch sight of her as she was leaving. After that, Hitachi no Suke didn't show up again for a long time, and none of us would have given her a second thought I'm sure.

Towards the middle of the twelfth month there was a great fall of snow. The maids collected a large mound of it on the veranda, so then we ladies decided we should have a real snow mountain built out in the garden. We summoned the servants and set them all to work under Her Majesty's orders. The groundsmen who had come in to clean got involved as well, and together they all set about creating an absolutely towering snow mountain. Some of the senior officials from the Empress's Office also gathered to give advice and enjoy the scene. The original three or four groundsmen had soon swelled to around twenty. Her Majesty even sent to ask the servants who were at home to come and help, informing them that everyone involved would receive three days extra pay, and the same amount would be deducted from all those who didn't come; some who heard this came running hastily to join in, though the message couldn't reach those whose homes were more distant.

When the construction was finally completed, the officials from the Empress's Office were summoned and each was given two large bundles of silk rolls. These they spread out on the veranda, and everyone in turn came and took a roll, bowed and tucked it into his belt, and retired. The senior courtiers, who were dressed in informal hunting costume for the job instead of their usual formal cloaks, remained behind.

'How long do you think it will last?' Her Majesty asked everyone. One guessed ten days, another suggested a little longer. Everyone gave opinions ranging over a week or two.

'What do you think?' Her Majesty then asked me.

'I think it will stay there until beyond the tenth day of the first month,' I replied.

Even Her Majesty thought this highly unlikely, and all the ladies were unanimous in declaring that it couldn't last beyond the end of the year at the very latest.

'Oh dear,' I thought privately, 'I've probably overestimated. I suppose it can't really last as long as that. I should have said something like the first day of the new year instead'—but I decided that even if I turned out to be wrong, I should stand by what I said, and I stubbornly continued to argue my case.

On the twentieth day it rained, but there was no sign of the snow mountain melting away. All that happened was that it lost a little of its height. I was beside myself with fervent prayers to the Kannon of White Mountain[3] to preserve it from melting.

On the day when the snow mountain was made, the Aide of Ceremonial Tadataka came to call. I put out a cushion for him, and during our talk he remarked, 'You know, there's not a place in the palace that hasn't built a snow mountain today. His Majesty has ordered one made in his garden, and they're

---

3. A sacred mountain famous for its perpetual snow. On its summit was an important shrine to Kannon, the Bodhisattva of Mercy who hears people in need.

busy making them in the Crown Prince's residence and in the Kōkiden and Kyōgokudono[4] as well.'

I then had someone nearby convey to him the following poem.

> Our singular snow mountain
> we thought was so uniquely ours
> has multiplied abroad
> and become merely commonplace
> as the common snow that falls.

He sat tilting his head admiringly over it for a while, then he finally said, 'It would be merely flippant of me to attempt to sully this marvellous poem with one in response. I shall simply tell the tale of it to everyone when we're gathered before His Majesty,' and he rose and departed. I must say this diffidence struck me as rather odd, in someone with his reputation for being a great poetry-lover.

When I told Her Majesty, she remarked, 'He must certainly have been deeply impressed with it.'

As the month drew to a close, the snow mountain seemed to have shrunk a little, but it still remained very high. One day around midday we'd gone out to sit on the veranda, when Hitachi no Suke suddenly appeared again.

'Why are you back?' we asked. 'We haven't seen you here for ages.'

'Well, the fact is I met with a misfortune,' she replied.

'What was it?' we asked.

'I shall tell you my thoughts at the time in question,' she said, and then she proceeded to recite, in ponderously drawn-out tones,

> 'Alas I am awash
> with envy at the gifts whose burden
> weights her till she limps—
> who is that "deep-sea fisher girl"
> to whom so many things are given?'

and with that she gave a nasty laugh. When no one deigned to look in her direction, she clambered on to the snow mountain and walked about for some time before she finally left.

After she had gone we sent word to Ukon telling her what had happened, and she made us laugh all over again when she replied, 'Why didn't you get someone to accompany her and bring her over here? What a shame! She must have climbed the snow mountain and walked round like that because you were ignoring her.'

The year ended without any change to our snow mountain. On the night of the first day of the new year, there was a great fall of snow.

Excellent! I thought. There'll be a fresh pile of snow for the mountain—but then Her Majesty decided that this wasn't fair. 'We must brush off the new snow and leave the original heap as it was,' she declared.

---

4. The home of Teishi's rival Shōshi, another wife of Emperor Ichijō; one of her ladies-in-waiting was Murasaki Shikibu, the author of *The Tale of Genji*.

Next morning when I went to my room very early, the chief retainer of the Office of the Empress's Household arrived, shivering with cold. On the sleeve of his night-watch cloak, which was a deep, almost cirron-leaf green, he held something wrapped in green paper, attached to a sprig of pine needles.

'Who is this from?' I inquired, and when he replied that it came from the Kamo High Priestess, I was filled with sudden delighted awe, and took it and carried it straight back to Her Majesty.

Her Majesty was still asleep when I arrived, and in order to get in I tugged a go-board table over to the lattice shutter facing her curtained dais, and stood on it while I struggled to raise the shutter. It was extremely heavy, and because I was only lifting one end of it, it grated against the next one, which woke Her Majesty.

'Why on earth are you doing that?' she inquired.

'A message from the Kamo High Priestess has arrived,' I replied. 'I simply had to get the shutter open so you would have it as early as possible.'

'Well, this certainly is early,' she said, getting up. She opened the package, and found two hare-mallets, the heads wrapped in imitation of hare-wands, decorated prettily with sprigs of mountain orange, creeping fern and mountain sedge. But there was no letter.

'I can't believe there would be no message,' said Her Majesty, searching, and then she discovered on one of the little pieces of paper that wrapped the mallet heads the following poem.

> When I went searching
> the mountain for the echoing ring
> of the woodsman's axe
> I found the tree he cut was for
> the festive hare-wands of this day.[5]

A delightful poem, and delightful too was the scene of Her Majesty composing her reply. In all her letters and replies to the High Priestess, you could see just how much trouble she took from the number of problems she had with her writing. To the man who had brought the message she gave a white-weave shift, and another of maroon which was I think in the plum combination, and it was lovely to see him making his way back through the snowy landscape with the robes over his shoulder. It's only a pity that I never discovered what Her Majesty wrote in reply.

As for the snow mountain, it showed no sign of melting away but continued to stand there, just as if it really was Koshi's famous snowy mountain. It now looked quite black with dirt, and was not a sight to please the eye, but I nevertheless felt elated at the thought of being proved right, and prayed that it could somehow be made to survive until the middle of the month. Everyone declared that it couldn't last beyond the end of the first week, and we were all waiting anxiously to witness the final outcome, when it was suddenly decided on the third day that Her Majesty would return to the imperial palace. I was terribly disappointed at the thought that I'd have to leave without ever knowing the moment of my mountain's final end, and others also said it was a great shame to

5. The first hare day of the year, when decorated sticks and poles were presented to members of the court and hung in rooms to ward off evil spirits.

have to leave now. Her Majesty agreed, and indeed I'd very much wanted her to witness that my guess had been right. But we had to leave and that was that.

There was great upheaval for the move, with Her Majesty's effects and all the other things being carried out, and in the midst of this I managed to call over to the veranda one of the gardeners who was living under a lean-to roof he had set up against the garden wall, and have a confidential word with him. 'You must take great care of this snow mountain, and make sure no children climb on it and destroy it. Keep a firm watch on it until the fifteenth. If it lasts till then, Her Majesty intends to reward you with a special gift, and you'll get high praise from me personally as well,' I said, and to persuade him further I heaped on him various leftovers, fruit and so on, though this would have enraged the kitchen maids and servants, who disliked him.

All this made him beam with pleasure. 'That's very easily done,' he assured me. 'I'll guard it carefully. The children will be sure to try and climb it.'

'You must forbid it,' I warned him, 'and if there's anyone who won't obey then let me know.'

I accompanied Her Majesty on her move to the palace, and stayed there until the seventh day, when I went home.

I was so anxious about my snow mountain while I was at the palace that I was constantly sending servants of various sorts, from the toilet cleaner to the head housekeeper, to keep the gardener up to the mark. On the seventh day I even sent along some of the leftovers from the Festival of Young Herbs feast, and everyone laughed at the tale of how reverently he'd received them.

Once I was back home the snow mountain continued to obsess me, and the first thing I did every morning was send someone over, just to keep him reminded of how very important it was. On the tenth day I was delighted to hear that enough still remained to last until the fifteenth. Day and night my constant stream of messengers continued, but then on the night of the thirteenth there was a terrific downpour of rain. I was beside myself, convinced that this would finally finish off my mountain. All that night I stayed up, lamenting that it couldn't possibly last another day or two. Those around me laughed and declared that I really had lost my mind. When one of our party left I leapt up and tried to rouse the servants, and flew into a rage when they refused to get up, but finally one emerged and I sent her off to bring a report.

'It's down to the size of a round cushion,' she reported. 'The gardener has looked after it most assiduously, and he hasn't let the children near it. He says it should last till tomorrow morning, and he's looking forward to his reward.' I was absolutely thrilled. I could hardly wait till the next day, when I decided I would compose a suitable poem and send it to Her Majesty with a container full of the snow. The anticipation was becoming quite unbearable.

The next morning I got up while it was still dark. I gave one of the servants a box and sent her off with the order to choose the whitest of the snow to put in it, and be careful to scrape away any that was dirty. But she was no sooner gone than back she came, dangling the empty container, to report that the last of the snow mountain had already disappeared. I was devastated. The clever poem that I had laboured and groaned over, and that I'd looked forward to being on everyone's lips, was to my horror suddenly quite worthless.

'How on earth could this have happened?' I said miserably. 'There was all that snow still there yesterday, and it's disappeared overnight!'

'The gardener was wringing his hands in despair,' replied the maid. 'He said that it was there until late last night, and he'd been so looking forward to getting his reward.'

In the midst of all the fuss, word arrived from Her Majesty, inquiring whether there was any snow left today. Thoroughly mortified, I replied, 'Please tell Her Majesty that I consider it a great victory that it was still there until yesterday evening, despite the fact that everyone predicted it couldn't last beyond the end of the year. But after all, my prediction would have been altogether too impressive if the snow had remained until the very day I guessed. During the night some spiteful person must have destroyed the last of it.'

This was the first subject I raised in Her Majesty's presence when I went back to the palace on the twentieth. I related to her how appalled I'd been to see the maid return with the empty container dangling from her hand—like the wandering performer's act with the empty lid, when he came on announcing 'the Buddha's thrown his body off Snow Mountain and all that's left is his hat'[6]—and I went on to explain how I'd planned to make a miniature snow mountain in the lid and send a poem with it, written exquisitely on white paper. Her Majesty laughed a great deal at my story, as did everyone else present.

'I fear I've committed a grave sin by destroying something you had so set your heart on,' Her Majesty then told me. 'To tell the truth, on the night of the fourteenth I sent some retainers there to remove it. When I read your message, I thought you were wonderfully clever to have guessed something like this had happened.'

The fellow apparently emerged wringing his hands and pleading, but he was told that it was an order from the Empress, and was forbidden to tell anyone from my place about it, on pain of having his house destroyed. They threw all the snow away near the south wall of the Left Palace Guards Office, and I gather they reported that it was packed down very hard, and there was a great deal of it. Her Majesty admitted that it would actually have lasted through even as far as the twentieth, and would no doubt have received some added snow from the first snowfall of the spring, too. Then she went on to relate that His Majesty had also heard about it, and had remarked to the senior courtiers that a great deal of thought had obviously gone into this contest of ours. 'Well then,' she said in conclusion, 'tell us the poem you'd prepared. After all, I've made my confession, and as you can see, you actually won your bet.'

The ladies added their voices to Her Majesty's request, but I replied sulkily, 'I don't see why I should be expected to turn around and tell you my poem, after the depressing things I've just heard'—and in truth I was by this time feeling thoroughly miserable.

At this point His Majesty arrived, and he said to me teasingly, 'I've always believed you were a favourite with Her Majesty, but I must say this has made me wonder.' This only served to depress me even more deeply, and by now I was close to tears.

'Oh dear, oh dear,' I moaned, 'life's so hard! And to think how overjoyed I was, too, about the snow that fell after we'd built the mountain, and then Her Majesty decided it shouldn't count, and ordered it removed.'

6. A comic image of absence, apparently referring to an act based on the well-known story that the Buddha threw himself off Snow Mountain in exchange for enlightenment.

Then His Majesty smiled and remarked, 'I suppose she just didn't want to see you win.'

* * *

104 *Things that are distressing to see*—Someone wearing a robe with the back seam hitched over to one side, or with the collar falling back to reveal the nape of the neck.

A woman who emerges with a child slung on her back to greet a special visitor.

A priest acting as Yin-Yang master, who conducts his purification ceremony with that little white paper cap[7] stuck on his forehead.

I do hate the sight of some swarthy, slovenly-looking woman with a hairpiece, lying about in broad daylight with a scrawny man with hair sprouting from his face. What kind of a picture do they think they make, lounging there for all to see? Of course this is not to say they should stay sitting upright all night for fear people will find them disgusting—no one can see them when it's dark, and besides, everyone else indulges in the same thing at night. The decent thing to do is to get up early once it's morning. No doubt it doesn't look quite as bad for people of high station to take daytime naps in summer, but anyone less than attractive will emerge from a nap with a face all greasy and bloated with sleep, and sometimes even a squashed cheek. How dreary for two such people to have to look each other in the face when they get up!

It's most distressing to see someone thin and swarthy dressed in a see-through gossamer-silk shift.

* * *

144 *Endearingly lovely things*—A baby's face painted on a gourd. A sparrow coming fluttering down to the nest when her babies are cheeping for her.

A little child of two or three is crawling rapidly along when his keen eye suddenly notices some tiny worthless thing lying nearby. He picks it up in his pretty little fingers, and shows it to the adults. This is very endearing to see. It's also endearing when a child with a shoulder-length 'nun's cut' hairstyle[8] that's falling into her eyes doesn't brush it away but instead tilts her head to tip it aside as she examines something.

A very young son of a noble family walking about dressed up in ceremonial costume. An enchanting little child who falls asleep in your arms while you're holding and playing with it is terribly endearing.

Things children use in doll play. A tiny lotus leaf that's been picked from a pond. A tiny *aoi*[9] leaf. In fact, absolutely anything that's tiny is endearing.

A very white, plump child of around two, who comes crawling out wearing a lavender silk-gauze robe with the sleeves hitched back, or a child walking about in a short robe that looks more long sleeves than robe. All these are endearing. And it's very endearing when a boy of eight or ten reads something aloud in his childish voice.

It's also enchanting to see a pretty little white chick, its lanky legs looking like legs poking out from under a short robe, cheeping loudly as it runs and pauses

7. A Buddhist priest should not wear the white paper cap of a Yin-Yang diviner in a Shinto ceremony.
8. That is, with long bangs, resembling the hair of women who shaved the crown of their head in a tonsure.
9. A plant used in Japanese heraldry.

here and there around someone's feet. Likewise, all scenes of chicks running about with the mother hen. The eggs of a spot-billed duck. A green-glass pot.

*　*　*

257 *Things that give you pleasure*—You've read the first volume of a tale you hadn't come across before, and are longing to go on with it—then you find the other volume. The rest of it can sometimes turn out to be disappointing, however.

Piecing back together a letter that someone has torn up and thrown away, and finding that you can read line after line of it.

It's extremely pleasing when you've had a puzzling dream which fills you with fear at what it may portend, and then you have it interpreted and it turns out to be quite harmless.

It's also wonderfully pleasing when you're in a large company of people in the presence of someone great, and she's talking, either about something in the past or on a matter she's only just heard about, some topic of the moment, and as she speaks it's you she singles out to look at.

Then there's the pleasing moment when you've heard that someone who matters a lot to you and who's far from you—perhaps in some distant place, or even simply elsewhere in the capital—has been taken ill, and you're worrying and wringing your hands over the uncertainty, when news arrives that the illness has taken a turn for the better.

Someone you love is praised by others, and some high-ranking person comments that his talents are 'not inconsiderable.'

When a poem that you've composed for some event, or in an exchange of poems, is talked of by everyone and noted down when they hear it. This hasn't yet happened to me personally, but I can imagine how it would feel.

It's very pleasing when someone you don't know well mentions an old poem or story that you haven't heard of, and then it comes up again in conversation with someone else. If you come across it later in something you're reading, there's the delightful moment when you cry, 'Oh is *that* where it comes from!', and you enjoy recalling the person's mention of it.

Managing to lay hands on some Michinoku or any good quality paper.

You feel very pleased with yourself when a person who rather overawes you asks you to supply the beginning or end of some bit of poem they quote, and you suddenly recall it. It so often happens that as soon as anyone asks you, even something you know perfectly well goes clean out of your head.

Finding something you need in a hurry.

How could you fail to feel pleased when you win at a matching game,[1] or some other kind of competition?

Managing to get the better of someone who's full of themselves and overconfident. This is even more pleasing if it's a man, rather than one of your own circle of gentlewomen. It's fun to be constantly on your guard because you're expecting him to try to get even with you, and it's also fun to have been fooled into relaxing your guard over time, as he continues to act quite unconcerned and pretend nothing's happened.

When someone you don't like meets with some misfortune, you're pleased even though you know this is wicked of you.

1. A popular diversion in which participants competed in matching objects such as shells, flowers, or paintings.

You've sent out your robes to be freshly glossed[2] for some event, and are holding your breath to see how they come out, when they're delivered looking absolutely beautiful. A comb that's come up delightfully with polishing is also pleasing. There are a lot of other things of this sort too.

It's very pleasing when you've finally recovered from a nasty illness that's plagued you day in, day out for months. This is even more the case when it's not your own illness but that of someone you love.

And it's wonderfully pleasing when a crowd of people are packed into the room in Her Majesty's presence, and she suddenly spies someone who's only just arrived at court, sitting rather withdrawn by a distant pillar, and beckons her over, whereupon everyone makes way and the girl is brought up and ensconced very close to Her Majesty.

* * *

529   *I have written in this book* things I have seen and thought, in the long idle hours spent at home, without ever dreaming that others would see it. Fearing that some of my foolish remarks could well strike others as excessive and objectionable, I did my best to keep it secret, but despite all my intentions I'm afraid it has come to light.

Palace Minister Korechika one day presented to the Empress a bundle of paper. 'What do you think we could write on this?' Her Majesty inquired. 'They are copying *Records of the Historian*[3] over at His Majesty's court.'

'This should be a "pillow,"[4] then,' I suggested.

'Very well, it's yours,' declared Her Majesty, and she handed it over to me.

I set to work with this boundless pile of paper to fill it to the last sheet with all manner of odd things, so no doubt there's much in these pages that makes no sense.

Overall, I have chosen to write about the things that delight, or that people find impressive, including poems as well as things such as trees, plants, birds, insects and so forth, and for this reason people may criticize it for not living up to expectations and only going to prove the limits of my own sensibility. But after all, I merely wrote for my personal amusement things that I myself have thought and felt, and I never intended that it should be placed alongside other books and judged on a par with them. I'm utterly perplexed to hear that people who've read my work have said it makes them feel humble in the face of it. Well, there you are, you can judge just how unimpressive someone is if they dislike things that most people like, and praise things that others condemn. Anyway, it does upset me that people have seen these pages.

When Captain of the Left Tsunefusa was still Governor of Ise, he came to visit me while I was back at home, and my book disconcertingly happened to be on the mat from the nearby corner that was put out for him. I scrambled to try and retrieve it, but he carried it off with him, and kept it for a very long time before returning it.

That seems to have been the moment when this book first became known—or so it is written.

---

2. Silk was made shiny by being beaten on special blocks.
3. The *Historical Records* by Sima Qian.
4. This concluding section explains the ori-

gins of *The Pillow Book* and of its title. A "pillow" might simply be a notebook for daily jottings kept at hand in some private place.

MURASAKI SHIKIBU

ca. 978–ca. 1014

The Tale of Genji is the undisputed masterpiece of Japanese prose and often considered the first great novel in the history of world literature. That it was written by an eleventh-century court lady is even more extraordinary. Virginia Woolf, who reviewed its first complete English translation—the masterful rendering by Arthur Waley—in 1925, responded to Murasaki Shikibu with the lonely empathy of an early twentieth-century woman author: "There was Sappho and a little group of women all writing poetry on a Greek island six hundred years before the birth of Christ. They fall silent. Then about the year 1000 we find a certain court lady, the Lady Murasaki, writing a very long and beautiful novel in Japan." Although originally written for a narrow circle of court aristocrats in Kyoto, *The Tale of Genji* has had unparalleled success in engaging generations of passionate readers and it is now uniquely representative of Japanese literature. Vast in scale and peopled by hundreds of characters, this thousand-page tale depicts the lives and loves of a former prince—Genji—who dies two-thirds through the book, and the lives and loves of his descendants. On a deeper level, *The Tale of Genji* is about the human ability to be touched by other people and by the outside world, about the tantalizing line between love and lust, and about the vulnerability of women in a male-dominated world. It celebrates the power of poetry, music, and dance to shape society and give depth to human life. Revered for its psychological insight, it captures a world that, however remote from our own, has always retained the sharp authenticity of real life. At its most basic, it chronicles the struggle with the most fundamental of human experiences: love, art, and death.

LIFE AND TIMES

The actual name of the author of *The Tale of Genji* is unknown. It was common at the time to name women after the office held by a male relative. "Shikibu" refers to the appointment her father held at the "Ministry of Ceremonial." The nickname "Murasaki" ("lavender," "purple") is based either on the heroine Murasaki in *The Tale of Genji* or on the color of wisteria, the emblematic flower of her clan. Murasaki Shikibu's ancestors had belonged to a branch of the Fujiwara ("wisteria fields") clan, which had managed since the tenth century to dominate the throne by ruling as regents on behalf of young emperors and marrying their daughters into the imperial family. Despite Murasaki's distinguished ancestry, her family eventually declined to the level of provincial governors. Her father had a mediocre career in the court administration, although he was known as a poet and scholar of Chinese literature. Through him Murasaki got a glimpse of life outside the Heian-era capital of Kyoto, when in her teens she accompanied him for a couple of years on one of his appointments in the provinces. After returning to the capital, Murasaki was briefly married to the much older Fujiwara no Nobutaka, a middle-ranking aristocrat. When he died in 1001, Murasaki was in her early twenties, now a widow with a two-year-old daughter. Murasaki probably started writing *The Tale of Genji* after the death of her husband. These early chapters won her a growing reputation and led to an invitation from Empress Shōshi around 1006 to serve as lady-in-waiting at the imperial court, where she remained until her death around 1014.

The flourishing of female literature during this time was in no small part a result of the efforts of the Fujiwara regents to fill the ranks of their daughters' entourages with the most talented and educated women. Shōshi was one of the consorts of Emperor Ichijō, and she was far more successful than her rival, Empress Teishi, whom **Sei Shōnagon**, the author of *The Pillow Book*, served. She bore Ichijō two emperors and her fortunes reflected the power of her father, the regent Fujiwara no Michinaga. Employment as ladies-in-waiting gave Heian women writers the financial support and leisure to produce literature that commanded the attention of society in the capital.

Murasaki had broad learning in Japanese vernacular literature—*waka* poetry, women's diaries, and tales—but also acquired a profound understanding of the Chinese classics (canonical texts) and Chinese poetry. While aristocratic women at the time were often knowledgeable in Chinese literature, they did not produce Chinese-style texts in the authoritative idiom of the male court bureaucracy and the Buddhist clergy, writing instead in the vernacular language. In her diary Murasaki confesses:

> When my brother, the Secretary at the Ministry of Ceremonial, was young and studied the Chinese classics, I used to listen to him and became unusually good at understanding those passages which he found too difficult to grasp. My father, a most learned man, was always lamenting this fact: "Just my luck!" he would say. "What a pity that she was not born a man!"

A father's admiration for his daughter's academic brilliance cannot conceal the fact that in Heian society, Chinese learning was truly valuable only for men.

In Heian Japan, men and women were strictly segregated and women's lives were extremely circumscribed. The role of a lady was to marry and bear children; and if she came from a suitably good family, she was apt to find herself a pawn in the marriage politics of the imperial court. A noblewoman's days were spent behind curtains and screens, hidden from the world (or from the male world). A man's first marriage often took place when he was still a boy of twelve or thirteen; women were even a year or two younger. Because of the ages of the spouses and the likelihood of the first marriage in particular being a political and economic arrangement, both husband and wife tended eventually to seek love elsewhere, although only men could have multiple marriage partners. The purpose of marriage was procreation, continuation of the family line, and the creation of advantageous alliances with other families. Ordinarily a man's several wives lived in different establishments. His first wife would typically remain in her parents' house. Initially, the young husband might take up residence there or merely visit. Sometimes her parents would furnish the newlyweds with a house of their own, though doing so was less common when the couple married at a young age and the maternal grandparents would be expected to assume many of the child-rearing duties. If in time a man took a second or third wife, he would usually live with his first (and main) wife and commute between the separate residences. It was in this world of gender asymmetries that Heian women's literature thrived. At the same time, Heian women used the status they had as female authors to voice how women suffered from their dependence on their husbands, lovers, and patrons.

An early sixteenth-century illustrated calligraphic excerpt from chapter 17, "The Picture Contest," of *The Tale of Genji*. The artwork is attributed to Reizei Tamehiro.

THE TALE OF GENJI

Although Genji's women play an important role in the tale, it is named after its male protagonist. He is the son of the reigning emperor and his beloved but low-ranking consort, Kiritsubo ("Paulownia Pavilion"). Her favor with the emperor makes her a target of vicious rivalry among the emperor's higher-ranking women, such as the Kokiden Consort, his principal wife. Genji's mother dies in despair when he is in his third year, and his father is eventually forced to remove him from the imperial line to protect him from the ill will of his other consorts. He makes the boy a commoner, bestowing the family name "Genji" on him. As Genji grows up his brilliance elicits sighs of admiration wherever he appears, and he is soon being called "the Radiant Prince." The emperor dotes on his remarkable son, who reminds him all the more painfully of his former favorite consort. He eventually finds solace in the young Fujitsubo, daughter of a previous emperor, who resembles Kiritsubo but is of highest rank.

With even more determination than his father, Genji embarks on a search for women who can replace the mother he barely remembers. His fatal attraction to Fujitsubo leads to one of his greatest transgressions. Fujitsubo gives birth to a son who later becomes emperor and whom everybody believes to be the son of Genji's father. Later, Fujitsubo's niece Murasaki becomes Genji's great love. Sometimes Genji's escapades with women of very high rank lead to disaster: after his affair with Oborozukiyo, who is the younger sister of his father's principal wife, the Kokiden consort (and thus his mortal enemy), he is forced into exile to the rustic countryside. Sometimes inattention, rather than sexual transgression, brings about disaster: Genji's failure to respond to the jealous passion of the lady at Rokujō, widow of a former crown prince, leads inexorably to the death of some of the most important women in his life.

Genji is charismatic, irresistible, and tantalizingly flawed. Charming and handsome, brilliant and ardent, rakish but faithful in his own way (unlike other men, he never abandons any woman he has loved), he is an extraordinary literary figure. Readers may hate Genji or adore him, but we can hardly deny that his creator has fashioned a character who is both larger than life and believably human.

The fifty-four-chapter tale falls broadly into three parts. The first thirty-three chapters describe Genji's career from his birth through his exile and his eventual glorious return to the capital. They focus on the various women with whom he becomes involved in his younger years. Chapters 34 through 41 treat the waning years of Genji's life, concluding with the death of Murasaki and Genji's own death. The remaining thirteen chapters, including the last ten so-called Uji chapters, move to the world of Kaoru, supposedly Genji's son by the Third Princess, and his friend Prince Niou, the son of Genji's daughter, the Akashi Empress. Featuring the two young men's rivalry over several women living in Uji, south of the capital of Kyoto, they draw the reader from the elegant capital to the countryside. Lacking the radiance of Genji's presence, this world is populated with compromised protagonists, darker entanglements with life's sufferings, and thinner hopes for salvation.

Though The Tale of Genji is a coherent whole, it can also be appreciated as a collection of interrelated episodes revolving around Genji, his women, and their descendants, in part because of how the work was composed. Since Murasaki wrote it over a span of a dozen years, probably starting with what eventually became chapter 5 ("Little Purple Gromwell," included here), the tale developed in thematic sequences. It first circulated in various shorter installments—single chapters or sequences—among Kyoto's court aristocracy. The sequences show how Murasaki's protagonists, interests, and narrative techniques evolved over time. The "Broom Cypress Sequence," for example, which includes chapters 2,

4, 6, and sequels in chapters 15 and 16, was apparently inserted later. Whereas the core chapters of the tale's first part show Genji dangerously in love with high-ranking women who were close to the emperor, in the "Broom Cypress Sequence" he pursues women of the middle and lower aristocracy. The key prelude to Genji's later conquests occurs in chapter 2 ("Broom Cypress," included here), when the seventeen-year-old Genji and his friends while away a rainy night in his quarters at the palace debating what makes the perfect woman. In the process, the young men trade stories of their experiences with women. Although Genji dozes off now and then, he takes away the lessons from that night and applies them to his pursuit of women in the following chapters of the sequence.

In The Tale of Genji Murasaki sometimes relied on conventions from earlier tales, so-called monogatari. A typical plot element was an illustrious aristocrat's discovery of a heroine in humble circumstances. This describes the situation of Genji's mother, and also many of Genji's own exploits. Liaisons between high-ranking men and humble women were far more popular in literary romances than in Heian-era reality. A real-life Genji would probably never have married somebody like the character Murasaki, orphaned and without appropriate family background. But in romantic tales, the total infatuation of an aristocrat with a lower-ranking woman was an expression of passion and emotional depth; for female readers it perhaps even inspired hope that they might find salvation and social mobility through the power of romantic love. Because of the social gap between Genji and his lovers, the tale's low-ranking heroines spend considerable energy agonizing about their lowly position and trying to cope with social marginalization. Another typical plot element of earlier tales is the pursuit of love in unexpected or forbidden places. There is no lack of such episodes in Genji's career; he strongly resembles the real-life Ariwara no Narihira (825–880), the epitome of a romantic lover and hero of the earlier *monogatari The Tales of Ise*.

The Tale of Genji displays the remarkable blend of Murasaki's talents. She was a gifted poet, inserting several hundred poems in the tale. Where modern readers might expect Genji and his lovers to exchange love letters in prose, Murasaki has them communicate through elaborate poems. Indeed, most of the protagonists are named after imagery from those poems, and until the early modern period readers studied *The Tale of Genji* to enhance their skills in poetry composition. Also, Murasaki was a perceptive reader of women's confessional diaries and a masterful prose stylist, relying on the nuanced expression of interiority developed by women diarists before her for the intimate psychological portrayal of *The Tale of Genji*'s fictional protagonists. Lastly, her expertise in Chinese literature inspired her to enrich recurring motifs with resonant references to Chinese poetry. In the first chapter she evokes "**The Song of Lasting Regret**" by the Tang poet **Bo Juyi**, which tells of the tragic love between a Chinese emperor and a low-ranking concubine, as a poignant analogy to the fate of Genji's mother; like a motif in music, Bo Juyi's gripping ballad keeps reappearing throughout the novel in various guises.

In its day *The Tale of Genji* was just another vernacular tale that, in the estimation of the learned elite, stood far below the Chinese-style writing by Heian men. Chinese learning—a coveted quality for a male aristocrat—was a dubious asset for a court lady. In her diary Murasaki tells how angry she was when somebody teased her for her Chinese learning and gave her the nickname "Our Lady of the Chronicles." But in fact this title should have pleased her: in "Fireflies" (chapter 25, included here) Genji discusses the worth of romantic tales with Tamakazura, his best friend's daughter, and she inspires him to argue that fiction is in some way more truthful than official Chinese-style histories such as the venerable *Chronicles of Japan*: vernacular tales tell the real stories that are left out of the Chinese-style histories.

Whether meant as a playful jibe or a serious polemical claim, Murasaki's bold comparison of popular vernacular tales to canonical Chinese-style histories facilitated the canonization of *The Tale of Genji* in later ages. *The Tale of Genji* became the subject of erudite scholastic commentaries; it inspired screen paintings and illustrated hand scrolls, Noh and puppet plays, poetry handbooks, parodies, and, more recently, woodblock prints, films, and manga (comic book) versions. This "Genji cult" is in part a result of the late-nineteenth-century promotion of *The Tale of Genji* from the status of a brilliant masterpiece to that of a modern national classic said to encapsulate Japanese sensibility. But leaving politics aside, one of the many reasons for *The Tale of Genji*'s timeless appeal is that it is a grand meditation on the emotional and psychological dynamics of love and loss. It seduces the reader with its extensive depictions of courtship and passion, but its ultimate theme is the deeper longing to find a common language through which to connect with another person.

Main Characters in *The Tale of Genji*

AKASHI EMPRESS, *daughter of Genji and the Akashi Lady; becomes empress by marrying one of Emperor Suzaku's sons, the last reigning emperor to appear in the tale*

AKASHI LADY, *daughter of the Akashi Novice; meets Genji during his exile and bears him a daughter who eventually becomes empress*

AKASHI NOVITIATE, *former governor of Harima, father of the Akashi Lady*

ASSISTANT HANDMAID, *Genji's aged and coquettish admirer*

BISHOP, *Murasaki's great-uncle, a distinguished Buddhist cleric*

EMPEROR SUZAKU, *Genji's elder half brother, son of the Kokiden Consort; succeeds the Kiritsubo Emperor on the throne*

EMPEROR REIZEI, *son of Genji and Fujitsubo, but believed to be the son of Genji's father; succeeds Suzaku as emperor*

FUJITSUBO, *daughter of an earlier emperor; Genji's father's empress with whom Genji has a son, the later Emperor Reizei*

GENJI'S WIFE, *daughter of the Minister of the Left; marries Genji at age 16, when Genji is 12*

HACHINOMIYA, *"Eighth Prince"; younger brother of Genji who lives as a saintly ascetic in Uji and is the father of the "Uji princesses" and Ukifune*

HIGH PRIESTESS OF ISE, *Akikonomu, the daughter of the Lady at Rokujō*

KAORU, *son of the Third Princess, Genji's wife, by Kashiwagi; friend of Niou and central protagonist of the "Uji chapters," named after his mysterious natural "fragrance"*

KASHIWAGI, *eldest son of Tō no Chūjō and actual father of Kaoru, believed to be Genji's son; his affair with the Third Princess leads to his early death*

KIRITSUBO EMPEROR, *Genji's father*

KOKIDEN CONSORT, *daughter of the Minister of the Right; mother of Emperor Suzaku and archenemy of Genji*

KOREMITSU, *Genji's foster brother and confidant*

LADY AT ROKUJŌ, *daughter of a Minister and widow of a deceased Heir Apparent; Genji's neglect of her has fatal consequences*

MINISTER OF THE LEFT, *father of Genji's wife and of Tō no Chūjō, Genji's friend*

MINISTER OF THE RIGHT, *father of the Kokiden Consort and Oborozukiyo*

MURASAKI, *unrecognized daughter of Prince Hyōbu and niece of Fujitsubo; raised by Genji, who later marries her*

NIOU, *imperial prince and son of the Akashi Empress, Genji's daughter, and the last reigning emperor to appear in the tale; friend of Kaoru and central protagonist of the "Uji chapters," named after his memorable "perfume"*

OBOROZUKIYO, *daughter of the Minister of the Right and younger sister of Kokiden; enters the service of Suzaku; Genji's affair with her leads to his exile*

PRINCE HYŌBU, *Fujitsubo's elder brother, Murasaki's father*

SOCHINOMIYA, *also "Prince Hotaru," Genji's half brother, who unsuccessfully courts Tamakazura*

TAMAKAZURA, *daughter of Tō no Chūjō by a low-ranking mistress; discovered by Genji, who installs her into his mansion and passes her off as his own daughter*

THIRD PRINCESS, *third daughter of Emperor Suzaku, who marries her to Genji; mother of Kaoru, whom people believe to be Genji's son, but whose actual father is Kashiwagi, the eldest son of Tō no Chūjō, with whom she has an affair*

TŌ NO CHŪJŌ, *son of the Minister of the Left and brother of Aoi; his name is the title of a post he occupies*

UJI PRINCESSES, *daughters of Hachinomiya, the younger brother of Genji who lives in Uji; the older of the princesses is also known as "Oigimi," the younger as "Naka no kimi"*

UKIFUNE, *unrecognized daughter of Hachinomiya and half-sister of the "Uji Princesses"*

YOKAWA BISHOP, *bishop at the large Enryakuji temple complex on Mount Hiei, northeast of Kyoto; discovers Ukifune and ordains her as a nun*

FROM THE TALE OF GENJI[1]

From Chapter I

Kiritsubo

THE LADY OF THE PAULOWNIA-COURTYARD CHAMBERS

In whose reign was it that a woman of rather undistinguished lineage captured the heart of the Emperor and enjoyed his favor above all the other imperial wives and concubines? Certain consorts, whose high noble status gave them a sense of vain entitlement, despised and reviled her as an unworthy upstart from the very moment she began her service. Ladies of lower rank were even more vexed, for they knew His Majesty would never bestow the same degree of affection and attention on them. As a result, the mere presence of this woman at morning rites or evening ceremonies seemed to provoke hostile reactions among her rivals, and the anxiety she suffered as a consequence of these ever-increasing displays of jealousy was such a heavy burden that gradually her health began to fail.

His Majesty could see how forlorn she was, how often she returned to her family home. He felt sorry for her and wanted to help, and though he could scarcely afford to ignore the admonitions of his advisers, his behavior eventually became the subject of palace gossip. Ranking courtiers and attendants found it difficult to stand by and observe the troubling situation, which they viewed as deplorable. They were fully aware that a similarly ill-fated romance had thrown the Chinese state into chaos.[2] Concern and consternation gradually spread through the court, since it appeared that nothing could be done. Many considered the relationship scandalous, so much so that some openly referred to the example of the Prize Consort Yang. The only thing that made it possible for the woman to continue to serve was the Emperor's gracious devotion.

The woman's father had risen to the third rank as a Major Counselor before he died. Her mother, the principal wife of her father, was a woman of old-fashioned upbringing and character who was well trained in the customs and rituals of the court. Thus, the reputation of her house was considered in no way inferior and did not suffer by comparison with the brilliance of the highest nobility. Unfortunately, her family had no patrons who could provide political support, and after her father's death there was no one she could rely on. In the end, she found herself at the mercy of events and with uncertain prospects.

Was she not, then, bound to the Emperor by some deep love from a previous life? For in spite of her travails, she eventually bore him a son—a pure radiant gem like nothing of this world. Following the child's birth His Majesty had to wait impatiently, wondering when he would finally be allowed to see the boy.

---

1. Translated by Dennis Washburn. Except where indicated, all notes are his. Murasaki Shikibu often alludes directly to works of poetry (both Chinese and Japanese), fiction, history, and court records. Most of these allusions are to Japanese poems compiled in imperial anthologies during the 10th and early 11th centuries. Notes throughout this selection cite the source of only some of these allusions.

2. The courtiers are referring to "Song of Lasting Regret" by the Tang dynasty poet Bai Juyi (722–846). The poem recounts the infatuation of the emperor Xuanzong (685–762) with Yang Guifei, which caused him to neglect affairs of state. His army revolted, and he was forced to execute his lover.

As soon as it could be ritually sanctioned, he had the infant brought from the home of the woman's mother, where the birth had taken place,[3] and the instant he gazed on the child's countenance he recognized a rare beauty.

Now, as it so happened, the Crown Prince[4] had been born three years earlier to the Kokiden Consort, who was the daughter of the Minister of the Right. As the unquestioned heir to the throne, the boy had many supporters and the courtiers all treated him with the utmost respect and deference. He was, however, no match for the radiant beauty of the newborn Prince; and even though the Emperor was bound to acknowledge the higher status of his older son and to favor him in public, in private he could not resist treating the younger Prince as his favorite and lavishing attention upon him.

The mother of the newborn Prince did not come from a family of the highest rank, but neither was she of such low status that she should have been constantly by the Emperor's side like a common servant. Certainly her reputation was flawless, and she comported herself with noble dignity, but because His Majesty obsessively kept her near him, willfully demanding that they not be separated, she had to be in attendance at all formal court performances or elegant entertainments. There were times when she would spend the night with him and then be obliged to continue in service the following day. Consequently, as one might expect, other courtiers came to look down on her not only as a person of no significance, but also as a woman who lacked any sense of propriety. Moreover, because the Emperor treated her with special regard following the birth of his second son, the Kokiden Consort and her supporters grew anxious; they worried about the effect of such an infatuation on the prospects of the Crown Prince and wondered if the younger Prince might not surpass his half brother in favor and usurp his position. The Kokiden Consort had been the Emperor's first wife. She had arrived at the palace before all the other women, and so His Majesty's feelings of affection for her were in no way ordinary. He considered her protests troubling, but he also had to acknowledge that she was deserving of sympathy, since she had given him two imperial princesses in addition to the Crown Prince.

Even though the mother of the newborn Prince relied on the Emperor's benevolence for protection, many of the ladies at court scorned her. She grew physically weak, and because she felt powerless and had no one to turn to for help, she suffered greatly because of his love.

Her chambers at the palace were in the Kiritsubo—named for its courtyard, which was graced with paulownia trees. Because the Kiritsubo was in the northeast corner of the palace, and thus separated from the Emperor's quarters in the Seiryōden, he would have to pass by the chambers of many of the other court ladies on his frequent visits to her. Their resentment of these displays was not at all unreasonable, and so it was decided that the woman herself would have to go more often to the Seiryōden. The more she went, however, the more her rivals would strew the covered passageways connecting the various parts of the palace with filth. It was an absolutely intolerable situation, for the hems of the robes of the accompanying attendants would be soiled. On other occasions,

---

3. It was customary for births to take place outside the palace in order to avoid defilement. A period of confinement for ritual purification usually followed a birth, which is why the Emperor has to wait to see his son.

4. Genji's half brother Suzaku [editor's note].

when the woman could not avoid taking the interior hallways, her rivals would arrange for the doors at both ends to be closed off so that she could neither proceed forward nor turn back, trapping her inside and making her feel utterly wretched. As the number of these cruel incidents mounted, His Majesty felt sorry that his beloved should have to suffer so and ordered that she be installed in the chambers of the Kōrōden, a hall next to the Seiryōden. To do so, however, he had to move the lady who had resided there from the very beginning of her service at court to other quarters, causing her to nurse a deep resentment that proved impossible to placate.

When the young Prince turned three, the court observed the ceremony of the donning of his first trousers. Employing all the treasures from the Imperial Storehouse and the Treasury, the event was every bit as lavish as the ceremony for the Crown Prince. Numerous objections were raised as a consequence of this ostentatious display, and everyone censured the ceremony as a breach of protocol. Fortunately, as the young Prince grew, his graceful appearance and matchless temperament became a source of wonder to all, and it was impossible for anyone to entirely resent him. Discerning courtiers who possessed the most refined sensibility could only gaze in amazement that such a child should have been born into this world.

During the summer of the year the young Prince turned three, his mother's health began to fail. She asked for permission to leave the court and return to her family home, but the Emperor would not hear of it and refused to let her go. She had been sickly and frail for some time, and so His Majesty had grown accustomed to seeing her in such a condition. "Wait a little while," he simply told her, "and let's see how you feel." Then, over the course of the next five or six days, she became seriously ill. The woman made a tearful entreaty, and at last she received permission to leave the palace. Even under these dire circumstances she was very careful to avoid any behavior that could be criticized as untoward or inappropriate. She decided to retire from the court in secret, leaving her young son behind.

Resigned to the fact that the life of his true love was approaching its end and mindful of the taboo against defiling the palace with death, His Majesty was nonetheless grief-stricken beyond words that the dictates of protocol prevented him from seeing her off. The woman's face, with its lambent beauty conveying that air of grace so precious to him, was now thin and wasted. She had tasted the sorrows of the world to the full, but as she slipped in and out of consciousness, she could not convey to him even those feelings that might have been put into words. The Emperor, who now realized that his beloved was on the verge of death, lost control and made all sorts of tearful vows to her, no longer able to distinguish past from future. She, however, could not respond to him. The expression of weariness in her eyes made her all the more alluringly vulnerable as she lay there in a semiconscious state. The Emperor was beside himself and had no idea what he should do. He had granted her the honor of leaving in a carriage drawn by servants, but when he returned to her chambers again, he simply could not bring himself to let her go.

"Didn't we swear an oath to journey together on the road to death? No matter what, I cannot let you abandon me," he said.

She was deeply moved by his display of sorrowful devotion. Though breathing with great difficulty, she still managed to compose a verse for him:

Now in deepest sorrow as I contemplate
Our diverging roads, this fork where we must part
How I long to walk the path of the living

"Had I known that things would turn out like this . . ."

She evidently wanted to say more to him, but her breathing was labored. She was so weak and in such pain the Emperor longed to keep her at the palace and see it through to the end, come what may. But when he received an urgent message informing him that the most skilled of priests had been called to her family home to chant the requisite prayers of healing for her that evening, His Majesty at last agreed that his beloved should leave the palace, unbearable as it was for him to make that decision.

His heart was full and he could not sleep as he impatiently waited for the short summer night to end. The messenger he sent had barely had time to get to the woman's home and return with news of her condition, yet His Majesty was assailed by a sense of dark foreboding.

As it turned out, when the messenger arrived at the woman's residence, he found the family distraught and weeping. "She passed away after midnight," they informed him. The messenger returned to the palace in a state of shock. The Emperor, stunned and shaken by the news, was so upset that he shut himself away from the rest of the court.

His Majesty desperately wanted to see the young Prince his beloved had left behind at the palace, but there was no precedent for permitting anyone to serve at court while having to wear robes of mourning. So it was decided that the boy should be sent from the palace to his mother's residence. Too young to fully comprehend what was going on, he knew from the way people around him were behaving, and from the Emperor's ceaseless tears, that something was terribly wrong. The death of loved ones is always a source of grief, but the little boy's puzzled expression only added to the unspeakable sadness of it all.

* * *

The days passed in a meaningless blur for the Emperor, who dutifully observed each of the seven-day ceremonies leading up to the forty-ninth day after the funeral. Despite the passage of time, His Majesty was so lost in grief he could find no comfort. He was indifferent to the consorts and ladies-in-waiting who attended him in the evenings and instead passed his days and nights distracted and disconsolate. For all who observed his grief, it was truly an autumn drenched by a dew of tears.

Over in the chambers of the Kokiden the mother of the Crown Prince and her faction remained implacably unforgiving. "Is he still so in love with her," she complained, "that even after her death he doesn't consider the feelings of others?" And indeed it was true that whenever the Emperor looked at the Crown Prince, his thoughts would inevitably drift in yearning to the younger Prince, and he would then dispatch his most trusted ladies-in-waiting or nurses to the family home of his late beloved to inquire after the boy.

* * *

The soughing of the wind, the chirring of insects . . . these brought only sadness to him. The quarters of the Kokiden Consort were close by on the north side of his private chambers in the Seiryōden. It had been a long time since she last came to serve him here, and on this particular evening, with the moon in full splendor, he could hear her indulging in musical entertainment to pass the night. The Emperor was appalled and found it quite unpleasant. The courtiers and ladies-in-waiting who observed his countenance at that moment listened uneasily as well. The Kokiden Consort was a proud and haughty woman who behaved as though she couldn't care less about His Majesty's grief.

* * *

The days and months passed, and the young Prince finally came back to the palace. He had grown so splendid and handsome that he no longer seemed to belong to this mortal world. His worried father, knowing that the beautiful die young, took the boy's good looks as an unlucky omen.

In the spring of the following year the time came for the Emperor to formally designate the heir apparent. He was seized by a desire to pass over the presumed Crown Prince, his son by the Kokiden Consort, and appoint his favored younger son instead, but he knew that the little Prince had no supporters and that the court would never accept such a move, which might prove dangerous to the boy. So in the end he went against his personal wishes and confirmed the Crown Prince as his heir apparent, all the while keeping his true feelings concealed. The courtiers remarked among themselves that no matter how much His Majesty preferred the younger son, he knew there were limits to his affection. When the Kokiden Consort caught wind of these rumors, she felt both relief and satisfaction.

The grandmother of the young Prince had long been sunk in a deep depression, and finding no means to console herself, she finally passed away. Was her death the answer to her prayers to be allowed to go to her daughter? The Emperor was once more plunged into grief beyond the measure of ordinary mortals. By this time the young Prince was almost six and was old enough now to understand what was happening. Deeply attached to his grandmother, he wept inconsolably. As she neared death, she recognized how accustomed her grandson had grown to being with her through the years, and she repeated over and over how sad she was to leave him alone in the world.

With both his mother and grandmother gone, the young Prince moved back to the palace for good. When he turned seven he underwent the ceremony of the First Reading, which initiated him into the study of the Chinese classics. The court had never known a child so precociously intelligent, and His Majesty, knowing how others felt and believing that talent and beauty die young, could not help but view such abilities with alarm.

"How could anyone possibly resent him now?" the Emperor declared. "Because he has lost his mother, I want him treated with affection."

Eventually even the Kokiden Consort and her attendants were won over, and whenever the young Prince accompanied his father to the Kokiden chambers, he would be permitted entry behind the curtains where the ladies-in-waiting were serving His Majesty. The fiercest warriors and most implacable enemies would have smiled had they seen him, and the ladies of the court were reluctant to let him out of their sight. The Kokiden Consort had given the Emperor two princesses as well, but neither of them could compare in beauty to this boy. The other consorts and ladies felt no inhibitions around him—indeed, they allowed him to catch glimpses of their faces—and his own appearance was so elegant that they would experience an embarrassed excitement whenever they saw him. All the courtiers considered him exceptionally splendid, a playmate to be treated with special deference.

His formal training included instruction on the koto and flute, and word of his talents echoed throughout the palace—though if I were to go into all the details about his abilities my account would seem exaggerated, and he would come across as too good to be true.

The Emperor learned that among the members of a mission from the Korean kingdom of Koryō was a diviner skilled at the art of physiognomy. An old edict by the Emperor Uda had forbidden the presence of foreigners within the palace, so His Majesty discreetly arranged to have the young Prince meet with this man at the Kōrōkan, the residence provided for foreign missions. The Major Controller of the Right assumed the role of guardian and accompanied the boy to the mission under the pretense that he was the father of the child. The diviner was both puzzled and astounded. He tilted his head back and forth, unable to believe that this child could really be the Major Controller's son.

"The young man's features tell me he is destined to be ruler of this country," the diviner declared, "and will perhaps even attain the supreme position of Emperor. Yet if that is what fate has in store for him, I foresee chaos and great sorrow for the court. On the other hand, if his destiny is to ascend to a position such as Chancellor and act as a guardian of imperial rule, then it appears he will be a great benefactor to the state. Still, I must say that judging by his features alone, the path leading to the Chancellorship seems less likely."

The Major Controller was himself a scholar of considerable learning and discernment, and his conversations with the men of the Korean mission were deeply engaging. The party composed and exchanged verses in Chinese, and because the mission planned to leave for home in a day or two, one of the diviner's poems expressed the joy at having met such a remarkable boy face-to-face and the sorrow of having to part from him so soon. In response to the heartfelt expression of this poem, the young Prince composed an accomplished verse of his own. The diviner praised his effort as auspicious and bestowed lavish gifts on him. In return, the diviner received splendid presents from the imperial household. Naturally, news of this encounter spread through the court. His Majesty did not let on that he knew anything about it, but the grandfather of the Crown Prince, who happened to be the Minister of the Right, caught wind of the gossip and, not knowing quite what to make of it, grew suspicious.

The Emperor in his wisdom had earlier sought out the opinion of a Japanese diviner, whose reading of the boy's physiognomy accorded with his own thinking at the time. His Majesty had been holding back on installing the young Prince in the line of succession, and was thus impressed by the perspicacity of the Korean diviner, who recognized the boy's imperial lineage. Even so, he could not be sure how long his own reign would last, and he hesitated to appoint his son prince-without-rank. He anxiously wondered whether the boy, who lacked support from his mother's family, would not end up precariously adrift once he was no longer in the line of succession. For that reason he determined that the boy's prospects might be better if he were made to serve as a loyal subject of the imperial court, and so he had his son tutored accordingly in the arts and in various fields of learning. The boy was so exceptionally bright it seemed a shame to demote him to commoner status, but the Emperor knew that designating his son heir apparent would invite the calumny and scorn of the court. He consulted yet another diviner who was wise in the ways of Indic astrology, and when this new reading proved to be in line with the others and with His Majesty's own thoughts on the matter as well, he decided to confer on the boy the clan name of Minamoto—Genji[5]—thereby making him a commoner.

Months and years passed, but there was never a moment when the Emperor forgot his love for the lady who had resided in the chambers looking out on the paulownia courtyard. Thinking he might find someone who could assuage his grief, he had women of appropriate breeding and talents brought before him. But it was all in vain, for where in the world could he expect to find her equal? Just when he had reached the point where he found everything tiresome and was contemplating retiring from the world, an Assistant Handmaid informed him of a young woman, the Fourth Princess of the previous Emperor, whose beauty was matchless, whose reputation at court was beyond reproof, and whose mother had raised her with extraordinary care and devotion. Since this Assistant Handmaid had once served at the court of the previous Emperor, she was familiar with the mother of this young woman and accustomed to waiting on her. In the course of her service she had been able to observe the Fourth Princess as she grew from childhood, and even now would occasionally see her.

"I have served at court for three successive reigns," she told the Emperor, "and I have never before seen anyone who even closely resembles the late lady of the Kiritsubo. The daughter of the former Empress, however, definitely puts me in mind of her. She is a woman of exquisite refinement and beauty."

Could this really be true? His Majesty, who could barely contain himself, began to make some discreet inquiries.

The mother of the Fourth Princess warned her daughter about the situation at the palace. "The Kokiden Consort is a vindictive woman. Just look at the unfortunate example of the lady in the Kiritsubo. The treatment she suffered was truly appalling." Unable to decide if she should allow her daughter to go to the palace, the mother was still struggling with the Emperor's request when suddenly she passed away.

Thinking that the Princess was now helpless and alone, His Majesty again approached the young lady. "I will think of you as an equal to my own daughters," he assured her. Her ladies-in-waiting, her supporters from her mother's family, and her older brother, Prince Hyōbu, who served in the Ministry of War, were all of the opinion that attending the Emperor would bring solace to her—and in any case it certainly would be preferable to remaining in her current wretched circumstances.

So it was that she was sent to the palace and installed in the Higyōsha, which was also called the Fujitsubo because its chambers looked out onto a courtyard graced with wisteria. The young woman was thereafter referred to as "Fujitsubo," and truly in face and figure she bore an uncanny resemblance to the deceased lady of the Kiritsubo. Fujitsubo, however, was of undeniably higher birth, and that status protected her from criticism, since the courtiers were predisposed to judge her a superior woman. Since she lacked no qualifications, the Emperor did not feel constrained in his relationship with her. The court had never accepted

5. The name "Genji" is the reading of the characters for Minamoto (*gen*) and "family name" (*shi/ji*).

His Majesty's love for the lady of the Kiritsubo, and so his affection for her was viewed as inappropriate and inopportune. The Emperor never wavered in his undying love for the lady of the paulownia-courtyard chambers, but it is a poignant fact of human nature that feelings change over time. Inevitably his attention shifted toward Fujitsubo, who, it seems, brought comfort to his heart.

Because the young Genji was always at his father's side, he was constantly in the presence of the women who attended His Majesty most frequently. These women grew familiar with the boy and gradually came to feel that they did not have to be reserved around him. Of course, none of the consorts considered herself inferior to the others, but even though each one was very attractive in her own individual way, there was no denying that they all had passed, or were on the verge of passing, the peak of their charms . . . all but Fujitsubo, that is. She still possessed the loveliness of youthful beauty and, try as she might to keep herself hidden away behind her screens, Genji, who was always nearby, would catch glimpses of her figure. He had no memory of his mother, and when he heard the head of the imperial household staff say that Fujitsubo looked just like her, his young heart ached with wistful longing—if only he could always be close to his father's new consort!

Genji and Fujitsubo were the two most precious people to the Emperor. "Do not be shy around the boy," His Majesty told Fujitsubo. "It may seem strange and curious, but I feel as though it is fitting for him to think of you as his mother. Do not think him discourteous, but cherish him for my sake. His face and expressions are so like his mother's . . . and since you resemble her so closely, you can hardly blame him for thinking of you the way he does."

After the Emperor made this request, Genji, in his boyish emotions, would try everything—even references to the transient blossoms of spring or the blazing leaves of autumn—to gain Fujitsubo's recognition of his yearning affection for her. When the Kokiden Consort learned of the unprecedented favoritism His Majesty was displaying toward these two, she once more grew cold and distant toward Fujitsubo and her retinue. Moreover, her earlier ominous dislike of Genji and his mother flared up again, and she found the boy repellent. Her son, the Crown Prince, was considered flawlessly handsome, and his reputation was above reproach. Nonetheless, he was no match for the lustrous beauty of Genji, who possessed an aura that prompted the courtiers to call him "the Radiant Prince." Because Fujitsubo was his equal in looks and in the affections of the Emperor, she came to be referred to as "the Princess of the Radiant Sun."

It pained the Emperor that his son would eventually grow out of his youthful good looks, but when Genji turned twelve, preparations were made for the coming-of-age ceremony in which his hair would be done up and his clothes and cap worn in the style of an adult. His Majesty personally tended to every little detail of the ceremony, adding touches that went beyond custom and set a new standard. The ceremony that had initiated the Crown Prince into manhood had been a spectacular affair held in the Shishinden, the great ceremonial hall of the palace. The Emperor wanted Genji's ceremony to be just as majestic and proper. He had various offices—including the Treasury and the Imperial Granaries—make formal preparations for the many banquets and celebrations that would follow the ceremony, and he left special instructions that no expense should be spared and that his directives should be carried out so as to make the occasion one of utmost splendor.

1256 | MURASAKI SHIKIBU

His Majesty was seated facing east under the eastern eaves of his residence in the Seiryōden, and the seats for Genji and the minister who would bestow the cap were located in front of him. Genji appeared before the Emperor at around four in the afternoon, during the Hour of the Monkey.[6] The lambent glow of his face, which was still framed on either side by the twin loops of his boyish hairdo, made his father feel all the more regretful about the change in appearance that was about to take place. The honor of trimming back Genji's hair fell to the Minister of the Treasury, whose face betrayed the pain he felt the moment he cut Genji's beautiful locks. The Emperor had a hard time keeping his emotions in check. *If only his mother were here to see this ceremony,* he thought, struggling to maintain his composure.

The capping ritual followed, and when that was finished, Genji withdrew to an antechamber to rest and change into the formal attire of an adult: an outer robe with the underarm vents sewn up. Stepping down into the garden east of the Seiryōden, he faced his father and performed obeisance, placing his ceremonial wand on the ground, rising and bowing left, right and left again, then sitting and repeating his actions to show his gratitude. He cut such a magnificent figure that all in attendance were moved to tears. As might be expected, the Emperor found it harder than the others to hide his feelings. At that moment the sad events of the past, which he normally kept himself from dwelling on, came flooding back. Since Genji was still at a tender age, His Majesty had fretted that cutting his locks and putting his hair up in the style of an adult man would spoil his looks. To his amazement the ceremony only added to Genji's aura of masculine beauty.

The Minister of the Left, who performed the capping ritual, had taken the younger sister of the Emperor as his principal wife. She gave him a daughter, whom he doted upon, raising her with the utmost care. The Minister was troubled when he learned that the Crown Prince evidently desired his daughter, because he was secretly planning to arrange a match for her with Genji. And so in the days leading up to the ceremony, he approached the Emperor with his proposal.

"I see," His Majesty replied. "Well . . . given that the boy seems to have no patrons for his coming-of-age ceremony, and since we have to select an aristocratic young woman to sleep with him on the night of his initiation, let's choose your daughter." Thus encouraged, the Minister followed through with his plans.

After the ceremony, Genji withdrew into the attendant's antechamber. As the party was making a celebratory toast in his honor, the Emperor gave permission for Genji, who had no rank, to sit at a place below the imperial princes but above the ministers. The Minister of the Left, who was seated next to him, casually dropped a few hints about his daughter, but Genji, who was still at an age when he felt diffident and embarrassed about such matters, did not respond.

An attendant from the imperial household staff brought a message from the Emperor to the Minister, requesting his presence. The Minister went to the imperial quarters, where a senior lady-in-waiting presented him with the appropriate gifts that custom demanded: a white oversized woman's robe made especially for this presentation, along with a set of three robes. His Majesty vented his pent-up emotions, presenting a cup of rice wine to the Minister and reminding him of his responsibilities toward Genji:

6. In premodern Japan the hours of the day, like the months, were designated by the signs of the Chinese zodiac. The Hour of the Monkey was about 3–5 p.m. [editor's note].

When you with purple cords first bound his hair
Did you not also bind your heart and swear
Eternal vows to give him your daughter

The Minister composed this reply:

So long as the deep purple of these cords that bind
Our hearts as tightly as your son's hair never fade
So our mutual vow will retain its deep hue

He stepped down from the long bridge that connected the imperial residence in the Seiryōden and the Ceremonial Court in the Shishinden and performed obeisance in the east garden. There he received a horse from the Left Division of the Imperial Stables and a falcon caged in a mew from the Office of the Chamberlain. Princes and nobles lined up along the foot of the stairs leading down from the Seiryōden into the east garden, and they each received gifts appropriate to their rank.

Decorative boxes of thin cypress wood filled with delicacies and baskets of fruit were among the items prepared for the Emperor that day. The Major Controller of the Right, who had acted earlier as Genji's guardian, had been put in charge of the presentations. The garden overflowed with trays stacked with rice cakes flavored with various fillings and with four-legged chests of Chinese-style lacquer stuffed with presents for the lower-ranking attendants—so many that their numbers surpassed even the presentations made at the coming-of-age ceremony held for the Crown Prince. Indeed, it was an incomparably magnificent affair.

That evening, Genji departed for the residence of the Minister of the Left, which was located on Sanjō Avenue. The ceremony welcoming Genji as groom and solemnizing his wedding was conducted with unprecedented attention to proper form. Feeling a touch of dread, the Minister was captivated by the masculine beauty of Genji, who still looked quite boyish. In contrast his daughter, who at sixteen was four years older than her new husband, was put off by Genji's youthfulness and considered their match inappropriate.

The Minister enjoyed the full confidence of the Emperor. After all, his principal wife, the mother of the bride, was His Majesty's full sister. Thus, the bride came from a distinguished line on both sides of her family. Moreover, the addition of Genji to the Minister's family diminished the prestige of his rival the Minister of the Right, who as grandfather of the Crown Prince would eventually assume power as Chancellor. The Minister of the Left had numerous children by several wives. His principal wife had given him, in addition to Genji's bride, a son who was now Middle Captain in the Inner Palace Guard. This young man, Tō no Chūjō,[7] was exceptionally handsome, and the Minister of the Right could hardly ignore such a promising prospect, even though he was not on good terms with the Minister of the Left, his main rival for power. He therefore arranged to marry the young Tō no Chūjō to his fourth daughter, who

---

7. I am following custom and using this name for Genji's close friend, brother-in-law, and rival. The name Tō no Chūjō refers to his positions as Middle Captain in the Inner Palace Guard (*Chūjō*) and in the Office of the Chamberlain. Like most of the male characters, he is identified by his position at court throughout the narrative, but since his positions and ranks change over time, it is easier to refer to him throughout by this initial appellation.

was his greatest treasure in the world. His regard for his son-in-law was every bit as strong as that given to Genji by the Minister of the Left. For their part, the two young men forged an ideal friendship.

Because the Emperor was always summoning him, Genji found it difficult to live at his wife's residence.[8] In his heart, he was obsessed with the matchless beauty of the Fujitsubo Consort, who seemed to be exactly the kind of woman he wanted to take as his wife. *Is there no one else like her?* he wondered. He found his bride to be a woman of great charm and proper training, but he was not really attracted to her. He had been drawn to Fujitsubo when he was a child, and the torment caused by his feelings for her was excruciating. Now that he was an adult, he was no longer permitted behind the curtains of the consorts. Whenever there was a musical entertainment, he would play the flute in accompaniment to Fujitsubo's koto, his notes subtly conveying his true feelings for her. The sound of her soft voice was a comfort to him, and the only time he felt happy was when he was at the palace. He would serve there for five or six days in succession, occasionally spending a mere two or three days at his wife's residence. His father-in-law attributed Genji's behavior to his youth and did not fault him for it, but instead continued to do all he could to offer support at court. He chose only the most exceptional ladies-in-waiting to serve his son-in-law and daughter, and he went out of his way to put on the musical entertainments that Genji so enjoyed and to show him every favor.

When Genji stayed at the palace, he took up residence in the Kiritsubo. The women who had once served his mother had not been dismissed and scattered, and so they were now assigned to wait on him. Orders were sent down to the Office of Palace Repairs and to the Bureau of Skilled Artisans to rebuild and expand the former residence of Genji's mother, a villa on Nijō Avenue. The project was to be carried out so splendidly that there would be no other villa like it. The setting of the surrounding woods and hills was already unparalleled, and when the garden pond was enlarged, the result was so eye-catching that it created a stir. Genji thought wistfully that such a villa would be the perfect residence for a wife who had all the qualities of his ideal woman, Fujitsubo.

It is said that it was the Korean diviner who, in his admiration, first bestowed on Genji the sobriquet Radiant Prince.

From Chapter II

Hahakigi

BROOM CYPRESS

The Radiant Prince—a splendid, if somewhat bombastic, title. In fact, his failings were so numerous that such a lofty sobriquet was perhaps misleading. He engaged in all sorts of flings and dalliances, but he sought to keep them secret out of fear that he would become fodder for gossips who delighted in circulating

---

8. Uxorilocal marriage arrangements were widespread in the Heian period, and thus it was common for a young nobleman to make his father-in-law's residence his primary abode [editor's note].

rumors about him and end up leaving to later generations a reputation as a careless, frivolous man. Genji was keen to avoid the censure of the court and, thus constrained, went about feigning a serious and earnest demeanor for a time, abstaining from all elegantly seductive or charming affairs. No doubt the Lesser Captain of Takano, that legendary lover, would have been amused.[9]

Genji was serving as Middle Captain in the Palace Guard at the time, and in fact he preferred being stationed there. Consequently, his visits to his wife, who resided at the estate of her father, the Minister of the Left, all but ceased. Although people expressed their suspicions about him, wondering if his heart wasn't in wild turmoil over a secret lover, Genji was not the sort who carried on common affairs impulsively or brazenly. There were rare occasions, however, when he strayed from his professed path of moderation, and he had an unfortunate tendency to become obsessed with relationships that brought him stress and pain, giving himself over entirely to behavior that could hardly be called proper.

During a stretch in the rainy season when there was no break in the clouds, a directional taboo[1] forced Genji to stay on and attend the Emperor for a longer than normal period. The members of the household of the Minister of the Left grew anxious and resentful at Genji's neglect of his wife, but they continued to arrange every detail of his wardrobe so that he would cut a remarkable figure at court. Moreover, the sons of the Minister, Genji's brothers-in law, would spend all their free time in Genji's palace quarters when they happened to be in service. One of these sons, Tō no Chūjō, was a Middle Captain who also served in the Office of the Chamberlain. He was a full sibling to Genji's wife—he and his sister had both been born to Princess Ōmiya—and of all the Minister's children he was closest to Genji and could behave in a more intimate and relaxed manner in his friend's presence at entertainments and amusements. Tō no Chūjō preferred the company of Genji because the residence that his own father-in-law, the Minister of the Right, had painstakingly provided and maintained for him and his wife was a dreary, uninspiring place. It must be added that he was fond of having affairs with other women.

Tō no Chūjō also had dazzlingly furnished quarters at his father's residence at Sanjō, but he was always accompanying Genji on his comings and goings. They were constantly together, day and night, pursuing the same interests and diversions, and he in no way lagged behind the Radiant Prince in his accomplishments. Because they were inseparable, it was natural that they did not stand on ceremony with one another. They never kept their innermost feelings hidden, but displayed an easygoing harmony whenever they spoke.

They had endured an especially tedious day, having spent the time in idleness on account of the interminable rain, and because the palace seemed practically deserted during the early evening hours, Genji's quarters took on a more relaxed atmosphere than usual. Drawing an oil lamp beside him, Genji perused some Chinese classics. Tō no Chūjō pulled out some letters written on paper of vari-

9. The tale of the amorous Lesser Captain of Takano referred to here has not survived.
1. A directional taboo, or prohibition, required a person to avoid traveling in a certain direction so as not to disturb gods whose movements over time were predictable (based on Chinese zodiacal and calendrical practices) and could be charted by the Bureau of Divination. Such prohibitions were often used as a convenient excuse for a gentleman to avoid meeting his wife or lover [editor's note].

ous hues from a small cabinet near him and was seized by the desire to read them. Genji would not allow that, but he did say, "I'll let you look at a few of the more appropriate ones . . . there are several I'd be ashamed for you to read."

Tō no Chūjō resented his friend's refusal. "But it's just those letters you don't feel free to share with me that I'm curious to see. I've exchanged many letters of the most common variety with ladies of all ranks, and at the time we were corresponding I couldn't wait to read them. Yet when I reread them now, the only ones really worthwhile were written when the women were being petulant or impatient with me for keeping them waiting."

Despite his protests, he knew full well that Genji would never have letters from high-ranking ladies—letters that had to be kept strictly confidential—lying scattered about in a commonplace cabinet like this where anyone could see them. Genji would certainly hide his most intriguing missives in a secret location, and would be comfortable sharing only those from easygoing ladies of decidedly second-rate backgrounds.

"Well, you certainly have a lot of them, don't you?" said Tō no Chūjō, who went on to interrogate Genji about the author of each of the missives. He found it amusing that his suppositions and guesses about the letters were sometimes right on the money, and other times wildly off the mark. Still, Genji gave very little away, and, by leading his friend on, he managed to disguise the identities of the letter writers.

"You must have a great number of letters at your place," said Genji. "I'd really like to take a peek at them. If you let me, I'll gladly open this cabinet to you."

"I have very few worth looking at," Tō no Chūjō answered. "You see, I've come to the realization that as far as women are concerned, there aren't many who are flawless enough to make you think *she's the one*. I've come across many who have passable skills in the arts, who can write flowing characters that create an impression of superficial elegance, who show a kind of facile understanding of how to respond in verse on certain occasions. Yet even when one chooses a woman on the basis of such accomplishments, she almost always fails to live up to the expectations created by her talents and disappoints in the end. She'll swell with pride, going on and on about her own accomplishments, looking down on others and, all in all, behaving rather foolishly. Her parents are always waiting on her, spoiling her with affection and lavishing attention, keeping their precious little princess hidden away in the recesses of their estates until some man hears about her extraordinary gifts and gets all worked up. Beautiful, young, and carefree, with little to distract her, she'll follow the lead of others, dedicate herself to some trivial diversion, and as a result acquire and perfect some skill. Naturally, those who look after her keep silent about her flaws, keeping up appearances and spreading plausible-sounding rumors that make her seem better than she really is. Since such rumors are all a man has to go on, can he really afford to assume the worst about her without actually meeting her? So a man goes about, wondering if she's the genuine article, and when they finally meet . . . well, it's rare that a woman actually lives up to her reputation."

Listening to Tō no Chūjō's lament, which gave the impression of a world-weary man who had experienced the shame of such disappointments, Genji smiled wryly. Although he knew that his friend's account of women was hardly the whole of the matter, he had had a few affairs that matched Tō no Chūjō's experiences.

"Can there really be women," Genji asked, "who lack even the most trivial merits?"

"I'm not saying that," Tō no Chūjō responded. "Who would be foolish enough to be drawn to a woman with absolutely no talent? A woman who has nothing to recommend her is as rare as one who is perfect in every way. My point is that a woman who is born into the nobility is raised with the greatest care, which includes concealing her many faults. So of course she's going to look superior to other women. A woman born into a family of middling rank will reveal her sensibility and habits of mind with a style and personality all her own, and so you would expect to discover various things that distinguish her from others. As for women of the lowest class . . . well, I'm not especially interested in learning anything about them."

Genji's curiosity was piqued by the worldly posture his friend had assumed. "I wonder about your standards. Can you really classify all women on the basis of just three levels? How do you discriminate between a woman born of a noble family . . . say rank three or above . . . whose social position has been ruined and whose rank has fallen so that it is indistinguishable from others, and a woman of less distinguished background . . . say rank four or lower . . . whose family has so prospered at court that they can now lavishly furnish her residence and adopt a smug attitude that proclaims their daughter inferior to no one?"

Just as Genji posed his question, the Warden of the Left Mounted Guard and the Junior Secretary from the Ministry of Rites showed up, explaining that directional prohibitions for that day were keeping them confined to the palace. They both had reputations as elegant lovers, and since they were also eloquent speakers—fluent, logical, and precise—Tō no Chūjō was eager to detain them and get their opinions on his idea of classifying women according to three levels. Their subsequent conversation touched upon topics of a highly questionable and even slightly disreputable nature.

The Warden addressed the matter straightaway. "A woman who is a parvenu will likely be judged by court society as inferior despite her rise in status, especially if her pedigree is not appropriate to her rank. On the other hand, a woman who may have a distinguished pedigree, but who lacks the means to make her way at court, will see her fortunes and position diminish over time, and her prospects and reputation crumble away until she cannot maintain her status in spite of her pride. Events will then conspire to make her situation more and more untenable. Looking at each of these types of women, I'm afraid we have to relegate them both to your middle category. Provincial governors toil away, tied up with petty people and affairs, but even among that lot, consigned to a middling station in life, there are various gradations that distinguish them. We live in an age when we sometimes find governors who are really not at all inferior, even though they come from the middle ranks. Actually, there are some of the fourth rank who are qualified to serve as a counselor, who have unsullied reputations and comfortable fortunes and prospects, and who are easier to take than some inexperienced or immature nobility of higher rank. There are many instances of such men who maintain splendid households where their daughters are nurtured with the utmost care. Nothing is lacking, nothing held back, no expense spared to raise them in the most dazzling manner . . . and as a result they grow into excellent young ladies who are beyond reproach. These women go into court service and many of them find unexpected good fortune, marrying above their station."

Genji smiled at that. "I guess that when all is said and done, the key is finding a girl from a rich family."

Tō no Chūjō responded petulantly. "Now you're talking nonsense. Such a remark is not worthy of you."

The Warden continued his disquisition: "The highborn lady who brings together both pedigree and public reputation, yet who in private lacks personal breeding and manners, is eccentric and not worth discussing. She's the type who makes you wonder in disappointment how she could have been brought up like that. Of course, it strikes you as perfectly natural when a woman's pedigree and reputation are in harmony and her character is flawless. So you assume that's the way things ought to be and aren't surprised by her, even though such a woman is a rarity. But perhaps I should set aside any discussion of the highest-ranking ladies, for someone as lowly as I could never be on their level.

"Beyond these types, you sometimes unexpectedly come across an adorable, defenseless girl whose existence is unknown to court society. She lives in a lonely, sublimely dilapidated residence shut away from the world behind a gate overgrown with weeds, and so of course you think of her as an exceptionally rare find. You're mysteriously drawn to her, your imagination stimulated by the things that make her different, and you wonder how she could have ended up in a place like that. Her father is likely to be some pathetic, overweight old man, her brothers probably all have unpleasant faces, and there in the women's quarters in the inner recesses of the residence . . . which, no matter how you try to imagine it, is nothing out of the ordinary . . . is a fiercely proud lady with all the refined demeanor of one who has somehow managed to acquire some accomplishments, even if she is not of the first rank and thus not all that much to talk about. And yet because you would never expect to find a woman like that in such a place, how could you not find her alluring? Of course, you can't compare the discovery of a woman like that to opting for a flawless woman of superior rank, but by the same token it is difficult to simply toss her aside."

The Warden glanced knowingly at the Junior Secretary, who, interpreting the expression as a subtle reference to the flawless reputation of his own sister, kept his counsel on the matter.

Genji seemed lost in thought: *I wonder about all this. Are there really women like that out in the world? After all, when I consider my wife, there don't seem to be any perfect women among the highest classes.*

Genji was dressed in an intentionally casual manner in an informal robe, minus trousers, over soft white under-robes. He had neglected to tie up the cords of his outer robes, and as he half-reclined amidst his books and papers in the dim shadows cast by the lamp, he cut such an attractive figure that the other men felt a desire to see him as a woman. He was so beautiful that pairing him with the very finest of the ladies at the court would fail to do him justice.

During the course of the young men's discussion of various types of women, the Warden remarked, "There are women who are flawless enough for a commonplace affair, but when the time comes to take a wife, you find it impossible to decide even if you have a large number of women to choose from. The same is true of men who serve at court and are expected to be rock-solid pillars of society. It proves quite difficult to produce a man of true worth and ability, and so no matter how gifted or clever he may be, in the end there will never be more than one or two who are fit to govern. That's why superior people command their inferiors, and inferiors follow their superiors, mutually accommodating each other to carry out public affairs.

"Now then, just consider the person who is to take charge of the private affairs of your household. It wouldn't do at all if she doesn't have the proper qualifications. That being the case, a man is naturally going to look around because he knows that a woman may possess some good qualities while lacking others. After all, it is rare to find one who, though maybe not perfect, is at least acceptable . . . and even a man who is not inclined to compare the appearance of one woman to another is going to take great care in making his decision, since the one he chooses will be his mate for life. All things being equal, he will take someone whose tastes match his own and who does not have the kind of flaws he must spend all his time correcting and setting in order. Well, this is all very hard, and a woman is not necessarily going to fulfill all of a man's expectations. That's why a man who does not allow his affections to stray, who focuses his attention on one woman and does not discard the karmic bonds of his first marriage vows, will always be seen as sincere, honest, and loyal. And a woman who is able to keep her husband from straying is the one we take to be refined and attractive.

"Given all that—how should I put this?—having observed all sorts of relationships in society, I can't help having doubts as to whether there is any woman who is perfectly elegant, or who can live up to the ideals in a man's heart. In the case of your lordships, what kind of woman could ever be worthy enough to meet your exalted standards? No doubt she would have to be young and beautiful and beyond reproach in every way. She would be well versed in composition, but her choice of words would be modest and her brushstrokes light and delicate, leaving you a little agitated and longing for a more revealing response. You are forced to wait, feeling unbearably impatient until that moment when you can get close enough to her to make your advances and exchange a few words. But she will say very little, speaking under her breath in a faint voice that shows how adept she is at concealing her flaws. Just when you think she is most pliant and feminine, she starts to fret about whether or not you really love her. And then when you humor her, she becomes flirtatious. This has to be the worst fault in women.

"Above all, a wife must never neglect her duty to assist her husband. A husband can get along well enough if a woman is not too emotionally demanding, does not make a big fuss over niceties, and doesn't give herself over to fashion. Of course, a man doesn't want a wife who is too serious, who busies herself with supporting her husband and managing the household to the extent that she keeps her hair swept back all the time, exposing her ears and making herself unattractive. A man who goes to work in the morning and returns home in the evening doesn't want to have to go to the trouble of talking with a stranger about the odd behavior of people he has encountered in public and private or about the good and bad things he has seen and heard. If he has a wife who is close to him and will listen to his stories and understand him, then doesn't he assume he should be able to discuss such matters with her? Maybe he suddenly recalls something and smiles, or perhaps tears come to his eyes, or maybe he relives some feeling of righteous indignation at something that happened to someone. Or he might have feelings that he just cannot keep to himself and thinks he might share them with her and ask her opinion. But if she is unattractive or too preoccupied to understand, he ends up turning away from her in disillusionment. Remembering something he has kept inside, a thought that makes him laugh or let out an audible sigh, he will mention it, almost as if speaking to himself, and all she will do is look up with a blank expression and reply, 'Did you just say something?' What man wouldn't regret marrying someone like that?

"When all is said and done, we men really should consider picking a completely childlike, compliant woman . . . a woman we can mold into an acceptable and flawless wife. Even when she gives you some cause for concern, you still have the feeling that there is some value in disciplining her. When you are with such a woman face to face, she is truly vulnerable and precious to you, and you are compelled to view her faults through forgiving eyes. Even so, there will be occasions when you have to be apart, and you tell her about something important that must be done, or give her some task, trivial or practical, that must be carried out to the letter. It will turn out that she cannot act on her own and is unable to do things as you instructed. This is really quite annoying and her unreliability will cause you no end of trouble. Why does it always seem that it's the cold, distant, slightly unpleasant woman who, depending on the occasion, is able to perform well in front of others and bring honor to your house?"

The Warden had tried to cover all aspects of the subject, but he was unable to come to any firm conclusions. Instead, he finished his analysis by heaving a great sigh. "Considering all of this," he continued, "you can't choose a wife solely on the basis of her family background, and certainly not on the basis of her looks alone. If you can find a woman who is not so strange or demure as to make you regret your choice, if she is serious through and through and has a quiet personality, then you ought to consider her dependable. Should she have any talents beyond these basic qualifications or be sweet-tempered, you should count yourself lucky. Even if she is deficient in certain respects, you shouldn't make unreasonable demands for her to improve. So long as she is morally upright and not fretful or jealous, then she will over time acquire an outward grace. Her comportment will be modest, she will protect her honor, and she will endure things she has a right to complain about, hiding her resentment behind feigned ignorance or pretending to be nonchalant.

"Unfortunately, there are cases where a woman can no longer suppress the emotions that have been building up inside her heart, and she will leave behind some fierce words that chill your soul, or compose a moving poem to which she has attached a memento that will remind you of her, then hide herself away in some village deep in the mountains or on a deserted strand along the shore. When I was a child I would hear stories like that, which the ladies-in-waiting would read aloud, and I found them so touching I was moved to tears. Now, when I think back on it, their tales seem frivolous and overly dramatic. A woman who casts aside a man who has deep feelings for her and runs off to hide in utter disregard of the husband's feelings, even when she has just cause for being upset, will stir anxieties that last a lifetime. The whole affair is extremely tiresome. Some people will praise her actions, saying how exquisitely profound her emotions are, and as a result her feelings of sad regret will accumulate to the point where she decides to become a nun. Having made up her mind, her heart seems pure and serene and she can no longer even consider returning to her former life. Her acquaintances come to call on her, telling her how melancholy it is that things should have come to this. When her husband hears of this he weeps, and the messenger and older ladies-in-waiting tell her what a shame it is and how sad that her husband has such deep feelings. The woman, who still has lingering affection for him, will then realize she had no reason to throw away his love. She will gather together the hair she had clipped from her forehead when she took vows as a nun and, feeling forlorn and helpless now that there is no turning back, will break down and cry. Though she had kept her emotions in check up to that moment, once she gives in to her feelings she is no longer able to hold back her tears whenever she considers her situation. Because she now seems to have so many regrets, the Buddha himself must look at her as one whose heart is tainted by base attachments. Halfhearted devotion to the Buddha is an even more certain path to Hell than being mired in the five evils of earthly existence.[2] Even if the marital bond was deep enough that the husband takes her back before she renounces the world, is there any couple that would not harbor at least some resentment upon recalling such an incident? For better or worse they live together as husband and wife, and their relationship is based on a deep karmic bond and shared emotions that can weather almost anything that might happen. Yet whenever a wife runs away, can any couple ever completely put aside their feelings of mutual reproach?

"It is folly for a wife to resent her husband, display her anger, and quarrel obsessively over some little affair he has had on the side. A man's affections may stray, but so long as he is still capable of the kind of feelings he had for her when they were first married, then she has good reason to think that their relationship has strong emotional bonds. If she makes a big fuss over his dalliances, however, those bonds may be cut for good.

"In general, then, a woman should be modest in all things. She should give a gentle hint when she knows something is going on that justifies her resentment. Or she should imply, without being spiteful, that there have been some occasions that have bothered her. If she behaves in such a way, her husband's regard for her will surely increase. Most of the time a man's wandering heart can be calmed by the guidance of his wife. A woman who is too lenient and turns a blind eye to her husband's behavior may in contrast seem easygoing and lovable, but in the end she will be dismissed as frivolous. As Bai Juyi put it, 'Who can tell where an unmoored ship will drift?'[3] Isn't that the truth?"

Tō no Chūjō nodded and replied, "Staying on the same subject, it's a serious matter when a person you like for their charm and sensitivity gives you cause to wonder if they can be trusted. Although people may choose to put up with their partner's wayward behavior and even fool themselves into believing they see some improvement, that doesn't mean that the wayward partner has reformed. In any case, when an indiscretion brings discord to a marriage, there is probably no better recourse than to calmly ignore it." His remarks described perfectly the situation of his own sister, which was no doubt his intention, and so it irritated him that her husband, Genji, was not joining in the discussion but was pretending to nod off instead.

2. In Buddhism the five evils are lust, wrath, greed, worldly attachment, and pride (ego).

3. A reference to a poem on marriage included in the collected writings of Bai (Bo) Juyi.

The Warden, who now found himself regarded as the expert on such matters, whinnied on and on. Tō no Chūjō, who wanted to hear what he had to say, assumed the role of disciple and listened eagerly.

"Compare women to artisans, if you will," the Warden continued. "For example, a woodworker may indulge his imagination and create all sorts of items . . . toys meant for a moment's diversion, objects not based on any model or pattern. These things look fashionable and amaze you with the cleverness of their construction, and insofar as they are new and different and in keeping with the times, they attract attention as modern and up-to-date and so have a certain charm. Yet when one has something of true beauty made properly . . . formal furnishings, say, or some decorative object for your residence that has a conventional form . . . the distinction between a maker of novelties and a master craftsman is plain for all to see. To take another example, there are many skilled painters at the palace, but when you have to pick one to do basic sketching for a work, it's hard to tell at a glance which ones are the truly skilled artists. Paintings that present startling scenes of the mountains on the Isle of Hōrai where the immortals dwell, or that show the stern visages of beasts from exotic lands or the faces of demons no man has ever seen, all give play to the imagination and astonish our eyes, since they bear no resemblance to the real world. Such works are fine, given what they are, and any painter should be able to execute them. But when it comes to realistically depicting scenes in the everyday world . . . mountain vistas, flowing streams, the appearance of our dwellings . . . what matters is the attention to detail and technique a master painter brings to his representation of both serenely commonplace objects and steep, rugged landscapes. Whether creating the impression that one is far removed from society by piling up layer upon layer of thick foliage, or giving one a sense of familiarity and comfort by foregrounding a garden enclosed by a bamboo fence, all such effects require a special power and grace far beyond the skills of an ordinary artist.

"Or take calligraphy. Even a person with no real knowledge of the art can add a flourish here and there to create the impression . . . at least at a cursory glance . . . that he has great talent, while a person who can in fact write with true skill and care may appear to lack the ability of a master. But when you compare the works of such people side by side, you can see that the latter is closer to the genuine thing. So it is with all trivial matters of art and pleasure. I know that when it comes to human emotions, it is even more the case that you cannot trust the affected elegance a woman puts on for show on a special occasion. Shall I tell you how I came by this knowledge, though I may have to speak indiscreetly about an affair?" He shifted a little closer, and Genji woke up. Tō no Chūjō was sitting across from him, his chin cupped in his hands, listening in earnest anticipation. It made for a charming tableau, resembling a scene in which a learned priest expounds on the ways of the world. It was the kind of moment, however, when young men find it hard to keep their relationships secret.

"Some time ago," the Warden resumed, "when I was still a very low-ranking official, I was quite taken with a young woman. But, as I presumed to mention to Your Highnesses earlier, she was not exceptionally beautiful, and so I decided in my youthful, fickle heart that I would not take her as my main wife. Though I thought of her as someone I could always turn to and rely on, there was something lacking, and I was sure I could do better. So I played around and cheated on her, and when she became distressingly jealous, she lost favor with me. I kept hoping that she would not be like that, and wanted her to be a little less sensitive. While I found it irksome that she was so unforgiving and suspicious, I was also puzzled that she had lost patience with a man of such a low rank as I. At the same time, I couldn't understand why she still had feelings for me. I often felt sorry for her, and so I eventually brought my tendency to stray under control.

"Her temperament was such that somehow or another she contrived to do her best for me, even in matters for which she had no innate ability. She prodded herself, ashamed of faults she didn't want others to see, and she earnestly supported me in every way, trying her best never to go against my wishes in even the slightest matter. At the beginning I had thought of her as a strong-willed woman, but in the end she was yielding and accommodating. She worried that she might put me off if she did not make herself attractive, and whenever she allowed herself to be seen by someone not close to her, she would fret about it, feeling that perhaps she had shamed her husband. She did her utmost to maintain her wifely virtue, and as we grew accustomed to living as husband and wife, I was not at all ill disposed toward her except for that one detestable flaw . . . her jealousy, which she could not control.

"At the time she seemed so absurdly obedient and fearful, I thought I should teach her a lesson . . . you know, shake her up a little so she would stop being jealous and mend her ways. So I pretended I was truly fed up and that we should break off our relationship. Since she had previously shown only a submissive attitude to me, I thought for sure I could teach her a lesson and intentionally treated her with wretched callousness. When, as usual, she got angry, I told her that if she were going to be so willful and disagreeable, I would put an end to our marriage and not meet her again despite the deep bond we shared as husband and wife. I said, 'If you really want us to separate, just keep harboring your baseless suspicions. But if you want us to have a long future together, then you have to accept that there will be hardships and try to not let things bother you. Rid yourself of your twisted disposition, and I will find you endearing. As soon as I work my way up at court and achieve respectable status, no other woman will ever compete with you for my devotion.' I thought I was being so clever in straightening her out with such assertive words, but she just smiled vaguely and replied, 'It doesn't bother or worry me that you are in a period in your life when you have neither status nor distinction, nor am I waiting impatiently for you to achieve success. But I find it painfully unbearable to have to always hide my feeling of wretchedness and rely on the uncertain hope that as the months and years go by the day will finally arrive when you reform your behavior. So the time has come when we must go our separate ways.' Her spiteful words made me very angry and I said a number of hateful things to her. At that point the woman, unable to control her passions, grabbed my hand and bit one of my fingers. I put on a show of outrage and, holding out my crooked finger, stalked out. 'Now that you've disfigured me like this,' I threatened, 'how can I possibly show myself at court? You yourself said I'm of no consequence, so now that you've done this, how do you expect me to get ahead? If this is how things are, then it looks like we really are through once and for all.' I composed a poem:

As I bend my wounded fingers counting
The times I called on you, your flaws it seems
Are not confined to jealousy alone

'You won't have me to resent anymore,' I said, and as expected she burst into tears and shot back:

Having counted in my heart the times
I showed restraint at your behavior
Now I have to take my hand from yours

"She challenged me in this manner, and even though I did not believe our relationship would really change, I drifted about seeing women here and there and let many days pass without once communicating with her. Then one night, near the end of the eleventh month, I was detained at the palace in order to rehearse music and dance for the Rinji Festival at the Kamo Shrine. A miserable sleet was falling that night, and as I was saying goodbye to my companions, who were going their separate ways, it occurred to me that I had no other place to go but hers. Sleeping at the palace seemed a dreary prospect, and the thought of visiting some woman who puts on an air of refined elegance chilled me to the bone. And so, all the while wondering what she thought about me, I went to peek in on her and see how she was faring. As I brushed the snow off myself, I felt constrained by feelings of embarrassment, and yet I hoped that perhaps tonight her icy resentment had thawed. The lamps had been dimmed and turned toward the walls, and softly padded robes had been plumped up and hung over a large filigree basket to be warmed and perfumed. The blinds were raised just as they were supposed to be, and the room gave the appearance that she had been waiting for me to return that very evening. Since everything was prepared just to my liking, I felt a swelling pride until I noticed she was nowhere to be found. Only the women who served her were there, as I had expected, and they told me she had gone to her parents' residence for the evening. She had left no elegant poem to rouse my interest, no word at all that she was anxious to see me. She had simply left and locked herself away, showing no consideration for me. I was quite let down and couldn't help wondering if her unyielding spitefulness wasn't implicitly signaling to me that I should go ahead and hate her if I wanted. The rooms gave no indication she was having an affair . . . was her aim to make me angry and suspicious of her? Yet the hues and stitching of the robes she had laid out for me were prepared with more than normal care, just as I would have wished. Clearly she was taking care to look after me even though she now assumed I had abandoned her.

"Things being the way they were, I figured she would never cut me off completely, and so I tried to downplay our spat and make up with her. And though she did not defy me by hiding herself away and making me run around looking for me or by replying in a way that would cause me embarrassment, still she told me, 'I cannot continue putting up with you the way you are now. If you reform and develop a more steady disposition, then maybe we can see each other.' Even though she spoke to me like that, I was convinced she could never leave me, and so I thought I'd let her stew a while longer to punish her. 'All right, then, let's do as you suggest,' I told her, showing her just how stubborn I could be. She suffered so much during that time that at last she died. I knew then that I should never have made light of her, and I can't help thinking now that it's good enough for a man if his wife is someone who is wholly dependable. It was always worthwhile talking to her, regardless of whether we were discussing some trivial, passing matter or an important issue. She was so skilled at dyeing cloth that it's no exaggeration to compare her to the goddess of fall foliage, Princess Tatsuta herself. And when it came to weaving, she was as skillful as the Celestial Weaver Maid we celebrate at Tanabata.[4] Gifted in such ways, she was an exceptional wife."

The Warden felt a keen sorrow at the memory. Tō no Chūjō tried to console him, saying, "Her weaving may have been unsurpassed, but her real virtue was following the example of the Celestial Weaver Maid, who faithfully keeps her vow of love with the Herdsman. The fact is, you cannot expect to find someone again whose weaving compares with that of Princess Tatsuta. When the passing flowers or autumn foliage are not in harmony with the hues of the season, they do not stand out as brightly, and their beauty dissipates. Women are just like that . . . their beauty passing out of season. That's why it's so difficult in this hard life to decide upon a wife."

These words acted as encouragement to the Warden, who promptly resumed his discussion. "After she died, I started calling on a woman whose family lineage was peerless and who seemed to have an exquisitely refined temperament. She wrote poetry in a flowing hand, was well trained in the plucking style of the koto, and sang like a master. I couldn't find any flaws in anything I saw or heard of her. She was also passably good-looking, and so even while I continued to be on familiar terms with the woman who bit my finger, I was also secretly visiting this other woman and eventually grew very attracted to her. After the death of my wife, while I was grieving and wondering what I should do, I came to the realization that nothing could be done for those who have died and started visiting the other woman more frequently. After I became familiar with her, I began to notice that she was somewhat ostentatious . . . and flirtatious. Since she did not seem to be the sort of woman I could trust, I began to keep my distance a little, and when I did so she started meeting another man in secret.

"It was an autumn evening during the tenth month. The moon was bright and seductive, and as I set out from the palace I encountered a certain high-ranking courtier. We got into my carriage together, and though I was intending to stay the night at the home of my father, who was a Major Counselor at the time, this courtier told me he was quite eager to stop by a certain place where a woman was waiting for him. Because the house he mentioned happened to be on the way to my father's house, I caught a glimpse of its garden through the fence and saw the moon shimmering on the surface of the pond. Finding it hard to pass by a dwelling where even the moon seemed to have taken up residence, I dismounted the carriage with the man. He apparently had had this sort of rendezvous before and seemed very excited when he sat down on the widely spaced

4. Tanabata is a festival on the seventh day of the seventh lunar month that celebrates the annual meeting of the young lovers Orihime (the Celestial Weaver Maid, i.e., the star Vega) and Hikoboshi (the Celestial Oxherd, i.e., the star Altair). Because their love distracted them from their heavenly responsibilities, they were separated by the Milky Way and are allowed to meet only once a year, crossing over a bridge formed by the wings of a flock of magpies. Princess Tatsuta (Tatsuta-hime) is the goddess of fall who weaves the brocade of autumn foliage on Mount Tatsuta. She is thus the patron goddess of weaving and dyeing.

boards of an open veranda near the inner gate. He struck a dashing pose as he gazed up at the moon. Chrysanthemums, their colors faded by the autumn frost, were arrayed gorgeously, and the scarlet profusion of scattered maple leaves rustling in the breeze looked magnificent. The man took out a flute from the breast fold of his robe and began to play various popular *saibara* such as 'The Shade Is Good.'[5] He also sang a few verses: 'Let us tarry awhile at the well of Asuka, the shade is good, the waters cool, the grasses inviting . . .' The woman inside accompanied him skillfully, having apparently readied her six-string koto. Her instrument reverberated clearly, and she played it flawlessly, softly, having tuned it to a folksy minor key, and the sound that wafted from the other side of the bamboo blinds seemed quite fashionably modern, a perfect accompaniment to the pure autumn moon. The man was charmed and impressed and moved closer to the blind. Alluding to a poem about visiting the abode of a beautiful woman, he tried to get a response from her, saying, 'I see no trace of anyone having disturbed the fallen leaves in your garden.' He picked some chrysanthemums and composed a poem:

> How lovely are the peerless moon
> And music here . . . yet do they draw
> None but coldhearted men to you

'I hear you have spoken ill of me. But never mind. Let me have one more song. When a person you want to encourage to listen is present, you should put all your skills on display.' The woman replied to his brazen bantering, affecting a disinterested voice:

> A leaf can never hope to stay the autumn breeze
> Any more than words or music could make tarry
> This flutist who accompanies the bitter wind

"She responded seductively, unaware that I was witness to her distasteful forwardness. She then switched to a larger thirteen-string koto tuned to the *ban-shiki* mode,[6] darker in tone and thus appropriate for the season. Her style of plucking was lively and contemporary, and yet even though her playing sparkled, listening to her left me feeling unsettled and embarrassed. When a lady you are seeing intimately from time to time goes out of her way to be fashionably elegant, she is certainly very alluring, at least on those infrequent occasions when you actually meet. But if on one of your rare visits a woman you are considering as a possible mate behaves too voluptuously, then you begin to grow wary and worry she might not be reliable after all. On the basis of what I observed that evening, I decided to end my affair with that lady.

"Though I was young and inexperienced at the time, when I look back and compare those two women, their capriciousness made them seem inscrutable and unreliable to me. And from now on I will likely be even more inclined to

5. The genre of music referred to here, the *saibara*, was a popular form in which the lyrics of folk songs (usually) were set to Chinese music. Lines from various *saibara* appear throughout the narrative.

6. This is one of six modes (or keys) used in *gagaku*, Japanese court music, which is based largely on the court music of Tang China. The various modes usually had seasonal or poetic associations.

feel that way about women. Your lordships may take delight only in the pleasures of those fragile and fleeting charms of a young lady whom poets would
liken to the dew on bush clover that scatters when you pluck the flower, or to
sleet on leaves of dwarf bamboo that melts away at your touch. But though you
may feel that way now, just wait another seven years, and when you reach my
age you will think the same way I do. Please take my poor, humble advice and
be careful with women who lead you on. They'll cheat on you and make you
look foolish in the eyes of others."

And so he advised them.

Tō no Chūjō continued to nod his head.

Genji smiled faintly, apparently agreeing with the Warden, then remarked,
"It seems in both cases your romantic escapades were awkward and unlucky."
They all had a good laugh.

Tō no Chūjō spoke up next: "I'd like to tell you about a foolish woman I knew.
I started seeing her in secret, and because it looked as though I would have to
keep seeing her on the sly, I didn't think our affair would last. But as we grew
intimate I came to have deeper feelings for her, and even though I could not
meet her very often, I simply couldn't get her out of my mind. Eventually our
relationship reached the stage where I could see she trusted me, and many times
I honestly thought if she depends on me so much, then there must be things I
do that upset her. If there were, however, she never let on about them. Even
when I did not visit her for long stretches, she did not jealously resent me or
think me inconsiderate. Instead, she kept up appearances morning and night,
as if she expected me every day. She was so meek and docile that I was moved
to pity and assured her that she could always rely on me.

"She had no parents and was quite lonely and helpless. That's why I found
it touching that she apparently thought of me as her provider. She was so
quiet and unassuming that I was unconcerned and let my guard down. But
then, during one of those long stretches when I did not call on her, she
received some rather deplorable messages from my wife's household . . . messages that implied threats against her. Unfortunately, I heard about that only
much later.

"I was unaware there had been such unpleasantness, and even though I had
not forgotten her, we went so long without exchanging a word that she grew
despondent. She was so wretched worrying over the baby girl I had fathered by
her that she sent me a wild pink, suggesting, I suppose, that the child was like
the flower, hidden from sight and easy to overlook." Tears welled up in Tō no
Chūjō's eyes.

"And the letter that accompanied the flower?" asked Genji.

"Nothing special, really," he replied. "She sent this poem:

> *The hedge around the hut of the mountain peasant*
> *Grows untended now . . . let fall your tender mercy*
> *Let it fall like dew and settle on this wild pink*[7]

---

7. The word I have translated as "wild pink" is
nadeshiko. In the two poems that follow immediately below, the word for wild pink is
tokonatsu. Although the two names refer to

the exact same flower, Murasaki Shikibu uses
both in this sequence of poems to distinguish
between mother and child. In the first poem,
nadeshiko refers to Tō no Chūjō's child by his

"With her verse fresh in my mind, I went to see her. She was as faithful and uncomplaining as ever, but her face was worn with care. It was autumn, and as she gazed out from her dilapidated house at the overgrown garden drenched in dew, her tearful expression seemed to vie in sadness with the melancholy chirring of the bell crickets. I felt as though I were part of some old romance:

> *I cannot judge which of these flowers is fairest*
> *Their colors mingling in never-ending summer*
> *But there is none dearer than my little wild pink*

"I turned my attention from the child and comforted the lady by reminding her of the old poem in which a lover promises to visit always, so that dust never settles on their bed.[8] She replied with this.

> *Autumn arrives and rough winds shake*
> *Dew from wild pinks and tears from sleeves*
> *That wipe dust from my lonely bed*

"She spoke casually, giving no hint that she harbored any serious resentment. Even when she wept, she seemed ashamed and awkward and tried to hide her face from me. It pained her to think that I might view her suffering as accusatory, and that attitude so reassured me about our relationship that I did not visit her again for a long time. During that interval she ran off, disappearing without a trace.

"She may still be alive somewhere, but her situation must be precarious and uncertain. If only she had given me some indication of how strongly attached she was to me at that moment when I was so moved by her plight, then she would never have had to run away like that. I would never have neglected her as I did but would have treated her properly, just like any other woman I called on, and looked after her forever. I cherished that little wild pink and so assumed I would always be able to visit her. But now I am unable to track her whereabouts. Certainly this woman is an example of the unreliable type you mentioned earlier. She appeared so unruffled, never letting on that she found my treatment of her cruel, but in the end my feelings for her, which had never waned, turned out to be nothing more than a futile, one-sided love. Now, even as I am slowly getting her out of my heart, I sometimes think about her, imagining that she has not forgotten me altogether . . . that there are evenings when she realizes she cannot blame anyone else for her predicament and her heart

---

lover, while in the second and third poems *tokonatsu* refers to the woman. Both *nadeshiko* and *tokonatsu* may be identified as other flowers (e.g., a carnation or a gillyflower), but both are generic names for pinks. I have chosen to use the name "wild pink" to suggest the well-worn theme in the tradition of Japanese literature that Murasaki Shikibu drew on of a beautiful lover who is discovered by a man in an out-of-the-way place, like a wildflower growing in a hidden spot. The two poems below also play on the word *tokonatsu,* which is a homophone for "never-ending summer," and

which has an element, *toko,* that is a homophone for "bed." [The mother appears in chapter 4 (*Yūgao*) as Genji's lover, the lady of the Evening Faces. The little girl is the future Tamakazura, who will later be taken in by Genji. In chapter 25, included below, she discusses with Genji the virtues and vices of romantic tales—Editor's note].
8. *Kokinshū* 167 (Ōshikōchi no Mitsune): "I long to stop even a mote of dust from settling on this bed of pinks that have come into bloom since first you and I lay on our bed."

smolders with regret. She is certainly the type of woman you cannot rely on or hold to for very long.

"Although a difficult woman is memorable, and thus hard to get out of your mind, when things do not go well and you find it troublesome to continue seeing her . . . as you found with the woman who bit your finger . . . you tire of the relationship. And a talented woman like your koto player is almost certain to be burdened by the sin of infidelity. As for the woman I spoke of, she was so utterly lacking in character that I have doubts about her as well. So I have reached the point where I find it impossible to choose which type of woman is best. It has proven difficult to compare each respective relationship between men and women in this manner. Where is the woman who could combine the virtues of the three women we discussed without inevitably bringing with her all their unmanageable flaws? Set your sights on the beautiful goddess of fortune, Kichijōten,[9] and not only will her holiness bore you stiff, but you'll end up reeking of incense to boot!"

The young men all laughed at that.

"But come now," Tō no Chūjō prodded the Junior Secretary from the Ministry of Rites. "There must be a few unusual affairs going on around your place. Tell us a little about them."

"Do you honestly think anything worth discussing happens in a place as lowly as mine?" the young man asked.

Tō no Chūjō remained insistent, however. He declared that he was waiting for a response, and so the Junior Secretary wracked his brain to come up with some tale.

"When I was still a student of letters in the Bureau of Education,[1] I happened to be calling on a clever young woman. Like the woman the Warden mentioned, she was a good companion. I could discuss official matters with her, and she was also deeply prudent when it came to the conduct of household affairs. Her brilliance would put an unprepared scholar to shame, and so it was hard to hold my own with her in any conversation we had.

"I began to attend an academy to study Chinese with a certain scholar who just happened to have many daughters. As things turned out, I became intimate with one of them, and when her father found out, he brought out some ceremonial sake cups and spoke to me in an overly suggestive tone, reciting a line from Bai Juyi's poem in praise of marriage: 'Listen while I recite a poem about the two paths of life.' You know the poem . . . the one that extols the virtues of a wife who comes from an impoverished home and urges the husband to cherish her. I hadn't actually fallen head over heels for the woman or anything like that, but I was mindful of her father's feelings. In any case I was beholden to him, and she was a kind and considerate support to me. Even during our pillow talk she would impart her knowledge of Chinese, teaching many crucial things I would need for my official position. Her own writing was clear, almost man-

9. Images of Kichijōten were common in Buddhist temples, and it was said that monks often fell in love with her [editor's note].

1. This official academy or university was loosely based on Chinese bureaucratic models and used to train young men for positions in the government. The course of study largely emphasized the Confucian canon and focused on the fields of Chinese classics, law, ethics, and letters (primarily history and poetry). It also provided instruction in practical fields such as mathematics and yin-yang studies (i.e., divination) [editor's note].

nish. She employed a precise, rational diction and never mixed the more feminine *kana* script with her Chinese characters. Naturally I couldn't break off the
relationship, because with her as my teacher I was able to learn how to write
halting verses in Chinese. Even now I can't forget the debt I owe her . . . but
then again, for a man like me who has no intellectual talents at all to have to
rely on a woman I was intimate with and have her witness my pathetic performances . . . well, it was too shameful. Your lordships, of course, would never
need such an efficient and rigorous helpmate. As for me, even though our relationship strikes me as trivial and regrettable now, at the same time she was
someone I was drawn to, perhaps as a result of a karmic bond from a former
life. It seems that men are really the feckless ones."

The moment he finished, both Genji and Tō no Chūjō cajoled him, saying,
"Well, well, a most intriguing lady indeed," in order to get him to finish up his
story. Knowing he was being led on, the Junior Secretary feigned distaste, a
comical sneer crinkling his nose as he continued.

"Now then, I did not go to see her for the longest time, and when I finally
dropped in on some errand, she was not at all the relaxed, familiar woman she
had once been, but instead stayed behind a bothersome screen when we met.
It seemed to me she was being peevish, which was foolish behavior, and so I
thought this might be the perfect opportunity to break up with her. Yet I knew
that such an intelligent woman would never hold a grudge for a frivolous reason. She understood the ways of the world and would not be resentful. She
spoke in a voice that sounded rushed and breathy. 'These past few months I
have been indisposed by a severe malady and prescribed a regimen of herbal
tonic concocted mainly of garlic. This has rendered me extremely malodorous
and incapable of meeting you tête-à-tête. Though we cannot meet directly, I
would be pleased to undertake any miscellaneous tasks you might request of
me.' Her words were so admirably learned, and so . . . manly. When I got up to
leave she was perhaps feeling anxious and restless, for she added in a screechy
voice, 'Please do come by when this odor has dissipated!' I felt very sorry to leave
without responding to her, but there was no reason to hang around and, to tell
the truth, the odor was getting to me. So I had no choice but to cast an imploring look at her as if to excuse myself. I sent this poem:

> On a night when the spider's busy spinning
> Foretold my arrival, why insist I wait
> And put me off till the smell of garlic fades

"'What sort of excuse are you giving me?' I asked. The words had barely left my
lips, and I was on the verge of making my escape, when her reply came chasing me
down:

> If my love could bring you every night,
> Why then should the daytime be so blinding
> Or this smell of garlic so offensive[2]

"You have to admit that she was certainly quick." He spoke so calmly that the
young nobles found the whole account implausibly sordid.

---

2. The poem plays on the word *hiru*, meaning   explains the Junior Secretary's admiration of
either "daytime" or "garlic." This wordplay   her quick wit [editor's note].

"A complete fabrication," they said, laughing. "Where could anyone ever find a woman like that? You might just as easily have gone off to meet a demon. The whole thing is unpleasantly weird." Flicking their thumbs with the nail of their index finger to indicate their pique, they chided the Junior Secretary and pressured him to tell them something better than that. But the young man just sat there and replied, "How can I serve you up anything stranger than that?"

The Warden interceded.

"Generally speaking," he said, "it is really pathetic how people of no importance, men or women, think they have to show off every last little thing they have learned. A woman who acquires knowledge of Chinese and has read the Three Histories or the Five Classics lacks all feminine charm. But then again, why should we assume that a woman, just because she's a woman, would go through life without acquiring any knowledge at all of public and private affairs? Though she may not receive any formal education, a woman who has even a modicum of intelligence will retain many things she sees and hears. Through such knowledge she may learn to write cursive Chinese characters, and the next thing you know she is sending stiffly written letters half-filled with Chinese script to other ladies who don't have a clue what to do with them. When you see such a woman you're filled with chagrin, wondering why she couldn't be a bit more soft-spoken and ladylike. She may not have intended to show off her learning in the letter, but of course as it is being read aloud in a halting, strained voice the whole thing seems calculated. There are many examples of this sort of behavior among the upper ranks of court ladies.

"A woman with aspirations to being a poet will become so obsessed with the art of composition that she'll insert allusions to felicitous old phrases even in the opening lines of her correspondence. She'll send off a poem at the most inopportune moments, which can be quite offputting. If the man doesn't reply, he's inconsiderate, and if he can't come up with an equally learned allusion, he looks ridiculous. For instance, at some seasonal festival, when a man is really busy . . . let's say on the morning of the Sweet Flag Festival in the fifth month when you don't have a moment to think calmly about anything . . . she whips out a poem with some fabulous allusion playing on the words 'sweet flag' and 'sweet eyes,' or some such nonsense. Or maybe it's the Chrysanthemum Festival, when you have no time at all to wrack your brains to come up with some difficult poem in Chinese as the occasion demands, and here she is sending you a lamentation that strains to play on the words 'chrysanthemum' and 'dew.'[3] The poem is not only unsuitable to the time and place but also a downright nuisance. What otherwise might have seemed a charming or moving poem at a subsequent reading ends up being totally inappropriate and not worth a second glance because of the manner in which it was sent. Composing a poem with no forethought is not very tactful.

"It is far easier to deal with a woman who has no talent for discerning the proper moment or season to compose, who does not put on airs and try to act

3. The Sweet Flag Festival, which fell on the fifth day of the Fifth Month, was celebrated at the court with equestrian and archery competitions. The Chrysanthemum Festival was observed on the ninth day of the Ninth Month; chrysanthemums were thought to possess properties that ensured a long life, and so on that day, the flowers were wrapped in thin cotton cloths that, once dampened with dew, were rubbed over the body to take advantage of chrysanthemums' supposed life-prolonging properties [editor's note].

refined in a way that leaves you wondering why she did what she did. In all cases a woman should pretend to be ignorant, even if she has a little learning. And when she has something to say, she should just focus on a couple of points and skip the rest."

While the Warden was droning on, Genji was preoccupied with thoughts of one particular woman. Comparing her to the women he had heard about this evening, he was moved to an even greater admiration, since she seemed to be that rare type who was neither extravagant nor lacking in any way.

There was no conclusion to their discussion, and in the end as daybreak neared their ramblings came to include some rather queer and disreputable stories.

* * *

From Chapter V

Wakamurasaki

LITTLE PURPLE GROMWELL

* * *

With no one to talk to and idle time to kill after the healing rites were completed, he stepped out under cover of the heavy evening mist and set off with Koremitsu toward the fence he had spotted earlier. Peering at the bishop's residence through gaps in the fence, he could see into a room on the near side that faced Amida's Pure Land[4] in the west. The blinds had been raised slightly, which allowed him to observe a nun performing religious devotions before her own personal image of Amida Buddha. She was apparently making an offering of flowers. Leaning against one of the central pillars, she had placed a sutra scroll on top of an armrest and was struggling to read the scripture. She did not look like a common woman. She was probably over forty, her complexion exceptionally fair and graceful. Though she was thin, her cheeks were plump, and the strands of her hair, which had been cut attractively to neatly frame the area around her eyes, struck Genji as more distinctively fashionable than the long hair that was the common style. Watching her, he was touched by her appearance.

Two pretty adult attendants, also neatly turned out, were with her, and some young girls were playing there, running in and out of the room. One of them, who must have been about ten years old, was wearing a white singlet under a soft, crinkled outer robe dyed the rich yellow of mountain rose and lined with a yellow fabric. She didn't look like the other girls at all; her features were so attractive that Genji could tell at once that she would grow up to be a woman of surpassing beauty. Her hair flowed out behind her, spreading open in the shape of a fan as she stood there, her face red from brushing tears away.

"What happened?" the nun asked her. "Did you get into a quarrel with the other girls?"

---

4. Devotees of Pure Land Buddhism believe that they will be reborn in the "Western Paradise" of the Buddha Amitabha [editor's note].

When the nun looked up to speak, Genji could see the resemblance in their faces and assumed that they must be mother and daughter.

"Inuki let my baby sparrow out of the cage and it flew away." The girl was pouting.

One of the young women sitting there said, "Careless as usual. Inuki's in for a real scolding this time. What a nuisance she is! So where did the sparrow go? It's such a darling little thing; it would be horrid if the crows get to it."

She stood up and went out, her hair quite long and luxuriant. *Certainly easy on the eyes,* Genji thought. Apparently her name was Shōnagon, and she was the nurse who looked after the little girl.

"How childish!" the nun said. "Really, this whole thing is just too petty. You pay no heed to me, even though I could pass away any day now, and instead go running about chasing after sparrows. How many times have I told you it's a sin in the sight of Buddha to capture living creatures. It's deplorable. Come over here!"

The girl knelt down beside her. Her face was remarkably sweet, her unplucked eyebrows had the most charming air about them, and the cut of her hair and the look of her forehead, with those bangs swept up so innocently, were unbearably cute. Genji couldn't stop gazing at her. *I'd really love to see her when she's grown up,* he mused. It occurred to him that his desire to see her grown up was kindled by her uncanny resemblance to Fujitsubo, the woman to whom his heart was eternally devoted. It was thus natural that his gaze would be drawn to the girl, and tears came to his eyes.

Stroking the child's hair, the nun told her, "You may not be fond of combing your hair, but it's so lovely. You're such a silly girl, and your childishness weighs heavily on my mind. Other children your age don't act like this. Even though your mother was only ten when her father passed away, she still understood everything going on around her. It won't be long before I die and you'll be left completely alone in the world. How will you ever manage to get by?"

Seeing the nun weep so bitterly, Genji felt a pang of sympathetic sorrow. The girl, with her childish emotions, stared at her grandmother, then hung her head and stared at the floor. Her hair came cascading down around her face. It was splendidly lustrous.

Just then the nun composed a verse:

> *The evanescent dewdrop tarries, reluctant*
> *To disappear into the sky and abandon*
> *The tender shoot of grass to its uncertain fate*

The other young woman, who was still sitting in the room, was now crying. "How true!" she said, and composed this reply:

> *How could the dewdrop disappear*
> *Without knowing the destiny*
> *Of the shoot of grass it clings to*

Just then the bishop entered and said, "What are you doing? You're clearly visible from the outside. Why, today of all days, are you out on the veranda? I just found out from the ascetic who lives up the mountain that His Lordship, Captain Genji, has arrived to receive treatment for his fever. He arrived in such secrecy that I knew nothing about it. I've been here all this time and didn't pay my respects to him."

"How awful," the nun said, lowering the blinds. "Has anyone seen us like this? We're not at all presentable."

"Don't you want to take this opportunity," asked the bishop, "to catch a glimpse of the Radiant Genji? After all, he has such a noble reputation at the court. His looks are enough to make even the heart of a monk who has renounced society forget the sorrows of life and desire to live on in this world. I shall send him a letter."

Upon hearing the bishop stand up to leave, Genji also retired, delighted at the thought that he had discovered such a gorgeous child under these circumstances. His amorous companions were always going out, and so they were skilled at finding the kind of unusual woman that one rarely meets at court. Genji, however, could only go out occasionally, and so he was even more delighted to have the unexpected good fortune to stumble across a girl like this. She was certainly lovely, but her beauty made him curious. Who was she? She resembled Fujitsubo so closely that he was completely taken with the notion that he might be able to make her a replacement for the woman he loved, keeping the girl by him mornings and evenings as a comfort to his heart.

Genji had withdrawn and was lying down and resting when a disciple of the bishop called out for Koremitsu. They were close by, so Genji could hear everything they said. The disciple was apparently reading aloud the bishop's message:

"I just now learned that His Lordship has passed by my residence, and though I was caught by surprise, I still should have called on you. However, as you know, I have secluded myself in this temple, and so I regret that you have traveled here in secret, for I could have made my abode, rough and humble though it is, ready for you. I feel this is truly unfortunate, for it was in no way my intention to slight you."

Genji sent back a reply:

"Starting around the tenth of this month I began suffering repeated bouts of ague. The attacks were so frequent I found them hard to bear, and so on the advice of others I came discreetly to see the ascetic here. I chose to keep my journey a strict secret, because if the ascetic's spells were ineffective for me, it would certainly damage his reputation. It would be a much greater pity if such a venerable ascetic were to fail than it would be if the healer were some ordinary priest, and so I wanted to exercise some caution. I shall go to your residence presently."

The bishop himself appeared soon after. Even though he was a priest, he had a reputation at court as a man of flawless breeding and dignity, and his bearing was enough to put people to shame. Genji, who was dressed in humble fashion, felt awkward before him. The bishop spoke of the time he had spent in seclusion here, and then insisted repeatedly that Genji pay him a visit.

"My house is but a rustic hut," he said, "not all that different from this abode here, but at least it will provide you a view of the cool stream there."

Genji felt embarrassed as he recalled the fawning manner in which the bishop had described his radiant looks to the women, who had never seen him. Still, he was eager to learn more about the lovely little girl, and so he went with the bishop.

Just as the bishop said, the garden at his residence exuded an air of elegance. The trees and grasses, which were familiar varieties, had been cultivated with special care. Because it was the night of the new moon, cressets had been set along the banks of the stream, the light from their fires reflecting in the water, and oil lamps were hung beneath the eaves. The room facing south at the front of the house had been cleaned and neatly prepared. The refined scent of incense wafted out from the interior and mingled with the scent of the ritual incense offered to the Buddha, suffusing the entire area around the residence. Genji's perfumed robes carried their own special scent, which the people in the house could not help but notice.

The reverend bishop instructed Genji on the evanescence of this world and on the worlds to come. Genji, with some trepidation, was forced to acknowledge to himself the gravity of his sin of loving Fujitsubo, and it was torment knowing he could do nothing about the one thing preoccupying his heart. It seemed that he was doomed to suffer obsessively on account of his sin for the rest of this life; and what made it worse for him was always imagining the kinds of terrible retribution that awaited him in future lives. He thought he would like to leave the base temptations of this world and retreat to a humble abode like this, but then he found it hard to concentrate on the bishop's lesson, since the alluring vision of that young girl he had spied on during the day lingered in his heart alongside the image of the woman, Fujitsubo, the girl so resembled.

"Who lives here?" Genji asked. "Upon arriving today, I was reminded of a dream I wanted to ask you about."

The bishop smiled. "So you want to suddenly change the subject to your dreams, do you? Well, you can ask, but I'm afraid I'll disappoint you. You probably didn't know the former Major Counselor, since he passed away some time ago, but his primary wife is my younger sister. After he died, she took religious vows and left her household to become a nun. She's been suffering from a variety of ailments recently, and since I no longer go back to the capital she has decided to go into seclusion, using my residence as her haven."

Genji said, "I've heard that the Major Counselor had a daughter. My motive in asking about her, by the way, is quite sincere. It is *not* frivolous curiosity."

"He did indeed. One daughter. Let's see . . . it's been more than ten years now since she died. The late Counselor intended to send her into service at the court, and so he raised her with the greatest care. When he passed away before he could realize his hopes and dreams, my sister ended up raising her daughter by herself. When the girl reached womanhood Prince Hyōbu, who was Minister of War at the time,[5] was able to conduct a clandestine affair with her, using one of her scheming ladies-in-waiting as his go-between. Prince Hyōbu's primary wife, however, was a woman of impeccable birth, and as a result my niece suffered various insults that brought worry and grief. She grew increasingly despondent day by day, until at last she died. I have witnessed with my own eyes how sick from worry a person can get."

Genji gathered from the bishop's story that the little girl he had seen was the granddaughter of the nun. The Prince in question was the older brother of Fujitsubo, which explained the resemblance between the woman Genji loved and

---

5. The name Prince Hyōbu is taken from the Ministry of War (*Hyōbushō*). Since this prince is identified by his position, I am using this name as a matter of convenience.

the little girl. Now he felt an even stronger desire to see the girl and make the child his own. She was possessed of both a noble lineage and extraordinary beauty, but she also had an obedient temperament and was not impudent or forward. He wanted to get close to her, raise and train her in accordance with his own desires and tastes, and then make her his wife.

"A sad tale, indeed," Genji remarked. Since he wanted to find out for sure what had become of the little girl he had seen earlier, he added, "Did your niece leave any children behind to remember her by?"

The bishop told him, "A child was born just before my niece died . . . a girl. The child is the cause of terrible worry for my sister, who as death approaches fears she will leave her granddaughter in an unsettled situation."

So she's the one I was looking at, Genji thought.

"I know this will sound like a bizarre request, but would you do me the kindness of asking the girl's grandmother to consider allowing me to take charge of the child? I have good reasons for this request. I do call upon my primary wife from time to time, but we really don't get along so well, and I live alone for the most part. You may not consider her the proper age for such an arrangement, and you may think I am motivated by some common, base desire. But if you do, you are being unkind and dishonoring my intentions."

"Such a proposition would normally be met with great joy, but the girl is still so innocent it would be difficult, would it not, to take her as a wife—even if the whole thing was done in jest? A woman becomes an adult when a husband looks after her, and so it is not my place to deal with the details concerning such a matter. If I may, I will consult with her grandmother and try to obtain an answer for you."

The bishop was so forbiddingly sincere and stiffly formal in his manner of speech that it made Genji's youthful spirit feel small, and he was unable to come up with a clever response.

"It's time," continued the bishop, "to perform my devotions before the shrine of Amida Buddha in the prayer hall. I have not finished early evening services yet, but I will call on you again when they are over."

The bishop left and Genji was feeling ill. It had started to rain, bringing a cooling breeze. Moreover, the water in the pool of a nearby waterfall had risen with the spring runoff, and the roar was clearly audible. He could just barely make out the sound of sleepy voices reciting sutras, a sound that sent chills through him. The atmosphere of the place would have affected even the most insensitive of people, and, coupled with his preoccupation with both Fujitsubo and the girl, it prevented him from getting any sleep at all. The bishop had told him that he was off to early evening devotions, but it was already late at night. Genji could clearly sense that the women who resided in the interior of the house were not asleep, and though they were trying to be quiet he could make out the clicking of rosary beads rubbing against an armrest and the elegant, inviting rustle of robes. Because they were near him, he slid open ever so slightly the center panels of the screens that had been set up outside his room and lightly tapped the palm of his hand with a fan in order to draw their attention. Apparently they thought it unlikely that anyone would be there, but at the same time they couldn't very well ignore his summons. He heard one of the women moving over toward him.

Apparently confused, she retreated a bit and said, "That's odd. I thought I heard something. I must be deluded."

Genji spoke up. "They say the guiding voice of the Buddha will never delude you or lead you astray, even in the darkest places."

His voice was so youthful and aristocratic that her own voice sounded hesitant and embarrassed in response. "Guiding to where?" she asked. "I'm not sure I understand you."

"You probably think something is amiss, which is reasonable, since I called out so suddenly. Please present the following to your mistress."

> *Glimpsing that sweet child so like a shoot of spring grass*
> *The sleeves of my traveling robes never dry out*
> *Damp as they are from dew and my own endless tears*

The woman responded, "You surely must know there's no one here who would accept that kind of message. To whom should I give it?"

"It so happens," Genji explained, "that I have reasons for my entreaty, and so I ask for your understanding."

The woman retreated back into the interior of the house and spoke with the nun, who was confused by the request. It was, after all, shocking in so many respects.

"Really, these young people and their modern ways!" she grumbled. "Apparently this lord is under the misapprehension that the girl is old enough to understand the relationship between men and women. And how did he come to hear about our poems that referred to her as 'spring grass'?"

She was confused but realized it would be rude to take an inordinately long time to respond. So she sent the following:

> *Are you comparing the dew-soaked pillow*
> *Of a single night's journey to these sleeves*
> *Covered by the moss of ancient mountains*

"Unlike your robes," she added, "it seems that mine will never dry."

"I'm not very experienced at communicating this way through a messenger," Genji answered. "Please forgive me, but I would be grateful if you would allow me a moment to speak with you about a serious matter."

The nun turned to her attendants. "I'm afraid he's mistakenly heard that the girl is older than she is. He seems such a high-ranking lord that I feel humbled before him. How should I respond?"

"You must answer him," one of her women advised. "It would be a pity if you made him feel awkward."

"Yes, I suppose you're right," the nun relented. "But if I were still a young woman, I'd find it rather improper to meet him. His words are so earnest they make me feel unworthy."

She rose and moved nearer to him.

"I realize that this is all quite sudden for you," Genji said, "and that under these circumstances you must think my request rash and immoderate. But I assure you, I have no base desires in my heart, and swear to you that the Amida Buddha himself understands the depths of my feelings, which you seem to find incomprehensible."

He spoke in a very respectful manner, since he himself was feeling awkward about raising the subject so directly in the presence of her quiet dignity.

"I must admit I never imagined that we would meet," the nun responded, "but that doesn't mean I consider the karmic bond between us to be shallow. Why should I, since we are speaking to one another like this?"

"I was moved when I heard about the painful struggles the girl has endured," Genji continued, "and wondered if you would consider me a substitute for the mother who has passed away. I was at a very tender age myself when I lost my mother and grandmother, the ones who should have looked after me most closely. As the months and years have passed I feel I have been living in a peculiar, drifting state. The girl's situation is so similar to my own that I sincerely ask permission to be her companion. Because I'm concerned about how you will interpret my request, I feel constrained in bringing it up. However, I'll have very few opportunities to approach you."

"I know I should be overjoyed by your request, but I'm reluctant to grant it. I don't know what you've heard about the girl, but isn't it possible that you are misinformed about how old she is? Insignificant though I am, the girl who lives here is completely dependent on me for support, and she's so young, I couldn't possibly agree to your request."

"I know all about her," Genji pressed his case. "If you'll just consider the depths of my feelings, which are anything but common, you will put your reservations aside."

In spite of his insistent pleadings, the nun was convinced that Genji was unaware of the inappropriateness of the request and would not give her assent. When the bishop returned, Genji at once closed up the folding screen. *Well, at least I've pleaded my case. At least I can feel relieved about that.*

With the arrival of dawn the sound of monks confessing their sins in the hall where they devotedly chanted the *Lotus Sutra* came drifting down the mountainside. Their voices mingled nobly with the roar of the waterfall.

Genji sent a verse to the bishop:

> *Voices of atonement waft down the mountain . . .*
> *As I awake from dreams and earthly desires*
> *The sound of falling waters calls forth my tears*

The bishop replied:

> *Purified in these mountain waters*
> *My own heart is unmoved by the sound*
> *That calls forth those tears that soak your sleeves*

"Have my own ears grown accustomed to the falling waters?" he added.

The sky brightened to reveal an overcast day. The continuous crying of mountain birds mingled together so that Genji could not tell from which direction they were coming. The various blossoms on the trees and grasses, whose names he did not know, were scattering in wild profusion, making it look as though someone had spread a brocade cloth over the landscape. He looked on in wonder at the deer ambling about, pausing here and there as they moved along. The scene was a diversion from his illness.

Normally, the old healer wasn't able to get out and about very easily, but somehow he managed to make his way to the bishop's residence and performed a protective spell. He was hoarse and missing so many teeth that his pronunciation was a little off, but he read the *dharani*[6] in a voice that possessed the august quality appropriate to a priest of great distinction and merit.

The party that would escort Genji back to the capital arrived and, after offering their congratulations on his cure, presented him with a message conveying best wishes from the Emperor. The bishop busily prepared delicacies not normally served at court, offering unusual types of fruits and nuts that had been harvested from various places, including the deep valley below.

"I have made a solemn vow to remain here for the year," the bishop told Genji, offering him some rice wine, "and so I will not be able to see you off. Ironically, my vow is now making me regret having to part with you."

"The waters of this mountain will remain in my heart. I have been undeservedly blessed by a gracious message from His Majesty, who is anxiously awaiting my return. However, I shall come here again before the season of spring blossoms has passed."

> *Returning to court, I shall tell them*
> *You must go see the mountain cherries*
> *Before the breeze scatters their petals*

Genji's manner of speaking and the tenor of his voice were dazzling.

The bishop replied:

> *The udumbara blooms once in three thousand years*
> *When a perfect lord appears*[7] *... having looked on you*
> *I no longer have eyes for those mountain cherries*

Genji smiled and sagely remarked, "The *Lotus Sutra* teaches that the flower of the udumbara blooms only once and in its proper time, which is quite rare. You flatter me."

The healer received the winecup and looked at Genji in tearful reverence:

> *The pine door waiting deep in the mountains*
> *Has now been opened so that I may see*
> *The face of a flower ne'er glimpsed before*

As a memento of their meeting, he presented Genji with a *tokko*.[8] The metal rod, with its diamond-shaped points at both ends, was one of the implements he used in his esoteric rituals to symbolize the strength and wisdom needed to break free of earthly desires.

The bishop also presented several appropriate gifts. One was a rosary made of embossed seeds from the fruit of the bodhi tree that the famed Prince Shōtoku had acquired from the Korean kingdom of Paekche. The rosary had been placed in a Chinese-style box that was wrapped up in a gauze pouch and attached to a

---

6. *Dharani* are spells or incantations used for meditation, healing, or protection. They consist of a phrase or line originally in Sanskrit that encapsulates a central teaching of a sacred text in Buddhism. Often the syllables in the phrase had no semantic force, but *dharani* were used as an aid in meditation and, in this case, as a

protective spell.
7. A Buddhist belief (the udumbara is a variety of fig) [editor's note].
8. This is an abbreviation of *tokkosho* (Sanskrit, *vajra*), a Buddhist ritual implement [editor's note].

branch of five-needle pine. Another gift was a set of medicine jars made of lapis lazuli, which were filled with medicines and attached to branches of wisteria and cherry.

Genji had arranged to have gifts and offerings brought from the capital for the healer and for the monks who had chanted sutras for him. He presented the required gifts to everyone there, even the woodcutters who lived in the vicinity, and after making an offering for continued sutra readings, he prepared to leave.

The bishop went inside with Genji's message and conveyed it directly to the nun. She replied to him, "No matter what he says, I couldn't possibly give him an answer now. If his heart is really set on the girl, then maybe we can consider it in four or five years."

The bishop agreed with her and told Genji how matters stood. Genji was deeply dissatisfied that the nun had thwarted his desires and responded by having one of the pages serving at the bishop's residence take a note to her:

> As I travel home through morning mists
> Having seen the flowers hue at dusk
> How painful to have to leave it now

Though the nun dashed off her reply, the brushstrokes were elegant and her characters truly graceful:

> It may be hard for the mist to leave the flower
> But gazing at the sky obscured by morning haze
> I can judge neither what it portends nor your aims

Just as Genji was about to board his carriage, a crowd of people, including his brothers-in-law, arrived from the palace to greet him.

"You left without bothering to tell any of us where you were going!" Tō no Chūjō complained.

He and his brothers had wanted to accompany Genji, and so they vented their grievances: "We would have loved to join you on your excursion here, but you heedlessly abandoned us. It would be a shame to return to the capital without resting for a while in the shade of these stunningly beautiful blossoms."

They all sat down on the moss in the shade of some craggy outcroppings and passed around the winecups. The cascading waterfall behind them made an elegant backdrop.

Tō no Chūjō pulled a flute from the breastfold of his robe and began to play clear, dulcet notes. Sachūben kept time by tapping a fan on the palm of his left hand and sang the line "West of the temple at Toyora" from the saibara "Kazuraki." The men in the party were all extraordinarily handsome, but Genji, still listless from his fever and leaning against a boulder, was incomparable. His looks were so awesomely superior that no one could take their eyes off him. Tō no Chūjō was gifted at playing the flute, so he had made certain to bring with him attendants who could accompany him on the double-reed hichiriki and the seventeen-pipe shō.[9]

9. The hichiriki is a type of flageolet. The shō is a mouth organ, similar to panpipes, made of bamboo.

The bishop brought out his own seven-string koto and insisted that Genji play it: "Please, just one song for us. I'd like to give the birds in the mountains a surprise."

Genji demurred, saying, "I'm not feeling all that strong."

Still, he managed to pluck out a not uncharming tune before they all set off. Even the humblest monks and pages wept tears of regret that Genji should be leaving so soon. Within the bishop's residence some of the older nuns, having never before seen a man of such extraordinary appearance, remarked, "He surely cannot be a person of this world."

The bishop wiped away a tear and said, "Ahh, it makes me terribly sad to think that such an impressive, handsome man should have been destined by his karma to be born during the final period of the Dharma in this troubled realm of the rising sun."[1]

To the little girl's innocent heart, Genji seemed a paragon of beauty.

"He is even more splendid than my father, the Captain of the Guards," she gushed.

"If that's how you feel," said one of the female attendants, "then why don't you become his child?"

The girl nodded, thinking how wonderful it would be if only she could. Subsequently, whenever she played with her Hina dolls[2] or drew pictures of the court, she pretended that the lord was the Radiant Genji, and she would dress him in the finest attire and treat him most solicitously.

Genji first went straight to the palace to inform his father of all that had happened in recent days. The Emperor thought his son looked thin and haggard and worried that it might be something serious. He asked Genji about the effectiveness of the venerable healer, and, on hearing the details, remarked graciously, "We must promote him to a more senior rank as a priest. He has apparently accumulated much merit through years of austerities, so why have we never heard of him before?"

The Minister of the Left arrived at the palace as well and spoke to his son-in-law: "I thought about coming to meet you, but since you had gone off in secret I hesitated, not knowing what you were doing. Why don't you come and spend a leisurely day or two at my residence? I can escort you there right away."

Genji did not feel much like going with him and left the palace reluctantly. The Minister had his own carriage brought around and humbled himself by getting in second. His deferential gesture was a polite way of showing the care and consideration with which he was treating his son-in-law, but it made Genji feel uncomfortable.

Once they arrived at the Minister's residence, Genji could see that they had made preparations for his visit. It had been a long time since they had last seen him, and in the interim they had refurbished everything, adding decorations so that the place shone like a burnished jewel. As usual, Genji's wife stayed in her

---

1. A reference to the doctrine of *mappō*, one of the Three Ages of Buddhism. *Mappō*, the age when the law or Dharma is corrupted, is the final historical stage of Buddhism. Although various timelines were given, the most widely accepted view was that *mappō* would begin 2,000 years after Sakyamuni Buddha's passing and last for 10,000 years. The first two ages are the age of the correct Dharma/Law and the age of the imitated Dharma. This doctrine was extremely influential during the Heian period, when it was believed that *mappō* would begin in the year 1052 C.E.
2. Dolls dressed as highborn men and women [editor's note].

quarters and did not come out to meet him. She finally appeared only after her father had coaxed her repeatedly. Genji watched as she sat there stiffly, not moving a muscle, so prim and proper, arranged like some fairy-tale princess in a painting.

I doubt if it would do any good to tell her what's in my heart, he brooded, *or to speak about my trip to the mountains, but it would be wonderful if she would just respond to me in a pleasant manner. Still, the plain truth is that she remains cold and remote in my presence, and we're becoming increasingly distant and estranged as the years go by.*

He considered the situation unfair and intolerable.

"Just once in a while I'd like to see you acting like a normal wife. I've been quite ill recently, but you couldn't be bothered to even ask how I was. I know that such callous behavior isn't rare for you, but I resent it all the same."

She paused for a moment, then responded, "Yes, I know how you feel. As the poet put it, 'How hurtful it is to be ignored.'" She cast a sidelong glance at him— an expression that gave her face an air of extreme reticence and an affect of grace and beauty.

"You so rarely speak to me," Genji shot back, "so why is it that when you do, you have to say such strange and unpleasant things? You cite the line 'How hurt-ful it is to be ignored,' but that poem referred to lovers having an affair, not to married couples. What a deplorable thing to say! You're always doing things to put me off, to make me feel awkward. And all the while I've tried various things hoping that the time will come when your attitude toward me changes. But now I see that you have grown even more distant. All right then, perhaps some day, in some life to come . . ."

He withdrew to their bedchamber for the night, but she did not follow after him. He couldn't bring himself to call for her, and so he sighed and lay down. He pretended to fall asleep, even though he was thoroughly disgruntled, his mind troubled by all the difficulties that may arise in relationships between men and women.

He couldn't get the girl out of his mind, and he was curious to see what that little shoot of grass would look like when she was fully grown. The nun, acting as the girl's grandmother, had not been at all unreasonable in thinking that the child was not an appropriate age for him. It would thus be difficult to make any hurried advances at this stage. So how could he contrive to bring her with him and always have her as a comfort and joy? The girl's father, Prince Hyōbu, was certainly a refined and graceful man, but his looks did not possess her lambent sheen. So how could it be that the girl bore such a striking family resemblance to Fujitsubo? Was it because the girl's father and aunt were both born to the same imperial consort? Mulling over these points, the family connections made him feel closer to her, and somehow his desires became more urgent.

The day after returning from his mountain retreat, Genji sent letters to the house in Kitayama. His letter to the bishop merely implied what his intentions were. In the letter to the nun he wrote:

> Awed and constrained by your august countenance, I was unable to express my thoughts clearly and openly to you. I would be overjoyed if you could at least understand that my decision to address you in this manner is evidence of the depth of my feelings and the sincerity of my motives.

He enclosed a letter to the girl as well, which he had folded up in a knot:

> *The vision of the mountain cherry*
> *Continues lingering inside me*
> *Though I left my feelings there with you*

"As Prince Motoyoshi put it, 'I fear the wind that blows in the night.'[3] I too worry that the wind might scatter the blossoms so that I may no longer view them."

The handwriting was of course magnificent, and even though the letter had been wrapped casually, to the eyes of the older people there it was startlingly beautiful. They were troubled and perplexed by the situation, unsure how to respond.

The nun sent a reply:

> I did not give your proposition any serious consideration after you left, and now, even though you have so graciously written to us, I have no idea how to respond. She is not even capable of writing the *Naniwazu*[4] in *kana* yet, and so even though she now has your letter, it really does no good.

> *You left your heart just before*
> *The mountain blossoms scatter*
> *Short-lived like your devotion*

"I am now all the more concerned," she added.

The bishop's reply was essentially the same, and Genji was frustrated. After a few days he sent Koremitsu off with the following instuctions: "There should be a person there, a nurse named Shōnagon. Meet her and find out what you can."

It's his nature, I suppose, Koremitsu thought. *He can never let anything go.* Koremitsu had caught only the briefest glimpse of the girl—and thought she looked very young—but it was pleasant to recall the moment he had seen her.

Receiving yet another letter of proposal from Genji, the bishop thanked Koremitsu, who then met with Shōnagon and conveyed Genji's wishes. He spoke in detail about Genji's feelings and told her about his status and circumstances. He was a smooth, glib talker and was able to put together quite a convincing case for his lord. For all that, the girl was absurdly young to be married off, and everyone there felt that the request was somehow ominous, even distasteful, and they wondered what Genji had in mind.

Genji had poured his soul into his letter, which was written with deep sincerity, and as he had done before, he included a folded note for the little girl:

"I know you do not yet write in cursive style, but still I long to see those characters you practice when you copy the lines: *My love for you is not shallow like the reflection of Mount Asaka you see when you peek into the mountain spring.*"[5]

---

3. *Shūishū* 29: "Anxious that the wind during the night may have scattered the blossoms of plum, I rise early to view them."
4. The *Naniwazu* refers to a poem in the *kana* preface to the *Kokinshū* that children in particular used, along with the poem on Mount Asaka that appears below, as a text to practice writing the *kana* syllabary: "The trees in bloom at the inlet of Naniwa announce that winter is over, spring has arrived! The trees in bloom!"
5. The place name Asaka plays on the homophone *asa*, meaning "shallow." The poem Genji cites that the girl would have practiced writing is from the *Man'yōshū*. The poems that follow make variations on similar lines in the *Kokin rokujō*, a *waka* anthology.

> *What does shallow Mount Asaka have to do*
> *With these deep feelings . . . why is the reflection*
> *Of your face in the mountain spring so distant*

The nun replied for the girl:

> *They say one feels regret after drawing water*
> *From a mountain spring . . . so how could you see the face*
> *Of a lover in a spring as shallow as this*

Before Koremitsu returned to Genji, Shōnagon, the girl's nurse, told him, "Once we have spent some time here and my young lady's grandmother is feeling better, we will travel to the capital and definitely be in touch with you then."

Genji was irritated and dissatisfied when he learned from Koremitsu's report that his proposal had been rejected.

Fujitsubo was ill and had withdrawn from the palace to her home. Genji could see his father's anxious, grieving expression, which aroused great feelings of pity. Yet he also considered it an opportunity, and was soon lost in a reverie, as if his spirit had drifted out of his body. He stopped calling on his various women and instead idled away the days at the palace or at his own villa, dreamily gazing out until evening, when he would then pester one of Fujitsubo's ladies-in-waiting, Ōmyōbu, to intercede on his behalf. It is not clear how she managed to arrange a tryst, but after some truly outrageous and exhausting machinations she pulled it off, and Genji was able at last to be with the woman he considered perfect. His meetings with her were so brief, however, they merely intensified the pain of his lonely yearnings. Were these trysts real, or were they a dream? He could no longer tell.

Her Highness was in a state of constant distraction, for she was all too aware that her unimaginable affair with Genji was genuinely shocking. She was determined to put an end to their relationship, since she found the prospect of continuing to meet him extremely unpleasant and depressing, and her appearance betrayed just how difficult it was for her to cope with the situation. Still, she somehow managed to maintain a sweet and familiar attitude toward Genji, and her dignified demeanor and discretion put him to shame. Her behavior only made him realize that there was no one like her in the world, that he could find no flaws in her—and that realization gave rise to a wistful anguish as he was left to wonder why it was that the woman who turned out to be his ideal was forbidden to him.

How could he possibly tell her all the things he wanted to say? He wished he might reside in obscurity in the perpetual darkness of the Kurabu Mountains. Unfortunately, his nights were short, and brought him nothing but sorrow and pain.

> *Though I am with you here and now*
> *So rare are these nights that I long*
> *To lose myself inside this dream*

He was sobbing now.

Feeling pity for him, she replied:

> *Will we not be forever the stuff of gossip . . .*
> *No one has ever suffered the anguish I feel*
> *Trapped in a dream from which I never awaken*

Fujitsubo's turmoil was understandable, and he felt ashamed before her. Ōmyōbu gathered up his robes and brought them to him.

Genji returned to his residence and spent a tearful day in bed. When he was told that Fujitsubo would no longer accept his messages, even though he knew she had always refused to read them anyway, he was hurt and could not focus his thoughts. He did not appear at court but locked himself away for two or three days. His Majesty was worried by his son's absence and wondered if something was wrong, if he had fallen ill again. In the face of what Genji had done with Fujitsubo, his father's concern terrified him.

Fujitsubo was distressed by her plight, and her illness, which had prompted her to withdraw from the palace in the first place, worsened. Messengers arrived one after another urging her to return, but she refused. There could be no doubt that she was not feeling normal, but no one knew what was wrong with her. As it turned out, she had already secretly surmised her condition, and the shock of realizing that she was expecting a child upset her. She was now panicked and confused. *What will become of me?* More and more, as the summer progressed, she refused to get up. She was now in her third month, and her condition was obvious. Her ladies-in-waiting observed this and grew worried and suspicious. She lamented that she should have to suffer such a strange and unhappy fate.

Because no one guessed what had actually happened, Fujitsubo's attendants were surprised to learn that their lady had said nothing to His Majesty until now. Only Fujitsubo knew, in her heart of hearts, what had happened. Her closest attendants, Ōmyōbu and Ben, the daughter of Fujitsubo's nurse, tended to her intimately in the bath, and so they had clearly seen her condition and recognized what was happening. They were troubled, because they knew they did not dare discuss the situation between themselves. Ōmyōbu in particular felt sad that her lady's inescapable karmic destiny had brought her to this pass. In order to explain the delay in reporting the pregnancy, they had no choice but to tell the Emperor that they had been beguiled by a spirit and had not recognized their mistress's condition right away. The women who served Fujitsubo all assumed that that was indeed the case, and the Emperor, overwhelmed with even more feelings of pity and concern, was constantly sending messengers to ask how she was doing. Their visits, however, only kept her in a constant state of dread and depression.

One night Genji had a weird and terrifying dream. He summoned a diviner who interpreted the dream to mean that Genji would become the father of an Emperor. This was shocking and unthinkable.

The diviner added, "Your dream also means that your fortunes are crossed and that you must exercise caution and good behavior."

Genji felt awkward, and so he told the diviner, "This isn't my dream. I have merely relayed to you what someone of very high rank told me. So until the dream actually comes true, don't say anything to anyone about it."

Genji was trying to make sense of things in his own mind, but when he heard that Fujitsubo was pregnant, he realized that her child might be what his dream portended. He sent increasingly desperate messages to Fujitsubo, but Ōmyōbu was now having second thoughts. Communicating like this was extremely risky and difficult, and she found that she could no longer act as a go-between for Genji. Even her brief one-line replies, which had always been infrequent at best, stopped altogether.

Fujitsubo returned to the palace in the seventh month. Because he had not seen her for so long, His Majesty's desire had only grown stronger, and he lavished his gracious affection on her. She was now a little plump, and her face had grown thin and careworn, but her appearance was truly, incomparably lovely. As he had done before, the Emperor would spend the whole day in her chambers. The early autumn sky signaled to them that it was the appropriate season for musical diversions, and so His Majesty was constantly calling for Genji, who had a talent for performance, to come and play various pieces on the koto or the flute. Genji had to struggle to keep his emotions in check on these occasions, though there were moments when his expression betrayed the feelings he found so hard to suppress. For her part, Fujitsubo would obsess over things she wished had turned out differently.

The health of the nun who had been staying at the mountain temple in Kitayama improved, and she finally returned to her residence in the capital. Genji inquired after her and sent her letters from time to time. It did not surprise him that in her replies she continued to refuse his proposition, but it didn't bother him that much because he was preoccupied by his concern with Fujitsubo and had little time to think much about other matters.

By the ninth month, as the end of autumn was approaching, Genji was lonely and depressed. A gorgeous moonlit evening inspired him at last to go to the place of a woman he had been secretly visiting. But then the weather changed—it turned stormy and a chill evening rain began to fall. The lady lived in the vicinity of Rokujō and Kyōgoku, and as he left the palace her place began to seem a little too distant. On the way he saw a weather-beaten house standing in the gloomy shade of an ancient grove of trees.

Koremitsu, who was accompanying Genji as usual, said, "That used to be the house of the late Major Counselor. I guess you should know that I visited it recently and learned that the nun has taken a turn for the worse. They have no idea what to do for her."

"What a pity," Genji replied. "I must pay her a visit. Why didn't you tell me about this earlier? Have a message taken to her."

Koremitsu sent one of the attendants in with instructions to say that Genji had arrived with the express purpose of calling on the nun. When the messenger entered and announced his lord's visit, the women were caught off guard.

One of them said, "This is most awkward. Our lady has been feeling much worse these last few days and couldn't possibly meet your lord."

It would have been rude and uncouth to send him away, however, so they prepared a space on the veranda under the eaves on the south side of the house and invited Genji to enter there.

"Frightfully untidy, I'm afraid," another of the women remarked, "but my lady wanted to show some gratitude for your visit. Your arrival was so unexpected, however, that you caught us unprepared. So please forgive the dark and gloomy atmosphere of this chamber."

The place did strike Genji as quite odd, but he answered, "I've been meaning to visit you all this time, but I refrained from doing so because I've been treated in such a way as to make me believe nothing would come of it. I'm anxious about you, having just learned that your illness has taken a turn for the worse."

"My ailments are no worse than usual, though I do sense now that I am nearing my end," the nun told him. "You have been gracious enough to call on me, but I'm not able to greet you directly. With regards to your proposal, the girl is still at an innocent age and lacks judgment, but once she is a little more mature, by all means think of her as you would any other woman and take her as one of your own. I'm so worried about leaving her behind in this world, isolated and helpless, that my anxiety creates a burden of attachment for me that will surely be a hindrance on the path to the salvation I pray for."

Because she was in a room close by, Genji could catch fragments of her weary voice.

"We are not worthy of this, and should be grateful for his attentions," she added. "If only the girl were old enough to be able to thank him properly."

Genji was keenly moved.

"If my feelings for the girl were truly shallow, then why would I embarrass myself by coming here and possibly looking lecherous? The moment I recognized there was some kind of karmic bond between us, I was deeply attracted to the girl and convinced to an almost mystical degree that our bond was not something that belonged to this world."

He turned to one of the attendants and continued, "My visit here may have been in vain, but may I ask for a word with the girl herself?"

"Oh, I don't know about that," one of the nun's attendants interjected. "She has been kept in the dark about all of this, and is now fast asleep."

Just as the woman spoke these words, the girl's voice could be heard from inside.

"Grandmama, Lord Genji is here . . . you know, the man who visited us at the temple? So why haven't you gone out to meet him?"

The women were all mortified and tried to hush the girl, but she protested, "Didn't Grandmama say that the sight of him was always a comfort to her?"

She spoke as if she were informing them of something that would benefit her grandmother. Genji was utterly charmed, but he had to be considerate of the bruised feelings of the flustered women there, and so he pretended he hadn't heard a thing. After politely bidding farewell and leaving his best wishes for them, he made his way home. *She may be a little girl*, he thought, *but I can't wait to see her after she's been properly trained.*

The next day Genji sent a most solicitous letter inquiring after the health of the nun. As always, he included a small folded letter for the girl:

> Hearing a young crane cry I long to go to it
> But my boat tangled among the reeds is hindered
> And I cannot leave this inlet to tend its needs

"As the poet put it, 'I always yearn to go back to the same person.'"[6]

Genji deliberately composed his note in a childish hand that was so delightful the women told the girl to imitate it in her copybook.

Shōnagon replied, "Our lady may not make it through the day, and we are preparing to take her back to the temple in Kitayama. She may not be able to express in this world her gratitude for your visit and your expressions of concern."

Genji felt very sad when he heard this.

6. *Kokinshū* 732 (Anonymous): "I always yearn to go back to the same person, like a little boat that has made its way through the channel and comes rowing home."

One autumn evening, when he was more preoccupied than ever with his longing for Fujitsubo, the woman who constantly tormented his heart, he felt his seemingly perverse desire to possess her little niece growing even stronger. He remembered a line from the nun's poem—"The evanescent dewdrop tarries, reluctant to disappear into the sky"—and thought lovingly of the girl. At the same time he was anxious and unsure, thinking that she might not live up to his expectations. An image of *wakamurasaki*[7]—a little purple gromwell—popped into his head:

> How I yearn to quickly pluck up and make my own
> That little purple gromwell sprouting in the wild
> With roots that share their color with wisteria

During the tenth month His Majesty decided to plan a visit to the Suzaku Palace. The dancers for the day of departure were to be selected from among sons of aristocratic families, high-ranking officials, and courtiers who had talents suitable for the occasion. From princes and ministers on down, each and every one practiced their skills. It was a hectic, busy time.

Because of all the preparations, it occurred to Genji that he had not contacted the nun in her mountain temple for some time. When at last he sent a messenger there, he received the following reply from the bishop:

"I am sorry to report that she passed away on the twentieth of last month. I know it is the reality of this world that we must all die, but still I cannot help mourning her."

After reading this, Genji experienced the poignant sorrow of the evanescent world and wondered what would become of the girl who had been the source of such worry for the nun. The girl was so young, she must be pining for her grandmother. Genji had vague memories of being left behind by his own mother, and so he sent his deepest condolences. Shōnagon composed a sympathetic reply.

Genji learned that after the twenty-day period of mourning and confinement was over, the girl came back to the capital and was now at the late nun's residence. He waited until a seemly period of time passed, then went to call on her one evening when he had some free time. The place was run-down and desolate, and there were few people about—the kind of place that would surely frighten a child. Genji was shown to the same space on the south side of the residence that they had used on his previous visit. He was moved to tears by Shōnagon's heartbreaking account of her mistress's final days.

"There is talk that the girl's father would have her come to his villa," Shōnagon told him. "But the nun was quite concerned about that prospect. After all, her own daughter, this child's late mother, found that household unbearably cruel and depressing. The girl is now at that in-between stage, no longer a child, but

7. The Japanese species of gromwell is a small plant that produces white flowers in the summer. Its purple roots were used to make dye for clothing. As in other cultures, purple was associated with royalty, and so I have translated *murasaki* as "purple gromwell" to indicate both the rustic image of the word and its imperial associations. The Japanese name for wisteria is *fuji*, alluding to the girl's aunt, Fujitsubo, and

suggesting by way of the color purple shared by the two plants the nature of their relationship. That is, since *murasaki* (or *wakamurasaki*) is the smaller, more rustic plant, Genji's poem acknowledges a difference in their relative status. His poem alludes to *Kokinshū* 867 (Anonymous): "Because of this one purple gromwell, I look on all the grasses in Musashino with tender feelings."

not old enough to really understand the motives of other people. And with all the other children at her father's residence, she is not likely to be welcomed with open arms, but will instead be belittled and treated as a stepchild. With so many indications that the girl will be badly served there, we are grateful for your passing words of kind consideration. Still, we cannot fathom your future intentions, and even though we should feel happy on occasions like this when you visit us, we remain extremely hesitant about your proposal . . . after all, the girl is simply not appropriate for you. Her character is immature and undeveloped, even for someone her age."

"Why do you continue to waver when I have repeatedly opened up to you like this? I know in my heart that my feelings of longing and pity, which her innocence stirs in me, are signs of a special bond between us from a former life. If I may, I would like to speak with her directly and tell her how I feel."

> *Seeing the young tangled seaweed struggle to grow*
> *Amidst reeds in the bay of Wakanoura*
> *Can the wave, once it has drawn near, recede again*

"It would be too hateful for the wave to have to withdraw now," Genji concluded.

Shōnagon answered, "You are truly gracious, my lord, but . . ."

> *If the algae at Wakanoura yielded*
> *Without knowing the true intentions of the wave*
> *Would it not be set adrift upon the shallows*[8]

"It just isn't reasonable."

The polished manner of her verse made it almost possible for Genji to forgive her refusal.

"Why does the day when we may finally meet never come?"[9] he murmured. The younger women in the house shivered in delight and admiration.

The little girl had been lying down, crying and grieving for her grandmother until her playmates told her, "A lord dressed in court robes has arrived. Perhaps it is the Prince, your father!"

She got up and went out to see for herself, calling out, "Shōnagon! Where is the nobleman in court robes? Is my father here?"

Her voice sounded achingly sweet as she approached.

"I'm not your father," said Genji, "but that doesn't mean you should treat me as a stranger. Come over here."

The girl immediately recognized his voice and realized that this was the splendid lord who had called on them before. Embarrassed that she had spoken improperly, she went over to her nurse and said, "I want to go now. I'm sleepy."

"Why do you want to hide from me? Please come over here and rest at my knees. Please, come closer."

"As you can see," said Shōnagon, pushing the girl toward him, "she really knows very little about the world."

8. Both poems play on the homophone *waka*, meaning "youthful."
9. Compare this *waka* poem by Fujiwara no Koremasa: "Though I keep my impatience a secret, as the years go by, why is it so hard to pass beyond the barrier gate of Ōsaka, the slope where we may finally meet?"

The girl sat innocently on the other side of the blinds from Genji, who put his hand through to search around for her. Her lustrous hair was draped over soft, rumpled robes, and even though he did not have a clear view of her, when he touched the rich thickness of the strands he imagined how attractive she must really be. When he tried to hold her hand she was put off that a stranger should have come so close to her and pulled away in fright.

"I told you I was sleepy," she said to Shōnagon.

At that moment Genji slipped inside the curtains and told her, "You must think of me now as the one you will rely upon. So please don't be distant or afraid."

His actions were upsetting to Shōnagon, who exclaimed, "What are you thinking, my lord, impetuously barging in here like this during a period of mourning? It's outrageous. You can talk to her all you like, but it won't do you any good. She's just too young to understand."

"You may be right," Genji answered, "but just what do you think I'm going to do with someone so young? Carefully observe the sincerity of my feelings, the purity of my heart, and you will realize that they are peerless, that you will find nothing like them in this world."

The wind was blowing violently and hail began to fall. It was a lonely, terrifying night.

"Why," Genji asked, tears in his eyes, "should she have to spend any more time in this isolated, deserted house?"

He couldn't stand the idea of going home and abandoning them here.

"Lower the shutters. It looks like it will be a frightful evening," he ordered. "I shall stand guard for you tonight. Please, everyone, gather closer to me."

With a remarkable air of familiarity about him, he went inside the curtained area where the girl slept. The women found his behavior shockingly abnormal, but they did not know what to do and did not even try to move from where they were sitting. Shōnagon couldn't stand it. She was beside herself, but she couldn't very well offer vehement objections or make a scene, and so she stayed put as well, sighing in lament.

The girl, not knowing what was going on, was truly scared and trembling. Genji felt sorry for her, thinking that her beautiful figure was shivering because of the cold, and he had a singlet brought in and wrapped around her. Genji knew perfectly well that his behavior was not normal, and so he spoke sensitively to the girl.

"You really must come with me. There are many gorgeous paintings at my residence and Hina court dolls to play with." His manner was kind and intimate as he spoke of things he was sure would appeal to her childish heart and allay her fears. Nonetheless, she still found it hard to sleep, and spent the night tossing and turning.

As the night wore on, the wind continued to gust and the women whispered among themselves:

"How forlorn we would have been had he not come here. If only they were a little closer in age, it would be so wonderful."

Shōnagon, worried about her charge, hovered just outside the curtains the whole time. When the wind began to die down a little, Genji got ready to go home. It was still dark, and he had a knowing look on his face, as if he were leaving some romantic tryst.

"Now that I've witnessed her situation with my own eyes," Genji said, "it's all too pathetic, and I will now be more anxious about her than ever. She should be moved to my residence, where I spend my days and nights in solitary reverie. How can she remain here like this? It's a wonder she isn't in a constant state of terror."

Shōnagon replied, "Prince Hyōbu has hinted that he would come for her, but that won't happen until after the forty-nine-day period of purification is complete."

"He *is* the one who really ought to look after her," Genji agreed, "but they have grown accustomed to living apart and the girl most likely regards him as much a stranger to her as I am. I may have only just met her today, but my feelings and motives are not shallow—indeed, they are far more worthy than her father's."

Genji stroked the girl's hair, then glanced back repeatedly at her as he made his way out.

* * *

Genji experienced a swirl of conflicting emotions. There would be gossip about what was going on,[1] and he would undoubtedly gain a reputation as a lecher. If the girl were of an age when she could understand these matters and consent to the relationship, then people would understand, and it would all seem normal. But she was not of that age, and if her father were to come searching for her, then Genji's own actions would be seen as wild and rash. Yet despite his reservations, if he were to let this opportunity slip away, he would have bitter regrets. And so he departed while it was still dark. His wife remained her usual sullen and distant self.

"I just remembered some pressing matters I have to attend to," Genji told her. "I shall return shortly."

After going to his own quarters in the house at Sanjō and changing his robes, he set off alone with Koremitsu, who was riding alongside the carriage on his horse. He left before the women attendants even realized he was gone.

He knocked on the gate and someone who had been apprised of the situation opened it. Genji had his carriage drawn inside quietly. Koremitsu tapped at the double doors in the corner of the main hall, then coughed as a signal. On hearing this, Shōnagon knew who was there and came out.

"My lord has arrived," Koremitsu announced.

"The girl is resting inside," Shōnagon told him. "Why have you come out so late at night?" She assumed they were stopping by on the way back from their previous rendezvous at the palace.

"I have something I must tell her before she is moved to her father's residence," Genji replied.

"Whatever would that be? And how could she possibly give you a clear answer?" Shōnagon laughed and began to withdraw.

Genji suddenly barged in, and Shōnagon was completely taken aback. "The older women are in there! They are absolutely unpresentable!"

"She's not awake yet, is she?" Genji said. "Well, then, I suppose I shall have to get her up. How can she remain asleep, oblivious to this lovely morning mist?"

1. That is, Genji's intentions to take away the girl [editor's note].

He barged straight into the girl's sleeping quarters. Shōnagon was so flabber-gasted that neither she nor her women could utter a peep in protest.

Genji picked up the girl, who was sleeping innocently, and woke her in his arms. She was still half asleep, and so she thought her father had come for her. Stroking her tangled hair, Genji said to her, "Come with me. I'm acting as a messenger for your father."

When she saw that it wasn't her father holding her, she was startled and fear-ful. "Come now, is that any way to act? I am just the same as your father." As he was carrying the girl out, Koremitsu, Shōnagon and the others all asked him what was happening.

"I told you I was worried about not being able to come here very often, and so I want to move her to my residence, which is much safer and more comfort-able. If she were cruelly taken away to her father's villa, it would be that much more difficult for us to communicate. One of you may accompany me if you wish."

Shōnagon, who was now frantic, replied, "But today is the worst possible time you could have chosen. What should I say when her father comes for her? If it is, as you say, truly fated for her to be your wife, then surely that is how things will turn out later on. As it is now, she is just too young, and you have given us no time to think about things, which is putting all of the attendants in an awk-ward position."

"Very well, then," Genji responded, "some of you may follow later."

He had his carriage brought around. Everyone there was stunned and at a loss as to what to do. The girl, who did not understand what was happening, was frightened and started to cry.

With no way to stop him, Shōnagon brought out the clothes she had been sewing the previous night and, changing into a not altogether unattractive robe herself, got into the carriage with him.

Genji's residence in Nijō was close by, and so they arrived before first light. The carriage was drawn up to the west hall and Genji alighted. He easily swept the girl up in his arms and brought her out.

Shōnagon wavered: "This is all like a dream. What should I be doing?"

"That's entirely up to you. Now that I've brought the young lady here, you may return if you wish. I'll be happy to have someone escort you back."

Shōnagon smiled bitterly at his words, for she had no choice but to resign herself to the situation. She got out of the carriage. This had all been so sud-den and outrageous that nothing could be done about it. She could not calm her heart. *What will her father say? And what about my young mistress? What will become of her? To have been left behind by all the people who loved her . . . it's just too much to bear.*

She could hardly hold back her tears, but she found a way to restrain herself, knowing that it would bring bad luck to cry on a momentous occasion like this.

The west hall was not usually inhabited, and there were no curtains or fur-nishings. Genji summoned Koremitsu and ordered him to have curtains, screens, and the like placed here and there where he indicated. He had the silk blinds hanging between the pillars around the inner chamber removed, and he had his attendants straighten up the room. When they were finished, he sent for robes and bedding from the east hall, then went in to rest. The girl now found the scene genuinely menacing and, uncertain about Genji's intentions, she began to tremble. Still, she managed not to cry out loud.

"I want to sleep with Shōnagon," she whimpered in a girlish voice.

"You must no longer sleep with her," Genji instructed, and the girl fell prostrate, weeping and feeling completely forlorn. Her nurse couldn't sleep either and stayed up all night lost in her thoughts.

As the dawn broke, Shōnagon studied her new surroundings. The residence and furnishings gave off a resplendent air—even the sand in the garden looked like jewels scattered all around. She remained hesitant, but it appeared that there were no other women serving in this hall. It was a pavilion where Genji would receive less intimate guests who called infrequently.

There were male servants just outside the bamboo blinds, and one of the men, who had heard that his lord had brought a woman here, was whispering to the others, "I wonder who she is? She must be someone extraordinary."

Cooked rice and water for their morning ablutions were brought in, and the sun was already high when they finally got up. Genji said, "This won't do at all. We have no one in service here. Choose those women at your former residence you would like to have as attendants for your young lady and I will send for them this evening."

Genji next summoned some page girls from the east hall, then told his servants, "Have these pages select several younger girls to serve over here."

Presently four captivating little girls appeared. The young lady was still asleep, her robes wrapped around her. Genji made her get up.

"This pouting and cold behavior will not do!" Genji scolded. "Would a man who is wild at heart have done all this for you? A woman must be kindhearted and obedient."

And with those words, from that moment on, her training began.

Her features were even more beautiful than when he had seen her from a distance. He spoke warmly to her, telling her stories and showing her all sorts of delightful pictures and playthings, which he had brought in for her, and did everything he could to soothe her feelings. Eventually she got up and inspected her quarters. She was wearing her dark mourning robes, soft and rumpled, and looked so adorable as she sat there with her innocent smile that Genji couldn't help smiling himself as he watched her.

Genji left for the east hall, and the young lady went over to the edge of the veranda and peeked out at the pond and the trees in the garden. She was fascinated by the grasses, which had been withered by the frost so that they looked like something out of a painting. A crowd of male courtiers of the fourth or fifth rank, none of whom she knew, bustled in and out, making her feel that she had come to some splendid world. She examined the captivating pictures on the folding screens and door panels, and with her childish disposition she was able quickly to comfort herself.

Genji did not go to the palace for two or three days so that he could spend time talking with the girl and making her feel at ease in her new surroundings. He wrote poems and drew pictures, presenting them to her with the thought that they might serve as a model for her own practice. He put them together to make a very charming collection. One of the poems, which he copied on purple-colored paper, was taken from *Kokin rokujō*:

> *I've never been there but lament my fate*
> *Each time I hear the name "Musashino"...*
> *The place where little* murasaki *grows*

The girl took up the sheet of paper and studied the unusual, exquisite brush-strokes. In smaller characters Genji had added his own verse:

> *Unable to cross Musashino's dewy plains*
> *I've yet to see the purple roots of the gromwell...*
> *How I long for the wisteria's little kin*

"Why don't you try writing something?" Genji encouraged her, though Fujit-subo was still obviously on his mind.

"But I can't write well," she protested, looking up at him. She was so lovely he couldn't help but smile.

"Even if you can't write well, you must at least try. You won't get better if you don't write anything. Let me show you."

He found it charming the way she held her brush and how she turned away from him when she wrote, and he thought it strange that he should have such feelings.

"I've made a mistake," she said, trying to keep him from seeing what she wrote. But he made her show it to him anyway.

> *I worry, unsure why you grieve...*
> *Tell me again which plant is it*
> *The one I am related to*

Her writing was quite immature, but he could see at once that she had the talent to be accomplished in composition. The lines of her brushstrokes were rich and gentle, and they resembled the hand of her late grandmother. If she practiced more modern models, he knew that she would be able to write very well.

He had court dolls and dollhouses made especially for her, and as they passed the time together he was able to distract himself from his painful longing for Fujitsubo.

The women who had remained behind at the girl's former residence were flus-tered and embarrassed when Prince Hyōbu came back and asked for his daughter, for they did not know what they should say to him. Genji had told them not to let anyone know what had happened—at least not for a while. Because Shōnagon agreed with him, she insisted that it was best to keep the matter quiet. Thus, all they could say to the father was that Shōnagon had taken his daughter into hiding, without telling them where.

Prince Hyōbu assumed that nothing could be done at this point, and he resigned himself to the situation. *Her grandmother was opposed to sending the girl to my residence, and so Shōnagon was moved to carry out her wishes, even if it meant going to this extreme. But why couldn't she just gently tell me that it would be too unbearable to move the girl, rather than willfully spiriting her away?*

When he left the house he said tearfully, "Let me know if you hear any news of her." This troubled the women.

He sent an inquiry to the bishop as well, but the bishop had no clue as to her whereabouts. Prince Hyōbu suffered longing and regret over the child's beauty, which would now go to waste. The enmity his primary wife had harbored toward the girl's mother had abated, and even she regretted that she would not be able to raise the child as she had hoped.

Gradually attendants arrived and gathered in the quarters of the girl—whom Genji called his little Murasaki. As a couple they possessed a rare, modern look. The youngest attendants and the little girls who were her playmates passed the time together without a care. Although there were lonely evenings when Genji was away and she cried out of yearning for her grandmother, she gave no thought at all to her father. From the beginning she had grown accustomed to not having him around, and she was now exceedingly close to the man who was her new father. Whenever he returned, she would be the first to go out to greet him. They would talk together lovingly, and she never felt distant or embarrassed when he held her to his bosom. Insofar as they looked like a father and a daughter, their behavior was quite endearing.

If a woman has a calculating heart and a troublesome disposition that makes an issue of everything, then a man has to take care that he not allow her emotions to lead her astray and keep her from fulfilling his desires. She will tend to be jealous and resentful, and difficulties he never imagined, such as a separation, will naturally arise. Murasaki, however, was an absolutely captivating companion for Genji. A real daughter, when she had reached this age, would not have been able to behave so intimately, to have gone to sleep or risen in such close proximity to him. Genji came to feel that his young Murasaki was a rare hidden treasure, his precious plaything.

From Chapter VII

Momiji no ga

AN IMPERIAL CELEBRATION OF AUTUMN FOLIAGE

The procession to the Suzaku Palace was set to take place sometime after the tenth day of the tenth month. Because it promised to be an unusually lavish event, the imperial consorts and ladies, who were not permitted to leave the palace, complained bitterly that they would not be able to see it. His Majesty was also disappointed that Fujitsubo would not be able to view the procession, and so he had the musicians and dancers perform a dress rehearsal in front of his living quarters in the Seiryōden.

Genji, a Captain in the Palace Guard, performed a dance called "Waves of the Blue Sea." His partner was Tō no Chūjō, who, as son of the Minister of the Left, was unquestionably superior to other men in terms of his looks and training. Performing next to Genji, however, he seemed like some nondescript tree deep in the mountains growing beside a cherry in full bloom. As the bright slanting rays of the setting sun shone down on them, the music swelled and the performance reached its climax. Genji was carefully following the prescribed form of the dance, but his movements and expressiveness were without peer.

The music paused and he recited the accompanying verse in Chinese by Ono no Takamura in a voice as sweet and ethereal as the cry of the Buddha's heavenly Kalavínka bird.[2] The Emperor was so moved by the performance that he brushed away a tear, while all the upper-ranking courtiers and princes were weeping. At the conclusion of Genji's recitation, the lively music, which had paused for him, started up again. Genji had twirled the sleeves of his robe around his arms at the very end of the verse, and he was now readjusting them, his face flushed, looking even more radiant than usual.

As auspiciously splendid as Genji's dance had been, the Kokiden Consort found it strangely disturbing and remarked, "His looks are enough to captivate the gods in the heavens. It seems weirdly unpleasant."

The younger women deplored her unkind words.

Fujitsubo might have enjoyed viewing the dance more had it not been for the terrible guilt she felt at having received the Emperor's gracious gift of ordering this rehearsal for her benefit. To make matters worse, she had to watch a dance performed by the very man with whom she had conducted her outrageous affair. The whole thing seemed like a dream to her. That evening she was in service to the Emperor in his chambers.

"Waves of the Blue Sea" had swept everything before it at the rehearsal that day.

"What did you think of it?" His Majesty asked Fujitsubo. She struggled to answer, but managed to stammer out, "It was certainly a special performance."

"Genji's partner did not look bad either," the Emperor continued. "When it comes to form and gesture, good breeding will out. Professional dancers, those who have some reputation, are no doubt skillful, but they cannot display the same natural, unaffected beauty and grace that we saw today. The two men performed so magnificently, I have to admit I'm worried that when they dance under the autumn foliage on the day of the procession, it might be a bit of a letdown. But never mind . . . I so wanted you to see the performance that I had them prepare for it."

The following morning Genji sent a note to Fujitsubo:

"How did I look yesterday? As I danced, my heart was being torn apart by an unrequited love such as the world has never known."

> *I should never have danced in your presence*
> *With thoughts so troubled . . . did you understand*
> *When, in wild abandon, I twirled my sleeves*

"I feel uncertain before your grace."

Unable to shake the captivating sight of his face and elegant dancing figure, Fujitsubo could not very well pretend she had not seen his note, and so she replied:

> *Chinese dancers conceived the "Waves of the Blue Sea"*
> *Twirling their sleeves so long ago and far away . . .*
> *But your every gesture touched me here and now*

"My heart is overflowing."

---

2. A bird mentioned in Buddhist sutras for its surpassingly beautiful voice, to which the Buddha's voice is often compared [editor's note].

Genji had not expected a reply, and so he was ecstatic. Smiling, he thought that her words, which displayed knowledge of ancient dance and foreign courts, showed she had already acquired the dignity expected of a future Empress. He unrolled the letter and pored over it as if it were some treasured sutra.

On the day of the procession the princes of the blood and all members of the court participated. Genji's older half brother, the Crown Prince, accompanied the Emperor. As custom demanded, two boats were rowed around the lake at the site of the performance. One boat, adorned with the head of a dragon, held performers playing Chinese court music, while the other boat, adorned with the head of a blue heron, carried performers playing Korean court music.[3] There were many varieties of Chinese and Korean dance, and the sound of musical instruments and drums reverberated in all directions. Genji had looked so spectacular at the rehearsal the previous evening that the Emperor's old fears that his son might be fated to die young were revived, and he had sutras read for Genji at various temples around the capital to ward off evil. Everyone at the court who heard about this was sympathetic and thought it a reasonable precaution—everyone, that is, except the Kokiden Consort, mother of the Crown Prince, who spitefully remarked: "Isn't this really taking things a bit too far?"

The Emperor had gathered and selected the most distinguished players from among courtiers of both high and low rank to serve as the flutists and drummers who would accompany "Waves of the Blue Sea." He had the performers divided into sides—those playing Chinese music on the left, those playing Korean music on the right. He then chose two Consultants from the Council of State, men who also served as the directors of the Left and Right Gate Guards, to conduct the Chinese and Korean music respectively. Prior to this performance each aristocratic house had sought out the most skilled dance instructors and secluded themselves away to practice under their tutelage.

The intermittent soughing of the wind in the pines mingled with the indescribably polished sound of forty musicians playing in the shade of tall trees in autumn foliage. Truly it sounded like a breeze blowing down from the deepest mountains, and amidst the multihued leaves that had fallen all around, the dazzling performance of "Waves of the Blue Sea" was sublime. The autumn leaves that had adorned Genji's headdress at the outset had dropped off as the dance proceeded. Having lost a little of its luster, the headdress was now suffering in comparison with Genji's lambent face. So the Consultant who was conducting the musicians of the Left plucked some of the chrysanthemums that had been placed in front of the Emperor and inserted them into the headdress.

As the day drew to a close, a chill evening drizzle began to fall, as if the scene had moved the very sky itself. The color of the chrysanthemums now adorning Genji's spectacular figure had faded slightly with the frost, and their beauty was beyond the power of words to describe. Genji himself was putting all his skill into his performance, dancing in a way that would never be equaled again. As he executed the final movements, retracing his steps just before he exited with a flourish, it seemed that an unearthly chill coursed through all of the spectators. Lower-class people were also watching from the shade of craggy rocks, or

3. The term for these boats is *ryōtōgekisu* (dragon head, blue heron head). In China it referred to a single boat with a carving of a drag-on's head at the prow and one of a blue heron's head at the stern, but in Japan it referred to a pair of boats.

from beneath the leaves falling from the mountain trees, and though one would hardly have imagined that they had the sensitivity to appreciate the performance, they were able to dimly recognize the sadness of transient beauty and wept accordingly.

The Fourth Prince, the Emperor's son by the Shōkyōden Consort, was still a boy. Nonetheless, his performance of "Dance of the Autumn Wind" proved to be the most spectacular event after Genji's dance. Because those two performances were so dazzling, everything that followed seemed bland by comparison, which put a damper on the whole affair.

That evening, both Genji and Tō no Chūjō were promoted—Genji to the senior third rank, which was rather an extraordinary rise given his previous status, and Tō no Chūjō to the lower division of the senior fourth rank, which was also an unusual rise. Other high-ranking courtiers had reason to rejoice as well, since those who deserved promotions received them. Since they had all benefited from Genji's success—his own rise having helped pull everyone up with him—it makes one curious to know just what virtue from a previous life now endowed him with the qualities that drew everyone's admiring eyes and caused hearts to be joyful.

At around the time of the procession Fujitsubo left the court and withdrew to her own residence. As always, Genji sought out every opportunity to see her, and consequently he was subjected to complaints from the Minister of the Left's household that he never visited his wife. Moreover, he learned that his wife was more distressed than usual because one of her attendants had reported to her that Genji had plucked a certain "wild grass"—meaning his little Murasaki—and that "he was keeping her in his villa at Nijō."

It's natural she would feel upset, Genji thought, *since she knows nothing at all about the situation or how young Murasaki is. Even so, why can't she just tell me how she feels and vent her resentments like a normal woman? I could then speak without reserve, tell her all the things I feel in my heart and put her mind at ease. But no, she has to be so damnably suspicious all the time. It's no wonder I find myself conducting these illicit affairs.*

Still, he had to admit that there were no flaws in his wife's appearance or manners that made him feel dissatisfied. And even though she did not understand his feelings for her, she was the first woman he had known, and so he could not help but regard her with special tenderness. He was sure that over time her attitude toward him would change and she would come to understand. After all, he had faith that, given her gentle and serious nature, she would naturally come around to him. The feelings he had for her were special and different from those he had for other women.

Murasaki was now comfortable with Genji. Possessed of both a virtuous character and attractive looks, she would innocently follow after Genji, clinging to him. For the moment, he was inclined not to give the people in his residence too much information about her, and he kept her in a separate wing of the villa, which he had done up in a lavish manner. He would visit her mornings and evenings, instructing her in all manner of things, copying out books for her to emulate in her writing practice. It made him feel as though he had taken in a daughter from some aristocratic household. He gave special care to setting up the household office and choosing the staff to serve her, so that she would never have cause for worry or complaint. Apart from Koremitsu, Genji kept everyone else in the dark about this woman he was treating so solicitously. Her father, Prince Hyōbu, had been unable to discover what had happened to her.

Murasaki would often reflect on the past, and she missed her grandmother terribly. For that reason Genji would try to divert her whenever he was at Nijō, and he even spent the night with her on occasion. Yet he was busy traveling here and there, visiting his many other women and going out during the evening, and so there were times when she would call after him and tell him how she ached to be with him. He found her unbearably sweet at those moments. Whenever he returned from two or three days of service at the palace, or from a visit with his wife at Sanjō, she would always look depressed. He found this distressing, and because he sometimes felt as though he were caring for a motherless child, he was no longer comfortable going out on his nighttime escapades. Upon hearing how well Genji was caring for the girl, the bishop at Kitayama was relieved and happy, even though he still considered the arrangement abnormal. Each time he conducted a memorial service for his sister, the late nun, Genji never failed to provide him with solemn, elaborate offerings.

Genji very much wanted to find out how Fujitsubo was doing. She had withdrawn to her own villa on Sanjō Avenue, and so he called on her there. He was met by several of her ladies-in-waiting—Ōmyōbu, Chūnagon and Nakatsukasa—and it bothered him that they acted so formally, clearly treating him as if he were a stranger. He stayed calm, keeping his feelings to himself as he exchanged pleasantries and court gossip with the women. Just then the Minister of War, Prince Hyōbu, arrived. When he learned that Genji was there as well, he granted him an audience. The Prince's elegant looks and bearing bespoke his high breeding, and Genji found his softly erotic, seductive manner so appealing that he imagined that the Prince would be a very alluring partner were he a woman. What's more, because the Prince was the older brother of Fujitsubo and the father of Murasaki, Genji felt a surge of intimacy with the man, speaking to him in a relaxed, warmly familiar way. Noticing that Genji was kindly opening up to him more than usual, the Prince found him quite enchanting. Unaware that Genji was now his son-in-law, he had a similar fantasy, imagining what Genji would be like as a woman.

Being Fujitsubo's older brother, he had the right to go in behind her curtains to speak to her when evening came. Genji was jealous of him, recalling the times when, as a little boy, he would be permitted to accompany his father behind Fujitsubo's curtains and address her face-to-face with no intermediaries. When he thought of the pain their separation caused him, he could hardly stand it.

"Though I should visit you more often," Genji said, "I normally don't have any reason to come here, so naturally I have neglected to stay in touch. Still, it would make me happy if you would send word should you ever need me to take care of something."

His manner was serious and he made no pretense of showing the usual charming warmth as he left Fujitsubo's residence. Ōmyōbu had been useless to Genji in arranging a meeting with Fujitsubo, and it was clear that Fujitsubo now regretted more than ever the karmic destiny that had brought them together. In the face of her mistress's coldhearted attitude, Ōmyōbu felt so ashamed, so at a loss, that as the days went by she found she was no longer able to help Genji in any way. Mutually lost in their unending torment, Fujitsubo and Genji realized how evanescent their bond had been.

Murasaki's nurse, Shōnagon, observed the wonderful though completely unexpected rapport that had developed between Genji and her young mistress and was convinced that their relationship was a blessing from the Buddha, to whom the old nun had constantly prayed and made hopeful offerings. Yet Shōnagon continued to be assailed with doubts about Murasaki's future.

Genji's wife is a woman of unquestionably high status and breeding, and he is involved with a number of other women as well. Surely when the girl comes of age someone will cause problems for her, will they not?

It was only because Genji seemed so devoted to Murasaki that Shōnagon felt she could trust him.

Murasaki was told that three months was an appropriately long period to wear robes of mourning for her grandmother, and so she put them away at the end of the twelfth month, just in time for the New Year. Having known no parent other than her grandmother, she was influenced by the old nun's tastes and continued to wear modest robes of plain crimson, purple, or yellow. In spite of these preferences, she was lovely—indeed, it could even be said that she was rather chic.

On the morning of the first day of the New Year, Genji peeked in on Murasaki's quarters on his way to court to attend the ceremony offering congratulations to the Emperor.

"Your change of attire makes you look more grown up than usual," he laughed, exuding a dazzlingly gentle and affectionate appeal.

Before he knew it, Murasaki was absorbed in arranging her Hina court dolls, setting out various accessories on a series of three-foot-long shelves and spreading the little dollhouses that had been made for her all around the room until it was overflowing with her playthings.

"That Inuki!" Murasaki grumbled. "Last night during the demon purification ritual, she was following the exorcist and got so excited by his mask and lance that she broke this. I've been trying to fix it."

Clearly she regarded this as a major crisis.

"She really is inconsiderate, isn't she?" Genji responded. "I'll have it repaired for you. You just remember that there is no crying or pouting today—it would bring bad luck."

His dashing looks, together with the grand size of his retinue, made his departure for court seem so ceremonious that the women attendants at his residence came out onto the veranda to see him off. Murasaki also stepped outside to watch him leave, then went back inside and dressed up her Genji doll to match the attire he was wearing to the palace.

"I hope you'll start acting a little more mature this year," Shōnagon scolded her charge. "Here you are, already past your tenth birthday, and you're still playing with these dolls. It just won't do. You have a husband now, and you really must start behaving more like a proper wife and looking more like a lady for him. You still can't stand for me to fix up your hair."

Shōnagon scolded Murasaki in order to shame the girl for always being so absorbed in her playthings. But the effect of her admonition was to make Murasaki finally understand her circumstances for the first time.

So he's my husband, is he? The attendants here all have husbands, but they're really ugly. Mine, on the other hand, is a dashing, handsome young man.

It may have been true that she was still attached to her playthings, but her newfound awareness of her relationship with Genji signaled that she was now a year older. The people who served at Genji's mansion had found her childish behavior, which could be quite pronounced at times, awkward and inappropriate, and yet they had no idea that she was in fact a wife in name only, for Genji had not had sex with her even though they slept together.

Following the ceremony at the palace, Genji went to the Minister of the Left's residence on Sanjō. His wife, as always, presented an icy, beautiful perfection that emitted not the slightest hint of demureness or endearing warmth. He felt uncomfortable in her presence.

"How happy it would make me if—this year, at least—you could change your attitude toward me so that we might have a little more normal relationship as husband and wife."

She, however, was in no mood for reconciliation. Having heard that he had set up another woman at his villa—evidently someone of great value worthy of his special attentions—she could not help feeling depressed and awkward around him. She struggled to act nonchalant, to pretend that she knew nothing about what was going on, and she found it hard, whenever he was intimate and unreserved, to remain stubborn and refuse to open up to him. Indeed, the gentle way she always responded had a special quality that set her apart from other women. Four years older than her husband, she was, at the age of twenty-two, now in her prime, and this was a problem for Genji because her flawless beauty and manners made him lose confidence when he was in her presence. There was nothing lacking in her, no flaws that he could detect anyway, and when he reflected on his own behavior he had to admit that her resentment was justified, since it was caused by those inexcusable affairs his fickle heart led him to pursue. After all, she was the only daughter of the Minister of the Left—a man who of all the nobles of similar rank had the weightiest reputation at court—and Princess Ōmiya, who was the younger sister of the Emperor. The greatest care had been lavished on his wife's upbringing, which meant that her sense of pride was exceptionally strong and that she would take even the most trivial slight or indiscretion as a serious and unpleasant injustice. This in turn made Genji resentful, wondering why it was that he was the one who always had to humor her pride. And so their hearts remained distant and unreconciled.

The Minister of the Left was disturbed by his son-in-law's fickleness, and yet whenever he saw Genji he would always forget his resentments, treat him deferentially, and do everything in his power to look after him. The following morning, as Genji was dressing and preparing to leave for court, the Minister dropped by to look in on him. Now that Genji had been promoted to the third rank, his father-in-law had ordered the servants to bring in a famous obi sash made of lacquered leather studded with gemstones that would show at the back of his robe and indicate his new status. He also had his servants straighten up the back of Genji's robes and was so particular about the choice of shoes it was almost as if he were putting them on Genji's feet himself. His solicitous behavior was somehow both touching and a little pathetic.

"Should I wear this on official occasions?" Genji asked. "The privy banquet will be held soon, on the Day of the Rat . . . is it the twenty-first or the twenty-third this year? Either way, I have to practice my Chinese verse for the event."

"I have better obi for events like that," the Minister sniffed. "This one just struck me as rather unusual-looking. That's all."

He pressed Genji to put it on, being almost religiously devoted to looking after him any way he could. Genji's appearances at Sanjō were certainly infrequent, but just to see this remarkable young man coming and going from his residence was a source of great joy and pride for the Minister.

Genji set off to make his New Year's round of visits. He did not have all that many places to call on: he paid his respects to the Emperor, to the Crown Prince, and to the former Emperor. He also dropped by Fujitsubo's villa on Sanjō.

"He's more remarkable than ever today. It's thrilling to realize that as he grows older, he's becoming even more handsome."

Fujitsubo's women were praising him up and down, and so she could not resist peeking through the gaps between her curtains to steal a glimpse. Immediately she was lost in her own troubled thoughts.

Her pregnancy was a source of considerable anxiety. Would she survive it? She was supposed to have given birth during the twelfth month, but here it was the New Year already. Her attendants were in a state of anticipation, thinking that surely their mistress would give birth sometime this month. Even His Majesty was having preparations made at court. But the first month passed with no indication that the birth was imminent, and rumors were now flying around court society. Was this delay the fault of some malign spirit? Such gossip made Fujitsubo feel even more miserable, for just as she was frightened by the possibility that she might die in childbirth, she was just as deathly afraid that the secret of her affair with Genji would be exposed. Her mental anguish eventually made her physically ill.

It was now increasingly clear to Genji that he was the father, and so to ward off evil spirits he discreetly ordered esoteric rites to be performed at various temples around the capital. He fully understood the evanescent nature of the world, but he could not help torturing himself with the thought that his relationship with Fujitsubo would end too soon and come to naught.

Then, sometime after the tenth of the second month, Fujitsubo gave birth to a Prince. The Emperor and all the people at Fujitsubo's residence in Sanjō were relieved and excited by this auspicious event, even if Genji and Fujitsubo were not. His Majesty had been praying for her to live a long life, yet now the thought of a long life was a burden to Fujitsubo, given all her cares. When rumors reached her that the Kokiden Consort had tried to curse her by praying for an unlucky birth, she realized that news of her death would have served as a source of amusement to some at the court. She drew strength and determination from that thought, and gradually her health and spirits improved.

The Emperor's desire to see the child as quickly as possible was boundless. Genji, who was keeping his feelings to himself, was also extremely anxious to see the child to confirm whether or not he was the father. Choosing a time when he knew there would be no one else around, he paid a visit to Fujitsubo.

"My father is eagerly waiting to see the child," Genji told her. "I thought I might take a look at the baby and then report to the Emperor."

"That's out of the question . . . he was just born and is not presentable in his present condition."

Fujitsubo quite reasonably refused, for there was no denying that the baby bore a shocking, almost otherworldly resemblance to Genji—a living reproduction.

Suffering from the demon of guilty conscience, Fujitsubo was convinced that anyone who saw the baby would instantly recognize the sin that she had committed with Genji. Since sanctimonious people were always eager to discover and condemn even the most minor of faults, what would they say about this? What would happen to her reputation? Dwelling on such possibilities, Fujitsubo was deeply distressed, body and soul.

Genji would meet with Ōmyōbu once in a while, doing his utmost through her to plead his case with Fujitsubo. Not surprisingly, his pleas fell on deaf ears.

He continually pestered her about the young Prince until finally Ōmyōbu told him, "Why must you insist on seeing him? You'll have your chance in due time." Even though she tried to reassure him, she seemed as troubled at heart as he.

Constrained by his surroundings, Genji could not speak frankly with Ōmyōbu.

"Will there ever be a time or conditions when I can speak directly to Fujitsubo, without having to rely on an intermediary?"

It was heartbreaking to see him on the verge of tears.

> What karmic bond forged in a former life
> Destined us to meet again in this world
> Only to find ourselves always apart

"I cannot understand these things," he lamented.

Having witnessed the torments her lady was experiencing, Ōmyōbu found it impossible, in the face of Genji's sadness, to curtly refuse him. She recalled the poem by Fujiwara no Kanesuke that evoked the "hearts of parents lost in darkness," and replied:

> The one looking on the child suffers regret
> The one who cannot see the child suffers grief . . .
> Must all parents wander lost in such darkness

"How sad that the birth of this child should keep your hearts from finding peace," she murmured.

With no means of communicating with Fujitsubo, Genji returned to his residence. Troubled by the possibility of idle chatter at the court, Fujitsubo told Ōmyōbu that she could no longer tolerate her leading Genji here; that was how she really felt. Wary that Ōmyōbu might bring Genji to her, she was no longer able to trust her lady-in-waiting as she had in the past, and stopped treating her as a confidante. She continued to treat Ōmyōbu kindly, so that no one would suspect anything was amiss, but there were times now when she appeared displeased by Ōmyōbu's conduct. Aware that she was estranged from Fujitsubo, Ōmyōbu felt sad that things had not turned out as she had expected.

The baby was taken to the palace during the fourth month. Larger than usual for a baby that age, the boy was already able to turn himself over. His face bore a striking resemblance to Genji's, but it never occurred to the Emperor that Genji might be the child's true father. Rather, he assumed that people who shared unparalleled good looks would naturally resemble one another. His affection and care for the baby were boundless. His affection for Genji also knew no limits, but the lack of recognition and support for Genji among the high-ranking courtiers had made it impossible for him to install Genji in the line of succession. He constantly regretted his decision, and it was a source of pain for him to now look on his son's mature bearing and features and have to think what a waste it was to have removed Genji from the imperial line. It was thus a source of consolation for him that Fujitsubo, the fourth daughter of the previous Emperor and a woman of unimpeachable status, had given him a son who possessed the same radiant beauty as Genji. He considered the child a flawless jewel and lavished the greatest care on him—attention that, for Fujitsubo, merely added to the guilt and anxiety filling her heart.

One day, when Genji decided to pass the time performing music in Fujitsubo's quarters at the palace, as was his wont, His Majesty joined them. He was carrying the infant Prince in his arms.

"I have many, many children," he remarked to Genji, "but you were the only one I was able to be with all day from the time you were this one's age. Maybe it's because this little one brings those days back to me that I think he looks so much like you. I wonder if all children look the same when they are very young?"

It was obvious that the Emperor found the child adorable.

Genji felt himself blanch. Fear, shame, elation, pity . . . all these emotions overwhelmed him to the point that he felt he was going to cry. The baby prattled and smiled, and looked almost preternaturally cute. Was it all that unreasonable or vain of Genji to think—assuming he really did resemble this child during his own infancy—that he himself must indeed have been incredibly precious? Fujitsubo could hardly stand to be there—she was so mortified that she began to perspire. At the same time Genji, who had been so eager to see the child, was unnerved in his presence, and the turmoil in his heart forced him to withdraw from Fujitsubo's quarters.

Genji returned to his Nijō villa, and after resting for a while to calm his nerves, he decided that he should pay a visit to his wife. Pinks were brightly blooming amidst the vibrant green of the plantings that seemed to cover the entire front garden, so he had one of them picked and sent to Ōmyōbu. There were so many things he had to write to Fujitsubo:

> Though I see you in him, the one so like this little pink,
> I cannot tell you so, and thus my heart knows no comfort
> My tears heavier than the dew on this flower's petals

"No matter how much I long to see the little one bloom, because our relationship was not meant to last in this vain world . . ."

His note must have been delivered at an opportune moment. Ōmyōbu showed it to Fujitsubo and encouraged her lady to write back:

"You really should answer him, even if, as Ōshikōchi no Mitsune put it, your response is no more than a mote of dust on the petal of a pink."[4]

Fujitsubo was deeply moved and sent back a simple poem written in the faintest of hands. Her characters looked as though she had pulled the brush away before finishing each stroke:

4. *Kokinshū* 167 (Ōshikōchi no Mitsune): "I long to stop even a mote of dust from settling on this bed of pinks that have come into bloom since first you and I lay on our bed." Mitsune's poem is alluded to in the *Hahakigi* chapter.

> *Though I may consider it the source*
> *Of the heavy dew that soaks my sleeves*
> *How could I discard this precious pink*

Ōmyōbu was overjoyed that her lady had responded, and she promptly delivered the poem to Genji. At that moment Genji was lying languidly, absently lost in melancholy thoughts, sure that his poem had been in vain and that no reply would be coming back to him. But as soon as he saw Ōmyōbu, his heart beat wildly and he was so happy he wept.

Feeling that it was not good for him to just lie around and mope, absorbed in his cares, he decided he should go to the west hall to see the one person who was his solace. His hair was mussed, he had carelessly tossed on a loose robe, and he was playing a sweetly nostalgic air on his flute when he looked in on Murasaki. She was reclining on an armrest, her elegant appearance calling to mind the image of pinks drenched in dew—perfectly lovely and cute. As enchanting as she looked, it turned out that she was nursing a new grudge against Genji. This was unusual for her, but there she was, sitting with her back toward him, annoyed that he had not come to see her sooner even though he had been in his quarters for some time. Genji moved over to the veranda at the edge of the room and knelt there.

"Come over here," Genji coaxed her, but she ignored him and continued to sulk.

She expressed her resentment toward him by murmuring lines from the *Man'yōshū*: "Is he like seaweed on the shore at high tide, which I long for so much, but see so seldom?"

She covered her mouth with the sleeve of her robe, apparently embarrassed at her own precociousness. Her gesture made her all the more adorable.

"Ahh, that's unfortunate . . . you've already learned how to complain just like an adult. Well, then, let me remind you of this poem: 'Were I to see you morning and night, just as often as the divers at Ise see the seaweed, would I not grow weary of you?'"[5]

He summoned a servant and had her bring in a thirteen-string koto for Murasaki to play.

"This instrument is difficult because the second string closest to you is thin and easily broken," Genji told her. He then tuned the instrument to a lower key to reduce the tension on the strings. He played a few short songs to test the tuning and then pushed the koto over in front of her. Murasaki found it impossible to continue sulking, and she played beautifully. She was still so small that she had to raise herself up and stretch to reach the strings, but he found the movements of her left hand, as she pressed the strings to make the instrument reverberate, delightfully refined. He instructed her by accompanying her on the flute. She had a quick memory and could pick up even the difficult keys in just one try. Clever, possessed of a sweet disposition, she was everything he had long hoped for in a woman. The court song "Hosoroguseri" may have had a peculiar-sounding title, but as Genji focused on playing it in his inimitable style, Murasaki

5. *Kokinshū* 683 (Anonymous).

accompanied him, skillfully keeping time to the rhythm even though she was so young.

Oil lamps were brought in and they passed the time poring over paintings together. He had mentioned earlier to his retinue that he intended to go out, and so a member of his escort began to cough to signal it was time to go.

"It looks like it might rain . . ." one of his guards remarked, and Murasaki at once became sullen and depressed, as she always did when Genji was about to leave.

She pushed the paintings away and lay facedown. Genji found her so endearing that he began to stroke her hair, which was spilling abundantly over her shoulders.

"I suppose you miss me when I'm away?" he asked her.

She nodded.

"I hate going even a single day without seeing you," Genji tried to comfort her, adding, "But since you are still a child, I have to ask you to be patient a little while longer and to not worry so. I have such fond feelings for you, but I must also consider the feelings of others and not offend those who may be jealous and resentful. Those women are troublesome, and that's why, for the present at least, I have to visit them as I do. When you are grown up I won't have to go out any-more, but for now I want to avoid the harm that might arise as a result of the jealousy of other women so that we might live a long life and be together as much as we desire."

Murasaki felt embarrassed to hear Genji speak about their relationship in such detail, and so she did not answer him. She drew herself up onto Genji's lap and went to sleep.

Genji felt terribly sorry for her and told his attendants, "I'll not be going out this evening." They all rose and withdrew, and he had his dinner, which he nor-mally ate in his own rooms, brought to her quarters instead.

He woke Murasaki and told her, "I'm not going out after all."

Her mood at once improved and she got up. They ate together, but Murasaki was still anxious about his plans and merely picked at her food.

"If you're not going out," she suggested, "then why not sleep here tonight?"

If it is so difficult for us to part at a moment like this, Genji mused, *then how much more difficult will it be when we have to part on the inevitable road of death?*

* * *

From Chapter IX

Aoi

LEAVES OF WILD GINGER

The court changed when His Majesty abdicated and the Crown Prince took the throne as Emperor Suzaku. The Kokiden faction, headed by the Minister of the Right, was now in ascendance, and Genji began to feel that everything was more difficult for him. Just before His Majesty stepped down, he had pro-moted his favored son to Major Captain of the Right—a rise in status that required the Radiant Prince, in keeping with the dignity of his new position, to begin showing more restraint in pursuing his frivolous nightly adventures. The result was that his many lovers began to complain more and more of his heartlessness. Was it in retribution for causing all these lamentations that Genji suffered from what he saw as the unending cruelty of Fujitsubo, who kept her distance from him? Now, more than ever, she served at the side of the Retired Emperor—almost as if she were some low-ranking attendant. This did not sit well with the Kokiden Consort, but she was now Imperial Mother and had to serve exclusively at the palace—an arrangement that was a source of considerable relief to Fujitsubo.

Depending on the occasion, the Retired Emperor would sponsor musical entertainments so lavish and spectacular that they became the talk of court society. He seemed more content now than when he had held power. The only thing lacking for him was Fujitsubo's little son, the new Crown Prince. He yearned to see the boy, who could not be by his side. Having long worried that Fujitsubo's son had no supporters at court, he asked Genji to look after the boy's affairs—a request that was of course awkward for Genji, but one that also made him happy.

At this point I must bring up another, entirely separate matter. At the time Emperor Suzaku ascended the throne, an imperial princess was appointed as the new High Priestess for the Imperial Shrine at Ise. The mother of this princess was the lady at Rokujō—the woman Genji had long been visiting discreetly—while the father was an imperial prince who had actually been ahead of Suzaku in the line of succession, but who had died before he could take the throne. Because the Princess was appointed High Priestess under these circumstances, the lady at Rokujō, who no longer had any confidence in the reliability of Genji's feelings, was greatly worried about her daughter's future. The girl was, after all, only thirteen and would be alone in Ise. Thus, the lady at Rokujō had for some time been giving serious consideration to leaving the capital herself and accompanying her daughter to the Imperial Shrine. When the Retired Emperor heard about her plans to leave, he was extremely upset and spoke sharply to Genji about the matter.

"Do I need to remind you," he scolded, "that she was the first wife of my late brother and would have been an Imperial Consort? He had special affection for her, but now I hear rumors about how carelessly you treat her, as if she were some ordinary woman. It's pathetic. I look on her daughter, the High Priestess, as one of my own, and so you must put an end to this frivolous behavior—not just for her sake, but for mine as well. If you persist in playing these irresponsible little games, then don't be surprised when your reputation is in ruins."

Genji could not deny that his father was speaking the truth. Thoroughly chastened, he refrained from answering, whereupon the Retired Emperor added, his tone a little softer, "Never do anything to dishonor or shame a woman. Treat them all gently and give them no cause to resent you."

With that admonition ringing in his ears, Genji humbly withdrew from his father's presence, terrified at the thought that a day might come when his father learned the truth about Genji's wildly reckless affair with Fujitsubo.

If his father was lecturing him about it, then obviously gossip about his affair with the lady at Rokujō had spread through the court. His promiscuity had damaged her honor and his own reputation. He could just imagine how terribly she must be suffering, but there was simply no way he could formally acknowledge their relationship. For one thing, the lady herself was embarrassed that at the age of twenty-nine she was having an affair with a man seven years younger. Moreover, she always tried to appear distant and aloof, and so Genji had grown more reserved with her. Now, however, everyone at court, even the Retired Emperor, knew what was going on, and she lamented that Genji's feelings for her were so shallow.

Genji had long been pursuing the daughter of Prince Shikibu—a lady he knew as Asagao, his Princess of the bellflowers. His efforts had so far proven futile, however, and when Princess Asagao heard rumors of his affair, she resolved never to end up like the lady at Rokujō and refused to give even the most perfunctory of replies to his vain entreaties. Even so, she showed a proper attitude and conducted herself in a way that would give no offense to Genji, and so he continued to consider her a woman of superior qualities.

Needless to say, the household of the Minister of the Left was not amused by Genji's restless disposition, but then again, since he showed no qualms about carrying on so openly, it would have been useless to have complained to him about it. His wife, for one, did not harbor any deep resentment toward him, not least because she was now pregnant and suffering most pitifully not only from morning sickness but also from anxiety over the dangers posed by the coming birth. Genji thought the pregnancy remarkable, and for the first time felt sympathy for his wife. Because everyone was so overjoyed for her, there was a concern that such happiness could invite bad fortune, and so various prayers and rituals of abstinence[6] were commissioned in order to ensure safe delivery for mother and child. With all these things going on, Genji had less and less time to even consider the feelings of his other women. He was especially mindful of the feelings of the lady at Rokujō, but despite his best intentions not to neglect her, his visits practically ceased altogether.

The High Priestess of the Kamo Shrine also stepped down at about that time, and her successor was the third daughter of the Retired Emperor by the Kokiden Consort. This girl was a special favorite of both parents, and it bothered them that unlike her siblings she would have to live isolated from court life. Unfortunately, there were no other princesses appropriate for the position. Although the rituals of investiture were austere, as was customary with Shinto shrines, they would nonetheless be solemn and grand. The Festival of the Kamo Shrine, which was held in the fourth month, was always a major event in the capital; those who accompanied the High Priestess's procession would decorate their carriages and headdresses with heart-shaped leaves of wild ginger[7] Because this year marked the new Priestess's inaugural procession, many attractions would be added to the public events already scheduled, and the festival, in keeping with the special status of the High Priestess, would be an especially glorious one.

A few days before the start of the Kamo Festival, twelve high-ranking officials were required to attend the Priestess during the procession to her ritual of

6. That is, periods of seclusion [editor's note].
7. *Aoi*, the Japanese name for wild ginger, is also a homophone for the words *au hi*, which means "the day we will meet." The combination of the heart-shaped leaves of the plant, which is an evergreen, and the romantic impli- cations of its name are played on later in this chapter in an exchange of poems between Genji and the older lady, Naishi, who appeared in the *Momiji no ga* chapter. Because much of this chapter centers on Genji's wife, she has been identified traditionally as Aoi.

purification, which took place on the banks of the Kamo River. Given the auspicious nature of the event, only men with honorable prospects and good looks were chosen for this task, and every detail of their appearance was carefully considered—from the color of the trains on their robes and the pattern of their trousers to the choice of horses and saddles. By special order of Emperor Suzaku, Genji was chosen to participate, and when those who planned to view the procession heard about this decision, they gave extra thought in advance to preparing and positioning their carriages along the route.

The thoroughfare of Ichijō was crammed with carriages and bustling with people. Viewing platforms had been erected at various sites and decorated with great care. Those decorations, together with the sleeves of the court ladies' robes, which trailed out from beneath the blinds set up on the platforms, created their own splendid spectacle.

Genji's wife rarely left her father's residence to go view events like this. Moreover, she had given no thought at all of going to view this particular procession, since she was feeling ill and nervous. Her younger attendants, however, all complained to her.

"What is my lady thinking? How could we ever hope to enjoy the beauty of the procession if we have to sneak off just to take a peak?"

"Ordinary folk, even the lowest woodcutters and hunters who have no connection with anyone in the procession, will be there to take in the sights. They'll especially want to catch a glimpse of your husband."

"People from distant provinces will bring their wives and children to take a look. So it's just not fair that we have to miss it!"

Princess Ōmiya, who, as the younger sister of the Retired Emperor, truly understood the importance of such matters, heard these complaints and urged her daughter to go.

"You've been feeling better recently, and your attendants will feel left out and dissatisfied if you don't."

And with that, all the women were suddenly informed, to their joy, that their lady would be going out after all.

Because the sun was already well up, they left without formally preparing the carriages in a manner befitting the status of the Minister's household. By the time they arrived, Ichijō Avenue was already packed with carriages lining both sides of the street, and it was difficult finding a place to park the imposing and dignified vehicles, unhitch the oxen, and set the shafts on their supports. Many noblewomen already had their carriages positioned there, and the male guards escorting Genji's wife decided to clear a space by pushing aside those that had no guardsmen protecting them.

Among the carriages that had been lined up in that space, two of them exuded a special air of refinement—informal in style, with roofs and blinds made of *hinoki*[8] wicker, slightly worn, but adorned with silk curtains. The women inside had obviously intended to remain inconspicuous. The fresh, vibrant colors of the cuffs of their sleeves, the hems of their skirts, and the ends of their singlets all peeked out coyly from beneath the blinds. The guards escorting Genji's wife were explicitly told not to touch these two carriages and warned, "This is not a carriage you can just push aside as you wish!" Unfortunately, the young men in

---

8. A Japanese evergreen used for various building purposes [editor's note].

both parties had been drinking too much, and in the end there was no way to prevent the situation from getting out of control. The older retainers from the Minister's household commanded the young men to desist, but they were unable to stop a fight from breaking out.

The lady at Rokujō, whose daughter would soon go off to serve as the Ise Priestess, had been thinking she might find relief from her tormented feelings about Genji by coming discreetly to view the procession for the Purification Ritual. Her attendants, aware of her desire to remain incognito, did not reveal her identity, but it was obvious to the men accompanying Genji's wife whose carriages they were moving.

"Don't let them talk to us like that," several of the men shouted. "They must think they can still rely on Lord Genji!"

Several of Genji's attendants had been assigned to accompany his wife's party. They all regarded this incident as most regrettable, but it would have been extremely awkward for them to intervene, and so they looked the other way. In the end, the carriages of Genji's wife and her attendants were positioned in the spaces that had been cleared away, and the carriages of the lady at Rokujō had been relegated to a place behind them, where she could neither see nor be seen. She was in an agony of anger and indignation, and now that her identity had been revealed, after having gone to such great lengths to conceal it out of concern that her shameful feelings for Genji might be exposed, there was no limit to the feelings of chagrin and remorse she suffered. Because the stands for her carriage shafts had been broken in the melee, they had to be propped up on the wheel hubs of some unknown carriages next to hers. It must have looked unsightly, and she was mortified, wondering vainly why she had ever decided to come here.

She no longer wanted to view the procession and wished instead to go home, but there was no space to move her carriage. Just then cries rang out from the crowd:

"They're on their way!"

Her resolve weakened, and now she wanted to wait until her cruel lover had passed. She recalled an ancient poem in which the Goddess of Ise asks a man to stop his horse at Sasanokuma to let it drink from the Hinokuma River—all so that she might have the chance to gaze upon him.[9] Anxious, she wondered if Genji would stop to acknowledge her . . . but no, he continued on, coldly passing by without so much as a glance in her direction. The turmoil in her heart was greater than ever. Genji feigned disinterest in the many carriages that lined the way, even though they were more splendidly decorated than usual, with the hems of robes spilling out from beneath the blinds as though the occupants were in competition with one another. Still, he did occasionally smile and give a sly, sidelong glance at certain carriages, and when he recognized the carriages of his father-in-law, he assumed a solemn expression as he passed. The men in his escort silently bowed to show their deep respect for Genji's wife. The Rokujō lady, overwhelmed by this display, which clearly demonstrated the inferiority of her status, could not have felt more wretched.

9. A sacred song for the Sun Goddess from *The Kokinshū*.

How cruel of those chill waters of lustration
To grant but a glimpse of your reflected image
Reminding me all the more of my wretched fate

She knew it would be disgraceful to weep in front of her women, so she comforted herself with the thought that she would have regretted passing up the opportunity to witness the radiance of his appearance and the beauty of his countenance on such a dazzling occasion.

The high-ranking nobles who accompanied the Kamo Priestess on the procession were superbly decked out in fine robes, each in keeping with his status at court, and attended by magnificent-looking escorts. The appearance of those of the highest rank was especially breathtaking, and yet, as remarkable as they were, they seemed to pale in comparison with Genji's radiance. One of the eight men in his retinue, which had been assembled just for this event, was a man of the sixth rank, a Lesser Captain in the Right Imperial Guard. It was most unusual to assign someone of his status to this kind of duty, but he was so remarkably good-looking that he was chosen anyway. The other men in Genji's escort were also dazzlingly resplendent, and Genji's appearance, which was always esteemed by the court, was so awe-inspiring that the very trees and grasses seemed to bow before him. Normally, it would be considered improper and unsightly for ladies of rank who, for the sake of modesty, wore veils beneath their deep-brimmed hats, or for nuns who had renounced the world to literally fall over one another in an effort to catch a glimpse of him. Today, however, was different, and no one reproved them. Women of the lower classes—their mouths drawn in where they were missing teeth, their hair tucked modestly inside their robes—jostled each other and made fools of themselves, clasping their hands to their foreheads in supplication to Genji. Vulgar men were grinning stupidly from ear to ear, unaware of how ridiculous their faces looked. Daughters of minor provincial officials, whom Genji would never so much as glance at, had arrived in their lavishly decorated carriages, hopelessly preening and posturing because they knew Genji would be passing by. So many amusing things to observe—including the many women who, having been favored by a covert visit from Genji, were now lamenting to themselves that they no longer belonged among the blessed few he favored.

Prince Shikibu, the Minister of Ceremonials, was viewing the procession from one of the platforms, and when he saw Genji, ominous thoughts came to him: *He has matured so, and his appearance is so truly spectacular that I fear he will attract the attention of gods and demons.*

Prince Shikibu's daughter, Princess Asagao, had exchanged many letters with Genji over several years and so she knew his sensibilities were anything but ordinary. Now that she was seeing his beauty for the first time, her heart was deeply moved.

A woman can be touched be a man's sincerity, she told herself, *even if he is rather ordinary-looking. How much more appealing, then, is the sincerity of a man whose looks are as stunning as his?*

Despite these sentiments, she was not inclined to allow her relationship with Genji to become any more familiar or intimate. Her younger attendants were all praising him so much they sounded uncouth, and she found it irritating to listen to them.

When the Kamo Festival proper was held a few days later, no one from the Minister of the Left's residence came out to view it. Genji had been informed of the quarrel between the carriages, and he felt sorry for the lady at Rokujō. He was also offended by his wife's conduct.

"It's a shame," he remarked, "that such a dignified person should show so little sympathy or kindness toward others. She probably never intended for such a thing to happen, and yet her temperament prevents her from even considering the possibility that women who share the kind of relationship she and the lady do should be mutually affectionate and supportive. No wonder her subordinates, who lack judgment and status, acted as outrageously as they did. As for the lady who suffered this insult, she has such a superior upbringing and is so sensitive to any slight that the whole sordid incident must have been terribly unpleasant for her."

Genji felt such pity that he went to Rokujō to visit the lady. She, however, was reluctant to meet him. Her daughter, after all, was still living in the residence while undergoing the rites of purification that would prepare her to serve as the High Priestess at Ise. Branches of the sacred *sakaki* tree[1] had been placed at all the corners and gates, and thus the lady did not feel comfortable letting Genji in to see her, since that would run the risk of defilement. Genji thought her precaution perfectly reasonable, but he still muttered to himself, "Why must things always be like this? Why do women have to flash their horns and quarrel?"

Genji retreated to his own residence at Nijō. On the day of the Kamo Festival he went with Murasaki to view the festivities. After ordering Koremitsu to prepare their carriages, he went over to the west hall.

"Will all your little ladies be going as well?" he teasingly asked, referring to Murasaki's playmates.

Observing her outfit and makeup, which exuded an exceptionally graceful air, he couldn't help smiling.

"Very well, then, shall we be going? Let's go view the festival together."

He stroked her hair, which looked even more lustrous than usual, and added, "It's been a while since you've had the ends trimmed. Today would be an auspicious time to do it." He summoned a scholar from the Bureau of Divination and asked him which hours that day would be lucky or unlucky for trimming hair. He then told Murasaki, "Have your little ladies come forth." He looked them over and found their childish figures delightfully charming. Their hair had been trimmed gorgeously and hung down in sharp relief over the outer trousers of their festive robes . . . altogether adorable. "I'll cut your hair," Genji said to Murasaki. "It's really thick, isn't it? What would become of it if you just let it grow out?" He found trimming her hair a little difficult. "Ladies with very long hair tend to cut the sidelocks that frame their foreheads a little shorter than the rest. I don't think you would look as attractive without short locks." When he finished with the trimming, Genji offered the obligatory benediction, expressing the hope that her hair might grow "a thousand fathoms."

Murasaki's nurse, Shonagon, had been watching them, her heart filled with gratitude. Genji composed and recited a verse:

1. *Sakaki* is a flowering evergreen tree native to Japan. It is sacred in the Shinto religion, and branches of *sakaki*, decorated with slips or streamers of paper, are used for ritual offerings and purifications.

> *I shall protect you, watching your hair grow*
> *Like strands of rippling seaweed stretching up*
> *From the thousand-fathomed depths of the sea*

Murasaki chose to write out her reply:

> *You swear love as deep as the thousand-fathomed sea*
> *Yet how am I to know that's true, since you wander*
> *Coming and going like uncertain, restless tides*

Such clever wit, and such youthful beauty. She's perfect, Genji thought.

So many sightseeing carriages had arrived for the Kamo Festival that there were not enough spaces to park them all this day as well. Because they were having trouble finding a place to stop, they pulled up near the parade grounds and pavilion where the Mounted Guard held their archery competition during the fifth month of each year.

"So many high-ranking officials have brought their carriages here, the area is really bustling," Genji said, sounding a little confounded and irritable. He had his carriage pause for a moment next to a lady's carriage that was not at all inelegant. The carriage was filled with occupants, and a fan was thrust out beckoning him over to them.

"Would you like to set your carriage here?" a woman asked. "We could make some space for you."

Genji was somewhat taken aback, wondering what kind of woman could be so coquettish. This spot, however, was an excellent place from which to view the festival parade, and so he decided to accept the invitation.

"How did you manage to come by this space?" he asked. "It's good enough to make people resent you, so I'll take you up on your offer."

The lady in the carriage then broke off a section of her stylish folding fan and wrote out the following:

> *Heart-shaped leaves of wild ginger adorn another*
> *Though their name promises some day we'll meet . . . vainly*
> *I waited for the Kamo gods to bless this day*

"I cannot pass beyond the ropes marking off that sacred space."

Genji recognized the handwriting. It was the old Assistant Handmaid, Naishi no suke. He found it shocking that someone her age should be flirting like a young woman. He was genuinely displeased and sent back a curt reply:

> *The feelings of one adorned with those heart-shaped leaves*
> *Are certainly fickle, since she can "meet this day"*
> *Any man she wants from among the eighty clans*

Naishi was filled with resentment when she received Genji's cruel response:

> *A bitter adornment, this wild ginger*
> *With its empty promise of meeting you . . .*
> *Mere leaves signifying vain and false hopes*

Many women, not just Naishi, experienced pangs of jealousy as they tried to guess the identity of the lady riding with Genji. They resented that for her sake he chose to keep his blinds down, because it denied them an opportunity to catch a glimpse of him. The women gossiped among themselves:

"He was so splendid-looking the day of the procession."

"Yes, but today's he's going about rather informally, don't you think?"

"Who is that riding with him? I wonder. She must be a special woman."

Genji remained disgruntled, thinking, *What a complete waste of time, exchanging verses that play on a subject like leaves of wild ginger.*

Anyone else would certainly have refrained from sending a note out of respect for the lady riding with him—but not someone as impudent as Naishi.

For her part, the lady at Rokujō had never in all her life experienced the kind of torment brought on recently by her dark, obsessive thoughts. She had, it is true, resigned herself to Genji's cruel neglect, but the thought of leaving him behind in order to go with her daughter to Ise brought on agonizing loneliness. She was also fully aware that she would be an object of derision at the court. Whenever she thought, wistfully, that perhaps she ought to stay behind in the capital, she would become anxious, for she knew that if she stayed she would expose herself to even more extreme levels of ridicule. Her days and nights were so filled with troubled thoughts that she couldn't help but recall the *Kokinshū* poem: "Am I a float on the line of the fisherman of Ise that my heart should be adrift like this, bobbing on the waves?"[2] Finding no relief from her obsessive, insecure state of mind, she fell ill.

Genji wasn't in the least concerned about her stated desire to accompany her daughter to Ise, and he never once tried to dissuade her by telling her that it was out of the question. Instead he remarked, rather sarcastically, "I understand. It's perfectly reasonable for you to find repugnant the prospect of continuing a relationship with a man as worthless as I. Yet no matter how unpleasant it may be for you now, if you were to stay with me to the end, your choice would prove that you're a woman of uncommonly deep sensibility, would it not?"

On hearing such hateful words, the lady withdrew even deeper into her dark thoughts. Distressed and depressed, she had decided to go see the procession only because she wanted some relief from her insecurity and indecisiveness. And then, when she did go, she found herself buffeted about, as if she were adrift on the violent rapids of the river of lustration.

While all of this was taking place, a malignant spirit was causing concern for everyone at the Minister of the Left's Sanjō residence. Genji's wife was suffering terribly, and under the circumstances it was not appropriate for him to be going around visiting his other women. Indeed, during this period he only rarely went to his own residence in Nijō. True, he had never warmed to his wife much, but he did consider her someone of special importance to him. He was wracked with grief that she should now be suffering so much as a consequence of her remarkable pregnancy, and he had prayers and rites performed for her in his own quarters at his father-in-law's residence.

Many souls of the deceased and spirits of living persons were exorcised and forced to reveal their names. One particular spirit, however, resisted all attempts to move it into the body of a medium and persisted in clinging fast to Genji's

2. Anonymous poem from *The Kokinshū*.

wife. It did no real harm, but it would not leave her body, even for a few moments. The deeply obsessive nature of this spirit, which would not obey the holiest of exorcists, made it clear that this was no commonplace possession. The attendants considered the various women Genji called on and whispered among themselves:

"Only the ladies at Rokujō and Nijō have a special place in his heart—perhaps their resentment is especially strong."

Diviners were brought in to confirm these suspicions, but they failed to do so. Whenever they questioned the spirits, they learned nothing that would suggest any of them was driven by revenge or hatred. There was the spirit of a former nurse and spirits that had haunted the families of the Minister and Princess Ōmiya for generations, but these had appeared simply because their daughter was in a fragile condition. None of them were really malicious but seemed to have shown up at random. Why, then, was Genji's wife constantly shouting out and weeping? She was always nauseous or had choking sensations, and she would writhe around as if in unbearable agony. Genji and her parents were frightened and upset, wondering how this would all turn out and worrying that she might die.

Because the Retired Emperor repeatedly sent messages of concern and graciously ordered prayers and rituals, her death would be all the more lamentable. Upon hearing that everyone at the court was worried, the lady at Rokujō was afflicted with the troubling thought that she was being diminished as sympathy for her rival grew. She had always had a jealous, competitive streak, but until that absurd quarrel over the carriages had unsettled her heart, it had never been as pronounced as it was now, and she felt a degree of resentment that no one at the Minister's household could have ever imagined.

The lady knew, as a result of her confused emotions, that her condition was not normal, and so she decided to undergo esoteric Buddhist healing rites. However, she had to move out of her residence and have the rites performed elsewhere in order to avoid defiling her daughter, who was still preparing to be the High Priestess of Ise. Genji heard about her plans and, moved to pity as he wondered how she was feeling, went to call on her. Because she was not at her usual residence in Rokujō, he had to be exceptionally discreet when he visited. He repeatedly asked her to overlook the way he had neglected her recently, pointing out that it was due to circumstances beyond his control. He even tried to elicit her sympathy by describing the terrible suffering of his wife.

"I'm not all that concerned about her myself," he said, "but I do feel sorry for her parents, who are upset and making rather too much of a fuss about it. So while she is in this condition, I really should stay close by her. If you could take all of these things into account, I would be very grateful."

Genji pleaded with her, but he could see from the expression on her face that she was suffering even more than usual, and he felt terribly sorry for her.

The lady had been moody and withdrawn that night, but when—in the welter of her yearnings and resentments—she saw how ravishing he looked as he prepared to leave at the crack of dawn, she was tempted to reconsider her decision to leave the capital with her daughter. At the same time, the lady was realistic enough to know that Genji, who already held that wife of his in high esteem, would feel even greater affection and lavish his attentions solely on *her* once the child was born. And when that happened, *she* would be left waiting, fretting impatiently over whether Genji would ever show up and knowing that whenever he did come to see her, it would be out of some lukewarm sense of duty or pity. Her tangled emotions opened her eyes afresh to the reality of her situation. After waiting all day for his morning-after letter, it finally arrived that evening—a short, curt note with no poem attached:

"Her condition had been improving recently, but now she has suffered a relapse, and I really must stay here."

She read the note and thought it was just another of his typical excuses. Even so, she sent a response:

> Intimate with love's path where dew has soaked my sleeves
> I followed too far . . . now my sad fate is to end
> Like a peasant planting fields, my robes soaked in mud

"Perhaps it is fitting to remind you of the old poem about the water of the mountain well. The poet, having tried to draw water from a well so shallow, regrets that she too gets nothing but damp sleeves."[3]

Genji pored over her response, marveling at the beauty of her script, which was far superior to everyone else's, and wondered why the world had to be so damnably complicated. He felt painfully torn—on the one hand, he couldn't simply abandon a woman of her sensibility and looks, and, on the other, there was no way he could settle on just one woman. He sent his reply well after dark:

"What do you mean that only your sleeves are damp? Your feelings for me must not be very deep."

> How shallow the path of love you follow
> That you merely dampen your sleeves with dew
> While I drench myself where the mud is deep

He added, among other things, "Do you imagine that my feelings for you are insincere, that I would not reply to you in person were my wife's condition not truly serious?"

At the Minister's residence the obsessive spirit was appearing more persistently and causing Genji's wife great distress. The lady at Rokujō then heard gossip to the effect that it was either her own living spirit or that of her late father. She gave the rumors careful consideration. Even though she had never wished ill fortune to befall others, she had often lamented her own bad luck, and she was aware that the living spirit of a person who is preoccupied with personal desires and attachments might wander from the body. She had lived for so many years convinced that she had suffered as much grief and anxiety as it was possible for one person to suffer, and now it was as if her soul had been torn asunder. That day when the foolish incident with the carriages occurred, she had been treated disdainfully, and *that woman*, Genji's wife, had in effect ignored her as though she were beneath contempt. After the procession to the Purification Ritual was over, her heart and mind lost their moorings and drifted, all on account of that one incident, and she found it truly difficult to calm her nerves.

Lately, whenever she dozed off, she began having a recurring dream. She would find herself in the beautifully appointed, luxurious quarters of some

3. Anonymous poem from an earlier *waka* anthology, the *Kokin waka rokujō*.

woman—Genji's wife, she assumed—and would then watch in horror as her living spirit, so completely different from her waking self, would move around the woman, pulling and tugging at her, and then, driven by menacingly obsessive emotions, violently striking and shaking her. Because of this recurring dream, the lady had many moments when she believed she was losing her grip on reality.

Ah, how horrible this is! What they say is true after all. A person's living spirit really can leave the body and wander about.[4] *And even if it isn't true in my case, people at the court prefer to speak ill of others, and this situation will provide fodder to those who relish spreading malicious gossip.*

Fearing that she would be notorious, the lady made a resolution to herself: *They say it's common for people to leave behind their obsessive attachments and resentments when they die. I've always considered such a thing deeply sinful and ominous, even when it has happened to people with whom I have no connections. But now there are rumors that it's my living spirit that's acting in such a grotesque, unearthly way. It must be retribution for the sins of a former life. I must never give another thought to that cruel man.*

She resolved over and over to put him out of her mind, but, try as she might, her resolutions were just another way to think about *him*.

As part of a series of purification rites in preparation for her departure for Ise, the daughter of the lady at Rokujō was to have moved during the previous year into a detached residence at the palace called the Shosai-in, which served as the pavilion of the First Lustration. However, there had been a number of complications, and so it was decided that she would not move into the pavilion until the autumn. Thereafter, in the ninth month, the Ise Priestess would move again, undergoing the Second Lustration at a temporary shrine built for this purpose on the plains of Sagano, famous for its lovely autumn vistas. The attendants in the residence at Rokujō thus had to make preparations for two purification rites, one right after the other. Their mistress, alas, was distracted and depressed and lying prone in her suffering, unable to rouse herself. This was no trivial matter for the ladies-in-waiting to the Priestess, since her mother's illness could be defiling, and so they commissioned prayers and rites. In truth, the lady didn't really seem all that sick, and as the days and months passed no one was sure exactly what was wrong or how serious it was. Genji was constantly inquiring after the lady's health, but because his wife—who was far more important to him—was suffering so much, he was burdened with seemingly endless concerns.

Because they assumed it was not yet time for Genji's wife to give birth, everyone at the Sanjō residence was caught off guard when she went into labor and appeared to be on the verge of delivering the child. More and more malignant spirits were drawn to her as the moment of the birth neared, and the number and intensity of the prayers and rites meant to assure a safe childbirth increased. Still, that one stubborn, obsessive spirit remained, more intransigent than ever. Even the most venerable of the priests found this spirit abnormal, and they were unable to exorcise it. As they tried to make the spirit show itself, their prayers finally forced it to speak to them through Genji's wife.

The spirit, in a weeping voice wracked with pain, pleaded with the priests, "Please stop for a moment. I have something I must say to Lord Genji."

---

4. *Kokinshū* 977 (Ōshikōchi Mitsune): "It must have wandered off, abandoning my body . . . this heart of mine that goes its own way, doing things I do not intend."

The attendants at once whispered among themselves, "Just as we thought; there's some reason for this after all."

Genji was shown in to where his wife was lying behind her curtains. Because she seemed to be near death, her parents withdrew a short distance away in case their daughter had some last words for her husband. The priests ceased their prayers and lowered their voices as they chanted the Kannon chapter of the *Lotus Sutra*. Their murmuring created an atmosphere at once uncanny and sublime. Genji lifted the curtains and looked in on his wife. There was something alluring about her as she lay there, her belly large and distended. Even someone with whom she had no connection at all would have been distracted gazing at her, so it was natural for Genji to feel overwhelmed with regret and sorrow. Her long, luxuriant black hair, which had been pulled back and tied up, stood out in vivid contrast to the white of her maternity robes. She was always so prim and proper that Genji had never found her special elegance all that attractive. Now, for the first time, as she lay there in her vulnerable, helpless condition, she struck him as not just precious but voluptuous. He took her hand.

"How terrible this is. Must you cause me to grieve so?"

He began to cry and could speak no further. She weakly raised her head and gazed at him with that expression that had hitherto always made him feel uncertain and inadequate in her presence. Tears filled her eyes, and when he gazed back at her—a woman who now seemed so accessible to him—how could he not be deeply touched?

Because she was crying so intensely, Genji assumed she was thinking of her poor, anxious parents and, on seeing him here like this, regretting that they would soon part.

"You mustn't brood so much about everything," Genji comforted her. "You don't feel well now, but you'll get better. And even if death should separate us, remember that husbands and wives are destined to meet in the next world. You have a deep bond with your father and mother, and no matter how many times you are reborn, that bond is never-ending. I am sure there will be a time when you will see them again."

"No, no, that's not why I'm crying. I'm crying because the exorcists' prayers hurt me so. I asked for you to come here so that I might have a moment of relief from them. I never imagined that I would come here in this form, but now I know the truth. The spirit of a person lost in obsessive longing will actually wander from the body." The voice that came from his wife's lips had a gentle, seductive familiarity. "Just as they did in ancient times . . ."

> Bind the hems of my robes
> To keep my grieving soul
> From wandering the skies

As he was listening to the voice, his wife's appearance changed and she no longer looked like herself. Genji was trying to comprehend this inexplicable, eerie phenomenon when he suddenly realized he was gazing on the countenance of the lady at Rokujō. He was horrified. He had dismissed out of hand the rumors claiming the spirit possessing his wife was the lady's, considering them nothing more than the idle gossip of vulgar, insensitive people. But he was witnessing the possession with his own eyes and understood now that such things did happen in this world. It was uncanny. *How wretched*, he thought. He then answered her, saying, "You sound like someone I know, but I'm not certain. Tell me who you are."

The spirit replied in a way that left no doubt it was *she*. To say that he was shocked would not do justice to the sense of horror he experienced. At the same time, the presence of the attendants made him feel awkward and embarrassed, since they might recognize that the spirit was the lady's.

When the voice grew a little more subdued, Genji's mother-in-law, thinking that her daughter was feeling more comfortable, brought in a hot medicinal infusion. The attendants raised his wife from behind and supported her in a squatting posture. She gave birth to a boy.

The joy everyone felt was boundless. In contrast, the malign spirits that had been forced into the mediums were raising a tremendous fuss, since they resented the safe delivery. There was still the afterbirth to worry about, but thanks to the numerous prayers and supplications to the Buddha, it was a normal birth. The abbot of the Enryakuji Temple on Mount Hiei and the other distinguished priests quickly withdrew, wiping the sweat from their proud, satisfied faces. All the women in the household were finally able to relax a little after so many days of worry and devoted service. They were sure that the worst was over; and even though new prayers and rites for the mother were ordered, for the moment the baby became the center of attention. Everyone let their guard down as they were absorbed in helping out with the remarkable child. The Retired Emperor, princes of the blood, and the highest-ranking officials all attended, without fail, the traditional banquets held on the third, fifth, seventh, and ninth nights following the birth. In joyous celebration, they brought with them exquisite and remarkable gifts of food and clothing, and because the child was a boy, the celebrations were all the more lively and auspicious.

When the lady at Rokujō learned about all of this, she grew agitated. She had heard that Genji's wife had been in a precarious state, but now, apparently, everything was fine, and she felt both jealous and disappointed. She continued to feel weird, as though she were not herself, and her robes reeked of the smell of the poppy seeds that exorcists burn to drive out a lingering spirit. Strangely, the smell would not dissipate, but continued to permeate her body no matter how often she tried washing her hair and changing her robes. She was disgusted with herself and worried what others might say or think. She couldn't very well discuss this with anyone, so she was forced to suffer in isolation, which only made her emotional turmoil worse. Genji was feeling somewhat calmer, but whenever he recalled the unpleasant moment when the lady's spirit had addressed him unbidden in that weird and shocking manner, he was reminded of the pain she was experiencing because he had not called on her in such a long time. He vacillated, thinking that perhaps he should visit her in person. But then every time he considered the idea of a visit, he couldn't help worrying that he might be appalled, wondering how she could have fallen into such a state. After considering all the options, he decided it would be best for her if he just sent a message.

Everyone was worried about the prognosis for Genji's wife, who had suffered so grievously, and kept a vigilant watch over her. Naturally, Genji stopped going out on his nightly amorous excursions, even though his wife was still quite sick and unable to see her husband in the customary manner. The baby boy was exceptionally handsome, and because there were worries that his looks might attract the resentful attention of malignant spirits, every effort was made from the moment of his birth to protect him and bring him up with the greatest care. Genji's father-in-law was tremendously pleased, since things had worked out as he had hoped. Though he continued to show concern over his daughter, who had not yet fully recovered, he assumed that her condition was simply the aftereffect of having been so ill and that there was no reason to be unduly alarmed.

On seeing the beauty of the eyes and features of the baby, who bore a striking resemblance to Fujitsubo's child, Genji thought lovingly of his other, unacknowledged son, the new Crown Prince, and he was seized with an unbearable desire to go to the palace to visit him.

"I've not been to the palace for some time, and that concerns me. Since my confinement ends today, I had better go there." He then added, with some resentment, "I wonder if I might speak to my wife directly, without a curtain between us? Why do we always have to be so formal with one another, especially now?"

"As you wish, my lord," one of the women responded. "Your relationship with my lady need not be so formal and distant. Though she is terribly weakened by her ordeal, there is no need to separate the two of you with screens or curtains."

The attendants brought in a cushion for him and placed it close to where his wife was lying. He went in, sat down, and began speaking to her. She answered from time to time, but she still seemed very weak. He remembered the state she had been in at that moment when he had been certain she was about to die. He now felt as if it had all been a dream. He spoke of the period when she had been in mortal danger, and it made his heart ache to think that she had been on the point of death, and to recall how she had stopped breathing, but then recovered and spoke to him so urgently.

"There is so much I want to tell you, but they say you are too weak and not up to it, so I'll let it go for now," he said. He reminded her to drink her medicine and showed her consideration in other ways as well. Her attendants were deeply impressed by his ministrations, amazed that he had learned such things.

Her appearance as she lay there was heartbreakingly sweet, so weak and pale that he could hardly tell if she were dead or alive. Her abundant hair was properly done up, and the strands that were lying across the pillow were incomparably elegant. He gazed possessively at her, feeling strange that in all their time together he should ever have found her deficient in any way.

"I must go visit my father, but I shall return quickly," Genji told her. "How happy it would make me if I could always gaze on you as I'm doing now. But your mother is constantly nearby, so out of deference to her I have refrained from seeing you directly, lest I be considered rash. You must do all you can to get well, then move back to your own chambers. One reason you are not improving may be that you have become too childishly dependent on others."

With these words he took his leave, put on splendid robes and went out. In the past she rarely saw him off, but this time she lay there watching him in rapt attention.

The Autumn Ceremonial for Court Promotions was scheduled for that evening, and because the Minister of the Left had to preside over the event, he too left his daughter at his Sanjō residence and headed for the palace. Each of his sons was hoping to receive a promotion, and since they didn't want to be separated from their father on this particular day, they all left with him.

As a result, there were very few people at the Minister's residence that evening, and while the villa was deserted a malignant spirit suddenly assaulted Genji's wife. The choking sensation she experienced made breathing difficult, and she was in great distress. She stopped breathing before there was time to inform those who had gone to the ceremony.

On hearing the news, everyone was stunned, and they left the palace not knowing where their feet were taking them. Though it was the evening of the Autumn Ceremonial, in the face of such a tragedy it would not have been appropriate to continue the event. The crisis had arisen in the middle of the night, and so they were unable to call for the abbot at Mount Hiei, or even for a distinguished priest. They had all relaxed and let their guard down, assuming that the worst was over, and because her death was so unexpected, the attendants at the Minister's residence were in a panic—confused, stumbling about, bumping into things. Messengers bearing condolences from various noble houses crowded into the residence at Sanjō, but there was no one to take their messages, and the whole house was shaking from the uproar. It was frightening to see how upset everyone was.

Because so many malignant spirits had possessed her, they followed prescribed custom and left her body lying there. They didn't disturb her or move the position of her pillow, lest her soul fail to find its way back should it try to return. They kept watch over her for two or three days, but when her appearance began to change, they realized they had reached the end, that she was indeed gone, and were overwhelmed by grief.

With his wife's tragic death coming on the heels of his shocking encounter with the living spirit of the lady at Rokujō, Genji was preoccupied with thoughts of the tiresome nature of this world, and as a result he felt put off by the words of condolences he received from people—even from women with whom he had a special relationship. Genji's father-in-law, the Minister of the Left, was deeply honored to receive condolences directly from the Retired Emperor. It was an honor that brought a moment of relief to his unremitting sorrow, and it left him crying tears of both joy and grief. On the advice of others, the Minister spared no expense or effort in commissioning mystery rites intended to revive his daughter, and though it was evident for all to see that her body was decaying away, in his distracted state he vainly persisted until there was nothing more to be done. When at last they took his daughter's body to be cremated on the plains of Toribeno, there were many heart-rending moments along the way.

* * *

At the Nijō villa his men and women were preparing for his arrival, cleaning and polishing. The senior attendants all appeared before him, and they vied to outdo one another in the splendor of their clothing and makeup. Genji couldn't help but be touched by the lively scene before him, which contrasted so starkly with the lonely, melancholy scene he had left behind at the Sanjō residence. He changed out of his mourning robes and went over to Murasaki's quarters in the west hall. The clothing and furnishings there had been changed with the advent of winter, and the rooms had a bright, fresh look to them. The outfits of the pretty women and girls there were pleasing to his eyes, and Murasaki's nurse,

Shōnagon, had made sure that all the preparations had been carried out to his complete satisfaction. Indeed, everything looked wonderful to him.

Murasaki was sweetly done up . . . truly lovely.

"It's been a long time," Genji began. "You've become quite the young lady."

He raised the lower half of the curtains to peek in on her, and when he did so she shyly turned away from him. Even so, he could see that her beauty was perfection itself. Glimpsing her profile in the lamplight, he could tell from her eyes and face that she looked exactly like Fujitsubo, the woman who had so possessed his heart, and he was overjoyed. He moved closer to her and spoke of all the things that had happened, and of how anxious he had been, wondering how she had fared during his period of mourning.

"I want to talk to you at leisure, tell you stories of all that took place while I was away. For the time being, however, I'll sleep in the east hall. Having just come out of mourning, it might be bad luck for me to stay here just now. But soon we will have all the time in the world to be together . . . so much so that you may come to regard me as a nuisance."

Shōnagon, who was listening in on them, was delighted by his words, but then she immediately began having anxious thoughts about the precarious position of her young charge. After all, Genji discreetly visited many highborn ladies, and it was also possible that he would be drawn to some new lady who might appear on the scene and take the place of his late wife. Shōnagon's suspicious nature was an unattractive trait, but her doubts were understandable, since her primary responsibility was to look after Murasaki.

Genji returned to his own chambers. One of his female attendants, Chūjō no kimi, massaged his legs, and he was finally able to relax and fall asleep. The next morning he sent a letter to his little son at Sanjō. The melancholy reply, obviously written for him by the boy's grandmother, filled him with inexhaustible grief.

With little to occupy him, Genji would lose himself in reveries of longing. Yet because he was reluctant to wander about on some random nocturnal adventure, he could not rouse himself to go out. His little Murasaki was now grown up and ideal in all respects. She looked spectacular, and he felt that now was the appropriate time to consummate their relationship. From time to time he would casually drop hints about their marriage, but she seemed to have no idea what he was talking about.

They whiled away the hours, relieving their tedium by playing Go or word games like *hentsugi*, writing down radicals or parts of a Chinese character and trying to guess which one it was. Murasaki had a clever and engaging personality, and she would demonstrate endearing talents in even the most trivial of pastimes. For several years he had driven all thoughts of taking her as a wife out of his mind, dismissing her talents as nothing more than the accomplishments of a precocious child. Now he could no longer control his passion— though he did feel pangs of guilt, since he was painfully aware of how innocent she was.

Her attendants assumed he would consummate their relationship at some point, but because he had always slept with her, there was simply no way for them to know when that moment would come. One morning Genji rose early, but Murasaki refused to get up. Her behavior worried her attendants.

"What's wrong?' they whispered. "She seems unusually out of sorts today."

Right before Genji returned to his own quarters, he placed just inside her curtains a box filled with inkstones, brushes, and paper, which she was to use for the customary morning-after letter.[5] When there was no one else around, Murasaki finally lifted her head and found his betrothal note folded in a love knot at her pillow. Still in a daze, she opened the letter.

> How strange that we have stayed apart so long
> Though we slept together night after night
> With only the robes we wore between us

The poem was written in a playful, spontaneous manner, as if he had allowed his emotions to carry him along. It had never crossed her mind that he might be the kind of man who harbored such thoughts about her, and she burned with shame when she recalled their sordid first night: *How could I have been so naive? How could I have ever trusted a man with such base intentions?*

Genji returned to her quarters at midday, peeking in through her curtains.

"Something seems to be bothering you . . . are you not well? It would be quite tedious for me if we weren't able to play Go today."

Murasaki was still lying face down. She pulled the bedding up over her face so that she would not have to look at him. When her attendants withdrew, Genji went over to her.

"Why are you acting so despondent? Are you displeased with me? I never imagined that you could be so cold. Your women must think this is all very queer."

He tugged her bedding away. She was bathed in perspiration, and tears had soaked the hair framing her forehead.

"Now this won't do at all!" Genji was put out. "Tears on the first day of your marriage? It's ominous . . . very inauspicious." He tried all sorts of things to cheer her up, but she thought him utterly horrid and refused to speak.

"All right, then, have it your way," he told her spitefully. "I won't come here any more if you insist on putting me to shame!"

He opened the box with the writing implements and checked inside. There was no reply note. *She's still a child after all*, he thought ruefully. He now felt sorry for her and decided to stay with her inside the curtains for the rest of the day. He passed the whole time trying to comfort her, but this proved difficult. Her refusal to warm up to him, however, merely made her look all the more precious to him.

It was the First Day of the Boar in the tenth month, when the moon rose in the north-northwest. The custom was to serve cakes made of pounded rice on this day, so as evening wore on and they reached the Hour of the Boar a little after 9:00 p.m., Genji had rice cakes shaped to look like baby pigs brought in to him and Murasaki. The boar was a symbol of fertility, but the First Day of the Boar was not an auspicious time for marriage. Moreover, Genji was still in mourning, and so he made sure their celebration was subdued, serving the rice cakes in Murasaki's quarters only. Observing the various colors of the rice cakes, which were flavored with beans, or chestnuts, or poppy, among other things, and nestled in cypress boxes, Genji remembered that he had to have white rice

---

5. After a couple's first night together the man was supposed to leave the woman a poem, to which she should respond [editor's note].

cakes prepared for tomorrow evening, the Third Night of their marriage. He stepped out and summoned Koremitsu.

"Have rice cakes brought here tomorrow," he ordered, "though not as many as today. This was not a particularly auspicious day for such things."

Seeing Genji's wry smile, Koremitsu caught on immediately. He did not press his lord on the matter, but simply replied with a perfectly serious expression on his face.

"Of course, my lord. It's most reasonable of you to choose an auspicious day to serve rice cakes." He then added, rather drolly, "Let's see . . . tomorrow is the Day of the Rat. Shall I tell them you're having rice cakes in the shape of baby mice to celebrate the event? And just how many will you need?"

"I suppose a third as many as we had today . . . that should be enough," Genji answered. And with that Koremitsu, who knew just what to do, withdrew. *He's certainly an experienced hand*, thought Genji. Koremitsu spoke of this to no one else, and had the rice cakes prepared at his own residence, without telling anyone why he needed them. He was so discreet, in fact, it was almost as if he had made them himself.

Genji was finding it so difficult to comfort Murasaki that he was at a loss. At the same time he was delighted when it occurred to him that, for the first time in her life, she must have felt like a stolen bride. With that realization came another.

She has been precious to me for many years, but my feelings for her during all that time were nothing compared to what I feel for her now. The heart is a peculiar thing. Now I find it impossible to be apart from her, even for a single night.

Koremitsu stealthily brought a box filled with the rice cakes Genji had ordered late the previous night. Deeply considerate and sensitive to the situation, Koremitsu thought it might be embarrassing for Murasaki if he asked her nurse, Shōnagon, to take the box into her chambers. So instead he summoned Shōnagon's daughter, Ben.

"Take this to your young mistress, and don't let anyone see you." He handed her an incense jar, inside of which he had hidden the box of rice cakes. "Now listen to me. This is a gift to celebrate an auspicious event, so you must set it beside her pillow. Be very careful. You must carry out my instructions to the letter." Ben thought that this request was suspicious, but she took the jar anyway.

"I have never," she insisted, "been unfaithful in serving my lady."

He cut her short.

"Don't use the word 'unfaithful.' The very uttering of it on an occasion like this is bad luck."

Ben considered the whole affair very odd, but she was young and really had no idea what Koremitsu was talking about. She placed the jar inside her lady's curtains next to her pillow. Genji, as he always did, explained the significance of the rice cakes to Murasaki.

Murasaki's attendants had known nothing about this. It wasn't until the next morning, when Genji had the box of rice cakes taken away, that they finally realized their lord had formally taken their young mistress as his wife. When could all of the dishes have been brought in? The stands on which the plates rested looked fabulous, their legs intricately carved in the shape of flowers. Various kinds of rice cakes had been specially prepared, and everything used for the

Third Night celebration—the silver plates, silver chopsticks, silver chopstick rests—had been exquisitely arranged. Shōnagon wondered, *Has he actually gone so far as to recognize her as his wife?* And when she saw it was true, she was profoundly grateful and wept at this proof of Genji's honorable intentions.

The other women were disappointed that they had not been let in on the secret, and they grumbled among themselves. "Of course it's wonderful that things have turned out like this, but why did our lord have to keep it secret? And that Koremitsu . . . whatever could he have been thinking?"

Following his marriage to Murasaki, Genji would feel so anxious about her whenever he went to the palace or called on the Retired Emperor, even for a short visit, that a vision of her would come to him and he would see her face. He found his own attraction to her mysterious. He received resentful letters from his other women enticing him to visit, and their notes did make him feel bad for them. But the very thought that such visits would be hard on his new bride troubled him. He recalled a line from an old *Man'yōshū* poem: "How can I endure a single night apart from you?"[6] He simply could not bring himself to go out on his nocturnal forays, but instead pretended he wasn't feeling well and was indisposed. He passed the time sending replies to his ladies along the lines of "I've been preoccupied of late with thoughts of the sad evanescence of this world. Once this mood of mine has passed, we shall, I assure you, meet again."

Oborozukiyo, the lady Genji associated with that evening of the misty moon, could not get him out of her mind. Her older sister, the Kokiden Consort, who was now the Imperial Mother, was extremely displeased to learn about this infatuation, and was further annoyed when her own father, the Minister of the Right, dismissed her concerns.

"Why should I be bothered about this?" he said. "If she realizes her heart's desire and becomes one of Genji's wives, I won't complain. After all, the woman who was most significant to him has apparently died."

The Kokiden Consort replied, "And what's wrong with her entering service in the women's quarters?" She seemed to have her heart firmly set on sending her younger sister to court to serve her son, Emperor Suzaku.

For his part, Genji did not consider Oborozukiyo just another woman, and he thought it a shame that she should be sent into service at the palace. At the present moment, however, he was not inclined to divide his attention among his women. He wanted to focus on Murasaki alone.

I'd better let it be, he thought. *Murasaki is good enough. Life is brief, and so I should just settle down with her. I must never again stir resentment in a woman.*

This train of thought brought back the incident with the lady at Rokujō. He had learned a fearful lesson. He was sorry for her, but now he could never feel comfortable recognizing her formally as a wife. *If she could be satisfied with continuing to meet as we have over the years, if she could go on being my companion, a woman who could talk with me on those occasions when it's natural and proper to do so, if we could just be a comfort to one another . . .*

As he mulled over their relationship, he realized that no matter how difficult she might be, she was someone he could not easily abandon.

* * *

6. Poem from *Man'yōshū*: "Now that we are betrothed, sharing a pillow of new grasses, how can I endure a single night apart from you?"

From Chapter X

Sakaki

A BRANCH OF SACRED EVERGREEN

The day of departure for the new High Priestess of Ise was drawing near, and her mother's heart was filled with melancholy and loneliness. Following the death of Genji's wife, whose special status the lady at Rokujō had found such an affront to her dignity, rumors spread around the court to the effect that now, at last, Genji would surely make her his primary wife. Even her own ladies-in-waiting were atwitter with anticipation at the possibility. Contrary to expectations, however, Genji's visits to the lady abruptly ceased altogether, and upon experiencing his shockingly cold behavior, the lady realized that something must have happened to truly upset him. She therefore resolved to abandon her lingering attachments and strengthened her resolve to accompany her daughter to Ise.

There was no precedent for a parent to accompany the High Priestess to Ise, but the lady, who wanted to distance herself from her troubled relationship with Genji, explained that she couldn't be separated from her daughter because the girl was simply too young to be on her own outside the capital. Hearing that the lady had decided to leave, Genji felt a twinge of remorse and exchanged with her a series of elegantly touching letters. The lady, however, was convinced that it was now too late for them and that they should not meet face to face. Genji would almost certainly consider her refusal hateful, but she was firmly resolved, heart and mind, for she knew it was inappropriate to do anything that would further disturb her troubled spirit and cause her more pain and suffering.

She would return occasionally to her villa on Rokujō, but she did so infrequently and in such secrecy that Genji was never able to learn when she was in residence there. Since she had moved out to the compound of the temporary shrine on the plains of Sagano—a place difficult for him to visit no matter how much he longed to go—they remained apart as days and months passed, even though he continued to be deeply concerned about her. On top of everything else, Genji's father was from time to time troubled by various ailments, which was unusual, and these additional worries burdened his heart and gave him no rest. Still, Genji was shamed by the prospect that the lady might think him cold and that people who heard about their relationship might consider him heartless, and so in spite of his travails he decided to go to the temporary shrine in Sagano. It was already the seventh day of the ninth month, and he assumed that their departure for Ise was imminent—perhaps in the next day or two. The lady was feeling restless, pressured by the numerous preparations she had to make for the departure. Now, on top of everything else, Genji was sending note after note begging to meet, if only for a moment. He told her that he would even stand outside her blinds. She struggled, unsure what to do, until she finally concluded that it would be excessively unfriendly not to meet him. She agreed to have him visit her secretly, but with a screen between them.

Once he had set out to cross the broad plains of Sagano, he was moved to sorrowful compassion. The autumn flowers were withering, and the lonely sound of the wind in the pine trees harmonized with the rasping cries of insects coming from the sere thickets of satin-tail grass. Faint notes of music, gentle and tender, were wafting faintly on the wind, though he could not quite make out the song or the kind of koto being played.

An escort of ten or so of Genji's most trusted guards accompanied him. In an effort to avoid attracting attention, his men had eschewed wearing formal robes. Genji, on the contrary, had not bothered to disguise himself, but had taken special care in preparing his attire. Because he looked so resplendent, he made the sophisticated, urbane young men traveling with him appreciate the profound beauty of the setting.

Why did I wait until now to come here? Genji reflected, bitterly regretting the time that had been lost.

A scattering of temporary dwellings roofed with wood-plank shingles stood inside a low, fragile, rustic-looking enclosure of brushwood. The *torii*[7] gate was made of logs that had not been stripped of their bark, creating an atmosphere of solemnity that, given the purpose of his visit, made him hesitate to enter such sacred ground. Here and there several Shinto clerics were coughing or clearing their throats in order to signal that Genji had arrived, and another group of priests stood talking amongst themselves. It was a different world altogether, one that struck Genji as strange and unfamiliar. The building where the ceremonial fire was kept constantly blazing was glowing faintly, and, since there were so few people about, stillness had settled over the compound. Genji felt a stab of keen sorrow when it occurred to him just how many days and months she had spent in isolation here, lost in her obsessive longings.

He withdrew, moving out of sight to what he assumed was the appropriate building on the north side of the main hall, and sent in a message to the lady announcing his arrival. He could hear intriguing sounds of people bustling about, but received only a reply from an intermediary. It irritated Genji that his lady showed no inclination to meet face to face, and so with great sincerity he spoke to her.

"If you could just appreciate how difficult and inappropriate it is for someone of my position to be coming here in secret like this, then you would not keep yourself apart from me, as if you had drawn a sacred straw rope between us. I wish to clear away the dark feelings and resentments that cloud my heart."

At that point her attendants interceded for him.

"Truly it would be a pity to leave him standing outside, looking so forlorn."

What should I do? the lady fretted. *I risk being shamed if I go out to meet him now, especially with my women watching . . . and even he might think it inappropriate for someone of my age.*

But as reluctant as she was to see him, she didn't want to seem cold or willfully aloof. In the end, the impression she made on his heart when she went out and sat behind her blind with much sighing and hesitation was one of magnificent refinement.

"May I be permitted to come up onto the veranda?" he asked, and stepped up.

His handsome figure and graceful movements gave off an incomparable radiance in the evening moonlight, which shone clearly into the space. They had reached the point in their relationship where he felt embarrassed to try to give some plausible excuse for all the months he had ignored her, so instead he presented her with a small branch of *sakaki*, the sacred evergreen, which he had

---

7. Gateway to a Shinto shrine [editor's note].

broken off on his way here. "Having made a signpost of my feelings, which, like the color of this sacred branch will never fade, I have entered this holy compound. And yet, how unfeeling you remain."

She responded with a poem:

> With no cedar trees to serve as signpost
> To guide you to this sacred enclosure
> Have you in error brought sakaki here[8]

Genji replied as follows:

> Thinking you might be where the shrine maiden dwells
> In longing I plucked this branch along the way
> Drawn by the fragrance of sacred evergreens

He felt constrained by the atmosphere of their surroundings, but he entered just inside her blind and leaned against one of the tie beams around the entrance.

During all those years when Genji ought to have followed the dictates of his heart and bestowed visits on her—a period during which the lady also thought longingly of him—his complacency, born of self-conceit, prevented him from feeling any sense of guilt or urgency about their relationship. Then, after he had been convinced in his heart that she was frighteningly flawed, his passion for her cooled to the point that now they were estranged. Yet as memories of their affair came back to him on the occasion of this extraordinary meeting, his heart was roiled by powerful emotions of sorrow and pity. Thinking of all that had happened and of all that was to come, he wept, brokenhearted. Although the lady seemed to be trying to steel herself, since she did not want her true feelings to show, she was unable to hold her emotions in check, and the sight of her struggling became more and more difficult for him to bear. As she looked at him, his appearance seemed to be telling her to reconsider her plans to leave the capital for Ise. Gazing into the sublime beauty of the sky—was it the early setting of the moon that made it seem so lovely?—his complaints spilled forth as he pleaded with her not to spurn his love. His pleas should have been enough to make the numerous hurts and resentments that had accumulated in her heart vanish. Indeed, even though she had finally resolved to make a clean break with him, now that they were meeting again her resolve began to crumble, and she found herself wavering.

Young noblemen accompanied one another on visits to this temporary shrine, and they cut remarkably splendid figures as they wandered about the garden there—a place they found difficult to leave. The scene before Genji and the lady was thus perfect, and there is simply no way to convey in writing all the words and feelings that these two, who had tasted sorrow to the full, shared with each other.

The sky was gradually growing light—its appearance seemed to have been made especially for them. Genji, who was finding it difficult to depart, took her hand and hesitated, overwhelmed by feelings of intimacy.

8. Anonymous poem from *The Kokinshū* "If you truly long for me, come to the foot of Mount Miwa, to my hut . . . to the gate where the sacred cedars stand."

> Partings at the break of dawn are always
> Soaked by the dew . . . but never have I known
> So sorrowful an autumn sky as this

A chill wind was blowing, and the raspy, mournful voices of bell crickets seemed to capture the mood of the moment. No one—not even a person untroubled by sad thoughts—could have passed by this scene without having been deeply affected. That being the case, it is hardly surprising, then, that the two of them, who were so distraught, found it hard to find the words for their poems of parting. Finally, she was able to reply:

> Parting in autumn is sorrow enough . . .
> Let me not hear as well the mournful cries
> Of bell crickets in fields of withered grass

Though he was filled with frustrations and regrets, it was no use obsessing over them; and so, wishing to avoid the gaze of others, Genji departed. His path was drenched in dew and tears.

The lady, unable to maintain a stoic bearing, was lost in melancholy reverie, staring sadly at the place where Genji had been just moments earlier. His visage, which had been faintly visible in the moonlight, and the lingering fragrance of his perfumed robes, made a deep impression on the young women in attendance, and their praise for him perhaps went beyond the bounds of what was proper.

"Is any journey worth abandoning a man like this?" they tearfully whispered among themselves, unaware of all that had taken place between Genji and their mistress.

His letter the next morning provided an unusually detailed account of his feelings, and though she found it difficult to resist his blandishments, she could not reverse herself and be indecisive once again. Thus, his letter came to naught. Genji was a man capable of unparalleled eloquence in expressing romantic emotions—even for affairs that didn't mean all that much to him—and so for a relationship that he could never have considered ordinary, it must have been all the more painful to have her reject him this way. He had magnificent robes and furnishings and goods of all sorts prepared and sent to her and her attendants for their journey, but she felt neither joy nor resentment at his show of concern. She was leaving behind a reputation as a frivolous and cruel woman, and as the day of departure drew near, she was now constantly regretting her situation, as if she were aware for the first time of the consequences of her actions. Her daughter, the High Priestess, had a youthful outlook on things, and she was happy that the departure date, which had been unsettled, was now firmly fixed. Naturally, gossip about the mother's unprecedented decision to accompany her daughter swirled about the court—some of it sympathetic, some sharply critical because of her relationship with Genji.

People whose status is such that they are never subjected to the barbed comments of others seem to have an easier time in life. Unfortunately, for those of high status who stand out in society, there are also many constraints on their behavior.

On the sixteenth day the Rite of Purification for the Ise Priestess was conducted at the Katsura River to the west of the capital. The ceremony was grander than most, in part because it was customary to choose men of high status and splendid reputations—a Consultant, for example, or a Middle Counselor—to serve as a member of her imperial escort. All of this of course reflected the interest that the Retired Emperor was taking in the matter.

Just as they were departing, a letter arrived from Genji revealing all the emotions he had not yet been able to fully express. He had addressed it "To the High Priestess, with Humble Reverence" and bound it with a ritual cord made of paper mulberry bark. "They say," he had written, "that the god of thunder himself has never sundered a relationship between lovers."[9]

> O Gods of the land of the Eight Isles
> If you feel pity, then judge kindly
> Two who taste in full parting's sorrow

"Thinking about you, I cannot help but feel depressed and dissatisfied."

Although she was extremely busy with her preparations, the High Priestess replied. Her Head of Household wrote out the response:

> Were the gods of our land to judge you
> Would they not first and foremost condemn
> The thoughtlessness of your heart and words

Genji was curious about the Ceremony of Parting and wanted to go to the palace, but he decided against it because he thought it would look pathetic for a man to be seeing off a lover who had rejected him. So, with nothing to occupy him, he was lost in his own thoughts. The High Priestess's reply poem was so mature that he had to smile as he read it. *She must be alluring beyond her years,* he thought, aroused to abnormal fantasies about her not as a Priestess but as a woman. His disposition always drew him toward relationships that were unusual and problematic.

How unfortunate that I wasn't able to see her when she was a child, he mused, *when I might have been able to get a good look at her. Oh well, nothing in this world is fixed forever, and so I should be able to meet her at some point.*

On the day of the Ceremony of Parting a large number of carriages lined up to view the procession, since it featured the presence of a lady and a daughter of exceptional beauty and breeding. At the Hour of the Monkey, around four o'clock in the afternoon, the procession arrived at the palace. The lady had last come here borne in a palanquin when she was to have become Empress. Her father had always aimed for her to reach the pinnacle of court society, but then her circumstances, which he had nurtured so carefully, suddenly changed. Upon seeing the palace now, after the collapse of her father's dreams, she was reminded of the mutability of all things in this world—a thought that moved her profoundly. She had come as the bride of the Crown Prince when she was sixteen and left the palace at twenty when he died. Now she was thirty, and upon seeing the ninefold palace again she composed a poem to herself:

> On this day, as much as I try to suppress
> Memories of all that happened long ago
> Unbearable sorrow lingers in my heart

---

9. Anonymous poem from *The Kokinshū*: "Would even the thunder-spirit who stomps and rages in the high plains of the heavens ever try to rend our love?"

The Ise Priestess had turned fourteen. She was exquisite, and her figure, properly attired for this occasion, was so stunningly beautiful that it raised concerns that she might draw the attention of gods or demons. The Emperor Suzaku was smitten by her, and when he placed the Comb of Parting in her hair, he could not hold back his emotions, and tears welled up in his eyes.

The carriages of the ladies accompanying the High Priestess to Ise were lined up along the compound of buildings housing the Eight Ministries under the Council of State. As they awaited departure the variegated hues of the sleeves of those ladies seated inside were spilling out from under the blinds, giving off a fresh appearance and vivacious charm. Many lords were feeling wistful regret, each of them seeing this moment as his own personal farewell to his parting lover.

The party set off after dark, and when they turned at Nijō Avenue onto the boulevard of Tōin, they passed by Genji's villa. Feeling great pity, Genji attached a poem to a branch of *sakaki* and sent it to the lady.

> *When you depart today will your sleeves be dampened*
> *By the Eighty Rapids at Suzuka River . . .*
> *Or by tears of regret for leaving me behind*

It was already quite dark when his letter arrived, and the lady was feeling rushed and flustered. Her reply, which she sent from the barrier gate at Ōsaka, did not reach him until the following day.

> *I cannot tell if my sleeves were dampened*
> *By the rapids at Suzuka River . . .*
> *Do your thoughts escort me to far Ise*

Though terse and hastily written, her calligraphy was interestingly elegant. Even so, he felt she should have written something that showed a little more depth of feeling for him. A thick fog had settled over everything, and as he stared out achingly at the misty early dawn, he whispered a poem to himself:

> *I gaze in longing toward the path you travel*
> *Hoping from afar that this year the autumn fog*
> *Will not hide Mount Osaka, where lovers meet*

He did not go over to the west hall to see Murasaki, but kept to himself, sunk in lonely, distracted thoughts. Compared to him, however, the lady on the road to Ise must surely have been suffering an even more exquisite agony.

Genji's father was ill, and by the tenth month his condition had become serious. Everyone in court society was concerned and grieving. Emperor Suzaku was so troubled that he personally called on his father. Although weakened by illness, the Retired Emperor asked repeatedly after the Crown Prince. He then spoke about Genji.

"When I'm gone I want you to continue thinking of him as an adviser in all matters of state, both great and small, just as when I was alive. In my opinion, you should not hesitate at all to entrust the government to him just because he is young. As the Korean diviner predicted, he is a man destined to rule the court. For that reason I was afraid that conflict might arise, and so I took him out of the line of succession and made him a commoner, with the idea that he would be of service to the throne. Do not go against my wishes on this matter."

Although there were numerous heartrending last requests, these are not the sort of things a woman should be relating, and I feel awkward having mentioned what little I have here. Emperor Suzaku was moved to sadness and gave repeated assurances that he would carry out his father's final instructions. He was so glorious in appearance and mature in demeanor that the Retired Emperor looked on him with joy and a sense of trust. Because the audience with his father was formal and public, Suzaku felt constrained, and he soon returned to the palace, regretting that many things had been left unsaid.

The Crown Prince had wanted to accompany Suzaku on his visit, but because it would have been too much excitement for the Retired Emperor, his visit was changed to another day. The boy was graceful and mature-looking beyond his years, and his longing to see his father had been building all throughout the illness. He was, in his innocence of the true circumstances of his birth, overjoyed when he was finally allowed to visit, and the scene of them together was touching. When the Retired Emperor saw Fujitsubo weeping disconsolately, his heart was filled with conflicting emotions. He spoke to the Crown Prince about all the things he should expect as future sovereign, but the boy was at such a tender age that the Retired Emperor couldn't help looking on him with a mix of concern and pity, and he repeatedly admonished Genji to be vigilant in attending to affairs of state and in looking after the interests of the Crown Prince. It was late at night when the boy left, and the tumultuous scene of his procession, which included virtually all of the upper ranking courtiers, was so grandly solemn that it was indistinguishable from that of Emperor Suzaku's. The Retired Emperor was sorry to see the boy go and dissatisfied that they had not had enough time together.

The Kokiden Consort also wanted to pay a visit, but the presence of Fujitsubo made her hesitate . . . and while she was vacillating, trying to decide what to do, the Retired Emperor passed away peacefully and with dignity. Many at the court were caught off guard and panicked. Even though the Retired Emperor had abdicated, he had maintained control of political power so the court would continue to function as it had during his reign. Suzaku, however, was still young, and his maternal grandfather, the Minister of the Right, was shallow, impulsive, and spiteful. Senior ministers and high-ranking nobles all fretted over what would become of the court under his control.

Fujitsubo and Genji had cause to be more distraught and uneasy than anyone. Observing that Genji's filial devotion in carrying out the subsequent memorial rites was much greater than that shown by the other princes, courtiers looked on him with pity and awe. Even in the unadorned robes of mourning, the extraordinary purity of his appearance stirred sympathy in onlookers. He had encountered misfortunes in consecutive years, and so he came to consider the world of the court vain and tedious. It occurred to him that the death of his father provided the perfect opportunity for him to withdraw from society and take religious vows, but because he was still bound by many relationships, he was not ready to do so just yet.

* * *

From Chapter XII

Suma

EXILE TO SUMA

* * *

Oborozukiyo[1] returned to court service in the seventh month. Suzaku had a strong lingering affection for her, and so he kept her near him as he had always done, acting as though he knew nothing of the imprecations directed at her by certain courtiers. He would on occasion reproach her for one reason or another while also offering tender vows of love. In both looks and bearing Suzaku possessed a youthful grace and elegance, and Oborozukiyo was certainly grateful for, and embarrassed by, his show of noblesse oblige. Yet her heart had room only for memories of Genji.

On one occasion, during a musical performance, Suzaku remarked, "It's at times like this that I miss Genji the most. I venture to say that there are many here who miss him even more than I. It seems as if the light has gone out of everything." He then added, "I have acted contrary to my father's wishes. I shall come to regret my sin." Tears welled up in his eyes, and at that moment Oborozukiyo could no longer restrain her own.

"I have learned from experience that the world is a tiresome place," he continued, "and no longer feel that I want to remain in it much longer. If I were no longer here, how would you feel about it? It makes me bitter to think that my death would not affect you nearly as much as the absence of one who still lives nearby. The poet who wrote the line 'while I am in this world'[2] did not express noble sentiments." His manner was so gentle, and his words suffused with such profound emotion, that tears began to stream down Oborozukiyo's cheeks.

"For whom do you weep?" Suzaku asked. "It makes me sad that you have yet to give me a child . . . it's as if something were missing in my life. I have considered adopting the Crown Prince as my father instructed me, but, given the enmity between my mother and the Fujitsubo Consort, it would cause too much trouble to do so."

Certain people were conducting affairs of state in a manner contrary to his wishes, but he was too young and weak-willed to resist, even though he was disappointed and bothered by many things, including Genji's exile, that had been carried out in his name.

At Suma the winds of autumn—the "season of anxious grief"[3]—were intensifying. Though his villa was some distance from the shore, each night the waves, which Middle Counselor Yukihira observed were stirred by winds blowing through the barrier pass, sounded as if they were breaking quite close. Genji had never experienced anything as affecting as the autumn in this place.

---

1. Genji's affair with her, described in pages not included here, forced him to leave the capital and go into exile to rustic Suma [editor's note].
2. Poem from an imperial *waka* collection, the *Shūishū* (Ōtomo no Momoyo): "What good would it do to die of longing? I want to be with my love for those days I am alive." The line *ikeru*

hi ("those days I am alive") is misquoted in the text as *ikeru yo* (literally, "the world I live in").
3. Anonymous poem from the *Kokinshū*: "Looking upon the light of the moon filtering through the trees, I see that autumn, season of anxious grief, has arrived."

He had only a few attendants with him. Because they were all asleep, he was lying awake by himself, his head propped up on his pillow, listening to the winds howling from every direction. Feeling as though the waves were crashing near his residence, tears welled up instinctively—so many that it seemed his pillow might float away. He tried playing his seven-string koto a little, but the music just made him feel even more frightened and alone, and so he abruptly stopped and murmured the following poem:

> Does the wind blow from where my loved ones mourn
> For I seem to hear in the sound of waves
> Voices crying in pain from loneliness

Hearing his poem, his attendants were startled awake. Seeing how splendid Genji looked, they were overcome by emotion, and as they arose unsteadily they were quietly wiping their noses to disguise their tears.

Genji wondered, *How must my attendants feel? For my sake alone they have come wandering with me to this sorry existence, having left behind their comfortable, familiar homes and parted with parents and siblings from whom even the briefest absence would be hard to bear.*

Such musings made him miserable, but then he realized that it must make his attendants feel forlorn to see him so downhearted like this. And so, during the days that followed, he diverted them with playful banter, and in moments of idle leisure he would make scrolls by gluing together pieces of paper of various hues and practice writing poems. He also drew remarkable-looking sketches and paintings on rare Chinese silk of patterned weave and used them to decorate the front panels of folding screens. Before he came to Suma he had heard about the views of the sea and mountains here, and he had imagined from afar what they looked like. Now that they were right before his eyes, he depicted those rocky shores—their incomparable beauty truly surpassed anything he had imagined—in charcoal sketches of unrivaled skill. A member of his escort remarked with impatient frustration, "If only we could summon the great masters Chieda and Tsunenori[4] and have them color in your sketches . . ." Genji's gentle, familiar behavior and splendid bearing helped his attendants forget the cares of the world. Four or five were in constant attendance, and they were overjoyed to be able to serve him in such close proximity.

One pleasant evening, when the garden flowers near the veranda were a riot of colors, Genji stepped out into a passageway that framed a view of the sea. As he stood there motionless for a few moments, he didn't look like an earthly being, given the odd juxtaposition of his beauty and the setting, and so the divine splendor of his appearance was eerily unsettling. His loose purple trousers, cinched at the ankles, were lined with a pale green; his robe was a soft white silk twill. His dark blue cloak was loosely tied, giving him a casual air as he began reciting in hushed tones the opening lines of his ritual devotions: "I, a disciple of Sakyamuni Buddha . . ."

He slowly chanted a sutra in a voice so sonorous that it too seemed like nothing of this world. From boats in the offing came voices of fishermen singing as they rowed over the waves. Viewed from a distance, the vague outlines of the

---

4. Tsunenori flourished during the reign of Emperor Murakami (946–67). Not much is known about Chieda.

boats resembled little birds floating on the sea, creating a lonesome effect. Just then a line of migrating geese flew overhead, their cries like the creaking of the oars, and Genji gazed out at the scene in rapt silence, his hands, white and lambent in contrast to the dark beads of his rosary, moving almost imperceptibly to brush away the tears running down his cheeks. His magnificent appearance gave comfort to his retainers, all of whom were yearning for their loved ones back home. Genji composed a verse:

> Is it because these wild geese, the first of autumn
> Were with the loved ones I miss in the capital
> That their cries echo mournfully across the skies

Yoshikiyo responded:

> Though not companions of mine from the past
> These geese crying out still stir memories
> One after another of my old life

Koremitsu also responded:

> Am I to consider these geese as companions
> On my exile when they willingly chose to leave
> Familiar homes for distant realms beyond the clouds

The Lesser Captain of the Right Palace Guard—the young man whose loyalty cost him a promising career—composed yet another poem:

> Even wild geese who leave familiar homes
> To migrate through distant skies find comfort
> So long as they are with their companions

"What would become of me if I were to lose sight of my companions?"

Although the Lesser Captain's father, who had once been Vice Governor of Iyo, had recently been appointed Vice Governor of Hitachi, the young man had decided not to accompany him, but went into exile with Genji instead. The choice must have caused him great distress, but he put on a brave front and pretended that nothing bothered him.

The full moon rose vivid and bright, bringing back memories to Genji. "That's right . . . tonight is the fifteenth." Staring up at the face of the moon, he lovingly imagined the music that would be playing on a night like this at the palace, with all the ladies gazing out at the night sky. When he murmured a line from Bai Juyi—"Feelings for acquaintances of old, now two thousand leagues distant"[5]—his attendants could not restrain their tears. With indescribable yearning he recalled the poem Fujitsubo sent him complaining about how the "ninefold mists" kept her from the palace. As memories of this and other moments came to him, he wept aloud. He heard a voice saying, "The hour is late." However, he could not bring himself to retire.

---

5. She is mentioned in passing in the *Hanachirusato* chapter.

> *As I gaze at the moon I am at peace*
> *Even if only briefly, for it shines*
> *On the distant palace I long to see*

He had warm recollections of a certain night when he had talked intimately with Emperor Suzaku about times past. *How closely he resembles our late father!* Genji whispered a line from a poem in Chinese by the exiled Sugawara no Michizane: "The robe bestowed on me by the Emperor is now with me here."[6] Truly the robe never left his sight but was always near him.

> *My sleeves both right and left are wet with tears*
> *Tears of bitter resentment on the one*
> *Tears of longing for you on the other*

* * *

As the days and months passed, there were many occasions back in the capital when the courtiers, Emperor Suzaku first among them, experienced pangs of wistful longing for Genji. The Crown Prince in particular constantly shed tears whenever he thought of him, so that his nurses, especially Myōbu, looked on with pity.

Fujitsubo, who had always been fearful about her son's position, was beside herself with anxiety now that Genji was not there to look after his interests. At the beginning of his exile the princes who were his half brothers and other high-ranking noblemen who had been close to him would send sympathetic notes inquiring how he was faring. Many at the court deemed these exchanges of heartfelt correspondence, which included poetry in Chinese, extraordinarily felicitous. When the Kokiden Consort learned about these letters, however, she harshly disparaged them.

"One might expect a man who has incurred official censure to find it a daily struggle just to savor the taste of food as he would like . . . but not Genji. He resides in an attractive villa, writing letters critical of the court, and like that traitorous official in the Qin dynasty, gets his sycophants to go along with everything he says. Why, they'd call a deer a horse if he told them to!"[7] When word spread of what she said and the asperity with which she spoke, people at the court were afraid, and no one wrote to Genji anymore.

The passage of time brought no comfort to Murasaki. When the women who had been serving Genji in the east hall moved to her quarters in the west hall, they had been skeptical of her, wondering why their lord would have brought such a young lady to his villa. But after they got to know her—her charming, endearing looks, her steady, sincere personality, her kindness and deep sensitivity—not one of them chose to leave. Those ladies-in-waiting of higher status and greater discernment were able once in a while to catch a glimpse of her behind her screens, and when they did they saw that their lord's preference for her over his other ladies was perfectly justified.

---

6. A line from a Chinese-style poem which Sugawara no Michizane wrote in exile when he looked at a robe he had received from the emperor while still at court. The poetry of famous Chinese and Japanese exiles, such as Bai (Bo) Juyi and Michizane, keeps Genji company during his own time in exile [editor's note].
7. This anecdote is related in Sima Qian's *Historical Records* [editor's note].

The longer Genji stayed at Suma, the more living apart from Murasaki became intolerable. Despite his torment, he rejected the idea of having her come to live with him in a place completely unsuitable for her: *How could I have her live in a place I myself consider retribution for past sins?* Everything in this province was so different from the capital. He had never before been exposed to the sight of lower-class people, who had no inkling of who he was, and they were a shock to his sensibilities—naturally he found them uncouth and beneath him. From time to time smoke would rise quite near his villa, and at first he imagined it was from the fires the fishermen used to extract salt. Later he learned it was smoke from smoldering brush that had been cleared on the mountain behind the villa. It was all such a marvel to him that he composed a poem:

> *Like brush burning at the huts of rustics*
> *My heart smolders with my constant yearnings*
> *For tidings from my loved one back at home*

* * *

Just when life was feeling most tiresome, Tō no Chūjō suddenly paid a visit. He may have been the son of the Minister of the Left, but he was also the husband of the younger sister of the Kokiden Consort, and so his career had not suffered. He was a man of sterling character and, having been promoted to Consultant at the third rank, he now possessed an impeccable reputation. Despite his good fortune, however, the palace was a dreary place for him with Genji gone, and at every event he found himself longing for his old friend. It finally reached the point where he no longer cared that he might become the subject of malicious gossip and censure, and he decided to venture to Suma. The moment he laid eyes on Genji he experienced a joy, mingled with a few tears, that he had not savored in a long time.

In Tō no Chūjō's eyes, the villa at Suma had a vaguely Chinese style about it. The setting was like something out of a painting, and the effect created by the fence of bamboo wattle, the stone steps, the pine pillars, all as rustic and simple as Bai Juyi's hut, was peculiarly charming. Eschewing royal colors, Genji was dressed without ostentation, wearing dark bluish-gray hunting cloak and trousers, cinched at the ankles, over a humble light red robe, creating the impression that he was a mountain peasant. Though Genji was intentionally dressed like a provincial, his looks were so dazzling that Tō no Chūjō couldn't help smiling. The personal effects he kept close at hand were simple and humble-looking, and his sitting room was completely exposed to view from the outside. The boards for Go and backgammon, the furnishings, and the pieces used for playing *tagi*[8] had all been fashioned intentionally to have an appropriately countrified look, while the implements used for the Buddhist rituals he practiced showed signs of his wholehearted devotion. Even the meal provided was prepared in an intriguing way in harmony with the setting.

Tō no Chūjō, spotting some fishermen carrying shellfish they had just harvested, summoned them over and asked them what it was like to live for so many years on these shores. They told him about the various hardships and worries that they had experienced, and though their babbling speech was in a rough

---

8. A game that is similar to tiddlywinks, except that the object is to flip stones onto a board instead of counters into a cup.

dialect he found hard to follow, he was nonetheless moved as he observed them—they made him realize that all people, no matter what their status, experienced similar emotions and were not that different. As a reward for the shell-fish, he adorned them with robes and other gifts, and the honor he bestowed on them made them think, if only for a moment, that the world was their oyster.

Genji's horses were stabled close by, and Tō no Chūjō watched in amazement as someone brought rice stalks from a strange-looking storehouse in the distance—apparently some kind of granary—to feed them. The scene reminded him of a line from the *saibara* "Asukai," from which he sang the words "the grasses are inviting." He then told Genji all that had happened during the months he had been away, alternately crying and laughing.

"My father," he said, "is always fretting over your son, and it makes him feel sad that the little one should be so innocent about what is happening in the world." Genji could hardly bear to think about the boy.

There is no way for me to record all that was said between them, and I can't even do justice to a small part of their conversation. They did not sleep that night but passed the time composing Chinese poetry until dawn. Still, even Tō no Chūjō had to be mindful of the consequences of rumors at the court, and so he hurried back to the capital at daybreak. Such haste made his departure all the harder for Genji to take. They took up their cups of wine and toasted one another, reciting together a line of verse composed by Bai Juyi to bid farewell to his friend, Yuan Zhen, who had visited the poet in exile: "Into the winecup in spring pour tears of drunken sorrow." All their companions wept with them, apparently in bitter regret that the two friends should have to part after so short a time together.

A formation of wild geese flew across the dimly lit sky. Genji composed the following:

> *In what spring will I be allowed at last*
> *To go and view the capital again . . .*
> *How I envy these geese returning home*

Tō no Chūjō could hardly bring himself to leave.

> *Will not the wild geese that leave unsated*
> *From this enchanting abode lose their way*
> *On the road to the capital in bloom*

The gifts from the capital were elegant and in good taste. In seeing off his guests, Genji showed his appreciation for them by making a present of a black horse.

"You may think it inauspicious to receive a memento from someone in exile," he said, "but, like me, this horse misses home, for he tends to neigh whenever he feels a breeze coming from the direction of the capital."[9] It was an exceptionally fine-looking steed.

"Keep these in remembrance of us," Tō no Chūjō replied, presenting Genji with several items, including a remarkable flute that had a reputation at court for its pure tonal qualities. All the same, he was careful not to give presents

9. Allusion to a Chinese poem in *Selections of Refined Literature* [editor's note].

that might invite censure. By now the sun was rising. Because it was already late to be starting off, he hurried away, flustered, glancing back over and over. How forlorn Genji looked as he saw the party off. "When will I see you again? Surely your exile won't last much longer."

Genji replied with a poem:

> *O crane, you who can soar so near the clouds*
> *Above the palace . . . look on one whose life*
> *Is pure and spotless as a day in spring*

"While I fully expect to return, it is difficult for people who suffer the misfortune of exile, even the wisest sages of the past, to mingle again successfully in court society, and so . . . well, I don't feel as though I want to see the capital again."

To no Chūjō answered with a verse of his own:

> *Longing for the companion who flew beside him*
> *Wing to wing, the solitary crane with no guide*
> *To help cries out within the clouds and the palace*

"Your absence is so painful, I now regret the good fortune of being your close friend." They had not had time to converse at their leisure, and his departure left such a void that Genji spent the rest of the day sunk in melancholy reverie.

On the Day of the Serpent, which fell during the first ten days of the third month, one of Genji's attendants, a person who took pride in his knowledge of such things, told him, "This is a day when a person who has the sort of cares that trouble you should perform rites of purification." And so Genji, who had wanted to go view the shore in any case, headed down to the sea. He had some simple soft blinds erected to create a temporary enclosure for himself, then summoned a diviner, a master of the way of yin-yang who traveled back and forth between the capital and this province. As part of the Purification Ritual, a large doll to which all defilements and malign spirits had been transferred was placed in a boat and set adrift on the waves. Watching it float away, Genji was reminded of his own fate.

> *Like a ritual doll drifting out*
> *Into an unknown expanse of sea*
> *I am overwhelmed by my sorrow*

Sitting in the midst of the bright, cheerful scenery, he looked indescribably handsome. The surface of the sea was serenely calm and gave no sign as to which way the currents were flowing, but as he pondered the flow of his own life, his past and his future, he composed another poem:

> *Surely the myriad deities*
> *Must take pity on me . . . after all*
> *Is what I have done truly a crime*

The wind suddenly picked up, and the skies darkened. People began bustling to get ready to leave, even though the Purification Ritual was not finished. Rain fell suddenly and violently, and his attendants were so flustered that they were unable to raise their parasols as they made their way back to the residence. The party had not prepared for this kind of storm; the wind, unlike anything they had seen before, blew away everything around them, and the waves broke with terrifying power, forcing everyone to flee before their fury. With each flash of lightning and crash of thunder, the surface of the sea shimmered like a silk quilt spread out before them. While the party struggled, barely managing to make it back, they feared they might be struck by lightning at any moment.

"I've never gone through anything like this!" said one of the attendants.

"Usually you see some signs that the wind is going to pick up. This is a shockingly rare occurrence," replied another.

Even as they spoke, stunned and dismayed, the thunder continued unabated, and the torrential rain fell so hard it seemed as though it would pierce through whatever it struck. *Is the world coming to an end?* they all wondered, feeling forlorn and confounded. All the while Genji was calmly reciting a sutra. The thunder lessened somewhat when darkness fell, but the wind howled on throughout the night.

When it seemed that the storm was subsiding, one of the attendants remarked, "Surely this is a sign of the power of all the prayers I've been offering."

"If it had gone on much longer," his companion added, "we would have been swallowed up by the waves for sure."

"I've heard that a tsunami can kill a person in an instant," someone else chimed in, "but I never knew anything like this could happen."

When dawn approached, everyone was finally able to fall asleep. Genji was also able to rest a little, but as he dozed off, someone—a person whose features he could not make out very clearly—approached him in a dream. "You have been summoned to the palace," the figure demanded, "so why have you not made an appearance?" The figure was walking about, apparently searching for him. Seeing this, Genji was startled awake. The Dragon King in the sea was known to be a connoisseur of genuine beauty, and so Genji realized he must have caught the deity's eye. The dream gave him such a horrifying, uncanny sensation that he could no longer stand residing in this abode by the sea.

From Chapter XIII

Akashi

THE LADY AT AKASHI

Several days passed, but the rain and wind did not let up, and the thunder did not abate. These endless hardships made Genji increasingly lonely and miserable, and under such circumstances, facing a dark past and bleak future, he could no longer put on a brave front.

What should I do? he asked himself as he pondered his situation. *If this storm drives me back to the capital before I receive a pardon, I'll be a laughingstock. Perhaps it would be best to leave here and seek out some abode deep in the mountains, leaving no trace of myself in the world.* But then he had second thoughts. *Even if I were to leave for the mountains, people would still gossip*

about me, saying that I retreated in a panic, driven off by the wind and waves.
Later generations would consider me utterly contemptible.

These thoughts weren't the only thing troubling him. The dream he had a few nights earlier, during which he had seen that foreboding figure, kept recurring. Day after day went by without a break in the clouds, and he grew increasingly anxious, fretting about what was happening in the capital and thinking abjectly that, if things continued like this, he would be cast utterly adrift. Yet because it was too stormy to even poke one's head outside, no one arrived from the capital to see him.

At last a messenger arrived from his Nijō villa. The man, who had rashly braved the weather, was soaked to the point of looking weird and unearthly. He was also of very humble station—had Genji passed such a person on the road at an earlier point in his life, he would not have recognized him as human and would have had his servants brush him aside. The fact that Genji now felt a deep kinship with such a man brought home just how far he had come down in the world and how much his self-esteem had collapsed.

The man carried a letter from Murasaki:

"This terrible, tedious storm goes on without end, making me feel as though the skies were closing me off from you even more than before, for now I cannot even gaze in your direction."

> *How fiercely must the winds blow across those strands*
> *During this time when endless waves drench the sleeves*
> *Of one who is longing for you from afar*

The account she gave of her anguish affected him greatly. After opening her letter, his mood turned to dark despair, and he felt like the poet whose river of tears "overflowed its banks."[1]

"Even in the capital," the messenger informed him, "people are viewing this storm as an eerie omen, and I've heard that they plan to hold a ritual congregation of the *Sutra for Benevolent Rulers* to protect against a disaster.[2] High-ranking officials who usually attend the palace to conduct affairs of state cannot do so because the roads are all blocked."

The messenger's way of speaking was stiff and unclear, but because Genji was curious about court matters, he was eager to learn more. He summoned the man to appear before him and questioned him further.

"Day after day the rain falls with no letup and the winds continue to gust," the messenger said. "Everyone is alarmed and amazed by this extraordinary weather. Of course, we haven't seen anything like what you've had here at Suma, what with hail falling so hard it drills into the ground and with this constant rumbling of thunder."

The expression on the man's face, which told of his surprise and fear of the terrible conditions at Suma, sharpened all the more the sense of isolation felt by Genji's attendants.

---

1. Poem from Ki no Tsurayuki's *Tosa Diary* included in this volume: "The river of tears has overflowed its banks and further dampens the sleeves of both the one who goes and the one who stays behind."

2. This congregation, called *Ninnōe*, was held in the palace in the fall and spring or in times of emergency to protect the realm.

As the storm raged on and on, Genji began to wonder if this might not be the end of the world . . . but then, the following morning, the wind picked up with even greater intensity, the tide surged, and waves broke violently on the shore, looking as if they might sweep away even the rocky crags and hills. No words could describe the booming thunder or the flashing lightning, which seemed to be crashing down right on top of them. Everyone was frightened out of his wits.

"What misdeed did we commit," bemoaned one retainer, "that we should suffer this tragic destiny? Must we die without seeing our parents again, without looking on the beloved faces of our wives and children?"

Genji regained his composure, resolute in the conviction that having committed no great crime his life would not end on these shores. Still, his attendants were in such a state of panic that he had an offering of multicolored strips of cloth made to the gods of the sea. He also made numerous supplications: "O deity of Sumiyoshi,"[3] he intoned, "you who calm and protect these nearby shores, if truly you are a manifestation of the Buddha taken form as the guardian divinity of this region, then deliver us from harm!" His attendants were deeply distressed by the prospect that not only they themselves but their lord as well would be swept into the sea and perish in this unheard-of fashion. A few of them gathered their courage as best they could and, regaining a sense of propriety, joined their voices in praying to the Buddha and the gods, each offering his own life in exchange for the safety of their lord. Turning in the direction of the Sumiyoshi Shrine, they made their supplications.

"Our lord was reared in the bosom of the Emperor's palace and had every sort of pleasure lavished upon him. Yet has not his profound compassion spread throughout this great realm of eight islands, lifting up and saving many who were mired in sin and impiety? What crime has he committed that he must now suffer retribution by drowning here amidst these foul, unjust waves and wind? You gods of Heaven and of Earth, show us clearly that you discern right from wrong! Though guiltless, he has been charged with crimes, stripped of office and rank, separated from home, driven into exile. Grieving anxiously morning and night, he has suffered this tragic fate . . . is he about to lose his life as well because of some sin in a former life, or some crime committed in this one? Gods and Buddha, if you are just, then put an end to our lordship's suffering!"

Genji once more offered prayers to the Dragon King and to the myriad gods of the sea, but the thunder only crashed all the more loudly, and lightning struck the gallery connecting Genji's quarters to the rest of the villa. Flames leapt up and the passageway caught on fire, throwing everyone into a state of panic. No one had enough wits about him to be able to deal with the situation, and so they had their lord move to the rear of the residence to a room that, from the looks of it, must have been the kitchen. Everyone, irrespective of rank, crowded into the space, and the thunder could barely be heard above the tumultuous din of the crying and shouting there. As the day ended, the sky was black as an inkstone.

Finally the winds gradually subsided, the rain tapered off, and sparkling stars were visible. Genji's attendants felt embarrassed for their lord, thinking it was an affront to his dignity to remain in a place as strange and disreputable as this,

---

3. A Shinto shrine near Osaka [editor's note].

and so they wanted to try to move him back to the main hall. They hesitated, however, debating what they should do.

One of them declared, "Even the quarters that escaped the fire have an ominous air about them. The people over there are in a state of shock, noisily stomping about, and the blinds have all been blown away."

Another attendant replied, "In that case, let's wait until morning."

All the while Genji was meditating and softly invoking the name of the Buddha. Feeling unsettled and restless, he mulled over all that had happened. After the moon rose he could make out clearly just how close to the villa the tide had surged. Pushing open a door of rough wattle and glancing outside, he gazed off toward the shore at the roiling surf left in the wake of the storm. No one in the immediate vicinity possessed the qualifications—sensitivity, proper judgment, ability to divine past and future—needed to make sense of all this and reliably sort things out. Instead, the only people to make their way to the villa were those strange, lowly fisherfolk, who gathered at a residence where they had heard a nobleman resides, babbling away in an unfamiliar dialect. Even though Genji considered them exceedingly bizarre, he couldn't very well have them chased away.

One of his attendants remarked, "If the wind hadn't subsided for a while, the high tide would have left nothing behind. The mercy of the gods is boundless!"

Feeling forlorn, he composed a verse:

> Had the gods of the sea shown no mercy
> Then the tide surging from all directions
> Would surely have swept me into the deep

Genji had maintained his composure throughout the tumult of the storm, but it had been terribly nerve-wracking and exhausting, and he began to doze off in spite of himself. The room he was using as a temporary shelter was so crude and rough that he could not lie down, so he slept while propping himself up against a pillar. As he did so, his late father came to him in a dream and stood before him, looking just as he did when he was alive.

"Why do you remain in such a strange, unseemly place as this?" His father took his hand and, pulling Genji to his feet, exhorted him: "Hurry now! Board a boat and leave these shores, following wherever the deity of Sumiyoshi may lead you!"

Genji felt overjoyed. "From the moment I was separated from your august presence," he said, "I have been beset with all manner of sorrows, so that now I feel I ought to end my life on this shore."

"Such rash thoughts simply will not do! All these trials are a mere trifle . . . retribution for some minor misdeeds. Though I committed no serious breach of conduct during my reign, I was unknowingly guilty of some misdeeds and have spent all my time after death atoning for them[4] without once giving any thought to matters of this world. But then I saw how deeply mired you are in your troubles here, and I could not bear it. I entered the sea and rose up to these shoals. Though I am now utterly exhausted, I must take this opportunity and hurry on

---

4. This statement by Genji's father is an apparent reference to a vision by the monk Nichizō, who saw the historical Emperor Daigo suffering the torments of Hell.

to the capital, where I will speak to Suzaku on your behalf." With that he rose to leave.

Genji was upset that his father was going away so soon, and because he wanted to accompany him, he began to weep. He looked up, but there was no one there—only the shining face of the moon. It had all felt so real, it hadn't felt like a dream at all. The lingering presence of his father remained, so palpable that Genji was profoundly moved by the sight of the wispy lines of clouds trailing across the night sky like traces of his father's ghostly presence. He had not seen his father's figure for many years, not even in his dreams. Now, even though he had glimpsed for only a few fleeting moments the face he had been longing so impatiently to see, the image continued to linger, hovering before his mind's eye. The poignant sense of gratitude he felt toward his father, who had flown to aid him when his life had reached its nadir and he was in despair and contemplating the end of his life, also made him look at the storm in a different, more positive light. The aftereffect of his dream was a boundless sense of happiness and relief that someone was looking out for him. His heart was full of conflicting emotions, and even though he had seen his father only in a dream, the turmoil in his heart distracted him from the sorrows of the waking world. He wanted to go back to sleep in hopes of seeing his father again, but the irritation he felt at himself for not responding to his father in more detail kept him from being able to close his eyes, and he stayed awake until dawn.

A small boat approached the shore and several men came toward the exile's abode. When one of Genji's retainers asked them to identify themselves, they answered, "The former Governor of Harima Province, a novitiate who has recently taken his vows, had this boat readied, and we journeyed here from the bay at Akashi. If Yoshikiyo, the Minamoto Lesser Counselor, is here, our lord would like to meet and discuss some matters at length."

Yoshikiyo was startled by their arrival and seemed not to know what to make of it.

"I was familiar with the man before he was a novitiate and still Governor of Harima and had opportunities to converse with him over the course of several years. However, we had a mutual falling-out over some trifling matter, and so it has been a long time since we exchanged any correspondence of a particularly personal nature. What business would bring him here over such rough seas?"

Genji's dream, especially his father's exhortation, was still vivid in his mind, and he told Yoshikiyo to hurry up and meet with the novitiate. So Yoshikiyo went down to the boat, scarcely believing that it had set out during the storm amidst such violent waves and wind.

"Earlier this month," the novitiate explained, "a remarkable-looking figure came to me in a dream and told me something incredible. 'On the thirteenth of this month,' he announced, 'I will give you a clear sign, so have a boat prepared and no matter what happens, make for Suma when the wind and waves subside.' Because he had informed me in advance, I did as instructed and had a boat ready. I waited as long as I could, until the ferocity of the rain and wind and thunder alarmed me and made me worry for the safety of your lord. Then it hit me that there have been many examples, even in other lands, in which a person who acted on his belief in a dream saved the state. Though your lord may have no use for my message, I could not let the appointed day spoken of in my dream pass without reporting these tidings to him. So I set out in the boat, and a miraculously favorable wind blew it along until we arrived at this strand. Truly this can only be a sign of divine favor. Is it possible that some sign was given to your lord here as well? If so, then please convey my words to him, ashamed though I am to beg your indulgence."

Yoshikiyo discreetly reported what he had heard.

Genji mulled over the information, turning over in his mind all things past and future—disturbing things he had seen in both his dreams and his waking life— that might be taken as signs from the gods: *If I hesitate out of fear that gossips will ruin my reputation by criticizing me for following after some eccentric novitiate, I could end up rejecting what might be genuine divine assistance. If that happened, I'd be an even greater laughingstock. It is hard enough to turn away from the advice of men . . . how much harder, then, to defy the gods. It's proper that I should be deferential, even in minor matters, and yield to the views of those higher in rank who are older, respected and trustworthy. A sage of old once advised that "one cannot be censured for following." In truth, I failed to heed those words, and as a result I've had to undergo many bitter, unprecedented hardships, including this life-threatening storm. In the face of all that, salvaging my reputation for posterity no longer seems so important. What's more, my father did admonish me in my dream, so why should I have any doubts about the novitiate's story?*

After deliberating in this way, Genji sent his reply: "Though I have encountered unheard-of difficulties in this unfamiliar province, no one from the capital has inquired after me. I have gazed after the sun and moon coursing through the sky to who knows where, and thought of them as my only companions from home . . . but now, to my great joy, a fisherman's boat arrives.[5] Is there a retreat on the shores of Akashi, some place where I might withdraw in peace?"

The novitiate's delight knew no bounds, and he expressed his deep gratitude.

"This is all fine and well," said a member of Genji's escort, "but our lord should go aboard before dawn so that he will not be seen."

Genji boarded the boat accompanied by the usual retinue of four or five of his most trusted attendants. The miraculous breeze that had brought the boat here picked up again, and they arrived at Akashi so quickly it was as if they had flown there. The shores of Suma and Akashi were separated by only a few miles, and so the journey would have been short in any case. Even so, the willfulness of the breeze seemed uncanny all the same.

What Yoshikiyo had told him years earlier was true—the scenery on the shores of Akashi was truly spectacular. For Genji, who was hoping for a peaceful sanctuary, the only distraction was the large number of people bustling about. The novitiate's estate extended from the waterfront up into the recesses of the hills, and he had brought together on his land all sorts of attractive buildings constructed with an eye to how well they suited the seasons and the topography—a thatched-roof cottage near the shore that would intensify the pleasures of viewing the four seasons, a magnificent meditation hall standing beside a stream flowing down out of the hills on a site perfect for performing ritual devotions and focusing one's thoughts on the next world, a row of granaries built to provide for the needs of this world and filled with the bountiful harvests of autumn

5. Poem by Ki no Tsurayuki: "To my great joy a fisherman's boat arrives, borne by a breeze that blows on one who has been soaked by waves."

in order to sustain the novitiate throughout his remaining years of life. Fearful of the recent tidal surges, the novitiate had moved his daughter and her entourage to a residence at the foot of the hills, allowing Genji to comfortably occupy the villa near the sea.

The sun was rising just as Genji was moving from the boat to a carriage. As soon as the novitiate caught a glimpse of him in the dim early morning light, he immediately forgot about his own advancing years and felt as though his life had been extended. With a beaming smile, he at once offered a prayer to the deity of Sumiyoshi. It seemed to him that he had been allowed to grasp the light of the sun and the moon in his hands, and so it seemed perfectly natural that he should busy himself tending to Genji's needs.

To capture the scene in a painting—not just the beauty of the setting, which goes without saying, but also the elegance of the buildings, the indescribable appearance of the grove of trees surrounding them, the rocks and plants in the gardens, the waters of the inlet—seemed impossible for anyone but the most inspired of artists. The residence here was much brighter and more cheerful than the villa at Suma Genji had occupied these many months, and the utterly charming furnishings brought back fond memories. The novitiate's lifestyle was, as Yoshikiyo had reported, no different from that enjoyed at the most distinguished aristocratic houses in the capital; indeed, the blinding brilliance of his lifestyle appeared, if anything, to be superior.

* * *

It was now the fourth month, and with the change of the seasons Genji was provided with superb new robes and silk curtains to hang around the dais in his sleeping quarters. He found the tendency of his host to obsess over every last detail when serving him somewhat pathetic and overdone. But, at the same time, he observed that the old man's proud dignity revealed a nobility of character, and so he allowed the novitiate to have his way in such matters.

Murasaki continued to send messages as frequently as ever. One quiet, calm moonlit evening, when a cloudless sky spread far into the distance over the sea, the scene brought to mind the water in the garden pond at his Nijō villa. He was filled with an ineffable yearning—a yearning for what or for whom he could not articulate. Before his eyes, off in the distance, was the island of Awaji. "Ah, how far away it seems . . . ,"[6] he murmured.

> *This moon illuminates the poignant beauty*
> *Of Awaji Island . . . ahh, how far it seems*
> *Bringing painful longings for my distant home*

He took his seven-string koto from its cover and plucked a few notes. He had not touched it for some time, and the sight of him aroused restless emotions in his attendants, who found their lord troublingly sad and beautiful.

Genji performed a tune titled "Kōryō,"[7] utilizing all his skills to produce an immaculate rendition. The music mingled with the rustling of the pines and

6. Poem by Ōshikōchi no Mitsune: "Ah, how far away it seemed . . . the moon I viewed at Awaji. Is it the special atmosphere of the setting here this evening that makes it look so near?"
7. A "secret" song composed by the legendary musician Reirin for the Yellow Emperor.

the rippling sound of the waves and wafted toward the lady's residence at the foot of the hill, sending shivers of delight through the refined young ladies-in-waiting there. The rustic denizens of that shore, who certainly were unable to recognize the song, walked along the beach feeling exhilarated, even though they ran the risk of catching cold in the sea breeze. Unable to restrain himself, the novitiate relaxed his devotions and hurried over to Genji's residence.

"It would seem I am still driven by memories to return to the world I supposedly left behind when I took my vows," he said, tears welling up. "The atmosphere conjured by your music, which draws me here this evening, is surely a harbinger of the Pure Land paradise I pray for in the coming life."

Memories came flooding back to Genji's heart as well . . . the musical entertainments celebrating various seasons at court . . . so-and-so playing the koto . . . such-and-such on the flute . . . the sound of voices singing in chorus . . . courtiers praising him lavishly for his own musical skills. How wonderful was the honor and respect shown to him by everyone from the Emperor on down; and of course how grand were the circumstances of those he loved and his own status back then. He felt like he was in a dream, and the overtones his koto produced as he played in that trancelike state conveyed an unearthly, frightening loneliness.

The novitiate could not help feeling maudlin, and he sent for a *biwa* lute[8] and a thirteen-string koto from the villa at the base of the hill. Playing the role of an itinerant priest performing on the lute, he played a couple of very charming, unusual tunes. He presented the thirteen-string koto to Genji, who played a little on the instrument. The novitiate marveled at how brilliantly talented the young lord was in a variety of arts. Even an instrument that does not produce an especially distinct timbre may, depending on the occasion, sound quite superior. As the music drifted across the waters stretching interminably into the distance, the stirring cry of a Water Rail—so like the rapping of some paramour at the gate of his beloved—rang out amidst the shadows of trees in rampant foliage more vivid and fresh than even the blossoms of spring or the leaves of autumn at their peak.

Genji was impressed by the novitiate's koto, which produced such unique tones, and by his host's own sweetly charming skills. "The thirteen-string koto is most delightful when played in a relaxed, informal style by a woman who exudes a gentle and intimate grace." Genji was referring to women in general, but the old novitiate, misinterpreting his intent, smiled and replied, "I'm not sure that any woman, no matter how gentle or graceful, could play better than Your Lordship. I myself learned to play under the tutelage of a disciple of the Engi period Emperor, Daigo,[9] but as you can see I'm not especially gifted, and so I've cast aside the things of this world. Still, whenever I was depressed I would play a little, and as a result there is someone here who learned the instrument by imitating me, and so her style naturally resembles Emperor Daigo's. Of course, I am just a humble mountain rustic, hard of hearing, and it may be that I am so used to the sound of the wind rustling in the pines that I can no longer tell the difference between it and the sound of the koto. Even so, would you

8. A four-stringed pear-shaped Japanese lute [editor's note].
9. Daigo (885–930) ruled 897–930 C.E. and his reign included the Engi period, from 901 to 923 C.E.

permit me to arrange for you to hear her in private?" His voice was tremulous, and he seemed to be on the verge of breaking down in tears.

"I should have known that in a place such as this, where people are accustomed to the superior music of nature, my performance would not sound like a koto. All very regrettable . . ." Genji pushed the instrument away. "It's odd, really, but since ancient times the thirteen-string koto has been considered a woman's instrument. Emperor Saga[1] passed down the techniques, and it is said that his daughter, the Fifth Princess, was the most skillful virtuoso of her age, though no one remains in her lineage to pass along that style of performance. Nowadays, for the most part, those who have achieved a reputation as master of the koto choose to approach this instrument superficially, as a pleasant diversion and no more. Thus, it's fascinating that an older style of performance should have survived, hidden away in a place like this. How will I manage to hear this person you spoke of?"

"There is nothing to prevent you from listening to her," the novitiate said. "You could even summon her. After all, if I may point to the story handed down by Bai Juyi, there was a woman, the wife of a merchant, who won praise for her talent with the lute . . . and what you said of the koto is true of the lute as well. In ancient times there were very few people who could calmly strum that instrument and reveal its true nature, but the lady I mentioned can play it exceptionally well, with a gentle charm and few hesitations. I'm not sure how she managed to learn the lute as well, but when I hear her music mingling with the sound of the waves, it sometimes brings on feelings of melancholy. At other times it provides a respite from my accumulating sorrows."

Delighted that the old man was a true connoisseur, Genji swapped instruments with him, exchanging the thirteen-string koto for the lute. As expected, the novitiate's skill on the koto was well above average. He played tunes in a style no longer heard in the modern world. His spectacular fingering showed a touch of continental flair, and the vibrato he produced with his left hand was deep and clear. Though they were not at Ise, Genji had one of his men, who had a fine voice, sing the line "Shall we pick up shells along the pristine shore?" from the *saibara* "The Sea at Ise," while he himself kept rhythm by using flat wooden clappers. From time to time he joined in the singing, and the novitiate would often pause to praise him. As the night wore on, the old man had unusual delicacies brought out and pressed wine upon everyone so that they would naturally forget the cares of the world.

The late night breeze off the shore was chilly, and the light of the setting moon seemed intensely clear. As the world grew quiet the novitiate opened up to Genji, telling him one small anecdote after another about all that had happened in his life—the burdens he had assumed when he first moved to Akashi and how he had devoted himself single-mindedly to his religious practice with the next life in mind. He even brought up, without prompting, his daughter's situation. Genji was amused by this show of paternal devotion, but at the same time he was also touched by the young lady's predicament.

"I hesitate to mention it," the old man continued, "but I wonder if your move to a strange province such as this—temporary though it may be—isn't the work of the gods and the Buddha who, by troubling your heart for a brief period, are

1. Ruled 809–823 C.E.

showing kindness and pity toward an old priest like me who has prayed to them for so long. I say this because it has been eighteen years since I first placed my faith in the deity of Sumiyoshi. From the time my daughter was a little girl I had ambitions for her, and so each spring and autumn, without fail, I go to pray at the Sumiyoshi Shrine. I practice my devotions day and night at each of the six prescribed times. But, rather than concentrating my prayers on the wish to be reborn on a lotus in the Pure Land, I ask that my ambitions for my daughter be fulfilled and that she be granted a noble position at court. Regrettably, sins from a previous life have brought me misfortune in this one, and I've become the miserable mountain peasant you see before you. My father was able to rise in status as a Minister of State, but I have ended up a rustic provincial. It grieves me to imagine what might become of my descendants, how low they might sink should my family's decline continue; that is why from the moment my daughter was born, I've invested all my hopes and expectations in her. As a consequence of my deep resolve to present her by any means possible to a high-ranking nobleman in the capital, I've rejected many suitors who wished to take her as a wife. Some of those suitors were men whose status was higher than mine, and I've suffered harsh treatment on account of their resentment of me. However, I don't consider that a hardship, and I admonish my daughter by reminding her that as long as I'm alive I'll look after her, even though, as you can see from the narrow cut of my sleeves, I don't have much wealth to give her. And I've told her that if I die while she is still young and unmarried, she should throw herself into the sea."

He broke down sobbing. He said so many other things besides, it is impossible to relate them all here. Genji was listening to all this during a period in his own life when he had been beset constantly with various problems, and so the old man's story invited tears of sympathy.

"Accused without basis and cast adrift in an unfamiliar land," Genji responded, "I have wracked my brain trying vainly to identify the misdeed I supposedly committed. But now, on hearing your tale this evening and reconsidering the matter, I'm deeply moved by the realization that we truly share a bond from a previous life that is anything but shallow. Why did you not tell me earlier that you knew all this? Once I had departed the capital I lost my attachments and came to find the fickleness of the world insipid and tiresome, and while passing the days and months pursuing only religious austerities, I grew disconsolate and melancholy. I heard faint reports about your daughter, but because it seemed likely that you would reject as inauspicious the suit of an exile without status, I had no confidence to even try. Now it appears that you are beckoning me to her quarters. To have her share my lonely bed would be a comfort."

The young lady's father was thrilled beyond measure at these words.

> Do you know as well what it means to sleep alone
> Then perhaps you understand the boredom she feels
> Waiting for the dawn on Akashi's lonely strand

"You may well appreciate," he added, "how much greater my own sense of melancholy has been, wearied as I am from years of concern over her." Now that he had finally spoken of his daughter, his body was trembling in agitation—though he did not lose his air of refinement and dignity.

"That may be," Genji replied, "but those who are accustomed to living on this bay may not appreciate how lonely it is for someone like me . . ."

> In lonely travel robes, on a pillow of grass
> I wait in sleepless grief for dawn at Akashi
> Unable to weave a dream and join my lover[2]

Genji was in dishabille; there is simply no way to describe how charming he looked at that moment.

The novitiate talked on and on at length about all sorts of things, but it would be annoying to record them all here. However, because I have not written down everything exactly as it happened or was spoken, I may have accentuated some of the man's more eccentric and stubborn characteristics.

With things going more or less as he had hoped, the novitiate felt as though a burden had been lifted from him. At around noon the following day, Genji sent a letter to the lady's residence at the base of the hill. He had given careful attention to the letter, thinking that the lady seemed on the one hand like someone of dauntingly superior talent who would be hard to approach, and on the other, like an unexpected find hidden away in this obscure location. He prepared the letter with exquisite care, writing on light brown Korean paper.

> Gazing sadly at the sky, is it near or far . . .
> How I want to pay a visit to those treetops
> At the abode obscured by mist and faint rumor

"My longing for you has overwhelmed my secret love."[3] Was that the full extent of his letter?

The novitiate had already arrived at his daughter's residence and was waiting with secret anticipation. Things were working out as expected, and by the time the letter arrived he had already arranged for refreshments for the messenger, plying him with wine until the man was embarrassingly drunk.

The lady took a long time to compose her reply. Her father entered her quarters and pressed her to answer, but she refused to listen to him. Intimidated by the brilliant wit of Genji's letter, she felt inadequate and ashamed to set her own hand to paper, which would expose the truth about her. Comparing his status to hers, it was obvious that the gulf separating them was enormous. She withdrew to lie down, telling her father that she wasn't feeling well. Unable to persuade his daughter and with his patience now exhausted, the novitiate wrote the reply for her:

"For a woman whose sleeves have about them the rustic air of the provinces, your graciousness brings a surfeit of happiness that is too much for her to bear. She is too overwhelmed even to read your letter, but observing her . . ."

---

2. This poem, like the one it answers, plays primarily on the word *akashi*—referring to the place name and to dawn breaking. Lovers would share robes as part of their bedding, and it was believed that this act ensured that they would meet in their dreams. Travel robes convey an image of sleeping alone, thus making it impossible to meet one's lover in a dream and intensifying the sense of loneliness.

3. Anonymous poem from *The Kokinshū*: "Though I never wanted to let the colors of my love show, my longing for you has overwhelmed my secret."

Lost in lonely thoughts, gazing sadly
At the same sky you are viewing now
Are not her feelings the same as yours

"Is my view of her perhaps too romantic?"

The note was written on Michinokuni paper, which lent it an old-fashioned aura, but Genji was a little surprised, shocked even, at the seductive allure of the calligraphy, which was embellished with refined flourishes. The novitiate had presented Genji's messenger with, among other things, an exceptionally fine set of women's robes.

The following day Genji sent another note: "I've never seen a letter by proxy before."[4]

How wretched my uncertain heart
Knowing there is no one who asks
"Do tell me, how are things with you"

"The difficulty of speaking of my feelings to one I have not yet seen . . ."

This time he used an extremely soft, thin paper, and his calligraphy was exquisite. Only a young lady who was excessively shy and introverted would have failed to appreciate it, and indeed when the Akashi lady saw it, she was amazed. Still, she remained convinced that the immeasurable difference in status between them made any relationship hopelessly unsustainable, and it made her cry to know that he was courting her even though she was of such inferior rank. She remained outwardly impassive, but this time she did as she was told and replied to him. Writing on heavily perfumed paper of light purple hue, her brush-strokes were thick and bold in some places, thin and wispy in others—a technique she employed to disguise any flaws in her hand.

How could you ever declare such feelings
To me, a person you have never met
Can rumors really trouble you so much

Her calligraphy and phrasing had an aristocratic flair not at all inferior to those of the most distinguished ladies.

Remembering all the exchanges he had engaged in with women back in the capital, Genji regarded the lady's letter with delight. Of course, he was mindful of prying eyes and of the censure he would surely suffer if he wrote too often, so he would let two or three days lapse between letters, and even then he corresponded only when he guessed that she might be experiencing emotions similar to his own—on an early evening passed in the quiet diversion of solitary idleness, for example, or a dawn that provided a scene of poignant beauty. Her replies on these occasions were always appropriate, and after thinking about her responses he concluded that she was a lady of discretion and noble character, and thus someone he very much wanted to meet. He asked Yoshikiyo to describe her and reacted with some distaste at the look on the young man's face as he did so—a look that seemed to say, *she belongs to me*—and he felt a twinge

---

4. The word Genji uses, *senjigaki*, refers to a letter dictated by the emperor or by an aristocrat.

of pity that his retainer's aspirations to win the lady for himself, which he had harbored for many years, would be thwarted right before his eyes. Genji believed, however, that he could justify his actions so long as the lady encouraged him to pursue a relationship. The problem was that she was proving even more aloof and proud than most highborn women. Genji found this kind of behavior damnably irritating, and so as time passed they began to engage in a contest of wills.

After crossing the barrier pass at Suma, his anxiety about Murasaki back in the capital only grew worse, and many times his resolve weakened as he wondered what to do—after all, being apart made it difficult to "bear this foolish game."[5] Should he have her come in secret to Akashi? Each time he asked himself this question, he ended up thinking better of it. No matter what happened, he believed that he would not spend many more years like this in exile, and so if he brought her here now, he would be criticized.

That same year the court witnessed many uncanny omens and disturbing incidents. On the evening of the thirteenth day of the third month—that is, the very day of the storm at Suma—thunder and lightning crashed, and wind and rain raged at the palace. During the night Emperor Suzaku dreamed that his father, the late Emperor, appeared below the steps leading out to the garden on the east side of the imperial quarters in the Seiryōden. His father was glaring at him, obviously in a foul mood, and so Suzaku sat up in a formal posture to show his respect. His father told him many things, and so must have said something about Genji. Suzaku was extremely frightened, but he was also moved to pity at the realization that his father's spirit had not yet been reborn in the Pure Land. Later, when he discussed his dream with his mother, the Kokiden Consort, she told him, "On nights when it rains and storms it's natural for you to dream of things that preoccupy your mind. A sovereign mustn't allow such trivial matters to upset him."

For some reason—perhaps because he had looked directly into his father's furious gaze—Suzaku began to have trouble with his eyes. His suffering was beyond endurance, and purification rites and exorcisms were performed constantly at both the palace and the residence of the Kokiden Consort.

Other incidents also brought grief to the palace. Suzaku's grandfather, the Minister of the Right who served as his Chancellor, suddenly died. Being advanced in years, his death was not unexpected or strange, but it was still a shock all the same, coming as it did after everything else that had happened. Then, on top of all this, the Kokiden Consort began to suffer from an unknown malady, and she grew weaker over time.

Occasionally Suzaku would give voice to his concerns, telling his mother, "If Genji has been exiled without just cause, then there is no escaping the conclusion that all of these problems are the result of karmic retribution. I think the time has come to restore him to his former rank."

The Kokiden Consort brushed aside his concerns and strongly admonished her son. "If you do that, you'll be criticized for lacking substance and lose respect. If you permit a man who has been expelled from the capital to return after less than three years, what will people say?" Her words made Suzaku waver, but as

<hr/>

5. Anonymous poem from *The Kokinshū*: "When I try to stay away and not meet you, just to see what will happen, my yearning is so great that I can no longer bear this foolish game."

the days and months continued to go by, the afflictions that he and his mother suffered grew ever more severe.

With the coming of autumn to Akashi, the sea breezes began to blow, stirring melancholy thoughts that were especially poignant. Genji was still sleeping in his solitary bed, but his loneliness was unbearable. He often spoke to the novitiate, telling the old man, "One way or another you will have to devise some pretext to have your daughter come here." Genji was convinced that it would be improper for him to go to her, and in any case the lady had shown no indication that she was inclined to meet him.

Only a provincial woman whose circumstances were utterly wretched, she thought, *would frivolously exchange vows as my father has encouraged me to do on the basis of some flimsy, seductive flattery from a man of the capital who has come here for a brief stay. He would never respect me or consider me one of his wives, and if I were to yield to him it would only add to my misery and woe, would it not? During this period of my life, while I remain a young, unmarried woman, my parents, who harbor these unattainable ambitions for me, seem to have placed their extravagant expectations for the future on very uncertain supports. And even if he did take me as a wife, wouldn't that merely add to their worries? So long as Genji remains at Akashi, the happiness I feel just exchanging letters with him is fortune enough for me. For many years I heard reports about him, and now I'm able to catch brief, indirect signs of his presence at a place where I never imagined I might meet such a man. I was told that his skill on the koto was peerless, and when I hear the notes from his instrument wafting to me on the breeze, I can guess what he is doing during the day. Now he has gone so far as to recognize my existence by courting me like this, and that is too great an honor, much more than someone like me, someone whose circumstances have been reduced to the status of the fisherfolk here, could ever deserve.*

As these thoughts raced through her mind, she felt more and more ashamed, and could not bring herself to even contemplate the possibility that she might have an intimate relationship with Genji.

Although the lady's parents were confident that the prayers they had offered over so many years would surely be answered, they also began to have ominous misgivings as they imagined how much sorrow they would experience if, having thoughtlessly rushed to give their daughter to Genji, there came a time when he no longer cared for her or counted her among his wives. They had heard how great and magnanimous he was, and yet how bitter would be their misery were he to abandon her! Relying upon the unseen Buddha and gods with no sign or proof of their blessing, knowing nothing of Genji's intentions or of their own daughter's karmic destiny, they tortured themselves with their obsessive worrying.

Genji was constantly pressing the novitiate. "If only I could hear the sound of her koto mingling with the sound of the autumn waves . . . what a waste, not to be able to listen to her play in this perfect season."

The novitiate ignored his wife's concerns and, without a word to his servants, secretly chose a propitious day to arrange a tryst. He went about busily sprucing up his daughter's quarters so that her rooms looked resplendent. Then, on the thirteenth day of the eighth month, with a nearly full moon shining gloriously, he sent a message to Genji that consisted of nothing more than a single line of verse: "On an evening too precious to waste."[6] Though Genji considered the wily old man a rather elegant pander, that didn't stop him from donning an informal cloak and setting out very late that night. A stylish carriage had been provided for him, but he thought it was too ostentatious for an occasion such as this and set out on horseback instead. His escort, which included only Koremitsu and a few attendants, was modest. He realized for the first time that the villa at the foot of the hill was farther away than he thought. From the road he could see all around the shore, and the moonlight reflecting off the inlets brought to mind an old verse describing such a scene as one to be viewed with "dear companions."[7] The words "dear companions" at once brought his beloved Murasaki to mind, and he immediately felt the urge to ride on past the villa and continue on to the capital. Instinctively, he muttered a poem to himself:

> Take flight, my stallion, with autumn moon reflecting
> Off your lustrous coat . . . carry me through cloudy skies
> So I may meet my love, if but for a moment

The villa of the Akashi lady, a stylish structure with many admirable touches, was set deep in a grove of trees. Whereas the residence near the shore that Genji was using was grand and attractive, the villa here was the kind of place where a person would lead a forlorn, solitary existence. Genji experienced a sweet, sublime sorrow at the thought that living here would allow him to contemplate to the full the sadness of life. The novitiate's handbell sounded a note of profound melancholy as it reverberated faintly from the meditation hall nearby and mingled with the soughing of the pines. The roots of the pine trees growing on the craggy rocks created a tasteful backdrop, and the chirruping of insects filled the garden. Genji glanced about, surveying the scene. The lady's quarters had been burnished with special care, and the door, made of exceptional wood, had been left open a crack so that the moonlight could stream in.

Genji stood uncertainly, hesitating before finally saying a few words of courtship. The lady, however, had been determined not to allow her relationship with him to become as intimate as this, and so she grew sullen and depressed, displaying a cold disposition that signaled she would not permit him to have his way.

She's getting above herself with these superior airs. Genji was irritated and resentful. *When a courtship has gone as far as ours, it is customary for the woman, even one whose high status makes her difficult to approach, to set aside her stubborn willfulness and yield. Could it be that she is belittling me for my loss of status? It would hardly be appropriate under the circumstances to force myself on her, but to lose a battle of wills with her would make me look pathetic.*

If only his handsome figure, confused and resentful, could have been displayed to a woman who was truly sensitive to beauty!

A curtain close by rustled and one of the silk streamers decorating it brushed lightly across the strings of a koto. The faint notes conjured in Genji's mind a pleasant image of the lady plucking the instrument, looking relaxed and unguarded. "Is this the koto I've heard so much about?" He asked her this and many other things besides, all trying to persuade her to play.

6. Poem by Minamoto no Saneakira: "On an evening too precious to waste, if only I could show the moon and the blossoms to one who understands, as I do, true beauty."

7. The source is not clear. An early commentary cites the following poem: "Shall we go to view it, dear companions . . . the moon's visage in the depths of the inlets at Tamatsushima?"

> If there were someone I could talk to
> Intimately, would I awaken
> From the dream that is this world of woe

She replied:

> Wandering just as I am, lost in the darkness
> Of a night without end, how could I speak to you
> Not knowing what is dream, what is reality

The dignified bearing of her figure, which he could barely make out in the dim light, put him very much in mind of the lady at Rokujō, who was now in Ise with her daughter.

Apparently the Akashi lady had not been prepared for his visit and, unaware of her father's machinations, had been caught off guard. It had never occurred to her that Genji might make such outrageous advances like this, and so she was quite flustered and upset. Moving into a room just off her private chambers, she somehow managed to securely latch the sliding door from the inside. Genji had no intention, it seemed, of trying to force the door open. Then again, how could he simply leave things as they were? The lady was aristocratic and tall, and her sense of propriety and dignity made Genji feel embarrassed and uncertain. Thinking about how their relationship had been destined by these strange circumstances, he was moved by the depth of the bond ordained by their karma. Surely his love for her would grow stronger the more intimate they became with one another.

He had come to loathe the long nights of autumn, which dragged on tediously for him in his solitary bed. But this night seemed to be rushing toward dawn, and so, mindful as ever that prying eyes might catch sight of his visit, he hurriedly left her, murmuring sweetly gentle words to her.

He discreetly dispatched the customary morning-after letter. His secrecy makes one wonder: was he bothered by a guilty conscience? The Akashi lady, worried about gossip, was equally careful to keep their affair secret, even from the others at her villa at the foot of the hill, and so she did not show the messenger bearing Genji's letter any special treatment or give him any lavish gifts. Her father deplored her aloof behavior.

Following this initial tryst, Genji would from time to time call on the lady in strictest secrecy. Their residences were separated by some distance, and there were nights when he was reluctant to venture out, concerned that he might encounter some of the local fishermen, who were by nature loquacious and prone to gossip. On those nights when he did not visit, the lady would be upset, taking his absence as proof that—just as she had imagined all along—his feelings for her were not sincere. Her father, seeing his daughter suffer and knowing that she had good reason for feeling the way she did, worried about how it would all turn out. He forgot about his devotions and his prayers for rebirth in paradise, unable to focus on anything besides waiting and listening for indications that Genji was calling on his daughter. It was truly pathetic that the heart of a man who had ostensibly taken religious vows could be so troubled by worldly affairs.

* * *

From Chapter XXV

Hotara

FIREFLIES

[*In omitted chapters, Genji is summoned back from exile, Reizei, Genji's son by Fujit-subo, becomes emperor, and the Akashi lady gives birth to a little girl, the future Akashi Empress. Genji finally persuades the Akashi Lady to move from the provinces to the capital and has Murasaki rear their daughter. Genji builds a mansion in the Rokujō area to accommodate his various women. He also takes in Tamakazura, the lost daughter of Tō no Chūjō, and is caught between fatherly and romantic feelings.*]

* * *

The rainy season continued for longer than usual this year, and because the women at Rokujō were bored and had no way to brighten either the skies or their mood, they passed the days and nights amusing themselves with illustrated tales. The Akashi lady prepared some stylish and interesting works of that type and sent them over to the quarters of her daughter, the Akashi Princess.[8]

Meanwhile, the lady in the west hall, Tamakazura, was more intrigued than the others by these stories, which she found fascinating and strange, perhaps because she had come from the provinces. Whatever the reason, she was utterly absorbed in reading them day and night. Quite a few of the young women who had been assigned to her quarters were proficient at reading and copying, and so she was able to collect quite a few texts describing the personal circumstances of a variety of remarkable characters. She couldn't tell if those stories were true or mere fiction, and, moreover, she couldn't find a single character whose cir-cumstances were similar to her own. It appeared as though the heroine Princess in *The Tale of Sumiyoshi*[9] experienced many remarkable incidents considered unusual as much in her own day as in the present. She compared the heroine's narrow escape from a forced marriage to the Chief Auditor to her own experi-ence with the loathsome Taifu no Gen.

Genji couldn't avoid seeing these illustrated tales, which were left scattered all around Tamakazura's quarters.

"Ahh . . . how tedious," he chided. "Women are by nature blithely content to allow others to deceive them. You know full well these tales have only the slight-est connection to reality, and yet you let your heart be moved by trivial words and get so caught up in the plots that you copy them out without giving a thought to the tangled mess your hair has become in this humid weather."

Genji smiled. "Of course, if we didn't have these old tales to read," he contin-ued, "we'd have nothing to divert us in our idle hours. What's more, even among this mass of falsehoods we find some stories that are properly written and exhibit enough sensitivity to make us imagine that they really happened. On the one hand, we may know that it's all silly, but we're still fascinated and affected by the fiction. When we read about some lovely princess lost in troubled thoughts, we're drawn to her story . . . or, when we encounter a tale that makes us wonder uncertainly if what it describes is really plausible or proper, we're nonetheless

---

8. Genji's daughter by the Akashi lady, [edi-tor's note].

9. A well-known tale in the author's time [edi-tor's note].

surprised and amazed that it could be told with such marvelous exaggeration. Of course, later on, when we come back to the tale in a calmer state of mind, we might dislike it or think it inappropriate . . . yet even then there may be aspects of the story that seem as charming to us as when we first read it. Recently, whenever I overhear one of the ladies-in-waiting reading to my little daughter, I'm struck by the realization that there are without doubt skilled storytellers in this world and that such tales must come from the mouths of people accustomed to spinning lies . . . but perhaps that is not the case?"

As soon as he spoke those words, Tamakazura shot back, "There is certainly no doubt that someone practiced at lying would be inclined to draw such a conclusion . . . for all sorts of reasons. I remain convinced, however, that these stories are quite truthful."

She pushed her inkstone away, and, when she did, Genji responded, "Have I been speaking rudely of your stories? Tales have provided a record of events in the world since the age of the gods, but histories of Japan like the *Nihongi*[1] give only partial accounts of the facts. The type of tales you are reading provide detailed descriptions that make more sense and follow the way of history."

Genji smiled again before continuing.

"A story may not relate things exactly as they happened out of consideration for the circumstances of its characters. Yet there are moments when one wants to pass on to later generations the appearance and condition of people living in the present—both the good and the bad. These are the subjects that people never tire of, no matter how many times they read about them. Thus, it's hard to keep such matters to oneself, and so you begin to tell stories about them. If you want to be upright and proper, then you will select only the good details to relate. Or, if you want to play to people's baser interests, then you will compile the strange and wondrous details of bad behavior. But in either case, you will always be speaking about things of this world. Styles of storytelling may differ in other lands, and even in Japan tales from the past certainly differ from those of the present . . . and of course there are distinctions between deep and shallow topics and themes. For that reason, the narrow-minded conclusion that all tales are falsehoods misses the heart of the matter. Even the Dharma, which was explicated for us through Sakyamuni's[2] splendidly pure heart, contains *hōben*, those parables that he told to illustrate the truth of the Law. There are many contradictory parts in the sutras that raise doubts in the mind of an unenlightened person. However, if you carefully consider the matter, you realize that all of the sutras have a single aim. The distinction between enlightenment and suffering is really no different from the distinction between the good and the bad in tales such as these. In the end, the correct view of the matter is that nothing is worthless." Genji was now claiming that tales were beneficial.

"Tell me, then," he concluded, "have you found any stories of piously foolish men like me among all your old scrolls? There couldn't possibly be any fictional princesses in this world who are as extremely aloof and heartless as you . . . who pretend not to notice anything. So, how about it? Shall we make a story unlike any other that has ever been told and pass it on to later generations?"

---

1. *Chronicles of Japan.* One of the two 8th-century chronicles of Japan, written in Sino-Japanese and modeled on the Chinese official histories, that told the history of the Japanese islands from the Age of the Gods to recent times [editor's note].

2. The Buddha (literally, "Sage of the Sakyas") [editor's note].

Genji sidled over to her. Tamakazura turned away from him, hiding her face in her collar, and said, "Even if we don't make a story together, the relationship we do have is so bizarre and unbelievable that it will likely never become the subject of court gossip."

"You think it's bizarre? Truly, there has never been a daughter as cruel as you." He had moved even closer, and his behavior was much too forward.

> Having a surfeit of cares and longings
> I seek answers for them in tales of old
> But find there no child as unfilial

"Even the teachings of Buddha admonish unfilial children," he added. When she refused to show her face, he began stroking her hair. As he did so, her resentment led her to reply:

> Though I have searched through all these ancient tales
> Truly I find no models in this world
> For parental feelings resembling yours

He felt ashamed when he heard her poem and went no further than stroking her hair. Given her situation, whatever would become of her?

Murasaki was also reading illustrated tales under the pretext that the Akashi Princess had requested them, and she was finding it hard to put them down. Looking at an illustration from *Tales of Kumano*[3] she remarked, "This is quite skillfully rendered." She gazed at the little girl, who was innocently taking a nap, and remembered when she was that age.

Genji studied the illustration. "How precocious children were back then. I was quite reserved by comparison when I was their age . . . a model of behavior, really." In truth, he was fond of being the model for all sorts of unheard-of behavior.

"You shouldn't be reading love stories in front of her," he continued. "She may not be all that intrigued by some young girl holding a secret love in her heart, but she is destined to be Empress, and it would be most unfortunate if she grew to accept the idea that it was normal for such affairs to actually take place." Had Tamakazura heard what he just said, she certainly would have taken umbrage at the difference in the way he treated his daughter and the way he treated her.

"People with shallow minds may imitate the behavior they read about in these stories, but they look rather pathetic when they do," Murasaki replied. "In *The Tale of the Hollow Tree*, the young Fujiwara Princess, Atemiya, is a prudent, dignified woman who never goes astray. However, her manner is stiff and unyielding, she lacks feminine grace, and her story ends up being just as bad an influence."

"People in real life seem to be the same," Genji said. "Everyone has their own way of doing things, but it's hard to strike a proper balance. A woman who has been brought up with the greatest care by parents who are not without breeding may grow up to be innocent and childlike, but the fact that she may also have many flaws will, sad to say, lead people to wonder what her parents were up to

---

3. This work has been lost.

and how they went about raising their daughter. On the other hand, when you see a young woman who in appearance and behavior is exactly what she should be for someone of her status, clearly her parents' efforts have paid off, and she brings honor to their house. If a young lady's nurses or attendants praise her to an absurd degree, then when her actions or words don't match her puffed-up reputation she will not seem as attractive. Parents should never let people who lack taste and judgment go about praising their daughters." He was determined to do everything in his power to ensure that his own daughter would avoid criticism.

Many of the tales depicted mean, vindictive stepmothers. He worried that the Akashi Princess might get the idea that all stepmothers were like those she read about. As a result, he took extra precaution when selecting stories and having clean copies and illustrations of them made for her.

* * *

From Chapter XL

Minori

THE RITES OF THE SACRED LAW

* * *

The following day she[4] was in pain and unable to get up, perhaps because she had overexerted herself by staying up throughout the dedication ceremony. At every similar event that she had attended over the years, she would wonder if *this day* would be the last time she would see the faces and figures of those who had gathered, the last time she would see them display their various talents or hear them play the koto or the flute. On such occasions, she would be moved even by the sight of faces normally beneath her notice. Her feelings were, of course, even stronger whenever she observed the other ladies at Rokujō. They were, after all, women with whom she shared both gentle rivalry and mutual affection, especially when they appeared together at some concert or diversion held in the summer or winter. Although no one can expect to remain for very long in this world, the thought that she would soon leave the other ladies behind, going forth all alone to an unknown destination, brought home to Murasaki the poignant sorrow of the evanescence of life.

When the dedication ceremony ended and each of the guests had begun to make his or her way home, she felt a twinge of regret that this would likely be the last time that she saw any of them. She sent a poem to Hanachirusato:[5]

> While my life, like these rites, must soon come to an end
> We may rely on the truth of the sacred law
> That karma will bind us through all the worlds to come[6]

4. Murasaki [editor's note].
5. One of Genji's ladies, also living in his Rokujō mansion [editor's note].
6. This poetic exchange gives the chapter its title. It should be noted, however, that the word

minori, which clearly means "rites" here, also refers to the Law (the Dharma), that is, the truth of the Buddha's teachings. That double sense operates implicitly in both poems.

Hanachirusato replied:

> *Even had these rites not been this magnificent*
> *They would still have forged a lasting bond between us*
> *Undeserving though I am, with little time left*

Immediately after the dedication ceremony, other solemn rites, such as the continuous reading of the *Lotus Sutra* and the ritual of confession and penance, were attentively performed. The esoteric healing rites that had been carried out every day over a long period showed no signs of helping Murasaki recover. Genji commissioned additional services at various holy sites and temples known for the efficaciousness of their prayers.

When summer arrived, Murasaki's fainting spells increased even though the weather was no hotter than usual. There were no alarming symptoms that one could point to as the source of her malaise. She was simply growing weaker, without ever suffering the sort of pain that caused others distress. Worried about what was to become of their mistress if she continued to weaken, her attendants observed her condition with regret and sorrow and fell into dark despair.

Because Murasaki's health was slowly failing, the Akashi Empress[7] withdrew from the palace and went to the Nijō villa. She was to take up residence in the east hall, and so Murasaki waited there to receive her. The ceremony greeting Her Majesty's arrival was nothing out of the ordinary, but Murasaki found everything about it moving, since she knew that she would never witness it again. She listened attentively as the name of each nobleman who had escorted the Akashi Empress—a very large group of senior officials indeed—was read out.

Since the two women had not seen each other for a long time, they seized this moment as a rare opportunity to speak intimately and at length. Genji arrived and said, "I feel like a bird evicted from its own nest. It's obvious that I'm of absolutely no use this evening. I'll take my leave and retire for the night." He went back to his quarters feeling quite happy to see Murasaki up and about— it was, however, only a brief moment of comfort for him.

"Since we will be staying in separate quarters," Murasaki said, "I would be deeply honored to have Your Majesty come to see me in the west hall. I know it is presumptuous of me to make such a request, but it is a considerable strain on me to leave my residence to visit you here." She stayed a while longer, and when the Akashi lady joined them, they continued their quiet, heartfelt conversation.

Murasaki had many things on her mind, but wisely she did not broach the subject of what would happen after her death. She calmly made a few passing references to the ephemeral nature of life, but the serious manner in which she talked made it clearer than any words she might have spoken just how sad and forlorn she felt. When she saw all of the children of the Akashi Empress, tears welled up and her face blushed with a most lovely glow. "I had so wanted to see each of them grow up . . . it would seem my heart regrets having so little time left."

Her Majesty wept as well and wondered why Murasaki had to be so fixated on death. The subject of their conversation shifted, providing Murasaki the

---

7. As noted above, Genji's daughter, the Akashi Princess who becomes the Kiritsubo Consort, has been elevated to the title of empress. The narrative does not explain when this event took place. From this point on, I will identify Genji's daughter as the Akashi Empress.

chance to speak about the ladies-in-waiting who had served her closely over the years. She did her best to avoid saying anything inauspicious, as if she were making last requests, but she felt sorry for her attendants, who would have nowhere else to turn once she was gone. "When I am no longer around," she remarked, "please remember to look after them." A sutra reading[8] was about to begin, and so Murasaki retired to her own quarters in the west hall.

As he walked around the villa, Niou, the Third Prince, had the most charming appearance of all Her Majesty's many children. During those intervals when Murasaki was feeling a little better, she would have him sit next to her and, when no one was around, ask him, "Would you remember me if I were not here?"

"I would miss you very much, Grandmama. You are much more important to me than Father or Mother! If you weren't here, I'd feel awful!" The way he rubbed his eyes to hide his tears was so adorable that she had to smile despite her sadness.

"When you are all grown up, you are to live here. And when the red plum and the cherry tree that grow in front of the west hall are in bloom in their respective seasons, you must not forget to view and enjoy them. At the appropriate times, you must make offerings of their branches to the Buddha in my memory."

The little boy nodded solemnly, then stared into Murasaki's face. Just as he was about to cry, he stood up and scampered off. She had raised him and the Third Princess with special consideration, and it filled her with pity and regret to know that she would not be able to help raise them to adulthood.

The heat of summer was so oppressive, she couldn't wait for the cool of autumn to arrive; and when it did, her spirits revived a little. Still, this was but a temporary respite, for even though the chill autumn winds were not yet blowing—cutting winds that bring only sorrows[9]—she was already spending her days in dewy tears.

The Akashi Empress was preparing to return to the palace. Murasaki wanted to ask her to stay on a little longer, even though such a request would overstep the bounds of propriety. It would also have been awkward, since His Majesty was now sending one messenger after another urging her to return. In the end, she didn't ask, and because she was so weak, she was unable to go to the east hall to see Her Majesty off. That was when the Empress took the extraordinary step of calling on her in the west hall. Murasaki was humbled and shamed that the Empress would deign to visit her, but she thought that it would have been senseless not to meet. Thus, she had special seating and furnishings prepared to receive her exalted guest.

Despite the fact that she was terribly emaciated, Murasaki still looked remarkable; the loss of weight had, if anything, distilled her beauty, which now possessed a boundless nobility and grace. Once, in the glorious flowering of her prime, her looks exuded to an almost excessive degree a lambent glow that was like the bright fragrance of blossoms. Now her infinitely cherished appearance,

8. This reading may be the *Sutra of Great Wisdom* (*Daihannyakyō*), which an empress would normally have performed during the second and eighth months (though the reading could be held on special occasions as well). However, the timing does not seem right here, and it is

likely that the sutra reading is part of the healing rites for Murasaki.
9. Poem by Izumi Shikibu: "What sort of wind is it, this wind that blows in autumn . . . how cutting it is, bringing only sorrow."

which brought to mind the transient nature of the mortal world, possessed a deeper loveliness, one that evoked incomparable feelings of compassion and sweet sorrow.

At dusk, a terrible, chilling wind began to blow, and just as she propped herself up on an armrest, thinking that she would gaze out at her garden, she saw Genji arriving.

"How good that you're able to get up today! Her Majesty's visit has apparently cheered you, has it not?"

She felt bad for him—he looked so happy whenever she was briefly feeling better that it moved her to imagine how devastated he would be when the end came.

> *How brief the moment when you see me sitting up*
> *As brief as the time that dew clings to bush clover*
> *Before being blown off and scattered by the wind*[1]

It was an apt comparison, for the dew clung precariously to the stems of bush clover in her garden that bent and sprang back with each gust of wind. Genji gazed out at the scene, and the melancholy desolation that accompanied this season was unbearable.

> *Our lives are like fragile dewdrops vying*
> *To disappear . . . would that no time elapse*
> *Between the first one to go and the last*

He could not brush all the tears from his eyes.

The Akashi Empress replied:

> *Who can look at this world, so like the droplets*
> *That cannot resist the blasts of autumn winds*
> *And think that only dew on the top leaves fades*

As they exchanged poems, Genji treasured the sight of these two women, ideal beauties both. Though he wished he could go on gazing at them like this for a thousand years, his heart ached, knowing that such a dream could never be fulfilled, for he had no way to keep his beloved from dying.

"You should leave now. I'm feeling very ill," Murasaki said. "It's terribly rude of me to say that I'm too ill to do anything for you." She pulled a standing curtain over and lay down so that they would not have to see her suffering. This time, it did not appear she would recover.

"What's wrong?" The Akashi Empress took Murasaki's hand and watched her tearfully. She looked every bit like a dewdrop fading away, and so they hurriedly sent off countless messengers to commission more sutra readings. There had been episodes like this in the past from which she had always recovered, but Genji suspected that the malignant spirit of the Rokujō lady might still be at work; accordingly, he did everything he could to protect Murasaki, ordering prayers and services to be held throughout the night. His efforts were in vain, however, for just as dawn approached her spirit vanished and she passed away.

---

1. Murasaki's poem plays on two senses of the word *oku*—"to be up/sit up" and "to settle."

The Akashi Empress thought it a sign of the boundless karmic bond she shared with Murasaki that she had not returned to the palace and was with the woman who had raised her until the very end. Neither she nor Genji could accept that her death was part of the natural order of things, that such partings were common to all. To them, her passing was singular and overwhelming, and so they felt as if they were wandering lost in the sort of dream one has in that twilight time between night and the dawn. No one there could make a rational judgment about anything. The attendants and other servants were completely stunned.

Genji suffered the most. Because he was upset and not thinking clearly, he summoned his son,[2] who was in attendance nearby, and had him move over in front of Murasaki's curtain.

"It appears that this is the end," he said. "It would be a great shame to go against her wishes at this point and not carry out what she had desired for so many years. The holy men who performed the healing rites and the priests reading scripture have all gone silent and have probably left, but some of them may still be here; tell one of them to cut her hair like a nun's. It won't do any good for her in this life, but if she shows a mark of her devotion to the Buddha, then at least she may rely on his mercy to comfort her on the dark path she is to follow. Is there some priest suitable for the task?"

Judging by his expression as he spoke, Genji was trying to be strong, but the color had drained from his face, and unable to bear his loss, he could not stop his tears. His son looked on in sympathy, thinking that his father's grief was perfectly understandable.

"Sometimes a malignant spirit will do this kind of thing just to torment the bereaved ones," said Genji's son. "What I mean is, the spirit may be making it appear that she is not breathing . . . that may be what's happening here. If that's the case, then it would be best to do what she wanted in any case, since according to the *Contemplation Sutra*,[3] making vows to uphold the precepts for even one day and night will lead to rebirth in Amida's Pure Land. Of course, if she *is* dead, simply cutting her hair at this point would have little benefit . . . it won't provide a light to guide her in the next world and would make the grief of those who look at her even worse. I wonder if it's for the best?"

He wanted to do all he could to make arrangements for the funeral and period of confinement, and so he summoned several priests from among those who had not yet withdrawn and were willing to serve during the weeks ahead. He also saw to all other necessary preparations.

Although he had longed for Murasaki for years after catching a glimpse of her on that morning after the autumn tempest, Genji's son had never harbored any improper or presumptuous fantasies about her. *In what world to come will I ever see her again as I did on that morning long ago? I never did hear her speak . . . not even a faint whisper.* Not a day had gone by since then when she hadn't been on his mind. *As it turns out, I will never hear her voice . . . and if*

2. Genji's oldest child from his first marriage. Long ago this son once caught an enthralling glimpse of his stepmother Murasaki, but has had no chance since to satisfy his yearning to see her again [editor's note].

3. The *Kanmuryōjukyō* is one of the three major scriptures of Pure Land Buddhism, along with the *Sutra of Infinite Life*, which is also known as the *Larger Pure Land Sutra*, and the *Amida Sutra*.

I'm ever to satisfy my hope of seeing her again, the only time to do so is right now, even if it means gazing at her lifeless form. He had been trying to control himself, since it would look odd if he exhibited excessive grief, but these thoughts brought him to tears. The attendants were loudly weeping and wailing, and Genji's son scolded them. "Really now, be still for a while!" As he spoke, he lifted one of the panels of Murasaki's standing curtain and peered inside. Because it was difficult to make things out in the dim light of early dawn, Genji had placed a lamp near Murasaki's bed and was gazing at her. He so regretted that such a lovely face would soon be no more—a face infinitely dear to him, one possessing such noble grace—it seemed that he no longer had the will to even try to hide his beloved from the gaze of his son, who was peeking in on this scene.

"Here she is, her face looking the same as ever . . . and yet it's obvious that she's no longer with us." Genji covered his face with his sleeves. His son, blinded by tears, could not see very well. To clear his vision, he closed his eyes tight and then opened them so that he could look at her; when he did, he was overcome by a feeling of sadness unlike anything he had ever known. He feared that he would lose his composure completely. Her hair was stretched out beside her, left just as it was when she died, incomparably lustrous and beautiful with not one strand of those thick, cascading tresses out of place. It no longer mattered to her that she was exposed to his gaze. In the bright glare of the lamplight, her complexion had an alabaster glow, and her face, needless to say, looked more pure and spotless than when she was alive, since she had always avoided being seen and concealed her real appearance under makeup. Gazing on her unique, extraordinary beauty, he wished that her soul, which had already departed, would soon return to her body—though he knew such a wish was unreasonable.

The women who had been her closest attendants were too overcome by grief to think clearly, and so Genji forced himself to calm down and set about making arrangements for the funeral. Although he had witnessed many sorrowful events in the past, he had no experience handling such matters directly himself. Undertaking this sad responsibility was like nothing else he had ever done in the past or would do in the future.

* * *

From Chapter XLI

Maboroshi

SPIRIT SUMMONER

Observing the bright cheer of the New Year season only served to make Genji's mood darker and more disordered. The sorrow that had completely overtaken his heart did not dissipate over time as might have been expected. Outside his quarters people were gathering for the customary seasonal visit, but he chose to remain inside his blinds, offering the excuse that he was not well. When Sochinomiya[4] arrived, Genji sent out a message saying that he preferred to meet in a private room in the interior of the residence. He included a poem with his note:

4. Genji's half brother, who unsuccessfully courts Tamakazura [editor's note].

> *The one who always lavished praise*
> *Upon these blossoms here is gone*
> *Why should spring care to visit me*

Tears welled up in Sochinomiya's eyes, and he replied:

> *Does the spring seek in vain the fragrance*
> *Of the red plum . . . are you suggesting*
> *It comes for common blossoms only*

Genji experienced a sense of deep nostalgia as he watched his younger brother strolling beneath the red plum trees. *Does anyone appreciate such beauty as deeply as Sochinomiya?* The blossoms were just barely open, and their fragrant glow was delightful. There was no music or entertainment this year—indeed, the celebrations were very different in form.

The ladies-in-waiting who had been in Murasaki's service for many years made no effort to change their wardrobes with the advent of the new season. Instead, they continued to wear dark robes of mourning. Their grief was hard to assuage, but since they remained devoted to Murasaki, they continued to serve Genji. It gave them a measure of comfort that he chose to stay with them in his quarters at the Nijō villa, where they could be near him, rather than going off to call on his other ladies at the Rokujō estate. After Murasaki died and Genji began sleeping by himself, he treated even those women whom he had previously regarded as lovers the same as any other attendant—though, to be sure, his relationship with them had never really been all that serious. He even had the women who served on duty at night withdraw to a spot some distance away from his sleeping chambers.

Whenever Genji was bored, he would reminisce about the old days. Though his devotion to following the path of Buddha had deepened and he had purged all traces of his former, fickle disposition, he would nevertheless recall things from the years he spent with Murasaki—especially the way she looked when her jealousy flared up over one of his passing affairs. *I suppose it made no difference whether my affairs were serious or mere dalliances . . . either way, they hurt her. Why did I have to be so impulsive? She got used to my peccadilloes as time went on and adopted an attitude of tolerance that allowed her to deal with them and to understand the true depth of my devotion to her. Though she never grew resentful or bore a grudge, she must have suffered from the turmoil in her heart, wondering with each passing affair what would become of her.* He was overcome by feelings of remorse and pity, and his heart was filled to bursting with shame and regret. Some of the women who most closely served him knew how their departed lady felt about Genji's betrayals, but they were circumspect about the subject, and would only discuss it with him in the most delicate terms.

Murasaki's face had betrayed no hint of her emotions when he brought the Third Princess[5] to Rokujō. Still, thinking back on it, he recalled how grief-stricken she looked during those moments when she sadly contemplated her wearisome existence. One time in particular—that snowy dawn following the Third Night with the Princess when Murasaki's spirit appeared at his pillow and he rushed

---

5. Third daughter of Emperor Suzaku, who marries her to Genji, much to Murasaki's dismay [editor's note].

back to her quarters—he remembered how he had tapped at her lattice shutter and was kept standing outside because no one could hear him; he had waited so long he thought he was going to freeze. Beneath those glowering skies, she had received him so sweetly and gently, hiding her tear-soaked sleeves from his view and doing everything she could to divert his attention from her own sorrow.

Every night until dawn, one thought ran through his mind over and over even in his dreams: *When will I be able to see her again . . . in what future world will we meet?* In the faint light of dawn Genji overheard a woman who must have been returning to his attendants' quarters saying, "My . . . it snowed heavily last night, didn't it?" Those words transported him back to that dawn long ago, and the loneliness that swept over him when he realized his beloved was not lying there beside him was shattering.

> *I long to melt like snow, to disappear*
> *From this world of sadness . . . but snow still falls*
> *And I still live on against my wishes*

To distract himself from sorrowful thoughts, Genji called for water to cleanse his hands and, as was now his custom, performed his devotions. The attendants stirred up the charcoal embers in the brazier, and then moved it closer to him. Two of the women, Chūnagon and Chūjō, sat nearby and talked with him. "Sleeping by myself last night, I felt lonelier than ever," Genji told them. "I still seem to be caught up in my attachments to this world, which I ought to understand well enough to renounce." He gazed off, lost in reverie. Then, as he glanced around, it occurred to him how sad these women would be and how much more grief they would have to endure were he to turn his back on the world. He privately continued his devotions out of sight, and anyone who heard the sublime beauty of his voice reading the sutras would have been moved to weep. One can only imagine the overwhelming feelings of those who were with him all the time, day and night. Their compassion for him was so great that they would not have been able to hold back the flood of tears even if their sleeves had been weirs.

"I was born into such a high station in life that I have lacked for nothing in this world," Genji remarked. "Yet I've always had the feeling that I was destined to experience more misfortune and regret than the average person. The Buddha has determined that I must know the truth about this world . . . that it is an ephemeral realm of woe. Throughout my long life, I pretended to ignore that truth. However, as I approach my final years and have had to experience the ultimate sorrow of witnessing my beloved's death, I now fully appreciate the nature of my karma and the limits of my desires. Since the fragile, dewlike bonds that tied me to this world have disappeared, I'm at peace. Still, I've grown closer to you now than when you were serving your late mistress, and so when it comes time to say my farewells I know that my heart will be in even greater agony than it is now. Our lives and loves are so fleeting . . . my mind is not right, for it is wrong of me to have such attachments."

He wiped his eyes in an effort to hide his tears, but he could not hold them back and they fell in spite of him. The women who witnessed his grief could not help but weep themselves. They each wanted to tell him how sorry they would be if he abandoned them, but their hearts were too full to say anything, and the conversation ended.

In moments of quiet solitude, Genji would have Murasaki's women sit nearby and converse with him either at dawn, following a sleepless night filled with regrets, or at dusk, following a day spent gazing off in pensive reverie. He did not look down on them as ordinary in any way; in fact, he had known one of the women, Chūjō, from the time she was a child. She had once been an object of his desire, and it must have been awkward for her when she first came to attend Murasaki, for soon after she began keeping her distance from Genji. For his part, he remembered how much Murasaki favored Chūjō over the other ladies-in-waiting, and it touched him to think of her now as a memento of his late beloved. Though he no longer considered her a sexual intimate, she had retained her attractive looks and personality. Indeed, because she resembled Murasaki a little, she was a living memorial, an evergreen planted beside a grave, and thus dearer to him than the other ladies-in-waiting.

Genji stopped meeting people with whom he felt no close affinity. Senior officials who were on good terms with him or his imperial brothers would often call on him at his estate, but he rarely met them directly. He even stayed behind his blinds when he spoke to his son.

If I agree to meet people, he had reasoned, *I risk exposing just how feeble-minded I've become over the past few months. Even if I'm in command of my faculties and keep my emotions in check. I'm likely to say something foolish, embarrass myself, and leave a bad reputation to later generations. I suppose that if people gossip about me and claim that I refuse to see anyone because I've grown senile, the effect on my reputation will be much the same. Still, it's far worse to have people witness my infirmities with their own eyes than to have them merely speculate about them.*

Genji was not yet ready to turn his back on the world. Biding his time and composing himself, he felt that he should wait to take vows, even during this period when people must be gossiping about how much he had changed. Whenever he made a rare, brief visit to one of his ladies—Akashi or Hanachirusato—he would be so overcome with emotion that tears would fall like rain. This was too shameful for him to bear and, consequently, he would let so much time elapse between visits or letters that the two ladies were always fretting about him.

The Akashi Empress returned to the palace, leaving the Third Prince, Niou, to comfort his lonely grandfather. "Grandmama Murasaki told me to give special attention to this tree," the boy announced, carefully tending the red plum in the garden that fronted the west hall of the Nijō villa. Genji was very touched watching him. It was the second month and the tops of the plum trees were in full bloom. Spring mists provided a delightful cover to those trees not yet in blossom. Hearing the cheerful voice of a warbler singing in the red plum tree just outside the west hall—a tree that also served as a memento of Murasaki— Genji stepped out to have a look. Walking about, he murmured a poem:

> *Feigning ignorance of her passing, the warbler*
> *Still comes to the house of the lady who planted*
> *This red plum tree and admired its fragrant blossoms*

It was now deep into the spring season, and the garden at the southeast residence at Rokujō looked just as spectacular as it did when Murasaki was still alive. However, Genji could no longer savor its beauty; just to look at it unsettled him and brought back all sorts of heartrending memories. His desire to go off to a remote spot deep in the mountains far removed from this world of woe—a place where he would not hear even the cry of a bird to remind him of spring[6]—only intensified. The sight of mountain roses and other flowers blooming in wild profusion suddenly brought dewy tears to his eyes.

The single-petal cherry blossoms had scattered already, the double-petal blossoms were past their peak, and the mountain cherries were now in bloom. The wisteria apparently darkened in color later than the cherries . . . Murasaki had had a good understanding of the plants in her garden, knowing which ones bloomed early, which ones late, and she had planted many varieties so that every season of the year would be filled with fragrant splendor. "My cherry is in bloom," Niou declared, referring to the one Murasaki had planted. "I'd hate it if the petals fell! There has to be some way to protect them . . . I know! I'll put a curtain around the tree, and so long as the cloth stays up, the wind won't be able to touch it!" The little boy's face showed just how clever he considered his plan to be. He was so precious-looking that Genji couldn't help but smile. "That's quite a good idea," he told his grandson. "You're much cleverer than the man who wanted to cover the sky with his sleeves!"[7] Genji considered this Prince his sole pleasure in life.

"We won't have much time to get to know one another. Life being what it is, regardless of how much time we may have together, the day will come when I'm no longer with you." Seeing his sentimental grandfather tear up as he was so wont to do recently, the boy was put off. "Grandmama Murasaki was always talking that way . . . I don't like it." Niou turned his face away, fingering his sleeves as he tried to hide his own tears.

Genji would often lean on the railing of the veranda just outside the corner of Murasaki's old quarters, lost in reverie as he gazed longingly around her garden or into the interior spaces beyond her blinds. Some of her women were still wearing mourning robes as a remembrance of their mistress; others wore robes of more everyday colors, though the pattern of their silks was plain and subdued. His own cloak was dyed an everyday hue, but its pattern was drab and inconspicuous. The furnishings and decorations were extremely austere—not much craftsmanship had gone into them, and they had such a forlorn air that he composed the following:

> *After I have renounced this world of woe*
> *Will it fall to ruin, this springtime hedge*
> *My departed love tenderly nurtured*

No one was forcing him to take vows, but, even so, his decision made him terribly sad.

Bored and with time on his hands, Genji went to pay a call on the Third Princess. Niou, carried by an attendant, accompanied him, and when they arrived, he ran around playing with the Third Princess's little boy, Kaoru. Still very much a child, it seemed that Niou had forgotten all about the scattering cherry blossoms that had so worried him earlier.

---

6. Anonymous poem from *The Kokinshū*: "Does she not know my feelings are as deep as those mountain recesses, where not even the cries of birds can be heard?"

7. Anonymous poem from the imperial anthology *The Gosenshū*: "If only I had sleeves wide enough to cover the heavens, I would not leave spring blossoms to the mercy of the wind."

The Third Princess was reading a sutra before the altar. She did not strike Genji as being especially devoted to the religious life, nor did she appear troubled at heart or regretful at having taken vows. She practiced her devotions quietly, without distraction, and Genji envied her ability to single-mindedly distance herself from the world. He deplored the fact that his own resolve to follow the religious life should be inferior to this shallow woman's. The flowers decorating the altar possessed a beguiling beauty in the dim twilight of dusk, prompting Genji to remark, "Now that the woman who was so attracted to the spring is gone, the colors of the blossoms have lost their charms for me. But seeing those flowers adorning the Buddha, I can't help finding them lovely. I've never seen the mountain roses in her garden bloom like they have this year . . . their petals are enormous! It's not a flower that one usually associates with refined elegance, but their vibrant colors are so exquisite and charming! How sad that they should be so much more lush and fragrant this spring, as if they were heedless of the fact that the one who planted them is gone."

The Third Princess offhandedly replied, "No spring comes to this dark valley . . ."[8]

Couldn't she have put it another way? Genji found her allusion tasteless and insensitive. It occurred to him that even at casual moments like this, Murasaki never once said or did anything that would cause him to think, I wish she hadn't done that. He tried conjuring up her appearance at different stages of her life, beginning from the time she was a child. A succession of images of her on various occasions in the past came to him one after another, reminding him of the wit and charm that had characterized her attitude, her behavior, and her manner of speech. Genji, who was now susceptible to teary sentimentality, was embarrassed that his memories should cause him to weep in the presence of the Third Princess.

The dusk, made indistinct by shimmering mists, was lovely to behold, and he decided to call on the Akashi lady. Since he had not looked in on her for some time, she was not expecting this visit and was caught by surprise. Still, she managed to receive him with grace and charm, which, to his eyes, made her look every bit the superior lady she was; and yet, try as he might, he could not control the natural inclination to compare her with Murasaki and note the differences in their personalities and talents. Recalling images of Murasaki ought to have brought some relief to him, but instead it merely increased his longing and sorrow, making it all the more difficult for him to find consolation.

The atmosphere of the quarters of his Akashi lady was very different from that of the apartments of the Third Princess, and Genji felt that here he could speak at ease about the old days. "I learned long ago that obsessing sorrowfully over a woman was certainly not proper, and in all my relationships I have tried to avoid attachments to this world. During the period of my life leading up to my exile—a time when people at the court were convinced that my fortunes were in decline—I thought things over carefully and concluded that there was nothing in particular to stop me from wandering off deep into the fields and mountains where I could take it on myself to abandon this world. But now in my

8. Poem by Kiyowara no Fukayabu from *The Kokinshū*: "Because spring comes not to this valley where no light shines, there are no lamentations for the scattering of blossoms."

twilight years, as I near the end of my life. I find myself entangled in bonds that will prove a hindrance to salvation. How frustrating to be weak-willed!"

Though he was speaking of his sorrows in general, the Akashi lady understood with pained sympathy the real reason why he was in such a mood. At that moment he seemed especially miserable to her.

"Even a person," she began, "who in the eyes of ordinary people appears to have nothing at all to regret, may in fact keep many bonds hidden away in their hearts. How could such a person possibly abandon those relationships with an easy conscience? Such ill-advised action would invite criticism for being frivolous and rash. When it comes to making a decision about a matter as serious as renouncing the world, it is best, in my opinion, to take your time, so that in the end you will make a deeply considered choice and bring peace and calm to your heart and mind. From what I know of past examples, they say it is never proper to renounce the world when your heart and mind are unsettled, when things have gone against your wishes and you find the world detestable. In your case, you should resist the impulse to take vows and hold off making such a life-changing decision until the children of the Akashi Empress are grown up and their positions truly secure. I would feel more at ease and happier if you would wait." The Akashi lady looked magnificent as she offered him her mature, sensible advice.

"You may be right," Genji replied, "but the deep wisdom that recommends taking time to think it over before renouncing the world may in fact prove the shallower choice." He went on to share with her things that had been on his mind for a long time. "The spring Fujitsubo passed away I felt just like the poet who wrote about those cherry trees blooming on the plains of Fukakusa.[9] I felt that way because I had seen her when I was young and was deeply moved by her beauty, which was apparent even to the court at large. Being more familiar with her than others, my grief was of course greater at the time of her death, but the special loss I felt was not due simply to our relationship as a man and woman . . . it grew out of feelings that were more complex than that. Now Murasaki has preceded me in death, and it is so hard to forget her that I find no way to console my heart. In this case, too, my grief is not simply the kind that comes when death severs a relationship between husband and wife. No, when I think back over the circumstances that led me to want to raise her from childhood, the way we grew old together, and how, in the end, I was left behind, the grief I feel arises out of all that happened between us and possesses a special quality that makes it too hard to bear. With all of the things that we experienced together—the sad and the sublime, the exquisite and the elegant, the amusing and the delightful—with such memories filling my thoughts, how could my grief be shallow?"

Genji shared his memories and talked about current happenings at the court until late that night. It occurred to him that he should stay with the Akashi lady until dawn, but instead he returned to his own quarters in the southeast residence. She could not help but be moved to sorrow and pity. For his part, he startled himself when he realized what a peculiar change had come over him.

9. Poem by Kamitsuke no Mineo from *The Kokinshū*: "If the cherry trees on the plains of Fukakusa have any feelings at all, for this year only let them put forth blossoms of mourning gray."

He set about his regular devotions, and in the middle of the night moved to his daytime quarters and lay down temporarily. When morning came, he sent a letter to the Akashi lady:

> *Crying on and on, wild geese head north, longing to return . . .*
> *I weep as well, longing to return, but in this sad world*
> *Nothing remains as it was and there is no place to rest*

She had resented his leaving her early the previous night, but seeing how much pain he was in, she realized that he was no longer himself. She put her own feelings aside, tears welling up in her eyes.

> *The water in the seedling paddy*
> *Where wild geese once gathered disappears*
> *And with it the flower's reflection*

Her calligraphy was lovely as ever.

For some reason, Genji recalled, Murasaki had never taken to her, though in her final years the two of them recognized their mutual interests and grew friendlier. Still, even after they realized that they were not a threat to each other and were able to establish a trusting relationship, Murasaki remained uncomfortable around her . . . and I was the only one who ever noticed how stiff and formal she was.

Whenever his loneliness became too much for him, Genji would suddenly drop in on the Akashi lady just to talk about everyday matters. Now, however, nothing remained of his former passion, and he showed no inclination to spend the night with her.

From her quarters in the northeast residence Hanachirusato sent new summer robes for the change of season. A poem was attached:

> *This day brings the start of the season . . .*
> *Will your heart be filled with memories*
> *As your old robes are exchanged for new*

Genji replied:

> *From this day forward, each time I put on these robes*
> *Diaphanous as cicada wings, the sorrows*
> *Of this fragile, fleeting world will only deepen*

During the fourth month, on the day of the Kamo Festival, the atmosphere at the Rokujō estate was so tedious that Genji told his female attendants, "It would make all of you feel better if you were to go off to see the sights today." Recalling how the Kamo Shrine looked during the festival, he added, "You will likely feel left out if you don't go. Perhaps it would be best if you returned discreetly to your family homes and then went to the festival from there."

Chūjō was taking a nap on the eastern side of Genji's quarters. When he stepped out and saw her lying there she got up, looking very dainty and adorable. The expression on her face was fresh and bright, and her hair, mussed from sleep, cascaded down and hid her face in a most charming fashion. Her trousers were dyed a scarlet hue tinged with yellow; her singlet was burnt orange and over it was an outer robe of dark gray and black. Her robes were not properly layered, since she had just got up from her nap, and her train and jacket had slipped down. While she casually pulled them back up, Genji picked up some of the sprigs of wild ginger that she had set aside in preparation for the festival. "What are these called?" he asked. "I've completely forgotten their name." Chūjō responded with a poem:

> Gods do not reveal themselves in a vessel choked with weeds
> Nor do you show yourself . . . so I adorned my hair with leaves
> That promise a tryst, only to find you forgot their name[1]

She seemed embarrassed as she spoke. Genji realized that what she said was true and felt sorry for her.

> Having now forsaken the things of this world
> Including the ways of love, is it sinful
> Of me to pluck off these leaves of wild ginger

Apparently Chūjō alone remained an object of Genji's affection.

With nothing else to do during the fifth month but gaze out at the endless rains of the season, Genji, sinking ever deeper into his brooding thoughts, was overcome with a sense of desolation. It was the tenth day of the month, and Genji's son was in attendance that evening. There was a rare break in the clouds, and the instant the bright moonlight broke through, the mandarin orange tree, which was then in full bloom, stood out vividly before their eyes. The fragrance of the tree wafted toward them on the breeze, stirring nostalgic memories. As they waited in anticipation for the sound of "the cuckoo's voice, which calls out for a thousand years,"[2] the clouds gathered again and suddenly took on an ominous appearance. They were startled when a driving rain began to fall and the wind accompanying the rain caused the lamps to flicker and nearly extinguished them. The sky seemed to have turned black. "The sound of the rain at the window."[3] Genji murmured these and other rather trite, common lines of old verse. Perhaps it was due to the atmosphere of the moment, but his son fervently wished that Murasaki had been there to hear his father's voice—truly a voice to be heard, as the old poem had it, "from my beloved's hedge."[4]

"Things aren't all that different now that I'm living by myself," Genji remarked, "but still, I feel strangely alone. Having grown accustomed to this solitary life, I wonder . . . even if I were to live in a hut deep in the mountains, would my heart really grow pure and tranquil?" He then called out to his attendants: "Bring

---

1. In addition to the oft-used play on the word *aoi*, the poem refers to a *yorube*, a sacred vessel containing water used in Shinto rituals to draw a god to its reflection. The comparison of Genji to a deity in this context is sexually suggestive: though the original text is coy, it leaves no doubt that he accepts the invitation, for in his reply poem he plays on the word *tsumi*, which means both "sin" and "to pluck."

2. Anonymous poem from *The Gosenshū*: "I hear the cuckoo's voice, which calls out for a thousand years amidst the orange blossoms, whose colors remain forever the same."
3. A reference to a poem included in the collected writings of Bo Juyi, the Tang Poet [editor's note].
4. The source of the poem is uncertain. It is cited in later commentaries.

food and refreshments here! I suppose it's much too late to summon some men to join us."

Genji's son could tell from the expression on his father's face as he gazed up distractedly toward the skies that the old man was in no mood for entertainment.[5] It was painful to see him in such a state, and he worried that his father's inability to take his mind off Murasaki was a lingering attachment that would make it difficult for him to purify and calm his heart. It occurred to him that if he himself found it so hard to forget Murasaki after only the briefest glimpse of her, how much more difficult must it be for his father?

"It seems like she left us only yesterday," he said, "but the first anniversary is already upon us. What sort of memorial service have you planned?"

Genji replied, "I don't plan to do anything out of the ordinary. This would be the right time to dedicate the mandala of Amida's paradise that she commissioned. She also had a large number of sutras prepared, and before she died she explained what she wanted done for the dedication to that bishop . . . I've forgotten his name . . . anyway, he knows what to do. If there are other details that need to be seen to, I'll just have to go along with whatever bishop what's-his-name recommends."

"She put a lot of thought into arranging these things ahead of time, and they'll certainly be a comfort to her in the afterlife. When I think back on it now, she was destined not to live long in this world, which makes it all the more regrettable that she left behind no children to remember her by."

"That may be," Genji said, "but of all my women, even those who are destined to live a long life, only a few gave me children. In that regard, I consider myself unlucky. It is you, my son, with all of your daughters, who will ensure that our family line flourishes."

Cognizant of his own tendency to break down over every little thing—a weakness he found difficult to conceal—Genji tried to avoid bringing up the past very often. Just then, the cuckoo that they had been waiting for gave a faint cry. Upon hearing it, Genji was unusually moved and whispered a line of verse: "How could it have known?"

> Is it yearning for the one who is gone
> That leads you back here, O mountain cuckoo
> Soaked by a sudden evening shower

Genji looked up ever more intently into the sky.

His son replied:

> Take this message with you, mountain cuckoo
> To one who is beloved of me . . . tell her
> The orange tree at home is in full bloom

Many of the women in attendance also composed poems, but I shall refrain from setting them down here. Genji's son stayed on in service—a task that he assumed from time to time because he felt sorry that his lonely father was now

---

5. Poem by Sakai no Hitozane from *The Kokinshū*: "The vaulting heavens are no memento for the lady I loved . . . why then, should I gaze distractedly up at the sky each time I long for you?"

sleeping by himself. He had many memories associated with these bedchambers—a place familiar to him now, but one that had been off limits while Murasaki was alive.

The following month, during the hottest season of the year, Genji stayed in a room cooled by the nearby pond. Looking at the lotus blooming profusely, the dew covering the many flowers brought back a line from a poem by Lady Ise: "How can there be so many tears?" He remained distracted, lost in his thoughts until the sun went down. Amidst the shrill cries of the cicadas, he sat by himself observing the pinks in the garden, which were aglow in the slanting light at sunset.[6] But they were no comfort to him.

> *Do these cicadas take this summer day*
> *A day I pass in idleness and tears*
> *As a pretext for incessant crying*

Swarms of fireflies reminded Genji of a line spoken by the Emperor in Bai Juyi's *Song of Everlasting Sorrow*:[7] "Here in the evening pavilion fireflies flit about, and I long for Yang Guifei." Reciting lines like this from old Chinese verse had now become habitual for him.

> *They at least know it is night, these flickering fireflies . . .*
> *But because my grief and sorrow are with me always*
> *I can no longer distinguish between night and day*

The seventh day of the seventh month arrived, and with it the festival of Tanabata. Genji did not have the heart to celebrate with the customary composition of verses in Chinese and Japanese. He did not call for music, but instead whiled away the time by gazing outside in idle reverie. There were no attendants to observe the meeting of the two celestial lovers, the weaver maiden and the oxherd. Late at night, Genji arose by himself in the dark and pushed open the hinged door at the corner of the hall. Dew had drenched the garden just below the veranda. He passed through the door into the walkway and, after looking around, went outside.

> *I look up to observe the heavenly lovers*
> *But their tryst belongs to a world beyond the clouds*
> *In this garden of parting, only dew remains*

* * *

---

6. Poem by Sosei from *The Kokinshū*: "Am I the only one who finds them moving . . . these Japanese pinks aglow in the light of sunset when crickets cry?"

7. Known in this anthology as "The Song of Lasting Regret."

From Chapter XLV

Hashihime

THE DIVINE PRINCESS AT UJI BRIDGE

In those days a certain aging prince of the blood, Hachinomiya[8] was living in obscurity, no longer counted as a member of court society. His mother was from a most distinguished family, and at one point there was hope that he might be named Crown Prince and attain the heights of glory. His circumstances, however, changed with the coming of a new sovereign, and as a consequence of certain incidents, he was censured and the court turned its back on him. All traces of his earlier aspirations faded. In the end, his supporters withdrew one after another, their hearts filled with bitter resentment, and he was left with no one to turn to either in public or in private. It seemed that he was utterly abandoned.

His principal wife was the daughter of a Minister who served long ago. Hachinomiya's many trials and tribulations left her feeling sad and forlorn whenever she recalled the ambitions her parents had for her, and yet she found comfort from the woes of the world in the intimate, unrivaled bond she shared with her husband over the years. Their mutual devotion was truly extraordinary.

Though they were married for many years, they had no children, and Prince Hachinomiya would often wistfully express his hope that somehow they might have an adorable child to relieve their loneliness and boredom. Then, miraculously, a beautiful little girl was born to them. Their joy was boundless, and they did everything they could to love and care for her. Soon after, Hachinomiya's wife was pregnant again; and though they wanted their second child to be a boy, they had another girl. Sadly, the mother suffered terribly from the effects of the birth and died. Her husband was in a state of shock and grief.

I have lived in a world that has brought me nothing but a surfeit of unbearable sorrows, Hachinomiya told himself, *but my attachment to the beauty and grace of the woman I loved kept me fettered to it . . . and now it's come to this. I'm on my own again, and the loneliness and tedium I suffer will be more intense than ever. Trying to raise two small daughters, constrained by my position as a Prince . . . I shall look a proper fool, utterly pathetic!*

He considered acting on his deepest wish by taking vows and renouncing the world, but he struggled terribly with the decision, hesitant to leave behind two girls who had no one to look after them. As he wavered, the months and years passed, and before he knew it, his daughters had grown to womanhood, lovely and ideal in looks and demeanor and a constant source of comfort to him.

The attendants who waited on the younger child did not serve her with whole-hearted devotion and were always whispering among themselves, "Really now, her birth was so inauspicious!" Her mother, however, had been deeply concerned over the little girl's future, which preoccupied her thoughts even when she was on the verge of death, fading in and out of consciousness. "Have pity and look

---

8. *Hachinomiya* means "the Eighth Prince." It is not in the original text at this point, but appears later when more of Hachinomiya's background is explained. I am introducing the name here in this fashion as a matter of convenience.

on her as a memento of me," she pleaded with her husband over and over. Thus, despite his resentment that the birth of the child had broken the karmic bond he shared with his wife from a previous life, he accepted that his beloved's death was meant to be. Remembering that his wife had begged him to the very end to look after and cherish the girl, he treated his second daughter as a precious treasure.

This younger girl was truly beautiful—so much so that it made people uneasy, since her looks might be ill-omened. Her older sister was quiet and thoughtful by nature, nobly refined and attractive in both appearance and manner. Of the two, the younger sister created the stronger impression as a woman of distinguished aristocratic lineage—a lady whom people were inclined to treat with tender favor. Their father, however, looked after each of them with equal consideration, though there were many things that he could not do for them given his straitened circumstances. As the years went by, his residence grew increasingly desolate, and the attendants, despairing of the bleak prospects facing their young mistresses, found the situation intolerable and began to leave one after another, scattering to other households. The younger sister's nurse, who had been selected without much consideration during the turmoil that followed the death of the mother, was a woman of shallow sensibility—as one might have expected given her breeding and low status—and she abandoned her charge when the girl was still quite young. As a result, the Prince had to bring her up entirely on his own.

The Prince's estate at the time was extensive and eye catching, and the vistas created by the pond and the landscaped hills in the garden remained as lovely as ever—except that now the garden was terribly overgrown. He would spend his idle days gazing out in reverie at the scene, but because there was no longer anyone on his household staff who could properly take care of the grounds, they were neglected. Lush green grasses and weeds grew in thick profusion while *shinobugusa* ferns,[9] whose very name makes one long for the past, spread under the eaves as though they were taking possession of the place. The colors and fragrances of the flowers of each season or of the autumn foliage often brought him comfort, since he had once enjoyed them with his beloved wife. However, as his estate grew ever more deserted and lonely and there were fewer and fewer people he could rely upon, he began to spend all of his time on his religious devotions, fastidiously looking after the decorations for the altar in his meditation hall.

He was frustrated that his circumstances bound him to the world against his wishes, and could only assume that the obstacles he faced in fulfilling his desire to renounce it all were the effects of his karmic destiny. As time went by, he grew ever more detached from relationships with women. *At this point in my life,* he wondered, *why should I act like other men and marry again?* He became a hermit in spirit. After losing his beloved wife, it never occurred to him—not even as an idle fancy—to give himself over to normal human emotions.

There were some who reproached him for his behavior: "Why must you insist on remaining alone? You certainly experienced more than a normal share of grief when your wife passed away, but to continue to dwell on your loss after all this time . . . well, you ought to show consideration for others and remarry like any

9. Literally "ferns of nostalgic longings."

other man. If you did, your neglected villa, which is an unsightly mess, would be in good shape in no time." He had many such reasonable suggestions from people here and there hoping to establish a connection with an imperial prince, but he paid no attention to any of their proposals.

Between periods of meditation and prayer, Hachinomiya would relax with his daughters; because they were getting older, he taught them how to play the koto and engaged them in trivial pastimes such as Go and *hentsugi*.[1] Observing the character of his daughters, he could see that the older sister was refined, serious and contemplative. The younger girl was sweet and gentle, and her shy, deferential air was most endearing. Each had distinctive merits.

* * *

A saintly ascetic who was a master of esoteric Buddhism lived in the mountains at Uji. He had a reputation as a most learned man, but he remained secluded and hardly ever appeared at court. When he learned that a prince of the blood was living alone nearby, doing noble religious practices and studying sutras, he thought him admirable and visited regularly. The ascetic elucidated the deeper meaning of the texts that Prince Hachinomiya had been studying for many years, bringing him to greater awareness of the vain mutability of the world. Despite his spiritual progress, Hachinomiya had to explain to the ascetic why he had not chosen the path of renunciation. "Though my heart is set on rebirth in the next world, where I may take my seat on the lotus and dwell in the unsullied pond of paradise, I am too anxious about leaving behind my young daughters to take priestly vows just yet."

As it turned out, this very same ascetic would, from time to time, travel to the capital to teach Retired Emperor Reizei about scripture and doctrinal matters. On one such occasion, after answering questions Reizei posed concerning the profound sutras they were reading, he took advantage of the opportunity to mention Hachinomiya.

"The Prince is very wise," the ascetic remarked, "and has gained a deep understanding of the teachings of the Buddha.[2] I believe he was truly born to follow the path of enlightenment . . . a saintly man who is sincerely dedicated to his devotions."

"But is it true that he has not yet become a priest?" Reizei asked. "The young men here refer to him as the earthbound saint . . . a most poignant situation."

Kaoru happened to be in service to Reizei at that moment and privately pondered what was being discussed: *I myself know full well the insipid nature of the world, but my practice of religious austerities is hardly enough to draw the attention of others. To my shame, I thoughtlessly let the time pass.* He listened intently to the conversation, wondering how it was that a man could become saintly while still living in this vulgar world.

"He originally intended to take priestly vows," the ascetic remarked, "but, as he once lamented to me, some trivial matters held him back, and now he finds that he cannot possibly abandon his poor daughters." Holy man though he was

1. This game is mentioned in the *Aoi* chapter. It involves writing down radicals or parts of a Chinese character and trying to guess the whole character.
2. The text uses the word *naikyō*, literally, "inner teachings," to distinguish Buddhism from the "outer teachings," *gaikyō*, which refers mainly to Confucian works. The use of this word reinforces Hachinomiya's political feck- lessness and his otherworldly preoccupations.

the ascetic was a connoisseur of the finer things. "When his daughters perform in concert," he added, "their captivating music vies with the sound of the rapids, putting one in mind of paradise!"

This praise of the young princesses had an old-fashioned ring to it that made Reizei smile.

"One would imagine that having grown up in the house of such a saintly man they would have been completely unfamiliar with secular diversions," he said. "What a delight to hear otherwise. He can't very well abandon them, being so worried about their future . . . apparently, he has a very difficult problem on his hands. If it happens that I should outlive him, even for a brief time, I wonder . . . would he give his daughters to me?"

Reizei was—or so people thought—the tenth son of the old Emperor, and thus Hachinomiya's younger half brother. He recalled the example of the cloistered Third Princess, whose father, Suzaku, had placed her in Genji's care. *If only I could have his daughters . . . they would be companions to me in my idleness.*

Kaoru's thoughts were focused not on the two princesses at Uji, as might have been expected of a young man, but on their father. He now wanted more than ever to meet and observe someone whose state of mind seemed so utterly devoted to religious practices. As the ascetic was preparing to return to his mountain retreat, Kaoru spoke to him and requested his help in arranging a visit. "I very much want to go there and study under Prince Hachinomiya's guidance, so please make some discreet inquiries on my behalf."

Reizei sent a message to Hachinomiya: "I have heard through an intermediary about the conditions in which you are living and have been greatly moved."

> *Though my heart, weary of this tiresome world*
> *Travels to the Uji mountains, the veil*
> *Of eightfold clouds you've drawn obscures my view*

The ascetic sent Reizei's messenger on ahead, and so the man reached Hachinomiya first. It was a rare occurrence for anyone, let alone a messenger from such a distinguished figure, to visit this humble abode in the shadow of the mountains. Hachinomiya was overjoyed and welcomed the man in a suitable manner, plying him with wine and local delicacies. He then composed his reply:

> *I did not cut all ties to purify my heart*
> *It's just that I grew weary of this world of woe*
> *And made a home of this but in Ujiyama*[3]

Because Hachinomiya refused to consider himself an enlightened holy man, it was clear that he harbored lingering resentments against the world. Reizei was deeply affected by the reply.

The ascetic conveyed to Hachinomiya Kaoru's profound desire to follow the path of the Buddha: "The young man told me that he has had an abiding inter-

---

3. Hachinomiya's poem alludes to a poem by Kisen from *The Kokinshū*. The play on Uji/ *ushi* will become a dominant, recurring element throughout the final chapters of the narrative. However, this poem also suggests that Hachinomiya did not voluntarily choose to follow the religious path at Uji and thus hints at a lingering bitterness that Reizei picks up on immediately [editor's note].

est since childhood in acquiring knowledge of the holy scriptures, but so long as he remains unavoidably caught up in the mundane world, he will be kept busy day and night with public and private matters. He said that someone as unimportant as he should have no cause to feel constrained about turning his back on the world, shutting himself away and studying. And yet his current life-style naturally causes him to neglect his devotions and give himself up to worldly diversions. That's why he spoke so earnestly to me, saying that after hearing about the admirable life you lead, he was eager to turn to you for religious guidance."

Hachinomiya replied at length: "Normally, the realization of the truth of mutability and the beginnings of an aversion to this world can be traced to some moment when a person suffers a reversal of fortune that makes him resentful and motivates him to pursue the path of religious devotion. It is thus remarkable that a young man like Kaoru, who has everything he wants, who has known no disappointments, should be so focused on the afterlife. In my case, perhaps it was destined that I should come to detest the world and turn to religion, as though the Buddha were giving me special encouragement. In the course of things, I was able to fulfill my wish to quietly practice my devotions; but now I sense that my life will soon come to an end without ever achieving any true spiritual enlightenment after all this time. Kaoru will be a companion in the study of the Dharma, but one who will put me to shame, since I'm all too aware that I've learned nothing of the past and future." He exchanged letters with Kaoru, and the young man set out to visit him.

In truth, the scene was even more poignantly desolate than what the ascetic had described. The villa was so simple and severe that it reminded Kaoru of a hermit's temporary grass hut. Other residences may be referred to in similar terms as mountain villas, but those are places of repose with their own special charms. Here, the violent roar of the rapids and crashing of waves made it seem impossible that one could forget one's cares, and with the fierce howling of the wind at night, there would not have been a moment to dream peaceful dreams. The appearance of the place moved Kaoru to speculate that Hachinomiya, who was determined to find enlightenment, may have found it easier to renounce the world in this environment, which had nothing appealing about it that might distract his attention from his devotions. *But what do his daughters think about it? It's certainly a far remove from the gentle, feminine places where princesses usually reside.*

A single sliding door separated the chapel from the daughters' quarters. Given the alluring atmosphere, a young man of amorous proclivities would have wanted to make advances to see how the young women might respond and thus find out what they were like. Kaoru, however, checked himself, thinking that to engage in suggestively playful banter would undermine the true purpose of his visit. After all, he had come to this place deep in the mountains with the intention of turning away from worldly desires. Thus, he sensitively focused on expressing his concern for Hachinomiya's difficult circumstances, and continued thereafter to visit again and again. Despite maintaining his connection with the vulgar world, Hachinomiya had gained profound insight from pursuing religious studies and austerities in his mountain retreat, and, just as Kaoru had hoped, he humbly shared his wisdom without ever flaunting his knowledge.

There are many holy men and learned priests in the world, but virtuous men at the rank of bishop or abbot are often officious and aloof. They are always busy, and so they tend to be curt and blunt in manner. Kaoru found them much too pompous and overweening to ask them to clearly explain the meanings and workings of things in the world. There were also disciples of Buddha, men at a much lower rank who had accrued great merit by practicing austerities and upholding the Precepts, but they were usually vulgar in appearance, rough in speech and uncouthly familiar in comportment. Kaoru was usually occupied with official duties during the daytime and had time to reflect on profound subjects only during the quiet evening hours. He thus found it altogether unpleasant to summon such boorish disciples close to his bedchambers to discuss the teachings. In contrast, Hachinomiya was truly refined and ennobled by his suffering. The words and expressions he used when discussing the teachings of the Buddha that the bishops and disciples lectured on were simpler and more familiar to Kaoru. Moreover, though he had not achieved an especially profound understanding of the scriptures, as a man whose karmic destiny was to be born a prince of the blood he had an unusually fine, innate grasp of the true nature of the world. The two men gradually grew closer. Kaoru began to wish he could be with his mentor all the time and longed to meet him during those periods when he was busy at court and could not go to Uji.

Reizei could see how highly Kaoru esteemed Prince Hachinomiya, and so he too began sending a constant stream of messages to Uji. Hardly a word had been spoken about Hachinomiya for years, but now gradually more and more visitors found their way to his lonely, desolate abode. Reizei would on appropriate occasions honor him with messages inquiring after his well-being, and Kaoru would take every opportunity to be of faithful service, seeing to both elegant celebrations and more serious, practical matters. In this way, three years passed.

It happened in late autumn, The seasonal Invocation of the Holy Name was at hand, and because the roar of the rapids at the fishing weir had been especially grating recently, Hachinomiya went up to the meditation hall at the temple where the ascetic lived to spend a week practicing his devotions.

While their father was gone, the two sisters felt more forlorn, bored, and depressed than ever. Kaoru, remembering that he had not called at Uji in some time, very discreetly set out during the wee hours of the night just as the predawn moon was rising. He had a very small escort and was dressed in a manner that would disguise his identity.

Because Hachinomiya's villa was on the near bank of the river, there was no need to arrange for a boat. Kaoru traveled on horseback; the closer he got to Uji, the denser the fog grew. As he made his way through undergrowth thick enough to obscure the path, he struggled against a fierce wind that shook the dew from the leaves of the trees. He was thoroughly soaked and chilled to the bone, but he couldn't complain, since he was the one who decided to come here. Having hardly ever set out on this sort of adventure, he felt sad and exhilarated at the same time.

> How much stranger than the dew dropping from leaves
> Helpless in the blasts sweeping down the mountain
> Are these tears of mine that fall so easily

He ordered his escort to be quiet lest they awaken some meddlesome mountain peasant. He also took care to minimize the clopping of his horse as he cut through fences of brush wattle or waded through murmuring streams. However, for all his caution, he could not disguise his fragrance, which was carried on the wind. At house after house people startled awake, wondering, *Whose fragrance do I smell?*[4]

As they neared the villa they heard chillingly sublime music, though they could not tell what the instruments were. *I have heard that Hachinomiya always plays in this manner, but I have never had the chance to hear his koto, so famous for its tonal beauty. What a stroke of luck that I should arrive at this moment!* With such thoughts in mind, Kaoru entered and realized that he had been hearing a *biwa* lute. The instrument was tuned to the *ōshiki* mode,[5] and though the song was an ordinary prelude used for tuning, in such a setting it had an otherworldly feel: the sound produced by the plectrum was pure and enchanting. A thirteen-string koto could be heard accompanying the *biwa* intermittently, and its graceful, feminine tone was deeply affecting.

He had concealed himself since he wanted to listen a while longer, but then a man—a guard or watchman of some sort who had clearly heard Kaoru's arrival—stepped out brusquely. "My lord has gone into retreat for certain reasons," the man said. "I shall have a messenger inform him that you are here."

"There's no need to bother with that." Kaoru replied. "I really mustn't intrude on him during the limited number of days he has to practice his devotions. It would, however, be a shame if after having drenched my robes getting here I should have to go back disappointed that it was all for naught. Please inform your mistresses about my situation . . . it would be some consolation to hear at least a word of pity from them."

A knowing smile spread over the man's unattractive face. "As you wish, my lord," he said, and started back inside.

"Wait a moment!" Kaoru called the man back. "I've heard from various people over the years how well the Prince's daughters play together and have been eager to hear them. This is a welcome chance for me. Is there no hidden corner nearby where I might conceal myself for a short time? I don't want my unexpected appearance to make them stop."

Even someone of rough, common sensibilities like the watchman could recognize from Kaoru's features and overall appearance that he was a remarkably impressive person—this despite his being dressed in hunting robes.

"They play all the time," the watchman informed him, "mornings and evenings when no one is around to hear them. But whenever someone calls from the capital, even a person of lower rank, they refuse to play at all. In fact, our lord has largely kept the presence of his daughters a secret, and he has made it clear that he does not want us to tell anyone that they live here."

Kaoru smiled and replied, "It's deplorable of Prince Hachinomiya to hide them away. Everyone praises him as a rare exemplar of virtue, yet here he is, behaving secretively. Be that as it may, take me to where I may listen to them. My

4. Poem by Sosei from *The Kokinshū*: "Whose fragrance do I smell? Someone has hung his purple trousers over mistflowers in the autumn fields."
5. This mode is equivalent to the key of A.

intentions are strictly honorable. How very strange that they should be living like this . . . in truth, they can hardly be considered normal."

"As you wish, my lord. Were I to refuse, I would be criticized afterward as a man of no judgment." So saying, he showed Kaoru to a spot in the garden in front of the residence that was closed off by a fence made of a lattice of bamboo. The watchman then called the escort into a gallery in the west hall and received them there himself.

A gate in the wattle fence appeared to lead to the residence beyond, and so Kaoru pushed it open a crack and peeked through. Gazing across the misty garden, enchanting in the pale light of the moon, he could see the two sisters sitting just inside their raised blinds. A page girl was seated on the veranda, looking thin and cold in her soft, shabby robe. Several grown-up attendants were sitting there as well, dressed in a similar manner. The sisters were seated inside in the aisle room. One of them was partially hidden behind a pillar. A *biwa* lute was set out in front of her and she was turning over the plectrum with her fingertips, toying with it. When the moon suddenly emerged from behind a cloud and brightly lit up the scene, she said, "I may not have a fan, but I can still call forth the moon with this."[6] The lovely glow of her face, which peeked out from behind the plectrum, was utterly adorable.

The other sister, who was reclining nearby, was leaning over a koto. "I've heard of people calling forth the setting sun,"[7] she said, "but you are certainly prone to some peculiar notions!" She was smiling, and her figure seemed a little more dignified and modestly refined.

"Even if this plectrum can't call forth the moon," her sister retorted, "that doesn't mean the *biwa* and the moon aren't connected!"[8] Their silly, sisterly exchanges touched Kaoru with their warmth and charm. They were not at all what he had imagined earlier from his distant vantage. Though he would on occasion hear younger ladies-in-waiting reading romances handed down from the past—stories that invariably included scenes involving characters like these two sisters—he himself had always remained skeptical, doubtful that such things could ever actually take place in real life. Yet here he was, finding himself irresistibly drawn to these young women. *It's true . . . remarkable things really do occur in out-of-the-way places in this world!*

6. Quotation from the *Japanese and Chinese Poems for Recitation* 587: "We raise a fan to call forth the moon, hidden behind mountain ranges; winds blow through the empty heavens, and we know them by the swaying trees." This allusion is especially noteworthy because the source of the verse is the *Zhi guan* (*On Cessation and Contemplation*) by the Chinese monk Chih-I (538–597), which was an important Tendai Buddhist text on meditation. The moon and wind stand for truth, which may be blocked from view or invisible to humankind until some evidence, expedient teaching, or symbol (such as a moon-shaped fan, or in this case a plectrum) makes them evident. Murasaki Shikibu is remarkably consistent in fitting poetic allusions to a narrative situation, and here she has the younger daughter cite a verse that reveals

the extent of the unusual influence of her religious father.

7. The playful reference here is to a Chinese-style *bugaku* dance called "The Masked Warrior King" (cf. the *Wakana* chapter, Part 2). As part of the dance a rod or baton was lifted toward the sun.

8. The plectrum could be stored by slipping it into a space between the tailpiece (*fukuju*, the piece of the instrument on the bottom front of the soundboard where the strings are attached) and the face of the soundboard. Beneath the tailpiece was a round acoustic hole called the "hidden moon" or "dark moon" (*ingetsu*), and so the younger sister is defending her poetic allusion by stressing a figurative relationship between the plectrum and the moon.

Because the fog was thick, he could not make the princesses out all that clearly. Just as he was hoping the moon would emerge from behind the clouds again, it appeared that someone stepped out from the interior of the residence and announced the arrival of a visitor, for the blinds were lowered immediately and everyone moved back inside. Neither sister look flustered; their quiet, gentle movements as they concealed themselves without so much as a rustle of their robes created an impression of endearing feminine softness, and he found their extreme elegance and courtly grace alluring.

Kaoru silently withdrew and then had a messenger rush back to the capital with orders to bring a carriage.

"I came at an inconvenient time," he told the homely watchman, "but as things turned out, my visit has given me joy and some small comfort from my cares. Inform your lord's daughters that I have arrived . . . and do be sure to let them know just how soaked I am as a result of my exertions." The man went off and delivered the message.

The two princesses, who never imagined that they might be spied on like this, were terribly embarrassed when they realized that Kaoru had possibly overheard their casual conversation. The breeze had earlier carried in a mysteriously wonderful fragrance, but because they had noticed it at an hour when a visitor was unlikely, they had not been at all alarmed. Their carelessness made them feel ashamed, and they didn't know what to do.

The attendant who was to deliver his message requesting an audience with the princesses struck Kaoru as much too young and inexperienced for the task. He thought that timing was crucial in all matters, and because the fog had not cleared yet, he took advantage of the moment to stride over to a spot in front of the blinds and kneel there. The unsophisticated young attendants had no idea what to say to him and seemed ill at ease even offering a cushion.

"It's discomfiting to be left outside these blinds," Kaoru said. "If my heart were really impulsive and shallow, would I have bothered traveling the rugged mountain path all the way here? This is a most peculiar welcome, I must say. Still, I would hope that if I were to come through the drenching dews over and over, you might at least recognize the sincerity of my feelings." He spoke in a genuinely earnest manner.

Not one of the younger attendants was capable of a smooth, coherent response—indeed, they felt so awkward and embarrassed that they wanted to disappear. As a result, some time passed while they went to wake up the more experienced women. The older sister, uncomfortable that the delay in replying would create the impression that they were teasing Kaoru, spoke up at last. "We are, as you can tell, inexperienced in such matters, so how could we pretend to know how to answer you?" She spoke in a hushed, reserved tone, her voice noble and gracious.

"I realize that it's customary for a woman to pretend that she knows nothing of the aching sorrow in a man's heart, even when she is all too aware of his feelings. But it's especially disappointing that you in particular should feign complete ignorance about me. I imagine that, since you reside in the house of a remarkable, enlightened man, you too have a clear understanding of the world. Thus, it would be best to use your wisdom to judge the depth or shallowness of my feelings, which are too powerful for me to keep hidden any longer. Must you cut me off, believing I am driven by wanton passions? There are some who have urged me to be more amorously inclined, but I stalwartly refuse to yield to such temptations. Reports about me must no doubt have reached you. How happy it would make me if I could turn to you as a companion, one who would listen in sympathy to my stories about tedious court society, or if you would come to trust me enough that I in turn could provide a diversion from your feelings of isolation and brooding sorrow." He said many other things besides. She, being diffident, found it hard to answer him and left it instead to an old attendant who had just been roused from sleep to respond in her place.

This older woman, who was known as Bennokimi, was anything but reticent.

"Really, now . . . this is unacceptable. How rude to leave his lordship seated in such a spot! He should be seated *inside* the blinds! These young women . . . they know nothing about protocol."

The two sisters felt ill at ease, since the voice speaking so bluntly was that of an old woman.

"It is exceedingly strange, you see," Bennokimi continued, "but due to the circumstances of my young mistresses' father, who is no longer counted as one who resides in this world, we receive neither visits nor expressions of concern from those people one might assume would still remember him. That's why your unexpected devotion to my lord is so moving, even to the heart of someone as insignificant as I am. My young mistresses feel grateful to you as well . . . it's just that they are shy and have a hard time expressing their emotions."

* * *

From Chapter XLVII

Agemaki

A BOWKNOT TIED IN MAIDEN'S LOOPS

* * *

Bennokimi informed Kaoru of all her mistress had said. *What is driving the Princess to turn her back on the world like this?* he wondered. *Did she learn the truth of the world's mutability at the side of her saintly father?* Because her heart seemed all the more in tune with his own, he could not despise her as someone who was making a pretense of her wisdom. "If that's how she feels," he said, "then naturally she would think it improper to see me now, even with a blind or curtain between us. But, come now . . . find some place where I may discreetly enter her private chambers." On hearing his words, Bennokimi set about complying with his orders. She dismissed most of the attendants early and told those ladies-in-waiting who were in on the plot to make preparations.

A little later that evening, the wind suddenly picked up and blew violently, causing the crude, rickety shutters to rattle and squeak. Kaoru was certain that the Princess would not be able to hear him enter her chambers because of all the noise, and so Bennokimi stealthily led him there. The old attendant was concerned that the Middle Counselor might make a mistake, since her mistresses were in the same room. However, the princesses were accustomed to sleeping together, and it might have seemed odd to ask them to retire to separate quarters. Besides, Bennokimi assumed that Kaoru was well enough acquainted with the sisters not to confuse them.

As it turned out, the older Princess was wide awake, fearful that something was afoot. As soon as she heard Kaoru enter, she quietly got up to make her escape, hurriedly slipping out through the curtains around her bedding. She felt terrible for her sister, who was innocently sleeping away, and it broke her heart to imagine what would happen. *If only we could hide together*, she thought— but it was too late to go back now. Trembling, she looked on in the dim, flickering lamplight as Kaoru, wearing only a single under robe, lifted one of the panels on the standing curtains and entered their bedchamber with an impudent expression, as if the place belonged to him. *How dreadful! What must my sister be thinking?*

With these thoughts running through her mind, she opened up a folding screen along the front of a crumbling wall and withdrew behind it, where she sat feeling miserable and uncomfortable. It was deeply upsetting to think that her sister, who had vehemently deplored the very idea of a future as wife of the Middle Counselor, might now mistakenly think she had planned this shocking tryst and hate her for it. As she reflected sadly that all of their troubles stemmed from having been left behind in this world with no one to support them, she had the sensation that she had last seen her father's figure departing for his retreat up the mountain only just this evening. She was filled with longing and grief.

When Kaoru entered the chambers and saw a woman sleeping alone, his heart leapt with joy, since it appeared that everything was going according to plan. But then it gradually became apparent that the woman was not the Princess he desired, but someone slightly more beautiful and alluring in appearance. Her shock and desperation as she startled from her slumbers made it clear that she had absolutely no idea what was happening, and he was moved to sympathy at her plight. At the same time, he was extremely angry, provoked by the callous behavior of the older sister who had fled into hiding. Though he could hardly deny that he was attracted to the younger Princess and did not want her to go to another man, he was nonetheless frustrated that his true desires were being denied. *I don't want the Princess to think I'm a man of fickle, shallow character, but I have no choice but to spend the night here. If it's my destiny after all to end up with the younger sister instead, well . . . it's not as though she's a complete stranger to me.* With those thoughts in mind, he regained his composure and, behaving the same way he did that earlier night with the Princess he loved, he did not force himself on her sister, but passed the time engaging in gentle, courtly conversation until dawn broke.

The older attendants, thinking that they had given the couple more than ample time, were just then questioning one another:

"Where has our younger mistress gone? This is very strange!"

"Oh well . . . she must have gone off for some reason. I'm sure she's fine."

Marriage proposals aside, Kaoru's remarkably splendid, attractive features and figure were enough to make the attendants feel their wrinkles would disappear just by gazing at him. One old woman, a toothless hag given to making unpleasant remarks, said, "Why must our older mistress be so aloof toward him? Perhaps she's been possessed by one of those fearsome gods that people always seem to be going on about."

"Really, now, watch what you say . . . such inauspicious words! Why would some spirit possess her? She acts like this because she was brought up far removed from people. With no one to advise her on how to behave appropriately, she feels awkward interacting with others. Just wait . . . once she gets used to having him around, she'll naturally warm to him soon enough."

"I just hope that she warms to him soon . . . I do so wish for her to fulfill her ideal destiny."

While the attendants were talking, they fell asleep one by one, and soon the discordant sounds of snoring and other noises reverberated.

A poet once claimed that the length of an autumn's night is "determined by one's companion."[9] Though this particular night had been awkward, unlike any other he had experienced, Kaoru still felt that the dawn arrived much too quickly. As he gazed at the younger Princess, who looked so fresh and lustrous that he could no longer decide which of the sisters was more attractive to him, he did not want to leave with his desires unsated. "Think lovingly of me as I think of you . . . and never emulate the behavior of one who is cold and heartless." He promised her as he left that they would meet again. It was all like a strange dream to him; while he was composing himself, thinking that he wanted to try again to be with the older Princess who had cruelly rejected him, he returned to his room, just as he had before, and lay down.

Bennokimi entered. "This is most peculiar," she remarked. "Where has my lady gone?" The younger Princess, mortified and dazed, continued to lie there trying to understand how all of this had come about. Recalling what had been said to her the day before, she was bitterly aggrieved by her sister's cruel scheming.

With the coming light of day the "cricket" emerged from her hiding place in the wall. She pitied her sister and was all too aware of how she must feel. The two of them could not bring themselves to speak to one another. The older Princess's thoughts were in chaos. *Now that we've both been exposed to his gaze, we've lost our air of mystery . . . what misery! From now on, we will never be able to relax or let down our guard.*

Bennokimi went over to the room where Kaoru was staying and learned about her mistress's shockingly stubborn rejection. The lady was too particular, given to brooding too deeply over her situation—so much so, indeed, that she made herself hateful. Bennokimi was stunned and most sorry for the Middle Counselor.

"Even when she rejected me before," Kaoru said, "I took comfort in thinking that there was still some hope that I might somehow persuade her . . . but what happened last night was utter humiliation. I ought to throw myself in the river. After observing just how troubled Hachinomiya was by the prospect of abandoning his daughters and leaving them on their own, I decided it wouldn't do for me to turn my back on this world and abandon them as well. Well, what's done is done . . . I shall never again consider either one of them an object of romantic interest. In return, they must never forget the anguish and bitterness they have caused me to suffer. Prince Niou remains unabashed in his pursuit of the younger sister, and if she were to yield to him I would fully understand

9. Poem by Ōshikōchi Mitsune from *The Kokinshū*: "How long and endless an autumn night feels has since ancient times been determined by one's companion."

her decision—all things being equal, it seems perfectly natural for her to seek out someone of the highest rank. In fact, her attitude is reasonable, which is why I feel ashamed and have no intention of subjecting myself ever again to the unpleasant, mocking gaze of the women here. I must insist, however, that you never divulge to anyone what a fool I've been." He vented his frustrations, then hurried off much earlier than normal.

"How sad for the both of them," the attendants whispered among themselves.

What happened with him? What if he grows spiteful and turns against my sister as well? The older Princess was brokenhearted, in utter misery. She deplored and resented the meddlesome ways of her women, who always acted against her wishes. While she was turning over these various thoughts in her mind, a letter arrived. She was bemused to find herself so uncharacteristically happy and grateful to receive a message from him. Almost as if he were unaware of the season, he had attached it to a bough covered almost entirely in green leaves, with only a single sprig displaying the crimson foliage of autumn.

> *How I long to ask the mountain goddess*
> *Who dyed the same branch different colors*
> *Which one of these two hues is the deeper*

He had controlled the angry resentment that had seemed so evident when he left, concealing it beneath a few words written on a letter wrapped up with an outer sheet of paper. It was obvious that he was prepared to let the incident pass as if nothing had happened, but she felt agitated and uneasy all the same. Her ladies-in-waiting were annoyingly insisting that she must respond, but she was in a quandary and found it difficult to write anything. It was too unpleasant to ask her younger sister to reply, since that would have been a tacit acknowledgment of last night's tryst with the Middle Counselor. And yet, if she herself wrote back, it would be as good as acknowledging her own affair with him. She finally managed the following:

> *I know not why the mountain goddess dyed this branch*
> *With two colors . . . but surely the leaves that have changed*
> *Hold the deeper hue that attracts your changing heart*

Though she had casually scribbled her reply, Kaoru was charmed, and his grudge against her faded away.

She has indicated to me over and over that even though as sisters they are two, at heart they are one, and she wants to yield and have me take the younger Princess in her place. Apparently, she's unhappy that I would not accept such an arrangement, and so she devised the scheme that she carried out last night. If her plans come to naught and I remain indifferent toward her younger sister, she may well come to pity her and think me cruelly insensitive . . . if that happens, it will be all the more difficult to win the lady I've truly wanted from the very beginning. Even the old lady-in-waiting who has served as my intermediary will very likely consider me rash and thoughtless. How I regret letting my heart be stained by love's passion . . . I resolved to renounce all attachments to this world, yet I was unable to achieve what I most desired.

Kaoru realized how ridiculous he would look to others. No, it was worse than that . . . he resembled some common lover who rows his laughable little boat back and forth to see the same woman over and over.[1] He spent the entire night lost in such reflections. The next morning, beneath a delightful dawn sky, he went to call on Niou.

After the Sanjō residence of the Third Princess burned down, Kaoru moved with his mother back to the Rokujō estate; because his quarters there were near the rooms Niou used when not at his Nijō villa, he was able to visit the Prince regularly. This arrangement pleased Niou very much. His residence at Rokujō, which was ideal for living a leisurely life untroubled by distractions, looked out from the veranda onto a front garden unlike any other—the same types of flowers grew there as elsewhere, the trees and grasses swayed in similar fashion, and yet somehow their shapes and elegant movements had a special appeal. Even the reflection of pure, clear moonlight in the garden stream looked like something out of an illustration.

Knowing Niou's fondness for such scenes, Kaoru had assumed that his friend would still be up when he arrived, and sure enough, he was. When Kaoru's distinctive scent came wafting in on the breeze, a startled Niou noted his arrival immediately and, putting on a court cloak, properly arranged himself before stepping out to greet his guest. Kaoru showed his respect by stopping partway up the front steps. Niou at once leaned against the railing and, without so much as a word inviting his friend to come up to the veranda, began making small talk. As they were chatting, something reminded Niou of the Uji villa, and he complained bitterly about how his proposal was being handled. His reproaches were a bit much for Kaoru, who was finding it so difficult to satisfy his own desires. Then it occurred to him that having Niou get his way might also work to his advantage by removing an obstacle to courting the older Princess, and so he spoke more openly than usual about what needed to be done.

Fog settled at a most inopportune moment in the predawn darkness. The sky took on a chill aspect, misty clouds obscured the moon, and the shadows of the trees presented an elegant gloominess in the faint light. Reminiscing about the poignant beauty of the Uji villa, Niou insisted to his friend, "You must take me there again in the very near future." Observing the obvious reluctance in Kaoru's expression, he playfully composed the following:

> Are you so petty that you'd rope off
> Those wide fields where maidenflowers bloom
> In order to keep others away

Kaoru replied in kind:

> Maidenflowers blooming in morning fields
> Covered in deep mists may only be seen
> By those whose hearts are truly drawn to them[2]

1. Anonymous poem from *The Kokinshū*: "I always yearn to go back to the same person, like a little boat that has made its way through the channel and comes rowing home."
2. Poem by Mibu no Tadamine from *The Kokinshū*: "Is it because maidenflowers find it painful to be viewed by men that they bloom hidden in the autumn mists?" Kaoru's poem mentions the place name Ashitanohara (in modern Nara Prefecture), which I have rendered according to its literal meaning, "morning fields," in keeping with the setting of this scene as a whole. Ashitanohara was famous for maidenflowers, but it was also associated with morning fog.

"These are no ordinary flowers," he added, as if intentionally trying to get a rise out of his friend—and, indeed, Niou was thoroughly irritated, exclaiming, "Ahh . . . how cheeky you are!"[3]

Niou had been talking like this about the younger Uji Princess for several years. Until last night Kaoru had been concerned about her looks, but now he considered it unlikely that Niou would be disappointed in her charms. He had also worried that her breeding and character might not meet expectations when seeing her up close, but evidently she had no flaws that might give cause for regret. He felt sorry for the older Princess, since it seemed unkind to undercut the plans that she was secretly making, but, regardless, he felt that he simply could not transfer his feelings from one sister to the other. *If I yield the younger Princess to Niou, neither he nor the woman I love will have any cause to resent me.*

Niou, who had no idea what Kaoru was secretly planning in his heart, was railing on about how his friend was selfishly intending to keep both Uji Princesses for himself. Kaoru found this amusing and couldn't resist tweaking his friend by assuming the role of father to the sisters. "It would be most unfortunate were you to cause her to suffer on account of your incorrigible tendency to pursue frivolous affairs."

"All right, then . . . I'll show you," Niou replied earnestly. "I've never been more devoted to anyone."

"That's all fine and well, but neither princess has shown the slightest indication that she's willing to give herself to you. This will be an excruciatingly difficult task to carry out," Kaoru said, then explained in detail just what needed to be done when they traveled together to Uji.

The twenty-eighth day of the month—the final day of the Equinox Festival—happened to be an auspicious one on the calendar. Kaoru, after privately making arrangements, decided that it would be the perfect time to make a secret excursion with Niou to the Uji villa. Niou's heart was so set on the younger Princess that there would have been no end of trouble had his mother, the Akashi Empress, found out about this adventure, for she certainly would have forbidden it. With that risk in mind, Kaoru went about the tricky task of planning the trip, all the while maintaining a nonchalant air, as if nothing out of the ordinary was afoot. The country estate of Genji's son was in the vicinity of Uji, and they had to be cautious and not attract attention when ferrying across the river. The need for secrecy also prompted Kaoru to forego staying over at some grand residence on the way. He chose instead to take Niou quietly to an inconspicuous residence of one of his retainers at a nearby manor, and then to go on to the Uji villa by himself. It was highly unlikely that anyone would notice them, but Kaoru did not want to give away the slightest hint of what he was up to—not even to that homely watchman who occasionally patrolled the grounds of the Uji villa.

As they always did whenever the arrival of the Middle Counselor was announced, the attendants bustled about preparing themselves to receive him. The princesses considered this something of a nuisance, with the older sister thinking, *I've made it abundantly clear that he should turn his fragrant atten-*

3. Poem by Bishop Henjō from *The Kokinshū*: "Ahh, how cheeky you are, you maidenflowers standing in autumn fields flaunting your seduc- tive charms . . . but blossoms too will soon fade."

tions to my sister . . . to the leaf that has changed colors. Will he finally come to understand? Meanwhile, the younger sister's thoughts were of a different order. I'm not the one he truly desires, so what does his visit today have to do with me? Still, she felt that she had to be on her guard, since she could no longer just blithely trust her sister—not after what had happened the night the Middle Counselor stole into her bedchambers. Indeed, her distrust was so great, she no longer spoke directly to the older Princess, but communicated through an intermediary. Her women were upset by this break between siblings, and they fretted over how it all might end.

Kaoru had Niou ride to the Uji villa on horseback. He then led him inside under cover of a dark, moonless night and summoned Bennokimi. "I must have a word with your older mistress," he said. "The way she insists on keeping her distance from me is deeply humiliating, but I cannot bring myself to just slink away and leave things between us as they are. I want you to show me to her chambers later this evening, just as you did before." His words struck Bennokimi as sincere, and he seemed to have no hidden motives. Thus, she agreed to go in and speak with the older Princess—after all, from her perspective it hardly mattered which of her mistresses he chose to take for his wife.

When the older Princess was informed of Kaoru's request, she was at once pleased and relieved. Just as I thought . . . he now prefers my sister. She had all of the sliding panel doors between the main chamber and the surrounding aisle rooms securely locked—all of them, that is, except for the ones that led to her younger sister's quarters. After taking that precaution, she received him.

"I must speak briefly with you," Kaoru began, "but it's awkward to have to speak as loudly as this, since others may hear what I have to say. Won't you open the panels just a bit? This is truly maddening."

"I can hear you perfectly well," she replied, leaving the doors locked.

But then she reconsidered. He must feel that he owes it to me to say something, since he has undergone a change of heart and doesn't want to offend me. What harm could it do at this point to see him? It's not like I haven't met him face to face before. It would be unkind of me to let the night pass without responding. With those thoughts in mind, she moved toward him and opened the panels.

At that moment, he reached through, grasped her sleeve, and while pulling on it to keep her from escaping, gave voice to all his complaints. She was mortified and immediately regretted her decision. How dreadful! Why did I ever agree to meet him? Still, she kept her wits and used all of her wiles to try to cajole and convince him to go to her sister instead. "You must not make a distinction, but consider us as one and the same." Kaoru found her demeanor, so sweet and pitiful as she pleaded earnestly with him, deeply affecting.

Niou, meanwhile, was doing just as he had been instructed. He drew near the door that Kaoru had used that earlier night, and then signaled Bennokimi by opening his fan. She showed him the way in, and as he entered he found it delightfully charming that she should be guiding him along a familiar path that another had obviously taken before him.

The older Princess, of course, knew nothing about Niou's presence, and so she continued trying to persuade Kaoru to go to her sister. Kaoru was amused but, at the same time, he felt sorry for her. He also recognized that if he said nothing about what was going on now, she would later come to resent his deception, and he would have no way to absolve himself of blame. He thus concluded that it was best to apprise her of the situation. "Prince Niou followed me tonight, and I was unable to turn him away. Evidently, he was able to enter furtively, without making a sound. That scheming old lady-in-waiting of yours, Bennokimi, has no doubt been speaking with him. Now that I've been rejected by both you and your sister, I'm destined to become a laughingstock at court."

The Princess was blindsided by this appalling turn of events, for it had never crossed her mind that something like this might occur. "I had no idea," she said, "just how far you were willing to go to carry out such an outrageous scheme. My lack of caution makes it obvious how feckless and naive I truly am, and you must take me for an utter fool." She was at a loss for words to describe her feelings at that moment.

"Nothing I say would make any difference now," Kaoru replied. "Even if I offer repeated explanations and apologies, they would not be enough. Go ahead . . . pinch and scratch me if you wish. Apparently, you were holding out hopes for a man of more distinguished lineage than I, but, as I know all too well, karmic destiny does not always work out exactly as our hearts might wish. That's why I sympathize with you now that Prince Niou has bestowed his affections on your sister . . . for I too am acquainted with the hopelessness that comes with being rejected and cast adrift with no haven. What is to be will be, and you should resign yourself to your fate. No matter how securely you may fasten these panels, no one believes our relationship is pure and chaste. Do you really imagine that the man who asked me to bring him to your sister is, at this moment, bothered by a conscience as full and troubled as ours?"

She was upset beyond words. Nonetheless, as it appeared that he might force the sliding panels open any moment, she maintained her composure, determined to calm his passions. "This 'karmic destiny' you speak of . . . it's not something tangible, not something I can see with my own eyes. I can't follow what you mean by such words, no matter how much I try. I feel as though a mist arising from tears of uncertainty[4] obscures and obstructs my path ahead. Trying to fathom your intentions toward me is unpleasant, like a bad dream. If future generations should ever speak of my sister and me, no doubt they will cite our story as an example of the foolishness of those easily deceived women who appear so often in ancient tales. Does Prince Niou possess the same degree of judgment and sincerity as someone who's capable of scheming the way you have? You've caused enough anguish and grief . . . don't confound me further. I don't expect to live much longer, but if I do, I shall speak to you when I'm feeling somewhat calmer. For now I must retire, since I'm really quite ill . . . it feels as though darkness has swept over me. Let go of my sleeves."

The reasonableness with which she pleaded with him despite being extremely upset made Kaoru feel at once ashamed of himself and protective. "I have gone to extraordinary lengths to respect and obey your wishes, my beloved . . . so much so that I've become obsessed, fixated on you. It seems that you find me inexpressibly despicable and unpleasant, and so there's nothing I can say to you. More and more, I've come to feel that I no longer want to live in this world."

4. Poem by Minamoto no Wataru from *The Gosenshū*: "That tears of uncertainty, of not knowing what the future brings, are sorrowful is due simply to the fact that they fall in plain sight".

He paused for a moment, then continued." Very well, then, since you are ill I shall let go . . . but please let me speak with you through your blinds. Do not completely abandon me."

When he released her sleeves, the Princess withdrew toward the interior of the room, but not all the way. Kaoru was moved by her gesture and said, "I shall spend the night here taking consolation from the fact that you have remained this near to me. It is more than I dared dream of, and so I swear I shall do nothing untoward." The roar of the rapids kept him awake, and a storm that raged in the middle of the night made him feel like a pheasant sleeping apart from his mate.[5] In that state of mind, he spent the night sleepless till dawn.

* * *

When the older Princess overheard her women gossiping, she felt her chest tighten in despair. *My sister's bond with Prince Niou is broken for good. So long as he had yet to decide on some distinguished lady to be his principal wife, he was probably content to use my sister as his plaything. He was no doubt mindful of what Kaoru and others might think of him, and so he offered up an endless string of pretty words professing his deep devotion.* She was convinced of Niou's deceitfulness. But that hardly mattered now, for who was she to resent his cruelty, given her own failures? More and more, she felt that there was no haven for her in this world, and she collapsed facedown, weeping.

In her frail condition, the Princess increasingly felt as though she should no longer go on living in this world. Although her attendants were not of such high status that she was ever constrained or awkward in their presence, it would be too painful to bear if they knew that she had overheard their gossip about Prince Niou's marriage. And so she lay down to sleep, pretending that she had heard nothing.

The younger Princess was napping, which apparently is something one does when longing for someone. It was adorable the way she slept with her arm as a pillow, her hair gathered at her head. The older Princess continued gazing at her sister's surpassing features; she grieved as her father's words of warning came back repeatedly: *Father, you surely have not sunk to those depths that await the deeply sinful . . . but, if you are not in Hell, then just where are you? Please come for us, call us to wherever you may be. You left us to our suffering and will not appear even in our dreams.*

The chill rain gave a terrifyingly lonely cast to the winter sky at dusk, and the sound of the wind blowing around the base of the trees was ineffable. Reclining on an armrest, pondering the past and the future, she cut an incomparably dignified and graceful figure. Even though her hair had not been properly groomed for a long time, perfect tresses draped down over her white robes.[6] She had a slight pallor from days of illness, but this merely added an alabaster glow to her complexion. The gentle curve of her eyes and forehead as she gazed

5. *Yamadori* (literally, "bird of the mountain") refers to a species of pheasant. The male and female supposedly roosted on separate slopes at the peak of a mountain, and so they became a poetic symbol of loneliness.
6. White robes were worn at times of illness or confinement. An example of this is found in the "Leaves of Wild Ginger" chapter at the time Genji's wife gives birth to his son. Page girls and ladies-in-waiting might wear white robes as well if they were in attendance at night.

pensively outside made one wish to show her to any man sensitive enough to appreciate such sublime beauty.

The younger Princess was startled out of her nap by a violent gust of wind. Her layers of clothing, which included robes in the mountain-rose style of fallen-leaf gold with a pale violet lining, as well as robes of pale blue lined with white, were bright and vibrant. Her face had a special glow as if it had been tinted, and she looked as if she didn't have a care in the world.

"I dreamed of our father just now," she said. "He appeared briefly just over there. He seemed terribly worried."

"After Father died," the older Princess replied, her grief now greater than ever, "I had so hoped that I would see him in my dreams . . . but he has never once appeared to me."

They both broke down and wept. The older Princess contemplated the world to come. *Of late Father has been on our minds constantly, and so he was bound to appear in a dream. How I long to go to him . . . but as a woman, I'm too deeply sinful.* She desperately wanted to obtain the magical incense from China that, when burned, enabled one to see the spirits of the dead.[7]

A messenger from Niou arrived late that night when it was pitch-black outside. The letter should have been a comfort to them, coming as it did when they were feeling so forlorn, but the younger Princess would not look at it right away.

"You must reply to him in a sweet, gentle manner," her older sister advised. "I am in a fragile condition and may not be around much longer, and so I worry that some someone even more cruel and inconsiderate than Prince Niou may appear and deal with you as he wishes. So long as the Prince thinks of you once in a while, no matter how rarely, I'm sure that no other man would dare have such evil designs on you. I know that it's difficult for you to accept this situation, but at least you can count on him for support and protection."

"Are you planning to abandon me? How horrible of you!" She pulled her sleeves completely over her face.

"The term of life is fixed, and death awaits us all," the older sister replied. "When Father died, I didn't want to live on after him for even a few brief moments. Despite my wishes, I lived on anyway. I know not if death will come tomorrow,[8] but even though I accept that the world is fleeting, I still grieve. After all, for whose sake do I value my life, if not for yours?"[9]

They pulled an oil lamp over and read the letter. As always, it was long and detailed.

> *The clouds that we sadly gaze at are the same*
> *As any other clouds . . . so why should these rains*
> *Increase my anxious yearning this winter night*

7. Poem 160 from *Collected Writings of Bo Juyi*. Bai (Bo) Juyi's poem retells the famous story of how, during the early Han dynasty, Emperor Wu, following the death of his imperial wife Li, had a Taoist adept prepare a special magical incense that when burned enabled Wu to see the figure of his beloved Li faintly in the smoke.

8. Poem by Ki no Tsurayuki, written on the death of Ki no Tomonori: "Though I may reflect on life, not knowing if death will come on the morrow, I grieve for one who did not live to see the evening of this day."

9. Poem from the personal collection of Lady Ise: "Scooping up water from a mountain spring gushing forth from rocky crags, I realize, for whose sake do I value my life if not for yours?"

Apparently, he had added conventional phrases such as "sleeves that have never been as drenched in my tears as they are now,"[1] but they were nothing more than common clichés. With the letter looking as if it had been scribbled out like some tiresome chore that Niou had to perform, the older Princess's resentment grew even greater. Still, his looks and figure were so splendid and his demeanor so elegant that it was natural that the younger Princess was still attracted to him. Indeed, the longer his absences, the more she missed him. In any case, Niou had made so many extravagant vows that she knew in her heart that he would never stop calling on her. For that reason alone her anger waned, and she remained devoted to him.

The messenger remarked, "I must be returning this evening," and pressed for a reply. The younger Princess gave him a poem and not a single word more.

> *The skies that I gaze upon from this village*
> *Pelted by hail, deep in mountain recesses*
> *Are, mornings and nights, ever dark and cloudy*

It was the final day of the tenth month, and Niou was disturbed to realize that yet another month had passed by since he last saw his love. Night after night, he kept telling himself that this was the night to go. However, something always prevented him, and he began to feel like a small boar caught up in countless reeds.[2] For one thing, the Gosechi Festival would be held early this year,[3] and as a result there were many stylish diversions throughout the palace that kept him occupied. Even though he did not deliberately neglect his Uji Princess, he allowed more time to slip, and she was left to suffer the unbearable loneliness of waiting for him. Nonetheless, even when he was having a passing affair with one of the ladies at court, she was constantly on his mind.

His mother, the Akashi Empress, brought up the matter of his engagement to the Minister's daughter, Roku no kimi. "If there's someone you love and want to call on, then once you have secured the steady support that a marriage like this promises, bring her in discreetly as one of your ladies and treat her with honor and respect."

"Let's wait awhile. I have things to consider," he replied, cutting her off.

Niou was concerned that his bride might truly end up suffering the indignity of becoming one of his "ladies," as his mother put it, and he wanted to avoid that outcome. But the anxious princesses at Uji did not know what was in his heart. As the days and months passed, they could only languish after him.

Appearances to the contrary, Niou is not the serious, trustworthy man that I took him to be. In his heart, Kaoru was sorry he ever vouched for the Prince, and now he very rarely visited Niou's quarters. He sent message after message

---

1. A poem from which this line is taken is cited in a later commentary, but the source is unknown.

2. Poem by Kakinomoto Hitomaro: "Unable to meet my love these days, I feel like a small boat trying to make port caught up in countless reeds."

3. The Gosechi Festival was held during the eleventh month. In most years, it was scheduled around the middle of the month on the second of the three Days of the Ox that occurred during that month (zodiacal days cycled around once every twelve days). However, in some years there were only two Days of the Ox, and, when that occurred, the festival was held on the first of those days.

to the Uji villa inquiring after the older Princess and learned that her condition had improved a little around the beginning of the eleventh month. Subsequently, during this busy season at the court, his time was entirely taken up with both public and private responsibilities, and he did not dispatch anyone for five or six days. Then, suddenly, he had an alarming premonition about the Princess's health; having no other recourse available to him, Kaoru dropped everything that he was supposed to do and went to Uji.

He had left orders that healing rites were to be conducted thoroughly with no letup, but the Princess had sent the ascetic back to his mountain retreat, insisting that she was feeling much better. There were few people attending her when Kaoru arrived, and so, as always, he summoned Bennokimi and asked about her mistress's condition.

"Her symptoms are vague," the old woman informed him, "and she doesn't seem to be suffering from anything serious . . . it's just that she won't eat anything, my lord. She's always been extremely delicate compared to most women, but ever since our young mistress's affair with Prince Niou began, her mood has darkened and she goes on refusing to even glance at the slightest piece of fruit. She's shockingly emaciated, and her condition seems hopeless now. I've experienced so much sorrow in my long life, but to have to witness this horror . . . I only hope that I may die first, before my mistress . . ." Understandably, words failed her and she broke down in tears.

"This is hard for me to hear. Why didn't you let me know sooner? I've been very busy recently at both the palace and the villa of Retired Emperor Reizei, and I was worried at not being able to ask after her for several days." He went into the Princess's chambers and sat down near her pillow. He tried to speak with her, but she was unable to answer, as if she had lost her voice.

"No one, not one person informed me that you have taken a turn for the worse," he said reprovingly. "It's deplorable! I was so worried, I left specific instructions to look after you, but what good did it do . . . it's too late now." He sent for the ascetic again and also summoned a large number of priests and healers who had a good reputation for the efficacy of their prayers. The healing rites and sutra readings were set to begin early the following morning, and so he ordered a great many of his own retainers and staff to come to Uji to assist with preparations. Soon the villa was bustling with people of both high and low station, and the attendants there took heart and felt reassured as all traces of their feeling of isolation faded.

When evening came, Kaoru was offered a simple meal of steamed rice gruel and then asked to retire to the guest rooms that he always used. He protested, insisting, "I want to stay close by to help nurse the Princess." Because the priests were seated in the aisle room to the south, he set up a folding screen in a space on the east side of his beloved's bedchamber, very near to her. The younger Princess was troubled by his presence, but her attendants had all concluded that the relationship between their older mistress and the Middle Counselor was far from ordinary; they could not bring themselves to cruelly keep him away from her. After the priests started the early evening services, they began a continuous reading of the *Lotus Sutra*. The twelve priests chanting the sutra all had sonorous voices, and the effect was nobly inspiring.

With lamps lit in the space on the south side, the interior of the Princess's room was dark. Kaoru lifted up one of the panels on her standing curtain and slipped just inside to look at his beloved. When he did so, two or three older attendants shifted closer to her. The younger sister quickly hid herself from his sight and, with so few people about, lay down feeling lonely and helpless.

"Why will you not speak to me?" Kaoru pleaded, taking her hand and startling her awake.

"I would like to talk to you, but it hurts whenever I talk," she said quietly, speaking under her breath. "You didn't come here for so long that I was worried. I would have regretted it had I passed away without being able to see you again."

"That I should have kept you waiting for me this long . . ." Kaoru began sobbing. He gently placed his hand on her forehead. She was a little feverish. "What sin did you commit to bring about this illness? It must be retribution for having made someone suffer," he said, speaking softly in her ear. As he went on to tell her all of the things that he felt for her, she began to find his words troublesome and embarrassing and covered her face. He gazed down at her frail, delicate body and felt his chest tighten at the thought of what it would feel like to have to look on her lifeless figure.

"I'm sure that it has been terribly trying for you to have to look after her for so long," he said to the younger sister. "Tonight I shall stand watch, so please try to get some rest."

She was concerned, but withdrew a short distance away on the assumption that the Middle Counselor must have reason to want to speak privately to his beloved.

Kaoru should not have addressed her face to face, but when he drew closer to look at her, the Princess, despite her embarrassment and discomfort, accepted that their relationship was destined by a bond they shared in a previous life. She also recognized his noble virtues. After all, compared to Prince Niou, the Middle Counselor was exceptionally kind, gentle and trustworthy. No . . . she simply couldn't be so cruel as to send him away now, for she did not want him to remember her after she died as willful or thoughtless.

All through the night, Kaoru ordered her women to prepare medicinal infusions, but she refused to take even a sip. Aghast at the situation, he was desperate beyond words, wondering if there was anything he could do to save her life.

The ascetic, who was napping after having performed services during the night, was startled by the sublime voices of the priests who arrived in the predawn hours and took over the continuous reading of the *Lotus Sutra*. Now awake, he chanted a *dharani* spell in a voice that, despite being hoarse and cracked from age, sounded mature and truly efficacious.

"How did the Princess get along last night?" he asked, and then began to reminisce tearfully about the late Hachinomiya, all the while blowing his nose over and over. "Which realm does he inhabit now? I always imagined that he would end up in paradise, despite the lingering attachment of his concern for his daughters, but recently I saw him in a dream . . . he was dressed in earthly robes and spoke quite distinctly to me. 'Because I detested the world and was deeply estranged from it,' he said. 'I had no desire to tarry in it for long. Yet, at the time of my death, some trivial worries distracted me from focusing on my salvation. To my bitter regret, the realm that I had hoped to attain still remains beyond me. Perform memorial rites to hasten my entry into paradise.' I couldn't think of what to do right away, and so I asked five or six of my disciples who happened to be performing services just then to chant the holy name. Then another idea occurred to me, and I sent them out in all directions to perform the Never-Disparaging austerity to teach that all people may attain Buddhahood."[4]

Kaoru wept bitterly as the ascetic spoke. The older Princess, who was already troubled, realized that she had committed a grave sin by hindering her father's salvation and wanted more than ever to just disappear completely. As she lay there listening to the ascetic, she thought, *Somehow I want to find Father's spirit while his destination is still unsettled and go together with him to the same place.*

The ascetic withdrew without saying much more. The priests who had been sent off a few days earlier to perform the Never-Disparaging austerity had gone to villages in the vicinity and even as far as the capital, but after laboring through rough winds at dawn, they sought out the place where the ascetic had summoned them. Kneeling at the center gate, they continued the reading of the *Lotus Sutra* in a most venerable manner. The final lines of the scripture, with their invocation to do good deeds for all sentient beings who are destined to become Buddhas, were especially moving. Kaoru, whose heart had long been drawn toward the path of enlightenment, found the scene unbearably affecting. The rustling of silk told him that the younger Princess, nervous and fretful about her sister's condition, had moved tentatively behind the standing curtain at the back of the room. He straightened himself up and assumed a more formal posture.

"How do those abject voices that never disparage sound to you?" Kaoru asked. "They may not have carried out an abject practice, but their humility is noble and awe-inspiring."

> Plovers cry mournfully at the water's edge
> Amidst an icy frost glinting bright and clear
> How desolate a sound in predawn twilight

He did not intone his verse, but spoke it as if he were simply conversing with her.

Something in his manner reminded the younger Princess of her cruel lover, prompting her to compare the two men in her mind. However, she found it difficult to reply directly to Kaoru, and so she gave her reply to Bennokimi to pass to him:

> Plovers calling out in the early dawn
> As they brush away the frost from their wings
> Do they understand my sad, pensive heart

4. This extreme religious austerity is called *jōfukyō* (literally, "never treat lightly"). Jōfukyō is the Japanese name of the bodhisattva Sadāparibhūta, who appears in the *Lotus Sutra*. Sadāparibhūta was the name of Sakyamuni in one of his previous lifetimes as a bodhisattva. He recognized the truth that all living beings could attain Buddhahood, and so he practiced humility before all he met (and suffered persecution as a result), saying that he could never disparage them because they possess the Buddha nature. Priests sent out on this austerity would go out and abject themselves before those they met, regardless of the person's status, as a way to teach this truth.

The old attendant was hardly an appropriate stand-in for her mistress, but she conveyed the poem with stylish grace. A trivial exchange, to be sure, but her response was warm and sensitive, even if she was retiring by nature. It disturbed him to wonder how he would feel if he had to be separated from her following the death of her sister.

Kaoru contemplated Prince Hachinomiya's appearance in the ascetic's dream, and after imagining what the troubled figures of the princesses must look like from their father's vantage on high, he commissioned sutra readings at the mountain temple above where Hachinomiya used to go into retreat. He also dispatched messengers to various temples here and there with requests for prayers and sent letters requesting leave from all of his public and private affairs. No rite of purification, prayer ceremony, or exorcism was overlooked in his effort to heal the Princess. Nonetheless, because her illness was not the result of some sinful behavior, nothing seemed to work.

If the Princess herself prayed to the Buddha for her recovery, she might have improved, but her thoughts were on different matters. *I must take this infirmity as my opportunity to die. He has now attended to me so closely—seen my face, touched me—that there is no longer any distance between us; now I have no excuse to treat him as anything other than my husband. Of course, even if he were to take me as his wife, the ardor that has driven him to treat me with such kindness would surely cool over time as we both grew familiar with one another, and I would be left in the end with nothing but uncertainty and heartache. No . . . if it turns out that I'm forced to live on, then I will use my illness as a pretext to take vows and become a nun. That is the only way to ensure that we stay together to the end, that our hearts remain as one forever.*

She was convinced that she must fulfill her wish one way or another, but she couldn't bring up the matter in such detail that others would catch on to her plans. Thus, she said to her sister, "I feel that my condition is more and more hopeless, but I've heard that taking vows to uphold the Precepts is very effective for healing and may extend my life. Would you please speak to the ascetic? He is a master of esoteric rites."

Her attendants wept and objected vociferously. "It's unthinkable," they told her. "The Middle Counselor is at his wits' end, frantic over your illness. He would be devastated if you did such a thing!" To the Princess's chagrin, they all found the idea outrageous and would not even mention it to the man they relied on for support.

Because Kaoru had withdrawn from the court and gone into seclusion like this, word spread and gentlemen soon arrived from the court to inquire after him. Seeing how concerned he was over the princess's illness, his retainers and those members of his staff who were close to him grieved for their lord, each offering prayers for her recovery.

When he realized that today was *Toyo no Akari*—"the Feast of the Glowing Harvest"—Kaoru's thoughts turned toward the capital. The winds at Uji were frightful, and the snow swirled about madly. The weather in the capital wouldn't be like this at all, and yet, while he himself had chosen to stay here to be with his beloved, his loneliness was unbearable. He gazed outside, lost in wistful thoughts. *Is she destined to die while the two of us remain strangers, never consummating our relationship? It's hard for me to accept such a fate, but I will not give voice to any bitterness. If only she could recover a little, display once more her sweet and gentle disposition even for a brief time, I would share with her all my thoughts and feelings!*

Evening fell at last on a gloomy, sunless day. He whispered the following to himself:

Deep in the mountains, beneath cloudy skies
I see no sunlight, no festive headbands
A season indeed to darken my heart[5]

The attendants were all encouraged that the Middle Counselor remained with them like this. He was seated as always near her pillow; when the rough winds caused the standing curtains to flutter, the younger Princess withdrew to a room in the interior to avoid being seen. Her unsightly old attendants followed after, their faces flushed in embarrassment as they too scurried to hide themselves. As they did so, Kaoru moved closer and spoke tearfully to his beloved. "How are you feeling? I have prayed for you with all my heart and soul, but none of it seems to be doing any good. It makes me feel desolate, not having heard even a word from you . . . I shall suffer terribly if you leave me behind."

Although the Princess was slipping in and out of consciousness, she still made sure that she kept her face hidden. "If I were feeling a little better, there is much I would like to tell you, but I regret for your sake that I must soon pass on."

Her demeanor told of the deep compassion that she felt for him, and he found it harder than ever to hold back his tears. He was reluctant to show any signs of sorrow, knowing that would be inauspicious, but he began sobbing anyway.

He kept watch over her, reflecting on their relationship. *What sort of bond did we share in a previous life? Despite my boundless love, I must be parted from her having tasted only a surfeit of bitter hardships. If she would reveal at least some small imperfection in herself, it might help temper the longings I will feel for her after she's gone.* To his eyes, she seemed more precious than ever, radiant and lovely. Her arms were terribly thin, her body wraithlike, but her complexion was still lustrous, pale, and graceful. In her soft white robes, with her bedcovers pushed to the side, she gave the impression of a court doll, hollow inside its robes, lying asleep. Her hair, which was not excessively thick or long, had been laid out just as it was. It spilled down over her pillow in shimmering undulations that had a delightfully charming air.

What will become of her in the end? Is there no possibility that she may live on? Must her beauty pass from the world? He would never again experience such profound regrets. She had been ill for so long and had not been properly groomed or dressed all that time, yet her looks were still far superior even to a woman who endlessly fusses over herself and remains unapproachable, lest someone see her unprepared. As he studied his beloved's face, he could not calm his fear that her spirit would soon slip away.

"If you should abandon me after all," he said, "I doubt that I will survive much longer myself. And if by chance I should live on for many years, I shall withdraw from the world and go off somewhere deep in the mountains. The one thing that might hold me back are the hardships your sister would face on her own." He was hoping to get some sort of response by mentioning her sister.

5. The poem plays on the word *hikage*, meaning "sunlight" and "headband" (referring to the headband worn by Gosechi dancers at the Feast of the Glowing Harvest).

The Princess pulled her sleeves away from her face a little.

"I always knew that my life would be brief, and so I could not accept your proposal. I don't want to die and leave you with memories of me as willful and unkind, but there was nothing else I could do. That's why I suggested that you think of the sister I leave behind in the same way you think of me. If you had not defied my wishes, I might have been at peace now . . . it is the one lingering regret that may yet keep me attached to this world and hinder my salvation."

"Am I fated to suffer the extremes of sorrow? I am by nature different from others . . . I was never attracted to worldly affairs of any kind. You're the only one that I have ever loved, so I simply could not do as you requested and take your sister instead. I regret that now and feel bad for you, but you need not worry about her."

Kaoru did his best to comfort and reassure her, but when her suffering seemed to grow more intense, he summoned the ascetic and other venerable priests and had them use all of their powers to perform healing rites and prayers. He himself offered heartfelt prayers to the Buddha.

Is it to encourage the rejection of this world that the gods and Buddha expressly allow so much grief and anguish in it? As he sat there gazing at her, she vanished before his eyes, fading like withering grasses in winter. He was mad with grief, frantically stamping his feet in frustration at not being able to call her back, oblivious to how others might view his behavior.

When the younger Princess realized that the end had come, she too was stunned and distraught at being left behind. Her attendants, who as usual were acting wise and in control, could see that their mistress was not in her right mind and escorted her out of the room, saying that it would bring bad luck if she were to remain near a defiling corpse.

This simply can't be happening, Kaoru told himself. *It must be a dream.* He brought the lamp closer to her face, which was still partly hidden by her sleeves. She looked as if she were asleep: nothing about her had changed, and she was lying there as beautiful as in life. He thought wistfully, *If only I could go on like this, looking upon her as I would the empty shell of a cicada!*[6]

In order to prepare the body for the funeral rites, her women combed and arranged her hair; the air around them was suffused with the warm, rich perfume that had always scented her hair when she was alive. Kaoru prayed to the Buddha. *She was a superior woman, unrivaled in this world. Is there nothing ordinary about her that would make it easier for me to accept her death . . . some small flaw at least? If you really are the guide who will show me how to renounce this world, then let me see something other than her beauty—something fearful and offputting about her corpse that will lessen my regrets and assuage my grief.*

His prayer served no purpose, however, for his yearning only grew more intense the more he gazed at her. Knowing that soon her body would have to be consigned to the flames, he set about making the proper arrangements for the services—but it was all much too much for him. He felt unsteady, drifting along as though he was walking through the air. When the last feeble-looking

6. Poem by Bishop Shōen from *The Kokinshū* composed after the burial of the Horikawa chancellor, Fujiwara no Mototsune, at Mount Fukakusa: "One finds comfort in gazing on the body, an empty shell of a cicada . . . send up at least a plume of smoke, Mount Fukakusa!"

traces of the pyre disappeared, so few plumes of smoke had risen to the sky that he was left feeling defeated and hopeless. He returned to the villa in a daze.

Many attendants secluded themselves at the villa for the period of confinement and mourning. Though their presence helped to relieve the loneliness a little, the younger Princess was so depressed and ashamed at how others viewed her that she herself did not seem to be among the living any more. Niou sent one message after another, but the Princess could not forget that her sister had died never wavering in her attitude that his neglect was unforgivably cruel. It was her woeful lot to be married to such an awful man.

Kaoru now found the world thoroughly wearisome, but though he was inclined finally to fulfill his most cherished wish and follow the path of the Buddha, he couldn't bring himself to take that step just yet. For one thing, he had his mother, the Third Princess, to consider. For another, he was troubled by the heartrending circumstances of the Princess at Uji. He mulled over the situation. *I should have done as the late Princess requested . . . I should have taken her sister as my wife and looked on her as a memento. But at the time she asked, I felt in my heart that I could never shift my affections, even though my beloved insisted that her heart was one with her sister's. Had I known that I would cause the younger Princess such misery by bringing Niou here, I would have married her instead. Had I done that, I might have found in my visits here some consolation for my unrequited love.*

He didn't go back to the capital for even a brief visit. Because he had thoroughly cut himself off and remained inconsolable in his seclusion, people at the court concluded that his affection for the late Princess had been anything but ordinary, and everyone, from the palace on down, sent letters expressing their condolences.

Empty days passed by. Kaoru arranged for the memorial services held every seven days, and he made sure they were each conducted in a most solemn and dignified manner. He showed extraordinary devotion to her memory, but since they had not been married, there were limits on what he could do. Forbidden by custom to change the color of his clothing, he would steal mournful glances at the black robes worn by those women who had been closest to their late mistress.

> It is useless for one not permitted to mourn
> To shed these blood-red tears, for they can never dye
> My crimson cloak gray in memory of my love

Kaoru cut a youthful, dashingly handsome figure as he gazed out lost in reverie, soaking his sleeves with his endless tears; the light crimson cloak he was permitted to wear seemed to glisten like melting ice. The attendants, peeking in to observe him, were all in tears.

"What's done is done, and I suppose it's useless now to lament the loss of our mistress . . . but it's truly regrettable that the Middle Counselor, who has been so close to this household over the years, will soon become an outsider to us all."

"What a strange, unexpected destiny has befallen him!"

"That a man as deeply thoughtful and kind as he should have been rejected by both of our ladies . . ."

Kaoru spoke to the younger Princess. "I think of you as a memento of the past, and from now on I hope that we might be able to speak freely with one another and that I may still call on you and be of service. Do not be aloof and treat me as a stranger."

The Princess, however, was still overwhelmed by her misfortunes and was too shy to meet or talk with him. She had always struck him as a little innocent and child-like, more open and noble compared to her sister, and yet to him she lacked the gentle warmth and beauty of spirit of the woman who had so touched his heart.

One day, when the skies were darkened by heavy snowfall, Kaoru passed the time from morning until evening staring blankly outside. That night the clouds cleared away, and the moon of the twelfth month—the moon that people always invoke as a symbol of chill desolation—shone clear and bright. He rolled up the blinds on the veranda to look up at it. The distant sound of the bell at the mountain temple echoed from high above, and as he strained to listen at his pillow, he heard it tolling out the close of day.[7]

> Not wishing to be left behind, to linger on
> I would follow the moon in its course . . . for this world
> Is not a realm I shall reside in forever

A stronger wind began to blow. When Kaoru got up to lower the shutters again, he glanced out into the garden. The ice at the water's edge, which was reflecting the image of the snow-covered mountains all around, sparkled brilliantly in the light of the moon. He could refurbish his villa on Sanjō in the capital all he liked, but nothing he could add to it would ever equal the scene before him.

If only she could come back to me, even for a moment, he thought, *I would talk with her about this sublime beauty!* His obsessive longing was simply too much to keep inside his breast.

> In my anguish over the loss of my beloved
> I long to vanish into the Snowy Mountains
> Leaving no trace while seeking the potion of death

If only there were some demon to teach me the second part of that verse of scripture, then I might well have an excuse to toss myself from some great height like that youth in the Snowy Mountains.[8] For someone who supposedly aspired to enlightenment in this way, his motivations were certainly less than pure.

---

7. Poem 978 from *Collected Writings of Bo Juyi:* "Straining to listen at my pillow, I hear the sound of the temple bell. I roll up the blinds and look out at the snow on the peaks." Anonymous poem from *The Shūishū:* "In grief and sorrow I listen to the sound of the temple bell as it tolls out the close of day."
8. In his poem and in this statement, Kaoru alludes to the story of Sessen Dōji (Youth of the Snow Mountains) that appears in the *Mahāparinirvāna Sutra* (the Nirvana sutra). Sessen Dōji, who was Sakyamuni in a previous life, is a young man seeking enlightenment by practicing austerities in the Himalaya Moun-

tains (the Snowy Mountains). The deity Śakra (Indra) decides to test the young man and approaches him disguised as a demon. He gives Sessen Dōji the first half of a Buddhist verse ("All is fleeting, nothing is constant/this is the law of birth and death") and offers the second half in exchange for his flesh and blood. The young man agrees, carves the verse into the stone wall of the cave that serves as his hermitage, then throws himself from a high place to fulfill the bargain. At that moment, Śakra changes back to his real form and saves Sessen Dōji.

Kaoru would summon the attendants and speak with them. At such times, he struck them as a paragon of noble virtue, gentle and deeply thoughtful. The younger ladies-in-waiting were completely smitten and thought him magnificent. The older women could only look at him and regret all the more what might have been.

"Our late mistress realized that Prince Niou was not trustworthy, and she was distressed at the prospect of being ridiculed. That's what made her ill."

"Yes, but she didn't want to let our young mistress know how worried she was, and so she kept her bitterness locked inside her heart and refused to eat anything—not even the smallest piece of fruit. She just grew weaker and weaker."

"On the surface she never gave any indication that she was deeply concerned about such things, but deep down she must have brooded endlessly over their situation."

"Her suffering began when all her hopes for her sister's future went awry and she realized that she had failed to live up to her father's admonition."

They went on sharing stories, relating what the late Princess had said on this or that occasion. With each anecdote, they invariably ended up breaking down and weeping.

Kaoru blamed his own folly for these tragedies and wanted to go back to the past and redo it. The world was unbearably trying to him, and he would spend sleepless nights immersing himself in prayer and meditation until dawn. Late one night as a heavy snow was falling, the shouts of men and the neighing of horses broke in on the freezing darkness. The venerable priests who had been commissioned for evening services were startled. Just as they were wondering what sort of men could have made their way here through the snow in the dead of night, Niou arrived, disguised in hunting robes and thoroughly soaked through. Kaoru knew by the impetuous rapping at the gate that it was the Prince, and so he withdrew and hid in a private space in the interior of the villa. The period of mourning and confinement had not yet passed, but Niou had been so fretful and impatient to see his Uji Princess that he had traveled all night long to get to her, struggling to make his way through the blizzard.

*   *   *

From Chapter XLIX

Yadoriki

TREES ENCOILED IN VINES OF IVY

*   *   *

The Uji Princess had never forgotten that peculiar night they spent together; having observed the workings of Kaoru's sincere, sensitive character—so unlike other men—did she wistfully imagine what might have been? A woman her age was no longer an inexperienced young girl, and when she compared the Middle Counselor to the man who had given her cause for resentment, she realized that Kaoru was far superior in all respects. Was that why, on this particular night, she took pity on him for having always kept her distance and, perhaps worried that she might come across as cold and inconsiderate, allowed him to be seated in the aisle room inside the veranda blinds? A standing curtain was set up inside the blinds of the main chambers, and she received him after withdrawing to the interior of the room.

"Although I did not receive an explicit invitation, I'm very happy to have been granted this rare permission to call on you," Kaoru began. "I wanted to come right away, but then I learned that the Prince might be returning and worried that it might prove awkward if I were here. So I decided to come today instead. Is it possible that, after all these years, you're showing some inclination to at last reward my earnest devotion to you? You've taken the remarkable step of relaxing your guard a little and allowing me inside your blinds."

The Princess still seem reserved toward him and had difficulty finding words to express what she wanted to say, but she finally replied with an air of modesty:

"It made me glad to hear about the memorial services the other day, and I would have regretted it if, as I always do, I simply kept my feelings to myself and let the occasion pass without somehow letting you know how much I appreciate all you've done." Because she had withdrawn so far back in her room, he could only catch faint snatches of her soft voice.

Feeling impatient and dissatisfied, he said, "You sound so distant. I should like permission to speak seriously with you about a certain worldly matter."

She thought his request reasonable, and his heart suddenly raced again at the sound of her moving closer toward him. He nonetheless exerted great self-control and maintained a nonchalant attitude. His manner of speech made it clear that he considered Niou's behavior inconsiderate. He criticized Niou and offered her words of comfort, talking to her soothingly on all sorts of subjects.

The Uji Princess could not openly voice her discontent with her marriage. Instead, she hinted indirectly, with few words, that she did not blame her misfortune on Niou so much as on her own karmic destiny.[9] She also expressed her heartfelt desire to go to the Uji villa for a brief visit.

"I'm afraid I can't decide on my own to help you," Kaoru replied. "It would be best to approach Prince Niou honestly and modestly with your request, and then do as he wishes. If you don't do that, he might misinterpret your motives a little, and it would be most unfortunate if he were then to consider you frivolous and untrustworthy. Once it's clear to him that he has nothing to be concerned about, then nothing will prevent me from accompanying you to Uji, and I will do all I can to be of service. The Prince knows full well that I am not like other men and that he can trust me completely."

While he was speaking with her, however, Kaoru did not for a moment forget his regrets, and he mentioned that he would like to go back to the past: "If only I could do it all over again."

It was growing dark, and the Princess was troubled that Kaoru showed no inclination to leave. "I'm not feeling all that well," she told him, "and so perhaps we might talk again some other time when I'm better."

9. The source of this line has not been definitively identified, but a later commentary cites the following poem: "Is my misfortune due to my woeful destiny or to his cruelty? I recall the little shrimp that live amid the seaweed the fishermen harvest and know it is my own fault." The poem plays on the word *warekara*, which may be read as the name of a species of shrimp or as a phrase meaning "I'm to blame."

He could tell from her movements that she was preparing to withdraw; because he desperately wanted her to stay, he said, as if to mollify her, "So tell me, then . . . when were you thinking of going to Uji? The paths must be terribly overgrown, and I shall have to have them cleared before then."

She stopped and paused for a moment. "This month will soon be over, so I was thinking perhaps the first of next month. But still, it seems best to keep the trip secret. If I were to ask Prince Niou for permission, it might lead to all sorts of troublesome complications."

Her voice was sweet and soft—so like her older sister's! He was assailed by memories and longings and could no longer restrain himself. He quietly stretched his arm through the blinds hanging next to the pillar he was leaning against and gently took hold of her sleeves.

Was this his intention all along? Ahh . . . how horrid he is! Not knowing what to say, she did not reply. Instead, she tried to move further back into the interior of the room. When she did so, he slipped further through the blinds—as if he had the run of the place!—and lay down beside her. "You have me all wrong, do you not?" he complained. "I was delighted when you said that you thought it best to travel to Uji secretly, and I entered because I wanted to ask if perhaps I hadn't misheard you. How unpleasant you are! You have no reason to be so cold and aloof."

She did not feel up to replying to him. Shocked by his behavior, she now detested him, though she remained sufficiently in control of her emotions to admonish his actions: "I never expected this sort of thing from you. What will my attendants think? Your behavior is atrocious!"

She was on the verge of tears—and with just cause. But though he felt sorry for her, he continued to plead his case: "Am I so outrageous that people would censure me? Meeting you face to face like this brings back memories of that night we spent together. A meeting your late sister approved, I might add. You think me shocking and atrocious, but your reaction is deeply offensive to me. You may rest assured that my intentions are in no way lascivious." He was very calm and gentle, but he talked on and on, telling her how keenly he felt the pain caused by the feelings of remorse he had kept inside himself for so many months.

She did not know what to do, since there was no indication that he was going to let go of her sleeves. It is difficult for me to convey just how frightened and disturbed she was. She felt more awkward and disgusted with him than she would have with a man who was a total stranger. When, at last, she began to cry, Kaoru said, "Why are you carrying on so? You're being childish, you know." She was adorable beyond words, and he felt bad for her, but at the same time her demeanor was so deeply thoughtful and prudent that it made him feel ashamed. He could see that she was even more mature and lovely than in the old days at Uji.

The yearnings that unsettle my heart this way are all the result of having given her up of my own volition to another man. Overwhelmed by self-reproach, he broke down in tears, sobbing.

Only two ladies-in-waiting were in close attendance that evening. Still, they would have been vigilant and would have been suspicious had a man with no relationship to the Princess—and thus no reason to be there—entered the main chamber. They would have drawn nearer, wondering what was happening. The

Middle Counselor, however, had been a confidant of their mistress for a long time, and if he was on familiar-enough terms to be allowed to speak directly and intimately with her, then the situation seemed perfectly acceptable. Indeed, given the circumstances at that moment, they felt uncomfortable being so near and pretended not to notice anything. They quietly withdrew, which made the Princess feel even more wretched. As for Kaoru, he was finding it extremely difficult to suppress the overpowering regrets he harbored for all that had happened in the past. Nonetheless, his matchless prudence, a virtue he had possessed since his youth, kept his passions in check, and he did not do as he wished with the Uji Princess. It wouldn't do to describe this scene in any greater detail. For Kaoru, the visit had proven completely pointless; because he was reluctant to be seen by others he withdrew, reflecting remorsefully on all he had done.

Kaoru had been under the impression that it was still early evening, but in fact dawn was approaching. He grew anxious that censorious eyes might see him leaving at this hour, worried not for his own reputation, but for that of the Uji Princess. *I'd heard rumors of late that she hasn't been feeling well, and now I understand why. She was extremely embarrassed that I saw her pregnancy belt,*[1] *and her reaction made me feel so bad that I did not take her. What a fool I am . . . as usual.*

Other thoughts, however, tempered these reflections. *And yet I never intended to do anything cruel. If, in a moment of weakness, I had given in to my baser instincts and forced myself on her, I'd never be able to feel at ease meeting her after that. Even if we carried on an affair, it would take tremendous effort on my part to arrange our secret trysts, and that would cause her to suffer the torment of constant dread.*

Despite these seemingly wise rationalizations, he could not completely repress his desires, and his unbeatable yearnings for her in the present moment[2] left him feeling utterly helpless. Come what may, he had to see her again, and yet his was a desire that would never be truly sated. He could not get the image of her out of his mind—the elegantly refined, enchanting figure that was even more willowy than in the old days at Uji. As a result, he had the sensation that she was always with him, and he could think of nothing else.

She very much wants to go back to Uji, and I would like to escort her there, but Niou would never permit such a thing. And if we went in secret against his wishes, it might well end in calamity. Is there any way I can get what I want without destroying our reputations? He lay there staring out blankly, lost in these pensive thoughts.

His letter to the Uji Princess arrived early in the morning in the predawn darkness. Just like his previous letters, it was folded so as to resemble a formal missive rather than a love note.

> All for naught did I travel o'er
> That dew-drenched path, the autumn sky
> Stirring memories of the past

1. This belt was a kind of sash (*obi*) worn low on the belly to provide support during pregnancy.
2. Anonymous poem from *The Gosenshū*: "How

must they have been, those times before ever we met? For when I cannot see you in the present moment, I yearn for you."

"Not understanding the reasons for your cruelty only makes it all the more intolerable. There are no words to describe how I feel."

Since she always replied to his letters, her women would surely take notice and think something amiss if she did not do so this time. However, it was too arduous a task for her to write a letter, and so she simply scribbled a note: "I received your letter. I am much too ill right now and cannot reply." When Kaoru read it, he was let down by its brevity. He longingly recalled her alluring air.

Now a little wiser in the ways of men and women, the Uji Princess did not consider Kaoru's behavior entirely shocking or despicable. For his part, when he recalled her demeanor at the moment she saw him off—her gentle kindness and humility, her complete lack of coldness, the warm familiarity with which she spoke—envy and sadness assailed his heart and he was disconsolate, tormented by conflicting emotions. He thought her far superior in every way from the young woman she was when he first saw her at Uji.

If, for some reason, Niou should ever be estranged from her, he fantasized, I would likely be the only person she could turn to for support. Yet even if that happened, it would not be easy for me to visit her openly. Instead, I would have to meet her in secret, and she would be my haven, the lasting object of my heart's desire, the woman I would love above all others.

How truly despicable that his heart should have been so fixated on her! Men may exude an air of kindness and sagacity, but they are cruelly fickle. Kaoru was sure that the sorrow over his lost love could never be assuaged, and yet here he was, suffering much worse over his love for her younger sister. Her attractiveness was all he could think about; when he heard someone mention that Niou would be returning to the Nijō villa that day, all his altruistic impulses to act as her support disappeared as his chest burned with jealous rancor.

* * *

From Chapter LIII

Tenarai

PRACTICING CALLIGRAPHY

In those days, there was an exceptionally pious priest residing at Yokawa on Mount Hiei[3]—a certain bishop whose name slips my mind. He had a mother who was over eighty years old and a younger sister who was in her fifties. Both of these women had become nuns, and together they undertook a pilgrimage to Hatsuse in fulfillment of a long-standing vow they had made to Kannon. Their traveling party included one of the bishop's closest and most highly regarded disciples, an ascetic who accompanied them in order to perform the dedication of sutras and images of the Buddha.

3. Yokawa, along with Tōdō (east pagoda) and Saitō (west pagoda), was one of three extensive compounds that comprised the important and influential monastic center of Enryakuji. Part of this temple's prestige derived from geomantic practices. Mount Hiei is located northeast of Kyoto. Northeast was considered a permanently unlucky direction, and it was thus believed that a holy site like Enryakuji protected the capital from evil influences.

After completing numerous acts of devotion, they started for home. Unfortunately, just as they were crossing the hills on the slope of Narasaka, the mother fell ill. Her condition caused tremendous apprehension among the attendants, who worried that their mistress might not be able to complete her pilgrimage. Thinking it best to rest for a day, the party stopped in the vicinity of Uji at the house of an acquaintance of the bishop. But then the old woman took a turn for the worse, and a messenger was immediately dispatched to Yokawa.

His Holiness had made a firm vow to remain in retreat for the year and not leave Mount Hiei. Nonetheless, he rushed to his aged mother's side, disturbed by the possibility that she might die on the road. Although his mother had lived such a long life that there would have been no need to feel any special regret about her passing, the bishop himself, along with his most efficacious disciples, raised a tremendous clamor as they performed healing rites.

The master of the house where they were lodging listened to this uproar with a worried expression: *What effect will the defiling presence of an ill, very old woman have as I purify myself in preparation for a pilgrimage to Mitake? What if she should die here?*

Upon hearing these concerns, the bishop recognized that his host had good reason to be anxious, and he felt sorry for being such an imposition. Moreover, the house was quite small and inconvenient. For these reasons, he decided that he would move his mother little by little whenever she felt well enough to travel. His plan, however, was thwarted when he learned that the direction to his mother's house was prohibited to them, blocked by the presence of the Middle Deity. He then remembered that an old imperial villa formerly used by the late Emperor Suzaku was nearby, just north of the Uji River.[4] Since His Holiness knew the steward who oversaw that estate, he sent a note requesting permission to stay there for a day or two.

"The steward and all the members of his household left yesterday on a pilgrimage to Hatsuse," reported the messenger, who had brought back with him the caretaker of the villa, an eccentric, ragged-looking old man.

"Yes, that's right," the caretaker affirmed. "The main hall is empty at the moment, so you must come right away before anyone else arrives. You see, pilgrims are always stopping by to lodge there."

"That sounds perfect," the bishop replied. "I know it's an imperial residence, but if no one is using it right now, we'll be able to rest at our leisure."

His Holiness sent some members of the party to inspect the site. The old caretaker was accustomed to looking after people who needed lodging, since visitors arrived regularly, and so he had already arranged to have plain and simple furnishings set out for the guests. The bishop then made his way over to the villa ahead of his mother and sister. The place had fallen into disrepair, and when His Holiness observed its frighteningly eerie atmosphere, he ordered his most saintly disciples to begin chanting sutras. The ascetic and one other disciple—a priest of equal rank and eminence—expressed their concern that something uncanny might happen in such a setting. Both men had experience with

---

4. This may be a reference to the real-life Emperor Suzaku (923–952), who used a villa near Uji as a retreat from the capital. However, since the association of fictional characters with real-life figures is a recurring feature of Murasaki Shikibu's narrative technique, it may be that the author is simply introducing new information about her character, Suzaku.

situations like this, and so they ordered the lighting of torches, a task they assigned to some lower-ranking monks whose burly appearance made them the appropriate choice for driving off lingering spirits.

The monks took up their torches and immediately set off to inspect the grounds behind the main hall, a neglected spot that people rarely approached. Warily peering into an eerie stand of trees that resembled a sacred grove at a shrine, they spotted something white amidst the undergrowth.

"What could that be?" The party froze in its tracks. Raising their torches higher, the men could make out the seated figure of a young lady.

"It must be a fox spirit in human form. Abhorrent creature! I'll make it show its true shape," one of the monks said, taking a few steps closer to the figure.

"Don't be rash! It could be a malevolent spirit," warned another who, just to be safe, was keeping his eyes fixed on the strange apparition and displaying the mudra[5] used to ward off evil. Had there been any hair on his head, he felt sure it would have been standing on end.

The fearless monk was undeterred, however, and moved closer to the strange figure to get a better look. It was a young lady with long, lustrous hair leaning against the thick gnarly roots of a tree. She was weeping most piteously.

"This is passing strange," he said. "I should like for His Holiness to have a look."

"Yes, indeed . . . exceedingly weird," replied one of his companions, who hurried off to inform the bishop of the unearthly discovery.

"I have long heard of fox spirits taking on human form, but I've never witnessed such a thing personally." So saying, the bishop left the main hall with the express intent of investigating the matter himself.

The bishop's mother and sister were now on their way to the villa, and the menial servants were busy tending to their responsibilities in the kitchen and living quarters as they hastened to make preparations for the arrival of their guests. As a result, the area behind the main hall remained deserted except for the four or five monks who were keeping an eye on the strange creature. They observed no change in its condition. Hours passed as they watched in doubtful wonder.

It will soon be dawn, and finally we shall see if it's human or something else. With that thought in mind, they recited the proper incantations in their hearts and formed the correct mudras. While they were doing so, the true nature of the creature became evident to the bishop.

"It's not a fox spirit, it's a young woman. She's human. Approach her and find out her name. She's obviously not dead. Probably someone left her body here thinking she had passed away, and she revived after they left. That must be what happened here, wouldn't you agree?"

"Why would anyone abandon a woman like this at an imperial villa?" one of the monks asked.

"Even if she *is* human, maybe she was bewitched by a fox spirit or wood sprite and tricked into following it here," suggested another.

5. Mudras were an important practice in Shingon Buddhism. Shingon esoteric practices during the Heian period were influential and had an impact on other Buddhist sects, including the Tendai Monastery at Enryakuji on Mount Hiei.

"Either way, this is most unfortunate. Her presence defiles this place, and your mother is just about to arrive."

The monks shouted for the caretaker. The echoing of their voices was eerily disturbing.

The disheveled old man emerged from the main hall, pushing the unkempt hair on his forehead back up under his cap.

"Does a young woman live close by? Look at what we've found," one of the monks said, pointing to the young lady.

"Must be the work of a fox," the caretaker replied. "Queer things happen from time to time in this grove. Why, just the year before last, in the autumn, a fox took a little child who lives on the estate . . . barely two years old, mind you . . . and left him in these woods. Nothing to be shocked about, really."

"Did the child die?"

"No, no, he's fine. Foxes like to alarm folks, but they don't do any real harm." The caretaker seemed utterly nonchalant about the matter, as if being bewitched by a fox spirit was the most natural thing in the world. Apparently, he was more preoccupied with preparing food for all the visitors who had arrived in the middle of the night.

"In that case," the bishop said, "we'd better check again to see if that's what befell this young lady."

The fearless monk who had confronted the apparition earlier approached once again and began tugging on one of the sleeves of the young lady's robes.

"Be you demon or deity, be you fox or woodland sprite, you cannot hope to conceal your identity in the presence of these most eminent priests. Announce yourself! Tell us your name!"

The woman buried her face in her sleeves and wept all the harder.

"Come now, insolent sprite or demon! Do you really think you can keep your true shape hidden?"

Though he was determined to get a better look at her face, the monk was steeling himself just in case this was one of those female demons with no eyes or nose that he had read about in ancient tales. Still, he felt that he had to put on a brave front with the bishop watching him, and so he tried to pull the woman's sleeves back. Whereupon she threw herself facedown, sobbing loudly.

The intrepid monk remained convinced that anything so unusual and suspicious could not be a creature of this world and that it would be best for them to continue observing it to see if any transformation took place. However, the weather was changing and there was no time for that. "A heavy storm is coming," he said. "If we leave the creature here like this, it will surely die and defile the residence. We should drive it away, outside the enclosure."

"She's obviously human," the bishop reassured him, "and it would be cruel to knowingly abandon her while she's alive. After all, it's natural for us to feel bad if we do nothing to help the fish that swim in the lakes or the deer that cry in the mountains when such creatures have been caught and are about to die. Human life is all too fleeting as it is, and so even if this young lady is destined to survive only a day or two more, we shouldn't begrudge her the time she has left. Perhaps a god or a demon possessed her, or maybe she was driven from her home, or deceived by someone plotting against her. Whatever the case, even if it seems that she's fated to die in this strange, pathetic manner, the Buddha would certainly show mercy to one in her situation. It is our duty to do no less. At the very least, we must try to help her. Give her medicinal infusions for a while. If she passes away after that, then I suppose there's not much more we could have done for her."

The bishop ordered the ascetic to pick up the young lady and carry her inside the villa. Some of the monks objected: "But Your Holiness . . . that's out of the question. To take a foul creature like this inside the villa will surely have a baleful effect on your mother, who's suffering enough as it is."

Others showed greater sympathy: "But if she *has* been bewitched by a shapeshifter, then it would be a grave sin to leave a living being out in this rain and allow her to pass away before our very eyes."

The menials would have raised a tremendous fuss and said all sorts of crude things had the monks brought the young lady into the main hall, and so they laid her down in an inconspicuous corner where people wouldn't be bustling in and out.

The carriages bearing the bishop's mother and his sister arrived at the villa. As soon as the women alighted, a clamor arose when, to everyone's alarm, it was discovered that the mother was feeling worse as a result of the strain of the journey. Only after things had settled down did the bishop turn his attention once more to the young lady.

"How's she doing?"

"Lethargic and unresponsive," one of the monks reported. "She doesn't even seem to be breathing at times. It's as if she's been possessed by a malevolent spirit and is no longer aware of herself or her surroundings."

"What are you two talking about?" asked the bishop's sister, who had overheard their conversation.

"I've witnessed many strange occurrences in my lifetime," the bishop answered, "but in all my sixty-plus years, this has to be one of the most unusual I've ever encountered."

Tears came to the nun's eyes as she listened to her brother explain what had happened.

"When we were staying at the temple in Hatsuse," she said, "I had a dream about a young lady. Could you describe this woman to me? May I see her?"

"By all means, go to her at once," the bishop replied. "She's resting just beyond the sliding doors on the east side."

The nun hurried over and peeked into the room. There wasn't a servant in sight. A woman was lying there, alone and abandoned. She seemed very young, but exuded an air of refined beauty. Dressed in crimson trousers over a singlet of white damask that was suffused with an ethereal scent, her appearance gave the impression of boundless grace and nobility.

"Why . . . she's the very image of my late lamented daughter," the nun gasped. Unable to stop her tears, she summoned her attendants and had them pick up the young lady and carry her to chambers further inside the villa. Of course, the attendants could not tell just by looking what tribulations this woman had endured, and so they carried out the nun's orders without fear or hesitation.

The young lady appeared to be lifeless, but then she opened her eyes ever so slightly.

"Say something," the nun implored. "Tell me who you are and how you ended up like this."

The young lady was silent. It seemed as though the nun's words were incomprehensible to her.

The nun picked up a cup containing a medicinal infusion and, with her own hands, tried to get the patient to drink. The lady, however, did not have the strength to take the medicine and seemed to be on the verge of breathing her last.

At that moment the nun turned in desperation to the saintly ascetic. "This infusion is no use. Her condition is worse than ever. She's going to die if we don't do something. Please, please perform a healing rite for her!"

"This is exactly what I was worried about," the ascetic replied. "I advised His Holiness against getting involved with such a strange and hopeless case." Despite these misgivings, the ascetic began chanting the *Heart Sutra* in order to appease the local deities before he commenced with the healing rites.[6]

The bishop stuck his head in and asked again, "How is she doing? Try to find out what sort of spirit is possessing her so that we may exorcise it."

The young lady was extremely weak, and it looked as if she might expire at any moment. "I don't think she'll last much longer," one of the attendants remarked.

"What a nuisance. If she dies, then we'll have to go into retreat. And all because of an unexpected defilement," grumbled another.

"You're right. It really *will* be a nuisance. What's more, she looks like she comes from a distinguished noble family, so even after we know for sure that she's dead, we won't be able to dispose of her body right away!"

"Be still," the nun scolded, "and make sure that no one hears about this matter! Any kind of gossip about this is bound to stir up trouble."

The nun kept constant vigil and was so preoccupied by her desire to save the young lady that she seemed to others to be more concerned about the threat to the well-being of a stranger than she was about the illness afflicting her own mother. Still, even though the young lady *was* an outsider, she was so extraordinarily beautiful that all of the attendants who saw her thought it would be terrible to just let her die. So moved, they fussed over her, doing all they could to be of assistance.

Weak as she was, she managed to open her eyes from time to time. Whenever she did, an endless stream of tears would pour forth.

"Ahh . . . how heartbreaking," cried the nun. "I believe the Buddha has brought you to me as a replacement for the beloved daughter whose death I continue to mourn. If you should die as well and this all comes to naught, then our chance encounter will have left me with nothing but one more bitter, painful memory. We must have been destined to meet. Perhaps we share a bond from a previous life. Please . . . won't you at least speak to me a little?"

The nun continued to plead in this fashion until, finally, the young lady replied in a thin whisper: "I may have survived, but I'm a woman of no importance,

---

6. The *Heart Sutra* is a central scripture of Mahāyāna Buddhism. The syncretic nature of religious belief at the time meant that even Buddhist priests had to be respectful of Shinto practices. The desire to maintain a proper balance between different religious systems is depicted at several points in the narrative.

and my life is worthless. Don't let anyone else see me. This evening, after darkness falls, throw me back into the river."

"You've uttered hardly a word to me since you were brought here, and so I suppose I should be thrilled to hear your voice. But what fearful things you say! Whatever could possess you to speak like that? And how did you come to be in those woods behind the villa?"

The young lady did not respond. The nun examined her body, looking for wounds or any sign of strange anomalies. Finding nothing out of the ordinary, she was at once shocked and saddened by the sight of such unblemished beauty, for it caused her to have doubts about the young lady, who might truly be a shape-shifter come to bewitch people and lead their hearts astray.

The bishop's party remained in retreat at the villa for two full days, and the unceasing reverberation of voices chanting prayers and healing rites for the two afflicted women left everyone on edge and feeling uneasy about the strange, suspicious events that had occurred.

A number of peasants living in the vicinity of the villa had once been in service to the bishop. When they learned that His Holiness was staying there, they came to pay their respects and express condolences for his mother's illness.

As the bishop was listening to them prattle on and on about trivial, everyday matters, one of the peasants offered an apology to him: "We're sorry that we couldn't be of service to you earlier, but you see, Lady Ukifune, a daughter of the late Prince Hachinomiya, died suddenly, without any prior indication that she was ill. Well, this lady was being courted by the Major Captain of the Right, and so I can assure you that her death caused quite a stir. We were so busy yesterday taking care of the funeral arrangements that we couldn't get away to see you until now."

The man's story got the bishop to thinking about the young lady who had been found in the grove behind the villa: *Is it possible that a demon snatched the soul of Hachinomiya's daughter and brought it here? Similar cases have been known to occur in the past.* His doubts were prompted by his observations over the past couple of days, for no matter how often he checked in on her, he never got the sense that she was really alive. There was something alarmingly sinister about her that greatly disturbed him—a precarious, ephemeral quality, as if she might suddenly disappear.

Several people questioned the peasant's story: "But the smoke and flames we observed last night didn't seem big enough for a proper funeral pyre."

"The rites were kept simple on purpose," the man explained. "If you ask me, it wasn't much of a ceremony." The peasants, who had been defiled by their proximity to death, were kept standing outside and were eventually sent away.

Some in the bishop's party began to gossip among themselves.

"The Major Captain was once enamored of Hachinomiya's eldest daughter, but she passed away several years ago. I wonder who that menial could have been referring to?"

"Now that the Major Captain has wed the Fujitsubo Princess,[7] do you really think it likely that he would give his heart to another woman?"

7. This "Second Princess" is the second daughter of the present emperor and is married to Kaoru. She resides in the "Chambers of the Wisteria Court" (Fujitsubo) [editor's note].

With his mother's condition improving and the direction toward her home no longer prohibited, the bishop decided that the party should make its way back, especially given how awkward it was to remain any longer in such a dreary, haunted place.

Several people wondered aloud about the decision: "But the young lady is still in such a delicate state," they pointed out. "Is she really up to the journey? The poor little thing may suffer terribly on the way."

Despite these concerns, two carriages were readied. The bishop's mother rode in the lead carriage and was accompanied by two other nuns who had been assigned to care for her. The young lady was placed in the second carriage and was accompanied by the bishop's sister and an attendant who stayed by her side throughout the trip.

Progress was slow and fitful, mainly because the party had to make frequent stops in order to prepare medicine for the young lady. Since the nuns resided in Ono on the lower slopes of Mount Hiei, their journey was a long one.

"We should have arranged to stop somewhere along the way," someone complained; and indeed, it was very late at night when they finally arrived.

The bishop looked after his mother, while his sister, the nun, tenderly cared for the young lady, whose identity remained unknown. Each of the nun's attendants took turns assisting her, taking the woman from the carriage and carrying her inside to rest. The bishop's mother was constantly beset by the infirmities of old age, and for a time her condition worsened as a result of the lingering effects of the journey. Nonetheless, she eventually recovered, and His Holiness was able to retire back up the mountain to his temple at Yokawa.

It was rather scandalous for a priest to be traveling in the company of a young woman, and so the bishop spoke not a word about his trip to those disciples who had not been with him to witness what had taken place. For her part, his sister made all of her attendants swear an oath of silence, for she feared that someone might come looking for the young lady.

How is it possible that someone who seems to be of such high status should have fallen so low and ended up in a place inhabited by rustics? The nun imagined several possibilities. *Did she fall ill while traveling on a pilgrimage, only to be betrayed and abandoned by a duplicitous stepmother? She has uttered nothing apart from that horrid request to be thrown into the river.*

The nun was extremely anxious, hoping that the patient would soon recover her health and faculties. Sadly, the young lady made no effort to get up, but remained lethargic and disoriented. Her condition was so alarming that survival seemed unlikely. Still, the nun couldn't bear the unpleasant thought of giving up, and so she revealed to others the dream she saw on her pilgrimage at Hatsuse. She also discreetly contacted the ascetic who had granted her pleas for healing rites when they were staying at the imperial villa in Uji and asked him to burn poppy seeds in an effort to exorcise any malicious spirits that might be lingering.

The rites of exorcism continued to be performed throughout the fourth and fifth months. Saddened and perplexed that nothing seemed to be helping, the nun sent a letter to the bishop:

Please come down to us again. Help this woman. That she has managed to hold on this long shows that it is not her destiny to die at this time. Whatever spirit or demon has possessed her will not let go. My dear brother, I know that you vowed to stay in retreat and not venture out, not even to the capital, but can there be any harm, would you really be breaking your vow, in coming to Ono?

After reading this heartrending message, His Holiness decided to leave his mountain retreat and descend to Ono. *What a curious affair! The young lady has survived so long . . . what if I had made a snap judgment to abandon her at that villa? My discovery of her there must have been the workings of a shared karmic bond, and so I must do my utmost to save her. If I fail, then I'll have to assume that she was fated to die after all.*

Receiving her brother with reverence and joy, the nun described to him the young lady's condition over the past few months: "A patient who's been ill as long as this would normally show the unpleasant effects, but she hasn't deteriorated at all. You can see that she's as youthful and lovely as ever . . . nothing of her appearance shows any sign of disfigurement. True, she does appear to be nearing death, and yet she continues to cling to life." The nun spoke with sincere intensity, weeping the whole time.

"From the moment I first saw her," the bishop replied, "I knew there was something out of the ordinary. Well . . . I shall see what I can do." He peeked in on the young lady, and then added, "She really is quite beautiful, isn't she! No doubt she was born with such features as a reward for good deeds performed in a previous life. What trespass could she have possibly committed to deserve this cruel fate? Have you heard anything that might explain what happened?"

"I've heard nothing . . . no rumors or gossip. I'm convinced that she's merciful Kannon's answer to my prayers."

"No, no, that's not right. There must exist some prior bond between people for karmic destiny to bring them together. Nothing happens by accident, so how could you think it possible, absent some necessary cause, for Kannon to have brought you someone who has no connection to you?" After voicing his priestly doubts about his sister's interpretation of events, he at once set about performing an exorcism.

The nun, who for her own reasons wanted to keep the young lady's presence a secret, felt that it would be awkward if word got out that her brother, who had declined to interrupt his vows even when summoned by the palace, had inexplicably left his mountain temple to go to the trouble of performing prayers and rites for a woman like this. The other priests in attendance shared the nun's concern, and they advised His Holiness to perform the rites quietly in order to keep them secret.

"I will hear no more of this, my noble disciples," the bishop replied. "I've proven to be a shameless priest, for I have broken many of the prohibitions that I'd sworn to uphold. Still, when it comes to women, I've never defiled myself or done anything that would merit censure. I'm over sixty now, and if at this point in my life I'm condemned for trying to save a young woman, then so be it. I would simply consider that my karmic destiny."

"But whenever vulgar rumormongers spread vicious gossip about a holy man of your high repute, that damages the Buddha's sacred teachings," the disciples said, voicing their displeasure.

The bishop made a gravely solemn vow: "If she shows no signs of improving while I am performing these incantations, then I swear I shall never do them again!" He persevered with the rites all through the night, and at dawn succeeded in driving out the stubborn spirit and forcing it into the body of a medium. The bishop and his disciple, the ascetic, wondered just what kind of creature had possessed the young lady, and they took turns continuing the rites in the hopes of pressing the spirit to reveal its situation and motives.

The spirit, which had for several months resisted revealing anything at all about its true nature, was finally overcome and began to shout and curse: "Once, my status was such that no one would ever have expected a man like me to end up in a place like this, subdued in this fashion. You see, long ago I was a monk who practiced austerities, but as a result of some petty resentments I harbored toward the world, I was unable to break free of my attachments and achieve salvation. While wandering adrift in the limbo between realms of existence, I came upon a place where several beautiful sisters resided, and I managed to steal the life of the eldest. Sometime later, I heard the young lady who lies here before you bemoaning her fate and insisting day and night that she wanted to die. One night, when she was alone in the pitch darkness, I took advantage of her despair to possess her. Alas, merciful Kannon protected her, allowing this saintly bishop to defeat me in the end. I shall leave you now!"

"Who are you? Announce yourself," the bishop demanded. However, the spirit's words were no longer intelligible, perhaps because the medium was exhausted.

Her mind and soul restored, the young lady regained her senses a little and glanced around the room. Surrounded by a throng of wizened old monks, she didn't recognize a single face. The sensation of having arrived in some strange, unknown land was profoundly unsettling. She tried recalling details from her past, but couldn't remember anything clearly—not the place where she lived, not even her own name.

All I remember is that I decided to throw myself in the river because it was unbearable to go on living. But where am I now? She struggled to make sense of fragmentary memories. *I was suffering dreadfully, lost in hopeless sorrow, but everyone around me was asleep. Stepping out through the hinged doors at the corner of some room, I felt the wind blowing wildly and heard the violent roar of a river. Frightened and alone, oblivious to past and future, I collapsed on the edge of the veranda and pondered uncertainly which way I should go. Having come this far, I felt ambivalent about going back inside, and as I sat there brooding, I kept telling myself that I should be resolute and leave this world behind once and for all, that it would be better to be devoured by demons than have anyone see me looking so foolish and pathetic. And then, at that moment, a radiantly handsome man approached and said, "Come with me, come to my home." I recall the feeling of being embraced in his arms, and then, just as I recognized him as the man whom people addressed as "Your Lordship,"*[8] *I must have fallen into a trance. When I came to and looked around, I was in an unfamiliar grove and the man had disappeared without a trace. I remember weeping bitterly as I realized that I had not, in the end, been able to die as I had wished. After that, I*

8. Although he is not explicitly named in the text, the implication is that Ukifune is recalling her relationship with Niou, who is depicted several times in the *Ukifune* chapter embracing her.

can't recall what happened, no matter how hard I try. I gather from what people have been saying that many days have passed since then. And to think, what a wretched-looking figure I must have presented to these strangers who were caring for me all that time.

During those days when she was sunk in that trancelike state, she had eaten at least a few morsels of food on occasion. Now, however, because she was ashamed and filled with remorse at the thought of having been resuscitated in this way, she fell into a deep depression and refused everything, even her medicine.

"Why must you remain so weak, seemingly unwilling to let us help you?" the nun tearfully pleaded. "I was so happy when your fever finally broke and you seemed to be feeling more yourself, but now . . ."

The nun kept a constant bedside vigil, lavishing attention on her patient. The attendants in residence also did everything they could to help, thinking it would be most regrettable if the young lady were to die under their care, especially seeing how fair and graceful of face and figure she was.

The young lady was grateful, but in her heart she continued to long for death. Still, she had managed to come back from the brink, clinging to life despite her ordeal, and because of her youthful vitality, she gradually regained the strength to raise her head, and eventually began to eat and take her medicine again. Despite this improvement, she also continued to lose weight, and her face looked increasingly gaunt.

The nun was happily anticipating a speedy recovery when the young lady said to her, "You must make me a nun. Otherwise, I can no longer go on living."

"It would be a great pity to alter such beauty as yours," the nun protested. "How can you ask me to do such a thing?"

As a compromise, the bishop snipped a few wisps of hair from the top of the young lady's head and had her take an oath swearing to uphold the Five Precepts.[9] This did not satisfy her, but being passive and yielding by nature, she couldn't bring herself to insist on being allowed to take the full formal vows that would make her a nun.

Setting off back up the mountain, the bishop gave instructions to his sister as he parted: "Let's leave it at this for now and focus on nursing her back to health."

The nun was overjoyed to have been entrusted with the care of this young lady, who seemed like a dream come true to her.[1] In her zeal, she would have her charge sit up and personally see to combing her hair, which, although it had been braided in a rather unsightly fashion and carelessly left that way during the long ordeal of spirit possession, was not especially tangled. By the time the nun finished, the young lady's tresses had a vibrant, lovely sheen. The presence of such beauty in a place with so many gray-haired nuns who all seemed to be just a year shy of one hundred[2] made everyone feel as though a dazzling,

9. The Five Precepts constitute a vow against killing, stealing, lying, promiscuity, and intemperance. The vows to become a true nun are more numerous.
1. The phrasing of this line calls to mind the dream the nun had at Hatsuse, implying that

her prayers were answered.
2. *Tales of Ise*, section 63: "The grizzled lady who is just a year shy of one hundred seems to be yearning for me, for the image of her face appears before my eyes."

wondrous angel had descended from the heavens. This stirred a sense of foreboding in the nun, who pressed the young lady to tell her more.

"Why do you seem so cold, keeping your distance from me even though I fret so terribly over you? Who are you? Where are you from? How did you end up in that grove?"

Feeling deeply ashamed at what the nun must think of her, the young lady replied, "I must have lost my memory while I was in that weird trance, for I have almost no recollection of anything that happened before that spirit possessed me. The only thing I can vaguely recall is sitting at the edge of a veranda, gazing blankly at a garden and thinking that I no longer wanted to live in this world. Suddenly, a man stepped out from beneath a large tree nearby. I have the feeling that he took me with him somewhere. After that, I can't remember a thing . . . I can't even remember who I am."

Her manner of speaking was sweetly endearing. She then broke down in tears as she added, "Whatever happens, I don't want anyone to find out that I'm still alive. It would be too much to bear if someone were to come looking for me."

Realizing how painful her questions must be, the nun felt that she could press the young lady no further. She was even more astounded than the old bamboo cutter must have been when he discovered the moon princess, Kaguyahime, inside a stalk of bamboo,[3] Knowing how that story ended, the nun was uneasy, wondering if this young lady like Kaguyahime, might disappear, like moonlight slipping through some narrow gap.

Now, the bishop's mother had come from a distinguished background, while his sister, the nun, had been the principal wife of a high-ranking official. The nun had given her husband a daughter, but when he passed away she was left to raise their only child on her own. She did everything she could for the girl, eventually arranging a promising marriage to a young groom of exceptional breeding. But then her daughter died as well. Heartbroken and despondent at being a childless widow, she took vows and withdrew to begin life at her mountain retreat in Ono.

Lamenting the tedium of her forlorn existence, the nun desperately wanted to find someone comparable in age and looks to her lost daughter—a keepsake of the one she mourned day and night. And then, quite unexpectedly, she was granted this young lady, who in face and figure was even lovelier than her own daughter. Hardly able to believe this was really happening, the nun was at once astonished and overjoyed. Although she herself was now in her fifties, she had retained a graceful beauty and dignified demeanor.

* * *

3. The divine protagonist of the *Tale of the Bamboo Cutter* who, after her adventures on Earth, ascends to heaven again [editor's note].

From Chapter LIII

Tenarai

PRACTICING CALLIGRAPHY

* * *

It may be awkward, but I must be brave and take advantage of this opportunity to ask His Holiness to administer vows to me. There's almost no one here to stop me, so the timing couldn't be better. With that in mind, Ukifune arose and addressed the bishop's mother.

"I'm seriously ill, so when your son, His Holiness, arrives, please inform him that I would like to take the vows that will make me a nun."

The senile old woman nodded in vague agreement.

Ukifune returned to her usual quarters. The nun was the only person who was permitted to comb her hair—Ukifune couldn't stand having anyone else touch it—and because she couldn't dress it herself, she simply loosened the cords and let it hang down a little. It made her sad to think that it was by her choice and no one else's that her mother would never again see her the way she looked now. She had been under the impression that her hair had thinned out as a result of the terrible ordeal she had been through, and yet, far from falling out, it was if anything thicker, a full six feet in length, and beautiful all the way to the ends. Each strand was fine and gave off a lovely sheen.

Ukifune recited a snatch of verse to herself: ". . . hoping that it would come to this."[4]

The bishop arrived at dusk. The aisle room facing south had been cleaned and cleared away, and soon a host of round shaven heads were scurrying about raising an alarming uproar that disturbed the normally quiet atmosphere of the place. His Holiness went over to his mother's quarters to ask after her.

"How have you been doing these past few months? I see that the rooms on the east side are vacant. Has my sister already left on her pilgrimage? Is that young lady still in residence here?"

"She is," the old nun replied. "She decided to remain here. She told me to tell you that she's not feeling well and that she wants to become a nun. She wants you to administer the vows."

The bishop arose and went over to the young lady's chambers. "Excuse me, are you in here?"

Because she was sitting behind a standing curtain when he called out, she moved closer to him by way of reply, her demeanor quiet and demure.

"From the moment I first met you under those startling circumstances, I felt certain that there must be a bond between us from some previous life. Since then, I have prayed devotedly for you. Of course, as a priest, it wouldn't do for me to call on you or send you letters without some reason to do so, and so naturally I have not kept in touch. How has it been, living among old women who have renounced the world? They must look frightfully strange to you, no?"

4. *The Gosenshū* 1240 (Bishop Henjō, written when he first took the tonsure): "Surely my mother never stroked my pitch-black hair hoping that it would come to this."

"It's depressing for me. Despite my desire to end my life, I continue to survive for reasons that remain a mystery. Please don't get me wrong . . . there's no way someone as foolish as I can adequately express the gratitude I feel for all the kindness you've shown on my behalf. It's just that I can no longer lead the sort of life expected of a woman. Please make me a nun. Even if I were to return to society, someone in my situation would never be able to settle into a normal relationship."

"But you have such a long future ahead of you," the bishop counseled her. "Why is your heart so firmly fixed on this one desire? Becoming a nun may instead lead to regrets and attachments that will only increase your sins. You may think yourself strong enough at the time you stir your heart to action and make the decision, but being a woman, your resolve will waver as the years go by, and you will face many impediments to salvation."

"From the time I was a child," Ukifune replied, "I knew only heartache and misfortune, and for that reason my mother even told me once that she had thought about making me a nun. Later, after I came to understand things a little better, I had no desire to live as a normal woman, but increasingly focused my thoughts and placed my hopes on the world to come. Now I feel as if I'm on the verge of collapse and that death is gradually drawing nearer. So I ask you again . . . please . . ." She was crying as she spoke.

It makes no sense. What could have made someone so beautiful despise her life so much? Even the spirit that possessed her said that she wanted to die. Making this connection, the bishop considered her request. *She certainly has good cause to feel the way she does. In fact, it's amazing that she's managed to live this long. Having been possessed once by such an evil creature, she's in terrible danger.*

"Despite my reservations, the Buddha himself[5] would praise the merits of your stated resolve. So who am I, a priest, to stand in your way? It is no trouble to administer the vows to you, but because I've been called out on an urgent matter, I have to go to the palace tonight. Starting tomorrow I must undertake healing rites for the First Princess. It will take about seven days to complete, and when I withdraw from the palace, I'll drop by here on the way back and perform the ceremony for you."

Ukifune was bitterly disappointed to hear that, for she knew that if the nun were back by then, she would most certainly object.

"I'm suffering just as much as when you administered to me the vows to uphold the Five Precepts. If my condition worsens, I fear that taking vows to become a nun will do no good at all. I would be grateful if you could do the ceremony today."

She was weeping so violently that she moved his pious heart to pity. "It's late, isn't it? In the old days I never gave a thought to going up and down this mountain, but as the years pass by it's getting harder for me to bear the strain, and so I thought I should rest here on my way to the palace. If you're really in such a hurry to take your vows, then I'll carry them out today."

Ukifune was overjoyed. She picked up a pair of scissors and pushed the lid of a comb box toward the bishop.

---

5. The text uses the phrase "the Three Treasures" (*sanbō*—the Buddha, the Dharma/Law, the priesthood), but in this context the word refers to the Buddha.

"Come here, my noble disciples," he called out.

The two monks who had first discovered the young lady happened to be accompanying the bishop, and when they entered the room he told them, "Prepare to cut her hair."

The ascetic thought this was a reasonable course of action. *She was in such a terrible state when we found her, it would seem cruel to force her to remain in society as a laywoman.* Nevertheless, the length of hair that she had laid out through the gaps in the curtain panels was so beautiful that he hesitated for a moment, reluctant to use the scissors.

At that moment, Shōshō was in her own room talking with her older brother, who was also an ascetic, while Saemon was receiving another of the priests who was a personal acquaintance of hers.[6] Because visits from people close to the nuns were so rare at this out-of-the-way place, both women were preoccupied entertaining their guests, leaving the page girl, Komoki, as the only one attending the young lady. When Komoki reported to them what was happening, Shōshō rushed in a panic over to Ukifune's chambers, where she found the bishop helping the young lady, who did not have proper religious attire, put on one of his own outer robes and a surplice for the ceremony.

"This is merely for the sake of form," he said. "Now, please face in the direction of your parents and pay obeisance to them."

Ukifune had no idea which way to turn, and with the memory of her mother being too much for her to bear, she wept.

"Oh my dear . . . how distressing!" Shōshō exclaimed. "Why are you taking such an ill-advised step? What will my mistress say when she returns?"

We've already begun the ceremony, His Holiness thought, *and now that we've come this far, such talk will only serve to upset the young lady and put her in the wrong frame of mind.* He admonished Shōshō, preventing her from saying anything more or coming any closer to interfere.

"Turning round and round, wandering through the Three Realms where all is in flux . . . ," the bishop chanted.

At last, I've cut myself off from all obligations and attachments, Ukifune mused. Still, as she recalled the debt she owed her mother, taking this step made her sad.

The bishop's disciple was having difficulty cutting her hair. "In a quiet moment," the ascetic said, "have the nuns trim it up for you."

His Holiness clipped the locks around her forehead. "Never regret the change in your appearance," he told the young lady, and then instructed her in the noble truths. They had all advised against rushing into this, but how happy she felt to have finally renounced the world. She felt that only by taking this step did she have a sign from the Buddha that surviving had been worthwhile after all.

The bishop and his entourage departed for the capital and the residence fell silent. As the evening breeze rustled outside, the nuns let the young woman know of their disappointment. "You've been living in this forlorn house for some time, and given your situation, we were expecting that you would soon be leading an auspicious life with the Middle Captain. But now that you've taken this

6. Two attendants to whom the nun had entrusted Ukifune [editor's note].

drastic action, how do you plan to spend the many years of life that remain to you? It makes even those of us who are old and decrepit sad to think that a normal life is over for a woman when she becomes a nun."

Despite their comments, at that moment Ukifune felt only relief and joy. She had come to the point where she couldn't imagine having to live on in this world and so, for her, becoming a nun was a wonderful thing, one that brightened her mood and lifted her burdens.

Early the next morning, however, she was ashamed to see her changed appearance, in part because no one around her had agreed with her decision, which they considered thoughtless. The ends of her hair had been cut so carelessly that they had suddenly gone all wild and uneven. Ukifune wanted someone to come in—preferably without making any snide or disapproving comments—and dress her hair properly, but because she was by nature shy and timid, she remained in her room with the blinds down to keep it dark.

She had never been able to express her most private feelings easily. Moreover, she now had no confidante to whom she could open up. Thus, all she could do when her emotions were too much for her to hold in was sit down in front of her ink-stone and pour her heart into the poems she would scribble out under the pretext of practicing her calligraphy.

> Yet again have I turned my back on this world . . .
> A world I once renounced, thinking of myself
> And those I knew as not among the living

"By taking these vows, I've made an end of it at last," she wrote. Still, looking at her own poem, her heart was filled with sorrow and pity.

> Over and over have I turned my back
> On a world that I have been determined
> To make an end of once and for all time

As she sat scribbling other poems that expressed similar sentiments, a letter from the Middle Captain arrived. The old nuns had been shocked and stunned about what had happened, and in the midst of the uproar someone had sent word to the Middle Captain. He thought it a great shame, but he was also filled with regret and disappointment. *She was deeply determined to take this step, and that must be why she kept her distance and refused to reply to me, since she probably wanted to avoid any frivolous exchanges. But even so, what a drastic thing to do! The night I mentioned how much I wanted to get a closer look at her hair, which seemed so alluring that time I caught a glimpse of it, I was told, "All in due time."*

He sent off a reply: "I don't know what to say to you."

> I must make haste, for I do not wish to be late
> And fail to board the fishing boat that from this world
> Rows away, bearing a nun to that distant shore[7]

7. This poem (and the reply that follows) plays on the word *ama*, which can mean both "fisherman (or diver)" and "nun."

Ukifune made an exception and agreed to read his note. In that moment of intense emotion, how must she have felt, moved by the thought that now, indeed, it was over? Along the edge of a mere scrap of paper, she wrote the following, again under the pretense of practicing her calligraphy:

> *Though her heart is leaving behind the shore*
> *Of this woeful world, the destination*
> *Of the nun's drifting bark remains unknown*

Shōshō wrapped the poem up to send to the Middle Captain.

"You should make a cleaner copy of it first," Ukifune said.

"But I might make an error if I do that," Shōshō replied, and sent it off just as it was.

It was a rare sight indeed to see a reply in the young lady's own hand. There are no words that can adequately describe the anguish the Middle Captain experienced.

The bishop's sister returned from her pilgrimage only to be deeply distressed to find out what had happened. "I'm aware that a woman in my position should be encouraging you for taking this step," she said to the young lady, "but you have so many years ahead of you, how are you going to get by? I have no idea how much longer I will live—I could pass away today or tomorrow—and so all my thoughts have been on ensuring that your future is secure once I'm gone. That's why I went to Hatsuse to pray to Kannon."

The nun was prostrate, writhing in grief. Ukifune found her extremely pitiful, but then she thought of her true mother and felt her heart break as she imagined just how terrible it must have been for a parent who had been left without even a body to mourn.

As usual, Ukifune was unresponsive and sat with her back to the nun. Because she looked so very tender and lovely, the nun couldn't hold back her tears as she remarked, "You certainly are a passive, fragile little thing!" She then made arrangements to provide her with the appropriate religious attire. A short outer robe and a surplice were tailored in the dark gray cloth that the nuns were accustomed to wearing. As the women there stitched the robes and tried them on the young lady, they vented their disappointment.

"She unexpectedly brought a radiant light to this mountain abode, and it was a joy to look at her every morning and evening. What a shame it's come to this!"

The women also expressed their resentment of the bishop and bitterly criticized his actions.

* * *

When the First Princess had completely recovered, the bishop returned to Yokawa. On the way he dropped by the residence in Ono, where he was met with a bitter outburst from his sister.

"You may have intended to set her on the path to salvation in the next life, but she is still young and beautiful, and if she comes to regret her decision, your rash actions will stir lingering attachments that will surely add to the burden of her sins. Why didn't you consult with me first? It's incomprehensible!" The nun's complaints, however, were useless at this point.

"You must now concentrate solely on your devotions," the bishop told Ukifune. "No one, neither the old nor the young, knows how long they have to live. The fact that you have rejected this world as a fleeting illusion is the proper frame of mind for someone in your situation."

His words were mortifying to Ukifune, for they were reminders that he had earlier witnessed her wretched condition.

The bishop brought out the damask, gauze and silk cloth he had received from Her Majesty as a reward for his services. "Take these," he told Ukifune, "and have a new habit made for you. So long as I'm alive, I'll do what I can to assist you. Nothing need worry you. We're all born creatures of this vulgar world, and insofar as we're pressured by our attachments and desire for its glories, it seems that all people find renunciation difficult. Why would anyone in your position, pursuing religious devotions in the midst of this forest, ever have cause to feel regret or shame?"

And so he instructed her, finishing with two lines from Bai Juyi: "Life is as thin and fragile as a leaf on a tree. The moon wanders through the sky until dawn breaks over the pines at the gate."[8] He may have been a monk, but to Ukifune, who sat there listening to him speak in his formidably elegant and erudite manner, he was saying things that she very much wanted to hear.

The wind, which blew all day long, sounded forlorn and melancholy. She heard the bishop saying, "On a day like this, even a hermit in the mountains is moved to weep aloud."

Am I not also a hermit now? Ukifune asked herself. *That must be the reason why I cannot stop my tears.*

She stood up and moved toward the edge of the veranda. Looking out at the valley spreading off into the distance, she saw a hunting party of men dressed in robes of various hues. Although they were heading up Mount Hiei, it was unusual for anyone to travel along the path that ran past the residence here. Once in a great while she might catch sight of a monk walking along from the direction of Kurodani, but to see a layperson out here was rarer still. Then she realized that the party belonged to the Middle Captain, who had been so aggrieved by her behavior.

He was visiting with the intent of making yet another of his complaints—useless though they were now—but because the autumn foliage was so delightful, having turned a deeper crimson here than in other places, he was enchanted, his mind distracted, from the moment he entered the valley.

How astonishing it would be to come across a beautiful woman in a place like this, he thought.

"I had some free time," he told the nun, "and feeling bored, I took to imagining how lovely the autumn leaves must look right now. Even your trees seem to beckon me to lodge for the night beneath their sheltering shade."

He was seated on the south-facing veranda, gazing around at the view. The nun, lachrymose as ever, composed the following:

8. Poem from *Collected Writings of Bo Juyi* [editor's note].

The chill blasts of late autumn sweep
The mountain's base, wither the trees
Leave no sheltering shade for you

The Middle Captain replied:

I know no one awaits me, but gazing
At the treetops in this mountain village
It is hard for me to just pass them by

He continued talking on and on about the young lady, though words could do nothing to win her now. "Do let me steal a glance of her to see how her appearance has changed," he pleaded with Shōshō. "You can at least do that much, as a token of the promise you once made to me."

Because he pressed her this way, Shōshō went inside, and when she saw how beautiful Ukifune looked, she felt the urge to do anything she could to show the young lady to the Middle Captain. Wearing subtly figured robes of simple, serene colors—light gray over pale orange-brown—she had a dainty physique, lithe and elegant, her face had a bright, modern appeal, and the ends of her hair, thick and abundant, spread across her back and shoulders like an opened multiribbed fan. Her fine complexion and delicate features gave off a lambent, rosy glow, as if she had applied her makeup with exquisite care.

Shōshō wanted to paint a picture to capture the scene of Ukifune performing her devotions, absorbed in reading a sutra with a rosary hanging from the frame of the standing curtain next to her.

Each time I see her like this, Shōshō reflected, *I'm moved to tears. And if I feel that way, how much more intense would be the reaction of a man whose heart was drawn to her?* Thinking that perhaps this was the appropriate moment to act, she let the Middle Captain know that there was a small opening just beneath the latch on the sliding door, and then moved aside the standing curtain that might otherwise have obstructed his view.

Seeing the young lady for the first time, the Middle Captain was filled with regret, resentment and sorrow, as if he himself were somehow to blame for what had happened. *I never once imagined that she was this beautiful. For a woman so extraordinary, so perfect in all respects, to have become a nun . . .* He could not contain his emotions and so he withdrew before she could hear him weeping madly, as if he had taken leave of his senses.

* * *

KAMO NO CHŌMEI

ca. 1155–1216

Retreating from civilization in times of crisis has a long history in East Asia. Since antiquity, there have been legends of extraordinary individuals who became recluses to stay true to themselves, or to their dynasties and lords. It was in the spirit of this tradition and in pursuit of Buddhism that Kamo no Chōmei decided to retreat into a mountain hut outside the capital, devoting himself to "An Account of a Ten-Foot-Square Hut." In this most poignant of Japanese essays on life in reclusion he evokes visions of disturbing destruction in the capital and of furtive pleasures in his mountain hut, attempting to come to terms with the impermanence of the world and the futility of people's attempts to find illusory stability in their houses, in their possessions, or in other people.

Chōmei came from the venerable Kamo family, a lineage of Shinto priests serving the Kamo Shrine north of Kyoto. Although he lost his father in his teens he received an extensive education in poetry and music. This earned him in 1201 a prestigious invitation from the retired Emperor GoToba to serve in the Imperial Poetry Office, the bureau that compiled imperial poetry anthologies in the tradition of **The Kokinshū**. Some of the poems he wrote at the time prefigure his later life of contemplation. In one composed for a poetry contest at court, which the emperor singled out for particular praise, Chōmei said:

> All night long,
> Alone in the deep mountains.
> But then: though clouded in sight,
> Shining through the needles of a
>   black pine,
> There is the moon of dawn.

In 1204, at around the age of fifty, Chōmei took Buddhist vows and retreated into the mountains. He had failed to receive a position at the Kamo Shrine, on which he had long pinned his hopes, and even the emperor's hasty creation of an alternative post at the shrine could not keep him in the capital. After a few years in Ōhara, northeast of Kyoto, he built a hut near Hino Mountain, southeast of Kyoto, where in 1212 he wrote "An Account of a Ten-Foot-Square Hut." In his time Chōmei was famous as a poet and the author of a manual of poetic lore, which contained his reflections on the poetic value of "mysterious depth" (*yūgen*). This notion later became a cardinal concept in the aesthetics of Zen, Noh theater, tea ceremony, linked verse, and haiku. Chōmei also compiled *Tales of Awakening,* a collection of Buddhist tales designed to guide people toward deeper understanding and salvation. But the work that has made him memorable for readers through the ages is undoubtedly the account of his life in reclusion.

Chōmei lived through the tumultuous decades of transition from the splendid aristocratic world of the Heian court in Kyoto (794–1185) to the austere medieval world of warrior rule, when shoguns—military rulers—took control over the disempowered imperial court and ruled the country from Kamakura near modern-day Tokyo. Experiencing this watershed moment of Japanese history was disorienting enough, but Chōmei and his contemporaries were convinced that they lived in the "Latter Day of the Law" (mappō)—the third and most degraded era of Buddhism. According to the cyclical cosmology developed in

Tang China (618–907), evil and disaster would prevail during this last period and the teachings of the historical Buddha (fifth century B.C.E.) would lose their power. Sensing such an age approaching, many aristocrats retreated to the countryside, took holy vows, and devoted themselves exclusively to holy practices or a contemplative life spent on literary and artistic pursuits.

Like Yoshida Kenkō's famous *Essays in Idleness*, which was written a good century later, Chōmei's "An Account of a Ten-Foot-Square Hut" belongs to the "recluse literature" produced by medieval writers who, when confronted with the chaos of life, took solace in Buddhism, poetry, and other artistic pursuits. The "Account" is written in an elegant mixture of Japanese and Chinese-style diction and rhetoric. It weds flamboyant poetic imagery to scholastic parallel phrasings, which are a hallmark of Buddhist literature. This hybrid style is emblematic of the nuanced tensions in Chōmei's life and work. He is an anxious victim, but also an ironic witness of his time. In moments of ironic distance he derides humans for their deluded efforts to build houses and amass possessions, offering us darkly beautiful images of destruction: fires unfolding like gorgeous fans, house shingles whirling through the air like alluring winter leaves.

Beautiful images also enable Chōmei to capture futility in less disturbing, more transcendental terms. You will never look at rivers quite in the same way once you have grasped the essay's memorable opening metaphors for impermanence: rivers, foam, dew, morning glories. But the attachments to the hut that Chōmei proudly calls his own, to the leather trunks that hold his books of poetry and music, to his musical instruments, and ultimately even to the idea of tranquillity in his recluse life seem to cause him equal amounts of pleasure and guilt. Although he counts out loud for his readers how he gradually downsized his livelihood from his family's large house to the mere ten squares of his recluse hut, the very sin of attachment to things remains. Does his recitation of the name of Amida Buddha, who promises rebirth in a western paradise, the "Pure Land," relieve him of his existential worries? Can writing, poetry, or music be a saving grace, although they too belong to the world of attachments that ultimately create suffering?

Written by an evocative recluse poet who had made a radical life choice during a tumultuous, transitional period, "An Account of a Ten-Foot-Square Hut" offers us shocking and pleasurable insights into the "ephemeral, locust-shell world" of Japan's Middle Ages.

An Account of a Ten-Foot-Square Hut[1]

The current of the flowing river does not cease, and yet the water is not the same water as before. The foam that floats on stagnant pools, now vanishing, now forming, never stays the same for long. So, too, it is with the people and dwellings of the world. In the capital, lovely as if paved with jewels, houses of the high and low, their ridges aligned and roof tiles contending, never disappear however many ages pass, and yet if we examine whether this is true, we will rarely find a house remaining as it used to be. Perhaps it burned down last year and has been rebuilt. Perhaps a large house has crumbled and become a small one. The people living inside the houses are no different. The place may be the same capital and the people numerous, but only one or two in twenty or

1. Translated by and with footnotes adapted from Anthony H. Chambers, who has supplied the bracketed material in the text.

thirty is someone I knew in the past. One will die in the morning and another will be born in the evening: such is the way of the world, and in this we are like the foam on the water. I know neither whence the newborn come nor whither go the dead. For whose sake do we trouble our minds over these temporary dwellings, and why do they delight our eyes? This, too, I do not understand. In competing for impermanence, dweller and dwelling are no different from the morning glory and the dew. Perhaps the dew will fall and the blossom linger. But even though it lingers, it will wither in the morning sun. Perhaps the blossom will wilt and the dew remain. But even though it remains, it will not wait for evening.

In the more than forty springs and autumns that have passed since I began to understand the nature of the world, I have seen many unexpected things. I think it was on the twenty-eighth of the Fourth Month of Angen 3 [1177]. Around eight o'clock on a windy, noisy night, a fire broke out in the southeastern part of the capital and spread to the northwest. Finally it reached Suzaku Gate, the Great Hall of State, the university, and the Popular Affairs Ministry, and in the space of a night they all turned to dust and ash. The source of the fire is said to have been the intersection of Higuchi and Tominokōji, in makeshift housing occupied by *bugaku* dancers.[2] Carried here and there in the violent wind, the fire spread outward like a fan unfolding. Distant houses choked on smoke; nearby, wind drove the flames against the ground. In the sky, ashes blown up by the wind reflected the light of the fire, while wind-scattered flames spread through the overarching red in leaps of one and two blocks. Those who were caught in the fire must have been frantic. Some choked on the smoke and collapsed; some were overtaken by the flames and died instantly. Some barely escaped with their lives but could not carry out their possessions. The Seven Rarities and ten thousand treasures[3] all were reduced to ashes. How great the losses must have been. At that time, the houses of sixteen high nobles burned, not to mention countless lesser homes. Altogether, it is said that fire engulfed one-third of the capital. Thousands of men and women died, and more horses, oxen, and the like than one can tell. All human endeavors are foolish, but among them, spending one's fortune and troubling one's mind to build a house in such a dangerous capital is particularly vain.

Then, in the Fourth Month of Jishō 4 [1180], a great whirlwind arose near the intersection of Nakanomikado and Kyōgoku and raged as far as the Rokujō District. Because it blew savagely for three or four blocks, not a single house within them, large or small, escaped destruction. Some were flattened; some were reduced to nothing more than posts and beams. Blowing gates away, the wind carried them four or five blocks and set them down; blowing fences away, it joined neighboring properties into one. Naturally, all the possessions inside these houses were lifted into the sky, while cypress bark, boards, and other roofing materials mingled in the wind like winter leaves. The whirlwind blew up dust as thick as smoke so that nothing could be seen, and in its dreadful roar no voices could be heard. One felt that even the winds of retribution in hell could be no worse than this. Not only were houses damaged or lost, but

2. Performers of a stately dance introduced from China.
3. Things of immense value. The "Seven Rari-

ties" named in Buddhist texts were precious substances (variously identified in different translations at different times).

countless men were injured or crippled in rebuilding them. As it moved toward the south-southwest, the wind was a cause of grief to many people. Whirlwinds often blow, but are they ever like this? It was something extraordinary. One feared that it might be a portent.

Then, in the Sixth Month of the same year, the capital was abruptly moved.[4] The relocation was completely unexpected. According to what I have heard, Kyoto was established as the capital more than four hundred years ago, during the reign of the Saga emperor. The relocation of the capital is not something that can be undertaken easily, for no special reason, and so it is only natural that the people were uneasy with this move and lamented together about it. Objections having no effect, however, the emperor, the ministers, and all the other high nobles moved. Of those who served at court, who would stay behind in the old capital? Those who vested their hopes in government appointments or in rank, or depended on the favor of their masters, wasted not a day in moving, while those who had missed their chance, who had been left behind by the world, and who had nothing to look forward to, stayed sorrowfully where they were. Dwellings, their eaves contending, went to ruin with the passing days. Houses were disassembled and floated down the Yodo River as the land turned into fields before one's eyes. Men's hearts changed; now they valued only horses and saddles. No one used oxen and carriages any more. People coveted property in the southwest and scorned manors in the northeast. At that time I had occasion to go to the new capital, in the province of Tsu. I saw that there was insufficient room to lay out a grid of streets and avenues, the area being small. To the north, the city pressed against the mountains and, to the south, dropped off toward the sea. The roar of waves never slackened; a violent wind blew in off the saltwater. The palace stood in the mountains. Did that hall of logs[5] look like this? It was novel and, in its way, elegant. Where did they erect the houses they had torn down day by day and brought downstream, constricting the river's flow? Open land was still plentiful, houses few. Even though the old capital had become a wasteland, the new capital was yet unfinished. Everyone felt like the drifting clouds. Those who had lived here before complained about losing their land. Those who had newly moved here bemoaned the pains of construction. In the streets, I saw that those who should have used carriages rode on horses, and most of those who should have dressed in court robes and headgear wore simple robes instead. The ways of the capital had changed abruptly; now they were no different from the ways of rustic samurai. I heard that these developments were portents of disorder in the land, and it turned out to be so: day by day the world grew more unsettled and the people more uneasy, and their fears proved to be well founded, so that in the winter of the same year the court returned to this capital.[6] But what became of all the houses that had been torn down? Not all of them were rebuilt as they had stood before.

4. Kiyomori, the overbearing leader of the Taira clan, had the capital temporarily moved from Kyoto to Fukuhara, near today's Kobe, in 1180. This was an unprecedented show of power by a warrior (samurai) clan against the imperial court. Events surrounding the rise and fall of the Taira (also called Heike) are told in the warrior epic The Tales of the Heike.
5. A primitive temporary palace of logs built by a 7th-century empress.
6. The court quickly returned from Fukuhara to Kyoto, and within a few years the Taira clan was exterminated.

I have heard that in venerable reigns of ancient times, emperors governed the nation with compassion: roofing his palace with thatch, Yao of China refrained from even trimming the eaves; seeing how thin the smoke that rose from the people's hearths, Nintoku of Japan[7] forgave even the lowest taxes. They did so because they took pity on the people and tried to help them. By measuring it against the past, we can know the state of the present.

Then, was it in the Yōwa era [1181–1182]?—long ago, and so I do not remember well, the world suffered a two-year famine, and dreadful things occurred. Droughts in spring and summer, typhoons and floods in fall—adversities followed one after another, and none of the five grains ripened. In vain the soil was turned in the spring and crops planted in the summer, but lost was the excitement of autumn harvests and of the winter laying-in. Consequently, people in the provinces abandoned their lands and wandered to other regions, or forgot their houses and went to live in the mountains. Various royal prayers were initiated and extraordinary Esoteric Buddhist rites were performed, to no effect whatever. It was the habit of the capital to depend on the countryside for everything, but nothing was making its way to the capital now. How long could the residents maintain their equanimity? As their endurance wore down, they tried to dispose of their valuables as if throwing them away, but no one showed any interest. The few who did engage in barter despised gold and cherished millet. Beggars lined the streets, their pleas and lamentations filling one's ears. In this way, the first year struggled to a close. Surely the new year would bring improvement, one thought, but on top of the famine came an epidemic, and conditions only got worse. The metaphor of fish in a shrinking pool fit the situation well, as people running out of food grew more desperate by the day. In the end, well-dressed men wearing lacquered sedge hats, their skirts wrapped around their legs, went intently begging house to house. One would see them walking, exhausted and confused, then collapse, their faces to the ground. The corpses of people who had starved to death lay along the earthen walls, and in the streets, their numbers were beyond reckoning. A stench filled the world, as no one knew how to dispose of so many corpses, and often one could not bear to look at the decomposing faces and bodies. There was not even room for horses and carriages to pass on the Kamo riverbed. As lowly peasants and woodcutters exhausted their strength, firewood, too, came to be in short supply, and so people with no other resources tore apart their own houses and carried off the lumber to sell at market. I heard that the value of what one man could carry was not enough to sustain him for a single day. Strangely, mixed in among the firewood were sticks bearing traces here and there of red lacquer, or of gold and silver leaf, because people with nowhere else to turn had stolen Buddhist images from old temples and ripped out temple furnishings, which they broke into pieces. I saw such cruel sights because I was born into this impure, evil age.[8] There were many pathetic sights as well. Of those who had wives or husbands from whom they could not part, the ones whose love was stronger always died first. The reason is that putting themselves second and pitying the others, they gave their mates what little food they found. So it was that when parents and

7. An early Chinese and an early Japanese emperor; both are known for benevolent rule and compassion toward the people.
8. The last of the three periods in Buddhist cosmology: the age of the "degenerated Law," when the teachings of the Buddha still survived but were no longer put into practice.

children lived together, the parents invariably died first. I also saw a small child who, not knowing that his mother was dead, lay beside her, sucking at her breast.

The eminent priest Ryūgyō of Ninna Temple,[9] grieving over these countless deaths, wrote the first letter of the Sanskrit alphabet on the foreheads of all the dead he saw, thereby linking them to the Buddha. Wanting to know how many had died, he counted the bodies he found during the Fourth and Fifth Months. Within the capital, between Ichijō on the north and Kujō on the south, between Kyōgoku on the east and Suzaku on the west, more than 42,300 corpses lay in the streets. Of course, many others died before and after this period, and if we include those on the Kamo riverbed, in Shirakawa, in the western half of the capital, and in the countryside beyond, their numbers would be limitless. How vast the numbers must have been, then, in all the provinces along the Seven Highways. I have heard that something of the sort occurred in the Chōjō era [1134], during the reign of Emperor Sutoku, but I do not know how things were then. What I saw before my own eyes was extraordinary.

Then—was it at about the same time?—a dreadful earthquake shook the land. The effects were remarkable. Mountains crumbled and dammed the rivers; the sea tilted and inundated the land. The earth split open and water gushed forth; boulders broke off and tumbled into valleys. Boats rowing near the shore were carried off on the waves; horses on the road knew not where to place their hooves. Around the capital, not a single shrine or temple survived intact. Some fell apart; others toppled over. Dust and ash rose like billows of smoke. The sound of the earth's movement and of houses collapsing was no different from thunder. People who were inside their houses might be crushed in a moment. Those who ran outside found the earth splitting asunder. Lacking wings, one could not fly into the sky. If one were a dragon, one would ride the clouds. I knew then that earthquakes were the most terrible of all the many terrifying things. The dreadful shaking stopped after a time, but the aftershocks continued. Not a day passed without twenty or thirty quakes strong enough to startle one under ordinary circumstances. As ten and twenty days elapsed, gradually the intervals grew longer—four or five a day, then two or three, one every other day, one in two or three days—but the aftershocks went on for perhaps three months. Of the four great elements, water, fire, and wind constantly bring disaster, but for its part, earth normally brings no calamity. In ancient times—was it during the Saikō era [855]?—there was a great earthquake and many terrible things occurred, such as the head falling from the Buddha at Tōdai Temple,[1] but, they say, even that was not as bad as this. Everyone spoke of futility, and the delusion in their hearts seemed to diminish a little at the time; but after days and months piled up and years went by, no one gave voice to such thoughts any longer.

All in all, life in this world is difficult; the fragility and transience of our bodies and dwellings are indeed as I have said. We cannot reckon the many ways in which we trouble our hearts according to where we live and in obedience to our status. He who is of trifling rank but lives near the gates of power cannot rejoice with abandon, however deep his happiness may be, and when his sorrow is keen, he does not wail aloud. Anxious about his every move, trembling with fear

9. A temple in Kyoto with close ties to the imperial family.
1. One of the great temples in Nara, the ancient capital before Kyoto was founded. The famous monumental Buddha statue in this temple is now known as the "Great Buddha." See the illustration on p. 1164.

no matter what he does, he is like a sparrow near a hawk's nest. One who is poor yet lives beside a wealthy house will grovel in and out, morning and evening, ashamed of his wretched figure. When he sees the envy that his wife, children, and servants feel for the neighbors, when he hears the rich family's disdain for him, his mind will be unsettled and never find peace. He who lives in a crowded place cannot escape damage from a fire nearby. He who lives outside the city contends with many difficulties as he goes back and forth and often suffers at the hands of robbers. The powerful man is consumed by greed; he who stands alone is mocked. Wealth brings many fears; poverty brings cruel hardship. Look to another for help and you will belong to him. Take someone under your wing, and your heart will be shackled by affection. Bend to the ways of the world and you will suffer. Bend not and you will look demented. Where can one live, and how can one behave to shelter this body briefly and to ease the heart for a moment?

I inherited my paternal grandmother's house and occupied it for some time. Then I lost my backing,[2] came down in the world, and even though the house was full of fond memories, I finally could live there no longer, and so I, past the age of thirty, resolved to build a hut. It was only one-tenth the size of my previous residence. Unable to construct a proper estate, I erected a house only for myself. I managed to build an earthen wall but lacked the means to raise a gate. Using bamboo posts, I sheltered my carriage. The place was not without its dangers whenever snow fell or the wind blew. Because the house was located near the riverbed, the threat of water damage was deep and the fear of robbers never ebbed. Altogether, I troubled my mind and endured life in this difficult world for more than thirty years. The disappointments I suffered during that time awakened me to my unfortunate lot.[3] Accordingly, when I greeted my fiftieth spring, I left my house and turned away from the world. I had no wife or children, and so there were no relatives whom it would have been difficult to leave behind. As I had neither office nor stipend, what was there for me to cling to? Vainly, I spent five springs and autumns living in seclusion among the clouds on Mount Ōhara.[4]

Reaching the age of sixty, when I seemed about to fade away like the dew, I constructed a new shelter for the remaining leaves of my life. I was like a traveler who builds a lodging for one night only or like an aged silkworm spinning its cocoon. The result was less than a hundredth the size of the residence of my middle age. In the course of things, years have piled up and my residences have steadily shrunk. This one is like no ordinary house. In area it is only ten feet square; in height, less than seven feet. Because I do not choose a particular place to live, I do not acquire land on which to build. I lay a foundation, put up a simple, makeshift roof, and secure each joint with a latch. This is so that I can easily move the building if anything dissatisfies me. How much bother can it be to reconstruct it? It fills only two carts, and there is no expense beyond payment for the porters.

Now, having hidden my tracks and gone into seclusion in the depths of Mount Hino,[5] I extended the eaves more than three feet to the east, making a convenient place to break and burn brushwood. On the south I made a bamboo

2. Probably a reference to the death of his father.

3. Chōmei came from a family of Shinto priests at the Kamo Shrine in Kyoto. He was greatly disappointed when he failed to secure a position at the shrine.

4. Northeast of the capital.

5. Southeast of the capital, where Chōmei wrote this account.

veranda, on the west of which I built a water-shelf for offerings to the Buddha, and to the north, behind a screen, I installed a painting of Amida Buddha, next to it hung Fugen,[6] and before it placed the Lotus Sutra. Along the east side I spread soft ferns, making a bed for the night. In the southwest, I constructed hanging shelves of bamboo and placed there three black leather trunks. In them I keep selected writings on Japanese poetry and music, and the *Essentials of Salvation*. A koto and a biwa[7] stand to one side. They are what are called a folding koto and a joined lute. Such is the state of my temporary hut. As for the location: to the south is a raised bamboo pipe. Piling up stones, I let water collect there. Because the woods are near, kindling is easy to gather. The name of the place is Toyama. Vines cover all tracks. Although the ravines are overgrown, the view is open to the west. The conditions are not unfavorable for contemplating the Pure Land of the West. In spring I see waves of wisteria. They glow in the west like lavender clouds. In summer I hear the cuckoo. Whenever I converse with him, he promises to guide me across the mountain path of death. In autumn the voices of twilight cicadas fill my ears. They sound as though they are mourning this ephemeral, locust-shell world. In winter I look with deep emotion upon the snow. Accumulating and melting, it can be compared to the effects of bad karma. When I tire of reciting the Buddha's name or lose interest in reading the sutras aloud, I rest as I please, I dawdle as I like. There is no one to stop me, no one before whom to feel ashamed. Although I have taken no vow of silence, I live alone and so surely can avoid committing transgressions of speech. Although I do not go out of my way to observe the rules that an ascetic must obey, what could lead me to break them, there being no distractions here? In the morning, I might gaze at the ships sailing to and from Okanoya, comparing myself to the whitecaps behind them, and compose verses in the elegant style of the novice-priest Manzei;[8] in the evening, when the wind rustles the leaves of the *katsura* trees, I might turn my thoughts to the Xunyang River and play my biwa in the way of Gen Totoku.[9] If my enthusiasm continues unabated, I might accompany the sound of the pines with "Autumn Winds" or play "Flowing Spring" to the sound of the water. Although I have no skill in these arts, I do not seek to please the ears of others. Playing to myself, singing to myself, I simply nourish my own mind.

At the foot of the mountain is another brushwood hut, the home of the caretaker of this mountain. A small child lives there. Now and then he comes to visit. When I have nothing else to do, I take a walk with him as my companion. He is ten years old; I am sixty. Despite the great difference in our ages, our pleasure is the same. Sometimes we pluck edible reed-flowers, pick pearberries, break off yam bulbils, or gather parsley. Sometimes we go to the paddies at the foot of the mountain, collect fallen ears of rice, and tie them into

6. A bodhisattva (enlightened being), widely worshipped by Japanese Buddhists; he is often shown seated on an elephant, symbolizing the slow and steady progress toward enlightenment. Amida Buddha presided over the Pure Land paradise, where anyone who appealed to him by reciting his name—as Chōmei does in the end of this account—could be reborn.
7. A pear-shaped four-stringed lute.
8. An 8th-century poet who took Buddhist

vows and thus a model for Chōmei, who alludes here to Manzei's best-known poem: "To what shall I compare the world? Whitecaps behind a ship that rows out at dawn." (Only a few of Chōmei's many allusions to Japanese and Chinese poems are cited in these notes.)
9. The founder (1016–1097) of a particular Japanese school of biwa playing. Xunyang River is where the Chinese poet Bo Juyi (772–846) wrote his famous "Ballad of the Lute."

sheaves. If the weather is fair, we climb to the peak and gaze at the distant sky above my former home, or look at Mount Kohata, the villages of Fushimi, Toba, and Hatsukashi. Because a fine view has no master,[1] nothing interferes with our pleasure. When walking is no problem and we feel like going somewhere far, we follow the ridges from here, crossing Mount Sumi, passing Kasatori, and visit the temple at Iwama or worship at the Ishiyama temple. Then again, we might make our way across Awazu Plain and go to see the site where Semimaru lived, or cross the Tanakami River and visit the grave of Sarumaru Dayū.[2] On our return, depending on the season, we break off branches of blossoming cherry, seek out autumn foliage, pick ferns, or gather fruit. Some we offer to the Buddha, and some we bring home to remind us of our outing. When the night is quiet, I look at the moon at the window and think fondly of my old friends; I hear the cries of the monkey and wet my sleeve with tears.[3] Fireflies in the grass might be taken for fishing flares at distant Maki Island; the rain at dawn sounds like a gale blowing the leaves of the trees. When I hear the pheasant's song I wonder whether it might not be the voice of my father or mother; when the deer from the ridge draws tamely near I know how far I have withdrawn from the world. Sometimes I dig up embers to keep me company when, as old men do, I waken in the night. This is not a fearful mountain, and so I listen closely to the owl's call. Thus from season to season the charms of mountain scenery are never exhausted. Of course one who thinks and understands more deeply than I would not be limited to these.

When I came to live in this place, I thought that I would stay for only a short time, but already five years have passed. Gradually my temporary hut has come to feel like home as dead leaves lie deep on the eaves and moss grows on the foundation. When news of the capital happens to reach me, I learn that many of high rank have passed away since I secluded myself on this mountain. There is no way to know how many of lower rank have died. How many houses have been lost in the frequent fires? Only a temporary hut is peaceful and free of worry. It may be small, but it has a bed on which to lie at night and a place in which to sit by day. Nothing is lacking to shelter one person. The hermit crab prefers a small shell. This is because he knows himself. The osprey lives on rugged shores. The reason is that he fears people. I am like them. Knowing myself and knowing the world, I have no ambitions, I do not strive. I simply seek tranquillity and enjoy the absence of care. It is common practice in the world that people do not always build dwellings for themselves. Some might build for their wives and children, their relations and followers, some for their intimates and friends. Some might build for their masters or teachers, even for valuables, oxen, and horses. I now have built a hut for myself. I do not build for others. The reason is that given the state of the world now and my own circumstances, there is neither anyone I should live with and look after, nor any dependable servant. Even if I had built a large place, whom would I shelter, whom would I have live in it?

When it comes to friends, people respect the wealthy and prefer the suave. They do not always love the warmhearted or the upright. Surely it is best simply to make friends with strings and woodwinds, blossoms and the moon. When it

1. From a couplet by Bo Juyi: "A fine view has no particular master. Mountains belong to those who love mountains."
2. Semimaru and Sarumaru were earlier Heian poets to whom many legends became attached.
3. In Chinese poetry, monkey cries are considered sad.

comes to servants, they value a large bonus and generous favors. They do not seek to be nurtured and loved, to work quietly and at ease. It is best simply to make my body my servant. How? If there is something to be done, I use my own body. This can be a nuisance, but it is easier than employing and looking after someone else. If I have to go out, I walk. This can be painful, but it is not as bad as troubling my mind over the horse, the saddle, the ox, the carriage. Now I divide my single body and use it in two ways. My hands are my servants, my legs my conveyance, and they do just as I wish. Because my mind understands my body's distress, I rest my body when it feels distressed, use it when it feels strong. [And] though I use it, I do not overwork it. When my body does not want to work, my mind is not annoyed. Needless to say, walking regularly and working regularly must promote good health. How can I idle the time away doing nothing? To trouble others is bad karma. Why should I borrow the strength of another? It is the same for clothing and food. Using what comes to hand, I cover my skin with clothing woven from the bark of wisteria vines and with a hempen quilt, and sustain my life with asters of the field and fruits of the trees on the peak. Because I do not mingle with others, I am not embarrassed by my appearance. Because food is scarce, my crude rewards taste good. My description of these pleasures is not directed at the wealthy. I am comparing my own past only with my present.

The Three Worlds exist only in the one mind.[4] If the mind is not at peace, elephants, horses, and the Seven Rarities will be worthless; palaces and pavilions will have no appeal. My present dwelling is a lonely, one-room hut, but I love it. When I happen to venture into the capital, I feel ashamed of my beggarly appearance, but when I come back and stay here, I pity those others who rush about in the worldly dust. Should anyone doubt what I am saying, I would ask them to look at the fishes and birds. A fish never tires of water. One who is not a fish cannot know a fish's mind. Birds prefer the forest. One who is not a bird cannot know a bird's mind. The savor of life in seclusion is the same. Who can understand it without living it?

Well, now, the moon of my life span is sinking in the sky; the time remaining to me nears the mountaintops. Soon I shall set out for the darkness of the Three Paths.[5] About what should I complain at this late date? The essence of the Buddha's teachings is that we should cling to nothing. Loving my grass hut is wrong. Attachment to my quiet, solitary way of life, too, must interfere with my enlightenment. Why then do I go on spending precious time relating useless pleasures?

Pondering this truth on a tranquil morning, just before dawn, I ask my mind: one leaves the world and enters the forest to cultivate the mind and practice the Way of the Buddha. In your case, however, although your appearance is that of a monk, your mind is clouded with desire. You have presumed to model your dwelling after none other than that of Vimalakirti, but your adherence to the discipline fails even to approach the efforts of Suddhipanthaka.[6] Is this

4. It is a basic Buddhist belief that the phenomena in the world are constructs of our minds, without objective existence. The "Three Worlds," in order of the level of enlightenment of their inhabitants, are the world of desire, the world of form, and the world of formlessness.
5. Human beings who had committed wrongs were believed to be reborn into one of three lesser "paths": as hell creatures, animals, or hungry ghosts.
6. The most foolish of the Buddha's disciples, who nevertheless ultimately achieved enlightenment. "Vimalakirti": a wealthy man who achieved enlightenment even without becoming a monk.

because poverty, a karmic retribution, torments your mind, or is it that a deluded mind had deranged you? At that time, my mind had no reply. I simply set my tongue to work halfheartedly reciting the name of the compassionate Amida Buddha two or three times, and that is all.

The monk Ren'in[7] wrote this late in the Third Month of Kenryaku 2 [1212], at his hut on Toyama.

7. Chōmei's religious name.

THE TALES OF THE HEIKE
fourteenth century

No other work in Japanese literature can match *The Tales of the Heike* in its appeal to the popular imagination. Besides helping to create the samurai ideal, it has offered its Japanese readers practically everything: heroic spirit, dramatic energy, vivid description, musical language, humor, and pathos. The tale re-creates events of the late twelfth century, which brought vast changes to Japanese political life, including the eclipse of the aristocracy and the rise and fall of great military clans. The tale's pitch-perfect rendering of the theme of evanescence—the notion that all who flourish are destined to fail and humankind is but dust before the wind—touches a chord that resonates throughout Japanese culture. As a result, *The Tales of the Heike* has influenced more writers in more subsequent genres, from medieval Noh plays to modern television dramas, than any other work of Japanese literature.

THE GENPEI WARS (1180–85)

The Tales of the Heike enshrined the memory of the Genpei Wars, fought between the Minamoto clan (whose Sino-Japanese designation was *Genji*) and the Taira clan (or *Heike* in Sino-Japanese). These wars marked the transition from the court-centered ancient period to the medieval period, which came to be dominated by military clans. At the beginning of the twelfth century the power of the court nobility was slowly declining, as the central bureaucracy and its local branches atrophied. A power vacuum began to form in the provinces, and the governors and their agents who had been deputized to maintain law and order gradually emerged as a warrior class. By the middle of the century the court administration was in paralysis. Retired emperors ruled behind the throne while the Fujiwara, which had been the most prominent clan of the courtly civil aristocracy, clung to a mere shred of its previous authority. The explosion that eventually ignited civil war was a dispute over imperial succession in 1156. The winner enlisted the support of the two most powerful military clans, but in so doing set in motion their rise as independent political forces within the capital. In a predictable sequence of events, the two clans began to quarrel, and the defeated house withdrew to the eastern provinces. This was the Minamoto, or Genji. The ascendant clan of the Taira, or Heike, remained in the capital, where it enjoyed twenty years of arrogant splendor before the Genji finally took revenge. Fighting began in 1180 and raged on for five years. When it was over, the Heike had been annihilated, and the Genji established a military dictatorship based in the northeastern city of Kamakura that would rule Japan for two centuries.

ORIGIN AND VERSIONS OF *THE TALES*

Most likely, *The Tales of the Heike* originated as a collection of stories written down by priests associated with Buddhist temples from the oral performances by minstrels, who were often blind. These minstrels traveled the countryside reciting the daring feats and tender passions of the famous warriors of the Genpei Wars, accompanying their recitation on the biwa (a pear-shaped lute). These chanters re-created their narrative with every performance. As a text meant for oral performance *The Tales of the Heike* came to be preserved in many versions, which differ considerably in content and style and sometimes reflect adaptation to local audiences. Eventually more than a hundred variants came into being, but the one that has become standard and is translated here is the version set down by a man named Kakuichi, himself a biwa minstrel, in 1371. He shaped the disparate materials into a unified text of literary merit, framed by Buddhist moral sentiments. The seductive blend of oral qualities and elegant literary craft in Kakuichi's version accounts for some of the most striking features of *The Tales of the Heike*: formulaic language and imagery, the use of repetition and variation,

structural contrast in the sequence of episodes and in the portrayal of protagonists, stress on action, exaggeration, lists of names or precedents, and the use of parables and analogies from Chinese and Japanese history to lend weight and antique flair to particular plot twists or character depictions.

BUDDHIST FRAMEWORK

The Tales of the Heike is not only a chronicle of the struggles between the Heike and Genji clans. It is also a profound reflection on the Buddhist law of retribution, which was at work in the spectacular rise and utter defeat of the Heike clan and its leader, Taira no Kiyomori. His arrogance and selfish caprice set in motion the events leading up to the Genpei Wars, and his horrible death, marked by violent convulsions and ominous fevers accompanied by insatiable thirst, prefigures the punishment that awaits him in hell as retribution for his actions in life. Although he dies in 1181, four years before the final defeat of his clan, Kiyomori's bad karma reaches beyond his grave, enables the Genji military successes, and induces the Heike's retreat from the capital and their final defeat in western Japan. Buddhist beliefs shape the broad narrative arch of *The Tales of the Heike* and the motivations of its protagonists. The awareness of the impermanence of all things, of the inevitability of disillusionment in life, and of the possibilities of awakening to the truth through Buddhist faith is the baseline of *The Tales* from its first to its final lines. Pure Land Buddhism, still today one of the most popular of the many schools of Buddhism, is particularly prominent in *The Tales of the Heike*. It promises its believers rebirth in a western paradise presided over by the Amida Buddha, the "Buddha of Infinite Light." Again and again characters in *The Tales of the Heike* will face west, inspired by the hope for rebirth into the Pure Land, and invoke the name of this Buddha in their last moments before execution, death in battle, or suicide. And women, servants, and samurai will wish to stay alive only so that they can continue to pray for their dead husbands' and masters' favorable rebirth in the Pure Land.

STRUCTURE AND PLOT

Divided into twelve books and a concluding "Initiates' Book," *The Tales of the Heike* unfolds in three parts. The first part, books 1 through 6 (sometimes called "chapters"), focuses on the flamboyant character of Kiyomori, the head of the Heike clan, and portrays his conflicts with Retired Emperor GoShirakawa and various members of the Genji clan. After Kiyomori's miserable death in book 6, attention turns in the second part (books 7 through 12) to the Genji clan and three of their leaders: Yoritomo, who commands the Genji in the northeast and will establish Japan's first shogunate in Kamakura after the defeat of the Heike in 1185; his cousin, the brutish Yoshinaka, who for a time holds the capital and is eliminated by Yoritomo in 1184, when his ambitions get out of hand; and Yoritomo's youthful and brilliant half brother Yoshitsune, who deals a crippling blow to the Heike in the surprise attack at Ichi-no-tani in 1184 (book 9) and masterminds their final rout—the naval battle at Dan-no-ura in 1185 (book 11). In this battle Kiyomori's widow, Emperor Antoku (Kiyomori's grandson by his daughter Kenreimon'in), and virtually all the men of the clan are sent to their deaths at sea. Yet, although the second part of *The Tales of the Heike* depicts the resurgence and triumphal victory of the Genji, the main focus of the narrative is on a series of Heike figures whose various deaths result from their forefather Kiyomori's evil deeds. The third part, the "Initiates' Book," is considered a text containing secret knowledge in certain schools of Heike performance. A self-contained tale, it takes us into the calm aftermath of the Genpei Wars, to the mountain temple north of Kyoto. There Kiyomori's daughter Kenreimon'in, now a nun, spends her life praying for the repose of the souls of her son, Emperor Antoku, and of the other dead Heike. The former empress's loneliness and nostalgia for the past is evoked in richly lyrical passages and dramatic poetic imagery. *The Tales of the Heike* ends with her death.

Although *The Tales of the Heike* unfolds its sprawling narrative in twelve books with numerous chapters, subplots and digressions, and a parade of hundreds of protagonists, many of whom figure only a few times and disappear without further trace, the work has a powerful unity due to its Buddhist framework. It starts with the sound of the bells of the world's first Buddhist monastery in India, which echo the "impermanence of all things" and the universal lesson that "the proud do not prevail for long but vanish like a spring night's dream." And it finds its proper closure on a reconciliatory note with the "Initiates' Book," when the nun, the only survivor of the slain Heike, performs pious service for the clan. In the end she finds peace with Retired Emperor GoShirakawa, who comes to visit her in the wilderness and for whom she recapitulates in tears her fate and the demise of her clan in Buddhist terms. *The Tales of the Heike* can thus be seen as an offering to the dead Heike—a narrative prayer for the peaceful repose of their souls. In a world where the dead were considered powerful forces who could wreak havoc and misfortune (and whose vengeance in such forms as natural disasters, epidemics, and catastrophes caused entire capitals to be abandoned in early Japan), such a pious offering was not just meaningful but necessary.

The Tales of the Heike belongs to the genre of "warrior tales." This genre flourished in the medieval period, when the military houses came to prominence, after the court-centered aristocratic world of the Heian Period (794–1185) had come to an end with the Genpei Wars. It includes anything from dry chronicles documenting particular uprisings or wars to highly lyrical warrior romances aimed at exploring the emotional experiences of the protagonists. Some of these tales were written from the perspective of the victors; others, like *The Tales of the Heike*, empathized with the tragedy of the defeated. Many of the warrior tales took shape over time at the hands of several compilers and include episodes that circulated separately in collections of anecdotes. While the fact-oriented warrior chronicles were largely written in the official idiom of Chinese-style prose, the psychological warrior romances used a mixed Chinese–Japanese style. This hybrid stood between the language of Heian romantic tales such as *The Tale of Genji*, filled with poetry and lyrical imagery, and Chinese-style official prose, as evoked by the inclusion of highly formal imperial edicts, letters and petitions, prayers, Buddhist homilies, and a large array of allusions to Chinese Classics and official histories. In this way the Heike warriors appear in more than one dimension, both as romantic protagonists, with complex psychology and touching entourages of women, children, and servants, and as displaced court officials fallen from grace and power.

The cultivation of the courtly arts of poetry and music is particularly central in *The Tales of the Heike*. Its battles display carnage but relatively little brutality. Tadanori, Kiyomori's brother, risks his life when he briefly returns to the capital, which the Heike had already left in haste, just to ask the famous poet Shunzei to include some of his poems in the imperial anthology that Shunzei had been commissioned to compile (book 7.16). The Genji who later kills Tadanori identifies him from a signed poem fastened to the dead man's quiver, and that death brings tears to friends and foes alike—a sign of how highly all regarded courtly refinement (book 9.14).

Still, *The Tales of the Heike* brims with military action. A common convention in the depiction of battle scenes is to parade the warriors in their splendid outfits before the audience's eyes. Each warrior's robe, sword, arrows, horse, and saddle are described in loving detail; red brocade was reserved for heroes of highest social status, while black or dark colors indicated that the warrior belonged to a lesser order. Before engaging a foe in battle a warrior would announce his name in a thundering voice: there was a direct relation between the enemy's social status and the glory that his killing would bring. The winner would take the head of the defeated to prove his valor and success in battle. The head trophy was a symbol of victory, but it also served to identify the defeated. Grueling recognition scenes, in which relatives or former lovers must identify a slain head, are an important plot element in *The Tales of the Heike*, heightening the audience's emotional empathy. Warriors are the work's main subject, yet its point of view is closer to that of the courtiers—as if, despite the loss of the aristocracy's political and economic viability, this was the only group considered capable of appreciating the sad implications of the tale. As the loser in history's upheaval, it could be counted on to identify with the fate of the Heike. But the story had a far broader appeal, as courtly values were becoming common currency. Earlier, the thought that life's glory is as brief as a spring night's dream could have been expressed only in court poetry or the prose of a noblewoman. Now it became a message for the illiterate masses, who listened to the minstrels' lute performances.

The Tales of the Heike are chanted to the plucking of the pear-shaped biwa, a four-stringed instrument with frets. The performance schools that survive today use an eighteenth-century musical score that fixed the music, rather than relying on the improvisational skills of the individual performer. The three basic performance styles are simple declamation, intoned recitation, and a more elaborate aria-like mode of exposition. Some of the recurrent melodic formulas correspond to the content of the passage: there is a formula for prayers or religious scenes, a formula for battle scenes, a specific formula for the performance of poems, and a formula for passages radiating elegance and dignity.

The popularity of *Heike* performances reached its peak in the fourteenth and early fifteenth centuries, when this previously humble form became an upper-class performance art; many of the blind minstrels traveled to perform before regional feudal lords and samurai, in addition to performing in services at Buddhist temples and at poetry and tea gatherings in the residences of the nobility in Kyoto. With the rise of Noh theater in the fourteenth century, Heike heroes found their way into the repertoire of warrior dramas. And they inspired plays of the Kabuki theater and puppet theater, new urban forms of entertainment that developed in the seventeenth century. As new media such as film, television, and manga appeared in the twentieth century, *The Tales of the Heike* has continued to be a fertile source of inspiration—and it will undoubtedly be drawn on in still-to-be-invented art forms of the future.

CHARACTERS IN *THE TALES OF THE HEIKE*

Imperial Family

GOSHIRAKAWA (1127–1192; reigned 1155–58), *Retired Emperor and head of the imperial clan*

TAKAKURA (1161–1181; reigned 1168–80), *Emperor and son of Retired Emperor GoShirakawa; father of Antoku*

ANTOKU (1178–1185; reigned 1180–85), *son of Emperor Takakura and Kenreimon'in; a child emperor, he is held by the Heike and drowns in the final battle at Dan-no-ura at age 7*

NUN OF THE SECOND RANK (ca. 1185), *Principal wife of Taira no Kiyomori and mother of Munemori, Shigehira, and Kenreimon'in; drowns in the final battle at Dan-no-ura*

The Taira Clan (Heike)

KIYOMORI (1118–1181), *Taira clan head*

SHIGEMORI (1138–1179), *eldest son of Kiyomori; until Kiyomori's early death a restraining influence on Kiyomori*

MUNEMORI (1147–1185), *son of Kiyomori and Nun of the Second Rank; Taira clan head after his father's death in 1181*

ATSUMORI (1169–1184), *nephew of Kiyomori; killed in the battle at Ichinotani*

TADANORI (1144–1184), *younger brother of Kiyomori; pupil of the famous poet Fujiwara no Shunzei; dies in the battle at Ichi-no-tani*

The Minamoto Clan (Genji)

YORITOMO (1147–1199), *leader of the Minamoto in eastern Japan and founder of the Kamakura shogunate*

YOSHITSUNE (1159–1189), *younger half brother of Yoritomo and one of the chief Minamoto commanders; defeats the Heike in the final battle at Dan-no-ura*

From The Tales of the Heike[1]

FROM BOOK ONE

The Bells of Gion Monastery (1.1)

The bells of the Gion monastery in India echo with the warning that all things are impermanent. The blossoms of the sala trees teach us through their hues that what flourishes must fade.[2] The proud do not prevail for long but vanish like a spring night's dream. In time the mighty, too, succumb: all are dust before the wind.

Long ago in a different land, Zhao Gao of the Qin dynasty in China, Wang Mang of the Han, Zhu Yi of the Liang, and An Lushan of the Tang all refused to be governed by former sovereigns. Pursuing every pleasure, deaf to admonitions, unaware of the chaos overtaking the realm, ignorant of the sufferings of the common people, before long they all alike met their downfall.

More recently in our own country there have been men like Masakado, Sumitomo, Gishin, and Nobuyori, each of them proud and fierce to the extreme. The tales told of the most recent of such men, Taira no Kiyomori, the lay priest of Rokuhara and at one time the prime minister, are beyond the power of words to describe or the mind to imagine.

Kiyomori was the oldest son and heir of Taira no Tadamori, the minister of punishments, and the grandson of Masamori, the governor of Sanuki. Masamori was a ninth-generation descendant of Prince Kazurahara, a first-rank prince and the minister of ceremonies, the fifth son of Emperor Kanmu.

FROM BOOK SIX

Summary   The selection from Book 6 takes us halfway into the tale, which to this point has largely been an account of the Heike (or Taira) clan's ascendancy. The clan controls half the provinces in Japan and enjoys sufficient military might to impose its will on the capital. As head of the clan, Kiyomori has attained the pinnacle of worldly success, been named Chancellor of the Realm, and been appointed to the most exalted of court ranks. His sons have also fared handsomely, and the clan possesses innumerable private estates and agricultural fields.

Yet Kiyomori abuses his power with such brutality that even his own son is repulsed. Shigemori, the hope of the future, confronts his father, urging restraint, but his voice goes unheard; after praying that either his father's heart be softened or his own life be cut short, he dies. Shigemori's untimely death is only one sign of the gods' apparent displeasure. The country is wracked with a series of natural disasters. Fires, tornadoes, and earthquakes are all interpreted as portents that Kiyomori is steering Japan toward some horrendous calamity. And indeed the remainder of Kiyomori's allotted time is beset with plot and counterplot, treachery and betrayal. He has lost the support of the powerful retired emperor and the bulk of the imperial family. Members of the aristocracy, who once saw Kiyomori as a protector, now revile him. The Buddhist temples stop their squabbling and unite their private armies against the hated despot. And

1. Translated by and with notes adapted from Burton Watson.
2. According to Buddhist legend, the Gion monastery, which was built by a rich merchant in a famous garden in India, was the first Buddhist monastery. The temple complex included a building known as Impermanence Hall. The Buddha died under the yellow blossoms of sala trees, which turned white to express their grief.

worst of all, Kiyomori's depredations have driven each of these former allies to embrace his most serious rival, the potent warrior house of the Minamoto, or Genji.

Yoritomo, head of the Genji clan, cuts a deal with the retired emperor. GoShirakawa agrees to pardon him for past offenses; in return, Yoritomo will lead his men against the Heike. Battle is joined in 1180. The war between the Heike and the Genji has begun, and rages inconclusively for a full year before the onset of Kiyomori's final illness.

The Death of Kiyomori (6.7)

After this, all the warriors of the island of Shikoku went over to the side of Kōno no Michinobu.[3] Reports also came that Tanzō, the superintendent of the Kumano Shrine,[4] had shifted his sympathies to the Genji side, despite the many kindnesses shown him by the Heike. All the provinces in the north and the east were thus rebelling against the Taira, and in the regions to the west and southwest of the capital the situation was the same. Report after report of uprisings in the outlying areas came to startle the ears of the Heike, and word repeatedly reached them of additional impending acts of rebellion. It seemed as though the "barbarian tribes to the east and west"[5] had suddenly risen up against them. The members of the Taira clan were not alone in thinking that the end of the world was close at hand. No truly thoughtful person could fail to dread the ominous turn of events.

On the twenty-third day of the Second Month, a council of the senior Taira nobles was convened. At that time Lord Munemori,[6] a former general of the right, spoke as follows: "We earlier tried to put down the rebels in the east, but the results were not all that we might have desired. This time I would like to be appointed commander in chief to move against them."

"What a splendid idea!" the other nobles exclaimed in obsequious assent. A directive was accordingly handed down from the retired emperor[7] appointing Lord Munemori commander in chief of an expedition against the traitorous elements in the eastern and northern provinces.[8] All the high ministers and courtiers who held military posts or were experienced in the use of arms were ordered to follow him.

---

3. A Genji supporter. His father has just been killed by a Heike partisan, and Michinobu's revenge rallies the warriors of Shikoku (one of the four main islands of Japan) to the side of the Genji. This is a serious setback for the Heike, because Shikoku lies in the southwestern portion of the country, where the clan has traditionally been strong.

4. One of the most important shrines in Japan, in an area that had long been under the sway of the Heike.

5. A Chinese phrase used to refer to all directions.

6. Kiyomori's son, successor to Shigemori.

7. Emperor GoShirakawa reigned only from 1155 to 1158, but until his death in 1192 he

had a considerably greater say in the government than the series of reigning emperors who succeeded him. Following the convention of the period he had abdicated early and assumed the status of "retired emperor," probably to gain more room for political maneuvers. At this point in the tale, GoShirakawa is nominally allied with the Heike, but only because he is in effect Kiyomori's hostage. On the surface, then, he does the Heike's bidding, when in fact he is in league with the Genji. The retired emperor is so duplicitous that, in the turmoil, it is hard at any given moment to tell whose side he is really on.

8. That is, against the Genji.

When word had already gotten abroad that Lord Munemori would set out on his mission to put down the Genji forces in the eastern provinces on the twenty-seventh day of the same month, his departure was canceled because of reports that Kiyomori, the lay priest and prime minister, was not in his customary good health.

On the following day, the twenty-eighth, it became known that Kiyomori was seriously ill, and people throughout the capital and at Rokuhara[9] whispered to one another, "This is just what we were afraid of!"

From the first day that Kiyomori took sick, he was unable to swallow anything, not even water. His body was as hot as though there were a fire burning inside it: those who attended him could scarcely come within twenty-five or thirty feet of him so great was the heat. All he could do was cry out, "I'm burning! I'm burning!" His affliction seemed quite unlike any ordinary illness.

Water from the Well of the Thousand-Arm Kannon on Mount Hiei[1] was brought to the capital and poured into a stone bathtub, and Kiyomori's body was lowered into it in hopes of cooling him. But the water began to bubble and boil furiously and, in a moment, had all gone up in steam. In another attempt to bring him some relief, wooden pipes were rigged in order to pour streams of water down on his body, but the water sizzled and sputtered as though it were landing on fiery rocks or metal, and virtually none of it reached his body. The little that did so burst into flames and burned, filling the room with black smoke and sending flames whirling upward.

Long ago, the eminent Buddhist priest Hōzō was said to have been invited by Enma, the king of hell, to visit the infernal regions. At that time he asked if he might see the place where his deceased mother had been reborn. Admiring his filial concern, Enma directed the hell wardens to conduct him to the Hell of Scorching Heat,[2] where Hōzō's mother was undergoing punishment. When Hōzō entered the iron gates of the hell, he saw flames leaping up like shooting stars, ascending hundreds of yojanas[3] into the air. The sight must have been much like what those attending Kiyomori in his sickness now witnessed.

Kiyomori's wife, the Nun of the Second Rank,[4] had a most fearful dream. It seemed that a carriage enveloped in raging flames had entered the gate of the mansion. Stationed at the front and rear of the carriage were creatures, some with the head of a horse, others with the head of an ox. To the front of the carriage was fastened an iron plaque inscribed with the single word *mu*, "never."

In her dream the Nun of the Second Rank asked, "Where has this carriage come from?"

---

9. An eternal district of the capital, where the Heike had their headquarters.

1. A source of holy water offerings for a nearby image of Thousand-Armed Kannon, a Buddhist deity known for compassion.

2. The hottest of the eight hells, reserved for punishing particularly egregious offenses, including murder, theft, lust, cruelty, and deceit.

3. A Hindu unit of distance (equivalent to several miles).

4. It was not unusual for members of the aristocratic and military classes to retire into religious life, often without fully renouncing their emotional attachments and worldly ambitions. Kiyomori himself took Buddhist vows in 1168, with no discernible difference in his conduct; and his wife, now a nun, has obviously not forsaken her husband.

"From the tribunal of King Enma," was the reply. "It has come to fetch His Lordship, the lay priest and prime minister of the Taira clan."

"And what does the plaque mean?" she asked.

"It means that because of the crime of burning the one-hundred-and-sixty-foot gilt-bronze image of the Buddha Vairochana in the realm of human beings,[5] King Enma's tribunal has decreed that the perpetrator shall fall into the depths of the Hell of Never-Ceasing Torment. The 'Never' of Never-Ceasing is written on it; the 'Ceasing' remains to be written."

The Nun of the Second Rank woke from her dream in alarm, her body bathed in perspiration, and when she told others of her dream, their hair stood on end just hearing about it. She made offerings of gold, silver, and the seven precious objects[6] to all the temples and shrines reputed to have power in such matters, even adding such items as horses, saddles, armor, helmets, bows, arrows, long swords, and short swords. But no matter how much she added as accompaniment to her supplications, they were wholly without effect. Kiyomori's sons and daughters gathered by his pillow and bedside, inquiring in anguish if there were something that could be done, but all their cries were in vain.

On the second day of the second intercalary month, the Nun of the Second Rank, braving the formidable heat, approached her husband's pillow and spoke through her tears. "With each day that passes, it seems to me, there is less hope for your recovery. If you have anything you wish to say before you depart this world, it would be good to speak now while your mind is still clear."

In earlier days the prime minister had always been brusque and forceful in manner, but now, tormented by pain, he had barely breath enough to utter these words. "Ever since the Hōgen and Heiji uprisings,[7] I have on numerous occasions put down those who showed themselves enemies of the throne, and I have received rewards and acclaim far surpassing what I deserve. I have had the honor to become the grandfather of a reigning emperor and to hold the office of prime minister, and the bounties showered on me extend to my sons and grandsons. There is nothing more whatsoever that I could wish for in this life. Only one regret remains to me—that I have yet to behold the severed head of that exile to the province of Izu, Minamoto no Yoritomo! When I have ceased to be, erect no temples or pagodas in my honor, conduct no memorial rites for me! But dispatch forces at once to strike at Yoritomo, cut off his head,

---

5. The Buddhist monasteries had already earned Kiyomori's ire by siding with the Genji. When the monks then mocked him in effigy, trampling a big wooden ball dubbed "Kiyomori's head," Kiyomori dispatched his troops. By the time the fighting was over, the two great temples of Nara, Kōfukuji and Tōdaiji, had been burned to the ground and an immense 53-foot bronze statue of the Buddha, known in Sanskrit as Vairocana and prized since its erection in the 8th century, had been completely destroyed. *The Tales of the Heike* describes Kiyomori as delighted with the results, but others at court are aghast at the level of destruction.

6. Precious substances mentioned in Bud-dhist texts (variously identified in different translations at different times).

7. The Hōgen Disturbance (1156) was a succession dispute in which the Heike and the Genji joined forces to support the then-reigning emperor, GoShirakawa. The Heiji Disturbance (1160) was a clash that arose between the two military clans when Retired Emperor GoShirakawa encountered a second challenge, this time from a faction that included the Genji. Under Kiyomori's command the Heike defeated the Genji; but Kiyomori made the tactical mistake of sparing the life of his enemy's 14-year-old son, Yoritomo, around whom the Genji would later rally to ultimately crush the Heike.

and hang it before my grave—that is all the ceremony that I ask!" Such were the deeply sinful words that he spoke!

On the fourth day of the same month, the illness continuing to torment him, Kiyomori's attendants thought to provide some slight relief by pouring water over a board and laying him on it, but this appeared to do no good whatsoever. Moaning in desperation, he fell to the floor and there suffered his final agonies. The sound of horses and carriages rushing about seemed to echo to the heavens and to make the very earth tremble. Even if the sovereign of the realm himself, the lord of ten thousand chariots, had passed away, there could not have been a greater commotion.

Kiyomori had turned sixty-four this year. He thus was not particularly advanced in age. But the life span decreed him by his actions in previous existences had abruptly come to an end. Hence the large-scale ceremonies and secret ceremonies performed on his behalf by the Buddhist priests failed to have any effect; the gods and the Three Treasures of Buddhism[8] ceased to shed their light on him; and the benevolent deities withdrew their guardianship.

And if even divine help was beyond his reach, how little could mere human beings do! Although tens of thousands of loyal troops stationed themselves inside his mansion and in the grounds around it, all eager to sacrifice themselves and to die in his place, they could not, even for an instant, hold at bay the deadly devil of impermanence, whose form is invisible to the eye and whose power is invincible. Kiyomori went all alone to the Shide Mountains of death, from which there is no return; alone he faced the sky on his journey over the River of Three Crossings to the land of the Yellow Springs.[9] And when he arrived there, only the evil deeds he had committed in past days, transformed now into hell wardens, were there to greet him. All in all, it was a pitiful business.

Since further action could not be postponed, on the seventh day of the same month Kiyomori's remains were cremated at Otagi in the capital. The Buddhist priest Enjitsu placed the ashes in a bag hung around his neck and journeyed with them down to the province of Settsu, where he deposited them in a grave on Sutra Island.

Kiyomori's name had been known throughout the land of Japan, and his might had set men trembling. But in the end his body was no more than a puff of smoke ascending in the sky above the capital, and his remains, after tarrying a little while, in time mingled with the sands of the shore where they were buried, dwindling at last into empty dust.

FROM *BOOK SEVEN*

Summary   With Kiyomori dead (1181), the Heike must depend for leadership on his feckless son Munemori. But cowardice and poor judgment are Munemori's most notable qualities, and the Heike position rapidly deteriorates. In the two years between the death of Kiyomori

---

8. That is, the Buddha, the Dharma (the Law or teachings of the Buddha), and the Sangha (the Buddhist spiritual community).
9. The Chinese underworld. The Shide Mountains were a range crossed by spirits of the dead

on their way to Enma's court of judgment. The River of Three Crossings had to be forded by human spirits on the seventh day after death, and the worst sinners were required to use the deepest, most difficult crossing.

and the events of Book 7, the Heike troops fall back before the Genji on both northern and eastern fronts. When Heike troops attempt a last stand in the mountains of the north, they are taken
by surprise and sent into a disastrous, headlong rout. The Genji leader Yoshinaka crushes a large
Heike force and heads for the capital. He enlists the help of the powerful monks at Mount Hiei,
northeast of Kyoto, who turns down the Heike's request for support. The Heike are forced to flee
west with Emperor Antoku, still a child, and the imperial regalia. Retired Emperor GoShirakawa
openly defects to the Genji and flees from the city in a different direction. Kiyomori's brother
Tadanori, a refined man and gifted poet, has to leave the capital together with the doomed
Heike. Knowing that he will soon meet his death, he returns once more to the capital in haste,
to convey a final wish to his former poetry teacher.

Tadanori Leaves the Capital (7.16)

Taira no Tadanori, the governor of Satsuma, returned once more to the capital,
although where he had been in the meantime is uncertain. Accompanied by
five mounted warriors and a page, a party of seven horsemen in all, he rode
along Gojō Avenue to the residence of Fujiwara no Shunzei.[1] The gate of
Shunzei's mansion was closed and showed little sign of opening.

When Tadanori announced his name, there was a bustle inside the gate, and
voices called out, "Those men who fled from the city have come back!" Tadanori dismounted from his horse and spoke in a loud voice. "There is no cause
for alarm. I have come back merely because I have something I would like to
say to His Lordship. You need not open the gate—if you could just have him
come here a moment. . . ."

"I was expecting this," said Shunzei. "I'm sure he won't make any trouble—
let him in."

The gate was opened and Shunzei confronted his caller, whose whole bearing conveyed an air of melancholy.

"You have been good enough to give me instruction for some years," said
Tadanori, "and I hope I have not been entirely unworthy of your kindness. But
the disturbances in the capital in the last two or three years and the uprisings
in the provinces have deeply affected all the members of my clan. Although
I have not intended in any way to neglect my poetry studies, I fear I have not
been as attentive to you as I should have been.

"The emperor has already left the capital, and the fortunes of my family
appear to have run out. I heard some time ago that you were going to compile
an anthology of poetry at the request of the retired emperor.[2] I had hoped that,
if you would be so kind as to give your assent, I might have perhaps one poem
included in it in fulfillment of my lifelong hopes. But then these disorders
descended on the world and the matter of the anthology had to be put aside, a
fact that grieves me deeply.

1. A prominent poet and scholar (1114–1204),
with whom Tadanori had studied poetry.
2. In 1183 Retired Emperor GoShirakawa had
appointed Shunzei as chief compiler of the seventh imperial poetry anthology. These anthologies were the most prestigious venue for poets
to gain reputation. (For selections from the first
imperial poetry anthology, *The Kokinshū*, see
above.)

"Should the state of the world become somewhat more settled, perhaps work on the anthology can be begun. I have here a scroll of poems. If in your kindness you could find even one of them to be worthy of inclusion, I will continue to rejoice long after I have gone to my grave and will forever be your guardian in the world beyond."

Reaching through the opening in his armor, Tadanori took out a scroll of poems and presented it to Lord Shunzei. From among the poems he had composed in recent years, he had selected some hundred or so that he thought were of superior quality and had brought them with him now that he was about to take final leave of the capital.

As Shunzei opened the scroll and looked at it, he said, "Since you see fit to leave me with this precious memento of your work, you may rest assured that I will not treat it lightly. Please have no doubts on that score. And that you should present it to me now, as a token of your deep concern for the art of poetry, makes the gesture more moving than ever—so much so that I can scarcely hold back the tears!"

Overjoyed at this response, Tadanori replied, "Perhaps I will find rest beneath the waves of the western ocean; perhaps my bones will be left to bleach on the mountain plain. Whatever may come, I can now take leave of this uncertain world without the least regret. And so I say good-bye!"

With these words he mounted his horse, knotted the cords of his helmet, and rode off toward the west. Shunzei stood gazing after until the figure had receded far into the distance. And then it seemed that he could hear Tadanori reciting in a voice loud enough to be heard from afar:

> Long is the journey before me—my thoughts race
> with the evening clouds over Wild Goose Mountain.

Deeply grieved at the parting, Shunzei wiped back the tears as he turned to reenter his house.

Later, after peace had been restored and Shunzei had begun compiling the anthology known as the *Senzaishū* [*The Collection of a Thousand Years*],[3] he recalled with deep emotion his farewell meeting with Tadanori and the words that the latter had spoken on that occasion. Among the poems that Tadanori had left behind were several that might have been included in the anthology. But since the anthology was being compiled by imperial command, Shunzei did not feel that he could refer to Tadanori by name. Instead, he selected one poem entitled "Blossoms in the Old Capital" and included it with the notation "author unknown." The poem read:

> In ruins now, the old capital of Shiga by the waves,
> yet the wild cherries of Nagara still bloom as before.[4]

Because Tadanori was among those branded as enemies of the sovereign, perhaps less might have been said about him. And yet there is great pathos in his story.

---

3. This imperial poetry collection was completed in 1188, after the fall of the Heike.
4. The poem refers to Ōmi, where Emperor Tenji had briefly built a capital and reigned from 668 to 671. For the earliest poem lamenting the fall of this ephemeral capital, and on the evanescence of things in general, see Kakinomoto no Hitomaro's poem, p. 1175 (from *The Manyōshū*).

The Flight from Fukuhara (7.20)

Palace Minister Munemori and the other Heike leaders, with the exception of Lord Koremori, took their wives and children with them when they left the capital. But for persons of less exalted station, such a course of action was impossible. They had to leave behind all their loved ones, never knowing when they might meet again. Even when the time of reunion is fixed, when promises have been made to return on such-and-such a day, at such-and-such an hour, how long is the interval of waiting! How much harder was it, then, for these people, this day their last together, the hour of parting even now at hand—little wonder that those departing and those left behind alike should wet their sleeves with tears.

Some followed the Heike leaders because they recalled how for generations their families had served under them, others because they could not forget great kindnesses bestowed in more recent years or days. But whether young or old, now they had nothing but backward glances, barely able to tear themselves away. Some would go to spend their days on distant sea paths or sleep by wave-lapped beaches, others to journey far afield over steep mountain passes, whipping their horses onward, manning the rudders of their boats, each with his own thoughts, his own memories as he made his way in flight.

When Palace Minister Munemori arrived at Fukuhara,[5] the site of the former capital, he summoned the more important samurai who served under him, several hundred men both young and old, and addressed them as follows: "Blessings imparted to us through good deeds piled up in the past have now run out; misfortunes born of accumulated evil press down on us. And so the gods have turned against us, and the retired emperor has cast us aside. We have left the imperial city and now are travelers on the highway, with nowhere to turn.

"But they say that even those who lodge for one night beneath the same tree are bound by karma from a former existence and that those who dip water from the same stream do so because of deep ties from other lifetimes. And how much deeper are the ties in our case! You are no mere one-day sojourners at our gate but retainers who have served our family for generation after generation. Ties of kinship link some of us, making us anything but strangers; generations of service in other cases have forged profound bonds between us. The prosperity of our clan in past times brought wave after wave of bounty to you, enabling you to fulfill your personal needs. Now, should you not consider how best to repay that debt of gratitude? The emperor, who gained his throne through observance of the Ten Good Precepts[6] in a previous existence, has departed from the capital, taking with him the three imperial regalia.[7] Wherever he may venture, to what-

---

5. The present city of Kōbe. It served briefly as a capital during late 1180, when Kiyomori, who had an estate there, insisted on removing the government from Kyoto. The move met with strong opposition, including from some members of his own clan; this resistance, combined with the aggression of the Genji in the east, forced Kiyomori to return the capital to its traditional location.
6. The avoidance of killing, stealing, adultery, lying, duplicitous language, slandering, equivocating, coveting, anger, and false views.

7. Objects viewed as symbols of the emperor's legitimacy and authority: a strand of jewels, a mirror, and a sword. In the Japanese creation myth, the sun goddess is said to have conferred the three regalia on her grandson as he was about to descend to the Japanese islands, establishing the imperial line. Here, the young emperor carries with him the sword and the jewels. The mirror is at Ise, the Shinto shrine honoring the ancestral gods of the imperial family (where it is said to remain to this day).

ever faraway wilderness, to whatever remote mountain recess, should we not wait for and attend him?"

The warriors, young and old alike in tears, replied, "Even lowly birds and beasts know how to repay a debt of kindness and show gratitude to those who have favored them. Why, then, should we, who are human beings, not be aware of what duty demands? For twenty years and more you have looked after our wives and children and tended to the wants of your followers—we owe everything to our lord's beneficence. Moreover, we are fighting men, bearers of arms, trained to life in the saddle—would we not count it a disgrace to be double-hearted? Therefore, wherever the ruler may go, be it beyond Japan to the lands of Silla or Paekche, Koguryo, or Pohai,[8] to the end of the clouds or the end of the sea, we will never cease to attend him!"

In different voices but speaking with one intent, they made their declaration, and all the Heike lords seemed heartened by their response.

The Heike spent one night at Fukuhara, their former home. It was the beginning of autumn and the moon was a waning crescent. In the late hours of the night, when the moon had set, all was quiet, and in the travelers' beds, mere makeshifts of grass, tears mingled with the dew, for everything around them moved them to sadness.

Not knowing when they might return here again, they gazed about them at the various spots where the late prime minister Kiyomori had built his capital.

For spring there had been the Flower-Viewing Knoll, for autumn, the Moon-Viewing Strand. The Hall of the Bubbling Spring, the Pine-Shaded Hall, the Riding Ground Hall, the two-story Viewing Stand Hall, the Snow-Viewing Palace, the Reed-Thatched Palace, the mansions of the nobles, the Temporary Imperial Palace built on orders from Lord Kunitsuna[9]—their roof tiles in the shape of mandarin ducks, their terraces of precious stone—all had in the course of three years fallen into ruin. Old moss covered the pathways, autumn grasses blocked the gates. Pine seedlings sprouted from the roof tiles, vines had overgrown the walls. Tall buildings leaned to one side, encrusted with moss; only pine winds passed there now. Window blinds had rotted away, leaving the sleeping rooms exposed to view, but only the moon looked in.

When dawn came, the Heike set fire to the imperial palace at Fukuhara, and Emperor Antoku and those accompanying him all took to the boats. Even though their departure was perhaps not as painful as that when they left the capital, it nevertheless filled them with regret.

The evening smoke rising up from the seaweed fires of the fisherfolk, the dawn cries of deer on the hillcrest, the sound of the waves washing ashore in cove after cove, the moon reflected in the tears on their sleeves, the crickets chirping in a thousand autumn grasses—all that they saw, all that they heard seemed to overwhelm them with feeling, leaving nothing that did not wound their spirits.

The more than one hundred thousand horsemen who only yesterday had set out bridle to bridle from the foot of Ōsaka Barrier today were a mere seven thousand souls casting off their mooring lines amid the waves of the western

8. Various parts of the Korean Peninsula and northeastern China.
9. Fujiwara Kunitsuna, a close supporter of the Taira, whose son Kiyokuni was adopted by Kiyomori. He was a member of the emperor's cabinet, or the council of state, ranking just below the three ministers of state.

ocean. The cloud-strewn sea was calm and still now, the bright day drawing to a close. The lone islands were veiled in evening mist, and the moon's rays floated on the water.

Cleaving the waves of distant inlets, drawn on by sea tides as they sped forward, the boats seemed to mount the clouds in mid-sky. By now the capital was even farther away than the clouds, so many were the mountains and rivers that had come between. "What a long way we've journeyed!" they thought, and there was no end to their tears.

Spying a flock of white birds resting on the waves, they exclaimed, "Ah yes! Ariwara no Narihira saw birds like these on the Sumida River and asked what they were called." They were called "capital birds,"[1] a name to stir sad memories in all who heard it.

The Heike departed from the capital on the twenty-fifth day of the Seventh Month, in the second year of the Juei era [1183].[2]

FROM BOOK NINE

Summary   In the capital, a new emperor has acceded to the throne to replace the child sovereign Antoku, whom the Heike took along. And Yoritomo, for his part, has gained both increased power and a certain legitimacy; Retired Emperor GoShirakawa has conferred on him the title of shogun (short for sei-i-tai shōgun, "barbarian-subduing commander").

Meanwhile, the Heike have regrouped along the Inland Sea, back in an area they have controlled for a century and flush with confidence. With the panic of the retreat behind them, they throw up defenses along the coast, secure control of the entrances to the Inland Sea, recruit supporters, and prepare to retake the capital.

The Attack from the Cliff (9.12)

After this, the other Genji warriors charged into the fray, the Chichibu, the Ashikaga, the Miura, the Kamakura, and the Inomata, Kodama, Noiyo, Yokoyama, Nishitō, Tsuzukitō, and Shinotō leagues, until all the Genji and Heike forces had closed in combat. The two sides repeatedly dashed into each other's ranks, calling out their names back and forth, shouting and clamoring until the hills resounded with their cries, the din of their charging horses echoing like thunder. The arrows whizzing back and forth resembled nothing so

---

1. A reference to a poem in *The Kokinshū* by Ariwara no Narihira (825–880), a famous poet and lover (and later a model for Prince Genji in *The Tale of Genji*), which came to embody the courtier's nostalgia for the capital. The poem is accompanied by the following headnote: "When they reached the bank of the Sumida River, which flows between the provinces of Musashi and Shimōsa, they were miserably homesick for the capital. They dismounted and stood for a time on the bank, thinking, 'How very far we have come!' The ferryman interrupted their laments. 'Come aboard quickly; it's getting late.' They got into the boat

and prepared to cross, all in wretched spirits, for there was not one among them who had not left someone dear to him in the city. A white bird with a red bill and red legs chanced to be frolicking near the river. Since it was a species unknown in the capital, none of them could identify it. 'What kind of bird is that?' they asked the ferryman. 'A capital-bird, of course,' he replied with an air of surprise. Then Narihira recited this poem. "If you are in truth / what your name seems to make you, / I will put to you, / capital-bird, this question: / do things go well with my love?"

2. The short reign of the child emperor Antoku.

much as torrents of rain. Some warriors, a wounded comrade on their backs, struggled to make their way toward the rear; others, despite being wounded, continued to fight while the mortally wounded fell dead where they were. Men rode side by side, grappling together and slashing at each other until one delivered a fatal stab to the other. Some held their foe down while they cut off his head; others, pinned down, had their heads lopped off in a like manner. Neither side revealed any weakness that its attackers could turn to advantage, and the Genji forces through their frontal attack alone did not seem to be able to gain victory.

Meanwhile, Yoshitsune had circled around to the rear and by dawn of the seventh day had climbed up to the region of Hiyodori Pass, preparing to swoop down on the Heike position at Ichi-no-tani. Just then, two stags and a doe, perhaps startled by the Genji horsemen, fled downhill in the direction of the Heike stronghold at Ichi-no-tani.

Catching sight of them, the Heike soldiers in the fort below exclaimed excitedly, "All the deer around here must have been so frightened of us that they fled far off into the mountains. That these deer would deliberately come toward a large force like ours seems highly peculiar! It must mean that the Genji are getting ready to charge down on us from above!"

Takechi Kiyonori, a man from Iyo Province, came forward. "Whatever it means," he said, "if they come from the direction of the enemy, we shouldn't let them by!" and he proceeded to fell the two stags with his bow and arrows, though he let the doe get away.

"What's the good of your shooting at deer!" objected Moritoshi of Etchū. "With just one of those arrows, you could have held off ten of the enemy. Killing is a sin to begin with, and then you waste arrows!" he grumbled.

Yoshitsune looked down over the Heike stronghold in the distance. "Try sending some of the horses down," he ordered. A few of the saddled horses were accordingly sent galloping down the slope. Some broke their legs and fell along the way, but others managed to reach the bottom without mishap. Three of them pulled up near the roof of Etchū Moritoshi's encampment and stood there trembling with fright.

Observing this, Yoshitsune announced, "If the riders are careful enough, the horses can get down without injury. Look lively, now—I'll show you how it's done!" Leading a force of thirty horsemen, he plummeted down the slope. The rest of the force followed, the incline so steep that the stirrups of the men in the rear clattered against the armor and helmets of those ahead of them. The ground was sandy, with scatterings of small rocks and stones, so that the riders fairly slid down for a distance of some seven hundred feet until they reached a shelflike stretch that halted their fall.

Peering down below, they could see only huge moss-shrouded rocks, a sheer drop of some hundred and forty or fifty feet. No way to go back where they had come from, no way to go forward that they could see, the men were utterly baffled, exclaiming, "This is the end!"

Just then, Sawara Yoshitsura came forward. "In Miura where I come from, we think nothing of galloping day and night over places like this just to get at a bird on the wing. This is a Miura-style racecourse!" he declared and led the way by plunging down the slope. The rest of the men followed. "Ei! Ei!" they cried in muffled voices, encouraging their horses on, the descent so terrifying that they kept their eyes closed as they went down. It seemed a feat impossible for mere human beings to accomplish, instead a performance by devils or spirits.

Halfway down, they began calling out their battle cries, and as the voices of the three thousand horsemen[3] came echoing back from the surrounding hills, they sounded like the shouts of one hundred thousand.

The men under Murakami Yasukuni began setting fires and before long had burned down all the Heike barracks and makeshift buildings. By chance, a strong wind was blowing and black smoke billowed through the air, throwing the Heike soldiers into such panic that they scrambled toward the beaches fronting the encampment, certain that in that direction lay their only hope for escape.

A number of boats were drawn up in readiness along the shore, but the fleeing troops were in such haste to board them that at times four or five hundred or even a thousand men, all fully armed, struggled to get into a single boat, impossible as that was. After advancing no more than three hundred and fifty yards from shore, three large vessels sank before the eyes of the onlookers.

Thereafter, the order went out: "Persons of rank are to be allowed aboard, underlings are not!" and swords and halberds were used to enforce it. But even after the order became known, men continued to cling to the boats that refused to take them, trying to climb aboard. As a result, a hand was cut off here, an arm severed at the elbow there, until the waters along the Ichi-no-tani shore turned crimson and the bodies floated side by side.

The Heike warrior Noritsune, the governor of Noto, had fought many battles and had never once been defeated, but what must have been his thoughts now? Mounted on his steed Usuguro, Gray Black, he fled westward. At the Akashi shore in Harima he boarded a boat and made his way across the straits to Yashima in Sanuki.[4]

The Death of Tadanori (9.14)

Taira no Tadanori, the governor of Satsuma, served as commanding general of the western flank at the battle of Ichi-no-tani. Dressed in a battle robe of dark blue brocade and armor laced with black silk, he rode a sturdy black horse fitted with a lacquer saddle flecked with gold. Surrounded by some hundred horsemen under his command, he was retiring from the engagement in a calm and unhurried manner, halting his horse now and then to parry with one of the enemy.

Okabe no Rokuyata, a member of the Inomata group of Genji warriors, spotted Tadanori and galloped after him in pursuit, urging his horse forward with spurs and whip and shouting, "Who goes there? Declare your name!"

"I'm a friend!" replied Tadanori, but as he turned to speak, he revealed enough of his face to make it apparent that his teeth were blackened.[5]

"Ha!" thought Rokuyata. "No one on our side looks like that! This must be one of the Taira lords." Overtaking Tadanori, he began to grapple with him. On

---

3. A good example of how the tale exaggerates for dramatic effect. Historical evidence suggests that Yoshitsune had about 100 men with him.

4. On the island of Shikoku, across the Inland Sea from Ichi-no-tani.
5. Identifying Tadanori as a noble and one of the Heike.

seeing this, the hundred horsemen under Tadanori, fighting men recruited from other provinces, fled as fast as they could, not one of them coming to his aid.

"Wretch!" exclaimed Tadanori. "You should have believed me when I said I was a friend!" Brought up in Kumano, a powerful man trained to act with lightning speed, Tadanori drew his sword and struck three blows at Rokuyata, two while the latter was still seated in the saddle and a third after he had unhorsed him. The first two glanced off Rokuyata's armor and did no harm. The third pierced his face, though not with sufficient force to kill him.

Tadanori pinned his attacker to the ground and was about to cut off his head when Rokuyata's page, rushing up from behind, drew his long sword and with one blow cut off Tadanori's arm at the elbow.

Tadanori realized this was the end. "Give me time enough for ten invocations of the Buddha!" he said. Gripping Rokuyata, he flung him a bow's length to the side. Then he faced west and, in a loud voice, recited these words: "His bright light illumines the worlds in the ten directions. Without fail He gathers up all living beings who recite His name!" He had scarcely concluded his recitation when Rokuyata approached from behind and struck off his head.

Rokuyata felt that the man had died like a true commanding general, but he still did not know his name. He found a slip of paper fastened to Tadanori's quiver, however, on which was written a poem entitled "On a Journey, Lodging Beneath the Blossoms." It read:

> Evening drawing on, I'll take lodging in the shade of this tree,
> and make its blossoms my host for the night.

The poem was signed "Tadanori."

Having thus learned who his opponent was, Rokuyata impaled the head on the tip of his long sword and, lifting it high up, declared in a loud voice, "You have heard much these days of this Taira lord, the governor of Satsuma—I, Okabe no Rokuyata Tadazumi, have killed him!"

When they heard Tadanori's name, the Taira and Genji warriors alike exclaimed, "What a pity! A man skilled both in arms and the practice of poetry, a true commanding general!" And there were none who did not wet their sleeve with tears.

The Death of Atsumori (9.16)

The Heike had lost the battle. "Those Taira lords will be heading for the shore in hopes of making their getaway by boat!" thought Kumagae Naozane to himself. "Fine! I'll go look for one of their generals to grapple with!" and he turned his horse in the direction of the beach.

As he did so, he spotted a lone warrior riding into the sea, making for the boats in the offing. He was wearing a battle robe of finely woven silk embroidered in a crane design, armor of light green lacing, and a horned helmet. He carried a sword with gilt fittings and a quiver whose arrows were fledged with black and white eagle feathers and held a rattan-wound bow in his hand. He was seated in a gold-rimmed saddle, astride a gray horse with white markings.

The lone warrior's horse had swum out about two hundred feet from the shore when Kumagae, waving with his fan, called out, "Ho there, General! I see you. Don't shame yourself by showing your back to an enemy. Come back!"

The rider, acknowledging the call, turned toward the beach. As he was about to ride up out of the waves, Kumagae drew alongside and grappled with him, dragging him from his horse. Pinning him down so as to cut off his head, Kumagae pushed aside his helmet. The face he saw was that of a young man of sixteen or seventeen, lightly powdered and with blackened teeth.

Gazing at the boy's handsome face, Kumagae realized that he was just the age of his own son Kojirō, and he could not bring himself to use his sword. "Who are you? Tell me your name and I'll let you go!" he said.

"Who are you?" asked the young man.

"No one of great importance—Kumagae Naozane of the province of Musashi."

"Then there's no need for me to tell you my name," the young man replied. "I'm worthy enough to be your opponent. When you take my head, ask someone who I am—they will know all right!"

"Spoken like a true general!" thought Kumagae. "But simply killing this one man can't change defeat into victory or victory into defeat. When my son Kojirō has even a slight injury, how much I worry about him! Just think how this boy's father will grieve when he hears that he's been killed! If only I could spare him."

But as he glanced quickly behind him, he saw some fifty Genji horsemen under Toi and Kajiwara coming toward him. Fighting back the tears, he said, "I'd like to let you go, but our forces are everywhere in sight—you could never get away. Rather than fall into someone else's hands, it's better that I kill you. I'll see that prayers are said for your salvation in the life to come."

"Just take my head and be quick about it!" the boy said.

Kumagae was so overcome with pity that he did not know where to strike. His eyes seemed to dim, his wits to desert him, and for a moment he hardly knew where he was. But then he realized that, for all his tears, no choice was left him, and he struck off the boy's head.

"We men who bear arms—how wretched is our lot!" he said. "If I had not been born of a warrior family, would I ever have faced a task like this? What a terrible thing I have done!" Again and again, he repeated the words as he raised his sleeve to brush the tears from his face.

After some time, aware that he must get on with the business, he removed the boy's armor and battle robe and wrapped the head in them. As he was doing so, he noticed a brocade bag with a flute in it that had been fastened to the boy's waist. "Ah, how pitiful!" he said. "Those people I heard at dawn this morning playing music in the enemy stronghold—he must have been one of them! Among all the ten thousand troops from the eastern provinces fighting on our side, is there anyone who carries a flute with him into battle? These highborn people—how gentle and refined they are!"

Later, when Kumagae's battle trophies were presented to Yoshitsune for inspection, there were none among the company who did not weep at the sight.

It was subsequently learned that the young man slain by Kumagae was Atsumori, the seventeen-year-old son of the master of the Palace Repair Office, Taira no Tsunemori. From that time onward, Kumagae's desire to become a Buddhist monk grew even stronger. The flute in question had been presented by Retired Emperor Toba to Atsumori's grandfather, Tadamori, who was a skilled player. From him it had been passed down to the son, Tsunemori, and in turn had been given to Atsumori because of his marked aptitude for the instrument. It was known by the name Saeda, Little Branch.

It is moving to think that for all their exaggerated phrases and flowery embellishments, even music and the arts can in the end lead a man to praise the Buddha way.

FROM *BOOK ELEVEN*

Summary   The final battle comes in 1185. The bulk of the Heike have gone no farther than several miles across the Inland Sea, to the island of Shikoku, when Yoshitsune strikes, and once again takes the Heike by surprise. With a mere hundred men in a few small boats and a storm brewing windward, the tactical genius braves the gale, making the daring calculation that it will carry them across before the enemy notices. The move is inspired, for the Heike expect an attack in fair weather. And the foul weather enables the Genji to make record time; what is normally a three-day crossing is over in six hours. Yoshitsune and his men hit land on the eastern side of the island. The enemy camp is above them, to the north. The small force rides through the night, again in record time, and surprises the Heike at daybreak. Yoshitsune lights fires to suggest a much larger expedition. Seeing the hills ablaze to their rear and the enemy approaching, the Heike, awaiting a frontal attack from the sea, assume they are outnumbered, and rush to their ships and abandon the island. On board the ships are Kiyomori's hapless son, Munemori; Kiyomori's widow, the Nun of Second Rank; their daughter, Kenreimon'in; and their grandson, the child emperor Antoku.

The Drowning of the Former Emperor (11.9)

By this time the Genji warriors had succeeded in boarding the Heike boats, shooting dead the sailors and helmsmen with their arrows or cutting them down with their swords. The bodies lay heaped in the bottom of the boats, and there was no longer anyone to keep the boats on course.

Taira no Tomomori boarded a small craft and made his way to the vessel in which the former emperor was riding. "This is what the world has come to!" he exclaimed. "Have all these unsightly things thrown into the sea!" Then he began racing from prow to stern, sweeping, mopping, dusting, and attempting with his own hands to put the boat into proper order.

"How goes the battle, Lord Tomomori?" asked the emperor's ladies-in-waiting, pressing him with questions.

"You'll have a chance to see some splendid gentlemen from the eastern region!" he replied with a cackling laugh.

"How can you joke at a time like this!" they protested, their voices joined in a chorus of shrieks and wails.

Observing the situation and evidently having been prepared for some time for such an eventuality, the Nun of the Second Rank, the emperor's grandmother, slipped a two-layer nun's robe over her head and tied her glossed silk trousers high at the waist. She placed the sacred jewel, one of the three imperial regalia, under her arm, thrust the sacred sword in her sash, and took the child emperor in her arms. "I may be a mere woman, but I have no intention of falling into the hands of the enemy! I will accompany my lord. All those of you who are resolved to fulfill your duty by doing likewise, quickly follow me!" So saying, she strode to the side of the boat.

The emperor had barely turned eight but had the bearing of someone much older than that. The beauty of his face and form seemed to radiate all around him. His shimmering black hair fell down the length of his back.

Startled and confused, he asked, "Grandma, where are you going to take me?"

Gazing at his innocent face and struggling to hold back her tears, the nun replied, "Don't you understand? In your previous life you were careful to observe the ten good rules of conduct,[6] and for that reason you were reborn in this life as a ruler of ten thousand chariots. But now evil entanglements have you in their power, and your days of good fortune have come to an end.

"First," she told him tearfully, "you must face east and bid farewell to the goddess of the Grand Shrine at Ise.[7] Then you must turn west and trust in Amida Buddha to come with his hosts to greet you and lead you to his Pure Land. Come now, turn your face to the west and recite the invocation of the Buddha's name.[8] This far-off land of ours is no bigger than a millet seed, a realm of sorrow and adversity. Let us leave it now and go together to a place of rejoicing, the paradise of the Pure Land!"

Dressed in a dove gray robe, his hair now done in boyish loops on either side of his head, the child, his face bathed in tears, pressed his small hands together, knelt down, and bowed first toward the east, taking his leave of the deity of the Ise Shrine. Then he turned toward the west and began chanting the *nenbutsu*, the invocation of Amida's name. The nun then took him in her arms. Comforting him, she said, "There's another capital down there beneath the waves!" So they plunged to the bottom of the thousand-fathom sea.

How pitiful that the spring winds of impermanence should so abruptly scatter the beauty of the blossoms; how heartless that the rough waves of reincarnation should engulf this tender body! Long Life is the name they give to the imperial palace, signaling that one should reside there for years unending; its gates are dubbed Ageless, a term that speaks of a reign forever young. Yet before he had reached the age of ten, this ruler ended as refuse on the ocean floor.

Ten past virtues rewarded with a throne, yet how fleeting was that prize! He who once was a dragon among the clouds now had become a fish in the depths of the sea. Dwelling once on terraces lofty as those of the god Brahma, in palaces like the Joyful Sight Citadel of the god Indra,[9] surrounded by great lords and ministers of state, a throng of kin and clansmen in his following, now in an instant ended his life beneath this boat, under these billows—sad, sad indeed!

6. That is, the ten commandments of Buddhism (see p. 1452, n. 6). The reward for adhering to these precepts is, rebirth in one of the Buddhist heavens or, for those whose fidelity is less than complete, rebirth in the human realm.
7. Where the ancestral gods of the imperial family are enshrined.

8. The Amida Buddha is revered as the ruler of the Pure Land, or Western Paradise, into which those who believe in him and recite his name are reborn.
9. A Buddhist deity who dwells on a lofty peak towering at the center of every world and battles pugnacious demons living by the sea. "Brahma": a Hindu god of creation.

The Imperial Lady Becomes a Nun (1)

Kenreimon'in took up residence in the Yoshida area, at the foot of the eastern hills, in a small hermitage belonging to a Buddhist monk of Nara named Kyōe. No one had lived there for many years, and the hut had fallen into disrepair. The garden was buried in weeds, and wild ferns sprouted by the eaves. The blinds had rotted away, leaving the sleeping room exposed to view and offering little shelter from the wind or rain. Although blossoms of one kind and another opened in season, no occupant was present to admire them; and although the moonlight streamed in night after night, no one sat up until dawn delighting in it.

In earlier times, Kenreimon'in had rested on a jeweled dais, brocade hangings surrounding her, but now, parted from all those who had meant anything to her, she resided in this shabby, half-decayed retreat. One can only surmise how forlorn her thoughts must have been. She was like a fish stranded on land, a bird that has been torn from its nest. Such was her present life that she recalled with longing those earlier days when her home had been no more than a boat tossing on the waves. Her thoughts, journeying far away over blue-billowed waters, rested once again on the distant clouds of the western sea. In her reed-thatched hut deep in moss, she wept to see the moonlight fill her garden by the eastern hills. Truly, no words can convey her sadness.

On the first day of the Fifth Month in the first year of the Bunji era [1185], Imperial Lady Kenreimon'in took the tonsure and became a nun.[1] The priest who administered the precepts to her was the Reverend Insei of Chōrakuji. In return she made an offering to him of an informal robe that had belonged to her son, the late emperor Antoku. He had worn the robe until his final days, and it still retained the fragrance of his body. She had brought it all the way with her when she returned to the capital from the western region, regarding it as a last memento of her child, and had supposed that whatever might come, she would never part with it. But since she had nothing else to serve as a gift, she offered it with a profusion of tears, hopeful that at the same time it might help her son attain buddhahood.

The Reverend Insei could find no words with which to acknowledge the offering but, wetting the black sleeves of his clerical robe, made his way from the room in tears. It is said that he had the robe remade into a holy banner to hang in front of the Buddha of Chōrakuji.

By imperial order when she was fifteen, Kenreimon'in had been appointed to serve in the palace, and when she was sixteen, she advanced to the position of imperial consort, attending at the emperor's side. At dawn she urged him to look to the official business of the court; when evening came she was his sole companion for the night. At the age of twenty-two she bore him a son, who was designated as the heir apparent, and when he ascended the throne she was honored with the palace appellation of Kenreimon'in.

Because she was not only the daughter of the lay priest and prime minister Kiyomori but the mother of the nation's ruler as well, she was held in the highest

---

1. The events of Kenreimon'in's last years, which constitute "The Initiates' Book," overlap with those of the preceding books.

respect by everyone in the realm. At the time of which we are speaking, she had reached the age of twenty-nine. Her complexion retained the freshness of peach or damson petals; her face had not lost its lotuslike beauty. But hair ornaments of kingfisher feathers were no longer of any use to her, for her hair had been shorn; her whole figure had suffered a change.

Despairing of this fickle world, Kenreimon'in had entered the true path of religion, but this had by no means brought an end to her sighs. While she could still recall how those she loved had sunk beneath the waves, the figure of her son, the late emperor, and her mother, the Nun of the Second Rank, remained to haunt her memory. She wondered why her own dewdrop existence had continued for so long, why she had lived on only to see such painful sights, and her tears flowed without end. Short as the Fifth Month nights were, she found them almost too long to endure, and since sleep was, by the nature of things, denied her, she could not hope to recapture the past even in her dreams. The lamp, its back to the wall, gave only a flicker of dying light, yet all night she lay awake listening to the mournful pelting of rain at the dark window.[2] The Shang-yang lady, imprisoned in Shangyang Palace, had endured similarly mournful nights, but her grief could hardly have been greater than Kenreimon'in's.

Perhaps to remind himself of the past, the previous owner of the retreat had planted an orange tree by the eaves,[3] and its blossoms now wafted their poignant fragrance on the breeze, while a cuckoo from the hills, lighting there, sang out two or three notes. Kenreimon'in, remembering an old poem, wrote the words on the lid of her inkstone box:

> Cuckoo, you come singing, tracing the orange tree's scent—
> is it because you yearn for someone now gone?

The ladies-in-waiting who had once attended her, but lacked the strength of character needed to drown themselves on the sea bottom as had the Nun of the Second Rank or the Third-Rank Lady of Echizen,[4] had been taken prisoner by the rough hands of the Genji warriors. Returned now to the capital where they had once lived, young and old alike had become nuns, their aspect wholly changed, their purpose in life utterly vanished. In remote valleys, among rocky cliffs, sites they had never even dreamed of in the past, they passed their days. The houses where they had dwelled before all had disappeared with the smoke of battle; mere traces of them remained, little by little overgrown with grasses of the field. No familiar figures came there anymore. They must have felt as desolate as those men in the Chinese tale who, having spent what they thought

---

2. A paraphrase from the poem "The White-Haired Lady of Shangyang" by Bo Juyi (772–846), a Chinese poet among the most popular in Japan. In "The Song of Lasting Regret," included in this volume, Bo Juyi tells the story of the tragic love between the Tang Emperor Xuanzong and his most beloved consort, Prized Consort Yang, who was executed before his eyes during a rebellion; the poem alluded to here focuses on one of the many ladies in the imperial harem who were forced to retire to the Shangyang Palace when Prized Consort Yang began to monopolize Emperor Xuanzong's affections.

3. An allusion to a poem in *The Kokinshū*: "Scenting the fragrance / of orange blossoms that await / the Fifth Month's coming, / I recall a perfumed sleeve / worn by someone long ago."

4. Who committed suicide after hearing of the death of her husband Michimori, Kiyomori's nephew.

was a mere half day in the realm of the immortals, returned to their old home to confront their seventh-generation descendants.[5]

And then, on the ninth day of the Seventh Month,[6] a severe earthquake toppled the tile-capped mud wall and rendered Kenreimon'in's dwelling, already dilapidated, even more ruinous and unsound, so that it was hardly fit for habitation. Worse off than the lady of Shangyang Palace, Kenreimon'in had no green-robed guard to stand at her gate. The hedges, now left untended, were laden with more dew than the lush meadow grasses, and insects, making themselves at home there, had already begun crying out their doleful chorus of complaints. As the fall nights grew longer, Kenreimon'in found herself more wakeful than ever, the hours passing with intolerable slowness. To the endless memories that haunted her were now added the sorrows of the autumn season, until it was almost more than she could bear. Since her whole world had undergone such drastic change, no one was left who might offer her so much as a passing word of consolation, no one to whom she might look for support.

The Move to Ōhara (2)

Although such was the case, the wives of the Reizei senior counselor, Takafusa, and of Lord Nobutaka, Kenreimon'in's younger sisters, while shunning public notice, managed to call on her in private. "In the old days I would never have dreamed that I might sometime be beholden to them for support!" exclaimed the imperial lady, moved to tears by their visit, and all the ladies in attendance shed tears as well.

The place where Kenreimon'in was living was not far from the capital, and the bustling road leading past it was full of prying eyes. She could not help feeling that fragile as her existence might be, mere dew before the wind, she might better live it out in some more remote mountain setting where distressing news of worldly affairs was less likely to reach her. She had been unable to find a suitable location, however, when a certain lady who had called on her mentioned that the Buddhist retreat known as Jakkō-in in the mountains of Ōhara was a very quiet spot.

A mountain village may be lonely, she thought to herself, recalling an old poem on the subject, but it is a better place to dwell than among the world's troubles and sorrows.[7] Having thus determined to move, she found that her sister, the wife of Lord Takafusa, could probably arrange for a palanquin and other necessities. Accordingly, in the first year of the Bunji era, as the Ninth Month was drawing to a close, she set off for the Jakkō-in in Ōhara.

As Kenreimon'in passed along the road, observing the hues of the autumn leaves on the trees all around her, she soon found the day coming to a close, perhaps all the sooner because she was entering the shade of the mountains.

---

5. In this legend, a traveler who spent half a year in the enchanted cottage of a mountain nymph returns home to find that his sons are dead and six generations have passed.
6. About six months after the Heike are defeated. Since spirits of the dead were held capable of returning to wreak havoc on the liv-

ing, it is widely assumed that this great earthquake is the Heike's revenge.
7. With a slight alteration, she quotes a poem in *The Kokinshū*: "It is true enough / that a mountain hermitage / offers small comfort, / yet life is far better there / than in the vexatious world."

The tolling of the evening bell from a temple in the fields sounded its somber note, and dew from the grasses along the way made her sleeves, already damp with tears, wetter than ever. A stormy wind began to blow, tumbling the leaves from the trees; the sky clouded over; and autumn showers began to fall. She could just catch the faint sad belling of a deer, and the half-audible lamentations of the insects. Everything contrived to fill her with a sense of desolation difficult to describe in words. Even in those earlier days, when her life had been a precarious journey from one cove or one island to another, she reflected sadly, she had never had such a feeling of hopelessness.

The retreat was in a lonely spot of moss-covered crags, the sort of place, she felt, where she could live out her days. As she looked about her, she noted that the bush clover in the dew-filled garden had been stripped of its leaves by frost, that the chrysanthemums by the hedge, past their prime, were faded and dry—all reflecting, it seemed, her own condition. Making her way to where the statue of the Buddha was enshrined, she said a prayer: "May the spirit of the late emperor attain perfect enlightenment; may he quickly gain the wisdom of the buddhas!" But even as she did so, the image of her dead son seemed to appear before her, and she wondered in what future existence she might be able to forget him.[8]

Next to the Jakkō-in she had a small building erected, ten feet square in size, with one room to sleep in and the other to house the image of the Buddha. Morning and evening, day and night, she performed her devotions in front of the image, ceaselessly intoning the Buddha's name over the long hours. In this way, always diligent, she passed the months and days.

On the fifteenth day of the Tenth Month, as evening was approaching, Kenreimon'in heard the sound of footsteps on the dried oak leaves that littered the garden. "Who could be coming to call at a place so far removed from the world as this?" she said, addressing her woman companion. "Go see who it is. If it is someone I should not see, I must hurry to take cover!" But when the woman went to look, she found that it was only a stag that had happened to pass by.

"Who was it?" asked Kenreimon'in, to which her companion, Lady Dainagon no Suke,[9] struggling to hold back her tears, replied with this poem:

> Who would tread a path to this rocky lair?
> It was a deer whose passing rustled the leaves of the oak.

Struck by the pathos of the situation, Kenreimon'in carefully inscribed the poem on the small sliding panel by her window.

During her drab and uneventful life, bitter as it was, she found many things that provided food for thought. The trees ranged before the eaves of her retreat suggested to her the seven rows of jewel-laden trees that are said to grow in the Western Paradise, and the water pooled in a crevice in the rocks brought to mind the wonderful water of eight blessings[1] to be found there. Spring blossoms, so easily scattered with the breeze, taught her a lesson in impermanence:

8. These two paragraphs in effect offer a digest of the conventional autumn imagery in classical Japanese poetry.
9. One of Emperor Antoku's nurses and a lady-in-waiting to Kenreimon'in.
1. According to one of the Buddhist sutras, a pond in the Pure Land has waters that possess eight virtues: purity, coolness, sweetness, softness, luster, peace, healing, and growth. The sutra also notes that paradise, or the Pure Land, is ringed with seven rows of trees having gold roots, copper-gilt trunks, white-gold branches, agate twigs, coral leaves, moonstone blossoms, and pearl fruit.

the autumn moon, so quickly hidden by its companion clouds, spoke of the transience of life. Those court ladies in the Zhaoyang Hall in China who admired the blossoms at dawn soon saw their petals blown away by the wind; those in the Changqiu Palace[2] who gazed at the evening moon had its brightness stolen from them by clouds. Once in the past, this lady too had lived in similar splendor, reclining on brocade bedclothes in chambers of gold and jade, and now in a hut of mere brushwood and woven vines—even strangers must weep for her.

Summary   After Kenreimon'in has lived in her hermitage for about half a year, Retired Emperor GoShirakawa decides to visit her. The journey to the mountain recesses of the little temple known as Jakkō-in proves arduous. The royal entourage, modestly limited to some dozen nobles, makes its way through the thick summer wilderness. When they come on the humble cottage, where the only visitors have been monkeys swinging in the trees, the retired emperor is astonished; and when Kenreimon'in descends from the mountain, where she has gone to pick wildflowers, GoShirakawa at first does not even recognize her. Tearfully, they reminisce, as the thoughts of better days rush in upon them. And then, in an incredible passage of just a few paragraphs, Kenreimon'in relives all the horrid experiences of her clan, which the tale has spent hundreds of pages chronicling. Neither Kenreimon'in nor the retired emperor can quite believe how the world has changed, how the fortunate have fallen. When she finishes, it is time for the ex-emperor to leave.

The Death of the Imperial Lady (5)

While they were speaking, the bell of the Jakkō-in sounded, signaling the close of the day, and the sun sank beyond the western hills. The retired emperor, reluctant though he was to leave, wiped away his tears and prepared to begin the journey back.

All her memories of the past brought back to her once more, Kenreimon'in could scarcely stem the flood of tears with her sleeve. She stood watching as the imperial entourage set out for the capital, watching until it was far in the distance. Then she turned to the image of the Buddha and, speaking through her tears, uttered this prayer: "May the spirit of the late emperor and the souls of all my clanspeople who perished attain complete and perfect enlightenment: may they quickly gain the wisdom of the Buddhas!"

In the past she had faced eastward with this petition: "Great Deity of the Grand Shrine of Ise and Great Bodhisattva Hachiman, may the Son of Heaven be blessed with most wonderful longevity, may he live a thousand autumns, ten thousand years!" But now she changed direction and, facing west with palms pressed together, in sorrow spoke these words: "May the souls of all those who have perished find their way to Amida's Pure Land!"

On the sliding panel of her sleeping room she had inscribed the following poems:

> When did my heart learn such ways?
> Of late I think so longingly of palace companions I once knew!

2. Two residences where the Chinese emperor's consorts lived during the Han Dynasty (206 B.C.E.–220 C.E.); the Chinese names impart a faded grandeur, and the characters with which they are written—the Brilliant Sun Pavilion (Zhaoyang Hall) and the Palace of Long Autumn [Nights] (Changqiu Palace)— enhance the poetic touch of the sentence.

> The past, too, has vanished like a dream—
> my days by this brushwood door cannot be long in number!

The following poem is reported to have been inscribed on a pillar of Kenreimon'in's retreat by Minister of the Left Sanesada, one of the officials who accompanied the retired emperor on his visit:

> You who in past times were likened to the moon—
> dwelling now deep in these faraway mountains, a light no longer
> shining—

Once, when Kenreimon'in was bathed in tears, overwhelmed by memories of the past and thoughts of the future, she heard the cry of a mountain cuckoo and wrote this poem:

> Come then, cuckoo, let us compare tears—
> I too do nothing but cry out in a world of pain

The Taira warriors who survived the Dan-no-ura hostilities and were taken prisoner were paraded through the main streets of the capital and then either beheaded or sent into exile far from their wives and children. With the exception of Taira no Yorimori,[3] not one escaped execution or was permitted to remain in the capital.

With regard to the forty or more Taira wives, no special punitive measures were taken—they were left to join their relatives or to seek aid from persons they had known in the past. But even those fortunate enough to find themselves seated within sumptuous hangings were not spared the winds of uncertainty, and those who ended in humble brushwood dwellings could not live free of dust and turmoil. Husbands and wives who had slept pillow to pillow now found themselves at the far ends of the sky. Parents and children who had nourished each other no longer even knew each other's whereabouts. Although their loving thoughts never for a moment ceased, lament as they might, they had somehow to endure these things.

And all of this came about because the lay priest and prime minister Taira no Kiyomori, holding the entire realm within the four seas in the palm of his hand, showed no respect for the ruler above or the slightest concern for the masses of common people below. He dealt out sentences of death or exile in any fashion that suited him, took no heed of how the world or those in it might view his actions—and this is what happened! There can be no room for doubt— it was the evil deeds of the father, the patriarch, that caused the heirs and offspring to suffer this retribution!

After some time had gone by, Kenreimon'in fell ill. Grasping the five-color cord[4] attached to the hand of Amida Buddha, the central figure in the sacred triad, she repeatedly invoked his name: "Hail to the Thus Come One Amida, lord of teachings of the Western Paradise—may you guide me there without fail!" The nuns Dainagon-no-suke and Awa-no-naishi attended her on her left and right, their voices raised in unrestrained weeping, for they sensed in their

---

3. Who abandoned his clan. Yorimori is richly rewarded by the Genji, both because he defected when the Heike fled the capital and because his mother was the one who persuaded the Heike to spare Yoritomo's life. He becomes a member of the emperor's cabinet.
4. At the hour of death, the cord would lead the faithful to the Pure Land.

grief that her end was now at hand. As the sound of the dying woman's recitations grew fainter and fainter, a purple cloud appeared from the west, the room became filled with a strange fragrance, and the strains of music could be heard in the sky. Human life has its limits, and that of the imperial lady ended in the middle days of the Second Month in the second year of the Kenkyū era [1191].

Her two female attendants, who from the time she became imperial consort had never once been parted from her, were beside themselves with grief at her passing, helpless though they were to avert it. The support on which they had depended from times past had now been snatched from them, and they were left destitute, yet even in that pitiable state they managed to hold memorial services each year on the anniversary of her death. And in due time they, too, we are told, imitating the example of the dragon king's daughter in her attainment of enlightenment and following in the footsteps of Queen Vaidehi,[5] fulfilled their long-cherished hopes for rebirth in the Pure Land.

5. The wife of an Indian king who embraced Buddhism. She is said to have entered the Pure Land after listening to the preaching of Prince Siddhārtha, the historical Buddha and founder of Buddhism. The Nāga king was a Buddhist deity in dragon form and protector of the faith; his daughter grasped the Buddhist doctrines and attained enlightenment at the remarkable age of seven.

Selected Bibliographies

I. Circling the Mediterranean: Europe and the Islamic World

On the idea of the Mediterranean, see the classic 1949 study by Fernand Braudel, *The Mediterranean and the Mediterranean World in the Age of Philip II*, trans. Siân Reynolds (1972–1973; rpt., 1996), as well as the increasingly influential work of Peregrine Horden and Nicholas Purcell, *The Corrupting Sea: A Study of Mediterranean History* (2000). On late antiquity and the early Middle Ages, see Peter Brown, *The World of Late Antiquity: From Marcus Aurelius to Muhammad* (1989), and Averil Cameron, *The Mediterranean World in Late Antiquity*, A.D. 395–600 (1993).

For an overview of medieval Islamic history, see John Esposito, *Oxford History of Islam* (2000); Albert Hourani, *A History of the Arab Peoples* (2002); Seyyed Hossein Nasr, *Islam: Religion, History and Civilization* (2003). Information on almost any subject can be found in P. J. Bearman et al., eds., *Encyclopaedia of Islam*, 12 vols. (2nd ed., 1960–2005). A useful account of Persian poetics is offered by Julie Scott Meisami, *Medieval Persian Court Poetry* (1987).

For a survey of Europe's history from the fall of Rome to the beginnings of the Renaissance, three classic and still valuable studies are R. W. Southern, *The Making of the Middle Ages* (1953); Charles Homer Haskins, *The Renaissance of the Twelfth Century* (1927); and J. W. Huizinga, *The Autumn of the Middle Ages* (1919), trans. Rodney J. Payton and Ulrich Mammitzsch (1996). For information on almost any topic pertaining to medieval Europe, see *The Dictionary of the Middle Ages*, gen. ed. Joseph Strayer, 13 vols. (1989), with *Supplement 1*, ed. William Chester Jordan (2003).

Classic overviews of medieval European literary history and its place within the discipline of world literature can be found in Ernst Robert Curtius, *European Literature and the Latin Middle Ages* (1948), trans. Willard Trask (1953), and Erich Auerbach, *Mimesis: The Representation of Reality in Western Literature* (1946), trans. Willard Trask (1953; rpt., 2003). On the literary interactions of the Islamic world and medieval Europe, see María Rosa Menocal, *The Arabic Role in Medieval Literary History* (1987), and the reappraisal of Menocal's work in *A Sea of Languages: Literature and Culture in the Pre-modern Mediterranean*, ed. Suzanne Conklin Akbari and Karla Mallette (2011).

Petrus Alfonsi
A full translation of the *Disciplina Clericalis* by Joseph Ramon Jones and John Esten Keller appears as *The Scholar's Guide* (1969). See the insightful biography by John Tolan, *Petrus Alfonsi and His Medieval Readers* (1993). For a reading of the *Disciplina Clericalis* that places it in the context of other medieval frame-tale narratives, see David A. Wacks, *Framing Iberia: "Maqāmāt" and Frametales in Medieval Spain* (2007).

Apuleius
Two accessible English translations of Apuleius's work include helpful introduction and notes: see

Apuleius, *The Golden Ass*, trans. P. G. Walsh (1994), and Apuleius, *The Golden Ass or Metamorphoses*, trans. E. J. Kenney (1998). For an overview of Apuleius's other works, see *Apuleius: Rhetorical Works*, ed. Stephen J. Harrison, John L. Hilton, and Vincent J. C. Hunink (2001), and for a biography of the writer in his social and intellectual context, see Stephen J. Harrison, *Apuleius: A Latin Sophist* (2000 [the 2004 paperback edition has an updated bibliography]). Offering a perspective more rooted in comparative literary history is John J. Winkler, *Auctor and Actor: A Narratological Reading of Apuleius's "The Golden Ass"* (1985; rev. ed., 1991).

Farid ud-Din Attar
For a full version of the poem, see Farid ud-Din Attar, *The Conference of the Birds*, trans. Sholeh Wolpé (2017); for thematic studies of the *Conference*, see Dick Davis, "The Journey as Paradigm: Literal and Metaphorical Travel in Attar's *Mantiq al-Tayr*," *Edebiyât*, n.s. 4.2 (1993); Dick Davis, "Sufism and Poetry: A Marriage of Convenience?" *Edebiyât*, n.s. 10.2 (1999); and Jerome W. Clinton, "The Downward Path to Wisdom: Gender and Archetype in the Story of Sheikh Sam'an," in *A Pearl in Wine: Essays on the Life, Music, and Sufism of Hazrat Inayat Khan*, ed. Pir Zia Inayat Khan (2001). For a biographical overview, see Benedikt Reinert, "Attar," in *Encyclopaedia Iranica*, ed. Ehsan Yarshater, vol. 3 (1989). On Attar's *Biographies of the Saints*, see Paul E. Losensky, "Words and Deeds: Message and Structure in 'Attar's *Tadhkirat al-awliya*'," in *'Attar and the Persian Sufi Tradition: The Art of Spiritual Flight*, ed. Leonard Lewisohn and Christopher Shackle (2006).

Augustine
A wonderful introduction and detailed notes can be found in the translation by Henry Chadwick (1991) and also the 3-volume edition and commentary by James J. O'Donnell (1992), both titled *Confessions*. O'Donnell's text is available online from the Stoa Consortium in cooperation with the Perseus Project at www.stoa.org/hippo/. For an account of Augustine's life by the foremost historian of early Christianity in the Roman Empire, see Peter Brown, *Augustine of Hippo: A Biography* (1967; 2nd ed., 2000). A provocative and engaging life of the bishop and saint appears in James J. O'Donnell, *Augustine: A New Biography* (2005). On Augustine's own reading practices and the reading communities that formed in his wake, see Brian Stock, *Augustine the Reader: Meditation, Self-Knowledge and the Ethics of Interpretation* (1996). A collection of scholarly essays that contextualize Augustine and his works in theological, historical, and cultural terms is *A Companion to Augustine* (2012) by Mark Vessey, with the assistance of Shelley Reid, ed.

Beowulf
See the invaluable guide to the poem by Andy Orchard, *A Critical Companion to 'Beowulf'* (2003). A useful collection of essays is Robert Bjork and John Niles, eds., *A Beowulf Handbook* (1997). For a broad view of Anglo-Saxon literature and culture, see Malcolm Godden and Michael Lapidge, eds., *The Cambridge Companion to Old English Literature* (1991).

The Christian Bible
A full text with useful notes can be found in *The New Oxford Annotated Bible: New Revised Standard Version*, ed. Michael D. Coogan, Marc Z. Brettler, Carol Newsom, and Pheme Perkins (4th ed., 2010). For a brief overview of the historical background of the Bible and the diverse reading communities that have made it their own, see John Riches, *The Bible: A Very Short Introduction* (2000). The poetic and artistic qualities of scripture are on view in *The Literary Guide to the Bible*, ed. Robert Alter and Frank Kermode (1987). A more idiosyncratic reading of the Bible, rooted in a deep knowledge of history but with the profound inquisitiveness of a science fiction writer, appears in Isaac Asimov, *Asimov's Guide to the Bible: The Old and New Testaments* (1981; rpt., 1988). An intriguing interpretation of the Bible as graphic novel is Siku's *The Manga Bible: From Genesis to Revelation* (2008).

Giovanni Boccaccio
The standard biography is Vittore Branca, *Boccaccio: The Man and His Works*, trans. Richard Monges and Dennis J. McAuliffe (1976). Useful guides to the *Decameron* include Giuseppe Mazzotta, *The World at Play in Boccaccio's "Decameron"* (1986); David Wallace, *Giovanni Boccaccio: "Decameron"* (1991); and Millicent Marcus, *An Allegory of Form: Literary Self-consciousness in the "Decameron"* (1979).

Geoffrey Chaucer
The most complete edition of Chaucer's poetry, with authoritative notes and commen-

tary, is *The Riverside Chaucer*, ed. Larry D. Benson (3rd ed., 1987). An engaging portrait of Chaucer and his times can be found in Donald R. Howard, *Chaucer: His Life, His Works, His World* (1987). On the manuscript history of the *Canterbury Tales* in historical context, see Derek Pearsall, *The Canterbury Tales* (1985), and for an art-historical perspective focused on the poem's interlocking structure, see V. A. Kolve, *Chaucer and the Imagery of Narrative: The First Five Canterbury Tales* (1984). On Chaucer's role in the premodern invention of the subject, see Lee Patterson, *Chaucer and the Subject of History* (1991). On sexuality and gender, including influential readings of the Wife of Bath and the Pardoner, see Carolyn Dinshaw, *Chaucer's Sexual Poetics* (1989).

Christine de Pizan

A full translation of Christine de Pizan's *City of Ladies* appears in Rosalind Brown-Grant, trans., *The Book of the City of Ladies* (1999); another popular translation of the same title is by Earl Jeffrey Richards (1982). *Christine de Pizan: Her Life and Works* (1984), by Charity Cannon Willard, is a highly readable biography of the author by a scholar who played a crucial role in reawakening modern readers' interest in Christine's writings. Well-chosen excerpts from Christine's numerous works of prose and poetry, accompanied by influential critical essays, appear in Renate Blumenfeld-Kosinski and Kevin Brownlee, ed. and trans., *The Selected Writings of Christine de Pizan* (1997). For an insightful study of the interrelation of the text and illuminated miniatures in Christine's manuscripts, see Sandra Hindman, *Christine de Pizan's "Epistre Othéa": Painting and Politics at the Court of Charles VI* (1986). A study of Christine de Pizan's *City of Ladies* in the light of premodern feminism is Maureen Quilligan's *The Allegory of Female Authority: Christine de Pizan's "Cité des Dames"* (1991).

Dante Alighieri

Charles Singleton's annotated translation of Dante's *Divine Comedy*, with facing-page Italian text, is unsurpassed (6 vols., 1970–1975; rpt., 1990–1991). See also Singleton's groundbreaking and still stimulating short studies *Commedia: Elements of Structure* (1954) and *Journey to Beatrice* (1958). Short articles on a range of topics appear in *The Dante Encyclopedia*, gen. ed. Richard Lansing (2000), and a synoptic view of the encyclopedic quality of the

Comedy is given in Giuseppe Mazzotta, *Dante's Vision and the Circle of Knowledge* (1993). The influence of Singleton remains strong in recent generations of Dante scholarship. Robert Pogue Harrison responds to Singleton's *Journey* in his *Body of Beatrice* (1988), while Teodolinda Barolini pushes back against the theologizing impulse of Singleton's work in *The Undivine Comedy: Detheologizing Dante* (1992). On Dante's relationship to his poetic forebears, from Virgil to the Occitan troubadours, see Teodolinda Barolini, *Dante's Poets: Textuality and Truth in the "Comedy"* (1984).

Abolqasem Ferdowsi

A complete version of the *Shahnameh* with an excellent introduction can be found in Abolqasem Ferdowsi, *Shahnameh: The Persian Book of Kings*, trans. Dick Davis (2006); for a fuller analysis of how the epic poem fits into Persian political history, see Davis, *Epic and Sedition: The Case of Ferdowsi's "Shahnameh"* (1992). A summary of Ferdowsi's life appears in Djalal Khaleghi-Motlagh, "Ferdowsi, Abu'l-Qasem: i. Life," in *Encyclopaedia Iranica*, ed. Ehsan Yarshater, vol. 9 (1999). For a broad overview of the place of Ferdowsi's epic in the traditions of oral poetry, see Olga Davidson, *Poet and Hero in the Persian Book of Kings* (1994), and Kumiko Yamamoto, *The Oral Background of Persian Epics: Storytelling and Poetry* (2003). On the interrelation of poetry and history writing in medieval Persia, viewed comparatively against medieval European literature, see Julie Scott Meisami, *Medieval Persian Court Poetry* (1987). See also Meisami, *Persian Historiography to the End of the Twelfth Century* (1999), especially her discussion of the *Shahnameh* itself; more generally, she provides a very useful framework for understanding the practice of writing history in medieval Persia.

Kebra Nagast

An excellent account of the continuities of Jewish and Islamic traditions within Ethiopian Christian culture can be found in Wendy Laura Belcher, "African Rewritings of the Jewish and Islamic Solomonic Tradition: The Triumph of the Queen of Sheba in the Ethiopian Fourteenth-Century Text *Kəbrä Nägäst*," in *Sacred Tropes: Tanakh, New Testament, and Qur'an as Literature and Culture*, ed. Roberta Sterman Sabbath (2009). For a short overview of the *Kebra Nagast*, see Paolo Marrassini,

"Kebra Nagast," in Encyclopaedia Aethiopica, gen. ed. Siegbert Uhlig, vol. 3 (2007). A wide-ranging perspective on the sources of the Kebra Nagast appears in Stuart C. Munro-Hay, Quest for the Ark of the Covenant: The True History of the Tablets of Moses (2005). On the intersection of Ethiopian literary history with pictorial art, focused specifically on the Kebra Nagast, see Denis Nosnitsin, "Ethiopian Literature in Ge'ez," in the richly illustrated Arise and Go Toward the South: 2000 Years of Christianity in Ethiopia, ed. Annegret Marx et al. (2007).

Marie de France

A full collection of Marie's lais appears in Dorothy Gilbert, trans., Marie de France: Poetry (2015). A still useful overview of her work is Emanuel J. Mickel, Jr., Marie de France (1974); for an insightful reading of Marie within the framework of medieval gender categories, see R. Howard Bloch, The Anonymous Marie de France (2003). An influential study of Marie's ouvre is Sharon Kinoshita and Peggy McCracken, Marie de France: A Critical Companion (2012).

Medieval Lyrics

On the Latin and vernacular lyrics of medieval Europe, see Peter Dronke, The Medieval Lyric (1968; 3rd ed., 1996). On Dante and other lyric poets of medieval Italy, see Robert Pogue Harrison, The Body of Beatrice (1988). On the Jewish poets of medieval Spain, see the wonderful study and sensitive translations to be found in Peter Cole, The Dream of the Poem: Hebrew Poetry from Muslim and Christian Spain, 950–1492 (2007). On the Arabic poetry of Spain in its cultural context, see Jerrilynn D. Dodds, María Rosa Menocal, and Abigail Krasner Balbale, The Arts of Intimacy: Christians, Jews, and Muslims in the Making of Castilian Culture (2008). For translations of Persian lyric poetry, see Dick Davis, Borrowed Ware: Medieval Persian Epigrams (1996) and The Faces of Love: Hafez and the Poets of Shiraz (2012). For a brilliant study of the resonance of medieval lyric with the poetics of modern popular music, see María Rosa Menocal, Shards of Love: Exile and the Origins of the Lyric (1994).

The Qur'an

An extraordinarily readable translation of the Qur'an with good annotations is M. A. S. Abdel Haleem, The Qur'an: A New Translation (2004).

See also his Understanding the Qur'an: Themes and Style (1999). A scholarly collection of essays appears in Jane Dammen McAuliffe, ed., The Cambridge Companion to the Qur'an (2009); for detailed information on specific topics, see also McAuliffe, ed., The Encyclopaedia of the Qur'an, 5 vols. (2001–2006). A useful overview is W. Montgomery Watt and Richard Bell, Introduction to the Qur'an (rev. ed., 2001). To get a sense of the rhythm and musicality of Qur'anic recitation, see Michael Sells, "Sound, Spirit, and Gender in the Qur'an" (1991), reprinted as an appendix to his Approaching the Qur'an: The Early Revelations (2nd ed., 2007), which includes a CD.

Sir Gawain and the Green Knight

For the text of the poem in Middle English, with excellent notes and introduction, see Sir Gawain and the Green Knight, ed. J. R. R. Tolkien and E. V. Gordon (2nd ed., rev., Norman Davis, 1967); see also Simon Armitage, trans., Sir Gawain and the Green Knight: A New Verse Translation (2007). A useful collection of essays on the works of the author of Sir Gawain and the Green Knight is Derek Brewer and Jonathan Gibson, eds., A Companion to the Gawain-Poet (1997). On the historical background, see John M. Bowers, The Politics of Pearl: Court Poetry in the Age of Richard II (2001). For an intriguing reading of the poem in the context of fourteenth-century philosophy, see Ross G. Arthur, Medieval Sign Theory and Sir Gawain and the Green Knight (1987).

Song of Roland

An edition of the poem with facing-page English translation, plus a separate volume of commentary, can be found in Gerald J. Brault, The Song of Roland: An Analytical Edition, 2 vols. (1978). For a well-written introduction to the epic with emphasis on the role of narratology, see Eugene Vance, Reading the Song of Roland (1970). On the context of emergent French nationalism and feudal politics, see Peter Haidu, The Subject of Violence: The "Song of Roland" and the Birth of the State (1993). For a reading of the Song of Roland in terms of European views of Islam, with a special focus on gender, see Sharon Kinoshita, Medieval Boundaries: Rethinking Difference in Old French Literature (2006), especially chap. 4. On the interrelation of the genres of epic and romance, see the lively analysis of Sarah Kay, The Chansons de geste in the Age of Romance (1995).

The Thousand and One Nights

The best short overview of the history of the *Nights'* composition and translation is Dwight F. Reynolds, "A Thousand and One Nights: A History of the Text and Its Reception," in *Arabic Literature in the Post-classical Period*, ed. Roger Allen and D. S. Richards (2006). The novelist Robert Irwin has published a widely available (but not always consistently reliable) guide called *The Arabian Nights: A Companion* (1994; rpt., 2004). The two best collections on the *Nights* focus respectively on the formation of the work and on its reception. The first is *The Arabian Nights Reader*, ed. Ulrich Marzolph (2006), which includes many of the crucial, groundbreaking scholarly articles on the *Nights* by such authors as Muhsin Mahdi, the modern editor of the Arabic text, and Nabia Abbott, the discoverer of the ninth-century manuscript fragment that is the first evidence of the work; the second, which offers some very useful correctives to Irwin, is *The Arabian Nights in Historical Context: Between East and West*, ed. Saree Makdisi and Felicity Nussbaum (2008).

Fruitful literary analyses of the *Nights* include Sandra Naddaff, *Arabesque: Narrative Structure and the Aesthetics of Repetition in the 1001 Nights* (1991), which features a comparative and theoretical literary analysis of the Porter and the Three Ladies group of tales, and David Pinault, *Story-telling Techniques in the Arabian Nights* (1992), which offers an excellent comparative analysis of the Syria and Cairo compilations of the *Nights* and their historical contexts. Provocative food for thought on the *Nights'* role in modern fiction, especially in magical realism, can be found in Jorge Luis Borges, "The Translators of *The Thousand and One Nights*" (1934), trans. Esther Allen, in *Selected Non-fictions* (in paper-

back as *The Total Library: Non-fiction, 1922–86*), ed. Eliot Weinberger (1999), and in *The Translation Studies Reader*, ed. Lawrence Venuti (2nd ed., 2004). Finally, http://journalofthenights.blogspot.com/ provides an appropriately abundant and fertile overview of everything imaginable responding to the *Nights*—adaptations (music, opera, theatre, film, video games, toys, etc.), recently published studies and articles, new translations, political issues (especially censorship), et cetera.

Travel and Encounter

An engaging overview of the many facets of travel writing can be found in Felipe Fernandez-Armesto, *Pathfinders: A Global History* (2006). For a historian's view of the evidence for Marco Polo's travels and the importance of his work as a source widely read at the dawn of the Age of Exploration, see John Larner, *Marco Polo and the Discovery of the World* (1999). Essays on Marco Polo's original text and on modern literary and cinematic adaptations of his work are available in *Marco Polo and the Encounter of East and West*, ed. Suzanne Conklin Akbari and Amilcare Iannucci (2008). On Ibn Battuta, a useful introduction by H. A. R. Gibb accompanies his translation of selections in *Travels in Asia and Africa, 1325–1354* (1929, with many reprints). A more detailed overview of the writer and his travels is provided by Ross E. Dunn, *The Adventures of Ibn Battuta, a Muslim Traveler of the Fourteenth Century* (1986; rev. ed., 2005). A biography of the anonymous author of *The Book of John Mandeville* and an overview of the work can be found in M. C. Seymour, *Sir John Mandeville* (1993); see also the brilliant study of *The Book of John Mandeville* in its many vernacular versions by Iain Macleod Higgins, *Writing East: The "Travels" of Sir John Mandeville* (1997).

II. India's Classical Age

Daniel H. H. Ingalls's *An Anthology of Sanskrit Court Poetry* (1965) still offers the best critical introduction to the classical lyric tradition; it also contains a complete, annotated translation of Vidyākara's eleventh-century *Subhāṣitaratnakośa*. *Theater of Memory: The Plays of Kālidāsa*, ed. Barbara Stoler Miller, (1984), and J. A. B. van Buitenen's *Tales of Ancient India* (1959) provide similar overviews of the classical dramatic and narrative genres, with translations of representative texts. A. Berridale Keith's *A History of Sanskrit Literature* (1928) remains a useful source of information. Sheldon Pollock's *The Language of the Gods in the World of Men: Sanskrit, Culture, and Power in Premodern India* (2006), which is more advanced, is the most comprehensive, up-to-date, and stimulating account of the world of Sanskrit literature and culture. Edward Dimock et al., *The Literatures of India: An*

Introduction (1974), and Sheldon Pollock, *Literary Cultures in History: Reconstructions from South Asia* (2003), include excellent discussions of the classical period in the context of other Indian literatures. General historical background is provided in Burton Stein, *A History of India* (1998), and Stanley Wolpert, *A New History of India* (8th ed., 2008); and a more detailed analysis appears in Upinder Singh, *A History of Ancient and Early Medieval India: From the Stone Age to the 12th Century* (2009).

Classical Sanskrit Lyric

Daniel H. H. Ingalls's *An Anthology of Sanskrit Court Poetry* (1965) provides the most balanced introduction to the classical Sanskrit lyric, containing a complete, annotated translation of Vidyākara's eleventh-century collection, *Subhāṣitaratnakośa*, and an excellent critical discussion. Barbara Stoler Miller's *Bhartṛhari: Poems* (1967) focuses on the multifaceted work of a single poet, translating 200 poems from his fifth-century *Satakatryam*. J. Moussaieff Masson and W. S. Merwin's *Sanskrit Love Poetry* (1977), an unusual collaboration between an American scholar of Sanskrit and an American poet, provides a more panoramic view, offering memorable examples from the second to the sixteenth century. Edward Dimock et al., *The Literatures of India: An Introduction* (1974), contains stimulating analyses by several scholars on the aesthetic, cultural, and historical dimensions of Sanskrit poetry. Martha Ann Selby, *Grow Long, Blessed Night: Love Poems from Classical India* (2000), compares the Sanskrit lyric to the lyric in early Prakrit and classical Tamil by presenting poems on a common theme.

Classical Tamil Lyric

A. K. Ramanujan's compilation, *Poems of Love and War: From the Eight Anthologies and the Ten Long Poems of Classical Tamil* (1985), is the most comprehensive literary and scholarly representation in English of classical Tamil poetry and poetics. His earlier collection, *The Interior Landscape: Love Poems from a Classical Tamil Anthology* (1967), offers a partial but more compact introduction to the subject. Two books by George L. Hart III, *The Poems of Ancient Tamil: Their Milieu and Their Sanskrit Counterparts* (1975) and *Poets of the Tamil Anthologies: Ancient Poems of Love and War* (1979), provide alternative translations and extended commentary in English. K. Kailasapathy's older work, *Tamil Heroic Poetry* (1968), offers a useful comparative perspective on classical Tamil poetry, as does Martha Ann Selby's more recent study, *Grow Long, Blessed Night: Love Poems from Classical India* (2000).

Kālidāsa

Theater of Memory: The Plays of Kālidāsa, ed. Barbara Stoler Miller, trans. Edwin Gerow, David Gitomer, and Barbara Stoler Miller (1984), provides the best translations of and commentary on Sanskrit drama and the classical Indian stage; it includes a detailed discussion of how the plays may have been performed. Other English versions of Kālidāsa's plays appear in Michael Coulson, *Three Sanskrit Plays* (1981), and Velcheru Narayana Rao and David Shulman, *How Úrvashi Was Won* (2009). Translations of Kālidāsa's poetry include Leonard Nathan, *The Transport of Love* (1976); Hank Heifetz, *The Origin of the Young God* (1985); and David Smith, *Birth of Kumāra* (2005).

Somadeva

C. H. Tawney's *The Kathá Sarit Ságara: or, Ocean of the Streams of Story*, 2 vols. (1880–1884), provides a complete translation, later edited with additional notes by N. M. Penzer (10 vols., 1924–1928; rpt., 1968). A selection of the stories, together with a critical discussion, is included in J. A. B. van Buitenen, *Tales of Ancient India* (1959). A new partial rendering, with an updated, contemporary perspective on Somadeva's classic, appears in Sir James Mallinson, *The Ocean of the Rivers of Story*, 2 vols. (2007–2009).

Viṣṇuśarman

Arthur W. Ryder's *The Pañchatantra* (1925; rpt., 1956) is a reliable rendering of the Sanskrit text, though its English style is now outdated. An alternative rendering, more recent but more uneven, is available in Chandra Rajan, *The Pañchatantra Viṣṇu Śarma* (1993). The history of the *Pañchatantra* and its transmission to the Middle East and Europe are discussed comprehensively in Joseph Jacobs, *History of the Aesopic Fable* (1889), and Maurice Winternitz, *A History of Indian Literature* (1963). Tales from the *Hitopadeśa*, another important ancient Indian source, are translated in *Animal Fables of India: Narayana's Hitopadesha, or, Friendly Counsel*, trans. Francis G. Hutchins (1985).

III. Medieval Chinese Literature

Two books by Mark Lewis, *China Between Empires: The Northern and Southern Dynasties* (2009) and *China's Cosmopolitan Empire: The Tang Dynasty* (2009), provide lively depictions of China's medieval world. Edward H. Schafer's *The Golden Peaches of Samarkand: A Study of T'ang Exotics* (1963) vividly evokes the multiethnic atmosphere of Tang culture.

For a general survey of medieval literature, see the relevant chapters in *The Cambridge History of Chinese Literature*, ed. Stephen Owen and Kang-i Sun Chang, 2 vols. (2010). On medieval poetry in particular, see Stephen Owen, *The Making of Early Chinese Classical Poetry* (2006); Kang-i Sun Chang, *Six Dynasties Poetry* (1986); and Kōjirō Yoshikawa, *An Introduction to Sung Poetry*, trans. Burton Watson (1967). Xiaofei Tian's *Beacon Fire and Shooting Star: The Literary Culture of the Liang (502–557)* (2008) is a compelling study of literary court culture in the South during the Period of Disunion.

Hanshan

Burton Watson, *Cold Mountain* (1962), contains lively translations of a selection of Hanshan's poetry. Excellent literary translations have been done by Gary Snyder, a poet associated with the Beat movement, in *Riprap and Cold Mountain Poems* (1965), and by Red Pine, *The Collected Songs of Cold Mountain* (1983; rev. ed., 2000). There is also a complete annotated translation by Robert Henricks, *The Poetry of Han-shan* (1990), who emphasizes the Buddhist dimension of the poetry. Paul Rouzer provides a broad context for Hanshan's poetry and gives extensive interpretations of his poems in *On Cold Mountain: A Buddhist Reading of the Hanshan Poems* (Seattle: University of Washington Press, 2016).

Li Qingzhao

Chapter 4 of *The Red Brush: Writing Women of Imperial China* (2004) by Idema Wilt and Beata Grant is devoted to Li Qingzhao's life and work. Pinqing Hu gives a portrait of her life in *Li Ch'ing-chao* (1966). A discussion of her "Afterword" can be found in Stephen Owen's *Remembrances: The Experience of the Past in Classical Chinese Literature* (1986). For a discussion of the development of the song lyric, see Kang-i Sun Chang's *The Evolution of Chinese Tz'u Poetry: From Late T'ang to Northern Sung* (1980). For a study of Li Qingzhao's image in her time and later ages consult Ronald Egan's *The Burden of Female Talent: the Poet Li Qingzhao and Her History in China* (2013). For more translations of Li Qingzhao's song lyrics, see James Cryer's *Plum Blossom: Poems of Li Ch'ing-chao* (1984), Sam Hamill's *The Lotus Lovers: Poems and Songs* (by Li Ye and Li Qin-gzhao) (1985), and Kenneth Rexroth and Ling Chung's *Li Ch'ing-chao: Complete Poems* (1979).

Literature about Literature

Stephen Owen's *Readings in Chinese Literary Thought* (1992) gives a captivating introduction to major works of Chinese literary thought and provides a bilingual translation of the original texts with detailed commentary. James Liu's *Chinese Theories of Literature* (1975) sketches major Chinese paradigms of the concept of literature. To explore literary thought in more recent times see *Modern Chinese Literary Thought: Writings on Literature, 1893–1945*, ed. Kirk Denton (1996). For scholarly essays on Chinese literary criticism in general see *Chinese Aesthetics and Literature: A Reader*, ed. Corinne H. Dale (2004). For a broader exploration of literary interpretation in Chinese and Western literatures, see Longxi Zhang's *The Tao and the Logos: Literary Hermeneutics, East and West* (1992).

Howard L. Goodman's *Ts'ao P'i Transcendent: The Political Culture of Dynasty-Founding in China at the End of the Han* (1998) traces Cao Pi's life as emperor and writer. For other translations of Lu Ji's rhapsody, see E. R. Hughes's *The Art of Letters: Lu Chi's "Wen fu,"* A.D. 302, A Translation and Comparative Study, with a forenote by I. A. Richards (1951), and Sam Hamill's *The Art of Writing: Lu Chi's Wen fu* (rev. ed., 1991).

Tang Poetry

Stephen Owen's *Traditional Chinese Poetry and Poetics: Omen of the World* (1985) provides a general introduction to Chinese poetry. For an anthology of guided readings in various genres of Chinese poetry, see Zongqi Cai's *How to Read Chinese Poetry: A Guided Anthology* (2008). To further explore the breadth and development of Tang poetry, see Stephen Owen's four magisterial studies: *The Poetry of the Early T'ang* (1977), *The Great Age of Chinese Poetry: The High T'ang* (1981), *The End of the Chinese 'Middle Ages': Essays in Mid-Tang Literary Culture* (1996), and *The Late Tang: Chinese Poetry of the Mid-Ninth Century (827–860)* (2006).

For translations of Wang Wei's poetry, see Pauline Yu's *The Poetry of Wang Wei: New Translations and Commentary* (1980), G. W. Robinson's *Poems of Wang Wei* (1973), and Vikram Seth's *Three Chinese Poets: Translations of Poems by Wang Wei, Li Bai, and Du Fu* (1992). For studies that explore Wang Wei's life, and his penchant for painting and Buddhism, see Marsha Wagner, *Wang Wei* (1981); Lewis Calvin and Dorothy Brush Walmsley, *Wang Wei, the Painter-Poet* (1968); and Jingqing Yang, *The Chan Interpretations of Wang Wei's Poetry: A Critical Review* (2007).

For translations of Li Bo's poetry, see Vikram Seth's *Three Chinese Poets: Translations of Poems by Wang Wei, Li Bai, and Du Fu* (1992). Paul W. Kroll's *Studies in Medieval Taoism and the Poetry of Li Po* (2009) and Paula Varsano's *Tracking the Banished Immortal: The Poetry of Li Bo and Its Critical Reception* (2003) are compelling studies of the poetry; Arthur Waley's *The Poetry and Career of Li Po, 701–762 A.D.* (1950) is a biography.

Among translations of Du Fu, David Hawkes's *A Little Primer of Tu Fu* (1967), an introductory bilingual edition of a few of the poems, is particularly recommended. For a complete bilingual translation of Du Fu's poetry see Stephen Owen's *The Poetry of Du Fu*, 6 volumes (2016). See also Burton Watson's *The Selected Poems of Du Fu* (2002). For studies of Du Fu's life and legacy see David McCraw's *Du Fu's Laments from the South* (1992) and Eva Shan Chou's *Reconsidering Tu Fu: Literary Greatness and Cultural Context* (1995).

For Bo Juyi's poetry, see Howard S. Levy's *Translations from Po Chü-i's Collected Works* (1978), David Hinton's *The Selected Poems of Po Chü-i* (1999), and Burton Watson's *Po Chü-i: Selected Poems* (2000). Arthur Waley's *The Life and Times of Po Chü-i* (1949) is a vivid evocation of Bo Juyi's life in his literary context.

Tao Qian

A. R. Davis's *T'ao Yüan-ming, A.D. 365–427, His Works and their Meaning*, 2 vols. (1984), and James Robert Hightower's *The Poetry of T'ao Ch'ien* (1970) provide complete translations of Tao Qian's poetry. Because his works circulated only in manuscript form for centuries before the advent of print, there are many different versions of his poems; Xiaofei Tian's *Tao Yuanming & Manuscript Culture: The Record of a Dusty Table* (2005) is a compelling study of how early editors adapted Tao Qian's pieces, based on their own image of him. Robert Ashmore's *The Transport of Reading: Text and Understanding in the World of Tao Qian (365–427)* (2010) discusses cultures of reading and interpretation in Tao Qian's work and time. Wendy Swartz's *Reading Tao Yuanming: Shifting Paradigms of Historical Reception (427–1900)* (2008) traces the changing images of Tao Qian from his death up until the twentieth century.

Yuan Zhen

You can read more Tang tales in Yang Xianyi and Gladys Yang's *Tang Dynasty Stories* (1986) and William H. Nienhauser Jr.'s *Tang Dynasty Tales: A Guided Reader* (2010). Stephen Owen's *The End of the Chinese 'Middle Ages': Essays in Mid-Tang Literary Culture* (1996) contains an excellent chapter on "The Story of Yingying." For a translation of the *Romance of the Western Chamber*, see Stephen H. West and Wilt L. Idema, *The Story of the Western Wing* (1995).

IV. Japan's Classical Age

To further explore early and medieval Japanese history see Conrad Schirokauer, David Lurie, and Suzanne Gay's *A Brief History of Japanese Civilization* (2nd ed., 2006) For a shorter treatment of Japanese history in the context of East Asia, Patricia Buckley Ebrey, Anne Walthall, and James B. Palais, *East Asia: A Cultural, Social, and Political History* (2nd ed., 2009), is recommended.

Traditional Japanese Literature: An Anthology, Beginnings to 1600, ed. Haruo Shirane (2007), and Donald Keene's Anthology of Japanese Literature: From the Earliest Era to the Mid-Nineteenth Century (1955) are great treasure troves of original early and medieval Japanese texts in English translation; see also Traditional Japanese Poetry: An Anthology, trans. Steven D. Carter (1991), and Classical Japanese Prose: An Anthology, ed. Helen Craig McCullough (1990). Lovers of travel literature will appreciate Donald Keene's Travelers of a Hundred Ages: The Japanese As Revealed Through 1,000 Years of Diaries (rev. ed., 1999). Keene presents a sweeping history of premodern Japanese literature in Seeds in the Heart: Japanese Literature from Earliest Times to the Late Sixteenth Century (1993). For a comprehensive history of Japanese literature see Cambridge History of Japanese Literature (2016), edited by Haruo Shirane, Tomi Suzuki, and David Lurie.

Earl Miner, Hiroko Odagiri, and Robert E. Morrell's The Princeton Companion to Classical Japanese Literature (1985) is a reliable reference work to the world of Japanese literature. Groundbreaking studies of the interplay between Chinese and Japanese cultural traditions in Japanese literature include David Pollack, The Fracture of Meaning: Japan's Synthesis of China from the Eighth Through the Eighteenth Centuries (1986); Thomas LaMarre, Uncovering Heian Japan: An Archaeology of Sensation and Inscription (2000); and Atsuko Sakaki, Obsessions with the Sino-Japanese Polarity in Japanese Literature (2005). Tomiko Yoda's Gender and National Literature: Heian Texts in the Constructions of Japanese Modernity (2004) is a compelling study of how Heian texts have influenced modern Japanese identity and self-understanding.

An Account of a Ten-Foot-Square Hut

Other translations include Donald Keene's "An Account of My Hut," in Anthology of Japanese Literature: From the Earliest Era to the Mid-Nineteenth Century (1955) and Yasuhiko Moriguchi and David Jenkins's Hōjōki: Visions of a Torn World (1996). Burton Watson's Four Huts: Asian Writings on the Simple Life (1994) presents Chōmei's essay together with three other famous texts by Chinese and Japanese poets on life in reclusion. Michele Marra compares Chōmei's and Kenkō's understanding of impermanence in "Semi-Recluses (tonseisha) and Impermanence (mujō): Kamo no Chōmei and Urabe Kenkō," Japanese Journal of Religious Studies (1984). For an exploration of Chōmei's work, see Thomas Blenman Hare's "Reading Kamo no Chōmei," Harvard Journal of Asiatic Studies (1989). Michele Marra's The Aesthetics of Discontent: Politics and Reclusion in Medieval Japanese Literature (1991) provides a broader view of Japanese medieval recluse literature.

The Man'yōshū

Good partial translations include Nippon Gakujutsu Shinkōkai's The Manyōshū, ed. Donald Keene (1965), Ian Hideo Levy's The Ten Thousand Leaves (1981), and Edwin Cranston's evocative translations in A Waka Anthology, vol. 1, The Gem-Glistening Cup (1993). Levy has also produced a detailed study of one poet, Hitomaro and the Birth of Japanese Lyricism (1984). Robert H. Brower and Earl Miner's Japanese Court Poetry (1961) contains a general study of the anthology, and Gary L. Ebersole's Ritual Poetry and the Politics of Death in Early Japan (1989) explores the religious and historical context of the anthology's poems on death and mourning.

Murasaki Shikibu

This anthology uses a new translation by Dennis Washburn; the three previous English translations of The Tale of Genji all have their partisans. The first English translation was published by Arthur Waley in installments between 1925 and 1933. Edward G. Seidensticker's The Tale of Genji (1976) is a beautiful translation, more faithful than Waley's. The translation by Royall Tyler (2001) is yet more faithful.

For a glimpse into the life of the author, see Murasaki Shikibu: Her Diary and Poetic Memoirs, trans. Richard Bowring (1982). Ivan Morris, The World of the Shining Prince: Court Life in Ancient Japan, with a new introduction by Barbara Ruch (1964; rpt., 1994), is a colorful account of the world that Murasaki and her characters inhabit.

The best brief introduction to the tale is Richard Bowring, *Murasaki Shikibu: "The Tale of Genji"* (1988). Two excellent longer studies are Norma Field, *The Splendor of Longing in the "Tale of Genji"* (1987), and Haruo Shirane, *The Bridge of Dreams: A Poetics of "The Tale of Genji"* (1987). *Envisioning "The Tale of Genji": Media, Gender, and Cultural Production* (2008), a collection of articles edited by Shirane, gives fascinating glimpses of how *The Tale of Genji* influenced later literature, art, and popular culture.

Poetry of the Heian Court

Robert Borgen's *Sugawara no Michizane and the Early Heian Court* (1986) is a detailed biography of Michizane and contains many translations from his poetry. For further translations of his poetry and of the Chinese-style imperial anthologies of the ninth century, see Judith N. Rabinovitch and Timothy R. Bradstock's *Dance of the Butterflies: Chinese Poetry from the Japanese Court Tradition* (2005) and Burton Watson's *Japanese Literature in Chinese*, 2 vols. (1975–1976).

Two complete translations of *The Kokinshū* are available in English: Helen Craig McCullough's *Kokin Wakashū: The First Imperial Anthology of Japanese Poetry, with "Tosa Nikki" and "Shinsen Waka"* (1985) and Laura Rasplica Rodd and Mary Catherine Henkenius's *Kokinshū: A Collection of Poems Ancient and Modern* (1984); Edwin A. Cranston's *A Waka Anthology*, vol. 2, *Grasses of Remembrance* (2006), contains selections from *The Kokinshū* with ample commentary. *Brocade by Night: "Kokin Wakashū" and the Court Style in Japanese Classical Poetry* (1985), McCullough's companion volume to her translation of the anthology, is a detailed study of the Chinese influences on Kokinshū poetry. On the interplay of poetry and politics at the Heian court, see Gustav Heldt's study *The Pursuit of Harmony: Poetry and Power in Early Heian Japan* (2008). Robert H. Brower and Earl Miner, *Japanese Court Poetry* (1961), is still the standard account of the development of the *waka* tradition in premodern Japan.

Sei Shōnagon

The selections printed in this anthology are taken from a complete translation by Meredith McKinney, *The Pillow Book* (2006). Other important translations include the pioneering translation of Arthur Waley, *The Pillow-Book of Sei Shōnagon* (1928); Ivan Morris, *The Pillow Book of Sei Shōnagon*, 2 vols. (1967) (the second volume contains useful notes and appendices); and the sampling in Helen Craig McCullough, *Classical Japanese Prose: An Anthology* (1990). Ivan Morris's *The World of the Shining Prince: Court Life in Ancient Japan* (1964), a colorful portrayal of the Heian period, will be helpful to readers of both *The Pillow Book* and *The Tale of Genji*.

The Tales of the Heike

In addition to Burton Watson's partial translation (2006) used for the selections in this anthology, Helen Craig McCullough's complete translation, *The Tale of the Heike* (1988), is recommended; it contains much useful background material and introductions to the work and its literary status. Paul Varley offers a helpful discussion of social issues in "Warriors as Courtiers: The Taira in *Heike monogatari*," in *Currents in Japanese Culture: Translations and Transformations*, ed. Amy Vladek Heinrich (1997). David T. Bialock's *Eccentric Spaces, Hidden Histories: Narrative, Ritual, and Royal Authority from "The Chronicles of Japan" to "The Tale of the Heike"* (2007) discusses *The Tales of the Heike* in its relation to Japanese and Chinese modes of history writing. Elizabeth Oyler's *Swords, Oaths, and Prophetic Visions: Authoring Warrior Rule in Medieval Japan* (2006), a compelling study of the relation between the rise of warrior rule and *The Tales of the Heike*, examines key protagonists and episodes from the text.

Ki no Tsurayuki

Complete translations of *Tosa Diary* include Helen Craig McCullough's *Kokin Wakashū: The First Imperial Anthology of Japanese Poetry, with "Tosa Nikki" and "Shinsen Waka"* (1985) and Earl Miner's *The Tosa Diary*, in his *Japanese Poetic Diaries* (1969).

McCullough's *Brocade by Night: "Kokin Wakashū" and the Court Style in Japanese Classical Poetry* (1985) focuses on *The Kokinshū* but also outlines the broader context of Tsurayuki's literary activities, and includes a discussion of *Tosa Diary*. Lynne Miyake, "The *Tosa Diary*: In the Interstices of Gender and Criticism," in *The Woman's Hand: Gender and Theory in Japanese Women's Writing*, ed. Paul Gordon Schalow and Janet A. Walker (1996), discusses Tsurayuki's diary in the context of gender issues.

Timeline

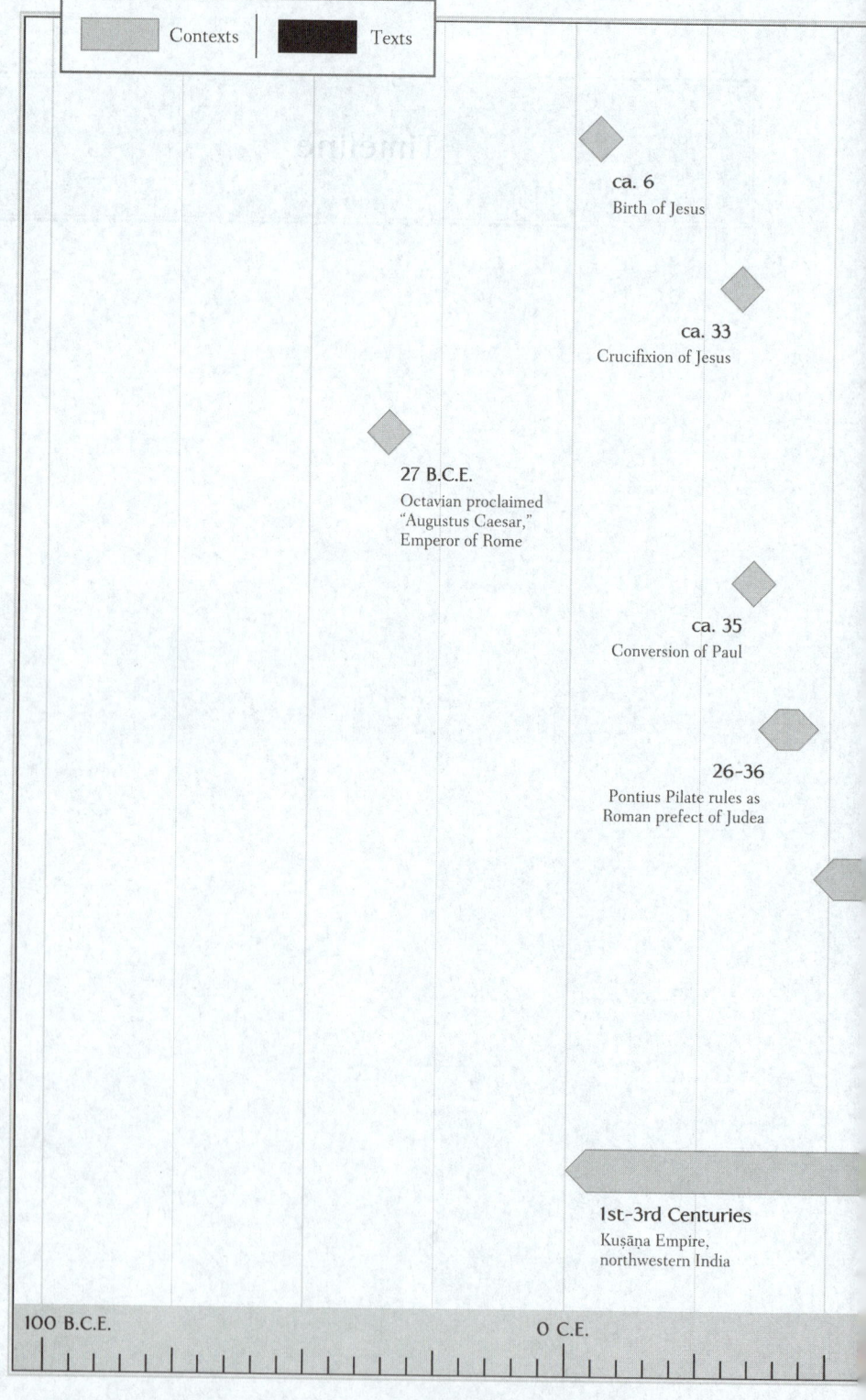

| Contexts | Texts |

ca. 6
Birth of Jesus

ca. 33
Crucifixion of Jesus

27 B.C.E.
Octavian proclaimed
"Augustus Caesar,"
Emperor of Rome

ca. 35
Conversion of Paul

26-36
Pontius Pilate rules as
Roman prefect of Judea

1st-3rd Centuries
Kuṣāṇa Empire,
northwestern India

100 B.C.E.   0 C.E.

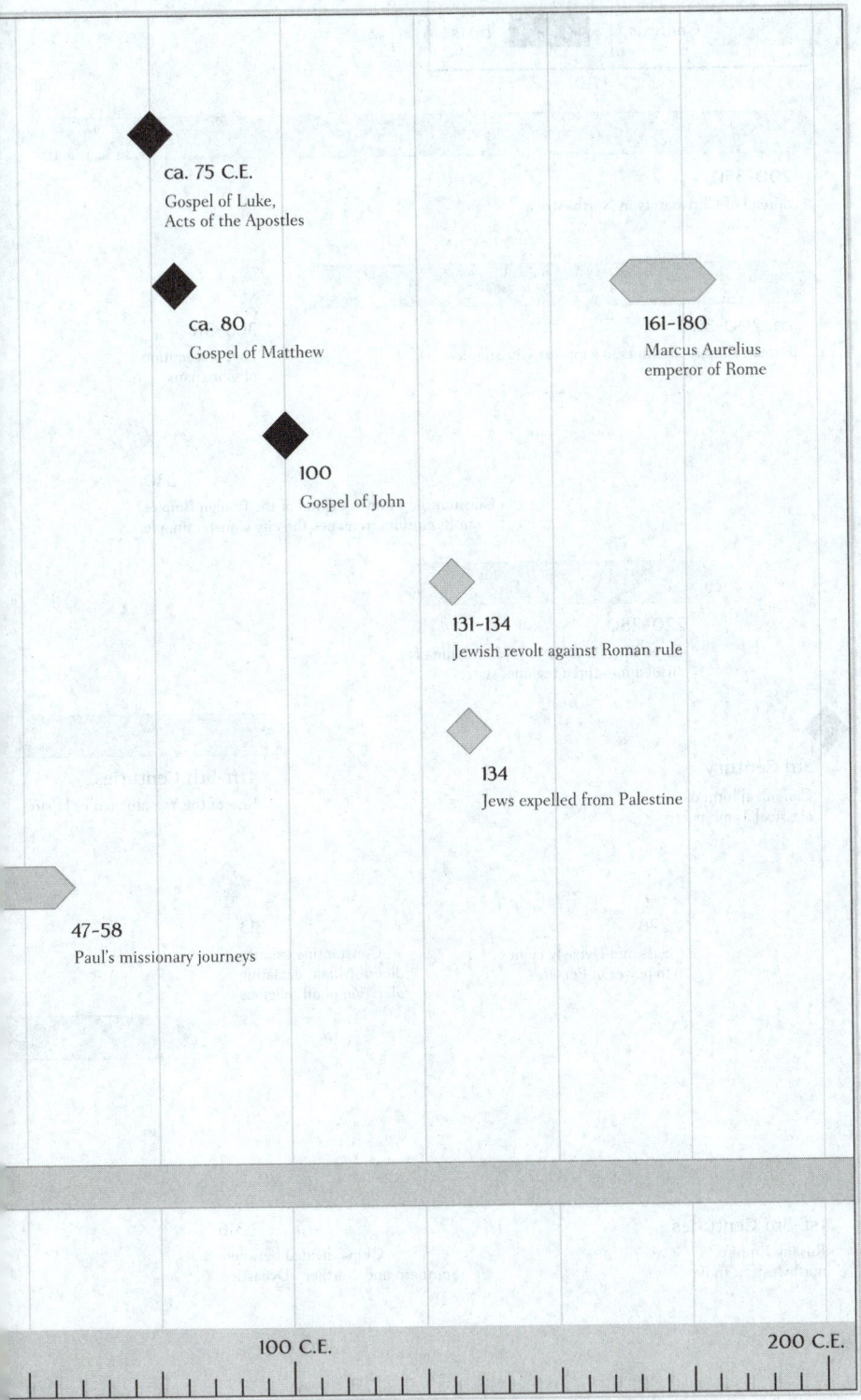

ca. 75 C.E.
Gospel of Luke,
Acts of the Apostles

ca. 80
Gospel of Matthew

161–180
Marcus Aurelius
emperor of Rome

100
Gospel of John

131–134
Jewish revolt against Roman rule

134
Jews expelled from Palestine

47–58
Paul's missionary journeys

100 C.E.

200 C.E.

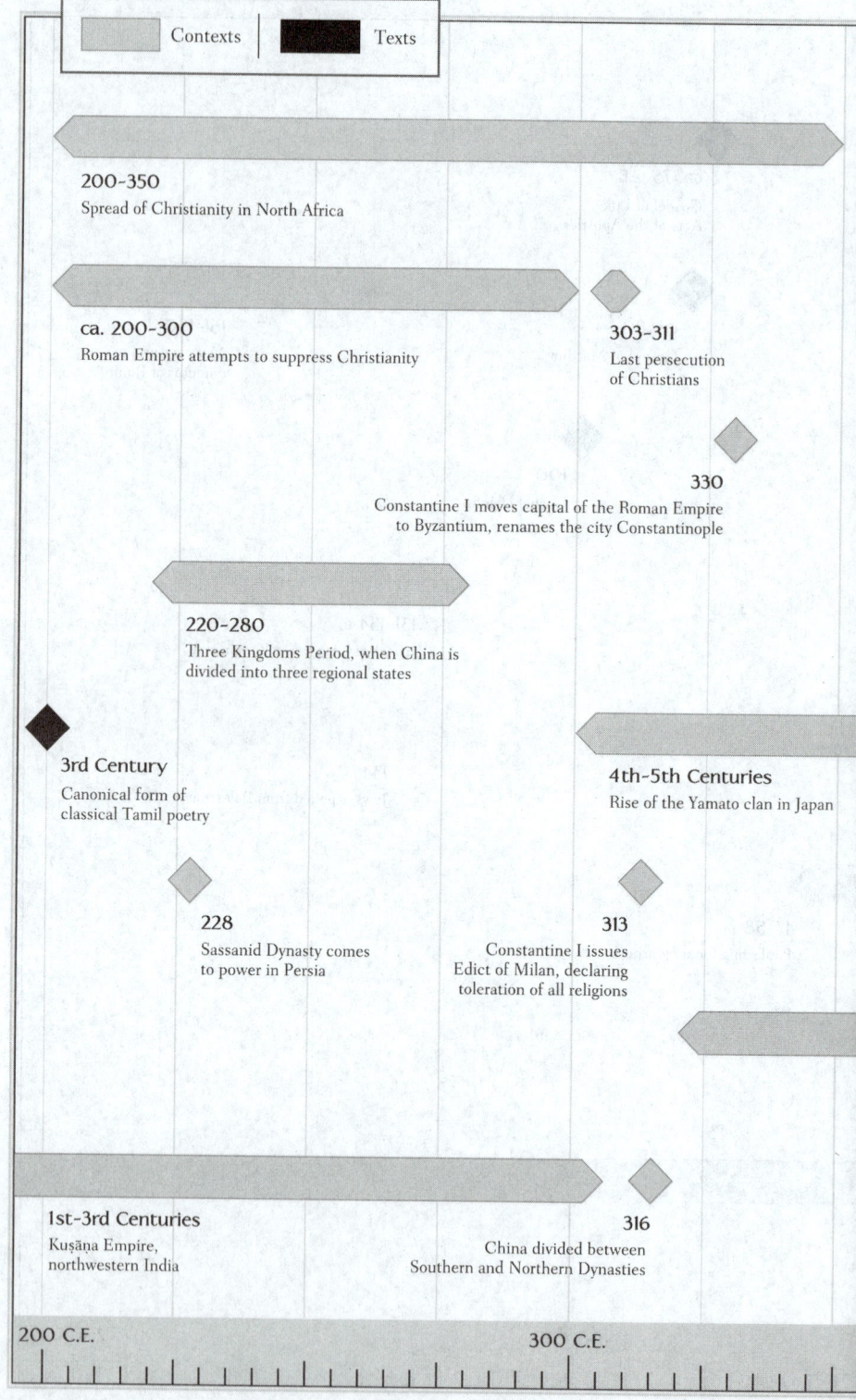

Contexts | Texts

200-350
Spread of Christianity in North Africa

ca. 200-300
Roman Empire attempts to suppress Christianity

303-311
Last persecution
of Christians

330
Constantine I moves capital of the Roman Empire
to Byzantium, renames the city Constantinople

220-280
Three Kingdoms Period, when China is
divided into three regional states

3rd Century
Canonical form of
classical Tamil poetry

4th-5th Centuries
Rise of the Yamato clan in Japan

228
Sassanid Dynasty comes
to power in Persia

313
Constantine I issues
Edict of Milan, declaring
toleration of all religions

1st-3rd Centuries
Kuṣāṇa Empire,
northwestern India

316
China divided between
Southern and Northern Dynasties

200 C.E.

300 C.E.

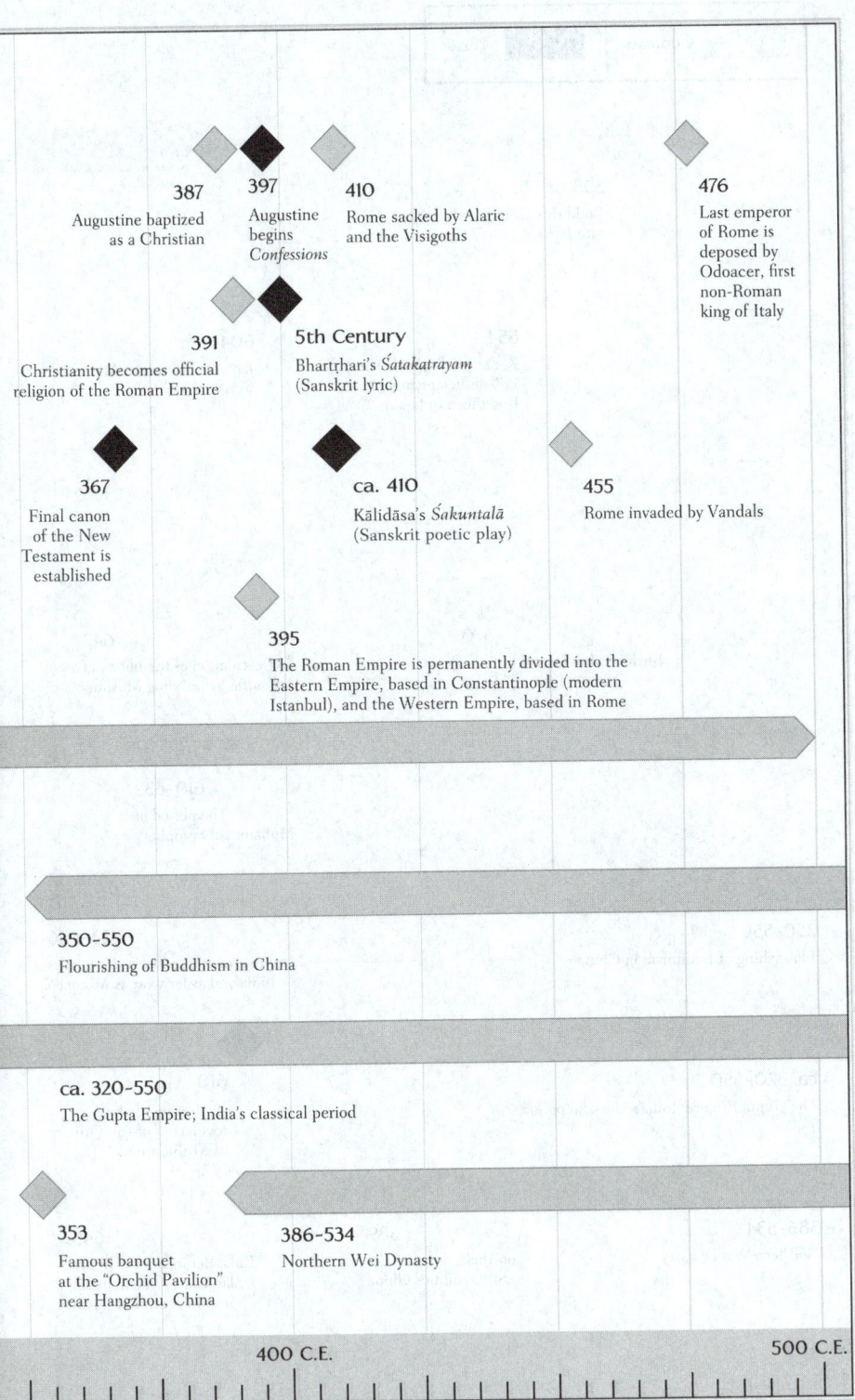

387
Augustine baptized
as a Christian

397
Augustine
begins
Confessions

410
Rome sacked by Alaric
and the Visigoths

476
Last emperor
of Rome is
deposed by
Odoacer, first
non-Roman
king of Italy

391
Christianity becomes official
religion of the Roman Empire

5th Century
Bhartṛhari's *Śatakatrayam*
(Sanskrit lyric)

367
Final canon
of the New
Testament is
established

ca. 410
Kālidāsa's *Śakuntalā*
(Sanskrit poetic play)

455
Rome invaded by Vandals

395
The Roman Empire is permanently divided into the
Eastern Empire, based in Constantinople (modern
Istanbul), and the Western Empire, based in Rome

350–550
Flourishing of Buddhism in China

ca. 320–550
The Gupta Empire; India's classical period

353
Famous banquet
at the "Orchid Pavilion"
near Hangzhou, China

386–534
Northern Wei Dynasty

400 C.E.

500 C.E.

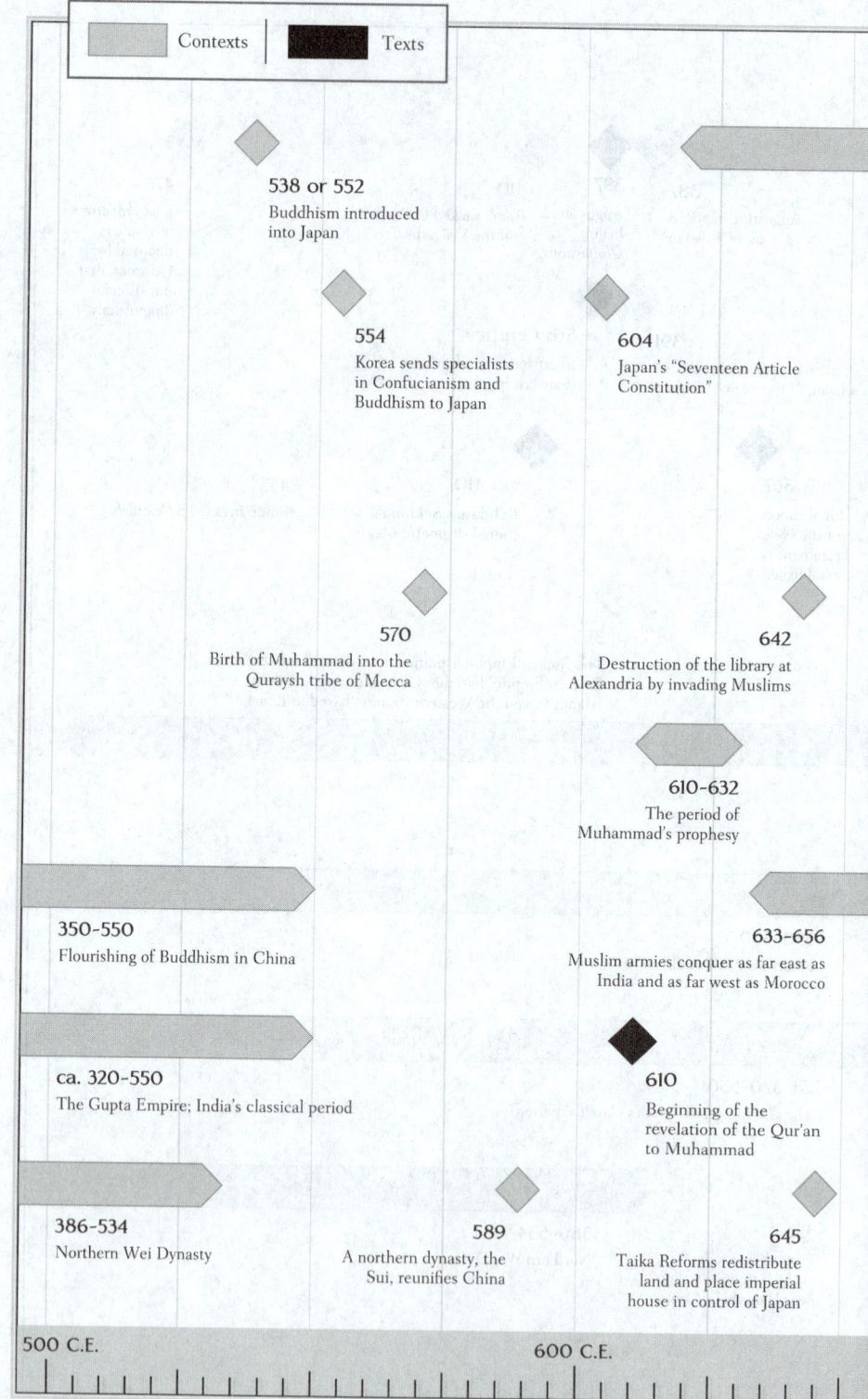

Contexts   Texts

538 or 552
Buddhism introduced
into Japan

554
Korea sends specialists
in Confucianism and
Buddhism to Japan

604
Japan's "Seventeen Article
Constitution"

570
Birth of Muhammad into the
Quraysh tribe of Mecca

642
Destruction of the library at
Alexandria by invading Muslims

610–632
The period of
Muhammad's prophesy

350–550
Flourishing of Buddhism in China

633–656
Muslim armies conquer as far east as
India and as far west as Morocco

ca. 320–550
The Gupta Empire; India's classical period

610
Beginning of the
revelation of the Qur'an
to Muhammad

386–534
Northern Wei Dynasty

589
A northern dynasty, the
Sui, reunifies China

645
Taika Reforms redistribute
land and place imperial
house in control of Japan

500 C.E.

600 C.E.

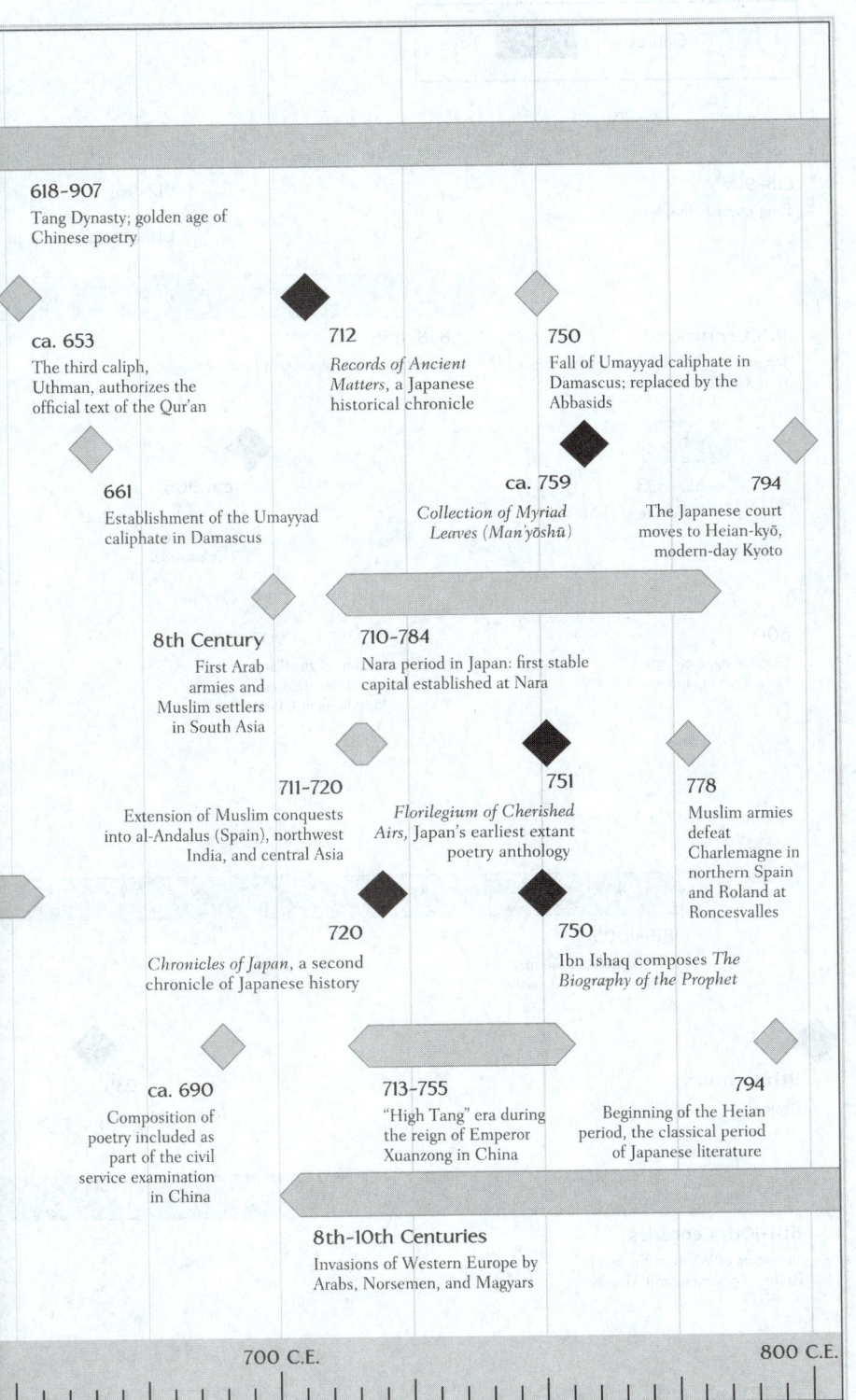

618–907
Tang Dynasty; golden age of Chinese poetry

ca. 653
The third caliph, Uthman, authorizes the official text of the Qur'an

712
Records of Ancient Matters, a Japanese historical chronicle

750
Fall of Umayyad caliphate in Damascus; replaced by the Abbasids

661
Establishment of the Umayyad caliphate in Damascus

ca. 759
Collection of Myriad Leaves (Man'yōshū)

794
The Japanese court moves to Heian-kyō, modern-day Kyoto

8th Century
First Arab armies and Muslim settlers in South Asia

710–784
Nara period in Japan: first stable capital established at Nara

711–720
Extension of Muslim conquests into al-Andalus (Spain), northwest India, and central Asia

751
Florilegium of Cherished Airs, Japan's earliest extant poetry anthology

778
Muslim armies defeat Charlemagne in northern Spain and Roland at Roncesvalles

720
Chronicles of Japan, a second chronicle of Japanese history

750
Ibn Ishaq composes *The Biography of the Prophet*

ca. 690
Composition of poetry included as part of the civil service examination in China

713–755
"High Tang" era during the reign of Emperor Xuanzong in China

794
Beginning of the Heian period, the classical period of Japanese literature

8th–10th Centuries
Invasions of Western Europe by Arabs, Norsemen, and Magyars

700 C.E.   800 C.E.

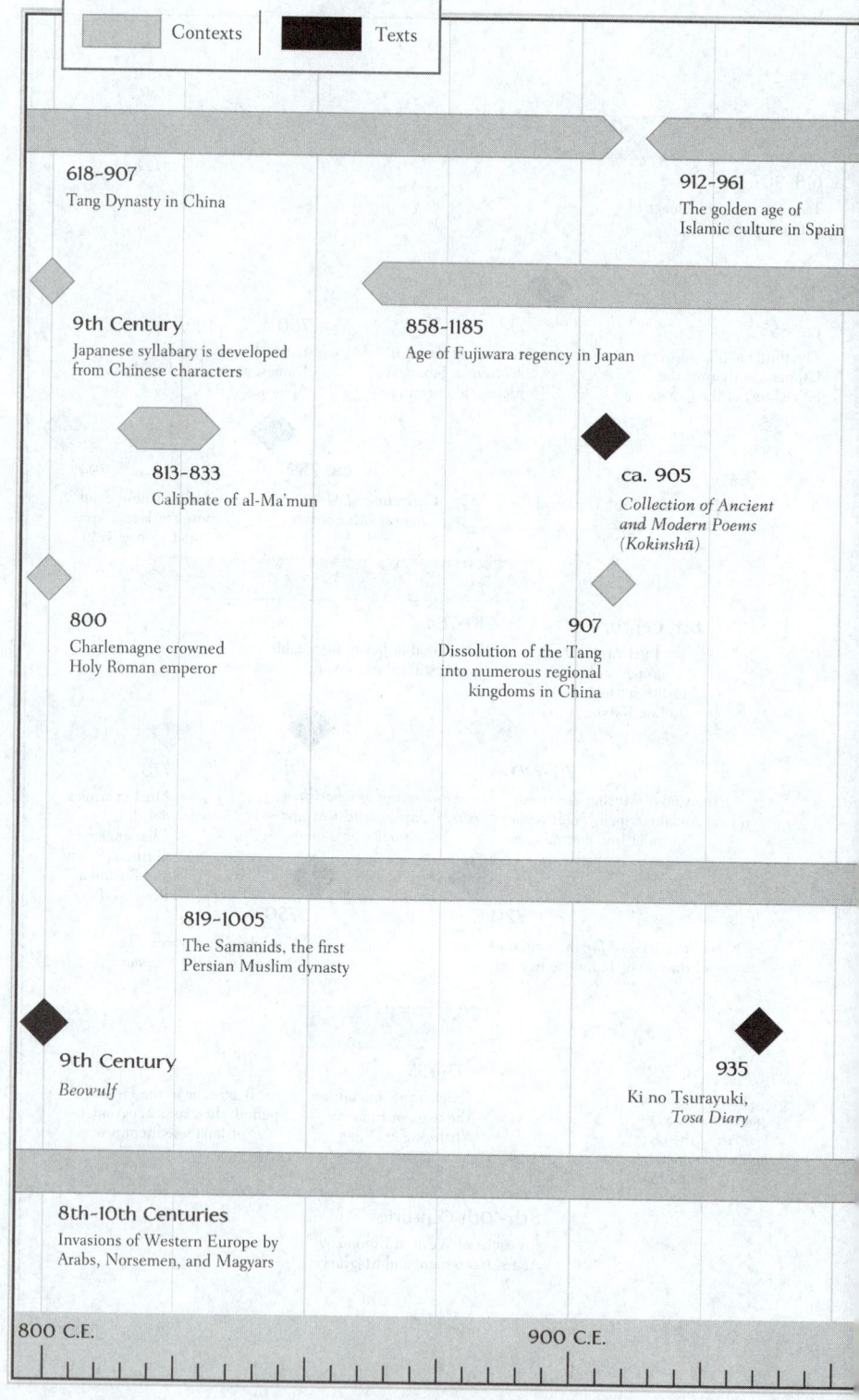

| Contexts | Texts |

618–907
Tang Dynasty in China

912–961
The golden age of
Islamic culture in Spain

9th Century
Japanese syllabary is developed
from Chinese characters

858–1185
Age of Fujiwara regency in Japan

813–833
Caliphate of al-Ma'mun

ca. 905
*Collection of Ancient
and Modern Poems
(Kokinshū)*

800
Charlemagne crowned
Holy Roman emperor

907
Dissolution of the Tang
into numerous regional
kingdoms in China

819–1005
The Samanids, the first
Persian Muslim dynasty

9th Century
Beowulf

935
Ki no Tsurayuki,
Tosa Diary

8th–10th Centuries
Invasions of Western Europe by
Arabs, Norsemen, and Magyars

800 C.E.

900 C.E.

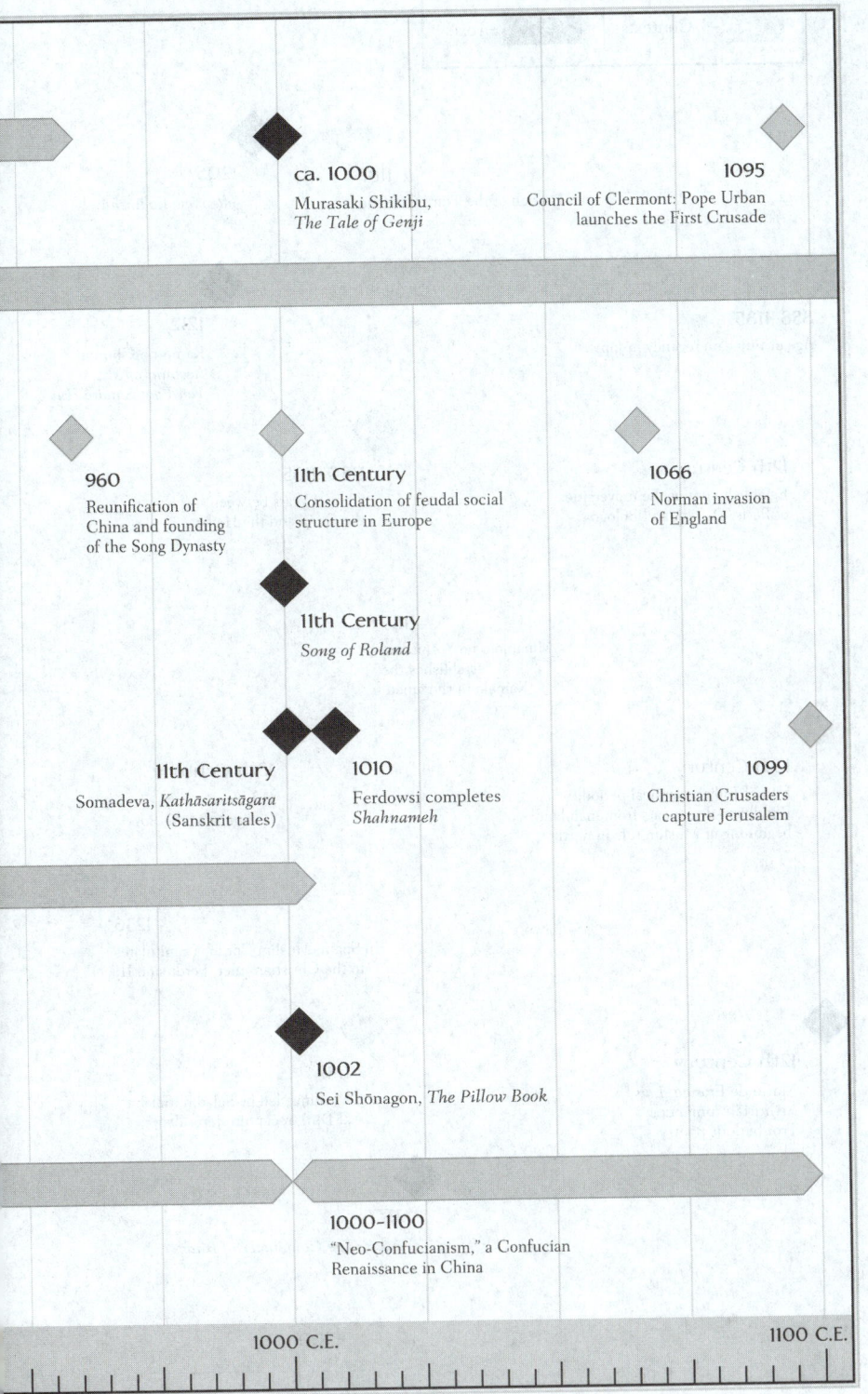

ca. 1000
Murasaki Shikibu,
The Tale of Genji

1095
Council of Clermont: Pope Urban
launches the First Crusade

960
Reunification of
China and founding
of the Song Dynasty

11th Century
Consolidation of feudal social
structure in Europe

1066
Norman invasion
of England

11th Century
Song of Roland

11th Century
Somadeva, *Kathāsaritsāgara*
(Sanskrit tales)

1010
Ferdowsi completes
Shahnameh

1099
Christian Crusaders
capture Jerusalem

1002
Sei Shōnagon, *The Pillow Book*

1000–1100
"Neo-Confucianism," a Confucian
Renaissance in China

1000 C.E.

1100 C.E.

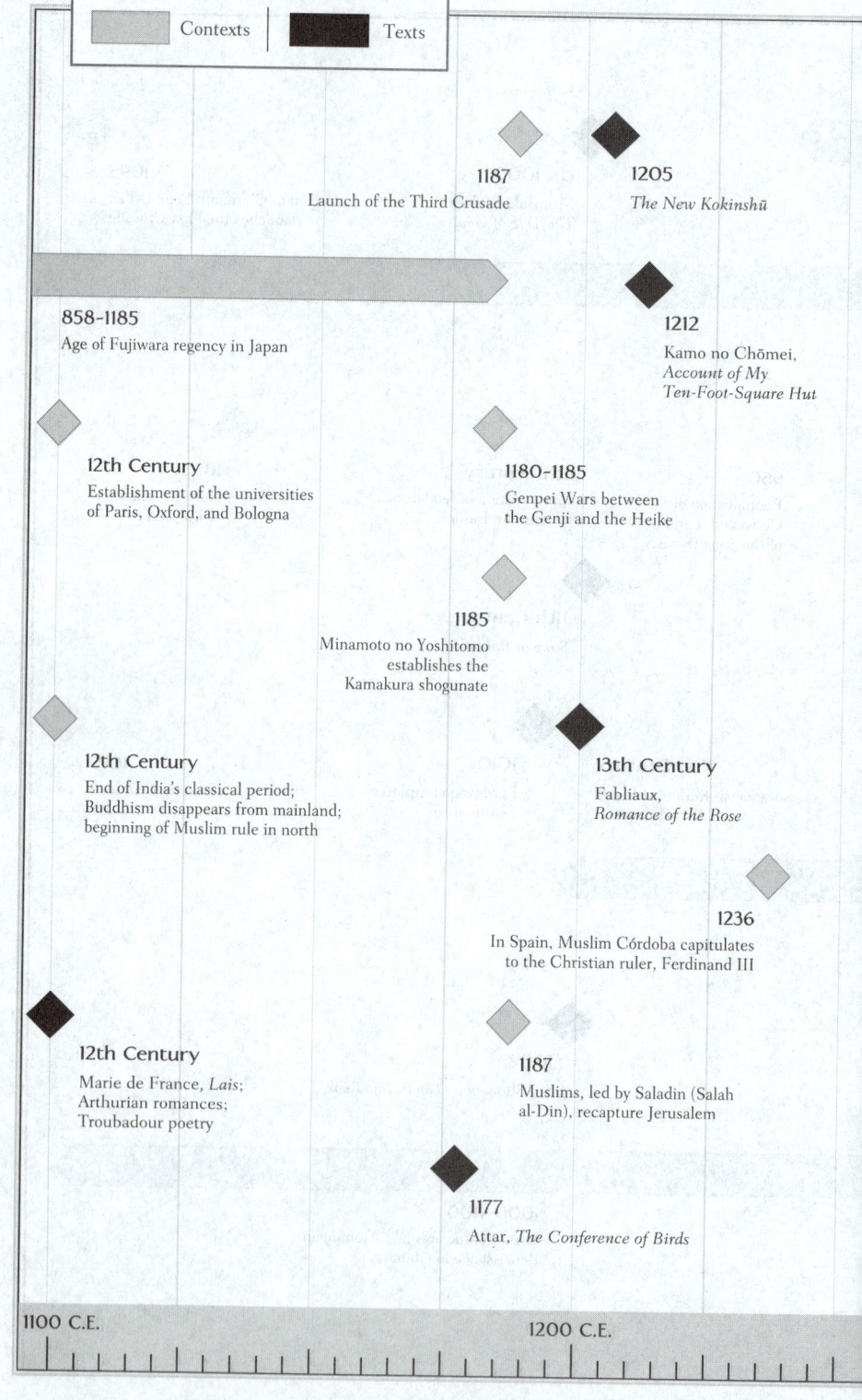

Contexts | Texts

1187
Launch of the Third Crusade

1205
The New Kokinshū

858–1185
Age of Fujiwara regency in Japan

1212
Kamo no Chōmei,
*Account of My
Ten-Foot-Square Hut*

12th Century
Establishment of the universities
of Paris, Oxford, and Bologna

1180–1185
Genpei Wars between
the Genji and the Heike

1185
Minamoto no Yoshitomo
establishes the
Kamakura shogunate

12th Century
End of India's classical period;
Buddhism disappears from mainland;
beginning of Muslim rule in north

13th Century
Fabliaux,
Romance of the Rose

1236
In Spain, Muslim Córdoba capitulates
to the Christian ruler, Ferdinand III

12th Century
Marie de France, *Lais*;
Arthurian romances;
Troubadour poetry

1187
Muslims, led by Saladin (Salah
al-Din), recapture Jerusalem

1177
Attar, *The Conference of Birds*

1100 C.E.   1200 C.E.

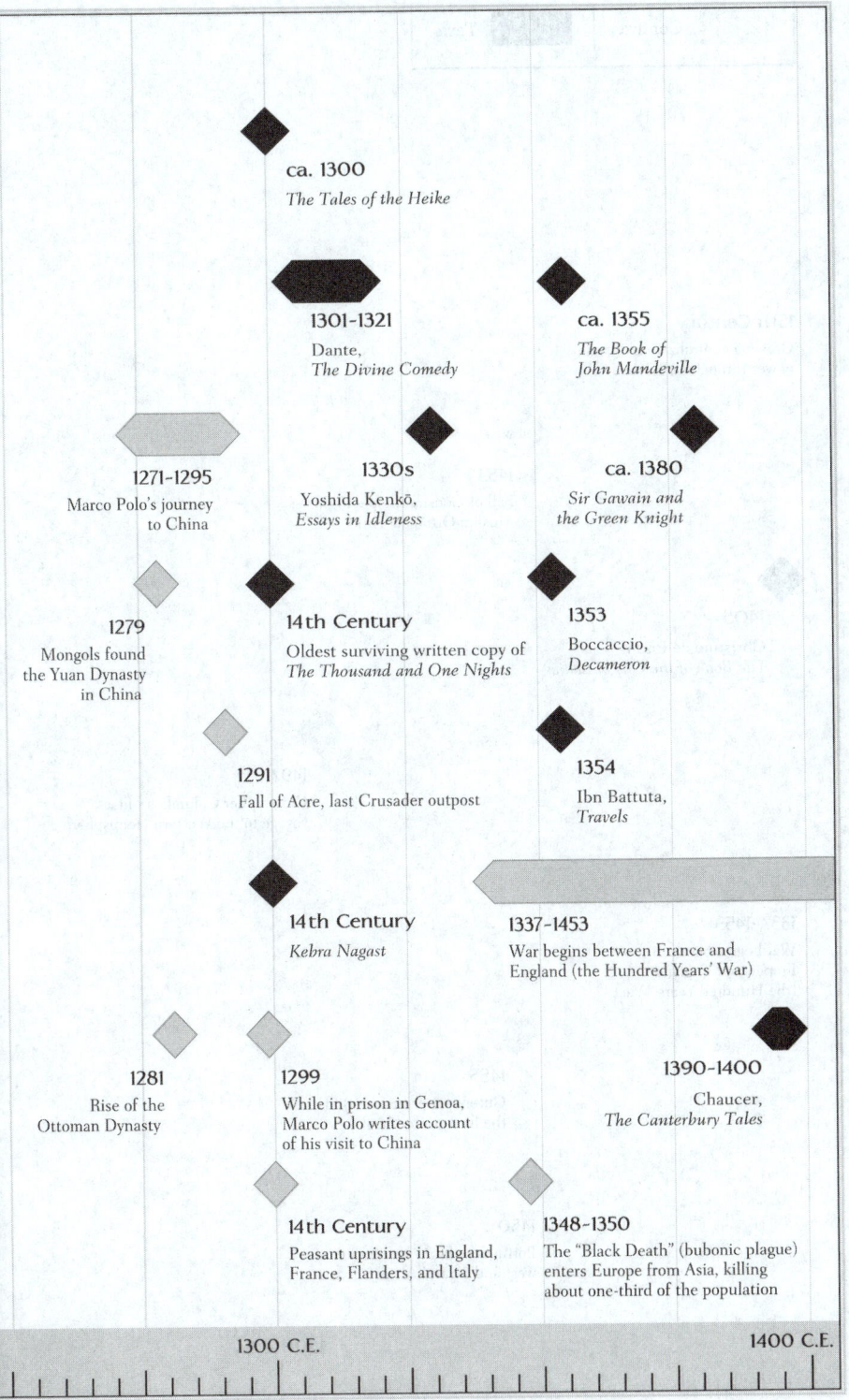

ca. 1300
The Tales of the Heike

1301-1321
Dante,
The Divine Comedy

ca. 1355
*The Book of
John Mandeville*

1271-1295
Marco Polo's journey
to China

1330s
Yoshida Kenkō,
Essays in Idleness

ca. 1380
*Sir Gawain and
the Green Knight*

1279
Mongols found
the Yuan Dynasty
in China

14th Century
Oldest surviving written copy of
The Thousand and One Nights

1353
Boccaccio,
Decameron

1291
Fall of Acre, last Crusader outpost

1354
Ibn Battuta,
Travels

14th Century
Kebra Nagast

1337-1453
War begins between France and
England (the Hundred Years' War)

1281
Rise of the
Ottoman Dynasty

1299
While in prison in Genoa,
Marco Polo writes account
of his visit to China

1390-1400
Chaucer,
The Canterbury Tales

14th Century
Peasant uprisings in England,
France, Flanders, and Italy

1348-1350
The "Black Death" (bubonic plague)
enters Europe from Asia, killing
about one-third of the population

1300 C.E.   1400 C.E.

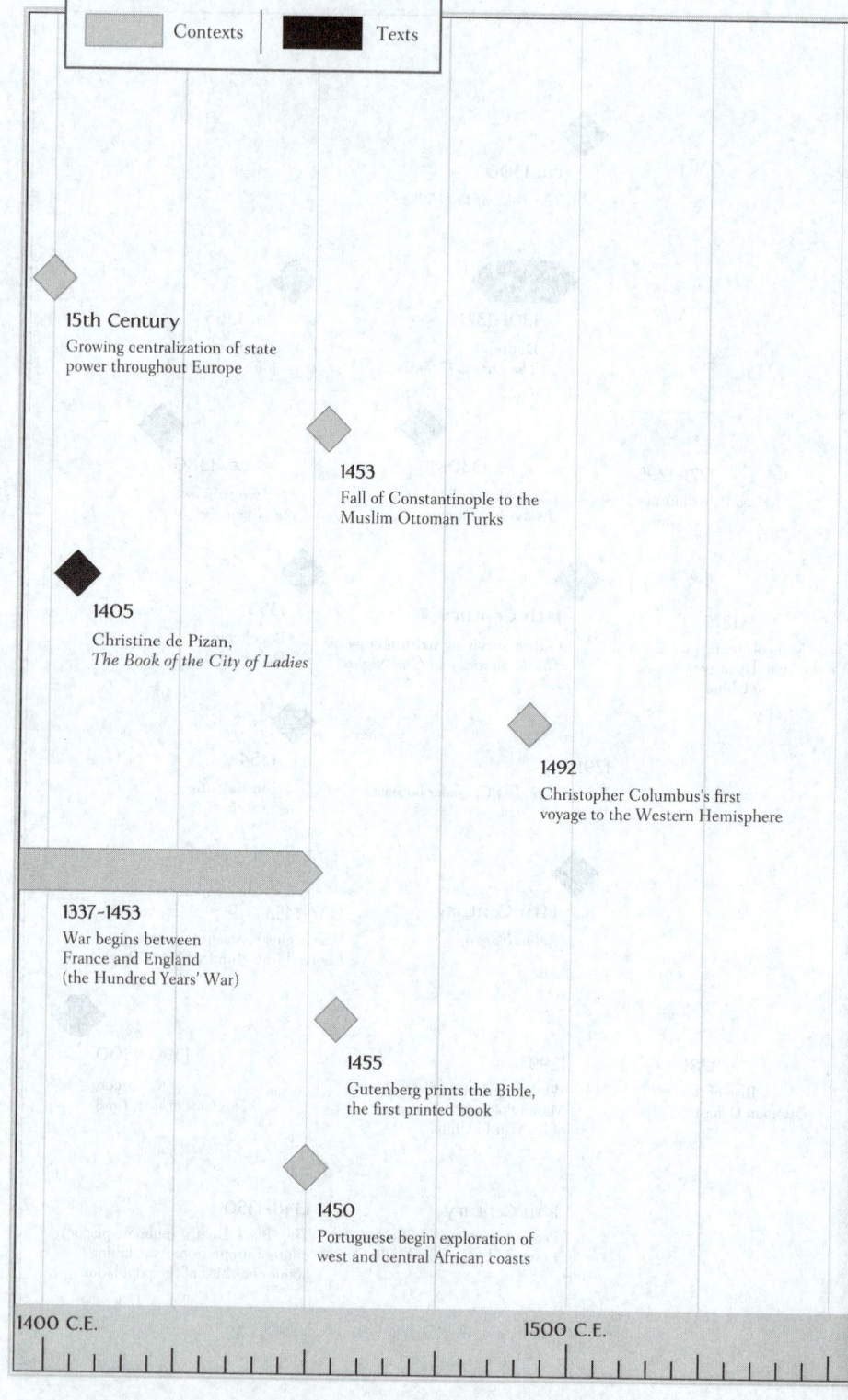

Contexts | Texts

15th Century
Growing centralization of state
power throughout Europe

1453
Fall of Constantinople to the
Muslim Ottoman Turks

1405
Christine de Pizan,
The Book of the City of Ladies

1492
Christopher Columbus's first
voyage to the Western Hemisphere

1337–1453
War begins between
France and England
(the Hundred Years' War)

1455
Gutenberg prints the Bible,
the first printed book

1450
Portuguese begin exploration of
west and central African coasts

1400 C.E.

1500 C.E.

Permissions Acknowledgments

Alexander the Wild: "Strawberry Picking," trans. by Peter Dronke from THE MEDIEVAL LYRIC, third ed., by Peter Dronke (1996). Reprinted by permission of the publisher Boydell & Brewer Ltd.

Petrus Alfonsi: From THE SCHOLAR'S GUIDE: A TRANSLATION OF THE TWELFTH-CENTURY DISCIPLINA CLERICALIS of Pedro Alfonso, trans. by Joseph Ramon Jones and John Esten Keller. Copyright © 1969 by The Pontifical Institute of Mediaeval Studies, Toronto, Canada. Reprinted by permission of the publisher.

Alfonso X: "The Scorpions," trans. by Peter Dronke from THE MEDIEVAL LYRIC, third ed., by Peter Dronke (1996). Reprinted by permission of the publisher Boydell & Brewer Ltd.

Apuleius: From THE GOLDEN ASS, trans. by P.G. Walsh (1999), pp.18–25, 47–54. By permission of Oxford University Press.

Muhyiddin Ibn 'Arabi: "Gentle Now, Doves" from STATIONS OF DESIRE: LOVE ELEGIES FROM IBN 'ARABI AND NEW POEMS, trans. by Michael Sells, copyright © 2000 by Michael A. Sells. Reprinted by permission of the publisher, IBIS Editions.

The Archpoet: "His Confession" from MEDIEVAL LATIN LYRICS by Helen Waddell. (London: Constable, 1929). Reprinted by permission of Constable & Robinson Ltd.

Farid ud-Din Attar: From THE CONFERENCE OF THE BIRDS, trans. by Sholeh Wolpé. Copyright © 2017 by Sholeh Wolpé. Used by permission of W. W. Norton & Company, Inc.

St. Augustine: From CONFESSIONS: A NEW TRANSLATION, trans. by Peter Constantine. Copyright © 2018 by Peter Constantine. Used by permission of Liveright Publishing Corp.

Avraham Ibn Ezra: "Elegy for a Son" from THE DREAM OF THE POEM: HEBREW POETRY FROM MUSLIM AND CHRISTIAN SPAIN 950–1492, trans. and ed. by Peter Cole. Copyright © 2007 by Princeton University Press. Reprinted by permission of Princeton University Press via the Copyright Clearance Center.

Bāṇa: Translations by Daniel H. Ingalls reprinted by permission of the publisher from AN ANTHOLOGY OF SANSKRIT COURT POETRY: VIDYAKARA'S SUBHSITARATNAKOSA, (Harvard Oriental Series, 44). Cambridge, Mass.: Harvard University Press. Copyright © 1965 by the President and Fellows of Harvard College. "[The horse rises, stretches its hind legs]," trans. by Vinay Dharwadker is reprinted by permission of the translator.

Beatrice of Dia: "A Lover's Prize," trans. by Peter Dronke from THE MEDIEVAL LYRIC, third ed., by Peter Dronke (1996). Reprinted by permission of the publisher Boydell & Brewer Ltd.

Beowulf: BEOWULF, trans. by Seamus Heaney. Copyright © 2000 by Seamus Heaney. Used by permission of W.W. Norton & Company, Inc.

Bhartṛhari: Translations by Vinay Dharwadker are reprinted by permission of the translator.

Bhavabhūtī: "[And as we talked together softly, secretly]" trans. by Daniel H. Ingalls is reprinted by permission of the publisher from AN ANTHOLOGY OF SANSKRIT COURT POETRY: VIDYAKARA'S SUBHSITARATNAKOSA, (Harvard Oriental Series, 44). Cambridge, Mass.: Harvard University Press. Copyright © 1965 by the President and Fellows of Harvard College. Translations by Vinay Dharwadker are reprinted with permission of the translator.

Bhāvakadevī: [As he came to bed the knot fell open of itself] is reprinted by permission of the publisher from AN ANTHOLOGY OF SANSKRIT COURT POETRY: VIDYAKARA'S SUBHSITAR-ATNAKOSA, trans. by Daniel H. Ingalls. (Harvard Oriental Series, 44). Cambridge, Mass.: Harvard University Press. Copyright © 1965 by the President and Fellows of Harvard College.

Bo Juyi: "The Song of Lasting Regret," trans. by Paul W. Kroll from THE COLUMBIA ANTHOLOGY OF TRADITIONAL CHINESE LITERATURE, ed. Victor H. Mair. Copyright © 1994 Columbia University Press. Reprinted with permission of the publisher. "[Chen Hong, An Account to Go with the 'Song of Lasting Pain']," "Salt Merchant's Wife (in hatred of profiteers)" and "On My Portrait" from AN ANTHOLOGY OF CHINESE LITERATURE: BEGINNINGS TO 1911, ed. and trans. by Stephen Owen. Copyright © 1996 by Stephen Owen and The Council for Cultural Planning and Development of the Executive Yuan of the Republic of China. Used by permission of W.W. Norton & Company, Inc.

Giovanni Boccaccio: From THE DECAMERON (Norton Critical Editions), trans. by Wayne A. Rebhorn. Copyright © 2013 by Wayne A. Rebhorn. Used by permission of W.W. Norton & Company, Inc.

Boethius: Reprinted by permission of the publishers and the Trustees of the Loeb Classical Library

Buitenen. Copyright © 1959 by The University of Chicago. Reprinted by permission of the University of Chicago Press.

The Song of Roland: From THE SONG OF ROLAND, trans. by Frederick Goldin. Copyright © 1978 by W.W. Norton & Company, Inc. Used by permission of W.W. Norton & Company, Inc.

Song of Summer: "Song of Summer," from THE CAMBRIDGE SONGS ed. and trans. by Jan M. Ziolkowksi. Copyright © 1998 by Jan M. Ziolkowski. Reprinted by permission of Medieval Renaissance Text and Studies and the translator.

Tales of the Heike: From TALES OF THE HEIKE, trans. by Burton Watson, ed. by Haruo Shirane. Copyright © 2005 by Columbia University Press. Reprinted with permission of the publisher.

Tao Qian: "Biography of Master Five Willows," trans. by Stephen Owen, is reprinted by permission of the publisher from REMEMBRANCES: THE EXPERIENCE OF THE PAST IN CLASSICAL CHINESE LITERATURE by Stephen Owen. Cambridge, Mass.: Harvard University Press. Copyright © 1986 by the President and Fellows of Harvard College. Poems from THE POETRY OF T'ao Ch'ien, trans. by James Robert Hightower (1970) are reprinted by permission of Oxford University Press.

The Thousand and One Nights: From THE ARABIAN NIGHTS: THE THOUSAND AND ONE NIGHTS, trans. by Husain Haddawy. Copyright © 1990 by W.W. Norton & Company, Inc. Used by permission of W.W. Norton & Company, Inc. [The Third Old Man's Tale], trans. by Jerome W. Clinton is reprinted by permission of the translator.

Vidyā: [Good neighbor wife, I beg you] is reprinted by permission of the publisher from AN ANTHOLOGY OF SANSKRIT COURT POETRY: VIDYAKARA'S SUBHSITARATNAKOSA, trans. by Daniel H. Ingalls (Harvard Oriental Series, 44). Cambridge, Mass.: Harvard University Press. Copyright © 1965 by the President and Fellows of Harvard College.

Vikaṭanitāmba: "[As he came to bed the knot fell open of itself]," is reprinted by permission of the publisher from AN ANTHOLOGY OF SANSKRIT COURT POETRY: VIDYAKARA'S SUBHSITARATNAKOSA, trans. by Daniel H. Ingalls. (Harvard Oriental Series, 44). Cambridge, Mass.: Harvard University Press. Copyright © 1965 by the President and Fellows of Harvard College.

Visnuśarman: Selections from THE PANCHATANTRA, ed. and trans. by Arthur W. Ryder. Copyright © 1925 by the University of Chicago; renewed 1953 by Mary E. and Winifred Ryder. Reprinted by permission of the University of Chicago Press. "The Ass without Ears or a Heart," from PANCATANTRA trans. by Patrick Olivelle, pp. 152–154. Reprinted by permission of Oxford University Press.

Walther von der Vogelweide: "Dancing Girl," trans. by Peter Dronke from THE MEDIEVAL LYRIC, third ed., by Peter Dronke (1996). Reprinted by permission of the publisher Boydell & Brewer Ltd.

Heinrich von Morungen: "The Wound of Love," trans. by Peter Dronke from THE MEDIEVAL LYRIC, third ed., by Peter Dronke (1996). Reprinted by permission of the publisher Boydell & Brewer Ltd.

Wang Wei: From THE POETRY OF WANG WEI, tr. Pauline Yu. Copyright © 1980 by Pauline Ruth Yu. Reprinted with permission of Indiana University Press.

Yogeśvara: Reprinted by permission of the publisher from AN ANTHOLOGY OF SANSKRIT COURT POETRY: VIDYAKARA'S SUBHSITARATNAKOSA, trans. by Daniel H. Ingalls (Harvard Oriental Series, 44). Cambridge, Mass.: Harvard University Press. Copyright © 1965 by the President and Fellows of Harvard College.

Yuan Zhen: "The Story of Ying-ying," trans. by James Robert Hightower, from TRADITIONAL CHINESE STORIES: THEMES AND VARIATIONS, edited by Y.W. Ma and Joseph S.M. Lau, copyright © 1986 by Cheng & Tsui Company, Inc. Used by permission of Cheng & Tsui Company, Inc.

IMAGES

2–3 Bpk Bildagentur/Bodleian Library, Oxford, Great Britain/Photo: Hermann Buresch/Art Resource, NY; **4** Bridgeman-Giraudon/Art Resource, NY; **6** Erich Lessing/Art Resource, NY; **10** SSPL/Science Museum/Art Resource, NY; **14** Wikimedia, public domain; **15** HIP/Art Resource, NY; **310–311** Art Resource, NY; **918–919** © 2011 The British Library; **946–947** Art Resource, NY; **951** Borromeo/Art Resource, NY; **954** © Rubin Museum of Art/Art Resource, NY; **968–969** David LeFranc/Gamma-Rapho via Getty Images; **1056–1057** Pictures from History/Bridgeman Images; **1082–1083** Image copyright © The Metropolitan Museum of Art. Image source: Art Resource, NY; **1085** Allen Lee Taylor/Getty Images; **1108–1109** Akg-images/Pictures From History; **1160–1161** De Agostini Picture Library/Bridgeman Images; **1164** © Sakamoto Photo Research Laboratory/CORBIS/Getty Images; **1166** The Art Archive/Private Collection Paris/Gianni Dagli Orti; **1186–1187** Chronicle/Alamy Stock Photo; **1244** © Harvard Art Museum/Art Resource, NY

COLOR INSERT

C1 Scala/Art Resource; **C2** © British Library Board/Robana/Art Resource, NY; **C3** Bpk Bildagentur/Museum fuer Islamische Kunst, Staatliche Museen, Berlin, Germany/Photo: Georg Niedermeiser/Art Resource, NY; **C4** © British Library Board/Robana/Art Resource, NY; **C5** Burstein Collection/CORBIS; **C6** Lebrecht Music & Arts/Corbis/Getty; **C7** © The Trustees of the British Museum/Art Resource, NY; **C8** Digital Image © 2017 Museum Associates/LACMA. Licensed by Art Resource, NY

Index